The IDG Books SECRETS® Advantage

Linux SECRETS is part of the SECRETS series of books brought to you by IDG Books Worldwide. We designed the SECRETS series because we know how much you appreciate insightful and comprehensive works from computer experts. Authorities in their respective areas, the authors of the SECRETS books have been selected for their ability to enrich your daily computing tasks.

The formula for a book in the SECRETS series is simple: Give an expert a forum to pass on his or her knowledge to readers. A SECRETS author, rather than the publishing company, directs the organization, pace, and treatment of the subject matter. SECRETS authors maintain close contact with end users through feedback from articles, training sessions, e-mail exchanges, user group participation, and consulting work. Because our authors know the realities of daily computer use and are directly tied to the reader, our SECRETS books have a strategic advantage.

SECRETS authors have the experience to approach a topic in the most efficient manner, and we know that you, the reader, will benefit from a "one-on-one" relationship with the author. Our research shows that readers make computer book purchases because they want expert advice on a product. Readers want to benefit from the author's experience, so the author's voice is always present in a SECRETS series book.

In addition, the author is free to include or recommend useful software in a SECRETS book. The software that accompanies a SECRETS book is not intended to be casual filler but is linked to the content, theme, or procedures of the book. We know that you will benefit from the included software.

You will find what you need in this book whether you read it from cover to cover, section by section, or simply one topic at a time. As a computer user, you deserve a comprehensive resource of answers. We at IDG Books Worldwide are proud to deliver that resource with *Linux SECRETS*.

Brenda McLaughlin
Publisher
Internet: YouTellUs@idgbooks.com

Linux
SECRETS®

Linux SECRETS®

by Naba Barkakati

IDG Books Worldwide, Inc.
An International Data Group Company

Foster City, CA ♦ Chicago, IL ♦ Indianapolis, IN
Braintree, MA ♦ Dallas, TX

Linux SECRETS®

Published by
IDG Books Worldwide, Inc.
An International Data Group Company
919 E. Hillsdale Blvd.
Suite 400
Foster City, CA 94404

Text, art, and software compilations copyright © 1996 by IDG Books Worldwide. All rights reserved. No part of this book, including interior design, cover design, and icons, may be reproduced or transmitted in any form, by any means (electronic, photocopying, recording, or otherwise) without the prior written permission of the publisher.

Library of Congress Catalog Card No.: 96-75004

ISBN: 1-56884-798-X

Printed in the United States of America

10 9 8 7 6 5 4 3 2 1

1B/SX/QS/ZW/IN

Distributed in the United States by IDG Books Worldwide, Inc.

Distributed by Macmillan Canada for Canada; by Computer and Technical Books for the Caribbean Basin; by Contemporanea de Ediciones for Venezuela; by Distribuidora Cuspide for Argentina; by CITEC for Brazil; by Ediciones ZETA S.C.R. Ltda. for Peru; by Editorial Limusa SA for Mexico; by Transworld Publishers Limited in the United Kingdom and Europe; by Al-Maiman Publishers & Distributors for Saudi Arabia; by Simron Pty. Ltd. for South Africa; by IDG Communications (HK) Ltd. for Hong Kong; by Toppan Company Ltd. for Japan; by Addison Wesley Publishing Company for Korea; by Longman Singapore Publishers Ltd. for Singapore, Malaysia, Thailand, and Indonesia; by Unalis Corporation for Taiwan; by WS Computer Publishing Company, Inc. for the Philippines; by WoodsLane Pty. Ltd. for Australia; by WoodsLane Enterprises Ltd. for New Zealand.

For general information on IDG Books Worldwide's books in the U.S., please call our Consumer Customer Service department at 800-762-2974. For reseller information, including discounts and premium sales, please call our Reseller Customer Service department at 800-434-3422.

For information on where to purchase IDG Books Worldwide's books outside the U.S., contact IDG Books Worldwide at 415-655-3021 or fax 415-655-3295.

For information on translations, contact Marc Jeffrey Mikulich, Director, Foreign & Subsidiary Rights, at IDG Books Worldwide, 415-655-3018 or fax 415-655-3295.

For sales inquiries and special prices for bulk quantities, write to the address above or call IDG Books Worldwide at 415-655-3200.

For information on using IDG Books Worldwide's books in the classroom, or ordering examination copies, contact the Education Office at 800-434-2086 or fax 817-251-8174.

For authorization to photocopy items for corporate, personal, or educational use, please contact Copyright Clearance Center, 222 Rosewood Drive, Danvers, MA 01923, or fax 508-750-4470.

Limit of Liability/Disclaimer of Warranty: Author and Publisher have used their best efforts in preparing this book. IDG Books Worldwide, Inc., and Author make no representation or warranties with respect to the accuracy or completeness of the contents of this book and specifically disclaim any implied warranties of merchantability or fitness for any particular purpose and shall in no event be liable for any loss of profit or any other commercial damage, including but not limited to special, incidental, consequential, or other damages.

Trademarks: All brand names and product names used in this book are trademarks, registered trademarks, or trade names of their respective holders. IDG Books Worldwide is not associated with any product or vendor mentioned in this book.

 is a trademark under exclusive license to IDG Books Worldwide, Inc., from International Data Group, Inc.

 SECRETS® is a registered trademark of IDG Books Worldwide, Inc.

About the Author

Naba Barkakati is an expert programmer and successful computer-book author who has experience in a wide variety of systems, ranging from MS-DOS and Windows to UNIX and the X Window System. He bought his first personal computer — an IBM PC-AT — in 1984 after graduating with a Ph.D. degree in electrical engineering from University of Maryland at College Park, Maryland. While pursuing a full-time career in engineering, Naba dreamed of writing software for the emerging PC software market. As luck would have it, instead of building a software empire like Microsoft, he ended up writing *The Waite Group's Microsoft C Bible* — one of the first 1,000-page tutorial-reference books that set a new trend in the computer-book-publishing industry.

Over the past eight years, Naba has written 18 computer books on topics ranging from Windows programming with Visual C++ to the X Window System. He is the author of several best-selling titles, such as *The Waite Group's Turbo C++ Bible*, *Object-Oriented Programming in C++*, *X Window System Programming*, *Visual C++ Developer's Guide*, and *Borland C++ 4 Developer's Guide*. His books have been translated into French, Polish, Greek, Japanese, and Korean.

Naba lives in North Potomac, Maryland, with his wife, Leha, and their children, Ivy, Emily, and Ashley.

Welcome to the world of IDG Books Worldwide.

IDG Books Worldwide, Inc., is a subsidiary of International Data Group, the world's largest publisher of computer-related information and the leading global provider of information services on information technology. IDG was founded more than 25 years ago and now employs more than 7,700 people worldwide. IDG publishes more than 250 computer publications in 67 countries (see listing below). More than 70 million people read one or more IDG publications each month.

Launched in 1990, IDG Books Worldwide is today the #1 publisher of best-selling computer books in the United States. We are proud to have received 8 awards from the Computer Press Association in recognition of editorial excellence and three from Computer Currents' First Annual Readers' Choice Awards, and our best-selling ...For Dummies® series has more than 19 million copies in print with translations in 28 languages. IDG Books Worldwide, through a joint venture with IDG's Hi-Tech Beijing, became the first U.S. publisher to publish a computer book in the People's Republic of China. In record time, IDG Books Worldwide has become the first choice for millions of readers around the world who want to learn how to better manage their businesses.

Our mission is simple: Every one of our books is designed to bring extra value and skill-building instructions to the reader. Our books are written by experts who understand and care about our readers. The knowledge base of our editorial staff comes from years of experience in publishing, education, and journalism — experience which we use to produce books for the '90s. In short, we care about books, so we attract the best people. We devote special attention to details such as audience, interior design, use of icons, and illustrations. And because we use an efficient process of authoring, editing, and desktop publishing our books electronically, we can spend more time ensuring superior content and spend less time on the technicalities of making books.

You can count on our commitment to deliver high-quality books at competitive prices on topics you want to read about. At IDG Books Worldwide, we continue in the IDG tradition of delivering quality for more than 25 years. You'll find no better book on a subject than one from IDG Books Worldwide.

John Kilcullen
President and CEO
IDG Books Worldwide, Inc.

IDG Books Worldwide, Inc., is a subsidiary of International Data Group, the world's largest publisher of computer-related information and the leading global provider of information services on information technology. International Data Group publishes over 250 computer publications in 67 countries. Seventy million people read one or more International Data Group publications each month. International Data Group's publications include: **ARGENTINA:** Computerworld Argentina, GamePro, Infoworld, PC World Argentina; **AUSTRALIA:** Australian Macworld, Client/Server Journal, Computer Living, Computerworld, Digital News, Network World, PC World, Publishing Essentials, Reseller; **AUSTRIA:** Computerwelt, PC TEST; **BELARUS:** PC World Belarus; **BELGIUM:** Data News; **BRAZIL:** Annuário de Informática, Computerworld Brazil, Connections, Super Game Power, Macworld, PC World Brazil, Publish Brazil, SUPERGAME; **BULGARIA:** Computerworld Bulgaria, Networkworld/Bulgaria, PC & MacWorld Bulgaria; **CANADA:** CIO Canada, ComputerWorld Canada, InfoCanada, Network World Canada, Reseller World; **CHILE:** Computerworld Chile, GamePro, PC World Chile; **COLUMBIA:** Computerworld Colombia, GamePro, PC World Colombia; **COSTA RICA:** PC World Costa Rica/Nicaragua; **THE CZECH AND SLOVAK REPUBLICS:** Computerworld Czechoslovakia, Elektronika Czechoslovakia, PC World Czechoslovakia; **DENMARK:** Communications World, Computerworld Danmark, Macworld Danmark, PC World Danmark, PC World Danmark Supplements, TECH World; **DOMINICAN REPUBLIC:** PC World Republica Dominicana; **ECUADOR:** PC World Ecuador, GamePro; **EGYPT:** Computerworld Middle East, PC World Middle East; **EL SALVADOR:** PC World Centro America; **FINLAND:** MikroPC, Tietoverkko, Tietoviikko; **FRANCE:** Distributique, Golden, Info PC, Le Guide du Monde Informatique, Le Monde Informatique, Reseaux & Telecoms; **GERMANY:** Computer Business, Computerwoche, Computerwoche Extra, Computerwoche Focus, Electronic Entertainment, GamePro, I/M Information Management, Macwelt, PC Welt; **GREECE:** GamePro, Macworld & Publish; **GUATEMALA:** PC World Centro America; **HONDURAS:** PC World Centro America; **HONG KONG:** Computerworld Hong Kong, PCWorld Hong Kong, Publish in Asia; **HUNGARY:** ABCD CD-ROM, Computerworld Szamitastechnika, PC & Mac World Hungary, PC-X Magazine; **INDIA:** Computerworld India, PC World India, Publish in Asia; **INDONESIA:** InfoKomputer PC World, Komputek Computerworld, Publish in Asia; **IRELAND:** ComputerScope, PC Live!; **ISRAEL:** PC World 32 BIT, People & Computers; **ITALY:** Computerworld Italia, Computerworld Italia Special Editions, Lotus Italia, Macworld Italia, Networking Italia, PC Shopping, PC World Italia, PC World/Walt Disney; **JAPAN:** Macworld Japan, Nikkei Personal Computing, SunWorld Japan, Windows World Japan; **KENYA:** East African Computer News; **KOREA:** Hi-Tech Information/Computerworld, Macworld Korea, PC World Korea; **MACEDONIA:** PC World Macedonia; **MALAYSIA:** Computerworld Malaysia, PC World Malaysia, Publish in Asia; **MEXICO:** Computerworld Mexico, GamePro, Macworld, PC World Mexico; **MYANMAR:** PC World Myanmar; **NETHERLANDS:** Computable, Computer! Totaal, LAN Magazine, Macworld, Net Magazine; **NEW ZEALAND:** Computer Buyer, Computerworld New Zealand, MTB, Network World, PC World New Zealand; **NICARAGUA:** PC World Costa Rica/Nicaragua; **NIGERIA:** PC World Africa; **NORWAY:** Computerworld Norge, Computerworld Privat, CW Rapport Klient/Tjener, CW Rapport Nettverk & Telecom, CW Rapport Offentlig Sektor, IDG's KURSGUIDE, Macworld Norge, Multimedia World, PC World Ekspress, PC World Nettverk, PC World Norge, PC World's Produktguide, Windows Spesial; **PAKISTAN:** Computerworld Pakistan, PC World Pakistan; **PANAMA:** GamePro, PC World Panama; **PARAGUAY:** PC World Paraguay; **P. R. OF CHINA:** China Computerworld, China Infoworld, Computer & Communication, Electronic Product World, Electronics Today, Game Camp, PC World China, Popular Computer Week, Software World, Telecom Product World; **PERU:** Computerworld Peru, GamePro, PC World Profesional Peru, PC World Peru; **POLAND:** Computerworld Poland, Computerworld Special Report, Macworld, Networld, PC World Komputer; **PHILIPPINES:** Computerworld Philippines, PC Digest, Publish in Asia; **PORTUGAL:** Cerebro/PC World, Correio Informático/Computerworld, Mac•In/PC•In Portugal; **PUERTO RICO:** PC World Puerto Rico; **ROMANIA:** Computerworld Romania, PC World Romania, Telecom Romania; **RUSSIA:** Computerworld Rossiya, Network World Russia, PC World Russia; **SINGAPORE:** Computerworld Singapore, PC World Singapore, Publish in Asia; **SLOVENIA:** MONITOR; **SOUTH AFRICA:** Computing S.A., Network World S.A., Software World; **SPAIN:** Computerworld España, COMUNICACIONES WORLD, Dealer World, Macworld España, PC World España; **SWEDEN:** CAP&Design, Computer Sweden, Corporate Computing, MacWorld, Maxi Data, MikroDatorn, Nätverk & Kommunikation, PC/Aktiv, PC World, Windows World; **SWITZERLAND:** Computerworld Schweiz, Macworld Schweiz, PCtip; **TAIWAN:** Computerworld Taiwan, Macworld Taiwan, PC World Taiwan, Windows World; **THAILAND:** Thai Computerworld, Publish in Asia; **TURKEY:** Computerworld Monitör, MACWORLD Turkiye, PC WORLD Turkiye; **UKRAINE:** Computerworld Kiev, Computers & Software Magazine, PC World Ukraine; **UNITED KINGDOM:** Acorn User, Amiga Action, Amiga Computing, Amiga, Appletalk, CD Powerplay, CD-ROM Now, Computing, Connexion, GamePro, Lotus Magazine, Macaction, Macworld, Open Computing, Parents and Computers, PC Home, PC Works, The WEB; **UNITED STATES:** Cable in the Classroom, CD Review, CIO Magazine, Computerworld, Computerworld Client/Server Journal, Digital Video Magazine, DOS World, Electronic InfoWorld, I-Way, Macworld, Maximize, MULTIMEDIA WORLD, Network World, PC World, PUBLISH, SWATPro Magazine, Video Event, WebMaster; **URUGUAY:** PC World Uruguay; **VENEZUELA:** Computerworld Venezuela, GamePro, PC World Venezuela; and **VIETNAM:** PC World Vietnam   10/17/95

Dedication

This book is dedicated to my wife, Leha, and daughters Ivy, Emily, and Ashley.

Credits

**Senior Vice President
and Group Publisher**
Brenda McLaughlin

Vice President and Publisher
Christopher J. Williams

Acquisitions Manager
Gregory Croy

Acquisitions Editor
Ellen L. Camm

Software Acquisitions Editor
Tracy Lehman Cramer

Marketing Manager
Melisa M. Duffy

Managing Editor
Andy Cummings

Editorial Assistant
Timothy Borek

Production Director
Beth Jenkins

Production Assistant
Jacalyn L. Pennywell

**Supervisor of
Project Coordination**
Cindy L. Phipps

Supervisor of Page Layout
Kathie S. Schnorr

Supervisor of Graphics and Design
Shelley Lea

Production Systems Specialist
Steve Peake

Reprint/Blueline Coordination
Tony Augsburger
Patricia R. Reynolds
Theresa Sánchez-Baker

Media/Archive Coordination
Leslie Popplewell
Melissa Stauffer
Michael Wilkey

Project Editor
Jim Grey

Copy Editor
Kathy Simpson

Technical Reviewer
Matt Hayden

Project Coordinator
Valery Bourke

Associate Project Coordinator
Debbie Sharpe

Graphics Coordination
Gina Scott
Carla Radzikinas
Angela F. Hunckler

Production Page Layout
Shawn Aylsworth
Brett Black
Cameron Booker
Linda M. Boyer
Elizabeth Cárdenas-Nelson
Kerri Cornell
Maridee V. Ennis
Todd Klemme
Jill Lyttle
Anna Rohrer
Kate Snell

Proofreaders
Peter J. Kuhns
Christine Meloy Beck
Carl Saff
Robert Springer

Indexer
Sharon Hilgenberg

Cover Design
Draper and Liew, Inc.

Acknowledgments

I am grateful to Greg Croy and Ellen Camm for getting me started on this book project. As the project editor, Jim Grey guided me through the manuscript-submission process and kept everything moving. I appreciate the guidance and support that all three of you gave me during this project.

I would like to thank Matt Hayden for reviewing the manuscript for technical accuracy. Matt also provided many useful suggestions for improving the book's content.

Thanks to everyone at IDG Books for transforming my raw manuscript into this well-edited and beautifully packaged book. In particular, thanks to Kathy Simpson for the thorough copy editing, and Tracy Cramer for taking care of the book's companion CD-ROM.

Of course, there would be no reason for this book if it were not for Linux. For this, we have Linus Torvalds and the legions of Linux developers around the world to thank.

Finally, and as always, I am most thankful to my wife, Leha, and my daughters, Ivy, Emily, and Ashley. It is their love and support that keeps me going.

(The Publisher would like to give special thanks to Patrick J. McGovern, without whom this book would not have been possible.)

Contents at a Glance

Introduction 1

Part I: Configuring Your Linux System 5
Chapter 1: Installing Linux 7
Chapter 2: Upgrading Linux 77

Part II: Running Linux 91
Chapter 3: An Overview of Linux 93
Chapter 4: Secrets of X under Linux 107
Chapter 5: Customizing Your Linux Startup 143
Chapter 6: Secrets of Linux Commands 181
Chapter 7: Secrets of DOS under Linux 231
Chapter 8: Scripting in Linux with Tcl/Tk 251

Part III: Exploiting Your Hardware in Linux 289
Chapter 9: Computers 291
Chapter 10: Video Cards and Monitors 315
Chapter 11: Disk Drives 335
Chapter 12: CD-ROM Drives and Sound Cards 363
Chapter 13: Keyboards and Pointing Devices 391
Chapter 14: Printers 407
Chapter 15: Modems 437
Chapter 16: Networks 469
Chapter 17: PC Cards 509

Part IV: Using Linux for Fun and Profit 521
Chapter 18: Dial-up Networking in Linux 523
Chapter 19: Setting Up a Linux Internet Host 557
Chapter 20: Running a World Wide Web Server on Linux 593
Chapter 21: Running a Business with Linux 631
Chapter 22: Developing Software in Linux 655
Chapter 23: X Programming in Linux 697
Chapter 24: Text Processing in Linux 755

Part V: The Best of Linux Applications 787
Chapter 25: Linux Applications Roundup 789
Appendix: Linux Resources 839

Index 843

Disc License Agreement and Installation Instructions 899

Reader Response Card ..... Back of Book

Table of Contents

Introduction 1
   Conventions Used in This Book 2
   Organization of the Book 3

Part I: Configuring Your Linux System 5

Chapter 1: Installing Linux 7
   Understanding the Linux Installation Process 9
   Preparing Your PC for Linux Installation 11
      Taking stock of your PC's components 11
         Processor 12
         Bus 12
         Memory 12
         Video card and monitor 13
         Hard drive 14
         Floppy drive 15
         Keyboard and mouse 16
         SCSI controller 16
         CD-ROM drive 17
         Sound card 18
         Network adapter 19
      Making a hardware checklist 20
      Partitioning your hard disk under MS-DOS 21
         Steps to repartition the hard disk 22
         Back up your hard disk 23
         Create a bootable floppy for MS-DOS 24
         Partition the hard disk with FDISK 25
            Check your hard disk's current partitioning information 26
            Delete the primary DOS partition 26
            Create a new DOS partition 27
            Make the DOS partition active 29
         Restore the MS-DOS partition 29
      Repartitioning with FIPS 29
      Creating the boot and root floppies 31
         Creating boot and root floppies under MS-DOS 32
            Creating the Linux boot floppy 33
            Creating the Linux root floppy 35

Booting Linux for Installation	36
Partitioning your hard disk under Linux	38
Disk names in Linux	38
Linux fdisk commands	39
Sample session with Linux fdisk	40
Special instructions for OS/2	42
Setting up a swap partition	43
Installing Linux from the Slackware CD-ROM	44
Adding the swap space	46
Selecting the target	46
Selecting the source	48
Selecting disk sets	50
Installing the disk sets	52
Disk set A	53
Disk set AP	54
Disk set D	55
Disk set E	56
Disk set F	57
Disk set K	57
Disk set N	57
Disk set Q	58
Disk set TCL	60
Disk set X	60
Disk set XAP	61
Disk set Y	62
Configuring some system components	63
Prepare the emergency boot disk	63
Set up the modem	64
Set up the mouse	64
Select screen font	64
Configure the floppy tape drive	65
Set the modem speed	65
Install LILO	65
Other configuration steps	68
Starting Linux for the First Time	69
Changing the password	69
Adding users	71
Changing the system name	72
Looking up the on-line documentation	72
Shutting down	75
Installing Linux in an MS-DOS Directory	75

Chapter 2: Upgrading Linux 77

Applying Kernel Patches 78
    Get the patches 78
    Apply the patches 81
    Rebuild the kernel 82
Upgrading from an Earlier Version of Slackware 87

Part II: Running Linux 91

Chapter 3: An Overview of Linux 93

Linux Versions 93
Linux as a UNIX Platform 94
X Window System in Linux 97
Linux Networking 98
    TCP/IP 99
    SLIP and PPP 100
    NFS 100
    UUCP 101
Linux System Administration 101
    System administration tasks 101
    Network administration tasks 102
DOS and Linux 103
Software Development in Linux 103
Linux as an Internet "On Ramp" 104

Chapter 4: Secrets of X under Linux 107

Understanding the X Window System 107
    Clients and servers 108
    Graphical user interfaces and X 109
    X on Linux 110
Setting up X on Linux 112
    Know your hardware before configuring XFree86 112
        Monitor 112
        Video card 113
        Mouse 114
    Use the xf86config program 114
    Check the XF86Config file 132
        Files section 133
        ServerFlags section 133
        Monitor section 133
        Device section 134
        Screen section 135
    Create an .xinitrc file 135

Running X 136
   Abort with Ctrl+Alt+Backspace 137
   Try different screen modes 138
   Quit from window manager 139
Getting Motif for Linux 140

Chapter 5: Customizing Your Linux Startup 143

Starting X Automatically at Login 143
Setting up a Graphical Login 145
   X Display Manager (xdm) 145
   The init process 146
      The /etc/inittab file 147
      The init command 149
   The .xsession file 150
   The initial set of applications 152
Customizing X 154
   Root-window appearance 154
      Screen color 155
      Screen-background image 156
      Cursor shape and color 158
   X resources 158
      Resource file 159
      Resource-naming convention 159
      Partial names for resources 160
      Location of resource file 162
      Common X resources 162
      Command-line options in X applications 163
         The -display option 163
         The -geometry option 163
         Options for window appearance 164
         Font specification 164
Customizing the fvwm Window Manager 165
   Overview of fvwm 165
   Input focus 168
   Desktop size 169
   Customizing menus 169
   Add-on modules in fvwm 172
   Emulating other window managers 173
Using and Customizing xterm 173
   Main features of xterm 173
   The main menu in xterm 174
   VT102 emulation 175
      Scrolling 175
      Cut-and-paste operations 176

VT102 menus 177
A termcap entry for xterm 178
Tektronix 4014 emulation 179

Chapter 6: Secrets of Linux Commands 181

The Bash Shell 181
    Command syntax 182
    Combination of commands 183
    I/O redirection 183
    Shell programs 184
    Environment variables 186
    Processes 187
    Background commands and virtual terminals 189
    Command completion in Bash 190
    Wildcards 190
    Command history 192
    Command editing 193
    Aliases 194
Linux Commands 195
    Linux directory layout 195
    Directory navigation 197
    Directory listing and permissions 199
    File manipulation 200
    Directory manipulation 201
    File finder 202
Shell Scripts in Bash 203
    A simple shell script 203
    Bash programming overview 204
        Variables 205
        Control structures 205
    Built-in functions in Bash 207
Perl as a Scripting Language 208
    Do I have Perl? 208
    Your first Perl script 210
    Perl overview 211
        Basic Perl syntax 211
        Variables 212
            Scalars 212
            Arrays 213
            Associative arrays 214
        Operators and expressions 215
        Regular expressions 216
        Flow-control statements 219
            Using if and unless 219
            Using while 220

    Using for and foreach 221
    Using goto 222
  Access to Linux 222
  File access 224
  Subroutines 225
  Built-in functions in Perl 226

Chapter 7: Secrets of DOS under Linux 231

  Mounting a DOS File System 231
    The mount command 232
    Mount DOS floppy disks 234
    The /etc/fstab file 235
  Using mtools 236
    Do I have mtools? 236
    The /etc/mtools file 237
    The mtools commands 238
    How to format a DOS floppy 239
  DOSEMU 240
    DOSEMU installation 241
    Read the manual 243
    Configure DOSEMU 243
      Edit /etc/dosemu.conf 244
      Initialize the hard disk image 244
      Start DOSEMU from the hard disk image 246
      List of users allowed to run DOSEMU 248

Chapter 8: Scripting in Linux with Tcl/Tk 251

  Introducing Tcl 252
    Your first Tcl script 252
    Tcl overview 253
    Basic Tcl syntax 254
      Substitutions 255
      Comments 256
      Braces and double quotation marks 257
  Variables 258
  Expressions 258
  Control-flow commands 259
    The if command 259
    The while command 260
    The for command 261
    The foreach command 261
    The switch command 262
  Tcl procedures 263
  Built-in Tcl commands 264

String manipulation in Tcl 267
Arrays 268
Environment variables 269
File operations in Tcl 269
Executing UNIX commands 271
Introducing Tk 272
"Hello, World!" in Tk 272
Tk widget basics 275
Naming widgets 277
Configuring widgets 278
Displaying widgets 279
The pack command 279
The place command 281
Binding actions to events 283
Keyboard events 285
Mouse events 286
Window events 287

Part III: Exploiting Your Hardware in Linux 289

Chapter 9: Computers 291

Basic Processor and Bus Types 291
Bus types 293
PCI-bus support in Linux 294
Some specific problems 295
System slowdown after memory is added 295
Cache not enabled for Cyrix 486DLC 296
Information from the /proc File System 296
The /proc/cpuinfo file 298
The /proc/pci file 299
Other information in the /proc file system 300
Linux on Laptops 301
Supported laptops 302
PCMCIA 302
Advanced Power Management 302
Sound on laptops 302
X on laptops 303
Information resources for specific laptops 307
Compaq laptops 308
NEC Versa laptops 309
Texas Instruments TravelMate 4000M 309
Installing Linux on a laptop without a CD-ROM drive 310
Installing Linux on a laptop with a CD-ROM drive 312

Chapter 10: Video Cards and Monitors 315

Video Cards and Monitors 315
    Raster-scan display 315
    Color display 317
    Color palette and resolution 317
    Video RAM 317
    Dot clock 317
    Importance of the video card and monitor to XFree86 318
X-Server Selection 319
XF86Config File Revisited 320
    Screen section 321
    Device section 322
    Monitor section 323
    Modeline computation 325
Common Video Cards 327
Accelerated Video Cards 328
    Diamond Viper and Orchid P9000 329
    ATI Mach8, Mach32, and Mach64 330
    S3 video cards 330
Commercial X Servers for XFree86 333

Chapter 11: Disk Drives 335

Disk Controller Types 335
Disk Drive Concepts 337
    Cylinders, heads, and sectors 337
    Master Boot Record (MBR) 338
    Partitions 338
    Linux device names for disks 338
Floppy Disks in Linux 339
Hard Disk Operations in Linux 339
    Altering disk partitions with FIPS 340
    Partitioning with fdisk 340
    Booting from the hard disk with LILO 341
        Installing LILO 342
        LILO's boot prompt 343
        Removing LILO 344
    Creating swap space 344
    Creating file systems 345
Specific Disk Problems in Linux 346
    Windows 95 and LILO 346
    Disks with more than 1,024 cylinders 346
    EIDE problems on PCI systems 348
    Error messages about inodes and blocks 349

SCSI Disk Controllers and Linux 349
    Cable and termination problems 350
    Adaptec AHA151x and Sound Blaster 16 SCSI 351
    Adaptec AHA154x, AMI FastDisk VLB, BusLogic, and DTC 329x 351
    Adaptec AHA174x 352
    Adaptec AHA274x, AHA284x, and AHA294x 352
    Allways IN2000 352
    EATA DPT Smartcache 353
    Future Domain 16x0 353
    NCR53c8xx SCSI Chip (PCI) 353
    Seagate ST0x and Future Domain TMC-8xx and TMC-9xx 354
    Pro Audio Spectrum PAS16 SCSI 355
    Trantor T128, T128F, and T228 355
    Ultrastor 14f (ISA), 24f (EISA), and 34f (VLB) 355
    Western Digital 7000 356
    Iomega Zip drive (SCSI) 356
    SCSI troubleshooting 357
        Problem booting with LILO 357
        SCSI device at all SCSI IDs 358
        SCSI device at all LUNs 358
        Sense errors on error-free SCSI device 359
        Networking kernel problems with SCSI device 359
        Device detected but not accessible 359
        SCSI lockup 360
        SCSI devices not found 360

Chapter 12: CD-ROM Drives and Sound Cards 363

CD-ROM Drives 364
    Supported CD-ROM drives 364
        ATAPI CD-ROM drives 365
        SCSI CD-ROM drives 365
        Proprietary CD-ROM drives 365
    CD-ROM troubleshooting 366
        CD-ROM drive not recognized after Linux installation 369
        Kernel configuration for specific CD-ROM drives 369
        IDE (ATAPI) CD-ROM troubles 370
        Boot-time parameters for CD-ROM drives 371
    CD-ROM device names 372
    CD-ROM drive use under Linux 373
        Mounting a CD-ROM 373
        Playing audio CDs in the CD-ROM drive 373
    Specific CD-ROM drive information 375
        The scd driver 375
        The IDE CD-ROM driver 376
        The sbpcd driver 376

The sonycd535 driver 377
The aztcd driver 378
The mcd driver 378
Sound Cards and Linux 379
Installing the sound driver 380
Configuring the sound driver 381
Learning sound-device names 383
Testing the sound card 384
Check sound-driver status 384
Try the sound card 385
Troubleshooting sound cards 386
Solving common sound-card problems 387
Works under DOS, but not under Linux 387
Can play sound, but not record 387
Pro Audio Spectrum PAS16 and Adaptec 1542 SCSI adapter 388
Sound Blaster AWE32 not supported 388

Chapter 13: Keyboards and Pointing Devices 391

Keyboards and Linux 391
Some keyboard terminology and notations 392
Keyboard layout 392
X keyboard terminology 393
Keyboard repeat delay and repeat rate 393
Keyboard map in Linux 394
Keyboard and XFree86 396
Specific keyboard questions in Linux 398
Turning on the Num Lock key 398
Gateway AnyKey keyboard 399
The Mouse and Linux 399
Mouse interfaces 399
Microsoft and Logitech busmouse interface 400
PS/2 Auxiliary Device interface 401
ATI-XL mouse 401
Mouse-device names 401
Mouse protocols 402
Mouse and XFree86 402
Protocol specification 403
Other mouse-configuration information 403
Mouse use in X 404
device not found error 405
device busy error 405
Mouse alternatives 406

Chapter 14: Printers 407

The PC, the Printer, and Linux 407
    Printer device name 407
    Spooling and print jobs 408
User's View of Printing in Linux 409
    Print with lpr 409
    Check print queue with lpq 410
    Cancel print job with lprm 410
    See printer status with lpc status 410
    Fancy printing 411
Behind-the-Scenes View of Printing 411
    Copying to printer: brute-force printing 412
    Spooling: a better way to print 412
    Spooling with a symbolic link 413
    Controlling printer with lpc 414
    Tracing a print request from lpr to printer 416
        lpr spools print jobs 416
        lpd sends print jobs to printer 417
    Knowing the spool directory 417
    Learning about /etc/printcap 418
        Basic structure of /etc/printcap 419
            Printer name 419
            Field types 420
        Fields in printcap entries 420
        Input-filter field 423
        Printer device 424
        Log file 424
        Suppress header and form feed 424
        Maximum size of print job 425
        Multiple printcap entries for one printer 425
Printer Setup and Configuration 425
    A printcap template 426
    Local-printer setup 428
    Remote-printer setup 428
Specific Printing Problems and Solutions 429
    Submit print job, but no output 429
    Problem printing on remote printer 430
    How to avoid the staircase effect 430
    How to filter a print job destined for a remote printer 431
    Graphics file gets truncated 432
    The lpr -i command does not indent output 432
    How to print PostScript files 432

Chapter 15: Modems 437

PC and Serial Ports 437
    UART 438
    Communications parameters 439
    Serial-port IRQs and I/O addresses 440
    Serial-device names in Linux 441
Modems 441
    RS-232C standard 442
        RS-232C cables 442
            Modem cable (DTE to DCE) 444
            Null modem cable (DTE to DTE) 445
            Cable choices 446
        Flow control 446
    Modem standards 446
    Modem commands (AT commands) 447
        The AT command line 448
        The A/ command 448
        Configuration commands 449
        Action commands 450
        The ATSr=n commands 451
        Online help 452
Linux and Modems 453
    Dialing out with a modem 453
        Hardware setup of modem 454
        Check Linux serial devices 454
        Dial out with a communications program 455
            Using seyon 455
            Using minicom 457
    Setting up Linux for dial-in 459
        Edit /etc/rc.d/rc.serial 459
        Update the uugetty configuration file 460
        Prepare the uugetty configuration file 461
        Start uugetty in /etc/inittab 463
        Test the dial-in setup 463
Terminals and Multiport Serial Boards 464
    Terminal on a serial port 464
    Multiport serial boards in Linux 465

Chapter 16: Networks 469

Networking Basics 469
    The OSI seven-layer model 470
    A simplified four-layer network model 471
    Network protocols 472
TCP/IP and the Internet 473
    RFCs 474

IP addresses 475
    Dotted-decimal addresses 475
    Address classes 475
    IP-address requests 477
    Next-generation IP (IPv6) 478
    Network mask 478
    Network address 479
    Subnets 479
TCP/IP routing 479
Domain Name System (DNS) 481
    Domain-name hierarchy 481
    Name servers 482
TCP/IP services 483
Ethernet and Linux 485
    Ethernet basics 485
    Address Resolution Protocol 487
    Ethernet cables 487
    Supported Ethernet cards 488
    Unsupported Ethernet cards 490
    Kernel support for Ethernet 490
    Ethernet autoprobing 491
    Network-device names 494
    Multiple Ethernet cards 494
TCP/IP Setup in Linux 495
    Configuring the kernel for TCP/IP 495
    Running netconfig 497
        Test the network 499
    TCP/IP configuration files 499
        The /etc/HOSTNAME file 500
        The /etc/hosts file 500
        The /etc/networks file 501
        The /etc/host.conf file 501
        The /etc/resolv.conf file 502
    Configuring networks at boot time 502
TCP/IP Diagnostics 503
    Checking the interfaces 503
    Checking the IP routing table 504
    Checking connectivity to a host 505
    Checking network status 505

Chapter 17: PC Cards 509

PC Card Basics 510
    PC Card physical specifications 510
    PC Card use 511
    PCMCIA standards 511
    PC Card terminology 511

PCMCIA Card Services for Linux 512
    Get the Card Services for Linux 512
    Unpack the Card Services software 515
    Build the Card Services software 516
    Supported cards 517
    Further reading 519

Part IV: Using Linux for Fun and Profit 521

Chapter 18: Dial-up Networking in Linux 523

Basics of Dial-up Networking 524
    Serial Line Internet Protocol (SLIP) 524
    Point-to-Point Protocol (PPP) 526
Making a SLIP Connection 527
    Verify SLIP support 528
    Obtain remote-system information 528
    Use dip to establish SLIP connection 529
        Running dip interactively 529
        Setting up a dip script 535
        Checking the SLIP connection 537
        Ending a SLIP connection 538
Connecting to a Remote Network as a PPP Client 539
    Check PPP support 539
    Gather information for PPP connection 539
    Use pppd with chat to make the PPP connection 540
        Using the chat program 540
            Timeouts 541
            Sub-expect sequences 541
            ABORT strings 541
            Escape sequences 542
        Using pppd with a chat script 543
            Typical pppd command line 543
            A PPP dial-up script 544
        Testing the PPP connection 545
        Ending the PPP connection 547
Routing Through the PPP Connection 548
    Learn to use the route command 549
    Enable IP forwarding in the kernel 550
    Make your system route to a remote gateway 550
    Make your system the gateway for your LAN 551
    Remote gateway must route to your LAN 551
Setting up a PPP Server 552

Chapter 19: Setting Up a Linux Internet Host 557

- What Is an Internet Host? 558
  - Exchanging e-mail 559
  - Participating in newsgroups 559
  - Locating and browsing information 560
  - Simple mail and news strategy 560
  - Mail and news software installation 560
- Setting Up and Using Mail 562
  - Mail software 563
  - sendmail configuration file 564
  - Mail-delivery test 565
  - Mail-delivery mechanism 567
- Setting Up and Using Newsgroups 568
  - How to read news 569
    - Set the NNTPSERVER environment variable 569
    - Create a .newsrc file 569
    - Run tin -r to read news 570
    - Alternative news reader: trn 572
  - Newsgroup hierarchy 577
  - Newsgroup subscription 579
  - How to post news 579
  - Did the article get out? 581
    - Post article with inews 582
    - Look for acknowledgments 583
- Using Secure Anonymous FTP 585
  - Try existing anonymous FTP service 586
  - Why worry about anonymous FTP? 587
  - Make anonymous FTP secure 588

Chapter 20: Running a World Wide Web Server on Linux 593

- What Is the World Wide Web? 594
  - Like a giant spider's web 594
  - Links and URLs 595
  - Hypertext Transfer Protocol (HTTP) 597
- Surfing the Net 601
  - Downloading the Web browsers 601
    - Netscape Navigator 601
    - NCSA Mosaic 604
  - A quick look at NCSA Mosaic 606
  - Take Netscape for a spin 608
    - Start Netscape 609
    - Netscape's user interface 609
- Setting Up a Web Server 611
  - Download the NCSA HTTPD software 611
  - Unpack the NCSA HTTPD software 614

Configure the NCSA HTTPD software	616
Edit httpd.conf	616
Edit srm.conf	619
Edit access.conf	622
Create the documents directory	625
Create the error-logs directory	625
Start the Web server	626
Try the Web server	626
More HTML resources	627

Chapter 21: Running a Business with Linux 631

This Chapter's Strategy	632
Role of Linux in a Business	632
What Linux offers	633
What Linux (apparently) lacks	634
Lack of personal-productivity applications	634
Lack of technical support	635
Specific Tasks for Linux	635
Workgroup server	636
Internet host	637
World Wide Web server	638
Using a Web server in a private LAN	639
Web-server configuration	639
Providing Web service	640
LAN Manager server	640
Installing Samba	641
Configuring Samba	642
Testing the Samba configuration file	644
Test with smbclient	645
LAN Manager client	647
Two steps to set up the printer	648
Add the printcap entry	648
Write a script to print with smbclient	648
Linux in Specific Businesses	649
Internet Service Provider	650
ISP equipment needs	650
Linux PC for ISP	651
UNIX software developer	652
Consultant	652

Chapter 22: Developing Software in Linux 655

Software Development Tools in Linux	656
info: the authoritative help on GNU tools	656

GNU C and C++ compilers 659
    Invoking GCC 660
    Compiling C++ programs 661
    Exploring GCC options 662
GNU make utility 665
    Makefile name 665
    The makefile 666
    Variables (or macros) 667
    Implicit rules 669
    A sample makefile 670
    How to run make 671
GNU debugger 673
    Preparing a program for debugging 673
    Running gdb 674
    Finding bugs with gdb 677
    Fixing bugs in gdb 679
Implications of GNU Licenses 680
    GNU General Public License 680
    GNU Library General Public License 681
Version Control 682
    Source-control tools in RCS 683
    Beginner's RCS 684
        Creating initial RCS files 684
        Using the archived files 685
        Identification keywords 686
    Other RCS commands 687
        Viewing the changes made so far 687
        Discarding changes made so far 687
        Viewing change history 688
        Examining identifier keywords 688
Linux Programming Topics 689
    Executable and Linking Format (ELF) 689
    Shared libraries in Linux applications 691
        Examining shared libraries that a program uses 691
        Creating a shared library 691
        Dynamically loading a shared library 694

Chapter 23: X Programming in Linux 697

Basic Motif Programming 698
    Step-by-step Motif programming 698
    A simple Motif program 699
    Makefile for a Motif program 700
    Widget resources 701
    Callback registration 703
    Event-handler registration 704

- Motif Widgets 705
  - Shell widgets 707
  - Primitive widgets 707
  - Manager widgets 710
- Xlib and Motif 712
  - An overview of Xlib 712
  - Xlib function overview 713
  - Common Xlib features 714
    - Header files 715
    - Naming conventions 715
    - Argument order in Xlib function calls 716
  - X server resources 716
    - Windows 717
    - Graphics contexts (GC) 717
    - Fonts 718
    - Cursors 718
    - Colormaps 718
    - Pixmaps 719
  - X event summary 719
  - Xlib programming topics 722
    - Setting cursor shape and color 722
    - Drawing graphics and text 724
      - Creating a GC 724
      - GC attributes 725
      - Drawing points 727
      - Drawing lines 728
      - Drawing and filling rectangles 729
      - Drawing polygons 730
      - Drawing arcs, circles, and ellipses 730
      - Drawing text 731
    - Using drawing functions in Motif 733
      - Display and window ID 733
      - GC creation in Motif 733
      - A Motif line-drawing program 734
    - Using color 740
      - Visuals 740
      - List of available visuals 741
      - X colormap 743
      - Colors from a colormap 743
      - Shared read-only color cells 744
      - Private read-write color cells 744
      - XColor structure 744
      - Read-only color cell allocation 745
      - Read-write color cell allocation 746
      - Free colormap 748

Displaying an image 748
　　Creating a pixmap 749
　　Drawing into a pixmap 750
　　Displaying a pixmap 750
　　Freeing pixmaps 750
　　Using bitmaps 751

Chapter 24: Text Processing in Linux 755

Text Editing with ed and vi 756
　Using ed 756
　　Invoking ed 756
　　Learning ed 757
　　A sample session with ed 757
　　Summary of ed commands 759
　Using vi 761
　　Setting the terminal type 761
　　Starting vi 762
　　Learning vi concepts 763
　　A sample session with vi 764
　　The vi command summary 765
Working with GNU Emacs 768
　Starting GNU Emacs 769
　Learning GNU Emacs 770
　Typing GNU Emacs commands 771
　Getting help 771
　Reading a file 774
　Moving around the buffer 774
　Inserting and deleting text 775
　Searching and replacing 776
　Copying and moving 777
　Saving changes 778
　Running a shell in GNU Emacs 779
Writing Man Pages with groff 779
　Try an existing man page 780
　Look at a man-page source 781
　Writing a sample man page 783
　Testing and installing the man page 784

Part V: The Best of Linux Applications 787

Chapter 25: Linux Applications Roundup 789

Editors 790
　GNU Emacs 790
　JED 791

  Joe 791
  Jove 791
  Vim 791
 Utilities 791
  DOSEMU 792
  GNU bc 792
  gzip 794
  ispell 795
  Midnight Commander 797
  patch 798
  sc 799
  Workbone 804
  Workman 804
  xcmap 804
  xfilemanager 805
  xfm 810
  xspread 815
 Graphics and Images 819
  XV 819
  XPaint 822
  Xfractint 824
  xfig 826
  Gnuplot 827
  Ghostscript 831
  Ghostview 835

Appendix: Linux Resources 839
 Web Pages 839
 Newsgroups 839
 Linux FTP Archive Sites 840
 Magazine 842

Index 843

Disc License Agreement and Installation Instructions 899

Reader Response Card .... Back of Book

Introduction

Over the past two years, a little-known UNIX clone called Linux has emerged to capture the hearts and minds of millions of UNIX devotees. Linux is a UNIX clone for Intel 80x86 systems that started with the work of Linus Torvalds of Finland. Over the course of a couple of years, Linux has grown into a full-fledged 32-bit operating system with features that rival those of commercial 80x86 UNIX systems, such as Solaris and SCO UNIX. To top it off, Linux — with all its source code — is available free of cost to anyone. All one has to do is download it from an Internet site or get it on a CD-ROM, for a nominal fee, from one of the many Linux CD-ROM vendors.

Linux certainly is an exception to the rule that "you get what you pay for." Even though Linux is free, it is no slouch when it comes to performance, features, and reliability. The robustness of Linux has to do with the way that it was developed. Many developers around the world collaborated over the Internet to add features. Incremental versions are continually being downloaded by users and tested in a variety of system configurations. Linux revisions go through much more rigorous beta testing than any commercial software does.

Since the release of Linux 1.0 on March 14, 1994, the number of Linux users around the world has grown exponentially. The estimated installed base is anywhere from 1 million to more than 5 million users worldwide.

Unlike many freely available software programs, Linux comes with extensive online information on topics such as installing and configuring the operating system for a wide variety of PCs and peripherals. A small group of hard-core Linux users are expert enough to productively use Linux with the online documentation alone. A much larger number of users, however, move to Linux with some specific purpose in mind (such as setting up a World Wide Web server or learning X programming). Also, a large number of Linux users use their system at home. For these new users, the documentation is not easy to use and typically does not cover the specific uses they have in mind.

Because of the growing popularity of Linux, several Linux books already are on the market. These books, however, are mostly reprints of the online documentation, focusing on the installation and configuration of Linux. Some books focus on "using Linux," but this coverage usually is a standard UNIX tutorial.

If you are beginning to use Linux, what you need is a practical guide that not only gets you going with the installation and setup of Linux, but also shows you how to use Linux for a specific task, such as an Internet host or a software development platform.

Linux SECRETS is a technical guide that is designed to address these needs. The book includes the latest version of the popular Slackware distribution of Linux on a CD-ROM, along with the standard installation and setup information. This book provides detailed technical information on installing and customizing Linux, including coverage of various types of computers and peripherals.

Then *Linux SECRETS* goes a step beyond the existing books and shows you how to use Linux as a solution to specific problems. Additionally, *Linux SECRETS* provides information on freely available software that runs under Linux and bundles a huge amount of this software — such as news and mail, graphics, and text utilities — on the book's companion CD-ROM.

The unique aspects of *Linux SECRETS* are the tips, techniques, shortcuts, and little-known facts about using Linux in various real-world tasks that range from simply learning UNIX to setting up a WWW server for your business.

By reading *Linux SECRETS*, you get the following benefits:

- Learn how to install and set up Linux
- Learn how to use various peripherals (video cards, hard disks, and network cards) in Linux
- Learn about dial-up networking (with SLIP and PPP) under Linux
- Get tips, techniques, and shortcuts for specific uses of Linux, such as:
    - Learn how to use Linux as an Internet host (WWW server and anonymous FTP server)
    - Understand how Linux and DOS can coexist
    - Learn UNIX on Linux
    - Learn C and C++ programming on Linux
    - Learn Motif programming on Linux
- Receive many Linux tools and utilities
- Learn about Linux resources that can serve as continuing sources of information in the ever-changing world of Linux

Conventions Used in This Book

Linux SECRETS uses a simple notational style. All listings, filenames, function names, variable names, and keywords are typeset in a `monospace font` for ease of reading. The first occurrences of new terms and concepts are in *italic*. Text you are directed to type is in **boldface**.

Each chapter starts with a short list of all the neat things that you learn in that chapter. The summary at the end of the chapter tells you a bit more about what the chapter covered.

Following the time-honored tradition of the IDG Books *SECRETS* series, I use icons to help you pinpoint useful information quickly. Following is what I had in mind for the icons:

The Note icon marks a general interesting fact — something that I thought you'd like to know.

The Tip icon marks things that you can do to make your job simpler — hints that you can try.

The Caution icon highlights potential pitfalls. With this icon, I'm telling you: Watch out! This could hurt your system!

The Cross Reference icon points out paragraphs that lead you to other chapters in the book for a deeper discussion of a topic.

The Secret icon marks facts that are not well-documented but important to know. It's not that no one knows this fact — it's just hard to find, and knowing this fact usually clears up many other questions that you may have.

The Wizard icon marks technical information that will be of interest to an advanced user.

Sidebars

This is a sidebar. I use sidebars throughout the book to highlight interesting, but not critical information. Sidebars explain concepts you may not have encountered before or give a little insight on a related topic. If you're in a hurry, you can safely skip the sidebars. On the other hand, if you find yourself flipping through the book looking for interesting information, you'll do well to search out the sidebars.

Organization of the Book

Linux SECRETS has 25 chapters, organized into five parts and an appendix:

Part I: **Configuring Your Linux System** includes two chapters that essentially guide the reader through the steps of installing Linux from the CD-ROM that is bundled with the book. The second chapter in this part describes how to apply patches and reconfigure the Linux kernel as new revisions become available.

Part II: **Running Linux** focuses on how to run Linux after it has been installed. Part II includes six chapters that explain how to set up the graphical interface with X, how to use Linux commands (which essentially are UNIX commands), how to access DOS from Linux, and how to use the Tcl/Tk scripting language for quick-and-dirty programming.

Part III: **Exploiting Your Hardware in Linux** provides all the information that a user needs to use various types of hardware in Linux. The hardware descriptions cover everything from the computer (processor, memory, and bus) to serial ports and PCMCIA cards.

Part IV: **Using Linux for Fun and Profit** has seven chapters that show how to use Linux for specific purposes, such as setting up an Internet host, running a World Wide Web server, developing software, and preparing documents.

Part V: **The Best of Linux Applications** has a single chapter that describes several popular Linux applications that are also on the book's companion CD-ROM.

Appendix A: **Linux Resources** lists resources on the Internet where the user can obtain the latest information about Linux.

If you are a new user, you should start in Part I with the installation of Linux from the CD-ROM. If you have already installed Linux, you might begin with Chapter 3, learning how to make the most of Linux in everyday use. If you have specific hardware questions, you should go directly to a relevant chapter in Part III. Part IV is meant to describe specific Linux uses. You should read the relevant chapters in Part IV to get going with specific tasks.

It's time to get started on your Linux adventure. Take out the companion CD-ROM, turn to Chapter 1, and let the fun begin. Before you know it, you'll be a Linux expert!

I hope you enjoy reading this book as much as I enjoyed writing it!

Part I
Configuring Your Linux System

Chapter 1: Installing Linux

Chapter 2: Upgrading Linux

Chapter 1
Installing Linux

In This Chapter

- Looking at the complete installation process for the Slackware Professional Linux CD-ROM that accompanies this book
- Looking at what you need to know about your PC's hardware before installing Linux
- Performing initial installation steps under Microsoft Windows or MS-DOS
- Booting Linux and installing the Slackware disk sets
- Running Linux for the first time
- Setting up Linux in an MS-DOS directory

Starting with the Intel 80386 processor, continuing with the 80486, and now with the Pentium and Pentium Pro, the computing power of PC processors continues to grow steadily. Processor clock speeds have increased from the 16 MHz 80386 of a few years ago to the 166 MHz Pentium of today. The IBM PC-AT-based Industry Standard Architecture (ISA) bus is being supplanted by the high-performance Peripheral Component Interconnect (PCI) bus. The hardware performance of a modern run-of-the-mill PC clearly is on par with that of workstations such as those from Hewlett-Packard and Sun.

When it comes to operating systems, however, PCs have not kept up with workstations. Many PCs still run 16-bit operating systems, such as MS-DOS or Windows 3.1, that do not fully exploit the 32-bit processing capabilities of the PC's processors. Workstations, on the other hand, run UNIX — a multitasking and multiuser operating system. (That means that the operating system can run several programs simultaneously and support more than one user at a time.) Typically, workstations also use the X Window System for a graphical user interface.

> **Differences between 16-bit and 32-bit operating systems**
>
> Intel 80386, 80486, and Pentium processors have 32-bit registers and can process data items 32 bits at a time. But 16-bit operating systems, such as MS-DOS and Windows 3.1, use only 16 low-order bits of the 32-bit registers (see figure) and work with data items in 16-bit chunks.
>
>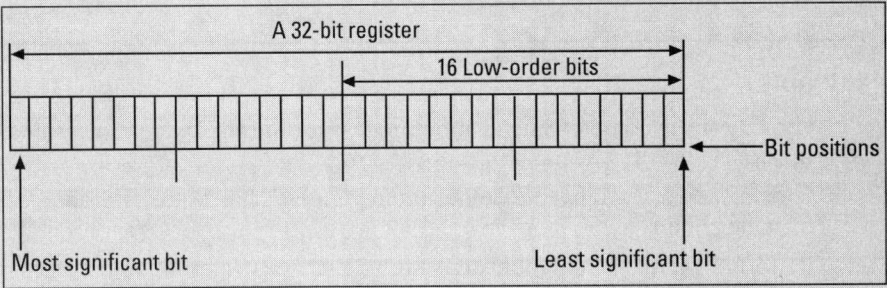
>
> Thirty-two-bit operating systems, such as Linux and Windows NT, exploit the 32-bit registers and process data 32 bits at a time. You need a 32-bit operating system such as Linux to exploit the capabilities of your PC's 32-bit processor.

UNIX has been available for PCs for quite some time, but you had to pay nearly as much for a fully configured commercial PC UNIX operating system as you did for the PC itself. This situation changed, however, when Linus Torvalds of the University of Helsinki in Finland decided to build a UNIX-like operating system for the PC. What started as a simple task-switching example, with two processes that printed AAAA... and BBBB... on a dumb terminal, has grown into a full-fledged multitasking and multiuser operating system that rivals the commercially available UNIX for Intel 80x86 systems. Many programmers around the world contributed code and collaborated to bring Linux to its current state. With the release of version 1.0 in March 1994, Linux became an operating system of choice for UNIX enthusiasts, as well as for people who are looking for a low-cost UNIX platform for a specific use such as developing software or running an Internet host.

After you overcome your initial fear of the unknown and install Linux, you will see how you can use Linux to turn your PC into a UNIX workstation. The best part is that you can get Linux free — just download it from one of several Internet sites. The best way for beginners and experts to get started, however, is to buy a book (such as this one) that comes with a Linux CD-ROM. This book is your complete guide to Linux. The book starts with installation and moves on to specific tasks (such as developing software or connecting to the Internet) that you may want to perform with your Linux PC.

Note

Installation can be one of the tricky steps in Linux, especially if you have a no-name IBM-compatible PC. You need some specific information about hardware, such as disk controller, video card, and CD-ROM drive. Linux controls the hardware through drivers, so you need to make sure that the current release of Linux includes drivers for your hardware. Because Linux is free, you cannot really demand — or expect — support for some specific hardware. Linux is, however, continually growing through collaboration among programmers throughout the world. If your hardware is popular enough, there's a good chance that someone has developed a driver for it. In any case, the Slackware Linux on the companion CD-ROM already supports such a wide variety of hardware that all your PC's peripherals probably are supported.

To get you started on your Linux experience, this chapter shows you how to install Linux from the companion CD-ROM. The chapter starts with an overview of the entire installation process; then it guides you step by step through the installation process.

Cross Reference

If you have installed Linux already, Chapter 2 shows you how to configure and upgrade Linux to take advantage of fixes or enhancements for the Linux operating system.

Understanding the Linux Installation Process

Before starting a big job, I always find it helpful to visualize the entire sequence of tasks that I must perform. The process is similar to studying a map before you drive to a place where you have never been. Linux installation can be a big job, especially if you run into snags. This section shows you the road map for the installation process. After reading this section, you should be mentally prepared to install Linux.

The exact steps for installing Linux may depend on the Linux *distribution* — the exact packaging of the operating system — that you are using. This book shows you the installation steps for the companion Slackware CD-ROM. You can use the following general procedure to completely install and configure Linux and the X Window System, which is the graphical user interface for Linux. Follow these steps:

1. Gather information about your PC's hardware before you install Linux. Linux accesses and uses various PC peripherals through software components called *drivers*. You have to make sure that the version of Linux that you are about to install has the necessary drivers for your system's hardware configuration. Conversely, if you do not have a system yet, look at the list of hardware supported by Linux, and make sure that you buy a PC with components that Linux supports.

2. You may have to perform a process known as *partitioning* to allocate parts of your hard disk for use by Linux. If you are lucky enough to have a spare hard disk, you may decide to keep MS-DOS and Windows on the first hard disk and install Linux on the second hard disk. If you have only one hard

disk, however, you may want to partition that disk into several parts. Use a part for DOS and Windows, and leave the rest for Linux. If you do not want to mess up your existing DOS and Windows setup, you can opt to install Linux in an MS-DOS directory. (As you will see, Linux is much more flexible than any commercial UNIX for Intel 80x86 systems. The ability to install Linux in an MS-DOS directory is just one of its flexibilities.)

3. Under DOS or Windows, create two floppy disks: the *Linux boot floppy* (or just *boot floppy*) and the *root floppy*. The boot floppy is used to boot your PC and start an initial version of the Linux operating system. The root floppy is the initial disk that contains some useful Linux files that you need to get the system ready for Linux. Basically, the root floppy provides the initial file system that Linux needs until you get the hard disk formatted and ready for Linux. You must select a boot floppy that supports the CD-ROM drive on your PC, because you are going to install Linux from the CD-ROM that accompanies this book.

4. Boot with the Linux boot floppy. When Linux asks for it, insert the root floppy. This procedure gives you a minimal Linux system that you can use to further prepare the system and install the rest of the files from the companion CD-ROM.

5. Prepare the hard disk partitions where you plan to install Linux. Typically, you need at least two partitions: one for the Linux files and the other for use as the *swap partition*, which is a form of virtual memory.

6. Type **setup** to start the Slackware Linux setup program. From this setup program, you format the hard disk partitions, indicate where Slackware Linux is located (in the CD-ROM drive), and specify where to install Linux (usually, on a hard disk partition). You also select various *disk sets* (so called because Linux used to be distributed on sets of floppy disks). Each disk set represents a part of Linux, from the base operating system to components such as the emacs editor, programming tools, the Tcl/Tk scripting language, and the X Window System. As the setup program installs the disk sets, it may ask you to confirm your choices or make further selections within a disk set.

7. After the disk sets are installed, the setup program takes you through a configuration process. You get a chance to create a new boot floppy in this step. You also configure your modem and mouse.

8. Use the boot floppy (created during installation) to reboot your PC. You will be able to log in with the user name root, with no password.

Caution

You must add a password for the root user, because root happens to be the most powerful user. The root user can perform any task, including dangerous ones such as deleting all the files from the system (see the "Changing Password" section later in this chapter).

9. Run the xf86config program to configure XFree86, the X Window System server for Linux.

10. If you find that Linux does not work properly with one or more of your system components (such as the CD-ROM drive or sound card), you may have to reconfigure the Linux operating system to add support for those system components.

The following sections guide you through the basic installation steps and the initial booting of Linux.

Your PC must have a CD-ROM drive — one that is supported by Linux — to install Linux from this book's companion CD-ROM.

Preparing Your PC for Linux Installation

Before you install Linux, you should prepare your PC for the installation. You can be in either of two situations:

- You already have a PC that runs one of the popular PC operating systems, such as MS-DOS, Microsoft Windows 3.1, Windows 95, Windows NT, or OS/2 Warp.
- You are about to buy a PC, and you plan to run Linux on that PC at least some of the time.

If you are about to purchase a PC, you are lucky because you can get a PC configured with peripherals that Linux supports. To pick a Linux-compatible configuration, all you have to do is consult the current list of hardware that Linux supports and then select a PC that includes only supported hardware components. You may have to explicitly ask the vendor for detailed information about peripherals such as the video card, CD-ROM drive, and networking card to ensure that you can use the peripherals under Linux. Selecting a PC with Linux-supported hardware greatly minimizes the potential for problems installing Linux. The next few sections list hardware that Linux supports.

If you want to install Linux on an existing PC, verify that the latest Linux distribution supports all the hardware on your PC. In other words, you have to take an inventory of your PC's hardware components and determine whether Linux currently supports any of them.

Taking stock of your PC's components

Like many other operating systems, Linux supports various types of hardware through device drivers. For each type of peripheral device, such as a networking card or a CD-ROM drive, Linux needs a driver. In fact, each kind of peripheral needs a separate driver. Because Linux is available free (or relatively inexpensively), and because many programmers scattered throughout the world cooperate to develop Linux, you cannot demand support for a specific kind of hardware. Your best bet is to hope that someone who can write a Linux driver has the same hardware that you do. In all likelihood, that person will write a driver, which eventually will find its way into a version of Linux; then you can use that hardware under Linux.

Cross Reference

Check the list of hardware that the version of Linux on the companion CD-ROM supports (I'll summarize this list in the next few sections). You can install and run Linux even if no Linux drivers are available for certain peripherals. At minimum, however, to install Linux from the companion CD-ROM, you must have a Linux-compatible processor, bus type, hard disk, keyboard, and CD-ROM drive. If you want to run the X Window System, you also must ensure that XFree86 (the X server for Linux) supports the mouse, the video card, and the monitor. (Chapter 4 tells you all about X.)

The following sections provide an overview of the hardware that the version of Linux on the companion CD-ROM supports.

Cross Reference

Chapters 9 through 17 cover all PC hardware in detail. Turn to those chapters for detailed information on whether Linux supports your system's unique hardware configuration. In chapters 9 through 17, you also can find information on how to get the most from your PC's hardware under Linux.

Processor

The *processor* is the central processing unit (CPU) — the integrated circuit chip that performs all the processing in the PC. At minimum, you need an Intel 80386 processor to run Linux. Any Intel 80386-, 80486-, and Pentium-compatible processor can run the Linux operating system. (The Linux code is not optimized for the Pentium processor, but the code runs fine on the Pentium, because the Pentium can run code meant for the 80386 or 80486.)

Note

You cannot run Linux on an 80286 PC; the 80286 is not a 32-bit processor.

Bus

The *bus* is the standard electrical connection between the processor and its peripherals. Several types of PC buses exist. The most popular bus is the Industry Standard Architecture (ISA) bus, formerly called the AT bus because IBM introduced it in the IBM PC-AT computer in 1984. Other buses include Extended Industry Standard Architecture (EISA); Video Local Bus (VLB); Micro Channel Architecture (MCA); and, most recently, Peripheral Component Interconnect (PCI).

Note

Linux supports all common PC buses except the MCA bus.

Memory

Commonly referred to as *random-access memory* or *RAM*, memory is not a factor in compatibility. You need at least 8MB of RAM to get good performance, however. Although you may be able to install and run Linux on a PC that has 4MB RAM, you cannot run the X Window System on that PC. The X Window System manages the graphical interface through an *X server*, which is a large program that needs a great deal of memory to run efficiently.

Secret

If you are buying a new PC, you should seriously consider getting 16MB of RAM. If you have an old PC with less than 8MB of RAM, you may want to add some more memory to bring the total up to 8MB. The more physical memory a system has, the more efficiently it runs multiple programs, because the programs can all fit in memory. Although Linux can use a part of the hard disk as virtual memory, such disk-based memory is much slower than physical memory. The amount of physical memory required depends on the size of the Linux operating system and any other software that you have to run all the time, such as the X Window System. Although Linux alone runs on 4MB of memory, you need at least 8MB to run X. Add to this any applications (such as editor or compiler) that you might run, and you'll soon see why you need 16MB of RAM for adequate performance.

Video card and monitor

Most PCs have what is known as Super VGA (Video Graphics Array) video cards. Linux works fine with all video cards in text mode. But when it comes to XFree86 — the Linux version of the X Window System — the story is quite different. If XFree86 does not support your video card explicitly, you have to work hard to get XFree86 configured for your video card.

The kind of monitor that you use is not particularly critical, but it must be capable of displaying at the screen resolutions that the video card uses, which are expressed in terms of the number of picture elements, or *pixels*, horizontally and vertically (such as 1024 by 768).

Generally, XFree86's support for a video card depends on the *video chipset* — the integrated circuit that controls the monitor and causes the monitor to display output. A video-card manufacturer, however, may use a video chipset in a nonstandard manner. In such a case, you need a special version of XFree86 to support that video card. To help you select a video card, following is a list of video cards that XFree86 version 3.1.2 (the version included on the companion CD-ROM) supports:

- ATI Mach8, ATI Mach32, and ATI Mach64
- ATI VGA Wonder series
- Compaq AVGA
- Diamond Viper VLB and Viper PCI (notice that these video cards were not supported until XFree86 3.1.1)
- Enhanced Graphics Adapter (EGA)
- Genoa GVGA
- Hercules monochrome
- Hyundai HGC-1280 monochrome
- IBM 8514/A, XGA, and XGA-II
- Orchid P9000
- Sigma LaserView PLUS monochrome
- Video 7 (also known as Headland Technologies HT216-32)

Part I: Configuring Your Linux System

- Video cards based on the Advance Logic AL2101, 2228, 2301, 2302, 2308, and 2401 chipsets
- Video cards based on the Chips & Technologies 65520, 65530, 65540, and 65545 chipsets
- Video cards based on the Cirrus Logic 5420, 542x, 5430, 5434, 62x5, 6420, and 6440 chipsets (x is any digit)
- Video cards based on the IIT AGX-010, 014, 015, and 016 chipsets
- Video cards based on the MX68000 and MX68010 chipsets
- Video cards based on the NCR 77C22, 77C22E, and 77C22E+ chipsets
- Video cards based on the OAK OTI-037, OTI-067, OTI-077, and OTI-087 chipsets
- Video cards based on the Cirrus 542x chipsets (x is any digit)

Cross Reference

- Video cards based on the S3 911, 924, 801, 805, 928, 864, 964, Trio32, and Trio64 chipsets (see Chapter 4 for a list of supported cards)
- Video cards based on the Weitek P9000 chipset
- Video cards based on the Trident TVGA8800, TVGA8900, and TVGA9000 chipsets
- Video cards based on the Tseng ET3000, ET4000, W32, W32i, and W32p chipsets
- Video cards based on the Western Digital WD90C31 and WD90C33 chipsets
- Video Graphics Array (VGA)
- Western Digital Paradise PVGA1 (uses WD90C00, WD90C10, WD90C11, WD90C24, WD90C30, WD90C31, and WD90C33 chipsets)

For the basic Linux installation, you do not have to worry about the video card. Detailed information about the video card becomes important when you want to configure XFree86.

Cross Reference

Chapter 4 tells you how to configure XFree86.

Hard drive

Linux supports any hard drive that your PC's Basic Input and Output System (BIOS) supports. In many older 386 and 486 PCs, you had to use a separate driver to access large hard drives — the system BIOS could not handle these drives. You can't install Linux on such systems. In short, Linux supports your hard drive only if the system BIOS supports the hard drive without any additional drivers.

For hard drives connected to your PC through a SCSI controller card, Linux must have a driver that enables the SCSI controller to access and use the hard drive. A summary of supported SCSI controllers appears in the "SCSI Controllers" section of this chapter.

Tip

The only remaining decision about the hard drive is its capacity. If you have an old PC, you may have a relatively low-capacity hard drive — perhaps as low as 100MB. Although you can install a workable Linux and X Window System within 100MB, doing so does not leave much room for MS-DOS or Windows, should you want to keep them. Therefore, if your old PC has an IDE interface and one small hard disk (100MB or smaller), you may want to add a second hard drive because most IDE controllers can support two hard drives. If you have a SCSI card, you can connect up to seven SCSI devices to it.

If you are buying a new PC, remember that a complete Linux installation (with all the Slackware disk sets) takes nearly 275MB of disk space. Get a large enough hard drive — at least 500MB. After all, even after you install all of Linux, you'll need room for your work. Also, you may want to reserve part of the disk for MS-DOS and Windows so that you have the option of booting either DOS or Linux.

Tip

If you can afford it, consider buying a second hard drive for Linux. A second drive makes the installation process considerably less risky, because you do not have to partition the drive on which MS-DOS and Windows may be installed.

Floppy drive

Linux drivers also use the PC BIOS to access the floppy drive. Therefore, your floppy drive is compatible with Linux. You do, however, have to boot Linux from a floppy during the installation. For this purpose, you need a high-density 5.25-inch (1.2MB-capacity) or 3.5-inch (1.44MB-capacity) floppy drive.

The PC BIOS

All IBM-compatible PCs come with a Basic Input and Output System (BIOS) built into read-only memory (ROM). The BIOS contains a set of input/output (I/O) functions for accessing the PC's peripheral devices, such as the keyboard, display, printer, serial port, and floppy or hard drive. Because the BIOS is present in all PCs, Linux drivers use the BIOS to access peripheral devices.

The BIOS is essentially software stored on ROM. As such, PC vendors revise and update the BIOS just like any software. The BIOS is typically revised to handle new devices such as new hard drives with much larger capacity than originally envisioned, or even new bus types such as PCI. BIOS revisions may also improve performance by doing various tasks more efficiently.

Because the BIOS is a crucial element in getting Linux to work with a PC's peripherals, you might consider a BIOS upgrade to get Linux going on an older 386 or 486 PC. The upgrade process involves replacing a pair of chips with new ones — you'll have to contact your PC's manufacturer to get new revisions of the BIOS chips compatible with your PC.

Keyboard and mouse

Linux supports any keyboard that already works with your PC. The mouse, however, needs explicit support in Linux. You need a mouse if you want to configure and run XFree86, the X Window System for Linux.

PCs have two kinds of mice: *serial mice* and *bus mice*. You connect a serial mouse to the serial port of the PC, but you connect a bus mouse directly to the PC bus.

Linux supports the following popular serial and bus mice:

- Microsoft serial mouse
- Mouse Systems serial mouse
- Logitech serial mouse
- Logitech bus mouse
- PS/2 bus mouse
- Microsoft bus mouse
- ATI XL Inport bus mouse
- QuickPort (C&T 82C710) mouse (used on TI Travelmate and Toshiba laptop PCs)

SCSI controller

The Small Computer System Interface, commonly called SCSI (and pronounced *scuzzy*), is a standard way of connecting many types of peripheral devices to a computer. You'll find SCSI in many kinds of computers, from high-end UNIX workstations to PCs. To use a SCSI device on your PC, you need a SCSI controller card that plugs into one of the connector slots on your PC's bus.

Typically, you connect hard drives and CD-ROM drives through a *SCSI controller*. A single controller allows you to connect up to seven SCSI devices to your PC. If you want to access and use a SCSI device under Linux, you have to make sure that Linux supports your SCSI controller card.

The Linux release on the companion CD-ROM already supports the following popular SCSI controllers:

- Adaptec AHA-1510 and AHA-152x (based on AIC-6260 or AIC-6360 chips; x is any digit) controllers for the ISA bus
- Adaptec AHA-154x (x is any digit) controllers for the ISA bus
- Adaptec AHA-174x (x is any digit) controllers for the EISA (Extended Industry Standard Architecture) bus
- Adaptec AHA-274x controller for the EISA bus and AHA-284x controller for the VLB (Vesa Local Bus); both cards use AIC-7770 chips

- Adaptec AVA-1505 and AVA-1515 controllers for the ISA bus (supported by the Adaptec 152*x* driver in Linux)
- Always IN2000
- AMI Fast Disk VLB/EISA (supported by the BusLogic driver in Linux)
- BusLogic SCSI controllers (all models)
- DPT Smartcache controllers for ISA, EISA, and PCI buses, including models PM2011, PM2012, PM2021, PM2022, PM2024, PM2122, PM2124, PM2322, PM3021, PM3222, and PM3224
- DTC 329*x* controller for the EISA bus (supported by the Adaptec 154*x* driver in Linux)
- Future Domain TMC-16*x*0 and TMC-3260 (PCI) SCSI controllers
- Future Domain TMC-8*xx* and TMC-950
- Pro Audio Spectrum 16 SCSI controller for ISA bus
- Qlogic FAS408 controller
- SCSI controllers based on the NCR 53c7*x*0 and 53c8*x*0 (for PCI bus) chipsets
- Seagate ST-01 and ST-02 controllers for ISA bus
- Sound Blaster 16 SCSI controller for ISA bus (supported by the Adaptec 152*x* driver in Linux)
- Trantor T128, T128F, and T228 controllers for ISA bus
- UltraStor 14F (for ISA bus), UltraStor 24F (for EISA bus), and UltraStor 34F (for VLB bus)
- Western Digital WD7000 SCSI controllers

This list keeps growing as Linux developers add support for new SCSI controllers. For a more complete list, check the on-line documentation included on the CD-ROM. The "Looking up the on-line documentation" section at the end of this chapter shows you how to find and use the on-line documentation.

CD-ROM drive

CD-ROM (Compact Disc Read-Only Memory) drives are popular because each CD-ROM can hold up to 650MB of data. This is a huge amount of storage, compared with a floppy disk or even a hard disk. CD-ROMs are reliable and inexpensive to manufacture. Vendors can use a CD-ROM to distribute a large amount of information at a reasonable cost.

This book provides Linux on a CD-ROM, so you need a CD-ROM drive to install the software. Most new PCs come with a CD-ROM drive. If the basic configuration does not include a CD-ROM drive, you can add one at a fraction of the cost of your PC — usually around two hundred U.S. dollars. If you have an older PC that doesn't have a CD-ROM drive, you need to buy one to install Linux from this book's companion CD-ROM.

On PCs, CD-ROM drives became popular over the past few years as users went for the multimedia experience. As you may know, in the context of the PC, *multimedia* refers to the use of multiple media — sound, images, animation, and video — in software applications. The sound card and CD-ROM drive were the two common elements of all multimedia software.

The combination of sound cards and CD-ROM drives has been so popular that many sound cards (such as Creative Labs' Sound Blaster Pro) can be purchased with a CD-ROM drive. You connect the CD-ROM drive with a cable to the sound card, which includes the appropriate hardware connector. Linux supports CD-ROM drives (such as the Sound Blaster Pro CD) that connect to a sound card.

Most other CD-ROM drives are SCSI devices that connect to a SCSI controller card. Linux supports a SCSI CD-ROM drive as long as it has a driver for the SCSI controller.

Following are some of the common CD-ROM drives that Linux supports:

- Any Enhanced Integrated Drive Electronics (EIDE) CD-ROM drive (also referred to as AT Attachment Packet Interface, or ATAPI drives)
- Any SCSI CD-ROM drive that can transfer data in blocks of 512 or 2,048 bytes (this includes most of the CD-ROM drives on the market)
- Aztech CDA268, Orchid CDS-3110, and Okano/Wearnes CDD-110
- Matsushita/Kotobuki/Panasonic CD-ROM drive models CR-521, CR-522, CR-523, CR-562, and CR-563 (the CD-ROM drives bundled with the Sound Blaster Pro sound card)
- Mitsumi CD-ROM drive
- Sony CDU31A, CDU33A, CDU-531, and CDU-535 drives

The Sound Blaster 16 sound card features one of two CD-ROM interfaces: a proprietary interface and a SCSI interface. Linux supports both interfaces, but you need to know which interface your Sound Blaster 16 board provides. You should find this information in the manual that accompanies the Sound Blaster 16 board.

You can connect an ATAPI CD-ROM drive to an IDE controller and treat it as a second hard drive. If you want a simple way to attach a CD-ROM drive to your PC and you don't need an additional hard drive, you might consider installing an ATAPI CD-ROM drive as a slave of the boot hard drive.

Sound card

On PCs, sound cards and CD-ROM drives go hand in hand because most CD-ROM-based multimedia programs include sound effects that you can enjoy only if you have a sound card. Under Linux, you also can play sound on the sound card. If you have a sound card, you can play audio CDs or play DOOM (a popular game) with full sound effects.

The version of Linux on the companion CD-ROM supports the following sound cards:

- 6850 UART (Universal Asynchronous Receiver Transmitter) MIDI (Musical Instrument Digital Interface)
- AdLib sound card
- ATI Stereo F/X (Sound Blaster-compatible)
- ECHO-PSS (Orchid SW32 and Cardinal DSP16)
- Ensoniq SoundScape (but you have to start DOS to initialize card)
- Gravis Ultrasound, Ultrasound MAX, and Ultrasound 16-bit sampling daughterboard
- Logitech SoundMan 16, SoundMan Games, and SoundMan Wave
- Media Vision Premium 3D Jazz16 (Sound Blaster Pro-compatible), Pro Audio Spectrum 16, and Pro Sonic 16 Jazz
- Microsoft Sound System (AD1848)
- MPU-401 MIDI
- Sound Galaxy NX Pro
- Sound Blaster, Sound Blaster 16, and Sound Blaster Pro
- ThunderBoard (Sound Blaster-compatible)
- WaveBlaster and other Sound Blaster 16 daughterboards

Network adapter

A network adapter is necessary only if you are going to connect your Linux PC to an Ethernet network, for example. Linux supports a variety of Ethernet network adapters. IBM's token-ring network is not yet supported, but a token-ring driver for Linux is in the works.

See Chapter 16 for more information on Linux's support for token-ring and other network adapters.

Following is a list of Ethernet cards that Linux supports:

- 3Com 3C503, 3C505, 3C507, 3C509 (ISA bus), and 3C579 (for EISA bus)
- Allied Telesis AT1500 and AT1700
- Ansel Communications AC3200 EISA
- Apricot Xen-II
- AT&T GIS WaveLAN
- AT-Lan-Tec and RealTek parallel-port Ethernet adapter
- Cabletron E21*xx* (*x* is any digit)
- D-Link DE600 and DE620 parallel-port Ethernet adapter
- Digital Equipment Corporation DEPCA and EtherWORKS

- Hewlett-Packard HP J2405A, PCLAN (27245 and 27*xxx* series), and PCLAN PLUS (27247B and 27252A)
- Intel EtherExpress
- Novell Ethernet NE1000 and NE2000
- PureData PDUC8028 and PDI8023
- Racal-Interlan NI5210 (based on the i82586 Ethernet chip), NI6510 (uses the AMD 7990 LANCE chip and does not work with more than 16MB of memory)
- Schneider & Koch G16
- SMC (Western Digital) WD8003, WD8013, SMC Elite, SMC Elite Plus, and SMC Elite 16 Ultra
- Zenith Z-Note and IBM ThinkPad 300 built-in Ethernet adapter

Tip

If you plan to use Linux on a stand-alone PC at home, you can use Serial Line Internet Protocol (SLIP) or Point-to-Point Protocol (PPP) to connect to the Internet over a dial-up connection through an Internet Service Provider. See Chapter 18 for details.

Making a hardware checklist

Now that you have seen a summary of various hardware peripherals that Linux supports, you should have a rough idea of whether you have the right PC hardware to use Linux. If you are buying a new PC to run Linux, the hardware list should help you decide the hardware configuration of the new PC.

To summarize, go through the following checklist to see whether you are ready to install Linux from this book's companion CD-ROM:

- Does your PC have an 80386 or better microprocessor, with the ISA, VLB, or PCI bus; at least 8MB of RAM; a high-density floppy drive; and a large hard drive (at least 500MB)?
- Does your PC have a CD-ROM drive that Linux supports? (You need a CD-ROM drive to install Linux from this book's companion CD-ROM.)

Tip

If you don't know what kind of CD-ROM drive you have, you should watch the system boot up in DOS and watch the DOS driver load — the driver usually displays a message with the brand of the CD-ROM drive.

- Can you get a second hard drive? (If so, you can install Linux on that hard drive. Installing Linux on a second drive prevents you from messing up your first hard drive, which usually has MS-DOS or Windows loaded on it.)
- If you have a SCSI controller with any SCSI devices that you want to use under Linux, is the SCSI controller supported by Linux?
- Is your video card supported by Linux? (If not, you won't be able to set up and run the X Window System.)
- Is your mouse supported by Linux? (If not, you won't be able to set up and run the X Window System.)

As the comments after the questions indicate, you do not necessarily have to answer each question yes. You must answer the first two items yes, however, because without that basic hardware configuration, Linux cannot run on your system.

If you plan to install Linux on a second hard disk, you do not have to go through the process of partitioning (dividing) your hard disk under MS-DOS. You should skip the next few sections and proceed to create the Linux boot and root floppy disks (see the "Creating the Boot and Root Floppies" section). Then you can boot Linux from a floppy disk and partition the second hard disk for use under Linux.

Partitioning your hard disk under MS-DOS

If your PC has a single hard disk drive, chances are that you have MS-DOS and Microsoft Windows installed on that drive. I recommend that you keep DOS and Windows installed on your system even if you want to work mostly in Linux. After all, you have to perform some of the Linux installation steps under DOS or Windows. Also, you can access the MS-DOS files from Linux. You get the best of both worlds if you keep DOS and Windows around when you install Linux.

Typically, your PC hard disk is set up as a single large drive, designated by a drive letter such as C. Unless you can scrounge up a second hard disk for your PC, or if you already have a second disk that you can spare, your first task is to divide your one and only hard disk to make room for Linux.

If you do not want to go through the process of partitioning your hard disk, you can install Linux in an MS-DOS directory. This option is a good way to try Linux before you install it in its own disk partition. Later in this chapter, I briefly describe how to install Linux in an MS-DOS directory (see the "Installing Linux in an MS-DOS Directory" section).

Working in MS-DOS before you install Linux

If you are a MS-DOS beginner, you may find it difficult to follow some of the Linux installation steps that you have to perform under MS-DOS. Following are some of the terms and concepts that you need to know to perform the necessary installation steps:

- *Boot floppy drive.* The first floppy drive (A) is the boot floppy drive. If you put a floppy disk in the A drive and turn on the power, your PC automatically tries to start from the floppy disk. This feature is built into the computer and does not depend on what operating system is installed on your system's hard disk. In most new systems, the A drive is a 3.5-inch floppy drive. Many older systems, however, use a 5.25-inch floppy drive as A. To install Linux, you need a high-density boot floppy drive.

- *Partitions.* A physical hard drive can be divided into several parts, each of which can be treated as a separate logical hard drive. Although most new PCs use the entire hard disk as a single drive, you can partition the disk into up to four sections, called the *four*

(continued)

(continued)

primary partitions. To install Linux on your hard disk, you have to create at least two partitions for Linux — one partition for the Linux file system and the other for swap space (virtual memory in which the contents of memory can be stored temporarily). If you want to keep MS-DOS and Windows in one partition and also install Linux, you need three partitions.

- *Repartitioning a hard disk*. If your hard disk has only one partition, the process of creating more partitions is referred to as *repartitioning*. To repartition a disk, you have to back up its contents. Use the MS-DOS FDISK command to delete the old partition and create several new ones, and then restore the old contents to one of the partitions. The Slackware Linux distribution (on this book's CD-ROM) includes an MS-DOS program called FIPS that you can use to repartition a hard disk without destroying the contents of the old partition. The utility is not guaranteed to work perfectly, however.

- *Formatting a disk*. The MS-DOS FDISK program only defines a section of the physical disk to be used by an operating system such as MS-DOS. You still have to prepare that section of disk before MS-DOS can use it to store files and directories.

- *Directories and files*. In MS-DOS, a drive is divided into directories. Each directory, in turn, can contain other directories and files. The file is where the actual information is stored. The directories help you organize your documents and programs. All files for the MS-DOS operating system, for example, usually are in the C:\DOS directory while all Windows files are in the C:\WINDOWS directory. The directory C:\WINDOWS\SYSTEM contains some special files that Windows needs. As you see, the backslash character is used as a separator between names of directories. The directory C:\ is known as the root directory; WINDOWS is a subdirectory of the root directory, and SYSTEM is a subdirectory of WINDOWS. Therefore, C:\WINDOWS\SYSTEM is two levels down from the root directory.

- *Filenames*. An MS-DOS filename consists of a name of 1 to 8 characters, followed by a period and then an extension that can have 0 to 3 characters. Therefore, README.TXT is an MS-DOS filename with the name README and the extension TXT. Executable programs have the COM or EXE extension, whereas DOC typically represents a document that can be opened by a word processing program.

- *MS-DOS commands*. You use MS-DOS through commands that you enter at a prompt. The MS-DOS command interpreter displays a prompt (usually the current drive and directory name, followed by a greater-than sign, such as C:\>). MS-DOS commands often have options that start with a slash. You can use the /S option with the FORMAT command, for example, to format and copy the system files to a disk.

Steps to repartition the hard disk

In the following sections, I assume that your PC has a single hard disk on which MS-DOS is already installed (Windows may be installed as well, but that does not matter in the task that you are about to perform.) To repartition the disk, you have to perform the following tasks:

1. Back up the contents of your hard disk.

    If you bought a new PC, you are lucky, because the hard disk should not have much data to back up.

2. Create an MS-DOS boot floppy (in Windows 95, create a startup disk by using the Add/Remove Programs option in the Control Panel).

   You use this floppy to start your PC and partition the hard disk.

3. Run FDISK from the floppy disk, and create the new partitions.

4. Format the MS-DOS partition, and restore the files from the backup that you created in step 1.

The next four sections guide you through these steps.

Back up your hard disk

Backing up the hard disk takes a long time, but there is just no safe way to repartition the hard disk without a backup. Slackware Linux, however, comes with a utility program called FIPS that can partition a hard disk without destroying the data that currently is on the disk.

How you back up your hard disk depends on what you have on your hard disk. If you have a new PC, the hard disk probably contains MS-DOS, Windows, and any other software that the vendor bundled with the system. If you have the original disks for DOS, Windows, and the bundled software, you may decide to skip the backup and reinstall everything after you create the new partitions. If you have an old PC, you may decide to back up only the directories that you cannot reinstall from original disks or CD-ROM. If you have a word processing program, for example, you don't have to back up that program's directory, because you can always install the program again.

To back up your hard disk, you can use the backup utility that comes with MS-DOS. In DOS versions 5.0 and earlier, use the BACKUP utility to back up all or some of the directories of your hard disk. In DOS versions 6.0 and later, use the MSBACKUP utility.

Tip

Whether you decide to back up everything or just the directories that you need, start by printing two files — CONFIG.SYS and AUTOEXEC.BAT — that are in your C drive's root directory. These files contain information that is crucial to getting your MS-DOS setup back to its previous state.

Partitioning your hard disk under Windows 95

If your system runs Windows 95, you still must follow the same steps to partition the hard disk as you would have under MS-DOS. The only difference is that you have to first create a startup disk by using the Add/Remove Programs option in the Control Panel, and then boot the PC with that startup disk. After that, you can run the FDISK program to create the new partitions.

Create a bootable floppy for MS-DOS

Usually, you turn on your PC's power, and the PC automatically loads the operating system (MS-DOS or Windows 95, for example) from the first hard drive: the C drive. If you put a floppy in the A drive and power up the PC, however, the PC loads the operating system from the floppy. If the floppy does not contain the operating system, you get this familiar message:

```
Non-System disk or disk error
Replace and strike any key when ready
```

This message tells you that the PC tried to load, but could not find, operating-system files on the floppy disk. Usually, you remove the floppy and press a key, and the PC boots from the hard drive.

To change the hard drive partitions, you actually want to boot the PC from the A drive. That way, you can be sure that the hard drive is not in use when you change its partitions. To create a bootable floppy, perform these steps:

1. Put a floppy disk in your A drive, and type the command **FORMAT A: /S**.

   MS-DOS prompts you with the following message:

   ```
   Insert new diskette for drive A
   and press ENTER when ready...
   ```

Caution

   The contents of the floppy are destroyed when you format the disk.

2. Press Enter, because you already have the disk in the A drive.

   MS-DOS formats the disk and places the necessary operating-system files on the disk (that's what the /S option of the FORMAT command does). DOS also prompts you for a Volume label; you can press Enter in response. Finally, DOS asks whether you want to format another disk; press **N** to indicate that you are done with formatting.

3. Copy other necessary files to the A drive.

   At minimum, you need to copy the FDISK.EXE program to the floppy so that you can use it to partition the hard disk and the FORMAT.COM program to format the new DOS partition. Use the following commands to copy the FDISK.EXE program to the floppy in A drive (text in parentheses is my comment):

   ```
   C:
   CD \DOS    (MS-DOS files usually are in \DOS)
   COPY FDISK.EXE A:
   COPY FORMAT.COM A:
   ```

Caution

   You also may need other programs to restore the backup that you created earlier. Those programs do not have to be on the boot floppy; just make sure that you have a copy of them on floppy disk somewhere.

4. Test the boot floppy.

   Close all running programs, put the newly created boot floppy in A drive, and press Ctrl+Alt+Delete to reboot your PC. MS-DOS should start, and you should see an A:\> prompt.

Partition the hard disk with FDISK

Now that you have successfully backed up your hard disk and prepared a bootable MS-DOS floppy, you can partition your hard disk. To begin this procedure, put the MS-DOS boot floppy in drive A, and restart your PC (press Ctrl+Alt+Delete, or turn the power off and then on). When you see the A:\> prompt, type **FDISK** and press Enter. FDISK runs and displays the screen shown in Figure 1-1.

Caution

Back up your hard disk before you use FDISK to repartition it (refer to "Back up your hard disk" earlier in this chapter). When you alter the partitions, you cannot access the old data on the disk. You can run FDISK, view the disk partitions, and exit without damaging your hard disk, but enter the commands carefully — you don't want to wipe out your hard drive's contents accidentally.

Tip

FDISK is available in all versions of MS-DOS and in Windows 95. (In Windows 95, you can start your PC in MS-DOS mode and use the FDISK command to repartition the disk.) In this session with FDISK, you delete a partition and create some new partitions.

Use the following strategy to repartition your hard disk:

1. Select FDISK menu option 4 to look at your hard disk's current partition information.

2. Select FDISK menu option 3 to delete the DOS partition.

3. Select FDISK menu option 1 to create a new, smaller DOS partition that leaves enough space for Linux (I'll discuss the size of partitions in the "Create New DOS Partition" section).

4. Select FDISK menu option 2, and mark the newly created DOS partition active.

```
                     MS-DOS Version 6
                   Fixed Disk Setup Program
              (C)Copyright Microsoft Corp. 1983 - 1993

                         FDISK Options

  Current fixed disk drive: 1

  Choose one of the following:

  1. Create DOS partition or Logical DOS Drive
  2. Set active partition
  3. Delete partition or Logical DOS Drive
  4. Display partition information
  5. Change current fixed disk drive


  Enter choice: [1]




  Press Esc to exit FDISK
```

Figure 1-1: FDISK's opening screen.

Later, you'll partition the rest of the disk under Linux as described in the "Partitioning Your Hard Disk under Linux" section.

Check your hard disk's current partitioning information

Before you delete the partition, press **4** and then press Enter to view the current partition information. Figure 1-2 shows the FDISK screen for a typical disk that contains a single DOS partition for the entire disk.

Disk 1 refers to the first physical hard disk on your system. The PRI DOS entry in the Type field indicates that the partition is a primary DOS partition — the partition that contains the files needed to boot MS-DOS. The entry in the Partition field tells you that this is the C drive in MS-DOS. You probably will have the same situation.

Delete the primary DOS partition

Press Esc to return to the FDISK main menu (refer to Figure 1-1). To delete the primary DOS partition, press **3** and then press Enter. FDISK displays another menu, shown in Figure 1-3.

You can delete several kinds of partitions. An extended partition, for example, is simply a partition that can be further subdivided into logical drives. Typically, however, when an entire disk is devoted to MS-DOS and Windows, you have only a primary DOS partition to delete.

To delete the primary DOS partition, press **1** and then press Enter. FDISK displays the screen shown in Figure 1-4, requesting confirmation that you really want to delete the partition.

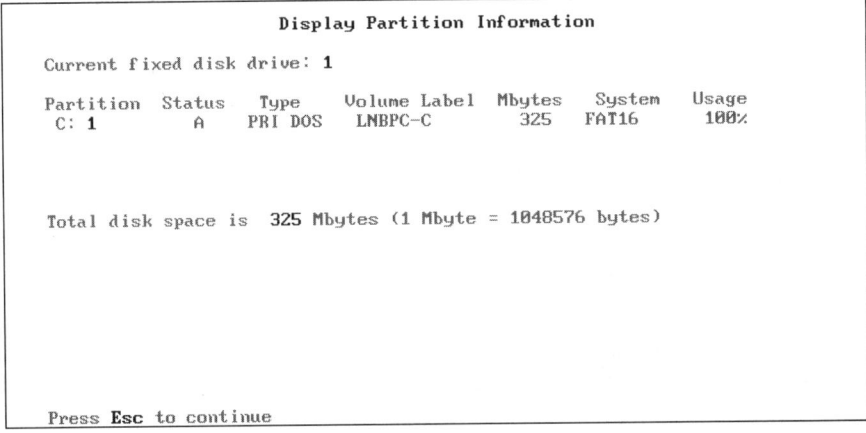

Figure 1-2: FDISK screen, showing typical partition information.

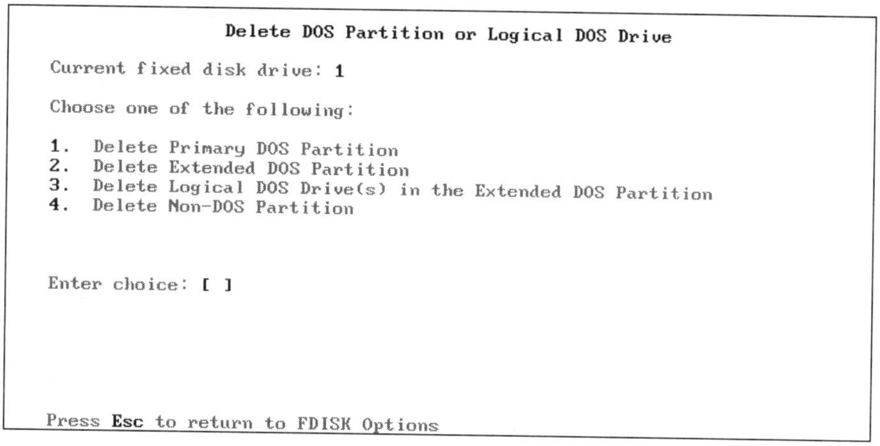

```
              Delete DOS Partition or Logical DOS Drive
Current fixed disk drive: 1

Choose one of the following:

  1. Delete Primary DOS Partition
  2. Delete Extended DOS Partition
  3. Delete Logical DOS Drive(s) in the Extended DOS Partition
  4. Delete Non-DOS Partition


  Enter choice: [ ]




  Press Esc to return to FDISK Options
```

Figure 1-3: FDISK screen, showing the options for deleting a partition.

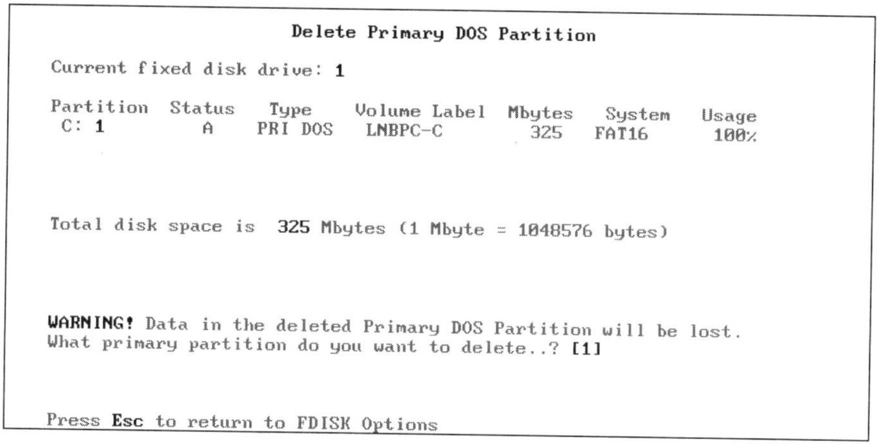

```
              Delete Primary DOS Partition
Current fixed disk drive: 1

Partition   Status   Type     Volume Label   Mbytes   System   Usage
C: 1          A      PRI DOS   LNBPC-C        325     FAT16    100%



Total disk space is  325 Mbytes (1 Mbyte = 1048576 bytes)



WARNING! Data in the deleted Primary DOS Partition will be lost.
What primary partition do you want to delete..? [1]


Press Esc to return to FDISK Options
```

Figure 1-4: FDISK screen, requesting confirmation before deleting the primary DOS partition.

Press Enter. FDISK deletes the partition and returns to the main screen shown in Figure 1-1.

Create a new DOS partition

In this step, you create the primary DOS partition again, but this time, you make it smaller. At this point, you have to decide how much disk space you want to leave aside for MS-DOS (and Windows) and how much you want to devote to Linux. The final choice depends on the total capacity of your hard disk and your planned use of Linux.

The following table shows a rough calculation of how much disk space you need:

Item	Amount (MB)
Complete Linux installation from companion CD-ROM	275
Linux swap space (for use in virtual memory)	16
User space for Linux (so that you can work in Linux)	60
MS-DOS/Windows	150
Total	501

If you have a 500MB hard disk, allocate 150MB to the primary DOS partition. Unfortunately, you may find 150MB to be inadequate for all your Windows applications. I assume that you want to use Linux in earnest, so I recommend setting aside enough disk space for Linux.

If you have a bigger-capacity disk (many new systems come with disks as large as 1GB, which is 1,000MB), keep these minimums in mind, and proportionately increase the sizes of the DOS and Linux partitions.

If you have a smaller-capacity disk — say, 300MB — go for a 200/100 split, with the DOS partition set at 100MB.

To create the new primary DOS partition, press **1** at the FDISK main screen (refer to Figure 1-1) and then press Enter. FDISK displays the menu shown in Figure 1-5.

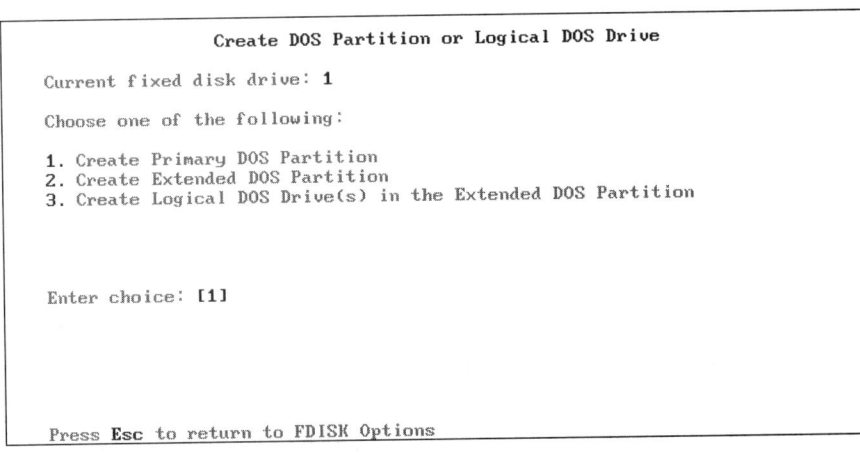

Figure 1-5: FDISK screen, with options for creating a partition.

Press Enter to indicate that you want to create a primary DOS partition. FDISK asks you for the partition's size, in megabytes. Specify the amount of space for the DOS partition, and press Enter. FDISK creates the primary DOS partition and returns to the main screen shown in Figure 1-1.

Make the DOS partition active

To boot from the primary DOS partition, you have to make it active. From FDISK's main screen (refer to Figure 1-1), press **2** and then press Enter. FDISK asks you for the partition that you want to make active. This should be the primary DOS partition that you just created. Press Enter to make that partition active.

Press Esc to quit FDISK. FDISK informs you that it will restart the PC. Leave the DOS boot floppy in the A drive, and press Enter. The PC reboots, and you again see the A:\> prompt.

Restore the MS-DOS partition

The new primary DOS partition will be your PC's C drive. Before you can use that drive, however, you have to format it. To format the C drive, type **FORMAT C: /S**. The FORMAT program displays a warning message; you can ignore it, because you are formatting a newly created partition on your hard disk.

After the new C drive is formatted, you have to restore the contents of the hard disk. If you had backed up only your files and not the DOS and Windows files, you have to start by installing MS-DOS on your newly formatted C drive. Typically, you have to boot the PC from the first DOS installation disk and follow the instructions.

If you have to install Windows, you can do so after you install DOS. To install Windows, insert the first installation disk into the floppy drive, and run the SETUP program from that floppy drive.

After you have MS-DOS and Windows installed on the C drive, you can use your backup program to restore all the files that you previously backed up from the hard disk. To complete this step, you have to follow the instructions that are appropriate for the backup program that you used. If you used the MSBACKUP program in DOS versions 6.0 or later, for example, you can use the same program to restore the files from the backup diskettes.

Repartitioning with FIPS

If you understand the partitions as being sections of the hard disk, you may wonder whether there is a way to "cordon off" the unused part of a hard disk and make a new partition out of that unused part without destroying any existing data. That very idea is behind a utility program called FIPS (The *F*irst *N*ondestructive *I*nteractive *P*artition *S*plitting Program). FIPS can split an existing DOS partition into two partitions.

Tip

Although you have no guarantee that FIPS will split a DOS partition successfully, you may consider using it to create room for Linux, especially if you have a brand-new PC with only DOS and Windows installed on the hard disk. In this case, even if something goes wrong with FIPS, you can simply reinstall DOS and Windows. I used FIPS to split the DOS partition on a new PC's hard disk and create room for Linux.

The FIPS.EXE program and related files are located in the \INSTALL\FIPS subdirectory of the companion CD-ROM. To use FIPS, follow these steps:

1. For FIPS to work, all used areas of the disk must be contiguous, or at least as tightly packed as possible. You can prepare the disk for FIPS by running a defragmenter (in MS-DOS 6.0 or later, use the program DEFRAG to defragment the disk). You also should check the hard disk for errors by running a program such as Norton Disk Doctor (in MS-DOS 6.2 or later, use SCANDISK). If you happen to have it, use Norton Speed Disk to defragment the hard disk because it's significantly faster than the DEFRAG utility.

2. Create a bootable floppy disk, using the command **FORMAT A: /S**.

3. Copy the following files from the CD-ROM to the formatted floppy (the following example assumes that D: is the CD-ROM drive):
   ```
   COPY D:\INSTALL\FIPS\FIPS.EXE A:
   COPY D:\INSTALL\FIPS\RESTORRB.EXE A:
   COPY D:\INSTALL\FIPS\ERRORS.TXT A:
   ```
   FIPS.EXE is the program that splits partitions. ERRORS.TXT is a list of FIPS error messages; you consult this list for an explanation of any error messages that FIPS displays. RESTORRB.EXE is a program that allows you to restore certain important parts of your hard disk from a backup of those areas created by FIPS.

4. Leave the bootable floppy in the A drive, and press Ctrl+Alt+Delete to reboot the PC. The PC boots from A and displays the A\> prompt.

5. Type **FIPS**. The FIPS program runs and shows you information about your hard disk. FIPS gives you an opportunity to save a backup copy of important disk areas before proceeding. After that, FIPS shows the first free cylinder where the new partition can start (as well as the size of the partition, in megabytes). Figure 1-6 shows the output of the FIPS program at this stage.

6. Use the left and right arrow keys to adjust the starting cylinder of the new partition (the one that results from splitting the existing partition) to change the partition size. Press the right arrow to increase the starting cylinder number (this leaves more room in the existing parition and reduces the size of the new partition you are creating).

```
Number of FATs: 2
Number of rootdirectory entries: 512
Number of sectors (short): 0
Media descriptor byte: F8h
Sectors per FAT: 130
Sectors per track: 63
Drive heads: 32
Hidden sectors: 63
Number of sectors (long): 816417
Physical drive number: 80h
Signature: 29h

Checking Bootsector ... OK
Checking FAT ... OK
Searching for free space ... OK

Do you want to make a backup copy of your root- and bootsector before
proceeding (y/n)? n

Enter start cylinder for new partition (399 - 404):

Use the cursor keys to choose the cylinder, <enter> to continue

Old partition          Cylinder          New Partition
   392.8 MB              399                 5.9 MB
```

Figure 1-6: The FIPS program prompting the user for new partition size.

7. When FIPS prompts you, press **c** to continue. FIPS displays some information about the disk and asks whether you want to write the new partition information to the disk.

8. Press **y**. FIPS writes the new partition table to the hard disk and then exits.

Remove the floppy disk from the A drive, and reboot the PC. When the system comes up, everything in your hard disk should be intact, but the C drive will be smaller. You have created a new partition from the unused parts of the old C drive.

You do not have to do anything with the newly created partition under DOS. Later, in the "Partitioning Your Hard Disk under Linux" section, you learn how to use the new partition under Linux.

Creating the boot and root floppies

After you repartition the hard disk, restore DOS and Windows, and make room on the hard disk for Linux, you can begin the next step of installing Linux from this book's CD-ROM: creating the Linux boot floppy and root floppy. (For this step, you should turn on your PC without any floppy disk in the A drive and then run DOS or Windows from the hard drive.)

Like the MS-DOS boot floppy, the Linux boot floppy is used to start your PC and start Linux. The *root floppy* is necessary because you do not yet have a hard disk for Linux. To prepare the hard disk partitions for Linux, you need Linux itself. The root floppy contains some files that you need to create the Linux partitions on your hard disk and install Linux to the hard disk.

After you have installed Linux, you will no longer need the boot and root floppy disks, except in the event of an emergency (when you have to reinstall Linux from the CD-ROM).

Creating boot and root floppies under MS-DOS

The boot disk is the initial version of Linux that you use to prepare the system and load the rest of Linux. The file to be copied to the Linux boot floppy is called the Linux *boot image*. You have to make sure that the boot image includes the drivers necessary to access your PC's CD-ROM drive. If your PC has a SCSI CD-ROM drive, for example, you need a boot image that includes support for your PC's SCSI controller. If you have a CD-ROM drive connected to a Sound Blaster Pro card, you should select the boot image that can access and read from the Sound Blaster Pro CD-ROM drive.

Note

Theoretically speaking, there could be a boot image that includes support for all possible CD-ROM drives, but the boot image would be too large to fit on a single floppy.

To create the Linux boot floppy under MS-DOS, follow these two general steps:

1. Select a boot image and a root image, depending on your PC's configuration, including the type of high-density floppy drive in your PC.

2. Use the RAWRITE.EXE program in the \INSTALL directory of the CD-ROM drive to copy the boot image and the root image to two separate floppy disks.

The following table shows the directories in which the boot and root images are located on the CD-ROM drive:

Directory	Images
BOOTDSKS.12	Boot images to create a 5.25-inch, 1.2MB Linux boot floppy
BOOTDSKS.144	Boot images to create a 3.5-inch, 1.44MB Linux boot floppy
ROOTDSKS	Root images to create either a 3.5-inch (1.44MB) or 5.25-inch (1.2MB) Linux root floppy

These directory names reflect the capacity of the floppy drives. A 5.25-inch high-density floppy has a capacity of 1.2MB, whereas a high-density 3.5-inch floppy can hold 1.44MB.

In the sections that follow, I assume that your PC has a 3.5-inch 1.44MB floppy drive, so I refer to the directories BOOTDSKS.144 and ROOTDSKS. You can follow the same steps to create 5.25-inch, 1.2MB-capacity boot and root floppies.

Tip

If your system runs Windows 95, open an MS-DOS window (select MS-DOS Prompt from the Programs area in the Start menu) and follow the steps shown in the next two sections.

Creating the Linux boot floppy

To make a Linux boot floppy, you have to select an appropriate boot image from the ones provided in the \BOOTDSKS.144 directory of the CD-ROM. Your choice of the boot image depends primarily on the type of CD-ROM drive that your PC has. After you initially boot Linux from its boot floppy, it must be capable of accessing the CD-ROM drive; otherwise, you won't be able to install the rest of Linux on your PC's hard disk.

Table 1-1 lists the boot-image filenames and the exact hardware configurations that they support.

Table 1-1   Linux boot-image filenames and usage guidelines

Filename	Usage guidelines
ACM206	Supports Integrated Drive Electronics (IDE) and SCSI hard drives and Phillips CM206 CD-ROM drive.
AGSCD	Supports IDE and SCSI hard drives and Goldstar R420 CD-ROM drive.
AHA2940	Supports IDE and the Adaptec AHA294x (where x is any digit) SCSI controller. Use this image to install from a CD-ROM drive connected to the AHA294x controller.
AOPTCD	Supports IDE and SCSI hard drives and Optics Storage 8000 AT CD-ROM drive.
ASJCD	Supports IDE and SCSI hard drives and Sanyo CDR-H94A CD-ROM drive.
AZTECH	Supports IDE and SCSI hard drives, as well as Aztech, Orchid, Okano, and Wearnes CD-ROM drives with proprietary interface. Use this image when you install Linux from one of these CD-ROM drives.
BARE	Supports only IDE hard drives. Use this image when you install Linux from floppy disks to an IDE hard drive.
CDU31A	Supports IDE and SCSI hard drives and Sony CDU31a or CDU33a CD-ROM drives with proprietary interface. Use this image when you install Linux from one of these CD-ROM drives.
CDU535	Supports IDE and SCSI hard drives and Sony CDU535 or CDU531 CD-ROM drives with proprietary interface. Use this image when you install Linux from one of these CD-ROM drives.
IDECD	Use this image when you install Linux from any CD-ROM drive with an IDE (also known as AT Attachment Packet Interface, or ATAPI) interface. You can install to any IDE or SCSI hard disk.
MITSUMI	Use this image when you install Linux from a Mitsumi CD-ROM drive (with its proprietary interface) to any IDE or SCSI hard disk.
NET	Supports IDE hard drives and TCP/IP networking. Use this image when you install Linux over a network (from another system on the network, for example) to an IDE drive.

(continued)

Table 1-1 *(continued)*

Filename	Usage guidelines
SBPCD	Supports IDE and SCSI hard drives, as well as Sound Blaster Pro CD-ROM drives (including models such as Panasonic, Matsushita, Kotobuki, TEAC CD-55A, and Lasermate) with a proprietary interface. Use this image when you install Linux from any of these Sound Blaster Pro CD-ROM drives.
SCSI	Supports IDE and SCSI hard drives and all SCSI CD-ROM drives. Use this image to install Linux from any SCSI CD-ROM drive (see also the AHA2940 image).
SCSINET1	Supports a selected set of SCSI controllers and TCP/IP networking. The SCSI controllers supported by this boot image are Adaptec AHA-152*x*, AHA-1542, AHA-1740, AHA-274*x*, and AHA-284*x*; Buslogic; EATA-DMA (DPT, NEC, and AT&T); Seagate ST-02; Future Domain TMC-8*xx*. Use this image when you install Linux over a network (from another system on the network, for example) to a SCSI hard drive that is attached to any of the supported controllers.
SCSINET2	Supports TCP/IP networking and the following SCSI controllers: Generic NCR5380; NCR 53c7 and NCR 8*xx*; Always IN2000; Pro Audio Spectrum 16 and QLogic; Trantor T128, T128F, and T228; Ultrastor; and 7000 FASST. Use this image when you install Linux over a network (from another system on the network, for example) to a SCSI hard drive that is attached to any of the supported controllers.
XT	Supports IDE and old IBM XT-style hard disks. Use this image when you install Linux from floppy disks to an XT-style disk.

Depending on your PC's hardware configuration, select one of these boot images. After you decide on a boot image, run the RAWRITE program directly from the CD-ROM. To do this, enter the following commands at the MS-DOS prompt (my comments are in parentheses, and your input is in boldface):

```
D:             (use the drive letter for the CD-ROM drive)
CD \BOOTDSKS.144
\INSTALL\RAWRITE
RaWrite 1.2 - Write disk file to raw floppy diskette

Enter source filename: SBPCD
Enter destination drive: A
Please insert a formatted diskette into drive A and press -ENTER- :
```

As instructed, you should put a formatted floppy into your PC's A drive and then press Enter. RAWRITE begins copying the selected boot-image file to the floppy. As the RAWRITE program works, it displays a status message. When the program finishes copying, it displays its final message, as follows:

```
Writing image to drive A. Press ^C to abort.
Track: 79  Head:  1 Sector: 16
Done.
```

You can take the Linux boot floppy out of the A drive and (if you haven't done so already) label it appropriately. A label such as Linux Boot Disk would be appropriate.

Make sure that you select the proper boot image — the one that supports your CD-ROM drive. You should select the boot image based on the CD-ROM's interface rather than the CD-ROM drive's model. On my PC, for example, I have a Mitsumi CD-ROM drive, but the drive uses an IDE (or ATAPI) interface. Therefore, I need the IDECD boot image, not the MITSUMI boot image; the MITSUMI image is for the Mitsumi proprietary interface.

Creating the Linux root floppy

The Linux root floppy contains the initial files needed to run some Linux commands. You start the PC with the boot floppy and then use the root floppy as your initial file system. To prepare the root floppy (like the boot floppy), you first have to select an appropriate root image. Table 1-2 lists the root images available in the \ROOTDSKS directory of the companion CD-ROM.

Table 1-2	Linux root-image filenames and usage guidelines
Filename	*Usage guidelines*
COLOR.GZ	Use this root image to install Linux. This root image includes full-color installation scripts and is the recommended root image for Slackware installation.
PCMCIA.GZ	Use this root image to install Linux on a laptop connected to a network through a PCMCIA Ethernet card. You'll need another system on the network that has the Slackware Linux distribution available on an NFS exported directory.
RESCUE.GZ	This root image is not really for installing Linux. Use this root image when you need a minimal Linux system to fix problems with your Linux PC. This root image contains utilities such as the `vi` editor and the `e2fsck` file system checker.
TAPE.GZ	Use this root image to install Linux from tape. (Be forewarned that installation from tape still is in the experimental stage.)
TEXT.GZ	This is a text-based install script.
UMSDOS.GZ	Use this root image when you install Linux in an MS-DOS directory. The performance is not as good as in a native Linux partition, but you do not have to repartition your hard disk.

The GZ file extension indicates that each root image is stored in a compressed form. You should copy them to the root floppy in the compressed form; the Linux kernel uncompresses the root image before using it (the kernel is on the boot floppy).

As you do with the boot floppy, select an appropriate root image — most probably, the COLOR.GZ file. Then run the RAWRITE program from the \INSTALL directory of the CD-ROM, and copy the selected root image to the floppy disk in the A drive.

Booting Linux for Installation

Now that you have the Linux boot and root floppies ready, you can start installing Linux from the CD-ROM on the non-DOS parititon of the hard drive.

To start Linux for installation, put the Linux boot floppy in your PC's A drive and restart your PC (either press the reset button or press Ctrl+Alt+Delete). Your PC goes through its normal startup sequence, such as checking memory and running the ROM BIOS code. Then the PC loads Linux from the floppy and displays this message:

```
Welcome to the Slackware Linux 3.0.0 bootkernel disk!
```

Following this message, a page of text informs you about some options that you can enter at the next prompt. At the end of the screen, you see this prompt:

```
boot:
```

Press Enter to continue. Linux continues to load and display information about the hardware that it finds in your PC.

Tip

Look carefully to see whether Linux has detected the CD-ROM drive. If not, you may have selected the wrong boot image. Look for information on your CD-ROM drive's interface, and pick a boot image that supports the interface. Remember that the brand name of the CD-ROM drive is not important — it's the interface that counts. If your Mitsumi CD-ROM drive has an IDE/ATAPI interface, for example, select the IDECD boot image, not the MITSUMI boot image.

Installing Linux over the network

You can install Linux from another system on a network, provided both systems are on the network and the other system has the Slackware distribution on a directory that's exported through the Network File System (NFS). To perform such an installation, you must be knowledgeable about NFS or ask the help of someone who manages the network. Create the boot and root floppy disks as usual, and select one of the boot images: NET, SCSINET1, or SCSINET2. After you use the boot and root floppies, you have to mount the NFS directory — the other system's directory containing the Slackware distribution. Then, you can proceed with the usual installation steps except designate the NFS directory as the source (instead of the CD-ROM drive).

Caution

If Linux does not detect the CD-ROM drive, remove the boot floppy and reboot your system with Windows 3.1 or Windows 95. Then, re-create the boot floppy with a boot image that supports your CD-ROM drive.

At the end of the information about the PC hardware, you see the following message:

```
VFS: Insert ramdisk floppy and press ENTER
```

Remove the Linux boot floppy from the A drive, and put the root floppy in its place. Then press Enter. Linux loads a small file system from the root floppy into memory. This system gives you access to some important Linux commands, including the Linux fdisk command, that you can use to prepare the hard disk partition for Linux.

After Linux loads the root floppy, it displays a message about the Slackware Linux installation disk that you are using to install Linux. Then Linux displays the following important information about the installation steps:

- You have to use the Linux fdisk utility to prepare hard disk partitions under Linux. You also should create a swap partition for use as virtual memory by Linux. (You learn how to create the swap partition later in the "Sample session with Linux fdisk" section.)

- If you use OS/2, you should create the Linux partitions (before booting Linux) with the OS/2 version of FDISK and then make the main Linux partition (not the swap partition) a boot partition, using the OS/2 Boot Manager. Then boot Linux, log in, run the Linux version of fdisk, and mark those partitions as Linux partitions (you soon learn how to mark a partition's type with Linux fdisk).

- If you have 4MB of memory or less, you must create and activate a Linux swap partition (you learn how to do this later in the "Setting up a swap partition" section).

- After you prepare the hard disk partitions and activate the swap partition, type **setup** to begin installing Linux. If you want to use a monochrome display, type **TERM=vt100** before you type the setup command.

At the end of this informative message, Linux prompts you to log in with the user name root, as follows:

```
You may now login as "root".
slackware login:
```

Type **root** and then press Enter. Linux should allow you to log in without any password. You see a brief welcome message and a pound-sign prompt:

```
#
```

The pound sign is the default prompt for the root user. At this point, you can enter Linux commands to perform the tasks that are necessary to install the rest of Linux.

All UNIX systems, including Linux, use root as the name of the *super user* — the user who has access to everything in the system. At this point, you are installing Linux, and you need access to everything in the system. Later, you can assign a password to the root user and also add yourself as a user so that you do not have to log in as root and inadvertently delete any important files.

Partitioning your hard disk under Linux

Like MS-DOS, Linux requires you to partition and prepare a hard disk before you can install Linux on the hard disk. You usually do not perform this step, because when you buy your PC from a vendor, the vendor takes care of preparing the hard disk and installing DOS and Windows on the hard disk. Because you are installing Linux from scratch, however, you have to perform this crucial step yourself. You have to prepare the hard disk partitions under Linux before you can install the rest of Linux. As you see in the following sections, this task is just a matter of following instructions.

Disk names in Linux

The first step is to learn how Linux refers to the various disks. Linux treats all devices as files and has actual files that represent each device. In Linux, these *device files* are located in the /dev directory. If you are new to UNIX, you may not yet know about UNIX filenames, but you will learn more as you continue to use Linux. If you know how MS-DOS filenames work, you will find that Linux filenames are similar, except that Linux filenames do not use drive letters (such as A and C), and substitute the slash (/) for the MS-DOS backslash (\) as the separator between directory names.

Because Linux treats a device as a file in the /dev directory, the hard disk names start with /dev. Table 1-3 lists the hard disk and floppy drive names that you may have to use.

Table 1-3	Hard disk and floppy drive names
Name	*Description*
/dev/hda	First Integrated Drive Electronics (IDE) drive (in DOS, usually the C drive)
/dev/hdb	Second IDE drive
/dev/sda	First Small Computer System Interface (SCSI) drive
/dev/sdb	Second SCSI drive
/dev/fd0	First floppy drive (the A drive in DOS)
/dev/fd1	Second floppy drive (the B drive in DOS)

Chapter 1: Installing Linux   39

When you use the Linux `fdisk` command to prepare the Linux partitions, you have to specify the disk drive by its device name as a command-line argument to the `fdisk` command. (If you type the `fdisk` command without any hard disk name, `fdisk` works with the first IDE drive: `/dev/hda`.)

Tip

If you are going to install Linux on part of your one and only hard drive (assuming that you reduced the size of the DOS partition and left some room for Linux), use `/dev/hda` as the device name. To install Linux on a second IDE hard disk, specify the device name `/dev/hdb` when you use the Linux `fdisk` command.

Linux `fdisk` commands

The Linux version of `fdisk` accepts simple single-letter commands. To see the commands, start `fdisk` with the following command:

fdisk /dev/hda *(to partition the second IDE drive, specify /dev/hdb as the argument)*

Caution

Unlike MS-DOS, Linux commands (as well as filenames and everything else) are case-sensitive. Therefore, you must enter the commands exactly as shown.

After you enter the `fdisk` command, Linux runs the `fdisk` program, which displays the following prompt:

```
Command (m for help):
```

You are supposed to enter single-letter commands. To see a list of these commands, press **m** and then press Enter. The `fdisk` program displays the following help message, which ends with a prompt:

```
Command action
   a   toggle a bootable flag
   c   toggle the dos compatibility flag
   d   delete a partition
   l   list known partition types
   m   print this menu
   n   add a new partition
   p   print the partition table
   q   quit without saving changes
   t   change a partition's system id
   u   change display/entry units
   v   verify the partition table
   w   write table to disk and exit
   x   extra functionality (experts only)

Command (m for help):
```

The help message shows you all the single-letter commands that you can use with `fdisk`. Of these commands, you mostly will use the following:

     p to see the current partition table

     d to delete a partition (in case you want to delete a non-Linux partition)

     n to create a new Linux partition

w to write the partition table to the disk and exit `fdisk`

q to exit `fdisk` without updating the partition table

Note

If you created the partitions under OS/2, you also have to use the **t** command to change the partition type.

If your disk has more than 1,024 cylinders, `fdisk` displays a warning message. The following example shows the warning message for a disk that has 1,656 cylinders (see Chapter 11 for more information on disks):

```
# fdisk /dev/hdb
The number of cylinders for this disk is set to 1656.
This is larger than 1024, and may cause problems with:
1) software that runs at boot time (e.g., LILO)
2) booting and partitioning software from other OSs
   (e.g., DOS FDISK, OS/2 FDISK)

Command (m for help):
```

In this example, `fdisk` is referring to MS-DOS's inability to handle more than 1,024 cylinders. All you have to do is make sure that the main Linux partition does not start above cylinder number 1,024.

Secret

The term *LILO* stands for *L*inux *Lo*ader, which is a small program that you can install to boot Linux. That program also must be located within the first 1,024 cylinders of your first hard disk.

Sample session with Linux `fdisk`

To show you how to use the Linux `fdisk` program to prepare the hard disk partitions, this section provides an example in which I prepare the Linux partitions on a new PC with a single 518MB hard disk.

To prepare the disk for use with Linux, I run the FIPS utility program (located in the \INSTALL\FIPS directory of the companion CD-ROM) to split the only DOS partition into two parts: a 398MB DOS partition (this PC was going to be mainly used under DOS and Windows) and a 120MB partition to be used for Linux. I felt relatively safe using FIPS, because the PC was brand-new and I could simply reinstall DOS and Windows if something went wrong when I split the DOS partition with FIPS. (FIPS is described in the "Repartitioning with FIPS" section earlier in this chapter.)

To prepare the Linux partitions, I boot Linux and then type **fdisk /dev/hda** to run `fdisk`. (When you use this command make sure that you use the correct disk name. Remember that /dev/hda is the equivalent of your DOS C drive and /dev/hdb is equivalent to your DOS D drive.) Then I press **p** to take a look at the current partition table, as follows:

```
Command (m for help): p

Disk /dev/hda: 32 heads, 63 sectors, 528 cylinders
Units = cylinders of 2016 * 512 bytes
```

```
   Device Boot   Begin   Start     End   Blocks   Id  System
/dev/hda1    *       1       1     405   408208+   6  DOS 16-bit >=32M
/dev/hda2          406     406     527   122976    6  DOS 16-bit >=32M

Command (m for help):
```

Because I used the FIPS utility program to split the single DOS partition, the disk has two DOS partitions. The asterisk (*) in the Boot column indicates that the first partition is the boot partition — the PC's C drive.

Tip

The Device column in `fdisk`'s listing of partitions shows how Linux names partitions. Linux constructs each partition name by appending the partition number (1 through 4, for the four primary partitions on a hard disk) to the disk's name. Therefore, Linux uses `/dev/hda1` and `/dev/hda2` as the names of the first two partitions on the first disk drive.

Because I know that the second DOS partition is empty, and I want to install Linux on that partition, I delete that partition, as follows:

```
Command (m for help): d
Partition number (1-4): 2
```

The `fdisk` program deletes the second partition and prompts me for the command again. I can press **p** to verify that the partition is gone. The `fdisk` program shows only the first DOS partition.

I want to set up two Linux partitions, as follows:

- A 16MB partition, to be used as the Linux swap partition
- Another, larger partition for the Linux file system, where Linux will be installed

I start with the 16MB swap partition. To create this partition, I use the following commands (my input is in boldface):

```
Command (m for help): n
Command action
   e   extended
   p   primary partition (1-4)
p
Partition number (1-4): 2
First cylinder (406-528): 406
Last cylinder or +size or +sizeM or +sizeK (406-528): +16M

Command (m for help):
```

The `fdisk` program prompts me for the partition type. Because there can be up to four primary partitions and I have only one DOS partition currently on the hard disk, I decide to create another primary partition and respond by pressing **p**. Then `fdisk` prompts me for the partition number. Because the first partition already exists, I enter **2** to indicate that this is the second partition. Next, `fdisk` requires the starting-cylinder number; the prompt shows the range of cylinder numbers available. I enter the lowest available cylinder number. Finally, `fdisk` needs the ending cylinder number or the size of the partition, in megabytes or kilobytes. I type **+16M** to create a 16MB partition.

To see whether the new partition has been created properly, I press **p**. The `fdisk` program displays the following partition table:

```
Disk /dev/hda: 32 heads, 63 sectors, 528 cylinders
Units = cylinders of 2016 * 512 bytes

    Device Boot    Begin    Start     End   Blocks    Id  System
/dev/hda1     *        1        1     405  408208+    6   DOS 16-bit >=32M
/dev/hda2            406      406     422   17136    83   Linux native

Command (m for help):
```

The System column indicates that the new partition (`/dev/hda2`) is *Linux native* and that the ID of the Linux partition is 83 (as shown in the Id column).

Tip

Notice the number of blocks in the partition that you intend to use as a swap partition. To make the swap partition ready to use, you have to perform another step, for which you need the swap partition's size, in number of blocks.

To create the main Linux partition, I repeat the steps, this time using the rest of the disk as the third primary partition (`/dev/hda3`), as follows:

```
Command (m for help): n
Command action
   e   extended
   p   primary partition (1-4)
p
Partition number (1-4): 3
First cylinder (511-528): 423
Last cylinder or +size or +sizeM or +sizeK (406-528): 527

Command (m for help): p

Disk /dev/hda: 32 heads, 63 sectors, 528 cylinders
Units = cylinders of 2016 * 512 bytes

    Device Boot    Begin    Start     End   Blocks    Id  System
/dev/hda1     *        1        1     405  408208+    6   DOS 16-bit >=32M
/dev/hda2            406      406     422   17136    83   Linux native
/dev/hda2            423      423     527  105840    83   Linux native

Command (m for help):
```

Next, I press **w** to write this partition table and exit `fdisk`. Even though `fdisk` displays a message suggesting that I reboot to ensure that the partition table is updated, I don't really have to do so.

Special instructions for OS/2

If you use the OS/2 Boot Manager, you should prepare the Linux partitions under OS/2. Then you should add the main Linux partition (the larger one that will hold all Linux files, not the smaller Linux swap partition) to the Boot Manager's table. Next, in Linux, you have to change the types of the OS/2 partitions that you plan to use for Linux.

To change the type of a partition, start `fdisk`, and use the **t** command. The `fdisk` program asks you for the partition number whose type you want to change, as well as for the hexadecimal code for the type. To change the type of partition number 2 to 83 (Linux native), for example, use `fdisk` as follows:

```
Command (m for help): t
Partition number (1-4): 2
Hex code (type L to list codes): 83
```

If you want to see the codes for all partition types that Linux understands, press **L** at the prompt. The `fdisk` program then lists all the known partition types. Of course, there really is no reason (other than curiosity) for you to learn about all the partition types. You may want to know, however, that code 83 indicates a Linux partition.

After entering the partition's type, make sure that you press **w** so that `fdisk` writes the changes to the disk before it exits.

Setting up a swap partition

Most advanced operating systems support the concept of *virtual memory*, in which part of your system's hard disk is used as an extension of the physical memory (RAM). When the operating system runs out of physical memory, it can move (or swap out) the contents of currently unneeded parts of RAM to make room for a program that needs more memory. As soon as the time comes to access anything in the swapped-out data, the operating system has to find something else to swap out and then swap in the required data from disk. This process of swapping data back and forth between the RAM and the disk is known as *paging*.

Because the disk is much slower than RAM, the system's performance is slower when the operating system has to perform a lot of paging, but virtual memory allows you to run programs that you otherwise would not be able to run.

Linux supports virtual memory and can make use of a swap partition, if you have one. If you have less than 4MB of memory, in fact, you cannot even go through the installation steps without first creating and setting up a swap partition.

When you created the Linux partitions, you should have created a swap partition for Linux. You have to perform three more steps: mark the partition as a swap partition, initialize the swap partition, and make Linux use it.

Marking a partition as a swap partition involves changing its type. You could have performed this step when you created the partition because you have to use `fdisk` to change a partition's type. Making the change now is easy enough, though. Suppose that you want to use the `/dev/hda2` partition as the swap partition. To mark that partition as a swap partition, start `fdisk` and use the following steps in `fdisk`:

```
Command (m for help): t
Partition number (1-4): 2
Hex code (type L to list codes): 82
Command (m for help): w
```

That procedure changes the swap partition's type to 82, which is the code for Linux swap partitions. Press **w** to write the new partition information to the disk.

Tip

You should change the type of the swap partition to 82 to ensure that the setup program can detect the swap partition and help you install the swap partition properly.

To initialize the swap partition, enter the following command:

```
# mkswap -c /dev/hda2 17136
```

Here, /dev/hda2 is the partition name for the swap partition, and 17136 is the block size of the swap partition. If you forgot the block size of the swap partition, you can simply run fdisk again and press **p** to see the partition table. Then quit fdisk by pressing **q**.

This command makes Linux use the swap partition for virtual memory:

```
# swapon /dev/hda2
```

When you run the setup program to install Linux, you have the option of setting up the swap partition. The setup program adds the swap partition's name in a special file named /etc/fstab. From then on, Linux sets up and uses the swap partition automatically whenever it boots.

Tip

The size of the swap partition depends on the amount of virtual memory you need. To Linux, the total amount of memory in your PC is the combined total of the swap partition's size and the amount of physical RAM. Although there is no formula to tell you how much virtual memory you need, the conventional wisdom is that you should have at least 16MB. That means, if your system has 8MB of physical RAM, you should create an 8MB swap partition. If you can spare the disk space, you may want to provide a total of 24 to 32MB of virtual memory. I typically use a 16MB swap partition on PCs with 8 to 16MB of physical RAM.

Note

In Linux, a single swap partition can be up to 128MB, but you can have up to 16 swap partitions in all. So you can have as much as 2,048MB (or 2GB) of swap space. All you have to do is run the mkswap and swapon commands for each swap partition that you create.

Installing Linux from the Slackware CD-ROM

Finally, you have completed all the prerequisites to install Linux on your PC: You have successfully booted Linux from a floppy disk, prepared the hard disk partitions, and set up a swap partition. The remaining step involves copying various Linux disk sets to the hard disk.

Compared with all the steps that you have been through, the actual installation step is relatively easy. All you have to do is type the following command:

```
# setup
```

This command displays a colorful text-based interface through which you complete the remaining installation steps (see Figure 1-7).

```
+ - - - - - - Slackware Linux Setup (version FD-3.0.0 ELF) - - - - - +
| Welcome to Slackware Linux Setup.                                   |
| Select an option below using the UP/DOWN keys and SPACE or ENTER.   |
| Alternate keys may also be used: '+', '-', and TAB.                 |
| + - - - - - - - - - - - - - - - - - - - - - - - - - - - - - - - + |
| |   HELP       Read the Slackware Setup HELP file                | |
| |   KEYMAP     Remap your keyboard if you're not using a US one  | |
| |   QUICK      Choose QUICK or VERBOSE install mode [now: VERBOSE]| |
| |   MAKE TAGS  Experts may customize tagfiles to preselect packages| |
| |   ADDSWAP    Set up your swap partition(s)                     | |
| |   TARGET     Set up your target partitions                     | |
| |   SOURCE     Select source media                               | |
| |   DISK SETS  Decide which disk sets you wish to install        | |
| |   INSTALL    Install selected disk sets                        | |
| |   CONFIGURE  Reconfigure your Linux system                     | |
| |   EXIT       Exit Slackware Linux Setup                        | |
| + - - - - - - - - - - - - - - - - - - - - - - - - - - - - - - - + |
+ - - - - - - - - - - - - - - - - - - - - - - - - - - - - - - - - - +
|                    < OK >      <Cancel>                             |
+ - - - - - - - - - - - - - - - - - - - - - - - - - - - - - - - - - +
```

Figure 1-7: Main menu of the Slackware Linux setup program.

To select an option, press the up- and down-arrow keys and then press Enter to activate the option. You also can press the first letter of an option to select that option. To read the help file, for example, press **H**; the setup program highlights the HELP option. Then press Enter to activate the HELP option.

In this menu, you should start with the ADDSWAP option. Because the setup program takes you from one option to the next automatically, you go through the following sequence:

- ADDSWAP to set up the swap space for Linux
- TARGET to tell the setup program where to put Linux
- SOURCE to tell the setup program where the Linux distribution is located (usually, the CD-ROM drive)
- DISK SETS to select the software packages that you want to install
- INSTALL to install the software
- CONFIGURE to configure some of the installed software

When you start with the ADDSWAP option, the setup program guides you through the rest automatically; you never have to return to the program's main menu.

Finally, select EXIT to quit the setup program.

A final note: Make sure that you use VERBOSE mode. In VERBOSE mode, the setup program displays the current install mode on the menu's QUICK option. To change to VERBOSE mode, press **Q** and then choose VERBOSE from the menu that appears.

Adding the swap space

Press **A** to select the ADDSWAP option; then press Enter. The setup program checks the partition table and locates any partition of type 82, which denotes a Linux swap partition. The program shows you the information about the swap partition and asks whether you want to install this as your system's swap partition. Press Enter to accept the default choice, Yes.

In the next two steps, the setup program offers to prepare the swap partition with the mkswap command and to turn swapping on with the swapon command. You already performed these steps before reaching this point in the installation, however. You should select No in response to the dialog boxes that offer to run mkswap and swapon.

Then the setup program displays a message indicating that the swap partition will be added to a file named /etc/fstab file. Addition of the swap partition to the /etc/fstab file ensures that, in the future, Linux automatically uses the swap partition whenever you boot Linux from the hard disk.

If you have more than one Linux swap partition (partitions of type 82) in the partition table, the setup program allows you to set up the others as well.

Selecting the target

After the swap-space configuration is finished, the setup program asks whether you want to continue with the next step: selecting the target, which refers to the partition where you want the setup program to install Linux. As it did with the swap partitions, the setup program checks the partition table, displays the disk partitions of type 83 (Linux native), and prompts you to enter the name of the partition where you want to install Linux. Type the partition name (for example, /dev/hda3) that you want to use as the root directory (/) of Linux.

The setup program then asks whether you want to format the partition. As you do with MS-DOS, you have to format a Linux partition before Linux can use it. The setup program offers three options:

```
Format   Quick format with no bad block checking
Check    Slow format that checks for bad blocks
No       No, do not format this partition
```

The default option is Format — a quick format. You can safely use the quick-format option for IDE and SCSI disks, because these disks avoid bad spots automatically. To accept the default option (Format Quick format), press Enter.

To format the partition, the setup program prompts you for information about inodes. Linux subdivides the disk partition into smaller blocks and assigns a number to each block. These blocks are the *inodes*. You are asked for the size of these blocks; the default is 4,096 bytes per inode. You should accept the default choice by pressing Enter.

If you are familiar with MS-DOS disk terminology, the Linux inodes are similar to clusters in MS-DOS. In MS-DOS, the cluster size increases as the size of the disk increases. In Linux, however, you can set the inode size to a small 4,096 bytes (4K) regardless of disk size.

The setup program then completes the formatting (which really *is* quick). If you have only one Linux partition, you are done with this step. If you have more than one Linux partition (you may have a second disk with a Linux partition), you can use all of them in Linux. All you have to do is decide which part of the Linux directory tree should be located on each partition — a process known in Linux as mounting a file system on a device (the disk partition is a device).

Suppose that you have two disks on your PC, and you have created Linux partitions on both disks. Figure 1-8 illustrates how you can mount different parts of the Linux directory tree (the file system) on these two partitions.

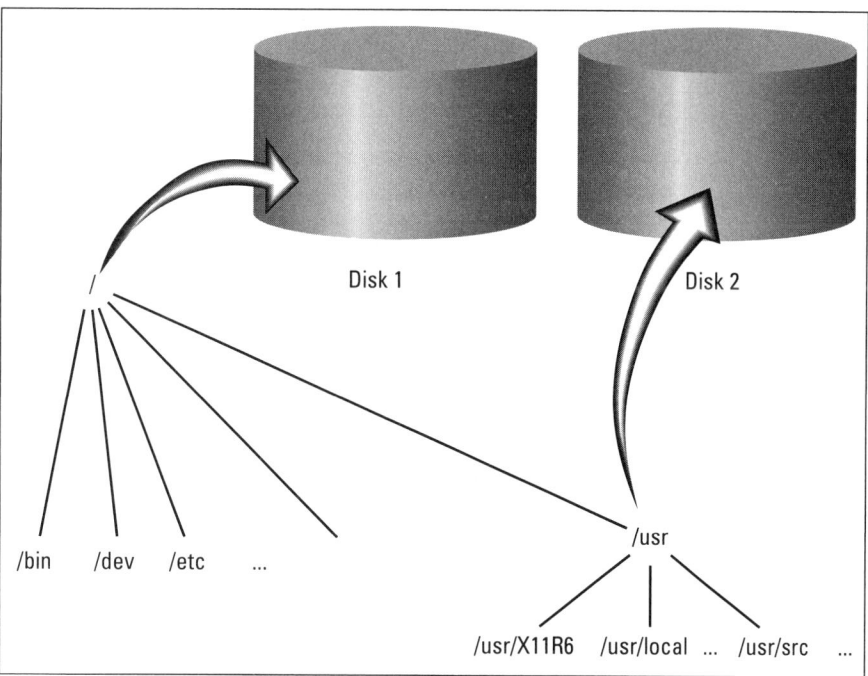

Figure 1-8: An example of mounting the Linux file system on two disk partitions.

When the setup program finishes formatting all Linux partitions, press **q** and then press Enter.

The setup program asks whether you want to access any existing DOS partition from Linux (of course, you don't see this option if your system has no DOS partition). Electing to access a DOS partition from Linux does not affect the system's performance, and you get the benefit of being able to copy files between Linux and DOS (you never know when you will need this capability). You should press Enter to say Yes to this question.

The setup program then prompts you to enter the name of the DOS or OS/2 partition. Type the name (such as `/dev/hda1`), and press Enter. Next, you have to decide where in the Linux file system you want to see the DOS partition (another way of saying this is "which part of the Linux file system is mounted on the DOS partition"). For example, you can enter `/dosc`; then you can access the DOS files in the `/dosc` directory in Linux. This mnemonic is good because the name dosc should remind you that this drive is the C drive under DOS.

The setup program informs you that a line will be added to the `/etc/fstab` file to allow you to access the DOS partition. You do not really need to understand the line to access the DOS files under Linux. Press Enter to continue.

If you have other DOS or OS/2 partitions, the setup program allows you to access each one from Linux. When you finish with the DOS and OS/2 partitions, press **q** and then press Enter to proceed to the next step.

Selecting the source

In the preceding section, you specified the destination of the installation process. Now the setup program displays a dialog box, asking whether you want to proceed to the next major installation step, which is selecting the source: the location of the Slackware Linux disk sets. Press Enter to continue.

The setup program displays five choices for the source of the Linux disk sets:

```
1   Install from a hard drive partition
2   Install from floppy disks
3   Install via NFS
4   Install from a pre-mounted directory
5   Install from CD-ROM
```

In the context of this book, the source is the CD-ROM drive, because you are installing Linux from the Slackware Linux CD-ROM that accompanies this book. You can, however, install Linux from four other sources, including floppy disks. The term *NFS* in the list refers to Network File System, which allows your system to access a disk on another system in a local-area network (for this procedure to work, however, you must use one of the boot images that support Ethernet networks). In this book, I focus on installing from the CD-ROM drive only. The steps for installing from other sources, however, are similar to the ones I describe.

Press **5** to indicate that the source is the CD-ROM drive; then press Enter. The setup program displays a selection of CD-ROM drives, as follows:

```
scan   Try to scan for your CD drive
1      SCSI (/dev/scd0 or /dev/scd1)
2      Sony CDU31A (/dev/sonycd)
3      Sony 531/535 (/dev/cdu535)
4      Mitsumi (/dev/mcd)
5      Sound Blaster Pro/Panasonic (/dev/sbpcd)
6      Aztech/Orchid/Okano/Wearnes with interface card
7      Most IDE-interface CD drives
```

Some entries in the list show the type of CD-ROM drive, as well as the Linux name for the device (for example, /dev/sbpcd for Sound Blaster Pro CD). Press the number that corresponds to your CD-ROM dive. If your CD-ROM drive has an IDE (also known as ATAPI) interface, for example, press **7** and then press Enter.

The next step depends on the CD-ROM drive type that you select. If you select an IDE-interface CD-ROM drive, for example, the setup program asks you to indicate which IDE device represents your CD-ROM drive, as follows:

```
scan       Try to scan for your drive
/dev/hda   Primary IDE drive 1
/dev/hdb   Primary IDE drive 2
/dev/hdc   Secondary IDE drive 1
/dev/hdd   Secondary IDE drive 2
```

If you watch the initial boot messages closely, you may notice the exact device name for the CD-ROM drive. If you are not sure, select the scan option and then press Enter. The setup program scans for a CD-ROM drive and indicates whether it finds any. If the setup program does not find a CD-ROM drive, you may have started with the wrong Linux boot image or specified the wrong type of CD-ROM drive. If the setup program indicates that it has found a CD-ROM drive, simply press Enter to continue.

When the setup program finds the CD-ROM drive, it asks you what type of installation you want. You have the following options:

```
help       Read the installation method help file
slakware   Normal installation to hard drive
slaktest   Link /usr -> /cdrom/usr to run mostly from CD
custom     Install from a custom directory
```

The slaktest option installs only a small part of Linux on your hard disk, leaving the rest on the CD-ROM. Although you can run Linux with most of the files on the CD-ROM, the performance is poor, because a CD-ROM's data-transfer rates are much slower than those of a hard disk. Still, you may decide to use the slaktest option if you have limited disk space.

If you have enough disk space (at least 300MB, if you install the Linux operating system and X Window System), select the slakware option and press Enter.

Selecting disk sets

After you go through the options for indicating the source, the setup program asks whether you want to continue to the next step: specifying which disk sets you want to install. Press Enter to accept the default option (Yes). The setup program then displays a Series Selection menu that lists the disk sets that you can install. You see only a small part of the list, but you can press the down-arrow key to scroll down the list to see more entries.

Press the up- and down-arrow keys to move from one item to another in the list. Each item is designated by a letter code (such as A or AP) and has a pair of square brackets next to the name; an X within the square brackets indicate that the disk set is selected. Press the spacebar to toggle a selection on or off.

The setup program installs the disk sets that have an X next to them. One disk set, which represents the base Linux operating system, is already selected; this disk set is required, so you should leave it alone. The setup program offers the following list of disk sets (the one marked with an X is the required disk set):

```
[ ] CUS   Also prompt for CUSTOM disk sets
[X] A     Base Linux system
[ ] AP    Various Applications that do not need X
[ ] D     Program Development (C, C++, Lisp, Perl, etc.)
[ ] E     GNU Emacs
[ ] F     FAQ lists, HOWTO documentation
[ ] K     Linux kernel source
[ ] N     Networking (TCP/IP, UUCP, Mail, News)

[ ] Q     Extra Linux kernels with UMSDOS/non-SCSI CD drivers
[ ] T     TeX typesetting software
[ ] TCL   Tcl/Tk script languages
[ ] X     XFree86 X Window System
[ ] XAP   X Applications
[ ] XD    X Server development kit
[ ] XV    XView (OpenLook Window Manager, apps)
[ ] Y     Games (that do not require X)
```

You should not install all the disk sets, because you may not need many programs. If you do not want to use TeX, for example, you do not have to install the T disk set. Even when you plan to use some software, such as the XFree86 X Window System, you may decide to forgo the XD disk set because you do not plan to develop any X server (this is the program that manages the display).

Note

To go through the material presented in this book, you should choose the disk sets A, AP, D, E, F, K, N, Q, TCL, X, XAP, and Y. The setup program subdivides each disk set into packages, and you can further select specific packages to install. This process is described in the following section.

To help you decide which packages to select, Table 1-4 provides an annotated list of the disk sets (with some recommendations on which ones to install).

Table 1-4	Linux disk sets
Set	*Contents*
A	This disk set contains the base Linux system that you must install. With this disk set alone, you can get Linux up and running. The setup program always installs this disk set.
AP	This disk set contains various Linux applications and files, such as on-line-manual pages, editors (such as jove, jed, joe, and vim), the Ghostscript PostScript interpreter, a few shells (command interpreters, such as zsh and ash), the groff text-formatting package, and the ispell spelling checker.
D	This disk set contains C and C++ software-development tools, including GNU C++, Objective C, GNU debugger, Common Lisp, the Perl scripting language, and the RCS revision control system.
E	This disk set contains the GNU Emacs editor and its supporting files. If you use GNU Emacs, install this disk set.
F	This disk set is a collection of files that contain frequently asked questions (or FAQs, as they commonly are called). Installing this set is helpful, because it enables you to look up answers to common questions in the FAQ files.
K	This disk set contains the source code for two versions of the Linux kernel: 1.2.13 and 1.3.20. Version 1.2.13 is the latest stable kernel whereas 1.3.20 is the latest development version. You should install the source files, because you need them to apply any fixes and rebuild the kernel. (*Kernel* refers to the core operating system, as opposed to all the supporting programs in an operating system. Therefore, Linux kernel source files contain the source code for the Linux operating system.)
N	This disk set contains networking software, including TCP/IP, Point-to-Point Protocol (PPP), dip (dial-up Internet Protocol), the netcfg TCP/IP configuration script, various electronic-mail programs (sendmail, elm, mailx, pine, and so on), and news software for reading USENET news (a bulletin-board system available on the Internet). If you want to use your Linux PC on a network, install this disk set. In Chapter 16, you learn more about networks. Note that the TCP/IP networking under Linux does not directly connect to a lot of PC LANs that use Netware or LAN Manager. In Chapter 21, you'll see how to connect a Linux PC to a LAN Manager network.
Q	This disk set includes various Linux kernels, each with support for a different set of CD-ROM drive and disk. You must pick a kernel from this set as the version of Linux to boot your PC. In the Series Selection menu, select this set. Then, during the installation, you should choose to install the kernel that includes support for your CD-ROM drive and for any SCSI controller that you may have on your PC.
T	This disk set contains the TeX (pronounced "tech," as in *technology*) document-formatting system. Install this disk set only if you know TeX and plan to use it.

Cross Reference

(continued)

Table 1-4 *(continued)*

TCL	This disk set contains the popular Tool Command Language (Tcl, pronounced "tickle") scripting language as well as Tk, the toolkit that you use to create graphical Tcl programs with the X Window System. Install this disk set because Chapter 8 of this book covers Tcl/Tk.
X	This disk set includes the XFree86 3.1.2 X Window System. Install this disk set. In Chapter 4, you will find information on configuring XFree86 for your mouse and video card.
XAP	This disk set contains various X applications, such as xpaint, xv, xfilemanager, and some X games. Install this disk set for use with XFree86.
XV	This disk set contains the XView toolkit — a library for use in building X applications with the OPEN LOOK graphical user interface. You should install this set if you plan to write X applications.
Y	This disk set contains a collection of well-known UNIX games (X is not required), such as Hangman, Dungeon, and Snake. The set also includes id Software's DOOM. (This game comes in two versions, one runs under X, and the other runs without X.) You may want to install this disk set just so you can try out DOOM.

Installing the disk sets

After you select the disk sets to install, press Enter. The setup program asks whether you want to go to the INSTALL option in the main menu. Press Enter to indicate Yes. The setup program then displays the following list of prompting modes:

```
Normal  Use the default tagfiles
Custom  Use custom tagfiles in the package directories
Path    Use tagfiles in the subdirectories of a custom path
None    Use no tagfiles - install everything
HELP    Read the prompt mode help file
```

Each disk set contains packages; you can *tag* (mark) these packages as ones that you want to install or skip. This information is stored in files that are known as *tagfiles*. When you use the default tagfiles, the setup program installs the packages that are mandatory and prompts you for the optional packages. You should press Enter to accept the default option (Normal).

Do not select the None option, which installs everything. The disk sets contain files that may conflict with one another, so it is a good idea to go through the packages one by one and select only those that your PC needs (depending on your PC's hardware configuration).

The setup program begins installing the packages from the CD-ROM. As installation proceeds, the setup program automatically installs any package that it considers to be mandatory, but it prompts you for the packages that are optional. For each optional package, the setup program shows you the package's name and a brief description. The program also tells you the disk space that the package requires. (Unfortunately, the setup program does not provide any running total of disk space used so far.)

To install a package, press Enter (because the default option is to install the package). If you do not want to install the package, press the down-arrow key and then press Enter.

Caution

When you respond to the prompts from the setup program, respond carefully, because you cannot go back and change any option.

The following sections provide a running summary of typical prompts that you can expect to see as the setup program installs disk sets A, AP, D, E, F, K, N, Q, TCL, X, XAP, and Y. Although you may see slightly different prompts if the Slackware Linux distribution is a later version than Slackware Pro Linux 3.0, the package names should give you a feel for what decisions you have to make during installation. I have added some recommendations about whether you should install a package or skip it:

Disk set A

idenet — a Linux kernel with support for IDE drives and Ethernet. Skip this package because it does not include support for a CD-ROM drive (which you want; after all, you are installing from a CD-ROM). You should pick a kernel from the Q disk set.

scsi — a Linux kernel with support for SCSI disks. Skip this one, and pick a kernel from the Q disk set.

getty — a package that enables users to log in through the serial port. Install it.

comms — contains file-transfer and serial-communications programs. Install it so that you can try these programs.

gpm — a program that provides General Purpose Mouse (GPM) support. Install it (but keep in mind that when gpm is used with a bus mouse, it may interfere with the X Window System; if this happens, you can simply stop the gpm program).

keytbls — software that allows you to *remap* keyboards (change the layout of the keyboard). You do not have to install this package if you are using the U.S. keyboard (but you should install it if you want to use a non-U.S. keyboard layout).

loadlin — a package that allows you to load Linux from the DOS command prompt (yes, Linux is really versatile). Install it so that you can boot Linux from DOS.

tcsh — a *shell* (command interpreter) patterned after the C shell. Install it, if you are interested. (If you plan to stick with the default Linux shell, known as bash, you can skip this shell.)

> ### What's GNU?
>
> *GNU*, which stands for *GNU Is Not UNIX*, is a project of the Free Software Foundation in Cambridge, Massachusetts, which aims to develop a free version of UNIX. Although that version of UNIX, called HURD, is not yet complete, the GNU project has already generated many high-quality programming tools, ranging from the `emacs` editor to the famous GNU C and C++ compilers (gcc and g++) that run on virtually any computer system. All GNU software and derivative work are covered by the GNU General Public License (GPL), which allows the author to copyright the software but gives everyone legal permission to copy, distribute, and modify the software. Linux is based on GNU code and was developed with the use of many GNU tools. The companion CD-ROM includes many of these GNU tools, which this book refers to at various times.

Disk set AP

jove — a text editor patterned after the `emacs` editor. Do not install it unless you already know jove. Later, you get a chance to install the GNU Emacs editor with disk set E.

man — the on-line-manual pages, which you should install.

termbin — a package that supports multiple sessions conducted over modem lines. Skip it unless you're using the computer as a dial-up server.

termnet — utility programs (such as tncftp, ttelnet, tfinger, and twhois) for the termbin package. Install it only if you installed termbin.

termsrc — contains source code that you have to upload to the other system (the system to which you want to connect) and then compile and build. If you plan to use termbin, you need this package. Do not install termscr if you skipped termbin and termnet.

diff — the GNU diff utility program to compare two files. You should install this package, because you can use it to apply *patches* (corrections) to source files.

ghostscr — the Ghostscript 2.6 software for viewing PostScript files. Install it if you want to try it.

gsfonts1 — fonts for Ghostscript. Install this package if you installed the ghost package.

jed — another editor. Skip it.

joe — yet another text editor with a WordStar-like command set. If you don't know WordStar (a popular word processor from the early days of the PC), you won't miss this one. Skip it.

sudo — a package that allows some users to execute commands as root. Skip it.

gsfonts2 — more Ghostscript fonts. Install this package only if you installed the ghost package.

zsh — yet another shell — a UNIX-command interpreter. Skip it.

Chapter 1: Installing Linux

ash — one more shell, a command interpreter that is compatible with the well-known Bourne shell. Skip it.

bc — a calculator program. This program needs very little disk space, so you should install it.

ftape — software for tape drives connected to the PC's floppy disk controller, such as the ones sold by Colorado Memory Systems. Install this package if you have a QIC-40- or QIC-80-format floppy tape drive.

gp9600 — a *script file* (a file that contains Linux commands) that allows you to set the modem speed. Install it if you plan to use a modem.

groff — the GNU document-formatting system. Install it if you plan to format documents.

manpgs — another set of on-line help pages. Install it.

mt_st — software for magnetic tapes with Small Computer System Interface (SCSI). Unless you have a SCSI tape drive, do not install this package.

sc — a spreadsheet program. Install it.

texinfo — a package that allows you to create on-line-manual pages and printed output from the same source file. No need to install it.

vim — another text editor, which is supposed to be an improved version of the vi editor. Skip it.

workbone — a text-based program that allows you to play audio CDs in the CD-ROM drive. Install it so that you can try it.

ispell — a spell-check program. Install it.

jpeg — software for reading and writing JPEG (Joint Photographic Experts Group) images. Install it if you plan to work with images.

mc — the Midnight Commander program, patterned after the popular DOS program Norton Commander. If you are familiar with Norton Commander, you may want to install this package.

shlbsvga — shared SVGA (Super VGA) graphics libraries. Install this package, because some graphics programs need the libraries.

Disk set D

Cross Reference

gcc270 — GNU C and C++ compilers and associated files with support for the new Executable and Linking Format (ELF). Install this package, because you need it to compile and build programs. You need this package even if you do not plan to write any programs, because you need it when you want to rebuild the Linux kernel after you apply a fix, for example. Chapter 2 shows you how to rebuild the Linux kernel.

byacc — the Berkeley YACC (stands for Yet Another Compiler Compiler) program that you can use to build compilers. You can skip it.

man2 — on-line-manual pages for system calls. Install it if you are going to write programs.

objc270 — the Objective C compiler. Objective C is an object-oriented extension to C. Unless you want to explore Objective C, you do not need to install this package.

p2c — a Pascal-to-C translator. No need to install it.

gdb — the GNU debugger. Install if you are developing software in Linux.

libgxx — the GNU library, including files for the GNU C++ compiler. Install it.

man3 — on-line-manual pages for the C library. Install it if you plan to write programs.

rcs — the GNU revision-control system (RCS). Install the package if you plan to develop software on your Linux PC.

f2c — a Fortran 77-to-C translator. No need to install it.

m4 — the GNU macro expander. Install it, because the sendmail package (for electronic mail) needs it.

ncurses — a screen-management library with support for color. Skip it.

svgalib — a video graphics library for many common video cards. You can skip it.

perl — the popular Perl (Practical Extraction Report Language) scripting language by Larry Wall. Install it, because you may find scripts that use Perl.

strace — a package that traces the execution of a command. Skip it.

bison — the GNU Bison parser generator (similar to the byacc package). Skip it.

Disk set E

emacsbin — various files for GNU Emacs 19.28. Install this package if you plan to use the `emacs` editor.

elispc1 — more files (part 1) for GNU Emacs. Install it if you installed emacsbin.

elispc2 — more files (part 2) for GNU Emacs. Install it if you installed emacsbin.

elisp1 — Lisp source code, part 1, for GNU Emacs. No need to install it.

elisp2 — Lisp source code, part 2, for GNU Emacs. No need to install it.

emacinfo — info files with documentation for GNU Emacs.

emac_nox — a scaled-down version of GNU Emacs that does not use X (you can still run it in a terminal window in the X Window System). Install this version if you are not going to install the X Window System.

Disk set F

All packages are mandatory, and the setup program installs them automatically.

Disk set K

lx1213_1 — Linux kernel source, part 1, for version 1.2.13. Install it.

lx1213_2 — Linux kernel source, part 2, for version 1.2.13. Install it.

lx1213_3 — Linux kernel source, part 3, for version 1.2.13. Install it.

lx1320_1 — Linux kernel source, part 1, for version 1.3.20. Skip it unless you feel like experimenting with version 1.3.20.

lx1320_2 — Linux kernel source, part 2, for version 1.3.20. Skip it unless you feel like experimenting with version 1.3.20.

lx1320_3 — Linux kernel source, part 3, for version 1.3.20. Skip it unless you feel like experimenting with version 1.3.20.

lx1320_4 — Linux kernel source, part 4, for version 1.3.20. Skip it unless you feel like experimenting with version 1.3.20.

Disk set N

elm — an interactive mail program. Install it.

netcfg — a script for configuring TCP/IP and mail. Install it.

rdist — a remote file-distribution program. Skip it.

tcpip — TCP/IP (Transmission Control Protocol/Internet Protocol) networking software. Install it.

deliver — software for local mail delivery. Skip it.

mailx — the Berkeley UNIX version of the mail program. Skip it.

pine — another mail program based on elm. Skip it.

sendmail — the Berkeley UNIX sendmail software. Install it.

smailcfg — configuration files for sendmail. Install it.

uucp — UNIX-to-UNIX Copy (UUCP) software. Install it.

cnews — software for managing USENET news — the bulletin-board system of the Internet. Install it.

dip — a dial-up IP connection handler. Install it.

inn — Internet news-transport software. Install it if you have access to a news server on the Internet.

Cross Reference

ppp — Point-to-Point Protocol (PPP) for Linux. Install it, because you can use it to connect to a Internet Service Provider. (See Chapter 18 for information on PPP.)

tin — a full-screen, threaded news-reader program (the term threaded refers to the news reader's ability to keep track of an article and all of its replies). Install it.

trn-nntp — software for reading news on a remote Network News Transfer Protocol (NNTP) server. Install it if you have access to a news server on the Internet (through an Internet Access Provider, for example).

trn — software for reading news from the local system. Install it.

bind — a name-server daemon. (Software that runs in the background is called a *daemon*.) Skip it unless you plan to run a name server (a program that converts the name of a system to its IP address).

nn-nntp — software for reading news via Network News Transfer Protocol (NNTP). Skip it if you installed trn-nntp.

nn-spool — software for reading news from the local system. Skip it if you installed trn.

Disk set Q

Tip

The packages in disk set Q have Linux kernels (the operating-system program). The kernel that you select from Q is the kernel used to boot Linux. You should choose only one kernel, and the selected kernel should support your PC's hard disk and CD-ROM drive.

To select a kernel smartly from disk set Q, select a package with a name similar to that of the boot image that you used in the Linux boot disk. Disk set Q has two separate packages for most of the boot images. Each package supports your CD-ROM drive, but the packages differ in terms of the list of supported SCSI controllers. If you used the IDECD boot image, for example, select the kernel from the package idecd1 or idecd2 (depending on your PC's SCSI controller, if any). When the setup program displays information about these packages, read the information carefully before you select one of them.

aztech1 — a Linux kernel with support for Aztech, Orchid, Okano, and Wearnes CD-ROM drives with proprietary interface; also supports Adaptec, Buslogic, EATA-DMA, Seagate, and Future Domain SCSI controllers. Install the package if it matches your CD-ROM drive and SCSI controller.

aztech2 — same as aztech1, but with support for NCR, Always, Pro Audio Spectrum, QLogic, Trantor, Ultrastor, and FASST SCSI controllers. Install the package if it matches your CD-ROM drive and SCSI controller.

bare — a Linux kernel with only IDE drive support. You probably do not want this one if you are already installing from a CD-ROM.

cdu31a1 — a Linux kernel that supports Sony CDU31a or CDU33a CD-ROM drives with proprietary interface; also supports Adaptec, Buslogic, EATA-DMA, Seagate, and Future Domain SCSI controllers. Install the package if it matches your CD-ROM drive and SCSI controller.

cdu31a2 — same as cdu31a1, but with support for NCR, Always, Pro Audio Spectrum, QLogic, Trantor, Ultrastor, and FASST SCSI controllers. Install the package if it matches your CD-ROM drive and SCSI controller.

cdu535_1 — a Linux kernel that supports Sony CDU535 or CDU531 CD-ROM drives with proprietary interface; also supports Adaptec, Buslogic, EATA-DMA, Seagate, and Future Domain SCSI controllers. Install the package if it matches your CD-ROM drive and SCSI controller.

cdu535_2 — same as cdu535_1, but with support for NCR, Always, Pro Audio Spectrum, QLogic, Trantor, Ultrastor, and FASST SCSI controllers. Install the package if it matches your CD-ROM drive and SCSI controller.

idecd1 — a Linux kernel that supports any CD-ROM drive (such as Sony, NEC, Mitsumi, Wearnes, and others) that connects to your PC through an IDE (also known as AT Attachment Packet Interface, or ATAPI) interface. The package also supports Adaptec, Buslogic, EATA-DMA, Seagate, and Future Domain SCSI controllers. Install the package if it matches your CD-ROM drive and SCSI controller.

idecd2 — same as idecd1, but with support for NCR, Always, Pro Audio Spectrum, QLogic, Trantor, Ultrastor, and FASST SCSI controllers. Install the package if it matches your CD-ROM drive and SCSI controller.

idenet — a Linux kernel with IDE hard disk and Ethernet support. You probably do not want this package, because it has no CD-ROM support.

mitsumi1 — a Linux kernel that supports Mitsumi CD-ROM drives with proprietary interface; also supports Adaptec, Buslogic, EATA-DMA, Seagate, and Future Domain SCSI controllers. Install the package if it matches your CD-ROM drive and SCSI controller.

mitsumi2 — same as mitsumi1, but with support for NCR, Always, Pro Audio Spectrum, QLogic, Trantor, Ultrastor, and FASST SCSI controllers. Install the package if it matches your CD-ROM drive and SCSI controller.

sbpcd1 — a Linux kernel that supports Sound Blaster Pro CD-ROM drives (connected via the Sound Blaster Pro interface); also supports Adaptec, Buslogic, EATA-DMA, Seagate, and Future Domain SCSI controllers. Install the package if it matches your CD-ROM drive and SCSI controller.

sbpcd2 — same as sbpcd1, but with support for NCR, Always, Pro Audio Spectrum, QLogic, Trantor, Ultrastor, and FASST SCSI controllers. Install the package if it matches your CD-ROM drive and SCSI controller.

scsi — a Linux kernel with IDE hard disk and all SCSI devices, including SCSI CD-ROM drives. Install the package if you have a SCSI CD-ROM drive.

scsinet1 — a Linux kernel that supports Ethernet and Adaptec, Buslogic, EATA-DMA, Seagate, and Future Domain SCSI controllers. You can use this package if you have one of these SCSI controllers and a SCSI CD-ROM drive.

scsinet2 — same as scsinet1, but with support for NCR, Always, Pro Audio Spectrum, QLogic, Trantor, Ultrastor, and FASST SCSI controllers. Install the package if it supports your SCSI controller and if you have a SCSI CD-ROM drive.

Part I: Configuring Your Linux System

xt — a Linux kernel with support for IDE and old IBM PC-XT hard drives. You probably do not want this package, because it does not support any CD-ROM drive.

Disk set TCL

tcl — the Tool Command Language (TCL) software developed by John Ousterhout. Install the package. Chapter 8 shows you how you might use Tcl and Tk.

tk — the toolkit for building X applications with Tcl. Install it.

Disk set X

The X server is the program that manages the display screen through the video card. From the X disk set, you should select an X server for your video card. The X server that you install becomes your default X server, so you should select the correct one, if possible. You need to know either the make of your video card or the chipset used in the video card. Based on this information, you should be able to select an appropriate X server. You learn how to configure the X server in Chapter 4.

x3128514 — an accelerated X server for video cards that use IBM 8514 chipsets.

x312agx — an accelerated X server for video cards that use the IIT AGX-015, AGX-016, and AGX-014 chipsets.

x312ma32 — an accelerated X server for video cards that use Mach32 chips.

x312ma8 — an accelerated X server for video cards that use Mach8 chips.

x312mono — a monochrome X server for video cards such as the Hercules monochrome card and VGA in monochrome mode.

x312p9k — an accelerated X server for video cards that use the Weitek P9000 chipset (Diamond Viper VLB, Diamond Viper PCI, Orchid P9000, and others).

x312s3 — an accelerated X server for video cards that use the S3 chipsets: 911, 924, 801, 805, 928, 864, 964, Trio32, and Trio64. (These chipsets represent a wide variety of brand names, such as Diamond Stealth 24 VLB, Diamond Stealth 64, Number Nine GXE64, Number Nine GXE64 PCI, and SPEA Mirage P64.)

x312svga — an X server for Super VGA (SVGA) video cards. This package should work with video cards based on chipsets such as Cirrus 542x, OAK OTI-037/67/77/87, Trident TVGA8900/9000, and Tseng ET3000/ET4000/W32.

fvwmicns — color icons for the fvwm window manager. Install this package.

x312ctrb — selected contributed programs for X Window System Version 11 Release 6 (X11R6): ico, listres, showfont, viewres, xbiff, xcalc, xditview, xedit, xev, xeyes, xfontsel, xgc, xload, xman, and xmessage. You should install these programs, because you can use them after you configure and run X.

Chapter 1: Installing Linux

x312vga — an X server for 16-color VGA cards. This package should work with all video cards, but you get the lowest common denominator — only 16 colors, as opposed to the 256 or more colors that most video cards provide.

x312w32 — an X server for video cards that use Tseng ET 4000/W32 chipsets.

Cross Reference

x312inc — header files (also known as *include files*) for writing X programs. Install the package, because this book covers X programming in Chapter 23.

x312ubin — the rstartd daemon (a program that runs all the time in the background), which allows you to start programs from another system on the network. Install it for experimentation.

oldlibs5 — the shared X libraries for the preceding release of X (X Window System Version 11, Release 5 — X11R5). Install the libraries, because some older programs (such as xv and DOOM) need them.

x312xtra — two experimental X servers named Xvfb and Xnest. No need to install these packages.

x312f75 — 75-dots-per-inch (*dpi*) fonts for X11R6. Install the package, because X programs need it.

fnt100_1 — 100-dpi fonts for X11R6, part 1. Install the package, because X programs need it.

fnt100_2 — 100-dpi fonts for X11R6, part 2. Install the package, because X programs need it.

fntbig1 — fonts for character sets such as Kanji, part 1. Skip it.

fntbig2 — fonts for character sets such as Kanji, part 2. Skip it.

fntbig3 — fonts for character sets such as Kanji, part 3. Skip it.

x312man — on-line-manual pages for X programs. Install the package.

x312doc — documentation for XFree86 3.1.2 X Window System. Install it.

x312fscl — Speedo and Type 1 scalable fonts for X. Install the package.

x312ma64 — an accelerated X server for video cards that use Mach64 chips.

Disk set XAP

gnuplot — a plotting package that works under X. You should install it.

gs_x11 — provides support for Ghostscript under X. Install it if you installed Ghostscript.

libgr — a shared graphics library with support for GIF, TIFF, and JPEG images. Install the package, because the xv image viewer needs the library.

seyon — a communications program that runs under X. Install it.

xfract — the xfractint program for drawing fractals. If you are interested in fractals, you should install this package.

gchess — a GNU chess game. Install it if you want to try it.

ghstview — a Ghostscript viewer for X. Install it if you installed Ghostscript.

x3270 — IBM 3270 terminal emulator under X. Install it only if you need it to access an IBM mainframe.

xfm — a file manager for the X Window System. Install this package so that you can try it.

xgames — games (such as xtetris and xmahjongg) that use X. Install the package.

xspread — a spreadsheet program. Install it.

xxgdb — a graphical interface for the GNU debugger. Install it if you plan to develop software on your Linux system.

xfileman — another file manager for X. Install it so that you can try it.

xpaint — the XPaint image-editing program for X. Install it.

xv — John Bradley's xv GIF, TIFF, JPEG, and PostScript image viewer for X. This program is provided as shareware; you are expected to register it if you plan to use it. Install this package so that you can try it.

Disk set Y

abuse1 — first part of ABUSE, a shareware arcade game from Crack Dot Com. Install it if you want to try it out (this is a beta version of the game).

abuse2 — second part of ABUSE, a shareware arcade game from Crack Dot Com. Install it if you installed abuse1.

bsdgames — old text-based games (such as backgammon, cribbage, Fish, Fortune, Hangman, Mille, Snake, and worm) from Berkeley UNIX. If you install this package, the setup program adds a call to Fortune in your login file so that you get a Fortune message when you log in. Install this package just so that you can see what games were like before graphical user interfaces came along.

sastroid — an astcroids game in which you shoot astcroids. Install it and give it a try.

tetris — Tetris for terminals. Try it, if you want (but xtetris looks better).

doomwad — game data file (part 1) for DOOM. Install it if you plan to install DOOM.

doom — DOOM for the console and for X. Install the package and try it, if you are curious.

doomwad2 — game data file (part 2) for DOOM. Install it if you installed DOOM.

Configuring some system components

After installing the selected disk sets, the setup program asks whether you want to configure your system. Press Enter to indicate Yes. As you see in this section, the configuration tasks include the following:

- Prepare an emergency boot disk
- Set up the modem
- Set up the mouse
- Select a screen font
- Set up the tape drive
- Set up the modem speed
- Configure and install the Linux Loader — LILO — that will load Linux when you power up your system
- Configure the network and mail software
- Set up the time zone for your system

A few of these configuration steps, such as creating a boot disk and installing the Linux Loader, are necessary because without them, you won't be able to start Linux. You can postpone some of the configuration tasks, such as configuring the network and mail software.

Cross Reference

A different type of system configuration involves customizing the Linux kernel to include support for the peripheral devices on your PC. That sort of configuration task is explained in Chapter 2.

Prepare the emergency boot disk

In the first step of configuring the system, the setup program recommends that you make a standard Linux boot disk. You can use this disk to boot your Linux system if the Linux kernel on the hard disk is damaged. Press Enter to accept the recommendation. The setup program then asks you to insert a formatted floppy into your PC's A drive and warns you that all data on that disk will be lost. You should place a formatted floppy in the A drive and press Enter.

The setup program copies the file vmlinuz from the Linux root directory — this happens to be the Linux kernel. After the setup program prepares the boot disk, remove the floppy from the A drive and label it appropriately (Linux Boot Disk will do).

You can use this boot disk to start Linux on your PC. Later, during this configuration step, you see how to place a Linux Loader program on your PC's C drive. That process, however, involves altering a critical part of the hard disk. If you do not feel comfortable with altering the hard disk, you can always boot Linux from the boot disk that you just created.

Set up the modem

After preparing the boot disk, the setup program offers to set up the modem. This step simply makes it possible to refer to the modem with a standard device name: /dev/modem. The setup program asks you for the serial port to which the modem is connected; then it creates a link from that device name (/dev/modem).

Establishing this link enables any software that uses the modem to assume that the device name is /dev/modem. Therefore, setting up the link is important. If you cannot immediately tell where your modem is connected, or if you enter a wrong serial port, you can correct the mistake later (when you are ready to use the modem).

To continue with this step, press Enter to answer Yes. The setup program asks you to select the serial port to which you have connected the modem. You have the following options:

```
cua0 com1: under DOS
cua1 com2: under DOS
cua2 com3: under DOS
cua3 com4: under DOS
```

Press the up- and down-arrow keys to highlight the modem's serial port, and press Enter. The setup program creates the link and prompts you to move to the next step.

Set up the mouse

In this step, the setup program asks whether you want to create a link from your mouse device to the standard device name /dev/mouse. Establishing this link allows any software that uses the mouse to refer to it by the standard name: /dev/mouse.

To proceed with this step, press Enter. The setup program displays the following list of mouse types:

```
1 Microsoft compatible serial mouse
2 C&T 82C710 or PS/2 style mouse (Auxiliary port)
3 Logitech Bus Mouse
4 ATI XL Bus Mouse
5 Microsoft Bus Mouse
6 Mouse Systems serial mouse
7 Logitech (MouseMan) serial mouse
```

Select your mouse type and then press Enter. If you select a serial mouse, you also have to indicate the serial port. The setup program establishes the link and proceeds to the next configuration step.

Select screen font

The setup program next allows you to customize the screen font — the font used to display the text screens. If you are happy with the appearance of the text that you see in the setup program's output, you can select No and skip this part.

If you want to use a different font, however, Linux offers quite a selection. To try them, select Yes and press Enter. The setup program displays a long list of fonts. To select a font, follow these steps:

1. Press the up- and down-arrow keys to select a font from the list and then press Enter. The setup program displays sample output in the selected font.

2. If you like the font and want to use it as the screen font, press Enter to indicate Yes. If you do not like the font, select No and press Enter. The setup program takes you back to the list of fonts, from which you can pick another. If you want to stick with the default font, press Esc while you are in the font-list menu.

Configure the floppy tape drive

If you installed the ftape package earlier, the setup program next asks whether you want to configure your floppy tape drive. If you have a QIC-40 or QIC-80 floppy drive on your system, press Enter to load the driver whenever Linux boots. If you do not have a floppy tape drive, select No and then press Enter.

Set the modem speed

Cross Reference

The setup program shows you a list of modem speeds, ranging from 300 to 38,400 baud. Select your modem's speed from the list and then press Enter. The setup program makes your selection the default speed of your modem. Chapter 15 tells you how to use the `setserial` command to alter the modem speed.

Install LILO

LILO stands for *Linux Loader* — a program that resides on your hard disk and starts Linux from the hard disk. If you have MS-DOS and Microsoft Windows, or OS/2, on your hard disk, you can configure LILO to load any of these operating systems as well.

Caution

When the setup program installs LILO on your PC's hard disk (the C drive), it overwrites the Master Boot Record (MBR), which is located in the first sector of the hard disk. If LILO is not configured properly, your PC may not be able to boot from the hard disk. LILO makes a backup copy of the original MBR, and you can use that backup to restore the hard disk to its working state. You have to run Linux, however, to restore the MBR from a backup. Therefore, you *must* make a Linux boot disk so that you have some means of starting Linux if LILO does not work.

To install LILO, first create a configuration file, named /etc/lilo.conf, from the setup program. That file contains information such as the list of disk partitions that LILO can use to boot different operating systems, the amount of time that LILO waits before booting the default operating system (the first disk partition is the default), and so on. You do not have to create the LILO configuration file manually; the setup program does the job for you.

Part I: Configuring Your Linux System

To configure and install LILO, the setup program offers the following options:

```
Begin    Start LILO configuration with a new LILO header
Linux    Add a Linux partition to the LILO config file
OS/2     Add an OS/2 partition to the LILO config file
DOS      Add a DOS partition to the LILO config file
Install  Install LILO
Recycle  Reinstall LILO using the existing lilo.conf
Skip     Skip LILO installation and exit this menu
View     View your current /etc/lilo.conf
Help     Read the Linux Loader help file
```

Select Begin, and press Enter. The setup program prompts you for any optional parameters that you may need when booting Linux. For some CD-ROM drives and hard drives, you may have to specify crucial information, such as the I/O address, as a command-line option to the Linux kernel. If you needed any parameters when initially booting Linux from the boot floppy, you need to enter the same parameters here. Most users need no optional parameters, so you can press Enter to continue.

The setup program then asks where you want to install LILO. You have the following options:

```
MBR     Use the Master Boot Record
Root    Use superblock of the root Linux partition
Floppy  Use a formatted floppy disk in the boot drive
```

If you select the first option, MBR, the setup program installs LILO on your C drive's Master Boot Record. This option is recommended, because the system boots quickly. The only problem is that LILO may fail to boot if something in its configuration file is wrong. You can, however, actually restore the MS-DOS boot record by booting from an MS-DOS boot floppy and using the FDISK /MBR command.

The Root option installs LILO in the Linux partition, which contains the root directory, not in the DOS C drive's MBR. Select this option if you are using the OS/2 Boot Manager to manage the operating systems that you want to boot. Add the Linux root partition to the Boot Manager's list of partitions; then install LILO in the Linux root partition.

For maximum safety, you may want to install LILO on a formatted floppy disk. If you install LILO on a floppy, you can boot from that floppy and get the same prompt that you get when LILO starts from your C drive's Master Boot Record. Select this option if you have an operating system such as Windows 95 on your hard disk and are not sure whether LILO will be able to boot Windows 95 properly.

Decide where you want to install LILO, select that option, and press Enter. The setup program then asks you to choose the amount of delay before LILO loads the default operating system. During that delay, you can type the name of the operating system to boot. If you have both DOS and Linux on your system, for example, during LILO's delay, you can indicate which of these operating systems you want to start.

Select a delay — say, 30 seconds — and press Enter. The setup program returns to the LILO installation menu.

Now you can select the first operating system that you want to boot. To select an operating system, follow these steps:

1. Select one of the operating systems — Linux, DOS, or OS/2 — from the LILO installation menu, and press Enter. The setup program prompts you for the name of the partition where the selected operating system is installed.

2. Enter the name of the partition where that operating system is installed, and press Enter. If you installed Linux in the partition /dev/hda3, for example, you type /dev/hda3. The setup program then asks for a short name for the partition.

3. Type a short but meaningful name such as **linux** for that partition, and press Enter. Later, when LILO loads, you can start that operating system by specifying the short name at LILO's boot prompt. When you specify the Linux partition, you might use linux as the short name for that partition. After you type the name and press Enter, the setup program returns to the LILO installation menu.

Select as many operating systems as you have on your system; then select Install from the LILO installation menu and press Enter. The setup program installs LILO and moves on to the next configuration step.

Tip

For a safe (in the sense that you do not alter the hard disk's Master Boot Record) but fast way to boot Linux, install LILO on a floppy disk and set the delay option to No Delay. Specify the Linux partition (on the hard disk) as the only partition to boot. Then you can use that LILO floppy to boot from your hard disk's Linux partition. This option is nearly as fast as booting from the hard disk, because only a small boot record is loaded from the floppy; that boot record immediately jumps to the hard disk to load the Linux kernel.

Restoring the Master Boot Record

The setup program creates a backup of the Master Boot Record before installing LILO on the MBR. If LILO fails to boot, you can restore the preceding MBR from the backup. Use a Linux boot floppy to start Linux (the floppy that you created at the beginning of the system-configuration step during Linux installation). Then enter the following command to uninstall LILO:

/sbin/lilo -u

This command works for LILO versions 0.14 and later. In response to this command, LILO restores the old boot sector. (The version of LILO included on the companion CD-ROM is newer than version 0.14.)

Other configuration steps

Cross Reference

Next, the setup program allows you to configure the network. You can perform these steps later, so you should answer No at this point. You learn more about networks in Chapter 16.

If you installed the General Purpose Mouse (gpm) package, the setup program asks whether you want to run gpm automatically when you boot Linux. The gpm program allows you to cut and paste text in text-mode display. If you have a bus mouse, you should answer No, because running gpm with a bus mouse may interfere with the XFree86 X Window System. If you have a serial mouse, you can go ahead and configure gpm to run when Linux starts.

Cross Reference

If you installed the sendmail package, the setup program asks whether you want to configure the Sendmail software. You can do this later, in Chapter 19; therefore, select Cancel and press Enter to continue.

Finally, you have to select the *time zone* — the difference between the local time and the current time at Greenwich, England, which is the standard reference time (also known as Greenwich Mean Time, or GMT). The setup program shows you a list of time zones, in terms of country or regions. You see time zones for many countries — including Australia, Brazil, Canada, Chile, Cuba, Egypt, Japan, Mexico, Poland, and Turkey — and for many regions of the United States. Press the up- and down-arrow keys to select your location. If you live on the East Coast of the United States, for example, you would select USA/Eastern. If your country is not listed, select one of the entries that designates the difference between your local time and GMT. After you select your time zone, press Enter.

The setup program then displays a message, indicating that system configuration is complete. Press Enter. The setup program displays its main menu. Press **E** to select Exit and then press Enter. You return to the Linux command prompt (#).

What is BogoMips?

When your Linux system boots, you notice a message such as `Calibrating delay loop.. ok - 30.22 BogoMips`, with some number before `BogoMips`. *BogoMips* is one of those words that confound new Linux users. This sidebar explains what it means.

As you may know, *MIPS* stands for *millions of instructions per second* — a measure of how fast your computer runs programs. (As such, MIPS is not a very good measure of performance, because comparing the MIPS of different types of computers is difficult.) BogoMips is *bogus MIPS*, which refers to an indication of the computer's speed. Linux uses the BogoMips number to calibrate a delay loop, in which the computer processes some instructions repeatedly until a specified amount of time has passed.

The BogoMips numbers can range anywhere from 1 to 40, depending on the type of processor (386, 486, or Pentium). A typical 33 MHz 80386DX system has a BogoMips of about 6, whereas a 66MHz 80486DX2/66 system shows a BogoMips of about 33. The BogoMips for Pentium systems is on par with (or slightly less than) that of 80486 processors, because the BogoMips calculation does not take advantage of any advanced features (such as the capability to execute instructions in parallel) of the Pentium. On my 75 MHz Pentium system, for example, Linux reports a BogoMips of 30.22.

Starting Linux for the First Time

After you complete the installation steps, press Ctrl+Alt+Delete to reboot the system. The PC goes through its normal power-up sequence and loads LILO from the C drive (you can tell, because the word `LILO` appears). When you configured LILO, if you specified the Linux partition as the first one, you can simply wait; after a specified amount of time, LILO boots Linux.

If you want to boot from another partition (such as DOS), press the Shift key. LILO displays the following prompt:

```
boot:
```

If you know the name of the bootable partition (the name that you assigned when you installed LILO), type that name. If you forget the partition name, press the Tab key; LILO displays the names of the available bootable partitions. Then you can type the name of the partition from which you want to boot the PC.

Cross Reference

After LILO boots Linux, you should see a long list of opening messages, including the names of the devices that Linux detects. One of the first few messages says `Calibrating delay loop.. ok - 30.22 BogoMips`; the number that precedes `BogoMips` depends on your system's processor type. *BogoMips* is a Linux jargon term that is the subject of countless discussions in various USENET newsgroups devoted to Linux. (USENET is a loose collection of computers that exchange electronic mail and news; you learn more about it in Chapters 18 and 19.) Linux uses the BogoMips measurement in situations in which the operating system has to wait for a specified period.

At the end of all the messages, you see the Linux login prompt, as follows:

```
Welcome to Linux 1.2.13.
darkstar login:
```

The word `darkstar` before the login prompt happens to be the default name of the system. Later, in the "Changing the system name" section, you'll see how to assign a different name to your system.

Because there are no other users at this point, type **root** to log in as the super user. Now you can perform a few initial chores and learn how to shut down your Linux system.

Changing the password

The root user is the super user in Linux. Right now, you do not need a password to log in as root. Because the super user can do anything in the system, you may want to assign a password for this account.

To change the password (or to add one), enter the Linux command `passwd`, as follows:

```
darkstar:´# passwd
Changing password for root
Enter new password:
```

Type the password that you want to use (it won't appear on-screen) and then press Enter. Linux asks for the password again, as follows:

```
Re-type new password:
```

Type the password again, and press Enter. If you enter the same password both times, Linux changes the password for the root user. Select a password that is easy for you to remember but that would be hard for other people to guess. To make a password harder to guess, include one or more special characters and numbers.

Caution

Make sure that you memorize the root password. If you forget the root password, you have to follow these steps to log in as root again:

1. Reboot Linux from the boot floppy that you used at the beginning of the installation.

2. Go through the root floppy as though you are about to install Linux again. When you get a prompt, you can log in as root without any password, just as you did at the beginning of the installation.

3. At the prompt, enter the command **mount -t ext2 /dev/hda3 /mnt** (replace /dev/hda3 with the name of the hard disk partition where you installed Linux).

4. Edit the file /mnt/etc/passwd with a text editor. At this point, you do not have access to any fancy editor, so type the following commands, pressing Enter after each command:

```
/mnt/bin/ed /mnt/etc/passwd
(ed displays the first line, which should start with root:)
1
i
root::0:0:root:/root:/bin/bash
.
2
.d
wq
```

I know that the commands are cryptic, but that's how the ed editor works, and at this point (because you booted from a minimal floppy-based Linux system), you really do not have access to any better editor. In the preceding session, make sure that when you type **1**, the ed editor displays the line that begins with root:.

5. Remove the Linux root floppy, and press Ctrl+Alt+Delete to reboot the PC, as usual. When Linux starts, you should be able to log in as root without any password.

As you may imagine, this situation clearly represents a security hole in Linux, because anyone with a boot disk can erase the root password and log in as root in this manner. On the other hand, without some means like this, it would be difficult to recover if you happen to forget the root password.

Adding users

When you log in as root for the first time, you also should create another user account. Even if you are the only user of the system, logging in as a less-privileged user is good practice, because that way, you cannot damage any important system files inadvertently. When necessary, you can log in as root and perform any system-administration tasks.

To add myself as a new user, for example, I would type the following at the Linux prompt (my input is in boldface, and my comments are in italics):

```
darkstar:~# adduser

Adding a new user. The user name should not exceed 8 characters
in length, or you may run info problems later.

Enter login name for new account (^C to quit): naba

Editing information for new user [naba]

Full Name: Naba Barkakati
GID [100]:         (The group ID. To accept the default, press Enter.)
Group 'users,' GID 100
First unused uid is 501

UID [501]:         (The user ID. To accept the default, press Enter.)

UID [501]:         (The user ID. To accept the default, press Enter.)

Home Directory [home/naba]:     (To accept the default, press Enter.)

Password [naba]:    (To accept the default, press Enter.)

Information for new user [naba]:
Home Directory: [/home/naba] Shell: [bin/bash]
uid: [501] gid: [100]

Is this correct? [y/N]: y

Adding login [naba] and making directory [/home/naba]

Adding files from /etc/skel directory:
./.kermrc -> /home/naba/./.kermrc
./.less -> /home/naba/./.less
./.lessrc -> /home/naba/./.lessrc
./.term -> /home/naba/./.term
./.term/termrc -> /home/naba/./.term/termrc
```

If you are willing to live with the defaults, all you really have to provide is the login name (the name that the user types at the login prompt) and the user's full name. The `adduser` command handles the rest of the chores of adding a new user. The default password for the user is the same as the login name, which you should ask the user to change as soon as possible.

Changing the system name

If you want to see a system name different from `darkstar`, you can set a name even before you fully configure the network. At the Linux prompt, type the command `netconfig`. The `netconfig` command displays an informative message about attempting to configure the network. Press Enter.

The `netconfig` command displays a dialog box, prompting you for the *host name* (the name of your system). Type the name that you want to use, and press Enter. In the next screen, `netconfig` asks you to enter the domain name for your system. For now, type **com**, and press Enter.

Cross Reference

The `netconfig` command asks whether you want to use loopback only. You learn more about loopback in Chapter 16. For now, press Enter to accept the default option (Yes). The `netconfig` command displays a message, saying that the network configuration is complete.

Press Enter to end the `netconfig` command and return to the Linux prompt.

The next time you reboot your system, the system name should change to the name that you set with the netconfig command.

Looking up the on-line documentation

In addition to the initial chores, you should know an important source of information in Linux. Every so often, you see instructions that ask you to enter a Linux command. After a while, you are bound to get to the point at which you vaguely recall a command's name, but you cannot remember the exact syntax of what you are supposed to type. This situation is where the Linux on-line-manual pages can come to your rescue.

You can view the manual page — commonly referred to as the *man page* — for a command by using the `man` command. (You do have to remember that command to be able to look up on-line help.) To view the man page for the `passwd` command, for example, type the following command:

```
man passwd
```

Linux displays the information page by page. Press the spacebar to move to the next page. When you finish, press **q** to return to the Linux command prompt.

Having touted the usefulness of the on-line help pages, I must point out that the term *Linux command* refers to any executable file, ranging from a script file that contains other Linux commands to standard Linux executable programs. Although man pages exist for most standard programs, many programs do not have any on-line help. If you type **man adduser**, for example, Linux responds as follows:

```
No manual entry for adduser
```

Nevertheless, whenever you are at a loss about some command, using the `man` command is worthwhile to see whether any on-line help for that command exists.

Chapter 1: Installing Linux

Another form of on-line documentation is the HOWTO files in the docs directory of the CD-ROM. The HOWTO files all have a -HOWTO suffix in the file name. Each file contains information about some area of Linux such as the hardware it supports or how to create a boot disk. Table 1-5 lists the HOWTO files in the docs directory of the companion CD-ROM.

Table 1-5	Linux HOWTO files
File	*Contents*
Bootdisk-HOWTO	How to create boot and root disks for Linux
BootPrompt-HOWTO	How to configure your kernel using commands typed at the boot prompt
Busmouse-HOWTO	How to get your bus mouse to work with Linux
CDROM-HOWTO	How to install, configure, and use CD-ROM drives with Linux
Commercial-HOWTO	A list of commercial software for Linux
Cyrillic-HOWTO	How to typeset and print documents in Russian
Danish-HOWTO	How to configure Linux for use with the Danish character set
Distribution-HOWTO	A list of Linux distributions available via mail order or FTP
DOSEMU-HOWTO	How to set up and use the MS-DOS emulator, DOSEMU
ELF-HOWTO	How to migrate your Linux system to compile and run programs in the ELF binary format (the version of Linux on the companion CD-ROM is already configured to run ELF binaries)
Ethernet-HOWTO	How to configure and use Ethernet network adapters with Linux
Firewall-HOWTO	How to set up an Internet firewall using Linux
Ftape-HOWTO	How to set up and use floppy tape drives (these drives connect to your PC through the floppy disk controller) with Linux
German-HOWTO	How to use Linux with the German character set (the document is in German)
HAM-HOWTO	Information about amateur radio software for Linux
Hardware-HOWTO	A list of hardware known to work with Linux
HOWTO-INDEX	Description of the HOWTO documents and an index of the current HOWTO documents about Linux
INFO-SHEET	An introduction to the Linux operating system
Installation-HOWTO	How to obtain and install the Linux software (describes Slackware version 2.0.1)

(continued)

Table 1-5 *(continued)*

File	Contents
JE-HOWTO	How to use JE, the Japanese Extensions for Linux
Kernel-HOWTO	How to upgrade and rebuild the Linux kernel
Keystroke-HOWTO	How to assign special actions to some keys on the keyboard
Mail-HOWTO	How to set up and maintain electronic mail in Linux
META-FAQ	A list of sources of information about Linux
MGR-HOWTO	How to use the MGR graphical windowing system in Linux
NET-2-HOWTO	How to install and configure TCP/IP networking in Linux
News-HOWTO	How to set up USENET news software in Linux
NIS-HOWTO	How to configure Network Information Service (NIS) in Linux
PCI-HOWTO	Information on Linux's support for the PCI bus architecture
PCMCIA-HOWTO	How to install and use PCMCIA Card Services in Linux
PPP-HOWTO	How to set up and use Point-to-Point Protocol (PPP) networking in Linux
Printing-HOWTO	How to set up printing in Linux
Printing-Usage-HOWTO	How to use the printing system in Linux
SCSI-HOWTO	Information about support for SCSI devices in Linux
SCSI-Programming-HOWTO	Information on programming the SCSI device driver in Linux (useful for programmers who want to add support for a new SCSI device in Linux)
Serial-HOWTO	How to set up serial communication devices in Linux
Sound-HOWTO	How to enable support for sound hardware in Linux
Term-HOWTO	How to set up and use the TERM communications package in Linux
Tips-HOWTO	A collection of tips
UMSDOS-HOWTO	How to install and use the UMSDOS filesystem that lets you install in an MS-DOS directory
UPS-HOWTO	How to use an uninterruptable power supply (UPS) with Linux
UUCP-HOWTO	How to set up and use the Unix-to-Unix Copy (UUCP) software in Linux
WRITING	Information on how to write and maintain a HOWTO document
XFree86-HOWTO	How to install and configure the XFree86 (X Window System Version 11 Release 6 — X11R6) in Linux

When you boot Linux, the CD-ROM drive is mounted at the directory /cdrom. Thus, you can access the directory containing the HOWTO files by typing **cd /cdrom/docs**.

After you change the directory, you can view a specific HOWTO file with the more command: **more CDROM-HOWTO**.

Shutting down

When you are ready to shut down Linux, you should do so in an orderly manner. Even if you are the sole user of a Linux system, several other programs usually are running in the background. Also, operating systems such as Linux try to optimize the way that they write data to the disk. Because disk access is relatively slow (compared with the time needed to access memory locations), data usually is held in memory and written to the disk in large chunks. Therefore, if you simply turn the power off, you run the risk that files will not be updated properly.

To shut down Linux, use the shutdown command. You have to log in as root to execute this command. After you log in as root, type the following command to halt the system:

```
shutdown -h now
```

The following message appears:

```
The system is going down NOW !!
```

After a few moments, you see a few more messages:

```
INIT: sending all processes the TERM signal...................
INIT: sending all processes the KILL signal..
Unmounting file systems.....
Done.

The system is halted
```

Now you can safely turn the power off.

If you want to reboot the system instead of halting it, use the shutdown command with the -r option, as follows:

```
shutdown -r now
```

Another way to restart the system quickly is to press Ctrl+Alt+Delete — the same key combination that you use to reboot a PC under DOS. Anyone can use the Ctrl+Alt+Delete sequence to reboot a Linux system from the console (that means the PC's keyboard, not a terminal connected to the serial port).

Installing Linux in an MS-DOS Directory

If you are uncomfortable with repartitioning the one and only hard disk on your PC, you can install Linux in a DOS directory. Many of the installation steps are the same as those that you follow to install Linux in its own partition, so start by reading the normal installation instructions first.

To install Linux in an MS-DOS directory, you still have to select a Linux boot image and create a boot floppy. You also need a root floppy, but you should select the file UMSDOS.GZ as the root image.

Start the installation process with the boot floppy; put the boot floppy in the A drive, and power up the PC. Press Enter when you see the `boot:` prompt. When you are prompted, place the root floppy (the one that contains the UMSDOS.GZ image) in the A drive, and press Enter. The minimal Linux system starts and prompts you to log in.

Log in as root (without any password); then type the **setup** command. The version of the setup program on the root floppy is meant for an UMSDOS installation. UMSDOS is a file system that builds a Linux file system in a MS-DOS directory. Basically, UMSDOS uses extra MS-DOS files to store information about a Linux file's attributes. A Linux file can have a much longer name than a DOS file, for example; the UMSDOS file system stores such information in a DOS file named `--linux-.---`.

The MS-DOS version of the setup program guides you through the installation process. In particular, you have to identify the MS-DOS disk partition as the target. The rest of the installation process is the same as installing on a Linux partition.

Summary

Linux is a UNIX-like operating system for Intel 80x86, Pentium, and compatible systems. The CD-ROM that accompanies this book includes the latest version of the popular Slackware Linux distribution. This chapter guides you through the process of installing Linux on your PC. The detailed information in this chapter includes:

▶ Information about your PC that you should gather before installing Linux

▶ The overall process of installing Slackware Professional Linux (including the X Window System) from the companion CD-ROM

▶ Steps that you perform under MS-DOS or Microsoft Windows before installing Linux

▶ How to initially boot Linux, partition the hard disk, and load the various disk sets from the companion CD-ROM

▶ Several ways in which you can boot Linux

▶ How to install Linux in an MS-DOS directory

▶ How to shut down a Linux system

Chapter 2
Upgrading Linux

In This Chapter

- Understanding the Linux kernel
- Building the Linux kernel
- Applying a kernel patch
- Upgrading from a previous version of Slackware Linux

An exciting aspect of Linux is the fact that many programmers are improving it constantly. Some programmers, for example, write drivers that add support for new hardware, such as a new CD-ROM drive or a new networking card. Another group of programmers adds support for more video cards to run the X Window System. The Linux development community makes all these innovations available to you in the form of fixes known as *patches* or through new versions of Linux.

Although you do not have to upgrade or modify the Linux operating system every time a new patch or a new version becomes available, sometimes you need to upgrade simply because the new version corrects some problems or supports your hardware better. Also, you may have to modify Linux right after the first installation to add support for a CD-ROM drive, for example.

To benefit from fixes and other improvements to Linux, you have to learn how to rebuild the Linux operating system — the Linux *kernel,* as it is commonly called. This chapter shows you how to apply a kernel patch and then how to rebuild the Linux kernel.

Kernel patch

The term *kernel* refers to the core Linux operating system — it is the program that makes your PC a Linux PC. The term *patch* refers to corrections. Putting the two together, you can see that *kernel patch* refers to corrections to the Linux operating system itself.

Linux comes with the source code, so the patches are alterations to the source code. When you apply a kernel patch, you change the Linux operating system's source code. After you make the changes, you have to rebuild Linux to put the changes into effect.

Applying Kernel Patches

Like any major software product, Linux has a version number that changes as new features are added. Typically, the version number has two parts: the *major version number* and the *minor version number*. MS-DOS 6.2, for example, has a major version number of 6 and a minor version number of 2. The minor version number changes as incremental improvements are made to the software; the major version number changes only when a significant change occurs.

In addition to the customary major and minor version numbers, Linux includes a third number that denotes the current patch level. Patches typically are corrections — changes made to code to fix errors.

When you boot Linux, the welcome message shows you the Linux version number and the patch level. You may, for example, see the following line:

```
Welcome to Linux 1.2.8.
```

This message tells you that the Linux version is 1.2 and that the patch level is 8.

Tip

Although the version number changes relatively slowly, a version such as 1.2 may contain many patches. You generally can find out about patches if you keep up with Linux developments by periodically reading USENET newsgroups that are devoted to Linux (such as `comp.os.linux.announce`).

Cross Reference

You need access to the Internet to read the USENET newsgroups; consult Chapters 18 and 19 for more information on connecting your Linux system to the Internet.

Get the patches

If you read about a kernel patch that fixes some problem that you may have had with Linux, you typically learn about the patch number as well. When you ask for help with some Linux problem by posting a message in a newsgroup (such as "I am running Linux 1.2.8, and my brand-new SCSI controller does not seem to work"), you may get replies saying that you should bring the kernel up to 1.2.11 because that new SCSI controller is supported at patch level 1.2.11.

To go from 1.2.8 to 1.2.11, you have two options:

- If it's available, get the complete Linux 1.2.11 kernel and install it.
- Get patches 9, 10, and 11 and apply them.

Tip

Typically, the entire kernel distribution is a large file (around 2.3MB) even in compressed form, whereas the patch files are less than 100K (many are around 10K). Therefore, it makes sense to download only the required patches and apply them. You have to get the patches over the Internet by using FTP (File Transfer Protocol).

Chapter 2: Upgrading Linux

Cross Reference

If you do not have Internet access, Chapters 18 and 19 explain how you can connect your system to the Internet using a modem (you have to sign up with an Internet Service Provider for the access).

Note

To explain the process of getting the patch files, I assume that your system is connected to the Internet and that you can use the `ftp` command to access any computer on the Internet.

The Linux kernel patches (as well as the latest versions of the kernel) are available from the FTP site `ftp.funet.fi` in Finland. That FTP site organizes the Linux kernels and associated patches by version number. All files for Linux version 1.2, for example, are in the `/pub/OS/Linux/PEOPLE/Linus/v1.2` directory. The kernel files and patches for version 1.2 are named as follows (I show only a few representative names):

```
linux-1.2.8.tar.gz  (compressed file containing the complete kernel for
                     Linux 1.2.8)
patch-1.2.9.gz      (compressed file containing patch 9 for version 1.2)
patch-1.2.10.gz     (compressed file containing patch 10 for version 1.2)
patch-1.2.11.gz     (compressed file containing patch 11 for version 1.2)
```

All Linux files typically are distributed in compressed format to minimize the amount of data that you have to transfer over the Internet. The `.gz` at the end of the file name tells you that this file was compressed with the `gzip` command. As you see later, you can decompress such a file by using the `gunzip` command (or the `gzip -d` command).

The best way to learn how to get and apply a patch is to see an example. Following is an example of how to get the relevant patch files to go from Linux version 1.2.8 to 1.2.11. The following sample session with the `ftp` program is based on my system's dial-up connection to the Internet (at a modem speed of 14,400 bits per second):

```
ftp ftp.funet.fi
Connected to nic.funet.fi.
220-Hello UNKNOWN at dcc0xxxx.slip.digex.net,
220-
220-Welcome to the FUNET archive.  Please login as 'anonymous' with
220-your E-mail address as the password to access the archive.
220-See the README file for more information about this archive.
220-
220-   All anonymous transfers are logged with your host name and
whatever you
220-  entered for the password. If you don't like this policy, discon-
nect now!
220-
220-
220-nic.funet.fi FTP server (Version 4.1385 problems@ftp.funet.fi)
ready.
220-There are 77 (max 196) archive users in your class at the moment.
220-Assuming 'login anonymous', other userids do vary.)
220-Local time is Wed Jul 26 19:50:55 1995 EET DST
```

```
220-
220 You can do "get README" even without logging in!
User (nic.funet.fi:(none)): anonymous
331 Guest login ok, give your E-mail address for password.
Password:
230-Guest 'naba@access.digex.net' login ok.
230-
230-           Finnish University and Research network FUNET
230-                      Archive FTP.FUNET.FI
230-
230-Most important file name suffixes are described at
README.FILETYPES
230-News about this system can be looked at README.NEWS
230-
230-Welcome, you are 114th archive user in your class (max 196).
230-Your class is named: The known world outside NORDUnet region
230-There are 170 users in all classes (max 590)
230-The maximum bandwidth allocated for you is limited.  It can be as
230-low as 500 B/s.  At this moment it would set to 15 kB/s.
230-
230-Local time is Wed Jul 26 18:20:17 1995 EET DST
230-
230-We have special access features, see file README
230-   It was last updated Sat Apr 22 17:50:19 1995 - 95.0 days ago
230
ftp> cd /pub/OS/Linux/PEOPLE/Linus/v1.2
ftp> ls -l
... (a portion of listing deleted)
-rw-r--r--   1 torvalds    2349983 May  3 08:27 linux-1.2.8.tar.gz
-rw-r--r--   1 torvalds    2352258 Jun  1 13:19 linux-1.2.9.tar.gz
-rw-r--r--   1 torvalds     107663 Jun  6 19:59 modules-1.2.8.tar.gz
-rw-r--r--   1 torvalds      26111 Mar 17 16:10 patch-1.2.1.gz
-rw-r--r--   1 torvalds      11639 Jun 12 19:28 patch-1.2.10.gz
-rw-r--r--   1 torvalds       3973 Jun 26 16:27 patch-1.2.11.gz
-rw-r--r--   1 torvalds       2268 Jul 25 13:03 patch-1.2.12.gz
-rw-r--r--   1 torvalds      42759 Mar 27 08:57 patch-1.2.2.gz
-rw-r--r--   1 torvalds       2198 Apr  2 12:09 patch-1.2.3.gz
-rw-r--r--   1 torvalds      12622 Apr  6 14:59 patch-1.2.4.gz
-rw-r--r--   1 torvalds      18838 Apr 12 21:53 patch-1.2.5.gz
-rw-r--r--   1 torvalds      29300 Apr 23 23:18 patch-1.2.6.gz
-rw-r--r--   1 torvalds      12639 Apr 29 11:27 patch-1.2.7.gz
-rw-r--r--   1 torvalds      90641 May  3 08:27 patch-1.2.8.gz
-rw-r--r--   1 torvalds      13300 Jun  1 13:19 patch-1.2.9.gz
-rw-r--r--   1 torvalds      14036 Mar  7 17:52 v1.1.95-1.2.0.patch.gz
226 Transfer complete.
1876 bytes received in 2.41 seconds (0.78 Kbytes/sec)
ftp> binary
200 Type set to I.
ftp> get patch-1.2.9.gz
200 PORT command successful.
150 Opening BINARY mode data connection for /pub/OS/Linux/PEOPLE/
Linus/v1.2/patch-1.2.9.gz (13300 bytes).
226 Transfer complete.
```

```
13300 bytes received in 9.45 seconds (1.41 Kbytes/sec)
ftp> get patch-1.2.10.gz
200 PORT command successful.
150 Opening BINARY mode data connection for /pub/OS/Linux/PEOPLE/
Linus/v1.2/patch-1.2.10.gz (11639 bytes).
226 Transfer complete.
11639 bytes received in 18.84 seconds (0.62 Kbytes/sec)
ftp> get patch-1.2.11.gz
200 PORT command successful.
150 Opening BINARY mode data connection for /pub/OS/Linux/PEOPLE/
Linus/v1.2/patch-1.2.11.gz (3973 bytes).
226 Transfer complete.
3973 bytes received in 7.91 seconds (0.50 Kbytes/sec)
ftp> bye
221-Goodbye, and thank you for using the FUNET archive.
```

Common practice is to use the login name *anonymous* when downloading software from an FTP site. Providing your e-mail address as the password also is customary. Then you follow these straightforward steps:

1. Use the `cd` command to change location to the directory where the files for the current version of Linux reside.

2. Type **ls -l** to see a listing of files in that directory. Look for files with *patch* in their name; these are the patch files.

3. Type **binary** to set file-transfer mode to binary.

4. Use the `get` command to download the necessary patch files one by one.

5. Type **bye** to quit the `ftp` program.

Next, you have to unpack the patch files and apply the patches.

Apply the patches

The `.gz` at the end of the patch file's name indicates that the files are compressed. Therefore, after you download the patches, you first have to decompress the file; then you can apply the patches. Follow these steps to apply the patches:

1. Copy the patch files to the `/usr/src` directory.

2. Type the following commands to decompress the patch files:
   ```
   cd /usr/src
   gunzip patch*.gz
   ```

3. Use the `patch` command to apply the patches one by one, as follows:
   ```
   patch -p0 < patch-1.2.9 2> err.9
   patch -p0 < patch-1.2.10 2> err.10
   patch -p0 < patch-1.2.11 2> err.11
   ```

The first command runs the patch utility with the file patch-1.2.9 as input and sends all output messages (including any error reports) to the file err.9.

After the commands have finished, check the err.9, err.10, and err.11 files to see whether any of the patches failed. One good way is to use the text-search tool grep to look for the occurrence of the string *fail,* as follows:

```
grep fail err.*
```

If grep finds any occurrence of the string *fail,* the patch was not successful, perhaps due to wrong command-line arguments.

Cross Reference

For now, just try the grep command as is; in Chapter 6, you learn more about grep and other Linux commands.

The patch commands change the source code of the Linux operating system to reflect any changes that the developers have made since version 1.2.8. After the last patch, the Linux source code should be at level 1.2.11. All you have to do next is rebuild the kernel; then your Linux system will be at version 1.2.11.

Caution

Before you rebuild the kernel, prepare an emergency boot floppy (see the "Prepare emergency boot disk" section of Chapter 1 for details). If the system does not boot after you rebuild the kernel, you can use that emergency boot floppy to start the system and repeat the process of building the kernel.

Rebuild the kernel

The expression *rebuild the kernel* refers to the task of creating a new binary file for the core Linux operating system. This binary file is the file that runs when Linux boots. You may have to build the kernel in the following circumstances:

- When you apply kernel patches (as you did in the preceding section), the operating system's source files are updated, and you have to rebuild the kernel and reboot the system to see the effects of the changes.

- When you want to add support for a new device (a sound card, for example), you have to configure the kernel and rebuild it. In this case, you select appropriate options to enable the sound driver for your sound card.

After you apply the patches, many source files (the ones indicated in the patch files) change. Now you have to rebuild the Linux kernel again from the revised source files. To rebuild the kernel, follow these steps:

1. Change the directory to /usr/src/linux by using the following command:

    ```
    cd /usr/src/linux
    ```

2. Configure the kernel. This step involves answering questions about the features that you want to include in your Linux system. In essence, you are building a copy of Linux with the mix-and-match features that you want. To configure the Linux kernel, all you have to do is type the make config command and then answer the subsequent questions.

Chapter 2: Upgrading Linux

In the following code, the default answer appears in brackets. To accept the default, press Enter.

Following is a complete session of kernel configuration for my PC (you must answer Yes to include support for any SCSI and CD-ROM interfaces that your system has). My comments are in italics.

```
make config

Kernel math emulation (CONFIG_MATH_EMULATION) [y]
Normal floppy disk support (CONFIG_BLK_DEV_FD) [y]
Normal (MFM/RLL) disk and IDE disk/cdrom support (CONFIG_ST506) [y]
    Use old disk-only driver for primary i/f (CONFIG_BLK_DEV_HD) [n]
    Use new IDE driver for primary/secondary i/f
(CONFIG_BLK_DEV_IDE) [y]
        Include support for IDE/ATAPI CDROMs (CONFIG_BLK_DEV_IDECD) [n] y
XT harddisk support (CONFIG_BLK_DEV_XD) [n]
Networking support (CONFIG_NET) [y]
Limit memory to low 16MB (CONFIG_MAX_16M) [n]
PCI bios support (CONFIG_PCI) [y]
    PCI bridge optimisation (experimental) (CONFIG_PCI_OPTIMIZE) [n]
System V IPC (CONFIG_SYSVIPC) [y]
Kernel support for ELF binaries (CONFIG_BINFMT_ELF) [y]
Use -m486 flag for 486-specific optimizations (CONFIG_M486) [y]

(Next comes a set of loadable module support:)
Set version information on all symbols for modules
(CONFIG_MODVERSIONS) [n]

(Following are networking options:)
TCP/IP networking (CONFIG_INET) [y]
IP forwarding/gatewaying (CONFIG_IP_FORWARD) [n] y
IP multicasting (CONFIG_IP_MULTICAST) [n]
IP firewalling (CONFIG_IP_FIREWALL) [n] y
IP accounting (CONFIG_IP_ACCT) [n]

(It's safe to leave the following untouched:)
PC/TCP compatibility mode (CONFIG_INET_PCTCP) [n]
Reverse ARP (CONFIG_INET_RARP) [n]
Assume subnets are local (CONFIG_INET_SNARL) [y]
Disable NAGLE algorithm (normally enabled) (CONFIG_TCP_NAGLE_OFF) [n]
The IPX protocol (CONFIG_IPX) [n]

(SCSI support:)
SCSI support? (CONFIG_SCSI) [y]

(SCSI support type: disk, tape, CDrom)
SCSI disk support (CONFIG_BLK_DEV_SD) [y]
SCSI tape support (CONFIG_CHR_DEV_ST) [y]
SCSI CDROM support (CONFIG_BLK_DEV_SR) [y]
SCSI generic support (CONFIG_CHR_DEV_SG) [n]
Some SCSI devices support multiple Logical unit numbers (LUNs)
Probe all LUNs on each SCSI device (CONFIG_SCSI_MULTI_LUN) [n]
```

```
(SCSI low-level drivers:)
Adaptec AHA152X support (CONFIG_SCSI_AHA152X) [y]
Adaptec AHA1542 support (CONFIG_SCSI_AHA1542) [y]
Adaptec AHA1740 support (CONFIG_SCSI_AHA1740) [y] n
Adaptec AHA274X/284X support (CONFIG_SCSI_AHA274X) [y] n
BusLogic SCSI support (CONFIG_SCSI_BUSLOGIC) [y] n
EATA-DMA (DPT, NEC&ATT for ISA, EISA, PCI) support
(CONFIG_SCSI_EATA_DMA) [y] n
UltraStor 14F/34F support (CONFIG_SCSI_U14_34F) [y] n
Future Domain 16xx SCSI support (CONFIG_SCSI_FUTURE_DOMAIN) [y] n
Generic NCR5380 SCSI support (CONFIG_SCSI_GENERIC_NCR5380) [y] n
NCR53c7,8xx SCSI support (CONFIG_SCSI_NCR53C7xx) [y] n
Always IN2000 SCSI support (test release) (CONFIG_SCSI_IN2000) [y] n
PAS16 SCSI support (CONFIG_SCSI_PAS16) [y] n
QLOGIC SCSI support (CONFIG_SCSI_QLOGIC) [y] n
Seagate ST-02 and Future Domain TMC-8xx SCSI support
(CONFIG_SCSI_SEAGATE) [y] n
Trantor T128/128F/228 SCSI support (CONFIG_SCSI_T128) [y] n
UltraStor SCSI support (CONFIG_SCSI_ULTRASTOR) [y] n
7000FASST SCSI support (CONFIG_SCSI_7000FASST) [y] n

(Network device:)
Network device support (CONFIG_NETDEVICES) [y]
Dummy net driver support (CONFIG_DUMMY) [y]
SLIP (serial line) support (CONFIG_SLIP) [y]
  CSLIP compressed headers (CONFIG_SLIP_COMPRESSED) [y]
  16 channels instead of 4 (SL_SLIP_LOTS) [n]
PPP (point-to-point) support (CONFIG_PPP) [y]
PLIP (parallel port) support (CONFIG_PLIP) [n]
Do you want to be offered ALPHA test drivers (CONFIG_NET_ALPHA) [n]
Western Digital/SMC cards (CONFIG_NET_VENDOR_SMC) [y] n
AMD LANCE and PCnet (AT1500 and NE2100) support (CONFIG_LANCE) [y] n
3COM cards (CONFIG_NET_VENDOR_3COM) [y]
3c501 support (CONFIG_EL1) [y] n
3c503 support (CONFIG_EL2) [y]
3c509/3c579 support (CONFIG_EL3) [y]
Other ISA cards (CONFIG_NET_ISA) [y] n
EISA, VLB, PCI and on board controllers (CONFIG_NET_EISA) [y] n
Pocket and portable adaptors (CONFIG_NET_POCKET) [n]

(CD-ROM drives -- not SCSI or non-IDE/ATAPI drives:)
Sony CDU31A/CDU33A CDROM driver support (CONFIG_CDU31A) [n]
Mitsumi (not IDE/ATAPI) CDROM driver support (CONFIG_MCD) [n]
Matsushita/Panasonic CDROM driver support (CONFIG_SBPCD) [n]
Aztach/Orchid/Okano/Wearnes (non IDE) CDROM support (CONFIG_AZTCD) [n]
Sony CDU535 CDROM driver support (CONFIG_CDU535) [n]

(File systems:)
Standard (minix) fs support (CONFIG_MINIX_FS) [y]
Extended fs support (CONFIG_EXT_FS) [n]
Second extended fs support (CONFIG_EXT2_FS) [y]
xiafs filesystem support (CONFIG_XIA_FS) [n]
msdos fs support (CONFIG_MSDOS_FS) [y]
umsdos: Unix like fs on top of std MSDOS FAT fs (CONFIG_UMSDOS_FS) [y]
```

```
/proc filesystem support (CONFIG_PROC_FS) [y]
NFS filesystem support (CONFIG_NFS_FS) [y]
ISO9660 cdrom filesystem support (CONFIG_ISO9660_FS) [y]
OS/2 HPFS filesystem support (read only) (CONFIG_HPFS_FS) [n]
System V and Coherent filesystem support (CONFIG_SYSV_FS) [n]

(Character devices:)
Cyclades async mux support (CONFIG_CYCLADES) [n]
Parallel printer support (CONFIG_PRINTER) [y]
Logitech busmouse support (CONFIG_BUSMOUSE) [n]
PS/2 mouse (aka "auxiliary device" support) (CONFIG_PSMOUSE) [y]
C&T 82C710 mouse support (as on TI Travelmate)
(CONFIG_82C710_MOUSE) [y] n
Microsoft busmouse support (CONFIG_MS_BUSMOUSE) [n]
ATIXL busmouse support (CONFIG_ATIXL_BUSMOUSE) [n]
QIC-02 tape support (CONFIG_QIC02_TAPE) [n]
QIC-117 tape support (CONFIG_FTAPE) [y]
   number of ftape buffers (NR_FTAPE_BUFFERS) [3]

(Sound:)
Sound card support (CONFIG_SOUND) [n] y

(Kernel hacking:)
Kernel profiling support (CONFIG_PROFILE) [n]
Verbose SCSI error reporting (kernel size +=12K)
(CONFIG_SCSI_CONSTANTS) [n] y

(At this point, the make utility compiles a program for sound
configuration:)
Compiling Sound Driver 2.90-2 for Linux
Configuring the sound driver
Do you want to include full version of the sound driver (n/y) ? n
Do you want to DISABLE the Sound Driver? n
The SoundBlaster, AdLib and ProAudioSpectrum
CARDS cannot be installed at the same time.

However the PAS16 has a SB emulator so you could select
the SoundBlaster DRIVER with it.
           - ProAudioSpectrum 16
           - SoundBlaster / SB Pro
             (Could be selected with a PAS16 also)
           - AdLib

Don't enable SoundBlaster if you have GUS at 0x220!

    ProAudioSpectrum 16 support (n/y) ? n
    SoundBlaster support (n/y) ? y

The following cards should work with any other cards.
CAUTION! Don't enable MPU-401 if you don't have it.
  Gravis Ultrasound support (n/y) ? n
  MPU-401 support (NOl for SB16) (n/y) ? n
  6850 UART Midi support (n/y) ? n
  Microsoft Sound System support (n/y) ? n
```

```
Select one or more of the following options
  SoundBlaster Pro support (y/n) ? y
  SoundBlaster 16 support (y/n) ? n
  /dev/dsp and /dev/audio support (_recommended_) (y/n) ? y
  MIDI interface support (y/n) ? n
  FM synthesizer (YM3812/OPL-3) support (y/n) ? n
Do you want support for the mixer of SG NX Pro ? n

I/O base for SB?
The factory default is 220
Enter the SB I/O base: 220

IRQ number for SoundBlaster?
The IRQ address is defined by the jumpers on your card.
The factory default is either 5 or 7 (depending on the model).
Valid values are 9(=2), 5, 7, and 10
Enter the value: 5

DMA channel for SoundBlaster?
For SB 1.0, 1.5 and 2.0 this MUST be 1
SB Pro supports DMA channels 0, 1 and 3 (jumper)
For SB16 give the 8 bit DMA# here
The default value is 1
Enter the value: 1

Select the DMA buffer size (4096, 16384, 32768 or 65536 bytes)
32768 is the recommended value for this configuration.
Enter the value: 32768
The DMA buffer size set to 32768
The sound driver is now configured.
```

The session ends with a message that you should proceed by typing the commands **make dep** and then **make clean**, followed by **make zlilo**, to complete the kernel rebuilding.

3. You should initiate the next three tasks with a single command line (Linux allows you to enter multiple semicolon-separated commands on the same line) so that you can type the line, press Enter, and then take a break, because that part takes a while.

   Depending on your system, making a new kernel can take anywhere from an hour to several hours. Type the following on a single line to initiate the process:

   `make dep; make clean; make zlilo`

   The `make dep` command determines which files have changed and what needs to be compiled again. The `make clean` command deletes old, un-needed files (such as old copies of the kernel). Finally, `make zlilo` creates the new kernel that can be loaded by LILO — the Linux Loader.

   If you do not use LILO and start Linux with a boot floppy instead, you should build the kernel boot image with the following command:

   `make dep; make clean; make zImage`

Then place a floppy disk in the A drive and type the following commands to create a new boot floppy:

```
fdformat /dev/fd0H1440
cd /usr/src/linux/arch/i386/boot
rdev -R zImage 1
cat zImage > /dev/fd0
```

The `rdev -R zImage 1` command ensures that the Linux hard disk partition is mounted in read-only mode, so that the file system can be checked properly before Linux starts up. Without that command, you get a warning message when you boot Linux from the boot floppy.

After everything is done and you are back at the Linux prompt, type the following command to reboot the system:

```
sync; sync
reboot
```

When the system reboots, you should see the following message before the login prompt:

```
Welcome to Linux 1.2.11.
```

Now your Linux system is at patch level 11.

If the system *hangs* (that means that nothing seems to happen — no output on the screen and no disk activity), you may have skipped a step during the kernel rebuild. Make sure that you performed all four of the following steps in the order shown:

```
make config
make dep
make clean
make zlilo    (or make zImage)
```

If the system does not boot after you rebuild the kernel, you should use an emergency boot disk (containing an earlier, but working, version of Linux) to start the system. Then, you can repeat the process of rebuilding the kernel, making sure that you follow all the steps correctly.

Upgrading from an Earlier Version of Slackware

New versions of the Slackware Linux distribution appear periodically, with enhanced performance, bug fixes, and support for new hardware. You may find that a new version includes a later release of XFree86 or has better support for some hardware in your system (such as a new SCSI controller).

Suppose that you install Linux along with many other packages from this book's companion Slackware Linux CD-ROM; then, a year or so later, you obtain a newer version of Slackware Linux. You have to upgrade your existing Slackware system with the new version.

You may not have realized it, but you have already seen a message that contains hints on how to upgrade an old Slackware system. After you boot Linux during the installation process and log in as the root user, Linux displays the following message (in addition to announcing the version of Linux):

```
If you're upgrading an existing Slackware system, you might want to
remove old packages before you run 'setup' to install the new ones. If
you don't, your system will still work but there might be some old files
left laying around on your drive.

Just mount your Linux partition under /mnt and type 'pkgtool'. If you
don't know how to mount your partitions, type 'pkgtool' and it will tell
you how it is done.

To start the main installation, type 'setup'.
```

Cross Reference

As the first two paragraphs of the message indicate, you are supposed to use the `pkgtool` utility to remove old packages (consult the installation process in Chapter 1 for a list of packages) before you run setup again and install new packages. As the message says, type **pkgtool** at the Linux prompt. Following is what that command displays:

```
# pkgtool

You can't run pkgtool from the rootdisk until you've mounted your Linux
partitions beneath /mnt. Here are some examples of this:

If your root partition is /dev/hda1, and is using ext2fs, you would type:
mount /dev/hda1 /mnt -t ext2

Then, supposing your /usr partition is /dev/hda2, you must do this:
mount /dev/hda2 /mnt/usr -t ext2

Please mount your Linux partitions and then run pkgtool again.

#
```

In fact, before you reach this point, you should have booted the old version of Linux from your hard disk and backed up any important files (such as any directories that contain work that you have done), just in case the upgrade process deletes or overwrites any files that you cannot recover easily.

If you have already backed up all your important files, also consider the possibility of simply erasing all old files and installing the new Slackware release from scratch. If you can do that, you avoid any potential problems due to errors such as forgetting to remove a package when you should have and mixing files from old distributions with new ones.

If you decide to remove the old packages and reinstall new ones, you should go ahead and mount all your Linux partitions, as the `pkgtool` message instructs you. After you mount the partitions, run `pkgtool` again, as follows:

```
# pkgtool
```

The `pkgtool` program displays a full-screen menu that contains the following options:

```
Current  Install packages from the current directory
Other    Install packages from some other directory
Floppy   Install packages from floppy disks
Remove   Remove packages that are currently installed
View     View list of files contained in a package
Exit     Exit Pkgtool
```

Press **R** to select Remove; then press Enter. The `pkgtool` program scans the mounted hard disk partitions for installed packages and shows you a list.

Press the up- and down-arrow keys to move up and down this list. To select a package for removal, press the spacebar until an *X* appears in the brackets before the package's name.

Cross Reference

After you select the packages to remove, press Enter. The `pkgtool` program removes the packages and exits. At the Linux prompt, type **setup** and then proceed to install the new packages, following the steps listed in the "Installing Linux from the Slackware CD" section of Chapter 1.

Summary

Linux was developed through the efforts of many programmers scattered around the globe. These programmers (and many new ones) continue to enhance Linux and to release bug fixes and new versions. From time to time, you may have to get some updates or bug fixes and rebuild the Linux kernel. This chapter provides detailed information on how to apply the fixes (known as *patches*) and how to upgrade to a new version of Linux. The next chapter will step back from the installation and configuration details and provide an overview of Linux and what you can do with your Linux PC.

By reading this chapter, you learn

- ▶ The term *kernel* refers to the core Linux operating system — this is the program that makes your PC a Linux PC.
- ▶ The Linux kernel is being improved continually to correct errors (these are the bug fixes) or add new functionality. Such updates are distributed in the form of patches — changes to specific Linux source files. You have to apply the patches and rebuild the kernel to benefit from any enhancements to the kernel.
- ▶ You can get the patches via FTP from `ftp.funet.fi` in the `/pub/OS/Linux/PEOPLE/Linus` directory. Look under the current version number for specific patches.
- ▶ The patches are distributed in compressed form — you should see this from the `.gz` suffix in the file name. You have to use the `gunzip` command to uncompress the patches.
- ▶ Copy the patches to the `/usr/src` directory and then use the `patch` command to apply the patches. This alters kernel's source code in the `/usr/src/linux` directory.
- ▶ Before rebuilding the kernel, you should prepare an emergency boot disk so that you can restart the system if something goes wrong with the kernel-rebuild process.
- ▶ To rebuild the kernel, change to the directory `/usr/src/linux` and then use the `make` utility. You have to follow the sequence: `make config; make dep; make clean; make zlilo` (in that order).

Part II
Running Linux

Chapter 3: An Overview of Linux

Chapter 4: Secrets of X under Linux

Chapter 5: Customizing Your Linux Startup

Chapter 6: Secrets of Linux Commands

Chapter 7: Secrets of DOS under Linux

Chapter 8: Scripting in Linux with Tcl/Tk

Chapter 3
An Overview of Linux

In This Chapter

- ▶ Looking at the current version of Linux and the version-numbering scheme
- ▶ Assessing Linux's suitability as a UNIX platform
- ▶ Understanding how X provides a graphical interface to Linux
- ▶ Understanding built-in networking capabilities of Linux
- ▶ Looking at the implications of Linux for network managers and system administrators
- ▶ Making DOS coexist with Linux
- ▶ Looking at the software-development tools in Linux
- ▶ Using Linux as your Internet "on ramp"

Now that you have successfully installed and configured Linux, you are ready to explore and use your Linux system. You probably had a specific use in mind when you first decided to install Linux on your PC. Whether you want to use Linux to develop software or just surf the Net, this book is your personal guide in your journey through the Linux maze. Even if you have a specific use in mind, you will find it very useful to get a detailed overview of Linux, complete with its high points and pitfalls. When you know more about Linux, you can be a smart user, employing Linux in ways that you may not have thought possible.

Accordingly, this chapter provides a broad-brushstroke picture of Linux. The chapter describes how you can get the most out of the built-in capabilities of Linux, such as networking, developing software, and running applications.

Linux Versions

After Linux version 1.0 was released on March 14, 1994, the loosely organized Linux development community adopted a version-number scheme. Versions 1.x.y, wherein x is an even number, are stable versions. The number y is the *patch level,* which is incremented as problems are fixed.

Note

Versions 1.*x.y* with an odd *x* are beta releases for developers only; they may be unstable, so you should not use these versions for day-to-day use. Developers add new features to these "odd" versions of Linux.

When this book was written, the latest stable version of Linux was 1.2.13, and developers were working on version 1.3.20. This book's companion CD-ROM contains the latest stable version of Linux available as of fall 1995.

Cross Reference

If you hear about a later version of Linux or about patches (corrections) to the current version that may help you, you can obtain the patches and rebuild the kernel easily by following the instructions in Chapter 2.

Linux as a UNIX Platform

Like other UNIX systems, Linux is a multiuser, multitasking operating system, which means that Linux allows multiple users to log in and run more than one program at the same time.

Linux is designed to comply with IEEE Std 1003.1-1988 (POSIX.1). This standard defines the functions that applications written in the C programming language use to access the services of the operating system for tasks ranging from opening a file to allocating memory. Although Linux conforms largely to the POSIX.1 standard, it has not actually been certified as such.

Along with POSIX compliance, Linux includes many features of other UNIX standards, such as the System V Interface Document (SVID) and the Berkeley Software Distribution (BSD) version of UNIX. Linux takes an eclectic approach, picking the most-needed features of several standard flavors of UNIX.

The POSIX standard

POSIX stands for *Portable Operating System Interface* (abbreviated as POSIX to make it sound like UNIX). The Institute of Electrical and Electronics Engineers (IEEE) began developing the POSIX standards to promote the portability of applications across UNIX environments. POSIX is not limited to UNIX, however. Many other operating systems, such as DEC VMS and Microsoft Windows NT, implement POSIX — in particular, IEEE Std. 1003.1-1990 or POSIX.1, which provides a source-level C-language Application Programming Interface (API) to the services of the operating system, such as reading and writing files. POSIX.1 has been accepted by the International Standards Organization (ISO) and is known as the ISO/IEC IS 9945-1:1990 standard.

Incidentally, the term POSIX is used interchangeably with the term P1003, which is how IEEE refers to the POSIX activities. Thus, POSIX.1 is the same as P1003.1.

In addition to POSIX.1, the POSIX family of standards includes standards ranging from POSIX.2 through POSIX.22, which are summarized as follows:

POSIX.1 — already a widely accepted standard for source-level portability. POSIX.1 provides a C-language Application Programming Interface (API) to the operating system. The IEEE and ISO have approved this standard. Over the past few years, POSIX.1 was expanded to include several other areas: POSIX.1a (system interface extensions), POSIX.1b (real-time), POSIX.1c (threads), POSIX.1d (real-time extensions), POSIX.1e (security), POSIX.1f (transparent file access), POSIX.1g (protocol independent services), POSIX.1h (fault tolerance).

POSIX.2 — a standard for shell and tools, which are, respectively, the command processor and the utility programs that an operating system must provide. The IEEE has approved this standard.

POSIX.3 — a standard for testing and verification. The IEEE has approved this standard.

POSIX.4 — a standard for real-time programming and *threads* (concurrently executing blocks of code within a program). This proposed standard has been incorporated into POSIX.1 as POSIX.1b (real-time), POSIX.1c (threads), and POSIX.1d (real-time extensions). POSIX.1b and POSIX 1.c have been approved by the IEEE.

POSIX.5 — an Ada-language API corresponding to POSIX.1. The IEEE and ISO have approved this standard.

POSIX.6 — a standard for system security. This standard has been moved to POSIX.1e and is work in progress.

POSIX.7 — a standard for system administration. This standard is now in a new area known as P1387.

POSIX.8 — a standard for networking, including (a) transparent file access, (b) protocol-independent network interface, (c) Remote Procedure Calls (RPC), and (d) protocol-dependent application interfaces for open system interconnect. This standard has been moved to POSIX.1f and it's not yet approved.

POSIX.9 — a FORTRAN language API corresponding to POSIX.1. The IEEE and ISO have approved this standard.

POSIX.10 — a standard for supercomputing Application Environment Profile (AEP). The IEEE has approved this standard.

POSIX.11 — was a proposed standard for Transaction Processing AEP. It has been removed from consideration.

POSIX.12 — a standard for protocol-independent services. This has been moved to POSIX.1g. (Work in progress.)

POSIX.13 — a standard for real-time application environment profile. (Work in progress.)

POSIX.14 — a standard for multiprocessing Application Environment Profile. (Work in progress.)

POSIX.15 — a standard for batch processing. (Work in progress.)

POSIX.16 — is a defunct standard.

POSIX.17 — a standard for directory services (X.400 and X.500). This has been moved to P1224.2, P1326.2, P1327.2, and P1328.2 (IEEE has approved these standards).

POSIX.18 — is the POSIX profile. (Work in progress.)

POSIX.19 — used to be the FORTRAN 90 binding for POSIX.1, but it has been deleted.

POSIX.20 — a standard for real-time extensions in Ada; it has been moved to POSIX.5b. (Work in progress.)

POSIX.21 — a standard for real-time distributed system communication. (Work in progress.)

POSIX.22 — a security framework guide. (Work in progress.)

For the latest information on the IEEE standards including POSIX, point your World Wide Web browser to http://stdsbbs.ieee.org/groups/pasc/sd11.html.

In addition to POSIX.1 compliance, Linux supports POSIX.2 (shell and utilities). POSIX.2 focuses on the operating system's command interpreter (commonly referred to as the *shell*) and a standard set of utility programs. If you know UNIX and have had some exposure to it, you know that UNIX takes a tools-oriented view of the operating system. A tool is available for almost anything that you want to do, and the shell allows you to combine several tools to perform tasks more complicated than those handled by the basic tools. The POSIX.2 standard maintains this tools-oriented view, providing the following features:

- A shell with a specified set of built-in commands and a programming syntax that can be used to write *shell programs* or scripts.

Cross Reference

- A standard set of utility programs — such as `sed`, `tr`, and `awk` — that can be called by shell scripts and applications. Even the `vi` editor and the `mailx` electronic-mail program are part of the standard set. You learn more about these utilities in Chapter 6.

- A set of C functions, such as `system` and `getenv`, that applications can use to access features of the shell.

- A set of utilities for developing shell applications (there is a C compiler for POSIX.2 called `c89`).

The default Linux shell is called *Bash,* which stands for *Bourne Again shell* — a reference to the *Bourne shell,* which has been the standard UNIX shell from its early days. Bash incorporates many of the features required by POSIX.2, and then some. Bash essentially inherits the features and functionality of the Bourne shell. In case of any discrepancy between the Bourne shell and POSIX.2, Bash follows POSIX.2. For stricter POSIX.2 compliance, Bash even includes a POSIX mode.

All in all, Linux can serve as a good platform for learning UNIX because it offers a standard set of UNIX commands (the POSIX.2 standard as well as the best features of both System V and BSD UNIX).

Linux's support for POSIX.1 and other common UNIX *system calls* (the functions that applications call) makes it an excellent system for software development. Another ingredient of modern workstation software — the X Window System — also is available in Linux, in the form of XFree86.

The availability of common productivity software — such as word-processing, spreadsheet, and database applications — is an area in which Linux is lacking. This situation is about to change, however. Many existing software packages (designed for UNIX workstations with the X Window System) can be readily ported to Linux, thanks to Linux's support for portable standards such as POSIX.1 and the X Window System.

Note

Another exciting development is the recent support for the Intel Binary Compatibility Standard (iBCS2) in Linux. The iBCS2 standard provides binary compatibility between applications developed on various UNIX systems meant for Intel x86 processors. For example, iBCS2 support should allow you to run WordPerfect for SCO UNIX on your Linux PC.

The iBCS2 support comes in the form of a loadable module (a loadable module is like a DOS TSR [terminate and stay resident] program) that you can load after booting Linux with the following command:

```
/sbin/insmod -f /usr/lib/modules/iBCS
```

The Slackware Linux distribution on the companion CD-ROM includes the iBCS2 modules and related documentation. According to the README file in /usr/doc/ibcs2 directory, the current iBCS2 module can load and run binary files from the following operating systems:

- SCO UNIX
- System V Release 4 UNIX for Intel processors (such as Unixware, Dell UNIX, and Interactive UNIX)
- Wyse V/386 UNIX
- Xenix V/386
- Xenix 286

Support for other operating systems such as 386BSD, FreeBSD, NetBSD, and BSDI/386 are also in the works.

X Window System in Linux

Let's face it — typing cryptic UNIX commands on a terminal is boring. Those of us who know the commands by heart may not realize it, but the installed base of UNIX is not going to increase significantly if we don't make the system easy to use. This is where the X Window System, or X for short, comes to the rescue.

X provides a standard mechanism for displaying device-independent bitmapped graphics. X also is a windowing system, enabling applications to organize their output in separate windows.

Although X provides the mechanism for windowed output, it does not offer any specific look and feel for applications. The look and feel comes from graphical user interfaces (GUIs), such as OSF/Motif and OPEN LOOK, that are based on the X Window System. Of these two GUIs, Motif has taken the lion's share of the market, but the OPEN LOOK interface continues to be available on workstations from Sun Microsystems.

Cross Reference

The Slackware Linux distribution on this book's CD-ROM comes with the X Window System in the form of XFree86 3.1.1 — an implementation of X11R6 (X Window System version 11, release 6, which is the latest release of X) for 80x86 systems. A key feature of XFree86 is its support for a wide variety of video cards available for today's PCs. As you learn in Chapter 4, XFree86 supports literally hundreds of PC video cards, ranging from the run-of-the-mill Super Video Graphics Adapter (SVGA) to accelerated graphics cards such as the ones based on the S3, Mach64, and Weitek P9000 video chipsets.

As for the GUI, Linux includes several *window managers* — special X programs that manage the windows in which other X programs display their output. The window managers typically add a border and a title bar to an X application's window.

Of the two common GUIs — OPEN LOOK and Motif — Linux includes the OPEN LOOK GUI in the form of the OPEN LOOK Window Manager (OLWM) and the XView toolkit, which you can use to create your own programs with the OPEN LOOK style.

Motif is dominant in the marketplace, but Motif does not come with Linux because the Open Software Foundation does not give away Motif for free. Like OPEN LOOK, Motif has a look and feel similar to that of Microsoft Windows, the Motif Window Manager (mwm), and the Motif toolkit for programmers. You can get Motif for Linux from several commercial vendors for about $150 (U.S.).

Although you have to pay extra to get Motif, if you need it for a project, a Linux PC with a copy of Motif still is an economical way to set up a software-development platform. If you have a consulting business, or if you want to develop X and Motif software at home, Linux definitely is the way to go.

Unlike Microsoft Windows or the Macintosh System software, Linux does not come with a powerful, graphic file manager, so you may not be able to escape the need to learn UNIX commands and use a terminal window under X to do your work. You can, however, use Linux and XFree86 to develop graphical software that's easy for everyone to use.

In the Linux distribution, you can see a sample of some graphical applications that run under X. The two programs worth mentioning relate to image display and editing. The first is the shareware program XV, by John Bradley; the other one is `xpaint`, by David Koblas.

Another important aspect of the X Window System is that you can run applications across the network. For example, you might run a graphical application on a server on the network but view that application's output and interact with it from your Linux desktop. In other words, with X, your Linux PC becomes a gateway to all the other systems on the network — from your Linux desktop you can run X applications anywhere on the network.

Cross Reference

Chapter 4 shows you how to set up XFree86 on your system, and Chapter 23 explains how to develop X applications on a Linux system.

Linux Networking

In this context, *networking* refers to all aspects of data exchange between one or more computers, ranging from the physical connection to the protocol for the actual data exchange. A *network protocol* is the method agreed upon by the sender and receiver for exchanging data across a network.

Different network protocols are used at different levels of the network. At the physical level — the level at which the data bits travel through a medium, such as a cable — protocols such as Ethernet and token-ring are used. Application programs don't really work at this physical level, however. Instead, they rely on protocols that operate on blocks of data. These protocols include Novell's Internet Packet Exchange (IPX) and the well-known Transmission Control Protocol/Internet Protocol (TCP/IP).

Cross Reference

The different levels of network protocols can be represented by a networking model such as the seven-layer Open Systems Interconnection (OSI) reference model, developed by the International Standards Organization (ISO). Chapter 16 includes a discussion of this model.

Standard network protocols such as TCP/IP have been key to the growth of interconnected computers, resulting in local as well as wide-area networks. Protocols have allowed interconnection of these smaller networks, and we now have interconnected networks that form an internetwork: the Internet.

TCP/IP

Networking has been a strength of UNIX since its early days. In particular, the well-known TCP/IP protocol suite has been an integral part of UNIX ever since TCP/IP appeared in BSD UNIX around 1982. By now, TCP/IP is the wide-area-networking protocol of choice in the global Internet.

Linux supports the TCP/IP protocol suite and includes all common network applications, such as `telnet`, `ftp`, and `rlogin`. At the physical-network level, Linux includes drivers for many Ethernet cards. Although token ring is not an integral part of Linux, token-ring drivers also are available from some developers through the Internet.

Cross Reference

You might say that Linux's support for TCP/IP — the dominant protocol suite of the Internet — comes naturally. The rapid development of Linux itself would not have been possible without the collaboration of so many developers from Europe and America. That collaboration, in turn, has been possible only because of the Internet. In Chapter 19, you learn how to set up TCP/IP networking and use the network software.

Linux also includes the Berkeley Sockets (so named because the socket interface was introduced in Berkeley UNIX around 1982) — a popular interface for network programming in TCP/IP networks. For those of you with C-programming experience, the Sockets interface consists of several C header files and several C functions that you call to set up connections and to send and receive data.

You can use the Berkeley Sockets programming interface to develop Internet tools such as World Wide Web (WWW) browsers. Because most TCP/IP programs include the Sockets interface (including those that are available for free at various Internet sites), and because Linux includes the sockets interface, it is easy to get these programs up and running on Linux.

SLIP and PPP

Not everyone has an Ethernet connection to the Internet — especially those of us who use Linux on our home PCs. There is, however, a way to connect to the Internet and communicate by using the TCP/IP protocol over a phone line and modem. What you need is a *server* — a system that has an Internet connection and that accepts a dial-in connection from your system.

Nowadays, commercial outfits known as *Internet Service Providers* (ISP) offer this type of service for a fee. If you don't want to pay for such a connection, find out whether a computer at your place of business provides this access. That option may not be unreasonable, especially if you are doing UNIX software development (for your company) on your Linux PC at home.

When you access the Internet through a server, that server runs either of two protocols:

- Serial Line Internet Protocol (SLIP)
- Point-to-Point Protocol (PPP)

Both protocols support TCP/IP over a dial-up line. SLIP is a simpler and older protocol than PPP, which has more features for establishing a connection. To establish a connection, your system must run the same protocol as the server.

Cross Reference

Linux supports both SLIP and PPP for dial-up Internet connections. You can turn your Linux system into a SLIP or PPP server so that other computers can dial into your computer and establish a TCP/IP connection over the phone line. Chapter 18 explains how to set up SLIP and PPP on your Linux system.

NFS

In the MS-DOS and Microsoft Windows world, you may be familiar with the concept of a *file server* — a system that maintains important files and allows all other systems on the network to access those files. Essentially, all PCs on the network share one or more central disks. In DOS and Windows, users see the file server's disk as being just another drive, with its own drive letter (such as U). In PC networks, file sharing typically is implemented with Novell NetWare or Microsoft LAN Manager protocols.

The concept of file sharing exists in UNIX as well. The *Network File System* (NFS) provides a standard way for a system to access another system's files over the network. To the user, the remote system's files appear to be in a directory on the local system.

Cross Reference

NFS is available in Linux; you can share your Linux system's directories with other systems that support NFS. The other systems that access your Linux system's files via NFS do not necessarily have to run UNIX; in fact, NFS is available on PCs as well. Therefore, you can use a Linux PC as the file server for a small workgroup of PCs that runs DOS and Windows. Chapter 21 further explores this idea of using a Linux PC as a file server.

UUCP

An old but important data-exchange protocol is UUCP (UNIX-to-UNIX Copy). This protocol continues to be a means of exchanging electronic mail and news. USENET news — the bulletin-board system (BBS) of the Internet — originated with UUCP. Computers that were connected to one another over phone lines and modems used UUCP to exchange mail messages, news items, and files. Essentially, the messages and news were relayed from one computer to another. That system was a low-cost way to deliver news and mail. Although today much of the e-mail and news travel over permanent network connections of the Internet, UUCP still allows many distant systems to use USENET news and e-mail, thereby allowing them to be part of the Internet community.

Linux includes UUCP. If your Linux system has a modem, and if you want to exchange files with another system via a dial-up connection, you can use UUCP. As part of its discussion of dial-up networking, Chapter 18 describes how to set up UUCP.

Linux System Administration

System administration refers to tasks that must be performed to keep a computer system up and running properly. Now that almost all computers are networked, another set of tasks is needed to keep the network up and running. These tasks are collectively called *network administration*. A site that has many computers probably has a full-time *system administrator* who takes care of all system- and network-administration tasks. Really large sites may have separate system-administration and network-administration personnel. If you are running Linux on a home PC or on a few systems in a small company, you probably are both the system administrator and the network administrator.

Linux includes all the basic commands and utilities needed for system and network administration. Chapter 6 briefly covers some of these commands. Chapters 18 and 19 describe the network-administration tools.

System administration tasks

As a system administrator, your typical tasks include the following:

- *Installing, configuring, and upgrading the operating system and various utilities.* You learned how to install Linux and the other software packages in Chapter 1. Chapter 2 shows you how to upgrade the operating system, and Chapter 4 covers the installation of the X Window System.

- *Adding and removing users.* As shown in the "Adding users" section of Chapter 1, you can use the Linux utility `adduser` to add a new user after you install Linux. If a user forgets the password, you have to use the `passwd` command to change the password.

- *Installing new software.* For the typical Linux software, which you get in source-code form, this task involves using tools such as `gunzip` (to uncompress the software), `tar` (to unpack the archive), and `make` (to build the executable programs).

- *Making backups.* You can use the `tar` program to archive one or more directories and to copy the archive to a floppy disk (if the archive is small enough) or to a tape (if you have a tape drive).

- *Mounting and dismounting file systems.* When you want to read an MS-DOS floppy disk, for example, you have to mount that disk's MS-DOS file system on one of the directories of the Linux file system. You have to use the `mount` command to accomplish this task.

- *Monitoring the system's performance.* You have to use a few utilities, such as `top` (to see where the processor is spending most of its time) and `free` (to see the amount of free and used memory in the system).

- *Starting and shutting down the system.* Although starting the system typically involves nothing more than powering up the PC, you do have to take some care when you want to shut down your Linux system. You should use the shutdown command to stop all programs before turning off your PC's power switch.

Network administration tasks

Typical network-administration tasks include the following:

Cross Reference

- *Adding network support to the kernel.* You may have to configure and build the Linux kernel so that it includes support for specific network adapters, as well as for SLIP and PPP. Chapter 2 guides you through the steps needed to configure and build the kernel.

- *Maintaining the network configuration files.* In Linux (as well as in other UNIX systems), the TCP/IP network is configured through several text files that you may have to edit to make networking work. You may have to edit one or more of the following files: `/etc/rc.d/rc.inet1`, `/etc/rc.d/rc.inet2`, `/etc/hosts`, `/etc/networks`, `/etc/host.conf`, `/etc/resolv.conf`, and `/etc/HOSTNAME`.

- *Setting up SLIP and PPP.* You use tools such as `dip` and `chat` to set up SLIP and PPP connections.

- *Monitoring network status.* You have to use tools such as `netstat` (to view information about active network connections) and `ping` (to make sure that a connection is working).

- *Configuring UUCP* (if you want to dial up another system and exchange e-mail or news). You may not use UUCP at all because nowadays most systems exchange e-mail and news with the TCP/IP protocol on the Internet.

DOS and Linux

As you probably know, MS-DOS and Microsoft Windows happen to be the most popular operating systems for 80386, 80486, and Pentium PCs. Because Linux started on 80386/80486 PCs, a connection between DOS and Linux has always existed. Typically, you start the Linux installation with some steps in DOS.

Linux has maintained its connection to DOS in several ways:

- Linux supports the MS-DOS file system. From Linux, you can access MS-DOS files on the hard disk or on a floppy disk.
- Linux includes a set of tools (called `mtools`) that manipulates MS-DOS files from within Linux.
- Work is progressing on an MS-DOS emulator (commonly referred to as DOSEMU) that uses the virtual 8086 mode of 80386 or better processors, much as Windows provides the capability to run a DOS session within a window.

The DOSEMU project has already shown some success, and many DOS applications (including WordPerfect 5.1 and FoxPro 2.0) have been shown to run under the DOS emulator.

An ongoing project called WINE is attempting to develop a Windows emulator for the X Window System under Linux. Actually, WINE lets you use your existing Windows 3.1 installation to run Windows 3.1 programs that you have installed on your PC's DOS partition.

Cross Reference

Chapter 7 describes how you can access DOS from Linux. The chapter also explains the use of the `mtools` utilities and provides information about DOSEMU and WINE.

Software Development in Linux

Of all the potential uses of Linux, software development fits Linux perfectly. Software-development tools such as the compiler and the libraries are included, because you need them anyway when you rebuild the Linux kernel. If you are already a UNIX software developer, you know UNIX, so you will feel right at home in Linux.

As far as the development environment goes, you have the same basic tools (such as an editor, a compiler, and a debugger) that you might use on other UNIX workstations, such as those from Hewlett-Packard (HP), Sun Microsystems, IBM, or Digital Equipment Corporation (DEC). Therefore, if you work by day on one of the mainstream UNIX workstations, you can use a Linux PC at home to duplicate that development environment at a fraction of the cost. Then you can either complete work projects at home or devote your time to software that you write for fun and then share on the Internet.

Just to give you a sense of Linux's software-development support, following is a list of various features that make Linux a productive software-development environment:

- GNU's C compiler, gcc, which can compile ANSI-standard C programs.
- GNU's C++ compiler (g++), which has support for AT&T C++ 3.0 features.
- The GNU debugger, gdb, which allows you to step through your program to find problems and to determine where and how a program failed. (The failed program's memory image is saved in a file named core; gdb can examine this file.)
- The GNU profiling utility, gprof, lets you determine the degree to which a piece of software uses your computer's processor time.
- GNU make and imake utilities, which enable you to manage the compiling and linking of large programs.
- Revision Control System (RCS), which maintains version information and control access to the source files so that two programmers don't modify the same source file inadvertently.
- GNU Emacs editor, which prepares source files and even launches a compile-link cycle to build the program.
- Perl scripting language, which is used to write scripts that tie together many smaller programs with UNIX commands to accomplish a specific task.
- The Tool Command Language and its X toolkit (Tcl/Tk), which allow you to prototype X applications rapidly.
- Dynamically linked shared libraries, which allow the actual program files to be much smaller, because all the library code that several programs may use is shared with only one copy loaded in the system's memory.
- POSIX.1 and POSIX.2 header files and libraries, which enable you to write portable programs.

Cross Reference

Chapter 22 covers software development in Linux. First, however, read Chapter 8 to learn about Tcl/Tk programming.

Linux as an Internet "On Ramp"

With all the attention that's being paid to Internet in popular media — newspapers and television — you must have heard about the Internet. Many of you already have access to the Internet and have experienced what it has to offer: electronic mail, newsgroups, and the World Wide Web (WWW or the Web). Whether you are in the "been there, done that" camp or "what's the Web?"

camp, you may be happy to learn that a Linux PC includes everything that you need to access the Internet. In fact, your PC can become a first-class citizen of the Internet, with its own Web server, on which you can publish any information that you want.

Although Linux includes TCP/IP and supporting network software with which you can set up your PC as an Internet host, there is one catch: First, you have to obtain a physical connection to the Internet. Your Linux PC has to be connected to another *node* (which can be another computer or a networking device, such as a router) on the Internet. This requirement is the stumbling block for many people — an Internet connection costs money, and the price goes up with the data-transfer rate.

Many commercial Internet Service Providers (ISPs) provide various forms of physical connections to the Internet. In the United States, if you are willing to spend between $15 and $30 a month, you can get an account on a SLIP or PPP server. Then you can run SLIP or PPP software on your Linux system, dial in using a modem, and connect to the Internet at data-transfer rates ranging from 14,400 bits per second (bps) to 28,800 bps, depending on your modem.

Although a dial-up connection is adequate for using your Linux system to access the Internet and to receive e-mail and read news, it may not be appropriate if you want your system to provide information to other people through the Web or FTP (file transfer protocol). For that purpose, you need a connection that is available 24 hours a day, because other systems may try to access your system at any time of day. For a few hundred dollars a month, you can get a dedicated SLIP or PPP connection and make your system a permanent presence on the Internet.

Another option for a small business — or for anyone who has a few networked PCs — is connecting a local-area network (LAN) to the Internet. You can run Linux on one of the PCs to accomplish this task. Typically, you would have an Ethernet LAN running TCP/IP connected to all of the PCs on the network including the Linux machine. The Linux PC sets up a SLIP or PPP connection to the Internet (via a dial-up or dedicated connection). You then can set up the Linux PC to act as a gateway between the Ethernet LAN and Internet so that the PCs on your LAN can access other systems on the Internet.

Cross Reference

In Chapter 19, you learn how to configure your Linux system to access the Internet. More important, you learn how to use a Linux PC as the gateway for your local network and the Internet.

Summary

When you get Linux going on your PC, you can turn your attention to the work that you plan to do with Linux. Whether you want to develop software or set up your PC as an Internet host, you can use Linux wisely if you know its overall capabilities. Accordingly, this chapter provides an overview of various aspects of Linux, ranging from software development to networking and system administration. The next chapter turns to another configuration task — it shows you how to configure and run the X Window System on your Linux PC. After you get X running, you'll have a graphical user interface for Linux.

By reading this chapter, you learn

▶ Linux developers use a version number scheme to help you understand what the versions mean. Versions 1.*x.y*, wherein *x* is an even number, are stable versions. The number *y* is the *patch level*, which is incremented as problems are fixed. Versions 1.*x.y* with an odd *x* are beta releases for developers only; they may be unstable.

▶ POSIX stands for *Portable Operating System Interface* (abbreviated as POSIX to make it sound like UNIX). The Institute of Electrical and Electronics Engineers (IEEE) began developing the POSIX standards to promote the portability of applications across UNIX environments.

▶ Linux is a UNIX look-alike operating system that conforms to most of the POSIX standard. As such, Linux is ideal as a low-cost UNIX system.

▶ The Linux distribution on the companion CD-ROM also includes an Intel Binary Compatibility Standard (iBCS2) module that you can load with the /sbin/insmod command. With the iBCS2 module, Linux can run binaries from other Intel x86 UNIX such as Unixware, SCO UNIX, Dell UNIX, Interactive UNIX, Xenix V/386, and Xenix 286.

▶ This book's Linux distribution comes with the XFree86 (X Window System Version 11 Release 6, or X11R6) software. After you install XFree86, you have a graphical user interface for Linux. Additionally, X lets you run applications across the network — that means you could run applications on another system on the network and have the output appear on your Linux PC's display.

▶ Linux supports TCP/IP networking well. TCP/IP is the networking protocol of choice on the Internet. Therefore, a Linux PC is ideal as an Internet host providing various Internet services such as FTP and World Wide Web. You can also use the Linux PC as your Internet ramp — connecting to an Internet Service Provider through dial-up TCP/IP connection and running a Web browser to "surf the Net."

▶ The Linux distribution includes all the software development tools necessary to write UNIX and X applications. You'll find the GNU C and C++ compiler for compiling source files, make for automating the compiling, gdb debugger to find bugs, and the Revision Control System (RCS) to manage various revisions of a file. Thus, a Linux PC serves as an ideal software developer's workstation.

Chapter 4

Secrets of X under Linux

In This Chapter

- ▶ Introducing the X Window System
- ▶ Setting up XFree86 under Linux
- ▶ Configuring XFree86
- ▶ Starting X
- ▶ Trying different video modes
- ▶ Getting Motif for Linux

If you have used the Macintosh System software or Microsoft Windows, you are familiar with the convenience of graphical user interfaces (GUIs). In the world of UNIX workstations, the GUI is not an integral part of the operating system. Instead, UNIX workstations typically provide Motif as the GUI. Motif, in turn, is built on a windowing system called the X Window System, or X for short. Linux also supports X — a version of X called XFree86 that is designed to work with your PC's video cards. For the GUI, Linux offers several window managers.

Cross Reference

This chapter explains the X Window System and provides the details to help you install XFree86 on your Linux system. The companion CD-ROM contains the XFree86 software, which you copied to your hard disk during the installation process shown in Chapter 1. In this chapter, you configure XFree86 and learn how to start X on your Linux PC. Additionally, you learn how to start some X applications automatically together with X.

Understanding the X Window System

The term *X Window System* is loosely applied to several components that facilitate window-based graphics output on a variety of bitmapped displays.

At the heart of X is the *X server* — a process (computer program) running on a computer that has a bitmapped display, a keyboard, and a mouse. Applications — *X clients* — that need to display output do so by communication with the X server by one of several possible interprocess communication mechanisms. The communication between the X clients and the X server follows a well-defined protocol: the *X protocol*. In addition to the X server, the clients, and the X protocol, the term *X* encompasses a library of routines, known as *Xlib,* that constitutes the C-language interface to the facilities of the X server.

Clients and servers

When you work with a typical X display, the X server runs on your computer and controls the monitor, keyboard, and mouse. The server responds to commands sent by X clients that open windows and draw in those windows. This arrangement is known as the *client/server model*. As the name implies, the server provides a service that the client requests. Usually, clients communicate with the server through a network, and client and server exchange data using a protocol that both understand.

Bitmapped graphics displays

Bitmapped graphics displays have two distinct components:

- A *video monitor* — usually, a cathode-ray tube (CRT) where the graphics output appears. The monitor often is referred to as the *display screen* or simply the *screen*.

- The *video card* (or *graphics card*) — either a plug-in card or some circuitry built into the system's motherboard that causes the output to appear by sending the appropriate signals to the monitor.

In a bitmapped graphics display, the monitor shows an array of dots (known as *pixels*), and the appearance of each pixel corresponds to the contents of a memory location in the video card (that's the *video memory*). For a black-and-white display in which each pixel is either bright or dark, a single bit of memory can store the state of a pixel. The term *bitmapped* refers to this correspondence between each bit in memory and a pixel on-screen.

For color displays, each pixel may have anywhere from 4 to 24 bits of memory. The number of bits per pixel also is referred to as the *depth*. The depth determines the number of colors that can be displayed on the monitor simultaneously. An 8-bit depth, for example, provides 256 simultaneous colors, because $2^8 = 256$.

PC video cards can work in different *video modes*, each with a specific depth. Most PC video cards include an 8-bit depth.

Bitmapped graphics is also called *raster graphics*, because the graphics that appear on the monitor are constructed from a large number of horizontal lines known as *raster lines*. These raster lines are generated by an electron beam sweeping back and forth on a phosphor-coated screen. Because each dot of phosphor, corresponding to a pixel, glows in proportion to the intensity of the beam, each line of the image can be generated by controlling the intensity of the beam as it scans across the screen. A monitor creates the illusion of a steady image by drawing the raster lines repeatedly. Most monitors redraw an entire screen of raster lines 50 to 90 times a second.

Color displays represent any color by using a combination of the three primary colors: red (R), green (G), and blue (B). The term *RGB value* often is used to specify a color in terms of the intensities of the primary colors. A color monitor uses three electron beams — one for each primary color. The screen of a color monitor has a repeated triangular pattern of red, green, and blue phosphor dots. Each phosphor glows in its color when the electron beam impinges on it. The video card sends signals to vary the intensity of the electron beams, thereby causing many shades of colors to be displayed on the monitor.

You may already have seen the client/server model in action. A *file server,* for example, stores files and allows clients to access and manipulate those files. Another common application, the *database server*, provides a centralized database from which clients retrieve data by sending queries. Similarly, the X display server offers graphics-display services to clients that send X protocol requests to the server.

One major difference exists between the X server and other servers, such as file and database servers. Whereas file servers and database servers usually are processes executing on remote machines, the X server is a process executing on the computer where the monitor is located. The X clients may run locally or on remote systems.

In the PC LAN's client/server model, applications are typically stored on a central server. Users access these server-based applications from client PCs. When you run an application from a PC, the application executes in your PC's processor. In the X client/server model, the situation is different. When you run an application, it actually runs in the server's processor — only the output appears at your Linux PC (which runs the X server). In other words, the X server runs at a location you typically associate with the client (as in client PC in a PC LAN). You should keep this distinction in mind when working with the X client/server model.

Graphical user interfaces and X

An application's user interface determines its appearance (look) and behavior (feel). When the user interface uses graphic objects, such as windows and menus, we call it a *graphical user interface* (many call it GUI — pronounced GOO-EY, for short). You also could call a GUI a point-and-click user interface, because users generally interact with a GUI by moving the mouse pointer on-screen and clicking the mouse button. To indicate consent to the closing of a file, for example, the user may click the mouse button while the mouse pointer is inside a box labeled OK.

Graphical user interfaces were developed at the Xerox Palo Alto Research Center (PARC). Subsequently, Apple Computer made such interfaces popular in its Lisa and Macintosh systems. Today, graphical interfaces are available for most systems. Microsoft Windows is available for most IBM-compatible PCs with 386 or better processors; Presentation Manager, for OS/2; and OSF/Motif and OPEN LOOK (built on X) for UNIX.

Most GUIs, including Motif and OPEN LOOK, have four components:

- Window system
- Window manager
- Toolkit
- Style guide

The graphical *window system* organizes graphics output on the display screen and performs basic text and graphics-drawing functions.

The *window manager* allows the user to move and resize windows. The window manager also is partly responsible for the appearance of the windows because it usually adds a decorative frame to the windows. Another important part of the window manager is the management of *input focus:* the mechanism by which the user can select one of several windows on-screen and make that one the current *active window* (the window with which the user intends to interact). This process is called giving the input focus to a window. For GUIs based on the X Window System, a window manager is an X client just like any other X application.

The third component, the *toolkit,* is a library of routines with a well-defined programming interface. This toolkit is primarily of interest to programmers because it allows programmers to write applications that use the facilities of the window system and have a consistent look and feel.

At first glance, you would think that these three components — the window system, the window manager, and the toolkit — are enough for a GUI. They are not. Unless programmers follow a common set of guidelines, the look and feel of applications built with a GUI may not be consistent. Therefore, a GUI has a crucial fourth component: the *style guide,* which specifies the appearance and behavior of an application's user interface.

You may feel that the requirement of following a style guide robs programmers of their creativity, but the style guide applies only to the common elements of applications' user interface. The guide establishes basic conventions such as the relative locations of the File, Edit, and Help pull-down menus and the meaning of mouse-button *bindings* (binding refers to the association of a button to a specific action, such as the appearance of a pop-up menu when the user clicks the right mouse button). The GUI does not impose any restrictions on the specific functions that an application performs. Programmers have ample opportunity to be creative in designing these application-specific parts.

X on Linux

The X Window System for Linux comes from the XFree86 project — a cooperative project of programmers who bring X to the PC. As a result, the Linux version of X is called XFree86.

The X server is responsible for displaying output on the monitor. As such, the server must access and use the video card. The PC world has such a wide variety of video cards that creating an X server that can work with all video cards is difficult. But common chipsets — integrated circuits — are used in many video cards. The XFree86 project provides several servers, each capable of working with a specific chipset.

> ### A short history of X
>
> The development of the X Window System started in 1984 at the Massachusetts Institute of Technology (MIT), under the auspices of the MIT Laboratory for Computer Science and MIT/Project Athena. From the beginning, X had industry support because DEC and IBM were involved in Project Athena. By early 1986, DEC introduced the first commercial implementation of X running on the VAXstation-II/GPX under the Ultrix operating system: X version 10, release 3 (X10R3). Soon X attracted the attention of other prominent workstation vendors, such as Hewlett-Packard, Apollo Computer (Apollo has since merged with Hewlett-Packard), Sun Microsystems, and Tektronix.
>
> Feedback from users of X10 urged project members to start a major redesign of the X protocol. While the design of what would become X Version 11 (X11) proceeded, X10R4 was released in December 1986. X10R4 was the last release of X version 10.
>
> In January 1987, during the first X technical conference, 11 major computer vendors announced a joint effort to support and standardize X11. The first release of X11 — X11R1 — became available in September 1987. To ensure continued evolution of X under the control of an open organization, the MIT X Consortium was formed in January 1988. Under the leadership of Robert W. Scheifler, one of the principal architects of X, the consortium has been a major reason for the success of X. Since then, control of the X Window System has been passed on to the X Consortium, Inc., a not-for-profit corporation.
>
> In March 1988, release 2 of X11 — X11R2 — became available. X11 release 3 — X11R3 — appeared in late October 1988. In January 1990, the MIT X Consortium released X11R4; X11R5 followed in August 1991.
>
> As X takes root in the workstation world, the X Consortium continues to improve X in several areas, including support for X programming by means of the C++ programming language and the addition of an object-based toolkit named Fresco, which was part of X11R6 (released in April 1994). Throughout these releases, the X11 protocol has remained unchanged. All enhancements have been made through the X11 protocol's capability to support extensions. At the time this book was written, the most prevalent version of X was X11R6.

Unfortunately, even when several vendors build video cards based on the same chipset, the vendors can configure the chipsets in unique ways. Therefore, the XFree86 servers still have to be tuned to handle each specific brand of video card. For this purpose, the XFree86 developers need detailed information about the video cards. Until recently, several well-known video-card vendors refused to release information about their cards. The growing installed base of Linux users, however, persuaded these vendors to release the necessary information to the XFree86 project. Therefore, XFree86 version 3.1.2 includes support for a large number of previously unsupported video cards.

 The version of XFree86 on the companion CD-ROM supports the commonly found Diamond SpeedStar series of video cards. The support became available when Diamond agreed to release technical information about the video cards to XFree86 developers.

Setting up X on Linux

You want to get X set up and going quickly, because without X, Linux has no GUI. If you are used to other graphical environments (perhaps on another UNIX workstation or on a PC running Microsoft Windows), you probably want a similar graphical environment on Linux.

If you plan to develop software on your Linux system, chances are that your software has a graphical component that has to be implemented and tested under X. You have to set up and run X to do this.

No matter what the reason, if you want to set up XFree86, you have to prepare a special configuration file, named XF86Config, that contains information about your hardware. XFree86 3.1.2 comes with a utility program called xf86config (same name as the configuration file, but in lowercase) that can help you create the XF86Config file.

The next few sections guide you through the process of configuring XFree86 and starting X on your Linux PC.

Know your hardware before configuring XFree86

To configure XFree86, you must know the hardware that X must access and use. From this chapter's brief introduction to X, you know that the X server controls the following hardware:

- Video card
- Monitor
- Keyboard
- Mouse

The X server needs information about these components to work properly.

Monitor

XFree86 controls the monitor through the video card. As such, an XFree86 server can cause a video card to send a wide range of signals to the monitor (to control how fast a raster line is drawn, for example, or how often the entire screen is redrawn). If a video card causes the monitor to perform some task beyond its capabilities (drawing each raster line much faster than it was designed to do, for example), the monitor may actually be damaged. To ensure that the signals from the video card are within the acceptable range for a monitor, XFree86 needs information about some key characteristics of the monitor.

At minimum, you have to provide the following information about the monitor:

- The range of acceptable horizontal synchronization frequencies. A typical range might be 30–64 kilohertz (kHz).

- The range of allowable vertical synchronization rates (also known as vertical refresh rates), such as 50–90 Hertz (Hz).
- If available, the bandwidth, in megahertz, such as 75 MHz.

Typically, the monitor's documentation includes all this information. If you bought your PC recently, you may still have the documentation. This suggestion may not be helpful, however, if your monitor is old; you may have misplaced the monitor's documentation.

If you lost your monitor's documentation, one way to find the information might be from your Microsoft Windows setup. If your system came with a Windows driver for the display, that driver may display information about the monitor. Also, the Norton System Information tool may provide this information as well.

Video card

XFree86 already provides X servers that are designed to work with a particular video chipset (the integrated circuit chips that generate the signals needed to control the monitor). To select the correct X server, you have to indicate what video chipset your video card uses.

Even within a family of video cards based on a specific chipset, many configurable parameters may vary from one card to another. Therefore, you also must specify the vendor name and the model of your video card.

At minimum, you have to provide the following information about the video card:

- Video chipset, such as S3 or ATI Mach64
- Vendor name and model, such as Diamond Stealth 64 VRAM, Number Nine GXE64, or ATI Graphics Xpression
- Amount of video RAM (random-access memory), such as 1MB or 2MB

Most PC vendors indicate only the make and model of the video card in advertisements; the ads rarely mention the video chipset. You should ask explicitly about the video chipset and for as much information as the vendor can provide about the video card model.

Tip

If you are going to use an old PC to run Linux, you could try to find this information by opening your computer's case and looking at the video card. The vendor name and model number may be inscribed on the card. For the video chipset, you have to look at the markings on the different chips on the video card and try to guess. On a video card, you may find a chip with the following markings (only part of the markings are shown here):

```
S3 Trio 64 (GACC 2)
86C764 - P
```

You might guess that this card uses the S3 chipset. In fact, markings on the chip show the 86C764 number as well (either in the full form or as 764). Now, if you can locate the vendor name and model of this card, you may be all set to configure the X server to run properly on your PC.

Mouse

The mouse is an integral part of a GUI because users indicate choices and perform tasks by pointing and clicking. The X server moves an on-screen pointer as you move the mouse. Also, the X server monitors all mouse clicks and sends these *mouse-click events* to the appropriate X client application — the one whose window contains the mouse pointer.

Although you may have set up the mouse during Linux installation, you still have to provide information about the mouse to the X server. The XFree86 X server needs a mouse to start; if the X server cannot access and control the mouse, it won't start.

To specify the mouse, you need to know the following things:

- The mouse type, such as Microsoft, Logitech, BusMouse, or PS/2-style mouse
- The type of connection between your mouse and the system — serial or bus
- The mouse device name. You can leave this as the generic name /dev/mouse, provided that you have set up a link between /dev/mouse and the actual mouse device; the actual device name depends on the type of mouse and where it is connected — the exact serial port for a serial mouse, for example.

You should not have any problem with the mouse as long as the mouse type and device names are correct.

Caution

If you have a bus mouse, you should know that running the gpm program (this program allows you to cut and paste text in text-mode display) may interfere with X. If you have a bus mouse, do not run gpm before starting X. To check if gpm is running, use the following command and look for a gpm process in the output:

```
ps -ax | grep gpm
```

If gpm is running, use the kill command to stop the program before you start X.

Use the xf86config program

The XFree86 X servers read and interpret the XF86Config file to find detailed information about your PC's monitor, video card, keyboard, and mouse. Additionally, the XF86Config file specifies the types of video modes that you want to use.

Until XFree86 3.1.2 came along, you had to edit a sample XF86Config file manually to configure the XFree86 X server. Now, however, a utility program called xf86config can generate a usable XF86Config file. The xf86config program asks you questions. As the following sample session with xf86config shows, you need to have some information about your PC's video card and monitor to answer these questions.

Chapter 4: Secrets of X under Linux   **115**

To run `xf86config`, log in as root and type **xf86config** at the Linux command prompt. The `xf86config` program displays a screen of text that includes the following information:

- The `XF86Config` file is in `/etc` or `/usr/X11R6/lib/X11`. A sample file is located in `/usr/X11R6/lib/X11`, which is configured for a standard Video Graphics Array (VGA) card and a monitor with 640 × 480 resolution.

- You can edit the sample `XF86Config` file or create a new one by continuing with `xf86config`.

- The file `/usr/X11R6/lib/X11/doc/README.Config` describes the configuration process.

- `README` files for specific video chipsets are located in the `/usr/X11R6/lib/X11/doc` directory.

- Before continuing with `xf86config`, you should know your video chipset and the amount of video memory.

After reading the preceding section, you should have found out all you could about your video card and monitor. Now press Enter to continue.

The `xf86config` program asks you to make sure that `/usr/X11R6/bin` is present in your `PATH` environment variable (the setting of this environment variable determines the order in which Linux searches for files). If you installed XFree86 from the companion CD-ROM, the directory name `/usr/X11` is a symbolic link — an alias — to the `/usr/X11R6` directory, which means that you can use the directory name `/usr/X11/bin` to refer to `/usr/X11R6/bin`.

The `xf86config` program also shows you the current setting of the `PATH` environment variable. You see that the `PATH` contains `/usr/X11/bin`, so you can press Enter to proceed to the next step.

The `xf86config` program asks you to specify a mouse protocol that determines how the X server communicates with the mouse. The program shows you the following list of choices:

```
1.  Microsoft compatible (2-button protocol)
2.  Mouse Systems (3-button protocol)
3.  Bus Mouse
4.  PS/2 Mouse
5.  Logitech Mouse (serial, old type, Logitech protocol)
6.  Logitech MouseMan (Microsoft compatible)
7.  MM Series
8.  MM HitTablet
```

Press the number that corresponds to your mouse type. If your mouse is connected to a PS/2 style port, for example, select 4. Press the appropriate number; then press Enter.

Caution

Note that it's the mouse interface that matters, not the actual brand of the mouse. After all, there are serial PS/2 style mice and Microsoft bus mice.

The `xf86config` program then asks the following:

```
Please answer the following question with either 'y' or 'n'.
Do you want to enable Emulate3Buttons?
```

If your mouse has two buttons, `xf86config` suggests that you enable Emulate3Buttons. Press **y** and then press Enter. If you enable Emulate3Buttons, you can simulate a middle button click by pressing both buttons simultaneously. Many X applications assume that the mouse has three buttons, so this feature comes in handy in the PC world where mice typically have two buttons.

Next, you have to specify the full device name for the mouse. During Linux installation, if you configured the mouse and created a link between your mouse device and the standard name `/dev/mouse`, you can press Enter. Otherwise, you should enter the device name for your mouse. For a serial mouse, use one of the following names:

- `/dev/ttyS0` for a mouse connected to COM1
- `/dev/ttyS1` for a mouse connected to COM2
- `/dev/ttyS2` for a mouse connected to COM3
- `/dev/ttyS3` for a mouse connected to COM4

For a bus mouse, use one of these names:

- `/dev/atibm` for ATI bus mouse
- `/dev/logibm` for Logitech bus mouse
- `/dev/inportbm` for Microsoft bus mouse
- `/dev/psaux` for any mouse connected to PS/2-style auxiliary port

Type the device name that corresponds to your mouse, and press Enter. You can enter an exact device name even if you created a link between `/dev/mouse` and your actual mouse device.

The `xf86config` program then asks whether you want to generate special characters when you work in X. To do this, you can bind the left Alt key to Meta and the right Alt key to ModeShift. (Meta and ModeShift are the standardized names of special keys used in X; you can associate the keys with any physical key on the keyboard.)

The program then asks the following:

```
Please answer the following question with either 'y' or 'n'.
Do you want to enable these bindings for the Alt keys? y
```

There is no harm in enabling these keys; therefore, press **y** and then press Enter to continue with the configuration.

Next, `xf86config` informs you that it needs two critical parameters of your monitor:

Chapter 4: Secrets of X under Linux 117

- Horizontal synchronization frequency — the number of times per second that the monitor can display horizontal raster lines, in kilohertz (kHz)

- Vertical synchronization rate — how many times a second the monitor can display the entire screen, in Hertz (Hz)

You can find this information in your monitor's manual.

Press Enter to continue. The `xf86config` program shows you the following options:

```
    hsync in kHz; monitor type with characteristic modes
 1  31.5; Standard VGA, 640x480 @ 60 Hz
 2  31.5 - 35.1; Super VGA, 800x600 @ 56 Hz
 3  31.5, 35.5; 8514 Compatible, 1024x768 @ 87 Hz interlaced (no
800x600)
 4  31.5, 35.15, 35.5; Super VGA, 1024x768 @ 87 Hz interlaced, 800x600
@ 56 Hz
 5  31.5 - 37.9; Extended Super VGA, 800x600 @ 60 Hz, 640x480 @ 72 Hz
 6  31.5 - 48.5; Non-Interlaced SVGA, 1024x768 @ 60 Hz, 800x600 @ 72
Hz
 7  31.5 - 57.0; High Frequency SVGA, 1024x768 @ 70 Hz
 8  31.5 - 64.3; Monitor that can do 1280x1024 @ 60 Hz
 9  31.5 - 79.0; Monitor that can do 1280x1024 @ 74 Hz
10  Enter your own horizontal sync range
```

You can enter the number that corresponds to your monitor, or type **10** to specify a range.

Caution

Do not specify a horizontal synchronization range that is beyond the capabilities of your monitor. A wrong value can damage the monitor.

Many monitor manuals provide a range of values for the horizontal synchronization rate. To enter a range of values, type **10** and then press Enter. The program prompts you for the range. Enter the range as two values separated by a minus sign. My monitor's documentation, for example, says that the horizontal synchronization range is 30–64 kHz, so I enter the following:

```
Horizontal sync range: 30-64
```

Next, `xf86config` prompts you for the vertical synchronization rate and gives you the following options:

```
1   50-70
2   50-90
3   50-100
4   40-150
5   Enter your own vertical sync range
```

If you know the range, press **5** and then press Enter. At the next prompt, enter the range for the vertical synchronization. My monitor's documentation shows this range to be 55–90 Hz, so I enter the following:

```
Vertical sync range: 55-90
```

Next, you have to enter an identifier for your monitor's definition. Typically, you can enter your monitor's make and model. You can enter anything here, because this information is simply used as an identifier in references to the monitor in another part of the XF86Config configuration file (the following section describes that file's layout). For my system's monitor, I respond as follows:

```
Enter an identifier for your monitor definition: Dell VS15X
Enter the vendor name of your monitor: Dell
Enter the model name of your monitor: VS15X
```

The next task is to configure the video-card settings. The xf86config program displays an explanatory message and asks this question:

```
Do you want to look at the card database? y
```

Press **y** and then press Enter. The program then displays a list of 124 cards. Press Enter after each screen to see the entire list. The complete list appears after this paragraph. The make, model, and chipset of the video card are crucial pieces of information that you need to select the correct XFree86 X server and configure it properly. You want to browse through this list to see whether X will work with your video card.

```
 0  928Movie                        S3-928
 1  AGX (generic)                   AGX
 2  ALG-5434(E)                     CL-GD5434
 3  ATI 8514 Ultra (no VGA)         ATI-Mach8
 4  ATI Expression                  ATI-Mach64
 5  ATI GUP Turbo                   ATI-Mach64
 6  ATI Graphics Ultra              ATI-Mach8
 7  ATI Graphics Ultra Pro          ATI-Mach32
 8  ATI Ultra Plus                  ATI-Mach32
 9  ATI WinTurbo                    ATI-Mach64
10  ATI Wonder SVGA                 ATI vgawonder
11  Actix GE32+ 2MB                 S3-801/805
12  Actix GE32i                     S3-805i
13  Actix GE64                      S3-864
14  Actix ProStar                   CL-GD5426/5428
15  Actix ProStar 64                CL-GD5434
16  Acumos AVGA3                    CL-GD5420/2/4/6/8/9
17  Avance Logic (generic)          Avance Logic

Enter a number to choose the corresponding card definition.
Press enter for the next page, q to continue configuration.

18  Boca Vortex                     AGX
19  Cardex Challenger (Pro)         ET4000/W32(i/p)
20  Cardex Cobra                    ET4000/W32(i/p)
21  Cirrus Logic GD542x             CL-GD5420/2/4/6/8/9
22  Cirrus Logic GD543x             CL-GD5430/5434
23  Cirrus Logic GD62xx (laptop)    CL-GD6205/15/25/35
24  Cirrus Logic GD64xx (laptop)    CL-GD6420/6440
25  DFI-WG1000                      CL-GD5420/2/4/6/8/9
26  DFI-WG5000                      ET4000/W32(i/p)
```

27	DFI-WG6000	WD90C33
28	Dell S3-805	S3-801/805
29	Diamond SpeedStar (Plus)	ET4000
30	Diamond SpeedStar 24X	WD90C31
31	Diamond SpeedStar 64	CL-GD5434
32	Diamond SpeedStar Pro (not SE)	CL-GD5426/28
33	Diamond SpeedStar Pro SE (CL-GD5430/5434)	CL-GD5430/5434
34	Diamond Stealth 24	S3-801/805
35	Diamond Stealth 32 (not fully supported)	ET4000/W32(i/p)

Enter a number to choose the corresponding card definition.
Press enter for the next page, q to continue configuration.

36	Diamond Stealth 64 DRAM with S3-SDAC	S3-864
37	Diamond Stealth 64 DRAM with S3-Trio64	S3-Trio64
38	Diamond Stealth 64 VRAM	S3-964
39	Diamond Stealth Pro	S3-928
40	Diamond Stealth VRAM	S3-911/924
41	Diamond Viper VLB 2Mb	Weitek 9000
42	EIZO (VRAM)	AGX
43	ET4000/W32, W32i, W32p (generic)	ET4000/W32(i/p)
44	Elsa Winner 1000	S3-928
45	Elsa Winner 1000 ISA	S3-805i
46	Elsa Winner 1000 PRO with S3-SDAC	S3-864
47	Elsa Winner 1000 PRO with STG or AT&T RAMDAC	S3-864
48	Elsa Winner 2000	S3-928
49	Elsa Winner 2000 Pro 4Mb	S3-964
50	Generic VGA compatible	Generic VGA
51	Genoa 8500VL(-28)	CL-GD5426/28
52	Genoa 8900 Phantom 32i	ET4000/W32(i/p)
53	Genoa Phantom 64i with S3-SDAC	S3-864

Enter a number to choose the corresponding card definition.
Press enter for the next page, q to continue configuration.

54	Hercules Dynamite Power	ET4000/W32(i/p)
55	Hercules Dynamite Pro	ET4000/W32i/p
56	Hercules Graphics Terminator 64	S3-964
57	Hercules Graphite HG210	AGX-014
58	Hercules Graphite Power	AGX-016
59	Hercules Graphite Pro	AGX-014/15/16
60	Hercules Graphite VL Pro HG720	AGX-015
61	Hercules Stingray	ALG-2228/2301 2302
62	Hercules Stingray 64	ARK2000PV
63	Hercules Stingray Pro	ARK1000PV
64	Intel 5430	CL-GD5430
65	LeadTek WinFast S200	ET4000/W32(i/p)
66	Miro Crystal 10SD with GenDAC	S3-801/805
67	Miro Crystal 16S	S3-928
68	Miro Crystal 20SD with ICD2061A (BIOS 2.xx)	S3-864
69	Miro Crystal 20SD with ICS2494 (BIOS 1.xx)	S3-864
70	Miro Crystal 20SD with S3-SDAC (BIOS 3.xx)	S3-864
71	Miro Crystal 20SV	S3-964

Enter a number to choose the corresponding card definition.
Press enter for the next page, q to continue configuration.

```
 72  Miro Crystal 40SV                              S3-964
 73  Miro Crystal 8S                                S3-801/805
 74  Number Nine GXE Level 12/14 2Mb                S3-928
 75  Number Nine GXE Level 16                       S3-928
 76  Number Nine GXE64                              S3-864
 77  Number Nine GXE64 Pro                          S3-964
 78  Number Nine GXE64 with S3-Trio64               S3-Trio64
 79  Oak (generic)                                  Oak-067/77/87
 80  Orchid Celsius                                 AGX
 81  Orchid Fahrenheit 1280                         S3-801
 82  Orchid Fahrenheit 1280                         S3-911/924
 83  Orchid Fahrenheit VA                           S3-801/805
 84  Orchid Fahrenheit-1280+                        S3-801/805
 85  Orchid Kelvin 64                               CL-GD5434
 86  Orchid Kelvin 64 VLB Rev A                     CL-GD5434
 87  Orchid Kelvin 64 VLB Rev B                     CL-GD5434
 88  Orchid P9000 VLB                               Weitek 9000
 89  Paradise Accelerator Value                     Oak OTI-087
```

Enter a number to choose the corresponding card definition.
Press enter for the next page, q to continue configuration.

```
 90  Paradise/WD 90CXX                              WD90CXX
 91  S3-801/805 (generic)                           S3-801/805
 92  S3-801/805 with ATT20c490 RAMDAC               S3-801/805
 93  S3-801/805 with ATT20c490 RAMDAC and ICD2061A  S3-801/805
 94  S3-801/805 with S3-GenDAC                      S3-801/805
 95  S3-864 (generic)                               S3-864
 96  S3-864 with ATT 20C498 or 21C498               S3-864
 97  S3-864 with SDAC (86C716)                      S3-864
 98  S3-911/924 (generic)                           S3-911/924
 99  S3-924 with SC1148 DAC                         S3-924
100  S3-928 (generic)                               S3-928
101  S3-964 (generic)                               S3-964
102  S3-Trio32 (generic)                            S3-Trio32
103  S3-Trio64 (generic)                            S3-Trio64
104  SPEA/V7 Mercury                                S3-928
105  SPEA/V7 Mirage P64                             S3-864
106  SPEA/V7 Mirage P64 with S3-Trio64              S3-Trio64
107  SPEA/V7 Mirage VFGA Plus                       ALG-2228
```

Enter a number to choose the corresponding card definition.
Press enter for the next page, q to continue configuration.

```
108  STB Horizon                                    CL-GD5426/28
109  STB LightSpeed                                 ET4000/W32(i/p)
110  STB Nitro                                      CL-GD5434
111  STB Pegasus                                    S3-928
112  STB Powergraph X-24                            S3-801/805
113  Sigma Concorde                                 ET4000/W32(i/p)
```

```
114  Spider Black Widow Plus                     AGX-016
115  Spider Tarantula 64                         S3-964
116  Spider VLB Plus                             CL-GD5428
117  TechWorks Thunderbolt                       ET4000/W32(i/p)
118  Trident 8900/9000 (generic)                 TVGA8900/9000
119  VI720                                       CL-GD5434
120  VidTech FastMax P20                         S3-864
121  VideoMagic PCI V864                         S3-864
122  ViewTop PCI                                 ET4000/W32(i/p)
123  WD 90C24 (laptop) (wd90c30 compatible)      WD90C24
124  WD 90C24A (laptop) (wd90c31 compatible)     WD90C24A

Enter a number to choose the corresponding card definition.
Press enter for the next page, q to continue configuration.
```

Select your video card by typing the appropriate number. One of my PCs, for example, has a Number Nine GXE64 video card with the S3-Trio64 chipset. For this PC, I type **78** and press Enter.

Tip

Each new release of XFree86 supports more video cards. The list in this section shows the cards that XFree86 3.1.2 supports. If your video card's vendor and model do not appear in the list, but you know the video chipset, try selecting the entry that corresponds to the generic chipset. If you have a video card based on the S3-Trio64 chipset, for example, but you do not know the make and model of the card, select card number 103 from the list.

After you enter your selection, xf86config displays some information (and any appropriate instructions) about the video card that you selected. When I select card number 78, for example, xf86config displays the following:

```
Your selected card definition:

Identifier: Number Nine GXE64 with S3-Trio64
Chipset:    S3-Trio64
Server:     XF86_S3
Do NOT probe clocks or use any Clocks line.

Press enter to continue, or ctrl-c to abort.
```

Notice the instruction that I should not probe clocks or use any Clocks line. If you see any instruction like this, keep it in mind as you continue with xf86config. If the program offers to probe clocks, for example, you should answer no. You don't really have to understand what the instruction means; simply follow it, and you should have an XF86Config file that works properly.

After you press Enter to continue, xf86config displays the following message, asking you to select an X server:

Now you must determine which server to run. Refer to the manpages and
other documentation. The following servers are available (they may not
all be installed on your system):

1   The XF86_Mono server. This a monochrome server that should work on
    any VGA-compatible card, in 640x480 (more on some SVGA chipsets).
2   The XF86_VGA16 server. This is a 16-color VGA server that should
    work on any VGA-compatible card.
3   The XF86_SVGA server. This is a 256 color SVGA server that sup-
    ports a number of SVGA chipsets. It is accelerated on some
    Cirrus and WD chipsets; it supports 16/32-bit color on certain
    Cirrus configurations.
4   The accelerated servers. These include XF86_S3, XF86_Mach32,
    XF86_Mach8, XF86_8514, XF86_P9000, XF86_AGX, XF86_W32 and
    XF86_Mach64.

These four server types correspond to the four different "Screen"
sections in XF86Config (vga2, vga16, svga, accel).

5   Choose the server from the card definition, XF86_S3.

Which one of these screen types do you intend to run by default (1-5)? **5**

If you specified your video card correctly, you should press 5 so that the server corresponds to the video card. The xf86config **program then displays the following message and question:**

The server to run is selected by changing the symbolic link 'X'. For
example, 'rm /usr/X11R6/bin/X; ln -s /usr/X11R6/bin/XF86_SVGA /usr/
X11R6/bin/X' selects the SVGA server.

The directory /var/X11R6/bin exists. On many Linux systems this is the
preferred location of the symbolic link 'X'. You can select the location when setting the symbolic link.

Please answer the following question with either 'y' or 'n'.
Do you want me to set the symbolic link? **y**

Do you want to set it to /var/X11R6/bin? **y**

Press y to answer yes to both questions. On the Slackware Linux installation, you should set the link X **in the** /var/X11R6/bin **directory. Even if you do not understand the meaning of these steps, you can safely answer y; the correct X server should run when you start X.**

Next, xf86config **asks how much video memory your video card has, as follows:**

How much video memory do you have on your video card:
1   256K
2   512K
3   1024K
4   2048K
5   4096K
6   Other

Most current video cards have at least 1MB (1,024K) of video memory. You need that much memory to display 256 colors at 1,024 × 768 resolution (1,024 pixels horizontally by 768 pixels vertically). Type the number that corresponds to the amount of memory in your video card and then press Enter.

Now you have to provide an identifier for your video card. Type the appropriate information for your card. Following is what I enter for my PC's video card:

```
Enter an identifier for your video card definition: Number Nine GXE64
Enter the vendor name of your video card: Number Nine
Enter the model (board) name of your video card: GXE64
```

The `xf86config` program then prompts you for some technical information that is especially useful for the accelerated servers. First, the program asks for a Clockchip setting. If you do not know this information, just press Enter to continue.

Next comes the Clocks line, which is a list of clock frequencies that the X server uses when it starts. Without a Clocks line, the X server determines the clock frequencies every time it starts. The X server can run in a *probeonly mode* (when started with the command `X -probeonly`), in which the server determines and displays the clock frequencies. Then you can place this information on a line in the `XF86Config` file. In fact, the `xf86config` program can run the X server in probeonly mode and get the clock values.

Before you decide to proceed, check to see whether your video card needs a Clocks line (recall the instructions that `xf86config` displays when you select a video card). Many video chipsets do not need a Clocks line. When I specify an S3 video card, for example, I get the following message:

```
The card definition says NOT to probe clocks.
Do you want me to run 'X -probeonly' now? n
```

Naturally, I press **n** to answer no. On the other hand, if your card can use a Clocks line, go ahead and press **y** to answer yes. The `xf86config` program runs the X server in probeonly mode, gets the clock values, and adds an appropriate Clocks line to the configuration file.

Next, the `xf86config` program displays several modes and asks you to make a selection, as follows:

```
For each depth, a list of modes (resolutions) is defined. The default
resolution that the server will start-up with will be the first listed
mode that can be supported by the monitor and card.
Currently it is set to:

"640x480" "800x600" 1024x768" for 8bpp
"640x480" "800x600" for 16bpp
"640x400" for 32bpp

Note that 16bpp and 32bpp are only supported on a few configurations.
Modes that cannot be supported due to monitor or clock constraints
will be automatically skipped by the server.
```

```
1  Change the modes for 8bpp (256 colors)
2  Change the modes for 16bpp (32K/64K colors)
3  Change the modes for 24bpp (24-bit color)
4  The modes are OK, continue.

Enter your choice: 4
```

The abbreviation bpp stands for *bits per pixel*. The depth of a mode is expressed by values such as 8bpp and 16bpp. You can safely select the last option and continue. Press **4** and then press Enter to accept the choices and proceed.

This step completes your session with `xf86config`. Then the program displays the following message, asking whether it can write the `XF86Config` file in the `/etc` directory:

```
I am going to write the XF86Config file now. make sure you don't
accidentally overwrite a previously configured one.

Shall I wrote it to: /etc/XF86Config? y
```

Press **y** and then press Enter. The `xf86config` program writes the configuration file and exits.

Cross Reference

If you are lucky, the `XF86Config` file generated by `xf86config` may be all that you need to run X with your PC's video card and monitor. Because of the potential for monitor damage if you make the wrong settings in the `XF86Config` file, you should use an editor to look through the configuration file (Chapter 24 describes the `vi` and GNU Emacs editors). The following listing shows the configuration file that the `xf86config` program generates after you go through the steps outlined in this section.

```
# File generated by xf86config.

#
# Copyright (c) 1994 by The XFree86 Project, Inc.
#
# Permission is hereby granted, free of charge, to any person obtaining a
# copy of this software and associated documentation files (the "Software"),
# to deal in the Software without restriction, including without limitation
# the rights to use, copy, modify, merge, publish, distribute, sublicense,
# and/or sell copies of the Software, and to permit persons to whom the
# Software is furnished to do so, subject to the following conditions:
#
# The above copyright notice and this permission notice shall be included in
# all copies or substantial portions of the Software.
#
# THE SOFTWARE IS PROVIDED "AS IS", WITHOUT WARRANTY OF ANY KIND, EXPRESS OR
# IMPLIED, INCLUDING BUT NOT LIMITED TO THE WARRANTIES OF MERCHANTABILITY,
# FITNESS FOR A PARTICULAR PURPOSE AND NONINFRINGEMENT.  IN NO EVENT SHALL
# THE XFREE86 PROJECT BE LIABLE FOR ANY CLAIM, DAMAGES OR OTHER LIABILITY,
# WHETHER IN AN ACTION OF CONTRACT, TORT OR OTHERWISE, ARISING FROM, OUT OF
# OR IN CONNECTION WITH THE SOFTWARE OR THE USE OR OTHER DEALINGS IN THE
# SOFTWARE.
#
# Except as contained in this notice, the name of the XFree86 Project shall
# not be used in advertising or otherwise to promote the sale, use or other
```

```
#  dealings in this Software without prior written authorization from the
#  XFree86 Project.
#

# **************************************************************************
# Refer to the XF86Config(4/5) man page for details about the format of
# this file.
# **************************************************************************

# **************************************************************************
# Files section.  This allows default font and rgb paths to be set
# **************************************************************************

Section "Files"

# The location of the RGB database.  Note, this is the name of the
# file minus the extension (like ".txt" or ".db").  There is normally
# no need to change the default.

    RgbPath     "/usr/X11R6/lib/X11/rgb"


# Multiple FontPath entries are allowed (which are concatenated together),
# as well as specifying multiple comma-separated entries in one FontPath
# command (or a combination of both methods)
#
# If you don't have a floating point coprocessor and emacs, Mosaic or other
# programs take long to start up, try moving the Type1 and Speedo directory
# to the end of this list (or comment them out).
#

    FontPath   "/usr/X11R6/lib/X11/fonts/misc/"
    FontPath   "/usr/X11R6/lib/X11/fonts/Type1/"
    FontPath   "/usr/X11R6/lib/X11/fonts/Speedo/"
    FontPath   "/usr/X11R6/lib/X11/fonts/75dpi/"
    FontPath   "/usr/X11R6/lib/X11/fonts/100dpi/"

EndSection

# **************************************************************************
# Server flags section.
# **************************************************************************

Section "ServerFlags"

# Uncomment this to cause a core dump at the spot where a signal is
# received.  This may leave the console in an unusable state, but may
# provide a better stack trace in the core dump to aid in debugging

#     NoTrapSignals

# Uncomment this to disable the <Ctrl><Alt><BS> server abort sequence
# This allows clients to receive this key event.
```

```
#       DontZap

# Uncomment this to disable the <Crtl><Alt><KP_+>/<KP_-> mode switching
# sequences.  This allows clients to receive these key events.

#       DontZoom

EndSection

# **********************************************************************
# Input devices
# **********************************************************************


# **********************************************************************
# Keyboard section
# **********************************************************************

Section "Keyboard"

    Protocol "Standard"

# when using XQUEUE, comment out the above line, and uncomment the
# following line

#       Protocol        "Xqueue"

    AutoRepeat      500 5
# Let the server do the NumLock processing.  This should only be required
# when using pre-R6 clients
#       ServerNumLock

# Specify which keyboard LEDs can be user-controlled (e.g., with xset(1))
#       Xleds       1 2 3

# To set the LeftAlt to Meta, RightAlt key to ModeShift,
# RightCtl key to Compose, and ScrollLock key to ModeLock:

    LeftAlt     Meta
    RightAlt    ModeShift
#   RightCtl    Compose
#   ScrollLock  ModeLock

EndSection


# **********************************************************************
# Pointer section
# **********************************************************************

Section "Pointer"
    Protocol    "PS/2"
    Device      "/dev/psaux"

# When using XQUEUE, comment out the above two lines, and uncomment
# the following line.
```

```
#       Protocol        "Xqueue"

# BaudRate and SampleRate are only for some Logitech mice
#       BaudRate        9600
#       SampleRate      150

# Emulate3Buttons is an option for 2-button Microsoft mice

    Emulate3Buttons

# ChordMiddle is an option for some 3-button Logitech mice

#       ChordMiddle

EndSection


# **************************************************************************
# Monitor section
# **************************************************************************

# Any number of monitor sections may be present

Section "Monitor"

    Identifier  "Dell VS15X"
    VendorName  "Dell"
    ModelName   "VS15X"

# Bandwidth is in MHz unless units are specified

#       Bandwidth       25.2

# HorizSync is in kHz unless units are specified.
# HorizSync may be a comma separated list of discrete values, or a
# comma separated list of ranges of values.
# NOTE: THE VALUES HERE ARE EXAMPLES ONLY.  REFER TO YOUR MONITOR'S
# USER MANUAL FOR THE CORRECT NUMBERS.

    HorizSync   30-64

#       HorizSync       30-64           # multisync
#       HorizSync       31.5, 35.2      # multiple fixed sync frequencies
#       HorizSync       15-25, 30-50    # multiple ranges of sync frequencies

# VertRefresh is in Hz unless units are specified.
# VertRefresh may be a comma separated list of discrete values, or a
# comma separated list of ranges of values.
# NOTE: THE VALUES HERE ARE EXAMPLES ONLY.  REFER TO YOUR MONITOR'S
# USER MANUAL FOR THE CORRECT NUMBERS.

    VertRefresh 55-90

# Modes can be specified in two formats.  A compact one-line format, or
```

```
# a multi-line format.

# These two are equivalent

#     ModeLine "1024x768i" 45 1024 1048 1208 1264 768 776 784 817 Interlace

#     Mode "1024x768i"
#         DotClock    45
#         HTimings    1024 1048 1208 1264
#         VTimings    768 776 784 817
#         Flags              "Interlace"
#     EndMode

# This is a set of standard mode timings. Modes that are out of monitor spec
# are automatically deleted by the server (provided the HorizSync and
# VertRefresh lines are correct), so there's no immediate need to
# delete mode timings (unless particular mode timings don't work on your
# monitor). With these modes, the best standard mode that your monitor
# and video card can support for a given resolution is automatically
# used.

# 640x400 @ 70 Hz, 31.5 kHz hsync
Modeline "640x400"    25.175 640  664  760  800   400  409  411  450
# 640x480 @ 60 Hz, 31.5 kHz hsync
Modeline "640x480"    25.175 640  664  760  800   480  491  493  525
# 800x600 @ 56 Hz, 35.15 kHz hsync
ModeLine "800x600"    36     800  824  896 1024   600  601  603  625
# 1024x768 @ 87 Hz interlaced, 35.5 kHz hsync
Modeline "1024x768"   44.9   1024 1048 1208 1264  768  776  784  817
Interlace

# 640x480 @ 72 Hz, 36.5 kHz hsync
Modeline "640x480"    31.5   640  680  720  864   480  488  491  521
# 800x600 @ 60 Hz, 37.8 kHz hsync
Modeline "800x600"    40     800  840  968 1056   600  601  605  628 +hsync
+vsync

# 800x600 @ 72 Hz, 48.0 kHz hsync
Modeline "800x600"    50     800  856  976 1040   600  637  643  666 +hsync
+vsync
# 1024x768 @ 60 Hz, 48.4 kHz hsync
Modeline "1024x768"   65     1024 1032 1176 1344  768  771  777  806 -hsync
-vsync

# 1024x768 @ 70 Hz, 56.5 kHz hsync
Modeline "1024x768"   75     1024 1048 1184 1328  768  771  777  806 -hsync
-vsync
# 1280x1024 @ 87 Hz interlaced, 51 kHz hsync
Modeline "1280x1024"  80     1280 1296 1512 1568 1024 1025 1037 1165
Interlace

# 1024x768 @ 76 Hz, 62.5 kHz hsync
Modeline "1024x768"   85     1024 1032 1152 1360  768  784  787  823
# 1280x1024 @ 61 Hz, 64.2 kHz hsync
Modeline "1280x1024"  110    1280 1328 1512 1712 1024 1025 1028 1054
```

```
# 1280x1024 @ 74 Hz, 78.85 kHz hsync
Modeline "1280x1024"    135     1280 1312 1456 1712   1024 1027 1030 1064

# Low-res Doublescan modes
# If your chipset does not support doublescan, you get a 'squashed'
# resolution like 320x400.

# 320x200 @ 70 Hz, 31.5 kHz hsync, 8:5 aspect ratio
Modeline "320x200"      12.588 320   336 384 400   200 204 205 225
Doublescan
# 320x240 @ 60 Hz, 31.5 kHz hsync, 4:3 aspect ratio
Modeline "320x240"      12.588 320   336 384 400   240 245 246 262
Doublescan
# 320x240 @ 72 Hz, 36.5 kHz hsync
Modeline "320x240"      15.750 320   336 384 400   240 244 246 262
Doublescan
# 400x300 @ 56 Hz, 35.2 kHz hsync, 4:3 aspect ratio
ModeLine "400x300"      18     400   416 448 512   300 301 602 312
Doublescan
# 400x300 @ 60 Hz, 37.8 kHz hsync
Modeline "400x300"      20     400   416 480 528   300 301 303 314
Doublescan
# 400x300 @ 72 Hz, 48.0 kHz hsync
Modeline "400x300"      25     400   424 488 520   300 319 322 333
Doublescan
# 480x300 @ 56 Hz, 35.2 kHz hsync, 8:5 aspect ratio
ModeLine "480x300"      21.656 480   496 536 616   300 301 302 312
Doublescan
# 480x300 @ 60 Hz, 37.8 kHz hsync
Modeline "480x300"      23.890 480   496 576 632   300 301 303 314
Doublescan
# 480x300 @ 63 Hz, 39.6 kHz hsync
Modeline "480x300"      25     480   496 576 632   300 301 303 314
Doublescan
# 480x300 @ 72 Hz, 48.0 kHz hsync
Modeline "480x300"      29.952 480   504 584 624   300 319 322 333
Doublescan

EndSection


# *************************************************************************
# Graphics device section
# *************************************************************************

# Any number of graphics device sections may be present

# Standard VGA Device:

Section "Device"
    Identifier      "Generic VGA"
    VendorName      "Unknown"
    BoardName       "Unknown"
    Chipset  "generic"
```

```
#     VideoRam        256

#     Clocks   25.2 28.3

EndSection

# Sample Device for accelerated server:

# Section "Device"
#     Identifier      "Actix GE32+ 2MB"
#     VendorName      "Actix"
#     BoardName       "GE32+"
#     Ramdac   "ATT20C490"
#     Dacspeed        110
#     Option   "dac_8_bit"
#     Clocks    25.0  28.0  40.0   0.0  50.0  77.0  36.0  45.0
#     Clocks   130.0 120.0  80.0  31.0 110.0  65.0  75.0  94.0
# EndSection

# Device configured by xf86config:

Section "Device"
    Identifier   "Number Nine GXE64 with S3-Trio64"
    VendorName   "Number Nine"
    BoardName    "GXE64"
    #VideoRam    1024
# Use Option "nolinear" if the server doesn't start up correctly
# (this avoids the linear framebuffer probe). If that fails try
# option "nomemaccess".
#
# Use Option "sw_cursor" if the server completely locked up
# several times while you're moving the mouse.
#
# Refer to /usr/X11R6/lib/doc/README.S3, and the XF86_S3 man page.
    # Insert Clocks lines here if appropriate
EndSection


# **********************************************************************
# Screen sections
# **********************************************************************

# The Colour SVGA server


Section "Screen"
    Driver      "svga"
    Device      "Generic VGA"
    #Device     "Number Nine GXE64 with S3-Trio64"
    Monitor     "Dell VS15X"
    Subsection "Display"
        Depth       8
        #Modes      "640x480" "800x600" "1024x768"
        ViewPort    0 0
        Virtual     320 200
        #Virtual    1024 768
```

```
        EndSubsection
EndSection

# The 16-color VGA server

Section "Screen"
    Driver      "vga16"
    Device      "Generic VGA"
    Monitor     "Dell VS15X"
    Subsection "Display"
        Modes       "640x480" "800x600"
        ViewPort    0 0
        Virtual     800 600
    EndSubsection
EndSection

# The Mono server

Section "Screen"
    Driver      "vga2"
    Device      "Generic VGA"
    Monitor     "Dell VS15X"
    Subsection "Display"
        Modes       "640x480" "800x600"
        ViewPort    0 0
        Virtual     800 600
    EndSubsection
EndSection

# The accelerated servers (S3, Mach32, Mach8, 8514, P9000, AGX, W32, Mach64)

Section "Screen"
    Driver      "accel"
    Device      "Number Nine GXE64 with S3-Trio64"
    Monitor     "Dell VS15X"
    Subsection "Display"
        Depth       8
        Modes       "640x480" "800x600" "1024x768"
        ViewPort    0 0
        Virtual     1024 768
    EndSubsection
    Subsection "Display"
        Depth       16
        Modes       "640x480" "800x600"
        ViewPort    0 0
        Virtual     800 600
    EndSubsection
    Subsection "Display"
        Depth       32
        Modes       "640x400"
        ViewPort    0 0
        Virtual     640 400
    EndSubsection
EndSection
```

Check the `XF86Config` file

When you run the `xf86config` utility program, you create an `XF86Config` file, such as the one shown in the previous listing; you also select an X server that is appropriate for your video card. The `XF86Config` file describes your video card, monitor, and mouse to the X server. By default, the X server first looks for the configuration file in the `/etc` directory (`/etc/XF86Config`), which is where the `xf86config` program places the file.

If you study the example `XF86Config` file, you see that the configuration file consists of several sections. Each section has the following format:

```
# This a comment
Section "SectionName"
    EntryName   EntryValue
    ...
    ...
    Subsection "SubsectionName"
        EntryName EntryValue
        ...
        ...
    EndSubsection
EndSection
```

Sections consist of a sequence of entries; each entry has a name and a value. A section may contain one or more subsections. A pound sign (#) at the beginning of a line marks a comment line.

The `XF86Config` file contains one or more of the following seven sections:

- *Files.* This section lists the *pathnames* (full directory names) of font files and the file that contains the color database, called the *RGB file*. RGB stands for red, green, and blue — the three primary components of color.

- *ServerFlags.* This section lists various X server options, such as DontZap (which means "do not allow the Ctrl+Alt+Backspace keystroke to terminate the X server") and DontZoom (means "do not accept special keystrokes to change screen resolution").

- *Keyboard.* This section specifies the type of keyboard and characteristics such as auto-repeat delay and rate.

- *Pointer.* This section lists information about the mouse, including its device name. (In the X Window System's terminology, the mouse is known as the *pointer*.)

- *Monitor.* This section includes the specifications of a monitor (such as horizontal and vertical synchronization rates) and a list of video modes that the monitor supports.

- *Device.* This section describes the characteristics of a video card (*graphics device*). The configuration file may have more than one Device section.

- *Screen.* This section describes a combination of a video card and monitor to be used by the X server. Typically, the configuration file has several Screen sections.

For the most part, you should not have to learn all the details of these sections; the `XF86Config` file should be your starting point. The next few sections summarize some of the important sections of the configuration file and give you guidelines on changes that you may have to make.

Files section

The Files section lists the location of some files that the X server needs. These files include

- A file that contains the color definitions (this file is called the RGB file)
- The locations of the fonts (each location is a directory)

You don't have to change the name of the RGB file. As for the font locations, make sure that each directory exists. These directories should exist, provided that you installed all the fonts during Linux installation. If a font directory does not exist, you have to remove that line from the configuration file or type # at the beginning of that line.

ServerFlags section

In this section, you can have one of the flags listed in Table 4-1; just place the word on a line.

Table 4-1   ServerFlags section flags

Flag	Meaning
`NoTrapSignals`	Used only for debugging.
`DontZap`	Causes the X server to ignore Ctrl+Alt+Backspace, which usually causes the X server to exit.
`DontZoom`	Causes the X server to ignore the Ctrl+Alt+Keypad + and Ctrl+Alt+Keypad – key combinations that otherwise would change the video modes. (*Keypad +* and *Keypad –* refer to the plus and minus keys in the numeric keypad.)

The configuration file generated by `xf86config` does not use any of these flags, so you should leave this section as is. Later, you will find the Ctrl+Alt+Backspace combination to be useful when the X server does not work or somehow hangs up. The Ctrl+Alt+Keypad + and Ctrl+Alt+Keypad – combinations are useful when you want to try different video modes without having to restart the X server.

Monitor section

The Monitor section is a crucial section of the `XF86Config` file because it lists some important technical data about the monitor. If you recently purchased your PC, you probably received a manual for the monitor. In that manual, you should find a Technical Specifications page. You need data from that page to fill out the Monitor section.

Make sure that the section contains an Identifier entry. Following is a typical entry:

```
Identifier    "Dell VS15X"
```

The Screen section, described later in this chapter, refers to this monitor by the name Dell VS15X.

Two other entries — HorizSync and VertRefresh — are very important. The HorizSync entry should specify the range of horizontal synchronization values; simply enter the range as specified in the monitor's manual. The unit for horizontal synchronization is kilohertz (kHz).

For VertRefresh, you should provide the range of vertical refresh frequencies (also listed as vertical synchronization in monitor manuals). The unit for vertical synchronization is Hertz (Hz).

For the Dell VS15X, the HorizSync and VertRefresh settings (obtained from the monitor's manual) are as follows:

```
# NOTE: THE VALUES HERE ARE EXAMPLES ONLY.  REFER TO YOUR MONITOR'S
# USER MANUAL FOR THE CORRECT NUMBERS.
HorizSync     30-64
VertRefresh   55-90
```

Following these two critical values, you see a large number of ModeLine entries. That list is a set of standard modelines; the X server picks the best standard mode from that set. You don't have to edit those lines.

Device section

The Device section specifies the video card and gives it a name (through the Identifier entry). The `xf86config` program generates a configuration file that contains a standard Device section for a VGA video card. You should check the Device section created with the input that you provided to `xf86config`. This section should contain a proper Identifier entry, such as the following:

```
Identifier    "Number Nine GXE64 with S3-Trio64"
```

The Screen section refers to this video card by the name shown in the Identifier entry. For many video cards, this section may not contain much more information because the X server (for that card) can automatically configure and use the card properly.

For some video cards, the Device section of the `XF86Config` file requires a Clocks entry that has a sequence of floating-point numbers as the value. These clocks are among the hardest things to fill in (although some video chipsets, such as S3-Trio64, do not need clocks). One way to get the clocks is to run the X server with the command `X -probeonly`. In fact, the `xf86config` program runs X this way and gets the clocks for you. All you have to do is press **y** when you see the following question:

```
Do you want me to run 'X -probeonly' now?
```

If your video card needs clocks in the Device section, this method is the easiest way to get the necessary values.

Screen section

Each Screen section specifies a Monitor and a Device to be used with a specific X server. You specify the Monitor and Device by the names shown in the respective Identifier entries. A Driver entry identifies the X server.

The `xf86config` program generates several Screen sections in the configuration file. Each Screen section is meant for a different X server, identified by the Driver entry. Table 4-2 lists the choices.

Table 4-2	Driver entries
Entry	*Purpose*
`accel`	X server for accelerated video chipsets (S3, Mach32, Mach64, P9000, 8514, AGX, and W32)
`svga`	X server for SuperVGA cards
`vga16`	X server for generic 16-color VGA
`vga2`	X server for monochrome VGA

Each Screen section also lists several Display subsections, which indicate the video modes (such as 640 × 480, for 640 pixels horizontally by 480 pixels vertically; 800 × 600; and 1,024 × 768). Each Display subsection also has a Depth entry that specifies the number of bits used for each pixel — bits per pixel or depth.

The current X server selects the Screen section whose Driver entry matches the X server's type (Super VGA or Accelerated, for example). You specify the X server during your session with the `xf86config` program.

Create an `.xinitrc` file

When you start the X Window System, you have to run the X server and then run some X client applications, which you then can use. You are supposed to start X with the command `startx`. This command starts the X server and, in turn, attempts to run a script file named `.xinitrc`, which is located in your home directory. To control what runs when you start X, you also should prepare a `.xinitrc` file in your home directory. In that file, you can specify what X applications get started.

To create a `.xinitrc` file, copy one of the example script files from your system's `/usr/X11R6/lib/X11/xinit` directory. You might use the following commands (my comments are in italics):

```
cd              (This changes the directory to your home directory)
cp /usr/X11R6/lib/X11/xinit/xinitrc.fvwm .xinitrc
```

Now you need to edit the `.xinitrc` file.

1. Type **vi .xinitrc** to start the vi editor and load .xinitrc.
2. To go to the end of the file, type **:$**. The vi editor displays the last part of the file.
3. Type **k** until you are on the line just above the one that says fvwm.
4. Type **A**. The vi editor positions the cursor at the end of the line, ready to accept text.
5. Press Enter and then type the following line:

   ```
   xterm -sb -name Linux &
   ```

   That line runs the xterm terminal emulator, with a scrollbar and the string *Linux* in the title bar.

6. Press Esc and then type **:wq** to save .xinitrc and exit vi.

Now you are ready to try X on your system.

Running X

After you have a complete XF86Config file, you are ready to start the X server and some X applications. To start X, run the startx script, which is a file that contains Linux commands. This script is in the /usr/X11/bin directory, but that directory should be in your PATH environment variable. Therefore, to run that script, type **startx**.

The startx script looks for another script file, named .xinitrc, in your home directory. If startx does not find any .xinitrc file in your home directory, it runs the default script /usr/X11R6/lib/X11/xinit/xinitrc. Notice that unlike the .xinitrc file in your home directory, the default script file does not have a period as the first character of its name.

The result of running startx depends on the commands in .xinitrc in your home directory. If you followed the instructions in the preceding section, .xinitrc should end with the following lines:

```
# start some nice programs
xsetroot -solid SteelBlue
xterm -sb -name Linux &
fvwm
```

The line with a leading pound sign (#) is a comment. The rest of the lines start separate X programs. The xsetroot program simply sets the color of the screen to a solid color named SteelBlue (the color is defined in the RGB file). The xterm command starts a terminal window — a window where you can enter further Linux commands. The ampersand at the end of that line means that xterm runs in the background. Finally, the last line starts the fvwm window manager, which lets you move windows around and resize them.

With this .xinitrc file, when you run startx, your screen should appear as shown in Figure 4-1.

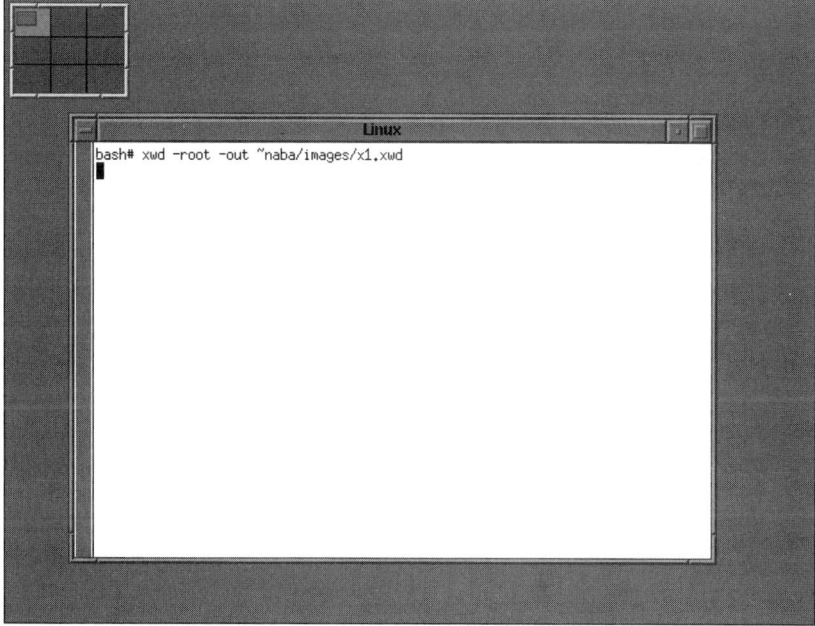

Figure 4-1: The initial X display, with the `fvwm` window manager and an `xterm` window.

Cross Reference

Now you can enter Linux commands at the prompt in the `xterm` window (the window that has *Linux* in the title bar). You learn more about customizing the X display in Chapter 5.

Tip

The X server quits when the `startx` script ends. The `startx` script, in turn, ends when its last command finishes. Always place the command that starts the window manager (such as `fvwm`) at the end of your `.xinitrc` file. That way, you can stop X and return to the text screen by quitting the window manager.

Abort with Ctrl+Alt+Backspace

Tip

If your monitor and video card are not properly specified in the `XF86Config` file, chances are that when you start X with the `startx` command, you do not see the X display shown in Figure 4-1. If you have problems such as a distorted display, or if the system appears to lock up, press Ctrl+Alt+Backspace to kill the X server and return to the text display. (In UNIX, the term *kill* refers to abnormally exiting a program. UNIX even has a `kill` command that stops errant programs.)

After you stop the X server, you can go through the `XF86Config` file again and try to figure out what may be wrong.

Try different screen modes

In your `XF86Config` file, if you look at the Screen section that applies to your X server, you notice several Display subsections. Each Display subsection lists the video modes that are supported for a specific depth — the number of bits in each pixel's value. An X server typically supports a depth of 8, which means that each pixel has an 8-bit value and that the server can display up to $2^8 = 256$ distinct colors. The Display subsection lists the video modes in terms of the display resolution, expressed in terms of the number of pixels horizontally and vertically.

The Screen section for the accelerated X server that I use for my S3-Trio64 video card, for example, shows the following Display subsection for the 8-bits-per-pixel depth:

```
# The accelerated servers (S3, Mach32, Mach8, 8514, P9000, AGX, W32,
Mach64)
Section "Screen"
    Driver      "accel"
    Device      "Number Nine GXE64 with S3-Trio64"
    Monitor     "Dell VS15X"
    Subsection "Display"
        Depth       8
        Modes       "640x480" "800x600" "1024x768"
        ViewPort    0 0
        Virtual     1024 768
    EndSubsection
    ...
EndSection
```

When the X server starts, it configures the video card at the resolution (in this case, 640 × 480, or 640 pixels horizontally by 480 pixels vertically) that corresponds to the first mode shown in the Modes entry, as follows:

```
        Modes       "640x480" "800x600" "1024x768"
```

You can try the other modes without having to exit the X server. Press Ctrl+Alt+Keypad + (*Keypad +* means the plus key in the numeric keypad). The X server switches to the next mode — in this case, 800 × 600. Press Ctrl+Alt+Keypad + again, and the X server switches to 1,024 × 768 mode. Therefore, when you press Ctrl+Alt+Keypad +, the X server cycles forward to the next mode listed in the Modes entry.

Tip

Press Ctrl+Alt+Keypad + several times, and make sure that the X server works in all video modes.

To cycle backward to the preceding mode, press Ctrl+Alt+Keypad – (*Keypad –* means the minus key in the numeric keypad). Therefore, if the X server is displaying in 800 × 600 mode and you press Ctrl+Alt+Keypad –, the server switches to 640 × 480 mode.

Tip

You can make the X server start in any of the supported modes. If you want the X server to start at the highest-resolution mode, simply change the Modes entry in the Screen section that corresponds to your X server (the Driver entry in the Screen section indicates the X server type) to the following:

```
    Modes       "1024x768" "800x600" "640x480"
```

Chapter 4: Secrets of X under Linux   **139**

Note

This change makes X start in 1,024 × 768 mode, which gives you much more screen area than 640 × 480 mode.

The screen resolutions in the Modes entry determine the following:

- The first resolution is the default resolution (the resolution in which the X server starts).

- When you alter screen resolutions, the X server scrolls through the resolutions in the order shown in the Modes entry. When you press Ctrl+Alt+Keypad+, the X server changes resolutions in the left to right order; the order is reversed when you press Ctrl+Alt+Keypad –.

Quit from window manager

To exit the X display and return to the text screen, you have to exit the last program that the .xinitrc script file started. This program should be the window manager — in this case, the fvwm window manager.

To quit the fvwm window manager, place the mouse pointer in a background area of the X display and click the left mouse button. The window manager displays a pop-up menu. Several of the menu items have arrows that point to the right; if you place the mouse pointer on one of these arrows, a cascade menu pops up.

Move the mouse pointer to the item labeled Exit fvwm, and place the pointer on top of the arrow pointing to the right. The fvwm window manager displays a submenu, as shown in Figure 4-2.

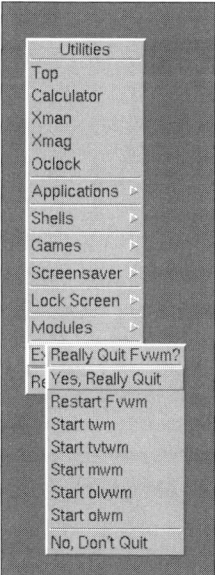

Figure 4-2: Quitting the fvwm window manager.

The submenu has an item that says Really Quit Fvwm?. Place the pointer on the item labeled Yes, Really Quit, and release the mouse button. The `fvwm` window manager quits, which in turn causes the `startx` script to end; then the X server exits. You should be back at the text screen, with a Linux command prompt.

Getting Motif for Linux

Unfortunately, Motif is not free — it is a commercial product licensed by the Open Software Foundation. Nevertheless, Motif is the most popular GUI on UNIX workstations. The Motif toolkit is widely used to develop graphical applications for UNIX workstations.

Several vendors have ported Motif to Linux and offer it as a product that you have to buy separately. Following are a few vendors that sell Motif for Linux:

- InfoMagic MOO-TIF Motif 2.0
  Typical street price: $99
  InfoMagic
  P.O. Box 30370
  Flagstaff, AZ 86003
  Phone: 520-526-9565
  Fax: 520-526-9573
  E-mail: info@infomagic.com

- SWiM Motif 2.0
  Typical street price: $149.95
  ACC Corporation
  136 Riverside Ave.
  Westport, CT 06880
  Phone: 203-454-3242
  Fax: 203-454-2582
  E-mail: info@acc-corp.com

- Metrolink Motif 2.0
  Typical street price: $199.95
  Metrolink, Inc.
  4711 North Powerline Rd.
  Fort Lauderdale, FL 33309
  Phone: 305-938-0283
  Fax: 305-938-1982
  E-mail: sales@metrolink.com

All these vendors sell the latest version of Motif (Motif 2.0). When you buy one of these packages, you get the following:

- The Motif Window Manager (`mwm`)
- The static and shared Motif libraries, which enable you to write Motif programs
- The Motif header files, for use in writing Motif programs
- Some documentation, utility programs, and sample programs

If you plan to develop applications that have the Motif look and feel, you should consider getting a copy of one of the commercial Motif packages.

Vendors typically distribute Motif for Linux on a CD-ROM. The installation steps vary from one vendor to another. In general, you have to copy some files from the CD-ROM to a temporary directory and then run an installation script that completes the installation.

Chapter 23 describes the Motif toolkit and shows you how to write Motif applications.

Summary

The X Window System, or X, is a popular window system that serves as the basis of graphical user interfaces and graphical output on most UNIX workstations. XFree86 is a free implementation of X for Intel 80x86 and compatible PCs. XFree86 works with a variety of video cards, but you have to configure it to use the appropriate parameters for your video card and monitor. This chapter shows you how to configure and run X on your Linux system. The next chapter turns to the subject of customizing and using the graphical user interface that X and the window manager provide.

By reading this chapter, you learn

- The X Window System is a network-transparent windowing system based on the client/server model. The X server, running on a workstation with a bitmapped graphics display, manages regions of the screen known as windows, where the output from X client applications appears. The X clients often run at remote systems, but their output appears on the local X display.

- The term graphical user interface (GUI) describes a user interface that makes use of windows, menus, and other graphical objects so that users can interact with the application by pointing and clicking mouse buttons. From an application developer's point of view, a GUI is a combination of a window manager, a style guide, and a library of routines (toolkit) that can be used to build the user interface.

- X provides the basic functions that can be used to build a GUI. Many GUIs are built upon X. Motif and OPEN LOOK are examples of such GUIs.

- XFree86 is the X Window System for Linux PCs and it comes with this book. When you install Linux from the CD-ROM, you also install XFree86.

- XFree86 3.1.2 supports a wide variety of video cards, including the commonly found Diamond brand video cards.

- Before you start X on your Linux PC, you have to configure XFree86 to work with your PC's video card, monitor, mouse, and keyboard.

- To configure XFree86, run the `xf86config` program. That program asks you for some information about your PC's video card, monitor, and mouse.

- You should specify the correct information about your monitor because incorrect information may cause damage to the monitor.

- The `xf86config` program creates the configuration file `/etc/XF86Config`. You must have this file ready before you start X.

- To start X, all you have to do is type `startx`. To automatically start an initial set of X applications, you should include commands to start these applications in a file named `.xinitrc` in your home directory.

- You can switch between different modes (screen resolutions such as $1,024 \times 768$ and 800×600) by pressing special key combinations: Ctrl+Alt+Keypad+ and Ctrl+Alt+Keypad–.

Chapter 5

Customizing Your Linux Startup

In This Chapter

- Following the steps in Linux startup
- Getting a graphical login prompt with `xdm`
- Starting a selected set of applications at startup
- Customizing the `fvwm` window manager
- Customizing and using the `xterm` terminal emulator

By now, you have installed Linux and X, and have had your first taste of Linux. You probably still log in at a text screen, however, and then start the X Window System manually. If you have any experience with the current generation of UNIX workstations or Microsoft Windows, you must be familiar with the convenience of a graphical interface. You also can set up Linux so that you work completely in the graphical environment provided by the X Window System.

This chapter explains how you can make your login prompt appear in a graphical window. You also learn some tricks for customizing the look and feel of `fvwm` — a popular window manager in Linux.

The Slackware Linux distribution includes a file manager that allows you to browse your system's files and directories and to start programs. You still need to use UNIX commands, however, to perform many tasks. While running X, you have to use the `xterm` terminal emulator to display a window in which you can enter UNIX commands. This chapter also describes the main features of the `xterm` terminal emulator and how to customize it.

Cross Reference

If you have not installed Linux and X yet, turn to Chapter 1 to install Linux and Chapter 4 to install X. Then return to this chapter to try the techniques shown in this chapter.

Starting X Automatically at Login

Right now, you have to log in at a text prompt and then type **startx** to start the X Window System. If you always log in and immediately switch to the graphical screen with the `startx` command, you can automate this task easily by adding the `startx` command to a special file that the Linux command processor — shell — executes automatically when you log in.

The default command processor in Linux is called *Bash,* which stands for *Bourne again shell.* When Bash starts, it reads and executes the commands in a file named /etc/profile. After processing the /etc/profile file, Bash processes one more file in your home directory, using the following logic:

1. If a file named .bash_profile exists in your home directory, Bash processes it.
2. If Bash does not find the .bash_profile file, it looks for and then processes the file named .bash_login, provided that the file exists.
3. If your home directory does not have .bash_profile or .bash_login, Bash looks for and processes the file named .profile.

Thus, to ensure that X starts automatically, you can create a file named .bash_profile in your home directory and place the startx command in it. There is, however, one problem with this solution. If your Linux system is on a network, you can log into your system over the network. When you log in over the network, however, you would not want to start X, because you won't be sitting in front of your monitor. That's because X will run at your monitor's location, even though you're not there.

Cross Reference

When you log into your Linux PC from the PC's keyboard (as opposed to logging in over the network), the commands in /etc/profile initialize an environment variable named TERM to the string console. To ensure that Bash executes the startx command only when you log in at the console (the term refers collectively to the PC's monitor and keyboard), you can put in the appropriate commands to have Bash run startx only when the TERM variable is set to console. You learn more about Bash commands in Chapter 6, but the following shows what you need in .bash_profile to start X when you log in at the console:

```
if [ "$TERM" = "console" ]; then
   startx
fi
```

A more interesting setup is when you stay entirely in a graphical environment. Even the login prompt is a dialog box. The next section explains how you can set up your Linux system to provide a graphical login screen.

Environment variable

An environment variable is simply a way to associate a name with a string. The shell has a standard set of environment variables. The environment variable named HOME, for example, is set to your home directory. How you define an environment variable depends on the shell that you use. In Bash (the default shell in Linux), you set an environment variable by using the following syntax:

NAME=Value; export NAME

NAME is the name of the environment variable, and Value is a string that denotes the value associated with NAME.

> **Processes**
>
> In UNIX, the term *process* refers to a program executing in memory and its associated environment. The environment includes the input and output files that belong to the program and a collection of environment variables. Essentially, you create a process whenever you type a command at the shell prompt. Of course, the shell (the command interpreter of the operating system) itself is just another process — one that creates new processes at your command.

Setting up a Graphical Login

To log in on many UNIX workstations (such as those from Hewlett-Packard or IBM), you have to type the name and password in a login dialog window. Setting up your Linux workstation so that it displays a graphical login screen is easy. In fact, the Linux CD-ROM comes with the X Display Manager (xdm) program, which is designed to handle user logins through a graphical interface.

X Display Manager (xdm)

The xdm program is similar to the processes getty and login, which are commonly used in UNIX systems (including Linux) to let a user log into the system.

When xdm runs, it reads various configuration parameters from a file named xdm-config, which usually is in the directory /usr/lib/X11/xdm. One of the parameters in this file is the name of another file, which specifies the displays on which xdm displays the login dialog window. This list usually is in the file /usr/lib/X11/xdm/Xservers.

The name of a display also indicates whether it is local or remote. Suppose that you want to use xdm to access your workstation from the local display. In this case, Xservers should contain the following line:

```
:0 local /usr/bin/X11/X
```

You specify the local display by the local keyword that follows the display number. In this case, you have to provide the complete pathname of the X server program.

For the default configuration (after you install Linux and X from the companion CD-ROM), xdm manages the login session as follows:

1. xdm starts the X server and executes the Xsetup_0 script from /usr/lib/X11/xdm. The default Xsetup_0 script runs the xconsole program, which opens a window in which all console messages appear.

2. xdm displays a dialog window that contains fields in which the user can enter a name and a password.

3. After a user enters a name and password and presses Enter, xdm verifies the password and executes the startup script /usr/lib/X11/xdm/GiveConsole.

4. xdm runs the Xsession script from the /usr/lib/X11/xdm directory. That script typically looks for another script file, named .xsession, in the user's home directory. This file is similar to the .xinitrc file that xinit uses after it starts the X server. The .xsession file should list the commands for starting selected X applications. Typically, this list includes the xterm terminal emulator. If no .xsession file exists, the Xsession script usually runs the script /usr/lib/X11/xinit/xinitrc.

5. From this point on, the user can interact with the system through the X display and through the window manager (started by the .xsession file or the systemwide script /usr/lib/X11/xinit/xinitrc).

6. When the user exits X (by quitting the window manager), xdm runs the /usr/lib/X11/xdm/TakeConsole script. At the end of this script, xdm returns to the login dialog window display and waits for another user to log on.

Although this brief description of xdm does not show you all the details, xdm provides a user-friendly interface for user login. Also, like many other X utility programs, xdm is highly configurable. For example, the names of the script files in the preceding list are the typical ones, but you can specify other names through the file named xdm-config, which, by default, also resides in the /usr/lib/X11/xdm directory.

When you install Linux and X from the companion CD-ROM, xdm is already configured to display a login dialog on your PC's monitor. If you want to experiment with xdm, you can log in as root and type **xdm** at the shell prompt. This command starts xdm, which in turn displays the login dialog window. At this point, you or any other user can log in by typing the user name and password in the dialog window. But you still do not have an arrangement in which xdm runs automatically as soon as Linux boots. You can create such an arrangement easily enough, but first, you need to understand a little bit about the way Linux runs programs after it boots.

The init process

Cross Reference

As you know from the installation steps in Chapter 1, when Linux boots, it loads and runs the core operating-system program from the disk. The core operating system, however, is designed to run other programs. A process named init is responsible for starting the initial set of processes on your Linux system.

What the init process starts depends on the following:

- The *run level,* which designates a system configuration in which only a selected group of processes exists

- The /etc/inittab file, a text file that specifies the processes to start at different run levels

Secret

The current run level, together with the contents of the /etc/inittab file, controls which processes init starts. Linux, for example, has eight run levels: S, 0, 1, 2, 3, 4, 5, and 6. By convention, some of these levels mean that specific processes run at that level. Run level S, for example, denotes a single-user, stand-alone system. The run level is set to 0 when the system is about to shut down. Run levels 1 through 6 are multiuser modes that have various levels of capabilities.

The initial default run level is 5. As the following section explains, you can change the default run level by editing a line in the /etc/inittab file.

The /etc/inittab file

The /etc/inittab file is the key to understanding the processes that init starts at various run levels. You can look at the contents of the file (you do not have to log in as root to do this) by using this command:

```
more /etc/inittab
```

Following are a few selected lines from the default /etc/inittab file:

```
# Lines starting with '#' are comments.

# Default run level.
id:5:initdefault:

# System initialization (runs when system boots).
si:S:sysinit:/etc/rc.d/rc.S

# Script to run when going single user.
su:S:wait:/etc/rc.d/rc.K

# Script to run when going multi user.
rc:123456:wait:/etc/rc.d/rc.M

# These lines start the processes that wait for users to log in

c1:12345:respawn:/sbin/agetty 38400 tty1
c2:12345:respawn:/sbin/agetty 38400 tty2
c3:45:respawn:/sbin/agetty 38400 tty3
c4:45:respawn:/sbin/agetty 38400 tty4
c5:45:respawn:/sbin/agetty 38400 tty5
c6:456:respawn:/sbin/agetty 38400 tty6

# Run level 4 starts xdm (see the script file /etc/rc.d/rc.4 for
details)

x1:4:wait:/etc/rc.d/rc.4
```

Lines that start with a pound sign (#) are comments. The first noncomment line in the /etc/inittab file specifies the default run level as follows:

```
id:5:initdefault:
```

Even though you do not know the syntax of the /etc/inittab file (and you really do not have to learn the syntax), you probably can guess that the 5 in that line denotes the default run level. Thus, if you want your system to be at run level 4 after startup, all you have to do is change 5 to 4.

Tip

Type **man inittab** to see the detailed syntax of the entries in the inittab file. The rest of this section briefly describes the inittab file format.

Each entry in the /etc/inittab file specifies a process that init should start one or more specified run levels — you simply list all the run levels at which the process should run. Each entry in the inittab file has four fields, separated by colons, in the following format:

id:runlevels:action:process

The fields have the following meanings:

- The *id* field is a unique two-character identifier. The init process uses this field internally.

- The *runlevels* field is a sequence of zero or more characters, each denoting a run level. The rc entry, for example, applies to run levels 1 through 6, so the *runlevels* field for this entry is 123456.

- The *action* field tells the init process what to do with that entry. If this field is initdefault, for example, init interprets the runlevels field as the default run level. If this field is set to wait, init starts the process specified in the *process* field and waits until that process exits.

- The *process* field specifies the process that init has to start. Of course, some settings of the *action* field require no process field. (When *action* is initdefault, for example, no need exists for a *process* field.)

The process often is specified in terms of a shell script, which in turn can start several processes. The rc entry, for example, is specified as follows:

rc:123456:wait:/etc/rc.d/rc.M

Cross Reference

This entry specifies that init should execute the file /etc/rc.d/rc.M after it processes this entry. If you look at the file /etc/.rc.d/rc.M, you notice that it is a script file. After you learn more about writing shell scripts in Chapter 6, you can study the file /etc/rc.d/rc.M to see what processes start in run levels 1 through 5.

Getting back to the subject of starting xdm for a graphical login, you cannot see any explicit reference to xdm in the /etc/inittab file except for the comment above the x1 entry, which is defined as follows:

x1:4:wait:/etc/rc.d/rc.4

As the 4 indicates, this entry takes effect only when the run level is 4 and it runs the file /etc/rc.d/rc.4. A look at the /etc/rc.d/rc.4 file reveals that it has only one command, as follows:

exec /usr/X11R6/bin/xdm -nodaemon

This command uses the shell's built-in `exec` command to start `xdm`. (No separate program named `exec` exists; `exec` is just a command that the shell understands.) Because of a symbolic link, `/usr/X11/bin/xdm` and `/usr/X11R6/bin/xdm` refer to the same program.

To start `xdm` automatically after Linux boots, all you have to do is edit the `/etc/inittab` file and change 5 in the following line to 4 (thereby changing the default run level to 4):

```
id:5:initdefault:
```

Caution

Before you edit the `/etc/inittab` file, you should know that any errors in this file may prevent Linux from starting up to a point at which you can log in. If you cannot log in, you cannot use your system. As the following section explains, you should try run level 4 with an `init 4` command before you actually change the default run level in the `/etc/inittab` file.

The `init` command

To try a new run level, you do not necessarily have to change the default run level in the `/etc/inittab` file. If you log in as `root`, you can change the run level (and, consequently, the set of processes that run in Linux) with the `init` command, which has the following format:

```
init runlevel
```

Here, `runlevel` must be a single character that denotes the run level that you want. To put the system in single-user mode, for example, you would type the following:

```
init s
```

Thus, if you want to try run level 4 (and see whether `xdm` works) without changing the `/etc/inittab` file, enter the following command at the shell prompt:

```
init 4
```

The system should end all current processes and enter run level 4. By default, the `init` command waits 20 seconds before stopping all current processes and starting the new processes for run level 4.

Wizard

To switch to run level 4 immediately, type the command **init -t0 4**. (The number after the `-t` option indicates the number of seconds that `init` waits before changing the run level.)

The `init` process switches to run level 6 and starts `xdm`. The `xdm` program in turn starts X and displays a graphical login dialog, as shown in Figure 5-1.

The text-entry cursor (it looks like a vertical bar) appears in the `login:` field. Type your login name and press Enter. The text cursor moves to the `Password:` field. Type your password and press Enter to complete the login process.

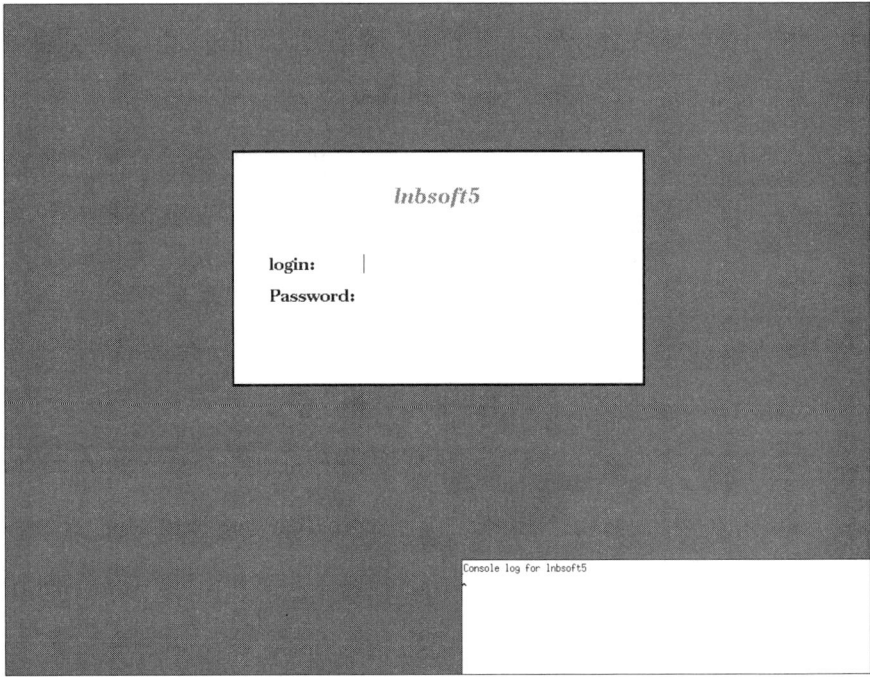

Figure 5-1: The xdm program displays a graphical login dialog.

The .xsession file

When you log in through the graphical login dialog, the xdm program runs the /usr/lib/X11/xdm/Xsession script, which in turn looks for and executes the .xsession script in your home directory. If you want to run some X applications automatically, all you have to do is create a .xsession file in your home directory and add to it commands that start the X applications that you want.

Cross Reference

In Chapter 4 you created a .xinitrc file in your home directory for a similar purpose: to run some X applications automatically when you start X with the startx command. In fact, a good way to create a .xsession file is to simply copy the .xinitrc file to .xsession with the cp command, as follows:

```
cd     (this ensures that you are in your home directory)
cp .xinitrc .xsession
```

The next time you log in, xdm executes your .xsession file, and any applications listed in the .xsession file start automatically.

You will find looking at the initial .xsession file to be helpful, because the contents of that file point to other ways of customizing your startup screen. Following is the initial .xsession file:

```
#!/bin/sh
# $XConsortium: xinitrc.cpp,v 1.4 91/08/22 11:41:34 rws Exp $

userresources=$HOME/.Xresources
usermodmap=$HOME/.Xmodmap
sysresources=/usr/X11R6/lib/X11/xinit/.Xresources
sysmodmap=/usr/X11R6/lib/X11/xinit/.Xmodmap

# merge in defaults and keymaps

if [ -f $sysresources ]; then
  xrdb -merge $sysresources
fi

if [ -f $sysmodmap ]; then
  xmodmap $sysmodmap
fi

if [ -f $userresources ]; then
  xrdb -merge $userresources
fi

if [ -f $usermodmap ]; then
  xmodmap $usermodmap
fi

# start some nice programs
xsetroot -solid SteelBlue
xterm -sb -sl 600 -name Linux -fn "10x20" -geometry +100+100 &
fvwm
```

This .xsession file is derived from the /etc/xinitrc file, with an extra line near the end that starts the xterm program in addition to the fvwm window manager.

You should notice the following items in the .xsession file:

- .xsession runs the xmodmap program with the .Xmodmap configuration file from /usr/X11R6/lib/X11/xinit or from your home directory. The xmodmap program maps a physical key on the keyboard, identified by a *keycode* (a number) to a virtual key (called a *keysym*) in X. To specify that the Backspace key (with a keycode of 22) maps to the Delete keysym, for example, you would create a .Xmodmap file in your home directory, with the file containing the following line:

    ```
    keycode 22 = Delete
    ```

- .xsession runs the xrdb program to load the X resources from the .Xresources file in /usr/X11R6/lib/X11/xinit or from your home directory. (You learn more about X resources in the section of the same name later in this chapter.)

- After setting the keymaps and loading the X resources, the .xsession script starts one or more X applications (at minimum, the xterm program) and ends the list with a window manager (in this case, fvwm).

- The ampersand (&) at the end of the xterm command line ensures that xterm is started as a background process and the .xsession script proceeds to the next line to start the fvwm window manager as well. (In UNIX, you can put an ampersand after any command to run that command as a background process.)

If you work in a language other than English, you may want to map keycodes to keymaps to accommodate the alphabet of your language. To specify the mapping between a keycode and a keysym (a keysym is a symbolic name for a key), you need to know the keycodes and the available keysyms. The file /usr/include/X11/keysymdef.h lists all available keysyms; each keysym name has an XK_ prefix that you must leave off when you refer to the keysym in a .Xmodmap file.

To see the keycode that corresponds to a key on the keyboard, type **xev** in an xterm window to run the xev utility program. Then press a key. The xev program displays information about that key, including its keycode.

The initial set of applications

By starting a number of applications from the .xsession file, you control the initial windows on your system's X screen. The sample .xsession file uses the following commands:

```
xsetroot -solid SteelBlue
xterm -sb -sl 600 -name Linux -fn "10x20" -geometry +100+100 &
fvwm
```

The first line runs the xsetroot program to set the screen's background color to a solid color named SteelBlue (the color is defined in the RGB color database file /usr/lib/X11/rgb.txt). The entire display screen is known as the *root window* in X — hence, the program that sets the root window's color is named xsetroot.

The second line starts the xterm terminal emulator program with the caption Linux in the title bar of the window. Essentially, xterm gives you a window that acts like a terminal connected to your system. A shell program monitors what you type in that window. Thus, you can interact with your Linux system through shell commands that you type in the xterm window. Everything that follows xterm in the following line constitutes command-line options that the xterm program accepts:

```
xterm -sb -sl 600 -name Linux -fn "10x20" -geometry +100+100 &
```

Because the xterm program is used often, this chapter covers the xterm command-line options in the "Using and Customizing xterm" section.

The last line in the .xsession program starts the fvwm window manager. Because the window manager adds a frame to each application's window, much of the screen's look and feel comes from the window manager. Later in this chapter, the "Customizing the fvwm Window Manager" section describes how to customize the fvwm window manager.

Chapter 5: Customizing Your Linux Startup   **153**

What is missing from this set of applications is a quick and easy way for new users to browse through files and directories and to start programs. You could use the xfm program, included on the companion CD-ROM, to fulfill this need. The xfm program is a file manager that displays the files and directories in a graphical format.

To set up xfm to run at startup, you should do the following:

1. At the shell prompt, type **xfm.install**. This command executes the xfm.install script from /usr/bin/X11. The script creates a .xfm directory in your home directory. In the .xfm directory, the script sets up some configuration files that the xfm program uses.

2. Edit the .xsession file, and add the following line before the line that starts the fvwm window manager:

   xfm &

The next time you log in after you make these changes, your X screen should have an appearance similar to Figure 5-2.

The xfm program displays two windows. The File Manager window shows the contents of the home directory, and the Applications window shows icons that represent commonly used applications. (The exact contents of your home directory, of course, will not match what appears in Figure 5-2.)

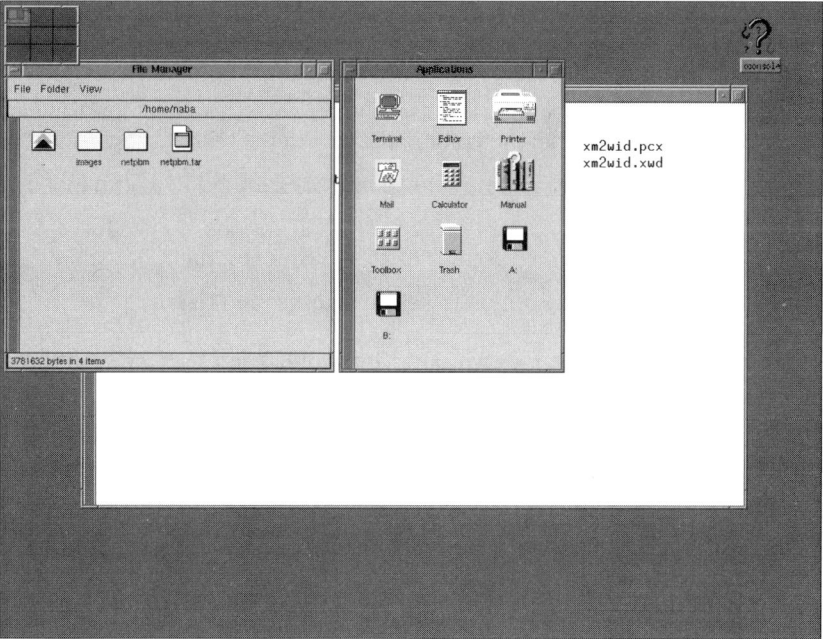

Figure 5-2: The initial X screen with an xterm window and the xfm file manager.

Cross Reference

The icons that appear in the Applications window depend on the xfm configuration files in the .xfm subdirectory of your login directory. Consult Chapter 25 for more information on the xfm configuration files and how to use xfm.

In Figure 5-2, the small window in the upper-left corner (the one with nine rectangles) belongs to the fvwm window manager. Through that window, fvwm offers nine separate work areas. You learn more about the features of the fvwm window manager later in the "Overview of fvwm" section of this chapter.

Customizing X

You can customize almost every part of the X display, ranging from the screen's background color to the default font for all applications. The basic philosophy of X (and of UNIX as well) is that the user should have the freedom to configure the software to suit his or her taste. Thus, X applications load various settings from a resource file. Each X application also accepts a set of standard command-line options. This section shows you the general techniques for customizing X applications. The section also provides specific information about the xterm terminal emulator and the fvwm window manager.

Root-window appearance

In X, the entire display screen is called the root window. A utility program named xsetroot allows you to tailor the appearance of the root window. With xsetroot, you can customize the screen as follows:

- Use the -solid option to set the screen to a solid color. You can specify the color by name; the color names are in the text file /usr/lib/X11/rgb.txt.
- Use the -bitmap option to set the background to a bitmapped graphic file.
- Use the -cursor or the -cursor_name options to specify a cursor shape when the mouse pointer rests anywhere on the root window.
- Use the -gray option to set the background to gray.

To customize the root window, you should run xsetroot from the command prompt and experiment with various options until you find an appearance that you like. Then you should put the appropriate xsetroot commands in your .xsession script.

If you have experience with the Macintosh or Windows 95 graphical environments, you realize that the tasks performed by the xsetroot command are similar to customizing your desktop from the Control Panel. Of course, in Macintosh and Windows 95, you use a GUI to customize the desktop. In X, you have to settle for a command-line program (xsetroot).

Screen color

In the current `.xsession` file, you have seen an example of how to set the screen's background color with the `xsetroot` program. To set the background to a solid `SteelBlue` color, for example, type the following command at a shell prompt in an `xterm` window:

```
xsetroot -solid SteelBlue
```

To try more colors, you have to know the names of the colors. The color definitions are in a text file named `/usr/lib/X11/rgb.txt`. To see a list of the color names, open that file with an editor or type the following command in an `xterm` window:

```
more /usr/lib/X11/rgb.txt
```

Following are some of the lines from the `rgb.txt` file:

```
255 255 255 white
  0   0   0 black
190 190 190 gray
 65 105 225 RoyalBlue
 70 130 180 SteelBlue
218 165  32 goldenrod
184 134  11 DarkGoldenrod
233 150 122 DarkSalmon
255 160 122 LightSalmon
```

As you might guess, the three numbers happen to be the intensity levels of the red (R), green (G), and blue (B) components of the color. The intensity levels range between 0 and 255.

Wizard

In addition to using the descriptive name for a color, you can specify a color as a hexadecimal number of six hexadecimal digits, which works out to two digits for each of the three components of a color: red (R), green (G), and blue (B). The digits in a six-digit hexadecimal RGB value of a color are interpreted from left to right, with the most significant pair of digits being assumed to be for R, the middle pair for G, and the least significant pair for B. The character # precedes the hexadecimal digits to signify a color specification in hexadecimal format. When you specify a color this way, you have to put the hexadecimal color value within quotation marks. You can use the hexadecimal format to specify any color that you want.

Table 5-1 lists some common colors expressed in hexadecimal format:

Table 5-1	Hexadecimal representations of common colors
Color	**Hexadecimal value**
black	#000000
red	#ff0000

(continued)

Table 5-1	*(continued)*
Color	Hexadecimal value
green	#00ff00
blue	#0000ff
yellow	#ffff00
cyan	#00ffff
magenta	#ff00ff
white	#ffffff

Now that you know how to specify any arbitrary color in hexadecimal RGB format, you can experiment with new colors. You can try a strange color for the screen background, for example, by using the following command:

```
xsetroot -solid "#ccb0b0"
```

If you want a simple gray background (which can be quite pleasing to the eye, if a bit unadventurous), you can get it by using this command:

```
xsetroot -gray
```

Screen-background image

You do not have to settle for a solid color as the screen background. You can use xsetroot with the -bitmap option to tile a monochrome bitmap image over the screen background. (Tiling means that copies of the bitmap are laid out one next to the other until the whole screen is covered — this is similar to the way you would cover a floor with physical tiles.) You can use the -fg and the -bg options to draw the image in the foreground color and fill the background with a selected background color.

Try the following command to set the screen background to an interesting pattern of the X logo:

```
xsetroot -bitmap /usr/include/X11/bitmaps/xlogo64 -fg "#cccccc" -bg "#c0c0c0"
```

The /usr/include/X11/bitmaps directory contains many more bitmap files that you can try as background images.

Although xsetroot cannot display a color image as the screen background, you can use the xv program to display an image file of your choice as the background. The xv program can handle quite a few image formats, including the popular formats GIF, PCX, BMP, JPEG, and TIFF. Suppose that you have a favorite image file called sunset.gif, which shows a beautiful sunset, and that you want to use this image as the backdrop on your X display. To accomplish this task, include the following command in your .xsession file:

```
xv -quit -quit -root -max @td/sunset.gif
```

Hexadecimal numbers

Even though you may not be familiar with the terminology, you're familiar with one number system from your everyday experience — the decimal number system. We express decimal numbers using the digits 0 through 9, and when writing values, we use the concepts of ones, tens, hundreds, and thousands. For example, consider the number 3,495. Using the concept of ones, tens, hundreds, and thousands, we can write this as:

3,495 = 3 Thousands + 4 Hundreds + 9 Tens + 5 Ones

or

$3,495 = 3 \times 10^3 + 4 \times 10^2 + 9 \times 10^1 + 5 \times 10^0$

The last form represents the number in powers of 10, which is the base or *radix* of the decimal number system.

The hexadecimal number system is similar to the decimal number system, except that the base is 16. To write a number in hexadecimal, you need 16 digits representing the values from 0 through 15 just as the decimal system uses the 10 digits 0 through 9. Here are the 16 hexadecimal digits:

Hexadecimal Digit	Decimal Value of Digit
0	0
1	1
2	2
3	3
4	4
5	5
6	6
7	7
8	8
9	9
a	10
b	11
c	12
d	13
e	14
f	15

As you can see, the letters a through f are used to represent the values 10 through 15, respectively. You can use either lower- or uppercase letters for the hexadecimal digits.

Knowing the similarity between the decimal and hexadecimal number systems, you can easily find the decimal equivalent of a hexadecimal number. For example, 1b in hexadecimal is $1 \times 16^1 + 11 \times 16^0 = 16 + 11 = 27$ in decimal.

This command assumes that the image file `sunset.gif` is in your home directory. (The `@td/` prefix in the filename indicates this fact.)

Tip

Avoid using colorful images as screen background; other X programs will run out of colors if you display a too-colorful image as the background. Remember that the typical 8-bit video card can display at most 256 colors. If the background image has anything more than 16 colors, you'll probably run into problems as you run other programs. In particular, programs like the Netscape Navigator Web browser also need colors to display all those images on most Web pages.

In addition to causing X to run out of colors, a color image background also uses up resources of the X server and may affect the system performance. Therefore, the safe solution is to use a solid color background for the screen background.

Cursor shape and color

With the `xsetroot` program, you can set the shape and color of the cursor when the pointer is resting anywhere on the root window. Inside an application's windows, the application controls the cursor shape and color.

Although you can use two bitmap files to define an arbitrarily shaped cursor, a simpler method is to select one of the predefined cursor shapes. You can use the `-cursor_name` option of the `xsetroot` program to specify a cursor. The cursor names are defined in the file `/usr/include/X11/cursorfont.h`. The names are meant for use in X programs, and each cursor name has an `XC_` prefix. You have to leave out the `XC_` prefix when you use the cursor name with the `xsetroot` program.

Following are a few cursor names:

`X_cursor`	A cursor shaped like an X (the default cursor)
`arrow`	An arrow pointing to the upper-right corner
`left_ptr`	An arrow pointing to the upper-left corner

The default cursor is a black `X_cursor`. To change the cursor to a white left arrow, type the following command:

```
xsetroot -cursor_name left_ptr -fg white -bg black
```

In the Macintosh and Windows 95 graphical environments, the cursor is a left-pointing arrow. If you are familiar with those environments, you might want to change the cursor to the left arrow.

X resources

Most X applications are highly configurable. You can alter the appearance and, to some extent, even the behavior of an X application. You can accomplish this task in two ways:

- Alter the application's default behavior through options you specify in the command line that starts the application.

- Specify values for options in a text file called a *resource file*. (X programmers use the term *resource* to refer to any user-configurable option in an application.)

For small UNIX utilities, a handful of command-line options may be enough to specify all user-configurable parameters of the program. X applications tend, however, to have a large number of variables that the user can set. An X application may have several windows, each of which may have a border, a background color, and a foreground color. Although an X application provides default values for these parameters, the user can override most of these values. In addition, the user can change the font for any text that is to be displayed in windows. X applications simply have too many variables for the user to set through command-line options alone. The creators of X recognized this problem and included the concept of a database of resources.

In an X application, the term *resource* refers to any parameter that affects the application's behavior or appearance. Accordingly, foreground and background colors, fonts, and size and placement of windows are typical resources. A resource does not have to be a parameter related to X; it can be anything that controls the behavior of an application and that can be specified by the user. An application might have a parameter named verbose, which, when set, enables printing of detailed information as it runs. In addition to the application's window size and location, verbose qualifies as being a resource of this application.

Resource file

You have to specify the resources for an X application in a text file known as a *resource file* or a *resource database*. The X resource database is a simple text file in which you can specify the value of various parameters in a well-defined format.

X resource files are not as complicated and sophisticated as a traditional database. The X resource database contains specifications of the form "all foreground colors are white," "xterm's background is light cyan," and so on.

X applications use a set of utility routines, collectively known as the *X resource manager,* to extract the value of precisely identified individual parameters from this rather imprecise database. Consider the query "what is the foreground color of the xterm application?" If you specified the foreground color of xterm in the resource file, the resource manager returns this value. If, however, the only specification for foreground color in the database is the general statement "all foreground colors are black," the value returned for xterm's foreground color is black.

Resource-naming convention

To specify an X application's resource values, such as foreground color, you have to know how to name a resource and how to specify the value for a resource.

The name of a resource depends on the name of the application and the names of its components, which usually are the major child windows. For applications that were built with the X toolkit (essentially, a library of user interface components), the components would be the names of widgets used to build the application.

Note

A *widget* is nothing more than a user interface component such as a push button, a list box, or a dialog box. An X toolkit such as the Motif toolkit provides the functions that programmers can use to create and use widgets in their programs.

The names of the application and its components can be of two types: *class name* and *instance name*. The class name indicates the general category of the application or component, whereas each individual copy has its own instance name.

The definition becomes clear if you consider a concrete example: the `xterm` application. This application is of the class `XTerm`, and the instance goes by the name `xterm`. The `xterm` application uses a component named `vt100` of class `VT100` (the `VT100` component emulates a VT102, but the internal name is VT100), which contains a component named `scrollbar` of the class `Scrollbar`. Now consider the following resources: the foreground color of the VT100 window and the visibility of the scrollbar in that window. In `xterm`, as in most X applications, the foreground color resource has the class name `Foreground` and the instance name `foreground`. The scrollbar's visibility is controlled by a Boolean variable named `on`.

Most X applications follow this convention of naming the class of a resource by capitalizing the first letter of its instance name. Names of applications follow this convention, which promotes some consistency among applications. The naming of the application, its components, and the resources, however, is entirely under the control of the application. (Toolkit-based applications, however, are somewhat constrained by the built-in names of predefined widgets.)

Now you can give these resources unique names in `xterm` and specify values for them. You can assign values for the foreground color of the VT100 window and the `on` variable of its scrollbar in the following manner:

```
xterm.vt100.foreground:      yellow
xterm.vt100.scrollbar.on:    true
```

This example illustrates the syntax of naming resources and giving their values. The name of a resource starts with the name of the application, followed by names of the components, each of which is separated from the next by a period (.). The resource name comes last, and the value of the resource follows a colon (:). You specify the value as a text string; it is up to the application to interpret that string. The resource manager has utility routines that can help the programmer with this task.

The names illustrated so far in this section are full instance names, showing the application and all its components. You also can have full class names, which for `xterm.vt100.foreground` is `XTerm.VT100.Foreground`. You obtain this name by replacing the instance name of each component with the corresponding class name.

Partial names for resources

The preceding section explains how to specify a resource by its full name, but the resource specification can be imprecise. You might indicate, for example, that all components of class VT100 should have a yellow foreground. You can accomplish this task by making the following entry in the resource database:

```
*VT100.Foreground:   yellow
```

Because there is no application name, this specification of the foreground color applies to the VT100 component used in any application. Similarly, to specify that the background color of every component of the `xterm` application be Navy, you would include the following line in the resource file:

```
xterm*background:Navy
```

To understand the resource-naming scheme, you have to know something about the inner workings of the X resource manager. By now, you probably have guessed that the X resource manager locates a resource's value by matching a precisely specified resource name with the imprecise entries in the resource database. The search algorithm used by the resource manager follows certain rules for matching a full resource name with the partial names in the resource database. Knowing the following rules can help you understand what kind of specification for a resource is precise enough to suit your needs:

- An asterisk (*) matches zero or more components of the name. Therefore, the query for `xterm.vt100.foreground` matches this entry:

  ```
  xterm*foreground:  yellow
  ```

- After the asterisk is accounted for, the application name, the component names, and the resource name (class or instance) must match the items present in the entry. Therefore, a query for `XTerm.VT100.Scrollbar.Background` matches this entry:

  ```
  xterm.vt100.scrollbar.background: Navy
  ```

  but not

  ```
  xterm.vt100.scrollbar.on: true
  ```

- More-specific resource specifications take precedence over less-specific settings. Entries with a period (.) take precedence over ones that have an asterisk (*). If you specify the following, everything in `xterm` has a Navy background, but the scrollbar has a white background:

  ```
  xterm*background: Navy
  xterm.vt100.scrollbar.background: white
  ```

- Instance names take precedence over class names. Thus, the specific entry `xterm*background` will override the one that uses class names: `XTerm*Background`.

- An entry with a class name or an instance name takes precedence over one that uses neither. In `xterm`, the value given in the entry `XTerm*Foreground` overrides that under the more general entry `*Foreground`.

- Names are matched from left to right, because the hierarchy of components of the name of a resource goes from left to right. In other words, when looking for the resource named `xterm.vt100.scrollbar.background`, the resource manager matches the entry

  ```
  xterm.vt100*background: white
  ```

  instead of

  ```
  xterm*scrollbar.background: Navy
  ```

  because `vt100` appears to the left of `scrollbar`.

Location of resource file

Most X applications load resource settings from several sources in a specific order. The applications look for a file named `/usr/lib/X11/app-defaults/AppClass`, in which `AppClass` is the class name of the application. Thus, `xterm` looks for its resources in `/usr/lib/X11/app-defaults/XTerm`.

Next, the application looks for a string named `RESOURCE_MANAGER`, which is attached to (associated with) the root window of the display in which the application's window appears. In X, a string associated with the root window is known as a *property* of the root window.

Tip

You can use the utility program `xprop` to see whether this property exists on your display's root window. Simply type **xprop -root**, and look for an entry labeled `RESOURCE_MANAGER(STRING)` in the output. The `xprop` utility also can read a resource file and load the contents into this property (as a long string).

If the `RESOURCE_MANAGER` property does not exist, the application reads the resource specifications from the `.Xdefaults` file in your home directory. Next, the application loads the resources (if any) specified by the file indicated by the environment variable `XENVIRONMENT`. If this variable is not set, the next source for resources is a file named `.Xdefaults-hostname` in your home directory. In this file, *hostname* is the name of the system on which the application is running.

You can, of course, override any of the resource specifications through command-line options.

If you want to see the effect of resources, following is an example of how you might do it. In your current `xterm` window, use an editor to create the file `xttest`, containing the following lines:

```
xterm.vt100.scrollBar:      true
*VT100.Foreground:          yellow
xterm.vt100.background:           Navy
xterm.vt100.scrollbar.background: white
```

Now type the following command, run the `xrdb` utility program, and load these settings into the `RESOURCE_MANAGER` property of the root window:

```
xrdb -load xttest
```

Type **xprop -root** to verify that the resources are loaded. Notice that the contents of the resource file are stored internally in the property `RESOURCE_MANAGER` as a very long string. Now start another `xterm` session with the command **xterm &**. You should see a new `xterm` window that has yellow characters on a Navy background except for the scrollbar, which has a white background.

Common X resources

By convention, all X applications have a standard set of resources. These resources include parameters such as foreground and background colors, window size and location (collectively known as *geometry*), and font. Table 5-2 lists some of the common X resources.

Table 5-2 Standard X resources

Instance Name	Class Name	Command-Line Option	Specifies
background	Background	-bg -background	Background color
borderColor	BorderColor	-bd -border	Border color
borderWidth	BorderWidth	-bw -borderwidth	Border width (in pixels)
display	Display	-d -display	Name of display
foreground	Foreground	-fg -foreground	Foreground color
font	Font	-fn -font	Font name
geometry	Geometry	-geometry	Size and location
title	Title	-title	Title string

Command-line options in X applications

In addition to resource databases, X applications accept command-line arguments. Table 5-2 shows the common command-line options for X applications. This section summarizes a few important command-line options.

The -display option

You use -display to specify the display on which the application's output should appear. (An X application can run on one system and display its output on a display connected to another system on a network.) If you are logged into a remote computer, for example, and you want to run the client xclock on that system, you can start it with a command like this:

```
xclock -display sysname:0 &
```

Here, *sysname* is the name of your system (the name that you see when you type the command **hostname** on your system).

The -geometry option

Another common option is -geometry, which you use to specify the size and location of an application's window. You have to specify the geometry in a standard format, as follows:

widthxheight[+-]xoffset[+-]yoffset

In this format, *width, height, xoffset,* and *yoffset* are numbers, and you have to pick one of the two signs shown in the brackets. The *width* and *height* values specify the size of the window, in pixels (except for xterm, for which you specify these values in number of columns and rows of text). The *xoffset* and *yoffset* values are also in pixels. The meaning of these two numbers depends on the application. In `xterm`, for example, a positive `xoffset` indicates the number of pixels by which the left side of the window is offset from the left side of the screen. A negative `xoffset`, on the other hand, specifies the number of pixels by which the right edge of the window is offset from the right edge of the screen. Similarly, positive and negative `yoffset` indicate the offsets of the top and bottom edges of the window, respectively.

You would type the following command to place a 80-character by 25-line `xterm` window at the upper-right corner of your screen, with a 16-pixel gap between the window's frame and the screen's top and right edges:

```
xterm -geometry 80x25-16+16 &
```

Options for window appearance

Several other command-line options determine the appearance of an application's window. These options specify the foreground color (`-fg`); the background color (`-bg`); the border color (`-bd`); and the border width (`-bw`), in pixels. You specify the colors by names that appear in the `/usr/lib/X11/rgb.txt file`. To start `xterm` with yellow characters on a Navy background, use the following command:

```
xterm -bg Navy -fg yellow &
```

If a color name includes embedded space, enter the name in quotes. To specify `light blue` as the background for `xterm`, use the following command:

```
xterm -bg "light blue" &
```

As explained in the "Screen color" section earlier in this chapter, you also can specify the color as a hexadecimal number with six hexadecimal digits. The digits in a six-digit hexadecimal RGB value of a color are interpreted from left to right, with the most significant pair of digits assumed to be for red (R), the middle pair for green (G), and the least-significant pair for blue (B). You have to place the # character in front of the hexadecimal digits to signify that the color specification is in hexadecimal format. You can try a strange color for `xterm`'s background by using the following command:

```
xterm -bg "#ccb0b0" &
```

Font specification

The font resource of an application controls the appearance of the text output. Like colors, fonts are specified by names. In X, the font names are very descriptive. Following is an example:

```
-adobe-courier-medium-r-normal--12-120-75-75 m 60-iso8859-1
```

For this font, `adobe` is the maker, `courier` is the family, and the font is of `medium` weight (it can be `bold`, for example). The `r` value indicates that the font is roman. An `i` at this position indicates italic, and `o` indicates oblique. The `normal` value is a parameter for character-width and spacing between characters; it also can be `condensed`, `narrow`, or `double`.

The numbers that follow the two dashes (--) indicate the font's size. `12` indicates the pixel size of the font, and `120` gives the size in tenths of a printer's point. The next two numbers, `75-75`, give the horizontal and vertical resolution for which the font is designed. The letter that follows the resolution (`m`) is the spacing; this value can be `m` for monospace or `p` for proportional. The next number, `60`, is the average width of all characters in this font, measured in tenths of a pixel (in this case, 6 pixels). The string `iso8859-1` identifies the character set of the font, as specified by the International Standards Organization (ISO). In this case, the character set is ISO Latin 1, a superset of the ASCII (American Standard Code for Information Interchange) character set.

Tip

You do not have to give the entire name when you specify a font in a resource file. You can use asterisks (`*`) for fields that can be arbitrary. Suppose that you want the VT100 window in `xterm` to use a medium-weight 12-point `courier` font. With a judicious sprinkling of asterisks, you can specify this font in the resource file as follows:

```
*VT100*Font: *courier-medium-r-normal--*120*
```

Customizing the `fvwm` Window Manager

A *window manager* is a special X client that takes care of interactions among windows for various clients on-screen. You need a window manager to control the placement and size of each client's window. Without a window manager, you cannot change a window's location or alter its size.

To see why a window manager is necessary, consider the case of two clients — A and B — that are displaying on the same screen. Neither client has any idea of the other's needs. Suppose that you run client B after A, and B takes over the entire screen (the root window) as its output window. At this point, A's window is obscured underneath B's, and you have no way to reach A's window.

A window manager provides you the means to switch from B to A, even when B is ill-behaved. The `fvwm` window manager adds a decorative frame to the main window of each application. This frame allows you to move and resize the windows. You can click and drag a corner of the frame to shrink B's window. The default window manager in Linux — `fvwm` — shows an outline of the window that changes in size as you move the mouse. This outline allows you to make the topmost window smaller to expose windows underneath it. Additionally, with `fvwm`, you can get a pull-down menu by clicking the upper-left corner of the window's frame (see Figure 5-3). This menu contains options that allow you to resize a window, reduce the window to an icon, and quit the application.

Overview of `fvwm`

The `fvwm` program is in the `/usr/X11/bin` directory. Typically, you start `fvwm` from a shell script such as `.xinitrc` or `.xsession`. When `fvwm` runs, it adds a frame (with a 3-D appearance) around each on-screen window.

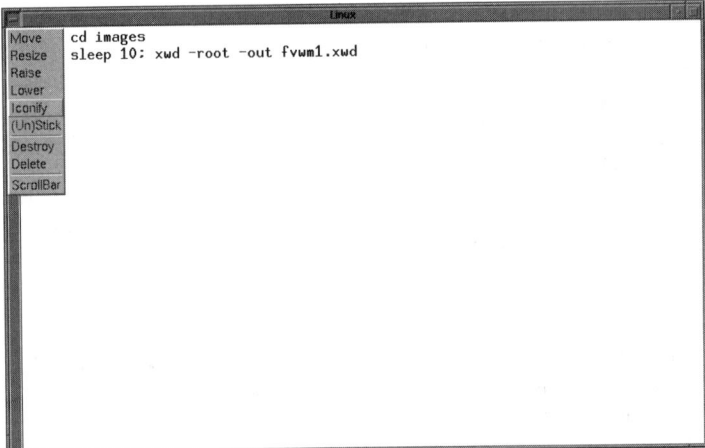

Figure 5-3: The `fvwm` window manager adds the frame and menu to this window.

The v in `fvwm` stands for *virtual;* `fvwm` provides a virtual desktop that is larger than the physical dimensions of your system's screen. By default, `fvwm` provides a virtual desktop that has nine pages, and each page has an area equal to the size of the X display screen. To help you navigate the virtual desktop, `fvwm` displays a small *pager window* in one corner of the screen, as shown in Figure 5-4.

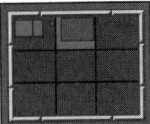

Figure 5-4: You can navigate the virtual desktop with the pager window.

To go to a specific page, click that page in the pager window. The pager window is a constant fixture on each page, because it is a *sticky* window. In `fvwm`, a sticky window always appears on each virtual screen page.

Secret

Even though you get many virtual screen pages, `fvwm`'s need for memory depends only on the number of windows. The size of the virtual desktop makes no difference in the amount of memory that `fvwm` uses. So you can use the virtual-desktop feature of `fvwm` without worrying about wasting memory.

As you read the following discussion of `fvwm`, remember that these descriptions correspond to the default settings of `fvwm` as defined by the resource file `/usr/lib/X11/system.fvwmrc`. As you will learn soon, you can easily customize `fvwm` to change its behavior. Therefore, do not be surprised if you find that `fvwm` in your system does not behave exactly as described in this section.

Under `fvwm`, if you click the left mouse button while the mouse pointer is anywhere in the root window, `fvwm` displays the Utilities menu, which you can customize. Typically, this menu lists items that start an application. Some of the menu items have an arrow; a submenu appears when you place the mouse pointer on the arrow. Figure 5-5 shows the default Utilities menu.

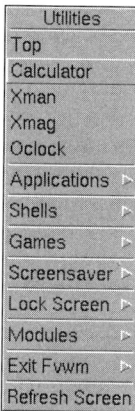

Figure 5-5: Click the left mouse button to view the Utilities menu in `fvwm`.

When you click the middle button of a three-button mouse (or simultaneously click the left and right buttons of a two-button mouse) while the mouse pointer is anywhere in the root window, `fvwm` displays the Window Ops menu. The default options in this menu let you manage the on-screen windows. An interesting option in this menu enables you to make a window sticky. If you make a window sticky, it appears in the same location on all virtual screen pages. Figure 5-6 shows the default Window Ops menu in `fvwm`.

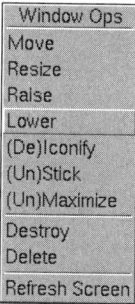

Figure 5-6: Click the middle button of a three-button mouse to view the Window Ops menu in `fvwm`.

Clicking the right mouse button while the mouse pointer is in the root window causes `fvwm` to display the CurrentDesk menu, which lists the titles of all available windows on the desktop. If you choose a window from the menu, `fvwm` makes that window current and moves the mouse pointer to that window. If the window happens to be on a different virtual screen page than the current one, `fvwm` also switches to that virtual screen. You can use the options in the CurrentDesk menu to jump to any window with a mouse click. Figure 5-7 shows a typical CurrentDesk menu.

CurrentDesk: 0	Geometry
1. Linux	0:+323+14x80x24
2. File Manager	0:-1019+70x400x350
3. Applications	0:-604+70x270x350
4. xconsole	(0:-490+610x480x130)

Figure 5-7: Click the right mouse button to view the CurrentDesk menu in `fvwm`.

You can customize `fvwm` through a configuration file that specifies settings in a format that `fvwm` accepts. If you start `fvwm` without any command-line options, `fvwm` by default looks in your home directory for a file named .fvwmrc, which is specified by the HOME environment variable. If no .fvwmrc file exists in your home directory, `fvwm` uses the contents of /usr/lib/X11/fvwm/system.fvwmrc to configure its menus and to bind the keys and mouse buttons to specific actions. If the /usr/lib/X11/fvwm/system.fvwmrc file is missing, `fvwm` simply exits.

Tip

The best way to customize `fvwm` is to start with a working configuration file. You should start with the systemwide file called system.fvwmrc, which is located in the directory /usr/lib/X11/fvwm. Copy this file to your home directory under the name .fvwmrc, and edit the file to alter one feature at a time. You can make the changes in an xterm window while you are running `fvwm`. After you make a change, choose the Utilities menu, then the Exit Fvwm submenu, and then the Restart Fvwm option. When `fvwm` restarts, it acts on your changes, and you can verify whether your modifications work properly. Following this approach, you can incrementally arrive at a configuration file that suits your needs.

Input focus

A window manager, such as `fvwm`, determines which window has the *input focus*. The window with input focus receives the keyboard events (that is, what you type). Deciding which window gets mouse events is easy — that window is the one that contains the mouse pointer. The keyboard, however, has no on-screen pointer to indicate which window should get the key presses. The X Window System solves this problem by specifying that all keystrokes go to the current focus window. The window manager lets you indicate which window gets the focus in one of two ways:

- Some window managers give the focus to the window that contains the mouse pointer. This method of letting the mouse location determine the focus is often referred to as the *focus follows pointer* (or the *pointer focus*) policy.

- Other window managers use the concept of a *listener window,* which is the window that has the focus. The user selects the listener window by moving the mouse pointer to it and clicking the mouse button. When it is selected, that window remains the focus window no matter where the mouse pointer moves. This type of focus assignment is called a *click-to-type* style of input-focus policy. Macintosh and Windows 95 use this click-to-type style of input focus.

You will find proponents of both styles, and you can have either style of keyboard focus with `fvwm`. The default focus style is click-to-type. The following line in the `.fvwmrc` file indicates this style:

```
ClickToFocus
```

If you want the focus to follow the mouse pointer, simply make this line a comment by placing a # at the start, as follows:

```
#ClickToFocus
```

Desktop size

Although a large virtual desktop does not waste any memory, you may find nine virtual screen pages to be more than you can use. The following line in the default configuration file causes `fvwm` to have a 3×3 grid of virtual screen pages:

```
DeskTopSize 3x3
```

If you want to have a 2×2 array of virtual screens (resulting in four virtual screens), all you have to do is change that line, as follows:

```
DeskTopSize 2x2
```

If, on the other hand, you want the four virtual screens to be laid out in a row, you can write the line as follows:

```
DeskTopSize 4x1
```

As you reduce the number of virtual screen pages, the pager window shrinks. When you have four screens in a row, the pager window becomes a slim horizontal panel, which you may find to be more appealing than the square window associated with a 3×3 desktop.

Customizing menus

The `fvwm` window manager displays pop-up menus when you click any mouse button while the mouse pointer is in the root window. These menus are defined in the configuration file. The best way to understand the format for menus is to look at a sample. Consider the configuration-file entries that generate the menu shown in Figure 5-5, earlier in this chapter. The following lines in the `/usr/lib/X11/fvwm/system.fvwmrc` file define this menu's layout:

```
Popup "Utilities"
    Title    "Utilities"
    Exec     "Top"         exec rxvt -font 7x14 -T Top -n Top -e top &
    Exec     "Calculator"  exec xcalc &
    Exec     "Xman"        exec xman &
    Exec     "Xmag"        exec xmag &
    Exec     "Oclock"      exec oclock &
    Nop      ""
    Popup    "Applications" Applications
    Nop      ""
    Popup    "Shells"      Shells
    Nop      ""
    Popup    "Games"       Games
    Nop      ""
    Popup    "Screensaver" Screensaver
    Nop      ""
    Popup    "Lock Screen" Screenlock
    Nop      ""
    Popup    "Modules"     Module-Popup
    Nop      ""
    Popup    "Exit Fvwm"   Quit-Verify
    Nop      ""
    Refresh  "Refresh Screen"
EndPopup
```

The first word in each line is a built-in function that fvwm understands. Then come the caption, in quotes (this is what appears in the menu), and any additional arguments required by the built-in function. Table 5-3 summarizes fvwm's built-in functions:

Table 5-3	fvwm's built-in functions
Function	**Purpose**
Beep	Causes the computer to beep.
CirculateDown [*name window_name*]	Moves input focus to the next window in the list or to the window whose name you provide as an argument.
CirculateUp [*name window_name*]	Moves input focus to the preceding window in the list or to the window whose name you provide as an argument.
Close	Closes the currently active window.
CursorMove *horizontal vertical*	Moves the mouse pointer to the specified horizontal and vertical page number on the desktop.
Delete	Sends a window-manager protocol message to a window, asking it to remove itself.
Desk *arg1 arg2*	Changes the current desktop.
Destroy	Destroys the window and terminates the application.

`Exec name command`	Executes a specified command. (*name* is what appears in the menu.)
`Focus`	Moves the focus to the window and raises the window to the top, if necessary.
`Function`	Binds a previously defined function to a key or a mouse button.
`Function FunctionName`	Starts the definition of a function.
`GotoPage x y`	Moves to page (x, y) on the desktop; page (0, 0) is the upper-left page.
`Iconify [value]`	Iconifies a window. (A positive value means that the window can only be iconified, not deiconified.)
`Lower`	Lowers a window in the stacking order (the order in which windows appear on-screen — one on top of another).
`Maximize [horizontal vertical]`	*Maximizes* a window (fills the screen).
`Module ModuleName`	Spawns (spawn means load and run a program) the specified module.
`Move`	Moves a window.
`Nop`	Does nothing. Use `Nop` to insert a blank line into the menu.
`Popup`	Binds a previously defined pop-up menu to a menu item.
`Popup PopupName`	Starts the definition of a pop-up menu.
`Quit`	Exits `fvwm` (and causes X to exit also).
`Raise`	Raises a window to the top of the stacking order.
`RaiseLower`	Alternately raises and lowers a window.
`Refresh`	Forces all windows on-screen to redraw themselves.
`Resize`	Resizes a window.
`Restart name WindowManagerName`	Restarts the window manager. `WindowManagerName` is the name of the executable file, and *name* is what appears in the menu.
`Scroll horizontal vertical`	Scrolls horizontally and vertically by a specified amount. (The amount is in terms of percentage of the page dimensions.)
`Stick`	Makes a window sticky so that it appears in the same location of every page of the desktop.
`Title`	Inserts a title into a menu.

(continued)

Table 5-3 *(continued)*

Function	Purpose
`TogglePage`	Disables automatic scrolling when the cursor moves beyond the edge of a page.
`Wait` *name*	Waits until a specified window appears on-screen.
`Warp` [*name window_name*]	Behaves the same way as `CirculateDown`, but the Warp command deiconifies an iconified window that is being brought to the top of other windows.
`WindowList` *arg1 arg2*	Creates and pops up a menu that lists the titles and geometries of all windows on the desktop.
`WindowsDesk` *new_desk*	Moves the window to the specified desktop.

The items labeled `Popup` cause other menus to pop up. In this case, the actions are other menu names. The Quit-Verify menu, for example, is defined as follows:

```
# This menu is invoked as a submenu - it allows you to quit,
# restart, or switch to another WM.
Popup "Quit-Verify"
     Title   "Really Quit Fvwm?"
     Quit    "Yes, Really Quit"
     Restart "Restart Fvwm"   fvwm
     Restart "Start twm"      twm
     Restart "Start tvtwm"    tvtwm
     Restart "Start mwm"      mwm
     Restart "Start olvwm"    /usr/openwin/bin/olvwm
     Restart "Start olwm"     /usr/openwin/bin/olwm
     Nop     ""
     Nop     "No, Don't Quit"
EndPopup
```

Add-on modules in `fvwm`

The `fvwm` window manager supports the concept of *add-on modules,* which are programs that `fvwm` starts as separate Linux processes. When `fvwm` starts a module, it sets up an interprocess communication mechanism known as *pipes;* the module uses the pipes to send commands to `fvwm` to execute. The commands from a module are in the form of text strings that `fvwm`'s command processor parses and executes. As far as `fvwm` is concerned, the commands from a module are no different from those sent by a mouse action, as specified in the .`fvwmrc` file. By supporting modules as separate communicating processes, `fvwm` allows users to extend its capabilities without affecting the integrity of `fvwm` itself.

A sample add-on module is the `GoodStuff` module, which you can start from `fvwm`'s Utilities menu. By default, the `GoodStuff` module provides a toolbar whose buttons can launch applications.

When `fvwm` tries to start a module, it looks for the module in the directories listed in the `ModulePath` option in the `.fvwmrc` file.

Emulating other window managers

In the `/usr/X11/lib/X11/fvwm/sample_configs` directory, you find several configuration files, each of which causes `fvwm` to emulate a different window manager. The file `4Dwm.fvwmrc` emulates the `4Dwm` window manager, which is available on Silicon Graphics workstations. The `4Dwm` window manager is similar to the Motif window manager.

The `mwm.fvwmrc` configuration file (also in the `/usr/X11/lib/X11/fvwm/sample_configs` directory) is meant to make `fvwm` behave like the Motif window manager.

To try any of these configuration files, copy the configuration file to the `.fvwmrc` file in your home directory; then start `fvwm` again to make the configuration file take effect.

Using and Customizing `xterm`

The one indispensable X application is the `xterm` terminal emulator. The window manager and `xterm` are the two applications that most users run when they start X on any workstation, including a Linux PC. By default, `xterm` emulates a VT102 terminal (24 lines × 80 columns). You interact with the UNIX shell in this window, just as you would in any alphanumeric terminal. (A *terminal* is a simple device, with a keyboard and a display, through which users access a host computer.) Character-oriented applications can run directly in this window. You also can start more `xterm` processes, thereby creating several terminals on the same screen. This section briefly describes `xterm` and shows you how to configure it to your liking.

The VT102 terminal window in `xterm` also is useful for starting X applications. Just type the application's name at the shell prompt in the `xterm` window.

In addition to the VT102 terminal, `xterm` can emulate the Tektronix 4014 graphics terminal. If you start `xterm` with the command `xterm -t`, it comes up in Tektronix 4014 mode.

Main features of `xterm`

The `xterm` application has several features that you don't see in a real VT102 or Tektronix 4014 terminal. (These terminals are not used much anymore, even though many communications programs emulate them.) These features include

- Pop-up menus for switching terminal modes and setting up other characteristics
- Support for cut-and-paste operations

- The option to change the foreground color, the background color, and the font used to display text
- Support for programmable keys

The main menu in xterm

The xterm window does not have a menu bar, but it provides pop-up menus. Position the mouse pointer in the xterm window; then press Ctrl and click the left mouse button simultaneously. The xterm program pops up the Main Options menu, shown in Figure 5-8.

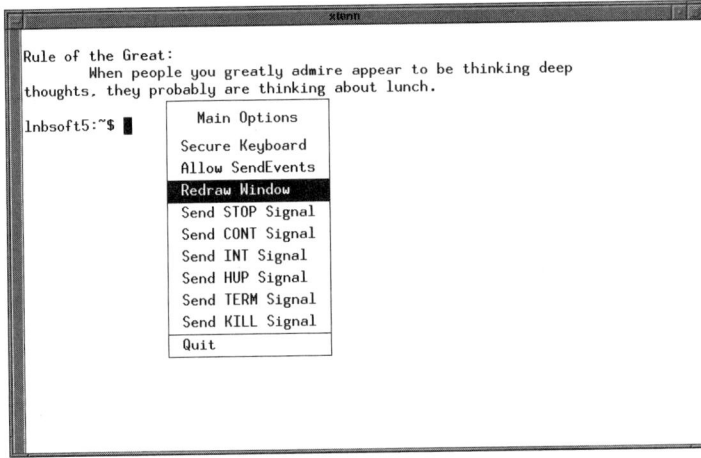

Figure 5-8: Pressing Ctrl and clicking the left mouse button activates xterm's main menu.

Figure 5-8 shows xterm's VT102 window, which is the window that you use almost exclusively when you run xterm.

The Main Options menu appears in both VT102 and Tektronix modes. You can use this menu as follows:

- Choose the Secure Keyboard option to ensure that keystrokes are delivered only to the xterm application, not to other X applications that are displaying at your workstation. If you are prompted for a password, first choose the Secure Keyboard option and then type the password. When you choose this option, a check appears next to the option name, and the xterm window appears in reverse video. This option is a *toggle,* which means that you can choose the option again to disable it.
- Choosing the Allow SendEvents option enables xterm to accept and interpret *synthetic events* (events that are not caused by the user's input) that other programs have sent. You should not choose this option, because allowing synthetic events makes xterm unsecure.

> ### Starting `xterm`
>
> If you want a new `xterm` window, you can start `xterm` from an existing `xterm` window. Simply type **xterm**, followed by any options (described in this section) and an ampersand (&). The ampersand causes the program to run in the background so that you can continue to type other commands. If you are running `fvwm`, you can get a new `xterm` window by following these steps:
>
> 1. With the mouse pointer in the root window, hold down the left mouse button on the root window. The `fvwm` window manager displays the Utilities menu.
>
> 2. While holding down the mouse button, move the mouse pointer to the Shells option. Then release the mouse button. The Shells menu appears, as shown in the following figure.
>
>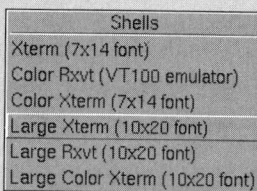
>
> 3. Select one of the `xterm` options from the menu. Each option runs `xterm` with different command-line options and provides different fonts.

- Choose the Redraw Window option to force `xterm` to redraw the contents of its window.

- Choose Send HUP Signal, Send KILL signal, or Quit to terminate `xterm`. The `xterm` window disappears from the screen. The difference among the options is in the UNIX signals that the options send to `xterm` to terminate it.

UNIX systems, including Linux, use signals to notify a process that a specific event has occurred. The SIGKILL and SIGHUP signals terminate a process.

VT102 emulation

In addition to providing a way to interact with the UNIX shell, emulating an alphanumeric terminal in a window has an added benefit: You can scroll back and look at old output, which you cannot do on a real VT102 terminal. If, for example, a directory listing displayed in response to the `ls` command is too long, you can scroll down the window's contents to view the lines that scrolled off the top of the VT102 window.

Another convenient feature of the VT102 window is that you can cut and paste text. If you type a long command that you need to repeat later, you can simply select the line and paste it as the new command.

Scrolling

Scrolling is not enabled by default. To enable scrolling, start `xterm` with this command:

```
xterm -sb &
```

The `-sb` option causes `xterm` to display a scrollbar attached to the left edge of the window.

You can scroll the VT102 window because, by default, `xterm` allocates a 64-line buffer to hold lines that are being sent to the terminal. Of these lines, only 24 usually are visible in the window. The scrollbar indicates the amount of text in this buffer by changing the size of the *thumb,* which is the highlighted area in the scrollbar. When the buffer is empty, the thumb fills the scrollbar. As text fills the buffer, the thumb gradually becomes smaller. To enlarge the size of the buffer, you can specify a new value in either of two ways:

- Use the `-sl` option when you start `xterm`. The command `xterm -sl 300 &`, for example, causes `xterm` to save the last 300 lines that scrolled off the window.

- Set the `saveLines` resource to the number of lines that you want to save. You can do this by placing the following line in the `.Xresources` file (assuming that you use `xdm` to log in as described earlier in this chapter) in your home directory:

    ```
    *saveLines: 300
    ```

To scroll back and forth to view the rest of the buffer, you have to bring the mouse pointer inside the scrollbar and then click a mouse button. If you have a three-button mouse, place the mouse pointer in the scrollbar and click the left mouse button to cause `xterm` to scroll the contents of the window up; click the right mouse button to scroll the contents down. You can see older output this way. Click the middle mouse button to scroll the window to a position that corresponds to the location of the mouse pointer in the scrollbar.

Tip

If you have a two-button mouse, click both buttons simultaneously to simulate clicking the middle button.

In other words, if you click the middle mouse button when the mouse pointer is at the top of the scrollbar, the `xterm` window shows the oldest 24 lines in the buffer. If you move the mouse while holding down the middle mouse button, the window's contents scroll in keeping with the mouse's movement.

Cut-and-paste operations

In `xterm`'s VT102 window, unlike the real terminal, you can cut and paste text. `xterm` has no explicit cut operation; instead, the convention is to use selections. When you select text in `xterm`, that text becomes the current selection. You then can paste the text into any application that can accept selections.

In `xterm`, you can select text in the following ways:

- Hold down the left mouse button and drag the mouse across the characters that you want to select. The selected text is highlighted as you drag the mouse.

- Double-click a word to select it.

- Click the right mouse button to select everything between the current location of the mouse pointer and the point where you last clicked the left mouse button.

Paste the selection into xterm by clicking the middle mouse button. The pasted text appears at the current insertion point in the terminal window.

A common use of cut-and-paste operations is to avoid typing long, repetitive commands. You can select the command and paste it at the command prompt by clicking the middle mouse button.

Another use of cut-and-paste capability is to start two xterm processes, each running an editor (for example, vi). Suppose that you are editing two files in the two editor sessions. You can select text in the window of one editor and paste that text into the other edit window by using the paste mechanism of xterm. (The editor that receives the pasted text has to be in insert mode for this procedure to work.)

VT102 menus

If you press Ctrl and click the middle mouse button while the mouse pointer is in the VT102 window, xterm displays the VT Options pop-up menu, shown in Figure 5-9.

This menu lets you set several features of the VT102 emulation. If you did not start xterm with the scrollbar enabled, for example, you can do so by choosing the Enable Scrollbar option from the VT Options menu.

The last section of the menu contains another important item. To switch to the Tektronix emulation mode, choose Switch to Tek Mode from the menu. To get back to the VT102 window, you have to choose the Hide Tek Window option from the Tektronix menu.

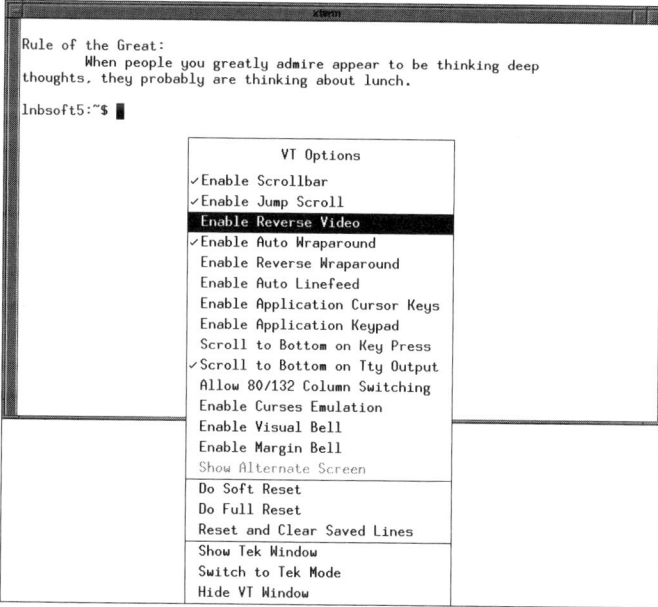

Figure 5-9: Pressing Ctrl and clicking the middle mouse button brings up xterm's VT Options menu.

Another menu in VT102 mode allows you to change the font that is used in the VT102 window. While the mouse pointer is in the VT102 window, press Ctrl and click the right mouse button. The `xterm` program displays the VT Fonts menu, shown in Figure 5-10.

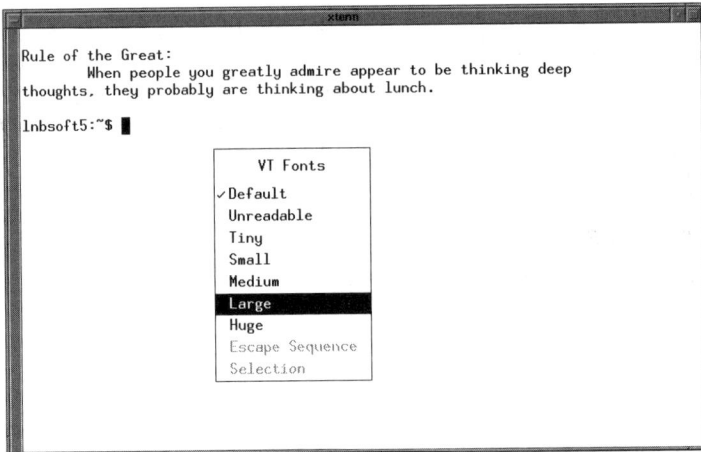

Figure 5-10: Pressing Ctrl and clicking the right mouse button brings up `xterm`'s VT Fonts menu.

Usually, the VT102 window uses the Default font. If you choose the Large option, for example, the VT102 window resizes, and its contents appear in a larger font. This option is helpful for large-screen displays (or when you set the screen resolution to 1,024 × 768), on which the Default font may be too small to use effectively.

A `termcap` **entry for** `xterm`

All alphanumeric terminals support programming that allows you to move the cursor, erase portions of the screen, and (sometimes) display characters in bold or reverse video. To perform these actions, you have to send to the terminal special sequences of characters, which usually start with the Escape character. As a result, these sequences often are called *escape sequences*.

UNIX uses a clever approach to programming alphanumeric terminals. Linux, as well as many other UNIX systems, stores the capabilities of various terminals in the `/etc/termcap` file. (The file is called `terminfo` in System V UNIX.) Each `termcap` entry identifies the terminal by name (for example, `vt100`, `ansi`, `tek4014`) and specifies the escape sequence necessary to activate each feature of the terminal.

Using this approach, you can add support for a new terminal by adding an entry for that terminal to the `termcap` file. The `termcap` entry for `xterm`'s VT102 emulation usually appears under the name `xterm`.

Most UNIX processes that must program the terminal extract the `termcap` entry for the terminal specified by the TERM environment variable. When you start `xterm`, the TERM environment variable is set to `xterm` automatically.

Tektronix 4014 emulation

The Tektronix 4014 emulation feature of xterm is useful for displaying output from older graphics programs that require the older Tektronix graphics terminal. If you are using or developing X applications, you are not likely to use this emulation mode, because X gives you much greater control of the display than the Tektronix 4014 does.

If you do get to Tektronix 4014 mode, you can interact with xterm by using the Tek Options menu, shown in Figure 5-11. This menu pops up when you press Ctrl and click the middle mouse button.

The most important item in this menu is the one labeled Hide Tek Window. Choose this item to get rid of the Tektronix window and revert to VT102 emulation.

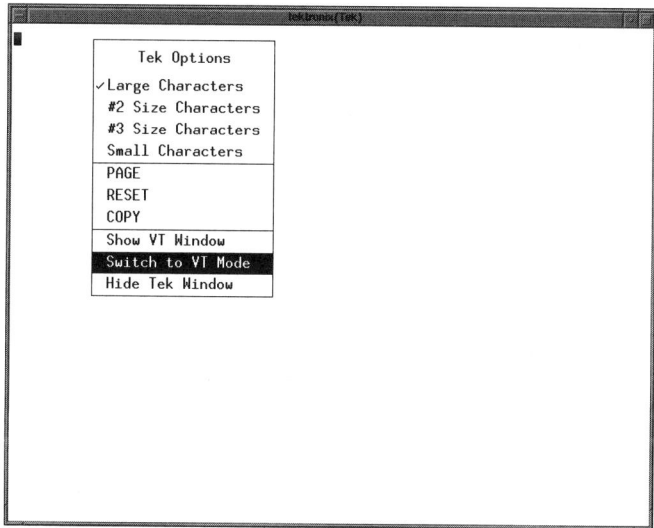

Figure 5-11: Pressing Ctrl and clicking the middle mouse button in Tektronix mode brings up the Tek Options menu.

Summary

Newcomers and old-timers alike can benefit from a graphical point-and-click user interface. This chapter shows you how to set up Linux to start in a graphical mode so that you can stay in the graphical environment. By reading this chapter, you learn the following:

- The X Window System includes a program named X Display Manager (xdm), which provides a graphical login prompt. When you understand how processes start in Linux, you can have xdm run every time you boot Linux.

- After Linux boots, a process named `init` starts all the other processes. The exact set of initial processes depends on the run level, which typically is a number ranging from 0 to 6. The `/etc/inittab` file specifies the processes that start in each run level.

- The `/etc/inittab` file specifies that the X Display Manager (xdm) program starts at run level 6. Therefore, you can start xdm running with the command `init 6`. This command is a good way to try xdm.

- After you log in, xdm automatically runs a script file named `.xsession` in your home directory. Therefore, you can start an initial set of X applications by placing appropriate commands in the `.xsession` file.

- The xterm terminal emulator, the xfm file manager, and the fvwm window manager constitute a good initial set of X applications to start at login. You can enter UNIX commands in the xterm window; use xfm to graphically browse directories and start programs; and use the fvwm window manager to move and resize windows.

- The window manager controls much of the look and feel of the X Window System's graphical environment. The fvwm window manager is highly customizable; its configuration is controlled by the `.fvwmrc` file in your home directory.

- You can easily customize most X applications, including the xterm terminal emulator. The customizable elements of an X application are known as *resources*. You can specify the values of resources in the `.Xresources` file in your home directory. Through resources, you can specify parameters such as background color, foreground color, and fonts.

Chapter 6
Secrets of Linux Commands

In This Chapter

- Understanding shells: the command interpreters of Linux
- Looking at Bash (the Bourne Again shell)
- Understanding the Linux directory structure
- Using Linux commands for working with files
- Writing shell scripts
- Automating common chores with a shell script
- Understanding the basics of Perl programming

Chapter 5 showed you how to work within a graphical environment in Linux. Unfortunately, you can't do everything from the graphical environment. It's not impossible to design a graphical interface that allows you to perform most chores, but Linux does not come with such a comprehensive graphical user interface. Therefore, even in the graphical environment of X, you often have to work in an xterm window, where you can use Linux commands to accomplish specific tasks.

You can have a variety of command interpreters, or *shells*, in Linux. This chapter introduces you to Bash: the Bourne Again Shell, which is the default shell in Linux. You learn some important shell commands and also see how to write simple *shell scripts*: a collection of shell commands stored in a file. When it comes to writing scripts, a language called Perl is gaining popularity among UNIX system administrators. Because you probably are the system administrator of your Linux system, this chapter also introduces you to Perl.

Cross Reference

I'll defer coverage of Tcl/Tk, another popular scripting language that you can use to build simple applications with a graphical interface, to Chapter 8.

The Bash Shell

If you have used MS-DOS, you may be familiar with COMMAND.COM: the DOS command interpreter. That program displays the infamous C:\> prompt. Linux provides a command interpreter that is similar to COMMAND.COM in DOS. In UNIX, the command interpreter traditionally is referred to as a *shell*.

The original UNIX shell was called the *Bourne shell,* and its executable program was named sh. The default Linux shell is Bash, and its program name is bash (you find it in the /bin directory). Bash is compatible with the original sh but includes many desirable features of other well-known shells, such as the C shell and the Korn shell. For example, Bash lets you recall commands that you entered previously, and it even completes partial commands.

The purpose of a shell such as Bash is to display a prompt and execute the command that you type at the keyboard. Some commands, such as cd (change directory) and pwd (print working directory), are built into Bash. Many more commands, such as cp (copy) and ls (list directory) are separate programs (meaning that a file that represents these commands resides in one of the directories on your system). As a user, however, you really do not have to know or care whether some command is built in or whether it is in the form of a separate executable program.

In addition to the standard Linux commands, Bash can execute any program that is stored in an executable file. Bash can even execute a shell script (a text file that contains one or more commands). As you learn later in the "Shell Scripts in Bash" section of this chapter, you can actually use the shell's built-in commands to write programs (also known as shell scripts).

The next few sections are designed to give you a feel for the various features of a shell, ranging from the general command syntax to the basics of shell programming. After you go through the overview, you can read more about selected topics in later sections.

Note

The discussions in this chapter assume that you are using Bash as your shell, because Bash is the shell that you get when you install Linux from the CD-ROM that accompanies this book.

Command syntax

Because a shell interprets what you type, it is important to know how the shell processes the text that you enter. All shell commands have the following general format:

```
command option1 option2 ... optionN
```

A single line of command commonly is referred to as a *command line.* On a command line, you enter a command followed by one or more options (or *arguments*) known as *command-line options* (or *command-line arguments*).

One basic rule is that you have to use a space or a tab to separate the command from the options. You must separate options with a space as well. If you want to use an option that contains embedded spaces, you have to put that option inside quotation marks. To search for my name in the password file, for example, I would enter the grep command as follows:

```
grep "Naba Barkakati" /etc/passwd
```

When grep prints the line with my name, it looks like this:

```
naba:Lgb7sOywtVswx:500:100:Naba Barkakati:/home/naba:/bin/bash
```

That line contains a great deal of information, the most interesting information (for purposes of this discussion) being the field that follows the last colon (:). That field shows the name of the shell that I am running.

The number and the format of the command-line options, of course, depend on the actual command. When you learn more about the commands, you see that the command-line options that control the behavior of a command are of the form -X, in which X is a single character.

Cross Reference

If a command is too long to fit on a single line, you can press the backslash (\) key, followed by Enter. Then you can continue entering the command on the next line. On the other hand, you can concatenate several shorter commands on a single line; just use the semicolon (;) as a separator between the commands. For example, when rebuilding the Linux kernel (as explained in Chapter 2) you can complete three sequential tasks by typing the following commands on a single line:

```
make dep; make clean; make zlilo
```

Combination of commands

Linux follows the UNIX philosophy of giving the user a toolbox of many simple commands. You can, however, combine these simple commands to create a more sophisticated command. Suppose that you want to find out whether a device file named sbpcd resides in your system's /dev directory. You look for the file because some documentation tells you that for a Sound Blaster Pro CD-ROM drive, you need that device file. You could use the command ls /dev to get a directory listing of the /dev directory and see whether anything that contains sbpcd appears in the listing. Unfortunately, the /dev directory has a great many entries, and it may be difficult to locate any item that has sbpcd in its name. You can, however, combine the ls command with grep and come up with a command that does exactly what you want, as follows:

```
ls /dev | grep sbpcd
```

The shell sends the output of the ls command (the directory listing) to the grep command, which searches for the string sbpcd. That vertical bar (|) is known as a *pipe* because it acts as a conduit between the two programs; the output of the first command becomes the input of the second one.

Note

Most Linux commands are designed in a way that allows the output of one command to be fed into the input of another. All you have to do is concatenate the commands, placing pipes between the commands.

I/O redirection

Linux commands that are designed to work together have a common feature: they always read from the *standard input* (usually, the keyboard) and write to the *standard output* (usually, the screen). If you want a command to read from a file, you can redirect the standard input to come from that file. Similarly, to save the output of a command in a file, you can redirect the standard output to a file. These features of the shell are called input and output redirection, or *I/O redirection*.

Using the following command, for example, you can search through all files in the /usr/include directory for the occurrence of the string "typedef" and then save that list in a file called typedef.out:

```
grep typedef /usr/include/* > typedef.out
```

This command also illustrates another feature of Bash. When you use an asterisk (*), Bash replaces the asterisk with a list of all the filenames in the specified directory. Thus, /usr/include/* means all the files in the /usr/include directory.

Shell programs

Tip

If you are not a programmer, you may feel apprehensive about programming. But shell programming can be as simple as storing a few commands in a file. In fact, you can have a useful shell program that has a single command.

While writing this book, for example, I had to capture screens from the X Window System and use the screen shots in figures. I used the X screen-capture program, xwd, to store the screen images in the X Window Dump (XWD) format. The book's production team, however, wanted the screen shots in PCX format. So I used the Netpbm toolkit to convert the XWD images to PCX format. To convert each file, I had to run two programs and delete a temporary file, as follows:

```
xwdtopnm < file.xwd > file.ppm
ppmtopcx < file.ppm > file.pcx
rm file.ppm
```

These commands assume that the programs xwdtopnm and ppmtopcx are in one of the directories listed in the PATH environment variable. By the way, xwdtopnm and ppntopcx are two programs in the Netpbm toolkit.

After converting a few XWD files to PCX format, I got tired of typing the same sequence of commands for each file. At that point, I prepared a file named topcx and saved the following lines in it:

```
xwdtopnm < $1.xwd > $1.ppm
ppmtopcx < $1.ppm > $1.pcx
rm $1.ppm
```

Then I made the file executable, using this command:

```
chmod +x topcx
```

Note

The chmod command lets you change the permission settings of a file. One of those settings determine whether the file is executable or not. The +x option means that you want to mark the file as an executable file. You need to do this because Bash will run only executable files.

Finally, I converted the file `figure1.xwd` to `figure1.pcx` by using the following command:

```
topcx figure1
```

The `topcx` file is called a *shell program*. When you run this shell program with the command `topcx figure1`, the shell substitutes `figure1` for each occurrence of `$1`.

That, in a nutshell, is why you might create shell programs: to have your Linux system perform repetitive chores.

Here is another interesting example of a shell program. Suppose that you occasionally have to use MS-DOS text files on your Linux system. Although you might expect to use a text file on any system without any problem, there is one catch: DOS uses a carriage return followed by a linefeed to mark the end of each line, whereas Linux (and other UNIX systems) uses only a linefeed. As a result, if you use the `vi` editor to open the DOS text file, you see ^M at the end of each line. That ^M stands for Ctrl-M, which is the carriage-return character.

On your Linux system, you can easily get rid of the extra carriage returns from the DOS text file by using the `tr` command with the `-d` option. Essentially, to convert the DOS text file `filename.dos` to a Linux text file named `filename.linux`, you type the following:

```
tr -d '\015' < filename.dos > filename.linux
```

In this command, `'\015'` denotes the ASCII code for the carriage-return character in octal notation.

You can use the `tr` command to translate or delete characters from its input. When you use `tr` with the `-d` option, it deletes all occurrences of a specific character from the input data. Following the `-d` option, you have to specify the character to be deleted. Like many UNIX utilities, `tr` reads the standard input and writes its output to standard output. As the sample command shows, you have to use input and output redirection to use `tr` to delete all occurrences of a character in a file and save the output in another file.

If you don't want to remember all this information every time you convert a DOS file to UNIX, store the following in a file named `dos2unix`:

```
tr -d '\015' < $1 > $2
```

Then make the file executable by using this command:

```
chmod +x dos2unix
```

That's it! Now you have a shell program named `dos2unix` that converts a DOS text file to a UNIX text file. If you have the MS-DOS partition mounted as `/dosc`, you can try the `dos2unix` shell program with the following command:

```
dos2unix /dosc/autoexec.bat aexec.bat
```

The command creates a file named `aexec.bat` in the current directory. If you open this file with the `vi` editor, you should not see any ^M characters at the ends of lines.

Note

If you are familiar with MS-DOS, you'll note that shell scripts are a lot like MS-DOS batch files. Except for some syntax differences, shell scripts are similar to DOS batch files.

Environment variables

The shell and other Linux commands need information to work properly. If you type a command and that command isn't one of that shell's built-in commands, the shell has to locate an executable file (whose name matches the command that you typed). The shell needs to know which directories to search for those files. Similarly, a text editor such as vi needs to know the type of terminal (even if the terminal happens to be xterm, which essentially emulates a terminal in a window).

One way to provide this kind of information to a program is through command-line options. If you use that approach, however, every time you start a program, you may have to enter many options. UNIX provides an elegant solution through *environment variables*.

An environment variable is nothing more than a name associated with a string. On my system, for example, the environment variable named PATH is defined as follows:

```
PATH=/usr/local/bin:/bin:/usr/bin:/usr/X11/bin:.
```

The string to the right of the equal sign is the value of the PATH environment variable. By convention, the PATH environment variable is a sequence of directory names, each name separated from the preceding one by a colon (:). The period at the end of the list of directories also denotes a directory; it represents the current directory.

When the shell has to search for a file, it simply searches the directories listed in the PATH environment variable. The shell searches the directories in PATH in order of their appearance. Therefore, if two programs have the same name, the shell executes the one that it finds first.

In a fashion similar to the shell's use of the PATH environment variable, an editor such as vi uses the value of the TERM environment variable to figure out how to display the file that you are editing with vi. To see the current setting of TERM, type the following command at the shell prompt:

```
echo $TERM
```

If you type this command in an xterm window, the output is as follows:

```
xterm
```

To define an environment variable in Bash, use the following syntax:

```
NAME=Value; export NAME
```

Here, `NAME` denotes the name of the environment variable, and `Value` is the string representing its value. Therefore, you set TERM to the value `xterm` by using the following command:

```
TERM=xterm; export TERM
```

With an environment variable like `PATH`, you typically want to append a new directory name to the existing definition, rather than define the `PATH` from scratch. The following example shows how you can accomplish this task:

```
PATH="$PATH:/usr/games"; export PATH
```

This command appends the string `:/usr/games` to the current definition of the `PATH` environment variable. The net effect is to add `/usr/games` to the list of directories in `PATH`.

`PATH` and `TERM` are only two of a handful of common environment variables. Table 6-1 lists some of the useful environment variables in Bash.

Table 6-1	Useful Bash environment variables
Environment variable	**Contents**
DISPLAY	The name of the display on which the X Window System displays output
HOME	Your home directory
LOGNAME	Your login name
PATH	The list of directories in which the shell looks for programs
PS1	The shell prompt (the default is `bash$` for all users except `root`; for `root`, the default prompt is `bash#`).
SHELL	Your shell (`SHELL=/bin/bash` for Bash)
TERM	The type of terminal

Processes

Every time the shell acts on a command that you type, it starts a *process*. The shell itself is a process; so are any scripts or programs that the shell executes. An example of such a program is the `fvwm` window manager. You can use the `ps` command to see a list of processes. When you type **ps**, for example, Bash shows you the current set of processes. Following is a typical report that I get when I enter the `ps` command in an `xterm` window:

```
bash$ ps
  PID TTY STAT  TIME COMMAND
  184 pp1 S     0:00 bash
  214 pp1 R     0:00 ps
```

In the default output format, the COMMAND column shows the commands that created the processes. This list shows the `bash` shell and the `ps` command as the processes.

Although the `ps` command shows only two processes, many more processes actually are running on your system. By default, the `ps` command shows only those processes that are associated with a terminal (including the `xterm` window). To see all your processes — even those that are not associated with any terminal — type the **ps -x** command. Following is the result of that command on my system:

```
bash$ ps -x
  PID TTY STAT   TIME COMMAND
  169 ?   S      0.00 sh /home/naba/.xsession
  182 ?   S      0:00 xfm
  183 ?   S      0:00 fvwm
  184 pp1 S      0:00 bash
  222 pp1 R      0:00 ps -x
```

This list shows the processes that the shell started when it processed the `.xsession` script in my home directory (`/home/naba`). That script contains commands that start the `xfm` (X file manager) and `fvwm` (window manager) processes.

Even the `ps -x` command does not give you a feel for all the processes that are running on a Linux system. What `ps -x` shows are the commands that you started, either directly or indirectly (through shell scripts that run automatically when you log in). To see the full complement of processes, use the `-a` option of the `ps` command together with the `-x` option, as follows:

```
ps -ax
```

I won't show the output of the command, because quite a few processes are running even when you are the only user on the system. You should expect to see 20 to 25 processes in the list.

Tip

The examples of the `ps` command show an interesting feature of Linux commands: most Linux commands take single-character options, each with a minus sign (you might think of this sign as being a hyphen) as prefix. When you want to use several options, type a hyphen and concatenate the option letters one after another. Therefore, `ps -ax` is equivalent to `ps -a -x`.

Secret

If you study the output of the `ps` command, you find that the first column has the heading PID and that it shows a number for each process. *PID* stands for *process ID* (identification), which is a sequential number assigned by the Linux kernel. If you look through the output of the `ps -ax` command, you should see that the `init` command is the first process; it has a PID or process number of 1. That's why `init` is referred to as the *mother of all processes*.

Tip

The process ID or process number is useful when you have to forcibly stop an errant process. Look at the output of the `ps -ax` command, and note the PID of the offending process. Then use the `kill` command with that process number. To stop process number 123, for example, type **kill -9 123**.

UNIX systems, including Linux, use signals to notify a process that a specific event has occurred. The kill command lets you send a signal to a process (identified by a process number). The -9 part of the kill command indicates the signal to be sent; 9 happens to be the number for the SIGKILL signal that causes a process to exit.

Background commands and virtual terminals

When you use MS-DOS, you have no choice but to wait for each command to complete before you enter the next command. (You can type ahead a bit, but the MS-DOS system can hold only a few characters in its internal buffer.) Linux, however, can handle multiple tasks at the same time. The only problem you may have is that the terminal or console will be tied up until a command completes.

If you are working in an xterm window, and a command takes too long to complete, you can open another xterm window and then continue to enter other commands and do your work. If you are working in text mode, however, and some command seems to take too long, you need some other way to access your system.

You can continue working in several ways while your Linux system handles a lengthy task:

- You can start a lengthy command *in the background*, which means that the shell starts the process corresponding to a command and immediately comes back to accept more commands. The shell does not wait for the command to complete; the command runs as a distinct process in the background. To start a process in the background, all you have to do is place an ampersand (&) at the end of a command line. When I want to run the topcx shell script to convert a large image file named image1.xwd to PCX format, for example, I run the script in the background by using the following command:

    ```
    topcx image1 &
    ```

- If a command (that you did not run in the background) seems to take a long time, press Ctrl-Z to stop it; then type **bg** to put that process in the background.

- Use the *virtual-terminal* feature of Linux. Even though your Linux system has only one physical terminal (the combination of monitor and keyboard is called the *terminal*), it gives you the appearance of having multiple terminals. The initial text screen is the first virtual terminal. Press Alt-F2 to get to the second virtual terminal, Alt-F3 for the third virtual terminal, and so on. From the X Window System, you have to press Ctrl-Alt-F1 to get to the first virtual terminal, Ctrl-Alt-F2 for the second one, and so on.

Tip

If you are using a graphical login with xdm (as explained in Chapter 5), press Ctrl-Alt-F6 to get the only working virtual terminal. To get back to the X display, press Ctrl-Alt-F2. You can use the virtual terminal to log in and kill processes that may be causing your X display screen to become unresponsive (if the mouse stops responding, for example).

Command completion in Bash

Many commands take a filename as an argument. When you want to browse through a file named /etc/XF86Config, for example, you type the following:

more /etc/XF86Config

That entry causes the more command to display the file /etc/XF86Config one screen at a time. For the commands that take a filename as an argument, Bash includes a feature that lets you type short filenames. All you have to type is the bare minimum — just the first few characters — to uniquely identify the file in its directory.

To see an example, type **more /etc/XF**, but don't press Enter yet; press Tab instead. Bash automatically completes the filename, so that the command becomes more /etc/XF86Config. Now press Enter to run the command.

Tip

Whenever you type a filename, press Tab after the first few characters of the filename. Bash probably can complete the filename, so that you don't have to type the entire name. If you have not entered enough characters to uniquely identify the file, Bash beeps. Just type a few more characters and press Tab again.

Wildcards

Another way to avoid typing too many filenames is to use *wildcards*: special characters, such as the asterisk (*) and question mark (?), that match one or more characters in a string. If you are familiar with MS-DOS, you may have used commands such as COPY *.* A: to copy all files from the current directory to the A drive. Bash accepts similar wildcards in filenames. In fact, Bash provides many more wildcard options than MS-DOS does.

Bash supports three types of wildcards:

- The asterisk (*) character matches one or more characters in a filename. Therefore, * denotes all files in a directory.
- The question mark (?) matches any single character.
- A set of characters in brackets match any single character from that set. The string [xX]*, for example, matches any filename that starts with x or X.

Wildcards are handy when you want to perform a task on a group of files. To copy all the files from a directory named /mnt to the current directory, for example, type the following:

cp /mnt/* .

> ### A surprising result of Bash following its wildcard rules
>
> When expanding the [...] wildcard format, if Bash does not find any filenames matching the format, it leaves the wildcard specification intact. The following example shows this behavior. (The example assumes that the directory currently does not have any file named `jimt`.) Type:
>
>   ls > jim[t]
>
> This command causes Bash to execute the `ls` command and send the output to a file. Bash tries to expand the wildcard filename `jim[t]`, but does not find any matching filenames. So, it leaves the filename alone. The net result is that Bash saves the output of the `ls` command in a file named `jim[t]`.
>
> Now type the following:
>
>   ls > jimt
>
> Bash runs `ls` and saves the output in a file named `jimt`.
>
> Next, try deleteing a file with a wildcard specification:
>
>   rm jim[t]
>
> In this case, Bash finds the `jimt` file whose name matches the wildcard specification. So Bach deletes the file named `jimt`.
>
> Now repeat the same `rm jim[t]` command again. Bash again tries to find filenames matching the `jim[t]` specification, but it won't find any files that match the specification (remember, you already deleted the file named `jimt`). So, Bash takes the filename `jim[t]` literally and ends up deleting the `jim[t]` file.
>
> Although it might seem confusing, Bash is working according to its rules — if Bash cannot find any matching filenames for a wildcard specification, it interprets the wildcard as a literal string.
>
> Thanks to my editor, Jim Grey, for reminding me about this behavior and providing this example.

Bash replaces the wildcard character * with the names of all the files in the `/mnt` directory. The period at the end of the command stands for the current directory.

You can use the asterisk with other parts of a filename to select a more specific group of files. Suppose that you want to use the `grep` command to search for the string `typedef struct` in all files in the `/usr/include` directory that meet the following criteria:

- The filename starts with `s`.
- The filename ends with `.h`.

The wildcard specification `s*.h` denotes all filenames that meet these criteria. Thus, you can perform the search with the following command:

    grep "typedef struct" /usr/include/s*.h

The string contains a space that you want the `grep` command to find, so you have to enclose that string in quotation marks. This method ensures that Bash does not try to interpret each word in the string as being a separate command-line argument.

Although the asterisk (*) matches any number of characters, the question mark (?) matches a single character. Suppose that you have four files — `image1.pcx`, `image2.pcx`, `image3.pcx`, and `image4.pcx` — in the current directory. To copy these files to the `/mnt` directory, use the following command:

```
cp image?.pcx /mnt
```

Bash replaces the single question mark with any single character and ends up copying the four files to `/mnt`.

The third wildcard format, [...], matches a single character from a specific set. Typically, you combine this format with other wildcards to narrow down the matching filenames to a smaller set. To see a list of all filenames in the `/etc/X11/xdm` directory that start with x or X, type the following command:

```
ls /etc/X11/xdm/[xX]*
```

Command history

To make it easy for you to repeat long commands, Bash stores up to 500 old commands. Essentially, Bash maintains a *command history* (a list of old commands). To see the command history, type **history**. Bash displays a numbered list of the old commands, including those that you entered during previous logins. That list may resemble the following:

```
1   cd
2   ls -a
3   vi .xsession
4   history
```

If the command list turns out to be too long, you may choose to see only the last few commands only. To see the last 10 commands only, type this command:

```
history 10
```

To repeat a command from the list that the `history` command shows, all you have to do is type an exclamation point (!), followed by that command's number. To repeat command number 3, type **!3**.

You also can repeat an old command without knowing its command number. Suppose that you typed **more /usr/lib/X11/xdm/xdm-config** a while ago, and now you want to look at that file again. To repeat the previous `more` command, simply type the following:

```
!more
```

Often, you want to repeat the last command that you typed, perhaps with a slight change. You may, for example, have displayed the contents of the directory by using the `ls -l` command. To repeat that command, type two exclamation points, as follows:

```
!!
```

Sometimes, you want to repeat the preceding command but add extra arguments to the command. Suppose that `ls -l` shows too many files. You can simply repeat that command but pipe the output through the `more` command, as follows:

```
!! | more
```

Bash replaces the two exclamation points with the preceding command and then appends `| more` to that command.

Tip
An easy way to recall previous commands is to press the up-arrow key, which causes Bash to go back in the list of commands. To move forward in the command history, press the down-arrow key.

Command editing

After you recall a command, you do not have to settle for the command as is; you can edit the command. Bash supports a wide variety of command-line editing commands. These commands are similar to those used by the `emacs` and `vi` editors.

Suppose that you wanted to look at the file `/etc/XF86Config`, but you typed the following:

```
more /etc/XF86config
```

After you press Enter and see an error message that says that there is no such file, you realize that the `c` in `config` should have been uppercase. Instead of typing the entire line, you can type the following editing command to fix the problem:

```
^con^Con
```

Bash interprets this command to mean that it should replace the string `con` with `Con` in the previous command.

By default, Bash allows you to edit the command-line using a small subset of commands supported by the `emacs` editor.

I am already familiar with `emacs`, so I use the `emacs` commands to edit commands. To bring back a previous command line, for example, I press Ctrl-P. Then I commonly use the following keystrokes to edit the command line:

- Ctrl-B to go backward a character
- Ctrl-F to go forward a character
- Ctrl-D to delete the character on which the text cursor rests

To insert text, I type the text. Although `emacs` has a huge selection of editing commands, you can edit Bash command lines adequately with the preceding small set.

Aliases

While configuring the Linux kernel and creating a new Linux boot floppy, I found myself changing the directory to /usr/src/linux/arch/i386/boot quite a few times. After typing that directory name twice, I immediately set up a shortcut, using Bash's alias feature. I typed the following command:

```
alias goboot='cd /usr/src/linux/arch/i386/boot'
```

I intentionally did not use any underscore characters or uppercase letters in goboot, because I wanted the alias to be quick and easy to type (and it had to mean something to me only). After I defined the alias, I could go to that directory by typing the following at the Bash prompt:

```
goboot
```

As you can see, an *alias* simply is an alternative (and, usually, shorter) name for a lengthy command. Bash replaces the alias with its definition and performs the equivalent command.

Tip

If you type the same long command often, you should define an alias for that command. To make sure that the alias is available whenever you log in, place the definition in the .bash_profile file in your home directory.

Many users use the alias feature to give more familiar names to common commands. If you are a DOS user, and you are used to the dir command to get a directory listing, you can simply define dir as an alias for ls (the Linux command that displays the directory listing), as follows:

```
alias dir=ls
```

Now you can type **dir** whenever you want to see a directory listing.

Another good use of alias is to redefine a dangerous command, such as rm, and make it safer. By default, the rm command deletes one or more specified files. If you type **rm *** by mistake, rm deletes all files in your current directory. I learned this the hard way the other day, when I wanted to delete all files that ended with .xwd. (These files were old screen images that I no longer needed.) I intended to type **rm *.xwd**, but somehow, I ended up typing **rm * .xwd**. I got the following message:

```
rm: .xwd: No such file or directory
```

At first I was puzzled by the message from rm, so I typed **ls** to see the directory's contents again. When the listing showed nothing, I realized that I had an extra space between the * and .xwd. All the files in that directory, of course, were gone forever.

The rm command provides the -i option, which asks for confirmation before deleting a file. To make that option a default, add the following alias definition to the .bash_profile file in your home directory:

```
alias rm='rm -i'
```

That's it! From now on, when you use `rm` to delete a file, the command first asks for confirmation, as follows:

```
rm .bash_profile
rm: remove '.bash_profile'? n
```

Press **y** to delete the file; otherwise, press **n**.

Linux Commands

The shell lets you run any Linux command, but you need to know the commands before you can run them. Because Linux is a UNIX clone, all Linux commands essentially are UNIX commands. Some of the most important commands are for moving around the Linux file system. This section summarizes these important commands. You can try these commands at the shell prompt in an `xterm` window.

Linux directory layout

Like any other operating system, Linux organizes information in files. The files are, in turn, contained in directories. A directory can have subdirectories, giving rise to a hierarchical structure. Unlike MS-DOS, in which you see individual drives, the Linux file system starts with a root directory; a single slash (/) denotes the root directory. Figure 6-1 shows the basic layout of the Linux file system, including the root directory and several important subdirectories.

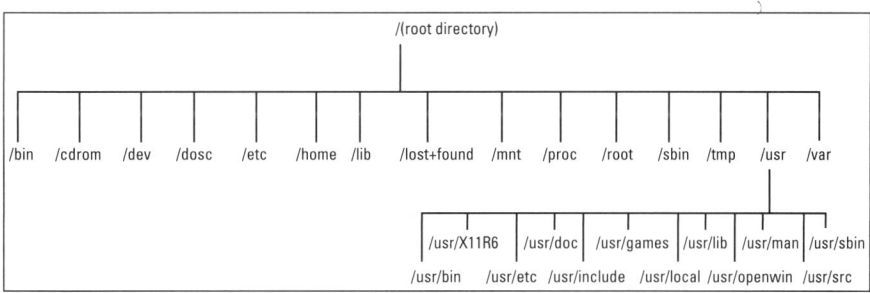

Figure 6-1: The Linux directory structure.

Many directories have specific purposes. If you know the purpose of specific directories, finding your way around the Linux directories is easier. Another benefit of knowing the typical use of directories is that you can guess where to look for specific types of files when you face a new situation. Table 6-2 briefly describes the directories in a Linux system.

Table 6-2	Linux system directories
Directory	Description
/	The root directory that forms the base of the file system. All files and directories are logically contained in the root directory, regardless of their physical locations.
/bin	Contains the executable programs that are part of the Linux operating system. Many Linux commands, such as cat, cp, ls, more, and tar, are located in /bin.
/cdrom	Directory where the CD-ROM drive typically is mounted. If you boot Linux with a CD-ROM in the CD-ROM drive, the init process automatically mounts the CD-ROM on the /cdrom directory.
/dev	Contains all device files. Linux treats each device as being a special file, and all such files are located in the device directory /dev.
/dosc	Directory where the MS-DOS partition is typically mounted (provided your system's hard disk has an MS-DOS partition).
/etc	Contains most system configuration files and the initialization scripts (in the /etc/rc.d subdirectory).
/home	Conventional location of the home directories of all users. User naba's home directory, for example, is /home/naba.
/lib	Contains library files for C and other programming languages.
/lost+found	Directory for lost files. Every disk partition has a lost+found directory.
/mnt	An empty directory, typically used to temporarily mount devices such as floppy disks and disk partitions.
/proc	A special directory that contains information about various parts of the Linux system.
/root	The home directory for the root user.
/sbin	Contains executable files representing commands that typically are used for system-administration tasks. Commands such as mount, halt, umount, and shutdown reside in the /sbin directory.
/tmp	Temporary directory that any user can use as a scratch directory (that means the contents of this directory are considered to be unimportant and is usually deleted every time the system boots).
/usr	Contains the subdirectories for many important programs, such as the X Window System, and online-manual pages.
/var	Contains various system definition files, as well as directories for holding transient information.

The /usr directory also contains a host of useful subdirectories. Table 6-3 lists a few of the important subdirectories in /usr.

Table 6-3	Important /usr subdirectories
Subdirectory	**Description**
/usr/X11R6	Contains the XFree86 (X Window System) software.
/usr/bin	Contains executable files for many more Linux commands, including utility programs that are commonly available in Linux but are not part of the core Linux operating system.
/usr/doc	Contains the documentation files for the Linux operating system, as well as many utility programs (such as the Bash shell, mtools, the xfm File Manager, and the xv image viewer).
/usr/games	Contains the Linux game collection, which includes games such as doom, dungeon, hangman, and snake.
/usr/include	Contains the header files (files with names ending in .h) for the C and C++ programming languages; also includes the X11 header files in the /usr/include/X11 directory.
/usr/lib	Contains the libraries for C and C++ programming languages; also contains the libraries for X and Tcl.
/usr/local	Contains local files. The /usr/local/bin directory, for example, is supposed to be the location of any executable program developed on your system.
/usr/man	Contains the online-manual pages (which you can read by using the man command).
/usr/openwin	Contains the OpenWindows software. The OPEN LOOK Window Manager (olwm), for example, is in the /usr/openwin/bin directory.
/usr/sbin	Contains many administrative commands, such as commands for electronic mail and networking.
/usr/src	Contains the source code for the Linux kernel (the core operating system).

Directory navigation

In Linux, when you log in as root, your home directory is /root. If you use the adduser command to add a new user, that user's home directory is in the /home directory. My home directory (when I log in as naba), for example, is /home/naba.

By default, you have permission to save files only in your home directory, but you can create subdirectories in your home directory to further organize your files.

A Linux shell such as Bash supports the concept of a *current directory*, which is the directory on which all file and directory commands operate. After you log in, for example, your current directory is the home directory. To see the current directory, use the pwd command.

To change the current directory, use the cd command. To change the current directory to /usr/doc, type the following:

cd /usr/doc

Then, to change the directory to the bash subdirectory in /usr/doc, type this command:

cd bash

Now, if you use the pwd command, that command shows /usr/doc/bash as the current directory. Therefore, you can refer to a directory's name in two ways:

- An absolute pathname (such as /usr/doc) that specifies the exact directory in the directory tree
- A relative directory name (such as bash, which means the bash subdirectory of the current directory)

If you type **cd bash** in /usr/doc, the current directory changes to /usr/doc/bash, but the same command in /home/naba tries to change the current directory to /home/naba/bash.

Use the cd command without any arguments to change the current directory to your home directory. Actually, the lone cd command changes the current directory to the directory listed in the HOME environment variable, but that environment variable contains your home directory by default.

Notice that the tilde character (~) also refers to the directory specified by the HOME environment variable. Thus, the command cd ~ changes the current directory to whatever directory the HOME environment variable specifies.

You can use a shortcut to refer to any user's home directory. Prefix a user's login name with a tilde (~) to refer to that user's home directory. Therefore, ~naba refers to the home directory of the user naba, and ~root is the home directory of the root user. If your system has a user with the login name ivy, you would type cd ~ivy to change to Ivy's home directory.

The directory names . and .. have special meanings. A single period (.) indicates the current directory, whereas two periods (..) indicate the parent directory. If the current directory is /usr/doc, for example, you can change the current directory to /usr by using this command:

cd ..

Directory listing and permissions

As you move around the Linux directories, you want to know the contents of a directory. You can get a directory listing by using the `ls` command. By default, the `ls` command, without any options, displays the contents of the current directory in a compact four-column format. If you log in as `root` and type **ls**, the `ls` command lists the contents of the `/root` directory in the following manner:

```
INSTALL       linux           lodlin15.zip  tmp
Mail          lodlin15.txt    mbox
```

From this listing, you cannot really tell whether an entry is a file or a directory. To see the complete details of a directory's contents, use the `-l` option with `ls`, as follows:

```
ls -l
```

For the `/root` directory, a typical output from `ls -l` is the following:

```
total 128
lrwxrwxrwx   1 root     root            8 Jul 21 14:06 INSTALL -> /var/adm
drwx------   2 root     root         1024 Jul 26 07:58 Mail
lrwxrwxrwx   1 root     root           14 Jul 21 14:06 linux -> /usr/src/linux
-rw-r--r--   1 root     root         4560 Sep 15  1994 lodlin15.txt
-rw-r--r--   1 root     root       115695 Sep 15  1994 lodlin15.zip
-rw-------   1 root     root         6858 Aug  4 00:03 mbox
drwxr-xr-x   2 root     root         1024 Jul 31 23:14 tmp
```

This listing shows considerable information about each directory entry, which can be a file or another directory. Looking at a line from the right column to the left, you see that the rightmost column shows the name of the directory entry. The date and time before the name show the date and time of the last modification to that file. Before the date and time comes the size of the file, in bytes.

The file's group and owner appear to the left of the column that shows the file's size. The next number indicates the number of links to the file. Finally, the leftmost column shows the file's *permission settings*, which determine who can read, write, or execute the file.

The first letter of the leftmost column has a special meaning, as the following list shows:

- If the first letter is `l`, the file is a symbolic link to another file.
- If the first letter is `d`, the file is a directory.
- If the first letter is a dash (–), the file is a normal file.

After that first letter, the leftmost column shows a sequence of nine characters, which appears as `rwxrwxrwx` when each letter is present (for example, see the entry named `linux`). Each letter indicates a specific permission, and a hyphen in place of a letter indicates no permission for a specific operation on the file. Think of these nine letters as being three groups of three letters (`rwx`), interpreted as follows:

- The leftmost group of rwx controls the read, write, and execute permission of the file's owner. In other words, if you see rwx in this position, the file's owner can read (r), write (w), and execute (x) the file. A hyphen in the place of a letter indicates no permission. Thus, the string rw- means that the owner has read and write permission but no execute permission. Typically, executable programs (including shell programs) have execute permission.
- The middle three rwx letters control the read, write, and execute permission of any user belonging to that file's group.
- The rightmost group of rwx letters controls the read, write, and execute permission of all other users (collectively referred to as the *world*).

Thus, a file with the permission setting rwx------ is accessible only to the file's owner, whereas the permission setting rwxr--r-- makes the file readable by everyone.

Tip

Use the chmod command to change the permission setting of a file. A shell program (or shell script), for example, typically is a text file that you prepare with a text editor. After saving the file, you have to make the file executable before you can run the script. To add execute permission to a script file named convert_images, for example, type the following:

chmod +x convert_images

This command adds the execute permission for owner, group, and world.

Secret

An interesting feature of the ls command is it does not list any file whose name begins with a period. To see these files, you must use the ls command with the -a option, as follows:

ls -a

File manipulation

You may often copy files from one directory to another. Use the cp command to perform this task. To copy the file /usr/lib/X11/fvwm/system.fvwmrc to the .fvwmrc file in your home directory, type the following:

cp /usr/lib/X11/fvwm/system.fvwmrc ~/.fvwmrc

If you want to copy a file to the current directory and retain the same name, use a period (.) as the second argument of the cp command. Thus, the following command copies the XF86Config file from the /etc directory to the current directory:

cp /etc/XF86Config .

The cp command makes a new copy of a file and leaves the original intact.

Another Linux command, mv, moves a file to a new location. The original copy is gone, and a new copy appears at the specified destination. One use of mv is to rename a file. If you want to change the name of the today.list to old.list, use the mv command, as follows:

mv today.list old.list

On the other hand, if you want to move the `today.list` file to the subdirectory named `saved`, you would use this command:

```
mv today.list saved
```

Wizard

An interesting feature of `mv` is you can use it to move entire directories, with all their subdirectories and files, to a new location. If you have a directory named `data` that contains many files and subdirectories, you can move that entire directory structure to `old_data` by using this command:

```
mv data old_data
```

Another common file operation is deleting a file. Use the `rm` command to delete a file. To delete a file named `old.list`, for example, type the following command:

```
rm old.list
```

Caution

Be careful with the `rm` command, in particular when you are logged in as `root`. Inadvertently deleting important files with `rm` is very easy. (See the "Aliases" section earlier in this chapter to learn how you can avoid accidentally clobbering files with the rm command.)

In addition to copying, renaming, and deleting files, you may want to view a file's contents. Use the `more` command to look at a text file a page at a time. To view the file `/etc/XF86Config`, for example, use this command:

```
more /etc/XF86Config
```

The `more` command pauses after each page, and you have to press the spacebar to move to the next page. Press Enter to move forward one line at a time in the file.

Another useful Linux command for file viewing is `less`. (The name is a play on the `more` command, because `less` does more than `more`.) Whereas `more` lets you move forward a page at a time, the `less` command allows you to move forward and backward through a file.

Directory manipulation

To organize files in your home directory, you have to create new directories. Use the `mkdir` command to create a directory. To create a directory named `images` in the current directory, type the following:

```
mkdir images
```

After you create the directory, you can use the `cd images` command to change to that directory.

When you no longer need a directory, use the `rmdir` command to delete it. You can delete a directory only when the directory is empty.

File finder

The `find` command locates files (and directories) that meet specified search criteria. The `find` command is one of the most useful Linux commands. The Linux version of the find command comes from GNU, and it has more extensive options than the standard UNIX version. I will show the syntax for the standard UNIX find command because that syntax works in Linux, and you can use the same format on other UNIX systems.

I have to admit that when I began using UNIX many years ago (I started with Berkeley UNIX in the early 1980s), I was confounded by the `find` command. I must have stayed with one basic syntax of `find` for a long time before graduating to more complex forms. The basic syntax that I learned first was for finding a file anywhere in the file system.

Suppose that you want to find any file or directory with a name that starts with `fvwm`. You can use `find` to perform this search, as follows:

```
find / -name "fvwm*" -print
```

This command tells `find` to start looking at the root directory (/), to look for filenames that match `fvwm*`, and to display the full pathname of any matching file.

Wizard

The `-print` option and the double quotation marks around the search string are not necessary in Linux. Therefore, you could have typed the preceding command as follows:

```
find / -name fvwm*
```

There is no harm in using the longer form, however; that's how you must use `find` in other UNIX systems. I will continue to show you `find` with the standard UNIX syntax.

You can use variations of this simple form of `find` to locate a file in any directory (as well as subdirectories contained in the directory). If you forget where in your home directory you stored all files named `awips*` (names that start with the string `awips`), you can search for the files by using the following command:

```
find ~ -name "awips*" -print
```

When you become comfortable with this syntax of `find`, you can start using other options of `find`. To find only specific types of files (such as directories), use the `-type` option. The following command displays all top-level directory names in your Linux system:

```
find / -type d -maxdepth 1 -print
```

You probably do not have to use the complex forms of `find` in a typical Linux system, but you can always look up the rest of the `find` options by using this command:

```
man find
```

Shell Scripts in Bash

The fundamental philosophy of UNIX is to give the user many small and specialized commands, along with the "plumbing" necessary to connect these commands. By plumbing, I mean the way that one command's output is used as a second command's input. Bash, the default shell in Linux, provides these plumbings in the form of I/O redirection and pipes. Bash also includes features such as the if statement, which runs commands only when a specific condition is true, and the for statement, which repeats commands a specified number of times. You can use these features of Bash to write programs called *shell scripts*.

Shell scripts are popular among system administrators. If you are a system administrator, you can build up a collection of custom shell scripts that help you automate tasks that you perform often. If the disk seems to be getting full, for example, you may want to find all files that exceed some size (say, 1MB) and that have not been accessed in the past 30 days. Additionally, you may want to send an e-mail message to all users who have large files, requesting that they try to archive and clean up those files. You can perform all these tasks with a shell script. You might start with the following find command to identify the large files:

```
find / -type f -atime +30 -size +1000k -exec ls -l {} \; > /tmp/largefiles
```

This command creates a file named /tmp/largefiles, which contains detailed information about the old files that are taking up too much space. After you get a list of the files, you can use a few other Linux commands — such as sort, cut, and sed — to prepare and send mail messages to users who have large files that they should try to clean up.

The following sections provide an overview of Bash programming.

Caution

As you try simple shell programs, don't name your sample programs test. Linux includes an important program named test (/usr/bin/test). This program is used in shell scripts to test for various conditions, such as whether a file exists and whether a file is readable. If you create a sample program named test, some scripts may end up calling your program instead of the system's test program.

A simple shell script

Earlier in this chapter, the "Shell Programs" section discussed how you can place often-used commands in a file and use the chmod command to make the file executable. Voilà — you have a shell script. Just as most Linux commands accept command-line options, a Bash script accepts command-line options. Inside the script, you can refer to the options as $1, $2, and so on. The special name $0 refers to the name of the script itself.

Consider the following Bash script:

```
#!/bin/sh
echo "This script's name is: $0"
echo Option 1: $1
echo Option 2: $2
```

The first line causes Linux to run the /bin/sh program, which subsequently processes the rest of the lines in the script. The name /bin/sh traditionally refers to the Bourne shell — the first UNIX shell. In Linux, /bin/sh is a symbolic link to /bin/bash, which is the executable program for Bash. Therefore, in Linux, Bourne shell scripts are run by Bash (which happens to be compatible with the Bourne shell).

If you save this simple script in a file named simple, and you make that file executable with the command chmod +x simple, you can run the script as follows:

```
simple
This script's name is: ./simple
Argument 1:
Argument 2:
```

The script file's name appears relative to the current directory, which is represented by a period. Because you ran the script without any arguments, the script does not display any arguments.

Now try running the script with a few arguments, as follows:

```
simple "This is one argument" second-argument third
This script's name is: ./simple
Argument 1: This is one argument
Argument 2: second-argument
```

As this example shows, the shell treats the entire string within double quotation marks as being a single argument. Otherwise, the shell uses spaces as separators between arguments on the command line.

Bash programming overview

Like any programming language, Bash includes the following features:

- Variables that store values, including special built-in variables for accessing command-line arguments passed to a shell script and other special values.
- The capability to evaluate expressions.

Learning more about shell programming

Although these sections provide an overview of shell programming, you have much more to learn about shell programming than this single chapter can teach. *UNIX SECRETS* by James Armstrong (IDG Books, 1996), is a source of information on all elements of UNIX commands, as well as shell programming.

- Control structures that allow you to loop over several shell commands or to execute some commands conditionally.

- The capability to define functions that can be called in many places within a script. Bash also includes many built-in functions that you can use in any script.

The next few sections illustrate some of Bash's programming features through simple examples. Because you are already running Bash, you can try the examples by typing them at the shell prompt in an `xterm` window.

Variables

Define variables in Bash just as you define environment variables. Thus, you might define a variable this way:

```
count=12    # note no embedded spaces allowed
```

To use a variable's value, prefix the variable's name with a dollar sign ($). $PATH, for example, is the value of the variable PATH (yes, the famous PATH environment variable). To display the value of the variable named count, you would use the following command:

```
echo $count
```

Bash has some special variables for accessing command-line arguments. In a shell script, $0 refers to the name of the shell script. The variables $1, $2, and so on refer to the command-line arguments. The variable $* stores all the command-line arguments as a single variable, and $? contains the exit status of the last command executed by the shell.

You also can prompt the user for input and use the `read` command to read the input into a variable. Following is an example:

```
echo -n "Enter value: "
read value
echo "You entered: $value"
```

Tip

The `-n` option stops the `echo` command from automatically adding a new line at the end of the string that it displays.

Control structures

In Bash scripts, the control structures — such as `if`, `case`, `for`, and `while` — depend on the exit status of a command to decide what to do next. When any command executes, it returns an *exit status*: a numeric value that indicates whether the command was successful. By convention, an exit status of zero means that the command succeeded. (Yes, you read it right: zero indicates success.) A non-zero exit status indicates that something went wrong with the command.

You might use a script that makes a backup copy of a file before opening it by using the `vi` editor in the following manner:

```
#!/bin/sh
if cp "$1" "~$1"
then
     vi "$1"
else
     echo "Failed to create backup copy"
fi
```

This script illustrates the syntax of the *if-then-else* structure and also shows how the exit status of the `cp` command is used by the `if` structure to decide the next action. If `cp` returns zero, the script invokes `vi` to edit the file; otherwise, the script displays a message and exits.

Tip

Don't forget the final `fi` that terminates the `if` structure. Forgetting `fi` is a common source of error in Bash scripts.

Bash includes the `test` command to let you evaluate any expression and use the expression's value as the exit status of the command. Suppose that you want a script that allows you to edit an existing file. Using `test`, you might write such a script as follows:

```
#!/bin/sh
if test -f "$1"
then
     vi "$1"
else
     echo "No such file"
fi
```

A shorter form of the `test` command leaves out `test` and places the command's options in brackets. Using this notation, you would write the preceding script as follows:

```
#!/bin/sh
if [ -f "$1" ]
then
     vi "$1"
else
     echo "No such file"
fi
```

Another common control structure is the `for` loop. The following script adds the numbers 1 through 10:

```
#!/bin/sh
sum=0
for i in 1 2 3 4 5 6 7 8 9 10
do
     sum=`expr $sum + $i`
done
echo "Sum = $sum"
```

This example also illustrates the use of the `expr` command to evaluate an expression.

Built-in functions in Bash

Bash has more than 50 built-in functions, including common functions such as `cd` and `pwd`, as well as many others that are not used frequently. You can use these built-in functions in any Bash script.

Although this chapter does not have enough space to cover all functions, the following listing shows all built-in Bash functions and their arguments. A comment next to each function summarizes its purpose. After looking through this information, if you want to learn more about one of these functions, you can consult the online manual for Bash by using the `man bash` command.

```
. filename [arguments]  # read and execute commands from a file
: [arguments]  # expand arguments but do not process them
[ expr ]  # evaluate expr and return zero status if expr is true
alias [name[=value] ...]  # define an alias
bg [jobspec]  # put specified job in background
bind [-m keymap] [-lvd] [-q name]  # bind a key sequence to a macro
break [n]  # exit from a for, while, or until loop
builtin shell-builtin [arguments]  # execute a shell built-in command
cd [dir]  # change current directory to dir
command [-pVv] cmd [arg ...]  # run the command cmd with arguments
continue [n]  # start the next iteration of the for, while, or until loop
declare [-frxi] [name[=value]]  # declare variables
dirs [-l] [+/-n]  #display list of currently remembered directories
echo [-neE] [arg ...]  # display the arguments on standard output
enable [-n] [-all] [name ...]  # enable or disable built-in commands
eval [arg ...]  # concatenate the arguments and execute as a command
exec [[-] command [arguments]]  # run command replacing the shell
exit [n]  # exit shell with the status code n
export [-nf] [name[=word]] ...  # export specified names to future processes
fc -s [pat=rep] [cmd]  # reexecute command after replacing pat with rep
fg [jobspec]  # put specified job in the foreground
getopts optstring name [args]  # get optional parameters (called in shell
scripts)
hash [-r] [name]  # remember full pathname of a specified command
help [pattern]  # display help about built-in commands
history [n]  # display past commands
jobs [-lnp] [ jobspec ... ]  # list active jobs
kill [-s sigspec | -sigspec] [pid | jobspec] ...  # send a specified signal to one
or more processes
let arg [arg ...]  # evaluate each argument and return 1 if last arg is 0
local [name[=value] ...]  # create local variable (used in shell functions)
logout  # exit a login shell.
popd [+/-n]  # remove entries from directory stack
pushd [dir]  # add directory to the top of the directory stack
pwd  # print the full pathname of the current working directory
read [-r] [name ...]  # read a line from standard input and parse it
readonly [-f] [name ...]  # mark the specified names as read-only
return [n]  # exit function with the return value n
set [--abefhkmnptuvxldCHP] [-o option] [arg ...]  # set various flags
shift [n]  # make the n+1 argument $1, n+2 argument $2, and so on
source filename [arguments]  # read and execute commands from a file
suspend [-f]  # stop execution until a SIGCONT signal is received
test expr  # evaluate expr and return zero if expr is true
```

```
times   # print the time spent running the shell and processes started from shell
trap [-l] [arg] [sigspec]   # execute arg when signal sigspec is received
type [-all] [-type | -path] name [name ...]   # indicate how each name is inter-
preted
typeset [-frxi] [name[=value]]   # declare variables
ulimit [-SHacdfmstpnuv [limit]]   # control resources available to shell
umask [-S] [mode]   # set file creation mask
unalias [-a] [name ...]   # remove name from alias list
unset [-fv] [name ...]   # remove definition of specified variables
wait [n]   # wait for a specified process to terminate
```

Perl as a Scripting Language

Officially, *Perl* stands for *Practical Extraction Report Language*. Perl was created by Larry Wall to extract information from text files and then use that information to prepare reports. Programs written in Perl, the language, are interpreted and executed by `perl`, the program. This book's companion CD-ROM includes the `perl` program; it should be installed on your system in the `/usr/bin` directory.

Cross Reference

Perl is available on a wide variety of computer systems because, like Linux, Perl can be distributed freely. Also, Perl is popular among many users and system administrators as a scripting language, which is why this section introduces Perl and shows its strengths. In Chapter 8, you learn about another scripting language (Tcl/Tk) that provides the capability to create graphical user interfaces for the scripts.

As you know by now, the term *script* simply is a synonym for *program*. Unlike programs written in programming languages such as C and C++, Perl programs do not have to be compiled; the `perl` program simply interprets and executes the Perl programs. The term *script* often is used for such interpreted programs written in a shell's programming language or in Perl. (Strictly speaking, `perl` does not simply interpret a Perl program; it converts the Perl program to an intermediate form before executing the program.)

Note

If you are familiar with shell programming or the C programming language, you can pick up Perl very quickly. If you have never programmed, becoming proficient in Perl may take a while. I encourage you to start with a small subset of Perl's features and ignore anything that you do not understand. Then you can slowly add Perl features to your repertoire as time goes by.

Do I have Perl?

Before you proceed with the Perl tutorial, check to see whether you have `perl` installed on your system. Type the following command:

```
which perl
```

The `which` command tells you whether it finds a specified program in the directories listed in the PATH environment variable. If `perl` is installed, you should see the following output:

```
/usr/bin/perl
```

If the `which` command complains that no such program exists in the current PATH, that message does not necessarily mean that you do not have `perl` installed; it may be that you do not have the `/usr/bin` directory in PATH. Check to ensure that `/usr/bin` is in PATH; either type **echo $PATH** or look at the message displayed by the `which` command (that message includes the directories in PATH). If `/usr/bin` is not in PATH, use the following command to redefine PATH:

```
PATH="$PATH:/usr/bin"; export PATH
```

Cross Reference

Now try the `which perl` command again. If you still get an error, you may not have installed `perl`. Log in as `root`, make sure that the companion CD-ROM is in the CD-ROM drive, and run the `setup` program. Then follow the on-screen directions, as well as the instructions in Chapter 1, to install `perl`.

If you have `perl` installed on your system, type the following command to see its version number:

```
perl -v
```

Following is typical output from that command:

```
This is perl, version 4.0 for Linux {36LA}-1j1-

$RCSfile: perl.c,v $$Revision: 4.0.1.8 $$Date: 1993/02/05 19:39:30 $
Patch level: 36

Copyright (c) 1989, 1990, 1991, Larry Wall

Perl may be copied only under the terms of either the Artistic License
or the GNU General Public License, which may be found in the Perl 4.0
source kit.
```

This output tells you that you have Perl version 4.0, patch level 36, and that Larry Wall, the originator of Perl, holds the copyright. Perl is freely distributed under the GNU General Public License, however.

The companion CD-ROM has version 5.001m of Perl. You can get the latest version of Perl via anonymous FTP (use the `ftp` program, and provide `anonymous` as the username) from one of the following sites on the Internet:

ftp.uu.net	137.39.1.2
ftp.netlabs.com	192.94.48.152
coombs.anu.edu.au	150.203.76.2 (Australia)
archive.cis.ohio-state.edu	128.146.8.52
jpl-devvax.jpl.nasa.gov	128.149.1.143
prep.ai.mit.edu	18.71.0.38
ftp.cs.ruu.nl	131.211.80.17 (Europe)

Your first Perl script

Perl has many features of C, and, as you may be aware, most books on C start with an example program that displays `Hello, World!` on your terminal. Because Perl is an interpreted language, you can accomplish this task directly from the command line. If you enter:

```
perl -e 'print "Hello, World!\n";'
```

the system responds:

```
Hello, World!
```

This command uses the `-e` option of the `perl` program to pass the Perl program as a command-line argument to the Perl interpreter. In this case, the following line constitutes the Perl program:

```
print "Hello, World!\n";
```

To convert this line to a script, all you have to do is place the line in a file and start the file with a directive to run the `perl` program (as you do in the shell scripts, in which you place a line such as `#!/bin/sh` to run the Bourne shell which will process the script).

To try a Perl script, follow these steps:

1. Use a text editor, such as `vi` or `emacs`, to save the following lines in the file named `hello`:

   ```
   #!/usr/bin/perl
   # This is a comment.
   print "Hello, World!\n";
   ```

2. Make the `hello` file executable by using the following command:

   ```
   chmod +x hello
   ```

3. Run the Perl script by typing the following at the shell prompt:

   ```
   hello
   Hello, World!
   ```

That's it! You have just written and tried your first Perl script.

Secret

Notice that the first line of a Perl script starts with `#!`, followed by the full pathname of the `perl` program. If the first line of a script starts with `#!`, the Linux kernel simply strips off the `#!`, appends the script file's name to the end, and runs the script. Thus, if the script file is named `hello` and the first line is `#!/usr/bin/perl`, Linux executes the following command:

```
/usr/bin/perl hello
```

> **More on Perl**
>
> This chapter devotes a few sections to Perl to give you an overview of Perl and show a few simple examples. However, this discussion does not do justice to Perl. If you want to use Perl as a tool, consult one of the following books on Perl:
>
> Larry Wall and Randal L. Schwartz, *Programming Perl* (O'Reilly & Associates, 1991)
>
> Randal L. Schwartz, *Learning Perl* (O'Reilly & Associates, 1993)
>
> Ellie Quigley, *PERL by Example* (Prentice Hall, 1995)
>
> The book by Perl originator Larry Wall and Randal Schwartz is the authoritative guide to Perl (although it may not be the best resource for learning Perl). The later book by Randal Schwartz focuses more on teaching Perl programming. Ellie Quigley's recent book teaches Perl with short but complete example programs.

Perl overview

Most programming languages, including Perl, have some common features:

- *Variables* to store different types of data. You can think of each variable as being a placeholder for data — kind of like a mailbox, with a name and room to store data. The content of the variable is its value.

- *Expressions* that combine variables by using *operators*. An expression might add several variables; another might extract a part of a string.

- *Statements* that perform some action, such as assigning a value to a variable or printing a string.

- *Flow-control statements* that allow statements to be executed in various orders, depending on the value of some expression. Typically, flow-control statements include for, do-while, while, and if-then-else statements.

- *Functions* (also called *subroutines* or *routines*) that allow you to group several statements and give them a name. This feature allows you to execute the same set of statements by invoking the function that represents those statements. Typically, a programming language provides some predefined functions.

The next few sections provide an overview of these major features of Perl and illustrate the features through simple examples.

Basic Perl syntax

Perl is free-form, like C; no constraints exist on exact placement of any keyword. Perl programs often are stored in files with names that end in .pl, but there is no restriction on the filenames that you can use.

As in C, each Perl statement ends with a semicolon (;). A pound sign (#) marks the start of a comment; the perl program disregards the rest of the line beginning with the pound sign.

Groups of Perl statements are enclosed in braces ({...}). This feature also is similar to C.

Variables

You don't have to declare Perl variables before using them, as you do in C. You can easily recognize a variable in a Perl script, because each variable name begins with a special character: an at symbol (@), a dollar sign ($), or a percent sign (%). This special character denotes the variable's type. The three variable types are

- *Scalar variables*, which represent the basic data types: integer, floating-point number, and string. A dollar sign ($) precedes a scalar variable. Following are some examples:

```
$maxlines = 256;
$title = "Linux Secrets";
```

- *Array variables*, which are collections of scalar variables. An array variable has an at symbol (@) as a prefix. Thus, the following are arrays:

```
@pages = (62, 26, 22, 24);
@commands = ("start", "stop", "draw", "exit");
```

- *Associative arrays*, which are collections of key-value pairs in which each key is a string and the value is any scalar variable. A percent-sign (%) prefix indicates an associative array. You can use associative arrays to associate a name with a value. You might store the amount of disk space used by each user in an associative array such as the following:

```
%disk_usage = ("root", 147178, "naba", 28547, "emily",
55, "ivy", 60);
```

Because each variable type has its own special character prefix, you can use the same name for different variable types. Thus, %disk_usage, @disk_usage, and $disk_usage can appear within the same Perl program.

Scalars

Scalar variables are the basic data type in Perl. Each scalar's name starts with a dollar sign ($). Typically, you start using a scalar with an assignment statement that initializes it. You can even use a variable without initializing it; the default value for numbers is zero, and the default value of a string is an empty string. If you want to see whether a scalar is defined, use the defined function as follows:

```
print "Name undefined!\n" if !(defined $name);
```

The expression (defined $name) is 1 if $name is defined. You can actually "undefine" a variable by using the undef function. You can undefine $name, for example, as follows:

```
undef $name;
```

Variables are evaluated according to context. Following is a script that initializes and prints a few variables:

```
#!/usr/bin/perl
$title = "Linux SECRETS";
$count1 = 450;
$count2 = 350;

$total = $count1 + $count2;

print "Title: $title -- $total pages\n";
```

When you run this Perl program, it produces the following output:

```
Title: Linux SECRETS -- 800 pages
```

As the Perl statements show, when the two numeric variables are added, their numeric values are used, but when the `$total` variable is printed, its string representation is displayed.

Another interesting part of Perl is that it evaluates all variables in a string within double quotation marks ("..."). On the other hand, if you write a string inside single quotation marks ('...'), Perl leaves that string untouched. If you were to write

```
print 'Title: $title -- $total pages\n';
```

with single quotes instead of double quotes, Perl would display

```
Title: $title -- $total pages\n
```

and not even generate a new line.

A useful Perl variable is `$_` (dollar sign followed by the underscore character). This special variable is known as the *default argument*. The Perl interpreter determines the value of `$_` depending on the context. When the Perl interpreter reads input from the standard input, `$_` holds the current input line; when the interpreter is searching, `$_` holds the default search pattern.

Arrays

An *array* is a collection of scalars. The array name starts with an at symbol (@). As in C, array subscripts start at zero. You can access the elements of an array with an index. Perl allocates space for arrays dynamically.

Consider the following simple script:

```
#!/usr/bin/perl
@commands = ("start", "stop", "draw" , "exit");

$numcmd = @commands;
print "There are $numcmd commands. The first command is: $commands[0]\n";
```

When you run the script, it produces the following output:

```
There are 4 commands. The first command is: start
```

As you can see, equating a scalar to the array sets the scalar to the number of elements in the array. The first element of the `@commands` array is referenced as `$commands[0]` because the index starts at zero. Thus, the fourth element in commands is `$commands[3]`.

Two special scalars are related to an array. The `$[` variable is the current base index, which is zero by default. The scalar `$#arrayname` (in which `arrayname` is the name of an array variable) has the last array index as the value. Thus, for the `@commands` array, `$#commands` is 3.

You can print an entire array with a simple `print` statement like this:

```
print "@commands\n";
```

When Perl executes this statement, it displays the following output:

```
start stop draw exit
```

Associative arrays

Associative-array variables, which are declared with a percent-sign (%) prefix, are unique features of Perl. Using associative arrays, you can index an array with a string such as a name. A good example of an associative array is the `%ENV` array that Perl automatically defines for you. In Perl, `%ENV` is the array of environment variables that you can access by using the environment-variable name as an index. The following Perl statement prints the current `PATH` environment variable:

```
print "PATH = $ENV{PATH}\n";
```

When Perl executes this statement, it prints the current setting of `PATH`. In contrast to regular arrays, you have to use braces to index into an associative array.

Perl has many built-in functions — such as `delete`, `each`, `keys`, and `values` — that enable you to access and manipulate associative arrays.

Predefined variables in Perl

Perl has several predefined variables that contain useful information that you may need in a Perl script. Following are a few important predefined variables:

`@ARGV` is an array of strings that contains the command-line options to the script. The first option is `$ARGV[0]`, the second one is `$ARGV[1]`, and so on.

`%ENV` is an associative array that contains the environment variables. You can access this array by using the environment-variable name as a key. Thus, `$ENV{HOME}` is the home directory, and `$ENV{PATH}` is the current search path that the shell uses to locate commands.

`$$` is the script's process ID.

`$<` is the user ID of the user who is running the script.

`$?` is the status returned by the last `system` call.

`$_` is the default argument for many functions.

`$0` is the name of the script.

Operators and expressions

Operators are used to combine and compare Perl variables. Typical mathematical operators are addition (+), subtraction (-), multiplication (*), and division (/). Perl provides nearly the same set of operators that C has. When you use operators to combine variables, you end up with *expressions*. Each expression has a value.

Following are some typical Perl expressions:

```
error < 0
$count == 10
$count + $i
$users[$i]
```

These expressions are examples of the *comparison operator* (the first two lines), the *arithmetic operator*, and the *array-index operator*.

Caution

In Perl, don't use the == operator to find out whether two strings match; the == operator works only with numbers. To test the equality of strings, Perl includes the FORTRAN-style eq operator. Use eq to see whether two strings are identical, as follows:

```
if ($input eq "stop") { exit; }
```

Other FORTRAN-style string comparison operators include ne (inequality), lt (less than), gt (greater than), le (less than or equal), and ge (greater than or equal). You also can use the cmp operator to compare two strings. The return value is –1, 0, or 1, depending on whether the first string is less than, equal to, or greater than the second one.

Perl also provides the following operators that are unique to itself. C lacks an exponentiation operator, which FORTRAN includes; Perl uses ** as the exponentiation operator. Thus, you can enter the following:

```
$x = 2;
$y = 3;
$z = $x**$y;   # z should be 8 (2 raised to the power 3)
$y **= 2; # y is now 9 (3 raised to the power 2)
```

You can initialize an array to null by using () — the *null-list operator* — as follows:

```
@commands = ();
```

The dot operator (.) allows you to concatenate two strings, as follows:

```
$part1 = "Hello, ";
$part2 = "World!";
$message = $part1.$part2;   # Now $message = "Hello, World!"
```

A curious but useful operator is the *repetition operator*, denoted by x=. You can use the x= operator to repeat a string a specified number of times. Suppose that you want to initialize a string to 65 asterisks (*). The following example shows how you can initialize the string with the x= operator:

```
$marker = "*";
$marker x= 65;   # Now $marker is a string of 65 asterisks
```

Another powerful operator in Perl is the *range operator*, which is represented by two periods (..). You can initialize an array easily by using the range operator. Following are some examples:

```
@numerals = (0..9);     # @numerals is the list 0, 1, 2, 3, 4, 5, 6, 7, 8 , 9
@alphabet = ('A'..'Z'); # @alphabet is the list of capital letters A through Z
```

Regular expressions

If you have used UNIX for a while, you probably know about the `grep` command, which allows you to search files for a pattern of strings. Following is a typical use of `grep` to locate all files that have any occurrences of the string `blaster` or `Blaster` on any line of all files with names that end in `.c`:

```
cd /usr/src/linux/drivers/block
grep "[bB]laster"  *.c
```

These commands produce this output on my system:

```
cdu31a.c:      { 0x230,      0 },     /* SoundBlaster 16 card */
sbpcd.c: *             SoundBlaster ("Pro" or "16 ASP" or compatible) cards
sbpcd.c:    0x230, 1, /* Soundblaster Pro and 16 (default) */
sbpcd.c:    0x250, 1, /* OmniCD default, Soundblaster Pro and 16 */
sbpcd.c:    0x270, 1, /* Soundblaster 16 */
sbpcd.c:    0x290, 1, /* Soundblaster 16 */
sbpcd.c:static char *str_sb = "SoundBlaster";
sbpcd.c:static char *str_sb_l = "soundblaster";
sbpcd.c: *                    sbpcd=0x230,SoundBlaster
sbpcd.c:            msg(DBG_INF,"   LILO boot: ...
sbpcd=0x230,SoundBlaster\n");
```

As you can see, `grep` found all occurrences of `blaster` and `Blaster` in the files whose names end in `.c`.

The `grep` command's `"[bB]laster"` argument is known as a *regular expression*, which is a pattern that matches a set of strings. You construct a regular expression with a small set of operators and rules that are similar to the ones for writing arithmetic expressions. A list of characters inside brackets ([...]), for example, matches any single character in the list. Thus, the regular expression `"[bB]laster"` is a set of two strings, as follows:

```
blaster    Blaster
```

Perl supports regular expressions just as the `grep` command does. Many other UNIX programs, such as the `vi` editor and `sed` (stream editor), also support regular expressions. The purpose of a regular expression is to search for a pattern of strings in a file. That's why editors support regular expressions.

Perl lets you construct complex regular expressions. The rules, however, are fairly simple. Essentially, the regular expression is a sequence of characters in which some characters have special meaning. Table 6-4 lists the basic rules of interpreting the characters.

Table 6-4   Rules for interpreting regular expression characters

Expression	Meaning
.	Matches any single character except new line
x*	Matches zero or more occurrences of the character x
x+	Matches one or more occurrences of the character x
x?	Matches zero or one occurrence of the character x
[...]	Matches any of the characters inside the brackets
x{n}	Matches exactly n occurrences of the character x
x{n,}	Matches n or more occurrences of the character x
x{,m}	Matches zero or, at most, m occurrences of the character x
x{n,m}	Matches at least n occurrences, but no more than m occurrences of the character x
$	Matches the end of a line
\0	Matches a null character
\b	Matches a backspace
\B	Matches any character that's not at the beginning or the end of a word
\b	Matches the beginning or end of a word — (when not inside brackets)
\cX	Matches Ctrl-x
\d	Matches a single digit
\D	Matches a nondigit character
\f	Matches a form feed
\n	Matches a new-line (line-feed) character
\ooo	Matches the octal value specified by the digits ooo (where each o is a digit between 0 and 7)
\r	Matches a carriage return
\S	Matches a non-white-space character
\s	Matches a white-space character (space, tab, or new line)
\t	Matches a tab
\W	Matches a nonalphanumeric character
\w	Matches an alphanumeric character
\xhh	Matches the hexadecimal value specified by the digits hh (where each h is a digit between 0 and f)
^	Matches the beginning of a line

If you want to match one of the characters $, |, *, ^, [,], \, and /, you have to place a backslash before them. Thus, you would type these characters as \$, \|, *, \^, \[, \], \\, and \/. Regular expressions often look confusing because of the preponderance of strange character sequences and the generous sprinkling of backslashes. As with anything else, however, you can start slow and use only a few of the features in the beginning.

So far, this section has summarized the syntax of regular expressions, but you have not yet seen how to use regular expressions in Perl. Typically, you place a regular expression within a pair of slashes and use the match (=~) or not-match (!~) operators to test a string. You can write a Perl script that performs the same search as the one done with grep earlier in this section. Follow these steps to complete this exercise:

1. Use an editor to type and save the following script in a file named lookup:

   ```
   #!/usr/bin/perl

   while (<STDIN>)
   {
       if ( $_ =~ /[bB]laster/ ) { print $_; }
   }
   ```

2. Make the lookup file executable by using the following command:

   ```
   chmod +x lookup
   ```

3. Try the script, using the following command:

   ```
   cat /usr/src/linux/drivers/block/sbpcd.c | lookup
   ```

   My system responds with this:

   ```
   *               SoundBlaster ("Pro" or "16 ASP" or compatible) cards
   0x230, 1, /* Soundblaster Pro and 16 (default) */
   0x250, 1, /* OmniCD default, Soundblaster Pro and 16 */
   0x270, 1, /* Soundblaster 16 */
   0x290, 1, /* Soundblaster 16 */
   static char *str_sb = "SoundBlaster";
   static char *str_sb_1 = "soundblaster";
   *               sbpcd=0x230,SoundBlaster
   msg(DBG_INF,"   LILO boot: ... sbpcd=0x230,SoundBlaster\n");
   ```

   The cat command feeds the contents of a specific file (which, as you know from the grep example, contains some lines with the regular expression) to the lookup script. The script simply applies Perl's regular expression-match operator (=~) and prints any matching line.

The $_ variable in the script needs some explanation. The <STDIN> expression gets a line from the standard input and, by default, stores that line in the $_ variable. Inside the while loop, the regular expression is matched against the $_ string. All the lookup script's work is done with this single Perl statement:

```
if ( $_ =~ /[bB]laster/ ) { print $_; }
```

This example illustrates how you might use a regular expression to search for occurrences of strings in a file.

After you use regular expressions for a while, you can better appreciate their power. The trick is to figure out exactly what regular expression performs the task that you have in mind. Following is a search that looks for all lines that begin with exactly seven spaces and end with a right parenthesis:

```
while (<STDIN>)
{
    if ( $_ =~ /\)\n/ && $_ =~ /^ {7}\S/ )  { print $_; }
}
```

Flow-control statements

So far, you have seen Perl statements that are meant to execute in a serial fashion, one after another. Perl also includes statements that let you control the flow of execution of the statements. You have already seen the `if` statement and a `while` loop. Perl includes a complete set of flow-control statements just like those in C, but with a few extra features.

Tip

In Perl, all conditional statements take the following form:

```
conditional-statement
{ Perl code to execute if conditional is true }
```

Notice that you *must* enclose within braces ({...}) the code that follows the conditional statement. The conditional statement checks the value of an expression to determine whether to execute the code within the braces. In Perl, as in C, any nonzero value is considered to be true, whereas a zero value means false.

The following sections briefly describe the syntax of the major conditional statements in Perl.

Using if and unless

The Perl `if` statement is similar to the C `if` statement. For example, an if statement might check a count to see whether the count exceeds a threshold, as follows:

```
if ( $count > 25 ) { print "Too many errors!\n"; }
```

You can add an `else` clause to the `if` statement, as follows:

```
if ($user eq "root")
{
    print "Starting simulation...\n";
}
else
{
    print "Sorry $user, you must be \"root\" to run this program.\n";
    exit;
}
```

If you know C, you can see that Perl's syntax looks quite a bit like C. Conditionals with the `if` statement can have zero or more `elsif` clauses to account for more alternatives, such as the following:

```
print "Enter version number:";     # prompt user for version number
$os_version = <STDIN>;             # read from standard input
chop $os_version;                  # get rid of newline at end line
# Check version number
if ($os_version >= 10 ) { print "No upgrade necessary\n";}
elsif ($os_version >= 6 && $os_version < 9) { print "Standard
upgrade\n";}
elsif ($os_version > 3 && $os_version < 6) { print "Reinstall\n";}
else { print "Sorry, cannot upgrade\n";}
```

Note

The `unless` statement is unique to Perl. This statement has the same form as `if`, including the use of `elsif` and `else` clauses. The difference is that `unless` executes its statement block only if the condition is false. You could, for example, use the following:

```
unless ($user eq "root")
{
    print "You must be \"root\" to run this program.\n";
    exit;
}
```

In this case, unless the string `user` is `"root"`, the script exits.

Using `while`

Use Perl's `while` statement for *looping* — repeating some processing until a condition becomes false. To read a line at a time from standard input and to process that line, you might use the following:

```
while ($in = <STDIN>)
{
# Code to process the line
    print $in;
}
```

Wizard

If you read from the standard input without any argument, Perl assigns the current line of standard input to the `$_` variable. Thus, you can write the preceding `while` loop as follows:

```
while (<STDIN>)
{
# Code to process the line
    print $_;
}
```

Perl's `while` statements are more versatile than those in C, because you can use almost anything as the condition to be tested. If you use an array as the condition, for example, the `while` loop executes until the array has no elements left, as in the following example:

```perl
# Assume @cmdarg has the current set of command arguments
while (@cmdarg)
{
    $arg = shift @cmdarg;       # extract one argument
# Code to process the current argument
    print $arg;
}
```

The `shift` function removes the first element of an array and returns that element.

You can skip to the end of a loop with the `next` keyword; the `last` keyword exits the loop. The following `while` loop adds the numbers from 1 to 10, skipping 5:

```perl
while (1)
{
    $i++;
    if($i == 5) { next;}   # Jump to the next iteration if $i is 5
    if($i > 10) { last;}   # When $i exceeds 10, end the loop
    $sum += $i;            # Add the numbers
}
# At this point $sum should be 50
```

Using `for` and `foreach`

Perl's `for` statement has a similar syntax to C's `for` statement. Use the `for` statement to execute a statement any number of times, based on the value of an expression. The syntax is as follows:

```perl
for (expr_1; expr_2; expr_3) { statement block }
```

expr_1 is evaluated one time, at the beginning of the loop, and the statement block is executed until expression expr_2 evaluates to zero. The third expression, expr_3, is evaluated after each execution of the statement block. You can omit any of the expressions, but you must include the semicolons. Also, the braces around the statement block are required. Following is an example that uses a `for` loop to add the numbers from 1 to 10:

```perl
for($i=0, $sum=0; $i <= 10; $sum += $i, $i++) {}
```

In this example, the actual work of adding the numbers is done in the third expression, and the statement controlled by the `for` loop is an empty block (`{}`).

The `foreach` statement is most appropriate for arrays. Following is the syntax:

```perl
foreach Variable (Array) { statement block }
```

The `foreach` statement assigns to `Variable` an element from the `Array` and executes the statement block. The `foreach` statement repeats this procedure until no array elements are left. The following `foreach` statement adds the numbers from 1 to 10:

```perl
foreach $i (1..10) { $sum += $i;}
```

Notice that I declare the array with the range operator (..). You also can use a list of comma-separated items as the array.

If you omit the `Variable` in a `foreach` statement, Perl implicitly uses the `$_` variable to hold the current array element. Thus, you could use the following:

```
foreach (1..10) { $sum += $_; }
```

Using `goto`

The `goto` statement transfers control to a statement label. Following is an example that prompts the user for a value and repeats the request if the value is not acceptable:

```
ReEnter:
print "Enter offset: ";
$offset = <STDIN>;
chop $offset;
unless ($offset > 0 && $offset < 512)
{
    print "Bad offset: $offset\n";
    goto ReEnter;
}
```

Access to Linux

You can execute any Linux command from Perl in several ways:

- Call the `system` function with a string that contains the Linux command that you want to execute.

- Enclose a Linux command within *backquotes* (`` ` ``), which also are known as *grave accents*. You can run a Linux command this way and capture its output.

- Call the `fork` function to copy the current script and process new commands in the child process (if a process starts another process then the new process is known as a *child process*).

- Call the `exec` function to overlay the current script with a new script or Linux command.

- Use `fork` and `exec` to provide shell-like behavior (monitor user input and process each user-entered command through a child process). This section presents a simple example of how to accomplish this task.

The simplest way to execute a Linux command in your script is to use the `system` function with the command in a string. After the `system` function returns, the exit code from the command is in the `$?` variable. You can easily write a simple Perl script that reads a string from the standard input and processes that string with the `system` function. Follow these steps:

1. Use a text editor to enter and save the following script in a file named `rcmd.pl`:

```
#!/usr/bin/perl
# Read user input and process command
```

```perl
$prompt = "Command (or \"exit\"): ";
print $prompt;

while (<STDIN>)
{
    chop;
    if ($_ eq "exit") { exit 0;}

# Execute command by calling system
    system $_;
    unless ($? == 0) {print "Error executing: $_\n";}
    print $prompt;
}
```

2. Make the `rcmd.pl` file executable, using the following command:

   ```
   chmod +x rcmd.pl
   ```

3. Run the script by typing **rcmd.pl** at the shell prompt. Following is some sample output from the `rcmd.pl` script (the output depends on what commands you enter):

   ```
   Command ("exit" to quit): ps
   PID TTY STAT  TIME COMMAND
     112 pp1 S      0:00 -bash
     195 pp1 S      0:00 perl ./rcmd.pl
     196 pp1 R      0:00 ps
   Command ("exit" to quit): exit
   ```

Another way to run UNIX commands is to use `fork` and `exec` in your Perl script. Following is an example script — `psh.pl` — that uses `fork` and `exec` to execute commands entered by the user:

```perl
#!/usr/bin/perl

# This is a simple script that uses "fork" and "exec" to
# runs a command entered by the user

$prompt = "Command (\"exit\" to quit): ";
print $prompt;

while (<STDIN>)
{
    chop;    # remove trailing newline
    if($_ eq "exit") { exit 0;}

    $status = fork;
    if($status)
    {
# In parent... wait for child process to finish...
        wait;
        print $prompt;
        next;
    }
    else
    {
        exec $_;
    }
}
```

The following example shows how the `psh.pl` script executes the `ps` command:

```
Command ("exit" to quit): ps
  PID TTY STAT   TIME COMMAND
  508 pp1 S      0:00 -bash
  527 pp2 S      0:02 -bash
 1514 pp2 S      0:00 perl ./psh.pl
 1515 pp2 R      0:00 ps
Command ("exit" to quit): exit
```

UNIX shells such as Bash use the `fork` and `exec` combination to run commands.

File access

You may have noticed the `<STDIN>` expression in various examples in this chapter. That's Perl's way of reading from a file. In Perl, a file is identified by a *file handle*, which is just another name for an identifier. Usually, file handles are in uppercase characters. `STDIN` happens to be a predefined file handle that denotes the standard input — by default, the keyboard. `STDOUT` and `STDERR` are the other two predefined file handles. `STDOUT` is used for printing to the terminal, and `STDERR` is used for printing error messages.

To read from a file, you write the file handle inside angle brackets (`<>`). Thus, `<STDIN>` reads a line from the standard input.

You can open other files by using the `open` function. The following example shows you how to open the `/etc/passwd` file for reading and to display the lines in that file:

```
open (PWDFILE, "/etc/passwd");       # PWDFILE is the file handle
while (<PWDFILE>) { print $_;}       # By default, input line is in $_
close PWDFILE;                        # Close the file
```

By default, the `open` function opens a file for reading. You can add special characters at the beginning of the filename to indicate other types of access. A `>` prefix opens the file for writing, whereas a `>>` prefix opens a file for appending. Following is a short script that reads the `/etc/passwd` file and creates a new file, named `output`, with a list of all users without any shell (the password entries for these users end with a `:` at the end of the line):

```
#!/usr/bin/perl
# Read /etc/passwd and create list of users without any shell

open (PWDFILE, "/etc/passwd");
open (RESULT, ">output");                    # open file for writing

while (<PWDFILE>)
{
    if ($_ =~ /:\n/) {print RESULT $_;}
}

close PWDFILE;
close RESULT;
```

After you execute this script, you should find a file named output in the current directory. Following is what the output file contains when this script is run on my Linux system:

```
bin:*:1:1:bin:/bin:
daemon:*:2:2:daemon:/sbin:
adm:*:3:4:adm:/var/adm:
lp:*:4:7:lp:/var/spool/lpd:
mail:*:8:12:mail:/var/spool/mail:
news:*:9:13:news:/usr/lib/news:
uucp:*:10:14:uucp:/var/spool/uucppublic:
games:*:12:100:games:/usr/games:
man:*:13:15:man:/usr/man:
nobody:*:-1:100:nobody:/dev/null:
```

One interesting filename prefix is the pipe character — the vertical bar (|). If you call open with a filename that begins with |, the rest of the filename is treated as a command. The Perl interpreter executes the command, and you can use print calls to send input to this command. The following Perl script sends a mail message to a list of users:

```
#!/usr/bin/perl
# Send mail to a list of users

foreach ("root", "naba")
{
    open (MAILPIPE, "| mail -s Greetings $_");
    print MAILPIPE "Remember to send in your weekly report today!\n";
    close MAILPIPE;
}
```

If a filename ends with a pipe character (|), that filename is executed as a command, and you can read that command's output with the angle brackets, as shown in the following example:

```
open (PSPIPE, "ps -ax |");
while (<PSPIPE>)
{
# Process the output of the ps command -- this example simply echoes each line
    print $_;
}
```

Subroutines

Although Perl includes a large assortment of built-in functions, you can add your own code modules, in the form of subroutines. In fact, the Perl distribution comes with a large set of subroutines. Following is a simple script that illustrates the syntax of subroutines in Perl:

```
#!/usr/bin/perl
sub hello
{
# Make local copies of the arguments from the @_ array
    local ($first,$last) = @_;
```

```
    print "Hello, $first $last\n";
}

$a = Jane;
$b = Doe;

&hello($a, $b);      # Call the subroutine
```

When you run this script, it displays the following output:

```
Hello, Jane Doe
```

Following are some points to note about subroutines:

- The subroutine receives its arguments in the array @_ (the at symbol, followed by an underscore character).
- Variables used in subroutines are global by default. Use the `local` function to create a local set of variables.
- Call a subroutine by placing an ampersand (&) before its name. Thus, subroutine `hello` is called by &hello.

If you want, you can put a subroutine in its own file. The `hello` subroutine, for example, can be in a file named `hello.pl`. When you place a subroutine in a file, remember to add a return value at the end of the file; just type **1;** at the end to return 1. Thus, the `hello.pl` file would be as follows:

```
sub hello
{
# Make local copies of the arguments from the @_ array
    local ($first,$last) = @_;

    print "Hello, $first $last\n";
}
1;       # return value
```

Then you have to write the script that uses the `hello` subroutine, as follows:

```
#!/usr/bin/perl
require 'hello.pl';   # include file with subroutine definition

$a = Jane;
$b = Doe;

&hello($a, $b);      # Call the subroutine
```

This script uses the `require` function to include the `hello.pl` file that actually contains the definition of the `hello` subroutine.

Built-in functions in Perl

Perl has more than 160 built-in functions, including functions that are similar to the ones in the C Run-Time Library as well as functions that access the operating system. You really need to go through the list of functions to see the breadth of capabilities available in Perl. Although this chapter does not have enough space to cover all functions, the listing that follows shows all Perl functions and their arguments. A comment next to each function summarizes its purpose. After looking through this information, if you want to learn more about one of these functions, you can consult the online manual for Perl by using the man perl command.

```
accept(NEWSOCKET,GENERICSOCKET)    # similar to UNIX accept
alarm(SECONDS)  # send SIGALARM signal
atan2(Y,X)    # arc tangent of Y/X
bind(SOCKET,NAME)  # similar to UNIX bind
binmode(FILEHANDLE)  # set file reading mode to binary
caller(EXPR)   # return context of current subroutine call
chdir(EXPR)   # change directory to directory specified by EXPR
chmod(LIST)   # change file permissions
chop(VARIABLE)   # chop off last character
chown(LIST)  # change file ownership
chroot(FILENAME)  # change root directory
close(FILEHANDLE)  # close specified file
closedir(DIRHANDLE)  # close directory structure opened by opendir
connect(SOCKET,NAME)   # similar to UNIX connect call
cos(EXPR)  # return cosine of angle
crypt(PLAINTEXT,SALT)    # encrypt text
dbmclose(ASSOC_ARRAY)   # close a database file
dbmopen(ASSOC,DBNAME,MODE)   # open a database file
defined(EXPR)   # return true if a variable is defined
delete $ASSOC{KEY}  # delete a value from an associative array
die(LIST)   # exit Perl program
do SUBROUTINE (LIST)   # call subroutine
each(ASSOC_ARRAY)   # return next key-value pair of associative array
eof(FILEHANDLE)  # return true if end-of-file is reached
eval(EXPR)  # evaluate specified expression
exec(LIST)  # execute system command
exit(EXPR)  # exit Perl program
exp(EXPR)   # return e to the power EXPR
fcntl(FILEHANDLE,FUNCTION,SCALAR)   # change properties of open file
fileno(FILEHANDLE)  # return file descriptor for a file handle
flock(FILEHANDLE,OPERATION)   # lock file
fork   # create a new child process
getc(FILEHANDLE)   # read next character from file
getgrgid(GID)  # similar to the UNIX getgrgid function
getgrnam(NAME)  # similar to the UNIX getgrnam function
gethostbyaddr(ADDR,ADDRTYPE)   # similar to UNIX gethostbyaddr function
gethostbyname(NAME)    # similar to UNIX gethostbyname function
getnetbyaddr(ADDR,ADDRTYPE)  # return network name for a network address
getnetbyname(NAME)  # return network address for a network name
getpeername(SOCKET)   # return name of other end of a network connection
getpgrp(PID)  # similar to UNIX getgrp function
getppid   # return process ID of parent process
getpriority(WHICH,WHO)  # return current priority
getprotobyname(NAME)   # return protocol number for a given name
getprotobynumber(NUMBER)   # return protocol name for a given number
getpwnam(NAME)   # return /etc/passwd entry for username
getpwuid(UID)   # return /etc/passwd entry for a given user ID
getservbyname(NAME,PROTO)   # return /etc/services entry for a given port name
getservbyport(PORT,PROTO)   # return /etc/services entry for a port number
getsockname(SOCKET)  # return socket address for a network connection
getsockopt(SOCKET,LEVEL,OPTNAME)   # return options associated with a socket
```

```
gmtime(EXPR)   # convert time to Greenwich Mean Time (GMT)
grep(EXPR,LIST)   # search LIST for occurrences of expression
hex(EXPR)   # return decimal value of hexadecimal EXPR
index(STR,SUBSTR)   # return position of first occurrence of a string
int(EXPR)   # return integer part of expression
ioctl(FILEHANDLE,FUNCTION,SCALAR)   # perform ioctl operation on file
join(EXPR,LIST)   # return single string by joining list elements
keys(ASSOC_ARRAY)   # return array of keys for an associative array
kill(LIST)   # terminate specified processes
length(EXPR)   # return length in number of characters
link(OLDFILE,NEWFILE)   # create NEWFILE as link for OLDFILE
listen(SOCKET,QUEUESIZE)   # wait for connections on a socket
local(LIST)   # make local list of variables
localtime(EXPR)   # convert binary time to local time
log(EXPR)   # return logarithm to base e
lstat(FILEHANDLE)   # return information about file
m/PATTERN/gio or /PATTERN/gio   # search a string for PATTERN
mkdir(FILENAME,MODE)   # create a new directory
msgctl(ID,CMD,ARG)   # perform operations on message queue
msgget(KEY,FLAGS)   # return message queue ID
msgrcv(ID,VAR,SIZE,TYPE,FLAGS)   # receive message from message queue
msgsnd(ID,MSG,FLAGS)   # send message to message queue
oct(EXPR)   # return decimal value for octal expression
open(FILEHANDLE,EXPR)   # open a file
opendir(DIRHANDLE,EXPR)   # open a directory structure for information
ord(EXPR)   # return ASCII code of first character in EXPR
pack(TEMPLATE,LIST)   # pack a list into a binary structure
pipe(READHANDLE,WRITEHANDLE)   # open a pipe for reading and writing
pop(ARRAY)   # remove and return last element of an array
print(FILEHANDLE LIST)   # print a string to a file
printf(FILEHANDLE LIST)   # print formatted string like C's printf
push(ARRAY,LIST)   # append values in LIST to end of ARRAY
rand(EXPR)   # return random value between 0 and EXPR
read(FILEHANDLE,SCALAR,LENGTH)   # read specified number of bytes from file
readdir(DIRHANDLE)   # read next entry in directory entry structure
readlink(EXPR)   # return value of a symbolic link
recv(SOCKET,SCALAR,LEN,FLAGS)   # receive message fron socket
rename(OLDNAME,NEWNAME)   # rename a file
require(EXPR)   # include file specified by EXPR
reset(EXPR)   # clear variables and arrays that start with specified names
reverse(LIST)   # reverse order of elements in LIST
rewinddir(DIRHANDLE)   # set position to beginning of directory structure
rindex(STR,SUBSTR)   # return last position of substring in string
rmdir(FILENAME)   # remove a directory
scalar(EXPR)   # evaluate expression as a scalar
seek(FILEHANDLE,POSITION,WHENCE)   # move to new location in file
seekdir(DIRHANDLE,POS)   # change position in directory structure
select(FILEHANDLE)   # set default file for reading and writing
select(RBITS,WBITS,EBITS,TIMEOUT)   # examine if file is ready for input or output
semctl(ID,SEMNUM,CMD,ARG)   # perform control operations on semaphore
semget(KEY,NSEMS,SIZE,FLAGS)   # return semaphore ID associated with KEY
semop(KEY,OPSTRING)   # perform specified operation on semaphore
send(SOCKET,MSG,FLAGS)   # send message to socket
```

```
setpgrp(PID,PGRP)  # set current process group
setpriority(WHICH,WHO,PRIORITY)  # set priority for a process
setsockopt(SOCKET,LEVEL,OPTNAME,OPTVAL)  # set options for a socket
shift(ARRAY)  # remove first value off the array and return it
shmctl(ID,CMD,ARG)  # perform control operations on shared memory
shmget(KEY,SIZE,FLAGS)  # return ID of shared memory segment
shmread(ID,VAR,POS,SIZE)  # read from shared memory
shmwrite(ID,STRING,POS,SIZE)  # write to shared memory
shutdown(SOCKET,HOW)  # shut down a socket connection to another process
sin(EXPR)  # return sine of angle EXPR (in radians)
sleep(EXPR)  # sleep for EXPR seconds
socket(SOCKET,DOMAIN,TYPE,PROTOCOL)  # open a socket of specified kind
socketpair(SOCKET1,SOCKET2,DOMAIN,TYPE,PROTOCOL)  # create pair of sockets
sort(LIST)  # sort list and return sorted list in an array
splice(ARRAY,OFFSET,LENGTH,LIST)  # replace some ARRAY elements with LIST
split(/PATTERN/,EXPR,LIMIT)  # split EXPR into array of strings
sprintf(FORMAT,LIST)  # format a string just like sprintf in C run-time library
sqrt(EXPR)  # return square root of EXPR
srand(EXPR)  # set seed for random number generation
stat(EXPR)  # return file statistics for file named EXPR
stat(FILEHANDLE)  # return file statistics for file specified by file handle
study(SCALAR)  # examine SCALAR in anticipation of doing pattern matches on SCALAR
substr(EXPR,OFFSET,LEN)  # return substring from the string EXPR
symlink(OLDFILE,NEWFILE)  # create the symbolic link NEWFILE to OLDFILE
syscall(LIST)  # make a system call specified by first element in LIST
sysread(FILEHANDLE,SCALAR,LENGTH,OFFSET)  # read from FILEHANDLE into SCALAR
system(LIST)  # execute the shell command in LIST
syswrite(FILEHANDLE,SCALAR,LENGTH,OFFSET)  # write from SCALAR to FILEHANDLE
tell(FILEHANDLE)  # return current file position in bytes from beginning of file
telldir(DIRHANDLE)  # return current position in the directory structure
time  # return number of seconds since 00:00:00 GMT 1/1/1970
times  # return time in seconds for this process
tr/SEARCHLIST/REPLACE_LIST/cds  # translate search list into replacement list
truncate(FILEHANDLE,LENGTH)  # truncate the file FILEHANDLE to a specified LENGTH
umask(EXPR)  # set the file creation mask
undef(EXPR)  # undefine a EXPR
unlink(LIST)  # delete the files specified by LIST
unpack(TEMPLATE,EXPR)  # unpack a string into an array and return the array
unshift(ARRAY,LIST)  # prepend LIST to beginning of ARRAY
utime(LIST)  # change access and modification times of files specified by LIST
values(ASSOC_ARRAY)  # return array containing all values from associative array
vec(EXPR,OFFSET,BITS)  # return element from the string EXPR (treated as vector)
wait  # wait for the child process to terminate
waitpid(PID,FLAGS)  # wait for a specified child process to terminate
wantarray  # return true if current context requires an array
warn(LIST)  # send warning message to STDERR
write(FILEHANDLE)  # write a formatted record to the file
```

Summary

Linux still is UNIX, and you have to learn to use a shell — a command interpreter — to perform many common tasks. Even when you use a graphical interface, you usually have to open an xterm terminal window and type commands at the shell prompt. This chapter focuses on Bash — the Bourne Again shell — as well as the scripting language Perl. By reading this chapter, you learn the following:

- Even when you stay in the graphical environment of the X Window System, you have to type Linux commands in an `xterm` window to perform many routine tasks.
- A shell is a program that runs commands for you. Bash is the default shell in Linux. Bash is compatible with the Bourne shell that comes with all other UNIX systems.
- The Linux directory structure is logically organized as a single tree, regardless of the physical location of subdirectories. Linux includes many commands for navigating directories and manipulating files.
- The `find` command provides a powerful way to locate all files that meet specific search criteria.
- A shell script is nothing more than a sequence of Linux commands in a file. Typically, you have to place a special line at the beginning of the script file and make it executable. Then you can run the script by typing its name at the shell prompt.
- Perl is a popular scripting language that comes on this book's companion CD-ROM. You can use Perl to write powerful scripts on your Linux system.
- Perl contains features comparable to those of other programming languages, such as C. A powerful feature of Perl is its capability to use regular expressions and to search files for occurrences of a search pattern.

Chapter 7

Secrets of DOS under Linux

In This Chapter
- Accessing a DOS partition from Linux
- Using the `mtools` utility programs to access and use DOS floppy disks
- Installing and exploring the capabilities of the DOSEMU DOS emulator

Typically, you install Linux on a PC that previously had DOS and Microsoft Windows installed on it. If you happen to work in DOS and Windows as well as in Linux, you probably want to access the DOS files from Linux. This chapter shows you how to mount and access MS-DOS disks, including floppy disks.

You also learn about a package called `mtools`, which allows you to access and use (copy, delete, and format) MS-DOS files (typically, on a floppy disk) in Linux.

Mounting a DOS File System

If you have MS-DOS and Microsoft Windows installed on your hard disk, you probably already have the DOS partition mounted under Linux. During installation (see Chapter 1), the setup program asks whether you want to access any DOS hard disk partition under Linux. The setup program finds these DOS partitions (and OS/2 partitions as well) by checking the hard disk's partition table and looking for any DOS partitions.

If you tell the setup program that you want to access the DOS partitions, the setup program asks you where you want to mount each DOS partition. (Mounting makes the DOS directory hierarchy appear as part of the Linux file system.) The default choice is to mount the first DOS partition as `/dosc`, the second one as `/dosd`, and so on. If you accept these defaults, the setup program performs the necessary steps to ensure that the DOS partitions are mounted automatically whenever you boot Linux.

Part II: Running Linux

Wizard

To see whether you already have your DOS hard disk partition mounted automatically, follow these steps (you do not have to be the `root` user to do this):

1. Use the `grep` command to look for the string `msdos` in the file `/etc/fstab`:

   ```
   grep msdos /etc/fstab
   /dev/hda1   /dosc   msdos   defaults   1   1
   ```

   I explain the file `/etc/fstab` in the "The `/etc/fstab` file" section of this chapter.

2. If the output shows one or more lines that contain `msdos`, your Linux system already mounts DOS hard disk partitions automatically. In this example, the output shows a matching line whose first field is the partition name `/dev/hda1` (first partition on the first IDE disk); the second field, `/dosc`, shows where that partition is mounted.

3. If the `grep` command does not show any lines that contain the string `msdos` in `/etc/fstab`, your system does not mount any DOS hard disk partitions automatically. An explanation, of course, may be that your hard disk does not have any DOS partitions.

Tip

Another quick way to find out about the mounted devices is to type **mount** (without any arguments) at the shell prompt. Following is the output of the `mount` command on my system:

```
/dev/hda3 on / type ext2 (rw)
/dev/sda2 on /usr type ext2 (rw)
/dev/hda1 on /dosc type msdos (rw)   (MS-DOS partition mounted on /dosc)
none on /proc type proc (rw)
/dev/hdc on /cdrom type iso9660 (ro)
/dev/sda1 on /dosd type msdos (rw)   (MS-DOS partition mounted on /dosd)
```

If you see any `msdos` in the output, those lines indicate MS-DOS file systems mounted on Linux. In this case, two MS-DOS partitions are mounted on the Linux directories `/dosc` and `/dosd`.

The following sections explain how the DOS partitions are mounted automatically. Even if you don't have any DOS partitions on your hard disk, you may want to learn how to access a DOS file system from Linux because you someday may have to access a DOS floppy disk under Linux. Understanding the concept of mounting is the key to using a DOS file system under Linux.

The `mount` command

Cross Reference

As Chapter 6 explains, Linux has a single file system that starts at the root directory, denoted by a single slash (`/`). Even if you have a separate hard disk (or multiple hard disk partitions on a single disk), the contents of those hard disks appear logically somewhere in the Linux file system. *Mounting* is the operation that you have to perform to cause a physical storage device (be it a hard disk partition or a CD-ROM) to appear as part of the Linux file system.

Chapter 7: Secrets of DOS under Linux   **233**

Many Linux systems have a small disk partition mounted on the root directory (/) and a larger partition mounted on the /usr directory. A larger partition is used for /usr because many software packages, including the X Window System, are installed under /usr.

You can use the mount command to manually mount a device on the Linux file system at a specified directory. That directory is referred to as the *mount point*. You can use any empty directory as the mount point. Like any UNIX command, mount has quite a few options. At the same time, you can get by with just a few options.

Note

Because mounting makes a physical device part of the Linux file system, only the root user is allowed to run the mount command. If you try to mount a device when you are not logged in as root, you get the following message:

```
mount: only root can do that
```

That message should tell you that you have to log in as root first.

Wizard

If you are not already logged in as root, use the su command to become root. When you type **su** without any argument, the shell assumes that you want to become root and prompts you for the root password, as follows:

```
bash$ su        (Become the root user)
Password:       (Enter root password)
bash#           (Now you are root)
```

After you enter the root password, the prompt changes to indicate that you are root.

As root, suppose that you want to mount the CD-ROM device (the name is /dev/cdrom) on the mount point /cdrom (which should already exist on your system). To do so, type the following command:

```
mount /dev/cdrom /cdrom
```

The mount command may report an error if the CD-ROM device is mounted already. Otherwise, the mount operation succeeds, and you can access the CD-ROM's contents through the /cdrom directory.

To mount a DOS partition, you use a similar format for the mount command, but you also should specify the type of file system on the DOS partition. If your DOS partition happens to be the first partition on your IDE (Integrated Drive Electronics) drive, and you want to mount it on /dosc, use the following mount command:

```
mount -t msdos /dev/hda1 /dosc
```

The -t msdos part of the mount command specifies that the device you are mounting — /dev/hda1 — has an MS-DOS file system. Linux has built-in support for MS-DOS files. Figure 7-1 illustrates the effect of this mount command.

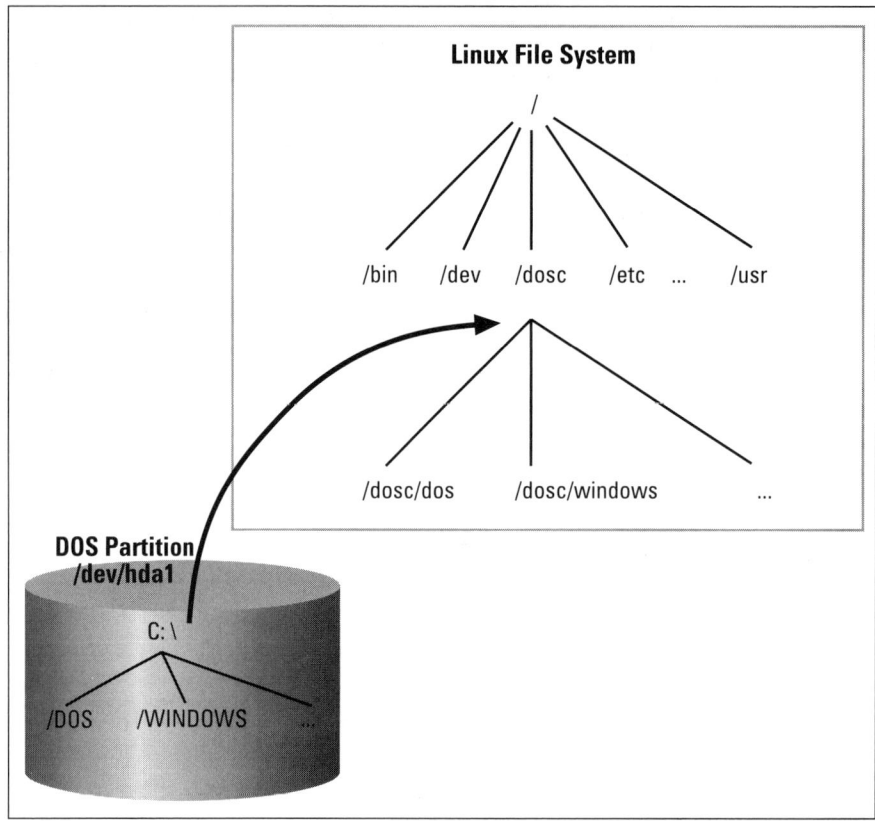

Figure 7-1: Mounting a DOS partition on the /dosc directory.

Figure 7-1 also shows how directories in your DOS partition are mapped to the Linux file system. What used to be the C:\DOS directory under DOS becomes /dosc/dos under Linux. Similarly, C:\WINDOWS now is /dosc/windows. You probably can see the pattern now. To convert a DOS filename to Linux (for this specific case when you mount the DOS partition on /dosc), do the following things:

- Change the DOS names to lowercase.
- Change C:\ to /dosc/.
- Change all backslashes (\) to slashes (/).

Mount DOS floppy disks

Just as you can mount a DOS hard disk partition under Linux, you can mount a DOS floppy disk. You have to log in as root, and you need to know the device name for the floppy drive. By default, Linux defines two generic floppy device names:

- `/dev/fd0`, which is the A drive (the first floppy drive)
- `/dev/fd1`, which is the B drive (the second floppy drive, if you have one)

As for the mount point, an existing directory named `/mnt` is specifically meant for this type of temporary mount operation. Thus, you can mount the DOS floppy disk on the `/mnt` directory with the following command:

```
mount -t msdos /dev/fd0 /mnt
```

After the floppy is mounted, you can copy files to and from the floppy by using Linux's copy command (**cp**). To copy the file `xtmenu1.pcx` from the current directory to the floppy, type the following:

```
cp xtmenu1.pcx /mnt
```

Similarly, to see the contents of the floppy disk, type the following:

```
ls /mnt
```

When you want to remove the floppy disk from the drive, you should first dismount the floppy drive. This action removes the association between the floppy disk's file system and the mount point on the Linux file system. Use the `umount` command to dismount a device, as follows:

```
umount /dev/fd0
```

The `/etc/fstab` file

Cross
Reference

In Linux, the `/etc` directory contains many text files that have configuration information for the system. As you learned in Chapter 5, for example, the `/etc/inittab` files contains information about what processes to start after Linux boots. The `/etc/fstab` file is one such configuration file — a text file containing information that the `mount` and `umount` commands use. Each line in the `/etc/fstab` file provides information about a device to be mounted on a directory in the Linux file system.

Following is the `/etc/fstab` file from a typical Linux system:

```
/dev/hda2     swap      swap      defaults   1  1
/dev/hda3     /         ext2      defaults   1  1
/dev/sda2     /usr      ext2      defaults   1  1
/dev/hda1     /dosc     msdos     defaults   1  1
none          /proc     proc      defaults   1  1
```

The first field on each line shows a device name, such as the hard disk partition. The second field is the mount point, and the third field indicates the type of file system on the device. You can ignore the last three fields for now.

The sample `/etc/fstab` file shows that the `/dev/hda2` device (the second partition on the first IDE hard disk) is used as a swap device for virtual memory, which is why both the mount point and the file-system type are set to `swap`. The last line shows another special file system: the `proc` file system, which Linux uses to store system information. The line on which `msdos` is the file-system type specifies that the DOS partition `/dev/hda1` should be mounted on `/dosc`.

Secret

The contents of the /etc/fstab file are used to mount various file systems in Linux automatically. During Linux startup, the init process executes a shell script that invokes mount with the -a option. This script causes mount to read the /etc/fstab file and mount all file systems listed in that file. Therefore, to mount a DOS partition automatically, you should add to the /etc/fstab file a line that contains the necessary information for mounting that partition. If you want to mount the DOS file system in the first partition of the first Small Computer System Interface (SCSI) disk on /dosd, for example, add the following line to /etc/fstab:

```
/dev/sda1    /dosd    msdos    defaults   1   1
```

Using mtools

The preceding sections show you one way to access the MS-DOS file system: mount the DOS hard disk or floppy disk by using the mount command; then use regular Linux commands, such as ls and cp. This approach of mounting a DOS file system is fine for hard disks. Linux can mount the DOS partition automatically at startup, and you can access the DOS directories on the hard disk whenever you need to.

If you want to get a quick directory listing of a DOS floppy disk, however, mounting can be tedious. First, you have to mount the floppy drive; then you have to use the ls command; finally, you must use the umount command before taking the floppy disk out of the drive.

This is where the mtools package comes to the rescue. The mtools package implements most common DOS commands; the commands have the same names as in DOS, except that you add an m prefix to each command. Thus, the command for getting a directory listing is mdir, and mcopy copies files. The best part of mtools is you do not have to mount the floppy disk to use the mtools commands.

Wizard

Because the mtools commands write to and read from the physical device (floppy disk), you have to log in as root to perform these commands. If you want any user to use the mtools commands, you have to alter the permission settings for the floppy drive devices. Use the following command to allow anyone to read from and write to the first floppy drive:

```
chmod o+rw /dev/fd0
```

Do I have mtools?

The mtools package comes with the Slackware Linux distribution on this book's companion CD-ROM. When you installed Linux, mtools was installed automatically as part of the base Linux. The mtools executable files are in the /usr/bin directory. To see whether you have mtools installed, type **ls /usr/bin/mdir** at the shell prompt. If the ls command shows that this file exists, you should have mtools available on your system.

To try `mtools`, follow these steps:

1. Log in as `root`, or type **su** and then enter the root password.
2. Place an MS-DOS floppy disk in your system's A drive.
3. Type **mdir**. You should see the directory of the floppy disk (in the standard DOS directory listing format).

The `/etc/mtools` file

The `mtools` package should work with the default setup, but if you get any errors, you should check the `/etc/mtools` file. That file contains the definitions of the drives (such as A and B) that the `mtools` utilities see. Following are the first few lines from the default `/etc/mtools` file:

```
# Parameters for the /usr/bin/mtools utilities
#
#
# Uncomment these if your boot drive is 1.44 MB, and your second drive
# is 1.2 MB:
#
A /dev/fd0 12 80 2 18 # 1.44 MB first floppy
A /dev/fd0 12 80 2 9 # low density
A /dev/fd0 12 0 0 0 # Generic autodetect
B /dev/fd1 12 80 2 15 # 1.2 MB second floppy
B /dev/fd1 12 40 2 9 # low density
B /dev/fd1 12 0 0 0 # Generic autodetect
#
# Uncomment these if your boot drive is 1.2 MB, and your second drive
# is 1.44 MB:
#
#A /dev/fd0 12 80 2 15 # 1.2 MB first floppy
#A /dev/fd0 12 40 2 9 # low density
#A /dev/fd0 12 0 0 0 # Generic autodetect
#B /dev/fd1 12 80 2 18 # 1.44 MB second floppy
#B /dev/fd1 12 80 2 9 # low density
#B /dev/fd1 12 0 0 0 # Generic autodetect
```

The pound sign (#) starts comments. Each line defines a drive letter and the associated Linux device name. The last three numbers on the line specify the number of tracks, the number of heads, and the number of sectors, in that order. If you want the `mtools` utilities to detect a floppy disk's characteristics automatically, you can use zeros in these fields.

If your system's A drive is a high-density 3.5-inch drive, you do not have to change anything in the default `/etc/mtools` file. Otherwise, comment the first few lines and uncomment the others (as instructed by the comment in the `/etc/mtools` file). To comment a line in the `/etc/mtools` file, simply place a pound sign (#) at the beginning of the line. To uncomment a line, remove the # character at the beginning of the line.

Although you can define C and D drives for your DOS hard disk partitions, you may want to access those partitions by mounting them with the Linux mount command. Because the hard disk partitions can be mounted automatically at startup, accessing them through the Linux commands should be just as easy.

The mtools commands

As explained earlier, the mtools package is a collection of utilities. So far, you have seen the command mdir — the mtools counterpart of the DIR command in DOS.

Tip

If you know the MS-DOS commands, using the mtools commands is very easy. Type the DOS command in lowercase, and remember to add m in front of each command. Because the Linux commands and filenames are case-sensitive, you must use all lowercase letters when you type mtools commands.

Table 7-1 summarizes the 13 commands available in mtools.

Table 7-1	The mtools commands	
Utility	MS-DOS Command	Action
mattrib	ATTRIB	Changes MS-DOS file-attribute flags
mcd	CD	Changes an MS-DOS directory
mcopy	COPY	Copies files between MS-DOS and Linux
mdel	DEL or ERASE	Deletes an MS-DOS file
mdir	DIR	Displays an MS-DOS directory listing
mformat	FORMAT	Places an MS-DOS file system on a low-level formatted floppy disk (use fdformat to low-level-format a floppy in Linux)
mlabel	LABEL	Initializes an MS-DOS volume label
mmd	MD or MKDIR	Creates an MS-DOS directory
mrd	RD or RMDIR	Deletes an MS-DOS directory
mread	COPY	Copies an MS-DOS file to a Linux file
mren	REN or RENAME	Renames an existing MS-DOS file
mtype	TYPE	Displays the contents of an MS-DOS file
mwrite	COPY	Copies a Linux file to MS-DOS

You can use the `mtools` commands just as you would use the corresponding real DOS command. For example, the `mdir` command works like the DIR command in DOS. The same goes for all the other `mtools` commands shown in Table 7-1. With regard to wildcard characters (such as *), you have to remember that the Linux shell is the first program to see your command. Therefore, if you do not want the shell to expand the wildcard character, you should use quotation marks around filenames that contain any wildcard characters. To copy all *.txt files from the A drive to your Linux directory, for example, use this command:

```
mcopy "a:*.txt"
```

If you leave off the quotation marks, the shell tries to expand the string `a:*.txt` with filenames from the current Linux directory and then tries to copy those files (if any) from the DOS floppy disk.

On the other hand, when you want to copy files from the Linux directory to the DOS floppy disk, you *do* want the shell to expand any wildcard characters. To copy all *.pcx files from the current Linux directory to the DOS floppy disk, for example, invoke `mcopy` this way:

```
mcopy *.pcx a:
```

The `mtools` utilities let you use the backslash character (\) as the directory separator, just as you would under DOS. Whenever you have a filename that contains the backslash character, you must enclose the string in double quotation marks. The following command copies a file from a subdirectory on the A drive to the current Linux directory:

```
mcopy "a:\test\sample.dat"
```

How to format a DOS floppy

Suppose that you run Linux on your home PC, and you no longer have MS-DOS installed on your system, but you have to copy some files on an MS-DOS floppy disk and take the disk to your office. If you already have a formatted MS-DOS floppy, you can simply mount that floppy and copy the file to the floppy by using the Linux `cp` command. What if you do not have any formatted DOS floppy? The `mtools` package again comes to the rescue.

Wizard

The `mtools` package provides the `mformat` utility, which can format a floppy disk for use under MS-DOS. Unlike the DOS `format` command that formats a floppy in a single step, the `mformat` command requires you to follow a two-step process to prepare the floppy disk, as shown in the following list:

1. Use the `fdformat` command (a Linux command) to low-level-format a floppy disk. The `fdformat` command expects the floppy device name to be the argument; the device name includes all the parameters necessary for formatting the floppy disk.

Figure 7-2 illustrates the device-naming convention for the floppy drive device. Based on the information shown in Figure 7-2, to format a 3.5-inch high-density floppy disk in your system's A drive, you use the following command:

```
fdformat /dev/fd0H1440
Double-sided, 80 tracks, 18 sec/track. Total capacity 1440 kB.
Formatting ... done
Verifying ... done
```

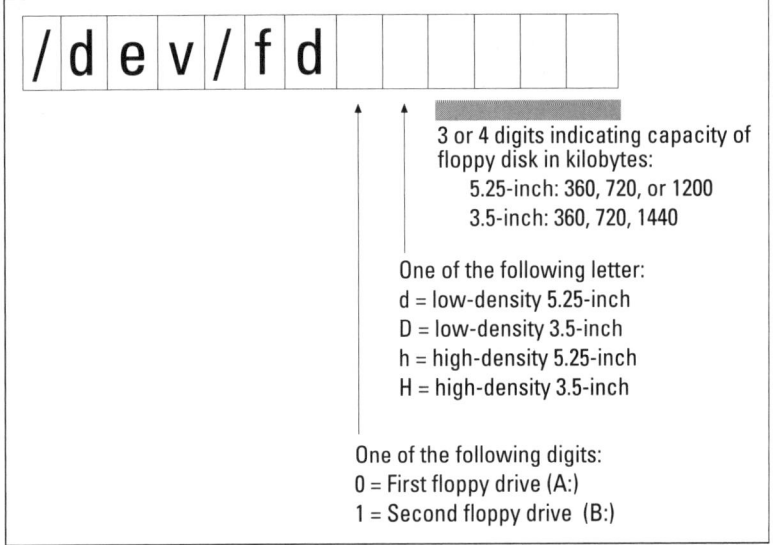

Figure 7-2: Naming convention for the floppy disk drive in Linux.

2. Use the `mformat` command to put an MS-DOS file system on the low-level-formatted floppy disk. If the floppy is in drive A, type the following command:

   ```
   mformat a
   ```

DOSEMU

Accessing DOS file systems with the Linux `mount` command or through the `mtools` utilities lets you exchange files with MS-DOS, but that capability does not help if you want to run a DOS program under Linux. As you might expect, Linux comes with a solution to this problem — you can use DOSEMU to create an MS-DOS environment within Linux.

Chapter 7: Secrets of DOS under Linux

Secret

Although DOSEMU stands for *DOS emulator*, it is really not an emulator. In fact, DOSEMU uses the same capabilities of the Intel 80x86 processor that Microsoft Windows 3.1 uses to run MS-DOS in a window. Beginning with the 80386, Intel 80x86 and Pentium processors support a *virtual-86 mode*, in which multiple virtual 8086 machines can exist on the same 80x86 processor. As you may recall, the 8086 is the 16-bit microprocessor that originally ran MS-DOS. Because DOSEMU uses virtual-86 mode, it can run DOS programs in their native form, without any need to emulate the 80x86 instruction set. You need a copy of MS-DOS (any version from 3.3 to 6.2) to run DOSEMU.

DOSEMU must simulate a DOS environment for DOS applications that want to directly access the system's resources, such as the keyboard, printer, serial port, display, and disk. A configuration file, `/etc/dosemu.conf`, controls the way that DOSEMU accesses various system resources.

Caution

Although this section introduces DOSEMU, you should know that DOSEMU still is under development. At this writing, the DOSEMU version was 0.60; it was not considered to be mature enough to have a 1.0 version number. Although DOSEMU is safe enough to try, you should be prepared to reboot your Linux system if anything goes wrong. Back up your important files before you try DOSEMU.

DOSEMU installation

Although the companion CD-ROM includes DOSEMU, you do not get any opportunity to install it when you first install Linux. DOSEMU is very easy to install. As you do with most Linux software, you copy the necessary files to your hard disk and then configure them. This section guides you through the installation process. Later in this chapter, the "Configure DOSEMU" section shows you how to configure DOSEMU.

To install DOSEMU, follow these steps:

1. If you are not already logged in as `root`, type the **su** command and provide the root password to become `root`.

2. Make sure that the companion CD-ROM is in the CD-ROM drive. If the CD-ROM is not mounted already, mount it by using the following command:

   ```
   mount /dev/cdrom /cdrom
   ```

3. Change the current directory to the root directory, as follows:

   ```
   cd /
   ```

4. Type the following command:

   ```
   tar -zxvf /cdrom/contrib/dosemu*.tgz
   ```

The final `tar` command decompresses the compressed DOSEMU archive and extracts the contents of the archive. I use a wildcard in the name because the name of the actual DOSEMU archive contains the current version number.

For version 0.60.1, the verbose output from the `tar` command shows the following information about the files extracted from the archive:

```
lnbsoft5:/# tar -zxvf /cdrom/contrib/dosemu*.tgz
./
usr/
usr/bin/
usr/bin/dos
usr/bin/xtermdos
usr/lib/
usr/lib/libdosemu-0.60.1
usr/X11R6/
usr/X11R6/lib/
usr/X11R6/lib/fonts/
usr/X11R6/lib/fonts/misc/
usr/X11R6/lib/fonts/misc/vga.pcf
usr/doc/
usr/doc/dosemu-0.60.1/
usr/doc/dosemu-0.60.1/ChangeLog
usr/doc/dosemu-0.60.1/alpha-test/
usr/doc/dosemu-0.60.1/alpha-test/Configure
usr/doc/dosemu-0.60.1/QuickStart
usr/doc/dosemu-0.60.1/doc/
usr/doc/dosemu-0.60.1/doc/Makefile
usr/doc/dosemu-0.60.1/doc/dosemu.texinfo
usr/doc/dosemu-0.60.1/doc/dos.1
usr/doc/dosemu-0.60.1/doc/announce-0.60
usr/doc/dosemu-0.60.1/doc/DPR
usr/doc/dosemu-0.60.1/doc/DANG
usr/doc/dosemu-0.60.1/doc/EMUsuccess.txt
usr/doc/dosemu-0.60.1/doc/dosemu.lsm
usr/doc/dosemu-0.60.1/doc/dosemu.info
usr/doc/dosemu-0.60.1/doc/README.CDROM
usr/doc/dosemu-0.60.1/doc/README.HOGTHRESHOLD
usr/doc/dosemu-0.60.1/doc/README.X
usr/doc/dosemu-0.60.1/doc/README.ibmset
usr/doc/dosemu-0.60.1/doc/README.mgarrot
usr/doc/dosemu-0.60.1/doc/README.video
usr/doc/dosemu-0.60.1/doc/DOSEMU-HOWTO.ps
usr/doc/dosemu-0.60.1/doc/DOSEMU-HOWTO.sgml
usr/doc/dosemu-0.60.1/doc/DOSEMU-HOWTO.txt
usr/doc/dosemu-0.60.1/doc/README.Windows
usr/doc/dosemu-0.60.1/doc/Known-Bugs
usr/doc/dosemu-0.60.1/doc/NOVELL-HOWTO.txt
usr/doc/dosemu-0.60.1/doc/DANG_CONFIG
usr/doc/dosemu-0.60.1/dosconfig
usr/doc/dosemu-0.60.1/dosemu.xpm
usr/doc/dosemu-0.60.1/examples/
usr/doc/dosemu-0.60.1/examples/Makefile
usr/doc/dosemu-0.60.1/examples/config.dist
usr/man/
usr/man/preformat/
usr/man/preformat/cat1/
usr/man/preformat/cat1/dos.1.gz
var/
var/lib/
```

```
var/lib/dosemu/
var/lib/dosemu/hdimage
install/
install/doinst.sh
etc/
etc/dosemu.conf
etc/dosemu.users
lnbsoft5:/#
```

All the files necessary for running DOSEMU should be installed in the appropriate directories after this `tar` command completes.

Read the manual

After you unpack the DOSEMU archive, you should read the documentation for information on how to set up and run DOSEMU. You should start with the `QuickStart` file (a text file) in the `/usr/doc/dosemu*` directory. (The exact directory name depends on the version of DOSEMU that you are using.) Use the following commands to browse this file:

```
cd /usr/doc/dosemu*
less QuickStart
```

The `less` command allows you to view the file a page at a time. `less` is similar to `more`, except that `less` allows you to go backward as well as forward.

Following are the key points that are explained in the `QuickStart` file:

- The file `/etc/dosemu.users` contains the names of users who are allowed to run DOSEMU. You should add to this file the names of any users who can run DOSEMU.

- You have to edit the DOSEMU configuration file `/etc/dosemu.conf` to reflect your system's configuration.

- You need a hard disk *image file* (a Linux file that DOSEMU treats as a DOS drive). This file is present when you install DOSEMU from this book's companion CD-ROM.

- To set up DOSEMU for the first time, you need an MS-DOS boot floppy that contains the files `FDISK.EXE` and `SYS.COM`. You can create this floppy under DOS, which must have come with your PC.

The following section shows you how to use the DOS floppy to set up the hard disk image. (That image file is used as the C drive under DOSEMU.)

Configure DOSEMU

The DOSEMU distribution on this book's companion CD-ROM comes nearly ready to run. You do have to go through some configuration steps, however, before you can run DOSEMU.

Edit /etc/dosemu.conf

You have to be logged in as root when you perform these configuration tasks. The first task is to edit the /etc/dosemu.conf file. Like most Linux configuration files, /etc/dosemu.conf is a text file. Comments start with a pound sign (#). The file already contains many commented lines, as well as instructions for each section.

To get started, you need to make the following changes:

1. Search for the string hdimage, and remove the comment symbol (#) at the beginning of that line so that it appears as follows:

   ```
   disk { image "/var/lib/dosemu/hdimage" }   # use diskimage file.
   ```

   This line refers to a Linux file /var/lib/dosemu/hdimage that serves as a disk under DOSEMU. The name hdimage stands for *hard disk image*. The first disk line in the /etc/dosemu.conf line defines the C drive under DOSEMU.

2. If you have a DOS partition that you want to access under DOSEMU, uncomment an appropriate line (or add a new one with the correct name of your DOS partition). My system's DOS partition is /dev/hda1, so I have the following disk line uncommented in /etc/dosemu.conf:

   ```
   disk { partition "/dev/hda1" readonly } # 1st partition on 1st IDE.
   ```

3. Find the FLOPPY DISKS section, and make sure that the floppy disk devices /dev/fd0 (first floppy drive) and /dev/fd1 (second floppy drive) are the correct size (threeinch or fiveinch). My system has only one 3.5-inch floppy drive; therefore, I have only one uncommented line in the FLOPPY DISKS section of the /etc/dosemu.conf file:

   ```
   floppy { device /dev/fd0 threeinch }
   ```

The /etc/dosemu.conf file contains many more options, but you do not have to configure everything right now. The first step is to get DOSEMU running; then you can turn to specific items such as how to make the printer work and how to access the serial port under DOSEMU.

Initialize the hard disk image

You can think of the hard disk image as being a raw hard disk; you have to format it and make it bootable before DOSEMU can boot off that hard disk image. To do this, you need a real MS-DOS boot floppy. You can create the boot floppy by using the MS-DOS installation that came with your PC.

To create a DOS boot floppy, you first have to boot your system under MS-DOS and then perform these steps:

1. Put a floppy disk in your A drive (all previous contents of the floppy will be destroyed when you format it), and type the command **FORMAT A: /S**. MS-DOS prompts you with the following message:

   ```
   Insert new diskette for drive A:
   and press ENTER when ready...
   ```

2. Press Enter because you already have the floppy disk in the A drive. MS-DOS formats the disk and places the necessary operating-system files on it (that's what the /S option of the FORMAT command does).

3. MS-DOS also prompts you for a Volume label; you can simply press Enter in response.

4. DOS asks whether you want to format another floppy disk. Type **N** to indicate that you are done formatting.

5. Copy FDISK.EXE and SYS.COM files to the floppy. You need these two programs to initialize the hard disk image under DOSEMU. Use the following commands to copy the FDISK.EXE and SYS.COM programs to the floppy in the A drive:

```
C:
CD \DOS (typically, the MS-DOS files are in the \DOS directory)
COPY FDISK.EXE A:
COPY SYS.COM A:
```

After you prepare the DOS boot floppy, restart Linux on your system, using your favorite method (LILO or a Linux boot floppy). Then log in as root.

Secret

Next, the DOSEMU documentation asks you to put the DOS boot floppy in the A drive and enter the dos -A command to start DOSEMU. This action, however, generates the following error message:

```
dos: cannot open shared library: /usr/lib/libdosemu
Check the LIBDOSEMU variable, default is /usr/lib/libdosemu
```

Sure enough, the /usr/lib/libdosemu file does not exist; instead, a similarly named file has the current version number appended to the name. To get around this error, create a symbolic link between the file /usr/lib/libdosemu and the similarly named file. Use the following commands to accomplish this task:

```
cd /usr/lib
ln -s libdosemu* libdosemu
```

After creating the symbolic link, you are ready to start DOSEMU from the DOS boot floppy. Type the following command at the shell prompt:

```
dos -A
```

After a brief pause, DOSEMU should boot off the A drive and prompt you for the current date and time (just as real DOS does). Press Enter twice to accept the default date and time. You are left with an A:\> prompt, as shown in Figure 7-3.

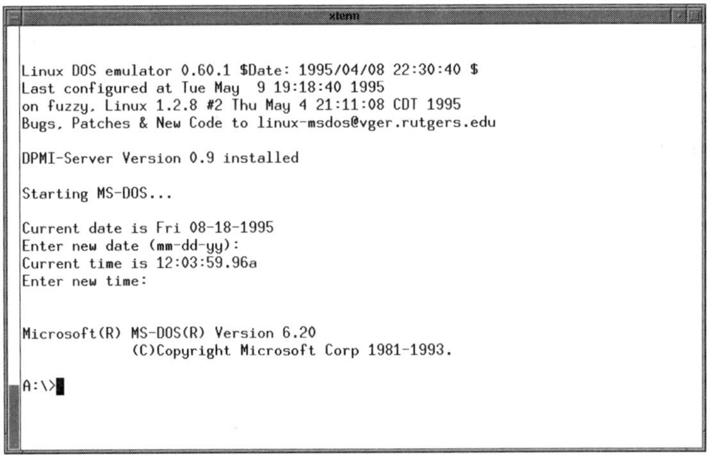

```
Linux DOS emulator 0.60.1 $Date: 1995/04/08 22:30:40 $
Last configured at Tue May  9 19:18:40 1995
on fuzzy, Linux 1.2.8 #2 Thu May 4 21:11:08 CDT 1995
Bugs, Patches & New Code to linux-msdos@vger.rutgers.edu

DPMI-Server Version 0.9 installed

Starting MS-DOS...

Current date is Fri 08-18-1995
Enter new date (mm-dd-yy):
Current time is 12:03:59.96a
Enter new time:


Microsoft(R) MS-DOS(R) Version 6.20
         (C)Copyright Microsoft Corp 1981-1993.

A:\>
```

Figure 7-3: Starting DOSEMU for the first time from a DOS boot floppy.

Try the DOS command `dir c:`. DOSEMU should display the contents of the C drive — actually, the hard disk image file that DOSEMU treats as the C drive. Your next task is to make this C drive bootable. To initialize the hard disk image (the C drive), perform these steps:

1. To initialize the master boot record of the C drive, type the following command:

    `A:\> fdisk /mbr`

2. Next, transfer the necessary system files to the hard disk image by using the following command:

    ```
    A:\> sys c:
    System transferred
    ```

After these two steps, the hard disk image (C drive in DOSEMU) should be bootable. Before you can test the hard disk image, exit DOSEMU by using this command:

`A:\> c:\exitemu`

Start DOSEMU from the hard disk image

After you get your hard disk image file set up properly, you should be able to boot directly from that image. Remove the DOS boot floppy from your system's A drive, and type **dos** at the shell prompt. DOSEMU should boot from the hard disk image and display the familiar `C:\>` prompt, as shown in Figure 7-4.

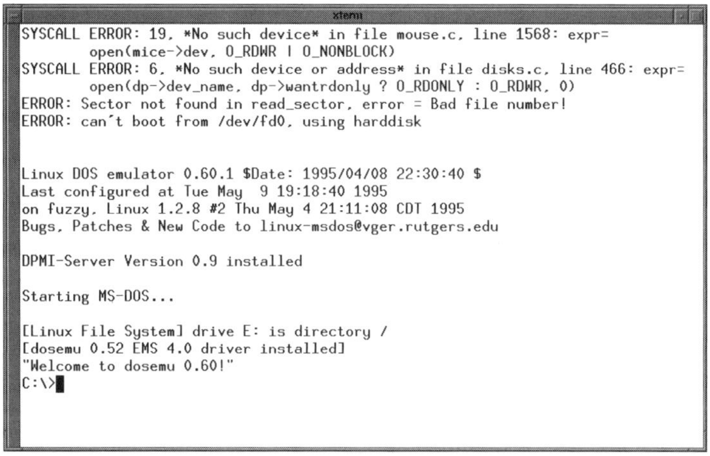

Chapter 7: Secrets of DOS under Linux   247

Figure 7-4: Booting DOSEMU from the hard disk image.

In Figure 7-4, you see DOSEMU reporting an error because it tries to boot from the A drive by default. (A `bootA` line in the `/etc/dosemu.conf` file specifies the A drive as the boot device.) When DOSEMU does not find any floppy in drive A, it boots from the hard disk image anyway, and you get the `C:\>` prompt. If you do not mind the initial error message, you can leave the `/etc/dosemu.conf` file as is.

If you type **dir**, you see that the hard disk image that works as the C drive is about 1MB. That's adequate because you can access your real DOS partition as well as your Linux partition. The C drive is used only to boot MS-DOS.

If you have a DOS partition on your hard disk, and you added an appropriate `disk` line in the `/etc/dosemu.conf` file, that partition should be the D drive under DOSEMU. Try the command `dir d:` and see what DOSEMU shows you. You should be able to run some simple DOS programs (such as the MS-DOS editor) from your hard disk's DOS partition. Figure 7-5 shows the MS-DOS editor running under a DOSEMU session in an `xterm` window.

Figure 7-5 shows the editor's Open dialog box (press Alt+F and then type **O** to open this dialog box). You can get a DOSlike screen if you start DOSEMU from a text-mode console instead of an `xterm` window.

When you are ready to quit DOSEMU, type **c:\exitemu** at the DOS prompt.

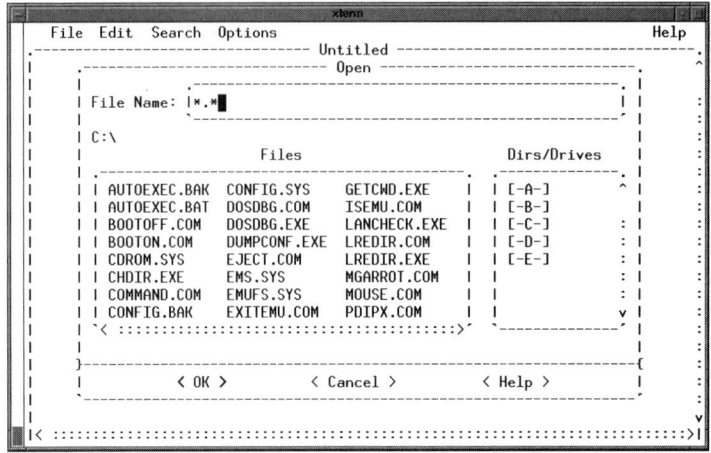

Figure 7-5: The Open dialog box of the MS-DOS editor, running under DOSEMU in an `xterm` window.

List of users allowed to run DOSEMU

The file `/etc/dosemu.users` contains the names of users who are allowed to run DOSEMU. By default, the `/etc/dosemu.users` file contains `root` as the only user who can run DOSEMU. If you want other users to run DOSEMU, you have to log in as `root` and add the other user names to the `/etc/dosemu.users` file.

Any unauthorized user who attempts to run DOSEMU gets an error message. When I log in as `naba` (my user name, which does not appear in the `/etc/dosemu.users` file), and I try to start DOSEMU with the `dos` command, DOSEMU displays the following message:

```
Sorry naba. You are not allowed to use DOSEMU. Contact System Admin.
```

Even if you are running Linux on your home PC, you may want to add your regular user name to the `/etc/dosemu.conf` file so that you do not have to log in as `root` just to run DOSEMU.

Summary

If your PC has a DOS partition in addition to the Linux partition, or if you work with DOS floppy disks, you can access the DOS files directly from Linux. You also can use the mtools utility programs to format and use a DOS floppy disk directly from Linux. Additionally, an ongoing project — DOSEMU — provides a DOS emulator that allows you to run DOS programs directly in Linux. By reading this chapter, you learn the following:

- Linux has built-in support for the MS-DOS file system. You can use the mount command to access a DOS partition or a DOS floppy from Linux. After mounting a DOS file system at a directory in your Linux system, you can use Linux commands such as ls and cp to manipulate the DOS files.

- When you installed Linux, following the directions in Chapter 1, you also installed a set of utility programs known as mtools. The mtools programs provide a convenient way to access MS-DOS files, especially floppy disks because you can use mtools commands without first having to mount the floppy disk. The mtools utilities include commands such as mdir and mcopy that work like the DOS commands DIR and COPY.

- This book's companion CD-ROM also includes a preliminary release of the DOSEMU DOS emulator that uses the Intel 80x86 processor's virtual-86 mode to run MS-DOS. You can install DOSEMU easily by decompressing and unpacking the DOSEMU archive directly from the CD-ROM. You need a copy of MS-DOS to set up DOSEMU. Although it is in its early stages of development, DOSEMU can run many existing DOS programs.

Chapter 8
Scripting in Linux with Tcl/Tk

In This Chapter

- Looking at Tcl/Tk
- Understanding Tcl syntax
- Writing Tcl scripts
- Building graphical interfaces for Tcl scripts with Tk
- Learning to use Tcl/Tk through examples

If you are already a C and X Window System programmer, you will be surprised by the ease with which you can create graphical applications with *Tcl* (Tool Command Language) and its associated X toolkit, *Tk* — collectively referred to as Tcl/Tk (pronounced "tickle/tee kay"). Tcl is a scripting language like Perl. The biggest strength of Tcl is its X toolkit, Tk, which allows you to develop scripts with graphical user interfaces.

When I started using Tcl/Tk, I was pleasantly surprised by how few lines of Tcl/Tk it takes to create a functioning graphical interface. To a newcomer, a Tcl/Tk script still looks rather complicated, but if you have used C-based toolkits such as Xt and Motif to write programs, you can appreciate the high-level nature of Tk. Creating a user-interface component such as a button is much simpler in Tk than in Motif. You still have to tend to many details, such as how to lay out the components of the user interface, but you can see results faster than you can with a C program that calls the Motif library.

Tip

If you have never programmed, don't avoid this chapter out of fear. The examples in this chapter teach you the basics of Tcl and Tk. You are bound to become a believer in Tcl/Tk after you see how quickly you can use Tcl/Tk's interpreter to create applications with graphical interfaces.

Whence Tcl/Tk?

John Ousterhout created Tcl and Tk when he was at the University of California at Berkeley. Tcl first appeared in 1989; Tk followed in 1991. Tcl/Tk are freely available for unrestricted use, including commercial use. At this writing, the Tcl version is 7.4; Tk is 4.0. This book's companion CD-ROM includes Tcl/Tk.

Introducing Tcl

Tcl stands for Tool Command Language and is pronounced "tickle." The creator of Tcl, John Ousterhout, intended Tcl to be a simple scripting language whose interpreter could be linked with any C program so that the C program could use Tcl scripts. The term *embeddable* refers to this property of Tcl: the capability of any C program to use the Tcl interpreter and run Tcl scripts.

The following sections provide an overview of Tcl, its syntax, and some of its important commands. Because Tcl underlies the Tk toolkit, you should become familiar with Tcl before jumping into Tk, although Tk undoubtedly is more fun, because you can use it to create graphical interfaces.

Your first Tcl script

Cross Reference

In Chapter 6, you saw how to write shell scripts and Perl scripts. You write Tcl scripts the same way. Unlike Perl, Tcl includes a shell — an interactive interpreter of Tcl commands. The Tcl shell program's name is tclsh; it should be in the /usr/bin directory.

When you log in, the PATH environment variable should include the /usr/bin directory. Thus, you can start the Tcl shell by typing **tclsh.** A percent sign (%) appears on the next line; this is the Tcl shell program's prompt. To see the version of Tcl that you have, type **info tclversion** at the Tcl shell prompt. The Tcl shell program responds by printing the version of Tcl.

Now you can interactively try the following Tcl program, which prints Hello, World! on the standard output (the display screen):

```
% puts "Hello, World!"
Hello, World!
%
```

Note

I did not show the shell prompt in previous chapters, but I show the TCL prompt (%) in this chapter's listings. That's because the TCL prompt looks different from the Bash prompt and that should tell you that you aren't working in Bash.

The Tcl shell immediately processes the Tcl command that you enter and displays the results; then it prompts you for the next input. At this point, you can type **exit** to quit the Tcl shell.

To prepare and run a Tcl script, follow these steps:

1. Use a text editor to enter and save the following lines in a file named hellotcl (this file will be the Tcl script):

   ```
   #!/usr/bin/tclsh
   # A simple Tcl script
   puts "Hello, World!"
   ```

2. Type the following command at the shell prompt to make the `hellotcl` file executable (that's what the `+x` in the `chmod` command means):

   ```
   chmod +x hellotcl
   ```

3. To run the `hellotcl` script, type the following at the shell prompt:

   ```
   hellotcl
   Hello, World!
   ```

You use these basic steps to create and run any Tcl script. You still have to learn the nuances of Tcl syntax, of course, as well as many rules. This section gets you started with an overview of Tcl.

Tcl overview

True to its name (Tool Command Language), Tcl consists of a set of commands that you can combine according to a set of rules. To write Tcl scripts, you have to understand two broad subjects:

- *Tcl syntax.* Tcl syntax is the set of rules that the Tcl command interpreter follows when it interprets a *command string* (a line that contains a command and its arguments).

More on Tcl/Tk

This chapter provides an overview of Tcl and Tk, highlights many key points, and shows simple examples. There simply is not enough room in this chapter to list all the information that you need to fully exploit the power of Tcl and Tk. Because of Tcl/Tk's popularity, you can find quite a few resources about it, ranging from books to FTP sites. Following is a short list of Tcl/Tk resources:

- **Books.** Two prominent books on Tcl/Tk are available. The first book is *Tcl and the Tk Toolkit* (Addison Wesley, 1994), by John K. Ousterhout, the originator of Tcl and Tk. John's book provides a broad overview of Tcl and Tk, including an explanation of the way that Tcl command strings are parsed. The other book is *Practical Programming in Tcl and Tk* (Prentice-Hall, 1995), by Brent B. Welch. This book provides more Tcl and Tk examples.

- **Internet resources.** Several FTP sites contain the latest Tcl and Tk distributions. The following list uses Uniform Resource Locator (URL) syntax. You can use a Web browser (such as Netscape, Mosaic, or Lynx) and enter the URL as shown. The browser then displays appropriate information about the contents of the site.

  ftp://ftp.cs.berkeley.edu/ucb/tcl
  ftp://ftp.ibp.fr/pub/tcl
  ftp://src.doc.ic.ac.uk/packages/tcl/
  ftp://ftp.luth.se/pub/unix/tcl/
  ftp://sunsite.unc.edu/pub/languages/tcl/
  ftp://ftp.funet.fi/pub/languages/tcl/

- *Tcl commands.* Although the syntax is the same for all commands, each individual Tcl command is meant to perform a specific task. To exploit Tcl fully, you have to know what commands are available and what each command does. The Tcl command set can be extended by applications. In fact, Tk itself is an extension of Tcl; Tk adds commands that manipulate components of graphical user interfaces.

Start by learning the Tcl syntax; a handful of rules that determine the way that each Tcl command is parsed. Because Tcl has many commands, learning all the commands can take a while. Even after you become proficient in the Tcl syntax and a small set of commands, you may need to keep a reference manual near by so that you can check the exact format of the arguments that each command requires.

Tcl commands include the following basic programming facilities that you expect from any programming language:

- *Variables* that store data. Each variable has a name and a value. Tcl also allows you to define arrays of variables.
- *Expressions* that combine values of variables with *operators*. An expression might add two variables, for example. Tcl uses the `expr` command to evaluate expressions.
- *Control-flow commands* that allow commands to be executed in various order, depending on the value of some expression. Tcl provides commands such as `for`, `foreach`, `break`, `continue`, `if`, `while`, and `return` to implement flow control in Tcl scripts.
- *Procedures* that let you group several commands and give them a name. Procedures also accept arguments. Tcl provides the `proc` command to allow you to define procedures. You can use a procedure to execute the same set of commands (usually, with different arguments) by invoking the procedure that represents those statements.

The next few sections provide an overview of the Tcl syntax and the core Tcl commands.

Basic Tcl syntax

To understand the basic Tcl syntax, you have to know a bit about how the Tcl interpreter processes each command string. The steps are as follows:

- The Tcl interpreter *parses* (breaks down) the command string into words.
- The Tcl interpreter applies rules to substitute values of variables and replace certain commands with their results.
- The Tcl interpreter executes the commands, taking the first word as the command name and calling a command procedure to execute the command. That command procedure receives the rest of the words as strings.

When writing Tcl command strings, you have to use *white space* (space or tab) to separate a command's name from its arguments. A new line or a semicolon (;) marks the end of a command string. You can put two commands on the same line, provided that you insert a semicolon after the first command. Thus, you can use the following:

```
puts Hello, ; puts World!
Hello,
World!
```

The resulting output appears on separate lines, because the `puts` command by default adds a new line.

Use a backslash at the end of a line to continue that command string on the next line. Thus, you could write a command string to print `Hello, World!` as follows:

```
puts "Hello, \
World!"
```

Substitutions

The Tcl interpreter replaces certain parts of the command string with an equivalent value. If you precede a variable's name with a dollar sign ($), for example, the interpreter replaces that word with the variable's value. As you learn in the "Variables" section, you can define a variable in a Tcl script by using the `set` command, as follows:

```
set count 100
```

This command defines a variable named `count` with the value `100`. Now suppose that you type the following:

```
puts $count
```

The interpreter first replaces `$count` with its value, which is `100`. Thus, that command string becomes

```
puts 100
```

When the interpreter executes the `puts` command, it prints `100`. This is an example of *variable substitution*.

In all, the Tcl interpreter supports three kinds of substitutions:

- *Variable substitution.* As the preceding example shows, if the Tcl interpreter finds a dollar sign ($), it replaces the dollar sign as well the following variable name with that variable's value.

- *Backslash substitution.* You can embed special characters, such as new line and tab, in a word by using backslash substitution. You simply type a backslash, followed by one or more characters; the interpreter replaces that sequence with a nonprintable character. These sequences are patterned after ANSI Standard C's escape sequences. Table 8-1, which follows this list, summarizes the backslash sequences that the Tcl interpreter understands.

- *Command substitution.* This type of substitution refers to the mechanism that allows you to specify that a command be evaluated and replaced by its result before the interpreter processes the command string. The command `string length "Hello, World!"`, for example, returns 13, which is the length of the string. To set a variable named `len` to the length of this string, type the following:

```
set len [string length "Hello, World!"]
```

The interpreter processes the command inside the brackets and replaces that part of the command string with the value of the command. Thus, this command becomes

```
set len 13
```

and the `set` command sets the `len` variable to 13.

Table 8-1	Backslash sequences in Tcl
Sequence	**Replacement character ***
\a	The bell character (0x7)
\b	Backspace (0x8)
\f	Form feed (0xc)
\n	New line (0xa)
\r	Carriage return (0xd)
\t	Horizontal tab (0x9)
\v	Vertical tab (0xb)
\<newline>	Replace the new line and white space on next line with a single space
\\	Interpret as a single backslash (\)
\"	Interpret as double quotation marks (")
\ooo	Use the value specified by the octal digits (up to three)
\xhh	Use the value specified by the hexadecimal digits (up to two)

* *Hexadecimal values shown in parentheses.*

Comments

A pound sign (#) marks the start of a comment; the Tcl interpreter disregards the rest of the command string, beginning with the pound sign. Tcl does, however, have a peculiar requirement on comments: you cannot start a comment within a command. The command string must end before you start a comment.

To understand this problem, try the following Tcl command at the `tclsh` prompt:

```
% puts "Hello, World!" # This is a comment
wrong # args: should be "puts" ?-nonewline? ?field? string
```

Essentially, the `puts` command processes the remainder of the line and complains about the number of arguments. The solution is to put a semicolon just before the pound sign (#), as follows:

```
% puts "Hello, World!" ;# This is a comment
Hello, World!
```

Tip

If you put comments at the end of a Tcl command, remember to precede the pound sign (#) with a semicolon (;). The semicolon terminates the preceding command and enables you to start a comment.

Braces and double quotation marks

You can use braces (`{...}`) and double quotation marks (`"..."`) to group several words. Use double quotes to pass arguments that contain an embedded space or a semicolon, which otherwise ends the command. The quotes are not part of the group of words; they simply serve to mark the beginning and end of a group of words. Following are some examples of using double quotes to group words:

```
% puts "Hello, World!"
Hello, World!
% puts "Enter 1; otherwise file won't be saved!"
Enter 1; otherwise file won't be saved!
```

When you group words with double quotes, all types of substitutions still take place, as illustrated by the following example:

```
% puts "There are [string length hello] characters in 'hello'"
There are 5 characters in 'hello'
```

The Tcl interpreter replaces everything inside the brackets with the result of the `string length hello` command, whose return value is the number of characters in `hello` (5).

You also can use braces to group words. The Tcl interpreter does not perform any substitution when you group words with braces (if you enclose words in double quotes, the interpreter does perform substitution). Consider the preceding example with braces instead of double quotes:

```
% puts {There are [string length hello] characters in 'hello'}
There are [string length hello] characters in 'hello'
```

As the result shows, the Tcl interpreter simply passes everything, unchanged, as a single argument.

Tip

Use braces as a grouping mechanism when you have to pass expressions to control commands, such as `while` loops, `for` loops, or procedures.

Variables

Everything is a string in Tcl. Variable names as well as values are stored as strings. To define a variable, use the built-in Tcl command `set`. The following commands, for example, define the variable `book` as "Linux SECRETS", the variable `year` as 1996, and the variable `price` as $39.99:

```
set book "Linux SECRETS"
set year 1996
set price \$39.99
```

To refer to the value of a variable, append a dollar sign (`$`) to the variable's name. Therefore, to print the variable `book`, use the following format:

```
% puts $book
Linux SECRETS
```

If you use `set` with a single argument, `set` returns the value of that argument. Thus, `set book` is equivalent to `$book`, as the following example shows:

```
% puts [set book]
Linux SECRETS
```

Expressions

You can write expressions by combining variables with mathematical operators, such as + (add), - (subtract), * (multiply), and / (divide). Here are some examples of expressions:

```
set count 1
$count+1
$count + 5 - 2
2 + 3.5
```

You can use numbers as well as variable names in expressions. You can use white space to enhance readability. Also, use parentheses to specify how you want the expressions to be evaluated.

In addition to the basic mathematical operators, Tcl includes several built-in mathematical functions such as `sin`, `cos`, `tan`, `log`, and `sqrt`. Call these functions just as you do in C, with arguments in parentheses, as follows:

```
set angle 1.5
2*sin($angle)
```

You also can use Boolean operators, such as ! (not), && (and), and or (||). Comparison operators — such as < (less than), > (greater than), <= (less than or equal to), == (equal to), and != (not equal to) — also are available. Expressions that use Boolean or comparison operators evaluate to 1 if true and 0 if false. You can write expressions such as the following:

```
count == 10
angle < 3.1415
```

Expressions are not commands by themselves. You can use expressions as arguments only for commands that accept expressions as arguments. The `if` and `while` commands, for example, expect expressions as arguments.

Tcl also provides the `expr` command to evaluate an expression. The following example shows how you might evaluate an expression in a Tcl command:

```
% set angle 1.5
1.5
% puts "Result = [expr 2*sin($angle)]"
Result = 1.99499
```

Although Tcl stores everything as a string, you have to use numbers where numbers are expected. If `book` is defined as `"Linux SECRETS"`, for example, you cannot write an expression `$book+1`, because it does not make sense.

Control-flow commands

Tcl's control-flow commands allow you to specify the order in which the Tcl interpreter executes commands. You can use the `if` command to test the value of an expression, and if the value is true (nonzero), you can make the interpreter execute a set of commands. Tcl includes control-flow commands that are similar to those in C, such as `if`, `for`, `while`, and `switch`. This section provides an overview of the control-flow commands.

Wizard

A Tcl control-flow command typically has a *command block* (a group of commands) that the control-flow command executes after evaluating an expression. To avoid substitutions (such as replacing variables with their values), you must enclose the entire command block in braces. The following `if-else` control-flow commands illustrate the style of braces that work properly:

```
if { expression } {
 # Commands to execute when expression is true
   command_1
     command_2
} else {
 # Commands to execute when expression is false
 # ...
}
```

You should follow this style of braces religiously in Tcl scripts. In particular, remember to include a space between the control-flow command (such as `if`) and the left brace ({) that follows the command.

The `if` command

In its simplest form, Tcl's `if` command evaluates an expression and executes a set of commands if that expression is nonzero (true). You might compare the value of a variable with a threshold as follows:

```
if { $errorCount > 25 } {
    puts "Too many errors!"
}
```

You can add an `else` clause to process commands if the expression evaluates to zero (false). Following is an example:

```
if { $user == "root" } {
    puts "Starting system setup ..."
} else {
    puts "Sorry, you must be \"root\" to run this program!"
}
```

Tcl's `if` command can be followed by zero or more `elseif` commands if you need to perform more complicated tests, such as the following:

```
puts -nonewline "Enter version number: "     ;# prompt user
set version [gets stdin]                     ;# read version number

if { $version >= 10 } {
   puts "No upgrade necessary"
} elseif { $version >= 6 && $version < 9} {
   puts "Standard upgrade"
} elseif { $version >= 3 && $version < 6} {
   puts "Reinstall"
} else {
   puts "Sorry, cannot upgrade"
}
```

The `while` command

The `while` command executes a block of commands until an expression becomes false. The following `while` loop keeps reading lines from the standard input until the user presses Ctrl+D:

```
while { [gets stdin line] != -1 } {
    puts $line
# Do whatever you need to do with $line
}
```

Although this `while` command looks simple, you should realize that it has two arguments inside two sets of braces. The first argument is the expression; the second argument contains the Tcl commands to be executed if the expression is true. You must always use braces to enclose both of these arguments. The braces prevent the Tcl interpreter from evaluating the contents; the `while` command is the one that processes what's inside the braces.

If you use a variable to keep count inside a `while` loop, you can use the `incr` command to increment that variable. You can skip to the end of a loop by using the `continue` command; the `break` command exits the loop. The following Tcl script uses a `while` loop to add all the numbers from 1 to 10 except 5:

```
#!/usr/bin/tclsh

set i 0
set sum 0
```

```
while { 1 } {
    incr i                        ;# increment i
    if {$i == 5} { continue }     ;# skip if i is 5
    if {$i > 10} {break }         ;# end loop if i exceed 10
    set sum [expr $sum+$i]        ;# otherwise, add i to sum
}
puts "Sum = $sum";
```

When you run this script, it should display the following result:

```
Sum = 50
```

The `for` command

Tcl's `for` command takes four arguments, which you should type in the following manner:

```
for {expr_1} { expr_2} { expr_3} {
    commands
}
```

The `for` command evaluates *expr_1* once at the beginning of the loop and executes the commands inside the final pair of braces until the expression *expr_2* evaluates to zero. The `for` command evaluates the third expression — *expr_3* — after each execution of the commands. You can omit any of the expressions, but you must use all the braces. The following example uses a `for` loop to add the numbers from 1 to 10:

```
#!/usr/bin/tclsh
for {set i 0; set sum 0} {$i <= 10} {set sum [expr $sum+$i]; incr i} {
}
puts "Sum = $sum";
```

When you run this script, it displays the following result:

```
Sum = 55
```

The `foreach` command

You may not have seen a command like `foreach` in C, but `foreach` is handy when you want to perform some action for each value in a list of variables. You can add a set of numbers with the `foreach` command as follows:

```
set sum 0
foreach i { 1 2 3 4 5 6 7 8 9 10} {
    set sum [expr $sum+$i]
}
puts "Sum = $sum"
```

If you have a list in a variable, you can use that variable's value in place of the list shown within the first pair of braces. Following is a `foreach` loop that echoes the strings in a list:

```
set users "root naba"
foreach user $users {
    puts "$user"
}
```

The `switch` command

Tcl's `switch` command is different from C's `switch` statement. Instead of evaluating a mathematical expression, Tcl's `switch` command compares a string with a set of patterns and executes a set of commands, depending on which pattern matched. Often, the pattern is expressed in terms of a regular expression.

Cross Reference

See Chapter 6 for an introduction to regular expressions.

The following script illustrates the syntax and a typical use of the `switch` command:

```
#!/usr/bin/tclsh
# This script reads commands from the user and processes
# the commands using a switch statement

set prompt "Enter command (\"quit\" to exit): "

puts -nonewline "$prompt"

while { [gets stdin cmd] != -1 } {
    switch -exact -- $cmd {
        quit    { puts "Bye!"; exit}
        start   { puts "Started"}
        stop    { puts "Stopped"}
        draw    { puts "Draw.."}
        default { puts "Unknown command: $cmd" }
    }
# prompt user again
    puts -nonewline $prompt
}
```

Following is a sample session with this script (user input is in boldface):

```
Enter command ("quit" to exit): help
Unknown command: help
Enter command ("quit" to exit): start
Started
Enter command ("quit" to exit): stop
Stopped
Enter command ("quit" to exit): quit
Bye!
```

As this example shows, the `switch` statement allows you to compare a string with a set of other strings and then activate a set of commands, depending on which pattern matches. In this example, the string is `$cmd` (which is initialized by reading the user's input with a `gets` command), and the patterns are literal strings: `quit`, `start`, `stop`, and `draw`. Following is a case of an exact match, as indicated by the `-exact` flag on the first line of the `switch` command:

```
switch -exact -- $cmd {
   ...
}
```

The two hyphens (--) immediately after the `-exact` flag mark the end of the flags. When you use the `switch` command, you should always use the double hyphens at the end of the flag to prevent the test string from matching a flag inadvertently.

You can use the `switch` command with the `-regexp` flag to compare a string with a regular expression, as in the following example:

```
# Assume that $cmd is the string to be matched

switch -regexp -- $cmd {
    ^q.*    { puts "Bye!"; exit}
    ^x.*    { puts "Something x..."}
    ^y.*    { puts "Something y..."}
    ^z.*    { puts "Something z..."}
    default { puts "Unknown command: $cmd" }
}
```

In this example, each regular expression has a similar form. The pattern `^z.*` means any string that starts with a single z, followed by any number of other characters.

Tcl procedures

You can use the `proc` command to add your own commands. Such commands are called *procedures*; the Tcl interpreter treats them just as though they were built-in Tcl commands. The following example shows how easy it is to write a procedure in Tcl:

```
#!/usr/bin/tclsh

proc total items {
    set sum 0
    foreach i $items {
        set sum [expr $sum+$i]
    }
    return $sum
}

set counts "5 4 3 5"
puts "Total = [total $counts]"
```

When you run this script, it prints the following:

```
Total = 17
```

In this example, the procedure's name is `total`, and it takes a list of numbers as the argument. The procedure receives the arguments in the variable named `items`. The body of the procedure extracts each item and returns a sum of the items. Thus, to add the numbers from 1 to 10, you have to call the `total` procedure as follows:

```
set sum1_10 [total {1 2 3 4 5 6 7 8 9 10}]
```

Secret

In a Tcl procedure, the argument name args has a special significance; if you use args as the argument name, you can pass a variable number of arguments to the procedure. If you change the total procedure's argument name from items to args, for example, you can call total this way:

```
set sum1_10 [total 1 2 3 4 5 6 7 8 9 10] ;# notice variable number of
                                                                arguments
```

If you want to access a *global variable* (a variable defined outside a procedure) in the Tcl procedure, you have to use the global command inside the procedure. The global command makes a global variable visible within the scope of a procedure. If a variable named theCanvas holds the current drawing area in a Tk (Tcl's X toolkit) program, a procedure that uses the theCanvas must include the following command:

```
global theCanvas
```

Built-in Tcl commands

You have seen many Tcl commands in the preceding examples. You should know the types of commands that are available in Tcl; this knowledge helps you decide which commands are most appropriate for the task at hand. Although this chapter does not have enough room to cover all Tcl commands, Table 8-2 summarizes Tcl's built-in commands.

Tip

To get online help on any Tcl command listed in Table 8-2, type **man 3**, followed by the command name. To get online help on the file command, for example, type **man 3 file**.

Table 8-2	Built-in Tcl commands
Command	Action
append	Appends an argument to a variable's value.
array	Performs various operations on an array variable.
break	Exits a loop command (such as while and for).
catch	Executes a script and traps errors to prevents errors from reaching the Tcl interpreter.
cd	Changes the current working directory.
close	Closes an open file.
concat	Joins two or more lists in a single list.
continue	Immediately begins the next iteration of a for or while loop.
eof	Checks to see whether end-of-file is reached in an open file.
error	Generates an error.

Command	Action
eval	Concatenates lists (as concat does) and then evaluates the resulting list as a Tcl script.
exec	Starts one or more processes that execute the command's arguments.
exit	Terminates the Tcl script.
expr	Evaluates an expression.
file	Checks filenames and attributes.
flush	Flushes buffered output to a file.
for	Implements a for loop.
foreach	Performs a specified action for each element in a list.
format	Formats output and stores it in a string (as the sprintf function in C does).
gets	Reads a line from a file.
glob	Returns the names of files that match a pattern (such as *.tcl).
global	Accesses global variables.
history	Provides access to the *history list* (the list of past Tcl commands).
if	Tests an expression and executes commands if the expression is true (nonzero).
incr	Increments the value of a variable.
info	Returns internal information about the Tcl interpreter.
join	Creates a string by joining all items in a list.
lappend	Appends elements to a list.
lindex	Returns an element from a list at a specified index. (Index 0 refers to the first element.)
linsert	Inserts elements into a list before a specified index.
list	Creates a list comprised of the specified arguments.
llength	Returns the number of elements in a list.
lrange	Returns a specified range of adjacent elements from a list.
lreplace	Replaces elements in a list with new elements.
lsearch	Searches a list for a particular element.
lsort	Sorts a list in a specified order.
open	Opens a file and returns a file identifier.
pid	Returns the process identifier (ID).

(continued)

Table 8-2 *(continued)*

Command	Action
proc	Defines a Tcl procedure.
puts	Sends characters to a file.
pwd	Returns the current working directory.
read	Reads a specified number of bytes from a file. (You can read the entire file.)
regexp	Matches a regular expression with a string.
regsub	Substitutes one regular expression pattern for another.
rename	Renames or deletes a command.
return	Returns a value from a Tcl procedure.
scan	Parses a string, using format specifiers patterned after C's sscanf function.
seek	Changes the *access position* (where the next input or output operation occurs) in an open file.
set	Sets a variable's value or returns its current value.
source	Reads a file and processes it as a Tcl script.
split	Breaks a string into a Tcl list.
string	Performs various operations on strings.
switch	Processes one of several blocks of commands, depending on which pattern matches a specified string.
tell	Returns the current access position for an open file.
time	Returns the total time needed to execute a script.
trace	Executes a specified set of Tcl commands whenever a variable is accessed.
unknown	Handles any unknown command. (The Tcl interpreter calls this command whenever it encounters any unknown command.)
unset	Removes the definition of one or more variables.
uplevel	Executes a script in a different context.
upvar	References a variable outside a procedure. (Used to implement the pass-by-reference style of procedure call, in which changing a procedure argument changes the original copy of the argument.)
while	Implements a while loop that executes a set of Tcl commands repeatedly as long as an expression evaluates to a nonzero value (true).

String manipulation in Tcl

If you browse through the Tcl commands listed in Table 8-2, you find a quite few Tcl commands — such as `append`, `join`, `split`, `string`, `regexp`, and `regsub` — that operate on strings. This section summarizes a few string-manipulation commands.

When you set a variable to a string, the Tcl interpreter considers that string to be a single entity, even if that string contains any embedded spaces or special characters. Sometimes, you need to access the string as a list of items. The `split` command is a handy way to separate a string into its components. The lines in the `/etc/passwd` file, for example, look like this:

```
root:NpYzwIeYYldcA:0:0:root:/root:/bin/bash
```

The line is composed of fields separated by colons (:). Suppose that you want to extract the first field from each line (because that field contains the login name). You can read the file a line at a time, split each line into a list, and extract the first element (the item at index 0) of each list. Following is a Tcl script that does this:

```
#!/usr/bin/tclsh

set fid [open "/etc/passwd" r]       ;# Open password file for read-only
                                        access

while { [gets $fid line] != -1 } {
    set fields [split $line ":"]     ;# this command splits the string
                                        into a list
# Just print out the first field
    puts [lindex $fields 0]          ;# lindex extracts an item at a
                                        specified index
}
```

When you run this script, it should print all the login names from your system's `/etc/passwd` file.

The `join` command is the opposite of `split`; you can use it to create a single string from the items in a list. Suppose that you have a list of six items, defined as follows:

```
set x {1 2 3 4 5 6}
```

When you join the elements, you can select what character you want to use between fields. To join the elements without anything in between them, use the following format:

```
set y [join $x ""]
```

Now the *y* string is `"123456"`.

The `string` command actually is a group of commands for working with strings, because the first argument of `string` specifies the operation to be performed.

The `string compare` command, for example, compares two strings. The `string compare` command returns zero when the two strings are identical. A return value of –1 indicates that the first string argument is lexicographically less than the second one, which means that it appears before the second one in a dictionary. Similarly, a 1 return value indicates that the first string is lexicographically greater than the second one. Thus, you might use `string compare` in an `if` command as follows:

```
if { [string compare $command "quit"] == 0} {
    puts "Exiting..."
    exit 0
}
```

Table 8-3 lists operations that you can perform with Tcl's `string` command:

Table 8-3   Operations you can perform with `string` in Tcl

String command	Description
`string compare string1 string2`	Returns `-1, 0, 1` after comparing strings
`string first string1 string2`	Returns index of the first occurrence of `string1` in `string2`
`string index string charIndex`	Returns the character at index `charIndex`
`string last string1 string2`	Returns index of the last occurrence of `string1` in `string2`
`string length string`	Returns the length of the string
`string match pattern string`	Returns `1` if the pattern matches the string and `0` if it does not
`string range string first last`	Returns a range of characters from `string`
`string tolower string`	Returns the string in lowercase characters
`string toupper string`	Returns the string in uppercase characters
`string trim string chars`	Returns the string after trimming the leading or trailing characters
`string trimleft string chars`	Returns the string after trimming the leading characters
`string trimright string chars`	Returns the string after trimming the trailing characters

Arrays

In Tcl, an *array* is a variable with a string index. An array contains elements; the string index of each element is called the *element name*. In other words, you can access an element of an array by using its name. Internally, Tcl implements arrays with an efficient data structure known as a *hash table*, which allows the Tcl interpreter to look up any array element in a relatively constant period of time.

You declare an array variable by using the `set` command. The following example shows how you might define the `disk_usage` array that holds the amount of disk space used by a system's users:

```
set disk_usage(root)     147178
set disk_usage(naba)     28574
set disk_usage(emily)    55
set disk_usage(ivy)      60
```

After you define the array, you can access its individual elements by element name, as in the following example:

```
set user "naba"
puts "Disk space used by $user = $disk_usage($user)K"
```

Environment variables

Tcl provides the environment variables in a predefined global array named `env`, with the environment-variable names used as element names. In other words, you can look up the value of an environment variable by using the variable name as an index. The following command prints the current `PATH`:

```
puts "$env(PATH)"
```

You can manipulate the environment variable array just as you do any other variables. You can add a new directory to `PATH`, for example, as follows:

```
set env(PATH) "$env(PATH):/usr/sbin"
```

Any changes to the environment variable do not affect the parent process (for example, the shell from which you started the Tcl script). Any new processes created by the script by means of the `exec` command, however, inherit the altered environment variable.

File operations in Tcl

Most of the examples presented so far in this chapter use Tcl's `puts` command to display output. By default, `puts` writes to the standard output: the `xterm` window, when you use X. You can write to a file, however, by providing a file identifier as the first argument of `puts`. To get a file identifier, you first have to open the file, using Tcl's `open` command. The following example shows how you would open a file, write a line of text to the file, and close the file:

```
set fid [open "testfile" w]     ;# open file named "testfile" for
                                   write operations
```

```
puts $fid "Testing 1..2..3"    ;# use file ID with puts to write to
                                  this file
close $fid                     ;# close the file
```

When you use `puts` to display a string on the standard output, you do not have to provide any file-identifier argument. Also, `puts` automatically appends a new-line character at the end of the string. If you do not want the new line, use `puts` with the `-nonewline` argument, as follows:

```
puts -nonewline "Command> "    ;# -nonewline is good for command
                                  prompts
```

Tip

Use `puts` with the `-nonewline` option to display command prompts in your Tcl script.

You also have seen the use of the `gets` command to read a line of input from the standard input. The following invocation of `gets`, for example, reads a line from the standard input (the command returns when you press Enter):

```
set line [gets stdin]          ;# read a line from standard input
```

The keyword `stdin` is a predefined file identifier that represents the standard input, which by default is your keyboard. Other predefined file IDs are `stdout`, for the standard output, and `stderr`, for the standard error-reporting device. By default, both `stdout` and `stderr` are connected to the display screen.

Following is a different way to call `gets` and read a line of input into a variable named `line`:

```
gets stdin line                ;# read a line of input into the line variable
```

To read from another file, you first should open the file for reading and then use `gets` with that file's ID. To read all lines from `/etc/passwd` and display them on the standard output, for example, you would use the following:

```
set fpass [open "/etc/passwd" r]   ;# open /etc/passwd for reading
while { [gets $fpass line] != -1} {  ;# read the lines in a while loop
    puts $line                       ;# and print each line
}
```

The `gets` command is good for reading text files because it works one line at a time; in fact, it looks for the new-line character as a marker that indicates the end of a line of text. If you want to read binary data, such as an image file, you should use the `read` command instead. To read and process a file in 2,048-byte chunks, you might use `read` in the following manner:

```
# Assume fid is the file ID of an open file
while { ![eof $fid]} {              ;# Until end-of-file is reached
    set buffer [read $fid 2048]     ;# read up to 2048 bytes into buffer
# process the data in buffer        ;# and process the buffer
}
```

Chapter 8: Scripting in Linux with Tcl/Tk

The second argument of the `read` command is the maximum number of bytes to be read. If you leave out this argument, the `read` command reads the entire file. You can use this feature to process entire text files. After reading the contents of the file, use the `split` command to separate the input data into lines of text. Following is an example:

```
set fid [open "/etc/passwd" r]         ;# open file for reading
set buffer [read $fid 100000]          ;# read entire file into buffer
split $buffer "\n"                     ;# split buffer into lines
foreach line $buffer {
    puts $line                         ;# do whatever you want with each
                                       line
}
```

If you want to process several files (such as all files whose names end with .tcl), use the `glob` command to expand a filename, such as *.tcl, into a list. Then you can use the `open` command to open and process each file in the following manner:

```
foreach filename [glob *.tcl] {        ;# use glob to create list
of filenames
    puts -nonewline $filename          ;# display the filename
(just for testing)
    set file [open $filename r]        ;# open that file
    gets $file line                    ;# read the first line
    puts $line                         ;# and print it (this is
only for testing)
# process rest of the file as necessary
    close $file                        ;# remember to close the file
}
```

This is a good example of how to use the `glob` command in a script.

Executing UNIX commands

Instead of duplicating the large number of UNIX commands, Tcl simply provides the mechanism to run any UNIX command. If you know UNIX commands, you can use them directly in Tcl scripts.

You use the `exec` command to execute a UNIX command in a Tcl script. In the command's simplest form, you provide the UNIX command as an argument of `exec`. To show the current directory listing, for example, type the following:

```
exec ls
```

The output appears on the standard output (the monitor) just as it does when you enter the `ls` command at the shell prompt.

When you run UNIX commands from the shell, you can redirect the input and output by using special characters, such as < (redirect input), > (redirect output), and | (pipe). These options are available in Tcl as well, because the `exec` command accepts a complete command line, including any input or output redirections. Thus, you can send the directory listing to a file named `dirlist` as follows:

```
exec ls > dirlist
```

Secret

Tcl's `exec` command does not expand wildcard characters (such as an asterisk) in filenames passed to a UNIX command. If you use wildcards in filenames, you have to perform an additional step: you must process the filename specification through the `glob` command to expand it properly before providing the command to `exec`. Additionally, you must pass the entire `exec` command to `eval` as an argument. To see a list of all files with names that end in `.tcl`, for example, you have to use the `exec` command with `glob` and feed the entire command to `eval` as follows:

```
eval exec ls [glob *.tcl]        ;# this is equivalent to the UNIX
                                 command "ls *.tcl"
```

Introducing Tk

Tk (pronounced "tee-kay") is an extension of Tcl. Tk provides an X Window System-based toolkit that you can use in Tcl scripts to build graphical user interfaces. As you might expect, Tk provides a set of about 35 Tcl commands beyond the core built-in set. You can use these Tk commands to create windows, menus, buttons, and other user-interface components and to provide a graphical user interface for your Tcl scripts.

Tk uses the X Window System for its graphic components, which are known as *widgets*. A widget represents a user-interface component, such as a button, scrollbar, menu, list, or even an entire text window. Tk widgets provide a Motif-like three-dimensional appearance.

Note

If you are familiar with the Motif widgets, you may know that Motif relies on the Xt Intrinsics — an X toolkit that is used to build widgets. Unlike Motif, the Tk toolkit is not based on any other toolkit; it uses only Xlib, which is the C-language library for the X Window System. The upshot is that you need only the freely available X Window System to use Tk.

As you do with anything new, you can best learn Tk through examples, which the following sections provide.

"Hello, World!" in Tk

Tk is a major-enough extension to Tcl that it has its own shell, called `wish` (the *wi*ndowing *sh*ell). The `wish` shell interprets all built-in Tcl commands, as well as the Tk commands. You must start X before you can run `wish`; after all, `wish` allows you to use X to create graphical interfaces.

The wish program should be in the /usr/bin directory, which should be in your PATH environment variable by default. To start wish, all you have to do is type the following at the shell prompt in an xterm window:

```
wish
%
```

The wish program displays its prompt (the percent sign) and also a small window, as shown in the upper-right corner of Figure 8-1.

wish provides an interactive prompt where you can enter Tk commands to create a graphical interface. As wish interprets the commands, it displays the resulting graphical interface in the window.

To see how this interactive creation of a graphical interface works, try the following commands at the wish prompt (type the part shown in boldface):

```
% label .msg -text "Hello, World!"
.msg
% button .bye -text "Bye" -command { exit }
.bye
% pack .msg .bye
%
```

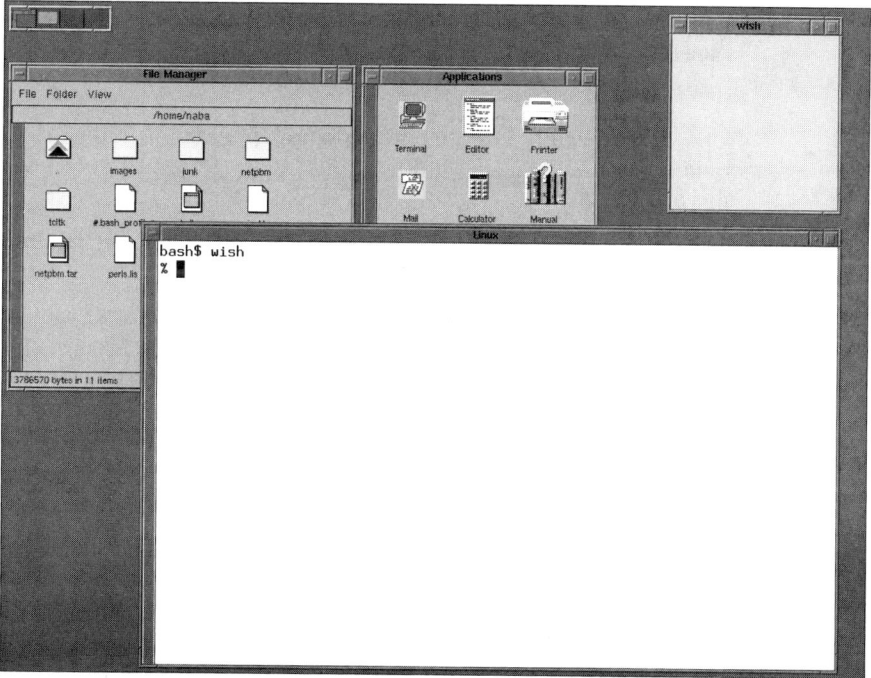

Figure 8-1: The result of running wish from an xterm window.

Figure 8-2 shows the result of these command; `wish` displays a `Hello, World!` label with a `Bye` button below it.

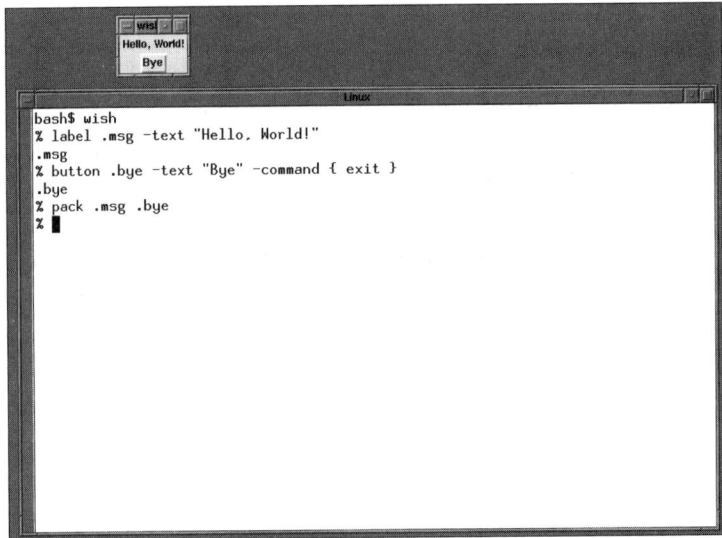

Figure 8-2: Interactively creating a label and a button in `wish`.

Notice that the label and the button do not appear until you enter the `pack` command. Also, the `wish` window shrinks to a size just large enough to hold the label and the button.

Click the `Bye` button; the `wish` program exits. The reason is that the `-command { exit }` argument of the `button` command associates the Tcl command `exit` with a click of the `Bye` button.

To create a Tk program or script that displays the `Hello, World!` label and the `Bye` button, all you have to do is place the Tk commands in a file, and add a special line at the beginning to ensure that the `wish` shell processes the file. To do so, follow these steps:

1. Use a text editor to enter and save the following lines in a file named `hellotk`:

    ```
    #!/usr/bin/wish -f
    # A simple Tk script
    label .msg -text "Hello, World!"
    button .bye -text "Bye" -command { exit }
    pack .msg .bye
    ```

Note

Notice the `-f` option in the first line. In Tk versions earlier than 4.0, you have to start `wish` with that option to make sure that it processes the script file. The flag is optional in Tk version 4.0 and later.

2. Type the following command at the shell prompt to make the `hellotk` file executable (that's what the +x in the `chmod` command means):

    ```
    chmod +x hellotk
    ```

3. To run the `hellotk` script, type the following at the shell prompt in an `xterm` window:

   `hellotk`

Figure 8-3 shows the window with a `Hello, World!` label and the `Bye` button that should appear when you run the `hellotk` script. Click the `Bye` button to close the window and end the script.

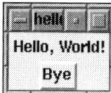

Figure 8-3: The result of running the `hellotk` script.

As this example shows, the basic steps for writing a Tk script are the same as those for creating and running any Tcl script. The only difference is that the Tk commands generate graphical output.

Tk widget basics

Now that you have been exposed to Tcl, you can begin writing Tk scripts. What you need to know are the Tk commands used to create and configure widgets.

Note

The term *widget* has the same meaning in Tk as it does in an X toolkit such as Motif — a widget is a user interface component such as a push button, list box, or dialog box.

In the example in the preceding section, you used a label and a button widget. The command for creating a widget is the same as the widget's name. Therefore, the `button` command creates a button widget, and `label` creates a label.

Tk has 13 other widget-creation commands, which are listed in Table 8-4.

Table 8-4	Tk commands for creating widgets
Command	**Action**
button	Creates a button widget.
canvas	Creates a canvas widget where you can display text, bitmaps, lines, boxes, polygons, and other widgets.
checkbutton	Creates a toggle button and associates it with a Tcl variable.
entry	Creates a one-line text-entry widget.
frame	Creates a frame widget that is capable of holding other widgets.

(continued)

Table 8-4 *(continued)*

Command	Action
label	Creates a read-only one-line label widget.
listbox	Creates a list-box widget that is capable of scrolling lines of text.
menu	Creates a menu.
menubutton	Creates a menu-button widget that pops up an associated menu when clicked.
message	Creates a read-only multiple-line message widget.
radiobutton	Creates a radio-button widget that is linked to a Tcl variable.
scale	Creates a scale widget that can use to adjust the value of a variable.
scrollbar	Creates a scrollbar widget that you can link to another widget.
text	Creates a text widget where the user can enter and edit text.
toplevel	Creates a top-level widget (a widget whose window is a child of the X Window System's root window).

As you create a widget, you can specify many of its characteristics as arguments of the command. You can, for example, create a blue button with a red label (test) and display the button by using the following commands:

```
button .b -text test -fg red -bg blue
pack .b
```

The pack command does not create a widget; rather, it positions a widget in relationship with others. Table 8-5 lists all the widget-manipulation commands.

Tip

To look up online help on any Tk command listed in Tables 8-4 and 8-5, type **man 3**, followed by the command name. To get online help on the file command, for example, type **man 3 file**.

Table 8-5   Tk commands for manipulating widgets

Command	Action
after	Executes a command after a specified amount of time elapses.
bind	Associates a Tcl command with an X event so that the Tcl command is automatically invoked whenever the X event occurs.
destroy	Destroys one or more widgets.
focus	Directs keyboard events to a particular window (gives that window the input focus).

Command	Action
grab	Confines pointer and keyboard events to a specified widget and its children.
lower	Lowers a window in the stacking order (the stacking order refers to the order in which various windows overlap one another on the display screen).
option	Provides access to the X resource database.
pack	Automatically positions widgets in a frame, based on specified constraints.
place	Allows manual positioning of a widget relative to another widget.
raise	Raises a window's position in the stacking order.
selection	Manipulates the X PRIMARY selection (the standard name of a selection in X).
send	Sends a Tcl command to a different Tk application (used for interprocess communications).
tk	Provides information about the internal state of the Tk interpreter.
tkerror	Handles any error that occurs in Tk applications (the interpreter calls this command when errors occur in Tk applications).
tkwait	Waits for an event such as the destruction of a window or a change in the value of a variable.
update	Processes all pending events and updates the display.
winfo	Returns information about a widget.
wm	Provides access to the window manager. (You can send commands to the window manager, requesting a size for your top-level window, for example.)

Naming widgets

From the example that creates a label and a button, you may have guessed that the argument that follows the widget-creation command is the widget's name. You may be wondering why all the names start with a period. You must have a period at the beginning of a widget's name. The reason for this widget-naming convention is that widgets are organized in a hierarchy.

Suppose that you have a main window that contains a menu bar, a text area, and a scrollbar. The menu bar has two buttons, labeled File and Help. Figure 8-4 shows this widget hierarchy as it appears on-screen and also shows how the widget names relate to this hierarchy.

The root of the hierarchy is the main window of the application; a single period (dot) is used to denote the main window. This main window is a child of the root window of the X display. Each child of the main window has a name that begins with a dot. Thus, .menu is a child of the main window.

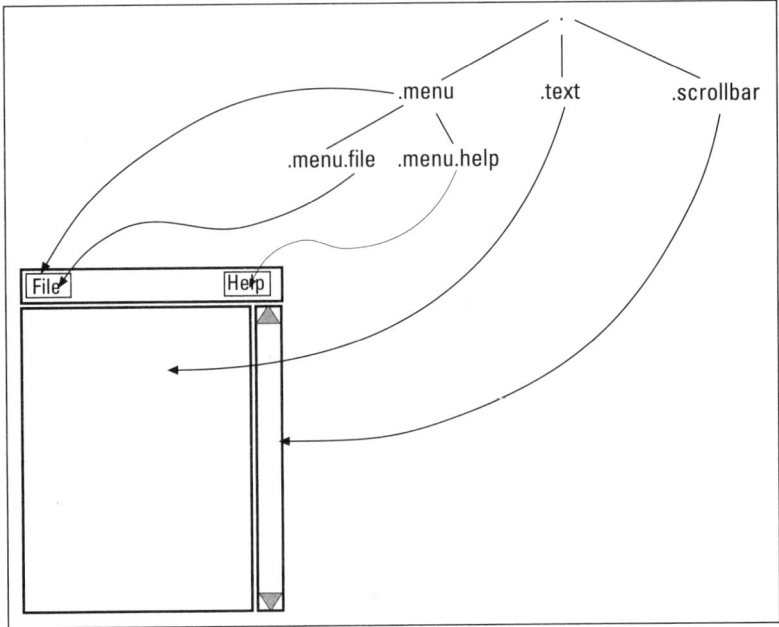

Figure 8-4: Relationship between widget names and widget hierarchy.

The names of other widgets depend on their positions in the hierarchy. The buttons in the menu bar have names — .menu.file and .menu.help — that indicate that they are child widgets of the .menu widget. As you create widgets, you specify the name of each widget, in turn defining the widget hierarchy.

If you think about it, you realize that the widget-naming scheme is similar to the pathname of a file in Linux. The period (.) in the widget names is analogous to the slash (/) in a file's pathname. In fact, the Tk documentation and online manual pages use the term *Tk pathname* to indicate the widget hierarchy.

Note

All widget names must start with a lowercase letter or a number. The name cannot include a period, because the period indicates the widget's location in the hierarchy. Names that start with an uppercase letter denote a class that is used in specifying resources; the meaning of the term *resources* is the same as in X.

Cross Reference

See Chapter 6 for a discussion of X resources and how they are specified.

Configuring widgets

Tk treats each widget name as a command name. You can perform operations on a specific widget by using that widget's name followed by arguments that make sense for that widget. If you have a button named .b, for example, use the following command to set that button's background to blue:

```
.b config -fg blue
```

Chapter 8: Scripting in Linux with Tcl/Tk

You can change the button's label to `Goodbye!` by using the following command:

`.b config -text Goodbye!`

The pairs of arguments `-fg blue` and `-text Goodbye!` specify the attributes of a widget. Each attribute name begins with a hyphen (`-`), as in `-text`. The next argument is that attribute's value.

Displaying widgets

Tk does not display a widget until you use a command to position the widget in the main window. You have to use a *geometry manager* — a Tk procedure that arranges one or more child widgets in a parent widget. Tk provides two geometry-management commands:

- The `place` command, which allows you to position a widget at a fixed location in the window of a designated master widget (which does not necessarily have to be a parent widget). The master widget is used as a reference — other widgets are positioned relative to the master widget. You also can specify relative positions, such as a horizontal position that is half the width of the master widget.

- The `pack` command, which arranges child widgets around the edges of the master window. You can specify which side of the parent the child widget is placed, as well as any extra space that you want to use around the child. As the name suggests, the `pack` command packs widgets together as tightly as possible.

Although the `pack` and `place` commands take many different options, their basic use is straightforward. My advice is that you start `wish`, create a few widgets, and try the `place` and `pack` commands to see their effects. After that, you can consult the online-manual page for the exact options whenever you need them.

Tip

The `pack` and `place` commands have a form — `pack forget` and `place forget` — that you can use to hide a widget. If you want to hide a button named `.btn1`, for example, use the command `pack forget .btn1`. To make the button reappear, use the `pack .btn1` command again.

The `pack` command

The `pack` command is the most commonly used geometry-management command in Tk. As some of the simple examples in this chapter show, to make a button named `.btn1` appear, you use `pack` as follows:

`pack .btn1`

You can specify several widget names on the same `pack` command line. To display the buttons `.btn1`, `.btn2`, and `.btn3`, arranged in a vertical line in that order, use the following:

`pack .btn1 .btn2 .btn3`

Table 8-6 summarizes the `pack` command's syntax. As Table 8-6 shows, you can position widgets and get information about the widget hierarchy. If you want a more complicated layout of widgets, you have to use the packing options shown in Table 8-7.

Table 8-6	Different forms of the `pack` command
Command	**Description**
`pack widgetNames options`	Packs the listed widgets according to the specified options (same as `pack configure`). Table 8-7 shows the list of available options.
`pack configure widgetNames options`	Packs the listed widgets according to the specified options.
`pack forget widgetNames`	Hides (*unpacks*) the specified widgets.
`pack info widget`	Returns the *packing configuration* (a list of options and values) of the specified `widget`.
`pack propagate widget boolean`	If `boolean` is 1, enables geometry propagation for the specified widget; otherwise, disables propagation. (When geometry propagation is enabled, the size of a widget's window is determined by the sizes of the widgets contained in that window.)
`pack slaves widget`	Returns the list of widgets managed by a specified `widget`.

Table 8-7	Options for packing widgets
Option	**Description**
`-after widgetName`	Places the widget that is being packed after the widget specified by `widgetName`.
`-anchor anchorPos`	Determines where the managed widget is placed. (Applies only when the containing widget is larger than the managed widget.) The `anchorPos` value can be `center`, `e`, `n`, `ne`, `nw`, `s`, `se`, `sw`, or `w`; the default is `center`.
`-before widgetName`	Places the widget that is being packed before the widget specified by `widgetName`.

Option	Description
-expand *boolean*	If *boolean* is 1, the contained widget expands to use any space left over in the containing widget.
-fill *style*	Indicates how to expand the containing widget if it gets bigger than what the widgets contained in it require. The *style* value can be both, none, x, or y.
-in *widgetName*	Indicates the widget in which the widgets specified in the pack command line are placed. If you do not use this option, widgets are packed in their parent widget (f.b is packed in .f).
-ipadx *amount*	Specifies extra horizontal space inside the widget that is being packed (in addition to the space that it already needs). The *amount* value is a number, in screen units.
-ipady *amount*	Specifies extra vertical space inside the widget that is being packed (in addition to the space that it already needs). The *amount* value is a number, in screen units.
-padx *amount*	Specifies extra horizontal space outside the border of the widget that is being packed. The *amount* value is a number, in screen units.
-pady *amount*	Specifies extra vertical space outside the border of the widget that is being packed. The *amount* value is a number, in screen units.
-side *sideName*	Packs against the specified side. The *sideName* value is bottom, left, right, or top; the default is top.

Tip

If you are wondering how to remember all these options, my advice is that you *not* remember them. You usually can get by with just a few of these options, and you will begin to remember these options after a while. To become familiar with what each option does, start wish, create a few widgets, and try packing them with different options. From then on, whenever you need the exact syntax of an option, consult the online manual by typing **man 3 pack** or simply **man pack**.

The place **command**

The place command is a simpler way to specify the placement of widgets, but you have to position all the windows yourself. You may find place to be simpler than pack, because the place command gives you direct control of the widget positions. On the other hand, direct control of widget placement is fine for a few windows, but it can get tedious in a hurry when you have many widgets in a user interface.

Using `place`, you can position a widget at a specific location. To place `.btn1` at the coordinate (100, 50) in its parent widget, use the following command:

```
place .btn1 -x 100 -y 50
```

A good use of `place` is to center a widget within its parent widget. For this purpose, you use the `-relx` and `-rely` options of `place`. If `.f` is a *frame widget* (a widget that contains other widgets), you can display it at the center of the parent window by using the following commands:

```
frame .f
button .f.b1 -text Configure
button .f.b2 -text Quit
pack .f.b1 .f.b2 -side left
place .f -relx 0.5 -rely 0.5 -anchor center
```

As the code fragment shows, the buttons inside the frame are packed with the `pack` command. Only the frame, `.f`, is positioned with the `place` command. The `-relx` and `-rely` options allow you to specify the relative positions in terms of a fraction of the containing widget's size. A zero value for `-relx` means the left edge; 1 is the right edge; and 0.5 means the middle.

Like `pack`, the `place` command has several forms, which are listed in Table 8-8. Also, `place` takes several options, which are summarized in Table 8-9. Use these options with the plain `place` command or `place configure` command.

Table 8-8	Forms of the `place` command
Command	**Description**
`place widgetNames options`	Positions the listed widgets according to the specified options (same as `place configure`). Table 8-9 shows the list of available options.
`place configure widgetNames options`	Positions the listed widgets according to the specified options.
`place forget widgetNames`	Stops managing the specified widgets and unmaps (hides) them.
`place info widget`	Returns the list of options and their values for the specified `widget`.
`place slaves widget`	Returns the list of widgets managed by the specified `widget`.

Table 8-9	Options for placing widgets
Option	Description
-anchor *anchorPos*	Specifies which point of the managed widget is placed in the specified position in the managing window. The *anchorPos* value can be center, e, n, ne, nw, s, se, sw, or w; the default is nw (upper-left corner).
-bordermode *bmode*	Indicates how the managing widget's borders are used when the managed widgets are positioned. The *bmode* value must be ignore, inside, or outside.
-height *size*	Specifies the height of the managed widget.
-in *widgetName*	Indicates the widget relative to which the positions of the widgets specified in the place command line are specified. If you do not use this option, widgets are placed relative to their parent widgets (.f.b is positioned relative to .f).
-relheight *fraction*	Specifies the height of the managed widget as a fraction of the managing widget. The fraction is a floating-point value.
-relwidth *fraction*	Specifies the width of the managed widget as a fraction of the managing widget. The fraction is a floating-point value.
-relx *fraction*	Specifies the horizontal position of the managed widget as a fraction of the managing widget's width. The fraction is a floating-point value; 0.0 means the left edge, and 1.0 means the right edge.
-rely *fraction*	Specifies the vertical position of the managed widget as a fraction of the managing widget's height. The fraction is a floating-point value; 0.0 means the top edge, and 1.0 means the bottom edge.
-x *coord*	Specifies the horizontal position of the managed widget's anchor point in the managing widget. The *coord* value is in screen coordinates.
-y *coord*	Specifies the vertical position of the managed widget's anchor point in the managing widget. The *coord* value is in screen coordinates.
-width *size*	Specifies the width of the managed widget.

Binding actions to events

When you write a program that has a graphical user interface, various program actions are initiated by events such as the user clicking a button in the user interface. In a Tk script, you indicate what the program does by associating actions with events. In this case, an *action* simply is a Tcl script that performs some task. In the case of a Quit button, for example, a logical action is the Tcl command exit that ends the Tk script.

For buttons, a simple way is to associate an action with a click of the button. Use the `-command` option of the `button` command to specify a Tcl command to be executed when the user clicks the button. The `exit` command is associated with the Quit button as follows:

```
button .b -text Quit -command { exit }
```

Tip

The braces are not necessary when you have only one Tcl command, but you can place more than one command inside the braces.

The `bind` command is the most general way to associate an action with an event. Following is the general syntax of the `bind` command:

```
bind widgetName <eventSpecification> TclCommand
```

The `widgetName` argument typically is the pathname of a widget, although you can bind an event to a class of widgets, such as all buttons. Typically, you have to consult online help to specify `eventSpecification`. (In this section, I show you an example and then explain event specifications.) The last argument — `TclCommand` — refers to the Tcl commands that you want to execute when the specified event occurs. These Tcl commands can be any Tcl script, ranging from a simple `puts` command to a complete Tcl script stored in a separate file.

To see a more detailed example of how to bind an action to an event, consider this scenario. You may have noticed that many Microsoft Windows applications sport a toolbar — essentially, a collection of buttons, each of which is meant to perform a specific task. Typically, each button bears an icon that indicates the purpose of the button. To help users learn the meaning of a button quickly, many Windows applications have a feature called *tool help*. If you place the mouse pointer on a button, a small window pops up, displaying a short help message that tells you what the button does.

You can use Tk to implement a similar tool-help feature. Follow these steps:

1. Create the button.

2. Prepare the help message as a label (preferably with a bright background, such as yellow).

3. When the mouse pointer enters a button, an `Enter` event occurs. Bind the `Enter` event to a command that makes the help label visible. Use the `place` command to position the label relative to the button so that the tool-help label always appears near the associated button.

   The following example shows how `bind` is used to associate the `place` command (shown within braces) with the `Enter` event:

   ```
   bind .f.b <Enter> { place .bh -in .f.b -relx 0.5 -rely 1.0 }
   ```

4. When the mouse pointer leaves the button, a `Leave` event occurs. Bind the `Leave` event to the `place forget` command to hide the help message, as follows:

   ```
   bind .f.b <Leave> { place forget .bh }
   ```

The following sample `toolhelp` script demonstrates how to implement tool help in Tk:

```
#!/usr/bin/wish -f
# Demonstrates a "tool help" window that appears when you
# place the mouse pointer inside the "File" button.

wm geometry . 100x60

frame .f
button .f.b -text File
label .bh -text "Open file"
.bh config -bg yellow

bind .f.b <Enter> { place .bh -in .f.b -relx 0.5 -rely 1.0 }
bind .f.b <Leave> { place forget .bh }

button .f.q -text Quit -command { exit }

pack .f.b .f.q -side left
pack .f -fill x
```

Make the `toolhelp` script file executable by using the `chmod +x toolhelp` command. Then run that script by typing **toolhelp** at the shell prompt in an `xterm` window. Figure 8-5 shows the window that results after you place the mouse pointer on the File button.

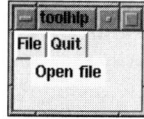

Figure 8-5: A Tk script that demonstrates how to implement tool-help messages.

When you use `bind` to associate a Tcl script with an event, you need to know how to specify the event. Most events are either keyboard events or mouse events. A smaller number of events are related to the state of a widget's window. `<Map>` and `<Unmap>` events, for example, occur when a widget is managed or unmanaged (when you use `pack forget` or `place forget`).

Keyboard events

There are two keyboard events:

- `<KeyPress>` occurs when you press a key.
- `<KeyRelease>` occurs when you release the key.

You can specify a keyboard event for a specific key by appending that key's keysym (which is the X Window System's standard name for a key) to the string `KeyPress-` and enclosing everything in angle brackets. The event associated with pressing the q key, for example, is specified by `<Keypress-q>`. Tk provides a shorter format for keyboard events. You can simply place the keysym inside angle brackets, as follows:

`<q>`

For most key presses, the event specification is straightforward. If you want to exit when the user presses Ctrl+C inside a widget named `.text`, use the `bind` command as follows:

```
bind .text <Control-c> exit
```

Following are some other commonly used keysyms:

```
BackSpace  comma  Down    dollar  Escape  exclam  Left  numbersign
period     Return Right   Tab     Up
```

Tip

Inside the Tcl commands that are bound to a key event, use the %A keyword to refer to the printable character that the user presses. For any nonprintable character, %A is replaced by { } (a pair of empty braces). The %W keyword is replaced by the name of the widget that receives the keypress. Thus, you can use the following code to insert text into a text widget:

```
# Assume .text1 is a text widget
bind .text <KeyPress> {
    if { "%A" != "{}"} { %W insert insert %A}
}
```

Remember that a widget's name itself is a command and that the command's argument depends on the type of widget. For a text widget, the command `%W insert insert %A` inserts the character into the text widget.

Mouse events

Use `<ButtonPress>` and `<ButtonRelease>` to denote mouse-button click and release events, respectively. You have to append the button number to make the event specific. Thus, the action of clicking the left mouse button (which is button 1 in X terminology) is denoted by `<ButtonPress-1>`. A shorthand notation for button presses is to leave out `Press`; thus, you can write `<Button-1>` to denote the event generated by clicking the left mouse button.

Tip

In the Tcl commands that are bound to a mouse event, the keywords %x and %y denote the x and y coordinates of the mouse pointer (relative to the widget's window) at the time of the mouse event. Thus, you can track the position of a mouse click of a widget as follows:

```
bind .text1 <Button-1> { puts "Click at (%x, %y) on widget: %W"}
```

Other mouse events include the `Enter` and `Leave` events, which occur when you move the mouse pointer into or out of a widget, respectively. These two events are denoted by `<Enter>` and `<Leave>`. The toolhelp example shown in "Binding actions to events" earlier in this chapter illustrates a way to use the `<Enter>` and `<Leave>` events.

Another event related to the mouse pointer is the `<Motion>` event, which occurs when you move the mouse pointer within a widget.

Window events

In addition to keyboard and mouse events, X includes many events that occur when a window is manipulated. The X server generates `<Map>` and `<Unmap>` events, for example, when a widget is displayed or hidden (by the `pack` or `place` command).

A `<Configure>` event occurs when the user resizes a window. Thus, you can bind a `<Configure>` event to a redisplay procedure that redraws the contents of a widget, based on the new size.

A `<Destroy>` event occurs when a window is about to be destroyed. You bind a procedure to the `<Destroy>` event and intercept requests to delete a window.

More information on the X Window System

Tk allows you to intercept many more X events. For information on these X events and other elements of the X Window System, consult one of the following books:

Naba Barkakati, *X Window System Programming*, Second Edition, SAMS, 1994.

O'Reilly & Associates, *Volume 1: Xlib Programming Manual*, O'Reilly & Associates, 1993.

O'Reilly & Associates, *Volume 2: Xlib Reference Manual*, O'Reilly & Associates, 1993.

Summary

The combination of Tool Command Language (Tcl) and its X Window System-based graphical toolkit, Tk, is ideal for quickly developing applications with a graphical interface. This chapter introduces Tcl/Tk through simple examples. By reading this chapter, you learn

- ▶ Tcl is an interpreted language with a set of commands that you can combine according to a set of rules. Tcl comes with the Slackware Linux distribution on the companion CD-ROM. You can install Tcl at the same time that you install Linux (see Chapter 1 for more information).

- ▶ You can learn the Tcl syntax and develop Tcl scripts interactively by running the Tcl command interpreter, `tclsh`, and entering Tcl commands at the `tclsh` prompt.

- ▶ Tcl includes built-in commands for most routine tasks, such as reading and writing files, manipulating strings, and running any UNIX command. Additionally, Tcl includes control-flow commands — such as `if`, `for`, and `while` — that enable you to control the sequence of commands processed by the interpreter. Finally, you can use Tcl's `proc` command to write new Tcl commands that use combinations of existing commands.

- ▶ Tk, the Tcl toolkit, is an extension of Tcl that uses the X Window System to allow you to build graphical user interfaces. Tk provides the three-dimensional appearance of Motif, but Tk does not require the Motif toolkit or any other X toolkit. Tk is built on Xlib, which is the C-language Application Programming Interface (API) for X.

- ▶ Tk includes commands for creating many common widgets (user-interface elements), such as button, label, text-entry, list-box, and scrollbar widgets. A widget-naming convention specifies the widget hierarchy (the organization of the widgets).

- ▶ To make the graphical interface active, you have to use the `bind` command to associate Tcl commands with specific keyboard and mouse events.

- ▶ You can interactively experiment with and create Tk programs by running `wish`, the windowing shell that can interpret all Tcl and Tk commands.

Part III
Exploiting Your Hardware in Linux

Chapter 9: Computers

Chapter 10: Video Cards and Monitors

Chapter 11: Disk Drives

Chapter 12: CD-ROM Drives and Sound Cards

Chapter 13: Keyboards and Pointing Devices

Chapter 14: Printers

Chapter 15: Modems

Chapter 16: Networks

Chapter 17: PC Cards

Chapter 9

Computers

In This Chapter
- Looking at different PC architectures: ISA, EISA, and MCA
- Using high-speed peripheral buses: VESA Local Bus (VLB) and Peripheral Component Interconnect (PCI)
- Using the /proc file system as a source of information
- Running Linux on laptop computers
- Installing Linux on laptop computers

Typically, after you install Linux by following the instructions in Chapter 1, you can begin using it without ever worrying about the details of your PC's architecture. You have to pay attention to the make and model of your computer and its internal details only if you run into problems during installation. At minimum, you may have to understand your PC's hardware architecture — whether it uses a PCI bus or a VLB bus, for example — to successfully install and use Linux on your PC. At worst, you may have to know specific details about your system's motherboard (the main circuit board in your system) — information such as the type of Integrated Drive Electronics (IDE) controller used on the motherboard. Other peripherals, such as the hard disk and the display, are equally important; I cover these hardware components in subsequent chapters.

In a sense, the title of this chapter is misleading because the term *computer* includes everything from the processor to the hard drive and the display. This chapter's goal is to provide information about the compatibility of Linux with specific processor and bus types (the bus is a standard physical connection method for peripherals). Because a laptop computer is a more tightly integrated system than a desktop computer, this chapter also provides information on running Linux on several popular brands of laptop computers.

Basic Processor and Bus Types

As you move from a simple operating system such as MS-DOS to a more complex one such as Linux, the exact details of your computer's hardware become more important because the operating system tries to make use of all features of the hardware. Most operating systems, including Linux, use device drivers to access and use hardware devices. However, some hardware, such as the system's processor and associated circuitry, must be supported by the Linux kernel — the core operating system.

Linux was developed for the Intel 80386 processor; the program uses what is known as the *protected mode* of that processor. MS-DOS uses the processor's *real mode,* in which the amount of addressable memory is limited to 1MB. In protected mode, 386 and better processors can access a large amount of memory (theoretically, up to 4GB).

Typical 386 architecture often limits 386-based PCs to run with at most 16MB of RAM. If you want to install more than 16MB RAM on a 386 PC, you may need a BIOS (Basic Input and Output System) ROM (Read-Only Memory) upgrade. For this, you have to contact your PC's manufacturer and get the new ROM chips. Then, you have to remove the old ROM BIOS chips and install the new ones before you install Linux. Because Linux runs quite well on a 386 with enough memory, upgrading the BIOS can be a worthwhile exercise to put your old 386 PCs to good use.

You need at least an 80386 system to run Linux. Linux runs on all variants of the 80386, 80486, and Pentium processors. Thus, you can run Linux on 386SX, 386DX, 386SL, 386SLC, 486SX, 486DX, 486SL, 486DX2, and 486DX4 processors from Intel. (This list does not include all variants of the 386 and 486 processors, but you get the idea.) Collectively, these processors are often referred to as the 80x86 family of processors. Linux also runs on 80x86-compatible processors from other vendors, such as Cyrix and AMD.

The 80x86 family of processors uses a *floating-point processor* (also known as a *math coprocessor*) to speed floating-point computations. In many 486 and Pentium processors, the floating-point processor is part of the basic processor. Linux uses the hardware floating-point processor, if available. Otherwise, Linux emulates the floating-point processor with software that is part of the Linux kernel.

Linux on other processors

Although the most widely distributed version of Linux is for Intel 80x86 and Pentium processors, developers are working on implementing Linux for systems based on other processors, such as the Motorola 68000 family, Digital Equipment Corporation's (DEC) Alpha AXP processor, the PowerPC processor, and the MIPS R4600 processor. You can find further information on these versions of Linux on the Internet. (You need a Web browser to access these Web pages; Chapter 20 explains how to use a Web browser.) Consult the following resources:

Linux for systems with Motorola 68000 processors: http://www-users.informatik.rwth-aachen.de/~hn/linux68k.html

Linux for DEC Alpha systems: ftp://ftp.dec.com/pub/DEC/Linux-Alpha/

Linux for systems with the MIPS processor: http://www.fnet.fr/linux-mips/

Linux for systems with the PowerPC processor: ftp://sunsite.unc.edu/pub/Linux/docs/ports/Linux-PowerPC-FAQ.gz

Bus types

The term *bus* refers to the collection of wires that carries signals between the PC's processor and any peripheral devices. After the processor, the bus is a critical hardware characteristic of a PC. Each type of bus specifies the meaning of various signals and the *protocol* (the order and timing of signals) for transferring data over the bus.

Each bus has a maximum rate of data transfer, which depends on how many bits of data the bus can carry at a time and on the *clock rate* — how many times a second the signal can change between two states (0 and 1). Like a processor's internal clock rate, the bus clock rate is expressed in megahertz (MHz). 1MHz means a million times a second.

Each bus type specifies the physical dimensions of the controller card, the number and purpose of the connectors, and the slot on the motherboard where you plug in the card. Your system's hard disk, for example, is connected to the motherboard by means of a disk-controller card that is compatible with the bus type of that motherboard.

Following are several popular bus types:

- The *Industry Standard Architecture (ISA) bus* is the most widely used bus; this bus was used in the original IBM PC-AT. The ISA bus can transfer data 16 bits at a time; it operates at an 8-MHz clock rate, which is slow compared with today's processors, which have clock rates in the 100-MHz range. Typically, the ISA bus can achieve a data-transfer rate of 5MB/sec (that's 5 megabytes per second).

- The *Video Electronics Standard Association (VESA) Local Bus,* or VLB, was designed for high-performance data transfer between the processor and the video card. The typical VLB transfer rate is 30MB/sec.

Caution

Note that early VLB systems often have a nonstandard implementation of the VESA local bus, which may cause problems with Linux.

- The *Micro Channel Architecture (MCA) bus* is IBM's proprietary bus, which first appeared in the PS/2 PCs. IBM designed this bus as a high-speed bus, but its proprietary nature kept it from being widely used in PCs.

- The *Extended Industry Standard Architecture (EISA) bus* came about as an alternative to the MCA bus with performance comparable to that of the MCA. The EISA bus is not widely used because the EISA bus peripheral cards are more expensive than their ISA bus counterparts. EISA bus performance is comparable with that of the VLB, transferring data at rates of 30MB/sec.

- The *Peripheral Component Interconnect (PCI) bus* is the latest high-performance bus; it operates at a clock rate of 33 MHz and can transfer up to 64 bits of data at a time. When a PCI bus is used to transfer 32 bits at a time, the 33-MHz clock rate implies that the bus can transfer data at the rate of $33 \times 4 = 132$MB per second (notice that 32 bits = 4 bytes). PCI is the up-and-coming standard; the current crop of Pentium PCs uses the PCI bus but also offers ISA bus slots so that you can continue to use ISA cards. Typically, the PCI bus achieves a data-transfer rate of 60MB/sec.

Linux supports ISA, VLB, EISA, and PCI buses; the version of Linux on the companion CD-ROM can be installed and run on systems that have any of these buses. Because a bus is meant for connecting peripherals to the system, the support for a bus implies that you can use peripherals that use controller cards of that bus type.

Of course, not all peripheral hardware (such as the graphics card and disk controller) for all these buses works under Linux. Each peripheral requires a driver, and the driver may not yet exist for some newer graphics cards or disk controllers. You can find more information about specific devices in Chapters 10 through 17.

The Linux kernel in this book's Slackware Linux distribution CD-ROM does not support IBM PS/2 systems that have the Micro Channel Architecture (MCA) bus. The primary problem in supporting a bus such as MCA is that someone has to develop the driver software needed to access peripherals such as disk drives and video cards. Some Linux developers are working on supporting the MCA bus. You can find a developer's release (not yet ready for general distribution) for PS/2s with ESDI (Enhanced Small Device Interface) hard drives at ftp://invaders.dcrl.nd.edu/pub/misc/.

PCI-bus support in Linux

The PCI bus is a relative newcomer, but it is rapidly becoming the bus of choice in all new systems, especially the Pentium-based PCs. One attraction is the high throughput of the bus. Additionally, the bus is processor-independent; a PCI interface card should work on a Pentium PC as well as on a DEC Alpha system, as long as both systems use the PCI bus. The PCI bus design also makes it easy to build PCI components that can go directly on the motherboard, thereby minimizing the cost of additional "glue logic" (that's extra electronic components required to make everything work) that other buses require.

Among the current crop of PCI motherboards, the emerging standard seems to be the ones based on the Intel Triton chipset. This chipset supports a special type of memory called EDO (extended data out) DRAM (dynamic random-access memory), which includes a cache within the memory chip. Most current Pentium PCs use Intel Triton motherboards with EDO DRAM together with an external 256K cache.

Typically, a PCI motherboard also has a built-in PCI video chipset and an IDE (Integrated Drive Electronics) interface for connecting IDE hard disks to the system. The PCI IDE interface is described further in Chapter 11.

XFree86 supports many PCI video cards — such as the ATI Graphics Pro Turbo, Diamond Viper PCI, and Number Nine GXE Pro PCI — as well as integrated video chipsets, such as S3 Trio32/Trio64.

The version of Linux on the companion CD-ROM includes PCI Probe code, which collects information about PCI devices on your system as Linux boots. You can see this information by issuing a `cat /proc/pci` command. (The `/proc` file system is explained in the "Information from the `/proc` File System" section of this chapter.)

Some specific problems

When you have problems installing or configuring Linux on a PC, most of those problems have to do with specific peripherals — disk controllers, video cards, the CD-ROM drive interface, and so on. A few problems, however, are directly related to the processor or the basic hardware architecture of the PC. This section points out a few such problems and suggests some solutions.

System slowdown after memory is added

This problem occurs when you add extra memory to your PC (go from 16MB to 32MB, for example) and expect a significant performance gain; instead, the system slows dramatically. The reason for this strange behavior is when you add memory, you also must make sure that the new memory is being cached.

Cache memory is very fast (and expensive) memory that keeps the processor working at full speed. (The *speed* of memory, incidentally, refers to how quickly the processor can get data in and out of that memory.) Typically, a system may have 128K or 256K of cache memory.

Ordinary memory (the kind you have in amounts of 4, 8, or 16MB) is too slow to keep up with today's fast processors. The cache memory acts as intermediate storage between the ordinary memory and the processor.

Secret

When you add memory, you have to make sure that the cache memory works with the new memory. The exact solution depends on your motherboard. Sometimes, the solution is a matter of running your PC's setup program and turning on an option to cache the new memory area, which may be switched off.

On some systems, you have to install the memory in specific physical sockets to ensure that all the memory is cached. Yet another solution may be to set *jumpers* — connectors between pins on the motherboard — to enable the caching.

Some motherboards cache a certain amount of memory, based on the amount of cache memory. Usually, a motherboard with a 256K cache should be able to handle the caching needs of the system. Even with a 256K cache, you still may have to set some jumpers or turn on some options to enable caching for all the memory. Check your system's documentation for any clues; a small motherboard manual may provide this information.

Cache not enabled for Cyrix 486DLC

The Cyrix 486 family of processors is a clone of the Intel 80486 family of processors. Like the various Intel 486 processors — 486DX, 486SX, 486SL, and so on — the Cyrix 486 family has several types of processors. Like the Intel 486 family, the Cyrix 486 chips also have an on-chip cache — a small amount of memory (anywhere from 1K to 16K) that's built into the chip. This cache stores instructions and data that are waiting to be processed.

Unlike the Intel 486 chips, however, some members of the Cyrix 486 family — in particular, the CX486DLC and CX486SLC processors — do not enable their on-chip caches by default. These processors rely on a motherboard with a BIOS that enables the cache. In other words, these Cyrix processors have a software-controlled cache that must be turned on. Without the cache, these Cyrix 486 processors do not perform much better than their 386 counterparts.

Secret

You have to apply a patch to the Linux kernel to turn on the cache in CX486DLC processors. The patch is in two parts: The first part adds the options for Cyrix processors to the kernel configuration script, and the second part adds the cache-enable code to the Linux bootstrap routines. If you have a Cyrix 486DLC or 486SLC system, you should get this patch from ftp://sunsite.unc.edu/pub/Linux/kernel/patches/CxPatch030.tar.z and apply it.

You don't need this patch if the Cyrix 486DLC processor is on a motherboard that enables the on-chip cache properly. Unfortunately, some such motherboards enable this cache properly only when you run DOS, which uses the BIOS on the motherboard. Thus, you may have to apply the patch even with Cyrix 486DLC-aware motherboards.

Information from the /proc File System

Wizard

You can find out a great deal about your computer by consulting the contents of a special file system known as the /proc file system. To use the /proc file system, of course, you must have Linux installed and running on your system. Still, knowing about the /proc file system is useful because it can help you determine exact information about your PC (at least, about what Linux thinks your PC has) in case you are adding a new device or rebuilding the kernel and trying to decide what types of features you should enable in the kernel.

The /proc file system is not a real directory on the disk but a collection of data structures in memory, managed by the Linux kernel, that appears to the user to be a set of directories and files. The purpose of /proc (also called the *process file system*) is to allow users to access information about the Linux kernel and the processes that are currently running on their system.

You can access the /proc file system just as you access any other directory, but you have to know the meaning of various files to interpret the information. Typically, you can use the cat or more command to view the contents of a file in /proc; the file's contents provide information about some part of the system.

As with any directory, you may want to start by looking at a detailed directory listing of /proc. To do so, type **ls -l /proc**. Following is typical output from my system:

```
ls -l /proc
total 0
dr-xr-xr-x   4 root    root         0 Sep 10 16:16 1/
dr-xr-xr-x   4 root    root         0 Sep 10 16:16 109/
dr-xr-xr-x   4 naba    users        0 Sep 10 16:16 110/
dr-xr-xr-x   4 naba    users        0 Sep 10 16:16 111/
dr-xr-xr-x   4 naba    users        0 Sep 10 16:16 112/
dr-xr-xr-x   4 root    root         0 Sep 10 16:16 25/
dr-xr-xr-x   4 root    root         0 Sep 10 16:16 38/
dr-xr-xr-x   4 root    root         0 Sep 10 16:16 40/
dr-xr-xr-x   4 bin     root         0 Sep 10 16:16 42/
dr-xr-xr-x   4 root    root         0 Sep 10 16:16 44/
dr-xr-xr-x   4 root    root         0 Sep 10 16:16 46/
dr-xr-xr-x   4 root    root         0 Sep 10 16:16 49/
dr-xr-xr-x   4 root    root         0 Sep 10 16:16 51/
dr-xr-xr-x   4 root    root         0 Sep 10 16:16 55/
dr-xr-xr-x   4 naba    users        0 Sep 10 16:16 557/
dr-xr-xr-x   4 root    root         0 Sep 10 16:16 6/
dr-xr-xr-x   4 root    root         0 Sep 10 16:16 7/
dr-xr-xr-x   4 root    root         0 Sep 10 16:16 75/
dr-xr-xr-x   4 root    root         0 Sep 10 16:16 837/
dr-xr-xr-x   4 naba    users        0 Sep 10 16:16 838/
dr-xr-xr-x   4 root    root         0 Sep 10 16:16 86/
dr-xr-xr-x   4 root    root         0 Sep 10 16:16 88/
dr-xr-xr-x   4 root    root         0 Sep 10 16:16 89/
dr-xr-xr-x   4 root    root         0 Sep 10 16:16 94/
dr-xr-xr-x   4 naba    users        0 Sep 10 16:18 957/
dr-xr-xr-x   4 naba    users        0 Sep 10 16:16 97/
-r--r--r--   1 root    root         0 Sep 10 16:16 cpuinfo
-r--r--r--   1 root    root         0 Sep 10 16:16 devices
-r--r--r--   1 root    root         0 Sep 10 16:16 dma
-r--r--r--   1 root    root         0 Sep 10 16:16 filesystems
-r--r--r--   1 root    root         0 Sep 10 16:16 interrupts
-r--r--r--   1 root    root         0 Sep 10 16:16 ioports
-r--------   1 root    root  16781312 Sep 10 16:16 kcore
-r--------   1 root    root         0 Sep  8 19:59 kmsg
-r--r--r--   1 root    root         0 Sep 10 16:16 ksyms
-r--r--r--   1 root    root         0 Sep 10 15:45 loadavg
-r--r--r--   1 root    root         0 Sep 10 16:16 meminfo
-r--r--r--   1 root    root         0 Sep 10 16:16 modules
dr-xr-xr-x   2 root    root         0 Sep 10 16:16 net/
-r--r--r--   1 root    root         0 Sep 10 16:16 pci
dr-xr-xr-x   4 naba    users        0 Sep 10 16:18 self/
-r--r--r--   1 root    root         0 Sep 10 16:16 stat
-r--r--r--   1 root    root         0 Sep 10 16:16 uptime
-r--r--r--   1 root    root         0 Sep 10 16:16 version
```

The first set of directories (indicated by the letter d at the beginning of the line) represents the processes that are currently running on your system. Each directory that corresponds to a process has the process ID (a number) as its name. The slash at the end of each directory name is not part of the name; it's a way to identify a directory.

Notice the large file named /proc/kcore; that file represents the entire physical memory of your system. As the next few sections show, the files in the /proc file system can help you find out a great deal about your system.

The /proc/cpuinfo file

Several files in /proc contain interesting information about your system's hardware. The /proc/cpuinfo file, for example, lists the key characteristics of your system, such as processor type and floating-point processor information.

Note

The term *CPU* stands for *central processing unit.* In the days of the mainframe and the minicomputer, the CPU really was a unit — like a cabinet. For a PC, however, the CPU is the microprocessor — the 486 or Pentium chip that's at the heart of the PC. Thus, the file that contains information about the processor (CPU) is named cpuinfo — a name derived from concatenating *cpu* with *info* (the short form of *information*). I am explaining this thought process because that's how programmers typically create short, cryptic names. After you see some of these names, you'll begin to guess their meanings more readily.

On my system, when I want to check out the /proc/cpuinfo file, I type **cat /proc/cpuinfo** and get the following output:

```
cat /proc/cpuinfo
cpu            : 586
model          : Pentium 90/100
mask           : E
vid            : GenuineIntel
fdiv_bug       : no
math           : yes
hlt            : yes
wp             : yes
Integrated NPU     : yes
Enhanced VM86      : yes
IO Breakpoints     : yes
4MB Pages      : yes
TS Counters    : yes
Pentium MSR    : yes
Mach. Ch. Exep.    : yes
CMPXCHGB8B     : yes
BogoMips       : 30.22
```

This output is from a Dell Dimension P75 (75 MHz Pentium) system from Dell Computer Corporation. The listing shows many interesting characteristics of the processor. Notice the line that starts with fdiv_bug. Remember the infamous Pentium floating-point-division bug? The bug is in an instruction called fdiv (for floating-point division). Thus, the fdiv_bug line indicates whether this particular Pentium has the bug (fortunately, my system's processor does not).

Cross Reference

The last line in the `/proc/cpuinfo` file shows the BogoMips (for more information on BogoMips, see the "What is BogoMips?" sidebar in Chapter 1) for the processor, as computed by the Linux kernel when it boots. BogoMips is something that Linux uses internally to time delay loops.

The `/proc/pci` file

If you have a PCI system (which most new Pentium systems are apt to be), you can check the `/proc/pci` file for information about the PCI devices on your system. As usual, type **cat /proc/pci** to see the information. Following is what I find on a Dell Pentium system with a PCI motherboard:

```
PCI devices found :
Bus 0 Device  1 Function 0.
  ISA bridge : VLSI 82C593-FC1 (rev 1).
Bus 0 Device 10 Function 0.
  VGA display controller : S3 Inc. Trio32/Trio64 (rev 0).
Bus 0 Device 13 Function 0.
  IDE controller : CMD 640A (rev 2). 8259's interrupt 14.
```

As the listing shows, the system has three PCI devices. The first device connects the PCI bus to the ISA bus. This system offers connectors for both ISA and PCI devices, but the motherboard uses a PCI bus; therefore, it needs a bridge between the PCI and ISA bus.

The second device is the video-display controller. This controller is a video card (or graphics card) that is built into the motherboard as a PCI device. Essentially, the motherboard contains the chips that are necessary to drive the monitor.

Note

Another PCI device is the interface to Integrated Drive Electronics (IDE) that are built into each IDE disk drive. Although the `/proc/pci` file shows this PCI device as an IDE controller, a more appropriate name would be *IDE interface* because the device-control functions actually are handled by the IDE circuitry built into each IDE drive. (The name *Integrated Drive Electronics* means that the electronics needed to control a drive are built into the drive itself.)

For each device, the `/proc/pci` file also shows the make and model of the device. The video controller, for example, is an S3 Trio32/Trio64 chipset. You can use information about the video chipset when you are configuring XFree86 to run on your system.

Secret

As the `/proc/pci` file shows, this Pentium system's IDE interface is the CMD 640A. The system's disk and CD-ROM drive are connected to the CMD640A. Although my system did not have any problems with the disk or the CD-ROM drive, some people have reported problems with the CMD 640 IDE controllers for the PCI bus. In particular, the CMD640 interface reportedly does not work reliably when drives are attached to the second interface. For the version of Linux on the companion CD-ROM, the workaround for any problems with the CMD 640 IDE interface involves placing the following line in the `/etc/lilo.conf` file:

```
append = "hda=serialize"
```

Other information in the /proc file system

Wizard

All peripheral devices (such as the hard disk, sound card, CD-ROM drive, modem, and printer) in your system need access to some system resources. Each device typically needs the following resources:

- *Interrupt Request (IRQ) number,* which the device uses to get the attention of the system's processor. You can think of the IRQ as being the direct line between a device and the processor. A limited number of IRQ lines are available, so a good possibility of conflict exists if you have too many peripheral devices in your system.

- *Input/Output Port address (I/O address),* which the processor uses to send data to and receive data from the peripheral device. A device typically needs a range of unique I/O addresses to work properly.

- *Direct Memory Access (DMA) channel,* which the device uses to access the system's memory directly, rather than going through the processor.

Some devices do not need DMA channels, but all devices need an IRQ number and the required range of I/O addresses.

Even Linux needs these resources — IRQ, I/O address, and DMA channel — for each device because the underlying hardware architecture dictates the need for these resources. Typically, if you have this information available for all hardware in your system, you can avoid problems that occur because of conflicting assignments of IRQ, I/O address, or DMA channel.

Cross Reference

When you rebuild the kernel (as explained in Chapter 2) to add support for a specific device, such as a particular sound card, you have to provide the necessary IRQ, DMA, and I/O addresses to configure Linux properly. For some devices, Linux can probe the device and determine this information.

Wizard

In addition to `/proc/cpuinfo` and `/proc/pci`, three files in the `/proc` file system contain information about the IRQ, DMA, and I/O addresses that are being used in your system. These files are

- `/proc/interrupts`, which contains information about the IRQs that are being used

- `/proc/dma`, which shows the DMA channels that are being used

- `/proc/ioports`, which lists the I/O port address ranges that are being used

As an example, following is the `/proc/interrupts` file for my system:

```
 0: 1077966   timer
 1:     413   keyboard
 2:       0 + cascade
10:     538   3c509
11:    1039   aha1542
12:     451   PS/2 Mouse
13:       1   math error
14:    4899 + ide0
15:      19 + ide1
```

The first number on each line is the IRQ (interrupt request number). A colon follows this number; then you see the total number of interrupts (for that IRQ) that have occurred so far. The text at the end of the line indicates the device that uses this IRQ. The device 3c509 refers to the 3Com 3C509 Ethernet card, and aha1542 is the Adaptec AHA1542 SCSI (Small Computer System Interface) controller card.

Following is the /proc/dma file for my system:

```
4: cascade
7: aha1542
```

As the listing shows, only two DMAs are in use. Many devices do not use direct memory access.

The /proc/ioports file contains more entries because each device needs I/O port addresses. The following listing shows the /proc/ioports file for my system (my comments are in italic):

```
0000-001f : dma1            Direct Memory Access (DMA) controller 1
0020-003f : pic1            Programmable Interrupt Controller (PIC) 1
0040-005f : timer
0060-0060 : kbd             Keyboard
0064-0064 : kbd             Keyboard
0070-007f : rtc             Real-time clock
0080-009f : dma page reg    DMA page register
00a0-00bf : pic2            Programmable Interrupt Controller (PIC) 2
00c0-00df : dma2            DMA controller 2
00f0-00f1 : npu             Floating-point processor (numeric processor
                            unit)
00f8-00ff : npu             Floating-point processor (numeric processor
                            unit)
0170-0177 : ide1            Integrated Drive Electronics interface 1
01f0-01f7 : ide0            ntegrated Drive Electronics interface 0
0210-021f : 3c509           3Com 3C509 Ethernet card
02f8-02ff : serial(auto)    Second serial port (COM2)
0330-0333 : aha1542         Adaptec AHA1542 SCSI controller card
0376-0376 : ide1            Integrated Drive Electronics interface 1
0378-037a : lp              Parallel port (for use by printer)
03d4-03d5 : ega+            Video controller (graphics card)
03f6-03f6 : ide0            Integrated Drive Electronics interface 0
03f8-03ff : serial(auto)    First serial port (COM1)
```

Linux on Laptops

Laptops are more integrated than are desktops; a laptop's video card, monitor, and hard disk are all built into a compact package. In other words, you cannot easily mix and match components in laptops as you do in desktop systems, so you have to make sure that Linux supports all components of your laptop system.

Chapters 10 through 17 of this book cover individual components, such as the video card and monitors. This section provides specific information about running Linux on laptop PCs.

Supported laptops

That section heading is just to get your attention because most laptops with Intel 80386 or better processors should be able to run plain Linux. If you want to install XFree86 (X Window System), however, you may have some trouble because the video card (on a laptop, video circuitry is built into the motherboard) and the pointing device have to be supported by XFree86.

PCMCIA

Laptops have a unique type of interface known as PCMCIA, which stands for Personal Computer Memory Card International Association. Beta software is available that allows you to use PCMCIA devices in Linux. The current PCMCIA drivers support many common PCMCIA controllers, such as Databook TCIC/2, Intel i82365SL, Cirrus PD67xx, and Vadem VG-468 chipsets.

Consult Chapter 17 for more information on PCMCIA support in Linux.

Advanced Power Management

Another laptop-specific feature is power management, which refers to the capability of a laptop to suspend its activities so as to conserve battery power. Laptops that have the Advanced Power Management (APM) capability can suspend and resume power-consuming components (such as the display and hard drive), as well as provide information on battery life.

You can obtain a Linux kernel patch from the Internet at ftp://tsx-11.mit.edu/pub/linux/packages/laptops/apm/. There, you should find an APM BIOS extensions package in a compressed tar archive. Use the steps outlined in Chapter 2 to incorporate the APM BIOS extensions into Linux. After that, you can get the battery level with the command `cat /proc/apm`.

Sound on laptops

Many high-end laptops come with built-in sound. Using the sound capabilities under Linux is a straightforward process, provided that you can figure out what type of sound card you have in the laptop. Chapter 12 covers sound cards in detail.

The type of sound card can vary even among laptop models from the same vendor. The NEC Versa P, for example, comes with a Sound Blaster Pro-compatible card. The NEC Versa M, on the other hand, has a Microsoft Sound System (MSS) card, which is not compatible with Sound Blaster.

Cross Reference

As you learn in Chapter 12, the typical setup for Sound Blaster Pro is I/O address 0x220 (that's 220 in hexadecimal notation; the 0x prefix indicates hexadecimal in the C programming language), IRQ 5, and DMA 1. Thus, on the NEC Versa P, you should configure the Linux kernel with a Sound Blaster Pro at I/O address 0x220, IRQ 5, and DMA 1. The Texas Instruments TravelMate 4000M has a built-in sound card that needs similar settings.

On the NEC Versa M, try the Microsoft Sound System at I/O address 0x530, IRQ 9, and DMA 3. As usual, you should check your laptop's documentation for clues about the make and model of the sound card before you set up sound support.

The bottom line is that you can set up Linux to support sound on a laptop the same way that you would for a desktop PC. The first step is finding out what type of sound card your laptop has. Of course, many laptops simply do not have sound capability, so this point may be moot for some laptop users.

X on laptops

Users have reported success in running Linux together with XFree86 on many 386, 486, and Pentium laptops. Until recently, to run X on a laptop, you had to settle for the standard 16-color VGA server (XF86_VGA16) because XFree86 did not support many of the popular video chipsets used in laptops. Many laptops support 640 × 480 resolution LCD screens with 256 colors, but the 16-color VGA server does not exploit the 256-color capability. You have to be able to run the Super VGA X server (XF86_SVGA) to use 256 colors on a laptop.

Table 9-1 lists the video chipsets used in many popular laptops. You should consult this list and read this section to learn more about running X on a specific laptop.

Table 9-1	List of laptop video chipsets
Laptop brand	Video chipset used
Aero Computers 8466T250	Cirrus Logic CL-GD6235AD
Altima Virage II	Western Digital WD90C24 series
Ambra N75	Chips & Technologies 65540
Amrel SLT	Cirrus Logic CL-GD6225/6235
AMS MediaPro	Western Digital WD90C24 series
AMS MediaPro II	Western Digital WD90C24 series
AMS SoundWave 486	Western Digital WD90C24 series
AMS TravelPro	Western Digital WD90C24 series
ARMNote TS30MC	Chips & Technologies 65540
ARMNote TS30PH	Chips & Technologies 65545

(continued)

Table 9-1 *(continued)*

Laptop brand	Video chipset used
Aspen Universa-CD	Chips & Technologies 65545
AST Ascentia 900N	Western Digital WD90C24 series
AST Ascentia 910N	Western Digital WD90C24 series
AST Ascentia 950N	Cirrus Logic CL-GD7543
AST PowerExec 4/25SL	Western Digital WD90C26
AstroNote SKD III	Chips & Technologies 65540
AT&T Globalyst 130	Chips & Technologies 65535
AT&T Globalyst 200S	Western Digital WD90C24 series
AT&T Globalyst 250P	Chips & Technologies 65545
Austin Business Audio 466C,D	Western Digital WD90C24 series
Austin Vista	Chips & Technologies 65540
Auston StepLite	Chips & Technologies 65535
BSI NP7657D	Chips & Technologies 65545
BSI NP7659T	Chips & Technologies 65545
BSI NP9549D	Chips & Technologies 65545
CAF Aqualite 2	Cirrus Logic CL-GD6225
Canon Innova 486NX	Chips & Technologies 65530
Canon Innova Book 200LS	Chips & Technologies 65545
Canon Notejet II 486c	Western Digital WD90C24 series
CompuAdd 450 ColorPro	Chips & Technologies 65535
CTX EzBook	Western Digital WD90C24 series
CTX EzNote	Western Digital WD90C24 series
Dell Latitude 475C	Western Digital WD90C24 series
Dell Latitude XP4100CX	Western Digital WD90C24 series
Dell Latitude XP450C,CX	Western Digital WD90C24 series
Dell Latitude XPi P75D	Cirrus Logic CL-GD7543
DFI MediaBook 5110T	Cirrus Logic CL-GD6440
Digital HiNote CT475	Chips & Technologies 65540
Digital HiNote Ultra CT475	Chips & Technologies 65545
Epson ActionNote 880CX	Chips & Technologies 65535
Ergo Powerbrick	Western Digital WD90C24 series
Ergo SubBrick 75	Chips & Technologies 65535

Everex StepNote D100	Chips & Technologies 65545
Everex StepNote P75	Chips & Technologies 65545
FutureMate FM309T	Chips & Technologies 65545
FutureMate FM559D	Chips & Technologies 65545
Gateway Colorbook DX4-75	Cirrus Logic CL-GD6235
Gateway ColorBook DX4/100	Chips & Technologies 65545
Gateway Handbook DX2-50	Chips & Technologies 65510
Gateway Liberty DX4/100	Chips & Technologies 65545
HP Omnibook 4000	Western Digital WD90C24 series
HyperData HP32Open	Cirrus Logic CL-GD6235
HyperData HyperBook 900A	Chips & Technologies 65545
IBM Thinkpad 350	Western Digital WD90C24 series
IBM Thinkpad 360	Western Digital WD90C24 series
IBM Thinkpad 701C	Chips & Technologies 65545
IBM Thinkpad 720	Western Digital WD90C24 series
IBM Thinkpad 750	Western Digital WD90C24 series
IBM Thinkpad 755	Western Digital WD90C24 series
Maximus MediaNote	Chips & Technologies 65540
Maximus PowerMax	Chips & Technologies 65545
MaxTech YesBook X-740C	Chips & Technologies 65540
MaxTech YesBook X-740T	Chips & Technologies 65540
Micro International HCP Pentium 3600D	Cirrus Logic CL-GD6440
Micro International HCP Pentium 6500	Cirrus Logic CL-GD6235AD
MicroExpress NP92DX4	Cirrus Logic CL-GD6440
Midwest Micro SoundBook II	Chips & Technologies 65545
Midwest Micro SoundBook Plus	Chips & Technologies 65545
Mitsuba Ninja II DX4-75	Chips & Technologies 65540
MPC CD-Book	Chips & Technologies 65540
MPC Touchnote	Western Digital WD90C24 series
NEC Versa M	Chips & Technologies 65545
NEC Versa P/75	Chips & Technologies 65545
NEC Versa/V	Western Digital WD90C24 series
Nova OpenNote	Chips & Technologies 65530

(continued)

Table 9-1 *(continued)*

Laptop brand	Video chipset used
Panasonic CF-V21P	Western Digital WD90C24 series
Panasonic V41	Chips & Technologies 65545
Sager NP3656D	Cirrus Logic CL-GD6440
Sager NP7659T	Chips & Technologies 65545
Sager NP9549A	Chips & Technologies 65545
Samsung NoteMaster S3945T	Western Digital WD90C24 series
Samsung SENS700	Western Digital WD90C24 series
Sceptre SoundX Series 3000	Chips & Technologies 65545
Sharp PC-3050	Chips & Technologies 65545
Sharp PC-8700/8900	Chips & Technologies 65545
TI (Texas Instruments) 4000E DX2/50	Cirrus Logic CL-GD6420
TI 4000E WinDX475	Cirrus Logic CL-GD6440
TI TravelMate 4000M series	Cirrus Logic CL-GD6440
TI TravelMate 5000	Cirrus Logic CL-GD7543
Toshiba 2150CS,CT	Western Digital WD90C24 series
Toshiba 4800CT	Western Digital WD90C24 series
Toshiba Portege T3400CT	Western Digital WD90C24 series
Toshiba Satellite Pro T2150CDT	Chips & Technologies 65545
Toshiba T2100CS	Chips & Technologies 65540
Toshiba T4700CT	Western Digital WD90C26
Toshiba T4900CT	Chips & Technologies 65545
Twinhead Slimnote 5100 series	Western Digital WD90C24 series
Twinhead Slimnote 8	Cirrus Logic CL-GD7542
Unisys Travel Asset	Western Digital WD90C24 series
Unisys Travel Partner	Western Digital WD90C24 series
Wedge Showbook EL	Chips & Technologies 65530
Wedge Showbook P5	Chips & Technologies 65545
Winbook XP	Western Digital WD90C24 series
Zenith ZDS Z-Lite 425SL	Chips & Technologies 65535
Zenith ZDS Z-Noteflex	Western Digital WD90C24 series
Zenith ZDS Z-Star EX	Chips & Technologies 65540
ZEOS Meridian 850A	Chips & Technologies 65545
ZEOS Meridian 850C	Chips & Technologies 65545

As Table 9-1 shows, most laptops use the following types of video chipsets:

- Western Digital WD90C24 series chips
- Chips & Technologies 655xx series chips
- Cirrus Logic CL-GD6440 and CL-GD7543

Of these chipsets, the XF86_SVGA server in XFree86 3.1.2 supports the following:

- Western Digital WD90C24 series chips
- Chips & Technologies 65520, 65530, 65540, and 65545 chipsets
- Cirrus Logic CL-GD6225, CL-GD6235, CL-GD420, and CL-GD6440 chipsets

In XFree86 3.1.1, the support for the WD90C24 chip was through its compatibility with the WD90C30. Beginning with XFree86 3.1.2, however, the XF86_SVGA server directly supports the WD90C24 chip. The WD90C26 chipset is not yet supported by the XF86_SVGA driver, however.

XFree86 3.1.2 supports most of the Cirrus Logic chipsets. One notable exception is CL-GD7543, which is used in several new laptops, such as Texas Instruments TravelMate 5000, AST Ascentia 950N, and Dell Latitude XPi P75D. Reportedly, the CL-GD7543 chipset may be compatible with CL-GD6235, which the XF86_SVGA driver already supports.

The Chips & Technologies 65545 is popular on high-end laptops, such as NEC Versa P and M. This chipset supports the Super VGA mode of 800 × 600 resolution with 256 colors (or gray levels, depending on the LCD screen).

Cross Reference

With the 65545, you should be able to run the XF86_SVGA server and drive the LCD at 640 × 480 resolution with 256 colors or gray levels. According to specifications, the 65545's dot clock (see the "Dot clock" section of Chapter 10 for more information on the dot clock) goes up to 65 MHz — good enough for a 1,024 × 768 resolution display at a 60-Hz refresh rate. The XF86_SVGA server, however, programs the 65545 at two dot clocks: 25.2 MHz and 28.3 MHz. (The commercial Accelerated-X server, from X Inside Inc., reportedly supports the 65545 at the rated 65-MHz dot clock.)

Caution

Although you can tinker with the `XF86Config` file and get X running on a laptop, you should remember that wrong settings in the configuration file could damage the laptop's LCD screen, the video chipset, or both.

Tip

If you plan to run X on a laptop, your best bet is to buy a laptop with the WD90C24 or CL-GD6440 chipsets; these chipsets are recent, and XFree86 3.1.2 supports them well.

Information resources for specific laptops

Although the basic Linux package should run on most laptops, getting all the features of a laptop working under Linux takes some effort. One problem seems to be the lack of technical information on specific chips used in the laptop — information such as the type of video chipset (so that you can configure XFree86).

Part III: Exploiting Your Hardware in Linux

Several users have documented their experiences with specific laptops and placed that information on the World Wide Web. Following are some information resources for specific laptops:

Laptop	Information resource
Compaq Contura Aero	http://domen.uninett.no/~hta/linux/aero faq.html
IBM ThinkPad	http://peipa.essex.ac.uk/tp-linux/tp linux.html
NEC Versa M and P	http://www.santafe.edu/~nelson/versa linux/
Tadpole P1000	http://peipa.essex.ac.uk/tadpole linux/tadpole linux.html

You can find general information about Linux on laptops at ftp://tsx-11.mit.edu/pub/linux/packages/laptops/.

The next few sections cover important information about running Linux on a few brands of laptops.

Compaq laptops

Linux is reported to work on the following Compaq laptop models:

- Compaq Contura Aero 486SLC/25
- Compaq Contura Aero 4/33C with 486SX processor
- Compaq LTE Lite 25c (25-MHz 486)
- Compaq 486/50 LTE laptop

The 486SL and 486SX chips do not have the floating-point unit (math coprocessor), so Linux has to emulate the floating-point processor. The same problem exists under DOS and Windows, of course, so it's not anything specific to Linux.

You'll get good performance with more memory — at least 8MB is recommended. Most older laptops come with only 4MB, which is not enough to run X.

To run X on these laptops, use the generic 16-color VGA X server (XF86_VGA16). To use the trackball as a pointer in X, specify a mouse connected to a PS/2-style auxiliary port (/dev/psaux). Also remember to disable the gpm (general purpose mouse) program because gpm interferes with X.

The Compaq laptops have PCMCIA slots and APM. Consult the "Advanced Power Management" section to learn where to get a Linux patch for APM.

NEC Versa laptops

Several users have reported good experiences with Linux and X on NEC Versa M and Versa P laptops. The Versa M comes in two configurations: 486 DX4/75 and 486 DX4/100. Versa P comes as a P/75 (75-MHz Pentium). These laptops support up to 40MB RAM; each type has an 810MB internal IDE hard disk, an 800 × 600 active matrix color display, and built-in sound. These laptops clearly are high-end models, both in features and in price (expect to pay between $4,000 and $5,500), so it shouldn't come as a surprise that Linux and X run well on these laptops.

Linux installation is straightforward, although you have to install from floppy disks. Thus, you have to copy the Linux distribution from the CD-ROM to a set of floppy disks, as explained in the "Installing Linux on a laptop without a CD-ROM drive" section.

When setting up Linux, make sure that you specify a PS/2-style mouse. Also specify the PS/2 mouse when you run `xf86config`, as explained in Chapter 4. By specifying the PS/2 mouse, you'll be able to use the NEC Versa trackball under X.

Texas Instruments TravelMate 4000M

Linux and X are reported to run on the Texas Instruments TravelMate 4000M laptop, which comes in 486DX4 75-MHz and 100-MHz models. The LCD screen is controlled by a Cirrus Logic CL-GD6440 chipset, which the XF86_SVGA server supports. The pointing device is a *trackpoint* (a small vertical stick that you move with your fingertip), which originally appeared in IBM Thinkpad laptops. When you configure XFree86, treat the trackpoint as a PS/2-style mouse (not as a C&T 82C710 mouse port, even though the TI TravelMate name is mentioned for that port).

TravelMate 4000M includes a built-in Adaptec AHA1510 SCSI controller, which should work fine under Linux as long as you select a kernel that supports the AHA152x SCSI controller. The SCSI controller does not have a BIOS, so that controller won't be detected by the SCSI driver automatically. Instead, you must provide the SCSI parameters at the boot prompt as follows:

```
aha152x=0x340,11,7,0
```

In the preceding example, 0x340 refers to the I/O address of the SCSI controller; 11 is its IRQ; and 7 is the DMA channel.

The TravelMate 4000M comes with built-in sound, in the form of a MediaVision Jazz16 sound card. This card is supposed to be compatible with Sound Blaster Pro, but you should install the latest VoxWare 3.0 sound driver that supports the Jazz16 directly. The sound-card settings are like those of the Sound Blaster Pro: I/O address 0x220, IRQ 5, and DMA 1. The MIDI port uses I/O address 0x330.

Caution

Before you use the VoxWare 3.0 sound drivers, you should know that these drivers may still be in the beta stage. Therefore, a chance exists that the system may crash when you use the sound drivers. Use these drivers at your own risk.

You also can buy a portable CD-ROM docking system with a double-speed CD-ROM drive, speakers, a separate battery, and a SCSI connection (to connect other SCSI peripherals). If you have the CD-ROM docking system, you can install Linux directly from this book's companion CD-ROM.

Secret

One reported "gotcha" during Linux installation on the TravelMate 4000M is your having to enter the no-hlt option at the boot prompt to make sure that the system does not hang while attempting to boot. By default, the Linux kernel executes a hlt instruction to halt the processor when there is nothing to do. During the boot process, the kernel tests the hlt instruction, which is where the kernel hangs in a TravelMate 4000M. With the no-hlt option, the kernel does not use the hlt instruction when idle. Nonuse of the hlt instruction defeats the advanced power-management concept of laptops (in which the processor stops completely when there is nothing to do).

Installing Linux on a laptop without a CD-ROM drive

If you plan to install Linux on a laptop, your first hurdle may be a lack of a CD-ROM drive. You'll have to find a PC with a CD-ROM drive so that you can copy the Linux distribution to a set of 3.5-inch high-density floppy disks.

Note

If you want to install the entire Slackware distribution from the book's companion CD-ROM, you need a total of 93 3.5-inch high-density floppy disks: 2 for the boot and root floppies, and 91 for the Slackware disk sets.

Tip

The files that you need to copy are organized in directories in the slakware directory of the companion CD-ROM. Each directory fits into a single 3.5-inch high-density floppy disk. A single disk set has one or more floppy disks. The A disk set, for example, has five disks in the directories A1, A2, A3, A4, and A5. To create the disks for this set, you put four MS-DOS-format floppy disks into the floppy drive, one at a time, and copy the contents of each directory to the disks, as follows (my comments are in italics):

```
D:     (change drive to the CD-ROM drive)
CD \SLAKWARE
       (put a formatted floppy in the 3.5-inch floppy drive)
COPY A1\*.* A:
       (take out floppy and put in a new one)
COPY A2\*.* A:
       (take out floppy and put in a new one)
COPY A3\*.* A:
       (take out floppy and put in a new one)
COPY A4\*.* A:
```

You have to repeat this process for each disk set. To help you plan and select the disk sets to load, Table 9-2 is a breakdown of the disk count, organized by disk sets.

Table 9-2 Breakdown of disks to create for laptop Linux installation

Disk set	Description	Directories	Number of disks needed
A	The base Linux system that you must install.	A1 through A5	5
AP	Text-based Linux applications.	AP1 through AP5	5
D	C and C++ software development tools.	D1 through D10	10
E	GNU Emacs editor and its supporting files.	E1 through E6	6
F	Frequently Asked Questions (FAQs).	F1 and F2	2
K	Linux kernel source files.	K1 and K5	5
N	Networking software, including TCP/IP, UUCP, Mail, and News.	N1 through N4	4
Q	Extra Linux kernel images and source.	Q1 through Q15	15
T	TeX document-formatting system.	T1 through T9	9
TCL	Tcl scripting language and Tk.	TCL1	1
X	XFree86 3.1.2 (X Window System).	X1 through X16	16
XAP	X applications, such as `xpaint` and `xv`.	XAP1 through XAP4	4
XD	X11 server development tools.	XD1 through XD3	3
XV	The XView toolkit and the OPEN LOOK window manager.	XV1 through XV3	3
Y	Games (including DOOM and Abuse).	Y1 through Y4	3

You can cut down on the number of floppy disks by selecting a small number of disk sets for the laptop. If you do not want X, for example, you can skip the sets TCL, X, XAP, XD, and XV, which account for 27 floppy disks.

Tip

Even if you do some C and C++ development and need networking support, you need only disk sets A, AP, D, K, and N. Those disk sets require a total 29 floppy disks — a much more manageable number than 91.

Secret

If you already have Linux installed on a desktop PC and want to create Linux floppy disk sets for a laptop (or for a friend), you should use the `makeflop` shell script to create the disks. Make sure that the companion CD-ROM is mounted. Change the working directory to the Slackware distribution directory on the CD-ROM, using the `cd /cdrom/slakware` command. Then type **makeflop** at the shell prompt and follow the instructions.

Cross Reference

After you have the floppy disks, you still need to go through the process of creating the boot and root floppies. For this step and subsequent installation procedures, you can follow the steps outlined in Chapter 1 because the steps are the same (except that you have to keep feeding in floppy disks).

Installing Linux on a laptop with a CD-ROM drive

Only recently have laptop computers begun to sport built-in CD-ROM drives. If you can afford one of these new systems, you may want to install Linux directly from this book's companion CD-ROM just as you would on a desktop system. The only potential problem is the possibility that Linux will not support the CD-ROM drive interface.

Cross Reference

If you are in the market for a laptop with a CD-ROM drive, make sure that Linux supports the CD-ROM drive interface. Consult Chapter 12 for information on the types of CD-ROM interfaces that Linux supports.

As an example, the Toshiba Satellite 2500CDT laptop reportedly has an ATAPI CD-ROM drive. Thus, you should be able to install Linux from the CD-ROM on this laptop.

Tip

As long as you have a laptop with a CD-ROM drive that Linux supports, you should be able to install Linux from this book's CD-ROM, following the instructions presented in Chapter 1.

Summary

Linux is much more dependent on the details of your PC's hardware than DOS is. To install and use Linux, you need to make sure that Linux supports various parts of your PC. This chapter focuses on Linux's compatibility with the most important part of your PC: the motherboard, which contains the processor and the bus, where you connect the peripheral devices, such as the hard disk, video card, and CD-ROM drive. By reading this chapter, you learn the following:

- Linux was designed for the Intel 80386 processor, and it currently supports all variants of 386, 486, and Pentium processors, including any compatible processors such as the ones from Cyrix and AMD. Some efforts are under way to port Linux to other processors, such as DEC Alpha AXP, MIPS, and PowerPC.

- A *bus* is a standard set of wires through which a peripheral device connects to the PC's motherboard. Several bus types exist: ISA, EISA, MCA, VLB, and PCI. Linux supports each of these bus types except the MCA, which is IBM's proprietary bus. The PCI bus is the emerging standard as the high-performance bus for new Pentium PCs.

- Linux includes the `/proc` file system as a convenient way for users to access information about the system. You can find out much about your system by looking at the files in `/proc`. The `/proc/devices` file, for example, lists all devices in your system, and `/proc/pci` shows the PCI devices in a PCI system.

- Laptops are a special breed of computer because all parts of a laptop — from the hard disk to the video card — are tightly integrated. Linux runs on many laptops. The main problem is support for laptop-specific features, such as Advanced Power Management (APM) and PCMCIA or PC card interfaces. Another problem is running X on a laptop because laptop video chipsets are not as well supported by XFree86 as are desktop PCs' video cards. Nevertheless, Linux and X run on a wide variety of laptops.

- Installing Linux on a laptop poses a challenge because laptops often lack a CD-ROM drive. To install Linux on a laptop that does not have a CD-ROM drive, you have to copy a selected set of Linux disk sets to 3.5-inch high-density floppy disks and then use the installation procedures outlined in Chapter 1. For a laptop that has a CD-ROM drive, all you have to do is make sure that Linux supports the CD-ROM drive.

Chapter 10

Video Cards and Monitors

In This Chapter

- ▶ Looking at different types of video cards and monitors
- ▶ Selecting an X server for your video card and monitor
- ▶ Specifying video-card and monitor configuration parameters for XFree86
- ▶ Looking at specific configuration information for various video cards

When you install Linux on a PC, the video card and the monitor do not matter much if you work only with text. The specific details of the video card and monitor become important if you want to use the graphical interface provided by the X Window System, or X for short. If you want to benefit from the ease of use afforded by graphical interfaces, you want to install X. When you install X, you need detailed information about your video card and monitor to make X work on your PC.

This chapter describes various common video cards and monitors, their attributes, and the nuances of getting X to work with the video card and monitor. You also learn how to specify some video-card and monitor parameters needed to configure X for Linux.

Video Cards and Monitors

The video card or graphics adapter contains the electronics that control the monitor. On most systems, the video card is in the form of a circuit board that plugs into a slot on your PC's motherboard. On many new systems, however, the motherboard contains the necessary graphics chipsets.

Raster-scan display

All video cards operate on the same principle: They store an image in video memory (also called *video RAM*, or *VRAM* for short) and generate the appropriate signals to display the image on the monitor's screen.

The *monitor* is the physical device that contains the display screen, where the graphic and text output appears. The *display screen* typically is a phosphor-coated glass tube on which an electron beam traces the output image. On laptop computers, the display screen is a Liquid Crystal Display (LCD) screen. More expensive laptops use active matrix display screens.

The image that appears on the monitor is made up of a large number of horizontal lines known as *raster lines*. An electron beam in the monitor generates the raster lines by sweeping back and forth on a phosphor-coated screen, as illustrated in Figure 10-1.

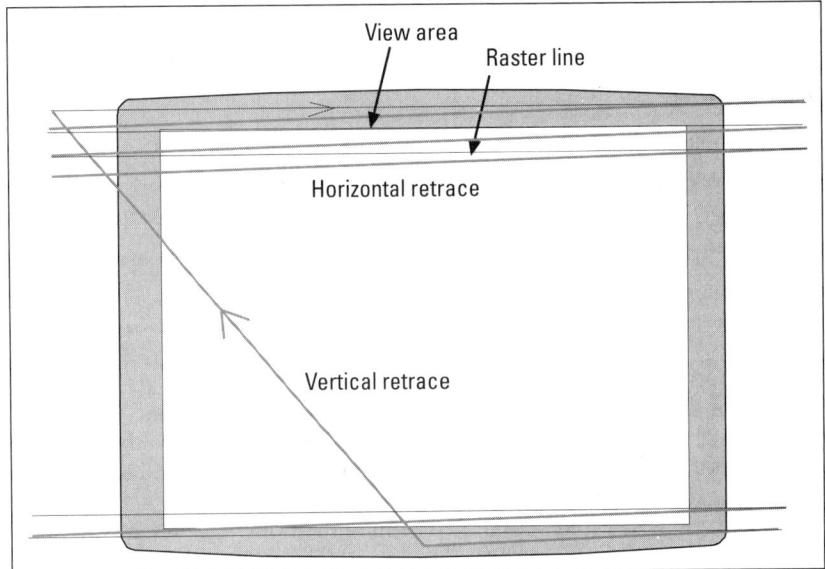

Figure 10-1: A typical raster scan display.

The phosphor on the screen glows in proportion to the intensity of the electron beam. The glowing dot on the screen represents a picture element, or *pixel*. Thus, a line of the image is generated by controlling the intensity of the beam as it scans across the screen. The phosphor fades in a while, but if the lines are redrawn repeatedly, our persistence of vision creates an illusion of a steady image. Most PC monitors redraw an entire screenful of raster lines 50 to 90 times a second.

As Figure 10-1 shows, the electron beam scans an area larger than the actual view area of the display screen, but the electron beam is active only when the beam is in the viewable area. Also, after reaching the end of a line, the beam has to return to the start of the next raster line. This part of the beam's motion is known as the *horizontal retrace*. Similarly, when the beam reaches the bottom of the screen, it has to return to the first line to start another cycle of drawing. This period is known as the *vertical retrace*. The beam's intensity is reduced (the beam is *blanked*) during horizontal and vertical retrace so that those lines do not appear on the screen.

Color display

Color display screens represent any color with a combination of the three primary colors: red (R), green (G), and blue (B). A color display uses three electron beams, one for each primary color.

The screen in a color display has a repeated triangular pattern of red, green, and blue phosphor dots. Each phosphor glows in its color when the electron beam strikes it. A perforated metal screen, known as a *shadow mask,* ensures that each electron beam strikes the correct colored phosphor. The video card varies the intensity of the red, green, and blue electron beams, thereby displaying many colors.

Color palette and resolution

Typically, a video card allows a palette of 256 colors, in which case each pixel's color is stored in an 8-bit value. The actual color (in terms of R, G, B components) that corresponds to a pixel's 8-bit value is determined by consulting a color lookup table, or *colormap.*

Many high-performance video cards allow 3 bytes of storage per pixel, so that each pixel's value can directly specify the RGB components that determine that pixel's color. These so-called 24-bit video cards provide true color display but require more video memory to store the entire image.

Note

The resolution of a display screen is expressed in terms of the number of visible dots (pixels) across a raster line and the total raster lines. A common resolution is 640 dots across by 480 lines vertically, which is commonly expressed as 640×480. Other common screen resolutions are 800×600, $1,024 \times 768$, and $1,280 \times 1,024$.

Video RAM

The video card stores the contents of the pixels in random-access memory (RAM) known as video RAM. The number of colors and the display resolution supported by a video card depend on the amount of video RAM. To store the information content of a 256-color $1,024 \times 768$ display screen, for example, the video card needs $1,024 \times 768$, or 786,432 bytes of video RAM (because an 8-bit pixel value represents 256 colors and 1 byte = 8 bits).

Typical video cards have 1MB, 2MB, or 4MB of video RAM. A video card with 1MB of video RAM can comfortably handle a 256-color, $1,024 \times 768$-resolution display.

Dot clock

You will run across the term *dot clock* when you configure a video card to work with XFree86 (the X Window System). *Dot clock* refers to the rate at which the video card can traverse the raster lines that make up a complete display screen. The value of the dot clock is expressed in terms of the number of dots drawn per second.

To get a rough idea of the dot clock, consider a 640 × 480 display, which has 640 × 480 = 307,200 dots (at least, the visible ones). To produce the appearance of a steady display, these dots should be repainted at least 72 times a second. Thus, the video card has to paint 640 × 480 × 72 = 22,118,400 dots a second. This rate amounts to approximately 22 million dots a second, which is expressed as a dot clock of 22 MHz (1 MHz = a million times a second).

In reality, an even higher dot clock is required for a 640 × 480 display refreshed at 72 Hz (which means 72 times a second) because the electron beam cannot turn around on a dime. As illustrated in Figure 10-1, the electron beam has to traverse a scan line beyond the visible number of dots before it can snap back to the beginning of the next line. The required dot clock for a 640 × 480 display at a 72-Hz refresh rate, for example, is 25.2 MHz.

As you must realize by now, a higher-resolution display requires even higher dot clocks. A 1,024 × 768 display at a 72-Hz refresh rate implies 1,024 × 768 × 72 = 56,623,104 dots per second, at minimum. Thus, you can tell that the dot clock necessary for a 1,024 × 768 display will be somewhat higher than 56.6 MHz.

Older video cards support a fixed set of dot clocks, but many advanced video cards include a programmable dot clock. When a video card has a programmable dot clock, the X server can set the video card to operate at any dot clock that lies in a range of acceptable values. For a video card with a programmable dot clock, however, you may need to specify the name of the chip that controls the dot clock (known as the *clock chip*).

Importance of the video card and monitor to XFree86

Linux will work with any video card-monitor combination in text mode. If a video card and monitor work under MS-DOS or Windows, the combination will also work under Linux in text mode. The story is different when you install XFree86, the X Window System for Linux. Because XFree86 controls the video card directly (MS-DOS typically uses standard predefined modes of the video card), getting XFree86 running with a specific video card takes more work.

The monitor also is important for XFree86. Electrical signals from the video card control the monitor, so the monitor must be compatible with the video card. The output on the monitor is produced by a rapidly moving electron beam that the video card's signals control. A monitor's compatibility with a video card has to do with how fast the video card attempts to move the electron beam on the display screen.

The resolutions supported by a video card-monitor combination depend on the amount of video memory on the card and on how fast the monitor's electron beam can move.

XFree86 gets the necessary information about the monitor and the video card from a special file named XF86Config, which usually is in the /etc directory.

X-Server Selection

XFree86 comes with several X servers, each of which is designed for a specific set of video cards. To select the X server to run, you need to know the type of video card that your PC has. For a new system, you can find this information by asking the PC's manufacturer. Ideally, you get information about the video card before you order the PC, so that you can be sure that Linux supports that video card.

If you have an older PC, determining the type of video card may be difficult. At minimum, you need to know what video chipset your system's video card uses. Even better is to know the manufacturer and model of the video card.

Tip

If you do not know anything about your system's video card, you still can run X. Assuming that your PC is of recent-enough vintage, chances are that its video card can emulate the original 16-color Video Graphics Array (VGA) video card. If you have run Microsoft Windows with the VGA driver, for example, you know that your video card works as a generic VGA. XFree86 includes an X server named XF86_VGA16, which is designed specifically for the generic 16-color, 640 × 480 VGA video mode. Although the 16-color VGA mode may not exploit the full capabilities of your system's video card, you can at least get going and use X.

XFree86 version 3.1.1 includes the following X servers (each of which is in the form of a separate executable program):

- XF86_8514 for video cards based on the IBM 8514/A
- XF86_AGX for video cards that use the AGX video chipset
- XF86_Mach32 for video cards that use the ATI Mach32 video chipset
- XF86_Mach64 for video cards that use the ATI Mach64 video chipset
- XF86_Mach8 for video cards that use the ATI Mach8 video chipset
- XF86_Mono for a video card operating in the monochrome video mode or 2-color VGA mode
- XF86_P9000 for video cards that use the Weitek P9000 chipset. Diamond Viper and Orchid P9000 video cards use this chipset.
- XF86_S3 for video cards that use the S3 chipset. Notice that not all S3-based video cards are supported; you still must have a card that this server explicitly supports.
- XF86_SVGA for a video card operating in Super VGA mode. This category includes a large selection of video cards based on many chipsets.
- XF86_VGA16 for a video card operating in 16-color VGA mode. You can use this X server with most video cards, including older VGA and EGA (Enhanced Graphics Adapter) cards.
- XF86_W32 for video cards that use the Tseng ET4000/W32 video chipset

This list of servers may grow in future versions of XFree86. You should check the README files in the `/usr/X11/lib/X11/doc` directory for the latest information about specific video cards.

Cross Reference

As explained in Chapter 4, you should run the `xf86config` utility program to set up XFree86 on your system. At that time, when you specify a video card, the `xf86config` program allows you to select an X server to run. After you select a specific X server, the `xf86config` program sets up `/var/X11R6/bin/X` as a symbolic link to the actual X server binary. To use the `XF86_S3` server, for example, the `xf86config` utility executes the following command:

```
ln -s /usr/X11R6/bin/XF86_S3 /var/X11R6/bin/X
```

Cross Reference

When you start X with the `startx` script or using `xdm` (as explained in Chapter 5), the X server that is symbolically linked to `/var/X11R6/bin/X` is the one that gets started. When the X server starts, it reads the contents of the `XF86Config` file (usually from the `/etc` directory) to configure the video card and the monitor.

`XF86Config` **File Revisited**

Cross Reference

When the X server starts, it finds information about the video card, monitor, keyboard, and mouse from the `XF86Config` file (usually in the `/etc` directory). In Chapter 4, I provided an overview of `/etc/XF86Config`, but I did not fully describe how to fill in several important sections of the file. This section examines `XF86Config` in terms of providing the appropriate information for specific video cards and monitors.

Cross Reference

As you learned in Chapter 4, `XF86Config` consists of several sections. Three sections in `XF86Config` deal with the video card and monitor:

- The `Screen` section combines a video card and monitor with the video modes to be used by a specific X server. Typically, `XF86Config` contains several `Screen` sections, one for each type of X server.

- The `Device` section describes the characteristics of a video card (also known as a *graphics device*). The configuration file may have several `Device` sections.

- The `Monitor` section lists the technical specifications of a monitor (such as the horizontal and vertical synchronization rates) and includes a list of video modes that the monitor supports.

Cross Reference

As explained in Chapter 4, you can create `XF86Config` by running the `xf86config` utility program. If you have your monitor's technical specifications handy, and your video card appears in the list that `xf86config` displays, the generated `XF86Config` file may work as is. You typically run into problems only when you attempt to use the full capabilities of advanced video cards. Later sections of this chapter describe how to use XFree86 with specific advanced video cards.

Screen **section**

The X server decides the settings of the video card and the monitor from the Screen section meant for that server. The X servers are grouped in four categories with the following names:

- vga2 refers to a video card-monitor combination operating in 2-color mode.
- vga16 means 16-color standard VGA mode.
- svga refers to Super VGA (256-color 640 × 480 mode).
- accel refers to all accelerated X servers. (The specific X server depends on the exact chipset; you select the server when you run the xf86config utility program.)

The Screen section specifies the X server that can use that section, as well as the names of a Device (video card) and a Monitor. Following is a Screen section meant for an accelerated X server:

```
# Screen for accelerated servers (S3, Mach32, Mach8, 8514, P9000, AGX,
W32, Mach64)
Section "Screen"
    Driver    "accel"
    Device    "Number Nine GXE64 with S3-Trio64"
    Monitor   "Dell VS15X"
    Subsection "Display"
        Depth      8
        Modes      "640x480" "800x600" "1024x768"
        ViewPort   0 0
        Virtual    1024 768
    EndSubsection
    Subsection "Display"
        Depth      16
        Modes      "640x480" "800x600"
        ViewPort   0 0
        Virtual    800 600
    EndSubsection
    Subsection "Display4"
        Depth      32
        Modes      "640x400"
        ViewPort   0 0
        Virtual    640 400
    EndSubsection
EndSection
```

Comment lines start with the pound sign (#). The section's definition is enclosed in the Section ... EndSection block.

The Driver line identifies the X server that should use this Screen section. Following the Device and Monitor names are several Display subsections. Each Display subsection applies to a specific Depth (the number of bits of storage per pixel, which also determines the number of colors that can be displayed at a time).

The X server automatically uses the first `Display` subsection in the `Screen` definition, but you can start the server with command-line options that specify a different `Depth`. If you start the X server with the `startx` command, you can use a `Depth` of 24 by issuing the following command:

```
startx -- -bpp 24
```

The `-bpp` option stands for bits per pixel, which is the same as `Depth`. Selecting a value for the `Depth` works provided that the video card and the monitor are capable of supporting that `Depth`.

The `Modes` line in the `Display` subsection lists the names of video modes that the monitor and video card can support. The names of these modes appear in the `Monitor` section of the `XF86Config` file.

If the video card has more memory than is needed to hold the information for all visible pixels in a specific mode, the X server can use the leftover memory to give the appearance of a much larger array of pixels than the 640 × 480 or 1,024 × 768 that may be specified by a video mode. In other words, you get a large virtual screen from which you can select a smaller area to view. The `Virtual` line indicates the size of this virtual screen, whereas `ViewPort` specifies which part of the virtual screen is mapped to the physical display.

Device **section**

The `Device` section of the `XF86Config` file provides information about the video card. For the standard VGA mode, `XF86Config` has a `Device` section that looks like this:

```
# Standard VGA Device:
Section "Device"
    Identifier      "Generic VGA"
    VendorName      "Unknown"
    BoardName "Unknown"
    Chipset     "generic"
#   VideoRam 256
#   Clocks   25.2 28.3
EndSection
```

Each line in the section provides some information about the video card. In this case, the `Identifier` indicates the type of video card; this identifier is used in the `Screen` section to refer to a specific video card.

`VendorName`, `BoardName`, and `Chipset` further specify the type of video card and the video chipset. For the standard VGA mode, the `VendorName`, `BoardName`, and `Chipset` do not matter. Neither do you have to specify the amount of video RAM (on the `VideoRam` line) or the allowable dot clocks (on the `Clocks` line).

For many video cards that do not have a programmable dot clock, the most important line in the `Device` section is the `Clocks` line. The values in this line indicate the dot clocks that the video card supports.

Chapter 10: Video Cards and Monitors

Tip

If you want, the `xf86config` program can run the X server with a special option (`-probeonly`), determine the dot clocks that the video card supports, and fill in the `Clocks` line in the `Device` section. All you have to do is answer yes when the `xf86config` program asks whether you want to run X in `-probeonly` mode. When the `X -probeonly` command is executed, the X server consults the `XF86Config` file. The X server does not probe for dot clocks if a `Clocks` line already exists. Also, the configuration file must have the `Keyboard` and `Pointer` sections specified correctly so that the X server can get to the point of probing the video card. In particular, if an error exists in the type of mouse device, `X -probeonly` fails.

In addition to the `Clocks` line, you can specify one or more flags meant for the X server for the type of video card that you are specifying in the `Device` section.

Monitor **section**

The `Monitor` section lists the technical specifications of the monitor: the bandwidth, the horizontal synchronization (or *horizontal sync*, for short) frequency, and vertical refresh rate. You can get these values from your monitor's manual.

Wizard

The horizontal-sync signal occurs at the end of each raster line; this signal moves the electron beam from the end of one line to the beginning of the next raster line. The horizontal-sync frequency essentially is the number of times per second that the monitor can trace a raster line on the display screen. If the monitor can display 480 lines (at 640 × 480 resolution, for example) and repaint the screen 72 times a second (a vertical refresh rate of 72 Hz), the horizontal-sync frequency is at least 480 × 72 = 34,560 times a second = 34,560 Hz = 34.56 kHz. The actual value is higher because the monitor always has to display more lines than are visible.

Caution

You have to be careful with the values of horizontal sync and vertical refresh; the X server uses these values to select what signals are sent from the video card. A monitor may be physically damaged if the video card sends signals that are beyond the monitor's specifications.

When you use the `xf86config` program to create the `XF86Config` file, the `xf86config` program gives you the option to select the horizontal-synchronization frequencies from a general list, such as standard VGA or a super VGA monitor. If you have no information about a monitor, you may want to start with a conservative setting for the horizontal sync, such as the value for a standard VGA monitor. (You do not have to enter the exact value of horizontal sync; just select the monitor type.)

Most new monitors are multisync monitors that support a range of horizontal-synchronization frequencies (as opposed to a fixed value). If you have the monitor's manual, you can specify the range of frequencies for the horizontal sync.

Note

The most important entries in the `Monitor` section are the `Modelines` lines, which list the video modes that are suitable for use with the monitor. Typically, most new users have questions about what to put in `Modelines`. Actually, you do not have to do much about the `Modelines`; the `xf86config` utility program generates an `XF86Config` file that includes a standard set of mode timings. As long as you specify the monitor's horizontal-sync and vertical-refresh rates correctly, the X server automatically selects the best video mode that your monitor and video card can support at a given resolution.

Following is a typical `Monitor` section (with most of the `Modelines` deleted):

```
Section "Monitor"

    Identifier  "Dell VS15X"
    VendorName  "Dell"
    ModelName   "VS15X"

# Bandwidth is in MHz unless units are specified
  Bandwidth  75.0

# HorizSync is in kHz unless units are specified.
# HorizSync may be a comma separated list of discrete values, or a
# comma separated list of ranges of values.
# NOTE: THE VALUES HERE ARE EXAMPLES ONLY. REFER TO YOUR MONITOR'S
# USER MANUAL FOR THE CORRECT NUMBERS.

    HorizSync   30-64

#   HorizSync       30-64     # multisync
#   HorizSync       31.5, 35.2 # multiple fixed sync frequencies
#   HorizSync       15-25, 30-50 # multiple ranges of sync frequencies

# VertRefresh is in Hz unless units are specified.
# VertRefresh may be a comma separated list of discrete values, or a
# comma separated list of ranges of values.
# NOTE: THE VALUES HERE ARE EXAMPLES ONLY. REFER TO YOUR MONITOR'S
# USER MANUAL FOR THE CORRECT NUMBERS.

    VertRefresh 55-90

# Modes can be specified in two formats. A compact one-line format, or
# a multi-line format.

# These two are equivalent

#   ModeLine "1024x768i" 45 1024 1048 1208 1264 768 776 784 817 Inter-
lace

#   Mode "1024x768i"
#       DotClock        45
#       HTimings        1024 1048 1208 1264
#       VTimings        768 776 784 817
#       Flags           "Interlace"
#   EndMode
```

```
# 640x400 @ 70 Hz, 31.5 kHz hsync
Modeline "640x400"    25.175 640 664 760 800  400 409 411 450
# (Modelines deleted)
EndSection
```

The `Monitor` section's `Identifier` field gives a name to this monitor; this name is used in the `Screen` section to refer to this monitor. You should fill in the `Bandwidth`, `HorizSync`, and `VertRefresh` lines with information from the monitor's manual (or select conservatively from the typical values that the `xf86config` program displays).

Modeline **computation**

Although you can live with the standard `Modelines` that `xf86config` generates, you may want to know the details of that line, in case you have to define a unique mode for a video card-monitor combination.

You typically specify a `Modeline` on a single line with the following syntax:

```
Modeline "name"   CLK   HRES HSS HSE HTOT   VRES VSS VSE VTOT  flags
```

You must fill in all arguments that appear in italics except the last argument, which is an optional keyword that indicates the type of the mode. The `flags` field, for example, can be `Interlace` for an interlaced mode (alternative raster lines are drawn through the image each time) or `DoubleScan` (each scan line is doubled). Other flags indicate the polarity of the sync signal. The values can be `+HSync`, `-HSync`, `+VSync`, or `-VSync`, depending on the polarities that you are specifying.

The meanings of the arguments on the `Modeline` are as follows:

- `"name"` is the name of this mode, in double quotes. Usually, the resolution of the mode is used as its name. Thus, you'll see mode names such as `"640x480"` and `"1024x768"`. These mode names are used in the `Display` subsection of the `Screen` section.

- `CLK` is the dot clock to be used for this mode. For a video card with a fixed set of dot clocks, the dot clock should be one of the values on the `Clocks` line in the `Device` section of the `XF86Config` file.

- `HRES HSS HSE HTOT` are the horizontal timing parameters. `HRES` is the horizontal resolution in terms of the number of pixels visible on a raster line. As Figure 10-1 shows, the actual number of pixels on a raster line exceed the number of visible pixels. `HTOT` is the total pixels on the line. `HSS` is where the horizontal-sync signal begins, and `HSE` is the pixel number where the horizontal-sync signal ends. The horizontal-sync signal moves the electron beam from one line to the next. For a 640 × 480 video mode, these four parameters might be 640 680 720 864. That sequence of numbers says that 864 pixels are on the raster lines but only 640 are visible. The horizontal-sync signal begins at pixel 680 and ends at pixel 864.

- VRES VSS VSE VTOT are the vertical timing parameters. VRES is the vertical resolution in terms of the number of visible raster lines on the display screen. As Figure 10-1 shows, the actual number of raster lines exceed the number of visible raster lines. VTOT is the total raster lines. VSS is the line number where the vertical-sync signal begins, and VSE is the line number where the vertical-sync signal ends. The vertical-sync signal moves the electron beam from the bottom of the screen to the beginning of the first line. For a 640 × 480 video mode, these four parameters might be 480 488 491 521.

From a monitor's manual, you can get two key parameters: the vertical refresh rate (in Hz) and the horizontal synchronization frequency (in kHz). The monitor's manual provides these two values as ranges of valid values. The vertical refresh rate typically is between 50 Hz and 90 Hz; the horizontal sync frequency can be anywhere from 30 kHz to 135 kHz. Following are two equations that define the relationship between the dot clock and some of the horizontal and vertical timing parameters on the Modeline:

```
CLK = RR * HTOT * VTOT
CLK = HSF * HTOT
```

In these equations, RR is a screen refresh rate that is within the range of vertical refresh rate of the monitor, and HSF is a horizontal-scan frequency supported by the monitor. Remember to convert everything to a common unit (for example, make sure that all values are in Hz) when you apply these formulas.

To define a mode, you can start with a desired refresh rate (RR), such as 72 Hz. For a given dot clock, you then can compute the product HTOT * VTOT from the first equation. Next, plug in a value for HSF that is within the range of supported horizontal-scan frequencies for the monitor. Because the dot clock is already known, you can compute HTOT from the second equation. After you know HTOT, you can determine VTOT because you already computed the product of HTOT * VTOT.

At this point, you know HTOT and VTOT. What you have to select are the arguments HSS, HSE, VSS, and VSE, which you need for the Modeline. Unfortunately, figuring out these four parameters requires some trial and error. You can pick the HRES and VRES values first (HRES and VRES determine the resolution of the mode). Then you have to select HSS and HSE to lie between HRES and HTOT and HSE > HSS. Similarly, VSS and VSE should be between VRES and VTOT and VSE > VSS.

If the display area looks small or not centered, you have to alter the values HSS, HSE, VSS, and VSE to tweak the display. Given that the default XF86Config file already includes the Modelines for many common video modes, you should simply provide the allowable ranges of vertical refresh rates and horizontal-sync frequencies for your monitor, and settle for one of the predefined modes.

Common Video Cards

XFree86 supports a wide variety of common video cards. Although the video card's brand name can be important, the video chipset is what matters most to the X server. XFree86 3.1.2 provides the XF86_SVGA server, for example, which supports video cards based on the following chipsets:

- Tseng ET3000, ET4000AX, and ET4000/W32
- Western Digital/Paradise PVGA1
- Western Digital WD90C00, WD90C10, WD90C11, WD90C24, WD90C30, WD90C31, and WD90C33
- Genoa GVGA
- Trident TVGA8800CS, TVGA8900B, TVGA8900C, TVGA8900CL, TVGA9000, TVGA9000i, TVGA9100B, TVGA9200CX, TVGA9320, TVGA9400CX, and TVGA9420
- ATI 18800, 18800-1, 28800-2, 28800-4, 28800-5, 28800-6, 68800-3, 68800-6, 68800AX, 68800LX, and 88800
- NCR 77C22, 77C22E, and 77C22E+
- Cirrus Logic CLGD5420, CLGD5422, CLGD5424, CLGD5426, CLGD5428, CLGD5429, CLGD5430, CLGD5434, CLGD6205, CLGD6215, CLGD6225, CLGD6235, and CLGD6420
- Chips & Technology 65520, 65530, 65540, and 65545
- Compaq AVGA
- OAK OTI067 and OTI077
- Avance Logic AL2101
- MX MX68000 and MX680010
- Video 7/Headland Technologies HT216-32

The XF86_SVGA server uses these video cards in Super VGA (SVGA) mode, typically at resolutions up to 1,024 × 768, with 256 colors.

For late-breaking news on specific video chipsets, consult the following files in the /usr/X11/lib/X11/doc directory:

README.ati describes the XF86_SVGA server's support for ATI VGA Wonder series video cards.

README.cirrus describes the XF86_SVGA server's support for Cirrus Logic's video chipsets, including support for some accelerated graphics capabilities. The file also describes the options that relate to the Cirrus chipsets.

README.trident describes the XF86_SVGA server's support for Trident video chipsets, including any options that affect the Trident chipsets.

`README.Video7` describes the XF86_SVGA server's support for the Headland Technologies HT216-32 chipset.

`README.WstDig` describes the XF86_SVGA server's support for Western Digital video chipsets, including the WD90C31 and WD90C33, with accelerated graphics capabilities.

Accelerated Video Cards

If you want faster graphics under X, you need an accelerated video card that uses special video chipsets. Quite a few accelerated video chipsets are available, and more will appear as PCs move to graphical operating systems such as Microsoft Windows and X Window System.

Following are some of the popular accelerated video chipsets:

- S3 chipsets (911, 924, 801, 805, 928, 864, 964, Trio32, and Trio64) are used in a wide variety of brand-name video cards, such as Diamond Stealth 24 VLB, Diamond Stealth 64, Number Nine GXE64, Number Nine GXE64 PCI, and SPEA Mirage P64. These chipsets are supported by the XF86_S3 server.

- The Weitek P9000 chipset is used in video boards such as Diamond Viper VLB, Diamond Viper PCI, and Orchid P9000. The chipset is supported by the XF86_P9000 server.

- ATI Mach8, Mach32, and Mach64 chipsets are used in ATI-brand video cards, such as ATI Graphics Xpression Mach64. These chipsets are supported by the XF86_Mach8, XF86_Mach32, and XF86_Mach64 server.

- Tseng ET4000/W32 chipsets are used by video cards such as Hercules Dynamite Pro VLB and Mirage ET4000/W32 VLB. These chipsets are supported by the XF86_W32 server.

- IBM 8514/A chipsets (and clones) are used by video cards such as IBM 8514/A and Western Digital WD9510-AT. These chipsets are supported by the XF86_8514 server.

- IIT AGX-014, AGX-015, and AGX-016 chipsets are used in video cards such as the Hercules Graphite series. These chipsets are supported by the XF86_AGX server.

- The accelerated features of the Cirrus Logic CLGD5420, CLGD5422, CLGD5424, CLGD5426, CLGD5428, CLGD5429, CLGD5430, CLGD5434, CLGD6205, CLGD6215, CLGD6225, and CLGD6235 chipsets are primarily used in the video cards integrated into laptops. These chipsets are supported directly by the XF86_SVGA server.

- The accelerated features of the Western Digital WD90C31 and WD90C33 chipsets are supported directly by the XF86_SVGA server.

- The accelerated features of the OAK OTI-087 chipset are supported directly by the XF86_SVGA server.

XFree86 includes a separate server for each accelerated chipset except the Cirrus, Western Digital, and OAK chipsets; these chipsets are directly supported by the XF86_SVGA server.

The following sections describe a few popular accelerated video cards and video chipsets. For late-breaking news on specific video chipsets, consult the following files in the `/usr/X11/lib/X11/doc` directory:

`README.agx` describes the XF86 AGX server, which supports a wide variety of video cards based on the IIT AGX video chipset.

`README.Oak` describes the XF86_SVGA server's support for video cards based on OAK Technologies Inc.'s OTI067, OTI077, and OTI087 chipsets.

`README.P9000` describes the XF86_P9000 server's support for the Weitek P9000 video chipset.

`README.S3` describes the XF86_S3 server that supports a wide variety of video cards based on the S3 video chipset.

`README.W32` describes the XF86_W32 server's support for video cards based on the ET4000/W32 series of chipsets.

Diamond Viper and Orchid P9000

Two versions of the Diamond Viper video card are available: Viper VLB for Video Local Bus, and Viper PCI for PCI systems. The Diamond Viper and Orchid P9000 video cards are based on the Weitek Power 9000 (P9000) video chipset, which the XF86_P9000 accelerated X server supports.

The XF86_P9000 server expects to find the name of the vendor on the `Chipset` line in the `Device` section of the `XF86Config` file. The server recognizes the following `Chipset` lines:

```
Chipset "viperpci"       # Diamond Viper PCI
Chipset "vipervlb"       # Diamond Viper VLB
Chipset "orchid_p9000"   # Orchid P9000
```

Historically, Linux did not support Diamond Video cards because Diamond did not freely provide technical information about its card; you had to sign a nondisclosure agreement to obtain such information. Since late 1994, however, Diamond has provided detailed technical information about its video cards to XFree86 developers without any restrictions. The net result is that all new Diamond video cards now are supported by XFree86. If you want to learn more about Diamond's support of XFree86, try http://www.diamondmm.com/linux.html on the World Wide Web.

Cross Reference

As explained in Chapter 4, the xf86config program generates the XF86Config file, based on your answers to a set of questions. One of these questions asks you to select your video card from a long list of video cards. Indicating a video card is enough to generate most of the entries for the XF86Config card. For some video chipsets, however, you have to provide more information for the server. For the Diamond Viper PCI card, for example, you have to specify two parameters in the XF86Config file:

- MemBase (the starting address of video memory)
- IOBase (the starting I/O address)

These parameters are PCI bus-specific parameters that the XF86_P9000 server cannot yet detect automatically. You need a program called scanpci, which reports these parameters. The scanpci program is available via FTP from ftp://ftp.XFree86.org/pub/XFree86/3.1.1/ScanPCI.

Use the numbers reported by scanpci to fill in the MemBase and IOBase lines in the Device section of the XF86Config file. A typical Device section for a Viper PCI card looks like this:

```
Section "Device"
  Identifier "ViperPCI"
  VendorName "Diamond"
  Chipset "viperpci"
  VideoRam 2048            # indicates 2MB video RAM
  MemBase 0x80000000       # use value reported by scanpci
  IOBase 0xe000            # use value reported by scanpci
EndSection
```

ATI Mach8, Mach32, and Mach64

ATI Mach8 and Mach32 are IBM 8514/A-compatible accelerated video chipsets. The XF86_Mach8 and XF86_Mach32 accelerated X servers support the ATI Mach8 and Mach32 based video cards, respectively.

ATI Mach64 is a more recent high-performance video chipset. Several brands of ATI video cards, such as ATI Graphics Pro Turbo and ATI Graphics Xpression, use the Mach64 video chipset. Many Pentium PCI systems use the ATI Graphics Xpression video card. The version of XFree86 on the companion CD-ROM includes the XF86_Mach64 server that supports the Mach64 video card.

Secret

Some ATI video cards, such as the ATI Graphics Ultra and Ultra Pro, come with a mouse port. This mouse port conforms to the Logitech bus mouse protocol. If you have a mouse connected to the ATI card's mouse port, you should install the Logitech busmouse driver.

S3 video cards

The S3 chipset is a popular accelerated video chipset that is used in many video boards. Table 10-1 shows the specific video cards (brand names) that the XF86_S3 server supports in XFree86 3.1.2 — the latest release of XFree86. The bits-per-pixel (BPP) column shows the maximum BPP supported for that card. When the BPP column shows 32, fthe 8- and 16-BPP modes are also supported.

Table 10-1 S3-based video cards supported by XFree86 3.1.2

S3 chipset	Bits per pixel (bpp)	Cards
801/805	16	Actix GE 32, Orchid Fahrenheit 1280+
801/805	16	STB PowerGraph X.24, JAX 8231, SPEA Mirage
805	16	Miro 10SD VLB/PCI, SPEA Mirage VLB
805	8	Diamond Stealth 24 VLB
928	16	Actix Ultra, SPEA Mercury VLB
928	32	ELSA Winner 1000 ISA/VLB/EISA, STB Pegasus VL, Number Nine GXE Level 10/11/12, Number Nine GXE Level 14/16
864	32	Actix GE 64 VLB, Miro 20SD (BIOS 1.x, BIOS 2.x, BIOS 3.x), ELSA Winner 1000 PRO VLB/PCI, ELSA Winner 1000 PRO, SPEA Mirage P64 DRAM (BIOS 4.x), Diamond Stealth 64 DRAM, Number Nine GXE64 PCI
864	16	SPEA Mirage P64 DRAM (BIOS 3.x), AT&T 21C498
964	32	Miro Crystal 20SV PCI, Diamond Stealth 64, SPEA Mercury 64, Number Nine GXE64 Pro VLB/PCI, Miro Crystal 40SV, Hercules Terminator 64
964	8	ELSA Winner 2000 PRO PCI
868	32	ELSA Winner 1000AVI
968	32	ELSA Winner 2000PRO/X, Diamond Stealth 64 Video VRAM, Genoa VideoBlitz III AVI, Hercules Terminator Pro 64, STB Velocity 64V, Number Nine FX Motion 771
732 (Trio32)	32	Diamond Stealth 64 DRAM SE, all Trio32-based cards
764 (Trio64)	32	SPEA Mirage P64 (BIOS 5.x), Diamond Stealth 64 DRAM, Number Nine FX Vision 330, STB PowerGraph 64, all Trio64-based cards

Although many video cards use the same S3 chipset, they differ in two significant areas:

- The clock chip that generates the dot clocks
- A chip, known as RAMDAC, that converts the contents of the video memory to analog signals sent to the monitor

Secret

When you select one of the supported S3-based video cards, you do not have to specify the clock chip or RAMDAC. If you come across a new S3-based video card whose name does not appear in the list of supported cards, you may be able to get the XF86_S3 server to work with that card by specifying its clock chip and RAMDAC in the Device section of the XF86Config file.

Most RAMDACs are detected automatically by the X server, but if you have a video card with the AT&T 20C490 RAMDAC, you should include the following line in the Device section of the XF86Config file:

```
RamDac "att20c490"
```

Table 10-2 lists the supported clock chips and the ClockChip line that you can use to specify the chip in the Device section of the Xf86Config file.

Table 10-2 Supported clock chips and the ClockChip **line**

Clock chip	ClockChip *line in* XF86Config
DCS2824-0 (Diamond, ICD2061A-compatible)	ClockChip "dcs2824"
ICD2061A	ClockChip "icd2061a"
ICS2595	ClockChip "ics2595"
ICS5300 GENDAC (86c708-compatible)	ClockChip "ics5300"
ICS5342 GENDAC	ClockChip "ics5342"
ICS9161A (ICD2061A-compatible)	ClockChip "ics9161a"
S3 86c708 GENDAC	ClockChip "s3gendac"
S3 86c716 SDAC	ClockChip "s3_sdac"
Sierra SC11412	ClockChip "sc11412"
TI3025	ClockChip "ti3025"

Commercial X Servers for XFree86

If XFree86 does not support your high-performance video card, you may have to look at a commercial X server. The price is between $100 and $200, but you'll get an X server that supports more cards than XFree86 does. For cards that XFree86 already supports, the commercial version may provide better performance than XFree86 does.

Two well-known commercial X servers are

- Metro-X from Metro Link Inc. For information, send e-mail to sales@metrolink.com.
- Accelerated-X from X Inside Inc. For information, send e-mail to info@xinside.com, or try the company's World Wide Web page at http://www.xinside.com/.

Following are examples of video cards that are supported by commercial X servers:

- Matrox MGA Millenium
- Number Nine Imagine 128
- Compaq QVision 2000
- Weitek P9100 chipset (used in video cards such as Diamond Viper Pro)
- Chips & Technologies 82C45x, 82C48x, and F655xx video chipsets

Many Pentium PCs are sold with these high-performance video cards. Although XFree86 probably will begin supporting at least some of these cards in the future, right now these commercial products allow you to exploit these video cards under X and Linux.

The commercial X servers also do a better job of supporting 16-, 24-, and 32-bits-per-pixel (bpp) modes better than the XFree86 servers do. These modes essentially refer to the number of colors that you can display on a monitor simultaneously. The 24-bpp mode allows 1 byte each for the RGB (red, green, and blue) components of color. The 32-bpp mode essentially is the 24-bpp mode, but the RGB value for a single pixel is stored in a 32-bit word, with 1 byte wasted. The term *24 bpp* is used to refer to the case in which the 24-bit RGB values are stored without wasting any space. As a result, the 24-bpp mode often is referred to as *24-bpp packed-pixel* mode.

Summary

Video cards and monitors don't matter much if you use Linux in text mode only. If you want to use the XFree86 X Window System, however, you have to pay attention to the video card and monitor. This chapter describes how XFree86 is configured and what types of video cards and monitors it supports. By reading this chapter, you learn the following:

- In a PC, the video card stores the array of pixels that constitutes the image that you see on-screen. The video card converts the pixel values to analog signals that drive the red (R), green (G), and blue (B) electron guns in a monitor. These RGB electron beams, in turn, paint the color image on the phosphor-coated display screen. The combination of the video card and monitor is important to the X Window System because the X server controls the video card directly and because the monitor must be capable of handling the signals that the video card generates.

- XFree86 includes several X servers, each designed for a specific category of video cards, ranging from the generic VGA to accelerated cards such as ATI Mach64 and S3. You have to select the X server based on the type of video card in your system, so you need to know what card you have before setting up XFree86.

- When the X server runs, it consults a configuration file named XF86Config (usually in the /etc directory) to select an appropriate video mode and to configure the video card and monitor for proper operation. Computing the valid video-mode parameters is complicated. As long as you know the technical specification of your monitor (such as horizontal-synchronization frequency and refresh rate), you do not need to compute the video-mode information.

- Video cards fall into two broad groups. All super VGA cards are controlled by the XF86_SVGA server; and the accelerated video cards have custom X servers, such as XF86_S3 and XF86_Mach64.

- XFree86 supports most of the popular high-performance video cards, but if your favorite video card is not on the supported list, you have to turn to a commercial vendor. For a small price, you can buy an X server for newer video cards, such as Number Nine Imagine 128 and Matrox MGA Millenium.

Chapter 11
Disk Drives

In This Chapter

- Surveying the different types of disk controllers that Linux supports
- Understanding disk drive concepts: cylinders, heads, and sectors (CHS)
- Understanding disk drive operations: partitioning and booting with LILO
- Understanding the 1,024-cylinder limit of BIOS
- Surveying SCSI disks that Linux supports
- Troubleshooting SCSI
- Using Iomega Zip drives in Linux
- Looking at known bugs in EIDE disk controllers for the PCI bus

When it comes to disk drives and Linux, what matters is whether Linux supports the *disk controller:* the card that connects the disk drive to your PC's motherboard. Linux supports most common disk controllers. This chapter gives you information on different disk controllers and specific details on how to install and run Linux on a system that has one or more of these controllers. In particular, a few of the newer PCI (Peripheral Component Interconnect) disk controllers have bugs that affect Linux. This chapter also describes some of the known problems with PCI disk controllers.

Disk Controller Types

The disk controller is the adapter card that acts as an intermediary between your PC's motherboard and one or more hard disk drives. Typically, you can connect up to two hard drives and two floppy drives to a single disk controller. The Small Computer System Interface (SCSI) controller is an exception to this norm; you can connect up to seven SCSI devices (anything that has a SCSI interface, such as a disk drive, CD-ROM drive, tape drive, or scanner).

Over the years, several types of hard disk controllers have appeared for the PC. Following are some of the disk controllers that you may find in a PC:

- *ST506* disk controllers, which originally appeared in IBM XT and AT computers, became the common disk controller of the PC industry in its early years (remember that the IBM PC-AT came out in 1984). Many PCs have disk controllers that are compatible with the ST506. Seagate's ST506 was the original hard drive for PCs; Western Digital's WD1003 was the controller card. Thus, these controllers are often referred to as being WD1003-compatible controllers. The original ST506 drives used a recording method known as Modified Frequency Modulation (MFM). Many ST506 disk controllers also support drives that use another type of data-recording technique, known as Run Length Limited (RLL).

- The *Integrated Drive Electronics* (IDE) interface emulates the ST506 interface. IDE drives, however, contain the necessary controller circuitry built into the drive itself. The motherboard typically contains an IDE interface for connecting the drive to the motherboard. IDE drives are now in widespread use in PCs. Nowadays, the term *AT Attachment* (ATA) is used to refer to IDE. The original IDE interface could support only two drives and it limited the maximum disk size to approximately 500MB. You needed third-party drivers to use disks larger than 500MB. Today's PCs with large disk drives use the Enhanced IDE interface (described next).

- The *Enhanced IDE* (EIDE) interface supports up to four internal IDE devices (which include hard drives as well as CD-ROM drives), and supports higher-capacity drives, and higher speeds of data transfer. Typical EIDE interfaces consist of two IDE interfaces: primary and secondary, each of which is capable of supporting up to two drives. EIDE interfaces are popular because of their low cost. Many PCs use the EIDE interface to connect both the hard disk and the CD-ROM drive to the PC's motherboard.

- The *Enhanced Small Device Interface* (ESDI) controllers emulate the ST506 interface but provide higher data-transfer rates.

- *Small Computer System Interface* (SCSI) controllers provide a separate bus onto which you can connect up to seven SCSI devices. You will find hard drives, CD-ROM drives, tape drives, and even scanners that support SCSI. You can connect multiple SCSI devices to the computer by daisy chaining the devices with a SCSI cable. All UNIX workstations (such as the ones from Hewlett-Packard, IBM, and Sun Microsystems) use SCSI. Lately, SCSI is becoming popular on PCs as well. The only drawback is that the SCSI controller is relatively expensive compared with EIDE controllers.

Linux supports all these common disk controllers. Even though several disk controllers appear in the preceding list, there are essentially two types of controllers: IDE (where IDE refers to all ST506-compatible interfaces) and SCSI. As explained in Chapter 1, you have to select a Linux kernel that supports the disk controller on your system. For most PCs, a kernel with IDE support is adequate.

Some systems have both an IDE interface and a SCSI interface. In that case, you need a kernel that supports SCSI as well as IDE.

Cross Reference

Most Pentium systems use a motherboard that supports the Peripheral Component Interconnect (PCI) bus. These PCI systems need SCSI adapter cards that plug into PCI bus slots and IDE interfaces that connect to the PCI bus. Because Linux only recently added support for the PCI bus, Linux still does not support all PCI peripherals. Additionally, some problems with specific PCI-interface hardware have been reported, probably because the PCI bus itself is fairly new. These initial problems notwithstanding, the PCI bus seems poised to become the dominant bus in the PC marketplace, replacing the old and outdated ISA bus. (Chapter 9 discusses various buses.)

Disk Drive Concepts

When you read about disk drives, you'll run into some terms and concepts that are unique to the world of hard disks. This section explains some of these concepts.

Cylinders, heads, and sectors

The physical organization of the disk is expressed in terms of cylinders, heads, and sectors. A hard disk consists of several platters of magnetic material. In physical terms, you can think of *cylinder, head*, and *sector* as meaning the following:

- A *cylinder* is one of a series of concentric rings on one side of a disk platter. Each side of the platter is divided into cylinders.

- The total number of *heads* is the number of sides of all the magnetic platters.

- A *sector* is a pie-shape wedge on the platter. Each cylinder is divided into sectors.

Any location on the disk can be expressed in terms of the cylinder, the head, and the sector. Identifying a disk location in terms of cylinder, head, and sector is known as *CHS addressing*.

Wizard

The physical *geometry* of a hard disk usually is expressed in terms of cylinders, heads, and sectors. A disk may have a geometry of 528/32/63, which means that the disk has 528 cylinders, 32 heads, and 63 sectors. Usually, each sector can store 512 bytes (or half a kilobyte) of data. Thus, the capacity of this disk is $(528 \times 32 \times 63) / 2$ kilobytes, or 532,224 kilobytes.

Note

PC hard disk controllers include a Read-Only Memory (ROM) Basic Input/Output System (BIOS) on the controller. By convention (and compatibility with the original IBM PC architecture), the BIOS uses CHS addressing to access the hard disk. The disk BIOS, however, uses a 10-bit value as the cylinder address. Because 10 bits can hold numbers between 0 and 1,023, the BIOS can address, at most, 1,024 cylinders.

Many large disks have more than 1,024 cylinders. To accommodate the 1,024-cylinder limit, the disk controllers have to resort to some tricks to handle disks with more than 1,024 cylinders. Later, in the "Disks with more than 1,024 cylinders" section, you read about problems with disks that have more than 1,024 cylinders.

Master Boot Record (MBR)

The first sector of the hard disk (cylinder 0, head 0, sector 1) is called the *Master Boot Record* (MBR). This 512-byte storage area contains important information about the disk, such as the partition table and a small amount of code that the PC's BIOS loads and runs when you boot the PC.

The small program in the MBR reads the partition table; determines which partition is active (that's just an attribute of a partition); reads the active partition's first sector, or *boot sector;* and runs whatever program resides in that boot sector. The program in a partition's boot sector usually loads whatever operating system is installed on that partition.

When you install the Linux Loader (LILO) on the hard disk, the LILO program resides on the hard disk's MBR.

Partitions

Partitions are a way of dividing up a hard disk and treating each part separately. By dividing your PC's hard disk into partitions, you can install different operating systems in different partitions. Even if you use the entire disk for Linux, you would, at minimum, need a partition that Linux can use as *swap space* — an extension of memory, so that you can have more virtual memory than the physical memory on your system.

Wizard

The Master Boot Record contains the partition table, starting at byte 446 (0x1be, which means 1be in hexadecimal). The partition table can have up to four 16-byte entries. Each 16-byte value defines a partition. Each partition is specified by a starting and an ending cylinder number. The partition entry also includes a type that identifies the operating system that created the partition. The concept of partitions is a convention that all PC-based operating systems, ranging from MS-DOS to Linux, follow.

In MS-DOS, you use the FDISK program to manipulate the partitions. Linux includes a program with the same name — fdisk (lowercase) — to alter the disk partitions.

Linux device names for disks

In Linux, each device is represented by a device file in the /dev directory. The device name for the hard disk depends on the type of disk controller. For IDE and EIDE drives, the device name is /dev/hda for the first disk, /dev/hdb for the second disk, and so on.

On an EIDE interface, if you have a hard disk on the primary interface and a CD-ROM drive on the secondary interface, the device names are /dev/hda for the hard disk drive and /dev/hdc for the CD-ROM drive.

The Linux disk drivers treat each disk partition as being a separate device. The first partition in the first IDE disk is /dev/hda1, the second partition is /dev/hda2, the third one is /dev/hda3, and so on. Similarly, the device names for the partitions on the second IDE drive are /dev/hdb1, /dev/hdb2, and so on.

The SCSI disk devices are named /dev/sda, /dev/sdb, and so on. If a SCSI device is a hard disk, its partitions are named by appending the partition number to the device name. Thus, the partitions of the first SCSI hard disk are named /dev/sda1, /dev/sda2, /dev/sda3, and so on.

Floppy Disks in Linux

Cross Reference

Chapter 7 describes several ways to access MS-DOS floppy disks under Linux; you can mount the floppy and use Linux commands, or use the mtools utility programs to read from or write to the floppy. You also can create a Linux file system on a floppy disk. In fact, you'll find Linux file systems on the boot and root floppies that you use to install Linux.

Formatting and creating a Linux file system on a floppy is a straightforward process. To format a 3.5-inch high-density floppy in the A drive, for example, use the following command:

fdformat /dev/fd0H1440

For a 5.25-inch high-density floppy, change the device name to /dev/fd0h1200. On the B drive, change the first 0 in the device name to 1.

Wizard

After you format the floppy, use the following command to create a Linux file system on the floppy:

mke2fs -m 0 /dev/fd0H1440 1440

The -m option is used to specify what percentage of blocks should be reserved for use by the *super user* (root). By specifying the -m 0 option, you ensure that mke2fs does not reserve any space on the floppy disk for the super user. If you do not explicitly specify the -m option, mke2fs reserves 5 percent of the disk space for the super user.

After you create the file system on the floppy drive, you can mount the floppy at a *mount point* (an empty directory) in the Linux file system. The following example shows how you would mount the floppy drive at the /mnt directory:

mount /dev/fd0H1440 /mnt

Now you can use Linux commands, such as cp and mv, to copy or move files to the floppy disk. Before you eject the floppy disk from the drive, use the following command to dismount the floppy:

umount /dev/fd0H1440

Hard Disk Operations in Linux

Cross Reference

You have to perform some disk operations to install and use Linux on your system. Chapter 1 explains some of the disk operations that you perform when you set up Linux. The next few sections provide some additional information about these disk operations.

Altering disk partitions with FIPS

When you first get a PC, the hard disk usually is set up as one huge partition, and DOS and Windows are already installed on it. (If you bought your PC recently, it probably came with Windows 95 preinstalled.) To install Linux, you have to start by creating at least two partitions for Linux: one for the swap space and the other for the Linux file system.

If you have original disks to reinstall the current operating system again (be it Windows 95 or MS-DOS and Windows 3.1), you can simply go ahead and repartition the disk. To do this, boot the PC, using a DOS boot floppy, and run the MS-DOS version of FDISK to delete the current partition and create new ones. Create three new partitions: one for DOS and Windows, one for Linux swap space, and one for the Linux file system. Then you have to reinstall DOS and Windows in their partition and install Linux on the other partition.

Cross Reference

If you do not want to go through the trouble of reinstalling DOS and Windows or Windows 95, you have to alter the existing partition somehow. FIPS, which can split an existing DOS partition into two separate partitions, allows you to perform this task. Chapter 1 describes how to use FIPS.

Partitioning with `fdisk`

Partitioning the disk involves creating several smaller logical devices within a single hard disk. Under MS-DOS, you would use the FDISK program to view and alter a disk's partition table. In Linux, the partitioning program is called `fdisk`.

Cross Reference

Chapter 1 explains how to use Linux and MS-DOS FDISK during Linux installation. I mention it here for the sake of completeness, to jog your memory about the `fdisk` program.

Even if you have already partitioned your hard disk, you can always run `fdisk` just to see the current partition table of a hard disk. If you have a SCSI disk drive with the device name /dev/sda, for example, you can look at its partition table with `fdisk` as follows:

```
fdisk /dev/sda
Command (m for help): m
Command action
   a   toggle a bootable flag
   c   toggle the dos compatibility flag
   d   delete a partition
   l   list known partition types
   m   print this menu
   n   add a new partition
   p   print the partition table
   q   quit without saving changes
   t   change a partition's system id
   u   change display/entry units
   v   verify the partition table
   w   write table to disk and exit
   x   extra functionality (experts only)
```

```
Command (m for help): p
Disk /dev/sda: 64 heads, 32 sectors, 500 cylinders
Units = cylinders of 2048 * 512 bytes

   Device Boot  Begin   Start    End   Blocks   Id  System
/dev/sda1            1       1    301  308208    6  DOS 16-bit >=32M
/dev/sda2          302     302    499  202752   83  Linux native

Command (m for help): q
```

The m command shows you a list of the single-letter commands that fdisk accepts. You can see the current partition table with a p command. This example's SCSI disk has two partitions: one for DOS and the other for Linux.

The Id field in the table of partitions printed by the fdisk program (when you type **p** at the fdisk prompt) is a number that denotes a partition type. If you want to see a list of all known partition types, type **l** (that's a lowercase L) at the fdisk prompt. Table 11-1 lists the partition types that Linux understands.

Table 11-1   Partition types known to Linux

Type	Description	Type	Description	Type	Description	Type	Description
0	Empty	8	AIX	75	PC/IX	b7	BSDI fs
1	DOS 12-bit FAT	9	AIX bootable	80	Old MINIX	b8	BSDI swap
2	XENIX root	a	OS/2 Boot Manager	81	Linux/MINIX	c7	Syrinx
3	XENIX usr	40	Venix 80286	82	Linux swap	db	CP/M
4	DOS 16-bit <32MB	51	Novell?	83	Linux native	e	DOS access
5	Extended	52	Microport	93	Amoeba	e3	DOS R/O
6	DOS 16-bit >=32MB	63	GNU HURD	94	Amoeba BBT	f2	DOS secondary
7	OS/2 HPFS	64	Novell	a5	BSD/386	ff	BBT

Booting from the hard disk with LILO

To automatically boot Linux from a hard disk, you need the Linux Loader (LILO). LILO is a boot loader program; OS/2 has an equivalent program, called Boot Manager. These programs usually reside in the Master Boot Record of a disk and are the first to get loaded. The boot loader program then, in turn, prompts you for the name of an operating system to start (which typically

Part III: Exploiting Your Hardware in Linux

means a disk partition from which to boot). Starting an operating system basically involves loading that operating system's main program into memory and running it. For Linux, this step involves loading the Linux kernel into memory and giving control to the kernel.

Cross Reference

LILO is much more than just Linux Loader; it also serves as a general-purpose boot manager that is capable of booting MS-DOS, OS/2, or Windows 95. Chapter 1 describes how you can install LILO on your hard disk during the Linux installation process. This section summarizes the LILO installation process if you do it outside the Linux setup program described in Chapter 1.

Tip

You'll find the LILO documentation in `/usr/doc/lilo` on your system. You should consult the README file in `/usr/doc/lilo` for the latest word on installing and configuring LILO. The following section provides only an overview.

Installing LILO

Cross Reference

Typically, you install LILO as part of the Linux installation process described in Chapter 1. The only time you have to repeat LILO configuration and installation is when you update the kernel or add a new operating system that you want to boot through LILO.

Installing LILO involves two basic steps:

1. Run the `/sbin/liloconfig` program to prepare the LILO configuration file, which contains information that is necessary for installing LILO. The default LILO configuration file is `/etc/lilo.conf`.

2. Run the `/sbin/lilo` program (referred to as the *map installer* in LILO's README file) to update the boot sector and create the `/boot/map` file, which contains information that LILO uses during the boot process.

To prepare the LILO configuration file, run `/sbin/liloconfig` as `root`. This program displays a menu that contains the following options:

```
/sbin/liloconfig

LILO INSTALLATION

LILO (the Linux Loader) is the program that allows booting Linux
directly from the hard drive. To install, you make a new LILO configu-
ration file by creating a new header and then adding at least one
bootable partition to the file. Once you've done this, you can select
the install option. Alternately, if you already have an /etc/
lilo.conf, you may reinstall using that. If you make a mistake, just
select (1) to start over.

1 - Start LILO configuration with a new LILO header
2 - Add a Linux partition to the LILO config file
3 - Add an OS/2 partition to the LILO config file
4 - Add a DOS partition to the LILO config file
```

```
5 — Install LILO
6 — Reinstall LILO using the existing lilo.conf
7 — Skip LILO installation and exit this menu
8 — View your current /etc/lilo.conf
9 — Read the Linux Loader HELP file

Which option would you like (1 - 9)?
```

This menu is similar to the LILO configuration menu that appears when you set up Linux by following the steps outlined in Chapter 1. The only difference is that the `liloconfig` program requires you to enter a number to indicate your choice.

The `liloconfig` program guides you through the process by asking questions. What you have to decide is what operating systems you want to boot with Linux and the names of the disk partitions where those operating systems reside.

When the LILO configuration file — /etc/lilo.conf — is ready, you can install LILO with the following command:

`/sbin/lilo`

The `lilo` program looks for the `lilo.conf` file in the `/etc` directory, interprets its contents, prepares the necessary boot and map files, and initializes the boot record of the device specified (by the `boot` line) in the configuration file. If the boot device is specified as a hard disk partition, for example, `lilo` sets up the boot sector of that disk partition.

The files in /usr/doc/lilo, especially /usr/doc/lilo/README, contain the latest information on LILO. You may want to check out that directory if you have a unique arrangement of hard disk partitions and want to find out whether you can use LILO to boot Linux.

Remember that you can always install LILO on a floppy. Also remember that the boot process is nearly as fast as booting from a hard disk, because after loading a 512-byte sector from the floppy, the boot process jumps to the hard disk partition where the Linux kernel resides.

LILO's boot prompt

LILO's boot prompt appears if one of the following things happens:

- You turn on Caps Lock or Scroll Lock.
- You press Alt, Shift, or Ctrl as the system boots.

If one of these conditions occurs, LILO displays the `boot:` prompt and waits for the name of a boot image to load. If you do not respond within a specified period (this value is stored in the /etc/lilo.conf file), LILO loads the default boot image (the first image in the /etc/lilo.conf file).

When you use LILO to boot Linux, you can specify the name of the Linux boot image, followed by one or more options. LILO passes these boot command-line options directly to the Linux kernel. As you read descriptions of various disk controllers, you'll find information on boot command-line options that you can use to specify various parameters of a device. These parameters typically include the I/O port address, IRQ, and DMA of a device. Notice that boot command-line options are always case sensitive.

Removing LILO

If you set up LILO on the hard disk's Master Boot Record but later want to remove it, you can do so easily, provided that you have MS-DOS version 5.0 or later. All you have to do is boot from a DOS boot floppy (place the boot floppy in drive A and then power up the PC) and run FDISK with the /MBR option. The FDISK/MBR command essentially restores the Master Boot Record to the format that MS-DOS uses. The next time you boot the PC, MS-DOS should start immediately.

Another way to uninstall LILO is to use LILO itself as follows:

```
/sbin/lilo -u
```

LILO replaces the MBR from a saved copy of the old boot sector, which LILO saves when you first install LILO.

Caution

Use the `/sbin/lilo -u` command only if you have installed LILO on your hard disk's MBR. When you use the `-u` option, LILO simply copies a file named `/boot/boot.nnnn` (nnnn is the device number, such as 0300 for the `/dev/hda` and 0800 for `/dev/sda`) to the disk's MBR. If you have been playing with LILO and an old boot file happens to be left over in the `/boot` directory, LILO might copy that file to the MBR. A bad MBR, of course, makes the disk unbootable. In such a case, boot from a DOS floppy and use the FDISK /MBR command to restore the MBR to boot DOS.

Creating swap space

Note

Swap space is a disk partition that Linux uses as an extension of its memory. When some memory-resident data is not needed immediately, Linux stores that data in the swap space. To create the swap space, you have to create a disk partition using `fdisk`. Make sure that you set the type of that disk partition to Linux swap. Typically, you can set up the swap partition and turn on swapping as you install Linux from this book's Slackware Linux.

Cross Reference

If you have to set up the swap space outside the installation program, you have to follow the procedure outlined in Chapter 1. The basic steps are to use the `mkswap` command to initialize the swap partition. You need the size of the swap partition (in number of blocks) before you use the `mkswap` command. Use the Linux `fdisk` program to find this information.

After `mkswap` finishes, use the `swapon` command to turn on swapping. Linux then begins to use the swap space.

Wizard

To ensure that Linux uses the swap space every time it boots, you have to add a line to the file `/etc/fstab` that indicates the swap partition's name. If the swap partition is `/dev/hda2`, for example, you would add the following line to `/etc/fstab`:

```
/dev/hda2       none        swap        sw
```

Secret

If you put a partition's name in /etc/fstab but forget to run mkswap on that partition, Linux displays the following error message:

```
Unable to find swap-space signature
```

The fix is to run mkswap to initialize the swap partition.

Creating file systems

Note

To use a disk partition in Linux, you have to create a file system on that partition. You can think of this procedure as formatting the partition for Linux. When you install Linux by following the steps described in Chapter 1, one of the steps creates the file system; the setup program actually asks you whether you want to format a partition. For a Linux partition, the setup program uses the mk2efs command to create a Linux file system.

Linux supports several types of file systems, including the following:

- *MS-DOS file system.* This DOS file system is based on the File Allocation Table (FAT). This type is designated by the keyword msdos.

- *Minix file system.* Minix is the original UNIX clone that inspired the creation of Linux. Linux started by using the Minix file system, which limits filenames to 14 or 30 characters. The minix keyword identifies this file-system type.

- *Extended file system.* This old Linux file system goes by the keyword ext. You should not use this file system anymore.

- *Second extended file system.* This system is the latest and greatest Linux file system. The keyword ext2 refers to this file-system type. You can use longer filenames in this file system.

Wizard

The setup program creates an ext2 file system on the Linux partition automatically. To create an ext2 file system manually, you have to use the mke2fs command. To use the mke2fs command, you need the number of blocks in the disk partition where you want to create the file system. Use the fdisk program to figure out the partition's size and then use the mke2fs command as follows:

```
mke2fs -c /dev/hda3 405040
```

This command creates an ext2 file system on the /dev/hda3 partition, which contains 308,040 blocks (each block is 1,024 bytes, or 1K). The -c option forces mke2fs to check for bad blocks (using a fast read-only test) before creating the file system.

When you install Linux on a hard disk that uses standard IDE, MFM, or RLL controllers, always install the ext2 file system and use the bad block-checking options when you create the file system.

Specific Disk Problems in Linux

Cross Reference

For most hard drives, installing Linux amounts to booting a Linux kernel that supports your system's hard disk controller, partitioning the disk under Linux, and loading the operating system and associated software onto the hard disk. You notice the hard disk only when you create the partitions (as explained in Chapter 1).

Whenever some part of the hard disk is out of the ordinary, however, you may run into problems when installing Linux. This section covers some of these problems and suggests solutions.

Windows 95 and LILO

Secret

On a PC that has both Linux and Windows 3.1 installed in separate partitions, you can use the Linux Loader (LILO) program to boot one or the other operating system. If you upgrade Windows 3.1 to Windows 95, you'll notice that Windows 95 wipes out LILO. Windows 95 overwrites the Master Boot Record with its own program, and LILO typically resides on the Master Boot Record. In this case, all you have to do is boot Linux using a boot floppy (you should have created the boot floppy during Linux installation), and then run /sbin/lilo to reinstall LILO.

Cross Reference

If you bought a new PC with Windows 95 preinstalled, all you have to do is install Linux by following the steps described in Chapter 1 (start with repartitioning the hard disk). When you come to the step that installs LILO, specify the operating systems and the disk partitions that LILO should configure for booting. When you specify partitions to boot, treat the Windows 95 disk partition as a DOS partition. After you finish installing Linux and LILO, you should be able to boot Windows 95 (assuming that you left it installed) or Linux by entering the name of the appropriate boot image at LILO's boot prompt.

Disks with more than 1,024 cylinders

Disks that have more than 1,024 cylinders were a problem in older Linux kernels. The version of Linux on the companion disk, however, should work fine with EIDE disks that have more than 1,024 cylinders, so you can safely ignore the discussions in this section.

Wizard

You can view a disk as being a collection of sectors, each of which is 512 bytes. The sectors are addressed in two ways:

- Linear Block Address (LBA), in which the sectors are numbered sequentially, starting at zero.

- Cylinder, Head, Sector (CHS) address, which is based on the physical construction of a hard disk, consisting of a stack of magnetic platters that rotate at high speed under read-write heads.

Old PC disk controllers and the Basic Input/Output System (BIOS) use physical CHS addresses to access the sectors on the disk. This arrangement worked fine until large disks started to appear on the market. The BIOS uses a 10-bit value as the cylinder number, which means that the BIOS can access, at most, 1,024 cylinders on a hard disk (because a 10-bit value lies between 0 and 1,023). Because of this limitation, any disk that has more than 1,024 cylinders is generally referred to as a *large disk* in the PC world.

Wizard

Most current hard disks tend to have 16 heads, 63 sectors, and a large number of cylinders. With a 1,024-cylinder limitation, the maximum disk size under BIOS is $16 \times 63 \times 1{,}024 = 1{,}0321{,}192$ sectors = 528,482,304 bytes (because each sector is 512 bytes long) = 504 MB (1MB = $1{,}024 \times 1{,}024$ bytes). As you well know, many current desktop PCs have 1GB disks. These disks typically come with the Enhanced IDE (EIDE) interface.

The EIDE interface handles large disks by playing with the number of cylinders and heads. One trick that EIDE BIOS uses is to halve the actual number of cylinders and double the number of heads. When the BIOS processes a disk-access request specified by CHS address, it automatically adjusts the cylinders and heads to access the correct sector on the disk. This adjustment is called *address translation*.

Linux gets a disk's geometry (number of cylinders, heads, and sectors) from the BIOS. If the BIOS does address translation, the reported values won't match the actual physical parameters of the disk. Unfortunately, Linux does not go through the BIOS to read from or write to the disk. When accessing the disk controller, Linux has to provide the CHS address with physically correct values. In other words, Linux has to perform address translation like the BIOS. Luckily, the Linux kernel on this book's companion disk already takes care of all the details and handles large disks properly.

You still may run into problems with large disks, however, not because Linux cannot handle large disks, but because on MS-DOS PCs, many older large hard disks are handled by special software that may conflict with Linux. Some large systems come with special software known as Disk Manager. The Disk Manager usually resides in the disk's Master Boot Record and may perform some "magic" to allow DOS to access the entire disk.

The only clean solution for such problems involves backing up your DOS files. Set the BIOS disk parameters to the correct disk parameters and then partition the disk under Linux. You can set aside the first partition for use under DOS (because DOS won't be able to access more than the first 1,024 cylinders), and create the necessary partitions for Linux beyond the DOS partition.

Because the Linux Loader (LILO) relies on BIOS, which cannot access more than 1,024 cylinders, you should try to create the Linux boot partition in the first 1,024 cylinders.

EIDE problems on PCI systems

The current crop of Pentium PCs uses the new PCI bus. With the new bus come new interfaces for disks. A common interface is the PCI EIDE controller to connect EIDE devices, such as hard disks and CD-ROM drives, to the PCI motherboard.

Secret

Recently, some users have reported data corruption in EIDE disks with some PCI EIDE controllers. Specifically, the affected systems have PCI motherboards with PCI EIDE controllers that use one of the following chips:

- RZ 1000
- CMD 640

To find out what type of PCI EIDE controller your system has, use the `cat /proc/pci` command (assuming, of course, that your system has a PCI bus).

Secret

The RZ 1000 is reported to cause two problems when reading from and writing to devices on the EIDE controller:

- In prefetch mode, reading from multiple sectors often fails. This problem is known as the prefetch bug.
- When the system sends status commands to the floppy drive, the chip responds to the requests and corrupts any hard disk or CD-ROM input or output operation that's in progress.

Secret

The CMD 640 suffers from the same problems as the RZ 1000, and then some. The CMD 640 also exhibits the following problems:

- Does not support simultaneous input and output operations on the primary and secondary IDE interfaces of the EIDE controller
- Does not support 32-bit write operations

These problems are reported only in multitasking 32-bit operating systems, such as OS/2 Warp and Linux. Windows NT uses the PCI EIDE controller in a different mode that does not suffer from these problems. The RZ 1000 and CMD 640 problems do not occur under MS-DOS, Windows 3.1, and Windows 95.

Wizard

The chips' vendors are aware of the problem, so new revisions of these chips should eliminate the bugs. In the meantime, you can take the following steps to avoid these bugs in Linux:

- Disable the prefetch buffer in your system's CMOS setup.
- If you have a CMD 640, provide the following option at the boot prompt:

    ```
    hda=serialize
    ```

    If you use LILO, add the following line to the `/etc/lilo.conf` file:

    ```
    option="hda=serialize"
    ```

Starting with kernel version 1.3.23 (the latest development version of Linux), Linux detects and works around these problems automatically. When you run that kernel, `/proc/pci` shows the CMD 640 controller as being buggy.

Error messages about inodes and blocks

Secret

If you get error messages about bad inodes or blocks during system startup, chances are that you did not shut down the system properly. Before powering off a Linux system, you should always log in as `root` and use the shutdown command to halt the system, as follows:

```
/sbin/shutdown -h now
```

After that, you must wait until you see a message that says that the system has halted. Only then you should turn the power off.

Because of our typical DOS experience of simply turning the power switch off, most of us are tempted to reach for the power switch to shut down the system (although somehow, I always remember to properly shut down other UNIX workstations, such as HP and Sun workstations).

If the system is not shut down properly, the file system may be damaged. When you boot the system the next time, it runs a file system-check program (`fsck`) that may fix the file system and boot the system. In some cases, however, `fsck` won't be able to fix the file system damage. You have no option but to reinitialize the file system, using the `mke2fs` command.

SCSI Disk Controllers and Linux

The remainder of this chapter explains using SCSI controllers under Linux.

SCSI (pronounced "scuzzy") is an increasingly popular interface for connecting up to seven different devices on the SCSI bus. Each device, and the SCSI controller, has a unique SCSI identifier (ID) in the range 0 through 7. The controller usually is set to SCSI ID 7; the other devices use numbers between 0 and 6. Typically, a SCSI hard disk is set to SCSI ID 0.

Linux supports the following SCSI controllers:

- Adaptec AHA-1510/152*x* (ISA) (AIC-6260/6360)
- Adaptec AHA-154*x* (ISA) (all models)
- Adaptec AHA-174*x* (EISA) (in enhanced mode)
- Adaptec AHA-274*x* (EISA) / 284*x* (VLB) (AIC-7770)
- Adaptec AHA-294*x* (PCI) (AIC-7870) (beginning in Linux version 1.3.6)
- Adaptec AVA-1505/1515 (ISA) (Adaptec 152*x*-compatible)
- Always IN2000
- AMI Fast Disk VLB/EISA (BusLogic-compatible)
- BusLogic (ISA/EISA/VLB/PCI) (all models)
- DPT PM2001 and PM2012A (EATA-PIO)
- DPT Smartcache (EATA-DMA) (ISA/EISA/PCI) (all models)
- DTC 329*x* (EISA) (Adaptec 154*x*-compatible)

Future Domain TMC-16x0 and TMC-3260 (PCI)

Future Domain TMC-8xx and TMC-950

NCR 5380 generic cards

NCR 53c7x0 and 53c8x0 (PCI)

Pro Audio Spectrum 16 SCSI (ISA)

Qlogic / Control Concepts SCSI/IDE (FAS408) (ISA/VLB/PCMCIA); the PCMCIA cards must boot DOS to initialize the card

Seagate ST-01/ST-02 (ISA)

Sound Blaster 16 SCSI-2 (Adaptec 152x-compatible) (ISA)

Trantor T128/T128F/T228 (ISA)

UltraStor 14F (ISA), 24F (EISA), and 34F (VLB)

Western Digital WD7000 SCSI

Linux currently does not support parallel-port SCSI adapters and non-Adaptec-compatible DTC boards (such as 327x and 328x).

When you configure the Linux kernel for SCSI support, the configuration program asks the following questions in regard to SCSI controller cards:

```
Adaptec AHA152X support (CONFIG_SCSI_AHA152X) [y] n
Adaptec AHA1542 support (CONFIG_SCSI_AHA1542) [y]
Adaptec AHA1740 support (CONFIG_SCSI_AHA1740) [y] n
Adaptec AHA274X/284X support (CONFIG_SCSI_AHA274X) [y] n
BusLogic SCSI support (CONFIG_SCSI_BUSLOGIC) [y] n
EATA-DMA (DPT, NEC&ATT for ISA, EISA, PCI) support
(CONFIG_SCSI_EATA_DMA) [y] n
UltraStor 14F/34F support (CONFIG_SCSI_U14_34F) [y] n
Future Domain 16xx SCSI support (CONFIG_SCSI_FUTURE_DOMAIN) [y] n
Generic NCR5380 SCSI support (CONFIG_SCSI_GENERIC_NCR5380) [y] n
NCR53c7,8xx SCSI support (CONFIG_SCSI_NCR53C7xx) [y] n
Always IN2000 SCSI support (test release) (CONFIG_SCSI_IN2000) [y] n
PAS16 SCSI support (CONFIG_SCSI_PAS16) [y] n
QLOGIC SCSI support (CONFIG_SCSI_QLOGIC) [y] n
Seagate ST-02 and Future Domain TMC-8xx SCSI support
(CONFIG_SCSI_SEAGATE) [y] n
Trantor T128/128F/228 SCSI support (CONFIG_SCSI_T128) [y] n
UltraStor SCSI support (CONFIG_SCSI_ULTRASTOR) [y] n
7000FASST SCSI support (CONFIG_SCSI_7000FASST) [y] n
```

Of these questions, you should answer yes (type **y**) only to the question that pertains to your make and model of SCSI card.

Cable and termination problems

The SCSI bus needs terminators at both ends to work reliably. A *terminator* is a set of resistors that indicates the end of the SCSI bus. One end is the controller card itself, which typically has the terminator. Each SCSI device has two SCSI connectors, so that you can daisy chain (connect one device to the next) several SCSI devices. You are supposed to place a terminator on the last connector on the chain.

Secret

Some SCSI controllers — such as Adaptec AHA 154xC, 154xCF, and 274x (x is any digit) — are sensitive to the type of cable and terminator you use. If the cables are not perfect or the terminator is not used properly, these SCSI cards may fail intermittently or may not work at all.

To avoid problems with overly sensitive SCSI cards, use cables that come from a reputable vendor, and use cables from the same vendor to connect all SCSI devices. The cables should be SCSI-2-compliant and should have an impedance of 132 ohms (a characteristic of the cable; all you have to do is make sure that the specified value is 132 ohms).

Adaptec AHA151x and Sound Blaster 16 SCSI

These ISA-bus SCSI cards include all SCSI controllers based on the AIC 6260 or 6360 chipset. Typical hardware parameters for these controllers include the following:

    BIOS addresses: 0xd8000, 0xdc000, 0xd0000, 0xd4000, 0xc8000, 0xcc000, 0xe0000, and 0xe4000

    I/O ports: 0x140 and 0x340

    IRQs: 9, 10, 11, and 12

    DMA channels: not used

Secret

Autoprobe works with boards that have a BIOS installed. For other boards, such as Adaptec 1510 and Sound Blaster 16 SCSI, use the boot option in this format:

`aha152x=IOPORT,IRQ,SCSI-ID,RECONNECT`

All right-side arguments are numbers. `IOPORT` is the I/O address, and if `RECONNECT` is nonzero, the driver is allowed to disconnect and reconnect the device. Usually, the `SCSI-ID` is 7, and `RECONNECT` is specified as 1. If an Adaptec AHA1510 card has I/O address 0x340 and IRQ 11, the boot option will be the following:

`aha152x=0x340,11,7,1`

Adaptec AHA154x, AMI FastDisk VLB, BusLogic, and DTC 329x

Typical hardware parameters of these ISA-bus SCSI controllers include the following:

    I/O ports: 0x330 and 0x334

    IRQs: 9, 10, 11, 12, 14, and 15

    DMA channels: 5, 6, and 7

Autoprobe works with these controllers; there is no need for a BIOS on the controller. The BusLogic SCSI controllers are software compatible with the Adaptec 1542. ISA, VLB, and EISA versions of BusLogic cards are available.

Secret

The newer Adaptec AHA154*x*C and AHA154*x*CF controller cards often generate unexpected errors; these controllers are very sensitive to cable and termination details.

If you encounter infinite timeout errors on Adaptec AHA154*x*C and 154*x*CF controllers, you may have to run the Adaptec setup program (which you do by pressing a specified key during power-up) and enable synchronous negotiation.

Adaptec AHA174*x*

This controller is an EISA-bus SCSI controller that Adaptec no longer sells. Older EISA bus systems may have this card. Following are the hardware parameters of the AHA174*x* card:

   Bus slots: 1–8

   I/O ports: EISA bus does not require preassigned I/O ports

   IRQs: 9, 10, 11, 12, 14, and 15

   DMA channels: EISA bus does not require preassigned I/O ports

The Linux driver can detect the card automatically without any problems. The driver also expects the card to be running in enhanced mode, as opposed to standard AHA1542 mode.

Adaptec AHA274*x*, AHA284*x*, and AHA294*x*

The Adaptec AHA274*x* controller is an EISA bus card; AHA284*x* is a VLB card; AHA294*x* is a new PCI bus card. The AHA274*x* driver supports all three cards. You should enable the BIOS on these controller cards.

Wizard

For the PCI controller to work, you must answer yes to the following question during kernel configuration:

```
PCI bios support (CONFIG_PCI) [y]
```

Allways IN2000

The Allways IN2000 is an ISA-bus controller card with the following parameters:

   I/O ports: 0x100, 0x110, 0x200, and 0x220

   IRQs: 10, 11, 14, and 15

   DMA: not used

The driver can detect the card automatically without any need for BIOS.

EATA DPT Smartcache

The Linux `eata_dma` SCSI driver supports all SCSI controllers that support the EATA-DMA protocol. The controllers include DPT PM2011, PM2012A, PM2012B, PM2021, PM2022, PM2024, PM2122, PM2124, PM2322, PM3021, PM3222, and PM3224.

Secret

The driver's autoprobe function works with all supported DPT cards. A common problem, however, is that the IDE driver detects the ST-506 interface of the EATA controller. If the IDE driver has a problem with the detected parameters and fails, you won't be able to access your IDE hardware. In this case, you should change the EATA board's parameters, such as the I/O address and the IRQ. In particular, don't use IRQs of 14 or 15, which are the IRQs of the primary and secondary IDE interfaces.

If you have a PCI controller such as DPT PM2024, PM2124, or PM3224, remember to enable PCI BIOS when you configure the kernel.

Future Domain 16x0

The Future Domain 16x0 SCSI controller uses the TMC-1800, TMC-18C30, TMC-8C50, or TMC-36C70 chip. These ISA-bus cards typically have the following configurations:

   BIOS addresses: 0xc8000, 0xca000, 0xce000, and 0xde000

   I/O ports: 0x140, 0x150, 0x160, and 0x170

   IRQs: 3, 5, 10, 11, 12, 14, and 15

   DMA: not used

The driver can probe and detect the hardware automatically, provided that the controller has a BIOS installed.

NCR53c8xx SCSI Chip (PCI)

NCR53c8xx refers to NCR53c810, NCR53c815, NCR53c820, and NCR53c825 — a series of low-cost SCSI chips for PCI motherboards. The version of Linux on the companion CD-ROM supports the NCR53c8xx. The driver can detect SCSI devices automatically, provided that the PCI BIOS is present. In fact, the driver needs the BIOS because it uses BIOS-initialized values in the registers of the NCR53c8xx.

Secret

A reported problem with the NCR53c8xx is that the chip works under DOS but fails under Linux, because it times out on a test due to a lost interrupt. A typical cause of this error is a mismatch between the IRQ setting in the hardware (typically set with a jumper) and the IRQ value stored in the CMOS setup (the setup program of your PC, the one that you can run during power-up). To correct the problem, check the following things:

- Make sure that the hardware IRQ setting matches that in the CMOS setup.
- If the NCR 53c8xx is on a board that has jumpers for selecting PCI interrupt lines (PCI has interrupt lines INTA, INTB, INTC, and INTD), make sure that only INTA is being used.
- If the PCI board has jumpers for selecting level-sensitive and edge-triggered interrupts, make sure that the board is using "level-sensitive" interrupts.

Secret

Another reported problem is system lockup when an S3 928 or Tseng ET4000/W32 PCI video chipset is used, due to problems in the video chipsets.

Secret

On a system that has an NCR53c8xx SCSI chip, you may encounter the following message:

```
scsi%d: IRQ0 not free, detaching
```

This message indicates that the PCI configuration register contains a zero. The reason may be a mismatch between the hardware IRQ and the value in CMOS, or a defective BIOS.

Because the NCR53c8xx is a PCI device, you must enable PCI support when you rebuild the Linux kernel.

Seagate ST0x and Future Domain TMC-8xx and TMC-9xx

Typical hardware parameters of these ISA-bus SCSI controllers include the following:

BIOS addresses: 0xc8000, 0xca000, 0xcc000, 0xce000, 0xdc000, and 0xde000

IRQs: 3 and 5

DMA channels: not used

When it tries to probe for the controller automatically, the driver probes only the BIOS addresses; it assumes that the IRQ is 5. Also, autoprobe works only if a BIOS is installed.

During boot, you can provide one of the following command lines to force detection of the controller:

```
st0x=BIOS-ADDRESS,IRQ
tmc8xx=BIOS-ADDRESS,IRQ
```

BIOS_ADDRESS is the BIOS address of the board, and IRQ is the interrupt-request channel.

Secret

Common problems with the ST01 or ST02 SCSI controller are timeouts when Linux accesses the disk that is connected to the controller, because the board's default settings disable interrupts. You should set jumpers (W3 on ST01 and JP3 on ST02) on the board to reenable interrupts. You also should select IRQ 5.

Chapter 11: Disk Drives

If you get errors when you try to run `fdisk` on a drive that is connected to Seagate or Future Domain controllers, you should use `fdisk`'s extra functions menu to specify the disk geometry (cylinders, heads, and sectors).

Pro Audio Spectrum PAS16 SCSI

The PAS16 SCSI refers to the SCSI interface on a Pro Audio Spectrum sound card. Following are the hardware-configuration parameters for the PAS16 SCSI:

I/O ports: 0x388, 0x384, 0x38x, and 0x288

IRQs: 10, 12, 14, and 15 (must be different from the IRQs used for sound)

DMA: not used for the SCSI portion of the card

The autoprobe function does not require BIOS. You can specify a command line at the boot prompt to specify the parameters of your PAS 16 SCSI. For a PAS 16 SCSI at I/O address 0x388 and IRQ 10, for example, use the following command line:

```
pas16=0x388,10
```

Trantor T128, T128F, and T228

These Trantor ISA-bus SCSI cards have the following configuration parameters:

BIOS addresses: 0xcc000, 00xc8000, 0xdc000, and 0xd8000

IRQs: on all boards, none, 3, 5, and 7; on T128F, 10, 12, 14, and 15

DMA: not used

The driver can autoprobe as long as a BIOS is installed. If one of these SCSI controllers does not have BIOS, or if the BIOS is disabled, you can specify the controller through a command line like the following:

```
t128=BIOS-ADDRESS,IRQ
```

BIOS-ADDRESS is the base address (not I/O address). For a controller with a BIOS address 0xcc000 and IRQ 5, for example, the command line is

```
t128=0xcc000,5
```

Use -1 for the *IRQ* if a controller does not have an IRQ; use -2 to make the driver probe the *IRQ*.

Ultrastor 14f (ISA), 24f (EISA), and 34f (VLB)

The Ultrastor SCSI cards have the following configuration parameters:

I/O ports: 0x130, 0x140, 0x210, 0x230, 0x240, 0x310, 0x330, and 0x340

IRQs: 10, 11, 14, and 15

DMA channels: 5, 6, and 7

Wizard

The autoprobe function works in all cases except when the I/O port address is 0x310. Because I/O port 0x310 is not supported by the autoprobe code, you should select a different I/O port address for the Ultrastor controller.

If you have a sound card, I/O port address 0x330 typically is used by the MIDI device. Use a different I/O port address for the Ultrastor card if you have a sound card in your PC. A good I/O port for the Ultrastor cards is 0x340.

The Ultrastor controllers support a WD1003 emulation mode, in which they can work with ST-506-interface disk drives. If you happen to have your Ultrastor controller in WD1003 mode, the Ultrastor SCSI driver will fail, displaying the following error message:

```
hd.c: ST-506 interface disk with more than 16 heads detected,
   probably due to non-standard sector translation.  Giving up.
   (disk %d: cyl-%d, sect=63, head=64)
```

You can fix this problem by setting the Ultrastor controller to its native SCSI mode.

Western Digital 7000

The hardware configurations for this ISA-bus SCSI controller are as follows:

BIOS address: 0xce000

I/O port: 0x350

IRQ: 15

DMA channel: 6

The driver can probe and detect the SCSI controller automatically, provided that the BIOS is installed.

Some revisions of the Western Digital 7000 controller may not work with the driver. Reportedly, revision 5 and later controllers work fine. Also, on the working controllers, the onboard SCSI chip should have an A suffix.

Iomega Zip drive (SCSI)

The Iomega Zip drive is a low-cost, removable disk drive that allows you to use floppylike disks, each of which is capable of holding 100 million characters. If you consider a megabyte to be 1,024 × 1,024 = 1,048,576 bytes, 100 million characters will be about 95MB. Unlike floppies, the Zip disks do not have a hardware write-protect tab, which means that you have to be careful when you initialize a disk or delete files.

Tip

The Zip drive comes in three versions: SCSI interface for Macintosh or MS-DOS and a parallel-port version. The parallel-port version of the Zip drive does not work with Linux. You can, however, access the parallel-port version of the Zip drive under DOSEMU (see Chapter 7 for more information on DOSEMU).

Both the DOS and Macintosh versions of the SCSI Iomega Zip drive should work under Linux. You can use an existing Linux-supported SCSI card (preferably, a simple Adaptec AHA152x-compatible card) to connect the Zip drive to your PC.

The Zip drive has switches to turn on termination (if it's the last device in the chain) and select SCSI ID (one of 5 or 6).

You also can connect the Zip drive to a separately sold Zip Zoom interface card — a low-end SCSI card that's compatible with the Adaptec AHA152*x* card. If you have a kernel that supports the AHA152*x*, and you use LILO, you can use the Zip drive with the following line added to the /etc/lilo.conf file:

```
append="aha152x=0x340,11,7,1"
```

Tip

To prepare the Zip disk for use under Linux, you should try it under DOS. Run the \SCSI\INSTALL program on the Iomega Tools disk. After that, the Zip disk should work under Linux.

Log in as root, and run /sbin/fdisk on the SCSI device that represents the Zip drive. If the Zip drive is the only SCSI device, it'll be /dev/sda, so you type the following:

```
/sbin/fdisk /dev/sda
```

Check the current partition, and set the type to Linux native. Then create an ext2 file system with the following command:

```
/sbin/mke2fs /dev/sda1
```

That command assumes that you are using the first partition of the Zip disk. You then can mount the Zip disk at an appropriate mount point and use the disk, as follows:

```
mount -text2 /dev/sda1 /mnt
```

The contents of the Zip disk will be in the /mnt directory. Before ejecting the disk, use the command umount /mnt to dismount the Zip disk.

SCSI troubleshooting

Most SCSI problems are due to bad cables or improper termination. You should check the cables and the terminator before trying anything else. The following sections list other common SCSI problems and their suggested fixes:

Problem booting with LILO

When booting from a SCSI hard disk, LILO may hang after displaying the letters LI. This problem occurs if the SCSI controller's BIOS and the Linux SCSI driver interpret the disk geometry differently.

Wizard

To fix this problem, add the linear keyword on a single line in the /etc/lilo.conf file. This keyword causes LILO to use Linear Block Addresses (LBA) instead of the physical cylinder-head-sector (CHS) addresses when it accesses the disk. LILO will use the disk geometry supplied by the BIOS and compute physical addresses at run time, which should work properly.

SCSI device at all SCSI IDs

If a SCSI device shows up at all possible SCSI IDs, you must have configured that device with the same SCSI ID as the SCSI controller (usually, 7). Change the ID of that device to another value. (Many devices have a simple switch for setting the SCSI ID; on many others, you have to change a jumper.)

SCSI device at all LUNs

If a SCSI device shows up at all possible SCSI Logical Unit Numbers (LUNs), the device probably has errors in the *firmware* — the built-in code in the device's SCSI interface. To verify these errors, first use the following command line during boot:

```
max_scsi_luns=1
```

Secret

If the device works with this option, you can add it to the list of blacklisted SCSI devices in the array of structures named blacklist in the file /usr/src/linux/drivers/scsi/scsi.c. The definition of that structure and the current contents of the array are as follows:

```
struct blist{
    char * vendor;
    char * model;
    char * revision; /* Latest revision known to be bad. Not currently used. */
    };

static struct blist blacklist[] =
{
    {"CHINON","CD-ROM CDS-431","H42"},  /* Locks up if polled for lun != 0 */
    {"CHINON","CD-ROM CDS-535","Q14"},  /* Lockup if polled for lun != 0 */
    {"DENON","DRD-25X","V"},   /* A cdrom that locks up when probed at lun != 0 */
    {"HITACHI","DK312C","CM81"},   /* Responds to all lun - dtg */
    {"HITACHI","DK314C","CR21" },  /* responds to all lun */
    {"IMS", "CDD521/10","2.06"},   /* Locks-up when LUN>0 polled. */
    {"MAXTOR","XT-3280","PR02"},   /* Locks-up when LUN>0 polled. */
    {"MAXTOR","XT-4380S","B3C"},   /* Locks-up when LUN>0 polled. */
    {"MAXTOR","MXT-1240S","I1.2"}, /* Locks up when LUN > 0 polled */
    {"MAXTOR","XT-4170S","B5A"},   /* Locks-up sometimes when LUN>0 polled. */
    {"MAXTOR","XT-8760S","B7B"},   /* guess what? */
    {"NEC","CD-ROM DRIVE:841","1.0"},  /* Locks-up when LUN>0 polled. */
    {"RODIME","RO3000S","2.33"},   /* Locks up if polled for lun != 0 */
    {"SEAGATE", "ST157N", "\004|j"}, /* causes failed REQUEST SENSE on lun 1 for aha152x
                             * controller, which causes SCSI code to reset bus.*/
    {"SEAGATE", "ST296","921"},    /* Responds to all lun */
    {"SONY","CD-ROM CDU-541","4.3d"},
    {"SONY","CD-ROM CDU-55S","1.0i"},
    {"TANDBERG","TDC 3600","U07"}, /* Locks up if polled for lun != 0 */
    {"TEAC","CD-ROM","1.06"},      /* causes failed REQUEST SENSE on lun 1 for seagate
                             * controller, which causes SCSI code to reset bus.*/
    {"TEXEL","CD-ROM","1.06"},     /* causes failed REQUEST SENSE on lun 1 for seagate
                             * controller, which causes SCSI code to reset bus.*/
    {"QUANTUM","LPS525S","3110"},/* Locks sometimes if polled for lun != 0 */
```

```
{"QUANTUM","PD1225S","3110"},/* Locks sometimes if polled for lun != 0 */
{"MEDIAVIS","CDR-H93MV","1.31"},  /* Locks up if polled for lun != 0 */
{"SANKYO", "CP525","6.64"},  /* causes failed REQ SENSE, extra reset */
{"HP", "C1750A", "3226"},    /* scanjet iic */
{"HP", "C1790A", ""},        /* scanjet iip */
{"HP", "C2500A", ""},        /* scanjet iicx */
{NULL, NULL, NULL}};  /* Marks the end of the list */
```

From this list, you get an idea of the types of SCSI devices that have the problem of showing up at all LUNs. If you have the same problem with a SCSI device, you can add that device's name to this list before the last line. You may not want to do this, however, if you are not familiar with the C programming language.

Sense errors on error-free SCSI device

The cause of this problem usually is bad cables or improper termination. Check all cables, and make sure that the SCSI bus is terminated at both ends.

Networking kernel problems with SCSI device

If a Linux kernel with networking support does not work with SCSI devices, the problem may be the autoprobe function of the networking drivers. The autoprobe capability is meant to detect the type of networking hardware automatically; the network drivers read from and write to specific I/O addresses during autoprobing. If an I/O address happens to be the same as that used by a SCSI device, the system may have a problem. In this case, you have to check the I/O address, IRQ, and DMA values of the network cards and of the SCSI controller, and make sure that no conflicts exist. Most SCSI controllers (and even network adapters) allow you to configure these parameters (I/O address, IRQ, and DMA) through setup software that comes with the adapter.

Device detected but not accessible

If the kernel detects a SCSI device (as reported in the boot messages, which you can see with `dmesg | more`) but you cannot access the device, the device file is missing from the /dev directory.

To add the device file, log in as `root`, change the directory to /dev, and then use the MAKEDEV script to create the device file. To add a device for a SCSI tape drive, for example, you would use the following command:

```
cd /dev
MAKEDEV st0
```

You can find more information about the MAKEDEV script with this command:

```
man MAKEDEV
```

SCSI lockup

If the SCSI system locks up, check the SCSI controller card, using any diagnostic software that came with the card (usually, the diagnostic software runs under DOS). Look for conflicts in I/O address, IRQ, or DMA with other cards. Some sound cards, for example, use a 16-bit DMA channel in addition to an 8-bit DMA; make sure that you did not inadvertently use the same 16-bit DMA for the SCSI card.

The Linux SCSI driver for some SCSI cards supports only one outstanding SCSI command at a time. With such a SCSI card, if a device such as a tape drive is busy rewinding, the system may not be able to access other SCSI devices (such as a hard disk or a CD-ROM drive) that are daisy chained with that tape drive. A solution to this problem is to add a second SCSI controller to take care of the tape drives.

SCSI devices not found

If the Linux kernel does not detect your SCSI devices at startup, you get the following message when Linux boots:

```
scsi : 0 hosts
```

If you see this message, but you know the SCSI devices are there (and that they work under DOS), the problem may be the lack of a BIOS on the SCSI controller; the autoprobe routines that detect SCSI devices rely on the BIOS.

This problem occurs for the following SCSI cards:

- Adaptec 152x, 151x, AIC-6260, and AIC-6360
- Future Domain 1680, TMC-950, and TMC-8xx
- Trantor T128, T128F, and T228F
- Seagate ST01 and ST02
- Western Digital 7000

Even if a SCSI controller has a BIOS, jumpers often are available for disabling the BIOS. If you disabled the BIOS for some reason, you may want to reenable it (read the documentation of your SCSI controller for directions) so that Linux can detect the SCSI devices automatically.

For a SCSI card, such as the Adaptec 151x, that does not have any BIOS, use the following command line during boot to force detection of the card:

```
aha152x=0x340,11,7,1
```

Summary

You need a hard disk to install Linux on your PC. In particular, to successfully install Linux, your PC's hard disk controller must be supported by Linux. This should not be a problem because Linux supports the popular IDE and Enhanced IDE interfaces, as well as the SCSI interface. This chapter describes how to install and use hard disks in Linux. By reading this chapter, you learn the following things:

- Linux's support for a specific hard disk drive depends on the disk controller used to connect that drive to the PC's motherboard. Linux supports the popular IDE (Integrated Drive Electronics), Enhanced IDE (EIDE), and SCSI disk controllers for ISA, EISA, VLB, and PCI buses. These disk controllers cover nearly all types of disks that PCs typically use.

- You have to partition a disk to install Linux, and when you install Linux, you have to create a swap space and set up a mechanism to boot Linux. You can use LILO to manage the boot process, even if you have multiple operating systems (such as DOS and Windows 95) on the disk.

- The disk controller sees the disk as being a collection of 512-byte sectors on magnetic platters that are mounted on a spindle and rotating under read-write heads. This physical construction of a hard disk gives rise to the view of a disk as a collection of cylinders, heads, and sectors (CHS). Linux likes to see the disk as being a sequence of sectors that can be addressed sequentially (Linear Block Address, or LBA).

- The PC's BIOS uses CHS addressing and limits the cylinder address to a 10-bit value, thus giving rise to a 1,024-cylinder limit on hard disk geometries. Because hardware constraints prevent disks from having more than 16 heads and 63 sectors, the BIOS can handle disks up to 504MB (1,024 × 16 × 63 sectors; each sector is 512 bytes). Newer large disks use some tricks to handle larger disks, but these tricks sometimes conflict with the way that Linux addresses disks. You generally are safe if you keep the DOS settings for the disk parameters such as number of cylinders, heads, and sectors.

- SCSI is popular because you can connect up to seven devices through a single SCSI controller. The only drawback is that the SCSI controller is relatively expensive compared with EIDE controllers.

- Linux supports a wide variety of SCSI controllers, including the popular Adaptec and BusLogic SCSI controllers.

- Many recent PCs have the PCI bus and PCI-bus EIDE controller chips built into the motherboard. Two of these EIDE controllers — RZ 1000 and CMD 640 — are reported to have some bugs that occur when you have multiple IDE devices on the EIDE controller. Some workarounds for these bugs exist.

- With a little effort, you should be able to use an Iomega Zip drive with Linux.

Chapter 12

CD-ROM Drives and Sound Cards

In This Chapter

- Looking at the different types of interfaces for CD-ROM drives
- Specifying Linux device names for CD-ROM drives and sound cards
- Using specific CD-ROM drives in Linux
- Fixing common problems with CD-ROM drives in Linux
- Looking at the brands of sound cards that Linux supports
- Including support for a specific sound card in Linux
- Testing and troubleshooting sound cards in Linux

If you have installed or are planning to install Linux from this book's companion CD-ROM, chances are that your system already has a CD-ROM drive. You probably are reading this chapter because you have questions about using your CD-ROM drive to install Linux. You should find answers to your questions in this chapter. As with other peripheral devices (such as a disk drive), the CD-ROM drive connects to your PC's motherboard through a controller board. Thus, the real issue of how to use a CD-ROM drive under Linux boils down to whether Linux includes a driver for that CD-ROM drive's interface. This chapter discusses various CD-ROM interfaces and explains which ones are supported under Linux.

I grouped CD-ROM drives with sound cards because many CD-ROM drives connect to the PC through interfaces built into sound cards. Vendors typically bundle CD-ROM drives and sound cards as a package, because you need both types of devices to enjoy multimedia software that uses sound, video, and animation. The CD-ROM provides the storage space needed to store the video clips, images, and sound files in a typical multimedia application. The sound card allows the PC to generate professional-quality sound — the other must-have ingredient in a multimedia application.

This chapter describes specific types of Linux-supported CD-ROM drives, categorized by interface type. You'll also find information about how to include support for specific sound cards in Linux.

CD-ROM Drives

Each CD-ROM can hold up to 650MB of data (the equivalent of about 450 high-density 3.5-inch floppy disks) and does not cost much to produce. The physical medium of the CD-ROM is the same as that used for audio compact discs (CDs): a polycarbonate disc with an aluminized layer. A laser reads the data, which is encoded in microscopic pits on the aluminized layer. CD-ROM media is more robust and reliable than other magnetic media, such as floppy disks. All these factors make CD-ROM an attractive medium for distributing data and programs. Most Linux books (including this one) bundle a CD-ROM with the entire Linux operating system and lots of popular software for Linux.

In that list of good properties of a CD-ROM — high capacity, low cost, and reliability — you don't see any mention of speed, because the data-transfer rates of CD-ROM drives are not as fast as those of hard disk drives. When CD-ROM drives first appeared, the drives could transfer data at rates of approximately 150K per second. These drives are known as *single-speed* (also referred to as *1X*) CD-ROM drives.

Double-speed (2X) CD-ROM drives, which provide data-transfer rates of 300K per second, now are widely available. Currently, most users opt for quad-speed (4X) CD-ROM drives, which can sustain data-transfer rates of up to 600K per second.

Note

Most CD-ROMs contain information in an ISO-9660 file system (formerly known as High Sierra). This file system supports only the MS-DOS-style 8.3 filenames, such as SLAKWARE.FAQ, which have an eight-character name and an optional three-character extension. An extension to the ISO-9660 file system, called the Rock Ridge Extensions, uses unused fields to support longer filenames and additional UNIX-style file attributes, such as ownership and symbolic links.

Most CD-ROM drives also typically let you play audio CDs via an external headphone jack. You also will find an output line that you can connect to the sound card so that you can play an audio CD on the speakers attached to the sound card.

Supported CD-ROM drives

As with hard disks, Linux's support for a CD-ROM drive depends on the interface through which that CD-ROM drive connects to the PC's motherboard. CD-ROM drives come with three popular types of interfaces:

- *AT Attachment Packet Interface (ATAPI).* ATAPI is a recent specification for accessing and controlling a CD-ROM drive that is connected to the PC through the AT Attachment (ATA). ATAPI is gaining popularity because it is built on the cheaper IDE interface. (ATA is the new name for IDE.)

- *Small Computer System Interface (SCSI).* SCSI is popular because of its relatively high data rates and its capability to support multiple devices. The only drawback is that you need a relatively expensive SCSI controller card for the PC.

- *Proprietary interfaces.* Many CD-ROM vendors provide their own proprietary interface between the CD-ROM drive and the PC's motherboard. Many sound cards include a built-in CD-ROM drive interface, which typically is a proprietary interface. The problem with proprietary interfaces is that someone has to develop a Linux driver specifically for each interface (as opposed to using a SCSI driver, for example, to access any SCSI device).

ATAPI CD-ROM drives

ATA (AT Attachment) is the official ANSI (American National Standards Institute) standard name for the commonplace IDE interface, which is commonly used to connect hard disk drives to the PC. ATAPI (ATA Packet Interface) is a protocol (similar to SCSI) for controlling storage devices such as CD-ROM drives and tape drives. Although ATAPI is relatively new, it is rapidly becoming the most popular type of interface for CD-ROM drives. ATAPI is based on the ATA (or IDE) interface and does not need any expensive controller card or cable. Also, an ATAPI CD-ROM can simply connect as the second drive on the same interface where the PC's hard drive is connected. That means the ATAPI CD-ROM drive does not require a separate interface card.

The Linux kernel includes an ATAPI driver that should work with any ATAPI CD-ROM drive. ATAPI CD-ROM drives are available from many vendors, such as Aztech, Mitsumi, NEC, Philips, Sony, and Toshiba. Nowadays, most PCs (such as those from Gateway and Dell) come configured with ATAPI CD-ROM drives.

If your system has an ATAPI CD-ROM drive, select the IDECD boot image; it contains the ATAPI driver that you need.

SCSI CD-ROM drives

Linux supports a SCSI CD-ROM drive connected to one of the supported SCSI controller cards (see Chapter 11 for more information). The only restriction is that the block size (for data transfers) of the SCSI CD-ROM drive should be 512 or 2,048 bytes, which cover the vast majority of CD-ROM drives on the market.

Some CD-ROM drives include a controller with a modified interface that's not fully SCSI compatible. This interface essentially amounts to being proprietary, and you cannot use such CD-ROM drives with the SCSI driver.

SCSI CD-ROM drives are available from many vendors, such as Plextor, Sanyo, and Toshiba.

Proprietary CD-ROM drives

Although the ATAPI and SCSI CD-ROM drives fall into neat categories and work well in Linux, the situation is much more confusing when it comes to CD-ROM drives with a proprietary interface. Following are some of the sources of confusion:

Secret

- Some vendors, such as Creative Labs (of Sound Blaster fame), have sold CD-ROM drives with all types of interfaces: ATAPI, SCSI, and a proprietary interface on a sound card. Thus, the vendor name alone does not mean anything; you have to know what type of interface the CD-ROM drive uses.

- PC vendors sometimes categorize the CD-ROM drive interface as being IDE, even though the interface really is proprietary. Like the IDE (or ATAPI) interface, the proprietary CD-ROM drive interface is low cost and popular. Often, a proprietary CD-ROM interface is incorrectly branded as an IDE interface.

As you may have guessed, proprietary CD-ROM drive interfaces are popular because they tend to be much simpler than SCSI, which was the primary alternative to proprietary interfaces before ATAPI came along. Because of the popularity of relatively inexpensive ATAPI, most new PCs do not use proprietary interfaces. Because a proprietary CD-ROM interface can be built into a sound card at little cost, however, many Linux users probably have PCs with a proprietary CD-ROM drive.

Table 12-1 lists CD-ROM drives with proprietary interfaces and the name of the drivers that you need to support those drives.

Table 12-1	CD-ROM drives with proprietary interfaces
Driver	CD-ROM drive
aztcd	Aztech CDA268, Orchid CDS-3110, Okano/Wearnes CDD-110
cdu31a	Sony CDU31A/CDU33A
cm206	Philips/LMS CM 206
gscd	GoldStar R420
mcd	Mitsumi CRMC LU005S, FX001
sbpcd	Matsushita/Panasonic (Panasonic CR-521, CR-522, CR-523, CR-562, and CR-563), Kotobuki, Creative Labs (CD-200), Longshine LCS-7260, Teac CD-55A
sonycd535	Sony CDU-535/CDU-531

CD-ROM troubleshooting

Secret

You need a CD-ROM drive that works under Linux to install Linux from this book's companion CD-ROM. When you install Linux by following the steps outlined in Chapter 1, start with a *boot image* (just another name for the Linux kernel) that includes the driver for your CD-ROM drive. Remember that the CD-ROM drive's interface is what counts, not the brand name. Thus, if you have a Mitsumi ATAPI CD-ROM drive, you need the boot image that supports IDE CD-ROM drives, *not* the boot image for Mitsumi drives.

Chapter 12: CD-ROM Drives and Sound Cards

When you try to install Linux or after you successfully install Linux, you may run into some problems with the CD-ROM drive. If Linux does not seem to recognize the CD-ROM drive, try the following steps to fix the problem:

Tip

1. If you have rebuilt the kernel with support for your CD-ROM drive, verify that you are indeed running the new kernel. To see the version number, use the `uname -a` command. Following is typical output from the `uname -a` command:

```
Linux lnbsoft 1.2.11 #1 Wed Jul 26 15:35:13 EDT 1995 i586
```

Cross Reference

This output of the `uname` command shows the kernel's version number as well as the date the kernel was built. If that date does not match the date when you rebuilt the kernel, you may not be running the new kernel. Go through the steps outlined in Chapter 2, and make sure that you have really installed the new kernel. One common problem is forgetting to reboot, so try that step as well.

2. Look at the contents of the `/proc/devices` file to verify that the CD-ROM device is present. Use the following procedure to view the contents of a `/proc/devices` file:

```
cat /proc/devices
Character devices:
 1 mem
 4 ttyp
 5 cua
 6 lp
 7 vcs
10 mouse
14 sound
Block devices:
 2 fd
 3 ide0
 8 sd
22 ide1
```

This listing corresponds to the devices on my system. You should look for the CD-ROM device in the list of block devices. I know that my CD-ROM drive is connected to the secondary IDE interface. The two IDE interfaces correspond to the devices `ide0` and `ide1` in `/proc/devices`. Because `ide1` appears in the listing, I know that the CD-ROM driver is in the kernel.

Tip

If you have a CD-ROM connected to a Sound Blaster Pro or compatible interface, look for a device number of 25 and a device name of `sbpcd`.

If you don't see a device that corresponds to your CD-ROM drive, you did not configure the kernel properly to include the sound driver. Reconfigure and rebuild the kernel, making sure that you include support for your CD-ROM drive.

3. Verify that the CD-ROM driver detected the CD-ROM drive when the system started. Use `dmesg | more` to look at the boot messages and see whether a line reports that the CD-ROM drive was found. On my system, which has an ATAPI CD-ROM drive, the message looks like this:

```
hdc: FX400_02, ATAPI, CDROM drive
```

Tip

If you find no boot message about the CD-ROM drive, make sure the CD-ROM is physically installed. For an external CD-ROM drive, make sure the drive is powered on and the cables are connected. Check any drive ID or jumpers, and make sure they are set correctly. You may want to first make sure the CD-ROM drive works under DOS; if the CD-ROM works under DOS, you can be sure that the drive is physically sound. Next, verify that you have rebuilt the kernel with support for the correct CD-ROM drive interface.

Wizard

4. Verify that you can read from the CD-ROM drive. Try the following command, and see whether the drive's activity light comes on (it should) and whether any error messages appear (there shouldn't be any):

```
dd bs=1024 count=5000 < /dev/cdrom > /dev/null
5000+0 records in
5000+0 records in
```

The `/dev/null` device is what you might call the "bit bucket." Output directed to `/dev/null` simply vanishes.

If the `dd` command does not work, the device file for the CD-ROM device may not be set properly. Use the `ls -l` command to view detailed information about your CD-ROM device. For an ATAPI CD-ROM drive on the secondary IDE interface, for example, I would look at `/dev/hdc` as follows:

```
ls -l /dev/hdc
brw-rw----   1 root     disk      22,   0 May  8 06:38 /dev/hdc
```

Notice the numbers 22 and 0, which are the major and minor device numbers. These numbers need to be corrected. (Later sections of this chapter list the device numbers for specific CD-ROM drivers.)

5. Verify that you can mount the CD-ROM. Place a good CD-ROM (such as the CD-ROM from this book) in the CD-ROM drive, and try to mount it by using the following command:

```
mount -t iso9660 -r /dev/cdrom /cdrom
```

If you can read from the CD-ROM drive with the `dd` command but cannot mount the CD-ROM, you may have configured the kernel without support for the ISO-9660 file system. To verify the currently supported file systems, use the following command:

```
cat /proc/filesystems
minix
ext2
umsdos
msdos
nodev     proc
nodev     nfs
iso9660
```

If you do not see `iso9660` listed, you have to rebuild the kernel and add support for the ISO-9660 file system.

Chapter 12: CD-ROM Drives and Sound Cards

Tip

6. If nothing works, you may want to read the latest CDROM-HOWTO document. To read the HOWTO document, run the `browse` program from the `/cdrom/browse` directory (you need this book's CD-ROM in the CD-ROM drive), and look at the contents of the directory `/usr/doc/faq/howto`.

If you still cannot get the CD-ROM drive to work under Linux, you may want to post a news item to one of the comp.os.linux newsgroups.

The following sections suggest solutions for a few more common problems.

CD-ROM drive not recognized after Linux installation

After you install Linux from the CD-ROM, you may run into a common problem: Even though you successfully installed Linux from the CD-ROM drive, you cannot get Linux to recognize the CD-ROM drive the next time you boot the system.

Secret

You run into this problem if you do not select the proper kernel when you install Linux. As explained in Chapter 1, you should select from disk set Q a package that contains a Linux kernel with support for your system's CD-ROM drive interface.

You can recover from the kernel's failure to recognize the CD-ROM drive by rebuilding the kernel. You probably want to do this anyway, because none of the Slackware kernels include support for sound cards by default. To add support for a sound card, you need to rebuild the kernel.

Cross Reference

Chapter 2 describes the steps that you must follow to rebuild the Linux kernel. During the step in which you configure the kernel with a `make config` command, the configuration program asks you questions about specific hardware in your PC. You should respond appropriately to include support for your CD-ROM drive. See the following section for specific information.

Kernel configuration for specific CD-ROM drives

If you have an ATAPI CD-ROM drive, you should answer yes to the following questions:

```
Normal (MFM/RLL) disk and IDE disk/cdrom support (CONFIG_ST506) [y]
Use old disk-only driver for primary i/f (CONFIG_BLK_DEV_HD) [n]
Use new IDE driver for primary/secondary i/f (CONFIG_BLK_DEV_IDE) [y]
Include support for IDE/ATAPI CDROMs (CONFIG_BLK_DEV_IDECD) [n] y
```

The default response is shown in brackets; y means yes, and n means no. You can accept the default by pressing Enter. Notice that you have to explicitly answer yes to include support for ATAPI CD-ROM drives.

For SCSI CD-ROM drives, answer yes to the following questions:

```
*** SCSI support
SCSI support? (CONFIG_SCSI) [y]
```

```
** SCSI support type (disk, tape, CDrom)
...
SCSI CDROM support (CONFIG_BLK_DEV_SR) [y]
```

Of course, you also must specify your SCSI controller type; otherwise, the SCSI CD-ROM won't work. If you have a Adaptec AHA1542 SCSI controller, for example, answer yes to the following question:

```
Adaptec AHA1542 support (CONFIG_SCSI_AHA1542) [y]
```

Tip

If your CD-ROM drive has a proprietary interface, you must enable support for that specific CD-ROM drive interface. Following is a sampling of the questions from the 1.2.11 kernel:

```
***CD-ROM drives (not SCSI or non IDE/ATAPI drives)
Sony CDU31A/CDU33A CDROM driver support (CONFIG_CDU31A) [n]
Mitsumi (not IDE/ATAPI) CDROM driver support (CONFIG_MCD) [n]
Matsushita/Panasonic CDROM driver support (CONFIG_SBPCD) [n]
Aztech/Orchid/Okano/Wearnes (non IDE) CDROM support (CONFIG_AZTCD) [n]
Sony CDU535 CDROM driver support (CONFIG_CDU535) [n]
```

Answer yes to the question about the specific CD-ROM drive in your PC. If you have a Mitsumi CD-ROM drive (with a proprietary interface, not ATAPI), for example, answer **y** to the line that starts with Mitsumi.

Newer versions of the Linux kernel support several other types of proprietary CD-ROM drive interfaces. Check the prompts carefully before answering these questions posed by the kernel-configuration program.

Tip

Because most CD-ROMs use the ISO-9660 file system, you also must enable support for this file system in the kernel. To do this, answer yes to the following question during kernel configuration:

```
ISO9660 cdrom filesystem support (CONFIG_ISO9660_FS) [y]
```

IDE (ATAPI) CD-ROM troubles

When a PC has an ATAPI CD-ROM drive, its ATA (IDE) adapter has two interfaces: primary and secondary, each of which is capable of supporting two drives. In Linux, the two primary devices are /dev/hda and /dev/hdb, which typically are used for hard disk drives. The secondary IDE devices are /dev/hdc and /dev/hdd. Thus, if you have an IDE hard drive connected to the primary interface and an IDE CD-ROM drive connected to the secondary interface, the hard drive will be /dev/hda, and the CD-ROM drive will be /dev/hdc.

Wizard

Of the two devices on an interface, one is designated as the master and the other as the slave. When only one IDE device is attached to an interface, it must be designated as the *master* (or *single*). Typically, the IDE device has a jumper (a connector that connects a pair of pins) to indicate whether the device is a master or a slave.

When a single IDE CD-ROM drive is connected to the secondary interface, you must set the jumper on the CD-ROM drive to make it a master. If you bought a PC with an IDE CD-ROM drive preinstalled, this jumper may already be set for you. If you run into a situation in which Linux refuses to recognize your IDE CD-ROM drive, however, you should check the CD-ROM drive's parameters, making sure that it uses the secondary IDE interface (IRQ 15 and I/O address 170H) and that it is set to be the master.

Secret

Some interface cards support more than two IDE interfaces. In such a case, you should know that the Linux IDE CD-ROM driver may not recognize anything but the primary and secondary IDE interfaces. The Creative Labs Sound Blaster 16 CD-ROM interface is, by default, set to be the fourth IDE interface. If you are connecting a CD-ROM drive to a Sound Blaster 16 for use in Linux, you have to set the jumpers on the Sound Blaster 16 so that the IDE interface is the secondary interface instead of the fourth interface.

Boot-time parameters for CD-ROM drives

Linux drivers normally find CD-ROM drives (and other peripherals) by *probing* (reading from and writing to various I/O addresses). Linux drivers also use any available information from the PC's CMOS memory. CMOS is a type of semiconductor. Each PC has a small amount of battery-backed, nonvolatile CMOS storage, where vital information about the PC, such as the number of types of disk drives, is stored. The real-time clock also is stored in the CMOS.

Wizard

One problem with probing is that it involves reading from or writing to specific I/O addresses. Depending on what device uses that I/O address, probing can cause the system to *hang* (become unresponsive). When the Sound Blaster Pro CD driver, sbpcd, probes for a CD-ROM drive, it may access an I/O address that may be used in an NE2000 Ethernet card, and if this happens, the system hangs.

To avoid probing, you can pass specific device parameters for the device corresponding to your CD-ROM drive at boot time.

If you have a CD-ROM drive with the Sound Blaster Pro CD interface, the device name is sbpcd, and you can provide settings at LILO's boot prompt as follows:

sbpcd=0x230,SoundBlaster

This command tells the sbpcd driver that the I/O address of the CD-ROM drive is 230H. The exact boot-time parameters for a device depend on that device driver. Later sections of this chapter provide specific boot-time parameters for CD-ROM device drivers.

Wizard

If you use LILO, you can put the boot-time parameters in the /etc/lilo.conf file in the following manner:

append = "sbpcd=0x230,SoundBlaster"

CD-ROM device names

Linux uses a unique device name for each type of CD-ROM interface. The CD-ROM devices are block devices like the disk device, such as /dev/hda and /dev/sda. Table 12-2 lists the CD-ROM device names.

Table 12-2	CD-ROM device names in Linux
Device name	**CD-ROM type**
/dev/sbpcd	Sound Blaster Pro CD-ROM drive interface
/dev/hdc	ATAPI CD-ROM drive on the secondary IDE interface on an EIDE controller
/dev/aztcd	Aztech proprietary CD-ROM drive interface
/dev/mcd	Mitsumi proprietary CD-ROM drive interface
/dev/sonycd535	Sony CDU-535/CDU-531 proprietary interface

By convention, the generic CD-ROM device /dev/cdrom is set up as a link to the actual CD-ROM device on your system. On my system, which has an ATAPI CD-ROM drive, a detailed listing of /dev/cdrom shows the following:

```
ls -l /dev/cdrom
lrwxrwxrwx 1 root   root    8 Sep 29 18:01 /dev/cdrom -> /dev/hdc
```

The output of ls indicates that /dev/cdrom is a symbolic link to /dev/hdc, which is the IDE block device. (The same device name is used for a disk or a CD-ROM drive connected to the interface.)

On the other hand, on my old 386 PC, the CD-ROM drive is on a Sound Blaster Pro card. In this case, a detailed listing of /dev/cdrom shows the following:

```
ls -l /dev/cdrom
lrwxrwxrwx 1 root   root   10 Sep 29 20:19 /dev/cdrom -> /dev/sbpcd
```

The convention of defining a symbolic link between the generic /dev/cdrom device to the actual CD-ROM device means that programs that use the CD-ROM drive can simply refer to the CD-ROM as /dev/cdrom and not worry about the actual type of CD-ROM drive interface. Because of the symbolic link between /dev/cdrom and the actual CD-ROM device, any input or output requests go directly to the actual CD-ROM driver that knows how to handle the request.

CD-ROM drive use under Linux

Cross Reference

As explained in Chapter 5, the `init` process and the shell scripts in the `/etc/rc.d` directory determine what processes run after Linux starts.

Secret

For the Linux distribution on this book's CD-ROM, a script called `/etc/rc.d/rc/cdrom` performs the following tasks:

- Automatically checks to see whether the system has a CD-ROM device
- If it finds a CD-ROM device, establishes a link between the device file and `/dev/cdrom` (so that you can refer to the CD-ROM device with a standard name regardless of what type of CD-ROM drive you have)
- If it finds a CD-ROM, mounts the file system on that CD-ROM at the location `/cdrom`

Thus, if you have a CD-ROM in the drive, you can automatically begin accessing that CD-ROM at the directory `/cdrom`. To see the contents of the CD-ROM, type **ls /cdrom**.

Tip

If you want to eject the CD-ROM and load a new one, you should first dismount the CD-ROM's file system by using the `umount` command. Type **umount /cdrom**. Then you can eject the CD-ROM by pressing the CD-ROM driver's eject button.

Caution

When you use removable media such as CD-ROMs or removable disks (even floppy disks), always use the `umount` command before you eject the removable disk or CD-ROM. For floppy disks, you have to dismount the floppy only if you previously mounted the floppy.

Mounting a CD-ROM

If you put a new CD-ROM in the drive, you must mount the CD-ROM before you can use it. Use the following command to mount the CD-ROM:

```
mount -t iso9660 -r /dev/cdrom /cdrom
```

The `-t` option specifies that the file system of the CD-ROM is ISO-9660 (which is true for a typical CD-ROM), and the `-r` option that indicates the CD-ROM is mounted as read-only.

Playing audio CDs in the CD-ROM drive

You need a special application to play audio CDs in the CD-ROM drive. You can install the following audio-CD applications from this book's companion CD-ROM:

- `workbone` is a text-based program that allows you to use the number pad (on the right side of the keyboard) as a control panel for playing the audio CD. This program is in the AP disk set.

- workman is an X11 application that provides a graphical control panel for playing the audio CD. This program is in the XV disk set, which contains OpenWindows applications.

Tip

Before using the workbone or workman program, make sure that you dismount any CD-ROM that is currently in the drive (use the umount /dev/cdrom command) and place an audio CD in the drive.

To use the workbone program, type **workbone -a**. Figure 12-1 shows the text-based user interface presented by workbone while running in an xterm window.

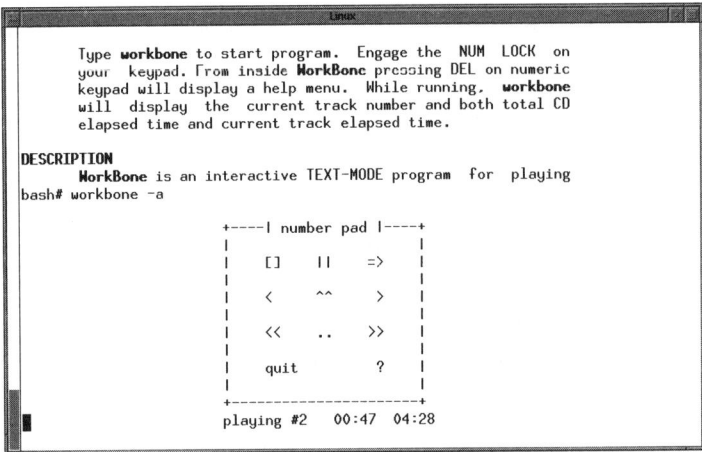

Figure 12-1: The text-based interface of the workbone program running in an xterm window.

The workman program needs the X Window System to run, so you should start it by typing **workman** at the shell prompt in an xterm window. Figure 12-2 shows the graphical user interface of workman.

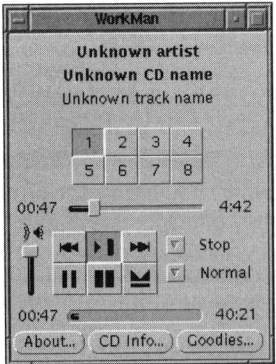

Figure 12-2: The graphical control panel of the workman program for playing audio CDs.

If you want to log in as a normal user and play audio CDs on the CD-ROM drive, you should first log in as `root` and set the permission settings on the CD-ROM device so that anyone can read the CD-ROM device. You have to set the permission for the actual CD-ROM device, not the generic `/dev/cdrom` device. To set the permission setting, follow these steps:

1. Log in as `root`. If you are already logged in, use the `su` command to assume the identity of the `root` user.

2. Determine the actual device name of the CD-ROM device. Type the following command:

   ```
   ls -l /dev/cdrom
   lrwxrwxrwx 1 root     root       8 Sep 22 19:32 /dev/cdrom -> /dev/hdc
   ```

   In the listing, you will find the name of the actual device next to `->` in the listing. In this case, the actual CD-ROM device is `/dev/hdc`.

3. Make the actual device readable by all users. To make `/dev/hdc` readable by all users, use the `chmod` command, as follows:

   ```
   chmod o+r /dev/hdc
   ```

4. Verify the permission settings of the actual CD-ROM device. You can check the permissions of `/dev/hdc` as follows:

   ```
   ls -l /dev/hdc
   brw-rw-r-- 1 root     disk    22,  0 May  8 06:38 /dev/hdc
   ```

   Notice the last three characters (`r--`) of the first column, which indicate that all users have read access to the device. Also notice the `b` at the beginning of the line, which indicates that the device is a block device (in a long listing, character devices have `c` as the first letter).

Specific CD-ROM drive information

In the following sections, I summarize information that is specific to some common device drivers. This information includes the name of the device file (such as `/dev/sbpcd` for a CD-ROM drive with Sound Blaster Pro interface), any boot parameters that the driver accepts, and any unique capabilities of the driver.

You should read the section that covers the CD-ROM interface of your CD-ROM drive.

The `scd` driver

The `scd` driver supports CD-ROM drives that connect to the PC through SCSI controller cards. The `scd` driver has the following characteristics:

```
Allows multiple CD-ROM drives: yes
Supports loadable module: yes
Can read audio frames: yes (CR-562 and CR-563 only)
```

```
Performs auto-probing: yes
Name of device file: /dev/scd0, major device number = 11
Device configuration file: /usr/include/linux/cdrom.h
Kernel option during make config: SCSI CDROM support?
Name of README file: none
```

Secret

The scd driver supports multiple CD-ROM drives on the SCSI bus. The names of the device files are /dev/scd0, /dev/scd1, /dev/scd2, and so on, with corresponding minor device numbers 0, 1, 2, and so on. All devices have the same major device number: 11.

The IDE CD-ROM driver

The IDE device driver supports all types of IDE devices, ranging from hard drives to CD-ROM drives. The driver finds the drives by auto probing and assigns device names in sequence: /dev/hda and /dev/hdb for drives on the primary IDE interface, and /dev/hdc and /dev/hdd for drives on the secondary IDE interface. A CD-ROM drive on the secondary IDE interface has the device name /dev/hdc. (Because the CD-ROM drive is slower than the hard disk, CD-ROM drives are connected to a separate IDE interface rather than being set up as a slave drive on the primary IDE interface.)

The IDE CD driver has the following characteristics:

```
Allows multiple CD-ROM drives: yes
Supports loadable module: no
Can read audio frames: no
Performs auto-probing: yes
Name of device file: /dev/hdc or /dev/hdd, major device number = 22
Device configuration file: /usr/include/linux/cdrom.h
Kernel option during make config:  Use new IDE driver for primary/
secondary i/f?
          Include support for IDE/ATAPI CDROMs?
Name of README file: /usr/src/linux/drivers/block/README.ide
```

The IDE CD driver accepts the following boot parameter:

```
hdc=cdrom
```

This parameter tells the IDE device driver that the first drive on the secondary IDE interface is a CD-ROM drive. If you have another CD-ROM drive on that interface, you might include the following boot parameter:

```
hdd=cdrom
```

The same IDE driver is used for both IDE hard disk drives as well as IDE (ATAPI) CD-ROM drives. The boot parameters are different for a hard drive.

The sbpcd driver

The sbpcd driver supports a variety of CD-ROM drives that connect to the PC through an interface that conforms to the proprietary interface used in Creative Labs Sound Blaster Pro sound cards.

The sbpcd driver has the following characteristics:

```
Allows multiple CD-ROM drives: yes
Supports loadable module: yes
Can read audio frames: yes (depends on the drive)
Performs auto-probing: yes
Name of device file: /dev/sbpcd, major device number = 25
Device configuration file: /usr/include/linux/sbpcd.h
Kernel option during make config: Matsushita/Panasonic CDROM support?
Name of README file: /usr/src/linux/drivers/block/README.sbpcd
```

The sbpcd driver accepts a boot parameter in this format:

sbpcd=*IOPORT*,*interface-type*

IOPORT is the I/O port address of the device in hexadecimal format (such as 0x230). *interface-type* is a single word that indicates the type of CD-ROM interface; it must be SoundBlaster, LaserMate, or SPEA.

If the device file /dev/sbpcd is missing, create it with the following mknod command:

mknod /dev/sbpcd b 25 0

The last three parameters specify the device type (b for block device), major device number (25 is the assigned number for /dev/sbpcd), and minor device number (0 for the first CD-ROM drive on the controller).

Secret

You can *daisy chain* (connect first to second, second to third, and so on) up to four drives per controller. Use minor device numbers 1 through 3 for the next three drives that you daisy chain to the first drive.

The sonycd535 driver

The sonycd535 driver supports Sony CDU-535 and CDU-531 CD-ROM drives that connect to the PC through Sony's proprietary interface card.

The sonycd535 driver has the following characteristics:

```
Allows multiple CD-ROM drives: no
Supports loadable module: yes
Can read audio frames: no
Performs auto-probing: no
Name of device file: /dev/sonycd535, major device number = 24
Device configuration file: /usr/include/linux/sonycd535.h
Kernel option during make config: Sony CDU535 CDROM driver support?
Name of README file: /usr/src/linux/drivers/block/README.sonycd535
```

This driver accepts the following boot parameter:

sonycd535=*IOPORT*

IOPORT is the I/O port address of the device in hexadecimal format (such as 0x320).

The `aztcd` driver

The `aztcd` driver supports Aztech CDA268, Orchid CD-3110, and Okano/Wearnes CDD110 CD-ROM drives that use a proprietary interface. Other CD-ROM drives from these vendors, such as Aztech CDA269, have the IDE interface; you have to use the IDE CD driver for those drives. The `aztcd` driver is only for the proprietary interface.

The `aztcd` driver has the following characteristics:

```
Allows multiple CD-ROM drives: no
Supports loadable module: yes
Can read audio frames: no
Performs auto-probing: no
Name of device file: /dev/aztcd, major device number = 29
Device configuration file: /usr/include/linux/aztcd.h
Kernel option during make config: Aztech/Orchid/Okano/Wearnes (non
IDE) CDROM support?
Name of README file: /usr/src/linux/drivers/block/README.aztcd
```

This driver accepts the following boot parameter:

`aztcd=IOPORT`

IOPORT is the I/O port address of the device in hexadecimal format (such as 0x320).

The `mcd` driver

Secret

The `mcd` driver supports Mitsumi CRMC-LU005S and CRMC-FX001 CD-ROM drives with the proprietary Mitsumi interface. Many new PCs use the Mitsumi CD-ROM drives but not the proprietary interface; instead, the current trend is to use the Mitsumi drives with the IDE (ATAPI) interface. Therefore, you should check carefully before selecting the `mcd` driver as the CD-ROM driver. If your PC has a Mitsumi CD-ROM driver, it's more likely to be an ATAPI drive than one that has the proprietary Mitsumi interface.

The `mcd` driver has the following characteristics:

```
Allows multiple CD-ROM drives: no
Supports loadable module: yes
Can read audio frames: no
Performs auto-probing: no
Name of device file: /dev/mcd, major device number = 23
Device configuration file: /usr/include/linux/mcd.h
Kernel option during make config: Mitsumi (not IDE/ATAPI) CDROM driver
support?
Name of README file: none
```

This driver accepts the following boot parameter:

`mcd=IOPORT,IRQ`

IOPORT is the I/O port address of the Mitsumi interface card in hexadecimal format (such as 0x340). *IRQ* is the interrupt request number used by that card.

Chapter 12: CD-ROM Drives and Sound Cards

Newer Linux kernels come with an experimental Mitsumi driver, `mcdx`, that provides additional capabilities. If the kernel includes this driver, you'll see the following question during kernel configuration:

```
Experimental Mitsumi support?
```

Remember that whenever you try any experimental drivers, you run the risk of damaging files or otherwise disrupting the use of your PC.

Sound Cards and Linux

Compared with those of the Apple Macintosh, the sound-generation capabilities of IBM-compatible PCs are rather limited. Essentially, all you can do with the PC's built-in speaker is play a single note; you can't even vary the loudness of the note.

You can greatly improve the sound-output capability of a PC by installing a sound card, such as the Sound Blaster, that can synthesize a wide range of sounds. The *sound card* is an adapter that plugs into a slot on your PC's motherboard and that includes the electronic circuitry needed to play and record sound. You can plug in speakers and a microphone to the back of a sound card. Many sound cards also include an interface through which you can connect a CD-ROM drive.

When a microphone is hooked up to the sound card, it can convert *analog* (continuously varying) sound waves into 8-bit or 16-bit numbers, sampling the wave at rates ranging from 4 kHz to 44 kHz (44,000 times a second). Higher sampling rates and a higher number of bits (16) provide better quality, but you need more disk space to store high-quality sound. Additionally, the sound card can convert digital sound samples to analog signals that you can play on a speaker.

Most sound cards, including the popular Sound Blaster, also support MIDI commands in addition to recording and playing back waveform sound. MIDI, which stands for *Musical Instrument Digital Interface,* is commonly used to record and play back musical sounds that can be created by a synthesizer. (Most sound cards have built-in synthesizers.)

Following is a list of sound cards that are currently supported by the Linux sound driver:

- 6850 UART MIDI
- Adlib (OPL2)
- Audio Excell DSP16
- Aztech Sound Galaxy NX Pro
- ECHO-PSS cards (Orchid SoundWave32, Cardinal DSP16)
- Ensoniq SoundScape

- Gravis Ultrasound
- Gravis Ultrasound 16-bit sampling daughterboard
- Gravis Ultrasound MAX
- Logitech SoundMan Games (SBPro, 44-kHz stereo support)
- Logitech SoundMan Wave (Jazz16/OPL4)
- Logitech SoundMan 16 (PAS-16-compatible)
- MPU-401 MIDI
- MediaTriX AudioTriX Pro
- Media Vision Premium 3D (Jazz16)
- Media Vision Pro Sonic 16 (Jazz)
- Media Vision Pro Audio Spectrum 16
- Microsoft Sound System (AD1848)
- OAK OTI-601D cards (Mozart)
- OPTi 82C928/82C929 cards (MAD16/MAD16 Pro)
- Sound Blaster
- Sound Blaster Pro
- Sound Blaster 16
- Wave Blaster (and other daughterboards)

Secret

Many sound cards include a built-in interface through which you can attach a CD-ROM drive. Linux needs a separate device driver to access a CD-ROM drive connected to a sound card; the sound driver does not have anything to do with the CD-ROM drive, even though the drive is attached to the sound card. Neither does the sound driver have anything to do with the joystick port that many sound cards include.

Installing the sound driver

Secret

Linux needs a driver to control the sound card. The initial Linux kernel (after you install Linux from the companion CD-ROM) does not include the sound driver. The directory `/usr/src/linux/drivers/sound` contains the source code for the sound driver. You have to rebuild the kernel to add support for your system's sound card.

Cross Reference

Chapter 2 walks you through the process of rebuilding the Linux kernel. As those steps show, when you configure the kernel with the `make config` command, you are prompted if you want to add support for a sound board. If you answer yes, the configuration process prompts you for further information about your sound card.

First, the configuration program asks whether you want to include support for specific sound cards. You should answer yes only for the actual brand of the sound card in your PC. After you indicate that you have a specific card, the configuration program may skip other cards that cannot coexist with the card that you selected.

After you select the sound cards that you want the sound driver to support, the configuration program asks for specific parameters for each selected card. You have to provide the I/O address, the IRQ, and the DMA channel number of the sound card. You should provide the same values for these parameters as they are set under DOS and Windows. You should be able to find the settings by reading the sound card's manual (a new PC with a sound card typically includes a small manual for the sound card).

My system has a Sound Blaster card. Under MS-DOS, the AUTOEXEC.BAT file contains the following command:

```
SET BLASTER=A220 I5 D1 H5 P300 T6
```

From my experience with Sound Blaster boards, I could determine from this SET command that the I/O address is 220 (hexadecimal), the IRQ is 5, and the DMA channel is 1. Thus, I provided these values when I configured the Linux kernel for sound-card support.

Cross Reference

After the sound driver is configured, you can finish rebuilding the kernel following the steps in Chapter 2. The new kernel should now support your system's sound card. I will discuss some troubleshooting suggestions in the "Troubleshooting sound cards" section later in this chapter.

Configuring the sound driver

During the configuration of the sound driver, you have to answer several questions that the configuration program asks. This section provides some guidelines for answering specific questions. Notice that the configuration program does not ask each and every question, because the exact sequence of questions depends on your earlier responses.

> **ProAudioSpectrum 16 support?** — You should answer yes (**y**) only if you have a Pro Audio Spectrum 16 (referred to as PAS16), ProAudio Studio 16, or Logitech SoundMan 16 sound card. In particular, don't answer yes if you have some other Media Vision or Logitech card, because those cards are not PAS16 compatible.
>
> **SoundBlaster support?** — Answer **y** if your PC's sound card is a Creative Labs Sound Blaster or one of many hardware-compatible clones such as Thunderboard. You should answer yes if a sound card claims to be Sound Blaster compatible.
>
> **Generic OPL2/OPL3 FM synthesizer support?** — You should answer **y** if your sound card has an FM chip made by Yamaha (OPL2/OPL3/OPL4). Answering yes usually is a safe choice.

Gravis Ultrasound support? — Answer **y** if your system's sound card is a Gravis Ultrasound (with a name such as GUS or GUS MAX). Although you can include GUS support without conflicts with other boards, the GUS driver consumes a great deal of memory. Therefore, you should answer **n** (no) if you don't have a GUS.

MPU-401 support (NOT for SB16)? — Although the Roland MPU401 MIDI interface is supported on many sound cards, the exact way of handling this interface varies from one card to another. You should answer **n** if your sound card does not have an MPU401 interface. It's safe to answer **y** if your sound card does indeed have a true MPU401 MIDI interface.

6850 UART Midi support? — You probably can answer **n** safely, because the 6850 UART interface is rarely used. UART stands for *Universal Asynchronous Receiver Transmitter,* a circuit that splits a byte into individual bits and recombines bits into bytes.

PSS (ECHO-ADI2111) support? — Answering **y** includes support for sound cards based on the PSS chipset. You should answer yes only if you have an Orchid SW32, Cardinal DSP16, or any other sound card based on the PSS chipset.

16-bit sampling option of GUS (not GUS MAX)? — The Gravis Ultrasound card has a daughterboard where you can install a card that provides 16-bit sampling. You should answer **n** if you have a GUS MAX card. If you answer **y**, support for GUS MAX is turned off automatically.

GUS MAX support? — If you have a GUS MAX sound card, answer **y** to this question.

Microsoft Sound System support? — You should answer **y** if you have the original Windows Sound System card made by Microsoft or Aztech SG 16 Pro (or NX16 Pro).

Ensoniq Soundscape support? — Answer **y** if your sound card is based on the Ensoniq SoundScape chipset. Several manufacturers — such as Ensoniq, Spea, and Reveal (Reveal also makes other cards) — use that chipset.

Sound Blaster Pro support? — Answer **y** if your card is a Sound Blaster Pro or a compatible card.

Sound Blaster 16 support? — Answer **y** to enable this support if your PC has a Sound Blaster 16 sound card.

/dev/dsp and /dev/audio support (usually required)? — Answer **y** so that the configuration program automatically creates the mount points: `/dev/dsp` and `/dev/audio`.

MIDI interface support? — Answer **y** to enable the MIDI devices (which have names such as `/dev/midiNN`, in which `NN` is a number) and allow access to the sound card through the `/dev/sequencer` and `/dev/music` devices. Answering yes affects any MPU401 and/or any MIDI-compatible devices.

FM synthesizer (YM3812/OPL-3) support? — You can safely answer this question **y**.

/dev/sequencer support? — If you answer **n**, the configuration program disables the /dev/sequencer and /dev/music devices.

Learning sound-device names

Like any other devices in Linux, the sound devices have files in the /dev directory with specific names. Table 12-3 lists the standard device filenames that provide sound capability in Linux (you may not have all devices on your system).

Table 12-3	Standard sound device filenames in Linux
Device filename	**Description**
/dev/audio	An audio device that is capable of playing Sun workstation-compatible audio files (typically with an .au extension). The device does not support all capabilities of the Sun workstation audio device but can play Sun audio files.
/dev/audio1	Sun workstation-compatible audio device for the second sound card (if any).
/dev/dsp	Digital signal-processing device that also can play Sun audio files.
/dev/midi	MIDI device.
/dev/mixer	Sound-mixer device.
/dev/mixer1	Second sound-mixer device.
/dev/pcaudio	Equivalent to /dev/audio, but plays on the PC's speaker. (You have to install a separate PC speaker driver, which is available from ftp://ftp.informatik.hu-berlin.de/pub/os/linux/hu-sound/.)
/dev/pcmixer	Equivalent to /dev/mixer, but plays on the PC's speaker. (You have to install a separate PC speaker driver, which is available from ftp://ftp.informatik.hu-berlin.de/pub/os/linux/hu-sound/.)
/dev/pcsp	Equivalent to /dev/dsp, but plays on the PC's speaker. (You have to install a separate PC speaker driver, which is available from ftp://ftp.informatik.hu-berlin.de/pub/os/linux/hu-sound/.)

(continued)

Table 12-3 *(continued)*

Device filename	Description
/dev/sequencer	MIDI sequencer device.
/dev/sndstat	A device that provides information about the sound driver (see the example in the "Check sound driver status" section).

Testing the sound card

After you enable support for your sound card and rebuild the Linux kernel, you should reboot the system (log in as `root`, and use the command `/sbin/shutdown -r now`). As Linux boots, you should see a message about the sound driver.

Tip

If the boot messages scroll by too fast to see, type the command `dmesg | more` to see these messages one screen at a time. Look for one or more lines that start with `snd`. On my system, for example, I have a Sound Blaster Pro sound card. The boot messages include the following line:

```
snd2 <SoundBlaster Pro 4.13> at 0x220 irq 5 drq 1
```

In this case, the text within the angle brackets shows the name of the sound card and the version number of the digital signal-processing circuitry on that card. The boot message about the sound device also shows an I/O address of 0x220 (220 in hexadecimal notation), an IRQ of 5, and a DMA channel (reported as `drq`) of 1.

Sometimes, the sound driver may print error or warning messages as the system boots. When you run the `dmesg` command, you should look for these messages as well.

Check sound-driver status

If you see the boot message about the sound driver, you can tell that sound support is included in the kernel. The sound driver comes with another way to check the status.

Secret

A special device named `/dev/sndstat` allows you to get information about the status of the sound driver. All you have to do is look at the contents of `/dev/sndstat`. On my system, I can see the status of the sound driver as follows:

```
cat /dev/sndstat
Sound Driver:2.90-2 (Wed Jul 26 15:27:19 EDT 1995 root@lnbsoft.com)
Config options: 1402

Installed drivers:
Type 2: SoundBlaster
```

Chapter 12: CD-ROM Drives and Sound Cards

```
Card config:
SoundBlaster at 0x220 irq 5 drq 1

PCM devices:
0: SoundBlaster Pro 4.13

Synth devices:

Midi devices:

MIDI Timers:

1 mixer(s) installed
```

The messages will be different on your system because you probably have a different sound card with different settings from mine. The /dev/sndstat device file, however, provides good diagnostic information about the sound driver.

Try the sound card

To test the sound driver, you should try playing a sound file. All you have to do is send the sound file to the sound device (/dev/audio) with the cat command. The sound device can play Sun's sound files, which usually have names that end with the .au extension. To play a sound file named piano-beep.au, you would type the following command:

Tip

```
cat piano-beep.au > /dev/audio
```

If you have the Slackware CD-ROM mounted, you will find several .au files in the directory /cdrom/live/usr/lib/lemacs-19.10/etc/sounds. Try the following command:

```
cat /cdrom/live/usr/lib/lemacs-19.10/etc/sounds/monkey.au > /dev/audio
```

If the sound file plays, your sound card is working properly.

If you have a microphone connected to your sound card, you also can try recording a ten-second sound file with the following command:

```
dd bs=8k count=10 </dev/audio >test.au
```

The dd command simply copies a specified amount of data from one file to another. In this case, the input file is the audio device (which records from the microphone), and the output file is the sound file. After recording the sound file, you can play it back by sending the data back to /dev/audio with the cat command.

Wizard

To use the sound card properly, you need some applications that allow you to play back and record sound files. Try one of the following Internet resources to locate sound-recording and playback applications for Linux:

- ftp://sunsite.unc.edu:/pub/Linux/apps/sound/
- ftp://tsx-11.mit.edu:/pub/linux/packages/sound/
- ftp://nic.funet.fi:/pub/OS/Linux/util/sound/

Troubleshooting sound cards

After you configure the sound driver and reboot, if the sound card does not produce any sound when you copy audio files to /dev/audio, try the following steps to determine and fix the problem:

1. Verify that you are running the kernel that you rebuilt with support for the sound card. To see the version number, use the uname -a command. Following is typical output from the uname -a command:

   ```
   Linux lnbsoft 1.2.11 #1 Wed Jul 26 15:35:13 EDT 1995 i586
   ```

   This string shows the kernel's version number, as well as the date when the kernel was built. If the date does not match the date when you rebuilt the kernel, you probably are not running the new kernel. Go through the steps outlined in Chapter 2, and make sure that you really installed the new kernel. One common problem is forgetting to reboot, so try that step as well.

2. Check to see whether the sound driver is included in the kernel. One way to check this is to look at the contents of the /proc/devices file. Following is an example:

   ```
   cat /proc/devices
   Character devices:
   1 mem
   4 ttyp
   5 cua
   6 lp
   7 vcs
   10 mouse
   14 sound
   Block devices:
   2 fd
   3 ide0
   8 sd
   22 ide1
   ```

   The listing should show character device 14, named sound. If you don't see this device, you did not configure the kernel properly to include the sound driver. Reconfigure and rebuild the kernel, making sure that you include support for your sound card.

3. Verify that the sound driver detected the sound card when the system started. Use dmesg | more to look at the boot messages, and check for a line reporting that the sound card was found. If the sound driver does not report the sound card, the sound card may not be installed and configured properly.

   First, make sure that the sound card works under DOS or Windows. Determine the I/O address, IRQ, and DMA channel, and then reconfigure the kernel to include support for your sound card with the same parameters as under DOS.

4. If nothing works, you may want to read the latest Sound-HOWTO document. To read the HOWTO document, run the `browse` program from the `/cdrom/browse` directory (you'll need this book's CD-ROM in the CD-ROM drive), and look at the contents of the directory `/usr/doc/faq/howto`.

Cross Reference

If you still can't get the sound card to work under Linux, you may want to post a news item to one of the comp.os.linux newsgroups. Chapter 19 discusses how to connect to the Internet and access the newsgroups.

Solving common sound-card problems

In addition to the basic sound-card driver configuration, you may run into problems with specific sound cards. This section provides hints for solving some common problems.

Works under DOS, but not under Linux

Secret

Many Sound Blaster-compatible cards work under MS-DOS and Microsoft Windows but do not work under Linux. A typical symptom is that everything appears to be fine — the sound driver is installed properly, and it reports the sound card with the correct parameters at startup — but you don't hear any sound when you copy a sound file to `/dev/audio`.

In this case, you have to initialize the sound card under DOS and Windows first. Try the following steps:

1. Boot the PC under DOS, and run Windows 3.1. If you have Windows 95, start Windows 95.

2. Run the Media Player application, and play some sound files under Windows.

3. Exit Windows, and reboot the PC. If you are running Windows 3.1, exit Windows and press Ctrl+Alt+Delete under DOS. In Windows 95, select the Start menu's Shut Down option, and select Reboot from the resulting dialog box.

4. Make sure that you reboot to Linux. If you use LILO, press Shift, and respond to the LILO prompt. If you use a Linux boot floppy, make sure that you place the boot floppy in the A drive before rebooting the PC.

After Linux boots, the sound driver should play the sound file successfully.

Can play sound, but not record

If you can play sound but not record, first make sure that you can record sound under DOS and Windows. That capability indicates that the sound card is capable of recording.

Then get a mixer program (from one of the FTP sites listed in the "Try the sound card" section), and use the mixer program to select the appropriate recording device, such as the microphone. You also may want to adjust the input gains to see if it helps.

Pro Audio Spectrum PAS16 and Adaptec 1542 SCSI adapter

Secret

The PAS16 sound card uses I/O address 330H (hexadecimal 330) as its MIDI port address. The Adaptec AHA 1542 SCSI card also can use I/O address 330H. Linux, however, can use the AHA 1542 at the base I/O address of 333H. To avoid I/O address conflict between the PAS16 and AHA 1542 SCSI card, set the SCSI card's I/O address to 333H.

Secret

Another potential problem is DMA conflicts between the PAS16 and the AHA 1542, which may halt the system with some memory error. The solution is to adjust two parameters — BUS ON and BUS OFF times — of the AHA 1542 SCSI card. Get the SCSISEL.EXE program from Adaptec through the Internet, run SCSISEL under DOS, and reduce the BUS ON time or increase the BUS OFF time until the problem goes away.

Sound Blaster AWE32 not supported

Linux does not support the E-mu MIDI synthesizer and the ASP chip on Sound Blaster AWE32 sound cards. The problem is that Creative Labs, the maker of the AWE32 card, has not released programming information about the E-mu and ASP chips.

Summary

Unlike many UNIX workstations, a typical PC nowadays comes with a CD-ROM drive and a sound card. The popularity of multimedia software fuels the demand for CD-ROM drives and sound capability in PCs. Additionally, many software packages, including Linux, come on CD-ROM. Linux supports CD-ROM drives and sound cards. This chapter describes the CD-ROM drives and sound cards that Linux supports, and shows you how to detect and correct some common sound-card and CD-ROM-drive installation problems. By reading this chapter, you learn the following:

▶ Linux's support for a specific CD-ROM drive depends on the interface used to connect that CD-ROM drive to the PC's motherboard. Linux supports the most popular ATAPI (IDE) and SCSI interfaces for CD-ROM drives, as well as many proprietary CD-ROM interfaces, such as Aztech, Sony, Mitsumi, and Sound Blaster Pro CD-ROM interface.

▶ New users often mistakenly select a CD-ROM driver based on the brand name of the CD-ROM drive; instead, they should select the CD-ROM driver that matches the CD-ROM's interface. Thus, a Mitsumi CD-ROM drive with an ATAPI interface requires the IDE driver, not the Mitsumi driver.

▶ The selection of the wrong Linux kernel often leads to the common problem of the CD-ROM drive not being recognized, even though you used it to install Linux from this book's companion CD-ROM. You have to rebuild the kernel to add support for your particular type of CD-ROM drive.

▶ Sound cards often include interfaces for CD-ROM drives and joysticks. The sound driver supports only the sound card's sound capabilities; you need separate drivers for the CD-ROM drive and the joystick.

▶ To use a sound card, you have to rebuild the Linux kernel, because none of the kernels on the companion CD-ROM includes support for sound. When you configure the kernel, you have to enable support for your sound card and provide information about the card's IRQ, I/O address, and DMA.

▶ You can use the /dev/audio and /dev/sndstat devices to check out the sound card after you rebuild the kernel and reboot the system with the new kernel.

Chapter 13

Keyboards and Pointing Devices

In This Chapter

- Adjusting the keyboard autorepeat delay and repeat rate in Linux
- Understanding the concept of the keyboard map
- Configuring the keyboard for some European languages
- Surveying the mouse interface types and mouse protocols Linux supports
- Configuring XFree86 to use various keyboards and mice

The keyboard and the mouse (or some other mouselike pointing device, such as a trackball) are the basic mechanisms for providing input to the computer. As far as hardware compatibility goes, Linux works with any keyboard that works under DOS. You may want to alter some characteristics of the keyboard, however, such as how fast it repeats a character when you hold down a key. You also may want to associate a different character set with the physical keys, especially if you use a language other than English. This chapter describes the keyboard-customization facilities of Linux.

You do not need a mouse (I'll use the term *mouse* to mean any pointing device, including a trackball) to run Linux. If, however, you install and use XFree86 (X Window System for Linux), you need a mouse. Several popular brands of mice and several types of interfaces (such as serial mouse or bus mouse) are available. In this chapter, you learn about the types of mouse interfaces and mouse protocols that Linux and X support.

Keyboards and Linux

The keyboard is one of those appendages of a PC that you can't do without but that you take for granted and don't think about much. If a keyboard works under DOS, it also should work under Linux. Thus, the make and model of a keyboard are not much of an issue.

You can, of course, customize some of the physical elements of the keyboard, such as the following:

- *Repeat delay.* If you hold down a key, the keyboard waits this amount of time before beginning to repeat that key.
- *Repeat rate.* The repeat rate is the rate at which the keyboard repeats a key.

Another area of customization has more to do with Linux than with the keyboard: how Linux interprets a keypress. You could make the Backspace key generate Ctrl-H by remapping the key (which means by changing how a physical keypress is mapped to an action).

The following sections show both types of keyboard customization: the physical characteristics and the mapping of keys to actions.

Some keyboard terminology and notations

In this chapter, you encounter references to specific keys (or combinations of keys) on the keyboard. This section provides a brief overview of the key names and other terminology associated with keyboards.

Keyboard layout

Keyboard layout refers to the way that the keys are laid out in the keyboard. Most PCs use a 101-key keyboard. Figure 13-1 shows the typical keyboard layout for a 101-key PC keyboard.

The basic alphabetic and numeric keys occupy most of the space on the keyboard. A set of 12 function keys, named F1 through F12, appears along the top edge of the keyboard. The numeric pad is the block of keys on the right side of the keyboard.

The upper-right corner of the keyboard has three status lights, called LEDs. (*LED* stands for *light-emitting diode*, an electronic part that displays the light.) The LEDs — labeled Num Lock, Caps Lock, and Scroll Lock — indicate whether the corresponding Lock key is pressed.

The Ctrl, Shift, and Alt keys are commonly referred to as the *modifier* keys. As you know, the keyboard has two of each of these keys. In Linux documentation, the right Alt key is referred to as the *AltGr* key.

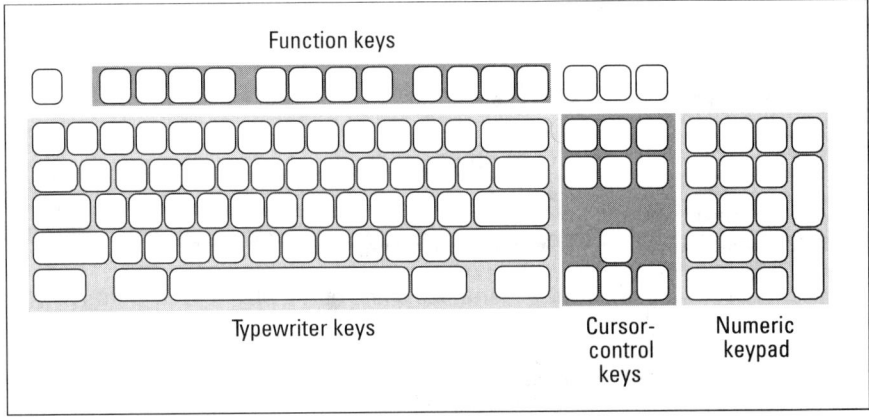

Figure 13-1: The keyboard layout for a 101-key PC keyboard.

Although many keys on the keyboard are labeled the same (the numbers on the number pad, for example, are the same as the numbers along the top row of the main block of keys), Linux assigns a unique keycode to each key on the keyboard. Typically, these keycodes go from 1 through the number of keys on the keyboard.

X keyboard terminology

The X Window System (X for short) also assigns a keycode to each key on the keyboard. Unfortunately, the X keycodes are not the same as the Linux keycodes. Internally, X translates the physical keycodes to keysyms, which represent symbolic names for keys.

Keys such as the Shift, Ctrl, Alt, and Caps Lock keys are known as *modifier keys* because they modify the meaning of the other keys. X supports up to five system-dependent modifier keys.

Keyboard repeat delay and repeat rate

When Linux boots, the kernel sets the keyboard repeat rate to the maximum allowed by a keyboard. Although the maximum repeat rate should be fine for most keyboards, in some cases, you may get multiple copies of a character all too easily because the repeat rate is too high. In such a case, you can use the `kbdrate` program to lower the keyboard repeat rate.

The `kbdrate` utility program allows you to manipulate the keyboard's repeat rate and the delay time — the amount of time for which a key must be depressed before the keyboard starts to repeat that key.

Following is the syntax of the `kbdrate` program:

```
kbdrate [-s] [-r rate] [-d delay]
```

All the arguments shown within brackets are optional. If you run `kbdrate` without any options, it works like this:

```
kbdrate
Typematic Rate set to 10.9 cps (delay = 250 mS)
```

That message from `kbdrate` means that the keyboard repeat rate (called Typematic Rate by IBM when the original PC came with these keyboards) is set to 10.9 characters per second (cps) and that the repeat delay is 250 milliseconds (ms). Thus, when the program is run without any options, `kbdrate` sets the repeat rate and delay to default values (these defaults were what IBM selected for the original PC keyboard).

You can set the rate with the `-r` option; the rate can lie between 2.0 and 30.0 cps. Usually, the keyboard allows a discrete set of values. A common set of possible values is 2.0, 2.1, 2.3, 2.5, 2.7, 3.0, 3.3, 3.7, 4.0, 4.3, 4.6, 5.0, 5.5, 6.0, 6.7, 7.5, 8.0, 8.6, 9.2, 10.0, 10.9, 12.0, 13.3, 15.0, 16.0, 17.1, 18.5, 20.0, 21.8, 24.0, 26.7, and 30.0 cps. When you specify a rate, the `kbdrate` program selects from this set a value that's less than or equal to what you request. Thus, if you enter `kbdrate -r 18.0`, `kbdrate` selects 17.1 as the rate.

Use the `-d` option to set the delay, which can be between 250 and 1,000 ms (or 1 second). Only four possible values are allowed: 250, 500, 750, and 1,000 ms.

The `-s` option causes `kbdrate` to do its job without displaying any messages.

The `kbdrate` program may not work with some keyboards. Reportedly, the program cannot set the repeat rate on the Gateway AnyKey keyboard.

Tip

When you run the X Window System, it takes over the control of the keyboard. Under X, you can run `kbdrate` (from an `xterm` window) and set the delay and repeat rate. X also comes with the `xset` utility program, which allows you to alter many user preferences for the keyboard, mouse, and display screen. Although `xset` does not allow you to set the repeat rate, you can turn the repeat feature on or off. To turn off keyboard repeat, type the following at the shell prompt in an `xterm` window:

```
xset r off
```

Try holding down a key; it should not repeat at all. To turn on the autorepeat feature, use this command:

```
xset r on
```

Keyboard map in Linux

You probably do not pay much attention to how the keyboard maps the physical keys to characters because for the English language, a one-to-one correspondence exists between the physical keys and the letters of the alphabet.

The situation is not as simple if your native language is not English and you need some special characters, such as characters with an umlaut (two dots above the letter), or other accented letters. To enter such letters from the keyboard, you have to change how a physical keypress is translated to characters in Linux. That conversion is referred to as the *keyboard map* or *keyboard translation*.

It's important to note that entering special letters from the keyboard involves two steps. First, you have to get Linux to interpret a keypress as the special character that you want; then you need a program that can display the special character. How a special character is displayed depends on the font.

Note

Linux includes two programs — `loadkeys` and `xmodmap` — to modify the way that a physical keypress is mapped to an action. What you use depends on whether you are running in text mode or the X Window System. When you work in a Linux virtual console (basically, the text screen), your keypresses are handled by the keyboard driver. In this case, you should use `loadkeys` to alter the keyboard translation.

When X is running, it takes over both the keyboard and the mouse. Therefore, you have to use a different utility program, `xmodmap`, to change the keyboard map. X consults the Linux key-translation tables at startup, however, so you get some consistency in keyboard translation between text mode and X.

In Linux, the keyboard driver consults a keyboard table to determine how to translate a physical keycode to a string of other codes or an action. You can load a keyboard-translation table with the `loadkeys` program.

Cross Reference

The `loadkeys` utility and a related program, `dumpkeys`, are in the `keytbls` package in the A disk set of the Slackware distribution in this book's CD-ROM. You have to install the `keytbls` package if you want to alter the keyboard-translation tables with `loadkeys`. Chapter 1 describes how to install specific packages when you install Linux from the CD-ROM.

The keyboard map is defined in a text file; the default keyboard map is in the `/usr/src/linux/drivers/char/defkeymap.map` file. The keyboard driver uses this table to convert physical keypresses to actions.

Tip

If you install the `keytbls` package, you'll find other keyboard-map files in the `/usr/lib/kbd/keytables` directory. Each file provides keyboard mapping for specific geographic regions or countries. The U.S. keyboard map, for example, is in the file `us.map`, and the map for Finland is in `fi.map`. To load a specific keyboard map, use the `loadkeys` program, as follows:

```
loadkeys fi.map
```

After that, if you press the minus key, you'll get the plus sign — just one symptom of a different mapping of the physical keys to characters. To revert to the default keyboard map, type **loadkeys -d** (which means load the default keyboard map).

You can, in fact, change keyboard mapping interactively from the command line. Consider a useless but illustrative example. Suppose that you want the A key to be interpreted as Q, and vice versa. That means that after remapping the keys, you have to press the key labeled A to enter the character Q (and press the Q key to enter A). Before the situation gets any more confusing, try typing the following at the shell prompt (this procedure won't work under X):

```
loadkeys
keycode 30 = +q
keycode 16 = +a
(press Ctrl+D to indicate end of input)
```

Now check out the result. Press the A and Q keys a couple of times, and verify that the meanings of those two keys have switched. `loadkeys` waits for you to enter lines of text, on each line you specify the action that corresponds to a physical keypress. The left side of the equal sign provides the keycode; the right side indicates the action for that keycode. A letter with a plus sign simply means that the keycode corresponds to that letter and that the letter should change case when the Shift or Caps Lock key is pressed.

Tip

Linux assigns a number — a keycode — to each key on the keyboard. You can use the `showkey` command to determine the keycode of any key on the keyboard. Just type `showkey` and press the key whose keycode you want to know.

Wizard

If you're setting up Linux for a non-U.S. keyboard map, you can initialize the keyboard map at startup. All you have to do is provide the shell script `/etc/rc.d/rc.keymap`; the `init` process runs this script file automatically at startup.

In the `/etc/rc.d/rc.keymap` file, use the `loadkeys` command with an appropriate keyboard map as the argument. To set up the keyboard with the Danish keyboard-translation table, you would use the following:

```
/usr/bin/loadkeys /usr/lib/kbd/keytables/dk.map
```

You can view the current keyboard-translation table with the `dumpkeys` program. If you type `dumpkeys` without any options, the program shows you the mapping from keycode to names of keys, and also shows what happens when you press a key along with other modifiers (such as Ctrl, Shift, and Alt).

Keyboard and XFree86

In XFree86, the X server controls the keyboard and the mouse. Thus, the X server needs some information about the keyboard. You have to provide this information in the `Keyboard` section of the `/etc/XF86Config` file — the configuration file for XFree86. A typical `Keyboard` section might look like this:

```
Section "Keyboard"
    Protocol      "Standard"
    AutoRepeat    500 5
    LeftAlt       Meta
    RightAlt      ModeShift
EndSection
```

Table 13-1 lists the options you can specify in the `Keyboard` section:

Table 13-1   XF86Config file keyboard section options

Option	Function
Protocol "*protocol-name*"	Specifies the keyboard protocol. Use `Standard` as the *protocol-name* in Linux. The other protocol name can be *Xqueue*, which is appropriate for other UNIX systems.
AutoRepeat *delay rate*	Sets the keyboard repeat delay and repeat rate (may not work on all systems). The delay is in milliseconds, and the rate is in characters per second.
ServerNumLock	Makes the X server handle the Num Lock key internally. This option was needed by versions of X before X11R6. You should not have to specify this option anymore because the version of X on the companion CD-ROM is X11R6.
LeftAlt *key*	Maps the left Alt key to the specified *key* (see text for list).
RightAlt *key*	Maps the right Alt key to the specified *key* (see text for list).
AltGr *key*	Maps the right Alt key to the specified *key* (see text for list).
ScrollLock *key*	Maps the Scroll Lock key to the specified *key* (see text for list).
RightCtl *key*	Maps the right Ctrl key to the specified *key* (see text for list).

Option	Function
XLeds x y z	Allows X applications to take control of the status lights (LEDs). Use numbers between 1 and 3 for x, y, and z.
VTSysReq	Causes X server to reserve the Alt+SysRq+Fn (Fn denotes a function-key number n) key sequence to switch virtual terminals (VTs). If you specify this line, it disables the default key sequence to switch VT (Ctrl+Alt+Fn).
VTInit "command"	Causes the X server to run the specified command with the shell (/bin/sh -c) after the X server opens its VT (virtual terminal).

You can use one of the following key names to specify the key mapping for the left and right Alt keys, Scroll Lock, and the right Ctrl key (these are names that the X server recognizes):

- Compose
- Control
- Meta
- ModeLock
- ModeShift
- ScrollLock

These are simply the standard names for keys in X. Each standard key is associated with a physical key on the keyboard. For example, what the X server calls the Meta key is actually the Alt key on the left hand side of the keyboard.

Following is the default mapping for the left and right Alt keys, Scroll Lock, and right Ctrl key:

- LeftAlt: Meta
- RightAlt (AltGr is a synonym for RightAlt): Meta
- RightCtl: Control
- ScrollLock: Compose

In X, the X server takes over the screen, the keyboard, and the mouse. The upshot is that X has its own scheme for mapping physical keypresses to various actions. Luckily, in Linux, XFree86 uses the Linux keyboard map to initialize its own keyboard map, thus ensuring some consistency between the two keyboard maps.

The X server decides the keycode to be generated for a specific physical key. Each key, including the modifiers, has a unique keycode. Although the keycode generated for the common alphanumeric keys may be the same for many workstations, it is not guaranteed to be so. Therefore, X applications do not use the raw keycode. Instead, the X server converts the keycode to meaningful characters by a two-step process:

- In the first step, the X server translates the keycode to a symbolic name, known as `keysym`. All meaningful combinations of a key and the modifiers have unique `keysym`s, which are constants defined in the header file `/usr/include/X11/keysymdef.h` (this file is for use in X applications). The `keysym` resulting from a single keypress depends on the state of the modifier keys as well as on the key itself. If you press the A key alone, you should get a lowercase a, but if you press A while the Shift key is down, the result should be an uppercase A. The `keysym` differentiates between these cases and assigns the names `XK_a` and `XK_A`, respectively, for lowercase and uppercase A.

- In the second step, the X server converts the `keysym` to an ASCII text string that the X application can use for displaying (and for saving in files). For most keys, this string would have a single character, but function keys (especially programmable ones) may generate multiple-character strings.

You can use the `xmodmap` utility program to modify the mapping of keycodes to `keysym`s. Suppose that you want to switch the meanings of the A and Q keys. To do that under X, place the following lines in a file named `xmodtest`:

```
keycode 38 = Q
keycode 24 = A
```

To make these definitions effective, type the following command in an `xterm` window:

```
xmodmap xmodtest
```

You'll find that the A and Q keys are swapped after this command executes.

The `xmodtest` file constitutes a simple X keyboard map. As in the Linux keyboard map, the term `keycode` means a physical key. The X number for a physical key, however, is different from the Linux number for that key. Typically, the X keycodes are eight more than the corresponding Linux keycode.

Specific keyboard questions in Linux

This section covers typical keyboard-related questions that you might have.

Turning on the Num Lock key

When the Num Lock key is set, you can use the number pad to enter numbers. Because the 101-key keyboard already has cursor keys as well as Page Up and Page Down keys, you may want to use the number pad for entering numbers only.

If you want to use the number pad this way, you may want to turn on the Num Lock key at system startup. To do this, you have to use the `setleds` (set LEDs, in which LED stands for light-emitting diode) program that comes with the `keytbls` package in disk set A. You have the option to install the `keytbls` package when you install Linux from this book's CD-ROM.

The `setleds` program changes the Num Lock, Caps Lock, and Scroll Lock settings. To turn on Num Lock at startup, use `setleds` in one of the script files that the `init` process runs when Linux starts. You can turn on the Num Lock key (and the associated LED) by placing the following shell commands in the `/etc/rc.d/rc.local` file:

```
for t in 1 2 3 4 5 6 7 8
do
  setleds +num < /dev/tty$t > /dev/null
done
```

The `+num` option causes `setleds` to turn on the Num Lock key; `setleds -num` turns off that key.

Gateway AnyKey keyboard

Secret

This keyboard has a built-in key-remapping capability, at a level even lower than the Linux keyboard driver. If this situation poses a problem, you should press the Ctrl+Alt+Suspend_Macro key combination to reset the keys to normal.

The Mouse and Linux

Although Linux allows you to use a mouse in text-mode display, you can do without a mouse if you plan to stick with text-mode displays only. If you want to use the graphical "point-and-click" interface provided by the X Window System, however, you must have a mouse. In fact, the X server won't start if it does not find the mouse device. Therefore, I'll discuss the mouse in the context of its use under XFree86.

Mouse interfaces

Secret

As with CD-ROM drives, the mouse interface is more important than the actual make and model of the mouse. To include support for a busmouse, you may have to rebuild the kernel. When you configure the kernel (see Chapter 2 for the procedure), the configuration program asks you to identify the type of mouse interfaces that you want to include with the kernel. Following are the configuration questions related to the mouse:

```
Logitech busmouse support (CONFIG_BUSMOUSE) [n]
PS/2 mouse (aka "auxiliary device" support) (CONFIG_PSMOUSE) [y]
C&T 82C710 mouse support (as on TI Travelmate) (CONFIG_82C710_MOUSE) [y]
Microsoft busmouse support (CONFIG_MS_BUSMOUSE) [n]
ATIXL busmouse support (CONFIG_ATIXL_BUSMOUSE) [n]
```

These questions essentially tell you the types of mouse interfaces that Linux supports.

In addition to using these special mouse interfaces, you can connect a mouse to the PC through a serial port. Thus, Linux offers the following mouse interfaces:

- Serial interface. Basically, the mouse is connected to a serial port just like a modem; Microsoft, Logitech, and Mouse Systems mice are available with the serial interface.

- PS/2 Auxiliary Device port. This mouse interface works through the keyboard controller.

- Microsoft Busmouse. This mouse is also known as the Inport mouse — it connects to an interface card that plugs into the bus on your PC's motherboard.

- Logitech Busmouse. This mouse is similar to Microsoft Busmouse, but Logitech mice follow a different protocol; that is, standard for data exchange between the mouse and the motherboard.

- ATI-XL Busmouse. This mouse is a variant of the Microsoft busmouse except that the ATI-XL busmouse comes with the ATI-XL video card that has a built-in interface for a mouse.

- Chips & Technology C&T 82C710 mouse. This interface is the QuickPort interface used on some laptops, such as Toshiba and older Texas Instruments TravelMates. The C&T 82C710 interface relies on the PS/2 interface. You need to include in the kernel support for both types of interfaces.

Most PCs use the PS/2 Auxiliary Device interface for the mouse. Among busmice, the Microsoft Busmouse interface is popular.

Secret

If you have a busmouse or a PS/2-style mouse, the Linux kernel identifies the mouse at startup. You can see the mouse name in the boot messages that the kernel displays. Check these boot messages with a `dmesg | more` command, and look for the mouse type that the kernel identifies. (You also can use `more /var/adm/messages` to browse through the boot messages.)

All mouse interfaces require the use of an IRQ, and some need an I/O port address. The serial ports COM1 and COM2 use IRQs 4 and 3, respectively. For a busmouse, the kernel uses a default IRQ of 5, which can conflict with the interrupt settings of other devices, such as sound cards and SCSI controllers.

Secret

The PS/2 auxiliary port always uses IRQ 12; you cannot change this setting. Therefore, if any other peripheral tries to use IRQ 12, you have to change that device's IRQ.

Microsoft and Logitech busmouse interface

This type of mouse connects to an interface card that plugs into the bus on your PC's motherboard. The mouse cord has a round nine-pin connector with a notch on one side; this type of connector is known as a nine-pin mini-DIN connector.

The Microsoft busmouse is also known as the InPort busmouse.

Secret

ATI Graphics Ultra and Ultra Pro video cards include a mouse port that's compatible with the Logitech busmouse interface. If you have a mouse connected to these ATI video cards, specify your mouse as a Logitech busmouse. Despite the ATI name, these mouse interfaces are not AT-XL busmice.

PS/2 Auxiliary Device interface

The PS/2-style mouse interface requires no expansion card. Instead, the mouse connects to the PS/2 Auxiliary Device port on the keyboard controller. The PS/2 mouse port uses a six-pin mini-DIN connector, just like the keyboard connector. The PS/2 auxiliary device is widely used in most new PCs. The PS/2 interface also is used in some laptops.

ATI-XL mouse

The ATI-XL video cards come with a mouse interface that's referred to as the ATI-XL busmouse. You probably won't have to bother with the ATI-XL busmouse unless you have an ATI-XL video card.

Mouse-device names

The mouse device is a character device just like the keyboard and the modem. Character devices transfer information one or more characters at a time, compared with block devices (such as hard disks), which transfer data in fixed-size blocks. For each supported mouse interface, Linux uses a special device name, as follows:

- /dev/atibm: ATI-XL busmouse
- /dev/inportbm: Microsoft InPort busmouse
- /dev/logibm: Logitech busmouse
- /dev/psaux: PS/2 auxiliary port for mouse
- /dev/ttyS0 and /dev/ttyS1: serial-port device names for COM1 and COM2 (used for serial mouse)

Wizard

By convention, the generic mouse device /dev/mouse is set up as a link to the actual mouse device on your system. On my system, which has a PS/2 auxiliary-port mouse, a detailed listing of /dev/mouse shows the following:

```
ls -l /dev/mouse
lrwxrwxrwx  1 root    root         5 Sep 28 17:40 /dev/mouse -> /dev/psaux
```

This listing indicates that /dev/mouse is a symbolic link to /dev/psaux, which represents the PS/2 auxiliary-device interface.

On the other hand, on my old 386 PC, the mouse is on the first serial port. In this case, a detailed listing of /dev/mouse shows the following:

```
ls -l /dev/mouse
lrwxrwxrwx  1 root    root        10 Jul 23 11:05 /dev/mouse -> /dev/ttyS0
```

The convention of linking /dev/mouse to the actual mouse device allows programs that use the mouse to use /dev/mouse to refer to the mouse device and not worry about the actual type of mouse. Because of the symbolic link between /dev/mouse and the actual device, any input or output requests go directly to the actual mouse driver that knows how to handle the request.

Mouse protocols

What with the mouse interface types and device names, you may be confused enough about using a mouse in Linux. But you need yet another piece of information to fully specify the mouse to XFree86: the mouse protocol.

Secret

The *mouse protocol* is the convention that the mouse uses to package information about mouse movement and button states (pressed or released). You can think of the mouse interface (such as serial, busmouse, or PS/2 Auxiliary) as being the physical data-exchange mechanism. The mouse protocol, on the other hand, is used by the recipient of the mouse data (button state or movement) to decipher that data and take action (such as moving the cursor on-screen).

The mouse protocol is important to XFree86 because the X server has to interpret and use the mouse data. You learn more about the protocols in the following section.

Mouse and XFree86

In XFree86, the recipient of the mouse data is the X server. At minimum, the X server needs two pieces of information about your mouse:

- The device name of your mouse. You can specify /dev/mouse, provided that /dev/mouse is symbolically linked to the actual mouse device.
- The protocol that the mouse uses to send reports of mouse movement and button positions.

For some mouse types, such as the Logitech serial mouse, the X server also needs information such as `BaudRate` and `SampleRate`. You also can specify other information, such as how to simulate a third mouse button on a two-button mouse (the typical type of mouse on PCs).

The X server expects to get this information from the /etc/XF86Config file — the configuration file for XFree86. Specifically, the `Pointer` section in that file specifies the mouse device and protocol. If you have a Microsoft serial mouse connected to COM1 (the first serial port on the PC), a bare-bones `Pointer` section in /etc/XF86Config looks like this:

```
Section "Pointer"
  Protocol "Microsoft"
  Device "/dev/ttyS0"
EndSection
```

The `Device` line specifies the device name for the mouse.

Protocol specification

The `Protocol` line indicates the mouse protocol. Following is the syntax of the `Protocol` line:

`Protocol "protocol-name"`

`protocol-name` is the name of a mouse protocol. (The double quotation marks are required.)

Table 13-2 lists the mouse-protocol names that XFree86 recognizes.

Table 13-2   Mouse-protocol names recognized by XFree86

Protocol name	Corresponding mouse type
BusMouse	Specify this protocol for the Microsoft and Logitech busmouse.
Logitech	Use this protocol for older Logitech serial mice. Newer Logitech mice use Microsoft or Mouseman protocol.
Microsoft	Use this protocol for Microsoft and other serial mice.
MMSeries	Use this protocol for MMSeries serial mice.
Mouseman	Specify this protocol for the Logitech Mouseman mouse.
MouseSystems	Use this protocol for MouseSystems mice.
PS/2	Specify this protocol for any mouse connected to the PS/2 auxiliary port.
MMHitTab	Use this protocol for the MouseMan HitTablet.
Xqueue	Use this protocol only if the `Keyboard` protocol also is set to `Xqueue`.
OSMouse	This protocol is for SCO UNIX (because XFree86 also works under SCO UNIX, a commercial brand of UNIX).

Other mouse-configuration information

Tip

Another option that you can specify in the `Pointer` section is the way that X handles the third mouse button. Many popular brands of PC mice have only two buttons, but X applications often expect three buttons on a mouse. One option is to click the left and right mouse buttons simultaneously to simulate a middle button. To simulate a middle button click with a simultaneous click of left and right buttons, you have to specify the following line in the `Pointer` section of the `XF86Config` file:

`Emulate3Buttons`

Some three-button mice, such as the Logitech Mouseman, send a simultaneous left- and right-button click when you click the middle button. To alert the X server about this situation, you have to add the following line in the configuration file:

```
ChordMiddle
```

In other words, even if you have a three-button mouse, the mouse may not report three distinct button states. You may have to use the ChordMiddle flag to ensure that the X server handles the middle-button click correctly.

Tip

For Logitech serial mice, you also have to specify the *baud rate* (the rate at which the mouse sends data) and the *sample rate* (how many mouse events occur per second). Following is a typical set of settings:

```
BaudRate 9600
SampleRate 150
```

Two other entries in the Pointer section of the XF86Config file are meant for MouseSystems mice that can operate in two protocol modes. Specify both of the following lines for a MouseSystems mouse:

```
ClearDTR
ClearRTS
```

Mouse use in X

The mouse features prominently in X applications because X is a graphical windowing system. How you use the mouse depends on the application. In Linux, you typically do not have many X applications (I mean applications such as word processing and spreadsheet applications). Typically, you have a window manager, such as fvwm, and one or more xterm windows on your screen. Now that Web browsers such as Mosaic and Netscape are all the rage, you also might have one of these graphical browsers running.

Most graphical applications respond to mouse events such as mouse clicks and double-clicks. The exact response depends on the application that receives the mouse event. You can perform several actions with the mouse. Following are the six basic actions that you would use to interact with a graphical X application:

- *Press* a mouse button by holding the button down without moving the mouse.

- *Release* a mouse button that you previously held down. The release of the button usually initiates some action.

- *Click* a mouse button by quickly pressing and releasing it.

- *Double-click* a mouse button by clicking it twice in rapid succession without moving the mouse.

- *Drag* the mouse pointer by pressing a mouse button and moving the mouse while holding down the button.

- *Move* the mouse pointer by moving the mouse without pressing any button.

The left mouse button commonly is used to indicate a selection. If a graphical interface shows a push button, you would activate that push button by clicking the left mouse button.

The `fvwm` window manager displays a pop-up menu — a different one for each button — when you click a mouse button while the mouse pointer is in the X root window. The frame around each window also belongs to the window manager. Thus, the window manager controls what happens when you click on the window frame by clicking any mouse button. If you click on the upper-right corner of a window frame, for example, `fvwm` displays a menu that allows you to move, resize, iconify, or even destroy the window.

If you have used Microsoft Windows or an Apple Macintosh, you probably are familiar with the "cut-and-paste" operation. You might select some text in one application, cut it, go to another application's window, and paste it there. X also supports the concept of cutting and pasting, but the exact steps depend on the X toolkit used to build an application. Under Motif (one of the popular graphical user interfaces), you cut and paste one way, but the same operation might be different under OPEN LOOK.

The `xterm` application supports cutting and pasting in a very simplistic manner. If you hold down the left mouse button and drag across any text in the `xterm` window, that text becomes the current selection. Then, if you click the middle mouse button in the same or another `xterm` window, that selection is pasted.

device not found **error**

When you start X (using the `startx` command), the X server may fail, displaying a message such as this:

```
device not found (/dev/mouse or /dev/psaux)
```

This message usually means that the device file (`/dev/psaux`, for example) does not exist for the mouse device. The `device not found` error can occur if you specify the wrong kind of mouse when you set up Linux. Suppose that you have a Microsoft mouse that plugs into the PS/2 auxiliary port. In this case, you must specify your mouse type as a PS/2 mouse, *not* as a Microsoft mouse (even though Microsoft may have made the mouse). Remember — what matters is the mouse interface type, not the make and model of the mouse.

device busy **error**

If you get a `device busy` error when you attempt to start X, another program may already be using the mouse device. A potential culprit is the `gpm` program, which allows you to use the mouse in text mode.

If you have a PS/2-style mouse, make sure that you do not run `gpm`. When installing Linux from the companion CD-ROM, if you install the `gpm` package, it adds a line in the `/etc/rc.d/rc.local` file to run `gpm` at startup. If you have a PS/2 mouse and you'll be running X, it's best to not install `gpm`.

If you install `gpm` and you have a PS/2 mouse, edit the `/etc/rc.d/rc.local` file to remove the lines that start `gpm`.

Mouse alternatives

Although I have not discussed other pointing devices explicitly, Linux and XFree86 can access and use other pointing devices, as long as those devices behave like mice.

The new ALPS GlidePoint pointing device, for example, works under Linux and X. All you have to do is set it up as a Microsoft serial mouse.

When you come across other pointing devices, your only problem will be determining whether that pointing device is compatible with any of the mouse types that Linux and X can use.

Many laptops use trackballs in place of mice. Trackballs often are compatible with the PS/2 mouse. Set up such a trackball as a PS/2 mouse, and give it a try.

Summary

Linux works with any keyboard that works under MS-DOS, and you can configure the keyboard for non-English languages. The mouse is not used much in text mode, but the XFree86 X Window System requires a mouse to run. XFree86 supports most major mouse types. This chapter describes how to use and configure the keyboard and mouse in Linux and X. By reading this chapter, you learn the following:

▶ The keyboard has two configurable parameters: the repeat delay (how long a wait occurs before a key starts repeating) and the repeat rate (how fast a key repeats when it is held down). You can set these parameters with the `kbdrate` program in Linux.

▶ To handle non-English languages, you have to change the keyboard mapping — the way that a physical key is interpreted as a character in an alphabet. You also have to make various applications accept and display the character. Many foreign languages use accents that the standard keyboard mapping ignores. You can, however, use the `loadkeys` program in text mode and `xmodmap` in X to change the keyboard mapping.

▶ The mouse is a necessity when you want to run XFree86, the X Window System for Linux. XFree86 supports most popular types of mouse interfaces, such as serial port, busmouse, and PS/2 auxiliary port. You identify the mouse interface by a device such as `/dev/psaux` for the PS/2 port and `/dev/ttyS0` for the COM1 serial port.

▶ *Mouse protocol* refers to formatting of mouse data (the way that the mouse reports mouse movements and button states). XFree86 supports several common mouse protocols from busmouse, PS/2-style, Microsoft, and Logitech mice.

▶ In the XFree86 configuration file, `/etc/XF86Config`, you have to provide information about the keyboard and the mouse in the `Keyboard` and `Pointer` sections, respectively.

Chapter 14
Printers

In This Chapter

- Printing from the user's point of view
- Spooling: The concept of a print queue
- Setting up the printing environment in Linux
- Understanding printing filters
- Printing PostScript files with Ghostscript
- Configuring a new printer in Linux

When you set up Linux on a PC, the printer probably is the last thing on your mind. First, you want to get Linux running on the PC. Then you may decide to make the modem work to dial up your office system or your Internet Service Provider. When you begin to depend more on Linux, however, you'll want to print text or PostScript files that you get from the network, and that's when you want to know how to make the printer work with Linux.

As you might guess, physically connecting a printer to the PC's parallel port is straightforward; that part does not depend on the operating system. The software setup for printing is the part that takes some effort. Accordingly, this chapter provides information on setting up the printing environment in Linux.

The PC, the Printer, and Linux

PCs typically come with one parallel port and two serial ports. The parallel port is so named because it can transfer 8 bits of data in parallel. The serial port, however, has to send data in bit-oriented serial manner. For example, an 8-bit byte is transferred as a sequence of 8 bits that go through the serial port one after another. The upshot is that the parallel port is much faster than the serial port.

Although a printer can connect to the PC through either the serial port or the parallel port, most users connect the printer to the PC's parallel port.

Printer device name

In MS-DOS, the first parallel port is called LPT1; the second one is LPT2. The serial ports are COM1 and COM2.

In Linux, the parallel ports have device names just like other devices, such as /dev/ttyS0 for the PC's first serial port or /dev/hda for the first IDE disk. The device names /dev/lp0 and /dev/lp1 refer to the first and second parallel ports, respectively.

Secret

Watch out, though — just because your PC has only one parallel port does not mean that Linux will use /dev/lp0 as the device name for that parallel port. When Linux boots, it displays information about the parallel port that it detects. Check the boot messages with dmesg | more to see what parallel-port device Linux detects. On my PC, which has a single parallel port, the boot message includes the following:

```
lp1 at 0x0378, using polling driver
```

Thus, for my Linux PC, the parallel port device is /dev/lp1.

Table 14-1 lists the parallel-port device names and device numbers in Linux:

Table 14-1	Parallel-port device names and numbers		
I/O address	Device name	Major device number	Minor device number
0x3bc	/dev/lp0	6	0
0x378	/dev/lp1	6	1
0x278	/dev/lp2	6	2

On most PCs, the LPT1 port uses the I/O address 0x378. Thus, the parallel port's device name is /dev/lp1, which is the device name that you'll use for a printer connected to that parallel port.

Spooling and print jobs

You may already be familiar with the concept of spooling from printing under Microsoft Windows. *Spooling* refers to the capability to print in the background. When you print from a word processor in Windows, for example, the output first goes to a file on the disk. Then, while you continue working with the word processor, a background process sends that output to the printer.

Note

The Linux printing environment, which consists of several programs that I'll describe later in this chapter, also supports spooling. The term *spool directory* refers to the directory that contains output files intended for the printer.

Note

The term *print job* refers to what you print with a single print command. The printing environment queues print jobs by storing them in the spool directory. A background process then can periodically send the print jobs from the spool directory to the printer.

Chapter 14: Printers

The Linux printing environment evolved from the printing facilities of the Berkeley Software Distribution (BSD) UNIX. As you become more knowledgeable about UNIX (or if you are a UNIX old-timer), you may find this bit of information to be useful, because it tells you the printing commands that you can use in Linux. If you don't know anything about BSD UNIX, don't worry; I explain the printing commands in the following section.

User's View of Printing in Linux

Before I describe how to set up your Linux system for printing, I'll provide an overview of the basic printing commands. You may not be able to try the printing commands until you actually set up the printing environment, but this section should give you a feel for how you would print in Linux (or in any BSD UNIX system, for that matter).

Print with `lpr`

In Linux, you use the `lpr` command to queue a print job. To print the file `rfc1789.txt`, you would type the following:

```
lpr rfc1789.txt
```

The `lpr` command copies the `rfc1789.txt` file to a spool directory (located in the `/var/spool` directory). Periodically, a print program known as `lpd` sends that file from the spool directory to the printer.

You can embellish that simple `lpr` command with some options. A common option is to indicate the type of printer with `-P`. If you have a Hewlett-Packard LaserJet printer named `hplj` (later in the "Learning about `/etc/printcap`" section, you'll see that the printer name appears in the `/etc/printcap` file), you print with the following command:

```
lpr -Phplj rfc1789.txt
```

In addition to the `-P` option of `lpr`, you can specify the default printer through the `PRINTER` environment variable. If your printer's name is `hplj`, you would use the following command to ensure that `lpr` sends all print jobs to the `hplj` printer:

```
PRINTER=hplj; export PRINTER
```

You may want to put the environment definition in the default `login` script for Bash. Just add a line like this to `/etc/profile`:

```
export PRINTER=hplj
```

This example assumes that your system's printer is named `hplj`; you should replace that name with whatever name you assign to your system's printer (you learn how to name a printer in the "Printer name" section).

Because the default `login` script — `/etc/profile` — is common to all `login`s that use the Bash shell, defining the `PRINTER` environment variable in `/etc/profile` saves everyone the trouble of having to specify the printer explicitly.

Check print queue with `lpq`

When `lpr` queues a print job, it does not print any messages. If you mistakenly print a large file and want to stop the print job before you waste too much paper, you have to use the `lpq` command to look at the current print jobs. Following is a typical listing of print jobs that you get with `lpq`:

```
lpq
lp is ready and printing
Rank    Owner   Job Files                   Total Size
active  naba     1  rfc1789.txt               14186 bytes
1st     leha     2  rfc1717.txt               46264 bytes
```

The word `active` in the Rank column indicates the job that's currently printing. The rest of the entries show jobs in the order in which they'll be printed. If you do not see your print job listed, it has finished printing.

Cancel print job with `lprm`

To remove a job from the print queue, use the `lprm` command. To stop print job number 1, you would type the following:

```
lprm 1
dfA001Aa00235 dequeued
cfA001Aa00235 dequeued
```

Tip

If you are in a hurry and want to cancel all print jobs that you have submitted so far, use `lprm` with a minus sign as the argument, as follows:

```
lprm -
```

See printer status with `lpc status`

To see the names of printers that are connected to your system, use the `lpc status` command. On a typical system, the `lpc status` command might show the following:

```
lpc status
lp:
    queuing is enabled
    printing is enabled
    no entries
    no daemon present
```

This sample output shows the status of a printer named `lp` — the default printer name used by print commands such as `lpr`, `lpq`, and `lprm` when you do not explicitly specify any printer name.

Wizard

The word `daemon` in the last line of the status message refers to the background process (called `lpd`) that takes care of the actual printing. In UNIX, the term *daemon* is used for background processes that monitor and perform many critical system functions. Typically, a daemon is started when the system boots, and the daemon processes run as long as the system is up. Most daemons have the capability to restart copies of themselves to handle specific tasks. Although this is not a rule, most daemons have names that end with `d`, such as `crond`, `syslogd`, `klogd`, `inetd`, `lpd` (that's the printer daemon), `rpc.mountd`, and `rpc.nfsd`.

Secret

You should not get worried about the fact that `lpc status` reports no daemon present for a printer; the daemon that controls a specific printer's queue goes away when the spool directory is empty. But there always is a master copy of the printer daemon, `lpd`, that monitors the spool directories. When you print anything on a specific printer with the `lpr` command, the master copy of `lpd` creates a new `lpd` process to take care of that printer's queue.

Fancy printing

So far, I've shown you the commands for sending a file to the printer. If you have a PostScript printer, you can send it a PostScript file to produce nicely formatted output.

Tip

If you want to print a text file with some additional formatting, such as a header and page number on each page, you can use the `pr` command. The idea is to use `pr` to format the text file and then send that output to `lpr`. Following is an example:

```
pr -h"Web Server Access Statistics" -l60 webstat.txt | lpr
```

This command line prints the file `webstat.txt` with the text `Web Server Access Statistics` added to the top of each page. The `-l60` option (lower-case L followed by 60) sets the length of each page to 60 lines.

Note

To do other types of typesetting, you can use text-processing programs such as TeX (which comes with Linux on this book's CD-ROM). Chapter 24 describes these typesetting systems and explains how to print typeset pages.

Nowadays, PostScript is a common format for documentation files for software, especially software that you download from the Internet. If you have PostScript files, you can preview and print them with the Ghostview program. (To try the program, type **ghostview** in an `xterm` window. You need the X Window System to run Ghostview.)

Behind-the-Scenes View of Printing

In Linux, the user's view of printing is based on the basic printing commands: `lpr`, `lpq`, `lprm`, and `lpc status`. You need a bit more information to understand how printing works behind the scenes. Like so many things in Linux, support for printing is all a matter of having the right files in the right places. You'll relate to this comment better after you have configured Linux for networking and set up dial-in modems, for example. In each case, you have to make sure that several configuration files appear in the correct places. The printing environment has the same need: configuration files that specify how printing occurs.

If you have experience with MS-DOS, you may have printed files by simply copying them to the printer port (LPT1, for example). You might think that a similar approach might be good enough for Linux. As you will see in the next section, such a brute force approach of copying a file to the physical printer port is not appropriate for a multiuser system like Linux. What you need is a way to queue print jobs and have a separate printing process take care of the printing.

Copying to printer: brute-force printing

If you have a printer connected to the `/dev/lp1` parallel port (you can find this information from the boot messages), you can print a text file simply by sending the file to the printer with the following command:

```
cat webstat.txt > /dev/lp1
```

This command would indeed produce a printout of the file `webstat.txt`, provided that the following conditions are true:

- You have to be logged in as `root` (Linux allows only `root` and certain processes direct access to physical devices, such as printers).
- The printer must be connected to the `/dev/lp1` port, powered up, and online.

The problem with copying a file directly to the printer device is that the command will complete only when the copying (which, in this case, is equivalent to printing) is done. For a large file, this process could take a while. In fact, if the printer is not turned on, the command will appear to hang (if this happens, just press Ctrl-C to abort the command).

Spooling: a better way to print

On a multitasking and multiuser system such as Linux, a better way to print is to *spool* the data: send the output to a file and then have a separate process send the output to the printer. That way, you can go on with your work while the printing takes place in the background. Also, if your system has more than one user, everyone can print on the same printer without worrying about whether the printer is available; the background printing process can take care of all the details.

That's how the Linux printing environment works. A directory, or *spool area*, is set up for each printer. Any data meant for a printer is stored in that printer's spool area, one file per print job. A background process called lpd — the printer daemon — constantly checks the spool area for new files. Whenever lpd finds a new file, it sends the file to the printer.

That spool area serves as the queue for the print jobs, each of which is a file in the spool directory.

Note

Although you typically would have only one printer connected to your PC, one strength of the Linux printing system (and of BSD UNIX printing) is the capability to print on a printer that's connected to another system on a network. Printing to such a remote printer is handled in the same fashion as printing to a local printer; a spool directory exists for the remote printer. The lpd program checks the remote printer's spool directory and sends any waiting files to that printer.

As explained earlier, the user-level command for spooling a file is lpr. When lpr runs, it copies the data for the printer to a file in the spool directory. Other user-level commands for working with print queues are lpq, lprm, and lpc. As this section describes, the program that completes the Linux printing environment is the printer daemon: lpd.

In addition to the five programs lpd, lpr, lpq, lprm, and lpc, a file named /etc/printcap plays a crucial role in the Linux printing environment.

Spooling with a symbolic link

When you use the lpr command to spool a file for printing, lpr copies that file to the spool directory. This situation can be a problem when you print a large file. The copying operation can take some time, and you will need disk space in the spool directory (in /usr/spool). If you are low on disk space, especially in the partition that contains the /usr directory tree, you may want to avoid the copy operation.

Tip

The lpr command provides the -s option, which sets up a symbolic link in the spool directory and makes the link refer to the file that you want to print. To print a large file, you could use lpr this way:

`lpr -s files.index`

Instead of copying files.index to the spool directory, lpr creates a symbolic link to that file (the symbolic link will be in the spool directory). You can create a symbolic link quickly, and the link uses almost no disk space compared with what the original file might use.

Caution

When you use the lpr -s command to spool a file by using a symbolic link, you have to watch out for an important side effect: because the symbolic link (in the spool directory) is only a reference to the actual file, you cannot edit or delete the original file until the printing is done.

Also, the `-s` option only stops `lpr` from copying the data file to the spool directory of the local system. If you submit a job for a remote printer, the data file is copied to the remote system's spool directory regardless of the `-s` option.

Controlling printer with `lpc`

All users can use the `lpc status` command to check the status of printers. If you log in as `root`, you can use `lpc` to perform many more printer-control functions, such as starting and stopping spooling, enabling and disabling printers, and rearranging the order of print jobs. You can use the second argument to `lpc` to perform a specific task or run `lpc` in interactive mode.

To run `lpc` in interactive mode, type **lpc** at the shell prompt. At the `lpc>` prompt, type **help** to see a list of commands that `lpc` understands. To get more help on a command, type **help** *command-name* (*command-name* should be replaced with one of the `lpc` commands). Following is a sample session with `lpc`:

```
lpc
lpc> help
Commands may be abbreviated. Commands are:

abort    enable   disable  help     restart  status   topq     ?
clean    exit     down     quit     start    stop     up
lpc> help status
status          show status of daemon and queue
lpc> q
```

Tip

For a specific operation, you can simply use the single-line syntax with `lpc` followed by one of the `lpc` commands and any necessary arguments. To stop the print-spooling daemon (`lpd`), move print job 39 to the top of the queue, and start spooling again, you would use the following commands (the example assumes that the printer's name is `hplj`):

```
lpc stop hplj
lpc topq 39
lpc start hplj
```

Tip

Table 14-2 lists the `lpc` commands that anyone can use.

Table 14-2	`lpc` commands that anyone can use
Command	**Description**
restart *printer-name*	Tries to restart the printer daemon (`lpd`). A user might try this command if the printer appears to be fine but nothing is printed, even though `lpq` shows jobs waiting in the spool area. Use `all` as the printer name if you want to restart all printers.
status *printer-name*	Displays the status of the specified printer. If you do not provide a printer name, this command shows the status of the printer named `lp` — the default printer.

Chapter 14: Printers **415**

Command	Description
`help command-name`	Provides help information on a specific `lpc` command.
`exit`	Exit `lpc` (use in interactive mode only).
`quit`	Exit `lpc` (use in interactive mode only).

Table 14-3 lists the `lpc` commands that only `root` can use.

Table 14-3   `lpc` **commands that only** `root` **can use**

Command	Description
`abort printer-name`	Behaves like `stop` but does not allow the current job to complete. When printing is restarted, the current job prints again.
`clean printer-name`	Removes all jobs, including the active job, from the printer's queue.
`disable printer-name`	Disables spooling of print jobs to a specified printer. When spooling is disabled, users can no longer use `lpr` to print.
`down printer-name message`	Disables spooling and stops the printer daemon from printing the spooled print jobs (combines the actions of `disable` and `stop`). The *message* will be displayed when users run the `lpq` command.
`enable printer-name`	Enables spooling of print jobs to a specified printer.
`start printer-name`	Enables the printer daemon so that it can begin printing any jobs in that printer's spool directory.
`stop printer-name`	Waits for the current print job to complete and then disables the printer daemon so that it stops printing the jobs in that printer's spool directory. When the printing is stopped, users can continue to issue the `lpr` command to print, but the actual output does not appear until the printer daemon is started with the `start` command.
`topq printer-name job-id`	Moves the specified print job to the beginning of the printer's queue. If you use a user name in place of *job-id*, all jobs that belong to that user are moved to the beginning of the queue.
`up printer-name`	Reverses the action of the `down` command, enables spooling, and starts the printer daemon (combines the actions of `enable` and `start`).

Tracing a print request from `lpr` to printer

A good way to understand the Linux printing environment is to trace a print request from the `lpr` command all the way to the actual output at the printer. Two programs, `lpr` and `lpd`, complete the printing process, as shown in Figure 14-1.

As Figure 14-1 shows, the two steps of the printing process are the following:

1. The `lpr` command takes the data to be sent to the printer and puts it in a file in the spool directory.

2. The `lpd` program finds the file in the spool directory and sends the file to the printer.

Both the `lpr` and `lpd` programs consult the `/etc/printcap` file for information about the printer.

`lpr` spools print jobs

The `lpr` program is the only program in Linux that queues print jobs. All other programs that need to print files do so by sending the data to `lpr` — usually with the shell's pipe mechanism, where you concatenate two commands with a vertical bar (|).

Each step involves many more details, of course. When `lpr` runs, it gathers information about the print job from three sources:

- Command-line options used with the `lpr` command
- Environment variables, such as PRINTER, that identify the printer where the output is to appear
- System defaults that provide information that `lpr` needs, such as the default printer name (`lp`)

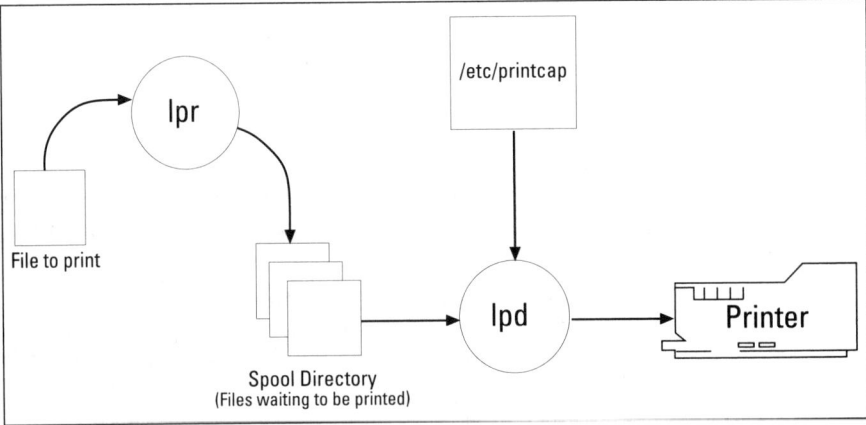

Figure 14-1: The printing process in Linux.

After lpr determines the destination printer's name, it looks up that printer in the system's printer database, /etc/printcap. Assuming that the printer has an entry in the /etc/printcap file, a field in that entry should tell lpr the name of the spool directory for that printer. Typically, the spool directory is /usr/spool/printername, but the directory name can be something else (although it's always in /usr/spool).

The lpr program creates two files in the spool directory:

- A file with a name that starts with cf, followed by an identifier (ID) for that print job. This file contains control information about the print job — information such as who submitted the job.

- A file that contains the actual data to be printed. This file's name starts with df, followed by the print job's number.

After lpr spools the files, it sends a signal to the lpd process. This signal tells lpd that a print job is waiting in a specific spool directory.

lpd **sends print jobs to printer**

The lpd process takes care of the actual printing — the act of sending a file to the printer. A copy of lpd is always running in the system, and you can check for its existence with the following command:

```
ps -ax | grep lpd
  48 ? S    0:00 /usr/sbin/lpd
```

If you don't see an lpd process running, you cannot use the Linux printing environment. You have to log in as root and type **/usr/sbin/lpd** to start the printer daemon.

Another characteristic of lpd is the fact that it creates copies of itself to handle print jobs in specific print queues.

After lpd receives a signal that there is a print job for a specific printer, it checks the /etc/printcap file to determine whether the specified printer is on your system or on another system on the network (remote printer). For a remote printer, your system's lpd establishes a link to the remote system's lpd, transfers both the control and data files to the remote system, and deletes those files from your system's spool directory.

If the printer is indeed connected to your system, lpd checks to see whether a copy of the printer daemon (also named lpd) is already running for that printer's queue. If not, lpd makes a copy of itself and sets up that copy to process print jobs in that printer's queue. The lpd for a specific printer's queue sends all waiting print jobs to the printer, one at a time.

Knowing the spool directory

The *spool directory* is where data destined for a printer accumulates in separate files before the lpd printer daemon sends those files to the printer. If you installed Slackware Linux from the companion CD-ROM, your system should have the spool directories in /usr/spool (which is a symbolic link to /var/spool).

By convention, the /usr/spool directory contains queues for various UNIX programs. Mail and news programs, for example, have their spool directories here.

Each type of printer should have its own spool directory. You'll find it helpful to name each spool directory with the printer's name as it appears in the /etc/printcap file (described in the following section). Thus, if you have an HP LaserJet printer named hplj, the spool directory will be /usr/spool/hplj.

Secret

Incidentally, a single printer may go by two different names. An HP LaserJet 4M printer, for example, might be used as a printer that understands HP's Printer Control Language (PCL) or PostScript. You might use printer names pcl and ps for the two ways in which you may access the LaserJet 4M printer. All these printer names appear in the /etc/printcap file, described in the following section.

Tip

Even remote printers need a spool directory on your system, because lpr first copies the files to the spool directory and then lpd sends those files to the remote printer.

Each printer's spool directory contains two files:

- The lock file, which contains information about the active job and ensures that only one lpd process prints the contents of this spool directory. The lpd process manipulates the permission settings of the lock file to enable or disable spooling for this printer.

- The status file, which contains a one-line message that describes the printer's state. The lpq command displays the message from the status file. You can change this message when you take down the printer with the lpc down command.

When you manually set up a new printer, you'll have to create a spool directory for the printer and set its permission appropriately. Later, the "Printer Setup and Configuration" section covers the printer setup and configuration steps in detail.

Learning about /etc/printcap

The /etc/printcap file is at the heart of Linux's printing environment. This text file (with cryptic syntax) describes the printer capabilities for various printers. The file must contain information about every printer that you can access from your system (including printers that are on the same network as your PC). No harm is done if the /etc/printcap file contains descriptions of printers that you do not actually have; the lpr and lpd programs consult the /etc/printcap file only to look up information for a specified printer.

Basic structure of /etc/printcap

The /etc/printcap file is modeled after the /etc/termcap file, which describes the capabilities of various types of terminals. To see the syntax of entries in /etc/printcap, you should start with an example. Following is a sample entry for an HP LaserJet printer:

```
# HP Laserjet printer
lp|hplj|Lasertjet-ADDL|HP Laserjet 4M in Advanced Development Lab:\
  :lp=/dev/lp1:\
  :sd=/usr/spool/lp1:\
  :mx#0:\
  :if=/usr/spool/lp1/hplj-if.pl:\
  :lf=/usr/spool/lp1/hplj-log:\
  :sh:
```

This example is a reasonably readable layout of an entry in the /etc/printcap file. The entry says the following things:

- Send the print job to printer device named /dev/lp1 (lp field).
- Store queued print jobs in the /usr/spool/lp1 directory (sd field).
- Do not limit the size of print jobs (mx field).
- Pass the print file through the filter (a command that reads from standard input and generates output on the standard output) named /usr/spool/lp1/hplj-if.pl (if field)
- Log errors in the file named /usr/spool/lp1/hplj-log, which must already exist for the error logging to work (lf field)
- Suppress headers — a separator page between print jobs (sh field)

Notice that you need a backslash (\) at the end of each line, because the entire entry is supposed to be a single line.

Caution

Make sure that you do not have any extra space after the backslash character at the end of a line. If a space or tab character appears after the backslash, the printing programs (lpr, lpd, and lpc) will not consider the following line to be a continuation. This error may cause printing to fail for a printer (even though the entry may look fine when you examine the /etc/printcap file).

As is true of most configuration files in Linux, the comment lines in /etc/printcap start with a pound-sign character (#).

Printer name

The first field of an entry (up to the first colon) lists the name of the printer and its aliases. Typically, each printer has three names:

- A short name with at most four characters (such as hplj)
- A longer name that indicates the printer's owner (such as LaserJet-ADDL)
- A descriptive name that should fully identify the printer to the users on your system (for example, HP LaserJet 4M in Advanced Development Lab)

Tip

If you print something with `lpr` without specifying a printer, that print job automatically goes to the system's default printer, named `lp`. Therefore, you should provide `lp` as the first name for the default printer.

Field types

After the names, the printer's entry has a sequence of fields. If you examine the sample entry, you notice that the fields are separated by colons (:). There are three types of fields:

- *String fields*, such as `lp` (which specify the printer's device name), are specified by the following syntax:

  `:field_name=string:`

  You can embed special characters in the string by using the backslash notation from the C programming language. To specify the form-feed character (which might be used to eject a page on the printer), you would use **\f**.

- *Number fields*, such as `mx` (which specify the size of print-job files), are specified as follows:

  `:field_name#number:`

- *Boolean fields*, such as `sh` (which suppress printing of a header page separating consecutive print jobs), are true when they appear in the printer's entry; otherwise, they are false.

Each field has a specific meaning. Through these fields, you control how output appears on the printer (for example, should the data file be processed by any intermediate program before output goes to the printer) and how errors are logged. The following sections further describe the fields in `/etc/printcap`.

Although the contents of `/etc/printcap` appear cryptic at first, when you know the basic format and the meaning of the various fields, you'll be able to understand and edit the file easily.

Tip

Subsequent sections provide all the information that you need to understand and add a new entry to the `/etc/printcap` file. If you need to look up information about the fields in the `/etc/printcap` file, you can do so easily with the following command:

`man printcap`

Fields in `printcap` entries

Before you learn about specific `printcap` (I'll refer to the `/etc/printcap` file with the generic name `printcap`) fields, consult Table 14-4, which provides an alphabetic list of the `printcap` fields. The Field column shows the two-character name of a field. The Type column shows the type of the field (string, number, or Boolean). The Default column shows the value assumed by `lpr` and `lpd` when the `printcap` entry does not specify this field. The Description column briefly describes the field.

Table 14-4   Alphabetic list of `printcap` fields

Field	Type	Default	Description
af	string	NULL	Name of accounting file
br	number	none	Baud rate (applies only if the lp field specifies a serial-port device)
cf	string	NULL	Name of cifplot data filter
df	string	NULL	Name of TeX data filter (DVI format)
fc	number	0	Flag bits to clear (applies only if the lp field specifies a serial-port device)
ff	string	\f (form feed)	String to send for a form feed
fo	Boolean	false	If specified, prints a form feed when device is opened
fs	number	0	Flag bits to set (applies only if the lp field specifies a serial port device)
gf	string	NULL	Name of graph data filter
hl	Boolean	false	If specified and if sh is not specified, prints the burst header page last (the *burst header page* separates one print job from another)
ic	Boolean	false	If specified, printer driver (identified by lp) supports control command to indent printout
if	string	NULL	Name of text filter, which is called once for each print job (you can use this to interpret the file and convert it to a format that is suitable for your printer)
lf	string	/dev/console	Name of file where errors are logged
lo	string	lock	Name of lock file
lp	string	/dev/lp	Device name to open to send output to printer
mx	number	1000	Maximum size of the print-job file (in KB); a value of 0 means unlimited size
nf	string	NULL	Name of ditroff (device-independent troff) data filter
of	string	NULL	Name of output-filtering program (called only if the if field is not specified and called only once)

(continued)

Table 14-4 *(continued)*

Field	Type	Default	Description
pc	number	200	Price per foot or page, in hundredths of cents
pl	number	66	Number of lines per page
pw	number	132	Page width, in number of characters
px	number	0	Page width in pixels (horizontal)
py	number	0	Page length in pixels (vertical)
rf	string	NULL	Name of filter for printing FORTRAN-style text files
rg	string	NULL	Restricted group; only members of listed groups can access the printer
rm	string	NULL	Name of system for remote printer
rp	string	lp	Remote printer name
rs	Boolean	false	If true, prints jobs submitted (from remote systems) by only those users with accounts on local system
rw	Boolean	false	If specified, opens the printer device for reading and writing
sb	Boolean	false	If specified, prints short banner (one line only)
sc	Boolean	false	If specified, does not print multiple copies
sd	string	/var/spool/lpd	Name of spool directory
sf	Boolean	false	If specified, does not print form feeds
sh	Boolean	false	If specified, does not print the burst page header
st	string	status	Name of status file
tf	string	NULL	Name of `troff` (typesetter) data filter
tr	string	NULL	Trailer string to print when the printer queues is emptied
vf	string	NULL	Name of raster image filter

As Table 14-4 shows, you can specify more than 35 fields for each `printcap` entry. For a typical entry in the `/etc/printcap` file, however, you have to specify only a few fields. The following nine are the most commonly used `printcap` fields:

- `if`: a string that specifies the input-filter name

- lf: a string that specifies the file where errors for this printer are logged
- lp: a string that specifies the device name for the printer (such as /dev/lp1)
- mx: a number that specifies the maximum allowable size (in 1K blocks) of a print file
- rm: a string that specifies the name of a remote computer
- rp: a string that specifies the name of a remote printer
- sd: a string that specifies the name of the spool directory for this printer
- sf: a Boolean that suppresses the form feed at the end of each job
- sh: a Boolean that suppresses the burst header page that appears between jobs

The next few sections further explain a few of these fields.

Input-filter field

The *input filter* is a shell script of an executable program that reads the print data from the standard input (stdin) and writes output to the standard output (stdout). The idea of the input filter is that it enables you to process a text file and convert it to a format that your printer needs.

The print daemon calls the specified input filter once for each print job. Suppose that you specified the if field this way:

```
:if=/usr/spool/lp1/hplj-if.pl:
```

If the file /usr/spool/lp1/hplj-if.pl is a Perl script, lpd invokes the filter with the following command line:

```
/usr/spool/lp1/hplj-if.pl [-c] -wwidth -llength -iindent -n login -h host acct-file
```

The brackets around the -c option indicate that it's optional. The -c option is used only if the user invoked the lpr command with a -l option (meaning pass all characters unchanged to the printer). Thus, if you were writing the input filter, you would assume the arguments to be the following:

Argument	Description
-c	Pass control characters literally to the printer (if the first argument is -c, the filter should simply copy the standard input to the standard output)
-wwidth	Page width, in number of characters per line (from the pw field in the printcap file)
-llength	Page length, in number of lines per page (from the pl field in the printcap file)
-iindent	Indent the output by printing indent number of blank spaces in front of each line

(continued)

Argument	Description
`-n login`	`login` name of the user who submitted the print job
`-h host`	Name of system where the user submitted the print job
`acct-file`	Name of accounting file from the `af` field in `printcap`

You'll see the use of input filters in the "How to avoid the staircase effect" section that describes how to avoid a "staircase" pattern when you print UNIX text files on a PC printer, which expects a carriage return–line feed pair at the end of each line.

Printer device

The printer-device field, `lp`, should specify the Linux device name for the port to which you connected the printer. For a local printer on the PC's parallel port, this field is `/dev/lp1` (or `/dev/lp0` on some older systems).

If your printer is on a serial port, specify the serial port's device name — `/dev/ttyS0` for COM1 and `/dev/ttyS1` for COM2 — as the string in the `lp` field.

Secret

When you set up a `printcap` entry for a remote printer, specify an empty `lp` field as follows:

`:lp=:`

Then, of course, you must specify the `rm` and `rp` fields, which specify the host name and the printer name for the remote printer; otherwise, `lpd` displays an error message, because it cannot find the printer device.

Secret

Another subtle use of the `lp` field is to set it to `/dev/null` — the universal "bit bucket" (nothing happens when data is sent to the `null` device). When you try a new `printcap` entry to see whether everything works, and you don't want to waste paper, just set the `lp` field of that `printcap` entry this way:

`:lp=/dev/null:`

Log file

The log-file field, `lf`, specifies the file to which `lpd` sends error messages. If you don't specify any file, error messages go to the console. Typically, you might specify a log file in the spool directory for the printer, as follows:

`:lf=/usr/spool/lp1/hplj-log:`

You can specify any file you want, but the specified file must exist; if it does not, `lpd` will not log errors.

Suppress header and form feed

Note

In the terminology of the Linux printing environment, the *burst header page* or *banner page* refers to a page that precedes a print job. By default, `lpd` generates a banner page and also sends a form feed to make sure that every print job starts on a new page.

You probably will not use header pages much if you're the only user of your Linux system. Also, most text-processing packages, such as TeX or `troff` (described in Chapter 24), already generate a form feed at the end of all the pages. Thus, the form feed sent by `lpd` causes an extra blank page, which is wasteful.

The two Boolean options `sh` and `sf` turn off the header page and form feed, respectively. All you have to do is place the two fields in the `printcap` entry, as follows:

```
:sh:\
:sf:
```

Maximum size of print job

You can use the `mx` field to limit the size of the print job. The size refers to the number of bytes in the spooled file. Before the advent of graphics and laser printers, this limit may have made sense. Nowadays, it's better not to specify this limit, because graphics files can turn out to be huge, even though the output may be only a few pages. To make sure that the size of spool files is limited only by available disk space, specify zero as the value of the `mx` field, as follows:

```
:mx#0:
```

If you want to make sure that spool files do not take up all your available disk space, put a file named `minfree` in the printer's spool directory (specified by the `sd` field). In the `minfree` file, specify the number of disk blocks (1K per block) that must be available for `lpr` to write spooled data in the spool directory.

Multiple `printcap` entries for one printer

As you begin to understand the `printcap` entries, you'll see that an entry specifies various processing options for the data that goes to the physical printer. If a printer can handle both PostScript and HP's Printer Control Language (PCL), for example, you can have two separate `printcap` entries: one for PostScript output and the other for PCL. Programs that generate PostScript could use the PostScript printer name, whereas those that "speak" PCL can send the output to the PCL printer.

Printer Setup and Configuration

After you install Linux from the companion CD-ROM, the installed kernel should already include support for parallel and serial ports. When you configure the kernel with the `make config` command (as explained in Chapter 2), you have to answer yes to the following question to include support for a parallel printer:

```
Parallel printer support (CONFIG_PRINTER) [y]
```

Apart from this, you do not have to do much with the kernel for printing. Where you have to spend some effort is in preparing the `printcap` entry for your printer.

A good way to learn to prepare a `printcap` entry is to try a sample entry.

A `printcap` template

In this section, I'll write a `printcap` entry for a printer named `sample`. Because the `/usr/spool/lp1` directory already exists, I decide to use that directory as the spool directory. To test the `printcap` entry without actually sending output to any printer, I'll use `/dev/null` as the printer device name and specify an input filter that copies the input data to a file.

With these assumptions, I wrote the following `printcap` entry and added it to the `/etc/printcap` file:

```
# A sample printcap template
sample|sample-printer|A sample printer that prints to a file:\
    :sd=/usr/spool/lp1:\
    :lp=/dev/null:\
    :if=/usr/spool/lp1/sample-if.tcl:\
    :lf=/usr/spool/lp1/sample-log:\
    :mx#0:\
    :sh:\
    :sf:
```

For error logging, I created the `/usr/spool/lp1/sample-log` file with the following commands (while I was logged in as `root`):

```
cd /usr/spool/lp1
touch sample-log
chgrp lp sample-log
chmod ug=rw,o=r sample-log
```

Next, I prepare the input filter, `/usr/spool/lp1/sample-if.tcl`. As you may have guessed from the filename, I wrote the input filter in Tcl. You can write the filter as a shell script or in Perl — whatever language you like. In fact, you can write the filter in C or C++. If you write the filter in C or C++, of course, you have to compile and link to create the executable file, the name of which is what you must specify in the `if` field of the `printcap` entry.

Following is the Tcl script file that serves as the input filter for the sample printer:

```
#!/usr/bin/tcl
#
# Sample input filter
#!/usr/bin/tcl
#
# Sample input filter
#
# Place in printer's spool directory and make it
# executable by world
# The filter is invoked with the following command line:
#
# <filter> [-c] -wWidth -lLength -iIndent -n Login -h Host AcctFile

# Open the file /tmp/sample.out
set outfile [open /tmp/sample.out w]
```

```
puts $outfile "----------------------------------------"
flush $outfile
exec date >@ $outfile
puts $outfile "----------------------------------------"

# Read from stdin and write to outfile

while { [gets stdin line] != -1} {
  puts $outfile $line
}

close $outfile
```

This filter simply writes the standard input to the file /tmp/sample.out, adding a header that shows the date and time of printing. Because the device name for the sample printcap entry is set to /dev/null, the /tmp/sample.out file will be the only proof that printing worked.

Notice that in a real input filter, the script would copy standard input to standard output, performing any necessary conversions (such as inserting extra characters on each line or indenting a line by a specified number of blank spaces).

To see the printcap entry for the sample printer in action, try the following command:

```
ls -l /usr/spool/lp1 | lpr -Psample
```

This command sends the directory listing of the /usr/spool/lp1 directory to lpr. The lpr command then spools that listing for printing on the sample printer (because of the -Psample option). After the print job is spooled, the lpd daemon invokes the input filter for the printer named sample. That filter (/usr/spool/lp1/sample-if.tcl), in turn, copies the directory listing to the /tmp/sample.out file.

To see whether everything worked, check the contents of the /tmp/sample.out file, as follows:

```
cat /tmp/sample.out
----------------------------------------
Wed Oct 4 21:53:18 EDT 1995
----------------------------------------
total 3
-rw-r--r--  1 root   lp       19 Oct 4 21:31 lock
-rwxr-xr-x  1 root   lp      657 Oct 4 21:26 sample-if.tcl*
-rw-rw-r--  1 root   lp        0 Oct 4 21:13 sample-log
-rw-rw-r--  1 root   root     29 Oct 4 21:31 status
```

As the output of the cat command shows, the /tmp/sample.out file appears to contain the expected output: the listing of the /usr/spool/lp1 directory, with a date stamp as the header.

Local-printer setup

The previous sections showed you various elements of the Linux printing environment, including a sample `printcap` entry and an input filter. With the information from the previous sections, you should be able to set up a new printer on your Linux PC. To set up a printer that is connected to your PC's `/dev/lp1` port, follow these steps:

1. Log in as `root`, because you need superuser privileges to complete the following steps.

Secret

2. Check to see that the printer daemon, `lpd`, is running. Use the command `ps -ax | grep lpd`, and see whether an `lpd` process is reported. If you installed Linux from this book's companion disk, the `lpd` daemon should be running on your system. The script file `/etc/rc.d/rc.M` starts the `lpd` program during boot.

3. Check to see whether the printing programs — `lpr`, `lpq`, `lprm`, and `lpc` — are in your system. These programs should be in the `/usr/bin` directory.

4. Create a spool directory for the new printer, or simply use `/usr/spool/lp1`, which should already exist in your system.

5. Open the `/etc/printcap` file, and add the `printcap` entry named `sample`, shown in the preceding section. Change the name (`sample`) to your printer's name (pick a short name that you can remember easily). Change the device name from `/dev/null` to `/dev/lp1` (your system's parallel port). Also remove the `if` field (you can add an input filter later, if necessary). Save the `/etc/printcap` file.

6. Make sure the printer is properly connected to the PC. Turn on its power switch, and make sure the printer is online.

7. Print a test page; just try `ls -l | lpr -Pprinter_name` (replace `printer_name` with your printer's name). The printout should appear on the printer.

8. If your Linux PC is on a network, and you want users from other systems to print on your printer, add the names of the remote systems to the file `/etc/hosts.lpd` (a text file). Simply add one host name per line for each remote host that can access your PC's printer.

Remote-printer setup

Suppose that your Linux PC is on a network. If you have access to a printer on another system on the network, you may be able to print on that remote printer. You still must set up a `printcap` entry in your system's `/etc/printcap` file before you can send print jobs to the remote system.

To set up a `printcap` entry for a remote printer, follow these steps:

1. In the local system's /etc/printcap file, add a new printcap entry with an empty lp field, the rm field set to the name of the remote system, and the rp field set to the name of the printer on the remote system. On my trusty old Sun SPARCStation IPC (since it runs BSD UNIX, it uses the same printer setup as Linux), I set up the following printcap entry to use the sample printer on my Pentium, running Linux (the system name is lnbsoft):

```
# A remote printer
lp|lnbsoft-sample|Remote printer on lnbsoft:\
   :lp=:\
   :sd=/usr/spool/lpd:\
   :rm=lnbsoft:\
   :rp=sample:\
   :mx#0:\
   :sh:\
   :sf:
```

WHEN RUNNING DNS might need to be FULLY DOMAINIZED: LNBSOFT, BUBBA, COM

Secret

2. In the remote system's /etc/hosts.lpd file, add the name of your local system. Thus, if I want to print on the lnbsoft system from my Sun workstation named lnbsun, I edit the /etc/hosts.lpd file on lnbsoft and add the following line:

    lnbsun

(Then reboot machine with HOSTS.LPD.)

Cross Reference

The /etc/hosts file on lnbsoft, of course, should include the IP address of lnbsun (you learn more about IP addresses in Chapter 16).

After completing these steps, you should be able to print on the remote system. From my Sun workstation, I printed on the sample printer on lnbsoft, and the result showed up in the file /tmp/sample.out on lnbsoft (because the sample printer is set up that way).

Specific Printing Problems and Solutions

Typically, you should be able to print text files readily. This section highlights some of the problems that you may encounter and suggests appropriate solutions.

Submit print job, but no output

This problem is one of the most frustrating ones. You submit a print job to a printer through lpr (make sure that you use the -P option to name the printer), and no error messages are reported, but nothing comes out of the printer. Try the following steps to identify the reason for the failure to print:

1. Check the physical printer. Make sure that it's connected to the PC, that the power is on, and that the printer is online.

2. Make sure that the printer is connected to the device specified in the lp field of the printer's printcap. Also make sure that the device is not /dev/null.

3. Run `lpq`, and make sure that the printer's queue shows the job that you submitted.

4. Type `lpc stat` to see the status of the printers, and make sure that printing and queuing are enabled for the printer.

5. Make sure that the printer daemon, `lpd`, is running. If not, type **lpd** to start the daemon.

Secret

6. Make sure that any input filter specified in the `printcap`'s `if` field is present in the correct directory and has execute permission. Check for error messages in the system log by using the following command:

   `tail /var/adm/syslog`

   If the messages include entries that say `cannot execv name-of-filter`, you can be sure that the filter does not exist or does not have the proper permission setting.

7. Check the file that you are trying to print. Some PostScript printers simply ignore plain-text files. (Filters are available that can convert plain text to PostScript. You may have to install such a filter.)

Problem printing on remote printer

Secret

If you submit a print job on a remote printer, and output does not appear on the remote printer, check the following fields in the `/etc/printcap` file on the remote system:

- See whether the `rg` field specifies groups that are allowed to print. If your username is not in that group, it may not be processed.

- See whether the `rs` field appears. If this field appears, you must have an account on the remote system to be able to print on the remote printer.

How to avoid the staircase effect

Secret

In UNIX, each line in a text file ends with a *newline* (line-feed) character. On typewriters, pressing the line-feed key advances the paper to the next line but does not bring the carriage to the edge of the paper; you have to press the carriage-return key to make that happen. If you were to print a UNIX text file on a typewriterlike device, the result would be something like the following:

```
Installed drivers:
          Type 2: Sound Blaster
                   Card config:
                            Sound Blaster at 0x220 irq 5 drq 1
```

As you can see, the lines of text look like a staircase — the origin of the term *staircase effect*.

MS-DOS and many PC printers behave like typewriters; each line of text must have both a carriage return and a line feed to advance properly to the next line on the paper. When you send a UNIX text file to a printer that expects a carriage-return–line-feed ending for each line, the resulting output shows the staircase effect.

You can avoid the staircase effect in two ways, both of which require an input filter:

- Some printers can be set to treat a line-feed (LF) character as a carriage return, followed by a line feed (CR+LF). The HP LaserJet and Deskjet family of printers, for example, can be programmed to treat a CR as CR+LF by sending the sequence Esc &k2G (the Escape character followed by &k2G). You can use an input filter to send this sequence to the printer at the beginning of the file.

- If the printer cannot be programmed to treat LF as CR+LF, you can write an input filter that converts each LF at the end of a line to CR, followed by LF.

Following is an input filter that sends the special printer command to LaserJet printers to enable the interpretation of LF as CR+LF:

```
#!/bin/bash
# Input filter for HP LaserJet and Deskjet printers to treat LF as
CR+LF

# Send command to make printer interpret LF as CR+LF
echo -ne \\033\&k2G

# Next command sends stdin to stdout
cat

# Next command sends a form feed at the end of the file
echo -ne \\f
```

If you save this shell script in the file /usr/spool/lp1/hplj-if.sh (and make it executable with the chmod +x command), you can use the filter by placing the following field in that printer's printcap entry:

```
:if=/usr/spool/lp1/hplj-if.sh:
```

How to filter a print job destined for a remote printer

After you use lpr to spool a print job for a remote printer (that has a printcap entry on your system), your system's lpd process immediately transfers the files associated with the print job to the remote system's lpd process. That means that even if you specify an input filter in the printcap for the remote printer, your system's lpd process does not apply any filter. Instead, the remote system's lpd process applies any filter specified in that system's /etc/printcap file.

If you do not have access to the remote system's /etc/printcap file to add an input filter, you can use a trick on your system to apply an input filter to the print job before it goes to the remote printer.

Create a dummy printcap entry that specifies the input filter you want to apply. In that input filter, do what you want with the data, and then pipe the data to the remote printer. If you want to add the programming sequence so that a remote HP printer interprets each line feed as a carriage return followed by a line feed, use a filter script such as the following:

```
#!/bin/bash
(
# Note that \033 is Esc in octal
  echo -ne \\033\&k2G
  cat
  echo -ne \\f
) | lpr -Php-remote -h -l
```

This example assumes that your system's /etc/printcap file refers to the remote printer as hp-remote.

Graphics file gets truncated

Graphics files can be quite large. If you have problems printing graphics files because they get truncated, check the printcap entry for the printer. If that entry does not have an mx field, the maximum size of a file in the spool directory is 1,000 blocks. Any file larger than 1,000 blocks is truncated automatically.

Secret

To avoid the truncation problem, add the following mx field to the printcap entry:

mx#0

This entry allows spool files to be as large as necessary.

The lpr -i command does not indent output

The -i option of the lpr command is supposed to indent the output by a specified amount. For that option to work, you must provide an input filter, because lpr simply passes the -i option to the input filter. You get indented output only if the input filter handles the -i option.

How to print PostScript files

If your printer is a PostScript printer, you can print a PostScript file simply by spooling the file to the printer. If you do not have a PostScript printer, you can use the Ghostscript program to print PostScript files on many types of printers. In fact, you can preview PostScript files with the Ghostview program, which uses Ghostscript to generate output suitable for displaying in an X window.

Chapter 14: Printers

Tip: The Ghostscript software is included on the companion CD-ROM. You have the option to install Ghostscript when you install Linux by following the steps outlined in Chapter 1.

Table 14-5 shows the output devices that Ghostscript 2.6.2 supports. As you can see, the output devices include hardware devices such as the display screen and printer as well as many popular image-file formats such as BMP and PCX.

Table 14-5	Ghostscript devices
Device name	**Description of output device**
`linux`	VGA display (uses the `libsvga` library)
`x11`	X window
`bj10e`	Canon BubbleJet BJ10e printer
`bj200`	Canon BubbleJet BJ200 printer
`cdeskjet`	HP DeskJet 500C color printer in 1-bit-per-pixel mode
`cdjcolor`	HP DeskJet 500C printer with 24-bits-per-pixel color and high-quality color (Floyd-Steinberg) dithering
`cdjmono`	HP DeskJet 500C printer in black-and-white mode
`cdj500`	HP DeskJet 500C printer (same as `cdjcolor`)
`cdj550`	HP DeskJet 550C printer
`declj250`	DEC LJ250 printer
`deskjet`	HP DeskJet and DeskJet Plus printer
`dfaxhigh`	DigiFAX (from DigiBoard, Inc.) software format
`dfaxlow`	Low- (normal) resolution DigiFAX format
`djet500`	HP DeskJet 500 printer
`djet500c`	HP DeskJet 500C printer
`epson`	Epson-compatible dot-matrix printers (9- or 24-pin)
`eps9high`	Epson-compatible 9-pin printer in triple-resolution (interleaved lines) mode
`epsonc`	Epson LQ-2550 and Fujitsu 3400/2400/1200 color printers
`escp2`	Epson printers, such as Stylus 800, that use ESC/P 2 language
`ibmpro`	IBM 9-pin Proprinter
`jetp3852`	IBM Jetprinter (Model #3852) inkjet color printer
`laserjet`	HP LaserJet printer
`la50`	DEC LA50 printer

(continued)

Table 14-5 *(continued)*

Device name	Description of output device
`la75`	DEC LA75 printer
`lbp8`	Canon LBP-8II laser printer
`ln03`	DEC LN03 printer
`lj250`	DEC LJ250 Companion color printer
`ljet2p`	HP LaserJet IID, IIP, and III printers with TIFF compression
`ljet3`	HP LaserJet III printer with Delta Row compression
`ljet4`	HP LaserJet 4 printer (default resolution of 600 dots per inch)
`ljetplus`	HP LaserJet Plus printer
`m8510`	C.Itoh M8510 printer
`necp6`	NEC P6, P6+, and P60 printers at 360x360-dpi resolution
`paintjet`	HP PaintJet color printer
`pj`	HP PaintJet XL printer
`pjxl`	HP PaintJet XL color printer
`pjxl300`	HP PaintJet XL300 color printer
`r4081`	Ricoh 4081 laser printer
`t4693d2`	Tektronix 4693d color printer; 2 bits per red (R), green (G), and blue (B) component
`t4693d4`	Tektronix 4693d color printer; 4 bits per RGB component
`t4693d8`	Tektronix 4693d color printer; 8 bits per RGB component
`tek4696`	Tektronix 4695 and 4696 inkjet plotter
`bit`	The "bit bucket" device (output does not appear anywhere)
`bmpmono`	Monochrome Microsoft Windows BMP file format
`bmp16`	4-bit (16-color EGA/VGA) Windows BMP file format
`bmp256`	8-bit (256-color) Windows BMP file format
`bmp16m`	24-bit Windows BMP file format
`pcxmono`	Monochrome PCX file format
`pcxgray`	8-bit gray scale PCX file format
`pcx16`	Older EGA/VGA 16-color PCX file format
`pcx256`	Newer 256-color PCX file format
`pbm`	Plain Portable Bitmap format
`pbmraw`	Raw Portable Bitmap format

Device name	Description of output device
pgm	Plain Portable Graymap format
pgmraw	Raw Portable Graymap format
ppm	Plain Portable Pixmap format
ppmraw	Raw Portable Pixmap format
tiffg3	International Telecommunications Union (ITU) standard Group 3 FAX format (TIFF/ F)

You run the Ghostscript program with the `gs` command. Use the `-sDEVICE=`*devicename* option to specify a device name. To interpret the PostScript file `testfile.ps` and produce output for an Epson dot-matrix printer, for example, you would type the following:

`gs -sDEVICE=epson testfile.ps`

Secret

To print PostScript files, you would define a `printcap` entry for a PostScript printer (typically, with a name such as `ps`) and specify an input filter for that entry. Then, in the input filter, you would use `gs` to create the output for your printer. If you have an HP DeskJet 550C printer, you would place the following line in the body of a shell script that serves as the input filter for the `printcap` entry for the HP DeskJet 550C:

`/usr/bin/gs -dSAFER -dNOPAUSE -q -sDEVICE=cdj550 -sOutputFile=-`

The `-sDEVICE=cdj550` option specifies that the output device is an HP DeskJet 550C. The `-sOutputFile=-` option sends the output to `stdout`, which is what the input filter should do: send its stream of output to the standard output (the printer daemon will send that output to the physical printer).

Summary

Printing under Linux is simple, provided that the printing environment is set up properly. You have to learn a small set of commands to submit a print job and check the status of pending print jobs. This chapter explains the Linux printing environment from the user's point of view and then explains how to set everything up as a system administrator. By reading this chapter, you learn the following things:

- In Linux, the printer's device name depends on the port to which you connect the printer. For a typical printer connected to the parallel port, the device name is /dev/lp0 or /dev/lp1, depending on the I/O address of the parallel port. If the printer is connected to the serial port, the device name is /dev/ttyS0 (for COM1) or /dev/ttyS1 (for COM2).
- As a user, you print with the lpr command, check the status of the print queue with lpq, cancel print jobs with lprm, and check the printer's status with lpc status.
- Behind the scenes, the lpr command copies the print file to a holding directory called the spool directory. A background process called lpd (the print daemon) sends the spooled print file to the printer.
- To set up the printing environment in Linux, you must have your printer defined in the /etc/printcap file. This file essentially specifies what to do when a print job is sent to the printer. Fields in the /etc/printcap file control various elements of printing, ranging from page size to whether a burst header page is printed before each print job.
- In /etc/printcap, you can specify an input filter (a process that reads from standard input and writes to standard output) through which all print jobs must pass. The input filter can send special commands to the printer or alter the print file as necessary.
- The staircase effect refers to the appearance of the printout when you print a UNIX text file (in which each line ends with a single line-feed character) on a PC printer, which expects lines to end with a carriage return–line feed pair. You can use an input filter to avoid the staircase effect.
- You can set up a printer entry in the /etc/printcap file so that the actual printing occurs on another system on the network.
- You can use the Ghostscript software (included on the companion CD-ROM) to view and print PostScript files. Many freely available software packages include documentation in PostScript format.

Chapter 15
Modems

In This Chapter

- Using the names of serial-port devices in Linux
- Understanding serial communications
- Looking at the RS-232C standard
- Understanding different types of modem standards, such as V.32bis and V.34
- Using the Hayes-standard AT command set used by modems
- Dialing out with a modem in Linux
- Setting up Linux for dial-in use
- Using multiport serial I/O boards in Linux

If you have installed Linux on your home PC, you may want to use a modem to dial out to your office system or a bulletin-board system (BBS). With the increasing popularity of the Internet, you also may want to connect to the Internet through the modem. To use a modem, you have to learn how Linux works with the PC's *serial ports* — the ports through which the modem communicates with the PC. You also need to get cables to connect the modem to the PC, select the proper serial device to use in Linux, and set up configuration files that control the communication parameters for the serial port.

Terminals — devices that have a display screen and a keyboard — also connect to the PC through the serial ports. In that sense, terminals are similar to modems. Terminals are ideal for simple data-entry tasks and often are used in point-of-sale systems. Linux also supports multiport serial boards that allow you to connect many terminals or modems to your PC running Linux.

This chapter explains how to connect, set up, and use modems and terminals. Much of the information applies to any device that is connected to the serial port, but some information is specific to modems. This chapter focuses primarily on modems because modems are more popular than terminals among Linux users.

PC and Serial Ports

If you have used communications software, such as Procomm or Crosstalk, under MS-DOS or Windows, you have used your PC's serial port. These communications programs transfer bytes of data from the PC to the modem over the serial port. The serial port is so named because each byte of data is sent *serially* — one bit at a time. Serial data communications comes with its own set of terminology. To understand how to set up the serial port, you need to understand the terminology.

UART

A chip named Universal Asynchronous Receiver/Transmitter (UART), which is at the heart of all serial communications hardware, takes care of converting each byte to a stream of ones and zeros. That stream of ones and zeros is then sent over the communications medium (for example, the telephone line). At the receiving end, another UART reconstitutes bytes of data from the stream of ones and zeros.

The original IBM PC's motherboard did not include any serial communications capability. Instead, the serial communications function was provided through a separate serial adapter card (or *serial board*) called the IBM Asynchronous Communications Adapter. This serial board used National Semiconductor's INS8250 UART chip.

Later, PCs began including the serial communications hardware on the motherboard, but the same 8250 or compatible UART was used for a long time. Still later, an improved version of the 8250 — the 16450 — was introduced, but the improvements were in the chip's fabrication details, not in the basic capability.

A problem with the 8250 and 16450 UARTs is that they do not have any way to buffer received characters. If the PC cannot keep up with the character stream, some characters may be lost. At high data-transfer rates (more than 9,600 bits per second), the PC may have trouble keeping up with the arrival of characters, especially with operating systems that keep the PC busy (such as Microsoft Windows).

The solution was to add a first-in-first-out (FIFO) buffer on the UART so that the PC can fall behind occasionally without losing any incoming characters. The newer 16550A UARTs have send and receive buffers, each of which is capable of storing up to 16 characters. The 16550A UART is compatible with the old 8250 and 16450, but it can support higher data-transfer rates because the built-in buffers can store incoming and outgoing characters directly on the UART.

On a historical note, National Semiconductor's original 16550 UART had the FIFO buffers, but the FIFO circuits had some bugs. The 16550A (and later versions of that UART) fixed the problems of the original 16550. By now, however, the 16550 name is often used in a generic manner to refer to UARTs that have onboard receive and transmit buffers. You don't have to worry about the distinctions between the 16550 and 16550A except for the original 16550 UARTs from National Semiconductor; those chips are marked NS16550 (without an A).

Linux supports PC serial ports and serial I/O boards that use a 8250, 16450, 16550, 16550A, or compatible UART. However, you really need a 16550A UART to keep up with today's high-speed modems, which can transfer data at rates of 14,400 and 28,800 bits per second. Most new Pentium PCs should already have 16550A UARTs. If you are buying a new PC to run Linux, you should check with the vendor and make sure that the serial interface uses 16550A UARTs.

Communications parameters

In serial communications, the transmission medium (such as the telephone line) is kept at a logical 1 (1 is represented by the presence of a signal on the line) when it is idle. In this case, the line is said to be *marking*. On the other hand, when the line is at a logical 0, it is said to be *spacing*. Thus, logical 1 and 0 are also referred to as MARK and SPACE, respectively.

A sequence of ones and zeros makes up a single 8-bit character, as shown in Figure 15-1.

As Figure 15-1 shows, a change in the condition of the line from MARK to SPACE indicates the start of a character. That change in line condition is referred to as the START bit. Following the START bit is a pattern of bits that represent the character and then a bit known as the PARITY bit. Finally, the line reverts to its idling MARK condition, which represents the STOP bit and indicates the end of the current character. The number of bits used to represent the character is known as the *word length* and usually is either seven or eight.

The PARITY bit is used to perform rudimentary error detection. When *even parity* is selected, for example, the parity bit is set so that the total number of ones in the current word is even (the logic is similar for odd parity). At the receiving end, the parity is recalculated and compared with the received parity bit. If the two disagree, the receiver declares a parity error. One problem of error detection with the parity check is that it can detect only errors that affect a single bit. The bit pattern 0100 0001 0 (the ASCII code for the letter *A*), for example, transmitted with an 8-bit word length and even parity, may change (due to noise in the telephone line) to 0100 0111 0 (ASCII *G*), but the receiver would not see the error, because the parity is still even. Thus, parity error detection is rarely used nowadays.

In serial communications, the transmitter and the receiver both must have some knowledge of how long each bit lasts; otherwise, they cannot detect the bits correctly. The duration of each bit is determined by data clocks at the receiver and the transmitter. Notice, however, that although the clocks at the receiver

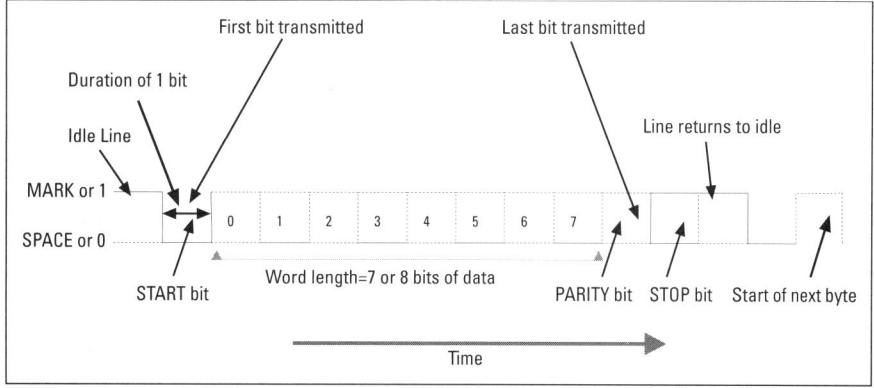

Figure 15-1: Format of a single character in serial communications.

and the transmitter must have the same frequency, they are not required to be synchronized. The START bit signals the receiver that a new character follows; the receiver then begins detecting the bits until it sees the STOP bit.

A particular condition of the line is sometimes used to gain the attention of the receiver. The normal state of the line is MARK (1), and the beginning of a character is indicated by a SPACE (0). If the line stays in the SPACE condition for a period of time longer than it would have taken to receive all the bits of a character, a BREAK is assumed to have occurred. When the receiver sees the BREAK condition, it can get ready to receive characters again.

The selection of the clock frequency depends on the *baud rate* (or simply *baud*), which refers to the number of times that the line changes state every second. Typically, the serial I/O hardware uses a clock rate of 16 times the baud rate so that the line is sampled often enough to detect a bit reliably.

The data-transfer rate is expressed in terms of *bits per second*, or *bps*. In the early days of modems, the data-transfer rate was the same as the baud rate — the rate of change of the line's state — because each line state carried a single bit of information. Nowadays, the modems use different technology that can send several bits of information each time the line state changes. In other words, you can get a high bps with a relatively low baud rate. Even the fastest modems today use a baud rate of 2400, even though the bits per second can be as high as 28,800.

Thus, the term *baud* and *bits per second* are not the same. Most of us, however, ignore the exact definition of *baud rate* and simply use the term *baud* to mean bits per second. Even though I'll stick to bps when I state data-transfer rates, you'll run across Linux settings that use the term *baud rate* to mean bps.

Serial-port IRQs and I/O addresses

The PC typically has two serial ports, called COM1 and COM2 in MS-DOS parlance. The PC also can support two more serial ports: COM3 and COM4. Because of these port names, the serial ports are often referred to as COM ports.

Like other devices, the serial ports need interrupt-request (IRQ) numbers and I/O port addresses. Two IRQs — 3 and 4 — are shared among the four COM ports. Table 15-1 lists the IRQs and I/O port addresses assigned to the four serial ports.

Table 15-1   IRQ and I/O port addresses assigned to serial ports

Port	IRQ	I/O address
COM1	4	0x3f8
COM2	3	0x2f8
COM3	4	0x3e8
COM4	3	0x2e8

Serial-device names in Linux

Like other devices in Linux, the serial-port devices are represented by device files in the /dev directory. Each serial port has two names: one for incoming connections and the other for outgoing connections. Table 15-2 lists the device names for incoming and outgoing serial ports, including the major and minor device numbers.

Table 15-2 Device names for incoming and outgoing serial ports

COM port	Device name	Major device number	Minor device number
Incoming COM1	/dev/ttyS0	4	64
Incoming COM2	/dev/ttyS1	4	65
Incoming COM3	/dev/ttyS2	4	66
Incoming COM4	/dev/ttyS3	4	67
Outgoing COM1	/dev/cua0	5	64
Outgoing COM2	/dev/cua1	5	65
Outgoing COM3	/dev/cua2	5	66
Outgoing COM4	/dev/cua3	5	67

Note

If you installed Linux from this book's companion CD-ROM, all these devices should already be in your system. In fact, if you check the /dev directory, you'll find many more /dev/ttyS* and /dev/cua* devices. Those device names are for *multiport serial boards* — serial interfaces that have more than one port (typically 4, 8, or 16 ports).

Modems

The term *modem* comes from *modulator/demodulator* — a device that converts digital signals, consisting of ones and zeros, to continuously varying analog signals that can be transmitted over telephone lines and radio waves. Thus, the modem is the intermediary between the digital world of the PC and the analog world of telephones.

Inside the PC, ones and zeros are represented with voltage levels, but signals carried over the telephone lines usually are tones of different frequencies. The modem sits between the UART and the telephone line, and makes data communication possible over the phone lines. The modem converts information back and forth between the voltage/no voltage representation of digital circuits and analog signals that are appropriate for transmission over phone lines.

The communication between the PC and the modem follows the RS-232C standard (often stated as RS-232, without the C). The communications protocol between two modems also follows one of several international modem standards. The next few sections briefly describe these standards.

RS-232C standard

The RS-232C standard, set forth by the Electrical Industry Association (EIA), specifies a prescribed method of information interchange between the modem and the PC's serial communication hardware.

Wizard

In EIA terminology, the modem is Data Communications Equipment (DCE), and the PC is considered to be Data Terminal Equipment (DTE). You'll see references to DCE and DTE in discussions of the RS-232C standard.

A modem can communicate in one of two modes:

- *Half-duplex mode*, in which data transmission can occur in only one direction at a time
- *Full-duplex mode*, which allows independent two-way communications

Most modems communicate in full-duplex mode.

RS-232C cables

The RS-232C standard also provides control signals, such as Request to Send (RTS) and Clear to Send (CTS), that can be used to coordinate the transmission and reception of data between the PC and the modem. The term *handshaking* refers to the coordination of the data exchange.

The handshaking signals, as well as data transmission and reception, occur through wires in the cable that connects the PC to the modem. The RS-232C specifies a 25-pin connector, with a specific function assigned to each pin.

Note

A typical modem has a female 25-pin, D-shell connector (called the DB-25 connector), whereas the PC's serial port provides a male 9-pin, D-shell (DB-9) connector. Thus, to connect a PC's serial port to a modem, you need a cable with a female DB-9 connector at one end and a male DB-25 connector at the other end. Figure 15-2 illustrates a typical PC-to-modem cable (often sold in computer stores under the label AT Modem Cable).

Some PCs have a DB-25 connector for the serial port. For these machines, you need a cable that has DB-25 connectors on both sides.

Chapter 15: Modems **443**

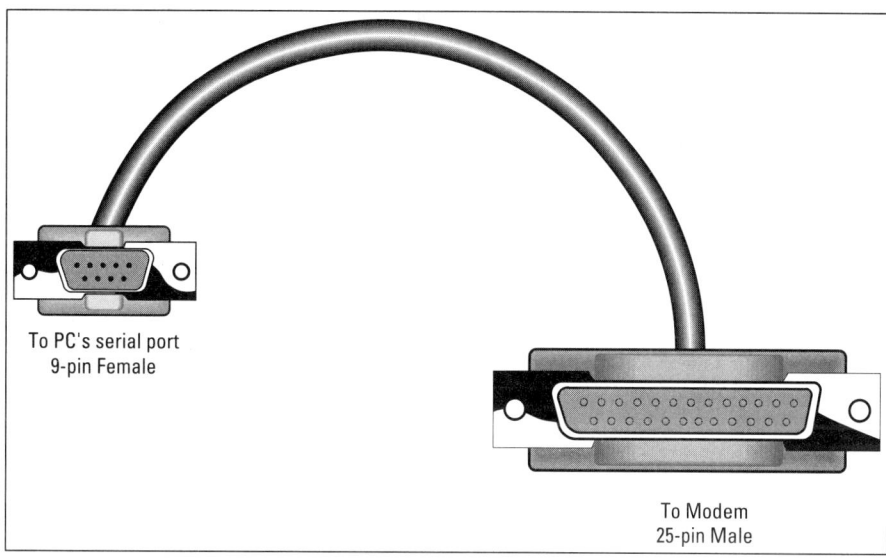

Figure 15-2: A typical cable for connecting a PC's serial port to a modem.

The RS-232C standard specifies the pins for the 25-pin connector. Figure 15-3 shows the DB-25 connector and pin assignments for IBM PC-compatible DB-25 male connectors.

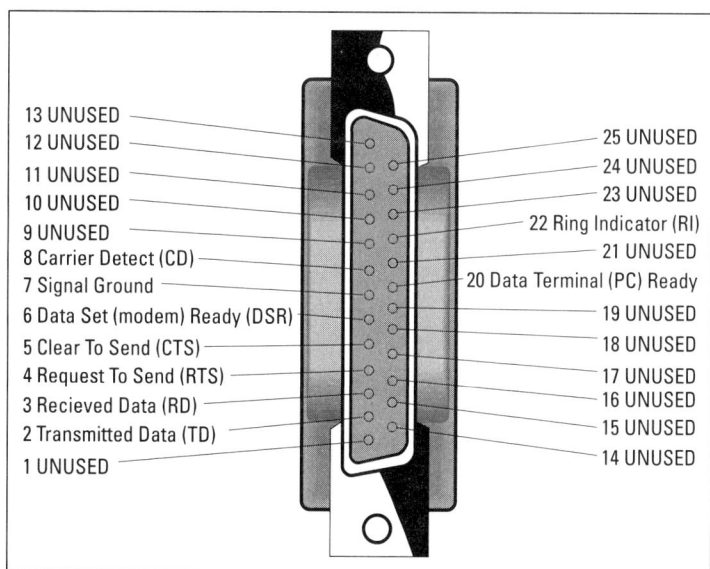

Figure 15-3: Pin assignments for the DB-25 serial connector.

Of the 25 pins available in a DB-25 connector, only 9 are used in the PC's serial port. In the Serial/Parallel Adapter card for the PC-AT, IBM decided to save space by introducing a DB-9 connector. The pin assignments for the DB-9 connector are shown in Figure 15-4.

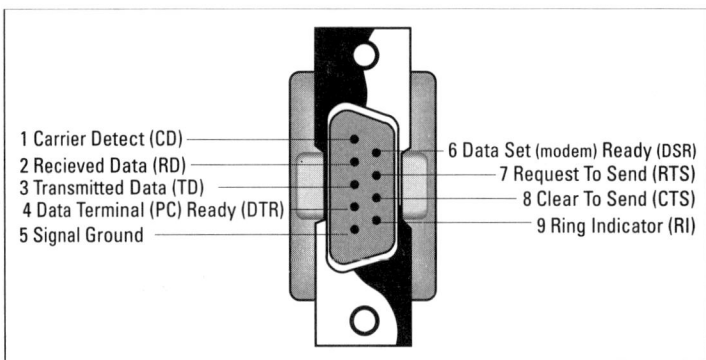

Figure 15-4: Pin assignments for the DB-9 serial connector used in PC serial ports.

Modem cable (DTE to DCE)

When you connect a PC (DTE) to a modem (DCE), the cable should connect the like signals at both ends like this (the arrow indicates the direction of data transfer on that line):

PC (DTE)	*Modem (DCE)*
TD (Transmit Data) ————————>	TD (Transmit Data)
RD (Receive Data) <————————	RD (Receive Data)
RTS (Request to Send) ————————>	RTS (Request to Send)
CTS (Clear to Send) <————————	CTS (Clear to Send)
DSR (Data Set Ready) <————————	DSR (Data Set Ready)
Signal Ground ————————	Signal Ground
CD (Carrier Detect) <————————	CD (Carrier Detect)
DTR (Data Terminal Ready) ————————>	DTR (Data Terminal Ready)
RI (Ring Indicator) <————————	RI (Ring Indicator)

A cable that has such connections is often called a *straight-through cable*, because it connects like signals to each other. If the connector at one end is DB-25 and the other one is DB-9, all you have to do is look up the pin numbers for each type of connector in Figure 15-3 and 15-4.

Null modem cable (DTE to DTE)

Wizard

If you want to connect two PCs through the serial port, you cannot use a straight-through cable, such as the one used to connect the PC to a modem. The reason is that each PC expects to send data on the TD line and receive data on the RD line. If both PCs send data on the same line, neither PC can hear the other. A solution is to create a cable that connects one PC's output (TD) to the other one's input (RD), and vice versa. Such a cable is known as a *null modem* cable.

Figure 15-5 shows the signal interconnections in a typical null modem cable. Instead of showing the pin numbers, I have shown the RS-232C signal names. The exact pin numbers depend on the type of connectors. You should consult Figures 15-3 and 15-4 for the pin numbers.

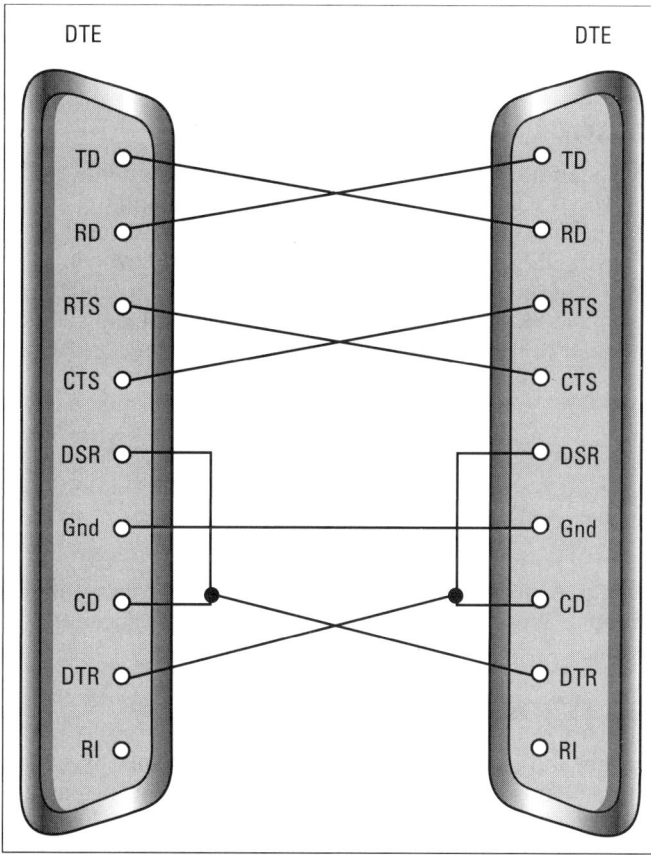

Figure 15-5: Signal interconnections in a typical null modem cable.

Cable choices

When you connect two devices that support RS-232C serial communications, the choice of cable depends on the type of each device: DTE or DCE. As I mentioned earlier, the PC is a DTE, and a modem is a DCE. Many printers and terminals are DTEs.

Use a straight-through modem cable to connect a DTE to a DCE. To connect a DTE to a DTE, you need a null modem cable. Many computer stores sell a smaller null modem adapter. You can connect two DTE devices by using a modem cable with a null modem adapter.

Secret

Notice that the serial interface on the HP Laserjet family of printers is configured as a DTE. Thus, you need a null modem-style cable to connect a PC's serial port to a Laserjet printer. Unfortunately, serial interface to printers introduces a further complication. Printer manufacturers interpret some of the RS-232C signals in a printer-specific manner. Thus, you may have to connect various signals in a specified manner to successfully use a printer with a serial interface.

Flow control

The RS-232C standard includes the RTS/CTS signals for hardware handshaking between the communicating devices (such as the PC and the modem). In addition to this hardware flow control, special ASCII control characters (Ctrl-Q/Ctrl-S, or XON/XOFF) are typically used to implement flow control in software. Flow control is necessary because sometimes either the sender or the receiver may not be able to keep up with the rate of data arrival and should be able to inform the other party to stop data transmission while it catches up to the other device.

Suppose that a receiver has a buffer to store incoming characters. As the buffer gets full, the receiver can send the XOFF character (Ctrl-S) to the transmitter, indicating that transmission should stop. If the transmitter understands the meaning of the XOFF character, it can stop sending data.

Then, when the receiver empties the buffer, it can send an XON (Ctrl-Q) to indicate that transmission can resume. This scheme of flow control is used in many communications programs, because the scheme is simple.

Modem standards

As the Internet and online services have grown in popularity, so has the demand for modems that offer high data-transfer rates. The early modems transferred data at the rate of 300 bits per second (bps), whereas the latest modems can transfer at rates of up to 28,800 bps — nearly a hundredfold increase in modem performance. To achieve these high data-transfer rates, modems use many tricks, including compressing the data before sending it. As you might expect, two modems can communicate successfully only if both modems understand how to interpret the signal that is being exchanged between the two. This is where the standard modem protocols come into play.

The International Telecommunications Union (ITU) has ratified several modem standards that are in use today. These standards have names that start with *V*. The latest standard is V.34, which supports data-transfer rates of 28,800 bps. Table 15-3 lists some of the common modem standards used today.

Table 15-3	Modem standards
Standard name	*Maximum data-transfer rate (bps)*
Bell 103	300
Bell 212A	1200
V.17 (Group III Fax)	14,400
V.21	300
V.22	1200
V.22bis	2400
V.23	1200
V.27ter (Group III Fax)	4800
V.29 (Group III Fax)	9600
V.32	9600
V.32bis	14,400
V.34	28,800

When you buy a modem, make sure that the modem conforms to these international standards. Increasingly, the V.34 28,800-bps modems are the norm, but V.32bis 14,400-bps modems also remain popular.

Modem commands (AT commands)

The now-famous AT command set first appeared in the 300-baud Hayes Smartmodem, a term coined and trademarked by Hayes Microcomputer Products, Inc. The Smartmodem worked in two distinct modes:

- *Command mode.* In this mode, characters sent from the PC (DTE) are interpreted as commands for the modem.

- *Online mode.* After receiving a dial command and establishing a connection, the modem sends all received data out on the phone lines.

The Hayes Smartmodem commands start with the two characters AT (for attention). The initial command set included those to dial a number, turn the modem's speaker on or off, and set the modem to answer an incoming call.

The AT command system has been widely copied by modem manufacturers, making the AT command mechanism a de-facto standard. Although virtually all modems use a core command set, each modem manufacturer has its own proprietary commands that control some of the exotic and advanced features of a modem.

Tip

I have found it very helpful to know at least a few of the AT commands for controlling a modem. Although many communications programs hide the details of the AT commands, you can end up in a situation in which the communications software is primitive — all that the software does is send the other modem whatever you type. In such situations, you can enter AT commands to set up the modem, dial out, and establish a connection. The following sections briefly cover the AT command set.

The AT command line

As the name implies, each command in the AT command set starts with the letters AT. Following these letters, you can enter one or more valid commands and then end the command line with a carriage return (press Enter on the PC's keyboard). Thus, the command line has the following format:

```
AT[command1][command2]...<CR>
```

[command1] and [command2] denote optional commands, each of which has appropriate arguments. The ending <CR> is a required carriage return.

Suppose that you want to use the following commands:

- The E command with an argument of 1 to force the modem to echo the commands
- The V command with 1 as the argument to make the modem provide verbose result codes (instead of numeric codes)

You can send these commands to the modem with the following AT command line:

```
ATE1V1
```

As you do with any AT command line, of course, you have to end this command by pressing Enter. If you enter this command through a communications software package, you see that the modem replies with the string OK.

Secret

All modems accept a minimum 40 characters per command line, in which the character count includes the AT and the final carriage return. Many modems, however, can accept up to 255 characters on an AT command line.

The A/ command

Every rule has an exception, and the A/ command is an exception to the AT command syntax. If you enter **A/** as the only command on a line by itself (no need to press Enter), the modem immediately repeats the last command line that it received.

Configuration commands

These commands specify how the modem should operate and how it responds to commands. Following are some useful configuration commands:

- *Echo commands.* ATE1 causes the modem to display a command as you type it; ATE0 disables the display of the command.

- *Speaker volume.* The ATLn (n is a number between 0 and 3) command sets the volume of the modem's built-in speaker. ATL0 and ATL1 set the volume low, ATL2 sets it medium, and ATL3 sets it high.

- *Speaker control.* ATMn, (n is a number between 0 and 2) controls whether and when the modem's speaker is turned on. ATM0 turns the speaker off, ATM1 turns it on until a call is established, and ATM2 turns it on always.

- *Quiet mode.* When quiet mode is enabled, the modem does not acknowledge commands or report call status. ATQ0 disables quiet mode, and causes the modem to respond to commands and show call status. ATQ1 enables quiet mode.

- *Verbose mode.* When verbose mode is enabled, the modem acknowledges commands and reports call status with words. Otherwise, the modem responds with numeric codes (which may be more suitable for communications software than for humans). The ATV1 command turns on verbose mode; ATV0 turns verbose mode off. A typical modem has the nine responses listed in Table 15-4.

Table 15-4	Responses from a typical modem
Numeric response	**Word response**
0	OK
1	CONNECT
2	RING
3	NO CARRIER
4	ERROR
5	CONNECT 1200
6	NO DIALTONE
7	BUSY
8	NO ANSWER

Most modems include several other responses to report successful connections at higher data rates.

- *Result code selection.* The ATXn command selects the type of reports that the modem should send back. The argument n can be one of the following:

```
0    CONNECT
1    CONNECT bits-per-sec
2    CONNECT bits-per-sec, NO DIALTONE
3    CONNECT bits-per-sec, BUSY
4    CONNECT bits-per-sec, NO DIALTONE, BUSY
```

- *View stored profiles.* Using AT&V causes the modem to display the current values of a selected set of configuration parameters and the values of internal registers. Some modems have nonvolatile memory to store groups of settings known as *profiles*. On such modems, AT&V displays the stored profiles.

Action commands

Each action command causes the modem to perform some action immediately. The most important action command is the dial command: ATDTnumber. Two other useful action commands are ATZn and AT&Fn, which reset the modem's configuration. Following are some of the important action commands:

- *Pulse dial.* The ATDPnumber command causes the modem to use the pulse dialing system to dial a specified phone number. The pulse dialing system was used by rotary telephones. Nowadays, you typically use the ATDT command to dial a number by using the tone dialing system.

- *Tone dial.* Use the ATDTnumber command to dial a specified phone number by using the tone dialing system. To dial the number 555-1234, for example, you use the command ATDT555-1234. You should enter whatever other digits you may need to dial the number that you want to reach. If you need to dial 9 to access an outside line, you simply use ATDT9,555-1234. The comma introduces a slight pause (typically, two seconds), which may be necessary to get an outside line.

- *Dial last number.* The ATDL command causes the modem to execute the last dial command.

- *Hook control.* The ATH command simulates the act of lifting or putting down the handset of a regular telephone. ATH0 hangs up the phone; ATH1 makes the modem go online (as though you had picked up the handset).

- *Answer call.* Use the ATA command to make the modem answer the phone. You can put the modem in answer mode (by setting register S0 to a nonzero value) so that it answers the phone when someone calls. With the ATA command, you can force the modem to answer the phone even if register S0 is set to 0 (which means that the modem won't answer the phone).

- *Return to online.* The ATO command returns the modem to online mode. Use this command after you press +++ (rapidly enter three plus signs in sequence) to take the modem offline.

- *Software reset.* If the modem stores configuration profiles in nonvolatile memory, you can recall one of the configuration profiles with the ATZn command (n is the number of the configuration profile). If you enter **ATZ** without any argument, the modem is reset. The ATZ command terminates any existing connection.

- *Factory-default setting.* The AT&F command causes the modem to restore the factory-default settings. Some modems take a numeric argument with AT&F; consult your modem's documentation for more information on the meaning of the numeric argument.

The ATSr=n commands

In addition to the AT command set, Hayes Smartmodem pioneered the use of internal modem registers to configure the modem. All current modems have a set of registers, called the *S registers*, that control many parts of the modem (including features that may be unique to a specific brand of modem).

Secret

A typical modem has anywhere from 30 to 60 S registers, denoted by S0, S1, S2, and so on. The ATSr=n command sets the S register numbered r to the value n. To view the current contents of the S register numbered r, use the ATSr? command.

Register S0, for example, contains the number of rings after which the modem answers the phone. When S0 is zero, the modem does not answer the phone at all. Following is how you might query and set the S0 register with the ATS command:

```
ATS0?
000

OK
ATS0=1
OK
ATS0?
001
```

Wizard

The exact set of S registers varies from one brand of modem to another, but most modems seem to provide and interpret the following 13 S registers in a consistent manner:

> S0 **Ring to Answer On** — The number of rings after which the modem answers the phone. When S0 is zero, the modem does not answer the phone.
>
> S1 **Counts Number of Rings** — The count of incoming rings. When S1 equals S0, the modem answers the phone (assuming that S0 is nonzero). The modem resets S1 to zero a few seconds after the last ring.
>
> S2 **Escape Code Character** — The character that is used as the escape sequence to switch the modem from online mode to command mode. The default value is 43, which is the ASCII code for the plus (+) character. To go from online mode to command mode, you have to enter this escape character three times in rapid succession.
>
> S3 **Carriage-Return Character** — The ASCII code of the character that is used as the carriage return (this character terminates the AT command lines). The default value is 13.
>
> S4 **Line-Feed Character** — The ASCII code of the character that is used as the line-feed character when the modem generates word responses to commands. The default value is 10.

S5 **Backspace Character** — The ASCII code of the character that is used as the backspace character. The modem echoes this character to implement the "erase preceding character" function. The default value is 8.

S6 **Wait Time for Dial Tone (seconds)** — The number of seconds to wait before dialing the first digit in a dial command. The default value is 2.

S7 **Wait Time for Carrier (seconds)** — The number of seconds that the modem waits for a carrier. If the modem does not detect a carrier after waiting for this many seconds, it displays the NO CARRIER message. The default value depends on the modem. Typically, the default is anywhere from 30 to 60.

S8 **Comma Time (seconds)** — The number of seconds to pause when the modem finds a comma in the phone number to dial. The default value is 2.

S9 **Carrier Detect Time (tenths of a second)** — The amount of time, in tenths of seconds, that the carrier must be present before the modem declares that a carrier has been detected. The default value is 6, which means that the carrier must be present for 0.6 seconds before the modem detects it.

S10 **Carrier Loss Time (tenths of a second)** — The amount of time, in tenths of seconds, that the carrier can be lost without causing the modem to disconnect. The default value is anywhere from 7 to 15, which means that the carrier can be lost for 0.7 to 1.5 seconds without causing a modem disconnect.

S11 **Dial-Tone Spacing (milliseconds)** — The duration of each dial tone and the spacing between adjacent tones. The default value typically is something between 50 and 100 milliseconds (50 is considered to be the minimum necessary for dial tones to be recognized by the phone system).

S12 **Escape Sequence Guard Time (fiftieths of a second)** — The amount of time, in fiftieths of a second, that must occur before and after the escape-code sequence (the default sequence is +++) that switches the modem from online mode to command mode. The default value is 50, which means that the guard time is 1 second.

Online help

Tip

In response to the AT$ command, USRobotics modems display online help information on the basic modem command sets. You'll find the help information instructive, because it shows you the breadth of commands that a typical modem accepts. Following is the response to the AT$ command from a USRobotics Sportster 28,800 Data/Fax Modem on my Linux PC (I entered the command on Seyon, which I'll describe briefly in the "Dial out with a communications program" section of this chapter):

```
AT$
HELP, Command Quick Reference (CTRL-S to Stop, CTRL-C to Cancel)
```

```
&$    HELP, Ampersand Commands       Mn       n=0 Speaker Off
A/    Repeat Last Command                     n=1 Speaker On Until CD
AT    Command Mode Prefix                     n=2 Speaker Always On
A     Answer Call                             n=3 Speaker Off During Dial
Bn    n=0 CCITT Answer Seq          On        n=0 Return Online
n=1   Reserved                                n=1 Return Online & Retrain
Dn    Dial a Telephone Number       n=2       Return Online & Speed Shift
n=0..9#*TPR,:"W@!()-                P         Pulse Dial
DL    Dial Last Phone Number        Qn        n=0 Result Codes Sent
DSn   Dial Stored Phone Number                n=1 Quiet (No Result Codes)
D$    HELP, Dial Commands                     n=2 Verbose/Quiet On Answer
En    n=0 No Command Echo           Sr=n      Sets Register "r" to "n"
n=1   Echo Command Chars            Sr?       Query Register "r"
Fn    n=0 Online Echo               S$        HELP, S Registers
n=1   No Online Echo                T         Tone Dial
Hn    n=0 On Hook (Hang Up)         Vn        n=0 Numeric Responses
n=1   Off Hook                                n=1 Verbal Responses
In    n=0 Product Code              Xn        n=0 Basic Result Codes
      n=1 Checksum                            n=1 Extended Result Codes
      n=2 RAM Test                            n=2-4 Advanced Result Codes
      n=4 Current Settings          Z         Software Reset
      n=5 NVRAM Settings            +++       Escape Code
      n=7 Product Configuration     $         HELP, Command Summary
      n=11 V.FC Link Screen
```

Linux and Modems

If you're using Linux at home or in a small office, you probably want to use the modem for one or more of the following reasons:

- To dial out to another computer (such as a bulletin-board system), an online service (such as CompuServe), or another UNIX system, perhaps at your university or company.

- To allow other people to dial in and use your Linux system. If your home PC runs Linux and you have a modem set up, you might even dial in to your home system from work.

- To use dial-up networking with Serial Internet Protocol (SLIP) or Point-to-Point Protocol (PPP) to connect to the Internet (typically, through an Internet Service Provider).

Cross Reference

In the following sections, I'll describe the first two uses of a modem: to dial in or dial out from your Linux PC. Dial-up networking with SLIP or PPP is an important topic by itself; Chapter 18 covers that subject in detail.

Dialing out with a modem

When you installed Linux from this book's companion CD-ROM, you automatically installed some tools that you can use to dial out from your Linux system with a modem. Before you can dial out, however, you have to make sure that you have a modem properly connected to one of the serial ports of your PC and that the Linux devices for the serial ports are set up correctly.

Hardware setup of modem

Make sure that your modem is properly connected to the power supply and that the modem is connected to the telephone line.

Buy the right type of cable to connect the modem to the PC. As explained in earlier sections of this chapter, you need a straight-through serial cable to connect the modem to the PC. The connectors at the ends of the cable depend on the type of serial connector on your PC. The modem end of the cable needs a male DB-25 connector. The PC end of the cable often is a female DB-9 connector, but some PCs need a female DB-25 connector at the PC end of the cable as well.

You can buy modem cables at most computer stores. In particular, the DB-9 to DB-25 modem cables are often sold under the label "AT Modem Cable."

Caution

If your PC's serial port is a DB-25, the connector at the back of the PC (not the one on the cable) is a male DB-25 connector. Don't confuse this connector with the parallel port's DB-25 connector, which is female. If you do use the wrong connector, no damage should occur except that serial communications won't work.

Tip

If your PC has an internal modem, all you have to do is make sure that the IRQ and I/O addresses are set properly (assuming that the modem card has jumpers for setting these values). For COM1, set the IRQ to 4 and the I/O address to 0x3f8; for COM2, the IRQ is 3 and the I/O address is 0x2f8. You also have to connect the phone line to a phone jack that's at the back of the internal-modem card.

Check Linux serial devices

Cross Reference

When you install Linux from this book's CD-ROM, then follow the directions in Chapter 1, the necessary Linux serial devices are automatically created for you. You should have two sets of devices: `/dev/cua*` (* is the port number), for dialing out through the modem; and `/dev/ttyS*`, for dialing in through the modem.

Wizard

The installation process creates the `/dev/cua*` file with a permission setting that does not allow everyone to read the device. If you want any user to be able to dial out with the modem, type the following command while you are logged in as `root`:

```
chmod o+rw /dev/cua*
```

This command gives all users access to the dial-out devices.

To verify that the appropriate serial devices indeed exist, type the following command and make sure that you see a similar listing on your system:

```
ls -l /dev/cua? /dev/ttyS?
crw-rw-rw-   1 root     uucp       5,  64 Oct  8 13:39 /dev/cua0
crw-rw-rw-   1 root     uucp       5,  65 Jul 17  1994 /dev/cua1
crw-rw-rw-   1 root     uucp       5,  66 Jul 17  1994 /dev/cua2
crw-rw-rw-   1 root     uucp       5,  67 Jul 17  1994 /dev/cua3
crw-rw-rw-   1 root     uucp       5,  68 Jul 17  1994 /dev/cua4
crw-rw-rw-   1 root     uucp       5,  69 Jul 17  1994 /dev/cua5
crw-rw-rw-   1 root     uucp       5,  70 Jul 17  1994 /dev/cua6
```

```
crw-rw-rw-   1 root     uucp       5,  71 Jul 17 1994 /dev/cua7
crw-rw-rw-   1 root     uucp       5,  72 Jul 17 1994 /dev/cua8
crw-rw-rw-   1 root     uucp       5,  73 Jul 17 1994 /dev/cua9
crw-rw-rw-   1 root     tty        4,  64 Jul 17 1994 /dev/ttyS0
crw-rw-rw-   1 root     tty        4,  65 Jul 17 1994 /dev/ttyS1
crw-rw-rw-   1 root     tty        4,  66 Jul 17 1994 /dev/ttyS2
crw-rw-rw-   1 root     tty        4,  67 Jul 17 1994 /dev/ttyS3
crw-rw-rw-   1 root     tty        4,  68 Jul 17 1994 /dev/ttyS4
crw-rw-rw-   1 root     tty        4,  69 Jul 17 1994 /dev/ttyS5
crw-rw-rw-   1 root     tty        4,  70 Jul 17 1994 /dev/ttyS6
crw-rw-rw-   1 root     tty        4,  71 Jul 17 1994 /dev/ttyS7
crw-rw-rw-   1 root     tty        4,  72 Jul 17 1994 /dev/ttyS8
crw-rw-rw-   1 root     tty        4,  73 Jul 17 1994 /dev/ttyS9
```

As the listing shows, you have more device files set up than you have serial ports on your system. Typically, you need the first four devices of each type — /dev/cua0 through /dev/cua3 and /dev/ttyS0 through /dev/ttyS3 — at most. Most users probably need only the first two sets of devices, because most PCs have only two serial ports. The other device files are for use with multiport serial boards, should you ever install one.

Dial out with a communications program

After you complete the physical installation of the modem and verify that the necessary Linux device files exist, you can try to dial out through the modem. The best approach is to use one of the serial communications programs included in the Linux distribution on this book's CD-ROM.

You have two choices of communication programs:

- seyon, developed by Muhammed M. Saggaf, is an X application that provides a graphical control panel for setting up the modem and an xterm terminal window where you can type commands for the modem or the remote computer (after you dial out with the modem). The seyon program uses xterm for terminal-emulation capability.

- minicom, created by Miquel van Smoorenburg, is a communications program with a text-based interface that you can run from a Linux virtual terminal or an xterm window. The minicom program emulates a VT102 terminal.

The following sections briefly describe both applications so that you can use one of them to try your modem.

Using seyon

To run seyon, type the following command at the shell prompt in an xterm window (you must start the X Window System to run seyon, because seyon uses X for its graphical interface):

```
seyon -modems /dev/cua0
```

After seyon starts, you see two windows, as shown in Figure 15-6.

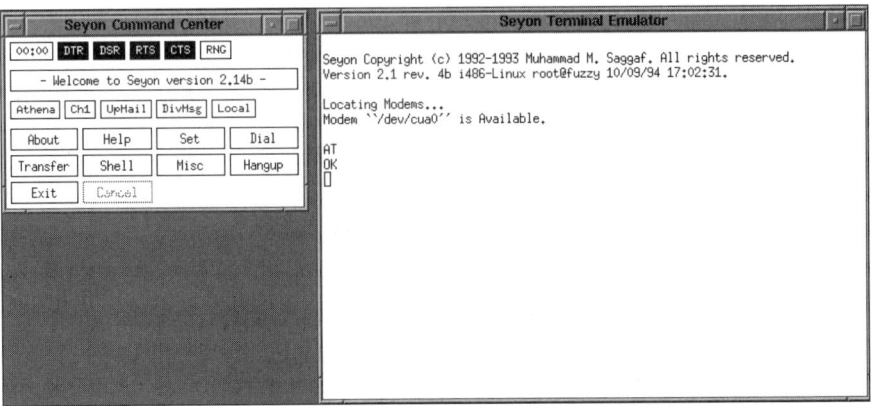

Figure 15-6: The `seyon` windows at startup.

The Seyon Command Center window provides a graphical interface that you use to set communications parameters, initiate file transfers, and even quit `seyon`. The Seyon Terminal Emulator window actually is an `xterm` window that `seyon` uses to provide the terminal window where you can type commands for the modem and the remote system (after the modem establishes a connection).

You use the Set button in the Seyon Command Center window to specify the communications parameters. If you click on Set, `seyon` brings up another window, as shown in Figure 15-7.

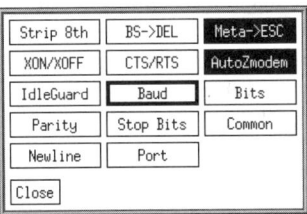

Figure 15-7: The window that appears when you click on the Set button in the Seyon Command Center.

From the window shown in Figure 15-7, you can specify various communications parameters. To set the data-transfer rate, for example, click on the Baud button. This button brings up another window, as shown in Figure 15-8.

After you specify the communications parameters, click on the Close button to close each dialog window.

To connect to a remote system, you can select Dial from the Seyon Command Center or type the modem commands in the Seyon Terminal Emulator window.

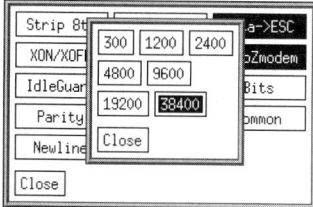

Figure 15-8: The dialog window where you specify the data-transfer rate (in bits per second).

Using `minicom`

To run `minicom`, type **minicom** at the shell prompt in an `xterm` window or in a Virtual Terminal screen. If you run `minicom` as a normal user (not `root`), `minicom` may display the following error message and exit:

```
minicom
Sorry naba. You are not allowed to use configuration dfl.
Ask your sysadm to add your name to /var/lib/minicom/minicom.users
```

As the message says, you have to log in as `root` and add the user name to the specified file. Copy one of the existing lines in the `/var/lib/minicom/minicom.users` file, and change the user name to your user name.

If your user name appears in the `/var/lib/minicom/minicom.users` file, you can run `minicom`. When `minicom` first runs, it resets the modem. Figure 15-9 shows the result of running `minicom` in an `xterm` window.

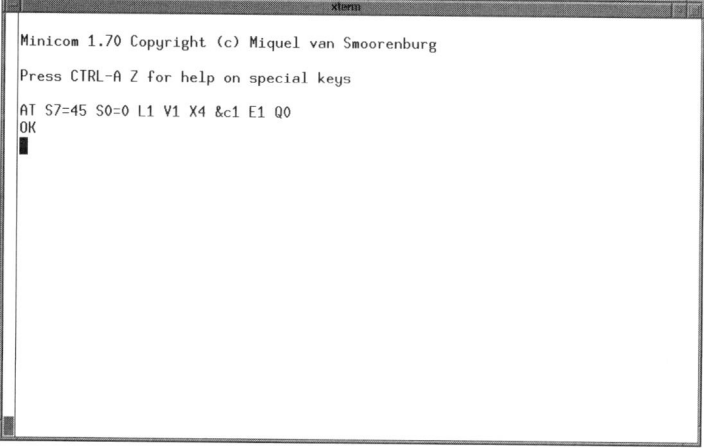

Figure 15-9: The initial `minicom` screen.

Part III: Exploiting Your Hardware in Linux

The `minicom` program is somewhat like another shareware communications program named Telix. As in that program, you can press Ctrl-A to get the attention of the `minicom` program. After you press Ctrl-A, if you press **Z**, a help screen appears in the form of a text window, as shown in Figure 15-10.

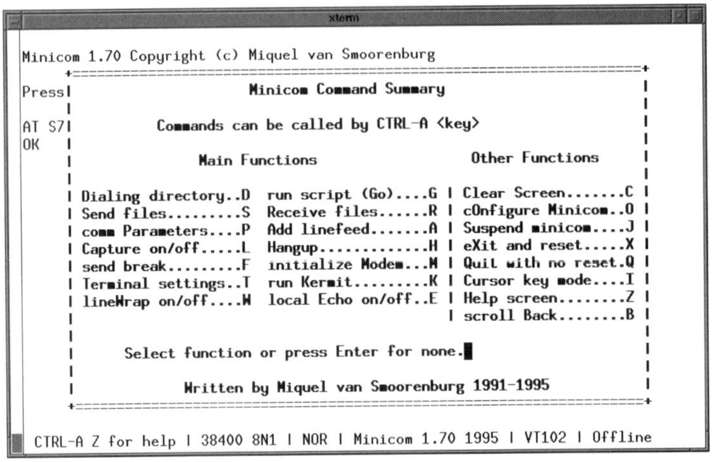

Figure 15-10: The `minicom` help screen.

Tip

In the help screen, you can get information about other `minicom` commands. From the help screen, press Enter to go back to online mode. In online mode, you can use the modem's AT commands to dial out. In particular, you can use the ATDT command to dial the phone number of another modem (for example, a BBS, a system at your office, or your Internet Service Provider's computer), as shown in Figure 15-11.

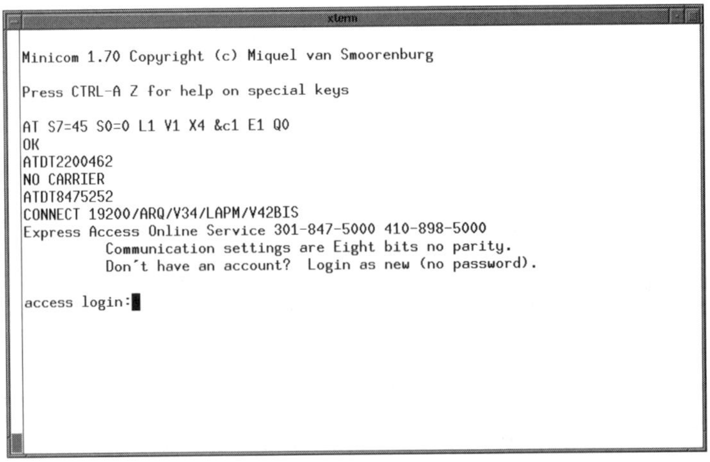

Figure 15-11: Dialing a remote system using `minicom`.

When you finish using `minicom`, press Ctrl-A and then type **X** to exit the program. Press Enter again in response to the `minicom` prompt, as shown in Figure 15-12.

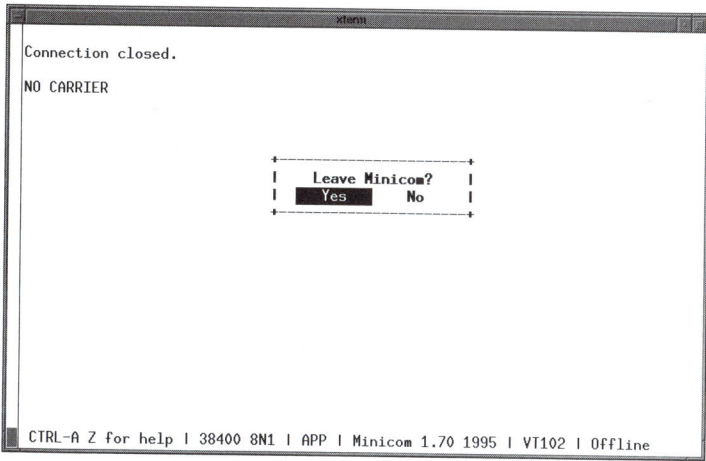

Figure 15-12: This `minicom` prompt appears when you press Ctrl-A and then type **X** to quit `minicom`.

Setting up Linux for dial-in

You can set up the same modem for dial-in as well as dial-out use (only one operation is allowed at any time, of course). The steps for setting up a modem for dial-in use involve setting up a program that monitors the serial port for any incoming calls; this program provides the `login` prompt. The generic name for these programs is `getty`. You can use the `uugetty` program that comes with the Linux distribution on this book's CD-ROM.

The next few sections explain how to set up a modem on COM1 for dial-in use. The Linux device name for that modem (when configured for incoming calls) is `/dev/ttyS0`.

Edit /etc/rc.d/rc.serial

When Linux starts, the `init` process executes the `/etc/rc.d/rc.serial` script during system initialization. Thus, you can configure the serial ports by putting the appropriate commands in the `/etc/rc.d/rc.serial` file.

Secret

If you have a high-speed modem, such as a 28,800-bps modem, you should put a command in the `rc.serial` file to run the `setserial` program and set the `spd_vhi` flag for COM1. Setting the `spd_vhi` flag allows your PC to communicate with the modem at a much higher speed than the modem might be using to connect with a remote system. Put the following line in the `rc.serial` file:

```
${SETSERIAL} /dev/cua0 spd_vhi
```

Secret

If your modem supports hardware that uses the RTS (Request to Send) and CTS (Clear to Send) signals, you should make use of them. Enable hardware handshaking for the modem with the `stty` command by placing the following command in the `rc.serial` file:

```
/bin/stty crtscts < /dev/cua0
```

Update the `uugetty` configuration file

The `uugetty` program checks the `/etc/gettydefs` file for information on speed and settings of a serial port (often referred to as a line). The entries in `/etc/gettydefs` also tell `uugetty` what `login` prompt it should display.

Wizard

The existing `/etc/gettydefs` file should work as is. You may, however, want to edit the `login` prompt. I use the following setting for a 28,800-bps modem:

```
# Modem locked at 38400 with hardware flow control (CRTSCTS):
#
38400# B38400 CS8 CRTSCTS # B38400 SANE -ISTRIP CRTSCTS #@S @L @B
login: #38400
```

The `/etc/gettydefs` file has many more settings, but I use only this one. The label `38400` at the beginning of the line is what I specify when I run `uugetty` on the `/dev/ttyS0` line.

The `CRTSCTS` flag indicates that the modem uses hardware flow control with the RTS/CTS signals (which I enabled with the `stty` command in the `/etc/rc.d/rc.serial` file).

This entry already existed in the `/etc/gettydefs` file; I simply added some more items for the `login` prompt (notice it near the end of the last line). In particular, you can use the following codes listed in Table 15-5 to display specific information in the `login` prompt:

Table 15-5	Some useful `/etc/gettydefs` codes
Code	**Meaning**
@B	The current data-transfer rate, in bits per second.
@D	The current date, in MM/DD/YY format.
@L	The serial line to which `uugetty` is attached (such as `ttyS0`).
@S	The name of the system (as shown by the `uname -n` command).
@T	The current time, in HH:MM:SS (24-hour) format.
@U	The number of currently logged-on users.
@V	The value of `VERSION` specified in the `uugetty` configuration file (`/etc/default/uugetty.ttyS0` for `uugetty` running on the `ttyS0` line). The default value is `/proc/version` (the version string for Linux).

Chapter 15: Modems

To display a single @ character in the `login` prompt, use either `\@` or `@@`. You can put other special characters in the `login` prompt by using the backslash escape. Table 15-6 lists some of the recognized escape characters. With these features, you can customize the `login` prompt to suit your needs.

Table 15-6	Escape characters in /etc/gettydefs
Character	Meaning
\\	A single backslash
\b	Backspace character (Ctrl-H)
\c	Stops newline at the end of a string
\f	Form feed (Ctrl-L)
\n	Newline character (Ctrl-J)
\r	Carriage return (Ctrl-M)
\s	Single space
\t	Single tab (Ctrl-I)
\nnn	ASCII character whose decimal value is nnn (if the number begins with 0, the value is assumed to be octal; if it begins with 0x, it's considered to be in hexadecimal)

Prepare the uugetty configuration file

The `uugetty` program has many parameters that you can tweak. In fact, you can specify separate options for `uugetty` on a per-line basis. These per-line configuration files are in the `/etc/default` directory. The name of each configuration file has the form `uugetty.line`, in which `line` is the device name for the line (without the `/dev` part). Thus, `/etc/default/uugetty.ttyS0` is the configuration file for the copy of `uugetty` that runs on the `/dev/ttyS0` line.

Here's what the `/etc/default/uugetty.ttyS0` file looks like for my system:

```
# Line to initialize (line name should not include /dev)
INITLINE=cua0
# Alternate lock file to check (if this lock file exists,
# then uugetty is restarted so that the modem is re-initialized
ALTLOCK=cua0
ALTLINE=cua0

# Timeout to disconnect if idle...
TIMEOUT=60
```

```
# Modem initialization string. Sets the modem not to auto-answer.
# When a call comes, uugetty will issue an ATA command to make
# the modem go online
# Format of these entries:
#   <expect> <send> ... (chat sequence)
INIT=""  \d+++\dAT\r OK\r\n ATH0\r OK\r\n AT\sM0\sE1\sQ0\sV1\sX4\sS0=0\s&C1\s&S0\r
OK\r\n

# Waitfor string. If this sequence of characters is received
# over the line, a call is detected.
WAITFOR=RING

# The following line is the connect chat sequence. This chat sequence is
performed
# after the WAITFOR string is found. The \A character automatically sets
# the baud rate to the characters that are found, so if you get the message
# CONNECT 2400, the baud rate is set to 2400 baud.
#
# format: <expect> <send> ... (chat sequence)
CONNECT=""  ATA\r CONNECT\s\A

# The next line sets the time to delay before sending the login banner
DELAY=1
```

The entries in this file control the way that uugetty initializes the modem, waits for a call, and answers with a login prompt.

The uugetty process uses the INIT string to initialize the modem. In this case, the initialization sequence issues the following modem commands:

Command	Purpose
ATM0	Turns speaker off
ATE1	Turns command echo on
ATQ0	Turns quiet mode off (so that the modem reports status)
ATV1	Turns verbose mode on
ATX4	Makes the modem report detailed result codes
ATS0=0	Turns auto-answer off (uugetty puts the modem online at the right moment with an ATA command)
AT&C1	Allows the modem to control the carrier-detect (CD) line (that line is turned on only after connect)
AT&S0	Turns the DSR (Data Set Ready) signal on and leaves it on

The uugetty process waits for the WAITFOR string before using the CONNECT string to initiate the connection. When the modem receives a call, it reports RING as the status. When uugetty receives the RING string, it issues the CONNECT string to the modem. The CONNECT string contains the command ATA, which puts the modem online.

After that, uugetty displays the contents of the file /etc/issue, followed by the login prompt. Then uugetty runs the /bin/login program to take care of the actual login.

Start uugetty in /etc/inittab

Wizard

Cross Reference

To ensure that uugetty runs when Linux starts, you have to put a line in the /etc/inittab file so that the init process starts uugetty automatically. Following is what I put in my system's /etc/inittab file to start a copy of uugetty on the /dev/ttyS0 line (for the modem on COM1):

```
# Serial line with dial-in modem
s1:456:respawn:/sbin/uugetty ttyS0 38400 vt100
```

This command ensures that uugetty runs in run levels 4, 5, and 6. (Refer to Chapter 5 for a discussion of run levels and /etc/inittab.)

The arguments to uugetty have the following meaning:

- ttyS0 specifies the line that uugetty monitors (ttyS0 means /dev/ttyS0)
- 38400 specifies the line speed (38400 must appear in the /etc/gettydefs file)
- vt100 specifies the terminal type (the terminal type must be an entry from the /etc/termcap file)

Test the dial-in setup

After you complete all the setup steps for uugetty and the modem, you have to make sure that the init process reexamines the /etc/inittab file and starts uugetty as specified in that file. To do this, log in as root and type the following command:

```
init q
```

After this command, you can test the dial-in modem. You may want to have a friend call your system and see whether login works. If you are lucky enough to have two phone lines (and more than one computer at home), you can dial out on one line and log in to the Linux system set up on the other line. On my system, here's what I get as a login prompt on a PC when I dial into my Linux system:

```
Welcome to Linux 1.2.11.

lnbsoft ttyS0 38400 login:
```

The /etc/gettydefs file on my system specifies the login prompt as follows:

```
@S @L @B login:
```

This line says the prompt should include the system name (@S), the line (@L), and the baud rate (@B). Notice what I see when I call into my system. The login prompt includes the system name (lnbsoft), line (tttyS0), and baud rate (38400), followed by the string login:.

Now your Linux system should be all set to allow users to log in through the dial-in modem.

Terminals and Multiport Serial Boards

The previous sections showed you in detail how to set up and use a modem in Linux for dialing out and letting other people dial in. The rest of this chapter briefly describes the steps involved in setting up terminals connected to the PC's serial port. You'll also find a list of multiport serial boards that Linux supports.

Note

You might want to use other MS-DOS PCs (especially older 286 PCs) as terminals connected to your Linux system. All you need on the PC is a serial communications package such as PROCOMM PLUS or Telix.

Terminal on a serial port

To set up a terminal on a serial port, you have to set up a `getty` process, just as you do when you set up a dial-in modem. Follow these steps:

1. Make sure that you used the correct serial cable to connect the terminal to the serial port. Most terminals need a null modem cable in which the TD (transmit data) and RD (receive data) signal lines are swapped in going from one end of the cable to the other. (See earlier sections of this chapter for further discussions of serial cables.)

2. Set up the terminal's communication parameters. The exact steps depend on the terminal type.

3. Edit `/etc/gettydefs`, and add a line for the terminal. If the terminal operates at 9600 bps, specify a line such as the following (the line that begins with a # is a comment):

   ```
   # 9600 bps connection to a terminal
   T9600# B9600 CS8 CLOCAL # B9600 SANE -ISTRIP CLOCAL #@S login: #T9600
   ```

   The most important part is the `CLOCAL` flag, which tells the `getty` process to ignore modem-control signals.

4. Edit `/etc/inittab` file, and add a line to start a `getty` process on the line that is connected to the terminal. If you have a VT100-compatible terminal on the line `ttyS1` (COM2), you might add the following line to your system's `/etc/inittab` file:

   ```
   s2:456:respawn:/sbin/getty ttyS1 T9600 vt100
   ```

5. Log in as `root`, and force the `init` process to reexamine the `/etc/inittab` file, as follows:

   ```
   init q
   ```

6. A `login` prompt should appear on the terminal, and you should be able to log in.

Multiport serial boards in Linux

If you plan to support a small business with a Linux PC and dumb terminals (because terminals are cheaper than complete PCs, although you also could use old PCs as terminals), you want more than two serial ports. With another serial board, the PC can support four serial ports. If you want more than four serial ports, you have to buy special serial I/O boards known as *multiport serial boards*. These boards typically support anywhere from 8 to 32 serial ports. The serial ports share one IRQ, but each port has a unique I/O address.

Tip

Many multiport serial boards use the 16450 or 16550A UARTs. When you buy a board, you may want to make sure that the UART is 16550A-compatible.

To add support for a specific multiport serial board, you have to uncomment appropriate lines in the /etc/rc.d/rc.serial file. Linux supports the following 16450 or 16550A UART-based multiport serial boards:

- AST FourPort and clones (4 ports)
- Accent Async-4 (4 ports)
- Arnet Multiport-8 (8 ports)
- Bell Technologies HUB6 (6 ports)
- Boca BB-1004 (4 ports), BB-1008 (8 ports), BB-2016 (16 ports)
- Boca IOAT66 (6 ports)
- Boca 2by4 (4 serial and 2 parallel ports)
- Computone ValuePort V4-ISA (AST FourPort-compatible)
- PC-COMM (4 ports)
- STB-4COM (4 ports)
- Twincom ACI/550
- Usenet Serial Board II (4 ports)

Notice that the Boca BB-1004 and BB-1008 boards do not support the Carrier Detect (CD) and Ring Indicator (RI) signals that are necessary to make dial-in modems work. Thus, you cannot use the BB-1004 and BB-1008 boards with dial-in modems.

Wizard

Some multiport serial boards use special processors instead of the 16450 or 16550A UART. These intelligent multiport serial boards require special drivers. Table 15-7 lists a few multiport serial boards and the locations of the drivers for Linux.

Table 15-7   Driver locations in Linux for multiport serial boards

Name	Ports	Driver location
Comtrol RocketPort	4, 8, 16, 32	ftp://tsx-11.mit.edu/pub/linux/packages/comtrol
Cyclades Cyclom	8, 16	ftp://sunsite.unc.edu/pub/Linux/kernel/patches/serial
DigiBoard PC/Xe	2, 4, 8, 16	ftp://ftp.digibd.com/digiline/drivers/linux
DigiBoard PC/Xi	8, 16	ftp://ftp.digibd.com/digiline/drivers/linux
Specialix SIO	4–32	ftp://sunsite.unc.edu/pub/Linux/kernel/patches/serial
Stallion EasyIO-4	4	ftp://sunsite.unc.edu/pub/Linux/kernel/patches/serial
Stallion EasyIO-8	8	ftp://sunsite.unc.edu/pub/Linux/kernel/patches/serial

Summary

Modems provide a convenient way to dial out and connect to other systems. You also can set up a modem to allow other people to dial into your Linux system. This chapter describes the use of modems in Linux. By reading this chapter, you learn the following:

- In Linux, the serial ports have two types of associated device files depending on whether you use the serial ports as outgoing or incoming devices. When you access the serial port to dial out with a modem, the device names are `/dev/cua0` and `/dev/cua1` for COM1 and COM2, respectively. On the other hand, COM1 and COM2 go by the device names `/dev/ttyS0` and `/dev/ttyS1` when they are used as incoming devices.

- The Universal Asynchronous Receiver Transmitter (UART) is at the heart of serial communications. The UART converts outgoing bytes into individual bits that the modem can convert to analog form and send over telephone lines; it also packs incoming bits into bytes. For high-speed communications, you need a National Semiconductor 16550A or compatible UART; these UARTs have 16-byte receive and transmit buffers to allow reliable data transmission in multitasking operating systems such as Linux — operating systems that may not be capable of monitoring the serial ports constantly.

- Serial communication involves several parameters, including baud rate (or bit rate), word length, parity, and number of stop bits. *Baud rate* actually refers to the number of times that the state of the transmission line changes each second, but it is commonly used to refer to the data-transmission rate (in bits per second, or bps).

- The RS-232C standard specifies how serial communication takes place between two devices. RS-232C refers to the modem as Data Communications Equipment (DCE), whereas the PC is called Data Terminal Equipment (DTE). The RS-232C standard also defines the pins of a serial cable.

- Several standards define the way that modems transmit signals over telephone lines. The International Telecommunications Union (ITU) has ratified several modem standards, including V.32bis for 14,400-bps and V.34 for 28,800-bps operation. You need two compatible modems at two ends of a line to establish a communications path.

- All modern modems understand a set of commands that start with the letters AT. This AT command set was developed by Hayes Microcomputer Products, Inc. You can set up a modem and dial out by using the AT commands.

- To dial out from Linux, you need a communications program. The companion CD-ROM includes two communications programs: `seyon` and `minicom`.

- To allow other people to dial into your Linux system through a modem, you have to run `uugetty` (or some other `getty` process) on the serial line with the modem. You also must set up some parameters in the `/etc/gettydefs` file. You typically start `uugetty` in the `/etc/inittab` file.

- You can connect a terminal to the serial port as long as you use an appropriate cable. Linux also supports several types of multiport serial I/O boards that allow you to connect several terminals or modems to your Linux PC.

Chapter 16

Networks

In This Chapter

▶ Understanding the OSI seven-layer network model

▶ Understanding network protocols and TCP/IP

▶ Understanding network and host addresses in the Internet Protocol (IP)

▶ Using Ethernet with Linux

▶ Setting up TCP/IP networking in Linux

▶ Using TCP/IP diagnostic commands in Linux

UNIX and networking go hand in hand. In particular, TCP/IP (Transmission Control Protocol/Internet Protocol) networking is practically synonymous with UNIX. As a UNIX clone, Linux includes extensive built-in networking capabilities. In particular, Linux supports TCP/IP networking over several physical interfaces, such as Ethernet cards, serial ports, and parallel ports.

You typically would use an Ethernet network for your local-area network (LAN) — at your office or even your home (if you happen to have several systems at home). TCP/IP networking over the serial port allows you to connect to other networks by dialing out over a modem. Linux supports both Serial Line Internet Protocol (SLIP) and Point-to-Point Protocol (PPP).

Cross Reference

This chapter focuses on Linux's support for Ethernet and TCP/IP. Although much of this applies to TCP/IP over the serial line, this chapter does not dwell on the specific details of dial-up networking; that topic is the focus of Chapter 18.

The chapter starts with a discussion of networking in general and TCP/IP in particular; then it covers the physical setup of an Ethernet LAN, including information on specific brands of Ethernet cards. Finally, the chapter turns to the subject of how to set up a TCP/IP network on a Linux system.

Cross Reference

Laptops often use PC cards for networking. Chapter 17 describes the PC cards that Linux supports.

Networking Basics

Like any other technical subject, networking is full of terminology and jargon that a newcomer might find daunting. This section introduces some basic concepts of networking, starting with a layered model of networking and proceeding to details of Ethernet and TCP/IP network protocols.

The OSI seven-layer model

A widely used conceptual model of networking is the seven-layer Open Systems Interconnection (OSI) reference model, developed by the International Standards Organization (ISO). The OSI reference model describes the flow of data between the physical connection to the network and the end-user application. Each layer is responsible for providing particular functionality, as shown in Figure 16-1.

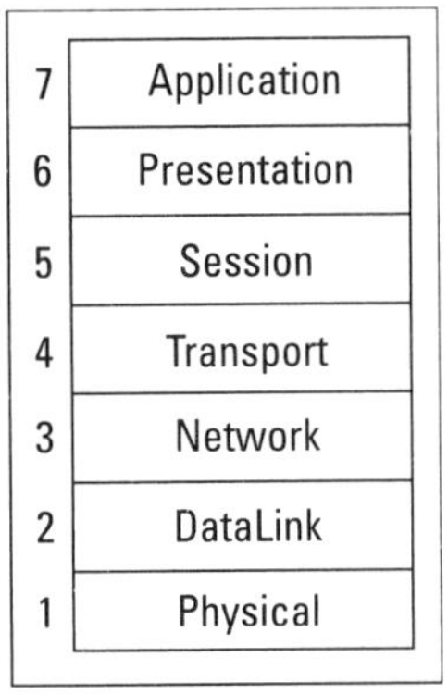

7	Application
6	Presentation
5	Session
4	Transport
3	Network
2	DataLink
1	Physical

Figure 16-1: OSI seven-layer reference model of networking.

As Figure 16-1 shows, the OSI layers are numbered from bottom to top. Basic functions, such as physically sending data bits through the network cable, are at the bottom, and functions that deal with higher-level abstractions of the data are at the top. The purpose of each layer is to provide services to the next-higher layer in a manner such that the higher layer does not have to know how the services are actually implemented.

The purposes of the seven layers in the OSI reference model are as follows:

- The *physical layer* transmits raw bits of data across the physical medium (the networking cable or electromagnetic waves, in case of wireless networks). This layer carries the data generated by all the higher layers. The physical layer deals with three physical components:
    - Network topology (such as bus or star), which specifies how various nodes of a network are physically connected
    - Transmission medium (such as RG-58 coaxial cable, shielded or unshielded twisted pair, fiber-optic cable, and microwave) that carries the actual signals representing data
    - Transmission technique (such as Carrier Sense Multiple Access with Collision Detection [CSMA/CD], used by Ethernet; and token-based techniques, used by token-ring and Fiber Distributed Data Interface [FDDI]), which defines the hardware protocols for data transfer

- The *data-link layer* deals with logical packets (or *frames*) of data. This layer packages raw bits from the physical layer into frames, the exact format of which depends on the type of network, such as Ethernet or Token Ring. The frames used by the data-link layer contain the physical addresses of the sender and the receiver of data.

- The *network layer* knows about the logical network addresses and how to translate logical addresses to physical ones. At the sending end, the network layer converts larger logical packets to smaller physical data frames. At the receiving end, the network layer reassembles the data frames into their original logical packet structure.

- The *transport layer* is responsible for the reliable delivery of messages that originate at the application layer. At the sending end, this layer divides long messages into several packets. At the receiving end, the transport layer reassembles the original messages and sends an acknowledgment of receipt. The transport layer also checks to make sure that data is received in the correct order and in a timely manner. In case of errors, the transport layer requests retransmission of data.

- The *session layer* allows applications on different computers to initiate, use, and terminate a connection (the connection is called a *session*). The session layer translates the names of systems to appropriate addresses (for example, IP addresses in TCP/IP networks).

- The *presentation layer* manages the format used to exchange data between networked computers. Data encryption and decryption, for example, would be in this layer. Most network protocols do not have a presentation layer.

- The *application layer* is the gateway through which application processes access network services. This layer represents services (such as file transfers, database access, and electronic mail) that directly support applications.

The OSI model is not specific to any hardware or software; it simply provides an architectural framework and gives us a common terminology for discussing various networking capabilities.

A simplified four-layer network model

The OSI seven-layer model is not a specification; it provides guidelines for organizing all network services. Most implementations adopt a layered model for networking services, and these layered models can be mapped to the OSI reference model. The TCP/IP networking model, for example, can be adequately represented by a simplified model.

Network-aware applications usually deal with the top three layers (session, presentation, and application) of the OSI seven-layer reference model. Thus, these three layers can be combined into a single layer called the application layer.

The bottom two layers of the OSI model — physical and data link — also can be combined into a single physical layer. These combinations result in a simplified four-layer model, as shown in Figure 16-2.

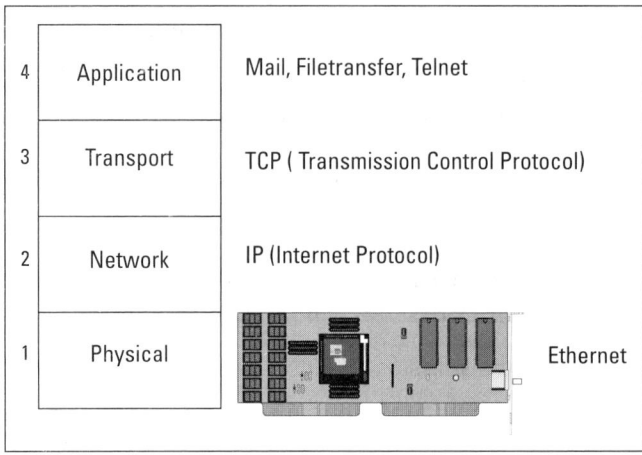

Figure 16-2: Simplified four-layer networking model.

At each of these layers, information is exchanged through one of many network protocols.

Network protocols

A *network protocol* refers to a detailed process agreed upon by the sender and receiver for exchanging data at a specific layer of the networking model. Thus, you would find the following protocols in the simplified four-layer network model of Figure 16-2:

- Physical-layer protocols, such as Ethernet, token ring, and FDDI.
- Network-layer protocols, such as the Internet Protocol (IP), which is part of the TCP/IP protocol suite.
- Transport-layer protocols, such as the Transmission Control Protocol (TCP) and User Datagram Protocol (UDP), that are part of the TCP/IP protocol suite.
- Application-layer protocols — such as File Transfer Protocol (FTP), Simple Mail Transfer Protocol (SMTP), Domain Name Service (DNS), telnet, and Simple Network Management Protocol (SNMP) — that are also part of the TCP/IP protocol suite.

The term *protocol suite* refers to a collection of two or more protocols from these layers that form the basis of a network. Some of the well-known protocol suites are

- IPX/SPX (Internet Packet Exchange/Sequenced Packet Exchange) protocol suite, used by Novell NetWare
- NetBIOS and NetBEUI (Network BIOS Extended User Interface)
- TCP/IP protocol suite

Of these protocol suites, you should be most interested in the TCP/IP protocol suite because that's what Linux and other UNIX systems support well.

In addition to the TCP/IP protocol, Linux also supports the IPX protocol, but not the SPX protocol necessary for NetWare. Linux's support for NetBIOS comes in the form of a software package named Samba, which is included in the companion CD-ROM and described in the "LAN Manager server" section of Chapter 21.

TCP/IP and the Internet

TCP/IP has become the protocol of choice on the Internet — the "network of networks" that evolved from ARPAnet, a packet-switching network that itself evolved from research initiated by the U.S. Government's Advanced Research Projects Agency (ARPA) in the 1970s. Subsequently, ARPA acquired a *Defense* prefix and became DARPA. Under the auspices of DARPA, the TCP/IP protocols emerged as a popular collection of protocols for *internetworking* — a term used to describe communication among networks.

TCP/IP has flourished for several reasons. A significant reason is that the protocol is an open protocol, which simply means that the technical descriptions of the protocol appear in public documents, so anyone can build a TCP/IP on his or her hardware and software.

Another, more important reason for TCP/IP's success is the availability of sample implementation. Instead of describing network architecture and protocols on paper, each component of the TCP/IP protocol suite began life as a specification with a sample implementation.

More on TCP/IP

This chapter gives you an overview of TCP/IP and Ethernet networking and then moves on to Linux-specific instructions for setting up TCP/IP networking. A single chapter simply isn't enough to provide all available information about TCP/IP. For more information on TCP/IP, consult one of the following books:

- Douglas E. Comer, *Internetworking with TCP/IP: Principles*, Protocols, and Architecture, Prentice-Hall, 1988

- W. Richard Stevens, *UNIX Network Programming*, Prentice-Hall, 1990

- Matthew Naugle, *Network Protocol Handbook*, McGraw-Hill, 1994

RFCs

Tip

The details of each TCP/IP protocol are described in documents known as Request for Comments (RFCs). These documents are freely distributed on the Internet. You can get the RFCs from ftp://rs.internic.net/rfc.

In fact, this notation of naming Internet resources in a uniform manner is itself documented in an RFC. The notation, known as the Uniform Resource Locator (URL), is described in RFC 1630, "Universal Resource Identifiers in WWW," written by T. Berners-Lee, the originator of the World Wide Web (WWW).

You can think of RFCs as being the working papers of the Internet research-and-development community. All Internet standards are published as RFCs. Many RFCs do not specify any standards, however; they are informational documents only.

The RFCs continue to evolve as new technology and techniques emerge. If you work in the networking area, you should keep an eye on the RFCs to monitor emerging networking protocols.

Important RFCs

Following are some of the RFCs that you may find interesting:

- RFC 768, "User Datagram Protocol (UDP)"
- RFC 791, "Internet Protocol (IP)"
- RFC 792, "Internet Control Message Protocol (ICMP)"
- RFC 793, "Transmission Control Protocol (TCP)"
- RFC 821, "Simple Mail Transfer Protocol (SMTP)"
- RFC 822, "Format for Electronic Mail Messages"
- RFC 950, "IP Subnet Extension"
- RFC 959, "File Transfer Protocol (FTP)"
- RFC 1034, "Domain Names: Concepts and Facilities"
- RFC 1058, "Routing Information Protocol (RIP)"
- RFC 1112, "Internet Group Multicast Protocol (IGMP)"
- RFC 1155, "Structure of Management Information (SMI)"
- RFC 1157, "Simple Network Management Protocol (SNMP)"
- RFC 1310, "The Internet Standards Process"
- RFC 1521, "Multipurpose Internet Mail Extensions (MIME)"
- RFC 1583, "Open Shortest Path First Routing V2 (OSPF2)"
- RFC 1661, "Point-to-Point Protocol (PPP)"
- RFC 1725, "Post Office Protocol, Version 3 (POP3)"
- RFC 1738, "Uniform Resource Locators (URL)"
- RFC 1739, "A Primer on Internet and TCP/IP Tools"
- RFC 1752, "The Recommendation for the IP Next Generation Protocol"
- RFC 1780, "Internet Official Protocol Standards"

IP addresses

When you have many computers on a network, you need a way to identify each one uniquely. In TCP/IP networking, the address of a computer is known as the *IP address*. Because TCP/IP deals with internetworking, the address is based on the concept of a network address and a host address. You might think of the idea of a network address and a host address as having to provide two addresses to uniquely identify a computer:

- The *network address*, which indicates the network on which the computer is located
- The *host address* of the computer on that network

Dotted-decimal addresses

The original IP address is a 4-byte (32-bit) value. The convention is to write each byte as a decimal value and to put a dot (.) after each number. Thus, you see network addresses such as 140.90.23.100. This way of writing IP addresses is known as *dotted-decimal* notation.

Address classes

The bits in an IP address are interpreted in the following manner:

```
<Network Address, Host Address>
```

In other words, a specified number of bits of the 32-bit IP address is considered to be a network address; the rest of the bits are interpreted as being a host address. The host address identifies your PC whereas the network address identifies the LAN to which your PC is connected.

To accommodate networks of various sizes (the network size is the number of computers in that network), the IP address includes the concept of several classes of network. There are five classes of IP addresses, named Class A through Class E, as shown in Figure 16-3.

Of the five address classes, only classes A, B, and C are used for addressing networks and hosts; class D and E addresses are reserved for special use.

Class A addresses support 126 networks, each with up to 16 million hosts. Although the network address is 7-bit, two values (0 and 127) have special meaning; therefore, you can have only 1 through 126 as Class A network addresses.

Class B addresses are for networks with up to 65,534 hosts. There can be, at most, 16,384 class B networks.

Class C addresses are for small organizations. Each class C address allows up to 254 hosts, and there can be about 2 million class C networks. If you are in a small company, you probably have one of the class C addresses.

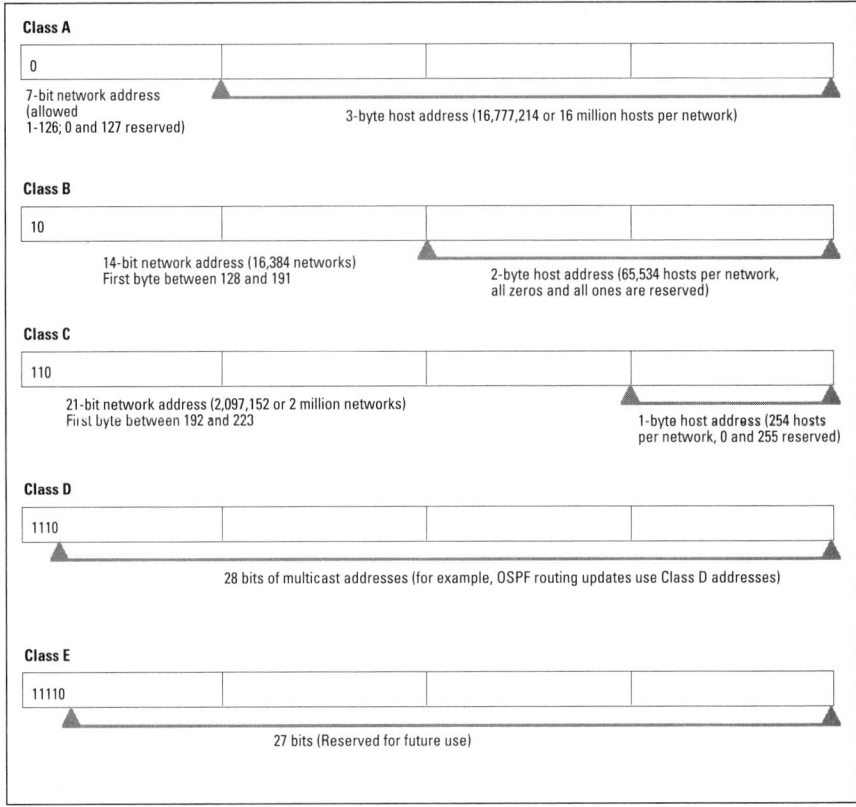

Figure 16-3: Classes of IP addresses.

You can tell the class of an IP address by the first number in the dotted-decimal notation, as follows:

- Class A addresses: 1.*xxx.xxx.xxx* through 126.*xxx.xxx.xxx*
- Class B addresses: 128.*xxx.xxx.xxx* through 191.*xxx.xxx.xxx*
- Class C addresses: 192.*xxx.xxx.xxx* through 223.*xxx.xxx.xxx*

Even within the five address classes, the following IP addresses have special meaning:

- An address with all zeros in the network portion of the address means the local network — the network where the message with this IP addresses originated. Thus, the address 0.0.0.200 means host number 200 on this class C network.

Chapter 16: Networks   **477**

- The class A address 127.*xxx.xxx.xxx* is used for *loopback* — communications within the same host. Conventionally, 127.0.0.1 is used as the loopback address. Processes that need to communicate through TCP with other processes on the same host use the loopback address to avoid having to send packets out on the network.

- Turning on all the bits in any part of the address means a broadcast message. The address 128.18.255.255, for example, means all hosts on the class B network 128.18. The address 255.255.255.255 is known as a limited broadcast; all workstations on the current network will receive the packet.

IP-address requests

If you are setting up an independent network of your own that will be connected to the Internet, you need unique IP addresses for your network. IP addresses are administered through the Network Information Center (NIC), at the following address:

> Network Solutions
> InterNIC Registration Services
> 505 Huntmar Park Drive
> Herndon, VA 22070
> Phone: (703) 742-4777
> Fax: (703) 742-4811

If you get your Internet access through an Internet Service Provider (ISP), you need not worry about getting IP addresses for your systems; your ISP will provide the necessary IP addresses.

If you already have Internet access someplace, you can get the application forms from ftp://rs.internic.net/templates

Download the appropriate application form (the form depends on whether your network is in the United States, Europe, or Asia), fill it in, and mail it to netreg@internic.net

Due to the explosive growth of the Internet, IP addresses are in great demand, and you will have to explain to the NIC why you need a network address, even if it's only a class C address. (I can tell you from recent personal experience that the NIC is really swamped with requests for IP addresses; it may take you a while to get an official network address.)

Until recently, anyone could get an IP address free. Due to a recent change, however, you'll have to pay a yearly fee of fifty dollars (U.S.) for your network's IP address.

If you do not plan to connect your network to the Internet, you really do not need a unique IP address. RFC 1597 ("Address Allocation for Private Networks") provides guidance on what IP addresses you can use within private networks (the term *private network* refers to any network that's not connected to the Internet). Three blocks of IP addresses are reserved for private networks:

- 10.0.0.0 to 10.255.255.255
- 172.16.0.0 to 172.16.255.255
- 192.168.0.0 to 192.168.255.255

You can use addresses from these blocks for your private network without having to coordinate with any organization.

Next-generation IP (IPv6)

At the time when the 4-byte IP address was created, the number of addresses seemed to be adequate. By now, however, class A and class B addresses are running out, and class C addresses are depleting at a fast rate. In addition, the proliferation of class C addresses has introduced a unique problem. Each class C address needs an entry in the network routing tables — the tables that contain information on how to locate any network in the Internet. Too many class C addresses means too many entries in the routing tables.

The Internet Engineering Task Force (IETF) recognized this problem in 1991, and work began then on the next-generation IP addressing scheme, named IPng. This standard was to eventually replace the old 4-byte addressing scheme (called IPv4, for IP version 4).

Note

Several alternative addressing schemes were proposed and debated. The final contender, with a 128-bit (16-byte) address, was dubbed IPv6 (for IP version 6). The latest news is that the IETF declared the core set of IPv6 addressing protocols to be an IETF Proposed Standard on September 18, 1995.

The IPv6 is designed to be an evolutionary step from IPv4. The proposed standard provides direct interoperability between hosts using the older IPv4 addresses and any new IPv6 hosts. The idea is that users can upgrade their systems to use IPv6 when they want and that network operators are free to upgrade their network hardware to use IPv6 without affecting current users of IPv4. Reportedly, a sample implementation of IPv6 is being developed for many operating systems, including Linux.

Secret

A 128-bit addressing scheme allows for 170,141,183,460,469,232,000,000,000,000,000,000 unique hosts! That should last us for a while!

Network mask

The *network mask* is an IP address that has 1s in the bits that correspond to the network address and 0s in all other bit positions. The class of your network address determines the network mask.

If you have a class C address, for example, the network mask is 255.255.255.0. Thus, class B networks have a network mask of 255.255.0.0, and class A networks have 255.0.0.0 as the network mask.

Network address

The *network address* is the bitwise-AND of the network mask with any IP address in your network. If the IP address of a system on your network is 206.197.168.200, and the network mask is 255.255.255.0, the network address is 206.197.168.0. As you may have noticed, the network address has a zero in the host-address area. When you request an IP address from NIC, you get a network address.

Subnets

If your site has a class B address, you get one network number, and that network can have up to 65,534 hosts. Even if you work for a megacorporation that has thousands of hosts, you may want to divide your network into smaller subnetworks (or *subnets*). If your organization has offices in several locations, for example, you may want each office to be on a separate network. You can do this by taking some bits from the host-address portion of the IP address and assigning those bits to the network address. This procedure is known as defining a subnet mask.

Essentially, you add more bits to the network mask. If you have a class B network, for example, the network mask would be 255.255.0.0. If you decide to divide your network into 128 subnetworks, each of which has 512 hosts, you would designate 7 bits from the host address space as the subnet address. Thus, the subnet mask becomes 255.255.254.0.

TCP/IP routing

Routing refers to the task of forwarding information from one network to another. Consider the two class C networks 206.197.168.0 and 164.109.10.0. You need a routing device to send packets from one of these networks to the other.

Secret

Because a routing device facilitates data exchange between two networks, it has two physical network connections, one on each network. Each network interface has its own IP address, and the routing device essentially passes packets back and forth between the two network interfaces. Figure 16-4 illustrates how a routing device has a physical presence in two networks and how each network interface has its own IP address.

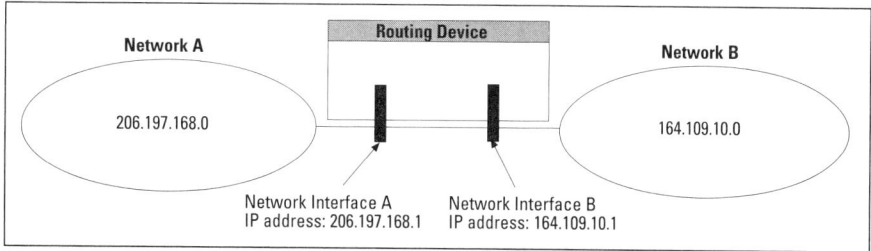

Figure 16-4: A routing device allows packet exchange between two networks.

The generic term *routing device* could be a general-purpose computer with two network interfaces or a dedicated device designed specifically for routing. Such dedicated routing devices are known as *routers*.

The generic term *gateway* also refers to any routing device. For good performance (high packet transfer rate), you want a dedicated router, whose sole purpose is to route packets of data in a network.

Later, when you learn how to set up a TCP/IP network in Linux, you'll run into the term *gateway*, which refers to a routing device regardless of whether the device is another PC or a router. As you'll learn in the "Enter Gateway Address" section, all you have to specify is the gateway's IP address on your network.

A single routing device, of course, does not connect all the networks in the world; packets get around in the Internet from one gateway to another. Any network connected to another network has a designated gateway. You can even have specific gateways for specific networks. As you'll learn later, a routing table keeps track of the gateway associated with an external network and the type of physical interface (such as Ethernet or Point-to-Point Protocol over serial line) for that network. A default gateway gets packets that are addressed to any unknown network.

In your local-area network, all packets addressed to another network go to your network's default gateway. If that gateway is physically connected to the destination network, the story ends there because the gateway can physically send the packets to the destination host. If that gateway does not know the destination network, however, it sends the packets to the next default gateway (the gateway for the other network on which your gateway also "lives"). In this way, packets travel from one gateway to the next until they reach the destination network (or you get an error message saying that the destination network is unreachable).

To send packets around in the network efficiently, routers exchange information (in the form of routing tables) so that each router can have a "map" of the network in its vicinity. Routers exchange information by using a routing protocol from a family of protocols known as Interior Gateway Protocol (IGP). A commonly used Interior Gateway Protocol is the Routing Information Protocol (RIP).

In TCP/IP routing, any time a packet passes through a router, it's considered to have made a *hop*. In RIP, the maximum size of the Internet is 15 hops. A network is considered to be unreachable from your network if a packet does not reach the destination network within 15 hops. In other words, any network more than 15 routers away is considered to be unreachable.

Within a single network, you don't need a router as long as you do not use any subnet mask to break the single IP network into several subnets. In that case, however, you'll have to set up routers to send packets from one subnet to another.

Domain Name System (DNS)

You can access any host computer in a TCP/IP network with an IP address. Remembering the IP addresses of even a few hosts of interest, however, is tedious. This fact was recognized from the beginning of TCP/IP, and the association between a host name and IP address was used. The concept is similar to that of a phone book, in which you can look up a telephone number by searching for a person's name.

In the beginning, the association between names and IP addresses was maintained in a text file named HOSTS.TXT at the Network Information Center (NIC), which was located in the Stanford Research Institute (SRI). This file contained the names and corresponding IP addresses of networks, hosts, and routers on the Internet. All hosts on the Internet used to transfer that file by FTP, or File Transfer Protocol. (Can you imagine all hosts getting a file from a single source in today's Internet?) As the number of Internet hosts increased, the single file idea became intractable. The hosts file was becoming difficult to maintain, and it was hard for all the hosts to update their hosts file in a timely manner. To alleviate the problem, RFCs 881, 882, and 883 introduced the concept and plans for Domain Name in November 1983. Eventually, this led to the Domain Name System (DNS) as we know it today (documented in RFCs 1032, 1033, 1034, and 1035).

Domain-name hierarchy

DNS provides a hierarchical naming system much like your postal address, which you can read as "your name" at "your street address" in "your city" in "your state" in "your country." If I know your full postal address, I would locate you by starting with your city in your country. Then I'd locate the street address to find your home, ring the doorbell, and ask for you by name.

DNS essentially provides an addressing scheme for an Internet host that is much like the postal address. The entire Internet is subdivided into several domains, such as gov, edu, com, mil, and net. Each domain is further subdivided into subdomains. Finally, within a subdomain, each host is given a symbolic name. To write a host's *fully qualified domain name*, you string together the host name, subdomain names, and domain name with dots (.) as separators. Following is the full domain name of a host named addlab in the subdomain nws within another subdomain noaa in the gov domain:
addlab.nws.noaa.gov

Figure 16-5 illustrates part of the Internet Domain Name System, showing the location of the host addlab.nws.noaa.gov.

For a commercial system in the com domain, the name of a host might be as simple as metrolink.com.

You can refer to a user on a system by appending an at sign (@), followed by the host's domain name, to the user name (the name under which the user logs in). Thus, you would refer to the user named sales at the host metrolink.com as sales@metrolink.com.

That's how you refer to users when you send electronic mail.

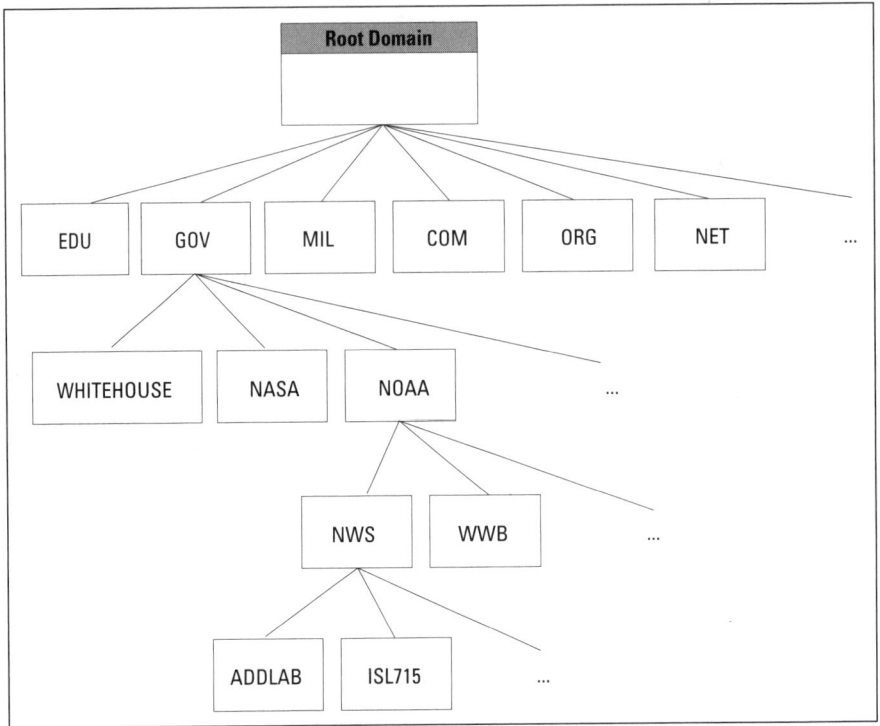

Figure 16-5: Part of the Internet domain-name hierarchy.

Name servers

TCP/IP network applications resolve a host name to an IP address by consulting a *name server*, which is another host that's accessible from your network. If you decide to use the Domain Name System (DNS) on your network, you have to set up a name server in your network or indicate a name server (by an IP address).

Later sections of this chapter discuss the configuration files /etc/host.conf and /etc/resolv.conf, through which you specify how host names would be converted to IP addresses. In particular, you specify the IP addresses of a name server in the /etc/resolv.conf file.

Tip

If you do not use DNS, you still can have host-name-to-IP-address mapping through a text file named /etc/hosts. The entries in a typical /etc/hosts file might look like the following example:

```
# This is a comment
127.0.0.1         localhost
206.197.168.2     lnbsun
206.197.168.50    lnb386
206.197.168.100   lnb486
206.197.168.150   lnbmac
206.197.168.200   lnbsoft
```

As the example shows, the file lists a host name for each IP address. The IP address and host names will be different for your system, of course.

One problem with relying on the /etc/hosts file for name lookup is that you have to replicate this file on each system on your network. This procedure can become a nuisance even in a network that has five or six systems.

TCP/IP services

The TCP/IP protocol suite has become the lingua franca of the Internet because many standard services are available on all systems that support TCP/IP. These services make the Internet tick by enabling the transfer of mail and news and by allowing remote logins. These services go by well-known names such as the following:

- ftp (File Transfer Protocol)
- http (Hypertext Transfer Protocol)
- smtp (Simple Mail Transfer Protocol)
- nntp (Network News Transfer Protocol)
- snmp (Simple Network Management Protocol)
- tftp (Trivial File Transfer Protocol)
- nfs (Network File System)

A well-known port is associated with each of these services. The TCP protocol uses this port to locate a service on any system. (A service is implemented by a *process* — a computer program running on a system.)

Like the /etc/hosts file, which stores the association between host names and IP addresses, the association between a service name and a port number (as well as a protocol) is stored in another text file, named /etc/services. Following are typical entries in an /etc/services file in Linux:

```
# Network services, Internet style
#
# Notice that it is currently the policy of IANA to assign a single
# well-known port number for both TCP and UDP; hence, most entries here
# have two entries even if the protocol doesn't support UDP operations.
# Updated from RFC 1340, "Assigned Numbers'' (July 1992). Not all
# ports are included, only the more common ones.
#
#   from: @(#)services    5.8 (Berkeley) 5/9/91
#    $Id: services,v 1.9 1993/11/08 19:49:15 cgd Exp $
#
tcpmux              1/tcp           # TCP port service multiplexer
echo                7/tcp
echo                7/udp
discard             9/tcp           sink null
```

```
discard         9/udp           sink null
systat          11/tcp          users
daytime         13/tcp
daytime         13/udp
netstat         15/tcp
qotd            17/tcp          quote
msp             18/tcp          # message send protocol
msp             18/udp          # message send protocol
chargen         19/tcp          ttytst source
chargen         19/udp          ttytst source
ftp             21/tcp
# 22 - unassigned
telnet          23/tcp
# 24 - private
smtp            25/tcp          mail
# 26 - unassigned
time            37/tcp          timserver
time            37/udp          timserver
rlp             39/udp          resource        # resource location
nameserver  42/tcp              name            # IEN 116
whois           43/tcp          nicname
domain          53/tcp          nameserver      # name-domain server
domain          53/udp          nameserver
mtp             57/tcp                          # deprecated
bootps          67/tcp          # BOOTP server
bootps          67/udp
bootpc          68/tcp          # BOOTP client
bootpc          68/udp
tftp            69/udp
gopher          70/tcp          # Internet Gopher
gopher          70/udp
rje             77/tcp          netrjs
finger          79/tcp
www             80/tcp          http    # World Wide Web HTTP
www             80/udp                  # HyperText Transfer Protocol
link            87/tcp          ttylink
kerberos        88/tcp          krb5    # Kerberos v5
kerberos        88/udp
supdup          95/tcp
# 100 - reserved
hostnames   101/tcp             hostname        # usually from sri-nic
iso-tsap    102/tcp             tsap            # part of ISODE.
csnet-ns    105/tcp             cso-ns  # also used by CSO name server
csnet-ns    105/udp             cso-ns
rtelnet         107/tcp         # Remote Telnet
rtelnet         107/udp
pop2        109/tcp             postoffice      # POP version 2
pop2        109/udp
pop3        110/tcp             # POP version 3
pop3        110/udp
sunrpc          111/tcp
sunrpc          111/udp
auth        113/tcp             tap ident authentication
sftp        115/tcp
uucp-path   117/tcp
```

```
nntp            119/tcp         readnews untp   # USENET News Transfer
Protocol
ntp             123/tcp
ntp             123/udp                         # Network Time Protocol
netbios-ns      137/tcp                         # NETBIOS Name Service
netbios-ns      137/udp
netbios-dgm     138/tcp                         # NETBIOS Datagram Service
netbios-dgm     138/udp
netbios-ssn     139/tcp                         # NETBIOS session service
netbios-ssn     139/udp
imap2                   143/tcp                         # Interim Mail
Access Proto v2
imap2                   143/udp
snmp            161/udp                         # Simple Net Mgmt Proto
snmp-trap       162/udp         snmptrap        # Traps for SNMP
cmip-man        163/tcp                         # ISO mgmt over IP (CMOT)
cmip-man        163/udp
cmip-agent      164/tcp
cmip-agent      164/udp
xdmcp                   177/tcp                         # X Display Mgr.
Control Proto
xdmcp                   177/udp
# Rest of the file not shown...
```

You'll find browsing through the entries in the /etc/services file to be instructive because the entries show the breadth of networking services available under TCP/IP.

Ethernet and Linux

TCP/IP is a fine protocol suite for networking, but before you can use TCP/IP, you have to set up the physical network. Ethernet is a good choice for the physical data-transport mechanism, for the following reasons:

- Ethernet is proven technology (it has been around since the early 1980s).
- Ethernet provides good data-transfer rates: a maximum rate of 10 million bits per second (10 Mbps).
- Ethernet hardware is relatively low-cost (PC Ethernet cards are approximately $100 U.S.).

Typically, Linux supports affordable hardware well, and Ethernet is no exception. The following sections describe the Ethernet cards that Linux supports and describe the physical setup of an Ethernet LAN.

Ethernet basics

Ethernet is a standard way to move packets of data between two or more computers connected to a single cable. (Larger networks are constructed by connecting multiple Ethernet segments with gateways.) Because a single wire is used, a protocol has to be used for sending and receiving data because only one data packet can exist on the cable at any time. An Ethernet LAN uses a data-transmission protocol known as *Carrier Sense Multiple Access/Collision Detection* (CSMA/CD) to ensure that multiple computers can share the single transmission cable. Ethernet controllers embedded in the computers follow the CSMA/CD protocol to transmit and receive Ethernet packets.

The idea behind the CSMA/CD protocol is similar to the way that you might have a conversation at a party. You listen for a pause (*carrier sense*) and talk when no one else is speaking. If you and another person begin talking at the same time, both of you realize the problem (*collision detection*) and pause for a moment; then one of you starts speaking again. As you know from experience, everything works out.

In an Ethernet LAN, each Ethernet controller checks the cable for presence of signals — that's the carrier-sense part. If the signal level is low, a controller sends its packets on the cable; the packet contains information about the sender and the intended recipient. All Ethernet controllers on the LAN listen to the signal, and the recipient receives the packet. If, somehow, two controllers send out a packet simultaneously, the signal level in the cable rises above a threshold, and the controllers know that a collision occurred (two packets were sent out at the same time). Both controllers wait for a random amount of time and then send their packets again.

Ethernet was invented in the early 1970s at the Xerox Palo Alto Research Center (PARC) by Robert M. Metcalfe. In the 1980s, Ethernet was standardized by a cooperative effort of three companies: Digital Equipment Corporation (DEC), Intel, and Xerox. Using the first initials of the company names, that Ethernet standard became known as the *DIX standard*. Later, the DIX standard was included in the 802-series standards developed by the Institute of Electrical and Electronics Engineers (IEEE). The Ethernet specification is formally known as IEEE 802.3 CSMA/CD, but people continue to call it Ethernet.

Wizard

Ethernet sends data in packets (also known as *frames*) with a standard format that consists of the following sequence of components:

- 8-byte preamble
- 6-byte destination address
- 6-byte source address
- 2-byte length of the data field
- 46- to 1,500-byte data field
- 4-byte frame-check sequence (used for error checking)

You don't need to know much about the innards of Ethernet packets except to note the 6-byte source and destination addresses. Each Ethernet controller has a unique 6-byte (48-bit) address. At the physical level, packets must be addressed with these 6-byte addresses.

Address Resolution Protocol

In an Ethernet LAN, two Ethernet controllers can communicate only if they know each other's 6-byte physical Ethernet address. You may wonder how IP addresses are mapped to physical addresses. This problem is solved by the Address Resolution Protocol (ARP), which specifies how to obtain the physical address that corresponds to an IP address. Essentially, when a packet has to be sent to an IP address, the TCP/IP protocol uses ARP to find the physical address of the destination.

When the packet is meant for an IP address outside your network, that packet is sent to the gateway that has a physical presence on your network and that, therefore, can respond to an ARP request for a physical address.

Ethernet cables

The original Ethernet standard used a thick coaxial cable, nearly half an inch in diameter. That wiring is called *thickwire* or *thick Ethernet*, although the IEEE 802.3 standard calls it 10BASE5. That designation means that the data-transmission rate is 10 megabits per second (10 Mbps), that the transmission is baseband (which simply means that the cable's signal-carrying capacity is devoted to transmitting Ethernet packets only), and that the total length of the cable can be no more than 500 meters. Thickwire was expensive, and the cable was rather unwieldy.

Nowadays, two other forms of Ethernet cabling are more popular. The first alternative to thick Ethernet cable is *thinwire*, or 10BASE2, which uses a thin, flexible coaxial cable. A thinwire Ethernet segment can be, at most, 185 meters long. The other, more recent alternative is Ethernet over unshielded twisted-pair cable (UTP), known as 10BASET.

To set up a 10BASET Ethernet, you need an Ethernet *hub* — a hardware box with phone jacks. You build the network by running twisted-pair wires from each PC's Ethernet card to this hub.

Thinwire has a feature that makes it attractive for small offices or home offices that have more than one PC. You can daisy-chain the thinwire cable from one PC to another and construct a small Ethernet LAN, as shown in Figure 16-6.

As Figure 16-6 shows, you need Ethernet cards in the PCs. The cards should have thinwire connectors, known as BNC connectors. You also need segments of thinwire cable (technically known as RG-58 thin coaxial cables with 50-ohm impedance). For each Ethernet card's BNC connector, you need a BNC T connector (so called because the connector looks like a *T*), and you need two 50-ohm terminators for the two end points of the Ethernet network. Then all you have to do to complete your own Ethernet LAN is connect the parts in the manner shown in Figure 16-6. I used this approach to connect several PCs and a workstation in my home office.

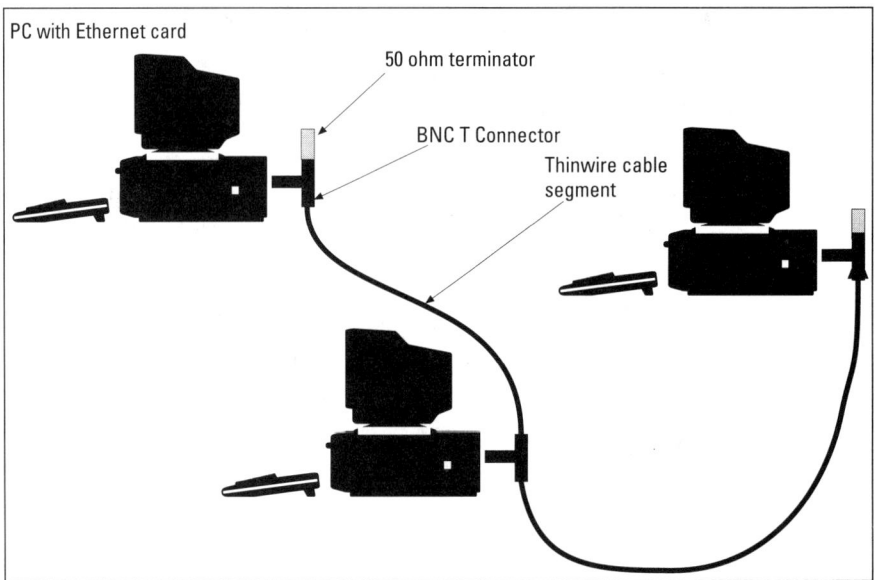

Figure 16-6: Constructing a small thinwire Ethernet LAN.

Note

Remember that you have to use the BNC T connectors and 50-ohm terminators even if you are connecting only two PCs on a LAN; you can't simply connect the two Ethernet cards with a cable.

Supported Ethernet cards

To set up an Ethernet LAN, you need an Ethernet card for each PC. Linux supports a wide variety of Ethernet cards for the PC. Following is a list of supported Ethernet cards in Linux kernel 1.2.8:

- 3Com 3C501 (obsolete and very slow)
- 3Com Etherlink 3C503, #C505, 3C507, 3C509, 3C509B, 3C579 (EISA)
- Allied Telesis AT1500 and AT1700
- AMD LANCE (79C960) and PCnet (AT1500, HP J2405A, NE1500, NE2100)
- Ansel Communications AC3200 (EISA)
- Apricot Xen-II onboard Ethernet
- AT&T GIS WaveLAB
- Cabletron E21xx
- DEC DE425 (EISA), DE434 (PCI), DE435 (PCI)
- DEC DEPCA and EtherWORKS
- HP PCLAN (27245 and other 27xxx series)

- HP PCLAN PLUS (27247B and 27252A)
- IBM ThinkPad 300 built-in Ethernet adapter
- Intel EtherExpress
- New Media Ethernet
- Novell Eagle NE1000 and NE2000
- PureData PDUC8028, PDI8023
- Racal-Interlan NI5210 (i82586 Ethernet chip)
- Racal-Interlan NI6510 (am7990 LANCE Ethernet chip; has problems with more than 16MB RAM)
- Schneider & Koch G16
- SMC Ultra
- WaveLAN
- Western Digital WD8003 (same as SMC Elite) and WD8013 (SMC Elite Plus)
- Zenith Z-Note

If you have upgraded the Linux kernel, the new kernel may support even more cards than the ones shown in this list.

If you have not bought a card yet, you want to buy a 16-bit card, not an 8-bit card. A 16-bit card transfers data faster and has a larger onboard buffer. The cards come with different types of connectors, as follows:

- A DB-15 connector for thick Ethernet. (You need an additional transceiver to connect thickwire to other types of Ethernet, such as thinwire or 10BASET.)
- A thinwire BNC connector.
- An RJ-45 connector for 10BASET. (The RJ-45 connector looks like a common RJ-11 phone jack, but the RJ-45 version is much larger.)

Tip

Nowadays, many Ethernet cards come with more than one, or all three, of these connectors. If you have a small office or a home office, I recommend that you buy an Ethernet card with a thinwire connector. Then you can set up an Ethernet LAN with a few RG58 coaxial cables, BNC T connectors, and 50-ohm terminators.

Thinwire is easy to set up, but it's not convenient to connect many PCs this way. One problem is that any break in the cable causes the entire network to come down.

To set up a 10BASET network, you need a separate hub with telephone jacks. A wire goes from each PC's Ethernet card to the hub, and the hub sets up the proper connections for Ethernet.

You can use Ethernet cards with a DB-15 thick Ethernet connector in a thinwire or 10BASET network. All you need is a transceiver that attaches to the DB-15 port and provides the right type of connector (BNC for thinwire and RJ-45 for 10BASET).

Tip

A better choice is to buy the newer "Combo" version of Ethernet cards that come with both thinwire and 10BASET transceivers built in; there is a BNC connector for a thinwire network and an RJ-45 jack for a 10BASET network.

Unsupported Ethernet cards

As you may realize by now, most device drivers in Linux exist because someone voluntarily wrote the code and provided it free to all of us. Of course, the developer can write a device driver only if the vendor provides technical information about the device without any restrictions (remember that the GNU Public License requires all source code to be freely available). Unfortunately, some hardware vendors refuse to provide technical information about their devices without a nondisclosure agreement. Many advanced video cards fall into this category, which is why many such video cards are not supported in Linux.

A few Ethernet-card vendors also refuse to provide technical information freely. At this writing, Cabletron and Xircom were two such vendors. Because of the lack of programming information, Cabletron and Xircom Ethernet cards are *not* supported in Linux. You need to watch out for these cards if you plan to run Linux on your PC.

Caution

The Cabletron E2100 card is supported only because it is a generic design based on the National Semiconductor DP8390 chip. Although a driver is available for Cabletron E2100, future fixes or enhancements may not be available for this driver.

Kernel support for Ethernet

When you follow the steps in Chapter 1 to install Linux from the companion CD-ROM, you have to select a kernel. Typically, these kernels already include support for some networking cards.

Tip

After you complete the Linux installation and reboot the system, you should check the boot messages to see whether your Ethernet card was detected. (If the boot messages flash by quickly, you can view them at your convenience with the `dmesg | more` command.) My PC, for example, has a 3Com 3C509 Ethernet card, and I see the following lines in the boot messages:

```
eth0: 3c509 at 0x210 tag 1, BNC port, address 00 20 af e8 a2 25,
IRQ 10.
3c509.c:1.03 10/8/94 becker@cesdis.gsfc.nasa.gov
```

The first line starts with the device name for the Ethernet device (eth0 means the first Ethernet card), followed by some identifying information about the card. The message also shows the I/O port address (0x210) and IRQ (10).

The second line, which starts with 3c509, shows information about the Ethernet driver that is being used. The line ends with the electronic-mail address of Donald J. Becker, the author of many Ethernet drivers in Linux.

Secret

If you do not see a message about your Ethernet card, you have to rebuild the kernel to enable support for your Ethernet card. Follow the steps outlined in Chapter 2 to rebuild the kernel. When you run make config to configure the kernel, the configuration program asks several questions (you answer yes or no) about what devices to support in the kernel. Because many devices conflict with one another, you should specify only those devices that you have installed on your system.

When I configured the kernel on my PC with a 3Com 3C509 Ethernet card, I answered the questions in the following manner:

```
Network device support (CONFIG_NETDEVICES) [y]
Dummy net driver support (CONFIG_DUMMY) [y]
SLIP (serial line) support (CONFIG_SLIP) [y]
 CSLIP compressed headers (CONFIG_SLIP_COMPRESSED) [y]
 16 channels instead of 4 (SL_SLIP_LOTS) [n]
PPP (point-to-point) support (CONFIG_PPP) [y]
PLIP (parallel port) support (CONFIG_PLIP) [n]
Do you want to be offered ALPHA test drivers (CONFIG_NET_ALPHA) [n]
Wester Digital/SMC cards (CONFIG_NET_VENDOR_SMC) [y] n
AMD LANCE and PCnet (AT1500 and NE2100) support (CONFIG_LANCE) [y] n
3COM cards (CONFIG_NET_VENDOR_3COM) [y]
3c501 support (CONFIG_EL1) [y] n
3c503 support (CONFIG_EL2) [y] n
3c509/3c579 support (CONFIG_EL3) [y]
Other ISA cards (CONFIG_NET_ISA) [y] n
EISA, VLB, PCI and on board controllers (CONFIG_NET_EISA) [y] n
Pocket and portable adapters (CONFIG_NET_POCKET) [n]
```

The default response appears in brackets at the end of each question; simply press Enter to accept the default. Otherwise, answer by typing **y** or **n** (to indicate yes or no, respectively).

Answer yes to the appropriate questions from that set of networking questions, and complete the kernel-rebuild process. The next time you boot the system, Linux should detect your Ethernet card.

Ethernet autoprobing

At boot time, a kernel with Ethernet support attempts to probe and detect the Ethernet card. The probing involves reading from and writing to specific I/O port addresses.

Although you specify a single I/O port address for a device, most devices use a block of I/O addresses for their operation. The I/O address that you specify is the *base address*; the rest of the I/O addresses are consecutive I/O ports, starting at the base address.

Secret

Depending on the number of I/O addresses used by a device, two devices may end up with overlaps in the range of I/O addresses that they use. The NE2000 (or NE2000) card, for example, uses 32 I/O ports (that's 0x20 in hexadecimal notation). If you select 0x360 as the base I/O address for an NE2000 card, the card uses the ports from 0x360 to 0x379. Unfortunately, the PC's parallel port (LPT1) uses the base I/O address of 0x378, and the secondary IDE controller uses the addresses 0x376 – 0x377. Thus, the NE1000 configured at 0x360 now has an overlap with the I/O addresses used by the first parallel port and the secondary IDE controller. In this case, you can prevent any problems by configuring the NE2000 card at a different I/O address, such as 0x280.

Such overlapping I/O port addresses causes problems because during autoprobing, the kernel may perform operations that might be harmless for some devices but that may cause another device to lock up the system. Typically, however, if your Ethernet card and other devices were working under DOS or Windows, you should have no problem with them under Linux (assuming, of course, that your Ethernet card is supported under Linux).

Secret

If your system hangs during autoprobe, you can exclude a specific range of I/O addresses from being probed. To exclude a range of addresses during autoprobing, use the `reserve` command during the LILO boot prompt. The `reserve` command has the following syntax:

`reserve=BASE-IO-PORT1,NUMPORTS1[,BASE-IO-PORT2,NUMPORTS2,...]`

Here, `BASE-IO-PORT1` is an I/O port address in hexadecimal notation (for example, 0x300), and `NUMPORTS1` is the number of ports (for example, 32) to be excluded when autoprobing. The arguments in brackets are optional; they are used to specify additional exclusion regions.

If you prevent a range of I/O addresses from being autoprobed, a device that may be at that address may not be detected. Thus, you must specify that device's parameters explicitly on the boot command-line.

For Ethernet cards, the LILO command for specifying device parameters is `ether`, which takes the following format:

`ether=IRQ,BASE-IO-PORT,PARAM-1,PARAM-2,NAME`

Table 16-1 explains the meanings of the arguments. All arguments are optional. The Ethernet driver takes the first non-numeric argument as `NAME`.

Chapter 16: Networks 493

Table 16-1   **Arguments for `ether`**

Argument	Meaning
IRQ	The IRQ of the Ethernet card. Specify a zero `IRQ` to make the driver autodetect the IRQ.
BASE-IO-PORT	The base I/O port address of the Ethernet card. Specify a zero `BASE-IO-PORT` to make the driver autodetect the base I/O port address.
PARAM-1	The meaning depends on the Ethernet driver. Some drivers use the least significant four bits of this value as the debug message level. The default is 0; set this argument to a value of 1 to 7 to indicate how verbose the debug messages should be (7 means most verbose). A value of 8 stops debug messages. The AMD LANCE driver uses the low-order four bits as the DMA channel.
PARAM-2	The meaning depends on the Ethernet driver. The 3Com 3c503 drivers use this value to select between an internal and external transceiver — 0 means the internal transceiver, and 1 means that the card uses an external transceiver connected to the DB-15 thick Ethernet port.
NAME	The name of the Ethernet driver (`eth0`, `eth1`, and so on). By default, the kernel uses `eth0` as the name of the first Ethernet card that it autoprobes. The kernel does not probe for more than one Ethernet card because that would increase any chance of conflicts with other devices during autoprobing.

Secret

If you have an Ethernet card at the I/O address 0x300 and do not want this card to be autoprobed, use a command line such as the following at the LILO boot prompt:

`reserve=0x300,32 ether=0,0x300,eth0`

The `reserve` command prevents 32 I/O ports starting at 0x300 from being autoprobed, whereas the `ether` command specifies the base I/O port address for the Ethernet card. The exact I/O addresses depend on your Ethernet card and the range of addresses for which an overlap with some other device exists. Most of the time, you should not have to use these commands.

Secret

A note about PCI cards: their I/O addresses and IRQs are assigned by the PCI BIOS when the system powers up. Thus, you cannot set the I/O address or IRQ of any PCI card through the LILO command line. Even if you specify these parameters through LILO commands, they are ignored for a PCI device.

Network-device names

For most devices, Linux uses files in the /dev directory. The networking devices, however, have names that are defined internally in the kernel; no files for these devices exist in the /dev directory. Following are the common network-device names in Linux:

- lo — the loopback device. This device is used for efficient handling of network packets that are sent from your system to itself (when, for example, an X client communicates with the X server on the same system).
- eth0 — the first Ethernet card. If you have more Ethernet cards, they get device names eth1, eth2, and so on.
- ppp0 — the first serial port configured for a point-to-point link to another computer, using Point-to-Point Protocol (PPP). If you have more serial ports configured for PPP networking, they are assigned device names ppp1, ppp2, and so on.
- sl0 — the first serial port configured for Serial Line Internet Protocol (SLIP) networking. SLIP is used for establishing a point-to-point link to a TCP/IP network. If you use a second serial port for SLIP, it gets the device name sl1.

You always have a loopback device (lo), whether or not you have any network. The loopback device passes data from one process to another without having to go out to a network. In fact, the whole idea of the loopback device is to allow network applications to work as long as the communicating processes are on the same system.

PPP is popular in dial-up networks, in which you use a modem to dial in to an Internet host (typically, a system at your work or your Internet Service Provider) and establish a connection to the Internet. Chapter 18 covers this subject in detail.

If you want to see the names of installed network devices on your system, try the following command:

cat /proc/net/dev

This command shows the network-device names, as well as statistics on the number of packets sent and received for a specific device.

Multiple Ethernet cards

You might use a Linux PC as a gateway between two Ethernet networks. In that case, you might have two Ethernet cards in the PC. The Linux kernel can support more than one Ethernet card; what it does *not* do is detect multiple cards automatically. The kernel looks for only the first Ethernet card. If you happen to have two Ethernet cards, you should specify the parameters of the cards on the LILO boot command line. (The two cards must have different IRQs and I/O addresses, of course.) Following is a typical boot command line for two Ethernet cards:

ether=10,0x220,eth0 ether=5,0x300,eth1

If you happen to have two Ethernet cards, you can place the necessary LILO boot parameters in the /etc/lilo.conf file so that you don't have to enter the arguments every time you boot Linux. For the preceding example, the line in /etc/lilo.conf looks like this:

```
append="ether=10,0x220,eth0 ether=5,0x300,eth1"
```

If you plan to use a Linux PC with two network interfaces as a TCP/IP gateway, you have to recompile the kernel with IP forwarding enabled. Chapter 2 explains how to rebuild the kernel. During the rebuild process, when you use the make config command, the following question appears (this is one of many questions):

```
IP forwarding/gatewaying (CONFIG_IP_FORWARD) [n]
```

You should answer **y** to enable IP forwarding.

TCP/IP Setup in Linux

Like almost everything else in Linux, TCP/IP setup is a matter of preparing a bunch of configuration files (text files that you can edit with any text editor). Most of these configuration files are in the /etc directory. The netconfig utility helps by hiding the details of the configuration. Nevertheless, it's better if you know the names of the files and their purposes so that you can edit the files manually, if necessary.

The next few sections show you how to set up TCP/IP for an Ethernet LAN. Chapter 17 covers dial-up networking under Linux, including topics such as PPP.

Before you look at TCP/IP setup, make sure that your system's Ethernet card is properly installed and detected by the Linux kernel.

Configuring the kernel for TCP/IP

The kernel configuration is the first step in setting up your system for TCP/IP. As shown in Chapter 2, the first step in kernel configuration involves the following commands:

```
cd /usr/src/linux
make config
```

The configuration program asks several questions about various system capabilities; some of these questions are about networking. Following are the first two sets of questions about networking (and some possible responses):

```
*** Networking options:
TCP/IP networking (CONFIG_INET) [y]
IP forwarding/gatewaying (CONFIG_IP_FORWARD) [n] y
IP multicasting (CONFIG_IP_MULTICAST) [n]
IP firewalling (CONFIG_IP_FIREWALL) [n] y
IP accounting (CONFIG_IP_ACCT) [n]
```

```
*** It is safe to leave these untouched
PC/TCP compatibility mode (CONFIG_INET_PCTCP) [n]
Reverse ARP (CONFIG_INET_RARP) [n]
Assume subnets are local (CONFIG_INET_SNARL) [y]
Disable NAGLE algorithm (normally enabled) (CONFIG_TCP_NAGLE_OFF) [n]
The IPX protocol (CONFIG_IPX) [n]
```

You can accept the default answer (shown in brackets at the end of each question) for almost all these questions. You should answer yes to enable IP forwarding if you want to use your Linux system as a gateway (or router) between two separate networks.

The following list explains the meanings of these configuration questions:

TCP/IP networking — This option enables support for the TCP/IP protocol suite in the kernel. You should answer yes to this question, even if you do not plan to set up a LAN. TCP/IP can be used even within a single system; the loopback device lo provides the data-transport mechanism to support TCP/IP exchanges between processes on the same PC.

IP forwarding/gatewaying — Answer yes to this question if you want to use your Linux system to forward TCP/IP packets to another network. The default is to disable IP forwarding. You should turn on IP forwarding if you want to connect your LAN to the Internet with a Linux PC running PPP.

IP multicasting — This question refers to the capability of the system to send and receive network packets addressed to a subset of hosts on the network. Some new Internet services, such as Internet Talk Radio, rely on multicasting. Even if you enable this feature, you need additional software to use the multicasting capabilities.

IP firewalling — If you answer yes to this question, the kernel allows networking software to selectively enable or disable access to groups of TCP/IP ports. You need additional software to control access to specific TCP/IP ports.

IP accounting — If you enable this feature, the kernel counts and records incoming and outgoing data volume (in bytes) on a per-port and per-address basis. You may want to use this feature if you use a Linux PC to provide Internet connectivity to other systems. You can use the IP accounting information to charge your customers based on the level of use.

PC/TCP compatibility mode — If your Linux system is on a LAN with other PCs, and some of those PCs run the PC/TCP networking software, you should answer yes to this question; it takes care of some problems that may occur when a PC running PC/TCP connects to your Linux PC.

Reverse ARP — ARP refers to Address Resolution Protocol, which is used to determine the physical Ethernet address that corresponds to an IP address. The opposite is Reverse ARP (or RARP) — a protocol that allows a system to say, "Here's my Ethernet address; somebody please give me an IP address." Some old Sun 3 workstations and other diskless workstations need RARP to work. Typically, you should not have to answer yes to this query.

Assume subnets are local — You should leave this option in its default setting of yes, which means that all of your subnets are directly connected to your Linux PC.

Disable NAGLE algorithm (normally enabled) — The NAGLE algorithm makes TCP/IP efficient by preventing the transmission of many small data packets. (Some TCP/IP programs, such as `telnet`, send single keystrokes in a separate TCP/IP packet.) When the NAGLE algorithm is enabled, it holds off smaller amounts of data until a larger packet can be assembled and sent. You should leave this option enabled.

The IPX protocol — Answer yes if you want to include support for the Internet Packet Exchange (IPX) protocol — part of the Xerox Network System (XNS) protocol. Novell NetWare uses IPX as its network layer. NetWare's transport layer is called Sequenced Packet Exchange (SPX); Linux does not include SPX support.

Running `netconfig`

After you make sure that the Linux kernel is properly configured for TCP/IP, you have to make sure that the appropriate configuration files exist. Slackware Linux (which is on the companion CD-ROM) includes a shell script named `netconfig` (in the `/sbin` directory) that helps you configure your system for TCP/IP and mail. You can run `netconfig` to begin the TCP/IP configuration and then fix any problems by editing specific configuration files described in later sections.

Tip

To run `netconfig`, log in as `root`, and use the following command:

`/sbin/netconfig`

The `netconfig` script displays a full-screen dialog box (in text mode) that informs you that the script will help you configure your system for TCP/IP and mail. Press Enter to continue. Next, `netconfig` guides you through the following steps, which are essential for TCP/IP and mail setup:

1. `netconfig` displays the Enter Hostname dialog box. You should enter a host name for your system and press Enter. You don't have to enter the fully qualified domain name (such as `lnbsoft.com`); enter only the host name (for example, **lnbsoft**).

2. `netconfig` displays the Enter Domain Name dialog box, requesting the domain name without any leading dot. You should enter the domain name for your system and press Enter. If your system's fully qualified domain name is `lnb386.lnbsoft.com`, for example, you would enter **lnbsoft.com** in this step.

3. `netconfig` displays the Loopback Only dialog box, asking you whether you plan to use TCP/IP through loopback only. I assume that you really do have a network, which is why you are reading this chapter. Therefore, you should press Tab to select the No option and then press Enter to proceed to the next step.

4. `netconfig` next displays the Enter Local IP Address dialog box, in which you should enter your system's IP address. As explained in the overview of TCP/IP earlier in this chapter, you need an IP address for each system on your LAN. If you are part of a larger corporate or government network, you should ask your local network administrator for an IP address. If you are a small business, you may want to request an IP address for your network from the Network Information Center (see the "IP-address requests" section for details).

   Enter the IP address in the text-entry area of the dialog box and then press Enter.

5. Next, `netconfig` displays the Enter Gateway Address dialog box, asking for the gateway address for your network. You should enter the address of any router or a PC designated as the gateway. If you do not have any gateway on the network, simply enter your PC's IP address again. Then press Enter to proceed to the next step.

6. `netconfig` now displays the Enter Netmask dialog box. The term *netmask* is simply a short form of network mask. The netmask looks like an IP address, but it has ones in the bit positions that correspond to the network address and zeros in the host-address part. (For a discussion of network and host addresses, consult the TCP/IP overview sections earlier in this chapter.) Thus, a class C address has a netmask of 255.255.255.0, whereas a class B network has 255.255.0.0 as the netmask.

   Enter the netmask for your network in the dialog box that the `netconfig` script displays. Most small companies probably have a class C IP address and, consequently, a netmask of 255.255.255.0.

7. `netconfig` displays the Use a Nameserver? dialog box, asking whether you plan to use a name server on the network. As long as your system has a gateway, you can specify the address of the appropriate name server for your domain. The name server translates host names to IP addresses.

   If you have a name server, press Enter to proceed. Otherwise, press Tab, followed by Enter, to answer no.

8. `netconfig` displays the Select Nameserver dialog box, which lists your system's IP address, its full host name, and the base host name. Enter the IP address of the name server. You can enter only one name server, but the dialog box tells you that you can add more name servers by editing the `/etc/resolv.conf` file. (You can tell from the message that the `/etc/resolv.conf` file contains the addresses of your domain's name servers.)

   You can use networking software without a name server. The only problem is that you won't be able to refer to systems by their names; you have to use the IP addresses.

   If you have a name server for your domain, type the IP address and then press Enter to continue.

9. Finally, netconfig displays the Network Setup Complete dialog box, informing you that the network setup is complete. If you reboot now, your system's TCP/IP network should begin to work.

Looking back through the steps, you can see that TCP/IP setup involves the following steps (I have filled in the configuration file names for your information):

1. Enter your system's host name and IP address, which are stored in the /etc/hosts file. The host name alone is stored in the /etc/HOSTNAME file.

2. Enter your gateway's IP address. This address is used in the /etc/rc.d/rc.inet1 file, which sets up the default gateway for your network.

3. Enter your network's netmask. This mask is used in the /etc/rc.d/rc.inet1 file to set up the routing table in your system. (The routing table tells the kernel how to send packets to other networks.) Your network's address (obtained by applying the netmask to the IP address) is stored in the /etc/networks file. Additionally, an interface configuration command (/sbin/ifconfig) is added to the /etc/rc.d/rc.inet1 file to ensure that the Ethernet interface is set up for the IP address of your system.

4. Enter the IP address of your domain's name server. This address is stored in the /etc/resolv.conf file.

Test the network

After you run netconfig, you may want to check to see whether the network is up and running. If you have not rebooted your system yet, you have to run /sbin/ifconfig to configure the Ethernet interface for your IP address. On a system whose IP address is 206.197.168.200, you would type the following command (you have to be logged in as root to do this):

```
/sbin/ifconfig eth0 206.197.168 netmask 255.255.255.0 broadcast
206.197.168.255
```

Tip

Now you should use the ping utility program to verify whether another system on your network is accessible. On my PC, I might try the following:

```
ping 206.197.168.50
PING 206.197.168.50 (206.197.168.50): 56 data bytes
64 bytes from 206.197.168.50: icmp_seq=0 ttl=32 time=3.4 ms
64 bytes from 206.197.168.50: icmp_seq=1 ttl=32 time=1.8 ms
64 bytes from 206.197.168.50: icmp_seq=2 ttl=32 time=1.8 ms
64 bytes from 206.197.168.50: icmp_seq=3 ttl=32 time=1.9 ms
        (press Ctrl-C here)
-- 206.197.168.50 ping statistics --
4 packets transmitted, 4 packets received, 0% packet loss
round-trip min/avg/max = 1.8/2.2/3.4 ms
```

If the ping command shows that other systems on your network are reachable, you can proceed to use other network programs, such as ftp and telnet.

TCP/IP configuration files

Running the netconfig script may be enough to get TCP/IP configured on your system. You may want to know the configuration files, however, so that you can edit the files if necessary. You can specify one name server through the `netconfig` script, for example, but you may want to add an alternative name server. To do so, you need to know about the `/etc/resolv.conf` file, which stores the IP addresses of name servers.

The following sections describe the basic TCP/IP configuration files.

The `/etc/HOSTNAME` file

The `/etc/HOSTNAME` file stores your system's host name. In this file, you should place your system's fully qualified domain name. On my system, the `/etc/HOSTNAME` file contains the following line:

```
lnbsoft.com
```

Many shell scripts in the `/etc` directory use the contents of the `/etc/HOSTNAME` file as your system's host name. The network initialization script (`/etc/rc.d/rc.inet1`) for example, uses the `/etc/HOSTNAME` file to determine the host name.

Secret

In Slackware Linux, if the `/etc/HOSTNAME` file does not exist, the `/etc/.rc.M` script (the multiuser startup script) creates the file and stores an arbitrary host name (something like `darkstar.frop.org`) in that file.

The `/etc/hosts` file

The `/etc/hosts` text file contains a list of IP addresses and host names for your local network. In the absence of a name server, any network program on your system consults this file to determine the IP address that corresponds to a host name.

Following is the `/etc/hosts` file from my system, showing the IP addresses and names of other hosts on my LAN:

```
#
# hosts      This file describes several host-name-to-address
#            mappings for the TCP/IP subsystem. It is mostly
#            used at boot time, when no name servers are running.
#            On small systems, this file can be used instead of a
#            "named" name server. Just add the names, addresses,
#            and any aliases to this file...
#
# By the way, Arnt Gulbrandsen <agulbra@nvg.unit.no> says that
# 127.0.0.1 should NEVER be named with the name of the machine. It
# causes problems for some (stupid) programs, irc and reputedly
# talk. :^)

# For loopbacking.
127.0.0.1       localhost

# Other hosts on the LAN
206.197.168.200    lnbsoft.com lnbsoft
206.197.168.50     lnb386
```

```
206.197.168.100      lnb486
206.197.168.150      lnbmac
206.197.168.2        lnbsun

# End of hosts.
```

As the example shows, each line in the file starts with an IP address, followed by the host name for that IP address. You can have more than one host name for a given IP address.

The /etc/networks file

The /etc/networks file is another text file that contains the names and IP addresses of networks. These network names are commonly used in the routing command (/sbin/route) to specify a network by name instead of its IP address. Following is a sample /etc/networks file from my system:

```
#
# networks    This file describes several net-name-to-address
#             mappings for the TCP/IP subsystem. It is mostly
#             used at boot time, when no name servers are running.
#

loopback    127.0.0.0
localnet    206.197.168.0

# End of networks.
```

The /etc/host.conf file

Linux uses a resolver library to obtain the IP address that corresponds to a host name. The /etc/host.conf file specifies how names are resolved. A typical /etc/host.conf file might contain the following lines:

```
order hosts, bind
multi on
```

The entries in the /etc/host.conf file tell the resolver library what services to use, in which order, to resolve names.

The order option indicates the order of services. The sample entry specifies that the resolver library should first consult the /etc/hosts file and then check the name server to resolve a name.

The multi option determines whether a host in the /etc/hosts file can have multiple IP addresses. Hosts that have more than one IP address are called *multihomed* because the presence of multiple IP addresses implies that the host has several network interfaces (the host "lives" in several networks simultaneously).

The /etc/resolv.conf file

The /etc/resolv.conf file is another text file used by the resolver — a library that determines the IP address for a host name. Following is a sample /etc/resolv.conf file:

```
domain com
nameserver 164.109.1.3
nameserver 164.109.10.23
```

The first line specifies your system's domain name. The nameserver line provides the IP addresses of name servers for your domain. If you have multiple name servers, you should list them on separate lines.

If you do not have any name server for your network, you can safely ignore this file. TCP/IP should still work, even though you may not be able to refer to hosts by name.

Configuring networks at boot time

You would want to start your network automatically every time you boot the system. For this to happen, you have to put the appropriate commands in one or more startup scripts. The init process runs immediately after Linux boots. The process consults the /etc/inittab file and then executes various commands (typically, shell scripts), depending on the current run level. In run level 5 — the multiuser level — /etc/inittab specifies that init should run the script file /etc/rc.d/rc.M.

In the /etc/rc.d/rc.M file, the section that sets up the network runs the scripts /etc/rc.d/rc.inet1 and /etc/rc.d/rc.inet2. Of these files, the rc.inet1 script performs the basic network setup; /etc/rc.inet2 starts several persistent network programs (called *daemons*).

If you run netconfig to set up the network, the /etc/rc.d/rc.inet1 file should already contain the commands needed to start the network. Specifically, the script file runs the following commands:

- /sbin/ifconfig, to configure any network interface on your system. At minimum, the loopback device (lo) is configured. If you have an Ethernet card, the eth0 device also is configured by a separate /sbin/ifconfig command.

- /sbin/route, to set up the routing tables for the network.

Following is the /etc/rc.d/rc.inet1 file from my system:

```
#! /bin/sh
#
# rc.inet1     This shell script boots up the base INET system.
#
# Version:     @(#)/etc/rc.d/rc.inet1  1.01  05/27/93
#
```

```
HOSTNAME=`cat /etc/HOSTNAME`

# Attach the loopback device.
/sbin/ifconfig lo 127.0.0.1
/sbin/route add -net 127.0.0.0

# IF YOU HAVE AN ETHERNET CONNECTION, use the lines below to configure the
# eth0 interface. If you're only using loopback or SLIP, don't include the
# rest of the lines in this file.

# Edit for your setup.
IPADDR="206.197.168.200"     # REPLACE with YOUR IP address!
NETMASK="255.255.255.0"      # REPLACE with YOUR netmask!
NETWORK="206.197.168.0"      # REPLACE with YOUR network address!
BROADCAST="206.197.168.255"  # REPLACE with YOUR broadcast address, if you
                             # have one. If not, leave blank and edit below.
GATEWAY="206.197.168.200"    # REPLACE with YOUR gateway address!

# Uncomment ONLY ONE of the three lines below. If one doesn't work, try again.
# /sbin/ifconfig eth0 ${IPADDR} netmask ${NETMASK} broadcast ${BROADCAST}
/sbin/ifconfig eth0 ${IPADDR} broadcast ${BROADCAST} netmask ${NETMASK}
# /sbin/ifconfig eth0 ${IPADDR} netmask ${NETMASK}

# Uncomment these to set up your IP routing table.
/sbin/route add -net ${NETWORK} netmask ${NETMASK}
/sbin/route add default gw ${GATEWAY} metric 1

# End of rc.inet1
```

If you have to edit this file manually, you should start by setting the variables IPADDR, NETMASK, BROADCAST, NETWORK, and GATEWAY at the beginning of the file. Then you can uncomment one of the lines that invoke /sbin/ifconfig to set up the Ethernet device (eth0). You also have to uncomment the lines that add the NETWORK and GATEWAY to the system's IP routing table.

TCP/IP Diagnostics

After you configure the kernel for Ethernet and TCP/IP, and you run netconfig to set up the TCP/IP network, you should be able to use various networking applications without any problem. The TCP/IP protocol suite includes several tools that help you monitor and diagnose problems.

Checking the interfaces

Use the /sbin/ifconfig command to view the currently configured network interfaces. The ifconfig command is used to configure a network interface (associate an IP address with a network device). If you run ifconfig without any command-line arguments, the command displays information about the current network interfaces. Following are a typical invocation of `ifconfig` and the resulting output:

```
/sbin/ifconfig
lo    Link encap:Local Loopback
      inet addr:127.0.0.1 Bcast:127.255.255.255 Mask:255.0.0.0
      UP BROADCAST LOOPBACK RUNNING MTU:2000 Metric:1
      RX packets:0 errors:0 dropped:0 overruns:0
      TX packets:12 errors:0 dropped:0 overruns:0

eth0  Link encap:10Mbps Ethernet HWaddr 00:20:AF:E8:A2:25
      inet addr:206.197.168.200 Bcast:206.197.168.255
Mask:255.255.255.0
      UP BROADCAST RUNNING MULTICAST MTU:1500 Metric:1
      RX packets:1356 errors:0 dropped:0 overruns:0
      TX packets:277 errors:0 dropped:0 overruns:0
      Interrupt:10 Base address:0x210
```

This output shows that two interfaces — the loopback interface (`lo`) and an Ethernet card (`eth0`) — are currently active on this system. For each interface, you get to see the IP address, as well as statistics on packets delivered and sent. For the Ethernet card, `ifconfig` also reports the IRQ (10) and the base I/O port address (0x210).

Checking the IP routing table

The other network configuration command, `/sbin/route`, also provides status information when it is run without any command-line argument. If you are having trouble checking a connection to another host (that you specify with an IP address), check the IP routing table to see whether a default gateway is specified. Then check the gateway's routing table to ensure that paths to an outside network appear in that routing table.

For my system, output from the `/sbin/route` command looks like this:

```
/sbin/route
 Kernel routing table
Destination     Gateway    Genmask         Flags MSS   Window Use Iface
localnet        *          255.255.255.0   U     1436  0      290 eth0
loopback        *          255.0.0.0       U     1936  0      12  lo
default         *          *               U     1436  0      0   eth0
```

As this routing table shows, the local network uses the `eth0` interface, and the default gateway happens to be this system (that's why a star appears in the `Gateway` column). As you see in Chapter 18, when I establish a PPP connection to the Internet, I specify a different gateway in the routing table.

Checking connectivity to a host

To check for a network path to a specific host, use the `ping` command. Ping is a widely used TCP/IP tool that uses a series of Internet Control Message Protocol (ICMP) messages. (ICMP provides for an Echo message to which every host responds.) Using the ICMP messages and replies, Ping can determine whether the other system is alive and compute the round-trip delay in communicating with that system.

The following example shows how I run `ping` to see whether one of the systems on my network is alive:

```
ping 206.197.168.50
PING 206.197.168.50 (206.197.168.50): 56 data bytes
64 bytes from 206.197.168.50: icmp_seq=0 ttl=32 time=3.4 ms
64 bytes from 206.197.168.50: icmp_seq=1 ttl=32 time=1.8 ms
64 bytes from 206.197.168.50: icmp_seq=2 ttl=32 time=1.8 ms
64 bytes from 206.197.168.50: icmp_seq=3 ttl=32 time=1.9 ms
        (press Ctrl-C here)
-- 206.197.168.50 ping statistics --
4 packets transmitted, 4 packets received, 0% packet loss
round-trip min/avg/max = 1.8/2.2/3.4 ms
```

On some systems, `ping` simply reports that a remote host is alive. You can still get the timing information with appropriate command-line arguments. In Linux, `ping` continues to run until you press Ctrl-C to stop it; then it displays summary statistics, showing the typical time it takes to send a packet between the two systems.

Checking network status

To check the status of the network, use the `netstat` command. This command displays the status of network connections of various types (such as TCP and UDP connections). You can view the status of the interfaces quickly with the `-i` option, as follows:

```
netstat -i
Kernel Interface table
Iface  MTU Met RX-OK RX-ERR RX-DRP RX-OVR TX-OK TX-ERR TX-DRP TX-OVR Flags
lo     2000  0     0      0      0      0    12      0      0      0 BLRU
eth0   1500  0  1537      0      0      0   461      0      0      0 BRU
```

In this case, the output shows the current status of the loopback and Ethernet interfaces. Table 16-2 describes the meanings of the columns.

Table 16-2 Columns in the kernel interface table

Column	Meaning
Iface	Name of the interface
MTU	Maximum Transfer Unit — the maximum number of bytes that a packet can contain
RX-OK, TX-OK	Number of error-free packets received (RX) or transmitted (TX)
RX-ERR, TX-ERR	Number of packets with errors
RX-DRP, TX-DRP	Number of dropped packets
RX-OVR, TX-OVR	Number of packets lost due to overflow
Flags	A = receive multicast, B — broadcast allowed, D = debugging turned on, L = loopback interface (notice the flag on lo), M = all packets received, N = trailers avoided, O = no ARP on this interface, P = point-to-point interface, R = interface is running, and U = interface is up

Another useful `netstat` option is `-t`, which shows all active TCP connections. Following is a typical result of `netstat -t` on one of my Linux PCs:

```
netstat -t
Active Internet connections
Proto Recv-Q Send-Q Local Address      Foreign Address     (State)      User
tcp      0      0 lnbsoft.com:telnet   lnb386:1057         ESTABLISHED  root
tcp      0      0 lnbsoft.com:ftp      lnb386:1056         ESTABLISHED  root
```

In this case, the output columns show the protocol (`Proto`), the number of bytes in receive and transmit queues (`Recv-Q, Send-Q`), the local TCP port in `hostname:service` format (`Local Address`), the remote port (`Foreign Address`), and the state of the connection.

Summary

Linux has extensive built-in support for TCP/IP and Ethernet networks. Thinwire Ethernet, which uses flexible RG-58 coaxial cables, provides a convenient way to set up a small network because you can simply daisy-chain the PCs together. This chapter explains the basics of TCP/IP and Ethernet; it also shows you how to set up TCP/IP networking on your Linux PC. By reading this chapter, you learn the following things:

▶ The OSI seven-layer model provides a framework for making various networks work together. The OSI layered model also sets the stage for various networking protocols.

▶ The Transmission Control Protocol and Internet Protocol (TCP/IP) originated from research initiated by the U.S. government's Advanced Research Projects Agency (APRA) in the 1970s. The modern Internet evolved from the networking technology developed during that time.

▶ All Internet protocols are documented in Request for Comments (RFC) documents. The RFCs are available from the Internet resource ftp://rs.internic.net/rfc. All standards are in RFCs, but many RFCs simply provide information to the Internet community.

▶ Internetworking is at the heart of the TCP/IP protocol; that is the purpose of the Internet Protocol. The TCP/IP protocol identifies a host with a 32-bit IP address that has two parts: a network address and a host address.

▶ An IP address typically is expressed in dotted-decimal notation, in which each byte's value is written in decimal format and separated from the adjacent byte by a dot (.). A typical IP address is 140.90.23.100.

▶ IP addresses are grouped in classes. Class A addresses use a 1-byte network address and 3 bytes for the host address; class B addresses use a 2-byte network and host address; and class C addresses use a 3-byte network address and a single byte for the host address. The values of the first byte indicate the type of address: 1-126 is class A, 128-191 is class B, and 192-223 is class C.

▶ The IP address space is filling rapidly. To alleviate this problem, the Internet Engineering Task Force has adopted a new 16-byte (128-bit) addressing scheme known as IPv6 (or IP version 6). Hosts that use the new IPv6 addresses will work with hosts that use the older IPv4 (32-bit) addresses.

▶ Ethernet is a popular physical data-transport mechanism. Several Ethernet standards exist, each of which uses a different type of cable. The 10BASE5 Ethernet (the original Ethernet) uses thick coaxial cables, 10BASE2 uses thin coaxial cables, and 10BASET uses unshielded twisted-pair (UTP) or telephone cables. Thinwire Ethernet (10BASE2) is easy to implement and convenient for small office networks.

▶ You need an Ethernet card on your PC to connect to an Ethernet network. Linux supports a wide variety of Ethernet cards. You should buy a 16-bit Ethernet card for good performance.

- Setting up TCP/IP on Linux requires setting up various configuration files. The `netconfig` script provides a convenient way to set up these files. You need some information — such as an IP address, the address of a gateway, and the address of a name server — to set up TCP/IP networking on your system. If you do not plan to connect your local network to the Internet, you can use a range of IP addresses (such as 192.168.0.0 to 192.168.255.255) without having to coordinate with any organization.

- Linux comes with many TCP/IP utilities, such as `ftp` (File Transfer Protocol) and `telnet` (for logging in to another system on the network).

- To diagnose TCP/IP networking problems, you can use the `ping`, `route`, and `netstat` commands.

Chapter 17

PC Cards

In This Chapter

- Introducing PCMCIA
- Understanding PC Cards
- Looking at typical uses of PC Cards
- Downloading the PCMCIA Card Services for Linux
- Installing the PCMCIA Card Services for Linux
- Looking at PC Cards that Card Services for Linux supports
- Obtaining the latest information about Card Services for Linux

PCMCIA stands for *Personal Computer Memory Card International Association*, an organization that standardized the interface for adding memory cards to laptop computers. Although originally conceived for memory cards, PCMCIA devices became popular for a wide variety of add-ons for laptops. Today, laptop computers use PCMCIA devices such as modems, network cards, SCSI controllers, and sound cards. Using Linux on a laptop means having to deal with the PCMCIA devices, or PC Cards, as they are called in the popular press nowadays. Thanks to the efforts of David Hinds, you can use PCMCIA devices under Linux with his PCMCIA Card Services for Linux. This software is available now and is being used by many people. This chapter briefly describes the PCMCIA support package for Linux.

Tip

The companion CD-ROM includes a version of the PCMCIA software in the A disk set. To get the latest version, you have to download the software yourself from the `/pub/Linux/kernel/pcmcia` directory at `sunsite.unc.edu`. You will find instructions in this chapter.

Note

I refer to the actual cards as *PC Cards*, because that's the proper name for the devices. PCMCIA refers to the industry organization that specifies the standard for PC Cards. I'll, however, use the term PCMCIA Card in one context — when referring to *PCMCIA Card Services for Linux*, which is the software that supports PC Cards in Linux.

PC Card Basics

PC Cards originated as static random-access memory (SRAM) and flash RAM cards that were used to store data on small laptop computers. The credit-card-size cards fit into a slot on the side of the laptop. The flash memory cards used electrically erasable programmable read-only memory (EEPROM) to provide laptops storage capability that might have been too small for other conventional storage media.

Vendors soon realized the convenience of the memory-card slot as a general-purpose expansion slot for laptop computers. The Personal Computer Memory Card International Association (PCMCIA) standardized various components of PC Cards including the electrical interface, card dimensions, and the card slot sizes. This standardization has contributed to the proliferation of PC Cards in the laptop market.

By now, PCMCIA slots are a common feature of almost all laptops. The memory card is a small part of the overall PC Card market. Most laptops provide the PCMCIA slots so that users can add hardware, such as fax/modems, sound cards, network cards, and even hard disks.

To learn more about PCMCIA (the association) and PC Card specifications, point your favorite World Wide Web browser at http://www.pc-card.com/.

PC Card physical specifications

PC Cards are classified in three different types, according to the thickness of the card. Following are the standard physical dimensions for each type of PC Card, in terms of width by length by thickness:

- Type I PC Card: 54 mm by 85.6 mm by 3.3 mm
- Type II PC Card: 54 mm by 85.6 mm by 5 mm
- Type III PC Card: 54 mm by 85.6 mm by 10.5 mm

All three types of PC Cards have the same length and width — the size of a standard credit card, except for corner rounding. The cards differ from credit cards in terms of thickness, and the card types are differentiated by thickness.

The term *form factor* is often used to refer to the dimensions of PC Cards.

All PC Cards use the same 68-pin connector. Because of this connector, a thinner card (Type I, for example) can be used in a thicker slot (Type II, for example). As you might guess, a thicker card cannot be used in a thinner slot, because you cannot physically insert the thick card into a thin slot.

PC Card use

Each type of PC Card is used for a specific type of application. Following are the typical applications of PC Cards, by card type:

- *Type I PC Card.* These thin cards are used for memory devices, such as static RAM (SRAM) and flash RAM.
- *Type II PC Card.* These cards are used for input and output (I/O) devices, such as fax/modems, network adapters, and sound cards.
- *Type III PC Card.* These cards are used for devices that need the thickness, such as hard disks with rotating components (hard to believe, isn't it!).

A PC Card can have a maximum length of 135.6 mm (that's slightly longer than 5 1/4 inches), which means that the card can extend outside the host. Extended cards are used in devices such as removable media, transceivers, and antennas.

PCMCIA standards

All these specifications are described in the PCMCIA Standard, of which there have been two major releases so far:

- *PCMCIA Standard Release 1.0 (June 1990).* The initial standard defined the 68-pin connector and Type I and Type II PC Cards. The standard also defined the Card Information Structure (CIS) that has been the basis for interoperability of PC Cards. The first release of the PCMCIA standard did not account for any I/O cards; only memory cards were considered.
- *PCMCIA Standard Release 2.0, 2.01, 2.1 (1991-94).* The second release of the standard defined an I/O interface for the 68-pin connector. Release 2.01 added the PC Card AT Attachment (ATA) specification and provided an initial version of the Card and Socket Services (CSS) specification. Release 2.1 further enhanced the Card and Socket Services specification.

PC Card terminology

As all laptop vendors adopt PC Card slots, the PC Card market has experienced explosive growth. Thanks to the PCMCIA standards, PC Card devices can be used in any PC Card slot. As you use PC Cards, you'll run into some terms that have special meaning for PC Cards. Following are some of these terms:

- *Card Information Structure (CIS)* describes the characteristics and capabilities of a PC Card so that the operating system or driver software can configure the card.
- *CardBus* is an electrical specification that describes the use of bus mastering technology and allows PC Cards to operate at up to 33 MHz.

- *Direct Memory Access (DMA)* has the same meaning as in other peripherals, but now PC Cards can use DMA technology.
- *Execute In Place (XIP)* refers to the feature that allows operating-system and application software to run directly from the PC Card without having to be loaded into the system's RAM (eliminating the need for too much system RAM).
- *Low Voltage Operation* refers to the capability of PC Cards to operate at 3.3 volts (as well as 5 volts). The connector has a physical key to ensure that you cannot inadvertently insert a 3.3-volt card into a 5-volt slot.
- *Multifunction Capability* allows a PC Card to support several functions. 3Com's 3C562, for example, is a 10BASET Ethernet card and a 28,800-bps modem in a Type II form-factor PC Card.
- *Plug and Play* allows you to insert or remove a PC Card while the system is turned on (this is known as *hot swapping*). Such hot swapping of PC Cards is done by making the power-connection pins the longest, so that the data lines disconnect before the power.
- *Power Management* refers to the capability of PC Cards to interface with the Advanced Power Management (APM) capabilities of laptops through the Card Services Specification.

PCMCIA Card Services for Linux

The standardization of PC Cards means that Linux developers can get their hands on the programming information that they need to write device drivers for PC Cards. In particular, the Card Services Specification provides an Application Programming Interface (API) that's independent of the hardware that controls the PC Card sockets — the receptacles or slots for PC Cards.

A related specification is the Socket Services Specification, which also provides an API to access the hardware that controls the sockets for PC Cards.

Luckily, you do not really have to learn about the PC Card and Socket Services APIs. David Hinds has already done the work in his PCMCIA Card Services for Linux, a beta software package that you can use to access PC Card devices under Linux. The following sections describe how to download and use the Card Services for Linux.

Get the Card Services for Linux

PCMCIA Card Services for Linux is not included on this book's companion CD-ROM, because it's beta software. If you want to install Linux on a laptop that has PCMCIA slots, however, you will want to get the software so that you can use PC Card devices under Linux. After all, the most exciting features of laptops, ranging from 28,800-bps modems to network cards, come in the form of PC Cards.

Chapter 17: PC Cards   513

Tip

The Card Services software package is available via FTP (File Transfer Protocol) in the /pub/Linux/kernel/pcmcia directory at sunsite.unc.edu, a well-known site where you'll find many other Linux software packages.

Cross Reference

You have to download the software over the Internet by using FTP. If you do not have Internet access, Chapter 18 explains how you can connect your system to the Internet via a dial-up modem (you have to sign up with an Internet Service Provider for the access).

Assuming that you are on a system that has access to the Internet, you can get the necessary files by following these steps:

1. To download the software, type the following command at the shell prompt:

   ftp sunsite.unc.edu

2. When you are prompted for a Name, type **anonymous** and press Enter.

Tip

3. At the Password prompt, type your e-mail address and press Enter. Generally, anything that you type is good enough, so don't worry if you don't have an e-mail address; just type your name and press Enter.

4. Change the directory to the location where Card Services for Linux is located. Use the following command at the ftp> prompt:

   cd /pub/Linux/kernel/pcmcia

5. If you are not on a UNIX system, type **binary** to use a binary mode of transfer. On UNIX systems, the default mode is binary, so you don't need to perform this step.

6. Get a listing of the directory with the following command:

   ftp> ls

Secret

7. You'll see several files with .tgz at the ends of their names. The .tgz at the end of the file means that the file is a tar archive that has been compressed with the gzip command. (You have to unarchive the file with a tar -zxvf command; the z flag tells tar to use the gunzip command to decompress the file before unarchiving.) Look for a filename that starts with pcmcia-cs-, followed by a version number.

8. Use the get command to download the file with the latest version number. When I downloaded the software, version 2.6.3a was the latest. Therefore, I used the following command to download the software:

   ftp> get pcmcia-cs-2.6.3a.tgz

   The file transfer can take anywhere from seconds to 15 minutes, depending on the data-transfer rate of your connection to Internet.

9. After the file transfer is done, type **bye** at the ftp> prompt to close the connection.

The following sample session shows how I used `ftp` to download version 2.6.3a of PCMCIA Card Services for Linux from sunsite.unc.edu (over a dial-up connection to the Internet through my Internet Service Provider):

```
ftp sunsite.unc.edu
Connected to sunsite.unc.edu.
220 calypso-2.oit.unc.edu FTP server (Version wu-2.4(39) Tue May 16 01:34:21 EDT
1995) ready.
Name (sunsite.unc.edu:root): anonymous
331 Guest login ok, send your complete e-mail address as password.
Password: (Enter your e-mail address here)
230-        WELCOME to UNC and SUN's anonymous ftp server
230-             University of North Carolina
230-           Office FOR Information Technology
230-              SunSITE.unc.edu
230-
230- For information on submitting software to this archive, retrieve
230-   /how.to.submit.
230-
230- We archive most of the SUN related USENET news groups here as well as
230- distributing SUN related announcements.
230-
230- Or telnet to sunsite and login as swais to test out a simple wais client.
230- Or telnet to sunsite and login as gopher to test out a sample gopher client.
230- Or telnet to sunsite and login as lynx to test out a sample WWW client.
230-
230- If you email to info@sunsite.unc.edu you will be sent help information
230- about how to use the different services sunsite provides.
230-
230- We use the Wuarchive experimental ftpd. if you "get" <directory>.tar.Z
230- or <file>.Z it will compress and/or tar it on the fly. Using ".gz" instead
230- of ".Z" will use the GNU zip (/pub/gnu/gzip*) instead, a superior
230- compression method.
230-
230- (currently <directory>.tar.gz and <directory>.tar.Z are broken. Either one
230- separately works though)
230-
230- Mail suggestions and questions to ftpkeeper@sunsite.unc.edu.
230-
230 Guest login ok, access restrictions apply.
Remote system type is UNIX.
Using binary mode to transfer files.
ftp> cd /pub/Linux/kernel/pcmcia
250 CWD command successful.
ftp> ls
200 PORT command successful.
150 Opening ASCII mode data connection for /bin/ls.
total 4202
drwxr-xr-x   5 67     25         1024 Sep 22 06:37 .
drwxr-xr-x  16 67     25         1024 Jul  5 14:19 ..
drwxr-xr-x   2 67     25          512 Oct  4 05:31 ALPHA
-r--r--r--   1 67     25        19691 Aug 10 13:58 CHANGES
lrwxrwxrwx   1 67     25           16 Jan 28  1995 PCMCIA-HOWTO -> doc/PCMCIA-HOWTO
```

```
-r--r--r--   1 67    25      1721 Jul 31 03:52 SUPPORTED.CARDS
drwxr-xr-x   2 67    25      1536 Sep 13 05:47 doc
drwxr-xr-x   2 67    25       512 Sep 22 06:37 extras
-r--r--r--   1 67    25     32578 Mar 23  1995 pc-2.4.9-2.5.0.diff.gz
-r--r--r--   1 67    25     21915 Apr  2  1995 pc-2.5.0-2.5.1.diff.gz
-r--r--r--   1 67    25      1893 Apr  3  1995 pc-2.5.1-2.5.2.diff.gz
-r--r--r--   1 67    25      1606 Apr  3  1995 pc-2.5.2-2.5.3.diff.gz
-r--r--r--   1 67    25      4812 Apr  5  1995 pc-2.5.3-2.5.4.diff.gz
-r--r--r--   1 67    25     27833 Apr  7  1995 pc-2.5.4-2.5.5.diff.gz
-r--r--r--   1 67    25     10163 Apr 14  1995 pc-2.5.5-2.5.6.diff.gz
-r--r--r--   1 67    25     71422 May 12 03:20 pc-2.5.6-2.6.0.diff.gz
-r--r--r--   1 67    25      7150 May 15 03:30 pc-2.6.0-2.6.1.diff.gz
-r--r--r--   1 67    25     55554 Jun  2 04:08 pc-2.6.1-2.6.2.diff.gz
-r--r--r--   1 67    25     71236 Jul 31 03:46 pc-2.6.2-2.6.3.diff.gz
-r--r--r--   1 67    25       368 Aug 10 14:00 pc-2.6.3-2.6.3a.diff.gz
-r--r--r--   1 67    25    426309 Jun  2 04:07 pcboot14.gz
-r--r--r--   1 67    25    325814 Apr 14  1995 pcmcia-cs-2.5.6.tgz
-r--r--r--   1 67    25    435672 Aug 10 13:58 pcmcia-cs-2.6.3a.tgz
-r--r--r--   1 67    25    570517 Jun  2 04:07 pcroot14.gz
226 Transfer complete.
ftp> get pcmcia-cs-2.6.3a.tgz
200 PORT command successful.
150 Opening BINARY mode data connection for pcmcia-cs-2.6.3a.tgz (435672 bytes).
226 Transfer complete.
435672 bytes received in 724 secs (0.59 Kbytes/sec)
ftp> bye
221 Goodbye.
```

Unpack the Card Services software

After you get the software, you have to uncompress and extract the files from the archive. What you get is the source code, so you should unpack the archive in the /usr/src directory. Follow these steps to unpack the PCMCIA Card Services software:

1. Log in as root. If you are logged in as another user, type **su** and provide the **root** password at the prompt.

2. Move the compressed tar file (files with the .tgz extension are tar files that have been compressed with gzip) to the /usr/src directory. From the directory that contains the downloaded file, type the following command:

    mv pcmcia-cs-2.6.3a.tgz /usr/src

3. Change the directory to /usr/src with this command:

    cd /usr/src

Tip

4. To uncompress and extract the files from the compressed tar archive, type the following command:

    tar -zxvf pcmcia-cs-2.6.3a.tgz

The last command unpacks the files from the file that you downloaded with ftp. For version 2.6.3, the tar command creates a directory named pcmcia-cs-2.6.3.

Build the Card Services software

After you unpack the Card Services software, you have to build it before you can use it. You need a Linux kernel later than 1.2.8 to use Card Services for Linux. If you installed Linux from this book's companion CD-ROM, you should be all set.

Cross Reference

You need the Linux source code tree to build the Card Services software. Again, if you followed the steps in Chapter 1, you should already have the Linux source tree (the *source tree* is the directory hierarchy containing the source files) on your system.

Secret

If you rebuild the kernel, watch out for the following (during the `make config` step, as explained in Chapter 2) if you plan to use the Card Services software:

- If you plan to use a PCMCIA Ethernet card, turn on networking support during kernel configuration, but do not include support for any Ethernet card (including the pocket and portable adapters).
- If you plan to use SLIP or PPP with PCMCIA modems, include SLIP and PPP support in the kernel.
- If you want to use a PCMCIA SCSI card, turn on support for SCSI as well as SCSI disk, CD-ROM, and tape support; but don't include support for any SCSI controller cards.

After you build the kernel with the appropriate options, follow these steps to build the PCMCIA Card Services (you have to log in as `root` for all these steps):

1. The Card Services software is in the form of loadable modules. Use the following command to build the loadable modules:

    ```
    cd /usr/src/linux
    make modules; make modules_install
    ```

2. Change the directory to where the PCMCIA Card Services software resides. Then type **make prereq** to see whether your system satisfies all the prerequisites for building and installing the Card Services software. Following are the commands, with typical output from `make prereq`:

    ```
    cd /usr/src/pcmcia-cs-2.6.3
    make prereq
    Checking directories...
      It looks like you have a BSD-ish init file setup.
    You'll need to edit /etc/rc.d/rc.M to invoke /etc/rc.d/rc.pcmcia
    so that PCMCIA services will start at boot time.
    The PCMCIA scripts will go in /etc/pcmcia.
    Linux source directory /usr/src/linux is OK.
    /var/run exists.

    Checking kernel version...
    Source tree is version 1.2.13, current kernel is 1.2.13
    Kernel build date matches source tree build date.
    Your kernel is recent enough.
    ```

As the output shows, the `make prereq` command tells you what you need to do to set up everything for the PCMCIA Card Services. For example, you have to add a line in /etc/rc.d/rc.M to call the script file /etc/rc.d/rc.pcmcia.

3. If the prerequisites are met, you can proceed to build the PCMCIA Card Services software. Type the following command to complete this step:

   ```
   make all; make install
   ```

   That command line should build the software and install it in appropriate locations. The install command puts the kernel modules in the directory /lib/modules/version-number/pcmcia, in which version-number is the Linux kernel's version number (such as 1.2.13). The cardmgr and cardctl programs are installed in /sbin. The make all step builds another program named cardinfo only if you have installed the X Window System and a public-domain Forms library. (You can get the Forms library via FTP from cb-iris.stanford.edu; the filename is /pub/pcmcia/extras/bxform-0.61.tgz.) If built, cardinfo is installed in /usr/bin/X11. The install command puts all necessary PCMCIA configuration files in the /etc/pcmcia directory and puts a script named rc.pcmcia in the /etc/rc.d directory.

4. Open the /etc/rc.d/rc.M file with a text editor, and add the following line to that file:

   ```
   /etc/rc.d/rc.pcmcia start
   ```

   This line ensures that the PCMCIA Card Services start properly when you boot the system. In particular, the rc.pcmcia script starts the cardmgr program, which handles all card-insertion and card-removal events. Running the cardmgr program allows you to "hot swap" PC Cards, so that you can insert and eject a card at any time.

Supported cards

Note

In the PCMCIA Card Services source directory, you'll find a file named SUPPORTED.CARDS. That file lists all the PCMCIA Cards that are known to work with at least one system.

PCMCIA Card Services version 2.6.3a supports these Ethernet PC Cards:

- Accton EN2212 EtherCard
- CNet CN30BC Ethernet
- D-Link DE-650
- EFA InfoExpress SPT EFA 205 10BASET
- EP-210 Ethernet
- Farallon Etherwave
- GVC NIC-2000P Ethernet Combo
- HYPERTEC HyperEnet

- IBM CreditCard Ethernet Adapter
- IC-Card Ethernet
- Katron PE-520 Ethernet
- Kingston KNE-PCM/M
- LANEED Ethernet
- Linksys EtherCard
- Maxtech PCN2000 Ethernet
- Network General "Sniffer"
- New Media Ethernet
- Novell/National NE4100 InfoMover
- PreMax PE-200 Ethernet
- Proteon Ethernet
- RPTI EP400 Ethernet
- Socket Communications Socket EA LAN Adapter
- Thomas-Conrad Ethernet
- 3Com 3c589 and 3c589B
- Volktek Ethernet

PCMCIA Card Services version 2.6.3a supports all modem PC Cards.

PCMCIA Card Services version 2.6.3a supports these memory PC Cards:

- Epson 2MB SRAM
- Intel Series 2 and Series 2+ Flash
- New Media SRAM

PCMCIA Card Services version 2.6.3a supports these SCSI adapter PC Cards:

- Adaptec APA-1460 SlimSCSI
- New Media Bus Toaster SCSI
- Qlogic FastSCSI

As the list shows, a variety of Ethernet cards and all modem cards are supported. Several PCMCIA SCSI adapters also are supported. For the latest list of supported cards, you should consult the SUPPORTED.CARDS file in the version of PCMCIA Card Services that you have downloaded.

Secret

Notice that Xircom Ethernet and Ethernet/Modem combo cards are not supported.

Further reading

Note

Because the PCMCIA Card Services software is still in beta release, you should consult the documentation included with the downloaded software for more information. In particular, you'll find a doc directory that contains the file PCMCIA-HOWTO.

This file contains the latest information about the Card Services software, including common problems and suggested fixes.

In particular, you should look through the PCMCIA-HOWTO file for any information that applies to your specific PC Card.

Summary

Developed as a way to attach memory cards to laptop computers, PC Cards have become a popular way to add new capabilities to laptops. If you use Linux on a laptop, you need some way to access the PC Cards. Dave Hinds's PCMCIA Card Services for Linux provides a way to use PC Cards under Linux. This chapter describes how to download and install the Card Services for Linux software. By reading this chapter, you learn

- PC Cards originated as credit-card-size memory devices that plugged into a slot on the side of a laptop computer and provided a data-storage medium.
- The Personal Computer Memory Card International Association (PCMCIA) standardized various parts of the PC Cards, including the electrical interface, the card dimensions, and the card-slot sizes.
- Nowadays, PC Cards are used widely in laptops as an expansion slot for many devices, such as network adapters, fax/modem cards, SCSI controllers, sound cards, and even hard disks.
- There are three types of PC Cards: Type I, II, and III. All types of cards have the same length and width (54 mm by 85.6 mm) — the size of a standard credit card. The types differ in thickness. Type I is the thinnest (3.3 mm), and Type III is the thickest (10.5 mm).
- If you want to use PC Cards under Linux, you have to get Dave Hinds's PCMCIA Card Services for Linux. This beta software is available via FTP from the /pub/Linux/kernel/pcmcia directory at sunsite.unc.edu.
- To build the software, you need to copy the software to the /usr/src directory, unpack the archive, and issue a few simple commands.
- You will find a list of supported PC Cards in the SUPPORTED.CARDS file.
- For the latest information about a specific PCMCIA device, consult the PCMCIA-HOWTO file that accompanies the Card Services for Linux software.

Part IV
Using Linux for Fun and Profit

Chapter 18: Dial-up Networking in Linux

Chapter 19: Setting up a Linux Internet Host

Chapter 20: Running a World Wide Web Server on Linux

Chapter 21: Running a Business with Linux

Chapter 22: Developing Software in Linux

Chapter 23: X Programming in Linux

Chapter 24: Text Processing in Linux

Chapter 18
Dial-up Networking in Linux

In This Chapter

- Understanding networking
- Understanding SLIP and PPP
- Establishing a SLIP connection
- Setting up PPP on your Linux PC
- Using PPP for data transport in TCP/IP networking
- Routing TCP/IP over a PPP connection
- Making your Linux system a PPP server

Previous parts of this book focus on Linux installation and setup on your PC. You learned how to install Linux on your system, configure the XFree86 X Window System, and set up Linux to use various types of hardware. This part of the book gets to the fun parts of Linux (and some business, too). The seven chapters in this part show you how to connect your Linux PC to the Internet; set up various Internet services, including a World Wide Web server; develop software; and even run a small business with Linux.

This chapter covers dial-up networking — one of the first steps that many of you perform to connect your Linux PC (and perhaps your own local-area network) to the Internet.

If you have a Linux system at home (or in a small office), you may want to use a modem to connect to the Internet. At the other end of the modem, you'll need a system that's already on the Internet. This system could be a system at your office, your university, or a commercial Internet Service Provider (ISP). That's what I mean by *dial-up networking* — establishing a network connection between your Linux PC and a remote computer through a dial-up modem.

This chapter describes the dial-up networking facilities in Linux, with particular emphasis on Point-to-Point Protocol (PPP) as the method of exchanging network packets over the dial-up connection.

Cross Reference

As you read this chapter, you should consult Chapter 16 for a discussion of networking, TCP/IP, the Internet, and terms such as Request for Comments (RFC).

Basics of Dial-up Networking

Cross Reference

Dial-up networking refers to connecting a PC to a remote network through a dial-up modem. A significant difference exists between dial-up networking and plain old serial communication. Both approaches use a modem to dial up another computer and establish a communication path, but the serial communication software (such as `Seyon` or `minicom`, described in Chapter 15) makes your computer act like a terminal connected to the remote computer. The dial-up connection is used exclusively by the serial communication software. You could not run another copy of the communication software and use the same modem connection, for example.

In dial-up networking, you run TCP/IP or other network-protocol software on your PC as well as on the remote system with which your PC has a dial-up communication path. That communication path simply forms one of the layers in the OSI seven-layer network model. The network protocols exchange data packets over the dial-up connection. You can use any number of network applications to communicate over the single dial-up connection. With dial-up networking, your PC truly becomes part of the network to which the remote computer belongs. (If the remote computer is not on a network, the dial-up networking creates a network that consists of the remote computer and your PC.) Thus, you can have any number of network applications, ranging from a Web browser to a `telnet` session, running at the same time, with all applications sharing the physical data-transport capabilities of the dial-up connection.

This chapter describes TCP/IP over a dial-up connection, because TCP/IP is the dominant protocol of the Internet and Linux has built-in support for TCP/IP. To be more accurate, I should say that the discussion in this chapter applies to TCP/IP over any point-to-point serial communication link. The "dial-up" part simply reflects the fact that most of us will use a modem to establish the point-to-point communication link to a remote computer.

Like TCP/IP networking over Ethernet, TCP/IP networking over a dial-up link is a matter of specifying the *protocol* — the convention — for packaging a network packet over the communication link. There are two popular protocols for TCP/IP networking over point-to-point serial communication links:

- Serial Line Internet Protocol (SLIP) is a simple protocol that specifies how to frame an IP packet on a serial line. SLIP is described in RFC 1055.
- Point-to-Point Protocol (PPP) is a more advanced protocol for establishing a TCP/IP connection over any point-to-point link, including dial-up serial links. RFC 1661 describes PPP.

I'll first provide an overview of SLIP and PPP; then I'll show you how to use SLIP, as well as PPP, to set up a network connection to a remote system.

Serial Line Internet Protocol (SLIP)

SLIP originated as a simple protocol for framing an *IP packet* — an Internet Protocol packet that consists of an IP header (that includes the source and destination IP addresses) followed by data (the data being sent from source to

Chapter 18: Dial-up Networking in Linux 525

destination). RFC 1055, "A Nonstandard for Transmission of IP Datagrams over Serial Lines: SLIP," Ronkey, 1988, describes SLIP. As the title of RFC 1055 suggests, SLIP is not an official Internet standard; it's a de-facto standard.

SLIP defines two special characters for framing IP packets:

- SLIP-END is octal 300 (decimal 192), and it marks the end of an IP packet.
- SLIP-ESC is octal 333 (decimal 219), and it is used to "escape" any SLIP-END or SLIP-ESC characters that are embedded in the packet (to ensure, for example, that a packet does not end prematurely because the IP packet happens to include a byte with decimal 192).

The protocol involves sending out the bytes of the IP packet one by one and marking the end of the packet with a SLIP-END character. The following convention is used to handle any SLIP-END and SLIP ESC characters that happen to be in the IP packet:

- Replace a SLIP-END character with SLIP-ESC, followed by octal 334 (decimal 220).
- Replace a SLIP-ESC character with SLIP-ESC, followed by octal 335 (decimal 221).

That's it! Based on the most popular implementation of SLIP from Berkeley UNIX, SLIP uses a few more conventions:

- Packets start and end with the SLIP-END character to ensure that each IP packet starts anew.
- The total size of the IP packet (including the IP header and data, but without the SLIP framing characters) is 1,006 bytes.

SLIP's simplicity has led to its popularity. SLIP has several shortcomings, however:

- Both ends of the SLIP connection have to know their IP addresses. Although some schemes have been worked out to allow dynamic assignment of IP addresses, the protocol does not have any provisions for address negotiation.
- Both ends of SLIP must use the same packet size, because the protocol does not allow the two ends to negotiate the packet size.
- SLIP has no support for data compression. (As you will learn later in this section, Compressed SLIP, or CSLIP, introduces data compression in SLIP.)
- There is no way to identify the packet type in SLIP. Accordingly, SLIP can carry only one protocol — the one that both ends of SLIP are hard-wired to use. A transport mechanism such as SLIP should carry packets of any protocol type.

The lack of data compression in SLIP was addressed by Compressed SLIP (CSLIP), which is described in RFC 1144, "Compressing TCP/IP Headers for Low-Speed Serial Links," Jacobson, 1990. CSLIP compresses TCP/IP header information, which tends to be repetitive in packets exchanged between the two ends of a SLIP connection. CSLIP does not compress the packet's data.

CSLIP is often referred to as the *Van Jacobson compression*, in recognition of CSLIP's author. Incidentally, PPP also supports the Van Jacobson TCP/IP header compression.

Point-to-Point Protocol (PPP)

PPP fixes the shortcomings of SLIP and defines a more complex protocol. Unlike SLIP, PPP is an official Internet standard; it is documented in RFC 1661, "The Point-to-Point Protocol," Simpson, 1994.

Wizard

PPP includes the following main components:

- A packet-framing mechanism that uses a modified version of the well-known High-Level Data Link Control (HDLC) protocol.
- A Link Control Protocol (LCP) to establish, configure, and test the data link.
- A Network Control Protocol (NCP) that allows PPP to carry more than one type of network packet — such as IP, IPX, and NetBEUI (Network BIOS Extended User Interface) — over the same connection.

PPP is gradually replacing SLIP as the protocol of choice for transporting packets over point-to-point links. In addition to the ubiquitous serial link, some versions of PPP work over several other types of point-to-point links. Some of the point-to-point links where PPP works include SONET (Synchronous Optical Network), X.25, and ISDN (Integrated Services Digital Network).

The PPP frame has a more complex structure than SLIP does. The PPP frame structure is based on ISO (International Standards Organization) standard 3309, "Data Communications — High-Level Data Link Control Procedures — Frame Structure," 1979. The High-Level Data Link Control (HDLC) protocol uses a special flag character to mark the beginning and the end of a frame. Figure 18-1 shows the structure of a complete PPP frame.

As Figure 18-1 shows, the PPP frames begin and end with a flag character whose value is always 0x7E (that's 7E in hexadecimal notation). The Address and Control fields come from HDLC; they have the fixed values of 0xFF and 0x03, respectively. The PPP data consists of a 2-byte protocol field. (Actually, this field can be only 1 byte; the length of the protocol field is negotiated with the Link Control Protocol.)

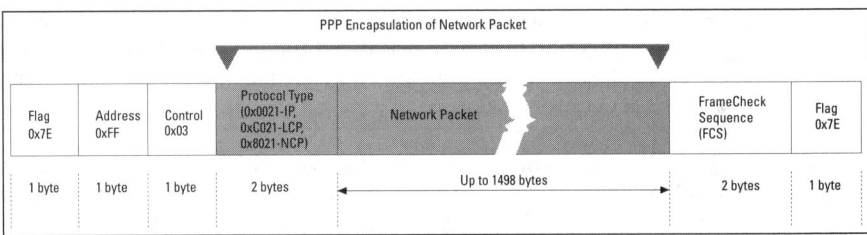

Figure 18-1: The format of a PPP frame.

Chapter 18: Dial-up Networking in Linux 527

Within the encapsulated network packet, PPP uses 0x7D as the escape character. To send a byte that has a special meaning (such as 0x7E, which marks the beginning and end of a frame), PPP uses the following steps:

- Embeds 0x7D in the data.
- Places the data byte being escaped.
- Toggles the sixth bit of that data byte.

Thus, if the PPP data includes 0x7E, that byte is replaced by the 2-byte sequence 0x7D, followed by 0x5E. (If you toggle the sixth bit of 0x7E or 0111 1110 in binary, you get 0x5E or 0101 1110 in binary.)

When you use PPP to set up a link between your Linux PC and a remote computer, your PC first sends LCP packets to set up the data link. After the physical data link is established and any optional parameters are negotiated, your PC sends NCP packets to select one or more network protocols to be used over that link. Thereafter, any of those network protocols can send packets over the PPP link.

You don't need to know the complete details of PPP to use it effectively. Later sections of this chapter describe how you can use PPP to establish a TCP/IP network connection to another computer.

Making a SLIP Connection

To set up a SLIP connection between your Linux PC and a remote system, both systems must support SLIP. Both ends also must run some SLIP software during the time when the connection is up.

To include SLIP in your Linux kernel, you should accept the default answers to the following questions during the kernel-configuration step (in which you type **make config**):

```
SLIP (serial line) support (CONFIG_SLIP) [y]
 CSLIP compressed headers (CONFIG_SLIP_COMPRESSED) [y]
 16 channels instead of 4 (SL_SLIP_LOTS) [n]
```

Chapter 2 describes how to configure and rebuild the kernel. You also need TCP/IP support in the kernel, of course.

Typically, the first step in establishing a SLIP connection is dialing up the remote system, logging in, and starting SLIP on the remote system. Then you must start SLIP at your end. After the two ends are running SLIP, you have the SLIP connection up. To use that connection, you also have to configure the interface (with the `ifconfig` command) and set up the routing (with the `route` command) so that network packets originating on your PC can reach their destination. You can do all these things through a program called `dip` (Dial-up IP Protocol Driver), which automates the process of setting up a SLIP connection. You learn how to use `dip` in the following sections.

Verify SLIP support

Secret

Before trying SLIP, you should verify that your kernel includes SLIP support. To see the currently configured network devices, type **cat /proc/net/dev.** For example, here's what I see on my system:

```
cat /proc/net/dev
Inter-|   Receive           |  Transmit
 face |packets errs drop fifo frame|packets errs drop fifo colls carrier
    lo:   0   0   0   0   0    12   0   0   0   0
 dummy: No statistics available.
  ppp0:   0   0   0   0   0     0   0   0   0   0
  ppp1:   0   0   0   0   0     0   0   0   0   0
  ppp2:   0   0   0   0   0     0   0   0   0   0
  ppp3:   0   0   0   0   0     0   0   0   0   0
   sl0:   0   0   0   0   0     0   0   0   0   0
   sl1:   0   0   0   0   0     0   0   0   0   0
   sl2:   0   0   0   0   0     0   0   0   0   0
   sl3:   0   0   0   0   0     0   0   0   0   0
  eth0:  72   0   0   0   0    81   0   0   0   0
```

The Interface column lists the names of the available network devices. As the names sl0 through sl3 indicate, this kernel supports four SLIP devices. The lo device is the loopback interface, eth0 refers to the Ethernet interface, and ppp0 through ppp3 are the PPP devices (described in later sections of this chapter).

Another source of information about networking support and SLIP is the collection of boot messages. Type **dmesg | more** to view the boot messages. If your kernel has SLIP support, you should see messages such as the following:

```
SLIP: version 0.8.3-NET3.019-NEWTTY (4 channels) (6 bit encapsulation enabled)
CSLIP: code copyright 1989 Regents of the University of California
```

These two lines refer to SLIP and Compressed SLIP (CSLIP) support, respectively. If you see these lines, you can assume that your kernel supports SLIP.

Obtain remote-system information

The exact mechanics of establishing a SLIP connection to a remote system depend on that system's setup. If you obtained a SLIP account from an Internet Service Provider (ISP), the ISP should give you the information that you need to establish a SLIP connection. At minimum, this information includes the following:

- The phone number that you must dial to connect to the remote computer.
- The user name and password that you have to use to log into the system.
- The IP addresses for both ends of the SLIP connection. Many ISPs provide a fixed (static) IP address, whereas other ISPs assign an IP address dynamically.

You'll also get the IP addresses of name servers (a name server translates names to IP addresses), a mail server, and a news server. These IP addresses are necessary when you begin to use Internet applications on your system; you don't need them during SLIP-connection setup.

Wizard

Typically, an ISP sets up a SLIP account for you in such a way that the SLIP software starts automatically after you log in. The ISP automatically starts SLIP by specifying that the SLIP software be run in place of a shell (such as /bin/bash) for that account name. An ordinary user might have an entry in /etc/passwd that looks like the following example:

```
naba:ZbW0xq2XfL03g:501:100:Naba Barkakati:/home/naba:/bin/bash
```

Colons (:) separate the fields in that line in /etc/passwd. The first field is the user name; the last two fields are the home directory and the shell (the program to run after that user logs in), respectively. For a SLIP account, the entry might be the following:

```
slipxxx:ZbW0xq2XfL03g:501:100:SLIP user xx:/tmp:/usr/bin/ppl
```

The user name may be something cryptic (slipxxx), the home directory might be /tmp, and the last field shows the name of the SLIP program on the remote system. On a Hewlett-Packard workstation, for example, /usr/bin/ppl is the point-to-point link software that establishes a SLIP connection.

If the remote system is at your office, you may have a separate SLIP login, or you could log in as a normal user and then start the SLIP software. You can automate this part of the process with the dip program that you would run on your Linux PC.

Use dip to establish SLIP connection

The dip (Dial-up IP Protocol Driver) program allows you to automate the steps involved in setting up a SLIP connection to a remote system. If you want, you can run dip in an interactive mode. The best way to use dip, however, is to prepare a *script file* (a text file that contains commands for dip) and then run dip with that script file as input. I'll show you how to set up a dip script in the "Setting up a dip script" section. First, however, try using some of the dip commands interactively.

Running dip interactively

Tip

To get a feel for dip's commands, run dip interactively. Start dip with the -t option, as follows:

```
lnbsoft:~$ /sbin/dip -t
DIP: Dialup IP Protocol Driver version 3.3.7n-uri (17 Apr 95)
Written by Fred N. van Kempen, MicroWalt Corporation.

DIP> help
DIP knows about the following commands:
```

```
beep    bootp   break   chatkey config
databits dec    default dial    echo
flush   get     goto    help    if
inc     init    mode    modem   netmask
parity  password proxyarp print port
quit    reset   securidf securid send
sleep   speed   stopbits term    timeout
wait
```

```
DIP> quit
lnbsoft:~$
```

Tip

When you run `dip` in interactive mode, you can use the `help` command to see a list of commands that `dip` accepts. If you have all the information, you could use `dip` in interactive mode and issue appropriate commands to dial a remote system, log in, and complete the SLIP connection. Table 18-1 lists the available `dip` commands, and shows the syntax and meaning of each command. You typically would use these commands in a `dip` script file.

Table 18-1	The dip commands
Command	**Meaning**
`beep [times]`	Beeps a specified number of times.
`bootp`	Uses BOOTP protocol to determine the local IP address. (BOOTP, or Bootstrap Protocol, defined in RFC 951, provides a way for a workstation to determine its IP address. The protocol was developed to allow a diskless workstation to find a host from which to download a boot file and execute.)
`break`	Sends a BREAK. (Refer to Chapter 15 for an explanation of BREAK.)
`chatkey keyword [value]`	Adds a keyword (and an associated value) to the list of modem responses that `dip` recognizes. `chatkey RING 10`, for example, associates the value 10 with the modem response `RING`.
`config [interface|routing] [pre|up|down|post] arguments`	Uses the specified interface and routing-table configuration parameters. By default, this command is disabled.
`databits 7|8`	Sets the number of data bits to 7 or 8 (you must specify one of the two values). The number of data bits also is referred to as *word length* in serial communications.

Chapter 18: Dial-up Networking in Linux

Command	Meaning
`dec $variable [number|$var2]`	Decrements the specified variable (`dip` uses a dollar-sign prefix with a name to denote a variable). You can provide a number or another variable to indicate the amount to be decremented. If you do not provide a number or a second variable, `dip` decrements the value of the variable by 1.
`default`	Sets up the default route to the remote system with which `dip` has established a connection. The default route is used to forward network packets that are addressed to any unknown network address.
`dial phonenum [num_seconds]`	Dials the specified phone number and waits the specified number of seconds to receive an answer. If you do not specify a number of seconds, `dip` uses 60 seconds as a timeout. After issuing the modem's dial command, `dip` parses the modem's reply and sets the variable named `$errlvl` according to the reply (0=OK, 1=CONNECT).
`echo on|off`	The command `echo on` enables the display of all modem replies and text being sent to the modem. (This command can help you debug `dip` scripts.) The `echo off` command disables this feature and makes `dip` work in silence. I like to see what's going on, so I always use `echo on` in `dip` scripts.
`exit [status]`	Exits the `dip` script with the specified status code (leaves the current SLIP connection intact and leaves `dip` running). You must exit a `dip` script in this manner after establishing a successful SLIP connection.
`flush`	Flushes the input that was read from the modem or terminal.
`get $variable [number|ask |remote [timeout] |$var2] ask`	Gets the value of a specified variable. Use the `ask` keyword to prompt the user for a value. Use a number to simply set the variable to that value. Use the `remote` keyword to read a value from the remote system. You also can provide the name of a second variable as the source of the value.

(continued)

Table 18-1 *(continued)*

Command	Meaning
`goto label`	Jumps to a specified label in the script. The label marks a location in the script. The syntax for a label is to write the label's text followed by a colon (:). You'll see an example of this in the "Setting up a `dip` script" section.
`help`	Prints help information (used in interactive mode).
`if expression goto label`	Tests the *expression* and jumps to the *label* if the expression is true. The expression is of the form `$variable operator constant`, in which `$variable` denotes a `dip` variable and *operator* is `==`, `!=`, `<`, `>`, `<=`, or `>=`. *constant* is a constant value.
`inc $variable [number $var2]`	Increments the specified variable. You can provide a number or another variable to indicate the amount to be incremented. If you do not provide a number or a second variable, `dip` increments the value of the variable by 1.
`init init_string`	Specifies the initialization string to be sent to the modem before `dip` executes the `dial` command. The default *init_string* is `ATE0 Q0 V1 X1`. (Refer to Chapter 15 for a list of Hayes-modem commands.)
`mode SLIP|CSLIP|PPP TERM`	Sets the protocol to be used for the connection. The default is SLIP. If your ISP supports Compressed SLIP, use the CSLIP mode.
`modem modem_type`	Specifies the type of modem. The only acceptable value is HAYES, which `dip` assumes by default.
`netmask xxx.xxx.xxx.xxx`	Specifies the netmask to be used in configuring the SLIP interface. (Refer to Chapter 16 for a discussion of TCP/IP terms, including netmask.)
`parity E|O|N`	Sets the parity to be used for serial communication. Use `E` for even, `O` for odd, and `N` for none.
`password`	Prompts the user for a password and then sends that password to the modem.

Command	Meaning
`proxyarp`	Sets up proxy ARP. (Described in RFC 1027, proxy ARP allows a host — which also must be a gateway — to stand in for other hosts.)
`print any_text [$variable]`	Prints the text, as well as the values of any variables.
`port device_name`	Specifies the device name of the serial port to which the modem is connected. You must provide the device name without the `/dev/` prefix. Thus, use `cua0` if the modem is on COM1.
`quit`	Exits `dip` with non-zero status.
`reset`	Sends the string +++, followed by ATZ, to the modem. (The three plus signs are used to get the modem's attention, and ATZ resets the modem.)
`securidf fixed_part`	Stores the fixed part of a SecureID password.
`securid`	Prompts the user for the variable part of a password generated by an ACE System SecureID card.
`send text [$variable]`	Sends the text, as well as the values of any variables, to the modem.
`skey [timeout|$variable]`	Makes `dip` look for an S/Key challenge from the remote system. (S/Key is an authentication system developed by Bellcore.)
`sleep num_seconds`	Waits the specified number of seconds.
`speed bits_per_second`	Sets the serial port's speed. (Provide a number in bits-per-second units.)
`stopbits 1|2`	Sets the number of stop bits for serial communication.
`term`	Makes `dip` go into terminal-emulation mode. This mode allows you to interact directly through the serial connection. You can press Ctrl-] to exit terminal mode.
`timeout num_seconds`	Sets the timeout value to a specified number of seconds. If no activity occurs for that number of seconds, `dip` breaks the connection and exits.
`wait text [timeout|$variable]`	Waits for specified text to arrive. The optional argument indicates how long `dip` should wait.

In addition to the commands, `dip` provides several built-in variables. Table 18-2 lists the built-in variables in `dip`.

Table 18-2	Built-in dip variables
Variable	**Description**
$errlvl	The result code of the last executed command. Zero indicates success; any other value indicates error.
$local	The host name of your Linux PC (the local system).
$locip	The IP address of your Linux PC.
$modem	The name of the modem. (The only supported value is HAYES.)
$mtu	The Maximum Transfer Unit — the maximum number of bytes that a packet can contain.
$port	The name of the serial device (for example, `cua0` for COM1) used for the SLIP connection.
$remote	The host name of the remote system — the other end of the SLIP connection.
$rmtip	The IP address of the remote end of the SLIP connection.
$speed	The data-transfer rate between your PC and the modem (in bits per second).

Tip

When you first try a SLIP connection, you may want to run `dip` in interactive mode and use its `term` command to log in and establish the connection. The following example shows how I log in as `root` on my Linux system and establish a SLIP connection with a remote HP workstation. (My input is in boldface; comments are in italics.)

```
lnbsoft:/home/naba/slip# dip -t
DIP: Dialup IP Protocol Driver version 3.3.7n-uri (17 Apr 95)
Written by Fred N. van Kempen, MicroWalt Corporation.

DIP> get $locip 140.90.23.195
DIP> get $rmtip 140.90.23.194
DIP> port cua0
DIP> speed 38400
DIP> term
[ Entering TERMINAL mode. Use CTRL-] to get back ]

NO CARRIER
ATZ
OK
ATDT5551212    (use appropriate phone number here)
CONNECT 21600/ARQ/V34/LAPM
```

```
GenericSysName [Release] (see /etc/issue)
 dialin login: naba   (use your login name here)
Password:   (type your password here)

(extraneous messages deleted)

You have mail.
TERM = (hp)   (press Enter)
0A/users/naba 21 % ppl
 ppl: starting for naba at Mon Oct 23 20:45:55 1995

/dev/ttyd01 38400 Linet=140.90.23.194 Rinet=140.90.23.195
Mask=255.255.255.0 SLIP
initialization complete, running protocol
   (Press Ctrl-] here)
[ Back to LOCAL mode. ]
DIP> default
DIP> mode SLIP
```

After the final mode SLIP command, `dip` exits, and the connection is completed. At this point, I can use network applications such as `telnet` or `ftp` to access the remote system. When I no longer need the SLIP connection, I log in as `root` again and type **dip -k cua0** to end the connection.

Notice that in `dip`'s interactive mode, you have to switch to a terminal mode (with the `term` command) to send commands to the modem. You have to be in terminal mode to send the dialing commands to the modem and to log into the remote system when you see the `login` prompt.

After you enter any commands needed by the remote system, you should revert to `dip`'s command mode by pressing Ctrl-]. Then you can complete the SLIP setup by entering the `default` command, followed by the `mode SLIP` command. The default command causes `dip` to set up a default route by using the SLIP connection (that means that any network packet with an unknown address goes to the SLIP connection). The `mode SLIP` command makes `dip` communicate with the remote end by using the SLIP protocol.

If your ISP supports Compressed SLIP, use the `mode CSLIP` command instead of `mode SLIP`.

Setting up a `dip` script

As the preceding section shows, you can establish a SLIP connection by running `dip` in interactive mode with the `-t` option. That approach is not convenient, however, if you want to make a SLIP connection regularly. If your ISP provides you fixed IP addresses for both ends of the SLIP connection, you can set up a script file that can set up the connection automatically. The script file contains commands for the `dip` program; you have to write the script according to the syntax required by the `dip` program.

If your `dip` script file is named `connect.dip` (it is common to use the `.dip` extension for script files meant for `dip`), you can use that file with `dip` by typing **dip connect**. This command causes the `dip` program to read and execute commands from the script file named `connect.dip`.

Note

The script file itself is essentially a sequence of commands for `dip`, much like the commands that you use when you run `dip` with the `-t` option. The only major difference is that you have to use the `send` command to send some text to the modem and use the `wait` command to look for specific text coming back from the remote system. Following is a `dip` script file that I use to connect to an HP workstation (I must use the `ppl` command manually to establish a point-to-point link that uses the SLIP protocol):

```
# File: connect.dip
#
# Establishes a dial-up SLIP connection.
#
# Naba Barkakati, 10/21/95

main:
# Echo everything so we can debug easily
  echo on

# Set up my IP address
  get $locip 140.90.23.195

# Set up the remote IP address
# NOTE: These are test values only -- you should use
# IP addresses specific to your case

  get $rmtip 140.90.23.194

# Set the netmask on sl0 to 255.255.255.0
  netmask 255.255.255.0

# Select the serial port and speed (my modem is on COM1, which
# is /dev/cua0 -- select yours appropriately)
  port cua0
  speed 38400

# Send initialization sequence to modem
  send ATZ\r
  wait OK 2
  send ATE1M1V1X4L3S0=0\&c1Q0DT5551212\r
  wait CONNECT 75

# Check the "errlvl"
  if $errlvl != 0 goto error

# We are connected. Log in.
login:
  wait ogin: 30
  if $errlvl != 0 goto no_login_prompt

# Send your user name (use your user ID on the next line)
  send your-username\r
  wait word: 10
```

```
# Send the passwrd (use your password on the next line)
  send your-password-here

# The following sequence depends on your system
# In this case, I am responding to a system's prompt for
# terminal name
  wait TERM 10
  send \r
  sleep 5
  send \r
  send \r
  wait some-text-in-the-prompt 30

# Start SLIP at the remote end
  print Sending command to start SLIP...
  send ppl\n
  wait some-text-indicating-SLIP-is-running 30

  default
  mode SLIP
# Print a message and exit
  print Connected... $locip -> $rmtip
  goto exit

no_login_prompt:
  print No login prompt...
  goto error

error:
  print CONNECT FAILED...
  quit 1

exit:
```

Notice that you must replace the items in italics with the text and numbers that are appropriate for your situation. In particular, if you obtained a SLIP account from an ISP, you must get the IP addresses and phone number from the ISP. Also, the exact steps for logging into the remote system will vary from one system to another.

Checking the SLIP connection

Tip

After the SLIP connection is set up, you can use the `ifconfig` command to see whether the SLIP device `sl0` is configured (`dip` does this for you). Following is typical output from the `ifconfig` command after you have SLIP up and running:

```
ifconfig
lo    Link encap:Local Loopback
      inet addr:127.0.0.1 Bcast:127.255.255.255 Mask:255.0.0.0
      UP BROADCAST LOOPBACK RUNNING MTU:2000 Metric:1
      RX packets:0 errors:0 dropped:0 overruns:0
      TX packets:25 errors:0 dropped:0 overruns:0
```

```
sl0     Link encap:Serial Line IP
        inet addr:140.90.23.195 P-t-P:140.90.23.194 Mask:255.255.255.0
        UP POINTOPOINT RUNNING MTU:296 Metric:1
        RX packets:4 errors:0 dropped:0 overruns:0
        TX packets:4 errors:0 dropped:0 overruns:0

eth0    Link encap:10Mbps Ethernet HWaddr 00:20:AF:E8:A2:25
        inet addr:206.197.168.200 Bcast:206.197.168.255
Mask:255.255.255.0
        UP BROADCAST RUNNING MULTICAST MTU:1500 Metric:1
        RX packets:2087 errors:0 dropped:0 overruns:0
        TX packets:543 errors:0 dropped:0 overruns:0
        Interrupt:10 Base address:0x210
```

Secret

Additionally, if you use the `default` command, `dip` adds a default route to the SLIP connection. To verify this, use the `route` command in the following manner:

```
/sbin/route -n
lnbsoft:~$ /sbin/route -n
Kernel routing table
Destination     Gateway         Genmask         Flags MSS   Window Use Iface
140.90.23.194   *               255.255.255.255 UH    232   0      98  sl0
206.197.168.0   *               255.255.255.0   U     1436  0      143 eth0
127.0.0.0       *               255.0.0.0       U     1936  0      108 lo
default         140.90.23.194   *               UG    232   0      390 sl0
```

As this listing shows, packets for the IP address 140.90.23.194 (which, in this case, is the remote end of the SLIP connection) are sent to the sl0 device — the SLIP device. The destination `default` (see the last line) refers to any network address. Packets meant for any network address (other than the ones specified in the entries in the routing table) are sent to the IP address 140.90.23.194 — the remote end of the SLIP connection. You need these routing-table entries so that your Linux system can communicate with the remote system.

Ending a SLIP connection

Tip

To end a SLIP connection, you have to use `dip` itself with the `-k` option followed by the serial device that is being used for the SLIP connection. Log in as `root`, and type the following command to close a SLIP connection on `/dev/cua0`:

```
dip -k cua0
DIP: Dialup IP Protocol Driver version 3.3.7n-uri (17 Apr 95)
Written by Fred N. van Kempen, MicroWalt Corporation.

DIP: process 951 killed.
```

Connecting to a Remote Network as a PPP Client

PPP is a more complex and more versatile protocol than SLIP, but the mechanics of connecting to a remote network with PPP are very similar to the steps that you use for SLIP. You still get IP addresses for the two ends of the PPP connection, a phone number to dial, and a user name you can use to log into the remote system.

Note

Just as the `dip` program helps you automate SLIP setup, you use two other programs — `pppd` and `chat` — to set up and configure a PPP connection. Before you try anything, your Linux kernel must include the PPP network devices.

Check PPP support

Secret

As with SLIP, you must have the kernel configured with PPP support. In the `make config` step of rebuilding the Linux kernel (consult Chapter 2 for details), you should accept the default yes answer to the following question about PPP support:

```
PPP (point-to-point) support (CONFIG_PPP) [y]
```

You can use the command `cat /proc/net/dev` to verify that PPP devices are available on your system. Typically, you should see four PPP devices listed: `ppp0`, `ppp1`, `ppp2`, and `ppp3`.

Secret

Additionally, when your system boots, the boot messages show whether PPP devices have been configured. Use the `dmesg | more` command to view the boot messages. You should see lines such as the following in the boot messages:

```
IP Protocols: ICMP, UDP, TCP
PPP: version 0.2.7 (4 channels) NEW_TTY_DRIVERS OPTIMIZE_FLAGS
TCP compression code copyright 1989 Regents of the University of
California
PPP line discipline registered.
```

Cross Reference

If you do not see any evidence of PPP support in the kernel, you should rebuild the kernel, using the steps in Chapter 2. Then you should make sure that you enable PPP support during the `make config` step.

Gather information for PPP connection

Note

Many ISPs (Internet Service Providers) provide PPP access to the Internet through one or more systems that the ISP maintains. If you sign up for such a service, the ISP should provide you the information that you need to make a PPP connection to the remote system. At minimum, this information should include the following:

- The IP address for your side of the connection. (This IP address will be associated with your PC's PPP interface — the serial port.)

- The IP address of the ISP's PPP interface. (This address may be listed as the "gateway" address, because this interface is your system's gateway to the Internet.)
- The phone number to dial to connect to the remote system.
- The user name and password that you must use to log into the remote system.

Most ISPs also provide the IP addresses of a name server, mail server, and news server. These addresses, however, are not important for the mechanics of setting up a PPP connection.

Use pppd with chat to make the PPP connection

To set up a PPP networking connection between two systems, you must have PPP software running at both ends. Typically, your ISP will provide you with an account that's set up so that the PPP software runs automatically upon login. In that case, all that remains is to start the PPP software on your system after you log into the remote system.

Note

Thus, the two basic steps for setting up a PPP connection are

1. Dial up and log into the remote system. (I'll assume that when you log in, the remote system starts its PPP software automatically.)
2. Start the PPP software on your Linux system.

Just as the dip program supports SLIP connection, the pppd program takes care of communicating with PPP over a dial-up line. Therefore, after you log in and start PPP software at the remote system, you have to run pppd on your Linux system.

Note

Incidentally, the pppd program's name stands for Point-to-Point Protocol Daemon. (In UNIX, the term *daemon* refers to a program that runs in the background and performs some useful task.) The pppd program actually provides an option through which you can invoke another program that actually establishes the serial communication and completes the remote login process.

In Linux, the common practice is to use pppd with the chat program. If you installed Linux from this book's companion CD-ROM, you'll find both pppd and chat programs in the /usr/lib/ppp directory on your Linux system.

Using the chat program

Note

You need to understand how chat works so that you can use it to automatically dial and log into the remote system. The chat program is designed to process a script that uses an *expect-send* pattern of text. The program looks for the *expect* string, and when it receives the *expect* string, chat sends the *send* string.

Chapter 18: Dial-up Networking in Linux

Suppose that I want `chat` to look for the string `login:` (which is how most UNIX systems prompt for a user name) and then send my user name (`naba`). Following that, I want `chat` to expect the `Password:` prompt and send out my password. I would use the following *expect-send* pairs to do this:

```
ogin: naba word: my-password
```

You may notice that I left out the leading `L` in the login prompt and some parts of the password prompt; the reason was to avoid being too specific, so that `chat` will succeed even if the received text is slightly different. After all, the login prompt may start with an uppercase `L`, or the first few characters of the `Password:` string may be garbled.

Timeouts

When it waits for an expected text string, `chat` uses a timeout feature. If the string does not arrive within the timeout period, `chat` moves to the next string. The default timeout value is 45 seconds. You can change the timeout with the TIMEOUT command, as follows:

```
TIMEOUT 10 ogin: naba TIMEOUT 5 word: my-password
```

In this case, the timeout period is 10 seconds when `chat` is waiting for the `login:` prompt. Then the timeout is changed to 5 seconds before `chat` looks for the `Password:` string.

Sub-expect sequences

The typical login sequence illustrates a simple case. A more complex case is when `chat` is looking for a login prompt, but none arrives within the timeout period. If you were logging in at a terminal, you would have pressed Enter to get another login prompt. You can simulate this behavior with `chat`'s *sub-expect sequences*, which start with two dashes. Following is an example:

```
ogin:--ogin: naba word: my-password
```

In this case, if `chat` does not receive the `login:` prompt within the timeout period, `chat` sends a single return (just as though you pressed Enter at the keyboard) and then looks for the `login:` prompt again.

ABORT strings

Most modems report the status of a connection as a string. For example, the modem might report `CONNECT` (which might be followed by the speed of connection) when successfully connected, `BUSY` if the remote phone is busy, or `NO CARRIER` if the modem does not get a dial tone from the phone.

You probably will want to stop the connection if the modem returns any status other than `CONNECT`. You can take care of this with `chat`'s ABORT command. The idea is to specify strings that should cause `chat` to abort the phone call. Following is an example:

```
ABORT BUSY ABORT "NO CARRIER" "" ATZ OK ATDT5551212
```

The first `ABORT BUSY` pair defines the `BUSY` string as an abort string. The next pair, `ABORT "NO CARRIER"`, defines another abort string. (Use quotation marks to enclose any string that includes spaces.)

After the two abort strings, you see two expect-send pairs. The first pair instructs chat to expect nothing (indicated by an empty string, "") and to send the ATZ command to reset the modem. The next expect-send pair causes chat to expect the string OK and to send the dialing command (ATDT, followed by a phone number) after the modem sends the OK string.

Escape sequences

In the expect-send strings, you can use special characters. Most special characters are denoted by a backslash prefix, which serves as the escape character. These special character sequences are traditionally called *escape sequences*. Table 18-3 lists the escape sequences that you can use in scripts for the chat program:

Table 18-3	chat escape sequences
Sequence	Description
" "	Two consecutive quotes mean an empty string. If you send an empty string, chat sends a single carriage-return character.
\b	A backspace character.
\c	Stops the new-line character at the end of the send string. You can send \c only at the end of a string.
\d	Delays for one second. You cannot use this sequence in the expect string.
\ddd	A byte that contains the specified octal value.
\K	Sends a BREAK signal (refer to Chapter 15). You cannot use this sequence in an expect string.
\n	A new-line (line-feed) character.
\N	Sends a null character (a byte with all zero bits). You cannot use this sequence in an expect string.
\p	Pauses for a tenth of a second. You cannot use this sequence in an expect string.
\q	Suppresses writing of the string to the /var/adm/syslog file. This sequence is not valid in an expect string.
\r	A carriage return.
\s	A space character. Use this sequence when you do not want to place quotes around the string.
\t	A tab character.
^C	A control character that corresponds to the letter that follows the caret. Thus, ^X means Ctrl-X.

Chapter 18: Dial-up Networking in Linux

You can use all these escape sequences in send strings, but as the comments indicate, you cannot use many sequences in expect strings.

Using pppd with a chat script

The actual details of PPP networking are handled by the PPP daemon program, pppd, which uses the PPP driver code in the Linux kernel to exchange TCP/IP packets over the serial port.

Note

You need to perform two basic steps to complete a PPP connection with a remote system:

1. Dial out, using your modem, and log into the remote system, using a user name and password provided by the remote system's owner. Typically, when you log into the remote system, that action should start the necessary PPP software at the remote end.

2. Start the PPP daemon (pppd) on your system to initiate and conduct a PPP session with the remote system.

The pppd program is designed to take care of both of these steps. Essentially, you use the chat program to perform the first step: dialing up and logging into the remote system. You do not have to run chat separately. Instead, you provide a chat script in the pppd command line; pppd invokes chat to process that script.

Tip

Typical pppd command line

In its simplest form, you can run pppd with a long command line that might look like the following:

```
/usr/lib/ppp/pppd connect "/usr/lib/ppp/chat chat-script" crtscts modem \
defaultroute 192.168.101.111:192.168.102.1 /dev/cua0 38400
```

The backslash at the end of the first line is used to continue the command on the next line. The actual pppd command line is even longer, because the chat-script part is a sequence of *expend-send* pairs. Here is what various parts of the pppd command line mean:

- The connect option instructs pppd to connect by executing the command within double quotes that follows the connect option. In the example, the command is shown without the enclosing quotation marks:

    ```
    /usr/lib/ppp/chat chat script
    ```

    The chat-script part may be a long sequence of expect-send pairs of strings that the chat program processes. You might implement a simple dial-up login script by using the following command to start chat:

    ```
    /usr/lib/ppp/chat "" ATZ OK ATDT5551212 CONNECT "" ogin: my-username \
    word: my-password
    ```

This `chat` script sends `ATZ` to reset the modem; waits for an `OK` and then sends a dial command (`ATDTphone-number`); waits for a `CONNECT` and then sends an empty string (a carriage return); waits for the `ogin:` string and sends `my-username` (which should be your PPP login name); and, finally, waits for the `word:` string and sends `my-password` (the password for your PPP login account).

Cross Reference

- The `crtscts` option instructs `pppd` to use the Request to Send (RTS) and Clear to Send (CTS) signals for hardware handshaking with the modem. (Consult Chapter 15, "Modems," for more information on RTS and CTS signals.)

- The `modem` option causes `pppd` to use and honor the modem control signals that reflect the modem's status.

- The `defaultroute` option instructs `pppd` to set up a default route entry on your system to use the remote system as the gateway. If you already have a default route set up (for your Ethernet LAN, for example), `pppd` does not set up the default route to the remote system.

- The two IP addresses instruct `pppd` to use the IP address 192.168.101.111 for the local interface and the IP address 192.168.102.1 for the remote end of the PPP connection. If the remote host assigns IP addresses dynamically, you can use 0.0.0.0 as your local IP address; `pppd` automatically uses the IP address assigned by the remote system.

- The device name tells `pppd` to dial out on the device `/dev/cua0` (COM1). If your modem is on COM2, use `/dev/cua1` as the device name.

- The last option causes `pppd` to set the modem's data rate (often called the *baud rate*) to 38,400 bps.

As this list shows, that single `pppd` command line packs a great deal of information. At the same time, however, that command does a great deal of work. After `pppd` establishes the connection to the remote system, your system becomes part of the remote network (provided that the remote system adds appropriate routing-table entries).

Caution

You should note one key point about the `pppd` command line: the entire `chat` command (which follows the `connect` option) is enclosed in quotes, but the `chat` command itself uses various strings in quotes. You have to remember to use a backslash-character prefix for those embedded quotes. The following example shows how a `chat` script looks in a `pppd` command line:

```
/usr/lib/ppp/pppd connect "/usr/lib/ppp/chat \"\" ATZ OK ATDT5551212 CONNECT \"\" \
ogin: my-username word: my-password"    (rest of command line not shown)
```

As this example shows, all embedded quotes need a backslash prefix.

A PPP dial-up script

Secret

If you are going to use `pppd` routinely, you probably do not want to type the command. You should prepare a shell script and start `pppd` from the script. If you save the script in a file named `dial-ppp`, for example, you can set up a PPP connection with the following command:

```
dial-ppp
```

Chapter 18: Dial-up Networking in Linux

Secret

That's what I do to connect my Linux PC to the Internet through my ISP. Here's a typical shell script to set up a PPP connection to a remote system:

```
#!/bin/sh
# A script to establish a dial-up PPP connection

# Shell variable with remote end's IP address
  RMTIP="192.168.102.1"

# If PPP link exists, then exit
  /sbin/ifconfig | grep $RMTIP >/dev/null && exit 0

# Other shell variables
# Set LOCIP to "" if your IP address is dynamically assigned
  LOCIP="192.168.101.111"
  PHONE="555-1212"
  DEVICE="/dev/cua0"
  SPEED="38400"
  PPP_LOGINNAME="my-username"
  PPP_PASSWORD="my-password"

  /usr/lib/ppp/pppd connect "/usr/lib/ppp/chat \
       ABORT \"NO CARRIER\" ABORT BUSY ABORT \"NO DIAL TONE\" \
       \"\" ATZ OK ATE1M1V1X4L3S0=0\&c1Q0DT$PHONE CONNECT \"\" \
       ogin:--ogin: $PPP_LOGINNAME word: $PPP_PASSWORD" \
         crtscts modem defaultroute $LOCIP:$RMTIP $DEVICE $SPEED
# End of script
```

Note

I replaced some sensitive information (such as phone number, user name, password, and IP addresses) with phony values. In the script, this information appears in italics. You should replace these parameters with ones that apply to your situation. If you have a PPP account with an ISP, the ISP should provide you this information (phone number, IP addresses, user name, and password).

Testing the PPP connection

If you have PPP access to another system (such as an ISP or a system at your employer's organization), you can set up a script as described in the preceding section and enjoy the benefits of full TCP/IP network access to another system. After you run the script, and after `pppd` completes the initial protocol exchanges to set up the connection, you can verify that the connection is up by typing the `ifconfig` command, which should show a listing like this:

```
/sbin/ifconfig
lo      Link encap:Local Loopback
        inet addr:127.0.0.1 Bcast:127.255.255.255 Mask:255.0.0.0
        UP BROADCAST LOOPBACK RUNNING MTU:2000 Metric:1
        RX packets:0 errors:0 dropped:0 overruns:0
        TX packets:12 errors:0 dropped:0 overruns:0

ppp0    Link encap:Point-Point Protocol
        inet addr:192.168.101.111 P-t-P:192.168.102.1 Mask:255.255.255.0
```

```
        UP POINTOPOINT RUNNING MTU:1500 Metric:1
        RX packets:2221 errors:0 dropped:0 overruns:0
        TX packets:2890 errors:0 dropped:0 overruns:0

eth0    Link encap:10Mbps Ethernet HWaddr 00:20:AF:E8:A2:25
        inet addr:206.197.168.200 Bcast:206.197.168.255
Mask:255.255.255.0
        UP BROADCAST RUNNING MULTICAST MTU:1500 Metric:1
        RX packets:2977 errors:0 dropped:0 overruns:0
        TX packets:3774 errors:0 dropped:0 overruns:0
        Interrupt:10 Base address:0x210
```

You should find the `ppp0` device listed in the output. The `ifconfig` output also shows the IP addresses of the local and remote ends of the PPP connection. This output confirms that the PPP device is up and running.

To verify that the routing table is set up correctly, use the `route` command without any arguments, as follows:

```
/sbin/route -n
Kernel routing table
Destination    Gateway         Genmask         Flags MSS   Window Use Iface
192.168.102.1  *               255.255.255.255 UH    1436  0      14  ppp0
localnet       *               255.255.255.0   U     1436  0      3749 eth0
loopback       *               255.0.0.0       U     1936  0      12  lo
default        192.168.102.1   *               UG    1436  0      2942 ppp0
```

In the routing table, the first line shows a route to the remote end's IP address; this one should be set to the `ppp0` device. Also, the default route should be set up so that the remote end of the PPP connection serves as the gateway for your system (as the last line of the routing table shows).

After checking the interface configuration (with the `ifconfig` command) and the routing table (with the `route` command), you should verify that you can reach some well-known host. If your ISP gave you the IP address of a name server or a mail server, you can try to ping those addresses. Otherwise, try to ping the IP address of a system at your workplace or your university.

Tip

The following example shows what you would see if you try the `ping` command:

```
ping 140.90.23.100
PING 140.90.23.100 (140.90.23.100): 56 data bytes
64 bytes from 140.90.23.100: icmp_seq=0 ttl=244 time=336.0 ms
64 bytes from 140.90.23.100: icmp_seq=1 ttl=244 time=290.2 ms
64 bytes from 140.90.23.100: icmp_seq=2 ttl=244 time=350.2 ms
64 bytes from 140.90.23.100: icmp_seq=3 ttl=244 time=300.2 ms
64 bytes from 140.90.23.100: icmp_seq=4 ttl=244 time=340.2 ms
64 bytes from 140.90.23.100: icmp_seq=5 ttl=244 time=290.2 ms

--- 140.90.23.100 ping statistics ---
6 packets transmitted, 6 packets received, 0% packet loss
round-trip min/avg/max = 290.2/317.8/350.2 ms
```

The time at the end of each line shows the round-trip time for a packet originating at your system to reach the designated IP address (140.90.23.100, in this case) and back to your system again. For PPP connection over dial-up lines, you'll see times in hundreds of milliseconds.

Incidentally, you do not have to have an account on a system to ping its IP address. Although a system may disable the automatic response to ping messages (ping uses Internet Control Message Protocol or ICMP messages), most systems respond to ping.

Ending the PPP connection

After pppd establishes a PPP connection, the link stays up as long as the PPP software at both ends continues to run. When you no longer need the PPP connection, you can end it by stopping the pppd process.

After setting up a PPP link, pppd creates a file in the /var/run directory where it stores the process ID of pppd. The filename is based on the PPP device name. For the first PPP link, the PPP device is ppp0, and the process ID file is /var/run/ppp0.pid. You can write a shell script to kill the pppd process by using the process ID stored in the /var/run/ppp0.pid file.

Secret

In fact, you do not really have to write your own shell script to end a PPP link. In the /usr/lib/ppp directory, you'll find a script named ppp-off that performs this task for you. Whenever you want to bring down the PPP link, log in as root and type **/usr/lib/ppp/ppp-off**.

This command ends the pppd process, which in turn cleans up the routing table.

Secret

The /usr/lib/ppp/ppp-off script looks like this:

```
#!/bin/sh

DEVICE=ppp0

#
# If the ppp0 pid file is presen, the program is running. Stop it.
if [ -r /var/run/$DEVICE.pid ]; then
    kill -INT `cat /var/run/$DEVICE.pid`
#
# If unsuccessful, ensure that the pid file is removed.
#
    if [ ! "$?" = "0" ]; then
            echo "removing stale $DEVICE pid file."
            rm -f /var/run/$DEVICE.pid
            exit 1
    fi
#
# Success. Terminate with proper status.
#
    echo "$DEVICE link terminated"
    exit 0
```

```
fi
#
# The link is not active
#
echo "$DEVICE link is not active"
exit 1
```

Notice that this script uses the command `cat /var/run/$DEVICE.pid` (`DEVICE` is defined as `ppp0`) to obtain the process ID of the `pppd` process. That process ID then is used as an argument in the `kill` command that terminates the `pppd` process.

Routing Through the PPP Connection

A common use of a PPP connection is to connect two geographically separated networks or, more commonly, to connect a small local-area network (LAN) to the Internet. In a typical scenario, you have a small Ethernet LAN that you want to connect to the Internet. You can do this with a Linux PC that has both an Ethernet card and a modem. The Linux system has a presence on your Ethernet LAN through its Ethernet-card interface. If you can establish a PPP connection to a system on the Internet, you can use the Linux PC as the gateway between your LAN and the remote system (which, presumably, is already connected to the Internet). Figure 18-2 illustrates such a scenario.

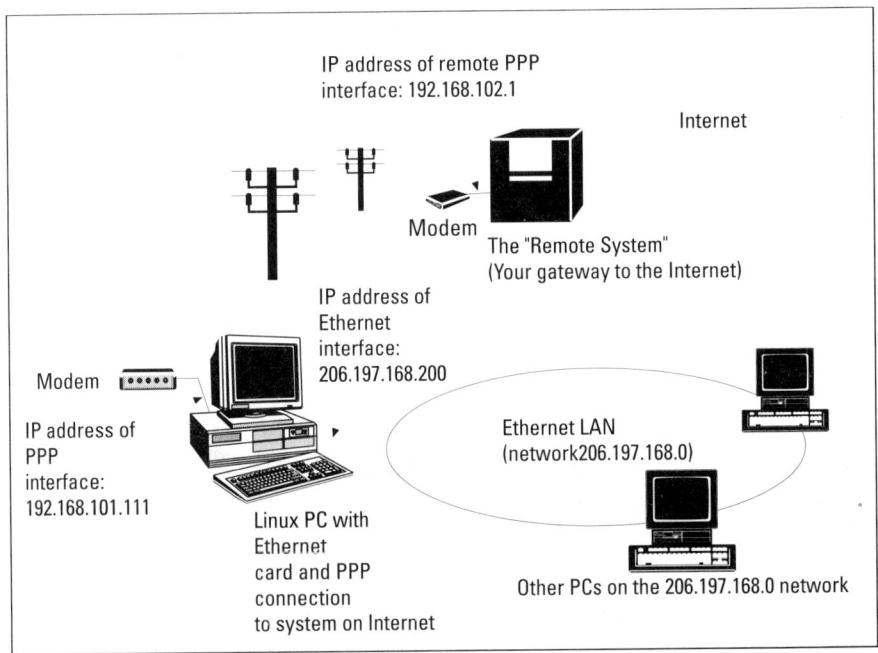

Figure 18-2: Connecting a LAN to the Internet.

Chapter 18: Dial-up Networking in Linux

In this case, you have a small Ethernet LAN with a few PCs and a class C IP address of 206.197.168.0. You have assigned 206.197.168.200 as the IP address of your Linux PC's Ethernet-card interface (you should do this with the `ifconfig` command in the `/etc/rc.d/rc.inet1` file).

The Linux PC also has a modem through which you establish a PPP connection to a remote system on the Internet. Both ends of the PPP connection have unique IP addresses. You want to ensure that the PCs on your Ethernet LAN can access the Internet. You want to use your Linux PC as a gateway to route network packets between the Ethernet LAN and the remote system, because the Linux PC is the only one that has both PPP and Ethernet interfaces. The following sections explain how to accomplish this goal.

Learn to use the `route` command

As you try to ensure that network packets can travel back and forth between your LAN and the Internet through a gateway, you realize the importance of the kernel routing table. You have to log in as `root` and use the `route` command to make any changes in the IP routing table.

A *route* specifies a path between two network nodes. A typical specification says something like this: "All packets for the 206.197.168.0 network should be sent to the Ethernet interface named `eth0`." With the `route` command, you'd specify this route as follows:

```
route add -net 206.197.168.0 eth0
```

That's a typical format of the `route` command, specifying the path to all hosts that belong to a network. If you have an Ethernet LAN, each system on the LAN has a routing entry of this form.

Another type of routing-table entry specifies the path to a specific host. When a PPP link is set up to remote IP address 192.168.102.1, for example, you might add to the routing table an entry that says, "Packets addressed to the IP address 192.168.102.1 should be sent to the `ppp0` device (the first PPP device)." To accomplish this task, use the following `route` command:

```
route add -host 192.168.102.1 ppp0
```

Finally, a third type of routing-table entry is for the *gateway* — an IP address that's used as the destination for any network address without an explicit route. If you have a PPP link, you may want to say, "Send any packet of unresolved address to the remote IP address of the PPP link." In other words, you want to use the remote end of the PPP connection as the gateway. If the remote IP address is 192.168.102.1, you can specify this address as the gateway by using the following `route` command:

```
route add default gw 192.168.102.1
```

If you find that you no longer need a route (for example, this can happen if a route's interface is a PPP link but the PPP link is down), you can delete that entry from the routing table by using the `route del` command. To remove the route to the IP address 192.168.102.1, use the following `route` command:

```
route del 192.168.102.1
```

If you type the `route` command without any arguments, the command displays the current routing table. If you want to see the entries in the form of IP addresses, instead of symbolic names, use the `route -n` command.

Enable IP forwarding in the kernel

The first step that you must take is to ensure that the Linux kernel on your system has IP forwarding enabled. This capability is not enabled by default. Therefore, you may have to reconfigure and rebuild the kernel to turn on IP forwarding.

Consult Chapter 2 for the steps that you must follow to reconfigure the kernel. In the step in which you type the `make config` command, you have to answer yes to the following question (among other questions related to TCP/IP networking):

```
*** Networking options:
TCP/IP networking (CONFIG_INET) [y]
IP forwarding/gatewaying (CONFIG_IP_FORWARD) [n] y
```

The letter in brackets indicates the default answer. As you can see, the default answer to the IP forwarding question is `n`, which means no. You must press `y` to indicate that you want IP forwarding support in the kernel.

When IP forwarding is enabled, the Linux kernel automatically forwards packets from one interface to another.

Make your system route to a remote gateway

If you use `pppd` to set up the PPP connection, you really do not have to do anything extra to designate the remote system as the gateway for your Linux PC. The `pppd` program automatically sets up two entries in the routing table:

- A host entry to the remote end of the PPP connection. For the IP addresses shown in Figure 18-2, the `route` command that adds this entry looks like the following:

```
route add -host 192.168.102.1 ppp0
```

This command tells the network software that all network packets addressed to 192.168.102.1 (the remote IP address) should be sent to the PPP interface.

- A default route entry with the remote IP address as the gateway. Again, using the IP addresses in Figure 18-2 as an example, the `route` command for this purpose is the following:

```
route add default gw 192.168.102.1
```

This command tells the network software to use 192.168.102.1 as the destination for all packets for which a route does not exist.

Chapter 18: Dial-up Networking in Linux

Caution

Watch out for one `pppd` behavior that may cause some problems. If a default route already exists, `pppd` does not overwrite that default route. This situation can occur if you have an Ethernet LAN with a router, and your system has a default route entry to the Ethernet router. For most people, this situation should not be a problem, but if you do not seem to be able to `ping` after establishing the PPP link, check the routing table (with a `route -n` command), and make sure that a default route to the remote end of the PPP connection exists.

If you have a PPP account with an ISP (Internet Service Provider), you should get the remote IP addresses from the ISP. Because the remote IP address is used as the gateway, the ISP's documentation often refers to the remote IP address as the *gateway address*.

Make your system the gateway for your LAN

Wizard

If you want to use the Linux PC as the path through which all other systems on your Ethernet LAN reach the Internet, you have to perform another task. On each of the systems on the Ethernet LAN, you must specify the Linux PC's IP address (on the Ethernet side; refer to Figure 18-2) as the gateway address.

How you specify a gateway address depends on the operating system and the TCP/IP networking software that you run on the systems on that Ethernet LAN. If those systems are PCs running Linux, use the following `route` command (after you log in as `root`):

```
route add default gw 206.197.168.200
```

If you run Windows 95, you have to set the TCP/IP properties from the Networking control panel and add the IP address 206.197.168.200 as a gateway.

By making your Linux PC the gateway for all systems on the Ethernet LAN, you ensure that the network software on each system knows what to do with network packets for the outside world: send the packets to your Linux PC. Then, your Linux PC can send the packets to its default route, which should be the remote system.

Remote gateway must route to your LAN

Secret

Unfortunately, Internet routing is a two-way street. Just as your system needs a path to the remote system, the remote system needs a route back to your network. I say "unfortunately" because you can control the routing at your end, but the routing-table entries at the other end of the link are in the hands of someone else. As a result, you are at the other person's mercy when it comes to getting proper IP routes set up so that your LAN can access the Internet.

Secret

Typically, if you get a PPP account from an ISP, the ISP will add a route to the IP address of your PPP interface. Because `pppd` adds a route in the other direction, your system should be able to access the Internet without any problems. The only problem that you'll have is putting your Ethernet LAN (assuming that you have one) on the Internet. You cannot successfully connect the LAN to the Internet unless the ISP's gateway has a route to your network. For the IP addresses shown in Figure 18-2, the remote system should route all network packets for the 206.197.168.0 network through the IP address of your Linux PC's PPP interface (which has the IP address 192.168.101.111). If the ISP runs a Linux system, you can accomplish this step with the following `route` command:

```
route add -net 206.197.168.0 192.168.101.111
```

It's entirely up to the ISP to decide whether to provide this route back to your network.

If you make arrangements with an ISP for a block of IP addresses for your Ethernet LAN, everything should be fine, because the ISP definitely will provide routing to any IP addresses known to it. The only problem is that the ISP probably will charge you extra if you want Internet access for more than one system.

If the remote system belongs to your employer or your university, you may be able to persuade the system administrator to add the appropriate routing-table entries in the remote system's gateway.

Setting up a PPP Server

The preceding sections describe how your Linux PC can establish a PPP link with another system that offers PPP service. After a PPP link is set up, both ends of the PPP link behave as peers. Before a PPP link is established, you can think of the end that initiates the dial-up connection as being the client, because that system asks for the connection. The other end provides the PPP connection when needed, so it's the PPP server.

If you want to allow other people to connect to your Linux PC by using PPP over a dial-up modem, follow these steps:

1. Follow the steps outlined in Chapter 15 to enable dial-up login on your system. Test this part to make sure that everything works; dial into your system from another computer and log in as a user. This step involves adding the following line to the `/etc/inittab` file:

   ```
   s1:456:respawn:/sbin/uugetty ttyS0 38400 vt100
   ```

2. Add a user name for the dial-up PPP connection — the user name under which the client system logs in. Upon login, the `pppd` program should run automatically. The following example shows how you might add a user named `pppuser` for this purpose:

   ```
   /usr/etc# /sbin/adduser

   Adding a new user. The username should not exceed 8 characters
   in length, or you may run into problems later.

   Enter login name for new account (^C to quit): pppuser

   Editing information for new user [pppuser]
   ```

```
Full Name: PPP Dialin User
GID [100]:
Group 'users', GID 100
First unused uid is 504

UID [504]:

Home Directory [/home/pppuser]: /tmp

Shell [/bin/bash]: /usr/etc/ppp-login

Password [pppuser]:

Information for new user [pppuser]:
Home directory: [/tmp] Shell: [/usr/etc/ppp-login]
uid: [504] gid: [100]

Is this correct? [y/N]: y

Adding login [pppuser] and making directory [/tmp]

Adding the files from the /etc/skel directory:
./.kermrc -> /tmp/./.kermrc
./.less -> /tmp/./.less
./.lessrc -> /tmp/./.lessrc
./.term/termrc -> /tmp/./.term/termrc
```

3. Prepare the /usr/etc/ppp-login script. This script is the "shell" for the PPP login account, which means this script is executed when the PPP user logs in. Thus, the script should start the pppd program with appropriate options. After you prepare the script, remember to make it executable. Following is a typical /usr/etc/ppp-login script:

```
#!/bin/sh
# A script to start PPP service for a login account

# Shell variables with IP addresses
  RMTIP="192.168.111.111"
  LOCIP="192.168.111.222"

  exec /usr/lib/ppp/pppd -detach silent modem \
          crtscts $LOCIP:$RMTIP
```

I tested this setup from a Windows 95 PC, and it worked; however, I had to type in the user name and password manually in a terminal window. In Windows 95 dial-up networking, you can turn on an option that displays a terminal window after the modems establish connection. Figure 18-3 shows the Windows 95 Dial-up Connection window, which shows the status of the PPP connection.

As the status window shows, the connection was established at 12,000 bps. In case you're curious, I used a 14,400-bps Zoom modem on the Windows 95 PC and a USRobotics 28,800-bps V.34 modem on the Linux PC. The two modems negotiated a connection at 12,000 bps.

Part IV: Using Linux for Fun and Profit

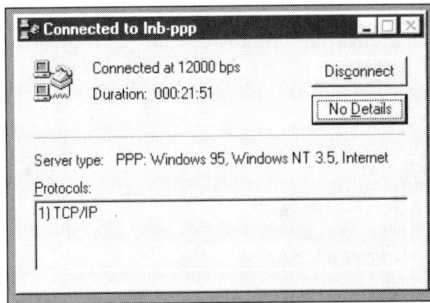

Figure 18-3: Windows 95 Dial-up Connection window, showing the status of the PPP connection.

After a connection is established, the /sbin/ifconfig command on the Linux PC shows the status of the connection as follows:

```
/sbin/ifconfig
lo      Link encap:Local Loopback
        inet addr:127.0.0.1 Bcast:127.255.255.255 Mask:255.0.0.0
        UP BROADCAST LOOPBACK RUNNING MTU:2000 Metric:1
        RX packets:0 errors:0 dropped:0 overruns:0
        TX packets:2921 errors:0 dropped:0 overruns:0

ppp0    Link encap:Point-Point Protocol
        inet addr:192.168.111.222 P-t-P:192.168.111.111
Mask:255.255.255.0
        UP POINTOPOINT RUNNING MTU:1500 Metric:1
        RX packets:9 errors:0 dropped:0 overruns:0
        TX packets:9 errors:0 dropped:0 overruns:0

eth0    Link encap:10Mbps Ethernet HWaddr 00:20:AF:E8:A2:25
        inet addr:206.197.168.200 Bcast:206.197.168.255
Mask:255.255.255.0
        UP BROADCAST RUNNING MULTICAST MTU:1500 Metric:1
        RX packets:23512 errors:5 dropped:5 overruns:6
        TX packets:28137 errors:0 dropped:0 overruns:0
        Interrupt:10 Base address:0x210
```

Notice the information for the ppp0 device. Additionally, the routing table on the Linux PC looks like this:

```
/sbin/route -n
Kernel routing table
Destination    Gateway     Genmask         Flags MSS   Window Use Iface
192.168.111.111 *          255.255.255.255 UH    1436  0      9   ppp0
206.197.168.0   *          255.255.255.0   U     1436  0      27713 eth0
127.0.0.0       *          255.0.0.0       U     1936  0      3417  lo
```

The first line shows the route to the remote PPP end through the ppp0 device. Following is what ping reported when I tried the connection:

```
dcc05211:/usr/etc# ping 192.168.111.111
PING 192.168.111.111 (192.168.111.111): 56 data bytes
```

```
64 bytes from 192.168.111.111: icmp_seq=0 ttl=32 time=347.3 ms
64 bytes from 192.168.111.111: icmp_seq=1 ttl=32 time=330.1 ms
64 bytes from 192.168.111.111: icmp_seq=2 ttl=32 time=320.1 ms
64 bytes from 192.168.111.111: icmp_seq=3 ttl=32 time=320.1 ms

-- 192.168.111.111 ping statistics --
4 packets transmitted, 4 packets received, 0% packet loss
round-trip min/avg/max = 320.1/329.4/347.3 ms
```

Running `ping` on the Windows 95 PC shows different times for the round trip, because the Windows 95 version of `ping` uses a smaller number of bytes, as the following example shows:

```
C:\>ping 192.168.111.222

Pinging 192.168.111.222 with 32 bytes of data:

Reply from 192.168.111.222: bytes=32 time=264ms TTL=255
Reply from 192.168.111.222: bytes=32 time=230ms TTL=255
Reply from 192.168.111.222: bytes=32 time=254ms TTL=255
Reply from 192.168.111.222: bytes=32 time=260ms TTL=255

C:\>
```

Notice that on the Windows 95 side, I `ping` the IP address of the other end of the connection.

Summary

Most of us do not have a direct connection to the high-bandwidth backbones of the Internet. Instead, we rely on dial-up modem connections to Internet Service Providers (ISPs), which in turn are connected to the backbones (typically provided by large telecommunications companies, such as Sprint and MCI). TCP/IP networking over serial lines is possible with SLIP and PPP. Software for both SLIP and PPP comes with Linux. This chapter explains what SLIP and PPP are, and shows you how to configure and use both of these protocols as the data-transport mechanism for TCP/IP networking. By reading this chapter, you learn:

- Serial communications with software such as Seyon or minicom (or something like ProComm, in the MS-DOS world) allows your PC to become a terminal to a remote host. That type of serial communication does not get you a full network connection, in which several network applications can use the same physical link to transfer data between your PC and the remote system.

- SLIP, or Serial Line Internet Protocol, was the first attempt at using the serial link as a data-transport layer for TCP/IP networking. Although simple, SLIP was deficient in many ways. Both ends needed to know the IP addresses, for example, and only one type of protocol could use a SLIP connection for packet transport.

- PPP, or Point-to-Point Protocol, is a more complex protocol for packet transport over any point-to-point link. PPP can carry packets of many protocols over the same link. PPP is the preferred way to establish a dial-up TCP/IP network connection with ISPs.

- A program named dip is used to establish a SLIP connection with a remote system.

- Setting up a PPP link involves two basic steps. First, you must use a utility program to dial the modem and make connection with the remote modem; then you have to start the PPP software on your system. The chat program is used with the pppd program to perform these two steps.

- When you connect your Linux PC to a remote system by using PPP, the PPP link is used as the default route on the Linux PC, because the PPP connection becomes the gateway to the rest of the Internet.

- You also can set up your Linux PC as a PPP server so that others may dial in and establish a PPP connection with your system. This chapter describes the steps for setting up a PPP server.

Chapter 19
Setting Up a Linux Internet Host

In This Chapter

- Understanding Internet hosts
- Looking at typical Internet services: mail, news, and `ftp`
- Setting up and testing mail
- Setting up and using news
- Posting news and verifying news distribution
- Setting up a secure anonymous FTP server

The Internet is all the rage now. Experts see it as the foundation of a new wave of computing, in which information is distributed and business is conducted over the network. Web browsers such as Mosaic and Netscape give us a glimpse of that new world of computing, where you can access information from anywhere in the world as easily as though it were right on your local disk.

You probably already are familiar with electronic mail (or e-mail) and news — the mainstay of the Internet. E-mail enables you to exchange messages and documents with anyone on the Internet. The newsgroups provide a bulletin-board system that spans the globe.

If you want to take advantage of Internet's offerings, you need access to the Internet. Whether you run a business or whether you are a Linux hobbyist, you'll find it beneficial to put your Linux PC on the Internet; you can set it up as an Internet host.

Note

I use the term *Internet host* for a system that has network access to the Internet — that means the Internet host can exchange TCP/IP network packets with any other computer on the Internet. Typically, your Linux system sets up a network connection to the Internet through a dial-up line by using SLIP or PPP. Chapter 18 explains SLIP and PPP and also shows you how to connect your Linux PC to the Internet.

To be an Internet host, however, your Linux PC needs more than just the network connection to the Internet. You also need to set up e-mail, `ftp`, and news. If you want to provide information to other users, you may want to set up your own Web server. Additionally, you may have to worry about security. After all, your system will be on the Internet, and anyone with Internet access can (in theory, at least) get to your system.

Note

This chapter focuses on the tasks that you might typically perform to set up your Linux PC as an Internet host. You learn how to set up e-mail, anonymous FTP (which enables anyone to download files from you, but in a reasonably secure manner), and newsgroups. This chapter also describes some ways of making your Internet host secure.

Setting up a Web server is a detailed process. I'll devote the next chapter to that topic.

What Is an Internet Host?

The meaning of the term *Internet host* depends on what you think *Internet* means. Technically speaking, the Internet is a worldwide network of networks. The term *internet* (without capitalization) is a short form of *internetworking* — the interconnection of networks. The Internet Protocol (IP) was designed with the idea of connecting networks. As you learned in Chapter 16, even IP addresses have a network part and a host part.

Wizard

Physically, the Internet is similar to a network of highways and roads. This similarity has prompted the popular press to dub the Internet the *Information Superhighway*. Just as the network of highways and roads includes some interstate highways, many state roads, and many more residential streets, the Internet has some very high-bandwidth networks (45-Mbps T3 backbones) and a large number of lower-capacity networks (ranging from 28,800-bps dial-up connections to 1.5-Mbps T1 links). The high-bandwidth network constitutes the backbone of the Internet.

Unlike commercial networks, such as CompuServe and America Online, the Internet is not run by a single organization; neither is it managed by any central computer. You can view the physical Internet as being a "network of networks" managed collectively by hundreds of cooperating organizations. I know that a collection of networks managed by hundreds of organization sounds amazing, but it works!

From the point of view of physical connectivity, an Internet host is any computer on a network that's part of the Internet. The user, however, judges an Internet host in terms of the services that it provides. Typically, users expect the following common services from an Internet host:

- *Electronic mail (e-mail).* From an Internet host, you can send e-mail to any other user on the Internet, using addresses such as president@whitehouse.gov.

- *Newsgroups.* You can read newsgroups and post news items to newsgroups with names such as comp.os.linux.networking or comp.os.linux.setup.

- *Information retrieval.* You can search for information with tools such as archie and gopher, and browse information with a Web browser. You also can download files with File Transfer Protocol (ftp). Reciprocally, users on other systems also can download files from your system, typically through a feature known as anonymous FTP. You learn how to set up anonymous FTP service in the "Secure Anonymous FTP" section of this chapter.

- *Remote access.* You can use `telnet` to log into another computer (the remote computer) on the Internet, assuming that you have access to that remote computer.

Some of the capabilities, such as being able to access a remote computer with `telnet` or `ftp`, is free when your Linux PC is connected to the Internet. For e-mail, newsgroups, and anonymous FTP, you have to perform some steps in Linux. Later sections of this chapter describe how to configure these Internet services.

Exchanging e-mail

One of the most common ways that people use the Internet is to keep in touch with friends, acquaintances, loved ones, and strangers through e-mail. If you have not used e-mail much, you may wonder why it is such a big deal. Even if you have used your company's internal e-mail system, you may not appreciate the convenience of Internet e-mail until you try it.

You may be surprised that you can send a message to a friend on the other coast and get back a reply within a couple of minutes. Essentially, you can send messages anywhere in the world from an Internet host, and that message typically makes its way to the destination within minutes — something that you cannot do with regular paper mail.

Because e-mail can be stored and forwarded, you can arrange to send and receive e-mail without making your Linux system a full-time host on the Internet. You won't get the benefits of nearly immediate delivery of messages, however, if your system is not an Internet host.

If you don't have a dedicated full-time Internet connection, you might consider using a service (such as LAN Soft in Columbus, OH) that allows dial-up Simple Mail Transfer Protocol (SMTP) connections. Some services will even dial your server when there's mail to be delivered to your address.

Participating in newsgroups

The Internet helps you communicate in many ways. With e-mail, you can exchange messages with people whom you already know. Sometimes, however, you may want to participate in group discussions. If you are looking for help in setting up XFree86 on an ATI Mach64 graphics card, for example, you may want to ask anyone who knows anything about this subject. For that sort of communication, you can post a message on the appropriate Internet newsgroup; someone is likely to give you an answer.

The Internet newsgroups are like the bulletin boards or forums on other online systems, such as CompuServe and America Online. You'll find a wide variety of newsgroups that cover subjects ranging from politics to computers. You can think of the Internet newsgroups as being a gathering place — a virtual meeting place where you can ask questions and discuss various issues.

Locating and browsing information

You may already have experienced sharing files among computers on a LAN (local-area network). Typically, a LAN has a server, and any user on the LAN can access and use the information in the files stored on that server.

Cross Reference

Being a collection of interconnected networks, the Internet also allows the Internet hosts — the computers on the Internet — to share information by using a variety of protocols. For example, the File Transfer Protocol (ftp) specifies how to select and download files from another computer on the Internet. You saw some examples of ftp in Chapter 2, where I explained how to download patches to the Linux kernel.

Note

Another, more recent information-sharing protocol is the Hypertext Transfer Protocol (http) that allows computers to exchange documents formatted in the Hypertext Markup Language (HTML). HTML and http form the foundation of the World Wide Web, where you can literally look at documents maintained on other computers on the Internet. You learn more about World Wide Web in Chapter 20.

Simple mail and news strategy

Although using mail and news is reasonably simple, both mail and news require some effort on your part to set up properly. To maintain newsgroups in particular, you need a great deal of disk space and access to a news server. You need a large amount of disk space because many newsgroups exist, and the volume of messages can be quite high. Also, the news articles must be purged periodically; otherwise, the disk will get filled. Even if you choose a small subset of newsgroups, you may need a hundred or so megabytes just to keep the news items on your system.

Tip

If you get your Internet access from an ISP (Internet Service Provider), the ISP gives you access to a mail server and a news server. Then you can use mail software that downloads messages from your mail server and use a news reader that reads newsgroups directly from the news server. If you are the lone user of your Linux PC, I strongly recommend this strategy for reading news.

Cross Reference

As you learn in Chapter 20, you can use a Web browser, such as Netscape, to read news and send mail, as well as access Web pages.

Mail and news software installation

During Linux installation from this book's companion CD-ROM, you have the option to install several packages for mail and news. If you did not install the mail and news software at that time, follow these steps to install the software:

1. Log in as root.
2. Make sure that this book's companion CD-ROM is mounted on the /cdrom directory.

Chapter 19: Setting Up a Linux Internet Host **561**

If not, first use the command `umount /dev/cdrom` to unmount any currently mounted CD-ROM. Then replace the CD-ROM in the drive with this book's companion CD-ROM and mount it with the `mount -r /dev/cdrom /cdrom` command.

3. Type **setup** at the shell prompt. The initial screen of the `setup` program appears.

4. From the initial `setup` screen, select the SOURCE option (press **S** or use the arrow keys to select the option); then press Enter. The Source Media Selection screen appears.

5. Select the option to install from the CD-ROM, then press Enter. The Select Installation Type screen appears.

6. Press Enter to select the default option of installing packages on your hard disk. A Continue? dialog box appears.

7. Press Enter to indicate Yes (that means you want to continue). The Series Selection dialog box appears.

8. Use the arrow keys to scroll down the list until you highlight the disk set N. Press the spacebar to select that disk set. Then press Enter. Another Continue? dialog box appears.

9. Press Enter to indicate Yes. The Select Prompting Mode dialog box appears.

10. Press Enter to select the default option (Normal).

11. From this point on, individual screens give you the option to install the following packages (in the order shown):

    - `elm` (mail user agent)
    - `netcfg` (the `netconfig` script)
    - `rdist` (remote file distribution)
    - `tcpip` (TCP/IP utilities)
    - `deliver` (local mail-delivery package)
    - `mailx` (mail user agent)
    - `pine` (a versatile mail and news program)
    - `sendmail` (a complex mail-transport agent)
    - `smailcfg` (`sendmail` configuration files)
    - `uucp` (UNIX-to-UNIX Copy protocol)
    - `cnews` (UUCP-based news program)
    - `dip` (Dial-up IP Program for SLIP networking)
    - `inn` (InterNetNews, a TCP/IP-based news program)
    - `ppp` (PPP for Linux)
    - `tin` (news reader)

- `trn-nntp` (news reader for a remote news server)
- `trn` (news reader for local news files)
- `bind` (name server utilities)
- `nn-nntp` (news reader for a remote news server)
- `nn-spool` (news reader for local news files)

You probably have installed many of these packages already. For this chapter, you need only the mail and news packages, so you should install `elm`, `sendmail`, `smailcfg`, `tin` and `trn-nntp` (as well as any other mail or news reader that you want to try). To install a package, press Enter. If you do not want to install a package, press the down-arrow key and then press Enter. After you go through all the package-installation screens, the Extra Configuration dialog box appears.

12. Press Tab to select No; then press Enter (because you do not want to perform other configurations now). The initial setup screen appears.

13. Press E to select Exit; then press Enter. The setup program exits.

Setting Up and Using Mail

Electronic mail — e-mail — is one of the most popular services on the Internet. Everyone likes the convenience of being able to send a message without having to play the game of "phone tag," in which you leave phone messages for each other without ever successfully making a contact by phone. When you send an e-mail message, it waits in the recipient's mailbox to be read at the recipient's convenience.

E-mail started as a simple mechanism in which messages were copied to a user's mailbox file. That simple mechanism is still used. In Linux, your mail messages are stored in the `/usr/spool/mail` directory, in a text file with the same name as your user name.

Messages still are addressed to a user name. That means that if John Doe logs in with the user name `jdoe`, e-mail to him is addressed to `jdoe`. The only other piece of information needed to uniquely identify the recipient is the fully qualified domain name of the recipient's system. Thus, if John Doe's system is named `someplace.net`, his complete e-mail address becomes `jdoe@someplace.net`. Given that address, anyone on the Internet can send e-mail to John Doe.

The Linux distribution on this book's companion CD-ROM comes with the software that you need to set up and use e-mail on your Linux system. The following sections guide you through the various steps of setting up and using e-mail on your Linux system.

Mail software

To set up and use e-mail on your Linux PC, you need two types of mail software:

- *Mail user agent* software allows you to read your mail messages, write replies, and compose new messages.

Note

- *Mail transport agent* software actually sends and receives mail message text. The exact method used for mail transport depends on the underlying network. In TCP/IP networks, the mail transport agent delivers mail by using the Simple Mail Transfer Protocol (SMTP). This book's Slackware Linux CD-ROM includes `sendmail`, a powerful and popular mail transport agent for TCP/IP networks.

Most mail transport agents run as *daemons* — background processes that run as long as your system is up. The reason is that you or another user on the system might send mail at any time, and the transport agent has to be there to deliver the mail to its destination. The mail user agent runs only when the user wants to check mail.

Wizard

Typically, a mail transport agent is started after the system boots. The system startup files for the Slackware Linux on this book's CD-ROM are set up so that the `sendmail` mail transport agent starts when the Linux system is in multiuser mode. In the file /etc/rc.d/rc.M, you'll find the following lines to start `sendmail`:

```
# Start the sendmail daemon:
if [ -x /usr/sbin/sendmail ]; then
 echo "Starting sendmail daemon (/usr/sbin/sendmail -bd -q 15m)..."
 /usr/sbin/sendmail -bd -q 15m
fi
```

These lines start `sendmail` with appropriate options if the executable file /usr/sbin/sendmail exists (it should exist if you install `sendmail`).

Because the system is already set up to start `sendmail` at boot time, all you have to do is use an appropriate `sendmail` configuration file to get e-mail going on your Linux system.

More on `sendmail`

This chapter shows you how to use a predefined `sendmail` configuration file to get e-mail going on your system. `sendmail`, however, is a very complex mail system. *sendmail,* by Bryan Costales with Eric Allman and Neil Rickert (O'Reilly & Associates, 1993), will help you learn how to configure `sendmail`.

sendmail **configuration file**

You cannot really try e-mail until the `sendmail` mail transport agent is configured properly, because mail cannot be sent or received if `sendmail` is not configured properly. `sendmail` has the reputation of being a complex but complete mail-delivery system. If you take a quick look at `sendmail`'s configuration file, `/etc/sendmail.cf`, you'll immediately agree that `sendmail` is indeed complex. Luckily, you do not have to become an expert on the `sendmail` configuration file (a whole book has been written on that subject; see the sidebar "More on `sendmail`"). All you need is one of the predefined configuration files from this book's companion CD-ROM.

Secret

When you install Linux by following the steps in Chapter 1, you get a chance to install `sendmail`. If you choose to install `sendmail`, the `setup` program also gives you a chance to configure `sendmail`. In Chapter 1, however, I did not walk you through the `sendmail` configuration step, which involves selecting a configuration file that is appropriate for your situation. To select a `sendmail` configuration file now, follow these steps:

1. Log in as `root`, and type **setup** at the shell prompt. The initial setup screen appears.

2. From the initial setup screen, select the CONFIGURE option (press **C** or use the arrow keys to select the option) and then press Enter.

3. The setup program displays a message about the configuration process. Press Enter to proceed.

4. This step allows you to create a boot disk. Press Tab to select No and then press Enter.

5. A message explains how you can start the system without the boot disk. Press Enter to continue.

6. This step asks whether you want to configure the modem. Press Tab to select No and then press Enter.

7. This step allows you to configure the mouse. Press Tab to select No and then press Enter.

8. This step allows you to select a custom screen font. Press Tab to select No and then press Enter.

9. This step allows you to select a modem speed. Press Tab to select Cancel and then press Enter.

10. This step asks whether you want to install LILO. Press Tab to select Cancel and then press Enter.

11. This step asks whether you want to configure the network. Press Tab to select No and then press Enter.

Secret

12. Finally, you reach the step in which you create a `sendmail` configuration file: `/etc/sendmail.cf`. You can choose among three files: a file that works if your system is connected to Internet and a name server is available; a file

for a network that does not have a name server; and a third file for a USENET system that relies on UUCP as the mail-transfer mechanism (see the "Newsgroups" section later in this chapter for a discussion of USENET). Because this chapter is about an Internet host, your system probably is on the Internet. Therefore, select the first `sendmail` configuration file and press Enter to continue.

13. This step allows you to select a time zone. Press Tab to select Cancel and then press Enter. You return to the initial setup screen.

14. Press **E** to select Exit and then press Enter to exit the setup program.

After installing the `sendmail.cf` file that expects an Internet connection and a name server, you should be able to send and receive e-mail from your Linux PC.

Secret

To ensure that mail delivery works correctly, you must make sure that your system's name matches what your ISP assigned to you. Although you can give your system any host name that you want, other systems can successfully deliver mail to your system only if your system's name is in the ISP's name server.

Mail-delivery test

On my system, I could send and receive mail immediately after selecting a `sendmail` configuration file. First, I made sure that my system's host name matched what my ISP assigned for my use. Then I used the `mail` command to compose and send a mail message to myself at a different address, as follows:

```
mail naba@access.digex.net
Subject: Testing e-mail
This is from my Linux PC.
.
EOT
```

The `mail` command runs a simple mail user agent. In this example, I specify the addressee — naba@access.digex.net — in the command line. The mail program prompts for a Subject line. Following the subject, I enter my message and end it with a line that starts with a period. After I end the message, the mail user agent passes the message to `sendmail` — the mail transport agent — for delivery to the specified address. Because my system was already connected to the Internet, `sendmail` delivered the mail message immediately.

To verify the delivery of mail, I used `telnet` to log into access.digex.net and then checked my mail, as follows:

```
access5% mail
Mail version SMI 4.0 Fri Oct 14 12:50:06 PDT 1994 Type ? for help.
"/usr/spool/mail/naba": 1 message 1 new
>N 1 naba@dcc05211.slip.digex.net  Mon Oct 30 20:45   11/648   Testing e-mail
Mail>
```

```
Message 1:
From naba@dcc05211.slip.digex.net Mon Oct 30 20:45:54 1995
Date: Mon, 30 Oct 1995 21:51:51 -0500
From: Naba Barkakati <naba@dcc05211.slip.digex.net>
To: naba@access.digex.net
Subject: Testing e-mail

This is from my Linux PC.

Mail>r
To: naba@dcc05211.slip.digex.net
Subject: Re: Testing e-mail

Received your message.
Cc:
Mail>q
Saved 1 message in /homea/naba/mbox
access5%
```

As you can verify from this listing, my mail message arrived at the destination. After reading the message, I pressed **r** to reply to the message. I typed a short reply and pressed Ctrl-D (that's how the mail program on access.digex.net expects messages to end). The mail program prompts for a carbon-copy list (addresses that should get a copy of the reply) with the text Cc:. I pressed Enter to indicate that I didn't want any carbon-copy addresses. At the mail prompt, I pressed **q** to quit the mail program.

After I logged out of access.digex.net, I checked mail again on my Linux PC to see whether my reply made its way back to the Linux PC. Here's how I read my mail on the Linux system:

```
dcc05211:~$ mail
Mail version 5.5 6/1/90. Type ? for help.
"/var/spool/mail/naba": 1 messages 1 new
 N 1 naba@access.digex.ne Mon Oct 30 21:53 12/678   "Re: Testing e-
mail"
& 1
Message 1:
From naba@access.digex.net Mon Oct 30 21:53:47 1995
Date: Mon, 30 Oct 1995 20:47:41 -0500
From: Naba Barkakati <naba@access.digex.net>
To: naba@dcc05211.slip.digex.net
Subject: Re: Testing e-mail

Received your message.

& q
Saved 1 message in mbox
Held 8 messages in /var/spool/mail/naba
dcc05211:~$
```

As the output shows, the reply reached my Linux system as well.

Tip

Thus, the initial `sendmail` configuration file from this book's companion CD-ROM should be adequate for sending and receiving e-mail, provided that your Linux system has an Internet connection.

Mail-delivery mechanism

On an Internet host, the `sendmail` mail transport agent delivers mail by using the Simple Mail Transfer Protocol (SMTP). SMTP is documented in RFC 821, "Simple Mail Transfer Protocol," Jonathan Postel, 1982.

Wizard

SMTP-based mail transport agents listen to the TCP port 25 and use a small set of text commands to interact with other mail transport agents. In fact, the commands are simple enough that you can use SMTP commands directly to send a mail message. The following example shows how I use SMTP commands to send a mail message to my account on the Linux PC from a `telnet` session running on another system on the local-area network:

```
telnet lnbsoft.com 25
220-lnbsoft.com Sendmail 8.6.12/8.6.9 ready at Mon, 30 Oct 1995
00:31:21 -0500
220 ESMTP spoken here
HELO
250 lnbsoft.com Hello lnb486 [206.197.168.100], pleased to meet you
MAIL FROM: naba@lnb486.lnbsoft.com
250 lnb486... Sender ok
RCPT TO: naba
250 naba... Recipient ok
DATA
354 Enter mail, end with "." on a line by itself
Testing ...1 2 3
Sending mail by telnet to port 25
.
250 AAA04325 Message accepted for delivery
QUIT
221 lnbsoft.com closing connection
```

The `telnet` command opens a `telnet` session to port 25 — the port where `sendmail` expects SMTP commands. The `sendmail` process on the Linux system immediately replies with an announcement.

I type **HELO** to introduce myself. The `sendmail` process replies with a greeting. To send the mail message, I start with the `MAIL FROM:` command that specifies the sender of the message (I enter the user name on the system from which I am sending the message).

Next, I use the `RCPT TO:` command to specify the recipient of the message. If I want to send the message to several recipients, all I have to do is provide each recipient's address with the `RCPT TO:` command.

To enter the mail message, I use the `DATA` command. In response to the `DATA` command, `sendmail` displays an instruction that I should end the message with a period on a line by itself. I enter the message and end it with a single period on a separate line. The `sendmail` process displays a message indicating that the message has been accepted for delivery. Finally, I quit the session with `sendmail` with the `QUIT` command.

Afterward, I log into my Linux system and check mail with the `mail` command. Following is what I see when I display the mail message that I sent through the sample SMTP session with `sendmail`:

```
Message 6:
From naba@lnb486.lnbsoft.com Mon Oct 30 00:32:28 1995
Date: Mon, 30 Oct 1995 00:31:38 -0500
From: naba@lnb486.lnbsoft.com
Apparently-To: naba@lnbsoft.com

Testing ...1 2 3
Sending mail by telnet to port 25
```

As this example shows, the SMTP commands are simple enough to understand. This example should help you understand how a mail transfer agent uses SMTP to transfer mail on the Internet.

Setting Up and Using Newsgroups

Newsgroups originated in *USENET* — a store-and-forward messaging network for exchanging electronic mail and news items. The USENET works like a telegraph in that news and mail are relayed from one system to another. In USENET, the systems are not on any network; they simply dial up and use the UNIX-to-UNIX Copy (UUCP) protocol to transfer text messages.

USENET is a very loosely connected collection of computers that has worked well and continues to be used because very little expense is involved in connecting to the USENET. All you need is a modem and a site that is willing to store and forward your mail and news. You have to set up UUCP on your system, but you do not need a sustained network connection; just a few phone calls are all it takes to keep the e-mail and news flowing. The downside is that you cannot use TCP/IP services, such as the World Wide Web, `telnet`, or `ftp`.

From its USENET origins, the newsgroups have migrated to the Internet. Instead of UUCP, the news is transported by means of the Network News Transfer Protocol (NNTP), which is described in RFC 977, "Network News Transfer Protocol: A Proposed Standard for the Stream-Based Transmission of News," B. Kantor and P. Lapsley, 1986.

Even though the news transport protocol has changed from UUCP to NNTP, the store-and-forward concept of news transfer still exists. Thus, if you want to get news on your Linux system, you have to find a news server from which your system can download news.

If you have signed up with an Internet Service Provider, the ISP should provide you access to a news server. Such Internet news servers communicate by using NNTP. Then you can use an NNTP-capable news reader, such as `tin`, to access the news server and read selected newsgroups. This is the easiest way to access news on your Linux Internet host.

Chapter 19: Setting Up a Linux Internet Host

For the following discussion, I'll assume that you have obtained access to a news server from your ISP.

How to read news

To read news, you need a *news reader* — a program that allows you to select a newsgroup and view the items in that newsgroup. You also need to understand the newsgroup hierarchy and naming convention, but I'll describe those details in the "Newsgroup hierarchy" section of this chapter. First, I want to show you how to read news from a news server.

Like mail programs, quite a few news readers are available. Most news readers support *threading*, which means organizing the replies to each article as a separate thread (sequence) of articles. Of these programs, the two most popular are

- The *threaded read news* program, `trn`, which is an improved version of `rn`, the venerable *read news* program (`rn`). This news reader is called "threaded" because it interconnects an article with any replies.

- The full-screen news reader program, `tin`. Like `trn`, `tin` supports *threading*.

Tip

This book's companion CD-ROM includes several news readers including both `trn` and `tin`. You may want to install both news readers and try each one before selecting the one that you like.

Set the NNTPSERVER environment variable

Secret

To read news from a news server by using NNTP, you have to define the NNTPSERVER environment variable. Define this environment variable to your news server's name. Both `tin` and `trn` news readers look up the NNTPSERVER environment variable for the name of the news server to contact.

For example, my news server's name is news.digex.net. Therefore, I define the NNTPSERVER variable this way:

```
NNTPSERVER=news.digex.net; export NNTPSERVER
```

Create a `.newsrc` file

Far too many newsgroups exist on the Internet. When a news reader starts, it has to know which newsgroups you want to read. Both the `tin` and `trn` news readers expect to find a list of the newsgroups in a file named `.newsrc` in your home directory.

To prepare the `.newsrc` file, you need to know how to name the newsgroups. You learn more about naming newsgroups in the "Newsgroup hierarchy" section of this chapter.

Tip

If you are interested in information about Linux, you might create a `.newsrc` file, specifying the following newsgroups:

```
comp.os.linux.networking:
comp.os.linux.answers:
comp.os.linux.misc:
comp.os.linux.announce:
comp.os.linux.setup:
comp.os.linux.hardware:
```

Each line shows the name of a newsgroup, followed by a colon. After you begin to read news, the news-reader program fills in article numbers following the newsgroup name.

Run `tin -r` to read news

As long as you have set the NNTPSERVER environment variable to your news server's name, you can use either of the news readers — `trn` or `tin` — to read the news. You can try reading the news with each of the news readers to decide which one you like best.

To read news with `tin`, use the following command:

```
tin -r
tin 1.2 PL2 [UNIX] (c) Copyright 1991-93 Iain Lea.
Connecting to news.digex.net...
Reading news active file...
Reading attributes file...
Reading newsgroups file...
```

Tip

The `-r` option causes `tin` to read news from a remote news server (the one that you specify through the NNTPSERVER environment variable). After `tin` starts, it connects to the news server and communicates by using NNTP. The `tin` news reader displays status messages as it progresses to the point at which it gathers the newsgroups listed in the `.newsrc` file in your home directory.

After obtaining information about the newsgroups from the news server, `tin` displays those newsgroups in a full-screen text menu, as shown in Figure 19-1.

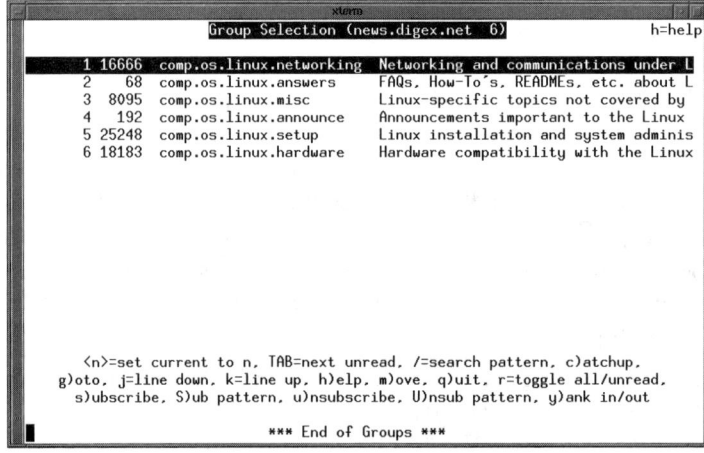

Figure 19-1: A typical newsgroup selection screen displayed by `tin`.

The list of newsgroups that you see depends on the contents of the .newsrc file in your home directory. Figure 19-1 shows tin's initial screen for my .newsrc file.

In tin's newsgroup selection screen, you see the list of newsgroups in the top half of the screen and some help information at the bottom of the screen. Initially, the first newsgroup is selected (it appears highlighted). Press **j** to go down the list; press **k** to go up. (Yes, the movement keys are the same as the ones used by the vi editor.) You also can press the up- and down-arrow keys to select a new newsgroup.

After you select a newsgroup to read, press Enter to view the list of articles in that newsgroup. Figure 19-2 shows the screen after I selected the comp.os.linux.announce newsgroup and pressed **j** to move down the list to an item of interest.

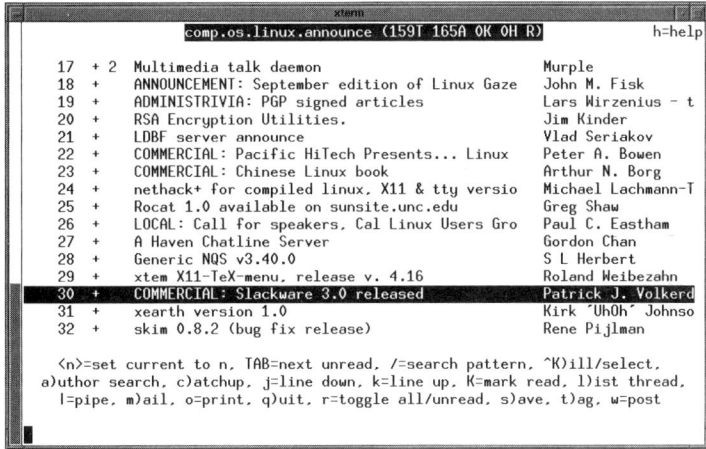

Figure 19-2: List of articles in a newsgroup (comp.os.linux.announce) as displayed by tin.

As the highlighted item in Figure 19-2 shows, I am interested in an item about Slackware 3.0 (the version of Slackware included on this book's companion CD-ROM). To read the item, I press Enter. The tin news reader downloads the article's text from the news server and displays it, as shown in Figure 19-3.

You can read the article's text one screen at a time. To view the next screen, press the space bar or Page Down. To return to the article selection menu, press **q**.

Pressing **q** again takes you back to the newsgroup selection screen. To quit tin, press **q** in the newsgroup selection screen.

```
┌─────────────────────────────── xterm ──────────────────────────────┐
│Sat, 30 Sep 1995 12:36:36    comp.os.linux.announce    Thread  30 of 159│
│Lines 192                 COMMERCIAL: Slackware 3.0 released   No responses│
│volkerdi@wcarchive.cdrom.com                        Patrick J. Volkerding at ?│
│                                                                    │
│     -----BEGIN PGP SIGNED MESSAGE-----                             │
│                                                                    │
│ Announcing the release of Slackware Linux 3.0 ELF!                 │
│                                                                    │
│ Slackware is a complete personal workstation operating system      │
│ based on the Linux kernel and an extensive collection of free      │
│ software and shareware from the net.                               │
│                                                                    │
│ Here are just a few of the new features in Slackware 3.0:          │
│                                                                    │
│ ELF binary format!                                                 │
│                                                                    │
│    This version uses the ELF binary format and shared libraries    │
│                                                                    │
│    <n>=set current to n, TAB=next unread, /=search pattern, ^K)ill/select,│
│       a)uthor search, B)ody search, c)atchup, f)ollowup, K=mark read,│
│       |=pipe, m)ail, o=print, q)uit, r)eply mail, s)ave, t)ag, w=post│
│                                                 --More--(12%) [1049/8093]│
└────────────────────────────────────────────────────────────────────┘
```

Figure 19-3: The `tin` news reader, displaying the text of a news article.

Although using `tin -r` to read news from a remote news server is painless, it can take a painfully long time for the news reader to download news overview and news items over a slower link. Even if you are using a PPP connection over a 28,800-bps modem, news reading over that PPP link is slow enough to make you wish for at least a 1.54-Mbps T1 link to your ISP.

Alternative news reader: `trn`

It's easy to read news with the `trn` news reader as well. To read news from an NNTP news server, you need a version of `trn` configured for NNTP news access. The `trn-nntp` package on disk set N of the companion CD-ROM includes the appropriate version of `trn`.

After you set the NNTPSERVER environment variable to the name of your news server, run `trn` as follows:

```
trn
Unread news in comp.os.linux.networking       3608 articles
Unread news in comp.os.linux.answers            66 articles
Unread news in comp.os.linux.misc             7905 articles
Unread news in comp.os.linux.announce          161 articles
Unread news in comp.os.linux.setup           25405 articles
etc.

Finding new newsgroups:

Newsgroup alt.binaries.warcraft not in .newsrc -- subscribe? [ynYN] N
(Ignoring alt.binaries.warcraft)
(Ignoring alt.fan.televisionx.sammi)
(Ignoring alt.music.utah-saints)
```

```
====== 3608 unread articles in comp.os.linux.networking -- read now?
[+ynq] n
====== 66 unread articles in comp.os.linux.answers -- read now? [+ynq]
Getting overview file.
```

The `trn` news reader downloads information about the newsgroups listed in the `.newsrc` file in your home directory. Then `trn` displays the number of articles for some of the newsgroups.

Tip

Because of the chaotic nature of the Internet, new newsgroups (especially the ones whose names begin with `alt`) are being added continually. If your `.newsrc` file does not contain the names of any recently added newsgroups, `trn` asks whether you want to subscribe the newsgroup. I generally press **N** (capital N) to indicate that I do not want to add any new newsgroup.

After displaying some messages about new newsgroups, `trn` prompts you with the name of the first newsgroup. To read that newsgroup, press **y** or Enter; to skip it, press **n**. To quit `trn`, press **q**.

If you select a newsgroup to read, `trn` gets an overview file for that newsgroup (that's the file with the list of articles in threaded order, so that each article is grouped with its replies). Then `trn` displays the list of articles in the selected newsgroup, as shown in Figure 19-4 for the `comp.os.linux.answers`.

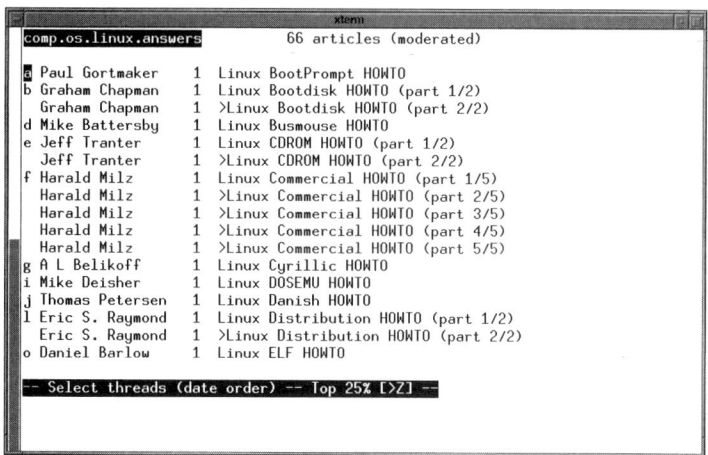

Figure 19-4: Threaded list of articles displayed by `trn`.

Each thread is identified by a letter that appears in the first column. To view a thread, use the arrow keys to select a thread letter and then press Enter. The `trn` news reader downloads and displays the first article of that thread.

While you read articles, you can use several `trn` commands to navigate the articles. The commands typically are single letters.

To see the `trn` commands that are available at any time, press **h**. Following is what you see when you press **h** after `trn` prompts you at the end of an article:

```
Article Selection commands:

n,SP  Find next unread article (follows discussion-tree in threaded
         groups).
N     Go to next article.
^N    Scan forward for next unread article with same subject in date
         order.
p,P,^P Same as n,N,^N, only going backwards.
_N,_P Go to the next/previous article numerically.
-     Go to previously displayed article.
<, >  Browse the previous/next selected thread. If no threads are
         selected, all threads that had unread news upon entry to the
         group are considered selected for browsing. Entering an empty
         group browses all threads.
[, ]  Go to article's parent/child (try left-/right-arrow also).
(, )  Go to article's previous/next sibling (try up-/down-arrow also).
{, }  Go to tree's root/leaf.
t     Display the entire article tree and all its subjects.
      number Go to specified article.
range{,range}:command{:command}
      Apply one or more commands to one or more ranges of articles.
      Ranges are of the form: number | number-number. You may use . for
      the current article, and $ for the last article.
      Valid commands are: e, j, m, M, s, S, t, T, |, +, ++, -, and --.
:cmd  Perform a command on all the selected articles.
::cmd Perform a command on all non-selected articles.
/pattern/modifiers
      Scan forward for article containing pattern in the subject line.
      (Use ?pat? to scan backwards; append f to scan from lines, h to
      scan whole headers, a to scan entire articles, r to scan read
      articles, c to make case-sensitive, t to scan from the top of the
      group.)
/pattern/modifiers:command{:command}
      Apply one or more commands to the set of articles matching
      pattern. Use a K modifier to save entire command to the KILL file
      for this newsgroup. Commands m and M, if first, imply an r
      modifier. Valid commands are the same as for the range command.
f,F   Submit a followup article (F = include this article).
r,R   Reply through net mail (R = include this article).
^F    Forward article through net mail.
e dir{|command}
      Extract to directory using /bin/sh, uudecode, unship, or command.
s ... Save to file or pipe via sh.
S ... Save via preferred shell.
w,W   Like s and S but save without the header.
| ... Same as s|...
C     Cancel this article, if yours.
^R,v  Restart article (v=verbose).
^X    Restart article, rot13 mode.
_C    Switch characterset conversion.
```

```
c       Catch up (mark all articles as read).
b       Back up one page.
^E      Display the last page of the article.
^L      Refresh the screen. You can get back to the pager with this.
X       Refresh screen in rot13 mode.
^       Go to first unread article. Disables subject search mode.
$       Go to end of newsgroup. Disables subject search mode.
#       Print last article number.
&       Print current values of command-line switches.
&switch {switch}
        Set or unset more switches.
&&      Print current macro definitions.
&&def   Define a new macro.
j       Junk this article (mark it read). Stays at end of article.
m       Mark article as still unread.
M       Mark article as read but to-return on group exit or Y command.
Y       Yank back articles marked as to-return via the M command.
k       Kill current subject (mark articles as read).
,       Mark current article and its replies as read.
J       Junk entire thread (mark all subjects as read in this thread).
A       Add current subject to memorized commands (selection or killing).
T       Add current (sub)thread to memorized commands (selection or
        killing).
K       Mark current subject as read, and save command in KILL file.
^K      Edit local KILL file (the one for this newsgroup).
=       List subjects of unread articles.
+       Start the selector in whatever mode it was last in.
_a      Start the article selector.
_s      Start the subject selector.
_t      Start the thread selector.
_T      Start the thread selector if threaded, else the subject selector.
U       Unread some news -- prompts for thread, subthread, all, or select.
u       Unsubscribe from this newsgroup.
q       Quit this newsgroup for now.
Q       Quit newsgroup, staying at current newsgroup.
```

These `trn` commands are the most commonly used commands for reading the articles in a newsgroup.

If you press **q** at an article, `trn` returns to the newsgroup selection level and displays a prompt such as the following:

```
====== 164 unread articles in comp.os.linux.announce -- read now?
[+ynq]
```

If you press **h** at this point, `trn` displays the following list of article selection commands:

```
Newsgroup Selection commands:

y    Do this newsgroup now.
SP   Do this newsgroup, executing the default command listed in []'s.
.cmd Do this newsgroup, executing cmd as first command.
```

(continued)

```
+       Enter this newsgroup through the selector (like typing .+<CR>).
=       Start this newsgroup, but list subjects before reading articles.
U       Enter this newsgroup by way of the "Set unread?" prompt.
u       Unsubscribe from this newsgroup.
t       Toggle the newsgroup between threaded and unthreaded reading.
c       Catch up (mark all articles as read).
A       Abandon read/unread changes to this newsgroup since you started
        trn.
n       Go to the next newsgroup with unread news.
N       Go to the next newsgroup.
p       Go to the previous newsgroup with unread news.
P       Go to the previous newsgroup.
-       Go to the previously displayed newsgroup.
1       Go to the first newsgroup.
^       Go to the first newsgroup with unread news.
$       Go to the end of newsgroups.
g name  Go to the named newsgroup. Subscribe to new newsgroups this way
        too.
/pat    Search forward for newsgroup matching pattern.
?pat    Search backward for newsgroup matching pattern.
        (Use * and ? style patterns. Append r to include read newsgroups.)
l pat   List unsubscribed newsgroups containing pattern.
m name  Move named newsgroup elsewhere (no name moves current
        newsgroup).
o pat   Only display newsgroups matching pattern. Omit pat to
        unrestrict.
O pat   Like o, but skip empty groups.
a pat   Like o, but also scans for unsubscribed newsgroups matching
        pattern.
L       List current .newsrc.
&       Print current command-line switch settings.
&switch {switch}
        Set (or unset) more command-line switches.
&&      Print current macro definitions.
&&def   Define a new macro.
!cmd    Shell escape.
q       Quit trn.
x       Quit, restoring .newsrc to its state at startup of trn.
^K      Edit the global KILL file. Use commands like /pattern/j to
        suppress pattern in every newsgroup.
v       Print version and the address for reporting bugs.
Macros:
^[OA    %(%m=[ap]?\(:%(%m=t?[:p))
^[OB    %(%m=[ap]?\):%(%m=t?]:n))
^[OC    %(%m=n?^j:%(%m=[ap]?\]:>))
^[OD    %(%m=[ap]?\[:<)
^[OM    ^C
^[[A    %(%m=[ap]?\(:%(%m=t?[:p))
^[[B    %(%m=[ap]?\):%(%m=t?]:n))
^[[C    %(%m=n?^j:%(%m=[ap]?\]:>))
^[[D    %(%m=[ap]?\[:<)
^[[M    ^C
```

The macros, listed at the end of the help list, define what happens when you press special keys, such as the up- and down-arrow keys.

As the list of article selection commands show, to quit `trn`, press **q** at the article selection prompt.

Newsgroup hierarchy

News items are organized into a hierarchy of newsgroups for ease of maintenance as well as ease of use. A typical newsgroup name looks like this:

comp.os.linux.announce

This name says that comp.os.linux.announce is a newsgroup for announcements (announce) about the Linux operating system (os.linux) and that these subjects fall under the broad category of computers (comp).

As you can see, the format of a newsgroup name is a sequence of words separated by periods. These words denote the hierarchy of the newsgroup.

To understand the newsgroup hierarchy, compare the newsgroup name with the path name of a file (such as `/usr/lib/news/bin/nntpget`) in Linux. Just as a file's path name shows the directory hierarchy of the file, the newsgroup name shows the newsgroup hierarchy. In file names, a slash (/) separates the names of directories; in a newsgroup's name, a period separates the different levels in the newsgroup hierarchy.

Tip

In a newsgroup name, the first word represents the newsgroup category. The comp.os.linux.announce newsgroup, for example, is in the comp category, whereas alt.books.technical is in the alt category.

Table 19-1 lists some of the major newsgroup categories:

Table 19-1	Major newsgroup categories
Category	Subject
alt	"Alternative" newsgroups (not subject to any rules), running the gamut from the mundane to the bizarre
bionet	Biology newsgroups
bit	Bitnet newsgroups
biz	Business newsgroups
clari	Clarinet news service (daily news)
comp	Computer hardware and software newsgroups
ieee	Newsgroups for the Institute of Electrical and Electronics Engineers

(continued)

Table 19-1 *(continued)*

Category	Subject
k12	Newsgroups devoted to elementary and secondary education
misc	Miscellaneous newsgroups
news	Newsgroups about Internet news administration
rec	Recreational and art newsgroups
sci	Science and engineering newsgroups
soc	Newsgroups for discussing social issues and various cultures
talk	Discussions of current issues (such as "talk radio")

This short list of categories is deceptive, because it does not really tell you about the wide-ranging variety of newsgroups available in each category. Because each newsgroup category contains several levels of subcategories, the overall count of newsgroups runs into several thousands. The comp category alone has more than 500 newsgroups.

Typically, you have to narrow your choice of newsgroups according to your interests. If you are interested in Linux, for example, you can pick one or more of the following newsgroups:

- **alt.uu.comp.os.linux.questions:** General Linux questions and answers.
- **comp.os.linux.admin:** Information about Linux system administration.
- **comp.os.linux.advocacy:** Discussions about promoting Linux.
- **comp.os.linux.announce:** Important announcements about Linux. This newsgroup is *moderated*, which means that you must mail the article to the moderator, who then posts it to the newsgroup.

Cross Reference

- **comp.os.linux.answers:** Questions and answers about Linux. All the Linux HOWTOs (see Chapter 1 for a list of Linux HOWTOs) are posted in this moderated newsgroup.
- **comp.os.linux.development:** Current Linux development work.
- **comp.os.linux.development.apps:** Linux application development.
- **comp.os.linux.development.system:** Linux operating-system development.
- **comp.os.linux.hardware:** Discussions about Linux and various types of hardware.
- **comp.os.linux.help:** Help with various areas of Linux.
- **comp.os.linux.misc:** Miscellaneous Linux-related topics.
- **comp.os.linux.networking:** Networking under Linux.

- **comp.os.linux.setup:** Linux setup and installation.
- **comp.os.linux.x:** Discussions about setting up and running the X Window System under Linux.

You really have to be selective about what newsgroups you read, because it's impossible to keep up with all the news, even in a specific area such as Linux. When you first install and set up Linux, you might read newsgroups such as comp.os.linux.setup., comp.os.linux.hardware, and comp.os.linux.x (especially if you run X). After you get Linux up and running, you may want to learn only about new things that are happening in Linux. For such information, you would read the comp.os.linux.announce newsgroup.

Newsgroup subscription

Unlike magazines or newspapers, newsgroups do not require you to actually subscribe to them; you can essentially read any newsgroup that is available on the news server. The news-server administrator may decide to exclude certain newsgroups, however, in which case you cannot read the excluded newsgroups.

Tip

The only step that comes close to subscription is the `.newsrc` file in your home directory. All news readers consult this file to determine which newsgroups you want to read. From inside the news reader, you can use a command such as g, followed by the newsgroup name (in the `trn` news reader), to subscribe to a newsgroup. When you subscribe to the newsgroup, the news reader simply adds the name of that newsgroup to the `.newsrc` file.

How to post news

You can use a news reader to post a news item (a new item or a reply to an old posting) to one or more newsgroups. The exact command for posting a news item depends on the news reader. In the `trn` news reader, follow these steps to post an article:

1. While you are reading an article in `trn`, press **f**. The news reader asks whether you are posting an unrelated topic (unrelated to the article that you were reading when you pressed **f**). Press **y** to answer yes, as follows:

    ```
    Are you starting an unrelated topic? [ynq] y
    ```

2. The news reader then prompts you for the subject of the new posting and the distribution. For this test posting, type a subject line with the word *ignore* in it. Otherwise, any site that receives your article will reply by mail to tell you that the article has reached the site; that's in keeping with the purpose of the misc.test newsgroup. For distribution, enter **na** to indicate North America, as follows:

    ```
    Subject: ignore no reply test
    Distribution: na
    ```

3. The news reader uses the `Postnews` program to post an article. If you are posting an article for the first time, you see the following message:

   ```
   (leaving cbreak mode; cwd=/usr/etc)
   ```

   ```
   I see you've never used this version of Pnews before. I will give
   you extra help this first time through, but then you must remember
   what you learned. If you don't understand any question, type h and
   a CR (carriage return) for help.
   ```

   ```
   If you've never posted an article to the net before, it is HIGHLY
   recommended that you read the netiquette document found in
   news.announce.newusers so that you'll know to avoid the commonest
   blunders. To do that, interrupt Pnews, get to the top-level prompt
   of [t]rn, and use the command "g news.announce.newusers" to go to
   that group.
   ```

4. After the message, the news reader asks whether you really want to post an article. Press **y** to continue.

   ```
   This program may post news to many machines.
   Are you absolutely sure that you want to do this? [ny] y
   ```

5. The news reader asks whether you have a file that you want to include as the news item with the following prompt:

   ```
   Prepared file to include [none]:
   ```

   Press Enter to continue.

6. The news reader prompts you for the name of your editor (the default is `vi`) with the following explanation and prompt:

   ```
   A temporary file has been created for you to edit. Be sure to leave at
   least one blank line between the header and the body of your message.
   (And until a certain bug is fixed all over the net, don't start the
   body of your message with any indentation, or it may get eaten.)
   ```

   ```
   Within the header may be fields that you don't understand. If you
   don't understand a field (or even if you do), you can simply leave
   it blank, and it will go away when the article is posted.
   ```

   ```
   Type return to get the default editor, or type the name of your
   favorite editor.
   ```

   ```
   Editor [/usr/bin/vi]:
   ```

   Press Enter to compose the news article with `vi`.

7. The news reader starts the `vi` editor. In the editor, you can fill in the name of the newsgroup and any other fields in the news article (including the body of the article). Following is what I filled in (shown in boldface):

   ```
   Newsgroups: misc.test
   Subject: ignore no reply test
   Summary:
   Expires:
   ```

```
Sender:
Followup-To:
Distribution: na
Organization: I need to put my ORGANIZATION here.
Keywords: test ignore
Cc:

Testing ignore
```

Notice that the name of the organization is something strange. You can edit the field to show your organization's name or define the `ORGANIZATION` environment variable (set it to your organization's name) before you start `trn`. After you finish editing the article, save it with the `:wq` command.

8. The news reader shows you the name (and a description) of the newsgroup where you are about to post the article. Then `trn` prompts you for a command. Press **s** to send the article. The interaction with the news reader goes like this:

```
Your article's newsgroup:
misc.test         For testing of network software. Very boring.

Check spelling, Send, Abort, Edit, or List? s
```

9. The `trn` news reader returns you to the article that you were reading when you started to post this article. Press **q** to quit the newsgroup that you have been reading.

10. Type **g misc.test** to subscribe to the `misc.test` newsgroup (that's where you just posted the new article).

11. Look at the latest article in `misc.test`, which should be the article that you just posted. Following is the article that I saw after I completed the test posting:

```
misc.test #98090 (28205 more)                              [1]
From: naba@lnbsoft.com (Naba Barkakati)
[1] ignore no reply test
Date: Thu Nov 02 22:46:27 EST 1995
Organization: I need to put my ORGANIZATION here.
Lines: 2
Distribution: na
Keywords: test ignore

Testing ignore

End of article 98090 (of 98090) -- what next? [npq]
```

Did the article get out?

If you post an article and read the newsgroup immediately, you'll see the new article, but that fact does not mean that the article has reached other sites on the Internet. After all, your posting shows up on your news server immediately because that's where you posted the article. Because of the store-and-forward model of news distribution, the news article gradually propagates from your news server to others around the world.

Secret

The misc.test newsgroup provides a way to see whether your news posting is really getting around. If you post to that newsgroup and do not include the word *ignore* in the subject, news servers will acknowledge receipt of the article by sending an e-mail message to the address listed in the `Reply-To` field of the article's header. The following section shows an example of how to use misc.test and another way to post a news article.

Post article with `inews`

The `inews` program allows you to send an article to a news server for distribution. Before using `inews`, place the name of your news server in the `/etc/nntpserver` file. Following is the line in my `/etc/nntpserver` file:

```
news.digex.net
```

Also, put the name of your system in the `/etc/uucpname` file. The name in this file has nothing to do with your host name (as used in the domain name system); you can use any name that you want. On my system, the `/etc/uucpname` file contains the following line:

```
lnbsoft.com
```

The `inews` software uses this name as the system name in the `Originator:` line of the posted news article.

Wizard

By default, `inews` reads the article from the standard input. Thus, you can post an article by running `inews` and typing the article's header and body. The following example shows how I posted a test article from my Linux system:

```
inews -h << EOF
> Newsgroups: misc.test
> From: naba@lnbsoft.com
> Subject: Testing
> Reply-To: naba@dcc05211.slip.digex.net
>
> This is a test message.
> EOF
```

I typed the text shown in boldface. As the example shows, you have to enter the following header fields:

- `Newsgroups:` List the newsgroups where the article should appear. In the example, I show only the misc.text newsgroup.
- `From:` Provide your name and address.
- `Subject:` Provide a one-line description of the article.
- `Reply-To:` Provide the e-mail address to which news servers should send acknowledgment of receipt.

After the headers, type the body of the article. Because of the way I ran `inews` (with the `<< EOF` ending), I end the article with the string `EOF` on a line by itself. After I end the article, `inews` sends the article on its way to my news server and, from there, to the rest of the Internet.

Look for acknowledgments

The reason for the existence of the misc.test newsgroup is to test whether your news postings are being propagated throughout the Internet properly. Most sites that receive a misc.test posting (one that does not include the word *ignore* in the subject line) send a mail message to the address shown in the `Reply-To:` line of the article's header.

As sites receive your posting, they automatically respond with e-mail messages. Following is the first message that I got from my test posting:

```
From usenet-bounceback@mathworks.com Tue Oct 31 01:20:02 1995
Date: Tue, 31 Oct 1995 00:13:58 -0500 (EST)
To: naba@dcc05211.slip.digex.net
From: usenet@mathworks.com (MathWorks Autoresponder)
Subject: Re: Testing
Reply-To: nobody@mathworks.com
Errors-To: usenet-bounceback@mathworks.com
References: <474baj$5g@news4.digex.net>
Newsgroups: misc.test
Precedence: junk

Your Usenet test article was received by news.mathworks.com on
Tue, Oct 31 00:13:58 EST here at The MathWorks, Inc. in Natick, MA.

You are receiving this message because you posted a test message to
the misc.test newsgroup.

The MathWorks news admin can be reached via e-mail at
usenet@mathworks.com.
Please note that we do not offer news access to sites outside of our
organization.

If you want to suppress this message in the future, include the word
"ignore" in the Subject: header of any subsequent articles.

You could also post your test articles with a Distribution: header of
"local" to prevent them from leaving your local machine, or you could
also ask your local newsadmin to create a local *.test group that will
not propagate outside of your organization.

The header of your message was:

 Path:
news.mathworks.com!newsfeed.internetmci.com!howland.reston.ans.net!news1.
digex.net!news3.digex.net!lnbsoft.com!naba
 From: naba@lnbsoft.com
 Newsgroups: misc.test
 Subject: Testing
```

```
Date: 31 Oct 1995 05:13:55 GMT
Organization: Express Access Online Communications, USA
Lines: 1
Message-ID: <474baj$5g@news4.digex.net>
Reply-To: naba@dcc05211.slip.digex.net
NNTP-Posting-Host: dcc05211.slip.digex.net
Originator: naba@lnbsoft.com
```

That message was only the beginning. Within minutes, my mailbox had about half a dozen replies from California and Florida; London, U.K.; Liege, Belgium; and Pohang, South Korea. Some of the replies, such as the following message from London, showed the time that it took for my posting to make it to that site. (It took nearly 4 minutes for the article to reach London from my home in Maryland.)

```
From news@news.demon.net Tue Oct 31 01:25:06 1995
From: Autoresponder <autoresponder@news.demon.net>
To: naba@dcc05211.slip.digex.net
Subject: Automatic reply to your test message
Organization: Demon Internet Ltd., London, UK
References: <474baj$5g@news4.digex.net>
In-Reply-To: <474baj$5g@news4.digex.net>
Date: Tue, 31 Oct 95 5:17:48 GMT


This message has been generated automatically in order to help
you track the propogation of your article in the test newsgroups.

If you do not wish any reply from this program, just include
the words "no reply" or its translation in French or German
in the subject line or in the first 5 lines of the body of
your article to the appropriate Usenet *.test newsgroup.

Your article took 3 minutes, 53 seconds to get here.

The header of your article was as follows:

> From: naba@lnbsoft.com
> Newsgroups: misc.test
> Subject: Testing
> Date: 31 Oct 1995 05:13:55 GMT
> Organization: Express Access Online Communications, USA
> Lines: 1
> Message-ID: <474baj$5g@news4.digex.net>
> Reply-To: naba@dcc05211.slip.digex.net
> Originator: naba@lnbsoft.com


and the first few lines of the body were:

> This is a test message.


If you have any questions about this software, please contact
Demon Internet Newsmaster <newsmaster@demon.net> for more information.
```

If you have your Linux host on the Internet, try posting to the misc.test newsgroup to verify that articles are getting out. You should be prepared to receive a dozen or so replies from various sites, acknowledging the arrival of your article at those sites.

Using Secure Anonymous FTP

Besides mail and news, anonymous FTP is a common service on an Internet host. You may be familiar with ftp (File Transfer Protocol), which you can use to transfer files from one system to another. When you use ftp to transfer files to or from a remote system, you have to log into the remote system before you can use ftp.

Anonymous FTP refers to the use of the user name anonymous, which anyone can use with FTP to transfer files from a system. Anonymous FTP is a common way to share files on the Internet. Chapter 2, "Upgrading Linux," explains how you can use anonymous FTP to download patches to Linux kernels from the Internet host named ftp.funet.fi.

If you have used anonymous FTP to download files from various Internet sites, you already know the convenience of that service. With anonymous FTP, you can make information available to anyone on the Internet. If you have a new Linux application that you want to share with the world, set up anonymous FTP on your Linux PC and place the software in an appropriate directory. After that, all you need to do is announce to the world (probably through a posting in the comp.os.linux.announce newsgroup) that you have a new program available. Now anyone can get the software from your system at his or her convenience.

Even if you run a for-profit business, you can use anonymous FTP to support your customers. If you sell some hardware or software product, you may want to provide technical information or software "fixes" through anonymous FTP.

Unfortunately, the convenience of anonymous FTP comes at a price. If you do not configure the anonymous FTP service properly, intruders and pranksters may gain access to your system. Some intruders may simply use your system's disk as a temporary holding place for various files; others may fill your disk with junk files, effectively making your system inoperable. At the other extreme, an intruder may gain user-level (or, worse, root-level) access to your system and do much more damage.

Note
If you installed Linux from this book's companion CD-ROM, you already have anonymous FTP available on your system. The default setup, however, does not employ all possible security precautions.

The following sections show you how to secure and test the anonymous FTP server on your Linux Internet host.

Try existing anonymous FTP service

You can try the existing anonymous FTP service from any Internet site or a system on your LAN — even from your Linux system.

Following is a sample anonymous FTP session from an Internet host to my Linux PC:

```
access5% ftp dcc05211.slip.digex.net
Connected to dcc05211.slip.digex.net.
220 dcc05211 FTP server (Version wu-2.4(1) Wed May 10 21:00:32 CDT 1995) ready.
Name (dcc05211.slip.digex.net:naba): anonymous
331 Guest login ok, send your complete e-mail address as password.
Password:           (I typed xx)
230-The response 'xx' is not valid
230-Next time please use your e-mail address as your password
230-       for example: joe@access5.digex.net
230-Welcome, archive user! This is an experimental FTP server. If have any
230-unusual problems, please report them via e-mail to root@dcc05211
230-If you do have problems, please try using a dash (-) as the first character
230-of your password -- this will turn off the continuation messages that may
230-be confusing your ftp client.
230-
230 Guest login ok, access restrictions apply.
ftp> ls -l
200 PORT command successful.
150 Opening ASCII mode data connection for /bin/ls.
total 7
drwxrwxr-x   2 root     wheel        1024 Sep 28 20:44 bin
drwxrwxr-x   2 root     wheel        1024 Sep 28 20:44 etc
drwxrwxr-x   2 root     wheel        1024 Dec  3 1993 incoming
drwxrwxr-x   2 root     wheel        1024 Nov 17 1993 lib
drwxrwxr-x   2 root     wheel        1024 Sep 28 20:44 pub
drwxrwxr-x   3 root     wheel        1024 Sep 28 20:44 usr
-rw-r--r--   1 root     root          312 Aug  1 1994 welcome.msg
226 Transfer complete.
remote: -l
442 bytes received in 0.18 seconds (2.4 Kbytes/s)
ftp> cd pub
250 CWD command successful.
ftp> ls -l
200 PORT command successful.
150 Opening ASCII mode data connection for /bin/ls.
total 0
-rwxrwxr-x   1 root     wheel           0 Jul 10 1993 dummy_test_file
226 Transfer complete.
remote: -l
81 bytes received in 0.059 seconds (1.3 Kbytes/s)
ftp> bye
221 Goodbye.
access5%
```

You can, however, easily avoid any potential problems with anonymous FTP by following a specified set of guidelines.

Why worry about anonymous FTP?

To understand why there are worries about the use of anonymous FTP, you have to know how `ftp` works. The `ftp` daemon listens to TCP port 21. Client `ftp` programs communicate with the server by using a set of text commands. Anyone can also communicate with the `ftp` daemon by running the `telnet` program and connecting to port 21. Following is a sample session with the default anonymous FTP setup on my Linux system (my input appears in boldface):

```
telnet dcc05211.slip.digex.net 21
Trying 204.192.70.170 ...
Connected to dcc05211.slip.digex.net.
Escape character is '^]'.
220 dcc05211 FTP server (Version wu-2.4(1) Wed May 10 21:00:32 CDT 1995) ready.
help
214-The following commands are recognized (* =>'s unimplemented).
   USER    PORT    STOR    MSAM*   RNTO    NLST    MKD     CDUP
   PASS    PASV    APPE    MRSQ*   ABOR    SITE    XMKD    XCUP
   ACCT*   TYPE    MLFL*   MRCP*   DELE    SYST    RMD     STOU
   SMNT*   STRU    MAIL*   ALLO    CWD     STAT    XRMD    SIZE
   REIN*   MODE    MSND*   REST    XCWD    HELP    PWD     MDTM
   QUIT    RETR    MSOM*   RNFR    LIST    NOOP    XPWD
214 Direct comments to ftp-bugs@dcc05211.
help site
214-The following SITE commands are recognized (* =>'s unimplemented).
   UMASK   CHMOD   GROUP   NEWER   INDEX   ALIAS   GROUPS
   IDLE    HELP    GPASS   MINFO   EXEC    CDPATH
214 Direct comments to ftp-bugs@dcc05211.
USER anonymous
331 Guest login ok, send your complete e-mail address as password.
PASS xx
230-The response 'xx' is not valid
230-Next time please use your e-mail address as your password
230-    for example: joe@access5.digex.net
230-Welcome, archive user! This is an experimental FTP server. If have any
230-unusual problems, please report them via e-mail to root@dcc05211
230-If you do have problems, please try using a dash (-) as the first character
230-of your password -- this will turn off the continuation messages that may
230-be confusing your ftp client.
230-
230 Guest login ok, access restrictions apply.
site exec ls -l
200-ls -l
200-total 7
200-drwxrwxr-x   2 root     wheel        1024 Sep 28 20:44 bin
200-drwxrwxr-x   2 root     wheel        1024 Sep 28 20:44 etc
200-drwxrwxr-x   2 root     wheel        1024 Dec  3 1993 incoming
200-drwxrwxr-x   2 root     wheel        1024 Nov 17 1993 lib
200-drwxrwxr-x   2 root     wheel        1024 Sep 28 20:44 pub
200-drwxrwxr-x   3 root     wheel        1024 Sep 28 20:44 usr
200--rw-r--r--   1 root     root          312 Aug  1 1994 welcome.msg
200 (end of 'ls -l')
```

```
quit
221 Goodbye.
Connection closed by foreign host.
```

Secret

This listing shows the ftp commands, including some potentially troublesome commands, such as SITE EXEC. In some older versions of ftp, this command can be used to gain shell access. Luckily, however, all known security holes have been fixed in the FTP server included on the companion CD-ROM.

Secret

Another typical problem with anonymous FTP is the permission settings of the home directory of the user named ftp — the user name for anyone who logs into ftp as anonymous. If /home/ftp — the home directory of the anonymous FTP user — is owned by ftp, anyone could use one of the SITE commands and create new files. The permission settings of the /home/ftp directory tree are what you have to fix to prevent any potential security problems with anonymous FTP.

Make anonymous FTP secure

To avoid any potential security problems with anonymous FTP, you should follow a specified set of guidelines. Following are the basic steps for making anonymous FTP secure:

1. Check the ownership of the /home/ftp directory and all its subdirectories and files.

2. Log in as root, and use the following commands:

   ```
   cd /home
   ls -1R ftp | more
   ```

3. Look through the resulting directory listing, and verify that all files are owned by root. This should be true for the default setup, provided that you installed Linux from this book's companion CD-ROM.

4. Change the ftp user's shell to /bin/false, because the ftp user does not need a shell to log in. Here's how to change the shell for the ftp user:

   ```
   chsh ftp
   Changing shell for ftp.
   New shell [/bin/true]: /bin/false
   warning: "/bin/false" is not listed as a valid shell.
   Shell changed.
   Ignore the warning from chsh.
   ```

5. Change the permission setting of the ftp user's home directory, denoted by ~ftp, to 555 (read and execute only), as follows:

   ```
   chmod 555 ~ftp
   ```

6. Change the permission setting of ~ftp/bin and ~ftp/etc to 111 (execute only). Also change the permission of the contents of ~ftp/bin to 111, as follows:

```
chmod 111 ~ftp/etc
chmod 111 ~ftp/bin
chmod 111 ~ftp/bin/*
```

7. Make sure that the `~ftp/etc/passwd` file does not contain any encrypted passwords; all password fields should be replaced with an asterisk. In particular, make sure that the `root` user does not have a blank password field, like this one:

```
root::0:0:root:/root:/bin/bash
```

Use a text editor, and put an asterisk between the first pair of colons, as follows:

```
root:*:0:0:root:/root:/bin/bash
```

8. Change the permission setting of all files in the `~ftp/etc` directory to 444 (read only), as follows:

```
chmod 444 ~ftp/etc/*
```

9. Change the permission settings of `~ftp/pub`, `~ftp/usr`, and `~ftp/lib` to 555, as follows:

```
chmod 555 ~ftp/pub
chmod 555 ~ftp/usr
chmod 555 ~ftp/lib
```

10. The `~ftp/incoming` directory allows anonymous `ftp` users to leave files on your system. You can make this directory somewhat secure by changing the permission settings of the `~ftp/incoming` directory to 1733, as follows:

```
chmod 1733 ~ftp/incoming
```

This permission setting allows anonymous users to copy files into this directory, but does not allow them to view the contents of the directory or delete any existing files.

11. Just to be safe, create zero-length `.rhosts` and `.forward` files in `~ftp`, and make them read-only, as follows:

```
touch ~ftp/.rhosts
touch ~ftp/.forward
chmod 400 ~ftp/.rhosts
chmod 400 ~ftp/.forward
```

More on Internet host security

The latest information on securing an Internet host is available on the Internet itself. Use a World Wide Web browser to access and read http://ciac.llnl.gov/ciac/documents/ciac2308.html. That document, which describes how to secure various Internet services, was prepared by the Computer Incident Advisory Capability (CIAC) of the U.S. Department of Energy. From that Web page, you'll be able to find other Internet resources on security.

Summary

The Internet is popular nowadays; Internet Service Providers (ISPs) are springing up all over the United States and in much of the world. Online services such as America Online and CompuServe now offer Internet mail and Web browsing, bringing even more people to the Internet. Because of its support for TCP/IP networking — the universal language of the Internet — a Linux PC is ideal as an Internet host. This chapter describes the typical services that are available on an Internet host and shows you how to configure these services — mail, news, and anonymous FTP — on a Linux PC. By reading this chapter, you learn the following:

- Although the Internet essentially is a "network of networks," it manifests itself differently, depending on how people use its capabilities. For most people, the Internet is the World Wide Web and electronic mail (e-mail), whereas many other people see it as being a place to read the newsgroups. Still other people use Internet applications such as `telnet` and `ftp` to access remote computers.

- World Wide Web, e-mail, newsgroups, and anonymous FTP are some of the important services available on an Internet host. This chapter describes how to set up e-mail, newsgroups, and anonymous FTP services on a Linux PC. (The World Wide Web is covered in the next chapter.)

- E-mail software comes in two parts: a mail transport agent, which physically sends and receives mail messages, and a mail user agent, which reads messages and prepares new messages.

- The companion CD-ROM includes several mail transfer agents and mail user agents. This chapter describes how to use `sendmail` as a mail transport agent.

- `sendmail` configuration is complex, but you can get going with the sample file provided on the CD-ROM. All you may need to do is set your Linux PC's host name properly.

- To read e-mail, you can use `mailx` or `elm`.

- Newsgroups originated in USENET, which is a store-and-forward network. News items travel around the world from one system to another. Nowadays, news is transported over the Internet by means of the Network News Transport Protocol (NNTP).

- Because thousands of newsgroups exist, storing all the news articles takes a great deal of disk space. Also, the articles must be purged periodically; otherwise, the disk will get filled. It's best to read news from a news server maintained by an Internet Service Provider (ISP).

- The companion CD-ROM includes several news readers, such as `tin` and `trn`. This chapter shows you how to use these news readers to read news from a designated news server.

- To read newsgroups from a news server, you should set the environment variable NNTPSERVER to the name of the news server.

- Anonymous FTP is another popular Internet service for distributing files. With anonymous FTP, anyone can use `ftp` with the anonymous user ID and download files from your system. Although anonymous FTP is useful for distributing data, it also poses a security risk if it is not set up properly.
- The default Linux installation includes an FTP server with anonymous FTP capabilities. This chapter guides you through the steps for making anonymous FTP secure.

Chapter 20

Running a World Wide Web Server on Linux

In This Chapter

- ▶ Understanding the World Wide Web
- ▶ Understanding URLs and hypertext links
- ▶ Understanding HTTP
- ▶ Surfing the Net
- ▶ Downloading and setting up Web-browser software
- ▶ Touring NCSA Mosaic and Netscape Navigator
- ▶ Downloading and setting up the NCSA Web server
- ▶ Understanding HTML
- ▶ Designing and building Web pages by using HTML
- ▶ Using transparent GIFs, image maps, and CGI script processing
- ▶ Creating interactive Web pages with forms

Chapters 18 and 19 showed you how to connect your Linux PC to the Internet (through an Internet Service Provider) and set up common Internet services — such as mail, news, and anonymous `ftp` — on your system. This chapter turns to one of the reasons why the Internet has become so popular in recent years: the World Wide Web (WWW, W3, or simply the Web), which provides a easy graphical way to browse and retrieve information from the Internet.

Note

As a system on the Internet, all your Linux system needs is a *Web browser* — an application that "knows" how to download and display Web documents — so that you can begin enjoying the benefits of the Web. You also can make information available to other users through *Web pages* — the common term for Web documents.

This chapter first explains what the World Wide Web is and describes the Hypertext Transfer Protocol (HTTP) — the information exchange protocol that makes the Web work. Then the chapter shows you how to download a Web browser, set up the browser, and use it. (I'll cover both the Netscape and Mosaic browsers.)

Next, the chapter turns to the use of the Web as a popular way to publish information on the Internet. This book's companion CD-ROM includes an HTTP server (that's the technical term for a Web server), which you could use simply by copying from the CD-ROM. However, I'll show you how to download and install the latest NCSA Web server. That way, you'll know where various files are supposed to go and how you should configure the server. This experience also will help you download and install new Web servers in the future.

Setting up the Web server is, of course, only a small part of publishing information on the Web. You also must provide the content in Hypertext Markup Language (HTML). The last part of this chapter gets you started with HTML authoring. You also learn about advanced HTML features, such as the use of forms to accept user input. After reading this chapter, you should be able to set up a Web server and provide some basic HTML content.

What Is the World Wide Web?

If you have used a network file server of any kind, you know the convenience of being able to access files that reside at a shared location. Using a word processing application that runs on your computer, you can easily open a document that physically resides on the file server.

Now imagine a word processor that allows you to open and view a document that resides on any computer on the Internet. You can view the document in its full glory, with formatted text and graphics. If the document makes a reference to another document (possibly residing on yet another computer), you can open that linked document by clicking the reference. That kind of easy access to distributed documents is essentially what the World Wide Web provides.

Of course, the documents have to be in a standard format, so that any computer (with appropriate Web software) can access and interpret the document. Additionally, a standard protocol is necessary for transferring Web documents from one system to another.

The standard Web document format is Hypertext Markup Language (HTML), and the standard protocol for exchanging Web documents is Hypertext Transfer Protocol (HTTP).

A *Web server* is the software that provides HTML documents to any client that makes the appropriate HTTP requests. A *Web browser* is the client software that actually downloads an HTML document from a Web server and displays the contents graphically.

Like a giant spider's web

The World Wide Web is the combination of the Web servers and the HTML documents that contain the information. In this view, the Web is like a giant book whose pages are scattered throughout the Internet. You use a Web browser running on your computer to view the pages, as illustrated in Figure 20-1.

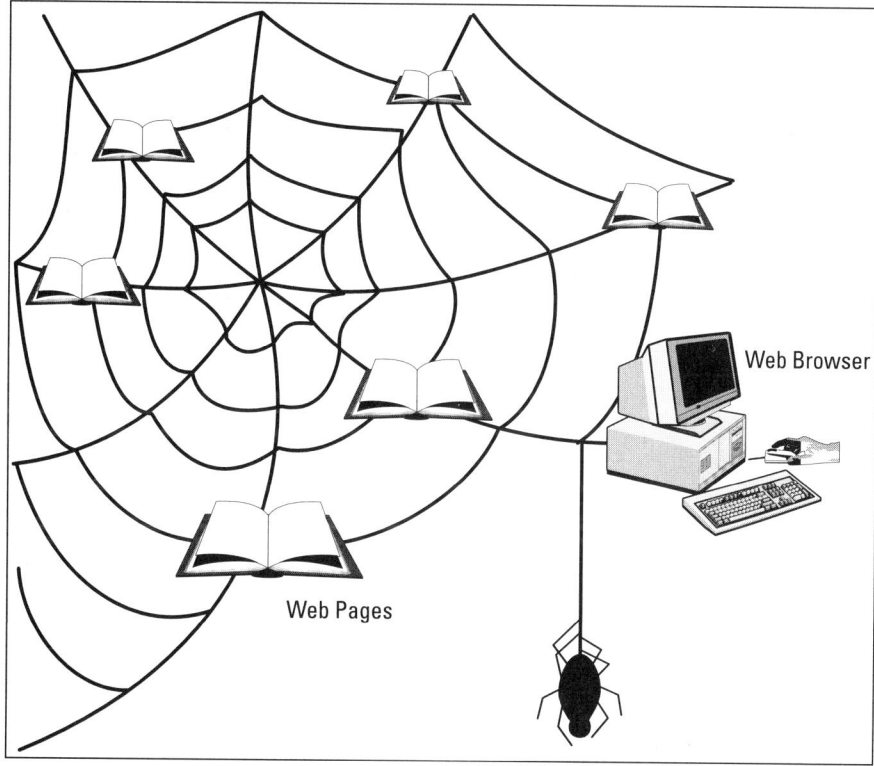

Figure 20-1: The World Wide Web is like thousands of pages, scattered across the network, that you can read from your computer by using a Web browser.

As Figure 20-1 shows, you can imagine that the pages — the HTML documents — are linked by network connections that resemble a giant spider's web, so you can see why the Web is called the Web. The "World Wide" part comes from the fact that the Web pages are scattered around the world.

Links and URLs

Like the pages of real books, Web pages contain text and graphics. Unlike real books, however, Web pages can contain multimedia information, such as video clips, digitized sound, and links to other Web pages that can actually take the user to the referenced Web page.

The *links* in a Web page are references to other Web pages that you can follow to go from one page to another. The Web browser displays these links as underlined text (in a different color) or images. Each link is like an instruction to the reader — something like "for more information, please consult Chapter 20," which you might find in a real book. In a Web page, all you have to do is click the link; then the Web browser brings up the referenced page, even if it's on a different computer.

Note

The links in a Web page are referred to as *hypertext* links, because when you click a link, the Web browser jumps to the Web page referenced by that link.

This arrangement brings up a question. In a real book, you might ask the reader to go to a specific chapter or page in the book. How does a hypertext link indicate the location of the referenced Web page? In the World Wide Web, each Web page has a special name, called a *Uniform Resource Locator (URL)*. A URL uniquely specifies the location of a file on a computer, as shown in Figure 20-2.

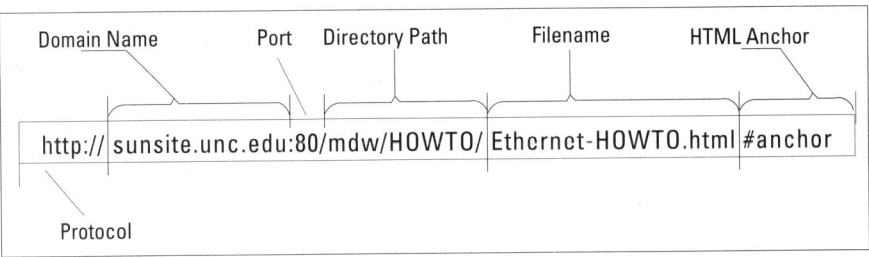

Figure 20-2: Various parts of a Uniform Resource Locator (URL).

As Figure 20-2 illustrates, a URL has the following sequence of components:

1. *Protocol.* The first field in the URL is the name of the protocol to be used to access the data that resides in the file specified by the URL. In Figure 20-2, the protocol is http://, which means that the URL specifies the location of a Web page. Following are the common protocol types and their meanings:

    - file:// specifies the name of a local file that is to be opened and displayed. You can use this file to view HTML files without having to connect to the Internet.
    - ftp:// specifies a file that is accessible through File Transfer Protocol (FTP).
    - gopher:// specifies a document and the name of a host system that runs the Gopher server from which the document is to be retrieved. (Gopher servers provide information by using a simple protocol.)
    - http:// specifies an HTML document that is accessible through Hypertext Transfer Protocol (HTTP).
    - mailto:// specifies an e-mail address that should be used to send an e-mail message.
    - news:// specifies a newsgroup that is to be read by means of Network News Transfer Protocol (NNTP).
    - telnet:// specifies a user name and a system name for remote login.
    - wais:// specifies the name of a Wide Area Information Server (WAIS) from which information is to be retrieved.

Cross Reference

2. *Domain name.* This part of the URL contains the fully qualified domain name of the computer on which the file specified by this URL resides. You also can specify an IP address (see Chapter 16 for more information on IP addresses) in this field.

3. *Port address.* This is the port address of the server that implements the protocol listed in the first part of the URL. This part of the URL is optional, because there are default ports for all protocols. The default port for HTTP, for example, is 80. Some sites, however, may configure the Web server to listen to a different port. In such a case, the URL must include the port address.

4. *Directory path.* This field is the directory path of the file that is being referenced in the URL. For Web pages, this field is the directory path of the HTML file.

5. *Filename.* This field is the name of the file. For Web pages, the filename typically ends with .html. If you omit the filename, the Web server returns a default file (often named index.html).

6. *HTML anchor.* This optional part of the URL is used to make the Web browser jump to a specific location in the file. If this part starts with a question mark (?) instead of a pound sign (#), the text following the question mark is taken to be a query. The Web server returns information based on such queries.

When you learn more about HTML in later sections of this chapter, you'll see how to associate a URL with a hypertext link.

Hypertext Transfer Protocol (HTTP)

Hypertext Transfer Protocol — the protocol that underlies the World Wide Web — is so named because Web pages include hypertext links. The *Transfer Protocol* part refers to the standard conventions for transferring a Web page across the network from one computer to another. Although you really do not have to understand HTTP to set up a Web server or use a Web browser, I think you'll find it instructive to know how the Web works.

Before I explain anything about HTTP, you should get a firsthand taste of HTTP. On most systems, the Web server listens to port 80 and responds to any HTTP requests sent to that port. Therefore, you can use the telnet program to connect to port 80 of a system (that has a Web server) and try out some HTTP commands.

To see an example of HTTP at work, follow these steps:

1. Make sure that your Linux PC's connection to the Internet is up and running. (If you use SLIP or PPP, for example, make sure that you have established the connection.)

2. Type the following command:

   ```
   telnet home.netscape.com 80
   ```

3. After you see the `Connected...` message, type the following HTTP command:

   ```
   GET /index.html
   ```

   In response to this HTTP command, the Web server returns the specified HTML file.

Notice that this example uses the old form of the GET command. In HTTP 1.0, the command lines are in the form shown below. (My comments are in italics.)

```
GET /index.html HTTP/1.0
Accept: (list the types of formats that you accept)
From: (provide your e-mail address)
(a blank line to indicate that you're done with your request)
```

Following is what I got when I tried the old form of the GET command on a well-known Web site:

```
dcc05211:~$ telnet home.netscape.com 80
Trying 198.95.251.30...
Connected to www1.netscape.com.
Escape character is '^]'.
GET /index.html
<TITLE>Welcome to Netscape</TITLE>
<BODY> <!-- /images/top_bg.gif -->

<CENTER>
<A HREF="/misc/home.map">
<IMG SRC="/images/home_igloo.gif" ISMAP WIDTH=468 HEIGHT=197
BORDER=0></A>
<P>
</CENTER>

<DL>

<A HREF="/comprod/mirror/index.html">
<IMG SRC="/comprod/mirror/images/now8.gif" HSPACE=10 VSPACE=10
ALIGN=RIGHT
WIDTH=88 HEIGHT=31 BORDER=1></A>
<DT>
<B>
N<FONT SIZE=-1>ETSCAPE</FONT>
N<FONT SIZE=-1>AVIGATOR</FONT>
B<FONT SIZE=-1>UGS</FONT>
B<FONT SIZE=-1>OUNTY</FONT>
</B>
<DD>
```

Chapter 20: Running a World Wide Web Server on Linux

```
Netscape <A HREF="/newsref/pr/newsrelease48.html">announces</A> a
program to reward users for finding and reporting bugs in the beta
release of <A HREF="/comprod/products/navigator/version_2.0/
index.html">Netscape Navigator 2.0</A>. Be sure to read <A HREF="/
comprod/products/navigator/version_2.0/contest_rules.html">the full
rules</A> and then <A HREF="/comprod/mirror/index.html">download </
A>Netscape 2.0 now.
<P>

<DT>
<B>
R<FONT SIZE=-1>EVENUE</FONT>
G<FONT SIZE=-1>ROWTH</FONT>
R<FONT SIZE=-1>EPORTED</FONT>
</B>
<DD>
Netscape <A HREF="/newsref/pr/newsrelease56.html">announces</A> rev-
enues totaling $20.8 million for the third quarter, a 75-percent
increase over the previous quarter.
<P>

................ (Lines deleted)

<HR SIZE=4>

<P>
<CENTER>
<A HREF="/misc/bottom.map"><IMG SRC="/images/navigation_bar.gif"
ISMAP BORDER=0 WIDTH=468 HEIGHT=32></a>
<P>

<FONT SIZE=-1><I>
Find out more about Netscape at <A HREF= "mailto:info@netscape.com">
info@netscape.com</A>, or call 415/528-2555.<BR>
Copyright &copy; 1995 Netscape Communications Corporation</I></FONT>
</CENTER>
<P>
<P>
</BODY>

Connection closed by foreign host.
```

When you try this example with `telnet`, you see the HTML as lines of text. If you were to view this HTML page with a Web browser, you would see the page in its graphical form, as shown in Figure 20-3.

If you don't have a Web browser, you learn how to download and set up a Web browser in the next few sections.

The example of HTTP commands shows the result of the GET command. GET happens to be the most common HTTP command, because GET causes the server to return a specified HTML document.

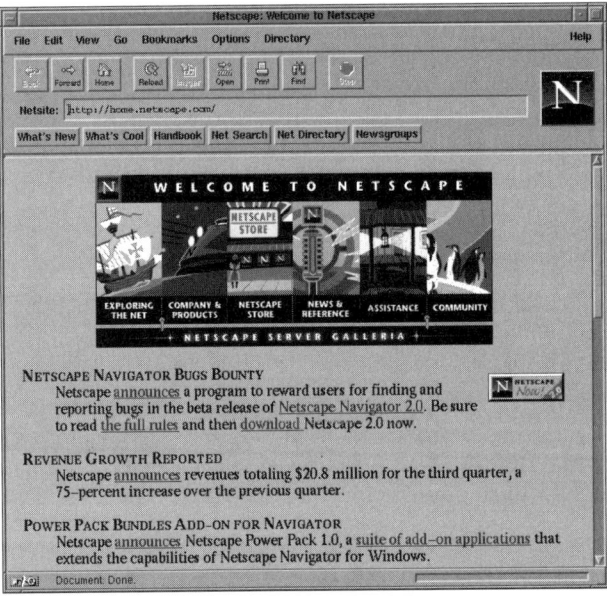

Figure 20-3: The `index.html` file from `home.netscape.com`, viewed with the Netscape Web browser. (Copyright © 1995-96, Netscape Communications Corporation)

The other two HTTP commands are HEAD and POST. The HEAD command is almost like GET; it causes the server to return everything in the document except the body. The POST command is used to send information to the server; it's up to the server to decide how to act on the information.

Is HTTP an Internet standard?

Despite its widespread use in the World Wide Web since the 1990, Hypertext Transfer Protocol (HTTP) is not yet an Internet standard. All Internet standards are distributed as Request for Comment (RFC); no RFC for HHTP exists yet. At this writing, an Internet Draft — a working document of the Internet Engineering Task Force (IETF) — is available. That Internet Draft, "Hypertext Transfer Protocol — HTTP/1.0," T. Berners-Lee, R. Fielding, and H. Frystyk, October 14, 1995, is in circulation. To learn more about HTTP/1.0 and other HTTP-related standards, use a Web browser to access http://www.w3.org/pub/WWW/Protocols/.

Surfing the Net

Like anything else, the World Wide Web is easier to understand after you have seen how it works. One of the best ways to learn about the Web is to go "surfing the Net" with a Web browser. Browsing Web pages is fun because the typical Web page contains both text and images. Also, browsing has an element of surprise; you can click the links and end up in unexpected Web pages. The links are the most curious aspect of the Web. You can start by looking at a page that shows today's weather, and a click later, you can be reading that week's issue of *Time* magazine online.

Before you can try anything, of course, you need a Web browser. (You also must have an Internet connection for your Linux system, but I am assuming that you have already taken care of that part.)

Downloading the Web browsers

You can choose two popular Web browsers for Linux:

- Netscape Navigator, from Netscape Communications Corporation
- NCSA Mosaic for the X Window System, from the National Center for Supercomputing Applications (NCSA) at the University of Illinois in Urbana-Champaign

Secret

Both Web browsers are copyrighted by their respective owners. Both products are available for free (at least for evaluation), but some constraints apply. You should read the respective licenses (which you can view online after you download and install the browsers) for details. Essentially, a commercial organization can use NCSA Mosaic for internal use without paying a fee. If you plan to use Netscape Navigator beyond a 90-day evaluation period, however, you need to buy a licensed copy of the browser.

I'll show you how to download both of these browsers. You can try them and then decide which one you like best.

Secret

Netscape Navigator

To download Netscape Navigator, follow these steps:

1. Make sure that your Linux system's Internet connection is up and running.

2. Type the following command (shown in boldface):

```
ftp ftp2.netscape.com

Connected to www3.netscape.com.
220 ftp3.netscape.com FTP server (Version wu-2.4(3) Tue Dec 27
    17:53:56 PST 1994) ready.
Name (ftp2.netscape.com:naba): anonymous
331 Guest login ok, send your complete e-mail address as password.
Password:
230-Welcome to the Netscape Communications Corporation FTP server.
```

```
230-
230-If you have any odd problems, try logging in with a minus sign (-)
230-as the first character of your password. This will turn off a
feature
230-that may be confusing your ftp client program.
230-
230-Please send any questions, comments, or problem reports about
230-this server to ftp@netscape.com.
230-
230 Guest login ok, access restrictions apply.
Remote system type is UNIX.
Using binary mode to transfer files.
```

3. At the `ftp>` prompt, type the following command (shown in boldface):

```
ftp> cd netscape/unix
250-This software is subject to a license agreement. Be sure to read and
250-agree to the license BEFORE you use the software.
250-
250-EXPORT
250-You may not download or otherwise export or re-export Netscape Software or
250-any underlying information or technology except in full compliance with
250-all United States and other applicable laws and regulations. In particular,
250-but without limitation, none of the Software or underlying information or
250-technology may be downloaded or otherwise exported or re-exported (i) into
250-(or to a national or resident of) Cuba, Haiti, Iraq, Libya, Yugoslavia,
250-North Korea, Iran, or Syria or (ii) to anyone on the US Treasury
250-Department's list of Specially Designated Nationals or the US Commerce
250-Department's Table of Deny Orders. By downloading the Software, you are
250-agreeing to the foregoing and you are representing and warranting that you
250-are not located in, under control of, or a national or resident of any
250-such country or on any such list.
250-
250-REDISTRIBUTION and MIRRORING
250-<font size=+2><b>Redistribution Not Permitted</b></font> --
250-unless you are an educational institution and want to mirror for your
250-faculty, staff and students. If you want to mirror, or are uncertain
250-about what to do, please see <a href="http://home.netscape.com/comprod/
mirror/mirror_application.html">
250-http://home.netscape.com/comprod/mirror/mirror_application.html</a>
250-or send email to <a href="mailto:mirror@netscape.com">mirror@netscape.com</a>.
250-
250-Please read the file README
250-  it was last modified on Fri Oct  6 02:02:27 1995 - 30 days ago
250 CWD command successful.
```

4. Type the `ls` command to view the file listing, as follows:

```
ftp> ls
200 PORT command successful.
150 Opening ASCII mode data connection for /bin/ls.
total 30785
drwxr-xr-x   2 root     sys           512 Oct  6 02:03 .
drwxr-xr-x   5 root     sys           512 Sep 28 00:25 ..
-rw-rw-r--   1 root     sys          1445 Sep 28 01:23 .message
```

Chapter 20: Running a World Wide Web Server on Linux

```
-rw-r--r--   1 999     999       11452 Sep 28 00:25 LICENSE
-rw-r--r--   1 999     999        8280 Oct  6 02:02 README
-rw-r--r--   1 999     999     2706463 Sep 28 00:21 netscape-v112-
   export.alpha-dec-osf2.0.tar.Z
-rw-r--r--   1 999     999     2193641 Sep 28 00:23 netscape-v112-
   export.hppa1.1-hp-hpux.tar.Z
-rw-r--r--   1 999     999     1669969 Sep 28 00:23 netscape-v112-
   export.i386-unknown-bsd.tar.Z
-rw-r--r--   1 999     999     1619612 Sep 28 00:21 netscape-v112-
   export.i486-unknown-linux.tar.Z
-rw-r--r--   1 999     999     1058513 Sep 28 00:22 netscape-v112-
   export.mips-sgi-irix5.2.tar.Z
-rw-r--r--   1 999     999     1023793 Sep 28 00:24 netscape-v112-
   export.rs6000-ibm-aix3.2.tar.Z
-rw-r--r--   1 999     999     1750883 Sep 28 00:20 netscape-v112-
   export.sparc-sun-solaris2.3.tar.Z
-rw-r--r--   1 999     999     3713749 Sep 28 00:19 netscape-v112-
   export.sparc-sun-sunos4.1.3_U1.tar.Z
226 Transfer complete.
```

5. Get the README and LICENSE files, as follows:

```
ftp> get README
200 PORT command successful.
150 Opening BINARY mode data connection for README (8280 bytes).
226 Transfer complete.
8280 bytes received in 3.12 secs (2.6 Kbytes/sec)
ftp> get LICENSE
200 PORT command successful.
150 Opening BINARY mode data connection for LICENSE (11452 bytes).
226 Transfer complete.
11452 bytes received in 3.82 secs (2.9 Kbytes/sec)
```

6. Set the file type to binary with the following command:

```
ftp> binary
200 Type set to I.
```

7. Get the Linux version of Netscape Navigator with the following command:

```
ftp> mget *linux*
mget netscape-v112-export.i486-unknown-linux.tar.Z? y
```

If you have a SLIP or PPP connection over a modem, this step will take a while, because that command downloads 1,619,612 bytes. (The file size may be different by the time you download Netscape.)

8. Type **bye** to quit `ftp`.

After completing the download, you have to decompress the file (the `.Z` at the end of the filename indicates that the file is compressed). Use the following command to decompress the file:

```
uncompress netscape-v112-export.i486-unknown-linux.tar.Z
```

Next, unpack the `tar` file with the following command:

```
tar xvf netscape-v112-export.i486-unknown-linux.tar
```

You'll find the `netscape` program, as well as several support files. In particular, you have to move the `nls` directory to the `/usr/X11R6/lib/X11` directory. Use the following command from the directory where you unpacked the Netscape files to accomplish this task:

```
mv nls /usr/X11R6/lib/X11
```

Finally, you should move the `netscape` program to a common directory, such as `/usr/local/bin`, so that any user can access it. From the directory where you unpacked Netscape, type this command:

```
mv netscape /usr/local/bin
```

That's it! You should be able to start Netscape Navigator by typing **netscape** in an `xterm` window. (Remember that you have to start X before running `netscape`, because Netscape uses the X Window System.)

NCSA Mosaic

To download NCSA Mosaic, follow these steps:

1. Make sure that your Linux system's Internet connection is up and running.

2. Type the following command (shown in boldface):

```
ftp ftp.ncsa.uiuc.edu
Connected to ftp.ncsa.uiuc.edu.
220 idunno FTP server (Version wu-2.4(25) Thu Aug 25 13:14:21 CDT 1994) ready.
Name (ftp.ncsa.uiuc.edu:naba): anonymous
331 Guest login ok, send your complete e-mail address as password.
Password:
230-
230-Welcome to NCSA's new anonymous FTP server! I hope you find what you are
230-  looking for. If you have any technical problems with the server,
230-  please e-mail to ftpadmin@ncsa.uiuc.edu. For other questions regarding
230-  NCSA software tools, please e-mail softdev@ncsa.uiuc.edu.
230-
230-The mail archive-server is no longer supported. Of course, if
230-  you can read this, you don't need it anyway.
230-
230-
230-Note to HyperFTP users: If you log in, and cannot list directories
230-  other than the top-level ones, enter a - as the first character of your
230-  password (e-mail address).
230-
230-If your ftp client has problems with receiving files from this server, send
230-  a - as the first character of your password (e-mail address).
230-
230-If you're ftp'ing from Delphi, please remember that the Delphi FTP client
230-  requires you to enclose case-sensitive directory and file names in double
230-  quote (") characters.
230-
230-You are user # 69 of an allowed 130 users.
230-
230-Please read the file README
230-  it was last modified on Tue Jan 3 18:54:35 1995 - 306 days ago
```

```
230-Please read the file README.FIRST
230- it was last modified on Thu Jan 12 17:53:58 1995 - 297 days ago
230 Guest login ok, access restrictions apply.
Remote system type is UNIX.
Using binary mode to transfer files.
```

3. At the `ftp>` prompt, type the following command (shown in boldface):

```
ftp> cd Mosaic/Unix/binaries
250 CWD command successful.
```

4. Type the `ls` command to view the file listing, as follows:

```
ftp> ls
200 PORT command successful.
150 Opening ASCII mode data connection for /bin/ls.
total 26
drwxr-xr-x   6 12873    wheel       2048 Oct 25 17:51 .
drwxr-xr-x   6 12873    wheel       2048 Dec 23 1994  ..
-rw-r--r--   1 12873    other        169 Oct 10 1994  .index
drwx------   2 101      10          2048 Jul  7 14:35 2.6
drwx------   2 18381    202         2048 Oct 26 11:14 2.7b
drwxr-xr-x   2 12873    wheel       2048 Aug 22 1994  app-defaults
drwxr-xr-x   7 15220    202         2048 Oct 25 17:50 old
226 Transfer complete.
```

Notice that there are two directories, named 2.6 and 2.7b. These names refer to the version numbers of Mosaic at this writing. Version 2.7b is a beta version. If you wanted to get version 2.6, you would type the following:

```
ftp> cd 2.6
250-Please read the file README-2.6
250- it was last modified on Fri Jul  7 14:31:14 1995 - 121 days ago
250-Please read the file README.solaris
250- it was last modified on Fri Jul  7 14:35:46 1995 - 121 days ago
250 CWD command successful.
```

5. View the directory listing with the `ls` command, as follows:

```
ftp> ls
200 PORT command successful.
150 Opening ASCII mode data connection for /bin/ls.
total 22596
drwx------   2 101      10          2048 Jul  7 14:35 .
drwxr-xr-x   6 12873    wheel       2048 Oct 25 17:51 ..
-rw-r--r--   1 101      10        936964 Jul  7 11:41 Mosaic-alpha-2.6.Z
-rw-r--r--   1 101      10       1111311 Jul  7 11:41 Mosaic-dec-2.6.Z
-rw-r--r--   1 101      10        853351 Jul  7 11:42 Mosaic-hp-2.6.Z
-rw-r--r--   1 101      10        797705 Jul  7 11:43 Mosaic-ibm-2.6.Z
-rw-r--r--   1 101      10        915718 Jul  7 11:44 Mosaic-indy-2.6.Z
-rw-r--r--   1 101      10        903973 Jul  7 11:59 Mosaic-linux-2.6.Z
-rw-r--r--   1 101      10        648431 Jul  7 11:44 Mosaic-sgi-2.6.Z
-rw-r--r--   1 101      10       1708074 Jul  7 11:45 Mosaic-solaris-23-2.6.Z
-rw-r--r--   1 101      10        809343 Jul  7 11:45 Mosaic-solaris-24-2.6.Z
-rw-r--r--   1 101      10       1427238 Jul  7 11:46 Mosaic-sun-2.6.Z
```

```
-rw-r--r--   1 101    10      1442713 Jul  7 11:47 Mosaic-sun-lresolv-2.6.Z
-rw-r--r--   1 101    10         1835 Jul  7 14:31 README-2.6
-rw-------   1 101    10          845 Jul  7 14:35 README.solaris
226 Transfer complete.
```

6. Set the file type to binary and download the Linux version of Mosaic with the following commands:

```
ftp> binary
200 Type set to I.
ftp> mget *linux*
mget Mosaic-linux-2.6.Z? y
```

7. When the file transfer is complete (which could take a while over a dial-up SLIP or PPP connection), type **bye** to quit the `ftp` program.

Next, you have to uncompress the `Mosaic-linux-2.6.Z` file with the following command:

`uncompress Mosaic-linux-2.6.Z`

Then you'll be left with the Mosaic 2.6 executable in the file named `Mosaic-linux-2.6`. Move this file to the `/usr/local/bin` directory under the name `mosaic`, as follows:

`mv Mosaic-linux-2.6 /usr/local/bin/mosaic`

Now you can run Mosaic by typing the **mosaic** command.

A quick look at NCSA Mosaic

Because Netscape Navigator is so popular, I plan to discuss it more extensively than Mosaic. Therefore, I'll describe Mosaic briefly and then move on to Netscape.

To run Mosaic, start X (with the startx command) and then type **mosaic** in an xterm window. After Mosaic starts, it displays the NCSA Mosaic Home Page from URL http://www.ncsa.uiuc.edu/SDG/Software/Mosaic/NCSAMosaicHome.html. Figure 20-4 shows the Mosaic browser displaying the IDG Books home page, http://www.idgbooks.com.

Mosaic is the original Web browser — the program that started all the current hoopla over the Internet. Before Mosaic, the Internet had the reputation of being hard to use. You had to know UNIX commands to use the Internet. Downloading an image or a document meant learning to use Internet applications such as `ftp`, which has its own command set. Then you had to unpack the files with the `tar` command (because files were often archived with the `tar` command) and find an appropriate viewer program to see the image or document. All these things changed when Mosaic came along in the spring of 1993.

Figure 20-4: IDG Books home page viewed in NCSA Mosaic.

With Mosaic, a single mouse click is all it takes to download and view a document with images. It was fortuitous that HTTP and HTML — the underpinnings of the World Wide Web — came together just as Mosaic 1.0 for the X Window System was developed and released to the Internet community in April 1993.

Mosaic development continues at NCSA, with versions available for Microsoft Windows as well as the Macintosh. At this writing, the current version of Mosaic is 2.6; 2.7 is in beta testing.

Mosaic is straightforward to use. The Mosaic window sports a Motif user interface, as shown in Figure 20-5.

Figure 20-5 also shows the major elements of the Mosaic interface. Like most Motif applications, Mosaic has a menu bar. The File pull-down menu includes an option to open a document specified by a URL.

The most important part of Mosaic's user interface is the document window, where Mosaic displays the Web page — the HTML document — with the embedded images and text. The hypertext links appear as underlined blue text.

Above the document window, Mosaic displays the title of the document and the URL — the address of the Web page. A globe appears in the top-right corner, below the menu bar. When Mosaic connects to a Web server, the globe spins to indicate ongoing network activity. You can interrupt the download by clicking this spinning globe.

Figure 20-5: Elements of the Mosaic window.

Below the document window, Mosaic displays a one-line status message. As it loads a Web page, Mosaic displays the size of each data item being downloaded. Each embedded image counts as a separate data item to be downloaded from the server.

A row of buttons in the button bar at the bottom of the Mosaic window provides quick access to commonly used menu items. After you browse a few Web pages, you can use the Back and Forward buttons to move around among those pages.

Take Netscape for a spin

Netscape is a successor to Mosaic in more ways than one. First, one of Mosaic's primary developers, Marc Andreessen, happens to be the force behind Netscape as well. Netscape improves on Mosaic in several ways, the most significant being the way that Netscape loads a Web page.

When a Web page includes embedded images, the browser has to download each image separately. Mosaic displays a Web page only after everything on that page has been downloaded. Netscape, on the other hand, begins displaying the page as soon as parts of it are available.

Netscape also finishes downloading a page faster, because it makes multiple connections with the Web server to download separate parts of the page in parallel. (This process puts more load on the Web server, but it's beneficial to the user.)

Start Netscape

To run Netscape, type **netscape** at the command line in an `xterm` window (you must start X before running Netscape). When Netscape starts, it automatically loads the Web page identified by http://home.netscape.com/.

If you compare this syntax with the URL syntax shown earlier in this chapter, you'll notice that this URL does not appear to have a filename. When a URL does not have a filename, the Web browser loads a default HTML file named `index.html`.

Typically, Web servers contain many Web pages that are organized in such a way that you can start at a main page and jump to the other pages. The main Web page on a Web server is known as the *home page*.

The URL `http://home.netscape.com/` represents the home page of Netscape Communications — the company that sells Netscape. Without a Web page, a Web browser cannot show anything. Netscape Communications provides a default Web page so that Netscape has something to show you when it first runs.

Netscape's user interface

Figure 20-6 shows the Netscape home page, as well as the main elements of the Netscape window.

If you compare the Netscape window shown in Figure 20-6 with the Mosaic window shown in Figure 20-5, you'll see many similarities. Like Mosaic, Netscape sports a Motif user interface. The Netscape window also has a title bar that shows the current document title, as well as a menu bar that contains all the standard menus (such as File and Edit).

As in the Mosaic window, the most important part of the Netscape window is the document window — the large area where Netscape displays the Web page with its text and images.

Immediately above the document window, you see three items that you can turn on or off from the Options menu:

- The *toolbar* gives you quick access to some common menu items. The Back and Forward buttons are for moving between Web pages that you've already seen; the Home button takes you to the Netscape home page; Reload forces the browser to download the current page again; Open allows you to open a new document specified by a URL; the Print button prints the current page; Find enables you to search the current document; and the Stop button allows you to stop loading a Web page.

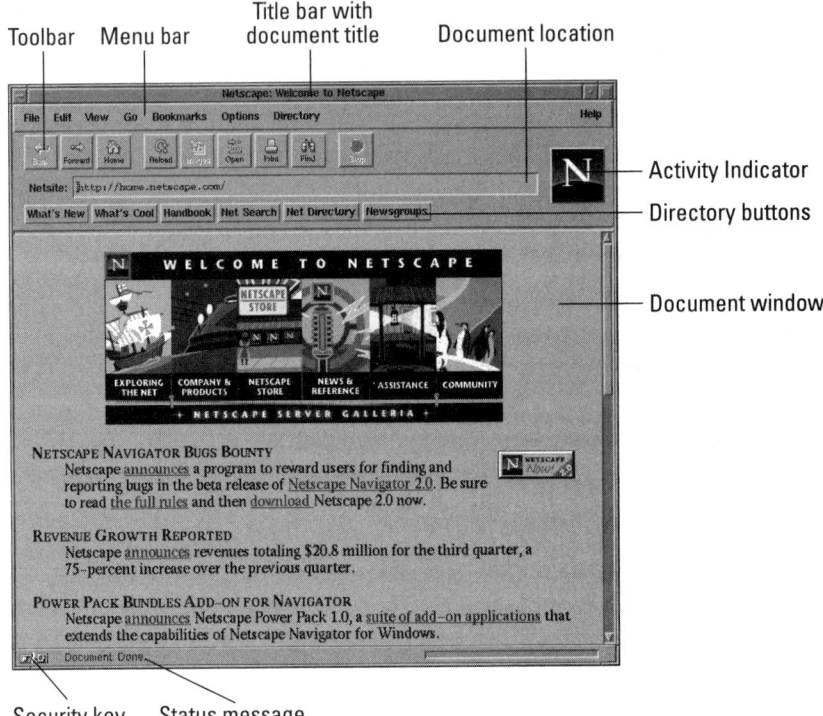

Figure 20-6: Elements of the Netscape window.

- The *document location* displays the location of the current Web page in the form of a URL.
- *Directory buttons* are shortcuts to items in the Directory menu. These buttons allow you to access specific Web pages quickly. The Net Search button, for example, brings up a Web page from which you can search for specific topics (by entering keywords in a text-entry area) whereas the Net Directory button takes you to the Internet Directory.

Secret

In the top-right corner of the Netscape window is the Activity Indicator button (marked with a large *N*). Netscape animates the Activity Indicator while it downloads a Web page. You can interrupt the download by clicking this button.

Secret

In the bottom-left corner of the Netscape window is a gold key — the *security key*. Netscape supports a secure version of the HTTP protocol. When Netscape connects to a Web server that supports secure HTTP, the security key appears whole. Otherwise, the security key is broken in two, signifying an insecure connection.

Netscape displays status messages in the area to the right of the security key. When Netscape is busy downloading a Web page, it displays the percentage of the document that it has downloaded.

Setting Up a Web Server

You probably already know how it feels to use the Web, but you may not know how to set up a Web server so that you, too, can provide information to the world through Web pages. To become an information provider on the Web, you have to run a Web server on your Linux PC on the Internet. You also have to prepare the Web pages — a task that may turn out to be more demanding than the server setup, as you'll see later in the "Building Web Pages" section of this chapter.

Note

Web servers provide information by using HTTP. Web servers are also known as HTTP daemons (because continuously running server processes are called *daemons* in UNIX) or HTTPD, for short. The Web server program usually is named `httpd`.

Among the freely available Web servers, the following two are the most popular:

- The CERN server is the original Web server. The server was developed at CERN, the European laboratory for particle physics, where the concepts of the Web and HTTP were invented. The CERN server is complex to set up but is very flexible.

Note

- The NCSA server is the most popular Web server on the Internet because it is the easiest free server to install and configure. Also, the NCSA server is reputed to be less demanding of system resources such as memory and processor time.

The following section describes how to download and set up the NCSA HTTPD software.

Download the NCSA HTTPD software

Secret

The NCSA HTTPD software is available from the `ftp` site `ftp.ncsa.uiuc.edu`. To download NCSA HTTPD, follow these steps:

1. Make sure that your Linux system is connected to the Internet.

2. Type the following commands, shown in boldface (my parenthetical comments are in italics):

```
ftp ftp.ncsa.uiuc.edu
Connected to ftp.ncsa.uiuc.edu.
220 larry FTP server (Version wu-2.4(25) Thu Aug 25 13:14:21 CDT 1994) ready.
Name (ftp.ncsa.uiuc.edu:naba): anonymous
331 Guest login ok, send your complete e-mail address as password.
Password:    (Type your e-mail address and then press Enter)
(lines deleted...)
```

3. At the `ftp>` prompt, type the following command, shown in boldface:

   ```
   ftp> cd Web/httpd/Unix/ncsa_httpd
   250-This directory contains NCSA's public domain HTTP server. The
   current
   250-release is 1.4. Comments to httpd@ncsa.uiuc.edu.
   250-
   250-All documentation is online in the World Wide Web under URL
   250-http://hoohoo.ncsa.uiuc.edu/
   250-
   250-
   250 CWD command successful.
   ```

4. Type the `ls` command to view the contents of this directory, as follows:

   ```
   ftp> ls
   200 PORT command successful.
   150 Opening ASCII mode data connection for /bin/ls.
   total 34
   drwxr-xr-x   7 12873    wheel        2048 Jun 22 19:29 .
   drwxr-xr-x   4 12873    wheel        2048 May 29 14:06 ..
   -rw-r--r--   1 12873    wheel          66 Jul  7 1994  .accountrc
   -rw-r--r--   1 12873    other         344 Aug 22 1994  .index
   -rw-r--r--   1 12873    wheel         212 May  3 1995  .message
   drwxr-xr-x   3 12873    wheel        2048 Jul  6 15:40 cgi
   drwxr-xr-x   2 12873    wheel        2048 May  2 1995 contrib
   lrwxr-xr-x   1 19038    wheel           9 May  2 1995 current -> httpd_1.4
   drwxr-xr-x   2 19019    202          2048 May  4 1995 documents
   -rw-r--r--   1 12873    wheel          61 Jul  7 1994 gsql.note
   drwxr-xr-x   2 19056    wsstaff      2048 Jun 22 19:10 httpd_1.4
   226 Transfer complete.
   ```

5. Change the directory to the current version, as follows:

   ```
   ftp> cd current
   250-Please read the file README
   250-  it was last modified on Thu Jun 22 19:28:09 1995 - 137 days ago
   250 CWD command successful.
   ```

6. Get a listing of that directory with the `ls` command, as follows:

   ```
   ftp> ls
   200 PORT command successful.
   150 Opening ASCII mode data connection for /bin/ls.
   total 10712
   drwxr-xr-x   2 19056    wsstaff      2048 Jun 22 19:10 .
   drwxr-xr-x   7 12873    wheel        2048 Jun 22 19:29 ..
   -rw-rw-r--   1 19056    wsstaff      3368 Jun 22 19:28 README
   -rwxr-xr-x   1 19056    wsstaff    113507 Jun 23 12:04
   httpd_1.4.2_aix3.2.5.Z
   -rw-r--r--   1 19056    wsstaff    377073 Jun 23 12:04
   httpd_1.4.2_aix3.2.5.tar.Z
   -rwxr-xr-x   1 19056    wsstaff     85261 Jun 23 12:04
   httpd_1.4.2_hpux9.0.5.Z
   -rw-r--r--   1 19056    wsstaff    304644 Jun 23 12:04
   httpd_1.4.2_hpux9.0.5.tar.Z
   ```

```
-rwxr-xr-x   1 19056    wsstaff    209641 Jun 23 12:04
httpd_1.4.2_irix4.0.5.Z
-rw-r--r--   1 19056    wsstaff    580755 Jun 23 12:04
httpd_1.4.2_irix4.0.5.tar.Z
-rwxr-xr-x   1 19056    wsstaff    108231 Jun 23 12:04
httpd_1.4.2_irix5.2.Z
-rw-r--r--   1 19056    wsstaff    333993 Jun 23 12:05
httpd_1.4.2_irix5.2.tar.Z
-rwxr-xr-x   1 19056    wsstaff     62597 Jun 23 12:05
httpd_1.4.2_linux.Z
-rw-r--r--   1 19056    wsstaff    694175 Jun 23 12:05
httpd_1.4.2_linux.tar.Z
-rwxr-xr-x   1 19056    wsstaff    133238 Jun 23 12:05
httpd_1.4.2_osf3.0.Z
-rw-r--r--   1 19056    wsstaff    379027 Jun 23 12:05
httpd_1.4.2_osf3.0.tar.Z
-rwxr-xr-x   1 19056    wsstaff     70743 Jun 23 12:05
httpd_1.4.2_solaris2.3.Z
-rw-r--r--   1 19056    wsstaff    303047 Jun 23 12:05
httpd_1.4.2_solaris2.3.tar.Z
-rwxr-xr-x   1 19056    wsstaff     70727 Jun 23 12:05
httpd_1.4.2_solaris2.4.Z
-rw-r--r--   1 19056    wsstaff    303213 Jun 23 12:05
httpd_1.4.2_solaris2.4.tar.Z
-rw-r--r--   1 19056    wsstaff    139070 Jun 23 12:05
httpd_1.4.2_source.tar.Z
-rwxr-xr-x   1 19056    wsstaff     72327 Jun 23 12:05
httpd_1.4.2_sunos4.1.3.Z
-rw-r--r--   1 19056    wsstaff    298136 Jun 23 12:05
httpd_1.4.2_sunos4.1.3.tar.Z
-rwxr-xr-x   1 19056    wsstaff    217343 Jun 23 12:05
httpd_1.4.2_ultrix4.0.Z
-rw-r--r--   1 19056    wsstaff    606639 Jun 23 12:05
httpd_1.4.2_ultrix4.0.tar.Z
226 Transfer complete.
```

7. Notice that two files have linux in their names. The smaller file is the NCSA HTTPD server binary; the httpd_1.4.2_linux.tar.Z file is larger because it contains the source code and other support files. You should download the .tar.Z file. Set the file type to binary and download the Linux version of the NCSA HTTPD with the following commands:

```
ftp> binary
200 Type set to I.
ftp> mget *linux.tar.Z
mget httpd_1.4.2_linux.tar.Z? y
```

8. After the file transfer is complete (which could take a few minutes over a dial-up SLIP or PPP connection), type **bye** to quit the ftp program.

After completing these steps, you have downloaded version 1.4.2 of NCSA HTTPD.

Unpack the NCSA HTTPD software

Secret

The `httpd_1.4.2_linux.tar.Z` file that you downloaded from NCSA's `ftp` server has to be decompressed and unpacked before you can use the HTTPD software. It's best to move this file to a directory where you plan to install the HTTPD software. The default installation directory is `/usr/local/etc/httpd`. Follow these steps to unpack the HTTPD software in its proper directory:

1. Assuming that you'll use the default installation directory for the HTTPD software, copy the downloaded file to the `/usr/local/etc` directory, as follows:

   ```
   mv httpd_1.4.2_linux.tar.Z /usr/local/etc
   ```

2. Change the directory to `/usr/local/etc` and decompress the file, as follows:

   ```
   cd /usr/local/etc
   uncompress httpd_1.4.2_linux.tar.Z
   ```

3. Use the `tar` command to extract the files from the archive in the following manner:

   ```
   tar xvf httpd_1.4.2_linux.tar
   httpd_1.4.2/
   httpd_1.4.2/Makefile
   httpd_1.4.2/README
   httpd_1.4.2/cgi-bin/
   httpd_1.4.2/cgi-bin/test-env
   httpd_1.4.2/cgi-bin/archie
   httpd_1.4.2/cgi-bin/calendar
   httpd_1.4.2/cgi-bin/date
   httpd_1.4.2/cgi-bin/finger
   httpd_1.4.2/cgi-bin/fortune
   httpd_1.4.2/cgi-bin/mail
   httpd_1.4.2/cgi-bin/nph-test-cgi
   httpd_1.4.2/cgi-bin/test-cgi
   httpd_1.4.2/cgi-bin/test-cgi.tcl
   httpd_1.4.2/cgi-bin/uptime
   httpd_1.4.2/cgi-bin/wais.pl
   httpd_1.4.2/cgi-bin/query
   httpd_1.4.2/cgi-bin/post-query
   httpd_1.4.2/cgi-bin/imagemap
   httpd_1.4.2/cgi-bin/jj
   httpd_1.4.2/cgi-bin/phf
   httpd_1.4.2/cgi-src/
   httpd_1.4.2/cgi-src/Makefile
   httpd_1.4.2/cgi-src/change-passwd.c
   httpd_1.4.2/cgi-src/imagemap.c
   httpd_1.4.2/cgi-src/jj.c
   httpd_1.4.2/cgi-src/phf.c
   httpd_1.4.2/cgi-src/post-query.c
   httpd_1.4.2/cgi-src/query.c
   httpd_1.4.2/cgi-src/util.c
   ```

```
httpd_1.4.2/conf/
httpd_1.4.2/conf/access.conf-dist
httpd_1.4.2/conf/httpd.conf-dist
httpd_1.4.2/conf/mime.types
httpd_1.4.2/conf/srm.conf-dist
httpd_1.4.2/icons/
httpd_1.4.2/icons/back.xbm
httpd_1.4.2/icons/ball.xbm
httpd_1.4.2/icons/binary.xbm
httpd_1.4.2/icons/blank.xbm
httpd_1.4.2/icons/ftp.xbm
httpd_1.4.2/icons/image.xbm
httpd_1.4.2/icons/index.xbm
httpd_1.4.2/icons/menu.xbm
httpd_1.4.2/icons/movie.xbm
httpd_1.4.2/icons/sound.xbm
httpd_1.4.2/icons/telnet.xbm
httpd_1.4.2/icons/text.xbm
httpd_1.4.2/icons/unknown.xbm
httpd_1.4.2/src/
httpd_1.4.2/src/Makefile
httpd_1.4.2/src/http_access.c
httpd_1.4.2/src/http_alias.c
httpd_1.4.2/src/http_auth.c
httpd_1.4.2/src/http_config.c
httpd_1.4.2/src/http_delete.c
httpd_1.4.2/src/http_dir.c
httpd_1.4.2/src/http_get.c
httpd_1.4.2/src/http_include.c
httpd_1.4.2/src/http_ipc.c
httpd_1.4.2/src/http_log.c
httpd_1.4.2/src/http_mime.c
httpd_1.4.2/src/http_post.c
httpd_1.4.2/src/http_put.c
httpd_1.4.2/src/http_request.c
httpd_1.4.2/src/oops
httpd_1.4.2/src/http_script.c
httpd_1.4.2/src/httpd.c
httpd_1.4.2/src/httpd.h
httpd_1.4.2/src/new.h
httpd_1.4.2/src/rfc931.c
httpd_1.4.2/src/util.c
httpd_1.4.2/support/
httpd_1.4.2/support/Makefile
httpd_1.4.2/support/change-passwd.readme
httpd_1.4.2/support/htpasswd.c
httpd_1.4.2/support/inc2shtml.c
httpd_1.4.2/support/unescape.c
httpd_1.4.2/support/htpasswd
httpd_1.4.2/support/unescape
httpd_1.4.2/support/inc2shtml
httpd_1.4.2/httpd
```

4. When `tar` unpacks the archive, it creates the `httpd_1.4.2` (which reflects the version of HTTPD) subdirectory in the `/usr/local/etc` directory. Rename that directory `httpd` with the `mv` command, as follows:

   `mv httpd_1.4.2 httpd`

Now you have the necessary files in the `/usr/local/etc/httpd` directory.

Configure the NCSA HTTPD software

After you install the NCSA HTTPD files in the `/usr/local/etc/httpd` directory, you have to prepare three configuration files in the `/usr/local/etc/httpd/conf` directory. In that directory, you'll find three files with the string `conf` in their names:

```
access.conf-dist
httpd.conf-dist
srm.conf-dist
```

These files are meant to be sample configuration files. Make copies of these files for use as the actual configuration files, as follows:

```
cp access.conf-dist access.conf
cp httpd.conf-dist httpd.conf
cp srm.conf-dist srm.conf
```

At this point, you have the following configuration files with the `.conf` extension:

- `access.conf` is the server access configuration file that controls who can access the Web server.
- `httpd.conf` is the basic HTTPD configuration file that controls how the HTTP daemon runs, where its files are, and what TCP/IP port the daemon uses.
- `srm.conf` is the server resource map file that tells the Web server (the HTTP daemon) how to serve the Web pages.

Each of these configuration files already contains most of the configuration items set up properly. You only need to fill in information that is specific to your system, such as the e-mail address of the *Webmaster* — the person who manages the Web server.

Edit `httpd.conf`

Start by editing `httpd.conf`, because this file is the basic HTTP daemon configuration file. In that file, make the following changes (use your favorite text editor to edit the file):

Secret

1. Find the line `ServerAdmin you@your.address`

2. Change `you@your.address` to the e-mail address of your system's Webmaster. (If you are the sole user of the system, provide your address here.)

Many more directives control the way that the Web server works. The following list summarizes the directives that you can use in the `httpd.conf` file. You can leave most of these directives in their default settings, but it's important to know about these directives if you are maintaining a Web server.

`ServerType` *type* — Specifies how the HTTP server is executed by Linux. The *type* can be `inetd` (to run the server through the `inetd` daemon) or `standalone` (to run the server as a stand-alone process). You should run the server stand-alone for better performance.

`Port` *num* — Specifies that the HTTP daemon should listen to port *num* (a number between 0 and 65,535) for requests from clients. The default port for HTTPD is 80. You should leave the port number at its default value, because clients assume the HHTP port to be 80. If your server does not use port 80, the URL for your server must specify the port number.

`User` *name [#id]* — Specifies the user name (or ID) used by the HTTP daemon when running in stand-alone mode. You can leave this directive at the default setting (`nobody`). If you specify a user ID, use a pound-sign (#) prefix for the numeric ID.

`Group` *name [#id]* — Specifies the group name (or ID) of the HTTP daemon when running in stand-alone mode.

`ServerAdmin` *webmaster@company.com* — Provides the server the e-mail address of the person who maintains the Web server. In case of errors, the server provides this address so that users can report errors.

`ServerRoot` *pathname* — Specifies the directory where you installed `httpd` (the directory where the `httpd` program resides). Most other files, including the Web pages, are expected to be in directories relative to the `ServerRoot`. The default `ServerRoot` is `/usr/local/etc/httpd`, but you can install HTTPD anywhere you want; all you need to do is set `ServerRoot` to that directory.

`ServerName` *www.company.com* — Sets the server's host name to *www.company.com* instead of its real host name. You cannot simply invent a name; the name must be a valid name from the Domain Name System (DNS) for your system.

`StartServers` *num* — Sets the number of child processes that start as soon as NCSA HTTPD runs. (The Linux version of NCSA HTTPD does not support this directive.)

`MaxServers` *num* — Sets the maximum number of children that `httpd` will launch to handle increased load. (The Linux version of NCSA HTTPD does not support this directive.)

`TimeOut` *numsec* — Sets the number of seconds that the server waits for a client to send a query after the client establishes connection. The default TimeOut is 1,200 seconds (20 minutes).

`ErrorLog` *filename* — Sets the file where `httpd` logs the errors that it encounters. The filename is taken to be relative to `ServerRoot`. The default `ErrorLog` is `logs/error_log`. For a `ServerRoot` of `/usr/local/etc/httpd`, the absolute location of the error log is `/usr/local/etc/httpd/logs/error_log`. Typical `ErrorLog` entries include events such as server restarts and any warning messages, such as the following:

```
[Sat Nov 11 17:07:54 1995] httpd: caught SIGHUP, restarting
This compile doesn't support StartServers on line 26 of /usr/
local/etc/httpd/conf/httpd.conf:
This compile doesn't support MaxServers on line 33 of /usr/local/
etc/httpd/conf/httpd.conf:
[Sat Nov 11 17:07:54 1995] httpd: successful restart
```

`TransferLog` *filename* — Sets the file where `httpd` records all client accesses (including failed accesses). The default `TransferLog` is `logs/access_log`. The following example shows how a typical access is recorded in the `TransferLog` file:

```
lnbsoft.com - - [10/Nov/1995:11:37:35 -0500] "GET /
HTTP/1.0" 200 660
lnbsoft.com - - [10/Nov/1995:11:37:36 -0500] "GET /
nbphotoi.gif HTTP/1.0" 200 9470
```

The first entry is for the text of the file; the second entry is for an embedded image. The last two items in a line shows the status code returned by the server, followed by the number of bytes sent by the server.

`AgentLog` *filename* — Sets the file where `httpd` records the name of the client software. The default `AgentLog` file is `logs/agent_log`. Following are some typical entries in the `AgentLog` file, showing records of accesses from various Netscape (which reports its name as Mozilla) and NCSA Mosaic browsers:

```
Mozilla/1.1N (Windows; I; 32bit)
Mozilla/1.12 (X11; I; Linux 1.2.13 i586)
NCSA_Mosaic/2.6 (X11;Linux 1.2.13 i586) libwww/2.12 modified
```

`RefererIgnore` *string* — Instructs `httpd` to ignore any `Referer` (the server that had a link to your page) whose `Referer` header contains the specified string. You should specify your own host name as the string, so that references between pages within the site are not recorded.

`PidFile` *filename* — Sets the file where `httpd` stores its process ID. The default `PidFile` is `logs/httpd.pid`. You can use this information to kill or restart the HTTP daemon. The following example shows how you would restart `httpd`:

```
kill -HUP 'cat /usr/local/etc/httpd/logs/httpd.pid'
```

This example assumes the default settings for `ServerRoot` and `PidFile`.

`AccessConfig` *filename* — Specifies the file that controls access to the server. The default `AccessConfig` file is `conf/access.conf`.

`ResourceConfig` *filename* — Specifies the resource configuration file that indicates the location of Web pages and the supported formats. The default `ResourceConfig` file is `conf/srm.conf`.

`TypesConfig` *filename* — Specifies the file that contains the mapping of file extensions to MIME data types. (MIME stands for *Multipurpose Internet Mail Extensions*, which defines a way to package attachments in a single message file.) The server reports these MIME types to clients. If you do not specify a `TypesConfig` directive, `httpd` assumes that the `TypesConfig` file is `conf/mime.types`. Following are a few lines from the default `mime.types` file:

```
(many lines deleted...)
audio/basic         au snd
audio/x-wav         wav
image/gif           gif
image/ief           ief
image/jpeg          jpeg jpg jpe
text/html           html htm
text/plain          txt
video/mpeg          mpeg mpg mpe
```

Each line shows the MIME type (such as `text/html`), followed by the file extensions for that type (`html` and `htm`).

`IdentityCheck off [on]` — Turns on or off the logging of the remote user name.

Edit `srm.conf`

The resource configuration file, `srm.conf` (the default filename), specifies the location of the Web pages, as well as how to specify the data types of various files. To get started, you can leave the directives at their default settings. These are the resource configuration directives for NCSA HTTPD version 1.4.2:

`DocumentRoot` *pathname* — Specifies the directory where the HTTP server finds the Web pages. The default `DocumentRoot` is `/usr/local/etc/httpd/htdocs`. If you place your HTML documents in another directory, set `DocumentRoot` to that directory.

`UserDir` *dirname* — Specifies the directory below a user's home directory where the HTTP server looks for the Web pages when a user name appears in the URL (in a URL such as `http://dcc05211.slip.digex.net/~naba/`, for example, which includes a user name with a tilde prefix). The default `UserDir` is `public_html`, which means that a user's Web pages will be in the `public_html` subdirectory of that user's home directory. If you do not want to allow users to have any Web pages, specify `DISABLED` as the directory name in the `UserDir` directive.

`DirectoryIndex` *filename* — Indicates the default file to be returned by the server when the client does not specify any document. The default `DirectoryIndex` is `index.html`. If `httpd` does not find this file, it returns an index (basically, a nice-looking listing of the files) of that directory.

`AccessFileName` *filename* — Specifies the name of the file that may appear in each directory that contains documents and that indicates who has permission to access the contents of that directory. The default `AccessFileName` is `.htaccess`. The syntax of this file is the same as that of the `access.conf` file, discussed in the following section.

`AddType` *type/subtype extension* — Associates a file extension with a MIME data type (of the form *type/subtype*, such as `text/plain` or `image/gif`). Thus, if you want to the server to treat files with the `.asc` extension as plain-text files, you would specify the following:

```
AddType text/plain asc
```

The default MIME types and extensions are listed in the `conf/mime.types` file.

`AddEncoding` *type extension* — Associates an encoding type with a file extension. If you want the server to mark files ending with `.gz` as encoded with the `x-gzip` encoding method (the standard name for the GZIP encoding), you would specify the following:

```
AddEncoding x-gzip gz
```

`DefaultType` *type/subtype* — Specifies the MIME type that the server should use if it cannot determine the type from the file extension. If you do not specify `DefaultType`, `httpd` assumes the MIME type to be `text/html`. In the default `srm.conf` file that you get from the companion CD-ROM, `DefaultType` is specified as `text/plain`.

`Redirect` *requested-file actual-URL* — Specifies that any requests for the *requested-file* be redirected to the *actual-URL*.

`Alias` *requested-dir actual-dir* — Specifies that the server use *actual-dir* to locate files in the *requested-dir* directory (in other words, *requested-dir* is an alias for *actual-dir*). If you want requests for `/images` directory to go to `/ftp/pub/images`, you would specify the following:

```
Alias /images /ftp/pub/images
```

`ScriptAlias` *requested-dir actual-dir* — Specifies the real name of the directory where scripts for the Common Gateway Interface (CGI) are located. (You learn about CGI in "Building Web Pages" later in this chapter.) The default `srm.conf` file contains the following directive:

```
ScriptAlias /cgi-bin/ /usr/local/etc/httpd/cgi-bin/
```

That directive means that when a Web browser requests a script such as `/cgi/bin/test-cgi`, the HTTP server runs the script `/usr/local/etc/httpd/cgi-bin/test-cgi`.

`FancyIndexing` *on [off]* — Enables or disables the display of fancy directory listings, with icons and file sizes.

`DefaultIcon` *iconfile* — Specifies the location of the default icon that the server should use for files that have no icon information. By default, `DefaultIcon` is `/icons/unknown.xbm`.

`ReadmeName` *filename* — Specifies the name of a README file whose contents are added to the end of an automatically generated directory listing. The default `ReadmeName` is README.

`HeaderName` *filename* — Specifies the name a header file whose contents are prepended to an automatically generated directory listing. The default `HeaderName` is HEADER.

`AddDescription "file description" filename` — Specifies that the *file description* string be displayed next to the specified *filename* in the directory listing. You can use a wildcard, such as `*.html`, as the *filename*.

`AddIcon` *iconfile extension1 extension2 ...* — Associates a icon with one or more file extensions. The following directive associates the icon file `/icons/movie.xbm` with the file extensions `.mpeg` and `.qt`:

`AddIcon /icons/movie.xbm .mpeg .qt`

`AddIconByType` *iconfile MIME-types* — Associates an icon with a group of file types specified as a wildcard form of MIME types (such as `text/*` or `image/*`). To associate an icon file of `/icons/text.xbm` with all `text` types, you would specify the following:

`AddIconByType (TXT,/icons/text.xbm) text/*`

This directive also tells the server to use TXT in place of the icon for clients that cannot accept images. (Browsers tell the server what types of data they can accept.)

`AddIconByEncoding` *iconfile encoding1 encoding2 ...* — Specifies an icon to be displayed for one or more encoding types (such as `x-compress` or `x-tar`).

`IndexIgnore` *filename1 filename2 ...* — Instructs the server to ignore the specified filenames (they typically have wildcards) when preparing a directory listings. To leave out README, HEADER, and all files with a leading period (.), you would specify the following:

`IndexIgnore */.??* */HEADER* */README*`

`IndexOptions` *option1 option2 ...* — Indicates the options that you want in the directory listing prepared by the server. Options can include one or more of the following:

- `FancyIndexing` turns on the fancy directory listing.
- `IconsAreLinks` makes the icons act like links.
- `ScanHTMLTitles` shows a description of HTML files.
- `SuppressLastModified` stops display of the last date of modification.
- `SuppressSize` stops display of the file size.
- `SuppressDescription` stops display of any file description.

`ErrorDocument` *errortype filename* — Specifies a file that the server should send when a error of a specific type occurs. If you do not have this directive, the server sends a built-in error message. The *errortype* can be one of the following:

- 302 - REDIRECT
- 400 - BAD_REQUEST
- 401 - AUTH_REQUIRED
- 403 - FORBIDDEN
- 404 - NOT_FOUND
- 500 - SERVER_ERROR
- 501 - NOT_IMPLEMENTED

Edit `access.conf`

The `access.conf` file allows you to control who can access different directories in the system. This file is the global access configuration file. In each directory, you can have another access configuration file with the name specified by the `AccessFileName` directive in the `srm.conf` file. (That per-directory access configuration file is named `.htaccess` by default.)

The sample `access.conf` file contains the following:

```
# access.conf: Global access configuration
# Online docs at http://hoohoo.ncsa.uiuc.edu/
# I suggest you consult them; this is important and confusing stuff.

# /usr/local/etc/httpd/ should be changed to whatever you set ServerRoot to.
<Directory /usr/local/etc/httpd/cgi-bin>
Options Indexes FollowSymLinks
</Directory>

# This should be changed to whatever you set DocumentRoot to.

<Directory /usr/local/etc/httpd/htdocs>

# This may also be "None", "All", or any combination of "Indexes",
# "Includes", or "FollowSymLinks"

Options Indexes FollowSymLinks

# This controls which options the .htaccess files in directories can
# override. Can also be "None", or any combination of "Options", "FileInfo",
# "AuthConfig", and "Limit"

AllowOverride All

# Controls who can get stuff from this server.
```

```
<Limit GET>
order allow,deny
allow from all
</Limit>

</Directory>

# You may place any other directories you wish to have access
# information for after this one.
```

As you may have noticed from the listing, the access configuration file has a different syntax than the server and resource configuration files. The layout and syntax of the access configuration file are similar to those of an HTML file. The file is organized in sections, with each section enclosed by opening and closing directives. There are two directives to define sections:

- Directory is used to group all the access control directives for a specified directory. A Directory section has the following format:

```
<Directory directory-name>
Other Directives
</Directory>
```

- Limit is used to specify which clients can access the contents of a directory. As the example access.conf file shows, one or more Limit sections appear inside a Directory section. A Limit section has the following format:

```
<Limit GET>
Other Directives (order, deny, allow, require)
</Limit>
```

The following example shows what the access control options for the cgi-bin directory look like:

```
<Directory /usr/local/etc/httpd/cgi-bin>
Options Indexes FollowSymLinks
</Directory>
```

The first line is the opening directive; the last line is the closing directive. In between, a single line lists the access control options that apply to the cgi-bin directory. In this case, there are two options:

- Indexes allows clients to request indexes (directory listings) for this directory.
- FollowSymLinks enables the server to follow symbolic links.

The following list describes some of the other access control directories. In particular, notice the AuthUserFile directive; you can have password-based access control for specific directories.

> Options *opt1 opt2* ... — Specifies the access control options for the directory section in which this directive appears. The options can be one or more of the following:
>
> - None disables all access control features.

- `All` turns on all features for the directory.
- `FollowSymLinks` enables the server to follow symbolic links.
- `SymLinksIfOwnerMatch` follows symbolic links only if the linked directory is owned by the same user as this directory.
- `ExecCGI` allows execution of CGI scripts in the directory.
- `Includes` allows server side include files in this directory.
- `Indexes` allows clients to request indexes (directory listings) for this directory.
- `IncludesNoExec` disables the exec feature.

`AllowOverride` *directive1 directive2* ... — Specifies which access control directives can be overridden on a per-directory basis. The directive list can have one or more of the following:

- `None` stops any directive from being overridden.
- `All` allows overriding of any directive on a per-directory basis.
- `Options` allows the use of the `Options` directive in the directory-level file.
- `FileInfo` allows the use of `AddType` and `AddEncoding` directives.
- `AuthConfig` allows the use of the `AuthName`, `AuthType`, `AuthUserFile`, and `AuthGroupFile` directives.
- `Limit` allows the use of `Limit` directives in a directory's access configuration file.

`AuthName` *name* — Specifies the authorization name for a directory.

`AuthType` *type* — Specifies the type of authorization to be used. The only supported authorization type is `Basic`.

`AuthUserFile` *filename* — Specifies the file where user names and passwords are stored for authorization. The following directive sets the authorization file to /usr/local/etc/httpd/conf/.htpasswd:

`AuthUserFile /usr/local/etc/httpd/conf/.htpasswd`

You have to create the authorization file with the `htpasswd` support program, located in the /usr/local/etc/httpd/support directory. To create the authorization file and add the password for a user named jdoe, you would specify the following:

```
/usr/local/etc/httpd/support/htpasswd -c /usr/local/etc/httpd/
conf\.htpasswd jdoe
Adding password for jdoe.
New password: (type the password)
Re-type new password: (type the same password again)
```

`AuthGroupFile` *filename* — Specifies the file to consult for a list of user groups for authentication.

Chapter 20: Running a World Wide Web Server on Linux

`order` *ord* — This directive appears only in a `Limit` section. The `order` *ord* directive specifies the order in which two other directives — `allow` and `deny` — are evaluated. The order can be one of the following:

- `deny,allow` evaluates the `deny` directive before `allow`.
- `allow,deny` evaluates the `allow` directive before `deny`.
- `mutual-failure` allows only those hosts that are in the `allow` list.

`deny from` *host1 host2...* — This directive, which appears only in a `Limit` section, specifies the hosts that are denied access.

`allow from` *host1 host2...* — This directive, which appears only in a `Limit` section, specifies the hosts that are allowed access. If you want all hosts in a specific domain to access the Web documents in a directory, you would specify the following:

```
<Limit GET>
order deny,allow
allow from .nws.noaa.gov
</Limit>
```

`require entity` *en1 en2...* — This directive, which appears only in a `Limit` section, specifies which users can access a directory. The `entity` can be one of the following:

- `user` allows only a list of named users.
- `group` allows only a list of named groups.
- `valid-user` allows all users listed in the `AuthUserFile` access to the directory (provided that they enter the correct password).

Create the documents directory

By default, all Web documents must be in the directory specified by the `DocumentRoot` directive in the resource configuration file (`srm.conf`). The default directory is `/usr/local/etc/httpd/htdocs`.

Secret

That directory does not exist, so you must create the directory; otherwise, `httpd` won't run. To create the directory, log in as `root` and type the following commands:

```
cd /usr/local/etc/httpd
mkdir htdocs
```

Create the error-logs directory

Secret

When `httpd` encounters errors it logs them in a file specified by the `ErrorLog` directive in the `httpd.conf` file. The default directory for the error log file is the `logs` subdirectory of the `ServerRootDirectory` — the directory where you installed the NCSA HTTPD software. For the default installation directory (`/usr/local/etc/httpd`), use the following commands to create the error-logs directory:

```
cd /usr/local/etc/httpd
mkdir logs
```

Start the Web server

After all these setup steps, you are ready to run the NCSA Web server, `httpd`. You can run `httpd` in two ways:

- *From `inetd`.* In this case, you have to specify the `httpd` program in the `/etc/inted.conf` file. Whenever a client attempts to connect to the HTTP port (80), the `inetd` daemon launches the `httpd` program.

- *Stand-alone.* In this case, you run the `httpd` program at system startup; it runs all the time as a daemon.

For best performance, you should run `httpd` in stand-alone mode because that way the server is always ready to respond to client requests.

To ensure that `httpd` runs whenever your system reboots, you should add a few lines to one of the scripts that the `init` process executes at startup. The `/etc/rc.d/rc.local` script is a good place to add these lines because that's where you are supposed to place any local initializations. Log in as `root`, and use your favorite text editor to add the following lines to the `/etc/rc.d/rc.local` file:

```
# Start the httpd
if [ -x /usr/local/etc/httpd/httpd ]; then
  echo -n " httpd"
  /usr/local/etc/httpd/httpd
else
  echo "NO httpd found!"
fi
```

These lines check for the existence of the Web server (`httpd`) and starts it, if it exists. Although you added these lines to the script, the script won't run until the system reboots. For now, start `httpd` by hand with the following command:

```
/usr/local/etc/httpd/httpd
```

If you don't see any error messages, the Web server should be running successfully.

Try the Web server

You need Web pages to use the Web server. After all, the Web server's job is to "serve" Web pages to its clients: the Web browsers. Even though you may not have any Web page yet, you can test the server manually to make sure that it's working. Follow these steps:

1. From a system on the Internet, type **telnet *your.system.domain* 80**, where *your.system.domain* is your Linux PCs fully-qualified domain name. (If you want to test the server without connecting to the Internet, use `localhost` as the system name.)

2. When you see the `Connected ...` message from `telnet`, type **HEAD / HTTP/ 1.0**. Then press Enter for an extra blank line.

These steps should generate a response from the Web server on your system. Following is what I got when I tried this procedure from a system on the Internet:

```
/users/naba 24 % telnet dcc05211.slip.digex.net 80
Trying...
Connected to dcc05211.slip.digex.net.
Escape character is '^]'.
HEAD / HTTP/1.0

HTTP/1.0 200 Document follows
Date: Tue, 07 Nov 1995 06:45:51 GMT
Server: NCSA/1.4.2
Content-type: text/html
Last-modified: Tue, 07 Nov 1995 06:43:58 GMT
Content-length: 660

Connection closed by foreign host.
/users/naba 25 %
```

As the listing shows, the server replies with information about the requested document and closes the connection after sending the reply.

More HTML resources

Because HTML works the same regardless of the oprating system, I'll refer you to some other sources of information on HTML. If you already have access to the Internet, the best way to learn more about HTML is to use the online resources. One of the best places to start is the following URL:

```
http://union.ncsa.uiuc.edu/HyperNews/get/www/html.html
```

What about Java?

If you keep up with Internet developments, you must have heard about Java — a new object-oriented programming language from Sun Microsystems for developing World Wide Web applications.

When you use a Java-enabled Web browser, clicking a link does more than simply download and display a "passive" document. With Java, the Web server can actually download a Java application (or *applet*) to your system and run it on your system. The process is sort of like an agent being sent to your system by the Web server. On your system, an interpreter executes the Java code. Because of the obvious worries of having a foreign application run on your system, Sun has designed many security features into Java.

Although Java is very new, several books about it are already on the market, and more are on their way. Due to the fluid nature of Java developments, however, your best bet is to look for the latest Java information on the Internet. A good place to start your search is http://java.sun.com/.

Following are a few other URLs that you can check for specific items:

- **HTML tutorial:** `http://www.ncsa.edu/demoweb/html-primer.html`
- **HTML language reference:** `http://union.ncsa.uiuc.edu/HyperNews/get/www/lang.html`
- **HTML forms (CGI):** `http://kuhttp.cc.ukans.edu/info/forms/forms-intro.html`
- **Official HTML information:** `http://www.w3.org/hypertext/WWW/MarkUp/MarkUp.html`

By now, far too many books have been written about all aspects of the Internet, including HTML authoring. For an easy guide to HTML, you should try *HTML For Dummies* (Ed Tittel and Steve James, IDG Books, 1995), or *Creating Cool Web Pages with HTML* (Dave Taylor, IDG Books, 1995).

Summary

The World Wide Web (WWW or the Web) has propelled the Internet into the mainstream because Web browsers make it easy for users to browse documents stored on various Internet hosts. Whether you run a small business or manage computer systems and networks for a company, chances are high that you have to set up and maintain a Web server. Because of its built-in networking support, a Linux PC makes an affordable World Wide Web server. This chapter describes how to set up and configure a Web server on a Linux PC. By reading this chapter, you learn the following things:

- The World Wide Web is possible because a standard format exists for documents and a standard protocol exists for transferring a document across the network. The document format is Hypertext Markup Language, or HTML. The standard document exchange protocol is Hypertext Transfer Protocol, or HTTP.

- The Web has a client-server architecture, with Web servers providing the HTML documents (often referred to as *Web pages*) to Web browser clients.

- To uniquely identify Web pages and other network resources, the Uniform Resource Locator (URL) syntax is used. A URL identifies the location of the document (machine name and directory), as well as the protocol to be used to transfer the document (such as `http` or `ftp`).

- Several well-known Web browsers are available. NCSA Mosaic (from the National Center for Supercomputing Applications at the University of Illinois in Urbana-Champaign) was the first popular Web browser. Currently, the most popular Web browser is Netscape Navigator (created by some of the developers of Mosaic).

- This chapter shows you how to download and set up both NCSA Mosaic and Netscape Navigator. Separate sections provide a tour of each browser. You should try a browser before tackling the task of setting up a Web server.

- Among Web servers, the two most popular are the CERN server and the NCSA HTTPD (HTTP Daemon) server.

- This chapter guides you through the steps of downloading the NCSA HTTPD software and getting it up and running on your Linux PC. Configuration files hold the key to setting up the NCSA HTTPD server.

- Although setting up the Web server takes some effort, that task is only a small part of publishing information on the World Wide Web. The more difficult part is preparing the content: the HTML documents.

- The last part of this chapter points to some sources of information on HTML.

Chapter 21
Running a Business with Linux

In This Chapter

- Understanding the role Linux can play in business
- Looking at tasks that are best suited for Linux
- Using a Linux PC as a LAN Manager server
- Printing from Linux on a LAN Manager printer
- Looking at business opportunities with Linux
- Using Linux in specific businesses

Because Linux is freely available, many people feel that Linux must not be good enough for a business. Some of the common reasons cited are the unsupported nature of Linux and the lack of business applications. These may be good reasons for some businesses to avoid Linux, but many small businesses can actually run entirely on Linux. By running a business, I mean taking care of all of your business chores such as keeping records and writing business correspondence.

Smaller technology companies with in-house UNIX expertise, for example, can manage to run the business with Linux. If you are a consultant providing a complete turnkey system for a point-of-sale application, you might be able to use Linux and keep the cost low enough to gain a competitive advantage. You may even consider providing the support necessary to assure your clients that they can count on the solution that you provide.

The situation is changing in other ways as well. Already, a company named Caldera, Inc. has started work on a commercial Linux distribution that includes a graphical desktop; productivity applications including WordPerfect for Linux; and the capability to access NetWare servers. Granted, all these features cost you some money, but the cost is still less than what you have to pay for a comparable package that does not use Linux.

Incidentally, Caldera, Inc. was started by Ray Noorda of Novell fame. Even though WordPerfect has been put up for sale by Novell, Caldera appears to be committed to supporting WordPerfect on Linux.

I won't describe the Caldera products in this chapter; you can find out more at the URL http://www.caldera.com. Instead, I'll focus on businesses that inherently have the types of technical personnel who can manage well with a "self-supported" operating system like Linux. In fact, many of the discussions in this chapter should give you ideas for new types of businesses — ones that build on the current popularity of the Internet and the World Wide Web.

This Chapter's Strategy

This chapter is not about a specific technical subject. After all, running a business has many facets, and in each area of business, there are many ways to do the job. Although this chapter focuses on areas that can benefit from the use of Linux, you still can use many different tools for each job. You, as the decision maker, have to decide what's right for your business.

To make this chapter's information more useful in your decision-making process, I'll use the following strategy:

- *Role of Linux in a business.* I'll briefly describe the types of business needs that Linux can address well and the ones for which Linux may not be the most cost-effective or appropriate solution.

- *Specific tasks for Linux.* I'll discuss several specific uses of Linux. You can think of these uses as being the menu from which you can pick and choose how you use Linux in your business.

- *Linux in specific businesses.* I'll home in on a few specific businesses in which Linux may work out well.

With the information presented this way, you should be able to decide how much of your business and exactly which parts you run with Linux.

Role of Linux in a Business

Many types of businesses exist, and within a specific business are many areas that can benefit from Linux PCs. If you are serious about using Linux in your business, think carefully about the areas in which you can best use Linux. Most businesses, for example, need productivity applications: word processors, spreadsheets, and the like. Linux is lacking in this area, even though applications such as the WingZ spreadsheet and WordPerfect for Linux have been announced. For these tasks, you may want to use PCs running Microsoft Windows 95 with commonly available PC productivity software.

On the other hand, when it comes to TCP/IP networking or UNIX software development, Linux provides all necessary software at no extra cost. Clearly, it makes sense to use Linux as a platform for networking, software development, or a Web server.

One attractive aspect of Linux is that it runs on the same PCs that you might use for Windows 95 or OS/2. In other words, you can standardize your business on low-cost and powerful PC hardware. Then choose Linux and other popular operating systems you'll need on your network (such as Windows 95, Windows NT, or OS/2) for the operating system. What you run on a specific PC depends on how that PC is used.

Linux is not for every kind of business; neither is it appropriate for all areas of a business. Think of Linux as being a tool for your business. Linux cannot be the one and only tool that your business needs. Just as a single tool does not work in all situations, Linux cannot solve all problems for a business. Even if you are a proponent of Linux, you should not try to make Linux the sole operating system for your entire business. Yes, you probably could do your business letters and memos in `troff`, but what's the point? For those tasks, you may as well go with the mass market and settle for WordPerfect or Microsoft Word for Windows.

Remember the phrase "the right tool for the right job." Select Linux for the jobs that it can do well.

What Linux offers

To decide what business needs Linux might fulfill in your business, you need to know exactly what Linux offers. When I talk about Linux, I mean a typical Linux software distribution, such as the one on this book's companion CD-ROM. Such a distribution includes much more than the basic operating system: utility programs; applications; entire add-on systems, such as the XFree86 X Window System; and compilers and interpreters for software development.

The Slackware 3.0 Linux distribution includes the following major components:

- Linux kernel 1.2.13, with built-in TCP/IP networking support and support for a wide variety of hardware, such as disk controllers, CD-ROM drives, Ethernet cards, and sound boards.

- Internet services such as SLIP/PPP networking, electronic mail (BSD `sendmail`, `deliver`, `elm`, `pine`), news (`tin`, `trn`, and `inn`), `telnet`, and `ftp`.

- Samba LAN Manager software for networking with PCs.

- XFree86 3.1.2 X Window System for graphical user interface and graphical applications.

- Executable and Linking Format (ELF) for binaries and shared libraries (important because ELF is the binary format used by Sun's Solaris and UNIX System V Release 4).

- Compilers and interpreters for many programming languages: GNU `gcc` 2.7.0 C and C++ compiler, GNU `g77-0.5.16` Fortran-77 compiler, BASIC, Perl 4 and Perl 5.001m (with ELF dynamic loading), Tcl 7.4 and Tk 4.0 scripting languages, Berkeley Yacc and GNU bison parser generators, `flex` 2.5.2 lexical analyzer generator, and GNU Common LISP 2.1.

- Intel Binary Compatibility Specification (iBCS) module, which allows binaries from several other operating systems to run on Linux. Currently, you can run binaries from the following systems on Linux: System V Release UNIX (such as Interactive, Unixware, and Dell UNIX), Any System V Release 3 UNIX system, SCO UNIX, Xenix V/386, and Xenix 286. Thus, you set up and use WordPerfect 6.0 for SCO on Linux.

- A plethora of applications and utilities, including the GNU Emacs editor, the `seyon` and `minicom` serial communication programs, and games.

- Text processing and typesetting software, such as TeX, LaTeX, and `groff`.

Tip

As you can see from this list, Linux clearly excels in two broad technology areas:

- TCP/IP networking and Internet services, including the World Wide Web service
- UNIX and X software development

These two areas have a common theme: the people who work in these areas tend to be computer-savvy. Thus, they are not worried about the apparent lack of technical support for Linux. In the next section, you'll see why I use the term *apparent* to describe the lack of a single source of technical support for Linux.

What Linux (apparently) lacks

I am not writing this section to complain about Linux's shortcomings. After all, you could pick any operating system or product (be it commercial or freeware), and find real or apparent shortcomings in each product. My goal is to point out the perceived shortcomings of Linux and explain how even those shortcomings can become business opportunities for someone like you — someone who has the technical knowledge necessary to install and configure Linux.

Lack of personal-productivity applications

When I mention the possibility of using Linux in a business, the immediate reaction that I get is that Linux does not have personal-productivity applications like the ones in Microsoft Office. (Microsoft Office is a collection of several applications: Microsoft Word, for word processing; Microsoft Excel, for spreadsheets; Microsoft PowerPoint, for presentation graphics; and Microsoft Access, for databases.)

This happens to be true — not that Linux does not have the technical foundation to support word processing or spreadsheet applications. It's just that no one has written a complete suite of applications for Linux. Although software packages for word processing and spreadsheet in Linux (such as WordPerfect and WingZ) are either planned or available, no popular suite of applications, like Microsoft Office in the Windows world, is available.

Note

I do not consider this situation to be a problem, however. If you follow the philosophy of selecting the right tool for the job, you should select the mainstream DOS or Windows applications for the word processing and spreadsheet tasks.

Lack of technical support

Another commonly cited shortcoming of Linux is that it requires someone with a reasonable level of computer knowledge to install and configure Linux. I argue that all UNIX operating systems require installation and maintenance by a knowledgeable person. In that respect, Linux is no different from the other UNIX systems.

The real complaint is that no single source of technical support for Linux is available. You cannot pick up the phone, dial a number, and talk to someone about any technical difficulties that you might have with Linux. Many businesses prefer the apparent stability and predictability of a commercial product that comes with technical support.

In reality, the technical support for a commercial product often means the privilege of being put on hold every time you call. Then, after you explain your problem, all you may get is a promise that someone will call you back. Nevertheless, many businesses turn away from Linux because it lacks technical support.

Secret

I consider this situation to be an apparent problem rather than a real one because the Linux newsgroups on the Internet typically have the answers to any questions that you might have. You can start by reading the Frequently Asked Questions (FAQ) for the Linux newsgroups. If your question has not yet been asked, you can simply post a news item, explaining your problem. Typically, you'll hear from someone within a day — probably the same amount of time that it takes for some of the commercial tech-support people to get back to you with an answer.

Tip

This business need for technical support can become the basis for your own business venture. You could be a consultant who provides technical support for Linux installation, setup, and configuration. It's up to you to decide what you want to offer through your business. You may want to sell preconfigured Linux workstations with several levels of technical support, for example.

Specific Tasks for Linux

Linux shines in many specific tasks that apply to various types of businesses. The next few sections briefly describe how you can use Linux for the following purposes:

- *Personal UNIX workstation.* If your organization uses UNIX workstations, and you cannot afford Sun or HP workstations for everyone, equip everyone with Linux PCs. They are affordable, and they make powerful UNIX machines.

- *Workgroup server.* Linux PCs can easily be configured for file and print sharing.
- *Internet host.* Linux itself originated in the Internet, and its internetworking capabilities make it an ideal Internet host. You can easily set up and use a Linux PC as a server on the Internet with mail, news, `ftp`, and `telnet` services.
- *World Wide Web server.* Download a freely available NCSA Web server onto a Linux PC connected to the Internet, and you could have a Web server up and running within an hour (especially if you follow the steps outlined in Chapter 20).
- *LAN Manager server/client.* With Samba (which comes on the companion CD-ROM), you can set up a Linux PC as a LAN Manager server. Samba makes it easy to use a Linux PC in a business that relies on LAN Manager for file and print sharing. Conversely, if you already have a LAN Manager server, you can make the Linux PC (with Samba) a client.
- *Developer's workstation.* A Linux PC makes an ideal workstation for UNIX and X developers. You can use your choice of languages, ranging from C and C++ to Tcl/Tk.

Workgroup server

A high-powered Pentium PC configured with Linux 1.2.13 (from this book's companion CD-ROM) makes a capable workgroup server. By *workgroup*, I mean a small LAN of perhaps a dozen or so PCs. If all the PCs run Linux, you can configure one Linux PC to be the file and print server, and have the other Linux PCs be the clients. The file sharing can be through Network File Sharing (NFS), which is built into Linux.

Secret

Sharing files through NFS is simple, involving two basic steps:

- On the server, export one or more directories by listing them in the `/etc/exports` file (`man exports` shows you the syntax).
- On each client PC, mount the directories exported by the server. Use the `mount` command to do this.

Cross Reference

You can enable print sharing by configuring a remote printer on each client Linux PC and setting up the physical printer as a local printer on the server. Chapter 14 describes how to set up remote and local printers in Linux.

Following is the hardware configuration of a typical Linux PC workgroup server:

- 120-MHz Pentium processor with 256K cache
- 16MB RAM
- 2GB hard disk
- PCI Video card and 17-inch monitor

Chapter 21: Running a Business with Linux   **637**

- IDE CD-ROM drive and 3.5-inch disk drive
- Ethernet card (such as 3Com 3C509)
- PCI and ISA slots
- One parallel port, two serial ports, keyboard, and mouse
- Uninterruptible Power Supply (UPS)

Tip

The UPS is important because all PCs on the LAN rely on the server.

If your LAN includes PCs running Windows for Workgroups, for example, you have to configure the Linux PC as a LAN Manager server. Later, the "LAN Manager Server" section of this chapter briefly mentions what software you should use to configure a Linux PC to work with LAN Manager.

Tip

Instead of simply using a Linux workgroup server for your business, of course, you could start a business that sells preconfigured Linux "workstations." The basic idea is to configure the Linux PC with appropriate hardware and software (Linux operating system, plus XFree86 and any necessary networking software) and to sell it bundled with on-site service. I have seen advertised prices in the $5,000 to $6,000 range for such Linux workstations.

Because Linux is freely available, this idea of selling a ready-to-run Linux workstation is a common one; therefore, you can expect quite a bit of competition in this area. You may be able to build up the business in your own area, however because you'll have the advantage of being able to provide in-person service. Of course, you can also provide support to businesses or individuals who run Linux on PCs that were purchased elsewhere.

Internet host

Cross Reference

Chapter 19 describes how you can configure a Linux PC as a host on the Internet. With an appropriate network connection to an Internet Service Provider, such a Linux PC can give your business an Internet presence.

An Internet host performs a collection of tasks. At minimum, those tasks include the following:

- *Electronic mail*, so that users can send and receive messages
- *News,* so that users can read and participate in discussions in various newsgroups
- *World Wide Web server*, to provide Web pages to other users on the Internet
- *Web browser,* to allow users to read Web pages from other sites
- *Anonymous* ftp, so that other users can download information that you provide (software fixes and technical information about your products, for example)

The Linux distribution on this book's CD-ROM comes with all the software necessary to set up these Internet services. For the most part, you have to do only minimal configuration to get everything going.

Secret

The primary reason for selecting Linux as an Internet host is the price/performance advantage that Linux holds over other UNIX systems. Linux runs on commodity PCs — a market in which the competition is intense and powerful Pentium PCs cost much less than comparable UNIX workstations. Install Linux from a distribution such as the one on this book's CD-ROM, and the Pentium PC is transformed into a powerful UNIX workstation that is comparable to ones from vendors such as Sun, HP, and IBM. My experience is that a Linux PC has more built-in capabilities than a commercial UNIX workstation, on which many features are options available at extra cost.

The bottom line is that a fully configured Linux PC costs much less than a similarly configured commercial UNIX workstation, yet the Linux PC offers performance comparable to that of other UNIX workstations. That's why a Linux PC is attractive as an Internet host.

In addition to the price/performance advantage, a Linux PC can act as a *firewall* — a system that isolates two networks, allowing only selected types of network data packets to pass between the two networks. When you connect a local-area network (LAN) to the Internet, you can use a firewall to isolate the LAN from the Internet at large.

World Wide Web server

Cross Reference

A Linux PC with an Internet connection serves as an ideal Web server for your business. Chapter 20 gives you detailed information on how to set up the Web server. Essentially, the task is as simple as downloading a file with `ftp`, unpacking it, and setting up a few configuration files. (The tougher job is developing the Web pages — the content for the World Wide Web.)

Many business already have a Web presence. For some businesses, the Web has been a profitable venture because of the online sales that it generates. An online flower shop, for example, reportedly is doing very well. For other businesses, sales have not yet materialized. Many companies are using the Web to distribute technical information (such as bug fixes, patches, and documentation) to their customers.

Tip

The consensus is that the Web certainly is a good tool for marketing and customer service, even though its potential for online commerce (the actual act of buying a product, for example) remains unrealized. The basic problem is in how the customer pays for the services or products. Some new businesses such as FIRST VIRTUAL (http://www.fv.com/) are attempting to create a secure Internet payment system.

Using a Web server in a private LAN

Secret

Many people do not realize that you can use the Web server inside a private LAN. Whenever I mention using the World Wide Web in a business, the immediate reaction is that it's too risky because the business LAN has to be connected to the Internet. Then I explain that there is no need to connect to the Internet to use popular network services such as the Web. It's possible (and useful) to set up a Web server and access it from browsers from inside a private LAN. I have five systems (a mix of PCs, a Macintosh, and an aging Sun workstation) on a LAN, and I use a Web server to share various information among the systems.

In a business, you might share documents — technical documents, status reports, meeting notes, and anything else — through a Web server, assuming that you have a TCP/IP network and Web browsers installed on all systems in the network.

Set up a Web server on a Linux PC that serves as your workgroup server, and place the documents on that server. You'll have to convert formatted documents to HTML format; many popular word processing programs, including WordPerfect and Microsoft Word for Windows, allow you to save documents in HTML format. From now on, users will be able to access the documents from their desktops through a Web browser.

Tip

Following are some ideas for using a Web server within a private LAN:

- Provide an online phone directory that employees can search through a form on a Web page.
- Distribute announcements on upcoming meetings and other events.
- Implement an electronic suggestion box, enabling employees to submit suggestions through a form on a Web page.
- Maintain a list of action items for various projects. Provide a form through which everyone can track the disposition of assigned work.
- Make important technical papers available through the Web server.

Web-server configuration

Linux makes efficient use of hardware, so you can implement a Linux-based Web server on affordable hardware. The following minimal hardware configuration works out well for a Web server:

- 486 DX2/66 or 75-MHz Pentium processor
- 16MB of RAM
- 500MB hard disk
- Ethernet card (for example, 3Com Etherlink III 3C509)

If you want dial-up connectivity to the Internet through an Internet Service Provider, you also need a 28,800-bps V.34 modem. If you are using the Web server in a self-contained local-area network, you don't need the modem.

Providing Web service

If you are an Internet Service Provider, you might use Linux PCs to provide Web servers to customers. Following are several possible Web services:

- *Web server at customer site.* Provide the customer a Linux PC and a dial-up PPP connection. Configure the Linux PC with a Web server. Also offer to prepare the Web pages for the customer. In this case, the limited bandwidth of the dial-up connection to the customer's site may be a bottleneck that limits the number and frequency of accesses that the Web server can support.

- *Dedicated Web server at ISP site.* Offer the customer a dedicated Linux PC with high-speed connection to the Internet located at your site. (I am assuming that, as an ISP, you have a high-bandwidth connection to the Internet.) This scenario should provide much better performance because the network connection can sustain many Web accesses simultaneously. The drawback of this scenario is that you have to charge the customer for a complete Linux PC; you also have to charge for the high-bandwidth Internet access because you are offering a dedicated system to the customer. Although high-priced, this service may appeal to large businesses that want a Web presence without the hassles of maintaining an Internet connection.

- *Individual Web pages.* Provide individual Web pages on a shared Linux PC that runs the Web server and that has the high-bandwidth Internet connection. In this case, you can spread the cost of the Linux PC and the Internet connection over several customers, so this service may be appropriate for individuals or small businesses that want a Web presence on the Internet without spending too much money.

LAN Manager server

If your business relies on LAN Manager for file and print sharing, you probably use Windows for Workgroups, Windows NT, or OS/2 in your servers and clients. You can move to a Linux PC as your server without losing the LAN Manager file and printer sharing because a Linux PC can be set up as a LAN Manager server. This book's companion CD-ROM includes the Samba software package, which performs that task.

Tip

After you install and configure Samba on your Linux PC, client PCs (running Windows for Workgroups, Windows 95, Windows NT, or OS/2) can access disks and printers on the Linux PC by using the Server Message Block (SMB) protocol, which is the underlying protocol in LAN Manager.

Tip

With the Samba package, you also can make your Linux PC a LAN Manager client, which means that the Linux PC can access disks and printers managed by a LAN Manager server. For example, I have my printer physically connected to a 486 PC running Windows 95, and other PCs use that printer through LAN Manager print sharing. I use Linux, however, on a Pentium PC that does not have its own printer. To print from the Linux PC, I use the Samba client to access the printer on the 486 PC that runs Windows 95.

The Samba software package has the following major components:

- `smbd` — the SMB server, which accepts connections from LAN Manager clients and provides file and print sharing services.
- `nmbd` — the NetBIOS name server, which clients use to look up servers. (NetBIOS stands for Network Basic Input/Output System — an interface that applications use to communicate with network transports such as TCP/IP.)
- `smbclient` — the LAN Manager client, which runs on Linux and allows Linux to access the files and printer on any LAN Manager server.
- `smb.conf` — the Samba configuration file used by the SMB server.
- `testparm` — a program that makes sure the Samba configuration file is correct.

Because I have not covered Samba elsewhere, the following sections describe how to install Samba from the companion CD-ROM and how to set up a printer on the Linux PC to print through LAN Manager.

Installing Samba

The latest distribution of Samba is on this book's companion CD-ROM. To install the software, follow these steps:

1. Log in as `root` because you have to copy files to various directories to which ordinary users do not have write access.

2. Make sure that the companion CD-ROM is in the drive and mounted. If not, use the `umount /dev/cdrom` command to dismount the current CD-ROM, replace it with the companion CD-ROM, and then mount it with the `mount -r /dev/cdrom /cdrom` command.

3. Change the directory to the root directory (`/`) and then use the `tar` command to unpack the Samba software. Following is an example of how the unpacking works for version 1.9.13 of Samba from the CD-ROM:

```
cd /
tar -zxvf /cdrom/contrib/samba*.tgz
./
 etc/
 etc/smb.conf.sampl
 usr/
```

```
usr/sbin/
usr/sbin/smbd
usr/sbin/smbclient
usr/sbin/nmbd
usr/sbin/testparm
usr/sbin/testprns
usr/sbin/smbrun
usr/sbin/smbstatus
usr/man/
usr/man/preformat/
usr/man/preformat/cat1/
usr/man/preformat/cat1/smbstatus.1.gz
usr/man/preformat/cat1/smbclient.1.gz
usr/man/preformat/cat1/smbrun.1.gz
usr/man/preformat/cat1/testparm.1.gz
usr/man/preformat/cat1/testprns.1.gz
usr/man/preformat/cat5/
usr/man/preformat/cat5/smb.conf.5.gz
usr/man/preformat/cat7/
usr/man/preformat/cat7/samba.7.gz
usr/man/preformat/cat8/
usr/man/preformat/cat8/smbd.8.gz
usr/man/preformat/cat8/nmbd.8.gz
usr/doc/
usr/doc/samba-1.9.13/
usr/doc/samba-1.9.13/BROWSING.txt
usr/doc/samba-1.9.13/COPYING
usr/doc/samba-1.9.13/HINTS.txt
usr/doc/samba-1.9.13/INSTALL.txt
usr/doc/samba-1.9.13/MIRRORS
usr/doc/samba-1.9.13/OS2.txt
usr/doc/samba-1.9.13/PROJECTS
usr/doc/samba-1.9.13/README
usr/doc/samba-1.9.13/SMBGuide.txt
usr/doc/samba-1.9.13/SPEED.txt
usr/doc/samba-1.9.13/THANKS
usr/doc/samba-1.9.13/WARP.txt
usr/doc/samba-1.9.13/WINNT.txt
usr/doc/samba-1.9.13/announce
usr/doc/samba-1.9.13/change-log
usr/doc/samba-1.9.13/history
usr/doc/samba-1.9.13/samba.faq
usr/doc/samba-1.9.13/smb.conf.sampl
usr/doc/samba-1.9.13/smbprint.sysv
```

This step completes the unpacking of the Samba software. The unpacking process puts various parts of the software in appropriate directories. Now all that you have to do to use Samba is configure it.

Configuring Samba

To set up the LAN Manager file and print sharing services, you have to provide a configuration file named /etc/smb.conf. The configuration file looks like a

Microsoft Windows 3.1 INI file, in case you are familiar with those files. Just to refresh your memory, the following example shows what part of a Windows 3.1 WIN.INI file looks like:

```
[windows]
; This is the "windows" section
; Comment lines start with a semicolon
NullPort=None
load=
run=
device=HP LaserJet 4/4M PostScript,PSCRIPT,LPT1:

[Desktop]
; This is the "Desktop" section
Wallpaper=(None)
TileWallpaper=0
WallpaperStyle=0
Pattern=(None)
Many lines deleted...
```

Secret

Like the Windows INI files, the /etc/smb.conf file consists of sections, with a list of parameters in each section. Each section of the smb.conf file begins with the name of the section in brackets. The section continues until the next section begins or the file ends.

Each line in a section specifies the value of a parameter, with the following syntax:

name = value

As in Windows INI files, comment lines begin with a semicolon (;). Following are a few typical sections of the Samba configuration file:

```
[homes]
; This section shares the home directory of each user
 comment = Home Directories
 browseable = no
read only = no
 create mode = 0750

[printers]
; This section specifies sharing of the printers
 comment = All Printers
 path = /usr/spool/lp1
 browseable = no
 printable = yes
 public = no
 writable = no
 create mode = 0700
Lines deleted...
```

Notice the similarity of these entries with those in Windows INI files.

Secret

The Samba software comes with a sample configuration file that you can edit to get started. To prepare the configuration file, follow these steps:

1. Log in as `root`.

2. Create an initial configuration file by copying the sample configuration file with the following command:

   ```
   cp /etc/smb.conf.sampl /etc/smb.conf
   ```

3. Use your favorite text editor to edit `/etc/smb.conf`.

4. In the `global` section, change the `guest account` line and the `workgroup` line, as follows:

   ```
   workgroup = LNB SOFTWARE ; set this to your workgroup's name
   guest account = ftp
   ```

5. Uncomment the lines in one of the `public` sections to provide access to a shared directory on the Linux PC, as follows:

   ```
   [public]
   path = /home/public
   public = yes
   only guest = yes
   writable = yes
   printable = no
   ```

This procedure should create a working `smb.conf` file.

Testing the Samba configuration file

To ensure that the Samba configuration file is correct, run the `testparm` program that comes with the Samba software. Following is the result of running `testparm` on my configuration file:

```
/usr/sbin/testparm
Load smb config files from /etc/smb.conf
Processing configuration file "/etc/smb.conf"
Processing section "[global]"
Processing section "[homes]"
Processing section "[printers]"
Processing section "[public]"
Loaded services file OK.
Press enter to see a dump of your service definitions (Press Enter)
(Long list of parameters and services deleted...)
```

If `testparm` reports syntax errors in the `smb.conf` file, you should edit the file to fix the problem. For detailed information about the contents of the `smb.conf` file, consult its online help by typing **man smb.conf**.

Test with smbclient

Secret

You should use the smbclient program to ensure that the LAN Manager server is working. One quick way to check is to use the -L option to view the list of services. Following is what I get when I run smbclient on my Linux PC:

```
/usr/sbin/smbclient -L lnbsoft
Server time is Fri Nov 10 11:54:24 1995
Timezone is UTC-5.0

Server=[lnbsoft] User=[naba] Workgroup=[LNB SOFTWARE] Domain=[LNB SOFTWARE]

    Sharename    Type      Comment
    ---------    ----      -------
    public       Disk
    smbpr        Printer   Prints on a LAN Manager printer
    sample       Printer   A sample printer that prints to a file
    hpj          Printer
    IPC$         IPC       IPC Service (Samba 1.9.13)
    naba         Disk      Home Directories

This machine does not have a browse list
```

The server name comes from the name associated with the IP address of my Linux PC's Ethernet interface. That name appears in the /etc/hosts file.

Secret

If you have other LAN Manager servers around, you can look at their services with the smbclient program. Following is what I get when I view the services on my 486 PC running Windows 95:

```
/usr/sbin/smbclient -L lnb486
Server time is Thu Nov 9 23:38:14 1995
Timezone is UTC-5.0

Server=[LNB486] User=[] Workgroup=[LNB SOFTWARE] Domain=[LNB SOFT-
WARE]

    Sharename    Type      Comment
    ---------    ----      -------
    F            Disk
    A            Disk
    D$           Disk
    E$           Disk
    LNB486_C     Disk
    PRINTER$     Disk
    HPLJ4M       Printer   Hp Laserjet 4M on Dell 486
    IPC$         IPC       Remote Inter Process Communication

This machine has a browse list:

    Server    Comment
    ------    -------
    LNB486    Naba Barkakati
```

Secret

You can do much more than simply look at resources with the `smbclient` program; you also can use `smbclient` to access a disk on a LAN Manager server, as well as send a file to a LAN Manager printer. The `smbclient` program is somewhat like `ftp` — you connect to a LAN Manager server and then use commands to get or put files and to send files to the printer.

The following example shows how I used `smbclient` to access a disk on my Windows 95 PC and view its directory:

```
/usr/sbin/smbclient \\\\lnb486\\f username password
Server time is Fri Nov 10 14:45:44 1995
Timezone is UTC-5.0
smb: \> dir
  SSTFQF.T           D      0        Mon Jan 16 10:12:42 1995
  WINDOWS.000        D      0        Fri Nov 25 18:09:14 1994
  MSVCRT20.DLL       A      243200   Fri Oct 28 12:00:00 1994
  WINDOWS.BAK        A      14103    Sat Mar 18 21:08:12 1995
  RECYCLED           DHS    0        Sat Nov 26 22:51:00 1994
  EXCHANGE           D      0        Sun Dec  4 20:54:02 1994
  PROGRA~1           DR     0        Sat Mar 18 16:44:38 1995

    51141 blocks of size 512. 9702 blocks available
smb: \> quit
```

To see a list of `smbclient` commands, type **help** at the prompt. Table 21-1 is a brief summary of `smbclient` commands.

Table 21-1	Some `smbclient` commands
Command	**Description**
!	Executes a shell command (remember that you run `smbclient` on Linux)
? cmd	Displays a list of commands or help on a specific command
cancel id	Cancels a print job identified by its ID
cd dir	Changes the remote directory
del file	Deletes the specified file
dir file	Displays the directory listing
exit	Logs off the LAN Manager server
get rfile lfile	Copies a remote file (rfile) to a local file (lfile)
help cmd	Provides help on a command (or displays a list of commands)
lcd newdir	Changes the local directory (on the Linux PC)
lowercase	Toggles automatic lowercase conversion of filenames when executing the get command

Command	Description
ls *files*	Lists files on the server
mask *name*	Applies a mask (such as *.c) to all file operations
md *dirname*	Makes a directory on the server
mget *name*	Gets all files with matching names (such as *.doc)
mkdir *dirname*	Makes a directory
mput *name*	Copies files from the Linux PC to the server
newer *file*	Gets only the files that are newer than the specified file
print *name*	Prints the named file
printmode *mode*	Sets the print mode (the mode must be text or graphics)
prompt	Toggles prompt mode off (similar to the command in ftp)
put *lfile rfile*	Copies a local file (*lfile*) to a remote file (*rfile*)
queue	Displays the print queue
quit	Logs off the LAN Manager server
rd *dir*	Deletes the specified directory on the server
recurse	Toggles directory recursion during file get and put operations
rm *name*	Deletes all files with the specified name
rmdir *name*	Deletes the specified directory
translate	Toggles text translation (converts a line feed to a carriage return–line-feed pair)

LAN Manager client

If you bring a Linux PC into an existing LAN Manager environment, you may have to use the Linux PC as a LAN Manager client because a server may already exist. As the preceding sections explain, the Samba software package includes the smbclient program, which allows your Linux PC to be a client in a LAN Manager network.

Cross Reference

In this section, I show you how to set up a printer on your Linux PC so that print jobs are sent to a specified LAN Manager server by means of the smbclient program. Chapter 14 describes how the printing system works in Linux. If you have questions about printing while reading this section, please consult that chapter.

Two steps to set up the printer

The basic idea is to define a new printer on your Linux PC so that when you print on that printer with the `lpr` command, the output actually appears on a specified network printer (managed by a LAN Manager server). This process involves two steps:

1. Add an entry for the printer to the `/etc/printcap` file, and specify an *input filter* (a script that gets to process the file that is being printed).

2. Write the script that runs `smbclient` and prints the file on a designated LAN Manager server.

Add the `printcap` entry

There are two key items to notice when you prepare the `printcap` entry that prints on a LAN Manager printer:

- Specify `/dev/null` as the printer device name because the actual printing occurs on a network printer.

- Specify an input filter that copies the input data to a file and then uses `smbclient` to send that file to the printer on a selected LAN Manager server.

Secret

Following is the `printcap` entry (in the `/etc/printcap` file) I used on my Linux PC to specify this printer:

```
lp|smbpr|Prints on a LAN Manager printer:\
:sd=/usr/spool/lp1:\
:lp=/dev/null:\
:if=/usr/spool/lp1/smbprint.tcl:\
:lf=/usr/spool/lp1/smbprint.log:\
:mx#0:\
:sh:\
:sf:
```

For error logging, I created the `/usr/spool/lp1/smbprint.log` file with the following commands (while I was logged in as `root`):

```
cd /usr/spool/lp1
touch smbprint.log
chgrp lp smbprint.log
chmod ug=rw,o=r smbprint.log
```

Write a script to print with `smbclient`

Next write the input filter — `/usr/spool/lp1/smbprint.tcl`, which performs the actual printing. As the extension suggests, I used Tcl to write the input filter. You could write the script in Perl or bash.

Secret

In the `smbprint.tcl` script, I decided to make a copy of the print job in a temporary file and then run `smbclient` to print that file. Following is the complete `/usr/spool/lp1/smbprint.tcl` script:

```
#!/usr/bin/tcl
#
# Tcl script to print on a LAN manager printer using smbclient.
# Place in printer's spool directory and make it executable
# by world.

# Open the file /tmp/smbprint.out
set outfile [open /tmp/smbprint.out w]

# Read from stdin and write to outfile

while { [gets stdin line] != -1} {
 puts $outfile $line
}

close $outfile

# Now prepare a script to run smbclient and print the file
set server "lnb486"
set printer "hplj4m"
set password ""

set outfile [open /tmp/printit w]
puts $outfile "#\!/bin/sh"
puts $outfile "echo print /tmp/smbprint.out | /usr/sbin/smbclient
\\\\\\\\$server\\\\$printer $password -N -P"
close $outfile

# Make the script executable
exec chmod +x /tmp/printit

# Now execute the script
exec /tmp/printit
# Delete the script
exec rm /tmp/printit
```

I wrote the script in a simple-minded manner: copy the print job to a temporary file, create a script that runs `smbclient` to print that file, and then run that script. I have been using this printer setup to print directly from Linux programs (such as Netscape) on that network printer.

Linux in Specific Businesses

In previous sections, I described several specific tasks for which Linux is an appropriate choice. The next few sections focus on specific businesses for which Linux makes the most sense. When I describe the use of Linux in a business, I'll mention which tasks you might consider performing with Linux.

Internet Service Provider

Cross Reference

The Internet Service Provider (ISP) is a relatively new type of business that has emerged as more and more individuals and businesses want to connect to the Internet. Many ISPs began by offering dial-up modem accounts to individual users in the early 1990s. Then, as the Internet became more popular, ISPs switched to offering SLIP and PPP over ISDN (Integrated Services Digital Network — an offering of the phone companies), and other high-speed connections that offer full TCP/IP networking. (Consult Chapter 18 for more information on SLIP and PPP.)

Secret

Nowadays, most ISPs maintain one or more T1 lines to larger telecommunications companies, such as Sprint and MCI. (A T1 link is capable of transmitting 1.54 million bits of data per second — more than 50 times faster than the data-transfer rate of 28,800-bps modems). Individual customers typically have SLIP/PPP connections over high-speed dial-up modems.

In addition to various telecommunications equipment (including modems), the ISP needs Internet hosts — the servers that handle the SLIP/PPP, as well as simple dial-in connections. This is where Linux comes in. With the built-in TCP/IP networking capabilities of Linux and its support for all types of network hardware, Linux PCs are ideal for this core aspect of the ISP business.

Note

If you look at the messages in the newsgroup `comp.os.linux.misc`, you'll see many messages about running an ISP business with Linux. You may be surprised to learn that many ISPs around the country are finding that Linux PCs are very capable Internet hosts.

Secret

I have used Windows NT, SunOS, HP-UX, and Linux, and I have found Linux to be the most flexible and fully featured operating system. The other operating systems aren't bad, but almost everything from a C or C++ compiler to the PPP support typically is an option. As you might guess, each option costs money. If you want to get started as an ISP within your budget, you can't go wrong with Linux PCs.

Tip

Although I briefly describe some areas of the ISP business in this section, you should browse the Internet and read the available information before deciding to take the plunge as an ISP. A good place to start is "Internet Access Frequently Asked Questions (FAQ)," maintained by David Dennis at http://www.amazing.com/internet/.

In that Web page, you'll find detailed information on all elements of the ISP business, from the viable types of network connections to accounting and billing practices.

ISP equipment needs

You can't run the ISP business on Linux PCs alone. Following is a typical assortment of equipment that you'll need to start business as an ISP:

- *A high-bandwidth connection to the Internet.* As an ISP, you'll go to one of the major telecommunication carriers for this service. For a small startup, this connection may be 56 Kbps, but a 1.54-Mbps T1 connection is more appropriate for a typical ISP.

- *A router* to direct network packets between your system and the rest of the Internet. Although Linux can serve as a router, that job is best left to a dedicated router.

- *Networking equipment* (such as CSU/DSU) that you may need to connect to your communications provider.

- *A terminal server* to handle the dial-up modems as well as SLIP/PPP connections. A Linux PC with a multiple-port serial board can handle this task, but the "right tool for the job" philosophy dictates that you use a terminal server for this task. Handling multiple dial-up modems requires constant attention of the processor. If the Linux PC is busy responding to arrival of data at the modem lines, it cannot adequately perform other tasks. On the other hand, a terminal server with a dedicated processor can easily handle the dial-up modems.

- *Phone lines for dial-up access,* which is how most of your customers access the system. For a small set of users, you need one phone line for every six to eight users; for a larger user base, 1 line for every 10 users is reported to be adequate.

- *Server PCs* (Internet hosts) for news, mail, World Wide Web, and user logins. This area is where Linux PCs come into play.

- *Uninterruptible Power Supply* (UPS) to continue operation or to gracefully shut down during power outages.

As this list of equipment shows, Linux PCs are most useful as servers. You typically need quite a few servers, each of which is dedicated to a specific service.

Linux PC for ISP

For the Internet servers, you want Pentium PCs configured with a large amount of RAM (32MB to 64MB) and disk storage (5GB to 10GB). The reason for the huge disk storage is USENET news. USENET news comes in huge volume, and you need enough storage to hold a few days' worth of news articles for all newsgroups.

Tip

You might also consider the new Pentium Pro systems that are aimed at the server market. The Pentium Pro is optimized for 32-bit operating systems such as Linux and Windows NT.

At minimum, you want two Linux PCs: one for logins, e-mail, and WWW, and the other for news. Each PC will need an Ethernet card because you'll have to network the servers locally.

As for user logins, a 66-MHz 486DX2 with 16MB RAM can handle up to 10 connections comfortably — about the same number of 14,400-bps modem connections that a 56-Kbps Internet connection should support. On the other hand, a 90-MHz Pentium with 32MB RAM can easily handle 20 to 40 connections. With a T1 connection to the Internet, you may be able to serve close to 100 dial-up customers because not everyone logs in at the same time.

One additional peripheral device that you need is a tape drive for backup. You may want to consider a 4mm DAT SCSI drive. These tapes are capable of backing up 2GB of data.

UNIX software developer

If your business develops applications for UNIX and X Window System, you should have the in-house technical know-how to install and set up Linux on PCs. Because Linux comes with a full set of software-development tools, a Linux PC can serve as the development workstation for each software developer.

Although the Linux software distribution comes with many programming languages, a Linux PC is ideal for developing UNIX applications. Nowadays, most applications are graphical, and on Linux, you'd use the XFree86 X Window System for graphics. The Linux distribution on the companion CD-ROM includes all necessary header files and libraries for developing X applications.

Tip

One item that you won't find on the companion CD-ROM is Motif — the graphical user interface that is built on top of X. Unfortunately, Motif is a licensed product of Open Software Foundation, and you have to buy it separately. Several vendors sell Motif for Linux; prices range from $100 to $200. (See Chapter 23 for further information.)

Incidentally, Linux PCs make ideal low-cost UNIX workstations for university students. Instead of having to share a VAX or some other large system with other users, each student can have a complete "UNIX workstation" with Linux PCs.

Consultant

As I explained earlier in this chapter, many businesses shy away from Linux because no single source of technical support exists for Linux. You could set yourself up as a Linux consultant to sell businesses on using Linux and then provide the necessary technical support.

Following are some of the ways that you can provide Linux-related service to businesses:

- Offer short courses on Linux installation and setup, as well as setting up a Linux Internet host and Web server
- Provide Linux PCs with bundled technical support as solutions to specific customer needs, such as Internet connectivity or a Web presence

Chapter 21: Running a Business with Linux 653

Tip: Instead of offering Linux technical support only, you should consider packaging a business solution based on Linux. For a given business need, you should be able to configure a Linux PC with appropriate free software from the Internet. Then you can sell that business system as a package that includes the hardware, the software, and support.

Tip: If you work with businesses that rely on Windows for Workgroups, propose a Linux PC with Samba software as a replacement LAN Manager server for the business. Again, sell the Linux LAN Manager server as a turnkey system with support.

Summary

Businesses often are reluctant to use Linux because it's not a supported product. Linux also has the reputation of being a hacker's dream, and no mainstream personal-productivity applications (such as word processors and spreadsheets) are available for Linux. Despite these perceived shortcomings, Linux actually has a great deal to offer, as long as it is used for the appropriate task. This chapter describes the role of Linux in business and describes some business uses of Linux. By reading this chapter, you learn the following things:

▶ Although Linux lacks mainstream productivity applications, such as word processing and spreadsheet software, the situation is about to change with the ongoing work at a new company named Caldera. WordPerfect for Linux and a spreadsheet named WingZ will be available for Linux soon.

▶ Linux excels in networking and software-development tools. To top it off, Linux can run on commodity PCs, which are much less expensive than Sun and HP workstations. Thus, Linux PCs are ideal Internet hosts and software-development workstations.

▶ The Slackware Linux distribution on the companion CD-ROM includes nearly all the networking and software-development tools that a business needs, for a nominal price (in this case, the price of the book).

▶ For PC networks that use LAN Manager, you can configure a Linux PC as a LAN Manager server; all you have to do is install the Samba software package from the companion CD-ROM. This chapter shows you how to install and use Samba.

▶ A Linux PC also can act as a LAN Manager client. As an example, this chapter describes how to use a LAN Manager printer from a Linux PC.

▶ Linux PCs are especially well suited to be servers in the Internet Service Provider (ISP) business. The built-in TCP/IP networking of Linux is a big plus in the ISP business.

▶ The perceived lack of Linux support can be a business opportunity to those who can install and maintain Linux. Another potential business is to sell Linux PCs configured with custom-developed or free software and designed to meet a specific business need. If they are bundled with technical support, such Linux PCs can be positioned as business solutions instead of just low-cost UNIX boxes.

Chapter 22
Developing Software in Linux

In This Chapter

- Looking at GCC: the GNU C and C++ compiler
- Using GNU `make` to automate software builds
- Using the GNU debugger: `gdb`
- Using RCS for version control
- Understanding GPL and LGPL
- Understanding ELF
- Dynamically loading and using a shared library

Many Linux users happen to be software developers. If you want to develop software as a hobby or want to add features to Linux, you'll find that Linux includes everything you need to create UNIX and X applications. You can use the GNU C and C++ compilers to write conventional programs (that you compile and link into an executable). Alternatively, you can use the Tcl/Tk scripting language to write interpreted graphical applications.

This chapter covers the general subject of software development on a Linux PC. The focus is not on any specific programming language. Instead, this chapter describes how to use various software development tools, such compilers, makefiles, and version-control systems.

The chapter also describes the implications of Free Software Foundation's GNU Public License on any plans you might have to develop Linux software. The reason you need to know this is because you'll be using GNU tools and GNU libraries to develop software in Linux.

I also cover the subject of dynamic linking and the recently adopted Executable and Linking Format (ELF), which makes dynamic linking easier. These topics are of interest to Linux programmers, because dynamic linking reduces the size of executables and may allow you to distribute your software in binary form, even if your software uses the GNU libraries.

Cross Reference

Developing X applications is a complex-enough subject to deserve an entire chapter. Accordingly, X programming on Linux is covered in Chapter 23.

Software Development Tools in Linux

Cross Reference

As expected, being a UNIX look-alike, Linux includes the traditional UNIX software development tools. By traditional tools, I mean the following:

- A text editor, such as vi or emacs, for editing the source code (described in Chapter 24).
- A C compiler for compiling and linking programs written in C — the programming language of choice for writing UNIX applications (although nowadays, many programmers are turning to C++). Linux includes GCC: the GNU C and C++ compiler.
- The GNU make utility for automating the *software build* process — the process of combining object modules into an executable or a library.
- A debugger for debugging programs. Linux includes the GNU debugger gdb, as well as xxgdb, a graphical interface to gdb.
- A version-control system to keep track of various revisions of a source file. Linux comes with RCS (Revision Control System).

Cross Reference

All these tools will be installed automatically if you install Linux from this book's companion CD-ROM, following the steps outlined in Chapter 1. The next few sections briefly describe how to use these tools to write applications for Linux.

info: the authoritative help on GNU tools

You may already have noticed that most of the Linux software development tools are from the Free Software Foundation's GNU project. The online documentation for all these tools come as info files. The info program is GNU's hypertext help system.

Tip

To see info in action, type **info** at the shell prompt or press Esc-x followed by **info** in GNU Emacs (you may also start info under GNU Emacs with the ctrl+h i command). I typically access info from GNU Emacs, because that way, I can look up online help while editing a program. Figure 22-1 shows the GNU Emacs window after I typed Esc-x **info**.

In info, the online help text is organized in nodes; each node represents information on a specific topic. The first line shows the header for that node.

Figure 22-1 shows the initial info screen, with a directory of topics. This directory itself is an info file: /usr/info/dir, a text file that contains some embedded special characters. Following are a few lines from the /usr/info/dir file that correspond to the screen shown in Figure 22-1:

```
-*- Text -*-
This is the file .../info/dir, which contains the topmost node of the
Info hierarchy. The first time you invoke Info, you start off
looking at that node, which is (dir)Top.
File: dir     Node: Top     This is the top of the INFO tree
  This (the Directory node) gives a menu of major topics. Typing "d"
  returns here, "q" exits, "?" lists all INFO commands, "h" gives a
  primer for first-timers, "mTexinfo<Return>" visits Texinfo topic, etc.
```

Chapter 22: Developing Software in Linux

```
File: dir         Node: Top      This is the top of the INFO tree
  This (the Directory node) gives a menu of major topics. Typing "d"
  returns here, "q" exits, "?" lists all INFO commands, "h" gives a
  primer for first-timers, "mTexinfo<Return>" visits Texinfo topic, etc.
  --- PLEASE ADD DOCUMENTATION TO THIS TREE. (See INFO topic first.) ---
* Menu: The list of major topics begins on the next line.

Developing in C and C++:
========================
* GCC: (gcc).            Information about the gcc Compiler
* CPP: (cpp).            The C Preprozessor
* Make: (make).          The GNU make Utility
* GDB: (gdb).            The GNU Debugger

Libraries and program generators:
=================================
* glibc: (libc).         The standard C runtime library.
* iostream: (iostream).  The GNU C++ iostream library.
* Libg++: (libg++).      The G++ Library
* gmp: (gmp).            GNU MP arbitrary precision arithmetic library.
* Regex: (regex).        The GNU regular expression library.
* Termcap: (termcap).    The termcap library, which enables application programs
                         to handle all types of character-display terminals.
* Gperf: (gperf).        Hash Gererator
* Bison: (bison).        bison, and not yacc
* Flex: (flex).          Fast lexical analyzer
* ipc: (ipc).            System V inter process communication system calls.
* M4: (m4).              GNU `m4' macro processor

Other languages:
================
* mst: (mst).            The GNU Smalltalk programming language.
* GAWK: (gawk).          The GNU version of awk
* Emacs Lisp: (elisp).   The language of emacs.
* CL: (cl).              Partial Common Lisp support for Emacs Lisp.

Using Emacs & Co.
=================
--%%-Info: (dir)Top      (Info Narrow)--Top------------------------------
Composing main Info directory...done
```

Figure 22-1: The GNU Emacs window, showing the result of the command Esc-x **info**.

```
 -- PLEASE ADD DOCUMENTATION TO THIS TREE. (See INFO topic first.) --
* Menu: The list of major topics begins on the next line.

Developing in C and C++:
========================
* GCC: (gcc).       Information about the gcc Compiler
* CPP: (cpp).       The C Preprocessor
* Make: (make).     The GNU make Utility
* GDB: (gdb).       The GNU Debugger
(...Lines deleted...)
```

If you compare this listing with the screen shown in Figure 22-1, you notice that info displays only the lines that follow the Ctrl+_ character. In your system, the /usr/info directory contains this info file as well as others with the text for each topic. These info files usually are stored in compressed format. You really don't have to know these details to use the info files.

Tip

You have to use several single-letter commands to navigate info files. The best way to learn the commands is to type **h** from the initial info directory, shown in Figure 22-1. After reading the help screens, type **d** to return to the initial directory of topics.

From the directory screen of Figure 22-1, type **m**, followed by the name of a menu item (shown in boldface with an asterisk prefix). To view the online help for GCC, for example, type **m** and then **gcc**. The `info` system in turn displays the top-level menu of items for GCC, as shown in Figure 22-2.

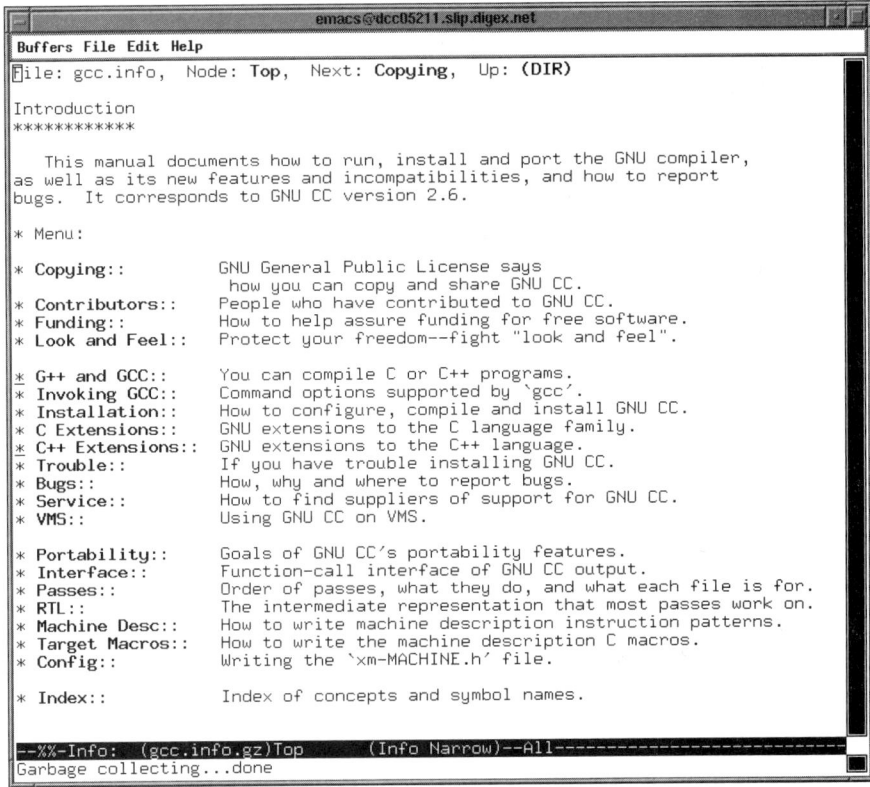

Figure 22-2: The GNU Emacs window, showing the top-level help on GCC.

You can explore further by typing **m**, followed by one of the menu items shown in Figure 22-2.

While you're at it, you may want to press the spacebar from the screen shown in Figure 22-2. That action displays the GNU General Public License (GPL), shown in Figure 22-3.

Linux and the `gcc` compiler itself are covered by the GPL, which requires distribution of the source code (that's why all Linux distributions come with source code). In the "Implications of GNU Licenses" section, you learn that you can still use GNU tools to develop commercial applications and distribute the applications in binary form (without source code) as long as they link with selected GNU libraries only.

Chapter 22: Developing Software in Linux

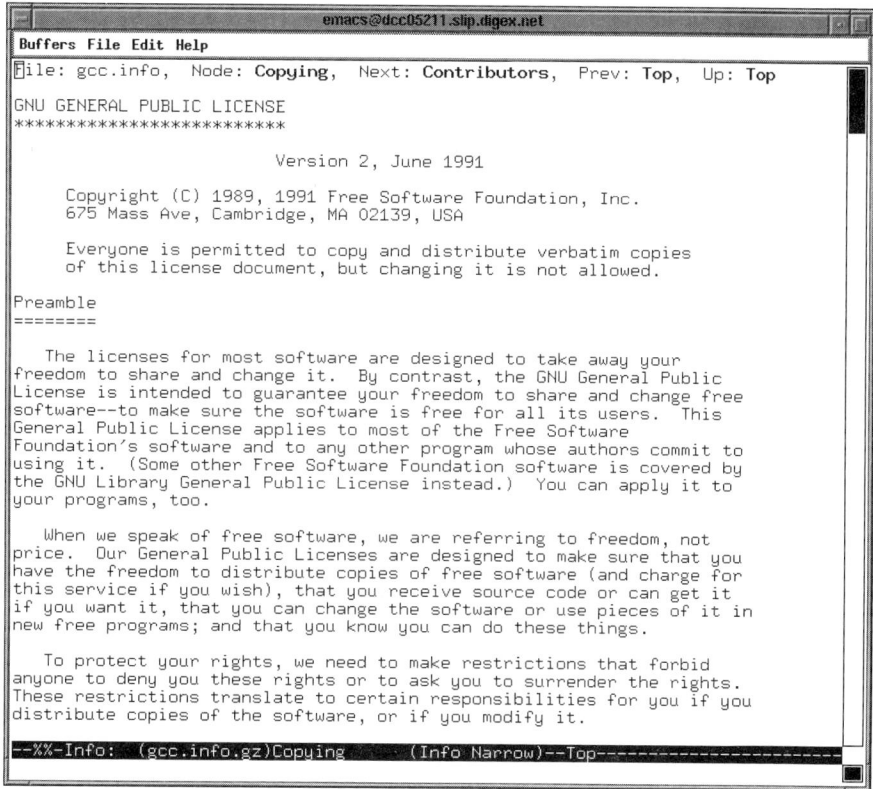

Figure 22-3: The GNU Emacs window, showing the first page of the GNU General Public License (GPL).

At any time in `info`, you can type **d** to go back to the `info` topic directory shown in Figure 22-1. From that screen, you can view help on other GNU tools, such as `make`, and the GNU debugger.

To quit `info`, type **q**.

GNU C and C++ compilers

The most important software development tool in Linux is GCC, which is the GNU C and C++ compiler. In fact, GCC can compile three languages: C, C++, and Objective-C (a language that has object-oriented extensions to C). You'd use the same `gcc` command to compile and link both C and C++ source files. The GCC compiler supports ANSI standard C, so you'll find it easy to port any ANSI C program to Linux. Additionally, if you've ever used a C compiler on other UNIX systems, you'll be right at home with GCC.

Invoking GCC

Use the gcc command to invoke GCC. By default, when you use the gcc command on a source file, GCC preprocesses, compiles, and links the executable. You can use GCC options to stop this process at an intermediate stage, however. For example, you might invoke gcc with the -c option to compile a source file and generate an object file, but not perform the link step.

Using GCC to compile and link a few C source files is very simple. Suppose that you want to compile and link a simple program made up of two source files. The following listing shows the file area.c: the main program that computes the area of a circle whose radius is specified through the command line.

```
#include <stdio.h>
#include <stdlib.h>

/* Function prototype */
double area_of_circle(double r);

void main(int argc, char **argv)
{
   if(argc < 2)
   {
     printf("Usage: %s radius\n", argv[0]);
     exit(1);
   }
   else
   {
     double radius = atof(argv[1]);
     double area = area_of_circle(radius);
     printf("Area of circle with radius %f = %f\n",
         radius, area);
   }
}
```

The following listing shows the file circle.c, which provides a function that computes the area of a circle.

```
#include <math.h>

#define SQUARE(x) ((x)*(x))

double area_of_circle(double r)
{
   return 4.0 * M_PI * SQUARE(r);
}
```

For such a simple program, of course, I could have placed everything in a single file, but this contrived example allows me to show you how to handle multiple files.

To compile these two programs and create an executable file named area, you might use the following command:

```
gcc -o area area.c circle.c
```

This particular invocation of GCC uses the -o option to specify the name of the executable file. (If you do not specify the name of an output file, GCC creates a file named a.out.)

If you have too many source files to compile and link, you want to compile the files individually and generate object files (with the .o extension). That way, when you change a source file, you need to compile only that single file and then link all the object files. The following example shows how you can separate the compile and link steps for the example program:

```
gcc -c area.c
gcc -c circle.c
gcc -o area area.o circle.o
```

The first two invocations of gcc with the -c option compile the source files. The third invocation links the object files into an executable named area.

In case you are curious, here's how you run the sample program (to compute the area of a circle with a radius of 1):

```
area 1
Area of circle with radius 1.000000 = 12.566371
```

Compiling C++ programs

GNU CC is a combined C and C++ compiler, so the gcc command also can compile C++ source files. GCC uses the file extension to determine whether a file is C or C++. C files have a lowercase .c extension, whereas C++ files end with .C or .cpp.

Although the gcc command can compile a C++ file, that command does not automatically link with various class libraries that C++ programs typically require. That's why it's easier to compile and link a C++ program with the g++ command, which invokes gcc with appropriate options.

Suppose that you want to compile the following simple C++ program stored in a file named hello.C (it's customary to use an uppercase C extension for C++ source files):

```
#include <iostream.h>

void main(void)
{
  cout << "Hello from Linux!" << endl;
}
```

To compile and link this program into an executable program named hello, you use the following command:

```
g++ -o hello hello.C
```

This command creates the hello executable, which you then can run as follows:

```
hello
Hello from Linux!
```

As you see in the following section, a host of GCC options control various parts of compiling C++ programs.

Exploring GCC options

Following is the basic syntax of the `gcc` command:

```
gcc options filenames
```

Each option starts with a hyphen (-) and usually has a long name, such as `-funsigned-char` or `-finline-functions`. Many commonly used options are short, however, such as `-c` to compile only and `-g` to generate debugging information (needed to debug the program with the GNU debugger).

You can best understand the GCC options by first viewing them in categories. Table 22-1 shows the GCC options organized by categories.

Table 22-1	GCC option categories
Category	**Options**
Controlling output	`-c -S -E -o FILE -pipe -v -x LANGUAGE -b MACHINE -V VERSION`
C language features	`-ansi -fallow-single-precision -fcond-mismatch -fno-asm -fno-builtin -fsigned-bitfields -fsigned-char -funsigned-bitfields -funsigned-char -fwritable-strings -traditional -traditional-cpp -trigraphs`
C++ language features	`-fall-virtual -fdollars-in-identifiers -felide-constructors -fenum-int-equiv -fexternal-templates -fhandle-signatures -fmemoize-lookups -fno-default-inline -fno-gnu-keywords -fnonnull-objects -foperator-names -fstrict-prototype -fthis-is-variable -nostdinc++ -traditional +eN`
Code generation	`-fcall-saved-REG -fcall-used-REG -ffixed-REG -finhibit-size-directive -fno-common -fno-ident -fno-gnu-linker -fpcc-struct-return -fpic -fPIC -freg-struct-return -fshared-data -fshort-enums -fshort-double -fvolatile -fvolatile-global -fverbose-asm -fpack-struct +e0 +e1`
Optimization	`-fcaller-saves -fcse-follow-jumps -fcse-skip-blocks -fdelayed-branch -fexpensive-optimizations -ffast-math -ffloat-store -fforce-addr -fforce-mem -finline-functions -fkeep-inline-functions -fno-default-inline -fno-defer-pop -fno-function-cse -fno-inline -fno-peephole -fomit-frame-pointer -frerun-cse-after-loop`

Category	Options
	`-fschedule-insns -fschedule-insns2 -fstrength-reduce -fthread-jumps -funroll-all-loops -funroll-loops -O -O0 -O1 -O2 -O3`
Debugging	`-a -dLETTERS -fpretend-float -g -gLEVEL -gcoff -gdwarf -gdwarf+ -ggdb -gstabs -gstabs+ -gxcoff -gxcoff+ -p -pg -print-file-name=LIBRARY -print-libgcc-file-name -print-prog-name=PROGRAM -print-search-dirs -save-temps`
Warning messages	`-fsyntax-only -pedantic -pedantic-errors -w -W -Wall -Waggregate-return -Wbad-function-cast -Wcast-align -Wcast-qual -Wchar-subscript -Wcomment -Wconversion -Wenum-clash -Werror -Wformat -Wid-clash-LEN -Wimplicit -Wimport -Winline -Wlarger-than-LEN -Wmissing-declarations -Wmissing-prototypes -Wnested-externs -Wno-import -Woverloaded-virtual -Wparentheses -Wpointer-arith -Wredundant-decls -Wreorder -Wreturn-type -Wshadow -Wstrict-prototypes -Wswitch -Wsynth -Wtemplate-debugging -Wtraditional -Wtrigraphs -Wuninitialized -Wunused -Wwrite-strings`
Preprocessor	`-AQUESTION(ANSWER) -C -dD -dM -dN -DMACRO[=DEFN] -E -H -idirafter DIR -IDIR -I- -include FILE -imacros FILE -iprefix FILE -iwithprefix DIR -iwithprefixbefore DIR -isystem DIR -M -MD -MM -MMD -MG -nostdinc -P -trigraphs -undef -UMACRO -Wp,OPTION`
Linker	`-LDIR -lLIBRARY -nostartfiles -nodefaultlibs -nostdlib -s -static -shared -symbolic -Wl,OPTION -Xlinker OPTION -u SYMBOL`
Intel 386/486 CPU	`-m486 -m386 -mieee-fp -mno-fancy-math-387 -mno-fp-ret-in-387 -msoft-float -msvr3-shlib -mno-wide-multiply -mrtd -malign-double -mreg-alloc=LIST -mregparm=NUM -malign-jumps=NUM -malign-loops=NUM -malign-functions=NUM`

Most of the options have positive and negative forms. `-fno-default-inline`, for example, is the negative form of `-fdefault-inline`. Table 22-1 shows only the default form of the options that can have both positive and negative forms.

Tip: Usually, you do not have to specify GCC options explicitly; the default settings are fine for most applications. Table 22-2 lists some of the GCC options that you might use.

Table 22-2	Commonly used GCC options
Option	Meaning
-ansi	Support ANSI standard C syntax only. (This option disables some GNU C specific features, such as the `asm` and `typeof` keywords.)
-c	Compile and generate object file only.
-DMACRO	Define the macro with the string "1" as its value.
-DMACRO=DEFN	Define the macro as `DEFN`.
-E	Run only the C preprocessor.
-fallow-single-precision	Perform all math operations in single precision.
-fpack-struct	Pack all structure members without any padding.
-fpcc-struct-return	Return all `struct` and `union` values in memory, rather than in registers. (Returning values this way is less efficient but compatible with other compilers.)
-fPIC	Generate position-independent code (PIC) that is suitable for use in a shared library.
-freg-struct-return	Return `struct` and `union` values in registers, when possible.
-g	Generate debugging information. (The GNU debugger can use this information.)
-IDIRECTORY	Search the specified directory for files that you include with the `#include` preprocessor directive.
-LDIRECTORY	Search the specified directory for libraries.
-lLIBRARY	Search the specified library when linking.
-m486	Optimize code for a 486. (This code also will run on a 386.)
-o FILE	Generate the specified output file (used to designate the name of an executable file).
-O0	Do not optimize.
O or -O1	Optimize the generated code.
-O2	Optimize even more.
-O3	Perform optimizations beyond those done for -O2.
-pedantic	Generate errors if any non-ANSI standard extensions are used.

Option	Meaning
`-pg`	Add extra code to program so that, when run, it generates information that the `gprof` program can use to display timing details for various parts of the program.
`-shared`	Generate a shared object file (typically used to create a shared library).
`-traditional`	Support traditional Kernighan & Ritchie C syntax only.
`-UMACRO`	Undefine the specified macro.
`-v`	Display the version number of GCC.
`-w`	Don't generate any warning messages.
`-Wl,OPTION`	Pass the `OPTION` string (containing multiple comma-separated options) to the linker. To create a shared library named `libXXX.so.1`, for example, you use the following flag: `-Wl,-soname,libXXX.so.1`

GNU `make` utility

When an application is made up of more than a few source files, compiling and linking the files by manually typing the `gcc` command is no longer convenient. Additionally, you do not want to compile every file whenever you change something in a single source file. This situation is what makes the GNU `make` utility so helpful.

The `make` utility works by reading and interpreting a *makefile*: a text file that you have to prepare according to a specified syntax. The makefile describes which files constitute a program and explains how to compile and link the files to build the program. Whenever you change one or more files, `make` determines which files should be recompiled and then issues the appropriate commands for compiling those files and rebuilding the program.

The `make` utility is, in fact, specified in Section 6.2 of the POSIX.2 standard (IEEE Standard 1003.2-1992) for shells and tools. GNU `make` conforms with the POSIX.2 standard.

Makefile name

By default, GNU `make` looks for a makefile with one of the following names, in the order shown:

- `GNUmakefile`
- `makefile`
- `Makefile`

In UNIX systems, it is customary to use `Makefile` as the name of the makefile, because it appears near the beginning of directory listings where the uppercase names appear before the lowercase ones.

When you download software from the Internet, you usually will find a `Makefile` together with the source files. To build the software, all you have to do is type **make** at the shell prompt; `make` takes care of all the steps necessary to build the software.

If your makefile does not have a standard name, such as `Makefile`, you have to use the `-f` option to specify the makefile's name. If your makefile is called `webprog.mak`, for example, you have to run `make` with the following command line:

```
make -f webprog.mak
```

GNU `make` also accepts several other command-line options, which are summarized in the "How to run `make`" section of this chapter.

The makefile

For a program that consists of several source and header files, the makefile specifies the following:

- The items to be created by `make` — usually, the object files and the executable. The term *target* is used for an item to be created.
- How the items (created by `make`) depend on other files.
- What commands should be executed to create each target.

Suppose that you have a C++ source file named `form.C` that contains the following preprocessor directive:

```
#include "form.h"   // Include header file
```

The object file `form.o` clearly depends on the source file `form.C` and the header file `form.h`. In addition to these dependencies, you must specify how `make` should convert the `form.C` file to the object file `form.o`. Suppose that you want `make` to invoke `g++` (because the source file is in C++) with the following options:

- `-c` (compile only)
- `-g` (generate debugging information)
- `-O2` (optimize some)

In the makefile, you can express this with the following rule:

```
# This a comment in the makefile
# The following lines indicate how form.o depends
# form.C and form.h and how to create form.o.

form.o: form.C form.h
    g++ -c -g -O2 form.C
```

In this example, the first noncomment line shows `form.o` as the *target* and `form.C` and `form.h` as the *dependent* files. The line following the dependency indicates how to build the target from its dependents.

The benefit of using `make` is that it prevents unnecessary compilations. After all, you could invoke g++ (or gcc) in a shell script to compile and link all the files that make up your application, but the shell script will compile everything, even if the compilations are unnecessary. GNU `make`, on the other hand, builds a target only if one or more of its dependents has changed since the last time the target was built. `make` verifies this change by examining the time of the last modification of the target and the dependents.

Note

Notice that `make` treats the target as the name of a goal to be achieved; the target does not have to be a file. You can have a rule such as the following:

```
clean:
    rm -f *.o
```

This rule specifies an abstract target named `clean` that does not depend on anything. This dependency statement says that to make `clean`, GNU `make` should invoke the command `rm -f *.o`, which deletes all files with the `.o` extension (these are the object files). Thus, the net effect of creating the target named `clean` is to delete the object files.

Variables (or macros)

In addition to the basic service of building targets from dependents, GNU `make` includes many nice features that make it easy for you to express the dependencies and rules for building a target from its dependents. If you need to compile a large number of C++ files with the same GCC options, for example, typing the options for each file would be tedious. You can avoid this task by defining a variable or macro in `make` as follows:

```
# Define macros for name of compiler
CXX= g++

# Define a macro for the GCC flags
CXXFLAGS= -O2 -g -m486

# A rule for building an object file
form.o: form.C form.h
    $(CXX) -c $(CXXFLAGS) form.C
```

In this example, `CXX` and `CXXFLAGS` are `make` variables. GNU `make` prefers to call them variables, but most UNIX `make` utilities call them macros.

To use a variable anywhere in the makefile, start with a dollar sign (`$`), followed by the variable within parentheses. GNU `make` replaces all occurrences of a variable with its definition; thus, it replaces all occurrences of `$(CXXFLAGS)` with the string `-O2 -g -m486`.

GNU `make` has several predefined variables that have special meanings. Table 22-3 lists these variables. In addition to the variables shown in Table 22-3, GNU `make` considers all environment variables to be predefined variables.

Table 22-3	Some predefined variables in GNU `make`
Variable	**Meaning**
`$%`	Member name for targets that are archives. If the target is `libDisp.a(image.o)`, for example, `$%` is `image.o`, and `$@` is `libDisp.a`.
`$*`	Name of the target file without the extension.
`$+`	Names of all dependent files with duplicate dependencies, listed in their order of occurrence.
`$<`	The name of the first dependent file.
`$?`	Names of all the dependent files (with spaces between the names) that are newer than the target.
`$@`	Complete name of the target.
`$^`	Names of all the dependent files, with spaces between the names. Duplicates are removed from the dependent file names.
`AR`	Name of the archive-maintaining program. (Default value: `ar`.)
`ARFLAGS`	Flags for the archive-maintaining program. (Default value: `rv`.)
`AS`	Name of the assembler program that converts the assembly language to object code. (Default value: `as`.)
`ASFLAGS`	Flags for the assembler.
`CC`	Name of the C compiler. (Default value: `cc`.)
`CFLAGS`	Flags to be passed to the C compiler.
`CO`	Name of the program that extracts a file from RCS. (Default value: `co`.)
`COFLAGS`	Flags for the RCS `co` program.
`CPP`	Name of the C preprocessor. (Default value: `$(CC) -E`.)
`CPPFLAGS`	Flags for the C preprocessor.
`CXX`	Name of the C++ compiler. (Default value: `g++`.)
`CXXFLAGS`	Flags to be passed to the C++ compiler.
`FC`	Name of the FORTRAN compiler. (Default value: `f77`.)
`FFLAGS`	Flags for the FORTRAN compiler.
`GET`	Name of the program to extract a file from SCCS. (Default value: `get`.)
`GFLAGS`	Flags for the SCCS `get` program.
`LDFLAGS`	Flags for the compiler when it is supposed to invoke the linker `ld`.
`LEX`	Name of the program to convert Lex grammar to C program. (Default value: `lex`.)
`LFLAGS`	Flags for Lex.

Variable	Meaning
MAKEINFO	Name of the program that converts Texinfo source files to `info` files. (Default value: `makeinfo`.)
RM	Name of the command to delete a file. (Default value: `rm -f`.)
TEX	Name of the program to generate TeX DVI files from TeX source files. (Default value: `tex`.)
TEXI2DVI	Name of the program to generate TeX DVI files from the Texinfo source. (Default value: `texi2dvi`.)
YACC	Name of the program to convert YACC grammars to C programs. (Default value: `yacc -r`.)
YFLAGS	Flags for `yacc`.

Implicit rules

GNU `make` also includes built-in or implicit rules that define how to create specific types of targets from various dependencies. An example of an implicit rule is the command that `make` should execute to generate an object file from a C source file.

GNU `make` supports two types of implicit rules:

- *Suffix rules.* Suffix rules are the old-fashioned way to define an implicit rule for `make`. A suffix rule defines how to convert a file that has one extension to a file that has another extension. Each suffix rule is defined with the target showing a pair of suffixes (file extensions). The suffix rule for converting a `.c` (C source) file to a `.o` (object) file, for example, might be written as follows:

    ```
    .c.o:
    $(CC) $(CFLAGS) $(CPPFLAGS) -c -o $@ $<
    ```

    This rule uses the predefined variables `CC`, `CFLAGS`, and `CPPFLAGS`. For filenames, the rule uses the variables `$@` (the complete name of the target) and `$<` (the name of the first dependent file).

- *Pattern rules.* These rules are more versatile, because you can specify more complex dependency rules with pattern rules. A pattern rule looks just like a regular rule, except that a single percent sign (%) appears in the target's name. The dependencies also use % to indicate how the dependency names relate to the target's name. The following pattern rule specifies how to convert any file `X.c` to a file `X.o`:

    ```
    %.o: %.c
    $(CC) $(CFLAGS) $(CPPFLAGS) -c -o $@ $<
    ```

GNU `make` has a large set of implicit rules, defined as both suffix and pattern rules. To see a list of all known variables and rules, run `make` with the following command:

```
make -p -f/dev/null
```

```
make: *** # GNU Make version 3.73, by Richard Stallman and Roland
McGrath.
# Copyright (C) 1988, 89, 90, 91, 92, 93, 94, 95 Free Software Founda-
tion, Inc.
# This is free software; see the source for copying conditions.
# There is NO warranty; not even for MERCHANTABILITY or FITNESS FOR A
# PARTICULAR PURPOSE.

No targets. Stop.

# Make data base, printed on Fri Nov 24 21:22:37 1995

# Variables
(lines deleted...)

# default
CC = cc
# default
OUTPUT_OPTION = -o $@
# default
COMPILE.c = $(CC) $(CFLAGS) $(CPPFLAGS) $(TARGET_ARCH) -c
(lines deleted...)

# Implicit Rules
 %.o: %.c
# commands to execute (built-in):
    $(COMPILE.c) $< $(OUTPUT_OPTION)
(lines deleted...)
```

The listing shows selected parts of the output displayed by GNU make when you use the -p option. The output includes the names of variables as well as implicit rules.

A sample makefile

You can write a makefile easily if you use GNU make's predefined variables and its built-in rules. Consider, for example, a makefile that creates the executable xdraw from three C source files (xdraw.c, xviewobj.c, and shapes.c) and two header files (xdraw.h and shapes.h). Assume that each source file includes one of the header files. Given these facts, here is what a sample makefile might look like:

```
#################################################################
# Sample makefile
# Comments start with '#'
#
#################################################################

# Use standard variables to define compile and link flags

CFLAGS= -g -O2

# Define the target "all"

all: xdraw
```

Chapter 22: Developing Software in Linux

```
OBJS=xdraw.o xviewobj.o shapes.o

xdraw: $(OBJS)

# Object files
xdraw.o: Makefile xdraw.c xdraw.h

xviewobj.o: Makefile xviewobj.c xdraw.h

shapes.o: Makefile shapes.c shapes.h
```

This makefile relies on GNU make's implicit rules. The conversion of .c files to .o files uses the built-in rule. The flags to the C compiler are passed by defining the variable CFLAGS.

Secret

The target named all is defined as the first target for a reason — if you run GNU make without specifying any targets in the command line (see the make syntax described in the following section), it builds the first target that it finds in the makefile. By defining the first target, all, as xdraw, you can ensure that make builds this executable file even if you do not explicitly specify it as a target. UNIX programmers traditionally use all as the name of the first target, but the target's name is immaterial; what matters is that it is the first target in the makefile.

If you have a directory that contains the appropriate source and header files, you can try the makefile. Here's what happens when I try the sample makefile:

```
make
cc -g -O2  -c xdraw.c -o xdraw.o
cc -g -O2  -c xviewobj.c -o xviewobj.o
cc -g -O2  -c shapes.c -o shapes.o
cc   xdraw.o xviewobj.o shapes.o   -o xdraw
```

As the output of make shows, it uses the cc command (which happens to be a symbolic link to GCC in your Linux system) with appropriate options to compile the source files and, finally, to link the objects to create the xdraw executable.

How to run make

Typically, you run make with a single command in the command line; that is, by typing **make**. When run this way, GNU make looks for a file named GNUmakefile, makefile, or Makefile — in that order. If make finds one of these makefiles, it builds the first target specified in that makefile. However, if make does not find an appropriate makefile, it displays the following error message and exits:

```
make: *** No targets specified and no makefile found. Stop.
```

If your makefile happens to have a different name from the default ones, you have to use the -f option to specify the makefile. The syntax of this make option is as follows (filename is the name of the makefile).

```
make -f filename
```

Even when you have a makefile with a default name such as Makefile, you may want to build a specific target out of several targets defined in the makefile. In that case, you have to run make with the following syntax:

```
make target
```

If the makefile contains the target named clean, you can build that target with the following command:

```
make clean
```

Another special syntax overrides the value of a make variable. For example, GNU make uses the CFLAGS variable to hold the flags used when compiling C files. You can override the value of this variable when you invoke make. Following is an example of how you can define CFLAGS to be the options -g -O2:

```
make CFLAGS="-g -O2"
```

In addition to these options, GNU make accepts several other command-line options. Table 22-4 lists the GNU make options.

Table 22-4   **Options for GNU** make

Option	Meaning
-b	Ignored, but accepted for compatibility with other versions of make
-C DIR	Change to the specified directory before reading the makefile
-d	Print debugging information
-e	Allow environment variables to override definitions of similarly named variables in the makefile
-f FILE	Read FILE as the makefile
-h	Display the list of make options
-i	Ignore all errors in commands executed when building a target
-I DIR	Search specified directory for included makefiles (the capability to include a file in a makefile is unique to GNU make)
-j NUM	Specifies the number of commands that make can run simultaneously
-k	Continue to build unrelated targets even if an error occurs when building one of the targets
-l LOAD	Don't start a new job if load average is at least LOAD (a floating-point number)
-m	Ignored, but accepted for compatibility with other versions of make
-n	Just print the commands to be executed, but do not execute them
-o FILE	Do not rebuild the file named FILE even if it is older than its dependents

Chapter 22: Developing Software in Linux

Option	Meaning
-p	Display the make database of variables and implicit rules
-q	Do not run anything, but return zero if all targets are up to date, one if anything needs updating, and two if an error occurs
-r	Get rid of all built-in rules
-s	Work silently (without displaying the commands as they are executed)
-t	Change the timestamp of the files without actually changing them
-v	Display the version number of make and a copyright notice
-w	Display the name of the working directory before and after processing the makefile
-W FILE	Assume that the specified file has been modified

GNU debugger

Although make automates the process of building a program, that task is the least of your worries when a program does not work correctly or when a program suddenly quits with an error message. You need a debugger to find the cause of program errors. This book's companion CD-ROM includes gdb: the versatile GNU debugger that has a command-line interface. gdb can debug C and C++ programs. The CD-ROM also includes xxgdb, an X Window System-based graphical front end for gdb.

Like any debugger, gdb allows you to perform typical debugging tasks, such as the following:

- Set breakpoint so that program execution stops at a specified line
- Watch the values of variables in the program
- Step through the program one line at a time
- Change variables in an attempt to fix errors

Preparing a program for debugging

If you want to debug a program with gdb, you have to ensure that the compiler generates and places debugging information in the executable. The debugging information contains the names of variables in your program and the mapping of addresses in the executable file to lines of code in the source file. gdb needs this information to perform its functions, such as stopping after executing a specified line of source code.

Tip

To ensure that the executable is properly prepared for debugging, use the -g option with GCC. You can do this by defining the variable CFLAGS in the makefile as follows:

```
CFLAGS= -g
```

Running gdb

The most common way to debug a program is to run gdb with the command

gdb *progname*

where progname is the name of the program's executable file. After it runs, gdb displays the following message and prompts you for a command:

```
GDB is free software and you are welcome to distribute copies of it
under certain conditions; type "show copying" to see the conditions.
There is absolutely no warranty for GDB; type "show warranty" for
details.
GDB 4.14 (i486-slackware-linux),
Copyright 1995 Free Software Foundation, Inc...
(gdb)
```

Tip

To see a list of gdb commands, type **help** at the prompt, as follows:

```
(gdb) help
List of classes of commands:

running -- Running the program
stack -- Examining the stack
data -- Examining data
breakpoints -- Making program stop at certain points
files -- Specifying and examining files
status -- Status inquiries
support -- Support facilities
user-defined -- User-defined commands
aliases -- Aliases of other commands
obscure -- Obscure features
internals -- Maintenance commands

Type "help" followed by a class name for a list of commands in that
class.
Type "help" followed by command name for full documentation.
Command name abbreviations are allowed if unambiguous.
(gdb)
```

The initial message displays the classes of gdb commands. You can get further help on a specific class of commands or a specific command by following the instructions. To see the list of commands that you would use to run the program that you are debugging, for example, type **help running**, as follows:

```
(gdb) help running
Running the program.

List of commands:

show args -- Show arguments to give program being debugged when it is
started
info handle -- What debugger does when program gets various signals
kill -- Kill execution of program being debugged
target -- Connect to a target machine or process
handle -- Specify how to handle a signal
```

Chapter 22: Developing Software in Linux

```
run -- Start debugged program
continue -- Continue program being debugged
jump -- Continue program being debugged at specified line or address
until -- Execute until the program reaches a source line greater than
the current
step -- Step program until it reaches a different source line
next -- Step program
finish -- Execute until selected stack frame returns
nexti -- Step one instruction
stepi -- Step one instruction exactly
signal -- Continue program giving it signal specified by the argument
detach -- Detach a process or file previously attached
attach -- Attach to a process or file outside of GDB
unset environment -- Cancel environment variable VAR for the program
--Type <return> to continue, or q <return> to quit--
```

Press Enter to see the rest of the list, as follows:

```
tty -- Set terminal for future runs of program being debugged
set environment -- Set environment variable value to give the program
set args -- Set arguments to give program being debugged when it is
started
thread -- Use this command to switch between threads
thread apply -- Apply a command to a list of threads
apply all -- Apply a command to all threads

Type "help" followed by command name for full documentation.
Command name abbreviations are allowed if unambiguous.
(gdb)
```

To quit gdb, type **q** and then press Enter.

gdb has a large number of commands, but you need only a few to find the cause of an error quickly. Table 22-5 lists the commonly used gdb commands.

Table 22-5	Commonly used gdb commands
Command	**Description**
break NUM	Set a breakpoint at the specified line number (the debugger stops at breakpoints).
bt	Display a trace of all stack frames. (This command shows you the sequence of function calls so far.)
clear	Delete the breakpoint at a specific line in a source file. clear FILENAME:NUMxdraw.c:8, for example, clears the breakpoint at line 8 of file xdraw.c.
continue	Continue running the program that is being debugged. (Use this command after the program has stopped due to a signal or breakpoint.)

(continued)

Table 22-5 *(continued)*

Command	Description
display EXPR	Display value of expression (consisting of variables defined in the program) each time the program stops.
file FILE	Load specified executable file for debugging.
help NAME	Display help on the command named NAME.
info break	Displays a list of current breakpoints, including information on how many times each breakpoint has been reached.
info files	Display detailed information about the file that is being debugged.
info func	Display all function names.
info local	Display information about local variables of current function.
info prog	Display the execution status of the program being debugged.
info var	Display all global and static variable names.
kill	End the program that you are currently debugging.
list	List a section of the source code.
make	Run the make utility to rebuild the executable without leaving gdb.
next	Advance one line of source code in the current function without stepping into other functions.
print EXPR	Show the value of the expression EXPR.
quit	Quit gdb.
run	Start running the currently loaded executable.
set variable VAR=VALUE	Set the value of the variable VAR to VALUE.
shell CMD	Execute a UNIX command CMD without leaving gdb.
step	Advance one line in the current function, stepping into other functions, if any.
watch VAR	Show the value of the variable named VAR whenever the value changes.
where	Display the call sequence. You can use this command to locate where your program died.
x/F ADDR	Examine the contents of the memory location at address ADDR in the format specified by the letter F, which can be o (octal), x (hex), d (decimal), u (unsigned decimal), t (binary), f (float), a (address), i (instruction), c (char), or s (string). You can append a letter indicating the size of data type to the format letter. Size letters are b (byte), h (halfword, 2 bytes), w (word, 4 bytes), and g (giant, 8 bytes). Typically, ADDR is the name of a variable or pointer.

Finding bugs with gdb

To understand how you can find bugs with gdb, you need to see an example. The procedure is easiest to show with a simple example, so I'll start with a rather contrived program that contains a typical bug.

Following is the program, which I stored in the file dbgtst.c:

```
#include <stdio.h>

static char buf[256];
void read_input(char *s);

void main(void)
{
  char *input = NULL; /* Just a pointer, no storage for string */

  read_input(input);

/* Process command. */
  printf("You typed: %s\n", input);

/* ... */
}

void read_input(char *s)
{
  printf("Command: ");
  gets(s);
}
```

This program's main function calls the read_input function to get a line of input from the user. The read_input function expects a character array in which it returns what the user types. In this example, however, main calls read_input with an uninitialized pointer — that's the bug in this simple program.

Build the program using gcc with the -g option, as follows:

```
gcc -g -o dbgtst dbgtst.c
```

To see the problem with this program, run it, as follows:

```
dbgtst
Command: test
Segmentation fault
```

The program dies with the Segmentation fault message. For this small program, you could find the cause by examining the source code. In a real-world application, however, you may not immediately know what caused the error. That's when you can use gdb to find the cause of the problem.

To use gdb to locate a bug, follow these steps:

1. Load the program under gdb. To load a program named dbgtst in gdb, **type the following:**

   gdb dbgtst
   ```
   GDB is free software and you are welcome to distribute copies of it
   under certain conditions; type "show copying" to see the condi-
   tions.
   There is absolutely no warranty for GDB; type "show warranty" for
   details.
   GDB 4.14 (i486-slackware-linux),
   Copyright 1995 Free Software Foundation, Inc...
   (gdb)
   ```

2. Run the program under gdb with the run command. If the program prompts for input, type the input text. The program should fail as it did before. Here's what happens with the dbgtst program:

   ```
   (gdb) run
   Starting program: /home/naba/swdev/dbg/dbgtst
   Command: test

   Program received signal SIGSEGV, Segmentation fault.
   _IO_gets (buf=0x0) at iogets.c:40
   iogets.c:40: No such file or directory.
   (gdb)
   ```

3. Use the where command to determine where the program died. For the dbgtst program, this command yields the following output:

   ```
   (gdb) where
   #0  _IO_gets (buf=0x0) at iogets.c:40
   #1  0x10e1 in read_input (s=0x0) at dbgtst.c:21
   #2  0x10a3 in main () at dbgtst.c:10
   (gdb)
   ```

   The output shows the sequence of function calls. Function call #0 — the most recent one — is to a C library function, gets. The gets call originated in the read_input function, which in turn was called from the main function.

4. Use the list command to inspect the lines of suspect source code. In dbgtst, you might start with line 21 of the dbgtst.c file, as follows:

   ```
   (gdb) list dbgtst.c:21
   16     }
   17
   18     void read_input(char *s)
   19     {
   20       printf("Command: ");
   21       gets(s);
   22     }
   (gdb)
   ```

   After looking at this listing, you should be able to tell that the problem may have been in the way that read_input was called. Then you'd list the lines around line 10 in dbgtst.c (which is where the read_input call originated), as follows:

   ```
   (gdb) list dbgtst.c:10
   ```

```
5
6    void main(void)
7    {
8      char *input = NULL; /* Just a pointer, no storage for string
*/
9
10     read_input(input);
11
12   /* Process command. */
13     printf("You typed: %s\n", input);
14
(gdb)
```

At this point, you should be able to narrow the problem down to the variable named input.

Fixing bugs in gdb

Sometimes, you can try a bug fix directly in gdb. For the example program in the preceding section, you can try this fix immediately after the problem dies with an error. Because the example is a contrived one, I have an extra buffer named buf defined in the dbgtst program, as follows:

```
static char buf[256];
```

I can fix the problem of the uninitialized pointer by setting the variable input to buf. The following session with gdb corrects the problem of uninitialized pointer (this example picks up immediately after the program has run and died due to the segmentation fault):

```
(gdb) file dbgtst
A program is being debugged already. Kill it? (y or n) y

Load new symbol table from "dbgtst"? (y or n) y
Reading symbols from dbgtst...
done.
(gdb) list
1    #include <stdio.h>
2
3    static char buf[256];
4    void read_input(char *s);
5
6    void main(void)
7    {
8      char *input = NULL; /* Just a pointer, no storage for string */
9
10     read_input(input);
(gdb) break 9
Breakpoint 1 at 0x109a: file dbgtst.c, line 9.
(gdb) run
Starting program: /home/naba/swdev/dbg/dbgtst
```

```
Breakpoint 1, main () at dbgtst.c:10
10        read_input(input);
(gdb) set var input=buf
(gdb) cont
Continuing.
Command: test
You typed: test

Program exited with code 020.
(gdb)
```

As the listing shows, if I stop the program just before `read_input` is called and set the variable named `input` to `buf` (which is a valid array of characters), the rest of the program runs fine.

After you try in `gdb` a fix that works, you can make the necessary changes to the source files and make the fix permanent.

Implications of GNU Licenses

There is a price to pay for the bounty of Linux — to protect its developers and users, Linux is distributed under the GNU GPL (General Public License), which stipulates the distribution of the source code.

This does not mean, however, that you cannot write commercial software for Linux that you want to distribute (either free or for a price) in binary form only. You can actually follow all the rules and still sell your Linux applications in binary form.

When writing applications on Linux, you should be aware of two licenses:

- GNU General Public License (GPL) governs many Linux programs, including the Linux kernel and GCC.
- GNU Library General Public License (LGPL) covers many Linux libraries.

Caution

The following sections provide an overview of these licenses and some suggestions on how to meet the requirements of the licenses. Because I am not a lawyer, however, you should not take anything in this book as constituting legal advice. As you'll see, the full text for these licenses is in text files on your Linux system; show these licenses to your legal counsel for a full interpretation and an assessment of applicability to your business.

GNU General Public License

You'll find the text of the GPL in a file named COPYING in various directories in your Linux system. For example, look for a directory named /usr/doc/binutils; you should find a file named COPYING there.

The GPL has nothing to do with whether you charge for the software or distribute it free; its thrust is to keep the software free for all users. GPL does this by requiring that the software be distributed in source-code form and stipulating that any user can copy and distribute the software to anyone else in source-code form. Additionally, everyone is reminded that the software comes with absolutely no warranty.

Software covered by GPL is not in the public domain; such software is always copyrighted, and the GPL spells out the restrictions on the software's copying and distribution. From a user's point of view, of course, GPL's restrictions are not really restrictions; they are benefits, because the user is guaranteed access to the source code.

Caution

If your application uses parts of any software covered by GPL, your application is considered to be a derived work, and it becomes covered by GPL, which means that you must distribute the source code to your application.

Although the Linux kernel is covered by GPL, GPL does not cover your applications that use the kernel services through system calls. Those applications are considered to be normal use of the kernel.

If you plan to distribute your application in binary form (just as most commercial software is distributed), you must make sure that your application does not use any parts of any software covered by GPL. Your application may end up using parts of other software when it calls functions in a library. Most libraries, however, are covered by a different GNU license, which is described in the following section.

You have to watch out for only a few library and utility programs that are covered by GPL. The GNU dbm (gdbm) database library is one of the prominent libraries covered by GPL. The GNU bison parser-generator tool is another utility covered by GPL. If you allow bison to generate code, that code is covered by GPL.

Secret

For the GNU dbm and GNU bison, you have other alternatives that are not covered by GPL. For a database library, you can use the Berkeley database library db in place of gdbm. For a parser-generator, you might use yacc instead of bison.

GNU Library General Public License

You'll find the text of the GNU LGPL in a file named COPYING.LIB, which is located in various directories in your Linux system. You can locate a copy by using the following find command:

```
find /usr -name "COPYING*" -print
```

This command lists all occurrences of COPYING and COPYING.LIB in your system. The COPYING file contains the GPL, whereas COPYING.LIB has the LGPL. Following are two locations of the COPYING.LIB file:

```
/usr/doc/gdb/COPYING.LIB
/usr/doc/binutils/COPYING.LIB
```

You can read the LGPL from any of these files.

The LGPL is intended to allow use of libraries in your applications even if you do not distribute source code for your application. The LGPL stipulates, however, that users must have access to the source code of the library that you used and that users can make use of modified versions of those libraries.

Most Linux libraries, including the C library (libc.a), are covered by LGPL. Thus, when you build your application on Linux with the GCC compiler, your application links with code from one or more libraries covered by LGPL. If you want to distribute your application in binary form only, you need to pay attention to LGPL.

Secret

One way to meet the intent of LGPL is to provide the object code for your application and a makefile that relinks your object files with any updated Linux libraries covered by LGPL.

Wizard

A better way to satisfy LGPL is to use *dynamic linking*, in which your application and the library are separate entities even though your application calls functions in the library when it runs. With dynamic linking, users immediately get the benefit of any updates to the libraries without ever having to relink the application.

Version Control

When you write applications with a few files, it might be simple enough to prepare a makefile to automate the software build process and not worry about keeping track of changes. Typically, for small projects, you might keep track of changes through comments at the beginning of a file.

The NCSA HTTPD software (World Wide Web server), for example, is maintained this way. A makefile is used to build the software. The comments in the source file reflect the changes made from one version to the next. Following is the first part of the main source file — httpd.c — for version 1.4.2 of NCSA HTTPD:

```
/*
 * httpd.c: simple http daemon for answering WWW file requests
 *
 * All code contained herein is covered by the Copyright as distributed
 * in the README file in the main directory of the distribution of
 * NCSA HTTPD.
 *
 *
 * 03-21-93 Rob McCool wrote original code (up to NCSA HTTPd 1.3)
 *
 * 03-06-95 blong
 * changed server number for child-alone processes to 0 and changed name
 *   of processes
 *
 * 03-10-95 blong
 *    Added numerous speed hacks proposed by Robert S. Thau (rst@ai.mit.edu)
 *    including set group before fork, and call gettime before to fork
 *    to set up libraries.
```

```
 *
 * 04-28-95 guillory
 *   Changed search pattern on child processes to better distribute load
 *
 * 04-30-95 blong
 *   added patch by Kevin Steves (stevesk@mayfield.hp.com) to fix
 *   rfc931 logging. We were passing sa_client, but this information
 *   wasn't known yet at the time of the pass to the child. Now uses
 *   getpeername in child_main to find this information.
 */

#include "httpd.h"
#include <sys/types.h>
#include <sys/param.h>
#include "new.h"
(lines deleted...)
```

This approach works well for a small project, but for larger software projects, you should use some tools that help you manage different versions of your applications. In fact, you can benefit from version-control tools even if you are the sole author of a small application. After some time passes, you may have trouble remembering what changes you made. Software version control can help you figure out these changes.

The Linux software distribution comes with RCS (Revision Control System), which is a collection of tools to help you control software revisions. The next few sections provide an overview of RCS and show you how to use it with some simple examples.

Source-control tools in RCS

Source control refers to the idea of saving a version of the source code so that you can recover a specific version or revision of a file whenever you need it. Essentially, when you modify a source file, the sequence goes something like this:

1. When you have an initial version of the source file, you archive it — place it under source control.

2. When you want to make any changes in the file, you first get a copy of the current revision. (When you get it this way, the tools should ensure that no one else can modify that revision.)

3. You make the changes in the source file, test the code, and store the modified file as a new revision.

4. The next time you want to make changes in the file, you start with the latest revision of the file.

RCS provides the tools that allow you to archive file revisions and update them in a controlled manner. Table 22-6 lists the tools.

Table 22-6	RCS tools
Tool	**Purpose**
`ci`	Creates a new revision of a file or add a working file to an RCS file.
`co`	Gets a working version of a file for reading. (`co -l` provides a working file and locks the original so that you can modify the working file.)
`ident`	Searches for identifiers in a file.
`merge`	Incorporates changes from two files into a third one.
`rcsdiff`	Compares a working file with its RCS file.
`rcsmerge`	Merges different revisions of a file.
`rlog`	Views the history of changes in a file.

Beginner's RCS

Suppose that you have just finished developing the initial working version of an application, and you want to use RCS to manage the revisions from now on. The following sections outline the steps that you'd follow to use RCS for your development effort.

Creating initial RCS files

The first step in managing source-file revisions with RCS is to allow RCS to archive the current revision of your files. Follow these steps to put the source file under the control of RCS:

1. In the directory where you keep your application's source files, create a subdirectory named RCS by typing **mkdir RCS**. If the RCS subdirectory exists, RCS archives file revisions in this directory.

2. In each file that you plan to place under revision control, add a comment with the following RCS identification keyword:

   `$Header$`

   In a C source file, for example, add the following:

   ```
   /*
    * $Id$
    */
   ```

   In a makefile, on the other hand, use the following:

   `# $Id$`

   RCS later expands these identifier keywords to include information about the file revision and date.

3. Check in each file with RCS, use the `ci` command, and provide a brief description of each file as prompted by `ci`. Following is how you might check in `Makefile`:

```
ci Makefile
RCS/Makefile,v  <-- Makefile
enter description, terminated with single '.' or end of file:
NOTE: This is NOT the log message!
>> Makefile for sample programs.
>> .
initial revision: 1.1
done
```

When a file is checked in, the `ci` command creates a corresponding RCS file in the RCS subdirectory. The RCS file's name is the same as the original file except for a ,v appended to the name. Thus, the RCS file for `Makefile` is `Makefile,v`. Also, `ci` deleted the original source file after it created the RCS file. To use or edit the file again, you have to extract it with the `co` command.

After you follow these steps, all your files will be safely stored in RCS files in the RCS subdirectory.

Using the archived files

Now suppose that you want to edit one of the files (for example, to add a new feature) and rebuild the application again. For starters, you need all the source files and the makefile for the compile and link step.

You should extract all these files with the `co` command for read-only access only (except for the file that you want to change, as you'll see soon). The `co` command is straightforward to use. To get a working copy of `Makefile` for read-only use, for example, use the following command:

```
co Makefile
RCS/Makefile,v  --> Makefile
revision 1.1
done
```

By default, this command looks for an RCS file named `RCS/Makefile,v` and creates a read-only working copy of it named `Makefile`.

You'll find a copy of `Makefile` in the directory. Examine that copy of `Makefile` to see what happened to that `$Header$` keyword that you added as a comment. Here's what my example `Makefile` shows:

```
# $Id: Makefile,v 1.1 1995/11/26 06:36:54 naba Exp $
```

As this example shows, RCS expands each identifier keyword into a string with information. The exact information depends on the identifier.

If you want to modify a file, you have to check it out with the `-l` option. If you want to check out a copy of the file `xmutil.c` for editing, use the following command:

```
co -l xmutil.c
RCS/xmutil.c,v  --> xmutil.c
revision 1.1 (locked)
don
```

If you compare this output with that from the previous example of `co`, you notice that the current output confirms that the RCS file is locked. No one else can modify the archived file until you check in the copy that you checked out for editing.

When you check out a file and put a lock on it, no one else can check out the same file for editing. Anyone can get a copy of the file for read-only use, however.

After you make changes in a file, you can check it in again with the `ci` command, just as you did when you created the RCS file.

Identification keywords

You can use the RCS identification keywords — each of which is a string delimited by dollar signs ($...$) — to record information in source files. RCS expands the `$Id$` keyword, for example, into summary information about the file, including the filename, revision number, date, and author. All you have to do is put the keyword in the file; RCS takes care of expanding that keyword into the appropriate information. Table 22-7 lists the identification keywords that RCS supports.

Table 22-7   Identification keywords supported by RCS

Keyword	Purpose
`$Author$`	The login ID of the user who checked in the revision.
`$Date$`	The date and time when the revision was checked in.
`$Header$`	Expands to summary information, including full path name of the RCS file, revision number, date, author, and the state of file revision.
`$Id$`	The same as `$Header$`, except that the RCS filename does not have any directory prefix.
`$Locker$`	The login ID of the user who locked the file (empty if the file is not currently locked).
`$Log$`	Expands to a log of changes made in the file.
`$RCSfile$`	The name of the RCS file without the directory names.
`$Revision$`	The revision number of the RCS file.
`$Source$`	Expands to the full path name of the RCS file.
`$State$`	Indicates the state of the file revision (whether it is locked or not).

At minimum, you may want to use the `$Id$` keyword in your files to include summary information about the latest revision.

RCS expands the identifier keywords anywhere in a file. Thus, you might "mark" an object file (and the executable that uses that object file) by placing the identifier keyword in a string variable. A common practice is to define a string named `rcsid` as follows:

```
static const char rcsid[] =
  "$Id";
```

Defining the `rcsid` string causes the object and executable file to contain a string such as the following:

```
$Id: xmutil.c,v 1.2 1995/11/26 06:31:20 naba Exp $
```

Other RCS commands

Most of the time, you will use the `ci` and `co` commands to maintain file revisions by using RCS. RCS, however, includes several other tools for managing various elements of revision control, such as comparing two revisions, viewing the history of changes, and examining identifiers in files.

Viewing the changes made so far

If you checked out a file for modification, you may want to know what changes you have made thus far. You can use the `rcsdiff` program to see a list of changes. If you've been editing a file named `xmutil.c`, for example, you can compare the working file against its RCS file with the following command:

```
rcsdiff xmutil.c
```

The `rcsdiff` program runs the UNIX `diff` utility to find the differences between the working file and the RCS file.

If necessary, you can even find the differences between two specific revisions of a file with a command such as the following:

```
rcsdiff -r1.1 -r1.2 xmutil.c
```

This command lists the differences between revision 1.1 and 1.2 of the file `xmutil.c`.

Discarding changes made so far

Sometimes, after you make some changes in a file, you realize that the changes are either wrong or unnecessary. In such a case, you want to discard the changes that you have made so far.

To discard changes, all you have to do is unlock the RCS file and then delete the working copy of the file. To unlock an RCS file, use the `rcs` command with the `-u` (unlock) option. The following command discards the current changes in the file named `xmutil.c`:

```
rcs -u xmutil.c
```

Another, more convenient way to discard changes is to overwrite the current working file with a copy of the old RCS file. To do this, use the `co` command with `-u` and `-f` flags, as follows:

```
co -f -u xmutil.c
```

The `-u` option unlocks the checked-out revision, and `-f` forces `co` to overwrite the working file with the older revision of that file.

Viewing change history

As you make changes in a file and keep checking in revisions, RCS maintains a log of changes. You can view this log with the `rlog` command. The following example shows how to view the log of changes for the file `xmutil.c`:

```
rlog xmutil.c

RCS file: RCS/xmutil.c,v
Working file: xmutil.c
head: 1.2
branch:
locks: strict
access list:
symbolic names:
comment leader: " * "
keyword substitution: kv
total revisions: 2;    selected revisions: 2
description:
Utility functions
----------------------------
revision 1.2
date: 1995/11/26 06:31:20;  author: naba;  state: Exp;  lines: +15 -1
minor revisions
----------------------------
revision 1.1
date: 1995/11/26 05:55:23;  author: naba;  state: Exp;
Initial revision
============================================================================
```

The first part of the `rlog` output displays some summary information about the RCS file. The lines following the `description:` line show the description that I entered when I created the RCS file. Following this description, you see an entry for each revision, with the most recent revision appearing first. Each revision's entry shows the date, the author, and a brief description entered by the author.

Examining identifier keywords

If you have any identifier keywords embedded in a file, you can view them with the `ident` command. If `Makefile` contains the `$Id$` keyword, you can examine the keyword with the following command:

```
ident Makefile
Makefile:
    $Id: Makefile,v 1.2 1995/11/26 06:36:54 naba Exp $
```

Chapter 22: Developing Software in Linux

Tip

If you define a string variable with a keyword that eventually gets embedded in a binary file (an object file or an executable file), you can use `ident` to view those identifiers as well. You can try `ident` in any binary file to see whether it contains any embedded keywords. Following is what I found when I tried `ident` in the file /usr/bin/co (the executable program for the co command):

```
ident /usr/bin/co
/usr/bin/co:
   $Id: rcsbase.h,v 5.20 1995/06/16 06:19:24 eggert Exp $
   $Id: co.c,v 5.18 1995/06/16 06:19:24 eggert Exp $
   $Id: rcslex.c,v 5.19 1995/06/16 06:19:24 eggert Exp $
   $Id: rcssyn.c,v 5.15 1995/06/16 06:19:24 eggert Exp $
   $Id: rcsgen.c,v 5.16 1995/06/16 06:19:24 eggert Exp $
   $Id: rcsedit.c,v 5.19 1995/06/16 06:19:24 eggert Exp $
   $Id: rcskeys.c,v 5.4 1995/06/16 06:19:24 eggert Exp $
   $Id: rcsmap.c,v 5.3 1995/06/16 06:19:24 eggert Exp $
   $Id: rcsrev.c,v 5.10 1995/06/16 06:19:24 eggert Exp $
   $Id: rcsutil.c,v 5.20 1995/06/16 06:19:24 eggert Exp $
   $Id: rcsfnms.c,v 5.16 1995/06/16 06:19:24 eggert Exp $
   $Id: maketime.c,v 5.11 1995/06/16 06:19:24 eggert Exp $
   $Id: partime.c,v 5.13 1995/06/16 06:19:24 eggert Exp $
   $Id: rcstime.c,v 1.4 1995/06/16 06:19:24 eggert Exp $
   $Id: rcskeep.c,v 5.10 1995/06/16 06:19:24 eggert Exp $
```

From this output, you can tell the exact versions of source files that were used to build this version of the co program.

Linux Programming Topics

Developing software under Linux is quite similar to developing software under any UNIX system. Most C and UNIX programming issues are generic and apply to all UNIX systems. There are, however, a few topics that you want to know about if you are developing software for Linux.

The most significant topic is the use of the new Executable and Linking Format (ELF) binary in Linux. The other topic — the use of dynamic linking in applications — is related to ELF. I also describe how you can exploit dynamic linking and how to create a dynamically linked library in Linux.

Executable and Linking Format (ELF)

If you have programmed in UNIX, you probably know that when you compile and link a program, the default executable file is named a.out. What you may not have realized is that a file format is associated with the a.out file. The operating system has to know this file format so that it can load and run an executable. Linux has been using the a.out format for its binaries ever since it originated.

Although the `a.out` format has served its purpose adequately, it has two shortcomings:

- Shared libraries are difficult to create.
- Dynamically loading a shared library is cumbersome.

The use of shared libraries is desirable because a shared library allows many executable programs to share the same block of code. Also, dynamic loading of modules is becoming increasingly popular because it allows an application to load blocks of code only when needed, thus reducing the memory requirement of the application.

Wizard

Meanwhile, the UNIX System Laboratories (USL) has developed a new binary format named Executable and Linking Format (ELF) for use in System V Release 4 (SVR4). The ELF format is much more flexible than the `a.out` format. In particular, ELF has the following advantages over the `a.out` format in Linux:

- Shared libraries for the ELF format are simpler to create. You compile all source files with the `gcc -fPIC -c` command and then link with a command such as the following, which creates the library `libXXX.so.1.0`:

    ```
    gcc -shared -Wl,-soname,libXXX.so.1 -o libXXX.so.1.0 *.o
    ```

- Dynamic loading (wherein a program loads code modules at runtime) is simpler. With dynamic loading, you can design an application to be extensible so that users can add new code in the form of shared libraries.

Because of ELF's increased flexibility, Linux developers (in particular, the GCC developers) decided to move to ELF as the standard binary-format Linux. By default, the new GCC compiler — `gcc` version 2.7 — generates ELF binaries.

Secret

Notice that GCC version 2.7 continues to use `a.out` as the default name of the executable file (used only if you do not specify an output filename with the `-o` option). Although the executable may be named `a.out`, the binary format is ELF and not the old `a.out` format.

Note

Wizard

The Slackware 3.0 and later versions of Linux distributions include ELF binaries and shared libraries. The companion CD-ROM includes a version of Linux with ELF support.

If you want to check the binary format of an executable file, use the `file` command. The following example shows how you would check the file type of `/bin/ls` (the executable file for the `ls` command):

```
file /bin/ls
/bin/ls: ELF 32-bit LSB executable i386 (386 and up) Version 1
```

On the other hand, the file command reports the following for an older `a.out` format executable, as follows:

```
file a.out
a.out: Linux/i386 demand-paged executable (QMAGIC) not stripped
```

Shared libraries in Linux applications

Most Linux programs use shared libraries. At minimum, most C programs use the C shared library `libc.so.X`, wherein X is a version number. When a program uses one or more shared libraries, you need the program's executable file, as well as all the shared libraries, to run the program. In other words, your program won't run if all shared libraries are not available on a system.

If you sell an application, you need to make sure that all necessary shared libraries are distributed with your software.

Examining shared libraries that a program uses

Use the `ldd` utility to determine what shared libraries an executable program needs. Following is what `ldd` reports for a typical C program compiled with `gcc` version 2.6.3 (the program uses the old `a.out` format):

```
ldd a.out
    libc.so.4 (DLL Jump 4.6p127) => /lib/libc.so.4.6.2
```

Notice the text in parentheses, `DLL Jump`. That text refers to the format for shared libraries in the old `a.out` binary format.

In the more recent ELF binary format, `ldd` reports the following for a typical C program (compiled and linked with `gcc` version 2.7.0):

```
ldd a.out
    libc.so.5 => /lib/libc.so.5.0.9
```

For a more complex program such as `xv` (ELF version), `ldd` shows more shared libraries, as follows:

```
ldd /usr/X11/bin/xv
    libX11.so.6 => /usr/X11R6/lib/libX11.so.6.0
    libtiff.so.1 => /usr/lib/libtiff.so.1.3
    libm.so.5 => /lib/libm.so.5.0.0
    libc.so.5 => /lib/libc.so.5.0.9
```

In this case, the required libraries include the X11 library (`libX11.so.6`), TIFF library (`libtiff.so.1`), Math library (`libm.so.5`), and C library (`libc.so.5`).

Thus, almost any Linux application requires shared libraries to run. Additionally, the shared libraries must have the same binary format as that used by an application.

Creating a shared library

With ELF, creating a shared library for your own application is simple enough. Suppose that you want to implement an object in the form of a shared library. A set of functions in the shared library will represent the object's interfaces. To use the object, you load its shared library and then invoke its interface functions (you learn how to do this in the following section).

Following is the C source code for this simple object, implemented as a shared library (you might also call it a dynamically linked library):

```c
/*-------------------------------------------------------------*/
/* File: dynobj.c
 *
 * Demonstrate use of dynamic linking.
 * Pretend this is an object that can be created by calling
 * init and destroyed by calling destroy.
 */
#include <stdio.h>
#include <stdlib.h>
#include <string.h>

/* Data structure for this object */
typedef struct OBJDATA
{
  char *name;
  int version;
} OBJDATA;

/*-------------------------------------------------------------*/
/* i n i t
 *
 * Initialize object (allocate storage).
 *
 */
void* init(char *name)
{
  OBJDATA *data = (OBJDATA*)calloc(1, sizeof(OBJDATA));
  if(name)
    data->name = malloc(strlen(name)+1);
  strcpy(data->name, name);

  printf("Created: %s\n", name);

  return data;
}
/*-------------------------------------------------------------*/
/* s h o w
 *
 * Show the object.
 *
 */
void show(void *data)
{
  OBJDATA *d = (OBJDATA*)data;
  printf("show: %s\n", d->name);
}
/*-------------------------------------------------------------*/
/* d e s t r o y
 *
 * Destroy the object (free all storage).
 *
 */
void destroy(void *data)
{
```

```
  OBJDATA *d = (OBJDATA*)data;
  if(d)
  {
    if(d->name)
    {
      printf("Destroying: %s\n", d->name);
      free(d->name);
    }
    free(d);
  }
}
```

The object offers three interface functions:

- `init` to allocate any necessary storage and initialize the object
- `show` to display the object (here, it simply prints a message)
- `destroy` to free any storage

To build the shared library named `libdobj.so`, follow these steps:

1. Compile all source files with the `-fPIC` flag. In this case, compile the `dynobj.c` file with the following command:

   ```
   gcc -fPIC -c dynobj.c
   ```

2. Link the objects into a shared library with the `-shared` flag, and provide appropriate flags for the linker. To create the shared library named `libdobj.so.1`, use the following:

   ```
   gcc -shared -Wl,-soname,libdobj.so.1 -o libdobj.so.1.0 dynobj.o
   ```

3. Set up a sequence of symbolic links so that programs that use the shared library can refer to it with a standard name. For the sample library, the standard name is `libdobj.so`, and the symbolic links are set up with the following commands:

   ```
   ln -s libdobj.so.1.0 libdobj.so.1
   ln -s libdobj.so.1 libdobj.so
   ```

4. When you test the shared library, define and export the `LD_LIBRARY_PATH` environment variable with the following command:

   ```
   export LD_LIBRARY_PATH='pwd':$LD_LIBRARY_PATH
   ```

After you test the shared library and are satisfied that the library works, you should copy it to a standard location, such as `/usr/local/lib`, and run the `ldconfig` utility to update the link between `libdobj.so.1` and `libdobj.so.1.0`. Following are the commands that you use to install your shared library for everyone's use (you have to be `root` to perform these steps):

```
cp libdobj.so.1.0 /usr/local/lib
/sbin/ldconfig
cd /usr/local/lib
ln -s libdobj.so.1 libdobj.so
```

Dynamically loading a shared library

ELF makes it simple to load a shared library in your program and use the functions within the shared library. The header file `<dlfcn.h>` declares the functions for loading and using a shared library. There are four functions for dynamic loading:

- `void *dlopen(const char *filename, int flag);` — Loads the shared library specified by `filename` and returns a handle for the library. The flag can be `RTD_LAZY` (resolve undefined symbols as the library's code is executed) or `RTD_NOW` (resolve all undefined symbols before `dlopen` returns and fail if all symbols are not defined). If `dlopen` fails, it returns `NULL`.

- `const char *dlerror (void);` — If `dlopen` fails, call `dlerror` to get a string that contains a description of the error.

- `void *dlsym (void *handle, char *symbol);` — Returns the address of the specified `symbol` (function name) from the shared library identified by the `handle` (that was returned by `dlopen`).

- `int dlclose (void *handle);` — Unloads the shared library if no one else is using it.

When you use any of these functions, include the header file `<dlfcn.h>` with the following preprocessor directive:

```
#include <dlfcn.h>
```

Following is a simple test program that shows how to load and use the object defined in the shared library `libdobj.so`, which you created in the preceding section:

```
/*-----------------------------------------------------------*/
/* File: dltest.c
 *
 * Test dynamic linking.
 *
 */
#include <dlfcn.h>   /* For the dynamic loading functions */
#include <stdio.h>

void main(void)
{
  void *dlobj;
  void * (*init_call)(char *name);
  void (*show_call)(void *data);
  void (*destroy_call)(void *data);

/* Open the shared library and set up the function pointers */
  if(dlobj = dlopen("libdobj.so.1",RTLD_LAZY))
  {
    void *data;

    init_call=dlsym(dlobj,"init");
    show_call=dlsym(dlobj,"show");
    destroy_call=dlsym(dlobj,"destroy");
```

```
/* Call the object interfaces */
    data = (*init_call)("Test Object");
    (*show_call)(data);
    (*destroy_call)(data);
  }
}
```

The program is straightforward: it loads the shared library, gets the pointers to the functions in the library, and calls the functions through the pointers.

You can compile and link this program in the usual way, except that you must link with the -ldl option so that you can use the functions declared in <dlfcn.h>. Following is how you build the program dltest:

```
gcc -o dltest dltest.c -ldl
```

To see the program in action, run dltest as follows:

```
dltest
Created: Test Object
show: Test Object
Destroying: Test Object
```

Although this procedure does not seem exciting, you now have a sample program that uses a shared library.

To see the benefit of using a shared library, go back to the preceding section, and make some changes in the shared library (print some other message in a function, for example). Rebuild the shared library alone. Then run dltest again. The resulting printout should show the effect of the changes that you made in the shared library, which means that you can update the shared library independent of the application.

Summary

Your Linux system comes loaded with all the tools that you need to develop software. In particular, you'll find all the GNU software development tools, such as GCC, the GNU debugger, GNU make, and the RCS version-control utility. This chapter describes these software development tools and show you how to use them. By reading this chapter, you learn

- The GNU tools comprise the software development environment on your Linux PC. These tools include GNU Emacs for text editing, GCC for compiling C and C++ programs, GNU make for automating software builds, the GNU debugger for debugging, and RCS for version control.

- A utility named info provides online help information on the GNU tools. You can run info alone or under GNU Emacs with the Ctrl+h I command.

- GCC is the GNU C and C++ compiler. You can use the gcc command to compile and link C programs. Use g++ to compile and link C++ programs.

- GCC has a plethora of options, but you need to use only a few. Some of the common options are -c (for compiling only) and -o (for specifying the name of the output executable file).

- The GNU make utility allows you to automate the build process. You specify the modules that compose an executable as well as any dependencies; make takes care of compiling only those files that need recompilation. The input file for make is known as a *makefile* and is commonly named Makefile.

- The GNU debugger allows you to locate errors in your programs. Use the gdb command to run the debugger. You have to compile the program with GCC's -g option to generate debugging information that the GNU debugger can use.

- When you use GNU tools to develop software (as you would in Linux), you should be aware of the GNU licenses: GNU General Public License (GPL) and GNU Library General Public License (LGPL). The GNU libraries are covered by LGPL. If you distribute your software in binary form, you should use dynamic linking to comply with the terms of the LGPL. You should not take anything in this book as constituting legal advice, of course; always consult your own legal counsel for a definitive answer.

- Version control is an important part of software development. In Linux, you get RCS (Revision Control System) to manage revisions of source files. With RCS, you use commands such as ci and co to manage source files. You can embed strings such as Id or $Header$ to mark the revision and date in your source files.

- Shared libraries are commonly used in Linux applications to reduce the memory requirement of executables. Applications are dynamically linked with a shared library at run-time, and many applications can share a single shared library.

- The Linux development community recently adopted the Executable and Linking Format (ELF), which makes dynamic linking simpler to program. This chapter shows an example of how to use dynamic linking in your own applications.

Chapter 23
X Programming in Linux

In This Chapter

- Understanding event-driven programming
- Understanding callback functions and event handlers
- Writing a Motif program
- Understanding Motif widgets
- Setting widget resources
- Using Xlib functions in Motif programs
- Summarizing X events
- Drawing text, graphics, and images in Motif programs

This chapter turns to another important programming topic: how to write applications with graphical user interfaces. This topic means writing X applications, because the X Window System happens to be the underlying windowing system on Linux.

The primary programming interface to the X Window System is the Xlib library of C functions. You can use Xlib functions to build graphical user interfaces with menus and buttons, using a hierarchy of windows, and display graphics, text, and images in these windows. Although you can do a great deal with Xlib, building complete programs by using Xlib functions alone is tedious. To build user interfaces without getting mired in details, you need utility functions and a collection of prefabricated user-interface components, such as buttons, menus, and scrollbars. Luckily, several X toolkits provide the tools that help you build user interfaces easily.

The current crop of X toolkits includes Open Software Foundation's Motif toolkit, Sun's XView, and OPEN LOOK Intrinsics Toolkit (OLIT), and the Athena Widgets, to name but a few. Of these, Motif happens to be the most popular toolkit for creating graphical user interfaces.

Note

Unfortunately, Motif is a licensed product of the Open Software Foundation, so the companion CD-ROM does not include Motif. If you want to develop Motif applications, you'll have to buy Motif separately. Nevertheless, I cover Motif programming in this chapter because if you are developing X applications at all, chances are that you'll have to use Motif.

This chapter provides a brief introduction to the Motif toolkit, which is based on the Xt Intrinsics. This chapter shows you how to create and manipulate widgets through the functions provided by the Xt Intrinsics. The latter part of the chapter provides an overview of the Motif widget set and describes how to use Xlib functions to draw in a Motif application.

Cross Reference

If you have not yet purchased Motif for your Linux system, Chapter 4 lists a few vendors of Motif for Linux.

Basic Motif Programming

The Motif toolkit provides a set of user interface components called *widgets*. You can think of each widget as being a window with some associated information, such as window dimensions and color. The *Xt Intrinsics*, a layer of data structures and functions built with Xlib, provides the necessary data structures for a widget. The Xt Intrinsics also automatically handles redrawing a widget's contents when needed.

Just as windows in X are organized in a parent–child hierarchy, with child windows contained within a parent's borders, Motif widgets are organized in a parent-child hierarchy.

If you have never written any applications with graphical user interfaces, you'll have to adapt to a new programming style when you write Motif applications. That new programming style is known as *event-driven programming*.

Note

In an event-driven program, you do not specify the exact sequence of tasks that the program must perform. Instead, you define many small functions, each of which is responsible for responding to an event such as "user has clicked the Save button." The event-driven program waits for events and processes each event by calling the corresponding event-handler function.

You'll understand event-driven programming best by going through the simple example presented in the following section.

Step-by-step Motif programming

To write any Motif program, you follow these steps:

1. Include the Motif header files, as follows:

    ```
    #include <Xm/Xm.h>

    /* Include header file of each widget you plan to use.
     * For example, here are the necessary header files for Form, Label,
     * and PushButton widgets.
     */

    #include <Xm/Form.h>
    #include <Xm/Label.h>
    #include <Xm/PushB.h>
    ```

2. Call the `XtAppInitialize` function to initialize the toolkit and create a top-level widget. This function returns an identifier (of the data type `Widget`) that represents the top-level widget.

3. Call `XtVaCreateManagedWidget` to create each widget and set the widget's internal variables, known as *resources*.

4. Call `XtAddCallback` to indicate what functions should be called to handle specific events occurring in a widget. These functions are known as *callback functions*. In a Motif program, all work is done in callback functions.

5. Call `XtRealizeWidget` with the identifier of the top-level widget as the argument. This action realizes (creates) all the widgets.

6. Call the `XtAppMainLoop` function to begin processing events.

This action gets the Motif program running.

A simple Motif program

The following listing shows a simple Motif program that displays a button. The program quits when the user clicks the button.

```
/*------------------------------------------------------------*/
/* File: xmquit.c
 *
 * An example program that displays a PushButton
 * inside a Form widget.
 *
 */

#include <Xm/Xm.h>
#include <Xm/Form.h>
#include <Xm/PushB.h>

/* Label for the push button */
static char label[] = "Press here to quit...";

/* Prototype of callback function */
static void cb_quit(Widget w, XtPointer client_data,
                    XtPointer call_data);

/*------------------------------------------------------------*/
void main(int argc, char **argv)
{
    XtAppContext app;
    Widget      toplevel, quit_button, form;
    XmString    xmlabel;

/* Initialize toolkit and create the top-level widget */
    toplevel = XtAppInitialize(&app, "XMquit", NULL, 0,
                   &argc, argv, NULL, NULL, 0);
```

```c
  /* Create the Form widget */
    form = XtCreateManagedWidget("Form", xmFormWidgetClass,
                toplevel, NULL, 0);

  /* Create the push button widget as a child of the Form
   * and set its label at the same time. This also shows
   * how to create a "Motif String (XmString)" and use it.
   */

    xmlabel = XmStringCreateLtoR(label,
                XmSTRING_DEFAULT_CHARSET),
    quit_button = XtVaCreateManagedWidget("Exit",
            xmPushButtonWidgetClass, form,
            XmNlabelString, xmlabel,
            NULL);
    XmStringFree(xmlabel);

  /* Set the callback function for this pushbutton */
    XtAddCallback(quit_button, XmNactivateCallback,
        cb_quit, NULL);

  /* Realize the widgets */
    XtRealizeWidget(toplevel);

  /* Start the event loop */
    XtAppMainLoop(app);
}
/*--------------------------------------------------------------*/
/* c b _ q u i t
 *
 * Function to be called when user presses and releases button
 * in the pushbutton.
 */
static void cb_quit(Widget w, XtPointer client_data,
            XtPointer call_data)
{
    XtCloseDisplay(XtDisplay(w));
    exit(0);
}
```

Makefile for a Motif program

Use the makefile shown in the following listing to compile and link the xmquit program. (You need Motif installed on your system.)

```
###############################################################
# Makefile to compile and link a Motif program on Linux

LDFLAGS= -lXm -lXt -lX11 -lXext

all: xmquit

xmquit.o: xmquit.c
```

```
xmquit: xmquit.o
    cc -o xmquit xmquit.o $(LDFLAGS)
```

Using the makefile in this section's code, type **make** to build the program, as follows:

```
make
cc  -c xmquit.c -o xmquit.o
cc -o xmquit xmquit.o -lXm -lXt -lX11 -lXext
```

To test the program, first make sure that X is running on your Linux PC. From an xterm window, type xmquit to run the program. Figure 23-1 shows the graphical interface displayed by the xmquit program.

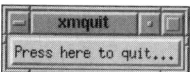

Figure 23-1: The output of the sample Motif program xmquit.

When you click the push button (by pressing and releasing the left mouse button with the pointer inside the push button's window), the program exits.

Widget resources

When you use a Motif widget in an application, you do not need to know the details of the widget's data structure. What you need is information about the configurable parameters of the widget. These parameters, known as the widget's *resources*, control its appearance and behavior. A widget's resources simply mean any configurable data used by that widget.

To be useful as a building block of user interfaces, a widget has to be highly configurable. A widget that allows the programmer to pick the foreground and background colors, for example, is much more useful than one that hard-wires these values.

As a programmer, you can set a widget's resources through an argument list. To do this, you first have to consult the widget's documentation and learn the names of the resources that you want to set. The resource names are constants, such as XmNwidth and XmNheight. You use the constants XmNwidth and XmNheight to refer to the width and height resources of a widget.

To set the values of resources through an argument list, specify the value of each resource in an Arg structure, which is defined in <X11/Intrinsic.h> with the following typedef statement:

```
typedef struct
{
  String   name;  /* Name of resource */
  XtArgVal value; /* Its value        */
} Arg, *ArgList;
```

The value of the resource is stored as an `XtArgVal` — a system-dependent data type that is capable of holding a pointer to any C variable. If the value of a resource is less than the size of `XtArgVal`, it is stored directly in the `value` field of `Arg`. Otherwise, the `value` field is a pointer to the resource's value.

When you create a widget, you can specify an array of `Arg` structures with the values of the resources that you want to set. You can prepare the array of resource values in two ways:

- Use a statically initialized array of `Arg` structures.
- Assign values at runtime by using the `XtSetArg` macro.

To see how to set resources, consider the `PushButton` widget. Suppose that you want to set the push button's width and height as well as its *label* — the text displayed on the button. The documentation of the `PushButton` widget tells you that the names of the resources are `XmNwidth`, `XmNheight`, and `XmNlabelString`. You also have to know that the string for `XmNlabelString` is not a simple C character array; it is a *compound string*, a special data type that you create by passing the string as an argument to a Motif utility routine (`XmStringCreateLtoR`).

With that information in hand, you can set the resource values with an `Arg` array as follows:

```
Arg      args[20];
Cardinal nargs;
XmString cstr;
.
.
.
cstr = XmStringCreateLtoR("WarnGen", XmSTRING_DEFAULT_CHARSET);
XtSetArg(args[nargs], XmNwidth, 160);      nargs++;
XtSetArg(args[nargs], XmNheight, 80);      nargs++;
XtSetArg(args[nargs], XmNlabelString, cstr); nargs++;
XmStringFree(cstr);
```

There is a reason why `nargs++` is not used in `XtSetArg` to increment the count of arguments; `XtSetArg` is defined as a macro in such a way that it uses the first argument twice. If you use `nargs++` in the first argument, the macro ends up incrementing `nargs` twice in each call. This situation is why most toolkit applications define the argument list as shown.

After you prepare the argument list, call the `XtCreateManagedWidget` function to create a widget and set its resources, as follows:

```
Arg      args[20];
Cardinal nargs;
Widget   toplevel, /* Previously-created top-level shell */
         pb1;      /* New push-button                    */
```

```
pb1 = XtCreateManagedWidget("WarnGen", xmPushButtonWidgetClass, toplevel,
                             args, nargs);
```

This procedure creates a new push button named `WarnGen` whose parent widget is `toplevel` and whose initial resource settings are in the array `args`.

You can avoid the tedious steps of specifying the resources one by one and then creating the widget. The Xt Intrinsics library includes the `XtVaCreateManagedWidget` function, which allows you to specify the resources and create the widget with a single function call. You can create a push button with specified width, height, and label, for example, by using the following call to `XtVaCreateManagedWidget`:

```
Widget  toplevel, /* Previously-created top-level shell */
        pb1;    /* New push-button           */
XmString label; /* Compound string to store label  */

/* First, create the compound string for the label */
xmlabel = XmStringCreateLtoR("WarnGen", XmSTRING_DEFAULT_CHARSET);

h_button = XtVaCreateManagedWidget("WarnGen",
           xmPushButtonWidgetClass, toplevel,
           XmNwidth,     200,
           XmNheight,    100,
           XmNlabelString, xmlabel,
           NULL);

/* Free the compound string (the Motif toolkit makes a copy) */
XmStringFree(xmlabel);
```

As the code fragment shows, `XtVaCreateManagedWidget` accepts a variable number of arguments, as follows:

- The first three arguments are required and are the same as those required by `XtCreateManagedWidget`. The first argument is the name of the widget, the second one is the widget class, and the third one specifies the parent widget.

- Following the three compulsory arguments comes a list of resource specifications. Each specification is in the form of a resource name followed by the value of that resource.

- A NULL resource name marks the end of this list.

Callback registration

Most Motif widgets include a class of resources known as *callbacks*, which are pointers to functions. You can set such a resource to one of your functions and have the widget call that function in response to one or more events. These functions go by the name of *callback functions* because the Motif toolkit calls them back when appropriate.

A widget typically has more than one type of callback resource, each type meant for functions to be called in a specific situation. A widget's callback resource actually is a list of functions rather than a single function. The widget calls all the callbacks when the conditions for that callback resource are met. The calling order is the same as the order in which you register the callbacks.

In the program listed under the heading "A simple Motif program," the function `cb_quit` is a callback function for the push button widget's `XmNactivateCallback` resource. According to the `PushButton` documentation, the widget calls the functions in the `XmNactivateCallback` resource when the user clicks the button. In addition to `XmNactivateCallback`, `PushButton` has two more callback resources:

- `XmNarmCallback` functions, called when the user clicks the button.
- `XmNdisarmCallback` list, called when the user releases the button.

As the example shows, you use the `XtAddCallback` function to add a function to a callback list of a widget. To add the `cb_quit` function to the `XmNactivateCallback` resource of the `quit_button` widget, use the following:

```
XtAddCallback(quit_button, XmNactivateCallback, cb_quit, NULL);
```

The last argument of `XtddCallback` — declared to be of type `XtPointer` — is a pointer to data that you want passed to the callback function when the widget calls it. The callback function, `cb_quit`, has the following prototype:

```
static void cb_quit(Widget w, XtPointer client_data, XtPointer call_data);
```

When the widget calls this function, the second argument will be whatever you passed to `XtAddCallback` as the last argument. The last argument passed to the callback function is the pointer to an `XmAnyCallbackStruct` structure, which is defined in `<Xm/Xm.h>` (refers to the file `/usr/include/Xm/Xm.h`) as follows:

```
typedef struct
{
    int    reason;  /* Indicates why callback was called  */
    XEvent *event;  /* Information on event that triggered callback */
} XmAnyCallbackStruct;
```

The `reason` field indicates why the widget called the callback function. You have to consult the widget's documentation to interpret the value of this field. The `event` field is a pointer to an `XEvent` structure with information on the event that triggered the callback.

Event-handler registration

Suppose that you want to allow the user to draw in a widget's window with the mouse. (Motif provides an `XmDrawingArea` widget for this purpose.) To program this capability, you want to catch the mouse click in the widget's window. The Motif toolkit allows you to do this by using a method similar to the callback resources used by widgets. Essentially, you can register your own event handler for selected events in a widget's window. Thereafter, when these events occur, the widget calls the registered event handler, giving you a chance to take some action.

Use the Xt Intrinsics function `XtAddEventHandler` to add an event handler. To add a function named `event_handler` as the handler for `ButtonPress` events in the `drawing` widget, you would use the following:

```
XtAddEventHandler(drawing, ButtonPressMask, FALSE,
        event_handler, NULL);
```

The first argument of `XtAddEventHandler` is the widget for which you are setting up an event handler. The second argument is an *event mask* (a bit pattern represented by a named constant value) that specifies the events for which the handler is invoked. The third argument is a Boolean value that should be set to `True` if you are setting the event handler for one of the X events — `ClientMessage`, `MappingNotify`, `SelectionClear`, or `SelectionRequest` — for which there is no event mask. In this case, set the second argument to `NoEventMask`. As in `XtAddCallback`, the last argument is a pointer to any data that you want to be passed back to the event handler when it is called.

You have to write the `event_handler` function according to the following prototype:

```
void event_handler(Widget w, XtPointer client_data, XEvent *event);
```

As this function prototype shows, the widget calls the event handler with three arguments:

- The first argument is the widget's ID.
- The second argument is the same pointer that you passed as the last argument of `XtAddEventHandler` when you registered this event handler.
- The third argument is a pointer to the `XEvent` structure that triggered the function call.

You'll find a summary of X events in the "X event summary" section.

Motif Widgets

A widget set is like any toolbox; before using the tools, you have to know what each one does. This section provides an overview of the Motif widgets so that you can learn the widget categories and what each category can do. You also should learn how to use important widgets in each category. Then you'll be able to pick the widgets that meet your needs and use them in your application. The next few sections provide an overview of the Motif widgets.

There are three distinct categories of Motif widgets:

- *Shell widgets* provide the top-level window for a Motif application. Pop-up dialog boxes also use shell widgets.

- *Primitive widgets* represent the stand-alone widgets, such as labels, push buttons, and scrollbars.
- *Manager widgets* can contain other widgets as children and manage the layout of the child widgets. This category includes forms, message boxes, and scrolled windows.

Note

All Motif widgets inherit the resources of a widget named Core. Knowing the resources of the Core widget is important, because its resources apply to every widget. Following is a list of the Core resources:

- XmNaccelerators is the translation table that binds a sequence of keyboard and mouse events to specific actions.
- XmNancestorSensitive is a Boolean variable that indicates whether the immediate parent of a widget receives input events. To alter this resource setting, call the XtSetSensitive function.
- XmNbackground is the background pixel value for the widget's window. The pixel value translates to an actual RGB (red-green-blue) color through the current colormap.
- XmNbackgroundPixmap is a pixmap (a block of memory that stores an array of pixel values) used to tile the widget's window.
- XmNborderColor and XmNborderPixmap are the colormap and pixmap for the border of the widget's window.
- XmNborderWidth is the width of the border of the widget's window.
- XmNcolormap is the colormap to be used by the widget's window.
- XmNdepth is the number of bits used for each pixel value in the widget's window. This value is set by Xt Intrinsics when the window is created.
- XmNdestroyCallback is the list of functions to be called when you destroy the widget by calling the XtDestroyWidget function.
- XmNheight and XmNwidth are the height and width of the widget's window, excluding the border width.
- XmNmappedWhenManaged is a flag that, when set to True, maps the widget's window as soon as the widget is realized and managed (the XtCreateManagedWidget function manages the widget). You can alter this flag by calling the XtSetMappedWhenManaged function.
- XmNscreen is a pointer to the Screen data structure that contains information about the physical display screen where the widget's window is displayed.
- XmNsensitive is a Boolean variable that, when True, causes Xt Intrinsics to dispatch mouse and keyboard events to the widget. To alter this resource, use the function XtSetSensitive.

- `XmNTranslations` is the *translation table* — a list of events with corresponding functions that are called when the specified events occur.
- `XmNx` and `XmNy` are the *x* and *y* coordinates of the upper-left corner of the widget's window, excluding the border. The coordinates are specified in the parent widget's coordinate frame.

Shell widgets

A shell widget manages only one child; its primary purpose is to set up the top-level window of an application. Xt Intrinsics provides several classes of shell widgets, the important of which are as follows:

- `TopLevelShell`
- `OverrideShell`
- `TransientShell`

When you call `XtAppInitialize`, Xt Intrinsics creates an instance of `ApplicationShell` widget, a subclass of `TopLevelShell`. The `ApplicationShell` and `TopLevelShell` widgets are used for normal top-level windows of applications. The window manager interacts with these top-level windows.

The `TransientShell` class is used for pop-up dialog boxes, which are top-level windows that the user can move but not resize to an icon. To create a dialog box, you actually use a subclass of `TransientShell` called `DialogShell`. Motif includes several "convenience functions" that enable you to create a `DialogShell` widget and place inside it another widget, such as a selection box or a message box. These convenience functions have names that start with `XmCreate` and end with `Dialog` (for example, `XmCreateFileSelectionDialog` or `XmCreateMessageDialog`).

The `OverrideShell` widget is a type of `Shell` widget that completely bypasses the window manager. The window manager does not put any frames around an `OverrideShell` widget. Motif defines a subclass of `OverrideShell` — `XmMenuShell` — to display pop-up menus. You can use the function `XmCreatePopupMenu` to create a `MenuShell` with a menu inside it.

Primitive widgets

All Motif primitive widgets are derived from the `XmPrimitive` class, which in turn is defined as a subclass of the `Core` class. The `XmPrimitive` class defines a standard set of resources that are inherited by all primitive widgets. In particular, the `XmPrimitive` class is responsible for the 3-D shading effect of Motif widgets.

Motif versions

The latest version of Motif is 2.0. Much of the UNIX world, however, still uses Motif version 1.2.x. One reason for the persistence of the older version of Motif is the Common Desktop Environment (CDE), which uses X11R5 and Motif 1.2 as the foundation. Motif 2.0 is what you get when you buy one of the commercially available versions of Motif for Linux.

Most Motif distributions include a sample program named `periodic` that displays a periodic table (remember the periodic table of elements in chemistry?) of widgets. Following is a screen shot of the periodic table of widgets for Motif 2.0.

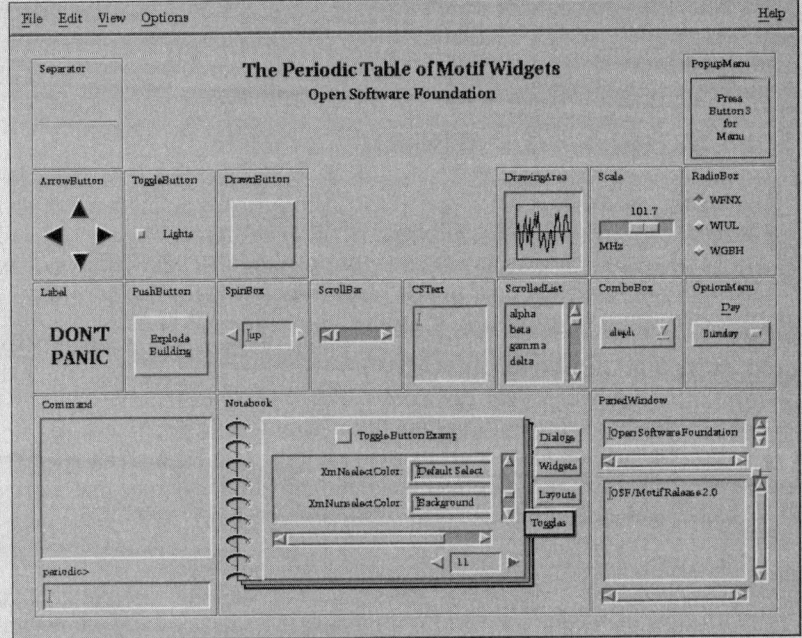

Compared with version 1.2.x, Motif 2.0 has the following new features:

- Addition of six new widgets: `CSText` (compound text editing), `ComboBox` (just like the Microsoft Windows `ComboBox`, a drop-down list with a text-editing area), `SpinButton` (two arrow buttons to cycle through choices), `IconGadget` (icon- and text-based list browser), `Container` (manages IconGadget widgets), and `Notebook` (displays information in a book with tabbed pages).

- Support of X Pixmap (XPM) image format for defining color icons.

- Unified support for cut and paste as well as drag and drop through the Uniform Transfer Model (UTM).

- Keyboard support for drag-and-drop operation.

- Use of the `XmRenderTable` property to support multiple fonts, colors, underlining, and tab stops in the `XmString` data type.

- Inclusion of the C++ classes `XmCxxPrimitive` and `XmCxxManager`, from which you can derive other C++ widget classes.

Note

The following eight primitive widgets are derived directly from the `XmPrimitive` class:

- `ArrowButton` displays a button with an arrow. You can specify the direction of the arrow.
- `CSText` displays and edits multiple lines of compound strings. The text can include multiple fonts, colors, underlined text, and embedded tabs.
- `Label` displays a string or a pixmap inside a window.
- `List` displays a list of text items from which the user can select one or more.
- `Sash` is used as a separator between two panes. The user can drag the sash to adjust the size of the panes.
- `ScrollBar` is a scrollbar with arrows at the two ends and a slider. Scrollbars can be horizontal or vertical.
- `Separator` is used to separate items in a menu.
- `Text` widget acts as a single or multiple-line editor.
- `TextField` displays a single line of editable text.

The functionality of the `Label` class is further specialized by the following subclasses:

- `CascadeButton` displays an associated pull-down menu when the user clicks the `CascadeButton`.
- `DrawnButton` is button that allows you to draw on it (so that you can display whatever you want on the button).
- `PushButton` is a standard push button.
- `TearOffButton` is a special push button that displays a tear-off menu.
- `ToggleButton` displays a string or a pixmap next to a small button. The button represents a state with two values: on or off. When the user clicks the button, it changes state.

All primitive widgets inherit the resources of the `XmPrimitive` class. Following are some of the important resources of the `XmPrimitive` class:

- `XmNbottomShadowColor` is the pixel value used to draw the bottom and right side of a primitive widget's shadow. These two sides are collectively called the *bottom shadow*.
- `XmNbottomShadowPixMap` is the pixmap used to draw the bottom shadow.
- `XmNforeground` is the foreground color to be used in the primitive widgets.
- `XmNhelpCallback` is the list of callbacks that can be bound to functions that provide context-sensitive help.
- `XmNhighlightColor` is the color used to highlight the widget's window. A push button, for example, is highlighted when the user clicks it.

- `XmNhighlightOnEnter` is a Boolean variable that, when set to `True`, asks the widget to highlight its window when the cursor enters the window (provided that the input focus follows the pointer; the window with the input focus gets the keyboard input). This resource is ignored if the user has to click to indicate input focus.

- `XmNhighlightPixmap` is the pixmap used to highlight the widget's window.

- `XmNhighlightThickness` is the thickness of the rectangle used to highlight the widget's window.

- `XmNnavigationType` is a constant that specifies how focus is assigned to the widget during keyboard traversal (keyboard traversal refers to the way the input focus moves from one widget to another as the user presses the Tab key); it can be `XmNONE`, `XmTAB_GROUP`, `XmSTICKY_TAB_GROUP`, or `XmEXCLUSIVE_TAB_GROUP`.

- `XmNshadowThickness` is the thickness of the shadow.

- `XmNtopShadowColor` is the color for the top shadow. Used only if `XmNtopShadowPixmap` is `NULL`.

- `XmNtopShadowPixmap` is the pixmap for the top shadow.

- `XmNtraversalOn` is a Boolean value that indicates whether the widget accepts keyboard inputs.

- `XmNunitType` is the measurement unit used for all values that specify dimensions in the widget. The default value is copied from a manager that owns the widget. Usually, the default unit is pixels (specified by the constant `XmPIXELS`). Motif allows you to work in device-independent units, if you prefer. You specify the unit with one of the constants: `XmPIXELS`, `Xm100TH_MILLIMETERS`, `Xm1000TH_INCHES`, `Xm100TH_POINTS`, or `Xm100TH_FONT_UNIT`, defined in the header file `<Xm/Xm.h>`. You can set `XmNunitType` to `Xm100TH_FONT_UNIT`, for example, to indicate that all dimensions are in terms of one hundredth of a font's unit. You can explicitly set the font unit with the `XmSetFontUnits` function.

- `XmNuserData` is a pointer that is not used internally. You can store a pointer to your own widget-specific data in this resource.

Manager widgets

The manager widgets are derived from the `XmManager` class — a subclass of the `Constraint` class that in turn inherits from the `Composite` class. A manager widget can act as a container for other child widgets and manage the layout of the children. Some manager widgets, such as `Form`, allow you to specify the layout in terms of constraints such as "attach this child widget to the left edge of the container."

All manager widgets inherit their resources from the `XmManager` class. The `XmManager` resources are similar to those of the `XmPrimitive` class.

Chapter 23: X Programming in Linux   711

Note

Following are a few important manager widgets:

- The Command widget is a type of SelectionBox that provides a command-history mechanism. There is a command-entry area where the user can type commands. When you execute a command by pressing Enter, that command string is saved in a history buffer, which is displayed in a scrollable list area. You can use the Command widget to accept user input for your command-driven applications.

- The DrawingArea widget provides an empty window where you can draw graphics or text (using Xlib functions as described in the "Xlib function overview" section later in this chapter).

- The FileSelectionBox widget is a special type of SelectionBox that displays a list of filenames in a list box. The widget has an area where the user can enter a *file filter*, which is a search string used to locate the files of interest. (*.c , for example, displays all filenames that end with .c.) The user's current selection is displayed in another box. At the bottom of the widget are four buttons labeled OK, Filter, Cancel, and Help.

- The Form widget supports complex layouts specified through certain resources that the widget attaches to each of its children. These resources are known as *constraint resources*; in effect, they provide a layout language that you can use to indicate how the child widgets are placed in the Form. Each constraint resource indicates the spatial relationship of a child widget to the Form or to another existing child widget.

- The Frame widget displays a frame (with 3-D shading) around a single child widget.

- The MainWindow widget provides a standard layout for the main window of an application. The MainWindow widget manages a combination of a menu bar, a Command widget, a DrawingArea widget, and scrollbars.

- The MessageBox widget displays a message and a row of three buttons labeled OK, Cancel, and Help.

- The PanedWindow widget lays out its children in panes, arranged vertically.

- The RowColumn widget arranges its children in rows and columns. You can use RowColumn widgets in menu bars and pull-down menus.

- The Scale widget displays an elongated rectangle with a slider that allows the user to enter a numerical value. You can set the minimum and maximum values for the scale and for floating-point values; you can specify the number of digits to follow the decimal point.

- The ScrolledWindow widget manages a work area (that can contain other widgets) and two scrollbars (horizontal and vertical).

- The SelectionBox widget displays a list of items in a scrollable box and provides an area where the current selection is displayed. The widget has three buttons labeled OK, Cancel, and Help. You can optionally turn on or off a fourth button labeled Apply.

Xlib and Motif

You can use the Motif widgets to build the user interface of a Motif application, but you cannot build most real-world applications with the Motif widgets alone. Suppose that your application is for viewing satellite images for weather forecasting. You can use Motif widgets to allow the user to select a satellite image and even prepare a scrollable viewing area to display the image. To actually display the image, however, you have to rely on Xlib functions. You use Xlib functions for displaying image, graphics, and text in Motif applications. Additionally, you may have to write code that responds to an X event.

Note

The bottom line is that you have to learn the basics of X programming with Xlib functions, even if you use the Motif toolkit to write most of your applications. The next few sections provide an overview of Xlib and X events. You'll also see an example of how to use Xlib drawing functions in a Motif application.

An overview of Xlib

The X Window System uses a client/server model to provide its services. The X server takes care of input and output at the display. X applications are the clients that use the capabilities of the server by sending X protocol requests. The X protocol requests are delivered over a communication link between the clients and the X server. For client and server running on different machines, this link is a network connection. If both client and server are on the same machine, the communication may be through a shared block of memory or some other interprocess communication (IPC) mechanism supported by the operating system.

Although you could conceivably write an X application that performs all input and output by sending X protocol requests to the server, doing so would be like programming a microprocessor directly in its machine language. To ease the programmer's job, the X Window System includes *Xlib*, a set of C language functions and macros that X applications can use to access the facilities of the X server.

Because Motif is based on X, a Motif application also is an X client; under the hood, a Motif application works by calling Xlib functions.

The primary purpose of Xlib is to provide an easy way for C programmers to send X protocol requests to the server. Xlib, however, is much more than just a set of functions with one-to-one correspondence to all possible X protocol requests; it also includes many convenience functions to ease the burden of handling common tasks while hiding the X protocol completely from the programmer. For example, only one X protocol request exists to create a window, but Xlib has two routines for creating windows: `XCreateSimpleWindow` and `XCreateWindow`, of which the first one is simpler than the second. Similarly, the foreground and background colors for a window are specified in a graphics context (GC). To set these colors, you simply call the Xlib routines `XSetForeground` and `XSetBackground`. Xlib takes care of setting up the proper protocol requests to change only these colors in the specified GC.

Xlib also includes many utility functions that don't have anything to do with interacting with the X server. Xlib utility functions help you get the user's choices from a resource file, manipulate screen images and bitmaps, translate names of colors to pixel values, and use the resource manager.

Xlib function overview

Broadly speaking, Xlib functions allow an application to open the X display (connect to the X server), create windows and draw in them, retrieve events, and finally close the display. If you are developing a Motif application, you can get by with a reasonably small number of Xlib functions. You do not have to worry about opening the display, for example, if you are using the Motif toolkit. In a Motif application, you primarily use the Xlib graphics, image, and text-output functions.

Table 23-1 summarizes the commonly used Xlib functions, grouped according to task. This list is by no means complete, yet it is rather long. As a Motif programmer, you do not have to learn all these functions; I am providing this list just to give you an overall view of Xlib's capabilities. For complete coverage of Xlib functions, consult the books listed in the "More Information on Xlib and Motif Programming" sidebar.

Table 23-1   Common Xlib functions grouped according to task

Task	Commonly used Xlib functions
Open/close X display	XOpenDisplay XCloseDisplay
Get user's choices	XGetDefault XrmInitialize XrmGetResource XrmParseCommand
Create/manage windows	XCreateSimpleWindow XCreateWindow XDestroyWindow XMapRaised XMapWindow XUnmapWindow XGetWindowAttributes XChangeWindowAttributes
Control window's size and position	XGeometry XGetGeometry XMoveWindow XResizeWindow XMoveResizeWindow XLowerWindow XRaiseWindow XCirculateSubWindows
Interact with window manager	XSetStandardProperties XGetWMHints XSetWMHints
Get and process events	XSelectInput XEventsQueued XNextEvent XPeekEvent
Synchronize with server	XFlush XSync XSynchronize
Handle errors	XGetErrorText XSetErrorHandler XSetIOErrorHandler

(continued)

Table 23-1 (continued)

Task	Commonly used Xlib functions
Manipulate graphics contexts	XCreateGC XChangeGC XCopyGC XFreeGC XSetForeground XSetState XSetBackground XSetFunction
Draw graphics	XDrawArc XDrawArcs XDrawLine XDrawLines XSetDashes XSetArcMode XDrawPoints XDrawPoint XDrawRectangle XDrawRectangles XFillArc XFillArcs XSetFillRule XFillRectangle XFillRectangles XFillPolygon XSetLineAttributes
Clear and copy areas	XClearWindow XClearArea XCopyArea XCopyPlane
Draw text	XLoadFont XLoadQueryFont XSetFont XUnloadFont XDrawString XDrawImageString XDrawText XTextWidth XListFonts
Use color	XDefaultColorMap XDefaultVisual XGetVisualInfo XParseColor XAllocColor XGetStandardColorMap XSetWindowColorMap XFreeColors
Display images	XCreatePixmap XFreePixmap XCreatePixmapFromBitmapData XReadBitmapFile XWriteBitmapFile XCreateImage XDestroyImage XGetImage XPutImage XGetPixel XPutPixel
Handle mouse and keyboard input	XQueryPointer XTranslateCoordinates XCreateFontCursor XDefineCursor XFreeCursor XUndefineCursor XGetMotionEvents XLookupString XRefreshKeyboardMapping XRebindKeysym
Interapplication communication	XInternAtom XChangeProperty XGetWindowProperty XDeleteProperty XSendEvent XGetSelectionOwner XSetSelectionOwner XConvertSelection

Common Xlib features

Although Xlib has a large number of functions, they share some common features. Knowing these common features can help you use Xlib effectively. The common features fall into the following categories:

- Common header files

- Function and data-structure naming conventions
- Order of arguments in function calls

Header files

If you use Xlib functions in a program, you have to include the following header files:

```
#include <X11/Xlib.h>
#include <X11/Xutil.h>
```

The first header file declares the Xlib functions and data structures. The second header file is used by the utility functions of Xlib. Additionally, you may need to include other header files, such as `<X11/cursorfont.h>`, if you use the standard cursor shapes.

When a header file is named this way (`<X11/Xlib.h>`), the compiler expects to find the file in the X11 subdirectory of the standard location for header files: the `/usr/include` directory. Thus, you'll find the file `<X11/Xlib.h>` in the `/usr/include/X11` directory of your system.

Naming conventions

Note

Xlib follows a consistent naming convention for all functions, macros, and data structures. When you know this naming scheme, you can often guess function names and avoid common typing errors. Following are the naming conventions:

- *Functions and macros.* The names of Xlib functions and macros are built by concatenating one or more words, with the first letter of each word capitalized (see Table 23-1 for examples). The names of functions begin with a capital X, but macro names never start with X. In fact, if a function and a macro work identically, the function's name is derived by adding an X prefix to the macro's name. The macro that returns the name of the current X display is `DisplayString`, for example, and the equivalent function is named `XDisplayString`.

More information on Xlib and motif programming

This chapter provides an overview of Motif programming and how Xlib functions are used in Motif applications. However, a single chapter is not enough to provide all the information that you need to fully exploit the power of Xlib and the Motif toolkit. Because of X and Motif's popularity, there are quite a few books on Xlib and Motif programming. For a more complete discussion of Xlib and the Motif toolkit, consult one of the following books:

Volume 1: Xlib Programming Manual, O'Reilly & Associates, O'Reilly & Associates, 1993

Volume 2: Xlib Reference Manual, O'Reilly & Associates, O'Reilly & Associates, 1993

Volume 6A: Motif Programming Manual, Second Edition, Dan Heller, Paula Ferguson and David Brennan, O'Reilly & Associates, 1994

Volume 6B: Motif Reference Manual, Paula Ferguson and David Brennan, O'Reilly & Associates, 1993

- *Data structures.* User-accessible data structures are named just like functions; their names begin with a capital X. Data-structure members are named in lowercase, with underscore characters (_) separating multiple words. The XImage data structure, for example, has an integer field named bits_per_pixel. This rule does not apply to data structures whose members are not to be accessed by the user. An example is the Display data structure, whose name does not begin with X because the user is not supposed to access the internals of this structure directly.

You can use these conventions to select names for your own data structures and functions so that they do not conflict with names in Xlib. You can use lowercase names for your variables and uppercase names for your macros. To be safe, you may decide to add a unique prefix (perhaps your organization's or your project's initials) to all your external functions and variables.

Argument order in Xlib function calls

In addition to the naming conventions, Xlib functions and macros order their arguments in a consistent manner. The arguments appear in the following order:

- *Display.* The display is the first argument of a function or a macro.
- *Windows, fonts, and other X server resources.* X server resources — such as window, font, and pixmap — appear immediately after the display argument. When several resources are used, windows and pixmaps precede all others. The graphics context (GC) appears last among the resources.
- *Source and destination.* Many functions perform tasks that involve taking something from one or more arguments (the source) and storing the result in other arguments (the destination). In these cases, the source arguments always precede the destination arguments.
- *x, y, width, and height.* Many functions take the position (*x*, *y*) and size (*width*, *height*) of windows or pixmaps as arguments. Among *x* and *y*, the *x* argument always precedes *y*, whereas *width* always comes before *height*. When all four arguments are present, the order is *x*, *y*, *width*, and *height*.
- *Bit mask.* Xlib has some functions that selectively change one or more members in a structure. You indicate the members that are being changed by setting bits in a *bit mask* (an integer variable in which each bit position corresponds to a member of the structure). When a function takes a bit mask as an argument, the mask always precedes the pointer to the structure.

Knowing the convention for argument order is even more helpful than knowing how functions are named. After you get familiar with a few Xlib functions, you can often guess the argument list for a function simply because you know these rules.

X server resources

Chapter 5 uses the term *resource* to mean user-customizable parameters in an application. In the context of the X server, however, *resource* signifies anything created at the request of an application. Thus, X resources include the following:

- Window
- Graphics context (GC)
- Font
- Cursor
- Colormap
- Pixmap

A large part of X programming involves creating and using these resources, because that is how an X or Motif application generates output in windows and accepts input from the mouse and keyboard.

Applications create resources by calling Xlib functions. When your program creates any of these resources, the Xlib function returns a resource ID — a 32-bit identifier (of type `unsigned long` in the C programming language). For your convenience, the header file `<X11/X.h>` uses the C `typedef` statement to define several synonyms — such as `Window`, `Font`, `Pixmap`, `Cursor`, and `Colormap` — for the resource identifiers. Thus, when you create a window, you can refer to the returned resource ID as a `Window`.

Windows

Among the resources of the X server, windows are the most important. The windows are the lifeblood of the X Window System. In X, a *window* is an area of the display screen where an application displays output and accepts input (mouse and keyboard). X allows windows to be nested in a parent–child hierarchy, with all child windows clipped at the boundary of the parent. Whenever an X application draws text or graphics, it must specify a window. Also, all inputs from the mouse and the keyboard are associated with a window. Xlib includes many functions for controlling the size, color, and the hierarchy of windows.

Graphics contexts (GC)

To avoid repeatedly sending graphics attributes to the server, X uses the concept of a *graphics context* (GC) — an X server resource that holds all graphics attributes, such as colors and font, that are necessary for drawing in a window. These graphics attributes control the appearance of the output. The advantage of this approach is that an application can create one or more GCs at the server, initialize them, and later use them for drawing in a window. Because a GC is identified by a resource identifier, you can ask the server to use a specific set of attributes by including a single graphics-context identifier in the drawing request instead of a variable number of graphics attributes.

To perform text output by using the Xlib text-output routine, `XDrawString`, you have to create the GC and set up the font and colors before calling `XDrawString`. You can use Xlib routines such as `XCreateGC` and `XChangeGC` to create and manipulate GCs.

Fonts

In X, a *font* refers to a collection of bitmaps (a pattern of ones and zeros) that represent the size and shape of characters from a set. The X server uses a font to display text in a window. When you call an Xlib function such as XDrawString to draw one or more characters, the server retrieves and draws the image corresponding to each character from the current font.

Cross Reference

X provides a large number of fonts with a standard naming convention. You have to load one of these fonts before drawing text in a window; otherwise, the server uses a default font. To specify a font, use a resource identifier of type Font. Chapter 5 summarizes the font-naming convention of X.

Cursors

The *cursor* represents the shape of the on-screen pointer that indicates the current position of the mouse. As you move the mouse, the cursor tracks the movement on-screen. A cursor is somewhat similar to a single character from a font. In fact, you can call Xlib's XCreateFontCursor function to create a new cursor by selecting one of the characters from a special cursor font. As with any other resource, when you create a cursor, you get back a resource identifier of type Cursor. After creating a cursor, you can assign it to a window by using the function XDefineCursor. If you do not define any cursor for a window, the X server uses the cursor of its parent.

Changing cursors is a useful way to inform users about the special purpose of a particular window. If a window manager allows you to resize a window by dragging the corners of a window's frame, for example, the window manager changes the cursor when the user has the mouse at the corners.

Colormaps

Note

An X display screen uses a block of memory, known as the *frame buffer* (or *video memory*), that is capable of storing a fixed number of bits (usually, 8) for each pixel on the screen. This number is the so-called *pixel value*. The color displayed at each pixel, on the other hand, is the result of varying the intensities of three closely located dots of the basic colors: red (R), green (G), and blue (B). The intensity of these three components is often referred to as the *RGB value* or the *RGB triplet*.

The *colormap* is the key to generating an RGB triplet from a pixel value — it maps a pixel value to an RGB color. For example, if the video memory stores 8-bit pixel values, a pixel can take one of 2^8, or 256, possible values. Thus, the colormap must have 256 entries, and each entry must show the intensities of the R, G, and B components.

When an X application uses colors, it works with pixel values. To ensure that a pixel value appears as the correct color, the application has to identify the colormap that is used to translate that pixel value to a color. The application does so through the colormap resource.

The video card in most systems can use only one colormap at a time — a situation that creates the notion of installing a colormap. If multiple applications install colormaps independently, the result will be chaos. The convention is that X applications should never install their own colormaps; instead, they should inform the window manager of the colormaps that they need. Given the right hints, the window manager will take care of installing the right colormap for each application.

Pixmaps

A *pixmap* is a block of memory in the X server in which you can draw just as you would in a window. In fact, window and pixmap resources are collectively known in X as *drawables*. All drawing functions accept drawables as arguments. What you draw in a pixmap does not appear on the display; to make the contents of a pixmap visible, you have to copy from the pixmap to a window. You can think of a pixmap as being an off-screen window — a two-dimensional array of pixel values that can be used to hold graphics images and fill patterns. If each pixel value in a pixmap is represented by a single bit, the pixmap is known as a bitmap.

X event summary

Everything in an X application happens in response to events received from the X server. When an application creates a window and makes it visible by mapping it, for example, the application cannot tell whether the server has actually finished preparing the window for output. To draw in that window, the application must wait for a specific event — an `Expose` event — from the server. All mouse and keyboard inputs from the user also arrive at the X application in the form of events.

Because the basic design of X does not impose any particular style of user interface, X events contain an extraordinary amount of detail. For example, you can get one mouse event when a mouse button is clicked and another when that button is released. For each event, you can find out (among other things) which button was involved, the window that contains the cursor, the time of the event, and the x and y coordinates of the cursor location. This level of detailed event reporting allows programmers to use X to implement any type of user interface.

X provides 33 events for handling everything from mouse and keyboard input to messages from other X clients. Table 23-2 summarizes the X events.

Table 23-2	Summary of X events
Event name	**Meaning**
Mouse events	
`ButtonPress`	Mouse button clicked with pointer in the window
`ButtonRelease`	Mouse button released with pointer in the window

(continued)

Table 23-2 *(continued)*

Event name	Meaning
Mouse events	
EnterNotify	Mouse pointer enters the window
LeaveNotify	Mouse pointer leaves the window
MotionNotify	Mouse moved after stopping
Keyboard events	
FocusIn	Window receives input focus (all subsequent keyboard events come to that window)
FocusOut	Window loses input focus
KeyMapNotify	Occurs after an EnterNotify or FocusIn event (this is how the X server informs the application of the state of the keys after these events)
KeyPress	Key pressed (when window has focus)
KeyRelease	Key released (when window has focus)
MappingNotify	Keyboard reconfigured (the mapping of a key to a string has changed)
Expose events	
Expose	Previously obscured window or part of window becomes visible
GraphicsExpose	During graphics copy operations, parts of the source image are obscured (means that the copied image is not complete)
NoExpose	Graphics copy is successfully completed
Colormap notification event	
ColormapNotify	Window's colormap has changed
Interclient communication events	
ClientMessage	Another client has sent a message, using the XSendEvent function
PropertyNotify	Property associated with the window has changed
SelectionClear	Window loses ownership of selection
SelectionNotify	Selection successfully converted
SelectionRequest	Selection needs conversion
Window-state notification events	
CirculateNotify	Window raised or lowered in the stacking order
ConfigureNotify	Window moved or resized, or position in the stacking order changed

Event name	Meaning
Window-state notification events	
CreateNotify	Window created
DestroyNotify	Window destroyed
GravityNotify	Window moved because its parent's size changed
MapNotify	Window mapped
ReparentNotify	Window's parent changed
UnmapNotify	Window unmapped
VisibilityNotify	Window's visibility changed (became visible or invisible)
Window-structure control events	
CirculateRequest	Request to raise or lower the window in the stacking order (used by window managers)
ConfigureRequest	Request to move, resize, or restack window (used by window managers)
MapRequest	Window about to be mapped (used by window managers)
ResizeRequest	Request to resize window (used by window managers)

The 33 X events shown in Table 23-2 can be broadly grouped in the following seven categories:

- *Mouse events.* The X server generates mouse events when the user clicks a mouse button or moves the mouse.

- *Keyboard events.* The server generates keyboard events when the user presses or releases any key on the keyboard. These events are delivered to an application only if a window owned by the application has the input focus. Usually, the window manager decides how the focus is transferred from one window to another. There are two common focus models: click a window to type in it (used by the Macintosh and Microsoft Windows), or allow the focus to follow the mouse pointer (which means that the focus is assigned to the window that contains the mouse pointer).

Secret

- *Expose events.* Of all X events, an Expose event is the most crucial; applications draw in their windows in response to this event. Almost all X applications request and process this event. (In Motif applications, most Expose events are handled behind the scenes, but you do have to take care of Expose events in DrawingArea widgets.) The GraphicsExpose and NoExpose events have to do with copying from one part of a window or a pixmap to another. These events allow applications to handle situations in which the source of the copy operation is obscured by another window and the contents of the obscured area are unavailable for copying.

- *Colormap notification event.* The server generates a `ColorMapNotify` event whenever an application changes the colormap associated with a window or installs a new colormap. Well-behaved X applications should handle the colormap changes through the window manager.

- *Interclient communication events.* These events send information from one X application to another. The concepts of property and selection are used for this purpose.

- *Window-state notification events.* The server generates these events whenever a window is moved or resized, or when its place in the stacking order is altered. These events are useful for keeping track of changes in the layout of windows on-screen. Typically, window managers use these events for this purpose; your application can use them, too, if you want to alter the size and position of the subwindows when the user resizes the topmost window.

- *Window-structure control events.* These events are used almost exclusively by window managers to intercept an application's attempt to change the layout of its windows. By monitoring the `MapRequest` event, for example, the window manager can tell when an application maps its topmost window. When this happens, the window manager can add its own frame to the window and places it at an appropriate location on-screen.

Xlib programming topics

When you write Motif applications, the Motif toolkit takes care of many window-creation and event-handling details for you. All that you typically provide are callback functions that perform application-specific tasks. You need to use only a small set of Xlib functions in a Motif application. The following sections provide an overview of the types of Xlib programming that you have to perform in a Motif application.

Setting cursor shape and color

The cursor determines the on-screen appearance of the mouse pointer. In X, a cursor is defined by the following parameters:

- Source bitmap
- Mask bitmap
- Foreground and background colors, specified as RGB values
- Hotspot (the point in the cursor's bitmap that defines the location of the pointer on-screen)

The bitmaps are small rectangular arrays of ones and zeros (usually, 16×16 or 32×32). When drawing the cursor, the X server paints the pixels that correspond to ones by using the foreground color, whereas pixels at locations with zeros appear in the background color. The mask bitmap determines the outline within which the cursor shape is drawn. The hotspot determines the pointer location. For many cursor shapes, the hotspot is at the center of the cursor's bitmap. For an arrow cursor, the hotspot is the point of the arrow.

Chapter 23: X Programming in Linux

You can assign a cursor to any window in your Motif application. The following example shows how you might create a new cursor from a standard cursor font and assign it to the window of a `DrawingArea` widget in a Motif application:

```
#include <X11/cursorfont.h>
Cursor xhair_cursor;
   .
   .
   .
/* Create a cross-hair cursor for the drawing area. Assume that
 * "drawing area" is the name of the DrawingArea widget.
 */
  xhair_cursor = XCreateFontCursor(XtDisplay(drawing_area),
                  XC_crosshair);
   .
   .
   .
/* Change the cursor shape in the DrawingArea (call this after the
 * widgets are realized.
 */
/* Realize all widgets */
  XtRealizeWidget(top_level);

/* Set the cursor for the DrawingArea widget's window */
  XDefineCursor(XtDisplay(drawing_area), XtWindow(drawing_area),
        xhair_cursor);

/* Free the cursor */
  XFreeCursor(XtDisplay(drawing_area), xhair_cursor);
```

After this is done, the cursor shape changes to the cross-hair cursor whenever the pointer enters the window `my_window`. This selection remains in effect until you undefine the cursor for that window by calling `XUndefineCursor`. When you remove the cursor from a window, the server displays the cursor of its parent when the pointer is in that window with an undefined cursor.

Notice that the second argument of `XCreateFontCursor` specifies the cursor shape with a symbolic name. These names are defined in the header file `<X11/cursorfont.h>`.

After assigning a cursor to a window, if you do not intend to refer to it anymore, you can free the cursor by calling `XFreeCursor`. Any window that displays this cursor will continue to do so; the server will get rid of the cursor only after that cursor is not defined for any window. After you undefine a cursor, you must not refer to that cursor's ID again.

When a cursor is created, it has, by default, a black foreground and a white background. To change the color of a cursor, use the `XRecolorCursor` function, as follows:

```
XColor fgcolor, bgcolor; /* Colors in XColor structure */
Cursor arrow_cursor;     /* Cursor whose color is set */

XRecolorCursor(theDisplay, arrow_cursor, &fgcolor, &bgcolor);
```

You have to allocate the foreground and background colors before using them in the `XRecolorCursor` function call.

You also can use your own source and mask bitmaps to define a custom cursor. After you have the two pixmaps (bitmaps are pixmaps of depth 1), you can use `XCreatePixmapCursor` to create a new cursor. This function needs the two pixmaps, the foreground and background colors, and the coordinates of the hotspot, as shown in the following example:

```
Display    *theDisplay;
Cursor     my_cursor;
Pixmap     source, mask;
XColor     fgcolor, bgcolor;
unsigned int x_hot, y_hot;

my_cursor = XCreatePixmapCursor(theDisplay, source, mask,
            &fgcolor, &bgcolor, x_hot, y_hot);
```

Another way to get a cursor is to select a specific character from a font and use the bitmap of that character as a cursor. Before using the font, you have to load the font by calling the `XLoadFont` function. Then you can create the cursor by using the function `XCreateGlyphCursor`.

Drawing graphics and text

To draw graphics or text in an X window, you have to create a *graphics context* (GC) — a data structure (resource) in which the X server stores graphics attributes such as background and foreground colors, line style, and font. The appearance of graphics and text is controlled by these attributes.

Creating a GC

To create a GC, use the Xlib function `XCreateGC`. This function takes four arguments, in the following order:

- A pointer to the X display
- The ID of a drawable (a `Window` or a `Pixmap` variable)
- An unsigned long bit mask that indicates which attributes of the GC you want to specify
- The address of a `XGCValues` structure

You specify various graphics attributes in the `XGCValues` structure and use the bit mask to indicate which members of the structure have valid values. Following is an example of how to call `XCreateGC`:

```
Display    *disp;
Drawable   win;
unsigned   long mask;
XGCValues  xgcv;
GC         gc;
```

```
/* Set values of selected members of xgcv, as needed.
 * Then set mask. This example sets the foreground and the
 * background pixels to the default white and black colors
 * for the screen.
 */
xgcv.foreground = WhitePixel(disp, DefaultScreen(disp));
xgcv.background = BlackPixel(disp, DefaultScreen(disp));
mask = GCForeground | GCBackground;

gc = XCreateGC(disp, win, mask, &xgcv);
```

Because a GC is a resource, it consumes memory in the X server. Therefore, you should free a GC when it is no longer needed. You can do so with the XFreeGC function, as follows:

```
Display *disp;
GC      gc;

XFreeGC(disp, gc);
```

The X server automatically frees all your application's resources (including GCs) when the application exits, so you need to explicitly destroy a GC only when you have created one for a temporary purpose.

GC attributes

Note

The X server maintains the GC, so you don't need to know the internal details of the GC. You specify the values of a GC's attributes through a XGCValues structure. The basic idea is to set the values of the attributes that you want and then to create a bit mask to indicate which attributes you are specifying. The X server uses the XGCValues structure together with the bit mask to determine which parts of a GC to change.

The definition of the XGCValues structure gives you an idea of what graphics attributes you can control. Following is how that structure is defined in the <X11/Xlib.h> header file:

```
typedef struct
{
  int        function;          /* Operation on pixels    */
  unsigned long plane_mask;     /* Bit planes affected    */
  unsigned long foreground;     /* Foreground pixel value */
  unsigned long background;     /* Background pixel value */
  int        line_width;        /* Line width (0 or more) */
  int        line_style;        /* One of: LineSolid,
                                   LineOnOffDash,
                                   LineDoubleDash         */
  int        cap_style;         /* One of: CapNotLast,
                                   CapButt, CapRound,
                                   CapProjecting          */
  int        join_style;        /* One of: JoinMiter,
                                   JoinRound, JoinBevel   */
  int        fill_style;        /* One of: FillSolid,
                                   FillTiled, FillStippled,
                                   FillOpaqueStippled     */
```

```
    int     fill_rule;          /* One of: EvenOddRule,
                                   WindingRule      */
    int     arc_mode;           /* One of: ArcChord,
                                   ArcPieSlice      */
    Pixmap  tile;               /* Pixmap for tiling    */
    Pixmap  stipple;            /* Bitmap for stippling */
    int     ts_x_origin;        /* x and y offset for tile*/
    int     ts_y_origin;        /* or stipple operations */
    Font    font;               /* Default font         */
    int     subwindow_mode;     /* One of: ClipByChildren,
                                   IncludeInferiors   */
    Bool    graphics_exposures; /* True=generate exposures*/
    int     clip_x_origin;      /* Origin of clip_mask  */
    int     clip_y_origin;
    Pixmap  clip_mask;          /* Bitmap for clipping  */
    int     dash_offset;        /* Controls dashed line */
    char    dashes;             /* Pattern of dashes    */
} XGCValues;
```

To set these attributes, you also need the name of the bit mask associated with each member of the XGCValues structure. Table 23-3 lists the bit masks used to select specific members of XGCValues. When you set multiple attributes, use a bitwise-OR (indicated by the C operator |) combination of the masks corresponding to the attributes that you want to set.

Table 23-3 also shows the default value of each attribute. When you create a GC without specifying any attribute values, the X server initializes the GC with the default attribute values.

Table 23-3   Bit-mask constants for GC attributes

Attribute name	Bit-mask constant	Description
function	GCFunction	Operation on pixels. (Default: overwrite existing pixels.)
plane_mask	GCPlaneMask	Bit planes affected. (Default: all bitplanes affected.)
foreground	GCForeground	Foreground pixel. (Default: 0.)
background	GCBackground	Background pixel. (Default: 1.)
line_width	GCLineWidth	Line width. (Default: 0.)
line_style	GCLineStyle	Line style. (Default: solid line.)
cap_style	GCCapStyle	How lines end. (Default: ends at end point without any projection.)
join_style	GCJoinStyle	How lines join. (Default: miter join.)
fill_style	GCFillStyle	Fill style. (Default: solid fill.)

Chapter 23: X Programming in Linux

Attribute name	Bit-mask constant	Description
fill_rule	GCFillRule	How figures are filled. (Default: fill using the even-odd rule, in which a point is inside if a line drawn from outside the figure crosses its edges an odd number of times.)
arc_mode	GCArcMode	Appearance of filled arcs as pie slices or closed with a chord. (Default: arcs filled as pie slices.)
tile	GCTile	Pixmap for tiling. (Default: pixmap filled with foreground pixel.)
stipple	GCStipple	Bitmap for stippling. (Default: bitmap of all ones.) The stipple pattern is like a stencil through which the foreground color is applied to a drawable.
ts_x_origin	GCTileStipXOrigin	x-offset for tiling or stippling. (Default: 0.)
ts_y_origin	GCTileStipYOrigin	y-offset for tiling or stippling. (Default: 0.)
font	GCFont	Default font for text output. (Default: depends on X server.)
subwindow_mode	GCSubwindowMode	Draw into children or not. (Default: do not draw into child windows.)
graphics_exposures	GCGraphicsExposures	Graphics exposure events generated if True. (Default: True.)
clip_x_origin	GCClipXOrigin	x-origin of clip_mask. (Default: 0.)
clip_y_origin	GCClipYOrigin	y-origin of clip_mask. (Default: 0.)
clip_mask	GCClipMask	Bitmap for clipping. (Default: no clip mask used.)
dash_offset	GCDashOffset	Starting point in dash pattern. (Default: 0.)
dashes	GCDashList	Pattern of dashes. (Default: pattern of 4 pixels on and then 4 off.)

Drawing points

The simplest graphics operations in X are to draw a point in a window or pixmap. You can draw a single point at the coordinates (x, y) with the following call:

```
Display *disp; /* The connection to the X server  */
Window  win;   /* The drawable—a window          */
GC      thisGC; /* Graphics context for the drawing */
int     x, y;  /* Point to be drawn              */

XDrawPoint(disp, win, thisGC, x, y);
```

The pixel at the location is set to the foreground color specified in the GC. Other attributes in the GC control the final appearance of the point. For example, the point is not drawn if it lies outside the clip mask.

Tip

If you want to draw a large number of points, all using the same GC, you can use the XDrawPoints function to draw them all at the same time with a single X protocol request. Store the points in an array of XPoint structures. The XPoint structure is defined in <X11/Xlib.h>, as follows:

```
typedef struct
{
    short x, y;   /* x and y coordinates of the point */
} XPoint;
```

You call XDrawPoints in the usual manner with a display, a drawable, and a GC as the first three arguments, as follows:

```
XPoint pt[10];
int    numpt = 10;
...
XDrawPoints(p_disp, window_1, thisGC, pt, numpt,
     CoordModeOrigin);
```

The three standard arguments are followed by the array of points and number of points. The last argument tells the server how to interpret the coordinates of the points in the array. You can specify one of the following constants:

- CoordModeOrigin means that the coordinates are relative to the origin of the window or the pixmap.
- CoordModePrevious is used when the coordinate of each point is given in terms of the x and y displacements from the preceding point. The first point is assumed to be relative to the origin of the window.

Drawing lines

Xlib includes three line-drawing functions:

- XDrawLine
- XDrawSegments
- XDrawLines

The XDrawLine function has the following calling syntax:

```
XDrawLine(disp, win, thisGC, x1, y1, x2, y2);
```

This function draws a line between the points (x1, y1) and (x2, y2) in the drawable named win, using the line attributes specified in the GC (thisGC).

XDrawSegments draws several possibly disjoint line segments, using the same graphics attributes. The segments are specified by means of the XSegment structure, which is defined in <X11/Xlib.h> as follows:

```
typedef struct
{
  short x1, y1; /* Coordinates of start-point of segment */
  short x2, y2; /* Coordinates of end-point of segment   */
} XSegment;
```

The following example shows how to use the `XDrawSegments` function to draw several line segments:

```
Display  *disp;
Window   window_1;
GC       thisGC;
XSegment lines[] =
{
  {50, 80, 150, 200},
  {10, 20, 35, 60},
  {250, 10, 200, 100}
};
int numsegs = sizeof(lines) / sizeof(XSegment);


XDrawSegments(disp, window_1, thisGC, lines, numsegs);
```

The `XDrawLines` function is similar to `XDrawPoints`, with one difference: `XDrawPoints` draws points, whereas `XDrawLines` connects them with a line. Call `XDrawLines` with the same arguments that you use for `XDrawPoints`.

Drawing and filling rectangles

Xlib includes several functions for drawing rectangles. The `XDrawRectangle` function is for drawing a rectangle, given the coordinates of its upper-left corner and its width and height. The function call is of the following form:

```
XDrawRectangle(disp, window, thisGC, x, y, width, height);
```

To draw the outline around the rectangle, this function draws the following lines:

- (x, y) to (x+width, y)
- (x+width, y) to (x+width, y+height)
- (x+width, y+height) to (x, y+height)
- (x, y+height) to (x,y)

You can use the same GC to draw several rectangles by calling `XDrawRectangles`, which expects an array of rectangles and their number as arguments, as follows:

```
XRectangle rect[]; /* Array of rectangles */
int        nrect;  /* Number of rectangles */

XDrawRectangles(disp, window, thisGC, rects, nrects);
```

The `XRectangle` function is a structure for storing the parameters of a rectangles. The function is defined in `<X11/Xlib.h>` as follows:

```
typedef struct
{
    short x, y;                        /* Upper-left corner */
    unsigned short width, height; /* Width and height */
} XRectangle;
```

You can draw a filled rectangle by calling the `XFillRectangle` function. Call this function the same way that you do `XDrawRectangle`, with exactly the same arguments. Notice that when you draw a filled rectangle, the width and height of the filled area are exactly the width and height specified in the call to `XFillRectangle`.

`XFillRectangles` is the function for drawing multiple filled rectangles. The function is analogous to `XDrawRectangles` and is called with the same arguments.

Drawing polygons

A *polygon* is a figure enclosed by multiple lines. To draw the outline of a polygon, use the `XDrawLines` function. For filled polygons, Xlib provides the `XFillPolygon` function, which has the following usage:

```
int shape; /* One of: Convex, NonConvex, or Complex    */
int mode;  /* One of: CoordModeOrigin or CoordModePrevious */

XPoint points[]; /* Vertices of the polygon */
int    numpoints; /* How many vertices      */

XFillPolygon(disp, win, thisGC, points, numpoints,
      shape, mode);
```

You have to specify the vertices of the polygon in an array of `XPoint` structures, just as you do when drawing multiple points with `XDrawPoints`. Also, the `mode` argument is interpreted the same way as it is for `XDrawPoints`.

The `shape` argument helps the server optimize the filling algorithm. Specify `Convex` for this argument only if your polygon is such that a line drawn between any two internal points lies entirely inside the polygon. (Triangles and rectangles, for example, are convex shapes.)

If the shape is not convex but none of the edges intersect, you should use `NonConvex` as the shape argument. For polygons that have intersecting edges, use `Complex`. Notice that if you are not sure about a polygon, you can safely specify `Complex` as the shape. The drawing process may be a bit slower, but the result will be correct.

The fill rule in the GC determines which points are filled by `XFillPolygon`. You can set the fill rule by calling `XSetFillRule`.

Drawing arcs, circles, and ellipses

In X, arcs, ellipses, and circles are handled by the arc-drawing functions: `XDrawArc` and `XDrawArcs`. You can think of the first function as being for a single arc and the latter as being for several arcs. Call the `XDrawArc` function like this:

```
XDrawArc(disp, window, gc, x, y, width, height, angle1, angle2);
```

You can think of an arc as being a part of an ellipse. Drawing an arc involves specifying the *bounding rectangle*, which is the smallest rectangle that completely encloses the ellipse to which the arc belongs. Specify the rectangle with the coordinates of the upper-left corner (x,y) and the dimensions of the rectangle (`width` and `height`). Indicate the angle where the arc starts (`angle1`), as well as its angular extent (`angle2`).

The X server draws the arc by starting at a point on the ellipse along the `angle1` line where `angle1` is measured counterclockwise, with zero degrees along the three o'clock line. Then the server traces over the ellipse in a counterclockwise direction until it covers the angular extent specified by `angle2`.

The angles `angle1` and `angle2` are integer values that specify angles in units of $1/64$-degree. Thus, to draw a 60-degree-wide arc starting at 30 degrees from the three o'clock direction, you would use the following call:

```
XDrawArc(p_disp, window, thisGC, x, y, width, height, 30*64, 60*64);
```

You can draw an ellipse by starting at zero degrees and specifying an extent of 360*64. If the width and height of the bounding rectangle are equal, you get a circle.

Drawing text

Cross Reference

To display text, you first need to select a font. In X, fonts are resources residing in the server. Applications have to load a font before using it. When the X server successfully loads a font, it returns a resource ID that the application subsequently uses to refer to that font. In Chapter 5, you learned how to name a font. When the name is known, you can load a font by calling the `XLoadFont` function as follows:

```
Display *disp;   /* Identifies the connection to the X server */
char    fontname[] = "*helvetica-bold-r*140*"; /* Font name */
Font    helvb14;                               /* Font id   */
.
.
.
if((helvb14 = XLoadFont(disp, fontname)) == None)
{
   fprintf(stderr, "Cannot load font: %s\n", fontname);
/* Handle error. Probably just use the default font */
/* ... */
}
```

When the `XLoadFont` function returns a nonzero value (meaning that the function is successful), you can start using the 14-point bold Helvetica font, shown in the example, by setting the font attribute of a GC. To do this, call `XSetFont` as follows:

```
XSetFont(disp, thisGC, helvb14);
```

Subsequently, whenever any text is drawn with this GC, the output will be in 14-point bold Helvetica.

Because fonts are server-resident resources, when your application no longer needs a font, you should release the font with the `XUnloadFont` function. This function call has the following form:

```
XUnloadFont(p_disp, helvb14);
```

Notice that if you have a GC with `helvb14` as the font, and you unload that font, the X server does not actually unload the font until that GC is destroyed.

After you have a GC with the appropriate font, your application can call one of the following functions to display text:

- `XDrawString(Display* display, Drawable d, GC gc, int x, int y, const char* string, int length);` — Draws text string in foreground color only.
- `XDrawImageString(Display* display, Drawable d, GC gc, int x, int y, const char* string, int length);` — Draws characters using both foreground and background colors.
- `XDrawText(Display* display, Drawable d, GC gc, int x, int y, XTextItem* items, int nitems);` — Draws several text strings on a line.

Each function draws several characters on a single line. The first two functions draw all the characters by using the font specified in the GC that you provide as an argument. The functions are called in the same way, as follows:

```
char string[]; /* String to be displayed     */
int  nchars;   /* Number of characters in string */

XDrawString(disp, window, thisGC, x, y, string, nchars);
XDrawImageString(disp, window, thisGC, x, y, string, nchars);
```

You specify a starting position, where the server places the origin of the first character's bitmap. Then the server copies the foreground pixel value (from the GC) to all pixels corresponding to ones in the bitmap. `XDrawString` does not alter the pixels where the bitmap is zero. `XDrawImageString`, on the other hand, also fills the pixels corresponding to zeros in each character's bitmap with the GC's background color (using the stipple or tile, if any).

Tip

If you want to use more than one font on the same line of text, use the `XDrawText` function. This function accepts the information about the string segments in a `XTextItem` structure, which is defined in `<X11/Xlib.h>` as follows:

```
typedef struct
{
  char *chars; /* Pointer to the string to be drawn      */
  int nchars;  /* Number of characters in string         */
  int delta;   /* Distance from last char of prev. string */
  Font font;   /* Font to be used (None means use GC's font) */
} XTextItem;
```

Each `XTextItem` structure contains information about a single chunk of text. The first two members identify the string and its length. The member named `delta` is an offset, in pixels, that is applied before drawing this string. The last member specifies the font to be used when drawing this string. When calling `XDrawText`, you have to provide the usual `Display` pointer, drawable, and GC, followed by the location where the string should appear and the strings in an array of `XTextItem` structures, as follows:

```
XTextItem text_chunks[]; /* Array of strings to be displayed */
int       numchunks;     /* Number of XTextItem structures   */

/* Initialize "text_chunks" first ... */

XDrawText(disp, window, thisGC, x, y, text_chunks, numchunks);
```

`XDrawText` displays each string by using the font specified in the `font` field of the corresponding `XTextItem` structure. The function does so by loading the font into the GC that you provide in the function call. If the `font` field in the `XTextItem` is set to `None`, `XDrawText` uses whatever font the GC happens to have.

Using drawing functions in Motif

To use Xlib functions in any application, you need the `Display` pointer, the window ID, and (for drawing functions) a graphics context (GC). Xt Intrinsics (the foundation on which Motif is built) provides macros and functions to get these parameters for any widget.

Display and window ID

Motif applications work with widgets, but most Xlib functions require a pointer to the `Display` structure and a window identifier as arguments. Given a widget ID, you can get the pointer to its `Display` structure by using the `XtDisplay` function. Similarly, the `XtWindow` function returns the ID of the window associated with a widget.

Suppose that you want to use the Xlib function `XClearWindow` to clear a widget's window. Given the widget ID `w`, you can do this with the following code fragment:

```
#include <X11/Intrinsics.h>

Widget   w;
Display *p_disp;
Window   win;

p_disp = XtDisplay(w);
win = XtWindow(w);
XClearWindow(p_disp, win);
```

The window ID returned by `XtWindow` will be `NULL` if the widget has not been realized. The `Display` pointer, however, is valid immediately after the widget is created if you call `XtCreateWidget` or another equivalent function.

GC creation in Motif

Note

To draw text and graphics in a widget's window, you have to create one or more GCs. When using Xlib alone, you use functions such as `XCreateGC`, `XCopyGC`, and `XChangeGC` to create and manipulate GCs. Xt Intrinsics provides the function

XtGetGC for creating GCs. This function tries to minimize the number of GC creations by keeping track of the GCs created by all the widgets in an application. Xt Intrinsics creates a new GC only when none of the existing ones has attributes that match what you request in the XtGetGC call.

When creating a GC for a widget, you should get the foreground and background pixel values from the widget's resources. That way, you will be using the foreground and background colors that the user may have specified for that widget in a resource file.

You get the value of a widget's resources by calling XtGetValues. The steps are similar to those involved in setting resource values. Suppose that you want the foreground and background colors for the DrawingArea widget named drawing_area. The following example shows how you can get these values and set up a GC with these attributes:

```
    Arg       args[20];
    Cardinal  narg;
    Widget    drawing_area;
    XGCValues xgcv;
    GC        theGC;
    int       fg, bg;

/* Retrieve the background and foreground
 * colors from the widget's resources.
 */
    narg = 0;
    XtSetArg(args[narg], XmNforeground, &fg); narg++;
    XtSetArg(args[narg], XmNbackground, &bg); narg++;
    XtGetValues(drawing_area, args, narg);

/* Now, define a GC with these colors */
    xgcv.foreground = fg;
    xgcv.background = bg;
    theGC = XtGetGC(drawing_area, GCForeground | GCBackground,
            &xgcv);
```

Notice that when you retrieve a resource's value, you provide the address of a variable in which XtGetValues places the value.

After you create the GC, you can manipulate it with Xlib functions. Notice, however, that the GC returned by XtGetGC is read-only; hence, you cannot change it. Use XCreateGC if you need a GC that you can change.

A Motif line-drawing program

The following listing shows xmlines, a Motif line-drawing program. The program can draw rubber-band figures. When the user first clicks the left mouse button in the drawing area, that marks one corner of the line. As the user moves the mouse while holding down the mouse button, the line appears to move in keeping with the mouse movement. The final line is drawn when the user releases the button.

```c
/*--------------------------------------------------------------*/
/* File: xmlines.c
 *
 * A Motif program that draws lines.
 */
/*--------------------------------------------------------------*/
#include <stdio.h>

#include <X11/Xlib.h>
#include <X11/Xutil.h>
#include <X11/cursorfont.h>

#include <Xm/Xm.h>
#include <Xm/RowColumn.h>
#include <Xm/MainW.h>
#include <Xm/DrawingA.h>

#define MAXARGS    20
#define MAXLINES   100
#define WIDTH      400
#define HEIGHT     300

static char message[] =
 "Hold down left mouse button, move, and then release.";
static int msglen = XtNumber(message) - 1;

/* Array of lines */

XSegment lines[MAXLINES];
int    numlines = 0;
int    curline = 0;

GC  theGC;    /* GC for regular drawing */
GC  xorGC;    /* GC used for rubber-band drawing */

Cursor xhair_cursor;

/* Function prototypes */

/* These are callbacks */
void start_rubberband(Widget w, XtPointer data, XEvent *p_event,
          Boolean *cdispatch);
void continue_rubberband(Widget w, XtPointer data, XEvent *p_event,
          Boolean *cdispatch);
void end_rubberband(Widget w, XtPointer data, XEvent *p_event,
          Boolean *cdispatch);

void handle_expose(Widget w, XtPointer client_data, XtPointer other);

/* This function draws the lines */
static void draw_line(Display *d, Window w, GC gc, int curline);

/*--------------------------------------------------------------*/
```

```c
void main(int argc, char **argv)
{
  Widget        top_level, main_window, drawing_area;
  Arg           args[MAXARGS];
  Cardinal      argcount;
  int           fg, bg;
  XGCValues     xgcv;
  XtAppContext  app;

/* Create the top-level shell widget and initialize the toolkit*/
  top_level = XtAppInitialize(&app, "XMlines", NULL, 0,
              &argc, argv, NULL, NULL, 0);

/* Next, the main window widget */
  argcount = 0;
  XtSetArg(args[argcount], XmNwidth, WIDTH);  argcount++;
  XtSetArg(args[argcount], XmNheight, HEIGHT); argcount++;
  main_window = XmCreateMainWindow(top_level, "Main",
                  args, argcount);
  XtManageChild(main_window);

/* Create the drawing area */
  argcount = 0;
  XtSetArg(args[argcount], XmNresizePolicy, XmRESIZE_ANY);
  argcount++;
  drawing_area = XmCreateDrawingArea(main_window,
              "drawing_area", args, argcount);
  XtManageChild(drawing_area);

/* Attach the drawing area to main window */
  XmMainWindowSetAreas(main_window, NULL, NULL, NULL,
            NULL, drawing_area);

/* Create the GCs. First retrieve the background and foreground
 * colors from the widget's resources.
 */
  argcount = 0;
  XtSetArg(args[argcount], XmNforeground, &fg); argcount++;
  XtSetArg(args[argcount], XmNbackground, &bg); argcount++;
  XtGetValues(drawing_area, args, argcount);

/* Define a GC with these colors */
  xgcv.foreground = fg;
  xgcv.background = bg;
  theGC = XtGetGC(drawing_area, GCForeground | GCBackground,
         &xgcv);
/* Set up a GC with exclusive-OR mode (for rubber-band drawing)*/
  xgcv.foreground = fg ^ bg;
  xgcv.background = bg;
  xgcv.function = GXxor;
  xorGC = XtGetGC(drawing_area, GCForeground |
          GCBackground | GCFunction, &xgcv);

/* Add callback to handle expose events for the drawing area */
  XtAddCallback(drawing_area, XmNexposeCallback, handle_expose,
         &drawing_area);
```

```c
/* Create a cross-hair cursor for the drawing area */
    xhair_cursor = XCreateFontCursor(XtDisplay(drawing_area),
                    XC_crosshair);

/* Add event handlers for button events to handle the drawing */
    XtAddEventHandler(drawing_area, ButtonPressMask, False,
            start_rubberband, NULL);
    XtAddEventHandler(drawing_area, ButtonMotionMask, False,
            continue_rubberband, NULL);
    XtAddEventHandler(drawing_area, ButtonReleaseMask, False,
            end_rubberband, NULL);

/* Realize all widgets */
    XtRealizeWidget(top_level);

/* Change the cursor for the drawing area */
    XDefineCursor(XtDisplay(drawing_area), XtWindow(drawing_area),
            xhair_cursor);

/* Set up a grab so that the cursor changes to a cross-hair and
 * is confined to the drawing_area while the mouse button is
 * pressed. This is done through what is known as a "grab"
 */
    XGrabButton(XtDisplay(drawing_area), AnyButton, AnyModifier,
        XtWindow(drawing_area), True, ButtonPressMask|
        ButtonMotionMask | ButtonReleaseMask,
        GrabModeAsync, GrabModeAsync,
        XtWindow(drawing_area), xhair_cursor);

/* Free the cursor */
    XFreeCursor(XtDisplay(drawing_area), xhair_cursor);

/* Start the main event-handling loop */
    XtAppMainLoop(app);
}
/*--------------------------------------------------------------*/
/* s t a r t _ r u b b e r b a n d
 *
 * Start of rubber-band line
 */
void start_rubberband(Widget w, XtPointer data, XEvent *p_event,
            Boolean *cdispatch)
{
    int x = p_event->xbutton.x,
        y = p_event->xbutton.y;

/* Crude check to ensure that we don't exceed array's capacity */
    if(numlines > MAXLINES-1) numlines = MAXLINES-1;
    curline = numlines;
    numlines++;

    lines[curline].x1 = x;
    lines[curline].y1 = y;
    lines[curline].x2 = x;
```

```c
        lines[curline].y2 = y;
        draw_line(XtDisplay(w), XtWindow(w), xorGC, curline);
}
/*----------------------------------------------------------------*/
/* c o n t i n u e _ r u b b e r b a n d
 *
 * Handle mouse movement while drawing a rubber-band line
 */
void continue_rubberband(Widget w, XtPointer data, XEvent *p_event,
            Boolean *cdispatch)
{
    int x = p_event->xbutton.x,
        y = p_event->xbutton.y;

/* Draw once at old location (to erase line) */
    draw_line(XtDisplay(w), XtWindow(w), xorGC, curline);

/* Now update end-point and redraw line */
    lines[curline].x2 = x;
    lines[curline].y2 = y;
    draw_line(XtDisplay(w), XtWindow(w), xorGC, curline);
}
/*----------------------------------------------------------------*/
/* e n d _ r u b b e r b a n d
 *
 * End of rubber-band drawing
 */
void end_rubberband(Widget w, XtPointer data, XEvent *p_event,
            Boolean *cdispatch)
{
    int x = p_event->xbutton.x,
        y = p_event->xbutton.y;

/* Draw once at old location (to erase line) */
    draw_line(XtDisplay(w), XtWindow(w), xorGC, curline);

/* Now update end-point and redraw line in normal GC */
    lines[curline].x2 = x;
    lines[curline].y2 = y;
    draw_line(XtDisplay(w), XtWindow(w), theGC, curline);
}
/*----------------------------------------------------------------*/
/* h a n d l e _ e x p o s e
 *
 * Expose event-handler for the drawing area
 */
void handle_expose(Widget w, XtPointer data, XtPointer other)
{
    XmDrawingAreaCallbackStruct *call_data =
            (XmDrawingAreaCallbackStruct*)other;
    XEvent *p_event = call_data->event;
    Window win = call_data->window;
    Display *p_display = XtDisplay(w);
```

```
      if(p_event->xexpose.count == 0)
      {
        int i;
/* Clear the window and draw the lines in the "lines" array*/
        XClearWindow(p_display, win);

        if(numlines > 0)
        {
           XDrawSegments(p_display, win, theGC, lines, numlines);
        }
      }

/* Display the message (this is an example of text output) */
      XDrawImageString(p_display, win, theGC, 50, 30, message,
             msglen);
}
/*------------------------------------------------------------------*/
/* d r a w _ l i n e
 *
 * Draw a specified line from the lines array.
 */
static void draw_line(Display *d, Window w, GC gc, int curline)
{
  int x1 = lines[curline].x1, y1 = lines[curline].y1,
      x2 = lines[curline].x2, y2 = lines[curline].y2;

  XDrawLine(d, w, gc, x1, y1, x2, y2);
}
```

To build the xmlines program, use the following command:

```
gcc -o xmlines xmlines.c -lXm -lXt -lX11 -lXext
```

Figure 23-2 shows the output of the xmlines program.

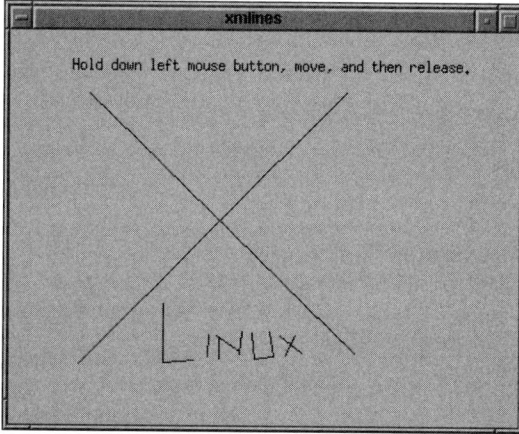

Figure 23-2: The output of the xmlines program, showing some lines.

Using color

X incorporates an abstract color model that captures most of the capabilities of common color graphics hardware. To use color in an X application, you need to understand the color model that X uses.

Visuals

X encapsulates the common features of the display hardware in a data structure called the `Visual`. X adds an important twist to encourage sharing of colormaps, however, by allowing colormaps to be read-only or read-write. Cells in the read-write colormaps can be changed dynamically, whereas read-only colormaps are fixed.

The class member of the `Visual` structure indicates the color capabilities of the underlying graphics display. Based on the classification of color and gray-scale displays together with X's notion of read-write and read-only colormaps, there are six distinct classes of `Visual`s, identified by the following names (defined in `<X11/X.h>`):

- `DirectColor` visually represents a display where the pixel value is decomposed into bit fields that index into individual colormaps for the R, G, B components. The colormap entries can be changed dynamically. This visual class is common among displays that have 24-bit planes.

- `TrueColor` displays are the same as `DirectColor`, but their colormaps are fixed.

- The `PseudoColor` visual class models a common type of display hardware — one in which each pixel value looks up an RGB value and in which the colormap can be modified at any time.

- `StaticColor` displays are similar to `PseudoColor`, except that the colormap cannot be modified.

- `GrayScale` visual represents a gray-scale monitor that allows the intensity map to be modified. The `GrayScale` visual is the gray-scale equivalent of the `PseudoColor` visual.

- `StaticGray` is similar to `GrayScale` but has a fixed gray-level map. Black-and-white (monochrome) displays are modeled by a `StaticGray` visual with a depth of 1.

Each screen in an X display has at least one associated visual structure. Many servers provide more than one visual for a screen. The server for an 8-bit display, for example, might provide a `PseudoColor` visual of depth 8 and a `StaticGray` visual of depth 1. Thus, windows on the same screen can be used as a color window or, in the case of `StaticGray`, as a monochrome one.

Even if a server supports multiple visuals, one of them is the default visual. You can refer to this default visual by using the macro `DefaultVisual(display,screen)`, which returns a pointer to the `Visual` structure of the specified screen in the X display identified by `display`.

List of available visuals

Tip

To see a list of visuals supported by the X server on your system, use the `xdpyinfo` utility. Following is the result of running `xdpyinfo` on a typical Linux system:

```
xdpyinfo -display :0.0
name of display:    :0.0
version number:    11.0
vendor string:    The XFree86 Project, Inc
vendor release number:    3110
maximum request size: 4194300 bytes
motion buffer size: 0
bitmap unit, bit order, padding:    32, LSBFirst, 32
image byte order:    LSBFirst
number of supported pixmap formats:    2
supported pixmap formats:
    depth 1, bits_per_pixel 1, scanline_pad 32
    depth 8, bits_per_pixel 8, scanline_pad 32
keycode range:    minimum 8, maximum 134
focus: window 0x100000d, revert to Parent
number of extensions:    9
    BIG-REQUESTS
    MIT-SCREEN-SAVER
    MIT-SHM
    MIT-SUNDRY-NONSTANDARD
    Multi-Buffering
    SHAPE
    SYNC
    XC-MISC
    XTEST
default screen number:    0
number of screens:    1

screen #0:
 dimensions:    1024x768 pixels (347x260 millimeters)
 resolution:    75x75 dots per inch
 depths (2):    1, 8
 root window id:    0x2a
 depth of root window:    8 planes
 number of colormaps:    minimum 1, maximum 1
 default colormap:    0x26
 default number of colormap cells:    256
 preallocated pixels:    black 1, white 0
 options:    backing-store YES, save-unders YES
 largest cursor:    64x64
 current input event mask:    0x50003d
   KeyPressMask        ButtonPressMask      ButtonReleaseMask
   EnterWindowMask     LeaveWindowMask      SubstructureRedirectMask
   PropertyChangeMask
 number of visuals:    6
 default visual id: 0x20
 visual:
```

```
visual id:    0x20
class:    PseudoColor
depth:    8 planes
available colormap entries:    256
red, green, blue masks:    0x0, 0x0, 0x0
significant bits in color specification:    6 bits
visual:
visual id:    0x21
class:    DirectColor
depth:    8 planes
available colormap entries:    8 per subfield
red, green, blue masks:    0x7, 0x38, 0xc0
significant bits in color specification:    6 bits
visual:
visual id:    0x22
class:    GrayScale
depth:    8 planes
available colormap entries:    256
red, green, blue masks:    0x0, 0x0, 0x0
significant bits in color specification:    6 bits
visual:
visual id:    0x23
class:    StaticColor
depth:    8 planes
available colormap entries:    256
red, green, blue masks:    0x7, 0x38, 0xc0
significant bits in color specification:    6 bits
visual:
visual id:    0x24
class:    TrueColor
depth:    8 planes
available colormap entries:    8 per subfield
red, green, blue masks:    0x7, 0x38, 0xc0
significant bits in color specification:    6 bits
visual:
visual id:    0x25
class:    StaticGray
depth:    8 planes
available colormap entries:    256
red, green, blue masks:    0x0, 0x0, 0x0
significant bits in color specification:    6 bits
```

The xdpyinfo program displays a great deal of information about the X server, including the number of visuals. The sample listing corresponds to a graphics card that uses 8 bits per pixel — a total 256 colors at a time. As xdpyinfo shows, the X server supports 6 visuals, the default one being an 8-bit PseudoColor visual.

Typically, you do not have to select any visual, because the default visual is adequate for most applications. If your system has a 24-bit graphics card and the default visual is 8-bit, however, you may want to explicitly select and use a 24-bit visual.

Chapter 23: X Programming in Linux

Secret

To use a nondefault visual in a Motif application, you have to specify the following resources of the top-level shell before the widget is realized:

- Visual type
- Colormap
- Depth

X colormap

In X, each window has an associated colormap that determines how the pixel values are translated into colors (or gray levels, in gray-scale monitors). Although the hardware may allow only one colormap, X allows each window to have its own colormap, as long as the visual class of the screen is not `TrueColor`, `StaticColor`, or `StaticGray`. Before the pixel values in a window are interpreted according to such a *virtual colormap*, that colormap has to be installed in the hardware colormap. You need a window manager to take care of this chore. By convention, most window managers implement a policy of installing a window's colormap in the hardware as soon as the window gains input focus.

A colormap is a resource of the X server. Normally, you do not have to create a new colormap for your application. When the server is started, it creates and installs a default colormap. The server normally defines only two color cells in this default colormap. The rest of the cells can be allocated and used by any X application.

Note

To use colors from a colormap, you first have to find the colormap's identifier, which is a variable of type `Colormap`. When you create a new colormap, you get back an ID. For the default colormap, the colormap's ID is returned by the macro `DefaultColormap(display, screen)`, which requires you to identify the display and the screen. You can use `DefaultScreen(display)` as the screen argument for `DefaultColormap`.

Colors from a colormap

When you use color in a Motif application, you have to specify a pixel value. The pixel value implies a particular color, depending on the contents of the colormap cell that it references. The first step in using a color in X is to obtain the index of a colormap cell that contains the red, green, and blue intensities that are appropriate for the color you want. To do this, you request that the X server allocate a colormap cell (in a specified colormap) with your color. When requesting a colormap cell, you provide the desired red, green, and blue levels; the X server returns an index that you can use as the pixel value corresponding to that color.

Note

Because many applications may use similar colors, X provides two ways to allocate colormap cells:

- Shared read-only cells
- Private read-write cells

Shared read-only color cells

You can allocate shared read-only cells in any visual class, but to allocate read-write cells, the visual class must allow the colormap to be altered. That means that the visual class has to be DirectColor, PseudoColor, or GrayScale.

For each colormap, the X server keeps track of the cells that are currently in use. When the server receives a request for a shared read-only cell in a colormap, it determines the closest color that the hardware can support; then it searches any previously allocated read-only cells in that colormap for one that may already contain that color. If the server finds such a cell, it returns the information about that cell. Otherwise, if the visual class permits writing to the colormap, the server allocates a new cell for read-only use, loads the requested color into the cell, and returns that information.

The nice thing about shared read-only colormap cells is that you can use them on any visual, but to allocate private read-write colormap cells, you have to make sure that the visual is DirectColor, PseudoColor, or GrayScale.

Private read-write color cells

Private read-write cells also have some advantages. These cells allow you to alter the mapping of pixel to color at any time. This capability can be useful for displaying images; you can change the colors of an image by altering the colormap entries without having to redraw the image with new pixel values.

Also, private colormap cells can be allocated in a single contiguous block so that the pixel values are in sequence. This capability can be useful if the application requires the displayed colors to relate to the pixel values in a well-defined way. An example is a satellite image displayed in a gray scale that associates a gray level to each data level in the satellite image.

XColor **structure**

When you are allocating colors or defining new colormap entries, you provide information about the color in an XColor structure, which is defined in <X11/Xlib.h> as follows:

```
typedef struct
{
  unsigned long pixel;  /* Pixel value (after allocation) */
  unsigned short red,   /* Red intensity (0 - 65,535)    */
                green,  /* Green intensity (0 - 65,535)  */
                blue;   /* Blue intensity (0 - 65,535)   */
  char          flags;  /* Used when storing colors      */
  char          pad;    /* Just so structure size is even */
};
```

You should specify a color by indicating the intensities of the RGB components in the fields red, green, and blue. These intensities range from 0 to 65,535; 0 implies no intensity, and 65,535 means full intensity. The server automatically scales these values to the range of intensities needed by the display screen's hardware.

The field named `pixel` is the pixel value that you use to display the color corresponding to the RGB value in red, green, and blue. When allocating a color, you provide the RGB values for the color; the X server returns the pixel value corresponding to the colormap cell with that color.

Read-only color cell allocation

Xlib provides two functions for allocating shared read-only colormap cells:

- `XAllocColor`
- `XAllocNamedColor`

The `XAllocColor` function requires that you define an `XColor` structure and then fill in the red, green, and blue fields with the RGB levels for the color that you want. You also have to specify the colormap in which you want to allocate the color. Typically, you use `XAllocColor` in conjunction with `XParseColor`, which accepts the name of a color and sets up the corresponding RGB values in an `XColor` structure.

Cross Reference

To allocate a light cyan color in the default colormap and use it as the background of a window, for example, you might use the following code (see Chapter 5 for information on naming colors in X applications):

```
Display    *disp;
XColor     color;
Colormap   default_cmap;
unsigned   long bgpixel;

default_cmap = DefaultColormap(disp, DefaultScreen(disp));

/* Try to allocate a "light cyan" colormap cell */

  if (XParseColor(disp, default_cmap, "light cyan", &color) == 0 ||
     XAllocColor(disp, default_cmap, &color) == 0)
  {
/* Use white background in case of failure */
     bgpixel = WhitePixel(disp, DefaultScreen(disp));
  }
  else
  {
/* Colormap cell successfully allocated */
     bgpixel = color.pixel;
  }
  .
  .
  .
/* Use "bgpixel" as background when creating the window */
```

First, `XParseColor` sets up the RGB values in color for the color named `light cyan`. Then `XAllocColor` requests a read-only color cell with that RGB value. If all goes well, both functions return nonzero values, and the pixel member of `color` contains the pixel value that you should use wherever you need the `light cyan` color. If the functions fail, you must include some means to handle the situation. In this example, if the allocation fails, the white color is used as the background color. The server always allocates the white and black colors in the default colormap. You can refer to these colors by using the macros `WhitePixel(display, screen)` and `BlackPixel(display, screen)`, respectively.

The X server provides a color database that applications can use to translate the textual names of colors into red, green, and blue intensities that are appropriate for that particular display screen. The functions `XParseColor` and `XAllocNamedColor` use this database.

`XAllocNamedColor` is similar to `XAllocColor`, except that it directly takes the name of a color as a string. When you use `XAllocNamedColor`, the earlier example of allocating a light-cyan cell becomes the following:

```
XColor exact; /* Exact RGB definition of color */

if (XAllocNamedColor(disp, default_cmap, "light cyan",
        &exact, &color) == 0)
{
/* Use white background in case of failure */
    bgpixel = WhitePixel(disp, DefaultScreen(disp));
}
    else
    {
/* Colormap cell successfully allocated */
    bgpixel = color.pixel;
}
```

`XAllocNamedColor` requires two `XColor` arguments. In the `XColor` structure named `exact`, `XAllocNamedColor` returns the exact RGB value for the requested color (from the database); in `color`, it returns the closest color supported by the hardware and the pixel value corresponding to the allocated colormap cell (when allocation succeeds).

Read-write color cell allocation

Note

Some applications need colors to be allocated in the colormap in a specific way. You can, for example, display a two-dimensional array of weather-satellite data as an image in which the color of each pixel represents a data point. When you display such an image, you may want all pixel values to appear in sequence so that you can easily map the data into colors. You also may want to alter the mapping of data to colors to bring out features of the data. This type of need is best handled by allocating a contiguous block of private read-write colormap cells.

Tip

To allocate read-write color cells, call the `XAllocColorCells` function. Before you use this function, of course, you must make sure that the screen's visual class allows alterations to the colormap (the class must be `DirectColor`, `PseudoColor`, or `GrayScale`).

Following is how you should call `XAllocColorCells`:

```
Display     *disp;
Colormap    cmap;        /* Colormap where cells are allocated*/
Bool        contig;      /* True = allocate contiguous planes */
```

```
unsigned long planes[]; /* Array to hold plane masks      */
unsigned int nplanes;   /* Number of planes to allocate   */
unsigned long pixels[]; /* Array to hold pixel values     */
unsigned int npixels;   /* Number of pixels to allocate   */

if(!XAllocColorCells(disp, cmap, contig, planes, nplanes, pixels,
npixels))
{
/* Error allocating color cells */
/* ... */
}
```

X requires you to specify the read-write colormap cells in a unique manner. You specify the number of pixel values (npixels) and the number of planes (nplanes); npixels must be positive, whereas nplanes can be zero or positive. In return, the server reserves npixels*2^nplanes colormap cells and returns the information about the usable cells in the arrays named pixels and planes. npixels values are returned in pixels, and nplanes bit masks are returned in the planes array.

Tip

If you want to allocate a single read-write color cell, you call XAllocColorCells as follows:

```
Display     *disp;
Colormap    cmap;    /* Colormap where cells are allocated*/
unsigned long pixels[1];

if(!XAllocColorCells(disp, cmap, False, NULL, 0, pixels, 1))
{
/* Error allocating color cells */
/* ... */
}
/* Successfully allocated color cell. The pixel value is pixels[0] */
```

Tip

After you call XAllocColorCells to allocate private read-write color cells, you must store colors in these cells before using them. Use XStoreColor to change the RGB value corresponding to a single pixel value; you have to use an XColor structure to do this. Set the red, green, and blue fields to the desired levels of the primary color. Set pixel to the pixel value of an allocated (read-write) cell. Then call XStoreColor as follows:

```
  Colormap colormap;
  XColor   color;
/* Assume that colorcell is a previously allocated read-write
 * cell. The following code stores "red" in this cell
 */
  color.pixel = colorcell;
  color.red = 65535;
  color.green = 0;
  color.blue = 0;
  color.flags = DoRed | DoGreen | DoBlue;
  XStoreColor(disp, colormap, &color);
```

The flags field in color indicates which of the primary color levels in the colormap cell should be updated.

Tip

To set a single colormap cell with a color identified by a name rather than the RGB components, you can use XStoreNamedColor. To set pixel value colorcell to red, you use the following:

```
XStoreNamedColor(p_disp, colormap, "red", colorcell,
        DoRed | DoGreen | DoBlue);
```

Tip

If you have several read-write colormap cells to initialize, you can use XStoreColors to store colors in them at the same time. As expected, this function takes an array of XColor structures and the number of such structures as arguments, as follows:

```
XColor colors[]; /* Array of colors    */
int    ncolors;  /* Number in colors array */
.
.
.
/* Set up the "colors" array before calling XStoreColors */

XStoreColors(p_disp, colormap, colors, ncolors);
```

Free colormap

Whether you use shared or private colormap cells, you should free the colors when they are no longer needed. When an application terminates, the X server automatically frees the colors used by that application. If your application allocates colors often (it may allocate colors every time an image is displayed in a window, for example), you should call XFreeColors to free the colors that you no longer need, as follows:

```
Display      *disp;
Colormap      colormap;      /* Cells freed in this colormap */
unsigned      long pixels[]; /* Identifies cells being freed */
int           numpix;        /* Number of cells being freed  */
unsigned      long planes;   /* Identifies planes being freed */

XFreeColors(disp, colormap, pixels, numpix, planes);
```

XFreeColors frees colors allocated by any of these functions: XAllocColor, XAllocNamedColor, XAllocColorCells, and XAllocColorPlanes. When you are freeing one or more read-only cells allocated by XAllocColor or XAllocNamedColor, provide the array of pixel values, their number, and a zero for the planes argument.

For private read-write cells, use a logical OR of the plane masks that were returned by an earlier call to XAllocColorCells.

Displaying an image

The X server supports images through pixmaps and bitmaps, whereas Xlib supports the XImage structure that allows you to manipulate images locally — on the system where your application is running, not at the server.

Creating a pixmap

A *pixmap* is a drawable, which means that you can draw into a pixmap just as you would in a window. Like a window, a pixmap can be thought of as being a rectangular array of pixels (a *raster*), with each location being capable of holding a pixel value. You also can view a pixmap as being several rectangular bit planes, with as many planes as there are bits in the pixel value.

For windows, the pixel values in the raster are being displayed constantly. The hardware reads the pixel values and translates them to colors or gray levels, depending on the capabilities of the display.

By contrast, the contents of a pixmap are not visible until they are copied into a window. Thus, you can think of a pixmap as being an off-screen drawing area — an area of memory where you can save a drawing or an image. In fact, you can prepare drawings in a pixmap and display them whenever they are needed by using the XCopyArea function.

Pixmaps are used primarily to draw images and to store patterns for tiling. Pixmaps used as tiles are small (usually, no larger than 32×32 pixels), but those that are used to store images may be quite large.

Like windows, pixmaps are resources maintained at the X server. Before using a pixmap, you have to create it by calling the Xlib function XCreatePixmap. This function returns a resource identifier of type Pixmap that you use when referring to the pixmap in subsequent drawing requests.

Suppose that you want to create a pixmap to draw some figures off-screen. You can create a pixmap with the following code:

```
Display   *disp;        /* Identifies the X display */
Window    root_win;     /* Root window's ID         */
Pixmap    pmap1;        /* Pixmap being created     */
unsigned  int width,    /* Width of pixmap (pixels) */
          height,       /* Height of pixmap (pixels) */
          depth;        /* Bits per pixel value     */
.
.
/* Create a pixmap */
  width = 100;
  height = 50;
  depth = DefaultDepth(disp, DefaultScreen(disp));
  root_win = RootWindow(disp, DefaultScreen(disp);

  pmap1 = XCreatePixmap(disp, root_win, width, height, depth);
```

When you create a pixmap, you specify its dimensions (*width* and *height*) and its *depth* (the number of bits in the pixel values that the pixmap should be able to store).

The second argument of XCreatePixmap must be an identifier of a previously created drawable. The X server uses this argument to determine the screen for which you are creating the pixmap. You can use the ID of any valid window or pixmap. A simple solution is to use the root window's ID.

Caution

In X, every window and pixmap is created for a specific screen. In a multiple-screen X display, you cannot copy a pixmap from one screen to a window in another, even if both have the same depth.

Drawing into a pixmap

When a valid pixmap is available, you can draw into it just as you would in a window. Following is how you draw some figures in a pixmap:

```
/* Draw into the pixmap (assume that the GC has been set up) */
    XFillRectangle(disp, pmap1, theGC, 10, 10, 20, 20);
    XFillArc(disp, pmap1, theGC, 30, 30, 20, 20, 0, 360*64);
```

As you do with windows, you have to provide a graphics context (GC) with all the graphics attributes, such as foreground and background colors. You use the same coordinate system with pixmaps as you do with windows — with the origin at the upper-left corner, the x-axis pointing to the right, and the y-axis pointing down.

Secret

A few minor differences exist between drawing into pixmaps and drawing in windows. The differences stem from the fact that windows are always displayed on-screen, but pixmaps are never displayed. One of the main differences is that windows have an associated background color, but pixmaps do not. Thus, you cannot fill the pixmap with the background color by calling `XClearArea`. Instead, you must use `XFillRectangle` to fill all pixels in the pixmap with the current background color. When you create a pixmap, its contents are undefined, so you should always fill it with a known value, such as the background color.

Pixmaps do not generate any events other than `GraphicsExpose` and `NoExpose` events that occur during copying between windows and pixmaps.

Displaying a pixmap

After you have created and drawn in a pixmap, you can display it by using the `XCopyArea` function. To display the pixmap `pmap1` in the window `win` at coordinates (x, y), for example, you use the following code:

```
/* Copy drawing from pixmap to the window */
    XCopyArea(p_disp, pmap1, win, theGC, 0, 0, width, height, x, y);
```

Freeing pixmaps

Because most X displays have limited off-screen memory, you should release pixmap resources as soon as you finish using them. You can free a pixmap by calling `XFreePixmap` as follows:

```
Pixmap pmap1;

/* Create pixmap "pmap1" and use it */
/* ... */

XFreePixmap(p_disp, pmap1);
```

All resources (including pixmaps) used by your application are automatically freed when your application exits. You have to free pixmaps explicitly only if you use several large pixmaps.

Using bitmaps

Note

A *bitmap* is a pixmap of depth 1. You create a bitmap by specifying depth 1 when you call the XCreatePixmap function. Because only 1 bit exists in each location of the bitmap, a bitmap is a pattern of ones and zeros.

Bitmaps are used somewhat differently from pixmaps. Because pixmaps store the entire pixel value, they usually are copied directly into windows and displayed. Bitmaps, however, are mostly used as stencils (or stipples) through which the background and foreground pixel values are applied to a drawable's raster. First, the bitmap is laid down over the raster of the drawable (repeating the bitmap, if necessary, to cover the entire raster). Then the foreground color is applied to all pixels where the bitmap (the stencil) has a one.

Another use of bitmaps is as a clip mask. The operation is similar to using the bitmap as a stencil, except that the graphics operations are performed only for those pixels in the raster that have a one in the bitmap pattern that is being used as the stencil.

Because of the special use of bitmaps, they are widely used even when the displays support more than one plane.

Although bitmaps are often used as stipples and clip masks, you also can display a bitmap directly in a window or copy it into a pixmap. Because the bitmap is depth 1 and the drawable (pixmap or window) may have a depth greater than 1, you cannot use the XCopyArea function to do this. Xlib provides another function, XCopyPlane, just for this purpose.

XCopyplane requires you to specify a rectangular area in a source bitmap and a destination drawable. The server copies the bitmap into the destination pixmap as follows: it uses the bitmap as a stencil and draws, using the foreground color (specified in a GC), those pixels in the drawable where the bitmap has ones.

You can identify the bitmap as being one of the planes in an arbitrary pixmap. To do this, you specify a mask with exactly 1 bit set to 1. That mask identifies a bit plane in the source pixmap. This bit plane is used as the stencil for the copy operation.

Following is some code that copies the bitmap that was read in by XReadBitmapFile into a window, using the current foreground color in a GC:

```
Display    disp;              /* Identifies the X display  */
Window     win;               /* Destination window        */
GC         theGC;             /* GC used for copying       */
Pixmap     my_bmp;            /* Bitmap created by function */
int        xh_bmp, yh_bmp;    /* Coordinates of hotspot    */
unsigned   int w_bmp, h_bmp;  /* Width and height of bitmap */
unsigned   long planemask;    /* Identifies source bitmap  */
int        xsrc, ysrc;        /* Corner of source rectangle */
int        xdest, ydest;      /* Copy to this point        */
  .
  .
  .
/* Read in bitmap using "XReadBitmapFile"
```

```
 * Assume that bitmap data is in a file named "testicon.xbm"
 */
root_win = RootWindow(disp, DefaultScreen(disp));

if(XReadBitmapFile(disp, root_win, "testicon.xbm",
        &w_bmp, &h_bmp, &my_bmp,
        &xh_bmp, &yh_bmp) != BitmapSuccess)
{
   fprintf(stderr, "Failed to read bitmap file!\n");
/* Exit if you cannot proceed */
 .
 .
 .
}
/* Bitmap "my_bmp" is ready to be used */

xsrc = 0;
ysrc = 0;
xdest = 10;
ydest = 10;
planemask = 1;

XCopyPlane(disp,my_bmp, win, theGC, xsrc, ysrc,
       w_bmp, h_bmp, xdest, ydest, planemask);
```

Notice that the mask that identifies the bitmap from `my_bmp` is set to 1, because `my_bmp` is already a bitmap and, as such, has only a 1 bit plane.

Summary

Nowadays, users expect most software to come with an easy-to-use graphical interface. In Linux, the graphical interface happens to be the X Window System — the standard for all UNIX workstations. X provides the basic windowing capability and graphical output capability, but not much more than that. The actual "look and feel" come from toolkits such as Motif. Motif is the de-facto standard graphical user interface for UNIX workstations. Although Linux does not come with Motif, you can buy Motif for as little as $100. Because Motif is the most commonly used graphical interface, this chapter provides an introduction to Motif programming. By reading this chapter, you learn:

▶ Xlib is the C function library that provides access to the basic capabilities of the X Window System. With Xlib, it's tedious to create even simple user-interface elements, such as buttons and menus. You need a higher-level toolkit, such as Motif, to easily build graphical user interfaces. (Some people would say that you need even a higher level of abstraction than Motif provides.)

▶ Motif relies on the X Toolkit Intrinsics, or Xt Intrinsics, which are a set of convenience functions for managing widgets — graphical user interface objects. Xt Intrinsics provides a basic set of widgets on which other widget sets (such as Motif) are built.

▶ Motif programs rely on widgets to implement the user interface. The look and feel of widgets are controlled by the settings of variables known as resources.

▶ A typical Motif program creates several widgets, sets their resources, and then runs a loop that processes events (such as input from the mouse and keyboard or a request to redraw the contents of a window). This style of programming is known as *event-driven programming*.

▶ The Motif widgets employ an object-oriented architecture (even though they were implemented in C) that uses inheritance to build on a basic set of widgets. The three basic types of widgets are shell, primitive, and manager.

▶ Most Motif distributions come with a sample program called `periodic`. You can view the widgets by running this demo program.

▶ Although Motif widgets make it easy to build user-interface elements such as buttons, menu bars, and list boxes, you still need to use the basic Xlib functions for displaying text, graphics, and images.

▶ The graphics context (GC) is at the heart of any graphics output that uses the X Window System. You specify all graphics attributes, such as color and font, through the GC.

▶ Pixmaps are off-screen blocks of memory where you can draw graphics and text just as you would in a window on the display screen. The X server manages the pixmaps.

▶ When you use Xlib drawing calls in Motif programs, you have to obtain an appropriate graphics context before making the Xlib calls.

Chapter 24
Text Processing in Linux

In This Chapter

- Editing text in Linux
- Using `ed`, the line editor
- Using `vi`, the full-screen text editor
- Editing text files with GNU Emacs
- Getting online help in GNU Emacs
- Understanding the format of a man page
- Preparing a man page with `groff`

Text processing refers to all areas of creating, editing, and formatting textual documents. The simplest form of text processing is preparing a plain-text file, which you have to do often, because most Linux configuration files are plain-text files. For this purpose, Linux offers a choice of text editors, ranging from the UNIX standard `vi` to the all-powerful GNU Emacs.

Cross Reference

To prepare formatted text in Linux, you have to use a markup language such as `groff`. With a markup language, you place special formatting commands in a plain-text file, and a formatting program processes the marked-up text file to generate the formatted document for printing or viewing. You may already be familiar with a more recent markup language called Hypertext Markup Language (HTML), which is used as the standard document format in the World Wide Web. (HTML is described in Chapter 20.)

Note

Even if you use a Microsoft Windows- or Macintosh-based "what you see is what you get" (often referred to as "whizzy whig" for the acronym WYSIWYG) application to prepare formatted text, you have to learn the rudiments of a markup language if you want to prepare a *man page* — online help text available through the `man` command.

This chapter describes the text-processing facilities in Linux. The chapter starts with the `ed`, `vi`, and GNU Emacs text editors. The latter half of the chapter describes how to use the `groff` text-formatting program to prepare a man page.

Text Editing with `ed` and `vi`

Text editing is an important part of all operating systems, including Linux. In Linux, you need to create and edit a variety of text files:

- System configuration files, including `/etc/fstab`, `/etc/hosts`, `/etc/inittab`, `/etc/XF86Config`, and many more
- User files, such as `.newsrc` and `.bash_profile`
- Mail messages and news articles
- Shell script files
- Perl and Tcl/Tk scripts
- C or C++ programs

All UNIX systems, including Linux, come with two text editors:

- `ed`, a line-oriented text editor that you can access as soon as the system boots
- `vi`, a full-screen text editor that supports the command set of an earlier editor named `ex`

In Linux, `vi` and `ex` are emulated by another text editor named `elvis`, but you can invoke the editor with the `vi` command.

Tip

Although `ed` and `vi` may be more cryptic than other, more graphical text editors, you should learn the basic editing commands of these two editors, because there are times when these may be the only editors available. When you run into some system problem and Linux refuses to boot from the hard disk, for example, you may have to boot from a floppy. In this case, you have to edit system files with the `ed` editor, because that editor is small enough to fit on the floppy.

As you see in the following sections, learning the basic text-editing commands of `ed` and `vi` isn't hard.

Using `ed`

Note

The `ed` text editor works with a *buffer* — an in-memory storage area where the actual text resides until you explicitly store the text in a file. You have to use `ed` only when you boot a minimal version of Linux (for example, from a boot floppy) and the system does not support full-screen mode.

Invoking `ed`

To invoke `ed`, use the following command syntax:

`ed [-] [-G] [-s] [-p`*prompt-string*`] [`*filename*`]`

The arguments shown in brackets are optional. The following list explains the arguments:

- `-` suppresses the printing of character counts and diagnostic messages.
- `-G` forces backward compatibility.
- `-s` means the same as the single hyphen.
- `-p prompt-string` sets the prompt string (the default is a null prompt string).
- `filename` is the name of the file to be edited.

Learning ed

When you use the `ed` editor, you work in one of two modes:

- *Command mode* is what you get by default. In this mode, anything that you type is interpreted as a command. As you see in the "Summary of ed commands" section, `ed` has a simple command set wherein each command consists of a single character.
- *Text-input mode* allows you to enter text into the buffer. You can enter input mode with the commands `a` (append), `c` (change), or `i` (insert). After entering lines of text, you can leave input mode by entering a period (.) on a line by itself.

Note

The `ed` editor works with the concept of the *current line* — the line to which `ed` applies the commands that you type. Each line has an address: the line number. You can apply a command to a range of lines by prefixing the command with an address range. The `p` command, for example, prints (displays) the current line. To see the first 10 lines, you use the following command:

```
1,10p
```

In a command, the period (.) refers to the current line, and the dollar sign ($) refers to the last line. Thus, the following command deletes all the lines from the current line to the last one:

```
.,$d
```

A sample session with ed

The following example shows how you might begin editing a file in `ed`:

```
ed -p: /etc/fstab
348
:
```

This example uses the `-p` option to set the prompt to the colon character (:) and opens the file `/etc/fstab` for editing. You may find turning on a prompt character to be helpful, because without the prompt, it's difficult to tell whether `ed` is in input mode or command mode.

The ed editor opens the file, reports the number of characters in the file (348), displays the prompt (:), and waits for a command.

After ed opens a file for editing, the current line is the last line of the file. To see the current line number, use the .= command, as follows:

```
:.=
6
```

This output tells you that the /etc/fstab file has six lines. (Your system's /etc/fstab file, of course, may have a different number of lines.) The following example shows how you can see all these lines:

```
:1,$p
/dev/hda2    swap    swap    defaults    1    1
/dev/hda3    /       ext2    defaults    1    1
/dev/sda2    /usr    ext2    defaults    1    1
/dev/hda1    /dosc   msdos   defaults    1    1
/dev/sda1    /dosd   msdos   defaults    1    1
none         /proc   proc    defaults    1    1
:
```

Tip

To go to a specific line, type the line number, as follows:

```
:1
/dev/hda2    swap    swap    defaults    1    1
:
```

The editor responds by displaying that line.

Suppose that you want to delete the line that contains dosc. To search for a string, type a slash (/), followed by the string that you want to locate, as follows:

```
:/dosc
/dev/hda1    /dosc   msdos   defaults    1    1
:
```

The editor locates the line that contains the string and then displays it. That line becomes the current line. To delete the line, use the d command, as follows:

```
:d
:p
/dev/sda1    /dosd   msdos   defaults    1    1
:
```

Tip

To replace a string with another, use the s command. To replace dosd with the single character d, for example, use the following command:

```
:s/dosd/d/
:p
/dev/sda1    /d      msdos   defaults    1    1
:
```

Chapter 24: Text Processing in Linux   **759**

Tip

To insert a line in front of the current line, use the i command, as follows:

```
:i
/dev/hda1     /c      msdos     defaults     1     1
.
:
```

You can enter as many lines as you want. After the last line, enter a period (.) on a line by itself. That period marks the end of text-input mode, and the editor switches over to command mode. In this case, you can tell that ed has switched to command mode because you see the prompt (:).

Tip

When you are happy with the changes, you can write them out to the file with the w command. If you want to save the changes and exit, you can simply type **wq** to perform both steps at the same time, as follows:

```
:wq
287
```

The ed editor saves the changes in the file, displays the number of characters that it has saved, and exits.

If you want to quit the editor without saving any changes, use the Q command.

Summary of ed commands

The sample session should give you an idea of how to use ed commands to perform the basic tasks of editing a text file. Table 24-1 lists all commonly used ed commands:

Table 24-1	Commonly used ed commands
Command	**Meaning**
!command	Execute a shell command
$	Go to last line in the buffer
%	Apply command that follows to all lines in the buffer (for example, %p prints all lines)
+	Go to next line
+N	Go to N-th next line (N is a number)
,	Apply command that follows to all lines in the buffer (for example, ,p prints all lines); similar to %
-	Go to preceding line
-N	Go to N-th previous line (N is a number)
.	Refer to the current line in the buffer

(continued)

Table 24-1 *(continued)*

Command	Meaning
/regex/	Search forward for the specified regular expression (see Chapter 6 for an introduction to regular expressions)
;	Refer to a range of lines: current through last line in the buffer
=	Print line number
?regex?	Search backward for the specified regular expression (see Chapter 6 for an introduction to regular expressions)
^	Go to the preceding line; also see the - command
^N	Go to the N-th previous line (where N is a number); also see the -N command
a	Append after current line
c	Change specified lines
d	Delete specified lines
e *file*	Edit file
f *file*	Change default filename
h	Display explanation of last error
H	Turn on verbose-mode error reporting
i	Insert text before current line
j	Join contiguous lines
kx	Mark line with letter x (later, the line can be referred to as 'x)
l	Print (display) lines
m	Move lines
N	Go to line number N
Newline	Display next line and make that line current
P	Toggle prompt mode on or off
q	Quit editor
Q	Quit editor without saving changes
r *file*	Read and insert contents of file after the current line
s/*old*/*new*/	Replace *old* string with *new*
Space N	A space, followed by N; Nth next line (N is a number)
u	Undo the last command
W *file*	Append contents of buffer to the end of the specified file
w *file*	Save buffer in the specified file (if no file is named, save in the default file — the file whose contents ed is currently editing)

Chapter 24: Text Processing in Linux

Tip

Notice that you can prefix most editing commands with a line number or an address range, expressed in terms of two line numbers separated by a comma; the command then applies to the specified lines. To append after the second line in the buffer, for example, you use the following command:

```
2a
Type lines of text. End with single period on a line.
.
```

To print lines 3 through 15, use this command:

```
3,15p
```

Although you may not use `ed` often, much of the command syntax carries over to the `vi` editor. As the following section on `vi` shows, in its command mode, `vi` accepts the commands that you use with `ed`.

Using vi

The `vi` editor is a full-screen text editor that allows you to view a file several lines at a time. Most UNIX systems, including Linux, comes with `vi`. Therefore, if you learn the basic features of `vi`, you'll be able to edit text files on almost any UNIX system.

Like the `ed` editor, `vi` works with a buffer. When `vi` edits a file, it reads the file into a buffer — a block of memory — and allows you to change the text in the buffer. The original file is not altered until you save the changes with a specific `vi` command.

Setting the terminal type

Before you start a full-screen text editor such as `vi`, you have to set the TERM environment variable to the terminal type (such as `vt100` or `xterm`). The `vi` editor uses the terminal type to look up the terminal's characteristics in the `/etc/termcap` file and then control the terminal in full-screen mode.

Tip

If you use `bash`, type the following command to set the terminal type to the Linux console (that's your PC's monitor in text mode):

```
TERM=console; export TERM
```

When you run X, you can still use `vi` in an `xterm` window. The `xterm` window's terminal type is `xterm`. When you start `xterm`, it automatically sets the TERM environment variable to `xterm`. Therefore, you should be able to use `vi` in an `xterm` window without explicitly setting the TERM variable.

Note

`vi` won't run if it does not recognize the terminal type. If you try to run `vi` without setting the TERM environment variable, you know immediately, because `vi` displays the following error message:

```
Unrecognized TERM type
```

Starting vi

Secret

On your Linux system, the `elvis` editor emulates what you see as `vi` on most other UNIX systems. You can, however, continue to use the `vi` name to run the editor, because a symbolic link exists between `vi` and `elvis`. To see this link, type the following `ls` command:

```
ls -l /usr/bin/vi
lrwxrwxrwx  1 root     root            5 Sep 28 16:21 /usr/bin/vi -> elvis*
```

If you want to consult the online manual pages for `vi`, use its real name and type the following command:

```
man elvis
```

To start the editor, however, you can use the `vi` name and run it with the following command syntax:

```
vi [flags] [+cmd] [filename]
```

The arguments shown in brackets are optional. The following list explains the arguments:

- *flags* are single-character flags that control the way that `vi` runs.
- *+cmd* causes `vi` to run the specified command after it starts. (You learn more about the commands in "The `vi` command summary" section.)
- *filename* is the name of the file to be edited.

The *flags* arguments can be one or more of the following:

- `-c` *cmd* executes the specified command before editing begins.
- `-e` starts in colon command mode (described in the following section).
- `-i` starts in input mode (described in the following section).
- `-m` causes the editor to search through the file for something that looks like an error message from a compiler.
- `-R` makes the file read-only so that you cannot accidentally overwrite the file.
- `-s` runs in safe mode, wherein many potentially harmful commands are turned off.
- `-v` starts in visual command mode (described in the following section).

Most of the time, however, you start `vi` with a filename as the only argument, as follows:

```
vi /etc/hosts
```

Another common way to start `vi` is to jump to a specific line number right at startup. To begin editing at line 96 of the file `xmbrowse.c`, for example, use the following command:

```
vi +96 xmbrowse.c
```

This way of starting `vi` is useful when you edit a source file after the compiler reports an error at a specific line number.

Learning `vi` concepts

When you edit a file with `vi`, the editor loads the file into a buffer, displays the first few lines of the file in a full-screen window, and positions the cursor on the first line. When you type the command **vi /etc/fstab** in an `xterm` window, for example, you get a full-screen text window, as shown in Figure 24-1.

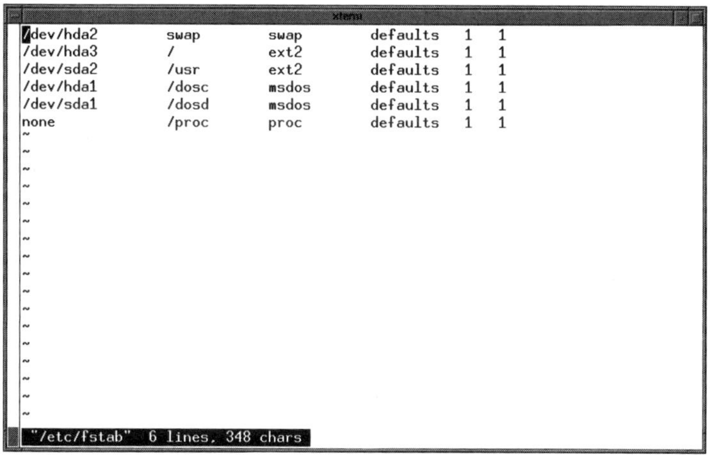

```
xterm
/dev/hda2      swap        swap      defaults   1   1
/dev/hda3      /           ext2      defaults   1   1
/dev/sda2      /usr        ext2      defaults   1   1
/dev/hda1      /dosc       msdos     defaults   1   1
/dev/sda1      /dosd       msdos     defaults   1   1
none           /proc       proc      defaults   1   1
~
~
~
~
~
~
~
~
~
~
~
~
~
~
"/etc/fstab"  6 lines, 348 chars
```

Figure 24-1: A file displayed in a full-screen text window by the `vi` (`elvis`) editor.

The last line shows information about the file, including the number of lines and the number of characters in the file. Later, this area is used as a command-entry area. The rest of the lines are used to display the file. If the file contains fewer lines than the window, `vi` displays the empty lines with a tilde (~) in the first column.

The current line is marked by the cursor, which appears as a small black rectangle. The cursor appears on top of a character. In Figure 24-1, the cursor is on the first character of the first line.

In `vi`, you work in one of three modes:

- *Visual command mode* is what you get by default. In this mode, anything that you type is interpreted as a command that applies to the line containing the cursor. The `vi` commands are similar to those of `ed` and are listed in "The `vi` command summary" section.
- *Colon command mode* allows you to read or write files, set `vi` options, and quit. All colon commands start with a colon (:). When you enter the colon, `vi` positions the cursor at the last line and allows you to type a command. The command takes effect when you press Enter.

- *Text input mode* allows you to enter text into the buffer. You can enter input mode with the command a (insert after cursor), A (append at end of line), or i (insert after cursor). After entering lines of text, you have to press Esc to leave input mode and re-enter visual command mode.

One problem with all these modes is that you cannot easily tell vi's current mode. It can frustrating to begin typing, only to realize that vi is not in input mode. The converse situation also is common, you may be typing text when you want to enter a command. If you want to make sure that vi is in command mode, just press Esc a few times. (Pressing Esc more than once doesn't hurt.)

A sample session with vi

To begin editing the file /etc/fstab, enter the following command:

```
vi /etc/fstab
```

Figure 24-1 shows the resulting display, with the first few lines of the file displayed in a full-screen text window. The last line shows the file's name and statistics: the number of lines and characters.

Note

The vi editor initially positions the cursor on the first character. One of the first things that you need to learn is how to move the cursor around. First, try the following commands (each command is a single letter; just type the letter, and vi responds):

- j moves the cursor one line down.
- k moves the cursor one line up.
- h moves the cursor one character to the left.
- l moves the cursor one character to the right.

Instead of moving one line or one character at a time, you can move around a word at a time. Try the following single-character commands for word-size cursor movement:

- w moves the cursor a word forward.
- b moves the cursor a word backward.

The last type of cursor movement is several lines at a time. Try the following commands, and see what happens:

- Ctrl-D moves down half a screen.
- Ctrl-U scrolls up half a screen.

The last two commands, of course, are not necessary when the file contains only a few lines. When you are editing large files, you'll find it handy to move around several lines at a time.

At any time, you can go to a specific line number. This situation is where a colon command comes in. To go to line 1, for example, type the following and then press Enter:

`:1`

When you type the colon, `vi` displays the colon on the last line of the screen. From then on, `vi` uses the text that you type as a command. You have to press Enter to submit the command to `vi`. In colon command mode, `vi` accepts all the commands that the `ed` editor accepts — and then some.

To search for a string, first type a slash (/). The `vi` editor displays the slash on the last line of the screen. Type the search string and then press Enter. The `vi` editor locates the string and positions the cursor at the beginning of that string. Thus, to locate the string `dosc` in the file `/etc/fstab`, type **/dosc**.

To delete the line that contains the cursor, type **dd** (that's two lowercase *d*s). The `vi` editor deletes that line of text and makes the next line the current one.

Tip

To begin entering text in front of the cursor, type **i** (a lowercase *i* all by itself). The `vi` editor switches to input mode. Now you can enter text. When you finish entering text, press Escape to return to visual command mode.

After you finish editing the file, you can save the changes in the file with the `:w` command. If you want to save the changes and exit, you can type **:wq** to perform both steps at the same time. The `vi` editor saves the changes in the file and exits.

If you want to quit the editor without saving any changes, use the `:q!` command.

The `vi` command summary

The sample editing session should give you a feel for the `vi` commands, especially the three modes:

- visual command mode (the default)
- input mode, which you enter by typing **a**, **A**, or **i**
- colon command mode, which you enter by typing a colon and then any commands

In addition to the few commands illustrated in the sample session, `vi` accepts a large number of commands. Table 24-2 lists the basic `vi` commands, organized by task.

Table 24-2	Basic `vi` commands
Command	Meaning
Insert text	
a	Insert text after the cursor
A	Insert text at the end of the current line
I	Insert text at the beginning of the current line
i	Insert text before the cursor
o	Open a line below the current line
O	Open a line above the current line
Ctrl-v	Insert any special character in input mode
Delete text	
D	Delete up to the end of the current line
dd	Delete the current line
dw	Delete from the cursor to the end of the following word
x	Delete the character on which the cursor rests
Change text	
C	Change up to the end of the current line
cc	Change the current line
cw	Change the word
J	Join the current line with the next one
r*x*	Replace the character under the cursor with *x* (*x* is any character)
~	Change character under the cursor to the opposite case
$	Move to the end of the current line
;	Repeat last f or F command
^	Move to the beginning of the current line
e	Move to the end of the current word
f*x*	Move cursor to the first occurrence of character *x* on the current line
F*x*	Move cursor to the last occurrence of character *x* on the current line
H	Move cursor to the top of the screen
h	Move one character to the left
j	Move one line down

Command	Meaning
Move cursor	
k	Move one line up
L	Move cursor to the end of the screen
l	Move one character to the right
M	Move cursor to the middle of the screen
N|	Move cursor to column N on current line
NG	Place cursor on line N
w	Move to the beginning of the following word
Mark a location	
`x	Move cursor to the beginning of the line that contains mark x
'x	Move cursor to mark x
mx	Mark the current location with the letter x
Scroll text	
Ctrl-b	Scroll backward by a full screen
Ctrl-d	Scroll forward by half a screen
Ctrl-f	Scroll forward by a full screen
Ctrl-u	Scroll backward by half a screen
Refresh screen	
Ctrl-l	Redraw screen
Cut and paste text	
"xNdd	Delete N lines and move them to buffer x (x is any single character)
"XNyy	Same as "xNyy, except that the yanked lines are appended to buffer x
"xNyy	Yank N (a number) lines into buffer x (x is any single character)
"xp	Put the yanked lines from buffer x after the current line
P	Put yanked line above the current line
p	Put yanked line below the current line
yy	Yank (copy) current line into an unnamed buffer
Colon commands	
:!command	Execute shell command
:e filename	Edit file
:f	Display filename and current line number

(continued)

Table 24-2 (continued)

Command	Meaning
Colon commands	
:N	Move to line N (N is a number)
:q	Quit editor
:q!	Quit without saving changes
:r filename	Read file and insert after current line
:w filename	Write buffer to file
:wq	Save changes and exit
Search text	
/string	Search forward for string
?string	Search backward for string
n	Find next string
View file information	
Ctrl-g	Show filename, size, and current line number
Miscellaneous	
u	Undo last command
Esc	End input mode and enter visual command mode

Working with GNU Emacs

Text editors are a matter of personal preference, and many UNIX users swear by GNU Emacs. Although it is intimidating at first, GNU Emacs is one of those software packages that grows on you; it has so many features that many users and programmers often perform all their tasks directly from within GNU Emacs.

Tip

A significant advantage of GNU Emacs is its availability on nearly every computer system imaginable, from MS-DOS PCs to any UNIX system. If a system does not have GNU Emacs, you can get it from one of many sites on the Internet. For your Linux system, you get GNU Emacs on the companion CD-ROM; you can choose to install it when you install Linux on your system. If you are just getting started with UNIX text editors, I recommend you learn to use GNU Emacs. That way you'll acquire a skill that you can use on any UNIX system.

Note

Because GNU Emacs is so versatile and powerful, describing it in detail could easily take an entire book; in fact, quite a few books on GNU Emacs are on the market. Most notably, O'Reilly & Associates has a GNU Emacs book, *Learning GNU Emacs*, that you may find to be useful.

On a text terminal, GNU Emacs runs in text-mode full-screen display. Under X, GNU Emacs runs in a window. Either way, the basic commands remain the same. The X version also allows you to position the cursor with the mouse.

The next few sections provide a brief introduction to the text-editing features of GNU Emacs.

Starting GNU Emacs

On the Linux console, you can start GNU Emacs by typing **emacs**. If you are running X, type **emacs &** in an xterm window to start GNU Emacs: This command launches the X window version of GNU Emacs in the background and allows you to continue other work in the xterm window.

When first started, GNU Emacs creates a buffer named *scratch* and displays a copyright message in a window, as shown in Figure 24-2.

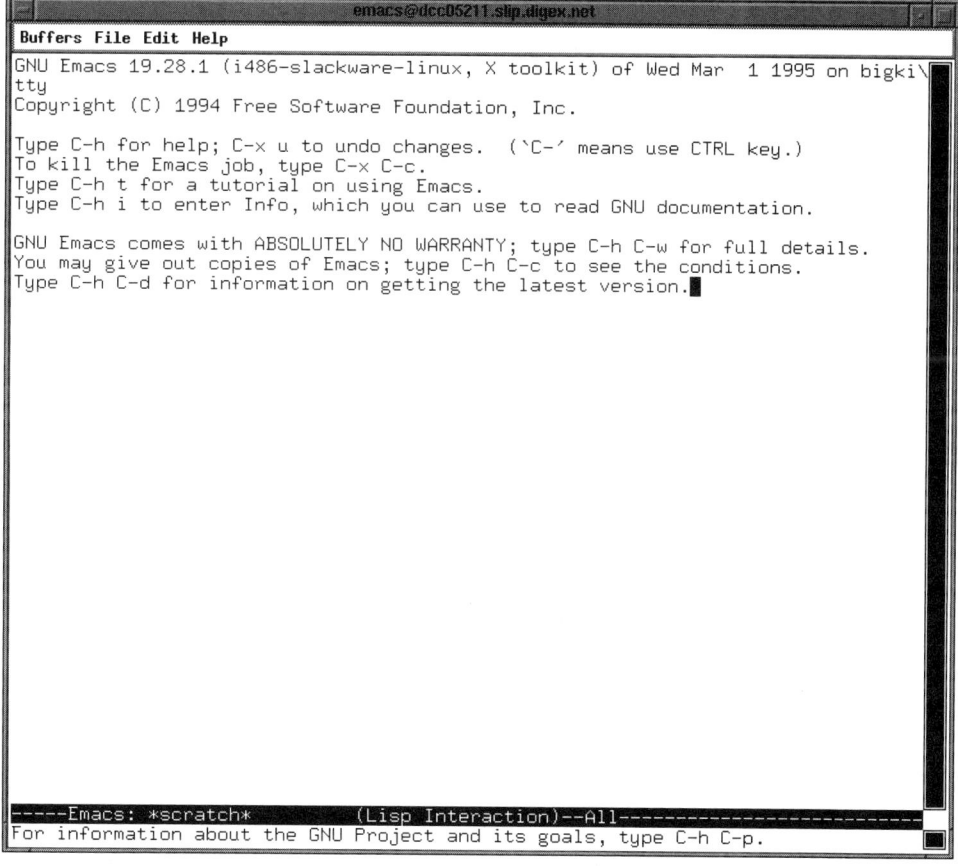

Figure 24-2: The initial window displayed by X version of GNU Emacs.

The initial GNU Emacs window also shows helpful information in the area where you normally edit the contents of a file. That information offers the following suggestions:

Cross Reference

- Press `C-h t` (press Ctrl-h, followed by t) to view an online tutorial on GNU Emacs.
- Press `C-h i` to start `info`, the online help system for all GNU software. Chapter 22 describes how to use `info`. (Hint: Type **m** and then **emacs** to see the information on GNU Emacs.)

The message also tells you that to quit GNU Emacs, you should press `C-x C-c` (that's Ctrl-x, followed by Ctrl-c). As you'll learn in the "Typing GNU Emacs commands" section, all GNU Emacs command keystrokes start with a control character or Escape (which is referred to as Meta and abbreviated as `M` in Emacs documentation).

Note

To be consistent with the GNU Emacs notation, I'll use the notation `C-x` for Ctrl-x and `M-x` for Escape-x (x is any character).

Learning GNU Emacs

I have used GNU Emacs extensively for years, but I feel that I have barely scratched the surface when it comes to using the full capabilities of GNU Emacs. As is true of anything else, your best bet is to start with a small subset of GNU Emacs commands. Then, as time goes by, you can gradually add to your repertoire of GNU Emacs commands and features.

GNU Emacs has some basic concepts that you'll find helpful to learn. Following are some of these concepts:

- Like other text editors (`vi` or `ed`), GNU Emacs uses a buffer to maintain the text you enter and change. You have to explicitly save the buffer to update the contents of the file.
- Unlike `vi` and `ed`, GNU Emacs does not require you to type any special command to enter text into the buffer. By default, anything that you type goes into the buffer.
- GNU Emacs uses the concept of a cursor marked by a block shape. When you type text, GNU Emacs inserts that text in front of the character on which the cursor rests.
- GNU Emacs has long, descriptive command names that are *bound to* (associated with) specific key sequences — these are the *key bindings* for the GNU Emacs commands. `C-x C-c`, for example, is bound to the GNU Emacs command `save-buffers-kill-emacs`.

Note

- All GNU Emacs key bindings start with a control character (for which you simultaneously press Ctrl and a character) or Escape.
- GNU Emacs uses several modes, each of which provides a specific type of editing environment. (In C mode, for example, GNU Emacs helps you by indenting the braces.)

Chapter 24: Text Processing in Linux   **771**

- In the GNU Emacs window, the last line is called the *minibuffer*; it displays all commands and filenames that you type. The line second to the bottom is called the *mode line*. On this line, GNU Emacs displays the name of the buffer and the current mode (the default mode is called Fundamental).

Tip

- You do not have to start GNU Emacs each time you want to edit a file. Rather, you start GNU Emacs and then open one or more files for editing. You save and close files that you finish editing.

- You can use many buffers in GNU Emacs, and you can cut and paste between buffers.

Typing GNU Emacs commands

GNU Emacs has an extensive set of commands in which each command has very long descriptive names, such as the following:

```
save-buffer save-buffers-kill-emacs scroll-up previous-line
```

Most of these commands, however, are bound to somewhat cryptic keystrokes. Otherwise, you'd have to type these long commands and wouldn't get much editing done.

Note

Although you can enter any of the descriptive commands in the minibuffer (at the bottom of the GNU Emacs window), the basic means of entering the commands is through special keystrokes. These keystrokes begin with one of the following characters:

- A control character that you enter by simultaneously pressing the Ctrl key and the character. In GNU Emacs documentation, each control character is abbreviated as `C-x` (x is a letter). In GNU Emacs online help, `Ctrl-v` is written as `C-v`.

- An Escape character. In GNU Emacs, the Escape key is abbreviated as the Meta key, or `M`. Thus, `Esc-v` (Escape, followed by the letter v) is written as `M-v`.

Most of the time, you'll be entering the control commands, which require you to press the Ctrl key together with a letter. `Ctrl-v` or `C-v`, for example, causes GNU Emacs to move forward one screen.

The commands with an `Esc` prefix are easier to enter, because you press the keys in sequence: first the Escape key and then the letter. `Esc v` or `M-v`, for example, causes GNU Emacs to move backward one screen of text. To enter this command, you press Escape first and then press **v**. Although the `Ctrl` and `Esc` commands may sound complicated, you can learn a basic set very quickly.

Getting help

The best source of information on GNU Emacs is GNU Emacs itself. For starters, GNU Emacs includes an online tutorial that teaches you the basics of GNU Emacs. To use the tutorial, type **C-h t**. GNU Emacs displays the initial screen of the tutorial in its window, as shown in Figure 24-3.

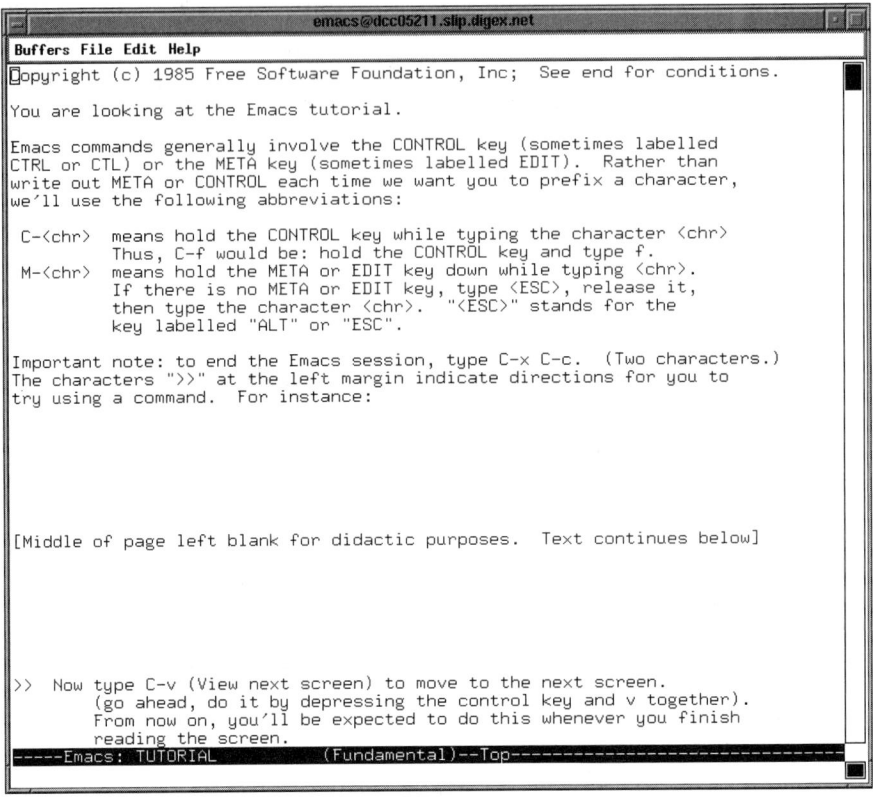

Figure 24-3: GNU Emacs displays the online tutorial when you press C-h t.

As the instructions toward the bottom of Figure 24-3 show, the tutorial guides you through the steps and asks you to try GNU Emacs commands. If you are new to GNU Emacs, you should go through the tutorial. Because the tutorial is hands-on, it'll give you a good feel for GNU Emacs.

In addition to the tutorial, you can look up the key bindings for various GNU Emacs commands. To see the key bindings, type **C-h b**. GNU Emacs splits the window and displays a list of key bindings in the bottom half, as shown in Figure 24-4.

Each line in the key binding shows the name of the key and the GNU Emacs command associated with that command. If you press the key, GNU Emacs executes the command that is bound to that key.

Figure 24-4 illustrates a feature of GNU Emacs: the capability to split its window into two or more parts. After splitting, each part becomes a separate window with its own buffer.

In Figure 24-4, you can scroll the key-binding list with the following keystrokes:

- C-x o switches to the other window (the bottom window, which shows the Help buffer with its key-bindings list).

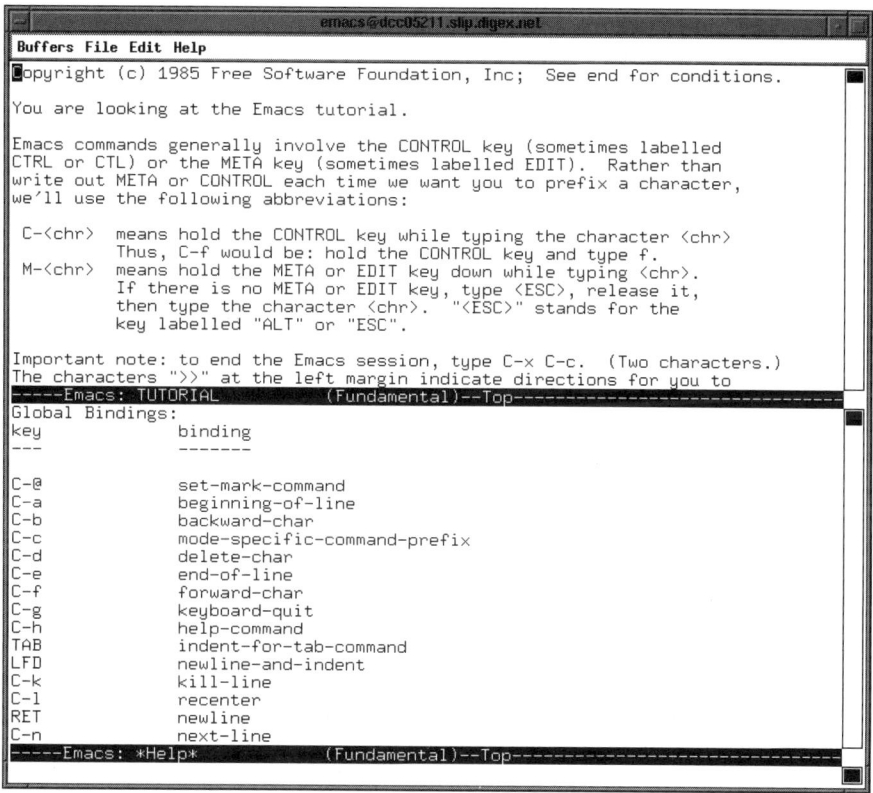

Figure 24-4: GNU Emacs displays the key bindings in a split window when you press C-h b.

- C-v scrolls the contents of the Help buffer.

Table 24-3 lists other GNU Emacs help commands.

Table 24-3	GNU Emacs help commands
Command	*Meaning*
C-h c	Prompts you for a key sequence and describes that sequence briefly
C-h f	Prompts you for a GNU Emacs command name and describes that command
C-h k	Prompts you for a key sequence and describes what that sequence does
C-h l	Displays the last 100 characters typed
C-h m	Displays current GNU Emacs mode
C-h s	Displays the syntax table for the current buffer
C-h v	Prompts for a variable name and describes that variable
C-h w	Prompts for a command and shows that command's key binding

Reading a file

After you start GNU Emacs, you can read in a file with the `C-x C-f` command. To open the file `/usr/src/linux/COPYING`, for example, follow these steps:

1. Press **C-x C-f**. GNU Emacs prompts you for a filename.
2. Type the filename **/usr/src/linux/COPYING** and press Enter. GNU Emacs reads the file into a buffer and displays that buffer in the window.

To open a file in the current directory, you do not have to type the full directory name; just type the filename. By default, GNU Emacs looks for the file in the current working directory.

Tip

You do not have to type the full filename in GNU Emacs; just enter the first few characters of the filename and then press Tab. If the partial name uniquely identifies a file, GNU Emacs completes the filename for you. You can use this shortcut feature to avoid typing long filenames.

Suppose that the current working directory contains the file `slack3-ls-laR`, which is the only file whose name starts with the substring `sla`. To load that file in GNU Emacs, press `C-x C-f`, type **sla**, and press Tab. GNU Emacs completes the filename and reads the file `slack3-ls-laR`.

Moving around the buffer

One of the first things that you have to do is move around in the buffer. The cursor marks the current spot in the buffer; anything that you type goes into the buffer in front of the character under the cursor. Thus, to insert text into a file, you have to read in the file, move the cursor to the desired spot, and type the text.

Tip

To move around the buffer, you need to move the cursor. You have to use control keys to move the cursor in any direction. The six basic cursor-movement commands are as follows:

- `C-b` moves the cursor backward one character.
- `C-f` moves the cursor forward one character.
- `C-n` moves the cursor to the following line (while trying to maintain the same column position as in the current line).
- `C-p` moves the cursor to the preceding line (while trying to maintain the same column position as in the current line).
- `C-a` moves the cursor to the beginning of the current line.
- `C-e` moves the cursor to the end of the current line.

If moving a character at a time is too slow, you can move a word at a time, using the following commands:

- `M-f` moves the cursor forward a word.
- `M-b` moves the cursor backward a word.

Tip

You can move in even bigger chunks through the buffer. The following commands allow you to move one screen at a time:

- C-v moves forward one screen.
- M-v moves backward one screen.

You can use two other simple cursor-movement commands for really big jumps:

- M-< (Escape, followed by the less-than key) moves the cursor to the beginning of the buffer.
- M-> (Escape, followed by the greater-than key) moves the cursor to the end of the buffer.

A time-saving feature of GNU Emacs enables you to repeat a command a specified number of times. Suppose that you want to move 13 characters forward. You can do so by pressing C-f 13 times or by typing **C-u 13 C-f**. The C-u command accepts a repeat count and repeats the next command that many times. If you don't provide a count and simply type a command after C-u, GNU Emacs repeats the command four times. Thus, C-u C-f means "move forward four characters."

Secret

One exception to the behavior of the C-u command exists: when you use C-u with the M-v or C-v command, GNU Emacs does not repeat the screen-scrolling commands. Instead, GNU Emacs scrolls the screen up or down by the specified count. Thus, if you press C-u 10 C-v, GNU Emacs scrolls down 10 lines (not 10 screens).

Inserting and deleting text

Because GNU Emacs does not have special command and insert modes like vi, to insert text in GNU Emacs, just begin typing. GNU Emacs inserts the text in front of the cursor. GNU Emacs, of course, interprets control characters and Esc as being the beginning of a command.

Tip

You can take advantage of the repeat-count feature to insert many copies of a character. I typically use the following line to separate sections of a C program:

/*---*/

I enter this line with the following key presses:

/* C-u 61 - */

Ignore the spaces; I don't really type them. I first type **/***. Then I press **C-u** and type **61**. Finally, I press the hyphen (-), followed by the ending ***/**.

You can delete text in GNU Emacs in the following ways:

- To delete the character in front of the cursor, press the Delete key.
- To delete the character on which the cursor rests, press C-d.

- To delete the word after the cursor, press M-d.
- To delete the word immediately before the cursor, press M-Delete.
- To delete from the cursor to the end of the line, press C-k. (GNU Emacs refers to this command as "kill the line.")

Tip

Whenever you delete anything more than a character, GNU Emacs saves it for you. Simply press C-y to get back the saved text.

You can undo a change with the C-x u command. Each time you press C-x u, GNU Emacs performs the undo operation for a previous command. To undo the effects of the last two commands, for example, press C-x u twice.

Searching and replacing

Every text editor has search-and-replace capability, and GNU Emacs is no exception. The two most common search commands are

- C-s string: incrementally search forward for string
- C-r string: incrementally search backward for string

When you press C-s to search forward, GNU Emacs prompts you for a search string in the minibuffer (the last line in the GNU Emacs window). As you enter the characters for the string, GNU Emacs jumps to the first occurrence of the string that you have typed so far. By the time you finish typing the search string, GNU Emacs will have positioned the cursor at the end of the next occurrence of the search string (provided, of course, that GNU Emacs finds the string).

To find the next occurrence of the string, simply press C-s again. To end the search, press Enter. You also can halt the search with cursor control commands, such as C-f or C-b.

Searching in the reverse direction works similarly; just press C-r instead of C-s.

GNU Emacs also allows you to replace an occurrence of one string with another. The two basic commands for replacing strings are replace-string and query-replace. The replace-string command replaces all occurrences of one string with another. The query-replace command works similarly, but GNU Emacs prompts you each time it's about to replace a string, allowing you to decide which strings actually get replaced.

The query-replace command is bound to the M-% (Escape, followed by %) key sequence. To perform a query-replace operation, first press M-%. GNU Emacs displays the following prompt in the minibuffer:

Query replace:

Enter the string that you want to replace — suppose that it's **1995** — and then press Enter. GNU Emacs prompts you for the replacement string, as follows:

Query replace 1995 with:

Enter the replacement string — say, **1996** — and press Enter. GNU Emacs moves the cursor to the next occurrence of the string to be replaced and displays a prompt in the minibuffer, as follows:

```
Query replacing 1995 with 1996: (? for help)
```

Type **y** or press the spacebar to allow GNU Emacs to replace the string. Otherwise, press **n** or Delete to stop GNU Emacs from replacing the string. In either case, GNU Emacs moves to the next occurrence of the string and repeats the prompt. When no more strings are left, GNU Emacs displays the following message in the minibuffer:

```
Done
```

No key binding exists for the `replace-string` command. You can type any GNU Emacs command, however, by following these steps:

1. Type **M-x**. GNU Emacs displays `M-x` in the minibuffer and waits for more text.
2. Type the GNU Emacs command, and press Enter. To use the `replace-string` command, for example, type **replace-string** and then press Enter.
3. For some commands, GNU Emacs prompts for further input; enter that input. When you use `replace-string`, for example, GNU Emacs first prompts for the string to be replaced and then for the replacement string.

When you type a GNU Emacs command with `M-x`, you can press the spacebar or the Tab key for command completion. To enter the `replace-string` command, for example, you might start by typing **repl** and then pressing the spacebar. That action causes GNU Emacs to display `replace-` and then pause. Type **s** and press the spacebar again. GNU Emacs displays `replace-string`. You then can use the command by pressing Enter. Try it; you'll see what I mean.

Copying and moving

Another common editing function is copying blocks of text and move that text to another location in the buffer. The first step in working with a block of text is defining the block.

In GNU Emacs, *block* is defined as being the text between a mark and the current cursor position. You can think of the *mark* as a physical marker placed in the buffer to mark a location. To set the mark, move the cursor to the beginning of the block and then press `C-@` or `C-Space` (press the Ctrl key together with the spacebar). GNU Emacs sets the mark at the current location and displays the following message in the minibuffer:

```
Mark set
```

After you set the mark, GNU Emacs treats the text between the mark and the current cursor location as a block. To copy the block, type the following:

```
M-w
```

That command copies the block to an internal storage area without deleting the block from the current buffer.

If you actually want to cut the block of text, use the following command:

`C-w`

That command deletes the block of text from the buffer and moves it to an internal storage area.

To insert the cut (or copied) text at any location, move the cursor to the insertion point and type the following:

`C-y`

That command causes GNU Emacs to paste the previously cut text in front of the cursor.

Between the cut and paste operations, you may switch from one buffer to another and thereby cut from one file and paste in another. To cut from one file and paste into another, follow these steps:

1. Open the first file with the `C-x C-f` command. For this exercise, assume that the first file's name is `first.txt`.
2. Open the second file with the `C-x C-f` command. For this exercise, assume that the second file's name is `second.txt`.
3. Change to the first buffer with the `C-x b first.txt` command.
4. Move the cursor to the beginning of the text to be copied, and press `C-Space`.
5. Move the cursor to the end of the block, and press `C-w` to cut the text.
6. Change to the second buffer with the `C-x b second.txt` command.
7. Move the cursor to the location where you want to insert the text, and press `C-y`. GNU Emacs inserts the previously cut text from the first buffer into the second one.

Saving changes

After you edit a buffer, you have to write those changes to a file to make them permanent. The GNU Emacs command for saving a buffer to its file is `C-x C-s`. This command saves the buffer to the file with the same name.

To save the buffer in another file, use the command `C-x C-w`. GNU Emacs prompts you for a filename. Type the filename and press Enter to save the buffer in that file. Unlike many DOS or Windows word processors, GNU Emacs does not automatically add a file extension. You have to provide the full filename.

Running a shell in GNU Emacs

Note

GNU Emacs is versatile enough to allow you to access anything in Linux from within a GNU Emacs session. One way to access anything in Linux is to run a shell session. You can do so with the GNU Emacs command named `shell`. To see how the `shell` command works, use M-x (press Escape, followed by **x**). GNU Emacs displays M-x in the minibuffer and waits for further input. Type **shell** and press Enter. GNU Emacs starts a new shell process and displays the shell prompt in the GNU Emacs window. Type any shell command that you want. The output appears in the GNU Emacs window.

You can continue to use the shell as long as you need it. All outputs from the commands go into the window where the shell prompt appears. When you no longer need the shell, type **exit**. That command terminates the shell process and returns you to GNU Emacs.

If you want to run a single shell command, use the M-! key binding. When you use M-!, GNU Emacs displays the following prompt in the minibuffer:

```
Shell command:
```

Type a shell command (such as **ls -l**) and press Enter. GNU Emacs executes that command and displays the resulting output in a separate window. To revert to a single-window display, type **C-x 1**. That command is Ctrl-x, followed by the number 1. The command instructs GNU Emacs to delete the other windows (excluding the one that contains the cursor).

Writing Man Pages with `groff`

Before the days of graphical interfaces, typesetting with the computer meant preparing a text file with embedded typesetting commands and then processing that marked-up text file with a computer program that generated commands for the output device: a printer or some other typesetter.

Cross Reference

As you know, such markup languages still exist. A prime example is Hypertext Markup Language (HTML), which is used to prepare World Wide Web pages. (See Chapter 20 for more information on HTML.)

In the late '70s and early '80s, I prepared all my correspondence and reports on a DEC VAX/VMS system, using a program named RUNOFF. That program formatted output for a line printer or a daisy-wheel printer. That VAX/VMS RUNOFF program accepted embedded commands like these:

```
.page size 58,80
.spacing 2
.no autojustify
```

As you might guess, the first command sets the number of lines per page and the number of characters on each line. The second command generates double-spaced output. The last command turns off justification. Essentially, I would pepper a text file with these commands, run it through RUNOFF, and send RUNOFF's output to the line printer. The resulting output looked as good as a typewritten document, which was good enough for most work in those days.

UNIX came with a more advanced typesetting program called `troff` (which stands for *typesetting runoff*) that could send output to a special device called a typesetter. A typesetter could produce much better output than a line printer. `troff` allows you to choose different fonts and to print text in bold and italic.

To handle output on simpler printers, UNIX also included `nroff` (which stands for *nontypesetting runoff*) to process `troff` files and generate output, ignore fancy output commands, and generate output on a line printer. `troff` typesetting is versatile enough that many computer books have been typeset with `troff`.

Now that nearly every computer has some sort of graphical interface (Microsoft Windows, Apple Macintosh, or the X Window System), most word-processing programs work in "what you see is what you get" mode, in which you get to work directly with the formatted document. Therefore, you probably won't have any reason to use `troff` for typesetting. `nroff` is still used for one important task, however: preparing man pages. The remainder of this chapter focuses on that purpose of `nroff`.

Note

The `groff` program is the GNU version of `troff` and `nroff`. With appropriate flags, you can use `groff` to typeset for several output devices, including any typewriterlike device.

Even if you do not use `groff` to prepare formatted documents (because using a PC-based word processor is more convenient), you may end up using `groff` to write the man page for any program that you write.

Man pages are the files that contain information users can view by typing the command `man progname`. This command shows online help information on `progname`. The subject of a man page can be anything from an overview of a software package to the programming information for a specific C function (for example, try `man fopen` on your Linux system).

After you go through an example, you'll realize that writing man pages in `groff` is quite simple.

Note

Before I describe the man-page preparation process, I should make it clear that you do not really use the `groff` program to prepare the man page. The man page is just a text file that contains embedded commands that `groff` recognizes. You might use `groff` to view a man page during preparation, but you can prepare a man page without ever running `groff`.

Try an existing man page

Before you write a man page, you should look at an existing man page. A brief example is the man page for `gnroff`, which is a command that emulates the behavior of `nroff` by using `groff`. Figure 24-5 shows the man page of `gnroff` in an `xterm` window.

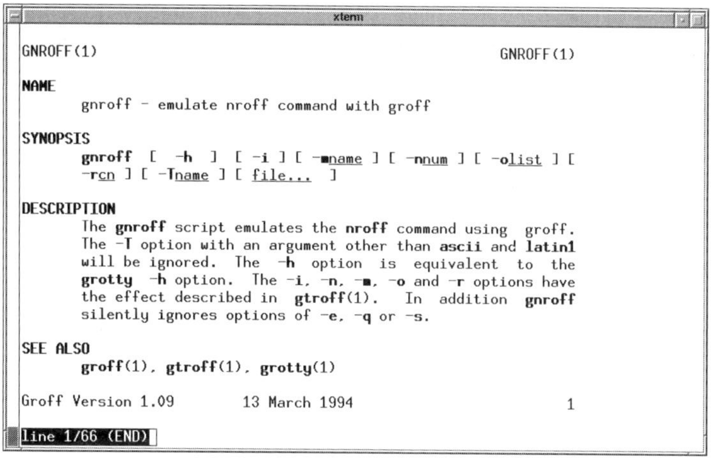

```
GNROFF(1)                                             GNROFF(1)

NAME
       gnroff - emulate nroff command with groff
SYNOPSIS
       gnroff [ -h ] [ -i ] [ -mname ] [ -nnum ] [ -olist ] [
       -rcn ] [ -Tname ] [ file... ]
DESCRIPTION
       The gnroff script emulates the nroff command using groff.
       The -T option with an argument other than ascii and latin1
       will be ignored.  The -h option is equivalent to the
       grotty -h option. The -i, -n, -m, -o and -r options have
       the effect described in gtroff(1).  In addition gnroff
       silently ignores options of -e, -q or -s.

SEE ALSO
       groff(1), gtroff(1), grotty(1)

Groff Version 1.09        13 March 1994                       1

line 1/66 (END)
```

Figure 24-5: Output of the `man gnroff` command in an `xterm` window.

In this case, you don't really have to pay attention to the exact content of the man page; all you care about is the layout. Take a moment to look over the layout. You'll notice the following things:

- The name of the command appears at the top of the man page. The number 1 that appears in parentheses next to the command's name denotes the section of the UNIX manual where this command belongs.

- The man page contains several sections, each of which appears in boldface. The text within the section is indented.

- In this example, the sections are NAME, SYNOPSIS, DESCRIPTION, and SEE ALSO. If you try a few more man pages, you'll see that some man pages have many more sections. Almost all man pages, however, have these four sections.

- Some text appears in boldface.

Look at a man-page source

After you view a man page with the `man` command, you should look at the original source file from which the `man` command generates the output. In your Linux system, the man-page source files are in several directories. These directory names appear as a colon-separated list in the environment variable MANPATH. To see the directory names, type the following command:

```
echo $MANPATH
/usr/local/man:/usr/man/preformat:/usr/man:/usr/X11/man:/usr/openwin/man
```

The second line shows a typical list of directories that contain man pages. Inside each of these directories, the files are organized in two sets of subdirectories. One set has the names `cat1`, `cat2`, and so on; the other set has the sequence of names `man1`, `man2`, and so on. The `mann` directories contain the raw source files (these are the files that you'll have to prepare by using `groff` syntax) for the man pages. When you first view a man page with the `man` command, the source in the `mann` directory is formatted, and a copy of that formatted file is saved in compressed form in the `catn` directory.

The source file for the `gnroff` man page is `/usr/man/man1/gnroff.1`. You should look at this file to see how the man page appears in its final form, as shown in Figure 24-5. Here is how you can look at the source file for the `gnroff` man page:

```
cd /usr/man/man1
cat gnroff.1
.TH GNROFF 1 "13 March 1994" "Groff Version 1.09"
.SH NAME
gnroff \- emulate nroff command with groff
.SH SYNOPSIS
.B gnroff
[
.B \-h
]
[
.B \-i
]
     ... Some lines deleted here
[
.I file\|.\|.\|.
]
.SH DESCRIPTION
The
.B gnroff
script emulates the
.B nroff
command using groff.
The
.B \-T
option with an argument other than
.B ascii
and
.B latin1
will be ignored.
          ... Some lines deleted here
.SH "SEE ALSO"
.BR groff (1),
.BR gtroff (1),
.BR grotty (1)
```

One interesting feature of the marked-up text file for the man page is the haphazard manner in which lines break. The formatting program `groff` (the `man` command uses `groff` to process the marked-up text file) fills up the lines of text and makes everything presentable.

Chapter 24: Text Processing in Linux

Most `groff` commands have to be on a line by themselves, and each such command starts with a period. You can, however, embed some `groff` font-control commands in the text; these embedded commands start with a backslash (\).

Note

Following is a summary of the commands that you see in the `gnroff` man-page source file:

- `.B` turns on boldface.
- `.BI` turns on boldface and then switches to italic.
- `.BR` turns on boldface and then changes to roman font.
- `.I` turns on italic.
- `.SH` is the start of a new section.
- `.TH` indicates the document title.

If you use these dot commands (by *dot commands*, I mean the commands that begin with a period or dot) to change the font, the man-page source file tends to have many short lines, because each dot command has to appear on a separate line. As the following section shows, you can use embedded font-change commands to produce a more readable source file.

Writing a sample man page

This section shows you how to write a man page for a sample application named `satview`. Assume that the `satview` program displays a satellite image in a window. The program has some options for specifying the map projection, the zoom level, and the name of the file that contains the satellite-image data.

Use a text editor to type the man-page source code shown in the following listing, and save it in a file named `satview.1`.

```
.TH SATVIEW 1 "Dec 10, 1995" "Satview Version 1.01"
.SH NAME
satview \- View satellite images.
.SH SYNOPSIS
\fBsatview\fP [-p \fIprojection\fP] [-m] [-z \fIzoomlevel\fP]
\fIfilename\fP
.SH DESCRIPTION
\fBsatview\fP displays the satellite image from \fIfilename\fP.
.SS Options
.TP
\fB-p \fIprojection\fR
Set the map projection (can be \fBL\fR for Lambert Conformal or
\fBP\fR for Polar Stereographic). The default is Lambert Conformal.
.TP
\fB-m\fP
Include a map in the satellite image.
.TP
```

```
\fB-z \fIzoomlevel\fR
Set the zoom level (can be one of: 2, 4, or 8). The default
zoomlevel is 1.
.TP
\fIfilename\fR
File containing satellite data.
.SH FILES
.TP
\fC/etc/satview.rc\fR
Initialization commands for \fBsatview\fR
.SH SEE ALSO
nexrad(1), contour(1)
.SH Bugs
At zoom levels greater than 2, map is not properly aligned with image.
```

The source file has the following significant features:

- The `.TH` tag indicates the man-page title, as well as the date and a version-number string. In the formatted man page, the version and date strings appear at the bottom of each page.
- This man page has six sections — `NAME`, `SYNOPSIS`, `DESCRIPTION`, `FILES`, `SEE ALSO`, and `Bugs` — each of which starts with the `.SH` tag.
- The `DESCRIPTION` has an `Options` subsection. The `.SS` tag indicates the beginning of a subsection.
- In the `Options` subsection, each item is listed with the `.TP` tag.
- The `\fB` command changes the font to boldface.
- `\fI` changes the font to italic.
- `\fR` changes the font to roman.
- `\fP` changes the font to its preceding setting.

With this information in hand, you should be able to understand the source code for this listing.

Testing and installing the man page

Tip

As you prepare the man-page file, you want to make sure that it is formatted correctly. To view the formatted output, you should use the following command:

```
groff -Tascii -man satview.1 | more
```

This command runs the `groff` command with the `ascii` typesetting device (that means produce plain ASCII output) and with the man-page macro set (that's what the `-man` option does).

If you find any formatting discrepancies, check the dot commands and any embedded font-change commands, and make sure that everything looks right.

After you are satisfied with the man-page format, you can make the man page available to everyone by copying the file to one of the directories in the MANPATH environment variable. You could install the man page with the following copy command:

```
cp satview /usr/man/man1
```

After that, try the man page with the following command:

```
man satview
```

Figure 24-6 shows the resulting output. Compare the output with the source file in satview.1 to see the effects of the commands on the final output. Notice that the italic command generates underlined output, because the terminal window cannot display an italic font.

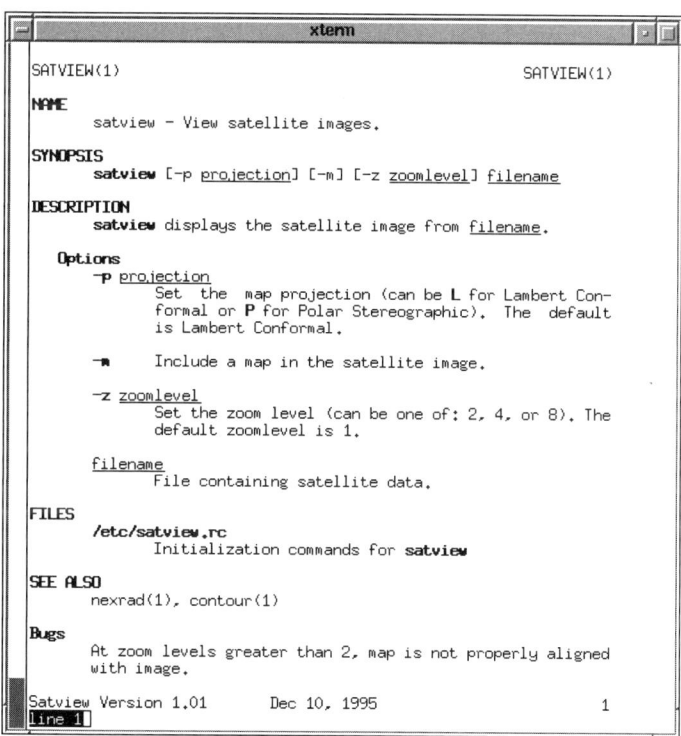

Figure 24-6: Output of the `man satview` command in an `xterm` window.

With the listing in this section as a guideline, you should now be able to write your own man pages.

Summary

The configuration of many Linux features depends on settings stored in text files. Therefore, you have to know how to edit text files to set up and maintain a Linux system. Another form of text processing involves typesetting and formatting text documents. Linux includes groff for this purpose. Nowadays, you're likely to use a PC to prepare formatted documents, but you still need to prepare one kind of formatted document: the man pages that provide online help on any software that you may write. Accordingly, this chapter shows you how to use several text editors and shows you how to prepare man pages by using groff. By reading this chapter, you learn:

▶ Linux includes a variety of text editors. It's important to learn ed and vi, because all UNIX systems come with these editors. Although the ed editor may be cryptic, you sometimes have to edit files when no other editor is available.

▶ The ed editor works on a text file a line at a time (which is why it's called a line editor). Each command takes the form of a range of lines, followed by a one-character command that applies to that range of lines.

▶ The vi editor is a full-screen editor that allows you to view a file several lines at a time. The vi editor has three modes: visual command mode, colon command mode, and input mode.

▶ In input mode, you can enter text. To change to input mode, press **i**, **a**, or **A**. To return to command mode, press Escape.

▶ In vi's colon command mode, you enter a colon (:) followed by a command that has the same syntax as ed commands.

▶ GNU Emacs is more than just an editor — it's also an environment in which you can perform most routine tasks.

▶ As an editor, GNU Emacs does not have any modes; whatever you type goes into the file. Commands begin with a control character (such as Ctrl-x) or Escape.

▶ To view the online tutorial, type Ctrl-h t in GNU Emacs.

▶ The groff utility is useful for formatting documents. groff provides the functionality of the standard UNIX nroff and troff utilities.

▶ Even though you may not prepare formatted documents in Linux (because it's easier to do so on a PC or a Macintosh), you still need to use groff to prepare man pages.

▶ The best way to learn to prepare a man page is to study an existing man page and mimic its style in your own man page. This chapter provides an example of how you might prepare a typical man page.

Part V
The Best of Linux Applications

Chapter 25: Linux Applications Roundup

Appendix: Linux Resources

Chapter 25
Linux Applications Roundup

The Slackware Linux distribution on this book's companion CD-ROM includes a number of applications. Many more Linux applications are available on the Internet. This chapter briefly describes many of the Linux applications on the companion CD-ROM. The purpose of this chapter is to introduce some of the applications so that you know they are available on the CD-ROM.

Following is a selected set of Linux applications from the CD-ROM, organized by category:

Category	*Applications*
Editors	GNU Emacs, elvis, JED, Joe, Jove, sed, Vim
Utilities	DOSEMU, GNU bc, gzip, ispell, Midnight Commander, patch, sc, Workbone, Workman, xcmap, xfilemanager, xfm, xspread
Graphics and images	XV, XPaint, Xfractint, Gnuplot, Ghostscript, Ghostview
Internet	dip, elm, nn, pine, pppd, rdist, sendmail, tin, trn, x3270
Serial communications	Minicom, Seyon
Programming	Bison, f2c, flex, Gawk, GCC, GNU Common List, p2c, Perl, RCS, Tcl/Tk, yacc
Text formatting	groff, TeX
Games	Abuse, DOOM, GNU Chess, xmahjongg, xtetris

This list is by no means comprehensive. The Linux distribution comes with a plethora of standard UNIX commands, for example, that are not shown in the list.

This chapter provides a brief summary of a smaller subset of these applications. In particular, I focus on some of the utility programs that were not covered in earlier chapters. Some applications, such as GNU Emacs and DOSEMU, are covered in detail elsewhere in the book. Also, entire categories of important applications, such as Internet applications, are covered in great detail in individual chapters.

Quite a few of the listed applications are automatically installed during the Linux installation process. For a few applications, you have to go through the trouble of installing them from the CD-ROM.

Notice that some of these applications are shareware; you are expected to register and pay a shareware fee if you plan to use the applications for your work. This information is noted where appropriate.

Editors

Cross Reference

You'll find several editors on the companion CD-ROM. If you install Linux by following the steps outlined in Chapter 1, you have the option of installing the following editors:

- GNU Emacs, the one and only original Emacs
- JED, a GNU Emacs-like editor
- JOE, a text editor with commands similar to those of WordStar
- JOVE, another GNU Emacs-like editor
- VIM, a vi-like editor

As you can see, most of these editors aspire to be either GNU Emacs or vi. The look-alikes typically are smaller in size and have fewer features.

GNU Emacs

The companion CD-ROM includes GNU Emacs version 19.29. GNU Emacs, which is one of the best-known GNU products, is distributed by Free Software Foundation. The CD-ROM includes two versions of GNU Emacs:

- The full version of GNU Emacs that works under X and provides menus for editing operations. You must have X installed to run this version. The binary is configured with the following options:

    ```
    --with-x11 --with-x-toolkit --prefix=/usr
    ```

- A version that is about 400K smaller than the full version of GNU Emacs, with the same functionality but without the support for X.

You can run the non-X version of GNU Emacs in an xterm window under X. The non-X version, however, is mainly for those users who do not have the X Window System installed on their systems.

Chapter 24 describes the features of GNU Emacs and shows how to use GNU Emacs for text-editing tasks.

JED

Like several of the other freely available text editors, this editor is named after its author, John E. Davis. JED is a powerful but small GNU Emacs-like editor that supports editing modes and reads info files. JED also can emulate other text editors, such as WordStar and the EDT editor of VAX/VMS systems. One of the unique features of JED is that you can actually edit binary files in JED.

Joe

The companion CD-ROM includes the Joe text editor version 2.2. Joe is named after its creator, Joseph H. Allen. The Joe editor uses commands similar to those of the popular PC word processor of yesteryear, WordStar.

Jove

Jove (the term stands for Jonathan's Own Version of Emacs) is another GNU Emacs-like editor. Jove works like GNU Emacs but is much smaller. In fact, Jove is available for the PC, which probably is where you can get the most benefit from a small GNU Emacs-like editor. On a capable system such as a Linux PC, the real GNU Emacs is a better choice. If you install and use Jove, you should use the `teachjove` tutorial program to learn more about it.

Vim

Vim stands for *Vi IM*proved. As the name implies, Vim is supposed to be an improved version of the standard UNIX text editor `vi`. The companion CD-ROM includes version 3.0 of Vim. In addition to the standard `vi` commands, Vim includes several new features such as several levels of undo, command-line history, and filename completion.

Cross Reference

Chapter 24 shows you how to use the `vi` editor. If you know `vi`, you can use Vim easily.

Utilities

This category is a catchall category for many helpful applications that come with the Linux distribution. The list is not exhaustive because I included only the most popular applications. The applications summarized in the following sections are

- DOSEMU, a DOS emulator for Linux
- GNU `bc`, an arbitrary precision calculator
- `gzip`, a utility for compressing and expanding files
- `ispell`, a full-screen interactive spelling checker

- `patch`, a utility for applying changes to a text file
- `sc`, a spreadsheet
- Workbone, a text-mode program for playing audio CDs
- Workman, an X-based program with a graphical interface for playing audio CDs
- `xcmap`, a program that displays the default colormap on X displays
- `xfilemanager`, an X-based UNIX file manager
- `xfm`, another X-based file manager
- `xspread`, a spreadsheet that runs under X (similar to `sc`)

DOSEMU

DOSEMU is a freely distributed DOS emulator — a program that you can run under Linux to get an MS-DOS environment. With DOSEMU, you can run DOS applications under Linux. DOSEMU is not installed by default. You'll find the DOSEMU software distribution in the `contrib` directory of the companion CD-ROM.

Cross Reference

To use DOSEMU, you first have to install it from the CD-ROM. Chapter 7 shows you how to install and use DOSEMU.

GNU `bc`

GNU `bc` allows you to enter arbitrary precision numbers and perform various calculations with these numbers. GNU `bc` implements the arbitrary precision-calculation capability specified by the POSIX P1003.2/D11 draft standard.

You'll get a chance to install GNU `bc` as part of a package during Linux installation from the companion CD-ROM.

If you have GNU `bc` installed, you should be able to run it with the following command:

```
bc
bc 1.03 (Nov 2, 1994)
Copyright (C) 1991, 1992, 1993, 1994 Free Software Foundation, Inc.
This is free software with ABSOLUTELY NO WARRANTY.
For details type 'warranty'.
```

After displaying the banner, `bc` waits for your input. Then you can enter numbers and expressions, using a syntax similar to that of the C programming language.

Numbers are the basic elements in `bc`. A number is treated as an arbitrary precision number with an integral and fractional part. You can enter numbers and evaluate expressions just the way that you write expressions in C, as the following example shows:

```
1.000000000000000033 + 0.1
1.100000000000000033
```

As soon as you enter an expression, bc evaluates the expression and displays the result.

You also can define variables and use them in expressions, as follows:

```
cost=119.95
tax_rate=0.05
total=(1+tax_rate)*cost
total
125.94
```

If you check this result with your calculator, you'll notice that bc truncates the result of multiplication (it does the same with division). If you want, you can retain more significant digits by setting the scale variable, as follows:

```
scale=10
total=(1+tax_rate)*cost
total
125.9475
```

In this case, the result has more significant digits.

The bc utility supports an entire programming language with a C-style syntax. You can write loops and conditional statements, and even define new functions with the define keyword. The following example shows how you might define a factorial function:

```
define factorial (n) {
  if(n <= 1) return (1);
  return (factorial(n-1)*n);
}
```

As you can see, the factorial function is recursive; it calls itself. Entering the lines as shown in the example is important. In particular, bc needs the open brace on the first line because that brace tells bc to continue reading input until it gets a closing brace.

After you define the factorial function, you can use it just as you might call a C function. Following are some examples:

```
factorial(3)
6
factorial(4)
24
factorial(10)
3628800
factorial(40)
815915283247897734345611269596115894272000000000
factorial(50)
30414093201713378043612608166064768844377641568960512000000000000
factorial(100)
9332621544394415268169923885626670049071596826438162146859296389521750\
9999322991560894146397615651828625369792082722375825118521091686400000\
00000000000000000000
```

As the example shows, you can use `bc` to represent as large a number as you want; no limit exists. When necessary, `bc` displays the result on multiple lines, with each continuation line ending in a backslash followed by a new line.

To quit `bc`, type the following command:

```
quit
```

To learn more about `bc`, consult its man pages by using the `man bc` command. After you learn about new features of `bc`, try them interactively.

gzip

The `gzip` program is the GNU zip compression utility that is used to compress all Linux software distributions. When you run `gzip` with a filename as argument, it reduces the file's size by using the Lempel-Ziv (LZ77) compression algorithm and stores the result in a file with the same name but with an additional `.gz` extension. Thus, if you compress a file with the `gzip files.tar` command, the result is a compressed file with the name `files.tar.gz`.

The same `gzip` program can decompress any file that was previously compressed by `gzip`. To decompress the file `files.tar.gz`, for example, you can simply type the following:

```
gzip -d files.tar
```

Notice that you do not have to explicitly type the `.gz` extension; `gzip` automatically appends a `.gz` extension when it is looking for the compressed file. After decompressing, the utility creates a new file with the name `files.tar`.

Instead of `gzip -d`, you can use the `gunzip` command to decompress a file, as follows:

```
gunzip files.tar
```

This command also looks for a file named `files.tar.gz` and decompresses the file, if found.

By default, `gzip` stores the original filename and timestamp in the compressed file. You can decompress a file with the `-N` option to restore the original filename and time stamp.

Following is the basic syntax of the `gzip` command:

```
gzip [-cdfhlLnNrtvV19] [-S .xxx] [file ...]
```

The options have the following meanings:

- `-c` writes output to standard output
- `-d` decompresses the file
- `-f` forces compression or decompression, even if file has multiple links or the corresponding file already exists

- `-h` displays a help screen and quits
- `-l` lists files sizes before and after compression
- `-L` displays the `gzip` license and quits
- `-n` stops `gzip` from storing the original filename in the compressed file
- `-N` restores original filename during decompression
- `-q` suppresses all warnings
- `-r` causes `gzip` to traverse the directory structure recursively and operate on all files
- `-S .xxx` causes `gzip` to use the suffix `.xxx` instead of `.gz`
- `-t` tests the integrity of a compressed file
- `-v` displays the name and percentage compression for each file
- `-V` displays version number and the compiler options used to build that version of `gzip`
- `-1` uses the fastest compression method (even though compression may not be as much)
- `-9` uses the slowest compression method (provides the most compression)
- `file ...` are one or more filenames (the files to be compressed or decompressed)

The `gzip` utility is installed automatically when you install Linux from the companion CD-ROM.

ispell

The `ispell` utility is an interactive spelling checker. When you install Linux from the companion CD-ROM, you get a chance to install `ispell`.

Using `ispell` is simple. Most of the time, you use `ispell` to check the spelling of words in a text file. To do so, simply type **ispell *filename*.** Suppose that you typed some notes and stored them in a text file named `notes`. To run the spell checker on that file, type the following command:

```
ispell notes
```

After `ispell` runs, it scans the file named `notes` until it finds a misspelled word (any word that is not in `ispell`'s dictionary). In the `notes` file, `ispell` may find the misspelled word *concensus*. Figure 25-1 shows how `ispell` reports this misspelling in the full-screen text window.

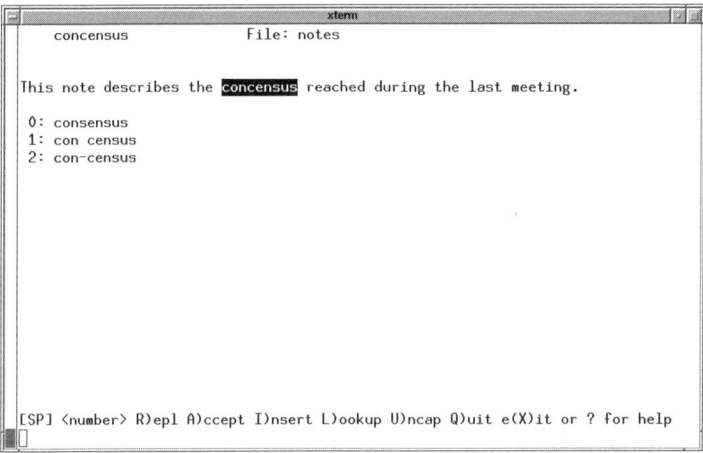

Figure 25-1: A misspelled word, with suggested spellings reported by `ispell`.

As Figure 25-1 shows, `ispell` shows you the misspelled word highlighted within the sentence where it occurs. Below that sentence, `ispell` lists possible corrections. In this case, the utility lists *consensus* — the right choice — as the first correction for *concensus*.

At the bottom of the screen, `ispell` displays the commands that you can enter. Following are the meanings of the items on the last line in Figure 25-1:

- `Space` means accept the word this time.
- `<number>` refers to the number of the suggested correction that you want to use. To replace the misspelled word with the correction numbered 0, simply type **0**.
- `R` means replace. `ispell` prompts for a replacement word.
- `A` means accept. `ispell` accepts the word for the rest of the file.
- `I` means insert. `ispell` accepts the word and also adds it to the user's private dictionary.
- `L` causes `ispell` to look up words in the system dictionary.
- `U` means accept the word and add a lowercase version to the user's private dictionary.
- `Q` causes `ispell` to quit immediately.
- `X` causes `ispell` to save the rest of the file, ignoring misspellings.
- `?` displays a help screen.

Additionally, you can enter a shell command with an exclamation-mark (`!`) prefix. If the screen gets messed up for any reason, press Ctrl-L to refresh the screen.

Midnight Commander

Midnight Commander is a file manager with a text-based interface, similar to Norton Commander for MS-DOS. You can use Midnight Commander to manage files and directories without having to learn UNIX commands. If you are not quite sure about all the UNIX commands, you may want to use Midnight Commander to perform file operations such as copy, rename, and delete. You can even view or edit a file with Midnight Commander.

When you install Linux from the companion CD-ROM, you get a chance to install Midnight Commander.

You can run Midnight Commander from the console or an `xterm` window. To start Midnight Commander, type **mc**.

Figure 25-2 shows typical output from Midnight Commander. In this case, the current directory happens to be the root directory (/).

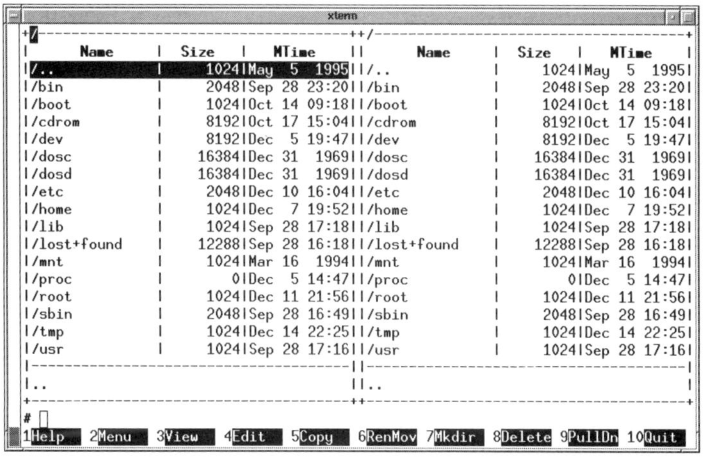

```
                                    xterm
+/-------------------------++/------------------------------+
|        Name    |  Size  |  MTime  ||       Name   |  Size  |  MTime    |
|/..             |  1024|May  5  1995||/..          |  1024|May  5  1995|
|/bin            |  2048|Sep 28 23:20||/bin         |  2048|Sep 28 23:20|
|/boot           |  1024|Oct 14 09:18||/boot        |  1024|Oct 14 09:18|
|/cdrom          |  8192|Oct 17 15:04||/cdrom       |  8192|Oct 17 15:04|
|/dev            |  8192|Dec  5 19:47||/dev         |  8192|Dec  5 19:47|
|/dosc           | 16384|Dec 31  1969||/dosc        | 16384|Dec 31  1969|
|/dosd           | 16384|Dec 31  1969||/dosd        | 16384|Dec 31  1969|
|/etc            |  2048|Dec 10 16:04||/etc         |  2048|Dec 10 16:04|
|/home           |  1024|Dec  7 19:52||/home        |  1024|Dec  7 19:52|
|/lib            |  1024|Sep 28 17:18||/lib         |  1024|Sep 28 17:18|
|/lost+found     | 12288|Sep 28 16:18||/lost+found  | 12288|Sep 28 16:18|
|/mnt            |  1024|Mar 16  1994||/mnt         |  1024|Mar 16  1994|
|/proc           |     0|Dec  5 14:47||/proc        |     0|Dec  5 14:47|
|/root           |  1024|Dec 11 21:56||/root        |  1024|Dec 11 21:56|
|/sbin           |  2048|Sep 28 16:49||/sbin        |  2048|Sep 28 16:49|
|/tmp            |  1024|Dec 14 22:25||/tmp         |  1024|Dec 14 22:25|
|/usr            |  1024|Sep 28 17:16||/usr         |  1024|Sep 28 17:16|
|----------------------------------||-------------------------------|
|..                                ||..                             |
+---------------------------------++-------------------------------+
#
1Help  2Menu  3View  4Edit  5Copy  6RenMov  7Mkdir  8Delete  9PullDn  10Quit
```

Figure 25-2: Midnight Commander display in an `xterm` window.

The display has two side-by-side directory listings. You can change the directory on either listing. The two side-by-side views allow you to perform operations such as copy or move between two directories.

At the bottom of the Midnight Commander display are 10 commands that vaguely resemble buttons in a graphical interface. These commands are the common operations that you can perform in the Midnight Commander window.

Midnight Commander responds to mouse input in a console window as well as an `xterm` window. That means that you can double-click a directory name to view that directory's contents in the Midnight Commander display. Also, you can click the commands (displayed in reverse video on the bottom edge of the Midnight Commander display) to activate them.

patch

The GNU `patch` utility is designed to apply *patches* (corrections) to files. The basic idea behind `patch` is that when you want to distribute changes in a file, you run the standard UNIX `diff` command and generate a `diff` file that indicates how the file should be changed; then you distribute that `diff` file to everyone who has the original file. The recipient runs the `patch` utility with the `diff` file as input, and `patch` makes the changes in the original files.

Cross Reference

The `patch` utility is installed automatically when you install Linux from the companion CD-ROM. Chapter 2 shows you how to use `patch` to apply changes to the Linux kernel sources when you upgrade the kernel from one version to the next.

You can learn more about `patch` through a simple example. Assume that you have a file named `original.txt` that contains the following text:

```
Version: 1.0

Revision history:
  12/15/95: Original file (NB)

This text file used as an example to illustrate how to use diff and
patch to update a file.
```

Suppose that you already distributed this file to several users. (Pretend that the file is the source file of a computer program.) After a while, you make some changes in this file. The new file, named `revised.txt`, looks like this:

```
Version: 1.1

Revision history:
  12/15/95: Original file (NB)
  3/15/96: Added a new line (LB)

This text file used as an example to illustrate how to use diff and
patch to update a file.

Something new added...
```

Now you want to provide these changes to your users so they can use the new file. Your first task is to create a `diff` file that captures the changes that you have made.

To create the `diff` file, run `diff` with the `-u` option, and specify the two filenames as arguments — the original file, followed by the revised one. Thus, the following command creates the `diff` file for the current example:

```
diff -u original.txt revised.txt > patch-1.1
```

This command creates the file `patch-1.1`, which is what you would distribute to your users who are currently using the file `original.txt`. This `diff` file also is referred to as the *patch file*.

When a user receives the patch file, all that he or she needs to do is put the patch file in the same directory where the file `original.txt` resides and then type the following command:

```
patch < patch-1.1
Hmm... Looks like a unified diff to me...
The text leading up to this was:
--------------------------
|-- original.txt    Fri Dec 15 16:08:57 1995
|+++ revised.txt    Fri Dec 15 16:10:33 1995
--------------------------
Patching file original.txt using Plan A...
Hunk #1 succeeded at 1.
done
```

The `patch` utility reports some helpful messages and applies the changes from the patch file. First, `patch` copies the `original.txt` file to `original.txt.orig`; then it applies the changes directly to the file `original.txt`. After `patch` finishes, the content of the `original.txt` file changes to the following:

```
Version: 1.1

Revision history:
  12/15/95: Original file (NB)
   3/15/96: Added a new line (LB)

This text file used as an example to illustrate how to use diff and
patch to update a file.

Something new added...
```

That example should give you a good idea of how to use the `patch` utility to update text files.

SC

The `sc` program is a spreadsheet program with a text-based full-screen display that's similar to Lotus 1-2-3. During Linux installation from the companion CD-ROM, you get a chance to install `sc`.

You can run `sc` from any terminal window. A good way to get started with `sc` is to use its online tutorial, which you can view in `sc` with the following command:

```
sc /usr/lib/sc/tutorial.sc
```

This command causes `sc` to open and display the `/usr/lib/sc/tutorial.sc` file, as shown in Figure 25-3.

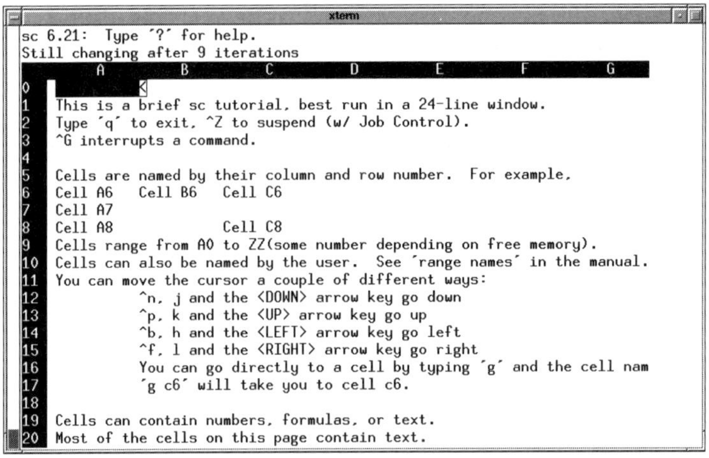

```
sc 6.21: Type '?' for help.
Still changing after 9 iterations
            A         B         C         D         E         F         G
 0
 1  This is a brief sc tutorial, best run in a 24-line window.
 2  Type 'q' to exit, ^Z to suspend (w/ Job Control).
 3  ^G interrupts a command.
 4
 5  Cells are named by their column and row number.  For example,
 6  Cell A6    Cell B6    Cell C6
 7  Cell A7
 8  Cell A8               Cell C8
 9  Cells range from A0 to ZZ(some number depending on free memory).
10  Cells can also be named by the user.  See 'range names' in the manual.
11  You can move the cursor a couple of different ways:
12          ^n, j and the <DOWN> arrow key go down
13          ^p, k and the <UP> arrow key go up
14          ^b, h and the <LEFT> arrow key go left
15          ^f, l and the <RIGHT> arrow key go right
16          You can go directly to a cell by typing 'g' and the cell nam
17          'g c6' will take you to cell c6.
18
19  Cells can contain numbers, formulas, or text.
20  Most of the cells on this page contain text.
```

Figure 25-3: The `sc` program displaying its tutorial in an `xterm` window.

The tutorial tells you how to use `sc`. If you are familiar with a spreadsheet program such as Lotus 1-2-3, you can start using `sc` very easily.

As the tutorial tells you, to exit `sc`, type **q**. To view the rest of the tutorial, use the arrow keys to scroll the display.

As you look at the `sc` display in Figure 25-3, you'll find it informative to look at the file `/usr/lib/sc/tutorial.sc` — the spreadsheet file that `sc` displays in Figure 25-3. Following are the first few lines of that file:

```
more /usr/lib/sc/tutorial.sc
# This data file was generated by the Spreadsheet Calculator.
# You almost certainly shouldn't edit it.

define "page5" A90
define "page1" A11
define "page2" A30
define "page3" A50
define "page4" A71
leftstring A1 = "This is a brief sc tutorial, best run in a 24-line
window."
leftstring A2 = "Type 'q' to exit, ^Z to suspend (w/ Job Control)."
leftstring A3 = "^G interrupts a command."
leftstring A5 = "Cells are named by their column and row number. For
example,"
leftstring A6 = "Cell A6"
leftstring B6 = "Cell B6"
leftstring C6 = "Cell C6"
leftstring A7 = "Cell A7"
leftstring A8 = "Cell A8"
leftstring C8 = "Cell C8"
leftstring A9 = "Cells range from A0 to ZZ(some number depending on
free memory)
."
```

```
leftstring A10 = "Cells can also be named by the user. See 'range
names' in the
manual."
(lines deleted...)
```

The spreadsheet file is a text file. If you compare this listing with what appears in Figure 25-3, you begin to see the syntax of how each cell's content is stored in the spreadsheet file.

Figure 25-3 also shows the basic layout of the `sc` display. The display is organized in four regions:

- The top line is for entering commands and displaying cell values.
- On the second line, `sc` displays messages.
- The third line shows the column letters; the first three columns on all other lines show the row number. Each column is marked by a letter (A, B, C, and so on), and each row has a number (0, 1, 2, and so on). Each cell is identified by its row letter and column number (A0, B0, A1, B1, and so on).
- The rest of the `sc` display is a window into the spreadsheet.

You can scroll through the spreadsheet cells by pressing the up-, down-, left-, and right-arrow keys. The current cell is always highlighted and marked by a less-than (<) sign.

A basic use of a spreadsheet is entering numbers or text into cells. To enter an item into a cell, move to the cell and then press one of the following keys, followed by the specified item type:

Key	Meaning
"	Centered string
+	Increment value by 1
-	Decrement value by 1
<	Left-justified string
=	Numeric constant, expression, or formula
>	Right-justified string
c	Copy marked cell to this cell
e	Edit numeric cell
E	Edit string in the cell
F	Format the cell's numeric value
m	Mark cell
x	Clear cell

To enter the numeric value 49.95 into cell C3, for example, first move to cell C3 and then type the following:

```
=49.95
```

To enter the value into the cell, press Enter.

Another common spreadsheet task is entering a formula in a cell. You enter the formula the same way that you enter a number: type = (equal sign), followed by the formula. Table 25-1 lists some of the formulas that sc recognizes:

Table 25-1   Commonly used sc formulas

Formula	Meaning
@abs(e)	Absolute value of expression e.
@acos(e)	Arc cosine of expression e.
@asin(e)	Arc sine of expression e.
@atan(e)	Arc tangent of expression e.
@atan2(e1,e2)	Arc tangent of e1/e2.
@avg(range)	Average value of all valid cells in the range.
@ceil(e)	Smallest integer not less than e.
@cos(e)	Cosine of expression e (assumed to be in radians).
@count(range)	Total number of all valid cells in the range.
@dtr(e)	Convert degrees to radians.
@eqs(se1,se2)	Result is 1 if string expression se1 has the same value as se2.
@exp(e)	Exponential of expression e.
@fabs(e)	Absolute value of expression e.
@floor(e)	The largest integer not greater than e.
@fv(p,r,n)	Future value of n payments of amount p at an interest rate of r. fv(100,0.004,120) evaluates to the future value of 120 monthly payments of $100, at an annual interest rate of 4.8 percent (0.004 per month).
@hypot(x,y)	Square root of $(x*x + y*y)$.
@ln(e)	Natural logarithm of expression e.
@log(e)	Base 10 logarithm of expression e.
@max(e1,e2,...)	Maximum of e1, e2, ...
@max(range)	Maximum value of all valid cells in the range.
@min(e1,e2,...)	Minimum of e1, e2, ...
@min(range)	Minimum value of all valid cells in the range.

Formula	Meaning
@now	Time, in the form of seconds elapsed since January 1, 1970 00:00.
@nval(se,e)	The numeric value of a named cell.
@pi	The value of the constant PI.
pi	The value of the constant PI.
@pmt(p,r,n)	Payments on principal p borrowed for a period of n at a rate of r. pmt(75000,0.005,180) evaluates to monthly payments on a $75,000 loan at 6 percent (0.005 per month) for 15 years (180 months).
@pow(e1,e2)	$e1$ raised to the power of $e2$.
@prod(range)	Product of all valid cells in the range.
@pv(p,r,n)	Present value of n payments of amount p at an interest rate of r. pv(100,0.006,120) evaluates to the amount that you can borrow at an annual interest rate of 7.2 percent (0.006 per month) if you pay $100 per month for 10 years (120 months).
@rnd(e)	Value of expression e rounded to the nearest integer.
@round(e,n)	Value of expression e rounded to n decimal places.
@rtd(e)	Convert radians to degrees.
@sin(e)	Sine of expression e (assumed to be in radians).
@sqrt(e)	Square root of expression e.
@stddev(range)	Standard deviation of all valid cells in the range.
@ston(se)	Convert string expression se to a numeric value.
@sum(range)	Sum of all valid cells in the range.
@tan(e)	Tangent of expression e (assumed to be in radians).

Some of these formulas accept a range. You have to specify a range with the following syntax:

Xm:Yn

X and *Y* are letters that indicate columns; *m* and *n* are row numbers. Thus, *Xm* is the starting cell, and *Yn* is the ending cell of the range. Following are some examples of ranges:

Range	Meaning
A45:A56	The cells in column A from row 45 to 56
A45:C56	All the cells in the rectangular area from column A to C and rows 45 through 56, inclusive

Thus, you would write the formula that denotes the sum of the cells A45 through A56 as follows:

```
@sum(A45:A56)
```

`sc` has many more features than I can describe in this brief section. If you need to use a spreadsheet in Linux, you should give `sc` a try. If you use the X Window System, you may want to use `xspread` instead; `xspread` is an improved version of `sc`.

Workbone

Workbone is an audio-CD-player program with a fairly intuitive text-based interface. (You'll find a brief mention of Workbone in Chapter 12.) To use Workbone, insert an audio CD into the CD-ROM drive, and type **workbone** to start the program. (You must make sure that the CD-ROM drive is not mounted, of course.)

Cross Reference

Your system must have a sound card, and you must include the sound-card drivers in Linux. Chapter 12 shows you how to modify the Linux kernel to include the sound driver.

Workman

Cross Reference

Workman is a fancier audio-CD-player program that runs under the X Window System. Workman sports an OPEN LOOK graphical user interface. Chapter 12 briefly describes Workman and shows a screen shot of the Workman window. You also should consult Chapter 12 to learn what you must do to install the CD-ROM drive and sound card on your Linux PC. You need both the sound card and the CD-ROM drive to use Workman.

Running Workman is simple. First, `umount` the CD-ROM drive, and remove any CD-ROM that may have been in the drive. Insert an audio CD into the CD-ROM drive. Then type **workman** in an `xterm` window. Workman runs and displays a graphical window through which you can play the audio CD.

xcmap

The `xcmap` program is an X application that displays the default colormap for an X display. If you install XFree86 — the X Window System for Linux — you get the `xcmap` utility installed automatically. Many other X utilities come with the X Window System, but I want to mention `xcmap` explicitly because it provides a helpful way to learn how color is being used in X.

To run `xcmap`, type **xcmap** in an `xterm` window. You can specify an initial size for the `xcmap` window with the `-geometry` option, as follows:

```
xcmap -geometry 320x320 &
```

This command starts `xcmap` with a window size 320 pixels wide by 320 pixels tall, as shown in Figure 25-4.

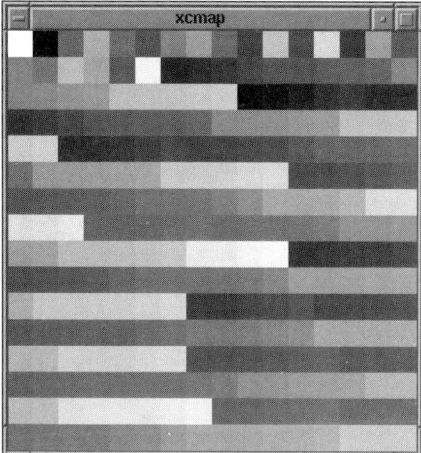

Figure 25-4: The `xcmap` program displaying the default colormap for an X display.

Figure 25-4 shows the `xcmap` output for an 8-bit X display. An 8-bit display has 256 colors in all, so the `xcmap` window is organized as a 16×16 grid of squares. Each square represents an entry in the colormap, and that square is filled with the color that corresponds to that colormap entry.

If you click any of these squares, `xcmap` displays the pixel value (the *pixel value* is the index of the colormap entry and can be a value between 0 and 255) and the red (R), green (G), and blue (B) components of the color that corresponds to that pixel value. The RGB values are shown as four-digit hexadecimal numbers. If the pixel value 232 is red, for example, clicking that square causes `xcmap` to display the following text along the top row:

```
Pix 232 = (#FFFF, #0000, #0000)
```

As you move the mouse pointer to other squares, the text display changes to show the RGB value for the square where the pointer rests. The text disappears as soon as you release the mouse button.

xfilemanager

The `xfilemanager` program runs under X and allows you to work with Linux directories and files through a graphical user interface. `xfilemanager` is one of two X-based file-manager programs on the companion CD-ROM; the other one is `xfm`, which is described in the following section. When you install Linux from this book's companion CD-ROM, you can choose to install `xfilemanager`; it's in the XAP disk set.

To run `xfilemanager`, type the following command in an `xterm` window (you have to start X to run `xfilemanager`):

```
xfilemanager &
```

Figure 25-5 shows the resulting `xfilemanager` window.

806   Part V: The Best of Linux Applications

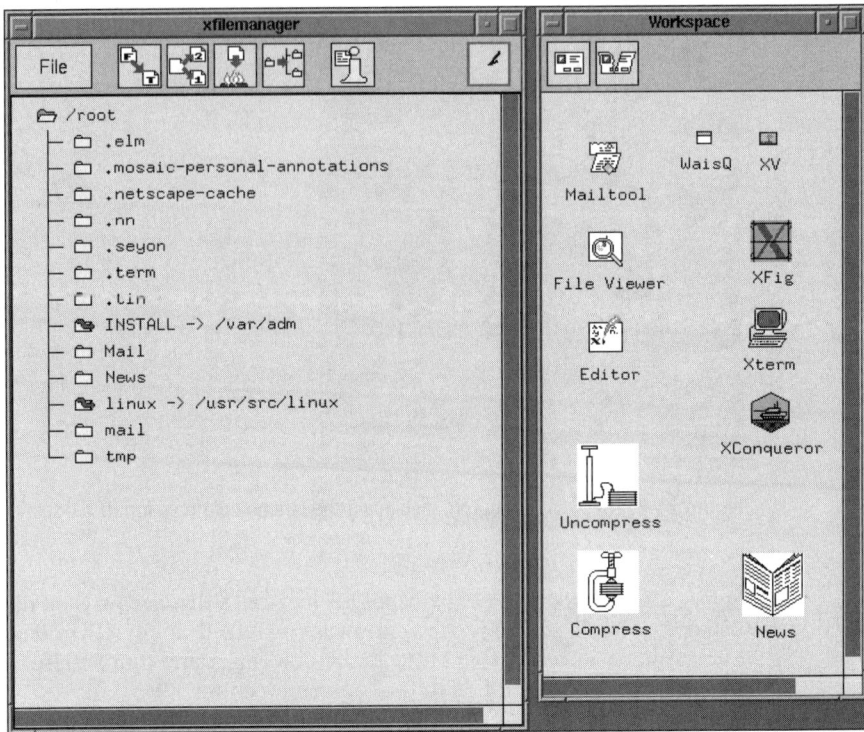

Figure 25-5: Initial windows of the `xfilemanager` program.

As Figure 25-5 shows, `xfilemanager` initially shows two separate windows:

- The `xfilemanager` window (I am referring to the windows by their titles) displays the directory tree of your home directory.
- The `Workspace` window shows several icons, each of which corresponds to an executable.

Each window has an icon bar along the top edge. In the `xfilemanager` window, the box labeled `File` is a pull-down menu. If you hold down the left mouse button on that item and move the mouse, a pull-down menu appears. That menu contains a `Quit` option that allows you to quit the `xfilemanager` program. The other icons in the icon bar allow you to initiate specific actions, such as copying or deleting a file. A single click of an icon activates the associated action.

If you look carefully, you notice that the `xfilemanager` window displays only the directory hierarchy; plain files are not shown. To view the contents of a directory, you have to double-click a directory name. Figure 25-6 shows the result of double-clicking the `.seyon` directory name.

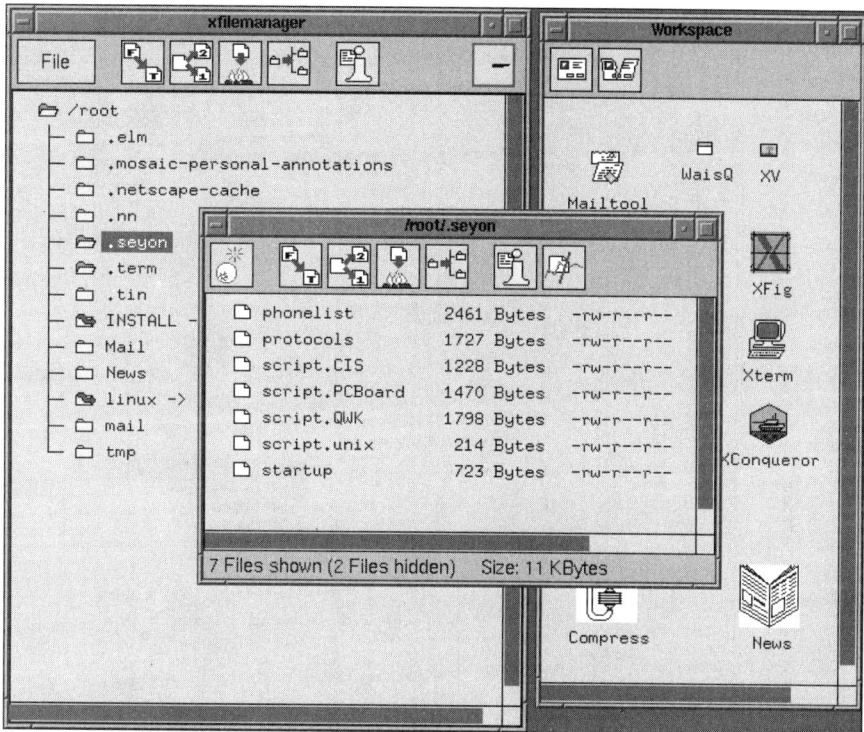

Figure 25-6: A window showing the contents of a selected directory.

If you want detailed information about a file, click that file's name and then click the yellow information icon (the one that looks like a lowercase *i*) in the icon bar. Figure 25-7 shows the resulting file-information window.

As Figure 25-7 shows, the file-information window displays the file's name, type, size, owner, and group. You can edit the owner and group, if you want. A matrix of rectangles shows the file's read/write/execute permissions for owner, group, and other. You can change the permission settings by clicking these rectangles. If you make changes, click Apply to make the changes effective. Otherwise, click Hide to get rid of the file-information window.

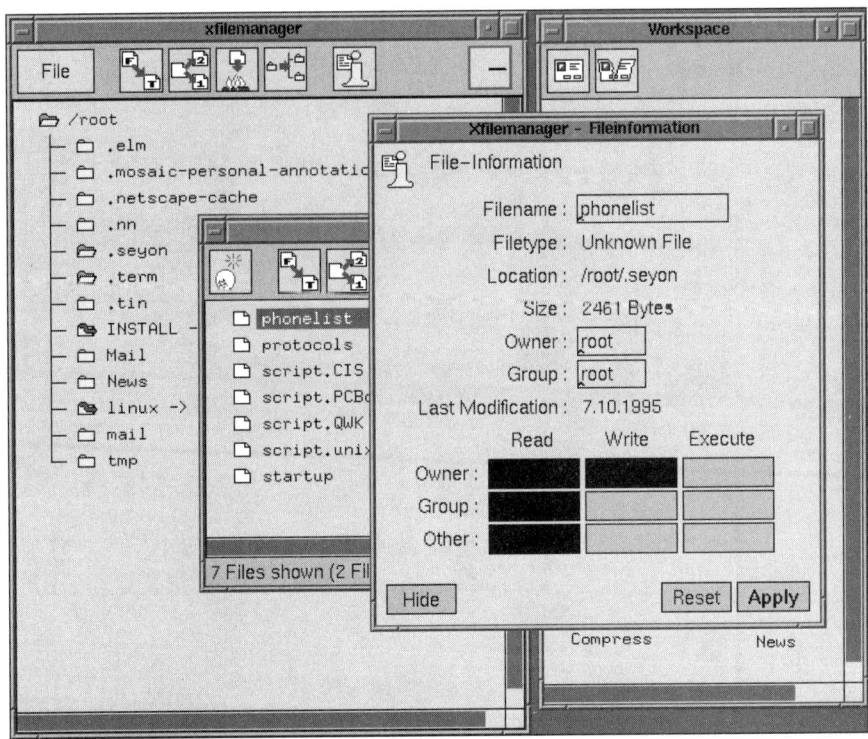

Figure 25-7: A window showing detailed information about a selected file.

A bomb icon (the first icon on the left edge of the icon bar) appears in the window that shows a directory's contents (see Figure 25-6). Clicking that icon gets rid of the window.

In the Workspace window, you have to double-click an icon to activate the associated executable program. The content of the Workspace window is determined by a text-configuration file. Following is the default Workspace window-configuration file:

/var/lib/xfilemanager/system.wsrc

Following is what the default file contains:

```
6 11 316 0 250 503
File Viewer:xmore:51 104:xmore.xpm:1 0 1
Editor:xedit:51 173:xedit.xpm:1 0 1
News:xrn:180 354:news.xbm:0 0 0
Mailtool:xmail:49 36:mail.xpm:0 0 0
WaisQ:xwaisq:127 29::0 0 0
XV:xv:177 30:file_pix.xpm:1 1 1
Compress:gzip:51 351:compressor.xbm:1 1 1
Uncompress:gunzip:51 270:decompressor.xbm:1 1 1
XFig:xfig:179 100:xdesigner.xpm:1 0 1
Xterm:xterm -sb:176 166:xterm.xpm:0 0 0
XConqueror:xconq -e 4 -M 100 100:178 230:xconq.xpm:0 0 0
```

Essentially, the lines in this file specify a label, an icon file (an X pixmap file with the `.xpm` extension), and the name of the executable program. You don't really have to understand this file because you can add new items to and delete items from the `Workspace` window by clicking one of the icons in its icon bar. If you make any changes, `xfilemanager` saves the configuration in a file named `.wsrc` in your home directory.

If you do not like to clutter your X display with too many windows, you may want to start `xfilemanager` with the `-singleWindow` option, as follows:

```
xfilemanager -single &
```

You do not have to type the full option string; typing `-single` is enough. Figure 25-8 shows the resulting single window displayed by the `xfilemanager` program.

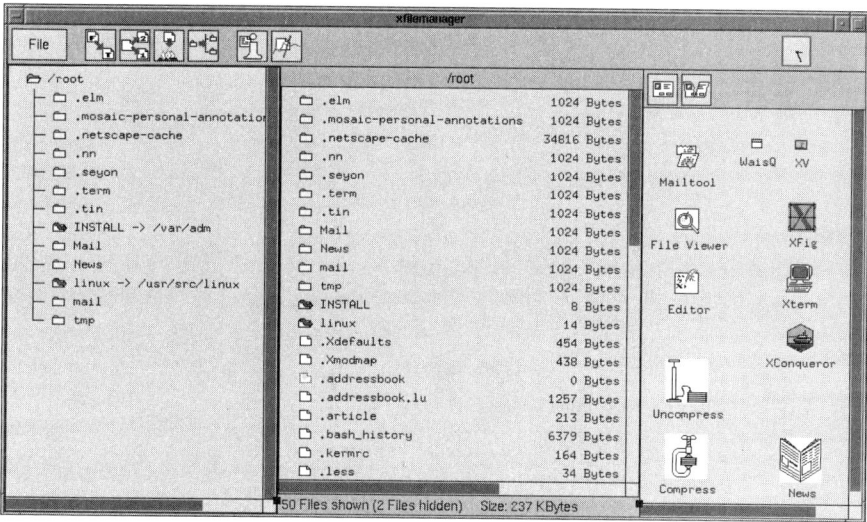

Figure 25-8: Initial windows of the `xfilemanager` program, when started with the single-window option.

Although I don't use `xfilemanager` often (I am already used to the UNIX commands, so I work from `xterm` windows), I prefer the less-cluttered look of single-window mode. In this case, you essentially get three windows packed into one large window.

The leftmost window shows the directory tree. The middle window shows the complete contents of the current directory. The rightmost window shows the workspace, with its icons.

In single-window mode, when you double-click a new directory in the left window, the middle window displays that directory's contents.

Cross Reference

Because `xfilemanager` is an X application, much of its look and feel are controlled by settings of resources. (X resources are discussed in Chapter 5.) The systemwide settings of `xfilemanager`'s resources are stored in the following file:

/usr/lib/X11/app-defaults/Xfilemanager

This file specifies the background color and font for specific parts of `xfilemanager` windows. Following are the first few lines of that file:

```
more /usr/lib/X11/app-defaults/Xfilemanager
*background:              grey90
*file_label.background:   grey80
*folder_form.background:  grey80
*folder_pane.background:  grey80
*folder_info.background:  grey80
*menu_form.background:    grey80
*quota_label.background:  grey80
*dir_pane.background:     grey80
*workspace_form.background:   grey80

*Command.background:      grey80
*Toggle.background:       grey80

*device_area.background:  grey80

*clock.background:        grey90
*clock.borderSize:        0.2
*clock.BorderColor:       steelblue

*iconFont:       8x13
*font:           -*-helvetica-medium-r-*-*-14-*-*-*-*-*-*-*
*dialog_accept.font:   -*-helvetica-bold-r-*-*-14-*-*-*-*-*-*-*
--More--(46%)
```

You can add resources to this file to alter the default behavior of `xfilemanager` (you have to log in as `root` to do this). If you want to make `xfilemanager` come up in single-window mode by default, for example, add the following line to this resource file:

```
*multiWindow:    FALSE
```

This brief discussion does not cover all the features of `xfilemanager`. The program also allows you to drag a file icon and drop it on an executable icon in the Workspace window, for example. If you plan to use a file manager, you can give `xfilemanager` a try and see whether you like it. If you don't like `xfilemanager`, you can always use `xfm`, which I describe in the following section.

xfm

The `xfm` program is another X-based file- and application-manager utility; the other one is `xfilemanager`, which is covered in the preceding section. When you first install Linux from this book's companion CD-ROM, you have the option to install `xfm`, which is in the XAP disk set.

Before you use `xfm`, you should run a script file — `/usr/bin/X11/xfm.install` — that installs some default configuration files in the `.xfm` subdirectory of your home directory (the script creates an `.xfm` directory, if it does not exist). Because the `/usr/bin/X11` directory usually is in your `PATH` environment variable, you should be able to run the `xfm` installation script with the following command:

```
xfm.install
Default configuration files installed.
```

After completing this step, you can start `xfm` in an `xterm` window by typing **xfm &**. Figure 25-9 shows the initial set of `xfm` windows.

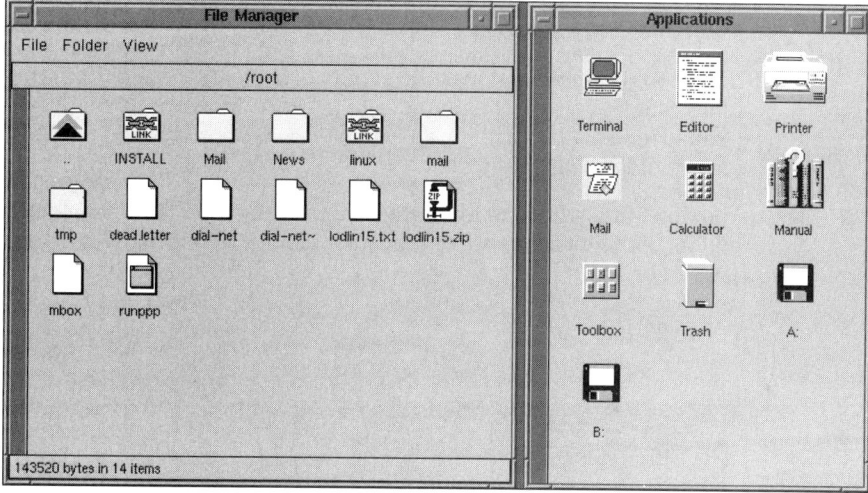

Figure 25-9: Initial windows of the `xfm` program.

The `File Manager` window shows the directories and files in the user's home directory. The directories appear as folders — a metaphor that is popular in many file managers, including recent ones such as the Explorer in Microsoft Windows 95.

The `Applications` window displays a set of icons that represent applications. The contents of the window depend on a text-configuration file: `˜/.xfm/xfm-apps` (located in the `.xfm` subdirectory of your home directory). The default `xfm-apps` file contains the following code:

```
#
# xfm applications file
# written by xfm Tue May 3 19:24:21 1994
#
##############################################

Terminal:::xterm.xpm:exec xterm:
Editor:::editor.xpm:exec emacs:exec emacs $*
Printer:::printer.xpm::exec lpr $*
Mail:::mail.xpm:exec xmailtool:
Calculator:::calc.xpm:exec xcalc:
Manual:::xman.xpm:exec xman:
Toolbox::.xfm/xfm-tools:xfm_appmgr.xpm:LOAD:
Trash::.trash:trash.xpm:OPEN:shift; mv -f -b -V numbered $* '/.trash
A\::/disk:a.disk.xpm:OPEN:
B\::/disk:b.disk.xpm:OPEN:
```

You should be able to guess the syntax of the xfm-apps file from this listing. Lines that begin with the pound sign (#) are comments. Other lines list a label, a pixmap icon file (with the .xpm extension), and a command to execute when the user double-clicks that icon.

You don't really have to learn the syntax of the xfm-apps file because you can edit its contents directly from the Applications window. When you right-click anywhere in the Applications window, a context-sensitive pop-up menu appears. If you right-click an icon, xfm displays the pop-up menu shown in Figure 25-10.

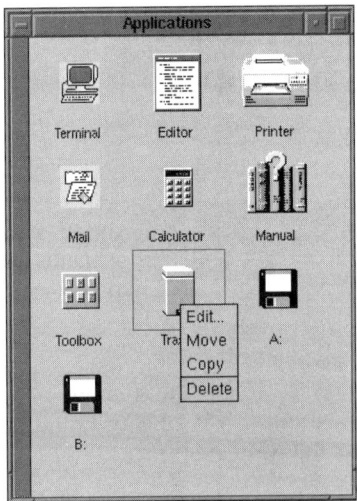

Figure 25-10: Pop-up menu that appears when you right-click an icon in the Applications window.

The pop-up menu allows you to perform one of several operations on the icon. If you right-click the Trash icon and then choose Edit from the pop-up menu, for example, xfm displays the dialog box shown in Figure 25-11.

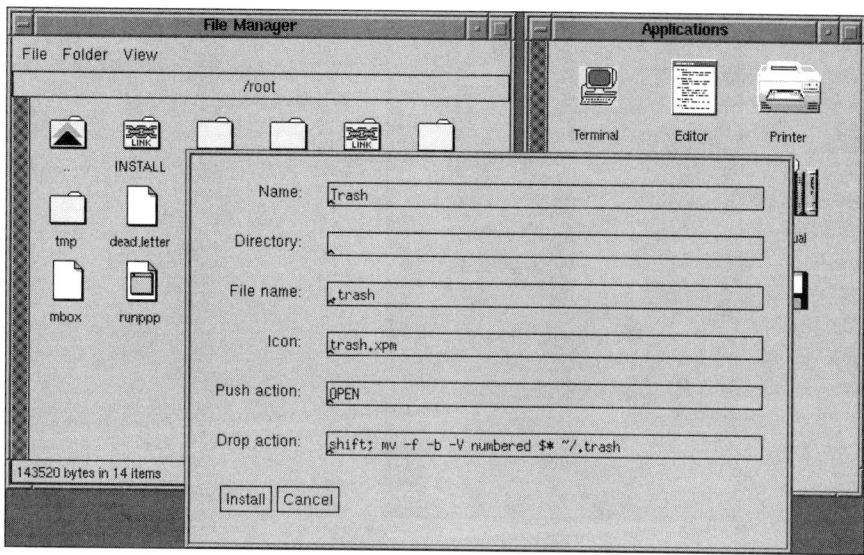

Figure 25-11: Editing the information for the Trash icon in the Applications window.

If you compare Figure 25-11 with the listing of the xfm-apps file, you see that the dialog box allows you to edit each field of the following line, which describes the Trash icon:

Trash::.trash:trash.xpm:OPEN:shift; mv -f -b -V numbered $* ~/.trash

After you edit any information in the dialog box shown in Figure 25-11, click Install to save it. Otherwise, click Cancel to dismiss the dialog box.

To add a new application to the Applications window, right-click an empty spot in the window. Figure 25-12 shows the pop-up menu that appears.

As Figure 25-12 shows, the pop-up menu allows you to add or remove applications. If you select Install from the pop-up menu, xfm displays the same dialog box shown in Figure 25-11, except that the fields are all empty. All you have to do is type the fields and then click the Install button.

You have to double-click an icon in the Applications window to launch the associated application.

In the File Manager window, xfm does not, by default, show any file or directory whose name begins with a period. By convention, these files are considered to be hidden files in UNIX. To view these hidden files, click the View label along the top edge of the window (the menu bar). From the pull-down View menu that appears, select Show hidden files. After that, xfm displays all files and directories, including the ones whose names begin with a period.

814   Part V: The Best of Linux Applications

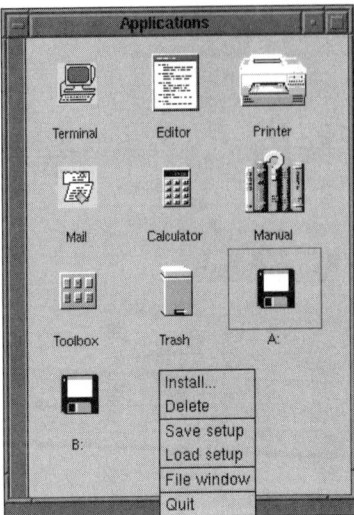

Figure 25-12: Pop-up menu that appears when you right-click an empty spot in the `Applications` window.

To view the contents of a directory, double-click that directory's name. The `File Manager` window shows the contents of that directory. To go back to the parent directory, double-click the folder that has two periods (..) as its label.

The `File Manager` window also supports context-sensitive pop-up menus that appear when you right-click an icon. Figure 25-13 shows the pop-up menu that appears when you right-click a file icon.

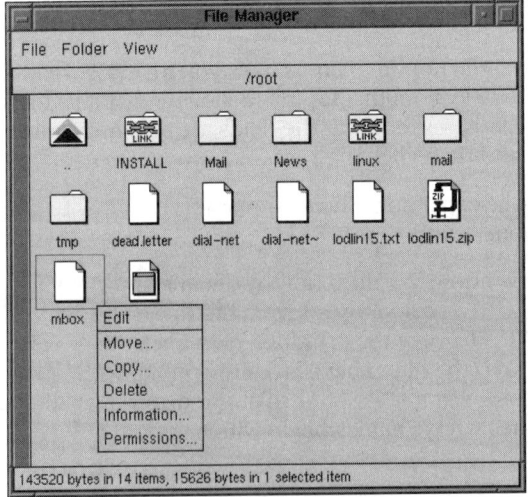

Figure 25-13: Pop-up menu that appears when you right-click an icon in the `File Manager` window.

You can use this pop-up menu to perform file operations such as copy, move, and delete. You also can view detailed information about the file and change its permission settings. To view file information, for example, select `Information` from the pop-up menu. Figure 25-14 shows the resulting dialog box, which displays information about the file that you right-clicked.

After viewing the file information, click the `Ok` button to dismiss the dialog box.

Finally, to quit `xfm`, select `Quit` from the `File` menu in the `File Manager` window. When `xfm` asks for confirmation, click the `Continue` button (if you really want to quit).

This brief overview does not do justice to all that `xfm` can do. You can, for example, configure the `Applications` window with your favorite applications by dragging and dropping icons of applications and scripts into the window. The best way to learn more about `xfm` is to start using it. If you plan to rely on a file manager, you should try both `xfm` and `xfilemanager`, and select one for long-term use.

xspread

The `xspread` program is a spreadsheet program that runs under the X Window System. You have to install and run X before you can use `xspread`.

You can choose to install `xspread` when you install Linux from the companion CD-ROM. The `xspread` program is in the XAP disk set, which contains several other X applications.

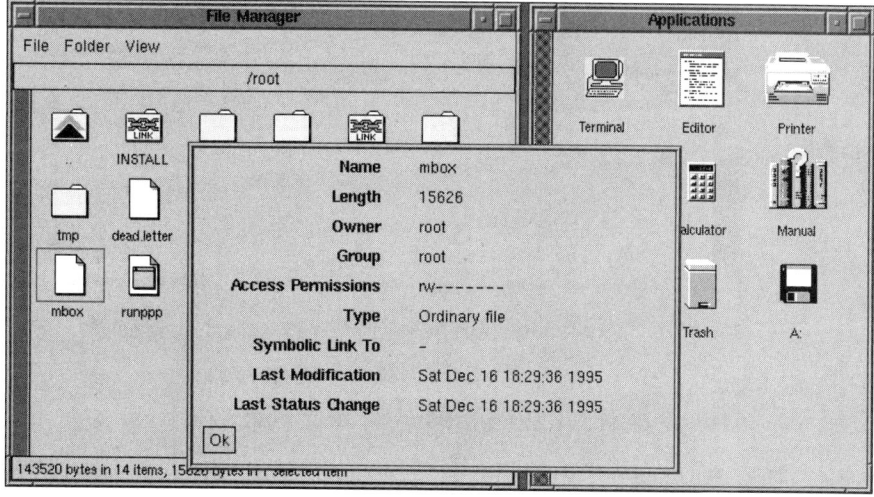

Figure 25-14: Dialog box with file information displayed by `xfm`.

The `xspread` program is based on the `sc` spreadsheet program (described earlier in this chapter). Like `sc`, `xspread` has commands that are similar to those of Lotus 1-2-3. You'll find the `xspread` documentation in the directory `/usr/doc/xspread`. In particular, if you have a PostScript printer, you should print the file `/usr/doc/xspread/xspread.ps` for a nicely formatted reference manual.

In the `/usr/doc/xspread` directory, you'll also find several sample files that you can use to try `xspread`'s features. To see `xspread` in action, type the following in an `xterm` window:

```
cd /usr/doc/xspread
xspread -font 10x20 demo_strval &
```

This command starts `xspread` and displays the `demo_strval` spreadsheet file, using a 10×20 font. I use the `-font` option to select a more legible font for the `xspread` window.

Although the `xspread` display looks very much like that of the `sc` program, some subtle but important differences exist. To see the differences, type a slash (/). Figure 25-15 shows the resulting `xspread` window.

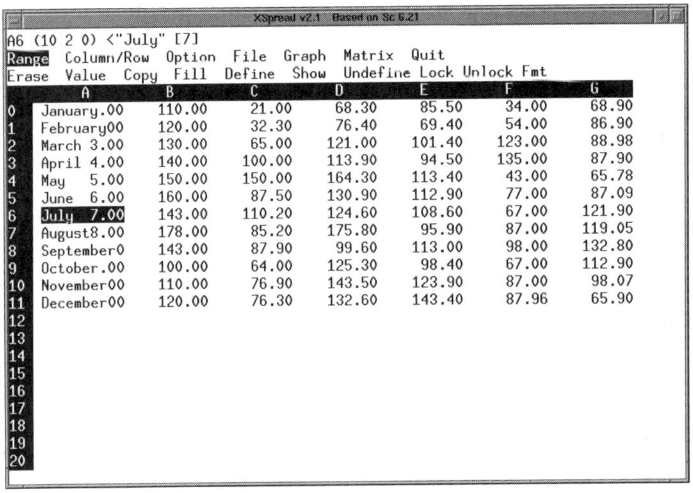

Figure 25-15: The `xspread` window displaying a sample spreadsheet file.

Like `sc`, `xspread` divides the spreadsheet window into four regions:

- The first region consists of the top three lines (unlike the first two lines in `sc`). On the first line, `xspread` displays the row–column address of the current cell and the contents of that cell. The second line is for messages or the slash (/) commands that appear when you press /, as shown in Figure 25-15. The third line shows the list of options for the currently selected slash command.

- The second region is the fourth line, which shows the column names, using letters such as A, B, C, and so on.
- The third region is the first three columns, starting at the fifth line and running down along the left edge of the window. This region shows the row numbers, such as 0, 1, 2, and so on.
- The rest of the xspread display constitutes the fourth region, which serves as a window into the spreadsheet. You work with the spreadsheet cells that appear in this region.

When it comes to entering values and formulas into the spreadsheet, the steps are the same as in sc. You should read the description of sc for an overview of the formulas.

The xspread program provides a more complete slash menu than sc does. In addition to the slash menu, xspread allows you to create different kinds of graphs from the spreadsheet data.

To see xspread's graphing capabilities, start with the spreadsheet shown in Figure 25-15 and then follow these steps:

1. Type **/G**. The xspread program displays the following slash menu:

   ```
   Type X A B C D E F Reset View Options
   ```

2. Type **t**. The xspread program displays the following slash menu:

   ```
   Line Bar XY Stack Bar Pie
   ```

3. Type **x** to select the XY option, which plots a point for each x-y value. The xspread program informs you that you have selected the XY plot and returns you to the slash menu of step 1.

4. Type **x**. The xspread program prompts you for the column that represents the x-axis values, as follows:

   ```
   Input column label for range X-- 2 character max.: b
   ```

5. Type the column name with x-axis values (in this case, B), and press Enter. The xspread program prompts for the starting row number in that column, as follows:

   ```
   Input starting row number, 200 max., for range X : 0
   ```

6. Type the row number, and press Enter. The xspread program now prompts for the ending row number, as follows:

   ```
   Input ending row number >= 0 for range X 11
   ```

7. Type the ending row number, and press Enter. The xspread program again displays the slash menu of step 1.

8. Type **A** (A through F represent the six possible y-axis variables that you can plot against one x variable). The xspread program prompts you for the column name of the A variable in the same way that it did for X in step 4.

9. Repeat steps 4–7 for the A variable. You return to the slash menu of step 1.
10. Type **o**. The xspread program displays the following slash menu:

    Legend Format Titles Grid Scale

11. Type **f**. The xspread program displays the following slash menu:

    Graph A B C D E F

12. Type **g**. The xspread program displays the following slash menu:

    Lines Symbols Both Neither

13. Type **s** to select the symbols style, in which the points are not joined by lines. The xspread program shows the slash menu of step 11.
14. Press Esc twice. The xspread program displays the slash menu of step 1.
15. Type **v**. The xspread program displays the x-y plot shown in Figure 25-16.
16. Type **q** to close the graph window and return to the xspread window.

These steps show some elements of the slash-menu system. To view the menu, type a slash (/); then type the first letter of a menu item to select that item. Instead of typing the letter, you can use the arrow keys to select a menu item or even click to select an item. When you select a menu item, another slash menu typically appears.

To go back up to a parent menu, press Esc. When you are at the topmost menu, pressing Esc causes the slash menu to disappear. The menu reappears when you press / again.

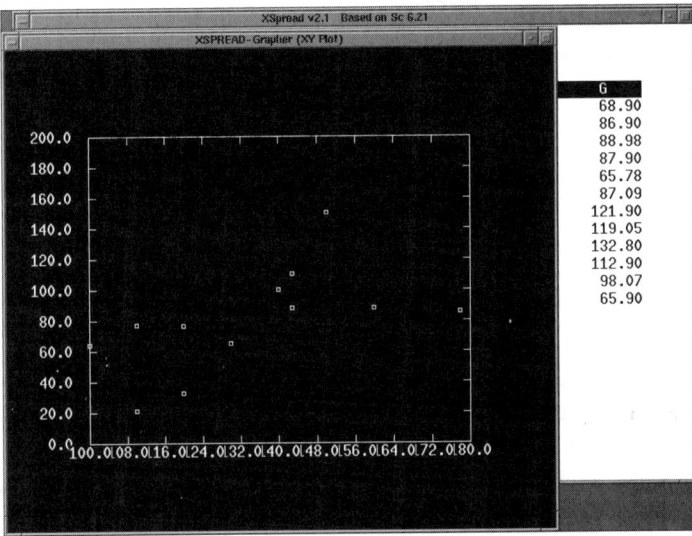

Figure 25-16: An x-y graph displayed by the xspread program.

You should consult the xspread documentation in /usr/doc/xspread for a full listing of all the slash commands.

Graphics and Images

The applications in this category allow you to prepare, view, modify, and print graphics and images. The following applications are summarized in this section:

- XV, a shareware program for viewing and manipulating many kinds of images
- XPaint, a bitmap painting program patterned after MacPaint
- Xfractint, Linux port of the DOS FRACTINT program that allows you to explore various types of fractals
- Xfig, a drawing program that is capable of producing engineering drawings
- Gnuplot, a plotting package
- Ghostscript, a PostScript interpreter that is capable of producing output on many devices, including output in various image-file formats
- Ghostview, an X application that serves as a front end to Ghostscript

XV

XV is an impressive shareware program for viewing nearly any kind of image (GIF, JPEG, Windows BMP, TIFF, PCX, and X11 Bitmap File, to name a few) on an X display. If you are interested in using the program, you should read the license information that appears in the accompanying documentation.

When you install Linux from the companion CD-ROM, you can choose to install XV as well; it's in the XAP disk set.

If XV is installed, you'll find its documentation in the /usr/doc/xv directory. In particular, you should find the file /usr/doc/xv/xvdocs.ps.gz. This file happens to be a compressed PostScript file. Copy the file to a convenient directory and then decompress it by typing **gunzip xvdocs.ps**. That command should create the xvdocs.ps file, which is nearly 4MB. That PostScript file is the XV manual.

XV has so many features that a brief description does not do it justice. You should find a PostScript printer and print the xvdocs.ps file. The documentation is nearly 130 pages long and contains many images; therefore, printing it may take a while.

You'll also find the license in the XV documentation. You should read the license to determine what you have to do if you plan to use XV for your work. Because XV is shareware, the author encourages you to give it a try and even distribute it to other users.

To try XV, type **xv &** in an xterm window (you have to run X to use XV). XV starts and displays its logo in an initial image window, as shown in Figure 25-17.

Figure 25-17: The initial XV image window.

The image window's title bar shows the XV version number and indicates that this copy is unregistered. The text in the window tells you to right-click to get the menu. If you right-click the image window, XV brings up the XV Controls window, shown in Figure 25-18.

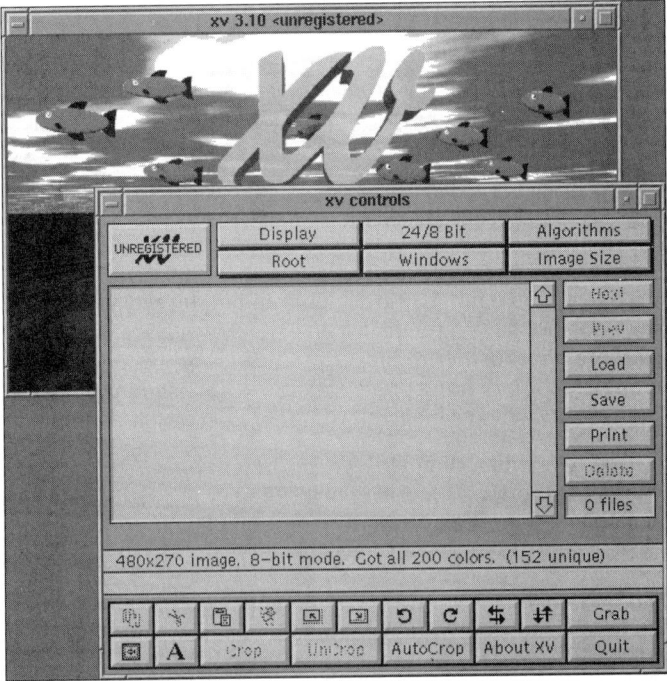

Figure 25-18: The XV Controls window.

As the name implies, the XV Controls window is the "control center" for XV; you perform all operations from this window.

If you have not read the license agreement already, click the About XV button in the XV Controls window. XV opens a text viewer window that displays the XV licensing information.

One common operation is loading an image. To do this, click the Load button in the XV Controls window. XV displays a file-selection dialog box, as shown in Figure 25-19.

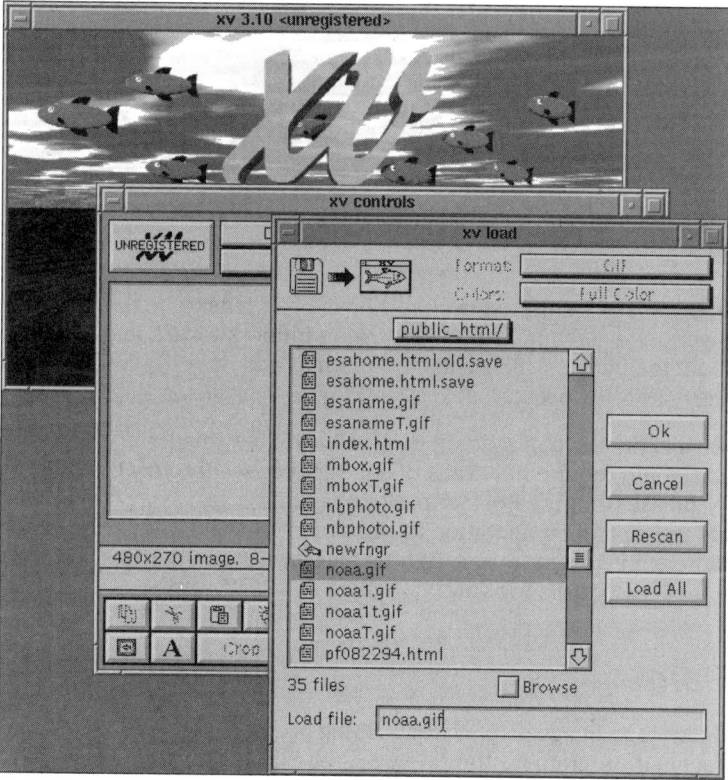

Figure 25-19: Selecting an image to view in XV.

Through the dialog box of Figure 25-19, you can select an image file from a directory. In Figure 25-19, the noaa.gif file is selected. From the .gif extension, you probably can guess that this is a GIF file, which XV can display.

To view the selected image file, click the Ok button. That action causes XV to load the image into the image window and to list the file's name in the XV Controls window, as shown in Figure 25-20.

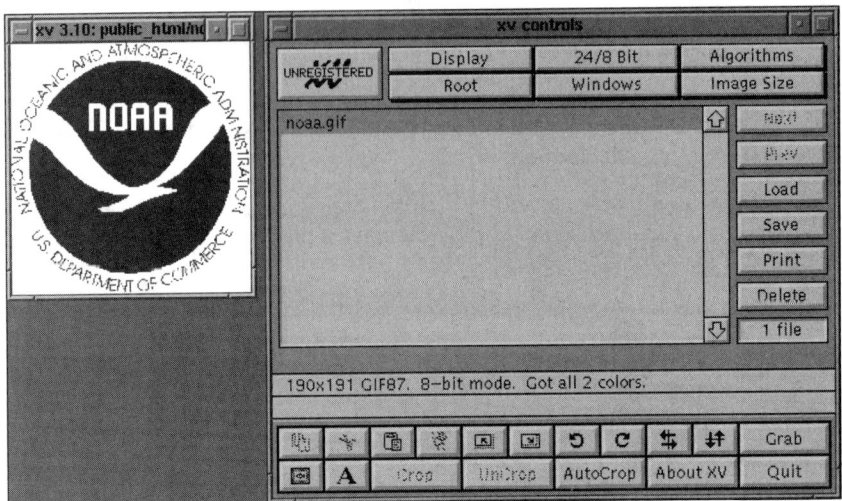

Figure 25-20: Loading the image into the image window in XV.

As the image window shows, this image happens to be the official seal of a U.S. government agency. The XV Controls window shows some detailed information about the image, which is in GIF87 format and has only two colors. The image size is 190×191 pixels.

You can do much more than just load and view images in XV, but describing all that would require hundreds of pages. If you want to try the other features of XV, please print the PostScript documentation (as described in this section), and use that documentation to learn more about XV. Another, equally effective approach is to simply dive right in and try various buttons and menu selections in the XV Controls window.

XPaint

XPaint is an image-display and -editing program patterned after the venerable MacPaint program for the Apple Macintosh. XPaint runs under the X Window System and allows you to view and edit bitmapped images in several formats, including GIF, X11 Pixmap (xpm), X11 Bitmap (xbm), and TIFF.

XPaint is included on this book's companion CD-ROM. You can choose to install XPaint when you install Linux from the companion CD-ROM.

To run XPaint, type **xpaint &** in an xterm window. XPaint runs and displays its toolbox window, as shown in Figure 25-21.

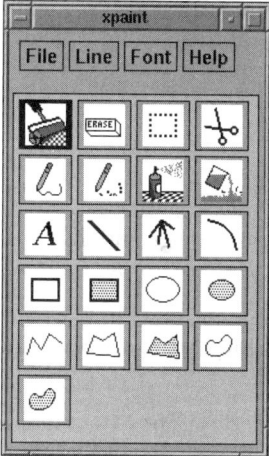

Figure 25-21: The image-editing toolbox in XPaint.

All image-loading and -editing operations start at the toolbox window. If you have used any image-editing program, you should not have any problem with the tools in the toolbox.

A menu bar that contains four items — File, Line, Font, and Help — appears at the top edge of the XPaint toolbox window. If you click any of these items, a pull-down menu appears, from which you can make further selections. The Help menu offers some online help information.

Figure 25-22 shows the result of selecting About from the Help menu.

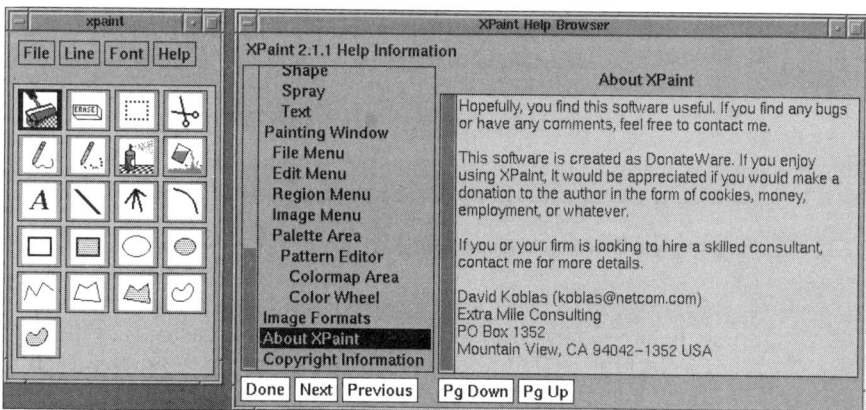

Figure 25-22: The About XPaint section of XPaint's online help.

The same window provides information on how to use various features of XPaint. Click the Next and Previous buttons (at the bottom edge of the Help window) to select a topic and look at its help information.

Xfractint

Xfractint is a fractal drawing program that allows you to choose among a wide variety of fractals and then generates the fractal image and displays it in a window. Xfractint is the X version of the popular DOS program FRACTINT.

Xfractint is in the XAP disk set on the companion CD-ROM. You can choose to install Xfractint when you install Linux by following the steps outlined in Chapter 1.

To try Xfractint, type **xfractint** in an xterm window. The Xfractint image window appears, and the xterm window displays the title screen of Xfractint. Press Enter to get to the main menu in the xterm window. At this point, the display appears as shown in Figure 25-23.

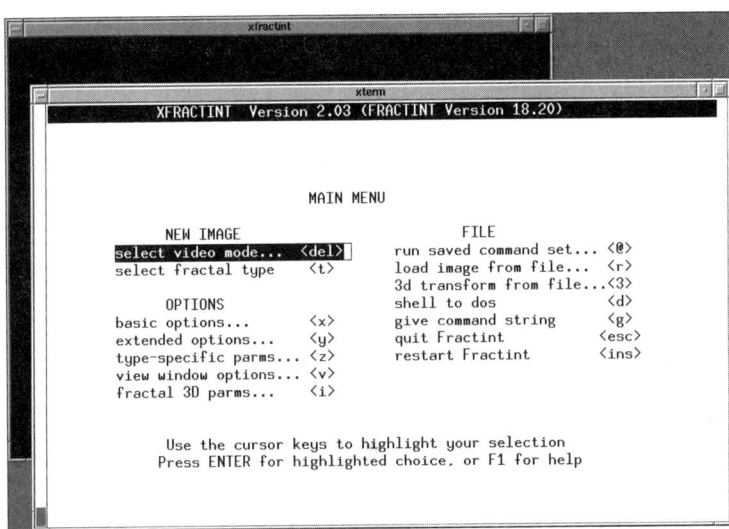

Figure 25-23: Initial Xfractint windows.

Use the arrow keys to select menu items. In this case, press the down-arrow key; select the select video mode option; and press Enter. Xfractint displays a menu of fractal types, as shown in Figure 25-24.

As the highlighted entry in Figure 25-24 indicates, the default selection is mandel, which stands for the classic Mandelbrot set fractal. To keep the default selection, press Enter. Xfractint displays a screen in which you can enter the parameters of the Mandelbrot set. Press Enter again to use the default values. Xfractint returns to the main menu shown in Figure 25-23. In the main menu, press Enter again. Xfractint computes and displays the fractal image in its image window, as shown in Figure 25-25.

To return to the main menu, press Esc; then press Esc again to quit Xfractint.

The whole purpose of Xfractint is to explore fractals. All you have to do is select a fractal type, set its parameters, and watch Xfractint display the fractal image.

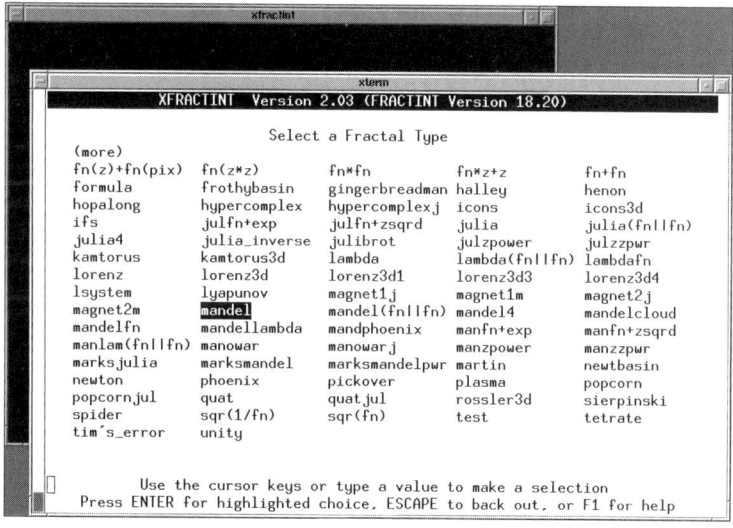

Figure 25-24: The choice of fractal types in Xfractint.

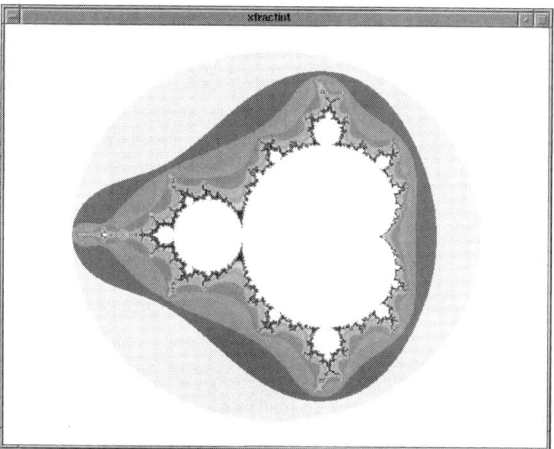

Figure 25-25: The classic Mandelbrot set fractal, being displayed by Xfractint.

xfig

The `xfig` program is an interactive drawing program that runs under X and that can generate encapsulated PostScript files that are suitable for inclusion in documents. On the companion CD-ROM, `xfig` is on the T disk set with the text-layout package TeX.

If you have installed TeX, you probably have `xfig` installed on your system. To try `xfig`, type **xfig &** in an xterm window. This command causes a rather large `xfig` window to appear. At the top edge of the window, you'll find a menu bar. To open an `xfig` drawing, click the `File` button. That action brings up a file-selection dialog box, through which you can change directories and locate `xfig` files (they usually have the `.fig` extension).

For your convenience, the `xfig` package includes a set of example `.fig` files in the `/usr/lib/texmf/xfig/examples` directory. Use `xfig`'s file-selection dialog box to locate this directory, and select one of the files. Figure 25-26 shows the file-selection dialog box with one of the `.fig` files selected.

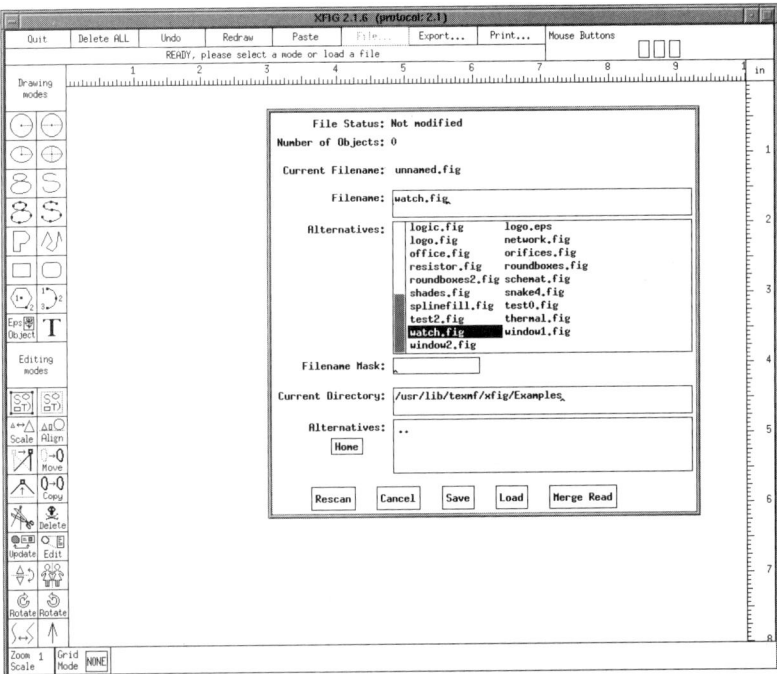

Figure 25-26: Selecting an example `.fig` file to load into `xfig`.

To load the selected .fig file into xfig, click the Load button. xfig loads and displays the figure, as shown in Figure 25-27.

As Figure 25-27 shows, in the hands of a skilled illustrator, xfig can produce impressive drawings.

As is true of any other tool, learning to use all the features of xfig takes some practice. If you are familiar with other drawing software, such as MacDraw (Macintosh) or CorelDRAW (PC), you should be able to use xfig without much trouble.

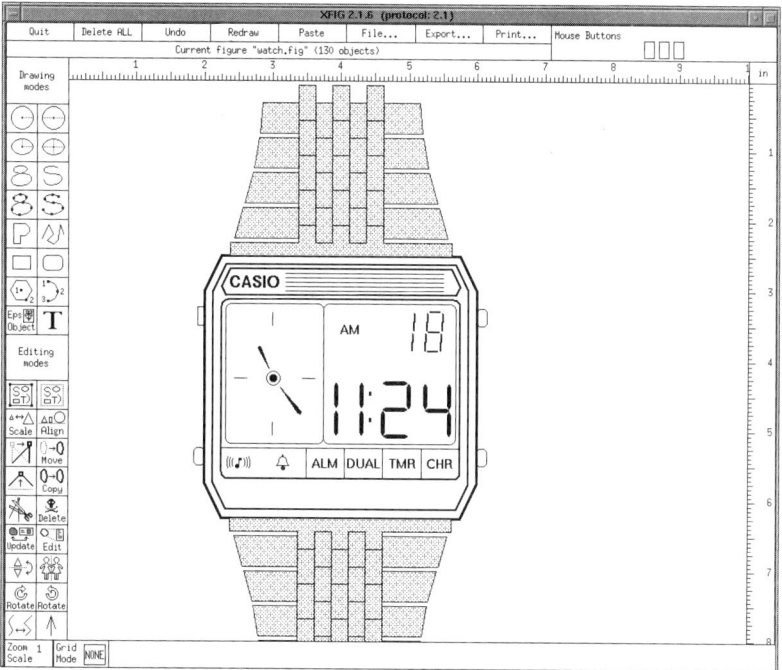

Figure 25-27: The watch.fig sample drawing being displayed in xfig.

Gnuplot

Gnuplot is an interactive plotting utility. You need to run Gnuplot under the X Window System because it uses an X window as the output device. Gnuplot is a command-line-driven program; it prompts you and accepts your input commands. In response to those commands, Gnuplot displays various types of plots. The output appears in an X window.

When you install Linux from the companion CD-ROM, you can choose to install Gnuplot as well; it appears in the XAP disk set.

Note

Incidentally, even though Gnuplot has *Gnu* in its name, it has nothing to do with GNU or the Free Software Foundation.

If Gnuplot is installed, you should be able to run it by typing **gnuplot** in an xterm window. Gnuplot displays an opening message and waits for further input at a prompt, as shown in Figure 25-28.

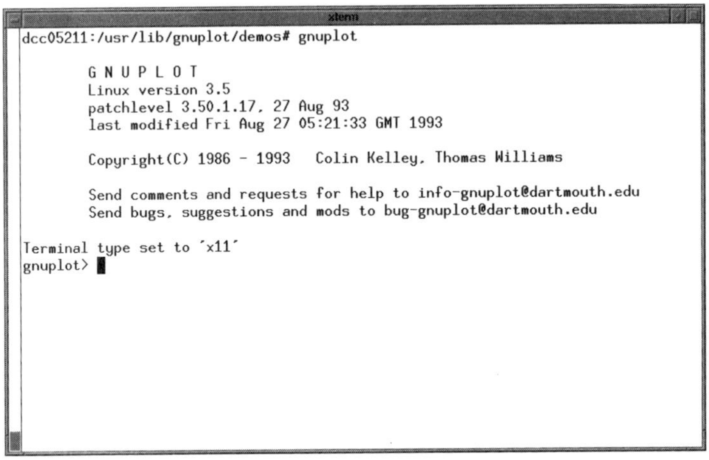

Figure 25-28: Running Gnuplot in an xterm window.

To see an immediate result, type the following Gnuplot command at the prompt:

```
plot sin(x)
```

Gnuplot opens an output window and displays a plot of the sine function, as shown in Figure 25-29.

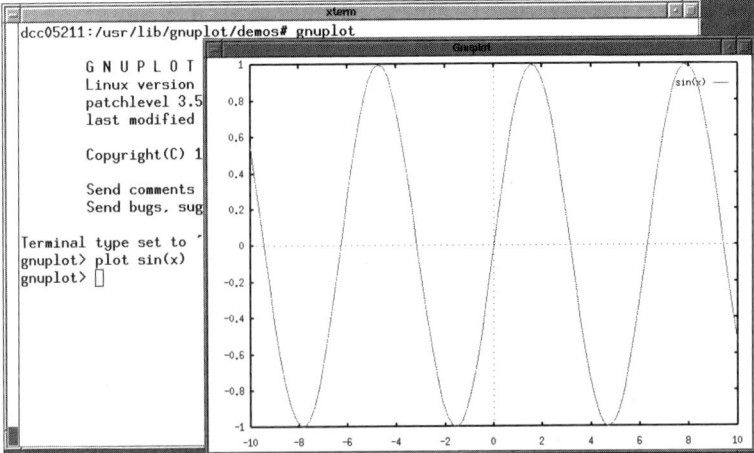

Figure 25-29: Plotting sin(x) in Gnuplot.

Chapter 25: Linux Applications Roundup   **829**

To quit Gnuplot, click the xterm window to make it active; then type **quit**. That example is a simple illustration of Gnuplot's capabilities.

At any time in Gnuplot, you can ask for online help. The help is similar to that in DEC's VAX/VMS system. To learn more about the plot command, for example, type **help plot** at the Gnuplot prompt. Figure 25-30 shows the resulting help information.

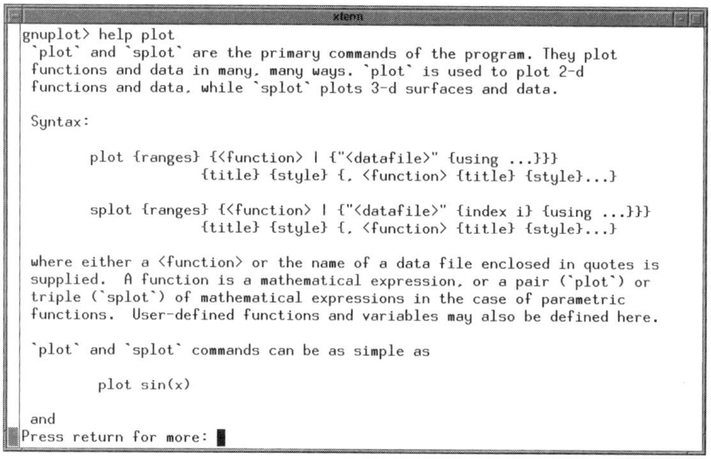

Figure 25-30: Online help in Gnuplot.

Gnuplot also comes with several example files that appear in the /usr/lib/gnuplot/demos directory of your system. To try these demo files, start Gnuplot with the following commands:

```
cd /usr/lib/gnuplot/demos
gnuplot
```

When the Gnuplot prompt appears, load one of the demo files (the ones with the .dem extension) with the load command. To load the world.dem file, for example, type **load "world.dem"**. The demo Gnuplot file displays a map of the world and then pauses until you press Enter. After you press Enter, Gnuplot displays the next plot, which happens to be a view of the earth in spherical coordinates, as shown in Figure 25-31.

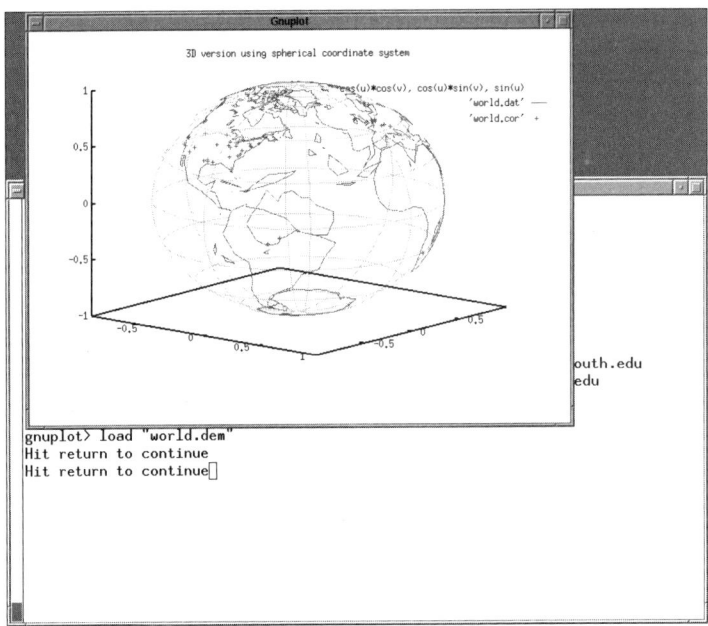

Figure 25-31: Trying the world.dem file in Gnuplot.

If you are curious about the world.dem file, here's what that file contains:

```
#
# $Id: world.demo 3.38.2.6 1992/11/14 02:25:21 woo Exp $
#
#
set title "Gnuplot Correspondences"
set nokey
set noborder
set noyzeroaxis
set noxtics
set noytics
#
# plot world map and correspondent locations as a +
plot 'world.dat' with lines 3 4, 'world.cor' with points 1 2
set title ""
set key
set border
set yzeroaxis
set xtics
set ytics
pause -1 "Hit return to continue"
#
# plot a '3D version using spherical coordinate system' of the world.
set angles degrees
set title "3D version using spherical coordinate system"
set view 70,40,,2.0
set mapping spherical
set parametric
```

```
set samples 32
set isosamples 9
set urange [-pi/2:pi/2]
set vrange [0:2*pi]
splot cos(u)*cos(v),cos(u)*sin(v),sin(u) with lines 5 6,\
'world.dat' with lines 3 4, 'world.cor' with points 1 2
pause -1 "Hit return to continue"
#
# plot a '3D version using cylindrical coordinate system' of the
world.
set title "3D version using cylindrical coordinate system"
set view 70,40,,2.0
set mapping cylindrical
set parametric
set samples 32
set isosamples 9
set urange [-pi:pi]
set vrange [-90:90]
splot cos(u),sin(u),v with lines 5 6,\
'world.dat' with lines 3 4, 'world.cor' with points 1 2
pause -1 "Hit return to continue"


#
# Clean up:
#
set noparametric
set mapping cartesian
set angles radians
set samples 100
set isosamples 10
set view 60,30,1,1
set xrange [-10:10]
set yrange [-10:10]
set zrange [-10:10]
set auto
set title "" 0,0
```

As the listing shows, the world.dem file consists of Gnuplot commands. You can learn a great deal about Gnuplot by trying each file and then studying the commands in the file.

Ghostscript

Ghostscript is a utility for previewing and printing PostScript documents. Ghostscript allows you to print PostScript documents on many non-PostScript devices.

At heart, Ghostscript is a nearly complete implementation of the PostScript language. Ghostscript includes the interpreter that processes PostScript input and generates output on an output device. A Ghostscript device can be a printer (or display screen), as well as an image-file format, such as BMP or PCX.

Ghostscript is distributed under the GNU General Public License but is copyrighted and maintained by Aladdin Enterprises. You can find the latest contact information in the `README` file in `/usr/lib/Ghostscript` directory. That directory also contains Ghostscript documentation and many example PostScript files.

The documentation in the `/usr/lib/Ghostscript/doc` directory includes the files listed in Table 25-2.

Table 25-2 Ghostscript documentation in `/usr/lib/Ghostscript/doc`

File	Description
`devices.doc`	Detailed description of a few printers for which Ghostscript can produce output.
`drivers.doc`	Description of the interface between Ghostscript and device drivers.
`fonts.doc`	Description of the fonts and font facilities supplied with Ghostscript.
`gs.1`	Man page for Ghostscript in `groff` format.
`hershey.doc`	Information about the Hershey fonts.
`history.doc`	History of changes to Ghostscript.
`humor.doc`	Humorous message about Ghostscript.
`language.doc`	Description of the Ghostscript language.
`lib.doc`	Description of the Ghostscript library — a collection of C functions that implement the primitive graphic capabilities of the Ghostscript language.
`make.doc`	Description of how to install Ghostscript and how to build Ghostscript executables from source code.
`NEWS`	Summary of recent changes to Ghostscript.
`ps2epsi.doc`	Description of the `ps2epsi` utility, which converts a Ghostscript file to Adobe's Encapsulated Postscript Interchange or EPSI format. (You can insert EPSI files into many word processors.)
`psfiles.doc`	Description of the `.ps` files in the Ghostscript distribution. (These files are in the `/usr/lib/Ghostscript` directory.)
`readme.doc`	Description of problems and new features in the current release of Ghostscript. (The companion CD-ROM includes version 2.6.2 of Ghostscript.)
`use.doc`	Description of how to use the Ghostscript language interpreter.
`xfonts.doc`	Description of the interface between Ghostscript and the routines that access externally supplied font and text-output facilities.

This list of documentation should give you an idea of Ghostscript's capabilities and what you get with the Ghostscript software distribution.

To run Ghostscript, type **gs** in an `xterm` window. Ghostscript brings up an empty window and displays the following text in the `xterm` window:

```
Initializing... done.
Ghostscript 2.6.2 (4/19/95)
Copyright (C) 1990-1995 Aladdin Enterprises, Menlo Park, CA.
 All rights reserved.
Ghostscript comes with NO WARRANTY: see the file COPYING for details.
GS>
```

At this point, you are interacting with the Ghostscript interpreter. Unless you know the Ghostscript language (which is like PostScript), you'll feel lost at this prompt. It's kind of like the `C:>` prompt under MS-DOS or the UNIX shell prompt at a terminal.

If you do have a PostScript file available, you can load and view it with a simple command. For example, try the following:

```
GS> (/usr/lib/Ghostscript/examples/golfer.ps) run
```

What you typed is a Ghostscript command that should cause Ghostscript to load the file `/usr/lib/Ghostscript/examples/golfer.ps` and process it. The result is a picture in Ghostscript's output window. After that, press Enter and type **quit** to exit Ghostscript.

Fortunately, you do not have to use Ghostscript at the interpreter level (unless you know PostScript well and want to try PostScript commands interactively). You typically use Ghostscript to load and view a PostScript file.

Ghostscript takes several command-line arguments, including the file to be loaded. To see a list of Ghostscript options, type the following command:

```
gs -h
Ghostscript version 2.6.2 (4/19/95)
Copyright (C) 1990-1995 Aladdin Enterprises, Menlo Park, CA.
Usage: gs [switches] [file1.ps file2.ps ...]
Available devices:
  x11 linux bj10e bj200 cdeskjet cdjcolor cdjmono cdj500
  cdj550 declj250 deskjet dfaxhigh dfaxlow djet500 djet500c epson
  eps9high epsonc escp2 ibmpro jetp3852 laserjet la50 la75
  lbp8 ln03 lj250 ljet2p ljet3 ljet4 ljetplus m8510
  necp6 paintjet pj pjxl pjxl300 r4081 t4693d2 t4693d4
  t4693d8 tek4696 bit bmpmono bmp16 bmp256 bmp16m pcxmono
  pcxgray pcx16 pcx256 pbm pbmraw pgm pgmraw ppm
  ppmraw tiffg3
Most frequently used switches: (you can use # in place of =)
  @<file>       treat file like part of the command line
                (to get around DOS command line limit)
  -d<name>[=<token>]  define name as token, or null if no token given
  -f<file>      read this file even if its name begins with - or @
  -g<width>x<height>  set width and height ('geometry'), in pixels
  -I<prefix>    add prefix to search path
  -q            'quiet' mode, suppress most messages
```

```
-r<res>          set resolution, in pixels per inch
-s<name>=<string>  define name as string
-sDEVICE=<devname>  select initial device
-sOutputFile=<file> select output file: embed %d for page #,
                 - means stdout, use |command to pipe
'-' alone as a file name means read from stdin non-interactively.
For more complete information, please read the use.doc file.
```

To see how Ghostscript renders a PostScript document, you can use any PostScript document that you may have available. One good solution is to use one of the sample PostScript files in the /usr/lib/Ghostscript/examples directory. Type the following command, for example, in an xterm window:

```
gs /usr/lib/Ghostscript/examples/golfer.ps
```

Ghostscript opens that file, processes its contents, and displays the output in another window, as shown in Figure 25-32.

Figure 25-32: Ghostscript displaying the file /usr/lib/Ghostscript/examples/golfer.ps.

In this case, the output happens to be a picture of a golfer. After displaying the output, Ghostscript displays the following message:

```
>>showpage, press <return> to continue<<
```

Press Enter to continue. For a multiple-page PostScript document, Ghostscript then shows the next page. After all the pages are displayed, you return to the Ghostscript prompt. Type **quit** to exit Ghostscript.

Ghostview

Ghostview is an X-based graphical front end to the Ghostscript interpreter. Ghostview is ideal for viewing and printing PostScript documents. For a long document, you can even print selected pages. You also can view the document at various levels of magnification (you can zoom in or out).

To run Ghostview, type **ghostview &** in an xterm window. This command causes the Ghostview window to appear. The window is divided into two parts. On the left side is a simple menu box that contains five buttons. The larger area on the right is the work area, where Ghostview displays the PostScript document.

Each of the buttons in the menu box pop up a menu when you click it. The following list explains what Ghostview's five pop-up menus offer:

- The File menu allows you to open a file, print all or a few pages, save specific pages, view the copyright notice, and quit Ghostview.
- The Page menu allows you to move around the pages of the document. You also can mark and unmark pages from this menu, which also includes an option for printing marked pages.
- The Magstep menu allows you to select the magnification step (magstep). The default is 0, which means what you see on-screen is what gets printed. The magnification is defined as 1.2 to the power magstep (1.2**magstep).
- The Orientation menu allows you to choose the display orientation (such as Portrait or Landscape).
- The Media menu is for selecting the size of paper that is to be used for printing. Table 25-3 lists the standard media names and sizes that appear in the Media menu.

Table 25-3   Standard media names and sizes in Ghostview

Medium name	Width × height*	Physical size (inches)
10x14	720×1,008	10×14
A3	842×1,190	
A4	595×842	
A5	420×595	
B4	729×1,032	
B5	516×729	
Executive	540×720	7.5×10
Folio	612×936	8.5×13
Ledger	1,224×792	17×11
Legal	612×1,008	8.5×14

(continued)

Table 25-3 (continued)

Medium name	Width × height*	Physical size (inches)
Letter	612×792	8.5×11
Quarto	610×780	
Statement	396×612	5.5×8.5
Tabloid	792×1,224	11×17

Width and height are in PostScript points; 1 inch = 72 points.

To load and view a PostScript document in Ghostview, click the `File` button and select `Open` from the pop-up menu. This action causes Ghostview to display a file-selection dialog box. Use this dialog box to select the file `tiger.ps` in the `/usr/lib/Ghostscript/examples` directory, as shown in Figure 25-33.

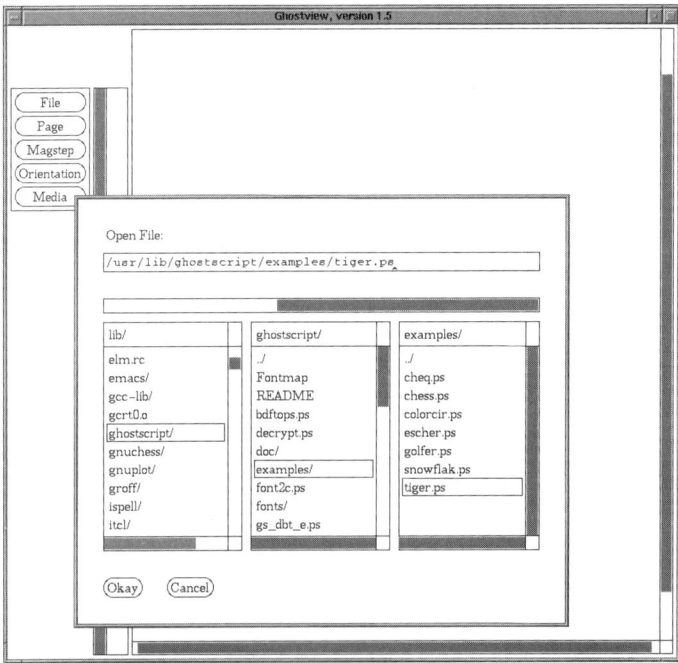

Figure 25-33: Selecting a file to open in Ghostview.

In Figure 25-33, you see the file-selection dialog box in the foreground; the Ghostview window appears in the background.

To open the selected file, click the Okay button in the file-selection dialog box shown in Figure 25-33. Ghostview opens the selected file, processes its contents, and displays the output in its window, as shown in Figure 25-34.

Figure 25-34: Ghostview displaying the file /usr/lib/Ghostscript/examples/tiger.ps.

In the upper-left corner of the window, Ghostview displays the current filename and date. Ghostview takes this information from the comments in the PostScript file itself, not from the timestamp of the file.

If you click anywhere in the output area, Ghostview displays a window with a zoomed-in (magnified) version of the area near where you clicked.

You also may want to try the Magstep menu to see how the output appears with various magstep choices. I found the magsteps to be particularly useful for reading PostScript documentation (for example, the documentation for the XV program) with Ghostview. I had to select a magstep of 2 to make the document legible on-screen.

Appendix
Linux Resources

This appendix lists some resources where you can get more information on specific topics. Most of the resources are on the Internet because that's where you can get the latest information. Often, you'll be able to download the files that you need for a specific task.

Some Internet resources appear in the standard Uniform Resource Locator (URL) syntax (Chapter 20 explains URLs). If you have used a Web browser such as Netscape Navigator or Mosaic, you probably are already familiar with URLs.

Web Pages

If you browse the Internet, you may have noticed that quite a few Web pages have Linux-related information. A good starting point is the following Linux page:

```
http://www.ssc.com/linux/
```

This page is maintained by SSC, Inc., the publisher of the *Linux Journal.* This page provides a starting point for locating information about Linux. In particular, this page links to a page that contains many links to other Linux-related Web pages. From this page, you can begin exploring specific sites, according to your immediate needs.

Another popular and definitive source of Linux information is the following URL:

```
http://sunsite.unc.edu/mdw/mdw.html
```

At this Web site, you can find many more pointers to other Linux resources on the Internet. In particular, you'll be able to browse and download the latest HOWTO documents from the `sunsite` Web page.

Newsgroups

To keep up with Linux developments, you really need access to the Internet and especially to the newsgroups. You'll find discussions on specific Linux-related topics in the following newsgroups:

- `alt.uu.comp.os.linux.questions` — General Linux questions and answers.
- `comp.os.linux.admin` — Information about Linux system administration.

- `comp.os.linux.advocacy` — Discussions about promoting Linux.
- `comp.os.linux.announce` — Important announcements about Linux. (This newsgroup is moderated, which means that you must mail an article to the moderator, who then posts it to the newsgroup.)
- `comp.os.linux.answers` — Questions and answers about Linux. (All the Linux HOWTOs are posted in this moderated newsgroup.)
- `comp.os.linux.development` — Current Linux development work.
- `comp.os.linux.development.apps` — Linux application development.
- `comp.os.linux.development.system` — Linux operating-system development.
- `comp.os.linux.hardware` — Discussions about Linux and various hardware.
- `comp.os.linux.help` — Help with various areas of Linux.
- `comp.os.linux.misc` — Miscellaneous Linux topics.
- `comp.os.linux.networking` — Networking under Linux.
- `comp.os.linux.setup` — Linux setup and installation.
- `comp.os.linux.x` — Discussions about setting up and running the X Window System under Linux.

Linux FTP Archive Sites

You can download Slackware Linux and other Linux distributions from one of several FTP sites around the world. In addition to the Linux distribution itself, these sites contain many other software packages that run under Linux. Table A-1 lists some of the Linux FTP sites around the world.

Table A-1	FTP sites with Linux archives
Site name	Directory
cnuce-arch.cnr.it	/pub/Linux/
dcs.muni.cz	/pub/UNIX/linux/
ftp.ba-mannheim.de	/pub/linux/mirror.sunsite/
ftp.cc.gatech.edu	/pub/linux/
ftp.cdrom.com	/pub/linux
ftp.cnr.it	/pub/Linux/
ftp.cps.cmich.edu	/pub/linux/sunsite/
ftp.cs.cuhk.hk	/pub/Linux/

Appendix: Linux Resources

Site name	Directory
ftp.cs.helsinki.fi	/pub/Software/Linux/Kernel
ftp.dfv.rwth-aachen.de	/pub/linux/sunsite/
ftp.dstc.edu.au	/pub/linux/
ftp.dungeon.com	/pub/linux/sunsite-mirror/
ftp.engr.uark.edu	/pub/linux/sunsite/
ftp.germany.eu.net	/pub/os/Linux/Mirror.SunSITE/
ftp.gwdg.de	/pub/linux/mirrors/sunsite/
ftp.infomagic.com	/pub/mirrors/linux/sunsite/
ftp.io.org	/pub/systems/linux
ftp.kfki.hu	/pub/linux/
ftp.linux.org	/pub/mirrors/sunsite/
ftp.loria.fr	/pub/linux/sunsite/
ftp.maths.warwick.ac.uk	/mirrors/linux/sunsite.unc-mirror/
ftp.metu.edu.tr	/pub/linux/sunsite/
ftp.nectec.or.th	/pub/mirrors/linux/
ftp.nus.sg	/pub/unix/Linux/
ftp.orst.edu	/pub/mirrors/sunsite.unc.edu/linux/
ftp.pht.com	/mirrors/linux/sunsite/
ftp.rge.com	/pub/systems/linux/sunsite/
ftp.rus.uni-stuttgart.de	/pub/unix/systems/linux/MIRROR.sunsite/
ftp.rz.uni-ulm.de	/pub/mirrors/linux/sunsite/
ftp.siriuscc.com	/pub/Linux/Sunsite
ftp.spin.ad.jp	/pub/linux/sunsite.unc.edu/
ftp.switch.ch	/mirror/linux/
ftp.tu-dresden.de	/pub/Linux/sunsite/
ftp.tu-graz.ac.at	/pub/Linux/
ftp.uni-erlangen.de	/pub/Linux/MIRROR.sunsite/
ftp.uni-paderborn.de	/pub/linux/sunsite/
ftp.uni-paderborn.de	/pub/Mirrors/sunsite.unc.edu/
ftp.uni-tuebingen.de	/pub/linux/Mirror.sunsite/
ftp.univ-angers.fr	/pub/linux/

(continued)

Table A-1 *(continued)*

Site name	Directory
ftp.wit.com	/systems/unix/linux/
ftp.yggdrasil.com	mirrors/sunsite/
pub.vse.cz	pub/386-unix/linux/
smug.student.adelaide.edu.au	/pub/sunsite.linux/
src.doc.ic.ac.uk	/packages/linux/sunsite.unc-mirror/
sunsite.unc.edu	/pub/Linux
tsx-11.mit.edu	/pub/linux
uiarchive.cso.uiuc.edu	/pub/systems/linux/sunsite

Magazine

The *Linux Journal* is the only magazine devoted entirely to Linux. Following is the contact information for this magazine:

Linux Journal
P.O. Box 85867
Seattle, WA 98145-1867 USA
Phone (voice): (206) 782-7733
Fax: (206) 782-7191
E-mail: subs@ssc.com

Index

Numbers & Symbols

.forward file, 589
.rhosts file, 580
$$ variable, 214
$0 variable, 205, 214
$< variable, 214
$? variable, 214
$_ variable, 214
%A keyword, 286
%ENV variable, 214
%W keyword, 286
%x keyword, 286
%y keyword, 286
/ directory, 196
1x1213_x packages, 57
1x1320_x packages, 57
3Com 3C503, 3C505, 3C507, and 3C509 (ISA bus) Ethernet cards, 19
3Com 3C579 (EISA bus) Ethernet cards, 19
4Dwm window manager, 173
4Dwm.fvwmrc file, 173
10BASE2 cable, 487
10BASE5 cable, 487
16-bit operating systems, 7–8
32-bit operating systems, 7–8
6850 UART (Universal Asynchronous Receiver Transmitter) MIDI (Musical Instrument Digital Interface) sound cards, 19
7000 FASST SCSI controllers, 34
80386 processors, 292
80486 processors, 292
80x86 family of processors, 292

A

a.out format, 689–691
abort command, 415
ABORT strings, 541
Abort XFree86 (Ctrl+Alt+Backspace) key combination, 138
absolute pathname, 198
abuse1 package, 62
abuse2 package, 62
Accelerated X, 333
access.conf file, 616
  editing, 622–625
access.conf-dist file, 616
ACM206 file, 33
actions binding to events, 283–287
active matrix display screens, 315
active window, 110
Adaptec AHA-1510 SCSI controllers for ISA bus, 16
Adaptec AHA-151x disk controllers, 351
Adaptec AHA-152x SCSI controller for ISA bus, 16, 34
Adaptec AHA-1542 SCSI controllers, 34, 388
Adaptec AHA-154x SCSI controller for ISA bus, 16, 351–352
Adaptec AHA-1740, AHA-274x, and AHA-284x SCSI controllers, 34
Adaptec AHA-174x SCSI controller for EISA (Extended Industry Standard Architecture) bus, 16, 352
Adaptec AHA-274x SCSI controller for EISA (Extended Industry Standard Architecture) bus, 16, 352
Adaptec AHA-284x SCSI controller for VLB (VESA Local Bus) bus, 16
Adaptec AHA-284x disk controllers, 352
Adaptec AHA-294x disk controllers, 352
Adaptec AHA-294x SCSI controllers, 33
Adaptec AVA-1505 SCSI controllers for ISA bus, 17
Adaptec AVA-1515 SCSI controllers for ISA bus, 17
address classes, 475–477
address translation, 347
ADDSWAP option, 45–46
adduser command, 71, 101, 197
AdLib sound cards, 19
administrative commands, 197
Advanced Logic-based video cards with AL2101, 2228, 2301, 2302, 2308 and 2401 chipsets, 14

aexec.bat file, 185
after command, 276
AGSCD file, 33
AHA2940 file, 33
aliases, 194
Allied Telesis AT1500 and AT1700 Ethernet cards, 19
Allman, Eric, 563
ALPS GlidePoint pointing device, 406
Always IN2000 SCSI controller, 17, 34, 352
AMI Fast Disk VLB/EISA SCSI controllers, 17, 351–352
Andreessen, Marc, 608
anonymous FTP
  reasons to worry about, 587–588
  secure, 585–589
  trying existing services, 586
Ansel Communications AC3200 EISA Ethernet cards, 19
AOPTCD file, 33
API (Application Programming Interface) PC cards, 512
APM (Advanced Power Management), 302
append command, 264
application-layer protocols, 472
applications, 51
  running across network, 98
Applications window, 153
Apricot Xen-II Ethernet cards, 19
archie, 558
arcs, 730–731
area.c file, 660
Arg structures, 702
@ARGV variable, 214
arithmetic operator, 215
Armstrong, James, 204
ARP (Address Resolution Protocol), 487
array command, 264
array-index operator, 215
arrays
  declaring variables, 269
  elements, 268–269
  executing multiple times, 221–222
  hash table, 269
  initializing, 215–216
  Tcl (Tool Command Language), 268–269
  variables, 212–214
asc file extension, 620
ash package, 55
ASJCD file, 33
associative arrays, 212, 214
asterisk (*) wildcard, 184, 190–191
AT commands, 447–451
  action, 450
  command line, 448
  configuration, 449–451
AT&T GIS WaveLAN Ethernet cards, 19
AT-Lan-Tec parallel-port Ethernet adapter, 19
ATAPI (AT Attachment Packet Interface) CD-ROM drives, 18, 364–365, 370–371
ATAPI (AT Attachment Packet Interface) interface, 33
ATI Graphics Pro Turbo video cards, 294
ATI Graphics Ultra Pro video cards, 330
ATI Graphics Ultra video cards, 330
ATI Graphics Xpression video card, 113
ATI Mach8 video cards, 13, 330
ATI Mach32 video cards, 13, 330
ATI Mach64 chipset, 113
ATI Mach64 video cards, 13, 330
ATI Stereo F/X sound cards, 19
ATI VGA Wonder series video cards, 13
ATI XL Inport mouse, 16, 401
ATSr=n commands, 451–452
au file extension, 385
audio CDs, 373–375
AUTOEXEC.BAT files, 23
awk program, 96
aztcd driver, 378
Aztech CD-ROM drives, 33
Aztech CDA268 CD-ROM drives, 18
AZTECH file, 33
aztechx packages, 58

B

background
  commands, 189
  images, 156–157
backing up hard disks, 23
backslash substitution, 255–256
BACKUP utility, 23
bandwith in megahertz, 113
BARE file, 33
bare package, 58
Barkakati, Naba, 287
base address, 492
base Linux system, 51
Bash (Bourne again shell), 96, 144, 181–182, 197
  aliases, 194
  background
    commands, 189

B

built-in functions, 207–208
combining commands, 183
command completion, 190
command history, 192–193
command syntax, 182–183
commands, 182
completing filename, 190
control structures, 205–206
defining functions, 205
editing commands, 193
environment variables,
  144, 186–187
evaluating expressions, 204
I/O redirection, 183–184
if-then-else structure, 206
processes, 187–189
programming overview,
  204–206
running, 204
searching for files, 186
shell programs, 184–186
shell scripts, 182, 203–204,
  206
variables, 204–205
virtual terminals, 189–190
wildcards, 190–192
bash_login file, 144
bash_profile file, 144, 194
baud rate, 440, 544
bc package, 55
beep command, 530
Berkeley Sockets
  interface, 99
Berkeley Software
  Distribution (BSD)
  version, 94
Berners-Lee, T., 474, 600
/bin directory, 196
binary command, 603
binary files
  from other operating
    systems, 97
  reading, 270–271
bind (name server utilities)
  program, 58, 562

bind command, 276, 284–286
BIOS (Basic Input and
  Output System), 15
bison program, 56
bitmapped, 108
bitmapped graphics, 751–752
  device-independent, 97
  displays, 108
bits per second (bps), 440
blocks, 349
BNC connectors, 487–488
BogoMIPS (bogus MIPS),
  68–69, 299
BOOKDSKS.12 directory, 32
boot disk, 63
boot floppy, 10, 36
  boot image, 32
  drive, 21
  Linux, 31–35
boot images, 32
  CD-ROM drives, 366
  NET, 36
  SCSINET1, 36
  SCSINET2, 36
Boot Manager, 341
boot sector, 338
bootable floppy, 24, 30
  ERRORS.TXT file, 30
  FDISK.EXE file, 24
  FIPS.EXE file, 30
  FORMAT.COM file, 24
  RESTORERB.EXE file, 30
  testing, 24
Bootdisk-HOWTO file, 73
BOOTDSKS.144 directory, 32
booting Linux for
  installation, 36–37
bootp command, 530
BootPrompt-HOWTO file, 73
bounding rectangle, 731
Bourne shell, 96, 182
bpp (bits per pixel), 124
braces ({...}), 257
brackets ([]) wildcard,
  190, 192

Bradley, John, 98
break command, 254, 260,
  264, 530
Brennan, David, 715
BSD (Berkeley Software
  Distribution) UNIX, 409
bsdgames package, 62
built-in functions
  Bash (Bourne again shell),
    207–208
  Perl (Practical Extraction
    Report Language),
    226–229
burst header page or banner
  page, 424–425
bus, 293
bus mouse, 16
  device name, 116
  gpm (General Purpose
    Mouse) program,
    68, 114
buses, 12, 291, 293–295
  clock rate, 293
  EISA (Extended Industry
    Standard Architecture),
    12, 293
  ISA (Industry Standard
    Architecture), 12, 293
  MCA (Micro Channel
    Architecture), 12, 293
  PCI (Peripheral Component
    Interconnect), 12,
    293–295
  protocol, 293
  VESA (Video Electronics
    Standard Association)
    Local Bus, 12, 293
business, 631–633
  consultant, 652–653
  developer's
    workstation, 636
  Internet host, 636–638
  ISP (Internet Service
    Provider), 650–652

(continued)

business *(continued)*
  LAN Manager client, 636, 647–649
  LAN Manager server, 636, 640–647
  personal productivity applications, 634–635
  personal UNIX workstation, 635
  role of Linux, 632–633
  specific Linux tasks, 635–636
  technical support lack, 635
  UNIX software developer, 652
  what Linux lacks, 634–635
  what Linux offers, 633–634
  workgroup server, 636–637
  WWW (World Wide Web) server, 636–640
BusLogic disk controllers, 351–352
BusLogic SCSI controllers, 17, 34
BusMouse, 114
Busmouse–HOWTO file, 73
button command, 275
  -command { exit } argument, 274
  -command option, 284
ButtonPress event, 286
ButtonRelease event, 286
byacc package, 55

C

c file extension, 661
C and C++
  header files, 197
  library files, 197
  software-development tools, 51
C functions, 96

C-language Application Programming Interface (API), 94
cables
  10BASE2, 487
  10BASE5, 487
  choices, 446
  DTE to DCE connectors, 444
  Ethernet, 487
  modems, 454
  null modem (DTE to DTE), 445
  RS-232C standard, 442–446
  straight-through, 444
  thick Ethernet, 487
  thickwire, 487
  thinwire, 487
Cabletron E2100 Ethernet card, 490
Cabletron E21xx Ethernet card, 19
cache memory, 295–296
callback functions, 699, 703–704
canvas command, 275
CardBus, 511
case control structure, 205
cat /proc/pci command, 348
cat command, 196, 218, 296, 385, 427
catch command, 264
Caution icon, 3
cb_quit function, 704
cc command, 671
cd command, 81–82, 182, 198, 201, 241, 264
cd function, 207
CD-ROM (Compact Disc Read-Only Memory)
  BOOTDSKS.12 directory, 32
  BOOTDSKS.144 directory, 32
  RAWRITE.EXE program, 32
  ROOTDSKS directory, 32

CD-ROM (Compact Disc Read-Only Memory) drives, 17–18, 363–364
  ATAPI (AT Attachment Packet Interface), 18, 33, 364–365, 370–371
  audio CDs, 373–375
  aztcd driver, 378
  Aztech, 33
  Aztech CDA268, 18
  boot image, 366
  boot-time parameters, 371
  connecting to sound cards, 18
  detecting, 36
  device names, 372
  directory mounted from, 196
  double-speed, 364
  ejecting CD-ROM, 373
  EIDE (Enhanced Integrated Drive Electronics), 18
  Goldstar R420, 33
  IDE, 49
  IDE driver, 376
  interface, 36
  kernel configurations, 369–370
  Kotobuki, 18, 34
  Lasermate, 34
  Linux usage, 373
  Matsushita, 18, 34
  mcd driver, 378
  mcdx driver, 379
  Mitsumi, 18, 33
  mounting CD-ROM, 373
  not detecting, 37
  not recognized after installation, 369
  Okano, 33
  Okano/Wearnes CDD-110, 18
  Optics Storage 8000 AT, 33
  Orchid, 33
  Orchid CDS-3110, 18

C

Panasonic, 18, 34
Phillips CM206, 33
probing, 371
proprietary interfaces,
    365–366
quad-speed, 364
Sanyo CDR-H94A, 33
sbpcd driver, 376–377
scd driver, 375–376
SCSI (Small Computer
    System Interface), 18,
    34, 364–365
single-speed, 364
slave to boot hard disk, 18
Sony CDU31a, CDU33a,
    CDU535 or CDU531,
    18, 33
sonycd35 driver, 377
Sound Blaster Pro CD,
    18, 34
supported, 364–366
TEAC CD-55a, 34
troubleshooting, 366–371
Wearnes, 33
CDE (Common Desktop
    Environment), 708
/cdrom directory, 196
CDROM-HOWTO file, 73, 369
CDU31A file, 33
cdu31ax packages, 58–59
CDU535 file, 33
cdu535_x packages, 59
central processing unit
    (CPU), 12
CERN server, 611
cgi-bin directory, 623
chat command, 102, 530
chat program
    ABORT strings, 541–542
    escape sequences, 542–543
    expect-send pattern of text,
        540–541
    pppd (Point-to-Point
        Protocol Daemon)
        program and, 540–544

sub-expect sequences, 541
    timeouts, 541
checkbutton command, 275
Chips & Technologies 655xx
    chipsets, 14, 307
Chips & Technologies
    chipsets, 333
chmod command, 184,
    200, 203
    +x option, 184–185, 204,
        274, 285
    o+rw option, 454
CHS (Cylinder, Head, Sector)
    address, 337, 346-347
ci command, 685–686
CIAC (Computer Incident
    Advisory Capa-
    bility), 589
circle.c file, 660
CirculateDown function, 170
CirculateUp function, 170
Cirrus Logic CL-GD6440, CL-
    GD7543 chipsets, 307
Cirrus Logic-based video
    cards, 14
Cirrus PD67xx chipsets, 302
CIS (Card Information
    Structure), 511
class name, 159–161
classes
    primitive widgets, 707,
        709–710
    shell widgets, 707
clean command, 415
click-to-type input focus, 169
client/server model, 108–109
client placement and size of
    window, 165
clock chip, 318
clock rate, 293
close command, 264
Close function, 170
CMD 640 IDE controllers, 299
cnews (UUCP-based news)
    program, 57, 561

co command, 685
    -f -u flags, 688
color
    display, 108, 317
    hexidecimal format,
        155–156
    X programming, 740–748
color palette, 317
COLOR.GZ file, 35, 36
colormap, 317, 718–719
    colors from, 743
    free, 748
    notification event, 722
    private read-write color
        cells, 744
    read-only color cell
        allocation, 745–746
    read-write color cell
        allocation, 746–748
    shared read-only color
        cells, 744
    XColor structure, 744–745
combining commands, 183
command block, 259
command history, 192–193
command line, 182
command mode, 447
command string
    substitutions, 255–256
    Tcl processor
        interpretation, 254–255
    white space, 255
command syntax, 182–183
command-line
    arguments, 182
    options, 182–183, 186
    X application options,
        163–164
commands
    accessing Linux from Perl,
        222–224
    administrative, 197
    aliases, 194
    arguments, 182

(continued)

commands *(continued)*
  asterisk (*) and, 184
  background, 189
  built-in Tcl (Tool
    Command Language),
    264–266
  case-sensitivity, 39
  combining, 183
  completion, 190
  concatenating, 183
  dangerous, 194–195
  dip (Dial-up IP Protocol
    Driver) program,
    530–533
  ed editor, 759–761
  editing, 193
  enclosing in back quotes
    ('), 222
  executable files, 197
  exit status, 205
  fdisk utility, 39–40
  filename as argument, 190
  gdb debugger, 674–676
  groff program, 783
  info program, 657–658
  Linux directory layout,
    195–202
  lpc program, 414–415
  manipulating widgets,
    276–277
  manual page, 72
  MS-DOS, 22
  mtools, 238–239
  multiple options, 188
  parsing, 254
  patch, 81–82
  pipe (|), 183
  printing, 409–411
  RCS (Revision Control
    System), 687–689
  repeating, 192
  repeating from command
    history, 192–193
  separating from
    arguments, 255
  separating from
    options, 182
  smbclient program,
    646–647
  standard input to standard
    output, 183
  Tcl (Tool Command
    Language), 254
  too long to fit on line, 183
  trn-nntp (threaded read
    news) program,
    574–576
  vi editor, 765–768
  widget creation, 275–276
Commercial-HOWTO file, 73
comms program, 53
communications programs
  minicom, 455, 457–459
  seyon, 455–456
comp.os.linux.announce
  newsgroup, 78
Compaq 486/50 LTE, 308
Compaq AVGA video
  cards, 13
Compaq Contura Aero
  4/33C, 308
Compaq Contura Aero
  485SLC/25, 308
Compaq LTE Lite 25C, 308
Compaq QVision 2000 video
  cards, 333
compare (cmp) operator, 215
comparison operator, 215
compound string, 702
computers, 291–292. *See also*
  PCs
  bus types, 291, 293–295
  Dell Dimension P75, 298
  laptops, 301–312
  PCI devices, 299
  /proc file system
    information, 296–301
  /proc/cpuinfo file
    information, 298–299
  /proc/pci file information,
    299
  processor information, 298–299
  processor types, 291–292
  processors, 295–296
  serial ports, 437–441
concat command, 264
conf file extension, 616
config command, 530
CONFIG.SYS file, 23
Configure event, 287
CONFIGURE option, 45
configuring
  DOSEMU (DOS emulator),
    243–244
  networks, 68
  software, 45
  system components, 63–68
  widgets, 278–279
  XFree86, 114–135
consultant, 652–653
continue command, 254,
  260, 264
control structures, 205–206
control-flow commands, 254,
  259–263
  command block, 259
COPY (DOS) command, 24
COPYING file, 680-681
copying files, 190-192, 200
COPYING.LIB file, 681
Core widget resources,
  706–707
Corner, Douglas E., 473
cos function, 258
Costales, Bryan, 563
cp command, 182, 190–192,
  196, 200, 206, 235–236
cpp file extension, 661
CPU (central processing
  unit), 298
Cross Reference icon, 3

CSLIP (Compressed SLIP), 525
CSMA/CD (Carrier Send Multiple Access/Collision Detection), 486
current directory, 198
Current Partition Table (p) command, 39–42, 44
CursorMove function, 170
cursors, 718
  shape and color, 158
  size and shape, 722–724
customizing
  fvwm window manager, 165–173
  xterm terminal emulator, 173–179
customizing startup, 150–154
  automatically starting X Windows System, 143–144
  graphical login, 145–154
  init process, 146–149
customizing X Windows System
  command-line X application options, 163–164
  cursor shape and color, 158
  resources, 158–163
  root window appearance, 154
  screen background image, 156–157
  screen color, 155–156
cut command, 203
cylinders, 337
  more than 1,024, 337, 346–347
Cyrillic-HOWTO file, 73
Cyrix 486DLC, 296

D

D-Link DE600 and DE620 parallel-port Ethernet adapter, 19
daemons, 411, 540
  mail transport agent programs, 563
Danish-HOWTO file, 73
DATA command, 567
data structure naming conventions, 716
database servers, 109
databits command, 530
Databook TCIC/2 chipsets, 302
dbgtst program, 678–679
DCE (Data Communications Equipment), 442
dd command, 368, 385
DEC Alpha systems processors, 292
dec command, 531
decimal numbers, 157
default command, 531, 535, 538
defined function, 212
DEFRAG program, 30
defragmenting hard disks, 30
Delete function, 170, 214
Delete Partition (d) command, 39
deleting files, 194–195, 201
deliver (local mail-delivery) program, 57, 561
Dell Dimension P75 computer, 298
Dennis, David, 650
depth, 108
Desk function, 170
desktop size, 169
destroy command, 276
Destroy event, 287

Destroy function, 170
/dev directory, 38, 196
/dev/fd0 floppy disk drive, 38
/dev/fd1 floppy disk drive, 38
/dev/hda hard disk, 38
/dev/hdb hard disk, 38
/dev/modem device name, 64
/dev/mouse device name, 64
/dev/null device, 368
/dev/sda hard disk, 38
/dev/sdb hard disk, 38
/dev/sndstat device, 384–385
/dosc directory, 196
developer's workstation, 636
device drivers, 11–12
device files, 38, 196
devices
  mounting file system on, 47
  resources, 300–301
  temporary directory for mounting, 196
dial phonenum command, 531
dial-up networking, 523
  basics, 524–527
  PPP (Point-to-Point Protocol), 526–527
  protocols, 524
  SLIP (Serial Line Internet Protocol), 524–526
dial.ppp script, 544–545
dialing in with modems
  /etc/rcc.d/rc.serial script, 459–460
  preparing uugetty configuration file, 461–463
  starting uugetty, 463
  testing dial-in setup, 463
  updating uugetty configuration file, 460–461

dialing out with modems, 453
  communications
    programs, 455–459
  hardware setup, 454
  Linux serial devices,
    454–455
Diamond SpeedStar series
  video cards, 111
Diamond Stealth 64
  VRAM, 113
Diamond Viper PCI video
  cards, 13, 294, 329–330
Diamond Viper VLB for
  Video Local Bus video
  cards, 13, 329–330
diff utility, 54, 687
Digital Corporation DEPCA
  Ethernet cards, 19
dip (Dial-up IP Protocol
  Driver) program, 57,
  527, 561
  built-in variables, 534
  commands, 530–533
  running interactively,
    529–535
  scripts, 529, 535–537
dip command, 102
dip file extension, 535
dir c: (DOS) command, 245
directories, 22, 195
  . (one period), 198
  .. (two periods), 198
  absolute pathname, 198
  backslash (\) character, 22
  CD-ROM drive mounted
    from, 196
  creation, 201
  current, 198
  device files, 196
  executable programs, 196
  file manipulation, 200–201
  finding, 202
  finding files, 202
  important programs, 196

information about Linux
  system, 196
initialization scripts, 196
listing, 199–200
l lost files, 196
manipulating, 201
moving, 201
MS-DOS partition mounted
  from, 196
navigation, 197–198
permissions, 199–200
programming language
  libraries, 196
relative directory
  name, 198
removing, 201
root, 22, 196
searching files for
  string, 184
system administration
  commands, 196
system configuration
  files, 196
system definition files, 196
temporary for mounting
  devices, 196
transient information, 196
users' home, 196
disable command, 415
disk controllers
  Adaptec AHA151x, 351
  Adaptec AHA154x, 351
  Adaptec AHA174x, 352
  Adaptec AHA274x, 352
  Adaptec AHA284x, 352
  Adaptec AHA294x, 352
  Allways IN2000, 352
  AMI FastDisk VLB, 351–352
  ATA (AT Attachment), 336
  BusLogic, 351–352
  DTC 329x, 351–352
  EATA DPT Smartcache, 353
  EIDE (Enhanced IDE),
    336, 348

ESDI (Enhanced Small
  Device Interface), 336
Future Domain 16x0, 353
Future Domain TMC-8xx
  and TMC-9xx, 354–355
IDE (Integrated Drive
  Electronics), 336
MFM (Modified Frequency
  Modulation), 336
NCR53c8xx SCSI chip,
  353–354
Pro Audio Spectrum PAS16
  SCSI, 355
RLL (Run Length Lim-
  ited), 336
ROM/BIOS (Read-Only
  Memory/Basic Input/
  Output System), 337
SCSI (Small Computer
  System Interface),
  335–336, 349–357
Seagate ST0x, 354
Sound Blaster 16 SCSI, 351
ST506, 336
Trantor T128, T128F, and
  T228, 355
types, 335–337
Ultrastor 14f, 24f, and 34f,
  355–356
Western Digital 7000, 356
disk names, 38–39
disk sets, 10, 53–57
  applications and files, 51
  base Linux system, 51
  C and C++ software-
    development tools, 51
  copying to hard disk, 44–62
  frequently asked questions
    (FAQs), 51
  installing, 52–62
  kernel source codes, 51
  kernels, 51

D–E

listing, 51–52
location, 48–49
mandatory, 57
networking software, 51
packages, 52–62
recommended, 50
selecting, 50–52
TeX document-formatting system, 51
Tool Command Language (Tcl), 52, 60
UNIX games, 52
X applications, 52
XFree86, 52
XView toolkit, 52
DISK SETS option, 45
disk-based memory, 13
disks, formatting, 22
DISPLAY environment variable, 187
display screens, 145, 315
resolution, 317
displaying images, 748–752
bitmaps, 751–752
pixmap, 749–750
Distribution-HOWTO file, 73
DIX standard, 486
<dlfcn.h> header file, 694–695
dltest.c file, 694
DMA (Direct Memory Access) channel, 300–301, 512
dmesg | more command, 367, 490, 539
DNS (Domain Name System), 481–483
DOC file extension, 22
doom game, 62, 197
doomwad package, 62
doomwad2 package, 62
DOS, connections to, 103
dos -A command, 245
DOS file system. *See also* MS-DOS

automatically mounting partitions, 232–234
boot floppy, 244–245
DOSEMU (DOS emulator), 240–248
/etc/fstab file, 235–236
floppy disks, 234–235
formatting DOS floppy, 239–240
implementing commands, 236
mounting, 231–240
mtools program, 236–240
programs running under Linux, 240–244
text files and deleting extra carriage returns, 185
dos2unix, 185
DOSEMU (DOS emulator), 103, 240–248, 792
accessing DOS partition, 244
authorized users, 248
configuring, 243–244
decompressing archive, 241–243
editing configuration file, 243
/etc/dosemu.conf file, 244
initializing hard disk image, 244–246
installing, 241
manual, 243
QuickStart file, 243
quitting, 247
running in xterm window, 247
starting from hard disk image, 246–248
users who are allowed to run, 243
DOSEMU-HOWTO file, 73
dot (.) operator, 215
dot clock, 317–318

dot commands, 783
dotted-decimal addresses, 475–476
double quotation marks ("..."), 257
down command, 415
DPT Smartcache SCSI controllers, 17
drivers, 9
CD-ROM, 32
DTC 329x disk controllers, 17, 351–352
DTE (Data Terminal Equipment), 442
dumpkeys program, 395–396
dungeon game, 197
dynamic linking, 682
shared libraries, 104

E

e-mail (electronic mail), 558
exchanging, 559
mail transport agent programs, 563
mail user agent programs, 563
setting up and using, 562–568
simple stragies for, 560
software, 563–567
software installation, 560–562
e2fsck system checker, 35
each function, 214
EATA DPT Smartcache disk controllers, 353
EATA-DMA SCSI controllers, 34
echo command, 205, 531
-n option, 205
ECHO-PSS (Orchid SW32 and Cardinal DSP16) sound cards, 19

ed editor
  buffer, 756
  command mode, 757
  commands, 759–761
  current line, 757
  current line number, 758
  displaying line, 758
  inserting lines, 759
  invoking, 756–757
  learning, 757
  replacing string, 758
  sample file editing, 757–759
  searching for string, 758
  text–input mode, 757
editors, 790–791
EEPROMS (electrically erasable programmable read-only memory), 510
EGA (Enhanced Graphics Adapter) video cards, 13
EIA (Electrical Industry Association), 442
EIDE (Enhanced Integrated Drive Electronics)
  CD–ROM drives, 18
  disk controllers, 336, 348
EISA (Extended Industry Standard Architecture) bus, 12, 293
electronic mail, 101
ELF (Executable and Linking Format), 689–690
  ldd utility, 691
  shared library creation, 691–693
ELF-HOWTO file, 73
elisp1 packages, 56
elisp2 packages, 56
elispc1 packages, 56
elispc2 packages, 56
ellipses, 730–731
elm (mail user agent) program, 57, 561

elseif command, 260
emacs. See GNU Emacs
emacinfo package, 56
emacsbin package, 56
emac_nox package, 56
emergency boot disk, 63, 82
enable command, 415
Ensoniq SoundScape sound cards, 19
Enter event, 284, 286
entry command, 275
environment variables, 144
  array of accessible, 214
  defining, 186–187
  Tcl (Tool Command Language), 269–271
eof command, 264
equal (eq) operator, 215
err.9 file, 82
err.10 file, 82
err.11 file, 82
error command, 264
error messages
  listing FIPS, 30
  Non-System disk or disk error, 24
ERRORS.TXT file, 30
escape sequences, 178, 542–543
ESDI (Enhanced Small Device Interface) disk controllers, 336
/etc directory, 115, 196
/etc/.rc./d/rc.M file, 148
/etc/.rc.M script, 500
/etc/default/uugetty.ttyS0 file, 461–462
/etc/dosemu.conf file, 241, 243–244
/etc/dosemu.users file, 243, 248
/etc/exports file, 636
/etc/fstab file, 44, 46, 232, 235–236, 344–345
/etc/gettydefs file, 460, 464

/etc/host.conf file, 482, 501
/etc/HOSTNAME file, 500
/etc/hosts file, 482–483, 500-501, 645
/etc/inittab file, 146–149, 463–464, 502, 552
  default run levels, 147–149
  fields, 148
/etc/inted.conf file, 626
/etc/lilo.conf file, 65, 343
/etc/mtools file, 237–238
/etc/networks file, 501
/etc/nntpserver file, 582
/etc/printcap file, 413, 418–425, 432, 648
  field types, 420
  fields in entries, 420–425
  input-filter field, 423–424
  multiple entries for printer, 425
  printer names, 419–420
  supressing header and form feed, 424–425
  template, 426, 427
/etc/profile file, 144
/etc/rc.d/rc.inet1 script, 502–503
/etc/rc.d/rc.inet2 script, 502
/etc/rc.d/rc.keymap script, 395–396
/etc/rc.d/rc.local script, 626
/etc/rc.d/rc.M script, 502, 563
/etc/rc.d/rc/cdrom script, 373
/etc/rcc.d/rc.serial script, 459–460, 465
/etc/resolv.conf file, 482, 502
/etc/sendmail.cf file, 564–565
/etc/services file, 483–485
/etc/smb.conf file, 642–644
/etc/termcap file, 178
/etc/uucpname file, 582
/etc/xinitrc file, 151
ether command, 492–493

E–F

Ethernet, 469
  ARP (Address Resolution Protocol), 487
  autoprobing, 491–493
  base address, 492
  basics, 485–486
  BNC connectors, 487–488
  cables, 487
  CSMA/CD (Carrier Send Multiple Access/Collision Detection), 486
  hardware, 19–20
  hub, 487
  kernel support, 490–491
  multiple Ethernet cards, 494–495
  network device names, 494
  packets, 486
  PCI cards, 493
  supported cards, 488–490
  thickwire, 487
  unsupported cards, 490
Ethernet cards, 488–490
  3Com 3C503, 3C505, 3C507, and 3C509 (ISA bus), 19
  3Com 3C579 (EISA bus), 19
  Allied Telesis AT1500 and AT1700, 19
  Ansel Communications AC3200 EISA, 19
  Apricot Xen–II, 19
  AT&T GIS WaveLAN, 19
  AT-Lan-Tec parallel-port Ethernet adapter, 19
  Cabletron E2100, 490
  Cabletron E21xx, 19
  connectors, 489
  D-Link DE600 and DE620 parallel-port Ethernet adapter, 19
  Digital Equipment Corporation DEPCA, 19
  drivers, 99
  EtherWORKS, 19
  Hewlett-Packard HP J2405A, 20
  IBM ThinkPad 300 built-in Ethernet adapter, 20
  Intel EtherExpress, 20
  multiple, 494–495
  Novell Ethernet NE1000 and NE2000, 20
  PCLAN (27245 and 27xxx series), 20
  PCLAN PLUS (27247B and 27252A), 20
  PureData PDUC8028 and PDI8023, 20
  Racal-Interlan NI5210 and NI6510, 20
  RealTek parallel-port Ethernet adapter, 19
  Schneider & Koch G16, 20
  SMC (Western Digital) WD8003, WD8013, SMC Elite, SMC Elite Plus, and SMC Elite 16 Ultra, 20
  unsupported, 490
  Zenith Z-Note, 20
Ethernet-HOWTO file, 73
EtherWORKS Ethernet cards, 19
eval command, 265, 272
even parity, 439
event mask, 705
event-driven programming, 698
event-handler registration, 704–705
events
  binding actions to, 283–287
  keyboard, 285–286
  mouse, 286–287
  window, 287
event_handler function, 705
EXE file extension, 22
exec command, 149–150, 265, 271–272
Exec function, 171, 222–223
executable files, 196
  checking binary format, 690
exit command, 265, 284, 415, 531
Exit fdisk (q) command, 40, 44
expose events, 721
expr command, 254, 259, 265
expressions, 211, 215–216, 254
  Boolean operators, 258
  evaluating, 204, 206, 259
  evaluating and executing commands, 259–260
  evaluating until it is zero, 261
  executing commands until it becomes false, 260–261
  functions, 258
  mathematical operators, 258
  regular, 216
  Tcl (Tool Command Language), 258–259
ext keyword, 345
ext2 keyword, 345
extended file system, 345

F

f2c package, 56
FAQs (Frequently Asked Questions), 51, 635
FAT (File Allocation Table), 345
fdformat command, 239–240, 339
FDISK (DOS) command, 25–28
  /MBR command, 344
  activating DOS partition, 28

(continued)

FDISK (DOS) command
    (continued)
  checking partition
    information, 26
  deleting primary DOS
    partition, 26
  new DOS partition, 27–28
fdisk command, 37, 39
fdisk utility, 37, 41, 338,
    340–341
  commands, 39–40
  Device column, 41
  listing commands, 39
  partition names, 41
  System column, 42
FDISK.EXE file, 24, 245
Ferguson, Paula, 715
Fielding, R., 600
FIFO (first-in-first-out)
    buffer, 438
file command, 265, 690
file handles, 224
File Manager window, 153
file servers, 100, 109
file systems, 345
filenames, 22, 38
  beginning or ending with
    (|), 225
  beginning with period
    (.), 200
  case-sensitivity, 39
  converting DOS to
    Linux, 234
  expanding into list, 271
  matching multiple
    characters, 190
  matching single character,
    190, 192
  matching specific set, 192
  treated as command, 225
files, 22, 51, 195
  confirmation before
    deleting, 194
  copying, 24, 190–192,
    200, 235
  copying to printer
    device, 412
  deleting, 194–195, 201
  devices as, 38
  finding, 202
  listing old unused, 203
  manipulating, 200–201
  moving, 200–201
  opening, 224
  operations, 269–271
  performing task on group,
    190–191
  Perl access, 224–225
  permission settings, 184,
    199–200
  printing, 409
  reading from, 224–225
  renaming, 200
  searching for, 186
  searching for pattern of
    strings, 216
  searching for string, 184,
    191
  specific types, 202
  viewing contents, 201
find command, 202–203, 681
  -print option, 202
  -type option, 202
FIPS (First Nondestructive
    Interactive Partition
    Splitting Program)
    utility, 22, 29–31, 40–41
  altering partitions, 340
  defragmenting hard disk
    before using, 30
  listing error messages, 30
  starting cylinder of
    partition, 30
FIPS.EXE file, 30
firewall, 638
Firewall-HOWTO file, 73
first floppy disk drive, 38
floppy disk drives, 15, 38
  boot, 21
  definitions of, 237
  high-density 5.25-inch or
    3.5-inch, 15
  naming conventions, 240
floppy disks, 339
  copying files to, 24
  formatting, 24, 339
  formatting DOS, 239–240
  mount point, 339
  mounting DOS, 234–235
floppy tape drive
    configuration, 65
flow control and RS-232
    standard, 446
flow-control statements, 211,
    219–222
flush command, 265, 531
fnt100_1 packages, 61
fut100_2 packages, 61
fntbig1 packages, 61
fntbig2 packages, 61
fntbig3 packages, 61
focus command, 276
focus follows pointer,
    168–169
Focus function, 171
fonts, 718, 731–733
  resource specifications,
    164–165
  VT102 terminal emula-
    tion, 178
for command, 254, 261, 265
for control structure, 205
for loop, 206
for statement, 203, 221
foreach command, 254, 261,
    265
foreach statement, 221–222
fork function, 222–223
form factor, 510
FORMAT A: /S (DOS)
    command, 24, 30, 244
format command, 265
FORMAT.COM file, 24
formatting
  disks, 22
  DOS floppy disk, 239–240
  floppy disks, 24

four primary partitions, 21–22
frame buffer, 718
frame command, 275
frame widget, 282
frames, 486
free utility, 102
Freeware Foundation, 54
Frystyk, H., 600
ftape package, 55
Ftape-HOWTO file, 73
ftp (File Transfer Protocol), 78–81, 99, 483, 558, 560, 585–589
  changing shell for user, 588
  commands, 81
FTP archive sites and Linux resources, 840, 841, 842
~ftp/bin file, 588
~ftp/etc directory, 588–589
~ftp/etc/passwd file, 589
~ftp/incoming directory, 589
~ftp/lib file, 589
~ftp/pub file, 589
~ftp/usr file, 589
ftp.funet.fi FTP site, 79
full-color installation scripts, 35
full-duplex mode, 442
Function function, 171
functions, 211
  defining, 205
  fvwm built-in, 170–172
  naming conventions, 715
Future Domain TMC-8xx and TMC-9xx disk controllers, 354–355
Future Domain TMC-8xx SCSI controllers, 17, 34
Future Domain TMC-950 SCSI controllers, 17
Future Domain TMC-16x0 SCSI controllers, 17, 353
Future Domain TMC-3260 (PCI) SCSI controllers, 17

fvwm window, 167
fvwm window manager, 137
  add-on modules, 172–173
  built-in functions, 170–172
  CurrentDesk menu, 168
  customizing, 165–173
  desktop size, 169
  emulating other window managers, 173
  GoodStuff module, 172
  input focus, 168
  menu customization, 169–172
  mouse buttons, 405
  overview, 165–168
  pager window, 166
  pipes, 172
  quitting from, 139
  starting, 151–152
  Utilities menu, 167, 175
  virtual desktop, 166
  Window Ops menu, 167
fvwmrc file, 168, 173
fvwmicns package, 60

G

g++ command, 661
g++ compiler, 104
gateway address, 551
Gateway AnyKey keyboard, 399
gateways, 480, 550–551, 549
gcc command, 660
  -g option, 677
  options, 662-665
gcc compiler, 104, 656, 659
  -c option, 660-661
  -g option, 661, 673
  invoking, 660–661
  linking and compiling C++ files, 661
  linking and compiling C files, 660–661
  options, 662–665
gcc270 package, 55
gchess package, 62
gdb debugger, 56, 104
  commands, 674–676
  finding bugs, 677–679
  fixing bugs, 679–680
  preparing programs for debugging, 673
  running, 674–676
gdbm (GNU dbm) database library, 681
Generic NCR5380 SCSI controllers, 34
Genoa GVGA video cards, 13
geometry manager, 279
German-HOWTO file, 73
get command, 513, 531, 598–599
getenv() function, 96
gets command, 262, 265, 270
getty program, 53, 459
ghostscr package, 54
Ghostscript program, 432, 831–834
  device names, 433–435
Ghostview program, 411, 432, 835–837
ghstview package, 62
glob command, 265, 271–272
global command, 264–265
global variables, 264
GNU (GNU is not UNIX) project, 54
  hypertext help system, 656–659
GNU bc utility, 792–794
GNU bison parser-generator tool, 681
GNU C and C++ compilers, 659–665
GNU debugger, 673–680

GNU Emacs, 51, 56, 104, 193, 768–790
  blocks, 777–778
  buffer, 770
  command completion, 777
  copying and moving text, 777–778
  cursor, 770
  entering text, 770
  help commands, 773
  inserting and deleting text, 775–776
  key bindings, 770, 772–773
  learning, 770–771
  mark, 777
  minibuffer, 771
  mode line, 771
  modes, 770
  moving around in buffer, 774–775
  online help, 771–772
  reading files, 774–775
  repeating commands, 775
  running shell, 779
  saving changes, 778
  scratch buffer, 769
  searching and replacing text, 776–777
  starting, 769–770
  typing commands, 771
  undoing changes, 776
GNU GPL (General Public License) implications, 54, 680–681
GNU LGPL (Library General Public License) implications, 681–682
GNU make utility, 656, 665–673
Gnuplot program, 61, 827–831
goboot command, 194
Goldstart R420 CD-ROM drives, 33
GoodStuff module, 172
gopher, 558
goto command, 532
goto statement, 222
GotoPage function, 171
gp9600 package, 55
gpm (General Purpose Mouse) program, 53, 405
  automatically running, 68
  bus mouse, 114
gprof utility, 104
grab command, 277
graphical login
  applications and File Manager windows, 153
  background color, 152
  browsing files and directories, 153
  starting programs, 153
  window acting like terminal to system, 152
graphical user interfaces (GUIs), 97-98, 107, 109–110, 272–275
  Macintosh, 109
  Microsoft Windows, 109
  OPEN LOOK, 98, 109
  OS/2 Presentation Manager, 109
  OSF/Motif, 98, 109
  style guide, 110
  toolkit, 110
  window manager, 110
  window system, 110
  workstations, 7
  X Windows System, 109–110
graphics, device-independent bitmapped, 97
graphics and images programs
  Ghostscript, 831–834
  Ghostview, 835–837
  Gnuplot, 827–831
  xfig, 826–827
  Xfractint, 824–825
  XPaint, 822–824
  XV, 819–822
graphics cards, 108
graphics contexts (GC), 717, 724–727
  attributes, 725–727
  bit-mask constants for attributes, 726–727
  Motif, 733–734
graphics device, 320
Gravis Ultrasound sound cards, 19
greater than (gt) operator, 215
Greenwich Mean Time (GMT), 68
grep command, 82, 182, 184, 191, 216, 232
  combining with ls command, 183
  [bB]laster argument, 216
groff program, 55, 779–785
  commands, 783
gsfonts1 packages, 54
gsfonts2 packages, 54
gs_x11 package, 61
GUI. See Graphical User Interfaces
gunzip command, 79, 81, 102
gz file extension, 35, 79, 81, 620
gzip command, 79
gzip utility, 794–795

H

half-duplex mode, 442
halt command, 196
HAM-HOWTO file, 73
handshaking, 442
hangman game, 197

H

hard disks, 335–337
  address translation, 347
  altering partitions with FIPS, 340
  backing up, 23
  bootable with DOSEMU (DOS emulator), 246
  booting from, 341–342
  capacity, 15
  checking for errors, 30
  CHS addressing, 337
  concepts, 337–339
  copying disk sets to, 44–62
  cylinders, 337
  defragmenting, 30
  directories, 22
  disk controllers, 335–337
  disk space requirements, 15
  fdisk program, 340–341
  files, 22
  first IDE (Integrated Drive Electronics), 38
  first SCSI (Small Computer System Interface), 38
  formatting, 22
  formatting partition, 29
  four primary partitions, 21–22
  geometry, 337
  heads, 337
  IDE (Integrated Drive Electronics), 33–34
  IDE controllers, 15
  image file, 243
  initializing image, 244–246
  initializing master boot record, 246
  inodes and block error messages, 349
  Linux names, 338–339
  Linux partitions, 38–44
  MBR (Master Boot Record), 338
  more than 1,024 cylinders, 40, 346–347
  names, 38
  old IBM XT-style, 34
  operations, 339–341
  partitioning, 9-10, 21–31, 238, 338, 340–341
  preparing partitions, 37
  problems, 346–349
  repartitioning, 22
  restoring from backup, 30
  SCSI, 33–34
  SCSI controller card, 14
  second IDE (Integrated Drive Electronics), 38
  second SCSI, 38
  sectors, 337
  starting DOSEMU (DOS emulator), 246–248
  swap partition, 10, 37, 41–44
  swap space, 344–345
  system BIOS support, 14
hardware, 9
  accessing peripherals with BIOS, 15
  buses, 12
  CD-ROM drives, 17–18
  checklist, 20–21
  drivers, 9
  floppy drives, 15
  hard disks, 14–15
  installation information, 36–37
  keyboards, 16
  memory, 12–13
  monitors, 13, 112–113
  mouse, 16, 114
  network adapters, 19–20
  processors, 12
  SCSI (Small Computer System Interface) controllers, 16–17
  sound cards, 18–19
  supported, 11–20
  video cards, 13–14, 112–113
  workgroup server, 636–637
  WWW (World Wide Web) server configuration, 639–640
  XFree86, 112–114
Hardware-HOWTO file, 73
hash table, 269
Hayes Smartmodem, 447
HDLC (High-Level Data Link Control), 526
HEAD command, 600
header files, 715
Headland Technologies HT216-32 video cards, 13
heads, 337
Heller, Dan, 715
hello script, 210
hello.pl script, 226
hellotcl script, 252–253
hellotk script, 274–275
Help (m) command, 39
help command, 415, 532
HELP file, 45
Hercules monochrome video cards, 13
Hewlett-Packard HP J2405A Ethernet cards, 20
hexadecimal numbers, 157
hexadecimal color format, 155–156
high-density 5.25-inch or 3.5-inch floppy drive, 15
Hinds, David, 509
history command, 192–193, 265
home directory, 187, 198
HOME environment variable, 187, 198
/home directory, 196
/home/ftp directory, 588
home page, 609
hops, 480
horizontal retrace, 316
horizontal sync, 323

horizontal synchronization
   frequencies, 112, 326
host address, 475
host name, 72
hosts
   multihomed, 501
   path for all, 549
   path to specific, 549
hot swapping, 512
HOWTO files, 73–75
html file extension, 597
HTML (Hypertext Markup
   Language), 560, 594
   resources, 627–628
HTTP (Hypertext Transfer
   Protocol), 483, 560, 594,
   597–600
HTTPD (HTTP daemon), 611
httpd.conf file, 616–619
httpd.conf-dist file, 616
httpd_1.4.2_linux.tar.Z file,
   613–614
hub, 487
HURD, 54
hypertext help system,
   656–659
hypertext links, 596
Hyundai HGC-1280
   monochrome video
   cards, 13

I

I/O addresses (Input/Output
   Port address), 300–301
   serial ports, 440
I/O redirection, 183–184
IBM 8514/A video card, 13
IBM Asynchronous
   Communications
   Adapter, 438
IBM ThinkPad, 308
IBM ThinkPad 300 built-in
   Ethernet adapter, 20

IBM token-ring networks, 19
IBM XGA video cards, 13
IBM XGA-II video cards, 13
ICMP (Internet Control
   Message Protocol)
   messages, 505
Iconify function, 171
icons used in this book, 3
IDE (Integrated Drive
   Electronics)
   CD-ROM drives, 49
   disk controllers, 15, 336
   driver, 376
   hard disks, 33–34, 38
IDECD file, 33
idecd1 packages, 59
idecd2 packages, 59
idenet package, 59
ident command, 688–689
IEEE (Institute of Electrical
   and Electronics
   Engineers), 94
   Std 1003.1-1988
      (POSIX.1), 94
IETF (Internet Engineering
   Task Force), 478, 600
if command, 254, 259, 265,
   532
   else clause, 260
if control structure, 205–206
if statement, 203, 219–220
   else clause, 219
   elseif clause, 220
If you're upgrading an
   existing Slackware
   system message, 88–89
ifconfig command, 527, 537,
   545, 547, 549
IGP (Interior Gateway
   Protocol), 480
IIT-based video cards with
   AGX-010, 014, 015, and
   016 chipsets, 14
image file, 243
imake utility, 104

in-then-else structure, 206
inc command, 532
incr command, 260, 265
indenet package, 53
index.html file, 609
inequality (ne) operator, 215
inews program, 582–584
info command, 265
info program
   commands, 657–658
   nodes, 656
INFO-SHEET file, 73
information retrieval,
   558, 560
Information Superhigh-
   way, 558
init command, 149, 532
   mother of all
      processes, 188
   q option, 463–464
init process, 146–149, 502
initialization scripts, 196
inn (InterNetNews) program,
   561
inn package, 57
inodes, 47, 349
InPort busmouse, 400
input data, separating into
   lines of text, 271
input filter, 423–424, 648
input focus, 110, 168
INSTALL option, 45
Installation-HOWTO file, 73
installing
   disk sets, 52–62
   DOSEMU (DOS
      emulator), 241
   LILO (Linux Loader), 65–67,
      342–343
   packages, 53–62
   Samba, 641–642
   software, 45
   sound driver, 380–381

I

installing Linux
  4MB of memory or less, 37
  boot floppy, 10, 36
  booting Linux for
    installation, 36–37
  configuring system
    components, 63–68
  detecting CD-ROM drive, 36
  disk sets, 10
  disk space, 15
  fdisk utility, 37
  from tape, 35
  hardware checklist, 20–21
  hardware drivers, 9
  hardware information,
    36–37
  laptop connected to
    network through
    PCMCIA Ethernet
    card, 35
  Linux boot floppy, 31–35
  Linux hard disk partitions,
    38–44
  Linux-supported hardware,
    12–20
  minimum system for
    installation, 10
  monochrome display, 37
  MS-DOS directory, 35,
    75–76
  networks, 36
  not detecting CD-ROM
    drive, 37
  partitioning hard disk,
    9–10, 21–31
  preparing PC for, 11–12
  recommended root
    image, 35
  reconfiguring system for
    components, 11
  root floppies, 10, 31–32,
    35–36
  setup program, 10
  Slackware CD-ROM, 44–62
  steps involved in, 9–11
  super user, 38
  swap partition, 10
  text-based install script, 35
  xf86config program, 10
instance name, 159–161
integrated video
  chipsets, 294
Intel 80286-compatible
  processors, 12
Intel 80386-compatible
  processor, 12
Intel 80486-compatible
  processor, 12
Intel Binary Compatibility
  Standard (iBCS2), 96–97
Intel EtherExpress Ethernet
  cards, 20
Intel i82365SL chipsets, 302
Intel Triton chipset, 294
interclient communication
  event, 722
International Standards
  Organization (ISO), 94,
  99, 165
Internet
  connecting LAN (local area
    network) to, 548–555
  connecting to, 100, 523
  ISP (Internet Service
    Provider), 477
  LANs (local area networks)
    connections, 105
  nodes, 105
  on ramp to, 104–105
  PPP (Point-to-Point
    Protocol), 20
  RFCs (Request for
    Comments), 474
  SLIP (Serial Line Internet
    Protocol), 20
  TCP/IP (Transmission
    Control Protocol/
    Internet Protocol),
    473–479
  USENET, 101
Internet Access Frequently
  Asked Questions
  (FAQ), 650
Internet hosts, 557–559,
  636–638
  defining, 558–559
  e-mail (electronic mail),
    558–568
  e-mail and newsgroup
    software installation,
    561, 562
  information retrieval,
    558–560
  newsgroups, 558–584
  remote access, 559
  secure anonymous FTP,
    584–589
  tasks, 637
internetworking, 473, 558
Iomega Zip drive (SCSI),
  356–357
IP (Internet Protocol)
  packet, 524
IP addresses
  address classes, 475–477
  dotted-decimal addresses,
    475–476
  host address, 475
  network address, 475, 479
  network mask, 478
  next-generation (IPv6), 478
  requests, 477–478
  subnets, 479
IPC (interprocess
  communication), 712
IPX (Internet Packet
  Exchange), 99
IPX/SPX (Internet Packet
  Exchange/Sequenced
  Packet Exchange)
  protocol suite, 473
IRQs (Interrupt Requests)
  number, 300–301
  serial ports, 440

ISA (Industry Standard Architecture) bus, 7, 12, 293
ISDN (Integrated Services Digital Network), 526
ISO (International Standards Organization), 470
　IEC IS 9945-1:1990 standard, 94
　standard 3309, 526
ISP (Internet Service Provider), 100, 477, 560, 650–652
　nodes, 105
　necessary equipment, 650–651
　PC requirements, 651–652
ispell utility, 55, 795–796
ITU (International Telecommunications Union), 447

J

James, Steve, 628
Java, 627
JE-HOWTO file, 74
JED editor, 54, 791
JOE editor, 54, 791
join command, 265, 267
Jove editor, 54, 791
jpeg package, 55

K

kbdrate program, 393–394
kernel, 51, 58–60, 77
　accessing information about, 296–301
　configuring, 82
　CX486DLC patch, 296
　deleting unneeded files, 86
　enabling IP forwarding, 550
　Ethernet support, 490–491
　file size for updating, 78
　rebuilding after patch, 82–87
　rebuilding and device support, 300–301
　recompiling changed files, 86
　routing table, 549
　source code, 51, 197
　TCP/IP configuration, 495–497
kernel patches
　applying, 81–82
　decompressing, 81
　file size, 78
　obtaining over Internet, 78–81
　rebuilding kernel, 82–87
　searching for string fail, 82
Kernel-HOWTO file, 74
keyboards, 16, 391
　events, 285–286, 721
　Gateway AnyKey, 399
　keycodes, 395
　keysyms, 393
　layout, 392–393
　LEDs (light-emitting diodes), 392
　logging into system, 144
　mapping, 151–152, 394–396
　modifier keys, 392
　repeat delay, 391–394
　repeat rate, 391–394
　special characters, 394
　translation, 394
　turning on Num Lock key, 398–399
　X Window System, 393
　XFree86, 396–398
keycode, 151–152, 395
KeyPress event, 285–286
KeyRelease event, 285–286
keys function, 214
Keystroke-HOWTO file, 74
keysym, 151–152, 285–286, 393, 398
keytbls program, 53, 395
kill command, 114, 188–189
Koblas, David, 98
Kotobuki CD-ROM drives, 34

L

Label class, 709
label command, 276
LAN (local area network)
　connecting to Internet, 105, 548–555
　remote gateway must route to, 551–552
　your system as gateway, 551
LAN Manager client, 636, 647–649
LAN Manager server, 636, 640–647
LAN Soft, 559
lappend command, 265
laptops
　APM (Advanced Power Management), 302
　Cirrus PD67xx chipsets, 302
　Databook TCIC/2 chipsets, 302
　display screens, 315
　information resources, 307–310
　installing Linux with CD-ROM drive, 312
　installing Linux without CD-ROM drive, 310–312
　Intel i82365SL chipsets, 302
　NEC Versa M, 302–303
　NEC Versa P, 302
　PCMCIA, 302
　sound, 302–303

L

supported, 302–310
Vadem VG-468 chipsets, 302
video chipsets, 303–307
XFree86, 303–307
Lasermate CD-ROM drives, 34
last keyword, 221
LBA (Linear Block Address), 346–347
LCD (Liquid Crystal Display) screens, 315
LCP (Link Control Protocol), 526
ldconfig utility, 693
ldd utility, 691
LD_LIBRARY_PATH environment variable, 693
Leave event, 284, 286
LEDs (light-emitting diodes), 392
less command, 201, 243
less than (lt) operator, 215
/lib directory, 196
libdobj.so shared library, 693
libgr package, 61
libgxx package, 56
LILO (Linux Loader), 40
  boot prompt, 343–344
  booting hard disks, 341–342
  configuration file, 342–343
  documentation, 342
  installing, 65–67, 342–344
  map installer, 342
  MBR (Master Boot Record), 338
  problems booting, 357
  removing, 344
  selecting operating systems, 67
  starting Linux for first time, 69
  Windows 95 and, 346

lindex command, 265
lines, 729
linsert command, 265
Linux
  as UNIX platform, 94–97
  changing source code, 77
  current patch level, 78
  disk space necessary for, 28
  documentation files, 197
  DOS under, 231–240
  Ethernet, 485–495
  information about system, 196
  installing, 7–68
  Intel Binary Compatibility Standard (iBCS2), 96–97
  Internet on-ramp, 104–105
  lack of software for, 96
  major components, 633–634
  major version number, 78
  minor version number, 78
  networking, 98–101
  overview, 93–105
  shutting down, 75
  software development, 103–104
  starting for first time, 69–75
  system administration, 101–102
  technical support lack, 635
  upgrading, 77–89
  versions, 93–94
  what it lacks, 634–635
Linux applications
  editors, 790–791
  graphics and images, 819–837
  utilities, 791–819
Linux directory layout commands, 195–202
Linux Journal, 842
Linux programming topics

ELF (Executable and Linking Format), 689–690
shared libraries, 691–695
Linux resources
  FTP archive sites, 840–842
  Linux Journal, 842
  newsgroups, 839–840
  Web pages, 839
list command, 678
List Partition Types (l) command, 43
listbox command, 276
listener windows, 169
llength command, 265
loadkeys program, 394–396
loadlin package, 53
local display, 145
local files, 197
local printer setup, 428
lock file, 418
log file, 424–425
log function, 258
login name, 187
login script, 409–410
login window, 145
Logitech bus mouse, 16
Logitech mouse, 114
Logitech serial mouse, 16
Logitech SoundMan 16 sound cards, 19
LOGNAME environment variable, 187
lookup script, 218
loopback, 72
looping, 220–221, 260
lost files, 196
/lost+found directory, 196
low voltage operation, 512
lower command, 277
Lower function, 171
lp default printer, 420
lpc program, 413–415
lpc status command, 410–411, 414

lpd daemon, 417–418, 427
lpd program, 413, 416–417
lpq command, 410
lpq program, 413
lpr command, 409, 416, 427, 648
  -i option, 432
  -P option, 409
  -s option, 413–414
  tracing print request, 416
lpr program, 413, 416–417
lprm command, 410
lprm program, 413
lrange command, 265
lreplace command, 265
ls command, 182, 192, 196, 199, 235–236, 602, 605, 612
  –a option, 200
  combining with grep command, 183
  –l option, 199, 368, 427
lsearch command, 265
lsort command, 265

M

m4 package, 56
macro naming conventions, 715
mail command, 565
MAIL FROM: command, 567
Mail–HOWTO file, 74
mailx (mail user agent) program, 57, 96, 561
major version number, 78
make clean command, 86
make command, 102
make config command, 82–83, 380, 425, 491, 550
make dep command, 86
make prereq command, 516
make utility, 104
  implicit rules, 669–670
  makefile, 665–667
  options, 672–673
  pattern rules, 669
  predefined variables, 668–669
  running, 671–672
  sample makefile, 670–671
  suffix rules, 669
  variables (macros), 667
make zImage command, 86
make zlilo command, 86
MAKEDEV script, 359
makefile
  dependent files, 667
  names, 665–666
  sample, 670–671
  specifications, 666–667
  target files, 667
makeflop script, 312
man 3 command, 276
man bash command, 207
man command, 72, 197, 781
man package, 54
man pages, 779–781
  existing, 780–781
  sample, 783–784
  source, 781–783
  testing and installing, 784–785
man perl command, 227–229
man2 package, 55
man3 package, 56
manager widgets, 706–711
MANPATH environment variable, 781
manpgs package, 55
Map event, 287
map installer, 342
marking, 439
match-string (==) operator, 215

math coprocessor, 292
Matrox MGA Millenium video cards, 333
Matsushita CD-ROM drives, 34
Matsushita/Kotobuki/ Panasonic models CR-521, CR-522, CR-523, CR-562, and CR-563 CD-ROM drives, 18
mattrib command, 238
Maximize function, 171
MBR (Master Boot Record), 65, 67, 338
mc package, 55
MCA (Micro Channel Architecture) bus, 293
mcd command, 238
mcd driver, 378
mcdx driver, 379
mcopy command, 238
mdel command, 238
mdir command, 238
Media Vision Premium 3D Jazz 16 (Sound Blaster Pro-compatible) sound cards, 19
memory
  4MB or less, 37
  disk-based, 13
  physical, 13
  requirements, 12–13
  speed, 295
  virtual, 13, 22, 43–44
menu command, 276
menubutton command, 276
menus
  fvwm customization, 169–172
  VT102 terminal emulation, 177–178
message command, 276
META–FAQ, 74

M

Metcalfe, Robert M., 486
Metro-X, 333
mformat command, 238, 240
mformat utility, 239–240
mget command, 603
MGR-HOWTO file, 74
Micro Channel Architecture (MCA) bus, 12
Microsoft and Logitech busmouse interface, 400–401
Microsoft bus mouse, 16
Microsoft mouse, 114
Microsoft serial mouse, 16
Microsoft Sound System (AD1848) sound cards, 19
MIDI (Musical Instrument Digital Interface), 379
Midnight Commander utility, 796
MIME (Multipurpose Internet Mail Extension), 619
minicom program, 455–459, 524
minimal Linux system, 35
Minix file system, 345
minix keyword, 345
minor version number, 78
MIPS (millions of instructions per second), 68
  processors, 292
misc.test newsgroup, 583–584
Mitsumi CD-ROM drives, 18, 33
MITSUMI file, 33
mitsumi1 packages, 59
mitsumi2 packages, 59
mk2efs command, 345
mkdir command, 201
mke2fs command, 339, 345
mkswap command, 44, 46, 344–345

mlabel command, 238
mmd command, 238
/mnt directory, 196
mode command, 532
mode SLIP command, 535
Modeline, 325–326
modem command, 532
modems, 437
  AT commands, 447–451
  ATSr=n commands, 451–452
  baud rate, 544
  cables, 454
  configuring, 10
  connectors, 442–444
  dialing in with, 459–463
  dialing out with, 453–459
  DTE to DCE connectors, 444
  full-duplex mode, 442
  half-duplex mode, 442
  Hayes Smartmodem, 447
  Linux and, 453–463
  null modem cables (DTE to DTE), 445
  RS-232C standard, 441–446
  S registers, 451–452
  setting up, 64
  speed, 65
  standards, 446–447
  USRobotics, 452–453
modifier keys, 392
Module function, 171
monitors, 13, 315–318
  bandwidth in megahertz, 113
  color, 108, 317
  display screen, 315
  horizontal retrace, 316
  horizontal sync, 323
  horizontal synchronization frequencies, 112, 326
  importance to XFree86, 318
  monochrome display, 37
  pixels, 13, 316

  raster lines, 108, 316
  resolution, 13, 317
  settings, 321–322
  shadow mask, 317
  technical specifications, 320, 323–325
  vertical refresh rate, 323, 326
  vertical retrace, 316
  vertical synchronization rates, 113
  video cards, 112
  video modes, 324
  XFree86, 112–113
more command, 75, 192, 196, 201, 296
  filename as argument, 190
Motif, 98, 140–141, 173
  basic programming, 698–705
  callback functions, 699
  callback registration, 703–704
  display and window ID, 733
  drawing functions, 733–739
  event-driven programming, 698
  event-handler registration, 704–705
  expose events, 721
  graphics context (GC), 733–734
  header files, 698
  line-drawing program, 734–739
  makefile for program, 700–701
  simple program, 699–700
  step-by-step programming, 698–699
  versions, 708
  widget resources, 701–703
  widgets, 698, 705–711
  Xlib and, 712–752
  Xt Intrinsics, 272, 698
Motion event, 287

Motorola 68000 processors, 292
mount -r command, 561, 641
mount command, 102, 196, 232–236, 339, 357, 368, 373, 636
　-a option, 236
　-t msdos option, 233
mount point, 233, 339
mounting, 232
　file system on device, 47
mouse, 16, 114, 399–401
　alternatives, 406
　ATI XL Inport, 16
　ATI-XL, 401
　basic actions, 404–405
　baud rate, 402, 404
　bus, 16
　BusMouse, 114
　busy, 405
　configuration information, 403
　configuring, 10
　connection type, 114
　device name, 114, 401–402
　interfaces, 399-401
　Logitech, 114
　Logitech bus, 16
　Logitech serial, 16
　Microsoft, 114
　Microsoft and Logitech busmouse interface, 400–401
　Microsoft bus, 16
　Microsoft serial, 16
　Mouse Systems serial, 16
　mouse-click events, 114
　not found, 405
　protocol specification, 403
　protocols, 402
　PS/2 auxiliary device interface, 401
　PS/2 bus, 16
　PS/2-style, 114
　QuickPort, 16
　sample rate, 402, 404
　serial, 16
　setting up, 64
　third button, 403
　type, 114
　XFree86, 402–405
mouse events, 286–287, 721
Mouse Systems serial mouse, 16
mouse-button bindings, 110
Move function, 171
moving files and directories, 200–201
mpeg file extension, 621
MPU-401 MIDI sound cards, 19
mrd command, 238
mread command, 238
mren command, 238
MS-DOS file system, 7, 345. *See also* DOS
　activating DOS partition, 28
　BACKUP utility, 23
　boot floppy drive, 21
　bootable floppy, 24
　clusters, 47
　commands, 22
　COPY command, 24
　DEFRAG program, 30
　directories, 22
　directory partition mounted from, 196
　FDISK command, 22
　file servers, 100
　filenames, 22
　files, 22
　formatting disks, 22
　four primary partitions, 21–22
　how much disk space to leave for, 27–28
　installing Linux in directory, 10, 35, 75–76
　Linux boot and root floppies, 32
　partition name, 48
　partitioning hard disks, 21–31
　repartitioning hard disks, 22
　restoring DOS partition, 29
　root directory, 22
　SCANDISK, 30
　subdirectories, 22
　swap space, 22
　UMSDS144 root image, 76
MS-DOS editor, 247
MSBACKUP, 29
msdos keyword, 345
mtools program, 103, 197, 339
　commands, 238–239
　directory separators, 239
　mformat utility, 239–240
　user access to, 236
　wildcards and filenames, 239
mtype command, 238
mt_st package, 55
multifunction capability, 512
multihomed, 501
multimedia, 18
multiple Ethernet cards, 494–495
multiport serial boards, 441, 464–466
mv command, 200–201
mwm.fvwmrc file, 173
mwrite command, 238
MX68000- and MX68010-based chipsets on video cards, 14

N

name servers, 482-483
native partitions, 42
Naugle, Matthew, 473

N

NCP (Network Control
    Protocol), 526
NCR 53c7 and NCR 8xx SCSI
    controllers, 34
NCR-based SCSI controllers
    with 53c7x0 and 53c8x0
    (for PCI) chipsets, 17
NCR-based video cards with
    NCR 77C22, 77C22E,
    77C22E+ chipsets, 14
NCR53c8xx SCSI chip,
    353–354
NCSA HTTPD (HTTP
    daemon) software
  configuring, 616–625
  documents directory, 625
  downloading, 611–613
  error–logs directory, 625
  starting, 626
  trying, 626–627
  unpacking, 614–616
  version control, 682–683
NCSA Mosaic for X Window
    System, 601
  document window, 607
  downloading, 604–606
  interrupting download, 607
  running, 606
  status message, 608
NCSA server
  configuring software,
    616–625
  downloading HTTPD
    software, 611–613
  starting, 626
  trying, 626–627
  unpacking software,
    614–616
ncurses package, 56
NEC Versa M laptop,
    302–303, 308–309
NEC Versa P laptop,
    302, 308–309

NET boot image, 36
NET file, 33
NET-2-HOWTO file, 74
NetBEUI (Network BIOS
    Extended User
    Interface) suite, 473
NetBIOS protocol suite, 473
netcfg program, 57, 561
netconfig command, 72
netconfig script, 495, 497–499
netmask command, 498, 532
Netscape Navigator, 608
  Activity Indicator, 610
  directory buttons, 610
  document location, 610
  document window,
    609–610
  downloading, 601–604
  security key, 610
  starting, 609
  toolbar, 609
  user interface, 609–610
netstat command, 102,
    505–506
network adapters, 19–20. *See
    also* Ethernet cards
network addresses, 475, 479
network administration,
    101–102
network mask, 478
network printer, 648
network protocols, 98–101
  application-layer, 472
  IPX (Internet Packet
    Exchange), 99
  network-layer, 472
  NFS (Network File
    System), 100
  physical-layer, 472
  PPP (Point-to-Point
    Protocol), 100
  protocol suites, 473
  SLIP (Serial Line Internet
    Protocol), 100

  TCP/IP (Transmission
    Control Protocol/
    Internet Protocol), 99
  transport-layer, 472
  UUCP (UNIX-to-UNIX
    Copy), 101
network topology, 470
network-layer protocols, 472
networking, 98–101
  basics, 469–473
  Internet connections, 100
  network protocols,
    472–473
  OSI (Open Systems
    Interconnect) seven-
    layer model, 470–471
  simplified four-layer model,
    471–472
  software, 51
  TCP/IP (Transmission
    Control Protocol/
    Internet Protocol), 469
  UNIX, 99
networks, 469
  configuring, 68
  configuring at boot time,
    502–503
  Ethernet, 469
  installing Linux, 36
  installing Linux over to IDE
    drive, 33
  laptop connected through
    PCMCIA Ethernet
    card, 35
  logging into system, 144
  NFS (Network File System),
    36
  printers, 413
  private, 477–478
  routing device, 479–480
  running applications
    across, 98
  SCSI hard disks, 34
New Partition (n) command,
    39

N

news readers, 569
News-HOWTO file, 74
newsgroups, 558, 561–562
   articles reaching other sites, 581–582
   hierarchy, 577–579
   Linux resources, 839–840
   major categories, 577–578
   news reader, 569
   .newsrc file, 569–579
   NNTPSERVER environment variable, 569
   participating in, 559
   posting news, 579–584
   reading news, 569–577
   simple strategies for, 560
   software installation, 560–562
   subscribing, 579
newsrc file, 569–579
next keyword, 221
Next XFree86 Mode (Ctrl+Alt+Keypad +) key combination, 138–139
next-generation IP addresses (IPv6), 478
NFS (Network File Sharing), 36, 48, 100, 483, 636
NIC (Network Information Center), 477, 481
NIS-HOWTO file, 74
nn-nntp (remote server news reader) program, 58, 562
nn-spool (local news reader), 58, 562
nntp (Network News Transfer Protocol), 483, 568
NNTPSERVER environment variable, 569, 572–573
nodes, 105
Non-System disk or disk error message, 24
Noorda, Ray, 631
Nop function, 171
Norton Utilities, 30
Note icon, 3
Novell Ethernet NE1000 and NE2000 Ethernet cards, 20
nroff (nontypesetting runoff) program, 780
null modem cables (DTE to DTE), 445
null-list () operator, 215
Number Nine GXE Pro PCI video cards, 294
Number Nine GXE64 video card, 113
Number Nine Imagine 128 video cards, 333

O

o file extension, 661
OAK-based video cards with OTI-037, OTI-067, OTI-077, and OTI-087 chipsets, 14
objc270 package, 56
Okano CD-ROM drives, 33
Okano/Wearnes CDD-110 CD-ROM drives, 18
old IBM XT-style hard disks, 34
oldlibs5 package, 61
on-line documentation
   command manual page, 72
   HOWTO files, 73–75
online mode, 447
online-manual pages, 197
open command, 265, 269, 271
open function, 224–225
OPEN LOOK Window Manager (OLWM), 97–98
OpenWindows, 197
operating systems
   16-bit, 7
   16-bit vs. 32-bit, 8
   32-bit, 7
   Linux, 8
   MS-DOS, 7
   Windows 3.1, 7
   Windows NT, 8
   workstations, 7
operators, 215–216
Optics Storage 8000 AT CD-ROM drives, 33
option command, 277
Orchid CD-ROM drives, 33
Orchid CDS-3110 CD-ROM drives, 18
Orchid P9000 video cards, 13, 329–330
ORGANIZATION environment variable, 581
OS/2
   Boot Manager, 37, 341
   Linux partitions, 42–43
   partition name, 48
   partition type, 40
   partitioning hard disks with FDISK, 37
OSF/Motif, 97
OSI (Open Systems Interconnect) seven-layer model, 99, 470–471
Ousterhout, John K., 251–253

P

p2c package, 56
pack command, 274, 276–277, 279–281
   options, 280–281
pack configure command, 280

P

pack forget command, 279–280
pack info command, 280
pack propagate command, 280
pack slaves command, 280
packages
  installing disk sets, 53–62
  tagging, 52
packets, 486
pager window, 166
paging, 43
Panasonic CD–ROM drives, 34
parent directory, 198
PARITY bit, 439
parity command, 532
partition names, 41
Partition Type (t) command, 40, 43
partitioning hard disks, 9–10
  bootable MS-DOS floppy, 24
  checking partition information, 26
  deleting primary DOS partition, 26
  disk names, 38–39
  FDISK program, 25–28
  FIPS (First Nondestructive Interactive Partition Splitting Program), 29–31
  formatting partition, 29
  inodes, 47
  Linux, 38–44
  marking type, 37
  native, 42
  new DOS partition, 27–28
  OS/2 and FDISK, 37
  restoring DOS partition, 29
  splitting DOS partition, 29–30
  without destroying existing data, 29–31

partitions, 21–22, 338, 340–341
  altering with FIPS, 340
  boot sector, 338
  file systems, 345
  mounting DOS automatically, 232–234
  swap space, 22
  types, 341
passwd command, 69, 72, 101
password command, 532
passwords
  changing, 69–70
  forgetting root password, 70
  root, 70
  root users, 10
  xterm terminal emulator, 174
patch command, 81–82
patch utility, 797–798
patches, 77
  current level, 78
  levels, 93
PATH environment variable, 115, 186–187, 252, 273
  current setting, 214
  finding listed programs, 209
  redefining, 209
pathnames in XF86Config file, 132
PC cards
  API (Application Programming Interface), 512
  CardBus, 511
  CIS (Card Information Structure), 511
  connectors, 510
  DMA (Direct Memory Access), 512
  EEPROMS (electrically erasable programmable read-only memory), 510

form factor, 510
low voltage operation, 512
multifunction capability, 512
physical specifications, 510
plug and play, 512
power management, 512
services, 512–517
supported, 517–518
terminology, 511–512
usage, 511
XIP (Execute in Place), 512
PCI (Peripheral Component Interconnect) bus, 7, 12, 293
  EIDE disk controller problems, 348
  Intel Triton chipset, 294
  Linux support, 294–295
PCI devices, 299
PCI motherboards, 294
PCI-HOWTO file, 74
PCLAN (27245 and 27xxx series) Ethernet cards, 20
PCLAN PLUS (27247B and 27252A) Ethernet cards, 20
PCMCIA (Personal Computer Memory Card International Association), 509–512. *See also* PC cards
PCMCIA Card Services program, 512–519
PCMCIA laptops, 302
PCMCIA-HOWTO file, 74, 519
PCMCIA.GZ file, 35
PCs. *See also* computers
  device drivers, 11–12
  Linux-supported hardware, 11–20
  preparing for Linux installation, 11–20

(continued)

PCs *(continued)*
    restarting, 36
    serial ports, 437–441
Pentium processors, 292
    PCI (Peripheral Component
        Interconnect) bus, 337
Pentium-compatible
    processor, 12
peripherals, 15–16
Perl (Practical Extraction
    Report Language),
    104, 181
    accessing Linux
        commands, 222–224
    as scripting language,
        208–222
    basic syntax, 211
    built-in functions, 226–229
    comments, 211
    expressions, 211, 215–216
    file access, 224–225
    flow-control statements,
        211, 219–222
    functions, 211
    operators, 215–216
    overview, 211–222
    predefined variables, 214
    regular expressions,
        216–219
    scripts, 213
    statements, 211
    subroutines, 225–226
    variables, 211–214
perl program, 56, 208
    -e option, 210
    hello script, 210
    latest versions, 209
    locating, 208–209
    passing as command-line
        argument to Perl, 210
    -v option, 209
permission settings, 199-200
personal productivity
    applications lack,
    634–635

personal UNIX work-
    station, 635
Phillips CM206 CD-ROM
    drives, 33
physical memory, 13
physical-layer protocols, 472
PID (process ID) number, 188
pid command, 265
pine (mail and news)
    program, 57, 561
ping command, 102, 505,
    547, 555
ping utility, 499
pipe (|), 183
pixel value, 718
pixels, 13, 108, 316
pixmaps, 719, 749
    displaying, 750
    drawing into, 750
    freeing, 750
pkgtool command, 88
pkgtool utility, 88-89
place command, 277, 279,
    281–284
    options, 283
place configure command,
    282
place forget command, 279,
    282, 284
place info command, 282
place slaves command, 282
plug and play, 512
pointer focus, 168–169
points, 727–728
polygons, 730
Popup function, 171
port command, 533
POSIX standards, 94–96
    POSIX.1 (Portable
        Operating System
        Interface), 94, 96, 104
    POSIX.2 (Portable
        Operating System
        Interface), 96, 104

POST command, 600
Postel, Jonathan, 567
Postnews program, 580
PostScript
    printers, 411
    printing files, 432–435
pound sign (#) default
    prompt, 37
power management, 512
PowerPC processors, 292
ppntopcx program, 184
PPP (Point-to-Point
    Protocol), 20, 100, 469,
    526–527
    checking support, 539
    connecting to remote
        network as client,
        539–548
    enable IP forwarding in
        kernel, 550
    ending connection,
        547–548
    gateway, 549
    gathering information for
        connection, 539–540
    HDLC (High-Level Data
        Link Control), 526
    LCP (Link Control
        Protocol), 526
    NCP (Network Control
        Protocol), 526
    paths, 549
    routing through, 548–550
    setting up server, 552–555
    system route to remote
        gateway, 550–551
    testing connection,
        545–547
ppp (PPP for Linux)
    program, 57, 561
PPP-HOWTO file, 74
pppd (Point-to-Point
    Protocol Daemon)
    program, 540–545,
    550–551

P

Index **869**

chat program and, 540–544
command line, 543–544
dial-up script, 544–545
pppd-off script, 547
pr command, 411
predefined variables, 214
Previous XFree86 Mode (Ctrl+Alt+Keypad –) key combination, 139
primitive widgets, 706–710
print any_text command, 533
print command, 214
print jobs, 408
  maximum size, 425
  spooling, 416–417
printer device, 424
PRINTER environment variable, 409–410, 416
printers, 407–411
  behind-the-scenes view, 411–412
  brute-force printing, 412
  canceling print job, 410
  capabilities, 418–425
  checking print queue, 410
  configuration, 425
  controlling, 414–415
  device names, 407–408
  /etc/printcap file, 418–427
  fancy printing, 411
  filtering print job for remote printer, 431–432
  local setup, 428
  multiple names, 418
  networks, 413
  not indenting output, 432
  PostScript, 411
  print jobs, 408
  printing PostScript files, 432–435
  problems printing on remote printer, 430
  remote setup, 428–430
  sending jobs to, 417
  setup, 425
  spool directory, 417–418
  spooling, 408, 412–413
  staircase effect, 430–431
  status, 410
  submitted print job, no output, 429–430
  symbolic-link spooling, 413–414
  tracing print request, 416
  truncated graphics files, 432
printing
  array variables, 214
  commands, 409–411
  CONFIG.SYS and AUTOEXEC.BAT files, 23
  files, 409
  PostScript files, 432–435
Printing-HOWTO file, 74
Printing-Usage-HOWTO file, 74
private LAN (local area network), 639
private networks, 477, 478
Pro Audio Spectrum 16 and QLogic SCSI controllers, 34
Pro Audio Spectrum 16 SCSI controller for ISA bus, 17
Pro Audio Spectrum 16 sound cards, 19, 388
Pro Audio Spectrum PAS16 SCSI, 355
Pro Audio Spectrum sound cards, 355
Pro Sonic 16 Jazz sound cards, 19
proc command, 254, 263–264, 266
/proc directory, 196
/proc file system, 296–301
/proc/cpuinfo file, 298–299
/proc/devices file, 367
/proc/dma file, 300–301
/proc/interrupts file, 300–301
/proc/ioports file, 300–301
/proc/pci file, 299
procedures, 254
  args argument, 264
  Tcl (Tool Command Language), 263–264
process file system, 296
processes, 145, 187–189
  accessing information about, 296–301
  forcibly stopping, 188
  listing, 187–188
  services, 483
  signals to notify of event, 189
processors, 12, 291–292
  80386, 292
  80486, 292
  80x86 family, 292
  cache not enabled for Cyrix 486DLC, 296
  computing power, 7
  DEC Alpha systems, 292
  floating–point, 292
  information about, 298–299
  Intel 80286-compatible, 12
  Intel 80386-compatible, 12
  Intel 80486-compatible, 12
  MIPS, 292
  Motorola 68000, 292
  Pentium, 292
  Pentium-compatible, 12
  PowerPC, 292
  slowdown after adding memory, 295
  specific problems, 295–296
profile file, 144
programming language libraries, 196
programs, 208
  describing files that make up, 665–666

(continued)

programs *(continued)*
  finding, 209
  running, 146–149
proprietary CD-ROM drives, 365–366
protected mode, 292
protocols, 293
  dial-up networking, 524
  mouse, 402
  URLs (Uniform Resource Locators), 596
proxyarp command, 533
ps command, 187–188, 224
PS/2 auxiliary device interface, 401
PS/2 bus mouse, 16
PS/2-style mouse, 114
PS1 environment variable, 187
psh.pl script, 223–224
PureData PDUC8082 and PDI8023 Ethernet cards, 20
PushButton widget, 702
puts command, 255, 257, 266, 269–270
pwd command, 182, 198, 266
pwd function, 207

Q

Qlogic FAS408 SCSI controller, 17
qt file extension, 621
question mark (?) wildcard, 190, 192
QuickPort mouse, 16
QuickStart file, 243
Quigley, Ellie, 211
quit command, 415, 533, 568
Quit function, 171

R

Racal-Interlan NI5210 and NI6510 Ethernet cards, 20
radiobutton command, 276
raise command, 277
Raise function, 171
RaiseLower function, 171
RAM (random-access memory), 12-13
range (..) operator, 216
raster graphics. *See* bitmapped graphics
raster lines, 108, 316
RAWRITE program, 34, 36
RAWRITE.EXE program, 32
rcmd.pl script, 222–223
RCPT TO: command, 567
RCS (Revision Control System), 104, 656
  archived files, 685–686
  basics, 684–687
  commands, 687–689
  discarding changes, 687–688
  examining identifier keywords, 688–689
  identification keywords, 686–687
  initial files, 684–685
  source-control tools, 683–684
  viewing change history, 688
  viewing changes, 687
rcs command, 687
rcs package, 56
RCS/Makefile.v file, 685
rcsdiff program, 687
rdev -R Image 1 command, 87
rdist (remote file distribution) program, 57, 561

read command, 205, 266, 270–271
README.agx file, 329
README.ati file, 327
README.cirrus file, 327
README.Oak file, 329
README.P9000 file, 329
README.S3 file, 329
README.trident file, 327
README.Video7 file, 328
README.W32 file, 329
README.WstDig file, 328
real mode, 292
RealTek parallel-port Ethernet adapter, 19
reboot command, 87
rectangles, 729–731
Refresh function, 171
regexp command, 266
regsub command, 266
regular expressions, 216, 218-219
relative directory name, 198
remote access, 559
remote display, 145
remote networks connecting as PPP client, 539-548
remote printer setup, 428, 429, 430
removable media, 373
rename command, 266
renaming system, 72
repartitioning hard disks, 22
repeat delay, 391, 393–394
repeat rate, 391, 393–394
repetition (x=) operator, 215
repetitive actions, 185
require function, 226
RESCUE.GZ file, 35
reserve command, 492–493
reset command, 533
Resize function, 171
resource database, 159
resource files, 158–159

resources
  class name, 159–161
  command-line X
    application options,
    163–164
  common, 162–163
  DMA (Direct Memory
    Access) channel, 300–
    301
  font specifications, 164–165
  I/O address (Input/Output
    Port address), 300–301
  instance name, 159–161
  IRQ (Interrupt Request)
    number, 300–301
  location, 162
  matching full and partial
    names, 161
  naming conventions,
    159–161
  partial names, 160–161
  precedence, 161
  viewing effect of, 162
restart command, 414
Restart function, 171
RESTORERB.EXE file, 30
return command, 254, 266
RFC (Request for Comment),
  474, 600
RGB triplet, 718
RGB (red, green, blue)
  value, 108
Rickert, Neil, 563
RIP (Routing Information
  Protocol), 480
rlog command, 99, 688
rm command, 194–195, 201
rmdir command, 201
rn (read news) program, 569
ROM/BIOS (Read-Only
  Memory/Basic Input/
  Output System), 337
/root directory, 196

root directory, 22, 195-196
root floppies, 10, 31-32,
  35–36
  loading small file system
    into memory, 37
root images, 35–36
root password, 70
root users
  assigning password, 38
  becoming, 233
  home directory, 196
  mount command, 233
  name, 10
  password, 10
  pound sign (#) default
    prompt, 37
root window, 152
  appearance, 154
  property, 162
ROOTDSKS directory, 32
route -n command, 551
route command, 538, 547,
  549–552
route del command, 549–550
routes, 549–550
routines, 211
routing, 479–480
routing table, 549
RS-232C standard
  cables, 442–446
  Clear to Send (CTS) control
    signal, 442
  connectors for modems,
    442–444
  flow control, 446
  handshaking, 442
  Request to Send (RTS)
    control signal, 442
run command, 678
run levels, 146–149

S

S3 Trio32/Trio64 integrated
  video chipset, 294
S3 video cards, 330–332
S3 video chipset, 113
Saggaf, Muhammed M., 455
Samba program
  components, 641
  configuring, 642–644
  installing, 641–642
  testing configuration
    file, 644
Sanyo CDR-H94A CD-ROM
  drives, 33
sastroid package, 62
saveLines resource, 176
/sbin directory, 196
/sbin/ifconfig command,
  502–503, 554
/sbin/lilo -u command, 344
/sbin/lilo program, 342
/sbin/liloconfig program,
  342–343
/sbin/route command,
  502, 504
sbpcd driver, 376–377
SBPCD file, 34
sbpcd1 packages, 59
sbpcd2 packages, 59
sc utility, 55, 798–804
scalar variables, 212–213
scale command, 276
scan command, 266
SCANDISK, 30
scanpci program, 330
scd driver, 375–376
Scheifler, Robert W., 111
Schneider and Koch G16
  Ethernet cards, 20
Schwartz, Randall, 211
SCO UNIX, 97
screen, 155–157

screen font, 64–65
scripts, 96, 208
   expect-send pattern of text, 540–541
   Tcl, 252–272
Scroll function, 171
scrollbar command, 276
SCSI (Small Computer System Interface)
   CD-ROM drives, 18, 34, 364–365
   device detected but not accessible, 359
   devices not found, 360
   disk controllers, 14, 16–17, 33–34, 335–336, 349–357
   hard disks, 33–34, 38, 357
   lockup, 360
   networking kernel problems with device, 359
   SCSI device at all LUNs (Logical Unit Numbers), 358–359
   SCSI device at all SCSI IDs, 358
   sense errors on error-free device, 359
   troubleshooting, 357–360
SCSI file, 34
scsi package, 53, 59
SCSI-HOWTO file, 74
SCSI-Programming-HOWTO file, 74
SCSINET1 boot image, 36, 59
SCSINET2 boot image, 34, 36
Scsinet1 package, 59
scsinet2 package, 59
Seagate ST-01 SCSI controllers for ISA bus, 17
Seagate ST-02 SCSI controllers for ISA bus, 17

Seagate ST0x disk controller, 354
second extended file system, 345
second floppy disk drive, 38
Second Virtual Terminal (Alt-F2) key combination, 189
Secret icon, 3
sectors, 337, 346–347
secure anonymous FTP, 585–589
securid command, 533
securidf command, 533
sed (stream editor), 96, 216
sed command, 203
seek command, 266
selection command, 277
send command, 277
send text command, 533
sendmail (complex mail-transport agent) program, 57, 561, 563
   configuration file, 564–565
   mail-delivery mechanism, 567–568
   mail-delivery test, 565-566
   SMTP (Simple Mail Transfer Protocol), 567–568
serial boards, 438
serial mouse, 16
   device name, 116
   gpm (General Purpose Mouse) package, 68
serial ports
   communications parameters, 439–440
   device names, 441
   I/O addresses, 440
   IRQs (Interrupt Requests), 440
   terminals, 464

UART (Universal Asynchronous Receiver/ Transmitter), 438
Serial-HOWTO file, 74
server, 100
services, 483–485
session file, 152
set command, 255, 258, 266, 269
setleds program, 398–399
setserial command, 65
setserial program, 459
setup command, 37, 44, 76
setup program, 10, 561
   accessing DOS partitions, 48
   adding swap space, 46
   ADDSWAP option, 45–46
   configuration process, 10
   CONFIGURE option, 45
   configuring system components, 63–68
   DISK SETS option, 45
   EXIT option, 46
   exiting, 46
   formatting partition, 46–47
   INSTALL option, 45, 52
   installing new packages, 89
   Linux distribution location, 45
   Master Boot Record (MBR), 67
   mounting DOS partitions, 231
   selecting disk sets, 50–52
   selecting source, 48–49
   selecting target, 46–48
   Series Selection menu, 50
   SOURCE option, 45
   tagfiles, 52
   TARGET option, 45
   UMSDOS installation, 76
   where to install Linux, 44–48

S

seyon program, 61, 455–456, 524
sh program, 182
shadow mask, 317
shared libraries
  creation, 691–693
  dynamically loading, 694–695
  examining, 691
shell, 96, 181
  developing applications for, 96
SHELL environment variable, 187
shell programs, 96, 184–186
shell prompt, 187
shell scripts, 181–182, 203, 205–206
  command-line options, 203
  running Bash shell, 204
  testing for conditions, 203
shell widgets, 705, 707
shift function, 221
shlbsvga package, 55
showkey command, 395
shutdown command, 75, 196
shutting down Linux, 75
Sigma LaserView PLUS monochrome video cards, 13
simple file, 204
simplified four-layer network model, 471–472
sin function, 258
SITE.EXEC command, 588
skey command, 533
Slackware CD-ROM, 9
  installing Linux from, 44–62
  XFree86 3.1.1, 97
sleep command, 533
SLIP (Serial Line Internet Protocol), 20, 100, 469, 524–526
  checking connection, 537–538

ending connection, 538
establishing connection, 529–537
making connections, 527–538
obtaining remote-system information, 528–529
shortcomings, 525
SLIP-END character, 525
SLIP-ESC character, 525
verifying support, 528
smailcfg (sendmail configuration files) program, 57, 561
smbclient program
  commands, 646, 647
  printcap entry, 648
  script for printing, 648, 649
SMC (Western Digital) WD8003, WD8013, SMC Elite, SMC Elite Plus, and SMC Elite 16 Ultra Ethernet cards, 20
SMTP (Simple Mail Transfer Protocol), 483, 559, 563
  sendmail program, 567–568
snake game, 197
soft command, 203
software, 45
software development, 103–104
  GNU GPL (General Public License), 680–681
  GNU LGPL (Library General Public License), 681–682
  Linux programming topics, 689–695
  RCS (Revision Control System) source-control tools, 683–684
  tools, 656–680
  version control, 682–689
SONET (Synchronous Optical Network), 526

Sony CDU31a or CDU33a CD-ROM drives, 18, 33
Sony CDU535 or CDU531 CD-ROM drives, 18, 33
sonycd35 driver, 377
sound and laptops, 302–303
Sound Blaster 16 daughterboards, 19
Sound Blaster 16 SCSI controller for ISA, 17
Sound Blaster 16 SCSI disk controllers, 351
Sound Blaster 16 sound cards, 18–19
Sound Blaster AWE32 sound cards, 388
Sound Blaster Pro, 18
Sound Blaster Pro CD CD-ROM drive, 18, 34
Sound Blaster Pro sound cards, 19
Sound Blaster sound cards, 19
sound cards, 18–19, 379
  Adaptec 1542 SCSI adapter, 388
  checking for sound driver, 386
  configuring sound driver, 381–383
  connecting CD-ROM drives, 18
  detected by sound driver, 386–387
  installing sound driver, 380–381
  Logitech SoundMan 16, 19
  MIDI (Musical Instrument Digital Interface), 379
  no sound from, 386
  play sound but not record, 387
  playing sound file, 385
  Pro Audio Spectrum, 355

(continued)

sound cards *(continued)*
  Pro Audio Spectrum 16, 19, 388
  Pro Sonic 16 Jazz, 19
  Sound Blaster 16, 18–19
  Sound Blaster AWE32, 388
  sound device names, 383–384
  sound-driver status, 384–385
  supported, 379–380
  testing, 384–385
  troubleshooting, 386–387
  work under DOS not Linux, 387
sound device names, 383–384
sound driver
  checking for, 386
  configuring, 381–383
    detecting sound card, 386–387
    installing, 380–381
    status, 384–385
Sound Galaxy NX Pro sound cards, 19
Sound-HOWTO file, 74
SoundMan Games sound cards, 19
SoundMan Wave sound cards, 19
source command, 266
SOURCE option, 45
source tree, 516
spacing, 439
special characters, 394
specific Linux business tasks, 635–636
speed command, 533
split command, 266–267, 271
spool area, 413
spool directory, 408, 417–418
spooling, 408, 412–413
  print jobs, 416–417
  symbolic-link, 413–414

sqrt function, 258
SRAM (static random-access memory), 510
srm.conf file, 616, 619–622
srm.conf-dist file, 616
ST506 disk controllers, 336
stable versions, 93–94
standard input, 183, 270
standard output, 183
Stanford Research Institute (SRI), 481
START bit, 439
start command, 415
starting Linux for first time
  adding users, 71
  changing password, 69–70
  LILO (Linux Loader), 69
  on-line documentation, 72–75
  renaming system, 72
startup, customizing, 143–154
startx command, 136, 143–144, 322, 606
startx script file, 136–137
statements, 211–222
status command, 414
status file, 418
STDERR file handle, 224
stderr keyword, 270
STDIN file handle, 224
stdin keyword, 270
STDOUT file handle, 224
stdout keyword, 270
Stevens, W. Richard, 473
Stick function, 171
sticky windows, 166–167
stopbits command, 533
strace package, 56
straight-through cables, 444
string command, 266–267
string compare command, 268
string first command, 268

string index command, 268
string last command, 268
string length command, 268
string length hello command, 257
string match command, 268
string range command, 268
string tolower command, 268
string toupper command, 268
string trim command, 268
string trimleft command, 268
string trimright command, 268
strings
  associating names with, 144
  comparing, 215, 268
  comparing with set of patterns, 262–263
  concatenating, 215
  from list items, 267
  manipulation, 267–268
  matching, 215
  repeating, 215
  searching file for pattern of, 216
  separating into components, 267
style guide, 110
su command, 233, 241
sub-expect sequences, 541
subdirectories, 22, 195
subnets, 479
subroutines, 211, 225–226
sudo package, 54
super user, 38
  logging in as, 69
Super VGA (Video Graphics Array) video cards, 13
supported hardware, 11–20
SUPPORTED.CARDS file, 517–518
svgalib package, 56

swap partition, 10, 37, 41–42
    adding to /etc/fstab file, 46
    number limitation, 44
    setting up, 43–44
    size of, 44
swap space, 22, 338
    adding, 46
    creating, 344–345
swapon command, 44, 46
switch command, 262–263, 266
symbolic-link spooling, 413–414
synthetic events, 174
SYS.COM file, 245
system
    administration, 101–102
    renaming, 72
    routing to remote gateway, 550–551
    user logging into, 145–146
system administrator, 101
system calls, 96
system components
    configuring, 63–68
    reconfiguring Linux for, 11
system configuration
    files, 196
    information, 235–236
system definition files, 196
system directories, 196–197
system function, 96, 222–223
System V Interface Document (SVID), 94
System V Release 4 for Intel processors, 97
system.fvwmrc file, 168

T

Tadpole P1000, 308
tagfiles, 52
tan function, 258
tape installation, 35
TAPE.GZ file, 35
tar command, 102, 196, 241, 606, 614
TARGET option, 45
Taylor, Dave, 628
Tcl (Tool Command Language), 52, 60, 104
    arrays, 268–269
    backslash substitution, 255–256
    basic syntax, 254–259
    braces ({...}), 257
    built-in commands, 264–266
    command string interpretation, 253
    command substitutions, 256
    commands, 254
    comments, 256–257
    control-flow commands, 254, 259–263
    double quotation marks ("..."), 257
    environment variables, 269
    executing UNIX commands, 271–272
    expressions, 254, 258–259
    file operations, 269–271
    grouping words, 257
    Internet resources, 253
    interpreter processing command strings, 254–255
    library files, 197
    overview, 253–266
    PATH environment variable, 252
    procedures, 254, 263–264
    prompt (%), 252
    scripts, 255
    string manipulation, 267–268
    substitutions, 255–256
    syntax, 253–254
    tclsh shell, 252
    variable substitution, 255
    variables, 254, 258
Tcl/Tk, 104, 251–287
tclsh shell, 252
TCP/IP (Transmission Control Protocol/Internet Protocol), 99, 469, 524
    Berkeley Sockets, 99
    configuration files, 499–502
    configuring kernel, 495–497
    connectivity to host, 505
    diagnostics, 503–506
    DNS (Domain Name System), 481–483
    interfaces, 503–504
    Internet and, 473–479
    IP addresses, 475–479
    network status, 505–506
    networking, 33-34
    PPP (Point-to-Point Protocol), 100
    RCFs (Request for Comments), 474
    routing, 479–480
    routing table, 504
    running netconfig, 497–499
    services, 483–485
    setup, 495–502
    SLIP (Serial Line Internet Protocol), 100
    testing network, 499
tcpip (TCP/IP utilities) program, 57, 561
tcsh package, 53
TEAC CD-55a CD-ROM drives, 34
Tektronix 4014 terminal emulation, 173, 179
Tektronix terminal emulation, 177
tell command, 266
telnet command, 567
telnet program, 99, 559, 597–599
term command, 533–535
TERM environment variable, 144, 178, 186–187, 761

Term-HOWTO file, 74
termbin package, 54
terminals, 173, 437, 464
   serial ports, 464
   type of, 187
   virtual, 189
terminator, 350–351
terminfor file, 178
termnet package, 54
termsrc package, 54
test command, 206
test program, 203
testparm program, 644
tetris package, 62
TeX document–formatting system, 51
TeX program, 411
Texas Instruments TravelMate 4000M, 309– 310
texinfo package, 55
text, 731–733
   editing, 756–779
   fonts, 731–733
text command, 276
text files, 270
text processing, 755, 786
text screens screen font, 64–65
text-based install script, 35
text-mode display, 68
TEXT.GZ file, 35
tftp (Trivial File Transfer Protocol), 483
tgz file extension, 513
The system is going down NOW! message, 75
thick Ethernet, 487
thickwire, 487
thinwire, 487
Third Virtual Terminal (Alt-F3) key combination, 189
threading, 569
thumb, 176

ThunderBoard (Sound Blaster-compatible) sound cards, 19
tiling, 156
time zone, 68
timeout command, 533, 541
tin (news reader) program, 58, 561, 570–572
tin -r command, 570–572
Tip icon, 3
Tips-HOWTO file, 74
Title function, 171
Tittel, Ed, 628
Tk (X Toolkit), 60
   geometry manager, 279
   online help, 276
   script creation, 274–275
   widget basics, 275–283
   widgets, 272
   wish (windowing shell), 272–275
   X Window System, 272
tk command, 277
Tk pathname, 278
Tk scripts
   binding actions to events, 283–287
   tool help, 284–285
tkerror command, 277
tkwait command, 277
/tmp directory, 196
TogglePage function, 172
toggles, 174
token ring, 99
tool help, 284–285
toolhelp script, 285
toolkit, 110
top utility, 102
topcx command, 189
topcx file, 184–185
toplevel command, 276
topq command, 415
Torvalds, Linus, 1, 8
Toshiba Satellite 2500CDT, 312
tr command, 185

tr program, 96
trace command, 266
trackballs, 406
trackpoint, 309
TransferLog file, 618
transmission medium, 470
transmission technique, 470
transport-layer protocols, 472
Trantor T128, T128F, and T228 disk controllers, 17, 34, 355
Trident-based video cards with TVGA8800, TVGA8900, and TVGA9000 chipset, 14
trn (threaded read news) program, 58, 562, 569, 570
trn-nntp (remote news server news reader) program, 562
trn-nntp (threaded read news) program, 58, 572–573, 577
   commands, 574–576
   posting news, 579–582
troff (typesetting runoff) program, 780
Tseng-based video cards with ET3000, ET4000, W32, W32i, and W32p chipsets, 14
TXT file extension, 22
Typematic Rate, 393

U

UART (Universal Asynchronous Receiver/Transmitter), 438
Ultrasound 16-bit sampling daughterboard sound cards, 19

U

Ultrasound MAX sound cards, 19
Ultrastor 14f, 24f, and 34f disk controllers, 17, 355, 356
Ultrastor SCSI controllers, 34
umount command, 196, 235, 339, 357, 373–374, 561, 641
UMSDOS file system, 76
UMSDOS-HOWTO file, 74
UMSDOS.GZ file, 35
uname -a command, 367
uname command, 386
undef function, 212
Undo (Ctrl-Z) key combination, 189
UNIX
  Berkeley Software Distribution (BSD) version, 94
  Bourne shell, 96
  commands, 271–272
  file sharing, 100
  games, 52
  networking, 99
  newline character, 430
  POSIX.1 (Portable Operating System Interface) standard, 94, 96
  POSIX.2 (Portable Operating System Interface) standard, 96
  shell, 96
  software developer, 652
  standard UNIX commands in Linux, 96
  system calls, 96
  System V Interface Document (SVID), 94
  TCP/IP (Transmission Control Protocol/Internet Protocol), 99
  tools-oriented view, 96
  X Windows and, 96
unknown command, 266
unless statement, 220
Unmap event, 287
unset command, 266
up command, 415
update command, 277
upgrading Linux, 77
  backing up important files before, 88
  earlier version of Slackware Linux, 87–89
  kernel patches, 78–87
  system hangs, 87
uplevel command, 266
UPS-HOWTO file, 74
upvar command, 266
URLs (Uniform Resource Locators), 474, 596–597
USENET, 69, 101, 568
users
  adding, 71
  exiting X Windows System, 146
  home directories, 196–197
  logging into system, 145, 146
USL (UNIX System Laboratories), 690
/usr directory, 196–197
/usr/bin directory, 236, 273
/usr/bin subdirectory, 197
/usr/doc subdirectory, 197
/usr/etc/ppp-login script, 553
/usr/games subdirectory, 197
/usr/include subdirectory, 197
/usr/include/X11/cursorfont.h file, 158
/usr/include/X11/keysymdef.h file, 152
/usr/info/dir file, 656
/usr/lib subdirectory, 197
/usr/lib/X11/app-defaults/AppClass file, 162
/usr/lib/X11/bitmaps directory, 156
/usr/lib/X11/fvwm/system.fvwm.rc file, 168
/usr/lib/X11/fvwm/system.fvwmrc file, 169
/usr/lib/X11/GiveConsole script, 146
/usr/lib/X11/rgb.txt file, 154–155
/usr/lib/X11/xdm/TakeConsole script, 146
/usr/lib/X11/xinitrc script, 146
/usr/lib/Xll/Xservers file, 145
/usr/local subdirectory, 197
/usr/man subdirectory, 197
/usr/openwin subdirectory, 197
/usr/sbin subdirectory, 197
/usr/spool/lpl/smbprint.log file, 648
/usr/spool/lpl/smbprint.tcl script, 648–649
/usr/src directory, 81, 197
/usr/src/linux directory, 82
/usr/X11/bin directory, 165
/usr/X11R6 subdirectory, 197
/usr/X11R6/lib/X11 directory, 115
/usr/X11R6/lib/X11/doc directory, 115
/usr/X11R6/X11/doc/README.Config file, 115
usr/lib/libdosemu file, 245
USRobotics modems, 452–453
utilities, 197
  DOSEMU, 792
  GNU bc, 7920–94
  gzip, 794–95
  ispell, 795–796
  Midnight Commander, 796
  patch, 797–798
  sc, 798–804

(continued)

utilities *(continued)*
  workbone, 804
  Workman, 804
  xcmap, 804–805
  xfilemanager, 805–810
  xfm, 810–815
  xspread, 815–819
uucp (UNIX-to-UNIX Copy protocol) program, 57, 101, 561
UUCP-HOWTO file, 74
uugetty program, 459
  displaying single @ character at login prompt, 461
  preparing configuration file, 461–463
  starting, 463
  testing dial-in setup, 463
  updating configuration file, 460–461

V

values function, 214
Van Jacobson compression, 526
van Smoorenburg, Miquel, 455
/var directory, 196
/var/lib/dosemu/hdimage file, 244
variables, 204–205, 211–214, 254
  array, 212–214
  associative arrays, 212, 214
  defining, 205, 255
  evaluating, 213
  incrementing, 260
  list of, 261
  predefined, 214
  reading input into, 205
  referring to value of, 258
  scalar, 212–213

subroutines, 226
substitution, 255
Tcl (Tool Command Language), 258
version control, 682–683
  RCS (Revision Control System), 683–689
versions, 93–94
vertical refresh rate, 113, 326
vertical retrace, 316
vertical synchronization rates, 113
VESA (Video Electronics Standard Association) Local Bus, 293
VFS: Insert ramdisk floppy and press enter message, 37
VGA (Video Graphics Array) video cards, 19, 319
vi editor, 35, 96, 193, 656, 756, 761
  colon command mode, 763
  commands, 765–768
  concepts, 763–764
  editing xinitrc script file, 136
  file information, 763
  full-screen window, 763
  jumping to line, 762, 765
  moving cursor, 764
  regular expressions, 216
  sample file editing, 764–765
  searching for string, 765
  setting terminal type, 761
  starting, 762–764
  symbolic link with elvis editor, 762
  TERM environment variable, 186
  text input mode, 764
  visual command mode, 763
Video 7 video cards, 13

video cards, 13–14, 108, 112, 315–318
  accelerated listing, 328–329
  amount of video RAM, 113
  ATI Graphics Pro Turbo, 294
  ATI Graphics Ultra, 330
  ATI Graphics Ultra Pro, 330
  ATI Graphics Xpression, 113
  ATI Mach8, 13, 330
  ATI Mach32, 13, 330
  ATI Mach64, 13, 113, 330
  ATI VGA Wonder series, 13
  characteristics, 320
  Chips & Technologies chipsets, 333
  color palette, 317
  Compaq AVGA, 13
  Compaq QVision 2000, 333
  Device section XF86Config file, 135
  Diamond SpeedStar series, 111
  Diamond Stealth 64 VRAM, 113
  Diamond Viper PCI, 13, 294, 329–330
  Diamond Viper VLB for VESA Local Bus, 13, 329–330
  dot clock, 317–318
  Enhanced Graphics Adapter (EGA), 13
  Genoa GVGA, 13
  Headland Technologies HT216-32, 13
  Hercules monochrome, 13
  Hyundai HGC-1280 monochrome, 13
  IBM 8514/A, 13
  IBM XGA, 13
  IBM XGA-II, 13
  importance to XFree86, 318

information about, 322–323
listing, 327
Matrox MGA Millenium, 333
Number Nine GXE Pro PCI, 294
Number Nine GXE64, 113
Number Nine Imagine 128, 333
Orchid P9000, 13, 329–330
S3, 113, 330–332
settings, 321–322
Sigma LaserView PLUS monochrome, 13
Super VGA (Video Graphics Array), 13
type, 322
VGA (Video Graphics Array), 319
Video 7, 13
video chipset, 13, 113
Video Graphics Array (VGA), 14
video modes, 108
VRAM (video RAM), 315, 317
Weitek P9100 chipsets, 333
Western Digital Paradise PVGA1, 14
X server selection, 319, 320
XFree86, 13–14, 113
XFree86 support, 111
video chipsets, 13, 307
Video Local Bus (VLB) bus, 12
video memory, 108, 718
video modes, 108
video monitor, 108
Vim editor, 791
vim package, 55
virtual, 166
virtual desktop, 166, 168
virtual memory, 13, 22, 43–44

virtual terminals, 189–190
virtual-86 mode, 241
visuals, 740
  colormap, 743–748
  listing available, 741–742
vmlinuz file, 63
VoxWare 3.0 sound drivers, 310
VRAM (video RAM), 315, 317
VT102 terminal emulation, 173, 175–178

W

Wait function, 172
wait text command, 533
Wall, Larry, 208–209, 211
Warm Boot (Alt+Ctrl+Delete) key combination, 24–25, 30, 36, 69
Warp function, 172
WaveBlaster sound cards, 19
Wearnes CD–ROM drives, 33
Web browsers, 593–594
  downloading, 601–606
  Java-enabled, 627
  NCSA Mosaic for the X Window System, 601, 604–608
  Netscape Navigator, 601–610
Web pages, 593
  links, 595–596
  Linux resources, 839
Web server, 594
Weitek P9000–based video cards, 14
Weitek P9100 chipset, 333
Welch, Brent B., 253
Welcome to the Slackware Linux 3.0.0 bootkernal disk! message, 36
Western Digital 7000 disk controllers, 356

Western Digital Paradise PVGA1 video card, 14
Western Digital WD7000 SCSI controllers, 17
Western Digital WD90C24 chipsets, 307
Western Digital-based video cards with WD90C31 and WD90C33 chipsets, 14
where command, 678
which command, 208–209
while command, 254, 259–261, 266
while control structure, 205
while statement, 220–222
white space, 255
widgets, 159–160, 272, 698
  basics, 275–283
  callback registration, 703–704
  configuring, 278–279
  constraint resources, 711
  Core, 706–707
  creation, 275–276
  displaying, 279–283
  file filter, 711
  frame, 282
  hiding, 279
  manager, 706, 710–711
  manipulating, 276–277
  naming, 277–278
  positioning, 276, 279
  primitive, 706–710
  resources, 701–703
  shell, 705–707
wildcards, 190–192
window events, 287
window manager, 98, 110, 165
window system, 110
window-state notification event, 722
window-structure control event, 722

WindowList function, 172
windows, 717
  click-to-type input focus, 169
  current, 168
  focus follows pointer (pointer focus), 168–169
  frames, 165
  input focus, 168–169
  listener, 169
  redrawing contents, 175
Windows 3.1, 7
Windows 95
  Add/Remove Programs option, 23
  boot and root directories, 32
  FDISK command, 25
  LILO (Linux Loader) and, 346
  partitioning hard disk, 23
  startup disk, 23
Windows NT, 8
WindowsDesk function, 172
WINE, 103
winfo command, 277
wish (windowing shell)
  -f option, 274
  displaying graphical user interfaces (GUIs), 273–275
  starting, 273
Wizard icon, 3
wm command, 277
word length, 439
workbone program, 55, 373–374, 804
workgroup, 636
workgroup server, 636–637
Workman utility, 374, 804
workstations, 7

Write Partition Table (w) command, 40, 42–44
WRITING file, 74
Writing image to drive A message, 34
WWW (World Wide Web)
  defining, 594–597
  HTML (Hypertext Markup Language), 594
  HTTP (Hypertext Transfer Protocol), 594–600
  links, 595–596
  URLs (Uniform Resource Locators), 596–597
  Web browsers, 601–610
WWW (World Wide Web) server, 636, 638
  CERN server, 611
  hardware configuration, 639–640
  home page, 609
  NCSA server, 611–614
  private LAN (local area network), 639
  providing Web service, 640
  setting up, 611–627
Wyse V/386 UNIX, 97

X

X applications, 52, 163–164
X clients, 107–109
X Consortium, Inc., 111
X Display Manager, 145–146, 148–150
X event summary, 719–722
X programming, 697
  color, 740–748
  colormap, 743–748
  Motif, 698–752
  visuals, 740–748
  X event summary, 719–722
X protocol, 107

X resource manager, 159, 161
X server, 12, 107–109, 333, 721–722
  listing, 319
  resources, 716–719
  running on client's computer, 109
  selection, 319–320
  video modes, 320
  XFree86, 110–111
X toolkit and widgets, 159–160
X Window System, 7, 287
  automatically running applications, 150–151
  automatically starting, 143–144
  customizing, 154–165
  display name, 187
  exiting, 146
  First Virtual Terminal (Ctrl–Alt–F1) key combination, 189
  Fresco toolkit, 111
  graphical user interfaces (GUIs), 97–98, 109–110, 153
  history, 111
  keyboard mapping, 394
  keyboards, 393
  library files, 197
  Linux, 110–141
  listing commands for starting applications, 146
  loading resources, 151
  OPEN LOOK, 97
  OSF/Motif, 97
  repeat delay, 394
  repeat rate, 394
  resources, 158–163
  root window, 152

X

running applications across network, 98
Second Virtual Terminal (Ctrl-Alt-F2) key combination, 189
seyon program, 455
UNIX platform and, 96
window manager, 110
X clients, 107–109
X Consortium, Inc., 111
X protocol, 107
X resource manager, 159
X server, 12, 107–109
X11R6, 97
xf86config server, 10
Xlib, 107, 272
<X11/Intrinsic.h> header file, 701
x3128514 package, 60
x312agx package, 60
x312ctrb package, 60
x312doc package, 61
x312f75 package, 61
x312fscl package, 61
x312inc package, 61
x312ma32 package, 60
x312ma64 package, 61
x312ma8 package, 60
x312mono package, 60
x312nam package, 61
x312p9k package, 60
x312s3 package, 60
x312svga package, 60
x312ubin package, 61
x312vga package, 61
x312w32 package, 61
x312xtra package, 61
x3270 package, 62
XAllocColor function, 745
XAllocColorCells function, 746, 747
XAllocNamedColor function, 746

XChangeGC function, 717, 733
XClearArea function, 750
XClearWindow function, 733
xcmap utility, 804–805
XColor structure, 744–745
xconsole program, 145
XCopyArea function, 749–751
XCopyGC function, 733
XCopyPlane function, 751
XCreateFontCursor function, 718, 723
XCreateGC function, 717, 724–725, 733–734
XCreateGlyphCursor function, 724
XCreatePixmap function, 749
XCreatePixmapCursor function, 724
XCreateSimpleWindow function, 712
XCreateWindow function, 712
XDefineCursor function, 718
xdm command, 146, 190
xdm program
  automatically starting, 149
  display name of login window, 145
  managing login session, 145–146
  .xsession file, 150–151
xdm-config file, 145
xdpyinfo program, 741–742
XDrawArc function, 730–731
XDrawArcs function, 730
XDrawImageString function, 732
XDrawLine function, 728
XDrawLines function, 728–730
XDrawPoints function, 728, 730

XDrawRectangle function, 729
XDrawRectangles function, 729
XDrawSegments function, 728–729
XDrawString function, 717–718, 732
XDrawText function, 732–733
Xenix 286, 97
Xenix V/386, 97
xev utility, 152
xf85config utility, 323
xf86config command, 115
XF86Config file, 112, 114, 324–326
  checking, 132–135
  Device section, 133–134, 320, 322–323
  different screen modes, 138–139
  DontZap option, 132–133
  DontZoom option, 132–133
  Driver entries, 135
  Files section, 132–133
  generating, 125–132
  graphics device, 133
  HorizSync entry, 134
  Indentifier entry, 134
  keyboard information, 396–397
  Keyboard section, 132
  ModeLine entries, 134
  Monitor section, 133–134, 320
  NoTrapSignals option, 133
  pathnames, 132
  pointer, 133
  Pointer section, 133
  RGB file, 132–133
  Screen section, 133, 135, 138–139, 320–325
  ServerFlags section, 132–134
  VertRefresh entry, 134

xf86config utility, 10, 112, 320
   /usr/X11R6/bin
      directory, 115
   Clockchipsetting, 123
   generating XF86Config file,
      124–132
   horizontal synchronization
      frequency, 117
   identifier for monitor
      definition, 118
   link X, 122
   Meta and ModeShift keys,
      116
   Modeline computation,
      325–326
   modes, 123–124
   monitor parameters,
      116–118
   monitor types, 117
   mouse device name, 116
   mouse protocol, 115
   PATH environment
      variable, 115
   probeonly mode for Clocks
      line, 123
   two–button mouse, 116
   vertical synchronization
      rate, 117
   video card identifier, 123
   video memory for video
      card, 122–123
   video–card settings, 118–
      121
   X server selection, 121–122
xfig program, 826–827
xfileman package, 62
xfilemanager utility, 805–810
XFillPolygon function, 730
XFillRectangle function, 730,
   750
XFillRectangles function, 730
xfm File Manager, 62, 153–
   154, 197, 810–815
xfm.install command, 153
xfract package, 62
Xfractint program, 824–825
XFree86, 12, 52, 96, 98, 107,
   110–111
   aborting, 138
   commercial X servers, 333
   configuring, 114–135
   device busy error, 405
   device not found error, 405
   directory for files, 197
   hardware, 112–114
   importance of video card
      and monitor, 318
   keyboards, 396–398
   keysyms, 398
   laptops, 303–307
   monitors, 112–113
   mouse, 402–405
   mouse–click events, 114
   PCI video cards, 294
   quitting, 139
   running, 136–137
   S3-based video cards
      supported, 331–332
   setting up, 112–135
   startx command, 136
   video cards, 13–14, 111,
      113
   X server, 110–111, 319
XFree86 3.1.1, 97
XFree86-HOWTO file, 74
XFreeColors function, 748
XFreeCursor function, 723
XFreeGC function, 725
XFreePixmap function, 750
xgames package, 62
.xinitrc file, 150
xinitrc script file, 136–137
XIP (Execute In Place), 512
Xlib library, 107, 272
   arcs, rectangles, and
      ellipses, 730–731
   colormaps, 718–719
   common features, 714–716
   cursor size and shape,
      722–724
   cursors, 718
   displaying images, 748–752
   drawing and filling
      rectangles, 729–730
   drawing graphics and text,
      727
   drawing lines, 728
   fonts, 718
   function argument order,
      716
   function overview, 713–714
   functions, 697
   graphics and text, 724–733
   graphics contexts (GC),
      717, 724–727
   header files, 715
   lines, 729
   Motif and, 712–752
   naming conventions,
      715–716
   overview, 712–713
   pixmaps, 719
   points, 727–728
   polygons, 730
   programming topics,
      722–733
   windows, 717
   X server resources,
      716–719
XLoadFont function, 724,
   731–732
XmCreatePopupMenu
   function, 707
XmDrawingArea widget, 704
XmManager class, 710
XmNActivateCallback
   resource, 704
XmNarmCallback resource,
   704

X–Z

XmNdisarmCallback resource, 704
Xmodemap configuration file, 151
xmodmap program, 151, 394, 398
xmodtest file, 398
XmPrimitive class, 707, 709–710
XmStringCreateLtoR utility, 702
XPaint program, 62, 98, 822–824
XParseColor function, 745–746
xprop utility, 162
xrdb program, 151, 162
XReadBitmapFile function, 751
XRecolorCursor function, 723–724
XRectangle function, 730
xsession file, 146, 150–151
  xv program, 156–157
  xsetroot commands, 154
XSetBackground function, 712
XSetFillRule function, 730
XSetForeground function, 712
xsetroot program, 137, 152, 154–156, 158
Xsetup_0 script, 145
xspread utility, 62, 815–819
XStoreColor function, 747
XStoreNamed Color, 748
Xt Intrinsics toolkit, 272, 698
xt package, 60
XtAddCallback function, 699, 704
XtAddEventHandler function, 705
XtAppInitialize function, 699, 707

XtAppMainLoop function, 699
XtCreateManagedWidget function, 702–703
XtDestroyWidget function, 706
XtDisplay function, 733
xterm program, 137, 152, 160, 176–177, 179
  accepting and interpreting synthetic events, 174
  basics, 173–174
  customizing, 173–179
  cutting and pasting, 405
  escape sequences, 178
  keystrokes delivered only to, 174
  Main Options menu, 174–175
  password, 174
  quitting, 175
  redrawing window contents, 175
  starting, 175
  switching to Tektronix emulation mode, 177
  viewing effect of resources, 162
  VT Fonts menu, 178
  VT Options pop–up menu, 177
  VT102 emulation, 175–177
xterm windows
  minicom program, 457
  writing output to, 269–270
XtGetGC function, 734
XtGetValues function, 734
XtRealizeWidget function, 699
XtSetArg macro, 702

XtSetMappedWhenManaged function, 706
XtSetSensitive function, 706
XtVaCreateManagedWidget function, 699, 703
XtWindow function, 733
XUndefineCursor function, 723
XUnloadFont function, 732
XV program, 62, 98, 156–157, 197, 819–822
XView toolkit, 52, 98
XWD (X Window Dump)
  converting to PCX file format, 184–185
xwd screen-capture program, 184
xwdtopnm program, 184
xxgdb debugger, 62, 656, 673

Y

You can't run pkgtool from the rootdisk message, 88
You may now log in as root message, 37

Z

Z file extension, 603
Zenith Z–Note Ethernet cards, 20
zsh package, 54

DUMMIES PRESS™

The Fun & Easy Way™ to learn about computers and more!

Windows® 3.11 For Dummies,® 3rd Edition
by Andy Rathbone
ISBN: 1-56884-370-4
$16.95 USA/
$22.95 Canada

Mutual Funds For Dummies™
by Eric Tyson
ISBN: 1-56884-226-0
$16.99 USA/
$22.99 Canada

DOS For Dummies,® 2nd Edition
by Dan Gookin
ISBN: 1-878058-75-4
$16.95 USA/
$22.95 Canada

The Internet For Dummies,® 2nd Edition
by John Levine & Carol Baroudi
ISBN: 1-56884-222-8
$19.99 USA/
$26.99 Canada

Personal Finance For Dummies™
by Eric Tyson
ISBN: 1-56884-150-7
$16.95 USA/
$22.95 Canada

PCs For Dummies,® 3rd Edition
by Dan Gookin & Andy Rathbone
ISBN: 1-56884-904-4
$16.99 USA/
$22.99 Canada

Macs® For Dummies,® 3rd Edition
by David Pogue
ISBN: 1-56884-239-2
$19.99 USA/
$26.99 Canada

The SAT® I For Dummies™
by Suzee Vlk
ISBN: 1-56884-213-9
$14.99 USA/
$20.99 Canada

Here's a complete listing of IDG Books' ...For Dummies® titles

Title	Author	ISBN	Price
DATABASE			
Access 2 For Dummies®	by Scott Palmer	ISBN: 1-56884-090-X	$19.95 USA/$26.95 Canada
Access Programming For Dummies®	by Rob Krumm	ISBN: 1-56884-091-8	$19.95 USA/$26.95 Canada
Approach 3 For Windows® For Dummies®	by Doug Lowe	ISBN: 1-56884-233-3	$19.99 USA/$26.99 Canada
dBASE For DOS For Dummies®	by Scott Palmer & Michael Stabler	ISBN: 1-56884-188-4	$19.95 USA/$26.95 Canada
dBASE For Windows® For Dummies®	by Scott Palmer	ISBN: 1-56884-179-5	$19.95 USA/$26.95 Canada
dBASE 5 For Windows® Programming For Dummies®	by Ted Coombs & Jason Coombs	ISBN: 1-56884-215-5	$19.99 USA/$26.99 Canada
FoxPro 2.6 For Windows® For Dummies®	by John Kaufeld	ISBN: 1-56884-187-6	$19.95 USA/$26.95 Canada
Paradox 5 For Windows® For Dummies®	by John Kaufeld	ISBN: 1-56884-185-X	$19.95 USA/$26.95 Canada
DESKTOP PUBLISHING/ILLUSTRATION/GRAPHICS			
CorelDRAW! 5 For Dummies®	by Deke McClelland	ISBN: 1-56884-157-4	$19.95 USA/$26.95 Canada
CorelDRAW! For Dummies®	by Deke McClelland	ISBN: 1-56884-042-X	$19.95 USA/$26.95 Canada
Desktop Publishing & Design For Dummies®	by Roger C. Parker	ISBN: 1-56884-234-1	$19.99 USA/$26.99 Canada
Harvard Graphics 2 For Windows® For Dummies®	by Roger C. Parker	ISBN: 1-56884-092-6	$19.95 USA/$26.95 Canada
PageMaker 5 For Macs® For Dummies®	by Galen Gruman & Deke McClelland	ISBN: 1-56884-178-7	$19.95 USA/$26.95 Canada
PageMaker 5 For Windows® For Dummies®	by Deke McClelland & Galen Gruman	ISBN: 1-56884-160-4	$19.95 USA/$26.95 Canada
Photoshop 3 For Macs® For Dummies®	by Deke McClelland	ISBN: 1-56884-208-2	$19.99 USA/$26.99 Canada
QuarkXPress 3.3 For Dummies®	by Galen Gruman & Barbara Assadi	ISBN: 1-56884-217-1	$19.99 USA/$26.99 Canada
FINANCE/PERSONAL FINANCE/TEST TAKING REFERENCE			
Everyday Math For Dummies™	by Charles Seiter	ISBN: 1-56884-248-1	$14.99 USA/$22.99 Canada
Personal Finance For Dummies™ For Canadians	by Eric Tyson & Tony Martin	ISBN: 1-56884-378-X	$18.99 USA/$24.99 Canada
QuickBooks 3 For Dummies®	by Stephen L. Nelson	ISBN: 1-56884-227-9	$19.99 USA/$26.99 Canada
Quicken 8 For DOS For Dummies,® 2nd Edition	by Stephen L. Nelson	ISBN: 1-56884-210-4	$19.95 USA/$26.95 Canada
Quicken 5 For Macs® For Dummies®	by Stephen L. Nelson	ISBN: 1-56884-211-2	$19.95 USA/$26.95 Canada
Quicken 4 For Windows® For Dummies,® 2nd Edition	by Stephen L. Nelson	ISBN: 1-56884-209-0	$19.95 USA/$26.95 Canada
Taxes For Dummies,™ 1995 Edition	by Eric Tyson & David J. Silverman	ISBN: 1-56884-220-1	$14.99 USA/$20.99 Canada
The GMAT® For Dummies™	by Suzee Vlk, Series Editor	ISBN: 1-56884-376-3	$14.99 USA/$20.99 Canada
The GRE® For Dummies™	by Suzee Vlk, Series Editor	ISBN: 1-56884-375-5	$14.99 USA/$20.99 Canada
Time Management For Dummies™	by Jeffrey J. Mayer	ISBN: 1-56884-360-7	$16.99 USA/$22.99 Canada
TurboTax For Windows® For Dummies®	by Gail A. Helsel, CPA	ISBN: 1-56884-228-7	$19.99 USA/$26.99 Canada
GROUPWARE/INTEGRATED			
ClarisWorks For Macs® For Dummies®	by Frank Higgins	ISBN: 1-56884-363-1	$19.99 USA/$26.99 Canada
Lotus Notes For Dummies®	by Pat Freeland & Stephen Londergan	ISBN: 1-56884-212-0	$19.95 USA/$26.95 Canada
Microsoft® Office 4 For Windows® For Dummies®	by Roger C. Parker	ISBN: 1-56884-183-3	$19.95 USA/$26.95 Canada
Microsoft® Works 3 For Windows® For Dummies®	by David C. Kay	ISBN: 1-56884-214-7	$19.99 USA/$26.99 Canada
SmartSuite 3 For Dummies®	by Jan Weingarten & John Weingarten	ISBN: 1-56884-367-4	$19.99 USA/$26.99 Canada
INTERNET/COMMUNICATIONS/NETWORKING			
America Online® For Dummies,® 2nd Edition	by John Kaufeld	ISBN: 1-56884-933-8	$19.99 USA/$26.99 Canada
CompuServe For Dummies,® 2nd Edition	by Wallace Wang	ISBN: 1-56884-937-0	$19.99 USA/$26.99 Canada
Modems For Dummies,® 2nd Edition	by Tina Rathbone	ISBN: 1-56884-223-6	$19.99 USA/$26.99 Canada
MORE Internet For Dummies®	by John R. Levine & Margaret Levine Young	ISBN: 1-56884-164-7	$19.95 USA/$26.95 Canada
MORE Modems & On-line Services For Dummies®	by Tina Rathbone	ISBN: 1-56884-365-8	$19.99 USA/$26.99 Canada
Mosaic For Dummies,® Windows Edition	by David Angell & Brent Heslop	ISBN: 1-56884-242-2	$19.99 USA/$26.99 Canada
NetWare For Dummies,® 2nd Edition	by Ed Tittel, Deni Connor & Earl Follis	ISBN: 1-56884-369-0	$19.99 USA/$26.99 Canada
Networking For Dummies®	by Doug Lowe	ISBN: 1-56884-079-9	$19.95 USA/$26.95 Canada
PROCOMM PLUS 2 For Windows® For Dummies®	by Wallace Wang	ISBN: 1-56884-219-8	$19.99 USA/$26.99 Canada
TCP/IP For Dummies®	by Marshall Wilensky & Candace Leiden	ISBN: 1-56884-241-4	$19.99 USA/$26.99 Canada

Microsoft and Windows are registered trademarks of Microsoft Corporation. Mac is a registered trademark of Apple Computer. SAT is a registered trademark of the College Entrance Examination Board. GMAT is a registered trademark of the Graduate Management Admission Council. GRE is a registered trademark of the Educational Testing Service. America Online is a registered trademark of America Online, Inc. The "...For Dummies Book Series" logo, the IDG Books Worldwide logos, Dummies Press, and The Fun & Easy Way are trademarks, and ---- For Dummies and ... For Dummies are registered trademarks under exclusive license to IDG Books Worldwide, Inc., from International Data Group, Inc.

For scholastic requests & educational orders please call Educational Sales at 1. 800. 434. 2086

FOR MORE INFO OR TO ORDER, PLEASE CALL ▶ 800. 762. 2974

For volume discounts & special orders please call Tony Real, Special Sales, at 415. 655. 3048

DUMMIES PRESS™

The Internet For Macs® For Dummies® 2nd Edition	by Charles Seiter	ISBN: 1-56884-371-2	$19.99 USA/$26.99 Canada
The Internet For Macs® For Dummies® Starter Kit	by Charles Seiter	ISBN: 1-56884-244-9	$29.99 USA/$39.99 Canada
The Internet For Macs® For Dummies® Starter Kit Bestseller Edition	by Charles Seiter	ISBN: 1-56884-245-7	$39.99 USA/$54.99 Canada
The Internet For Windows® For Dummies® Starter Kit	by John R. Levine & Margaret Levine Young	ISBN: 1-56884-237-6	$34.99 USA/$44.99 Canada
The Internet For Windows® For Dummies® Starter Kit, Bestseller Edition	by John R. Levine & Margaret Levine Young	ISBN: 1-56884-246-5	$39.99 USA/$54.99 Canada

MACINTOSH

Mac® Programming For Dummies®	by Dan Parks Sydow	ISBN: 1-56884-173-6	$19.95 USA/$26.95 Canada
Macintosh® System 7.5 For Dummies®	by Bob LeVitus	ISBN: 1-56884-197-3	$19.95 USA/$26.95 Canada
MORE Macs® For Dummies®	by David Pogue	ISBN: 1-56884-087-X	$19.95 USA/$26.95 Canada
PageMaker 5 For Macs® For Dummies®	by Galen Gruman & Deke McClelland	ISBN: 1-56884-178-7	$19.95 USA/$26.95 Canada
QuarkXPress 3.3 For Dummies®	by Galen Gruman & Barbara Assadi	ISBN: 1-56884-217-1	$19.99 USA/$26.99 Canada
Upgrading and Fixing Macs® For Dummies®	by Kearney Rietmann & Frank Higgins	ISBN: 1-56884-189-2	$19.95 USA/$26.95 Canada

MULTIMEDIA

Multimedia & CD-ROMs For Dummies® 2nd Edition	by Andy Rathbone	ISBN: 1-56884-907-9	$19.99 USA/$26.99 Canada
Multimedia & CD-ROMs For Dummies® Interactive Multimedia Value Pack, 2nd Edition	by Andy Rathbone	ISBN: 1-56884-909-5	$29.99 USA/$39.99 Canada

OPERATING SYSTEMS:

DOS

MORE DOS For Dummies®	by Dan Gookin	ISBN: 1-56884-046-2	$19.95 USA/$26.95 Canada
OS/2® Warp For Dummies® 2nd Edition	by Andy Rathbone	ISBN: 1-56884-205-8	$19.99 USA/$26.99 Canada

UNIX

MORE UNIX® For Dummies®	by John R. Levine & Margaret Levine Young	ISBN: 1-56884-361-5	$19.99 USA/$26.99 Canada
UNIX® For Dummies®	by John R. Levine & Margaret Levine Young	ISBN: 1-878058-58-4	$19.95 USA/$26.95 Canada

WINDOWS

MORE Windows® For Dummies® 2nd Edition	by Andy Rathbone	ISBN: 1-56884-048-9	$19.95 USA/$26.95 Canada
Windows® 95 For Dummies®	by Andy Rathbone	ISBN: 1-56884-240-6	$19.99 USA/$26.99 Canada

PCS/HARDWARE

Illustrated Computer Dictionary For Dummies® 2nd Edition	by Dan Gookin & Wallace Wang	ISBN: 1-56884-218-X	$12.95 USA/$16.95 Canada
Upgrading and Fixing PCs For Dummies® 2nd Edition	by Andy Rathbone	ISBN: 1-56884-903-6	$19.99 USA/$26.99 Canada

PRESENTATION/AUTOCAD

AutoCAD For Dummies®	by Bud Smith	ISBN: 1-56884-191-4	$19.95 USA/$26.95 Canada
PowerPoint 4 For Windows® For Dummies®	by Doug Lowe	ISBN: 1-56884-161-2	$16.99 USA/$22.99 Canada

PROGRAMMING

Borland C++ For Dummies®	by Michael Hyman	ISBN: 1-56884-162-0	$19.95 USA/$26.95 Canada
C For Dummies® Volume 1	by Dan Gookin	ISBN: 1-878058-78-9	$19.95 USA/$26.95 Canada
C++ For Dummies®	by Stephen R. Davis	ISBN: 1-56884-163-9	$19.95 USA/$26.95 Canada
Delphi Programming For Dummies®	by Neil Rubenking	ISBN: 1-56884-200-7	$19.99 USA/$26.99 Canada
Mac® Programming For Dummies®	by Dan Parks Sydow	ISBN: 1-56884-173-6	$19.95 USA/$26.95 Canada
PowerBuilder 4 Programming For Dummies®	by Ted Coombs & Jason Coombs	ISBN: 1-56884-325-9	$19.99 USA/$26.99 Canada
QBasic Programming For Dummies®	by Douglas Hergert	ISBN: 1-56884-093-4	$19.95 USA/$26.95 Canada
Visual Basic 3 For Dummies®	by Wallace Wang	ISBN: 1-56884-076-4	$19.95 USA/$26.95 Canada
Visual Basic "X" For Dummies®	by Wallace Wang	ISBN: 1-56884-230-9	$19.99 USA/$26.99 Canada
Visual C++ 2 For Dummies®	by Michael Hyman & Bob Arnson	ISBN: 1-56884-328-3	$19.99 USA/$26.99 Canada
Windows® 95 Programming For Dummies®	by S. Randy Davis	ISBN: 1-56884-327-5	$19.99 USA/$26.99 Canada

SPREADSHEET

1-2-3 For Dummies®	by Greg Harvey	ISBN: 1-878058-60-6	$16.95 USA/$22.95 Canada
1-2-3 For Windows® 5 For Dummies® 2nd Edition	by John Walkenbach	ISBN: 1-56884-216-3	$16.95 USA/$22.95 Canada
Excel 5 For Macs® For Dummies®	by Greg Harvey	ISBN: 1-56884-186-8	$19.95 USA/$26.95 Canada
Excel For Dummies® 2nd Edition	by Greg Harvey	ISBN: 1-56884-050-0	$16.95 USA/$22.95 Canada
MORE 1-2-3 For DOS For Dummies®	by John Weingarten	ISBN: 1-56884-224-4	$19.99 USA/$26.99 Canada
MORE Excel 5 For Windows® For Dummies®	by Greg Harvey	ISBN: 1-56884-207-4	$19.95 USA/$26.95 Canada
Quattro Pro 6 For Windows® For Dummies®	by John Walkenbach	ISBN: 1-56884-174-4	$19.95 USA/$26.95 Canada
Quattro Pro For DOS For Dummies®	by John Walkenbach	ISBN: 1-56884-023-3	$16.95 USA/$22.95 Canada

UTILITIES

Norton Utilities 8 For Dummies®	by Beth Slick	ISBN: 1-56884-166-3	$19.95 USA/$26.95 Canada

VCRS/CAMCORDERS

VCRs & Camcorders For Dummies™	by Gordon McComb & Andy Rathbone	ISBN: 1-56884-229-5	$14.99 USA/$20.99 Canada

WORD PROCESSING

Ami Pro For Dummies®	by Jim Meade	ISBN: 1-56884-049-7	$19.95 USA/$26.95 Canada
MORE Word For Windows® 6 For Dummies®	by Doug Lowe	ISBN: 1-56884-165-5	$19.95 USA/$26.95 Canada
MORE WordPerfect® 6 For Windows® For Dummies®	by Margaret Levine Young & David C. Kay	ISBN: 1-56884-206-6	$19.95 USA/$26.95 Canada
MORE WordPerfect® 6 For DOS For Dummies®	by Wallace Wang, edited by Dan Gookin	ISBN: 1-56884-047-0	$19.95 USA/$26.95 Canada
Word 6 For Macs® For Dummies®	by Dan Gookin	ISBN: 1-56884-190-6	$19.95 USA/$26.95 Canada
Word For Windows® 6 For Dummies®	by Dan Gookin	ISBN: 1-56884-075-6	$16.95 USA/$22.95 Canada
Word For Windows® For Dummies®	by Dan Gookin & Ray Werner	ISBN: 1-878058-86-X	$16.95 USA/$22.95 Canada
WordPerfect® 6 For DOS For Dummies®	by Dan Gookin	ISBN: 1-878058-77-0	$16.95 USA/$22.95 Canada
WordPerfect® 6.1 For Windows® For Dummies® 2nd Edition	by Margaret Levine Young & David Kay	ISBN: 1-56884-243-0	$16.95 USA/$22.95 Canada
WordPerfect® For Dummies®	by Dan Gookin	ISBN: 1-878058-52-5	$16.95 USA/$22.95 Canada

Windows is a registered trademark of Microsoft Corporation. Mac is a registered trademark of Apple Computer. OS/2 is a registered trademark of IBM. UNIX is a registered trademark of AT&T. WordPerfect is a registered trademark of Novell. The "...For Dummies Book Series" logo, the IDG Books Worldwide logos, Dummies Press, and The Fun & Easy Way are trademarks, and ---- For Dummies and ... For Dummies are registered trademarks under exclusive license to IDG Books Worldwide, Inc., from International Data Group, Inc.

For scholastic requests & educational orders please call Educational Sales at 1. 800. 434. 2086

FOR MORE INFO OR TO ORDER, PLEASE CALL ▶ 800. 762. 2974

For volume discounts & special orders please call Tony Real, Special Sales, at 415. 655. 3048

DUMMIES PRESS™ QUICK REFERENCES

Fun, Fast, & Cheap!™

The Internet For Macs® For Dummies® Quick Reference
by Charles Seiter
ISBN: 1-56884-967-2
$9.99 USA/$12.99 Canada

Windows® 95 For Dummies® Quick Reference
by Greg Harvey
ISBN: 1-56884-964-8
$9.99 USA/$12.99 Canada

Photoshop 3 For Macs® For Dummies® Quick Reference
by Deke McClelland
ISBN: 1-56884-968-0
$9.99 USA/$12.99 Canada

WordPerfect® For DOS For Dummies® Quick Reference
by Greg Harvey
ISBN: 1-56884-009-8
$8.95 USA/$12.95 Canada

Title	Author	ISBN	Price
DATABASE			
Access 2 For Dummies® Quick Reference	by Stuart J. Stuple	ISBN: 1-56884-167-1	$8.95 USA/$11.95 Canada
dBASE 5 For DOS For Dummies® Quick Reference	by Barrie Sosinsky	ISBN: 1-56884-954-0	$9.99 USA/$12.99 Canada
dBASE 5 For Windows® For Dummies® Quick Reference	by Stuart J. Stuple	ISBN: 1-56884-953-2	$9.99 USA/$12.99 Canada
Paradox 5 For Windows® For Dummies® Quick Reference	by Scott Palmer	ISBN: 1-56884-960-5	$9.99 USA/$12.99 Canada
DESKTOP PUBLISHING/ILLUSTRATION/GRAPHICS			
CorelDRAW! 5 For Dummies® Quick Reference	by Raymond E. Werner	ISBN: 1-56884-952-4	$9.99 USA/$12.99 Canada
Harvard Graphics For Windows® For Dummies® Quick Reference	by Raymond E. Werner	ISBN: 1-56884-962-1	$9.99 USA/$12.99 Canada
Photoshop 3 For Macs® For Dummies® Quick Reference	by Deke McClelland	ISBN: 1-56884-968-0	$9.99 USA/$12.99 Canada
FINANCE/PERSONAL FINANCE			
Quicken 4 For Windows® For Dummies® Quick Reference	by Stephen L. Nelson	ISBN: 1-56884-950-8	$9.95 USA/$12.95 Canada
GROUPWARE/INTEGRATED			
Microsoft® Office 4 For Windows® For Dummies® Quick Reference	by Doug Lowe	ISBN: 1-56884-958-3	$9.99 USA/$12.99 Canada
Microsoft® Works 3 For Windows® For Dummies® Quick Reference	by Michael Partington	ISBN: 1-56884-959-1	$9.99 USA/$12.99 Canada
INTERNET/COMMUNICATIONS/NETWORKING			
The Internet For Dummies® Quick Reference	by John R. Levine & Margaret Levine Young	ISBN: 1-56884-168-X	$8.95 USA/$11.95 Canada
MACINTOSH			
Macintosh® System 7.5 For Dummies® Quick Reference	by Stuart J. Stuple	ISBN: 1-56884-956-7	$9.99 USA/$12.99 Canada
OPERATING SYSTEMS:			
DOS			
DOS For Dummies® Quick Reference	by Greg Harvey	ISBN: 1-56884-007-1	$8.95 USA/$11.95 Canada
UNIX			
UNIX® For Dummies® Quick Reference	by John R. Levine & Margaret Levine Young	ISBN: 1-56884-094-2	$8.95 USA/$11.95 Canada
WINDOWS			
Windows® 3.1 For Dummies® Quick Reference, 2nd Edition	by Greg Harvey	ISBN: 1-56884-951-6	$8.95 USA/$11.95 Canada
PCs/HARDWARE			
Memory Management For Dummies® Quick Reference	by Doug Lowe	ISBN: 1-56884-362-3	$9.99 USA/$12.99 Canada
PRESENTATION/AUTOCAD			
AutoCAD For Dummies® Quick Reference	by Ellen Finkelstein	ISBN: 1-56884-198-1	$9.95 USA/$12.95 Canada
SPREADSHEET			
1-2-3 For Dummies® Quick Reference	by John Walkenbach	ISBN: 1-56884-027-6	$8.95 USA/$11.95 Canada
1-2-3 For Windows® 5 For Dummies® Quick Reference	by John Walkenbach	ISBN: 1-56884-957-5	$9.95 USA/$12.95 Canada
Excel For Windows® For Dummies® Quick Reference, 2nd Edition	by John Walkenbach	ISBN: 1-56884-096-9	$8.95 USA/$11.95 Canada
Quattro Pro 6 For Windows® For Dummies® Quick Reference	by Stuart J. Stuple	ISBN: 1-56884-172-8	$9.95 USA/$12.95 Canada
WORD PROCESSING			
Word For Windows® 6 For Dummies® Quick Reference	by George Lynch	ISBN: 1-56884-095-0	$8.95 USA/$11.95 Canada
Word For Windows® For Dummies® Quick Reference	by George Lynch	ISBN: 1-56884-029-2	$8.95 USA/$11.95 Canada
WordPerfect® 6.1 For Windows® For Dummies® Quick Reference, 2nd Edition	by Greg Harvey	ISBN: 1-56884-966-4	$9.99 USA/$12.99/Canada

Microsoft and Windows are registered trademarks of Microsoft Corporation. Mac and Macintosh are registered trademarks of Apple Computer. UNIX is a registered trademark of AT&T. WordPerfect is a registered trademark of Novell. The "...For Dummies Book Series" logo, the IDG Books Worldwide logos, Dummies Press, The Fun & Easy Way, and Fun, Fast, & Cheap! are trademarks, and ---- For Dummies and ... For Dummies are registered trademarks under exclusive license to IDG Books Worldwide, Inc., from International Data Group, Inc.

For scholastic requests & educational orders please call Educational Sales at 1. 800. 434. 2086

FOR MORE INFO OR TO ORDER, PLEASE CALL ▶ 800. 762. 2974

For volume discounts & special orders please call Tony Real, Special Sales, at 415. 655. 3048

PC PRESS

Windows® 3.1 SECRETS™
by Brian Livingston
ISBN: 1-878058-43-6
$39.95 USA/$52.95 Canada
Includes software.

MORE Windows® 3.1 SECRETS™
by Brian Livingston
ISBN: 1-56884-019-5
$39.95 USA/$52.95 Canada
Includes software.

Windows® GIZMOS™
by Brian Livingston
& Margie Livingston
ISBN: 1-878058-66-5
$39.95 USA/$52.95 Canada
Includes software.

Windows® 3.1 Connectivity SECRETS™
by Runnoe Connally,
David Rorabaugh,
& Sheldon Hall
ISBN: 1-56884-030-6
$49.95 USA/$64.95 Canada
Includes software.

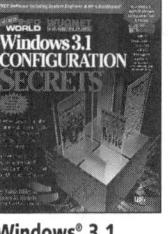

Windows® 3.1 Configuration SECRETS™
by Valda Hilley
& James Blakely
ISBN: 1-56884-026-8
$49.95 USA/$64.95 Canada
Includes software.

Internet SECRETS™
by John Levine
& Carol Baroudi
ISBN: 1-56884-452-2
$39.99 USA/$54.99 Canada
Includes software.

Internet GIZMOS™ For Windows®
by Joel Diamond,
Howard Sobel,
& Valda Hilley
ISBN: 1-56884-451-4
$39.99 USA/$54.99 Canada
Includes software.

Network Security SECRETS™
by David Stang
& Sylvia Moon
ISBN: 1-56884-021-7
Int'l. ISBN: 1-56884-151-5
$49.95 USA/$64.95 Canada
Includes software.

PC SECRETS™
by Caroline M. Halliday
ISBN: 1-878058-49-5
$39.95 USA/$52.95 Canada
Includes software.

WordPerfect® 6 SECRETS™
by Roger C. Parker
& David A. Holzgang
ISBN: 1-56884-040-3
$39.95 USA/$52.95 Canada
Includes software.

DOS 6 SECRETS™
by Robert D. Ainsbury
ISBN: 1-878058-70-3
$39.95 USA/$52.95 Canada
Includes software.

Paradox 4 Power Programming SECRETS,™ 2nd Edition
by Gregory B. Salcedo
& Martin W. Rudy
ISBN: 1-878058-54-1
$44.95 USA/$59.95 Canada
Includes software.

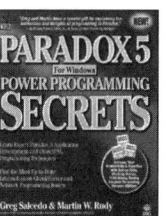

Paradox 5 For Windows® Power Programming SECRETS™
by Gregory B. Salcedo
& Martin W. Rudy
ISBN: 1-56884-085-3
$44.95 USA/$59.95 Canada
Includes software.

Hard Disk SECRETS™
by John M. Goodman,
Ph.D.
ISBN: 1-878058-64-9
$39.95 USA/$52.95 Canada
Includes software.

WordPerfect® 6 For Windows® Tips & Techniques Revealed
by David A. Holzgang
& Roger C. Parker
ISBN: 1-56884-202-3
$39.95 USA/$52.95 Canada
Includes software.

Excel 5 For Windows® Power Programming Techniques
by John Walkenbach
ISBN: 1-56884-303-8
$39.95 USA/$52.95 Canada
Includes software.

Windows is a registered trademark of Microsoft Corporation. WordPerfect is a registered trademark of Novell. ----SECRETS, ----GIZMOS, and the IDG Books Worldwide logos are trademarks, and ...SECRETS is a registered trademark under exclusive license to IDG Books Worldwide, Inc., from International Data Group, Inc.

For scholastic requests & educational orders please call Educational Sales, at 1. 800. 434. 2086

FOR MORE INFO OR TO ORDER, PLEASE CALL ▶ 800. 762. 2974

For volume discounts & special orders please call Tony Real, Special Sales, at 415. 655. 3048

PC PRESS

"A lot easier to use than the book Excel gives you!"

Lisa Schmeckpeper, New Berlin, WI, on PC World Excel 5 For Windows Handbook

Official Hayes Modem Communications Companion
by Caroline M. Halliday

ISBN: 1-56884-072-1
$29.95 USA/$39.95 Canada
Includes software.

1,001 Komputer Answers from Kim Komando
by Kim Komando

ISBN: 1-56884-460-3
$29.99 USA/$39.99 Canada
Includes software.

PC World DOS 6 Handbook, 2nd Edition
by John Socha, Clint Hicks, & Devra Hall

ISBN: 1-878058-79-7
$34.95 USA/$44.95 Canada
Includes software.

PC World Word For Windows® 6 Handbook
by Brent Heslop & David Angell

ISBN: 1-56884-054-3
$34.95 USA/$44.95 Canada
Includes software.

PC World Microsoft® Access 2 Bible, 2nd Edition
by Cary N. Prague & Michael R. Irwin

ISBN: 1-56884-086-1
$39.95 USA/$52.95 Canada
Includes software.

PC World Excel 5 For Windows® Handbook, 2nd Edition
by John Walkenbach & Dave Maguiness

ISBN: 1-56884-056-X
$34.95 USA/$44.95 Canada
Includes software.

PC World WordPerfect® 6 Handbook
by Greg Harvey

ISBN: 1-878058-80-0
$34.95 USA/$44.95 Canada
Includes software.

QuarkXPress For Windows® Designer Handbook
by Barbara Assadi & Galen Gruman

ISBN: 1-878058-45-2
$29.95 USA/$39.95 Canada

Official XTree Companion, 3rd Edition
by Beth Slick

ISBN: 1-878058-57-6
$19.95 USA/$26.95 Canada

PC World DOS 6 Command Reference and Problem Solver
by John Socha & Devra Hall

ISBN: 1-56884-055-1
$24.95 USA/$32.95 Canada

Client/Server Strategies™: A Survival Guide for Corporate Reengineers
by David Vaskevitch

ISBN: 1-56884-064-0
$29.95 USA/$39.95 Canada

"PC World Word For Windows 6 Handbook is very easy to follow with lots of 'hands on' examples. The 'Task at a Glance' is very helpful!"

Jacqueline Martens, Tacoma, WA

"Thanks for publishing this book! It's the best money I've spent this year!"

Robert D. Templeton, Ft. Worth, TX, on MORE Windows 3.1 SECRETS

Microsoft and Windows are registered trademarks of Microsoft Corporation. WordPerfect is a registered trademark of Novell. ----STRATEGIES and the IDG Books Worldwide logos are trademarks under exclusive license to IDG Books Worldwide, Inc., from International Data Group, Inc.

For scholastic requests & educational orders please call Educational Sales, at 1. 800. 434. 2086

FOR MORE INFO OR TO ORDER, PLEASE CALL ▶ 800. 762. 2974

For volume discounts & special orders please call Tony Real, Special Sales, at 415. 655. 3048

MACWORLD® PRESS

Macworld® Mac® & Power Mac SECRETS™, 2nd Edition
by David Pogue & Joseph Schorr

This is the definitive Mac reference for those who want to become power users! Includes three disks with 9MB of software!

ISBN: 1-56884-175-2
$39.95 USA/$54.95 Canada

Includes 3 disks chock full of software.

Macworld® Mac® FAQs™
by David Pogue

Written by the hottest Macintosh author around, David Pogue, *Macworld Mac FAQs* gives users the ultimate Mac reference. Hundreds of Mac questions and answers side-by-side, right at your fingertips, and organized into six easy-to-reference sections with lots of sidebars and diagrams.

ISBN: 1-56884-480-8
$19.99 USA/$26.99 Canada

Macworld® System 7.5 Bible, 3rd Edition
by Lon Poole

ISBN: 1-56884-098-5
$29.95 USA/$39.95 Canada

Macworld® ClarisWorks 3.0 Companion, 3rd Edition
by Steven A. Schwartz

ISBN: 1-56884-481-6
$24.99 USA/$34.99 Canada

Macworld® Complete Mac® Handbook Plus Interactive CD, 3rd Edition
by Jim Heid

ISBN: 1-56884-192-2
$39.95 USA/$54.95 Canada

Includes an interactive CD-ROM.

Macworld® Ultimate Mac® CD-ROM
by Jim Heid

ISBN: 1-56884-477-8
$19.99 USA/$26.99 Canada

CD-ROM includes version 2.0 of QuickTime, and over 65 MB of the best shareware, freeware, fonts, sounds, and more!

Macworld® Networking Bible, 2nd Edition
by Dave Kosiur & Joel M. Snyder

ISBN: 1-56884-194-9
$29.95 USA/$39.95 Canada

Macworld® Photoshop 3 Bible, 2nd Edition
by Deke McClelland

ISBN: 1-56884-158-2
$39.95 USA/$54.95 Canada

Includes stunning CD-ROM with add-ons, digitized photos and more.

Macworld® Photoshop 2.5 Bible
by Deke McClelland

ISBN: 1-56884-022-5
$29.95 USA/$39.95 Canada

Macworld® FreeHand 4 Bible
by Deke McClelland

ISBN: 1-56884-170-1
$29.95 USA/$39.95 Canada

Macworld® Illustrator 5.0/5.5 Bible
by Ted Alspach

ISBN: 1-56884-097-7
$39.95 USA/$54.95 Canada

Includes CD-ROM with QuickTime tutorials.

Mac is a registered trademark of Apple Computer. Macworld is a registered trademark of International Data Group, Inc. ----SECRETS, and ----FAQs are trademarks under exclusive license to IDG Books Worldwide, Inc., from International Data Group, Inc.

For scholastic requests & educational orders please call Educational Sales, at 1. 800. 434. 2086

FOR MORE INFO OR TO ORDER, PLEASE CALL ▶ 800. 762. 2974

For volume discounts & special orders please call Tony Real, Special Sales, at 415. 655. 3048

MACWORLD® PRESS

10/31/95

"*Macworld Complete Mac Handbook Plus CD* covered everything I could think of and more!"

Peter Tsakiris, New York, NY

"Very useful for PageMaker beginners and veterans alike—contains a wealth of tips and tricks to make you a faster, more powerful PageMaker user."

Paul Brainerd, President and founder, Aldus Corporation

"Thanks for the best computer book I've ever read—*Photoshop 2.5 Bible*. Best $30 I ever spent. I *love* the detailed index....Yours blows them all out of the water. This is a great book. We must enlighten the masses!"

Kevin Lisankie, Chicago, Illinois

"*Macworld Guide to ClarisWorks 2* is the easiest computer book to read that I have ever found!"

Steven Hanson, Lutz, FL

"...thanks to the *Macworld Excel 5 Companion, 2nd Edition* occupying a permanent position next to my computer, I'll be able to tap more of Excel's power."

Lauren Black, Lab Director, *Macworld* Magazine

Macworld® QuarkXPress 3.2/3.3 Bible
by Barbara Assadi & Galen Gruman

ISBN: 1-878058-85-1
$39.95 USA/$52.95 Canada

Includes disk with QuarkXPress XTensions and scripts.

Macworld® PageMaker 5 Bible
by Craig Danuloff

ISBN: 1-878058-84-3
$39.95 USA/$52.95 Canada

Includes 2 disks with PageMaker utilities, clip art, and more.

Macworld® FileMaker Pro 2.0/2.1 Bible
by Steven A. Schwartz

ISBN: 1-56884-201-5
$34.95 USA/$46.95 Canada

Includes disk with ready-to-run data bases.

Macworld® Word 6 Companion, 2nd Edition
by Jim Heid

ISBN: 1-56884-082-9
$24.95 USA/$34.95 Canada

NEWBRIDGE BOOK CLUB SELECTION

Macworld® Guide To Microsoft® Word 5/5.1
by Jim Heid

ISBN: 1-878058-39-8
$22.95 USA/$29.95 Canada

Macworld® ClarisWorks 2.0/2.1 Companion, 2nd Edition
by Steven A. Schwartz

ISBN: 1-56884-180-9
$24.95 USA/$34.95 Canada

Macworld® Guide To Microsoft® Works 3
by Barrie Sosinsky

ISBN: 1-878058-42-8
$22.95 USA/$29.95 Canada

Macworld® Excel 5 Companion, 2nd Edition
by Chris Van Buren & David Maguiness

ISBN: 1-56884-081-0
$24.95 USA/$34.95 Canada

NEWBRIDGE BOOK CLUB SELECTION

Macworld® Guide To Microsoft® Excel 4
by David Maguiness

ISBN: 1-878058-40-1
$22.95 USA/$29.95 Canada

Microsoft is a registered trademark of Microsoft Corporation. Macworld is a registered trademark of International Data Group, Inc.

For scholastic requests & educational orders please call Educational Sales, at 1. 800. 434. 2086

FOR MORE INFO OR TO ORDER, PLEASE CALL ▶ 800 762 2974

For volume discounts & special orders please call Tony Real, Special Sales, at 415. 655. 3048

PROFESSIONAL PUBLISHING GROUP

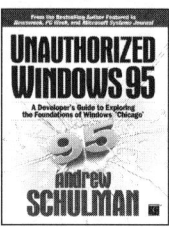

Unauthorized Windows® 95: A Developer's Guide to Exploring the Foundations of Windows "Chicago"
by Andrew Schulman

ISBN: 1-56884-169-8
$29.99 USA/$39.99 Canada

Unauthorized Windows® 95 Developer's Resource Kit
by Andrew Schulman

ISBN: 1-56884-305-4
$39.99 USA/$54.99 Canada

Best of the Net
by Seth Godin

ISBN: 1-56884-313-5
$22.99 USA/$32.99 Canada

Detour: The Truth About the Information Superhighway
by Michael Sullivan-Trainor

ISBN: 1-56884-307-0
$22.99 USA/$32.99 Canada

PowerPC Programming For Intel Programmers
by Kip McClanahan

ISBN: 1-56884-306-2
$49.99 USA/$64.99 Canada

Foundations™ of Visual C++ Programming For Windows® 95
by Paul Yao & Joseph Yao

ISBN: 1-56884-321-6
$39.99 USA/$54.99 Canada

Heavy Metal™ Visual C++ Programming
by Steve Holzner

ISBN: 1-56884-196-5
$39.95 USA/$54.95 Canada

Heavy Metal™ OLE 2.0 Programming
by Steve Holzner

ISBN: 1-56884-301-1
$39.95 USA/$54.95 Canada

Lotus Notes Application Development Handbook
by Erica Kerwien

ISBN: 1-56884-308-9
$39.99 USA/$54.99 Canada

The Internet Direct Connect Kit
by Peter John Harrison

ISBN: 1-56884-135-3
$29.95 USA/$39.95 Canada

Macworld® Ultimate Mac® Programming
by Dave Mark

ISBN: 1-56884-195-7
$39.95 USA/$54.95 Canada

The UNIX®-Haters Handbook
by Simson Garfinkel, Daniel Weise, & Steven Strassmann

ISBN: 1-56884-203-1
$16.95 USA/$22.95 Canada

Learn C++ Today!
by Martin Rinehart

ISBN: 1-56884-310-0
34.99 USA/$44.99 Canada

Type & Learn™ C
by Tom Swan

ISBN: 1-56884-073-X
34.95 USA/$44.95 Canada

Type & Learn™ Windows® Programming
by Tom Swan

ISBN: 1-56884-071-3
34.95 USA/$44.95 Canada

Windows is a registered trademark of Microsoft Corporation. Mac is a registered trademark of Apple Computer. UNIX is a registered trademark of AT&T. Macworld is a registered trademark of International Data Group, Inc. Foundations of ----, Heavy Metal, Type & Learn, and the IDG Books Worldwide logos are trademarks under exclusive license to IDG Books Worldwide, Inc., from International Data Group, Inc.

For scholastic requests & educational orders please call Educational Sales, at 1. 800. 434. 2086

FOR MORE INFO OR TO ORDER, PLEASE CALL ▶ 800. 762. 2974

For volume discounts & special orders please call Tony Real, Special Sales, at 415. 655. 3048

DUMMIES PRESS™ PROGRAMMING BOOKS

10/31/95

COMPUTER BOOK SERIES FROM IDG

For Dummies who want to program...

Delphi Programming For Dummies®
by Neil Rubenking
ISBN: 1-56884-200-7
$19.95 USA/$26.99 Canada

Access Programming For Dummies®
by Rob Krumm
ISBN: 1-56884-091-8
$19.95 USA/$26.95 Canada

TCP/IP For Dummies®
by Marshall Wilensky & Candace Leiden
ISBN: 1-56884-241-4
$19.99 USA/$26.99 Canada

HTML For Dummies®
by Ed Tittel & Carl de Cordova
ISBN: 1-56884-330-5
$29.99 USA/$39.99 Canada

Windows® 95 Programming For Dummies®
by S. Randy Davis
ISBN: 1-56884-327-5
$19.99 USA/$26.99 Canada

Mac® Programming For Dummies®
by Dan Parks Sydow
ISBN: 1-56884-173-6
$19.95 USA/$26.95 Canada

PowerBuilder 4 Programming For Dummies®
by Ted Coombs & Jason Coombs
ISBN: 1-56884-325-9
$19.99 USA/$26.99 Canada

Visual Basic 3 For Dummies®
by Wallace Wang
ISBN: 1-56884-076-4
$19.95 USA/$26.95 Canada
Covers version 3.

ISDN For Dummies®
by David Angell
ISBN: 1-56884-331-3
$19.99 USA/$26.99 Canada

Visual C++ "2" For Dummies®
by Michael Hyman & Bob Arnson
ISBN: 1-56884-328-3
$19.99 USA/$26.99 Canada

Borland C++ For Dummies®
by Michael Hyman
ISBN: 1-56884-162-0
$19.95 USA/$26.95 Canada

C For Dummies,® Volume I
by Dan Gookin
ISBN: 1-878058-78-9
$19.95 USA/$26.95 Canada

C++ For Dummies®
by Stephen R. Davis
ISBN: 1-56884-163-9
$19.95 USA/$26.95 Canada

QBasic Programming For Dummies®
by Douglas Hergert
ISBN: 1-56884-093-4
$19.95 USA/$26.95 Canada

dBase 5 For Windows® Programming For Dummies®
by Ted Coombs & Jason Coombs
ISBN: 1-56884-215-5
$19.99 USA/$26.99 Canada

Windows is a registered trademark of Microsoft Corporation. Mac is a registered trademark of Apple Computer. Dummies Press, the "...For Dummies Book Series" logo, and the IDG Books Worldwide logos are trademarks, and ----For Dummies, ... For Dummies and the "...For Dummies Computer Book Series" logo are registered trademarks under exclusive license to IDG Books Worldwide, Inc., from International Data Group, Inc.

For scholastic requests & educational orders please call Educational Sales, at 1. 800. 434. 2086

FOR MORE INFO OR TO ORDER, PLEASE CALL ▶ 800. 762. 2974

For volume discounts & special orders please call Tony Real, Special Sales, at 415. 655. 3048

PC PRESS

Official Hayes Modem Communications Companion
by Caroline M. Halliday

ISBN: 1-56884-072-1
$29.95 USA/$39.95 Canada

Includes software.

1,001 Komputer Answers from Kim Komando
by Kim Komando

ISBN: 1-56884-460-3
$29.95 USA/$39.99 Canada

Includes software.

PC World Excel 5 For Windows® Handbook, 2nd Edition
by John Walkenbach & Dave Maguiness

ISBN: 1-56884-056-X
$34.95 USA/$44.95 Canada

Includes software

PC World WordPerfect® 6 Handbook
by Greg Harvey

ISBN: 1-878058-80-0
$34.95 USA/$44.95 Canada

Includes software.

PC World DOS 6 Command Reference and Problem Solver
by John Socha & Devra Hall

ISBN: 1-56884-055-1
$24.95 USA/$32.95 Canada

NATIONAL BESTSELLER!

Client/Server Strategies™: A Survival Guide for Corporate Reengineers
by David Vaskevitch

SUPER STAR

ISBN: 1-56884-064-0
$29.95 USA/$39.95 Canada

Internet SECRETS™
by John Levine & Carol Baroudi

ISBN: 1-56884-452-2
$39.95 USA/$54.99 Canada

Includes software.

Network Security SECRETS™
by David Stang & Sylvia Moon

ISBN: 1-56884-021-7
Int'l. ISBN: 1-56884-151-5
$49.95 USA/$64.95 Canada

Includes software.

PC SECRETS™
by Caroline M. Halliday

ISBN: 1-878058-49-5
$39.95 USA/$52.95 Canada

Includes software.

Here's a complete listing of PC Press Titles

Title	Author	ISBN	Price
BBS SECRETS™	by Ray Werner	ISBN: 1-56884-491-3	$39.99 USA/$54.99 Canada
Creating Cool Web Pages with HTML	by Dave Taylor	ISBN: 1-56884-454-9	$19.99 USA/$26.99 Canada
DOS 6 SECRETS™	by Robert D. Ainsbury	ISBN: 1-878058-70-3	$39.95 USA/$52.95 Canada
Excel 5 For Windows® Power Programming Techniques	by John Walkenbach	ISBN: 1-56884-303-8	$39.95 USA/$52.95 Canada
Hard Disk SECRETS™	by John M. Goodman, Ph.D.	ISBN: 1-878058-64-9	$39.95 USA/$52.95 Canada
Internet GIZMOS™ For Windows®	by Joel Diamond, Howard Sobel, & Valda Hilley	ISBN: 1-56884-451-4	$39.99 USA/$54.99 Canada
Making Multimedia Work	by Michael Goodwin	ISBN: 1-56884-468-9	$19.99 USA/$26.99 Canada
MORE Windows® 3.1 SECRETS™	by Brian Livingston	ISBN: 1-56884-019-5	$39.95 USA/$52.95 Canada
Official XTree Companion 3rd Edition	by Beth Slick	ISBN: 1-878058-57-6	$19.95 USA/$26.95 Canada
Paradox 4 Power Programming SECRETS™, 2nd Edition	by Gregory B. Salcedo & Martin W. Rudy	ISBN: 1-878058-54-1	$44.95 USA/$59.95 Canada
Paradox 5 For Windows® Power Programming SECRETS™	by Gregory B. Salcedo & Martin W. Rudy	ISBN: 1-878058-85-3	$44.95 USA/$59.95 Canada
PC World DOS 6 Handbook, 2nd Edition	by John Socha, Clint Hicks & Devra Hall	ISBN: 1-878058-79-7	$34.95 USA/$44.95 Canada
PC World Microsoft® Access 2 Bible, 2nd Edition	by Cary N. Prague & Michael R. Irwin	ISBN: 1-56884-086-1	$39.95 USA/$52.95 Canada
PC World Word For Windows® 6 Handbook	by Brent Heslop & David Angell	ISBN: 1-56884-054-3	$34.95 USA/$44.95 Canada
QuarkXPress For Windows® Designer Handbook	by Barbara Assadi & Galen Gruman	ISBN: 1-878058-45-2	$29.95 USA/$39.95 Canada
Windows® 3.1 Configuration SECRETS™	by Valda Hilley & James Blakely	ISBN: 1-56884-026-8	$49.95 USA/$64.95 Canada
Windows® 3.1 Connectivity SECRETS™	by Runnoe Connally, David Rorabaugh & Sheldon Hall	ISBN: 1-56884-030-6	$49.95 USA/$64.95 Canada
Windows® 3.1 SECRETS™	by Brian Livingston	ISBN: 1-878058-43-6	$39.95 USA/$52.95 Canada
Windows® 95 A.S.A.P.	by Dan Gookin	ISBN: 1-56884-483-2	$24.99 USA/$34.99 Canada
Windows® 95 Bible	by Alan Simpson	ISBN: 1-56884-074-8	$29.95 USA/$39.99 Canada
Windows® 95 SECRETS™	by Brian Livingston	ISBN: 1-56884-453-0	$39.95 USA/$54.99 Canada
Windows® GIZMOS™	by Brian Livingston & Margie Livingston	ISBN: 1-878058-66-5	$39.95 USA/$52.95 Canada
WordPerfect® 6 For Windows® Tips & Techniques Revealed	by David A. Holzgang & Roger C. Parker	ISBN: 1-56884-202-3	$39.95 USA/$52.95 Canada
WordPerfect® 6 SECRETS™	by Roger C. Parker & David A. Holzgang	ISBN: 1-56884-040-3	$39.95 USA/$52.95 Canada

Microsoft and Windows are registered trademarks of Microsoft Corporation. WordPerfect is a registered trademark of Novell. ----SECRETS, ----STRATEGIES, and the IDG Books Worldwide logos are trademarks and ...SECRETS is a registered trademark under exclusive license to IDG Books Worldwide, Inc., from International Data Group, Inc.

For scholastic requests & educational orders please call Educational Sales, at 1. 800. 434. 2086

FOR MORE INFO OR TO ORDER, PLEASE CALL ▶ 800. 762. 2974

For volume discounts & special orders please call Tony Real, Special Sales, at 415. 655. 3048

Colliders and Neutrinos

The Window into
Physics beyond the
Standard Model

Colliders and Neutrinos

The Window into Physics beyond the Standard Model

Editors

Sally Dawson
Brookhaven National Laboratory, USA

Rabindra N. Mohapatra
University of Maryland, USA

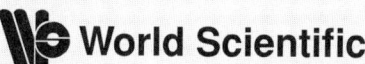

NEW JERSEY · LONDON · SINGAPORE · BEIJING · SHANGHAI · HONG KONG · TAIPEI · CHENNAI

Published by

World Scientific Publishing Co. Pte. Ltd.
5 Toh Tuck Link, Singapore 596224
USA office: 27 Warren Street, Suite 401-402, Hackensack, NJ 07601
UK office: 57 Shelton Street, Covent Garden, London WC2H 9HE

British Library Cataloguing-in-Publication Data
A catalogue record for this book is available from the British Library.

Images on cover design are from www.interactions.org and
http://cdsweb.cern.ch/collection/Photos?ln=en

COLLIDERS AND NEUTRINOS
The Window into Physics beyond the Standard Model

Copyright © 2008 by World Scientific Publishing Co. Pte. Ltd.

All rights reserved. This book, or parts thereof, may not be reproduced in any form or by any means, electronic or mechanical, including photocopying, recording or any information storage and retrieval system now known or to be invented, without written permission from the Publisher.

For photocopying of material in this volume, please pay a copying fee through the Copyright Clearance Center, Inc., 222 Rosewood Drive, Danvers, MA 01923, USA. In this case permission to photocopy is not required from the publisher.

ISBN-13 978-981-281-925-3
ISBN-10 981-281-925-8

Printed in Singapore by B & JO Enterprise

Preface

With many experimental undertakings in particle physics around the corner such as the Large Hadron Collider at CERN, many neutrino experiments are under way and in the horizon, with aspirations for perhaps an International Linear Collider in the not too distant future. The field of particle physics is poised to take a giant leap into unravelling the unknown world of new particles and forces in the coming decades, and build on its success of the past four decades. Combined with the spectacular developments in the field of cosmology, which has perhaps already given us the standard model of the universe and begging for new ideas from particle theory for a deeper understanding of observations, the promise of major breakthroughs and deep insights have filled the air. Many exciting ideas such as supersymmetry, extra dimensions and grand unification are reaching a stage of maturity waiting to be tested. We may also learn about the true nature of the dark constituent of the universe, as well as about the happenings at the early moments of the Big Bang embodied in the ideas of inflation. These discoveries may also provide a better understanding of the formation of structure and evolution of stars and galaxies.

In order to prepare for this new era, the TASI summer school has always been structured to bring to Ph. D. students in the US and abroad the latest ideas and information in a cogent and pedagogical manner, so as to build the intellectual base for tackling the new theoretical challenges that will emerge and are already emerging. The 2006 TASI school was charged with bringing the new phenomenological, cosmological and model building frontier to the students and researchers of tomorrow. With this in mind, we decided to focus on two main themes: Colliders and Neutrinos at the frontier of Physics and inviting experts in the related fields to lecture at the school.

Acknowledgments

We are grateful to all the speakers for taking time out of their busy schedule to prepare lectures and interact with students and contribute to the success of the school. We are especially grateful to those who submitted the written version of the lectures that can be an invaluable educational resource for students both now and in future. We thank Susan Spika and Elizabeth Price for efficient secretarial assistance before and during TASI, Abdul Bachri and Sogee Spinner for organizing the student seminars, Erin DePree and Nicholas Setzer for designing and distributing the TASI06 tee-shirts and Thomas Degrand for organizing the hikes. We thank the National Science Foundation, the Department of Energy, and the University of Colorado for financial and material support. We are very grateful to Prof. K. T. Mahanthappa for superb organization and for being a wonderful host.

Sally Dawson
Rabindra N. Mohapatra

Contents

Preface	v
Extra Dimensions *K. Agashe*	1
The International Linear Collider *M. Battaglia*	49
Astrophysical Aspects of Neutrinos *J. F. Beacom*	101
Leptogenesis *M.-C. Chen*	123
Neutrino Experiments *J. M. Conrad*	177
String Theory, String Model-Building, and String Phenomenology — A Practical Introduction *K. R. Dienes*	255
Theoretical Aspects of Neutrino Masses and Mixings *R. N. Mohapatra*	379
Searching for the Higgs Boson *D. Rainwater*	435
Z' Phenomenology and the LHC *T. G. Rizzo*	537
Neutrinoless Double Beta Decay *P. Vogel*	577
Supersymmetry in Elementary Particle Physics *M. E. Peskin*	609

Chapter 1

Extra Dimensions

Kaustubh Agashe

*Department of Physics, Syracuse University,
Syracuse, NY 13244, USA*[*]

We begin with a discussion of a model with a *flat* extra dimension which addresses the flavor hierarchy of the Standard Model (SM) using profiles for the SM fermions in the extra dimension. We then show how flavor violation and contributions to the electroweak precision tests can be suppressed [even with $O(\text{TeV})$ mass scale for the new particles] in this framework by suitable modifications to the basic model. Finally, we briefly discuss a model with a *warped* extra dimension in which all the SM fields propagate and we sketch how this model "mimics" the earlier model in a flat extra dimension. In this process, we outline a "complete" model addressing the Planck-weak as well as the flavor hierarchy problems of the SM.

1.1. Introduction

Extra dimensions is a vast subject so that it is difficult to give a complete review in 5 lectures. The reader is referred to excellent lectures on this subject already available such as references [1–4] among others. Similarly, the list of references given here is incomplete and the reader is referred to the other lectures for more references.

We begin with some (no doubt this is an incomplete list) motivations for studying models with extra dimensions:

(i) Extra dimensional models can address or solve many of the problems of the Standard Model (SM): for example, the various hi-

---

[*]After August 1, 2007:
Maryland Center for Fundamental Physics,
Department of Physics,
University of Maryland,
College Park, MD 20742, USA

erarchies unexplained in the SM – that between the Planck and electroweak scales [often called the "(big) hierarchy problem"] and also among the quark and lepton masses and mixing angles (often called the flavor hierarchy). We will show how both these problems are solved using extra dimensions in these lectures.

Extra dimensional models can also provide particle physics candidates for the dark matter of the universe (such a particle is absent in the SM). We will *not* address this point in these lectures.

(ii) Extra dimensions seem to occur in (and in fact are a necessary ingredient of) String Theory, the only known, complete theory of quantum gravity (see K. Dienes' lectures at this and earlier summer schools).

(iii) Although we will *not* refer to this point again, it turns out [5] that, under certain circumstances, extra dimensional theories can be a (weakly coupled) "dual" description of strongly coupled four-dimensional ($4D$) theories as per the correspondence between $5D$ anti-de Sitter (AdS) spaces and $4D$ conformal field theories (CFT's) [6].

The goal of these lectures is a discussion of the theory and phenomenology of some types of extra dimensional models, especially their applications to solving some of the problems of the SM of particle physics. The main concept to be gleaned from these lectures is that

- extra dimensions appear as a tower of particles (or modes) from the $4D$ point of view (a la the standard problem of a particle in $1D$ box studied in quantum mechanics).

The lightest mode (which is often massless and hence is called the zero-mode) is identified with the observed or the SM particles. Whereas, the heavier ones are called Kaluza-Klein (KK) modes and appear as new particles (beyond the SM). It is these particles which play a crucial role in solving problems of the SM, for example they could be candidates for dark matter of the universe or these particles can cut-off the quadratically divergent quantum corrections to the Higgs mass. These particles also give rise to a variety of signals in high-energy collider (i.e., via their on-shell or real production) and in low-energy experiments (via their off-shell or virtual effects). This is especially true if the masses of these KK modes are around the TeV scale, as would be the case if the extra dimension is relevant to explaining the Planck-weak hierarchy.

Here is a rough outline of the lectures. In lecture 1, we begin with the basics of KK decomposition in *flat* spacetime with one extra dimension compactified on a circle. We will show how obtaining chiral fermions requires an *orbifold* compactification instead of a circle. In lecture 2, we will consider a simple solution to the flavor hierarchy using the profiles of the SM fermions in the extra dimension. However, we will see that such a scenario results in too large contributions to flavor changing neutral current (FCNC) processes (which are ruled out by experimental data) if the KK scale is around the TeV scale – this is often called a flavor *problem*. Then, in lecture 3, we will consider a solution to this flavor problem based on the idea of large kinetic terms (for $5D$ fields) localized on a "brane". Another kind of measurement of properties of the SM particles (not involving flavor violation), called Electroweak Precision Tests, will be also be studied in this lecture, including the problem of large contributions to one such observable called the T (or ρ) parameter. In lecture 4, we will solve this problem of the T parameter by implementing a "custodial isospin" symmetry in the extra dimension. We will then briefly discuss some collider phenomenology of such models and some questions which are unanswered in these models. Finally, we will briefly study models based on *warped* spacetime in lecture 5, indicating how such models "mimic" the models in *flat* spacetime (with large brane kinetic terms) studied in the previous lectures. We will sketch how some of the open questions mentioned in lecture 4 can be addressed in the warped setting, resulting in a "complete" model.

1.2. Lecture 1

1.2.1. *Basics of Kaluza-Klein Decomposition*

Consider the following $5D$ action for a (real) scalar field (here and henceforth, the coordinates x^μ will denote the usual $4D$ and the coordinate y will denote the extra dimension):

$$S_{5D} = \int d^4x \int dy \left[(\partial^M \Phi)(\partial_M \Phi) - M^2 \Phi \Phi \right] \quad (1.1)$$

Since gravitational law falls off as $1/r^2$ and not $1/r^3$ at long distances, it is clear that we must compactify the extra dimension. Suppose we compactify the extra dimension on a circle (S^1), i.e., with y unrestricted ($-\infty < y < \infty$), but with y identified with $y + 2\pi R$.[a] We

---
[a]Equivalently, we can restrict the range of y: $0 \leq y \leq 2\pi R$, imposing the condition that $y = 0$ same as $y = 2\pi R$.

impose periodic boundary conditions on the fields as well, i.e., we require $\Phi(y = 2\pi R) = \Phi(y)$. Then, we can (Fourier) expand the $5D$ scalar field as follows:

$$\Phi = \frac{1}{\sqrt{2\pi R}} \sum_{n=-\infty}^{n=+\infty} \phi^{(n)}(x) e^{iny/R} \quad (1.2)$$

where the coefficient in front has been chosen for proper normalization.

Substituting this expansion into S_{5D} and using the orthonormality of profiles of the Fourier modes in the extra dimension (i.e., $e^{iny/R}$) to integrate over the extra dimension, we obtain the following $4D$ action:

$$S_{4D} = \int d^4x \sum_n \left[\left(\partial_\mu \phi^{(n)} \right) \left(\partial^\mu \phi^{(n)} \right) - \left(M^2 + \frac{n^2}{R^2} \right) \phi^{(n)} \phi^{(n)} \right] \quad (1.3)$$

This implies that from the $4D$ point of view the $5D$ scalar field appears as an (infinite) tower of $4D$ fields which are called the Kaluza-Klein (KK) modes: $\phi^{(n)}$ with mass^2, $m_n^2 = M^2 + n^2/R^2$ (note that the n^2/R^2 contribution to the KK masses arises from ∂_5 acting on the profiles) [see Fig. 1.1(a)].

The lightest or zero-mode ($n = 0$) has mass M (strictly speaking it is massless only for $M = 0$). The non-zero KK modes start at $\sim 1/R$ (for the case $M \ll 1/R$) which is often called the *compactification scale*. We can easily generalize to the case of δ extra dimensions, each of which

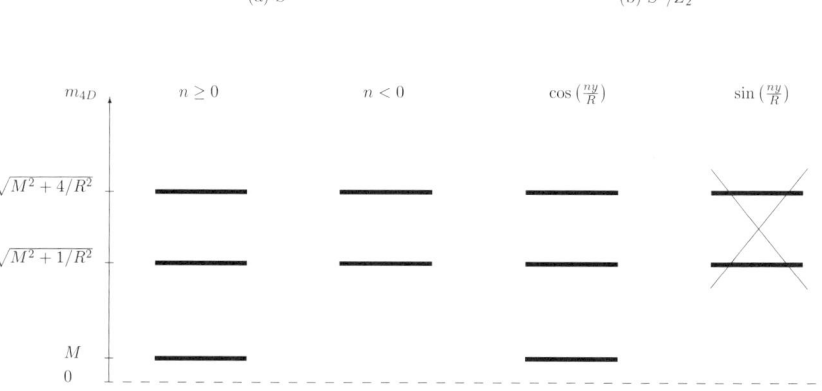

Fig. 1.1. KK decomposition of a $5D$ scalar on a circle (a) and an orbifold (b), choosing even parity.

Fig. 1.2. Going from a circle to an orbifold using Z_2 symmetry

is compactified on a circle of same radius to obtain the spectrum: $m_n^2 = M^2 + \sum_{i=1}^{\delta} n_i^2/R^2$. However, in these lectures, *we will restrict to only one extra dimension*.

Thus, we see that the signature of an extra dimension from the 4D point of view is the appearance of infinite tower of KK modes: to repeat, the lightest (zero)-modes is identified with the SM particle and the heavier ones (KK modes) appear as new particles beyond the SM.

1.2.2. *Orbifold*

Mathematically speaking, a circle is a (smooth) manifold since it has no special points. We can "mod out" this smooth manifold by a discrete symmetry to obtain an "orbifold". Specifically, we impose the discrete (Z_2) identification: $y \leftrightarrow -y$ in addition to $y \equiv y + 2\pi R$. Thus, the physical or fundamental domain extends only from $y = 0$ to $y = \pi R$[b] – this compactification is denoted by S^1/Z_2: see Fig. 1.2.

The endpoints of the orbifold ($y = 0, \pi R$) do *not* transform under Z_2 and hence are called *fixed* points of the orbifold. Also, note that the end points of this extra dimension are not identified with each other either by the periodicity condition $y \equiv y + 2\pi R$ (unlike the endpoints $y = 0, 2\pi R$ on S^1) or by the Z_2 symmetry.

Let us consider how the KK decomposition is modified in going from a circle to an orbifold. We can rewrite the earlier KK decomposition in terms of functions which are even and odd under $y \to -y$:

$$\Phi(x,y) = \frac{1}{\sqrt{2\pi R}}\phi^{(0)} + \sum_{n=1}^{\infty} \frac{1}{\sqrt{\pi R}}\left[\phi_+^{(n)}\cos\frac{ny}{R} + \phi_-^{(n)}\sin\frac{ny}{R}\right] \quad (1.4)$$

with the identification $\phi_\pm^{(n>0)} \equiv 1(i)/\sqrt{2}\left(\phi^{(n)} \pm \phi^{(-n)}\right)$.

---
[b]Equivalently, we can still pretend that it extends from $y = 0$ to $y = 2\pi R$ as before, but with the region $y = \pi R$ to $y = 2\pi R$ *not* being independent of the region $y = 0$ to $y = \pi R$.

We must require the physics, i.e., S_{5D}, to be invariant under $y \to -y$. For this purpose, we assign an (intrinsic) parity transformation to Φ:

$$\Phi(x, -y) = P\Phi(x, y) \tag{1.5}$$

with $P = \pm 1$, i.e., Φ being even or odd. This assignment sets $\phi_-^{(n>0)} = 0$ for $P = +1$ and $\phi_+^{(n)} = 0$ [including $\phi^{(0)}$] for $P = -1$ see Fig. 1.1(b).

Thus, a summary of orbifold compactification is that[c]: (i) it reduces the number of modes by a factor of 2 and (ii) it removes or projects out the *zero*-mode for the case of the $5D$ field being *odd* under the parity.

1.2.3. Fermions on a Circle: Chirality Problem

One possible representation of the $5D$ Clifford algebra for fermions:

$$\{\Gamma_M, \Gamma_N\} = 2\eta_{MN} \tag{1.6}$$

is provided by the usual Dirac (4×4) matrices

$$\Gamma_\mu = \gamma_\mu, \quad \Gamma_5 = -i\gamma_5 \tag{1.7}$$

Thus, we see that the smallest (irreducible) representation for $5D$ fermions has 4 (complex) components (cf. 2-component complex or Weyl spinor in $4D$, where the 2×2 Pauli matrices form a representation of Clifford algebra).

Consider the following $5D$ action for fermions

$$S_{5D} = \bar{\Psi}\left(i\partial_M \Gamma^M - M\right)\Psi \tag{1.8}$$

When the extra dimension is compactified on a circle, we can plug in the usual decomposition $\Psi_{\alpha=1-4} = \sum_n \psi_\alpha^{(n)} e^{iny/R}$ to find the $4D$ action:

$$S_{4D} = \sum_n \bar{\psi}^{(n)}\left(i\gamma_\mu \partial^\mu - M - in/R\right)\psi^{(n)} \tag{1.9}$$

Thus, we obtain a tower of Dirac (4-component) spinors from the $4D$ point of view: $m_n^2 = M^2 + n^2/R^2$: see Fig. 1.3(a).

---

[c]We will see later how an orbifold is "useful" in the case of $5D$ fermion/gauge fields because of these properties.

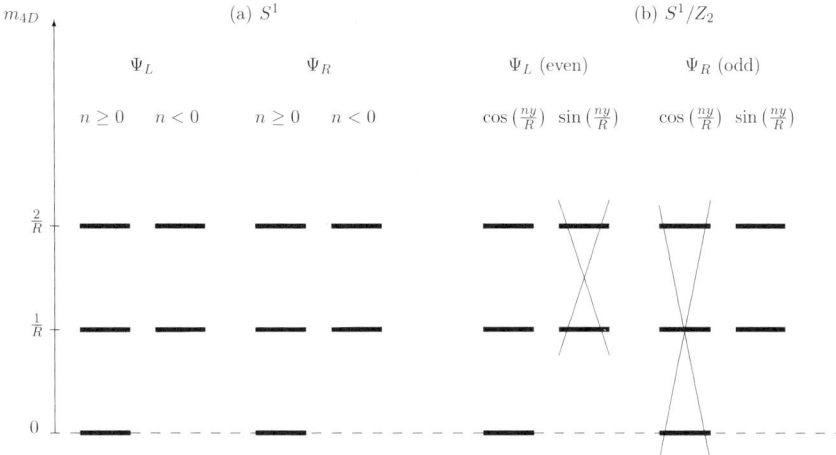

Fig. 1.3. KK decomposition for a $5D$ fermion on a circle (a) and an orbifold (b) with even parity for Ψ_L.

Consider the case $M = 0$. We see that there are *non*-chiral massless (or zero) modes: explicitly, in the Weyl representation of Dirac matrices, i.e.,

$$\gamma_\mu = \begin{pmatrix} \mathbf{0} & \sigma_\mu \\ \sigma_\mu & \mathbf{0} \end{pmatrix} \tag{1.10}$$

$$\gamma_5 = \begin{pmatrix} \mathbf{1} & \mathbf{0} \\ \mathbf{0} & -\mathbf{1} \end{pmatrix} \tag{1.11}$$

$$\sigma_\mu = (\sigma_{i=1..3}, \mathbf{1}), \tag{1.12}$$

$\psi^{(0)}_{\alpha=1-4}$ decomposes as $\sim \left[\psi^{(0)}_L (\alpha = 1, 2), \psi^{(0)}_R (\alpha = 3, 4) \right]$, where L (R) refers to left (right) chirality (or helicity) under the $4D$ Lorentz transformation. The problem is that if the $5D$ fermion transforms under some $5D$ gauge symmetry, then the L and R (massless) chiralities (zero-modes) transform identically under this gauge symmetry. Hence, such a scenario cannot correspond to the SM, where the fermions are known to be chiral, i.e., the left-handed (LH) and right-handed (RH) ones transform as doublets and singlets, respectively under the $SU(2)_{weak}$ gauge symmetry.

1.2.4. *Fermion Chirality from Orbifold*

We can obtain chiral fermions by compactifying the $5D$ theory on an orbifold instead of a circle as follows. Suppose we choose Ψ_L to be even under the Z_2 parity. Then, Ψ_R must be odd since the $5D$ action contains the term $\bar{\Psi}\Gamma^5 \partial_5 \Psi \ni \Psi_L^\dagger \partial_5 \Psi_R$, which must be even so that the $5D$ action is Z_2-invariant (note that ∂_5 is odd under parity).

We obtain the following decomposition:

$$\Psi_{L\ (R)} \sim \sum_n \psi^{(n)}_{L\ (R)} \cos \frac{ny}{R} \left(\sin \frac{ny}{R} \right) \qquad (1.13)$$

Thus, (for case of the $5D$ mass, $M = 0^{\text{d}}$) we get a massless zero-mode only for Ψ_L (even field): see Fig. 1.3(b). Of course, we could have chosen Ψ_R to be even instead to obtain a RH zero-mode.

1.3. Lecture 2

1.3.1. *Zero-Mode Fermion Profiles*

We see that the massless (chiral) mode on an orbifold has a *flat* profile [see Eq. (1.13)]. So, if all the SM fermions have $M = 0$, then the extra dimension does not provide any resolution of the flavor hierarchy, i.e., we need to put hierarchies in $5D$ Yukawa couplings (similar to the situation in the SM) in order to obtain hierarchies in the $4D$ Yukawa couplings.

We must then consider modifying the profiles of the fermion zero-modes in order to solve the flavor hierarchy problem using the extra dimension. We can try adding a bare mass term: $\bar{\Psi}\Psi = \Psi_L^\dagger \Psi_R + h.c.$, but such a mass term breaks the Z_2 symmetry (again since $\Psi_{L,R}$ transform oppositely under the parity). The solution to this problem [7] is to couple the $5D$ fermion to a Z_2-odd scalar with the following $5D$ Lagrangian:

$$\mathcal{L}_{5D} = \bar{\Psi}\left(i\partial_M \Gamma^M - h\Phi\right)\Psi$$
$$+ (\partial_M \Phi)^2 - \lambda \left(\Phi^2 - V^2\right)^2 \qquad (1.14)$$

The point is that the potential $V(\Phi) = \lambda \left(\Phi^2 - V^2\right)^2$ forces a vacuum expectation value (vev) for Φ which is a constant in y in-between the endpoints of the extra dimension (often called the "bulk"). However, such a vev tends to "clash" with $\Phi = 0$ at the endpoints (as required by the scalar being odd under the Z_2 parity). As a result, we obtain a (approximately) "kink-anti-kink" profile for the scalar vev (see references [7] for more details) as in Fig. 1.4. Such a profile for the scalar vev is equivalent to adding a Z_2-*odd* $5D$ mass for the fermion. The point is that with such a scalar vev

---

[d]We will see in the next section that only a "special" form of mass term is allowed on an orbifold.

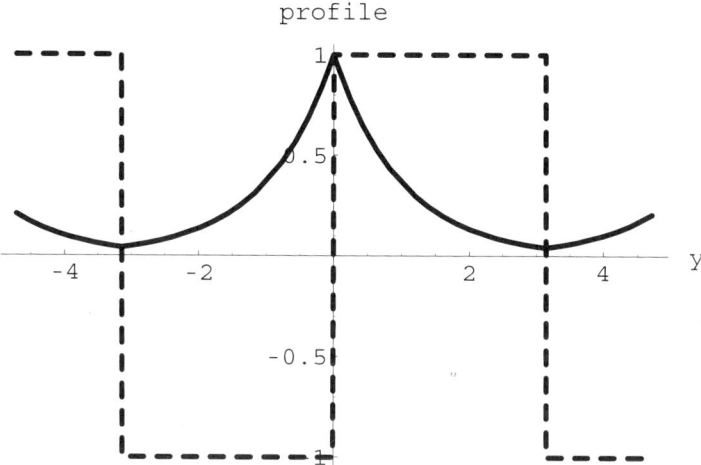

Fig. 1.4. Profile of odd mass term (dashed line) and fermion zero-mode (solid line). Here and henceforth, we set radius of extra dimension, $R = 1$ in all figures.

we have a *spontaneous* breaking of the Z_2 symmetry – recall that it is this Z_2 symmetry which prevented us from writing such a mass term to begin with, i.e., a *bare* mass term would correspond to an *explicit* breaking of this symmetry.

Let us then consider how the KK decomposition is modified in the presence of such an (odd) bulk fermion mass term. The $5D$ action is

$$S_{5D} = \bar{\Psi}\left[i\partial_M \Gamma^M + M\epsilon(y)\right]\Psi \qquad (1.15)$$

where $\epsilon(y) = +1(-1)$ for $\pi R > y > 0 (-\pi R < y < 0)$. It is easy to see that the eigenmodes are no longer *single* sin or cos, but instead are linear *combinations* of these basis functions. Hence, we have to work harder to obtain the eigenmodes.

1.3.2. General Procedure for KK Reduction

We will now take a slight detour to discuss the procedure to obtain the KK decomposition for a general $5D$ action and return to apply this procedure to the above $5D$ fermion case.

For simplicity, consider a $5D$ scalar field decomposed into modes as follows: $\Phi(x, y) = \sum_n \phi^{(n)}(x) f_n(y)$. Plug this expansion into the simple

5D action:
$$S_{5D} = \int d^4x \int dy \left[(\partial^M \Phi)(\partial_M \Phi) - M^2 \Phi\Phi \right] \quad (1.16)$$

We *require* that, *after* integrating over the extra dimension, we get

$$S_{4D} = \int d^4x \sum_n \left[\left(\partial_\mu \phi^{(n)}\right)\left(\partial^\mu \phi^{(n)}\right) - \left(M^2 + \frac{n^2}{R^2}\right) \phi^{(n)} \phi^{(n)} \right] \quad (1.17)$$

so that we can interpret $\phi^{(n)}$'s as particles (KK modes) from the $4D$ point of view.

This requirement gives us the following two equations: matching kinetic terms in S_{4D} of Eq. (1.17) to the ∂_μ (or $4D$) part of the kinetic term obtained from S_{5D} gives us the following:

(i) orthonormality condition

$$\int dy f_n^*(y) f_n(y) = 1 \quad (1.18)$$

whereas matching the mass terms in S_{4D} of Eq. (1.17) to the $5D$ mass term (M) and the action of ∂_5 on the profiles in S_{5D} gives us the

(ii) differential equation:

$$\partial_y^2 f_n(y) - M^2 f_n^2(y) = -m_n^2 f_n^2(y) \quad (1.19)$$

Thus the KK decomposition reduces to an eigenvalue problem, solving which gives us the KK masses (eigenvalues) m_n and their profiles $f_n(y)$ (eigenfunctions). This is very reminiscent of solving the problem of Schroedinger equation for a particle in a $1D$ box in quantum mechanics.

For the above simple case of a $5D$ scalar with a bulk mass, we get the following solutions to the differential equation [i.e., Eq. (1.19)]: $f_n(y) \sim e^{\pm i \sqrt{m_n^2 - M^2} y}$ for $m_n^2 \geq M^2$. In addition, the periodicity condition, i.e., $f_n(y) = f_n(y + 2\pi R)$ requires $\sqrt{m_n^2 - M^2} = n^2/R^2$ so that $m_n^2 = M^2 + n^2/R^2$ (as before). The reader should think about the possibility $m_n^2 < M^2$ (where we get exponentially rising or decaying profiles) to show that we cannot satisfy the continuity of derivative at $y = 0, \pi R$ in this case and hence we cannot have such solutions for a scalar.

The above procedure can be generalized to more complicated $5D$ actions and for other spin fields.

1.3.3. *Solution to Flavor Puzzle*

Next, we return to the problem of the KK decomposition of a $5D$ fermion with the (odd) mass term and with $\Psi_{L\ (R)}$ being even (odd) under Z_2 parity. As outlined above, we plug $\Psi_{L,R} = \psi^{(n)}(x) f_{L,R\ n}(y)$ into S_{5D} to obtain the differential equations:

$$\left[-\partial_5 + M\epsilon(y) \right] f_{L\ n} = m_n f_R \qquad (1.20)$$

$$\left[\partial_5 + M\epsilon(y) \right] f_{R\ n} = m_n f_L \qquad (1.21)$$

Note that (as mentioned before) cos or sin are solutions only for $M = 0$, but not for $M \neq 0$ [On a circle, the mass term M has no $\epsilon(y)$ so that $f_{L,R\ n} \sim e^{iny/R}$ are indeed solutions.].

It is easy to solve for the zero-mode profile ($m_n = 0$) even for $M \neq 0$ (the $m_n \neq 0$ case is difficult to solve due to the two differential equations being coupled):

$$\begin{aligned} f_{L\ 0}(y) &= Ne^{My} \quad (0 \leq y \leq \pi R) \\ &= Ne^{-My} \quad (0 \geq y \geq -\pi R) \end{aligned} \qquad (1.22)$$

(N is a normalization factor: see exercise 1 in appendix).

Note that for RH modes, $f_{R\ 0} \sim e^{\mp My}$ solves the eigenvalue equation, but it clashes with vanishing of $f_{R\ 0}(y)$ at $y = 0, \pi R$ as required by Ψ_R being odd under Z_2 parity. Thus, as expected from the parity choice, there is no RH zero-mode. Note that there is a discontinuity in the derivative of $f_{L\ 0}$ at $y = 0, \pi R$ (Fig. 1.4), which precisely matches the $\epsilon(y)$ term (cf. scalar case earlier where such profiles cannot satisfy the requirement of continuity of derivative at the fixed points). The point is that $M \neq 0$ still gives a mass*less* fermion mode (unlike for a scalar).

We will now see how the flavor hierarchy can be accounted for without any large hierarchies in the $5D$ theory: see exercise 1 and Fig. 1.5. For simplicity, suppose the SM Higgs field is localized at $y = \pi R$ (each end of the extra dimension is often called a "brane", motivated by String Theory) and add the following coupling of $5D$ fermions to it:

$$S_{5D} \ni \int d^4x\, dy\, \delta(y - \pi R) H \Psi_L \Psi'_R \lambda_{5D} \qquad (1.23)$$

where Ψ and Ψ' are two *different* $5D$ fermion fields which are $SU(2)_L$ doublets and singlets with M, M' being their $5D$ masses, respectively. Note that Ψ_L and Ψ'_R are chosen to be even under Z_2 so that they give the LH and RH zero-modes, respectively. Since Ψ_R and Ψ'_L vanish at the $y = \pi R$

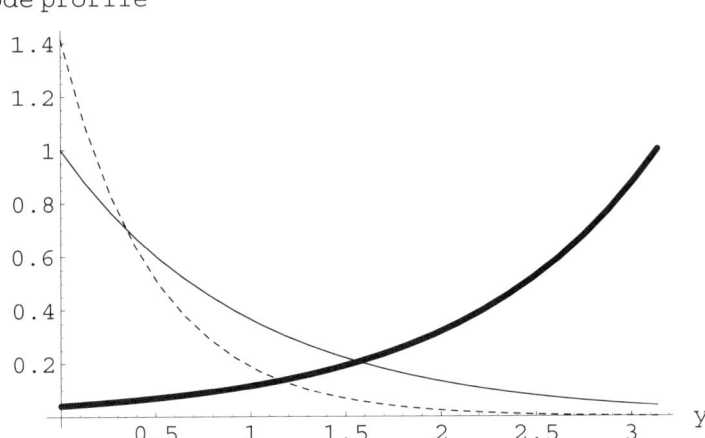

Fig. 1.5. Profiles for down (dashed line: 5D mass, $M = -2$), strange (thin solid line: $M = -1$) and top quarks (thick solid line: $M = +1$). The SM Higgs is localized on the $y = \pi R$ brane.

brane, they do not couple to the Higgs as seen in Eq. (1.23). Plugging in the zero-mode profiles, we obtain the effective 4D Yukawa coupling, i.e., $\lambda_{4D} H \psi_L^{(0)} \psi_R'^{(0)}$:

$$\lambda_{4D} \approx \lambda_{5D} \times f_{L\,0}(\pi R) f_{R\,0}(\pi R)$$
$$\propto \lambda_{5D} e^{(M-M')} \quad (1.24)$$

Let us consider the hierarchy between the down (d) and strange (s) quark masses for example. For simplicity, we set λ_{5D} to be the same for d, s and also $M = -M'$ for each quark to obtain (up to small dependence of normalization on M's)

$$\frac{m_d}{m_s} \sim e^{2\Delta M \pi R}$$
$$\sim 1/100 \text{ which is the required, i.e., experimental value} \quad (1.25)$$

so that $\Delta M \equiv M_d - M_s \sim -2$ [for example, $M_d = -3, M_s = -1$] in units of $1/(\pi R)$ suffices to obtain the hierarchy in 4D masses (or Yukawa couplings).

The crucial point is that we did not invoke any large hierarchies in the 5D or fundamental parameters (M or λ_{5D}), but we can still obtain large hierarchies in the 4D Yukawa couplings.

1.3.4. *Intermediate Summary: Basic Concepts*

Before moving on, let us summarize:

(i) A $5D$ field appears as a tower of KK modes from $4D$ point of view, with each mode having a profile in the extra dimension.
(ii) The profiles and the KK masses are obtained by solving an eigenvalue problem (or wave equations in $5D$ space-time).
(iii) The coupling of particles (i.e., zero and KK modes) is proportional to the overlap of their profiles in the extra dimension.

1.3.5. *Gauge Field on a Circle*

Next, we consider $5D$ gauge fields with the following $5D$ action[e]:

$$S_{5D} = \int d^4x dy \frac{1}{4} \mathcal{F}_{MN} \mathcal{F}^{MN} \tag{1.26}$$

$$= \int d^4x dy \frac{1}{4} \left(\mathcal{F}_{\mu\nu} \mathcal{F}^{\mu\nu} + \mathcal{F}_{\mu 5} \mathcal{F}^{\mu 5} \right) \tag{1.27}$$

with

$$\mathcal{A}_M = \mathcal{A}_\mu + \mathcal{A}_5 \tag{1.28}$$

As usual, the KK decomposition is achieved by plugging in the expansion $\mathcal{A}_{\mu,\,5} = \sum_n A^{(n)}_{\mu,\,5} f_{\mu,\,5\,n}(y)$ into S_{5D}. It is easy to see that this procedure is similar to that for a $5D$ scalar, up to the presence of Lorentz index and gauge fixing. It is straightforward to include the Lorentz index in the KK decomposition, but there are subtleties with gauge fixing – we will not go into details of the latter issue in these lectures (for a discussion of this issue, see, for example, 1st reference in [3]).

The end result is that, on a circle, both $\mathcal{A}_\mu$ and $\mathcal{A}_5$ components have zero-modes – the former is a vector, whereas the latter is a scalar from the $4D$ point of view: see Fig. 1.6(a).

Thus, we encounter a *unification of spins* in the sense that massless $4D$ scalars can be obtained from $5D$ gauge fields. If the $4D$ scalar $A_5^{(0)}$ remains massless, then it will result in an extra long range force which would be ruled out by experiments. However, this scalar does acquire a mass from

---
[e]Once the SM fermions propagate in the extra dimension, we can show that the SM gauge fields also have to do the same to preserve gauge invariance.

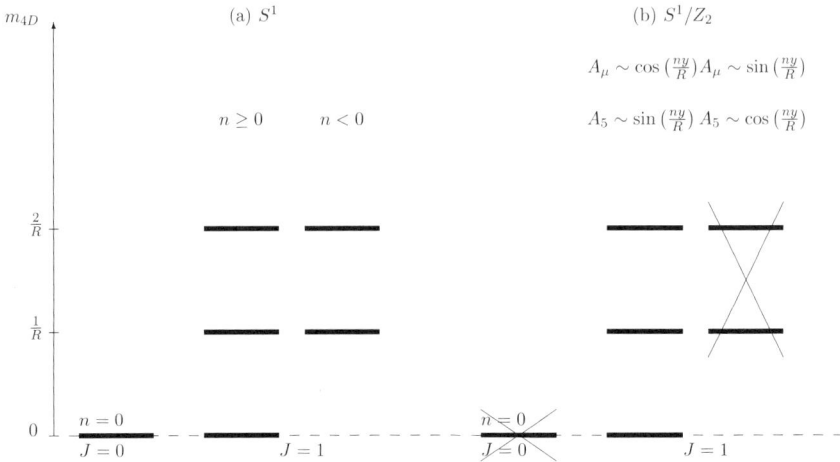

Fig. 1.6. KK decomposition for a 5D gauge field on a circle (a) and on a orbifold (b) with choice of even parity for $\mathcal{A}_\mu$.

loop corrections (see lecture 5) so that such a light scalar (almost zero-mode) might not be a *robust* problem (unlike the chirality problem with fermions on a circle).

1.3.6. *Gauge Field on an Orbifold*

In any case, it is possible to get rid of the $\mathcal{A}_5$ zero-mode using orbifold compactification as follows. Notice that for

$$\mathcal{F}_{\mu 5} = \partial_\mu \mathcal{A}_5 - \partial_5 \mathcal{A}_\mu \tag{1.29}$$

to have a well-defined Z_2 parity, we have two choices:

(i) $\mathcal{A}_\mu$ is even – it has a zero-mode which is identified with the SM gauge boson – which implies that $\mathcal{A}_5$ is odd and so does not have a zero-mode [see Fig. 1.6(b)] or

(ii) $\mathcal{A}_\mu$ is odd (no zero-mode gauge boson) so that $\mathcal{A}_5$ is even and has a zero-mode.

As we will see later, the $\mathcal{A}_5$ zero-mode in case (ii) can play the role of SM Higgs, but for now, we will make the choice (i), i.e., $\mathcal{A}_{\mu\,(5)}$ is even (odd) so that we do have a zero-mode (i.e., SM) gauge boson.

Hence, we obtain the following KK decomposition for this gauge field on an orbifold [Fig. 1.6(b)]:

$$f_{\mu\,0} = \frac{1}{\sqrt{2\pi R}} \quad \text{(i.e., a flat profile)} \tag{1.30}$$

$$f_{\mu\,n}(y) = \frac{1}{\sqrt{\pi R}} \cos ny/R \tag{1.31}$$

$$f_{5\,n}(y) = \frac{1}{\sqrt{\pi R}} \sin ny/R \tag{1.32}$$

We have normalized the modes over $-\pi R \leq y \leq +\pi R$, even though the physical domain is from $y = 0$ to $y = \pi R$. We can show that $A_\mu^{(n\neq 0)}$ "eats" $A_5^{(n)}$ to form a massive spin-1 gauge boson from the following mass terms

$$\mathcal{F}_{\mu 5}^2 \ni \partial_\mu A_5 \partial_5 \mathcal{A}^\mu \tag{1.33}$$

$$\sim \sum_n A_\mu^{(n)} \partial^\mu A_5^{(n)} \partial_y f_{\mu\,n}(y) \tag{1.34}$$

These mass terms mixing $A_\mu^{(n)}$ and $A_5^{(n)}$ are similar to the ones in the SM: $W_\mu \partial^\mu H \langle H \rangle$ (which indicate that the longitudinal polarization of W is the unphysical component of Higgs, i.e., the equivalence theorem).

1.3.7. Couplings of Gauge Modes

We now calculate the couplings of the various gauge modes to the matter particles (in this case fermions) based on their profiles. We can show that the coupling of zero-mode is the same to all fermion modes (whether zero or KK):

$$\int d^4x\, dy\, \bar{\Psi}\Gamma^M \left(\partial_M + g_5 \mathcal{A}_M\right) \Psi \ni \sum_n \bar{\psi}_L^{(n)} \gamma^\mu \psi_L^{(n)} \times \int dy\, f_{L\,n}^2(y)$$

$$\left(\partial_\mu + A_\mu^{(0)} \frac{g_5}{\sqrt{2\pi R}}\right) \tag{1.35}$$

$$= \bar{\psi}_L^{(n)} \gamma^\mu \psi_L^{(n)} \left(\partial_\mu + g_4 A_\mu^{(0)}\right)$$

$$\text{(for all } n\text{)} \tag{1.36}$$

with

$$g_4 \text{ (or } g_{SM}\text{)} = \frac{g_5}{\sqrt{2\pi R}} \tag{1.37}$$

The point is that the profile of the gauge zero-mode is flat so that the overlap integrals appearing in the kinetic term for fermion mode and in the coupling to gauge zero-mode are identical. This universality of the zero-mode gauge coupling is actually guaranteed by $4D$ gauge invariance.

However, the couplings of zero-mode fermions to gauge KK modes (coming from the overlap of profiles) are *non*-universal, i.e., these couplings depend on the $5D$ fermion mass (see Fig. 1.7):

$$g(n, M) = g_5 \int dy \left(Ne^{-My}\right)^2 \times f_{\mu\,n}(y) \tag{1.38}$$

$$\equiv g_4 \times a(n, M) \tag{1.39}$$

where a is an $O(1)$ quantity (see exercise 1). The reason is that the gauge KK profile is not flat (unlike for zero-mode) or equivalently there is no analog of $4D$ gauge invariance for the massive (KK) gauge modes.

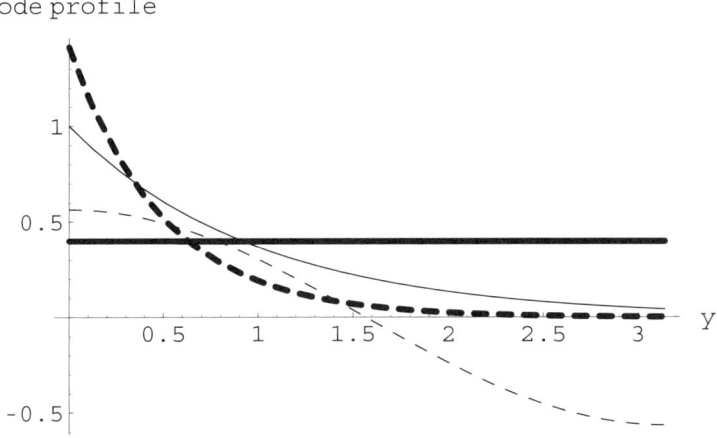

Fig. 1.7. Profiles for down (thick dashed line) and strange (thin solid line) quarks and the gauge zero-mode (thick solid line) and 1st KK mode (thin dashed line). The SM Higgs is localized on the $y = \pi R$ brane.

1.3.8. *Flavor Problem from Gauge KK Modes*

Such non-universal couplings of gauge KK modes to fermion zero-modes results in flavor violation as follows [8]. The point is that the couplings of the gauge KK modes to zero-mode fermions are flavor *diagonal*, but non-universal in the interaction (or weak) basis:

$$g_4 \left(\bar{d}_{L\,\text{weak}} \;\; \bar{s}_{L\,\text{weak}}\right) \begin{pmatrix} a_d & 0 \\ 0 & a_s \end{pmatrix} \gamma^\mu A_\mu^{(n)} \begin{pmatrix} d_{L\,\text{weak}} \\ s_{L\,\text{weak}} \end{pmatrix} \tag{1.40}$$

which results in the appearance of flavor violating couplings *after* a unitary rotation to the mass basis:

$$...g_4 D_L^\dagger \text{diag}(a_d, a_s) D_L... \to g_4 (a_s - a_d)(D_L)_{12} \times$$
$$\bar{d}_{L\,\text{mass}} \gamma^\mu A_\mu^{(n)} s_{L\,\text{mass}} \quad (1.41)$$

where D_L is the unitary transformation to go from the interaction (or weak) basis to the mass basis (for left-handed down-type quarks).

Hence, we obtain a contribution to, for example, $K - \bar{K}$ mixing amplitude:

$$\mathcal{M}_{KK} \sim \frac{g_4^2}{M_{KK}^2} (a_s - a_d)^2 (D_L)_{12}^2 \quad (1.42)$$

The SM contribution to $K - \bar{K}$ mixing amplitude has a suppression mechanism (see below):

$$\mathcal{M}_{SM} \sim \frac{g_4^4}{16\pi^2} \frac{m_c^2}{M_W^4} (V_{us} V_{ud})^2 \quad (1.43)$$

where $V_{us,\,ud}$ are the Cabibbo-Kobayashi-Maskawa (CKM) mixing angles. Since the data agrees with the SM prediction, we must require the KK contribution to be smaller than the SM one and hence we can set a bound on the KK mass. Using

$$(a_s - a_d) \sim O(1/10) \quad (1.44)$$

(see exercise 1), i.e., the fact that the couplings of gauge KK modes to down and strange quarks are $O(1)$ different, we get

$$M_{KK} \gtrsim 20 \text{ TeV} \quad (1.45)$$

assuming that the the D_L mixing angles are of order the CKM mixing angles. Such a large KK mass scale could result in a tension with a solution to the Planck-weak hierarchy problem: we would like the KK scale to be $\sim$ TeV for this purpose (we will see later how the KK mass scale is related to the EW scale).

For completeness, we briefly review FCNC's in the SM below. We begin with the transformation of quarks from weak to mass basis. The Yukawa couplings of the SM fermions to the Higgs (or the mass terms) are 3×3 complex matrices (denoted by M_d in the down quark sector) in the generation space. Such matrices can be diagonalized by *bi*-unitary transformations, $D_{L,R}$. For simplicity, consider the 2 generation case (this analysis can be easily generalized to the case of 3 generations), where this transformation can be explicitly written as

$$\left(\bar{d}_{L\,\text{weak}} \; \bar{s}_{L\,\text{weak}} \right) (M_d)_{2\times 2} \begin{pmatrix} d_{R\,\text{weak}} \\ s_{R\,\text{weak}} \end{pmatrix}$$
$$= \left(\bar{d}_{L\,\text{mass}} \; \bar{s}_{L\,\text{mass}} \right) M_d^{\text{diag.}} \begin{pmatrix} d_{R\,\text{mass}} \\ s_{R\,\text{mass}} \end{pmatrix} \quad (1.46)$$

where

$$\begin{pmatrix} d_{L,R\,\text{weak}} \\ s_{L,R\,\text{weak}} \end{pmatrix} = D_{L,R} \begin{pmatrix} d_{L,R\,\text{mass}} \\ s_{L,R\,\text{mass}} \end{pmatrix} \quad (1.47)$$

$$M_d^{\text{diag.}} \equiv D_L^\dagger M_d D_R$$
$$= \begin{pmatrix} m_d & 0 \\ 0 & m_s \end{pmatrix} \quad (1.48)$$

There are no tree-level FCNC in the SM since the gluon, γ and Z vertices preserve flavor in spite of the above transformations. Of course, the reason is that the couplings of gluon, γ and Z in the weak (or interaction) basis are universal. Explicitly,

$$g_Z \left(-\frac{1}{2} + \frac{1}{3}\sin^2\theta_W \right) \left(\bar{d}_{L\,\text{weak}} \; \bar{s}_{L\,\text{weak}} \right) Z_\mu \gamma^\mu \begin{pmatrix} 1 & 0 \\ 0 & 1 \end{pmatrix} \begin{pmatrix} d_{L\,\text{weak}} \\ s_{L\,\text{weak}} \end{pmatrix}$$
$$= \ldots \left(\bar{d}_{L\,\text{mass}} \; \bar{s}_{L\,\text{mass}} \right) Z_\mu \gamma^\mu D_L^\dagger \begin{pmatrix} 1 & 0 \\ 0 & 1 \end{pmatrix} D_L \begin{pmatrix} d_{L\,\text{mass}} \\ s_{L\,\text{mass}} \end{pmatrix}$$
$$= \ldots \sum_{i=d,s} \bar{d}^i_{L\,\text{mass}} Z_\mu \gamma^\mu d^i_{L\,\text{mass}} \quad (1.49)$$

as compared to Eqs. (1.40) and (1.41).

However, the charged current (W) couplings *are* non-diagonal in the mass basis:

$$\frac{g}{\sqrt{2}} \left(\bar{u}_{L\,\text{weak}} \; \bar{c}_{L\,\text{weak}} \right) W_\mu \gamma^\mu \begin{pmatrix} 1 & 0 \\ 0 & 1 \end{pmatrix} \begin{pmatrix} d_{L\,\text{weak}} \\ s_{L\,\text{weak}} \end{pmatrix}$$
$$= \ldots \left(\bar{u}_{L\,\text{mass}} \; \bar{c}_{L\,\text{mass}} \right) W_\mu \gamma^\mu U_L^\dagger \begin{pmatrix} 1 & 0 \\ 0 & 1 \end{pmatrix} D_L \begin{pmatrix} d_{L\,\text{mass}} \\ s_{L\,\text{mass}} \end{pmatrix}$$
$$= \ldots \sum_{i=u,c\; j=d,s} \bar{u}^i_{L\,\text{mass}} W^\mu \gamma_\mu V_{CKM\;ij} d^j_{L\,\text{mass}} \quad (1.50)$$

where the CKM matrix

$$V_{CKM} \equiv U_L^\dagger D_L$$
$$\neq 1 \qquad (1.51)$$

since the transformations in the up and down sectors are, in general, not related. Hence, the charged currents do convert up-type quark of one generation to a down-type quark of a *different* generation. So, we can use the charged current interactions more than once, i.e., in loop diagrams, to change one down-type quark to another down-type quark, for example, to obtain a $\Delta S = 2$ process via a box diagram.

Naively, we can estimate the size of this box diagram

$$\mathcal{M}_{SM} \sim g_2^4 \int \frac{d^4k}{(2\pi)^4} V^*_{CKM\ is} V^*_{CKM\ js} V_{CKM\ id} V_{CKM\ jd} \frac{1}{\slashed{k}-m_i} \frac{1}{\slashed{k}-m_j} \frac{1}{k^2-M_W^2}$$

$$\sim g_2^4 \left(V_{us} V_{cd}\right)^2 \frac{1}{16\pi^2 M_W^2} \qquad (1.52)$$

(neglecting $m_{i,j}$ in the up quark propagators: more on this assumption below) which turns out to be too large compared to the experimental value!

However, this is where the Glashow-Iliopoulos-Maiani (or GIM) mechanism comes in. Using the unitarity of the CKM matrix,

$$\sum_i V^\dagger_{si} V_{id} = 0, \qquad (1.53)$$

we find that $\mathcal{M}_{SM}$ vanishes if $m_i = m_j$, in particular if we neglect the quark masses as we did above. Hence, the amplitude must be proportional to the non-degeneracy of the up-type quark masses, i.e., for the two generation case we find that

$$\mathcal{M}_{SM} \sim \frac{g_2^4}{16\pi^2} \left(V_{us} V_{cd}\right)^2 \frac{m_c^2 - m_u^2}{M_W^4} \qquad (1.54)$$

which was used earlier in Eq. (1.43). The point is that we get an extra suppression of $\sim m_c^2/M_W^2 \sim 10^{-4}$ compared to the naive estimate in 2nd line of Eq. (1.52).

1.4. Lecture 3

As we saw in the previous lecture, the extra dimensional model which addresses the flavor hierarchy does *not* have analog of the GIM suppression in the gauge KK contribution to flavor violation. The reason is that the couplings of the strange and down quarks to the gauge KK modes, denoted by $a_{s,d}$ (in units of g_4), are $O(1)$, and different.

In order to solve this problem, we would like to modify the gauge KK profile, for example, a more favorable picture would be as in Fig. 1.8, where gauge KK modes are localized near the $y = \pi R$ brane whereas light fermions are localized near the $y = 0$ brane as usual. The point is that in this case couplings of fermions to the gauge KK modes (even though still non-universal) are $\ll 1$ (in units of g_4) so that the FCNC's are suppressed. So, the question is how to modify KK decomposition in general and, in particular, how to obtain the profiles as in Fig. 1.8.

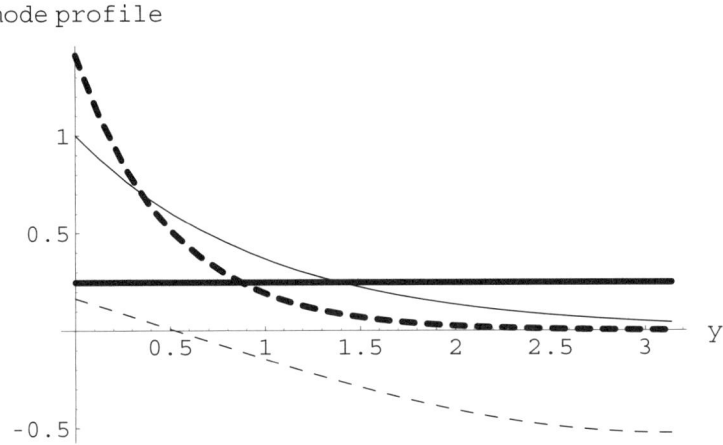

Fig. 1.8. Same as Fig. 1.7, but with brane kinetic term, $r/R = 10$, for gauge fields on $y = 0$ brane.

1.4.1. Brane Kinetic Terms

We consider a modification to the extra dimensional model by adding interactions for the $5D$ gauge fields which are localized at the fixed points (branes). The point is that such interactions are allowed for an orbifold, but not on a circle, where there are no such "special" points in the extra dimension. In fact, consistency of the model at the quantum level requires the presence of such terms since such terms are generated by loops even if they are absent at tree-level [9].

Specifically, we study the Lagrangian:

$$\mathcal{L}_{5D} = -\frac{1}{4}\Big[\mathcal{F}_{MN}\mathcal{F}^{MN} + \delta(y)r\mathcal{F}_{\mu\nu}\mathcal{F}^{\mu\nu}\Big]$$
$$+ \bar{\Psi}\left(\partial_M + g_5\mathcal{A}_M\right)\Gamma^M\Psi \quad (1.55)$$

Simple dimensional analysis gives $\left[\mathcal{A}_M\right] = 3/2$, $\left[\Psi\right] = 2$, $\left[g_5\right] = -1/2$ (here $[...]$ denotes mass dimension) so that the brane kinetic term has mass dimension -1 (i.e., it has dimension of a length) and is therefore denoted by r.

It is sometimes convenient to use a different normalization for $\mathcal{A}_M$: $\mathcal{A}_M \to \hat{\mathcal{A}}_M/g_5$ in terms of which the action is:

$$\mathcal{L}_{5D} = -\frac{1}{4}\Big[\frac{1}{g_5^2}\hat{\mathcal{F}}_{MN}\hat{\mathcal{F}}^{MN} + \delta(y)\frac{r}{g_5^2}\hat{\mathcal{F}}_{\mu\nu}\hat{\mathcal{F}}^{\mu\nu}\Big]$$
$$+ \bar{\Psi}\left(\partial_M + \hat{\mathcal{A}}_M\right)\Gamma^M\Psi \quad (1.56)$$

With this normalization, we have $\left[\hat{\mathcal{A}}_M\right] = 1$ (as in $4D$) so that the brane kinetic term is dimensionless: we can then define a brane-localized "coupling" as $1/g_{\text{brane}}^2 \equiv r/g_5^2$.

We will now study how the KK decomposition is modified in the presence of these brane kinetic terms. Consider the case of a scalar field for simplicity (the gauge case which we are really interested in is similar). Here, we will only give a summary: for details, see exercise 2 and reference [10] for example.

Following the procedure outlined in lecture 2, we find that the orthonormality condition is modified (relative to the case of no brane terms):

$$\int dy f_n^*(y) f_m(y)\Big[1 + r\delta(y)\Big] = \delta_{mn} \quad (1.57)$$

and the profiles and mass eigenvalues are given by solving the differential equation:

$$\Big[\partial_y^2 + m_n^2 + r\delta(y)m_n^2\Big] f_n(y) = 0 \quad (1.58)$$

The solutions $f_n(y)$ of this equation are linear combination of sin and cos, in particular, a *different* one for $y = 0$ to $y = \pi R$ and $y = -\pi R$ to $y = 0$.

In addition, in order to solve for the coefficients of sin, cos in these linear combinations, we must impose conditions such as continuity of $f_n(y)$ at $y = 0$, periodicity of $f_n(y)$ and matching the discontinuity in derivative of $f_n(y)$ to $\delta(y)$ in Eq. (1.57).

1.4.2. *Couplings of gauge modes*

It turns out that the zero-mode of the gauge field continues to have a flat profile: only its normalization affected by brane term such that

$$g_4 = \frac{g_5}{\sqrt{r + 2\pi R}} \quad (1.59)$$

For large brane kinetic terms,

$$g_4 \approx \frac{g_5}{\sqrt{r}} \quad (1.60)$$

Let us now consider couplings of gauge KK modes to particles localized on the branes in the limit of large brane terms. We find that

(i) the coupling of gauge KK mode to a particle (say light SM fermion) localized at $y = 0$ is *suppressed* (compared to zero-mode): $g_5 \times f_n(0) \sim g_4/\sqrt{r/R}$.

(ii) Whereas, the coupling to particles (such as the Higgs) localized at $y = \pi R$ is *enhanced* compared to the zero-mode (or SM) gauge coupling : $g_5 \times f_n(\pi R) \sim g_4 \times \sqrt{r/R}$

The intuitive understanding is that large brane kinetic terms "repel" gauge KK mode from that brane (see Fig. 1.8).

1.4.3. *Solution to Flavor* **Problem**

In reality, the light SM fermions are not exactly localized at the $y = 0$ brane, but we find a similar suppression in their coupling to gauge KK mode for the actual profiles of the light fermions which are exponentials *peaked* at $y = 0$. Hence, based on the rough size of the coupling mentioned in point (i) above, we can show that FCNC's from exchange of gauge KK modes are suppressed by a factor of r/R relative to the case of without brane kinetic terms, i.e., large brane kinetic terms provide an *analog* of GIM suppression in the SM.

One might wonder if we are introducing a new hierarchy since we need $r/R \gg 1$. However, that's not really the case since a mild hierarchy of $O(10)$ is enough. In fact, we will see in lecture 5 how we can *effectively* obtain the same effect as that of such large brane kinetic terms in a *warped* extra dimension without introducing *any* brane terms and therefore any hierarchy in the $5D$ theory at all.

1.4.4. *Electroweak Precision Tests*

Having seen how to suppress contributions of the gauge KK modes to FCNC's, we will now consider their contributions to flavor-*preserving* observables called electroweak precision tests (EWPT). There are 3 such effects which we discuss in turn.

1.4.4.1. *4-fermion operators*

Tree-level exchange of gauge KK modes also generates flavor-preserving 4-fermion operators, Fig. 1.9. We can compare these effects to SM (i.e., zero-mode) Z exchange which has coefficient $\sim g_Z^2/m_Z^2$ and use the fact that the experimental data on these operators agrees with the SM prediction at the $\sim 0.1\%$ level. For $r = 0$ (no brane term), we found that gauge KK coupling $\approx \sqrt{2} g_4$ for fermions localized at $y = 0$ (recall that light fermions are localized near $y = 0$) so that we obtain a limit of $m_{KK} \gtrsim$ a few TeV. However, for large brane kinetic terms, the gauge KK couplings and hence the coefficients of these operators are further suppressed by a factor of $\sim r/R$ so that $m_{KK} \sim$ TeV is *easily* allowed by the data.

The other 2 effects originate from the mixing of zero and KK modes for W, Z via the Higgs vev which we now discuss. The gauge group in the bulk is $SU(2)_L \times U(1)_Y$. We first perform the KK decomposition (i.e., obtain zero and KK modes) for $W_{i=1,2,3}$ and B (hypercharge) setting $v = 0$. At this level, there is no kinetic or mass mixing between these modes.

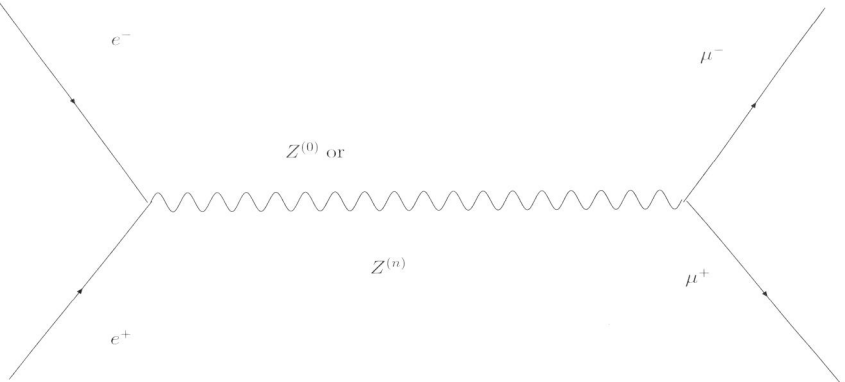

Fig. 1.9. 4-fermion operators generated by exchange of zero and KK modes of Z.

Next, we turn on the Higgs vev. For $v \neq 0$, we obtain masses for zero-modes of B and W_i and mass *mixing* between W_3 and B zero-modes (as in the SM). We define photon and Z zero-modes, $Z_\mu^{(0)}$ and $A_\mu^{(0)}$, to be combinations of $W_3^{(0)}$ and $B^{(0)}$ such that the *zero*-mode mass mixing is diagonalized (as in the SM). We first define the zero-mode gauge couplings (we neglect the brane terms for simplicity here, but it is straightforward to include them): $g_{W^{(0)}} = g_{5\,2}/\sqrt{2\pi R}$, $g_{Z^{(0)}} = g_{5\,Z}/\sqrt{2\pi R}$, where $(g_{5\,Z}^2 = g_{5\,2}^2 + g_5'^2)$. The weak mixing angle between $W_3^{(0)}$ and $B^{(0)}$, i.e., $\sin^2 \theta_W$ is the ratio of these zero-mode gauge couplings.

It turns out to be convenient to define the KK modes, $Z^{(n)}$ and $A^{(n)}$ ($n \neq 0$), using *same* (0-mode) mixing angles. The reason is that with this definition, the KK photon modes $A_\mu^{(n)}$ do not couple to Higgs (just like zero-mode) and hence decouple from the other modes.

However, the crucial point is that the $W^\pm$ zero mode mixes with the KK modes of $W^\pm$ via mass terms coming from the Higgs vev localized at $y = \pi R$ (similarly for Z). Therefore, the mass eigenstates, i.e., SM $W^\pm$ and Z, are *admixtures* of zero and KK modes. To understand this effect, we can diagonalize the 2×2 mass matrix (for zero and 1st KK mode) for simplicity (see exercise 3).

1.4.4.2. *Shift in coupling of SM fermions to Z*

The above zero-KK mode mixing for W, Z induced by Higgs vev results in a shift in the coupling of SM W, Z to a fermion localized at $y = 0$ from the pure zero-mode coupling, i.e., SM Z has a (small) KK Z component so that $g_Z = g_{Z^{(0)}} + \delta g_Z$. We can estimate this effect via mass insertion diagrams as in Fig. 1.10 which are valid for $v \times$ couplings $\ll m_{KK}$ to find $\delta g_Z / g_{Z^{(0)}} \sim g_{Z^{(0)}}^2 v^2 / m_{KK}^2$: see exercise 3 for a more accurate calculation. Note that there is *no* enhancement in δg_Z for large brane kinetic terms ($r/R \gg 1$). The point is that the enhancement in the coupling (relative to the zero-mode coupling) at the Higgs-KK Z vertex cancels the suppression in the coupling at the fermion-KK Z vertex (cf. the effect on the W, Z masses below). Just like the case of 4-fermion operators, the measured couplings of SM fermions to Z agree with the SM prediction at the $\sim 0.1\%$ level so that we obtain a limit of $m_{KK} \stackrel{>}{\sim}$ a few TeV.

1.4.4.3. *Shift in ratio of W and Z masses or ρ parameter*

The mixing of zero and KK W modes induced by the Higgs vev also results in a shift in SM W mass from the pure zero-mode mass (a similar effect

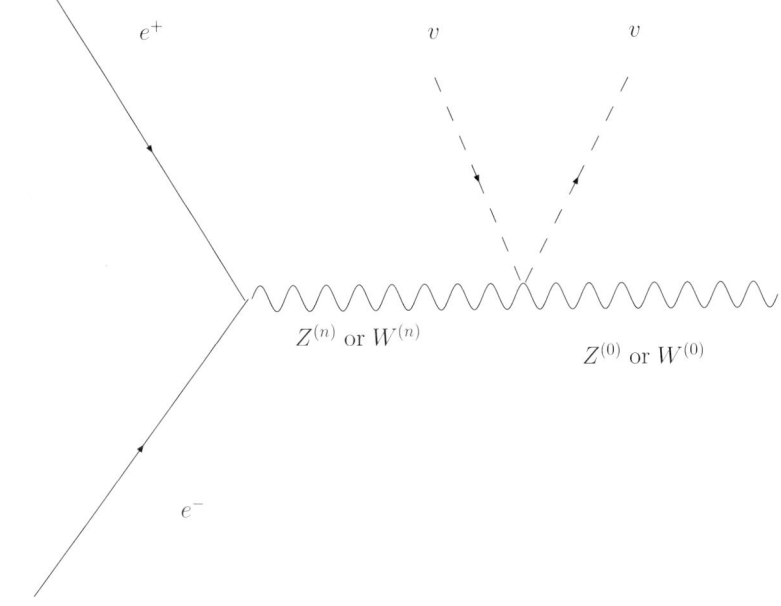

Fig. 1.10. Shift in the coupling of a SM fermion to SM Z from the zero-mode gauge coupling due to the mixing of zero and KK modes of Z.

also happens for SM Z) as in Fig. 1.11:

$$M_W^2 = M_{W^{(0)}}^2 + \delta M_W^2, \text{ where} \quad (1.61)$$

$$M_{W^{(0)}}^2 = \frac{1}{4} g_{W^{(0)}}^2 v^2 \quad (1.62)$$

$$\delta M_W^2 \sim g_{W^{(0)}}^4 \frac{v^4}{m_{KK}^2} \frac{r}{R} \quad (1.63)$$

This effect, in turn, shifts the ρ parameter defined as

$$\rho = \frac{M_W^2}{M_Z^2} \times \frac{g_Z^2}{g_2^2} \quad (1.64)$$

The point is that $\rho = 1$ in the SM (at the tree-level) and $\Delta \rho_{expt.} \equiv \rho_{expt.} - 1 \sim 10^{-3}$. Actually, there is a subtlety in this definition for the 5D model due to the fact that the couplings of the Z boson to the SM fermions are also modified from the pure zero-mode Z coupling: $g_Z = g_{Z^{(0)}} + \delta g_Z$. However, as we discussed earlier, $\delta g_{Z,\,W}$ are not enhanced by $r/R \gg 1$ so that we

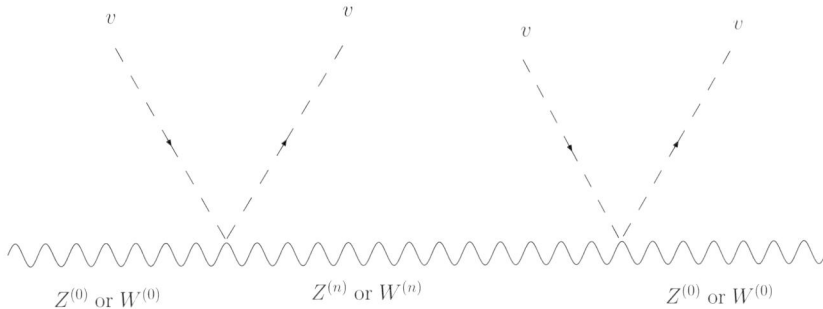

Fig. 1.11. Shift in the masses of SM W, Z from the zero-mode masses due to the mixing of zero and KK modes.

can set $g_Z \approx g_{Z^{(0)}}$ in $\Delta\rho$ to find

$$\delta\rho \equiv \rho - 1 \sim \left(g_{Z^{(0)}}^2 - g_{W^{(0)}}^2\right) \frac{v^2}{m_{KK}^2} \times \frac{r}{R} \qquad (1.65)$$

The crucial point is that $\Delta\rho$ is *enhanced* by the presence of large brane kinetic terms such that we must require $m_{KK} \gtrsim 10$ TeV for $r/R \sim 10$ (as needed to solve the flavor problem).

1.5. Lecture 4

In this lecture, we will show how to solve the problem of large corrections to the ρ parameter discussed in lecture 3. For this purpose, we have to introduce a "custodial isospin" symmetry in the extra dimension. We will then discuss some signals of this extra dimensional scenario.

1.5.1. *Custodial Isospin in SM*

We will first review why $\rho = 1$ in the SM at the tree-level. The starting point is that the Higgs potential, $V(|H|)$ in the SM with the *complex* doublet Higgs written as

$$H = (h_1, h_2, h_3, h_4) \qquad (1.66)$$

has a global $SO(4)$ symmetry (corresponding to rotations among the 4 *real* fields, h_i). Moreover, $SO(4)$ is isomorphic to $SU(2) \times SU(2)$ – one of these $SU(2)$'s in fact corresponds to the usual gauged $SU(2)_L$ group and the other one is usually denoted by $SU(2)_R$. The crucial point is that the global symmetry of the Higgs potential is enhanced compared to the gauged $SU(2)_L$ symmetry. The Higgs vev:

$$\langle H \rangle = (0, 0, 0, v) \tag{1.67}$$

breaks the global $SO(4)$ symmetry of the Higgs sector (in isolation) to $SO(3)$ – the gauged $SU(2)_L$ symmetry is broken in this process so that the W_i^L gauge bosons acquire masses. The unbroken $SO(3)$ symmetry (which is global) is isomorphic to an $SU(2)$ – clearly this unbroken $SU(2)$ is the *diagonal* subgroup of the 2 original $SU(2)$'s and is often called *custodial isospin*. It is this remnant symmetry which enforces equal masses for $W_{i=1,2,3}^L$.

Of course, W_3^L only mixes with B (there is no mixing for $W_L^\pm$). This mixing results in the neutral mass, $M_Z^2 = 1/4 \, v^2 \left(g_2^2 + g'^2 \right)$, not being equal to the charged mass, $M_W^2 = 1/4 \, v^2 g_2^2$. That is the reason why there is a factor of g_Z^2/g_2^2 in the definition $\rho = M_W^2/M_Z^2 \, g_Z^2/g_2^2$: this factor takes the "violation of custodial symmetry" due to the gauging of hypercharge into account.

1.5.2. *Custodial Isospin* Violation *in* 5D

Based on the above discussion, the sizable $\Delta \rho$ in the 5D model signals violation of custodial isospin symmetry somewhere in the 5D theory. First we begin with identifying the precise origin of custodial isospin *violation* and then we will come up with a solution to this problem. As we saw in lecture 3, $\Delta \rho$ from gauge KK modes $\propto \left(g_{Z^{(0)}}^2 - g_{W^{(0)}}^2 \right) \sim g_{B^{(0)}}^2$ just as in the SM. So, the origin of large $\Delta \rho$ or custodial isospin violation seems to be similar to that in the SM, i.e., it is due to gauging of hypercharge and the resulting mixing of W_3 with B. However, the point is that there are *additional* mixing effects (compared to the SM) in the 5D model due to the presence of KK modes (the mixing of zero-modes amongst each other is same as in the SM). In particular, $W_{L\,3}^{(0)} - B^{(n)}$ mixing occurs only in neutral sector and has no charged counterpart, whereas $W_L^{(0)} - W_L^{(n)}$ mixing is symmetric between charged and neutral sectors.

The origin of this dichotomy between charged and neutral sectors is the fact that the symmetry gauged in 5D is same as in the SM, i.e., $SU(2)_L \times U(1)_Y$, so that we have KK modes only for $W_L^{3,\,\pm}$ and B: there are no charged partners for the B KK modes. This new effect (the custodial isospin violation due to B KK modes) is not taken into account by the factor of g_Z^2/g_2^2 in the definition of ρ – the point is that this factor only accounts for the mixing only amongst *zero*-modes, i.e., the $W_{L\,3}^{(0)} - B^{(0)}$

mixing. To repeat, $W_{L\,3}^{(0)} - W_{L\,3}^{(n)}$ mixing *does* have a counterpart in the charged sector. Moreover, $W_{L\,3}^{(0)} - B^{(n)}$ mass term $\sim g_{W^{(0)}} g_5' \times f_n(\pi R) v^2 \sim g_{W^{(0)}} g_{B^{(0)}} v^2 \sqrt{r/R}$ so that this effect is *enhanced* for large brane terms!

1.5.3. *Custodial Isospin* Symmetry *in* 5D

It is clear that we need *extra* charged KK modes to partner $B^{(n)}$ if we wish to suppress $\Delta\rho$. We can achieve this goal by promoting the hypercharge gauge boson to be a triplet. Hence, we can restore custodial isospin symmetry in the 5D model by enlarging the 5D *gauge* symmetry to $SU(2)_L \times SU(2)_R$ [11]. It turns out that we need something like $SU(2)_L \times SU(2)_R \times U(1)_{B-L}$ to obtain the correct fermion hypercharges as follows. Hypercharge is identified with a subgroup of $U(1)_R$ and $U(1)_{B-L}$: $Y = T_{3R} + (B-L)/2$, with $T_{3R} = \pm 1/2$ for $(u,d)_R$ and $(\nu, e)_R$ and $B - L = 1/3, -1$ for q, l (it is easy to check that this reproduces the SM hypercharges). Note that we still have extra neutral KK modes from $U(1)_{B-L}$ (which have no charged counterpart), but these KK modes do not couple to Higgs since the Higgs has $B - L$ charge of zero: only KK $W_{L,R}^{3,\pm}$ couple to Higgs such that the KK exchanges which give the shifts in masses respect custodial isospin (i.e., they are the same in the charged and the neutral channels).

Of course, we must break $SU(2)_R \times U(1)_{B-L}$ down to $U(1)_Y$, i.e., we must require that there are no zero-modes for $W_R^\pm$ and the extra $U(1)$ which is the combination of $U(1)_R$ and $U(1)_{B-L}$ orthogonal to $U(1)_Y$. However, this breaking must (approximately) preserve degeneracy for (at least the lighter) $W_R^\pm$ and W_R^3 modes such that $\Delta\rho$ continues to be (at least approximately) protected. It is clear that for this purpose we require degeneracy in both the mass of these modes and their coupling to the Higgs. This might seem to be challenging at first, but note that, for large brane kinetic terms ($r/R \gg 1$), KK modes are localized near $y = \pi R$. Therefore, if we break custodial isospin on the $y = 0$ brane, then the degeneracy between W_R^3 and $W_R^\pm$ is not significantly affected by this breaking. Specifically, we write down a *large* mass term for $W_R^\pm$ and the extra $U(1)$ at $y = 0$ which can originate from a localized scalar vev (different from the SM Higgs). We can show that this is equivalent to requiring vanishing of these gauge fields at $y = 0$ (odd or Dirichlet boundary condition: section 3.3 of reference [2]). This illustrates the general idea that breaking a 5D gauge symmetry by a large mass term localized on a brane is equivalent to breaking by boundary condition.

1.5.4. *Signals*

Let us consider some of the signals of this extra-dimensional set-up. A quick glance at Fig. 1.8 tells us that the coupling of gauge KK modes to top quark is enhanced compared to the SM couplings, whereas the couplings to the light SM fermions are suppressed (all based on the profiles for these modes).

We begin with real production of gauge KK modes, for example, the KK gluon. Due to the $\sim$ TeV mass for these particles, it is clear that we have to consider such a process at the Large Hadron Collider (LHC). Based on the above couplings, we typically find a broad resonance decaying into top pairs making it a challenge to distinguish the signal from SM background. It turns out that due to a constraint from a shift in the $Z \to \bar{b}b$ coupling,[f] we cannot localize b_L and hence its partner t_L too close to the Higgs brane, forcing us to localize t_R near the Higgs brane in order to obtain the large top mass. Hence the KK gluon dominantly decays to RH top quark. We can use this fact (and noting that the SM $t\bar{t}$ production is approximately same for LH and RH top quarks) for the purpose of signal versus background discrimination [12]. It is easy to distinguish this signal for the extra dimension from SUSY: there is no missing energy (at least in this process) and top quark is treated as "special" in the sense that it has a larger coupling (than the other SM fermions) to the new particles, namely KK modes, unlike in SUSY.

We can also consider *virtual* exchange of gauge KK modes.

(i) In analogy with the shift in the coupling of SM fermion to the Z that we considered earlier, we see that $\bar{t}tZ$ is shifted compared to the SM prediction (or compared to $\bar{u}uZ$ and $\bar{c}cZ$) since top quark (up quark) is localized near $y = \pi R$ ($y = 0$) brane. Such an effect can be easily measured at the International Linear Collider (ILC) [13].

(ii) From the above discussion, it is clear that the couplings of the top and charm quarks to the KK Z are diagonal, but not universal in the weak or interaction basis. Once we rotate to the mass basis, there is a flavor violating coupling to KK Z to the top and the charm quark. In turn, this effect induces a flavor violating coupling

---

[f]This shift in the coupling originates from diagrams similar to the ones we considered earlier for the shift in coupling of SM fermion to the Z: see Fig. 1.10. Such shifts are enhanced if SM fermion is localized near $y = \pi R$ brane, where gauge KK mode is peaked.

of the *SM Z* to the top and charm quarks (via mixing of KK and zero-mode *Z*), resulting in a flavor violating decay of the top quark: $t \to cZ$. Such decays can be probed at the LHC [14].

1.5.5. *Summary of Model and Unanswered Questions*

So, far we have considered a model with the SM gauge and fermion propagating in the bulk of a *flat* extra dimension, with the Higgs localized on or near one of the branes. The other SM particles (gauge bosons and fermions) are identified with zero-modes of the corresponding $5D$ fields.

We have seen that a solution to the flavor hierarchy of the SM is possible using profiles for the SM fermions (again, these are the zero-modes of the $5D$ fields) in the extra dimension; in particular, top and bottom quarks can be localized near the Higgs brane, whereas the 1st and 2nd generation (or light) fermions can be localized near the other brane. Moreover, the resulting flavor problem due to non-universal couplings of gauge KK modes to the SM fermions (for a few TeV KK scale) can be ameliorated with large brane kinetic terms for $5D$ gauge fields on *non*-Higgs brane (i.e., where the light fermions are localized).

We also studied constraints from electroweak precision tests on this set-up and found that these constraints can also be satisfied for $m_{KK} \sim$ TeV, provided there is a custodial isospin symmetry in the bulk to protect the observable related to the ratio of W/Z masses (the ρ parameter).

This set-up still leaves some questions unanswered:

(i) We have assumed so far that $m_{KK} \sim$ TeV, but why is it $\ll M_{Pl}$?
(ii) Is there a mild hierarchy problem associated with having large brane kinetic terms? Moreover, it seems a bit arbitrary that such terms appear only at $y = 0$ brane (where light SM fermions are localized) and not at $y = \pi R$.

We will see in the next lecture that both these questions can be answered by using a *warped* geometry (instead of flat extra dimension).

Furthermore,

(iii) Why does Higgs have a negative (mass)^2 or why does electroweak symmetry breaking (EWSB) occur? What sets this mass scale? Specifically, can the hierarchy $m_H \ll M_{Pl}$ be due to some dynamics giving $m_H \sim m_{KK}$ which, in turn, is $\sim$ TeV?
(iv) Why is the Higgs localized on or near one of the branes?

These questions will be answered by a *combination* of Higgs being A_5, i.e., the 5th component of bulk gauge field and warped geometry.

1.6. Lecture 5

In this lecture, we will be brief: for details and a more complete set of references, see the excellent set of lectures by Sundrum [3].

1.6.1. *Warped Extra Dimension (RS1)*

We begin with a review of the original Randall-Sundrum model (RS1) [15]: see Fig. 1.12. It consists of an extra-dimensional interval ($y = 0$ to πR as before), but with the gravitational action containing a bulk cosmological constant (CC) and brane tensions (localized or 4D CC's):

$$S_{5D} = \int d^4x dy \sqrt{-\det G}\left(M_5^3 \mathcal{R}_5 - \Lambda\right)$$

$$S_{brane\ 1,\ 2} = \int d^4x \sqrt{-\det g_{1,\ 2}} T_{1,\ 2} \qquad (1.68)$$

with $g_{\mu\nu\ 1}(x) = G_{\mu\nu}(x, y = 0)$ and $g_{\mu\nu\ 2}(x) = G_{\mu\nu}(x, y = \pi R)$, where $g_{\mu\nu}$'s are the induced metrics on the branes and G_{MN} is the bulk metric. Also, M_5 is the 5D Planck scale and $\mathcal{R}_5$ is the 5D Ricci scalar.

With the following two fine-tunings:

$$T_1 = -T_2 = 24k M_5^3, \qquad (1.69)$$

where the (curvature) scale, k is defined using $\Lambda = 24k^2 M_5^3$, we obtain a flat (or Minkowski), but y-dependent 4D metric as a solution of the 5D Einstein's equations:

$$(ds)^2 = e^{-2ky} \eta_{\mu\nu}(dx)^\mu (dx)^\nu + (dy)^2 \qquad (1.70)$$

Thus, the geometry is that of a slice of anti-de Sitter space in 5D (AdS$_5$). The y-dependent coefficient of the 4D metric, i.e., e^{-ky} is called the "warp factor".

4D gravity: The 4D graviton (which is the zero-mode of the 5D gravitational) corresponds to fluctuations around the flat spacetime background, i.e., $g^{(0)}_{\mu\nu}(x) \approx \eta_{\mu\nu} + h^{(0)}_{\mu\nu}(x)$. As usual, we plug this fluctuation into the 5D action and integrate over the extra dimensional coordinate to find an effective 4D action for $g^{(0)}_{\mu\nu}(x)$:

$$S_{4D} = \frac{M_5^3}{k}\left(1 - e^{-2k\pi R}\right) \int d^4x \sqrt{-\det g^{(0)}} \mathcal{R}_4[g^{(0)}] \qquad (1.71)$$

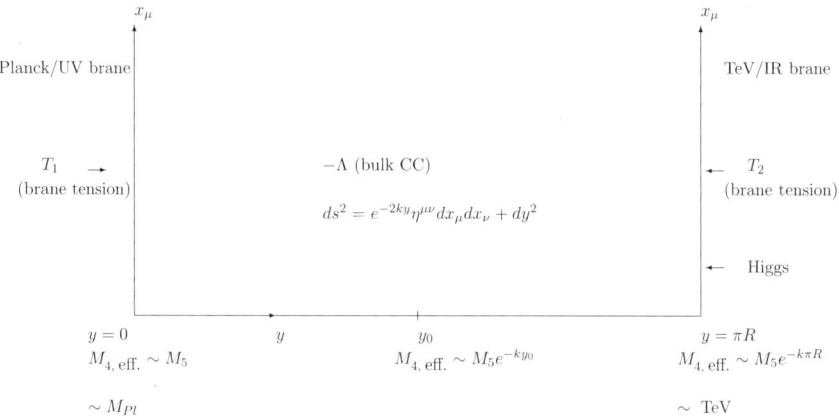

Fig. 1.12. The Randall-Sundrum (RS1) model.

from which we can deduce the $4D$ Planck scale:

$$M_{Pl}^2 = \frac{M_5^3}{k}\left(1 - e^{-2k\pi R}\right)$$
$$\approx \frac{M_5^3}{k} \text{ for } kR \gg 1 \qquad (1.72)$$

We choose $k \lesssim M_5$ so that the higher curvature terms in the $5D$ action are small and hence can be neglected. Thus, we get the following order of magnitudes for the various mass scales:

$$k \lesssim M_5 \lesssim M_{Pl} \sim 10^{18} \text{ GeV} \qquad (1.73)$$

It turns out that the $4D$ graviton is (automatically) localized near $y = 0$ (which is hence called the Planck or UV brane) - that is why the $4D$ Planck scale is finite even if we go to the decompactified limit of $R \to \infty$ in Eq. (1.72). Specifically, its profile is $\sim e^{-2ky}$.

1.6.2. *Solution to Planck-Weak Hierarchy*

The motivation for the RS1 model is to solve the Planck-weak hierarchy problem. Let us now see how this model achieves it. Assume that a $4D$ Higgs field is localized on the $y = \pi R$ brane which is hence called the TeV or IR brane:

$$S_{\text{Higgs}} = \int d^4x \sqrt{-\det g_2} \Big[g^{\mu\nu}_{\text{ind.}} \, \partial_\mu H \partial_\nu H \\ - \lambda \left(|H|^2 - v_0^2 \right)^2 \Big] \qquad (1.74)$$

where the natural size for v_0 is the 5D gravity or fundamental scale (M_5). Using the metric induced on the TeV brane, $g_{\mu\nu\,2} = G_{\mu\nu}(y = \pi R) = g^{(0)}_{\mu\nu} e^{-2k\pi R}$, the action for the Higgs field becomes

$$S_{\text{Higgs}} = \int d^4x \sqrt{-\det g^{(0)}} \Big[e^{-2k\pi R} g^{(0)\,\mu\nu} \partial_\mu H \partial_\nu H \\ - e^{-4k\pi R} \lambda \left(|H|^2 - v_0^2 \right)^2 \Big] \qquad (1.75)$$

Now comes the crucial point: we must rescale the Higgs field to go to canonical normalization, $H \equiv \hat{H} e^{k\pi R}$, which results in

$$S_{\text{Higgs}} = \int d^4x \sqrt{\det g^{(0)}} \Big[g^{(0)\,\mu\nu} \partial_\mu \hat{H} \partial_\nu \hat{H} \\ - \lambda \left(|\hat{H}|^2 - v_0^2 e^{-2k\pi R} \right)^2 \Big] \qquad (1.76)$$

Note that the Higgs mass is "warped-down" to $\sim$ TeV from the 5D (or the 4D) Planck scale if we have the following *modest* hierarchy between the radius (or the proper distance) of the extra dimension and the AdS curvature scale.

$$k\pi R \sim \log\left(M_{Pl}/\text{TeV}\right) \\ \sim 30 \text{ or} \\ R \sim \frac{10}{k} \qquad (1.77)$$

Moreover, the quartic coupling is unchanged and hence the Higgs vev (or weak scale) is also at the TeV scale, assuming $\lambda \sim O(1)$.

Note that the radius of the extra dimension is not a fundamental or 5D parameter, rather it is determined by the dynamics of the theory. Hence, in order to have complete solution to the hierarchy problem (without any hidden fine-tuning), we must show that the radius can be stabilized at the required size without further (large) fine-tuning of parameters of the 5D theory. In fact, stabilization of such a radius can be achieved using a bulk scalar (Goldberger-Wise mechanism) [16], provided we invoke a *mild* hierarchy $M^2/k^2 \sim O(1/10)$, where M is the 5D mass of the scalar.

Thus, we see that the Planck-weak hierarchy can be obtained from $O(10)$ hierarchy in the fundamental or $5D$ theory! In general, a large ("exponential") hierarchy for the $4D$ mass scales can be obtained from a small hierarchy in the $5D$ parameters.

The central feature of a warped extra dimension is that the *effective $4D$ mass scale depends on position* in the extra dimension. In order to have a more intuitive understanding of this feature, consider the position $y \sim y_0$ where the metric is:

$$(ds)^2_{y \sim y_0} \sim e^{-2ky_0} \eta_{\mu\nu} (dx)^\mu (dx)^\nu + (dy)^2 \quad (1.78)$$

In terms of the rescaled coordinate and mass scale: $\hat{x} \equiv e^{-ky_0} x$, $\hat{m}_{4D} \equiv e^{ky_0} m_{4D}$, we get

$$(ds)^2_{y \sim y_0} \sim \eta_{\mu\nu} (d\hat{x})^\mu (d\hat{x})^\nu + (dy)^2 \quad (1.79)$$

The advantage of the new coordinates $\hat{x}$ is that we have a "flat" metric in terms of it so that we expect $\hat{m}_{4D} \sim m_{5D}$ (such a relationship is valid in the absence of warping). Converting back to original mass scales, we find $m_{4D} \sim e^{-ky_0} m_{5D}$, i.e., $4D$ mass scales are warped compared to $5D$ mass scales. *An analogy with the expanding Universe is useful*: just as $3D$ space expands with time, in the warped extra dimension, the $4D$ space-*time* "expands" (or contracts) with motion along the 5th dimension.

1.6.3. *Summary of RS1*

The preceding discussion leads us to the "master equation" for a warped extra dimension:

$$M_{4,\,\text{eff.}}(y) \sim M_5 \times e^{-ky}$$

relating the effective $4D$ mass scales on the left-hand side (LHS) of the above equation to the fundamental or $5D$ mass scale on the right-hand side (RHS) by the warp factor. Applying it to the case of the $4D$ graviton localized at $y \sim 0$, we get

$$M_{Pl} \sim M_5 \quad (1.80)$$

so that we must choose the $5D$ Planck scale to be

$$M_5 \sim 10^{18}\,\text{GeV} \quad (1.81)$$

Whereas, the Higgs sector is localized at $y \sim \pi R$ so that

$$M_{\text{weak}} \sim M_5 \times e^{-k\pi R} \quad (1.82)$$

so that

$$M_{\text{weak}} \sim \text{TeV} \quad (1.83)$$

provided we have a mild hierarchy

$$k\pi R \sim \log(M_{Pl}/\text{TeV})$$
$$\sim 30 \quad (1.84)$$

1.6.4. *Similarity with* Flat *TeV-Size Extra Dimension with Large Brane Terms*

In the original RS1, it was assumed that the entire SM, i.e., including fermion and gauge fields, is localized on the TeV brane. However, it was subsequently realized that, in oder to solve the Planck-weak hierarchy problem, only the SM Higgs boson has to be localized on or near the TeV brane – the masses of non-Higgs fields, i.e., fermions and gauge bosons, are protected by gauge and chiral symmetries, respectively.

So, we are led to consider RS1 with the SM gauge [17] and fermion fields [18] propagating in the bulk (with the Higgs still being on or near the TeV brane). It turns out that the profiles for the SM fermions in the bulk can address the flavor hierarchy just as in the case of flat extra dimension. Moreover, solving the wave equation in curved spacetime, we can show [17–19] that all KK modes are localized near the IR brane (that too automatically, i.e., with*out* actual brane terms) and the KK masses are given by $m_{KK} \sim k e^{-k\pi R}$ and *not* $1/R$ [note that, based on Eqs. (1.73) and (1.77) $1/R$ is of the size of the $4D$ Planck scale!]. Hence, we find $m_{KK} \sim$ TeV given the choice of parameters to solve the Planck-weak hierarchy problem! A very rough intuition for localization of KK modes near the TeV brane is that the KK modes can minimize their mass by "living" near IR brane, where all mass scales are warped down. In this sense, the warped extra dimension "mimics" large brane kinetic terms of flat geometry – recall that the large brane kinetic terms in a flat extra dimension result in a similar localization of KK modes. In addition, the hierarchy $m_{KK} \ll M_{Pl}$ is explained by the warped geometry. This addresses the 1st and 2nd questions outlined at the end of the previous lecture.

Because of this localization of KK modes near the TeV brane, we find that the solution to the flavor problem and the discussion of the electroweak precision tests (including custodial isospin) goes through (roughly) as in the case of a flat extra dimension.

1.6.5. Unification of Spins: Higgs as A_5

We now return to the other (3rd and 4th) questions asked at the end of the previous lecture, namely, what sets the scale of EWSB or Higgs mass and why is Higgs localized on the TeV brane?

We will show in this and the next subsection that obtaining the SM Higgs as the 5th component of $5D$ gauge field (or A_5) can resolve the 3rd question and then outline in the final subsection how combining the idea of Higgs as A_5 with the warped geometry answers the 4th question, resulting in a "complete" model.

As a warm-up for the idea of Higgs as A_5 (see the review [20] for references), consider an $SU(2)$ gauge theory in an extra dimension which is compactified on a circle (S^1). As we saw earlier, for $n \neq 0$, the $A_\mu^{(n)}$ modes "eat" $A_5^{(n)}$ modes to form massive spin-1 states. Moreover, there is a (massless) zero-mode A_5, which is in adjoint representation of $SU(2)$, i.e., it is charged under the $SU(2)$ gauge symmetry. We can introduce an $SU(2)$ doublet fermion in the bulk which will acquire a Yukawa coupling $\sim g$ to the A_5 zero-mode from the interaction $\bar{\Psi}_L A_5 \Psi_R$ coming from the $5D$ covariant derivative. Hence, this scenario is often called "Gauge-Yukawa unification".

Note that this scalar has no potential at the tree-level since it is part of a $5D$ gauge field. We will now discuss the potential for A_5 zero-mode induced by loop effects to find that it is *finite*. Naively, the scalar (mass)^2 gets quadratically divergent loop corrections: $m^2_{A_5^{(0)}} \sim g_4^2 / \left(16\pi^2\right) \Lambda_{UV}^2$. However, from the $5D$ point of view, it is clear that $5D$ gauge invariance protects the A_5 scalar mass from receiving divergent loop corrections (there is no counter-term to absorb such divergences and so these must be absent). The reader is referred to the 1st reference in [3] for a detailed calculation of $m^2_{A_5^{(0)}}$ coming from a fermion loop for the simpler case of a $U(1)$ gauge field in the bulk. The summary is that loop contributions to $m^2_{A_5^{(0)}}$ are "cut-off" by R^{-1}:

$$m^2_{A_5^{(0)}} \sim \frac{g_4^2}{16\pi^2} R^{-2} \quad (1.85)$$

Intuitively, the understanding is that A_5 behaves as a "regular" scalar till $E \sim R^{-1}$: see Fig. 1.13(a). Beyond these energies, the quantum corrections "realize" that A_5 is part of a $5D$ gauge field. Therefore, the loop contributions from $E \gtrsim R^{-1}$ are highly suppressed, in particular, there is no divergence. Thinking in terms of KK modes, there is a cancellation in the loop diagram among the different modes. We can then ask: what

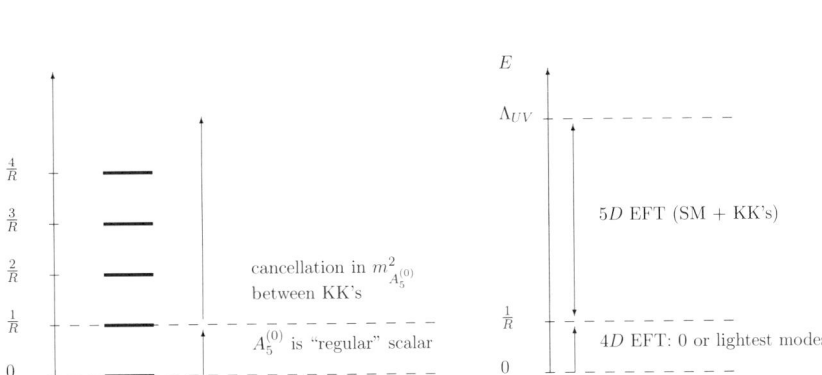

Fig. 1.13. Contributions to mass of A_5 (a) and various energy scales in the $5D$ model (b).

did we gain relative to a "regular" scalar (which is not an A_5 zero-mode, but is localized on a brane or originates in a $5D$ scalar field)? To answer this question, we need to know what is Λ_{UV}, the scale which cuts of the divergence in the case of a regular scalar. The $4D$ SM (without gravity) is renormalizable so that the cut-off is the Planck scale (where quantum gravity becomes important). However, the $5D$ *gauge theory*, even without gravity, *is non-renormalizable* and therefore must be defined with a cut-off (which is not related to the Planck scale): see Fig. 1.13(b). The reason is that the $5D$ gauge coupling constant is dimensionful so that the $5D$ loop expansion grows with energy: $g_5^2 E / \left(16\pi^2\right)$. Since we cannot extrapolate the $5D$ gauge theory beyond the energy scale where the loop expansion parameter becomes ~ 1, we must introduce a cut-off at this scale:

$$\Lambda_{UV} \sim \frac{16\pi^2}{g_5^2}$$
$$\sim \frac{16\pi}{g_4^2} R^{-1} \qquad (1.86)$$

where we have set the brane terms to be small so that $g_4 \sim g_5/sqrtR$. Note that this cut-off is not much larger than the compactification scale since $g_4 \sim 1$ in the SM. Thus, we find that $m^2_{A_5^{(0)}}$ is suppressed relative to the mass^2 in the case of a regular scalar by $\sim (\Lambda_{UV} R)^2 \sim \left(16\pi/g_4^2\right)^2$: we *do* gain by going to A_5.

Next, we discuss how to use A_5 for *radiative symmetry breaking (often called Hosotani mechanism)* [21]. Continuing with the case of $SU(2)$ on S^1, we see that a vev for the A_5 zero-mode, $\langle A_5^{(0)} \rangle$ can break $SU(2)$ gauge symmetry to a $U(1)$ gauge symmetry. The point is that fermion loops typically give $m^2_{A_5^{(0)}} < 0$, whereas gauge loops are of opposite sign. However, the fermion contributions can win if the number of fermion degrees of freedom is larger than that of gauge bosons.

Thus, we have a "cartoon" of the SM in the following sense. We can identify the $SU(2)$ gauge group that we considered above with the SM W's. We will then get $M_{W^\pm} \sim R^{-1}$ (coming from $\langle A_5 \rangle$), whereas W_3 [corresponding to the unbroken $U(1)$ gauge symmetry] remains massless (it is the "photon"). Finally, the $\bar{\Psi}_L A_5 \Psi_R$ coupling mentioned above gives a fermion mass $M_{\psi^{(0)}} \sim R^{-1} \sim M_W$ which is roughly correct for top quark (since $m_t \sim M_W$).

Of course, this model is far from being realistic:

(i). We must require $1/R \gg 100$ GeV since we have not seen any KK modes in experiments so far which have probed energy scales up to $\sim$ TeV (either directly in the highest energy colliders or indirectly via virtual effects of new particles). To satisfy this constraint, we can fine-tune the fermion versus the gauge loop contributions to A_5 mass such that $M_{W^\pm}$ or $\langle A_5 \rangle \sim 100$ GeV $\ll R^{-1}$.

(ii). More importantly, we do not have fermion chirality on a circle.

1.6.6. *Towards Realistic Higgs as A_5: Chirality and Enlarging the Gauge Group*

As we saw earlier, we can obtain chiral fermions by going to an orbifold: S^1/Z_2. However, if we require A_μ of $SU(2)$ to be even under Z_2 (such that we get a corresponding zero-mode, i.e., a massless 4D gauge boson), then the A_5's are necessarily odd. Thus, we lose the scalar zero-mode. In any case, the scalar was in the adjoint representation of $SU(2)$, whereas we need a doublet for EW symmetry breaking.

The trick is to enlarge the gauge group to $SU(3)$ and to break it down to $SU(2) \times U(1)$ by boundary condition as follows. Choose the following parities under Z_2 for the fundamental representation

$$\begin{pmatrix} \\ 3 \\ \end{pmatrix} \to P \begin{pmatrix} \\ 3 \\ \end{pmatrix}, \text{ where}$$

$$P = \begin{pmatrix} + & & \\ & + & \\ & & - \end{pmatrix} \tag{1.87}$$

Given this parity choice, can derive the transformation of any other representation under Z_2. For example, consider fields in the adjoint representation, Φ_a ($a = 1...8$), written as a 3×3 matrix, $\Phi_a T^a$, where T^a's are generators of the fundamental representation. This matrix transforms as

$$\begin{pmatrix} \\ 8 \\ \end{pmatrix} \to P^\dagger \begin{pmatrix} \\ 8 \\ \end{pmatrix} P \sim \begin{pmatrix} + & + & - \\ + & + & - \\ - & - & + \end{pmatrix} \tag{1.88}$$

This implies that if the A_μ's belonging to $SU(2) \times U(1)$ are chosen to be even (and hence have a zero-mode), then the A_μ's of the coset group $SU(3)/[SU(2) \times U(1)]$ are odd (i.e., do not have a zero-mode). This choice of parities thus achieves the desired breaking pattern $SU(3) \to SU(2) \times U(1)$. Moreover, the A_5's of $SU(3)/[SU(2) \times U(1)]$ are even, giving us a scalar zero-mode which is a doublet of the unbroken $SU(2)$ group as desired.

Furthermore, just like in the case of the breaking $SU(2) \to U(1)$ discussed earlier, the breaking of $SU(2) \times U(1)$ can be achieved by vev of A_5 which is generated by loop corrections. Moreover, due to usage of fundamental representation for this radiative symmetry breaking, the rank of the gauge group is also broken, i.e., we have an unbroken $U(1)$ symmetry.

A 5D fermion which is a triplet of $SU(3)$ gives zero-modes for LH $SU(2)$ doublet *and* RH singlet:

$$\Psi_L = \begin{pmatrix} \Psi_L^D\ + \\ \Psi_L^S\ - \end{pmatrix}$$

$$\Psi_R = \begin{pmatrix} \Psi_R^D\ - \\ \Psi_R^S\ + \end{pmatrix} \tag{1.89}$$

where D and S denote $SU(2)$ doublet and singlet, respectively – recall that the parities of the RH and LH fields must be opposite. Moreover, the Yukawa coupling for the zero-mode fermions comes from the interaction $\bar{\Psi}_L^D A_5 \Psi_R^S$. Thus, we are getting closer to the SM!

1.6.7. *Realistic Higgs as* A_5 *in* **Warped Extra Dimension**

When we construct the previous model in a warped extra dimension, it turns out that the $A_5^{(0)}$ is automatically localized near the TeV brane [22] – recall that in order to solve the hierarchy problem, we would like the Higgs to be localized precisely there. Thus, A_5 zero-mode is an excellent candidate for SM Higgs!

As "finishing touches", we can add an extra $U(1)$ to obtain the correct hypercharges for the fermions and similarly a custodial isospin symmetry to protect the ρ parameter [23]. Also, it turns out that the Ψ_L^D and Ψ_R^S have (effectively) "opposite" sign of $5D$ mass, M (recall that this mass is not coming from $\langle A_5^{(0)} \rangle$) in the sense that if the LH zero-mode is localized near $y = 0$, then the RH zero-mode must be near $y = \pi R$ (or vice versa): see exercise 1. To relax this constraint, i.e., to obtain more freedom in localization of LH versus RH zero-modes, we can instead obtain LH and RH SM fermions as zero-modes of different bulk multiplets. However, then the question arises: since A_5 only couples fermions within the same fermionic multiplet, how do we obtain Yukawa couplings? The solution is to mix fermionic multiplets by adding mass terms localized at the endpoints of the extra dimension.

1.6.8. *Epilogue*

Due to lack of time, we have not considered other extra dimensional models with connections to the weak scale (and gravitational aspects of extra dimensional models in general). Here, we give a summary of the essential features of these other models: for details, see the references below and other lectures [1–4]. Arkani-Hamed, Dimopoulos and Dvali (ADD) proposed a scenario where only gravity propagates in extra dimensions, with all the SM fields localized on a brane [24]. The idea is that the fundamental or higher-dimensional gravity scale is $\sim$ TeV (and not the $4D$ Planck scale), while the weakness of gravity (or largeness of $4D$ or observed Planck scale) is accounted for by diluting the strength of gravity using extra dimensions which are much larger in size than the fundamental length scale, i.e., $R \gg 1/$ TeV. The crucial point is that the gravitational force law has been tested only for distances larger than $O(100)\,\mu m$ so that such very large extra dimensions could be consistent with current experiments. Only the graviton has KK modes in this framework, that too very light, resulting in interesting phenomenology both from real and virtual production of these KK modes. These KK modes couple with the usual $4D$ gravitational strength, but their large multiplicity can compensate for this very weak coupling.

At the other extreme is the model called Universal Extra Dimensions (UED) [25]. This scenario has a flat extra dimension(s) in which *all* the SM fields (including Higgs) propagate. The $5D$ fields have no brane localized interactions at the tree-level: of course, loops will generate small brane terms. Moreover, there are no $5D$ masses for fermions and Higgs so that profiles for all zero-modes (including all fermions, gauge fields and Higgs) are flat. Hence, we do not have a solution to the flavor hierarchy of the SM unlike in the scenario considered in these lectures. The motivation for UED is more phenomenological: there is a remnant of extra dimensional momentum or KK number conservation (dubbed KK parity) which forbids a coupling of a *single* lightest (level-1 and in general, odd level) KK mode to SM particles. Such a coupling *is* allowed for level-2 (and in general, even level) KK modes, but it is still suppressed by the small (loop-induced size) of brane kinetic terms.[g] Hence, the contributions from KK exchange to precision tests are suppressed (in particular, tree-level exchange of odd level modes is forbidden), *easily* allowing KK mass scale *below* a TeV for level-1 and even level-2 modes (cf. the lower limit of *a few* TeV in the scenario studied in these lectures). Thus, KK modes can be more easily produced at colliders (even though it is clear that the odd level KK modes have to be pair produced). Moreover, the lightest KK particle (LKP) is stable and can be a good dark matter candidate [26].

Finally, we mention the $5D$ Higgsless models [27], where EW symmetry itself is broken by boundary conditions like the breaking of $5D$ custodial isospin symmetry mentioned in lecture 4 [or the breaking $SU(3) \to SU(2) \times U(1)$ considered in lecture 5 in order to obtain Higgs as A_5]. The idea is that there is no light Higgs in the spectrum in order to unitarize WW scattering, which is instead accomplished by exchange of gauge KK modes. These KK modes then must have mass $\lesssim 1$ TeV. It turns out that due to such a low KK scale, the simplest such models are severely constrained by precision tests, but it is possible to avoid some of these constraints by suitable model-building.

---

[g]This coupling does not preserve KK number conservation or extra dimensional translation invariance and hence must arise from interactions localized on the branes which violate these symmetries.

Acknowledgments

KA was supported in part by the U. S. DOE under Contract no. DE-FG-02-85ER 40231 and would like to thank organizers of the summer school for the invitation to give lectures and all the students at the summer school for a wonderful and stimulating experience.

Appendix A. Excercises

A.1. Exercise 1

A.1.1. *Zero-Mode Fermion and 4D Yukawa Coupling*

Show that the normalized profile for LH zero-mode fermion (i.e., choosing Ψ_L to be even) is (lecture 2):

$$f_{L\,0}(y) = \sqrt{\frac{M}{e^{2M\pi R}-1}} e^{My} \quad (0 \leq y \leq \pi R)$$
$$= \sqrt{\frac{M}{e^{2M\pi R}-1}} e^{-My} \quad (0 \geq y \geq -\pi R) \tag{A.1}$$

where the normalization is over $0 \leq y \leq 2\pi R$ (even though the physical domain is from $y = 0$ to $y = \pi R$). Similarly, if we choose Ψ_R to be even instead of Ψ_L, then the RH zero-mode profile is

$$f_{R\,0}(y) = \sqrt{\frac{-M}{e^{-2M\pi R}-1}} e^{-My} \quad (0 \leq y \leq \pi R)$$
$$= \sqrt{\frac{-M}{e^{-2M\pi R}-1}} e^{+My} \quad (0 \geq y \geq -\pi R) \tag{A.2}$$

Note the opposite sign of M in the LH versus RH zero-mode profiles [following from Eqs. (1.20) and 1.21)]. Assuming that the SM Higgs field is localized at $y = \pi R$, we see that we need $M < 0$ (> 0) for LH (RH) fermion to obtain small fermion wavefunction at the location of the Higgs and hence small 4D Yukawa couplings for light fermions (1st and 2nd generations). So, we can neglect $e^{\pm M\pi R}$ compared to 1 wherever appropriate.

The zero-mode (4D or SM) Yukawa coupling in terms of the 5D Yukawa coupling: $\int dy d^4 x \delta(y) \lambda_{5D} H \Psi_L \Psi'_R$ [where Ψ_L is $SU(2)_L$ doublet and Ψ'_R is $SU(2)_L$ singlet] is:

$$\lambda_{4D} \approx \lambda_{5D} M e^{2M\pi R} \tag{A.3}$$

and the $4D$ mass of fermion is

$$m \approx \lambda_{4D} v, \tag{A.4}$$

where, for simplicity, we assume equal size of 5D masses, i.e., $M = -M'$, for doublet and singlet fermions.

A.1.2. Coupling of Zero-mode Fermion to Gauge KK mode: No Brane Kinetic Terms

The profile for n^{th} gauge KK mode ($m_n = n/R$) is:

$$f_n(y) = \frac{1}{\sqrt{\pi R}} \cos(m_n y) \tag{A.5}$$

Calculate the coupling of zero-mode fermion to gauge KK modes in terms of the coupling of zero-mode gauge field (i.e., SM gauge coupling), $g_4 \equiv g_5/\sqrt{2\pi R}$:

$$g(n, M) = g_4 a(n, M) \tag{A.6}$$

You should obtain:

$$a(n, M) \approx \sqrt{2} \frac{4M^2}{4M^2 + (n/R)^2} \tag{A.7}$$

Use $m_{d,s} = 1$ MeV, 100 MeV and the Higgs vev $v \approx 100$ GeV. Assume, for simplicity, that $\lambda_{5D} M = 1$ for both s, d – otherwise, we have to solve a transcendental equation to obtain M (given the 4D Yukawa coupling). Calculate the 5D masses $M_{s,d}$ and show that $a(1, M_s) - a(1, M_d) \approx 0.1$.

Compare $K - \bar{K}$ mixing from KK Z exchange as in lecture 2

$$\frac{g_Z^2}{m_{KK}^2} \left[a(1, M_s) - a(1, M_d) \right]^2 (\text{mixing angle})^2 \tag{A.8}$$

to the SM amplitude

$$\frac{g_2^4}{16\pi^2} \frac{m_c^2}{M_W^4} (\text{mixing angle})^2 \tag{A.9}$$

to obtain bound on m_{KK} of ≈ 20 TeV, using $g_Z \approx 0.75$ and $g_2 \approx 0.65$ for the SM Z and $SU(2)_L$ gauge couplings.

It turns out that another observable called ϵ_K (which is the imaginary or CP-violating part of the above $K - \bar{K}$ mixing amplitude) gives a stronger bound on KK mass scale of ~ 100 TeV.

A.2. Exercise 2

A.2.1. *General Brane Kinetic Terms*

The Lagrangian is

$$\mathcal{L}_{5D} \ni -\frac{1}{4}\mathcal{F}_{MN}\mathcal{F}^{MN} - \frac{1}{4}\delta(y)r\mathcal{F}_{\mu\nu}\mathcal{F}^{\mu\nu} \quad (A.10)$$

where r has dimension of length.

Go through the derivation outlined in lecture 3, i.e., f_n satisfies the orthonormality condition:

$$\int dy f_n^*(y) f_m(y) \left[1 + r\delta(y)\right] = \delta_{mn} \quad (A.11)$$

and the differential equation:

$$\left[\partial_y^2 + m_n^2\left(1 + r\delta(y)\right)\right] f_n(y) = 0 \quad (A.12)$$

The solution is

$$\begin{aligned} f_n(y) &= a_n \cos(m_n y) + b_n \sin(m_n y) \text{ for } y \geq 0 \\ &= \tilde{a}_n \cos(m_n y) + \tilde{b}_n \sin(m_n y) \text{ for } y \leq 0 \end{aligned} \quad (A.13)$$

Use the following 4 conditions to obtain relations between coefficients a, b's and to solve for m_n: (i) continuity at $y = 0$, (ii) discontinuity in derivative matches brane term, (iii) f_n is even and (iv) periodicity of f_n. In particular, condition (iv) is satisfied by repeating (or copying) f_n between $-\pi R$ and πR to between πR and $3\pi R$ and so on. However, continuity of f_n at $y = \pi R$ has to be imposed and similarly that of derivative of f_n (assuming no brane kinetic term at $y = \pi R$).

You should find

$$\begin{aligned} a_n &= \tilde{a}_n \\ \frac{b_n}{a_n} &= -\frac{rm_n}{2} \\ b_n &= -\tilde{b}_n \\ \frac{b_n}{a_n} &= \tan(m_n \pi R) \end{aligned} \quad (A.14)$$

so that eigenvalues are solutions to

$$\tan(m_n \pi R) = -\frac{rm_n}{2} \quad (A.15)$$

Finally, calculate

$$\frac{1}{a_n^2} = \pi R \left(1 + \frac{1}{4}r^2 m_n^2 + \frac{r}{2\pi R}\right) \quad \text{(A.16)}$$

from normalization.

A.2.2. Large *Brane Kinetic Terms*

Verify approximate results shown in lecture 3 for large brane kinetic terms, $r/R \gg 1$, namely,

(i) $m_n \approx (n + 1/2)/R$,

(ii) $1/g_4^2 \approx r/g_5^2$

and for lightest KK modes (small n)

(iii) coupling of a fermion localized at $y = 0$ to gauge KK mode $\sim g_4/\sqrt{r/R}$

(iv) coupling of gauge KK mode to a fermion/Higgs field localized on $y = \pi R$ brane $\sim g_4 \sqrt{r/R}$.

We can generalize these couplings of gauge KK mode to the case of a zero-mode fermion with a profile in the bulk – it's just that we have to do an overlap integral as in problem 2 of exercise 1. Calculate the new $a(1, M_s) - a(1, M_d)$. For $r/R \gg 1$, show that it is smaller than before (i.e., without brane terms) so that $K - \bar{K}$ mixing is suppressed and a lower KK mass scale is allowed.

A.3. Exercise 3

As discussed in lecture 3, the zero and KK modes of Z are defined by setting the Higgs vev to zero. However, due to non-zero Higgs vev, the zero and KK modes of Z mix via mass terms – kinetic terms are still diagonal. The $Z^{(0)}$-$Z^{(1)}$ (i.e., 1st KK mode of Z) mass matrix is:

$$\mathcal{L}_{mass} \ni \begin{pmatrix} Z_\mu^{(0)} & Z_\mu^{(1)} \end{pmatrix} \begin{pmatrix} m^2 & \Delta m^2 \\ \Delta m^2 & M^2 \end{pmatrix} \begin{pmatrix} Z^{\mu \, (0)} \\ Z^{\mu \, (1)} \end{pmatrix} \quad \text{(A.17)}$$

where $m^2 = 1/4\, g_{Z^{(0)}}^2 v^2$, mixing term $\Delta m^2 = 1/4\, g_{Z^{(0)}} g_{5\,Z} f_1(\pi R)\, v^2$ and $M^2 = m_{KK}^2 + 1/4\, g_{5\,Z}^2 f_1^2(\pi R)\, v^2$. Here, $f_1(\pi R)$ is wavefunction of $Z^{(1)}$ evaluated at the Higgs brane ($y = \pi R$). Also, $g_{Z^{(0)}} = g_{5\,Z}/\sqrt{2\pi R + r}$ denotes the coupling of $Z^{(0)}$ (where r is the brane kinetic term at $y = 0$) and $g_{5\,Z} = \sqrt{g_{5\,2}^2 + g_5'^{\,2}}$ denotes the 5D coupling of Z, with $g_{5\,2}$ and g_5' being the 5D gauge couplings of $SU(2)$ and $U(1)_Y$, respectively (assume, for simplicity, the same brane kinetic term r for all gauge fields).

Diagonalize this mass matrix, assuming $v^2/m_{KK}^2 \times$ gauge couplings $\ll 1$ where appropriate, i.e., determine

(i) the unitary transformation to go from $\left(Z^{(0)} Z^{(1)}\right)$ to physical basis and

(ii) the eigenvalues of the mass matrix.

There are 2 effects of this diagonalization.

A.3.1. *Shift in Coupling of a Fermion to Z*

Given couplings of a fermion to $Z^{(0)}$ and $Z^{(1)}$ (KK basis)

$$\mathcal{L}_{coupling} \ni \bar{\psi}\gamma^\mu(g, G) \begin{pmatrix} Z_\mu^{(0)} \\ Z_\mu^{(1)} \end{pmatrix} \psi \tag{A.18}$$

use the above unitary transformation to calculate the couplings to the fermion in the physical basis, denoted by Z_{light} (which is SM Z) and Z_{heavy}.

Specifically, calculate the coupling of a fermion localized at $y = 0$ to the SM Z using $g = g_{Z^{(0)}}$ and $G = g_{5\,Z} f_1(0)$ in the above equation, where $f_1(0)$ is wavefunction of $Z^{(1)}$ evaluated at the fermion brane ($y = 0$).

Verify that the shift in the coupling of this fermion to the SM Z from the zero-mode Z coupling (i.e., $g_{Z^{(0)}}$) is as shown in lecture 3: $\delta g_Z/g_{Z^{(0)}} \sim g_{Z^{(0)}}^2 v^2/m_{KK}^2$, in particular, that there is *no* enhancement for large brane kinetic terms, $r/R \gg 1$.

A.3.2. *Shift in Z mass*

The lighter eigenvalue of mass matrix is the SM Z mass. Verify that the shift in the SM Z mass from the purely zero-mode mass, i.e., $1/4 g_{Z^{(0)}}^2 v^2$, is as shown in lecture 3, in particular, that there *is* an enhancement in this shift due to $r/R \gg 1$ (when the shift is expressed in terms of $g_{Z^{(0)}}$).

References

[1] K. Dienes, this summer school proceedings and http://scipp.ucsc.edu/haber/tasi_proceedings/dienes.ps.

[2] C. Csaki, arXiv:hep-ph/0404096.

[3] R. Sundrum, arXiv:hep-th/0508134; http://www-conf.slac.stanford.edu/ssi/2005/lec_notes/ Sundrum1/default.htm
(+ "...Sundrum2..." and "...Sundrum3...")

[4] G. D. Kribs, arXiv:hep-ph/0605325.

[5] N. Arkani-Hamed, M. Porrati and L. Randall, JHEP **0108**, 017 (2001) [arXiv:hep-th/0012148]; R. Rattazzi and A. Zaffaroni, JHEP **0104**, 021 (2001) [arXiv:hep-th/0012248].

[6] J. M. Maldacena, Adv. Theor. Math. Phys. **2**, 231 (1998) [Int. J. Theor. Phys. **38**, 1113 (1999)] [arXiv:hep-th/9711200]; S. S. Gubser, I. R. Klebanov and A. M. Polyakov, Phys. Lett. B **428**, 105 (1998) [arXiv:hep-th/9802109]; E. Witten, Adv. Theor. Math. Phys. **2**, 253 (1998) [arXiv:hep-th/9802150].

[7] H. Georgi, A. K. Grant and G. Hailu, Phys. Rev. D **63**, 064027 (2001) [arXiv:hep-ph/0007350]. For further discussion, see, for example, D. E. Kaplan and T. M. P. Tait, JHEP **0111**, 051 (2001) [arXiv:hep-ph/0110126].

[8] A. Delgado, A. Pomarol and M. Quiros, JHEP **0001**, 030 (2000) [arXiv:hep-ph/9911252].

[9] H. Georgi, A. K. Grant and G. Hailu, Phys. Lett. B **506**, 207 (2001) [arXiv:hep-ph/0012379]. For further discussion, see, for example, H. C. Cheng, K. T. Matchev and M. Schmaltz, Phys. Rev. D **66**, 036005 (2002) [arXiv:hep-ph/0204342].

[10] M. Carena, T. M. P. Tait and C. E. M. Wagner, Acta Phys. Polon. B **33**, 2355 (2002) [arXiv:hep-ph/0207056].

[11] K. Agashe, A. Delgado, M. J. May and R. Sundrum, JHEP **0308**, 050 (2003) [arXiv:hep-ph/0308036].

[12] K. Agashe, A. Belyaev, T. Krupovnickas, G. Perez and J. Virzi, arXiv:hep-ph/0612015; B. Lillie, L. Randall and L. T. Wang, arXiv:hep-ph/0701166.

[13] See, for example, F. del Aguila and J. Santiago, Phys. Lett. B **493**, 175 (2000) [arXiv:hep-ph/0008143] and section 4.1 of A. Juste *et al.*, arXiv:hep-ph/0601112.

[14] K. Agashe, G. Perez and A. Soni, Phys. Rev. D **75**, 015002 (2007) [arXiv:hep-ph/0606293].

[15] L. Randall and R. Sundrum, Phys. Rev. Lett. **83**, 3370 (1999) [arXiv:hep-ph/9905221].

[16] W. D. Goldberger and M. B. Wise, Phys. Rev. Lett. **83**, 4922 (1999) [arXiv:hep-ph/9907447].

[17] H. Davoudiasl, J. L. Hewett and T. G. Rizzo, Phys. Lett. B **473**, 43 (2000) [arXiv:hep-ph/9911262]; A. Pomarol, Phys. Lett. B **486**, 153 (2000) [arXiv:hep-ph/9911294]; S. Chang, J. Hisano, H. Nakano, N. Okada and M. Yamaguchi, Phys. Rev. D **62**, 084025 (2000) [arXiv:hep-ph/9912498].

[18] Y. Grossman and M. Neubert, Phys. Lett. B **474**, 361 (2000) [arXiv:hep-

ph/9912408]; T. Gherghetta and A. Pomarol, Nucl. Phys. B **586**, 141 (2000) [arXiv:hep-ph/0003129].
[19] L. Randall and R. Sundrum, Phys. Rev. Lett. **83**, 4690 (1999) [arXiv:hep-th/9906064].
[20] M. Quiros, arXiv:hep-ph/0302189.
[21] Y. Hosotani, Phys. Lett. B **126**, 309 (1983); Phys. Lett. B **129**, 193 (1983) and Annals Phys. **190**, 233 (1989).
[22] R. Contino, Y. Nomura and A. Pomarol, Nucl. Phys. B **671**, 148 (2003) [arXiv:hep-ph/0306259];
[23] K. Agashe, R. Contino and A. Pomarol, Nucl. Phys. B **719**, 165 (2005) [arXiv:hep-ph/0412089].
[24] N. Arkani-Hamed, S. Dimopoulos and G. R. Dvali, Phys. Lett. B **429**, 263 (1998) [arXiv:hep-ph/9803315]; I. Antoniadis, N. Arkani-Hamed, S. Dimopoulos and G. R. Dvali, Phys. Lett. B **436**, 257 (1998) [arXiv:hep-ph/9804398]; N. Arkani-Hamed, S. Dimopoulos and G. R. Dvali, Phys. Rev. D **59**, 086004 (1999) [arXiv:hep-ph/9807344].
[25] T. Appelquist, H. C. Cheng and B. A. Dobrescu, Phys. Rev. D **64**, 035002 (2001) [arXiv:hep-ph/0012100].
[26] G. Servant and T. M. P. Tait, Nucl. Phys. B **650**, 391 (2003) [arXiv:hep-ph/0206071] and New J. Phys. **4**, 99 (2002) [arXiv:hep-ph/0209262]; H. C. Cheng, J. L. Feng and K. T. Matchev, Phys. Rev. Lett. **89** (2002) 211301 [arXiv:hep-ph/0207125].
[27] C. Csaki, C. Grojean, H. Murayama, L. Pilo and J. Terning, Phys. Rev. D **69**, 055006 (2004) [arXiv:hep-ph/0305237]; C. Csaki, C. Grojean, L. Pilo and J. Terning, Phys. Rev. Lett. **92**, 101802 (2004) [arXiv:hep-ph/0308038]; for a review, see C. Csaki, J. Hubisz and P. Meade, arXiv:hep-ph/0510275.

Chapter 2

The International Linear Collider

Marco Battaglia

Department of Physics, University of California at Berkeley and Lawrence Berkeley National Laboratory Berkeley, CA 94720, USA
MBattaglia@lbl.gov

The International Linear Collider (ILC) is the next large scale project in accelerator particle physics. Colliding electrons with positrons at energies from 0.3 TeV up to about 1 TeV, the ILC is expected to provide the accuracy needed to complement the LHC data and extend the sensitivity to new phenomena at the high energy frontier and answer some of the fundamental questions in particle physics and in its relation to Cosmology. This paper reviews some highlights of the ILC physics program and of the major challenges for the accelerator and detector design.

2.1. Introduction

Accelerator particle physics is completing a successful cycle of precision tests of the Standard Model of electro-weak interactions (SM). After the discovery of the W and Z bosons at the $Sp\bar{p}S$ hadron collider at CERN, the concurrent operation of hadron and e^+e^- colliders has provided a large set of precision data and new observations. Two e^+e^- colliders, the SLAC Linear Collider (SLC) at the Stanford Linear Accelerator Center (SLAC) and the Large Electron Positron (LEP) collider at the European Organization for Nuclear Research (CERN), operated throughout the 1990's and enabled the study of the properties of the Z boson in great detail. Operation at LEP up to 209 GeV, the highest collision energy ever achieved in electron-positron collisions, provided detailed information on the properties of W bosons and the strongest lower bounds on the mass of the Higgs boson and of several supersymmetric particles. The collision of point-like, elementary particles at a well-defined and tunable energy offers advantages for precision measurements, as those conducted at LEP and SLC, over proton colliders. On the other hand experiments at hadron machines, such as the Tevatron $p\bar{p}$ collider at Fermilab, have enjoyed higher constituent energies. The CDF and D0 experiments eventually observed the direct production of top quarks, whose mass had been predicted on the basis of precision data obtained at LEP and SLC.

While we await the commissioning and operation of the LHC pp collider at CERN, the next stage in experimentation at lepton colliders is actively under study. For more than two decades, studies for a high-luminosity accelerator, able to collide electrons with positrons at energies of the order of 1 TeV, are being carried out world-wide.

2.2. The path towards the ILC

The concept of an e^+e^- linear collider dates back to a paper by Maury Tigner[1] published in 1965, when the physics potential of e^+e^- collisions had not yet been appreciated in full. This seminal paper envisaged collisions at 3-4 GeV with a luminosity competitive with that of the SPEAR ring at SLAC, i.e. 3×10^{30} cm^{-2} s^{-1}. *A possible scheme to obtain e^-e^- and e^+e^- collisions at energies of hundreds of GeV* is the title of a paper[2] by Ugo Amaldi published a decade later in 1976, which sketches the linear collider concept with a design close to that now developed for the ILC. The

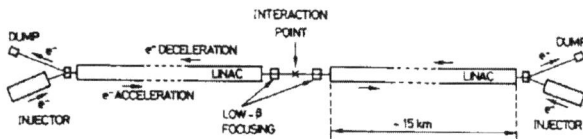

Fig. 2.1. The linear collider layout as sketched in 1975 in one of the figures of Ref. 2. The paper discussed the possibility to achieve e^-e^- and e^+e^- collisions at 0.3 TeV using superconducting linacs with a gradient of 10 MV/m.

parameters for a linear collider, clearly recognised as the successors of e^+e^- storage rings on the way to high energies, were discussed by Burt Richter at the IEEE conference in San Francisco in 1979[3] and soon after came the proposal for the *Single Pass Collider Project* which would become SLC at SLAC.

From 1985, the CERN Long Range Planning Committee considered an e^+e^- linear collider, based on the CLIC[4] design, able to deliver collisions at 2 TeV with 10^{33} cm^{-2} s^{-1} luminosity, *vis-a-vis* a hadron collider, with proton-proton collisions at 16 TeV and luminosity of 1.4×10^{33} cm^{-2} s^{-1}, as a candidate for the new CERN project after LEP. That review process eventually led to the decision to build the LHC, but it marked an important step to establish the potential of a high energy e^+e^- collider. It is important to note that it was through the contributions of several theorists, including John Ellis, Michael Peskin, Gordon Kane and others, that the requirements in terms of energy and luminosity for a linear collider became clearer in the mid 1980's.[5] The SLC project gave an important proof of principle for a high energy linear collider and the experience gained has shaped the subsequent designs in quite a significant way.

After a decade marked by important progress in the R&D of the basic components and the setup of advanced test facilities, designs of four different concepts emerged: TESLA, based on superconducting RF cavities, the NLC/JLC-X, based on high frequency (11.4 GHz) room-temperature copper cavities, JLC-C, based on lower frequency (5.7 GHz) conventional cavities and CLIC, a multi-TeV collider based on a different beam acceleration technique, the two-beam scheme with transfer structures operating at 30 GHz. Accelerator R&D had reached the maturity to assess the technical feasibility of a linear collider project and take an informed choice of the most advantageous RF technology. The designs were considered by the International Linear Collider Technical Review Committee (ILC-TRC), originally formed in 1994 and re-convened by the International Committee for Future Accelerators (ICFA) in 2001 under the chairmanship of Greg A. Loew. The ILC-TRC assessed their status using common criteria, identified outstanding items needing R&D effort and suggested areas of collaboration. The TRC report was released in February 2003[6] and the committee found that there were *no insurmountable show-stoppers to build TESLA, NLC/JLC-X or JLC-C in the next few years and CLIC in a more distant future, given enough resources*. Nonetheless, significant R&D remained to be done. At this stage, it became clear that, to make further progress, the international effort towards a linear collider should be focused on a single design. ICFA gave mandate to an International Technology Recommendation Panel (ITRP), chaired by Barry Barish, to make a definite recommendation for a RF technology that would be the basis of a global project. In August 2004 the ITRP made the recommendation in favour of superconducting RF cavities.[7] The technology choice, which was promptly accepted by all laboratories and groups involved in the R&D process, is regarded as a major step towards the realization of the linear collider project. Soon after it, a truly world-wide, centrally managed design effort, the Global Design Effort (GDE),[8] a team of more than 60 persons, started, with the aim to produce an ILC Reference Design Report by beginning of 2007 and an ILC Technical Design Report by end of 2008. The GDE responsibility now covers the detailed design concept, performance assessments, reliable international costing, industrialization plan, siting analysis, as well as detector concepts and scope. A further important step has been achieved with release of the Reference Design Report in February 2007.[9] This report includes a preliminary value estimate of the cost for the ILC in its present design and at the present level of engineering and industrialisation. The value estimate is structured in three parts: 1.78 Billion ILC Value Units for site-related costs, such as those of tunneling in a specific region, 4.87 Billion ILC Value Units for the value of the high technology and conventional components and 13,000 person-years for the required supporting manpower. For this estimate the conversion factor is 1 ILC Value Unit = 1 US Dollar = 0.83 Euro = 117 Yen. This estimate, which is comparable to the LHC cost, when the pre-existing facilities, such as the LEP tunnel, are included, provides guidance for optimisation of both the design and the R&D to be done during the engineering phase, due to start in Fall 2007.

Technical progress was paralleled by increasing support for the ILC in the scientific community. At the 2001 APS workshop *The Future of Physics* held in Snowmass, CO, a consensus emerged for the ILC as the right project for the next large scale facility in particle physics. This consensus resonated and expanded in a number of statements by highly influential scientific advisory panels world-wide. The ILC role in the future of scientific research was recognised by the OECD Consultative Group on High Energy Physics,[10] while the DOE Office of Science ranked the ILC as its top mid-term project. More recently the EPP 2010 panel of the US National Academy of Sciences, in a report titled *Elementary Particle Physics in the 21st Century* has endorsed the ILC as the next major experimental facility to be built and its role in elucidating the physics at the high energy frontier, independently from the LHC findings.[11] Nowadays, the ILC is broadly regarded as the highest priority for a future large facility in particle physics, needed to extend and complement the LHC discoveries with the accuracy which is crucial to understand the nature of New Physics, test fundamental properties at the high energy scale and establish their relation to other fields in physical sciences, such as Cosmology. A matching program of physics studies and detector R&D efforts has been in place for the past decade and it is now developing new, accurate and cost effective detector designs from proof of concepts towards that stage of engineering readiness, needed for being adopted in the ILC experiments.

2.3. ILC Accelerator Parameters

2.3.1. *ILC Energy*

The first question which emerges in defining the ILC parameters is the required centre-of-mass energy $\sqrt{s}$. It is here where we most need physics guidance to define the next thresholds at, and beyond, the electro-weak scale. The only threshold which, at present, is well defined numerically is that of top-quark pair production at $\sqrt{s} \simeq 350$ GeV. Beyond it, there is a strong prejudice, supported by precision electro-weak and other data, that the Higgs boson should be light and new physics thresholds may exist between the electro-weak scale and approximately 1 TeV. If indeed the SM Higgs boson exists and the electro-weak data is not affected by new physics, its mass M_H is expected to be below 200 GeV as discussed in section 2.4.1. Taking into account that the Higgs main production process is in association with a Z^0 boson, the maximum of the $e^+e^- \to H^0 Z^0$ cross section varies from $\sqrt{s} = 240$ GeV to 350 GeV for 120 GeV $< M_H <$ 200 GeV. On the other hand, we know that the current SM needs to be extended by some New Physics. Models of electroweak symmetry breaking contain new particles in the energy domain below 1 TeV. More specifically, if Supersymmetry exists and it is responsible for the dark matter observed in the Universe, we expect that a significant fraction of the supersymmetric spectrum would be accessible at $\sqrt{s} = 0.5$-1.0 TeV. In particular, the ILC should be able to study in detail those particles determining the dark matter relic density in the Universe by operating at energies not exceeding 1 TeV, as discussed in section 2.4.2. Another useful perspective on the ILC energy is an analysis of the mass scale sensitivity for new physics vs. the $\sqrt{s}$ energy for lepton and hadron colliders in view of their synergy. The study of electro-weak processes at the highest available energy offers a window on mass scales well beyond its kinematic reach. A comparison of the mass-scale sensitivity for various new physics scenarios as a function of the centre-of-mass energy for e^+e^- and pp collisions is given in section 2.4.3. These and similar considerations, emerged in the course of the world-wide studies on physics at the ILC, motivate the choice of $\sqrt{s} = 0.5$ TeV as the reference energy parameter, but requiring the ILC to be able to operate, with substantial luminosity, at 0.3 TeV as well and to be upgradable up to approximately 1 TeV.

It is useful to consider these energies in an historical perspective. In 1954 Enrico Fermi gave a talk at the American Physical Society, of which he was chair, titled *What can we learn with high energy accelerators ?*. In that talk Fermi considered a proton accelerator with a radius equal to that of Earth and 2 T bending magnets, thus reaching a beam energy of 5×10^{15} eV.[12] Stanley Livingstone, who had built with Ernest O. Lawrence the first circular accelerator at Berkeley in 1930, had formulated an empirical linear scaling law for the available centre-of-mass energy vs. the construction year and cost. Using Livingstone curve, Fermi predicted that such an accelerator could be built in 1994 at a cost of 170 billion $. We have learned that, not only such accelerator could not be built, but accelerator physics has irrevocably fallen off the Livingstone curve, even in its revised version, which includes data up to the 1980's. As horizons expanded, each step has involved more and more technical challenges and has required more resources. The future promises to be along this same path. This underlines the need of coherent and responsible long term planning while sustaining a rich R&D program in both accelerator and detector techniques.

The accelerator envisaged by Enrico Fermi was a circular machine, as the almost totality of machines operating at the high energy frontier still are. Now, as it is well known, charged particles undergoing a centripetal acceleration $a = v^2/R$ radiate at rate $P = \frac{1}{6\pi\epsilon_0} \frac{e^2 a^2}{c^3} \gamma^4$. If the radius R is kept constant, the energy loss is the above rate P times $t = 2\pi R/v$, the time spent in the bending section of the accelerator. The energy loss for electrons is $W = 8.85 \times 10^{-5} \frac{E^4 (\text{GeV}^4)}{R(\text{km})}$ MeV per turn while for protons is $W = 7.8 \times 10^{-3} \frac{E^4 (\text{TeV}^4)}{R(\text{km})}$ keV per turn. Since the energy transferred per turn by the RF cavities to the beam is constant, $G \times 2R \times F$, where G is the cavity gradient and F the tunnel fill factor, for each value of the accelerator ring radius R there exists a maximum energy E_{max} beyond which the energy loss exceeds the energy transferred. In practice, before this value of E_{max} is reached, the real energy limit is set by the power dumped by the beam as synchrotron radiation. To make a quantitative example, in the case of the LEP ring, with a radius $R = 4.3$ km, a beam of energy $E_{beam} = 250$ GeV, would lose 80 GeV/turn. Gunther Voss is thought to be the author of a plot comparing the guessed cost of a storage ring and a linear collider as a function of the e^+e^- centre-of-mass energy. A $\sqrt{s} = 500$ GeV storage ring, which would have costed an estimated 14 billions CHF in 1970's is aptly labelled as the Crazytron.[13] LEP filled the last window of opportunity for a storage ring at the high energy frontier. Beyond LEP-2 energies the design must be a linear collider, where no bending is applied to the accelerated particles. Still the accelerator length is limited by a number of constraints which include costs, alignment and siting. Therefore, technology still defines the maximum reachable energy at the ILC.

The ILC design is based on superconducting (s.c.) radio-frequency (RF) cavities. While s.c. cavities had been considered already in the 1960's, it was Ugo Amaldi to first propose a fully s.c. linear collider in 1975.[2] By the early

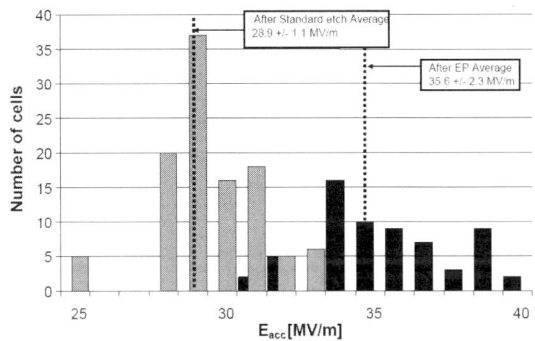

Fig. 2.2. Distributions of gradients measured for pure niobium, nine-cell cavities. After electro-polishing an average gradient in excess to 35 MV/m has been obtained.

1990's, s.c. cavities equipped already one accelerator, TRISTAN at KEK in Japan, while two further projects were in progress, CEBAF at Cornell and the LEP-2 upgrade at CERN. LEP-2 employed a total of 288 s.c. RF cavities, providing an average gradient of 7.2 MV/m. It was the visionary effort of Bjorn Wijk to promote, from 1990, the TESLA collaboration, with the aim to develop s.c. RF cavities pushing the gradient higher by a factor of five and the production costs down by a factor of four, thus reducing the cost per MV by a factor of twenty. Such reduction in cost was absolutely necessary to make a high energy collider, based on s.c. cavities, feasible. Within less than a decade 1.3 GHz, pure niobium cavities achieved gradients in excess to 35 MV/m. This opened the way to their application to a e^+e^- linear collider, able to reach centre-of-mass energies of the order of 1 TeV, as presented in detail in the TESLA proposal published in 2001[14] and recommended for the ILC by the ITRP in 2004.[7]

Today, the ILC baseline design aims at matching technical feasibility to cost optimisation. One of the major goals of the current effort in the ILC design is to understand enough about its costs to provide a reliable

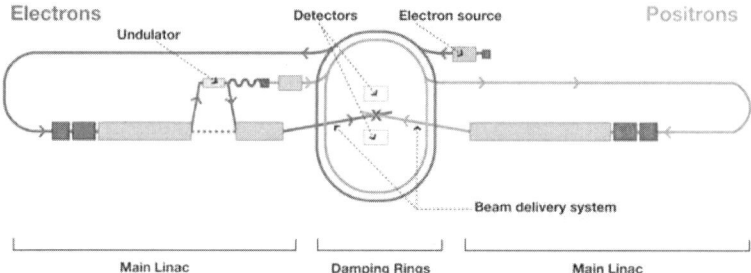

Fig. 2.3. Schematic layout of the International Linear Collider. This diagram reflects the recommendations of the Baseline Configuration Document, a report published in December 2005 that outlines the general design of the machine. (Credit ILC Global Design Effort)

indication of the scale of funding required to carry out the ILC project. Preparing a reliable cost estimate for a project to be carried out as a truly world-wide effort at the stage of a conceptual design that still lacks much of the detailed engineering designs as well as agreements for responsibility and cost sharing between the partners and a precise industrialisation plan is a great challenge. Still having good cost information as soon as possible, to initiate negotiations with the funding agencies is of great importance. An interesting example of the details entering in this process is the optimisation of the cost vs. cavity gradient for a 0.5 TeV collider. The site length scales inversely with the gradient G while the cost of the cryogenics scales as G^2/Q_0 resulting in a minimum cost for a gradient of 40 MW/m, corresponding to a tunnel length of 40 km, and a fractional cost increase of 10 % for gradients of 25 MV/m or 57 MV/m. The chosen gradient of 35 MV/m, which is matched by the average performance of the most recent prototypes after electro-polishing, gives a total tunnel length of 44 km with a cost increment from the minimum of just 1 %.

Beyond 1 TeV, the extension of conventional RF technology is more speculative. In order to attain collisions at energies in excess of about 1 TeV, with high luminosity, significantly higher gradients are necessary. As the gradient of s.c. cavities is limited below $\sim$ 50 MV/m, other avenues should be explored. The CLIC technology,[15] currently being developed at CERN and elsewhere, may offer gradients of the order of 150 MV/m,[16] allowing collision energies in the range 3-5 TeV with a luminosity of 10^{35} cm^{-2} s^{-1}, which would support a compelling physics

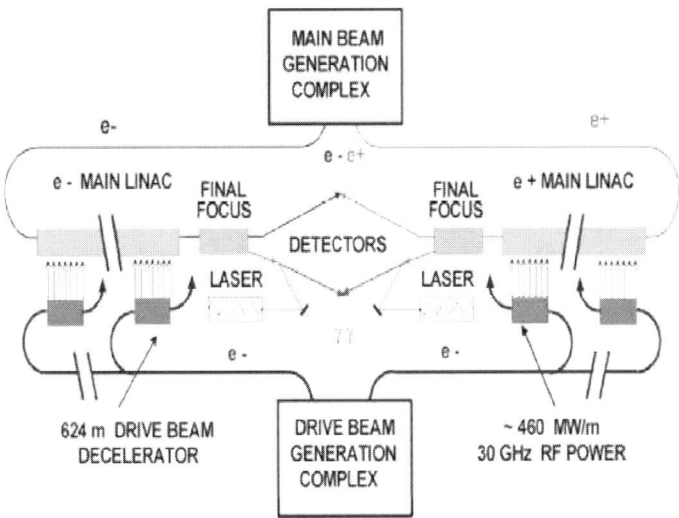

Fig. 2.4. Schematics of the overall layout of the CLIC complex for e^+e^- collisions at $\sqrt{s} = 3$ TeV. (from Ref. 17)

program.[17] While RF cavities are limited to accelerating fields of order of 100-200 MV/m, or below, laser-wakefield accelerators are capable, in principle, of producing fields of 10-100 GV/m. Recently a 1 GeV e^- beam has been accelerated over just 3.3 cm using a 40 TW peak-power laser pulse,[18] thus opening a possible path towards ultra-high energies in e^+e^- collisions in some more distant future.

2.3.2. ILC Luminosity

The choice of a linear collider, rather than a circular storage ring, while solving the problem of the maximum reachable energy, introduces the challenge of achieving collisions with the required luminosity. The luminosity, $\mathcal{L}$, defined as the proportionality factor between the number of events produced and the process cross section σ, has requirements which depend on the typical values of s-channel cross sections and so scale as $1/s$. First luminosity requirements were already outlined in the 1980s[19,20] as $\mathcal{L} \simeq \frac{2E_{beam}}{\text{TeV}} \times 10^{33}$ cm^{-2} s^{-1}, based on the estimated discovery potential. But in the present vision of the ILC role in probing the high energy frontier new requirements must be considered. One example is the precision study of electro-weak processes to look for deviations from the SM predictions, due to effect of new physics at high scales. The $e^+e^- \to b\bar{b}$ cross section at 1 TeV is just 96 fb, so this would corresponds to less than 10^3 events per year at 10^{33} cm^{-2} s^{-1}, which is certainly insufficient for the kind of precision measurements which we expect from the ILC. Another example is offered by one of the reactions most unique to the ILC: the double-Higgs production $e^+e^- \to HHZ$ sensitive to the Higgs self-coupling, which has a cross section of order of only 0.2 fb at 0.5 TeV. Therefore a luminosity of 10^{34} cm^{-2} s^{-1} or more is required as baseline parameter.

The luminosity can be expressed as a function of the accelerator parameters as:

$$\mathcal{L} = f_{rep} n_b \frac{N^2}{4\pi \sigma_x \sigma_y}. \qquad (2.1)$$

Now, since in a linear machine the beams are collided only once and then dumped, the collision frequency, f_{rep}, is small and high luminosity should be achieved by increasing the number of particles in a bunch N, the number of bunches n_b and decreasing the transverse beam size σ. Viable values for N are limited by wake-field effects and the ILC parameters have the same number of electrons in a bunch as LEP had, though it aims at a luminosity three orders of magnitude higher. Therefore, the increase must come from a larger number of bunches and a smaller transverse beam size. The generation of beams of small transverse size, their preservation during acceleration and their focusing to spots of nanometer size at the interaction region presents powerful challenges which the ILC design must solve. A small beam size also induces beam-beam interactions. On one hand the beam self-focusing, due to the electrostatic attraction of particles of opposite charges enhances the luminosity. But beam-beam interactions also result in an increase of beamstrahlung with a larger energy spread of the colliding particles, a degraded luminosity spectrum and higher backgrounds. Beamstrahlung is energy loss due to particle radiation triggered by the trajectory bending in the interactions with the charged particles in the incoming bunch.[21] The mean beamstrahlung energy loss, which has to be minimised, is given by:

$$\delta_{BS} \simeq 0.86 \frac{e r_e^3}{2 m_0 c^2} \frac{E_{cm}}{\sigma_z} \frac{N_b^2}{(\sigma_x + \sigma_y)^2}. \qquad (2.2)$$

Since the luminosity scales as $\frac{1}{\sigma_x \sigma_y}$, while the beamstrahlung energy loss scales as $\frac{1}{\sigma_x + \sigma_y}$, it is advantageous to choose a large beam aspect ratio, with the vertical beam size much smaller than the horizontal component. The parameter optimisation for luminosity can be further understood by expressing the luminosity in terms of beam power $P = f_{rep}NE_{cm} = \eta P_{AC}$ and beamstrahlung energy loss as:

$$\mathcal{L} \propto \frac{\eta P_{AC}}{E_{cm}} \sqrt{\frac{\delta_{BS}}{\epsilon_y}} H_D \qquad (2.3)$$

which highlights the dependence on the cavity efficiency η and the total power P_{AC}. The H_D term is the pinch enhancement factor, that accounts for the bunch attraction in the collisions of oppositely charged beams. In summary, since the amount of available power is necessarily limited, the main handles on luminosity are η and ϵ_y. The efficiency for transferring power from the plug to the beam is naturally higher for s.c. than for conventional copper cavities, so more relaxed collision parameters can be adopted for a s.c. linear collider delivering the same luminosity. The main beam parameters for the ILC baseline design are given in Table 2.1.

Table 2.1. ILC baseline design beam parameters.

Parameter	$\sqrt{s}$ 0.5 TeV	$\sqrt{s}$ 1.0 TeV
Luminosity L (10^{34} cm^{-2}s^{-1})	2.0	2.8
Frequency (Hz)	5.0	5.0
Nb. of particles (10^{10})	2.0	2.0
Nb. of bunches N_b	2820	2820
Bunch spacing (ns)	308	308
Vertical beam size σ_y (nm)	5.7	3.5
Beamstrahlung Parameter δ_{BS}	0.022	0.050
H_D	1.7	1.5

2.4. ILC Physics Highlights

The ILC physics program, as we can anticipate it at present, is broad and diverse, compelling and challenging. The ILC is being designed for operation at 0.5 TeV with the potential to span the largest range of collision energies, from the Z^0 peak at 0.091 TeV up to 1 TeV, collide electrons with positrons, but optionally also electrons with electrons, photons with photons and photons with electrons, and combine various polarization states of the electron and positron beams. Various reports discussing the linear collider physics case, including results of detailed physics studies, have been published in the last few years.[5,17,22–26] Here, I shall focus on three of the main ILC physics themes: the detailed study of the Higgs boson profile, the determination of neutralino dark matter density in the Universe from accelerator data, and the sensitivity to new phenomena beyond the ILC kinematic reach, through the analysis of two-fermion production, at the highest $\sqrt{s}$ energy. Results discussed in the following have been obtained mostly using realistic, yet parametric simulation of the detector response. Only few analyses have been carried out which include the full set of physics and machine-induced backgrounds on fully simulated and reconstructed events. With the progress of the activities of detector concepts and the definition of well-defined benchmark processes, this is becoming one of the priorities for the continuation of physics and detector studies.

2.4.1. *The Higgs Profile at the ILC*

Explaining the origin of mass is one of the great scientific quests of our time. The SM addresses this question by the Higgs mechanism.[27] The first direct manifestation of the Higgs mechanism through the Higgs sector will be the existence of at least one Higgs boson. The observation of a new spin-0 particle would represent a first sign that the Higgs mechanism of mass generation is indeed realised in Nature. This has motivated a large experimental effort, from LEP-2 to the Tevatron and, soon, the LHC, actively backed-up by new and more accurate theoretical predictions. After a Higgs discovery, which we anticipate will be possible at the LHC, full validation of the Higgs mechanism can only be established by an accurate study of the Higgs boson production and decay properties. It is here where the ILC potential in precision physics will be crucial for the validation of the Higgs mechanism, through a detailed study of the Higgs profile.[31]

The details of this study depend on the Higgs boson mass, M_H. In the SM, $M_H = \sqrt{2\lambda}v$ where the Higgs field expectation value v is determined as $(\sqrt{2}G_F)^{-1/2} \approx 246$ GeV, while the Higgs self-coupling λ is not specified, leaving the mass as a free parameter. However, we have strong indications that M_H must be light. The Higgs self-coupling behaviour at high energies,[28] the Higgs field contribution to precision electro-weak data[30] and the results of direct searches at LEP-2[29] at $\sqrt{s} \geq 206$ GeV, all point towards a light Higgs boson. In particular, the study of precision electro-weak data, which are sensitive to the Higgs mass logarithmic contribution to radiative corrections, is based on several independent observables, including masses (m_{top}, M_W, M_Z), lepton and quark asymmetries at the Z^0 pole, Z^0 line-shape and partial decay widths. The fit to eighteen observables results in a 95% C.L. upper limit for the Higgs mass of 166 GeV, which becomes 199 GeV when the lower limit from the direct searches at LEP-2, $M_H > 114.4$ GeV, is included. As a result, current data indicates that the Higgs boson mass should be in the range 114 GeV $< M_H <$ 199 GeV. It is encouraging to observe that if the same fit is repeated, but excluding this time m_{top} or M_W, the results for their values, 178^{+12}_{-9} GeV and 80.361±0.020 GeV respectively, are in very good agreement with the those obtained the direct determinations, $m_{top} = 171.4 \pm 2.1$ GeV and $M_W = 80.392 \pm 0.029$ GeV.

At the ILC the Higgs boson can be observed in the Higgs-strahlung production process $e^+e^- \to HZ$ with $Z \to \ell^+\ell^-$, independent of its decay mode, by the distinctive peak in the di-lepton recoil mass distribution. A data set of 500 fb^{-1} at $\sqrt{s} = 350$ GeV, corresponding to four years of ILC running, provides a sample of 3500-2200 Higgs particles produced in the di-lepton HZ channel, for $M_H = 120$-200 GeV. Taking into account the SM backgrounds, dominated by $e^+e^- \to Z^0Z^0$ and W^+W^- production, the Higgs boson observability is guaranteed up to its production kinematical limit, independent of its decays. This sets the ILC aside from the LHC, since the ILC sensitivity to the Higgs boson does not depend on its detailed properties.

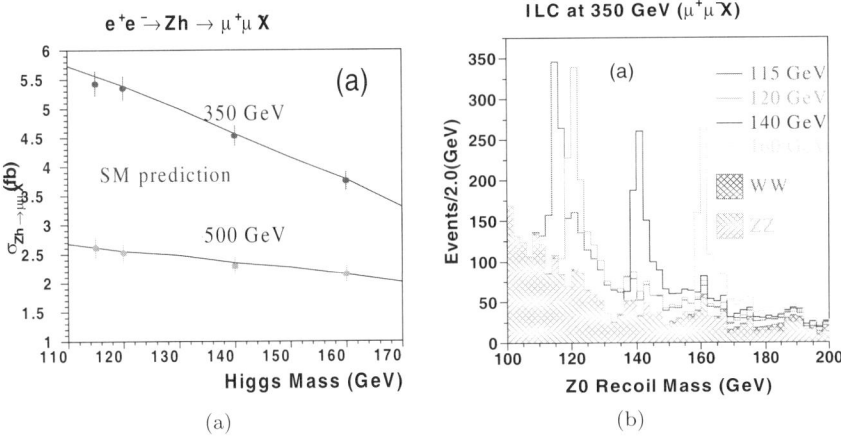

Fig. 2.5. The Higgs-strahlung process at the ILC. (a) $e^+e^- \to HZ$ cross section vs. M_H for $\sqrt{s} = 0.35$ TeV and 0.5 TeV, (b) reconstructed $\mu^+\mu^-$ recoil mass for various values of the Higgs boson mass (Credit: ALCPG Study Group).

After observation of a new particle with properties compatible with those of the Higgs boson, a significant experimental and theoretical effort will be needed to verify that this is indeed the boson of the scalar field responsible for the electro-weak symmetry breaking and the generation of mass. Outlining the Higgs boson profile, through the determination of its mass, width, quantum numbers, couplings to gauge bosons and fermions and the reconstruction of the Higgs potential, stands as a most challenging, yet compelling, physics program. The ILC, with its large data sets at different centre-of-mass energies and beam polarisation conditions, the high resolution detectors providing unprecedented accuracy on the reconstruction of the event properties and the use of advanced analysis techniques, developed from those successfully adopted at LEP and SLC, promises to promote Higgs physics into the domain of precision measurements. Since the Higgs mass M_H is not predicted by theory, it is of great interest to measure it precisely. Once this mass, and thus λ, is fixed, the profile of the Higgs particle is uniquely determined in the SM. In most scenarios we expect the LHC to determine the Higgs mass with a good accuracy. At the ILC, this measurement can be refined by exploiting the kinematical characteristics of the Higgs-strahlung production process $e^+e^- \to Z^* \to H^0 Z^0$ where the Z^0 can be reconstructed in both its leptonic and hadronic decay modes. The $\ell^+\ell^-$ recoil mass for leptonic Z^0 decays yields an accuracy of 110 MeV for 500 fb^{-1} of data, without any requirement on the nature of the Higgs decays. Further improvement can be obtained by explicitly selecting $H \to b\bar{b}$ (WW) for $M_H \leq (>)$ 140 GeV. Here a kinematical 5-C fit, imposing energy and momentum conservation and the mass of a jet pair to correspond to M_Z, achieves an accuracy of 40 to 90 MeV for 120$< M_H <$ 180 GeV.[32]

The total decay width of the Higgs boson is predicted to be too narrow to be resolved experimentally for Higgs boson masses below the ZZ threshold. On the contrary, above $\simeq$ 200 GeV, the total width can be measured directly from the reconstructed width of the recoil mass peak, as discussed below. For the lower mass range, indirect methods must be applied. In general, the total width is given by $\Gamma_{tot} = \Gamma_X/\mathrm{BR}(H \to X)$. Whenever Γ_X can be determined independently of the corresponding branching fraction, a measurement of Γ_{tot} can be carried out. The most convenient choice is the extraction of Γ_H from the measurements of the WW fusion cross section and the $H \to WW^*$ decay branching fraction . A relative precision of 6% to 13% on the width of the Higgs boson can be obtained at the ILC with this technique, for masses between 120 GeV and 160 GeV. The spin, parity

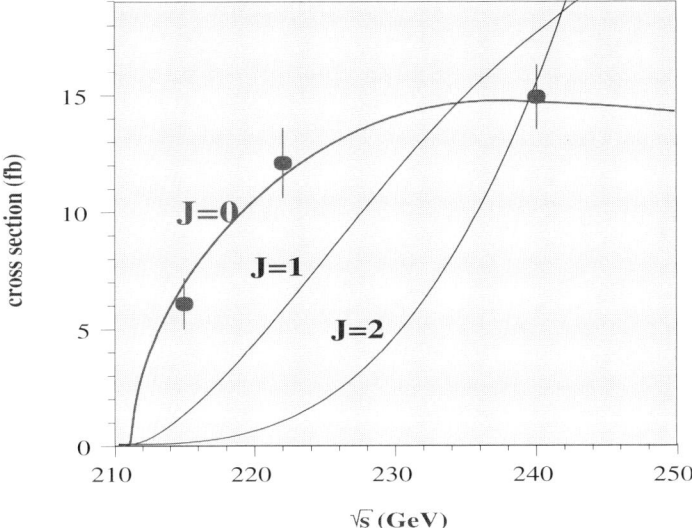

Fig. 2.6. Determination of the Higgs boson spin from a scan of the $e^+e^- \to HZ$ cross section at threshold at the ILC (from Ref. 23).

and charge-conjugation quantum numbers J^{PC} of Higgs bosons can be determined at the ILC in a model-independent way. Already the observation of either $\gamma\gamma \to H$ production or $H \to \gamma\gamma$ decay sets $J \neq 1$ and $C = +$. The angular dependence $\frac{d\sigma_{ZH}}{d\theta} \propto \sin^2\theta$ and the rise of the Higgs-strahlung cross section:

$$\sigma_{ZH} \propto \beta \sim \sqrt{s - (M_H + M_Z)^2} \quad (2.4)$$

allows to determine $J^P = 0^+$ and distinguish the SM Higgs from a CP-odd 0^{-+} state A^0, or a CP-violating mixture of the two.[33,34] But where the ILC has a most unique potential is in verifying that the Higgs boson does its job of providing gauge bosons, quarks and leptons with their masses. This requires to precisely test the relation $g_{HXX} \propto m_X$ between the Yukawa couplings, g_{HXX}, and the corresponding particle masses, m_X. In fact, the SM Higgs couplings to fermion pairs $g_{Hff} = m_f/v$ are fully determined by the fermion mass m_f. The corresponding decay partial widths only depend on these couplings and on the Higgs boson mass, QCD corrections do not represent a significant source of uncertainty.[35] Therefore, their accurate determination will represent a comprehensive test of the Higgs mechanism of mass generation.[36] Further, observing deviations of the measured values

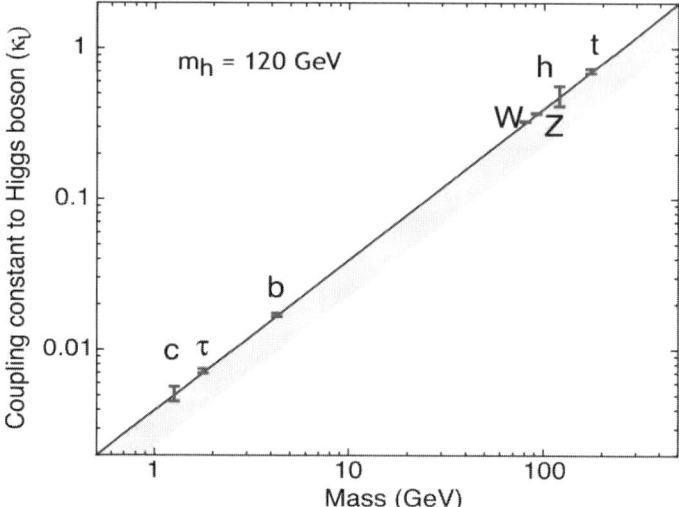

Fig. 2.7. Particle couplings to the Higgs field, for a 120 GeV boson, as a function of the particle masses. The error bars show the expected ILC accuracy in determining each of the couplings. The dark line is the SM prediction, while the shaded gray area shows the range of predictions from theories of new physics beyond the SM with extra dimensions (Credit: ACFA ILC Study Group).

from the SM predictions will probe the structure of the Higgs sector and may reveal a non-minimal implementation of the Higgs model or the effect of new physics inducing a shift of the Higgs couplings.[37–39] The accuracy of these measurements relies on the performances of jet flavour tagging and thus mostly on the Vertex Tracker, making this analysis an important benchmark for optimising the detector design. It is important to ensure that the ILC sensitivity extends over a wide range of Higgs boson masses and that a significant accuracy is achieved for most particle species. Here, the ILC adds the precision which establishes the key elements of the Higgs mechanism. It is important to point out that these tests are becoming more stringent now that the B-factories have greatly improved the determination of the b- and c-quark masses. When one of these studies was first presented in 1999,[40] the b quark mass was known to ± 0.11 GeV and the charm mass to ± 0.13 GeV, with the expectation that e^+e^- B-factory and LHC data could reduce these uncertainties by a factor of two by the time the ILC data would be analysed. Today, the analysis of a fraction of the BaBar data[41] has already brought these uncertainties down to 0.07 GeV for

m_b and, more importantly, 0.09 GeV for m_c, using the spectral moments technique in semi-leptonic B decays, which had been pioneered on CLEO[42] and DELPHI data.[43] Extrapolating to the anticipated total statistics to be collected at PEP-II and KEKB, we can now confidently expect that the b quark mass should be known to better than ± 0.05 GeV and the charm mass to better than ± 0.06 GeV. This translates into less than ± 0.4 % and ± 6.5 % relative uncertainty in computing the Higgs SM couplings to b and c quarks, respectively, and motivates enhanced experimental precision in the determination of these couplings at the ILC. Detailed simulation shows that these accuracy can be matched by the ILC.[44,47]

While much of the emphasis on the ILC capabilities in the study of the Higgs profile is for a light Higgs scenario, preferred by the current electro-weak data and richer in decay modes, the ILC has also the potential of precisely mapping out the Higgs boson properties for heavier masses. If the Higgs boson turns out to weigh of order 200 GeV, the 95% C.L. upper limit indicated by electro-weak fits, or even heavier, the analysis of the recoil mass in $e^+e^- \to HZ$ at $\sqrt{s} = 0.5$ TeV allows to precisely determine M_H, Γ_H and the Higgs-strahlung cross section. Even for $M_H = 240$ GeV, the mass can be determined to a 10^{-3} accuracy and, more importantly, the total width measured about 10% accuracy. Decays of Higgs bosons produced in $e^+e^- \to H\nu\bar{\nu}$ give access to the Higgs couplings. The importance of the WW-

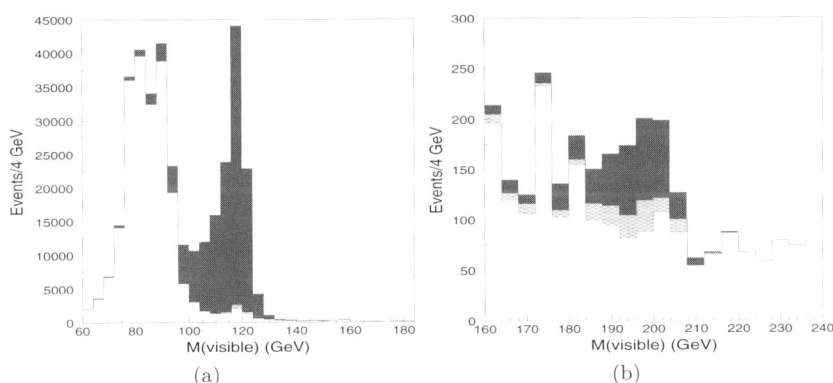

Fig. 2.8. $H \to b\bar{b}$ signal after full event selection at the ILC for (a) $M_H = 120$ GeV and (b) $M_H = 200$ GeV (from Ref. 47).

fusion process $e^+e^- \to H^0\nu\bar{\nu}$ to probe rare Higgs decays at higher energies, emerged in the physics study for a multi-TeV linear collider.[45] Since this cross section increases as $log\frac{s}{M_H^2}$, it becomes dominant around $\sqrt{s} = 1$ TeV. Detailed studies have been performed and show that 1 ab^{-1} of data at $\sqrt{s} = 1$ TeV, corresponding to three to four years of ILC running, can significantly improve the determination of the Higgs couplings, especially for the larger values of M_H.[46,47] WW and ZZ couplings can be determined with relative accuracies of 3 % and 5 % respectively, while the coupling to $b\bar{b}$ pairs, a rare decay with a branching fraction of just 2×10^{-3} at such large masses, can be determined to 4 % to 14 % for 180 GeV $< M_H <$ 220 GeV. This measurement is of great importance, since it would offer the only opportunity to learn about the fermion couplings of such an heavy Higgs boson, and it is unique to a linear collider.

A most distinctive feature of the Higgs mechanism is the shape of the Higgs potential:

$$V(\Phi) = -\frac{\mu^2}{2}\Phi^2 + \frac{\lambda}{4}\Phi^4 \qquad (2.5)$$

with $v = \sqrt{\frac{\mu^2}{\lambda}}$. In the SM, the triple Higgs coupling, $g_{HHH} = 3\lambda v$, is related to the Higgs mass, M_H, through the relation

$$g_{HHH} = \frac{3}{2}\frac{M_H^2}{v}. \qquad (2.6)$$

By determining g_{HHH}, the above relation can be tested. The ILC has access to the triple Higgs coupling through the double Higgs production processes $e^+e^- \rightarrow HHZ$ and $e^+e^- \rightarrow HH\nu\nu$.[48] Deviations from the SM relation for the strength of the Higgs self-coupling arise in models with an extended Higgs sector.[49] The extraction of g_{HHH} is made difficult by their tiny cross sections and by the dilution effect, due to diagrams leading to the same double Higgs final states, but not sensitive to the triple Higgs vertex. This makes the determination of g_{HHH} a genuine experimental *tour de force*. Other modes, such as $e^+e^- \rightarrow HHb\bar{b}$, have also been recently proposed[50] but signal yields are too small to provide any precise data. Operating at $\sqrt{s} = 0.5$ TeV the ILC can measure the HHZ production cross section to about 15% accuracy, if the Higgs boson mass is 120 GeV, corresponding to a fractional accuracy on g_{HHH} of 23%.[51] Improvements can be obtained first by introducing observables sensitive to the presence of the triple Higgs vertex and then by performing the analysis at higher energies where the $HH\nu\bar{\nu}$ channel contributes.[52] In the HHZ process events from diagrams containing the HHH vertex exhibit a lower invariant mass of the HH system compared to double-Higgstrahlung events. When

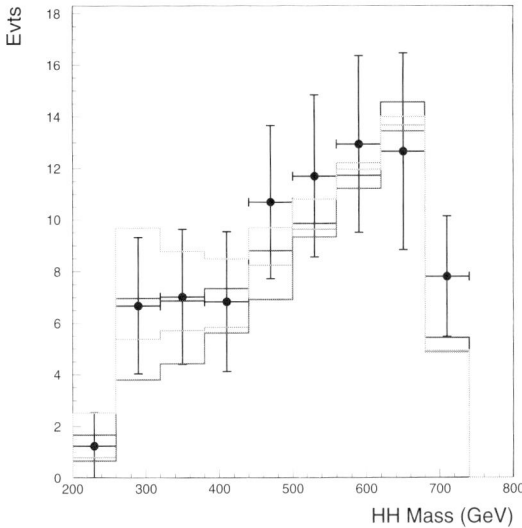

Fig. 2.9. Invariant mass of the HH system in $e^+e^- \to HHZ$ events reconstructed with 1 ab^{-1} of data at 0.8 TeV. The histograms show the predicted distribution for various values of g_{HHH} demonstrating that the low mass region is sensitive to the contribution of the triple Higgs vertex.

the M_{HH} spectrum is fitted, a relative statistical accuracy of ±0.20 can be obtained with 1 ab^{-1} at $\sqrt{s} = 0.5$ TeV. The availability of beam polarization increases the HHZ cross section by a factor of two and that for $HH\nu\bar{\nu}$ by a factor of four, thus offering a further possible significant improvement to the final accuracy. The ILC and, possibly, a multi-TeV e^+e^- collider represent a unique opportunity for carrying out this fundamental measurement. In fact, preliminary studies show that, the analysis of double Higgs production at the LHC is only possible after a luminosity upgrade and, even then, beyond the observation of double Higgs production, it would provide only a very limited information on the triple-Higgs coupling.[53,54]

2.4.2. *Understanding Dark Matter at the ILC*

The search for new physics beyond the Standard Model has a central role in the science program of future colliders. It is instructive to contrast the LHC and the ILC in terms of their potential in such searches. Running

Table 2.2. Summary of the accuracies on the determination of the Higgs boson profile at the ILC. Results are given for a 350-500 GeV ILC with $\mathcal{L}=0.5$ ab^{-1}. Further improvements, expected from a 1 TeV ILC are also shown for some of the measurements.

	M_H (GeV)	$\delta(X)/X$ ILC-500 0.5 ab^{-1} | ILC-1000 1 ab^{-1}
$\delta M_H/M$	120-180	(3-5) $\times 10^{-4}$
$\delta\Gamma_{tot}/\Gamma$	120-200	0.03- -- | 0.03 - 0.05
$\delta g_{HWW}/g$	120-240	0.01-0.03 | 0.01 - 0.01
$\delta g_{HZZ}/g$	120-240	0.01-0.05
$\delta g_{Htt}/g$	120-200	0.02- -- | 0.06 - 0.13
$\delta g_{Hbb}/g$	120-200	0.01-0.06 | 0.01 - 0.05
$\delta g_{Hcc}/g$	120-140	0.06-0.12
$\delta g_{H\tau\tau}/g$	120-140	0.03-0.05
$\delta g_{H\mu\mu}/g$	120-140	0.15 | 0.04-0.06
CP test	120	0.03
$\delta g_{HHH}/g$	120	0.20 | 0.1

at $\sqrt{s} \leq 1$ TeV the ILC might appear to be limited in reach, somewhere within the energy domain being probed by the Tevatron and that to be accessed by LHC. And yet its potential for fully understanding the new physics, which the LHC might have manifested, and for probing the high energy frontier beyond the boundaries explored in hadron collisions is of paramount importance. There are several examples of how the ILC will be essential for understanding new physics. They address scenarios where signals of physics beyond the SM, as observed at the LHC, may be insufficient to decide on the nature of the new phenomena. One such example, which has been studied in some details, is the case of Supersymmetry and Universal Extra Dimensions (UED), two very different models of new physics leading to the very same experimental signature: fermion pairs plus missing energy. Here, the limited analytical power of the LHC may leave us undecided,[56,57] while a single spin measurement performed at the ILC precisely identifies the nature of the observed particles.[58] But the ILC capability to fully understand the implications of new physics, through fundamental measurements performed with high accuracy, is manifested also in scenarios where the LHC could observe a significant fraction of the new particle spectrum. An especially compelling example, which can be studied quantitatively, is offered by Supersymmetry in relation to Dark Matter (DM). Dark Matter has been established as a major component of the Universe. We know from several independent observations, including the cosmic microwave background (CMB), supernovas (SNs) and galaxy clusters, that DM is responsible for approximately 20 % of the energy density of the universe. Yet, none of the SM particles can be responsible for it and the observation of DM is likely the first direct signal of new physics beyond the SM. Several particles and objects have been nominated as candidates for DM. They span a wide range of masses, from 10^{-5} eV, in the case of axions, to 10^{-5} solar masses, for primordial black holes. Cosmology tells us that a significant fraction of the Universe mass consists of DM, but does not provide clues on its nature. Particle physics tells us that New Physics must exist at, or just beyond, the EW scale and new symmetries may result in new, stable particles. Establishing the inter-relations between physics at the microscopic scale and phenomena at cosmological scale will represent a major theme for physics in the next decades. The ILC will be able to play a key role in elucidating these inter-relations. Out of these many possibilities, there is a class of models which is especially attractive since its existence is independently motivated and DM, at about the observed density, arises naturally. These are extensions of the SM, which include an extra symmetry protecting the lightest particle in the new sector from decaying into ordinary SM states. The lightest particle becomes stable and can be chosen to be neutral. Such a particle is called a weakly interacting massive particle (WIMP) and arises in Supersymmetry with conserved R-parity (SUSY) but also in Extra Dimensions with KK-parity (UED).[66] Current cosmological data, mostly through the WMAP satellite measurements of the CMB, determine the DM density in the Universe with a 6 % relative accuracy.[59] By the next decade, the PLANCK satellite will push this uncertainty to $\simeq$ 1 %, or below.[60] Additional astrophysical data manifest a possible evidence of DM annihilation. The EGRET data show excess of γ emission in the inner galaxy, which has been interpreted as due to DM[61] and the WMAP data itself may show a signal of synchrotron emission in the Galactic center.[62] These data, if confirmed, may be used to further constrain the DM properties. Ground-based DM searches are also approaching the stage where their sensitivity is at the level predicted by Supersymmetry for some combinations of parameters.[63] The next decades promise to be a time when accelerator experiments will provide new breakthroughs and highly accurate data to gain new insights, not only on fundamental questions in particle physics, but also in cosmology, when studied alongside the observations from satellites and other experiments. The questions on the nature and the origin of DM offer a prime example of the synergies of new experiments at hadron and lepton colliders, at satellites and ground-based DM experiments.

It is essential to study, in well defined, yet general enough, models, which are the properties of the new physics sector, such as masses and couplings, most important to determine the resulting relic density of the DM particles. Models exist which allow to link the microscopic particle properties to the present DM density in the Universe, with mild assumptions. If DM consists of WIMPs, they are abundantly produced in the very early Universe when $T \simeq (t(\text{sec}))^{-1/2} > 100$ GeV and their interaction cross section is large enough that they were in thermal equilibrium for some period in the early universe. The DM relic density can be determined by solving the Boltzmann equation governing the evolution of their phase space number density.[64] It can be shown that, by taking the WMAP result for the DM relic density in units of the Universe critical density, $\Omega_{DM}h^2$, the thermal averaged DM annihilation cross section times the co-moving velocity, $<\sigma v>$, should be $\simeq 0.9$. From this result, the mass of the DM candidate can be estimated as:

$$M_{DM} = \sqrt{\frac{\pi \alpha^2}{8 <\sigma v>}} \simeq 100 \text{ GeV}. \qquad (2.7)$$

A particle with mass $M = \mathcal{O}(100 \text{ GeV})$ and weak cross section would naturally give the measured DM density. It is quite suggestive that new physics, responsible for the breaking of electro-weak symmetry, also introduce a WIMP of about that mass. In fact, in essentially every model of electroweak symmetry breaking, it is possible to add a discrete symmetry that makes the lightest new particle stable. Often, this discrete symmetry is required for other reasons. For example, in Supersymmetry, the conserved R parity is needed to eliminate rapid proton decay. In other cases, such as models with TeV-scale extra dimensions, the discrete symmetry is a natural consequence of the underlying geometry.

Data on DM density already set rather stringent constraints on the parameters of Supersymmetry, if the lightest neutralino χ_1^0 is indeed responsible for saturating the amount of DM observed in the Universe. It is useful to discuss the different scenarios, where neutralino DM density is compatible with the WMAP result, in terms of parameter choices in the context of the constrained MSSM (cMSSM), to understand how the measurements that the ILC provides can establish the relation between new physics and

DM. The cMSSM reduces the number of free parameters to just five: the common scalar mass, m_0, the common gaugino mass, $m_{1/2}$, the ratio of the vacuum expectation values of the two Higgs fields, $\tan\beta$, the sign of the Higgsino mass parameter, μ, and the common trilinear coupling, A_0. It is a remarkable feature of this model that, as these parameters, defined at the unification scale, are evolved down to lower energies, the electroweak symmetry is broken spontaneously and masses for the $W^\pm$ and Z^0 bosons generated automatically. As this model is simple and defined by a small number of parameters, it is well suited for phenomenological studies. The cosmologically interesting regions in the m_0 - $m_{1/2}$ parameter plane are shown in Figure 2.10. As we move away from the bulk region, at small values of m_0 and $m_{1/2}$, which is already severely constrained by LEP-2 data, the masses of supersymmetric particles increase and so does the dark matter density. It is therefore necessary to have an annihilation process, which could efficiently remove neutralinos in the early universe, to restore the DM density to the value measured by WMAP. Different processes define three main regions: i) the focus point region, where the χ^0_1 contains an admixture of the supersymmetric partner of a neutral Higgs boson and annihilates to W^+W^- and Z^0Z^0, ii) the co-annihilation region, where the lightest slepton has a mass very close to $M_{\chi^0_1}$, iii) the A annihilation funnel, where $M(\chi^0_1)$ is approximately half that of the heavy A^0 Higgs boson, providing efficient s-channel annihilation, $\chi\chi \to A$. In each of these regions, researchers at the ILC will be confronted with several different measurements and significantly different event signatures.

Table 2.3. cMSSM parameters of benchmark points.

Point	m_0	$m_{1/2}$	$\tan\beta$	A_0	$Sgn(\mu)$	$M(t)$
LCC1	100	250	10	-100	+	178
LCC2	3280	300	10	0	+	175
LCC3	210	360	40	0	+	178
LCC4	380	420	53	0	+	178

It is interesting to observe that the DM constraint, reduces the dimensionality of the cMSSM plane, by one unit, since the allowed regions are tiny lines in the m_0 - $m_{1/2}$ plane, evolve with $\tan\beta$ and depend only very weakly on A_0.[65] Representative benchmark points have been defined and their parameters are summarised in Table 2.3. Even though these points have been defined in a specific supersymmetric model, their phenomenol-

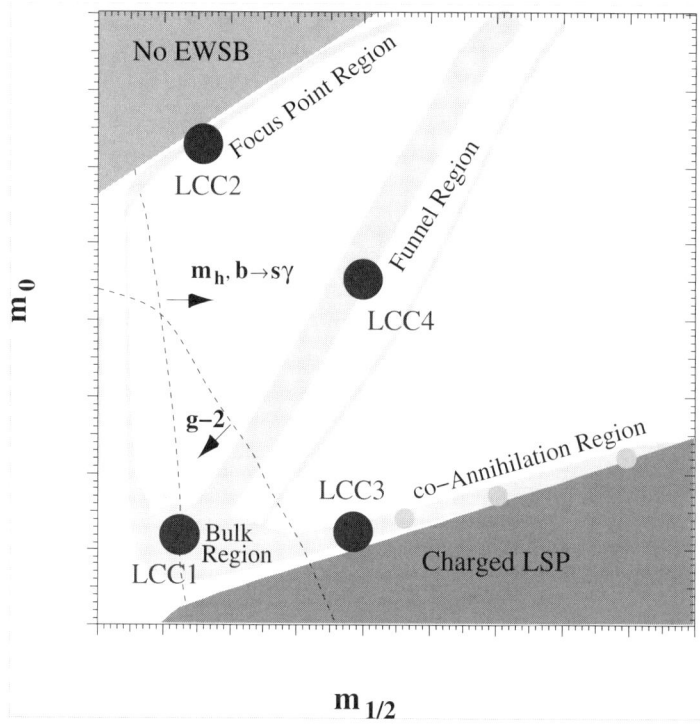

Fig. 2.10. The DM-favoured regions in the m_0 - $m_{1/2}$ plane of the cMSSM and existing constraints. The precise locations of these regions vary with the $\tan\beta$ parameter and therefore the axis are given without units. The indicative locations of the four benchmark points adopted, are also given. Lower limits on the Higgs boson mass and, in a portion of the parameter space, the measurement of the $b \to s\gamma$ decay branching fraction, exclude the region at low values of $m_{1/2}$. A discrepancy of the measured anomalous magnetic moment of the muon value with the SM prediction would favour the region on the left of the curve labeled $g-2$.

ogy is common to the more general supersymmetric solutions and we shall soon discuss the extension of results derived in this constrained model to the general MSSM. There are several features which are common to all these regions. First, the relic density depends on the mass of the lightest neutralino and of few additional particles, close in mass to it. The heavier part of the SUSY spectrum decouples from the value of $\Omega_\chi h^2$. This is of particular importance for the ILC. Running at $\sqrt{s} \leq 1$ TeV, the ILC will not be able to study supersymmetric particles exceeding $\simeq$450-490 GeV, in particular scalar quarks and heavy Higgs bosons in some regions of the parameter phase space. But, independently of the LHC results, the ILC will either observe and measure these particles if they may be relevant to determine the relic DM density, or it will set bounds that ensure their decoupling. A second important observation is that $\Omega_\chi h^2$ typically depends on SUSY parameters which can be fixed by accurate measurements of particle masses, particle mass splittings, decay branching fractions and production cross sections. In some instances the availability of polarised beams is advantageous. The LHC can often make precise measurements of some particles, but it is difficult for the LHC experiments to assemble the complete set of parameters needed to reconstruct annihilation cross section. It is also typical of supersymmetry spectra to contain light particles that may be very difficult to observe in the hadron collider environment. The ILC, in contrast, provides just the right setting to obtain both types of measurements. Again, it is not necessary for the ILC to match the energy of the LHC, only that it provides enough energy to see the lightest charged particles of the new sector.

Rather detailed ILC analyses of the relevant channels for each benchmark point have been performed,[67–70] based on parametric simulation, which includes realistic detector performances and effects of the ILC beam characteristics. It has been assumed that the ILC will be able to provide collisions at centre-of-mass energies from 0.3 TeV to 0.5 TeV with an integrated luminosity of 500 fb^{-1} in a first phase of operation and then its collision energy can raised to 1 TeV to provide an additional data set of 1 ab^{-1}, corresponding to an additional three to four years of running. Results are summarised in terms of the estimated accuracies on masses and mass differences in Table 2.4.

In order to estimate the implications of these ILC measurements on the estimation of neutralino dark DM density $\Omega_\chi h^2$, broad scans of the multi-parameter supersymmetric phase space need to be performed. For each benchmark point, the soft parameters (masses and couplings) at the electroweak scale can be computed with the full 2-loop renormalization group equations and threshold corrections using `Isajet 7.69`.[71] Supersymmetric loop corrections to the Yukawa couplings can also be included. The electroweak-scale MSSM parameters are extracted from the high scale cMSSM parameters. The dark matter density $\Omega_\chi h^2$ can be estimated using the `DarkSUSY`[72] and `Micromegas`[73] programs. These programs use the same `Isajet` code to determine the particle spectrum and couplings, including the running Yukawa couplings, and compute the thermally averaged cross section for neutralino annihilation, including co-annihilation and solve the equation describing the evolution of the number density for the DM candi-

Table 2.4. Summary of the accuracies (in GeV) on the main mass determinations by the ILC at 0.5 TeV for the four benchmark points. Results in [] brackets also include ILC data at 1 TeV.

Observable	LCC1	LCC2	LCC3	LCC4
$\delta M(\tilde{\chi}_1^0)$	± 0.05	± 1.0	± 0.1	[± 1.4]
$\delta M(\tilde{e}_R)$	± 0.05	-	[± 1.0]	[± 0.6]
$\delta M(\tilde{\tau}_1)$	± 0.3	-	± 0.5	± 0.9
$\delta M(\tilde{\tau}_2)$	± 1.1	-	-	-
$\delta(M(\mu_R) - M(\tilde{\chi}_1^0))$	± 0.2		[±0.2]	± 0.6
$\delta(M(\tilde{\tau}_1) - M(\tilde{\chi}_1^0))$	0.3	-	± 1.0	± 1.0
$\delta(M(\tilde{\tau}_2) - M(\tilde{\chi}_1^0))$	± 1.1		[± 3.0]	
$\delta(M(\tilde{\chi}_2^0) - M(\tilde{\chi}_1^0))$	± 0.07	± 0.3	± 0.6	[± 1.8]
$\delta(M(\tilde{\chi}_3^0) - M(\tilde{\chi}_1^0))$	± 4.0	± 0.2	[± 2.0]	[± 2.0]
$\delta(M(\tilde{\chi}_1^+) - M(\tilde{\chi}_1^0))$	± 0.6	± 0.25	[± 0.7]	± 2.0
$\delta(M(\tilde{\chi}_2^+) - M(\tilde{\chi}_1^+))$	[± 3.0]	-	[± 2.0]	± 2.0
$\delta M(A^0)$	[± 1.5]	-	[± 0.8]	[± 0.8]
$\delta \Gamma(A^0)$		-	[± 1.2]	[± 1.2]

date. While the assumptions of the cMSSM are quite helpful for defining a set of benchmark points, the cMSSM is not representative of the generic MSSM, since it implies several mass relations, and its assumptions have no strong physics justification. Therefore, in studying the accuracy on $\Omega_\chi h^2$, the full set of MSSM parameters must be scanned in an uncorrelated way and the mass spectrum evaluated for each parameter set. A detailed study has recently been performed.[74] I summarise here some of the findings, Table 2.5 gives results for the neutralino relic density estimates in MSSM for the LHC, the ILC at 0.5 TeV and the ILC at 1 TeV.

The LCC1 point is in the bulk region and the model contains light sleptons, with masses just above that of the lightest neutralino. The most

Table 2.5. Summary of the relative accuracy $\frac{\delta \Omega_\chi h^2}{\Omega_\chi h^2}$ for the four benchmark points obtained with full SUSY scans.

Benchmark Point	Ωh^2	LHC	ILC 0.5 TeV	ILC 1.0 TeV
LCC1	0.192	0.072	0.018	0.024
LCC2	0.109	0.820	0.140	0.076
LCC3	0.101	1.670	0.500	0.180
LCC4	0.114	4.050	0.850	0.190

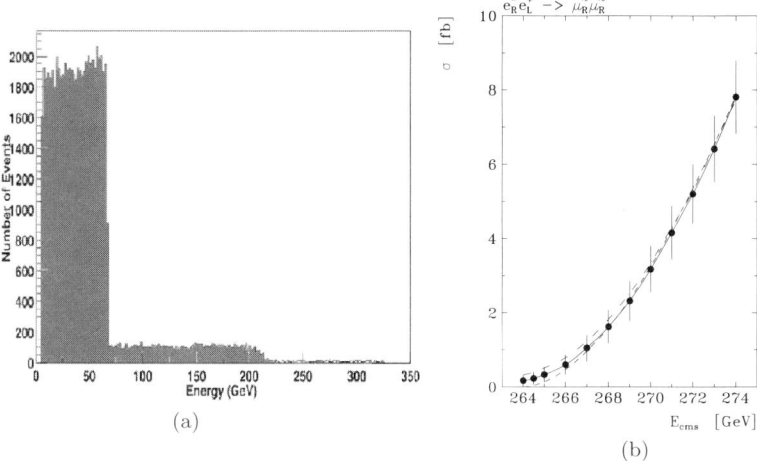

Fig. 2.11. Mass reconstruction at ILC: (a) momentum endpoint in $\tilde{\mu} \to \mu\chi_1^0$ (from Ref. 76) and (b) threshold scan for $e^+e^- \to \tilde{\mu}^+\tilde{\mu}^-$ (from Ref. 23)

important annihilation reactions are those with t-channel slepton exchange. At the LHC, many of the SUSY spectrum parameters can be determined from kinematic constraints. At the ILC masses can be determined both by the two-body decay kinematics of the pair-produced SUSY particles and by dedicated threshold scans. Let us consider the two body decay of a scalar quark $\tilde{q} \to q\chi_1^0$. If the scalar quarks are pair produced $e^+e^- \to \tilde{q}\tilde{q}$, $E_{\tilde{q}} = E_{beam}$ and the χ_1^0 escapes undetected, only the q (and the $\bar{q}$) are observed in the detector. In a 1994 paper, J. Feng and D. Finnell[75] pointed out that the minimum and maximum energy of production for the quark can be related to the mass difference between the scalar quark $\tilde{q}$ and the χ_1^0:

$$E_{max,\,min} = \frac{E_{beam}}{2}\left(1 \pm \sqrt{1 - \frac{m_{\tilde{q}}^2}{E_{beam}^2}}\right)\left(1 - \frac{m_\chi^2}{m_{\tilde{q}}^2}\right). \quad (2.8)$$

The method can also be extended to slepton decays $\tilde{\ell} \to \ell\chi_1^0$, which share the same topology, and allows to determine slepton mass once that of the neutralino is known or determine a relation between the masses and get $m_{\chi_1^0}$ if that of the slepton can be independently measured. The measurement requires a precise determination of the endpoint energies of the lepton momentum spectrum, E_{min} and E_{max}. It can be shown that accuracy is limited by beamstrahlung, affecting the knowledge of E_{beam} in the equation above, more than by the finite momentum resolution, $\delta p/p$ of the detector. The ILC has a second, and even more precise, method for mass measurements. The possibility to precisely tune the collision energy allows to perform scans of the onset of the cross section for a specific SUSY particle pair production process. The particle mass and width can be extracted from a fit to the signal event yield as function of $\sqrt{s}$. The accuracy depends rather weakly on the number of points, N, adopted in the scan and it appears that concentrating the total luminosity at two or three different energies close to the threshold is optimal.[77,78] The mass accuracy, δm can be parametrised as:

$$\delta m \simeq \Delta E \frac{1 + 0.36/\sqrt{N}}{\sqrt{18NL\sigma}} \tag{2.9}$$

for S-wave processes, where the cross section rises as β and as

$$\delta m \simeq \Delta E \frac{1}{N^{1/4}} \frac{1 + 0.38/\sqrt{N}}{\sqrt{2.6NL\sigma}} \tag{2.10}$$

for P-wave processes, where the cross section rises as β^3. The combination of these measurements allows the ILC to determine the χ_1^0 mass to ± 0.05 GeV, which is two orders of magnitude better than the anticipated LHC accuracy, while the mass difference between the $\tilde{\tau}_1$ and the χ_1^0 can be measured to ± 0.3 GeV, which is more than a factor ten better. Extension of ILC operation to 1 TeV gives access to the $e^+e^- \to H^0 A^0$ process. As a result of the precision of these measurements, the ILC data at 0.5 TeV will allow to predict the neutralino relic density to ± 2 % and the addition of 1.0 TeV data will improve it to ± 0.25 %. It is suggestive that this accuracy is comparable, or better, than that expected by the improved CMB survey by the PLANCK mission. For comparison, the LHC data should provide a ± 7 % accuracy. This already a remarkable result, due the fact that, a large number of measurements will be available at the LHC and SUSY decay chains can be reconstructed. Still, the overall mass scale remains uncertain at the LHC. The direct mass measurements on the ILC data remove this uncertainty.

The LCC1 point is characterised by the relatively low SUSY mass scale, most of the particles can be observed at the LHC and their masses accurately measured at the ILC. However, in more general scenarios, the information available from both collider will be more limited. This is the case at

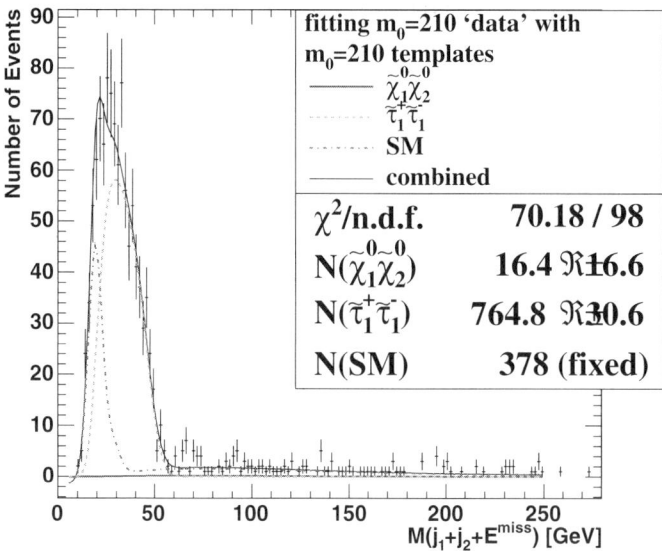

Fig. 2.12. DM-motivated SUSY $\tilde{\tau}$ reconstruction at ILC: determination of the stau-neutralino mass difference from a reconstruction of $e^+e^- \to \tilde{\tau}_1\tilde{\tau}_1$ at 0.5 TeV for LCC3 (from Ref. 69).

the LCC2 point, located in the focus point region, where masses of scalar quarks, sleptons and heavy Higgs bosons are very large, typically beyond the ILC but also the LHC reach, while gauginos masses are of the order of few hundreds GeV, thus within the kinematical domain of the ILC. In this specific scenario, the LHC will observe the SUSY process $\tilde{g} \to q\bar{q}\chi$ and the subsequent neutralino and chargino decays. Still the neutralino relic density can only be constrained within $\pm 40\%$ and the hypothesis $\Omega_\chi h^2 = 0$, namely that the neutralino does not contribute to the observed dark matter density in the universe, cannot be ruled out, based only on LHC data. At a 0.5 TeV collider, the main SUSY reactions are $e^+e^- \to \chi_1^+\chi_1^-$ and $e^+e^- \to \chi_2^0\chi_3^0$. Operation at 1 TeV gives access also to $e^+e^- \to \chi_2^+\chi_2^-$ and $e^+e^- \to \chi_3^0\chi_4^0$. Not only the gaugino mass splittings but also the polarised neutralino and chargino production cross section can be accurately determined at the ILC.[68] These measurements fix the gaugino-Higgsino mixing angles, which play a major role in determining the neutralino relic density. The decoupling of the heavier, inaccessible part of the SUSY spectrum, can be insured with the data at the highest energy. The combined ILC

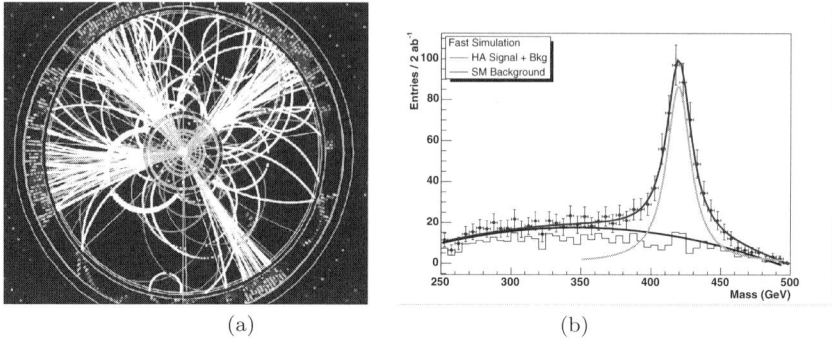

Fig. 2.13. DM-motivated SUSY Higgs reconstruction at ILC: (a) an event $e^+e^- \to A^0 H^0 \to b\bar{b}b\bar{b}$ at 1 TeV in the LDC detector and (b) di-jet invariant mass spectrum for $e^+e^- \to A^0 H^0 \to b\bar{b}b\bar{b}$ at 1 TeV for LCC4 (from Ref. 70).

data at 0.5 TeV and 1 TeV provide an estimate of the neutralino relic density to ±8 % accuracy, which matches the current WMAP precision. The characteristics featured by the LCC2 point persist, while the SUSY masses increase, provided the gaugino-Higgsino mixing angle remains large enough. This DM-motivated region extends to SUSY masses which eventually exceed the LHC reach, highlighting an intriguing region of parameters where the ILC can still observe sizable production of supersymmetric particle, compatible with dark matter data, while the LHC may report no signals of New Physics.[82]

Instead, the last two points considered, LCC3 and LCC4, are representative of those regions where the neutralino relic density is determined by accidental relationships between particle masses. Other such regions may also be motivated by baryogenesis constraints.[83] The determination of the neutralino relic density, in such scenarios, depends crucially on the precision of spectroscopic measurements, due to the large sensitivity on masses and couplings. The conclusions of the current studies are that the LHC data do not provide quantitative constraints. On the contrary, the ILC can obtain interesting precision, especially when high energy data is available.

The LCC3 point is in the so-called $\tilde{\tau}$ co-annihilation region. Here, the mass difference between the lightest neutralino, χ_1^0, and the lightest scalar tau, $\tilde{\tau}_1$, is small enough that $\tilde{\tau}_1 \chi_1^0 \to \tau\gamma$ can effectively remove neutralinos in the early universe. The relative density of $\tilde{\tau}$ particles to neutralinos scales as $e^{-\frac{m_{\tilde{\tau}} - m_\chi}{m_\chi}}$, so this scenario tightly constrain the $m_{\tilde{\tau}} - m_\chi$ mass difference. Here, the precise mass determinations characteristic of LCC1 will not be

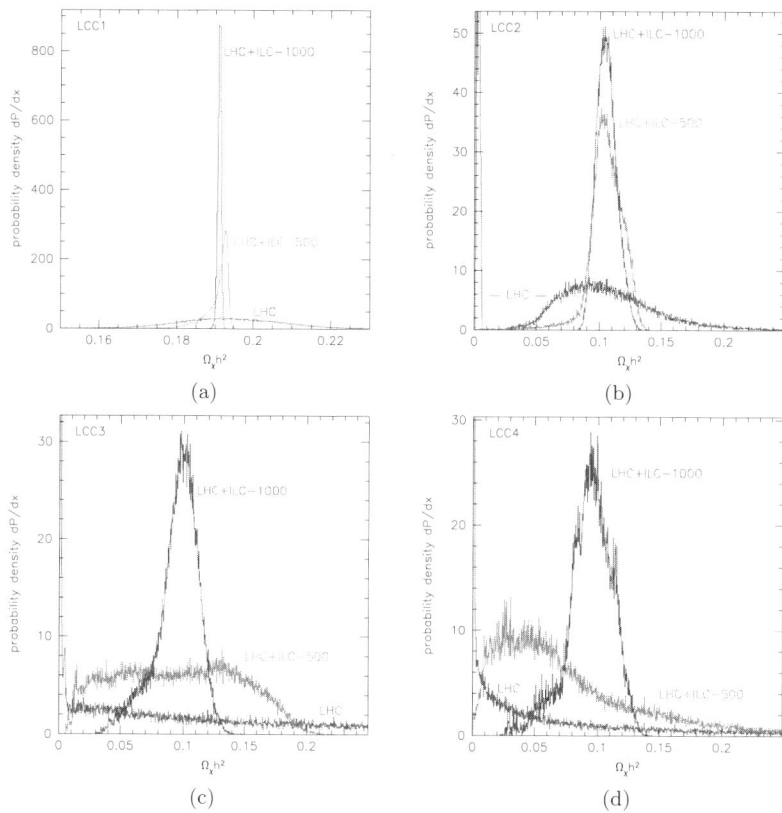

Fig. 2.14. Relic DM density determination based on simulation from LHC, ILC at 0.5 TeV and ILC at 1.0 TeV for the four SUSY benchmark points studied: a) LCC1, b) LCC2, c) LCC3 and d) LCC4. The plots show the probability density functions of the Ωh^2 values corresponding to MSSM points compatible with the accelerator data (from Ref. 74).

available: at 0.5 TeV, the ILC will observe a single final state, $\tau^+\tau^- + E_{missing}$, from the two accessible SUSY processes,[69] $e^+e^- \to \tilde{\tau}_1\tilde{\tau}_1$, $\tilde{\tau} \to \tau\chi_1^0$ and $e^+e^- \to \chi_1^0\chi_2^0$, $\chi_2^0 \to \chi_1^0\tilde{\tau} \to \chi_1^0\chi_1^0\tau\tau$. The signal topology consists of two τ-jets and missing energy. Background processes, such as $e^+e^- \to ZZ$ can be suppressed using cuts on event shape variables. The mass splitting can be determined by a study of the distribution of the invariant mass of the system made by the two τ-jets and the missing energy vector, $M_{j_1 j_2 E_{missing}}$. In this variable, the remaining SM background is confined to low values and the shape and upper endpoint of the $\tilde{\tau}_1\tilde{\tau}_1$ contribution depends on the stau-neutralino mass difference, $\Delta M = M_{\tilde{\tau}_1} - M_{\chi_1^0}$. Templates functions can be generated for different values of ΔM and the mass difference is extracted by a χ^2 fit of these templates to the "data". As the ΔM value decreases, the energy available to the τ leptons decreases. Since τ decays involve neutrinos, additional energy is lost from detection. When the $\tau\tau$ system becomes soft, the four fermion background process $ee \to ee\tau\tau$, the so-called $\gamma\gamma$ background which has cross sections at the nb level, makes its detection increasingly difficult. What makes possible to reject these $\gamma\gamma$ events is the presence of the two energetic primary electrons at small angle w.r.t. the beamline.[79] This is a significant challenge for low angle calorimetry, since the electron has to be detected in an hostile environment populated by a large number of other electrons, of lower energy, arising from pairs created during the bunch collision.[80,81] A detailed study,[69] performed for a statistics of 500 fb^{-1}, shows that values of ΔM as small as 5 GeV can be measured at the ILC, provided the primary electrons can be vetoed down to 17 mrad. In the specific case of the LCC3 point, where the mass splitting, ΔM, is 10.8 GeV, an accuracy of 1 GeV can be achieved. Heavier gauginos, as well as the A^0 boson, become accessible operating the ILC at 1 TeV. These data constrain both the mixing angles and $\tan \beta$. As a result the neutralino relic density can be estimated with an 18 % accuracy. Finally, the LCC4 point, chosen in the A funnel, has the DM density controlled by the $\chi\chi \to A$ process. This point is rather instructive in terms of the discovery-driven evolution of a possible experimental program at the ILC. The ILC can obtain the neutralino and $\tilde{\tau}$ masses at 0.5 TeV, following the same technique as for LCC3. We would also expect LHC experiments to have observed the A^0 boson, but it is unlikely M_A could be determined accurately in pp collisions, since the available observation mode is the decay in τ lepton pairs. At this stage, it would be apparent that the mass relation between the neutralino mass, accurately measured by the ILC at 0.5 TeV, and the A boson mass, from the LHC data, is compatible with $M_A \simeq 2M_\chi$, as required for the s-channel annihilation process to be effective. Three more measurements have to be performed at the ILC: the A^0 mass, M_A, and width Γ_A and the μ parameter, which is accessible through the mass splitting between heavier neutralinos, χ_3^0, χ_4^0 and the lighter χ_1^0, χ_2^0. All these measurements are available by operating the ILC at 1 TeV. M_A and Γ_A can be determined by studying the A^0 production in association with a H^0 boson, in the reaction $e^+e^- \to A^0 H^0 \to b\bar{b}b\bar{b}$. This process results in spectacular events with four b jets, emitted almost symmetrically, due to low energy carried by the heavy Higgs bosons (see Figure 2.13a). The cross section, for the parameters of LCC4 corresponding to $M_A = 419$ GeV, is just 0.9 fb highlighting the need of large luminosity at the highest energy. Jet flavour tagging and event shape analysis significantly reduces the major multi-jet backgrounds, such as WW, ZZ and $t\bar{t}$. The SM $b\bar{b}b\bar{b}$ electro-weak background has a cross section of $\sim$3 fb, but since it includes Z^0 or h^0 as intermediate states it can be efficiently removed by event shape and mass cuts. After event selection, the A^0 mass and width must be reconstructed from the measured di-jet invariant masses. This is achieved by pairing jets in the way that minimises the resulting di-jet mass difference, since the masses of the A and H bosons are expected to be degenerate within a few GeV, and the di-jet masses are computed by imposing constraints on energy and momentum conservation to improve the achievable resolution and gain sensitivity to the boson natural width (see Figure 2.13b). The result is a determination of the A mass to 0.2 % and of its width to $\simeq$15 % if a sample of 2 ab^{-1} of data can be collected. The full set of ILC data provides a neutralino relic density evaluation with 19 % relative accuracy. The full details of how these numbers were obtained can be found in Ref.[74].

SUSY offers a compelling example for investigating the complementarity in the search and discovery of new particles and in the study of their properties at the LHC and ILC. The connection to cosmology, through the study of dark matter brings precise requirements in terms of accuracy and completeness of the anticipated measurements and puts emphasis on scenarios at the edges of the parameter phase space. The interplay of satellite, ground-based and collider experiments in cosmology and particle physics will be unique and it will lead us to learn more about the structure of our Galaxy and of the Universe as well as of the underlying fundamental laws of the elementary particles. This quest will represent an major effort for science in the next several decades. The scenarios discussed above highlight the essential role of the ILC in this context. It will testing whether the particles observed at accelerators are responsible for making up a sizeable fraction of the mass of the Universe, through precision spectroscopic measurements. The data obtained at the ILC will effectively remove most particle physics uncertainties and become a solid ground for studying dark matter in our galaxy through direct and indirect detection experiments.[84]

2.4.3. *Indirect Sensitivity to New Physics at the ILC*

Beyond Supersymmetry there is a wide range of physics scenarios invoking new phenomena at, and beyond, the TeV scale. These may explain the origin of electro-weak symmetry breaking, if there is no light elementary Higgs boson, stabilise the SM, if SUSY is not realised in nature, or embed the SM in a theory of grand unification. The ILC, operating at high energy, represents an ideal laboratory for studying this New Physics in ways that are complementary to the LHC.[85,86] Not only it may directly produce some of the new particles predicted by these theories, the ILC also retains an indirect sensitivity, through precision measurements of virtual corrections to electro-weak observables, when the new particle masses exceed the available centre-of-mass energy.

One of the simplest of such SM extensions consists of the introduction of an additional $U(1)$ gauge symmetry, as predicted in some grand unified theories.[87,88] The extra Z' boson, associated to the symmetry, naturally mixes with the SM Z^0. The mixing angle is already strongly constrained, by precision electroweak data, and can be of the order of few mrad at most, while direct searches at Tevatron for a new Z' boson set a lower limit on its mass around 800 GeV, which may reach 1 TeV by the time the LHC will start searching for such a state. The search for an extended gauge sector offers an interesting framework for studying the ILC sensitivity to scales beyond those directly accessible. It also raises the issue of the discrimination between different models, once a signal would be detected. The main classes of models with additional Z' bosons include E_6 inspired models and left-right models (LR). In the E_6 models, the Z' fermion couplings depend on the angle, θ_6, defining the embedding of the extra $U(1)$ in the E_6 group. At the ILC, the indirect sensitivity to the mass of the new boson, $M_{Z'}$, can be parametrised in terms of the available integrated luminosity, $\mathcal{L}$, and centre-of-mass energy, $\sqrt{s}$. A scaling law for large values of $M_{Z'}$ can be obtained by considering the effect of the $Z' - \gamma$ interference in the two fermion production cross section $\sigma(e^+e^- \to f\bar{f})$ ($\sigma_{f\bar{f}}$ in the following). For $s << M_{Z'}^2$ and assuming the uncertainties $\delta\sigma$ to be statistically dominated, we obtain the following scaling for the difference between the SM cross section and that in presence of the Z', in units of the statistical accuracy:

$$\frac{|\sigma_{f\bar{f}}^{SM} - \sigma_{f\bar{f}}^{SM+Z'}|}{\delta\sigma} \propto \frac{1}{M_{Z'}^2}\sqrt{s\mathcal{L}} \qquad (2.11)$$

from which we can derive that the indirect sensitivity to the Z' mass scales with the square of the centre-of-mass energy and the luminosity as:

$$M_{Z'} \propto (s\mathcal{L})^{1/4}. \qquad (2.12)$$

In a full analysis, the observables sensitive to new physics contribution in two-fermion production are the cross section $\sigma_{f\bar{f}}$, the forward-backward asymmetries $A_{FB}^{f\bar{f}}$ and the left-right asymmetries $A_{LR}^{f\bar{f}}$. The ILC gives us the possibility to study a large number of reactions, $e_R^+ e_L^-$, $e_R^+ e_R^-$ → $(u\bar{u} + d\bar{d})$, $s\bar{s}$, $c\bar{c}$, $b\bar{b}$, $t\bar{t}$, e^+e^-, $\mu^+\mu^-$, $\tau^+\tau^-$ with final states of well defined flavour and, in several cases, helicity. In order to achieve this, jet flavour tagging is essential to separate b quarks from lighter quarks and c quarks from both b and light quarks. Jet-charge and vertex-charge reconstruction allows then to tell the quark from the antiquark produced in the same event.[89,90] Similarly to LEP and SLC analyses, the forward-backward asymmetry can be obtained from a fit to the flow of the jet charge Q^{jet}, defined as $Q^{jet} = \frac{\sum_i q_i |p_i T|^k}{\sum_i |p_i T|^k}$, where q_i is the particle charge, p_i its momentum, T the jet thrust axis and the sum is extended to all the particles in a given jet. Another possible technique uses the charge of secondary particles to determine the vertex charge and thus the quark charge. The application of this technique to the ILC has been studied in some details in relation to the optimisation of the Vertex Tracker.[91] At ILC energies, the $e^+e^- \to f\bar{f}$ cross sections are significantly reduced, compared to those at LEP and SLC: at 1 TeV the cross section $\sigma(e^+e^- \to b\bar{b})$ is only 100 fb, so high luminosity is essential and new experimental issues emerge. At 1 TeV, the ILC beamstrahlung parameter doubles compared to 0.5 TeV, beam-beam effects becoming important, and the primary e^+e^- collision is accompanied by $\gamma\gamma \to$ hadrons interactions.[92] Being mostly confined in the forward regions, this background may reduce the polar angle acceptance for quark flavour tagging and dilute the jet charge separation using jet charge techniques. The statistical accuracy for the determination of $\sigma_{f\bar{f}}$, $A_{FB}^{f\bar{f}}$ and $A_{LR}^{f\bar{f}}$ has been studied, for $\mu^+\mu^-$ and $b\bar{b}$, taking the ILC parameters at $\sqrt{s} =$ 1 TeV. The additional particles from the $\gamma\gamma$ background cause a broadening of the Q^{jet} distribution and thus a dilution of the quark charge separation. Detailed full simulation and reconstruction is needed to fully understand these effects. Despite these backgrounds, the anticipated experimental accuracy in the determination of the electro-weak observables in two-fermion processes at 1 TeV is of the order of a few percent, confirming the ILC role as the precision machine. Several scenarios of new physics have been investigated.[93,94] The analysis of the cross section and asymmetries at 1 TeV would reveal the existence of an additional Z' boson up to $\simeq$ 6-15 TeV, depending on its couplings. As a comparison the LHC direct sensitivity extends up to approximately 4-5 TeV. The ILC indirect sensitivity also extends to different models on new physics, such as 5-dimensional exten-

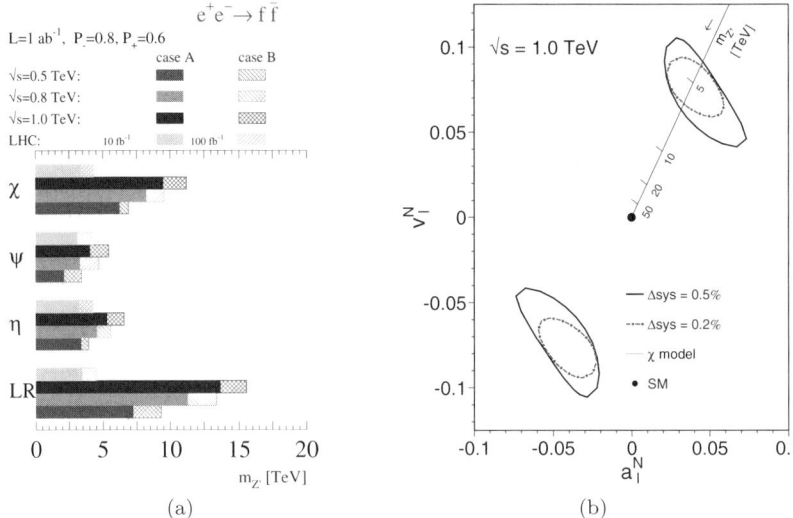

Fig. 2.15. Indirect sensitivity to Z' bosons at ILC: (a) mass sensitivity to different Z' models for 1 ab^{-1} of data at different centre-of-mass energies compared to that of LHC and (b) accuracy on leptonic couplings for a 5 TeV Z' boson (from Ref. 23)

sion of the SM with fermions on the boundary for a compactification where scales up to about 30 TeV can be explored. Finally, fermion compositeness or the exchange of very heavy new particles can be described in terms of effective four-fermion contact interactions.[96] The interaction depends on a scale $\Lambda = M_X/g$, where M_X is the mass of the new particle and g the coupling. Limits to this scale Λ can be set up to $\simeq 100$ TeV, which shows that the ILC sensitivity to new phenomena can exceed its centre-of-mass energy by a significant factor. In order to maximise this indirect sensitivity to new physics, the precision of the SM predictions should match the experimental accuracy. Now, at TeV energies, well above the electroweak scale, the ILC will face the effects of large non-perturbative corrections. Large logarithms $\propto \alpha^n \, log^{2n}(M^2/s)$ arise from the exchange of collinear, soft gauge bosons and are known as Sudakov logarithms.[95] At 1 TeV the logarithmically enhanced W corrections to $\sigma_{b\bar{b}}$, of the form $\alpha \, log^2(M_W^2/s)$ and $\alpha \, log(M_W^2/s)$ amount to 19% and -4% respectively. The effect of these large logarithmic corrections has been studied in some details.[17,97] It will be essential to promote a program of studies to reduce these theoretical uncertainties, to fully exploit the ILC potential in these studies.

2.4.4. Run Plan Scenario

One of the points of strength of the ILC is in its remarkable flexibility of running conditions. Not only the centre-of-mass energy can be changed over approximately an order of magnitude, but the beam particle and their polarization state can be varied to suit the need of the physics processes under study. At the same time, the ILC program is most diversified and data taken at the same centre-of-mass energy may be used for very different analyses, such as precise top mass determination, Higgs boson studies and reconstruction of SUSY decays. This has raised concerns whether the claimed ILC accuracies can be all achieved with a finite amount of data. A dedicated study was performed in 2001, under the guidance of Paul Grannis, taking two physics scenarios with Supersymmetry realised at relatively low mass, one being the LCC1 benchmark point, rich in pair-produced particles and requiring detailed threshold scans.[98] The study assumes a realistic profile for the delivered luminosity, which increases from 10 fb^{-1} in the first year to 200 fb^{-1} in the fifth year and 250 fb^{-1} afterward, for a total integrated equivalent luminosity $\int \mathcal{L} = 1$ ab^{-1}. The proposed run plan starts at the assumed maximum energy of 0.5 TeV for a first determination of the sparticle masses through the end-point study and then scans the relevant thresholds, including $t\bar{t}$ in short runs with tuned polarization states. A summary is given in Table 2.6. This plan devotes approximately

Table 2.6. ILC Run plan scenario for LCC1.

Beams	$\sqrt{s}$ (TeV)	Pol.	$\int \mathcal{L}$ (fb^{-1})	Comments
e^+e^-	0.500	L/R	335	Sit at max. energy for sparticle endpoint measurements
e^+e^-	0.270	L/R	100	Scan $\chi_1^0\chi_2^0$ (R pol.) and $\tilde{\tau}_1\tilde{\tau}_1$ (L pol.)
e^+e^-	0.285	R	50	Scan $\tilde{\mu}_R\tilde{\mu}_R$
e^+e^-	0.350	L/R	40	Scan $t\bar{t}$, $\tilde{e}_R\tilde{e}_L$ (L& R pol.), $\chi_1^+\chi_1^-$ (L pol.)
e^+e^-	0.410	L/R	100	Scan $\tilde{\tau}_2\tilde{\tau}_2$
e^-e^-	0.285	RR	10	Scan for $\tilde{e}_R$ mass

two third of the total luminosity at, or near, the maximum energy, so the program will be sensitive to unexpected new phenomena at high energy, while providing accurate measurements of masses through dedicated scans.

2.5. Sensors and Detectors for the ILC

The development of the ILC accelerator components and the definition of its physics case has been paralleled by a continuing effort in detector design and sensor R&D. This effort is motivated by the need to design and construct detectors which match the ILC promise to provide extremely accurate measurements over a broad range of collision energies and event topologies. It is important to stress that, despite more than a decade of detector R&D for the LHC experiments, much still needs to be done to obtain sensors matching the ILC requirements. While the focus of the LHC-motivated R&D has been on sensor radiation hardness and high trigger rate, the ILC, with its more benign background conditions and lower interaction cross sections, admits sensors of new technology which, in turn, have better granularity, smaller thickness and much improved resolution. Sensor R&D and detector design are being carried out world-wide and are starting deploying prototype detector modules on test beamlines.

2.5.1. *Detector Concepts*

The conceptual design effort for an optimal detector for the ILC interaction region has probed a wide spectrum of options which span from a spherical detector structure to improved versions of more orthodox barrel-shaped detectors. These studies have been influenced by the experience with SLD at the SLC, ALEPH, DELPHI and OPAL at LEP, but also with ATLAS and CMS at the LHC. The emphasis on accurate reconstruction of the particle flow in hadronic events and thus of the energy of partons is common to all designs. The main tracker technology drives the detector designs presently being studied. Four detector concepts have emerged, named GLD, LDC, SiD and 4th Concept.[99] A large volume, 3D continuous tracking volume in a Time Projection Chamber is the centerpiece of the GLD, the LDC and the so-called 4th Concept designs. The TPC is followed by an highly segmented electro-magnetic calorimeter for which these three concepts are contemplating different technologies A discrete tracker made of layers of high precision Silicon microstrip detectors, and a larger solenoidal field, which allows to reduce the radius, and thus the size, of the calorimeter is being studied in the context of the SiD design. Dedicated detector design studies are being carried out internationally[100,101] to optimise, through physics benchmarks,[102] the integrated detector concepts. Such design activities provide a bridge from physics studies to the assessment of priorities

Fig. 2.16. View of the four ILC detector concepts presently being studied: GLD (upper left), LDC (upper right), SiD (lower left) and 4th Concept (lower right).

in detector R&D and are evolving towards the completion of engineered design reports at the end of this decade, synchronously with that foreseen for the ILC accelerator.

2.5.2. Vertexing and Tracking

The vertex and main tracker detectors must provide jet flavour identification and track momentum determination with the accuracy which makes the ILC such a unique facility for particle physics. The resolution in extrapolating charged particle trajectories to their production point, the so-called impact parameter, is dictated by the need to distinguish Higgs boson decays to $c\bar{c}$ from those to $b\bar{b}$ pairs, but also $\tau^+\tau^-$ and gluon pairs, as discussed in section 2.4.1. In addition, vertex charge measurements put emphasis on precise extrapolation of particle tracks down to very low momenta. Tagging of events with multiple b jets, such as $e^+e^- \to H^0 A^0 \to b\bar{b}b\bar{b}$, discussed in section 2.4.2, underscores the need of high tagging efficiency, ϵ_b, since the overall efficiency scales as ϵ_b^N, where N is the number of jets to be tagged. This is best achieved by analysing the secondary vertex structures in hadronic jets. A B meson, from a Higgs boson produced at 0.5 TeV, has an average energy of $x_B\sqrt{s}/4 \simeq 100$ GeV, where $x_B \simeq 0.7$ represents the average b fragmentation function, or a γ value of $\simeq 70$. Since $c\tau \simeq 500$ μm, the average decay distance $\beta\gamma c\tau$ is 3.5 mm and the average impact parameter, $\beta\gamma c\tau \sin\theta$, is 0.5 mm. In comparison, a D meson from a $H \to c\bar{c}$ decay has a decay length of 1.3 mm. More importantly, the average charged decay multiplicity for a B meson is 5.1, while for a D meson is 2.7. Turning these numbers into performance requirements sets the target accuracy for the asymptotic term a and the multiple scattering term b defining the track extrapolation resolution in the formula

$$\sigma_{\text{extrapolation}} = a \oplus \frac{b}{p_t} \qquad (2.13)$$

The ILC target values are compared to those achieved by the DELPHI experiment at LEP, those expected for ATLAS at the LHC and the best performance ever achieved at a collider experiment, that of SLD, in Table 2.7. This comparison shows that the improvements required for ILC

Table 2.7. Values for the asymptotic term a and multiple scattering term b defining the track extrapolation resolution required for the ILC compared to those obtained by other collider experiments.

Experiment	a (μm)	b (μm/GeV)
ILC	5	10
DELPHI	28	65
ATLAS	15	75
SLD	8	33

on state-of-the-art technology is a factor 2-5 on asymptotic resolution and another factor 3-7 on the multiple scattering term.

At the ILC, particle tracks in highly collimated jets contribute a local track density on the innermost layer of 0.2-1.0 hits mm^{-2} at 0.5 TeV, to reach 0.4-1.5 hits mm^{-2} at 1.0 TeV. Machine-induced backgrounds, mostly pairs, add about 3-4 hits mm^{-2}, assuming that the detector integrates 80 consecutive bunch crossings in a train. These values are comparable to, or even exceed, those expected on the innermost layer of the LHC detectors: 0.03 hits mm^{-2} for proton collisions in ATLAS and 0.9 hits mm^{-2} for heavy ion collisions in ALICE. Occupancy and point resolution set the pixel size to 20x20 μm^2 or less. The impact parameter accuracy sets the layer material budget to $\leq 0.15\%$ X_0/layer. This motivates the development of thin monolithic pixel sensors. Charge coupled devices (CCD) have been a prototype architecture after the success of the SLD VXD3.[103] However, to match the ILC requirements in terms of radiation hardness and readout speed significant R&D is needed. New technologies, such as CMOS active pixels,[104] SOI[105] and DEPFET[106] sensors, are emerging as promising, competitive alternatives, supported by an intensive sensor R&D effort promoted for the ILC.[107]

The process $e^+e^- \to H^0 Z^0$, $H^0 \to X$, $Z^0 \to \ell^+\ell^-$ gives access to Higgs production, irrespective of the Higgs decay properties. Lepton momenta must be measured very accurately for the recoil mass resolution to be limited by the irreducible smearing due to beamstrahlung. Since the centre-of-mass energy $\sqrt{s} = E_H + E_Z$ is known and the total momentum $p_H + p_Z = 0$, the Higgs mass, M_H can be written as:

$$M_H^2 = E_H^2 - p_H^2 = (\sqrt{s} - E_Z)^2 - p_Z^2 = s + E_Z^2 - 2\sqrt{s}E_Z - p_Z^2 = s - 2\sqrt{s}E_Z + M_Z^2 \quad (2.14)$$

In the decay $Z^0 \to \mu^+\mu^-$, $E_Z = E_{\mu^+} + E_{\mu^-}$ so that the resolution on M_H depends on that on the muon momentum. In quantitative terms the resolution required is

$$\delta p/p^2 < 2 \times 10^{-5} \quad (2.15)$$

A comparison with the performance of trackers at LEP and LHC is given in Table 2.8. The ability to tag Higgs bosons, independent on their decay mode

Table 2.8. Values for the momentum resolution $\delta p/p^2$ for the main tracker and the full tracking system at ILC, LEP and LHC. These values do not include the vertex constraint.

Experiment	Main Tracker Only	Full Tracker
ILC	1.5×10^{-4}	5×10^{-5}
ALEPH	1.2×10^{-3}	5×10^{-4}
ATLAS	–	2×10^{-4}

is central to the ILC program in Higgs physics. A degraded momentum resolution would correspond to larger background, mostly from $e^+e^- \to$

ZZ^*, being accepted in the Higgs signal sample. This degrades the accuracy on the determination of the Higgs couplings both in terms of statistical and systematic uncertainties. The particle momentum is measured through its bending radius R in the solenoidal magnetic field, B. The error on the curvature, $k = 1/R$, for a particle track of high momentum, measured at N equidistant points with an accuracy, σ, over a length L, applying the constraint that it does originate at the primary vertex (as for the leptons from the Z^0 in the Higgstrahlung reaction) is given by:[108]

$$\delta k = \frac{\sigma}{L^2} \sqrt{\frac{320}{N+4}} \qquad (2.16)$$

This shows that the same momentum resolution can be achieved either by a large number of measurements, each of moderate accuracy, as in the case of a continuous gaseous tracker, or by a small number of points measured with high accuracy, as in the case of a discrete Si tracker. Continuous tracking capability over a large area, with timing information and specific ionization measurement, and its robust performance make the Time Projection Chamber an attractive option for precision tracking at the ILC. The introduction of Micro Pattern Gaseous Detectors[109,110] (MPGD) offers significant improvements in terms of reduced $E \times B$, larger gains, ion suppression and faster, narrower signals providing better space resolution. Improving on the space resolution requires an optimal sampling of the collected charge, while the high solenoidal magnetic field reduces the diffusion effects. Several paths are presently being explored with small size prototypes operated on beamlines and in large magnetic fields.[111,112]

A multi-layered Si strip detector tracker in an high B field may offer a competitive $\delta p/p^2$ resolution with reduced material budget and afford a smaller radius ECAL, thus reducing the overall detector cost. This is the main rationale promoting the development of an all-Si concept for the main tracker, which follows the spirit of the design of the CMS detector at LHC. Dedicated conceptual design and module R&D is being carried out as a world-wide program.[113] There is also considerable R&D required for the engineering of detector ladders, addressing such issues as mechanical stability and integration of cooling and electrical services. These modules may also be considered as supplemental tracking devices in a TPC-based design to provide extra space points, with high resolution, and in endcap tracking planes. Assessing the required detector performance involves realistic simulation and reconstruction code accounting for inefficiencies, noise, overlaps and backgrounds.

2.5.3. Calorimetry

The ILC physics program requires precise measurements of multi-jet hadronic events, in particular di-jet invariant masses to identify W, Z and Higgs bosons, through their hadronic decays. An especially demanding reaction is $e^+e^- \rightarrow Z^0 H^0 H^0$, which provides access to the triple Higgs coupling as discussed in section 2.4.1. The large background from $e^+e^- \rightarrow Z^0 Z^0 Z^0$ can be reduced only by an efficient H^0/Z^0 separation, based on their masses. This impacts the parton energy resolution through the measurement of hadronic jets. Detailed simulation[51] shows that a jet energy resolution $\frac{\sigma_{E_{jet}}}{E_{jet}} \simeq \frac{0.30}{\sqrt{E}}$ is required, in order to achieve an interesting resolution on the g_{HHH} coupling. The analysis of other processes, such as $e^+e^- \rightarrow W^+W^-\nu\bar{\nu}$ and Higgs hadronic decays, leads to similar conclusions.[115] In the case of the determination of $H^0 \rightarrow W^+W^-$ branching fractions, the statistical accuracy degrades by 22 % when changing the jet energy resolution from $\frac{0.30}{\sqrt{E}}$ to $\frac{0.60}{\sqrt{E}}$. Such performance is unprecedented

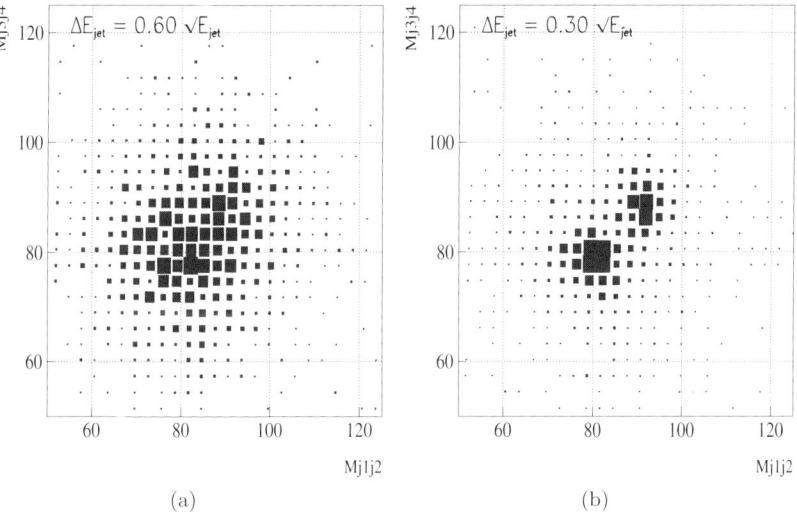

Fig. 2.17. $W^\pm$ and Z^0 gauge boson pair production separation at the ILC: invariant mass of the first di-jet pair vs. that of the second for a sample of WW and ZZ for two different assumptions on the jet energy resolution (a) $\frac{0.30}{\sqrt{E}}$ and (b) $\frac{0.60}{\sqrt{E}}$ (from Ref. 114).

and requires the development of an advanced calorimeter design as well as new reconstruction strategies. The most promising approach is based on the *particle flow algorithm* (PFA). The energy of each particle in an hadronic jet is determined based on the information of the detector which can measure it to the best accuracy. In the case of charged particles, this is achieved by measuring the particle bending in the solenoidal field with the main tracker. Electromagnetic neutrals (γ and π^0) are measured in the electromagnetic calorimeter and hadronic neutrals (K_L^0, n) in the hadronic calorimeter. The jet energy is then obtained by summing these energies:

$$E_{jet} = E_{charged} + E_{em\ neutral} + E_{had\ neutral} \qquad (2.17)$$

each being measured in a specialised detector. The resolution is given by:

$$\sigma_{E_{jet}}^2 = \sigma_{charged}^2 + \sigma_{em\ neutral}^2 + \sigma_{had\ neutral}^2 + \sigma_{confusion}^2. \qquad (2.18)$$

Assuming the anticipated momentum resolution, $\sigma_E \simeq 0.11/\sqrt{E}$ for the e.m. calorimeter, $\sigma_E \simeq 0.40/\sqrt{E}$ for the hadronic calorimeter and the fractions of charged, e.m. neutral and hadronic neutral energy in an hadronic jet we get:

$$\sigma_{charged}^2 \simeq (0.02\text{GeV})^2 \frac{1}{10} \sum \frac{E_{charged}^4}{(10\text{GeV})^4} \qquad (2.19)$$

$$\sigma_{em\ neutral}^2 \simeq (0.6\text{GeV})^2 \frac{E_{jet}}{100\text{GeV}} \qquad (2.20)$$

$$\sigma_{had\ neutral}^2 \simeq (1.3\text{GeV})^2 \frac{E_{jet}}{100\text{GeV}} \qquad (2.21)$$

In case of perfect energy-particle association this would correspond to a jet resolution $\simeq 0.14/\sqrt{E}$. But a major source of resolution loss turns out to be the confusion term, $\sigma_{confusion}$, which originates from inefficiencies, double-counting and fakes, which need to be minimised by an efficient pattern recognition. This strategy was pioneered by the ALEPH experiment at LEP, where a resolution $\simeq 0.60/\sqrt{E}$ was obtained, starting from the stochastic resolutions of $\sigma_E \simeq 0.18/\sqrt{E}$ for the e.m. calorimeter, and $\sigma_E \simeq 0.85/\sqrt{E}$ for the hadronic calorimeter.[116] At hadron colliders, the possible improvement from using tracking information together with calorimetric measurements is limited, due to underlying events and the shower core size. On the contrary, at the ILC these limitations can be overcome, by developing an imaging calorimeter, where spatial resolution becomes as important as energy resolution. The minimisation of the confusion rate can then be obtained by choosing a large solenoidal field, B, and calorimeter radius, R, to increase the separation between charged and neutral particles

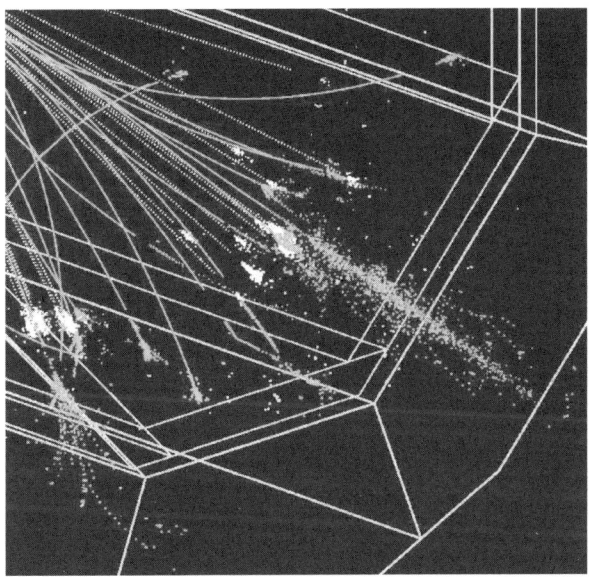

Fig. 2.18. Visualisation of the imaging calorimeter for the ILC: simulated response of a SiW calorimeter to a jet from $e^+e^- \to W^+W^- \to jets$ at $\sqrt{s}$=0.8 TeV.

in dense jets, a small Moliere radius, R_M, for the e.m. calorimeter, to reduce the transverse shower spread and small cells, R_{pixel}, with large longitudinal segmentation. The distance between a neutral and a charged particle, of transverse momentum p_t, at the entrance of the e.m. calorimeter located at a radius R is given by $0.15BR^2/p_t$, where B is the solenoidal magnetic field. A useful figure of merit of the detector in terms of the particle flow reconstruction capability is then offered by:

$$\frac{BR^2}{R_M^2 R_{pixel}^2} \qquad (2.22)$$

which is a measure of the particle separation capability. The value of BR^2 is limited to about 60 Tm^2 by the mechanical stability. An optimal material in terms of Moliere radius is Tungsten, with $R_M = 9$ mm. In four-jet events at $\sqrt{s}$=0.8 TeV, there are on average 28 GeV per di-jet carried by photons, which are deposited within 2.5 cm from a charged particle at the e.m. calorimeter radius. With pixel cells of order of 1×1 cm^2 to ensure sufficient transverse segmentation and 30 to 40 layers in depth, the e.m. calorimeter would consists of up to 30 M channels and 3000 m^2 of active Si. Due to the large amount of channels and the wish to use an absorber with the smallest possible Moliere radius, the e.m. calorimeter is the main cost-driver of the ILC detector and its optimisation in terms of performance and cost requires a significant R&D effort. A Silicon-Tungsten calorimeter (SiW) was first proposed in the framework of the TESLA study[114,117] and it is currently being pursued by large R&D collaborations in both Europe and the US. Alternative technologies are also being studied by the GLD and the 4th Concept. This R&D program involves design, prototyping and tests with high energy particle beams and it is being carried out world-wide,[118-120] supported by efforts on detailed simulation and reconstruction.

2.6. Epilogue

The ILC promises to complement and expand the probe into the TeV scale beyond the LHC capabilities, matching and improving its energy reach while adding precision. Its physics program will address many of the fundamental questions of today's physics from the origin of mass, to the nature of Dark Matter. After more than two decades of intense R&D carried out world-wide, the e^+e^- linear collider, with centre-of-mass energies up to 1 TeV, has become technically feasible and a costed reference design is now available. Detectors matching the precision requirements of its anticipated physics program are being developed in an intense R&D effort carried out world-wide. Now, theoretical predictions matching the anticipated experimental accuracies are crucially needed, as well as further clues on what physics scenarios could be unveiled by signals that the LHC may soon be observing. These will contribute to further define the physics landscape for the ILC. A TeV-scale electron-positron linear collider is an essential component of the research program that will provide in the next decades new insights into the structure of space, time, matter and energy. Thanks to the efforts of many groups from laboratories and universities around the world, the technology for achieving this goal is now in hand, and the prospects for the ILC success are extraordinarily bright.

Acknowledgments

I am grateful to the TASI organisers, in particular to Sally Dawson and Rabindra N. Mohapatra, for their invitation and the excellent organization. I am indebted to many colleagues who have shared with me both the excitement of the ILC physics studies and detector R&D, over many years, as well as many of the results included in this article. I would like to mention here Ugo Amaldi, Timothy Barklow, Genevieve Belanger, Devis Contarato, Stefania De Curtis, Jean-Pierre Delahaye, Albert De Roeck, Klaus Desch, Daniele Dominici, John Ellis, JoAnne Hewett, Konstantin Matchev, Michael Peskin and Tom Rizzo. I am also grateful to Barry Barish, JoAnne Hewett, Mark Oreglia and Michael Peskin for reviewing the manuscript and their suggestions.

This work was supported in part by the Director, Office of Science, of the U.S. Department of Energy under Contract No.DE-AC02-05CH11231.

References

1. M. Tigner, *Nuovo Cim.*, **37** 1228 (1965).
2. U. Amaldi, *Phys. Lett.* **B61** 313 (1976).
3. B. Richter, IEEE Trans. Nucl. Sci. **26**, 4261 (1979).
4. W. Schnell, *A Two Stage Rf Linear Collider Using A Superconducting Drive Linac*, CERN-LEP-RF/86-06 (1976).
5. C. r. Ahn et al., *Opportunities and Requirements for Experimentation at a Very High-Eenergy e^+e^- Collider*, SLAC-0329 (1988).
6. G. Loew (editor), *International Linear Collider Technical Review Committee: Second Report*, SLAC-R-606 (2003).
7. http://www.ligo.caltech.edu/~skammer/ITRP_Home.html
8. http://www.linearcollider.org/
9. http://media.linearcollider.org/rdr_draft_v1.pdf
10. Report of the OECD Consultative Group on High-Energy Physics, June 2002 (http://www.oecd.org/dataoecd/2/32/1944269.pdf)
11. http://www7.nationalacademies.org/bpa/EPP2010.html
12. L. Maiani, prepared for the *9th International Symposium on Neutrino Telescopes*, Venice, Italy, 6-9 March 2001.
13. D. Treille, *Nucl. Phys. Proc. Suppl.* **109B**, 1 (2002).
14. R. Brinkmann, K. Flottmann, J. Rossbach, P. Schmueser, N. Walker and H. Weise (editors), *TESLA: The superconducting electron positron linear collider with an integrated X-ray laser laboratory. Technical design report.*, DESY-01-011B (2001).
15. R. W. Assmann et al., *A 3-TeV e^+e^- linear collider based on CLIC technology*, CERN-2000-008 (2000).
16. W. Wuensch, *Progress in Understanding the High-Gradient Limitations of Accelerating Structures*, CLIC-Note-706 (2007).
17. M. Battaglia, A. De Roeck, J. Ellis and D. Schulte (editors), *Physics at the CLIC multi-TeV linear collider: Report of the CLIC Physics Working Group*, CERN-2004-005 (2004) and arXiv:hep-ph/0412251.
18. W.P. Leemans et al., *Nature Physics* **2** 696 (2006).
19. B. Richter, SLAC-PUB-2854 (1981)
20. U. Amaldi, *Summary talk given at Workshop on Physics at Future Accelerators, La Thuile, Italy, Jan 7-13, 1987*, CERN-EP/87-95 (1987).

21. R. J. Noble, Nucl. Instrum. Meth. A **256**, 427 (1987).
22. H. Murayama and M. E. Peskin, Ann. Rev. Nucl. Part. Sci. **46**, 533 (1996) [arXiv:hep-ex/9606003].
23. J. A. Aguilar-Saavedra et al. [ECFA/DESY LC Physics Working Group], *TESLA Technical Design Report Part III: Physics at an e+e- Linear Collider*, DESY-2001-011C (2001) and arXiv:hep-ph/0106315.
24. T. Abe et al. [American Linear Collider Working Group], *Linear collider physics resource book for Snowmass 2001*, SLAC-R-570 (2001).
25. K. Abe et al. [ACFA Linear Collider Working Group], *Particle physics experiments at JLC*, KEK-REPORT-2001-11 (2001) and arXiv:hep-ph/0109166.
26. S. Dawson and M. Oreglia, Ann. Rev. Nucl. Part. Sci. **54**, 269 (2004) [arXiv:hep-ph/0403015].
27. P.W. Higgs, *Phys. Rev. Lett.* **12** 132 (1964); idem, *Phys. Rev.* **145** 1156 (1966); F. Englert and R. Brout, *Phys. Rev. Lett.* **13** 321 (1964); G.S. Guralnik, C.R. Hagen and T.W. Kibble, *Phys. Rev. Lett.* **13** 585 (1964).
28. A. Hasenfratz et al., *Phys. Lett.* **B199** 531 (1987); M. Lüscher and P. Weisz, *Phys. Lett.* **B212** 472 (1988); M. Göckeler et al., *Nucl. Phys.* **B404** 517 (1993).
29. R. Barate et al. [LEP Working Group for Higgs boson searches], *Phys. Lett.* B **565**, 61 (2003) [arXiv:hep-ex/0306033].
30. LEP Electroweak Working Group, Report CERN-PH-EP-2006 (2006), arXiv:hep-ex/0612034 and subsequent updates available at http://lepewwg.web.cern.ch/LEPEWWG/.
31. S. Heinemeyer et al., arXiv:hep-ph/0511332.
32. P. Garcia-Abia, W. Lohmann and A. Raspereza, Note LC-PHSM-2000-062 (2000).
33. D. J. Miller, S. Y. Choi, B. Eberle, M. M. Muhlleitner and P. M. Zerwas, Phys. Lett. B **505**, 149 (2001) [arXiv:hep-ph/0102023].
34. M. Schumacher, Note LC-PHSM-2001-003 (2001).
35. A. Djouadi, M. Spira and P. M. Zerwas, Z. Phys. C **70**, 427 (1996) [arXiv:hep-ph/9511344].
36. M. D. Hildreth, T. L. Barklow and D. L. Burke, Phys. Rev. D **49**, 3441 (1994).
37. M. Carena, H. E. Haber, H. E. Logan and S. Mrenna, Phys. Rev. D **65**, 055005 (2002) [Erratum-ibid. D **65**, 099902 (2002)] [arXiv:hep-ph/0106116].
38. K. Desch, E. Gross, S. Heinemeyer, G. Weiglein and L. Zivkovic, JHEP **0409**, 062 (2004) [arXiv:hep-ph/0406322].
39. M. Battaglia, D. Dominici, J. F. Gunion and J. D. Wells, arXiv:hep-ph/0402062.
40. M. Battaglia, arXiv:hep-ph/9910271.
41. B. Aubert et al. [BABAR Collaboration], *Phys. Rev. Lett.* **93**, 011803 (2004) [arXiv:hep-ex/0404017].
42. C. W. Bauer, Z. Ligeti, M. Luke and A. V. Manohar, *Phys. Rev.* **D67**, 054012 (2003) [arXiv:hep-ph/0210027].
43. M. Battaglia et al., *Phys. Lett.* **B556**, 41 (2003) [arXiv:hep-ph/0210319].

44. T. Kuhl, prepared for the *International Conference on Linear Colliders (LCWS 04)*, Paris, France, 19-24 April 2004.
45. M. Battaglia and A. De Roeck, arXiv:hep-ph/0211207.
46. M. Battaglia, arXiv:hep-ph/0211461.
47. T. L. Barklow, arXiv:hep-ph/0312268.
48. A. Djouadi, W. Kilian, M. Muhlleitner and P. M. Zerwas, *Eur. Phys. J.* **C10** (1999) 27 [arXiv:hep-ph/9903229].
49. S. Kanemura, Y. Okada, E. Senaha and C. P. Yuan, Phys. Rev. D **70**, 115002 (2004) [arXiv:hep-ph/0408364].
50. A. Gutierrez-Rodriguez, M. A. Hernandez-Ruiz and O. A. Sampayo, arXiv:hep-ph/0601238.
51. C. Castanier, P. Gay, P. Lutz and J. Orloff, arXiv:hep-ex/0101028.
52. M. Battaglia, E. Boos and W. M. Yao, in *Proc. of the APS/DPF/DPB Summer Study on the Future of Particle Physics (Snowmass 2001)* ed. N. Graf, E3016, [arXiv:hep-ph/0111276].
53. U. Baur, T. Plehn and D. L. Rainwater, *Phys. Rev.* **D67**, 033003 (2003) [arXiv:hep-ph/0211224].
54. U. Baur, T. Plehn and D. L. Rainwater, *Phys. Rev.* **D69**, 053004 (2004) [arXiv:hep-ph/0310056].
55. T. L. Barklow, arXiv:hep-ph/0411221.
56. A. Datta, K. Kong and K. T. Matchev, Phys. Rev. D **72**, 096006 (2005) [Erratum-ibid. D **72**, 119901 (2005)] [arXiv:hep-ph/0509246].
57. J. M. Smillie and B. R. Webber, JHEP **0510**, 069 (2005) [arXiv:hep-ph/0507170].
58. M. Battaglia, A. Datta, A. De Roeck, K. Kong and K. T. Matchev, JHEP **0507**, 033 (2005) [arXiv:hep-ph/0502041].
59. D. N. Spergel et al. [WMAP Collaboration], Astrophys. J. Suppl. **148**, 175 (2003) [arXiv:astro-ph/0302209]
60. J. R. Bond, G. Efstathiou and M. Tegmark, Mon. Not. Roy. Astron. Soc. **291**, L33 (1997) [arXiv:astro-ph/9702100]
61. W. de Boer, C. Sander, V. Zhukov, A. V. Gladyshev and D. I. Kazakov, Astron. Astrophys. **444**, 51 (2005) [arXiv:astro-ph/0508617].
62. D. P. Finkbeiner, arXiv:astro-ph/0409027.
63. D. S. Akerib *et al.* [CDMS Collaboration], Phys. Rev. Lett. **96**, 011302 (2006) [arXiv:astro-ph/0509259].
64. R. J. Scherrer and M. S. Turner, Phys. Rev. D **33**, 1585 (1986) [Erratum-ibid. D **34**, 3263 (1986)].
65. M. Battaglia, A. De Roeck, J. R. Ellis, F. Gianotti, K. A. Olive and L. Pape, Eur. Phys. J. C **33**, 273 (2004) [arXiv:hep-ph/0306219].
66. K. Kong and K. T. Matchev, JHEP **0601**, 038 (2006) [arXiv:hep-ph/0509119].
67. G. Weiglein *et al.* [LHC/LC Study Group], arXiv:hep-ph/0410364.
68. R. Gray *et al.*, arXiv:hep-ex/0507008.
69. V. Khotilovich, R. Arnowitt, B. Dutta and T. Kamon, Phys. Lett. B **618**, 182 (2005) [arXiv:hep-ph/0503165].
70. M. Battaglia, arXiv:hep-ph/0410123.

71. F. E. Paige, S. D. Protopescu, H. Baer and X. Tata, arXiv:hep-ph/0312045.
72. P. Gondolo, J. Edsjo, P. Ullio, L. Bergstrom, M. Schelke and E. A. Baltz, JCAP **0407**, 008 (2004) [arXiv:astro-ph/0406204].
73. G. Belanger, F. Boudjema, A. Pukhov and A. Semenov, arXiv:hep-ph/0607059.
74. E. A. Baltz, M. Battaglia, M. E. Peskin and T. Wizansky, Phys. Rev. D **74**, 103521 (2006) [arXiv:hep-ph/0602187].
75. J. L. Feng and D. E. Finnell, Phys. Rev. D **49**, 2369 (1994) [arXiv:hep-ph/9310211].
76. G. A. Moortgat-Pick *et al.*, arXiv:hep-ph/0507011, based on work of U. Nauenberg *et al.*.
77. G. A. Blair, in *Proc. of the APS/DPF/DPB Summer Study on the Future of Particle Physics (Snowmass 2001)* ed. N. Graf, E3019.
78. H. U. Martyn and G. A. Blair, Note LC-TH-2000-023.
79. P. Bambade, M. Berggren, F. Richard and Z. Zhang, arXiv:hep-ph/0406010.
80. P. Chen and V. I. Telnov, Phys. Rev. Lett. **63**, 1796 (1989).
81. T. Tauchi, K. Yokoya and P. Chen, Part. Accel. **41**, 29 (1993).
82. H. Baer, A. Belyaev, T. Krupovnickas and X. Tata, JHEP **0402**, 007 (2004) [arXiv:hep-ph/0311351].
83. C. Balazs, M. Carena and C. E. M. Wagner, Phys. Rev. D **70**, 015007 (2004) [arXiv:hep-ph/0403224].
84. J. L. Feng, in Proc. of the *2005 Int. Linear Collider Workshop (LCWS 2005)*, Stanford, California, 18-22 Mar 2005, pp 0013 and [arXiv:hep-ph/0509309].
85. M. Battaglia *et al.*, in *Physics and Experiments with Future Linear e^+e^- Colliders*, (A. Para and H.E. Fisk editors), AIP Conference Proceedings, New York, 2001, 607 [arXix:hep-ph/0101114].
86. D. Dominici, arXiv:hep-ph/0110084.
87. J. L. Hewett, arXiv:hep-ph/9308321.
88. T. G. Rizzo, arXiv:hep-ph/0610104.
89. K. Ackerstaff *et al.* [OPAL Collaboration], Z. Phys. C **75**, 385 (1997).
90. K. Abe *et al.* [SLD Collaboration], Phys. Rev. Lett. **94**, 091801 (2005) [arXiv:hep-ex/0410042].
91. S. Hillert [LCFI Collaboration], *In the Proceedings of 2005 International Linear Collider Workshop (LCWS 2005), Stanford, California, 18-22 Mar 2005, pp 0313*.
92. P. Chen, T. L. Barklow and M. E. Peskin, Phys. Rev. D **49**, 3209 (1994) [arXiv:hep-ph/9305247].
93. S. Riemann, arXiv:hep-ph/9710564.
94. M. Battaglia, S. De Curtis, D. Dominici and S. Riemann, in *Proc. of the APS/DPF/DPB Summer Study on the Future of Particle Physics (Snowmass 2001)* ed. N. Graf, E3020, [arXiv:hep-ph/0112270].
95. M. Melles, Phys. Rept. **375**, 219 (2003) [arXiv:hep-ph/0104232].
96. E. Eichten, K. D. Lane and M. E. Peskin, Phys. Rev. Lett. **50**, 811 (1983).
97. P. Ciafaloni and D. Comelli, Phys. Lett. B **476**, 49 (2000) [arXiv:hep-ph/9910278].

98. M. Battaglia *et al.*, in *Proc. of the APS/DPF/DPB Summer Study on the Future of Particle Physics (Snowmass 2001)* ed. N. Graf, E3006, [arXiv:hep-ph/0201177].
99. http://physics.uoregon.edu/~lc/wwstudy/concepts/
100. T. Behnke, *In the Proceedings of 2005 International Linear Collider Workshop (LCWS 2005), Stanford, California, 18-22 Mar 2005, pp 0006.*
101. K. Abe *et al.* [GLD Concept Study Group], arXiv:physics/0607154.
102. M. Battaglia, T. Barklow, M. Peskin, Y. Okada, S. Yamashita and P. Zerwas, *In the Proceedings of 2005 International Linear Collider Workshop (LCWS 2005), Stanford, California, 18-22 Mar 2005, pp 1602* [arXiv:hep-ex/0603010].
103. T. Abe [SLD Collaboration], Nucl. Instrum. Meth. A **447** (2000) 90 [arXiv:hep-ex/9909048].
104. R. Turchetta *et al.*, Nucl. Instrum. Meth. A **458** (2001) 677.
105. J. Marczewski *et al.*, Nucl. Instrum. Meth. A **549** (2005) 112.
106. R. H. Richter *et al.*, Nucl. Instrum. Meth. A **511** (2003) 250.
107. M. Battaglia, Nucl. Instrum. Meth. A **530**, 33 (2004) [arXiv:physics/0312039].
108. W.-M. Yao *et al*, J. Phys. G **33**, 1 (2006)
109. Y. Giomataris, P. Rebourgeard, J. P. Robert and G. Charpak, Nucl. Instrum. Meth. A **376**, 29 (1996).
110. F. Sauli, Nucl. Instrum. Meth. A **386**, 531 (1997).
111. S. Kappler *et al.*, IEEE Trans. Nucl. Sci. **51**, 1039 (2004).
112. P. Colas *et al.*, Nucl. Instrum. Meth. A **535**, 506 (2004).
113. J. Kroseberg *et al.*, arXiv:physics/0511039.
114. T. Behnke, S. Bertolucci, R. D. Heuer and R. Settles, *TESLA Technical design report. Pt. 4: A detector for TESLA* DESY-01-011 (2001).
115. J. C. Brient and H. Videau, in *Proc. of the APS/DPF/DPB Summer Study on the Future of Particle Physics (Snowmass 2001)* ed. N. Graf, E3047, [arXiv:hep-ex/0202004].
116. D. Buskulic *et al.* [ALEPH Collaboration], Nucl. Instrum. Meth. A **360**, 481 (1995).
117. H. Videau, *Prepared for 5th International Linear Collider Workshop (LCWS 2000), Fermilab, Batavia, Illinois, 24-28 Oct 2000*
118. D. Strom *et al.*, IEEE Trans. Nucl. Sci. **52**, 868 (2005).
119. G. Mavromanolakis, *In the Proceedings of 2005 International Linear Collider Workshop (LCWS 2005), Stanford, California, 18-22 Mar 2005, pp 0906* [arXiv:physics/0510181].
120. D. Strom *et al.*, *In the Proceedings of 2005 International Linear Collider Workshop (LCWS 2005), Stanford, California, 18-22 Mar 2005, pp 0908.*

Chapter 3

Astrophysical Aspects of Neutrinos

John F. Beacom

Center for Cosmology and Astro-Particle Physics,
Departments of Physics and Astronomy,
191 W. Woodruff Ave., Columbus, OH 43210, USA

Neutrino astronomy is on the verge of discovering new sources, and this will lead to important advances in astrophysics, cosmology, particle physics, and nuclear physics. This paper is meant for non-experts, so that they might understand the basic issues in this field.

3.1. General Introduction

It has long been appreciated that neutrino astronomy would have unique advantages. The principal one, due to the weak interactions of neutrinos, is that they would be able to penetrate even great column densities of matter. This could be in dense sources themselves, like stars, supernovae, or active galactic nuclei. It could also be across the universe itself. Of course, the small interaction cross section is also the curse of neutrino astronomy, and to date, only two extraterrestrial sources have been observed: the Sun, and Supernova 1987A. That's it.

However, a new generation of detectors is coming online, and their capabilities are significantly better than anything built before. Additionally, a great deal of theoretical effort, taking advantage of the very rapid increases in the quality and quantity of astrophysical data, has refined estimates of predicted fluxes. The basic message is that the detector capabilities appear to have nearly met the theoretical predictions, and that the next decade should see several exciting first discoveries.

For these two talks, I was asked to introduce the topics of supernova neutrinos and high-energy neutrinos. See the other talks in this volume for more about these and related topics. To increase the probability of this paper being read, I have condensed the material covered in my computer presentation, focusing on the basic framework instead of the details. In the actual lectures, I made extensive use of the blackboard, and of interaction with the students through questions from them (and to them). It isn't possible to represent that here. I thank the students for their active participation, and hope that they've all solved the suggested problems!

3.2. PART ONE: Supernova Neutrinos

3.2.1. *Preamble*

Over the centuries, supernovae, which appear as bright stars and then disappear within a few months, have amazed and confused us. We're still amazed, and as Fermi said, we're still confused, just on a higher level. The historical observations of supernovae were of rare objects in our own Milky Way Galaxy (here and elsewhere, "Galaxy" is used for the Milky Way, and "galaxy" for the generic case). Now that we know their distances, we know that supernovae are extremely luminous in the optical, in fact comparable to the starlight from the whole host galaxy. But that's not the half of it, literally. If you had neutrino-detecting eyes, you'd see the neutrino burst from a single core-collapse supernova outshine the steady-state neutrino emission from all the stars in a galaxy (the analog of solar neutrinos) by a factor more like 10^{15} (that's a lot!). This is what enabled the detection of about 20 neutrinos from Supernova (SN) 1987A, despite its great distance.

A good general rule in decoding physical processes is "Follow the energy," much like "Follow the money" for understanding certain human endeavors. For core-collapse supernovae, this means the neutrinos, while for thermonuclear supernovae, this means the gamma rays. These are the direct messengers that reveal the details of the explosions. In the following, I'll discuss this in more detail, mostly focusing on the "observational" perspective, since it's easy to be convinced that observing these direct messengers is important, while hard to think of how to actually do it. As I will emphasize, this is much more than just astronomy for its own sake: these data play a crucial role in testing the properties of neutrinos, and more generally, in probing light degrees of freedom beyond the Standard Model.

3.2.2. *Introduction*

Stars form from the collapse and fragmentation of gas clouds, and empirically, the stellar Initial Mass Function is something like $dn/dm \sim m^{-2.35}$, where $m = M_{\text{star}}/M_{\text{sun}}$, as first pointed out by Salpeter in 1955, and refined by many authors since. You'll notice that this distribution is not renormalizable, but don't start worrying about dimensional regularization – a simple cutoff near $m = 0.1$ is enough for our purposes. What is the fate of these stars? There are two interesting broad categories. The "types" are observational distinctions, based on spectral lines, but the divisions below are based on the physical mechanisms.

- **Thermonuclear (Type Ia) supernovae**
  These have progenitors with $m \sim 3$–8, and live for $\sim$ Gyr. The interesting case is when the progenitor has ended its nuclear fusion processes at the stage of being a carbon/oxygen white dwarf, while it has a binary companion that donates mass through accretion. Once the mass of the progenitor grows above the Chandrasekhar mass of $m = 1.4$, this carbon and oxygen will explosively burn all the way up to elements near iron, generating a tremendous amount of energy. The most important isotope produced is ^{56}Ni, which decays to ^{56}Co with $\tau = 9$ days, which then decays to stable ^{56}Fe with $\tau = 110$ days. These decays produce MeV gamma rays and positrons that power the optical light curve. Indeed, a plot of luminosity versus time directly shows the two exponential components.

- **Core-collapse (Type II/Ib/Ic) supernovae**
  These have progenitors with $m \sim 8$–40, and live for less than ~ 0.1 Gyr. Importantly, the dynamics depend only on single stars, and not whether they happen to be in binaries or not. As you know, the source of stellar energy is nuclear fusion reactions, which burn light elements into progressively heavier ones, until elements near iron are reached, and the reactions stop being exothermic. Until that point, as each nuclear fuel is exhausted, the star contracts until the core is hot and dense enough to ignite the next one (remember, these reactions are suppressed by the Coulomb barrier). The cutoff of $m \sim 8$ denotes the requirement of being able to burn all the way up to iron. So what happens at that point? Once there is a $m \sim 1.4$ iron core, it is no longer generating nuclear energy, but it could support itself by electron degeneracy pressure, except for the fact that the massive envelope of the star is weighing down on it. As discussed below, this leads to the collapse of the core and the formation of a hot and dense proto-neutron star, which cools primarily by neutrino emission over a timescale of seconds.

In both cases, a tremendous amount of energy is released in a time that is very short compared to the lifetimes of stars, the resulting optical displays are crudely similar, and shell remnants are left behind. For thermonuclear supernovae, the source of the energy is nuclear fusion reactions, primarily revealed by the gamma rays from nuclear decays. The neutrino emission is subdominant, and no compact remnant is left behind. For core-collapse supernovae (often referred to as type-II supernovae, even when this is inclusive of types Ib and Ic as well), the source of the energy is gravitational, and is primarily revealed by the neutrinos emitted from the newly-formed neutron star (which may ultimately become a black hole). There is also gamma-ray emission, but it is subdominant compared to the neutrinos. Finally, one interesting fact is that for both categories of supernova, the explosion energy is about 10^{51} erg, known as 1 "f.o.e." (fifty-one erg) or 1 "Bethe." Note that this is about $10^{-3} Mc^2$ for 1 solar mass of material.

The neutrino and gamma-ray emissions from supernovae could in principle be detected from individual objects, or as diffuse glows from all past supernovae. Although low-mass stars are much more common than high-mass stars, type Ia supernovae are more rare than core-collapse supernovae by a factor of several, due to the requirement of being in a suitable binary. Before we get into details, here's where things stand on observations of the direct messengers.

- **Gamma rays from thermonuclear supernovae**
  These have never been robustly detected from individual objects, though in a few cases the COMPTEL instrument set interesting limits. While a diffuse background of gamma rays is seen in the MeV range (and beyond), it is now thought that supernovae do not contribute significantly, making it more of a mystery what does.

- **Neutrinos from core-collapse supernovae**
  These have been seen just once, from SN 1987A, but only with about 20 events. No diffuse background of neutrinos has been seen yet, placing interestingly tight limits on the contribution from supernovae.

For particle physicists, the primary interest is on two points. If neutrinos have unexpected properties, or if there are new light particles that effectively carry away energy, then the neutrino emission per supernova could be altered. If there are processes in the universe that produce MeV gamma rays, directly or after redshifting, e.g., dark matter decay, then these may explain the observed gamma-ray background.

Now let's turn to the basics of the neutrino emission from core-collapse supernovae. The gravitational binding energy release can be simply estimated. The gravitational self-energy of a constant-density sphere is $(3/5)G_N M^2/R$, and so

$$\Delta E \simeq \frac{3}{5}\frac{G_N M_{NS}^2}{R_{NS}} - \frac{3}{5}\frac{G_N M_{NS}^2}{R_{core}} \simeq 3\times 10^{53} \text{ erg} \simeq 2\times 10^{59} \text{ MeV},$$

using the observed facts that neutron stars have masses of about $m = 1.4$ and radii of about 10 km. Note that the second term in the difference is negligible. This is a tremendous amount of energy, trapped inside a very dense object, and so no particles can escape and carry away energy except neutrinos. In fact, even the neutrinos must diffuse out, as the density is high enough to counteract the smallness of their interaction cross sections.

The core collapses until it reaches near-nuclear densities, at which point it cannot proceed further, and hitting this wall creates an outgoing shock. If successful, the shock will propagate though the envelope of the star, lifting it off and creating the optical supernova. If not, it will stall, and then the inflow of further material will lead to black hole formation and no optical supernova.

The neutrinos are emitted from the core, within seconds of the collapse, and carry nearly the full binding energy release noted above. It takes perhaps hours or days for the shock to break through the envelope and begin the optical supernova, which is then bright for months. Importantly, the neutrinos are received *before* the light. It's not that they are tachyons, but rather just that they were emitted first. The kinetic energy of the supernova ejecta is only $\sim 1\%$ of the total energy, and the energy in the optical emission is even less. The neutrinos are the most interesting, since they carry most of the energy, are emitted in the shortest and earliest time, and come from the densest regions. Other than gravitational waves, which have yet to be observed, only neutrinos can reveal the inner dynamics of the core collapse process.

As noted, the neutrinos diffuse through the proto-neutron star, meaning that they leave on a longer timescale and with lower energies than they would if it were less dense. It is typically assumed that the neutrino emission per flavor (all six, counting neutrinos and antineutrinos) is comparable. That is, each takes about 1/6 of the binding energy, and has thermal spectral with average energies of 10–20 MeV. There is a vast literature about

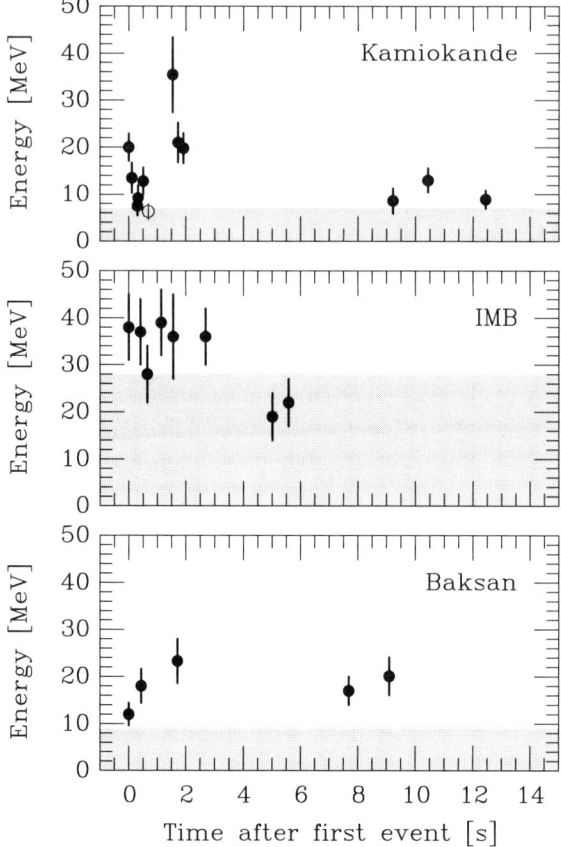

Fig. 3.1. Scatterplots of the neutrino events associated with SN1987A, as seen in the Kamiokande [2], IMB [3], and Baksan [4] detectors. The shaded regions indicate the nominal detector energy thresholds. Figure taken from Ref. [5].

the differences between flavors, and using this to test neutrino mixing, but this is beyond our scope.

The SN 1987A data are shown in Fig. 3.1. These are consistent with mostly being signal events due to inverse beta decay on free protons, $\bar{\nu}_e + p \to e^+ + n$. This reaction channel is special due to its large cross section, and the fact that the outgoing positron carries nearly the full antineutrino energy. The other flavors are much harder to detect. The first thing to notice is that the duration of the burst was about 10 seconds. The second is that the typical energies were low tens of MeV. (This is complicated somewhat by the nontrivial response function of the detectors, especially IMB, which was only effective at the highest energies.) At zeroth order, the Kamiokande and IMB data are consistent with each other and theoretical expectations. The Baksan data are quite puzzling, as this detector was about ten times smaller than Kamiokande, and thus they should have seen ~ 1 event; probably detector backgrounds were present.

The most important message is that these data are consistent with the picture of slow diffusion out of a very hot and dense object, i.e., with the birth of a neutron star, as is suggested also by the total energetics, assuming a comparable neutrino emission per flavor. You can easily estimate the number of detected events yourself, using the total energy noted above, the inverse beta cross section, and the distance of 50 kpc. (Interestingly, there is still no good astronomical evidence for such a compact object in the SN 1987A remnant.) This kind of basic confirmation of the explosion mechanism is what can do with such a small number of neutrino events.

How can we gather more supernova neutrinos? There are three possibilities. First, **Milky Way** objects, with $D \simeq 10$ kpc. Taking into account the fact that we have much larger detectors now, and assuming a typical distance in the Milky Way, we expect about 10^4 detected events in Super-Kamiokande. Unfortunately, the frequency is probably only 2 or 3 times per century, but we might get lucky. It will be very obvious if it happens. Second, **Nearby** objects with $D \sim 10$ Mpc or less. For these, one would need a much larger detector, at the 1 Mton scale, and the number of detected events per supenova is ~ 1. On the other hand, the frequency is about once per year. To reduce backgrounds, this would require a coincident detection of say two or more neutrinos, or one neutrino and the optical signal. Third, **Distant** objects from redshifts $z \sim 1$–2 or less. As a crude guide to how this works, imagine a supernova at a distance such that the expected number of detected events in Super-Kamiokande is 10^{-6}. Almost all of the time, nothing happens, but for one supernova in a million, one neutrino will be detected. This seems crazy until you realize that the supernova rate of the universe is a few per second. Putting this together more carefully leads to an expectation of several detected supernova events per year in Super-Kamiokande (these will be uncorrelated with the optical supernovae, due to the nearly isotropic nature of the detection cross section). A strong rejection of detector backgrounds is required to make this work.

Of these three detection modes, I'll focus on the last, as it is the least familiar.

3.2.3. Supernovae in the Milky Way

At present, the flagship supernova neutrino detector is Super-Kamiokande, which is located in a deep mine in Japan. It is the largest detector with the ability to separate individual supernova neutrino events from detector backgrounds. Its huge fiducial volume contains 22.5 kton of ultrapure water. Relativistic charged particles in a material emit optical Čerenkov radiation, which is detected by photomultiplier tubes around the periphery.

With $\sim 10^4$ events detected for a Milky Way supernova, the Super-Kamiokande data could be used to map out the details of the neutrino spectrum and luminosity profile. Additionally, other neutrino detection reactions, for which the yields are at the 1–10% level in comparison to inverse beta decay, would become important, revealing more about the flavors besides $\bar{\nu}_e$. The aspects of detecting a Milky Way supernova are very interesting, and have been extensively discussed elsewhere.

3.2.4. Supernovae in Nearby Galaxies

If Super-Kamiokande can detect 10^4 events at a supernova distance of 10 kpc, then it can expect to detect 1 event for a supernova distance of 1 Mpc, somewhat larger than the distance to the M31 (Andromeda) and M33 (Triangulum) galaxies. Unfortunately, a single event isn't exciting by itself, and anyway, these galaxies appear to have even lower supernova rates than the Milky Way. Still, it makes one wonder about greater distances. The number of galaxies in each new radial shell in distance increases like D^2, while the flux of each falls like $1/D^2$. As mentioned, one can beat even small Poisson expectations with enough tries, so this is intriguing.

An estimate based on the known nearby galaxies shows that the supernova rate with 10 Mpc should be about one per year, and this is shown in Fig. 3.2. In fact, the observed rates in the past few years have been even higher. A detailed calculation shows that a larger detector than Super-Kamiokande, something more on the 1 Mton scale, could detect about one supernova neutrino per year. (Such detectors are being considered for proton decay studies and as targets for long-baseline neutrino beams.) That seems like a small rate, but bear in mind that in the twenty years since SN 1987A, exactly zero supernova neutrinos have been (identifiably) detected. To reduce backgrounds, these nearby supernovae would need a coincidence of at least two neutrinos or one neutrino and the optical signal. Perhaps most importantly, the detection of even a single neutrino would fix the start time of the collapse to about ten seconds, compared to the precision

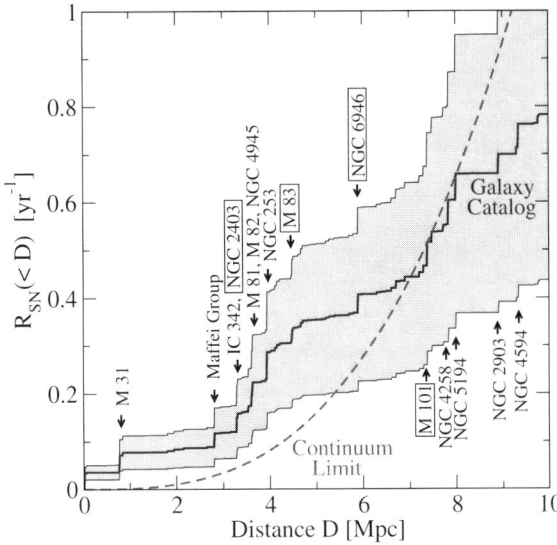

Fig. 3.2. The predicted cumulative supernova rate for nearby galaxies is shown by the blue line, and its uncertainty by the grey band (together denoted as "Galaxy Catalog"). The redshift $z = 0$ limit of the cosmic supernova rate is also shown ("Continuum Limit"). The observed local supernova rate in recent years has been higher than either prediction. Figure taken from Ref. [6].

of about one day that might be determined from the optical signal. This would be very useful for refining the window in which to look for a faint gravitational wave signal.

Related to this is an effort called NO SWEAT (Neutrino-Oriented Supernova Whole-Earth Telescope), led by Avishay Gal-Yam, to use a network of telescopes worldwide to find all supernovae in nearby galaxies.

3.2.5. *DSNB: First Good Limit*

The star formation rate was larger in the past, and in particular, was about 10 times larger at redshift $z \simeq 1$ than it is today. Since the lifetimes of massive stars are short, the core-collapse supernova rate should closely follow the evolution of the star formation rate, up to a constant factor. This gives more weight to distant supernovae than if the rate were constant. On the other hand, for supernova beyond $z \sim 1$, the neutrinos are so redshifted that their detection probabilities are too low (at lower energy, the detection cross section goes down while the detector background rates increase).

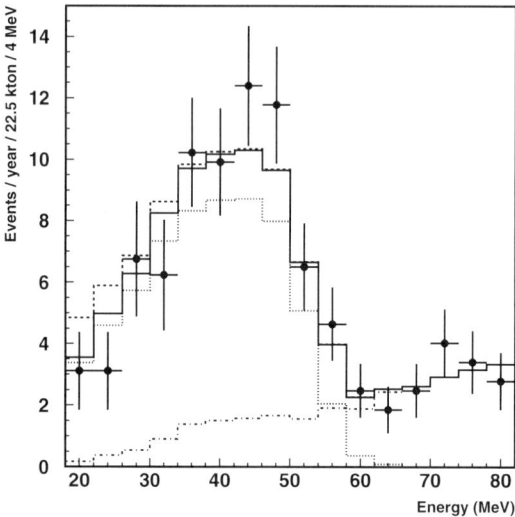

Fig. 3.3. The event spectrum measured in Super-Kamiokande is denoted by the points with error bars. The solid line indicates the expected total detector background rate (the dotted component is due to muon neutrinos, and the dot-dashed component is due to electron neutrinos). The dashed line above the solid line indicates how large of an excess due to DSNB events could be present, given the statistical uncertainties. Figure taken from Ref. [7].

Integrating the neutrino emission per supernova with the evolving supernova rate, and taking into account the cosmological factors, the accumulated spectrum of all past supernovae can be calculated. This is known as the Diffuse Supernova Neutrino Background (DSNB), or sometimes as relic supernova neutrinos (which is a confusing and deprecated term, i.e., these have nothing to do with the 2 K relic background of neutrinos that decoupled just before big-bang nucleosynthesis).

In 2000, a paper by Kaplinghat, Steigman, and Walker calculated the largest plausible DSNB flux, and found it to be 2.2 cm^{-2} s^{-1} for electron antineutrinos above 19.3 MeV. This was about 100 times smaller than the existing limit from Kamiokande, so the prospects for detection didn't look great. Other calculations with reasonable inputs (by modern standards) gave results that were a few to several times smaller.

In 2003, the Super-Kamiokande collaboration published a limit that was 1.2 in the above units. This was a milestone, because it showed for the first time that there was hope of reaching the range in which a detection might be made. Still, as shown in Fig. 3.3, there are large detector backgrounds that make it difficult to identify the DSNB signal. Note that for a background-limited search, like this one, to improve the signal sensitivity by a factor of 3 takes a factor 9 more statistics. Since this figure was based on 4 years of data, this would take a long time to collect (comparable to the wait for a Galactic supernova!).

3.2.6. *DSNB: Detection with Gadolinium*

In order to make progress, it is necessary to find a way to eliminate or at least severely reduce the detector background. Mark Vagins (a member of the Super-Kamiokande collaboration) and I decided to put our heads together to find a way to isolate the DSNB signal. This resulted in a 2004 article in Physical Review Letters, though we were forced to remove the code name of the project, "GADZOOKS!," from the title and text (but see the arXiv version). Recall that the detection reaction is $\bar{\nu}_e + p \to e^+ + n$, and that at present, only the positron is detected. We realized that the key was to detect the neutron in time and space coincidence with the positron. This is an old idea, and was used by Reines and Cowan in the first detection of neutrinos (antineutrinos from a nuclear reactor).

Saying that we had to detect the neutron was the easy part. It was more challenging to find a way to do this in a water-based detector, where normally the neutrons capture on free protons. That produces a 2.2 MeV gamma ray that Compton scatters electrons, but they are too low in energy to be detectable. We pointed out that the required neutron tagging might be possible by using a 0.2% admixture of dissolved gadolinium trichloride ($GdCl_3$). Gadolinium has a huge neutron capture cross section, and produces an 8 MeV gamma-ray cascade that reconstructs as an equivalent single electron of about 5 MeV, which is readily detectable.

The really hard part was in establishing that this technique might be possible in practice, which involved raising and answering many difficult technical questions. (Among them, finding a suitable water-soluble compound of gadolinium.) Somewhat to our surprise, we found no obvious obstacles. Mark Vagins has been leading a detailed research and development effort, and so far, the prospects look very good.

In Fig. 3.4, the spectra expected in Super-Kamiokande if gadolinium is added are shown. The atmospheric neutrino backgrounds mentioned above are reduced by a factor of about 5. Additionally, backgrounds at lower energies are severely reduced, allowing the use of a much lower threshold

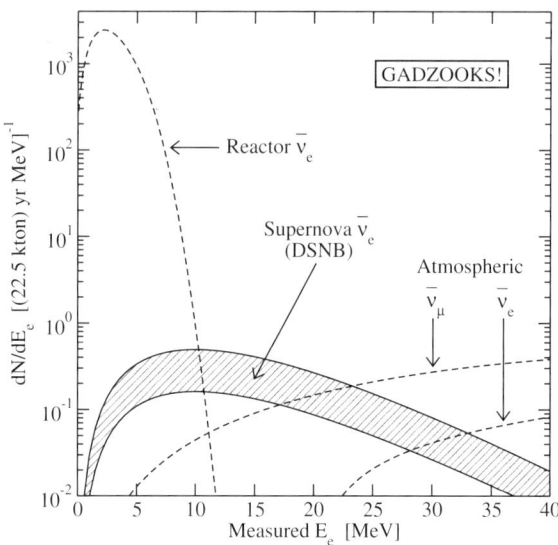

Fig. 3.4. The DSNB signal and detector backgrounds expected in Super-Kamiokande if gadolinium is added. Figure taken from Ref. [8].

energy. At moderate energies, it should be possible to cleanly identify DSNB signal events.

3.2.7. DSNB: Astrophysical Impact

Now let's return to the predicted DSNB spectrum. If either the assumed star formation rate or the neutrino emission per supernova were too large, then the predicted DSNB flux would already be ruled out the the Super-Kamiokande data.

Even since the time of the Super-Kamiokande limit, the astrophysical data have improved substantially. Andrew Hopkins and I synthesized a wide variety of data to constrain the star formation and supernova rate histories. An example fit is shown in Fig. 3.5. The uncertainty band is much more narrow now than it was just a few years ago. The normalization of the cosmic star formation rate depends on dust corrections. If the true star formation rate were even somewhat larger than determined here, then the DSNB neutrino flux would be too large relative to the Super-Kamiokande limit. The only way out would be to require a substantially lower neutrino emission per supernova.

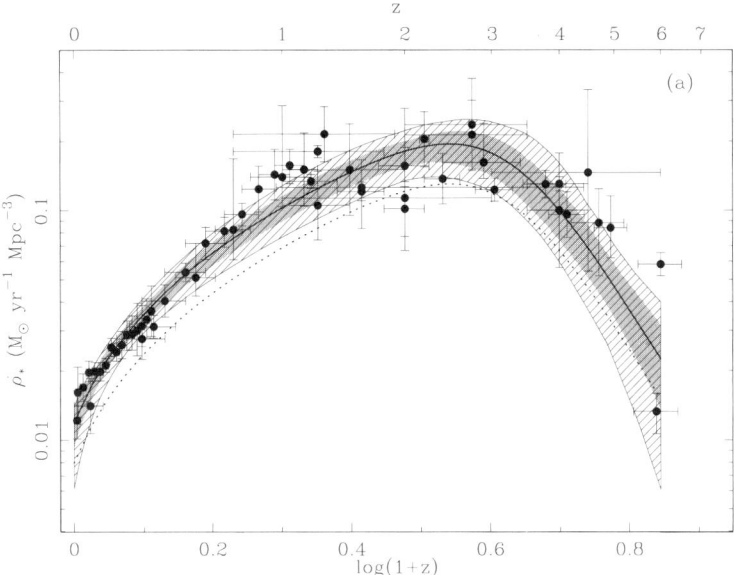

Fig. 3.5. The star formation rate history, with selected data shown by points and the fit and uncertainty shown by the bands. Figure taken from Ref. [9].

The corresponding calculated supernova rates are in good agreement with data. As an interesting aside, it was shown that the diffuse gamma-ray background from type Ia supernovae is too small to account for the observed data in the MeV range. That is particularly significant because many limits on exotic particle physics depend on just this energy range.

3.2.8. Back to the Scene of the Crime: SN 1987A

If we now know the star formation history, then the only remaining unknown is the neutrino emission per supernova. Hasan Yüksel, Shin'ichiro Ando, and I considered how well the Super-Kamiokande data already restrict the neutrino emission per supernova. The emission models are usually parametrized in terms of the time-integrated luminosity (or portion of the binding energy release) and the average energy per neutrino (related to the temperature of the spectrum). I mentioned above that the Kamiokande and IMB data on the emission from SN 1987A were mostly consistent. In fact, when fitted with thermal spectra, there are some discrepancies.

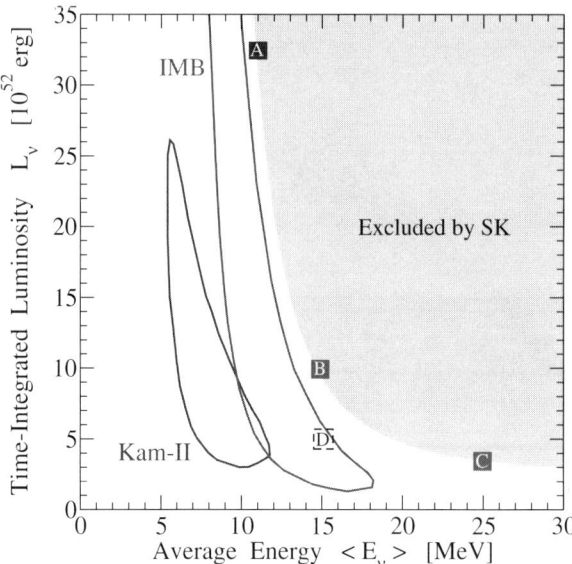

Fig. 3.6. The contours labeled Kam-II and IMB are the allowed regions from the SN 1987A data, assuming a thermal spectrum [10]. The shaded region is what is already excluded by the non-observation of a DSNB signal in Super-Kamiokande. Figure taken from Ref. [11].

In Fig. 3.6, I show that the DSNB data are probing neutrino emission parameters only slightly larger than those deduced from the SN 1987A data. With reduced detector backgrounds, the DSNB spectrum would be a new way to measure the neutrino emission per supernova.

3.2.9. *Conclusions*

Why is understanding supernovae interesting and important? For particle physics, it is to test the properties of neutrinos, and to search for new low-mass particles that cool the proto-neutron star. For nuclear physics, it is to constrain the neutron star equation of state and to shed light on the formation of the elements. For astrophysics, it is to understand the stellar life and death cycles and to understand the supernova mechanisms. For cosmology, it is to better understand the details of whether type Ia supernovae are standard candles, and to probe the origins of the gamma-ray and neutrino backgrounds. With more data, we can't lose.

3.3. PART TWO: High-Energy Neutrinos

3.3.1. *Introduction*

Now that we've covered the specific example of supernova neutrinos, let's step back and comment on the general status and outlook in neutrino astrophysics.

Unique among the Standard Model fermions, neutrinos are neutral, and more generally, have only weak interactions. This makes them potentially sensitive to even very feeble postulated new interactions. While the discovery of neutrino mass and mixing was "new physics" beyond the minimal Standard Model, the discovery of any new interactions would be a much more radical step, as it would require new particles as well.

This is one reason that we're interested in neutrinos. The other, already discussed, is that they will be especially powerful probes of astrophysical objects, once these neutrinos are detected. Already with the neutrinos from the Sun and SN 1987A, the scientific return was very rich: not only confirmation of the physics of their interiors, but also a crucial piece in the discovery of neutrino mass and mixing. Ray Davis and Masatoshi Koshiba shared in the 2002 Nobel Prize for this work, and their citation reads, "...for pioneering contributions to astrophysics, in particular for the detection of cosmic neutrinos...."

The general achievements in neutrino physics in just the recent past might be summarized as follows. The **cosmological** results are the consistency of big-bang nucleosynthesis yields with three flavors of neutrinos, and the exclusion of neutrinos as the (hot) dark matter. In both cases, these facts have been established independently in the laboratory as well. The **astrophysical** results are the discovery of neutrinos from SN 1987A and the solution of the solar neutrino problem. The **fundamental** results are the discovery of neutrino mass and mixing, and the clear exclusion of a huge range of formerly allowed models of exotic neutrino properties.

One of the lessons from this list is that we need data from new sources to make new discoveries, and that those discoveries may have a broader impact than initially thought. Astrophysical sources reach extremes of density, distance, and energy, and this will allow unprecedented tests of neutrino properties, for example.

We can identify three frontiers where new sources will likely be discovered soon. By the rough energy scale of the neutrinos, we might call these the MeV (10^{-6} TeV) scale, the TeV scale, and the EeV (10^6 TeV) scale. At the MeV scale, the focus is on the **Visible Universe**, i.e., stars and supernovae, and Super-Kamiokande is the main detector. At the TeV scale, the focus is on the **Nonthermal Universe**, i.e., jets powered by black holes, and the primary detector is AMANDA, which is being succeeded by IceCube. At the EeV scale, the focus is on the **Extreme Universe**, i.e., at the energy frontier of the highest-energy cosmic rays, and one of the key detectors is ANITA.

Why do we think that high-energy neutrinos even exist? First, because cosmic rays (probably mostly protons) are observed at energies as high as 10^{20} eV, and they are increasingly abundant down to at least the GeV range. Something is accelerating these cosmic rays, and it is very likely that these sources also produce neutrinos. Second, because extragalactic gamma-ray sources have been observed with energies up to about 10 TeV (and galactic sources up to about 100 TeV). Again, something is producing these particles, and in large fluxes, and it is likely that neutrinos are also produced.

So then why do we need neutrinos? The problem with cosmic rays is that they are easily deflected by magnetic fields, and so only their isotropic flux has been observed, making the identification of their sources very difficult. The problem with photons is that they are easily attenuated: a TeV gamma ray colliding with an eV starlight photon is able to produce an electron-positron pair. Thus at high energies, only nearby objects can be seen.

High-energy neutrinos can be made through either proton-proton or proton-photon collisions, depending on energies. In either case, pions are readily produced, and typically comparable numbers of neutral and charged pions are made. Neutral pions decay as $\pi^0 \to \gamma + \gamma$, and charged pions decay as $\pi^+ \to \mu^+ + \nu_\mu$, followed by $\mu^+ \to e^+ + \nu_e + \bar{\nu}_\mu$ (with obvious changes for the charge conjugate). This is the **hadronic** mechanism for producing gamma rays and neutrinos. There is also a **leptonic** mechanism, based on the inverse Compton scattering reaction $e^- + \gamma \to \gamma + e^-$, where fast electrons collide with low-energy photons and promote them to high-energy gamma rays. Note that the leptonic process produces no neutrinos. It is a major mystery whether the observed high energy gamma-ray sources are powered by the hadronic or leptonic mechanism. This is a key to uncovering the sources of the cosmic rays.

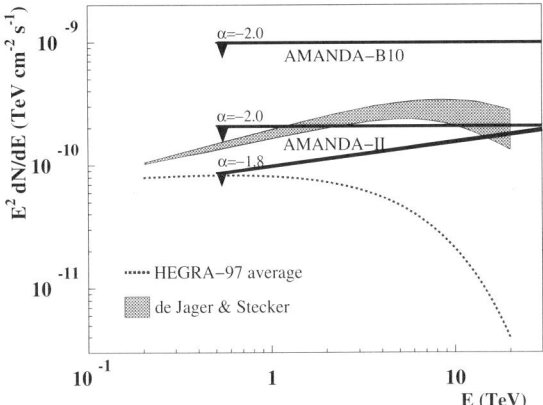

Fig. 3.7. The dotted line is based on gamma-ray observations of the nearby AGN Markarian 501 by the HEGRA experiment, and the shaded band is a calculation that removes the assumed affects of attenuation en route. The labeled solid lines indicate AMANDA limits on the neutrino flux. This object flares, and the gamma ray and neutrino data are not contemporaneous. Figure taken from Ref. [12].

3.3.2. Sources and Detection at ~ 1 TeV

At the simplest level, hadronic sources produce nearly equal fluxes of gamma rays and neutrinos (the corrections due to multiplicities, decay energies, and neutrino mixing can be easily taken into account). Therefore, the observed gamma-ray spectrum of an object like an AGN is a strong predictor of the neutrino spectrum, if the source is hadronic (if it is leptonic, then the neutrino flux will be zero). Any attenuation of the gamma-ray spectrum en route would mean that the neutrino flux would be even larger. An example is illustrated in Fig. 3.7, where it is shown that the neutrino detectors are now approaching the required level of flux sensitivity.

For hadronic sources, the initial neutrino flavor ratios (adding neutrinos and antineutrinos) are $\phi_e : \phi_\mu : \phi_\tau = 1 : 2 : 0$, following simply from the pion and muon decay chains. After vacuum neutrino mixing en route, these will become $\phi_e : \phi_\mu : \phi_\tau = 1 : 1 : 1$.

Of all flavors, the muon neutrinos are the easiest to detect and identify. Through charged-current deep inelastic scattering reactions, these produce muons that carry most of the neutrino energy, and which have only a very small deflection from the neutrino direction. Muons and other charged particles produce optical Čerenkov radiation in the detector, which is registered by photomultiplier tubes throughout the volume. Muons produce

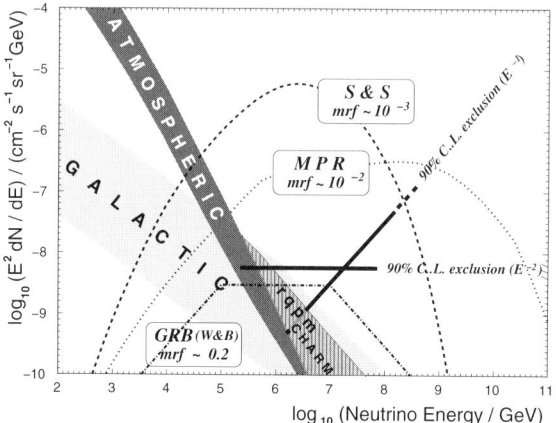

Fig. 3.8. The sensitivity of IceCube is marked with heavy solid lines, as labeled. The broken lines indicate various astrophysical diffuse flux models. The shaded regions indicate the atmospheric neutrino, prompt/charm component thereof, and Galactic neutrino backgrounds. Figure taken from Ref. [13].

spectacular long tracks that can range through the kilometer of the detector and beyond. The detection of electron and tau neutrinos is interesting and important too, but beyond our scope here.

To screen out enormous backgrounds from downgoing atmospheric muons, these detectors only look for upgoing events. Since muons cannot pass through Earth, these muons must have been created just below the detector by upgoing neutrinos. Even after this, there are backgrounds due to atmospheric neutrinos, themselves produced on the other side of Earth, and thus hardly extraterrestrial.

An astrophysical point source can be identified as an excess in a given direction, whereas the atmospheric neutrino background is smoothly varying. Transient point sources are even easier to recognize. On the other hand, diffuse astrophysical neutrino fluxes are quite hard to separate from the atmospheric neutrino background. The principal technique is that the former are believed to have spectra close to E^{-2}, while the latter is closer to E^{-3}, and steeper at higher energies. Thus at high energies the astrophysical diffuse fluxes should emerge as dominant. Once cannot go too high in energy – the event rates get too low, and Earth becomes opaque to neutrinos at around 100 TeV. An example of the diffuse flux sensitivity of IceCube is shown in Fig. 3.8.

3.3.3. Testing Neutrino Properties

As an example of a novel neutrino property that could be tested once astrophysical sources are observed, consider neutrino decay. Why should neutrinos decay? Other than the fact that there is no interaction that can cause fast neutrino decay, why shouldn't they decay? The other massive fermions all decay into the lowest-mass generation in their family. (Neutrinos can too, via the weak interaction, but it is exceedingly slow.) We'll consider simply neutrino disappearance, i.e., that the other particle in the decay of one neutrino mass eigenstate to another is too weakly interacting to be detected. It is quite hard to test for the effects of such decays.

Decay will deplete the original flux as

$$\exp\left(-t/\tau_{lab}\right) = \exp\left(-\frac{L}{E} \times \frac{m}{\tau}\right),$$

where L is distance, E the energy, m the mass, and τ the proper lifetime. For the Sun, the τ/m scale that can be probed is up to about 10^{-4} s/eV. On the other hand, for distant astrophysical sources of TeV neutrinos, L/E may be such that τ/m up to about 10^{+4} s/eV is relevant!

How can we tell if decay has occurred, if the neutrino fluxes are uncertain? As mentioned, the flavor ratios after vacuum oscillations are expected to be $\phi_e : \phi_\mu : \phi_\tau = 1 : 1 : 1$. However, it is among the mass eigenstates, not the flavor eigenstates, where decays take place. Suppose that the heaviest two mass eigenstates have decayed, leaving only the lightest mass eigenstate. What is its flavor composition? In the normal hierarchy, it has flavor ratios $\phi_e : \phi_\mu : \phi_\tau \sim 5 : 1 : 1$, whereas in the inverted hierarchy, they are $\sim 0 : 1 : 1$. In either case, they are quite distinct from the no-decay case, and the flavor identification capabilities of IceCube should be able to distinguish these possibilities.

3.3.4. Sources and Detection at $\sim 10^6$ TeV

Cosmic rays have been observed at energies above 10^{20} eV, and there are no good answers as to what astrophysical accelerators may have produced them. However, this becomes even more puzzling when it is noted that the universe should be opaque to protons above about 3×10^{19} eV traveling over more than 100 Mpc. There are no obvious sources within that distance.

The process by which protons are attenuated is $p + \gamma \to p + \pi^0, n + \pi^+$, where both final states are possible, and the target photon is from the cosmic microwave background. As with the hadronic processes discussed

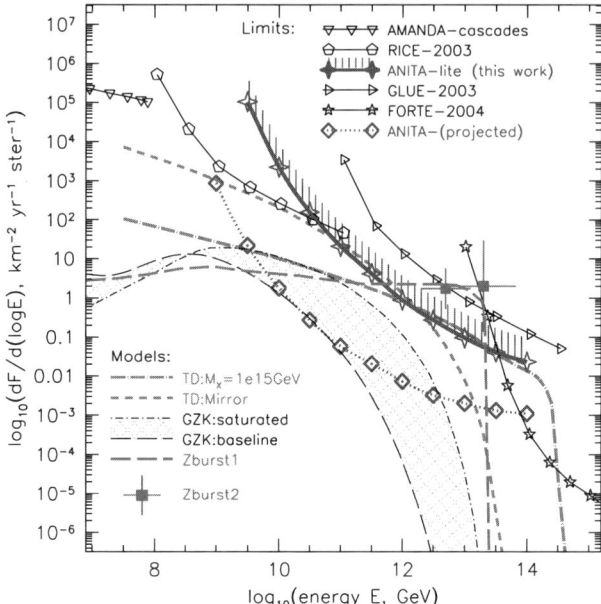

Fig. 3.9. Real and projected neutrino flux sensitivities of various experiments (lines with points), along with various models (as labeled). Figure taken from Ref. [14].

above, the neutral pion decays produce gamma rays and the charged pion decays produce neutrinos. The gamma rays are themselves attenuated, but the neutrino flux builds up when integrating over sources everywhere in the universe. Since the attenuation process for the protons is called the GZK process (Greisen-Zatsepin-Kuzmin), these are called GZK neutrinos. Typical energies are in the EeV range, and an isotropic diffuse flux is expected.

New experiments are being deployed to search for the GZK neutrino flux, as shown in Fig. 3.9. Unlike IceCube, which is based on optical Čerenkov radiation, ANITA and other experiments are based on radio Čerenkov radiation that is emitted coherently from the whole shower initiated by a neutrino in the ice or other transparent medium. ANITA is using the Antarctic ice cap as the detector, and is observing it with radio antennas mounted on a balloon. So far, detector backgrounds appear to be negligible, meaning that it should be straightforward to improve the signal sensitivity with more exposure.

In Fig. 3.10, I show the results of a very recent calculation of the expected GZK neutrino fluxes.

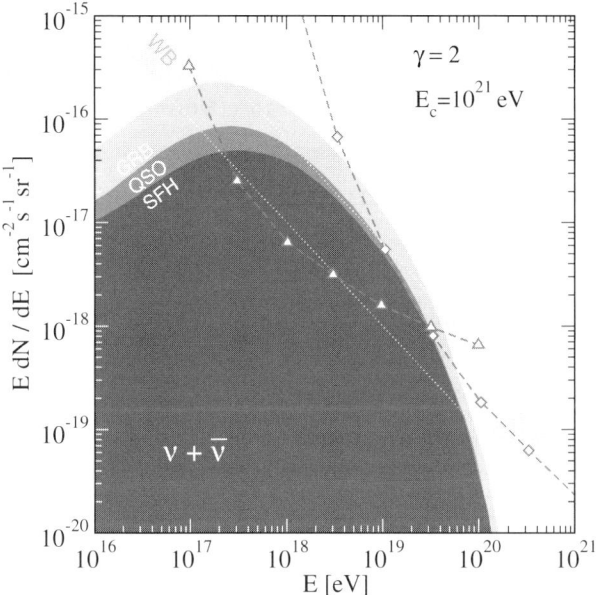

Fig. 3.10. Predicted GZK neutrino fluxes, assuming that ultrahigh energy cosmic rays are produced in gamma-ray bursts, and according to how the latter rate evolves with redshift (i.e., following the star formation rate alone, or rising like that of the quasars, or depending on both the star formation rate and the evolving local metallicity. The "WB" band is the Waxman-Bahcall bound. The curves with points are projected sensitivities for ANITA (upper) and ARIANNA (lower). Figure taken from Ref. [15].

Interestingly, when adjusted for the neutrino-quark center of mass energy, the detection reactions are probing above the TeV scale, opening the prospect of sensitivity to new physics in the detection alone.

3.3.5. *Conclusions*

So far, zero high-energy astrophysical neutrinos have been detected. However, the near-term prospects are very good, and are strongly motivated by measured data on high-energy protons and photons. Still, this will not be easy, and large detectors with strong background rejection will be needed. If successful, these experiments will make important astrophysical discoveries, e.g., whether gamma-ray sources are based on the hadronic or leptonic mechanisms, the origins of cosmic rays at all energies, etc. We might even learn something new about neutrinos in the process!

Acknowledgments

JFB was supported by National Science Foundation CAREER grant PHY-0547102, and by CCAPP at the Ohio State University.

References

[1] **Disclaimer:** I have been very light on referencing, in fact only noting the sources of the figures shown, to make the paper more readable.
[2] K. Hirata *et al.*, Phys. Rev. Lett. **58**, 1490 (1987).
[3] R. M. Bionta *et al.*, Phys. Rev. Lett. **58**, 1494 (1987).
[4] E. N. Alekseev, L. N. Alekseeva, I. V. Krivosheina and V. I. Volchenko, Phys. Lett. B **205**, 209 (1988).
[5] G. G. Raffelt, Ann. Rev. Nucl. Part. Sci. **49**, 163 (1999) [arXiv:hep-ph/9903472].
[6] S. Ando, J. F. Beacom and H. Yuksel, Phys. Rev. Lett. **95**, 171101 (2005) [arXiv:astro-ph/0503321].
[7] M. Malek *et al.*, Phys. Rev. Lett. **90**, 061101 (2003) [arXiv:hep-ex/0209028].
[8] J. F. Beacom and M. R. Vagins, Phys. Rev. Lett. **93**, 171101 (2004) [arXiv:hep-ph/0309300].
[9] A. M. Hopkins and J. F. Beacom, Astrophys. J. **651**, 142 (2006) [arXiv:astro-ph/0601463].
[10] B. Jegerlehner, F. Neubig and G. Raffelt, Phys. Rev. D **54**, 1194 (1996) [arXiv:astro-ph/9601111]; A. Mirizzi and G. G. Raffelt, Phys. Rev. D **72**, 063001 (2005) [arXiv:astro-ph/0508612].
[11] H. Yuksel, S. Ando and J. F. Beacom, Phys. Rev. C **74**, 015803 (2006) [arXiv:astro-ph/0509297].
[12] J. Ahrens *et al.*, Phys. Rev. Lett. **92**, 071102 (2004) [arXiv:astro-ph/0309585].
[13] J. Ahrens *et al.*, Astropart. Phys. **20**, 507 (2004) [arXiv:astro-ph/0305196].
[14] S. W. Barwick *et al.*, Phys. Rev. Lett. **96**, 171101 (2006) [arXiv:astro-ph/0512265].
[15] H. Yuksel and M. D. Kistler, Phys. Rev. D **75**, 083004 (2007) [arXiv:astro-ph/0610481].

Chapter 4

Leptogenesis

Mu-Chun Chen

*Theoretical Physics Department, Fermi National Accelerator Laboratory
Batavia, IL 60510-0500, U.S.A.
and
Department of Physics & Astronomy, University of California
Irvine, CA 92697-4575, U.S.A.*[*]
muchunc@uci.edu

The origin of the asymmetry between matter and anti-matter of the Universe has been one of the great challenges in particle physics and cosmology. Leptogenesis as a mechanism for generating the cosmological baryon asymmetry of the Universe has gained significant interests ever since the advent of the evidence of non-zero neutrino masses. In these lectures presented at TASI 2006, I review various realizations of leptogenesis and allude to recent developments in this subject.

4.1. Introduction

The understanding of the origin of the cosmological baryon asymmetry has been a challenge for both particle physics and cosmology. In an expanding Universe, which leads to departure from thermal equilibrium, a baryon asymmetry can be generated dynamically by charge-conjugation (C), charge-parity (CP) and baryon (B) number violating interactions among quarks and leptons. Possible realizations of these conditions have been studied for decades, starting with detailed investigation in the context of grand unified theories. The recent advent of the evidence of non-zero neutrino masses has led to a significant amount of work in leptogenesis. This subject is of special interests because the baryon asymmetry in this scenario is in principle entirely determined by the properties of the neutrinos.

---

[*]Address after January 1, 2007.

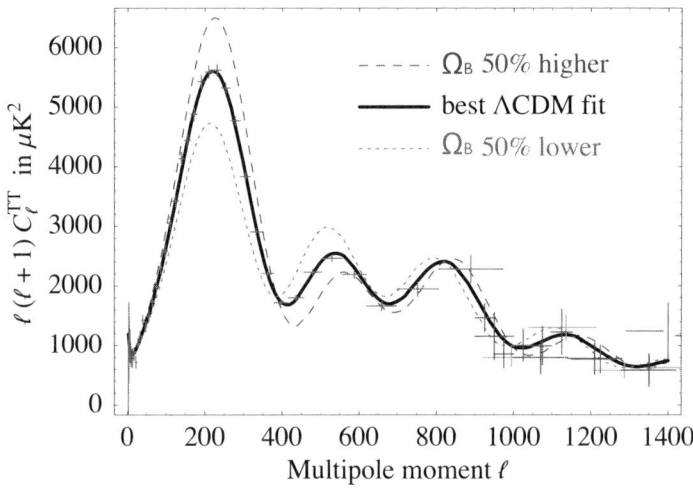

Fig. 4.1. The power spectrum anisotropies defined in Eqs. 4.2 and 4.3 as a function of the multiple moment, l. Figure taken from Ref. [2].

In these lectures, I discuss some basic ingredients of leptogenesis as well as recent developments in this subject.

These lectures are organized as follows: In Sec. 4.1, I review the basic ingredients needed for the generation of baryon asymmetry and describe various mechanisms for baryogenesis and the problems in these mechanisms. In Sec. 4.2, I introduce the standard leptogenesis and Dirac leptogenesis as well as the problem of gravitino over-production that exists in these standard scenarios when supersymmetry is incorporated. This is followed by Sec. 4.3, in which several alternative mechanisms that have been invented to alleviate the gravitino over-production problem are discussed. Section 4.4 focuses on the subject of connecting leptogenesis with low energy leptonic CP violating processes. Section 4.5 concludes these lectures with discussions on the recent developments. For exiting reviews on the subject of leptogenesis and on baryogenesis in general, see *e.g.* Refs. [1–4] and [5–7].

4.1.1. *Evidence of Baryon Number Asymmetry*

One of the main successes of the standard early Universe cosmology is the predictions for the abundances of the light elements, D, ^{3}He, ^{4}He and ^{7}Li. (For a review, see, Ref. [8]. See also Scott Dodelson's lectures.) Agreement between theory and observation is obtained for a certain range of parameter, η_B, which is the ratio of the baryon number density, n_B, to photon density, n_γ,

$$\eta_B^{\text{BBN}} = \frac{n_B}{n_\gamma} = (2.6 - 6.2) \times 10^{-10} \ . \tag{4.1}$$

The Cosmic Microwave Background (CMB) is not a perfectly isotropic radiation bath. These small temperature anisotropies are usually analyzed by decomposing the signal into spherical harmonics, in terms of the spherical polar angles θ and ϕ on the sky, as

$$\frac{\Delta T}{T} = \sum_{l,m} a_{lm} Y_{lm}(\theta, \phi) \ , \tag{4.2}$$

where a_{lm} are the expansion coefficients. The CMB power spectrum is defined by

$$C_l = \langle |a_{lm}|^2 \rangle \ , \tag{4.3}$$

and it is conventional to plot the quantity $l(l+1)C_l$ against l. The CMB measurements indicate that the temperature of the Universe at present is $T_{now} \sim 3°K$. Due to the Bose-Einstein statistics, the number density of the photon, n_γ, scales as T^3. Together, these give a photon number density at present to be roughly $400/\text{cm}^3$. It is more difficult to count the baryon number density, because only some fraction of the baryons form stars and other luminous objects. There are two indirect probes that point to the same baryon density. The measurement of CMB anisotropies probe the acoustic oscillations of the baryon/photon fluid, which happened around photon last scattering. Figure 4.1 illustrates how the amount of anisotropies depends on n_B/n_γ. The baryon number density, $n_B \sim 1/\text{m}^3$, is obtained from the anisotropic in CMB, which indicates the baryon density Ω_B to be 0.044. Another indirect probe is the Big Bang Nucleosynthesis (BBN), whose predictions depend on n_B/n_γ through the processes shown in Fig. 4.2. It is measured independently from the primordial nucleosynthesis of the light elements. The value for n_B/n_γ deduced from primordial Deuterium abundance agrees with that obtained by WMAP [9]. For ^{4}He and ^{7}Li, there are nevertheless discrepancies which may be due to the under-estimated errors. Combining WMAP measurement and the Deuterium abundance gives,

$$\frac{n_B}{n_\gamma} \equiv \eta_B = (6.1 \pm 0.3) \times 10^{-10} \ . \tag{4.4}$$

4.1.2. Sakharov's Conditions

A matter-anti-matter asymmetry can be dynamically generated in an expanding Universe if the particle interactions and the cosmological evolution satisfy the three Sakharov's conditions [10]: (*i*) baryon number violation; (*ii*) C and CP violation; (*iii*) departure from thermal equilibrium.

4.1.2.1. Baryon Number Violation

As we start from a baryon symmetric Universe ($B = 0$), to evolve to a Universe where $B \neq 0$, baryon number violation is necessary. Baryon number violation occurs naturally in Grand Unified Theories (GUT), because quarks and leptons are unified in the same irreducible representations. It is thus possible to have gauge bosons and scalars mediating interactions among fermions having different baryon numbers. In the SM, on the other hand, the baryon number and the lepton number are accidental symmetries. It is thus not possible to violate these symmetries at the tree level. t'Hooft realized that [11] the non-perturbative instanton effects may give rise to processes that violate $(B + L)$, but conserve $(B - L)$. Classically, B and L are conserved,

$$B = \int d^3 x J_0^B(x), \quad L = \int d^3 x J_0^L(x), \qquad (4.5)$$

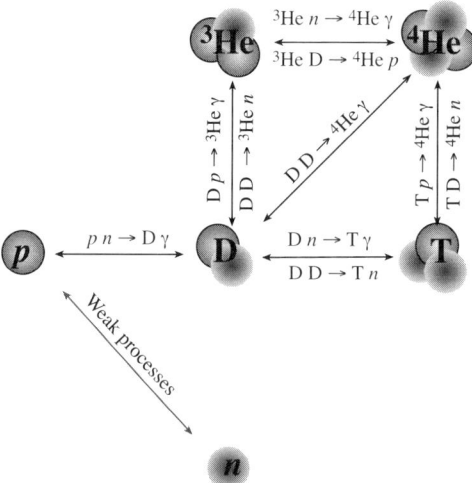

Fig. 4.2. Main reactions that determine the primordial abundances of the light elements. Figure taken from Ref. [2].

Table 4.1. Standard model fermions and their B and L charges.

	$q_L = \begin{pmatrix} u \\ d \end{pmatrix}_L$	u_L^c	d_L^c	$\ell_L = \begin{pmatrix} \nu \\ e \end{pmatrix}_L$	e_L^c
B	1/3	-1/3	-1/3	0	0
L	0	0	0	1	-1

where the currents associated with B and L are given by,

$$J_\mu^B = \frac{1}{3} \sum_i \left(\overline{q}_{L_i} \gamma_\mu q_{L_i} - \overline{u}_{L_i}^c \gamma_\mu u_{L_i}^c - \overline{d}_{L_i}^c \gamma_\mu d_{L_i}^c \right) , \qquad (4.6)$$

$$J_\mu^L = \sum_i \left(\overline{\ell}_{L_i} \gamma_\mu \ell_{L_i} - \overline{e}_{L_i}^c \gamma_\mu e_{L_i}^c \right) . \qquad (4.7)$$

Here q_L refers to the $SU(2)_L$ doublet quarks, while u_L and d_L refer to the $SU(2)_L$ singlet quarks. Similarly, ℓ_L refers to the $SU(2)_L$ lepton doublets and e_L refers to the $SU(2)_L$ charged lepton singlets. The B and L numbers of these fermions are summarized in Table 4.1. The subscript i is the generation index. Even though B and L are individually conserved at the tree level, the Adler-Bell-Jackiw (ABJ) triangular anomalies [12] nevertheless do not vanish, and thus B and L are anomalous [13] at the quantum level through the interactions with the electroweak gauge fields in the triangle diagrams (see, for example Ref. [14] for details). In other words, the divergences of the currents associated with B and L do not vanish at the quantum level, and they are given by

$$\partial_\mu J_B^\mu = \partial_\mu J_L^\mu = \frac{N_f}{32\pi^2} \left(g^2 W_{\mu\nu}^p \widetilde{W}^{p\mu\nu} - g'^2 B_{\mu\nu} \widetilde{B}^{\mu\nu} \right) , \qquad (4.8)$$

where $W_{\mu\nu}$ and $B_{\mu\nu}$ are the $SU(2)_L$ and $U(1)_Y$ field strengths,

$$W_{\mu\nu}^p = \partial_\mu W_\nu^p - \partial_\nu W_\mu^p \qquad (4.9)$$

$$B_{\mu\nu} = \partial_\mu B_\nu - \partial_\nu B_\mu , \qquad (4.10)$$

respectively, with corresponding gauge coupling constants being g and g', and N_f is the number of fermion generations. As $\partial^\mu (J_\mu^B - J_\mu^L) = 0$, $(B-L)$ is conserved. However, $(B+L)$ is violated with the divergence of the current given by,

$$\partial^\mu (J_\mu^B + J_\mu^L) = 2 N_F \partial_\mu K^\mu , \qquad (4.11)$$

where

$$K^\mu = -\frac{g^2}{32\pi^2} 2\epsilon^{\mu\nu\rho\sigma} W_\nu^p (\partial_\rho W_\sigma^p + \frac{g}{3}\epsilon^{pqr} W_\rho^q W_\sigma^r) \quad (4.12)$$
$$+ \frac{g'^2}{32\pi^2}\epsilon^{\mu\nu\rho\sigma} B_\nu B_{\rho\sigma} \; .$$

This violation is due to the vacuum structure of non-abelian gauge theories. Change in B and L numbers are related to change in topological charges,

$$B(t_f) - B(t_i) = \int_{t_i}^{t_f} dt \int d^3x \, \partial^\mu J_\mu^B \quad (4.13)$$
$$= N_f [N_{cs}(t_f) - N_{cs}(t_i)] \; ,$$

where the topological charge of the gauge field (*i.e.* the Chern-Simons number) N_{cs} is given by,

$$N_{cs}(t) = \frac{g^3}{96\pi^2} \int d^3x \epsilon_{ijk} \epsilon^{IJK} W^{Ii} W^{Jj} W^{Kk} \; . \quad (4.14)$$

There are therefore infinitely many degenerate ground states with $\Delta N_{cs} = \pm 1, \pm 2, \ldots$, separated by a potential barrier, as depicted by Fig. 4.3. In semi-classical approximation, the probability of tunneling be-

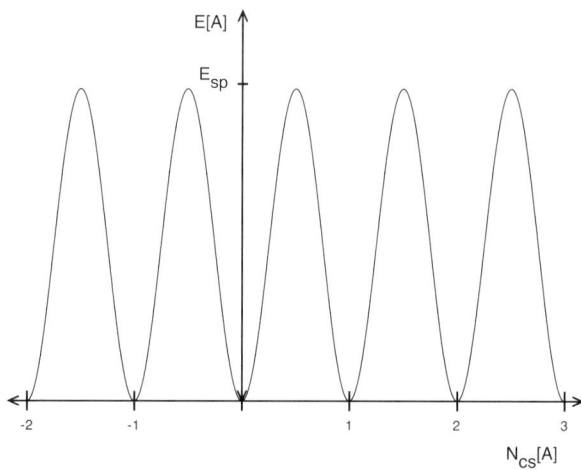

Fig. 4.3. The energy dependence of the gauge configurations A as a function of the Chern-Simons number, $N_{cs}[A]$. Sphalerons correspond to the saddle points, *i.e.* maxima of the potential.

tween neighboring vacua is determined by the instanton configurations. In

SM, as there are three generations of fermions, $\Delta B = \Delta L = N_f \Delta N_{cs} = \pm 3n$, with n being an positive integer. In other words, the vacuum to vacuum transition changes ΔB and ΔL by multiples of 3 units. As a result, the $SU(2)$ instantons lead to the following effective operator at the lowest order,

$$\mathcal{O}_{B+L} = \prod_{i=1,2,3} (q_{L_i} q_{L_i} q_{L_i} \ell_{L_i}), \quad (4.15)$$

which gives 12 fermion interactions, such as,

$$\bar{u} + \bar{d} + \bar{c} \to d + 2s + 2b + t + \nu_e + \nu_\mu + \nu_\tau. \quad (4.16)$$

At zero temperature, the transition rate is given by, $\Gamma \sim e^{-S_{int}} = e^{-4\pi/\alpha} = \mathcal{O}(10^{-165})$ [11]. The resulting transition rate is exponentially suppressed and thus it is negligible. In thermal bath, however, things can be quite different. It was pointed out by Kuzmin, Rubakov and Shaposhnikov [15] that, in thermal bath, the transitions between different gauge vacua can be made not by tunneling but through thermal fluctuations over the barrier. When temperatures are larger than the height of the barrier, the suppression due to the Boltzmann factor disappear completely, and thus the $(B+L)$ violating processes can occur at a significant rate and they can be in equilibrium in the expanding Universe. The transition rate at finite temperature in the electroweak theory is determined by the sphaleron configurations [16], which are static configurations that correspond to unstable solutions to the equations of motion. In other words, the sphaleron configurations are saddle points of the field energy of the gauge-Higgs system, as depicted in Fig. 4.3. They possess Chern-Simons number equal to $1/2$ and have energy

$$E_{sp}(T) \simeq \frac{8\pi}{g} \langle H(T) \rangle, \quad (4.17)$$

which is proportional to the Higgs vacuum expectation value (vev), $\langle H(T) \rangle$, at finite temperature T. Below the electroweak phase transition temperature, $T < T_{EW}$, (i.e. in the Higgs phase), the transition rate per unit volume is [17]

$$\frac{\Gamma_{B+L}}{V} = k \frac{M_W^7}{(\alpha T)^3} e^{-\beta E_{ph}(T)} \sim e^{\frac{-M_W}{\alpha k T}}, \quad (4.18)$$

where M_W is the mass of the W gauge boson and k is the Boltzmann constant. The transition rate is thus still very suppressed. This result can be extrapolated to high temperature symmetric phase. It was found that, in the symmetric phase, $T \geq T_{EW}$, the transition rate is [18]

$$\frac{\Gamma_{B+L}}{V} \sim \alpha^5 \ln \alpha^{-1} T^4 , \qquad (4.19)$$

where α is the fine-structure constant. Thus for $T > T_{EW}$, baryon number violating processes can be unsuppressed and profuse.

4.1.2.2. C and CP Violation

To illustrate the point that both C and CP violation are necessary in order to have baryogenesis, consider the case [19] in which superheavy X boson have baryon number violating interactions as summarized in Table 4.2. The

Table 4.2. Baryon number violating decays of the superheavy X boson in the toy model.

process	branching fraction	ΔB
$X \to qq$	α	2/3
$X \to \bar{q}\ell$	$1 - \alpha$	-1/3
$\overline{X} \to \bar{q}\bar{q}$	$\bar{\alpha}$	-2/3
$\overline{X} \to q\ell$	$1 - \bar{\alpha}$	1/3

baryon numbers produced by the decays of X and $\overline{X}$ are,

$$B_X = \alpha \left(\frac{2}{3}\right) + (1 - \alpha)\left(-\frac{1}{3}\right) = \alpha - \frac{1}{3} , \qquad (4.20)$$

$$B_{\overline{X}} = \bar{\alpha}\left(-\frac{2}{3}\right) + (1 - \bar{\alpha})\left(\frac{1}{3}\right) = -\left(\bar{\alpha} - \frac{1}{3}\right) , \qquad (4.21)$$

respectively. The net baryon number produced by the decays of the X, $\overline{X}$ pair is then,

$$\epsilon \equiv B_X + B_{\overline{X}} = (\alpha - \bar{\alpha}) . \qquad (4.22)$$

If C or CP is conserved, $\alpha = \bar{\alpha}$, it then leads to vanishing total baryon number, $\epsilon = 0$.

To be more concrete, consider a toy model [19] which consists of four fermions, $f_{1,\ldots 4}$, and two heavy scalar fields, X and Y. The interactions among these fields are described by the following Lagrangian,

$$\mathcal{L} = g_1 X f_2^\dagger f_1 + g_2 X f_4^\dagger f_3 + g_3 Y f_1^\dagger f_3 + g_4 Y f_2^\dagger f_4 + h.c. , \qquad (4.23)$$

where $g_{1,...,4}$ are the coupling constants. The Lagrangian $\mathcal{L}$ leads to the following decay processes,

$$X \to \overline{f}_1 + f_2, \overline{f}_3 + f_4 , \tag{4.24}$$

$$Y \to \overline{f}_3 + f_1, \overline{f}_4 + f_2 , \tag{4.25}$$

and the tree level diagrams of these decay processes are shown in Fig. 4.4. At the tree level, the decay rate of $X \to \overline{f}_1 + f_2$ is,

$$\Gamma(X \to \overline{f}_1 + f_2) = |g_1|^2 I_X , \tag{4.26}$$

where I_X is the phase space factor. For the conjugate process $\overline{X} \to f_1 + \overline{f}_2$, the decay rate is,

$$\Gamma(\overline{X} \to f_1 + \overline{f}_2) = |g_1^*|^2 I_{\overline{X}} . \tag{4.27}$$

As the phase space factors I_X and $I_{\overline{X}}$ are equal, no asymmetry can be generated at the tree level.

At the one-loop level, there are additional diagrams, as shown in Fig. 4.5, that have to be taken into account. Including these one-loop contributions, the decay rates for $X \to \overline{f}_1 + f_2$ and $\overline{X} \to f_1 + \overline{f}_2$ become,

$$\Gamma(X \to \overline{f}_1 + f_2) = g_1 g_2^* g_3 g_4^* I_{XY} + c.c. , \tag{4.28}$$

$$\Gamma(\overline{X} \to f_1 + \overline{f}_2) = g_1^* g_2 g_3^* g_4 I_{XY} + c.c. , \tag{4.29}$$

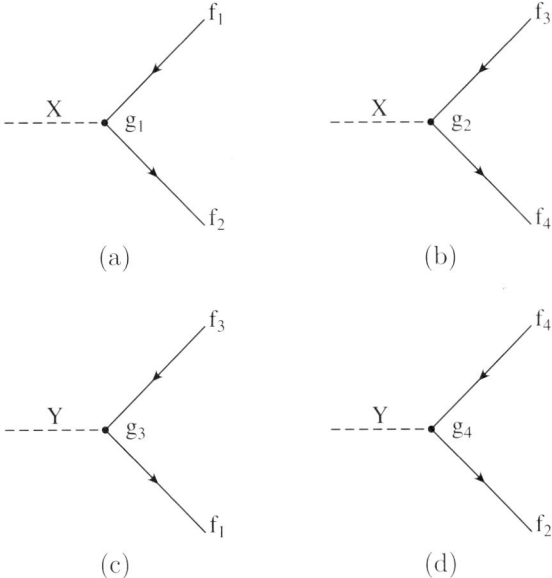

Fig. 4.4. Tree level diagrams for the decays of the heavy scalar fields, X and Y.

where c.c. stands for complex conjugation. Now I_{XY} includes both the phase space factors as well as kinematic factors arising from integrating over the internal loop momentum due to the exchange of J in I decay. If fermions $f_{1,...4}$ are allowed to propagate on-shell, then the factor I_{XY} is complex. Therefore,

$$\Gamma(X \to \overline{f}_1 + f_2) - \Gamma(\overline{X} \to f_1 + \overline{f}_2) = 4\,\text{Im}(I_{XY})\text{Im}(g_1^* g_2 g_3^* g_4). \quad (4.30)$$

Similarly, for the decay mode, $X \to \overline{f}_3 + f_4$, we have,

$$\Gamma(X \to \overline{f}_3 f_4) - \Gamma(\overline{X} \to f_3 + \overline{f}_4) = -4\,\text{Im}(I_{XY})\text{Im}(g_1^* g_2 g_3^* g_4). \quad (4.31)$$

Note that, in addition to the one-loop diagrams shown in Fig. 4.5, there are also diagrams that involve the same boson as the decaying one. However, contributions to the asymmetry from these diagrams vanish as the interference term in this case is proportional to $Im(g_i g_i^* g_i g_i^*) = 0$. The total baryon number asymmetry due to X decays is thus given by,

$$\epsilon_X = \frac{(B_1 - B_2)\Delta\Gamma(X \to \overline{f}_1 + f_2) + (B_4 - B_3)\Delta\Gamma(X \to \overline{f}_3 + f_4)}{\Gamma_X}, \quad (4.32)$$

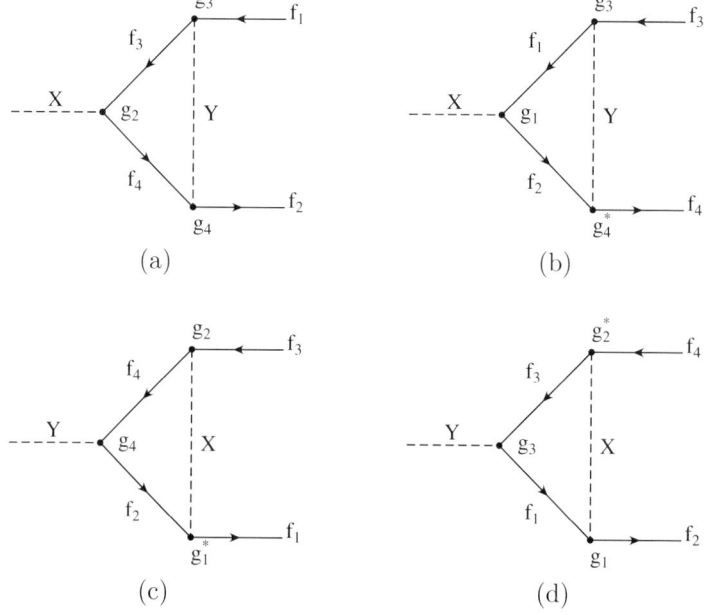

Fig. 4.5. One loop diagrams for the decays of the heavy scalar fields, X and Y, that contribute to the asymmetry.

where

$$\Delta\Gamma(X \to \overline{f}_1 + f_2) = \Gamma(X \to \overline{f}_1 + f_2) - \Gamma(\overline{X} \to f_1 + \overline{f}_2), \quad (4.33)$$
$$\Delta\Gamma(X \to \overline{f}_3 + f_4) = \Gamma(X \to \overline{f}_3 + f_4) - \Gamma(\overline{X} \to f_3 + \overline{f}_4). \quad (4.34)$$

Similar expression can be derived for the Y decays. The total asymmetries due to the decays of the superheavy bosons, X and Y, are then given, respectively, by

$$\epsilon_X = \frac{4}{\Gamma_X}\text{Im}(I_{XY})\text{Im}(g_1^* g_2 g_3^* g_4)[(B_4 - B_3) - (B_2 - B_1)], \quad (4.35)$$
$$\epsilon_Y = \frac{4}{\Gamma_Y}\text{Im}(I'_{XY})\text{Im}(g_1^* g_2 g_3^* g_4)[(B_2 - B_4) - (B_1 - B_3)]. \quad (4.36)$$

By inspecting Eq. 4.35 and 4.36, it is clear that the following three conditions must be satisfied to have a non-zero total asymmetry, $\epsilon = \epsilon_X + \epsilon_Y$:

- The presence of the two baryon number violating bosons, each of which has to have mass greater than the sum of the masses of the fermions in the internal loop;
- The coupling constants have to be complex. The C and CP violation then arise from the interference between the tree level and one-loop diagrams. In general, the asymmetry generated is proportional to $\epsilon \sim \alpha^n$, with n being the number of loops in the lowest order diagram that give non-zero asymmetry and $\alpha \sim g^2/4\pi$;
- The heavy particles X and Y must have non-degenerate masses. Otherwise, $\epsilon_X = -\epsilon_Y$, which leads to vanishing total asymmetry, ϵ.

4.1.2.3. *Departure from Thermal Equilibrium*

The baryon number B is odd under the C and CP transformations. Using this property of B together with the requirement that the Hamiltonian, H, commutes with CPT, the third condition can be seen by calculating the average of B in equilibrium at temperature $T = 1/\beta$,

$$< B >_T = \text{Tr}[e^{-\beta H} B] = \text{Tr}[(CPT)(CPT)^{-1} e^{-\beta H} B)] \quad (4.37)$$
$$= \text{Tr}[e^{-\beta H}(CPT)^{-1} B (CPT)] = -\text{Tr}[e^{-\beta H} B].$$

In equilibrium, the average $< B >_T$ thus vanishes, and there is no generation of net baryon number. Different mechanisms for baryogenesis differ in the way the departure from thermal equilibrium is realized. There are three possible ways to achieve departure from thermal equilibrium that have been utilized in baryogenesis mechanisms:

- Out-of-equilibrium decay of heavy particles: GUT Baryogenesis, Leptogenesis;
- EW phase transition: EW Baryogenesis;
- Dynamics of topological defects.

In leptogenesis, the departure from thermal equilibrium is achieved through the out-of-equilibrium decays of heavy particles in an expanding Universe. If the decay rate Γ_X of some superheavy particles X with mass M_X at the time when they become non-relativistic (*i.e.* $T \sim M_X$) is much smaller than the expansion rate of the Universe, the X particles cannot decay on the time scale of the expansion. The X particles will then remain their initial thermal abundance, $n_X = n_{\overline{X}} \sim n_\gamma \sim T^3$, for $T \lesssim M_X$. In other words, at some temperature $T > M_X$, the superheavy particles X are so weakly interacting that they cannot catch up with the expansion of the Universe. Hence they decouple from the thermal bath while still being relativistic. At the time of the decoupling, $n_X \sim n_{\overline{X}} \sim T^3$. Therefore, they populate the Universe at $T \simeq M_X$ with abundance much larger than their abundance in equilibrium. Recall that in equilibrium,

$$n_X = n_{\overline{X}} \simeq n_\gamma \quad \text{for} \quad T \gtrsim M_X, \tag{4.38}$$

$$n_X = n_{\overline{X}} \simeq (M_X T)^{3/2} e^{-M_X/T} \ll n_\gamma \quad \text{for} \quad T \lesssim M_X. \tag{4.39}$$

This over-abundance at temperature below M_X, as shown in Fig. 4.6, is the departure from thermal equilibrium needed to produce a final non-vanishing baryon asymmetry, when the heavy states, X, undergo B and CP violating decays. The scale of rates of these decay processes involving X and $\overline{X}$ relative to the expansion rate of the Universe is determined by M_X,

$$\frac{\Gamma}{H} \propto \frac{1}{M_X}. \tag{4.40}$$

The out-of-equilibrium condition, $\Gamma < H$, thus requires very heavy states: for gauge bosons, $M_X \gtrsim (10^{15-16})$ GeV; for scalars, $M_X \gtrsim (10^{10-16})$ GeV, assuming these heavy particles decay through renormalizable operators. Precise computation of the abundance is carried out by solving the Boltzmann equations (more details in Sec. 4.2.1.2).

4.1.3. Relating Baryon and Lepton Asymmetries

One more ingredient that is needed for leptogenesis is to relate lepton number asymmetry to the baryon number asymmetry, at the high temperature, symmetric phase of the SM [1]. In a weakly coupled plasma with temperature T and volume V, a chemical potential μ_i can be assigned to each of the quark, lepton and Higgs fields, i. There are therefore $5N_f + 1$ chemical potentials in the SM with one Higgs doublet and N_f generations of fermions. The corresponding partition function is given by,

$$Z(\mu, T, V) = \text{Tr}[e^{-\beta(H - \sum_i \mu_i Q_i)}] \qquad (4.41)$$

where $\beta = 1/T$, H is the Hamiltonian and Q_i is the charge operator for the corresponding field. The asymmetry in particle and antiparticle number densities is given by the derivative of the thermal-dynamical potential,

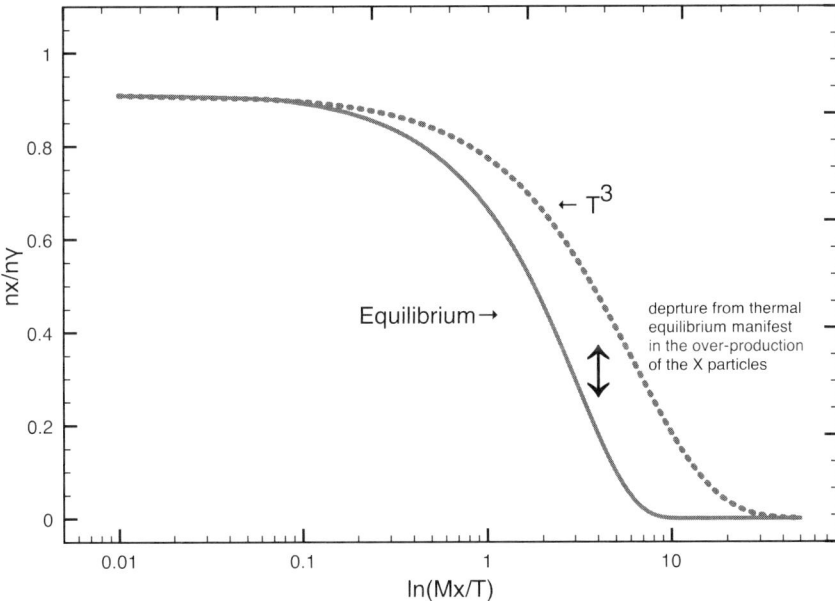

Fig. 4.6. The distribution of the X particles in thermal equilibrium (blue curve) follows Eq. 4.38 and 4.39. When departure from the thermal equilibrium occurs, the distribution of the X particles remains the same as the thermal distribution (red dashed curve).

$\Omega(\mu, T)$, as

$$n_i - \overline{n}_i = -\frac{\partial \Omega(\mu, T)}{\partial \mu_i}, \qquad (4.42)$$

where $\Omega(\mu, T)$ is defined as,

$$\Omega(\mu, T) = -\frac{T}{V} \ln Z(\mu, T, V). \qquad (4.43)$$

For a non-interacting gas of massless particles, assuming $\beta\mu_i \ll 1$,

$$n_i - \overline{n}_i = \frac{1}{6} g T^3 \begin{cases} \beta\mu_i + \mathcal{O}((\beta\mu_i)^3), & \text{fermions} \\ 2\beta\mu_i + \mathcal{O}((\beta\mu_i)^3), & \text{bosons}. \end{cases} \qquad (4.44)$$

In the high temperature plasma, quarks, leptons and Higgs interact via the guage and Yukawa couplings. In addition, there are non-perturbative sphaleron processes. All these processes give rise to constraints among various chemical potentials in thermal equilibrium. These include [1]:

(1) The effective 12-fermion interactions $\mathcal{O}_{B+L}$ induced by the sphalerons give rise to the following relation,

$$\sum_i (3\mu_{q_i} + \mu_{\ell_i}) = 0. \qquad (4.45)$$

(2) The SU(3) QCD instanton processes lead to interactions between LH and RH quarks. These interactions are described by the operator, $\prod_i (q_{L_i} q_{L_i} u_{R_i}^c d_{R_i}^c)$. When in equilibrium, they lead to,

$$\sum_i (2\mu_{q_i} - \mu_{u_i} - \mu_{d_i}) = 0. \qquad (4.46)$$

(3) Total hypercharge of the plasma has to vanish at all temperatures. This gives,

$$\sum_i \left(\mu_{q_i} + 2\mu_{u_i} - \mu_{d_i} - \mu_{\ell_i} - \mu_{e_i} + \frac{2}{N_f} \mu_H \right) = 0. \qquad (4.47)$$

(4) The Yukawa interactions yield the following relations among chemical potential of the LH and RH fermions,

$$\mu_{q_i} - \mu_H - \mu_{d_j} = 0, \qquad (4.48)$$
$$\mu_{q_i} + \mu_H - \mu_{u_j} = 0, \qquad (4.49)$$
$$\mu_{\ell_i} - \mu_H - \mu_{e_j} = 0. \qquad (4.50)$$

From Eq. (4.44), the baryon number density $n_B = \frac{1}{6}gBT^2$ and lepton number density $n_L = \frac{1}{6}gL_iT^2$, where L_i is the individual lepton flavor number with $i = (e,\mu,\tau)$, can be expanded in terms of the chemical potentials. Hence

$$B = \sum_i (2\mu_{q_i} + \mu_{u_i} + \mu_{d_i}) \tag{4.51}$$

$$L = \sum_i L_i, \quad L_i = 2\mu_{\ell_i} + \mu_{e_i}. \tag{4.52}$$

Consider the case where all Yukawa interactions are in equilibrium. The asymmetry $(L_i - B/N_f)$ is then preserved. If we further assume equilibrium among different generations, $\mu_{\ell_i} \equiv \mu_\ell$ and $\mu_{q_i} \equiv \mu_q$, together with the sphaleron and hypercharge constraints, all the chemical potentials can then be expressed in terms of μ_ℓ,

$$\mu_e = \frac{2N_f + 3}{6N_f + 3}\mu_\ell, \quad \mu_d = -\frac{6N_f + 1}{6N_f + 3}\mu_\ell, \quad \mu_u = \frac{2N_f - 1}{6N_f + 3}\mu_\ell$$
$$\mu_q = -\frac{1}{3}\mu_\ell, \quad \mu_H = \frac{4N_f}{6N_f + 3}\mu_\ell. \tag{4.53}$$

The corresponding B and L asymmetries are

$$B = -\frac{4}{3}N_f\mu_\ell, \tag{4.54}$$

$$L = \frac{14N_f^2 + 9N_f}{6N_f + 3}\mu_\ell. \tag{4.55}$$

Thus B, L and $B - L$ are related by:

$$B = c_s(B - L), \quad L = (c_s - 1)(B - L), \tag{4.56}$$

where

$$c_s = \frac{8N_f + 4}{22N_f + 13}. \tag{4.57}$$

For models with N_H Higgses, the parameter c_s is given by,

$$c_s = \frac{8N_f + 4N_H}{22N_f + 13N_H}. \tag{4.58}$$

For $T = 100$ GeV $\sim 10^{12}$ GeV, which is of interest of baryogenesis, gauge interactions are in equilibrium. Nevertheless, the Yukawa interactions are in equilibrium only in a more restricted temperature range. But these effects are generally small, and thus will be neglected in these lectures. These effects have been investigated recently; they will be discussed in Sec. 4.5.

4.1.4. *Mechanisms for Baryogenesis and Their Problems*

There have been many mechanisms for baryogenesis proposed. Each has attractive and problematic aspects, which we discuss below.

4.1.4.1. *GUT Baryongenesis*

The GUT baryogenesis was the first implementation of Sakharov's B-number generation idea. The B-number violation is an unavoidable consequence in grand unified models, as quarks and leptons are unified in the same representation of a single group. Furthermore, sufficient amount of CP violation can be incorporated naturally in GUT models, as there exist many possible complex phases, in addition to those that are present in the SM. The relevant time scales of the decays of heavy gauge bosons or scalars are slow, compared to the expansion rate of the Universe at early epoch of the cosmic evolution. The decays of these heavy particles are thus inherently out-of-equilibrium.

Even though GUT models naturally encompass all three Sakharov's conditions, there are also challenges these models face. First of all, to generate sufficient baryon number asymmetry requires high reheating temperature. This in turn leads to dangerous production of relic particles, such as gravitinos (see Sec. 4.2.3). As the relevant physics scale $M_{GUT} \sim 10^{16}$ GeV is far above the electroweak scale, it is also very hard to test GUT models experimentally using colliders. The electroweak theory ensures that there are copious B-violating processes between the GUT scale and the electroweak scale. These sphaleron processes violate $B+L$, but conserve $B-L$. Therefore, unless a GUT mechanism generates an excess of $B-L$, any baryon asymmetry produced will be equilibrated to zero by the sphaleron effects. As $U(1)_{B-L}$ is a gauged subgroup of $SO(10)$, GUT models based on $SO(10)$ are especially attractive for baryogenesis.

4.1.4.2. *EW Baryogenesis*

In electroweak baryogenesis, the departure from thermal equilibrium is provided by strong first order phase transition. The nice feature of this mechanism is that it can be probed in collider experiments. On the other hand, the allowed parameter space is very small. It requires more CP violation than what is provided in the SM. Even though there are additional sources of CP violation in MSSM, the requirement of strong first order phase transition translates into a stringent bound on the Higgs mass, $m_H \lesssim 120$ GeV.

To obtain a Higgs mass of this order, the stop mass needs to be smaller than, or of the order of, the top quark mass, which implies fine-tuning in the model parameters.

4.1.4.3. Affleck-Dine Baryogensis

The Affleck-Dine baryogenesis [20] involves cosmological evolution of scalar fields which carry B charges. It is most naturally implemented in SUSY theories. Nevertheless, this mechanism faces the same challenges as in GUT baryogenesis and in EW baryogenesis.

4.1.5. Sources of CP Violation

In the SM, C is maximally broken, since only LH electron couples to the $SU(2)_L$ gauge fields. Furthermore, CP is not an exact symmetry in weak interaction, as observed in the Kaon and B-meson systems. The charged current in the weak interaction basis is given by,

$$\mathcal{L}_W = \frac{g}{\sqrt{2}} \overline{U}_L \gamma^\mu D_L W_\mu + h.c. , \qquad (4.59)$$

where $U_L = (u, c, t)_L$ and $D_L = (d, s, b)_L$. Quark mass matrices can be diagonalized by bi-unitary transformations,

$$\mathrm{diag}(m_u, m_c, m_t) = V_L^u M^u V_R^u , \qquad (4.60)$$

$$\mathrm{diag}(m_d, m_s, m_d) = V_L^d M^d V_R^d . \qquad (4.61)$$

Thus the charged current interaction in the mass eigenstates reads,

$$\mathcal{L}_W = \frac{g}{\sqrt{2}} \overline{U}'_L U_{CKM} \gamma^\mu D'_L W_\mu + h.c. , \qquad (4.62)$$

where $U'_L \equiv V_L^u U_L$ and $D'_L \equiv V_L^d D_L$ are the mass eigenstates, and $U_{CKM} \equiv V_L^u (V_L^d)^\dagger$ is the CKM matrix. For three families of fermions, the unitary matrix K can be parameterized by three angles and six phases. Out of these six phases, five of them can be reabsorbed by redefining the wave functions of the quarks. There is hence only one physical phase in the CKM matrix. This is the only source of CP violation in the SM. It turns out that this particular source is not strong enough to accommodate the observed matter-antimatter asymmetry. The relevant effects can be parameterized by [21],

$$B \simeq \frac{\alpha_w^4 T^3}{s} \delta_{CP} \simeq 10^{-8} \delta_{CP} , \qquad (4.63)$$

where δ_{CP} is the suppression factor due to CP violation in the SM. Since CP violation vanishes when any two of the quarks with equal charge have degenerate masses, a naive estimate gives the effects of CP violation of the size

$$A_{CP} = (m_t^2 - m_c^2)(m_c^2 - m_u^2)(m_u^2 - m_t^2) \qquad (4.64)$$
$$\cdot (m_b^2 - m_s^2)(m_s^2 - m_d^2)(m_d^2 - m_b^2) \cdot J \; .$$

Here the proportionality constant J is the usual Jarlskog invariant, which is a parameterization independent measure of CP violation in the quark sector. Together with the fact that A_{CP} is of mass (thus temperature) dimension 12, this leads to the following value for δ_{CP}, which is a dimensionless quantity,

$$\delta_{CP} \simeq \frac{A_{CP}}{T_C^{12}} \simeq 10^{-20} \; , \qquad (4.65)$$

and T_C is the temperature of the electroweak phase transition. The baryon number asymmetry due to the phase in the CKM matrix is therefore of the order of $B \sim 10^{-28}$, which is too small to account for the observed $B \sim 10^{-10}$.

In MSSM, there are new sources of CP violation due to the presence of the soft SUSY breaking sector. The superpotential of the MSSM is given by,

$$W = \mu \hat{H}_1 \hat{H}_2 + h^u \hat{H}_2 \hat{Q} \hat{u}^c + h^d \hat{H}_1 \hat{Q} \hat{d}^c + h^e \hat{H}_1 \hat{L} \hat{e}^c \; . \qquad (4.66)$$

The soft SUSY breaking sector has the following parameters:

- tri-linear couplings: $\Gamma^u H_2 \widetilde{Q} \tilde{c}^c + \Gamma^d H_1 \widetilde{Q} \tilde{d}^c + \Gamma^e H_1 \widetilde{L} \tilde{e}^c + h.c.$, where $\Gamma^{(u,d,e)} \equiv A^{(u,d,e)} \cdot h^{(u,d,e)}$;
- bi-linear coupling in the Higgs sector: $\mu B H_1 H_2$;
- gaugino masses: M_i for $i = 1, 2, 3$ (one for each gauge group);
- soft scalar masses: $\widetilde{m}_f$.

In the constrained MSSM (CMSSM) model with mSUGRA boundary conditions at the GUT scale, a universal value is assumed for the tri-linear coupling constants, $A^{(u,d,e)} = A$. Similarly, the gaugino masses and scalar masses are universal, $M_i = M$, and $\widetilde{m}_f = \widetilde{m}$. Two phases may be removed by redefining the phase of $\hat{H}_2$ such that the phase of μ is opposite to the phase of B. As a result, the product μB is real. Furthermore, the phase of M can be removed by R-symmetry transformation. This then modifies the tri-linear couplings by an additional factor of $e^{-\phi_M}$, while other coupling constants are invariant under the R-symmetry transformation. There are thus two physical phases remain,

$$\phi_A = \text{Arg}(AM), \quad \phi_\mu = -\text{Arg}(B) . \quad (4.67)$$

These phases are relevant in soft leptogenesis, which is discussed in Sec. 4.3.2.

If the neutrinos are massive, the leptonic charged current interaction in the mass eigenstates of the leptons is given by,

$$\mathcal{L}_W = \frac{g}{\sqrt{2}} \bar{\nu}'_L U^\dagger_{MNS} \gamma^\mu \ell'_L W_\mu + h.c. , \quad (4.68)$$

where $U_{MNS} = (V^\nu_L)^\dagger V^e_L$. (For a review on physics of the massive neutrinos, see, e.g. Refs. [22] and [23]. See also Rabi Mohapatra's lectures.) The matrices V^ν_L and V^e_L diagonalize the effective neutrino mass matrix and the charged lepton mass matrix, respectively. If neutrinos are Majorana particles, which is the case if small neutrino mass is explained by the seesaw mechanism [24], the Majorana condition then forbids the phase redefinition of ν_R. Unlike in the CKM matrix, in this case only three of the six complex phases can be absorbed, and there are thus two additional physical phases in the lepton sector if neutrinos are Majorana fermions. And due to this reason, CP violation can occur in the lepton sector with only two families. (Recall that in the quark sector, CP violation can occur only when the number of famalies is at least three). The MNS matrix can be parameterized as a CKM-like matrix and a diagonal phase matrix,

$$U_{MNS} = \begin{pmatrix} c_{12}c_{13} & s_{12}c_{13} & s_{13}e^{-i\delta} \\ -s_{12}c_{23} - c_{12}s_{23}s_{13}e^{i\delta} & c_{12}c_{23} - s_{12}s_{23}s_{13}e^{i\delta} & s_{23}c_{13} \\ s_{12}s_{23} - c_{12}c_{23}s_{13}e^{i\delta} & -c_{12}s_{23} - s_{12}c_{23}s_{13}e^{i\delta} & c_{23}c_{13} \end{pmatrix}$$
$$\cdot \begin{pmatrix} 1 & & \\ & e^{i\alpha_{21}/2} & \\ & & e^{i\alpha_{31}/2} \end{pmatrix} . \quad (4.69)$$

The Dirac phase δ affects neutrino oscillation (see Boris Kayser's lectures),

$$P(\nu_\alpha \to \nu_\beta) = \delta_{\alpha\beta} - 4 \sum_{i>j} \text{Re}(U_{\alpha i} U_{\beta j} U^*_{\alpha j} U^*_{\beta i}) \sin^2\left(\Delta m^2_{ij} \frac{L}{4E}\right) \quad (4.70)$$
$$+ 2 \sum_{i>j} J^{\text{lep}}_{\text{CP}} \sin^2\left(\Delta m^2_{ij} \frac{L}{4E}\right)$$

where the parameterization invariant CP violation measure, the leptonic Jarlskog invariant J_{CP}^{lep}, is given by,

$$J_{CP}^{\text{lep}} = -\frac{Im(H_{12}H_{23}H_{31})}{\Delta m_{21}^2 \Delta m_{32}^2 \Delta m_{31}^2}, \quad H \equiv (M_\nu^{eff})(M_\nu^{eff})^\dagger . \quad (4.71)$$

The two Majorana phases, α_{21} and α_{31}, affect neutrino double decay (see Petr Vogel's lectures). Their dependence in the neutrinoless double beta decay matrix element is,

$$|\langle m_{ee}\rangle|^2 = m_1^2 |U_{e1}|^4 + m_2^2 |U_{e2}|^4 + m_3^2 |U_{e3}|^4 \quad (4.72)$$
$$+ 2m_1 m_2 |U_{e1}|^2 |U_{e2}|^2 \cos\alpha_{21}$$
$$+ 2m_1 m_3 |U_{e1}|^2 |U_{e3}|^2 \cos\alpha_{31}$$
$$+ 2m_2 m_3 |U_{e2}|^2 |U_{e3}|^2 \cos(\alpha_{31} - \alpha_{21}) .$$

The Lagrangian at high energy that describe the lepton sector of the SM in the presence of the right-handed neurinos, ν_{R_i}, is given by,

$$\mathcal{L} = \overline{\ell}_{L_i} i\gamma^\mu \partial_\mu \ell_{L_i} + \overline{e}_{R_i} i\gamma^\mu \partial_\mu e_{R_i} + \overline{N}_{R_i} i\gamma^\mu \partial_\mu N_{R_i} \quad (4.73)$$
$$+ f_{ij} \overline{e}_{R_i} \ell_{L_j} H^\dagger + h_{ij} \overline{N}_{R_i} \ell_{L_j} H - \frac{1}{2} M_{ij} N_{R_i} N_{R_j} + h.c. .$$

Without loose of generality, in the basis where f_{ij} and M_{ij} are diagonal, the Yukawa matrix h_{ij} is in general a complex matrix. For 3 families, h has nine phases. Out of these nine phases, three can be absorbed into wave functions of ℓ_{L_i}. Therefore, there are six physical phases remain. Furthermore, a real h_{ij} can be diagonalized by a bi-unitary transformation, which is defined in terms of six mixing angles. After integrating out the heavy Majorana neutrinos, the effective Lagrangian that describes the neutrino sector below the seesaw scale is,

$$\mathcal{L}_{eff} = \overline{\ell}_{L_i} i\gamma^\mu \partial_\mu \ell_{L_i} + \overline{e}_{R_i} i\gamma^\mu \partial_\mu e_{R_i} + f_{ii} \overline{e}_{R_i} \ell_{L_i} H^\dagger \quad (4.74)$$
$$+ \frac{1}{2} \sum_k h_{ik}^T h_{kj} \ell_{L_i} \ell_{L_j} \frac{H^2}{M_k} + h.c. .$$

This leads to an effective neutrino Majorana mass matrix whose parameters can be measured at the oscillation experiments. As Majorana mass matrix is symmetric, for three families, it has six independent complex elements and thus six complex phases. Out of these six phases, three of them can be absorbed into the wave functions of the charged leptons. Hence at low energy, there are only three physical phases and three mixing angles in the lepton sector. Going from high energy to low energy, the numbers of mixing angles and phases are thus reduced by half. Due to the presence of the additional mixing angles and complex phases in the heavy neutrino sector, it is generally not possible to connect leptogenesis with low energy CP violation. However, in some specific models, such connection can be established. This will be discussed in more details in Sec. 4.4.

4.2. Standard Leptogenesis

4.2.1. *Standard Leptogenesis (Majorana Neutrinos)*

As mentioned in the previous section, baryon number violation arises naturally in many grand unified theories. In the GUT baryogenesis, the asymmetry is generated through the decays of heavy gauge bosons (denoted by "V" in the following) or leptoquarks (denoted by "S" in the following), which are particles that carry both B and L numbers. In GUTs based on $SU(5)$, the heavy gauge bosons or heavy leptoquarks have the following B-non-conserving decays,

$$V \to \bar{\ell}_L u_R^c, \qquad B = -1/3, \quad B-L = 2/3 \qquad (4.75)$$
$$V \to q_L d_R^c, \qquad B = 2/3, \quad B-L = 2/3 \qquad (4.76)$$
$$S \to \bar{\ell}_L \bar{q}_L, \qquad B = -1/3, \quad B-L = 2/3 \qquad (4.77)$$
$$S \to q_L q_L, \qquad B = 2/3, \quad B-L = 2/3. \qquad (4.78)$$

Since $(B-L)$ is conserved, *i.e.* the heavy particles V and S both carry $(B-L)$ charges $2/3$, no $(B-L)$ can be generated dynamically. In addition, due to the sphaleron processes, $\langle B \rangle = \langle B-L \rangle = 0$. In $SO(10)$, $(B-L)$ is spontaneously broken, as it is a gauged subgroup of $SO(10)$. Heavy particles X with $M_X < M_{B-L}$ can then generate a $(B-L)$ asymmetry through their decays. Nevertheless, for $M_X \sim M_{GUT} \sim 10^{15}$ GeV, the CP asymmetry is highly suppressed. Furthermore, one also has to worry about the large reheating temperature $T_{RH} \sim M_{GUT}$ after the inflation, the realization of thermal equilibrium, and in supersymmetric case, the gravitino problem. These difficulties in GUT baryogenesis had led to a lot of interests in EW baryogenesis, which also has its own disadvantages as discussed in Sec. 4.1.4.

The recent advent of the evidence of neutrino masses from various neutrino oscillation experiments opens up a new possibility of generating the asymmetry through the decay of the heavy neutrinos [25]. A particular attractive framework in which small neutrino masses can naturally arise is GUT based on $SO(10)$ (for a review, see, *i.e.* Ref. [22]). $SO(10)$ GUT models accommodate the existence of RH neutrinos,

$$\psi(16) = (q_L, u_R^c, e_R^c, d_R^c, \ell_L, \nu_R^c), \quad (4.79)$$

which is unified along with the fifteen known fermions of each family into a single 16-dimensional spinor representation. For hierarchical fermion masses, one easily has

$$M_N \ll M_{B-L} \sim M_{GUT}, \quad (4.80)$$

where $N = \nu_R + \nu_R^c$ is a Majorana fermion. The decays of the right-handed neutrino,

$$N \to \ell H, \quad N \to \overline{\ell}\,\overline{H}, \quad (4.81)$$

where H is the $SU(2)$ Higgs doublet, can lead to a lepton number asymmetry. After the sphaleron processes, the lepton number asymmetry is then converted into a baryon number asymmetry.

The most general Lagrangian involving charged leptons and neutrinos is given by,

$$\mathcal{L}_Y = f_{ij}\overline{e}_{R_i}\ell_{L_j}H^\dagger + h_{ij}\overline{\nu}_{R_i}\ell_{L_j}H - \frac{1}{2}(M_R)_{ij}\overline{\nu}_{R_i}^c\nu_{R_j} + h.c.. \quad (4.82)$$

As the RH neutrinos are singlets under the SM gauge group, Majorana masses for the RH neutrinos are allowed by the gauge invariance. Upon the electroweak symmetry breaking, the SM Higgs doublet gets a VEV, $\langle H \rangle = v$, and the charged leptons and the neutrino Dirac masses, which are much smaller than the RH neutrino Majorana masses, are generated,

$$m_\ell = fv, \quad m_D = hv \ll M_R. \quad (4.83)$$

The neutrino sector is therefore described by a 2×2 seesaw matrix as,

$$\begin{pmatrix} 0 & m_D \\ m_D^T & M_R \end{pmatrix}. \quad (4.84)$$

Diagonalizing this 2×2 seesaw matrix, the light and heavy neutrino mass eigenstates are obtained as,

$$\nu \simeq V_\nu^T \nu_L + V_\nu^* \nu_L^c, \quad N \simeq \nu_R + \nu_R^c \quad (4.85)$$

with corresponding masses

$$m_\nu \simeq -V_\nu^T m_D^T \frac{1}{M_R} m_D V_\nu, \quad m_N \simeq M_R. \quad (4.86)$$

Here the unitary matrix V_ν is the diagonalization matrix of the neutrino Dirac matrix.

At temperature $T < M_R$, RH neutrinos can generate a lepton number asymmetry by means of out-of-equilibrium decays. The sphaleron processes then convert ΔL into ΔB.

4.2.1.1. *The Asymmetry*

At the tree level, the ith RH neutrino decays into the Higgs doublet and the charged lepton doublet of α flavor, $N_i \to H + \ell_\alpha$, where $\alpha = (e, \mu, \tau)$. The total width of this decay is,

$$\Gamma_{D_i} = \sum_\alpha [\Gamma(N_i \to H + \ell_\alpha) + \Gamma(N_i \to \overline{H} + \overline{\ell}_\alpha)] \qquad (4.87)$$

$$= \frac{1}{8\pi}(hh^\dagger)_{ii} M_i .$$

Suppose that the lepton number violating interactions of the lightest right-handed neutrino, N_1, wash out any lepton number asymmetry generated in the decay of $N_{2,3}$ at temperatures $T \gg M_1$. (For effects due to the decays of $N_{2,3}$, see Ref. [26].) In this case with N_1 decay dominating, the final asymmetry only depends on the dynamics of N_1. The out-of-equilibrium condition requires that the total width for N_1 decay, Γ_{D_1}, to be smaller compared to the expansion rate of the Universe at temperature $T = M_1$,

$$\Gamma_{D_1} < H \bigg|_{T=M_1} . \qquad (4.88)$$

That is, the heavy neutrinos are not able to follow the rapid change of the equilibrium particle distribution, once the temperature dropped below the mass M_1. Eventually, heavy neutrinos will decay, and a lepton asymmetry is generated due to the CP asymmetry that arises through the interference of the tree level and one-loop diagrams, as shown in Fig. 4.7,

$$\epsilon_1 = \frac{\sum_\alpha [\Gamma(N_1 \to \ell_\alpha H) - \Gamma(N_1 \to \overline{\ell}_\alpha \overline{H})]}{\sum_\alpha [\Gamma(N_1 \to \ell_\alpha H) + \Gamma(N_1 \to \overline{\ell}_\alpha \overline{H})]} \qquad (4.89)$$

$$\simeq \frac{1}{8\pi} \frac{1}{(h_\nu h_\nu)_{11}} \sum_{i=2,3} \text{Im}\{(h_\nu h_\nu^\dagger)^2_{1i}\} \cdot \left[f\left(\frac{M_i^2}{M_1^2}\right) + g\left(\frac{M_i^2}{M_1^2}\right) \right] .$$

In Fig. 4.7, the diagram (b) is the one-lop vertex correction, which gives the term, $f(x)$, in Eq. 4.89 after carrying out the loop integration,

$$f(x) = \sqrt{x}\left[1 - (1+x)\ln\left(\frac{1+x}{x}\right)\right] . \qquad (4.90)$$

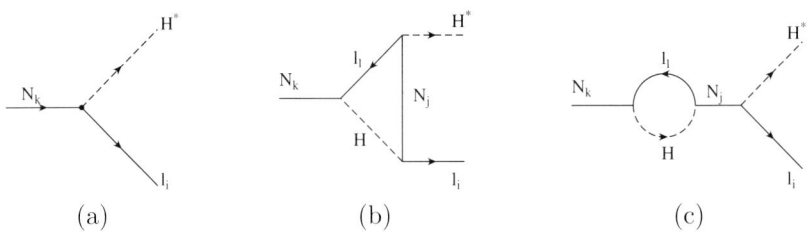

Fig. 4.7. Diagrams in SM with RH neutrinos that contribute to the lepton number asymmetry through the decays of the RH neutrinos. The asymmetry is generated due to the interference of the tree-level diagram (a) and the one-loop vertex correction (b) and self-energy (c) diagrams.

Diagram (c) is the one-loop self-energy. For $|M_i - M_1| \gg |\Gamma_i - \Gamma_1|$, the self-energy diagram gives the term

$$g(x) \equiv \frac{\sqrt{x}}{1-x}, \qquad (4.91)$$

in Eq. 4.89. For hierarchical RH neutrino masses, $M_1 \ll M_2, M_3$, the asymmetry is then given by,

$$\epsilon_1 \simeq -\frac{3}{8\pi} \frac{1}{(h_\nu h_\nu^\dagger)_{11}} \sum_{i=2,3} \text{Im}\{(h_\nu h_\nu^\dagger)_{1i}^2\} \frac{M_1}{M_i}. \qquad (4.92)$$

Note that when N_k and N_j in the self-energy diagram (c) have near degenerate masses, there can be resonant enhancement in the contributions from the self-energy diagram to the asymmetry. Such resonant effect can allow M_1 to be much lower while still generating sufficient amount of the lepton number asymmetry. This will be discussed in Sec. 4.3.1.

To prevent the generated asymmetry given in Eq. 4.89 from being washed out by the inverse decay and scattering processes, the decay of the RH neutrinos has to be out-of-equilibrium. In other words, the condition

$$r \equiv \frac{\Gamma_1}{H|_{T=M_1}} = \frac{M_{pl}}{(1.7)(32\pi)\sqrt{g_*}} \frac{(h_\nu h_\nu^\dagger)_{11}}{M_1} < 1, \qquad (4.93)$$

has to be satisfied. This leads to the following constraint on the effective light neutrino mass

$$\widetilde{m}_1 \equiv (h_\nu h_\nu^\dagger)_{11} \frac{v^2}{M_1} \simeq 4\sqrt{g_*} \frac{v^2}{M_{pl}} \frac{\Gamma_{D_1}}{H}\bigg|_{T=M_1} < 10^{-3} \text{ eV}, \qquad (4.94)$$

where g_* is the number of relativistic degrees of freedom. For SM, $g_* \simeq 106.75$, while for MSSM, $g_* \simeq 228.75$. The wash-out effect is parameterized by the coefficient κ, and the final amount of lepton asymmetry is given by,

$$Y_L \equiv \frac{n_L - \bar{n}_L}{s} = \kappa \frac{\epsilon_1}{g_*} , \qquad (4.95)$$

where κ parameterizes the amount of wash-out due to the inverse decays and scattering processes. The amount of wash-out depends on the size of the parameter r:

(1) If $r \ll 1$ for decay temperature $T_D \lesssim M_X$, the inverse decay and 2-2 scattering are impotent. In this case, the inverse decay width is given by,

$$\frac{\Gamma_{ID}}{H} \sim \left(\frac{M_X}{T}\right)^{3/2} e^{-M_X/T} \cdot r , \qquad (4.96)$$

while the width for the scattering processes is,

$$\frac{\Gamma_S}{H} \sim \alpha \left(\frac{T}{M_X}\right)^5 \cdot r . \qquad (4.97)$$

Thus the inverse decays and scattering processes can be safely ignored, and the asymmetry ΔB produced by decays is not destroyed by the asymmetry $-\Delta B$ produced in inverse decays and scatterings. At $T \simeq T_D$, the number density of the heavy particles X has thermal distribution, $n_X \simeq n_{\bar{X}} \simeq n_\gamma$. Thus the net baryon neumber density produced by out-of-equilibrium decays is

$$n_L = \epsilon_1 \cdot n_X \simeq \epsilon_1 \cdot n_\gamma . \qquad (4.98)$$

(2) For $r \gg 1$, the abundance of X and $\bar{X}$ follows the equilibrium values, and there is no departure from thermal equilibrium. As a result, no lepton number may evolve, and the net lepton asymmetry vanishes,

$$\frac{n_\ell - n_{\bar{\ell}}}{dt} + 3H(n_\ell - n_{\bar{\ell}}) = \Delta \gamma^{eq} = 0 . \qquad (4.99)$$

In general, for $1 < r < 10$, there could still be sizable asymmetry. The wash out effects due to inverse decay and lepton number violating scattering processes together with the time evolution of the system is then accounted for by the factor κ, which is obtained by solving the Boltzmann equations

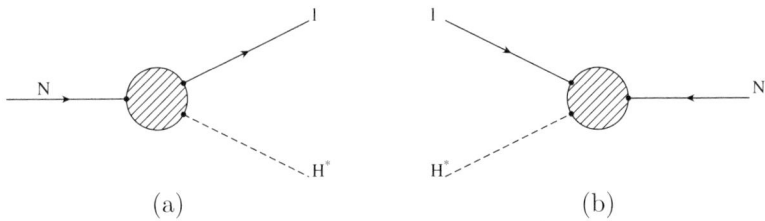

Fig. 4.8. Decay and inverse decay processes in the thermal bath.

for the system (see next section). An approximation is given by [19],

$$10^6 \lesssim r : \kappa = (0.1r)^{1/2} e^{-\frac{4}{3}(0.1)^{1/4}} \quad (<10^{-7}) \quad (4.100)$$

$$10 \lesssim r \lesssim 10^6 : \kappa = \frac{0.3}{r(\ln r)^{0.8}} \quad (10^{-2} \sim 10^{-7}) \quad (4.101)$$

$$0 \lesssim r \lesssim 10 : \kappa = \frac{1}{2\sqrt{r^2+9}} \quad (10^{-1} \sim 10^{-2}). \quad (4.102)$$

The EW sphaleron effects then convert Y_L into Y_B,

$$Y_B \equiv \frac{n_B - n_{\overline{B}}}{s} = c Y_{B-L} = \frac{c}{c-1} Y_L, \quad (4.103)$$

where c is the conversion factor derived in Sec. 4.1.3.

4.2.1.2. Boltzmann Equations

As the decays of RH neutrinos are out-of-equilibrium processes, they are generally treated by Boltzmann equations. Main processes in the thermal bath that are relevant for leptogenesis include,

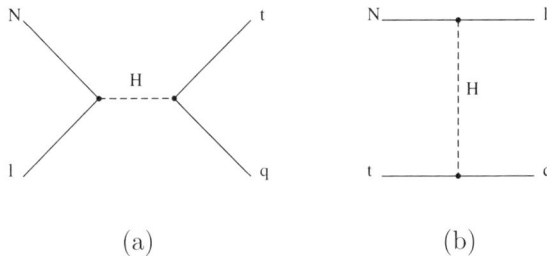

Fig. 4.9. The $\Delta L = 1$ scattering processes in the thermal bath.

(1) decay of N (Fig. 4.8 (a)):

$$N \to \ell + H, \qquad N \to \overline{\ell} + \overline{H} \quad (4.104)$$

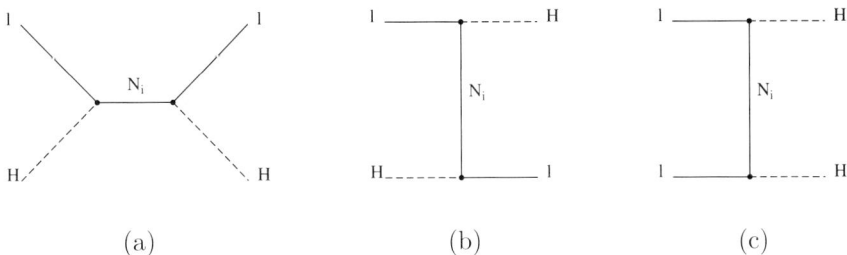

Fig. 4.10. The $\Delta L = 2$ scattering processes in the thermal bath.

(2) inverse decay of N (Fig. 4.8 (b)):

$$\ell + H \to N, \qquad \overline{\ell} + \overline{H} \to N \qquad (4.105)$$

(3) 2-2 scattering: These include the following $\Delta L = 1$ scattering processes (Fig. 4.9),

$$[\text{s-channel}]: \quad N_1 \ell \leftrightarrow t\overline{q} \;,\quad N_1 \overline{\ell} \leftrightarrow \overline{t}\,q \qquad (4.106)$$

$$[\text{t-channel}]: \quad N_1 t \leftrightarrow \overline{\ell}\,q \;,\quad N_1 \overline{t} \leftrightarrow \ell\,\overline{q} \qquad (4.107)$$

and $\Delta L = 2$ scattering processes (Fig. 4.10),

$$\ell H \leftrightarrow \overline{\ell}\,\overline{H} \;,\quad \ell\ell \leftrightarrow \overline{H}\,\overline{H},\; \overline{\ell}\,\overline{\ell} \leftrightarrow H H \,. \qquad (4.108)$$

Basically, at temperatures $T \gtrsim M_1$, these $\Delta L = 1$ and $\Delta L = 2$ processes have to be strong enough to keep N_1 in equilibrium. Yet at temperature $T \lesssim M_1$, these processes have to be weak enough to allow N_1 to generate an asymmetry.

The Boltzmann equations that govern the evolutions of the RH neutrino number density and $B - L$ number density are given by [27],

$$\frac{dN_{N_1}}{dz} = -(D + S)(N_{N_1} - N_{N_1}^{eq}) \qquad (4.109)$$

$$\frac{dN_{B-L}}{dz} = -\epsilon_1 D(N_{N_1} - N_{N_1}^{eq}) - W N_{B-L} \,, \qquad (4.110)$$

where

$$(D, S, W) \equiv \frac{(\Gamma_D, \Gamma_S, \Gamma_W)}{Hz}, \quad z = \frac{M_1}{T} \,. \qquad (4.111)$$

Here Γ_D includes both decay and inverse decay, Γ_S includes $\Delta L = 1$ scattering processes and Γ_W includes inverse decay and $\Delta L = 1$, $\Delta L = 2$

scattering processes. The N_1 abundance is affected by the decay, inverse decay and the $\Delta L = 1$ scattering processes. It is manifest in Eq. 4.110 that the N_1 decay is the source for $(B - L)$, while the inverse decay and the $\Delta L = 1, 2$ scattering processes wash out the asymmetry. The generic behavior of the solutions to the Boltzmann equations is shown in Fig. 4.11.

4.2.1.3. *Bounds on Neutrino Masses*

In the case with strongly hierarchical right-handed neutrino masses, when the asymmetry ϵ_1 due to the decay of the lightest right-handed neutrino, N_1, contribute dominantly to the total asymmetry, leptogenesis becomes very predictive [1, 4, 27], provided that N_1 decays at temperature $T \gtrsim 10^{12}$ GeV. In particular, various bounds on the neutrino masses can be obtained.

For strongly hierarchyical masses, $M_1/M_2 \ll 1$, there is an upper bound

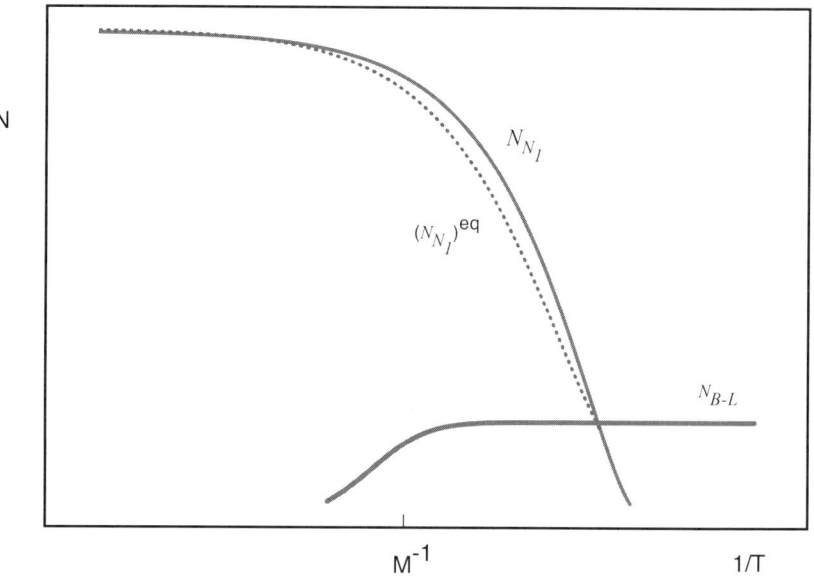

Fig. 4.11. Generic behavior of the solutions to Boltzmann equations. Here the functions N_{N_1} (red solid curve) and N_{B-L} (green solid curve) are solutions to Eq. 4.109 and 4.110. The function $(N_{N_1})^{eq}$ (blue dotted curve) is the equilibrium particle distribution.

on ϵ_1 [29], called the "Davidson-Ibarra" bound,

$$|\epsilon_1| \leq \frac{3}{16\pi} \frac{M_1(m_3 - m_2)}{v^2} \equiv \epsilon_1^{DI}, \qquad (4.112)$$

which is obtained by expanding ϵ_1 to leading order in M_1/M_2. Becuase $|m_3 - m_2| \leq \sqrt{\Delta m_{32}^2} \sim 0.05$ eV, a lower bound on M_1 then follows,

$$M_1 \geq 2 \times 10^9 \text{ GeV}. \qquad (4.113)$$

This bound in turn implies a lower bound on the reheating temperature, T_{RH}, and is in conflict with the upper bound from gravitino over production constraints if supersymmetry is incorporated. We will come back to this in Sec. 4.2.3. One should note that, in the presence of degenerate light neutrinos, the leading terms in an expansion of ϵ_1 in M_1/M_2 and M_1/M_3 vanish. However, the next to leading order terms do not vanish and in this case one has [30],

$$|\epsilon_1| \lesssim \text{Max}\left(\epsilon^{DI}, \frac{M_3^3}{M_1 M_2^2}\right). \qquad (4.114)$$

By requiring that there is no substantial washout effects, bounds on light neutrino masses can be derived. To have significant amount of baryon asymmetry, the effective mass $\tilde{m}_1$ defined in Eq. 4.94 cannot be too large. Generally $\tilde{m}_1 \lesssim 0.1 - 0.2$ is required. As the mass of the lightest active neutrino $m_1 \lesssim \tilde{m}_1$, an upper bound on m_1 thus ensues. By further requiring the $\Delta L = 2$ washout effects be consistent with successful leptogenesis impose a bound on,

$$\sqrt{(m_1^2 + m_2^2 + m_3^2)} \lesssim (0.1 - 0.2) \text{ eV}, \qquad (4.115)$$

which is of the same order as the bound on $\tilde{m}_1$. From these bounds, the absolute mass scale of neutrino masses is thus known up to a factor of ~ 3 to be in the range, $0.05 \lesssim m_3 \lesssim 0.15$ eV [4], if the observed baryonic asymmetry indeed originates from leptogenesis through the decay of N_1.

4.2.2. Dirac Leptogenesis

In the standard leptogenesis discussed in the previous section, neutrinos acquire their masses through the seesaw mechanism. The decays of the heavy right-handed neutrinos produce a non-zero lepton number asymmetry, $\Delta L \neq 0$. The electroweak sphaleron effects then convert ΔL partially into ΔB. This standard scenario relies crucially on the violation of lepton number, which is due to the presence of the heavy Majorana masses for the right-handed neutrinos.

It was pointed out [31] that leptogenesis can be implemented even in the case when neutrinos are Dirac fermions which acquire small masses through highly suppressed Yukawa couplings without violating lepton number. The realization of this depends critically on the following three characteristics of the sphaleron effects: (i) only the left-handed particles couple to the sphalerons; (ii) the sphalerons change $(B+L)$ but not $(B-L)$; (iii) the sphaleron effects are in equilibrium for $T \gtrsim T_{EW}$.

As the sphelarons couple only to the left-handed fermions, one may speculate that as long as the lepton number stored in the right-handed fermions can survive below the electroweak phase transition, a net lepton number may be generated even with $L = 0$ initially. The Yukawa couplings of the SM quarks and leptons to the Higgs boson lead to rapid left-right equilibration so that as the sphaleron effects deplete the left-handed $(B+L)$, the right-handed $(B+L)$ is converted to fill the void and therefore it is also depleted. So with $B = L = 0$ initially, no baryon asymmetry can be generated for the SM quarks and leptons. For the neutrinos, on the other hand, the left-right equilibration can occur at a much longer time scale compared to the electroweak epoch when the sphaleron washout is in effect. The left-right conversion for the neutrinos involves the Dirac Yukawa couplings, $\lambda \bar{\ell}_L H \nu_R$, where λ is the Yukawa coupling constant, and the rate for these conversion processes scales as,

$$\Gamma_{LR} \sim \lambda^2 T \,. \tag{4.116}$$

For the left-right conversion not to be in equilibrium at temperatures above some critical temperature T_{eq}, requires that

$$\Gamma_{LR} \lesssim H \,, \quad \text{for} \quad T > T_{eq} \,, \tag{4.117}$$

where the Hubble constant scales as,

$$H \sim \frac{T^2}{M_{\text{Pl}}} \,. \tag{4.118}$$

Hence the left-right equilibration can occur at a much later time, $T \lesssim T_{eq} \ll T_{EW}$, provided,

$$\lambda^2 \lesssim \frac{T_{eq}}{M_{\text{Pl}}} \ll \frac{T_{EW}}{M_{\text{Pl}}} \,. \tag{4.119}$$

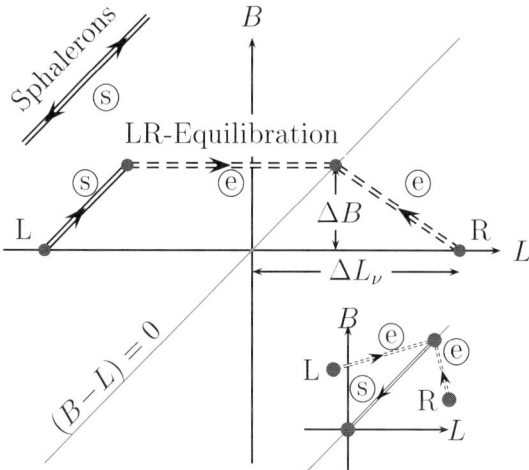

Fig. 4.12. With sufficiently small Yukawa couplings, the left-right equilibration occurs at a much later time, well below the electroweak phase transition temperature. It is therefore possible to generate a non-zero baryon number even if $B = L = 0$ initially. For the SM particles, as shown in the insert for comparison, the left-right equilibration takes place completely before or during the sphaleron processes. Thus no net baryon number can be generated if $B - L = 0$ initially. Figure taken from Ref [31].

With $M_{\text{Pl}} \sim 10^{19}$ GeV and $T_{EW} \sim 10^2$ GeV, this condition then translates into

$$\lambda < 10^{-(8\sim 9)} \, . \tag{4.120}$$

Thus for neutrino Dirac masses $m_D < 10$ keV, which is consistent with all experimental observations, the left-right equilibration does not occur until the temperature of the Universe drops to much below the temperature of the electroweak phase transition, and the lepton number stored in the right-handed neutrinos can then survive the wash-out due to the sphalerons [31].

Once we accept this, the Dirac leptogenesis then works as follows. Suppose that some processes initially produce a negative lepton number (ΔL_L), which is stored in the left-handed neutrinos, and a positive lepton number (ΔL_R), which is stored in the right-handed neutrinos. Because sphalerons only couple to the left-handed particles, part of the negative lepton number stored in left-handed neutrinos get converted into a positive baryon number by the electroweak anomaly. This negative lepton number ΔL_L with reduced magnitude eventually equilibrates with the positive lepton number, ΔL_R when the temperature of the Universe drops to $T \ll T_{EW}$. Because the equilibrating processes conserve both the baryon number B and the lepton number L separately, they result in a Universe with a total positive baryon number and a total positive lepton number. And hence a net baryon number can be generated even with $B = L = 0$ initially.

Such small neutrino Dirac Yukawa couplings required to implement Dirac leptogensis are realized in a SUSY model proposed in Ref. [32].

4.2.3. Gravitino Problem

For leptogenesis to be effective, as shown in Sec. 4.2.1.3, the mass of the lightest RH neutrino has to be $M_1 > 2 \times 10^9$ GeV. Figure 4.13 shows the lower bound on the lightest RH neutrino mass as a function of the low energy effective lightest neutrino mass, $\widetilde{m}_1$ [28, 33]. If RH neutrinos are produced thermally, the reheating temperature has to be greater than the right-handed neutrino mass, $T_{RH} > M_R$. This thus implies that $T_{RH} > 2 \times 10^9$ GeV, in order to generate sufficient baryon number asymmetry. Such a high reheating temperature is problematic as it could lead to overproduction of light states, such as gravitinos [34, 35]. If gravitinos are stable (i.e. LSP),

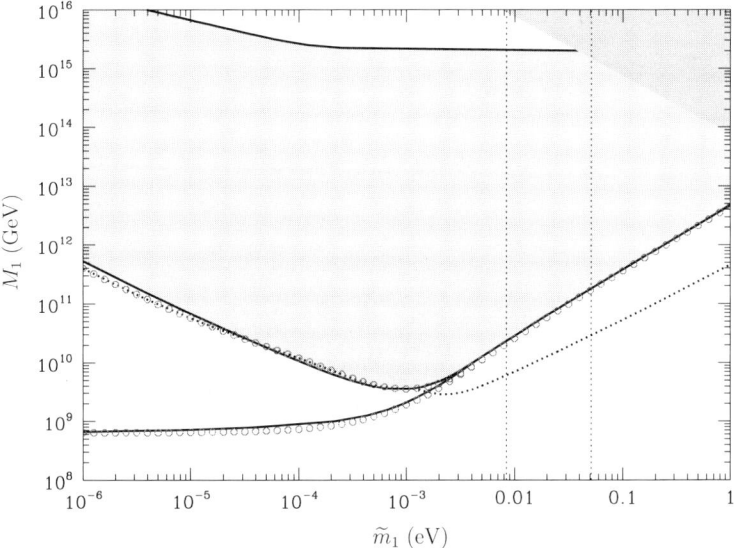

Fig. 4.13. Lower bound on the lightest RH neutrino mass, M_1 (circles) and the initial temperature, T_i (dotted line), for $m_1 = 0$ and $\eta_B^{CMB} = 6 \times 10^{-10}$. The red circles (solid lines) denote the analytical (numerical) results. The vertical dashed lines indicate the range ($\sqrt{\Delta m_{\text{sol}}^2}$, $\sqrt{\Delta m_{\text{atm}}^2}$). Figure taken from Ref. [28].

Table 4.3. Photo-dissociation reactions that the high energy photons can participate in. The light elements may be destroyed through these reactions and thus their abundance may be changed.

reaction	threshold (MeV)
$D + \gamma \to n + p$	2.225
$T + \gamma \to n + D$	6.257
$T + \gamma \to p + n + n$	8.482
$^3He + \gamma \to p + D$	5.494
$^4He + \gamma \to p + T$	19.815
$^4He + \gamma \to n + {}^3He$	20.578
$^4He + \gamma \to p + n + D$	26.072

WMAP constraint on DM leads to stringent bound on gluino mass for any given gravitino mass $m_{3/2}$ and reheating temperature T_{RH}. (Bounds on other gaugino masses can also be obtained as discussed in [36].) On the other hand, if gravitinos are unstable, it has long lifetime and can decay during and after the BBN, and may have the following three effects on BBN [1]:

(1) These decays can speed up cosmic expansion, and increase the neutron to proton ratio and thus the ^{4}He abundance;
(2) Radiation decay of gravitinos, $\psi \to \gamma + \tilde{\gamma}$, increases the photon density and thus reduces the n_B/n_γ ratio;
(3) High energy photons emitted in gravitino decays can destroy light elements (D, T, ^{3}He, ^{4}He) through photo-dissociation reactions such as those given in Table 4.3;

The gravitino number density, $n_{3/2}$, during the thermalization stage after the inflation is governed by the following Boltzmann equation [35],

$$\frac{d}{dt}n_{3/2} + 3Hn_{3/2} \simeq \left\langle \sum_{\text{tot}} v \right\rangle \cdot n_{\text{light}}^2 \qquad (4.121)$$

where $\sum_{\text{tot}} \sim 1/M_{\text{Pl}}^2$ is the total cross section determining the production rate of gravitinos and $n_{\text{light}} \sim T^3$ is the number density of light particles in the thermal bath. As the thermalization is very fast, the friction term $3Hn_{3/2}$ in the above Boltzmann equation can be neglected. Using the fact that the Universe is radiation dominant, $H \sim t^{-1} \sim T^2/M_{\text{Pl}}$, it follows that,

$$n_{3/2} \sim \frac{T^4}{M_{\text{Pl}}}, \qquad (4.122)$$

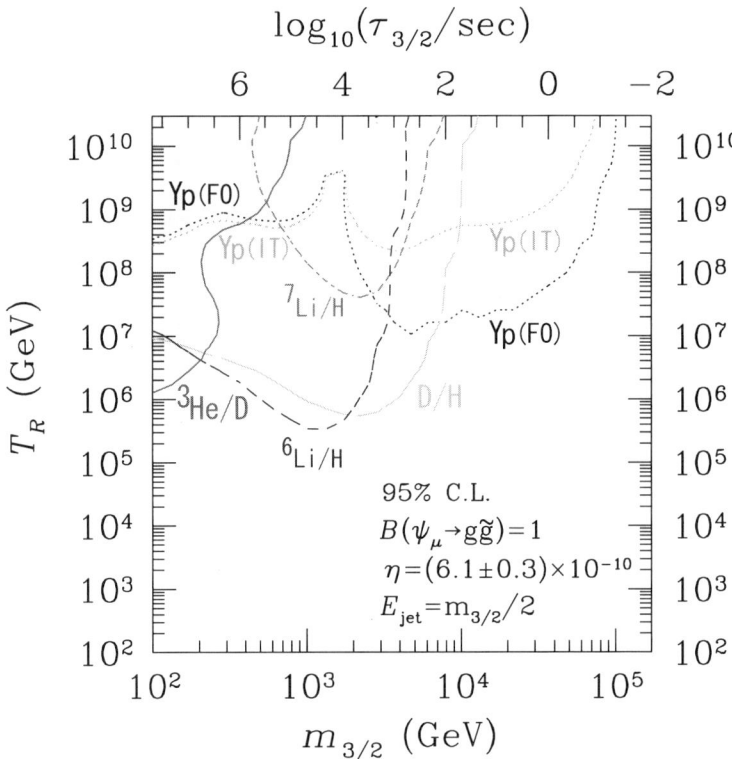

Fig. 4.14. Upper bound on reheating temperature as a function of the gravitino mass, for the case when gravitino dominant decays into a gluon-gluino pair. Figure taken from Ref. [37].

and the number density at thermalization in unit of entropy then reads,

$$\frac{n_{3/2}}{s} \simeq 10^{-2} \frac{T_{RH}}{M_{\mathrm{Pl}}} \ . \tag{4.123}$$

The observed abundances for various light elements are,

$$0.22 < Y_p = (\rho_{^4He}/\rho_B)_p < 0.24 \ , \tag{4.124}$$

$$(n_D/n_H) > 1.8 \times 10^{-5} \ , \tag{4.125}$$

$$\left(\frac{n_D + n_{^3He}}{n_H}\right)_p < 10^{-4} \ . \tag{4.126}$$

Table 4.4. Upper bound on the reheating temperature for different values of gravitino mass.

Gravitino mass $m_{3/2}$	Upper bound on T_R
$\lesssim 100$ GeV	10^{6-7} GeV
100 GeV -1 TeV	10^{7-9} GeV
1 TeV -3 TeV	10^{9-12} GeV
3 TeV -10 TeV	10^{12} GeV

The most stringent constraint is from the abundance of (D + ^{3}He) which requires the gravitino number density to be

$$\frac{n_{3/2}}{s} \simeq 10^{-2}\frac{T_{RH}}{M_{\text{Pl}}} \lesssim 10^{-12} \,. \qquad (4.127)$$

The constraint $T_{RH} < 10^{8-9}$ GeV then follows. More recently, it has been shown that, for hadronic decay modes, $\psi \to g + \tilde{g}$, the bounds are even more stringent, $T_R < 10^{6-7}$ GeV, for gravitino mass $m_{3/2} \sim 100$ GeV [37]. Fig. 4.14 shows the upper bound on the reheating temperature, T_R, for different values of gravitino mass, $m_{3/2}$. Table 4.4 summarizes the numerical results for the upper bound on T_R for various values of $m_{3/2}$. It has also been pointed out [38] that including recent constraint from ^6Li, a new upper bound $T_R < 10^7$ GeV can be derived for the case of gravitino LSP in the constrained minimal supersymmetric Standard Model (CMSSM).

There is therefore a conflict between generation of sufficient amount of leptogenesis and not overly producing gravitinos. To avoid these conflicts, various non-standard scenarios for leptogenesis have been proposed. These are discussed in the next section.

4.3. Non-standard Scenarios

There are a few non-standard scenarios proposed to evade the gravitino over-production problem. In these new scenarios, the conflicts between leptogenesis and gravitino over-production problem are overcome by, (i) resonant enhancement in the self-energy diagrams due to near degenerate right-handed neutrino masses (resonant leptogenesis); (ii) relaxing the relation between the lepton number asymmetry and the right-handed neutrino mass (soft leptogenesis); (iii) relaxing the relation between the reheating temperature and the right-handed neutrino mass (non-thermal leptogenesis). These scenarios are discussed below.

4.3.1. Resonant Leptogenesis

Recall that in the standard leptogenesis discussed in Sec. 4.2, contributions to the CP asymmetry is due to the interference between the tree-level and the one-loop diagrams, that include the vertex correction and self-energy diagrams. It was pointed out in Ref. [39] that in the limit $M_{N_i} - M_{N_j} \ll M_{N_i}$, the self-energy diagrams dominate,

$$\epsilon_{N_i}^{\text{Self}} = \frac{Im[(h_\nu h_\nu^\dagger)_{ij}]^2}{(h_\nu h_\nu^\dagger)_{ii}(h_\nu h_\nu^\dagger)_{jj}} \left[\frac{(M_i^2 - M_j^2)M_i\Gamma_{N_j}}{(M_i^2 - M_j^2)^2 + M_i^2\Gamma_{N_j}^2} \right]. \tag{4.128}$$

When the lightest two RH neutrinos have near degenerate masses, $M_1^2 - M_2^2 \sim \Gamma_{N_2}^2$, the asymmetry can be enhanced. To be more specific, CP asymmetry of $\mathcal{O}(1)$ is possible, when

$$M_1 - M_2 \sim \frac{1}{2}\Gamma_{N_{1,2}}, \quad \text{assuming} \quad \frac{Im(h_\nu h_\nu^\dagger)_{12}^2}{(h_\nu h_\nu^\dagger)_{11}(h_\nu h_\nu^\dagger)_{22}} \sim 1. \tag{4.129}$$

Due to this resonant effect, the bound on the RH neutrino mass scale from the requirement of generating sufficient lepton number asymmetry can be significantly lower. It has been shown that sufficient baryogenesis can be obtained even with $M_{1,2} \sim$ TeV [40].

4.3.2. Soft Leptogenesis

CP violation in leptogenesis can arise in two ways: it can arise in decays, which is the case in standard leptogenesis described in the previous section. It can also arise in mixing. An example of this is the soft leptogenesis. Recall that in the Kaon system, non-vanishing CP violation exists due to the mismatch between CP eigenstates and mass eigenstates (for a review, see for example, Ref. [41]). The CP eigenstates of the K^0 system are $\frac{1}{\sqrt{2}}(|K^0\rangle \pm |\overline{K}^0\rangle)$. The time evolution of the $(K^0, \overline{K}^0)$ system is described by the following Schrödinger equation,

$$\frac{d}{dt}\begin{pmatrix} K^0 \\ \overline{K}^0 \end{pmatrix} = \mathcal{H}\begin{pmatrix} K^0 \\ \overline{K}^0 \end{pmatrix} \tag{4.130}$$

where the Hamiltanian $\mathcal{H}$ is given by $\mathcal{H} = \mathcal{M} - \frac{i}{2}\mathcal{A}$. Here, the off-diagonal matrix element $\mathcal{M}_{12}$ describes the dispersive part of the transition amplitude, while the element $\mathcal{A}_{12}$ gives the absorptive part of the amplitude. The physical (mass) eigenstates, $|K_{L,S}\rangle$, are given in terms of the flavor eigenstates, $|K^0\rangle$ and $|\overline{K}^0\rangle$, as

$$|K_L\rangle = p|K^0\rangle + q|\overline{K}^0\rangle \qquad (4.131)$$

$$|K_S\rangle = p|K^0\rangle - q|\overline{K}^0\rangle . \qquad (4.132)$$

To have non-vanishing CP violation requires that there exists a mismatch between the CP eigenstates and the physical eigenstates. This in turn implies,

$$\left|\frac{q}{p}\right| \neq 1, \quad \text{where} \quad \left(\frac{q}{p}\right)^2 = \left(\frac{2\mathcal{M}_{12}^* - i\mathcal{A}_{12}^*}{2\mathcal{M}_{12} - i\mathcal{A}_{12}}\right). \qquad (4.133)$$

For soft leptogenesis, the relevant soft SUSY Lagrangian that involves lightest RH sneutrinos $\widetilde{\nu}_{R_1}$ is the following,

$$-\mathcal{L}_{soft} = \left(\frac{1}{2} B M_1 \widetilde{\nu}_{R_1} \widetilde{\nu}_{R_1} + A \mathcal{Y}_{1i} \widetilde{L}_i \widetilde{\nu}_{R_1} H_u + h.c.\right)$$
$$+ \widetilde{m}^2 \widetilde{\nu}_{R_1}^\dagger \widetilde{\nu}_{R_1} . \qquad (4.134)$$

This soft SUSY Lagrangian and the superpotential that involves the lightest RH neutrino, N_1,

$$W = M_1 N_1 N_1 + \mathcal{Y}_{1i} L_i N_1 H_u \qquad (4.135)$$

give rise to the following interactions

$$-\mathcal{L}_\mathcal{A} = \widetilde{\nu}_{R_1}(M_1 Y_{1i}^* \widetilde{\ell}_i^* H_u^* + \mathcal{Y}_{1i} \overline{H}_u \ell_L^i + A \mathcal{Y}_{1i} \widetilde{\ell}_i H_u) + h.c. \quad , \qquad (4.136)$$

and mass terms (to leading order in soft SUSY breaking terms),

$$-\mathcal{L}_\mathcal{M} = (M_1^2 \widetilde{\nu}_{R_1}^\dagger \widetilde{\nu}_{R_1} + \frac{1}{2} B M_1 \widetilde{\nu}_{R_1} \widetilde{\nu}_{R_1}) + h.c. . \qquad (4.137)$$

Diagonalization of the mass matrix $\mathcal{M}$ for the two states $\widetilde{\nu}_{R_1}$ and $\widetilde{\nu}_{R_1}^\dagger$ leads to eigenstates $\widetilde{N}_+$ and $\widetilde{N}_-$ with masses,

$$M_\pm \simeq M_1 \left(1 \pm \frac{|B|}{2M_1}\right), \qquad (4.138)$$

where the leading order term M_1 is the F-term contribution from the superpotential (RH neutrino mass term) and the mass difference between the two mass eigenstates $\widetilde{N}_+$ and $\widetilde{N}_-$ is induced by the SUSY breaking B term. The time evolution of the $\widetilde{\nu}_{R_1}$-$\widetilde{\nu}_{R_1}^\dagger$ system is governed by the Schrödinger equation,

$$\frac{d}{dt}\begin{pmatrix} \widetilde{\nu}_{R_1} \\ \widetilde{\nu}_{R_1}^\dagger \end{pmatrix} = \mathcal{H} \begin{pmatrix} \widetilde{\nu}_{R_1} \\ \widetilde{\nu}_{R_1}^\dagger \end{pmatrix}, \qquad (4.139)$$

where the Hamiltonian is $\mathcal{H} = \mathcal{M} - \frac{i}{2}\mathcal{A}$ with $\mathcal{M}$ and $\mathcal{A}$ being [42, 43],

$$\mathcal{M} = \begin{pmatrix} 1 & \frac{B^*}{2M_1} \\ \frac{B}{2M_1} & 1 \end{pmatrix} M_1 \,, \tag{4.140}$$

$$\mathcal{A} = \begin{pmatrix} 1 & \frac{A^*}{M_1} \\ \frac{A}{M_1} & 1 \end{pmatrix} \Gamma_1 \,. \tag{4.141}$$

For the decay of the lightest RH sneutrino, $\widetilde{\nu}_{R_1}$, the total decay width Γ_1 is given by, in the basis where both the charged lepton mass matrix and the RH neutrino mass matrix are diagonal,

$$\Gamma_1 = \frac{1}{4\pi}(\mathcal{Y}_\nu \mathcal{Y}_\nu^\dagger)_{11} M_1 \,. \tag{4.142}$$

The eigenstates of the Hamiltonian $\mathcal{H}$ are $\widetilde{N}'_\pm = p\widetilde{N} \pm q\widetilde{N}^\dagger$, where $|p|^2 + |q|^2 = 1$. The ratio q/p is given in terms of $\mathcal{M}$ and Γ_1 as,

$$\left(\frac{q}{p}\right)^2 = \frac{2\mathcal{M}_{12}^* - i\mathcal{A}_{12}^*}{2\mathcal{M}_{12} - i\mathcal{A}_{12}} \simeq 1 + \text{Im}\left(\frac{2\Gamma_1 A}{BM_1}\right), \tag{4.143}$$

in the limit $\mathcal{A}_{12} \ll \mathcal{M}_{12}$. Similar to the $K^0 - \overline{K}^0$ system, the source of CP violation in the lepton number asymmetry considered here is due to the CP violation in the mixing which occurs when the two neutral mass eigenstates ($\widetilde{N}_+, \widetilde{N}_-$), are different from the interaction eigenstates, ($\widetilde{N}'_+, \widetilde{N}'_-$). Therefore CP violation in mixing is present as long as the quantity $|q/p| \neq 1$, which requires

$$\text{Im}\left(\frac{A\Gamma_1}{M_1 B}\right) \neq 0 \,. \tag{4.144}$$

For this to occur, SUSY breaking, *i.e.* non-vanishing A and B, is required. As the relative phase between the parameters A and B can be rotated away by an $U(1)_R$-rotation as discussed in Sec. 4.1.5, without loss of generality we assume from now on that the remaining physical phase is solely coming from the tri-linear coupling, A.

The total lepton number asymmetry integrated over time, ϵ, is defined as the ratio of the difference to the sum of the decay widths Γ for $\widetilde{\nu}_{R_1}$ and $\widetilde{\nu}_{R_1}^\dagger$ into final states of the slepton doublet $\widetilde{L}$ and the Higgs doublet H, or the lepton doublet L and the Higgsino $\widetilde{H}$ or their conjugates,

$$\epsilon = \frac{\sum_f \int_0^\infty [\Gamma(\widetilde{\nu}_{R_1}, \widetilde{\nu}_{R_1}^\dagger \to f) - \Gamma(\widetilde{\nu}_{R_1}, \widetilde{\nu}_{R_1}^\dagger \to \overline{f})]}{\sum_f \int_0^\infty [\Gamma(\widetilde{\nu}_{R_1}, \widetilde{\nu}_{R_1}^\dagger \to f) + \Gamma(\widetilde{\nu}_{R_1}, \widetilde{\nu}_{R_1}^\dagger \to \overline{f})]} \,. \tag{4.145}$$

Here the final states $f = (\tilde{L}\,H)$, $(L\,\tilde{H})$ have lepton number $+1$, and $\bar{f}$ denotes their conjugate, $(\tilde{L}^\dagger\,H^\dagger)$, $(\bar{L}\,\tilde{\bar{H}})$, which have lepton number -1. After carrying out the time integration, the total CP asymmetry is [42, 43],

$$\epsilon = \left(\frac{4\Gamma_1 B}{\Gamma_1^2 + 4B^2}\right)\frac{\text{Im}(A)}{M_1}\delta_{B-F} \qquad (4.146)$$

where the additional factor δ_{B-F} takes into account the thermal effects due to the difference between the occupation numbers of bosons and fermions [44].

The final result for the baryon asymmetry is [42, 43],

$$\begin{aligned}\frac{n_B}{s} &\simeq -c_s\, d_{\tilde{\nu}_R}\, \epsilon\, \kappa\,, \\ &\simeq -1.48 \times 10^{-3} \epsilon\, \kappa\,, \\ &\simeq -(1.48 \times 10^{-3})\left(\frac{\text{Im}(A)}{M_1}\right) R\, \delta_{B-F}\, \kappa\,, \qquad (4.147)\end{aligned}$$

where $d_{\tilde{\nu}_R}$ in the first line is the density of the lightest sneutrino in equilibrium in units of entropy density, and is given by, $d_{\tilde{\nu}_R} = 45\zeta(3)/(\pi^4 g_*)$; the factor c_s, which characterizes the amount of $B - L$ asymmetry being converted into the baryon asymmetry Y_B, is defined in Eq. 4.57. The parameter κ is the efficiency factor given in Sec. 4.2.1.2. The resonance factor R is defined as the following ratio,

$$R \equiv \frac{4\Gamma_1 B}{\Gamma_1^2 + 4B^2}\,, \qquad (4.148)$$

which gives a value equal to one when the resonance condition, $\Gamma_1 = 2|B|$, is satisfied, leading to maximal CP asymmetry. As Γ_1 is of the order of $\mathcal{O}(0.1 - 1)$ GeV, to satisfy the resonance condition, a small value for $B \ll \tilde{m}$ is thus needed. Such a small value of B can be generated by some dynamical relaxation mechanisms [45] in which B vanishes in the leading order. A small value of $B \sim \tilde{m}^2/M_1$ is then generated by an operator $\int d^4\theta Z Z^\dagger N_1^2/M_{pl}^2$ in the Kähler potential, where Z is the SUSY breaking spurion field, $Z = \theta^2\, \tilde{m} M_{pl}$ [43]. In a specific SO(10) model constructed in Refs. [46, 47], it has been shown that with the parameter $B' \equiv \sqrt{BM_1}$ having the size of the natural SUSY breaking scale $\sqrt{\tilde{m}^2} \sim \mathcal{O}(1)$ TeV, a small value for B required by the resonance condition $B \sim \Gamma_1 \sim \mathcal{O}(0.1)$ GeV can be obtained.

4.3.3. Non-thermal Leptogenesis

The conflict between generating sufficient leptogenesis and not overly producing gravitinos in thermal leptogenesis arises due to strong dependence of the reheating temperature T_R on the lightest RH mass, M_{R_1}, in thermal leptogenesis. This problem may be avoided if the relation between the reheating temperature and the lightest RH neutrino mass is loosened. This is the case if the primordial RH neutrinos are produced non-thermally. One possible way to have non-thermal leptogenesis is to generate the primordial right-handed neutrinos through the inflaton decay [48].

Inflation solves the horizon and flatness problem, and it accounts for the origin of density fluctuations. Assume that the inflaton decays dominantly into a pair of lightest RH neutrinos, $\Phi \to N_1 + N_1$. For this decay to occur, the inflaton mass m_Φ has to be greater than $2M_1$. For simplicity, let us also assume that the decay modes into $N_{2,3}$ are energetically forbidden. The produced N_1 in inflaton decay then subsequently decays into $H + \ell_L$ and $H^\dagger + \ell_L^\dagger$. The out-of-equilibrium condition is automatically satisfied, if $T_R < M_1$. The CP asymmetry is generated by the interference of tree level and one-loop diagrams,

$$\epsilon = -\frac{3}{8\pi}\frac{M_1}{\langle H \rangle^2} m_3 \delta_{eff}, \qquad (4.149)$$

where δ_{eff} is given in terms of the neutrino Yukawa matrix elements and light neutrino masses as,

$$\delta_{eff} = \frac{Im\left\{h_{13}^2 + \frac{m_2}{m_3}h_{12}^2 + \frac{m_1}{m_3}h_{11}^2\right\}}{\left|h_{13}\right|^2 + \left|h_{12}\right|^2 + \left|h_{11}\right|^2}. \qquad (4.150)$$

Numerically, the asymmetry is given by [48],

$$\epsilon \simeq -2 \times 10^{-6}\left(\frac{M_1}{10^{10}\text{ GeV}}\right)\left(\frac{m_3}{0.05\text{ eV}}\right)\delta_{eff}. \qquad (4.151)$$

The chain decays $\Phi \to N_1 + N_1$ and $N_1 \to H + \ell_L$ or $H^\dagger + \ell_L^\dagger$ reheat the Universe producing not only the lepton number asymmetry but also the entropy for the thermal bath. Taking such effects into account, the ratio of lepton number to entropy density after the reheating [48] is then,

$$\frac{n_L}{s} \simeq -\frac{3}{2}\epsilon\frac{T_R}{m_\Phi} \simeq 3 \times 10^{-10}\left(\frac{T_R}{10^6\text{ GeV}}\right)\left(\frac{M_1}{m_\Phi}\right)\left(\frac{m_3}{0.05\text{ eV}}\right), \qquad (4.152)$$

assuming $\delta_{eff} = 1$. The ratio $n_B/s \sim 10^{-10}$ can thus be obtained with $M_1 \lesssim m_\Phi$, and $T_R \lesssim 10^6$ GeV.

4.4. Connection between leptogenesis and neutrino oscillation

As mentioned in Sec. 4.1.5, there is generally no connection between low energy CP violating processes, such as CP violation in neutrino oscillation and in neutrinoless double beta decay, and leptogenesis, which occurs at very high energy scale. This is due to the extra phases and mixing angles present in the heavy neutrino sector. One way to establish such connection is by reducing the inter-family couplings (equivalently, by imposing texture zero in the Yukawa matrix). This is the case for the 3×2 seesaw model. A more powerful way to obtain such connection is to have all CP violation, both low energy and high energy, come from the same origin. This ensues if CP violation occurs spontaneously. Below we described these two models in which such connection does exist.

4.4.1. *Models with Two Right-Handed Neutrinos*

One type of models where there exists connection between CP violating processes at high and low energies is models with only two RH neutrinos. In this case, the neutrino Dirac mass matrix is a 3×2 matrix. This 3×2 Yukawa matrix has six complex parameters, and hence six phases, out of which, three can be absorbed by the wave functions of the three charged leptons. Even though, the reduction in the number of right-handed neutrinos reduces the number of CP phases in high energy, it also reduces the number of CP phases at low energy to two. There is therefor still one high energy phase that cannot be determined by measuring the low energy phases. However, if one further assumes that the 3 Yukawa matrix has two zeros, there is then only one CP phase in the Yukawa matrix, making the existence of the connection possible.

The existence of two right-handed neutrinos is required by the cancellation of Witten anomaly, if a global leptonic $SU(2)$ family symmetry is imposed [49]. (For implications of non-anomalous gauge symmetry for neutrino masses, see Ref. [50]. This model provided the interesting possibility of probing the neutrino sector at the colliders through their couplings to the Z' gauge boson [51].) Along this line, Frampton, Glashow and Yanagida proposed a model, which has the following Lagrangian [52],

$$\mathcal{L} = \frac{1}{2}(N_1 N_2)\begin{pmatrix} M_1 & 0 \\ 0 & M_2 \end{pmatrix}\begin{pmatrix} N_1 \\ N_2 \end{pmatrix} + (N_1 N_2)\begin{pmatrix} a & a' & 0 \\ 0 & b & b' \end{pmatrix}\begin{pmatrix} \ell_1 \\ \ell_2 \\ \ell_3 \end{pmatrix} H + h.c.,$$
(4.153)

with the Yukawa matrix having two zeros in the $N_1 - \ell_3$ and $N_2 - \ell_1$ couplings. The effective neutrino mass matrix due to this Lagrangian is obtained, using the see-saw formula,

$$\begin{pmatrix} \frac{a^2}{M_1} & \frac{aa'}{M_1} & 0 \\ \frac{aa'}{M_1} & \frac{a'^2}{M_1} + \frac{b^2}{M_2} & \frac{bb'}{M_2} \\ 0 & \frac{bb'}{M_2} & \frac{b'^2}{M_2} \end{pmatrix},$$
(4.154)

where a, b, b' are real and $a' = |a'|e^{i\delta}$. By takinging all of them to be real, with the choice $a' = \sqrt{2}a$ and $b = b'$, and assuming $a^2/M_1 \ll b^2/M_2$, the effective neutrino masses and mixing matrix are obtained

$$m_{\nu_1} = 0, \quad m_{\nu_2} = \frac{2a^2}{M_1}, \quad m_{\nu_3} = \frac{2b^2}{M_2}$$
(4.155)

$$U = \begin{pmatrix} 1/\sqrt{2} & 1/\sqrt{2} & 0 \\ -1/2 & 1/2 & 1/\sqrt{2} \\ 1/2 & -1/2 & 1/\sqrt{2} \end{pmatrix} \times \begin{pmatrix} 1 & 0 & 0 \\ 0 & \cos\theta & \sin\theta \\ 0 & -\sin\theta & \cos\theta \end{pmatrix},$$
(4.156)

where $\theta \simeq m_{\nu_2}/\sqrt{2}m_{\nu_3}$, and the observed bi-large mixing angles and Δm_{atm}^2 and $\Delta m_\odot^2$ can be accommodated. An interesting feature of this model is that the sign of the baryon number asymmetry ($B \propto \xi_B = Y^2 a^2 b^2 \sin 2\delta$) is related to the sign of the CP violation in neutrino oscillation (ξ_{osc}) in the following way

$$\xi_{osc} = -\frac{a^4 b^4}{M_1^3 M_2^3}(2 + Y^2)\xi_B \propto -B$$
(4.157)

assuming the baryon number asymmetry is resulting from leptogenesis due to the decay of the lighter one of the two heavy neutrinos, N_1. This idea can be realized in a $SO(10)$ with additional singlets [53].

4.4.2. Models with Spontaneous CP Violation (& Triplet Leptogenesis)

The second type of models in which relation between leptogenesis and low energy CP violation exists is the minimal left-right symmetric model with spontaneous CP violation (SCPV) [54]. The left-right (LR) model [55] is based on the gauge group, $SU(3)_c \times SU(2)_L \times SU(2)_R \times U(1)_{B-L} \times P$, where the parity P acts on the two $SU(2)$'s. (See also Kaladi Babu's lectures.) In this model, the electric charge Q can be understood as the sum of the two T^3 quantum numbers of the $SU(2)$ gauge groups,

$$Q = T_{3,L} + T_{3,R} + \frac{1}{2}(B - L) . \qquad (4.158)$$

The *minimal* LR model has the following particle content: In the fermion sector, the iso-singlet quarks form a doublet under $SU(2)_R$, and similarly for e_R and ν_R,

$$Q_{i,L} = \begin{pmatrix} u \\ d \end{pmatrix}_{i,L} \sim (1/2, 0, 1/3), \qquad Q_{i,R} = \begin{pmatrix} u \\ d \end{pmatrix}_{i,R} \sim (0, 1/2, 1/3),$$

$$L_{i,L} = \begin{pmatrix} e \\ \nu \end{pmatrix}_{i,L} \sim (1/2, 0, -1), \qquad L_{i,R} = \begin{pmatrix} e \\ \nu \end{pmatrix}_{i,R} \sim (0, 1/2, -1) .$$

In the scalar sector, there is a bi-doublet and one triplet for each of the $SU(2)$'s,

$$\Phi = \begin{pmatrix} \phi_1^0 & \phi_2^+ \\ \phi_1^- & \phi_2^0 \end{pmatrix} \sim (1/2, 1/2, 0)$$

$$\Delta_L = \begin{pmatrix} \Delta_L^+/\sqrt{2} & \Delta_L^{++} \\ \Delta_L^0 & -\Delta_L^+/\sqrt{2} \end{pmatrix} \sim (1, 0, 2)$$

$$\Delta_R = \begin{pmatrix} \Delta_R^+/\sqrt{2} & \Delta_R^{++} \\ \Delta_R^0 & -\Delta_R^+/\sqrt{2} \end{pmatrix} \sim (0, 1, 2) .$$

Under the parity P, these fields transform as,

$$\Psi_L \leftrightarrow \Psi_R, \quad \Delta_L \leftrightarrow \Delta_R, \quad \Phi \leftrightarrow \Phi^\dagger . \qquad (4.159)$$

The VEV of the $SU(2)_R$ breaks the left-right symmetry down to the SM gauge group,

$$SU(3)_c \times SU(2)_L \times SU(2)_R \times U(1)_{B-L} \times P$$
$$\to SU(3)_c \times SU(2)_L \times U(1)_Y , \qquad (4.160)$$

and the subsequent breaking of the electroweak symmetry is achieved by the bi-doublet VEV. In general,

$$\langle \Phi \rangle = \begin{pmatrix} \kappa e^{i\alpha_\kappa} & 0 \\ 0 & \kappa' e^{i\alpha_{\kappa'}} \end{pmatrix}, \qquad (4.161)$$

$$\langle \Delta_L \rangle = \begin{pmatrix} 0 & 0 \\ v_L e^{i\alpha_L} & 0 \end{pmatrix}, \quad \langle \Delta_R \rangle = \begin{pmatrix} 0 & 0 \\ v_R e^{i\alpha_R} & 0 \end{pmatrix} .$$

To get realistic SM gauge boson masses, the VEV's of the bi-doublet Higgs must satisfy $v^2 \equiv |\kappa|^2 + |\kappa'|^2 \simeq 2M_w^2/g^2 \simeq (174 \text{ GeV})^2$. Generally, a non-vanishing VEV for the $SU(2)_L$ triplet Higgs is induced, and it is suppressed by the heavy $SU(2)_R$ breaking scale similar to the see-saw mechanism for the neutrinos,

$$<\Delta_L> = \begin{pmatrix} 0 & 0 \\ v_L e^{i\alpha_L} & 0 \end{pmatrix}, \qquad v_L v_R = \beta |\kappa|^2, \qquad (4.162)$$

where the parameter β is a function of the order $\mathcal{O}(1)$ coupling constants in the scalar potential and v_R, v_L, κ and κ' are positive real numbers in the above equations. (The presence of a triplet Higgs in warped extra dimensions can provide a natural way to generate small Majorana masses for the neutrinos [56].) Due to this see-saw suppression, for a $SU(2)_R$ breaking scale as high as 10^{15} GeV, which is required by the smallness of the neutrino masses, the induced $SU(2)_L$ triplet VEV is well below the upper bound set by the electroweak precision constraints [57]. The scalar potential that gives rise to the vacuum alignment described can be found in Ref. [58].

The Yukawa sector of the model is given by $\mathcal{L}_{Yuk} = \mathcal{L}_q + \mathcal{L}_\ell$, where $\mathcal{L}_q$ and $\mathcal{L}_\ell$ are the Yukawa interactions in the quark and lepton sectors, respectively. The Lagrangian for quark Yukawa interactions is given by,

$$-\mathcal{L}_q = \overline{Q}_{i,R}(F_{ij}\Phi + G_{ij}\tilde{\Phi})Q_{j,L} + h.c. \qquad (4.163)$$

where $\tilde{\Phi} \equiv \tau_2 \Phi^* \tau_2$. In general, F_{ij} and G_{ij} are Hermitian to preseve left-right symmetry. Because of our assumption of SCPV with complex vacuum expectation values, the matrices F_{ij} and G_{ij} are real. The Yukawa interactions responsible for generating the lepton masses are summarized in the following Lagrangian, $\mathcal{L}_\ell$,

$$\begin{aligned} -\mathcal{L}_\ell = &\; \overline{L}_{i,R}(P_{ij}\Phi + R_{ij}\tilde{\Phi})L_{j,L} \\ &+ i f_{ij}(L_{i,L}^T C \tau_2 \Delta_L L_{j,L} + L_{i,R}^T C \tau_2 \Delta_R L_{j,R}) + h.c. , \end{aligned} \qquad (4.164)$$

where $\mathcal{C}$ is the Dirac charge conjugation operator, and the matrices P_{ij}, R_{ij} and f_{ij} are real due to the assumption of SCPV. Note that the Majorana mass terms $L_{i,L}^T \Delta_L L_{j,L}$ and $L_{i,R}^T \Delta_R L_{j,R}$ have identical coupling because the Lagrangian must be invariant under interchanging $L \leftrightarrow R$. The complete Lagrangian of the model is invariant under the unitary transformation, under which the matter fields transform as

$$\psi_L \to U_L \psi_L, \qquad \psi_R \to U_R \psi_R \qquad (4.165)$$

where $\psi_{L,R}$ are left-handed (right-handed) fermions, and the scalar fields transform according to

$$\Phi \to U_R \Phi U_L^\dagger, \qquad \Delta_L \to U_L^* \Delta_L U_L^\dagger, \qquad \Delta_R \to U_R^* \Delta_R U_R^\dagger \qquad (4.166)$$

with the unitary transformations U_L and U_R being

$$U_L = \begin{pmatrix} e^{i\gamma_L} & 0 \\ 0 & e^{-i\gamma_L} \end{pmatrix}, \qquad U_R = \begin{pmatrix} e^{i\gamma_R} & 0 \\ 0 & e^{-i\gamma_R} \end{pmatrix}. \qquad (4.167)$$

Under these unitary transformations, the VEV's transform as

$$\kappa \to \kappa e^{-i(\gamma_L - \gamma_R)}, \qquad \kappa' \to \kappa' e^{i(\gamma_L - \gamma_R)}, \qquad (4.168)$$
$$v_L \to v_L e^{-2i\gamma_L}, \qquad v_R \to v_R e^{-2i\gamma_R}.$$

Thus by re-defining the phases of matter fields with the choice of $\gamma_R = \alpha_R/2$ and $\gamma_L = \alpha_\kappa + \alpha_R/2$ in the unitary matrices U_L and U_R, we can rotate away two of the complex phases in the VEV's of the scalar fields and are left with only two genuine CP violating phases, $\alpha_{\kappa'}$ and α_L,

$$<\Phi> = \begin{pmatrix} \kappa & 0 \\ 0 & \kappa' e^{i\alpha_{\kappa'}} \end{pmatrix}, \qquad (4.169)$$

$$<\Delta_L> = \begin{pmatrix} 0 & 0 \\ v_L e^{i\alpha_L} & 0 \end{pmatrix}, \qquad <\Delta_R> = \begin{pmatrix} 0 & 0 \\ v_R & 0 \end{pmatrix}.$$

The quark Yukawa interaction $\mathcal{L}_q$ gives rise to quark masses after the bi-doublet acquires VEV's

$$M_u = \kappa F_{ij} + \kappa' e^{-i\alpha_{\kappa'}} G_{ij}, \qquad M_d = \kappa' e^{i\alpha_{\kappa'}} F_{ij} + \kappa G_{ij}. \qquad (4.170)$$

Thus the relative phase in the two VEV's in the SU(2) bi-doublet, $\alpha_{\kappa'}$, gives rise to the CP violating phase in the CKM matrix. To obtain realistic quark masses and CKM matrix elements, it has been shown that the VEV's of the bi-doublet have to satisfy $\kappa/\kappa' \simeq m_t/m_b \gg 1$ [59]. When the triplets and the bi-doublet acquire VEV's, we obtain the following mass terms for the leptons

$$M_e = \kappa' e^{i\alpha_{\kappa'}} P_{ij} + \kappa R_{ij}, \qquad M_\nu^{Dirac} = \kappa P_{ij} + \kappa' e^{-i\alpha_{\kappa'}} R_{ij} \qquad (4.171)$$
$$M_\nu^{RR} = v_R f_{ij}, \qquad M_\nu^{LL} = v_L e^{i\alpha_L} f_{ij}. \qquad (4.172)$$

The effective neutrino mass matrix, M_ν^{eff}, which arises from the Type-II seesaw mechanism, is thus given by

$$M_\nu^{eff} = M_\nu^{II} - M_\nu^I = \left(f e^{i\alpha_L} - \frac{1}{\beta} P^T f^{-1} P\right) v_L, \quad (4.173)$$

$$M_\nu^I = (M_\nu^{Dirac})^T (M_\nu^{RR})^{-1} (M_\nu^{Dirac}) \quad (4.174)$$

$$= (\kappa P + \kappa' e^{-i\alpha_{\kappa'}} R)^T (v_R f)^{-1} (\kappa P + \kappa' e^{-i\alpha_{\kappa'}} R)$$

$$\simeq \frac{v_L}{\beta} P^T f^{-1} P,$$

$$M_\nu^I = v_L e^{i\alpha_L} f. \quad (4.175)$$

Consequently, the connection between CP violation in the quark sector and that in the lepton sector, which is made through the phase $\alpha_{\kappa'}$, appears only at the sub-leading order, $\mathcal{O}(\kappa'/\kappa)$, thus making this connection rather weak. We will neglect these sub-leading order terms, and there is thus only one phase, α_L, that is responsible for all leptonic CP violation.

The three low energy phases δ, α_{21}, α_{31}, in the MNS matrix are therefore functions of the single fundamental phase, α_L. Neutrino oscillation probabilities depend on the Dirac phase through the leptonic Jarlskog invariant, which is proportional to $\sin \alpha_L$, $J_{CP}^\ell \propto \sin \alpha_L$. There are two ways to generate lepton number asymmetry. One is through the decay of the $SU(2)_L$ triplet Higgs, $\Delta^* \to \ell + \ell$, and the corresponding asymmetry is given by,

$$\epsilon = \frac{\Gamma(\Delta_L^* \to \ell + \ell) - \Gamma(\Delta_L \to \overline{\ell} + \overline{\ell})}{\Gamma(\Delta_L^* \to \ell + \ell) + \Gamma(\Delta_L \to \overline{\ell} + \overline{\ell})}. \quad (4.176)$$

The asymmetry can also be generated through the decay of the lightest RH neutrinos, $N_1 \to \ell + H^\dagger$, and the asymmetry in this case is,

$$\epsilon = \frac{\Gamma(N_1 \to \ell + H^\dagger) - \Gamma(N_1 \to \overline{\ell} + H)}{\Gamma(N_1 \to \ell + H^\dagger) + \Gamma(N_1 \to \overline{\ell} + H)}. \quad (4.177)$$

Whether N_1 decay dominates or Δ_L decay dominates depends upon if N_1 is heavier or lighter than Δ_L. As the mass of the triplet Higgs is typically at the scale of the LR breaking scale, it is naturally heavier than the lightest RH neutrino. As a result, N_1 decay dominates. With the particle content of this model, there are three diagrams at one loop that contribute to leptogeiesis, as shown in Fig. 4.15. The contribution from diagram (a) and (b) mediated by charged lepton and Higgs doublet, which appear also in standard leptogenesis with SM particle content, is given by [60],

$$\epsilon^{N_1} = \frac{3}{16\pi} \left(\frac{M_{R_1}}{v^2}\right) \cdot \frac{\text{Im}\left(\mathcal{M}_D \left(M_\nu^I\right)^* \mathcal{M}_D^T\right)_{11}}{(\mathcal{M}_D \mathcal{M}_D^\dagger)_{11}}. \quad (4.178)$$

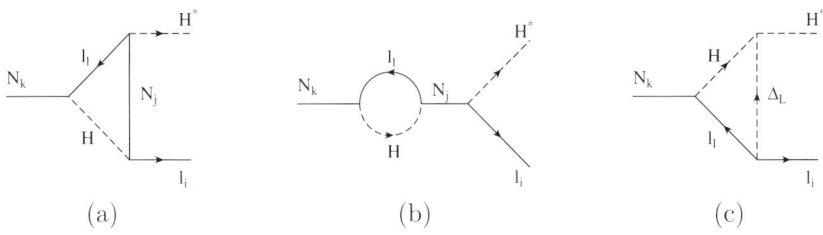

Fig. 4.15. Diagrams in the minimal left-right model that contribute to the lepton number asymmetry through the decay of the RH neutrinos.

Now, there is one additional one-loop diagram, Fig. 4.15 (c), mediated by the $SU(2)_L$ triplet Higgs. It contributes to the decay amplitude of the right-handed neutrino into a doublet Higgs and a charged lepton, which gives an additional contribution to the lepton number asymmetry [60],

$$\epsilon^{\Delta_L} = \frac{3}{16\pi}\left(\frac{M_{R_1}}{v^2}\right) \cdot \frac{\text{Im}(\mathcal{M}_D(M_\nu^{II})^*\mathcal{M}_D^T)_{11}}{(\mathcal{M}_D\mathcal{M}_D^\dagger)_{11}}, \quad (4.179)$$

where $\mathcal{M}_D$ is the neutrino Dirac mass term in the basis where the RH neutrino Majorana mass term is real and diagonal,

$$\mathcal{M}_D = O_R M_D, \quad f^{\text{diag}} = O_R f O_R^T. \quad (4.180)$$

Because there is no phase present in either $M_D = P\kappa$ or M_ν^I or O_R, the quantity $\mathcal{M}_D\left(M_\nu^I\right)^*\mathcal{M}_D^T$ is real, leading to a vanishing ϵ^{N_1}. This statement is true for *any* chosen unitary transformations U_L and U_R defined in Eq. (4.167). On the other hand, the contribution, ϵ^{Δ_L}, due to the diagram mediated by the $SU(2)_R$ triplet is proportional to $\sin\alpha_L$.

As all leptonic CP violation in this model come from one single origin, that is, the phase in the VEV of the LH triplet, $\langle\Delta_L\rangle$, strong correlation between leptogenesis and low energy CP violating processes can thus be established. In particular, both J_{CP}^ℓ and ϵ are proportional to $\sin\alpha_L$.

It has been found recently that, by lowering the left-right symmetry breaking scale with an additional $U(1)$ symmetry, the link between CP violation in the quark sector and that in the lepton sector can also be established [61].

4.5. Recent Progress and Concluding Remarks

Leptogenesis provides a very appealing way to generate the observed cosmological baryonic asymmetry. It has gained a significant amount of interests ever since the advent of the evidence of non-zero neutrino masses. In this scenario, the baryonic asymmetry is closely connected to the properties of the neutrinos, and the fact that the required neutrino mass scale for successful leptogenesis is similar to the scale observed in neutrino oscillations makes leptogenesis a very plausible source for the cosmological baryonic asymmetry. Even though there is so far no direct way to test leptogenesis, the search for leptonic CP violation in neutrino oscillations at very long baseline experiments [66] and to look for lepton number violation in neutrinoless double beta decay will inevitably further the credibility of leptogenesis as a source of the baryon asymmetry.

The recent developments in the subject of leptogenesis have been focused on the role of flavor. Recall that the total asymmetry given in Eq. 4.89 have summed over all three flavor indices,

$$\epsilon_1 = \sum_{\alpha=e,\mu,\tau} \epsilon^{\alpha\alpha}, \qquad (4.181)$$

where $\epsilon^{\alpha\alpha}$ is the CP asymmetry in the α-flavor. Correspondingly, previous solutions to the Boltzmann equations have summed over all the three flavors, e, μ, τ, and thus they did not include flavor dependence [62],

$$\frac{d(Y_{N_1} - Y^{eq}_{N_1})}{dz} = -\frac{z}{sH(M_1)}(\gamma_D + \gamma_{\Delta L=1})\left(\frac{Y_{N_1}}{Y^{eq}_{N_1}} - 1\right) \qquad (4.182)$$
$$- \frac{dY^{eq}_{N_1}}{dz},$$

$$\frac{dY_L}{dz} = \frac{z}{sH(M_1)}\left[\left(\frac{Y_{N_1}}{Y^{eq}_{N_1}} - 1\right)\epsilon_1\gamma_D \qquad (4.183)\right.$$
$$\left. + -\frac{Y_L}{Y^{eq}_L}(\gamma_D\gamma_{\Delta L=1} + \gamma_{\Delta L=2})\right],$$

where Y_{N_1} and Y_L are the number density of the lightest right-handed neutrino N_1 and of the lepton number asymmetry, respectively, and γ's are the decay rates for the processes specified in the subscripts. It has recently been pointed out that flavor effects matter if heavy neutrino masses are hierarchical [62]. The Yukawa interactions of all three flavors, e, μ and τ, reach equilibrium at different temperatures. These temperatures are determined by the size of the Yukawa couplings, λ, as

$$\lambda^2 M_{Pl} = T_{eq}. \qquad (4.184)$$

Due to the relative large coupling constant, the τ Yukawa interactions reach equilibrium at $T \sim 10^{12}$ GeV, while the muon Yukawa interactions reach equilibrium at $T \sim 10^9$ GeV. If leptogenesis takes place at $T \sim M_1 > 10^{12}$ GeV, the Yukawa interactions of all three lepton flavors are out of equilibrium, and hence the three flavors are indistinguishable. In particular, the washout factor is universal for all three flavors. However, if leptogenesis takes place at temperature below 10^{12} GeV, which is generally the case for hierarchical right-handed neutrino masses, the three flavors are distinguishable and thus their effects should be included in the Boltzmann equations properly. Instead of a single evolution function for Y_L as given in Eq. 4.183, one should consider the evolution of the lepton number asymmetry, $Y^{\alpha\alpha}$, which is due to the decay of the lightest right-handed neutrino into charged lepton of flavor α with the corresponding asymmetry given by $\epsilon^{\alpha\alpha}$ and decay rate given by $\gamma_D^{\alpha\alpha}$ [62],

$$\frac{dY^{\alpha\alpha}}{dz} = \frac{z}{sH(M_1)}\left[\left(\frac{Y_{N_1}}{Y_{N_1}^{eq}} - 1\right)\epsilon^{\alpha\alpha}(\gamma_D^{\alpha\alpha} + \gamma_{\Delta L=1}) \right.$$
$$\left. - \frac{Y^{\alpha\alpha}}{Y_L^{eq}}(\gamma_D^{\alpha\alpha} + \gamma_{\Delta L=1})\right], \qquad (4.185)$$

Note that in the above equation, there is no summation over the flavor index, α. By properly including the flavor effects, the amount of leptogenesis may be enhanced by a factor of 2 to 3 [62].

Except for the specific types of models [52, 54] discussed in Sec. 4.4, the general lack of connection between leptogenesis and low energy CP violation translates into the fact that the observation of the leptonic Dirac or Majorana phases at low energy does not imply non-vanishing leptogenesis. This statement is weakened in a framework when the right-handed neutrino sector is CP invariant and when the flavor effects are important [63]. This is elucidate by introducing the "orthogonal parametrization" for neutrino Dirac Yukawa matrix [64],

$$h = \frac{1}{v}M^{1/2}Rm^{1/2}U^\dagger, \qquad (4.186)$$

where $m = \text{diag}(m_1, m_2, m_3)$ is the diagonal matrix of the light neutrino masses, M is the diagonal matrix of the right-handed neutrino masses and U is the MNS matrix. The orthogonal matrix R is defined by this equation as $R = vM^{-1/2}hUm^{-1/2}$. In the basis where the right-handed neutrino mass matrix and the charged lepton mass matrix are diagonal, the neutrino Dirac Yukawa matrix can be written as $h = V_R^{\nu\dagger}\text{diag}(h_1, h_2, h_3)V_L^\nu$. Therefore, the low energy CP violation in the lepton sector can arise from either the left-handed sector through V_L^ν, the right-handed sector through V_R^ν, or from both. From $hh^\dagger v^2 = V_R^{\nu\dagger}\text{diag}(h_1^2, h_2^2, h_3^2)V_R^\nu v^2 = M^{1/2}RmR^\dagger M^{1/2}$, it can be seen that the phases of R are related to those in the right-handed sector through V_R^ν. The asymmetry ϵ_1 given in Eq. 4.89, which is derived with one-flavor approximation, can be rewritten as follows [65],

$$\epsilon_1 = -\frac{3M_1}{16\pi v^2} \frac{\text{Im}\left(\sum_\rho m_\rho^2 R_{1\rho}^2\right)}{\sum_\beta m_\beta |R_{1\beta}|^2} \ . \tag{4.187}$$

Assuming the right-handed sector is CP invariant, low energy CP phases can then arise entirely from the left-handed sector and thus are irrelevant for ϵ_1, which vanishes because the orthogonal matrix R is real. If leptogenesis takes place at $T < 10^{12}$ GeV, the flavor effects must be taken into account. In this case the asymmetry in each flavor is given by [65],

$$\epsilon_\alpha = -\frac{3M_1}{16\pi v^2} \frac{\text{Im}\left(\sum_{\beta\rho} m_\beta^{1/2} m_\rho^{3/2} U_{\alpha\beta}^* U_{\alpha\rho} R_{1\beta} R_{1\rho}\right)}{\sum_\beta m_\beta |R_{1\beta}|^2} \ . \tag{4.188}$$

The contribution of each of these individual asymmetries to the total asymmetry is then weighted by the corresponding washout factor. Therefore, barring accidental cancellations, the presence of the MNS matrix elements in Eq. 4.188 signifies the need for low energy CP violation in order to have leptogenesis. Hence if leptonic CP violation in neutrino oscillations is observed at future very long baseline experiments [66] and if lepton number violation is established by observing neutrinoless double beta decay, it would even more strongly suggest than it has been that leptogenesis be the source for the origin of the cosmological baryon asymmetry.

Finally, a fundamental problem in the current treatment of leptogenesis is the fact that the Boltzmann equations utilized in the present calculations are purely classical treatment. However, the collision terms are zero-temperature S-matrix elements which involve quantum interference. In addition, the time evolution of the system should be treated quantum mechanically. These lead to the need of quantum Boltzmann equations which is based on Closed-Time-Path (**CTP**) formalism [67]. A more detailed discussion on this issue can be found in Refs. [6, 68].

Acknowledgments

I would like to thank the organizers, Sally Dawson, K. T. Mahanthappa and Rabi Mohapatra for inviting me to lecture and for organizing such an intellectually stimulating TASI summer school, which has been a very essential experience for graduate students in theoretical high energy physics.

I would also like to thank the student participants for their interesting questions and for their enthusiastic participation at the school.

References

[1] W. Buchmuller, R. D. Peccei and T. Yanagida, Ann. Rev. Nucl. Part. Sci. **55**, 311 (2005).
[2] A. Strumia, hep-ph/0608347.
[3] E. Nardi, hep-ph/0702033.
[4] Y. Nir, hep-ph/0702199.
[5] A. Riotto and M. Trodden, Ann. Rev. Nucl. Part. Sci. **49**, 35 (1999); M. Trodden and S. M. Carroll, "*TASI Lectures: Introduction to Cosmology*", published in *Boulder 2002, Particle Physics and Cosmology*, 703-793, the proceedings of the Theoretical Advanced Study Institute in Elementary Particle Physics – Particle Physics and Cosmology: The Quest for Physics Beyond the Standard Model(s), Boulder, Colorado, 2-28 Jun 2002, World Scientific, astro-ph/0401547.
[6] A. Riotto, hep-ph/9807454.
[7] M. Trodden, hep-ph/0411301.
[8] C. J. Copi, D. N. Schramm and M. S. Turner, Science **267**, 192 (1995).
[9] C. L. Bennett *et al.*, Astrophys. J. Suppl. **148**, 1 (2003).
[10] A. D. Sakharov, Pisma Zh. Eksp. Teor. Fiz. **5**, 32 (1967) [JETP Lett. **5**, 24 (1967); Sov. Phys. Usp. **34**, 392 (1991)].
[11] G. 't Hooft, Phys. Rev. Lett. **37**, 8 (1976); G. 't Hooft, Phys. Rev. **D14**, 3432 (1976) [Erratum-ibid. **D18**, 2199 (1978)].
[12] S. L. Adler, Phys. Rev. **177**, 2426 (1969); J. S. Bell and R. Jackiw, Nuovo Cimento **51**, 47 (1969).
[13] S. Dimopoulos and L. Susskind, Phys. Rev. **D18**, 4500 (1978); N. S. Manton, Phys. Rev. **D28**, 2019 (1983).
[14] T. P. Cheng and L. F. Li, "*Gauge Theory Of Elementary Particle Physics*", Oxford, UK: Clarendon (Oxford Science Publications), 536 pages, (1984).
[15] V. A. Kuzmin, V. A. Rubakov and M. E. Shaposhnikov, Phys. Lett. **B155**, 36 (1985).
[16] F. R. Klinkhamer and N. S. Manton, Phys. Rev. **D30**, 2212 (1984).
[17] P. Arnold and L. D. McLerran, Phys. Rev. **D36**, 581 (1987).
[18] P. Arnold, D. Son and L. G. Yaffe, Phys. Rev. **D55**, 6264 (1997); P. Arnold, D. T. Son and L. G. Yaffe, Phys. Rev. **D59**, 105020 (1999); D. Bodeker, Phys. Lett. **B426**, 351 (1998); D. Bodeker, Nucl. Phys. **B559**, 502 (1999); D. Bodeker, Nucl. Phys. **B559**, 502 (1999).
[19] E. W. Kolb and M. S. Turner, "The Early Universe," Redwood City, USA: Addison-Wesley (1988) 719 pp., (Frontier in Physics, 70).
[20] I. Affleck and M. Dine, Nucl. Phys. **B249**, 361 (1985).
[21] M. E. Shaposhnikov, JETP Lett. **44**, 465 (1986) [Pisma Zh. Eksp. Teor. Fiz. **44**, 364 (1986)]. see also, G. R. Farrar and M. E. Shaposhnikov, Phys. Rev. Lett. **70**, 2833 (1993) [Erratum-ibid. **71**, 210 (1993)].

[22] M.-C. Chen and K. T. Mahanthappa, Int. J. Mod. Phys. **A18**, 5819 (2003); M.-C. Chen and K. T. Mahanthappa, AIP Conf. Proc. **721**, 269 (2004) hep-ph/0311034.
[23] A. de Gouvea, in the proceedings of Theoretical Advance Study Institute in Elementary Particle Physics (TASI 2004): *Physics in D >= 4*, 197 - 258 pp, Boulder, Colorado, 6 Jun - 2 Jul 2004, hep-ph/0411274; R. N. Mohapatra *et al.*, hep-ph/0412099; R. N. Mohapatra *et al.*, hep-ph/0510213; C. H. Albright and M.-C. Chen, Phys. Rev. **D74**, 113006 (2006).
[24] P. Minkowski, Phys. Lett. **B67**, 421 (1977); M. Gell-Mann, P. Ramond and R. Slansky, in *Supergravity*, eds. D. Freedman and P. Van Niuwenhuizen (North Holland, Amsterdam, 1979), p. 315; T. Yanagida, in *Proceedings of the Workshop on Unified Theories and Baryon Number in the Universe*, eds. O. Sawada and A. Sugamoto (KEK, Tsukuba, Japan, 1979); S. L. Glashow in *1979 Cargèse Lectures in Physics – Quarks and Leptons*, eds. M. Lévy *et al.* (Plenum, New York, 1980), p. 707. See also R. N. Mohapatra and G. Senjanović, Phys. Rev. Lett. **44**, 912 (1980); J. Schechter and J.W.F. Valle, Phys. Rev. **D22**, 2227 (1980).
[25] M. Fukugita and T. Yanagida, Phys. Lett. **B174**, 45 (1986); M. A. Luty, Phys. Rev. **D45**, 455 (1992); M. Plumacher, Z. Phys. **C74**, 549 (1997); W. Buchmuller and M. Plumacher, Phys. Lett. **B389**, 73 (1996).
[26] S. Blanchet and P. Di Bari, JCAP **0606**, 023 (2006); G. Engelhard, Y. Grossman, E. Nardi and Y. Nir, hep-ph/0612187.
[27] W. Buchmuller, P. Di Bari and M. Plumacher, Nucl. Phys. **B643**, 367 (2002); R. Barbieri, P. Creminelli, A. Strumia and N. Tetradis, Nucl. Phys. **B575**, 61 (2000).
[28] W. Buchmuller, P. Di Bari and M. Plumacher, Annals Phys. **315**, 305 (2005).
[29] S. Davidson and A. Ibarra, Phys. Lett. **B535**, 25 (2002).
[30] T. Hambye, Y. Lin, A. Notari, M. Papucci and A. Strumia, Nucl. Phys. **B695**, 169 (2004).
[31] K. Dick, M. Lindner, M. Ratz and D. Wright, Phys. Rev. Lett. **84**, 4039 (2000).
[32] H. Murayama and A. Pierce, Phys. Rev. Lett. **89**, 271601 (2002).
[33] W. Buchmuller, P. Di Bari and M. Plumacher, Phys. Lett. **B547**, 128 (2002); S. Davidson and A. Ibarra, Phys. Lett. **B535**, 25 (2002); G. F. Giudice, A. Notari, M. Raidal, A. Riotto and A. Strumia, Nucl. Phys. **B685**, 89 (2004).
[34] M. Y. Khlopov and A. D. Linde, Phys. Lett. **B138**, 265 (1984); B. A. Campbell, S. Davidson and K. A. Olive, Nucl. Phys. **B399**, 111 (1993); S. Sarkar, hep-ph/9510369. G. G. Ross and S. Sarkar, Nucl. Phys. **B461**, 597 (1996); M. Y. Khlopov, *"Cosmoparticle Physics"*, 577p, World Scientific, Singapore (1999).
[35] G. F. Giudice, A. Riotto and I. Tkachev, JHEP **9911**, 036 (1999).
[36] J. Pradler and F. D. Steffen, Phys. Rev. **D75**, 023509 (2007).
[37] M. Kawasaki, K. Kohri and T. Moroi, Phys. Rev. **D71**, 083502 (2005).
[38] J. Pradler and F. D. Steffen, to appear in Phys. Lett. **B**, hep-ph/0612291.
[39] A. Pilaftsis, Phys. Rev. **D56**, 5431 (1997).

[40] A. Pilaftsis and T. E. J. Underwood, Nucl. Phys. **B692**, 303 (2004).
[41] Y. Nir, hep-ph/0109090.
[42] Y. Grossman, T. Kashti, Y. Nir and E. Roulet, Phys. Rev. Lett. **91**, 251801 (2003); L. Boubekeur, hep-ph/0208003. L. Boubekeur, T. Hambye and G. Senjanovic, Phys. Rev. Lett. **93**, 111601 (2004); Y. Grossman, T. Kashti, Y. Nir and E. Roulet, JHEP **0411**, 080 (2004).
[43] G. D'Ambrosio, G. F. Giudice and M. Raidal, Phys. Lett. **B575**, 75 (2003).
[44] L. Covi, N. Rius, E. Roulet and F. Vissani, Phys. Rev. **D57**, 93 (1998).
[45] M. Yamaguchi and K. Yoshioka, Phys. Lett. **B543**, 189 (2002).
[46] M.-C. Chen and K. T. Mahanthappa, Phys. Rev. **D62**, 113007 (2000); *ibid.* **65**, 053010 (2002); *ibid.* **68**, 017301 (2003).
[47] M.-C. Chen and K. T. Mahanthappa, Phys. Rev. **D70**, 113013 (2004).
[48] M. Fujii, K. Hamaguchi and T. Yanagida, Phys. Rev. **D65**, 115012 (2002)
[49] R. Kuchimanchi and R. N. Mohapatra, Phys. Rev. **D66**, 051301 (2002); Phys. Lett. **B552**, 198 (2003).
[50] M.-C. Chen, A. de Gouvea and B. A. Dobrescu, Phys. Rev. **D75**, 055009 (2007).
[51] T. G. Rizzo, hep-ph/0610104.
[52] P. H. Frampton, S. L. Glashow and T. Yanagida, Phys. Lett. **B548**, 119 (2002).
[53] S. Raby, Phys. Lett. **B561**, 119 (2003).
[54] M.-C. Chen and K. T. Mahanthappa, Phys. Rev. **D71**, 035001 (2005).
[55] J. C. Pati and A. Salam, Phys. Rev. **D10**, 275 (1974); R. N. Mohapatra and J. C. Pati, Phys. Rev. **D11**, 566 (1975); R. N. Mohapatra and J. C. Pati, Phys. Rev. **D11**, 2558 (1975); G. Senjanovic and R. N. Mohapatra, Phys. Rev. **D12**, 1502 (1975).
[56] M.-C. Chen, Phys. Rev. **D71**, 113010 (2005).
[57] T. Blank and W. Hollik, Nucl. Phys. **B514**, 113 (1998); M. Czakon, M. Zralek and J. Gluza, Nucl. Phys. **B573**, 57 (2000); M. Czakon, J. Gluza, F. Jegerlehner and M. Zralek, Eur. Phys. J. **C13**, 275 (2000); M.-C. Chen and S. Dawson, Phys. Rev. **D70**, 015003 (2004); M.-C. Chen, S. Dawson and T. Krupovnickas, Int. J. Mod. Phys. **A21**, 4045 (2006); M.-C. Chen, Mod. Phys. Lett. **A21**, 621 (2006); M.-C. Chen, S. Dawson and T. Krupovnickas, Phys. Rev. **D74**, 035001 (2006).
[58] N. G. Deshpande, J. F. Gunion, B. Kayser and F. I. Olness, Phys. Rev. **D44**, 837 (1991); Y. Rodriguez and C. Quimbay, Nucl. Phys. **B637**, 219 (2002).
[59] P. Ball, J. M. Frere and J. Matias, Nucl. Phys. **B572**, 3 (2000).
[60] S. Antusch and S. F. King, Phys. Lett. **B597**, 199 (2004); A. S. Joshipura, E. A. Paschos and W. Rodejohann, Nucl. Phys. **B611**, 227 (2001); T. Hambye and G. Senjanovic, Phys. Lett. **B582**, 73 (2004); W. Rodejohann, Phys. Rev. **D70**, 073010 (2004)
[61] M.-C. Chen and K. T. Mahanthappa, Phys. Rev. **D75**, 015001 (2007).
[62] R. Barbieri, P. Creminelli, A. Strumia and N. Tetradis, Nucl. Phys. **B575**, 61 (2000); A. Abada, S. Davidson, A. Ibarra, F. X. Josse-Michaux, M. Losada and A. Riotto, JHEP **0609**, 010 (2006); A. Abada, S. Davidson, F. X. Josse-Michaux, M. Losada and A. Riotto, JCAP **0604**, 004 (2006).

[63] E. Nardi, Y. Nir, E. Roulet and J. Racker, JHEP **0601**, 164 (2006).
[64] J. A. Casas and A. Ibarra, Nucl. Phys. **B618**, 171 (2001).
[65] S. Pascoli, S. T. Petcov and A. Riotto, hep-ph/0609125; S. Pascoli, S. T. Petcov and A. Riotto, hep-ph/0611338.
[66] W. J. Marciano, hep-ph/0108181; M. V. Diwan et al., Phys. Rev. **D68**, 012002 (2003).
[67] K. T. Mahanthappa, Phys. Rev. **126**, 329 (1962); P. M. Bakshi and K. T. Mahanthappa, J. Math. Phys. **4**, 1 (1963); ibid. 12 (1963).
[68] A. De Simone and A. Riotto, hep-ph/0703175.

Chapter 5

Neutrino Experiments

J. M. Conrad

Department of Physics,
Columbia University,
New York, NY

This article is a summary of four introductory lectures on "Neutrino Experiments," given at the 2006 TASI summer school. The purpose was to sketch out the present questions in neutrino physics, and discuss the experiments that can address them. The ideas were then explored in depth by later lecturers.

This article begins with an overview of neutrinos in the Standard Model and what we know about these particles today. This is followed by a discussion of the direction of the field, divided into the three themes identified in the *APS Study on the Future of Neutrino Physics*.[1] This APS study represented the culmination of a year-long effort by the neutrino community to come to a consensus on future directions. The report is recommended reading for students, along with the accompanying working group white papers, especially the Theory Group Whitepaper.[2]

While these lectures used the APS Neutrino Study themes as the core, the emphasis here is different from the APS report. The point of a summer school is to teach specific ideas rather than provide a perfectly balanced overview of the field. The result is that, with apologies, some experiments were necessarily left out of the discussion. Students are referred to the Neutrino Oscillation Industry Website[3] for a complete list of all neutrino experiments, by category.

5.1. Neutrinos As We Knew Them

Neutrinos are different from the other fermions. Even before the recent evidence of neutrino mass, neutrinos were peculiar members of the Standard

Model. They are the only fermions

- to carry no electric charge.
- for which we have no evidence of a right-handed partner.
- that are defined as massless.

These ideas are connected by the fact that, unlike other spin 1/2 particles, neutrinos can only interact through the weak interaction.

Even though the Standard Model picture is now demonstrably wrong, this theoretical framework provides a good place to start the discussion. This section begins by expanding on the Standard Model picture of the neutrino sketched above. It then discusses how neutrinos interact. This is followed by an overview of neutrino sources and detectors.

5.1.1. Neutrinos in the Standard Model

Neutrinos are the only Standard Model fermions to interact strictly via the weak interaction. This proceeds through two types of boson exchange. Exchange of the Z^0 is called the neutral current (NC) interaction. Exchange of the $W^\pm$ is called the charged current (CC) interaction. When a W is emitted, charge conservation at the vertex requires that a charged lepton exits the interaction. We know the family of an incoming neutrino by the charged partner which exits the CC interaction. For example, a scattered electron tags a ν_e interaction, a μ tags a ν_μ interaction, and a τ tags a ν_τ interaction. The neutrino always emits the W^+ and the antineutrino always emits the W^- in the CC interaction. In order to conserve charge at the lower vertex, the CC interaction is flavor-changing for target quarks. For example, in a neutrino interaction, if a neutron, n, absorbs a W^+, a proton, p, will exit the interaction. The W has converted a d quark to a u quark. The first two diagrams shown on Fig. 5.1 illustrate a NC and a CC interaction, respectively.

In 1989, measurements of the Z^0 width at LEP[4] and SLD[5] determined that there are only three families of light-mass weakly-interacting neutrinos, although we will explore this question in more depth in section 3 of these lectures. These are the ν_e, the ν_μ, and the ν_τ. The interactions of the ν_e and ν_μ have been shown to be consistent with the Standard Model weak interaction. Until recently, there has only been indirect evidence for the ν_τ through the decay of the τ meson. In July 2000, however, the DoNuT Experiment (E872) at Fermilab presented direct evidence for ν_τ interactions.[6]

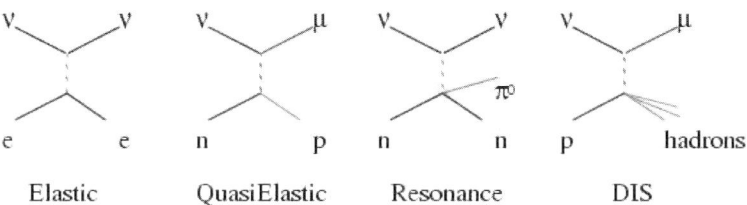

Fig. 5.1. Examples of the four types of neutrino interactions which appear throughout this discussion and are defined in Sec. 5.1.2. The first two diagrams show an NC and CC interaction, respectively.

Within the Standard Model, neutrinos are massless. This assumption is consistent with direct experimental observation. It is also an outcome of the feature of "handedness" associated with neutrinos. To understand handedness, it is simplest to begin by discussing "helicity," since for massless particles helicity and handedness are identical.

For a spin 1/2 Dirac particle, helicity is the projection of a particle's spin (Σ) along its direction of motion $\hat{p}$, with operator $\Sigma \cdot \hat{p}$. Helicity has two possible states: spin aligned opposite the direction of motion (negative, or "left helicity") and spin aligned along the direction of motion (positive or "right helicity"). If a particle is massive, then the sign of the helicity of the particle will be frame dependent. When one boosts to a frame where one is moving faster than the particle, the sign of the momentum will change but the spin will not, and therefore the helicity will flip. For massless particles, which must travel at the speed of light, one cannot boost to a frame where helicity changes sign.

Handedness (or chirality) is the Lorentz invariant (*i.e.*, frame-independent) analogue of helicity for both massless and massive Dirac particles. There are two states: "left handed" (LH) and "right handed" (RH). For the case of massless particles, including Standard Model neutrinos, helicity and handedness are identical. A massless fermion is either purely LH or RH, and, in principle, can appear in either state. Massive particles have both RH and LH components. A helicity eigenstate for a massive particle is a combination of handedness states. It is only in the high energy limit, where particles are effectively massless, that handedness and helicity coincide for massive fermions. Nevertheless, people tend to use the terms "helicity" and "handedness" interchangeably. Unlike the electromagnetic and strong interactions, the weak interaction involving neutrinos has a definite preferred handedness.

In 1956, it was shown that neutrinos are LH and outgoing antineutrinos are RH.[7] This effect is called "parity violation." If neutrinos respected parity, then an equal number of LH and RH neutrinos should have been produced in the 1956 experiment. The fact that all neutrinos are LH and all antineutrinos are RH means that, unlike all of the other fermions in the Standard Model, parity appears to be maximally violated for this particle. This is clearly very strange.

We need a method to enforce parity violation within the weak interaction theory. To this end, consider a fermion wavefunction, ψ, broken up into its LH and RH components:

$$\psi = \psi_L + \psi_R. \quad (5.1)$$

We can introduce a projection operator which selects out each component:

$$\gamma^5 \psi_{L,R} = \mp \psi_{L,R}. \quad (5.2)$$

To force the correct handedness in calculations involving the weak interaction, we can require a factor of $(1 - \gamma^5)/2$ at every weak vertex involving a neutrino. As a result of this factor, which corresponds to the LH projection operator, we often say the charged weak interaction (W exchange) is "left handed."

Note that by approaching the problem this way, RH neutrinos (and LH antineutrinos) could in principle exist but be undetected because they do not interact. They will not interact via the electromagnetic interactions because they are neutral, or via the strong interaction because they are leptons. RH Dirac neutrinos do not couple to the Standard Model W, because this interaction is "left handed," as discussed above. Because they are non-interacting, they are called "sterile neutrinos." By definition, the Standard Model has no RH neutrino.

With no RH partner, the neutrino can have no Dirac mass term in the Lagrangian. To see this, note that the free-particle Lagrangian for a massive, spin 1/2 particle is

$$\mathcal{L} = i\overline{\psi}\gamma_\mu \partial^\mu \psi - m\overline{\psi}\psi. \quad (5.3)$$

However, $\overline{\psi}\psi$ can be rewritten using

$$\psi_{L,R} = 1/2(1 \mp \gamma^5)\psi, \quad (5.4)$$

$$\overline{\psi}_{L,R} = 1/2\overline{\psi}(1 \pm \gamma^5), \quad (5.5)$$

giving

$$\overline{\psi}\psi = \overline{\psi}\left[\frac{1+\gamma^5}{2} + \frac{1-\gamma^5}{2}\right]\left[\frac{1+\gamma^5}{2} + \frac{1-\gamma^5}{2}\right]\psi = \overline{\psi}_L \psi_R + \overline{\psi}_R \psi_L. \quad (5.6)$$

In other words, an $m\bar{\psi}\psi$ ("mass") term in a Lagrangian mixes RH and LH states of the fermion. If the fermions have only one handedness (like νs), then the Dirac mass term will automatically vanish. In the Standard Model, there is no Dirac mass term for neutrinos.

5.1.2. Neutrino Interactions

Neutrino interactions in the Standard Model come in four basic types. Figure 5.1 shows examples of the four interactions. In *Elastic* scattering, "what goes is what comes out," just like two billiard balls colliding. An example is a NC interaction where the target is does not go into an excited state or break up, e.g., $\nu_e + n \to \nu_e + n$. A more complicated example is electron-neutrino scattering from electrons, where the W exchange yields a final state which is indistinguishable from the Z exchange on an event-by-event basis, so this is categorized as an elastic scatter. *Quasi-elastic* scattering is, generally, the CC analogue to elastic scattering. Exchange of the W causes the incoming lepton and the target to change flavors, but the target does not go into an excited state or break apart. An example is $\nu_\mu + n \to \mu + p$. *Single pion* production may be caused by either NC or CC interactions. In resonant single pion production, the target becomes a Δ which decays to emit a pion. In coherent scattering, there is little momentum exchange with the nucleon and a single pion is produced diffractively in the forward direction. The case of NC single π^0 production is particularly important, because this forms a background in many neutrino oscillation searches. Finally, *DIS*, or Deep Inelastic Scattering, is the case where there is large 4-momentum exchange, breaking the nucleon apart. One can have NC or CC deep inelastic scattering.

Figure 5.2 summarizes the low energy behavior of σ/E for CC events (solid line), as predicted by the NUANCE neutrino event generator.[9] The quasi-elastic, single pion and deep inelastic contributions are indicated by the broken curves. The data indicate the state of the art for neutrino cross section measurements. One can see that if precision neutrino studies are to be pursued in the MeV to few GeV range, that more accurate measurements are essential. The MiniBooNE,[10] SciBooNE,[11] and MINERvA[12] experiments are expected to improve the situation in the near future.

Above a few GeV, the total neutrino cross section rises linearly with energy. The total cross section is the sum of many partial cross sections: quasi-elastic + single pion + two pions + three pions + etc. As the energy increases, each of these cross sections sequentially "turns on" and then

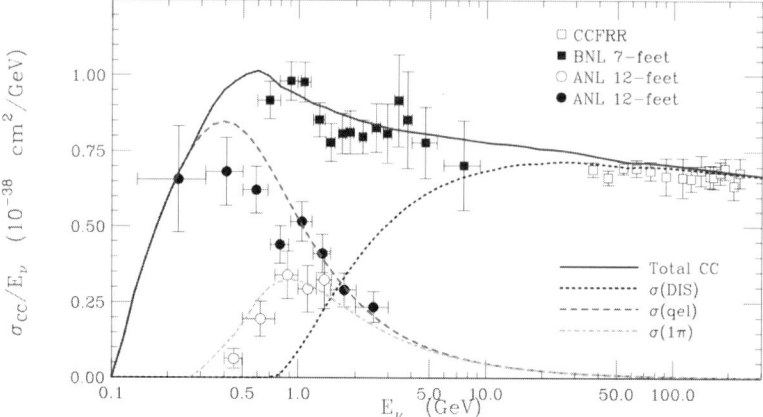

Fig. 5.2. Current status of ν_μ CC cross section measurements in the 1 to 100 GeV range. This plot shows σ/E, thus removing the linear energy dependence at high energies. Note the low energy cut-off due to the muon mass suppression. Components of the total cross section are indicated by the curves.[8]

becomes constant with energy. Thus the sum, which is the total cross section, increases continuously and linearly with E.

Nevertheless, even at high energies, this interaction is called "weak" for good reason. The total cross section for most neutrino scattering experiments is small. For 100 GeV ν_μ interactions with electrons, the cross section is $\sim 10^{-40}$ cm^2. For 100 GeV ν_μ interactions with nucleons, the cross section is $\sim 10^{-36}$ cm^2. This is many orders of magnitude less than the strong interaction. For example, for pp scattering, the cross section is $\sim 10^{-25}$ cm^2. The result is that a 100 GeV neutrino will have a mean free path in iron of 3×10^9 meters. Thus most neutrinos which hit the Earth travel through without interacting. It is only at ultra-high energies that the Earth becomes opaque to neutrinos, as discussed in Sec. 5.3.3.2.

In principle, the interactions of the ν_e, ν_μ, and ν_τ should be identical ("universal"). In practice, the mass differences of the outgoing leptons lead to considerable differences in the behavior of the cross sections. In the CC interaction, you must have enough CM energy to actually produce the outgoing charged lepton. Just above mass threshold, there is very little phase space for producing the lepton, and so production will be highly suppressed. The cross section increases in a non-linear manner until well above threshold. Consider, for example, a comparison of the ν_e and ν_μ CC quasielastic cross section on carbon, shown in Fig. 5.3. At very low energy

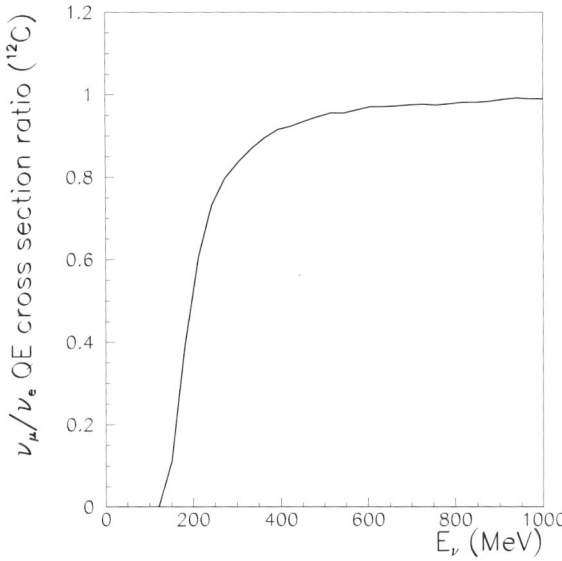

Fig. 5.3. The ratio of the ν_e to ν_μ CC cross sections as a function of neutrino energy, showing the suppression due to the lepton mass.

the CC ν_μ cross section is zero, while the ν_e cross section is non-zero, because the 105 MeV muon cannot be produced. The ratio approaches one at about 1 GeV. A similar effect occurs for the ν_τ CC interaction cross sections. The mass of the τ is 1.8 GeV, resulting in a cross section which is zero below 3.5 GeV and suppressed relative to the total ν_μ CC scattering cross section for ν_τ beam energies beyond 100 GeV. At 100 GeV, which corresponds to a center-of-mass energy of $\sqrt{2ME} \approx 14$ GeV, there is still a 25% reduction in the total CC ν_τ interaction rate compared to ν_μ due to leptonic mass suppression.

For low energy neutrino sources, the CC interaction may also be suppressed due to conversion of the nucleon at the lower vertex. For example, the CC interaction commonly called "inverse beta decay" (IBD), $\bar{\nu}_e p \to e^+ n$, which is crucial to reactor neutrino experiments, has a threshold of 1.084 MeV, driven by the mass difference between the proton and the neutron plus the mass of the positron. In the case of bound nuclei, the energy transferred in a CC interaction must overcome the binding energy difference between the incoming and outgoing nucleus as well as the mass suppression due to the charged lepton. This leads to nuclear-dependent

Table 5.1. Reactions from the Sun producing neutrinos.

Common Terminology	Reaction
"pp neutrinos"	$p + p \to\, ^2\text{H} + e^- + \nu_e$
"pep neutrinos"	$p + e^- + p \to\, ^2\text{H} + \nu_e$
"^{7}Be neutrinos"	$^7\text{Be} + e^- \to\, ^7\text{Li} + \nu_e$
"^{8}B neutrinos"	$^8\text{B} \to\, ^8\text{Be}^* + e^+ + \nu_e$
"hep neutrinos"	$^3\text{He} + p \to\, ^4\text{He} + e^+ + \nu_e$

thresholds for the CC interaction. For example:

$$^{35}\text{Cl}(75.8\%) \to\, ^{35}\text{Ar}: \quad 5.967 \text{ MeV};$$
$$^{37}\text{Cl}(24.2\%) \to\, ^{37}\text{Ar}: \quad 0.813 \text{ MeV};$$
$$^{69}\text{Ga}(60.1\%) \to\, ^{69}\text{Ge}: \quad 2.227 \text{ MeV};$$
$$^{71}\text{Ga}(39.9\%) \to\, ^{71}\text{Ge}: \quad 0.232 \text{ MeV}.$$

are the thresholds for isotopes which have been used as targets in past solar neutrino (ν_e) detectors.[14–16]

In discussing neutrino scattering at higher energies, several kinematic quantities are used to describe events. The squared center of mass energy is represented by the Mandelstam variable, s. The energy transferred by the boson is ν, and $y = \nu/E_\nu$ is the fractional energy transfer, or "inelasticity." The distribution of events as a function of y depends on the helicity. For neutrino scattering from quarks, the y-dependence is flat, but for antineutrinos, the differential cross section is peaked at low y. The variable Q^2 is the negative squared four-momentum transfer. Deep inelastic scattering begins to occur at $Q^2 \sim 1$ GeV^2. If x is the fractional momentum carried by a struck quark in a deep inelastic scatter, then $x = Q^2/2M\nu$, where M is the target mass. Elastic and quasielastic scattering occur at $x = 1$, hence $Q^2 = 2M\nu \approx sxy$, valid for large s.

5.1.3. *Sources of Neutrinos*

With such a small interaction probability, it is clear that intense neutrino sources are needed to have high statistics in a neutrino experiment. The primary sources of neutrino for interactions observed on Earth are the Sun, cosmic-ray interactions, reactors, and accelerator beams.

At present, there are two intense sources in the few MeV range that allow for low energy neutrino interaction studies. First, the interactions in the Sun produce a pure ν_e flux, as listed in Table 5.1. The energy distribution of neutrinos produced by these reactions is shown in Fig. 5.4. The sensitivity

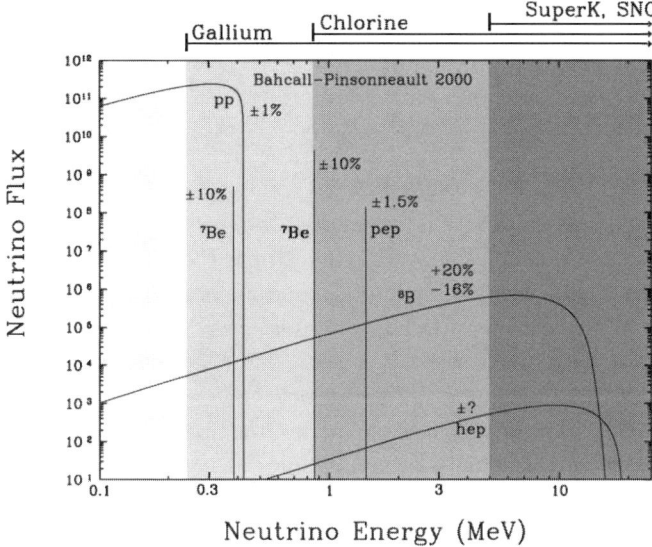

Fig. 5.4. The flux predicted by the Standard Solar Model.[13] The sensitivity of past solar neutrino detectors varies due to CC threshold in the target material.[14–16] The thresholds for various experiments is shown at the top of the plot.

of various solar neutrino experiments, due to the CC threshold, is shown at the top of the figure. There is no observable antineutrino content. The best limit on the solar neutrino $\bar{\nu}_e/\nu_e$ ratio for $E_\nu > 8.3$ MeV is 2.8×10^{-4} at 90% CL.[17] The second source is from reactors. In contrast to the Sun, reactors produce a nearly pure $\bar{\nu}_e$ flux. The energy peaks from ~ 3 to 7 MeV. Neutrinos from β decay of accelerated isotopes could, in principle, represent a third intense source of neutrinos in the MeV range (or higher), once the technical issues involved in designing such an accelerator are overcome. Such a "beta beam" would produce a very pure ν_e or $\bar{\nu}_e$ beam, depending on the accelerated isotope.[18]

At present, higher energy experiments use neutrinos produced at accelerators and in the atmosphere. In both cases, neutrinos are dominantly produced via meson decays. In the atmospheric case, cosmic rays hit atmospheric nuclei producing a shower of mesons which may decay to neutrinos along their path through the atmosphere to Earth. In a conventional neutrino beam, protons impinge on a target, usually beryllium or carbon, producing secondary mesons. In many experiments, the charged mesons are focussed (bent) toward the direction of the experiment with a magnetic

Table 5.2. Common sources of neutrinos in atmospheric and accelerator experiments.

2-body pion decay	$\pi^+ \to \mu^+ \nu_\mu,\ \pi^- \to \mu^- \bar{\nu}_\mu$
2-body kaon decay	$K^+ \to \mu^+ \nu_\mu,\ K^- \to \mu^- \bar{\nu}_\mu$
muon decay	$\mu^+ \to e^+ \bar{\nu}_\mu \nu_e,\ \mu^- \to e^- \nu_\mu \bar{\nu}_e$
K_{e3} decay	$K^+ \to \pi^0 e^+ \nu_e,\ K^- \to \pi^0 e^- \bar{\nu}_e,\ K^0 \to \pi^- e^+ \nu_e,\ K^0 \to \pi^+ e^- \bar{\nu}_e$

device called a horn. These devices are sign-selecting – they will focus one charge-sign and defocus the other – and so produce beams which are dominantly neutrinos or antineutrinos depending on the sign-selection. The beamline will have a long secondary meson decay region, which may be air or vaccuum. This is followed by a beam dump and an extended region of dirt or shielding to remove all particles except neutrinos. There are excellent reviews of methods of making accelerator-produced neutrino beams.[19] Table 5.2 summarizes the common sources of neutrino production in the atmosphere and conventional accelerator based beams.

Many atmospheric and accelerator-based neutrino experiments are designed to study 100 MeV to 10 GeV neutrinos. The atmospheric neutrino flux drops as a power-law with energy, and the 1 to 10 GeV range dominates the event rate. Accelerator beams can be tuned to a specific energy range and, using present facilities, can extend to as high as 500 GeV. From the viewpoint of sheer statistics, one should use the highest energy neutrino beam which is practical for the physics to be addressed, since the cross section rises linearly with energy. However, lower neutrino energy beams, from $\sim$ 1 to 10 GeV, are typically used for oscillation experiments. In these experiments, having a cleanly identified lepton in a low multiplicity event trumps sheer rate, and so $\sim$ 1 GeV beams are selected to assure that CCQE and single pion events dominate the interactions.

Both atmospheric and accelerator based neutrino sources are dominantly ν_μ-flavor. The main source of these neutrinos is pion decay. To understand why pions preferentially decay to produce ν_μ rather than ν_e, consider the case of pion decay to a lepton and an antineutrino: $\pi^- \to \ell^- \bar{\nu}_\ell$. The pion has spin zero and so the spins of the outgoing leptons from the decay must be opposite from angular momentum conservation. In the center of mass of the pion, this implies that both the antineutrino and the charged lepton have spin projected along the direction of motion ("right" or "positive" helicity). However, this is a weak decay, where the W only couples to the RH antineutrino and the LH component of the charged particle. The amplitude for the LH component to have right-helicity is proportional to m/E. Thus it is very small for an electron compared to the muon, producing a significant suppression for decays to electrons. Calculating the expected branching ratios:

$$R_{theory} = \frac{\Gamma(\pi^\pm \to e^\pm \nu_e)}{\Gamma(\pi^\pm \to \mu^\pm \nu_\mu)} \quad (5.7)$$

$$= \left(\frac{m_e}{m_\mu}\right)^2 \left(\frac{m_\pi^2 - m_e^2}{m_\pi^2 - m_\mu^2}\right)^2 \quad (5.8)$$

$$= 1.23 \times 10^{-4}; \quad (5.9)$$

This compares well to the data:[20] $R_{exp} = (1.230 \pm 0.004) \times 10^{-4}$.

The above discussion assumed the neutrino was massless. If the neutrino is massive, then it too can be produced with wrong helicity with an amplitude proportional to m_ν/E and thus a probability proportional to $(m_\nu/E)^2$. As discussed in Sec. 5.2.2, below, neutrino mass is limited to be very small ($\sim$ eV) and thus the rate of wrong-helicity neutrino production is too low a level for any chance of observation in the near future.

Depending on the energy, there may also be significant neutrino production from kaon decays. The charged kaon preferentially decays to the ν_μ for the same reason as the charged pion. However, for equal energy mesons, the kinematic limit for a neutrino from K^+ decay is much higher than for π^+ decay: $E_\nu^{\max,K} = 0.98 E_K$ compared to $E_\nu^{\max,\pi} = 0.43 E_\pi$. Thus the neutrinos from kaon decays can be isolated by studying the highest energy component of a beam. Figure 5.5 shows the contributions of pion and kaon decays to the ν_μ flux in the MiniBooNE experiment, which uses an 8 GeV primary proton beam.

Electron neutrino flavors are produced in these beams through $K \to \pi \nu_e e$ (called "Ke3") decay and through the decay of the muons which were produced in the pion decay. These are three-body decays which avoid substantial helicity suppression. Helicity does, however, affect the energy spectrum of the outgoing decay products. In an accelerator-based experiment, the level of electron-flavor content can be regulated, at some level, by the choice of primary beam energy and the length of the decay region. A low primary beam energy will suppress kaon production because of the relatively high mass of this meson (494 MeV). A short decay pipe will suppress ν_e from μ decay, which tends to occur downstream, because it is produced in a multi-step decay chain ($\pi \to \mu \to \nu_e$). Both of these methods of suppressing ν_e production also lead to a reduction in the ν_μ production rate, so an experimenter must balance competing goals in the beam design. In the case of atmospheric neutrinos, the ratio is roughly 2:1 for ν_μ:ν_e, though the fraction ν_e's changes with energy (see Fig. 5.6). The atmospheric flux

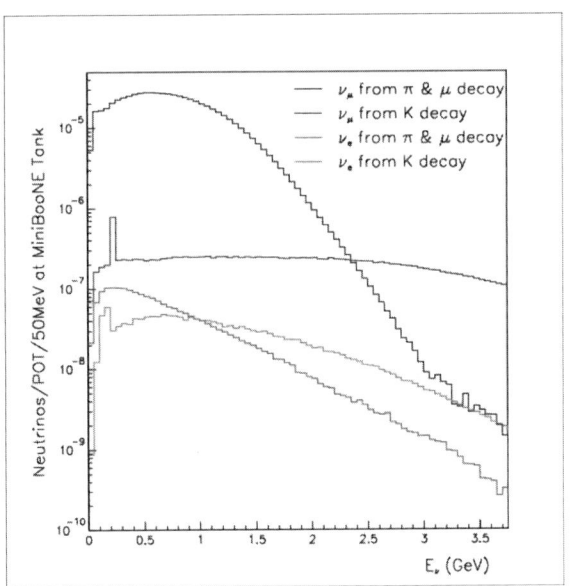

Fig. 5.5. The contributions from pion and kaon production to the total predicted ν_μ flux in the MiniBooNE experiment. The spikes at low energy in the K-produced fluxes are due to decays of stopped kaons in the beam dump.[10]

depends on the location of the detector because charged particle are bent by the Earth's magnetic field. The variation between fluxes at the Kamioka mine in Japan and Soudan mine in Minnesota are shown in Fig. 5.6.

As we move to a precision era in neutrino physics, precise "first-principles" predictions of the flux are becoming very important. For conventional accelerator-based neutrino beams and for the atmospheric flux, this requires well-measured cross-sections for production of secondary pions and kaons. This has motivated a range of secondary production experiments. The kinematic coverage is shown on Fig. 5.7.

The future of high intensity ν_μ and ν_e beams is likely to lie in beams produced from muon decay. Because of the potential for very high intensity, these beams are called "Neutrino Factories." The concept is very attractive because it produces beams which are very pure ν_μ and $\bar{\nu}_e$ from μ^- and vice versa from μ^+. Each flavor has no "wrong sign" (antineutrino-in-neutrino-beam or neutrino-in-antineutrino beam) background. However, neutrino factory designs[18] necessarily produce high energy neutrinos, since the muons must be accelerated to high energies in order to live long enough to be captured and circulated in an accelerator. The Neutrino Factory is

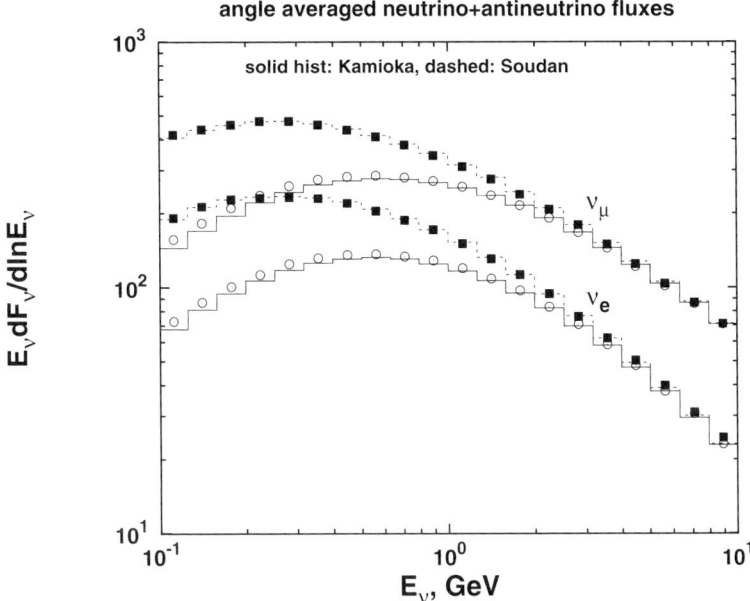

Fig. 5.6. The variation in the atmospheric neutrino flavor content as a function of energy for two locations, Japan (solid line, open circles) and Minnesota (dashed line, closed squares). The points are from a full 3-dimensional monte carlo of the flux, while the histograms are from a simpler model.[21]

seen as a promising first machine for testing ideas for a muon collider,[18] and thus has attracted interest beyond the neutrino community.

A beam enriched in ν_τ can be produced by impinging very high energy protons on a target to produce D_s-mesons which are sufficiently massive to decay to $\tau \nu_\tau$. The τ lepton is very massive, at 1.8 GeV, compared to the muon, at 106 MeV, and thus helicity considerations for the D_s decay strongly favor the $\tau \nu_\tau$ mode compared to $\mu \nu_\mu$, by a ratio of about 10:1. The τ then subsequently decays, also producing ν_τs.

Unfortunately, because of the short lifetime, it is not possible to separate D_s mesons from the other mesons prolifically produced by the primary interaction. As a result, the beam is dominated by the ν_μs produced by decays of other mesons. To reduce the production of ν_μ, experiments use a "beam dump" design where protons hit a very thick target where pions can be absorbed before decaying. The only enriched-ν_τ beam created to date was developed by DoNuT.[6] They used an 800 GeV proton on a beam dump, to produce a ratio of ν_e:ν_μ:ν_τ of about 6:9:1.

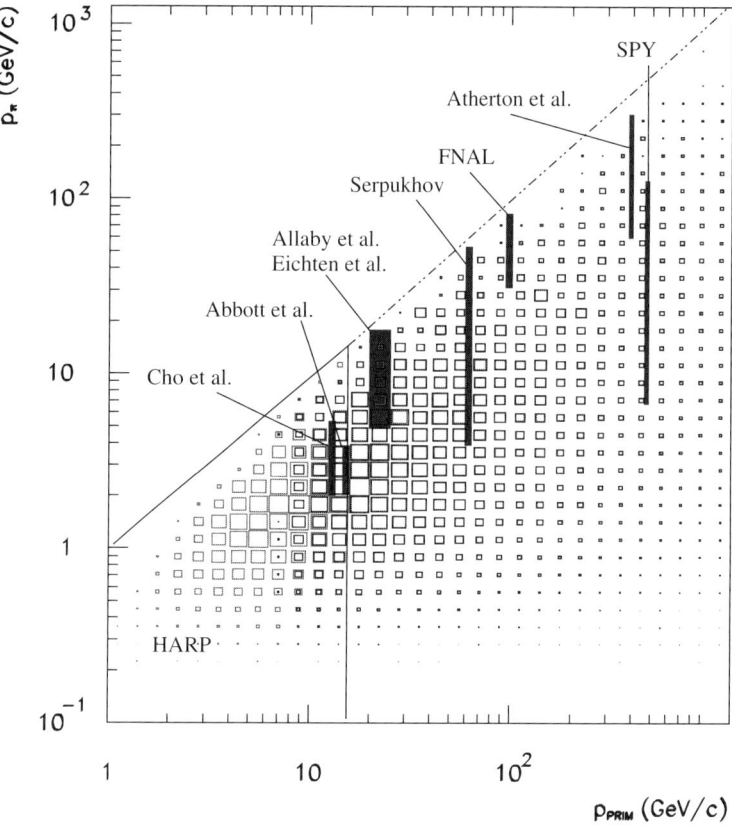

Fig. 5.7. The kinematic range covered by recent experiments measuring secondary pion and kaon production.[24]

5.1.4. *Typical Neutrino Detectors*

Because neutrinos interact so weakly, the options for detectors are limited to designs which can be constructed on a massive scale. There are several general styles in use today: unsegmented scintillator detectors, unsegmented Cerenkov detectors, segmented scintillator-and-iron calorimeters, and segmented scinitillator trackers. The most promising future technology is the noble-element based detector, which is effectively an electronic bubble chamber. Liquid argon detectors are likely to be the first large-scale working example of such technology. There are a few variations on these five themes, which are considered in later sections in the context of the measurement.

Unsegmented scintillator detectors are typically used for low energy antineutrino experiments. Recent examples include Chooz,[25] KamLAND[26] and LSND.[27] These consist of large tanks of liquid scintillator surrounded by phototubes. Usually the scintillator is oil based, hence the target material is CH_2 and its associated electrons. Often the tubes are in an pure oil buffer. This reduce backgrounds from radiation emitted from the glass which would excite scintillator. The free protons in the oil provide a target for the interaction, $\bar{\nu}_e p \to e^+ n$, which is the key for reactor experiments. The reaction threshold for this interaction is 1.806 MeV due to the mass differences between the proton and neutron and the mass of the positron. The scintillation light from the e^+, as well as light from the Compton scattering of the 0.511 MeV annihilation photons provide an initial ("prompt") signal. This is followed by n capture to produce deuterium and a 2.2 MeV. This sequence – positron followed by neutron capture – provides a clean signal for the interaction. Doping the liquid scintillator with gadolinium substantially increases the neutron capture cross section as well as the visible energy produced in the form of gammas upon neutron capture.

Unsegmented scintillator detectors are now being introduced for low energy solar neutrino measurements at Borexino,[28] KamLAND[29] and SNO+.[30] These provide energy information on an event-by-event basis, unlike most past solar neutrino experiments, such as Homestake,[14] SAGE[15] and GallEx,[16] which intergrated over time and energy. However, these are very difficult experiments to perform because a neutron is not produced and so the scattering does not produce a two-fold coincidence, but only a prompt flash of light.

Environmental backgrounds are by far the most important issue in low energy experiments. These fall into two categories: naturally occurring radioactivity and muon-induced backgrounds. To get a sense for what is expected, Fig. 5.8 shows the visible energy distribution of singles events from the KamLAND experiment with the sources of environmental background identified. The naturally occurring radioactive contaminants mainly populate the low energy range of Fig. 5.8, with isotopes from the U and Th chain extending to the highest energies. These isotopes must be kept under control by maintaining very high standards of cleanliness. The second source of environmental background, the β-decays of isotopes produced by cosmic ray muons. These dominate the background for $E_{vible} > 4$ MeV (see Fig. 5.8). These can only be eliminated by shielding the detector from cosmic rays. As a result, we must build deep underground laboratories with many thousands of meters-water-equivalent ("mwe") of rock shielding.

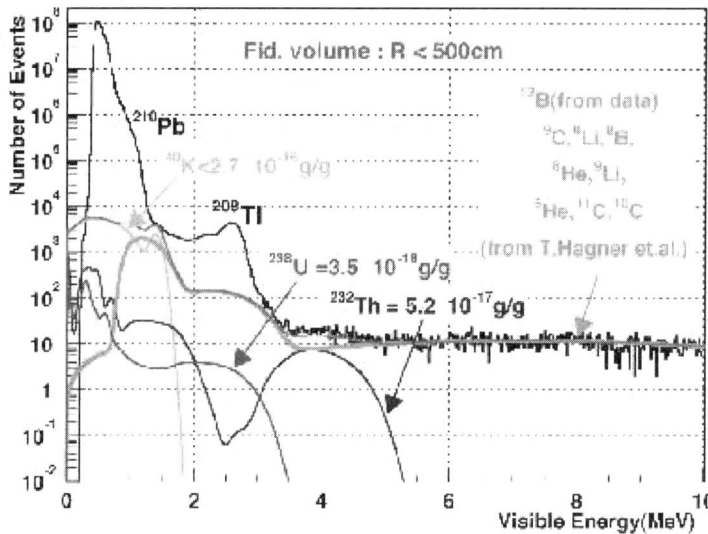

Fig. 5.8. Energy distribution and sources of singles events in KamLAND as a function of visible energy.[31]

In these scintillator detectors, the CC interaction with the carbon in the oil (which produces either nitrogen or boron depending on whether the scatterer is a neutrino or antineutrino) has a significantly higher energy threshold than scattering from free protons. $\nu_e + C \to e^- + N$ has a threshold energy of 13.369 MeV, which arises from the carbon-nitrogen mass difference (plus the mass of the electron). In the case of both reactor and solar neutrinos, the flux cuts off below this energy threshold.

Existing unsegmented Cerenkov detectors include MiniBooNE,[32] Super K,[33] and AMANDA.[34] These detectors make use of a target which is a large volume of a clear medium (undoped oil, water and ice, respectively) surrounded by or interspersed with phototubes. Undoped oil has the advantages of a larger refractive index, leading to larger Cerenkov opening angle, and of not requiring a purification system to remove living organisms. Water is the only affordable medium once a detector is larger than a few ktons. For ultra-high energy neutrino experiments, a vast natural target is needed. Sea water[35] and ice[34] have been used. Ice is, to date, more successful because it does not suffer from backgrounds from bioluminescence.

In most cases of these detectors, the tubes surround the medium and the projected image of the Cerenkov ring is used for particle identification.

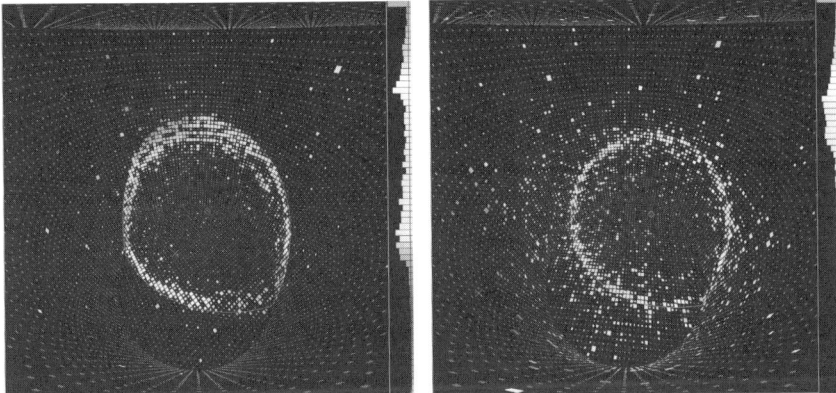

Fig. 5.9. An example of a muon ring (left) and electron ring (right) in the Super K Cerenkov detector.[33]

To understand how this works, first consider the case of a perfect, short track. This will project a ring with a sharp inner and outer edge onto the phototubes. Next consider an electron produced in a ν_e CC quasielastic interaction. Because the electron is low mass, it will multiple scatter and easily bremsstrahlung, smearing the light projected on the tubes and producing a "fuzzy" ring. A muon produced by a CC quasileastic ν_μ interaction is heavier and thus will produce a sharper outer edge to the ring. For the same visible energy, the track will also extend farther, filling the interior of the ring, and perhaps exit the tank. Fig. 5.9 compares an electron and muon ring observed in the Super K detector. If the muon stops within the tank and subsequently decays, the resulting "michel electron" provides an added tag for particle identification. In the case of the μ^-, 18% will capture in water, and thus have no michel electron tag, while only 8% will capture in oil.

Scintillator and iron calorimeters provide affordable detection for ν_μ interactions in the range of ~1 GeV and higher. Recent examples include the MINOS[36] and NuTeV[37] experiments. In these detectors, the iron provides the target, while the scintillator provides information on energy deposition per unit length. This allows separation between the hadronic shower, which occurs in both NC and CC events, and the minimum ionizing track of an outgoing muon, which occurs in CC events. Transverse information can be obtained if segmented scintillator strips are used, or if drift chambers are interspersed. The light from scintillator strips is transported to tubes by mirrored wave-length-shifting fibers. Transverse information improves

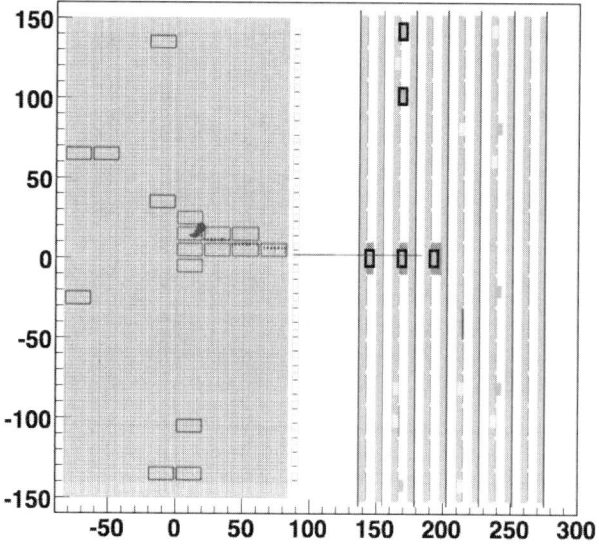

Fig. 5.10. A CCQE($\nu_\mu + n \to \mu + p$) event observed in the SciBooNE detector. The long, minimum-ionizing red track is identified as the muon, the short, heavily-ionizing red track is identifed as the proton.[11]

separation of electromagnetic and hadronic showers. The iron can be magnetized to allow separation of neutrino and antineutrino events based on the charge of the outgoing lepton.

In all three of the above detector designs, it is difficult to reconstruct multi-particle events. Tracking is not an option for an unsegmented scintillator detector. Cerenkov detectors can typically resolve two tracks per event. Segmented calorimeters reduce multiple hadrons to a shower, obscuring any track-by-track information other than from muons.

To address the problem of track reconstruction in low energy ($\lesssim 1$ GeV), low multiplicity events, there has been a move toward all-scintillator tracking detectors. This began with the SciBar detector in K2K.[38] This detector used scintillator strips, as in MINOS, but without interspersing iron. As a result, low energy (few MeV) tracks were clearly observable and quasielastic and single pion events could be fully reconstructed. SciBar has since been incorporated into the SciBooNE experiment at Fermilab.[11] The CCQE event in SciBooNE, shown in Fig. 5.10, makes clear the benefits of fine segmentation. The position of the vertex and the short track from the proton are well-resolved in the SciBar detector (green region). The technology has been taken further by the MINERvA experiment, which has attained 2 mm resolution with their prototype.[39] Scibar and MINERvA are relatively small (few ton) detectors. The first very large scale application of this technology will be NOvA, which is a future 15 kton detector.[40] This detector will use PVC tubes filled with liquid scintillator, which is more cost-effective than extruded scintillator strips for very large detectors. Their design also loops the wave-length shifting fiber, so that there are, effectively, two perfectly mirrored fibers are in each cell. This elegant solution increases the collected light by a factor of four, which is necessary for ~ 15 m strips.

The most promising new technology for high resolution track reconstruction in neutrino physics is the liquid argon TPC. A TPC, or time projection chamber, uses drift chambers to track in the x and y views and drift time to determine the z view. Liquid argon (LAr), which provides the massive target for the neutrino interaction, also scintillates, providing the start for the drift-time measurement. A key point for future neutrino experiments is the high efficiency for identifying electron showers (expected to be 80-90%) with a rejection factor of 70 for NC π^0 events. In particular, these detectors can differentiate between converted photons and electrons through the dE/dx in the first few centimeters of the track. Typical energy resolution for an electromagnetic shower is $3\%/\sqrt{E}$.

There is a great deal of activity on development of LAr detectors. Data have been taken successfully on a 50 liter LArTPC prototype in the NOMAD neutrino beam at CERN, resulting in reconstruction of $\sim$100 CC quasielastic events.[41] Also, recently, a 600 ton Icarus module has been commissioned at Gran Sasso.[42] A 0.8 ton LAr test detector will begin taking data at Fermilab in January, 2008.[43] As discussed in Sec. 5.3.2, the microBooNE experiment is a proposed 100 ton detector which would take data in 2010.[44] In principle, these detectors can be scaled up to tens of ktons, as is discussed in the "Ash River Proposal".[45]

5.2. Neutrinos As We Know Them Now

The recent discovery of neutrino oscillations requires that we reconsider the Standard Model Lagrangian of Sec. 5.1.1. It must now incorporate, preferably in a motivated fashion, both neutrino mass and neutrino mixing. This represents both a challenge and an opportunity for the theory, which I will discuss in the following section. This section concentrates on the experimental discovery. It is interesting to note that while neither neutrino mass nor mixing were "needed" in the Standard Model theory, both are required for the discovery of neutrino oscillations. The probability for neutrino oscillations will be zero unless *both* effects are present.

The outcome of the observation of neutrino oscillations is typically summarized by the statement that "neutrinos have mass." To be clear: we still have no direct measurement of neutrino mass. At this point, we have clear evidence of mass differences between neutrinos from the observation of neutrino oscillations. A mass difference between two neutrinos necessarily implies that at least one of the neutrinos has non-zero mass. All experimental evidence indicates that the actual values of the neutrino masses are tiny in comparison to the masses of the charged fermions. At the end of this section, attempts at direct measurement of neutrino mass are described.

5.2.1. *Neutrino Oscillations*

Recent results on neutrino oscillations provide indisputable evidence that there is a spectrum of masses for neutrinos. In this section, I describe the formalism for neutrino oscillations, and then review the experimental results which have now been confirmed at the 5σ level. This is covered briefly because these results are well known and covered extensively elsewhere.[2]

5.2.1.1. *The Basic Formalism*

Neutrino oscillations requires that neutrinos have mass, that the difference between the masses be small, and that the mass eigenstates be different from the weak interaction eigenstates. In this case, the weak eigenstates can be written as mixtures of the mass eigenstates. For example, in a simple 2-neutrino model:

$$\nu_e = \cos\theta\, \nu_1 + \sin\theta\, \nu_2$$
$$\nu_\mu = -\sin\theta\, \nu_1 + \cos\theta\, \nu_2$$

where θ is the "mixing angle." In this case, a pure flavor (weak) eigenstate born through a weak decay can oscillate into another flavor as the state propagates in space. This oscillation is due to the fact that each of the mass eigenstate components propagates with different frequencies if the masses are different, $\Delta m^2 = |m_2^2 - m_1^2| > 0$. In such a two-component model, the oscillation probability for $\nu_\mu \to \nu_e$ oscillations is then given by:

$$\text{Prob}\,(\nu_\mu \to \nu_e) = \sin^2 2\theta\, \sin^2\left(\frac{1.27\,\Delta m^2\,(\text{eV}^2)\,L\,(\text{km})}{E\,(\text{GeV})}\right), \quad (5.10)$$

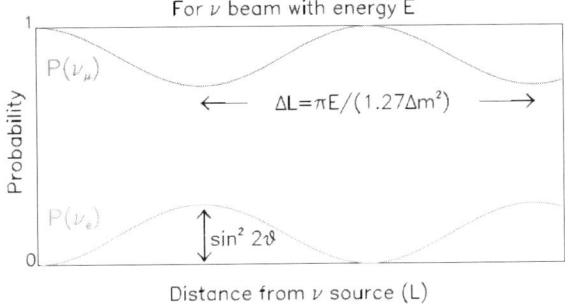

Fig. 5.11. Example of neutrino oscillations as a function of distance from the source, L. The wavelength depends upon the experimental parameters L and E (neutrino energy) and the fundamental parameter Δm^2. The amplitude of the oscillation is constrained by the mixing term, $\sin^2 2\theta$.

where L is the distance from the source, and E is the neutrino energy. As shown in Fig. 5.11, the oscillation wavelength will depend upon L, E, and Δm^2. The amplitude will depend upon $\sin^2 2\theta$.

Neutrino oscillations only occur if the two mass states involved have sufficiently small Δm^2 that the neutrino flavor is produced in a superposition of two mass states. If the mass splitting is sufficiently large, a given neutrino flavor would be produced in one or the other of the two mass eigenstates and interference (i.e., oscillations) would not occur.

Most neutrino oscillation analyses consider only two-generation mixing scenarios, but the more general case includes oscillations among all three neutrino species. This can be expressed as:

$$\begin{pmatrix} \nu_e \\ \nu_\mu \\ \nu_\tau \end{pmatrix} = \begin{pmatrix} U_{e1} & U_{e2} & U_{e3} \\ U_{\mu 1} & U_{\mu 2} & U_{\mu 3} \\ U_{\tau 1} & U_{\tau 2} & U_{\tau 3} \end{pmatrix} \begin{pmatrix} \nu_1 \\ \nu_2 \\ \nu_3 \end{pmatrix}.$$

This formalism is analogous to the quark sector, where strong and weak eigenstates are not identical and the resultant mixing is described conventionally by a unitary mixing matrix. The oscillation probability is then:

$$\text{Prob}\,(\nu_\alpha \rightarrow \nu_\beta) = \delta_{\alpha\beta} - 4 \sum_{j>i} U_{\alpha i} U^*_{\beta i} U^*_{\alpha j} U_{\beta j} \sin^2\left(\frac{1.27\,\Delta m^2_{ij}\,L}{E}\right), \quad (5.11)$$

where $\Delta m^2_{ij} = m_j^2 - m_i^2$, α and β are flavor-state indices (e, μ, τ) and i and j are mass-state indices $(1, 2, 3)$.

For three neutrino mass states, there are three different Δm^2 parameters, although only two are independent since the two small Δm^2 parameters must sum to the largest. The neutrino mass states, ν_1, ν_2 and ν_3 are defined such that the difference between ν_1 and ν_2 always represents the smallest splitting. However, the mass of ν_3 relative to ν_1 and ν_2 is arbitrary and so the sign of the Δm^2 parameters which include the third mass state may be positive or negative. That is, if $\nu_3 > \nu_1, \nu_2$, then Δm_{23}^2 will be positive, but if $\nu_1, \nu_2 > \nu_3$, then Δm_{23}^2 will be negative. The former is called a "normal mass hierarchy" and the latter is the "inverted mass hierarchy." At this point, the sign is irrelevant because Δm^2 appears in a term which is squared. However, in Sec. 5.3.1, this point will become important.

The mixing matrix above can be described in terms of three mixing angles, θ_{12}, θ_{13} and θ_{23}:

$$U = \begin{pmatrix} c_{12}c_{13} & s_{12}c_{13} & s_{13} \\ -s_{12}c_{23} - c_{12}s_{23}s_{13} & c_{12}c_{23} - s_{12}s_{23}s_{13} & s_{23}c_{13} \\ s_{12}s_{23} - c_{12}c_{23}s_{13} & -c_{12}s_{23} - s_{12}c_{23}s_{13} & c_{23}c_{13} \end{pmatrix}, \quad (5.12)$$

where $c_{ij} \equiv \cos\theta_{ij}$ and $s_{ij} \equiv \sin\theta_{ij}$, with i and j referring to the mass states. In fits to the oscillation parameters, people variously quote the results in terms of the matrix element of U, sin-squared of the given angle, sin-squared of twice the angle and a variety of other forms, all of which are related. Using the 13 case as an example, the quoted parameters are related by:

$$U_{e3}^2 \approx \sin^2\theta_{13} \approx \frac{1}{4}\sin^2 2\theta_{13}. \quad (5.13)$$

Thus, in total, there are five free parameters in the simplest three-neutrino oscillation model, which can be taken to be Δm_{12}^2, Δm_{23}^2, θ_{12}, θ_{13} and θ_{23}.

Although in general there will be mixing among all three flavors of neutrinos, two-generation mixing is often assumed for simplicity. If the mass scales are quite different ($m_3 \gg m_2 \gg m_1$, for example), then the oscillation phenomena tend to decouple and the two-generation mixing model is a good approximation in limited regions. In this case, each transition can be described by a two-generation mixing equation. However, it is possible that experimental results interpreted within the two-generation mixing formalism may indicate very different Δm^2 scales with quite different apparent strengths for the same oscillation. This is because, as is evident from equation 5.11, multiple terms involving different mixing strengths and Δm^2 values contribute to the transition probability for $\nu_\alpha \to \nu_\beta$.

5.2.1.2. Matter Effects

The probability for neutrino oscillations is modified in the presence of matter. This is true in any material, however the idea was first explored for neutrino oscillations in the Sun, by Mikheyev, Smirnov and Wolfenstein. Therefore, matter effects are often called "MSW" effects.[46] In general, matter effects arise in neutrino-electron scattering. The electron neutrino flavor experiences both CC and NC elastic forward-scattering with electrons. However, the ν_μ and ν_τ experience only NC forward-scattering, because creation of the μ or τ is kinematically forbidden or suppressed (e.g. $\nu_\mu + e^- \to \nu_e + \mu^-$). This difference produces the matter effect.

For neutrinos propagating through a constant density of electrons, if V_e is the elastic forward scattering potential for the ν_e component, and V_{other} is the potential for the other neutrino flavors, then the additional scattering potential is

$$V = V_e - V_{other} = \sqrt{2} G_F n_e, \quad (5.14)$$

where G_F is the Fermi constant and n_e is the electron density. This potential modifies the Hamiltonian, so that, if H_0 is the vacuum Hamiltonian, then in matter the Hamiltonian is $H_0 + V$. This means that the eigenstates are modified from those of a vacuum, ν_1 and ν_2, to become ν_{1m} and ν_{2m}. Effectively, the neutrino mass spectrum is not the same as in vacuum. The solutions to the Hamiltonian are also modified. From this, one can see that the presence of electrons may substantially change the oscillatory behavior of neutrinos.

The simplest outcome is that matter induces a shift in the mass state, which is a combination of flavor eigenstates, propagates through the material. This leads to a change in the oscillation probability:

$$\text{Prob}(\nu_e \to \nu_\mu) = \left(\sin^2 2\theta / W^2\right) \sin^2 \left(1.27 W \Delta m^2 L / E\right) \quad (5.15)$$

where $W^2 = \sin^2 2\theta + (\sqrt{2} G_F n_e (2E/\Delta m^2) - \cos 2\theta)^2$ (Note that in a vacuum, where $n_e = 0$, this reduces to equation 5.10.) From this, one can see that if a neutrino, passing through matter, encounters an optimal density of electrons, a "resonance," or large enhancement of the oscillation probability, can occur. The Sun has a wide range of electron densities and thus is a prime candidate for causing matter effects. Also, neutrinos traveling through the Earth's core, which has a high electron density, might experience matter effects. This will produce a "day-night effect," or siderial variation, for neutrinos from the Sun.

For situations like the Sun, with very high electron densities which vary with the position of the neutrino (and hence the time which the neutrino has lived), the situation is complex. If the electron density is high and the density variation occurs slowly, or adiabatically, then transition (not oscillation!) between flavors in the mass state can occur as the neutrino propagates. Thus it is possible for neutrinos to be produced in the core of the Sun in a given mass and flavor state, and slowly evolve in flavor content until the neutrino exits the Sun, still in the same mass state. In other words, in the Sun, a ν_e produced in a mass eigenstate $\nu_{2m}(r)$, which depends on the local electron density at radius r, propagates as a ν_{2m} until it reaches the $r = R_{solar}$, where $\nu_{2m}(R_{solar}) = \nu_2$. This peculiar effect is called the Large Mixing Angle MSW solution.

5.2.1.3. Designing an Oscillation Experiment

From equation 5.10, one can see that three important issues confront the designer of the ideal neutrino experiment. First, if one is searching for oscillations in the very small Δm^2 region, then large L/E must be chosen in order to enhance the $\sin^2(1.27\Delta m^2 L/E)$ term. However if L/E is too large in comparison to Δm^2, then oscillations occur rapidly. Because experiments have finite resolution on L and E, and a spread in beam energies, the $\sin^2(1.27\Delta m^2 L/E)$ averages to $1/2$ when $\Delta m^2 \gg L/E$ and one loses sensitivity to Δm^2. Finally, because the probability is directly proportional to $\sin^2 2\theta$, if the mixing angle is small, then high statistics are required to observe an oscillation signal.

There are two types of oscillation searches: "disappearance" and "appearance." To be simplistic, consider a pure source of neutrinos of type x. In a disappearance experiment, one looks for a deficit in the expected flux of ν_x. This requires accurate knowledge of the flux, which is often difficult to predict from first principles. Therefore, most modern disappearance experiments employ a near-far detector design. The near detector measures the flux prior to oscillation (the design goal is to effectively locate it at $L = 0$ in Fig. 5.11). This is then used to predict the unoscillated event rate in the far detector. A deficit compared to prediction indicates disappearance. Appearance experiments search for $\nu_\alpha \to \nu_\beta$ by directly observing interactions of neutrinos of type β. The case for oscillations is most persuasive if the deficit or excess has the (L/E) dependence predicted by the neutrino oscillation formula (equation 5.10).

The "sensitivity" of an experiment is defined as the average expected limit if the experiment were performed many times with no true signal (only background). Let us consider the sensitivity for a hypothetical perfect (no-systematic error) disappearance neutrino oscillation experiment with N events. A typical choice of confidence level is 90%, so in this case, the limiting probability, assuming there is no signal, is

$$P = \sigma\sqrt{N}/N. \qquad (5.16)$$

There are two possible choices of σ associated with a 90% CL sensitivity, depending on the underlying philosophy. If one assumes there is no signal in the data, then one quotes the sensitivity based on 90% of a single-sided Gaussian, which is $\sigma = 1.28$. If the philosophy is that there is a signal which is too small to measure, then one quotes the sensitivity using $\sigma = 1.64$, which is appropriate for a double-sided Gaussian. Historically, $\sigma = 1.28$ was used in most publications. Physicists engage in arguments as to which is most correct, but what is most important from a practical point of view is for the reader to understand what was used. The reader can always scale between 1.28 and 1.64 depending on personal opinion.

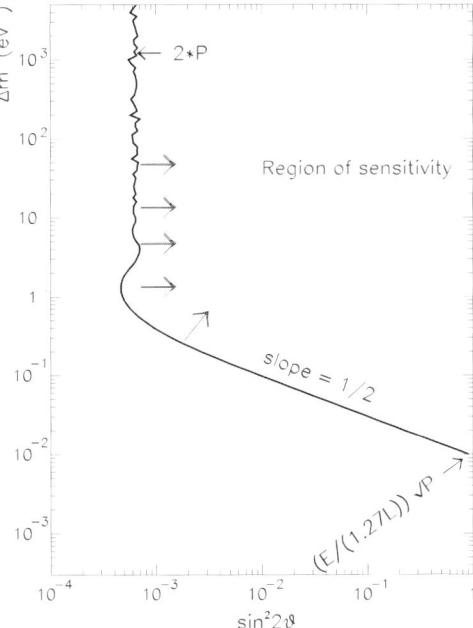

Fig. 5.12. An illustration of the sensitivity of an imaginary oscillation experiment. The region of sensitivity for an experiment depends on the oscillation probability, P, where one can set a limit at some confidence level. Most experiments use 90% CL. The boundaries depend on P, L and E.

There is only one measurement, P, and there are two unknowns, Δm^2 and $\sin^2 2\theta$; so this translates to a region of sensitivity within $\Delta m^2 - \sin^2 2\theta$ space. This is typically indicated by a solid line, with the allowed region on the right on a plot (see illustration in Fig 5.12). For the perfect (no-systematic error) experiment, the high Δm^2 limit on $\sin^2 2\theta$ is driven by the statistics. On the other hand, the L and E of the experiment drive the low Δm^2 limit, which depends on the fourth root of the statistics. If our perfect experiment had seen a signal, the indications of neutrino oscillations would appear as "allowed regions," or shaded areas on plots of Δm^2 vs. $\sin^2 2\theta$.

This rule of thumb – that statistics drives the $\sin^2 2\theta$-reach and L/E drives the Δm^2 reach – becomes more complicated when systematics are considered. The imperfections of a real experiment affect the limits which can be set. Systematic uncertainties in the efficiencies and backgrounds reduce the sensitivity of a given experiment. Background sources introduce multiple flavors of neutrinos in the beam. Misidentification of the interacting neutrino flavor in the detector can mimic oscillation signatures. In addition, systematic uncertainties in the relative acceptance versus distance and energy need to be understood and included in the analysis of the data.

For a real experiment, with both statistical and systematic errors, finding the sensitivity and final limit or allowed region requires a fit to the data. The data are compared to the expectation for oscillation across the range of oscillation parameters, and the set of parameters where the agreement is good to 90% CL are chosen. Historically, there are three main approaches which have been used in fits. The first method is the "single sided raster scan." In this case one chooses a Δm^2 value and scans through the $sin^2 2\theta$-space to find the 90% CL limit. The second method, the "global scan," explores Δm^2- and $sin^2 2\theta$-space simultaneously. Thus there are two parameters to fit and two degrees of freedom. The third method is the frequentist, or "Feldman-Cousins" approach,[47] in which one simulates "fake-experiments" for each Δm^2 and $sin^2 2\theta$ point, and determines the limit where, in 90% of the cases, no signal is observed. Each method has pros and cons and the choice is something of a matter of taste. As with the question of a single- or double-sided gaussian, what is important is to compare sensitivities, limits, and signals from like methods.

It is possible for an experiment which does not observe a signal to set a limit which is better than the sensitivity. This occurs if the experiment observed a downward fluctuation in the background. In this case, a limit is hard to interpret. The latest standard practice is to show the sensitivity and the limit on plots, and the readers can draw their own interpretation.[47]

5.2.1.4. *Experimental Evidence for Oscillations*

Two separate allowed regions in Δm^2-and-$\sin^2 2\theta$ -space for neutrino oscillations have been observed at the $> 5\sigma$ level. These are called the "Atmospheric Δm^2" and "Solar Δm^2" regions. The names are historical, as will be seen below. Many reviews have been written on these results (see, for example,,[2],[48] and[49]) and so here the results are briefly outlined.

The highest Δm^2 signal was first observed using neutrinos produced in the upper atmosphere. These atmospheric neutrinos are produced through collisions of cosmic rays with the atmosphere. The neutrinos are detected through their charged–current interactions in detectors on the Earth's surface.

The first evidence for atmospheric neutrino oscillations came from the Kamioka[50] and IMB[51] experiments. This was followed by the convincing case presented by the Super K experiment.[53] These were single detector experiments observing atmospheric neutrino interactions as a function of zenith angle (see Fig. 5.13). Several striking features were observed. The first was that the ν_μ flavor neutrinos showed clear evidence of disappearance while the ν_e flavor CC scatters were in good agreement with prediction. The second striking observation was that the apparent mixing was nearly maximal. In other words, the experiments were seeing a 50% reduction of the ν_μ event rate compared to expectation.

Complications in the analysis arise from the difficulty in understanding production of atmospheric neutrinos (affecting the understanding of E) and in the accurate reconstruction of events as a function of zenith angle (affecting knowledge of L). The Δm^2 extracted from the Kamoiokande data is an order of magnitude higher than that extracted from the Super K data, indicating a clear systematic effect. Thus, it was absolutely crucial for accelerator-based "long-baseline" neutrino experiments to confirm this result. In these experiments, the L is well defined by the distance from source to detector, and the E is well understood from a near detector measurement.

The challenge for long-baseline experiments is that the L/E required to access the atmospheric signal is on the order of 1000 km/GeV. If the beam is relatively low energy, so that the easy-to-reconstruct CCQE interaction dominates the events, then L is on the order of 1000 km. This leads to two major technical challenges. First, because the Earth is a sphere, if the source and detector are to be located on (or near) the surface, the beam must be directed downward, into the Earth. Engineering a beamline at a

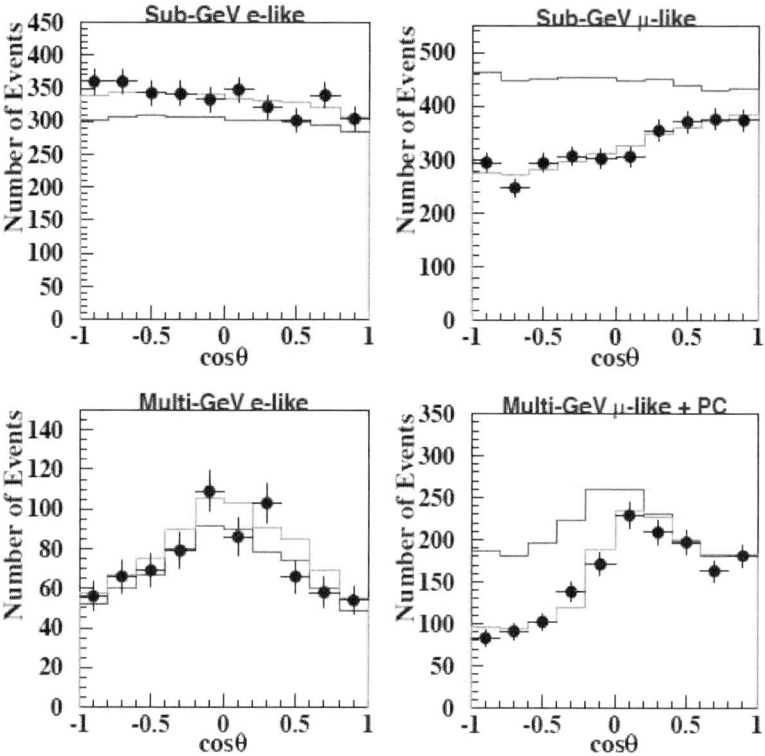

Fig. 5.13. Event rates observed in Super K as a function of zenith angle for two energy ranges. Candidate ν_e events are on the left, ν_μ are on the right. The red line indicates the predicted rate. The green line is the best fit including oscillations.[52]

steep angle requires overcoming substantial hurdles in tunneling. Second, the beam spreads as it travels outward from the source, resulting in low intensity at the detector. Therefore, very high rates are needed. However, these challenges have now been overcome at three accelerator complexes: KEK, FNAL and CERN, and a new long-baseline beam from the JPARC facility will be available soon. Making use of these lines, initial confirmation of the atmospheric neutrino deficit came from the KEK-to-Kamiokande (K2K) long baseline experiment.[54] This has since been followed up by the MINOS experiment to high precision.[55,56]

In the atmospheric data, the ν_e CC signal is in agreement with expectation, and in the long-baseline experiments, no ν_e excess has been observed. Therefore, one cannot interpret this oscillation signal as $\nu_\mu \to \nu_e$. This leaves only $\nu_\mu \to \nu_\tau$ as an explanation for the deficit in a three-neutrino model. Observation of ν_τ CC interactions is experimentally difficult in these experiments for a number of reasons. First, the L/E of the signal is such that for lengths available to present experiments, the energy of the beam must be low ($\lesssim$ 10 GeV). As discussed in Sec. 5.1.2, because the τ mass is 1.8 GeV, there is substantial mass suppression for τ production at low energies, so the CC event rate is low. Second, the τ decays quickly, leaving behind a complicated event structure which can be easily confused with ν_μ and ν_e low multiplicity interactions in calorimeter or Cerenkov detectors. The difficulty of identifying ν_τ events even in a specialized emulsion-based detector with a high energy neutrino beam, was made clear by the DoNuT experiment,[6] which provided the first, and so far only, direct observation of CC ν_τ interactions. Thus, while some studies claim observation of ν_τ CC interactions in SuperK,[57] these results are not very convincing to this author. Fortunately, a specialized experiment called OPERA,[58] which is an emulsion-based long-baseline detector, is presently taking data. The average energy of the CNGS beam used by this experiment is 17 GeV, sufficiently high to produce ν_τ CC events. This experiment is expected to observe $\sim$ 15 events in 5 years of running if the atmospheric neutrino deficit is due to $\nu_\mu \to \nu_\tau$ with $\Delta m^2 = 2.5 \times 10^{-3}$ eV^2.[59]

The lower Δm^2 signal is called the "Solar Neutrino Deficit," as it was first observed as a low rate of observed ν_e's from the Sun. The first observation of this effect was a ν_e deficit observed using a Cl target[14] by Ray Davis and collaborators at Homestake, using $\nu_e + \text{Cl} \to e + \text{Ar}$. Only about 1/3 of the total expected neutrino event rate was observed. By 1999, four additional experiments had confirmed these observations. The GALLEX[16] and SAGE[15] experiments confirmed a deficit for CC electron neutrino interactions in a Ga target producing Ge. The Super Kamiokande experiment observed a deficit for $\nu_e + e \to \nu_e + e$ reactions in water.[22] The deficit is shown on Fig. 5.14, indicated by the blue points. This plot shows the ratio to the Standard Solar Model prediction, which is indicated by the solid line at unity.

A few aspects of the initial solar neutrino deficit studies should be noted. First, the three types of experiments, chlorine-based, gallium-based, and water-based, measured different levels of deficit. Given that each type of nucleus has a different low energy threshold for observation of CC events, as previously discussed, one can interpret the varying levels of deficit as an energy dependent effect. Second, all of the above experiments rely upon the CC interaction. The energy of neutrinos from the Sun is so low, that

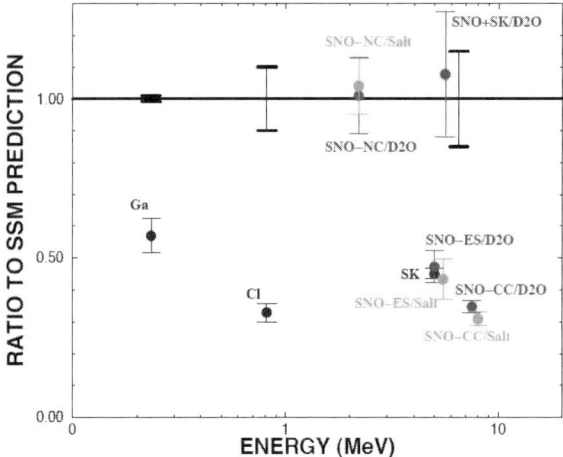

Fig. 5.14. Ratio of observed event rates in solar neutrino experiments compared to the Standard Solar Model. Experiments are plotted at the average energy of the detected signal, which varies due to detection threshold. Black error bars indicate Standard Solar Model error.[23]

should ν_μ or ν_τ be produced through oscillations, the CC interaction could not occur. This is because of the relatively high mass of the μ (106 MeV) and the τ (1.8 GeV). Thus all of these experiments can observe that ν_es disappeared, but they cannot observe if the neutrinos reappear as one of the other flavors. This makes a decisive statement that the effect is due to neutrino oscillations problematic.

For some time, people argued the apparent deficit was due to an incomplete picture of solar processes. The two important theoretical issues related to the solar neutrino fluxes were the fusion cross sections and the temperature of the solar interior. A comprehensive analysis of the available information on nuclear fusion cross sections important to solar processes has been compiled[60] and shows that the important cross sections are well-known. Results in helioseismology provided an important further test of the "Standard Solar Model".[61] The Sun is a resonant cavity, with oscillation frequencies dependent upon P/ρ, the ratio of pressure to density. Helioseismological data confirmed the SSM prediction of U to better than 0.1%.[62] With the results of these studies, most physicists were convinced that the Standard Solar Model was substantially correct. The error bars on the black line at unity in Fig. 5.14 shows the side of the estimated systematic error on the Standard Solar Model.

Interpreting the results as neutrino oscillations resulted in a complicated picture. The vacuum oscillation probability, calculated using equation 5.10, results in allowed regions of Δm^2 which are very low ($\Delta m^2 \sim 10^{-10} \text{eV}^2$). This is because the energy of the neutrinos is only a few MeV, and the Sun to the Earth pathlength is very long ($\sim 10^{11}$m) . On the other hand, the Sun has high electron content and density, so matter effects (Sec. 5.2.1.2) could interfere with the picture, allowing higher true values of Δm^2. The MSW effect yielded two solutions in fits to the data. One was at mixing angles of $\sim 10^{-3}$. Until very recently, this was regarded as the most likely solution based on analogy with mixing in the quark sector. The other solution gave a very large, although not maximal, mixing angle.

Two dramatic results of the early 2000's demonstrated that the solar neutrino deficit was due to oscillations with the MSW effect and with large mixing angle. The first result was from the SNO experiment.[63] SNO used a D_2O target which allowed for measurement of both CC ν_e interactions as well as $\nu + d \rightarrow \nu + n + p$. In the former measurement, SNO sees a deficit consistent with the other measurements within an oscillation interpretation, and which yields a ν_e flux of $(1.76 \pm 0.05(\text{stat}) \pm 0.09(\text{sys})) \times 10^6/\text{cm}^2\text{s}$.[64] The later measurement is an NC interaction, and thus is flavor-blind. It yields a total NC flux of $(5.09^{+0.44}_{-0.43}(\text{stat})^{+0.46}_{-0.43}(\text{sys})) \times 10^6/\text{cm}^2 s$[64] which can be compared with the theoretical prediction of $(5.69 \pm 0.91) \times 10^6/\text{cm}^2\text{s}$.[65] In other words, SNO observed the expected total event rate, within errors. This implied that the ν_es are oscillating to neutrinos which participate in the NC interaction, ν_μs and/or ν_τs, with the total $\nu_\mu + \nu_\tau$ flux equal to $(3.41 \pm 0.45(\text{stat})^{+0.48}_{-0.45}(\text{sys})) \times 10^6/\text{cm}^2 s$.[64] The results of two runs of the SNO experiment are shown by the red and green points on Fig. 5.14. The second result was from the KamLAND experiment. This was a reactor-based experiment located in Japan. Using many reactors which were hundreds of kilometers away, the KamLAND experiment was able to reach $L/E \sim 10^{-6}$ m/MeV. This covered the MSW allowed-Δm^2 solution. The statistics were on the order of hundreds of events, but this was enough to probe the large mixing-angle MSW solution. KamLAND expected 365 events and observed 258 events, and thus had clear evidence for oscillations with large mixing, $\tan^2\theta = 0.40^{+0.010}_{-0.07}$ and relatively high Δm^2, of $7.9^{+0.6}_{-0.5} \times 10^{-5}$ eV^2.[66] The energy distribution of the events observed in KamLAND is shown in Fig. 5.15.

Based on the atmospheric and solar studies, there are two squared mass differences: Δm^2_{solar} and Δm^2_{atmos}. The smaller is identified with the mass splitting between ν_1 and ν_2: $\Delta m^2_{12} = \Delta m^2_{solar}$. The atmospheric deficit

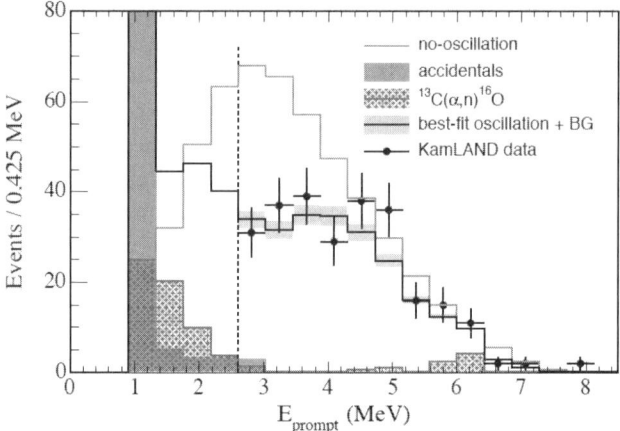

Fig. 5.15. Events in KamLAND as a function of energy. The grey line indicates the expectation for no oscillation.[66]

measures a combination of Δm_{23}^2 and Δm_{13}^2. However, since $\Delta m_{13}^2 = \Delta m_{12}^2 + \Delta m_{23}^2$ and Δm_{12}^2 is small, $\Delta m_{13}^2 \approx \Delta m_{23}^2 \approx \Delta m_{atmos}^2$.

A recent global analysis of the data[67] from the above experiments yields a consistent picture for three neutrino oscillations with five free parameters. The mass differences are: $\Delta m_{12}^2 = (7.9 \pm 0.3) \times 10^{-5} \text{eV}^2$ and $|\Delta m_{13}^2| = (2.5^{+0.20}_{-0.25}) \times 10^{-5} \text{eV}^2$, where the absolute value is indicated in the second case because the sign (i.e. the mass hierarchy) is unknown. The two well-measured mixing angles are determined to be: $\sin^2 \theta_{12} = 0.30^{+0.02}_{-0.03}$ and $\sin^2 \theta_{23} = 0.50^{+0.08}_{-0.07}$. One mixing angle, θ_{13} is yet to be measured, but a limit of $\sin^2 \theta_{13} < 0.025$ can be placed based on global fits.

Based on the measurements, the mixing matrix of Eq. 5.12, translates roughly into:

$$U = \begin{pmatrix} 0.8 & 0.5 & ? \\ 0.4 & 0.6 & 0.7 \\ 0.4 & 0.6 & 0.7 \end{pmatrix}. \quad (5.17)$$

This matrix, with its large off-diagonal components, looks very different from the quark-sector mixing matrix where the off-diagonal elements are all relatively small. In this matrix, the "odd element out" is U_{e3} which is clearly substantially smaller than the others. At this point, there is no consensus on what this matrix may be telling us about the larger theory, but there is a sense that the value of θ_{13} is an important clue. Theories which attempt to explain this matrix tend to fall into two classes – those where

Table 5.3. Selected predictions for $\sin^2 2\theta_{13}$.[104]

Model(s)	Refs.	approximate $\sin^2 2\theta_{13}$
Minimal SO(10)	68	0.13
Orbifold SO(10)	69	0.04
SO(10) + Flavor symmetry	70	$1.2 \cdot 10^{-6}$
	71	$7.8 \cdot 10^{-4}$
	72–74	0.01 .. 0.04
	75–77	0.09 .. 0.18
SO(10) + Texture	78	$4 \cdot 10^{-4}$ .. 0.01
	79	0.04
$SU(2)_L \times SU(2)_R \times SU(4)_c$	80	0.09
Flavor symmetries	81–83	0
	84,85,94	$\lesssim 0.004$
	87–89	10^{-4} .. 0.02
	90–94	0.04 .. 0.15
Textures	95	$4 \cdot 10^{-4}$ .. 0.01
	96–99	0.03 .. 0.15
3×2 see-saw	100	0.04
Anarchy	101	> 0.04
Renormalization group enhancement	102	0.03 .. 0.04
M-Theory model	103	10^{-4}

θ_{13} is just below the present limit and those with very small values. As an illustration of this point, Table 5.3 shows order of magnitude predictions for a variety of theories. Thus a measurement of $\sin^2 2\theta_{13}$ which is greater than about 1%, or a limit at this level, can point the way to the larger theory.

The best method for measuring θ_{13} is from reactor experiments which constrain this oscillation by searching for $\bar{\nu}_e$ disappearance. The oscillation probability is given by:

$$P_{reactor} \simeq \sin^2 2\theta_{13} \sin^2 \Delta + \alpha^2 \Delta^2 \cos^4 \theta_{13} \sin^2 2\theta_{12}, \quad (5.18)$$

with

$$\alpha \equiv \Delta m_{21}^2 / \Delta m_{23}^2 \quad (5.19)$$

$$\Delta \equiv \Delta m_{31}^2 L/(4E_\nu). \quad (5.20)$$

Events are detected through the inverse beta decay (IBD) interaction. The CHOOZ experiment,[25] with a baseline of 1.1 km and typical neutrino event energies between 3 and 5 MeV $\langle E \rangle = 3.5$ MeV) has set the best reactor-based limit to date, of $\sin^2 2\theta_{13} < 0.27$ at $\Delta m^2 = 2.5 \times 10^{-3}$ eV^2. This limit can be improved with a global fit, as quoted above.

Significant improvement is expected from the upcoming round of reactor experiments results due to introducing a near-far detector design. The near detector measures the unoscillated event rate, and the far detector is used to search for a deficit as a function of energy. The Double Chooz experiment, beginning in 2009, is expected to reach $\sin^2 2\theta_{13} \sim 0.03$.[105] This will be followed by the Daya Bay experiment which will reach ~ 0.01.[106]

5.2.2. *Direct Measurements of Neutrino Mass*

For neutrinos, there are no mass measurements, only mass limits. Observations of neutrino oscillations are sensitive to the mass differences between neutrinos, not the actual mass of the neutrino. Therefore, they do not fall into the category of a "direct measurement". One can, however, use these oscillation results to estimate the required sensitivity for a direct mass measurement. The upper limit comes from assuming that one of the neutrino masses is exactly zero. Given that the largest Δm^2 is $\sim 3 \times 10^{-3}$ eV^2, this implies there is a neutrino with mass $\sqrt{\Delta m^2} \sim 0.05$ eV. The mass of the neutrino can be directly measured from decay kinematics and from time of flight from supernovae. Neither method has reached the 0.05 eV range yet, although the next generation of decay-based experiments comes close.

We know from neutrino oscillations that there is a very poor correspondence between neutrino flavors and neutrino masses, *i.e.*, the mixings are large. However, it is easiest to conduct the discussion of these limits in terms of specific flavors. Thus, what is actually being studied is an average mass associated with each flavor. For example, for the ν_e mass measured from β decay, which will be expanded upon below, what is actually probed is:

$$m_\beta = \sqrt{\Sigma_i |U_{ei}|^2 m_i^2}. \qquad (5.21)$$

The simplest method for measuring neutrino mass is applied to the ν_μ. The mass is obtained from the 2-body decay-at-rest kinematics of $\pi \to \mu\nu_\mu$. One begins in the center of mass with the 4-vector relationship: $p_\pi = p_\mu + p_\nu$. Squaring and solving for neutrino mass gives: $m_\nu^2 = m_\pi^2 + m_\mu^2 - \sqrt{4m_\pi^2(|\mathbf{p}_\mu|^2 + m_\mu^2)}$. From this, one can see that this technique requires accurate measurement of the muon momentum, $\mathbf{p}_\mu$, as well as the masses of the muon, m_μ and the pion, m_π. In fact, the uncertainty on the mass of the pion is what dominates the ν_μ mass measurement. As a result, a limit is set at $m_{\nu_\mu} < 170$ keV.[107,108]

The mass for the ν_τ is obtained from the kinematics of τ decays. The τ typically decays to many hadrons. However, the four vectors for each of the hadrons can be summed. Then the decay can be treated as a two-body

Table 5.4. Overview of ν_e squared mass measurements.

Experiment	measured m^2 (eV^2)	limit (eV), 95% C.L.	Year
Mainz[110]	-0.6± 2.2± 2.1	2.2	2004
Troitsk[111]	-1.0 ± 3.0± 2.1	2.5	2000
Mainz[112]	-3.7 ± 5.3 ± 2.1	2.8	2000
LLNL[113]	- 130 ± 20± 15	7.0	1995
CIAE[114]	- 31 ± 75± 48	12.4	1995
Zurich[115]	-24 ± 48± 61	11.7	1992
Tokyo INS[116]	- 65 ± 85± 65	13.1	1991
Los Alamos[117]	- 147 ± 68± 41	9.3	1991

problem with the neutrino as one 4-vector and the sum of the hadrons as the other vector. At this point, the same method described for the ν_μ can be applied. Measurements are again error-limited, so a limit on the mass is placed. The best limit, which is $m_{\nu_\tau} < 18.2$ MeV, comes from fits to $\tau^- \to 2\pi^-\pi^+\nu_\tau$ and $\tau^- \to 3\pi^-2\pi^+(\pi^0)\nu_\tau$ decays observed by the ALEPH experiment.[109]

The experimental situation for the ν_e mass measurement is more complicated. The endpoint of the electron energy spectrum from tritium β decay is used to determine the mass. Just as in the case of the ν_μ and ν_τ, the experiments measure a value of m^2. The problem is that the measurements have been systematically negative. A review of measurements, as a function of time, is given in Table 5.4. Recent measurements at Troitsk[111] and Mainz[112] are negative, but in agreement with zero. Following the Particle Data Group prescription for setting limit in the case of an unphysical results, $m^2 = 0$ is assumed, with the quoted errors. Based on these results, one can extract a limit of approximately < 2 eV for the mass of the ν_e.

The next big step in the measurement of neutrino mass from decay kinematics will come from the Katrin Experiment.[118] Katrin will use tritium beta decay to measure the mass of the neutrino to 0.2 eV. This does not reach the range of 0.05 eV, which our simplistic argument presented at the top of this section indicated. However, that argument assumed that the lightest neutrino had zero mass. A small offset from zero easily boosts the spectrum into the range observable by Katrin. On the other hand, Katrin is sensitive to only electron flavor. Thus, its sensitivity depends up on the amount of mixing of ν_e within the heaviest neutrino.

Another method for measuring neutrino mass from simple kinematics is to use time of flight for neutrinos from supernovae. Neutrinos carry away $\sim 99\%$ of the energy from a supernova. The mass limit is obtained from the spread in the propagation times of the neutrinos. The propagation time for a single neutrino is given by

$$t_{obs} - t_{emit} = t_0\left(1 + \frac{m^2}{2E^2}\right) \quad (5.22)$$

where t_0 is the time required for light to reach Earth from the supernova. Because the neutrinos escape from a supernova before the photons, we do not know t_{emit}. But we can obtain the time difference between 2 events:

$$\Delta t_{obs} - \Delta t_{emit} \approx \frac{t_0 m^2}{2}\left(\frac{1}{E_1^2} - \frac{1}{E_2^2}\right). \quad (5.23)$$

using the assumption that all neutrinos are emitted at the same time, one can obtain a mass limit of ~ 30 eV from the ~ 20 events observed from SN1987a at 2 sites.[119,120]

This is actually an oversimplified argument. The models for neutrino emission are actually quite complicated. The pulse of neutrinos has a prompt peak followed by a broader secondary peak with a long tail distributed over an interval which can be 4 s or more. The prompt peak is from "neutronization" and is mainly ν_e, while all three neutrino flavors populate the secondary peak. However, the rate of ν_e escape is slower compared to ν_μ and ν_τ produced at the same time, because the ν_es can experience CC interactions, while the kinematic suppression from the charged lepton mass prevents this for the other flavors. However, when all of the aspects of the modeling are put together, the bottom line remains the same: it will be possible to set stringent mass limits if we observe neutrinos from nearby supernovae.

Some argue that cosmology provides a "direct measurement." Cosmological fits have sensitivity to neutrino masses, but the results are dependent on the cosmological parameters[121] and the model for relic neutrino production. There are many examples of models with low relic neutrino densities which would significantly change the present interpretation of the cosmological data.[122] In the opinion of the author, until these issues are settled, cosmological measurements cannot convincingly compete with kinematic decays and supernova measurements, despite aggressive claims.

5.3. Neutrinos We Would Like to Meet

Now that we know that neutrinos have mass, and thus are outside of expectations, the obvious question is: "what other Beyond Standard Model properties do they possess?" *The APS Study on the Future of Neutrino Physics* focussed on this question. The plan for attack was divided into three fronts: (1) Neutrinos and the New Paradigm, (2) Neutrinos and the Unexpected and 3) Neutrinos and the Cosmos. The remainder of this paper follows this structure.

The consequences of the discovery of neutrino mass leads to a rich array of ideas. It is was beyond the scope of these lectures to cover the entire spectrum. So, in each of the three areas, two topics are chosen for extensive discussion. The reader is referred to the study[1] and the accompanying theory white paper[2] for further ideas.

5.3.1. *Neutrinos and the New Paradigm*

The first step in creating a "New Standard Model" is to incorporate neutrino mass. The simplest method is to introduce a Dirac mass, by analogy with the electron. This allows us to introduce a small neutrino mass, simply by arguing that the coupling to the Higgs is remarkably small. However, the unlikely smallness of the coupling has pushed theorists to look for other approaches. Among the oldest of these ideas is that neutrinos may be "Majorana particles," *i.e.*, they are their own antiparticle. This leads to a new type of mass term in the Lagrangian. Through the "see-saw" mechanism, which fits well with Grand Unified Theories, this can also give a motivation for the apparently small value of the neutrino masses.

A direct consequence of the Majorana See-Saw Model is a heavy neutrino, with mass near the GUT scale. Because the heavy neutrino gets its mass through the Majorana rather than Dirac term of the Lagrangian, this neutrino was massive during the earliest periods of the universe, before the electroweak phase transition. The decays of such a heavy lepton could be CP violating. This would provide a mechanism for producing the observed matter-antimatter imbalance seen today.

The tidiness of the the above theoretical ideas has caused this paradigm to emerge as the consensus favorite for the "New Standard Model." However, there is absolutely no experimental evidence for this theory at this time. We have no evidence for the Majorana nature of neutrinos. Nor do we have any evidence for CP violation in the neutrino system. The great challenge of the next few years, then, is to find any sign at all that this theory is correct.

This section reviews how one introduces mass into the Lagrangian. The search for evidence of the Majorana nature of neutrinos though neutrinoless double beta decay is considered. Then, the prospects for finding evidence for CP violation is considered.

5.3.1.1. *How Neutrinos Might Get Their Mass*

The simplest assumption is that the neutrino mass should appear in the Lagrangian in the same way as for the charged fermions – via a Dirac mass term. In general, the Dirac mass term in the Lagrangian will be of the form

$$m(\bar{\psi}_L \psi_R + \bar{\psi}_R \psi_L). \quad (5.24)$$

From the arguments presented in eqs. 5.1 through 5.6, we saw that the scalar "mass" term mixes the RH and LH states of the fermion. If the fermion has only one chirality, then the Dirac mass term will automatically vanish. For this reason, a standard Dirac mass term for the neutrino will require the RH neutrino and LH antineutrino states.

To motivate the mass term, the most straightforward approach is to use the Higgs mechanism, as was done for the electron in the Standard Model. In the case of the electron, when we introduce a spin-0 Higgs doublet ,(h^0, h^+), into the Lagrangian, we find terms like:

$$g_e \bar{\psi}_{e_R}(\psi_{\nu_L}(h^+)^\dagger + \psi_{e_L}(h^0)^\dagger) + h.c., \quad (5.25)$$

where g_e is the coupling constant and "h.c." is the Hermetian conjugate. The piece of this term proportional to $\bar{\psi}_{e_R}\psi_{e_L}(h^0)^\dagger$, combined with its Hermetian conjugate, can be identified with the Dirac mass term, $m_e \bar{\psi}_e \psi_e$. We set $\langle h^0 \rangle = v/\sqrt{2}$, so that we obtain $g\langle h^0 \rangle \bar{\psi}_e \psi_e$ and $m_e = g_e v/\sqrt{2}$. This is the Standard Model method for conveniently converting the *ad hoc* electron mass, m_e, into an *ad hoc* coupling to the Higgs, g_e and a vacuum expectation value (VEV) for the Higgs, v. Following the same procedure for neutrinos allows us to identify the Dirac mass term with $m_\nu = g_\nu v/\sqrt{2}$. The VEV, v, has to be the same as for all other leptons. Therefore, the small mass must come from a very small coupling, g_ν. This implies that $g_e > 5 \times 10^4 g_\nu$.

There are several troublesome features to this procedure. The first issue which is often raised is:

- Why would the Higgs coupling vary across eleven orders of magnitude (the approximate ratio of the neutrino mass to the top quark mass)?

In fact, this question is rather odd. Disregarding the neutrinos, the masses of the charged fermions varies across six orders of magnitude (from the electron mass to the top mass). If six orders of magnitude do not bother anyone, why should eleven? Turning this around, if the Higgs couplings alreay seemed stretched in the charged fermion case, the neutrinos stretch the argument much further. This leads to the second troublesome issue,

- Physically, what is occurring?

The Higgs mechanism really gives little physical insight. While it does introduce mass, it has simply shifted the arbitrariness of the magnitude of the mass into an arbitrary coupling to a new field.

These two questions have led theorists to look at other explanations for small neutrino mass. It has been noted that neutrinos have the unique feature of carrying no electric or strong charge. Thus, neutrinos, alone among the Standard Model fermions, may be their own antiparticle, *i.e.* they may be Majorana particles. The nice consequence of this is a somewhat more motivated theory of mass for neutrinos.

To understand this, first consider what is meant to be a Dirac versus a Majorana particle. If neutrinos are Dirac particles, then the ν and the $\bar{\nu}$ are distinct particles, just as the electron and positron are distinct. The particle, ν has lepton number $+1$ and the antiparticle, $\bar{\nu}$ has lepton number -1. Lepton number is conserved in an interaction. Thus, using the muon family as an example, νs ($L = +1$) must produce μ^- ($L = +1$) and $\bar{\nu}$s ($L = -1$) must produce μ^+ ($L = -1$). The alternative viewpoint is that the ν and $\bar{\nu}$ are two helicity states of the same "Majorana" particle, which we can call "ν^{maj}." The π^+ decay produces the left-handed ν^{maj} and the π^- decay produces the right-handed ν^{maj}. This model explains all of the data without invoking lepton number and has the nice feature of economy of total particles and quantum numbers, but it renders the neutrino different from all other Standard Model fermions.

Saying that the neutrino is its own antiparticle is equivalent to saying that the neutrino is its own charge conjugate, $\psi^c = \psi$. The operators which appear in the Lagrangian for the neutrino in this case are the set $(\psi_L, \psi_R, \psi_L^c, \psi_R^c)$ and $(\bar{\psi}_L, \bar{\psi}_R, \bar{\psi}^c{}_L, \bar{\psi}^c{}_R)$. Certain bilinear combinations of these in the Lagrangian can be identified as Dirac masses (*i.e.* $m(\bar{\psi}_L\psi_R + ...)$). However, we also get a set of terms of the form:

$$(M_L/2)(\bar{\psi}_L{}^c\psi_L) + (M_R/2)(\bar{\psi}_R{}^c\psi_R) + \cdots \qquad (5.26)$$

These are the "Majorana mass terms," which mix the pair of charge-conjugate states of the fermion. If the particle is not its own charge conjugate, then these terms automatically vanish and we are left with only the Dirac terms. Dirac particles have no Majorana mass terms, but Majorana particles will have Dirac mass terms.

The mass terms of the Lagrangian can be written in matrix form:

$$(1/2)(\bar{\psi}_L^c \ \bar{\psi}_R) \begin{pmatrix} M_L & m \\ m & M_R \end{pmatrix} \begin{pmatrix} \psi_L \\ \psi_R^c \end{pmatrix} + h.c., \quad (5.27)$$

The Dirac mass, m, is on the off-diagonal elements, while the Majorana mass constants, M_L, M_R are on the diagonal. To obtain the physical masses, one diagonalizes the matrix.

One can now invoke "see-saw models" which motivate small observable neutrino masses. It turns out that GUT's motivate mass matrices that look like[124]:

$$\begin{pmatrix} 0 & m_\nu \\ m_\nu & M \end{pmatrix}, \quad (5.28)$$

with $m_\nu \ll M$. When you diagonalize this matrix to obtain the physical masses, this results in two states which can be measured experimentally:

$$m_{light} \approx m_\nu^2/M, \quad (5.29)$$

$$m_{heavy} \approx M \quad (5.30)$$

Grand Unified Theories favor very large masses for the "heavy neutrino" (often called a "neutral heavy lepton"). It is argued that it is most "natural" to have M be at the GUT scale. If $M \sim 10^{25}$ eV, and $m_{light} < 1$ eV, as observed, then $m_\nu \sim 10^{12}$ eV, or is at the TeV scale. This is rather high compared to masses of other leptons, but not so far beyond the top quark mass to regard the connection as crazy. So while some arbitrariness remains in this model, nevertheless there is a general feeling in the theory community that this is an improvement.

In this theory neutrinos have only approximate handedness, where the light neutrino is mostly LH with a very small admixture of RH and the neutral heavy lepton is essentially RH. Thus we have a LH neutrino which is light, which matches observations, and a RH neutrino which is not yet observed because it is far too massive.

5.3.1.2. *Majorana vs. Dirac?*

How can we experimentally tell the difference between the Dirac (ν, $\bar{\nu}$) and Majorana (ν^{maj}) scenarios? One can imagine a straight-forward thought experiment. First, produce left-handed neutrinos in π^+ decays. These may be νs or they may be ν_{LH}^{maj}s. Next, run the neutrino through a magic helicity-flipping device. If the neutrinos are Majorana, then what comes out of the flipping-device will be ν_{RH}^{maj}. These particles will behave like antineutrinos when they interact, showing the expected RH y-dependence for the cross section. But if the initial neutrino beam is Dirac, then what comes out of the flipping-device will be right-handed νs, which are sterile. They do not interact at all. Such a helicity-flipping experiment is presently essentially impossible to implement. If neutrinos do have mass, then they may have an extremely tiny magnetic moment and a very intense magnetic field could flip their helicity. But the design requirements of such an experiment are far beyond our capability at the moment. Therefore, at the moment, we do not know if neutrinos are Majorana or Dirac in nature.

Instead, experimentalists are pursing a different route. The Majorana nature of the neutrino can lead to an effect called neutrinoless double β decay: $(Z, A) \to (Z+2, A)+(e^-e^-)$. This is a beyond-the-Standard Model analogue to double β decay: $(Z, A) \to (Z+2, A) + (e^-e^-\bar{\nu}_e\bar{\nu}_e)$. Double β decay is a standard nuclear decay process with a very low rate because there is a suppression proportional to $(G_F \cos\theta_C)^4$. Therefore, in most cases, if the weak decay is possible, single β decay ($(Z, A) \to (Z+1, A) + e^- + \bar{\nu}_e$) will dominate. However, there are 13 nuclei, including ^{136}Xe $\to$ ^{136}Ba and ^{76}Ge $\to^{76}$ Se, for which single β decay is energetically disallowed. In these cases double β decay with two neutrinos has been observed.[123] If the neutrino were its own antiparticle, then the neutrinos produced in the double β decay process could annihilate, yielding neutrinoless double β decay.

If there are Majorana neutrinos, then the amplitude for $0\nu\beta\beta$ is proportional to the square of

$$m_{0\nu\beta\beta} = \sum U_{ei}^2 m_i. \qquad (5.31)$$

This should be contrasted with Eq. 5.21. The $0\nu\beta\beta$ searches are probing different effective masses than the direct searches and the two results yield complementary information. Like the direct searches, the possibility of seeing $0\nu\beta\beta$ depends on the amount of electron-flavor mixed in the most massive neutrino state. If this is small, then the rate of decay will be very low. Thus the hierarchy of the neutrino states affects our ability to observe $0\nu\beta\beta$. To completely untangle the Dirac vs. Majorana question, three different experiments – direct mass measurement, hierarchy measurement and $0\nu\beta\beta$ measurement – may be required.[2]

Extracting $m_{0\nu\beta\beta}$ from a measured half-life leads to a theoretical error from the nuclear matrix element calculations. A favored style of calculation uses the "QRPA" (Quasiparticle Random Phase Approximation)[125–128] model. Using ^{100}Mo as an example, different matrix elements from QRPA

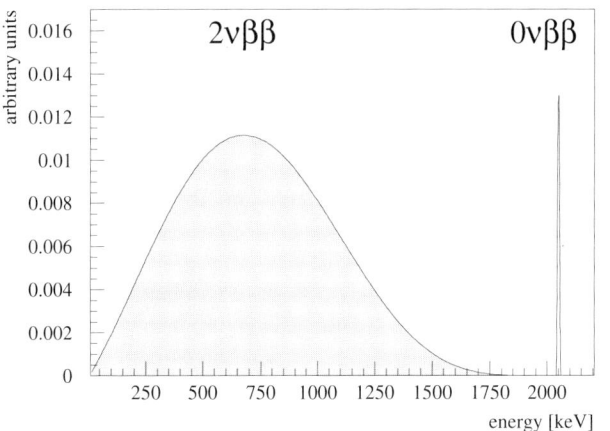

Fig. 5.16. Spectrum for two-neutrino double β decay and expected peak for neutrinoless double β decay.

calculations cause $m_{0\nu\beta\beta}$ to vary by up to 2 eV for a half-life of 4.5×10^{23} years.[129] So the error is significant.

The $0\nu\beta\beta$ events must be separated from the standard two-neutrino double β ($2\nu\beta\beta$) decay background. This can be done through simple kinematics cuts. The two-body nature of $0\nu\beta\beta$ decay will cause a peak at the endpoint of the $2\nu\beta\beta$ decay (4-body) spectrum, as shown in Fig. 5.16. An advantage of observing $2\nu\beta\beta$, however, is that measurement of its half-life allows direct measurement of the matrix element. At this point the $2\nu\beta\beta$ decay spectrum has been observed in 10 elements. In some cases, such as ^{100}Mo, the the $2\nu\beta\beta$ half-life is well measured and can be used to constrain nuclear matrix element calculation. For this case, NEMO-3 reports a half life of $(7.68 \pm 0.02(\text{stat}) \pm 0.54(\text{sys})) \times 10^{18}$ y.[130]

At present, no signal for $0\nu\beta\beta$ decay has been clearly observed. The present 90% CL limit on the lifetime from CUORICINO on ^{130}Te is 1.8×10^{24} years, corresponding to limit of $m_{0\nu\beta\beta} < 0.2 - 1.1$ eV.[131] The NEMO-3 experiment has set 90% CL limits of 4.6×10^{23} and 1.0×10^{23} on ^{100}Mo and ^{82}Se, respectively.[129] The corresponding limits on $m_{0\nu\beta\beta}$ are 0.7-2.8 eV and 1.7-4.9 eV.[129] There is a candidate signal observed at 4.2σ from a Germanium detector,[132] although the statistical significance is under debate.[2] The measured half-life was 1.19×10^{25} years. Until this result is confirmed by further experiments, it is best to reserve judgment.

Luckily, a range of future $0\nu\beta\beta$ decay experiments are on the horizon. These are expected to probe an order of magnitude further in lifetimes.

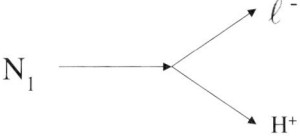

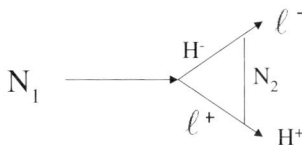

Fig. 5.17. Example of two diagrams for Neutral Heavy Lepton decay which can interfere to produce CP violation.

In particular, the germanium-based GERDA experiment,[133] will turn on soon and will address the existence of the possible signal. CUORE,[134] SuperNEMO,[135] EXO,[136] Majorana[137] and Moon[138] will extend the search even further using a wide range of elements. The reach of these near future $0\nu\beta\beta$ covers the prediction for the inverted mass hierarchy.

5.3.1.3. CP Violation in the Neutrino Sector

An intriguing aspect of the "new Standard Model" is the heavy GUT-scale neutrinos which gain mass through the Majorana terms in the Lagrangian. There could be more than one, and likely, given the trend in the Standard Model, there would be three, so we can label these N_1, N_2 and N_3. These heavy neutrinos have mass prior to the electroweak phase transition in which the Dirac terms appear. As a result, prior to the electroweak phase transition, decays shown in Fig. 5.17 are possible. Both decays produce the same final state, $N_1 \to \ell H$, where ℓ and H are oppositely charged. These diagrams interfere, and can lead to a different decay rate to ℓ^- and ℓ^+, which is CP violation.

This form of CP violation would lead to a lepton asymmetry in the early universe which could be transferred into a baryon asymmetry. A mechanism for this already appears in the Standard Model, in which but B, baryon number, and L, lepton number are not conserved, but the difference, $B-L$, is exactly conserved. B and L violation occurs in transitions between vacuum states at high energies, called the "sphaleron process." Variations on this mechanism, called "leptogenesis," may explain the matter-antimatter asymmetry we see today.

N_1, N_2, and N_3 are far too massive to be produced at accelerators in the near future. Thus observing CP violation in their decays is out of the question. However, observing CP violation in the light neutrino sector would be a plausible hint that the theory is correct.

To incorporate CP violation into the three-light-neutrino model, the leptonic mixing matrix is expanded and written as: $U^{with\ CP} = VK$. In this case, V is very similar to the U of Eq. 5.12, but with a CP violating phase, δ:

$$V = \begin{pmatrix} c_{12}c_{13} & s_{12}c_{13} & s_{13}e^{-i\delta} \\ -s_{12}c_{23} - c_{12}s_{23}s_{13}e^{i\delta} & c_{12}c_{23} - s_{12}s_{23}s_{13}e^{i\delta} & s_{23}c_{13} \\ s_{12}s_{23} - c_{12}c_{23}s_{13}e^{i\delta} & -c_{12}s_{23} - s_{12}c_{23}s_{13}e^{i\delta} & c_{23}c_{13} \end{pmatrix}. \tag{5.32}$$

This is analogous to the CKM matrix of the quark sector. The other term,

$$K = \text{diag}\left(1, e^{i\phi_1}, e^{i(\phi_2+\delta)}\right) \tag{5.33}$$

has two further CP violating phases, ϕ_1 and ϕ_2.

Now, we potentially have three non-zero CP violating parameters in the light neutrino sector, δ, ϕ_1 and ϕ_2, as well as one or more CP violating parameters in the heavy neutrino sector, where the number depends upon the total number of N. In the Lagrangian, these all come from a matrix of Yukawa coupling constants. In principle, all of these phases can take on the full range of values, including exactly zero. However, it is difficult to motivate a theory in which some are nonzero and some are exactly zero. It is expected that these parameters will either all have non-zero values or all be precisely zero. If the latter case, then the difference between the lepton sector, with no CP violation, and quark sector, with clear CP violation, must be motivated. As a result, observation of CP violation in the light neutrino sector is regarded as the "smoking gun" to CP violation in the heavy sector.

Returning to the light neutrino sector, how can the CP phases be measured? The ϕ phases arise as a direct consequence of the Majorana nature of neutrinos. Therefore, in principle, the the ϕ phase associated with the electron family is accessible in neutrinoless double beta decay. In practice, this will be extremely hard to measure because this term manifests itself as a change in the sum in Eq. 5.31, which is proportional to the $0\nu\beta\beta$ decay amplitude. Thus one seeks to measure a deviation of the (as-yet-unmeasured) $0\nu\beta\beta$ lifetime from the prediction which depends upon the mixing angles (with relatively large errors at present), the (unknown) neutrino masses, and the (poorly known) nuclear matrix element. Even if the effect is large, observation of the effect is clearly hopeless in the near future. On the other hand, δ, the "Dirac" CP violating term in V may be accessible though oscillation searches.

CP violation searches involve observing a difference in oscillation probability for neutrinos and antineutrinos. Only appearance experiments can observe CP violation. A difference between oscillations of neutrinos and antineutrinos in disappearance searches is CPT violating. In oscillation appearance searches, the K matrix does not affect the oscillation probability because this diagonal matrix is multiplied by its complex conjugate. On the other hand, non-zero δ can be observed. To test for non-zero δ, the oscillation probability must depend upon the U_{e3} component of Eq. 5.32. In other words, the search needs to involve transitions from or to electron flavor and involve the mass state ν_3. This combination of requirements – appearance signal, electron flavor involvement, and ν_3 mass state involvement – leads to one experimental option at present: comparison of $\nu_\mu \to \nu_e$ to $\bar{\nu}_\mu \to \bar{\nu}_e$ at the atmospheric Δm^2, which is Δm_{13}^2. The oscillation probability is given by:

$$P_{long-baseline} \simeq \sin^2 2\theta_{13} \sin^2 \theta_{23} \sin^2 \Delta$$
$$\mp \alpha \sin 2\theta_{13} \sin \delta_{CP} \cos \theta_{13} \sin 2\theta_{12} \sin 2\theta_{23} \sin^3 \Delta$$
$$+ \alpha \sin 2\theta_{13} \cos \delta_{CP} \cos \theta_{13} \sin 2\theta_{12} \sin 2\theta_{23} \cos \Delta \sin^2 \Delta$$
$$+ \alpha^2 \cos^2 \theta_{23} \sin^2 2\theta_{12} \sin^2 \Delta, \quad (5.34)$$

where α and Δ are defined in Eq. 5.20. The second term is negative for neutrino scattering and positive for antineutrino scattering.

Unfortunately, Eq. 5.34 convolutes two unknown parameters, the sign of Δm_{13}^2 (the mass hierarchy) and the value of θ_{13}, with the parameter, δ, that we want to measure. The problem of the mass hierarchy can be mitigated by the experimental design. The sign of $\Delta m_{13}^2 = m_3^2 - m_1^2$ affects the terms where Δm^2 is not squared. These terms arise from matter effects and can so be reduced if the pathlength in matter is relatively short. For long baseline experiments, which must shoot the beam through the Earth, this means that L must be relatively short. In order to retain the same L/E and, hence, the same sensitivity to Δm_{13}^2, E must be comparably reduced. On the other hand, the problem of θ_{13} cannot be mitigated. From Eq. 5.32, one sees that we are in the unfortunate situation of having the CP violating term multiplied by $\sin \theta_{13}$. The smaller this factor, the harder it will be to extract δ. If $\sin^2 2\theta_{13}$ is smaller than ~ 0.01 at 90% CL, then substantial improvements in beams and detectors will be required.

Equation 5.34 also depends on two other as-yet-poorly understood parameters, θ_{23} and the magnitude of Δm_{23}^2. Disappearance experiments measure $\sin^2 2\theta_{23} = 1.00^{+0.16}_{-0.14}$,[67] thus there is an ambiguity as to whether θ_{23}, is larger or smaller than 45°. Δm_{23}^2 is only known to about 10%.[56,67] This measurement is extracted from the location of the "dip" in the rate versus L/E distribution of disappearance experiments, and is already systematics-dominated. Improvement requires experiments with better energy resolution[56] and better understanding of the CCQE and background cross sections.[139] These errors lend a significant error to the analysis.

Lastly, it is difficult to measure a ν_e signal which is at the $\sim 1\%$ level. Most ν_μ beams have a substantial ν_e intrinsic contamination from μ and K decays. Given that θ_{13} is small, this contamination is a serious issue. One solution to this problem is to go to an off-axis beam design. This relies on the tight correlation between energy and off-axis angle, θ, in two-body decays. For pion decay, which dominates most beams,

$$E_\nu = \frac{0.43 E_\pi}{1 + \gamma^2 \theta^2}, \qquad (5.35)$$

where $\gamma = E_\pi/m_\pi$ is the Lorentz boost factor. The solution for two-body K decay replaces 0.43 with 0.96. Thus at $\theta = 0$, the relationship between E_ν and E_π is linear. However, for larger θ, above a moderate energy threshold, all values of E_π map to the same E_ν. This is illustrated in Fig. 5.18. The result is that an off axis ν_μ beam which comes largely from pion decay is tightly peaked in energy while the ν_e intrinsic background is spread across a range of energies. This also helps to reduce ν_μ events which are misreconstructed as ν_e scatters, such as NC π^0 production where a photon is lost. These "mis-ids" tend to be spread across a range of energies, since the true energy is misreconstructed. Thus a peaked signal, as one expects from an off-axis beam, is helpful in separating signal and background.

The major problem with this design is that off axis beams have substantially lower flux. The flux scales[140] as:

$$F = \left(\frac{2\gamma}{1+\gamma^2\theta^2}\right)^2 A/4\pi z^2. \qquad (5.36)$$

In this equation, A is the area of the detector and z is the distance to the detector. Two future long baseline experiments, NOvA[40] and T2K[141] are proposing off-axis beams for a $\nu_\mu \to \nu_e$ search. Because of the low flux, very large detectors are required.

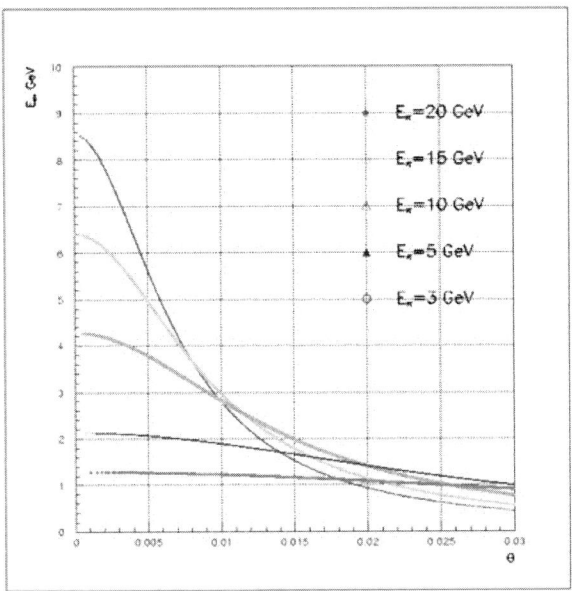

Fig. 5.18. Neutrino energy versus angle off-axis for various values of pion energy. In this example one can see that for moderate off-axis angles, between 15-30 mrad, all pion energies between 3 and 20 GeV map to approximately 1 GeV neutrino energy.

In summary, the path to a test for non-zero δ is clear but will take several steps and requires some luck. First, a clean measure θ_{13} from Double Chooz and Daya Bay is needed. If $\sin^2 2\theta_{13} < 0.005$ at 90% CL, then a significant measurement of CP violation is unlikely to be possible in the near future. At the same time, improvements in the θ_{23} and Δm^2_{23} from disappearance ($\nu_\mu \to \nu_\mu$) measurements at MINOS and T2K will improve the situation. T2K and NOvA[40] may be able to make a first exploration of CP parameter space, from ν_e appearance measurements, depending on statistics. NOvA may also be able to address the mass hierarchy question. This will open up the possibility of measuring CP violation to the next generation of very long baseline experiments.[142] The most sensitive of these use a beam originating at Fermilab and a LAr detector located at Ash River, Minnesota[45] or a Cerenkov or LAr detector located at the Deep Underground Science Laboratory at Homestake.[143]

At some point in the future, a beta beam or a neutrino factory beam could provide an intense source of ν_e and $\bar{\nu}_e$ fluxes, allowing comparison of $\nu_e \to \nu_\mu$ to $\bar{\nu}_e \to \bar{\nu}_\mu$. In this case one would search for events with wrong-sign muons in a calorimeter-style detector. This would be a striking signature with low background, especially in the case of a beta beam. This could allow a very precise measurement of δ.[144]

5.3.2. Neutrinos and the Unexpected

While it is nice to have a tidy, well-motivated theory of neutrino masses, it is disconcerting to have essentially no experimental evidence for this theory. Moreover, neutrino theories have a history of being incorrect. Only a decade ago, most theorists would have told you that neutrinos have no mass. Those who thought neutrinos might have mass believed it would be relatively large (> 5 eV), explaining dark matter. Most theorists also believed that if the solar neutrinos were experiencing oscillations, the correct solution would be the small mixing angle MSW solution, because the mixing matrix should look like the quark matrix. Using the same logic, the atmospheric neutrino deficit, which could only correspond to large mixing angle, was routinely dismissed as an experimental effect.

On the basis of this, it is wise not to constrain ourselves to the "New Paradigm." The reason the APS neutrino study chose to devote a chapter to "the Unexpected" was to emphasize the importance of being open to what nature is telling us about neutrinos. There are two ways to approach this idea: (1) the theory-driven approach: explore for properties which could, theoretically, exist and (2) the experiment-driven approach: follow up on anomalous results which have been observed.

For lack of time, I will only briefly consider two examples of the first case: searching for a neutrino magnetic moment and searching for CPT violation. In the Standard Model, the neutrino magnetic moment is expected to be $\sim 10^{-19}\mu_B$. Laboratory experiments and astrophysical limits are many orders of magnitude away from this level.[145] Nevertheless, if a new experiment could advance this measurement by an order of magnitude, that would be worth pursuing. A more startling discovery would be a difference in the oscillation disappearance probability of neutrinos versus antineutrinos. In a three-neutrino model, a difference in the rate of disappearance of neutrinos and antineutrinos would imply CPT violation. MINOS will be the next experiment to pursue such a search.[36] If CPT violation were discovered we would need to rethink the very basis of our theory. However, there are theorists exploring these ideas.

The remainder of this section will focus on the second approach, exploring "anomalies" which have appeared in various experiments. Physicists today are always cautious about pursuing deviations from the Standard Model. Most do not, in the end, point to new physics. The Standard Model has been very resilient Most anomalies are arguably more likely due to systematic effects or statistical fluctuations, than to new physics. However, those which do "pan out" completely change the way we think. The solar neutrino deficit is a perfect example. So, if a new, unexpected result withstands questions by the community on the systematics of the experiment, then the anomaly becomes worth pursuing further.

There are several examples of $> 3\sigma$ unexpected results in the neutrino sector which are worth pursuing and two cases are covered here. The first, the LSND anomaly, is being actively pursued. The second, the NuTeV anomaly, will require a new experiment. Unlike most of the topics in these lectures, the NuTeV anomaly is not directly related to neutrino oscillations and neutrino mass, and so expands the discussion, which has so far been rather narrowly focussed.

Along with the known discrepancies which have reached the level of full-fledged anomalies, there are also examples of "unexpected results to watch." These results which have not yet reached the 3σ level, but are showing interesting trends. For example, unconstrained fits to atmospheric oscillation data from a wide range of experiments consistently result in $\sin^2 2\theta_{23}$ best fit value greater than unity. While in each case, the best fit is $\sim 1\sigma$ from unity, it is the trend which is interesting, since the experiments involved are all very different. There is simply not enough space to cover this and other examples of "results to watch."

The take-away message of this section is: the neutrino sector is a rich place for new physics to appear, and physicists need to be alert and open-minded to what nature is saying.

5.3.2.1. *The LSND Anomaly*

The LSND experiment ran at the LAMPF accelerator at Los Alamos National Laboratory between 1993 and 1998. The decay-at-rest (DAR) beam was produced by impinging 800 MeV protons on a beam dump. These produced π^+s which stop and decay to produce μ^+s, which also stop and decay to produce $\bar{\nu}_\mu$ and ν_e. These were studied in the range of 20 to 55 MeV. The π^-s capture, so the beam has a $< 8 \times 10^{-4}$ contamination of $\bar{\nu}_e$. The neutrino events were observed in a detector located 30 m downstream of the beam dump. 1220 phototubes surrounded the periphery of a

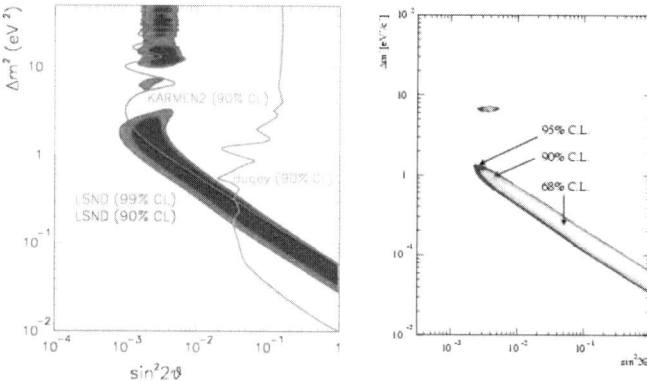

Fig. 5.19. Left: LSND allowed range compared to short baseline experiment limits. Right: Allowed range from the Karmen-LSND joint analysis.[149]

cylindrical detector filled with 167 tons of mineral oil, lightly doped with scintillator. The signature of a $\bar{\nu}_e$ appearance was $\bar{\nu}_e + p \to e^+ n$. This resulted in a two-component signature: the initial Cerenkov and scintillation light associated with the e^+, followed later by the scintillation light from the n capture on hydrogen, producing a 2.2 MeV γ. The experiment observed $87.9 \pm 22.4 \pm 6.0$ events, a 4σ excess[146] above expectation.

LSND is a short baseline experiment, with an $L/E \sim 1$ m/MeV. Thus, from the two-generation oscillation formula, Eq. 5.10, one can see that this experiment is sensitive to $\Delta m^2 \geq 0.1$ eV^2. Other experiments have searched for oscillations at high Δm^2, and the two most relevant to LSND are Karmen[147] and Bugey.[148] The KARMEN experiment, which also used a DAR muon beam and was located 17.7 m from the beam dump, had sensitivity to address only a portion of the LSND region, and did not see a signal there. Since the design of the experiments are very similar, one can think of the Karmen experiment as a "near detector," which measures the flux before oscillation. The results were combined in a joint analysis performed by collaborators from both experiments; the allowed range for oscillations is shown in Figure 5.19.[149] The Bugey experiment was a reactor-based $\bar{\nu}_e$ disappearance search which set a limit on oscillations. Because this is disappearance and not explicitly $\bar{\nu}_e \to \bar{\nu}_\mu$, its limit is applicable to LSND in many, but not all, oscillation models. This limit is shown in Figure 5.19.

Why can't we fit LSND into the three-neutrino theory? The LSND signal cannot be accommodated within the standard three-neutrino picture, given the solar and atmospheric oscillations. To see the incompatibility, first consider the case where the oscillation signals de-couple into, effectively, two-generation oscillations (Eq. 5.10). For three generations, then $\Delta m_{31}^2 = \Delta m_{32}^2 + \Delta m_{21}^2$, which is clearly not the the case for these three signals. The more general case allows the atmospheric result to be due to a mixture of high (LSND-range) and low (solar-range) Δm^2 values. In order for this model to succeed, the atmospheric Δm^2 from a shape analysis must shift up from its present value of $\sim 2 \times 10^{-3}$ eV^2 and the chlorine experiment must have overestimated the deficit of ^{7}Be solar neutrinos. However, the largest clash between data and this model arises from the Super-K ν_e events. This model requires that Super-K has missed a ν_e appearance signal of approximately the same size and shape as the ν_μ deficit before detector smearing and cuts. Neutrino measurements are experimentally difficult and parameters do sometimes shift with time as systematics are better understood, but it seems unlikely that all of the above results could change sufficiently to accommodate LSND.

Sterile Neutrinos as a Solution Additional neutrinos which do not interact via exchange of W or Z are called "sterile;" they may mix with active neutrinos, and thereby can be produced in neutrino oscillations. Experimental evidence of this would be the disappearance of the active flavor from the beam. In contrast to the GUT-scale sterile neutrinos we have already discussed, the sterile neutrinos which could explain LSND must be light (in the eV range), and this narrows the class of acceptable theories. Nevertheless, a number of possible explanations remain.[150]

Sterile neutrinos solve the LSND problem by adding extra mass splittings. The additional mass states must be mostly sterile, with only a small admixture of the active flavors in order to accommodate the limits on sterile neutrinos from the atmospheric and solar experiments. In principle, one might expect three sterile neutrinos. In practice, the data cannot constrain information on more than two sterile neutrinos. Therefore these are called "3+2" models. The method for fitting the data is described in reference.[151] One is fitting for two additional mass splittings, Δm_{14}^2 and Δm_{15}^2. In the fit, the three mostly active neutrinos are approximated as degenerate. The mixing matrix is also expanded by two rows and two columns.

The data that drive the fits are the "short baseline" experiments that provide information on high Δm^2 oscillations, summarized in Table 5.5. The combination of $\bar{\nu}_\mu \to \bar{\nu}_e$ (LSND,[146] Karmen II[147]), $\nu_\mu \to \nu_e$ (NOMAD[152]), ν_μ disappearance (CDHS,[153] CCFR84[154]), and ν_e disappearance

Table 5.5. Results used in 3 + 2 fit. $\sin^2 2\theta$ limit is 90% CL

Channel	Experiment	Lowest Δm^2	$\sin^2 2\theta$ at high Δm^2	Best reach in $\sin^2 2\theta$
$\nu_\mu \to \nu_e$	LSND	0.03 eV^2	$> 2.5 \times 10^{-3}$	$> 1.2 \times 10^{-3}$
	KARMEN	0.06 eV^2	$< 1.7 \times 10^{-3}$	$< 1.0 \times 10^{-3}$
	NOMAD	0.4 eV^2	$< 1.4 \times 10^{-3}$	$< 1.0 \times 10^{-3}$
ν_e disappearance	Bugey	0.01 eV^2	$< 1.4 \times 10^{-1}$	$< 1.3 \times 10^{-2}$
	Chooz	0.0001 eV^2	$< 1.0 \times 10^{-1}$	$< 5 \times 10^{-2}$
ν_μ disappearance	CCFR84	6 eV^2	NA	$< 2 \times 10^{-1}$
	CDHS	0.3 eV^2	NA	$< 5.3 \times 10^{-1}$

(Bugey,[148] CHOOZ[25]) must all be accommodated within the model. A constraint for Super K ν_μ disappearance is also included. None of the short baseline experiments except for LSND provide evidence for oscillations beyond 3σ. However, it should be noted that CDHS has a 2σ (statistical and systematic, combined) effect consistent with a high Δm^2 sterile neutrino when the data are fit for a shape dependence, and Bugey has a 1σ pull at $\Delta m^2 \sim 1\text{eV}^2$. As a result, these two experiments define the best fit combination of high and low Δm^2 for the 3+2 model. However, there are acceptable solutions with a combination of low Δm^2 values. The best fit,[151] has $\Delta m^2_{14} = 0.92$ eV^2, $\Delta m^2_{15} = 22$ eV^2, although there are combinations which work with two relatively low Δm^2 values. A wide range of mixing angles can be accommodated, and the best fit has $U_{e4} = 0.121$, $U_{\mu 4} = 0.204$, $U_{e5} = 0.036$ and $U_{\mu 4} = 0.224$. The other mixing angles involving the sterile states are not probed by the ν_μ disappearance, ν_e disappearance and $\nu_\mu \to \nu_e$ appearance experiments listed above. There is 30% compatibility for all other experiments and LSND.

Introducing extra neutrinos, including sterile ones, would have cosmological implications, compounded if the extra neutrinos have significant mass (>1 eV). However, there are several ways around the problem. The first is to note that while the best fit requires a high mass sterile neutrino, there are low-mass fits which work within the 3+2 model. The second is to observe that there are a variety of classes of theories where the neutrinos do not thermalize in the early universe.[122] In this case, there is no conflict with the cosmological data, since the cosmological neutrino abundance is substantially reduced.

If more than one Δm^2 contributes to an oscillation appearance signal, then the data can be sensitive to a CP-violating phase in the mixing matrix. Experimentally, for this to occur, the Δm^2 values must be within less than about two orders of magnitude of one another.

In 3+2 CP-violating models:[155]

$$P(\overset{(-)}{\nu_\mu} \to \overset{(-)}{\nu_e}) = 4|U_{e4}|^2|U_{\mu4}|^2 \sin^2 x_{41}$$
$$+ 4|U_{e5}|^2|U_{\mu5}|^2 \sin^2 x_{51}$$
$$+ 8|U_{e4}||U_{\mu4}||U_{e5}||U_{\mu5}|$$
$$\sin x_{41} \sin x_{51} \cos(x_{54} \mp \phi_{54}), \quad (5.37)$$

where in the last line, the negative sign is for neutrino oscillations and the positive sign is for antineutrino oscillations, and defined:

$$x_{ji} \equiv 1.27 \Delta m_{ji}^2 L/E, \quad \phi_{54} \equiv arg(U_{e4}^* U_{\mu 4} U_{e5} U_{\mu 5}^*).$$

Thus the oscillation probability is affected by CP violation through the term ϕ_{54}. The CP conserving cases are $\phi_{54} = 0$ and 180 degrees.

MiniBooNE First Results The main purpose of the MiniBooNE experiment was to resolve the question of the LSND signal. First results of this experiment, presented in April, 2007, considered those explanations with a high expectation for $\nu_\mu \to \nu_e$ oscillations. This includes the CP conserving 3+2 model and many cases of CP violating 3+2 models described above. As will be described below, the first results are incompatible with $\nu_\mu \to \nu_e$ oscillations, but show an unexpected low energy excess, very much in keeping with the subsection title of "Neutrinos and the Unexpected."

The MiniBooNE experiment uses the Fermilab Booster Neutrino Beam, which is produced from 8 GeV protons incident on a beryllium target located within a magnetic focusing horn. The current of the horn can be reversed such that the beam is dominantly neutrinos or antineutrinos. The first results are from neutrino running. The MiniBooNE detector is located $L = 541$ m from the primary target, and the neutrino flux has average energy of ~ 0.75 GeV. The detector is located 541 m from the front of the beryllium target and consists of a spherical tank of radius 610 cm that is covered on the inside by 1520 8-inch photomultiplier tubes and filled with 800 tons of pure mineral oil (CH_2). Neutrino events in the detector produce both Cerenkov and scintillation light.

In order to test the LSND result, the MiniBooNE design maintains $L/E \sim 1$ m/MeV while substantially changing the systematic errors associated with the experiment. This is accomplished by increasing both L and E by an order of magnitude from the LSND design. This changes the source of the neutrinos (ν_μ from energetic pions rather than $\bar{\nu}_\mu$ from stopped muons), the signature for the signal, and the major backgrounds in the detector. In its first run, in neutrino mode, MiniBooNE collected over a million clean, neutrino events. About 99.5% of the MiniBooNE neutrino events are estimated to be ν_μ-induced, while 0.5% are estimated to be due to "intrinsic" ν_e background in the beam.

The initial MiniBooNE results were analyzed within an appearance-only, two neutrino oscillation context. While the LSND signal must be a result of a more complex oscillation model, in most cases a $\nu_\mu \to \nu_e$-like oscillation signal is predicted. After the complete ν_e event selection is applied, the total background was estimated to be 358 ± 35 events, while 163 ± 21 signal events were expected for the LSND central expectation of 0.26% $\nu_\mu \to \nu_e$ transmutation.

The top plot of Fig. 5.20 shows candidate ν_e events as a function of reconstructed neutrino energy (E_ν^{QE}). The vertical dashed line indicates the minimum E_ν^{QE} used in the two-neutrino oscillation analysis. There is no significant excess of events ($22\pm19\pm35$ events) for $475 < E_\nu^{QE} < 1250$ MeV; however, an excess of events ($96\pm17\pm20$ events) is observed below 475 MeV. In the top plot, the points show the statistical error, while the histogram is the expected background with systematic errors from all sources. The background subtracted excess as a function of E_ν^{QE} is shown in the bottom plot, where the points represent the data with total errors. Oscillation scenarios are indicated by the histograms.

The low-energy excess cannot be explained by a two-neutrino oscillation model, and its source is under investigation. The low energy events isolated by the cuts, including the excess events, are single-ring and electromagnetic-like, with no unusual detection issues. The low energy excess events are neither consistent with the spatial nor energy distributions of photons coming from interactions outside of the tank. Nor are they consistent with the energy distribution from single photons from radiative Δ decays ($\Delta \to N+\gamma$). Mis-identification of π^0 events is well constrained in MiniBooNE by the rate of reconstructed π^0 events, studied as a function of π^0 momentum.[156] This rate would need to be mis-measured by well over a factor of three to explain the excess, far outside of the error of the analysis.

With that said, as shown in Fig. 5.20, the excess is not in agreement with a simple two-neutrino $\nu_\mu \to \nu_e$ oscillation signal. This figure shows the predicted spectrum when the best-fit two-neutrino oscillation signal is added to the predicted background. The bottom panel of the figure shows background-subtracted data with the best-fit two-neutrino oscillation and two oscillation points from the favored LSND region.

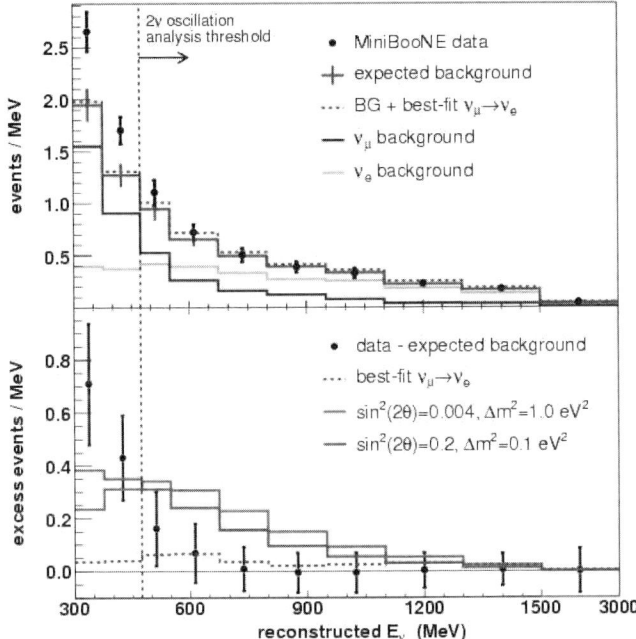

Fig. 5.20. The top plot shows the number of candidate ν_e events as a function of E_ν^{QE}. Also shown are the best-fit oscillation spectrum (dashed histogram) and the background contributions from ν_μ and ν_e events. The bottom plot shows the number of events with the predicted background subtracted as a function of E_ν^{QE}. The two histograms correspond to LSND solutions at high and low Δm^2.

A single-sided raster scan to a two neutrino appearance-only oscillation model is used in the energy range $475 < E_\nu^{QE} < 3000$ MeV to find the 90% CL limit corresponding to $\Delta \chi^2 = \chi^2_{limit} - \chi^2_{bestfit} = 1.64$. As shown by the top plot in Fig. 5.21, the LSND 90% CL allowed region is excluded at the 90% CL. A joint analysis as a function of Δm^2, using a combined χ^2 of the best fit values and errors for LSND and MiniBooNE, excludes at 98% CL two-neutrino appearance-only oscillations as an explanation of the LSND anomaly. The bottom plot of Fig. 5.21 shows limits from the KARMEN[147] and Bugey[148] experiments. This is plot represents an example of the problem of apples-to-apples comparisons raised in Sec. . The MiniBooNE and Bugey curves are 1-sided upper limits on $\sin^2 2\theta$ corresponding to $\Delta \chi^2 = 1.64$ – hence directly comparable – while the published KARMEN curve is a "Feldman Cousins" contour.

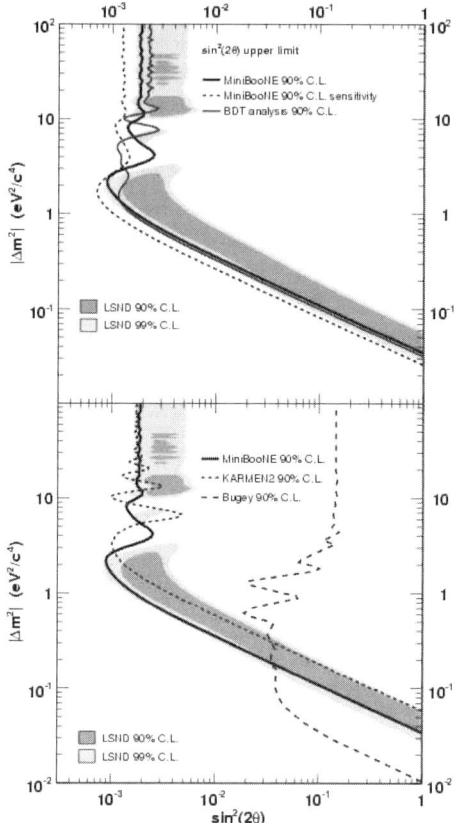

Fig. 5.21. The top plot shows the $\nu_\mu \to \nu_e$ MiniBooNE 90% CL limit (thick solid curve) and sensitivity (dashed curve) for events with $475 < E_\nu^{QE} < 3000$ MeV. Also shown is the limit from a second cross-check analysis (thin solid curve). The bottom plot shows the limits from the KARMEN[147] and Bugey[148] experiments. The shaded areas show the 90% and 99% CL allowed regions from the LSND experiment.

Next Steps From the initial MiniBooNE result, one can draw two conclusions: (1) there is excellent agreement between data and prediction in the analysis region originally defined for the two-neutrino oscillation search and (2) there is a presently unexplained discrepancy with data lying above background at low energy. This combination of information severely limits models seeking to explain the LSND anomaly.

Interpreting the MiniBooNE data as appearance-only and combining this result with other data in a 3+2 fit does not give a satisfactory result.[157] While MiniBooNE and LSND are compatible if CP violation is allowed in the 3+2 model, there is tension between these results and the ν_μ disappearance experiments. This might be addressed if a 3+2 interpretation of the MiniBooNE result were expanded to include the possibility of ν_μ disappearance and intrinsic ν_e disappearance. This analysis is underway by the MiniBooNE collaboration.[158] Most likely, if a good fit is obtained in a 3+2 scenario, it will require some level of CP violation. Mini-BooNE is presently collecting data in antineutrino mode. However, this is a small data set ($\sim 2 \times 10^{20}$ protons on target producing the beam) and future running to reach roughly three times the statistics will be required to make a decisive statement. Other, alternative explanations are also being explored[159–161].

An upcoming result which will shed light on the question is the analysis of the MiniBooNE data from the NuMI beam. This beam is 110 mrad off-axis, with a π peak of average ν_μ energy of about 200 MeV and a K peak of about 2 GeV, and a length of 750 m. If an excess of events is observed in this analysis, this rules out mis-estimate of intrinsic ν_e in the Booster Neutrino Beam as the source of the MiniBooNE excess. Results from this study are expected in autumn, 2007.

If the unexplained excess persists after the above studies, then it will be valuable to introduce a detector which can differentiate between electrons and photons. That is the goal of MicroBooNE,[44] which uses a Liquid argon TPC (LArTPC) detector. This is particularly sensitive at low energies and nearly background-free. Specifically, this detector has a ν_e efficiency $> 80\%$ and rejects photons efficiently through dE/dx deposition in the first ~ 2 cm of the shower. With these qualities the detector can be an order of magnitude smaller in size than MiniBooNE, making quick construction feasible. A proposal for this experiment will be submitted to the Fermilab PAC in autumn 2007.

5.3.2.2. *The NuTeV Anomaly*

Neutrino scattering measurements offer a unique tool to probe the electroweak interactions of the Standard Model (SM). The NuTeV anomaly is a 3σ deviation of $\sin^2\theta_W$ from the Standard Model prediction.[162] $\sin^2\theta_W$ parameterizes the mixing between the weak interaction Z boson and the photon in electroweak theory. Deviations of measurements of this parameter, and its partner parameter, ρ, the relative coupling strength of the neutral-to-charged-current interactions, may indicate Beyond-Standard-Model physics. This section also highlights that fact that new neutrino

Table 5.6. left and right handed coupling constants.

f	ℓ_f	r_f
e^-	$-\frac{1}{2} + \sin^2\theta_W$	$\sin^2\theta_W$
u, c	$\frac{1}{2} - \frac{2}{3}\sin^2\theta_W$	$-\frac{2}{3}\sin^2\theta_W$
d, s	$-\frac{1}{2} + \frac{1}{3}\sin^2\theta_W$	$\frac{1}{3}\sin^2\theta_W$

properties may be revealed in TeV-scale interactions at LHC, which has not been addressed previously.

The NuTeV experiment represents a departure from the previous train of thought in several ways. NuTeV was a deep inelastic neutrino scattering experiment, and thus is performed at significantly higher energy than the experiments previously discussed. Also, while NuTeV did an oscillation search, it was mainly designed for another purpose: precision measurement of electroweak parameters. We will focus on that purpose here. As a result, this analysis allows new issues related to neutrino physics to be brought into the discussion.

$\sin^2\theta_W$ in Neutrino Scattering and Other Experiments

In neutrino scattering, the neutral current cross section depends upon $\sin^2\theta_W$. The dependence is a function of the neutrino flavor and the target. NuTeV was a muon-neutrino-flavor scattering experiment. In this case, the NC cross sections for scattering from a light fermion target are:

$$\frac{d\sigma(\nu_\mu f \to \nu_\mu f)}{dy} = \frac{G_F^2 s}{\pi} \left(\ell_f^2 + r_f^2(1-y)^2\right)\left(1 + \frac{sy}{M_Z^2}\right)^{-2}, \quad (5.38)$$

$$\frac{d\sigma(\bar{\nu}_\mu f \to \bar{\nu}_\mu f)}{dy} = \frac{G_F^2 s}{\pi} \left(\ell_f^2(1-y)^2 + r_f^2\right)\left(1 + \frac{sy}{M_Z^2}\right)^{-2}. \quad (5.39)$$

In this equation, f is the type of light fermion: $f = e^-, u, d, s, c$. Several constants appear: G_F is the Fermi constant, M_Z is the mass of the Z. The two kinematic variables are: s, the effective center of mass energy, which depends on the mass of f and y, the inelasticity (see definitions in Sec. 5.1.2). ℓ_f, r_f are left and right handed coupling constants which are given in Table 5.6.

While neutrino scattering has traditionally been a method for measuring $\sin^2\theta_W$, the "Standard Model Prediction" quoted in literature comes from the very precise measurements made by the LEP and SLD experiments, which have been summarized by the Electroweak Working Group.[163] $\sin^2\theta_W$ appears in various measurements from e^+e^- scattering at the Z pole. An example which leads to a highly precise measurement is the "left-right asymmetry" measured from polarized scattering at SLD:

$A_{LR} = (\sigma_L - \sigma_R)/(\sigma_L + \sigma_R)$ where σ_L and σ_R refer to the scattering cross sections for left- and right- polarized electrons, respectively. In this case the asymmetry is given by:

$$A_{LR}(Z^0) \equiv \frac{\left(\frac{1}{2} - \sin^2\theta_W^{((\text{eff})}\right)^2 - \sin^4\theta_W^{(\text{eff})}}{\left(\frac{1}{2} - \sin^2\theta_W(\text{eff})\right)^2 + \sin^4\theta_W^{(\text{eff})}}, \quad (5.40)$$

When comparing quoted values of the weak mixing angle $\sin^2\theta_W$, care must be taken because this parameter is defined in various ways. The simplest definition is the "on shell" description:

$$1 - M_W^2/M_Z^2 \equiv \sin^2\theta_W^{(\text{on-shell})}. \quad (5.41)$$

This is the definition commonly used in neutrino physics. In the discussion which follows, if not explicitly labeled, the on-shell definition for $\sin^2\theta_W$ is used. A variation on this definition uses the renormalized masses at some arbitrary scale μ which is usually taken to be M_Z:

$$1 - M_W(\mu)^2/M_Z(\mu)^2 \equiv \sin^2\theta_W^{(\overline{\text{MS}})}. \quad (5.42)$$

However, the LEP experiments used the "effective" weak mixing angle which is related to the vector and axial vector couplings:

$$\frac{1}{4}(1 - g_V^l/g_A^l) \equiv \sin^2\theta_W^{(\text{eff})}. \quad (5.43)$$

This is what appears in Eq. 5.40 above. One must convert between definitions, which have different radiative corrections and renormalization prescriptions, in order to make comparisons.

The parameter $\sin^2\theta_W$ evolves with Q^2, the squared 4-momentum transfer of the interaction. Fig. 5.22 illustrates this evolution. The highest Q^2 measurements are from LEP and SLD, with $Q^2 = M_Z^2$. There are several types of experiments, including neutrino experiments, which measure $\sin^2\theta_W$ with $Q^2 \ll m_Z^2$. NuTeV was performed at $Q^2 = 1$ to 140 GeV^2, $\langle Q_\nu^2 \rangle = 26$ GeV^2, $\langle Q_{\bar\nu}^2 \rangle = 15$ GeV^2. The lowest Q^2 measurements are from studies of atomic parity violation in the nucleus[164] (APV), which arises due to the electroweak interference of the photon and the Z in the boson exchange between the electrons and the nucleus. This samples $Q^2 \sim 0$. At higher Q^2, there is the result from SLAC E158, a Møller scattering experiment at average $Q^2 = 0.026$ GeV^2.[165] Using the measurements at the Z-pole with $Q^2 = M_z^2$ to fix the value of $\sin^2\theta_W$, and evolving to low Q^2, Fig. 5.22[166] shows that APV and SLAC E158 are in agreement with the Standard Model.

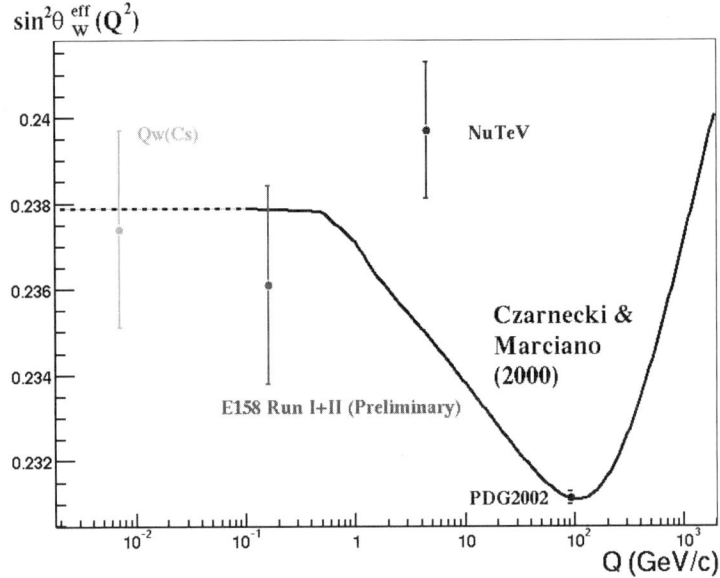

Fig. 5.22. Measurements of $\sin^2 \theta_W$ as a function of Q.[166] The curve shows the Standard Model expectation.

NuTeV is strikingly off the prediction of Fig. 5.22. Neutrino scattering may measure a different result because new physics enters the neutrino process differently than the other experiments. Compared to the colliders, neutrino physics measures different combinations of couplings. Also neutrino scattering explores new physics through moderate space-like momentum transfer, as opposed to the time-like scattering at the colliders. With respect to the lower energy experiments, the radiative corrections to neutrino interactions allow sensitivity to high-mass particles which are complementary to the APV and Møller-scattering corrections.

The NuTeV Result The NuTeV experiment provides the most precise measurement of $\sin^2 \theta_W$ from neutrino experiments. The measurement relied upon deep inelastic scatter (DIS). It was performed using a "Paschos-Wolfenstein style"[167] analysis which is designed to minimize the systematic errors which come from our understanding of parton distributions and masses.

This method requires separated ν and $\bar{\nu}$ beams. In this case, the following ratios could be formed:

$$R^\nu = \frac{\sigma^\nu_{NC}}{\sigma^\nu_{CC}} \tag{5.44}$$

$$R^{\bar\nu} = \frac{\sigma^{\bar\nu}_{NC}}{\sigma^{\bar\nu}_{CC}} \tag{5.45}$$

$$\tag{5.46}$$

Paschos and Wolfenstein[167] recast these as:

$$R^- = \frac{\sigma^\nu_{NC} - \sigma^{\bar\nu}_{NC}}{\sigma^\nu_{CC} - \sigma^{\bar\nu}_{CC}} = \frac{R^\nu - rR^{\bar\nu}}{1-r}, \tag{5.47}$$

where $r = \sigma^{\bar\nu}_{CC}/\sigma^\nu_{CC}$. In the case of R^-, many systematics cancel to first order. In particular, the quark and antiquark seas for u, d, s, and c, which are less precisely known than the valence quark distributions, will cancel. Charm production only enters through $d_{valence}$ which is Cabbibo suppressed and at high x, thus the error from the charm mass is greatly reduced. One can also form R^+, but this will have much larger systematic errors, and so the strength of the NuTeV analysis lies in the measurement of R^-.

According to the "Paschos-Wolfenstein" method, an experiment should run in neutrino and antineutrino mode, categorize the events as CC or NC DIS, and then form R^- to extract $\sin^2\theta_W$. This requires identifying the CC or NC events properly in NuTeV's iron-scintillator/drift-chamber calorimeter. Most CC DIS events have an exiting muon, which causes a long string of hits in the scintillator and are therefore called "long." Most NC DIS events are relatively "short" hadronic showers. However, there are exceptions to these rules. A CC event caused by interaction of an intrinsic ν_e in the beam will appear short. An NC shower which contains a pion-decay-in-flight, producing a muon, may appear long. The connection between long vs. short and CC vs. NC must be made via Monte Carlo.

NuTeV measurement is in agreement with past neutrino scattering results, although these have much larger errors. However, the NuTeV result is in disagreement with the global fits to the electroweak data which give a Standard Model value of $\sin^2\theta_W = 0.2227$.[162]

Explanations In the case of any anomaly, it is best to start with the commonplace explanations. Three explanations for the NuTeV anomaly that are "within the Standard Model" have been proposed: the QCD-order of the analysis, isospin violation, and the strange sea asymmetry. The NuTeV analysis was not performed at a full NLO level. However, the effect of going to NLO on NuTeV can be estimated,[168] and the expected pull is away from the Standard Model. The NuTeV analysis assumed isospin symmetry, that is, $u(x)^p = d(x)^n$ and $d(x)^p = u(x)^n$. Various models for isospin violation have been studied and their pulls range from less than 1σ away from the Standard Model to $\sim 1\sigma$ toward the Standard Model.[169] Variations in the strange sea can either pull the result toward or away from the Standard Model expectation,[169] but not by more than one sigma.

With respect to Beyond-Standard-Model explanations, Chapter 14 of the APS Neutrino Study White Paper on Neutrino Theory[2] is dedicated to "The Physics of NuTeV" and provides an excellent summary. The discussion presented here is drawn from this source.

The NuTeV measurements of R^ν and $R^{\bar{\nu}}$, the NC-to-CC cross sections, are low compared to expectation. For this to be a Beyond-Standard-Model effect, it therefore requires introduction of new physics that suppresses the NC rate with respect to the CC rate. Two types of models produce this effect and remain consistent with the other electroweak measurements: (1) models which affect only the Z couplings, e.g., the introduction of a heavy Z' boson which interferes with the Standard Model Z; or (2) models which affect only the neutrino couplings, e.g., the introduction of moderate mass neutral heavy leptons which mix with the neutrino.

Any Z' model invoked to explain NuTeV must selectively suppress NC neutrino scattering, without significantly affecting the other electroweak measurements. This rules out most models, which tend to increase the NC scattering rate. Examples of successful models are those where the Z' couples to $B - 3L_\mu$[170] or to $L_\mu - L_\tau$.[171]

Moderate-mass neutral heavy leptons, a.k.a. "neutrissimos," can also produce the desired effect. Suppression of the coupling comes from intergenerational mixing of heavy states, so that the ν_μ is a mixture:

$$\nu_\mu = (\cos\alpha)\nu_{\text{light}} + (\sin\alpha)\nu_{\text{heavy}}. \tag{5.48}$$

The $Z\nu_\mu\nu_\mu$ coupling is modified by $\cos^2\alpha$ and the $W\mu\nu_\mu$ coupling is modified by $\cos\alpha$. Neutrissimos may have masses as light as ~ 100 GeV.[172] These new particles can play the role of the seesaw right-handed neutrinos, as long as one is willing to admit large tuning among the neutrino Yukawa couplings.[172] So this offers an alternative to the GUT-mass heavy neutrino model discussed in Sec. 5.3.1.

If neutrissimos exist, they would be expected to show up in other precision experiments. One must avoid the constraints on mixing from $0\nu\beta\beta$ (recall Eq. 5.31 to see why these experiments have sensitivity to the mixing). These experiment place a limit of $|U_{e4}|^2$ at less than a few $\times 10^{-5}$ for a 100 GeV right-handed neutrino. Rare pion and tau decays constrain $|U_{\mu 4}|^2$ to be less than 0.004 and $|U_{\tau 4}|^2$ to be less than 0.006, respectively.

Neutrissimos would be produced at LHC, thus neutrino physics can be done at the highest energy scales! However, they may be difficult to observe. One would naturally look for a signal of missing energy. However, neutrissiomos will not necessarily decay invisibly; for example one can have $N \to \ell + W$ and the W may decay to either two jets or a neutrino–charged-lepton pair. Only the latter case has missing energy. This may make them difficult to identify.

If the neutrissimo is a Majorana particle, then these could provide a clue to the mechanism for leptogenesis. The present models of leptogenesis require very high mass scales for the neutral lepton. However, theorists are identifying ways to modify the model to accommodate lower masses.[173] There also may be a wide mass spectrum for these particles, with one very heavy case that accommodates standard leptogenesis models, while the others have masses in the range observable at LHC.[174]

NuSOnG and Other Possibilities A new round of precision electroweak measurements can be motivated by the NuTeV anomaly as well as the imminent turn-on of LHC. These measurements are best done using neutrino-electron scattering, because this removes the quark-model related questions discussed in the previous section. Two possible methods for such a measurement are ν_μ scattering with higher statistics, using a NuTeV-style beam, or a $\bar{\nu}_e$s scattering measurement from a reactor. In either case, to provide a competitive measurement, the error from the best present neutrino-electron scattering measurement, from CHARM II, must be reduced by a factor of five.

The NuSOnG (Neutrino Scattering On Glass) Experiment[175] is proposed to run using a ν_μ beam produced by 800 GeV protons on target from the TeVatron. The plan is to use a design which is inspired by the CHARM II experiment: a target of SiO_2 in one quarter radiation length panels, with proportional tubes or scintillator to allow event reconstruction. The detector will have a 2.6 kton fiducial volume. The major technical challenge of such an experiment is in achieving the required rates from the TeVatron, as $\times 20$ the rate of NuTeV proton delivery is required.

Alternatively, a measurement of the weak mixing angle using antineutrinos from reactors may be possible.[176] The weak mixing angle can be extracted from the purely leptonic $\bar{\nu}_e e$ "elastic scatter" (ES) rate, which is normalized using the $\bar{\nu}_e p$ "inverse beta decay" (IBD) events, to reduce the error on the flux. Thus, a hydrocarbon (scintillator oil) based detector, which has free proton targets for the IBD events, is ideal. Gadolinium (Gd) doping is necessary for a high rate of neutron capture, which constitutes the signal for the IBD events. A window in visible energy of 3 to 5 MeV is selected to reduce backgrounds from contaminants in the oil and cosmic-muon-induced isotopes. In this energy range, the dominant contamination comes from the progeny of the uranium and thorium chain. This would clearly be an ambitious, state-of-the-art measurement, but could be done at a new reactor experiment where the detector is in close proximity to the source and had high shielding from cosmic rays.

5.3.3. Neutrinos and the Cosmos

Neutrinos are ubiquitous in the universe, and their presence and interactions must be incorporated into astrophysical and cosmological models. Nearly any new neutrino property will have direct consequences in these fields, which must be examined. As an illustrative example, the first discussion considers the impact of introducing of relatively light sterile neutrinos to the theory. Sterile neutrinos with keV-scale masses can explain dark matter as well other astrophysical questions.

As we improve our capability for detecting astrophysical neutrinos, these become a new source of neutrinos for study. The second example is a case in point: the search for ultra-high energy sources of neutrinos. The discovery of such sources would be of great interest to astrophysics, and the particle physics we can do with such a "beam" is remarkable.

While this section concentrates on the unknown, it is interesting to note that the known astrophysical sources of neutrinos are sufficiently intense that these neutrinos are already a possible background to other physics measurements. An example is the case of dark matter searches, which aim to measure cross sections as small as 10^{-46} cm^2. These experiments will have to contend with the background from coherent scattering ($\nu + N \to \nu + N$) of solar neutrinos, which has a cross section of 10^{-39} cm^2 and which produces a recoil nucleon that is very much like the expected dark matter signal.[177]

5.3.3.1. *Neutrinos as Dark Matter*

From the mid-1980's through mid-90's a 5 eV ν_τ was considered a likely candidate for dark matter. This was the motivation for the Chorus and NOMAD search for $\nu_\mu \to \nu_\tau$ oscillations in the > 10 eV^2 range[178,179] as well as the proposed COSMOS experiment.[180]

In the late 90's and early 2000's, two measurements led to a shift in opinion about neutrinos as candidates for dark matter. The first was the Super-K confirmation of ν_μ oscillations. As discussed in Sec. 5.2.1.4, the cleanest explanation, which fits within a three-neutrino model, is that this effect is $\nu_\mu \to \nu_\tau$. Combining this information with the direct limit on the ν_e implied that neutrinos were unlikely to have masses in the 5 to 10 eV range, as required for dark matter. Also, at the same time, studies of the large scale structure of the universe indicated that dark matter must be non-relativistic, or "cold." Relativistic, or "hot dark matter," like neutrinos, would smooth the large scale structure far beyond observations.[181]

The idea of neutrinos as dark matter candidates fell into disfavor. For some time, the more likely solution was assumed to be WIMPs, Weakly Interacting Massive Particles. The "weak" in this name is somewhat confusing, since it does not refer strictly to the weak interaction – other Beyond-Standard-Model interactions are involved. It is simply meant to say that the interaction rate is very low.

For some time, the lightest supersymmetric particle has been the most favored candidate for the WIMP. However, this is now starting to be questioned, as no evidence for supersymmetry has been observed at colliders.[182] This makes the formulation of the theory more awkward, and SUSY explanations for dark matter have been pushed from the "Minimal Super Symmetric Model" to the "Next-to-Minimal Super Symmetric Model," and even this is challenged.[183] If supersymmetry does not show up at LHC, then a new explanation for dark matter must be found.

As a result, neutrino models are being reconsidered.[184–193] The new models involve neutrinos which are mostly sterile, with a very tiny mixing with the light flavors and with keV masses (0.5 keV $< m_\nu <$ 15 keV and $\sin^2 2\theta \geq 10^{-12}$). Because of the high mass, they are not relativistic and are regarded as "warm" or "cold." At high mass, the large scale structure limits are much less stringent. A recent analysis from the Sloan Digital Sky Survey (SDSS) finds that a sterile neutrino mass above 9 keV can reproduce the power spectrum.[194] Only tiny mixing with the active neutrinos is required in order to produce the dark matter. With such small mixings, this model

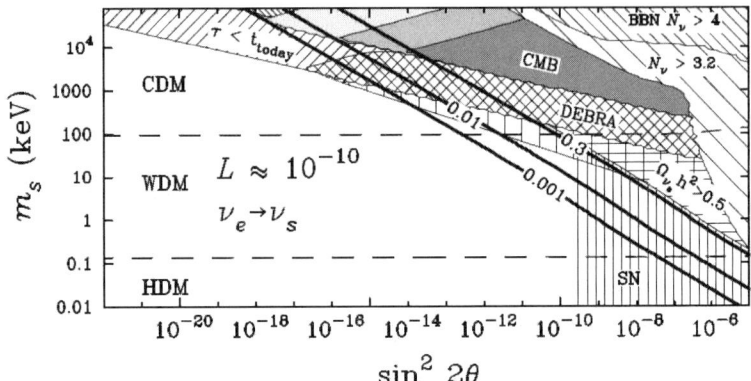

Fig. 5.23. Bounds for $\nu_e \to \nu_s$ oscillations from astrophysics and cosmology. Allowed regions for neutrino cold, warm and hot dark matter are shown.[187]

easily evades all accelerator-based bounds on $\nu_e \to \nu_s$ oscillations. As shown in Fig. 5.23, this model also escapes the cosmological limits on $\nu_e \to \nu_s$ from the CMB measurements, from Big Bang Nucleosynthesis (BBN), and supernova limits (SN), assuming negligible lepton number asymmetry, L, in the early universe.

Currently the only constraints on keV sterile neutrinos come from X-ray astronomy[193] which are searching for evidence of radiative decay of the massive neutrino into a lighter state, $\nu_2 \to \nu_1 + \gamma$. This proceeds through loop diagrams where the photon is coupling to a W or a charged lepton in the loop.[195] Because this is a 2-body decay, one is searching for a spectral line in the x-ray region. For a Dirac-type sterile neutrinos of mass m_s the decay rate is given by:

$$\Gamma_\gamma(m_s) = 1.36 \times 10^{-29} \mathrm{s}^{-1} \left(\frac{\sin^2 2\theta}{10^{-7}}\right) \left(\frac{m_s}{1\mathrm{keV}}\right)^5, \qquad (5.49)$$

which is clearly tiny, even for a keV scale neutrino. This is important as the dark matter neutrinos must be stable on the scale of the lifetime of the universe. No signal has been observed and the current mass limit, from the Chandra X-ray telescope observations, ranges from >3 to >6 keV depending on model assumptions.

Having motivated a keV-mass sterile state using dark matter, one can explore the consequences in other areas of cosmology and astrophysics. The small mixing allows these neutrinos to evade bounds from big bang nucleosynthesis.[196] Their presence may be beneficial to models of supernova explosions and pulsar kicks, as discussed below.

The existence of these neutrinos may improve the supernova models substantially. The problem faced by most models is that the supernova stalls and fails to explode. As modest increase in neutrino luminosity during the epoch when the stalled bounce shock is being reheated ($t_{\rm pb} < 1\,{\rm s}$) will incite the explosion.[197] As the supernova occurs, neutrinos will oscillate and even be affected by MSW resonances. If neutrinos oscillate to a sterile state, then their transport-mean-free-paths become larger. This increases the neutrino luminosity at the neutrino sphere and makes "the difference between a dud and an explosion."[197]

Also, sterile neutrinos in the 1 to 20 keV mass range can also be used to explain the origin of pulsar motion. Pulsars are known to have large velocities, from 100 to 1600 km/s. This is a much higher velocity than an ordinary star which typically has 30 km/s. Pulsars also have very high angular velocities. Apparently, there is some mechanism to give pulsars a substantial "kick" at birth, which sends them off with high translational and rotational velocities. One explanation for the kick is an asymmetric neutrino emission of sterile neutrinos during or moments after the explosion which forms the pulsar.[196] An asymmetry in neutrino emission occurs because the "urca reactions"

$$\nu_e + n \leftrightarrow p + e^-, \tag{5.50}$$

$$\bar{\nu}_e + p \leftrightarrow n + e^+, \tag{5.51}$$

are affected by magnetic fields which trap electrons and positrons. If the neutrinos oscillate to a sterile state, they stream out of the pulsar. If the sterile neutrinos have high mass, they can provide a significant kick. There are a number of solutions, either with standard neutrino oscillations, as described by Eq. 5.10 or with an MSW-type resonance. All require a sterile state in the 1 to 20 keV range with very small mixing, compatible with the dark matter scenario described above.

In summary, this is an example of how introducing a new neutrino property, *i.e.* sterile companions to the known neutrinos, can have a major impact on astrophysical models. This is an interesting case in point, because it is unlikely that these neutrinos will be observable in particle physics experiments in the near future. At present, the only detection method is through X-ray emission due to the radiative decay. Thus this is, at the moment, an example of a neutrino property which is entirely motivated and explored in the context of astrophysics.

5.3.3.2. *Ultra High Energy Neutrinos*

All of the experiments so-far discussed have used neutrino sources in the energy range of a few MeV to many GeV. We do not know how to produce neutrino beams at higher energies. However, nature clearly has high energy acceleration mechanisms, because cosmic rays with energies of 10^8 GeV have been measured. A new generation of neutrino experiments is now looking for neutrinos at these energies and beyond. These include AMANDA,[34] ICEcube,[198] Antares,[35] and Anita.[199]

These experiments make use of the fact that the Earth is opaque to ultra-high energy neutrinos. The apparent weakness of the weak interaction, which is due to the suppression by the mass of the W in the propagator term, is reduced as the neutrino energy increases. Amazingly, when you reach neutrino energies of 10^{17} eV, the Earth becomes opaque to neutrinos. To see this, recalling the kinematic variables defined in Sec. 5.1.2, consider the following back-of-the-envelope calculation. For a 10^8 GeV ν, $s = 2ME_\nu = 2 \times 10^8$ GeV^2. Most interactions occur at low x; and at these energies $x_{typical} \sim 0.001$. For neutrino interactions, the average y is 0.5. Therefore, using $Q^2 = sxy$, we find $Q^2_{typical} = (2 \times 10^8)(1 \times 10^{-3})(0.5) = 1 \times 10^5$ Gev^2. The propagator term goes as

$$\left(\frac{M_W^2}{M_W^2 + Q^2}\right)^2 = \left(\frac{1}{1 + Q^2/M_W^2}\right)^2 \approx \frac{M_W^4}{Q^4}, \quad (5.52)$$

which is approximately 10^{-3} for our "typical" case. The typical cross section $\sigma_{typical}$ is:
$E \times (\sigma_{tot}/E) \times (\text{prop term}) = 10^8(\text{GeV})(0.6 \times 10^{-38}\text{cm}^2/\text{GeV})10^{-3}$
$= 0.6 \times 10^{-33}\text{cm}^2$. From this we can extract the interaction length, λ_0, on iron, by scaling from hadronic interactions, which tells us that at 30 mb ($= 0.3 \times 10^{-25}$ cm^2), $1\lambda_0 \sim 10$ cm. This implies that λ_0 for our very high energy νs is $\approx 5 \times 10^3$ km. However, the Earth is a few $\times 10^4$ km. Thus all of the neutrinos interact; the Earth is opaque to them.

This opens up the opportunity to instrument the Earth and use it as a neutrino target. One option is to choose a transparent region of the Earth, ice or water, and instrument it like a traditional neutrino detector. This has been the design chosen by AMANDA, ICECube and Antares, which use phototubes to sense the Cerenkov light produced when charged particles from neutrino interactions traverse the material. The largest of these detectors are on the order of $(1 \text{ km})^3$ of instrumented area. The second method exploits the Askaryan effect[200] in electromagnetic showers. Electron and positron scattering in matter have different cross sections. As the electromangetic shower develops, this difference leads to a negative charge asymmetry, inducing strong strong coherent Cerenkov radiation in the radio range. The pulse has unique and easy-to-distinguish broadband (0.2 - 1.1 GHz) spectral and polarization properties which can be received by detecting antennas launched above the target area. In ice, the radio attenuation length is 1 km. The Anita Experiment, which uses such a detector, can view 2×10^6 km^3 of volume. This makes it by far the world's largest tonnage experiment.

Neutrinos with energies above 10^4 GeV have yet to be observed. However, they are expected to accompany ultra high energy cosmic rays, which have been observed. Nearly all potential sources of ultra-high energy cosmic rays are predicted to produce protons, neutrinos, and gamma rays at roughly comparable levels. Ultra high energy protons, which have been observed by the HiRes[201] and Auger[202] experiments are guaranteed sources of neutrinos through the Gresein-Zatsepi-Kuzmin (GZK) interaction. In this effect, protons above $E_{GZK} = 6 \times 10^{10}$ GeV scatter from the cosmic microwave background: $p\gamma \to \Delta^+ \to n\pi^+$. This degrades the energy of protons above E_{GZK}, leading to an apparent cutoff in the flux called the "GZK cutoff." There are several Δ resonances and the CMB photons have an energy distribution, so the cutoff is not sharp. But it has been clearly observed by both HiRes and Auger.[203] As a result, ultra-high energy pions are produced and these must decay to ultra-high-energy neutrinos. There may be other, more exotic mechanisms for producing an ultra-high energy flux, possibly with energies beyond the GZK cutoff. Since, unlike the protons, these neutrinos do not interact with the cosmic microwave background, they can traverse long distances and can be messengers of distant point sources.

There many reviews of the exotic physics one can do with ultra high energy neutrino interactions. The opportunities include[204] gravitational lensing of neutrinos, the search for bumps or steps in the NC/CC ratio, the influence of new physics on neutrino oscillations at high energies, the search for neutrino decays, neutrino interaction with dark matter WIMPs, and the annihilation of the ultra high energy neutrinos by the cosmic neutrino background. This final example is interesting because significant limits have been set by Anita-lite, a small prototype for Anita that flew only 18.4 days. This illustrates the power of even a small experiment entering an unexplored frontier of particle physics.

The 1 eV mass neutrino implied by the LSND anomaly could be a candidate for the source of the ultra-high energy cosmic rays observed on Earth.[205] This neutrino, if produced at ultra-high energies, could annihilate on the cosmic neutrino background producing a "Z-burst" of ultra high energy hadrons. This was offered as an explanation for ultra-high energy cosmic which were observed by the AGASA experiment.[206] Scaling from the AGASA rate, a prediction for the flux of ultra-high neutrinos in the energy range of $10^{18.5} < E_\nu < 10^{23.5}$ eV for Z-burst models was made.[207,208] Based on this flux, Anita-lite was predicted to see between 5 and 50 events at >99% CL. During its short run, this prototype detector observed no events in the energy range and therefore could definitively rule out this model.[209] Shortly thereafter, the AGASA events were shown to be due to energy miscalibration.[210]

5.4. Conclusions

The goal of this review was to sketch out the present questions in neutrino physics, and discuss the experiments that can address them. Along the way, I have highlighted the experimental techniques and challenges. I have also tried to briefly touch on technological advances expected in the near future. This text followed the structure of the set of lectures entitled "Neutrino Experiments," given at the 2006 TASI Summer School.

Neutrino physics is an amalgam of astrophysics, cosmology, nuclear physics, and particle physics, making the field diverse and exciting, but hard to review comprehensively. In this paper, I have tried to touch on examples which are particularly instructive and have been forced to leave out a wide range of other interesting points. What should be clear, however, is that the recent discoveries by neutrino experiments have opened up a wide range of interesting questions and opportunities. This promises to be a rich field of research for both theorists and experimentalists for years to come.

Acknowledgments

I wish to thank A. Aguilar-Arevalo, G. Karagiorgi, B. Kayser, P. Nienaber, J. Spitz, and E. Zimmerman for their suggestions concerning this text.

References

1. https://www.interactions.org/cms/?pid=1009695

2. R.N. Mohapatra, et al., hep-ph/050213v2, 2005.
3. http://neutrinooscillation.org/
4. D. Decamp, et al., CERN-EP/89-169, Phys.Lett.B235:399, 1990.
5. H. Band, et al., SLAC-PUB-4990, published in the Proceedings of the Fourth Family of Quarks ,and Leptons, Santa Monica, CA, Feb 23-25, 1989.
6. http://fn872.fnal.gov/
7. C.S. Wu, et al. Phys. Rev. 105, 1413, 1957.
8. P. Lipari, Nucl. Phys. Proc. Suppl. **112**, 274 (2002) [arXiv:hep-ph/0207172].
9. D. Casper, Nucl. Phys. Proc. Suppl. 112:161, 2002.
10. http://www-boone.fnal.gov.
11. http://www-sciboone.fnal.gov/
12. http://minerva.fnal.gov/
13. http://www.sns.ias.edu/~jnb.
14. R. Davis, Prog. Part. Nucl. Phys. **32**, 13 (1994); B. T. Cleveland et al., Astrophys. J. **496**, 505 (1998).
15. J. N. Abdurashitov et al. [SAGE Collaboration], J. Exp. Theor. Phys. **95**, 181 (2002) [Zh. Eksp. Teor. Fiz. **122**, 211 (2002)] [arXiv:astro-ph/0204245].
16. W. Hampel et al. [GALLEX Collaboration], Phys. Lett. B **447**, 127 (1999).
17. K. Eguchi et al. [KamLAND Collaboration], Phys. Rev. Lett. **92**, 071301 (2004) [arXiv:hep-ex/0310047].
18. C. H. Albright et al. [Neutrino Factory/Muon Collider Collaboration], arXiv:physics/0411123.
19. See, for eaxmple, S. E. Kopp, Phys. Rept. **439**, 101 (2007) [arXiv:physics/0609129].
20. D.E. Groom et al, The European Physical Journal C15: 1, 2000.
21. G. D. Barr, T. K. Gaisser, P. Lipari, S. Robbins and T. Stanev, Phys. Rev. D **70**, 023006 (2004) [arXiv:astro-ph/0403630].
22. J. Hosaka et al. [Super-Kamkiokande Collaboration], Phys. Rev. D **73**, 112001 (2006) [arXiv:hep-ex/0508053].
23. H. Back et al., arXiv:hep-ex/0412016.
24. G. D. Barr, T. K. Gaisser, S. Robbins and T. Stanev, Phys. Rev. D **74**, 094009 (2006) [arXiv:astro-ph/0611266].
25. M. Apollonio et al., Eur. Phys. J. C **27**, 331 (2003) [arXiv:hep-ex/0301017].
26. T. Araki et al. [KamLAND Collaboration], [arXiv:hep-ex/0406035].
27. C. Athanassopoulos et al. [LSND Collaboration], Nucl. Instrum. Meth. A **388**, 149 (1997) [arXiv:nucl-ex/9605002].
28. http://pupgg.princeton.edu/ borexino/welcome.html
29. K. Nakamura [KamLAND Collaboration], AIP Conf. Proc. **721**, 12 (2004).
30. C. Kraus [SNO+ Collaboration], Prog. Part. Nucl. Phys. **57**, 150 (2006).
31. Karsten Heager, private communication.
32. E. Church et al. [BooNe Collaboration], "A proposal for an experiment to measure muon-neutrino → electron-neutrino oscillations and muon-neutrino disappearance at the Fermilab Booster: BooNE," FERMILAB-PROPOSAL-0898;
33. http://www-sk.icrr.u-tokyo.ac.jp/sk/index.html
34. http://amanda.berkeley.edu/

35. http://antares.in2p3.fr/
36. http://www-numi.fnal.gov/
37. http://www-e815.fnal.gov/
38. S. Yamamoto et al., IEEE Trans. Nucl. Sci. **52**, 2992 (2005).
39. A. Pla-Dalmau, A. D. Bross, V. V. Rykalin and B. M. Wood [MINERvA Collaboration],
40. http://www-nova.fnal.gov/
41. A. Curioni, et al., hep-ex/0603009.
42. S.Amerio, et al., NIM A527: 329, 2004.
43. http://t962.fnal.gov/
44. http://www.fnal.gov/directorate/Longrange/Steering_Public/community_letters.html, see letter 15: "MicroBooNE - Fleming and Willis," June 12, 2007.
45. http://www.fnal.gov/directorate/Longrange/Steering_Public/community_letters.html, see letter 14: "Neutrino Expt with 5kton LAr TPC" Fleming and Rameika, June 12, 2007; D. Finley et al.,
46. L. Wolfenstein, Phys. Rev. D17, 2369 (1978); D20, 2634 (1979); S. P. Mikheyev and A. Yu. Smirnov, Yad. Fiz. 42, 1441 (1985) [Sov. J. Nucl. Phys. 42, 913 (1986)]; Nuovo Cimento 9C, 17 (1986).
47. G. J. Feldman and R. D. Cousins, Phys. Rev. D **57**, 3873 (1998) [arXiv:physics/9711021].
48. T. Schwetz, Acta Phys. Polon. B **36**, 3203 (2005) [arXiv:hep-ph/0510331].
49. B. Kayser, "Neutrino Mass, Mixing, and Flavor Change," available from the PDG website: http://pdg.lbl.gov/2007/reviews/contents_sports.html, W.-M. Yao, et al., J. Phys. G **33**, 1 (2006).
50. Y. Totsuka, Nucl. Phys. A663, 218 (2000); Y.Fukuda, et al. Phys. Rev. Lett. 81, 1562 (1998)
51. D. Casper et al., Phys. Rev. Lett. **66**, 2561 (1991); R. Becker-Szendy et al., Phys. Rev. Lett. **69**, 1010 (1992).
52. E. Kearns, talk presented at Neutrino 2004.
53. Y. Fukuda et al. [Super-Kamiokande Collaboration], Phys. Lett. B **433**, 9 (1998) [arXiv:hep-ex/9803006]; Phys. Lett. B **436**, 33 (1998) [arXiv:hep-ex/9805006]; Phys. Rev. Lett. **81**, 1562 (1998) [arXiv:hep-ex/9807003]; Phys. Rev. Lett. **82**, 2644 (1999) [arXiv:hep-ex/9812014]; Phys. Lett. B **467**, 185 (1999) [arXiv:hep-ex/9908049]; Y. Ashie et al. [Super-Kamiokande Collaboration], Phys. Rev. D **71**, 112005 (2005) [arXiv:hep-ex/0501064].
54. S. H. Ahn et al. [K2K Collaboration], Phys. Lett. B **511**, 178 (2001) [arXiv:hep-ex/0103001]; Phys. Rev. Lett. **90**, 041801 (2003) [arXiv:hep-ex/0212007]; Phys. Rev. D **74**, 072003 (2006) [arXiv:hep-ex/0606032].
55. D. G. Michael et al. [MINOS Collaboration], [arXiv:hep-ex/0607088].
56. N. Saoulidou for the MINOS Collaboration, http://theory.fnal.gov/jetp/ July 19, 2007.
57. A. Habig [Super-Kamiokande Collaboration], arXiv:hep-ex/0106025.
58. http://www.cern.ch/opera.
59. J. Marteau [for the OPERA collaboration], arXiv:0706.1699 [hep-ex].

60. E. G. Adelberger et al. , "Solar Fusion Cross Sections," To be published in Rev. Mod. Phys., Oct. 1998, astro-ph/9805121.
61. For example, J. Christensen-Dalsgaard et al. , Science **272** 1286 (1996).
62. For example, Castellani et al. , Nucl. Phys. Proc. Suppl. **70** 301 (1998).
63. http://www.sno.phy.queensu.ca.
64. B. Aharmim et al. [SNO Collaboration], arXiv:nucl-ex/0610020.
65. J. N. Bahcall, M. H. Pinsonneault and S. Basu, Astrophys. J. **555**, 990 (2001) [arXiv:astro-ph/0010346].
66. T. Araki et al. [KamLAND Collaboration], Phys. Rev. Lett. **94**, 081801 (2005) [arXiv:hep-ex/0406035].
67. T. Schwetz, Phys. Scripta **T127**, 1 (2006) [arXiv:hep-ph/0606060].
68. H. S. Goh, R. N. Mohapatra and S. P. Ng, Phys. Rev. D **68**, 115008 (2003) [arXiv:hep-ph/0308197].
69. T. Asaka, W. Buchmuller and L. Covi, Phys. Lett. B **563**, 209 (2003) [arXiv:hep-ph/0304142].
70. K. S. Babu, J. C. Pati and F. Wilczek, Nucl. Phys. B **566**, 33 (2000) [arXiv:hep-ph/9812538].
71. C. H. Albright and S. M. Barr, Phys. Rev. D **64**, 073010 (2001) [arXiv:hep-ph/0104294].
72. T. Blazek, S. Raby and K. Tobe, Phys. Rev. D **62**, 055001 (2000) [arXiv:hep-ph/9912482].
73. G. G. Ross and L. Velasco-Sevilla, Nucl. Phys. B **653**, 3 (2003) [arXiv:hep-ph/0208218].
74. S. Raby, Phys. Lett. B **561**, 119 (2003) [arXiv:hep-ph/0302027].
75. R. Kitano and Y. Mimura, Phys. Rev. D **63**, 016008 (2001) [arXiv:hep-ph/0008269].
76. N. Maekawa, arXiv:astro-ph/0010559.
77. M. C. Chen and K. T. Mahanthappa, Phys. Rev. D **68**, 017301 (2003) [arXiv:hep-ph/0212375].
78. M. Bando and M. Obara, Prog. Theor. Phys. **109**, 995 (2003) [arXiv:hep-ph/0302034].
79. W. Buchmuller and D. Wyler, Phys. Lett. B **521**, 291 (2001) [arXiv:hep-ph/0108216].
80. P. H. Frampton and R. N. Mohapatra, JHEP **0501**, 025 (2005) [arXiv:hep-ph/0407139].
81. W. Grimus and L. Lavoura, JHEP **0107**, 045 (2001) [arXiv:hep-ph/0105212].
82. W. Grimus and L. Lavoura, Phys. Lett. B **572**, 189 (2003) [arXiv:hep-ph/0305046].
83. W. Grimus, A. S. Joshipura, S. Kaneko, L. Lavoura and M. Tanimoto, JHEP **0407**, 078 (2004) [arXiv:hep-ph/0407112].
84. M. C. Chen and K. T. Mahanthappa, arXiv:hep-ph/0409165.
85. I. Aizawa, M. Ishiguro, T. Kitabayashi and M. Yasue, Phys. Rev. D **70**, 015011 (2004) [arXiv:hep-ph/0405201].
86. R. N. Mohapatra, Pramana **63**, 1295 (2004).

87. S. Antusch and S. F. King, Nucl. Phys. B **705**, 239 (2005) [arXiv:hep-ph/0402121].
88. S. Antusch and S. F. King, Phys. Lett. B **591**, 104 (2004) [arXiv:hep-ph/0403053].
89. W. Rodejohann and Z. z. Xing, Phys. Lett. B **601**, 176 (2004) [arXiv:hep-ph/0408195].
90. K. S. Babu, E. Ma and J. W. F. Valle, Phys. Lett. B **552**, 207 (2003) [arXiv:hep-ph/0206292].
91. T. Ohlsson and G. Seidl, Nucl. Phys. B **643**, 247 (2002) [arXiv:hep-ph/0206087].
92. S. F. King and G. G. Ross, Phys. Lett. B **574**, 239 (2003) [arXiv:hep-ph/0307190].
93. Q. Shafi and Z. Tavartkiladze, Phys. Lett. B **594**, 177 (2004) [arXiv:hep-ph/0401235].
94. R. N. Mohapatra, JHEP **0410**, 027 (2004) [arXiv:hep-ph/0408187].
95. M. Bando, S. Kaneko, M. Obara and M. Tanimoto, Phys. Lett. B **580**, 229 (2004) [arXiv:hep-ph/0309310].
96. M. Honda, S. Kaneko and M. Tanimoto, JHEP **0309**, 028 (2003) [arXiv:hep-ph/0303227].
97. R. F. Lebed and D. R. Martin, Phys. Rev. D **70**, 013004 (2004) [arXiv:hep-ph/0312219].
98. A. Ibarra and G. G. Ross, Phys. Lett. B **575**, 279 (2003) [arXiv:hep-ph/0307051].
99. P. F. Harrison and W. G. Scott, Phys. Lett. B **594**, 324 (2004) [arXiv:hep-ph/0403278].
100. P. H. Frampton, S. L. Glashow and T. Yanagida, Phys. Lett. B **548**, 119 (2002) [arXiv:hep-ph/0208157].
101. A. de Gouvea and H. Murayama, Phys. Lett. B **573**, 94 (2003) [arXiv:hep-ph/0301050].
102. R. N. Mohapatra, M. K. Parida and G. Rajasekaran, Phys. Rev. D **69**, 053007 (2004) [arXiv:hep-ph/0301234].
103. R. Arnowitt, B. Dutta and B. Hu, Nucl. Phys. B **682**, 347 (2004) [arXiv:hep-th/0309033].
104. M. G. Albrow et al., arXiv:hep-ex/0509019.
105. http://doublechooz.in2p3.fr/
106. http://dayawane.ihep.ac.cn/
107. K. Assamagan, et al., Phys.Rev.D53:6065, 1996.
108. B. Jeckelman, et al., PL B3555 326, 1994.
109. Barate, et al, EPJ C2 395, 1998.
110. C. Kraus et al., Eur. Phys. J. C **40**, 447 (2005) [arXiv:hep-ex/0412056].
111. V. M. Lobashev, et al., Phys.Atom.Nucl.63: 962, 2000.
112. J. Bonn, et al., Phys. Atom. Nucl.63:969, 2000.
113. W. Stoeffl, et al., PRL 75: 3237, 1995.
114. C. Ching, et al., Int. Journ Mod. Phys. A10: 2841, 1995.
115. E. Holzschuh, et al., Phys. Lett., B287: 381, 1992.
116. H. Kawakami, et al., Phys. Lett., B256: 105, 1991.

117. H. Robertson, *et al.*, Phys.Rev.Lett.67: 957, 1991; H. Robertson, PR D33: R6, 1991.
118. http://www-ik.fzk.de/ katrin/index.html
119. R. Bionta, *et al.*, PRL 58: 1494, 1987.
120. K. Hirata, *et al.*, PRL 58: 1490, 1987.
121. S. Hannestad, Prog. Part. Nucl. Phys. **57**, 309 (2006) [arXiv:astro-ph/0511595].
122. J.F. Beacom, N. F. Bell, S. Dodelson, astro-ph/0404585; Z. Chacko, L. J. Hall, S. J. Oliver, M. Perelstein, hep-ph/0405067; K. Abazajian, N. F. Bell, G. M. Fuller and Y. Y. Y. Wong, astro-ph/0410175.
123. A. Alessandrello, *et al.*, Phys. Lett. B486: 13, 2000; L. DeBraekelee, *et al.*, Phys. Atom Nucl 63:1214, 2000; R. Arnold, *et al.*, Nucl. Phys. A678:341, 2000; M. Alston-Garnjost, *et al.*, PR C55: 474, 1997; A. DeSilva, *et al.*, PR C56:2451, 1997; M. Gunther, *et al.*, PR D55:54, 1997; Arnold, *et al.*, Z. Phys. C72: 239, 1996; A. Balysh, *et al.*, PRL 77:5186, 1996.
124. A good discussion of GUT motivation for the sea-saw model appears in Kayser, Gibrat-Debu, and Perrier, *The Physics of Massive Neutrinos*, World Scientific Lecture Notes in Physics, 25, World Scientific Publishing, 1989.
125. V. A. Rodin, A. Faessler, F. Simkovic and P. Vogel, arXiv:nucl-th/0503063.
126. F. Simkovic, G. Pantis, J. D. Vergados and A. Faessler, Phys. Rev. C **60**, 055502 (1999) [arXiv:hep-ph/9905509].
127. M. Aunola and J. Suhonen, Czech. J. Phys. **48**, 145 (1998); M. Aunola and J. Suhonen, Czech. J. Phys. **48**, 145 (1998).
128. S. Stoica and H. V. Klapdor-Kleingrothaus, Nucl. Phys. A **694**, 269 (2001).
129. R. Arnold *et al.* [NEMO Collaboration], Phys. Rev. Lett. **95**, 182302 (2005) [arXiv:hep-ex/0507083].
130. R. Arnold *et al.* [the NEMO Collaboration], JETP Lett. **80**, 377 (2004) [Pisma Zh. Eksp. Teor. Fiz. **80**, 429 (2004)] [arXiv:hep-ex/0410021].
131. O. Cremonesi *et al.* [CUORICINO Collaboration], Phys. Atom. Nucl. **69** (2006) 2083.
132. H. V. Klapdor-Kleingrothaus, I. V. Krivosheina, A. Dietz and O. Chkvorets, Phys. Lett. B **586**, 198 (2004) [arXiv:hep-ph/0404088].
133. S. Schonert *et al.* [GERDA Collaboration], Phys. Atom. Nucl. **69**, 2101 (2006).
134. http://crio.mib.infn.it/wigmi/pages/cuore.php
135. http://nemo.in2p3.fr/supernemo/
136. http://0-www-project.slac.stanford.edu.ilsprod.lib.neu.edu/exo/
137. http://majorana.pnl.gov/
138. M. Nomachi *et al.*, Nucl. Phys. Proc. Suppl. **138**, 221 (2005).
139. C. Walter, Talk given at NuINT07, https://indico.fnal.gov/conferenceOtherViews.py?view=standard&confId=804, Session 1.
140. D. S. Ayres *et al.* [NOvA Collaboration], arXiv:hep-ex/0503053.
141. http://jnusrv01.kek.jp/public/t2k/
142. V. Barger *et al.*, arXiv:0705.4396 [hep-ph].
143. V. Barger, P. Huber, D. Marfatia and W. Winter, arXiv:hep-ph/0703029.
144. V. Barger, P. Huber, D. Marfatia and W. Winter, arXiv:hep-ph/0703029.

145. A. B. Balantekin, AIP Conf. Proc. **847**, 128 (2006) [arXiv:hep-ph/0601113];
146. A. Aguilar *et al.*, Phys. Rev. D **64**
147. B. Armbruster *et al.*, Phys. Rev. D **65** (2002) 112001.
148. B. Achkar *et al.*, Nucl. Phys. B **434** (1995) 503.
149. E. D. Church, K. Eitel, G. B. Mills,
150. B.H.J. McKellar, *et al.* hep-ph/0106121; R.N. Mohapatra, Phys. Rev. D **64** 091301, 2001; hep-ph/0107264; A. Ioannisian and J.W.F. Valle, Phys. Rev. D **63** 073002, 2001; E. Ma, G. Rajasekaran, and U. Sarkar, Phys. Lett. B **495** 363-368, 2000; hep-ph/0006340; Z. Berezhiani and R. Mohapatra, Phys. Rev. D **52** 6607, 1995; R. Fardon, A.E. Nelson, and N. Weiner, arXiv:astro-ph/0309800.
151. M. Sorel, J. Conrad, and M. Shaevitz, Phys. Rev. D70:073004,2004, hep-ph/0305255.
152. P. Astier, *et al.* Phys. Lett. B570:19, 2003; hep-ex/0306037.
153. F. Dydak *et al.*, Phys. Lett. B **134** 281, 1984..
154. I.E. Stockdale *et al.*, Phys. Rev. Lett. **52**, 1384 (1984); Z. Phys. C **27**, 53 (1985).
155. G. Karagiorgi, A. Aguilar-Arevalo, J. M. Conrad, M. H. Shaevitz, K. Whisnant, M. Sorel and V. Barger, Phys. Rev. D **75**, 013011 (2007) [arXiv:hep-ph/0609177].
156. A. Aguilar-Arevalo, *et al.*, paper in preparation. See also talk by J. Link, NuInt07.
157. M. Maltoni and T. Schwetz, arXiv:0705.0107 [hep-ph].
158. Paper in preparatuon, See talk at NuFact07 website: http://fphy.hep.okayama-u.ac.jp/nufact07/
159. T. Katori, A. Kostelecky and R. Tayloe, Phys. Rev. D **74**, 105009 (2006) [arXiv:hep-ph/0606154].
160. H. Pas, S. Pakvasa and T. J. Weiler, AIP Conf. Proc. **903**, 315 (2007) [arXiv:hep-ph/0611263].
161. X. Q. Li, Y. Liu and Z. T. Wei, arXiv:0707.2285 [hep-ph].
162. G. P. Zeller *et al.* Phys. Rev. Lett., **88** 091802, 2002.
163. http://lepewwg.web.cern.ch/LEPEWWG/
164. S. C. Bennett and Carl E. Wieman, Phys. Rev. Lett., **82** 2484–2487, 1999.
165. P. L. Anthony *et al.* [SLAC E158 Collaboration], Phys. Rev. Lett. **95**, 081601 (2005) [arXiv:hep-ex/0504049].
166. http://www.slac.stanford.edu/exp/e158/
167. E. A. Paschos and L. Wolfenstein, Phys. Rev. D **7**, 91 (1973).
168. K. S. McFarland and S. O. Moch, arXiv:hep-ph/0306052; S. Kretzer and M. H. Reno, Phys. Rev. D **69**, 034002 (2004) [arXiv:hep-ph/0307023]; B. A. Dobrescu and R. K. Ellis, Phys. Rev. D **69**, 114014 (2004) [arXiv:hep-ph/0310154].
169. M. Gluck, P. Jimenez-Delgado and E. Reya, arXiv:hep-ph/0501169; F. M. Steffens and K. Tsushima, Phys. Rev. D **70**, 094040 (2004) [arXiv:hep-ph/0408018]; J. T. Londergan and A. W. Thomas, arXiv:hep-ph/0407247; A. D. Martin, R. G. Roberts, W. J. Stirling and R. S. Thorne, Eur. Phys. J. C **39**, 155 (2005) [arXiv:hep-ph/0411040].

170. S. Davidson, J. Phys. G **29**, 2001 (2003) [arXiv:hep-ph/0209316].
171. E. Ma, D. P. Roy and S. Roy, Phys. Lett. B **525**, 101 (2002) [arXiv:hep-ph/0110146].
172. A. de Gouvea, arXiv:0706.1732 [hep-ph].
173. N. Sahu and U. A. Yajnik, Phys. Rev. D **71**, 023507 (2005) [arXiv:hep-ph/0410075].
174. A. de Gouvea, J. Jenkins and N. Vasudevan, Phys. Rev. D **75**, 013003 (2007) [arXiv:hep-ph/0608147].
175. http://www.fnal.gov/directorate/Longrange/Steering_Public/community_letters.html, see letter 3: "Precision Neutrino Scattering at the TeVatron - Conrad and Fisher," June 12, 2007. An expression of Interest is in preparation.
176. J. M. Conrad, J. M. Link and M. H. Shaevitz, Phys. Rev. D **71**, 073013 (2005) [arXiv:hep-ex/0403048].
177. J. Monroe and P. Fisher, arXiv:0706.3019 [astro-ph].
178. E. Eskut et al. [CHORUS Collaboration], Phys. Lett. B **497**, 8 (2001).
179. P. Astier et al. [NOMAD Collaboration], Nucl. Phys. B **611**, 3 (2001) [arXiv:hep-ex/0106102].
180. K. Kodama et al., 'Muon-neutrino to tau-neutrino oscillations: Proposal," FERMILAB-PROPOSAL-0803.
181. S. Bonometto, New Astron. Rev. **43**, 169 (1999).
182. M. Carena, D. Hooper and A. Vallinotto, Phys. Rev. D **75**, 055010 (2007) [arXiv:hep-ph/0611065]; D. Hooper and A. M. Taylor, JCAP **0703**, 017 (2007) [arXiv:hep-ph/0607086].
183. D. G. Cerdeno, E. Gabrielli, D. E. Lopez-Fogliani, C. Munoz and A. M. Teixeira, JCAP **0706**, 008 (2007) [arXiv:hep-ph/0701271].
184. S. Colombi, S. Dodelson and L. M. Widrow, Astrophys. J. **458**, 1 (1996) [arXiv:astro-ph/9505029]; S. Dodelson and L. M. Widrow, Phys. Rev. Lett. **72**, 17 (1994) [arXiv:hep-ph/9303287].
185. T. Asaka, M. Shaposhnikov and A. Kusenko, Phys. Lett. B **638**, 401 (2006) [arXiv:hep-ph/0602150].
186. X. D. Shi and G. M. Fuller, Phys. Rev. Lett. **83**, 3120 (1999) [arXiv:astro-ph/9904041].
187. K. Abazajian, G. M. Fuller and M. Patel, Phys. Rev. D **64**, 023501 (2001) [arXiv:astro-ph/0101524].
188. A. D. Dolgov and S. H. Hansen, arXiv:hep-ph/0103118.
189. A. D. Dolgov and S. H. Hansen, arXiv:hep-ph/0103118.
190. K. Abazajian, Phys. Rev. D **73**, 063506 (2006) [arXiv:astro-ph/0511630].
191. P. L. Biermann and A. Kusenko, Phys. Rev. Lett. **96**, 091301 (2006) [arXiv:astro-ph/0601004].
192. K. Abazajian and S. M. Koushiappas, Phys. Rev. D **74**, 023527 (2006) [arXiv:astro-ph/0605271].
193. K. N. Abazajian, M. Markevitch, S. M. Koushiappas and R. C. Hickox, Phys. Rev. D **75**, 063511 (2007) [arXiv:astro-ph/0611144].
194. P, McDonald, et al., Astrophys. J. Suppl. **163**, 80 (2006), astro-ph/0405013.
195. P. B. Pal and L. Wolfenstein, Phys. Rev. D **25**, 766 (1982).

196. G. M. Fuller, A. Kusenko, I. Mocioiu and S. Pascoli, Phys. Rev. D **68**, 103002 (2003) [arXiv:astro-ph/0307267].
197. J. Hidaka and G. M. Fuller, Phys. Rev. D **74**, 125015 (2006) [arXiv:astro-ph/0609425].
198. http://icecube.wisc.edu/
199. http://amanda.uci.edu/ anita/
200. G. A. Askaryan, JETP Lett. **50**, 478 (1989) [Pisma Zh. Eksp. Teor. Fiz. **50**, 446 (1989)].
201. S. Westerhoff [HiRes Collaboration], AIP Conf. Proc. **698**, 370 (2004).
202. http://www.auger.org/
203. R. Abbasi *et al.* [HiRes Collaboration], arXiv:astro-ph/0703099.
204. C. Quigg, arXiv:astro-ph/0603372.
205. T. J. Weiler, Astropart. Phys. 11:303 (1999).
206. http://www-akeno.icrr.u-tokyo.ac.jp/AGASA/
207. Z. Fodor, S. D. Katz and A. Ringwald, arXiv:hep-ph/0210123.
208. O. Kalashev, G. Gelmini and D. Semikoz, arXiv:0706.3847 [astro-ph].
209. S. W. Barwick *et al.* [ANITA Collaboration], Phys. Rev. Lett. **96**, 171101 (2006) [arXiv:astro-ph/0512265].
210. B. M. Connolly, S. Y. BenZvi, C. B. Finley, A. C. O'Neill and S. Westerhoff, Phys. Rev. D **74**, 043001 (2006) [arXiv:astro-ph/0606343].

Chapter 6

String Theory, String Model-Building, and String Phenomenology — A Practical Introduction

Keith R. Dienes

Department of Physics, University of Arizona, Tucson, AZ 85721, USA
dienes@physics.arizona.edu

> This is the written version of an introductory self-contained course on string model-building and string phenomenology given at the 2006 TASI summer school. No prior knowledge of string theory is assumed. The goal is to provide a practical, "how-to" manual on string theory, string model-building, and string phenomenology with a minimum of mathematics. These notes cover the construction of bosonic strings, superstrings, and heterotic strings prior to compactification. These notes also develop the ten-dimensional free-fermionic construction. A final lecture discusses general features of heterotic string models, Type I (open) string models, and recent trends of string phenomenology. and general features of low-energy string phenomenology.

6.0. Introduction

These lectures were delivered at the 2006 Theoretical Advanced Study Institute (TASI), to an audience of graduate students whose interests were primarily oriented towards high-energy phenomenology. Indeed, this school had a stated focus on neutrino physics, and consequently my goal was to present string theory in a way that ultimately might explain how a specific particle such as a neutrino might ultimately emerge from string theory. Of course, string theory contains a lot more than neutrino physics (and also, in some ways, a lot less!), and in the course of these lectures I will not really focus so much on neutrinos as on string theory as a whole. Nevertheless, I will continue to keep neutrinos as a running theme throughout these lectures as a way of reminding ourselves that our discussion of string theory is ultimately aimed at understanding something real and observable, such as an actual neutrino.

The title of these lectures indicates that these lectures are meant to serve as a practical introduction to string theory, string model-building, and string phenomenology. Let me explain, in a rough sense, what each of these words is meant to convey. We are all familiar with quantum field theory, which is a *language* through which we might construct particular *models* of physics (such as the Standard Model or the Minimal Supersymmetric Standard Model). Such models then have certain physical characteristics, certain *phenomenologies*. String theory, at least as I shall try to present it, can likewise be considered as a *language* for discussing physics: in this sense it replaces quantum field theory (a language based on point-particle physics) with a new language suitable for theories whose fundamental objects are the one-dimensional extended objects known as *strings*. However, from this perspective, string theory is still only a language: it is still necessary to take the next step and *use* this language to construct *models* that describe the everyday world. Therefore, although I will attempt to give a self-contained introduction to the language of string theory, these lectures will primarily focus on the model-building aspects of string theory and on the resulting phenomenologies that these models have. While there already exist many excellent reviews of string theory, there are relatively few that focus on its model-building and phenomenological aspects. These lecture notes will therefore hopefully help to fill the gap, especially for those readers who might care less for the formal aspects of string theory and more for their phenomenological implications.

Finally, I should explain the word "practical" which also appears in the title. The word "practical" refers to actual *practice* — the things that practitioners actually need to know in order to build *bona-fide* string models and/or comprehend their low-energy properties. Of course, string theory is a rich and beautiful subject, with many mathematical aspects that are compelling and ultimately essential for a deep understanding of the subject. However, the goal of these lectures is simply to present the basic features of string theory with a minimum of mathematics — as stated in the abstract, I am seeking to provide a "how-to" manual which cuts the subject to the bone and conveys only that information which will be important for phenomenology. Therefore, in many places the omissions will be substantial. Certainly they do not do justice to the subject. However, these lectures were designed for phenomenologically-oriented graduate students whose desire (I hope) was to learn something of string theory without being deluged by mathematical formalism. It is with them in mind that I designed these lectures to be as elementary as feasible, and to "get to the physics" as rapidly as possible. Therefore, I now issue the following

> **Warning:** These lectures are meant to cover a considerable amount of introductory material very rapidly and without mathematical sophistication. The purpose is to advance quickly to the model-building and phenomenological aspects of string theory, while still conveying an intuitive flavor of the essential issues. The target audience consists of people who have had no prior exposure to string theory, and who wish to understand the basic concepts from a purely phenomenological perspective.

Hopefully, the students came away with a sense that string theory is a real part of physics, one with direct relevance for the real world. Perhaps the reader will too. If so, then these lectures will have served their purpose.

6.1. Lecture #1: Why strings? — an overview

Why should we be interested in string theory? In this lecture, we shall review our present state of knowledge about the underlying constituents of matter, and discuss how string theory has the potential to extend that knowledge in a profoundly new direction. Since this lecture is meant only as an overview, we shall keep the discussion at an extremely superficial level and seek to present the intuitive *flavor* of string theory rather than its substance. We shall deal with the substance in subsequent lectures.

6.1.1. *From atoms to the Standard Model: A quick review*

Certainly we do not need to understand string theory in order to appreciate modern high-energy particle physics, or to understand or interpret the results of collider experiments. Why then should one study string theory, a subject whose connections to observable phenomena are usually considered rather tenuous at best?

The primary reason, of course, is that the goal of high-energy physics has always been to uncover the fundamental "elements" or building-blocks of the natural world. These consist of both the fundamental *particles* that make up the *matter*, and the fundamental *forces* that describe their *interactions*. In this way, we hope to expose the underlying laws of physics in their simplest forms.

But what is "fundamental"? Clearly, the answer depends on the energy scale, or equivalently the inverse length scale, at which these constituents are being probed. In order to establish our frame of reference, recall that 1 eV $\approx 1.6 \times 10^{-19}$ Joules $\approx (10^{-7}$ meters$)^{-1}$. At the eV scale, the fundamental objects are atoms, or nuclei plus electrons. But it turns out that there are many different types of atoms or nuclei — indeed, they fill out an entire periodic table, the complexity but regularity of which suggests a deeper substructure. And indeed such a deeper substructure exists: at the keV to MeV scale, the nuclei are no longer fundamental, but decompose into new fundamental objects — protons and neutrons. Thus, at this energy scale, the fundamental objects are protons, neutrons, and electrons. But once again, it is found that there are many different "types" of protons and neutrons — collectively they are called *hadrons*, and include not only the proton (p) and neutron (n), but also the pions (π), kaons (K), rho (ρ), omega (Ω), and so forth. Indeed, the "periodic table of the elements" at this energy scale is nothing but the Particle Properties Data Book! But once again, the complexity and regularity of these "elementary" particles suggests a deeper substructure, and indeed such a substructure is found, this time at the GeV scale: the proton and neutron are just made of two kinds of *quarks*, the so-called up and down quarks. Thus, at the GeV scale, the fundamental objects are up quarks, down quarks, and electrons. But once again complexity emerges: it turns out that there are many different "types" (flavors) of quarks: up, down, strange, charm, top, and bottom. Likewise, there are many different "types" of electrons (collectively called *leptons*): the electron, the muon, the tau, and their associated neutrinos. And indeed, once again there is a mysterious pattern, usually referred to as a family or generational structure. This once again suggests a deeper substructure.

Unfortunately, this is as far as we've come. Indeed, all of our present-day knowledge down to this energy scale is gathered together into the so-called *Standard Model* of particle physics. The primary features of the Standard Model are as follows. The fundamental *particles* are the quarks and leptons. They are all fermions, and are arranged into three generations of doublets:

$$\text{quarks}: \begin{pmatrix} u \\ d \end{pmatrix}, \begin{pmatrix} c \\ s \end{pmatrix}, \begin{pmatrix} t \\ b \end{pmatrix}$$

$$\text{leptons}: \begin{pmatrix} \nu_e \\ e \end{pmatrix}, \begin{pmatrix} \nu_\mu \\ \mu \end{pmatrix}, \begin{pmatrix} \nu_\tau \\ \tau \end{pmatrix}. \tag{6.1.1}$$

The fundamental *forces* also come in three varieties. First, there is the strong (or "color") force, associated with the non-abelian Lie group $SU(3)$.

Its fine-structure constant is $\alpha_3 \approx 1/8$ (as measured at energy scales of approximately 100 GeV), and it is responsible for binding quarks together to form hadrons and nuclei. As such, it is felt only by quarks. Its mediators or carriers are called *gluons*. Second, there is the electroweak force, associated with the non-abelian Lie group $SU(2)$. Its fine-structure constant is $\alpha_2 \approx 1/30$ (indeed, weaker than the strong force!), and it is responsible for β-decay. Unlike the strong force, it is felt by *all* of the fundamental particles. Finally, there is the "hypercharge" force, associated with the abelian Lie group $U(1)$, with fine-structure constant $\alpha_1 \approx 1/59$. Once again, this force is felt by essentially *all* particles, both quarks and leptons. The carriers of the latter two forces are the photon as well as the $W^\pm$ and Z particles. Indeed, ordinary electromagnetism is a combination of the electroweak and hypercharge forces, and is the survivor of electroweak symmetry breaking. This breaking is induced by the one remaining particle of the Standard Model, a boson called the *Higgs particle*. An excellent introduction to the physics of the Standard Model can be found in the TASI lectures of G. Altarelli (this volume).

6.1.2. *Beyond the Standard Model: Two popular ideas*

Is that all there is? Clearly, there are lots of reasons to believe in something deeper! First, the Standard Model contains many *arbitrary parameters*, such as the masses and "mixings" of fundamental particles. All of these must ultimately be *fit* to data rather than *explained*. Second, there are many *conceptual* questions. *Why* are there three generations? *Why* are there three kinds of forces? *Why* do these forces have different strengths and ranges? A fundamental theory should explain these features. Finally, there is also another force which we have not yet mentioned: the *gravitational* force. How do we incorporate the gravitational force into this framework? In other words, how do we "quantize" gravity?

There is only one conclusion we can draw from this state of affairs. Just as in each previous case, there must still be a deeper underlying principle. It is important to stress that this is not simply an issue of academic interest. Rather, it is one of practical importance, because the next generation of particle accelerators are being built right now! (Two of the most prominent that will be exploring physics beyond the Standard Model are Fermilab, where upgrades to the TeVatron are being implemented, and CERN, where construction of the Large Hadron Collider (LHC) is already underway.) The pressing question, therefore, is: What do we expect to see at these machines? What will high-energy physics be focusing on over the next ten to twenty years? It turns out that there are two very popular sets of ideas, both of which are thoroughly reviewed in the TASI lectures of N. Polonsky.

6.1.2.1. *Low-energy supersymmetry*

The first idea is *supersymmetry* (SUSY). This refers to a new kind of symmetry in physics, one which relates bosons (particles with integer spin) to fermions (particles with half-integer spin). Thus, for every known particle, there is a predicted new particle, its so-called superpartner:

$$\begin{aligned} \text{quarks} &\iff \textit{squarks} \\ \text{leptons} &\iff \textit{sleptons} \\ \text{gauge bosons} &\iff \textit{gauginos} \,. \end{aligned} \qquad (6.1.2)$$

Clearly, this implies the existence of a *lot* of new particles and a *lot* of new interactions! Why then go through all this trouble?

Well, it turns out that supersymmetry can provide a number of striking benefits. First, through supersymmetry, we can explain the relative strengths of the forces ("gauge coupling unification"). Second, we can explain the origin of electroweak symmetry breaking. Third, supersymmetry has a number of favorable cosmological implications (for example, supersymmetry provides a natural set of dark-matter candidates). Finally, it turns out that supersymmetry is the only known answer to certain difficult theoretical puzzles in the Standard Model (chief among them the so-called "gauge hierarchy problem", *i.e.*, the difficulty of explaining the lightness of the Higgs particle, or equivalently to difficulty of explaining the stability of the scale of electroweak symmetry breaking against radiative corrections). In order to serve as an explanation of the gauge hierarchy problem, the energy scale associated with supersymmetry must not be too much higher than the scale of electroweak symmetry breaking. This is therefore called "low-energy supersymmetry", which refers to the common expectation that superparticles should exist at or near the TeV-scale.

Supersymmetry is a beautiful theory, both phenomenologically and mathematically. But it is *not* observed in nature. Therefore, supersymmetry must be broken. The problem, however, is that supersymmetry is very robust! It turns out to be quite hard to find mechanisms that can easily ("spontaneously") break supersymmetry at the expected energy scales. Therefore, we are faced with a major unsolved problem: *How do we break supersymmetry?* Indeed, we often have to resort to introducing

SUSY-breaking by hand, which requires the introduction of *many* additional unknown parameters. This is quite unpleasant, not only from an aesthetic point of view but also a phenomenological (predictive) point of view. However, it is often possible to consider only a minimal supersymmetric extension to the Standard Model (the so-called MSSM) where a minimal number of supersymmetry-breaking parameters are chosen.

6.1.2.2. *Grand unification*

The second popular idea for physics beyond the Standard Model concerns so-called *Grand Unified Theories* (GUTs). This refers to an attempt to realize the different forces and particles in nature as different "faces" or "aspects" of a single GUT force and a single GUT particle. An electromagnetic analogy here might be useful. Recall that the electric force is felt or caused by static charges, and that the magnetic force is felt or caused by moving charges. Are these therefore different forces? As we know, the answer is most definitely "no": we can Lorentz-boost from a rest frame to a moving frame, whereupon the distinction between the electric and magnetic forces melts away and these forces become intertwined. Thus, we conclude that the electric and magnetic forces are merely different aspects of *one* force, the "electromagnetic" force.

Is the same true for the strong, electroweak, and hypercharge forces? Is there a single "strong-weak-hypercharge" GUT force?

At first glance, this doesn't seem possible, because these different forces have different strengths. Recall their fine-structure constants: $\alpha_1 \approx 1/59$, $\alpha_2 \approx 1/30$, and $\alpha_3 \approx 1/8$. However, also recall that in quantum field theory, the strengths of forces ultimately depend on the energy scale through which they are measured. To see why this is so, let us think of placing a positive charge next to a dielectric. The positive charge draws some negative charge from within the dielectric towards it, so that the dielectric medium partially screens the positive charge. Therefore, in a rough sense, the less of the dielectric we see (*i.e.*, the more finely resolved our experimental apparatus to probe the original positive charge), the stronger our original positive charge seems to be. Thus, we see that at shorter distances (corresponding to higher energies), our electric charges (and therefore the corresponding electric forces) appear to be stronger. If this dielectric analogy serves as a good model for the results of a true quantum field-theoretic calculation (and in this case it does), we conclude that the electric force appears to grow stronger with increasing energy.

Of course, this is just a mechanical analogy. However, in the supersymmetric Standard Model, it turns out that the quantum field-theoretic vacuum itself indeed behaves like a dielectric for the hypercharge and weak forces. However, for the strong force, it behaves as an *anti*-dielectric. Thus, while the hypercharge and electroweak forces become *stronger* at higher energies, the strong force becomes *weaker* at higher energies. (This latter feature is the celebrated phenomenon of *asymptotic freedom*.) Together, these observations imply that these three forces have a chance of *unifying* at some energy scale if their strengths become equal, and indeed, carrying out the appropriate calculations, one finds the results shown in Fig. 6.1. We see from this figure that the forces appear to unify at the scale

$$M_{\rm GUT} \approx 2 \times 10^{16} \text{ GeV} .\qquad(6.1.3)$$

This would then be the natural energy scale for grand unification. Note that this unification also requires the existence of weak-scale supersymmetry in the form of weak-scale superpartners. Without such superpartners, the evolution of these fine-structure constants as a function of the energy scale is different, and they fail to unify at any scale. This then serves as another motivation for weak-scale supersymmetry.

GUTs would have numerous important effects on particle physics. First, by their very nature, they would imply new interactions that can mix the three fundamental forces. Second, this in turn implies that GUTs naturally lead to new, rare decays of particles. The most famous example of this is proton decay, the rate for which is experimentally known to be exceedingly small (since the proton lifetime is $\tau_p \gtrsim 10^{32}$ years). Third, GUTs would naturally explain the quantum numbers of all of the fundamental particles. Along the way, GUTs would also explain charge quantization. GUTs might also explain the origins of fermion mass. Finally, because they generally lead to baryon-number violation, GUTs even have the potential to explain the cosmological baryon/anti-baryon asymmetry. By combining GUTs with supersymmetry in the context of SUSY GUTs, it might then be possible to realize the attractive features of GUTs simultaneously with those of supersymmetry in a single theory.

Both the SUSY idea and the GUT idea are very compelling. Certainly, the SUSY idea (and indirectly the GUT idea, through measurements of proton decay and other rare decays) will be the focus of experimental high-energy physics over the next 20 years. But high-energy theorists also have plenty of work to do — we must build theories in order to interpret the

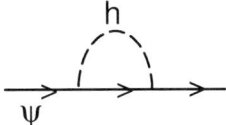

Fig. 6.1. One-loop evolution of the gauge couplings within the Minimal Supersymmetric Standard Model (MSSM), assuming supersymmetric thresholds at the Z scale. Here $\alpha_1 \equiv (5/3)\alpha_Y$, where α_Y is the hypercharge coupling in the conventional normalization. The relative width of each line reflects current experimental uncertainties.

data. But *how* do we build realistic SUSY theories? *How* do we build realistic GUT theories? *How* do we incorporate gravity?

Clearly, the possibilities seem endless. And even the SUSY or GUT ideas have not answered our most fundamental questions, such as why there are three gauge forces, or why there are three generations. Therefore, it is natural to hope that there is yet a deeper principle that can provide some theoretical guidance. And that's where string theory comes in.

6.1.3. *So what is string theory?*

The basic premise of string theory is very simple: all elementary particles are really closed vibrating loops of energy called *strings*. The length scale of these loops of energy is on the order of 10^{-35} meters (corresponding to 10^{19} GeV), so it is not possible to probe this stringy structure directly.

This idea has great power, because it provides a way to unify all of the particles and forces in nature. Specifically, each different elementary particle can be viewed as corresponding to a different vibrational mode of the string. A pictorial representation of this idea is given in Fig. 6.2, where we are schematically associating higher vibrational string modes with string loops containing more "wiggles". From the point of view of a low-energy observer who cannot make out this stringy structure, the different excitations each appear to be point particles. However, to such an observer, the states with more underlying "wiggles" appear to have higher spin. Thus, in this way we find that string theory predicts not only spin-1/2 and spin-1 states (which can be associated with the fermions and gauge bosons of the Standard Model respectively), but also a spin-2 state (which can naturally be associated with the graviton). Thus, through string theory, we see that the gauge interactions, particles, *and also gravity* are unified into a common quantized description as corresponding to different excitation modes of a single fundamental entity, the string itself.

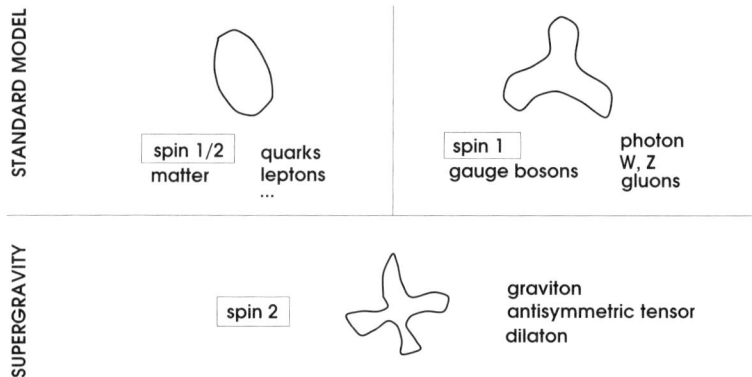

Fig. 6.2. The basic hypothesis of string theory is that the different elementary particles correspond to the different vibrational modes of a single fundamental entity, a closed loop of energy called a string. In this way one obtains not only spin-1/2 and spin-1 states which can be associated with the matter and gauge bosons of the Standard Model, but also a spin-2 state which can be identified with the graviton. Thus, string theory provides a way of unifying the Standard Model with gravity.

Of course, this is not the end of the story. Just as a violin string has an infinite number of harmonics, so too does a string give rise to an infinite tower of states corresponding to higher and higher vibrational modes. Since it takes more and more energy to excite these higher vibrational string modes, such states are increasingly massive. Indeed, because the fundamental string scale is on the order of $M_{\text{string}} \approx 10^{18}$ GeV, these string states are quantized in units of M_{string}. The states which we have illustrated in Fig. 6.2 are all *massless* with respect to M_{string}, and correspond, in some sense, to the ground states of the string. These are the so-called "observable states", and include not only the (supersymmetric) Standard Model and (super)gravity, but also may include various additional states (often called "hidden-sector states" which contain their own matter and gauge particles). However, there also exists an infinite tower of massive states with masses $M_n \approx \sqrt{n} M_{\text{string}}$, $n \in \mathbb{Z}^+$. In most discussions of the phenomenological properties of string theory, these massive states are ignored (since they are so heavy), and one concentrates on the phenomenology of the massless states. One then presumes that they accrue (relatively small) masses through other means, such as through radiative corrections.

Nevertheless, the passage from point particles to strings has tremendous consequences. Not only have we replaced the physics of zero-dimensional objects (elementary point particles) with the physics of one-dimensional objects (strings), but we have also replaced the physics of the one-dimensional worldlines that they sweep out with the physics of two-dimensional so-called *worldsheets*. Likewise, we have replaced the physics of Feynman diagrams with the physics of two-dimensional *manifolds*, so that a tree diagram corresponds to a genus-zero manifold (a sphere) and a one-loop diagram corresponds to a genus-one manifold (a torus). These comparisons are illustrated in Fig. 6.3. Note that the latter descriptions as spheres and tori correspond to shrinking the external strings to points, essentially "pinching off" the external legs. This is a valid description for reasons to be discussed in Lecture #2.

This is clearly a new language for doing physics. However, as we have seen, because string theory also includes gravity (which is exceedingly weak compared with the other forces), its fundamental mass scale is very high. Indeed, since the fundamental energy scale for gravity is the Planck mass

$$M_{\text{Planck}} \equiv \sqrt{\frac{\hbar c}{G_N}} \approx 10^{19} \text{ GeV} \approx (10^{-33} \text{ cm.})^{-1} \;, \tag{6.1.4}$$

the string scale must also be very high. Indeed, to a first approximation, it turns out that

$$M_{\text{string}} \approx g_{\text{string}} M_{\text{Planck}} \tag{6.1.5}$$

where g_{string} is the string coupling constant, typically assumed to be $\sim \mathcal{O}(1)$. Thus, we see that string theory is ultimately a theory of Planck-scale physics.

There are lots of "formal" reasons for being excited about string theory. First, it turns out that string theory requires the existence of extra space-time dimensions in order to be consistent, and consequently we now have to consider physics in different numbers of dimensions as well as all sorts of geometric questions pertaining to different possible "compactification" scenarios. Second, string theory gives us a new perspective on the structure of spacetime itself. For example, string theory gives rise to many novel Planck-scale effects. One of these is called T-duality: the physics of a closed string in a spacetime one of whose dimensions is compactified on a circle of radius R turns out to be *equivalent* to the physics of the same string in a spacetime in which the radius is M_{string}^2/R. Thus, T-duality interchanges large radii and small radii, and suggests that our naïve view of spacetime and its linear hierarchy of energy and length scales cannot ultimately be correct. Third, string theory also provides new types of strong/weak coupling dualities. These have proven useful for elucidating the strong-coupling

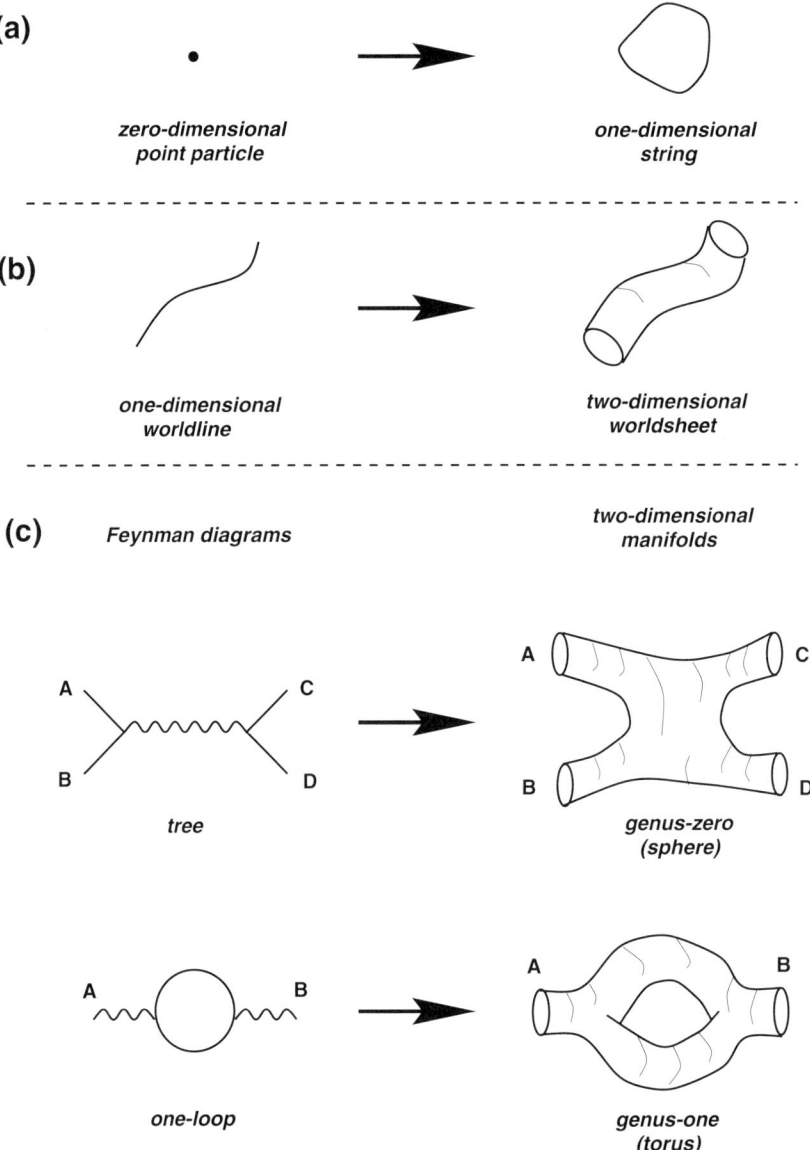

Fig. 6.3. In string theory, we replace (a) zero-dimensional elementary particles with one-dimensional strings; (b) one-dimensional worldlines with two-dimensional worldsheets; and (c) Feynman diagrams with two-dimensional manifolds. For example, tree diagrams correspond to genus-zero manifolds (spheres), and one-loop diagrams correspond to genus-one manifolds (tori).

dynamics of not only string theory, but also *field* theory. Finally, there have even been novel applications to black-hole physics. The most famous example of this is the fact that various non-perturbative string structures called D-branes have provided the first *statistical* (*i.e.*, microscopic) derivation of the Bekenstein-Hawking entropy formula $S = A/4$ that relates the entropy S of a black hole to its surface area A. Indeed, the above list only begins to scratch the surface of all of the many exciting recent formal developments in string theory.

But we are phenomenologists, so it is natural to ask about the rest of high-energy physics. How does string theory connect with the rest of particle physics?

Some of the answers to this question have already been given above. We have seen, in particular, that string theory is capable of reproducing the Standard Model as its low-energy limit. Moreover, as we have also seen, the Standard Model naturally emerges coupled with gravity. Furthermore, in many cases this entire structure is also joined with *supersymmetry*. Finally, this entire structure is also often joined with many properties of GUTs (such as gauge coupling unification). All of this comes out of the low-energy limit of string theory, in some sense automatically.

There are also many other benefits to considering the application of string theory to particle physics. First, string theory provides us with new kinds of symmetries (so-called "worldsheet symmetries") which lead to powerful new constraints on the resulting low-energy phenomenology. Second, in principle* string theory has *no free parameters*, which leads to a very predictive theory. Third, string theory has no divergences — in some sense, string theory is a completely *finite* theory in which many of the troublesome divergences associated with field theory are simply absent. Finally, it

---

*In this connection, we hasten to emphasize the phrase "in principle". Unfortunately, our relative inability to understand the non-perturbative structure of string theory often means that the pragmatic consequences of having no free parameters cannot be realized, and in practice one is often forced to introduce many parameters to reflect our ignorance of the underlying dynamics. This will be discussed in subsequent lectures. This situation is rather analogous to one that arises in the MSSM: we do not know how supersymmetry is broken, so we typically parametrize our ignorance through the introduction of various supersymmetry-breaking parameters. Likewise, in string theory, there are analogous questions which come under the heading of "vacuum selection": we do not know how the non-perturbative dynamics of string theory selects a particular vacuum state. Thus, in order to proceed to make phenomenological predictions, we are often forced to *assume* a certain vacuum state, or to parametrize the vacuum via the introduction of essentially unfixed parameters. The important point, however, is that string theory is a complete theory in that it should *in principle*, by virtue of its dynamics, uniquely fix the values of all of its fundamental parameters.

turns out that string theory can even give rise to a new perspective on the Standard Model itself, and often provides new and simpler ways to perform calculations.

These last three points (absence of free parameters, absence of divergences, and new ways to perform calculations) are truly remarkable. Therefore, let us pause to explain in an intuitive way why these features arise. First, let us explain why string theory has fewer free parameters. To do this, let us consider a Feynman diagram for a typical tree-level decay $A \to B+C$, as shown in Fig. 6.4(a). In field theory, such a process depends on many separate parameters ultimately associated with the separate propagators and vertices. Specifically, even though the propagators are determined once the masses and spins of the particles are specified, there still remains an *independent* choice as to the form of the vertex interaction. Thus, in a given field theory, there still remain many independent parameters to choose. In string theory, by contrast, there is no sharp distinction between propagators and vertices; they melt into each other, and are essentially the same. Thus, once the propagators are determined, the vertices are also intrinsically determined. This is one of the underlying reasons why string theory contains fewer free parameters than field theory.

Next, let us discuss why string theory is more finite than field theory. To do this, let us consider a typical one-loop Feynman diagram, as shown in Fig. 6.4(b). In field theory, the virtual interactions occur at sharp spacetime locations x and y. This is ultimately the origin of the ultraviolet (*i.e.*, short-distance) divergence as $x \to y$. In string theory, by contrast, we have seen that there are no such sharp interaction points — essentially the interaction is "smoothed out" by the presence of the string. Thus, there is no sense in which the dangerous $x \to y$ limit exists, for there are no precise means by which one can define such interaction locations x and y. It is in this manner that string theory automatically removes ultraviolet divergences: the string itself, through its extended geometry, acts as a (Planck-scale) ultraviolet regulator.

Finally, let us discuss why string theory can often give us simpler ways to perform calculations than in field theory. To do this, let us consider the total tree-level amplitude for a typical process $A + B \to C + D$, as illustrated in Fig. 6.4(c). As we know, in field theory there are two separate topologies of Feynman diagram that must be separately considered: the s-channel diagram and the t-channel diagram. In general, at any given order, there are many separate diagrams to evaluate, and one often finds that great simplifications and cancellations occur only when these individual

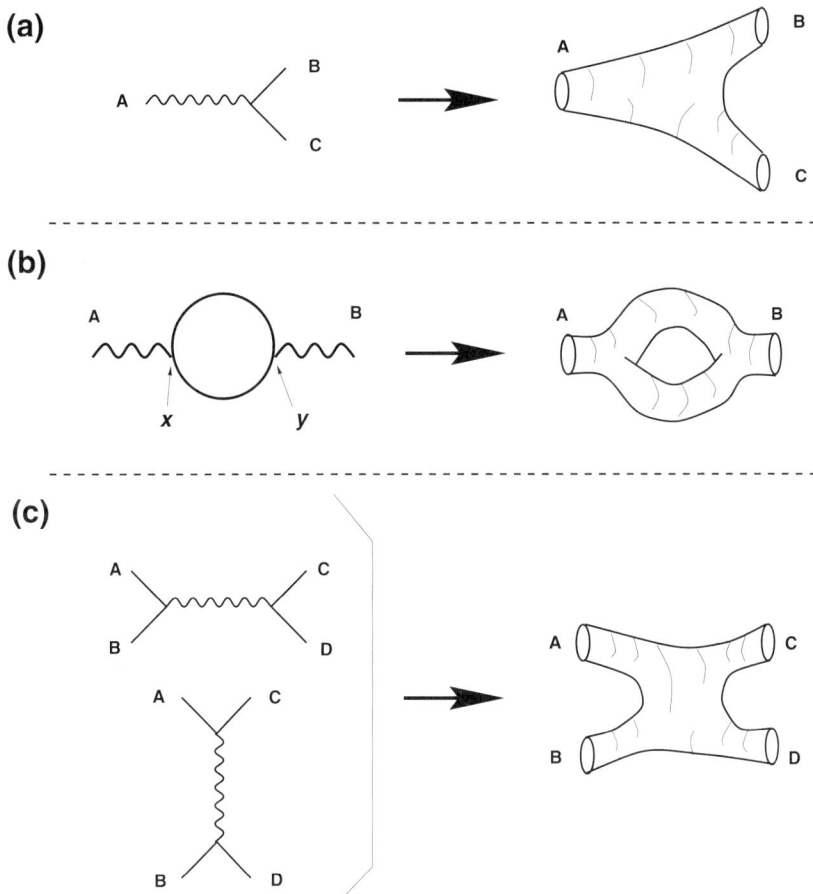

Fig. 6.4. (a) Illustration of the fact that string propagators and string vertices are not independent. (b) Illustration of the fact that string theory lacks many of the ultraviolet divergences that arise in field theory from the short-distance limit $x \to y$. (c) Illustration of the fact that one string diagram often comprises many field-theoretic diagrams.

contributions are added together. In string theory, by contrast, there is only *one* corresponding diagram to evaluate at any given order. Thus, the sorts of simplifications or cancellations that might occur in field theory are automatically "built into" string theory from the very beginning. In some sense, string theory manages to find a way to reorganize the field-theory diagrams in a perturbative expansion in a useful and potentially profitable way. Indeed, this observation has even led to the development of many new techniques for evaluating complicated field-theoretic processes, particularly in QCD where the number of diagrams and the number of terms in each diagram can easily grow to otherwise unmanageable proportions.

We thus see that in a number of ways, string theory is a very useful language in which we might consider thinking about particle physics. Indeed, in various aspects (such as finiteness, fewer parameters, *etc.*) it is superior to field theory. But overall, the fundamental fact remains that if we are thinking about strings, we are abandoning our usual four-dimensional point of view of particle physics. Specifically, since each different particle in spacetime is now interpreted as a different quantum mode excitation of an underlying string, we see that four-dimensional (spacetime) physics is now ultimately the consequence of two-dimensional (worldsheet) physics. Thus, everything we ordinarily focus on in field theory (such as the four-dimensional particle spectrum, the gauge symmetries, the couplings, *etc.*) are now all ultimately determined or constrained by worldsheet symmetries.

And this brings us to string phenomenology.

6.1.4. *So what is string phenomenology?*

In order to understand what string phenomenology is, we can draw a useful analogy. Just as we are replacing the *language* of high-energy physics from field theory to string theory, we likewise replace field-theory phenomenology with string-theory phenomenology. The goals of string phenomenology are of course the same as those of ordinary field-theory phenomenology: both seek to reproduce, explain, and predict observable phenomena, and both seek to suggest or constrain new physics at even higher energy scales. Indeed, only the language in which we will carry out this procedure has changed. Thus, in some sense, string phenomenology is the "art" of using the new insights from string theory in order to understand, explain, and predict what physics at the next energy scale is going to look like. Or, recalling that string theory is ultimately a theory of Planck-scale physics, we can say that string phenomenology is the "interplay" or "meeting-ground" between Planck-scale physics and GeV-scale physics.

It is important to understand that we are not abandoning field theory completely. Nor would we want to. Field theory automatically incorporates many desirable features such as causality, spin-statistics relations, and CPT invariance (which in turn implies the existence of antiparticles). These are all generic predictions of field theory, and are the underlying reasons why field theory is the appropriate language for particle physics. However, since string theory ultimately reduces to field theory in its low-energy limit, all of these features will still be retained in string theory. Moreover, as we have seen, string theory *additionally* predicts or explains gravity, supersymmetry, and the absence of ultraviolet divergences. Furthermore, as we shall see, string theory also automatically predicts the existence of gauge symmetry, and even incorporates features such as gauge coupling unification. These are all generic predictions of string theory. It is for these reasons to believe that a change in language from field theory to string theory might be useful.

String theory will also provide us with new tools for model-building, new mechanisms and new guiding principles. Let us give some examples. In field theory, there are many well-known ideas that are part and parcel of the model-building game: one must enforce ABJ anomaly cancellation (to preserve gauge symmetries); one can employ the Higgs mechanism (to generate spontaneous symmetry breaking and give masses to particles); one has the GIM mechanism (to preserve flavor symmetries); and one has supersymmetry (to cancel quadratic divergences). Likewise, in string theory there are analogous sets of ideas, many of which are extensions of their field-theory counterparts. For example, one has the so-called "Green-Schwarz" mechanism for anomaly cancellation (to preserve gauge symmetries); one has string vacuum shifting via pseudo-anomalous $U(1)$ gauge symmetries (to generate spontaneous symmetry breaking and generate particle masses); one has spacetime compactification (to generate gauge symmetries); one has hidden string sectors (to break supersymmetry and impose selection rules); and one has massive towers of string states (to enforce finiteness). Thus, model-building proceeds, but with a different set of principles.

There is also a much more subtle effect of changing our language from field theory to string theory. Ultimately, since four-dimensional physics is now derived from an underlying two-dimensional (worldsheet) theory, string phenomenology is ultimately much more constrained than field-theory phenomenology. One given worldsheet symmetry, which might serve as an "input", can have various seemingly unrelated effects in the resulting spacetime phenomenological "output". Thus, string theory not only leads to unexpected connections or correlations between seemingly disparate spacetime phenomena, but can also give rise to entirely new phenomenological scenarios that could not have been anticipated within field theory alone. We will see many examples of this in the coming lectures.

Thus, we see that string phenomenology does many things and has many goals:

- to provide a new framework for addressing and answering numerous phenomenological questions;
- to provide a rigorous test of string theory as a theory of physics;
- to explore the interplay between worldsheet physics and spacetime physics (*i.e.*, to ultimately determine which "patterns" of low-energy phenomenology are allowed or consistent with being realized as the low-energy limit of an underlying string theory); and
- to augment field theories of "low-energy" physics into the string framework so as to give them the full benefits of the language of string theory.

Because of these different roles, string phenomenology occupies a rather central position in high-energy physics: it allows the transmission of ideas from high-scale string theory to guide "low"-scale particle physics, and vice versa. This situation is illustrated in Fig. 6.5. At the lowest energies (lower left), string phenomenology has direct relevance for the Standard Model, where it can potentially explain features such as the choice of the gauge group, the number of generations, and numerous other parameters such as the masses and mixings of Standard-Model particles. At slightly higher energies (lower right), we see that string phenomenology can also suggest or constrain various extensions to the Standard Model, such as SUSY and SUSY-breaking, grand unification, and hidden-sector physics. At the highest energies (upper left), string phenomenology is also concerned with the more formal aspects of string theory: such important questions include string vacuum selection, non-perturbative string dynamics, string duality, and new mathematical structures and techniques. And string phenomenology even has relevance outside the strict confines of particle physics. For example, string theory should have a profound impact on cosmology (upper right), where important stringy issues include the role of the dilaton, the effects of many other light degrees of freedom (the so-called *moduli*), the possibility of extra spacetime dimensions, the cosmological constant problem, and even more exotic ideas such as topology change. As illustrated in Fig. 6.5, string phenomenology sits at the center of this web of ideas. Exploring the connections between the different corners of this figure is, therefore, the job of the string phenomenologist. Indeed, through string phenomenology, one "uses" string theory in order to open a window into the possibilities for physics beyond the Standard Model.

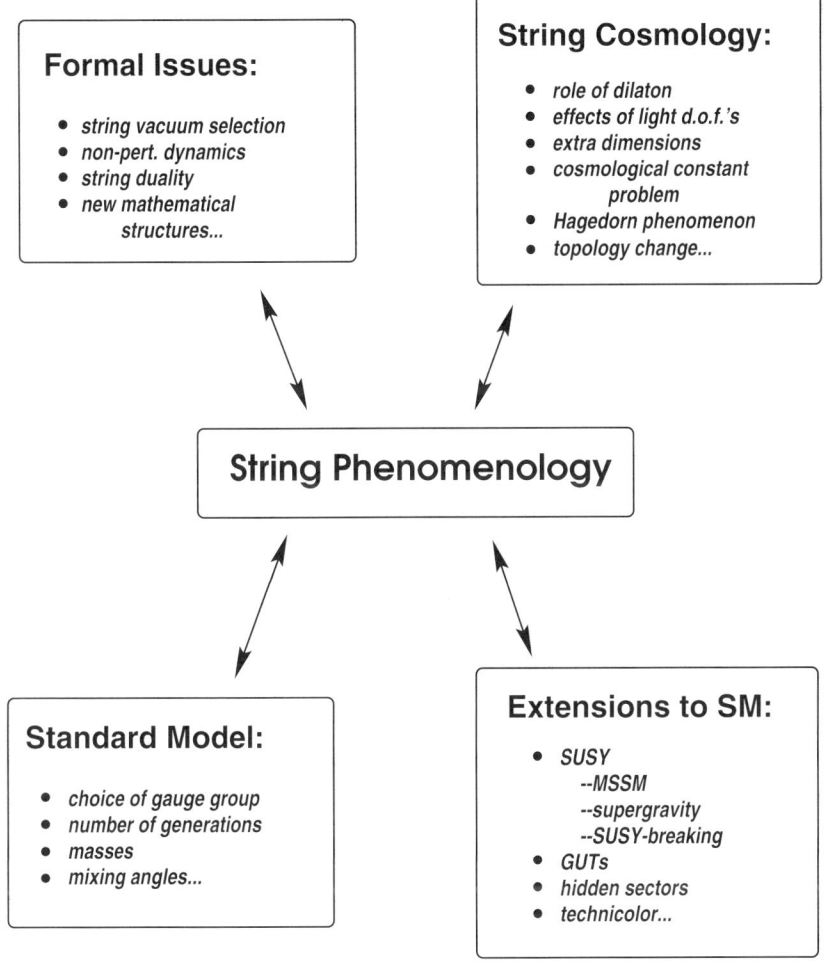

Fig. 6.5. String phenomenology is the central "meeting-ground" between Standard-Model physics, extensions to the Standard Model, formal string issues, and string cosmology.

6.1.5. *Plan of these lectures*

For much of the past decade, string phenomenology has been practiced assuming a particular type of underlying string theory, the so-called *perturbative heterotic string*. Therefore, this string will be the focal point of most of these lectures. However, it turns out that the heterotic string is built directly on the foundations of two other kinds of strings, the *bosonic string* and *Type II superstring*. Indeed, in a sense to be made more precise in Lecture #5, one can view the heterotic string as the "sum" of the bosonic string and the superstring string. Therefore, in these lectures, we will have to start at the beginning by studying first the bosonic string, then the Type II string, and finally the heterotic string. Indeed, this situation is analogous to the way in which one often studies quantum field theory: first one learns how to quantize the Klein-Gordon field, then the Dirac field, and finally the gauge field. In a certain sense, the bosonic string is the analogue of the Klein-Gordon field, while the Type II superstring is the analogue of the Dirac field and the heterotic string is the analogue of the gauge field. Of course, this analogy is only a pedagogical organizational one, since the heterotic string itself will ultimately contain *all* of the phenomenological properties (*e.g.*, scalars, fermions, and gauge symmetries) that we desire.

In Lecture #2, we will therefore give a brief introduction to the bosonic string, stopping only long enough to develop the ideas and techniques we will need for later applications. In Lectures #3 and #4, we will then proceed to develop the Type II superstring, once again focusing on only those aspects that will be useful for later applications. Finally, in Lecture #5, we will arrive at our destination: the heterotic string. In Lecture #6 we will construct some ten-dimensional heterotic string models, and in Lecture #7 we will develop a useful set of rules for heterotic string model-building.

It is important to note, however, that all of string phenomenology is not based on the heterotic string. Particularly over the past decade, there has been a profound shift in our understanding of both string theory and its phenomenological implications. One of the consequences of this so-called "second superstring revolution" has been a new emphasis on yet another class of strings, the *Type I (open) strings*. Within this class, so-called *intersecting D-brane models* have shown great promise in yielding chiral, Standard-Model-like spectra. Indeed, there has even emerged a new superstructure which promises to relate all of these strings to each other: this structure is called *M-theory*, and is deeply tied to many non-perturbative aspects of string theory which are still being understood. Needless to say, these recent developments have the potential to completely change the way we think about string theory and string phenomenology. We will therefore discuss some of these modern developments in the final Lecture #8. Nevertheless, the bulk of these lectures will primarily be focused on the more traditional aspects of string phenomenology that concern the weakly coupled heterotic string. Indeed, this affords the best introduction to string theory and string phenomenology, regardless of the future directions that string theory and string phenomenology might ultimately take.

We also remind the reader that our goal here is to provide an introduction to string theory that avoids mathematical complications wherever possible, and which "gets to the physics" as rapidly as possible. Therefore, in many places, we will simply assert a mathematical result to be true, leaving its derivation to be found in various textbooks on the subject. For this purpose, we recommend Volume I of the textbook *Superstring Theory*, by M.B. Green, J.H. Schwarz, and E. Witten (henceforth to be referred to as GSW[†]). In fact, our initial approach will be very similar to that of GSW, and we will continually refer back to this textbook as we proceed. Another recommended textbook with a more modern mathematical perspective is *Introduction to String Theory*, by J. Polchinski. Likewise, *A First Course in String Theory* by B. Zwiebach is particularly useful for students who may lack a full background in relativistic quantum field theory.

6.2. Lecture #2: Strings and their spectra: The bosonic string

6.2.1. *The action*

We begin by studying the simplest string of all: the bosonic string. As we discussed in Lecture #1, the physics of a string is ultimately described by the shape it takes (*e.g.*, its vibrational mode of oscillation) as it propagates through an external spacetime and thereby sweeps out a two-dimensional worldsheet. Therefore, we must first have a way of describing the shape of this worldsheet. To this end, we parametrize the worldsheet by two worldsheet coordinates (σ_1, σ_2) as illustrated in Fig. 6.6, and describe the embedding of this worldsheet into the external spacetime by giving the spacetime coordinates X^μ of any location (σ_1, σ_2) on the worldsheet. Thus, the physics of the string is ultimately encapsulated in the embedding functions $X^\mu(\sigma_1, \sigma_2)$, where $\mu = 0, 1, ..., D-1$. Here D is the total spacetime dimension, which we shall keep arbitrary for now.

Given these embedding functions, we can attempt to write down an appropriate action for the string. To do this, we first note that as we might

---

[†]Not to be confused with another great GSW trio, namely Glashow, Salam, and Weinberg. One can only hope that someday string theory will be as well-established, both theoretically and experimentally, as the GSW electroweak theory. This may sound a bit optimistic, but a possible new *experimental* direction for string theory and string phenomenology will be discussed in Lecture #8 in the context of the brane world.

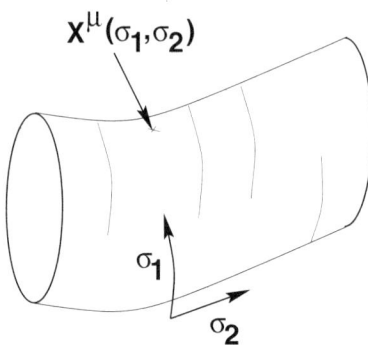

Fig. 6.6. The string worldsheet can be parametrized by two worldsheet coordinates (σ_1, σ_2). Thus, the location in the external spacetime of any point on the string worldsheet is described by a set of functions $X^\mu(\sigma_1, \sigma_2)$. It is convenient to think of σ_1 as a spacelike worldsheet coordinate, and σ_2 as a timelike worldsheet coordinate.

expect, strings have *tension* — *i.e.*, strings generically have a non-zero energy per unit length. In other words, it takes energy to stretch a string and to give the worldsheet a larger area. Thus, as the string propagates along in spacetime, we expect on physical grounds that this string should choose a configuration that minimizes the area of the worldsheet. This leads us to identify the string action with the area of the corresponding worldsheet. Indeed, this results in the so-called *Nambu-Goto action*, which involves a non-trivial square root of the X^μ coordinates. For certain calculational purposes, however, this square root is often problematic. Fortunately, however, there exists an alternative action, the so-called *Polyakov action*, which is classically equivalent to the Nambu-Goto action but which does not involve fractional powers of the X coordinates. This action is given by

$$ S = -\frac{1}{4\pi\alpha'} \int d^2\sigma \sqrt{h}\, h^{\alpha\beta}\, g_{\mu\nu}\, \partial_\alpha X^\mu \partial_\beta X^\nu \,. \qquad (6.2.1) $$

Here $g_{\mu\nu}$ is the metric of the external spacetime, $h_{\alpha\beta}$ is the metric of the worldsheet, the worldsheet derivative is given by $\partial_\alpha \equiv \partial/\partial\sigma^\alpha$, and $h \equiv \det h_{\alpha\beta}$. In the prefactor, α' is a dimensionful constant (called the *Regge slope*) with units of (length)^2. Since these units are equivalent to length/energy, we see that α' is an inverse tension, and indeed the string tension T turns out to be related to α' via $T = (2\pi\alpha')^{-1}$. We shall discuss the numerical value of α' below. Note that the action (6.2.1) is manifestly spacetime Lorentz-invariant.

Before proceeding further, it may be useful to draw an analogy between this action and the analogous action for a *point* particle propagating through spacetime and sweeping out a *worldline* rather than a worldsheet. The worldline can be parametrized by a single coordinate σ, which functions as a proper time along the worldline. The point-particle action can then be written in the form

$$S_{\text{point particle}} = \tfrac{1}{2} \int d\sigma \, \left(e^{-1} g_{\mu\nu} \partial_\sigma X^\mu \partial_\sigma X^\nu - e\hat{m}^2 \right) \qquad (6.2.2)$$

where $\hat{m}$ is the mass of the point particle and where $e(\sigma)$ is an auxiliary field (a so-called *einbein*). Solving for $e(\sigma)$ through its equation of motion and substituting back into (6.2.2) yields an action proportional to the length of the worldline and involving a square root. Thus, we see that the string action (6.2.1) is nothing but the generalization of the point-particle action (6.2.2), where we have associated

$$e^{-1}(\sigma) \iff h^{\alpha\beta}(\sigma_1, \sigma_2) \,, \qquad \hat{m} = 0 \,. \qquad (6.2.3)$$

In other words, the string action (6.2.1) is the two-dimensional generalization of the action of a *massless* point particle, where the worldsheet metric functions as an auxiliary field (a "zweibein"). This masslessness property will be crucial shortly.

It is now possible to make some simplifications. Perhaps the most obvious is to restrict our attention to a flat spacetime and take $g_{\mu\nu} = \eta_{\mu\nu}$. We shall do this throughout these lectures. A much more subtle simplification, however, is to simplify the worldsheet metric. Let us therefore pause to discuss how this can be done.

One of the first things we realize is that the ultimate physics of the string should not depend on the particular choice of coordinate system (σ_1, σ_2) on the string worldsheet. After all, on purely physical grounds, we know that the particular choice of worldsheet coordinate system cannot have a physical effect, for the same worldsheet geometry can ultimately be described using an infinite variety of coordinate systems which differ from each other through relative reparametrizations or rescalings. (Indeed, in the point-particle case, we are likewise free to reparametrize our proper-time variable along the particle worldline.) Therefore, the string action should have a symmetry that makes it invariant under reparametrizations and rescalings of the worldsheet coordinates. Note, in particular, that the invariance under *rescalings* follows from the fact that we chose our string action (6.2.1) to generalize that of a *massless* point particle. In other words, we have taken $\hat{m} = 0$ in (6.2.3). While it is possible to add terms to the action of the bosonic string which mimic the effects of possible mass terms and which explicitly break the scale invariance of the bosonic string, we shall not need to consider such theories in these lectures.

The symmetry that comprises both reparametrizations and rescalings of the worldsheet coordinates is called *conformal symmetry*, and the bosonic string action (6.2.1) is thus said to be "conformally invariant". Clearly, this symmetry must hold not only at the classical level, but also at the quantum level, for we would not have a consistent theory if this symmetry were broken by quantum anomalies. Conformal invariance of the action is a very powerful physical tool which will play an important role throughout these lectures, and indeed the mathematical structure underlying conformal symmetry and its implications is a deep and beautiful subject which we will not have time or space to discuss here. A recommended starting point is *Applied Conformal Field Theory* (Proceedings of Les Houches, Session XLIX, 1988), by P. Ginsparg. Therefore, in order to proceed, we will have to make the first of many "great leaps", and take certain results on faith. Our first great leap will therefore be the following:

Great Leap #1: Conformal invariance of the string action allows us to replace the string metric $h_{\alpha\beta}$ with the two-dimensional Minkowski metric $\eta_{\alpha\beta}$ without loss of generality.

This then results in the simplified bosonic string action

$$S = -\frac{1}{4\pi\alpha'} \int d^2\sigma \, \partial_\alpha X^\mu \partial^\alpha X_\mu \; . \tag{6.2.4}$$

Looking at the action (6.2.4), we see that it has two possible interpretations. The first interpretation is the one that we have already been following: minimizing this action is classically equivalent to minimizing the worldsheet area. This follows directly from the interpretation of $X^\mu(\sigma_1, \sigma_2)$ as the *spacetime coordinates* of a given worldsheet position (σ_1, σ_2). Note that this action is invariant under $SO(D-1,1)$ Lorentz transformations of the spacetime coordinates, with the index μ interpreted as a spacetime vector index relative to the Lorentz group. We shall refer to this as the *spacetime interpretation*.

There is, however, a completely different interpretation of (6.2.4): this is the action of a *two-dimensional quantum field theory* where the two dimensions refer to the worldsheet coordinates and where the "fields" are nothing but the functions $X^\mu(\sigma_1, \sigma_2)$, $\mu = 0, 1, ..., D-1$. Indeed, we see that these spacetime coordinate functions are simply a collection of D different massless bosonic Klein-Gordon fields which happen to exhibit an internal $SO(D-1,1)$ rotation symmetry (analogous to a gauge symmetry) between them. In such a case, the index μ is simply an internal symmetry index which tells us that the X^μ fields transform as vectors with respect to the internal $SO(D-1,1)$ symmetry. We shall refer to this as the *worldsheet interpretation*. Indeed, it is because this string action contains only bosonic worldsheet fields that we call this the *bosonic string*. In such a description, spacetime is not a fundamental concept but rather a "derived" concept: it results from the interpretation of various worldsheet fields as spacetime coordinates, and from the interpretation of an internal symmetry as a spacetime Lorentz symmetry. It is indeed remarkable that such different interpretations can be made of the same physics, and we shall often go back and forth between these different worldsheet and spacetime points of view.

Given these two descriptions of the action, we can also understand the origin of the Regge slope parameter α' on dimensional grounds. Let us first take the worldsheet point of view, so that our length dimensions are determined with respect to the coordinates (σ_1, σ_2). In such a case, we know that the ordinary Klein-Gordon action does not require any dimensionful prefactor, for $\int d^2\sigma (\partial_\alpha X^\mu)^2$ is indeed dimensionless when the Klein-Gordon field X^μ is itself dimensionless. However, from the spacetime point of view, we see that X^μ cannot be dimensionless, for we ultimately need to interpret this field as a spacetime coordinate with units of length. Thus, we are forced to compensate by inserting a dimensionful prefactor α' in front of the action. In other words, *the need for the dimensionful prefactor α' arises from the need to interpret our dimensionless (scale-free) worldsheet theory as a dimensionful (spacetime) theory.* Or, to put it slightly differently, the parameter α' is the dimensionful conversion factor that describes the overall scale of the embedding of the dimensionless worldsheet physics into the dimensionful spacetime. We shall see this phenomenon very often throughout these lectures: the worldsheet physics is by itself scale-invariant (since it generalizes the physics of a massless point particle with $\hat{m} = 0$), and it is only in the conversion to dimensionful *spacetime* quantities that the overall scale α' plays a role. Thus, α' sets the overall spacetime mass scale of string theory, often called the *string scale*:

$$M_{\text{string}} \equiv \frac{1}{\sqrt{\alpha'}} . \tag{6.2.5}$$

A priori, this mass scale is unfixed, but we shall see shortly how this scale is ultimately determined.

Now that we have established the worldsheet picture and the spacetime picture, it is easy to see how they are related to each other: each quantum excitation of the Klein-Gordon worldsheet fields X^μ corresponds to a different particle in spacetime. Thus, the study of string theory can be reduced to the study of a two-dimensional quantum field theory! For example, particle scattering amplitudes in spacetime can be re-interpreted as the correlation functions of our two-dimensional worldsheet fields, evaluated on various two-dimensional manifolds. Of course, as we have stated above, this is not just *any* two-dimensional quantum field theory, for physical consistency also requires the presence of conformal symmetry. Thus, from this point of view, string theory is the study of two-dimensional *conformal* field theories. In two dimensions, it turns out conformal symmetry is extremely powerful, for it gives rise to an infinite number of conserved currents. Indeed, two-dimensional conformal symmetry is often sufficiently powerful to permit the *exact* evaluation for many scattering amplitudes.

In the case in question, the particular conformal field theory that concerns us is that of D free massless bosonic fields X^μ, $\mu = 0, 1, ..., D-1$. However, just as with any symmetry, there is always the danger of quantum anomalies. Nevertheless, it is straightforward to show that

> **Great Leap #2:** Conformal invariance of the string action is preserved at the quantum level (*i.e.*, all quantum anomalies are cancelled) if and only if $D = 26$.

This is clearly a big result, and we will not have space to provide a proper mathematical derivation of this fact. At the very least, however, we can give a guide as to the most useful way of thinking about this result. Note that our D bosonic fields are identical to each other and essentially decoupled from each other. Therefore, each contributes the same amount to any potential anomaly. This amount is called the *central charge*, and the central charge c of each bosonic field X will be denoted c_X. It turns out that $c_X = 1$, and therefore the total central charge from the D bosonic fields is $c_{\text{fields}} = D$. However, it can be shown that there also exists a "background" central charge (*i.e.*, a background quantum anomaly) of magnitude $c_{\text{background}} = -26$. Thus, the total anomaly is cancelled only if $D = 26$. Clearly, the most mysterious part of this discussion is the origin of this "background" central charge. In technical terms, it reflects the contributions of the conformal ghosts that arose when we used the conformal symmetry to set (or "gauge-fix") the worldsheet metric $h_{\alpha\beta} \to \eta_{\alpha\beta}$. However, all we will need to know for the future is that the value of the "background" anomaly $c_{\text{background}}$ depends on only the particular symmetry of the worldsheet action that we are dealing with. In the present case, this worldsheet symmetry is simply conformal invariance, and the corresponding background central charge corresponding to conformal invariance is $c_{\text{background}} = -26$. Therefore, we see that the total conformal anomaly is cancelled only if $D = 26$. This is typically called the *critical dimension* of the bosonic string.

We see, then, that string theory is able to determine the spacetime dimension as the result of an *anomaly cancellation argument*! It is worth reflecting on how this happened by considering an analogous situation in field theory, namely the cancellation of the triangle axial anomaly. We know that this anomaly is cancelled only for very particular combinations of particle representations (*e.g.*, we require complete generations of Standard-Model fields, with three colors of quark for every lepton). So we are used to the idea that anomalies are extremely sensitive to the field content of the theory. In string theory, however, we have seen that the analogous worldsheet field content is parametrized by the spacetime dimension. More worldsheeet fields correspond to more spacetime dimensions. Therefore, just as triangle anomaly cancellation requires three colors, conformal anomaly cancellation requires 26 dimensions.

Of course, our world does not consist of 26 flat spacetime dimensions, and we shall ultimately need to find a way of reducing this to a four-dimensional theory. For now, however, we can just think of the present bosonic string as a 26-dimensional toy model.

6.2.2. *Quantizing the bosonic string*

Let us now quantize this theory. Having already noted that the action (6.2.4) is nothing but the action of a set of 26 Klein-Gordon fields X^μ, we already know how to proceed: in the usual fashion, we introduce a Fourier-expansion of the fields X^μ, and interpret the coefficients of this expansion as creation and annihilation operators obeying canonical quantization relations.

Because we ultimately wish to interpret the fields X^μ as spacetime coordinates, we must first impose the constraint

$$X^\mu(\sigma_1 + \pi, \sigma_2) = X^\mu(\sigma_1, \sigma_2) \tag{6.2.6}$$

where we have chosen to normalize the length of the closed string as π. In other words, the spacetime coordinates must be single-valued as we make one complete circuit around the closed string. This is the first place where we have essentially incorporated the requirement that we are dealing with closed strings whose topology is that of a circle. Moreover, because of this topology (and because of the linear nature of the wave equation resulting from the action (6.2.4)), we know that we can also decompose any possible quantum excitation of the wiggling string into a superposition of modes that travel clockwise around the string (in the direction of, say, decreasing σ_1) and those that travel counter-clockwise (in the direction of increasing σ_1). These are respectively called *left-movers* and *right-movers*. We can therefore decompose each of our Klein-Gordon fields into the form

$$X^\mu(\sigma_1, \sigma_2) = X_L^\mu(\sigma_1 + \sigma_2) + X_R^\mu(\sigma_1 - \sigma_2) . \tag{6.2.7}$$

The most general mode-expansion consistent with the boundary condition (6.2.6) is then

$$X^\mu(\sigma_1, \sigma_2) = x^\mu + \ell^2 p^\mu \sigma_2 + \frac{i}{2}\ell \sum_{n \neq 0} \left[\frac{\alpha_n^\mu}{n} e^{-2in(\sigma_1+\sigma_2)} + \frac{\tilde{\alpha}_n^\mu}{n} e^{+2in(\sigma_1-\sigma_2)} \right],$$
$$\tag{6.2.8}$$

which decomposes into

$$X_L^\mu(\sigma_1 + \sigma_2) = \tfrac{1}{2}x^\mu + \frac{\ell^2}{2} p^\mu (\sigma_1 + \sigma_2) + \frac{i}{2}\ell \sum_{n \neq 0} \frac{\alpha_n^\mu}{n} e^{-2in(\sigma_1+\sigma_2)}$$

$$X_R^\mu(\sigma_1 - \sigma_2) = \tfrac{1}{2}x^\mu - \frac{\ell^2}{2} p^\mu (\sigma_1 - \sigma_2) + \frac{i}{2}\ell \sum_{n \neq 0} \frac{\tilde{\alpha}_n^\mu}{n} e^{+2in(\sigma_1-\sigma_2)} \quad (6.2.9)$$

Here $\ell \equiv \sqrt{2\alpha'}$ is a fundamental length that has been inserted on dimensional grounds.

It is easy to interpret the different terms in (6.2.8) and (6.2.9). Clearly the final terms in each line represent the internal quantum vibrational oscillations of the string, where α_n^μ and $\tilde{\alpha}_n^\mu$ are the left-moving and right-moving creation/annihilation operators corresponding to vibrational modes of a given frequency n. We shall discuss these operators shortly. Note that the contribution from the "zero-mode" has been separated out and written explicitly in the form $x^\mu \pm \tfrac{1}{2}\ell^2(\sigma_1 \pm \sigma_2)$ for the left- and right-movers respectively. In the case when there are no quantum excitations (so that we can ignore the final exponential terms), these "zero-modes" are all that remain of the mode-expansion, whereupon we see from (6.2.8) that the total X^μ field takes the form $X^\mu = x^\mu + \ell^2 p^\mu \sigma_2$. Interpreting σ_2 as the timelike coordinate on the string worldsheet, we thus see that x^μ is nothing but the center-of-mass position of the string, and p^μ its center-of-mass momentum.

Let us now consider the quantization rules that we must impose. The first one (for the zero-modes) is easy: we simply impose the usual commutation relation $[x^\mu, p^\nu] = i\hbar \eta^{\mu\nu}$. We shall henceforth set $\hbar = 1$. The excited modes also have a similar commutation relation. First, note that because the X fields are interpreted as spacetime coordinates, they are necessarily *real*. This implies that we must identify $\alpha^\mu_{-n} = (\alpha^\mu_n)^\dagger$, with a similar result for the right-moving oscillator modes. In other words, the negative modes *create* excitations, while the positive modes *annihilate* the same excitations. Given this, we then can immediately write down the commutation relation for the creation/annihilation operators:

$$[\alpha^\mu_m, \alpha^\nu_n] = m\, \delta_{m+n}\, \eta^{\mu\nu}\,, \qquad [\tilde{\alpha}^\mu_m, \tilde{\alpha}^\nu_n] = m\, \delta_{m+n}\, \eta^{\mu\nu}\,. \qquad (6.2.10)$$

Here we have introduced the notation $\delta_x = \delta_{x,0} \equiv 1$ if $x = 0$, and $\equiv 0$ if $x \neq 0$. Note that these are exactly the harmonic oscillator commutation relations, except that we have rescaled each mode α_n by its corresponding frequency n in (6.2.9). Thus, $a_n \equiv \alpha_n/\sqrt{n}$ obey the usual harmonic oscillator commutation relations. This rescaling has become conventional in string theory, and we shall retain it here. Likewise, it is often conventional to define the zero-mode $\alpha^\mu_0 \equiv \frac{1}{2}\sqrt{\alpha'}p^\mu$.

Given this mode-expansion, we can now construct the corresponding number operators

$$n > 0: \qquad N_n = \frac{1}{n}\alpha^\mu_{-n}\alpha_{n\mu}\,, \qquad \tilde{N}_n = \frac{1}{n}\tilde{\alpha}^\mu_{-n}\tilde{\alpha}_{n\mu} \qquad (6.2.11)$$

which count the number of excitations of the nth frequency modes of the string. Once again, this is completely analogous to the harmonic-oscillator creation/annihilation modes, after we take into account the rescaling $\alpha_n \equiv \sqrt{n}a_n$ and the hermiticity condition $\alpha_{-n} = \alpha^\dagger_n$.

Likewise, we can also write down the total *energy* of the system. To do this, let us consider the different contributions to the total energy. First, there is the energy associated with the internal quantum vibrational oscillations of the string. As we might expect, this is given by

$$L_0^{(\text{osc})} \equiv \sum_{n=1}^{\infty} n N_n = \sum_{n=1}^{\infty} \alpha^\mu_{-n}\alpha_{n\mu}$$

$$\bar{L}_0^{(\text{osc})} \equiv \sum_{n=1}^{\infty} n \tilde{N}_n = \sum_{n=1}^{\infty} \tilde{\alpha}^\mu_{-n}\tilde{\alpha}_{n\mu}\,. \qquad (6.2.12)$$

For convenience, we are defining these energy operators in such a way that they are dimensionless numbers (*i.e.*, they are *worldsheet* energies). These L_0 operators are often called *Virasoro generators*, which are more generally defined $L_m \equiv \sum_n \alpha^\mu_{m-n} \alpha_{n\mu}$. These generators are nothing but the different frequency modes of the total worldsheet stress-energy tensor, and together they satisfy the so-called *Virasoro algebra*. We shall only consider L_0 in these lectures.

Next, there is the energy of the zero-modes, which correspond to the net center-of-mass motion of the string. This is given by

$$L_0^{(\text{com})} \equiv \alpha_0^\mu \alpha_{0\mu} = \frac{\alpha'}{4} p^\mu p_\mu$$
$$\bar{L}_0^{(\text{com})} \equiv \tilde{\alpha}_0^\mu \tilde{\alpha}_{0\mu} = \frac{\alpha'}{4} p^\mu p_\mu \; . \qquad (6.2.13)$$

Note that factors of α' must appear in order to counter-balance the fact that the center-of-mass momentum p^μ is a spacetime quantity, and hence dimensionful.

Finally, there is the possibility of an overall non-zero vacuum energy for both the left-movers and the right-movers. In other words, there is no reason to assume that the vacuum state (the state without any excitations) is exactly at zero energy. This is important, of course, since string theory is ultimately a theory which will contain gravity, and it is precisely in theories containing gravity that the overall zero of energy becomes important. Indeed, mathematically, one can imagine that due to the commutation relations (6.2.10), there can be an overall normal-ordering ambiguity in the definitions in (6.2.12), and this overall normal-ordering constant would be our "vacuum energy".

Thus, denoting the left- and right-moving vacuum energies as $a_{L,R}$, we have the total left- and right-moving energies

$$H \equiv L_0^{(\text{com})} + L_0^{(\text{osc})} + a_L \; , \qquad \bar{H} \equiv \bar{L}_0^{(\text{com})} + \bar{L}_0^{(\text{osc})} + a_R \; . \qquad (6.2.14)$$

These are the total worldsheet Hamiltonians.

Clearly, the important thing to do at this stage is to determine the vacuum energies $a_{L,R}$. Of course, the symmetry between left-movers and right-movers requires $a_L = a_R$. Calculating this vacuum energy can be done in numerous ways, each of which would take too much space for our purposes. Once again, we refer the reader to Chapter 2 of GSW, where a full calculation is given. Therefore, it is time for another

Great Leap #3: Conformal invariance of the string action implies that $a_L = a_R = -1$.

Finally, in order to determine the total *spacetime mass* of a given string state, we must have a *mass-shell condition* for the string. Rather than provide a rigorous derivation (for which we again refer the curious reader to GSW), we can instead give an intuitive argument which suggests the proper answer. In a quantum field theory of point particles, the mass $\hat{m}$ is a parameter that appears in the Lagrangian through an explicit mass term that might be generated in some separate manner, *e.g.*, through the Higgs mechanism. Since a point particle has no internal degrees of freedom beyond those associated with its center-of-mass motion, such a mass parameter $\hat{m}$ would then be directly identified with M, the resulting physical mass of the particle. Such a physical mass M is the quantity satisfying the condition $p^\mu p_\mu = -M^2$, or equivalently the condition $L_0^{(\text{com})} = \bar{L}_0^{(\text{com})} = -\alpha' M^2/4$. In the special case of a massless particle (for which $\hat{m} = M = 0$), this mass-shell condition then takes the simple form $L_0^{(\text{com})} = \bar{L}_0^{(\text{com})} = 0$.

A similar condition emerges in string theory. We have already seen that our string action (6.2.1) generalizes that of a massless particle, which again suggests that our effective Lagrangian mass parameter $\hat{m}$ vanishes. Indeed, as we have discussed, this is the root of the scale invariance of the string action (6.2.1). However, unlike the point-particle case, a string *does* have additional, purely internal degrees of freedom — these are the oscillations of the string itself, whose additional energy contributions are represented by $L_0^{(\text{osc})}$, $\bar{L}_0^{(\text{osc})}$, and $a_{L,R}$. Thus, even though $\hat{m} = 0$, the resulting string state can still have a non-zero physical mass M in spacetime. Indeed, just as the mass-shell condition for massless point particles is given by $L_0^{(\text{com})} = \bar{L}_0^{(\text{com})} = 0$, the mass-shell condition for our scale-invariant string is generalized to $H = \bar{H} = 0$. This then becomes our scale-invariant mass-shell condition in string theory. Of course, spacetime Lorentz invariance still allows us to identify the physical spacetime mass M of a given string state via the relations $L_0^{(\text{com})} = \bar{L}_0^{(\text{com})} = -\alpha' M^2/4$. Thus, the string mass-shell conditions $H = \bar{H} = 0$ lead to the identifications

$$\frac{1}{4}\alpha' M^2 = L_0^{(\text{osc})} - 1, \qquad \frac{1}{4}\alpha' M^2 = \bar{L}_0^{(\text{osc})} - 1. \qquad (6.2.15)$$

Note that these two conditions can also be written in the form

$$\alpha' M^2 = 2\left(L_0^{(\text{osc})} + \bar{L}_0^{(\text{osc})} - 2\right) \qquad (6.2.16)$$

where we must obey the constraint

$$L_0^{(\text{osc})} = \bar{L}_0^{(\text{osc})} . \tag{6.2.17}$$

Interpreting the conditions (6.2.16) and (6.2.17) is easy. The condition (6.2.16) simply tells us that the physical spacetime mass M of a given string state (and thus the square of its center-of-mass momentum) is generated *solely* from its internal left- and right-moving vibrational excitations. The condition (6.2.17), by contrast, tells us that the mass of the string must come *equally* from left-moving and right-moving excitations. The latter condition (6.2.17) is often referred to as the *level-matching condition*, since it implies that a given string oscillator state is considered to be "on shell" (or "physical") only if the total excitation level of the left-movers matches the total excitation level of the right-movers. This condition implies that the string does not have an unbalanced "wobbling", for if such a wobbling existed, it could ultimately be used to determine a preferred coordinate system on the worldsheet (thereby breaking conformal invariance). Indeed, demanding invariance under shifts in the σ_1 variable leads directly to the condition (6.2.17). We remark, however, that states not satisfying (6.2.17) are nevertheless important for understanding the "off-shell" or "virtual" structure of string theory. Such "virtual" states contribute, for example, within loop amplitudes. In these lectures, however, we shall focus on only the so-called "tree-level" string spectrum for which the level-matching constraint (6.2.17) is imposed and the corresponding physical masses are given by (6.2.16).

6.2.3. *The spectrum of the bosonic string*

Having discussed the quantization of the bosonic string, we can now examine its spectrum. The procedure is simple: we simply consider all possible combinations of left- and right-moving mode excitations of the string worldsheet, subject to the level-matching constraint (6.2.17), and then we tensor these left- and right-moving states together to form the total resulting string state. The spacetime mass of this string state is then given by (6.2.16), and the properties of the state are deduced directly from the underlying vibrational configuration of the string.

The simplest state, of course, is the string vacuum state

$$|0\rangle_R \otimes |0\rangle_L \tag{6.2.18}$$

in which the right- and left-moving vacuum states are tensored together. This state trivially satisfies (6.2.17), which indicates that this state is indeed part of the physical string spectrum. Unfortunately, we see from (6.2.16) that this state has a negative squared mass — *i.e.*, the spacetime mass of this state is imaginary! This state is thus a *tachyon*. Making sense of this string state is problematic, and is one of the reasons that we shall not ultimately be interested in the bosonic string.

Let us continue, however. The first excited string state is

$$\tilde{\alpha}^{\mu}_{-1}|0\rangle_R \otimes \alpha^{\nu}_{-1}|0\rangle_L \ . \tag{6.2.19}$$

This state has $L_0^{(\text{osc})} = \bar{L}_0^{(\text{osc})} = 1$, and according to (6.2.16) is therefore massless. As evident from its Lorentz index structure, this state transforms under the spacetime Lorentz group as the tensor product of two spin-one Lorentz vectors. We can therefore decompose this tensor product into a spin-two state (the symmetric traceless component), a spin-one state (the antisymmetric component), and a spin-zero state (the trace). Mathematically, this is equivalent to the tensor-product rule for Lorentz transverse $SO(24)$ vector representations:

$$\mathbf{V}_{24} \otimes \mathbf{V}_{24} \ = \ \mathbf{1} \ \oplus \ \mathbf{276} \ \oplus \ \mathbf{299} \tag{6.2.20}$$

where $\mathbf{V}_8$ is the eight-dimensional vector representation, and where the $\mathbf{1}$ representation is the spin-zero state, the $\mathbf{276}$ representation is the spin-one state, and the $\mathbf{299}$ representation is the spin-two state.

How can we interpret these states? A massless spin-two state must, by Lorentz invariance, have equations of motion which are equivalent to the Einstein field equations of general relativity. Thus, we are forced to identify the spin-two (traceless symmetric) component of the state (6.2.19) as the *graviton* $g_{\mu\nu}$, which is the spin-two mediator of the gravitational interactions. The spin-one (antisymmetric) state within (6.2.19) is an antisymmetric tensor field, often denoted $B_{\mu\nu}$, and the spin-zero (trace) component is the so-called *dilaton*, denoted ϕ. Together, $(g_{\mu\nu}, B_{\mu\nu}, \phi)$ are called the *gravity multiplet*.

By identifying (6.2.19) with the gravity multiplet, we see that string theory becomes a theory that contains gravity! This in turn allows us to determine the value of our previously unfixed mass scale α'. We shall now sketch how this happens (with details available in GSW). It turns out that if one calculates loop amplitudes in string theory, one finds that $e^{-\phi}$ serves as a loop expansion parameter (*i.e.*, higher-loop amplitudes come multiplied by more powers of $e^{-\phi}$). Given this observation, it is natural to identify the string coupling constant as the vacuum expectation value of the dilaton:

$$g_{\text{string}} \ = \ e^{-\langle\phi\rangle} \ . \tag{6.2.21}$$

This string coupling constant describes the strength of string interactions. Given this definition, we then find that the graviton state couples to matter with the expected gravitational strength only if we choose

$$\alpha' = \frac{G_{\text{Newton}}}{g_{\text{string}}^2} \qquad (6.2.22)$$

where G_{Newton} is Newton's constant. Substituting this result into (6.2.5), we then find

$$M_{\text{string}} = g_{\text{string}} M_{\text{Planck}}, \qquad (6.2.23)$$

where $M_{\text{Planck}} \equiv 1/\sqrt{G_{\text{Newton}}}$. Thus, because it contains gravity, string theory becomes a theory whose fundamental mass scale is related to the Planck scale.

We can also construct more and more massive string states. Ultimately, these fill out an infinite tower of string states. It is clear that such additional states all have $\alpha' M^2 > 0$. Given the above value for α', this implies that these additional states all have Planck-scale masses. Such Planck-scale excited states are therefore not of direct relevance for string phenomenology. Let us note, however, one interesting fact about these states. For any given spacetime mass level M, the string state with maximum spin is achieved by exciting only the lowest vibrational modes α_{-1}^μ and $\tilde{\alpha}_{-1}^\mu$. We thus find that for a given spacetime mass M, the maximum spin $J_{\max}$ that can be realized is

$$\alpha' M^2 = 2J_{\max} - 4. \qquad (6.2.24)$$

For example, we see that the maximum spin that can be realized for a massless state is $J = 2$ (the graviton). The relation (6.2.24) was originally observed for hadron resonances, and historically gave rise to the so-called "dual resonance models" (which eventually became modern string theory). In such dual resonance models, the relation (6.2.24) describes a so-called "Regge trajectory", with α' serving as the so-called "Regge slope". It is for this reason that in modern string theory, we continue to refer to α' as the Regge slope.

Before concluding, let us briefly mention one further important issue. In ordinary four-dimensional quantum field theory, we know that a massless spin-one state (*e.g.*, a photon) naïvely has four distinct states (corresponding to the four components of a vector field A^μ). However, the underlying gauge invariance allows us to make a unitary gauge choice wherein only two of these states (the two helicity states) are truly physical. The timelike and longitudinal states decouple, leaving only the transverse components. In the above description of the string spectrum, however, we have taken a covariant approach analogous to the description of a photon as a four-component vector. One might then wonder which of these states are truly physical. This issue is an important one in string theory, and once again we cannot here provide a proper proof. We shall therefore make recourse to another

> **Great Leap #4:** The physical string states are those which are realized by exciting the oscillator modes of only the *transverse* coordinates X^i ($i = 1, ..., 24$).

Proving this statement requires showing that even after we have used conformal invariance to set the string worldsheet metric to $\eta_{\alpha\beta}$, there still remains sufficient freedom to make a further "gauge" choice wherein we set the oscillator modes of the timelike and longitudinal spacetime coordinates to zero. This gauge choice, which is called *light-cone gauge*, is thus the analogue of unitary gauge in quantum field theory, and essentially tells us that only the 24 transverse coordinates correspond to physical degrees of freedom in the string worldsheet action. An important by-product of this fact is that every remaining string state has a non-negative norm. This is non-trivial. For example, if our metric signature is chosen such that $\eta^{00} = -1$, then the state $\alpha_{-n}^{\mu=0}|0\rangle$ has a negative norm. However, one can demonstrate that in light-cone gauge all resulting states are physical and have non-negative norm.

6.2.4. *Summary*

Let us quickly review those features of the bosonic string that we shall need to bear in mind in subsequent lectures. We shall separate these features into worldsheet features and spacetime features.

Worldsheet: The worldsheet fields consist of D copies of the left- and right-moving spacetime coordinates X_L^μ and X_R^μ (the worldsheet bosons). The fact that these X coordinates are periodic as we traverse the closed string loop implies that they have integer modings α_n and $\tilde{\alpha}_n$, where $n \in \mathbb{Z}$. The relevant worldsheet symmetry is conformal invariance, which tells us that the number of these X^μ fields is $D = 26$ and also tells us that the vacuum energy corresponding to these fields is $a_L = a_R = -1$. As we have stated above, a useful way to think about these results is to imagine that there is a "background" conformal anomaly $c_{\text{background}} = -26$, and that each X^μ field makes a contribution $c_X = 1$. In general, the "background" conformal anomaly is only a function of the relevant worldsheet symmetry (in this case conformal invariance), and it will always remain true that $c_X = 1$. Thus, cancellation of the conformal anomaly requires $D = 26$. A similar interpretation can also be given to the vacuum energy. When calculating the vacuum energies, only the physical (*i.e.*, transverse) fields are relevant. It is a general result that each X field contributes $a_X = -1/24$ to the vacuum energy. Therefore, we find $a_L = a_R = 24 a_X = -1$.

Spacetime: The above worldsheet theory leads to the following features in spacetime. We find that the *spacetime dimension* (often called the *critical* spacetime dimension) is 26. The spectrum consists of a spinless tachyon, as well as a massless gravity multiplet consisting of the graviton $g_{\mu\nu}$, the antisymmetric tensor $B_{\mu\nu}$, and the dilaton ϕ. There is also an infinite tower of massive (Planck-scale) string states.

Comments: Two remarkable things have happened. First, we have a theory of quantized gravity! The graviton has emerged as the quantum excitation of a closed string. This alone is very exciting, but also somewhat mysterious. We started by assuming a closed string propagating through an external, fixed, flat spacetime. But this string itself includes a graviton mode, which implies a distortion in that background spacetime. This then acts back to change the worldsheet theory. Thus, in some sense, the string itself not only "creates" the spacetime in which it propagates, but is then affected by this change in the spacetime geometry. This coupling or interplay between the string and its spacetime is not fully understood, and is clearly at the heart of the many mysterious features of string theory as a theory of quantum gravity.

A second remarkable thing has also happened, although we have not demonstrated it explicitly. As indicated in (6.2.21), a coupling constant has been determined *not* as a free parameter, but rather *dynamically* as the vacuum expectation of a string field. It is in this sense that string theory contains no free parameters, and that all parameters such as coupling constants are determined dynamically.

There are, however, a number of drawbacks to this bosonic string theory. First, it contains a tachyonic state. We must somehow find a way to eliminate this. Second, all string excitations are spacetime *bosons* (*i.e.*, they have integer spin). We must find a way to obtain spacetime fermions. Third, there are no massless spin-one states (which we would wish to associate with gauge fields). Thus, there are no gauge symmetries. It is for these reasons that we shall go on to consider more complicated string theories.

And finally, there is another major drawback that we need to be aware of. Although it is compelling that the string coupling g_{string} is in principle determined dynamically, as the vacuum expectation value of the dilaton scalar field, in practice we do not understand how to calculate the potential of the dilaton field and thereby deduce its vacuum expectation value. In the bosonic string we are considering here, the dilaton potential $V(\phi)$ is actually divergent for all $\phi < \infty$, and so this question cannot be meaningfully addressed. However, even in the more realistic string theories to be discussed, this potential is either completely flat (as happens in a supersymmetric context), or generally takes a shape that sends $\langle\phi\rangle \to \infty$. This is the famous *dilaton runaway problem*. Solving this problem is perhaps one of the most important (unsolved) problems in string phenomenology.

How can we remedy these features? One possibility is prompted by the appearance of the tachyon. In ordinary quantum field theory, the existence of a tachyon (a state with a negative mass-squared) signals that the vacuum has been misidentified (as in the Higgs mechanism); the theory then "rolls" to a different vacuum configuration in which the tachyon is eliminated. So it is natural to speculate that perhaps the bosonic string theory also "rolls" to a new vacuum in such a way that the tachyon is no longer present and the dilaton is stabilized. Perhaps fermions and gauge fields might also appear in this new vacuum, as desired. However, as we have already indicated, it is not known how the bosonic string behaves in this context. We do not know if there exists a new ("stable") vacuum to roll to, and if so, what its properties might be. Of course, knowing the potential $V(\phi)$ would be extremely useful, yet as we indicated this potential is naïvely divergent and therefore requires some knowledge of the non-perturbative structure of string theory. So (at least for the time being) this option does not appear promising.

A second possibility, then, is simply to abandon the bosonic string and attempt to construct a new string theory altogether. And this is what we shall now do.

6.3. Lecture #3: Neutrinos are fermions: The superstring

As we saw in the last lecture, the bosonic string has two glaring failures: it contains a tachyon, and it does not give rise to spacetime fermions. Both of these features are troubling, especially since the announced goal of these lectures is to derive a neutrino from string theory, and we know that the neutrino is a fermionic object. We therefore seek to construct a new string theory which can give rise to excitations with half-integer spins.

6.3.1. *The action*

We have already seen that string theories are defined by their two-dimensional worldsheet actions. Thus, in order to construct a new string theory, we must construct a new worldsheet action. At the very least, this action should contain that of the bosonic string, since we still wish to retain the spacetime interpretatation that we had previously. Thus, our only option is to *introduce additional worldsheet fields* into the action:

$$S = -\frac{1}{4\pi\alpha'} \int d^2\sigma \; (\partial_\alpha X^\mu \partial^\alpha X_\mu + ...) \; . \qquad (6.3.1)$$

What new fields can we add? If our goal is to produce spacetime fermions, a natural guess would be to add worldsheet fermions! These would complement the worldsheet bosonic fields X^μ that are already present. For the moment, let us denote such fermionic fields schematically as ψ. We would then attempt to consider an action of the form

$$S = -\frac{1}{4\pi\alpha'} \int d^2\sigma \; \left(\partial_\alpha X^\mu \partial^\alpha X_\mu + \bar\psi i \rho^\alpha \partial_\alpha \psi\right) \; . \qquad (6.3.2)$$

Here $\psi(\sigma_1, \sigma_2)$ represents our two-dimensional fermionic fields, and ρ^α are an appropriate set of two-dimensional Dirac matrices (the analogues of the γ^μ matrices in four dimensions).

We then face a number of questions. First, how many ψ fields must we add? Second, what kinds of worldsheet fermions should these be? Should they be Dirac fermions, or Majorana fermions, or Majorana-Weyl fermions? Third, how should these two-dimensional spinors ψ transform under the (internal) $SO(D-1,1)$ spacetime Lorentz symmetry? We already know that the X^μ fields, for example, transform as vectors under this symmetry. Note that it is not obvious that the ψ fields should necessarily transform as spinors under $SO(D-1,1)$ and carry a spacetime spinor index. In particular, all we know thus far is that the ψ fields transform as spinors under worldsheet *two-dimensional* Lorentz transformations. This does not *a priori* give us any information about their *spacetime* transformation properties.

There is also another potential worry that appears if we try to add new worldsheet fields. We have already seen in the bosonic string that worldsheet conformal invariance was sufficiently powerful a symmetry to allow us to choose a light-cone gauge and thereby eliminate all negative-norm states. However, the presence of new worldsheet fields implies the existence of new quantum excitation modes in the resulting string spectrum, and some of these new states may also have negative norm. Thus, conformal symmetry may no longer be sufficient (and indeed would not be sufficient) to allow us to eliminate these states as well.

It turns out that all of these questions have a common answer: we can impose an extra symmetry beyond simple worldsheet conformal invariance. Indeed, the extra symmetry that we shall impose is nothing but worldsheet (*i.e.*, two-dimensional) *supersymmetry*. Specifically, we shall require that the ψ fields be the two-dimensional superpartners of the X fields, so that the resulting action has a manifest worldsheet (two-dimensional) supersymmetry.* This new theory will be called the *superstring*.

It is important to stress that this supersymmetry that we will be discussing is *not* the spacetime supersymmetry that might be seen in the next round of accelerator experiments. Instead, this is a *worldsheet* supersymmetry which stems directly from the worldsheet interpretation of the original Polyakov action (6.2.4), and which relates the worldsheet bosons X to worldsheet fermions ψ via a worldsheet supercurrent J.

Imposing this worldsheet supersymmetry then answers all of the questions we previously raised. How many ψ fields? The answer is D, one for each boson X^μ. What kind of ψ spinor? The answer is a Majorana (two-component) spinor. How does the ψ field transform under the $SO(D-1,1)$ spacetime Lorentz symmetry? The answer is that the ψ field must transform as a *vector* under the Lorentz symmetry, since the X^μ field (for which it is the worldsheet superpartner) also transforms as a vector. In other words, the *worldsheet* supersymmetry commutes with the *spacetime* Lorentz symmetry, and thus does not change the Lorentz index structure.

---

*We remark that this is only one possible choice, and will ultimately lead us to the so-called Ramond/Neveu-Schwarz (RNS) formalism. Another possible choice would be to demand *spacetime* supersymmetry, and to imagine that the ψ fields are the Grassmann coordinates θ of a super-spacetime. This possibility would then lead to the so-called Green-Schwarz (GS) formalism. It turns out that these two formalisms are ultimately equivalent, however, and both provide suitable descriptions of the resulting superstring theory. This equivalence is possible because the RNS superstring ultimately also has spacetime supersymmetry (as we shall discover below). In these lectures, however, we shall restrict our attention to the RNS formulation in which the ψ fields are *worldsheet* (rather than spacetime) superpartners of the X^μ fields. Aside from being more useful for string phenomenology, the RNS formalism has the philosophical advantage that it treats the *string* as the fundamental object, with the spacetime structure emerging as a *derived consequence*. The RNS formalism thus reinforces one of the central themes of these lectures, namely that we define a string theory by its worldsheet properties alone, and then deduce the spacetime effects of these properties as consequences. The GS formalism, on the other hand, has the benefit of being manifestly spacetime supersymmetric from the very beginning.

Thus, the ψ fields transform as spacetime vectors, and carry a spacetime vector index: $\psi^\mu(\sigma_1,\sigma_2)$.

This last point may initially seem confusing, so we reiterate: the ψ fields are worldsheet fermions, but spacetime bosons! They transform as spinors under worldsheet Lorentz transformations, but as vectors under the spacetime Lorentz transformations.

Given this, we can now explicitly write down the superstring action:

$$S = -\frac{1}{4\pi\alpha'}\int d^2\sigma\,\left(\partial_\alpha X^\mu \partial^\alpha X_\mu - i\bar\psi_\mu \rho^\alpha \partial_\alpha \psi^\mu\right)\,. \tag{6.3.3}$$

Our worldsheet fields are $X^\mu(\sigma_1,\sigma_2)$ and $\psi^\mu(\sigma_1,\sigma_2)$, and the μ index (with $\mu=0,1,2,...,D-1$) is a vector index with respect to the internal symmetry $SO(D-1,1)$. From the worldsheet perspective, each X^μ is a scalar field (containing one component), while each ψ^μ is a two-component spinor. The ρ^α are two-dimensional Dirac matrices satisfying the two-dimensional Clifford algebra $\{\rho^\alpha,\rho^\beta\}=-2\eta^{\alpha\beta}$, and $\bar\psi \equiv \psi^\dagger \rho^0$. One can then show that the action (6.3.3) is invariant under the worldsheet supersymmetry transformations $\delta X^\mu = \bar\epsilon\psi^\mu$, $\delta\psi^\mu = -i\rho^\alpha \epsilon \partial_\alpha X^\mu$, where ϵ is a constant anticommuting spinor that parametrizes the "magnitude" of the supersymmetry transformation. The corresponding generator of this worldsheet supersymmetry transformation is the worldsheet supercurrent $J_\alpha = \frac{1}{2}\rho^\beta \rho_\alpha \psi^\mu \partial_\beta X_\mu$.

It is convenient to choose a particular Weyl (chiral) representation for the two-dimensional ρ^α matrices:

$$\rho^0 = \begin{pmatrix} 0 & -i \\ i & 0 \end{pmatrix},\quad \rho^1 = \begin{pmatrix} 0 & i \\ i & 0 \end{pmatrix} \Longrightarrow \rho^0\rho^1 = \begin{pmatrix} 1 & 0 \\ 0 & -1 \end{pmatrix}\,. \tag{6.3.4}$$

Here the product $\rho^0\rho^1$ plays the role of the chirality operator (the analogue of γ_5 in four dimensions), and thus in this basis we can identify the upper and lower components of the two-component Majorana spinor ψ as being left-moving and right-moving respectively. Our worldsheet action (6.3.3) then decomposes into the form

$$S = -\frac{1}{4\pi\alpha'}\int d^2\sigma\,\left(\partial_\alpha X^\mu \partial^\alpha X_\mu - \psi_{\mu R}\partial_- \psi^\mu_R - \psi_{\mu L}\partial_+ \psi^\mu_L\right) \tag{6.3.5}$$

where $\partial_\pm$ are derivatives with respect to the left- and right-moving worldsheet coordinates $\sigma_1 \pm \sigma_2$. The worldsheet content of this theory therefore consists of D left-moving worldsheet bosons X_L, D right-moving worldsheet bosons X_R, D left-moving worldsheet Majorana-Weyl (one-component) fermions ψ_L, and D right-moving worldsheet Majorana-Weyl (one-component) fermions ψ_R. There are two worldsheet supercurrents in this theory:

$$J_L = \psi_{\mu L} \, \partial_+ X^\mu_L \,, \qquad J_R = \psi_{\mu R} \, \partial_- X^\mu_R \,. \qquad (6.3.6)$$

Note that our original goal in constructing the superstring had been to obtain spacetime fermions. However, it may seem from the above that we have failed in this regard, since we have only introduced new fields ψ which themselves are spacetime vectors. How then are we to obtain spacetime fermions? It turns out that this will happen in a surprising way.

Let us proceed to analyze this string following the same steps as we used for the bosonic string. First, we see that our worldsheet symmetry has been enlarged: rather than simply have conformal invariance, we now have conformal invariance *plus* worldsheet supersymmetry. Together, this is called *superconformal invariance*, which is a much larger symmetry than conformal invariance alone.

This enlargement of the worldsheet symmetry changes many of the features of the resulting string. The most profound is the value of the spacetime dimension D. Recall from our discussion of the bosonic string that associated with each worldsheet symmetry there is a particular "background" conformal (central charge) anomaly, and that it is necessary to choose a sufficient number of worldsheet fields so as to cancel this anomaly and ensure that conformal invariance is maintained even at the quantum level. The same argument applies here as well, except that

> **Great Leap #5:** The "background" conformal anomaly associated with *superconformal* invariance is not $c = -26$ but rather $c = -15$. Likewise, the conformal anomaly contribution from each worldsheet Majorana fermion is $c = 1/2$.

We can understand the origin of the "background" conformal anomaly $c = -15$ as follows. Just as in the bosonic string, a certain contribution $c = -26$ is attributable to the conformal ghosts resulting from conformal gauge fixing. The new feature here is that we now have an additional contribution $+11$ which is attributable to the worldsheet *superpartners* of these ghosts. Together, this produces a background anomaly $c = -15$. What this means is that we must choose the number D of worldsheet bosons and fermions such that this "background" anomaly is cancelled. We have already seen that the anomaly contribution from each worldsheet boson X^μ is $c_X = 1$. Since the anomaly contribution from each Majorana fermion is $c_\psi = 1/2$, we must satisfy

$$D\left(1 + \tfrac{1}{2}\right) - 15 = 0 \quad \implies \quad D = 10 \;. \tag{6.3.7}$$

Thus, we see that the critical dimension of the superstring is $D = 10$ rather than $D = 26$. Moreover, just as for the bosonic string, the *super*conformal symmetry of the superstring worldsheet action again allows us to choose a light-cone gauge in which only *eight* transverse bosons and *eight* transverse fermions represent the truly physical propagating worldsheet fields.

6.3.2. *Quantizing the superstring*

Let us now quantize the superstring, just as we did for the bosonic string. The boundary conditions (6.2.6) for the X^μ fields remain valid even for the superstring, since the X^μ continue to have the interpretation of spacetime coordinates. Therefore the mode-expansions (6.2.9) continue to apply.

The only new feature, then, is the mode-expansion for the fermionic fields ψ^μ. However, unlike the bosonic fields X^μ which must be periodic because of their interpretation as spacetime coordinates, these fermionic fields ψ^μ do not have any immediate interpretation in spacetime. Therefore, the only boundary conditions that might be imposed on these fields are those that are required directly from the symmetries of the action. In particular, we must choose boundary conditions for the ψ^μ fields so as to maintain the single-valuedness of the action as we traverse the closed string (*i.e.*, as $\sigma_1 \to \sigma_1 + \pi$), and so as to maintain the worldsheet supersymmetry of the action (whose algebra includes a requirement that the supercurrent square to the Hamiltonian, *i.e.*, $J \cdot J \sim H$). It turns out that are only two choices of boundary conditions that satisfy these requirements. One possibility is that the ψ^μ fields are periodic under $\sigma_1 \to \sigma_1 + \pi$:

$$\text{Ramond:} \quad \psi^\mu(\sigma_1 + \pi, \sigma_2) \;=\; + \,\psi^\mu(\sigma_1, \sigma_2) \;. \tag{6.3.8}$$

Such periodic boundary conditions are typically called "Ramond" (R) boundary conditions, after P. Ramond (who introduced these fermionic boundary conditions in 1971). The second possibility is that the ψ^μ fields are *anti*-periodic under $\sigma_1 \to \sigma_1 + \pi$:

$$\text{Neveu-Schwarz:} \quad \psi^\mu(\sigma_1 + \pi, \sigma_2) \;=\; - \,\psi^\mu(\sigma_1, \sigma_2) \;. \tag{6.3.9}$$

Such periodic boundary conditions are typically called "Neveu-Schwarz" (NS) boundary conditions, after A. Neveu and J. Schwarz (who introduced these fermionic boundary conditions in 1971). As we shall see in Lecture

#4, both of these boundary conditions are ultimately required for the self-consistency of the superstring.

In the case of periodic (Ramond) boundary conditions, the mode-expansion of the ψ^μ field resembles that of the X^μ field:

$$\text{Ramond:} \quad \psi_L^\mu(\sigma_1 + \sigma_2) = \sum_{n \in \mathbb{Z}} b_n^\mu \, e^{-2in(\sigma_1+\sigma_2)}$$

$$\psi_R^\mu(\sigma_1 - \sigma_2) = \sum_{n \in \mathbb{Z}} \tilde{b}_n^\mu \, e^{+2in(\sigma_1-\sigma_2)} \; . \quad (6.3.10)$$

Here $b_n^\mu, \tilde{b}_n^\mu$ are the (fermionic) creation and annihilation operators, satisfying the *anti*-commutation relations

$$\{b_m^\mu, b_n^\nu\} = \eta^{\mu\nu} \delta_{m+n} \quad (6.3.11)$$

where we recall the hermiticity condition $b_{-n}^\mu = (b_n^\mu)^\dagger$. The same relations hold for the right-moving modes as well. This hermiticity condition follows from the fact that the ψ fields are Majorana (*i.e.*, real) fields. Note that unlike the bosonic mode-expansion (6.2.9), we have joined the zero-modes together with the excited modes in (6.3.10).[†] There is also no "center-of-mass" term in the mode-expansion (a fermionic analogue of x^μ) because the ψ fields are Grassmann variables and thus lack a classical limit. Finally, also note that unlike the bosonic α_n^μ modes, which are rescaled relative to the usual harmonic oscillator modes by powers of the mode frequency n, the fermionic b_n^μ modes are defined without this rescaling and hence satisfy the usual harmonic-oscillator commutation relations (6.3.11) directly. This too is traditional in string theory.

In the case of anti-periodic (Neveu-Schwarz) boundary conditions, the mode-expansion of the ψ^μ field involves *half-integer* rather than integer modes:

$$\text{Neveu-Schwarz:} \quad \psi_L^\mu(\sigma_1 + \sigma_2) = \sum_{r \in \mathbb{Z}+1/2} b_r^\mu \, e^{-2ir(\sigma_1+\sigma_2)}$$

$$\psi_R^\mu(\sigma_1 - \sigma_2) = \sum_{r \in \mathbb{Z}+1/2} \tilde{b}_r^\mu \, e^{+2ir(\sigma_1-\sigma_2)} \; . \quad (6.3.12)$$

[†]We are cheating slightly here, since the treatment of Ramond zero-modes for Majorana worldsheet fermions is actually quite subtle. In some sense, each Majorana fermion has only "half" a zero-mode. We will provide a rigorous discussion of this fact in Lecture #5. In the meantime, it will suffice to ignore this subtlety.

Once again, $b_r^\mu, \tilde{b}_r^\mu$ are the (fermionic) creation and annihilation operators, satisfying the *anti*-commutation relations

$$\{b_r^\mu, b_s^\nu\} = \eta^{\mu\nu}\delta_{r+s} \qquad (6.3.13)$$

where we have the hermiticity condition $b_{-r}^\mu = (b_r^\mu)^\dagger$.

The expressions for the total energy of a given string configuration now receive contributions from not only the bosonic oscillator modes, as in (6.2.12), but also the fermionic oscillator modes. These new contributions are given by

$$\text{R:} \qquad L_0^{(\text{osc})} = \sum_{n=0}^{\infty} n\, b_{-n}^\mu b_{n\mu}$$

$$\text{NS:} \qquad L_0^{(\text{osc})} = \sum_{r=1/2}^{\infty} r\, b_{-r}^\mu b_{r\mu}\,, \qquad (6.3.14)$$

with similar expressions for the right-movers.

Finally, we must consider the vacuum energies a_L and a_R for the superstring. Recall that for the bosonic string, each of the 24 transverse X^μ fields contributed $a_X = -1/24$, yielding a total of $a_L = a_R = -1$. This contribution from each bosonic field remains the same for the superstring, so we continue to have $a_X = -1/24$. It therefore only remains to determine the vacuum-energy contributions from the worldsheet Majorana fermions, and it is found that

> **Great Leap #6:** Each Ramond fermion contributes vacuum energy $a_\psi = +1/24$, whereas each Neveu-Schwarz fermion contributes vacuum energy $a_\psi = -1/48$.

We thus see that like the bosons, the Neveu-Schwarz fermions contribute negative vacuum energies, while Ramond fermions contribute positive vacuum energies.

Given these mode-expansions and commutation relations, it is instructive to consider the Fock space of an individual Ramond (R) or Neveu-Schwarz (NS) fermion. It turns out to be simplest to consider the Fock space of an individual (left- or right-moving) NS fermion first. The two lowest-lying states are

$$\begin{array}{lll}
\text{vacuum:} & |0\rangle & L_0^{(\text{osc})} = 0 \\
\text{first-excited state:} & b_{-1/2}|0\rangle & L_0^{(\text{osc})} = 1/2\,.
\end{array} \qquad (6.3.15)$$

Note that relative to the vacuum, all further excited states are reached through only half-integer excitations. Also note that the vacuum of the NS Fock space is unique, just like that of the bosons X^μ. What this means is that from the spacetime perspective, the vacuum is spinless (and hence a spacetime bosonic state), and that all subsequent excitations of the vacuum are also spacetime bosons. Recall, in this connection, that the fermion mode operators b are only fermionic from the worldsheet perspective; they are still bosonic operators (just like the fields ψ^μ themselves) relative to *spacetime* Lorentz symmetries.

Let us now consider the corresponding Fock space for the Ramond fermions with periodic boundary conditions. Once again, we have a tower of states

$$\text{vacuum:} \quad |0\rangle \quad L_0^{(\text{osc})} = 0$$
$$\text{first-excited state:} \quad b_{-1}|0\rangle \quad L_0^{(\text{osc})} = 1 \qquad (6.3.16)$$

which now continues upwards through integer, rather than half-integer, steps. However, in this case it is important to observe that we also have a *zero-mode* in the theory. The existence of this zero-mode means that it is possible to excite this zero-mode without increasing the overall energy of the state. We therefore have the additional tower of states

$$\text{vacuum:} \quad b_0^\dagger|0\rangle \quad L_0^{(\text{osc})} = 0$$
$$\text{first-excited state:} \quad b_{-1}b_0^\dagger|0\rangle \quad L_0^{(\text{osc})} = 1 \; . \qquad (6.3.17)$$

(Note that b_0 and $b_0^\dagger$ are equivalant.) In other words, combining (6.3.16) and (6.3.17), we see that the Ramond vacuum consists of *two degenerate states*,

$$|0\rangle \quad \text{and} \quad b_0^\dagger|0\rangle \; , \qquad (6.3.18)$$

and that all further excitations maintain this two-fold degeneracy.

How can we interpret this two-fold degeneracy of the Ramond vacuum? It may seem, at first, that both of the states in (6.3.18) cannot be considered as the true vacuum, because the second state in (6.3.18) appears to be realized as a zero-mode excitation of the first. However, let us define the first state in (6.3.18) as $|V_0\rangle$ and let us also define $|V_1\rangle \equiv \sqrt{2}b_0^\dagger|0\rangle$, which is a rescaling of the second state in (6.3.18). Then using (6.3.11), it is easy to show that

$$|V_1\rangle = \sqrt{2}b_0^\dagger|V_0\rangle \; , \quad |V_0\rangle = \sqrt{2}b_0^\dagger|V_1\rangle \; . \qquad (6.3.19)$$

Thus, we see that neither state in (6.3.18) is more fundamental than the other, and there exists an unbroken symmetry between them — they are realized as zero-mode excitations of each other. The interpretation of this fact is that the true Ramond vacuum state is a two-component object, a spacetime spinor! It then follows that all of the excited states in the Ramond spectrum are also spacetime spinors, since they are realized as non-zero-mode excitations of a spinorial ground state.

Of course, the above discussion is only suggestive, since we have not proven that these two vacuum states actually form a Lorentz spinor representation with respect to the spacetime Lorentz algebra. However, it is easy to see that this is indeed the case. Observe from (6.3.11) that the zero-modes satisfy the algebra $\{b_0^\mu, b_0^\nu\} = \eta^{\mu\nu}$. Thus, if we define $\Gamma^\mu \equiv \sqrt{2}ib_0^\mu$, then we see that $\{\Gamma^\mu, \Gamma^\nu\} = -2\eta^{\mu\nu}$, which is nothing but the spacetime Clifford algebra. In other words, the zero-modes act as spinorial gamma-matrices. This implies that all states built upon such a vacuum state will transform in spinor representations of the spacetime Lorentz symmetry group $SO(D-1,1)$, and hence will be spacetime fermions.

This is a remarkable result. Even though we have introduced worldsheet ψ^μ fields which are spacetime bosons and which carry a spacetime Lorentz *vector* index, the algebra of zero-modes in the case of Ramond boundary conditions has managed to change these vector indices into spinor indices and thereby produce spacetime fermions. Of course, this is completely analogous to what happens in the usual four-dimensional Dirac equation, where the γ^μ matrices are matrices in a spinor space but nevertheless carry vector indices. Thus, we see that by choosing Ramond boundary conditions for worldsheet fermions, string theory affords us with the same possibility. We therefore now see that string theory can indeed give rise to spacetime fermions: while excitations of worldsheet Neveu-Schwarz fermions give rise to spacetime bosons, excitations of worldsheet Ramond fermions give rise to spacetime fermions.

6.4. Lecture #4: Some famous superstrings

The next step is to determine the spectrum of the full superstring, just as we did for the bosonic string. However, the presence of two possibilities (Neveu-Schwarz and Ramond) for the modings of the fermions introduces several new complications relative to the bosonic string, and enables us to make different choices for what kind of superstring we wish to construct. These different choices are typically called different "string models", and so we are finally in a position to begin to discuss string model-building. That is the subject of the present lecture.

6.4.1. *String sectors*

Recall from the previous lecture that in light-cone gauge, the worldsheet field content of the ten-dimensional superstring consists of eight right-moving bosons X_R, eight right-moving Majorana-Weyl (one-component) fermions ψ_R, and a similar set of left-moving fields X_L and ψ_L. The bosons X_L and X_R must have periodic (integer) modings because of their interpretation as spacetime coordinates, but their worldsheet fermionic superpartners ψ_L and ψ_R can have either Ramond (periodic, integer) or Neveu-Schwarz (anti-periodic, half-integer) modings. The question then immediately arises: What rules govern the possible self-consistent choices of fermion modings? *A priori*, the appearance of 16 distinct fermions would seem to lead to 2^{16} different choices.

It is easy to see that not all possibilities are allowed, however. One quick way to see this is to realize that if some of the right-moving fermions had different periodicities than other right-moving fermions, then these different periodicities would necessarily break spacetime Lorentz invariance because these fermions carry a spacetime vector index μ. A similar situation would also hold for the left-moving fermions. This would then imply that all of the right-moving fermions should have the same periodicity as each other, and that all of the left-moving fermions should have the same periodicity as each other (though not necessarily the same as that of the right-moving fermions). However, this argument is not really satisfactory because we do not necessarily wish to preserve the full *ten*-dimensional Lorentz invariance (or even its eight-dimensional transverse subgroup); after all, our sole phenomenological requirement is that *four*-dimensional Lorentz invariance must be maintained. Moreover, it goes against the spirit of string theory (as we have been presenting it) that we should demand a certain phenomenological property of the resulting *spacetime* physics when formulating our worldsheet theory. In string theory the spacetime physics is a *consequence* of the worldsheet physics, and we would ultimately like to base our worldsheet choices directly on worldsheet symmetries.

Fortunately, it is easy to find a worldsheet argument that leads to the same constraint. Recall that the worldsheet symmetry that we must maintain is superconformal invariance. The worldsheet supersymmetry that makes up superconformal invariance is generated by the two worldsheet supercurrents given in (6.3.6). Because these two supercurrents are also worldsheet fermionic, they may also be either periodic or anti-periodic as we traverse the closed string. Indeed, each individual term $\psi^\mu \partial X_\mu$ in these supercurrents will have the periodicity property of the fermion ψ^μ. However, in order for each of these supercurrents J_R and J_L to have a unique, well-defined periodicity as we traverse the closed string, we see that it is necessary that all right-moving fermions have the same periodicity as each other, and that all left-moving fermions have the same periodicity as each other. This is required in order to preserve worldsheet supersymmetry. Thus, we have our first constraints on fermion modings:

- All right-moving fermions ψ_R^μ must have the same periodicity as each other, either Ramond or Neveu-Schwarz.
- All left-moving fermions ψ_L^μ must have the same periodicity as each other, either Ramond or Neveu-Schwarz.

Note that there is no requirement that the right- and left-moving periodicities be the same.

Table 6.1. The four possible sectors of the ten-dimensional superstring, numbered 1 through 4. Here 'NS' and 'R' respectively indicate Neveu-Schwarz (anti-periodic) and Ramond (periodic) boundary conditions for worldsheet fermions, and a_R and a_L respectively denote the corresponding right- and left-moving vacuum energies.

#	$\psi_R^{i=1,\ldots,8}$	$\psi_L^{i=1,\ldots,8}$	a_R	a_L
1	NS	NS	$-1/2$	$-1/2$
2	R	R	0	0
3	R	NS	0	$-1/2$
4	NS	R	$-1/2$	0

Given these constraints, we see that we are left with four distinct periodicity choices for our sixteen Majorana-Weyl worldsheet fermions, as shown in Table 6.1. Each individual choice is called a *sector* or *spin structure* of the superstring, so we see that the ten-dimensional superstring has four possible sectors. For future convenience, these sectors have been numbered in Table 6.1. We have also indicated the corresponding right- and left-moving vacuum energies of these sectors. Recall from the previous lecture (in particular, Great Leap #6) that the vacuum-energy contribution of each Ramond fermion is $+1/24$, while that of each Neveu-Schwarz fermion is $-1/48$ and that of each worldsheet boson is $-1/24$. Therefore, generally assuming $n_{\rm NS}$ Neveu-Schwarz fermions and $n_{\rm R}$ Ramond fermions, we can add these individual contributions to find

$$a \;=\; -\frac{1}{24}\left(8 - n_{\rm R} + \tfrac{1}{2} n_{\rm NS}\right) \;=\; -\frac{n_{\rm NS}}{16}\;. \qquad (6.4.1)$$

The second equality results from setting $n_{\rm R} = 8 - n_{\rm NS}$. Of course, as discussed above, in the ten-dimensional superstring we are restricted to the cases $n_{\rm NS} = 0, 8$ for both the right- and left-moving fermions.

6.4.2. *Modular invariance and GSO projections*

The next question that arises is whether we are free to pick any one of these sectors to construct our superstring theory, or whether we must consider all of them together, superposing the spectrum from each sector separately in order to construct the full superstring spectrum. What rules govern the choices of sectors?

Ultimately, it turns out that a special form of conformal invariance known as *modular invariance* will give us the answer. In keeping with the spirit of these lectures, we will not be able to provide a proper mathematical discussion of modular invariance. (Indeed, doing so would require a preliminary discussion of string partition functions and the modular group.) However, we can discuss the relevance and implications of modular invariance at a conceptual level.

Recall from Lecture #2 that our string actions always have a certain symmetry known as conformal invariance, which reflects the fact that the action should be invariant under *local* reparametrizations and rescalings of the coordinates (σ_1, σ_2) that parametrize the string worldsheet. For *tree*-level string interactions, demanding this *local* symmetry is sufficient to ensure that the resulting physics is indeed invariant under arbitrary coordinate reparametrizations. This is because any tree-level string interaction has the topology of a sphere (a genus-zero surface, with no handles), and on a sphere it can be shown that any possible net coordinate reparametrization can be generated or "built up" in small steps as the cumulative effect of small, local coordinate reparametrizations. Geometrically, this is equivalent to saying that any closed loop on the surface of a sphere can be continuously shrunk to a point, as illustrated in Fig. 6.7(a), by sliding the loop along the surface of the sphere towards one side. Thus, demanding invariance under *local* coordinate reparametrizations (*i.e.*, conformal invariance) by itself is sufficient to guarantee consistency for tree-level string amplitudes.

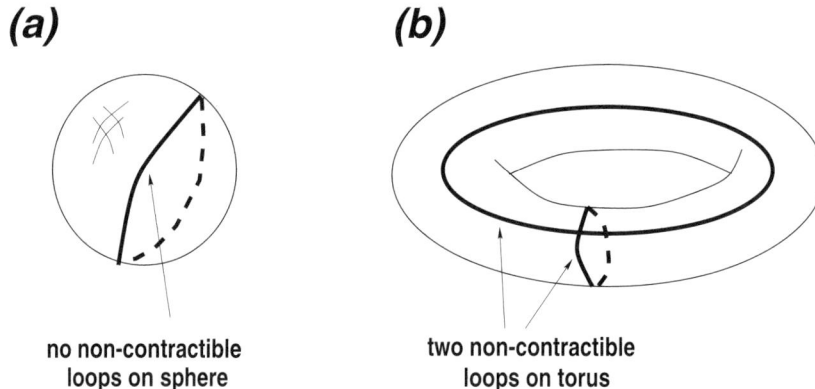

(a) no non-contractible loops on sphere

(b) two non-contractible loops on torus

Fig. 6.7. (a) On a sphere, all closed loops can be continuously shrunk to a point. (b) On a torus, there exist two topologically distinct non-contractible loops.

However, this situation changes drastically if we now consider one-loop amplitudes. As discussed in Lecture #1, these amplitudes have the worldsheet topology of a *torus* (a genus-*one* surface), and we see from Fig. 6.7(b) that on a torus there exist *two* types of closed loops that cannot be continuously shrunk to a point. Such loops are said to be *non-contractible*, which is indeed the defining property of such higher-genus surfaces. The presence of these non-contractible loops means that for torus diagrams, there exist possible coordinate reparametrizations that *cannot* be built up from local coordinate reparametrizations alone. Indeed, these reparametrizations non-trivially involve "large", discrete mappings around these non-contractible loops. Thus, we see that demanding conformal invariance alone is not sufficient to ensure that one-loop string amplitudes are truly invariant under worldsheet coordinate reparametrizations: we must also demand an invariance under these "large" discrete mappings around these non-contractible loops. This additional global invariance is called "modular invariance", and just like conformal invariance, it too stems from our need to maintain the overall invariance of the string under reparametrizations and rescalings of the worldsheet coordinates.

One might wonder, at this stage, why we are suddenly worrying about modular invariance, whereas we did not need to consider modular invariance in Lecture #2 when we discussed the bosonic string. The truth of the matter is that we must *always* consider modular invariance in addition to conformal invariance, regardless of the type of (closed) string we are discussing. However, in the simple case of the 26-dimensional bosonic string, it turns out that all amplitudes are trivially modular-invariant, so we did not need to make recourse to modular invariance in order to distinguish between different possibilities. However, for the superstring (and particularly for the heterotic string to be discussed later), the possible sector choices become quite numerous, and it turns out that modular invariance is the powerful tool by which we are able to narrow down the self-consistent possibilities.

What, then, are the effects of modular invariance? It turns out that at the level of string model-building, modular invariance has two primary effects:

- it forces us to consider only certain selected *sets* or *combinations* of underlying sectors, and
- it produces new *constraints* (beyond the level-matching constraint $L_0 = \bar{L}_0$) that govern which Fock-space excitations are allowed in each sector.

These new constraints are called *GSO constraints*, after F. Gliozzi, J. Scherk, and D. Olive who first imposed some of these constraints in 1977. The important point is that these conditions stem directly from modular invariance, and thus they follow from the worldsheet physics of the string and do not represent any additional arbitrary input. We will provide many explicit examples of such combinations and constraints shortly.

In order to construct a fully consistent string model, therefore, our procedure is as follows. First, we must determine which are the allowed sectors that need to be considered as part of our set. For each of these sectors in our allowed set, we then determine the corresponding Fock space of physical states by applying not only the usual level-matching constraint, but also the GSO constraints appropriate for that sector. In this way each underlying sector then gives rise to a different Fock space of states, and the full Hilbert space of states for the full string theory (*i.e.*, for the resulting string "model") is nothing but the direct sum of these different Fock spaces corresponding to each of the underlying sectors in the specified set. This then yields a fully self-consistent (and in particular, modular-invariant) theory.

This is an important point, so it is worth repeating: the full Hilbert space of string states is given by the direct sum of the different Fock spaces corresponding to different underlying boundary conditions for worldsheet fields. In order to better understand this fact, an analogy with QCD may be useful. Recall that Yang-Mills quantum field theory contains non-perturbative instanton solutions, and therefore one can imagine doing quantum field theory in an n-instanton background $|n\rangle$. Of course, as we know, the full vacuum state of QCD is not composed of any one of these $|n\rangle$ vacua by itself, but rather by an appropriately weighted *combination* of these vacua:

$$|\theta\rangle = \sum_n e^{in\theta} |n\rangle . \qquad (6.4.2)$$

This is the famous θ-vacuum of QCD. The situation that we now face in string theory is somewhat analogous. The fact that the string worldsheet fermions can have different boundary conditions (thereby giving rise to different sectors) is in some sense analogous to the fact that QCD can have different instanton backgrounds. Indeed, each underlying string sector is analogous to a different n-instanton vacuum state $|n\rangle$, and the different "combinations of sectors" that we are now being forced to consider are analogous to the different QCD θ-vacua. In this sense, then, each different "string model" that we will be constructing can be viewed as a different θ-vacuum of string theory! Of course, this analogy with the QCD θ-vacuum can take us only so far. One important difference is that whereas the θ-vacuum necessarily involves *all* of the $|n\rangle$ states regardless of the value of θ, in string theory our "vacuum" may consist of more complicated combinations of sectors which may or may not include all possible sectors. In fact, the more sectors that are included in our "combination of sectors", the more GSO constraints there are for each sector. But the important lesson that emerges from all of this is that no single sector by itself forms a consistent string vacuum; rather, we must select an appropriate combination of sectors and add together their corresponding Fock spaces in order to produce the fully self-consistent string model.

In Lecture #7, we shall provide an explicit set of rules which will enable us to quickly determine the appropriate sector combinations and GSO constraints that can be chosen in order to yield self-consistent theories. For the time being, however, we shall defer a discussion of these rules and proceed directly with the construction of actual string models in order to deduce their physical properties. Therefore, even though we shall simply assert certain sector combinations and GSO projections to be required by modular invariance, we stress that all of these features can (and ultimately will) be derived using the rules to be presented in Lecture #7.

6.4.3. Ten-dimensional superstring models

In the case of the ten-dimensional superstring, we have already seen that the four possible sectors are listed in Table 6.1. It then only remains to determine the particular sector combinations and GSO constraints that are required by modular invariance. In this case, it turns out that there are only two possible combinations or sets of sectors that can be considered:

- we consider the contributions from only Sectors #1 and #2, or
- we consider the contributions from *all* Sectors #1 through #4.

Moreover, for each of the above cases, it turns out that there are two possible choices of GSO projections that may be imposed in each sector. Thus, combining all of these possibilities, we see that there are four distinct possible superstring "models" that can be constructed in ten dimensions. We shall therefore now turn to a construction of these models.

6.4.3.1. *The Type 0 strings*

Let us begin by considering the first option, taking our set of sectors to consist only of Sectors #1 and #2. For each of these sectors, we need to determine the appropriate GSO constraints that must be applied in addition to the usual level-matching constraint. In order to write down these GSO constraints, let us first recall that for a given left-moving worldsheet fermion (with either Ramond or Neveu-Schwarz boundary conditions), the corresponding number operator is defined by

$$\text{R}: \quad N^{(i)} = \sum_{n=0}^{\infty} b^i_{-n} b_{ni}$$

$$\text{NS}: \quad N^{(i)} = \sum_{r=1/2}^{\infty} b^i_{-r} b_{ri} \,. \quad (6.4.3)$$

Here the index $i = 1, ..., 8$ labels the individual fermion. For right-moving fermions, the analogous number operators $\bar{N}^{(i)}$ are constructed using the right-moving mode operators $\tilde{b}_n, \tilde{b}_r$. Let us also define N_L and N_R respectively as the total left- and right-moving number operators, *i.e.*,

$$N_L \equiv \sum_{i=1}^{8} N^{(i)}, \quad N_R \equiv \sum_{i=1}^{8} \bar{N}^{(i)} \,. \quad (6.4.4)$$

Note that these number operators are defined to include only the contributions of the worldsheet *fermions*, and in particular do not include the contributions of the worldsheet bosons. It then turns out (and we shall see in Lecture #7) that if we choose our set of sectors to consist only of Sectors #1 and #2, then the appropriate GSO constraints in each sector are as follows:

$$\text{Sector \#1:} \qquad N_L - N_R = \text{even}$$
$$\text{Sector \#2:} \qquad N_L - N_R = \left\{ \begin{array}{c} \text{odd} \\ \text{even} \end{array} \right\} . \qquad (6.4.5)$$

In the second line, we have used a brace notation to indicate a further choice: we can choose to impose *either* the 'odd' constraint, or the 'even' constraint. As we shall see, this is a residual choice that is not fixed by modular invariance (or by any other worldsheet symmetry), leading to two equally valid possibilities. Thus, we see that if we choose our set of sectors to consist of only Sectors #1 and #2, then this leads to *two different string models* depending on our subsequent choice of which GSO constraint we choose to impose in (6.4.5).

Let us now determine the spectra of these two models, beginning with the states that arise from Sector #1. Note that in this sector, both models have the same states (because both models have the same GSO constraint for Sector #1). As with the bosonic string, our procedure is to consider all possible excitations of the worldsheet fields (in this case, the worldsheet fermions as well as the worldsheet bosons). These excitations are subject to the level-matching constraint $L_0 = \bar{L}_0$ (which ensures that the total bosonic and fermionic worldsheet *energy* is distributed equally between left- and right-moving excitations) and the GSO constraint $N_L - N_R = \text{even}$ (which is a constraint on the worldsheet *number* operators of the worldsheet fermions only). In general, the mass-shell condition for the superstring is

$$\alpha' M^2 = 2 (L_0 + \bar{L}_0 + a_L + a_R) \qquad (6.4.6)$$

where a_L and a_R are the individual left- and right-moving vacuum energies, and where L_0 and $\bar{L}_0$ include the contributions from not only the worldsheet bosons, but also the worldsheet fermions. Note from Table 6.1 that the left- and right-moving vacuum energies in Sector #1 are $a_L = a_R = -1/2$.

We see that the tachyonic vacuum state $|0\rangle_R \otimes |0\rangle_L$ satisfies both constraints, and thus it remains in the spectrum. However, unlike the tachyon in the bosonic string (which has spacetime mass $\alpha' M^2 = -4$), we see from (6.4.6) that the tachyonic state in the superstring has spacetime mass $\alpha' M^2 = -2$. This is the result of the smaller (less negative) vacuum energy of the superstring compared to that of the bosonic string.

Because the vacuum energies in Sector #1 are $a_L = a_R = -1/2$, we see that massless states cannot be obtained by exciting the quantum modes of worldsheet bosons, for each of these excitations would add a full unit of energy. Instead, massless states can be obtained only by adding a half-unit of energy. Fortunately, this is possible in Sector #1 because in this sector, all worldsheet fermions have Neveu-Schwarz boundary conditions and therefore have half-integer modings. The first excited states in Sector #1 are therefore

$$\tilde{b}^{\mu}_{-1/2}|0\rangle_R \otimes b^{\nu}_{-1/2}|0\rangle_L \ . \tag{6.4.7}$$

Note that these states satisfy both the level-matching constraint (since $L_0 = \bar{L}_0 = 1/2$) as well as the GSO constraint (since $N_L = N_R = 1$). The interpretation of these states is precisely the same as in the bosonic string: these states give us the gravity multiplet, consisting of the graviton $g_{\mu\nu}$, dilaton ϕ, and anti-symmetric tensor $B_{\mu\nu}$. Mathematically, this is equivalent to the tensor-product rule for Lorentz transverse $SO(8)$ vector representations:

$$\mathbf{V}_8 \otimes \mathbf{V}_8 \ = \ \mathbf{1} \ \oplus \ \mathbf{28} \ \oplus \ \mathbf{35} \tag{6.4.8}$$

where $\mathbf{V}_8$ is the eight-dimensional vector representation, and where the **1** representation is the spin-zero state, the **28** representation is the spin-one state, and the **35** representation is the spin-two state. It is indeed a general principle that *all* weakly coupled closed strings contain at least these massless states, and this is a useful cross-check of the GSO constraints.

Let us now turn to the states from Sector #2. Before concerning ourselves with the implication of the GSO constraints in (6.4.5), let us first understand the general structure of the states from this sector. In this sector, the vacuum energy (according to Table 6.1) is $(a_R, a_L) = (0, 0)$, so we see immediately that this sector contains no tachyons. Indeed, the ground state is already massless, so all that will concern us here is the nature of this ground state. As we discussed at the end of Lecture #3, the left- and right-moving ground states in this sector are each spacetime *spinors* since all worldsheet fermions in this sector have Ramond boundary conditions. Because the nature of these spinors will be important to us, let us pause to review some properties of these spinors.

Since we are considering these ten-dimensional strings in light-cone gauge, the Lorentz group that concerns us here is the transverse ("little") Lorentz group $SO(8)$. In general, the groups $SO(2n)$ share a number of properties. Their smallest representations, of course, are simply the identity representations. These are singlets, which will be denoted **1**. The next representations are the vector representations, which are $(2n)$-dimensional, and which will be denoted $\mathbf{V}_{2n}$. Along with these are the spinor representations, which are (2^{n-1})-dimensional. In general, there are two types of spinor representations, **S** and **C**, the so-called "spinor" and "conjugate spinor" representations. In the special case of $SO(8)$, the vector, spinor, and conjugate spinor representations are all eight-dimensional, and will be denoted $\mathbf{V}_8$, $\mathbf{S}_8$, and $\mathbf{C}_8$ respectively. The distinction between $\mathbf{S}_8$ and $\mathbf{C}_8$ is one of spacetime *chirality*, but the choice of which is to be associated with a given physical chirality is a matter of convention.

The ground state of Sector #2 has the structure

$$\{\tilde{b}_0^\mu\} |0\rangle_R \otimes \{b_0^\nu\} |0\rangle_L \qquad (6.4.9)$$

where the notation $\{b_0^\mu\}$ (and similarly for the right-movers) indicates that each of the individual Ramond zero-modes can be either excited or not excited.

How can we interpret (6.4.9) physically? This issue is actually quite subtle, and we shall not have the space to give a proper discussion. Moreover, as we have already indicated, we are not giving a fully rigorous treatment of Ramond zero-modes in these lectures, since our aim is to focus more on the physics than the formalism. However, it is possible to understand the appropriate physical interpretation intuitively. First, let us *count* the number of states in (6.4.9). A priori, it would seem that we have 2^{16} individual states, since each Ramond fermion zero-mode can either be excited or not excited. However, this is not correct because (as we shall discuss more completely in Lecture #5, and as we have already hinted in the footnote in Sec. 3.2), one should really count only one zero-mode per *pair* of Ramond Majorana-Weyl fermions. Thus, we can imagine that there are only four independent zero-modes for the right-movers, and four for the left-movers. Therefore, (6.4.9) consists of only $2^8 = 128$ states.

All combinations of these zero-mode excitations already satisfy the level-matching constraint (since $L_0 = \bar{L}_0 = 0$). Imposing either of the GSO constraints for Sector #2 in (6.4.5) then reduces the number of allowed states by a factor of two. Specifically, if we impose the constraint $N_L - N_R = $ odd, then we can choose only an even number of right-moving zero-mode excitations together with an odd number of left-moving zero-mode excitations, or an odd number of right-moving excitations together with an even number of left-moving excitations. Choosing the constraint $N_L - N_R = $

even has the opposite effect, pairing even numbers of excitations for left- and right-movers with each other, and likewise pairing odd numbers with each other.

Interpreting these results is therefore quite simple. As we discussed at the end of Lecture #3, the left-moving states and right-moving states are spacetime spinors, and we have already seen that there are two possible spinors, $\mathbf{S}_8$ and $\mathbf{C}_8$. At this stage, the names assigned to each are arbitrary, so we shall now establish the following convention: spinors realized by an even number of zero-mode excitations will be identified with $\mathbf{C}_8$, and those realized by an odd number of zero-mode excitations will be identified with $\mathbf{S}_8$. Of course, only the relative difference between these two spinors is physically significant (having the interpretation of spacetime chirality).

Given these definitions, we see that if we choose the first GSO constraint $N_L - N_R =$ odd, the 128 states in (6.4.9) decompose into

$$(\bar{\mathbf{C}}_8 \otimes \mathbf{S}_8) \oplus (\bar{\mathbf{S}}_8 \otimes \mathbf{C}_8) , \quad (6.4.10)$$

whereas if we choose the second GSO constraint $N_L - N_R =$ even, these states instead decompose into

$$(\bar{\mathbf{C}}_8 \otimes \mathbf{C}_8) \oplus (\bar{\mathbf{S}}_8 \otimes \mathbf{S}_8) . \quad (6.4.11)$$

If we wish to further decompose these states into representations of the Lorentz group, we can use the $SO(8)$ tensor-product relations

$$\mathbf{S}_8 \otimes \mathbf{S}_8 = \mathbf{1} \oplus \mathbf{28} \oplus \mathbf{35'}$$
$$\mathbf{C}_8 \otimes \mathbf{C}_8 = \mathbf{1} \oplus \mathbf{28} \oplus \mathbf{35''}$$
$$\mathbf{S}_8 \otimes \mathbf{C}_8 = \mathbf{V}_8 \oplus \mathbf{56} . \quad (6.4.12)$$

Here the **28** representation is the anti-symmetric component of the spinor tensor product (spin-one), while the **35'** and **35''** representations are the symmetric components of the spinor tensor product (also spin-one). (These latter representations are not to be confused with the spin-two **35** graviton representation in (6.4.8).) Likewise, the **56** is a certain vectorial (spin-one) higher-dimensional representation.* However, for our present purposes it

---
*For the mathematically inclined reader, we can succinctly describe all of these states as follows. Recall that a given representation is called a p-form if it can be realized as the totally anti-symmetric combination within the tensor product of p different vector indices of $SO(8)$, with resulting dimension $8 \times 7 \times 6 \times ... \times (9-p)/p!$. Using this language, we see that singlet states are zero-forms, the **28** representations are two-forms, and the **35'** and **35''** representations are "self-dual" four-forms. (The self-duality condition eliminates exactly half of the degrees of freedom in the four-form.) Likewise, the $\mathbf{V}_8$ state is a one-form, and the **56** representation is a three-form. These different forms (and the

will be sufficient to think of these states in the tensor-product forms (6.4.10) and (6.4.11). Note that in each case, the tensor product of two spacetime fermionic (spinor) states produces a spacetime bosonic state. Thus, just as in Sector #1, the states emerging in Sector #2 are spacetime bosons.

Thus, summarizing, we see that the spectra of our two resulting superstring models are as follows. First, from Sector #1, we have the tachyonic state $|0\rangle_R \otimes |0\rangle_L$. In the notation of $SO(8)$ Lorentz representations, this state may be denoted $\bar{\mathbf{1}} \otimes \mathbf{1}$; this tachyon is a Lorentz singlet. Next, we have the massless gravity multiplet. In the notation of $SO(8)$ Lorentz representations, this state takes the form $\bar{\mathbf{V}}_8 \otimes \mathbf{V}_8$. Finally, from Sector #2, we have massless states whose form depends on the particular choice of the GSO projection. In the first case, we have the states given in (6.4.10), while in the second case, we have the states given in (6.4.11). There are then, as usual, an infinite tower of massive (Planck-scale) states above these.

The string model produced by the first GSO projection is called the *Type 0A* string model, and the second is called the *Type 0B* string model. Collectively, these are sometimes simply called the Type 0 strings. As we see, both of these strings are tachyonic, and moreover they contain only bosonic states. Furthermore, as is evident from (6.4.10) and (6.4.11), both of these strings are non-chiral. In other words, they are invariant under the transposition $\mathbf{S}_8 \leftrightarrow \mathbf{C}_8$ for the left- and right-movers. These string theories were first constructed by N. Seiberg and E. Witten in 1985. Although not relevant for phenomenology, they are currently proving to have an important role in understanding certain non-perturbative aspects of non-supersymmetric string theory.

6.4.3.2. *The Type II strings*

Let us now turn to the second choice outlined at the beginning of Sec. 4.3, namely the case in which we consider the contributions from *all* of the sectors in Table 6.1. This will result in the so-called *Type II strings*. As we discussed at the end of Sec. 4.2, it is a general property that the larger the set of sectors that we consider, the more GSO constraints there are that must be imposed in each sector. Thus, the introduction of new sectors generally leads to new GSO constraints in each of the sectors (old and new), and likewise the introduction of new GSO constraints in a given sector requires the introduction of entire new sectors to compensate.

---

so-called *D-branes* whose existence they imply) are important when considering the non-perturbative structure of these string theories.

It turns out (and we shall see explicitly in Lecture #7) that if we consider the full set of sectors in Table 6.1, then the appropriate GSO constraints in each sector are given as follows:

$$\begin{aligned}
\text{Sector \#1:} \quad & N_L - N_R = \text{odd}, \quad N_R = \text{odd} \\
\text{Sector \#2:} \quad & N_L - N_R = \left\{\begin{array}{c}\text{odd}\\ \text{even}\end{array}\right\}, \quad N_R = \text{odd} \\
\text{Sector \#3:} \quad & N_L - N_R = \text{even}, \quad N_R = \text{odd} \\
\text{Sector \#4:} \quad & N_L - N_R = \left\{\begin{array}{c}\text{odd}\\ \text{even}\end{array}\right\}, \quad N_R = \text{odd}.
\end{aligned} \quad (6.4.13)$$

Note that in each case where a choice is possible, these choices are correlated: we simultaneously choose either the top lines within all braces, or the bottom lines. Thus, once again there are two sets of GSO conditions that can be imposed, resulting in two distinct string models.

Before proceeding further, it is useful to note the *pattern* of these GSO projections. In the case of the Type 0 strings, we considered only Sectors #1 and #2; as shown in Table 6.1, these were the sectors for which the right-moving fermions were always identical to the left-moving fermions and shared the same boundary conditions. The corresponding GSO projections in (6.4.5) likewise did not distinguish between right- and left-moving fermions. (In this context, note that the GSO projections in (6.4.5) can equivalently be written with minus signs replaced by plus signs.) Thus, in some sense, the Type 0 strings are symmetric under exchange of left- and right-movers. However, for the Type II strings, we have now introduced two additional sectors (Sectors #3 and #4) whose structure explicitly breaks this symmetry between left- and right-movers. No longer does each sector individually exhibit this left/right symmetry. As we see from (6.4.13), the effect of this breaking is to introduce additional GSO conditions which mirror this broken symmetry by becoming sensitive to right- or left-moving number operators *by themselves*. The technical word for this breaking of symmetry is "twisting" or "orbifolding", for by including Sectors #3 and #4, we see that we have twisted the left-movers relative to the right-movers by allowing them to have oppositely moded boundary conditions. Thus, the Type II strings that will result can be viewed as twisted (or orbifolded) versions of the Type 0 strings. This twisting procedure ultimately serves as the means by which more and more complicated (and more and more phenomenologically realistic) string models may be constructed, and will be discussed more fully in Lecture #7.

Given the GSO constraints in (6.4.13), we can proceed to determine the resulting spectrum just as we did for the Type 0 strings. Let us begin with Sector #1 (this is often called the "NS-NS sector"). Because the boundary conditions of the worldsheet fermions are the same in this sector as they were for the Type 0 strings, the possible states that arise are the same as they were for the Type 0 strings, and consist of the tachyon $|0\rangle_R \otimes |0\rangle_L$ as well as the gravity multiplet (6.4.7). The only difference is that we must now impose the additional GSO constraint $N_R = $ odd. It is immediately clear that the effect of this new GSO constraint is that *the tachyon is projected out of the spectrum*, while the gravity multiplet is retained. Thus, by "twisting" the Type 0 strings in just this way, we have succeeded in curing one of the major problems of the bosonic and Type 0 strings, namely the appearance of tachyons. Moreover, we have done this *without* eliminating the desirable gravity multiplet.

Let us now consider the states from Sector #2 (this is often called the "Ramond-Ramond" sector). Once again, if we impose only the first GSO constraint in (6.4.13), we obtain the states in either (6.4.10) or (6.4.11). Imposing the additional GSO constraint in (6.4.13) then enables us to project out half of these states, so that we retain only the states

$$\bar{\mathbf{S}}_8 \otimes \begin{Bmatrix} \mathbf{C}_8 \\ \mathbf{S}_8 \end{Bmatrix} . \tag{6.4.14}$$

These states are spacetime bosons.

Finally, let us consider the states that arise in the new Sectors #3 and #4. In Sector #4, the vacuum energy is $(a_R, a_L) = (-1/2, 0)$. Therefore, in order to have level-matching ($L_0 = \bar{L}_0$), we see that we are immediately forced to excite a half-unit of energy for the right-movers while not increasing the energy of the left-movers. This is the only way to produce a massless state. This also ensures that this sector does not give rise to tachyons. Fortunately, since the right-moving fermions have Neveu-Schwarz boundary conditions in this sector, these fermions have half-integer modings, and thus by exciting their lowest modes we can indeed introduce a half-unit of energy. The left-moving fermions have Ramond boundary conditions in this sector, and hence their ground state is the Ramond zero-mode state. The massless states in Sector #4 therefore take the form

$$\tilde{b}^\mu_{-1/2} |0\rangle_R \otimes \{b^\nu_0\} |0\rangle_L . \tag{6.4.15}$$

At this stage, of course, these states satisfy only the level-matching constraint. Imposing the GSO constraints then leaves us with the state in which we excite only an even (or odd) number of left-moving Ramond zero modes.

How can we interpret this state? First, we notice that this state is a spacetime *fermion* because it results from tensoring a right-moving Neveu-Schwarz state with a left-moving Ramond state. Thus, we now have a string theory that contains spacetime fermions! This is yet another benefit of performing the "twist" that takes us from the Type 0 strings to the Type II strings. However, let us examine this state a bit more closely. Clearly, it has the Lorentz structure

$$\overline{\mathbf{V}_8} \otimes \begin{Bmatrix} \mathbf{C}_8 \\ \mathbf{S}_8 \end{Bmatrix} \qquad (6.4.16)$$

where we have retained the spinor-labelling conventions that we employed for the Type 0 strings. The relevant tensor-product decompositions in this case are given by

$$\overline{\mathbf{V}_8} \otimes \mathbf{C}_8 = \mathbf{S}_8 \oplus \mathbf{56}'$$
$$\overline{\mathbf{V}_8} \otimes \mathbf{S}_8 = \mathbf{C}_8 \oplus \mathbf{56}'' \qquad (6.4.17)$$

where the $\mathbf{S}_8$ and $\mathbf{C}_8$ representations are spin-1/2 and where the $\mathbf{56}'$ and $\mathbf{56}''$ representations are spin-3/2. Thus, we see that the Type II strings contain a massless, spin-3/2 object! Just as a massless spin-two object satisfies the Einstein field equations and must be interpreted as the graviton, a massless spin-3/2 object must be interpreted as a *gravitino* — i.e., a superpartner of the graviton. This implies that this string not only gives rise to spacetime bosons *and* fermions, but actually gives rise a spectrum which exhibits *spacetime supersymmetry*! This is yet another phenomenologically compelling feature.

Finally, let us now consider Sector #3. This sector has vacuum energies $(a_R, a_L) = (0, -1/2)$, so now we must excite right-moving zero-modes and left-moving $b^\mu_{-1/2}$ modes. This then leads to states of the form

$$\{\tilde{b}^\mu_0\}|0\rangle_R \otimes b^\nu_{-1/2}|0\rangle_L , \qquad (6.4.18)$$

and imposing the GSO projections results in states with the Lorentz structure $\bar{\mathbf{S}}_8 \otimes \mathbf{V}_8$. Once again, this also contains a gravitino!

So what do we have in the end? The first choice of GSO projections results in the so-called *Type IIA string*, while the second choice results in the *Type IIB string*. Both of these strings are tachyon-free, and their spectra contain both bosons and fermions. Moreover, these strings exhibit *spacetime* supersymmetry. This is most easily seen in the following suggestive way. Let us collect together the states from all four sectors, retaining our Lorentz-structure tensor-product notation:

$$\overline{\mathbf{V}}_8 \otimes \mathbf{V}_8 , \quad \overline{\mathbf{S}}_8 \otimes \left\{ \begin{array}{c} \mathbf{C}_8 \\ \mathbf{S}_8 \end{array} \right\} , \quad \overline{\mathbf{V}}_8 \otimes \left\{ \begin{array}{c} \mathbf{C}_8 \\ \mathbf{S}_8 \end{array} \right\} , \quad \overline{\mathbf{S}}_8 \otimes \mathbf{V}_8 . \quad (6.4.19)$$

Together, this collection of states can be written in the factorized form

$$\left(\overline{\mathbf{V}}_8 \oplus \overline{\mathbf{S}}_8 \right) \otimes \left(\mathbf{V}_8 \oplus \left\{ \begin{array}{c} \mathbf{C}_8 \\ \mathbf{S}_8 \end{array} \right\} \right) . \quad (6.4.20)$$

We thus see that there are *two* spacetime supersymmetries exhibited in this massless spectrum: the first exchanges $\overline{\mathbf{V}}_8 \leftrightarrow \overline{\mathbf{S}}_8$ amongst the right-movers, while the second exchanges

$$\mathbf{V}_8 \leftrightarrow \left\{ \begin{array}{c} \mathbf{C}_8 \\ \mathbf{S}_8 \end{array} \right\} \quad (6.4.21)$$

amongst the left-movers. Thus, the massless spectrum exhibits $N = 2$ supersymmetry. This is, of course, consistent with the appearance of two gravitinos in the massless spectrum (one from Sector #3 and one from Sector #4). Another way to understand this $N = 2$ supersymmetry is to realize that the first supersymmetry relates the bosonic states in Sector #1 to the fermionic states in Sector #3 (and the bosons in Sector #2 to the fermions in Sector #4), while the second supersymmetry relates the bosons in Sector #1 to the fermions in Sector #4 (and the bosons in Sector #2 to the fermions in Sector #3). In either case, we thus see that we have two independent spacetime supersymmetries.

It is important to note that we did not demand spacetime supersymmetry when constructing the superstring. We merely introduced *worldsheet* supersymmetry, and found that spacetime supersymmetry emerged naturally as the result of certain GSO projections. This further illustrates the fact that in string theory, spacetime properties such as supersymmetry emerge only as the consequences of deeper, more fundamental *worldsheet* symmetries. Another important point is that the same "twist" which eliminated the tachyon has introduced spacetime supersymmetry. While this is certainly an interesting phenomenon that arises for ten-dimensional superstrings, it is certainly *not* a general property that the elimination of the tachyon requires spacetime supersymmetry. In particular, we shall see in Lecture #6 that it is possible to construct string theories whose tree-level spectra lack spacetime supersymmetry but nevertheless are tachyon-free.

One might question whether we have really demonstrated the existence of $N = 2$ supersymmetry, since we have examined only the massless spectrum. However, it can be shown that any unitary theory which contains a massless spin-$3/2$ state necessarily exhibits supersymmetry, and hence must be supersymmetric at all mass levels (*i.e.*, for all massive, excited states as well). Of course, this is still not a proof, since we do not *a priori* know (and would therefore need to verify) that string theory is a consistent theory in this sense. However, it is possible to construct (two) explicit spacetime supercurrent operators and to demonstrate that they commute with the full (massless and massive) spectrum of the string. Another approach (as indicated in the footnote in Sec. 3.1) is to develop an alternative formulation of the superstring in which *spacetime* (rather than worldsheet) supersymmetry is manifest at the level of the string action, and to demonstrate the equivalence of the two formulations. Indeed, both approaches have been successfully carried out, thereby demonstrating that the Type II spectrum is indeed $N = 2$ supersymmetric. It is for this reason that these strings are referred to as Type II strings.

One important distinction between these two strings is their chirality. The Type IIA string, as we see, contains two supersymmetries of opposite chiralities, interchanging $\bar{\mathbf{V}}_8 \leftrightarrow \bar{\mathbf{S}}_8$ for the right-movers and $\mathbf{V}_8 \leftrightarrow \mathbf{C}_8$ for the left-movers. Equivalently, the two gravitinos associated with these supersymmetries are of opposite chiralities (because the $\mathbf{56'}$ and $\mathbf{56''}$ representations in (6.4.17) are of opposite chiralities). Because it contains supersymmetries of both chiralities, this string is ultimately non-chiral, and its low-energy (field-theoretic) limit consists of so-called *Type IIA supergravity* (whose discovery predates that of the Type IIA string). It is for this reason that this string is called the Type IIA string. The Type IIB string, by contrast, contains two supersymmetries (or two gravitinos) of the *same* chirality, exchanging $\bar{\mathbf{V}}_8 \leftrightarrow \bar{\mathbf{S}}_8$ and $\mathbf{V}_8 \leftrightarrow \mathbf{S}_8$ respectively. Thus, this string theory is *chiral*, and has a low-energy field-theoretic limit consisting of Type IIB supergravity.

We conclude, then, that by introducing a twist relative to the Type 0 strings, we have constructed a set of strings (the Type IIA and Type IIB strings) that exhibit a number of compelling features: they are tachyon-free, they contain both bosons and fermions in their spacetime spectra, they contain gravity, and they are spacetime $N = 2$ supersymmetric. Despite this success, however, there is still something that we lack: we do not, as yet, have gauge symmetries. Specifically, there are no gauge bosons (such as photons, gluons, or W and Z particles). Likewise, there are no states which carry gauge charges. Therefore, once again, we shall need to construct a new kind of string.

6.5. Lecture #5: Neutrinos have gauge charges: The heterotic string

6.5.1. Motivation and alternative approaches

Thus far in these lectures, we have shown how string theory can give rise to quantized gravity, spacetime bosons and fermions, spacetime supersymmetry, and tachyon-free spectra. There is, however, one important phenomenological feature that is still missing: *gauge symmetry*. In other words, we wish to have massless gauge bosons, *i.e.*, spacetime vectors that transform in the adjoint representation of some internal symmetry group. As a side issue, we would also like to find a way of breaking $N=2$ supersymmetry to $N=1$ supersymmetry (if our goal is to reproduce the MSSM) or even to $N=0$ supersymmetry (if our goal is to reproduce the Standard Model).

It is worth considering why such gauge-boson states fail to appear for the ten-dimensional Type II strings discussed in the previous lecture. The problem is the following. In order to produce worldsheet bosons, we are restricted to considering only the NS-NS or Ramond-Ramond sectors (Sectors #1 and #2 in Table 6.1). In the NS-NS sector (Sector #1), the vacuum energy is $(a_R, a_L) = (-1/2, -1/2)$, so we must excite the half-energy fermionic mode oscillators $\tilde{b}^\mu_{-1/2}, b^\mu_{-1/2}$ for the both the left- and right-movers. This produces a state with *two* vector indices rather than one, and as we see from the vector-vector tensor-product decomposition in (6.4.8), this does not contain a vectorial state. In the Ramond-Ramond sector (Sector #2), by contrast, the vacuum energy is $(a_R, a_L) = (0, 0)$, which implies that our massless states comprise the tensor product of two Ramond spinors as in (6.4.10) for the Type IIA string, or as in (6.4.11) for the Type IIB string. In the case of the Type IIB string, we see from (6.4.12) that the tensor product $\bar{\mathbf{S}}_8 \otimes \mathbf{S}_8$ does not contain a vector state $\mathbf{V}_8$. Thus, the Type IIB string contains no massless vectors. In the case of the Type IIA string, we observe from (6.4.17) that indeed $\bar{\mathbf{S}}_8 \otimes \mathbf{C}_8 \supset \mathbf{V}_8$, and thus the Type IIA string does contain a massless vector. (This state is often called a "Ramond-Ramond gauge boson".) However, the $U(1)$ "gauge" symmetry associated with this state is too small to contain the Standard-Model gauge group, and moreover it can be shown that no states in the perturbative spectrum of the Type IIA string spectrum can carry this Ramond-Ramond charge.*

In each case, the fundamental obstruction that we face is that we need to generate representations of a *gauge group* (*i.e.*, an internal symmetry group) that is *different* from the Lorentz group. Until now, all of our worldsheet fields (such as $X^\mu_{L,R}$ and $\psi^\mu_{L,R}$) have carried Lorentz indices associated with the $SO(D-1,1)$ Lorentz symmetry. In order to produce a separate gauge symmetry, we therefore need fields which do *not* carry a Lorentz index but which carry a purely internal index. (Note that these fields cannot carry a Lorentz index because we ultimately want our gauge symmetries to commute with the Lorentz symmetries.)

How can we do this? One idea is to *compactify* the Type II strings that we constructed in the previous lecture. Although this approach ultimately fails for phenomenological reasons, it will be instructive to briefly explain this idea. Recall that for the superstring, the critical dimension $D = 10$ emerges as the result of an anomaly cancellation argument: each worldsheet boson X contributes $c_X = 1$, each Majorana fermion ψ^μ contributes $c_\psi = 1/2$, and thus ten copies of each are necessary in order to cancel the "background" central charge associated with the worldsheet superconformal symmetry. But, even though we require ten bosons and ten fermions, there is no reason why we must endow *all* of them with Lorentz vector indices μ. Since we are ultimately interested in four-dimensional string theories, one natural idea is to consider these ten bosons and ten fermions in two groups, four with indices $\mu = 0, 1, 2, 3$, and the remaining six with purely internal indices $i = 1, ..., 6$. This internal symmetry could then be interpreted as a gauge symmetry.

This idea is in fact reminiscent of the original Kaluza-Klein idea whereby gauge symmetries are realized from higher-dimensional gravitational theories upon compactification. Moreover, this idea does succeed in producing gauge bosons (and gauge symmetries) in dimensions $D < 10$. However, the problem is that this idea fails to produce *enough* gauge symmetry. Specifically, although we obtain gauge symmetries that are large enough to contain the Standard Model gauge symmetry $SU(3) \times SU(2) \times U(1)$, we cannot obtain massless representations that simultaneously transform as

---

*Despite this fact, Ramond-Ramond charge plays a crucial role in recent developments concerning string duality. While none of the states in the *perturbative* Type IIA string spectrum carry Ramond-Ramond charge, these strings also contain non-trivial *solitonic* states (so-called *D-branes*) which do carry Ramond-Ramond charge. We shall briefly discuss D-branes in Lecture #8.

triplets of $SU(3)$ and doublets of $SU(2)$. Such "quark" representations are required phenomenologically. Thus, even though this compactification idea is interesting as a way of generating certain amounts of gauge symmetry, it cannot be used in order to save the superstring.

What we require, then, is a different way of introducing worldsheet fields without Lorentz vector indices. Since we will (temporarily) abandon the idea of removing Lorentz indices from our ten worldsheet bosons and fermions, what this means is that we require a way of obtaining *even more worldsheet fields* in ten dimensions. In other words, if we want bigger gauge symmetries in $D = 4$, then we require more than six extra fields with internal indices i, which in turn means that we already want extra fields even in the original ten-dimensional interpretation.

But how can we introduce extra worldsheet fields without violating our previous conformal anomaly cancellation arguments? Just adding extra fields will reintroduce the conformal anomaly at the quantum level.

6.5.2. *The heterotic string: Constructing the action*

The idea, of course, is to abandon the Type II string and proceed to construct a new kind of string that can accomplish the goal. This string is called the *heterotic* string, and it is this string that will be our focus for the remainder of these lectures. This string was first introduced by D. Gross, J. Harvey, E. Martinec, and R. Rohm in 1985, and for more than a decade dominated (and still continues to play a pivotal role in) discussions of string phenomenology.

Let us begin by recalling the action of the bosonic string:

$$S_{\text{bosonic}} = -\frac{1}{4\pi\alpha'} \int d^2\sigma \left\{ (\partial_- X_R^\mu)^2 + (\partial_+ X_L^\mu)^2 \right\} . \qquad (6.5.1)$$

Here the worldsheet symmetry is simply conformal invariance, which requires that we take $\mu = 0, 1, ..., 25$ in order to cancel the conformal anomaly. Clearly, this action contains lots of worldsheet fields. However, we saw in Lecture #2 that this string does not give rise to spacetime fermions.

Next, we considered the superstring, whose action is given by:

$$S_{\text{super}} = -\frac{1}{4\pi\alpha'} \int d^2\sigma \left\{ (\partial_- X_R^\mu)^2 - \psi_R^\mu \partial_- \psi_{R\mu} + (\partial_+ X_L^\mu)^2 - \psi_L^\mu \partial_+ \psi_{L\mu} \right\} . \qquad (6.5.2)$$

Here the worldsheet symmetry is *superconformal* invariance, which requires that we take $\mu = 0, 1, ..., 9$ in order to cancel the superconformal anomaly. Unlike the bosonic string, this string gives rise to spacetime fermions. But as we have just explained, this string does not contain enough worldsheet fields to give rise to appropriate gauge symmetries.

Clearly, each of these strings has an advantage lacked by the other. The natural solution, then, is to attempt to "weld" them together, to "crossbreed" them in such a way as to retain the desirable attributes of each. But how can this be done?

The fundamental observation is that we are always dealing with *closed* strings, and for closed strings, we have seen that the left- and right-moving modes are essentially independent of each other and form separate theories. Indeed, only the level-matching constraint $L_0 = \bar{L}_0$ serves to relate these two halves to each other, but even this constraint applies at the level of the physical Fock space rather than the level of the action. Therefore, since these two halves are essentially independent, a natural idea is to construct a new hybrid string whose left-moving half is the left-moving half of the bosonic string, but whose right-moving half is the right-moving half of the superstring. As we shall see, this fundamental idea is just what we need. The resulting string is therefore called a *heterotic* string, where the prefex *hetero-* indicates the joining of two different things.

Given this idea, let us now see how the action for the heterotic string can be constructed. We shall do this in three successive attempts. Our first attempt would be to write an action of the form

$$S = -\frac{1}{4\pi\alpha'} \int d^2\sigma \left\{ (\partial_- X_R^\mu)^2 - \psi_R^\mu \partial_- \psi_{R\mu} + (\partial_+ X_L^\mu)^2 \right\}. \quad (6.5.3)$$

In this case, the worldsheet symmetry would be conformal invariance for the left-movers, but superconformal invariance for the right-movers.

But what is the spacetime dimension of such a string? If we consider the right-moving sector, then just as in the superstring we would require $D = 10$, so that $\mu = 0, 1, ..., 9$. But given this, how do we interpret the left-moving side of the heterotic string? On the left-moving side, cancellation of the *conformal* (rather than superconformal) anomaly requires that we still retain 26 X_L fields! But if only ten of these fields are spacetime coordinates, then the remaining sixteen must be mere internal scalar fields. In other words, rather than carry the μ index (which would imply that these X fields would transform as vectors under the spacetime Lorentz group $SO(9,1)$), these sixteen extra fields must instead carry a purely internal index $i = 1, ..., 16$. So our second attempt at writing a heterotic string action would result in an action of the form

$$S = -\frac{1}{4\pi\alpha'} \int d^2\sigma \left\{ (\partial_- X_R^\mu)^2 - \psi_R^\mu \partial_- \psi_{R\mu} + (\partial_+ X_L^\mu)^2 + (\partial_+ X_L^i)^2 \right\} \quad (6.5.4)$$

where we have explicitly separated the left-moving bosons into two groups, with $\mu = 0, 1, ..., 9$ and $i = 1, ..., 16$.

But there still remains a subtlety. We cannot simply *decide* to remove the μ index from the X fields and make no other changes, because these X^i fields would continue to have a mode-expansion of the form (6.2.9) with the μ index replaced by an internal index i. While the interpretation of the oscillation exponential terms in (6.2.9) is not problematic, how would we interpret the "zero-mode" terms $x^i + \ell^2 p^i (\sigma_1 + \sigma_2)$? In the case of the spacetime coordinate fields X^μ, recall that these "zero-mode" quantities x^i and p^i are interpreted as the center-of-mass position and momentum of the string. But for purely internal fields X^i, this interpretation is problematic. To clarify this difficulty, let us consider the worldsheet energy $L_0^{(\text{com})}$ associated with these degrees of freedom, as in (6.2.13). Just as in the case of the spacetime coordinates X^μ, these worldsheet energies for the X^i fields would *a priori* take *continuous* values, thereby leading to a continuous spectrum even in $D = 10$. A continuous spectrum, of course, indicates nothing but the appearance of extra spacetime dimensions, so even though we may have replaced the index μ with the index i, we have not really solved the fundamental problem that there are too many uncompactified degrees of freedom amongst the left-movers.

Therefore, we still must find a way to replace this continuous spectrum with a discrete one. Because the following discussion is slightly technical and outside the main line of the development of the heterotic string action, we shall separate it from the main flow of the text. The reader uninterested in the following details can skip them completely and proceed directly to the resumption of the main text.

> In order to eliminate this continuous spectrum, we must compactify these extra sixteen dimensions. This is analogous to discretizing the continuous spectrum of a free particle (plane wave) by localizing it in a box. In the present case, we can choose to compactify each of these extra spacetime "coordinates" X^i on a circle of radius R_i. What this means, operationally, is that we make the fol-

lowing topological identification in *spacetime*:

$$X^i \iff X^i + 2\pi R_i \; . \tag{6.5.5}$$

For simplicity (and as we shall see, without loss of generality), we shall take $R_i = R$ for all i. Thus, rather than demand simple periodicity of the X^i "coordinates" as in (6.2.6) as we traverse the closed string worldsheet, we must allow for the more general possibility

$$X^i(\sigma_1+\pi,\sigma_2) = X^i(\sigma_1,\sigma_2)+2\pi n_i R \; , \quad n_i \in \mathbb{Z} \tag{6.5.6}$$

where the integer n_i is called the "winding number". The interpretation of this condition is that as we traverse the closed string once on the *worldsheet* (*i.e.*, as $\sigma_1 \to \sigma_1 + \pi$), the spacetime "coordinate" field X^i traverses the compactified spacetime circle n_i times. In other words, the closed string "winds" around the ith compactified *spacetime* circle n_i times. Because of this compactification, we see that the momentum p^i is now quantized (as we would expect for any particle in a periodic box of length R), and is restricted to take the values $p^i = m_i/R$, $m_i \in \mathbb{Z}$. Indeed, working out the most general mode-expansion consistent with (6.5.6), we find that a given such coordinate X^i takes the form

$$X(\sigma_1,\sigma_2) = x + 2nR\sigma_1 + \ell^2 \frac{m}{R}\sigma_2 + \text{oscillators} \; , \tag{6.5.7}$$

where $\ell \equiv \sqrt{2\alpha'}$ is our fundamental length scale and where 'oscillators' generically denotes the higher frequency modes. This decomposes into left- and right-moving components

$$X_{L,R}(\sigma_1 \pm \sigma_2) = \tfrac{1}{2}x + \left(\frac{\alpha' m}{R} \pm nR\right)(\sigma_2 \pm \sigma_1) + \text{oscillators} \; . \tag{6.5.8}$$

Comparing (6.5.8) with (6.2.9) enables us to identify the left- and right-moving compactified momenta

$$p_{L,R} \equiv \frac{m}{R} \pm \frac{nR}{\alpha'} \; . \tag{6.5.9}$$

We would then simply keep X_L in our heterotic theory.

Let us pause here to note an interesting phenomenon: this mode-expansion is invariant under the simultaneous exchange $R \leftrightarrow \alpha'/R$, $m \leftrightarrow n$. This is a so-called *T-duality*. What this means is that unlike point particles, strings cannot distinguish between extremely large spacetime compactification radii and extremely small spacetime compactification radii. Indeed, although the usual momentum m/R is extremely small in the first case and extremely large in the second, we see from the above mode-expansions that there is another contribution to the momentum, a "winding-mode momentum" nR/α', which compensates by growing large in the first case and small in the second. Since there is no physical way of distinguishing between these two types of momenta, the string spectrum is ultimately invariant under this T-duality symmetry. This duality underlies many of the unexpected physical properties of strings relative to point particles, and has important (and still not well-understood) implications for string cosmology. More importantly, however, this duality dramatically illustrates the breakdown of the traditional (field-theoretic) view of the linearly ordered progression of length scales and energy scales as we approach the string scale.

Having succeeded in avoiding the consequences of a continuous momentum p^i, our final question is the size of the radius R. It would certainly be aesthetically undesirable if we were forced to incorporate a new, fundamental, unfixed parameter R into our string theory. Fortunately, it turns out that in $D = 10$, there are only a very restricted set of possibilities that lead to consistent theories, and these restrictions imply that we can restrict our attention to the simple case $R = \ell = \sqrt{2\alpha'}$ *without loss of generality*. Thus, we see that R can be taken to be at the string scale, and hence essentially unobservable to "low-energy" measurements.

In order to see what is special about this radius, recall that the conformal anomaly contribution for each worldsheet boson is $c_X = 1$, while the conformal anomaly contribution for each worldsheet Majorana (real) fermion is $c_\psi = 1/2$. This suggests that the spectrum of a single compactified boson X might somehow be related to the spectrum of two Majorana fermions ψ_1, ψ_2, and this is indeed the case. Such a relation is typically referred to as a "boson-fermion equivalence" (which is possible in two dimensions because the usual spin-statistics distinction between bosons and fermions does not apply in two dimensions). In general, the spectrum of a compactified boson is identical to the spectrum of two Majorana fermions which are *coupled* to each other in a radius-dependent manner, and $R = \sqrt{2\alpha'}$ is the only value of the radius for which this coupling vanishes. Thus, if X is compactified on a circle of radius $R = \sqrt{2\alpha'}$, then the spectrum of quantum excitations of X is identical to the spectrum of quantum excitations of two *free* Majorana fermions ψ_1, ψ_2 (or equivalently those of one *complex* fermion $\Psi \equiv \psi_1 + i\psi_2$).[†] In fact, at a mathematical level, it turns out that this equivalence takes the form of an actual *equality* between the product $\psi_1 \psi_2$ and the partial derivative ∂X. Note, however, that while this specific radius is special from the point of view of boson/fermion equivalence, this is *not* the self-dual radius with respect to the T-duality transformation $R \leftrightarrow \alpha'/R$.

The upshot, then, is that in the action (6.5.4), we are free to replace the worldsheet bosons X^i ($i = 1, ..., 16$) with *complex* worldsheet fermions Ψ^i ($i = 1, ..., 16$). For ten-dimensional heterotic strings, we shall see that this replacement can be made *without loss of generality*. This replacement suffices to make the center-of-mass "momenta" associated with the X^i fields discrete rather than continuous, as we require. Given this, the final action for the heterotic string takes the form:

$$S_{\text{heterotic}} = -\frac{1}{4\pi\alpha'} \int d^2\sigma \left\{ (\partial_+ X_L^\mu)^2 - \bar{\Psi}_L^i \partial_+ \Psi_L^i + (\partial_- X_R^\mu)^2 - \psi_R^\mu \partial_- \psi_{R\mu} \right\}$$
(6.5.10)

[†]We are again cheating slightly here. The rigorous statement is that we must compactify the X boson on a so-called $\mathbb{Z}_2$ orbifold with this radius in order for the spectrum of X to be identical to that of two free Majorana fermions. The equivalence between these bosonic and fermionic systems can be demonstrated explicitly at the level of their full underlying left/right two-dimensional conformal field theories. By contrast, compactifying X on a *circle* of this radius yields the spectrum of a single *complex* fermion, and the full left/right conformal field theory corresponding to a single complex fermion actually differs from that corresponding to two real fermions. These distinctions between circles and orbifolds, and likewise between a single complex fermion and two real fermions, will not be relevant for what follows.

where ψ_R are Majorana-Weyl (real) right-moving worldsheet fermions, where Ψ_L are complex Weyl left-moving fermions, and where $\mu = 0, 1, ..., 9$ and $i = 1, ..., 16$.

6.5.3. Quantizing the heterotic string

The next step, then, is to quantize the worldsheet fields of the heterotic string. The quantization of the bosonic fields X^μ and worldsheet Majorana fermions ψ_R^μ was discussed in previous lectures, and does not change in this new setting. The only new feature, then, are the mode-expansion and quantization rules for the *complex* fermions Ψ_L^i.

Once again, there are two possible mode expansions for the left-moving complex fermions Ψ, depending on whether we choose Neveu-Schwarz (antiperiodic) or Ramond (periodic) boundary conditions.[‡] In the case of antiperiodic boundary conditions, recall that our mode-expansion (6.3.12) for left-moving *real* (Majorana) fermions can be written in the form

$$\psi(\sigma_1 + \sigma_2) = \sum_{r=1/2}^{\infty} \left[b_r e^{-ir(\sigma_1+\sigma_2)} + b_r^\dagger e^{+ir(\sigma_1+\sigma_2)} \right] \quad (6.5.11)$$

where we recall the hermiticity condition $b_{-r} = b_r^\dagger$. Thus, for a left-moving *complex* fermion, our analogous mode-expansion takes the form

$$\Psi(\sigma_1 + \sigma_2) = \sum_{r=1/2}^{\infty} \left[b_r e^{-ir(\sigma_1+\sigma_2)} + d_r^\dagger e^{+ir(\sigma_1+\sigma_2)} \right] \quad (6.5.12)$$

which of course implies

$$\Psi^\dagger(\sigma_1 + \sigma_2) = \sum_{r=1/2}^{\infty} \left[b_r^\dagger e^{+ir(\sigma_1+\sigma_2)} + d_r e^{-ir(\sigma_1+\sigma_2)} \right] \quad . \quad (6.5.13)$$

For $r > 0$, b_r destroys fermionic excitations and $b_r^\dagger$ creates them, while d_r destroys *anti-fermionic* excitations and $d_r^\dagger$ creates them. Thus, as expected, the only new feature is the presence of twice as many mode degrees of freedom, one set associated with fermionic excitations and the other

---
[‡] Because there is no worldsheet supersymmetry that relates these left-moving fermions to corresponding left-moving bosons X^μ, more general boundary conditions may actually be imposed in this case. However, for heterotic strings in ten dimensions, it turns out that we can restrict our attention to periodic or anti-periodic boundary conditions without loss of generality. Fermions with generalized worldsheet boundary conditions will be discussed further in Lecture #7.

with their anti-fermionic counterparts. These modes satisfy the usual anti-commutation relations

$$\{b_r^\dagger, b_s\} = \{d_r^\dagger, d_s\} = \delta_{rs} . \tag{6.5.14}$$

The corresponding number operator and worldsheet energy contributions are then given by

$$N = \sum_{r=1/2}^{\infty} \left(b_r^\dagger b_r - d_r^\dagger d_r\right)$$

$$L_0 = \sum_{r=1/2}^{\infty} r\left(b_r^\dagger b_r + d_r^\dagger d_r\right) . \tag{6.5.15}$$

Note that the anti-particle excitations *subtract* from the number operator yet *add* to the total energy. Finally, as expected, the vacuum energy contribution from each complex Neveu-Schwarz fermion is twice that for each real Neveu-Schwarz fermion: $a_\Psi = 2a_\psi = -1/24$.

The Ramond case, of course, is more subtle because of the zero-mode. It turns out that the complex-fermion mode-expansion is given by

$$\Psi(\sigma_1 + \sigma_2) = \sum_{n=1}^{\infty} [b_n e^{-in(\sigma_1+\sigma_2)} + d_n^\dagger e^{+in(\sigma_1+\sigma_2)}] + b_0$$

$$\Psi^\dagger(\sigma_1 + \sigma_2) = \sum_{n=1}^{\infty} [b_n^\dagger e^{+in(\sigma_1+\sigma_2)} + d_n e^{-in(\sigma_1+\sigma_2)}] + b_0^\dagger , \tag{6.5.16}$$

with the anti-commutation relations

$$\{b_m^\dagger, b_n\} = \{d_m^\dagger, d_n\} = \delta_{mn} . \tag{6.5.17}$$

In (6.5.16), we have explicitly separated out the zero-mode from the higher-frequency modes. The number operator and worldsheet energy conributions are given by

$$N = \sum_{r=1/2}^{\infty} \left(b_r^\dagger b_r - d_r^\dagger d_r\right) + b_0^\dagger b_0$$

$$L_0 = \sum_{r=1/2}^{\infty} r\left(b_r^\dagger b_r + d_r^\dagger d_r\right) . \tag{6.5.18}$$

Note that there is no worldsheet energy contribution from the zero-modes. Finally, the vacuum energy contribution from each complex Ramond fermion is twice that for each real Ramond fermion: $a_\Psi = 2a_\psi = +1/12$.

One might wonder, at first, why there is no *anti-particle* zero-mode d_0. However, such an anti-particle zero-mode d_0 would be *equivalent* to the *particle* zero-mode b_0. The easiest way to see this is to realize that ultimately (6.5.16) represents a Fourier-decomposition of the $\Psi(\sigma_1+\sigma_2)$ into different harmonic frequencies (exponentials). By its very nature, the zero-mode is the constant term in such a decomposition (since it corresponds to zero frequency), and this constant term is nothing but b_0. However, there can only be *one* degree of freedom associated with a given constant term. Having an additional zero-mode d_0 would thus represent a redundant (non-independent) degree of freedom. Of course, whether we associate b_0 or d_0 with the constant term is purely a matter of convention.

Given this observation, we are finally in a position to explain our counting of zero-mode states in Lectures #3 and #4. Since there is only one zero-mode degree of freedom for each *complex* worldsheet fermion, there can really be only "half" a zero-mode for each *real* worldsheet fermion. This explains the footnote in Sec. 3.2, and also explains why (in the paragraph following (6.4.9)) we counted only one zero-mode excitation per *pair* of Majorana fermions. This also explains why, ultimately, the treatment of the Ramond zero-mode for a *real* worldsheet fermion is rather subtle: essentially we must take a "square root" of the complex Ramond zero-mode b_0. There does exist a consistent method for taking this square root, but this is beyond the scope of these lectures. For our purposes, it will simply be sufficient to recall that there is only one zero-mode state for each complex worldsheet fermion, or for each pair of real worldsheet fermions.

6.6. Lecture #6: Some famous heterotic strings

Our next step is to construct actual heterotic string *models*, just as we did for the superstring. This will be the subject of the present lecture.

6.6.1. *General overview*

Before plunging into details, it is worthwhile to consider the general features that will govern the construction of our heterotic string models. Recall from the previous lecture that the worldsheet fields of the heterotic string in light-cone gauge consist of eight right-moving worldsheet bosons X_R^μ, eight left-moving worldsheet bosons X_L^μ, eight right-moving Majorana (real) worldsheet fermions ψ_R^μ, and sixteen left-moving complex worldsheet fermions Ψ_L^i ($i = 1, ..., 16$).

The role of the right-moving fermions ψ_R^μ is the same as in the superstring: if they have Neveu-Schwarz modings, the corresponding states are spacetime bosons, and if they Ramond modings, the corresponding states are spacetime fermions. Indeed, by properly stitching these sectors together, it may also be possible to obtain spacetime supersymmetry (as in the superstring). Note that unlike the superstring, however, these boson/fermion identifications hold *regardless* of the modings of the left-moving complex fermions Ψ_L^i. This is because only the right-moving fermions carry spacetime Lorentz indices μ, and hence only these fermions determine the representations of the spacetime Lorentz algebra.

The role of the left-moving complex fermions Ψ_L^i is analogous. Because they carry internal indices rather than spacetime Lorentz indices, the symmetries they carry are also internal, and as we shall see, they can be interpreted as gauge symmetries. Indeed, these Ψ_L^i fields are precisely the internal fields we were hoping to obtain in Sec. 5.1. When they have Neveu-Schwarz modings, these fermions provide "vectorial" (scalar, vector, tensor) representations of the internal gauge symmetry. When they have Ramond modings, by contrast, they provide "spinorial" representations of the internal gauge symmetry. Thus, we expect a rich gauge representation structure in these models as well.

As with the superstring, different models can be constructed depending on how the different modings are joined together to form our set of underlying sectors, and how the corresponding GSO constraints are implemented. We shall construct explicit models below. But it is already apparent that the heterotic string contains all the ingredients we require for successful phenomenology. By choosing certain combinations of right-moving fermionic modings with left-moving fermionic modings, we can control which gauge-group representations are bosonic and which are fermionic. Moreover, by choosing the relative modings *amongst* the left-moving complex fermions, we can even control the gauge group that is ultimately produced.

6.6.2. *Sectors and GSO constraints*

Just as in the superstring, we begin the process of model-building by choosing an appropriate set of underlying sectors and corresponding GSO constraints. Moreover, just as in the superstring, we know that preservation of the right-moving worldsheet supersymmetry (or equivalently spacetime Lorentz invariance) requires that we choose our eight right-moving fermions ψ_R^μ to all have the same boundary condition in each sector. This implies that we can, if we wish, combine these right-moving fermions to form four complex right-moving fermions which we can denote Ψ_R^μ. (We retain the index μ to remind ourselves that these fields carry indices with respect to the spacetime Lorentz algebra, even though strictly speaking only the real fields ψ_R^μ carry such vectorial indices.) However, unlike the superstring, there is no longer any such restriction on the boundary conditions of the left-moving fermions Ψ_L^μ. Thus, there remains substantial freedom in choosing the boundary conditions of these left-moving fermions. Ultimately this choice becomes the choice of the gauge group for the particular model in question.

In the next lecture, we shall provide a detailed discussion of the rules by which one can choose these boundary conditions and determine their associated GSO constraints. Therefore, for the time being, we shall simply restrict our attention to the sectors listed in Table 6.2. Note that the corresponding vacuum energies are also listed in Table 6.2. In order to compute these energies, we can continue to use the middle expression in (6.4.1) where we recall that n_R and n_{NS} count the number of *real* worldsheet fermions. Thus, for complex fermions, these numbers are doubled.

Table 6.2. Eight possible sectors for ten-dimensional heterotic strings, numbered 1 through 8. Here 'NS' and 'R' respectively indicate Neveu-Schwarz (anti-periodic) and Ramond (periodic) boundary conditions for worldsheet fermions, and a_R and a_L respectively denote the corresponding right- and left-moving vacuum energies.

#	$\psi_R^{i=1,\ldots,8}$	$\Psi_L^{i=1,\ldots,8}$	$\Psi_L^{i=9,\ldots,16}$	a_R	a_L
1	NS	NS		$-1/2$	-1
2	R	R		0	$+1$
3	NS	R		$-1/2$	$+1$
4	R	NS		0	-1
5	NS	NS	R	$-1/2$	0
6	NS	R	NS	$-1/2$	0
7	R	NS	R	0	0
8	R	R	NS	0	0

Before proceeding further, we can immediately deduce some physical properties of the string states that would emerge in each sector. First, we see that Sector #1 is the only sector from which tachyons can possibly emerge. This is because the level-matching constraints prevent tachyons in any other sector (*i.e.*, there is no other sector which for which both a_L and a_R are negative). Second, we observe that Sectors #2 and #3 cannot give rise to massless states. This again follows from the level-matching constraints, and implies that (for phenomenological purposes) we will not need to consider the states arising in these sectors. Finally, we observe that Sectors #1,3,5,6 give rise to spacetime bosons, while Sectors #2,4,7,8 give rise to spacetime fermions.

In some sense, Sectors #1–4 are the direct analogues of the four possible sectors in Table 6.1 for the superstring. Thus, the heterotic models that result from these sectors will be the analogues of the Type 0 and Type II superstring models. However, the additional Sectors #5–8 represent new sectors that arise only for heterotic strings. We hasten to add that these sectors are not unique, and others could equally well have been chosen. We will discuss these possibilities in the next lecture.

The next issue we face is to determine which *combinations* of sectors form self-consistent sets. It turns out (following the rules to be discussed in Lecture #7) that there are three different possibilities:

- Case A: we consider Sectors #1 and #2 by themselves;
- Case B: we consider Sectors #1 through #4 by themselves; or
- Case C: we consider *all* Sectors #1 through #8.

For each of these cases, there is then a different set of GSO constraints for each sector. As we have seen in our discussion of the superstring, the more sectors we have in our model, the more GSO constraints there are in each sector. In particular, each time the number of sectors doubles, the number of GSO constraints in each sector increases by one. For completeness, Table 6.3 lists the GSO constraints that apply in each sector for each of these three cases.

Once again, observe the *pattern* of the GSO constraints. In Case A, we have only Sectors #1 and #2, for which all right-moving and left-moving boundary conditions are identical. Thus, the GSO constraints that apply in Case A combine N_L and N_R together. (Recall that since $N_{L,R} \in \mathbb{Z}$, we can just as easily write the GSO constraint for Case A as $N_L + N_R =$ odd.) When we move from Case A to Case B, we introduce two new sectors (Sectors #3 and #4 in Table 6.2) which "twist" the boundary conditions of the right-movers relative to those of the left-movers. This has the effect of introducing a new GSO constraint in each sector, one which distinguishes separately between N_L and N_R. Finally, when we move from Case B to Case C, we introduce four new sectors (Sectors #5 through #8) which introduce an additional "twist" that distinguishes between the first eight left-moving fermions $\Psi_L^{i=1,\ldots,8}$ and the second eight left-moving fermions

$\Psi_L^{i=9,\ldots,16}$. The corresponding new GSO constraint in each sector is then one which is sensitive only to $^{(8)}N_L \equiv \sum_{i=1}^{8} N^{(i)}$. This suggests (and we shall see explicitly in Lecture #7) that the set of sectors is deeply correlated with the set of GSO constraints that are applied in each sector: each new "twist" introduces both a new set of sectors and a new GSO constraint in each sector. The fact that we are considering only Ramond or Neveu-Schwarz boundary conditions for our left-moving complex fermions Ψ_L^i means that each successive twist doubles the number of sectors and introduces one new GSO constraint in each sector. These are called $\mathbb{Z}_2$ twists. If we were to consider more general "multi-periodic" boundary conditions for the left-moving fermions (which is possible because they are not related to the left-moving worldsheet bosons by worldsheet supersymmetry), then we could introduce so-called "higher-order" twists that would result in more complicated GSO constraints. However, it turns out that in ten dimensions, we lose no generality by restricting our attention to such $\mathbb{Z}_2$ twists.

6.6.3. *Four ten-dimensional heterotic string models*

It is apparent from Table 6.3 that Case A and Case B each correspond to one heterotic string model, while Case C corresponds to two separate heterotic string models. Thus, the GSO constraints in Table 6.3 together give rise to four distinct heterotic string models. In the remainder of this lecture, we shall work out the physical properties of these four models.

6.6.3.1. *The non-supersymmetric SO(32) string*

Let us begin by considering Case A, which consists of only Sectors #1 and #2. Only Sector #1 (the so-called "NS-NS sector") can contain massless states. As indicated in Table 6.1, the vacuum energy in this sector is $(a_R, a_L) = (-1/2, -1)$. Thus, at the bare minimum, the level-matching constraint $L_0 = \bar{L}_0$ forces us to excite at least a half-unit of energy on the left-moving side. This can be accomplished by exciting any of the left-moving half-unit fermionic modes, since in this sector the left-moving fermions all have Neveu-Schwarz boundary conditions and thus contain half-integer modings. This produces the 32 possible states

$$|0\rangle_R \otimes b^i_{-1/2}|0\rangle_L \quad \text{and} \quad |0\rangle_R \otimes d^i_{-1/2}|0\rangle_L . \tag{6.6.1}$$

Note that these states also satisfy the single applicable GSO constraint $N_L - N_R =$ odd, so they remain in the spectrum. From (6.4.6), we see that these states are tachyonic with $\alpha' M^2 = -2$.

Table 6.3. GSO constraints for each of the eight heterotic string sectors in Table 6.2. Here the notation $^{(8)}N_L \equiv \sum_{i=1}^{8} N^{(i)}$ indicates the total left-moving number operator for only the first *eight* left-moving complex fermions. As before, the braces indicate different *correlated* choices of GSO projections, so that we simultaneously choose either the upper choice or the lower choice for all sets.

Sector #	Case A	Case B	Case C
1	$N_L - N_R =$ odd	$N_L - N_R =$ odd $N_L =$ even	$N_L - N_R =$ odd $N_L =$ even $^{(8)}N_L =$ even
2	$N_L - N_R =$ odd	$N_L - N_R =$ odd $N_L =$ even	$N_L - N_R =$ odd $N_L =$ even $^{(8)}N_L =$ even
3	—	$N_L - N_R =$ odd $N_L =$ even	$N_L - N_R =$ odd $N_L =$ even $^{(8)}N_L = \left\{ \begin{array}{c} \text{odd} \\ \text{even} \end{array} \right\}$
4	—	$N_L - N_R =$ odd $N_L =$ even	$N_L - N_R =$ odd $N_L =$ even $^{(8)}N_L = \left\{ \begin{array}{c} \text{odd} \\ \text{even} \end{array} \right\}$
5	—	—	$N_L - N_R =$ odd $N_L = \left\{ \begin{array}{c} \text{odd} \\ \text{even} \end{array} \right\}$ $^{(8)}N_L = \left\{ \begin{array}{c} \text{odd} \\ \text{even} \end{array} \right\}$
6	—	—	$N_L - N_R =$ odd $N_L = \left\{ \begin{array}{c} \text{odd} \\ \text{even} \end{array} \right\}$ $^{(8)}N_L =$ even
7	—	—	$N_L - N_R =$ odd $N_L = \left\{ \begin{array}{c} \text{odd} \\ \text{even} \end{array} \right\}$ $^{(8)}N_L =$ even
8	—	—	$N_L - N_R =$ odd $N_L = \left\{ \begin{array}{c} \text{odd} \\ \text{even} \end{array} \right\}$ $^{(8)}N_L = \left\{ \begin{array}{c} \text{odd} \\ \text{even} \end{array} \right\}$

Further states are realized by exciting higher worldsheet modes. Because our worldsheet modes are quantized in minimum half-integer steps, we see that the next excited states in this model are massless. These states come in two varieties:

$$\tilde{b}^{\mu}_{-1/2}|0\rangle_R \otimes \alpha^{\nu}_{-1}|0\rangle_L \qquad (6.6.2)$$

and

$$\tilde{b}^{\mu}_{-1/2}|0\rangle_R \otimes \begin{cases} b^i_{-1/2} b^j_{-1/2} |0\rangle_L \\ b^i_{-1/2} d^j_{-1/2} |0\rangle_L \\ d^i_{-1/2} b^j_{-1/2} |0\rangle_L \\ d^i_{-1/2} d^j_{-1/2} |0\rangle_L \end{cases} . \quad (6.6.3)$$

In (6.6.2), we have excited the lowest mode of the left-moving worldsheet boson X^{μ}_L, whereas in (6.6.3) we have excited two of the lowest modes of the left-moving fermions $\Psi^{i,j}_L$. Note that it is possible to excite both the particle and anti-particle modes from the same fermion Ψ^i, and thus there is no restriction that $i \neq j$. Also note that all of these states in (6.6.2) and (6.6.3) satisfy the GSO constraint $N_L - N_R = $ odd. While $N_R = 1$ in all cases, we have $N_L = 0$ in (6.6.2) (since the number operators are defined not to include the contributions from worldsheet bosons), and $N_L = 2$ in (6.6.3).

How do we interpret these states? Once again, the states (6.6.2) are easily recognized as our gravity multiplet, consisting of the spin-two graviton $g_{\mu\nu}$, the spin-one anti-symmetric tensor $B_{\mu\nu}$, and the spin-zero dilaton ϕ. It is interesting to note that this state (6.6.2) is realized as a hybrid of the gravity multiplet state in the bosonic string (6.2.19) and in the superstring (6.4.7). This reflects the underlying construction of the heterotic string, and ensures that the heterotic string, like its predecessors, is also a theory of quantized gravity. Once again, the appearance of the gravity multiplet is a useful cross-check of the GSO constraints.

The states in (6.6.3) have a different interpretation, however. Clearly, their Lorentz structure indicates that they are massless Lorentz vectors. Thus, they are to be interpreted as spacetime *gauge bosons*. Thus, we see that the heterotic string has succeeded in providing us with spacetime gauge symmetry, just as we had originally hoped.

But what is the gauge group? Of course, the gauge group is ultimately determined from the i, j indices, and since (in Cases A and B) we have not destroyed the rotational symmetry in the space of the 16 complex left-moving fermions Ψ^i_L (or the 32 real left-moving fermions into which they can be decomposed), we immediately suspect that the gauge symmetry should be $SO(32)$. There are number of ways to deduce that this is correct. Perhaps the easiest way is simply to *count* the gauge boson states in (6.6.3). If we restrict our attention to the cases $i \neq j$, then there are $(2 \cdot 16)(2 \cdot 15)/2$ states. The first factor $(2 \cdot 16)$ reflects the fact that for each of the 16 possible choices of Ψ_L^i, we can excite either the fermion or anti-fermion mode. The second factor $(2 \cdot 15)$ reflects the same set of options for the second fermion Ψ_L^j, and we divide by two as the interchange symmetry factor. There are also the cases with $i = j$: from such cases we obtain 16 possible states, reflecting the 16 different fermions Ψ_L^i whose fermion and anti-fermion modes are jointly excited. The total number of states is then

$$\frac{(2 \cdot 16)(2 \cdot 15)}{2} + 16 = 496 = \dim SO(32) \,. \tag{6.6.4}$$

Of course, the above counting method for determining the gauge group is hardly precise, for there are a number of gauge groups with the same overall dimension (and we shall come across another such gauge group very soon). We therefore require a more sophisticated method which also generalizes to more complicated cases. By definition, of course, the gauge group can be determined by explicitly examining the charges of the gauge boson states and determining which Lie algebra (*i.e.*, which root system) they fill out. We therefore need a way of determining the charges of the gauge boson states. Since our gauge symmetry is ultimately associated with the left-moving worldsheet fermions Ψ_L^i, the relevant current in this case is simply the worldsheet current $J^i \equiv \bar{\Psi}_L^i \Psi_L^i$. From this, we can deduce the associated charge Q_i. It turns out that

Great Leap #7: The charge associated with each worldsheet fermion Ψ_L^i for a given string state with fermionic excitation number $N^{(i)}$ is given by $Q_i \equiv N^{(i)} + q_i$. Here q_i is a "background" charge which is 0 if Ψ_L^i is a Neveu-Schwarz fermion and $-1/2$ if Ψ_L^i is a Ramond fermion.

Given this result, we can easily deduce the gauge group for the case in question. For simplicity, let us first imagine that there are only *two* left-moving fermions $\Psi_L^{i=1,2}$. In this case, (6.6.3) reduces to six states:

$$b_{-1/2}^1 b_{-1/2}^2 |0\rangle_L \,, \quad b_{-1/2}^1 d_{-1/2}^2 |0\rangle_L \,, \quad d_{-1/2}^1 b_{-1/2}^2 |0\rangle_L \,,$$
$$d_{-1/2}^1 d_{-1/2}^2 |0\rangle_L \,, \quad b_{-1/2}^1 d_{-1/2}^1 |0\rangle_L \,, \quad b_{-1/2}^2 d_{-1/2}^2 |0\rangle_L \,. \tag{6.6.5}$$

For each of these states, there are two charges, Q_1 and Q_2, associated with each of the two complex fermions. If we denote these states as A through F respectively, we can plot the charges of these six states as in Fig. 6.8. The resulting diagram is easily recognized as the root system (or equivalently the weight system of the adjoint representation) of the Lie group $SO(4)$. Generalizing from two complex fermions to n complex fermions analogously

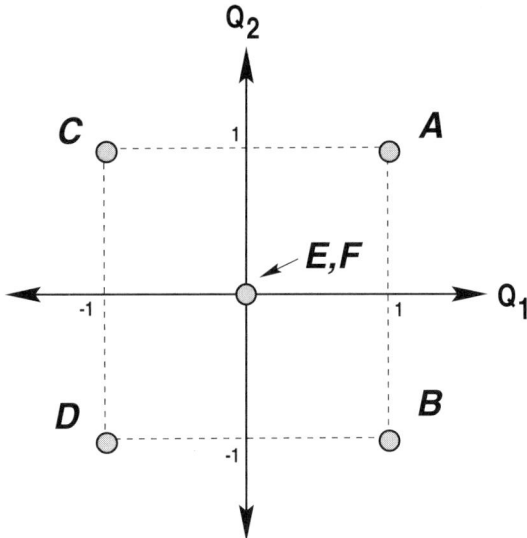

Fig. 6.8. The two-dimensional "charge lattice" associated with the six string states A through F in (6.6.5). Note that the two states E and F fill out the Cartan subalgebra of the root system. For a ten-dimensional heterotic string, the charge lattice is always sixteen-dimensional (generally implying a gauge group of rank 16), with a Cartan subalgebra consisting of sixteen gauge boson states.

yields the gauge group $SO(2n)$, provided that all n complex fermions have the same modings. Thus, in the case of 16 complex fermions, we find the gauge group $SO(32)$.

Note that this argument suffices to show that the gauge bosons fill out the adjoint representation of $SO(32)$. However, it does not demonstrate that all other string states in the model fall into representations of this gauge group. Of course, this is required for the consistency of the string. However, such a result can indeed be proven mathematically by constructing the current operators associated with the gauge group in question (as discussed above), and demonstrating that all states surviving the appropriate GSO constraints transform appropriately under these currents. For example, the 32 tachyonic states in (6.6.1) transform in the vector representation of $SO(32)$, and the gravity multiplet (6.6.2) transforms as a singlet of $SO(32)$ (as it must). However, a proof that this holds for all states in both the massless and massive string spectrum is beyond the scope of these lectures.

We should also point out that what emerges in such closed string theories is not simply the algebra associated the gauge symmetry in question, but rather an infinite-dimensional extension (or "affinization") of it. Such affine Lie algebras are discussed in Ginsparg (reference given at the end of Lecture #1), and play an important role in the consistency and phenomenology of such heterotic string theories.

To summarize, then, we see that Case A results in a tachyonic string model with quantum gravity and $SO(32)$ gauge symmetry. In addition to 32 scalar tachyons transforming in the vector representation of $SO(32)$, this model contains massless gauge bosons transforming in the adjoint representation of $SO(32)$ as well as the usual gravity multiplet. This non-supersymmetric $SO(32)$ heterotic string model is the heterotic analogue of the Type 0 string models in Lecture #4.

6.6.3.2. *The supersymmetric SO(32) string*

Let us now proceed to Case B. In this case there are four sectors (#1 through #4 in Table 6.2), and we must impose the GSO constraints listed in the second column of Table 6.3.

Let us begin by considering the states from Sector #1. These are the same as those considered in Case A, except that we must now impose the additional GSO constraint N_L = even. This projects out the tachyonic states (6.6.1), but preserves the gravity multiplet as well as the gauge bosons.

As we discussed previously, Sectors #2 and #3 contain no massless states. Therefore, all that remains is to consider the states from Sector #4. Here the vacuum energy is $(a_R, a_L) = (0, -1)$. The right-moving ground state in this sector is the Ramond zero-mode ground state, which we have previously denoted $\{\tilde{b}_0^\mu\}|0\rangle_R$, and thus massless states are realized only through non-zero excitations of the left-movers. The possible states are

$$\{\tilde{b}_0^\mu\}|0\rangle_R \otimes \begin{cases} \alpha^\nu_{-1}|0\rangle_L \\ b^i_{-1/2} b^j_{-1/2}|0\rangle_L \\ b^i_{-1/2} d^j_{-1/2}|0\rangle_L \\ d^i_{-1/2} b^j_{-1/2}|0\rangle_L \\ d^i_{-1/2} d^j_{-1/2}|0\rangle_L \ . \end{cases} \quad (6.6.6)$$

In each case, the GSO constraints imply that we can excite only an odd number of right-moving zero-modes. According to our previous conventions, this indicates that the right-moving ground state corresponds to the spacetime Lorentz spinor $\bar{\mathbf{S}}_8$ (rather than the conjugate spinor $\bar{\mathbf{C}}_8$).

It is, by now, easy to interpret the states in (6.6.6). The first state provides the superpartner states to the gravity multiplet, and contains a gravitino. This implies that the model has spacetime supersymmetry. Likewise, the remaining states correspond to the superpartners of the $SO(32)$ gauge bosons, and contain the $SO(32)$ gauginos. The chirality of these spinor states is fixed by the GSO constraint and the right-moving ground state $\bar{\mathbf{S}}_8$.

Summarizing, we see that this model therefore consists of the following states. We shall describe these states using the notation $\bar{R}_1 \otimes (R_2; R_3)$ where R_1, R_2 are representations of the spacetime Lorentz group, and where R_3 is a representation of the $SO(32)$ gauge group. These states consist of

$$\bar{\mathbf{V}}_8 \otimes (\mathbf{V}_8; \mathbf{1}) , \quad \bar{\mathbf{V}}_8 \otimes (\mathbf{1}; \mathbf{adj}) , \quad \bar{\mathbf{S}}_8 \otimes (\mathbf{V}_8; \mathbf{1}) , \quad \bar{\mathbf{S}}_8 \otimes (\mathbf{1}; \mathbf{adj}) , \quad (6.6.7)$$

where the first and third states form the $N = 1$ supergravity multiplet and the second and fourth states form the $SO(32)$ gauge boson supermultiplet. Together these states can be written in the factorized form

$$(\bar{\mathbf{V}}_8 \oplus \bar{\mathbf{S}}_8) \otimes \{(\mathbf{V}_8; \mathbf{1}) \oplus (\mathbf{1}; \mathbf{adj})\} , \quad (6.6.8)$$

thereby explicitly exhibiting the supersymmetry $\bar{\mathbf{V}}_8 \leftrightarrow \bar{\mathbf{S}}_8$.

This string is the famous supersymmetric $SO(32)$ heterotic string. Although not directly relevant for string phenomenology, this string plays a vital role in recent developments in string duality (to be discussed briefly in Lecture #8).

6.6.3.3. *The $SO(16) \times SO(16)$ and $E_8 \times E_8$ strings*

Let us now proceed to Case C. As discussed in Sec. 6.2, this case differs from Case B because we have now "twisted" the second group of eight left-moving complex worldsheet fermions relative to the first set. *A priori*, it is easy to imagine that this twist will break the gauge symmetry $SO(32) \to SO(16) \times SO(16)$. However, there a few surprises still in store for us.

We begin in Sector #1, which previously gave rise to the states given in (6.6.2) and (6.6.3). Introducing the third GSO constraint [8] $N_L \equiv \sum_{i=1}^{8} N^{(i)} =$ even does not affect the gravity multiplet (6.6.2), but has a drastic effect on the remaining gauge boson states. We now see that we cannot excite arbitrary combinations of (i, j) fermions; instead we must choose either $(i, j) = 1, ..., 8$ or $(i, j) = 9, ..., 16$. In string-theory parlance, all of the other states have been "projected out of the spectrum". It is in this manner that we remove gauge boson states and break gauge symmetries in string theory. (There are other methods for doing this in string theory, but this is the only method at tree-level.) It is easy to see (following the arguments given above) that the remaining gauge boson states fill out the adjoint representation of two copies of $SO(16)$, and thus the gauge group is *a priori* $SO(16) \times SO(16)$. Therefore, we shall henceforth denote our string states in the notation $\bar{R}_1 \otimes (R_2; R_3, R_4)$ where $\bar{R}_1, R_2$ are the representations of the Lorentz group from the right- and left-movers, and where R_3, R_4 are the representations with respect to the two gauge group factors of $SO(16)$ respectively. Thus, we see that Sector #1 gives rise to the states

$$\bar{\mathbf{V}}_8 \otimes (\mathbf{V}_8; \mathbf{1}, \mathbf{1}) \, , \quad \bar{\mathbf{V}}_8 \otimes (\mathbf{1}; \mathbf{adj}, \mathbf{1}) \, , \quad \bar{\mathbf{V}}_8 \otimes (\mathbf{1}; \mathbf{1}, \mathbf{adj}) \, , \qquad (6.6.9)$$

where the first states form the gravity multiplet and the second and third states are the $SO(16) \times SO(16)$ gauge bosons.

As before, Sectors #2 and #3 do not give rise to massless states. Let us now consider what happens in Sector #4. The states that previously emerged in Sector #4 are given in (6.6.6). We now must impose the remaining GSO constraint $^{(8)}N_L = \left\{ \begin{matrix} \text{odd} \\ \text{even} \end{matrix} \right\}$. Let us consider each case separately. If we impose the odd choice, then the gravitino state in (6.6.6) is projected out of the spectrum, indicating that *supersymmetry is broken*. Likewise, we find that the gaugino states are also affected: we can now excite only those states for which $i = 1, ..., 8$ and $j = 9, ..., 16$. This spinor state transforms in the $(\mathbf{16}, \mathbf{16})$ representation of $SO(16) \times SO(16)$ (*i.e.*, as the vector-vector bifundamental). By contrast, if we impose the even choice, then the gravitino state in (6.6.6) remains in the spectrum, indicating that *supersymmetry is preserved*. Likewise, the gaugino states are affected only by the new requirement that either $i, j = 1, ..., 8$ or $i, j = 9, ..., 16$. Thus, the new GSO projection projects our $SO(32)$ gauginos down to $SO(16) \times SO(16)$ gauginos, as expected. Summarizing, we find that in the "even" case, the states from Sector #4 are

$$\bar{\mathbf{S}}_8 \otimes (\mathbf{V}_8; \mathbf{1}, \mathbf{1}) \, , \quad \bar{\mathbf{S}}_8 \otimes (\mathbf{1}; \mathbf{adj}, \mathbf{1}) \, , \quad \bar{\mathbf{S}}_8 \otimes (\mathbf{1}; \mathbf{1}, \mathbf{adj}) \, . \qquad (6.6.10)$$

Let us now consider Sector #5. As indicated in Table 6.2, in this sector the vacuum energy is $(a_R, a_L) = (-1/2, 0)$ and the first eight left-moving complex fermions are Neveu-Schwarz while the second eight are Ramond. Choosing the "odd" GSO constraints projects all possible massless states out of the spectrum (because there is no simultaneous solution to all three GSO constraints in the "odd" case). By contrast, choosing the "even" GSO constraints yields the states

$$\tilde{b}^{\mu}_{-1/2}|0\rangle_R \otimes \{b^i_0\}|0\rangle_L \qquad (i=9,...,16) \qquad (6.6.11)$$

where we must choose an even number of zero-mode excitations on the left-moving side. This produces a massless vector state which transforms in a (128-dimensional) *spinorial* representation of the second $SO(16)$ gauge group factor. Following our previous conventions, we shall refer to this spinor as $\mathbf{C}_{128}$ rather than its conjugate $\mathbf{S}_{128}$. This state can therefore be denoted as

$$\overline{\mathbf{V}}_8 \otimes (\mathbf{1};\mathbf{1},\mathbf{C}_{128}) . \qquad (6.6.12)$$

We shall discuss the physical interpretation of this state shortly.

Sector #6 is similar to Sector #5, except that now the first eight left-moving complex fermions are Ramond and the second eight are Neveu-Schwarz. In a similar way we then find that there are no states in the "odd" case, while in the "even" case we find the states

$$\overline{\mathbf{V}}_8 \otimes (\mathbf{1};\mathbf{C}_{128},\mathbf{1}) . \qquad (6.6.13)$$

We now turn to Sector #7. Here the vacuum energy is $(a_R,a_L) = (0,0)$, which implies that if we restrict our attention to massless states, we can tolerate only zero-mode excitations amongst both the left- and right-movers. In the "odd" case, we find the states

$$\{\tilde{b}^{\mu}_0\}|0\rangle_R \otimes \{b^i_0\}|0\rangle_L \qquad (i=9,...,16) \qquad (6.6.14)$$

where the GSO projections restrict us to an even number of zero-mode excitations on the right-moving side and an odd number on the left-moving side. According to our conventions, this produces the state $\overline{\mathbf{C}}_8 \otimes (\mathbf{1};\mathbf{1},\mathbf{S}_{128})$. In the "even" case, by contrast, we are restricted to (6.6.14) where now we must have an even number of zero-mode excitations on the right-moving side and an odd number of the left-moving side. This produces the state

$$\overline{\mathbf{S}}_8 \otimes (\mathbf{1};\mathbf{1},\mathbf{C}_{128}) . \qquad (6.6.15)$$

Finally, in Sector #8, we similiarly find the states $\overline{\mathbf{C}}_8 \otimes (\mathbf{1};\mathbf{S}_{128},\mathbf{1})$ in the "odd" case and

$$\overline{\mathbf{S}}_8 \otimes (\mathbf{1};\mathbf{C}_{128},\mathbf{1}) \qquad (6.6.16)$$

in the "even" case.

What are we to make of these results? Collecting our states for the "odd" case, we find a string model with the following massless spectrum:

$$\bar{V}_8 \otimes (V_8; 1, 1) \,, \quad \bar{V}_8 \otimes (1; \mathbf{adj}, 1) \,, \quad \bar{V}_8 \otimes (1; 1, \mathbf{adj})$$
$$\bar{S}_8 \otimes (1; V_{16}, V_{16}) \,, \quad \bar{C}_8 \otimes (1; S_{128}, 1) \,, \quad \bar{C}_8 \otimes (1; 1, S_{128}) \,. \quad (6.6.17)$$

This is clearly a non-supersymmetric spectrum consisting of a gravity multiplet, vector bosons transforming of the adjoint of $SO(16) \times SO(16)$, one spinor transforming as a vector-vector bifundamental with respect to the gauge group, and two additional spinors of opposite chirality transforming in the spinor representations of the gauge group. This is the non-supersymmetric $SO(16) \times SO(16)$ heterotic string model, first constructed in 1986. Note that this spectrum configuration is anomaly-free, as required for a self-consistent string theory. Also note that this string is tachyon-free even though it is non-supersymmetric. This example thus proves that *not all non-supersymmetric strings have tachyons* (although it is certainly true that all supersymmetric strings lack tachyons). While this is the only non-supersymmetric tachyon-free heterotic string in ten dimensions, there exist a plethora of such strings in lower dimensions. We shall discuss some of the properties of such strings in Lecture #8, but this raises an interesting issue: Does string theory *predict* spacetime supersymmetry? As this example makes clear, string theory certainly does not predict spacetime supersymmetry on the basis of tachyon-avoidance. However, the general answer to this question is unknown.

Even more interesting is the model that results in the "even" case. Collecting our states from (6.6.9), (6.6.10), (6.6.12), (6.6.13), (6.6.15), and (6.6.16), we find that the total massless spectrum of this string can be written in the factorized form

$$(\bar{V}_8 \oplus \bar{S}_8) \otimes \{(V_8; 1, 1) \oplus (1; \{\mathbf{adj} \oplus C_{128}\}, 1) \oplus (1; 1, \{\mathbf{adj} \oplus C_{128}\})\} \,. \quad (6.6.18)$$

The appearance of the right-moving factor $\bar{V}_8 \oplus \bar{S}_8$ indicates that this model has $N = 1$ supersymmetry, as expected from the appearance of a single gravitino in the massless spectrum. The left-moving factor, by contrast, contains three terms. The first term combines with the right-moving factor to produce the supergravity multiplet. The second two terms formerly gave rise to the $SO(16) \times SO(16)$ gauge supermultiplet. However, we now see that for each $SO(16)$ gauge group factor, the massless vector states transform in the $\mathbf{adj} \oplus C_{128}$ representation rather than simply in the $\mathbf{adj}$ representation. While the $\mathbf{adj}$ contribution is easy to interpret (giving rise to the usual gauge bosons of $SO(16)$), the extra massless vector states transforming in the $\mathbf{C}_{128}$ representation of each gauge group factor appear to cause an inconsistency, for we know that all massless vector states must be interpreted as gauge bosons, and hence such states can only transform in the adjoint representation. Thus, the only possible way that this string can be consistent is if the massless vector states in this model somehow combine to fill out the adjoint representation of some *other* group G:

$$\mathbf{adj}_{SO(16)} \oplus \mathbf{C}_{128} \stackrel{?}{=} \mathbf{adj}_G \ . \tag{6.6.19}$$

Remarkably, this is precisely what occurs: the group G is nothing but the exceptional Lie group E_8! Indeed, the 120 states of the adjoint representation of $SO(16)$ together with the 128 states of the spinor representation of $SO(16)$ combine to produce the 248 states of the adjoint representation of E_8! In string parlance, we thus say that the presence of the "twisted" states (6.6.12), (6.6.13), (6.6.15), and (6.6.16) has *enhanced* the total gauge group from $SO(16) \times SO(16)$ to $E_8 \times E_8$. This, then, is the famous supersymmetric $E_8 \times E_8$ heterotic string.

Unlike the supersymmetric $SO(32)$ string, this string is generally considered to have excellent phenomenological prospects. It has $N = 1$ spacetime supersymmetry, quantum gravity, and an $E_8 \times E_8$ gauge symmetry. E_8 is a compelling gauge group for phenomenology because it contains E_6 as a subgroup, and E_6 is a group that contains chiral representations which can be associated with grand unification and which thereby contain all of the particle content of the Standard Model. (Of course, it is still necessary to obtain actual *matter* representations from this string, but these can arise upon compactification.) Moreover, while we can imagine the Standard Model to reside entirely within one of the E_8 gauge group factors, the other factor may be interpreted as a "hidden" sector which can also have important phenomenological uses (such as triggering supersymmetry breaking, providing dark-matter candidates, and enforcing string selection rules). Thus, historically, much of the original work in string phenomenology began with a study of the compactification of this model down to four dimensions. However, it is possible to construct heterotic string models directly in four dimensions, and to obtain models which do not necessarily have an interpretation as arising via the compactification of any particular string model in ten dimensions. Thus, as we shall see, the prospects for phenomenological heterotic string model-building are broader than merely studying the compactifications of the $E_8 \times E_8$ heterotic string.

6.6.4. More ten-dimensional heterotic strings

So far, we have constructed four heterotic string models in ten dimensions. Of these, two have spacetime supersymmetry, and two do not. However, it is readily apparent that further models can be constructed by introducing further "twists" which further enlarge the set of sectors in Table 6.2 and which further break the gauge group into smaller factors (or which break the original $SO(32)$ gauge group in entirely different ways). The question that arises, then, is whether there exist other ten-dimensional heterotic strings with spacetime supersymmetry, or whether there exist other non-supersymmetric strings in ten dimensions that are tachyon-free. The answer to both questions turns out to be "no". A complete list of ten-dimensional heterotic strings is given in Table 6.4.

Table 6.4. The complete set of ten-dimensional heterotic string models. Two have spacetime supersymmetry, one is non-supersymmetric but tachyon-free, and the remaining six are non-supersymmetric and tachyonic.

gauge group	spacetime SUSY?	tachyon-free?
$SO(32)$	yes	yes
$E_8 \times E_8$	yes	yes
$SO(16) \times SO(16)$	no	yes
$SO(32)$	no	no
$SO(16) \times E_8$	no	no
$SO(8) \times SO(24)$	no	no
$(E_7)^2 \times [SU(2)]^2$	no	no
$U(16)$	no	no
E_8	no	no

The presence of the last string in Table 6.4 might seem surprising. After all, the rank of the gauge group for this string is only eight rather than sixteen, which implies that its construction must differ substantially from that of the previous strings. It turns out that this is indeed the case.* We briefly indicate in Lecture #7 how such strings may be constructed.

---

*Unlike the other ten-dimensional heterotic strings, this string involves splitting each complex worldsheet fermion into a pair of two real worldsheet fermions and then introducing relative "twists" within each pair. In technical language, this results in a gauge group whose rank is reduced but whose so-called *affine level* is increased relative to those of the other strings. This increase in the affine level is important for string GUT model-building, and will be discussed in subsequent lectures.

6.7. Lecture #7: Rules for string model-building

In the last several lectures, we constructed many different string models. Amongst the superstring models, we constructed the Type 0A, Type 0B, Type IIA, and Type IIB models, while amongst the heterotic string models, we constructed the non-supersymmetric $SO(32)$ model, the non-supersymmetric $SO(16) \times SO(16)$ model, and the supersymmetric $SO(32)$ and $E_8 \times E_8$ models. In each case, we simply *asserted* a set of sectors (combinations of Neveu-Schwarz and Ramond modings) and a set of GSO constraints in each sector. Of course, each of these sets of sectors and GSO constraints conspires to yield a self-consistent string model, and occasionally it is even possible to see intuitively which choices can lead to self-consistent string models. However, we ultimately wish to construct semi-realistic string models where the groups are broken down to much smaller pieces than we have been dealing with thus far (*e.g.*, $SU(3) \times SU(2) \times U(1)$, or even $SU(5)$ or $SO(10)$), and this is going to require more complicated twists than we have thus far been using. Furthermore, all of our string models thus far have been in ten dimensions, yet we are ultimately going to wish to compactify our string models to four dimensions. It turns out that this will introduce even further choices for modings, twists, and their associated GSO projections. (In geometric language, these further choices amount the choice of compactification manifold.)

The question that arises, then, is to determine the minimal set of parameters that govern these choices. What we require is a way to *systematize* the whole process of string model-construction, so that we will know precisely which choices govern the construction of a string model and guarantee its internal self-consistency. In other words, we require *rules for string model-building*. This is the subject of the present lecture.

Once we learn the rules for the construction of ten-dimensional string models, it will be relatively straightforward to generalize these rules for the construction of models in four dimensions. We will then have the tools whereby we may finally construct semi-realistic four-dimensional string models.

6.7.1. *Generating the sector combinations: The 20-dimensional lattice*

The first issue we face is that of choosing the appropriate sector combinations. For example, let us recall the possible heterotic string sectors in

Table 6.2. As we discussed in Sec. 6.2, this set of sectors permits only three distinct sector combinations: either we choose Sectors #1 and #2 only, or we choose Sectors #1 through #4 only, or we choose Sectors #1 through #8. How can we know which combinations are allowed, and which sectors are required in each grouping? In Sec. 6.2, we discussed how modular invariance ultimately governs these choices. Here, however, we shall develop a rule which we can use in order to deduce these sector combinations rather quickly and which can easily be generalized to more complicated situations.

First, let us introduce some notation. Since it is rather awkward to consider left-moving complex fermions Ψ_L^i at the same time as right-moving *real* (Majorana) fermions ψ_R^μ, let us "complexify" our right-moving Majorana fermions so that *all* of our worldsheet fermions are complex. This means that instead of having eight left-moving real fermions ψ_R^μ in light-cone gauge, we have instead four complex ones Ψ_R^μ formed by pairing the left-moving real fermions in groups of two. (We retain the index μ to remind ourselves that these fields carry indices with respect to the spacetime Lorentz algebra, even though strictly speaking it is only their real component fields ψ_R^μ that carry such vectorial indices.)

We also need a more general notation for discussing the possible boundary conditions and modings that any such complex worldsheet fermion can take. In general, we can parametrize any possible worldsheet boundary condition in the form

$$\Psi(\sigma_1 + \pi, \sigma_2) = -e^{-2\pi i v} \Psi(\sigma_1, \sigma_2) \qquad (6.7.1)$$

where $-\frac{1}{2} \leq v < \frac{1}{2}$. Thus the quantity v parametrizes the boundary condition of the individual fermion, with

$$\begin{aligned} v = 0: & \quad \text{anti-periodic} \quad \text{(Neveu-Schwarz)} \\ v = -1/2: & \quad \text{periodic} \quad \text{(Ramond)} \,. \end{aligned} \qquad (6.7.2)$$

General values of v correspond to so-called "multi-periodic fermions". For example, the general moding of a multi-periodic left-moving complex fermion is given by

$$\Psi_L(\sigma_1 + \sigma_2) = \sum_{n=1}^{\infty} \left[b_{n+v-1/2} e^{-i(n+v-1/2)(\sigma_1+\sigma_2)} \right.$$
$$\left. + d^\dagger_{n-v-1/2} e^{+i(n-v-1/2)(\sigma_1+\sigma_2)} \right], \quad (6.7.3)$$

and the corresponding number operator and worldsheet energy are defined accordingly. Note that these modings generalize those given in Sec. 5.3.

Likewise, the vacuum energy contribution from such a fermion is given by

$$a_\Psi = \frac{1}{2}\left(v^2 - \frac{1}{12}\right) . \qquad (6.7.4)$$

This too generalizes our previous results.

In ten dimensions, it turns out that we lose no generality by considering only the specific cases $v = 0, -\frac{1}{2}$ for all worldsheet fermions. What this means is that all self-consistent ten-dimensional string models can ultimately be realized using worldsheet fermions with only Neveu-Schwarz or Ramond boundary conditions. In lower dimensions, by contrast, other choices are possible. Therefore, even though we shall primarily focus our attention on the cases $v \in \{0, -\frac{1}{2}\}$, we shall develop our formalism in such a way that it holds for arbitrary values of v.

Given this parametrization, we can describe the boundary conditions within any sector rather succinctly by specifying twenty v-values, four for the complex right-movers Ψ_R^μ and sixteen for the complex left-movers Ψ_L^i. We can group these twenty v-values to form a "boundary-condition" vector

$$\mathbf{V} = [\bar{v}_1, \bar{v}_2, \bar{v}_3, \bar{v}_4 \,|\, v_1, ..., v_{16}] , \qquad (6.7.5)$$

and thus we may associate a vector with each underyling string sector. For example, the sectors in Table 6.2 now correspond to the vectors shown in Table 6.5. Note that in Table 6.5, we have used a shorthand notation in which superscripts indicate repeated components. We have also dropped the minus signs from the Ramond entries $v = -\frac{1}{2}$. We stress, however, that even though we shall no longer explicitly indicate the Ramond minus sign, it should continue to be implicitly understood for all Ramond boundary conditions. (This minus sign can play an important role for string models in lower dimensions.)

What, then, are the self-consistent combinations of sectors? Recall from the previous lecture that the first self-consistent combination of sectors comprises Sectors #1 and #2 only. Let us therefore study this simplest combination. Sector #1 (the so-called NS-NS sector) corresponds to the *zero-vector* $\mathbf{0}$, the vector whose entries all vanish. Thus, in this sense, we might associate the NS-NS sector with the *origin* in a twenty-dimensional vector space. Sector #2 (the so-called Ramond-Ramond sector) then corresponds to some other point in the vector space which is some distance away from the origin. Let us call this other location $\mathbf{V}_0 \equiv [(\frac{1}{2})^4 | (\frac{1}{2})^{16}]$.

If we were to consider $\mathbf{V}_0$ to be a lattice basis vector, a natural question would be to determine the lattice that is generated by this basis vector.

Table 6.5. The eight possible sectors for ten-dimensional heterotic strings from Table 6.2, written in the boundary-condition vector notation of (6.7.5). Here the superscripts indicate repeated components, and we have dropped the minus sign for Ramond boundary conditions.

Sector #	V
1	$[(0)^4 \mid (0)^{16}]$
2	$[(\frac{1}{2})^4 \mid (\frac{1}{2})^{16}]$
3	$[(0)^4 \mid (\frac{1}{2})^{16}]$
4	$[(\frac{1}{2})^4 \mid (0)^{16}]$
5	$[(0)^4 \mid (0)^8(\frac{1}{2})^8]$
6	$[(0)^4 \mid (\frac{1}{2})^8(0)^8]$
7	$[(\frac{1}{2})^4 \mid (0)^8(\frac{1}{2})^8]$
8	$[(\frac{1}{2})^4 \mid (\frac{1}{2})^8(0)^8]$

Because there is only one such non-zero vector, this would clearly be a one-dimensional "lattice". Since $\mathbf{V}_0 \equiv [(\frac{1}{2})^4 \mid (\frac{1}{2})^{16}]$, the next point in the lattice would be $2\mathbf{V}_0 \equiv [(1)^4 \mid (1)^{16}]$. How can we interpret this point? Recall from (6.7.1) that the components of such vectors (*i.e.*, the values of v) are defined only modulo 1 (*i.e.*, they are restricted to the unit interval $-\frac{1}{2} \leq v < \frac{1}{2}$). Thus, we see that $v = 1$ is physically the same as $v = 0$, once again implying a Neveu-Schwarz boundary condition. In other words, we should only add our vectors *modulo 1*. Given this, we find that $2\mathbf{V}_0 \stackrel{1}{=} \mathbf{0}$, where we have introduced the notation $\stackrel{1}{=}$ to indicate equality modulo 1. Likewise, $3\mathbf{V}_0 \stackrel{1}{=} \mathbf{V}_0$, and so forth. Thus, we see that $\mathbf{V}_0$ generates a "lattice" consisting of only two physically distinct "points":

$$\{\mathbf{0}, \mathbf{V}_0\} \ . \tag{6.7.6}$$

However, these are precisely the two "points" that comprised our first self-consistent set of sectors (Case A in Lecture #6), and which led to our first string model!

It turns out that this is a general property: *All self-consistent choices of string sectors are those that correspond to the "points" in a twenty-dimensional lattice generated by a set of basis vectors.* To illustrate this principle, let us consider the next case (Case B in Lecture #6). In this case, we included only Sectors #1 through #4. This indicates that we need a larger lattice, which in turn implies the existence of not just the single lattice-generating basis vector $\mathbf{V}_0$, but also an additional basis vector $\mathbf{V}_1$.

One choice is:
$$\mathbf{V}_0 = [(\tfrac{1}{2})^4 \,|\, (\tfrac{1}{2})^{16}]$$
$$\mathbf{V}_1 = [(0)^4 \,|\, (\tfrac{1}{2})^{16}] \,. \qquad (6.7.7)$$

Using these choices, we can see that indeed all four of these sectors can be generated as the different "points" in the resulting lattice: Sector #1 corresponds to the origin $\mathbf{0}$, Sector #2 corresponds to $\mathbf{V}_0$ itself, Sector #3 corresponds to $\mathbf{V}_1$ itself, and Sector #4 corresponds to the remaining lattice point $\mathbf{V}_0 + \mathbf{V}_1$. Note that no other points exist in this lattice, since $2\mathbf{V}_0 \stackrel{1}{=} 2\mathbf{V}_1 \stackrel{1}{=} \mathbf{0}$. Thus, we see that the introduction of the additional basis vector $\mathbf{V}_1$ is physically equivalent to the "twist" that shifts the boundary conditions of the left-moving fermions relative to those of the right-moving fermions in Sectors #3 and #4.

Finally, let us consider the full set (Case C) consisting of Sectors #1 through #8. It is easy to see that this set is generated by the *three* basis vectors:
$$\mathbf{V}_0 = [(\tfrac{1}{2})^4 \,|\, (\tfrac{1}{2})^{16}]$$
$$\mathbf{V}_1 = [(0)^4 \,|\, (\tfrac{1}{2})^{16}]$$
$$\mathbf{V}_2 = [(0)^4 \,|\, (\tfrac{1}{2})^8 (0)^8] \,. \qquad (6.7.8)$$

Once again, the introduction of the new basis vector $\mathbf{V}_2$ implements the "twist" that separates the boundary conditions of the first set of eight left-moving fermions from those of the second set.

This procedure can be continued. Each additional basis vector introduces a new twist, increases the size of the resulting lattice, and leads to the introduction of new physical string sectors (so-called "twisted sectors"). For example, one further basis vector that might be introduced is $\mathbf{V}_3 \equiv [(0)^4 | (\tfrac{1}{2})^4 (0)^4 (\tfrac{1}{2})^4 (0)^4]$. This vector would have the effect of introducing a further twist amongst the left-moving fermions within each group of eight.

Clearly, given a set of N basis vectors $\mathbf{V}_i$ ($i = 0, ..., N-1$), the procedure for generating the full set of resulting string sectors is to consider all possible lattice vectors $\sum_{i=0}^{N-1} \alpha_i \mathbf{V}_i$ where $\alpha_i \in \{0, 1\}$. Note that this restriction on the values of α_i assumes that we are considering only Neveu-Schwarz or Ramond boundary conditions for the worldsheet fermions; generalizations to multi-periodic fermions will be discussed shortly. We shall henceforth denote a given string sector as $\alpha\mathbf{V} \equiv \sum_i \alpha_i \mathbf{V}_i$. For example, the NS-NS sector (*i.e.*, Sector #1) always corresponds to $\alpha = (0, 0, ...)$ and the Ramond-Ramond sector (*i.e.*, Sector #2) corresponds to $\alpha = (1, 0, ...)$.

At this stage, we now know how to generate the full set of underlying string sectors once we are given a "primordial" set of basis vectors $\mathbf{V}_i$. The next issue that arises is to determine the rules that govern the allowed choices of these basis vectors. Of course, we have already derived one such rule: each basis vector $\mathbf{V}_i$ must take the form

$$\mathbf{V}_i = [(\bar{v})^4 \,|\, v_1, ..., v_{16}] \tag{6.7.9}$$

where the right-moving fermions all have *same* moding $\bar{v} \in \{0, -\frac{1}{2}\}$. Indeed, as we saw in Lectures #5 and #6, this requirement is necessary for the preservation of the right-moving worldsheet supersymmetry (so that the right-moving worldsheet supercurrent has a unique moding in each sector). This is also necessary for the preservation of spacetime Lorentz invariance, since the right-moving worldsheet fermions carry Lorentz spacetime indices.

As we might expect, there are still several additional conditions that our basis vectors $\mathbf{V}_i$ must satisfy. But before we can discuss these conditions, we must turn to the generation of the GSO constraints in each sector.

6.7.2. *Generating the GSO constraints*

We have already seen in previous lectures that the appearance of new string sectors is correlated with the appearance of new GSO constraints in each sector. We are now in a position to formulate this correlation more precisely: *in each string sector, there is one GSO projection for each basis vector*. Our task, then, is to find a simple way to generate the exact forms of these GSO projections.

Let us return to Case A, and consider the model consisting of only Sectors #1 and #2. As we have seen above, this model is generated by the single basis vector $\mathbf{V}_0 \equiv [(\frac{1}{2})^4|(\frac{1}{2})^{16}]$, resulting in the two sectors $\mathbf{0}$ (Sector #1) and $\mathbf{V}_0$ (Sector #2). In each of these sectors, recall from Table 6.3 that we then had the single GSO constraint $N_L - N_R =$ odd, or equivalently

$$\sum_{i=1}^{16} N^{(i)} - \sum_{j=1}^{4} \bar{N}^{(j)} = \text{odd} . \tag{6.7.10}$$

(Here we have used the j-index to span our four complex right-moving fermions, while the i-index spans our sixteen complex left-moving fermions.) It is this GSO constraint that we now wish to write in a more transparent manner.

Given our success in using the lattice idea and modular arithmetic in order to generate the complete set of string sectors, let us attempt to write (6.7.10) in a form that makes use of both ideas. Let us first concentrate on the modular arithmetic idea. Since all of our basis vectors are defined only modulo one, let us cast (6.7.10) into the form of a modulo-one relation. Since (6.7.10) is already a modulo-two relation, this can be achieved by dividing by two:

$$\tfrac{1}{2}\sum_{i=1}^{16} N^{(i)} - \tfrac{1}{2}\sum_{j=1}^{4} N^{(j)} \stackrel{1}{=} \tfrac{1}{2} \qquad (6.7.11)$$

where we have used the notation $\stackrel{1}{=}$ to indicate equality modulo 1.

Let us now try to incorporate the lattice idea. To do this, let us make a *vector* out of our twenty number operators:

$$\mathbf{N} \equiv [\bar{N}^{(1)}, \bar{N}^{(2)}, \bar{N}^{(3)}, \bar{N}^{(4)} \,|\, N^{(1)}, ..., N^{(16)}] \,. \qquad (6.7.12)$$

Clearly, each different possible string state in a given sector corresponds to a different **N**-vector, and the physical (surviving) string states are those satisfying (6.7.11). Let us now attempt to write (6.7.11) in a vector notation. Neglecting the minus sign in (6.7.11) for the moment, we see that (6.7.11) involves a sum of vector components, which reminds us of a vector dot product. Thus, if we define the "signature" of our twenty-dimensional lattice to be $[(-)^4 \,|\, (+)^{16}]$, we can write (6.7.11) in the form of a vector dot product:

$$[(\tfrac{1}{2})^4 \,|\, (\tfrac{1}{2})^{16}] \cdot \mathbf{N} \stackrel{1}{=} \tfrac{1}{2} \qquad (6.7.13)$$

where we have introduced a vector each of whose components is equal to $\tfrac{1}{2}$. However, this vector is nothing but $\mathbf{V}_0$, the basis vector that generates the lattice for this model! Thus, we see that if our model is generated by the basis vector $\mathbf{V}_0$, then in each of the resulting sectors $\{\mathbf{0}, \mathbf{V}_0\}$ the GSO projections take the form

$$\mathbf{V}_0 \cdot \mathbf{N} \stackrel{1}{=} \tfrac{1}{2} \,. \qquad (6.7.14)$$

This produces the non-supersymmetric $SO(32)$ string model from Lecture #6!

Let us now consider Case B, consisting of Sectors #1 through #4. As we saw in Lecture #6, this produces the *supersymmetric $SO(32)$* heterotic string model, and is generated by the set of two basis vectors given in (6.7.7). In each of the four resulting sectors $\{\mathbf{0}, \mathbf{V}_0, \mathbf{V}_1, \mathbf{V}_0 + \mathbf{V}_1\}$, the *two*

GSO projections were $N_L - N_R =$ odd and $N_L =$ even. (Recall Table 6.3.) These now take the form

$$\mathbf{V}_0 \cdot \mathbf{N} \stackrel{1}{=} \tfrac{1}{2}, \qquad \mathbf{V}_1 \cdot \mathbf{N} \stackrel{1}{=} \tfrac{1}{2}. \qquad (6.7.15)$$

Similarly, Case C is generated by the *three* basis vectors in (6.7.8), and the three GSO constraints in each sector take the general form

$$N_L - N_R = ..., \qquad N_L = ..., \qquad {}^{(8)}N_L = ... \qquad (6.7.16)$$

Here ${}^{(8)}N_L \equiv \sum_{i=1}^{8} N^{(i)}$, and we shall momentarily defer a discussion of the values of the right sides of these constraint equations. We then find that these three GSO constraints take the general forms

$$\mathbf{V}_0 \cdot \mathbf{N} \stackrel{1}{=} ..., \qquad \mathbf{V}_1 \cdot \mathbf{N} \stackrel{1}{=} ..., \qquad \mathbf{V}_2 \cdot \mathbf{N} \stackrel{1}{=} ... . \qquad (6.7.17)$$

Depending on the right sides of these equations, this generates either the supersymmetric $E_8 \times E_8$ string or the non-supersymmetric $SO(16) \times SO(16)$ string.

The final question, then, is to determine what appears on the right sides of these GSO constraint equations. In general, this will be some value x which satisfies $-\tfrac{1}{2} \leq x < \tfrac{1}{2}$. This x-value is called a *GSO projection phase*, and is generally different for each sector. Thus, we know that x must itself depend on α, where (as discussed in Sec. 7.1) α parametrizes the particular sector in question. We also know from our prior experience (in particular, from Table 6.3) that x must also contain some additional *free* parameters because we occasionally still had the freedom to make choices such as $\{\text{evenodd}\}$ when constructing our GSO constraints.

It turns out the final result is the following. Within any given string sector $\alpha \mathbf{V} \equiv \sum_{i=0}^{N-1} \alpha_i \mathbf{V}_i$, the states that survive are those whose number operator vectors $\mathbf{N}$ satisfy the equations

$$\mathbf{V}_i \cdot \mathbf{N} \stackrel{1}{=} \sum_{j=0}^{N-1} k_{ij} \alpha_j + s_i - \mathbf{V}_i \cdot (\alpha \mathbf{V}), \qquad 0 \leq i \leq N-1. \qquad (6.7.18)$$

This is therefore the full set of GSO constraint equations for the sector $\alpha \mathbf{V}$. In (6.7.18), the notation is as follows. There are N different equations here, depending on the value of i. In the last term, the dot product $\mathbf{V}_i \cdot (\alpha \mathbf{V})$ is the dot product between $\mathbf{V}_i$ and the sector $\alpha \mathbf{V}$ for which the GSO constraint is being applied. In the second-to-last term, s_i is defined as the first component (*i.e.*, the first of the right-moving components) of the vector $\mathbf{V}_i$:

$$s_i \equiv \mathbf{V}_i^{(1)}. \qquad (6.7.19)$$

Thus s_i parametrizes the *spacetime statistics* of the sector $\mathbf{V}_i$, with $s_i = 0$ indicating spacetime bosons and $s_i = -\frac{1}{2}$ indicating spacetime fermions. Likewise, the sum $\sum \alpha_i s_i$ (mod 1) indicates the statistics of the sector $\alpha \mathbf{V}$. In the remaining term, k_{ij} denotes a certain $N \times N$ matrix of numbers (so-called *GSO projection phases*) satisfying $-\frac{1}{2} \leq k_{ij} < \frac{1}{2}$. These are therefore the remaining degrees of freedom that enter into our GSO constraints. In the case of $\mathbb{Z}_2$ twists (for which all fermionic boundary conditions have either Neveu-Schwarz or Ramond boundary conditions), one has $k_{ij} \in \{0, -\frac{1}{2}\}$ only. The case of multi-periodic fermions will be discussed shortly.

Thus, if we are given a set of parameters $\{\mathbf{V}_i, k_{ij}\}$, we can now generate the resulting string model and the entire corresponding spectrum! These parameters are ultimately the parameters that physically describe a given string model.

6.7.3. *Self-consistency constraints*

We finally turn to the remaining question: what determines how the parameters $\{\mathbf{V}_i, k_{ij}\}$ are to be chosen? What are the rules that guarantee a self-consistent choice?

Clearly, as we have discussed earlier, modular invariance is one of many symmetries that govern these choices. Other requirements for self-consistency include proper spacetime spin-statistics relations (so that all Ramond states are indeed anti-commuting spacetime fermions, and all Neveu-Schwarz states are commuting spacetime bosons) and physically sensible GSO projections (so that unitarity is not violated, among other things). It is important to stress that these are not *additional* constraints that need to be imposed in order to guarantee the consistency of the string in spacetime; rather these constraints are intrinsic to string theory itself at the worldsheet level, emerging as string self-consistency constraints, and together imply these features in spacetime.

We have already discussed the first contraint that governs the choices of the basis vectors: they must all have the form (6.7.9), with all right-moving fermions sharing the same boundary condition. Second, these vectors must all be linearly independent with respect to addition (modulo 1); otherwise, at least one of these vectors is redundant. The third constraint also turns out to be quite simple: among our set of basis vectors, we must always start with the vector

$$\mathbf{V}_0 \equiv [(\tfrac{1}{2})^4 \,|\, (\tfrac{1}{2})^{16}] \,. \qquad (6.7.20)$$

The presence of this vector ensures that the resulting string model contains at least a Ramond-Ramond sector in addition to a NS-NS sector.

The remaining constraints serve to correlate the $\mathbf{V}_i$ vectors with the GSO projection phases k_{ij}, and take the form:

$$k_{ij} + k_{ji} \stackrel{1}{=} \mathbf{V}_i \cdot \mathbf{V}_j$$
$$k_{ii} + k_{i0} \stackrel{1}{=} \tfrac{1}{2}\mathbf{V}_i \cdot \mathbf{V}_i - s_i \,. \quad (6.7.21)$$

Note that given a set of boundary condition vectors $\mathbf{V}_i$, the constraints (6.7.21) imply that only the elements k_{ij} with $i > j$ are independent parameters. The first equation in (6.7.21) then enables us to uniquely determine k_{ij} with $i < j$, and the second equation in (6.7.21) enables us to uniquely determine the diagonal elements k_{ii}.

6.7.4. *Summary, examples, and generalizations*

Let us now summarize the rules for heterotic string model-building in $D = 10$. We begin by choosing a set of linearly independent basis vectors $\mathbf{V}_i$ ($i = 0, ..., N - 1$) and a corresponding matrix of GSO projection phases k_{ij} ($i, j = 0, ..., N - 1$). Our set of basis vectors may be as large as we desire; since each vector corresponds to an additional twist, larger sets of vectors lead to more complicated string models. Among our choice of basis vectors must always appear the vector $\mathbf{V}_0$ defined in (6.7.20), and every basis vector is required to have the form (6.7.9). We must also ensure that our choices of basis vectors $\mathbf{V}_i$ and GSO projection phases k_{ij} are properly *correlated* according to (6.7.21). If there does not exist a solution for k_{ij}, then our original choice of $\mathbf{V}_i$ must be discarded or repaired. These are the only constraints that govern the choices of the parameters $\{\mathbf{V}_i, k_{ij}\}$.

Given such a self-consistent choice of parameters $\{\mathbf{V}_i, k_{ij}\}$, we are then guaranteed to have a self-consistent string model. The different sectors of this model are generated as all combinations $\sum_i \alpha_i \mathbf{V}_i$ that fill out the twenty-dimensional lattice, where $\alpha_i \in \{0, 1\}$. In each sector $\alpha\mathbf{V} \equiv \sum_i \alpha_i \mathbf{V}_i$, the allowed states are then those whose number operator vectors $\mathbf{N}$ simultaneously satisfy the constraints (6.7.18) for $i = 0, ..., N-1$. This is often called the *spectrum-generating formula*.

It is straightforward to see how this formalism can be applied in practice. We shall leave it as an exercise to verify that the choice

$$\mathbf{V}_0 \equiv [(\tfrac{1}{2})^4 \,|\, (\tfrac{1}{2})^{16}]\,, \quad k_{00} = (0) \quad (6.7.22)$$

generates the non-supersymmetric $SO(32)$ heterotic string model; that the choice

$$\begin{cases} \mathbf{V}_0 \equiv [(\tfrac{1}{2})^4 \,|\, (\tfrac{1}{2})^{16}] \\ \mathbf{V}_1 \equiv [(0)^4 \,|\, (\tfrac{1}{2})^{16}] \end{cases} \qquad k_{ij} = \begin{pmatrix} 0 & 0 \\ 0 & 0 \end{pmatrix} \qquad (6.7.23)$$

generates the *supersymmetric* $SO(32)$ heterotic string model; and that the choices

$$\begin{cases} \mathbf{V}_0 \equiv [(\tfrac{1}{2})^4 \,|\, (\tfrac{1}{2})^{16}] \\ \mathbf{V}_1 \equiv [(0)^4 \,|\, (\tfrac{1}{2})^{16}] \\ \mathbf{V}_2 \equiv [(0)^4 \,|\, (\tfrac{1}{2})^8 (0)^8] \end{cases} \qquad k_{ij} = \begin{pmatrix} 0 & 0 & 0 \\ 0 & 0 & k \\ 0 & k & 0 \end{pmatrix} \qquad (6.7.24)$$

generate the supersymmetric $E_8 \times E_8$ string model if we choose $k = 0$, and the non-supersymmetric $SO(16) \times SO(16)$ string model if we choose $k = 1/2$. Indeed, it is a general property that if we choose our vector $\mathbf{V}_1$ as above, then spacetime supersymmetry is preserved if $k_{i0} = k_{i1}$ for all $i = 0, 1, ..., N-1$, and broken otherwise. Thus, we see that we now have a very compact notation and procedure for generating and analyzing ten-dimensional heterotic string models! We should also stress that these are not the only parameter choices of $\{\mathbf{V}_i, k_{ij}\}$ that will lead to these models. In fact, there is often a great redundancy in this procedure, so that a given physical string model can have many different representations in terms of the worldsheet parameters $\{\mathbf{V}_i, k_{ij}\}$. However, a given set of parameters always corresponds to a single, unique, self-consistent string model in spacetime.

The formalism that we have presented in this lecture is called the "free-fermionic construction", and was developed in 1986 by H. Kawai, D.C. Lewellen, and S.-H.H. Tye and by I. Antoniadis, C. Bachas, and C. Kounnas. The name stems from the fact that the fundamental degrees of freedom on the string worldsheet (in addition to the spacetime coordinate fields X^μ) are taken to be the free fermionic fields Ψ. Even though we have presented this formalism for the case of ten-dimensional heterotic strings, there also exists a straightforward generalization of this formalism to *four-dimensional* heterotic string models.

As we have indicated, this formalism also carries over directly to the case of multi-periodic complex fermions for which the boundary condition parameter v in (6.7.1) can be an arbitrary rational number in the range $-\tfrac{1}{2} \leq v < \tfrac{1}{2}$. For each resulting boundary-condition vector $\mathbf{V}_i$, let us define

m_i to be the smallest integer such that if we multiply each element in $\mathbf{V}_i$ by m_i, we obtain a vector of integer entries. In general, m_i is called the "order" of the vector $\mathbf{V}_i$, and is also the order of the corresponding physical twist introduced by that vector. For example, in the case of only Neveu-Schwarz or Ramond fermions, we have $m_i = 2$ for all i, implying only $\mathbb{Z}_2$ twists. Nevertheless, even for general multi-periodic boundary conditions, the above constraints continue to apply exactly as written. Indeed, the only small change is that we now must take $\alpha_i \in \{0, 1, ..., m_i - 1\}$ when generating our lattice of corresponding string sectors. Likewise, each GSO projection phase k_{ij} must now also be chosen such that $m_j k_{ij} \in \mathbb{Z}$.

In this regard, it is important to note that the only fermions which can possibly have such generalized boundary conditions are those which are *not* the worldsheet superpartners of worldsheet bosons. This restriction arises because the structure of the worldsheet supersymmetry algebra itself restricts the corresponding fermions to have only Neveu-Schwarz or Ramond boundary conditions. For example, in the case of the ten-dimensional heterotic string, only the left-moving worldsheet fermions are *a priori* permitted to have generalized boundary conditions. By contrast, the right-moving fermions are restricted by the right-moving worldsheet supersymmetry algebra to have either Neveu-Schwarz or Ramond boundary conditions. This in turn implies that $s_i \in \{0, -\frac{1}{2}\}$, so that a given string sector continues to give rise to only spacetime bosons or spacetime fermions. Also note that although we are capable *in principle* of utilizing multi-periodic fermions while constructing ten-dimensional heterotic string models, in practice it turns out that this does not lead to new models which are physically distinct from those using only Ramond or Neveu-Schwarz fermions. It is for this reason that we can ultimately restrict ourselves to these simpler boundary conditions in ten dimensions without loss of generality. In lower dimensions, by contrast, this is no longer true, and the number of possible models grows dramatically.

This formalism can also be carried over to the case of ten-dimensional *superstrings* (rather than heterotic strings). For superstrings, the boundary-condition vectors take the simpler form

$$\mathbf{V}_i = [(\bar{v})^4 \,|\, (v)^4] \qquad (6.7.25)$$

where $v, \bar{v} \in \{0, \frac{1}{2}\}$. Our mandatory vector $\mathbf{V}_0$ then takes the form $[(\frac{1}{2})^4 | (\frac{1}{2})^4]$, and we define $s_i \equiv v + \bar{v} \pmod 1$ as our new spacetime statistics parameter, replacing (6.7.19). The results (6.7.21) and (6.7.18) then continue to apply directly. Of course, this formalism is fairly trivial in the case of *ten-dimensional* superstrings, for the maximal set of linearly independent basis vectors of the form (6.7.25) consists of only $\mathbf{V}_0$ and $\mathbf{V}_1 \equiv [(0)^4|(\frac{1}{2})^4]$. As we have seen in Lecture #4, this results in only four distinct superstring models in ten dimensions: omitting $\mathbf{V}_1$ from our basis set generates the Type 0 models, while including $\mathbf{V}_1$ in our basis set generates the Type II models. However, just as for the heterotic strings, this formalism can also be generalized to the case of four-dimensional superstring models where the possibilities become much richer.

It turns out that the free-fermionic formalism can be extended still further. For example, one can also extend this formalism to compactifications of the *bosonic* string. Moreover, one can even extend this formalism to special types of superstring and heterotic string models whose worldsheet actions must be represented in terms of real rather than complex fermions. Likewise, there even exist generalizations to string models involving non-free worldsheet fermions (*i.e.*, models whose worldsheet actions involve additional Thirring-type interactions between the worldsheet fermions). In fact, even though there exist alternative model-construction formalisms that do not involve free worldsheet fermions at all, the free-fermionic construction can often yield models that are physically equivalent to those that are constructed through these other means.

How general, then, is the free-fermionic construction? It turns out that for *ten-dimensional* string models, this construction is completely general. What this means is that all known physically consistent superstring and heterotic string models in ten dimensions can be realized via this construction (*i.e.*, as stemming from an underlying set of free-fermionic parameters $\{\mathbf{V}_i, k_{ij}\}$). In lower dimensions, by contrast, this construction is *not* completely general — there exist self-consistent lower-dimensional string models which cannot be written or constructed in this manner. However, the free-fermionic construction does comprise a *vast set* of semi-realistic string models. Moreover, the free-fermionic construction has the great advantage that the rules for construction are relatively simple, and that they enable one to *systematically* construct many string models and examine their phenomenological properties. Indeed, many computer programs have been written that use this formalism in order to scan the space of string models and analyze their low-energy phenomenologies. Thus, for these reasons, the free-fermionic construction has played a very useful role as the underlying method through which the majority of string model-building has historically been pursued.

6.7.5. *Assessment:*

At this point, it is perhaps useful to assess the position in which we now find ourselves. Clearly, through these constructions, we are able to produce *many* string models. In fact, as we shall see, the number of self-consistent string models in $D < 10$ is virtually infinite, and there exists a whole space of such models. This space of models is called a *moduli space*, where the so-called moduli are various continuous parameters which can be adjusted in order to yield different models. (Of course, we have seen that we have only discrete parameter choices in ten dimensions, but these parameters can become continuous in lower dimensions.) Moreover, each of these models has a completely different spacetime phenomenology. What, then, is the use of string theory as an "ultimate" theory, if it does not lead to a single, unique model with a unique low-energy phenomenology?

To answer this question, we should recall our discussion at the beginning of these lectures. Just as field theory is a language for building certain models (one of which, say, is the Standard Model), string theory is a new and deeper language by which we might also build models. The advantages of using this new language, as discussed in Lecture #1, include the fact that our resulting models incorporate quantum gravity and Planck-scale physics. Of course, in field theory, many parameters enter into the choice of model-building. These parameters include the choice of fields (for example, the choice of the gauge group, and whether or not to have spacetime supersymmetry), the number of fields (for example, the number of generations), the masses of particles, their mixing angles, and so forth. These are all *spacetime* parameters. In string theory, by contrast, we do not choose these spacetime parameters; we instead choose a set of *worldsheet* parameters. For example, in the free-fermionic construction, we choose the parameters $\{\mathbf{V}_i, k_{ij}\}$. All of the phenomenological properties in spacetime are then derived as consequences of these more fundamental choices. But still, just as in field theory, we are faced with the difficult task of model-building.

Is this progress, then? While opinions on this question may differ, one can argue that the answer is still definitely "yes". Recall that quantum gravity is automatically included in these string models. This is one of the benefits of model-building on the worldsheet rather than in spacetime. Also recall that string theory is a finite theory, and does not contain the sorts of ultraviolet divergences that plague us in field theory. This is another benefit of worldsheet, rather than spacetime, model-building. Moreover, worldsheet model-building ultimately involves choosing *fewer* parameters than we would have to choose in field theory — for example, we have seen that an entire infinite tower of string states, their gauge groups and charges and spins, are all ultimately encoded in a few underlying worldsheet parameters such as $\{\mathbf{V}_i, k_{ij}\}$. Furthermore, because of this drastic reduction in the number of free parameters, string phenomenology is in many ways more tightly constrained than ordinary field-theoretic phenomenology. Thus, it is in this way that string theory can guide our choices and expectations for physics beyond the Standard Model. Indeed, from a string perspective, we see that we should favor only those patterns of spacetime physics that can ultimately be derived from an underlying set of worldsheet parameters such as $\{\mathbf{V}_i, k_{ij}\}$. These would then serve as a "minimal set" of parameters which would govern all of spacetime physics!

Of course, at a theoretical or philosophical level, this state of affairs is still somewhat unsatisfactory. After all, we still do not know *which* self-consistent choice of string parameters ultimately corresponds to reality. However, *in principle*, string theory should be able to predict this dynamically. Indeed, even though there exists a whole moduli space of self-consistent string models, there should exist an energy or potential function in this space (*i.e.*, some function $V(\{\phi\})$ of all the moduli $\{\phi\}$) which should dynamically select a particular point in moduli space (*e.g.*, as a local or global minimum of V). This would then fix all of the moduli to specific values, or equivalently (in the language of the free-fermionic construction) tell us which choices of parameters $\{\mathbf{V}_i, k_{ij}\}$ are preferred dynamically.

Unfortunately, we do not understand the dynamics of string theory well enough to carry out such an ambitious undertaking. Certainly, at the level of perturbative (weakly coupled) string theory, we have no way to distinguish amongst the possible low-energy models by calculating such a function $V(\{\phi\})$. This is particularly true for string models exhibiting spacetime supersymmetry, for which $V = 0$ exactly to all orders in perturbation theory. Even if the spacetime supersymmetry is broken, the resulting potential $V(\{\phi\})$ often turns out not to have a stable minimum. This is the so-called "runaway problem", to be discussed further in Lecture #8. Of course, one might hope that recent advances in understanding the *non-perturbative* structure of string theory will ultimately be able to provide guidance in this direction. However, as we shall discuss briefly in Lecture #8, although these non-perturbative insights (particularly those concerning string duality) have thus far changed our understanding of the size and shape of this moduli space, they have not yet succeeded in leading us to an explanation of which points in this moduli space are dynamically selected.

So where do we stand? As string phenomenologists, we can do two things. First, we can pursue *model-building*: we can search through the moduli space of self-consistent string models in order to determine how close to realistic spacetime physics we can come. This is, in some sense, a direct test of string theory as a phenomenological theory of physics. Of course, this approach to string phenomenology is ultimately limited by many factors: we have no assurance that our model-construction techniques are sufficiently powerful or general to include the "correct" string model (assuming that one exists); we have no assurance that our model-construction techniques will not lead to physically distinct models which nevertheless "agree" as far as their testable low-energy predictions are concerned; and we have no assurance that the most important phenomenological features that describe our low-energy world (such as the pattern of supersymmetry-breaking) are to be found in perturbative string theory rather than in non-perturbative string theory. For example, it may well be (and it has indeed been argued) that the true underlying string theory that describes nature is one which is intrinsically non-perturbative, and which would therefore be beyond the reach of the sorts of approaches typically followed in studies of string phenomenology.

Another option, then, is to temporarily abandon string model-building somewhat, and to seek to extract general phenomenological theorems or correlations about spacetime physics that follow directly from the general structure of string theory itself. Clearly, we would wish such information to be *model-independent*, *i.e.*, independent of our particular location in moduli space or the values of particular string parameters such as $\{\mathbf{V}_i, k_{ij}\}$. For example, if some particular configuration of spacetime physics (some pattern of low-energy phenomenology) can be shown to be inconsistent with being realized from an underlying set of $\{\mathbf{V}_i, k_{ij}\}$ parameters, and if such a demonstration can be made to transcend the particular free-fermionic construction so that it relies on only the primordial string symmetries themselves, then such patterns of phenomenology can be ruled out. In this way, one can still use string theory in order to narrow the list of possibilities for physics at higher energies, and to correlate various seemingly disconnected phenomenological features with each other. Such correlations would then be viewed as "predictions" from string theory, and we shall see many examples of this phenomenon in subsequent lectures.

In summary, then, we have seen that there exist powerful ways of constructing string models and surveying their low-energy phenomenologies, but that this leads to the problem of selecting the true model (*i.e.*, the true "ground state" or "vacuum") of string theory. Despite recent advances in understanding various non-perturbative aspects of string theory, our inability to answer the fundamental question of vacuum selection persists. Until this challenge is overcome, string phenomenology therefore must content itself with answering questions of a *relative* nature (such as questions concerning relative *patterns* of phenomenology) rather than the sorts of absolute questions (such as calculating the mass of the electron) that one would also ideally like to ask. Nevertheless, as we shall see, string theory can still provide us with considerable guidance for physics beyond the Standard Model.

6.8. Lecture #8: A final lecture

Up to this point, we have primarily discussed string *model-building* — *i.e.*, the art of building string models. Hopefully, we have given the reader some sense of the complexity of the many constraints that are involved. In this final lecture, however, we shall depart from the somewhat "linear" development we have followed thus far in order to discuss *string phenomenology* — the study of the low-energy physical attributes of these models.

In the first part of this final lecture, we shall outline some general properties of four-dimensional heterotic string models. Then, we shall contrast these with the phenomenological properties of open-string D-brane models. Finally, we shall provide general comments concerning string phenomenology as a whole, and conclude with a brief discussion of some new, recent directions in string phenomenology.

6.8.1. *General properties of perturbative $D = 4$ heterotic string models*

In previous lectures, we have discussed the construction of perturbative heterotic string models. Here, we shall now turn the general low-energy properties that emerge from these constructions.

First, such models all have big gauge groups. For perturbative heterotic strings in four dimensions, we find that

$$\text{rank}(G) \leq 22 \ . \tag{6.8.1}$$

This is the four-dimensional analogue of the observation that the maximum rank in 10 dimensions is 16, such as for the $SO(32)$ and $E_8 \times E_8$ heterotic strings. The additional six units of rank emerge from the Kaluza-Klein reduction from $D = 10$ to $D = 4$.

If the string model in question is "realistic", then typically we can write

$$G = G_1 \times G_2 \qquad (6.8.2)$$

where G_1 contains $SU(3) \times SU(2) \times U(1)_{\text{hypercharge}}$. Here G_1 is called the "observable-sector" gauge group: *e.g.*, G_1 could be $SU(3) \times SU(2) \times U(1)$, $SO(6) \times SO(4)$, $SU(5)$, $SO(10)$, E_6, *etc.* By contrast, G_2 is called the "hidden-sector" gauge group.

Second, there are typically lots of massless ("observable") states! These can be classified into several categories:

- Typical representations will carry charges under both G_1 and G_2 (*i.e.*, transform as non-singlet representations of these groups). In general, we will only have spinors, vectors (*i.e.*, fundamentals), and adjoints at the massless string level. (This is indeed a theorem: the allowed representations are closely tied to something called the "affine level" of the gauge group.) These states will typically fall into two subsets. First, there may be states that can be identified as (MS)SM quarks and leptons. In such cases, all gauge symmetry groups under which the SM gauge particles transform as singlets are considered to be part of G_2, *i.e.*, the hidden sector. Second, there can be extra states *beyond* the (MS)SM. There will typically be a lot of such states as well. They may be identified as exotic quarks and leptons. They will typically have fractional electric charge. This could cause problems (see below).
- Many gauge-*singlet* states (*i.e.*, states carrying no gauge charges) will also exist in the string model. For example, such states include the graviton, antisymmetric tensor, and dilaton ϕ. Recall that $g_{\text{string}} \sim \exp(-\langle\phi\rangle)$. Thus, the dilaton must be stabilized to yield a fixed value for the string coupling, and to avoid the so-called "dilaton runaway problem" (wherein $\langle\phi\rangle \to \infty$, or $g_{\text{string}} \to 0$).

The dilaton is just one example of a generic class of Lorentz-singlet particles called string "moduli". The effective potential for such models is *flat* to all orders in perturbation theory. Thus, non-perturbative string effects must somehow introduce a potential for these fields, *i.e.*, lift the degeneracy of string "ground states" and select a string vacuum. But how does this happen? This is a major unsolved problem, with lots of ideas in the literature. This is critically important for string phenomenology, since the vevs of the moduli set the values for gauge couplings, particle masses, and so forth. Without knowing the values of these couplings, the best we can look for is string-constrained *patterns* (textures) in these parameters.

Third, there will be infinite towers of Planck-scale string states! These states come in increasingly larger representations of gauge groups, and likewise have higher and higher Lorentz spins. These states are the means by which string theory maintains finiteness. They propagate in all string loop diagrams, and their contributions cancel the divergences of the massless states. They are the result of conformal invariance (really its one-loop extension, called "modular invariance").

One interesting fact about these states is that the number of such massive states with spacetime mass M grows *exponentially*:

$$g_M \sim \exp(cM\sqrt{\alpha'}) \qquad (6.8.3)$$

where c is a fixed positive constant. One of the implications of an exponentially growing degeneracy is as follows. Let us consider the thermodynamic partition function:

$$Z \equiv \sum_M g_M \exp(-M/kT) \qquad (6.8.4)$$

where T is the temperature and k is Boltzmann's constant. This gives:

$$Z = \sum_M \exp[M(c\sqrt{\alpha'} - 1/kT)] \,. \qquad (6.8.5)$$

Thus, if T is bigger than a critical value

$$T_c \equiv (kc\sqrt{\alpha'})^{-1} \,, \qquad (6.8.6)$$

then the thermodynamic partition function *diverges*! This is the so-called "Hagedorn" phenomenon.

Does this signal a phase transition? Or is there instead a limiting ("Hagedorn") temperature for string theory beyond which one cannot go? What happens to a box of strings (*i.e.*, the "universe") if we pump in lots of energy and try to raise the temperature?

The answers to these questions are really not known. The current belief is that we have a phase transition in which all extra energy gets dumped into long string modes. But the nature of this phase transition is generally unclear. Indeed, this Hagedorn phenomenon is one of the central hallmarks of the the subject of *string thermodynamics*. As might be imagined, this subject is of critical importance for string cosmology and for string-based studies of the early universe.

Fourth, such heterotic string models will typically give rise to a single "pseudo-anomalous" $U(1)$ gauge group! Recall that in field theory, given a set of states with $U(1)$ charges Q_i, we must have $\sum_i Q_i = 0$ in order to cancel axial (triangle) anomalies. In particular, certainly the hypercharge $U(1)$ must be anomaly-free.

However, in (many/most) heterotic string models, gauge groups are big and there can be *extra* $U(1)$ gauge groups. One finds, upon summing over massless spectrum, that *one* of these gauge groups, typically denoted $U(1)_X$, has corresponding states with charges Q_X such that $\sum Q_X \neq 0$. Thus, from the field-theory point of view, this $U(1)_X$ appears to be anomalous!

In fact, however, this gauge group is not anomalous (since string theory is always anomaly-free); there are extra contributions to the apparent anomaly which come from anomalous transformations of the string "axion field" (related to the antisymmetric tensor $B_{\mu\nu}$) which cancel this anomaly. This is an intrinsically "stringy" mechanism (called the Green-Schwarz mechanism) for cancelling an anomaly.

Fifth, such models typically give rise to automatic gauge coupling unification (regardless of existence of any GUT symmetry in the string model). In fact, the gauge couplings are even unified with the gravitational coupling!

It is easy to understand why this is the case. Recall that our original "untwisted" four-dimensional heterotic string model has a "unified" gauge group $SO(44)$, with one gauge gauge coupling whose value is set by the dilaton vev. (This is the analogue of $SO(32)$ in ten dimensions.) When we break subsequently break the gauge symmetry by introducing twists ("orbifolding"), this does not affect the gauge couplings. They are still all set by the same dilaton vev (ultimately because there is only *one* dilaton to which all gauge groups can couple). Thus, gauge coupling unification is automatic in heterotic string theory.

One important question is the *scale* of the unification. Clearly, by dimensional analysis, this can be nothing but the string scale. At tree-level, we have already seen in Lecture #1 that the string scale is given by $M_{\text{string}} = g_{\text{string}} M_{\text{Planck}}$. However, work by Kaplunovsky has shown that at one-loop order, and with the usual GUT assumption of $g_{\text{string}} \approx 0.7$, this result is shifted down to an approximate value, $M_{\text{string}} \approx 5.27 \times 10^{17}$ GeV. This is generally a problem, since the expected GUT value for the unification scale is $M_{\text{GUT}} = 2 \times 10^{16}$ GeV. How then do we explain this factor-of-20 discrepancy between M_{string} and M_{GUT}? This is currently an open question, with many potential solutions. A comprehensive review of this subject can be found in K.R. Dienes, Phys Reports 287 (1997) 447 = hep-th/9602045.

Sixth, such models typically give rise to states with fractional electric charge. We already referred to this above. Indeed, extra states beyond the MSSM will typically have $SU(2) \times U(1)$ quantum numbers which imply non-integer values for the electric charge. In fact, one can prove (see theorem by A.N. Schellekens) that if the model has a gauge symmetry $SU(3) \times SU(2) \times U(1)$ rather than a GUT, then the string will *necessarily* give rise to such fractionally charged states. This is a result of conformal invariance and modular invariance.

One possible resolution to this problem is that such fractionally charged states might be able to *confine* to form integer-charged states under the influence of non-abelian gauge symmetries beyond the SM. However, if this is not possible in a given string model, then that model is generally considered to be phenomenologically inconsistent.

General theorems exist which enable one to classify the different types of fractional charges one can expect to find in a given string model and which can be "confined" away. (We refer the reader to papers by Schellekens; also by Dienes, Faraggi, March-Russell.)

Seventh, it turns out that such string models *cannot* contain any exact global symmetries! For example, in heterotic string theory, baryon- and lepton-number conservation, as well as other discrete symmetries, must all be parts of *local* symmetries (gauge symmetries) or be only approximate symmetries (*i.e.*, accidental).

Eighth, such heterotic string models will either exhibit spacetime supersymmetry, or they will be non-supersymmetric. If non-supersymmetric, however, they nevertheless have a hidden symmetry called a "misaligned supersymmetry" which governs how the bosons and fermions are arranged at all mass levels so that finiteness is preserved, even without SUSY. Even the supertraces, when evaluated over the entire Fock space of string states, continue to vanish. [References include K.R. Dienes, Nucl. Phys. B429 (1994) 533; K.R. Dienes, M. Moshe, and R.C. Myers, Phys. Rev. Lett. 74 (1995) 4767.]

However, it is not known whether such non-supersymmetric strings can ever be stable beyond tree level. This is an important open question in string theory. However, if such stable non-SUSY strings exist, then this could provide a whole new framework for thinking about the gauge hierarchy problem, SUSY-breaking, questions of finiteness, the role of effective field theories and in particular the massive Planck-scale states, and gauge coupling unification. This may even provide an alternative, "stringy" approach towards the hierarchy problem which does not involve either supersymmetry or extra spacetime dimensions. [For some speculative ideas along this direction, see K.R. Dienes, hep-th/0104274.]

Ninth, the spacetime string spectrum can exhibit certain dualities. Indeed, there are several kinds of duality which, taken together, form an interconnected web of relations between different kinds of string theories.

- One kind of duality is called "T-duality". Consider string #1, compactified on a circle of radius R, and string #2, compactified on a circle of radius $\sqrt{\alpha'}/R$. It turns out that these strings are indistinguishable, in the sense that they have exactly the same spacetime spectrum! What would be considered a momentum state in string #1 would be considered a winding-mode state in string #2, and vice versa. This is clearly a very "stringy" symmetry! In fact, this symmetry transcends the mere tree-level spectrum, and holds to all orders. It also applies for all correlation functions, scattering amplitudes, both perturbatively and even non-perturbatively. This is an exact symmetry of closed string theories.

   One important implication of T-duality is that closed string theory (unlike point-particle field theory) cannot distinguish between large and small compactification radii! An interesting question is what this might imply about string cosmology. Likewise, what are the implications about our ultimate ability to derive *effective field theories* from the string?

- There are also other kinds of dualities which exist amongst the different string theories. For example, there is a duality called "S-duality" which flips the sign of the dilaton and thus relates theories at weak coupling to theories at strong coupling! Under such a mapping, perturbative string states (such as the ones we have been considering all along) are exchanged with non-perturbative string states (which have not considered at all, but which are "solitons" = D-branes in the theory). Under this mapping, for example, the $SO(32)$ heterotic (closed) string theory is mapped into the $SO(32)$ Type I (open) string theory. Combined with T-duality, one finds that all the different kinds of ten-dimensional strings are ultimately related to each other, becoming part of a larger superstructure called "M-theory".

The study of string dualities is a vast subject which easily deserves its own lectures, and which comprises the so-called "second" superstring revolution, dating from 1995. Indeed, insights have enabled us, in many cases, to "solve" for the strong-behavior of string theory!

I cannot give a proper introduction to M-theory here, but I will simply give some general comments. M-theory is a conjectured eleven-dimensional theory (of strings? of membranes? – we don't know) which can be *defined* through its three fundamental properties:

- The low-energy limit of M-theory is eleven-dimensional SUGRA (recall that $D = 11$ is the maximum dimension for SUGRA).
- Compactifying M-theory on a circle of radius R yields the Type IIA string with a coupling that is a growing function of R. So, at strong coupling, the Type IIA string begins to "see" an extra dimension and become eleven-dimensional.
- Compactifying M-theory on a line segment of length L yields the $E_8 \times E_8$ heterotic string with a coupling that grows with L. This is why one does not see this 11th dimension in studies of the perturbative heterotic string: the very act of taking the string coupling to be small reduces the 11th dimension to zero size!

Studying M-theory and its compactifications (and its phenomenological properties, such as how SUSY-breaking may be realized in this framework) has been a hot topic in the string literature. In particular, one may ask whether it is possible to compactify M-theory to four dimensions in ways that do *not* pass through an intermediate realization in terms of a $D = 10$ heterotic string, thereby constructing new classes of four-dimensional string models? The answer is to this question is 'yes'. Thus, even without knowing the precise nature of M-theory, it has already been possible to use insights gleaned from the mere existence of such a theory in order to generate new classes of string models.

Taken together, these developments have led to the realization that many of our cherished "fundamental" string symmetries (such as conformal invariance, modular invariance, etc.) are only *effective* weak-coupling symmetries, applicable only for closed strings. Thus, as the string coupling grows in closed string theories, we expect to see *deviations* from the constraints that come from these symmetries. This could be very useful in "freeing up" certain undesirable predictions of string phenomenology, even within closed strings.

6.8.2. General properties of $D = 4$ open-string models

Many of the above phenomenological features of heterotic strings change when one deals with Type I theories (*i.e.*, theories which include *open* strings). Some of the most viable models in this class that have chiral spectra include so-called "intersecting D-brane Models" as well as models with D-branes at singularities. Unfortunately, we do not have the space here to discuss such constructions. However, there are excellent reviews available, In particular, we refer the reader to R. Blumenhagen, M. Cvetic, P. Langacker, and G. Shiu, hep-th/0502005 and to M. Grana, hep-th/0509003.

There are many reasons to examine such Type I theories. Of course, they are interesting in their own right since they are among the possible allowed string constructions. However, as a result of the various string dualities discussed above, such strings often represent the strong-coupling limits of the heterotic models (this is "heterotic/Type I duality", a component of S-duality). Thus, by studying Type I string models, one is often really analyzing the strong-coupling limit of a closed heterotic string model.

We cannot provide a complete discussion of such Type I models here. However, the basic ideas are simple. Unlike heterotic string models, which realize their gauge symmetries along the closed strings through Kaluza-Klein reductions from 10 or 26 dimensions (as discussed above), gauge symmetries are realized in open strings through so-called "Chan-Paton factors" which reside at the endpoints of the open strings. These are the analogues of "quarks" at the ends of the open strings, and they carry the gauge charges associated with the string states.

Nowadays these Chan-Paton factors are reinterpreted as the labels associated with D-branes, so that open strings are considered to have endpoints which are restricted to lie on D-branes. Indeed, one definition of a D-brane is that it represents a solitonic membrane-like object on which an open strings can end. A single D-brane corresponds to a $U(1)$ gauge symmetry (the corresponding photon being represented by an open string which starts and ends on the brane), while non-abelian $U(N)$ gauge symmetries are realized through stacks of N coincident D-branes. In such configurations, the non-abelian gauge bosons are realized as strings which start and end on different D-branes within the stack. The Higgs mechanism (by which certain gauge symmetries can be broken and certain corresponding gauge bosons get heavy) can be realized in this framework by separating branes within the stack; those strings which start and end on different D-branes get stretched as a result of this separation, and thus become massive as a result of the tension involved in that stretching.

In general, within such constructions, one might realize the Standard Model through an $SU(3)$ stack of D-branes and an $SU(2)$ stack of D-branes. In such a scenario, quarks (which carrying non-trivial $SU(3)$ and $U(2)$ gauge charges) would be represented by strings stretching from the $SU(3)$ stack to the $SU(2)$ stack; such states can indeed be light (or massless) if these stacks of branes intersect, and the strings lie near that intersection. Of course, gravitational physics continues to be represented by closed strings which, having no endpoints, are not tied to particular branes and can therefore propagate freely in the "bulk". In general, only those states which are neutral with respect to all gauge symmetries (such as gravitons) are permitted to wander freely in the entire volume both within and transverse to the branes. In certain constructions, other possible closed-string states might include right-handed neutrinos (which are also completely neutral with respect to all Standard-Model gauge symmetries).

In general, the requirements of spacetime supersymmetry imply that the theory contain combinations of D-branes of only certain dimensionalities; likewise, the relative positions and/or geometric intersections of these D-branes are highly constrained. There are also generally other extended objects in these theories (beyond D-branes): these include anti-Dbranes, orientifold planes, and other types of branes (such as NS branes). Anomaly cancellation considerations end up playing a huge role in determining which configurations of all of these objects are required to form self-consistent string models.

Other than these constraints, however, one has tremendous freedom in designing D-brane configurations, compactifying the theory, wrapping the D-branes around the compactification manifolds, and so forth. This is then the art of Type I model building. Because of the tremendous range of allowed D-brane configurations and dimensionalities, and because the closed-string and open-string sectors have very different properties, Type I string phenomenology turns out to be *very rich* and *unconstrained* compared to heterotic string phenomenology.

In particular, even without providing details concerning such constructions, it is possible to summarize some of the major phenomenological differences between these string models and the closed (heterotic) strings discussed above.

First, the rank of the gauge group no longer restricted to 22! Indeed, non-perturbative effects can give rise to new gauge interactions that can increase the total rank beyond 22, and there is no bound to how large these gauge groups can become! (You can decide for yourself whether you consider this to be a good thing...)

Second, the fundamental scale of the theory (M_{string}) is no longer tied to M_{Planck}. The usual heterotic relation $M_{\text{string}} = g_{\text{string}} M_{\text{Planck}}$ no longer applies to open strings. The reason is that for closed strings, both gauge forces and the gravitational force emerge together. However, for Type I strings, the gravitational force emerges from the closed-string sector, while the gauge forces typically emerge from the open-string sectors. This difference introduces an undetermined "rescaling" factor between the different sectors, and therefore allows one to "dial" M_{string} as we wish in such theories. [For more details, see Chapter 10 of K.R. Dienes, Phys Reports 287 (1997) 447 = hep-th/9602045, which summarizes the original proposal of Witten: E. Witten, Nucl Phys B 471, 135 (1996)]. One could conceivably dial the Type I string scale all the way down to the TeV range – see, *e.g.*, J. Lykken, PRD 54, 3693 (1996); K.R. Dienes, E. Dudas, T. Gherghetta, Nucl. Phys. B537, 47 (1999); G. Shiu, S.-H.H. Tye, Nucl. Phys. B548, 180 (1999).

This freedom to adjust the string scale and realize the Standard Model as an open string living on a brane while gravitational fields correspond to closed strings living in the bulk is the primary reason why Type I strings provide the natural realization (and inspiration) for extra-dimensional "brane-world" scenarios.

Third, for weakly coupled heterotic strings, there is only one dilaton-like field which couples to all gauge groups and matter fields in a universal way. However, in Type I theories there can generally be *multiple* dilaton-like fields.

Fourth, for Type I theories, gauge coupling unification is no longer automatic. This is a consequence of the existence of multiple dilaton-like fields. Each gauge coupling can be determined by the vev of a different dilaton field, and likewise the gauge theories living on different D-branes can experience different transverse volumes which also affect the values of their respective gauge couplings.

Fifth, in heterotic strings, there was only one anomalous $U(1)$ because there was only one dilaton to cancel this anomaly through the Green-Scwharz mechanism. However, in Type I theories there can be multiple anomalous $U(1)$'s because the presence of multiple dilatons in Type I theories implies that there can be a generalized Green-Schwarz mechanism which cancels multiple $U(1)$ anomalies.

Sixth, it turns out that whole new types of spacetime compactifications are possible. In heterotic strings, one must compactify on a so-called "Calabi-Yau" manifold if one wishes to preserve N=1 spacetime supersymmetry. (See Polchinski's textbook for a complete discussion: technically CY manifolds are six-dimensional complex manifolds with $SU(3)$ holonomy or equivalently vanishing first Chern class.) While the simple cases of tori (and orbifolds thereof) are well understood, the general full class of CY manifolds is not well understood (not even classified by mathematicians) and it is hard to perform detailed calculations of the resulting low-energy phenomenologies that emerge when heterotic strings are compactified on such spaces.

Type I string models are different. Because the matter arises locally (on branes) rather than globally (in the bulk), the compactification geometry is less constrained. For example, chirality no longer requires compactification on an orbifold, since chirality can instead emerge directly from D-brane intersections even when the compactification space is a smooth manifold.

For further discussions of these differences between the phenomenologies of open and closed strings, good references are: L.E. Ibanez, hep-th/9804236; F. Quevedo, Trieste String School Lectures, March 2002.

6.8.3. *String model-building and string phenomenology: General practice and goals*

Having discussed the different types of phenomenological features of these different types of string models, we now outline the basic way in which the string model-building game is played. Of course, the following steps are merely caricatures, with many details omitted. Nevertheless, they do indicate the rough methodology that a string phenomenologist must follow in order to claim to have a realistic string model.

The first step, as always, is to build the candidate string model itself. We have discussed how to do this in great detail in previous lectures. This is the string "model-building" aspect of string phenomenology. How one goes about doing this will depend on the particular string framework one has in mind, whether closed or open strings are involved, whether one is dealing with perturbative or non-perturbative constructions, and so forth. Each construction will carry with it its own constraints, its own techniques, and its own unique advantages and difficulties.

Once one has a particular string model in hand, one then extracts the gauge symmetry, the particle content (massless spectrum only, if one cares only about questions pertaining to observable low-energy states), and all associated charges and couplings.

The next step, if necessary (such as in heterotic strings), is to do a so-called "string vacuum shift". This is a technical step. Recall that there often exists a pseudo-anomalous $U(1)_X$ gauge symmetry. Although this is not really anomalous, it leads to an effective Fayet-Iliopoulos D-term which can break spacetime SUSY and destabilize the string vacuum. So, in order to "fix" this problem, one shifts the ground state slightly: one assigns a vev to certain moduli in the theory in order to break the $U(1)_X$ gauge symmetry and cancel the D-term. This makes the model stable again. This vev may often also break other gauge symmetries in addition to $U(1)_X$. It also can generate intermediate mass scales for various light states in the string model.

The third step is to write down an effective Lagrangian of these light fields that are derived from the string. Typically we will write something of the form

$$\mathcal{L} = \mathcal{L}_{\text{SUGRA}} + \mathcal{L}_{\text{matter}} + \mathcal{L}_{\text{couplings}} \,. \tag{6.8.7}$$

These different pieces are as follows.

- $\mathcal{L}_{\text{SUGRA}}$: This must be appropriate for the given model in question, e.g., $N = 0$ (non-susy), or $N = 1$, or Type IIA or IIB SUGRA, etc.
- $\mathcal{L}_{\text{matter}}$: This will consist of the kinetic terms for all light fields (including an appropriate dilaton dependence).
- $\mathcal{L}_{\text{couplings}}$: Here, we must include all couplings allowed by string symmetries, given the charges that these states have under both observable and hidden-sector gauge symmetries (i.e., selection rules). These will include renormalizable *and* non-renormalizable couplings, where the non-renormalizable ones are suppressed by powers of the string scale M_{string}. In principle, one should calculate the coefficients that pre-multiply these terms by explicitly evaluating the appropriate corresponding string diagrams.

All together, this is the "effective Lagrangian from the string model". One must make sure that it is consistent with all string symmetries (*e.g.*, T-duality, S-duality, others) if you are going to ask physics questions for which those symmetries are likely to be important.

The final step is to proceed to analyze the physics of the string model by analyzing the effective field theory of the effective Lagrangian derived from the string. We treat this Lagrangian as describing the physics at the string scale, and use RGE's to pass to lower energy scales (as we would in ordinary field theory). Along the way (*i.e.*, at intermediate scales), various new features can arise. For example, although Standard Model gauge groups will hopefully stay perturbative, the *hidden-sector* gauge couplings *may*, depending on the particle content, become strong and non-perturbative at some intermediate scale. This can trigger the corresponding gauginos to condense ("gaugino condensation"). which in turn can trigger SUSY-breaking. This is indeed an elegant string-inspired but field-theoretic means of breaking SUSY at intermediate energy scales. Likewise, extra matter beyond the MSSM (with masses determined by vacuum shifting, as discussed) can decouple. Clearly, the analysis for this sep is generally very model-dependent!

Ultimately, we seek to reproduce the low-energy world at the TeV-scale — *i.e.*, we wish to reproduce the Standard Model, and then study the phenomenological implications of the extra string-inspired particles or interactions that are predicted at higher scales. For example, one might construct string GUT models (realizing standard field-theory GUT scenarios from string theory), or realize the Standard Model directly at the string scale without an intervening GUT, or...

Given this procedure as outlined, one might wonder what the goals of string phenomenology ultimately are. Is it sufficient to try to construct semi-realistic string models, or are there are other goals as well? While a conversation on this topic can easily yield as many opinions as there are people in the conversation, the following represent the personal opinions of your humble lecturer. Therefore, the reader is forewarned about the potential bias of the lecturer.

Clearly, one important and undeniable goal must be to try to construct realistic string models, *i.e.*, to see how far one can really "push" the embedding of the low-energy world into string theory, to test the extent to which one can really make string theory consistent with the real world.

Unfortunately, this is very model-dependent. Also, given the large (infinite) "moduli" space of all possible string models, it is hard (impossible?) to believe that we would really be lucky enough to stumble across the right string model (assuming one exists).

Also, although we discussed one particular method of model-construction in these lectures (the so-called "free-fermionic construction" for closed strings), its applications and scope are limited (it essentially only hits discrete points in moduli space). They are points of enhanced symmetry, so they may indeed be special, but we don't know the structure of moduli space well enough to have a feeling for whether other, more compelling points might exist. And for open strings, we have seen the possibilities are even more varied!

Therefore, an alternative goal might be to try to uncover *model-independent* phenomenological truths from string theory. For example, one might ask questions such as

- What "patterns" of low-energy phenomenology are consistent with coming from or being realized from an underlying string theory?
- What "patterns" of low-energy phenomenology can be excluded?
- What sorts of "correlations" does string theory predict between phenomenological features that would otherwise appear to be completely independent from a field theory point of view? As an example, string theory predicts correlations between gauge groups and fractional charges, *etc.* These correlations are ultimately the reflections of the deeper string symmetries (*i.e.*, worldsheet symmetries) from which all spacetime physics is ultimately derived. For further editorializing along these lines, see the comments about the string landscape at the end of this lecture. In this way, we can then ask the question:
- What *guidance* does string theory provide for answering or addressing questions of physics beyond the Standard Model?

Of course, string theory also has the potential to provide insights of a completely different nature. For example, just as field theory provides certain mechanisms for addressing long-standing questions of particle physics, string theory (viewed as a general theory of extended objects) has the potential to provide new, additional, intrinsically geometric mechanisms for solving some of these same problems. Moreover, these mechanisms may also be able to generate new approaches to solving long-statnding problems that ordinary field theories based on point particles cannot reach. Thus, string phenomenology may be able to enlarge the domain of problems that a particle physicist might hope to address, and provide new tools for this endeavor.

But finally, perhaps the most important unresolved problem within string phenomenology is to understand what selects the string vacuum. Clearly, in order to make full progress in our understanding of string theory and its low-energy phenomenological predictions, we must eventually uncover the dynamics (presumably non-perturbative or semi-perturbative, or involving a mix of perturbative and non-perturbative physics) which ultimately pushes the universe towards the true ground state of string theory, the one in which we live.

Progress along these lines will be very hard, but is very important. Perhaps insight will come (or even may be coming) from recent developments in string duality. This problem seems tied up with the whole issue of how SUSY is broken, and the cosmological constant problem, so it is likely to take some time.

6.8.4. *New/current directions in string phenomenology*

We close this final lecture with a brief discussion of three new/current directions in string phenomenology. Once again, the following list is hardly complete. However, it does capture several of the main thrusts of string phenomenology research over the past few years, and the directions which are likely to hold the attention of string phenonenologists for the forseeable future.

Large-radius compactifications / TeV-scale strings

Many of you probably consider higher-dimensional "brane world" scenarios as something separate from string theory. But in truth, much of this work is really a branch of string phenomenology: one is studying the properties of string theories in a corner of the parameter space where the compactification radii are large, or where the Standard Model is restricted to a brane (stack) as in Type I models! Indeed, the whole setup of much of this work (SM restricted to a brane, gravity propagating in the bulk, and so forth) really emerges from Type I string theories where the SM is realized through open strings (whose endpoints therefore must lie on D-branes) and the graviton is realized through closed strings (which have no endpoints and which are therefore free to wander throughout the full higher-dimensional spacetime).

Thus, when one studies issues of flavor physics or develops new higher-dimensional mechanisms for understanding hierarchies, supersymmetry breaking, proton stability, *etc*, one is really developing an understanding of the phenomenology of open strings in a particular corner of compactification parameter space! In other words, the *brane world* is nothing but a branch of string phenomenology, studied through an effective field theory approach which might ultimately emerge from an underlying (Type I) string.

In addition to Kaustubh Agashe's excellent lectures on this subject at this year's TASI school, I recommend (of course) my own TASI 2002 lectures on the brane world: K.R. Dienes, 2002 TASI Lectures: New Directions for New Dimensions: An Introduction to Kaluza-Klein Theory, Large Extra Dimensions, and the Brane World", available at http://scipp.ucsc.edu/haber/tasi_proceedings/dienes.ps.

Flux compactifications

Another line of intense research in recent years concerns the possibility of so-called *flux compactifications*. There are compactifications in which various background fluxes associated with different p-form gauge fields in the theory are actually turned on. (Previous work had always assumed that such fluxes were zero.) It turns out that turning on such fluxes has a number of important effects. For example, the constraints on the allowed compactification geometries are modified, and the extra flux contributions allow us to go beyond the simple class of Calabi-Yau compactifications.

However, the most important phenomenological aspect of such flux compactifications is that they provide a framework leading to new methods of moduli stabilization. Indeed, within the framework of flux compactifications, it has been been possible to build semi-realistic string models in which the vast majority of complex and Kähler moduli are completely frozen!

Flux compactifications thus provide a new arena in which to address the all-important issues of moduli stabilization and vacuum selection. Indeed, work of Kachru, Kallosh, Linde, and Trivedi (KKLT) has even provided a framework in which it might be possible to realize meta-stable string vacua with deSitter (dS) geometries. This is of critical importance if string theory is to make contact with cosmological evolution.

The string theory "landscape"

Finally, as we have seen repeatedly throughout these lectures, one of the most serious problems faced by practitioners of string phenomenology is the multitude of possible, self-consistent string vacua. That there exist large numbers of potential string solutions has been known since the earliest days of string theory; these result from the large numbers of possible ways in which one may choose an appropriate compactification manifold (or orbifold), an appropriate set of background fields and fluxes, and appropriate expectation values for the plethora of additional moduli to which string theories generically give rise. Although historically these string solutions were not completely stabilized, it was tacitly anticipated for many years that some unknown vacuum stabilization mechanism would ultimately lead to a unique vacuum state. Unfortunately, recent developments suggest that there continue to exist huge numbers of self-consistent string solutions (*i.e.*, string "models" or "vacua") even after stabilization. Thus, a picture emerges in which there exist huge numbers of possible string vacua, all potentially stable (or sufficiently metastable), with apparently no dynamical principle to select amongst them. Indeed, each of these potential vacua can be viewed as sitting at the local minimum of a complex terrain of possible string solutions dominated by hills and valleys. This terrain has come to be known as the "string-theory landscape".

The existence of such a landscape has tremendous practical significance because, as we have seen, the specific low-energy phenomenology that can be expected to emerge from string theory depends critically on the particular choice of vacuum state. Detailed quantities such as particle masses and mixings, and even more general quantities and structures such as the choice of gauge group, number of chiral particle generations, magnitude of the supersymmetry-breaking scale, and even the cosmological constant can be expected to vary significantly from one vacuum solution to the next. Thus, in the absence of some sort of vacuum selection principle, it is natural to tackle a secondary but perhaps more tractable question concerning whether there might exist generic string-derived correlations between different phenomenological features. In this way, one can still hope to extract phenomenological predictions from string theory.

Over the past two years, this idea has triggered a surge of activity concerning the *statistical* properties of the landscape. Investigations along these lines have focused on diverse phenomenological issues including the value of the supersymmetry-breaking scale, the value of the cosmological constant, and the preferred rank of the corresponding gauge groups, the prevalence of the Standard-Model gauge group, and possible numbers of chiral generations. Discussions of the landscape have also led to various theoretical paradigm shifts, ranging from alternative landscape-based notions of naturalness and novel cosmological inflationary scenarios to the use of anthropic arguments to constrain the set of viable string vacua. There have even been proposals for field-theoretic analogues of the string-theory landscape, as well as discussions concerning whether a landscape of sufficiently stable string vacua actually exists.

The implications of a landscape (if it exists) have been hotly debated in the string community. Undoubtedly, if the string landscape exists, it is a very rich place, full of unanticipated properties and characteristics. Nevertheless, at the very least, the possible existence of such a landscape has focused the attention of the string community on the fundamental question which has plagued string theory over the past twenty years, namely the issue of vacuum selection.

One might argue that the landscape is simply too large to permit any reasonable analysis. Indeed, one might even argue that if such a landscape exists, string theory is doomed as a predictive theory of physics, and that the answers to some of the most fundamental questions in physics might find their answers in random environmental selection (or as the result of cosmological chance).

However, it is also true that the direct examination of actual string models uncovers features and behaviors that might not otherwise be expected. Moreover, through direct enumeration, we gain valuable experience in the construction and analysis of phenomenologically viable string vacua. Finally, as string phenomenologists, we must ultimately come to terms with the landscape (if it exists). Just as in other fields ranging from astrophysics and botany all the way to zoology, the first step in the analysis of a large data set is enumeration and classification. Indeed, this is how science begins. Thus, properly interpreted, statistical landscape studies might be useful and relevant in this overall endeavor of connecting string theory to the real world.

Acknowledgments

I would like to thank the organizers of the 2006 TASI school, especially Sally Dawson, Rabi Mohapatra, and K.T. Mahanthappa, for their invitation to visit Boulder, Colorado, and deliver these lectures in such a pleasant and stimulating environment. I would also like to thank Sally and Rabi for their extreme patience waiting for the written version of these lectures to appear. But most importantly, I also wish to thank the TASI students themselves for their questions and sustained interest in these lectures. There is nothing more pleasant for a lecturer than an enthusiastic and inquisitive audience. This work was supported in part by the U.S. National Science Foundation under Grant PHY/0301998, by the U.S. Department of Energy under Grant DE-FG02-04ER-41298, and by a Research Innovation Award from Research Corporation.

Chapter 7

Theoretical Aspects of Neutrino Masses and Mixings

R. N. Mohapatra

Department of Physics, University of Maryland, College Park, MD, 20742, USA

Neutrino oscillation experiments have yielded valuable information on the nature of neutrino masses and mixings and have provided the first glimpse of new physics beyond the standard model. Even though we are far from a complete understanding of the new physics implied by them, some tell-tale hints are emerging which have narrowed the direction of the new physics and have provided some insight into the flavor problem. In these lectures, I provide a panoramic overview of the current thinkings in neutrino model building.

7.1. Introduction

For a long time, it was believed that neutrinos are massless, spin half particles, making them drastically different from their other standard model spin half cousins such as the charged leptons (e, μ, τ) and the quarks (u, d, s, c, t, b), which are known to have mass. This myth has however been shattered by the accumulating evidence for neutrino mass from the solar and atmospheric neutrino observations compiled in the nineties as well as several terrestrial experiments in the new century. One must therefore now be free to look beyond the massless neutrino idea to explore new physics as we proceed to understand the neutrino mass.

The possibility of a nonzero neutrino mass at phenomenological level goes back almost 50 years. In the context of gauge theories, they were discussed extensively in the 70's and 80's long before there was any firm evidence for it. For instance the left-right symmetric theories of weak interactions introduced in 1974 and discussed in those days in connection with the structure of neutral current weak interactions, predicted nonzero neutrino mass as a necessary consequence of parity invariance and quark lepton symmetry.

The existence of a nonzero neutrino mass makes neutrinos more like the quarks, and allows for mixing between the different neutrino species leading to the phenomenon of neutrino oscillation, an idea first discussed by Pontecorvo[1] and Maki et al.[1] in the 1960's, unleasing a whole new realm of particle physics phenomena to explore beyond the standard model. At the present time, we are of course far from a complete picture of the masses and mixings of the various neutrinos and cannot therefore have a full outline of the theory of neutrino masses. However there exist enough information that we can surmise some viable possibilities for the theories beyond the standard model. Combined with other ideas outside the neutrino arena such as supersymmetry and unification, the possibility narrows even further. Many clever experiments now under way will soon clarify or rule out many of the allowed models. In these lectures, I give a panoramic view of what we may have learned about physics beyond the standard model and new symmetries of flavor as we attempt to understand neutrino masses.[2]

For simplicity, I will focus on a widely discussed framework for understanding of the small neutrino masses, the seesaw mechanism, which employs a minimal extension of the standard model by adding two or three right handed neutrinos, which are super-heavy and Majorana type. I will touch briefly on some specific models that are based on the above general framework but attempt to provide an understanding of the detailed mass and mixing patterns using family symmetries which must supplement the seesaw mechanism. We will also present a class of SO(10) grand unified theories where there is no need for family symmetries to understand large mixings. These works are instructive for several reasons: first they provide an existence proof that this is a sensible way to proceed in tackling the hard problem of understanding large lepton mixings; second they often illustrate the kind of assumptions needed and through that provide a unique insight into which directions the next step should be; finally of course nature may be generous in picking one of those models as the final message bearer.

The fact that the neutrino has no electric charge endows it with certain properties not shared by other fermions of the standard model. One can write two kinds of Lorentz invariant mass terms for the neutrino, the Dirac and Majorana masses, whereas for the charged fermions, conservation of electric charge allows only Dirac type mass terms. In the four component notation for the fermions, the Dirac mass has the form $\bar{\psi}\psi$, whereas the Majorana mass is of the form $\psi^T C^{-1} \psi$, where ψ is the four component spinor and C is the charge conjugation matrix. One can also discuss the two different kinds of mass terms using the two component notation for the spinors, which provides a very useful way to discuss neutrino masses. We therefore present some of the salient concepts behind the two component description of the neutrino.

7.1.1. *Two component notation for neutrinos*

Before we start the discussion of the 2-component neutrino, let us write down the Dirac equation for an electron:[3]

$$i\gamma^\lambda \partial_\lambda \psi - m\psi = 0 \tag{7.1}$$

This equation follows from a free Lagrangian

$$\mathcal{L} = i\bar\psi \gamma^\lambda \partial_\lambda \psi - m\bar\psi \psi \tag{7.2}$$

and leads to the relativistic energy momentum relation $p^\lambda p_\lambda = m^2$ for the spin-half particle only if the four γ_λ's anticommute. If we take γ_λ's to be $n \times n$ matrices, the smallest value of n for which four anticommuting matrices exist is four. Therefore ψ must be a four component spinor. The physical meaning of the four components is as follows: two components for particle spin up and down and same for the antiparticle.

A spin-half particle is said to be a Majorana particle if the spinor field ψ satisfies the condition of being self charge conjugate, i.e.

$$\psi = \psi^c \equiv C\bar\psi^T, \tag{7.3}$$

where C is the charge conjugation matrix and has the property $C\gamma_\lambda C^{-1} = -\gamma^{\lambda T}$. This constraint reduces the number of independent components of the spinor by a factor of two, since the particle and the antiparticle are now the same particle. Using this condition, the mass term in the Lagrangian in Eq. (2) can be written as $\psi^T C^{-1} \psi$, where we have used the fact that C is a unitary matrix. Writing the mass term in this way makes it clear that if a field carries a $U(1)$ charge and the theory is invariant under those $U(1)$ transformations, then the mass term breaks this symmetry. This means that one cannot impose the Majorana condition on a particle that has a gauge charge. Since the neutrinos do not have electric charge, they can be Majorana particles unlike the quarks, electron or the muon. It is of course well known that the gauge boson interactions in a gauge theory Lagrangian conserve a global $U(1)$ symmetry known as lepton number with the neutrino and electron carrying the same lepton number. If lepton number were to be established as an exact symmetry of nature, the Majorana mass for the neutrino would be forbidden and the neutrino, like the electron, would be a Dirac particle.

The properties of a Majorana fermion can be seen in its free field expansion in terms of creation and annihilation operators:

$$\psi(x) = \int \frac{d^3p}{\sqrt{(2\pi)^3 2E_p}} \Sigma_s \left(a_s(\mathbf{p}) u_s(\mathbf{p}) e^{-ip\cdot x} + a_s^\dagger v_s(\mathbf{p}) e^{ip\cdot x} \right). \quad (7.4)$$

In the gamma matrix convention where $\gamma_i = \begin{pmatrix} 0 & \sigma_i \\ -\sigma_i & 0 \end{pmatrix}$ and $\gamma_0 = \begin{pmatrix} 0 & \mathbf{I} \\ \mathbf{I} & 0 \end{pmatrix}$, the u_s and v_s are given by

$$u_s(\mathbf{p}) = \frac{m}{\sqrt{E}} \begin{pmatrix} \alpha_s \\ \frac{E - \sigma \cdot \mathbf{p}}{m} \alpha_s \end{pmatrix} \quad (7.5)$$

and

$$v_s(\mathbf{p}) = \frac{m}{\sqrt{E}} \begin{pmatrix} -\frac{E + \sigma \cdot \mathbf{p}}{m} \alpha_s' \\ \alpha_s' \end{pmatrix}. \quad (7.6)$$

α_s and α_s' are two component spinors.

If we choose $\alpha_s' = \sigma_2 \alpha_s$, we get the relation among the spinors $u_s(\mathbf{p})$ and $v_s(\mathbf{p})$ $C\gamma_0 u_s^*(\mathbf{p}) = v_s(\mathbf{p})$ and the Majorana condition follows. Note that if ψ were to describe a Dirac spinor, then we would have had a different creation operator $b^\dagger$ in the second term in the free field expansion above.

The origin of the two component neutrino is rooted in the isomorphism between the Lorentz group and the SL(2, C) group. The latter is defined as the set of 2×2 complex matrices with unit determinant, whose generators satisfy the same Lie algebra as that of the Lorentz group. Its basic representations are 2 and 2^* dimensional. These are the spinor representations and can be used to describe spin half particles.

We can therefore write the familiar 4-component Dirac spinor used in the text books to describe an electron can be written as $\psi = \begin{pmatrix} \phi \\ i\sigma_2 \chi^* \end{pmatrix}$, where χ and ϕ two two component spinors. A Dirac mass is the given by $\chi^T \sigma_2 \phi$ whereas a Majorana mass is given by $\chi^T \sigma_2 \chi$, where σ_a are the Pauli matrices. To make correspondence with the four component notation, we point out that ϕ and $i\sigma_2 \chi^*$ are nothing but the ψ_L and ψ_R respectively. It is then clear that χ and ϕ have opposite electric charges; therefore the Dirac mass $\chi^T \sigma_2 \phi$ maintains electric charge conservation (as well as any other kind of charge like lepton number etc.).

2-component neutrino is described by the following Lagrangian:

$$\mathcal{L} = \nu^\dagger i \sigma^\lambda \partial_\lambda \nu - \frac{im}{2} e^{i\delta} \nu^T \sigma_2 \nu + \frac{im}{2} e^{-i\delta} \nu^\dagger \sigma_2 \nu^*. \quad (7.7)$$

This leads to the following equation of motion for the field χ

$$i\sigma^\lambda \partial_\lambda \chi - im\sigma_2 \chi^* = 0. \tag{7.8}$$

As is conventionally done in field theories, we can now give a free field expansion of the two component Majorana field in terms of the creation and annihilation operators:

$$\chi(x,t) = \sum_{p,s}[a_{\mathbf{p},s}\alpha_{p,s}e^{-ip.x} + a^\dagger_{\mathbf{p},s}\beta_{p,s}e^{ip.x}], \tag{7.9}$$

where the sum on s goes over the spin up and down states.

Exercise 1: Using the field equations for a free massive two component Majorana spinor, show that its expansion in terms of the creation and annihilation operators and two component spinors $\alpha = \begin{pmatrix} 1 \\ 0 \end{pmatrix}$ and $\beta = \begin{pmatrix} 0 \\ 1 \end{pmatrix}$ is given by the following expression:

$$\chi(x,t) = \sum_p [a_{\mathbf{p},+}e^{-ip.x} - a^\dagger_{\mathbf{p},-}e^{ip.x}\alpha]\sqrt{E+p}$$
$$+ \sum_p [a_{\mathbf{p},-}e^{-p.x} + a^\dagger_{\mathbf{p},+}e^{ip.x}\alpha]\sqrt{E-p}. \tag{7.10}$$

Note that in a beta decay process, where a neutron is annihilated and proton is created, the leptonic weak current that is involved is $\bar{e}\nu$ (dropping gamma matrices); therefore, along with the electron, what is created predominantly is a right handed particle (with a wave function α), the amplitude being of order $\sqrt{E+p} \approx \sqrt{2E}$. This is the right handed anti-neutrino. The left handed neutrino is produced with a much smaller amplitude $\sqrt{E-p} \approx m_\nu/E$. Similarly, in the fusion reaction in the core of the Sun, what is produced is a left handed state of the neutrino with a very tiny i.e. $O(m_\nu/E)$ admixture of the right handed helicity (or the "anti-neutrino" component).

7.1.2. *Neutrinoless double beta decay and neutrino Majorana mass*

As already noted a Majorana neutrino breaks lepton number by two units. This has the experimentally testable prediction that it leads to the process of neutrino-less double beta decay, that involves the decay of an even-even nucleus i.e. $(Z,N) \to (Z+2, N-2) + 2e^-$. We will now show by using the above property of the Majorana neutrino that if light neutrino exchange is responsible for this process, then the amplitude is proportional to the neutrino mass.

Double beta decay involves the change of two neutrons to two protons and therefore has to be a second order weak interaction process. Since each weak interaction process emits an antineutrino, in second order weak interaction, the final state will involve two anti-neutrinos. But in neutrino-less double beta decay, there are no neutrinos in the final state; therefore the two neutrinos must go into the vacuum state. Vacuum state by definition has no spin whereas the antineutrino emitted in a beta decay has spin. Consider the antineutrino from one of the decays: it must be predominantly right handed. But to disappear into vacuum, it must combine with a lefthanded antineutrino so that the left and right handed spin projections add up to zero. In the previous paragraph, we showed that the fraction of left handed spin projection in a neutrino emitted in beta decay is m_ν/E. Therefore, $\bar{\nu}_e\bar{\nu}_e \to |0>$ must be proportional to the neutrino mass. Thus neutrino-less double beta decay is therefore a very sensitive measure of neutrino mass.

7.1.3. *Neutrino mass in two component notation*

Let us now discuss the general neutrino mass for Majorana neutrinos. We saw earlier that for Majorana neutrinos, there are two different ways to write a mass term consistent with relativistic invariance. This richness in the possibility for neutrino masses also has a down side in the sense that in general, there are more parameters describing the masses of the neutrinos than those for the quarks and leptons. For instance for the electron and quarks, dynamics (electric charge conservation) reduces the number of parameters in their mass matrix. As an example, using the two component notation for all fermions, for the case of two two component spinors, a charged fermion mass will be described only by one parameters whereas for a neutrino, there will be three parameters. This difference increases rapidly e.g. for 2N spinors, to describe charged fermion masses, we need N^2 parameters (ignoring CP violation) whereas for neutrinos, we need $\frac{2N(2N+1)}{2}$ parameters. What is more interesting is that for a neutrino like particle, one can have both even and odd number of two component objects and have a consistent theory.

In this article, we will use two component notation for neutrinos. Thus when we say that there are N neutrinos, we will mean N two-component neutrinos.

In the two component language, all massive neutrinos are Majorana particles and what is conventionally called a Dirac neutrino is really a very specific choice of mass parameters for the Majorana neutrino. Let us give some examples: If there is only one two component neutrino (we will drop the prefix two component henceforth), it can have a mass $m\nu^T \sigma_2 \nu$ (to be called $\equiv m\nu\nu$ in shorthanded notation). The neutrino is now a self conjugate object which can be seen if we write an equivalent 4-component spinor ψ:

$$\psi = \begin{pmatrix} \nu \\ i\sigma_2 \nu^* \end{pmatrix} \quad (7.11)$$

Note that this 4-component spinor satisfies the condition

$$\psi = \psi^c \equiv C\bar{\psi}^T \quad (7.12)$$

This condition implies that the neutrino is its own anti-particle, a fact more transparent in the four- rather than the two-component notation. The above exercise illustrates an important point i.e. given any two component spinor, one can always write a self conjugate (or Majorana) 4-component spinor. Whether a particle is really its own antiparticle or not is therefore determined by its interactions. To see this for the electrons, one may solve the following exercise i.e. if we wrote two Majorana spinors using the two two-component spinors that describe the electron, then until we turn on the electromagnetic interactions and the mass term, we will not know whether the electron is its own antiparticle or not. Once we turn on the electromagnetism, this ambiguity is resolved since electric charge conservation will allow a mass term that connects the two 2-component spinors and no mass term connecting either of the two component spinors with themselves.

Let us now go one step further and consider two 2-component neutrinos (ν_1, ν_2). The general mass matrix for this case is given by:

$$\mathcal{M}_{2\times 2} = \begin{pmatrix} m_1 & m_3 \\ m_3 & m_2 \end{pmatrix} \quad (7.13)$$

Note first that this is a symmetric matrix and can be diagonalised by orthogonal transformations. The eigen-states which will be certain admixtures of the original neutrinos now describe self conjugate particles. One can look at some special cases:

Case i:

If we have $m_{1,2} = 0$ and $m_3 \neq 0$, then one can assign a charge $+1$ to ν_1 and -1 to ν_2 under some $U(1)$ symmetry other than electromagnetism and the theory is invariant under this extra $U(1)$ symmetry which can be identified as the lepton number and the particle is then called a Dirac neutrino. The point to be noted is that the Dirac neutrino is a special case of for two Majorana neutrinos. In fact instead of calling this a Dirac neutrino, we could call this a case with two Majorana neutrinos with equal and opposite (in sign) mass. Since a complex mass term in general refers to its C transformation property (i.e. $\psi^c = e^{i\delta_m}\psi$, (where δ_m is the phase of the complex mass term), the two two-component fields of a Dirac neutrino having opposite sign mass would be equivalent to having opposite charge conjugation properties.

Case ii:

If we have $m_{1,2} \ll m_3$, this case is called pseudo-Dirac neutrino since this is a slight departure from case (i). In reality, in this case also the neutrinos are Majorana neutrinos with their masses $\pm m_0 + \delta$ with $\delta \ll m_0$. The two component neutrinos will be maximally mixed. Thus this case is of great current physical interest in view of the atmospheric (and perhaps solar) neutrino data.

Case iii:

There is third case where one may have $m_1 = 0$ and $m_3 \ll m_2$. In this case the eigenvalues of the neutrino mass matrix are given respectively by: $m_\nu \simeq -\frac{m_3^2}{m_2}$ and $M \simeq m_2$. One may wonder under what conditions such a situation may arise in a realistic gauge model. It turns out that if ν_1 transforms as an $SU(2)_L$ doublet and ν_2 is an $SU(2)_L$ singlet, then the value of m_3 is limited by the weak scale whereas m_2 has no such limit and $m_1 = 0$ if the theory has no $SU(2)_L$ triplet field (as for instance is the case in the standard model). Choosing $m_2 \gg m_3$ then provides a natural way to understand the smallness of the neutrino masses. This is known as the seesaw mechanism.[4] Since this case is very different from the case (i) and (ii), it is generally said that in grand unified theories, one expects the neutrinos to be Majorana particles. The reason is that in most grand unified theories there is a higher scale which under appropriate situations provides a natural home for the large mass m_2.

While we have so far used only two neutrinos to exemplify the various cases including the seesaw mechanism, these discussions generalize when $m_{1,2,3}$ are each $N \times N$ matrices (which we denote by $m_3 \equiv m_D$ and $m_2 \equiv M_R$). For example, the seesaw formula for this general situation can be written as

$$\mathcal{M}_\nu \simeq m_1 - m_D^T M_R^{-1} m_D \qquad (7.14)$$

where the subscripts D and R are used in anticipation of their origin in gauge theories where M_D turns out to be the Dirac matrix and M_R is the mass matrix of the right handed neutrinos and all eigenvalues of M_R are much larger than the elements of M_D. It is also worth pointing out that Eq. 7.14 can be written in a more general form where the Dirac matrices are not necessarily square matrices but $N \times M$ matrices with $N \neq M$. We give such examples below.

Although there is no experimental proof that the neutrino is a Majorana particle, the general belief is that since the seesaw mechanism provides such a simple way to understand the glaring differences between the masses of the neutrinos and the charged fermions, neutrino is indeed most likely to be a Majorana particles as implied by it.

Even though in many situations, the difference between the Dirac and Majorana neutrinos is not manifest, there are some physical processes where differences becomes explicit: one such process is when the two neutrinos annihilate. For Dirac neutrinos, the particle and the antiparticle are distinct and therefore their annihilation is not restricted by Pauli principle in any manner. However, for the case of Majorana neutrinos, the identity of neutrinos and antineutrinos plays an important role and one finds that the annihilation to the Z-bosons occurs only via the P-waves. Similarly in the decay of the neutrino to any final state, the decay rate for the Majorana neutrino is a factor of two higher than for the Dirac neutrino.

7.1.4. *Experimental indications for neutrino masses*

There have been other lectures at this school on the experimental evidences for neutrino masses and their analyses to determine the current favorite values for the various mass differences as well as mixing angles. I will therefore only summarize the main results: (For detailed discussion and references, see[5] and lectures by J. Conrad[6]).

The evidence for neutrino masses and mixings have come from neutrino oscillation experiments involving neutrinos from the Sun, the cosmic rays as well as from accelerators. Neutrino oscillation is a phenomenon where neutrinos of one flavor transmute to neutrinos of another flavor. Since such transmutation can occur only if the neutrinos have masses and mixings, these experiments provide evidence for neutrino mass. To see this, note the expression for vacuum oscillation probability for neutrinos of a given energy E that have travelled a distance L is given by:

$$P_{\alpha\beta} = \sum_{i,j} |U_{\alpha i} U^*_{\beta i} U^*_{\alpha j} U_{\beta j}| \cos\left(\frac{\Delta_{ij} L}{2E} - \phi_{\alpha\beta,ij}\right) \qquad (7.15)$$

This can be derived on the basis of simple quantum mechanical superposition principle and the equations of time evolution of free particles. The observed neutrino oscillation probabilities therefore yield information about the mass difference squares of the neutrinos ($\Delta_{ij} = m_i^2 - m_j^2$) and mixing angles $U_{\alpha i}$. If the neutrino propagates in dense matter, the oscillation probability is changed by the so-called Mikheyev-Smirnov-Wolfenstein effect however the new probability depends on the same parameters i.e. mass difference square and the $U_{\alpha i}$ in addition to depending on the density of matter through which neutrinos travel. The analysis of the data for the atmospheric neutrinos where the neutrino propagates in vacuum and that for solar neutrinos where the effect of dense matter in the Sun is included lead to the following picture values for mass differences and mixings:

7.1.4.1. *Atmospheric neutrinos:*

The Super-Kamiokande experiment observed the oscillations of the atmospheric muon neutrinos to tau neutrinos (although the tau neutrinos from the oscillations have not been confirmed yet). This oscillation of ν_μ to ν_τ has now been confirmed by the accelerator observations in the K2K and the MINOS experiments. From the existing data several important conclusions can be drawn: (i) the data cannot be fit assuming oscillation between ν_μ and ν_e nor $\nu_\mu - \nu_s$, where ν_s is a sterile neutrino which does not any direct weak interaction; (ii) the oscillation scenario that fit the data best is $\nu_\mu - \nu_\tau$ for the mass and mixing parameters

$$\Delta m^2_{\nu_\mu - \nu_\tau} \simeq (2 - 8) \times 10^{-3} \text{ eV}^2; \tag{7.16}$$

$$in^2 2\theta_{\mu-\tau} \geq 0.92$$

7.1.4.2. *Solar neutrinos*

The second evidence for neutrino oscillation comes from the several experiments that have observed a deficit in the flux of neutrinos from the Sun as compared to the predictions of the standard solar model championed by Bahcall and his collaborators[5] and more recently studied by many groups. The experiments responsible for this discovery are the Chlorine experiment of Ray Davis, Kamiokande, Gallex, SAGE, Super-Kamiokande, SNO, GNO experiments conducted at the Homestake mine, Kamioka in Japan, Gran Sasso in Italy and Baksan in Russia and Sudbery in Canada respectively.

The different experiments see different parts of the solar neutrino spectrum. The details of these considerations are discussed in other lectures.

As far as the final state goes, it can either be one of the two remaining active neutrinos, ν_μ and ν_τ or it can be the sterile neutrino ν_s. SNO neutral current data announced recently has very strongly constrained the second possibility (i.e. the sterile neutrino in the final state). The global analyses of all solar neutrino data seem to favor the so called large mixing angle MSW solution with parameters: $\Delta m^2 \simeq 1.2 \times 10^{-5} - 3.1 \times 10^{-4} \mathrm{eV}^2$; $\sin^2 2\theta \simeq 0.58 - 0.95$.

This result has been confirmed by the terrestrial KamLand experiment which looked for oscillation for reactor neutrinos from several reactors with a detector at an average distance of about 100 Km from the various sources. It eliminated solutions to the solar neutrino puzzle based e.g. on spin flavor precession as well as the so called low solution and confirmed the large angle MSW resolution as the most plausible one.

7.1.4.3. Search for the mixing angle θ_{13}

The remaining mixing angle θ_{13} has been probed by the reactor experiments that used the French reactor CHOOZ and the US reactor in Palo-Verde by looking for the oscillation of reactor electron anti-neutrinos with a detector at a distance of about a kilo-meter. In the simple three neutrino picture, the dominant oscillation in this case would be to the tau neutrinos since $\Delta m_{31}^2 \gg \Delta m_{21}^2$. The absence of a signal put an upper limit on the mixing angle of about $\theta_{13} \leq 0.17$. There are several reactor as well as long baseline experiments now being prepared which will conduct a higher precision search for θ_{13} during the next decade.[7]

7.1.4.4. LSND and MiniBooNe

Finally, we come to the last indication of neutrino oscillation from the Los Alamos Liquid Scintillation Detector (LSND)[6] experiment, where neutrino oscillations both from a stopped muon (DAR) as well as the one accompanying the muon in pion decay (known as the DIF) have been observed. The evidence from the DAR is statistically more significant and is an oscillation from $\bar{\nu}_\mu$ to $\bar{\nu}_e$. The mass and mixing parameter range that fits data is[6]:

$$LSND: \Delta m^2 \simeq 0.2 - 2 eV^2; \sin^2 2\theta \simeq 0.003 - 0.03 \quad (7.17)$$

There are also points at higher masses specifically at 6 eV^2 which are also allowed by the present LSND data for small mixings. KARMEN experiment at the Rutherford laboratory has very strongly constrained the allowed parameter range of the LSND data. Recently the Miniboone experiment at Fermilab has announced the results of its search for $\nu_\mu - \nu_e$ oscillation. They have not found any evidence for oscillation with characteristic mass diffrerence square in the eV range.[8,9]

7.1.4.5. *Neutrino-less double beta decay and Tritium decay experiment*

Oscillation experiments only depend on the difference of mass squares of the different neutrinos and the mixing angles. Therefore, in order to have a complete picture of neutrino masses, we need other experiments. Two such experiments are the neutrino-less double beta decay searches and the search for neutrino mass from the analysis of the end point of the electron energy spectrum in tritium beta decay. They have been discussed at this institute by P. Vogel,[11] which is referred to for more details and references.

Neutrino-less double beta decay measures the following combination of masses and mixing angles:

$$<m>_{\beta\beta} = \sum_i U_{ei}^2 m_i \qquad (7.18)$$

Therefore naively speaking it is sensitive to the overall neutrino mass scale. But in practice, as we will see below, for the case of both normal and inverted hierarchies, it is unlikely to settle the question of the overall mass scale at the presently contemplated level of sensitivity in double beta decay searches. Only if the neutrino mass patterns are inverse hierarchical does one expect a visible signal in $\beta\beta_{0\nu}$ decay. We do not get into great details into this issue except to mention that in drawing any conclusions about neutrino mass from this process, one has to first have a good calculation of nuclear matrix elements of the various nuclei involves such as ^{76}Ge, ^{136}Xe, ^{100}Mo etc.; secondly, another confusing issue has to do with alternative physics contributions to $\beta\beta_{0\nu}$ which are unrelated to neutrino mass. Nevertheless, neutrino-less double beta decay is a fundamental experiment and a nonzero signal will establish the important result that neutrino is a Majorana particle and that lepton number symmetry is violated. Regardless of whether it tells us anything about the neutrino masses, it would provide an indication in favor of the seesaw mechanism. Presently two experiments

Heidelberg-Moscow and IGEX that use enriched ^{76}Ge have published limits of ≤ 0.3 eV. More recently, evidence for a double beta signal in the Heidelberg-Moscow data has been claimed.[12] Several experiments are now under planning e.g. EXO, Majorana and Cuore etc. which are expected to improve the sensitivity to the Majorana mass of the neutrino to the level of 20 milli-eV. This can for example test the hypothesis that neutrino mass ordering may be inverted if they are Majorana fermions.

Another important result in further understanding of neutrino mass physics could come from the tritium end point searches for neutrino masses. This experiment will measure the parameter $m_\nu = \sqrt{\sum_i |U_{ei}|^2 m_i^2}$. This involves a different combination of masses and mixing angles than $<m>_{\beta\beta}$. Presently, the KATRIN proposal for a high sensitive search for for m_ν has been made and it is expected that it can reach a sensitivity of 0.2 eV.

A third source of information on neutrino mass will come from cosmology, where more detailed study of structure in the universe is expected to provide an upper limit on $\sum_i m_i$ of less than an eV. Present WMAP data appears to provide a limit of $\sum_i m_{\nu_i} \leq 0.6 - 1$ eV.[13]

Our goal now is to study the theoretical implications of these discoveries. We will proceed towards this goal in the following manner: we will isolate the mass patterns that fit the above data and search for patterns and symmetries that lead to observed mixing angles. We then look for plausible models that can first lead to the general feature that neutrinos have tiny masses; then we would try to understand in simple manner some of the features indicated by data in the hope that these general ideas will be part of our final understanding of the neutrino masses. As mentioned earlier on, to understand the neutrino masses one has to go beyond the standard model. First we will sharpen what we mean by this statement. Then we will present some ideas which may form the basic framework for constructing the detailed models.

7.2. Physics of neutrino mass

There are two distinct aspects to neutrino mass physics: first is the absolute overall magnitude and second is the flavor structure. Understanding the first will reveal the gross features of the new physics such as the presence of a new symmetry and its scale responsible for the smallness of neutrino mass compared to masses of other fundamental fermions, whereas understanding the flavor pattern is likely to throw light on possible new family symmetries of matter which may in turn be relevant to unravelling the mystery of quark flavor. It could be (probably likely) that both are related to each other.

To begin this discussion, we first list the puzzles of neutrino mass physics; we then discuss the neutrino mass matrix which is the starting point of many attempts to understand the neutrino mixings and then discuss ideas that have been proposed to understand these patterns before going to a discussion of the overall scale.

7.2.1. *Puzzles of neutrino mass physics*

The present neutrino discoveries have posed a list of puzzles for physics beyond the standard model, whose resolution will provide an unmistakable path beyond it. Below we give a list of these puzzles.

- *Ultra-light-ness of neutrinos:* Why are the neutrino masses so much lighter than the quark and charged lepton masses?
- *Bi-large mixing:* How to understand simultaneously two large mixing angles one for the $\mu - \tau$ and another for $e - \mu$?
- *Smallness of $\Delta m_\odot^2 / \Delta m_A^2$:* Experimentally, $\Delta m_\odot^2 \simeq 10^{-2} \Delta m_A^2$. How does one understand this in a natural manner?
- *Smallness of U_{e3}:* The reactor results also seem to indicate that the angle $\theta_{13} \equiv U_{e3}$ is a very small number. One must also understand this in a framework that simultaneously explains all other puzzles.

Possible other puzzles include a proper understanding of neutrino mass degeneracy if there is a large positive signal for the neutrinoless double beta decay and of course, when we have evidence for CP violating phases in the mass matrix, we must understand their magnitude.

In order to take the first step towards understanding these puzzles, we discuss the flavor pattern of leptons that may be at the root of large mixings and defer the discussion of the origin of mass scale to the next section and finally focus on specific unification models which address both the issues as examples how one may proceed to unravel the grand picture of physics beyond standard model inspired by neutrino physics. It could of course be that large neutrino mixings result from a joint effect of both the charged lepton and the neutrino matrix since $U_{PMNS} = U_l^\dagger U_\nu$ and we do not know apriori whether the large neutrino mixings come from the charged lepton sector or the neutrino sector or both. However, we first follow the line of thinking that in the fundamental theory, charged lepton mass matrix is diagonal or near diagonal and all mixings result from the neutrino mass matrix. This point of view is not so unreasonable since charged lepton mass matrix is likely to be similar to the quark sector and the small observed CKM mixings pretty much guarantees that quark mass matrices are near diagonal. We will also present grand unified models where this conjecture is borne out.

7.2.2. Notation

We will assume two component neutrinos and therefore their masses will in general be Majorana type. Let us also give our notation to facilitate further discussion: the neutrinos emitted in weak processes such as the beta decay or muon decay are weak eigenstates and are not mass eigenstates. The mass eigenstates determine how a neutrino state evolves in time. Similarly, in the detection process, it is the weak eigenstate that is picked out. This is of course the key idea behind neutrino oscillation and the formula presented in the last section. To set the notation, let us express the weak eigenstates in terms of the mass eigenstates. We will denote the weak eigenstate by the symbol α, β or simply e, μ, τ etc whereas the mass eigenstate will be denoted by the symbols i, j, k etc. To relate the weak eigenstates to the mass eigenstates, let us start with the mass terms in the Lagrangian for the neutrino and the charged leptons:

$$\mathcal{L}_m = \nu_L^T \mathcal{M}_\nu \nu_L + \bar{E}_L M_\ell E_R + h.c. \qquad (7.19)$$

Here the ν and E which denote the column vectors for neutrinos and charged leptons are in the weak basis. To go to the mass basis, we diagonalize these matrices as follows:

$$U_L^T \mathcal{M}_\nu U_L = d_\nu \qquad (7.20)$$
$$V_L M_\ell V_R^\dagger = d_\ell$$

The physical neutrino mixing matrix is then given by:

$$\mathbf{U} = V_L U_L \qquad (7.21)$$

$\mathbf{U}_{\alpha i}$ and relate the two sets of eigenstates (weak and mass) as follows:

$$\begin{pmatrix} \nu_e \\ \nu_\mu \\ \nu_\tau \end{pmatrix} = U \begin{pmatrix} \nu_1 \\ \nu_2 \\ \nu_3 \end{pmatrix} \qquad (7.22)$$

Using this equation, one can derive the well known oscillation formulae for the survival probability of a particular weak eigenstate α discussed in the previous section.

To see the general structure of the mixing matrix **U**, let us recall that the matrix $\mathcal{M}_\nu$ is complex and symmetric and therefore has six complex parameters describing it for the case of three generations. But since the neutrino is described by a complex field, we can redefine the phases of three fields to remove three parameters. That leaves nine parameters. In terms of observables, there are three mass eigenvalues (m_1, m_2, m_3) and three mixing angles and phases in the mixing matrix **U**. The three phases can be split into one Dirac phase, which is analogous to the phase in the quark mixing matrix and two Majorana phases. We can then write the matrix **U** as

$$\mathbf{U} = U^{(0)} \begin{pmatrix} 1 & & \\ & e^{i\phi_1} & \\ & & e^{i\phi_2} \end{pmatrix} \qquad (7.23)$$

The matrix $\mathbf{U}^{(0)}$ has three real angles $\theta_{12}, \theta_{23}, \theta_{13}$ and a phase. The goal of experiments is to determine all nine of these parameters. The knowledge of the nine observables allows one to construct the mass matrix for the neutrinos and from there one can go in search of the new physics beyond the standard model that leads to such a mass matrix.

The neutrino mass observables given above can be separated into two classes: (i) oscillation observables and (ii) non-oscillation observables. The first class of observables are those accessible to neutrino oscillation experiments and are the two mass differences $\Delta m_\odot^2$ and Δm_A^2; three mixing angles θ_{12} (or $\theta_\odot$); θ_{23} (or θ_A) and θ_{13} (the reactor angle, also called U_{e3}) and the CP phase δ in $U^{(0)}$. The remaining three observables i.e. the lightest mass of the three neutrinos and the two Majorana phases $\phi_{1,2}$ can only be probed by nonoscillation experiments such as $\beta\beta_{0\nu}$ decay, beta decay spectrum at the endpoint and cosmological observations etc.

7.3. Neutrino mixing matrix and mass patterns

A good starting point for the exploration of new physics such as new symmetries, new scaleshidden in neutrino observations is to construct the neutrino mass matrix in the basis where the charged leptons are mass eigenstates (or near mass eigen states.) One can then look for symmetries which could be responsible for this form of the neutrino mass matrix in extensions of the standard model.

In order to construct the neutrino mass matrix, we will use the following experimental numbers: $\Delta m_A^2 \simeq 0.0021$ eV^2; for solar neutrinos, it gives $\Delta m_\odot^2 \simeq (7.21 - 8.63) \times 10^{-5}$ eV^2. It also provides information on the angles in **U** which can be summarized by the following mixing matrix (neglecting all CP phases):

$$\mathbf{U} = \begin{pmatrix} c & s & \epsilon \\ -\frac{s+c\epsilon}{\sqrt{2}} & \frac{c-s\epsilon}{\sqrt{2}} & \frac{1}{\sqrt{2}} \\ -\frac{s-c\epsilon}{\sqrt{2}} & \frac{-c-s\epsilon}{\sqrt{2}} & \frac{1}{\sqrt{2}} \end{pmatrix} \qquad (7.24)$$

where from the discussion above $\epsilon \leq 0.17$; $s = \sin\theta_{12}$ is in the range $0.267 \leq \sin^2\theta_{12} \leq 0.371$ with the central value being near 0.314. We have chosen the atmospheric mixing angle θ_{23} to be maximal.

A particularly interesting form of the mixing matrix which seems to be in accord with data is the so-called tri-bi-maximal form[15] where:

$$U_{PMNS} = \begin{pmatrix} \sqrt{\frac{2}{3}} & \frac{1}{\sqrt{3}} & 0 \\ -\frac{1}{\sqrt{6}} & \frac{1}{\sqrt{3}} & \frac{1}{\sqrt{2}} \\ -\frac{1}{\sqrt{6}} & \frac{1}{\sqrt{3}} & -\frac{1}{\sqrt{2}} \end{pmatrix} \qquad (7.25)$$

As far as the mass pattern goes however, there are three possibilities:

- (i) normal hierarchy: $m_1 \ll m_2 \ll m_3$;
- (ii) inverted hierarchy: $m_1 \simeq -m_2 \gg m_3$ and
- (iii) approximately degenerate pattern[14] $m_1 \simeq m_2 \simeq m_3$,

where m_i are the eigenvalues of the neutrino mass matrix. In the first case, the atmospheric and the solar neutrino data give direct information on m_3 and m_2 respectively. On the other hand, in the last case, the mass differences between the first and the second eigenvalues will be chosen to fit the solar neutrino data and the second and the third to fit the atmospheric neutrino data.

7.3.1. *Neutrino mass textures*

From the mixing matrix in Eq. 7.24, we can write down the allowed neutrino mass matrix for any arbitrary mass pattern assuming the neutrino is a Majorana fermion. Denoting the matrix elements of $\mathcal{M}_\nu$ as $\mu_{\alpha\beta}$ for $\alpha, \beta =$

1, 2, 3, we have (Recall that $\mu_{\alpha\beta} = \mu_{\beta\alpha}$):

$$\mu_{11} = [c^2 m_1 + s^2 m_2 + \epsilon^2 m_3]$$
$$\mu_{12} = \frac{1}{\sqrt{2}}[-c(s+c\epsilon)m_1 + s(c-s\epsilon)m_2 + \epsilon m_3]$$
$$\mu_{13} = \frac{1}{\sqrt{2}}[-c(s-c\epsilon)m_1 - s(c+s\epsilon)m_2 + \epsilon m_3]$$
$$\mu_{22} = \frac{1}{2}[(s+c\epsilon)^2 m_1 + (c-s\epsilon)^2 m_2 + m_3] \quad (7.26)$$
$$\mu_{23} = \frac{1}{2}[-(s^2 - c^2\epsilon^2)m_1 - (c^2 - s^2\epsilon^2)m_2 + m_3]$$
$$\mu_{33} = \frac{1}{2}[(s-c\epsilon)^2 m_1 + (c+s\epsilon)^2 m_2 + m_3].$$

In certain limits for the mixing angles in the above mass matrix, symmetries leptons can manifest. Below I give some examples:

7.3.2. $\mu - \tau$ exchange symmetry

The current observations that θ_{23} is very close to maximal (with $\theta_{23} = \frac{\pi}{4}$ being the best fit solution in many analyses) and the fact that θ_{13} could be vanishing can be understood if the neutrino Majorana mass matix has a Z_2 symmetry that interchanges $\mu - \tau$.[16] The corresponding mass matrix is the special case of the matrix below with $c = 1$, and $a = b$.

$$\mathcal{M}_\nu = \sqrt{\Delta m_A^2} \begin{pmatrix} d\epsilon^n & b\epsilon & a\epsilon \\ b\epsilon & 1+\epsilon & 1 \\ a\epsilon & 1 & 1+c\epsilon \end{pmatrix} \quad (7.27)$$

where a, b, c, d are parameters of order one and $\epsilon \sim \sqrt{\frac{\Delta m_\odot^2}{\Delta m_A^2}} \sim 0.2$. Since at the moment it is not certain whether $\mu - \tau$ symmetry is exact or approximate, the mass matrix in Eq. 7.27 includes small breaking terms characterized by $a \neq b$ and $c \neq 1$. These small departures lead to non-zero values for θ_{13} and $\theta_{23} - \frac{\pi}{4}$ which are correlated with each other.[17] We have ignored leptonic CP violation in this discussion. One can have other ways of introducing $\mu - \tau$ symmetry breaking using CP phases.[18]

Overall, this symmetry has a good chance be part of the final theory of neutrino mixing since there seems to be good experimental support for it. This has therefore led to a great deal of model building activity[19] most of whom predict departures from the exact symmetry limit and can provide insight into which way to proceed in assimilating this symmetry as part of the quark-lepton world.

7.3.3. *Mass matrix for tri-bi-maximal mixing and associated approximate flavor symmetries*

In the $\mu - \tau$ symmetric models, the value of the solar mixing angle θ_{12} remains large but arbitrary. The indication that the value of $\sin\theta_{12} \simeq \frac{1}{\sqrt{3}}$ may be an indication of higher symmetries of the lepton world. This is called tri-bi-maximal mixing pattern.[15] Clearly these must have $\mu - \tau$ symmetry as a subgroup. A typical neutrino mass matrix that leads to the tri-bi-maximal mixing pattern is:

$$\mathcal{M}_\nu = \begin{pmatrix} a & b & b \\ b & a+c & b-c \\ b & b-c & a+c \end{pmatrix} \tag{7.28}$$

where a, b, c are arbitrary parameters. The charged lepton mass matrix is chosen to be diagonal. Diagonalizing this matrix leads to the U_{PMNS} in the tri-bi-maximal form and the neutrino masses: $m_1 = a - b$; $m_2 = a + 2b$ and $m_3 = a - b + 2c$. Clearly if $a \simeq b \ll c$, we get a normal hierarchy for masses. A symmetry that has been found to lead to this mass matrix is S_3.[20]

Another way to get the tri-bi-maximal form is to use specific forms for the charged lepton and neutrino mass matrices in such a way that the combined diagonalization leads to the desired lepton mixing matrix. An example is to have a charged lepton mass matrix of the form:

$$\mathcal{M}_\nu = \begin{pmatrix} a & 0 & 0 \\ 0 & a & b \\ 0 & b & a \end{pmatrix}$$

$$M_\ell = \tfrac{1}{\sqrt{3}} \begin{pmatrix} 1 & 1 & 1 \\ 1 & \omega^2 & \omega \\ 1 & \omega & \omega^2 \end{pmatrix} \begin{pmatrix} m_e & 0 & 0 \\ 0 & m_\mu & 0 \\ 0 & 0 & m_\tau \end{pmatrix} \tag{7.29}$$

where $\omega = e^{\frac{2\pi i}{3}}$. This for may appear much too contrived to arise from some symmetries, but remarkably enough it has been shown that this can emerge under certain assumptions if the assumed symmetry is A_4,[21] which is group of even permutations of four elements.

Detailed theory for all these cases involves many Higgs multiplets and probably should not be taken literally but the important message is the presence of the hidden symmetry and its implications. Generally such symmetries are hard to grand unify and further research along this direction is going to be important.

7.3.4. Inverted hierarchy and $L_e - L_\mu - L_\tau$ symmetry

In this sub-section, we consider another interesting clue to model building present in neutrino data if the mass arrangement is inverted. It starts with the observation that if the neutrino mass matrix has the form

$$\mathcal{M}_\nu = \begin{pmatrix} 0 & A & A \\ A & 0 & 0 \\ A & 0b & 0 \end{pmatrix} \quad (7.30)$$

this leads to two degenerate neutrinos with mass $\pm\sqrt{2}A$ and one massless neutrino. The atmospheric mass difference is given by $\Delta m_A^2 = 2A^2$ and mixing angle $\theta_A = \pi/4$. As far as the solar ν_e oscillation is concerned, the $\sin^2 2\theta_\odot = 1$ but $\Delta m_\odot^2 = 0$. While this is unphysical, this raises the hope that as corrections to this mass matrix are taken into account, it may be possible understand the smallness of $\Delta m_\odot^2/\Delta m_A^2$ naturally.

In fact this hope is fortified by the observation that this mass matrix has the leptonic symmetry $L_e - L_\mu - L_\tau$; therefore one might hope that as this symmetry is broken by small terms, one will end up with a situation that fits data well.

This question was studied in two papers.[25,26] To proceed with the discussion, let us consider the following mass matrix for neutrinos where small $L_e - L_\mu - L_\tau$ violating terms have been added.

$$\mathcal{M}_\nu = m \begin{pmatrix} z & c & s \\ c & y & d \\ s & d & x \end{pmatrix}. \quad (7.31)$$

The charged lepton mass matrix is chosen to have a diagonal form in this basis and $L_e - L_\mu - L_\tau$ symmetric. In the perturbative approximation, there are sum rules involving the neutrino observables and the elements of the neutrino mass matrix,[26] which first of all imply (i) a close connection between the measured value of the solar mixing angle and the neutrino mass measured in neutrino-less double beta decay; (ii) the present values for the solar mixing angle can be used to predict the $m_{\beta\beta}$ for a value of the $\Delta m_\odot^2$. For instance, for $\sin^2 2\theta_\odot = 0.9$, we would predict $(\frac{\Delta m_\odot^2}{4\Delta m_A^2} - z) = 0.3$. For small $\Delta m_\odot^2$, this implies $m_{\beta\beta} \simeq 0.01$ eV. This is expected to be within the reach of new double beta decay experiments contemplated.[27] In fact now there exist more thorough numerical analyses[23] of general $L_e - L_\mu - L_\tau$ broken models which imply that the inverted hierarchy for neutrinos can be tested in neutrinoless double beta experiments in the next decade or so. This way of breaking $L_e - L_\mu - L_\tau$ symmetry also implies a value for $\sin^2 2\theta_{12} \geq 0.9$, which is now almost ruled out. Of course there could be other ways of breaking this symmetry using charged lepton sector etc. which can still lead to lower solar angle.

If the value of $\sin^2 2\theta_\odot$ is ultimately determined to be less than 0.9, the question one may ask is whether the idea of $L_e - L_\mu - L_\tau$ symmetry is dead. The answer is in the negative since so far we have explored the breaking of $L_e - L_\mu - L_\tau$ symmetry only in the neutrino mass matrix. It was shown in[25] that if the symmetry is broken in the charged lepton mass, one can lower the $\sin^2 2\theta_\odot$ as long as the value of U_{e3} is sizable. However given the present upper limit on U_{e3}, the smallest value is somewhere around $\sin^2 2\theta_\odot \simeq 0.8$.

7.3.5. *Scale invariant mass matrix*

Most of the above forms for the mass matrices are scale dependent in the sense that once radiative corrections are taken into account, their forms can change. This is specially relevant because in many theories neutrino mass matrix is predicted at a high scale due to physics at this scale. They have to be extrapolated to the weak scale to compare with experiments. This process relies on the nature of physics between the neutrino mass generation scale and the weak scale. Thus connection between fundamental physics responsible for neutrino masses and observations gets interrupted. Luckily the radiative correction effects are not significant if neutrino mass hierarchy is normal (see discussion later). However both for inverted and degenerate spectra, they are. It is therefore interesting to search for neutrino flavor structure that is not affected by such effects. One such form arises when the neutrino mass matrices satisfy certain scaling properties.[28] An example of such a mass matrix is:

$$\mathcal{M}_\nu = m_0 \begin{pmatrix} A & B & B/c \\ B & D & D/c \\ B/c & D/c & D/c^2 \end{pmatrix}. \tag{7.32}$$

It is called $\mu - \tau$ scaling whose most important phenomenological is that it leads to an inverted hierarchy with $m_3 = 0$ and $U_{e3} = 0$. Atmospheric neutrino mixing is governed by the "scaling factor" c via $\tan^2 \theta_{23} = 1/c^2$, i.e., is in general non-maximal because c is naturally of order, but not equal to, one. These results are scale independent predictions and do not depend on extraneous physics between the neutrino mass generation scale and the weak scale. It is interesting to note that current data analyzes (though at the present stage statistically not very significant) yield non-maximal $\tan^2\theta_{23} = 0.89$ as the best-fit point.[5]

7.3.6. *CP violation*

A not very well explored aspect of neutrino physics at the moment is CP violation in lepton physics. Unlike the quark sector, CP violation for Majorana neutrinos allows for more phases than in the quark sector. Since the Majorana neutrino mass matrix is symmetric, for N generations of neutrinos, there are in general $\frac{N(N+1)}{2}$ phases in it. When the mass matrix is diagonalized, these phases will appear in the unitary matrix U_L that does the diagonalization (i.e. $U^T\mathcal{M}_\nu U_L = d_\nu$). If we are working in a basis where the charged lepton mass matrix is diagonal, then U_L is the leptonic weak mixing matrix. As we saw this has $N(N+1)/2$ phases. Out of them, redefinition of the charged lepton fields in the weak current allows the removal of N phases; so there are $N(N-1)/2$ phases in the neutrino masses. In the quark sector, both up and down fields could be redefined allowing for the number of physical phases that appear in the end to be smaller. However for Majorana neutrinos, redefinition of the fields does not remove the phases entirely from the theory but rather shifts them to other places where they can manifest themselves physically.[29] The detailed discussion of CP violation is in other lectures at this school.

7.4. Neutrino mass scale and physics beyond the standard model

In the standard model (SM), the neutrino mass vanishes to all orders in perturbation theory as well as nonperturbatively implying that observation of neutrino masses is the first laboratory evidence for physics beyond the standard model. To clarify this point, note that the SM is based on the gauge group $SU(3)_c \times SU(2)_L \times U(1)_Y$ under which the quarks and leptons, Higgs bosons and gauge bosons transform as described in the Table I.

Table I

Field	gauge transformation
Quarks Q_L	$(3, 2, \frac{1}{3})$
Righthanded up quarks u_R	$(3, 1, \frac{4}{3})$
Righthanded down quarks d_R	$(3, 1, -\frac{2}{3})$
Lefthanded Leptons L	$(1, 2 - 1)$
Righthanded leptons e_R	$(1, 1, -2)$
Higgs Boson **H**	$(1, 2, +1)$
Color Gauge Fields G_a	$(8, 1, 0)$
Weak Gauge Fields $W^\pm, Z, \gamma$	$(1, 3 + 1, 0)$

Table caption: The assignment of particles to the standard model gauge group $SU(3)_c \times SU(2)_L \times U(1)_Y$.

The electro-weak symmetry $SU(2)_L \times U(1)_Y$ is broken by the vacuum expectation of the Higgs doublet $<H^0> = \frac{v_{wk}}{\sqrt{2}} \simeq 186$ GeV, which gives mass to the gauge bosons. The fermion masses arise from the Yukawa couplings:

$$\mathcal{L}_Y = h_u \bar{Q}_L H u_R + h_d \bar{Q}_L \tilde{H} d_R + h_e \bar{L} \tilde{H} e_R + h.c. \qquad (7.33)$$

when H^0 acquires a vev. Note that since there are no right handed neutrinos in the theory, there is no term in Eq. 7.33 that can give mass to the neutrinos. Thus they remain massless at the tree level.

There are several questions that arise at this stage. What happens when one goes beyond the above simple tree level approximation? Secondly, do non-perturbative effects change this tree level result? Finally, how to judge whether this result will be modified when the quantum gravity effects are included?

The first and second questions are easily answered by using the B-L symmetry of the standard model. The point is that since the standard model has no $SU(2)_L$ singlet neutrino-like field, the only possible mass terms that are allowed by Lorentz invariance are of the form $\nu_{iL}^T C^{-1} \nu_{jL}$, where i, j stand for the generation index and C is the Lorentz charge conjugation matrix. Since the ν_{iL} is part of the $SU(2)_L$ doublet field and has lepton number +1, the above neutrino mass term transforms as an $SU(2)_L$ triplet and furthermore, it violates total lepton number (defined as $L \equiv L_e + L_\mu + L_\tau$) by two units. However, a quick look at the standard model Lagrangian convinces one that the model has exact lepton number symmetry after symmetry breaking; therefore such terms can never arise in perturbation theory. Thus to all orders in perturbation theory, the neutrinos are massless. As far as the nonperturbative effects go, the only known source is the weak instanton effects. Such effects could change the result if they broke the lepton number symmetry. One way to see if such breaking occurs is to look for anomalies in lepton number current conservation from triangle diagrams. Indeed it is easy to convince oneself that $\partial_\mu j_\ell^\mu = cW\tilde{W} + c'B\tilde{B}$ due to the contribution of the leptons to the triangle involving the lepton number current and W's or B's. Luckily, it turns out that the anomaly contribution to the baryon number current nonconservation has also an identical form, so that the $B-L$ current j_{B-L}^μ is conserved to all orders in the gauge couplings. As a consequence, nonperturbative effects from the gauge sector cannot induce $B-L$ violation. Since the neutrino mass operator described above violates also $B-L$, this proves that neutrino masses remain zero even in the presence of nonperturbative effects.

Let us now turn to the effect of gravity. Clearly as long as we treat gravity in perturbation theory, the above symmetry arguments hold since all gravity coupling respect $B-L$ symmetry. However, once nonperturbative gravitational effects e.g black holes and worm holes are included, there is no guarantee that global symmetries will be respected in the low energy theory. The intuitive way to appreciate the argument is to note that throwing baryons into a black hole does not lead to any detectable consequence except through a net change in the baryon number of the universe. Since one can throw in an arbitrary number of baryons into the black hole, an arbitrary information loss about the net number of missing baryons would prevent us from defining a baryon number of the visible universe- thus baryon number in the presence of a black hole can not be an exact symmetry. Similar arguments can be made for any global charge such as lepton number in the standard model. A field theoretic parameterization of this statement is that the effective low energy Lagrangian for the standard model in the presence of black holes and worm holes etc must contain baryon and lepton number violating terms. In the context of the standard model, the only such terms that one can construct are nonrenormalizable terms of the form $LHLH/M_{P\ell}$. After gauge symmetry breaking, they lead to neutrino masses; however these masses are at most of order $v_{wk}^2/M_{P\ell} \simeq 10^{-5}$ eV.[30] But as we discussed in the previous section, in order to solve the atmospheric neutrino problem, one needs masses at least three orders of magnitude higher.

Thus one must seek physics beyond the standard model to explain observed evidences for neutrino masses. While there are many possibilities that lead to small neutrino masses of both Majorana as well as Dirac kind, here we focus on the possibility that there is a heavy right handed neutrino (or neutrinos) that lead to a small neutrino mass. The resulting mechanism is known as the seesaw mechanism[4] and leads to neutrino being a Majorana particle.

The nature and origin of the seesaw mechanism can also be tested in other experiments and we will discuss them below. This will be dependent on the kind of operators that play a role in generating neutrino masses. If the leading order operator is of dimension 5, then the scale necessarily is very high (of order 10^{12} GeV or greater). On the other hand, in theories with extra space dimensions, this operator may be forbidden and one may be forced to go to higher dimensional operators, in which case the scale could be lower or it could be that neutrino Dirac Yukawa couplings are of order 10^{-6} (similar to the electron Yukawa coupling in the standard model) in which case even the seesaw scale could be in the TeV range.

The seesaw mechanism raises a very important question: since we require the mass of the right handed neutrino to be much less than the Planck scale, a key question is "what symmetry keeps the right handed neutrino mass lighter?" We will give two examples of symmetries that can do this.

7.4.1. *Seesaw and the right handed neutrino*

The simplest possibility extension of the standard model that leads to nonzero mass for the neutrino is one where only a right handed neutrino is added to the standard model. In this case ν_L and ν_R can form a mass term; but apriori, this mass term is like the mass terms for charged leptons or quark masses and will therefore involve the weak scale. If we call the corresponding Yukawa coupling to be Y_ν, then the neutrino mass is $m_D = Y_\nu v/\sqrt{2}$. For a neutrino mass in the eV range requires that $Y_\nu \simeq 10^{-11}$ or less which is far below even the small electron Yukawa coupling of SM. Introduction of such small coupling constants into a theory is generally considered unnatural and a sound theory must find a symmetry reason for such smallness. As already already alluded to before, seesaw mechanism,[4] where we introduce a singlet Majorana mass term for the right handed neutrino is one way to achieve this goal. The effective mass terms for the (ν_L, ν_R) system is given by (suppressing the generation index):

$$\mathcal{L}_m = m_D^* \bar{\nu}_L \nu_R + M_R^* \nu_R^T C^{-1} \nu_R + h.c. \qquad (7.34)$$

where $m_D = Y_\nu v_{wk}$, Y_ν is the lepton doublet coupling to the right handed neutrinos (defined as $\bar{\nu}_R Y_\nu L$) . Suppose we write ν spinor in terms of its two component spinors as $\nu = \begin{pmatrix} \nu \\ i\sigma_2 N^* \end{pmatrix}$, then $\nu_L = \begin{pmatrix} \nu \\ 0 \end{pmatrix}$ and $\nu_R = \begin{pmatrix} 0 \\ i\sigma_2 N^* \end{pmatrix}$. This gives remembering that $\gamma_0 = \begin{pmatrix} 0 & I \\ I & 0 \end{pmatrix}$ and $C^{-1} = \begin{pmatrix} i\sigma_2 & 0 \\ 0 & -i\sigma_2 \end{pmatrix}$

$$\mathcal{L}_m = im_D^* \nu^\dagger \sigma_2 N^* + iM_R^* N^\dagger \sigma_2 N^* + h.c. \tag{7.35}$$

. We can write the neutrino mass matrix as:

$$\mathcal{L}_m = i \begin{pmatrix} \nu^T & N^T \end{pmatrix} \sigma_2 \mathbf{M} \begin{pmatrix} \nu \\ N \end{pmatrix} + h.c. \tag{7.36}$$

where $\mathbf{M}$ has the form:

$$\mathbf{M} = \begin{pmatrix} 0 & m_D \\ m_D^T & M_R \end{pmatrix} \tag{7.37}$$

Since M_R is not constrained by the standard model symmetries, it is natural to choose it to be at a scale much higher than the weak scale. Now diagonalizing this mass matrix, we get a set of heavy eigenstate N_R and a set of light eigenstates with mass matrix given by:

$$\mathcal{M}_\nu \simeq -m_D^T M_R^{-1} m_D \tag{7.38}$$

This provides a natural way to understand a small neutrino mass without any unnatural adjustment of parameters of a theory. In a subsequent section, we will discuss a theory which connects the scale M_R to a new symmetry of nature beyond the standard model. This formula for neutrino masses is called type I seesaw formula.

7.4.1.1. Why is $M_R \ll M_{P\ell}$?

The question "why $M_R \ll M_{P\ell}$?" is in many ways similar to the question in the standard model i.e. "why is $M_{Higgs} \ll M_{P\ell}$?" It is well known that searches for answer to this latter question has led to many interesting possibilities for physics beyond the standard model including supersymmetry, extra dimensions and technicolor. It is hoped that answering this question for ν_R can also lead us to new insight into new symmetries beyond the standard model. There are two interesting answers to our question that I will elaborate later on.

$B - L$:

If one adds three right handed neutrinos to implement the seesaw mechanism, the model admits an anomaly free new symmetry i.e. $B-L$. One can therefore extend the standard model symmetry to either $SU(2)_L \times U(1)_{I_{3R}} \times U(1)_{B-L}$ or its left-right symmetric extension $SU(2)_L \times SU(2)_R \times U(1)_{B-L}$. In either case the right handed neutrino carries the B-L quantum number and its Majorana mass breaks this symmetry. Therefore, the mass of the ν_R can at most be the scale of $B - L$ symmetry breaking, hence answering the question "why $M_{\nu_R} \ll M_{P\ell}$?".

$SU(2)_H$:

While local $B - L$ is perhaps the most straight forward and natural symmetry that keeps ν_R lighter than the Planck scale, another possibility has recently been suggested in Ref. 24. The main observation here is that is the standard model is extended by including a local $SU(2)_H$ symmetry acting on the first two lepton generations including the right handed charged leptons, then global Witten anomaly freedom dictates that there must be at least two right handed neutrinos which transform as a doublet under the $SU(2)_H$ local symmetry. In this class of models, in the limit of exact $SU(2)_H$ symmetry, the ν_R's are massless and as soon as the $SU(2)_H$ symmetry is broken, they pick up mass. Therefore "lightness" of the ν_R's compared to the Planck scale in these models is related to an $SU(2)_H$ symmetry. These comments are elaborated with explicit examples later on in this review.

7.4.2. Double seesaw mechanism with ν_R and B-L singlet neutral fermions

As we saw from the previous discussion, the conventional seesaw mechanism requires rather high mass for the right handed neutrino and therefore a correspondingly high scale for B-L symmetry breaking. The right handed neutrinos are B-L non-singlet fields. There is however no way at present to know what the scale of B-L symmetry breaking is. For lower B-L scale models, one must either find a mechanism to suppress the Dirac mass in the conventional seesaw formula or extend the theory some other way. A particularly simple way is to introduce, B-L singlet heavy neutrinos S and use a double seesaw mechanism suggested in Ref. 31 where one writes a three by three neutrino mass matrix in the basis (ν, N, S) of the form:

$$M = \begin{pmatrix} 0 & m_D & 0 \\ m_D & 0 & M \\ 0 & M & \mu \end{pmatrix} \qquad (7.39)$$

This comes from an effective mass Lagrangian of the form:

$$\mathcal{L}'_m = m_D^\dagger \bar{\nu}_L N_R + M^\dagger \bar{N}_R S + \mu S_L^T C^{-1} S_L + h.c. \qquad (7.40)$$

It is possible to have extra symmetries that guarantees the above form for the Lagrangian. (It will be a good exercise to discover these symmetries.) For the case $\mu \ll M \approx M_{B-L}$, (where M_{B-L} is the $B - L$ breaking scale) this matrix has one light and two heavy neutrinos per generation and the latter two form a pseudo-Dirac pair with mass of order M_{B-L}. The important thing for us is that the light mass eigenvalue is given by $m_D^2 \mu / M^2$; for $m_D \approx \mu \simeq$ GeV, a 10 TeV $B - L$ scale is enough to give neutrino masses in the eV range. For the case of three generations, the formula for the light neutrino mass matrix is given by:

$$\mathcal{M}_\nu = m_D^T M^{-1} \mu M^{-1} m_D. \qquad (7.41)$$

7.4.3. *High mass Higgs triplet induced neutrino masses*

As already noted, one way to generate nonzero neutrino masses without using righthanded neutrinos is to extend the standard model by the addition of an $SU(2)_L$ triplet Higgs field with $Y = 2$ so that the electric charge profile of the members of the multiplet is given as follows: $(\Delta^{++}, \Delta^+, \Delta^0)$. This allows an additional Yukawa coupling of the form $f_L L^T \tau_2 \tau L.\Delta$, where the Δ^0 couples to the neutrinos. Clearly Δ field has $L = 2$. When Δ^0 field has a nonzero vev, it breaks lepton number by two units and leads to Majorana mass for the neutrinos. There are two questions that arise now: one, how does the vev arise in a model and how does one understand the smallness of the neutrino masses in this scheme. There are two answers to the first question: One can maintain exact lepton number symmetry in the model and generate the vev of the triplet field via the usual "mexican hat" potential. There are two problems with this case. This leads to the triplet Majoron which has been ruled out by LEP data on Z-width. In any case, in this model smallness of the neutrino mass is not naturally understood.

Another way to generate the induced vev is to keep a large but positive mass (M_Δ) for the triplet Higgs boson and allowing for a lepton number violating coupling $M\Delta^* HH$.[2] In this case, minimization of the potential induces a vev for the Δ^0 field when the doublet field acquires a vev[36]:

$$v_T \equiv <\Delta^0> = \frac{Mv_{wk}^2}{M_\Delta^2} \qquad (7.42)$$

Since the mass of the Δ field is invariant under $SU(2)_L \times U(1)_Y$, it can be very large connected perhaps with some new scale of physics. If we assume that $M_\Delta \sim M \sim 10^{13}$ GeV or so, we get $v_T \sim$ eV. Now in the Yukawa coupling $f_L L^T \tau_2 \tau L.\Delta$, since the Δ^0 couples to the neutrinos, its vev leads to a neutrino mass We will see later when we discuss the seesaw models that unlike those models, the neutrino mass in this case is not hierarchically dependent on the charged fermion masses. Note further the high mass suppression in Eq. 7.42 leading to a new kind of seesaw suppression. This is called type II seesaw.

7.5. Left right symmetric unification: a natural realization of the seesaw

Let us now explore the implications of including the righthanded neutrinos into the extensions of the standard model to understand the small neutrino mass by the seesaw mechanism. As already emphasized, if we assume that there are no new symmetries beyond the standard model, the right handed neutrino will have a natural mass of order of the Planck scale making the light neutrino masses too small to be of interest in understanding the observed oscillations. We must therefore search for new symmetries that can keep the RH neutrinos at a lower scale than the Planck scale. A new symmetry always helps in making this natural.

To study this question, let us note that the inclusion of the right handed neutrinos transforms the dynamics of the gauge models in a profound way. To clarify what we mean, note that in the standard model (that does not contain a ν_R) the $B - L$ symmetry is only linearly anomaly free i.e. $\text{Tr}[(B-L)Q_a^2] = 0$ where Q_a are the gauge generators of the standard model but $\text{Tr}(B-L)^3 \neq 0$. This means that $B - L$ is only a global symmetry and cannot be gauged. However as soon as the ν_R is added to the standard model, one gets $\text{Tr}[(B-L)^3] = 0$ implying that the B-L symmetry is now gaugeable and one could choose the gauge group of nature to be either $SU(2)_L \times U(1)_{I_{3R}} \times U(1)_{B-L}$ or $SU(2)_L \times SU(2)_R \times U(1)_{B-L}$, the latter being the gauge group of the left-right symmetric models.[37] Furthermore the presence of the ν_R makes the model quark lepton symmetric and leads to a Gell-Mann-Nishijima like formula for the electric charges[39] i.e.

$$Q = I_{3L} + I_{3R} + \frac{B-L}{2} \quad (7.43)$$

The advantage of this formula over the charge formula in the standard model charge formula is that in this case all entries have a physical meaning. Furthermore, it leads naturally to Majorana nature of neutrinos as can be seen by looking at the distance scale where the $SU(2)_L \times U(1)_Y$ symmetry is valid but the left-right gauge group is broken. In that case, one gets

$$\Delta Q = 0 = \Delta I_{3L} : \quad (7.44)$$
$$\Delta I_{3R} = -\Delta \frac{B-L}{2}$$

We see that if the Higgs fields that break the left-right gauge group carry righthanded isospin of one, one must have $|\Delta L| = 2$ which means that the neutrino mass must be Majorana type and the theory will break lepton number by two units.

Let us now proceed to give a few details of the left-right symmetric model and demonstrate how the seesaw mechanism emerges in this model.

The gauge group of the theory is $SU(2)_L \times SU(2)_R \times U(1)_{B-L}$ with quarks and leptons transforming as doublets under $SU(2)_{L,R}$. In Table II, we denote the quark, lepton and Higgs fields in the theory along with their transformation properties under the gauge group.

Table II

Fields	$SU(2)_L \times SU(2)_R \times U(1)_{B-L}$ representation
Q_L	$(2,1,+\frac{1}{3})$
Q_R	$(1,2,\frac{1}{3})$
L_L	$(2,1,-1)$
L_R	$(1,2,-1)$
ϕ	$(2,2,0)$
Δ_L	$(3,1,+2)$
Δ_R	$(1,3,+2)$

Table caption Assignment of the fermion and Higgs fields to the representation of the left-right symmetry group.

The first task is to specify how the left-right symmetry group breaks to the standard model i.e. how one breaks the $SU(2)_R \times U(1)_{B-L}$ symmetry so that the successes of the standard model including the observed predominant V-A structure of weak interactions at low energies is reproduced. Another question of naturalness that also arises simultaneously is that since the charged fermions and the neutrinos are treated completely symmetrically (quark-lepton symmetry) in this model, how does one understand the smallness of the neutrino masses compared to the other fermion masses.

It turns out that both the above problems of the LR model have a common solution. The process of spontaneous breaking of the $SU(2)_R$ symmetry that suppresses the V+A currents at low energies also solves the problem of ultralight neutrino masses. To see this let us write the Higgs fields explicitly:

$$\Delta = \begin{pmatrix} \Delta^+/\sqrt{2} & \Delta^{++} \\ \Delta^0 & -\Delta^+/\sqrt{2} \end{pmatrix}; \quad \phi = \begin{pmatrix} \phi_1^0 & \phi_2^+ \\ \phi_1^- & \phi_2^0 \end{pmatrix} \quad (7.45)$$

All these Higgs fields have Yukawa couplings to the fermions given symbolically as below.

$$\begin{aligned} \mathcal{L}_Y &= h_1 \bar{L}_L \phi L_R + h_2 \bar{L}_L \tilde{\phi} L_R \\ &+ h'_1 \bar{Q}_L \phi Q_R + h'_2 \bar{Q}_L \tilde{\phi} Q_R \\ &+ f(L_L L_L \Delta_L + L_R L_R \Delta_R) + h.c. \end{aligned} \quad (7.46)$$

The $SU(2)_R \times U(1)_{B-L}$ is broken down to the standard model hypercharge $U(1)_Y$ by choosing $<\Delta_R^0> = v_R \neq 0$ since this carries both $SU(2)_R$ and $U(1)_{B-L}$ quantum numbers. It gives mass to the charged and neutral righthanded gauge bosons i.e. $M_{W_R} = gv_R$ and $M_{Z'} = \sqrt{2}gv_R \cos\theta_W/\sqrt{\cos 2\theta_W}$. Thus by adjusting the value of v_R one can suppress the right handed current effects in both neutral and charged current interactions arbitrarily leading to an effective near maximal left-handed form for the charged current weak interactions.

The fact that at the same time the neutrino masses also become small can be seen by looking at the form of the Yukawa couplings. Note that the f-term leads to a mass for the right handed neutrinos only at the scale v_R. Next as we break the standard model symmetry by turning on the vev's for the ϕ fields as $Diag <\phi> = (\kappa, \kappa')$, we not only give masses to the W_L and the Z bosons but also to the quarks and the leptons. In the neutrino sector the above Yukawa couplings after $SU(2)_L$ breaking by $<\phi>\neq 0$ lead to the so called Dirac masses for the neutrino connecting the left and right handed neutrinos. In the two component neutrino language, this leads to the following mass matrix for the ν, N using the notation earlier with the four component $\nu = \begin{pmatrix} \nu \\ i\sigma_2 N^* \end{pmatrix}$.

$$M = \begin{pmatrix} 0 & h\kappa \\ h\kappa & fv_R \end{pmatrix} \quad (7.47)$$

Note that m_D in previous discussions of the seesaw formula (see Eq. ()) is given by $m_D = h\kappa$, which links it to the weak scale and the mass of the RH neutrinos is given by $M_R = fv_R$, which is linked to the local B-L symmetry. This justifies keeping RH neutrino mass at a scale lower than the Planck mass. It is therefore fair to assume that seesaw mechanism coupled with observations of neutrino oscillations are a strong indication of the existence of a local B-L symmetry far below the Planck scale.

By diagonalizing this 2×2 matrix, we get the light neutrino eigenvalue to be $m_\nu \simeq \frac{(h\kappa)^2}{fv_R}$ and the heavy one to be fv_R. Note that typical charged fermion masses are given by $h'\kappa$ etc. So since $v_R \gg \kappa, \kappa'$, the light neutrino mass is automatically suppressed. This way of suppressing the neutrino masses is called the seesaw mechanism.[4] Thus in one stroke, one explains the smallness of the neutrino mass as well as the suppression of the V+A currents.

In deriving the above seesaw formula for neutrino masses, it has been assumed that the vev of the lefthanded triplet is zero so that the $\nu_L \nu_L$ entry of the neutrino mass matrix is zero. However, in most explicit models such as the left-right model which provide an explicit derivation of this formula, there is an induced vev for the Δ_L^0 of order $<\Delta_L^0> = v_T \simeq \frac{v_{wk}^2}{v_R}$. In the left-right models, this this arises from the presence of a coupling in the Higgs potential of the form $\Delta_L \phi \Delta_R^\dagger \phi^\dagger$. In the presence of the Δ_L vev, the seesaw formula undergoes a fundamental change and takes the form

$$M_\nu = fv_L - h_\nu^T f_R^{-1} h_\nu \left(\frac{v_{wk}^2}{v_R}\right) \quad (7.48)$$

which includes both the type I and the type II seesaw contributions. In Fig. 1, the two mdiagrams responsible for type I and type II seesaw are given:

This left-right symmetric seesaw formula has recently been shown to exhibit some interesting duality properties[38] which can perhaps be used to restrict some of the arbitrariness in its applications.

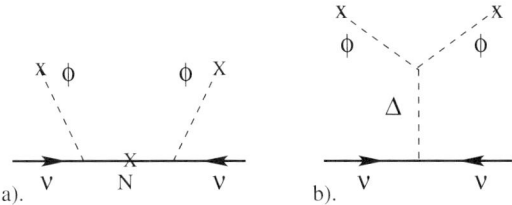

Fig. 7.1. The type I and type II contribution to seesaw formula for neutrino masses.

Note that in the type I seesaw formula, what appears is the square of the Dirac neutrino mass matrix which in general expected to have the same hierarchical structure as the corresponding charged fermion mass matrix. In fact in some specific GUT models such as SO(10), $M_D = M_u$. This is the origin of the common statement that neutrino masses given by the seesaw formula are hierarchical i.e. $m_{\nu_e} \ll m_{\nu_\mu} \ll m_{\nu_\tau}$ and even a more model dependent statement that $m_{\nu_e} : m_{\nu_\mu} : m_{\nu_\tau} = m_u^2 : m_c^2 : m_t^2$.

On the other hand if one uses the type II seesaw formula, there is no reason to expect a hierarchy and in fact if the neutrino masses turn out to be degenerate as discussed before as one possibility, one possible way to understand this may be to use the type II seesaw formula.

Secondly, the type II seesaw formula is a reflection of the parity invariance of the theory at high energies. Evidence for it would point more strongly towards left-right symmetry at high energies.

7.5.1. *Understanding detailed mixing pattern for neutrinos using the seesaw formula*

Let us now address the question: to what extent one can understand the details of the neutrino masses and mixings using the seesaw formulae. The answer to this question is quite model dependent. While there exist many models which fit the observations, none (except a few) are completely predictive and almost always they need to invoke new symmetries or new assumptions. The problem in general is that the seesaw formula of type I, has 12 parameters in the absence of CP violation (six parameters for a symmetric Dirac mass matrix and six for the M_R) which is why its predictive power is so limited. In the presence of CP violation, the number of parameters double making the situation worse. Specific predictions can be made only under additional assumptions.

For instance, in a class of seesaw models based on the SO(10) group that embodies the left-right symmetric unification model or the $SU(4)$-color, the mass the tau neutrino mass can be estimated provided one assumes the normal mass hierarchy for neutrinos and a certain parameter accompanying a higher dimensional operator to be of order one. To see this, let us assume that in the SO(10) theory, the B-L symmetry is broken by a **16**-dim. Higgs boson. The RH neutrino mass in such a model arises from the nonrenormalizable operator $\lambda(\mathbf{16_F \overline{16}_H})^2/\mathbf{M_{P\ell}}$. In a supersymmetric theory, if **16**-Higgs is also responsible for GUT symmetry breaking, then after symmetry breaking, one obtains the RH neutrino mass $M_R \simeq \lambda(2 \times 10^{16})^2/M_{P\ell} \simeq 4\lambda 10^{14}$ GeV. In models with $SU(4)_c$ symmetry, $m_{\nu_\tau,D} \simeq m_t(M_U) \sim 100$ GeV. Using the seesaw formula then, one obtains for $\lambda = 1$, tau neutrino mass $m_{\nu_\tau} \simeq 0.025$ eV, which is close to the presently preferred value of 0.05 eV. The situation with respect to other neutrino masses is however less certain and here one has to make assumptions.

The situation with respect to mixing angles is much more complicated. In generic seesaw models, one needs additional family symmetries to understand the largeness of both solar and atmospheric mixing angles, as has been commented before. It could of course very well be that the Dirac coupling in the seesaw formula is similar to the quark Yukawas but large neutrino mixings owe their origin to the flavor structure of right handed neutrino mass matrix. Or it could be that it is the type II seesaw term (the triplet Higgs contribution) dominates the neutrino mass decoupling neutrino masses completely from the charged lepton and quark mixings.

Essentially, one has to arrive at matrices similar to the above examples. There are however some exceptional situations such as in a class of minimal SO(10) models described below where the overall unification constraints on Yukawa textures is enough to explain desired large mixings, without the need for any family symmetry.

7.5.2. *General consequences of the seesaw formula for neutrino masses*

In this section, we will consider some implications of the seesaw mechanism for understanding neutrino masses. We will discuss two main points. One is the nature of the right handed neutrino spectrum as dictated by the seesaw mechanism and secondly, ways to get an approximate $L_e - L_\mu - L_\tau$ symmetric neutrino mass matrix using the seesaw mechanism and its possible implications for physics beyond the standard model.[33]

For this purpose, we use the type I seesaw formula along with the assumption of a diagonal Dirac neutrino mass matrix to obtain the right handed neutrino mass matrix M_R:

$$\mathcal{M}_{R,ij} = m_{D,i}\mu_{ij}^{-1}m_{D,j} \qquad (7.49)$$

with

$$\begin{aligned}
\mu_{11}^{-1} &= \frac{c^2}{m_1} + \frac{s^2}{m_2} + \frac{\epsilon^2}{m_3} \\
\mu_{12}^{-1} &= -\frac{c(s+c\epsilon)}{\sqrt{2}m_1} + \frac{s(c-s\epsilon)}{\sqrt{2}m_2} + \frac{\epsilon}{\sqrt{2}m_3} \\
\mu_{13}^{-1} &= \frac{c(s-c\epsilon)}{\sqrt{2}m_1} - \frac{s(c+s\epsilon)}{\sqrt{2}m_2} + \frac{\epsilon}{\sqrt{2}m_3} \\
\mu_{22}^{-1} &= \frac{(s+c\epsilon)^2}{2m_1} + \frac{(c_s\epsilon)^2}{2m_2} + \frac{1}{2m_3} \\
\mu_{23}^{-1} &= -\frac{(s^2-c^2\epsilon^2)}{2m_1} - \frac{(c^2-s^2\epsilon^2)}{2m_2} + \frac{1}{2m_3} \\
\mu_{33}^{-1} &= \frac{(s-c\epsilon)^2}{2m_1} + \frac{(c+s\epsilon)^2}{2m_2} + \frac{1}{2m_3}.
\end{aligned} \qquad (7.50)$$

Since for the cases of normal and inverted hierarchy, we have no information on the mass of the lightest neutrino m_1, we could assume it in principle to be quite small. In that case, the above equation enables us to conclude that quite likely one of the three right handed neutrinos is much heavier than the other two, leading to the so-called two right handed neutrino dominance model.[32] The situation is of course completely different for the degenerate case. This kind of separation of the RH neutrino spectrum is very suggestive of a symmetry. In fact we have recently argued that,[24] this indicates the possible existence of an $SU(2)_H$ horizontal symmetry, that leads in the simplest case to an inverted mass pattern for light neutrinos. A scenario which realizes this is given below.

7.5.2.1. *Approximate $L_e - L_\mu - L_\tau$ symmetric mass matrix from seesaw*

In this section, we discuss how an approximate $L_e - L_\mu - L_\tau$ symmetric neutrino mass matrix may arise within a seesaw framework. Consider a simple extension of the standard model by adding two additional singlet right handed neutrinos,[34] N_1, N_2 assigning them $L_e - L_\mu - L_\tau$ quantum numbers of $+1$ and -1 respectively. Denoting the standard model lepton doublets by $\psi_{e,\mu,\tau}$, the $L_e - L_\mu - L_\tau$ symmetry allows the following new couplings to the Lagrangian of the standard model:

$$\mathcal{L}' = (h_3\bar{\psi}_\tau + h_2\bar{\psi}_\mu)HN_2 + h_1\bar{\psi}_e HN_1 + MN_1^T C^{-1}N_2 + h.c. \quad (7.51)$$

where H is the Higgs doublet of the standard model; C^{-1} is the Dirac charge conjugation matrix. We add to it the symmetry breaking mass terms for the right handed neutrinos, which are soft terms, i.e.

$$\mathcal{L}_B = \epsilon(M_1 N_1^T C^{-1} N_1 + M_2 N_2^T C^{-1} N_2) + h.c. \quad (7.52)$$

with $\epsilon \ll 1$. These terms break $L_e - L_\mu - L_\tau$ by two units but since they are dimension 3 terms, they are soft and do not induce any

with $\epsilon \ll 1$. These terms break $L_e - L_\mu - L_\tau$ by two units but since they are dimension 3 terms, they are soft and do not induce any new terms into the theory.

It is clear from the resulting mass matrix for the ν_L, N system that the linear combination $h_2\nu_\tau - h_3\nu_\mu$) is massless and the atmospheric oscillation angle is given by $tan\theta_A = h_2/h_3$; for $h_3 \sim h_2$, the θ_A is maximal. The seesaw mass matrix then takes the following form (in the basis $(\nu_e, \tilde{\nu}_\mu, N_1, N_2)$ with $\tilde{\nu}_\mu \equiv h_2\nu_\mu + h_3\nu_\tau$):

$$M = \begin{pmatrix} 0 & 0 & m_1 & 0 \\ 0 & 0 & 0 & m_2 \\ m_1 & 0 & \epsilon M_1 & M \\ 0 & m_2 & M & \epsilon M_2 \end{pmatrix} \quad (7.53)$$

The diagonalization of this mass matrix leads to the mass matrix of the form discussed before.

7.5.2.2. Tri-bi-maximal mixing from seesaw

In this section, we present an example of a seesaw model for the mass matrix for neutrinos (Eq. 7.28) that leads to the tri-bi-maximal mixing.[35] It was shown that the Majorana neutrino mass matrix in 7.28 can be realized in a combined type I type II seesaw model with soft-broken S_3 family symmetry for leptons. The type II contribution comes from an S_3 invariant coupling of lepton doublets to the triplet field Δ i.e. $f_{\alpha\beta}L_\alpha L_\beta\Delta$. The most general S_3 invariant form for f is:

$$f = \begin{pmatrix} f_a & f_b & f_b \\ f_b & f_a & f_b \\ f_b & f_b & f_a \end{pmatrix} \quad (7.54)$$

After the triplet Higgs field Δ gets vev and decouples, its contribution to the light neutrino mass can written as

$$M_{II} = \begin{pmatrix} a' & b' & b' \\ b' & a' & b' \\ b' & b' & a' \end{pmatrix} \qquad (7.55)$$

where $a' = \frac{v^2 \sin^2\beta \lambda}{M_T} f_a$ and $b' = \frac{v^2 \sin^2\beta \lambda}{M_T} f_b$. We denote M_T as the mass of the triplet Higgs and λ as the coupling constant between the triplet and doublets in the superpotential.

Coming to the type I contribution, the Dirac mass matrix for neutrinos comes from an S_3 invariant Yukawa coupling of the form:

$$\mathcal{L}_D = h_\nu [\overline{\nu_{R1}} H(L_e - L_\mu) + \overline{\nu_{R2}} H(L_\mu - L_\tau) \\ + \overline{\nu_{R3}} H(L_\tau - L_e)] + h.c. \qquad (7.56)$$

leading to

$$Y_\nu = \begin{pmatrix} h & -h & 0 \\ 0 & h & -h \\ -h & 0 & h \end{pmatrix}. \qquad (7.57)$$

In the limit of $|M_{R1,R3}| \gg |M_{R2}|$, where a single right-handed neutrino dominates the type I contribution, the mixed type I+II seesaw formula

$$\mathcal{M}_\nu = M_{II} - M_D^T M_{\nu R}^{-1} M_D, \qquad (7.58)$$

then leads to Eq. 7.28 which gives the tri-bi-maximal mixing matrix. It turns out that,[35] the charged lepton mass matrix in this case can be made diagonal if one of the two lepton Yukawa couplings is set to zero.

7.6. Neutrino mass and grand unification

One of the interesting features of the seesaw mechanism is that if one assumes the Dirac masses to be roughly of order of the up-quark masses, then the atmospheric neutrino mass difference would directly measure the mass of m_3 and can be used to get a rough idea of how high the seesaw scale is. In order to do this one can use the rough relation $m_{\nu_3} \sim \frac{m_t^2}{M_R}$ which then yields $M_R \sim 10^{14}$ GeV. This is of course not a rigorous argument at all and can therefore only be used as a suggestive one. If however one takes this seriously, then it suggests that the seesaw scale could be related to the scale of grand unification which from arguments of coupling constant unification is also of order 10^{16} GeV. In view of other theoretical arguments in favor of GUTs, one may try to understand the neutrino masses within a grand unified theory framework.

The minimal GUT group that appears to have many desirable properties is the SO(10) group,[41] whose spinor representation is **16** dimensional and is just right for all then SM fermions of one generation plus the right handed neutrino needed for implementing the seesaw mechanism. This has therefore been extensively studied as a way to understand neutrino properties.

7.6.1. *SO(10) Grand Unification of seesaw mechanism and predictions for neutrino masses*

In addition to the fermion unification by the **16** dimensional spinor representation, SO(10) contains the B-L as a subgroup and seesaw mechanism requires that the process of symmetry breaking down to the standard model must break the B-L at a high scale. One implication of this is a natural understanding of the seesaw scale as being connected to the GUT scale. Secondly in the context of supersymmetric SO(10) models, the way B-L breaks has profound consequences for low energy physics. For instance, if B-L is broken by a Higgs field belonging to the **16** dimensional Higgs field, then the field that acquires a nonzero vev has the quantum numbers of the ν_R field i.e. B-L breaks by one unit. In this case higher dimensional operators of the form $\Psi\Psi\Psi\Psi_H$ will lead to R-parity violating operators in the effective low energy MSSM theory such as $QLd^c, u^c d^c d^c$ etc which can lead to large breaking of lepton and baryon number symmetry and hence unacceptable rates for proton decay. This theory also has no dark matter candidate without making additional assumptions. Furthermore, since non-renormalizable operators are an essential part of this approach, there are many more parameters, making it non-predictive in the absence of additional assumptions.[42]

On the other hand, one may break B-L by a **126** dimensional Higgs field.[43,44] The member of this multiplet that acquires vev has $B - L = 2$ and leaves R-parity as an automatic symmetry of the low energy Lagrangian. This then gives a naturally stable dark matter. Furthermore, in this approach, since one considers only renormalizable couplings, the number of Yukawa parameters are quite limited so that the model is quite predictive.[43] The predictivity clearly arises from one irreducible **16** dimensional spinor multiplet containing all fermions of each family or complete fermion unification.

In order to study the predictions of the model, we first note that since the SO(10) model contains the left-right subgroup, the seesaw formula takes the modified form as in Eq.7.48 that we repeat below.[36]

$$M_\nu = fv_L - h_\nu^T f_R^{-1} h_\nu \left(\frac{v_{wk}^2}{v_R}\right) \qquad (7.59)$$

It turns out that if the B-L symmetry is broken by **16** Higgs fields, the first term in the type II seesaw (effective triplet vev induced term) becomes very small compared to the type I term. On the other hand, if B-L is broken by a **126** field, then the first term in the type II seesaw formula is not necessarily small and can in principle dominate in the seesaw formula. As we discuss below, this leads to predictions for neutrino masses and mixings that are in excellent agreement with experiments.

The basic ingredients of this model[43] are that one considers only two Higgs multiplets that contribute to fermion masses i.e. one **10** and one **126**. A unique property of the **126** multiplet is that it not only breaks the B-L symmetry and therefore contributes to right handed neutrino masses, but it also contributes to charged fermion masses by virtue of the fact that it contains MSSM doublets which mix with those from the **10** dimensional multiplets and survive down to the MSSM scale. This leads to a tremendous reduction of the number of arbitrary parameters.

There are only two Yukawa coupling matrices in this model: (i) h for the **10** Higgs and (ii) f for the **126** Higgs. SO(10) has the property that the Yukawa couplings involving the **10** and **126** Higgs representations are symmetric. Therefore if we assume that CP violation arises from other sectors of the theory (e.g. squark masses) and work in a basis where one of these two sets of Yukawa coupling matrices is diagonal, then it will have only nine parameters. Noting the fact that the (2,2,15) submultiplet of **126** has a pair of standard model doublets that contributes to charged fermion masses, one can write the quark and lepton mass matrices as follows[43]:

$$\begin{aligned} M_u &= h\kappa_u + fv_u \\ M_d &= h\kappa_d + fv_d \\ M_\ell &= h\kappa_d - 3fv_d \\ M_{\nu_D} &= h\kappa_u - 3fv_u \end{aligned} \qquad (7.60)$$

where $\kappa_{u,d}$ are the vev's of the up and down standard model type Higgs fields in the **10** multiplet and $v_{u,d}$ are the corresponding vevs for the same doublets in **126**. Note that there are 13 parameters in the above equations and there are 13 inputs (six quark masses, three lepton masses and three quark mixing angles and weak scale). Thus all parameters of the model that go into fermion masses are determined.

To determine the light neutrino masses, we use the seesaw formula in Eq. 7.48, where the **f** is nothing but the **126** Yukawa coupling. Thus all parameters that give neutrino mixings except an overall scale are determined. A simple way to see how large mixings arise in this model is to note that when the triplet term dominates the seesaw formula, we have the neutrino mass matrix $M_\nu \propto f$, where f matrix is the **126** coupling to fermions discussed earlier.

$$M_\nu = c(M_d - M_\ell) \qquad (7.61)$$

All the quark mixing effects are then in the up quark mass matrix i.e. $M_u = U_{CKM}^T M_u^d U_{CKM}$. Note further that the minimality of the Higgs content leads to the following sum-rule among the mass matrices:

$$k\tilde{M}_\ell = r\tilde{M}_d + \tilde{M}_u \qquad (7.62)$$

where the tilde denotes the fact that we have made the mass matrices dimensionless by dividing them by the heaviest mass of the species. We then find that we have

$$M_{d,\ell} \approx m_{b,\tau} \begin{pmatrix} \lambda^3 & \lambda^3 & \lambda^3 \\ \lambda^3 & \lambda^2 & \lambda^2 \\ \lambda^3 & \lambda^2 & 1 \end{pmatrix} \qquad (7.63)$$

where $\lambda \sim 0.22$ and the matrix elements are supposed to give only the approximate order of magnitude. An important consequence of the relation between the charged lepton and the quark mass matrices in Eq. 7.62 is that the charged lepton contribution to the neutrino mixing matrix i.e. $U_\ell \simeq \mathbf{1} + O(\lambda)$ or close to identity matrix. As a result the neutrino mixing matrix is given by $U_{PMNS} = U_\ell^\dagger U_\nu \simeq U_\nu$, since in U_ℓ, all mixing angles are small. Thus the dominant contribution to large mixings will come from U_ν, which in turn will be dictated by the sum rule in Eq. 7.61.

As we extrapolate the quark masses to the GUT scale, due to the fact that $m_b - m_\tau \approx m_\tau \lambda^2$ for a wide range of values of $\tan\beta$, the neutrino mass matrix $M_\nu = c(M_d - M_\ell)$ takes roughly the form

$$M_\nu = c(M_d - M_\ell) \approx m_0 \begin{pmatrix} \lambda^3 & \lambda^3 & \lambda^3 \\ \lambda^3 & \lambda^2 & \lambda^2 \\ \lambda^3 & \lambda^2 & \lambda^2 \end{pmatrix} \qquad (7.64)$$

It is easy to see that both the θ_{12} (solar angle) and θ_{23} (the atmospheric angle) are now large. The detailed magnitudes of these angles of course depend on the details of the quark masses at the GUT scale. Using the extrapolated values of the quark masses and mixing angles to the GUT scale, the predictions of this model for various oscillation parameters are given in.[26] Some of the salient features are: (i) the atmospheric mixing angle θ_{23} is not maximal and the maximum value for it is around 38^0; (ii) the prediction for $sin\theta_{13} \equiv U_{e3}$ is near 0.18, a value within the reach of MINOS as well as other planned Long Base Line neutrino experiments such as Numi-Off-Axis, JPARC etc.

7.6.2. *CP violation in the minimal SO(10) model*

In the discussion given above, it was assumed that CP violation is non-CKM type and resides in the soft SUSY breaking terms of the Lagrangian. The overwhelming evidence from experiments seem to be that CP violation is perhaps of CKM type with CKM phase of about 60^0. Success of the above approach in understanding neutrino mixings suggests that we should consider extending the above simple model to accommodate CKM CP violation. Several such attempts have been made in recent literature.[19,47]

One approach discussed by us[47] employs a slight extension of the **10+126** model by adding a **120** Higgs field. A further Z_2 symmetry is imposed in such a way that the **10** and **126** couplings are real whereas the **120** couplings turn out to be imaginary. This will add a new piece to all fermion masses but in such a way that the $b-\tau$ mass convergence still leads to large atmospheric mixing as in the 10+126 case.

The new model is still predictive in the neutrino sector. Of the three new parameters, one is determined by the CP violating quark phase. the two others are determined by the solar mixing angle and the solar mass difference squared. Therefore we lose the prediction for these parameters. However, we can predict in addition to θ_A which is now close to maximal, $\theta_{13} \geq 0.1$ (see figure below) and the Dirac phase for the neutrinos, also close to 90°.

In the above discussion, we assumed type II seesaw terms to dominate.

This model has been reanalyzed using type I seesaw term to dominant in a recent paper[19] and a fit to the fermion masses as well as neutrino mixings exists for this case.

Finally, a few comments on what really will constitute a true test of the grand unification theories: a key prediction of simple grand unified theories such as $SU(5)$ and $SO(10)$ is the existence of proton decay. In supersymmetric theories, proton decay turns from an exciting prediction to somewhat of a challenge since the presence of super-partners at the TeV scale generates "dangerous" operators such as $\tilde{Q}\tilde{Q}QL/M_U$ which could lead to very rapid proton decay. In fact it is the appearance of these kind of operators that has ruled out minimal SUSY $SU(5)$ model. For this reason, in the last two papers by us,[47] a Yukawa texture was chosen that is in accord with current experimental bounds on proton lifetime resulting from dimension five operators as the one given above and a fit to neutrino masses as well as charged fermions etc was found with type II seesaw. A proton decay check is therefore needed for the type I fit to fermions carried out in Ref. 48 and proton decay predictions for the model of[47] need to be worked out.

7.6.3. *Type II seesaw and Quasi-degenerate neutrinos*

In this subsection we like to discuss some issues related to the degenerate neutrino hypothesis, which will be necessary if there is evidence for neutrinoless double beta decay at a significant level(see for example the recent results from the Heidelberg-Moscow group[12]) and assuming that no other physics such as R-parity breaking or doubly charged Higgs etc are not the source of this effect). Thus it is appropriate to discuss how such models can arise in theoretical schemes and how stable they are under radiative corrections.

There are two aspects to this question: one is whether the degeneracy arises within a gauge theory framework without arbitrary adjustment of parameters and the second aspect being that given such a degeneracy arises at some scale naturally in a field theory, is this mass degeneracy stable under renormali9zation group extrapolation to the weak scale where we need the degeneracy to be present. In this section we comment on the first aspect.

It was pointed out long ago[14] that degenerate neutrinos arise naturally in models that employ the type II seesaw since the first term in the mass formula is not connected to the charged fermion masses. One way that has been discussed is to consider schemes where one uses symmetries such as $SO(3)$ or $SU(2)$ or permutation symmetry S_4 so that the Majorana Yukawa couplings f_i are all equal. This then leads to the dominant contribution to all neutrinos being equal. This symmetry however must be broken in the charged fermion sector in order to explain the observed quark and lepton masses. Such models consistent with known data have been constructed based on $SO(10)$ as well as other groups. The interesting point about the $SO(10)$ realization is that the dominant contributions to the Δm^2's in this model comes from the second term in the type II seesaw formula which in simple models is hierarchical. It is of course known that if the MSW solution to the solar neutrino puzzle is the right solution (or an energy independent solution), then we have $\Delta m^2_{solar} \ll \Delta m^2_{ATMOS}$. In fact if we use the fact true in SO(10) models that $M_u = M_D$, then we have $\Delta m^2_{ATMOS} \simeq m_0 \frac{m_t^2}{fv_R}$ and $\Delta m^2_{SOLAR} \simeq m_0 \frac{m_c^2}{fv_R}$ where m_0 is the common mass for the three neutrinos. It is interesting that for $m_0 \sim$ few eV and $fv_R \approx 10^{15}$ GeV, both the Δm^2's are of right order to the required values.

Outside the seesaw framework, there could also be electroweak symmetries that guarantee the mass degeneracy.

The second question of stability under RGE of such a pattern is discussed in a subsequent section.

7.7. Some other consequences of seesaw paradigm

Generic seesaw models have several other important implications that we go into now. For simplicity, we first consider the type I seesaw formula 7.38. The first question one can ask is that given low energy information, to what extent we can discover the high scale physics associated with the seesaw mechanism such as the spectrum of right handed neutrinos, the structure of the Dirac mass matrix m_D (or equivalently Y_ν). A simple parameter counting shows that the neutrino masses and mixings (including CP phases) are characterized by nine observables whereas seesaw formula involves eighteen parameters (in the basis where RH neutrinos are mass eigenstates, there are three masses and 15 parameters characterizing m_D. Thus we need nine more pieces of low energy inputs to completely determine the seesaw physics (granted that all observables in the neutrino mass matrix are determined). Radiative leptonic decays such as $\mu \to e + \gamma, \tau \to \mu, e + \gamma$ including both CP violating and conserving channels could provide six pieces of information; three electric dipole moments of the charged leptons could provide the remaining three. Thus in principle, all the seesaw parameters could be determined from low energy observations.

In discussing the connection between high scale and low scale physics for neutrinos, it is often convenient to use a parameterization suggested by Casas and Ibarra.[49]

$$Y_\nu v_{wk} = iM_R^{1/2} O (\mathcal{M}_\nu^d)^{1/2} U^\dagger \qquad (7.65)$$

where O is a complex matrix with the property that $OO^T = 1$[49] and U is the neutrino mixing matrix; M_ν^d is the diagonal neutrino mass matrix. The set of matrices O in fact form a group analogous to the complex extension of the Lorentz group. Note that six parameters (or three complex angles) characterize O, three needed each for M_R and $\mathcal{M}_\nu$ and six for U giving a total of 18 as we counted above. In special cases where there are symmetries e.g. $\mu - \tau$ symmetry, the number of complex angles in reduces to only one making the direct connection between high and low energy phases somewhat closer.

For the case of type II seesaw, the corresponding relation is:

$$Y_\nu v_{wk} = iM_R^{1/2} O[U^* \mathcal{M}_\nu^d U^\dagger - M_R \zeta]^{1/2} \quad (7.66)$$

where $\zeta = \frac{v_L}{v_R}$.

It is clear from Eq.7.65 that in general the neutrino mixing matrix is only indirectly related to the details of Y_ν due to the unknown matrix O. In a given model however, when Y_ν is given, O and U get related.

7.7.1. *SUSY seesaw and lepton flavor violation*

In the standard model, the masslessness of the neutrino implies that that there is no lepton flavor changing effects unlike in the quark sector. Thus the leptons are completely "flavor sterile" and do not throw any light on the flavor puzzle. Once one includes the right handed neutrinos N_R one for each family, there is lepton mixing and this activates the lepton flavor. A simple phenomenological consequence of this "flavor activation" is that there appear lepton flavor changing effects such as $\mu \to e + \gamma$, $\tau \to e, \mu + \gamma$ etc. However, a simple estimate of the one loop contribution to such effects shows that the amplitude is of order

$$A(\ell_j \to \ell_i + \gamma) \simeq \frac{eG_F m_{\ell_j} m_e m_\nu^2}{\pi^2 m_W^2} \mu_B \quad (7.67)$$

This leads to an unobservable branching ratio (of order $\sim 10^{-40}$) for the rare radiative decay modes for the leptons given above.

The situation however changes drastically as soon as the seesaw mechanism for neutrino masses is combined with supersymmetry. It has been noted in many papers already that in supersymmetric theories, the lepton flavor changing effects get significantly enhanced. They arise from the the mixings among sleptons (superpartners of leptons) of different flavor caused by the renormalization group extrapolations which via loop diagrams lead to lepton flavor violating (LFV) effects at low energies.[50]

The way this happens is as follows. In the simplest N=1 supergravity models,[51] the supersymmetry breaking terms at the Planck scale are taken to have only few parameters: a universal scalar mass m_0, universal A terms, one gaugino mass $m_{1/2}$ for all three types of gauginos. Clearly, a universal scalar mass implies that at Planck scale, there is no flavor violation anywhere except in the Yukawa couplings (or when the Yukawa terms are diagonalized, in the CKM angles). However as we extrapolate this theory to the weak scale, the flavor mixings in the Yukawa interactions induce non universal flavor violating scalar mass terms (i.e. flavor violating slepton and squark mass terms). In the absence of neutrino masses, the Yukawa matrices for leptons can be diagonalized so that there is no flavor violation in the lepton sector even after extrapolation down to the weak scale. On the other hand, when neutrino mixings are present or when the quarks and leptons are unified in such a way that this diagonalization becomes impossible, there is no basis where all leptonic flavor mixings can be made to disappear. In fact, in the most general case, of the three matrices Y_ℓ, the charged lepton coupling matrix, Y_ν, RH neutrino Yukawa coupling and M_{N_R}, the matrix characterizing the heavy RH neutrino mixing, only one can be diagonalizd by an appropriate choice of basis and the flavor mixing in the other two remain. In a somewhat restricted case where the right handed neutrinos do not have any interaction other than the Yukawa interaction and an interaction that generates the Majorana mass for the right handed neutrino, one can only diagonalize two out of the three matrices (i.e. Y_ν, Y_ℓ and M_R). Thus there will always be lepton flavor violating terms in the basic Lagrangian, no matter what basis one chooses. These LFV terms can then induce mixings between the sleptons of different flavor and lead to LFV processes. If we keep the M_ℓ diagonal by choice of basis, searches for LFV processes such as $\tau \to \mu + \gamma$ and/or $\mu \to e + \gamma$ can throw light on the RH neutrino mixings/or family mixings in M_D, as has already been observed.

Since in the absence of CP violation, there are at least six mixing angles (nine if M_D is not symmetric) in the seesaw formula and only three are observable in neutrino oscillation, to get useful information on the fundamental high scale theory from LFV processes, it is assumed that M_{N_R} is diagonal so that one has a direct correlation between the observed neutrino mixings and the fundamental high scale paramters of the theory. The important point is that the flavor mixings in Y_ν then reflect themselves in the slepton mixings that lead to the LFV processes via the RGEs.

From the point of view of the LFV analysis, there are essentially two classes of neutrino mass models that need to be considered: (i) the first class is where it is assumed that the RH neutrino mass M_{N_R} is either a mass term in the basic Lagrangian or arises from nonrenormalizable terms such as $\nu^c \chi^{c2}/M_{P\ell}$, as in a class of SO(10) models; (we will such models Dirac type) and (ii) a second class where the Majorana mass of the right handed neutrino itself arises from a renormalizable Yukawa coupling e.g. $f\nu^c\nu^c\Delta$ (we will call them Majorana type models). In Dirac type models, in principle, one could decide to have all the flavor mixing effects in the right handed neutrino mass matrix and keep the Y_ν diagonal. In that case, RGEs would not induce any LFV effects. However we will bar this possibility and consider the case where all flavor mixings are in the Y_ν so that RGEs can induce LFV effects . In Majorana type models on the other hand, there will always be an LFV effect, although its magnitude will depend on the choice of the seesaw scale (v_{BL}).

Examples of class two models are models for neutrino mixings such as SO(10) with a **126** Higgs field[43] or models with a triplet Higgs, whose vev is the seesaw scale.

In both these examples, the equations that determine the extent of lepton flavor violation in leading order, for the case $A = 0$ are:

$$\frac{dm_L^2}{dt} \simeq \frac{1}{16\pi^2}[3m_0^2(Y_\nu^\dagger Y_\nu)] \qquad (7.68)$$

In the Majorana case, this equation will have contributions from the renormalizable f couplings that give Majorana masses to the right handed neutrinos[52] in the sense that generation mixing elements in Y_ν will be generated by f's even if they were absent in the beginning. Using these equations, one can obtain the branching ratios for the radiative lepton flavor violating processes using the formula below:

$$\mathcal{L} = iem_j \left(\bar{\ell}_{jL}\sigma_{\mu\nu}\ell_{iR}C_L + \bar{\ell}_{jR}\sigma_{\mu\nu}\ell_{iL}C_R\right) F^{\mu\nu} + h.c. \qquad (7.69)$$

then the Branching ratio for the decay $\ell_j \to \ell_i + \gamma$ is given by the formula

$$B(\ell_j \to \ell_i + \gamma) = \frac{48\pi^3 \alpha_{em}}{G_F^2}(|C_L|^2 + |C_R|^2)B(\ell_j \to \ell_i + 2\nu). \qquad (7.70)$$

7.7.2. *Renormalization group evolution of the neutrino mass matrix*

In the seesaw models for neutrino masses, the neutrino mass arises from the effective operator

$$\mathcal{O}_\nu = -\frac{1}{4}\kappa_{\alpha\beta}\frac{L_\alpha H L_\beta H}{M} \qquad (7.71)$$

after symmetry breaking $< H^0 > \neq 0$; here L and H are the leptonic and weak doublets respectively. α and β denote the weak flavor index. The matrix κ becomes the neutrino mass matrix after symmetry breaking i.e. $< H^0 > \neq 0$. This operator is defined at the scale M since it arises after the heavy field N_R is integrated out. On the other hand, in conventional oscillation experiments, the neutrino masses and mixings being probed are at the weak scale. One must therefore extrapolate the operator down from the seesaw scale M to the weak scale M_Z.[53] The form of the renormalization group extrapolation of course depends on the details of the theory. For simplicity we will consider only the supersymmetric theories, where the only contributions come from the wave function renormalization and is therefore easy to calculate. The equation governing the extrapolation of the $\kappa_{\alpha\beta}$ matrix is given in the case of MSSM by:

$$\frac{d\kappa}{dt} = [-3g_2^2 + 6Tr(Y_u^\dagger Y_u)]\kappa + \frac{1}{2}[\kappa(Y_e^\dagger Y_e) + (Y_e^\dagger Y_e)\kappa] \qquad (7.72)$$

We note two kinds of effects on the neutrino mass matrix from the above formula: (i) one that is flavor independent and (ii) a part that is flavor specific. If we work in a basis where the charged leptons are diagonal, then the resulting correction to the neutrino mass matrox is given by:

$$\mathcal{M}_\nu(M_Z) = (1+\delta)\mathcal{M}(M_{B-L})(1+\delta) \qquad (7.73)$$

where δ is a diagonal matrix with matrix elements $\delta_{\alpha\alpha} \simeq -\frac{m_\alpha^2 \tan^2\beta}{16\pi^2 v^2}$. In more complicated theories, the corrections will be different. Let us now study some implications of this corrections. For this first note that in the MSSM, this effect can be sizable if $\tan\beta$ is large (of order 10 or bigger).

7.7.3. Radiative magnification of neutrino mixing angles

A major puzzle of quark lepton physics is the diverse nature of the mixing angles. Whereas in the quark sector the mixing angles are small, for the neutrinos they are large. One possible suggestion in this connection is that perhaps the mixing angles in both quark and lepton sectors at similar at some high scale; but due to renormalization effects, they may become magnified at low scales. It was shown in Ref. 54 that this indeed happens if the neutrino spectrum os degenerate. This can be seen in a simple way for the $\nu_\mu - \nu_\tau$ sector.[54]

Let us start with the mass matrix in the flavor basis:

$$\mathcal{M}_{\mathcal{F}} = U^* \mathcal{M}_{\mathcal{D}} U^\dagger$$
$$= \begin{pmatrix} C_\theta & S_\theta \\ -S_\theta & C_\theta \end{pmatrix} \begin{pmatrix} m_1 & 0 \\ 0 & m_2 e^{-i\phi} \end{pmatrix} \begin{pmatrix} C_\theta & -S_\theta \\ S_\theta & C_\theta \end{pmatrix}. \quad (7.74)$$

Let us examine the situation when $\phi = 0$ (i.e. CP is conserved), which corresponds to the case when the neutrinos ν_1 and ν_2 are in the same CP eigenstate. Due to the presence of radiative corrections to m_1 and m_2, the matrix $\mathcal{M}_{\mathcal{F}}$ gets modified to

$$\mathcal{M}_{\mathcal{F}} \to \begin{pmatrix} 1+\delta_\alpha & 0 \\ 0 & 1+\delta_\beta \end{pmatrix} \mathcal{M}_{\mathcal{F}} \begin{pmatrix} 1+\delta_\alpha & 0 \\ 0 & 1+\delta_\beta \end{pmatrix}. \quad (7.75)$$

The mixing angle $\bar{\theta}$ that now diagonalizes the matrix $\mathcal{M}_{\mathcal{F}}$ at the low scale μ (after radiative corrections) can be related to the old mixing angle θ through the following expression:

$$\tan 2\bar{\theta} = \tan 2\theta \, (1 + \delta_\alpha + \delta_\beta) \, \frac{1}{\lambda}, \quad (7.76)$$

where

$$\lambda \equiv \frac{(m_2 - m_1)C_{2\theta} + 2\delta_\beta(m_1 S_\theta^2 + m_2 C_\theta^2) - 2\delta_\alpha(m_1 C_\theta^2 + m_2 S_\theta^2)}{(m_2 - m_1)C_{2\theta}}. \quad (7.77)$$

If

$$(m_1 - m_2) C_{2\theta} = 2\delta_\beta(m_1 S_\theta^2 + m_2 C_\theta^2) - 2\delta_\alpha(m_1 C_\theta^2 + m_2 S_\theta^2), \quad (7.78)$$

then $\lambda = 0$ or equivalently $\bar{\theta} = \pi/4$; i.e. maximal mixing. Given the mass heirarchy of the charged leptons: $m_{l_\alpha} \ll m_{l_\beta}$, we expect $|\delta_\alpha| \ll |\delta_\beta|$, which reduces (7.78) to a simpler form:

$$\epsilon = \frac{\delta m C_{2\theta}}{(m_1 S_\theta^2 + m_2 C_\theta^2)} \quad (7.79)$$

In the case of MSSM, the radiative magnification condition can be satisfied provided provided

$$h_\tau(MSSM) \approx \sqrt{\frac{8\pi^2 |\Delta m^2(\Lambda)| C_{2\theta}}{\ln(\frac{\Lambda}{\mu}) m^2}}. \quad (7.80)$$

For $\Delta m^2 | simeq \Delta m_A^2$, this condition can be satisfied for a very wide range of $\tan\beta$.

It is important to emphasize that this magnification occurs only if at the seesaw scale the neutrino masses are nearly degenerate. A similar mechanism using the right handed neutrino Yukawa couplings instead of the charged lepton ones has been carried out recently.[55] Here two conditions must be satisfied: (i) the neutrino spectrum must be nearly degenerate (i.e. $m_1 \simeq m_2$ as in Ref. 54) and (ii) there must be a hierarchy between the right handed neutrinos.

7.7.3.1. *An explicit example of a neutrino mass matrix unstable under RGE*

In this section, we give an explicit example of a neutrino mass matrix unstable under RGE effects. Consider the following mass matrix with degenerate neutrino masses and a bimaximal mixing.[56]

$$\mathcal{M}_\nu = \begin{pmatrix} 0 & \frac{1}{\sqrt{2}} & \frac{1}{\sqrt{2}} \\ \frac{1}{\sqrt{2}} & \frac{1}{2} & -\frac{1}{2} \\ \frac{1}{\sqrt{2}} & \frac{1}{2} & \frac{1}{2} \end{pmatrix} \tag{7.81}$$

The eigenvalues of this mass matrix are $(1, -1, 1)$ and the eigenvectors:

$$V_1 = \begin{pmatrix} 0 \\ \frac{1}{\sqrt{2}} \\ \frac{1}{\sqrt{2}} \end{pmatrix}; V_2 = \begin{pmatrix} \frac{1}{\sqrt{2}} \\ -\frac{1}{2} \\ -\frac{1}{2} \end{pmatrix}; V_3 = \begin{pmatrix} \frac{1}{\sqrt{2}} \\ \frac{1}{2} \\ \frac{1}{2} \end{pmatrix} \tag{7.82}$$

After RGE to the weak scale, the mass matrix becomes

$$\mathcal{M}_\nu = \begin{pmatrix} 0 & \frac{1}{\sqrt{2}} & \frac{1}{\sqrt{2}}(1+\delta) \\ \frac{1}{\sqrt{2}} & \frac{1}{2} & -\frac{1}{2}(1+\delta) \\ \frac{1}{\sqrt{2}}(1+\delta) & \frac{1}{2}(1+\delta) & \frac{1}{2}(1+2\delta) \end{pmatrix} \tag{7.83}$$

It turns out that the eigenvectors of this matrix become totally different and are given by:

$$V_1 = \begin{pmatrix} \frac{1}{\sqrt{3}} \\ \frac{2}{\sqrt{3}} \\ 0 \end{pmatrix}; V_2 = \begin{pmatrix} \frac{1}{\sqrt{2}} \\ -\frac{1}{2} \\ -\frac{1}{2} \end{pmatrix}; V_3 = \begin{pmatrix} \frac{1}{\sqrt{6}} \\ -\frac{1}{2\sqrt{3}} \\ \frac{\sqrt{3}}{2} \end{pmatrix} \tag{7.84}$$

We thus see that the neutrino mixing pattern has become totally altered, although the eigenvalues are only slightly perturbed from their unperturbed value.

7.7.4. *Seesaw paradigm and leptogenesis*

Finally let us comment that in models where the light neutrino mass is understood via the seesaw mechanism using heavy right handed neutrinos, there is a very simple mechanism for the generation of baryon asymmetry of the universe. Since the righthanded neutrino has a high mass, it decays at a high temperature which in combination with CP violation in Y_ν generates a lepton asymmetry.[57] This lepton asymmetry is converted to baryon asymmetry via the sphaleron effects[58] above the electroweak phase transition temperature since sphalerons break B+L conservation. It also turns out that one of the necessary conditions for sufficient leptogenesis is that the right handed neutrinos must be heavy as is required by the seesaw mechanism. To see this note that one of Sakharov conditions for leptogenesis is that the right handed neutrino decay must be slower than the expansion rate of the universe at the temperature $T \sim M_{N_R}$. The corresponding condition is:

$$\frac{h_\ell^2 M_{N_R}}{16\pi} \leq \sqrt{g^*}\frac{M_{N_R}^2}{M_{P\ell}} \tag{7.85}$$

This implies that $M_{N_R} \geq \frac{h_\ell^2 M_{P\ell}}{16\pi\sqrt{g^*}}$. Translating this into a reliable bound on the masses of the right handed neutrinos is quite model dependent since the Yukawa texture i.e. h_ℓ values in the above equation depends on the particular way to understand large mixings as well as the neutrino mass hierarchy.

To proceed further, we start with the expression for lepton asymmetry in these scenarios:[59]

$$\varepsilon_i^I = -\frac{1}{8\pi}\frac{1}{[Y_\nu Y_\nu^\dagger]_{ii}}\sum_j \mathrm{Im}[Y_\nu Y_\nu^\dagger]_{ij}^2 F\left(\frac{M_j^2}{M_i^2}\right), \tag{7.86}$$

One can draw several conclusions from this expression: first using Eq. 7.65 and 7.86, we see that, ε_i^I is independent of the low energy CP phases. This implies that in principle observation of CP violation in neutrino oscillation may not throw any light on the origin of matter.

Second point to notice is that for hierarchical masses for RH neutrinos i.e. $M_1 \ll M_{2,3}$, one can write 7.86 as

$$\varepsilon_i^I = -\frac{1}{8\pi}\frac{1}{[Y_\nu Y_\nu^\dagger]_{ii}}\sum_j \mathrm{Im}[Y_\nu \mathcal{M}_\nu^* Y_\nu^T]_{ii}. \tag{7.87}$$

From this it follows that if the neutrino masses are strictly degenerate, then using 7.65, it is easy to see that $\varepsilon_i^I = 0$. This is an interesting result although this cannot strictly be used to rule out the possibility of degenerate neutrino masses since, it is more natural (as emphasized earlier) for a degenerate neutrino spectrum to arise from a type II seesaw rather than type I seesaw which has been used in drawing this conclusion.

Another consequence of 7.86 is that combining 7.85 and 7.86, it is possible to obtain a reliable lower bound on the lightest RH neutrino mass[60] and it turns out to be: $M_{N_1} \geq 10^9$ GeV. This is bound is somewhat strengthened if one further demands that there is a $\mu - \tau$ exchange symmetry in the left as well as the right handed neutrino sector for which there is some observational indication (since θ_{13} appears to be very small). The bound then becomes $M_{N_1} \geq 6 \times 10^9$ GeV.[61]

In the presence of triplet contributions to seesaw (type II), there are new contributions to the lepton asymmetry given by: The type II contribution has been calculated and is given in Refs. 45 and 62 to be

$$\varepsilon_i^{II} = \frac{3}{8\pi} \frac{\text{Im}[Y_\nu f^* Y_\nu^T \mu]_{ii}}{[Y_\nu Y_\nu^\dagger]_{ii} M_i} \ln\left(1 + \frac{M_i^2}{M_T^2}\right), \quad (7.88)$$

where $\mu \equiv \lambda M_T$ and λ is the coupling between triplet and two doublets in the superpotential and f is the triplet coupling to leptons. Thus baryogenesis via leptogenesis is a very sensitive way to probe the neutrino mass mechanisms. For more details on this see the lectures by M. C. Chen.[63]

7.8. Conclusions and outlook

In summary, the neutrino oscillation experiments have provided the first evidence for new physics beyond the standard model. The field of neutrino physics, along with the search for the origin of mass, dark matter has therefore become central to the study of new physics at the TeV scale and beyond. Another area which is foremost in the minds of many theorists is supersymmetry which stabilizes the Higgs mass, provides a way to understand the electro-weak symmetry breaking and possibly a dark matter candidate. In discussing consequences of seesaw mechanism as well as in seeking theories of neutrino mass, we have assumed supersymmetry. An exception is the last section, where we consider low scale extra dimensional models for understanding Higgs mass and its possibility as an alternative to seesaw mechanism.

What have we learned so far? One thing that seems very clear is that there is probably a set of three right handed neutrinos which restore quark lepton symmetry to physics; secondly there must be a local $B-L$ symmetry at some high scale beyond the standard model that keeps the RH neutrinos so far below the Planck scale. While there are very appealing arguments that the scale of $B - L$ symmetry is close to 10^{14}-10^{16} GeV's, in models with extra dimensions, one cannot rule out the possibility that it is around a few TeVs, although the present TeV scale models generally require many near TeV particles with sometimes undesirable consequences for flavor violation. Third thing that one may suspect is that the right handed neutrino spectrum may be split into a heavier one and two others which are nearby. If this suspicion is confirmed, that would point towards an $SU(2)_H$ horizontal symmetry or perhaps even an $SU(3)_H$ symmetry which breaks into an $SU(2)_H$ symmetry (although simple anomaly considerations prefer the first alternative).

The correct theory should explain:

(i) Why both the solar mixing angle is large and atmospheric mixing angle maximal?

(ii) Why the $\Delta m^2_\odot \ll \Delta m^2_A$ and what is responsible for the smallness of U_{e3}? While in the inverted hierarchy models and models with $\mu - \tau$ symmetry, the smallness of U_{e3} is natural, in general it is not. In fact high precision search for U_{e3} may hold the clue to possible family symmetries vrs simple grad unification.

(iii) What is the nature of CP phases in the lepton sector and what is their relation to the CP phases possibly responsible for baryogenesis via leptogenesis?

(iv) What is the complete mass spectrum for neutrinos?

These and other questions are likely to prove to be very exciting challenges to both theory and experiment in neutrino physics for the next two decades. These lectures are meant to be a very cursory overview of what seems to be the simplest way to understand neutrino masses and mixings i.e. seesaw mechanism and some related physics. Even at that, only a few selected topics are covered and for more details and references, we refer the reader to other excellent reviews in the literature.

Acknowledgment

This work is supported by the National Science Foundation grant number PHY-0354401. The author is grateful to K. T. Mahanthappa and the organizing committee of TASI 2006 for the invitation to co-direct the school and providing the unique opportunity to engage in many lively interactions with the students.

References

1. B. Pontecorvo, Sov. Phys. JETP **6**, 429 (1958); Z. Maki, M. Nakagawa, S. Sakata, Prog. Theor. Phys. **28**, 870 (1962).
2. For a recent review of new physics from neutrinos, see R. N. Mohapatra and A. Yu Smirnov, Ann. Rev. Nucl. and Part. Sc. **56**, 569 (2006); G. Altarelli, arXiv:0711.0161 [hep-ph].
3. We follow the discussion in B. Kayser and R. N. Mohapatra, in *Current Aspects of Neutrino Physics*, ed. D. Caldwell (Springer, 2001); pp.17.
4. P. Minkowski, Phys. Lett. **B 67**, 421(1977); M. Gell-Mann, P. Ramond and R. Slansky, in *Supergravity*, eds. P. van Niewenhuizen and D.Z. Freedman (North Holland 1979); T. Yanagida, in Proceedings of *Workshop on Unified Theory and Baryon number in the Universe*, eds. O. Sawada and A. Sugamoto (KEK 1979); S. L. Glashow, Erice lectures (1979); R. N. Mohapatra and G. Senjanović, Phys. Rev. Lett. **44**, 912 (1980).
5. M. C. Gonzalez-Garcia and M. Maltoni, arXiv:0704.1800 [hep-ph].
6. J. Conrad, lectures at this institute.
7. E. Abouzaid *et al.*, LBNL-56599.
8. A. A. Aguilar-Arevalo *et al.* [The MiniBooNE Collaboration], Phys. Rev. Lett. **98**, 231801 (2007)
9. For a theoretical analysis of MiniBooNe experiment in terms of sterile neutrinos, see M. Maltoni and T. Schwetz, arXiv:0705.0107 [hep-ph].
10. For a history, see H. Klapdor-Kleingrothaus, *Sixty years of double beta decay*, World Scientific (1999).
11. P. Vogel, TASI 2006 lectures, this volume.
12. H. Klapdor-Kleingrothaus *et al.*, Mod. Phys. Lett. **A16**, 2409 (2001).
13. S. Hannestad, Phys. Rev. Lett. **95**, 221301 (2005); U. Seljak, A. Slosar and P. McDonald, JCAP **0610**, 014 (2006); For a review and more references, see O. Elgaroy, hep-ph/0612097.
14. D. Caldwell and R. N. Mohapatra, Phys. Rev. **D 48**, 3259 (1993); A. Joshipura, Phys. Rev. **D51**, 1321 (1995).
15. L. Wolfenstein, Phys. Rev. **D 18**, 958 (1978); P. F. Harrison, D. Perkins and W. G. Scott, Phys. Lett. **B 530**, 167 (2002); P. F. Harrison and W. G. Scott, Phys. lett. **B 535**, 163 (2002); Z. z. Xing, Phys. Lett. **B 533**, 85 (2002); X. G. He and A. Zee, Phys. Lett. B **560**, 87 (2003).
16. T. Fukuyama and H. Nishiura, hep-ph/9702253; R. N. Mohapatra and S. Nussinov, Phys. Rev. **D 60**, 013002 (1999); E. Ma and M. Raidal, Phys. Rev. Lett. **87**, 011802 (2001); C. S. Lam, hep-ph/0104116.
17. W. Grimus, A. S.Joshipura, S. Kaneko, L. Lavoura, H. Sawanaka, M. Tanimoto, hep-ph/0408123; R. N. Mohapatra, SLAC Summer Inst. lecture; http://www-conf.slac.stanford.edu/ssi/2004; hep-ph/0408187; JHEP, **0410**, 027 (2004); A. de Gouvea, Phys. Rev. **D69**, 093007 (2004).
18. R. N. Mohapatra and W. Rodejohann, Phys. Rev. **D 72**, 053001 (2005); T. Kitabayashi and M. Yasue, Phys. Lett,. **B 621**, 133 (2005).
19. A. Ghosal, hep-ph/0304090; W. Grimus and L. Lavoura, hep-ph/0305046; 0309050; K. Matsuda and H. Nishiura, hep-ph/0511338; A. Joshipura, hep-

ph/0512252; R. N. Mohapatra, S. Nasri and H. Yu, Phys. Lett. **B 636**, 114 (2006).
20. F. Caravaglios and S. Morisi, hep-ph/0503234; R. N. Mohapatra, S. Nasri and H. Yu, Phys. Lett. **B 639**, 318 (2006); O. Felix, A. Mondragon, M. Mondragon and E. Peinado, hep-ph/0610061. .
21. E. Ma, Phys. Rev. **D70**, 031901R (2004); **D 72**, 037301 (2005); K. S. Babu and X. G. He, hep-ph/0507217; G. Altarelli and F. Feruglio, Nucl. Phys. **B720**, 64 (2005); A. Zee, Phys. Lett. **B630**, 58 (2005).
22. S. Petcov, Phys. Lett. **B110**, 245 (1982); R. Barbieri, L. J. Hall, D. R. Smith, A. Strumia and N. Weiner, JHEP **9812**, 017 (1998); A. Joshipura and S. Rindani, Eur.Phys.J. **C14**, 85 (2000); R. N. Mohapatra, A. Perez-Lorenzana, C. A. de S. Pires, Phys. Lett. **B474**, 355 (2000); Q. Shafi and Z. Tavartkiladze, Phys. Lett. **B 482**, 1451 (2000);T. Kitabayashi and M. Yasue, Phys. Rev. **D 63**, 095002 (2001); Phys. Lett. **B 508**, 85 (2001); hep-ph/0110303; L. Lavoura, Phys. Rev. D 62, 093011 (2000); W. Grimus and L. Lavoura, Phys. Rev. D 62, 093012 (2000); J. High Energy Phys. 09, 007 (2000); J. High Energy Phys. 07, 045 (2001); R. N. Mohapatra, Phys. Rev. **D 64**, 091301 (2001). K. S. Babu and R. N. Mohapatra, Phys. Lett. **B 532**, 77 (2002); H. S. Goh, R. N. Mohapatra and S.-P. Ng, Phys. Lett. **B542**, 116 (2002)); Duane A. Dicus, Hong-Jian He, John N. Ng, Phys. Lett. **B 536**, 83 (2002); G. Altarelli and R. Franceschini, JHEP **0603**, 047 (2006).
23. F. Feruglio, A. Strumia and F. Vissani, Nucl. Phys. B **637**, 345 (2002); S. Pascoli, S.T. Petcov and L. Wolfenstein, Phys. Lett. **B524** (2002) 319; S. Pascoli, S. T. Petcov and W. Rodejohann, Phys. Lett. B **558**, 141 (2003).
24. R. Kuchimanchi and R. N. Mohapatra, hep-ph/0107110 Phys. Rev. **D 66**, 051301 (2002); and hep-ph/0107373.
25. K. S. Babu and R. N. Mohapatra, Phys. Lett. **B 532**, 77 (2002).
26. H. S. Goh, R. N. Mohapatra and S.-P. Ng, ref..[22]
27. GENIUS collaboration, H. Klapdor-Kleingrothaus *et al.*, J. Phys. G. **G 24**, 483 (1998); CUORE collaboration, E. Fiorini, Phys. Rep. **307**, 309 (1998); MAJORANA collaboration, C. E. Aalseth *et al.* hep-ex/0201021; EXO collaboration, G. Gratta *et al.* Invited talk at the *Neutrino miniworkshop at INT, Seattle*, April, 2002; MOON collaboration, H. Ejiri *et al.* Phys. Rev. lett. **85**, 2917 (2000); For a review, see O. Cremonesi, Proceedings of *Neutrino 2002*, Munchen.
28. R. N. Mohapatra and W. Rodejohann, Phys. Lett. B **644**, 59 (2007); A. Blum, R. N. Mohapatra and W. Rodejohann, arXiv:0706.3801 [hep-ph].
29. B. Kayser, in *CP violation*, ed. C. Jarlskog (World Scientific, 1988), p. 334; A. Barroso and J. Maalampi, Phys. Lett. **132B**, 355 (1983).
30. R. Barbieri, J. Ellis and M. K. Gaillard, Phys. Lett. **90 B**, 249 (1980); E. Akhmedov, Z. Berezhiani and G. Senjanović, Phys. Rev. Lett. **69**, 3013 (1992).
31. R. N. Mohapatra, Phys. Rev. lett. **56**, 561 (1986); R. N. Mohapatra and J. W. F. Valle, Phys. Rev. **D 34**, 1642 (1986).
32. S. F. King, JHEP **0209**, 011 (2002); S. F. King and N. N. Singh, Nucl. Phys. B **591**, 3 (2000).

33. For discussions of the seesaw formula and attempts to understand neutrino mixings see E. Akhmedov, G. Branco and M. Rebelo, Phys. Rev. lett. **84**, 3535 (2000); G. Altarelli, F. Feruglio and I. Masina, Phys. Lett. B **472**, 382 (2000); D. Falcone, hep-ph/0204335; M. Jezabek and P. Urban, hep-ph/0206080.
34. W. Grimus and L. Lavoura, Phys. Rev. **D 62**, 093012 (2000); JHEP **07**, 045 (2001).
35. R. N. Mohapatra, S. Nasri and H. Yu, Phys. Lett. **B 639**, 318 (2006).
36. G. Lazarides, Q. Shafi and C. Wetterich, Nucl.Phys.**B181**, 287 (1981); R. N. Mohapatra and G. Senjanović, Phys. Rev. **D 23**, 165 (1981).
37. J. C. Pati and A. Salam, Phys. Rev. **D10**, 275 (1974); R. N. Mohapatra and J. C. Pati, Phys. Rev. **D 11**, 566, 2558 (1975); G. Senjanović and R. N. Mohapatra, Phys. Rev. **D 12**, 1502 (1975).
38. E. K. Akhmedov and M. Frigerio, Phys. Rev. Lett. **96**, 061802 (2006);P. Hosteins, S. Lavignac and C. A. Savoy, Nucl. Phys. B **755**, 137 (2006); E. K. Akhmedov, M. Blennow, T. Hallgren, T. Konstandin and T. Ohlsson, arXiv:hep-ph/0612194.
39. R. N. Mohapatra and R. E. Marshak, Phys. Lett. **B 91**, 222 (1980); A. Davidson, Phys. Rev. **D20**, 776 (1979).
40. See for instance, R. N. Mohapatra, *Unification and Supersymmetry*, 3rd edition, Springer-Verlag, 2002.
41. H. Georgi, in *Particles and Fields*, (ed. C. Carlson), A. I. P. (1975); H. Fritzsch and P. Minkowski, Ann. Phys. **93**, 193 (1975).
42. C. Albright, K. S. Babu and S. Barr, Phys. Rev. lett. **81**, 1167 (1998); C. Albright and S. Barr, Phys. Rev. **D 58**, 013002 (1998); K. S. Babu, J. C. Pati and F. Wilczek, hep-ph/9812538; X. Ji, Y. Li and R. N. Mohapatra, Phys. Lett. **B 633**, 755 (2006).
43. K. S. Babu and R. N. Mohapatra, Phys. Rev. Lett. **70**, 2845 (1993).
44. C. S. Aulakh and R. N. Mohapatra, Phys. Rev. **D 28**, 217 (1983); D. G. Lee and R. N. Mohapatra, Phys. Rev. **D 51**, 1353 (1995); Y. Achiman, hep-ph/9812389; arXiv:hep-ph/0612138; M. Bando, T. Kugo and K. Yoshioka, Phys. Rev. Lett. **80**, 3004 (1998); K. Oda, E. Takasugi, M. Tanaka and M. Yoshimura, Phys. Rev. **D59**, 055001 (1999); M. C. Chen and K. T. Mahanthappa, Phys. Rev. **D 62** , 113007 (2000); T. Fukuyama and N. Okada, hep-ph/0206118; T. Fukuyama, Y. Koide, K. Matsuda and H. Nishiura, Phys. Rev. **D 65**, 033008 (2002); B. Bajc, A. Melfo, G. Senjanovic and F. Vissani, Phys. Lett. **B 634**, 272 (2006); C. S. Aulakh and S. K. garg, hep-ph/0512224; K. S. Babu and C. macesanu, Phys. Rev. **D 72**, 115003 (2005); S. Bertolini, M. Malinsky and T. Schwetz, Phys. Rev. **D 73**, 115012 (2006).
45. B. Bajc, G. Senjanović and F. Vissani, Phys. Rev. Lett. **90**, 051802 (2003) hep-ph/0210207.
46. H. S. Goh, R. N. Mohapatra and S. P. Ng, Phys. Lett. B **570**, 215 (2003) [arXiv:hep-ph/0303055].
47. B. Dutta, Y. Mimura and R. N. Mohapatra, hep-ph/0406262, Phys. Lett. **B 603** , 35 (2004) ; Phys. Rev. Lett. **94**, 091804 (2005); Phys. Rev. **D 72**, 075009 (2005).

48. W. Grimus and H. Kuhbock, hep-ph/0612132.
49. J. A. Casas and A. Ibarra, Nucl. Phys. B **618**, 171 (2001).
50. F. Borzumati and A. Masiero, Phys. Rev. Lett. **57**, 961 (1986); A. Masiero, S. Vempati and O. Vives, hep-ph/0209303.
51. A. H. Chamseddine, R. Arnowitt and P. Nath, Phys. Rev. Lett. **49**, 970 (1982); R. Barbieri, S. Ferrara and C. A. Savoy, Phys. Lett. B **119**, 343 (1982).
52. K. S. Babu, B. Dutta and R. N. Mohapatra, Phys. Rev. **D67**, 076006 (2003).
53. K.S. Babu, C.N. Leung and J. Pantaleone, Phys. Lett. **B319**, 191 (1993); P.H. Chankowski and Z. Pluciennik, Phys. Lett. **B316**, 312 (1993); S. Antusch, M. Drees, J. Kersten, M. Lindner and M. Ratz Phys. Lett. **B519**, 238 (2001).
54. K. R. S. Balaji, A. Dighe, R. N. Mohapatra and M. K. Parida, Phys. Rev. Lett. **84**, 5034 (2000); Phys. Lett. B **481**, 33 (2000); R. N. Mohapatra, M. K. Parida and G. Rajasekaran, Phys. Rev. **D 69**, 053007 (2004); S. Agarwalla *et al.* hep-ph/0611225.
55. S. Antusch, J. Kersten, M. Lindner and M. Ratz, hep-ph/0206078.
56. H. Georgi and S. L. Glashow, hep-ph/9808293.
57. M. Fukugita and T. Yanagida, Phys. Lett. **74 B**, 45 (1986).
58. V. Kuzmin, V. Rubakov and M. Shaposnikov. Phys. Lett. **185B**, 36 (1985).
59. W. Buchmuller, P. Di Bari and M. Plumacher, Nucl. Phys. B **643**, 367 (2002).
60. S. Davidson and A. Ibarra, Nucl. Phys. **B 648**, 345 (2003).
61. R. N. Mohapatra, S. Nasri and H. Yu, Phys. Lett. **B615**, 231 (2005).
62. T. Hambye and G. Senjanovic, Phys. Lett. B **582**, 73 (2004); S. Antusch and S. F. King, Phys. Lett. B **597**, 199 (2004).
63. M. C. Chen, this volume.

Chapter 8

Searching for the Higgs Boson

D. Rainwater

*Dept. of Physics and Astronomy, University of Rochester,
Rochester, NY, USA*

These lectures on Higgs boson collider searches were presented at TASI 2006. I first review the Standard Model searches: what LEP did, prospects for Tevatron searches, the program planned for LHC, and some of the possibilities at a future ILC. I then cover in-depth what comes after a candidate discovery at LHC: the various measurements one has to make to determine exactly what the Higgs sector is. Finally, I discuss the MSSM extension to the Higgs sector.

8.1. Introduction

Despite all the remarkable progress made early in the 21st century formulating possible explanations for the weakness of gravity relative to the other forces, the nature of dark matter (and dark energy), what drove cosmological inflation, why neutrino masses are so small, and what might unify the gauge forces, we still have not yet answered the supposedly more readily accessible problem of electroweak symmetry breaking. Just what, exactly, gives mass to the weak gauge bosons and the known fermions? Is it weakly-coupled and spontaneous, involving fundamental scalars, or strongly-coupled, involving composite scalars? Is the flavor problem linked? Do we discover the physics behind dark matter (and *its* mass), gauge unification and flavor at the same time? Or are those disconnected problems?

Our starting point is unitarity, the conservation of probability: the weak interaction of the Standard Model (SM) of particle physics violates it at about 1 TeV [1]. The theory demands at least one new propagating scalar state with gauge coupling to weak bosons to keep this under control. The same problem holds for fermion–boson interactions [2–5], only at much higher energy, so is generally less often discussed.[a] While the variety of explanations for electroweak symmetry breaking (EWSB) is vast, what we call the Standard Model (SM) assumes the existence of a single fundamental scalar field which spontaneously acquires a vacuum expectation value to generate all fermion and boson masses. It is a remarkably compact and elegant explanation, simple in the extreme. Yet while it tidies up the immediate necessities of the SM, it suffers from glaring theoretical pathologies that drive much of the model-building behind more ambitious explanations.

Numerous lectures and review articles already exist, covering the SM Higgs sector and the minimal supersymmetric (MSSM) extension [6–9], which are useful both for learning nitty-gritty theoretical details and serving as formulae references. These lectures are instead a crash-course tour of theory in practical application: previous, present and planned Higgs searches, what happens after a candidate Higgs discovery, and an overview of MSSM Higgs phenomenology as a perturbation of that for SM Higgs. They are not comprehensive, but do provide a solid grounding in the basics of Higgs hunting. They should be read only after one has become intimate with the SM Higgs sector and its underlying theoretical issues. Within TASI 2006, this means you should already have studied Sally Dawson's lectures. After both of these you should also be able to explain to your friends how we look for a Higgs boson at colliders (if they care), how to confirm it's a Higgs and figure out what variety it is (since we care), and describe how some basic extensions to the SM Higgs sector behave as a function of their parameter space (nature might not care for the SM).

Herein I'll assume that nature prefers fundamental scalars and spontaneous symmetry breaking. This is a strong bias, but one that provides a solid framework for phenomenology. The ambitious student who wants to really learn all the varieties of EWSB should also study strong dynamics [16], dimensional deconstruction [17], extra-dimensional Higgsless constructions [18] and the Little Higgs [19] and Twin Higgs mechanisms [20]. In many of these classes of theories the Higgs sector appears to be very SM-like, but in some no Higgs appears and one instead would pay great attention to weak boson scattering around a TeV.

---

[a]The original study [2] was clearly incorrect, but the correct line of reasoning is a work in progress [3–5].

8.2. Collider searches for the Standard Model Higgs

Even though the SM Higgs sector doesn't explain flavor (why all the fermion masses are scattered about over 12 orders of magnitude in energy) and has a disconcerting radiative stability problem that surely must involve new physics beyond the SM, it's a suitable jumping-off point for formulating Higgs phenomenology. That is, the study of physical phenomena associated with a theory, exploring the connection between theory and experiment. Without this connection, experiments would not make sense and theory would flail about, untested. To survey SM Higgs collider physics we need to recall a few fundamentals about the SM Higgs boson.

1. The Higgs boson unitarizes weak boson scattering, $VV \to VV$, so its interaction with weak bosons is very strictly defined to be the electroweak gauge coupling times the vacuum expectation value (vev); i.e., proportional to the weak boson masses.
2. The Higgs also unitarizes $VV \to f\bar{f}$ scattering, so its fermion couplings (except ν_i) are proportional to the fermion mass, with a strictly defined universal coefficient.
3. Because of the coupling strengths, the Higgs is dominantly produced by or in association with massive particles (including loop-induced processes, as we'll see in Sec. 8.2.1.1), and prefers to decay to the most massive particles kinematically allowed.
4. The Higgs boson mass itself is a free parameter[b], but influences EW observables, so we can fit EW precision data to make a prediction for its mass.

We may thus define the SM Higgs sector by its vacuum expectation value, v, measured via M_W, G_F, etc., and the known electroweak gauge couplings; 9 Yukawa couplings (fermion mass parameters, ignoring neutrinos and CKM mixing angles); and one free parameter, M_H.

Prior to the Large Electron Positron (LEP) collider era starting around 1990, Higgs searches involved looking for resonances amongst the low energy hadronic spectra in e^+e^- collisions. These were in fact non-trivial searches, mostly involving decays of hadrons to Higgs plus a photon, but are generally regarded as comprehensive and set a lower mass bound of $M_H \gtrsim 3$ GeV.

Higgs hunting in the 1990s was owned by LEP, an e^+e^- collider at CERN which steadily marched up in energy over the decade. It found no

---
[b]We know it is not massless, due to the absence of additional long-range forces.

Higgs bosons[c]. Attention then turned to the long-delayed Tevatron Run II program, proton–antiproton collisions at 2 TeV, which got off to a shaky start but is now performing splendidly. It so far sees nothing Higgs-like, either, but has not yet gathered enough data to be able to say much. The proton–proton Large Hadron Collider (LHC) at CERN is also many years behind schedule, but its construction is now nearing completion and we may expect physics data within a few years.

Our survey begins with LEP from a historical perspective and some general statements about Higgs boson behavior as a function of its mass. Next we turn our attention to the ongoing Tev2 search, for which the prospects hinge critically on machine performance. Then we delve into the intricacies of LHC Higgs pheno, which is far more complicated than either LEP or Tevatron, yet essentially guarantees an answer to our burning questions.

8.2.1. *The LEP Higgs search*

An obvious question to ask is, can we produce the Higgs directly in e^+e^- collisions? We could then probe Higgs masses up to our machine energy, which for LEP-II eventually reached 209 GeV. Recalling that the Higgs–electron coupling is proportional to the electron mass, which is quite a bit smaller than the electroweak vev of 246 GeV, the coupling strength is about 1.5×10^{-6}, or teeny-tiny in technical parlance. A quick calculation reveals that it would take about 4 years running full-tilt to produce just one Higgs boson. This one event would have to be distinguished from the general scattering cross section to fermion pairs in the SM, which is beyond hopeless.

Instead, we think of what process involves something massive, with vastly larger Higgs coupling, so that the interaction rate is large enough to produce a statistically useful number of Higgs bosons. The two obvious possibilities are $e^+e^- \to W^+W^-H$ (two W's required for charge conservation) and $e^+e^- \to ZH$. The first process will obviously have less reach in M_H as the two W bosons require far more energy than a single Z boson to produce. LEP Higgs searches therefore focused on the latter process, shown as a Feynman diagram in Fig. 8.1: the electron and positron annihilate to form a virtual Z, far above its mass shell, which returns on-shell by spitting off a Higgs boson. This process is generically known as Higgsstrahlung, analogous to bremsstrahlung radiation. Both the Higgs and

---

[c]This may be a somewhat controversial statement, depending on what lunch table you're sitting at. See Sec. 8.2.1.3.

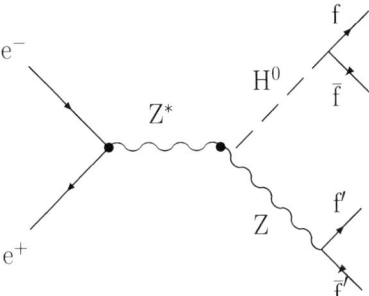

Fig. 8.1. Feynman diagram for the process $e^+e^- \to ZH$ with subsequent Higgs and Z boson decays to fermion pairs. All LEP Higgs searches were based primarily on this process, with various fermion combinations in the final state composing the different search channels.

Z immediately decay to an asymptotic final state of SM particles. For the Higgs this is preferentially to the most massive kinematically-allowed pair, while Z decays are governed by the fermion gauge couplings.[d] In brief, the Z decays 70% of the time to jets, 20% of the time invisibly (to neutrinos, which the detectors can't see), and about 10% to charged leptons, which are the most distinctive, "clean" objects in a detector.

8.2.1.1. *Momentary diversion: Higgs decays*

What, precisely, are the Higgs branching ratios (BRs)? To find these, we first need the Higgs partial widths; that is, the inverse decay rates to each final state kinematically allowed. Everyone should calculate these once as an exercise.

Let's start with the easiest case: Higgs decay to fermion pairs, which is a very simple matrix element. The general result at tree-level is:

$$\Gamma_{f\bar{f}} = \frac{N_c G_F m_f^2 M_H}{4\sqrt{2}\,\pi} \beta^3 \quad \text{where } \beta = \sqrt{1 - \frac{4m_f^2}{M_H^2}} \quad (8.1)$$

One factor of the fermion velocity β comes from the matrix element and two factors come from the phase space. I emphasize that this is at tree-level because there are significant QCD corrections to colored fermions. The bulk of these corrections are absorbed into a running mass (see Ref. [8]). For

---

[d]See the PDG [21] for Z boson branching ratios, which you should memorize.

calculations we should always use $m_q(M_H)$, the quark mass renormalized to the Higgs mass scale, rather than the quark pole mass. Programs such as HDECAY [22] will calculate these automatically given SM parameter inputs, greatly simplifying practical phenomenology.

Note that the partial width to fermions is linear in M_H, modulo the cubic fermion velocity dependence, which steepens the ascent with M_H near threshold. Partial widths for various Higgs decays are shown in Fig. 8.2. While the total Higgs width above fermion thresholds grows with Higgs mass, Higgs total widths below W pair threshold are on the order of tens of MeV – quite narrow. The only complicated partial width to fermions is that for top quarks, for which we must treat the fermions as virtual (at least near threshold) and use the matrix elements to the full six-fermion final state, integrated over phase space. This is slightly more complicated, but easily performed numerically.

Before the decay to top quarks is kinematically allowed, however, the decays to weak bosons turn on. A few W/Z widths above threshold the W and Z may be treated as on-shell asymptotic final states, making

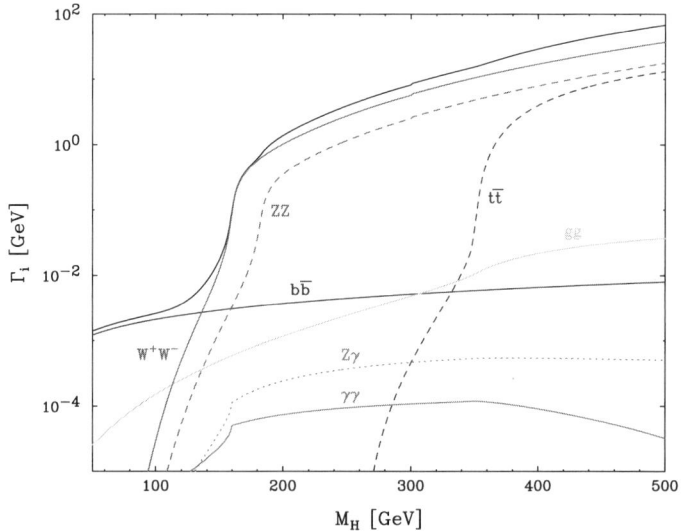

Fig. 8.2. Select Standard Model Higgs boson partial widths, as a function of mass, M_H. Individual partial widths are labeled, while the total width (sum of all partial widths, some minor ones not shown) is the black curve. Widths calculated with HDECAY [22].

the partial width calculation easier. We find:

$$\Gamma_{VV} = \frac{G_F M_H^3}{16\sqrt{2}\pi} \delta_V \beta \left(1 - x_V + \frac{3}{4}x_V^2\right) \text{ where } \begin{cases} \delta_{W,Z} = 2, 1 \\ \beta = \sqrt{1 - x_V} \\ x_V = \frac{4M_V^2}{M_H^2} \end{cases} \quad (8.2)$$

The factor of β comes from phase space, while the matrix elements give the more complicated function of x_V. The partial width is dominantly cubic in M_H, although the factors of beta and x_V enhance this somewhat near threshold, as in the fermion case. We can see this in Fig. 8.2: the partial widths to VV gradually flatten out to cubic behavior above threshold. The reason for this stronger M_H dependence compared to fermions is that a longitudinal massive boson wavefunction is proportional to its energy in the high-energy limit, which enhances the coupling by a factor E/M_V. (Recall that it is this property of massive gauge bosons that requires the Higgs, lest their scattering amplitude rise as E^2/M_V^2, violating unitarity. The Higgs in fact generates the longitudinal modes.) This much stronger dependence on M_H leads to a very rapid total width growth with M_H, which reaches 1 GeV around $M_H = 190$ GeV. We'll return to this when discussing Higgs couplings measurements in Sec. 8.3.3. The bottom line is that bosons "win" compared to fermions. Thus, even though the top quark has a larger mass than W or Z, it cannot compete for partial width and thus BR. Note that the partial widths to VV are non-trivial below threshold: the W and Z are unstable and therefore have finite widths; they may be produced off-shell. The Higgs can decay to these virtual states because its coupling is proportional to the daughter pole masses (or, in the case of quarks, the running masses), not the virtual q^2, which can be much smaller. Below threshold the analytical expressions are known [23] (see Ref. [7] for a summary), but are not particularly insightful to derive as an exercise.

The astute reader will have noticed by now that Fig. 8.2 contains curves for Higgs partial widths to *massless* final states! (Have another look if you didn't notice.) We know the Higgs couples to particles proportional to their masses, so this requires some explanation. Recall that loop-induced transitions can occur at higher orders in perturbation theory. Such interactions typically are important to calculate only when a tree-level interaction doesn't exist. They are responsible for rare decays of various mesons, for instance, and are in some cases sensitive to new physics which may appear in the loop. Here, we consider only SM particles in the loop. Which ones

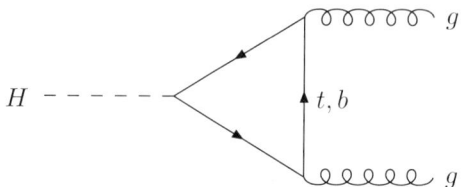

Fig. 8.3. Feynman diagram for the loop-induced process $H \to gg$ in the SM. All quarks enter the loop, but contribute according to their Yukawa coupling squared (mass squared). In the SM, only the top quark is important.

are important? Recall also once again that the Higgs boson couples proportional to particle mass. Thus, the top quark and EW gauge bosons are most important. For $H \to gg$, then, that means only the top quark, while for $H \to \gamma\gamma$ it is both the top quark and W loops (there is no $ZZ\gamma$ vertex). The $H \to gg$ expression (for the Feynman diagram of Fig. 8.3) is [24]:

$$\Gamma_{gg} = \frac{\alpha_s^2 G_F M_H^3}{16\sqrt{2}\,\pi^3} \left| \sum_i \tau_i [1 + (1-\tau_i)f(\tau_i)] \right|^2 \quad (8.3)$$

$$\text{with} \quad \tau_i = \frac{4m_f^2}{M_H^2} \quad \text{and} \quad f(\tau) = \begin{cases} \left[\sin^{-1}\sqrt{1/\tau}\right]^2 & \tau \geq 1 \\ -\frac{1}{4}\left[\ln\frac{1+\sqrt{1-\tau}}{1-\sqrt{1-\tau}} - i\pi\right]^2 & \tau < 1 \end{cases} \quad (8.4)$$

which is for a general quark in the loop with SM Yukawa coupling. It's easy to see that in the SM the b quark contribution, which is second in size to that of the top quark, is inconsequential. Remember to use the running mass $m_f(M_H)$ to take into account the largest QCD effects. When you derive this expression yourself as an exercise, take care to solve the loop integral in $d > 4$ dimensions, otherwise you miss a finite piece. The $H \to \gamma\gamma, Z\gamma$ expressions have a similar form [25], but with two loop functions, since it can also be mediated a W boson loop (which interferes destructively with the top quark loop!):

$$\Gamma_{\gamma\gamma} = \frac{\alpha^2 G_F M_H^3}{128\sqrt{2}\,\pi^3} \left| \sum_i N_{c,i} Q_i^2 F_i \right|^2 \quad (8.5)$$

$$F_1 = 2 + 3\tau[1 + (2-\tau)f(\tau)], \quad F_{1/2} = -2\tau[1 + (1-\tau)f(\tau)], \quad F_0 = \tau[1 - \tau f(\tau)] \quad (8.6)$$

where $N_{c,i}$ is the number of colors, Q_i the charge, and F_j the particle's spin.

Now look again more closely at Fig. 8.2. The important feature to notice is that these loop-induced partial widths are ostensibly proportional to M_H^3, like the decays to gauge bosons. However, the contents of the brackets, specifically the $f(\tau_i)$ function, can alter this in non-obvious ways. For $H \to gg$, Fig. 8.2 shows a slightly more than cubic dependence at low masses, leveling of to approximately M_H^3, and flattening out to approximately quadratic a bit above the top quark pair threshold. We see from Eq. 8.3 that the functional form changes at that threshold, albeit fairly smoothly, by picking up a constant imaginary piece when the top quarks in the loop can be on-shell.

The partial widths to $\gamma\gamma$ and $Z\gamma$ behave very differently than gg. For M_H below W pair threshold, the interference between top quark and W loops produces an extremely sharp rise with M_H, which transitions to something slightly more than linear in M_H at W pair threshold where the W bosons in the loop go on-shell. There is is a smoother transition at the top quark pair threshold, where they can similarly go on-shell. The $\gamma\gamma$ and $Z\gamma$ partial widths behave differently because of the different $t\bar{t}\gamma$ and $t\bar{t}Z$ couplings: the partial width to $Z\gamma$ at large M_H is almost a constant, but falls off for $\gamma\gamma$ almost inverse cubic in M_H.

Once we've calculated all the various possible partial widths, we sum them up to find the Higgs total width. Each BR is then simply the ratio Γ_i/Γ_{tot}. These are shown in Fig. 8.4; note the log scale. If it wasn't obvious from the partial width discussion, it should be now: near thresholds, properly including finite width effects can be very important to get the BRs correct. Observe how the BR to WW^* (at least one W is necessarily off-shell) is 50% at $M_H = 140$ GeV, 20 GeV below W pair threshold. BR($H \to b\bar{b}$)~BR($H \to W^+W^-$) at $M_H = 136$ GeV.

8.2.1.2. *A brief word on statistics – the simple view*

Now that we understand the basics of Higgs decay, and production in electron-positron collisions, we should take a moment to consider statistics. The reason we must resort to statistics is that particle detectors are imperfect instruments. It is impossible to precisely measure the energy of all outgoing particles in every collision. The calorimeters are sampling devices, which means they don't capture all the energy; rather they're calibrated to give an accurate central value at large statistics, with some Gaussian uncertainty about the mean for any single event. Excess energy can also appear, due to cosmic rays, beam–gas or beam secondary interactions. Quark final

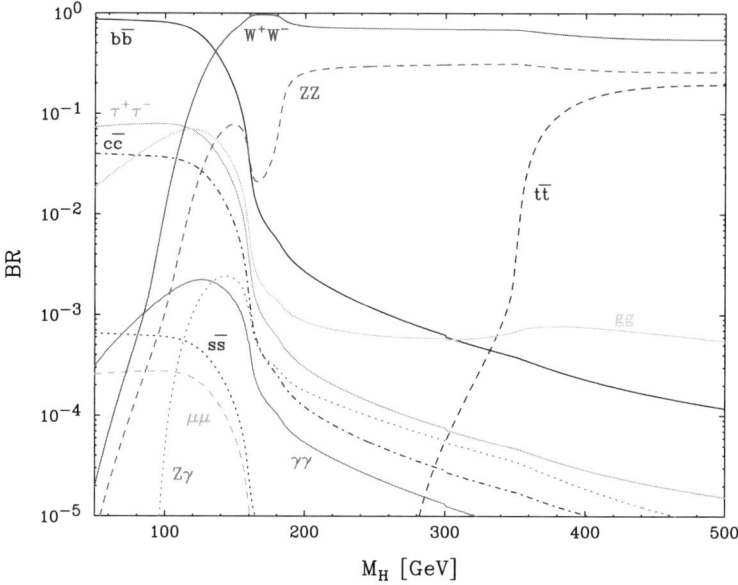

Fig. 8.4. Select Standard Model Higgs boson branching ratios as a function of mass, M_H [22]. The Higgs prefers to decay to the most massive possible final state. The ratio of fermionic branching ratios are proportional to fermion masses squared, modulo color factors and radiative corrections.

states hadronize, resulting in the true final state in the detector (a jet) being far more complicated and difficult even to identify uniquely. The electronics can suffer hiccups, and software *always* has bugs, leading to imperfect analysis. Thus, we would never see two or three events at precisely the Higgs mass of, say, 122.6288... GeV, and pop the champagne. Rather, we'll get a distribution of masses and have to identify the central value and its associated uncertainty.

In any experiment, event counts are quantum rolls of the dice. For a sufficient number of events, they also follow a Gaussian distribution about the true mean:

$$f(x; \mu, \sigma) = \frac{1}{\sigma\sqrt{2\pi}} \exp\left(-\frac{(x-\mu)^2}{2\sigma^2}\right) \quad (8.7)$$

The statistical uncertainty in the rate then goes as $1/\sqrt{N}$, where N is the number of events. This is "one sigma" of uncertainty: 68.2% of identically-conducted experiments would obtain N within $\sigma \approx \pm\sqrt{N}$ about $\mu = N_{\text{true}}$, representing the true cross section. Figure 8.5 shows the fractional prob-

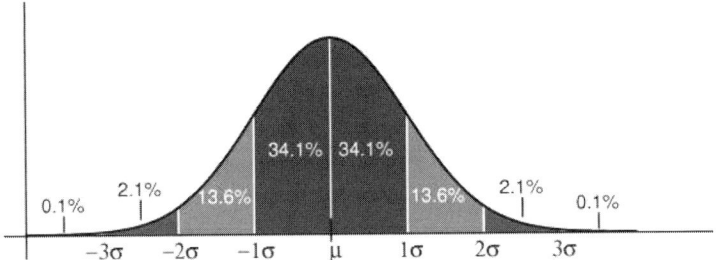

Fig. 8.5. Gaussian distribution about a mean μ, showing the fractional probability of events within one, two and three standard deviations of the mean.

abilities for various "sigma", or number of standard deviations from the true mean. To claim observation of a signal deviating from our expected background, we generally use a 5σ criteria for discovery. This means, if systematic errors have been properly accounted for, that there is only a 0.00006% chance that the signal is due to a statistical fluctuation. However, this threshold is subjective, and you will often hear colleagues take 4σ or even 3σ deviations seriously. Since particle physics has seen dozens of three sigma deviations come and go over the decades, I would encourage you to regard 3σ as "getting interesting", and 4σ as "pay close attention and ask lots of questions about systematics".

Because SM processes can produce the same final state as any ZH combined BR, we must know accurately what the background rate is for each signal channel (final state) and how it is distributed in invariant mass, then look for a statistically significant fluctuation from the expected background over a fixed window region. The size of the window is determined by detector resolution: the better the detector, the narrower the window, so the smaller the background, yielding a better signal-to-background rate. Generally, the window is adjusted to accept one or two standard deviations of the hypothesized signal (68–95%).

Analyses are then defined by two different Gaussians: that governing how many signal (and background) events were produced, and that parameterizing the detector's measurement abilities. The event count N in our above expression is the actual number of events observed, in an experiment. But in performing calculations ahead of time for expected signal and background, it is variously taken as just B, the number of background events expected, or $S + B$, expected signal included, depending on the relative sizes of S and B. For doing phenomenology, trying to decide which signals to study and calculate more precisely, the distinction is often ignored.

The statistical picture I've outlined here is quite simplified. Not all experiments have sufficient numbers of events to describe their data by Gaussians – Poisson statistics may be more appropriate. (An excellent text on statistics for HEP is Ref. [26].) Not all detector effects are Gaussian-distributed. Nevertheless, it gets across the main point: multiple sources of randomness introduce a level of uncertainty that must be parameterized by statistics. Only when the probability of a random background fluctuation up or down to the observed number of events is small enough, perhaps in some distribution, can signal observation be claimed. Exactly where this line lies is admittedly a little hazy, but there's certainly a point of several sigmas at which everybody would agree.

8.2.1.3. LEP Higgs data and results

Now to the actual LEP search. Electrons and positrons have only electroweak interactions, so backgrounds and a potential Higgs signal are qualitatively of the same size. (We'll see shortly in Sec. 8.2.2 how this is not so at a hadron collider, which has colored initial states.) LEP thus had the ability to examine almost all Z and H decay combinations: $b\bar{b}jj$, $b\bar{b}\ell^+\ell^-$, $b\bar{b}\nu\bar{\nu}$, $\tau^+\tau^-jj$, $jjjj$, etc. The largest of these is $b\bar{b}jj$, as it combines the largest BRs of both the Z and H. It's closely followed by $b\bar{b}\nu\bar{\nu}$, since a Z will go to neutrinos 20% of the time. Neutrinos are missing energy, however, so not precisely measured, making it possible that any observed missing energy didn't in fact come from a Z. Jets are much less well-measured than leptons, so a narrower mass window can be used for the Z in $b\bar{b}\ell^+\ell^-$ events than $b\bar{b}jj$; the smaller backgrounds in the narrower window might beat the smaller statistics of the leptonic final state.

The exact details of each LEP search channel are not so important, as lack of observation means we're more interested in channels' signal and background attributes at hadron colliders. For these lectures I just present the final LEP result combining all four experiments. The interested student should read Eilam Gross' "Higgs Statistics for Pedestrians", which goes into much more depth, and with wonderful clarity [27].

The money plot is shown in Fig. 8.6. It shows the expected confidence level (CL) for the signal+background hypothesis as a function of Higgs mass. The thin solid horizontal line at CL=0.05 signifies a 5% probability that a true signal together with the background would have fluctuated down

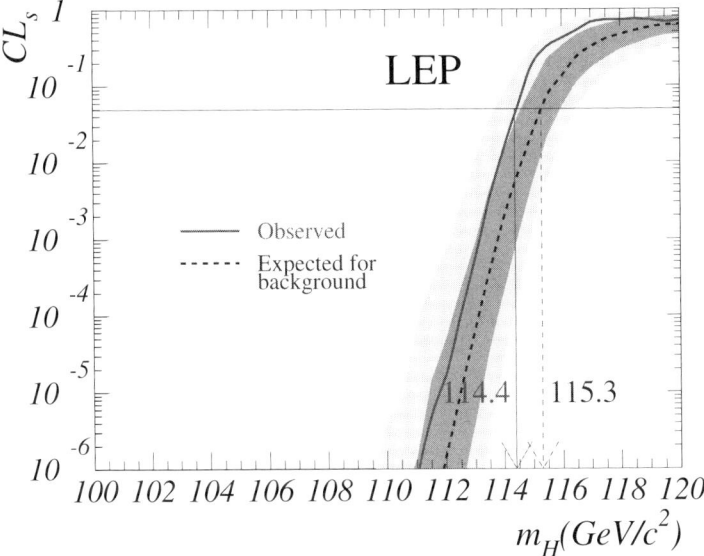

Fig. 8.6. Four-experiment combined result of the LEP Standard Model Higgs search. No signal was observed, establishing a lower limit of 114.4 GeV. See text of Ref. [27] for explanation.

in number of events to not be discriminated from the expected background. The green and yellow regions are the 1σ and 2σ *expected* uncertainty bands as a function of M_H, taking into account all sources of uncertainty, calculational as well as detector effects. Where the central value (dashed curve) crosses 0.05 defines the 95% CL expected exclusion (lower mass limit). This is essentially the available collision energy minus the Z mass minus a few extra GeV to account for the Z finite width – it may be produced slightly off-shell with some usable rate. The solid red curve is the actual experimental result, which is slightly above the experimental result everywhere, meaning that the experiments gathered a couple more events than expected in the 115-116 GeV mass bin.

The end of LEP running involved a certain amount of histrionics. At first, the number of excess event at the kinematic machine limit was a few, but more careful analyses removed most of these. For example, one particularly notorious event originally included in one experiment's analysis had more energy than the beam delivered. Another experiment removed a candidate event because some of the outgoing particles traveled down a poorly-instrumented region of the detector which was not normally used in

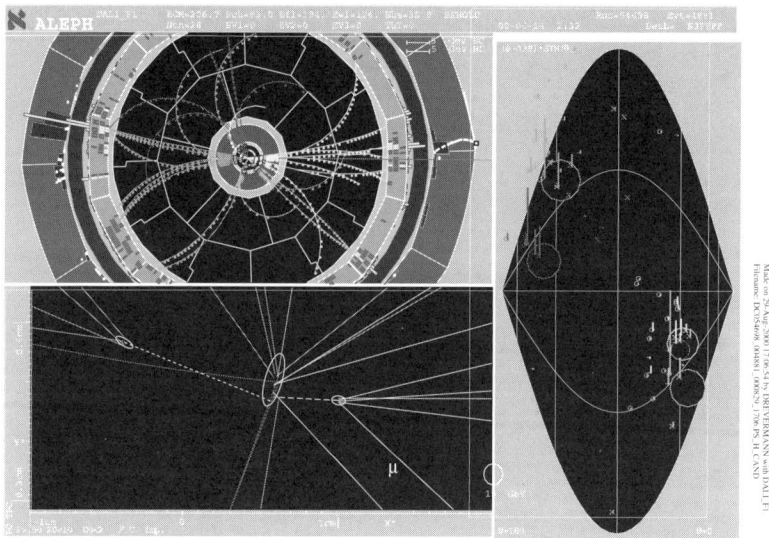

Fig. 8.7. Event display of an interesting candidate $Z \to jj$, $H \to b\bar{b}$ event in the Aleph detector at the end of LEP-II running and at the machine's kinematic limit [28].

analysis. The final, most credible enumeration was one candidate event in one experiment, show in Fig. 8.7.

8.2.2. Prospects at Tevatron

With the end of the LEP era, all eyes turned to Run II of the upgraded Fermilab Tevatron. Its energy increased from 1.8 to 1.96 GeV, and is expected to gather many tens of times the amount of data in Run I. Higgs-hunting hopes were high [29], although it was clear that the machine and both detectors have to perform exceptionally well to have a chance, as Tevatron's Higgs mass reach will not be all that great, and will have significant observability gaps in the mass region expected from precision EW data.

To understand the details and issues, we first need to identify how a Higgs boson may be produced in proton-antiproton collisions. Like the electron, the light quarks have too small a mass (Yukawa coupling) to produce a Higgs directly with any useful rate, discernible against the large QCD backgrounds produced in hadron collisions.[e] Quarks may annihilate, however, to EW gauge bosons, which have large coupling to the Higgs; and

---

[e]For example, $H \to b\bar{b}$ is the dominant BR of a light Higgs, but QCD b jet pair production in hadron collisions is many orders of magnitude larger. Cf. Fig. 8.10.

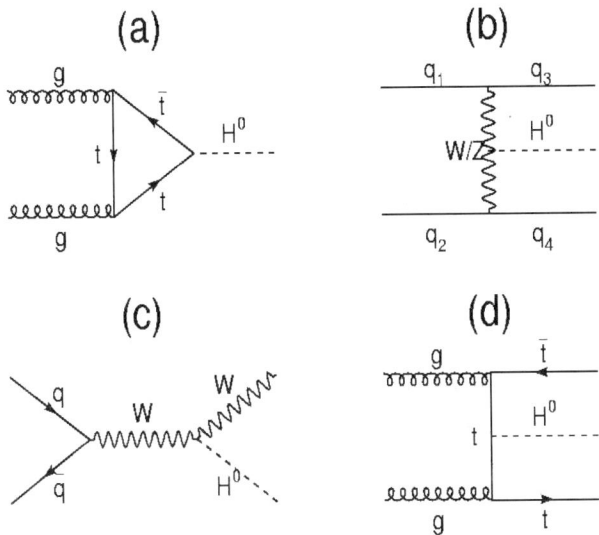

Fig. 8.8. Feynman diagrams for the four dominant Higgs production processes at a hadron collider.

likewise to a top quark pair. Incoming quarks may also emit a pair of gauge bosons which fuse to form a Higgs, a process known as weak boson fusion (WBF). But high energy protons also possess a large gluon content; recall that gluons have a loop-induced coupling to the Higgs. Figure 8.8 displays Feynman diagrams for all four of these processes at hadron colliders. The questions are, what are their relative sizes, and what are their backgrounds? Because of the partonic nature of hadron collisions, the Higgs couplings are not enough to tell us the relative sizes; we also need to take into account incoming parton fluxes and final state phase space – single Higgs production is much less greedy than $t\bar{t}H$ associated production, for instance. In addition, the internal propagator structure of the processes is important: WH,ZH bremsstrahlung are s-channel suppressed, but no other process is.

The various rates, updated in 2006 with the latest theoretical calculations [30, 31], are shown in Fig. 8.9 for a light SM Higgs boson. Students not already familiar with hadron collider Higgs physics will probably be surprised to learn that $gg \to H$, gluon fusion Higgs production, dominates at Tevatron energy. This is partly because the coupling is actually not all that small, partly because high-energy protons contain a plethora of gluons, and partly because there is no propagator suppression, and much less phase space suppression, compared to other processes. Higgsstrahlung

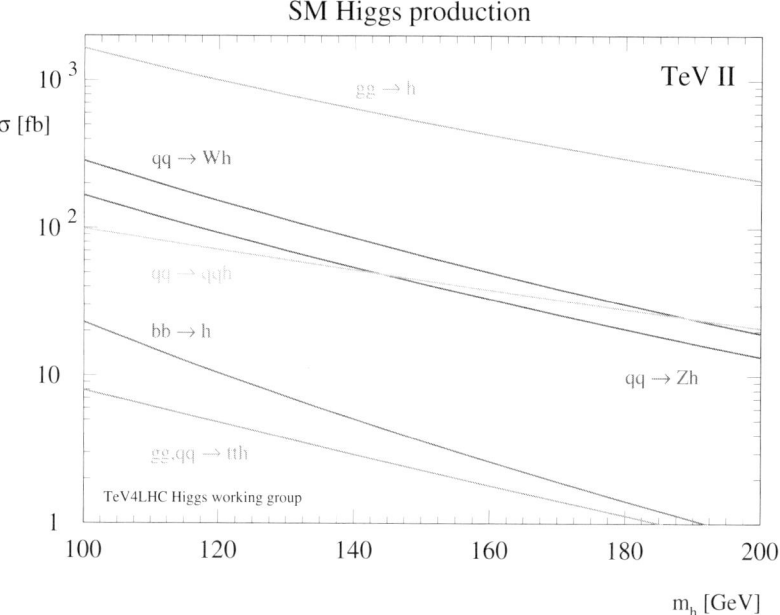

Fig. 8.9. Cross sections for Higgs production in various channels at Tevatron Run II ($\sqrt{s} = 2$ TeV). Note the log scale. Figure from the Tev4LHC Higgs working group [30].

(Fig. 8.8(c)) is still important at Tevatron, analogous to LEP. Note that the smaller cross sections have more complicated final states, therefore potentially less background, and possibly distinctive kinematic distributions that could assist in separating a signal from the background. It's not obvious that the largest rate is the most useful channel! Considering that the Higgs decays predominantly to different final states as a function of its mass, it's also not obvious that the optimal channel at one mass is optimal for all masses. In fact, that's definitely not the case.

Not knowing the answer, we naturally start by considering the largest cross section times branching ratio, $gg \to H \to b\bar{b}$. Just how large is the background, QCD $pp \to b\bar{b}$ production? Figure 8.10 shows a variety of SM cross section for hadron collisions of various energy, and marks off in particular Tevatron and LHC. (The discontinuity in some curves is because Tevatron is $p\bar{p}$ and LHC is pp.) We immediately notice that the $b\bar{b}$ inclusive rate is almost nine orders of magnitude larger than inclusive $H \to b\bar{b}$. Of course the background will be smaller in a finite window about the Higgs mass. But jets are not so well-measured, necessitating a fairly large window,

proton - (anti)proton cross sections

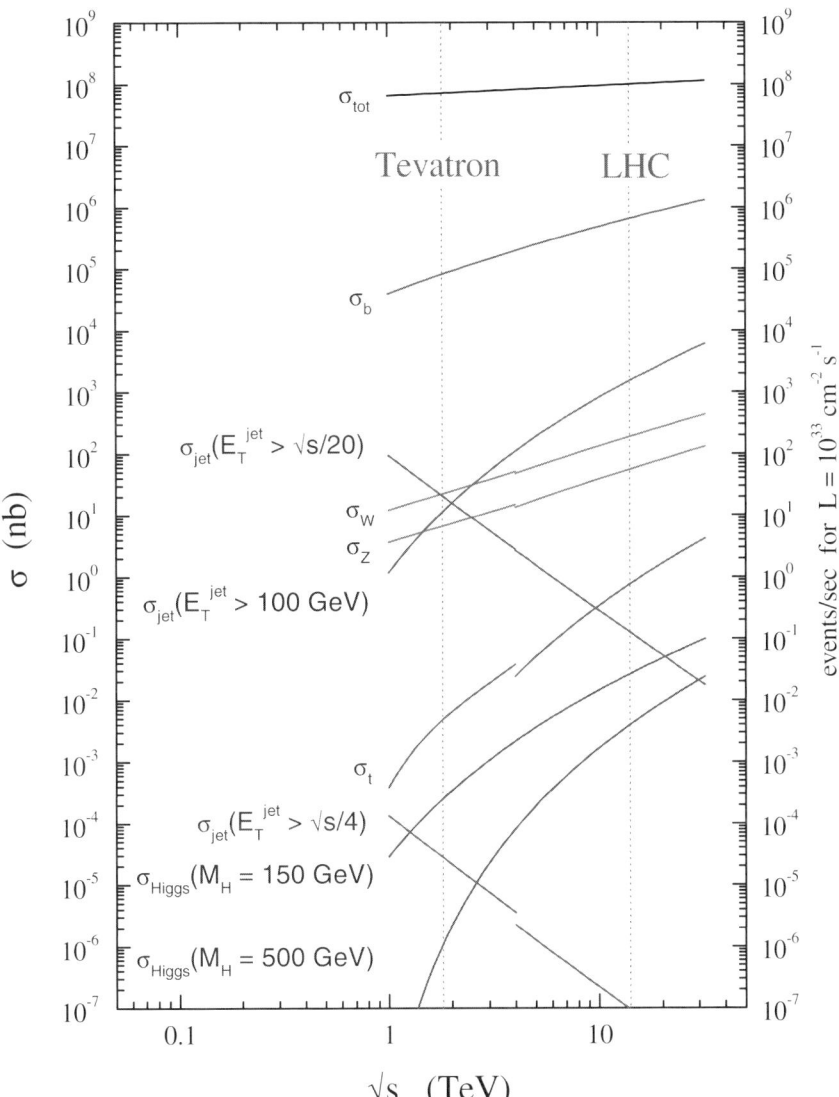

Fig. 8.10. Various SM "standard candle" cross sections at hadron colliders of varying energy, with Tevatron and LHC marked in particular. Note the log scale. Discontinuities are due to the difference between $p\bar{p}$ for Tevatron and pp for LHC. Figure from Ref. [32].

~15–20 GeV either side of the central value. We lose only a few orders of magnitude of the background, taking us from "laughable" to just terminally hopeless.

The general rule of thumb at hadron collider experiments is to require a final state with at least one high-energy lepton. This means lower backgrounds because the event had at least some EW component, such as a W or Z, or came from a massive object, such as the top quark, which is not produced in such great abundance due to phase space suppression.

Tevatron's Higgs search is rate-limited. We can see this by multiplying the 150 GeV Higgs cross section from Fig. 8.9 by the expected integrated luminosity of 4–8 fb^{-1} during Run II. Because of this, and the very low efficiency of identifying final-state taus in a hadron collider environment (unlike at LEP), Tevatron's experiments CDF and DØ focus on the $H \to b\bar{b}$ final state where that decay dominates the BR, and Higgsstrahlung to obtain the lepton tag. For larger Higgs masses, where $H \to W^+W^-$ dominates, gluon fusion Higgs production is the largest rate, but Higgsstrahlung has some analyzing power. To summarize [29]:

$M_H \lesssim 140$ GeV: $H \to b\bar{b}$ dominates, so we use:

- $WH \to \ell^\pm \nu b\bar{b}$
- $ZH \to \ell^+\ell^- b\bar{b}$
- $WH, ZH \to jjb\bar{b}$
- $ZH \to \nu\bar{\nu}b\bar{b}$

$M_H \gtrsim 140$ GeV: $H \to W^+W^-$ dominates, so we use:

- $gg \to H \to W^+W^-$ (dileptons)
- $WH \to W^\pm W^+W^-$ (2ℓ and 3ℓ channels)

8.2.2.1. $VH, H \to b\bar{b}$ at Tevatron

While a lepton tag gets rid of most QCD backgrounds, it doesn't automatically eliminate top quarks: they decay to Wb, thus the event often contains one lepton and two jets, or two leptons and missing energy, in addition to the b jet pair. This is the same final state as our Higgs signal, with either extra jets or transverse energy imbalance. Kinematic cuts help, but because the detectors are imperfect some top quark events will leak through. Jet mismeasurement gives fake missing energy, for example (and is one of the most difficult uncertainties to quantify in a hadron collider experiment). In addition, QCD initial-state radiation from the incoming partons can give extra jets. Thus top quark and Higgs signal events qualitatively become very similar. To control this further the experiments have to look at other observables, such as angular distributions of the b jets and leptons. Other backgrounds to consider are QCD $Wb\bar{b}$ production, weak bosons pairs where one decays to $b\bar{b}$ (and thus has invariant mass close to the Higgs signal window).

Figure 8.11 shows the results of a CDF simulation study of WH and ZH Higgsstrahlung events at Run II for $M_H = 115$ GeV (right at the LEP Higgs limit) [33]. First note how the top quark pair and diboson backgrounds peak very close to the Higgs mass. Eyeballing the plots and simplistically applying our knowledge of Gaussian statistics, we could easily believe that this could yield a four or five sigma signal, perhaps combined with DØ results. However, carefully observe that the shape of the invariant mass distribution for background alone and with signal are extremely similar: they are both steeply falling; the Higgs signal is not a stand-out peak above a fairly flat background. Therein lies a hidden systematic! This means that we must understand the kinematic-differential shape of the QCD backgrounds to a very high degree of confidence. This is not just knowing the SM background at higher orders in QCD, differentially, but also the detector response. This criticality is not appreciated in most discussions of a potential discovery at Tevatron. It should be obvious that an excess in one of these channels would cause a scramble of cross-checking and probably further theoretical work to ensure confidence, in spite of the statistics alone. We'll run into this feature again with one of the LHC channels in Sec. 8.2.3.1, but quantified.

CDF has in fact already observed an interesting candidate Higgs event in Run II, in the first few hundred pb^{-1}. It is in the $ZH \to \nu\bar{\nu}b\bar{b}$ channel (a b jet pair plus missing transverse energy). The event display and key kinematic information are shown in Fig. 8.12. Given the very low b jet pair invariant mass, it's much more likely that the event came from EW ZZ or QCD $Zb\bar{b}$ production (cf. Fig. 8.11). It therefore doesn't generate the kind of excitement that the handful of events at LEP did. Nevertheless, finding this event was a milestone, showing that CDF could perform such an analysis and find Higgs-like events with good efficiency.

Table 8.1 summarizes the 2000 Tevatron Higgs Working Group Report predictions for Higgsstrahlung reach in Run II [29]. The results are quoted for one detector and per fb^{-1}, hence the rather small significances. CDF and DØ will eventually combine results, giving a factor of two in statistics. However, it's not known how much data they'll eventually collect by 2009 or 2010, when LHC is expected to have first physics results and CDF & DØ

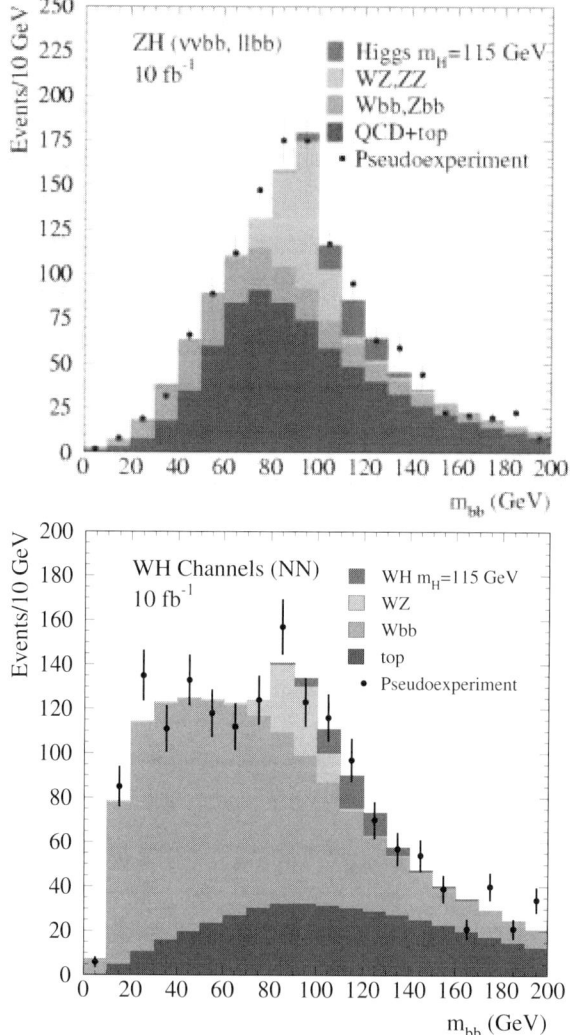

Fig. 8.11. CDF simulations of a 115 GeV signal at Tevatron Run II in ZH (left) and WH (right) Higgsstrahlung production with Higgs decays $H \to b\bar{b}$ and assuming 10 fb^{-1} is collected [33].

detector degradation becomes an issue. Fairly low Higgs masses are shown, because when the report was written nobody expected LEP to perform as well as it did, greatly exceeding its anticipated search reach. It should be obvious that a clear discovery would require a large amount of data,

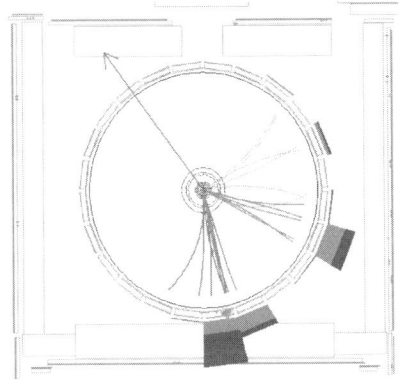
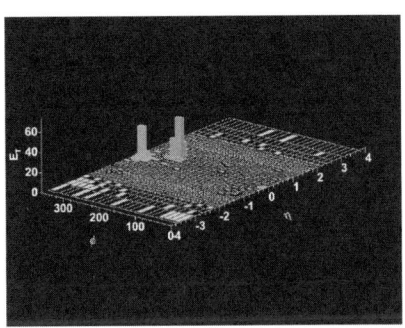

Two b-tagged jets

Jet$_1$ E$_T$= 100.3 GeV
Jet$_2$ E$_T$= 54.7 GeV

m$_{jj}$= 82 GeV

Missing E$_T$=145 GeV

Could be ZZ

Fig. 8.12. Interesting $bb\not{p}_T$ event at CDF in Tevatron Run II [34].

Table 8.1. Predicted signal significances at Tevatron Run II, for one detector and 1 fb^{-1}, for various $VH, H \to b\bar{b}$ searches, taken from Ref. [29].

Channel	Rate	\multicolumn{5}{c}{Higgs Mass (GeV/c^2)}
		90	100	110	120	130
$\ell^{\pm}\nu b\bar{b}$	S	8.7	9.0	4.8	4.4	3.7
	B	28	39	19	26	46
	$S/\sqrt{B}$	1.6	1.4	1.1	0.9	0.5
$\nu\bar{\nu}b\bar{b}$	S	12	8	6.3	4.7	3.9
	B	123	70	55	45	47
	$S/\sqrt{B}$	1.1	1.0	0.8	0.7	0.6
$\ell^+\ell^- b\bar{b}$	S	1.2	0.9	0.8	0.8	0.6
	B	2.9	1.9	2.3	2.8	1.9
	$S/\sqrt{B}$	0.7	0.7	0.5	0.5	0.4
$q\bar{q}b\bar{b}$	S	8.1	5.6	3.5	2.5	1.3
	B	6800	3600	2800	2300	2000
	$S/\sqrt{B}$	0.10	0.09	0.07	0.05	0.03

combining multiple channels, and the Higgs boson happening to be fairly light; not to mention the QCD shape systematic concern I described earlier (but is not quantified). In spite of this apparent pessimism, however, CDF and DØ seem to be performing modestly better than expected – higher

8.2.2.2. $gg \to H \to W^+W^-$ at Tevatron

For $M_H \gtrsim 140$ GeV, a SM Higgs will decay mostly to W pairs (cf. Fig. 8.4), which has a decent rate to dileptons and has very little SM background – essentially just EW W pair production, with some background from top quark pairs where both b jets are lost. This channel has some special characteristics due to how the Higgs decay proceeds. There is a marked angular correlation between the outgoing leptons which differs from the SM backgrounds: they prefer to be emitted together, that is close to the same flight direction in the center-of-mass frame [35].

To understand this correlation, consider what happens if the Higgs decays to a pair of transversely-polarized W bosons. For W decays, the lepton angle with respect to the $W^\pm$ spin follows a $(1 \pm \cos\theta_{\ell\pm})^2$ distribution. That is, the positively-charged lepton prefers to be emitted with the W spin, while the negatively-charged lepton prefers to be emitted opposite the W spin. Since the Higgs is a scalar (spin-0), the W spins are anti-correlated, thus the leptons are preferentially emitted in the same direction. For longitudinal W bosons, the lepton follows a $\sin^2\theta_\ell$ distribution. The W spins are still correlated, however, and the matrix element squared (an excellent exercise for the student) is proportional to $(p_{\ell^-} \cdot p_\nu)(p_{\ell^+} \cdot p_{\bar\nu})$. Since a charged lepton and neutrino are emitted back-to-back in the W rest frame, this is again maximized for the charged leptons emitted together. This correlation is shown visually by the schematic of Fig. 8.13. Projected onto the azimuthal plane (transverse to the beam), its efficacy is shown in Fig. 8.14 by comparison to various backgrounds [29, 36].

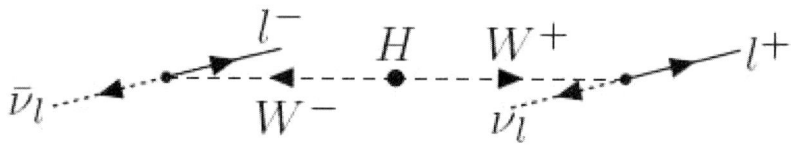

Fig. 8.13. Diagram showing the preferred flight direction of charged leptons in $H \to \ell^+\nu\ell^-\bar\nu$.

In addition to this angular correlation, we may also construct a transverse mass (M_T) for the system, despite the fact that two neutrinos go missing [37]. We first write down the transverse energy (p_T) of the dilepton and missing transverse energy ($\not{E}_T$) systems,

$$E_{T_{\ell^+\ell^-}} = \sqrt{\vec{p}_{T_{\ell^+\ell^-}}^2 + m_{\ell^+\ell^-}^2}, \qquad \not{E}_T = \sqrt{\vec{\not{p}}_T^2 + m_{\ell^+\ell^-}^2} \qquad (8.8)$$

where I've substituted the dilepton invariant mass $m_{\ell^+\ell^-}^2$ for $m_{\nu\bar{\nu}}^2$. This is exact at $H \to WW$ threshold, and is a very good approximation for Higgs masses below about 200 GeV and where this decay mode is open. The W pair transverse mass is now straightforward:

$$M_{T_{WW}} = \sqrt{(\not{E}_T + E_{T_{\ell^+\ell^-}})^2 - (\vec{p}_{T_{\ell^+\ell^-}} + \vec{\not{p}}_T)^2} \qquad (8.9)$$

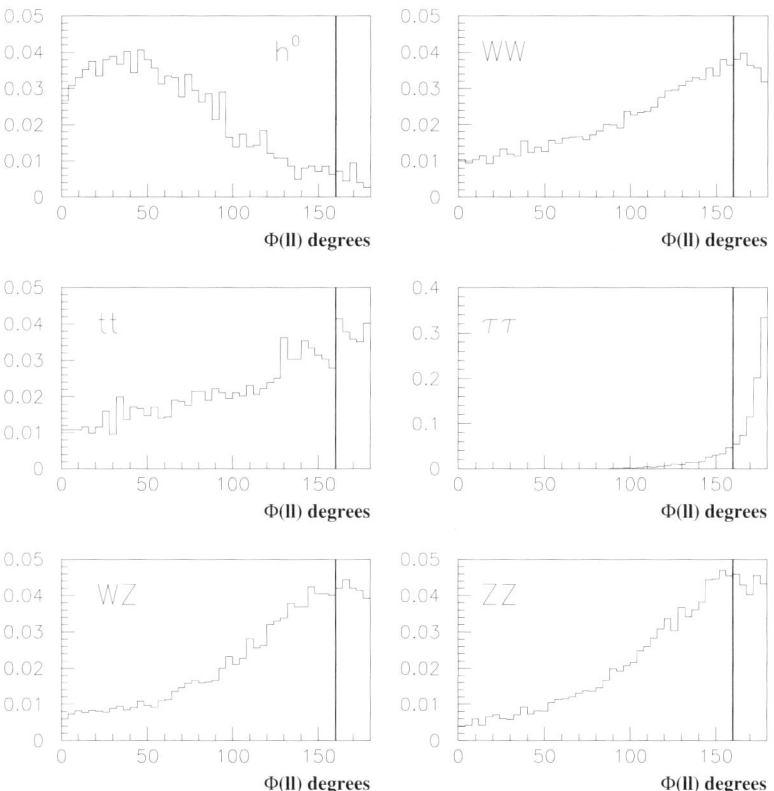

Fig. 8.14. Dilepton azimuthal angular correlation for a $H \to W^+W^- \to \ell^+\nu\ell^-\bar{\nu}$ signal and its backgrounds. The efficacy of the cut (vertical line) can easily be estimated visually. From the Tevatron Run II Higgs Working Group Report [29].

This gives a nice Jacobian peak for the Higgs signal, modulo detector missing-transverse-energy resolution, whereas the SM backgrounds tend to be comparatively flat.

Utilizing these techniques gives Tevatron some reach for a heavier Higgs boson, mostly in the mass range $150 \lesssim M_H \lesssim 180$ GeV, where the BR to WW is significant and the Higgs production rate is not too small.

8.2.2.3. Tevatron Higgs summary expectations

Tevatron Higgs physics expectations have changed since the 2000 Report, as DØ and CDF have better understood their detectors and made analysis improvements. As yet, the only progress summary is from 2003, shown in Fig. 8.15. It compares the original Report's findings, shown by the thick curves, with improved findings for the low-mass region, shown by the thinner lines. However, the new results do not yet include systematic uncertainties, which may be considerable. We should expect some form of a new summary expectation sometime in 2007. A final note on the undiscussed WBF production mode: some study has been done (see Sec. II.C.4 of Ref. [29]), but DØ and CDF both lack sufficient coverage of the forward region to use this mode. This is not the case at LHC.

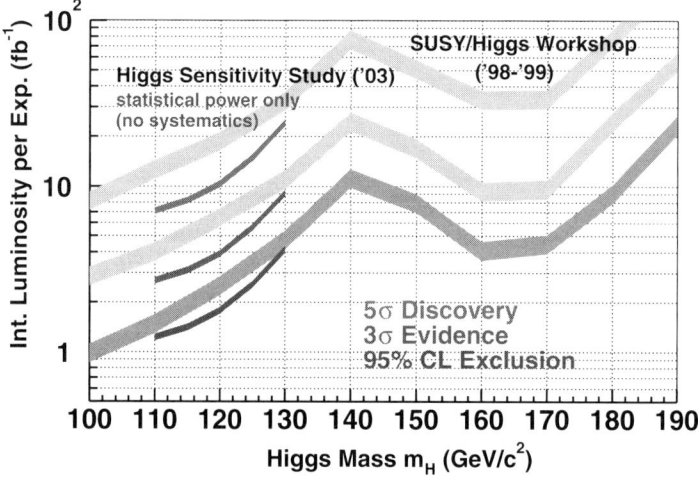

Fig. 8.15. Expected required integrated luminosity per experiment required in Run II to observe a SM Higgs as a function of M_H [33].

Run II now has about 1 fb^{-1} of analyzed data, and a Higgs search summary progress report is available in Ref. [38], which updates each channel's expectations.

8.2.3. *Higgs at LHC*

Higgs physics at LHC will be similar to that at Tevatron. There is the slight difference that LHC will be pp collisions rather than $p\bar{p}$. The biggest difference, however, is the increased energy, from 2 to 14 TeV. Particle production in the 100 GeV mass range will be at far lower Feynman x, where the gluon density is much larger than the quark density. In fact, it's useful (for Higgs physics) to think of the LHC as a gluon collider to first order. The ratio between gluon fusion Higgs production and Higgsstrahlung is thus larger than at Tevatron. Figure 8.16 displays the various SM Higgs cross sections, only over a much larger range of M_H – at LHC, large-M_H cross sections are not trivially small, compared to at the Tevatron. There are huge QCD corrections to the $gg \to H$ rate (also at Tevatron), but these

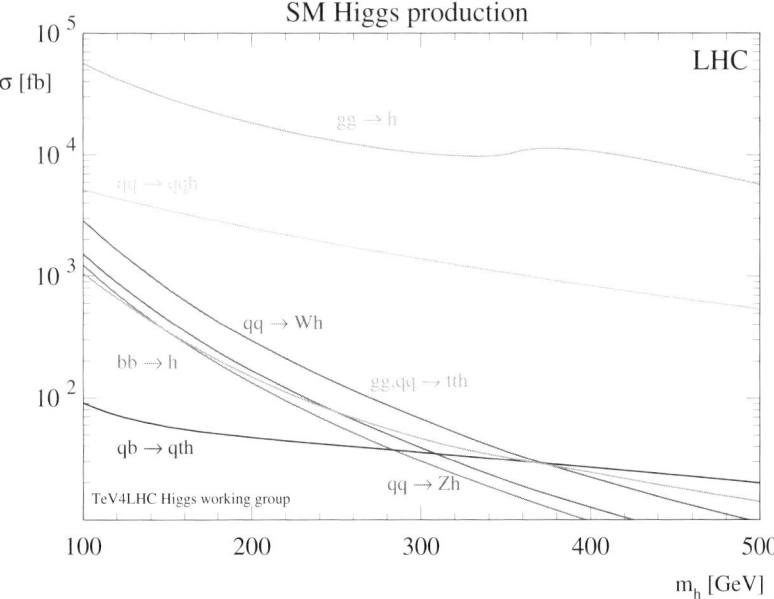

Fig. 8.16. Cross sections for Higgs production in various channels at LHC ($\sqrt{s} = 14$ TeV) [30].

are now known at NNLO and under control [39] (and included in Fig. 8.16). They don't affect the basic phenomenology, however. Knowing that LHC is plans to collect several hundred fb^{-1} of data, a quick calculation reveals that the LHC will truly be a Higgs factory, producing hundreds of thousands of light Higgs bosons, or tens of thousands if it's heavy.

Looking back at Fig. 8.10, we see that while the Higgs cross section rises quite steeply with collision energy ($gg \to H$ is basically a QCD process), so do important backgrounds like top quark production. The inclusive b cross section is still too large to access to $gg \to H \to b\bar{b}$, but note that the EW gauge boson cross sections do not rise as swiftly with energy. Immediately we realize that channels like $gg \to H \to W^+W^-$ should have a much better signal-to-background (S/B) ratio. (In fact it suffers from non-trivial single-top quark [40] and $gg \to W^+W^-$ [41] backgrounds, but is still an excellent channel for $M_H \gtrsim 150$ GeV.) The figure does not show cross sections like $Wb\bar{b}$ or $Zb\bar{b}$, which grow QCD-like and thus become a terminal problem for WH and ZH channels.

Obviously there are a few significant differences between Tevatron and LHC with implications for Higgs physics. We'll lose access to WH and ZH at low mass, at least for Higgs decay to b jets. What about rare decays, since the production rate is large? The $t\bar{t}H$ cross section is large and would yield a healthy event rate. It's complexity is distinctive, so one might speculate that perhaps it could be useful. WBF production is also accessible due to better detectors, and likewise its more complex signature is worthy of a look. It will in fact turn out to be perhaps the best production mode at LHC.

As with Tevatron, we need to understand both the signal and background for each Higgs channel we wish to examine. As a prelude to Chapter 8.3, Higgs measurements, at LHC we won't want to just find the Higgs in one mode. Rather, we'll want to observe it in as many production and decay modes as possible, to study all its properties, such as couplings.

8.2.3.1. $t\bar{t}H, H \to b\bar{b}$

Let's begin by discussing a very complex channel, top quark associated production at low mass, $t\bar{t}H, H \to b\bar{b}$. This was studied early on in the ATLAS TDR [42] and in various obscure CMS notes, and found to be a sure-fire way to find a light Higgs. Figure 8.17 shows a schematic of such an event, with multiple b jets from both top quarks and the Higgs, at least one lepton from a W for triggering, and possibly extra soft jets from QCD

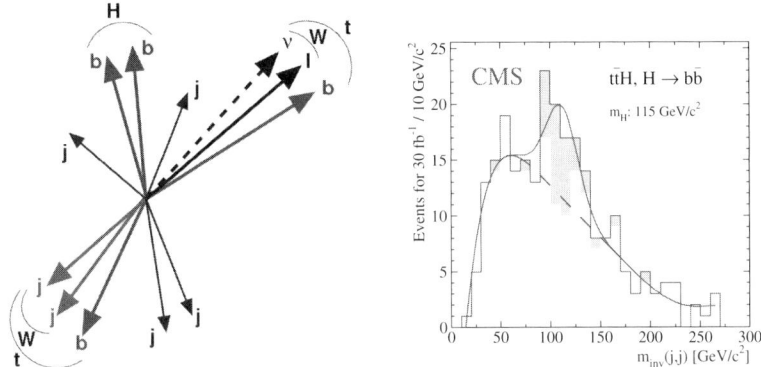

Fig. 8.17. Left: schematic of the outgoing particles in a typical $t\bar{t}H, H \to b\bar{b}$ event at LHC [47]. Right: early CMS study expectations for a $b\bar{b}$ mass peak in such events, for $M_H = 115$ GeV [44, 45].

radiation. The schematic is a bit fanciful in the neatness of separation of the decay products, but is useful to get an idea of what's going on.

These early studies [42–45] were too ambitious, however. The backgrounds to this signal are $t\bar{t}b\bar{b}$ and $t\bar{t}jj$[f] production, pure QCD processes. The extra (b) jets must be fairly energetic, or hard, because the signal is a 100+ GeV-mass object which decays to essentially massless objects. Despite this being a known problem [46], these backgrounds were calculated using the soft/collinear approximation for extra jet emission implemented in standard Monte Carlo tools such as PYTHIA or HERWIG. This greatly underestimated the backgrounds.

The left panel of Fig. 8.18 shows the results of a repeated study by ATLAS using a proper background calculation [47]. (Recent CMS studies found similar results, and the new CMS TDR [48] does not even bother to discuss this channel.) There is no longer any clearly-visible mass peak, and S/B is now about 1/6, much poorer. While the figure reflects only 1/10 of the expected total integrated luminosity at LHC, statistics is not the problem. Rather, it is systematic: uncertainty on the exact shape of the QCD backgrounds.

Therein lies the sleeping dragon. Now is a good time to explain how systematic errors may enter our estimate of signal significance. Our simple

---

[f]Non-b jets can fake b jets with a probability of about 1% or a little less.

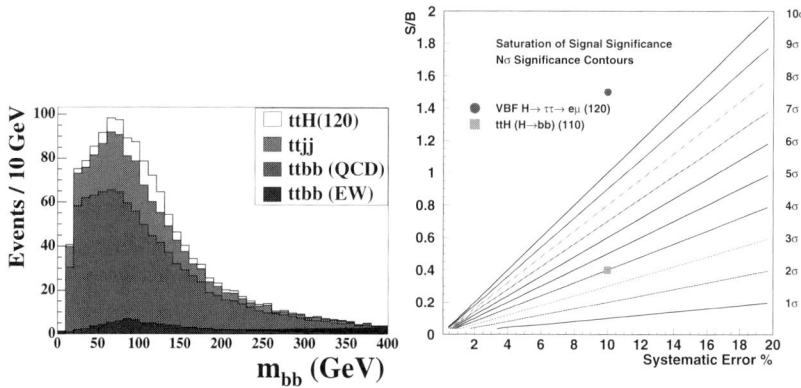

Fig. 8.18. Left: results of a more up-to-date ATLAS studying of $t\bar{t}H, H \to b\bar{b}$ production at LHC, for 30 fb^{-1} of data and a Higgs mass of $M_H = 120$ GeV [47]. The QCD backgrounds were calculated with exact matrix elements rather than in the soft/collinear approximation. Right: maximum achievable signal significance for two LHC Higgs channels as a function of S/B and shape systematic uncertainty $\triangle$ [49], as discussed in the text.

formula is modified:

$$\frac{S}{\sqrt{B}} \to \frac{S}{\sqrt{B(1+B\triangle^2)}} \xrightarrow{\mathcal{L}\to\infty} \frac{S/B}{\triangle} \qquad (8.10)$$

where $\triangle$ is the shape uncertainty in the background, a kind of normalization uncertainty. In the limit of infinite data, if S/B is fixed (which it is), signal significance saturates. The only way around this is to perform higher-order calculations of the background to reduce $\triangle$ (and hope you understand the residual theoretical uncertainties). The right panel of Fig. 8.18 shows the spectrum of possibilities [49]. For the known 10% QCD shape systematic for $t\bar{t}H$, even an infinite amount of data would never be able to grant us more than about a 3σ significance. This could still potentially be useful for a coupling measurement, albeit poorly, but will not be a discovery channel unless higher-order QCD calculations can improve the situation. Calculating even just $t\bar{t}b\bar{b}$ at NLO is currently beyond the state of the art, but is likely to become feasible within a few years.

While I don't discuss it here, top quark associated Higgs production does show some promise for the rare Higgs decays to photons. Photons are very clean, well-measured, and the detectors have good rejection against QCD jet fakes. The final word probably hasn't been written on this, but the CMS TDR [48] does have updated simulation results which the interested student may read up on.

8.2.3.2. $gg \to H \to \gamma\gamma$

We've just seen that QCD can be a really annoying problem for Higgs hunting at LHC. A logical alternative for a low-mass Higgs is to look for its rare decays to EW objects, e.g. photons. The BR is at about the two per-mille level for a light Higgs, $110 \lesssim M_H \lesssim 140$ GeV. The LHC will certainly produce enough Higgses, but what are the backgrounds like?

It turns out that the loop-induced QCD process $gg \to \gamma\gamma$ is a non-trivial contribution, but we also have to worry about single and double jet fakes from QCD $j\gamma$ and jj production. This occurs when a leading π^0 from jet fragmentation goes to photons, depositing most of the energy in the EM calorimeter, thereby looking like a real photon. Fortunately, because photons and jets are massless, the invariant mass distribution obeys a very linear $1/m_{\gamma\gamma}$ falloff in our region of interest. The experiments can in that case normalize the background very precisely from the sidebands, where we know there is no Higgs signal. Shape systematics are not much of a concern, thus avoiding the pitfalls of the $t\bar{t}H, H \to b\bar{b}$ case.

Figure 8.19 shows the results of an ATLAS study for this channel using 30 fb^{-1} of data [42], 1/10 of the LHC run program or 3 years at low-luminosity running. The exact expectations are still uncertain, mostly due to an ongoing factor of two uncertainty in the fake jet rejection efficiency. A conservative estimate shows that this channel isn't likely to be the first

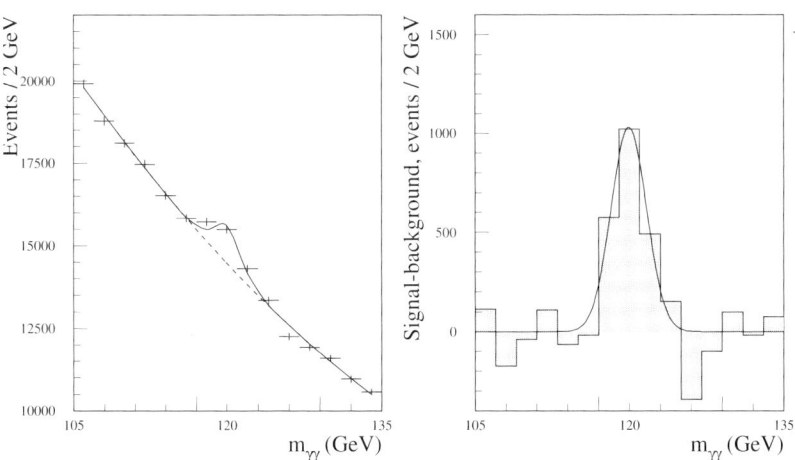

Fig. 8.19. ATLAS simulation of $gg \to H \to \gamma\gamma$ at LHC for $M_H = 120$ GeV and 30 fb^{-1} of data [42]. The right panel is the mass distribution after background subtraction, normalized from sidebands.

discovery mode, but would be crucial for measuring the Higgs mass precisely at low M_H, to about 1% [42, 48]. Photon energy calibration nonlinearity in the detector may be an issue for the ultimate precision, but is generally regarded as minor. We'll come back to this point in Chapter 8.3 on Higgs property measurements.

While I focus here on the SM, keep in mind that because $H \to \gamma\gamma$ is a rare decay, it can be very sensitive to new physics. Recall that the coupling is induced via both top quark and W loops which mostly cancel. Depending on how the new physics alters couplings, or what new particles appear in the loop, the partial width could be greatly suppressed or enhanced. (Anticipating Chapter 8.4, the interested student could peruse Ref. [51] and references therein to see how this can happen in supersymmetry.)

8.2.3.3. *Weak boson fusion Higgs production*

Let us explore this other production mechanism I said isn't accessible at Tevatron, weak boson fusion (WBF). It was long ignored for LHC light Higgs phenomenology because its rate is about an order of magnitude smaller than $gg \to H$ there. However, it has quite distinctive kinematics and QCD properties that make it easy to suppress backgrounds, for all Higgs decay channels. The process itself is described by an incoming pair of quark partons which brem a pair of weak gauge bosons, which fuse to produce a Higgs; see Fig. 8.20.

The first distinctive characteristic of WBF[g] is that the quarks scatter with significant transverse momentum, and will show up as far forward and backward jets in the hadronic calorimeters of CMS and ATLAS. The Higgs boson is produced centrally, however, so its decay products, regardless of decay mode, typically show up in the central detector region. This is shown in the lego plot schematic in the right panel of Fig. 8.20[h].

The reason for this scattering behavior comes from the W (or Z) propagator, $1/(Q^2 - M^2)$. For t-channel processes, Q^2 is necessarily always negative. Thus the propagator suppresses the amplitude least when Q^2 is small. For small Q^2, we have $Q^2 = (p_f - p_i)^2 \approx E_q^2(1-x)\theta^2$, where x is

---

[g]Some experimentalists refer to this as vector boson fusion (VBF), even though the vector QCD boson (gluon) process of Fig. 8.22 is not included. This will cause increasing confusion as time goes by.

[h]The angle ϕ is the azimuthal angle perpendicular to the beam axis. Pseudorapidity η is a boost-invariant description the polar scattering angle, $\eta = -\log(\tan\frac{\theta}{2})$. The lego plot is a Cartesian map of the finite-resolution detector in these coordinates, as if the detector had been sliced lengthwise and unrolled.

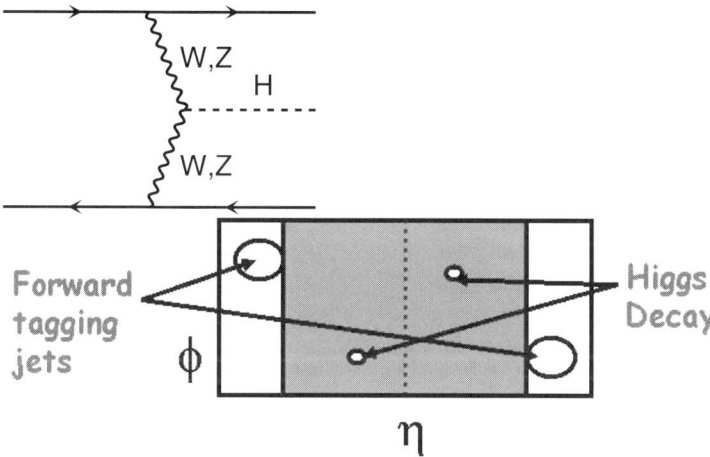

Fig. 8.20. WBF Higgs production Feynman diagram and lego plot schematic of a typical event.

the fraction of incoming quark energy the weak boson takes with it, and is small. Thus θ prefers to be small, translating into large pseudorapidity. One quark will be scattered in the far forward detector, the other far backward, and the pseudorapidity separation between them will tend to be large. We call these "tagging" jets. QCD processes with an extra EW object(s) which mimics a Higgs decay, on the other hand, have a fundamentally different propagator structure and prefer larger scattering angles [52, 53], including at NLO [54]. The differences between the two are shown in Fig. 8.21 [55].

The second distinctive characteristic is QCD radiation [56]. Additional jet activity in WBF prefers to be forward of the scattered quarks. This is because it occurs via bremsstrahlung off color charge, which is scattered at small angles, with no connection between them. In contrast, QCD production always involves color charge being exchanged between the incoming partons: acceleration through 180 degrees. QCD bremsstrahlung thus takes place over large angles, covering the central region. Central jet activity can be vetoed, giving large background suppression [57]. We won't discuss it further, due to theoretical uncertainties; the interested student may learn more from Ref. [58].

We'll see in the next few subsections that WBF Higgs channels are extremely powerful even without a central jet (minijet) veto[i]. Eventually

---

[i]A technical topic outside our present scope: see Refs. [53, 57–59] and the literature they reference.

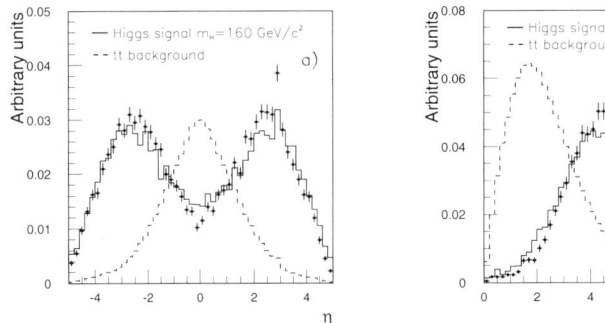

Fig. 8.21. Tagging jet rapidity (left) and separation (right) for WBF Higgs production v. QCD $t\bar{t}$ production [55].

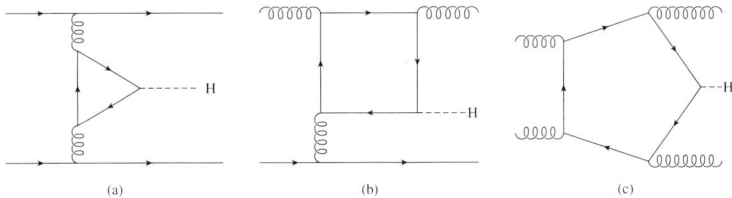

Fig. 8.22. Representative Feynman diagrams for gluon fusion Higgs plus two jets production [60].

a veto will be used, after calibration from observing EW v. QCD Zjj production in the early running of LHC [53]. There is however another lingering theoretical uncertainty, coming from Higgs production itself!

QCD Higgs production via loop-induced couplings may itself give rise to two forward tagging jets, which would then fall into the WBF Higgs sample [60]. Some representative Feynman diagrams for this process are shown in Fig. 8.22. After imposing WBF-type kinematic cuts (far forward/backward, well-separated jets, central Higgs decay products), this contribution to the WBF sample adds about another third for a light Higgs, or doubles it for a very heavy Higgs, $M_H \gtrsim 350$ GeV, as shown in the left panel of Fig. 8.23. The residual QCD theoretical cross section uncertainty is about a factor of two, however, and being QCD it will produce far more central jets, which will be vetoed to reject QCD backgrounds. Naïvely, then, gluon fusion Hjj is an $\sim 10\%$ contribution to WBF, but with a huge uncertainty.

This contribution is a mixed blessing. It's part of the signal, so would hasten discovery. Yet it creates confusion, since at some point we want

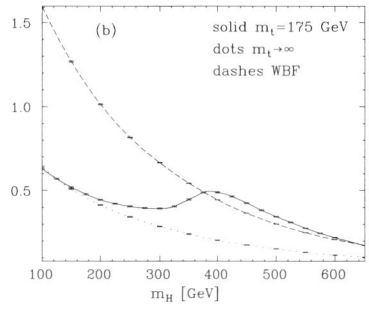 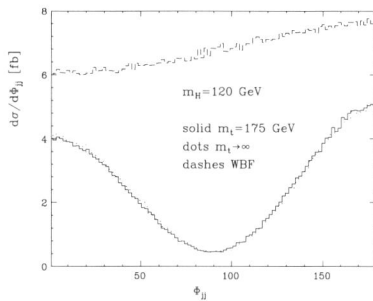

Fig. 8.23. Left: WBF and gluon fusion contributions to the forward-tagged Hjj sample at LHC. Right: azimuthal angular distributions for the same two processes, showing distinctive differences. Figures taken from Ref. [60].

to measure couplings, and the WBF and gluon fusion components arise from different couplings. Fortunately, there is a difference! WBF produces an almost-flat distribution in ϕ_{jj}, the azimuthal tagging jet separation, but gluon fusion has a suppression at 90 degrees [60]; cf. right panel of Fig. 8.23.

8.2.3.4. Weak boson fusion $H \to \tau^+\tau^-$

Now we know that the WBF signature can strongly suppress QCD backgrounds because of its unique kinematic characteristics. We expect that $H \to \gamma\gamma$ is visible in WBF [48, 61, 62], but being a rare decay in a smaller-rate channel, it's not expected to lead to discovery. Rather, it would be a useful additional channel for couplings measurements. Let's now instead discuss a decay mode we haven't yet considered, $H \to \tau^+\tau^-$. This is subdominant to $H \to b\bar{b}$ in the light Higgs region, $M_H \lesssim 150$ GeV, but the backgrounds are more EW than QCD. We thus have some hope to see it, whereas $H \to b\bar{b}$ remains frustratingly hopeless.

We first have to realize that taus decay to a variety of final states:

- 35% $\tau \to \ell\nu_\ell\nu_\tau$, ID efficiency $\epsilon_\ell \sim 90\%$
- 50% $\tau \to h_1\nu_\tau$ "1-prong" hadronic (one charged track), ID efficiency $\epsilon_h \sim 25\%$
- 15% $\tau \to h_3\nu_\tau$ "3-prong" hadronic (three charged tracks), which are thrown away

The obvious problem is that with at least two neutrinos escaping, the Higgs cannot be reconstructed from its decay products. Or can it?

Let's assume the taus decay collinearly. This is an excellent approximation: since 50+ GeV energy taus have far more energy than their mass, so their decay products are highly collimated. We then have two unknowns, x_+ and x_-, the fractions of tau energy that the charged particles take with them. What experiment measures is missing transverse energy in the x and y directions. Two unknowns with two measurements is exactly solvable. For our system this gives [63]:

$$m^2_{\tau^+\tau^-} = \frac{m^2_{\ell^+\ell^-}}{x_+x_-} + 2m^2_\tau \qquad (8.11)$$

(an excellent exercise for all students to get a grip on kinematics and useful tricks at hadron colliders). An important note is that this doesn't work for back-to-back taus (the derivation will reveal why), but WBF Higgses are typically kicked out with about 100 GeV of p_T, so this almost never happens in WBF. This trick can't be used in the bulk of $gg \to H$ events because there it is produced mostly at rest with nearly all taus back-to-back.

We need a lepton trigger, so consider two channels: $\tau^+\tau^- \to \ell^\pm h$ and $\tau^+\tau^- \to \ell^+\ell'^-$ ($\ell = e, \mu$). The main backgrounds are EW and QCD Zjj production (really Z/γ^*), top quark pairs, EW & QCD $WWjj$ and QCD $b\bar{b}jj$ production. But after reconstruction, the non-Z backgrounds look very different than the signal in x_+-x_- space, as shown in Fig. 8.24.

ATLAS and CMS have both studied these channels with full detector simulation and WBF kinematic cuts, but no minijet veto, and found extremely promising results [55]. Figure 8.25 shows invariant mass distributions for a reconstructed Higgs in the two different decay channels, assuming only 30 fb^{-1} of data. The Higgs peak is easily seen above the backgrounds and away from the Z pole. Mass resolution is expected to be a few GeV.

But this joint study by CMS and ATLAS [55] is not the best we can do. The joint study ignored the minijet veto, for instance. While that will assuredly improve the situation further, we're just not sure precisely how much. Putting this aside for the moment, there are yet further tricks to play to improve the situation.

The leading idea zeroes in on the fact that missing transverse momentum ($\not{p}_T$) has some uncertainty due to jet energy mismeasurement (those imperfect detectors). Using a χ^2 test, one determines which is more likely: $Z \to \tau^+\tau^-$ or $H \to \tau^+\tau^-$, *using a fixed Higgs mass constraint* [65]. Examining the schematics in Fig. 8.26, we see this is tantamount to deciding which fit is closer to the center of the $\not{p}_T$ uncertainty region. Early indications are that this technique would improve S/B by about a factor *four*, in addition to recovering some signal lost using more traditional strict kinematic cuts on x_+ and x_- (recall Fig. 8.24). This would approximately halve

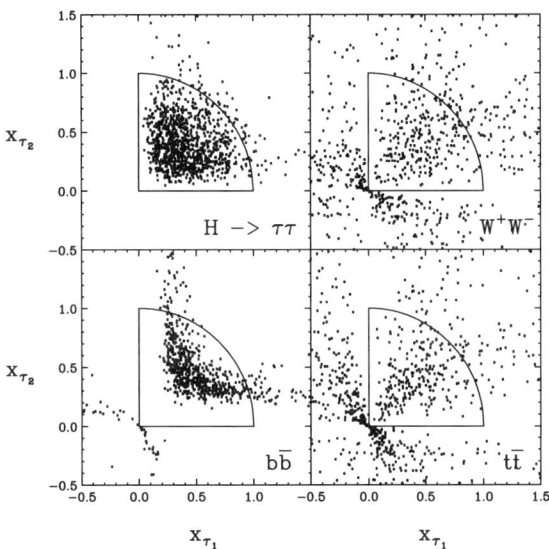

Fig. 8.24. Reconstructed x_+ v. x_- (x_1, x_2) for a WBF $H \to \tau^+\tau^-$ signal v. non-Z backgrounds [64].

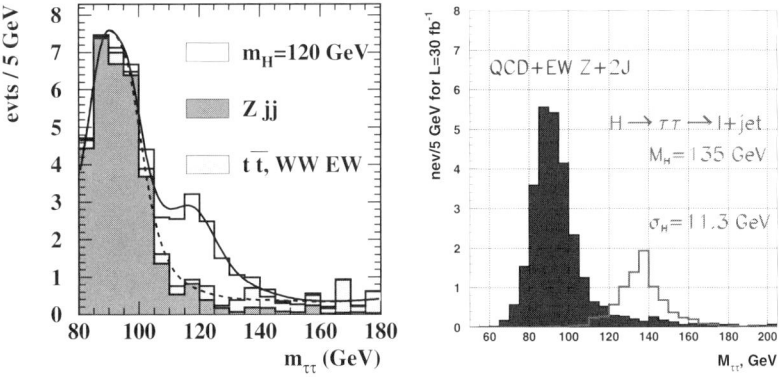

Fig. 8.25. ATLAS (left) and CMS (right) simulations of WBF $H \to \tau^+\tau^-$ events after 30 fb^{-1} of data at LHC. The Higgs resonance clearly stands out from the background. Figures from Ref. [55].

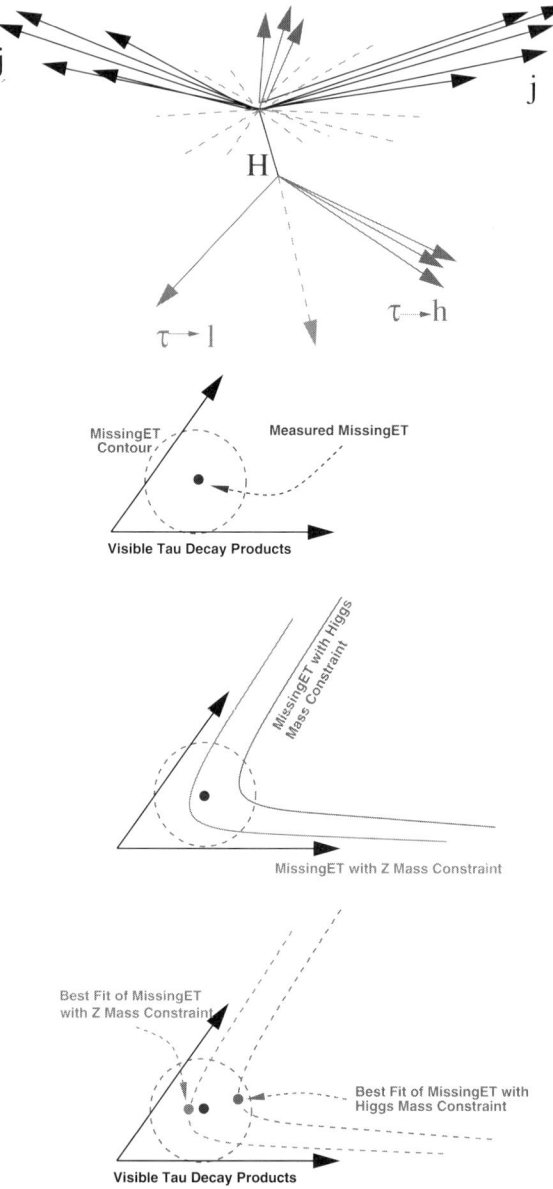

Fig. 8.26. Top: schematic azimuthal projection of WBF $H \to \tau^+\tau^-$ events at LHC. Bottom: diagram illustrating the 1σ uncertainty region (due to jet mismeasurement) of missing p_T, and how a Z mass or Higgs mass hypothesis can be best fit using a χ^2 test. Figures from Ref. [50].

the data required to discover a light SM Higgs boson using this channel. Keep it in mind when we see the current official discovery expectations in Sec. 8.2.3.7. Further improvements might also be expected from neural-net type analyses, which are coming to the fore now that Tevatron has demonstrated their viability.

A final word on systematic uncertainties. Unlike the tortuous case of $t\bar{t}H, H \to b\bar{b}$, we don't have to worry about shape systematics here. The dominant background is Zjj production. We can separately examine $Z \to ee, \mu\mu$, which produces an extremely sharp, clean peak, precisely calibrating Zjj production in Monte Carlo. The only uncertainty then is tau decay modeling, which is very well understood from the LEP era.

8.2.3.5. Weak boson fusion $H \to W^+W^-$

A natural question to ask is, how well does WBF Higgs hunting work for $M_H \gtrsim 140$ GeV, where $H \to W^+W^-$ dominates? We should expect fairly well, since it's the production process characteristics that supply most of the background suppression, leaving us only to look for separated reconstructed mass peaks.

For $H \to W^+W^-$ we'll consider only the dilepton channel, as it has relatively low backgrounds, while QCD gives a large rate for the other possible channel, one central lepton plus two central jets (and the minijet veto will likely not work). We'll therefore rely on exactly the same angular correlations and transverse mass variable we encountered in the Tevatron case [37] (cf. Eqs. 8.8,8.9). The only critical distinction is then $e\mu$ v. ee, $\mu\mu$ samples, as the latter have a continuum background (Z^*/γ^*). These are not too much of a concern, however.

Without going too much into detail, I'll simply say that top quarks are a major background, and they have the largest uncertainty. The largest component comes from $t\bar{t}j$ production, where the extra hard parton is far forward and ID'd as one tagging jet; a b jet from top decay gives the other tagging jet, and the other b jet is unobserved. This background requires care to simulate, because the soft/collinear approximation in standard codes is no good. There is also a significant contribution from single-top production, and off-shell effects are crucial to simulate, which is not normally an issue for backgrounds at LHC [66]. Work is still needed in this area to be fully prepared for this particular search channel. Fortunately, we may expect an NLO calculation of $t\bar{t}j$ before LHC start [67].

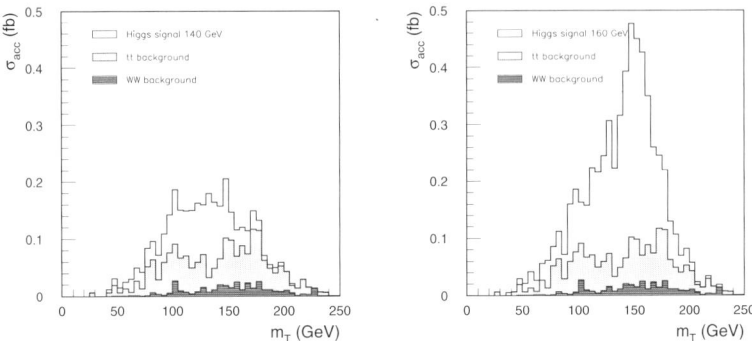

Fig. 8.27. ATLAS simulations of WBF $H \to W^+W^-$ events after 30 fb^{-1} of data at LHC for $M_H = 140$ GeV (left) and 160 GeV (right). The Higgs signal clearly stands out from the background in both cases, although the Jacobian peak is easier to identify closer to threshold. Figures taken from Ref. [55].

Figure 8.27 shows the results of the same ATLAS/CMS joint WBF Higgs study for this channel [55]. The results are extremely positive, with $S/B > 1/1$ without a minijet veto over a large mass range; even for $M_H = 120$ GeV, $S/B \sim 1/2$, allowing for Higgs observation even down to the LEP limit in this channel. The transverse mass variable works extremely well for Higgs masses near WW threshold, and reasonably well for lower masses, where the W bosons are off-shell.

8.2.3.6. $t\bar{t}H, H \to W^+W^-$ at higher mass

A late entry to the Higgs game at LHC is top quark associated production, but with Higgs decaying to W bosons. Representative Feynman diagrams are shown in Fig. 8.28. Obviously this is intended to apply to larger Higgs masses, but turns out to work fairly well even below W pair threshold [68, 69]. The key is to use same-sign dilepton and trilepton subsamples. The backgrounds then don't come from pure QCD production, rather from mixed QCD-EW top quark pairs plus W, Z/γ^*, W^+W^-, etc. We would be especially eager to observe this channel because, if the HWW coupling is measured elsewhere, it provides the only viable direct measurement of the top quark Yukawa coupling. More on this in Chapter 8.3.

A noteworthy features of this channel is that while the $t\bar{t}H$ cross section falls with increasing M_H, BR($H \to W^+W^-$) rises with increasing M_H in our mass region of interest, and the two trends coincidentally approximately balance each other. From a final-state rate perspective, this channel is

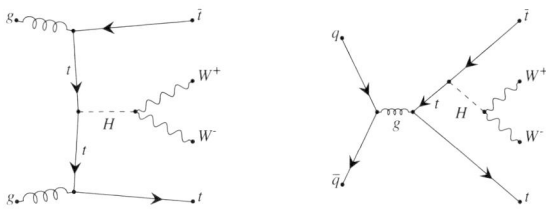

Fig. 8.28. Representative Feynman diagrams for $t\bar{t}H, H \to W^+W^-$ production at LHC.

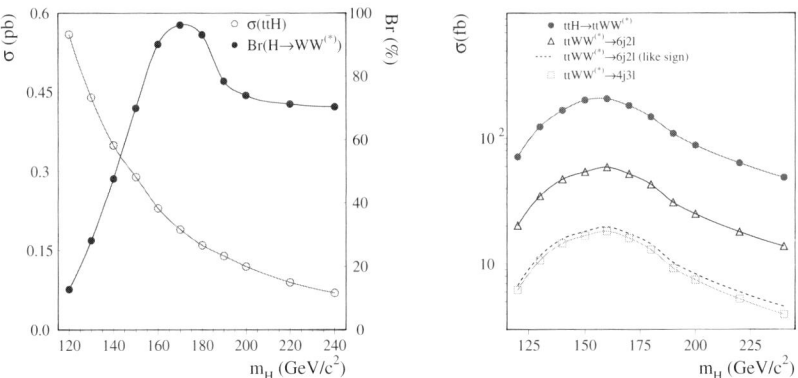

Fig. 8.29. Left: $t\bar{t}H$ cross section and BR($H \to W^+W^-$) as a function of M_H. Right: the cross section to three different final states after top quark and Higgs decays. Figures from Ref. [69].

approximately constant over a wide mass range, up to about 200 GeV. Figure 8.29 shows this numerically. Figure 8.30 shows ATLAS's expected statistical uncertainty on the top quark Yukawa coupling. It ranges from about 20% over a broad mass range for 30 fb^{-1} of data, to about 10% from the full LHC run. Systematic uncertainties are currently unexplored.

8.2.3.7. *LHC Higgs in a nutshell*

LHC Higgs phenomenology has come a long way in the decade since the first comprehensive studies were reported (e.g. the ATLAS TDR [42]). The old studies give a seriously misleading picture of LHC capabilities. Students should refer to newer ATLAS Notes and the new CMS TDR [48]. Solid

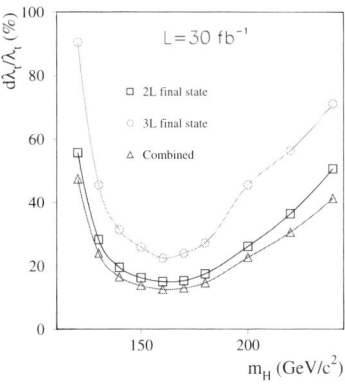 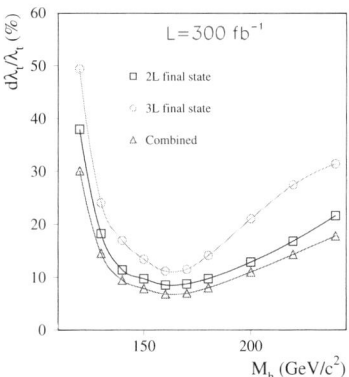

Fig. 8.30. ATLAS prediction [69] for the top quark Yukawa coupling measurement uncertainty (statistical only) from $t\bar{t}H, H \to W^+W^-$, for separate leptonic final-state channels and combined.

grounds exist for expecting even more improvements. Fig. 8.31 summarizes ATLAS's projections for multiple Higgs channels as a function of Higgs mass. Note especially the new dominance of WBF channels and degradation of $t\bar{t}H$.

8.3. Is it the Standard Model Higgs?

Imagine yourself in 2010 (hey, we're optimists!), squished shoulder-to-shoulder in the CERN auditorium, waiting for the speaker to get to the punchline. Rumors have been circulating for months about excess events showing up in some light Higgs channels, but not all that would be expected. LHC has 40 fb^{-1}, after all. Your experimental friends tell you that both collaborations have been scrambling madly, independent groups cross-checking the original first analyses. Then the null result slides start passing by. No diphoton peaks anywhere. Nothing in the WW or ZZ channels. Even CMS's invisible Higgs search (WBF – tagging jets with no central objects at all) doesn't show anything. Numerous standard MSSM Higgs results fly by, invariant mass spectra fitting the SM predictions perfectly. The audience becomes restless, irritated. People around you mutter that there must not be a Higgs after all. But you realize that the speaker skipped mention of the WBF $H \to \tau^+\tau^-$ channel. Then suddenly it appears, and there's a peak above the Z pole, centered around 125 GeV, broader than

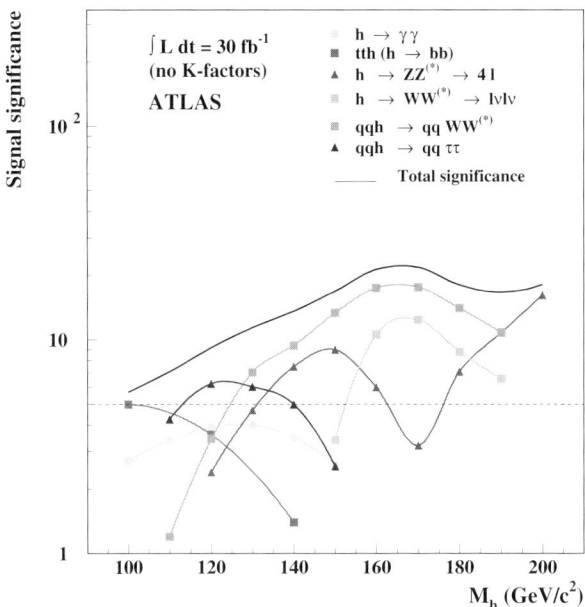

Fig. 8.31. ATLAS significance projections in multiple Higgs channels w/ 30 fb^{-1} of LHC data [55].

you'd expect but the speaker says something about resolution will improve with further refinement of the tau reconstruction algorithms. It's also a too-small rate, less than half what's expected.

So what is this beast? The bump showed up in a Higgs search channel, but at that mass it should have shown up in several others as well. If it's Standard Model, that is. At 125 GeV there should be $H \to W^+W^-$ in WBF, and $H \to \gamma\gamma$ both inclusively and in WBF, although maybe they're still marginal. Photons turned out to be hard at first, and QCD predictions weren't quite on the mark. Quite a few people are on their cell phones already. You hear a dozen different exclamations, ranging from "We found the Higgs!" to "The Standard Model is dead!". Quite obviously this is a new physics discovery, but what exactly is going on?

By now you should get the point of this imaginary scenario: finding a new bump is merely the start of real physics. For numerous reasons you've heard at this summer school, some better than others, finding a SM Higgs really isn't very likely. But as we'll see in Chapter 8.4, SM Higgs phenomenology is a superb base for beyond-the-SM (BSM) Higgs sectors. They're variations on a theme in some sense, with the occasional special channel thrown in, like the invisible Higgs search alluded to above. Our job will be to figure out what any new resonance is. But how do we go about doing that in a systematic way that's useful to theorists for constructing the New Standard Model?

For starters, we want to know the complete set of quantum numbers for any Higgs candidate we find. Standard Model expectations will probably prejudice us as to what they are (roughly, at least) based on which search channel a bump shows up in. But for the scenario above, I can envision at least three very reasonable yet completely different models that would give that kind of a result in early LHC running. We should keep in mind that further data may reveal more resonances – not everything is easy to see against backgrounds, or is produced with enough rate to emerge with only 1/10 of the planned LHC data. In some cases we would have to wait much longer, using data from the planned LHC luminosity upgrade (SLHC) [70]. New physics could also mean new quantum numbers that we don't yet know about, so we should be prepared to expand our list of measurements needed to sort out the theory, and spend time *now* thinking about what kinds of observables are even possible at the LHC. Some measurements will almost certainly require the clean environment of a future high-energy electron-positron machine like an ILC [71, 72]. The most complete picture would emerge only after combining results [73], which could take than a decade. In the meantime we might get a good picture of the new physics, but not its details.

Let's prepare a preliminary list of quantum numbers we need to measure for a candidate Higgs resonance, which I'll generically call ϕ. In brackets is the SM expectation. I'll order them in increasing level of difficulty. (See also the review article of Ref. [74].)

- electric charge [neutral]
- color charge [neutral]
- mass [free parameter]
- spin [0]
- CP [even]
- gauge coupling (g_{WWH}) [$SU(2)_L$ with tensor structure $g^{\mu\nu}$]
- Yukawa couplings [m_f/v]
- spontaneous symmetry breaking potential (self-couplings) [fixed by the mass]

Of course, the first two of those, electric and color charge, are known immediately from the decay products. (A non-color-singlet scalar is a radically different beast than the SM Higgs and would have dramatically different couplings and signatures.) Mass is also almost immediate, with some level of uncertainty that depends almost purely on detector effects. Spin and CP are related to some degree, and not entirely straightforward if the Higgs sector is non-minimal and contains CP violation. Gauge and Yukawa couplings are generally regarded as the most crucial observables, and in some sense I would agree. However, I would argue that the linchpin of spontaneous symmetry breaking (SSB) is the existence of a Higgs potential, which requires Higgs self-couplings. Measuring these and finding they match to some gauge theory with a SSB Higgs sector would to me be the most definitive proof of SSB, and strongly suggest that the Higgs is a fundamental scalar, not composite. It is also the most difficult task – perhaps not even possible.

A cautionary note: the results I show in this section are in general applicable only to the Standard Model Higgs! This point is often lost in many presentations highlighting the capabilities of various experiments, but it is very easy to understand. For example, if for some reason the Higgs sector has suppressed couplings to colored fermions, then any measurement of, say, the b Yukawa coupling, will be less precise, simply because the signal rate is lower, yet the background remains fixed. It's statistics!

8.3.1. *Mass measurement*

As already noted, our Higgs hunt pretty much gets us this quantum number immediately, but with some slop driven by detector performance. We want to measure it as accurately as possible, but in practice a GeV or so is good enough, because theoretical uncertainties in parameter fits tend to dominate for most BSM physics. (This is a long-standing problem in SUSY scenarios, for example. It may be that we need to know the Higgs mass theoretical prediction to four loops [75]; at present only a partial three-loop calculation is known [76], and only two-loop results exist in usable code [77].) Figure 8.32 shows the CMS and ILC expected Higgs mass precision as a function of M_H [78]. It varies, of course, because different decay modes are accessible at different M_H, and detector resolution depends on the final state. In general, photon pairs ($H \to \gamma\gamma$) and four leptons coming from Z pairs ($H \to ZZ \to \ell^+\ell^-\ell'^+\ell'^-$) will give the most precise measurement. As a rule of thumb, we may expect per-mille precision over a broad mass range, translating typically to a few hundred MeV.

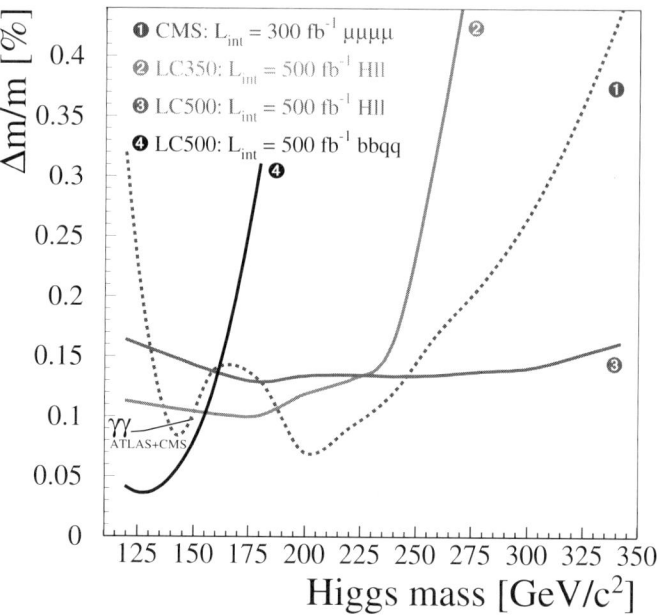

Fig. 8.32. Expected SM Higgs mass precision at LHC (for CMS; ATLAS will be slightly different but comparable) and a future ILC, as a function of Higgs mass [78].

8.3.2. *Spin & CP measurement*

Spin and CP (J^{PC}) experimental measurements are linked, because both require angular distributions to obtain. Numerous techniques have been proposed to address this, with significant overlap but also some unique features with each method. I'll highlight the leading proposals which garner the most attention from LHC experimentalists today.

From the observed final state we can tell that the Higgs candidate is a boson. We'll start by assuming that it may be spin 0, 1 or 2, but no higher[j]. Then we recall that the Yang-Landau Theorem [80] forbids a coupling between three $S=1$ bosons if two of them are identical. Thus, if we observe $\phi \to \gamma\gamma$, then our new object cannot be spin-1, and $C=1$. For the very curious student who wants to delve deeper, there is a recent report on CP Higgs studies at colliders [81].

---

[j]$S \geq 3$ fundamental particles are believed to have deep problems in renormalizable field theory [79].

8.3.2.1. Nelson technique

The first method is the oldest, developed by Nelson [82]. It assumes the object is a scalar or pseudoscalar[k] and relies on the decay angular distributions to a pair of EW gauge bosons, which decay further. The most practical aspect relevant for LHC Higgs physics is in essence a measurement of the relative azimuthal angle between the decay planes of two Z bosons in turn coming from the scalar decay, in the scalar particle's rest frame. See Fig. 8.33 for clarity. One bins the data in this distribution and fits to the equation:

$$F(\phi) = 1 + \alpha \cos(\phi) + \beta \cos(2\phi) \tag{8.12}$$

For a scalar, such as the SM Higgs, the coefficients α and β are functions of the scalar mass, and further we have the constraint that $\alpha(M_\phi) > \frac{1}{4}$. In contrast, for a pseudoscalar, $\alpha = 0$ and $\beta = -0.25$, independent of the mass.

Reference [83] was the first to apply this to the LHC Higgs physics program using detector simulation. Assuming 100 fb^{-1} of data, the study found that LHC could readily distinguish a SM Higgs from a pseudoscalar for $M_H > 200$ GeV, and from a spin-1 boson of either CP state from a little above that, but not right at 200 GeV; see Fig. 8.34. Applying this technique to $M_H < 200$ but above ZZ threshold was not examined.

As a practical matter, $H \to ZZ^{(*)}$ observation is assured only for both Z bosons decaying to leptons (e or μ), where there is essentially zero background. Unfortunately, this is an extremely tiny branching ratio, only 0.05% of all $H \to ZZ$ events. Some studies consider $jj\ell^+\ell^-$ channels, which is a ten-times larger sample, in an attempt to increase statistics, but this suffers from non-trivial QCD backgrounds.

8.3.2.2. CMMZ technique

Reference [84] provides an extension to the Nelson technique below ZZ threshold. Its full analysis is far more in-depth, discussing the angular behavior of the matrix elements for arbitrary boson spin and parity. It first demonstrates how objects of odd normality (spin times parity) can be discriminated via angular distributions, but for even normality require a further discriminant. That is, a $J^P = 2^+$ boson could mimic a SM Higgs in angular distribution below ZZ threshold. (Exotic higher spin states can

---

[k]A pseudoscalar doesn't couple at tree-level to W or Z, but can have a (large) loop-induced coupling.

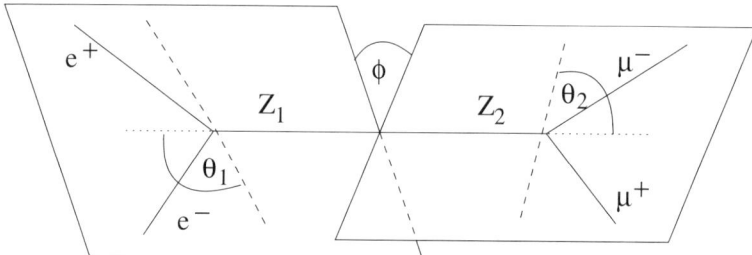

Fig. 8.33. Schematic of the azimuthal angle between the decay planes of Z bosons arising from massive scalar decay. All angles are in the scalar rest frame. Figure from Ref. [83].

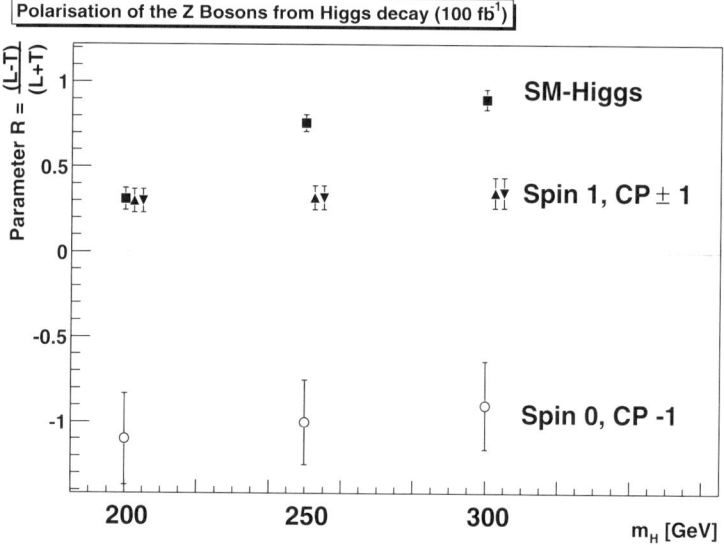

Fig. 8.34. Results of the LHC expectations spin/CP study of Ref. [83], showing how a SM Higgs could be distinguished from a pseudoscalar or spin-1 boson as a function of M_H.

be trivially ruled out via the lack of angular correlation between the beam and the object's flight direction.)

The key discriminant is the differential partial decay rate for the off-shell Z boson[1] It depends on the invariant mass of the final-state lepton

---
[1]Typically only one Z boson is off-shell for $M_H < 2M_Z$, but this ceases to be a good approximation at much lower (but observable) masses.

pair and is linear in Z^* velocity:

$$\frac{d\Gamma_H}{dM_*^2} \sim \beta \sim \sqrt{(M_H - M_Z)^2 - M_*^2} \qquad (8.13)$$

Figure 8.35 shows the predicted distributions for 150 GeV spin-0,1,2 even-normality objects as a function of M_*, the off-shellness of the $Z^*\ell^+\ell^-$. The histogram represents about 200 events that a SM Higgs would give in this channel after 300 fb^{-1} of data at LHC. Unfortunately there are no error bars, although one can estimate the statistical uncertainty for each bin as $\sqrt{N}$ and observe that the measurement is likely not spectacular. We can expect that CMS and ATLAS will eventually get around to quantifying the discriminating power, but it would not be surprising to learn that this measurement requires far more data, e.g. at the upgraded SLHC [70].

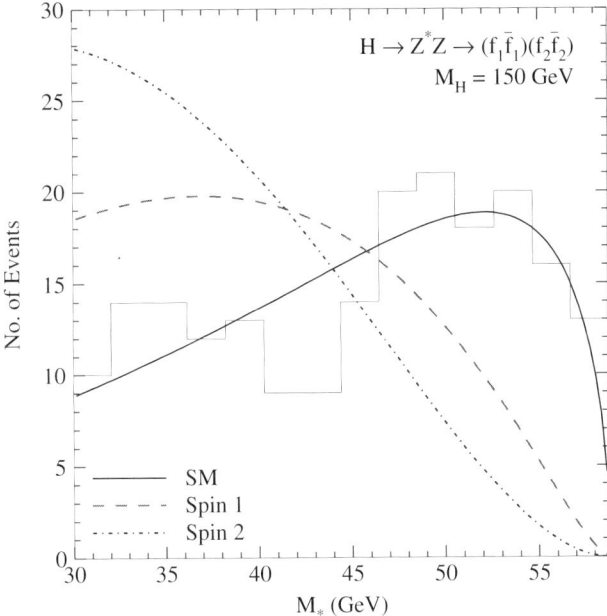

Fig. 8.35. Differential decay rate as a function of dilepton invariant mass of the off-shell Z^* in ZZ events, for a 150 GeV SM Higgs v. spin-1 and spin-2 objects of even normality and the same mass. The histogram is the SM Higgs case for 300 fb^{-1} of data at LHC. Figure from Ref. [84].

8.3.2.3. *CP and gauge vertex structure via WBF*

A third technique [85] takes a different approach, but addressing spin and CP in a slightly different way. Rather than examine Higgs decays, it notes that WBF Higgs production is observable for *any* Higgs mass, regardless of decay mode. Furthermore, the same HVV vertex appears on the production side for all masses, also independent of decay. More precisely, this vertex has the structure $g^{\mu\nu}HV_\mu V_\nu$ ($V = W, Z$). This tensor structure is not gauge invariant by itself. It must come from a gauge-invariant kinetic term $(D_\mu\Phi)^\dagger(D^\mu\Phi)$. Identifying it in experiment would go a long way to establishing that the scalar field is a remnant of spontaneous symmetry breaking.

For a scalar field which couples via higher-dimensional operators to two gauge bosons, however, we may write down the CP-even and CP-odd gauge-invariant D6 operators [86]:

$$\mathcal{L}_6 = \frac{g^2}{2\Lambda_{6,e}}(\Phi^\dagger\Phi)W^+_{\mu\nu}W^{-\mu\nu} + \frac{g^2}{2\Lambda_{6,o}}(\Phi^\dagger\Phi)\widetilde{W}^+_{\mu\nu}W^{-\mu\nu} \qquad (8.14)$$

where Λ_6 is the scale of new physics that is integrated out, $W^{\mu\nu}$ is the W boson field strength tensor, and $\widetilde{W} = \epsilon_{\alpha\beta\mu\nu}W^{\alpha\beta}$ is its dual. After expanding Φ with a vev and radial excitation, we obtain two D5 operators:

$$\mathcal{L}_5 = \frac{1}{\Lambda_{5,e}}HW^+_{\mu\nu}W^{-\mu\nu} + \frac{1}{\Lambda_{5,o}}H\widetilde{W}^+_{\mu\nu}W^{-\mu\nu} \qquad (8.15)$$

where Λ_5 are dimensionful but now parameterize both the D6 coefficients and the Φ vev.

These two D5 operators produce very distinctive matrix element behavior. Recalling that the external gauge bosons in WBF are actually virtual and connect to external fermion currents, the initial-state scattered quarks, we derive the following approximate relations for the CP-even operator, using $J_{1,2}$ for the incoming fermion currents:

$$\mathcal{M}_{e,5} \propto \frac{1}{\Lambda_{e,5}}J_1^\mu J_2^\nu\left[g_{\mu\nu}(q_1\cdot q_2) - q_{1,\nu}q_{2,\mu}\right] \sim \frac{1}{\Lambda_{e,5}}[J_1^0 J_2^0 - J_1^3 J_2^3]\,\vec{p}_T^{\,j1}\cdot\vec{p}_T^{\,j2} \qquad (8.16)$$

That is, the amplitude is proportional to the tagging jets' transverse momentum dot product. This is easy to measure experimentally – we just plot the azimuthal angular distribution, i.e. angular separation in the plane perpendicular to the beam. It will be minimal, nearly zero, for $\phi_{jj} = \pi/4$. In contrast, the $g^{\mu\nu}$ tensor structure of the SM Higgs mechanism does not correlate the tagging jets. The CP-odd D5 operator is different and more

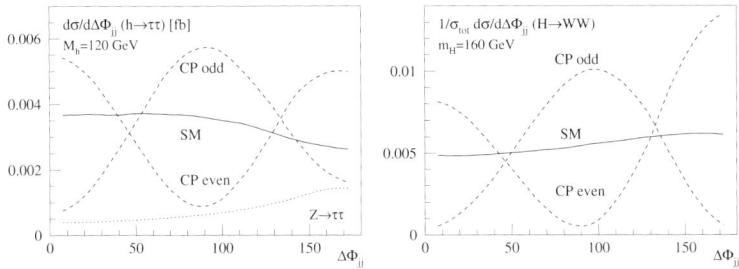

Fig. 8.36. Azimuthal angular distributions of the tagging jets in WBF production of a SM Higgs v. scalar field coupled to weak bosons via CP-even/odd D6 operators. The dotted line in the left panel is the SM background, which is added to the signal curves. Figures from Ref. [85].

complex, but may be understood by noting that it contains a Levi-Civita tensor $\epsilon^{\mu\nu\rho\delta}$ connecting the external fermion momenta. This is non-zero only when the four external momenta are independent, i.e. not coplanar. Thus this distribution will be zero for $\phi_{jj} = 0, \pi$.

Figure 8.36 shows the results of a parton-level simulation for scalars in both the mass range where decays to taus would be used, and where $\phi \to W^+W^-$ dominates. The SM signal curve is not entirely flat due to kinematic cuts imposed on the final state to ID all objects. The D5 operators produce behavior qualitatively distinct from spontaneous symmetry breaking, with minima for the distributions exactly where expected, and orthogonal from each other. It would be essentially trivial to distinguish the cases from each other shortly after discovery, regardless of M_H and the particular channel used to discover the Higgs candidate. A key requirement for this, of course, is that the discovery searches don't use this distribution to separate signal from background.

Now, what happens if the Higgs indeed arises from SSB, but new physics generates sizable D6 operators? Since $H_{\rm SM}$ is CP-even, a CP-even D5 operator would interfere with the SM amplitude, while a CP-odd contribution would remain independent. This is illustrated in the left panel of Fig. 8.37. The obvious thing to do is create an asymmetry observable sensitive to this interference:

$$A_\phi = \frac{\sigma(\Delta\phi_{jj} < \pi/2) - \sigma(\Delta\phi_{jj} > \pi/2)}{\sigma(\Delta\phi_{jj} < \pi/2) + \sigma(\Delta\phi_{jj} > \pi/2)} \qquad (8.17)$$

With only 100 fb^{-1} of data at LHC (one experiment), this asymmetry would have access to $\Lambda_6 \sim 1$ TeV, which is itself within the reach of LHC,

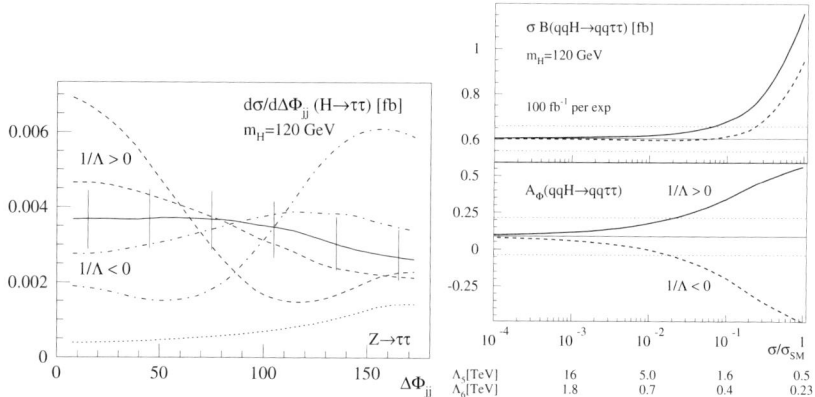

Fig. 8.37. Left: As in Fig. 8.36, but with interference between the SM Higgs and a CP-even D5 operator. Right: the effective reach in $\Lambda_{5,e}$ for 100 fb^{-1} at LHC, using only the rate information (top) or the asymmetry (bottom). Figures from Ref. [85].

likely resulting in new physics observation directly. One caveat: the study Ref. [85] was done before the $gg \to Hgg$ contamination [60] was known, which will complicate this measurement.

8.3.2.4. Spin and CP at an ILC

The much cleaner, low-background environment of e^+e^- collisions would be an excellent environment to study a new resonance's spin and CP properties. J^{PC} can in fact be determined completely model-independently. Recalling the LEP search, the canonical production mechanism is $e^+e^- \to ZH$. We would identify the Z via its decay to leptons, and sum over all Higgs decays (this is possible using the recoil mass technique, coming up in Sec. 8.3.4). J and P are completely determined by a combination of the cross section rise at threshold and the polar angle of the Z flight direction in the lab, shown in the left panel of Fig. 8.38. The differential cross section is [71]:

$$\frac{d\sigma}{d\cos\theta_Z} \propto \beta\big[1 + a\beta^2 \sin^2\theta_Z + b\eta\beta\cos\theta_Z + \eta^2\beta^2(1 + \cos^2\theta_Z)\big] \quad (8.18)$$

where a and b depend on the EW couplings and Z boson mass, η is a general pseudoscalar (loop-induced) coupling and β is the velocity. Far more sophisticated analyses techniques exist, often called "optimal observable" analyses [87], but are only for the terminally curious.

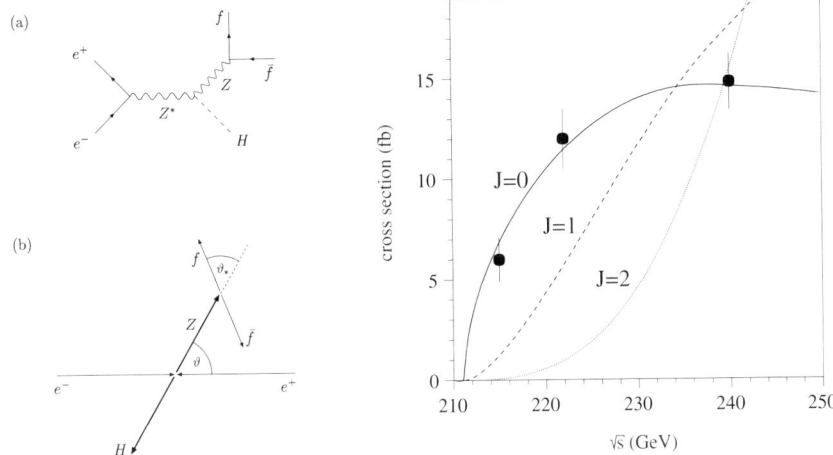

Fig. 8.38. Left: Feynman diagram for $e^+e^- \to ZH$ and schematic [88] showing the analyzing angles. Right: curves showing the threshold rate dependence for $J = 0, 1, 2$ states in this channel [71].

If one would have the liberty to perform a threshold scan of $Z\phi$ production at an ILC, distinguishing given-normality $J = 0, 1, 2$ states is straightforward due to their different β-dependence. For $J = 0$ it is linear, but for higher spin is higher-power in β [88]. The qualitative behavior is shown in the right panel of Fig. 8.38, complete with error bars for the SM Higgs case. However, while the physics is solid, experiments in the past have generally proved to be a horse race for highest energy, so there is no guarantee that one would have threshold scan data available. The angular distribution fortunately works at all energies.

8.3.3. *Higgs couplings at LHC*

Now to something much harder. It's commonly believed that LHC cannot measure Higgs couplings, only ratios of BRs [42]. This is incorrect, but requires a little explanation to understand why people previously believed in a limitation.

First, let me state that the LHC doesn't measure couplings or any other quantum number directly. It measures *rates*. (This is true for any particle physics experiment.) From those we extract various $\sigma_i \cdot \mathrm{BR}_j$ by removing detector, soft QCD and phase space effects, among other things, using Monte Carlo simulations based on known physics inputs.

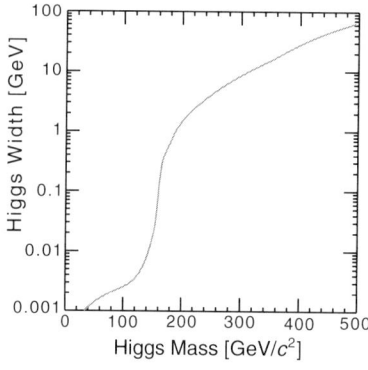 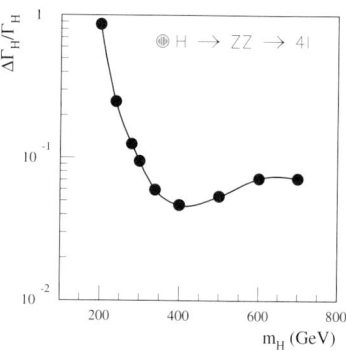

Fig. 8.39. Left: Standard Model Higgs total width as a function of M_H. Right: expected experimental precision on Γ_H at ATLAS using the $gg \to H \to ZZ \to 4\ell$ channel [42] (CMS similar).

Second, we note that for a light Higgs, which has a very small width (cf. Sec. 8.2.1.1), the Higgs production cross section is proportional to the partial width for Higgs decay to the initial state (the Narrow Width Approximation, NWA). That is, $\sigma_{gg \to H} \propto \Gamma_{H \to gg}$. Similarly, $\sigma_{\text{WBF}} \propto \Gamma_{H \to W^+W^-}$. The student who has never seen this may easily derive it by recalling the definition of cross section and partial decay width – they share the same matrix elements and differ only by phase space factors[m]. Typically we abbreviate these partial widths with a subscript identifying the final state particle, thus we have Γ_g, Γ_γ, Γ_b, etc. Since a BR is just the partial decay width over the total width, we then write:

$$(\sigma_H \cdot \text{BR})_i \propto \left(\frac{\Gamma_p \Gamma_d}{\Gamma_H}\right)_i \quad (8.19)$$

where Γ_p and Γ_d are the "production" and decay widths, respectively.

Third, count up the number of observables we have and measurements we can make. Assuming we have a decay channel for each possible Higgs decay (which we don't), we're still one short: Γ_H, the total width. Now, if the width is large enough, larger than detector resolution, we can measure it directly. Figure 8.39 shows that this can happen only for $M_H \gtrsim 230$ GeV or so [42], far above where EW precision data suggests we'll find the (SM) Higgs. Below this mass range, we have to think of something else.

---

[m] Well, slightly more than that in the case of WBF, but the argument holds after careful consideration.

In the SM, we know precisely what Γ_H is: the sum of all the partial widths. For the moment let's assume we have access to all possible decays or partial widths via production, ignore the super-rare decay modes to first- and second-generation fermions. This is a mild assumption, because if for some reason the muon or electron Yukawa were anywhere close to that of taus, where it might contribute to the total width, it would immediately be observable. The list of possible measurements we can form from accessible $(\sigma \cdot \text{BR})_{i,exp}$ is:

$$X_\gamma, X_\tau, X_W, X_Z, Y_\gamma, Y_W, Y_Z, Z_b, Z_\gamma, Z_W \qquad (8.20)$$

where X_i correspond to WBF channels, Y_i are inclusive Higgs production, and Z_i are top quark associated production[n] We could easily add measurements like X_μ, Y_e, etc. if we wanted, because measuring zero for any observable is still a measurement – it simply places a constraint on that combination of partial widths or couplings.

In the original implementation of this idea [89], the authors noted that the $t\bar{t}H, H \to b\bar{b}$ channel won't work, so there is no access at LHC to Γ_b. However, there is access to Γ_τ. In the SM, the b and τ Yukawa couplings are related by $r_b = \Gamma_b/\Gamma_\tau = 3c_{\text{QCD}} m_b^2/m_\tau^2$, where c_{QCD} contains QCD higher-order corrections and phase space effects. Γ_W and Γ_Z are furthermore related by $SU(2)_L$, although we don't need to use it. Now write down the derived quantity

$$\widetilde{\Gamma}_W = X_\tau(1 + r_b) + X_W + X_Z + X_\gamma + \widetilde{X}_g = \left(\sum \Gamma_i\right)\frac{\Gamma_W}{\Gamma_H} = (1-\epsilon)\Gamma_W \qquad (8.21)$$

where $\widetilde{X}_g$ is constructed from X_W, X_γ, Y_W and Y_γ. Although Γ_γ is an infinitesimal contribution to Γ_H, it is important as above, and it contains both the top quark Yukawa and W gauge-Higgs couplings. Our error is contained in ϵ and is typically small. This provides a good <u>lower</u> bound on Γ_W from data. The total width is then

$$\Gamma_H = \frac{\widetilde{\Gamma}_W^2}{X_W} \qquad (8.22)$$

and the error goes as $(1-\epsilon)^{-2}$. Assuming systematic uncertainties of 5% on WBF and 20% on inclusive production, this would achieve about a 10% measurement of Γ_W and $10-20\%$ on the total width for $M_H < 200$ GeV.

---

[n]For this case, we actually use the Yukawa coupling squared (y_t^2) instead of Γ_t, because decays to top quarks is kinematically forbidden. But this is irrelevant for our argument.

Voilà! We have circumvented the naïve problem of not enough independent measurements. The astute observer should immediately protest, however, and rightly so. The result is achieved with a little too much confidence that the SM is correct. Not only does the trick rely on a very strong assumption about the b Yukawa coupling, but there could be funny business in the up-quark sector, giving a large partial width to e.g. charm quarks, which would not be observable either via production (too little initial-state charm, and anyhow unidentifiable) or decay (charm can't be efficiently tagged). Nevertheless, this was a useful exercise, because a much more rigorous, model-independent method is closely based on it.

The more sophisticated method is a powerful least-likelihood fit to data using a more accurate relation than Eq. 8.19 between data and theory [90]:

$$\sigma_H \cdot \mathrm{BR}(H \to xx) = \frac{\sigma_H^{\mathrm{SM}}}{\Gamma_p^{\mathrm{SM}}} \cdot \boxed{\frac{\Gamma_p \Gamma_d}{\Gamma_H}} \qquad (8.23)$$

where the partial widths in the box are the true values to be extracted from data, and the $(\sigma/\Gamma)_{\mathrm{SM}}$ ratio in front quantifies all effects shoved into Monte Carlo using SM values: phase space, QCD corrections, detector, etc. As before, the "sum" of all channels provides a solid lower bound on Γ_H, simply because some rate in each of a number of channels requires some minimum coupling. But these are found by a fit, rather than theory assumptions. It also properly takes into account all theory and experimental systematic and statistical uncertainties assigned to each channel. We then need only a firm upper bound on Γ_H and the fit then extracts *absolute* couplings (transformed from the partial widths). This bound comes from unitarity: the gauge-Higgs coupling can be depressed via mixing in any multi-doublet model, as well as any number of additional singlets, but it cannot exceed the SM value, which is strictly defined by unitarity. Thus $\Gamma_V \leq \Gamma_V^{\mathrm{SM}}$. (This bound is invalid in triplet models, but these have other characteristics which should make themselves apparent in experiment.) The WBF $H \to W^+W^-$ channel then provides an upper limit on Γ_H via its measurement of Γ_V^2/Γ_H.

The method can be further armored against BSM alterations by including the invisible Higgs channel, allowing additional loop contributions, and so on. Of course, the more possible deviations one allows, the larger the fit uncertainties become. We see this in the differences between the left and right panels of Fig. 8.40 [90]. It is obvious that LHC's weakness is lack of access to $H \to b\bar{b}$. Nevertheless, LHC can measure absolute Higgs couplings with useful constraints on BSM physics. This is especially

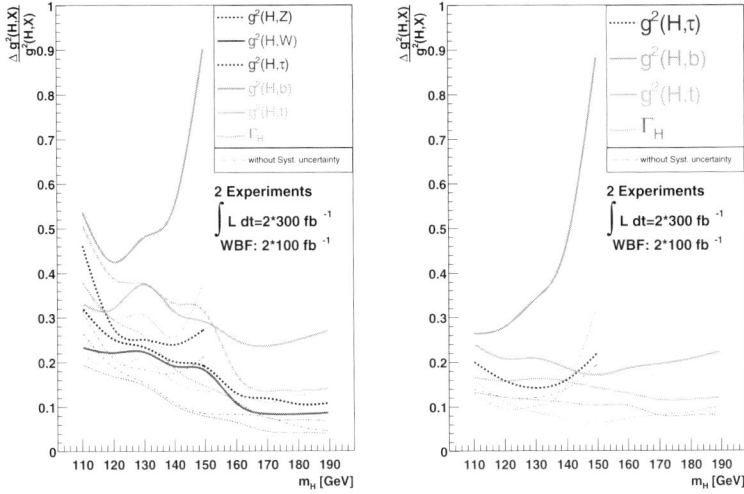

Fig. 8.40. Left: a least likelihood general fit on simulated LHC data, with no additional assumptions about the Higgs sector. Right: the fit assuming no new particles appear in Higgs loop-induced decays, and the gauge-Higgs coupling fixed exactly to the SM value. Figures from Ref. [90].

true for $M_H \gtrsim 150$ GeV, where LHC can achieve $\mathcal{O}(10\%)$ precision on the gauge-Higgs couplings and the total width.

The fit as implemented in Ref. [90] fixes M_H. This is a slight cheat, since for some M_H the BRs change quite rapidly, and a 1-2 GeV uncertainty can lead to a lot of slop in the coupling extraction. This is especially critical for the Higgs sector of the Minimal Supersymmetric Standard Model (MSSM). Eventually a fit to M_H will also have to be included, which will degrade measurement precision somewhat.

At the same time, there is cause for optimism. The results of Fig. 8.40 were based on very conservative, almost pessimistic assumptions: overly-large systematic errors, WBF not being possible at all at high-luminosity running, no minijet veto for WBF (cf. Sec. 8.2.3.3), and lack of progress in higher-order QCD calculations for signals and backgrounds. The reality is that significant progress has been made regarding QCD corrections, and we'll see one example shortly. Also, everyone knows that the minijet veto is a qualitatively correct aspect of the physics, we just can't accurately predict its impact. Early LHC data from Zjj production should take care of this. Furthermore, ATLAS and CMS experimentalists fully expect WBF to work at high-luminosity LHC running, they just don't have full simulation results for the probable efficiencies. Also, we may expect far better performance in the WBF $H \to \tau^+\tau^-$ channels as discussed in Sec. 8.2.3.4. Finally, if new physics exists up to a few TeV, it will be observable and we can take it into accounts in Higgs loop-induced decays.

Now to QCD corrections. Ref. [90] used large QCD uncertainties for $\sigma_{gg \to H}$ and Γ_g, 20% each, which is the correct NNLO uncertainty for each by itself. However, these two quantities appear as a ratio in our observables formula, Eq. 8.23. As pointed out in Ref. [91], most of these uncertainties drop out in the ratio. The reason for this is that the QCD corrections to the cross section and partial width are largely the same:

$$\Gamma \sim \alpha_s^2(\mu_R) C_1^2(\mu_R)[1 + \alpha_s(\mu_R) X_1 + ...] \qquad (8.24)$$

$$\sigma \sim \alpha_s^2(\mu_R) C_1^2(\mu_R)[1 + \alpha_s(\mu_R) Y_1 + ...] \qquad (8.25)$$

The correct uncertainty on the ratio is 5%, which will have an enormous impact on the fits of Fig. 8.40. We eagerly await new results from this and other improvements!

8.3.4. *Higgs couplings at an ILC*

Measuring Higgs couplings at an e^+e^- collider would be far more straightforward and rely on far fewer theoretical assumptions. Between that and being a colorless collision environment, it would also involve far fewer systematic uncertainties. I'll outline the basic idea.

In fixed-beam collisions it's possible to measure the *total ZH* production rate. To see this, we just apply a little relativistic kinematics, rewriting the invariant M_H^2:

$$M_H^2 = p_H^2 = (p_+ + p_- - p_Z)^2 = s + M_Z^2 - 2E_Z\sqrt{s} \qquad (8.26)$$

We see that observing the Higgs and measuring its total rate boils down to observing Z bosons via their extremely sharp dimuon peak and plotting this recoil mass. Figure 8.41 shows what the resulting event rate looks like in this distribution. The Higgs peak is clearly visible and sidebands allow one to subtract the SM background in the signal region. This captures all possible Higgs decays, even though that aren't taggable or even identifiable, simply by ignoring everything in the event except for the Z dimuons.

Simulations [71] suggest that the recoil mass technique would allow for about a 2.5% absolute measurement of the ZH rate. Since the cross section depends on the Z–Higgs coupling squared, the coupling uncertainty is then about a percent.

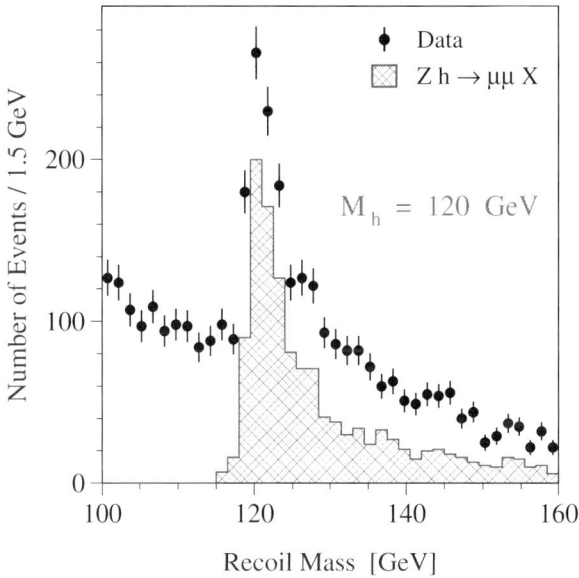

Fig. 8.41. Event rate of the recoil mass for $e^+e^- \to \mu^+\mu^- + X$ at a future high-energy linear collider. ZH production will fall into this sample, but the Higgs decays are ignored, thus capturing the total Higgs production rate. (Figure modified from Ref. [92] for a public talk by one of the authors.)

Getting from this one coupling and the total rate to any other coupling is formulaic:

1. In the total rate, measure the best branching ratios, whatever they may be. Depending on the mass and detector performance, that's likely one of $b\bar{b}$, $\gamma\gamma$ or W^+W^- decays.
2. Now look in WBF Higgs production[o] with the Higgs decaying to the same best final state. This yields the partial width Γ_W.
3. Calculate the total Higgs width as $\Gamma_W/BR(H \to W^+W^-)$.
4. Any other measured BR now gives that individual partial width, therefore the relevant coupling (or couplings for some loop-induced decays).

Table 8.2 enumerates the results of ILC simulation for select M_H [93]. (Clearly more thorough work should be done here.) There are a few noteworthy features. First, $H \to b\bar{b}$ would be accessible even as a rare BR at

---

[o]For a linear collider this is both $e^+e^- \to e^+e^-H$ and $e^+e^- \to \nu\bar{\nu}H$, since e and ν are distinguishable. Experimentally they become two different analyses.

Table 8.2. Estimated precision on various SM Higgs partial widths for a few select values of M_H, from measurements at a future e^+e^- collider [93].

M_H (GeV)	120	140	160	180	200	220
Decay	Relative precision on Γ_i (%)					
$b\bar{b}$	1.9	2.6	6.5	12.0	17.0	28.0
$c\bar{c}$	8.1	19.0				
$\tau^+\tau^-$	5.0	8.0				
gg	4.8	14.0				
W^+W^-	3.6	2.5	2.1			
ZZ				16.9		
$\gamma\gamma$	23.0					
$Z\gamma$		27.0				

larger M_H, due to the nearly QCD-free collision environment. Second, a weak measurement of $H \to c\bar{c}$ should be possible, for the same reason, and due to the superior b v. c resolution of the next generation of collider detectors. Third, $H \to jj$ is also accessible. This would be attributed to gg, which is a mild theoretical assumption. It is in principle sanity-checkable by the absence of an anomalous high-x Higgs production rate at LHC, which would come from sea or valence quarks and a non-SM coupling to lighter fermions (which would be difficult to accommodate theoretically, so not expected).

But what about the top Yukawa coupling? Its anticipated value of approximately one is curious enough to warrant special attention. A light Higgs can't decay to top quark pairs, so we'd have to rely on top quark associated production, as at LHC but without all the nasty QCD backgrounds. However, the event rate is far lower than at LHC and would require an 800 GeV machine collecting 1000 fb^{-1} [94], the planned lifetime of a next-generation second-stage machine (justifying my previous statement about the drive to go to maximum energy and sit there). One study combined expected LHC and ILC results [73, 95], and there are more recent results for ILC, summarized in Fig. 8.42 [96]. SLHC and an ILC would be complementary, granting superb coverage of M_H for a y_t measurement at the 10% level.

More sophisticated LC Higgs coupling analyses exist [87], but aren't often reviewed. They use a more complicated "optimal observables" (detailed kinematic shape information, for example) scheme. It's more powerful, but doesn't lend itself to the simplistic formulaic approach I just discussed.

I should emphasize that the results I reviewed are relevant only for the Standard Model. If the Higgs sector is non-minimal, or any new physics

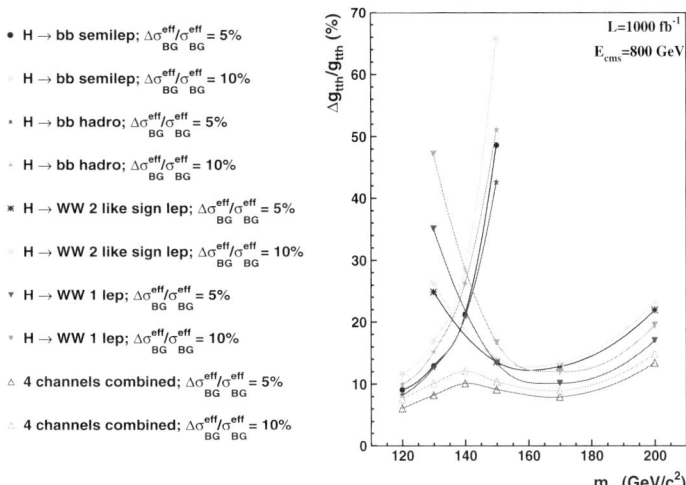

Fig. 8.42. Top Yukawa coupling measurement expectations for a future 800 GeV e^+e^- collider [96].

appears at the weak scale, it could result in altered couplings (and usually does; see Chapter 8.4). If they're suppressed, the event rate goes down, resulting in greater uncertainty. This is often glossed over or ignored in discussions of Higgs phenomenology, but is a potential reality and something we'd just have to lump. Nevertheless, it should be clear by now that an ILC would be a spectacular experiment for precision Higgs measurements.

8.3.5. Higgs potential

Finally we arrive at the most difficult Higgs property to test, the potential. This is the hallmark of spontaneous symmetry breaking, thus ranks at least as high in priority as finding Yukawa couplings proportional to fermion masses. To see what's involved, let's review the SM Higgs potential. The potential is normally written as:

$$V(\Phi) = \mu^2 \Phi^\dagger \Phi + \lambda (\Phi^\dagger \Phi)^2 \tag{8.27}$$

where Φ is our $SU(2)_L$ complex doublet of scalar fields. The Higgs spontaneous symmetry-breaking mechanism is what happens to the Lagrangian when $\mu^2 < 0$ and the field's global minimum shifts to $v = \sqrt{-\mu^2/\lambda}$. We then expand $\Phi \to v + H(x)$ (ignoring the Goldstone modes which you learned about in Sally Dawson's lectures) where $H(x)$ is the radial excitation, the physical Higgs boson. The Higgs mass squared is then $2v^2\lambda$, and is the only free parameter, although constrained (weakly) by EW precision fits. The student performing this expansion will also notice HHH and $HHHH$ Lagrangian terms, which are self-interactions of the Higgs boson. The three- and four-point couplings are $-6v\lambda$ and -6λ, respectively[p].

To measure the potential is to measure these self-couplings and check their relation to the measured Higgs mass. Our phenomenological approach is to rewire the Higgs potential in terms of independent parameters and the Higgs candidate field η_H:

$$V(\eta_H) = \frac{1}{2} M_H^2 \eta_H^2 + \lambda v \eta_H^3 + \frac{1}{4}\tilde{\lambda}\eta_H^4 \qquad (8.28)$$

λ and $\tilde{\lambda}$ are now free parameters, which we measure from the direct production rate of HH and HHH events. This will ultimately be a voyage of frustration.

8.3.5.1. HH production at LHC

We begin with Higgs pairs at LHC. The dominant production mechanism is gluon fusion, $gg \to HH$ [97–99]. The Feynman diagrams are shown in Fig. 8.43. The first diagram is off-shell single Higgs production which split via the three-point self-coupling to a pair of on-shell Higgses, which then decay promptly. The second diagram is a box (four-point) loop contribution which involves only the top quark Yukawa coupling. Interestingly, the two diagrams interfere destructively and have a rather large cancellation. This means the rate is small [100], as shown in Fig. 8.44, making our life difficult with a small statistical sample. On the other hand, the destructive interference will turn out to be crucial to making constructive statements about the self-coupling λ.

The left panel of Fig. 8.44 tells us that we can expect $\mathcal{O}(10k)$ light Higgs pair events per detector over the expected 300 fb^{-1} lifetime of the first LHC run, and ten times that at SLHC. That sounds like a lot, but keep in mind that both Higgses have to decay to a final state we can observe, which will reduce the captured rate to something much smaller. Then we have to consider what backgrounds affect each candidate channel.

The right panel of Fig. 8.44 shows selected Higgs pair branching ratios. At low mass, decays to b pairs dominate, as expected, while for $M_H \gtrsim 135$ GeV mass it's W pairs. We can immediately discount the $4b$ final state

---
[p]Don't forget the identical-particle combinatorial factors.

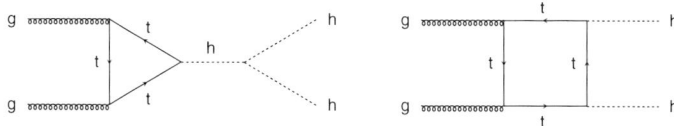

Fig. 8.43. Feynman diagrams for the dominant Higgs pair production rate at LHC, $gg \to HH$.

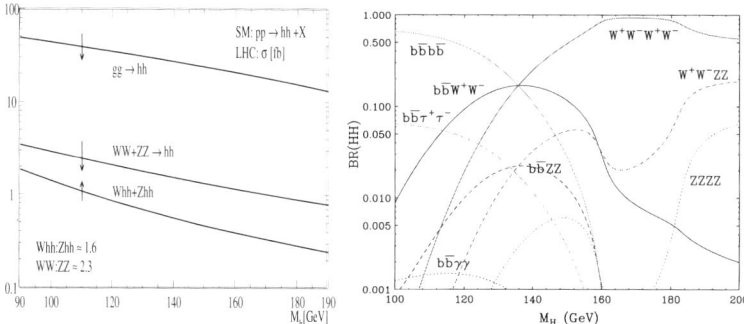

Fig. 8.44. Left: Higgs pair production cross sections at LHC as a function of M_H [100]. Arrows show the change of the cross section as λ is increase, and the tips are at one-half and twice the SM value. Right: Higgs pair branching ratios as a function of M_H, calculated using HDECAY [22].

as hopeless, based on what we already learned about QCD backgrounds – but $4W$ is promising for higher masses. The next-largest mode from those two is $b\bar{b}W^+W^-$, which unfortunately is the same final state as the far larger top quark pair cross section. A few minutes' investigation causes this to be discarded, even after trying various invariant mass constraints; b pair mass resolution is just not good enough. The $b\bar{b}\tau^+\tau^-$ mode has very low backgrounds, comparable to the signal, but suffers hugely from lack of statistics, due to low efficiency for subsequent tau decays. However, the rare decay mode $b\bar{b}\gamma\gamma$ is extremely clean and worth further consideration at low masses.

$HH \to W^+W^-W^+W^-$ at LHC

$HH \to W^+W^-W^+W^-$ has myriad decays, but for triggering purposes and to get away from QCD background sources of leptons (like top quarks) we need to select special multilepton final states [101]. The most likely

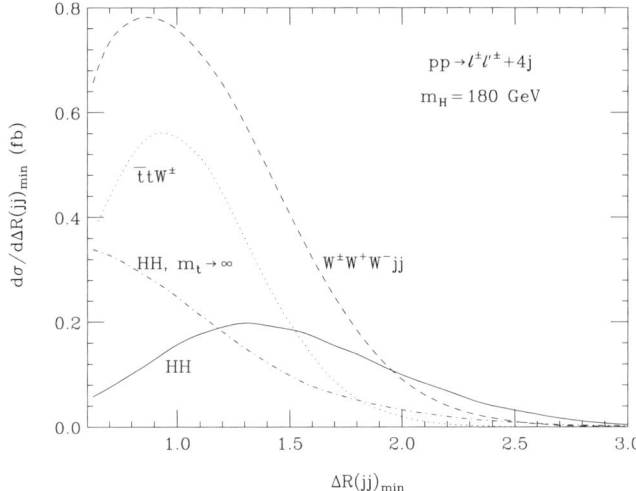

Fig. 8.45. Differential cross section as a function of the minimum jet pair lego plot separation for $\ell^+\ell^- + 4j$ at events at LHC. The solid curve is the correct distribution using exact matrix elements for HH, while the dash-dotted curve comes from effective-Lagrangian matrix elements where the top quark mass is taken to infinity. Figure taken from Ref. [101].

accessible channels are same-sign lepton pairs, $\ell^\pm\ell^\pm + 4j$, and three leptons, $\ell^+\ell^-\ell^\pm + 2j$, since the principal QCD SM backgrounds can't easily mimic them. Note that because of multiple neutrinos departing the detector unobserved, complete reconstruction is not possible. The principle backgrounds are $WWWjj$, $t\bar{t}W$, $t\bar{t}j$, $t\bar{t}Z/\gamma^*$ and $WZ + 4j$, but we also need to consider $t\bar{t}t\bar{t}$, $4W$, $W^+W^- + 4j$, W^+W^-Zjj as well as double parton scattering and overlapping events. The calculation of all of these is technical so I won't go into it, rather simply mention a few noteworthy points.

The first is a warning about using the $gg \to HH$ effective Lagrangian in practical calculations. It is still a mystery why the leading term in the $\sqrt{\hat{s}}/m_t$ expansion [97] should get the overall rate so close that of an exact calculation [98], but it does. Because of that, nobody has ever bothered to calculate higher-order terms in the effective Lagrangian expansion; in any case, the exact results are available, as well as NLO in QCD [99]. However, the leading terms in the expansion cancel too much close to threshold, yielding incorrect kinematics [101], as can be seen from Fig. 8.45. One should thus use only the exact matrix element results for practical $gg \to HH$ phenomenology.

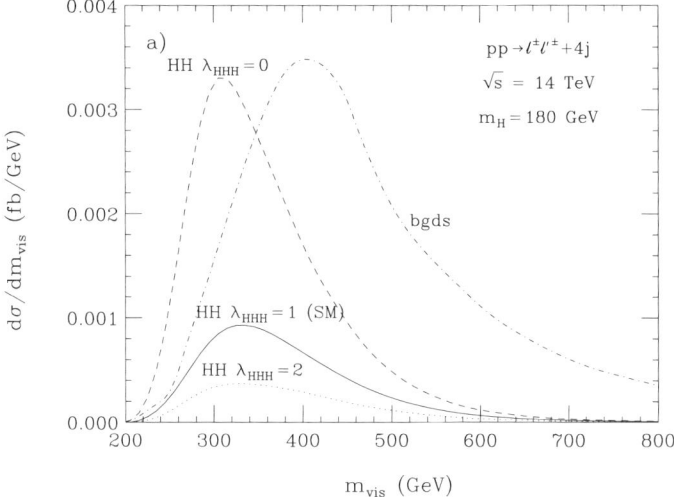

Fig. 8.46. Visible invariant mass distribution for same-sign dilepton plus four jet event at LHC [101]. All SM backgrounds are summed into one curve, while the $gg \to HH$ signal is shown separately, for the SM value of self-coupling λ, twice that value, and zero.

The second point is that our main systematic uncertainties will be our limited knowledge of the top quark Yukawa coupling, which drives the production rate, and the BR to W^+W^-, which drive the decay fraction. These must be known very precisely for any measurement to be useful.

We will need a discriminating observable to separate signal from background. We can speculate that nearly all the signal's kinematic information is encoded in the invariant mass of the visible final state particles, so let's construct a new variable, m_{vis}:

$$m_{vis}^2 = \left[\sum_i E_i\right]^2 - \left[\sum_i \mathbf{p}_i\right]^2 \quad (8.29)$$

where i are all the leptons and jets in the event. We suspect a difference because the signal is a two-body process, which is threshold-like, while the backgrounds are multi-body processes which peak at much larger m_{vis} than the sum of their heavy resonances' masses.

Figure 8.46 displays the fruits of parameterizing our ignorance (or rather, the detector's). The separation between signal and background is exactly as expected: the signal peaks much lower, allowing a χ^2 fit to distinguish it from the backgrounds. But the plot also reveals a saving grace

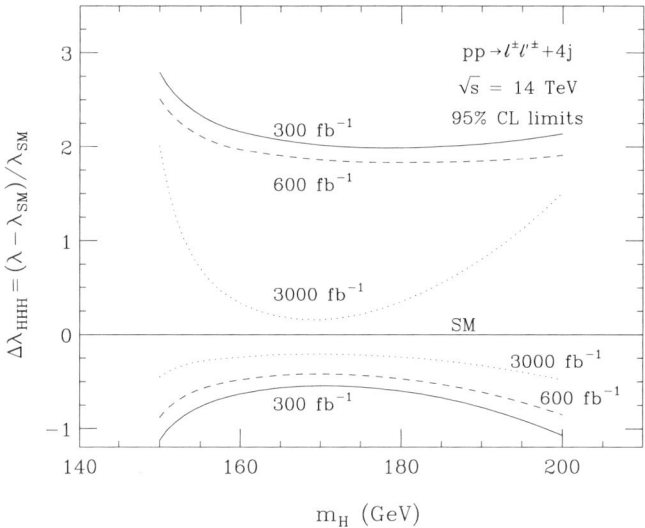

Fig. 8.47. 95% CL limits achievable at LHC on the shifted Higgs triple self-coupling (see text), $\triangle\lambda$, for LHC and SLHC expected luminosities [101].

in the destructive interference between triangle and box loop diagrams. If spontaneous symmetry breaking isn't the right description and there is no Higgs potential, then $\lambda = 0$ and the lack of destructive interference gives a wildly larger signal cross section, which is far easier to observe.

Figure 8.47 summarizes the results of Ref. [101]. It plots 95% CL limits on the shifted self-coupling, $\triangle\lambda = (\lambda - \lambda_{SM})/\lambda_{SM}$. This is somewhat easier to understand: zero is the SM, and -1 corresponds to no self-coupling, or no potential. For $M_H > 150$ GeV, the LHC can exclude $\lambda = 0$ at (for some M_H much greater than) 2σ with only the LHC. After SLHC running, this becomes a $20 - 30\%$ measurement, if other systematics are under control. Here, they're assumed to be smaller than the statistical uncertainty.

Another potential systematics issue is minimum bias, the presence of extra jets in an event which don't come from the primary hard scattering. Here, they could be confused with jets from the W bosons, causing a distortion of m_{vis}. ATLAS has investigated this and found it to not be a concern – the shape of m_{vis} for the signal remains largely unaltered [102].

$HH \to b\bar{b}\gamma\gamma$ at LHC

We've already ruled out as viable the vast majority of Higgs pair BRs for $M_H \lesssim 150$ GeV due to QCD backgrounds or too-small efficiencies.

Table 8.3. The major ID efficiencies and fake photon rejection factors at LHC. Note the two values for $P_{j\to\gamma}$, which represent the current uncertainty in detector capability for fake photon rejection. The true value won't be known until data is collected. See Ref. [103] for details.

	ϵ_γ	ϵ_μ	$P_{c\to b}$	$P_{j\to b}$	$P_{j\to\gamma}^{hi}$	$P_{j\to\gamma}^{lo}$
LHC	80%	90%	1/13	1/140	1/1600	1/2500
SLHC	80%	90%	1/13	1/23	1/1600	1/2500

However, the rare decay mode to $b\bar{b}\gamma\gamma$ is worth a closer look [103]. There are many backgrounds to consider, coming from b or c jets plus photons, or other jets which fake photons, just as in the single Higgs to photon pairs case. Table 8.3 highlights the major ID efficiencies and fake photon rejection factors at LHC and SLHC relevant for us. The backgrounds are all calculable at LO, but with significant uncertainties, probably a factor of two or more. However, that won't be a concern as we can identify distributions useful for measuring the background in the non-signal region. Note that with this channel we can completely reconstruct both Higgs bosons.

The background QCD uncertainties have a work-around. There are two angular distributions in the lego plot which look very different for the signal, principally because scalars decay isotropically and thus are uncorrelated, while the QCD backgrounds have spin correlations. The two distributions are shown in Fig. 8.48. The differences are rather dramatic (and even more so in 2-D distributions). Tevatron's experiments CDF and DØ have used such a pseudo-sideband analysis for some time to measure a background in a non-signal region to normalize their Monte Carlo tools, then extrapolating

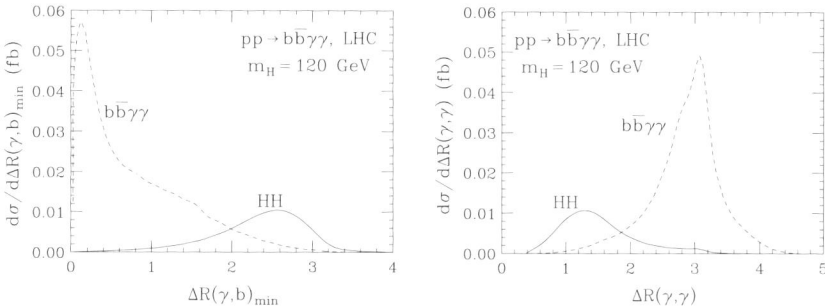

Fig. 8.48. Angular separations in the lego plot for b jets and photons in $gg \to HH \to b\bar{b}\gamma\gamma$ signal events and background at the LHC. Figures from Ref. [103].

Table 8.4. Expected event rates after ID efficiencies and all kinematic cuts for $b\bar{b}\gamma\gamma$ events at LHC (SLHC), two detectors and 600(6000) fb^{-1} of data [103]. LHC assumes only one b tag, while SLHC requires two. Note the increased fake rate at SLHC.

	HH	$b\bar{b}\gamma\gamma$	$c\bar{c}\gamma\gamma$	$b\bar{b}\gamma j$	$c\bar{c}\gamma j$	$jj\gamma\gamma$	$b\bar{b}jj$	$c\bar{c}jj$	γjjj	$jjjj$	$\sum$(bkg)	S/B
LHC	6	2	1	1	0	5	0	0	1	1	11	1/2
SLHC	21	6	0	4	0	6	1	0	1	1	20	1/1

to the signal region to perform a background subtraction. The technique is viable because QCD radiative corrections *in general* do not significantly alter angular distributions.

Table 8.4 summarizes the results of Ref. [103]. It gives event rates expected with 600(6000) fb^{-1} of data (two detectors) at LHC(SLHC). SLHC would not get ten times as many events because of lower efficiency of having to tag two b jets instead of only one, to overcome the low fake jet rejection rate in a high-luminosity environment. First, note that fake b jets or fake photons are the largest background: the measurement would be significantly hampered by detector limitations. Second, while the S/B ratio is excellent, the overall event rate is extremely small, definitely in the non-Gaussian statistics regime.

SLHC could make a useful statement about λ, ultimately achieving limits on $\Delta\lambda$ of about ± 0.5, but this is not such a strong statement. It could at best generally confirm the SM picture of spontaneous symmetry breaking and perhaps rule out wildly different scenarios, but would never be particularly satisfying. On the other hand, it's strong encouragement for ATLAS and CMS to push the envelope on tagging efficiency and fake rejection, especially for the detector upgrades necessary for SLHC. Doing studies like this well ahead of time is useful for this reason, our present case being a perfect example.

8.3.5.2. *HH production at an ILC*

While (S)LHC clearly has access to Higgs pair production and thus λ for $M_H > 150$ GeV, it would disappoint at lower masses. We should see if a future linear collider could also give a precision measurement for λ as it could for (most) other Higgs couplings.

For e^+e^- collisions below about 1 TeV, double Higgsstrahlung is the largest source of Higgs pairs. The Feynman diagrams appear in Fig. 8.49, while the cross sections as a function of M_H for 500 and 800 GeV collisions [104] are found in Fig. 8.50, which also shows the cross sections times

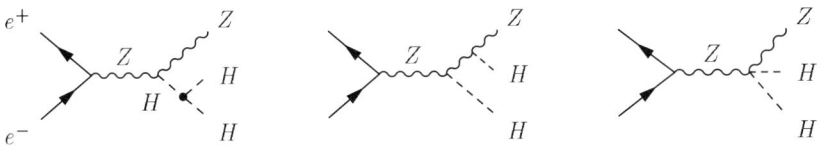

Fig. 8.49. Feynman diagrams for double Higgsstrahlung at a future linear collider, $e^+e^- \to HH$.

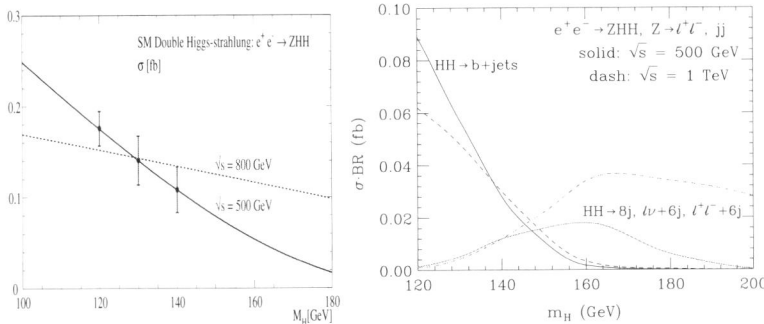

Fig. 8.50. Left: the double Higgsstrahlung cross section as a function of M_H for 500 and 800 GeV e^+e^- collisions [104]. Right: the cross section times BR at 500 GeV and 1 TeV e^+e^- collisions, for the dominant final state BRs as a function of M_H [105].

BRs for the dominant final states over the range of Higgs masses. Roughly, this corresponds to $4b$ and $4W$ final state. The former is very steeply falling with M_H, but the latter is much flatter over the 100–200 GeV mass region, suggesting broader access if at all visible.

The parton-level studies performed so far [105] are fairly encouraging. As shown in Fig. 8.51, an ILC could achieve about a $20-30\%$ measurement of λ over a broad mass range, with somewhat worse performance around $M_H \sim 140$ GeV, where the $b\bar{b}$ and W^+W^- BRs are roughly equal. Interestingly, for a lower Higgs mass, the analysis prefers lower machine energy, while the opposite is true at least to a small degree at higher mass. This is largely a phase space effect for the 3-body production mechanism. Also, SLHC is superior for $M_H \gtrsim 150$ GeV (largely due to better statistics), with an important caveat: controlling systematics in $gg \to HH \to 4W$ at LHC would require precision input from ILC for the Higgs couplings and BRs. This is an excellent example of synergy between experiments.

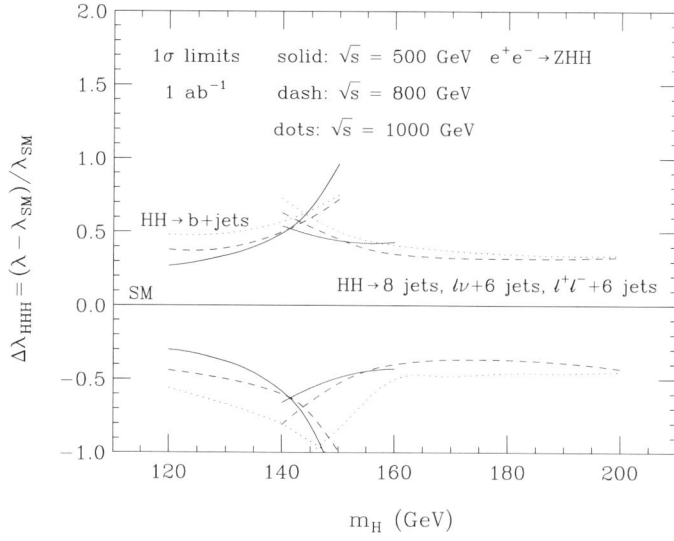

Fig. 8.51. Estimated achievable limits in the shifted self-coupling $\triangle\lambda$ (see Sec. 8.3.5.1) at future e^+e^- colliders of various energy, as a function of M_H [105].

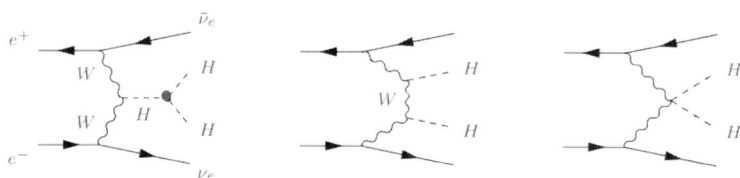

Fig. 8.52. Representative Feynman diagrams for the WBF process $e^+e^- \to \nu\bar{\nu}HH$.

Double Higgsstrahlung is not the only source of Higgs pairs at an e^+e^- collider, however. In fact, as the energy increases, WBF Higgs pair production becomes more and more important. Representative Feynman diagrams for $e^+e^- \to \nu\bar{\nu}HH$ are shown in Fig. 8.52. A preliminary analysis [106] for CLIC [107], a second-generation $1-5$ TeV e^+e^- collider collecting 5000 fb^{-1}, found rather interesting results, summarized graphically in Fig. 8.53. The principal finding is that no matter how high the collision energy goes, and regardless of Higgs mass, the precision on λ bottoms out at $10-15\%$. This is because the self-coupling has an s-channel suppression, and its contributions becomes washed out as by other diagrams as $\sqrt{s}$

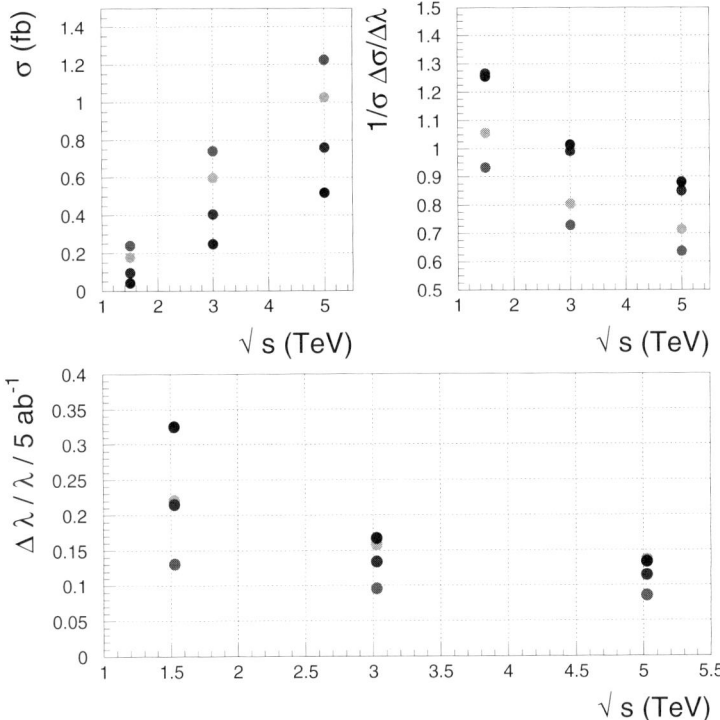

Fig. 8.53. The results of Ref. [106] for WBF HH production at CLIC, a second-generation multi-TeV e^+e^- collider. The plot labels are self-explanatory, while the colors are for various Higgs masses: 120 GeV in red, 140 GeV in blue, 180 GeV in green and 240 GeV in black.

increases. A corollary, though, is that CLIC could potentially achieve better precision than SLHC for larger M_H, although this may be marginal. Much more detailed work would be required for both SLHC and CLIC, as well as experience at LHC and SLHC to determine its true potential, to make conclusive statements.

8.3.5.3. *Electroweak corrections to* λ

One final word on the trilinear self-coupling λ: Ref. [108] calculated the leading 1-loop top quark EW corrections to λ_{SM}. Their principal SM result is:

$$\lambda_{HHH}^{eff} = \frac{M_H^2}{2v^2} \left[1 - \frac{N_C}{3\pi^2} \frac{m_t^4}{v^2 M_H^2} + ... \right] \tag{8.30}$$

The correction is $-10\%(-4\%)$ for $M_H = 120(180)$ GeV, non-trivial for smaller Higgs masses, but those are excluded in the SM. This correction should obviously be taken into account in any future analysis, should the Higgs be found. But it should be clear that neither (S)LHC nor ILC will be sensitive to it. Even CLIC would have only marginal sensitivity, and then only for low M_H.

Non-minimal Higgs sectors and new physics effects can tell a very different story, however, as we'll see, coming up in Secs. 8.4.1 and 8.4.5.

8.3.5.4. HHH production anywhere

The trilinear self-coupling λ is only part of our phenomenological Higgs potential of Eq. 8.28, though. We also need to measure $\tilde{\lambda}$, the quartic self-coupling. In some sense this is equally important to measuring λ. Recall the structure of the Higgs potential: λ allows the global minimum to be away from zero, but a non-zero (and positive) $\tilde{\lambda}$ is required to keep the potential bounded from below. We can't really convince ourselves that the potential structure of Eq. 8.27 is the right picture without a measurement of both these ingredients. We've just seen that probing λ is extremely challenging. Just how difficult is this likely to be for $\tilde{\lambda}$?

For e^+e^- collisions we already know this is hopeless: the HHH rate is both too low and its dependence on $\tilde{\lambda}$ too weak [104]. However, the situation at (S)LHC was only very recently investigated [109, 110]. The authors calculated the $gg \to HHH$ cross section, which involves Feynman diagrams like those of Fig. 8.54. Note the appearance of numerous diagrams dependent on the trilinear self-coupling, in addition to diagrams dependent only on y_t.

The results of the study are shown in Fig. 8.55, *for a 200 TeV VLHC*. They're rather deflating because the cross section is miserably small. A challenge to the student: find a three-Higgs BR to a final state that could be observed at a VLHC, where the rate is not laughable. Good luck! In addition, the right panel shows that any variation of the trilinear coupling

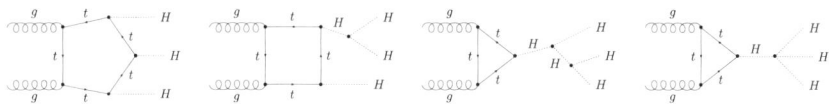

Fig. 8.54. Representative Feynman diagrams for $gg \to HHH$.

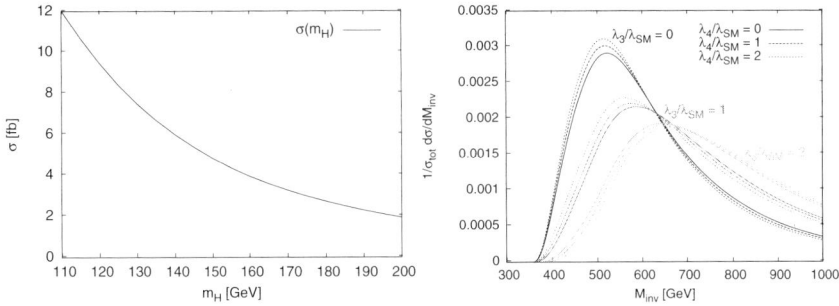

Fig. 8.55. Left: 200 TeV VLHC $gg \to HHH$ cross section as a function of M_H. Right: differential cross section as a function of M_{HHH} for three values each of λ and $\tilde{\lambda}$. Figures from Ref. [109].

λ completely swamps variation of the quartic $\tilde{\lambda}$, whose own variation is already infinitesimal.

In summary, it appears that we will likely never achieve a complete picture of the Higgs potential. This of course applies only to the Standard Model. Coming up in Chapter 8.4 we're going to see that for BSM physics the situation is even more discouraging.

8.4. Beyond-the-SM Higgs sectors

Now that we know how the Standard Model Higgs sector works – how it could be discovered and measured at LHC – it's natural to think about other possibilities for EWSB. The SM Higgs is elegant in its simplicity, but as you know from Sally Dawson's SM lectures, it's probably too minimal – nagging theoretical questions remain about Higgs mass stability, flavor (ignoring this is kind of a black eye), neutrino masses (another black eye), and so on. Because new physics that could explain dark matter is likely to also lie at the TeV scale, most model building makes an attempt to incorporate solutions to some of these other problems along with EWSB. The literature is vast, but let's try to roughly classify some of the major ideas to get a handle on the variations.

The broadest two categories of classes are weakly-coupled new physics which can be handled with perturbation theory, and strongly-coupled or "strong dynamics" models which are penetrable in some cases, others not. These include QCD-inspired theories like Technicolor [10, 11] (or more properly Extended [12, 13] or Walking [14] Technicolor, which can handle a top quark mass very different from the other quark masses) and Topcolorassisted Technicolor [15] ("TC2"), which incorporates additional weakly-coupled gauge structure. Strong dynamics assumes that some TeV-scale massive or heavier fermions' attraction became strong at low energy scales, eventually causing their condensation to mesonic states (Technipions, Technirho, Technieta, etc.), the neutral scalars of which can incite EWSB via their $SU(2)_L$ gauge interactions. Strong dynamics scenarios are beyond the scope of these lectures, however, so I leave it for the interested student to study the excellent review article of Ref. [111].

While strong dynamics theories are Higgsless in some sense, meaning no fundamental scalar fields, the terms is usually reserved for a new class of models where the EW symmetry is broken using boundary conditions on gauge boson wavefunctions propagating in finite extra dimensions (see e.g. Refs. [18, 112]). We'll also skip these.

There is far more theoretical effort expended on weakly-coupled EWSB, which is mostly variations on what we can add to the single Higgs doublet of the SM:

① 1HDM + invisible (high-scale) new physics, hidden from direct detection
② CP-conserving 2HDM: 4 types (minimal supersymmetry, MSSM, is Type II)
③ CP-violating 2HDM
④ Higgs singlet(s) (e.g. next-to-minimal supersymmetry, NMSSM)
⑤ Higgs triplets (often appear in Grand Unified Theories)
⑥ Little Higgs models: $SU(2)_L \times U(1)_Y$ is part of larger gauge and global group

The first item, new high-scale physics hidden from direct detection, sounds like a cheat. It actually involves an important aspect of phenomenology: effective Lagrangians from higher-dimensional operators. We'll come back to these in a moment. Two Higgs doublets instead of one is an idea with multiple sources. For instance, one doublet could give mass to the leptons and the other to the quarks, or one to the up-type fermions and the other to the down-type, etc. We'll return to these after effective operators. Additional Higgs singlets likewise have a variety of reasons for being written down, but usually it's just "we can do it, so we will". We'll skip these. Higgs triplets originated from natural appearance in left-right symmetric GUTs. They're a bit exotic and typically have issues with precision EW data, but are interesting in that they predict the existence of doubly-charged Higgs states $H^{\pm\pm}$, and a tree-level $H^\pm W^\mp Z$ coupling, which must be zero in most Higgs-doublet models. It would therefore stand out experimentally. For all these cases I don't have time to cover, the Higgs Hunter's Guide is the best place to start to learn more [6].

Little Higgs theories, on the other hand, are different in that they necessarily involve new scalar *and* gauge structure arising from an enlarged global symmetry from which the SM emerges, as well as additional matter content. Interestingly, in these models the Higgs looks very much like the SM Higgs, but with $\mathcal{O}(v^2/F^2)$ corrections, where F is typically a few TeV, parametrically 4π larger than the EW scale. The smallness of v^2/F^2 could make it very difficult to measure Little Higgs corrections to Higgs observables. These models are probably ultimately strongly-coupled at a scale $\Lambda \sim 4\pi F$, but this is an open question. If nature chose this course, the most interesting physics is the new gauge boson and matter fields that appears at a scale F. Refs. [19] provide nice overviews and simple explanations of the two primary Little Higgs mechanisms.

8.4.1. *Higher-dimensional operators*

The new physics responsible for dark matter, flavor, neutrino masses, etc., might very well be too massive to produce directly at colliders. This the dreaded SM-Higgs-only scenario, where LHC sees nothing new. It would really be an invitation to take a more rigorous look at all data – new physics effects might still appear as small deviations in precision observables.

The standard way of parameterizing this is to write down all the possible Lagrangian operators with the heavy fields integrated out which preserve $SU(3)_c \times SU(2)_L \times U(1)_Y$ gauge invariance. This was done over two decades ago for operators up to dimension six [86]. Although not often emphasized in today's phenomenology, I consider this paper a must-read for all students.

Let's begin by considering the possible operators involving only the SM Higgs doublet. There are two, of dimension six:

$$\mathcal{O}_1 = \frac{1}{2} \partial_\mu (\Phi^\dagger \Phi) \partial^\mu (\Phi^\dagger \Phi) \qquad \& \qquad \mathcal{O}_2 = -\frac{1}{3} (\Phi^\dagger \Phi)^3 \qquad (8.31)$$

for the effective Lagrangian contribution

$$\mathcal{L}_{6D,\Phi} = \sum_{i=1}^{2} \frac{f_i}{\Lambda^2} \mathcal{O}_i , \quad f_i > 0 \qquad (8.32)$$

Λ must be at least a couple TeV, otherwise we'd likely observe it directly at LHC. If you've somewhere seen an alternative effective theory for the

Higgs potential written as

$$V_{\text{eff}} = \sum_{n=0} \frac{\lambda_n}{\Lambda^{2n}}\left(|\Phi|^2 - \frac{v^2}{2}\right)^{2+n} \quad (8.33)$$

the operators written above correspond to the $n=1$ term in this expansion.

$\mathcal{O}_1$ modifies the Higgs kinetic term, while $\mathcal{O}_2$ modifies the EW vev, v:

$$\mathcal{L}_{\text{kin}} = \frac{1}{2}\partial_\mu\phi\,\partial^\mu\phi + \frac{1}{2}f_1\frac{v^2}{\Lambda^2}\partial_\mu\phi\,\partial^\mu\phi, \quad \frac{v^2}{2} \approx \frac{v_0^2}{2}\left(1 - \frac{f_2}{4\lambda}\frac{v_0^2}{\Lambda^2}\right) \quad (8.34)$$

where v is what G_F measures. We must also canonically normalize the physical Higgs field: $\phi = NH$ with $N = 1/(1 + f_1\frac{v^2}{\Lambda^2})$.

This results in a number of alterations to masses and couplings [113]. First, the Higgs mass itself receives corrections from the expected value, given λ:

$$M_H^2 = 2\lambda v^2\left(1 - f_1\frac{v^2}{\Lambda^2} + \frac{f_2}{2\lambda}\frac{v^2}{\Lambda^2}\right) \quad (8.35)$$

where the f_2 term is independent of λ. Next, Higgs gauge couplings receive v^2/Λ^2 shifts:

$$\frac{1}{2}g^2 v\left(1 - \frac{f_1}{2}\frac{v^2}{\Lambda^2}\right)HW_\mu^+W^{-\mu} \quad \frac{1}{4}g^2\left(1 - f_1\frac{v^2}{\Lambda^2}\right)HHW_\mu^+W^{-\mu}$$
$$\frac{1}{2}\frac{g^2}{c_W}v\left(1 - \frac{f_1}{2}\frac{v^2}{\Lambda^2}\right)HZ_\mu Z^\mu \quad \frac{1}{4}\frac{g^2}{c_W}\left(1 - f_1\frac{v^2}{\Lambda^2}\right)HHZ_\mu Z^\mu \quad (8.36)$$

Finally, the Higgs boson self-couplings are (phases vary with Feynman rule convention):

$$|\lambda_{3H}| = \frac{3m_H^2}{v}\left[\left(1 - \frac{f_1}{2}\frac{v^2}{\Lambda^2} + \frac{2f_2}{3}\frac{v^2}{M_H^2}\frac{v^2}{\Lambda^2}\right) + \frac{2f_1}{3M_H^2}\frac{v^2}{\Lambda^2}\sum_{i<j}^{3} p_i \cdot p_j\right] \quad (8.37)$$

$$|\lambda_{4H}| = \frac{3m_H^2}{v^2}\left[\left(1 - f_1\frac{v^2}{\Lambda^2} + 4f_2\frac{v^2}{M_H^2}\frac{v^2}{\Lambda^2}\right) + \frac{2f_1}{3M_H^2}\frac{v^2}{\Lambda^2}\sum_{i<j}^{4} p_i \cdot p_j\right] \quad (8.38)$$

Note that $\mathcal{O}_1$ and $\mathcal{O}_2$ both enter here, but more importantly there are momentum-dependent terms, which are typical of higher-dimensional operators. The effect of these terms would be anomalous high-p_T Higgses in pair production.

Only one phenomenological analysis exists for these effects, and only for precision experiments at a future ILC and CLIC [113]. In this study, measurements are expressed in terms of $a_i = f_i v^2/\Lambda^2$, since f_i and Λ

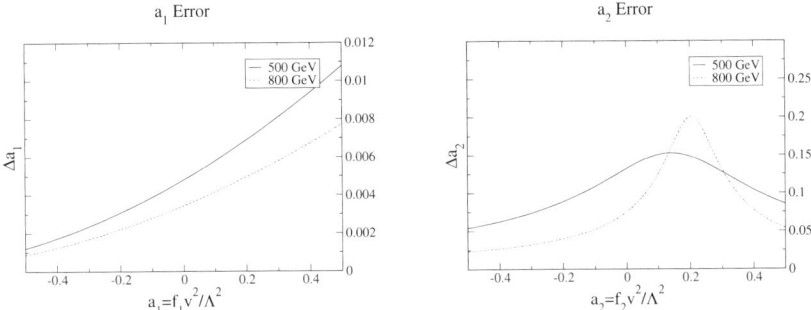

Fig. 8.56. Achievable uncertainty on measurements of the a_1 (left) and a_2 (right) coefficients of Eq. 8.31 (also see text) at a future ILC for 500 and 800 GeV running [113].

can't be easily separated from so few measurements. Higgsstrahlung, double Higgsstrahlung and WBF Higgs pair production together measure a combination of a_1 and a_2.

Figure 8.56 shows the expected achievable uncertainties (not limits!) on a_1 and a_2 at a future ILC. For $f_1 = 1$, this corresponds to a reach in Λ of about 4 TeV, possibly out of the reach of LHC depending on what might be directly produced. For $f_2 = 1$, however, this corresponds to only about $\Lambda \sim 0.8$ TeV, easily accessible at LHC. Put another way, an ILC could have access to new high-scale physics via altered Higgs–gauge boson couplings, but not via Higgs self-couplings. This is in line with what we'd come to expect, as HH production is much smaller. The shapes of the uncertainty curves in the figures depend on what values of the operator coefficients add to or subtract from the signal, with the added feature that the momentum dependence of the Higgs self-couplings that the $\mathcal{O}_1$ operator introduces changes to kinematic distributions.

In addition to the Higgs-only D6 operators, there are a handful of operators involving the Higgs and gauge boson fields together [86]:

$$O_{WW} = (\phi^\dagger \phi)\left[W^+_{\mu\nu} W^{-\mu\nu} + \tfrac{1}{2} W^3_{\mu\nu} W^{3\mu\nu}\right]$$
$$O_{BB} = (\phi^\dagger \phi) B_{\mu\nu} B^{\mu\nu}$$
$$O_{BW} = B^{\mu\nu}\left[(\phi^\dagger \sigma^3 \phi) W^3_{\mu\nu} + \sqrt{2}\left[(\phi^\dagger T^+ \phi) W^+_{\mu\nu} + (\phi^\dagger T^- \phi) W^-_{\mu\nu}\right]\right]$$
$$O_B = (D^\mu \phi)^\dagger (D^\nu \phi) B_{\mu\nu}$$
$$O_W = (D^\mu \phi)^\dagger \left[\sigma^3 (D^\nu \phi) W^3_{\mu\nu} + \sqrt{2}\left[T^+ (D^\nu \phi) W^+_{\mu\nu} + T^- (D^\nu \phi) W^-_{\mu\nu}\right]\right]$$
$$O_{\Phi,1} = (D_\mu \phi)^\dagger \phi \phi^\dagger (D^\mu \phi)$$

These induce momentum-dependent $HHVV$ vertices, so could be studied at an ILC or CLIC in the same manner as the Higgs-only couplings, as well as with rare Higgs decays [114], but in general they're highly constrained by EW precisions observables (S, ρ, g_{VVV}) [115]. Interestingly, it appears there has not been an update of the EW constraints on these operators since 1997 [116], although there are predictions for limits at an ILC [117]. There is, however, a new analysis for WBF Higgs at LHC includes the effects of some of these operators and finds that they would be encoded in the tagging jet azimuthal separation [118].

There is also a set of D6 operators involving the Higgs, fermion and gauge boson fields [86]:

$$\begin{aligned}
O_{d\phi} &= (\phi^\dagger \phi)(\bar{q} d \phi) \\
O_{\phi d} &= i(\phi^\dagger D_\mu \phi)(\bar{d}\gamma^\mu d) \\
O_{\bar{D}d} &= (D_\mu \bar{q} d) D^\mu \phi \\
O_{\phi q}^{(1)} &= i(\phi^\dagger D_\mu \phi)(\bar{q}\gamma^\mu q) \\
O_{\phi\phi} &= i(\phi^\dagger \epsilon D_\mu \phi)(\bar{u}\gamma^\mu d) \\
O_{dW} &= (\bar{q}\sigma^{\mu\nu}\sigma^i d)\phi W^i_{\mu\nu} \\
O_{\phi q}^{(3)} &= i(\phi^\dagger D_\mu \sigma^i \phi)(\bar{q}\gamma^\mu \sigma^i q) \\
O_{Dd} &= (\bar{q} D_\mu d) D^\mu \phi \quad O_{dB} = (\bar{q}\sigma^{\mu\nu} d)\phi B_{\mu\nu}
\end{aligned} \quad (8.39)$$

Some of these are constrained by precise LEP measurements of $Zb\bar{b}$, $\gamma b\bar{b}$ couplings, but not severely. They would give interesting rare Higgs decays like $H \to b\bar{b}Z, b\bar{b}\gamma$. Their phenomenology for LHC and even ILC is not really studied. Thus, I can't say to what scale they might be sensitive given a SM Higgs discovery with nothing else observed.

8.4.2. Two-Higgs doublet models (2HDMs)

The most-often studied extension to the SM Higgs sector is the two-Higgs doublet model (2HDM) [6, 119]. That is, we add one additional $SU(2)_L$ doublet. Both of the doublets acquire a vev. For now let's assume CP conservation and work with in the real-vev basis. Counting degrees of freedom, four per complex doublet, and knowing that three modes are "eaten" to give the $W^\pm$ and Z their masses, after SSB there must be five physical states. Two of them will necessarily be charged ($H^\pm$) regardless of how we assigned hypercharge to each doublet, leaving the other three neutral. Of those, two (h, H) will be CP-even and one will be CP-odd (A), the last of which won't couple to the weak bosons at tree level. The general 2HDM potential is quite messy [6, 120], so we'll not discuss it.

Recall the primary role of the Higgs sector: to restore unitarity to weak boson scattering. This requires the gauge coupling to WW to be exactly $\frac{1}{2}g_W^2 v$, where v is what we measure with G_F. In the amplitude, then, the coupling squared is $\frac{1}{4}g_W^4 v^2$. With two vevs, there is the automatic constraint $v_1^2 + v_2^2 \equiv v^2$ [121]. The ratio is $\tan\beta \equiv \frac{v_2}{v_1}$. The CP-even mass eigenstates, which couple to the weak bosons, thus boil down to simply mixing:

$$h = \sqrt{2}[-(\text{Re}\phi_1^0 - v_1)\sin\alpha + (\text{Re}\phi_2^0 - v_2)\cos\alpha] \quad (8.40)$$
$$H = \sqrt{2}[\ (\text{Re}\phi_1^0 - v_1)\cos\alpha + (\text{Re}\phi_2^0 - v_2)\sin\alpha] \quad (8.41)$$

where α is the angle which diagonalizes the 2×2 mixing matrix. The Higgs sector is typically defined by α, $\tan\beta$ and the potential parameters which govern the self-couplings. Some models are defined instead by M_A and M_Z.

Let's pause for a moment to reflect on what would happen if we introduced CP violation [119]. This is a well-motivated exercise since there isn't enough CP violation in the SM model to account for baryogenesis in the early universe. The most immediate impact is that h, H and A now mix. M_A is supposed to parameterize the pseudoscalar pole, but it's now mixed into three physical states, so it becomes ill-defined. Instead, we typically use the charged Higgs mass. It would be logical to use $M_{H^\pm}$ for CP-conserving scenarios as well, but this is one of those historical accidents that has too much momentum to change.

Regarding the fermions, we can apportion the two doublets in four general ways [6]:

    I   only Φ_2 couples to fermions

   II Φ_1 couples to down-type, Φ_2 to up-type fermions

  III Φ_1 couples to down quarks, Φ_2 to up quarks and down leptons

  IV Φ_1 couples to quarks, Φ_2 to leptons

Types III and IV induce flavor-changing neutral currents (FCNCs), which are highly constrained, thus these models are not much studied any more. Types I and II are qualitatively different and worth a quick look at the differences in their couplings, shown in Table 8.5[q]. Because of which doublet gives the down-type fermions their masses, those Yukawa couplings to h and

---

[q]Note that various references use different phase conventions for the Lagrangian. The important distinction is the phase between Higgs couplings, and a reference SM coupling such as $ee\gamma$. I use positive terms in the covariant derivative and drop the overall superfluous factor of i typical of most Lagrangians.

Table 8.5. Fermion and gauge boson couplings in Type I (upper) and II (lower) 2HDMs.

Φ	$\dfrac{g_{\Phi u\bar{u}}}{g_f}$	$\dfrac{g_{\Phi d\bar{d}}}{g_f}$	$\dfrac{g_{\Phi VV}}{g_V}$	$\dfrac{g_{\Phi ZA}}{g_V}$
h	$-\dfrac{\cos\alpha}{\sin\beta}$	$-\dfrac{\cos\alpha}{\sin\beta}$	$\sin(\beta-\alpha)$	$-\dfrac{1}{2}i\cos(\beta-\alpha)$
H	$-\dfrac{\sin\alpha}{\sin\beta}$	$-\dfrac{\sin\alpha}{\sin\beta}$	$\cos(\beta-\alpha)$	$\dfrac{1}{2}i\sin(\beta-\alpha)$
A	$-i\gamma_5\cot\beta$	$i\gamma_5\cot\beta$	0	0
h	$-\dfrac{\cos\alpha}{\sin\beta}$	$\dfrac{\sin\alpha}{\cos\beta}$	$\sin(\beta-\alpha)$	$-\dfrac{1}{2}i\cos(\beta-\alpha)$
H	$-\dfrac{\sin\alpha}{\sin\beta}$	$-\dfrac{\cos\alpha}{\cos\beta}$	$\cos(\beta-\alpha)$	$\dfrac{1}{2}i\sin(\beta-\alpha)$
A	$-i\gamma_5\cot\beta$	$-i\gamma_5\tan\beta$	0	0

H are swapped between models, with a phase factor from mixing. Similarly, the $Af\bar{f}$ coupling is inverted and changes sign: $\cot\beta \to -\tan\beta$. The gauge coupling for h and H, of course, are unaffected by the Yukawa couplings and are fixed to $\sin(\beta-\alpha)$ and $\cos(\beta-\alpha)$. (The sum of their squares in the amplitude must equal 1!)

The charged Higgs Yukawa couplings are slightly different yet. The left-handed coupling is proportional to the up-type Yukawa coupling, and the right-handed coupling the down-type Yukawa, *for an out-flowing H^-*. The reverse is true for an outflowing H^+. We have:

$$g_{H-D\bar{U}} = \frac{g}{2\sqrt{2}M_W}\left[m_U\cot\beta(1+\gamma_5) - m_D\cot\beta(1-\gamma_5)\right] \quad (8.42)$$

$$g_{H-D\bar{U}} = \frac{g}{2\sqrt{2}M_W}\left[m_U\cot\beta(1+\gamma_5) + m_D\tan\beta(1-\gamma_5)\right] \quad (8.43)$$

where H^- flows out, D is incoming and $\bar{U}$ is outgoing.

8.4.3. *Type II 2HDM in the MSSM*

At this point we should focus on the Type II 2HDM, because that's the one required to appear in the MSSM[r] (see Ref. [123] for a detailed description). Model I will have similar features, modulo the couplings swaps given in Table 8.5, so is understandable by analogy. We'll spend the remaining

---
[r] A superpotential can't be constructed from conjugate fields, else the supersymmetry transformations aren't preserved. For an excellent SUSY tutorial, see Ref. [122].

portion discussing only SUSY Higgs phenomenology, and specifically minimal SUSY, the MSSM. However, by the end it should be apparent that extended Higgs sectors may often be treated as variations on a theme, with much of the phenomenology based on the same collider signatures.

The MSSM imposes tree-level constraints on the Higgs potential which require the various λ to be gauge parameters (MSSM extensions add non-gauge terms). We'll come back to what the potential looks like in Sec. 8.4.5 and study its phenomenology, and for now simply examine the implication of this structure on the mass spectrum. Because we consider only the CP-conserving case here, we can get away with using M_A as an input. The others will be $\tan\beta$ as discussed before, the average top squark mass M_S, and an encoded trilinear mixing parameter for the top sector, X_t. This last one is important because of the large top Yukawa corrections the MSSM Higgs sector receives. The values 0 and $\sqrt{6}\,M_S$ are referred to as "no mixing" and "maximal mixing", because they extremize the loop corrections. The $h - H$ mixing angle is

$$\alpha = \frac{1}{2}\tan^{-1}\left[\tan 2\beta \frac{M_A^2 + M_Z^2}{M_A^2 - M_Z^2}\right], \qquad -\frac{\pi}{2} \leq \alpha \leq 0 \qquad (8.44)$$

to first order. The CP-even masses are given by:

$$M_{H,h}^2 = \frac{1}{2}\left(M_A^2 + M_Z^2 \pm \sqrt{(M_A^2 + M_Z^2)^2 + 4M_A^2 M_Z^2 \sin^2(2\beta)}\right)$$
$$+ \frac{3}{8\pi^2}\cos^2\alpha\, y_t^2 m_t^2 \left[\log\frac{M_S^2}{m_t^2} + \frac{X_t^2}{M_S^2}\left(1 - \frac{X_t^2}{12 M_S^2}\right)\right] \quad \text{for } M_h \text{ only}$$
(8.45)

where the top Yukawa correction can be significant, a couple tens of GeV. The charged Higgs mass is rather more simple:

$$M_{H^\pm}^2 = M_A^2 + M_W^2 \qquad (8.46)$$

These equations exhibit the interesting property of h decoupling with increasing pseudoscalar mass: for large M_A the heavy states H, A and $H^\pm$ tend to be closely degenerate, and the light h has an asymptotic maximum mass which depends mostly on $\tan\beta$. We see this behavior, along with a plateau effect for M_h and M_H, in Fig. 8.57. There is always at least one CP-even Higgs boson in the mass region $90 \lesssim M_\phi \lesssim 145$ GeV, assuming perturbativity to high scales. For large M_A, toward the decoupling region, it is the lighter state, h, but at low M_A it is the heavier state, H. The transition region is sharper for larger $\tan\beta$.

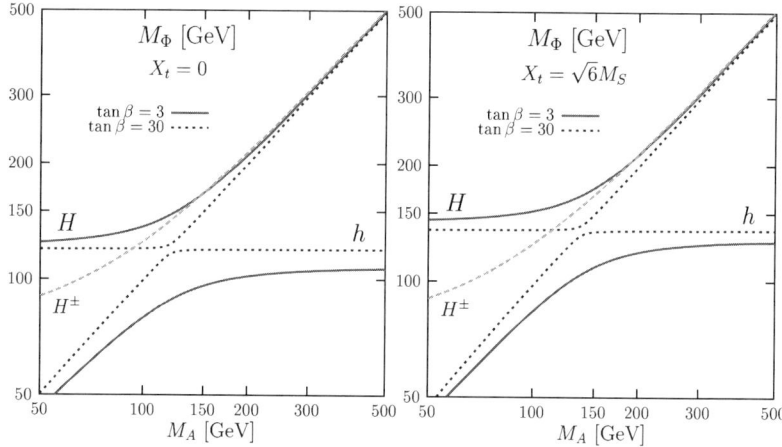

Fig. 8.57. MSSM Higgs boson masses as a function of pseudoscalar mass M_A and two choices of $\tan\beta$, for no (left) and maximal (right) mixing (X_t parameter; see text). Figures from Ref. [7].

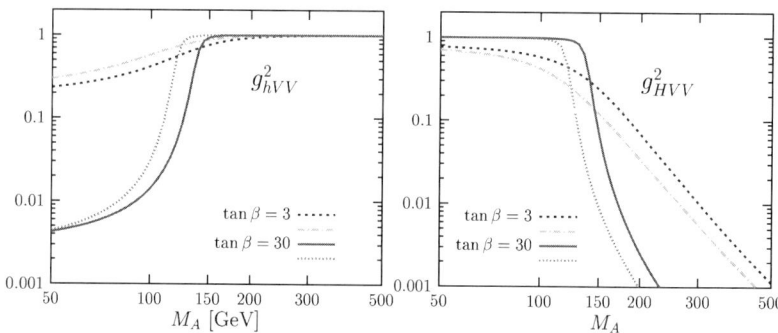

Fig. 8.58. MSSM CP-even Higgs boson couplings to the weak gauge bosons as a function of M_A and for two choices of $\tan\beta$, and for no mixing (darker colors) and maximal mixing (lighter colors). Figures from Ref. [7].

The mass spectrum is not the only feature to exhibit the decoupling and transition behavior, however. Both the gauge and Yukawa couplings do the same. The $VV\phi$ couplings are shown in Fig. 8.58. By comparison with Fig. 8.57, we easily see that when either h or H is in its plateau mass region, it holds most of the gauge coupling; $\sin(\beta-\alpha) \to 1$ or $\cos(\beta-\alpha) \to 1$. In the transition region, the two states share the gauge coupling, and both are of comparable importance in unitarity cancellation. As with the mass spectrum, and by now as anticipated, the transition region is sharper for larger $\tan\beta$. Hold these two figures in your mind, as they are going to play an extremely important phenomenological role shortly.

Using just trigonometry, let's rewrite the Yukawa couplings of Table 8.5 to see better how they depend on M_A and $\tan\beta$:

$$\begin{aligned}
g_{hu\bar{u}} &= -\frac{\cos\alpha}{\sin\beta} Y_u = -[\sin(\beta-\alpha) + \cot\beta\cos(\beta-\alpha)]\, Y_u \\
g_{hd\bar{d}} &= \frac{\sin\alpha}{\cos\beta} Y_d = -[\sin(\beta-\alpha) - \tan\beta\cos(\beta-\alpha)]\, Y_d \\
g_{Hu\bar{u}} &= -\frac{\sin\alpha}{\sin\beta} Y_u = -[\cos(\beta-\alpha) - \cot\beta\sin(\beta-\alpha)]\, Y_u \\
g_{Hd\bar{d}} &= -\frac{\cos\alpha}{\cos\beta} Y_d = -[\cos(\beta-\alpha) + \tan\beta\sin(\beta-\alpha)]\, Y_d
\end{aligned} \quad (8.47)$$

This is a far more convenient form, since $\tan\beta$ is an input and $\sin(\beta-\alpha)/\cos(\beta-\alpha)$ is the reduced h/H gauge coupling. These are both natural, convenient parameters to describe production cross sections and decay partial widths (thus branching ratios), rather than the CP-even mixing angle and $\sin\beta$ or $\cos\beta$, or their inverses. Check Fig. 8.59 to see if you agree.

These are the most salient features of the MSSM Higgs sector, sufficient to understand the bulk of MSSM Higgs phenomenology. For a more in-depth discussion, especially of why SUSY imposes these constraints, and for more detailed formulae, see Refs. [7, 123].

Now that we know the couplings, we can obtain cross sections for h and H production simply as correction factors to the SM channels of equal mass. There is no WBF or W/Z-associated pseudoscalar production, but there is both $gg \to A$ inclusive and top quark associated production, $t\bar{t}A$, which are easily obtained if one inserts the γ_5 factor into the loop derivation for $gg \to A$ [7]. The charged Higgs is a special case as there is no SM analogue; we'll discuss this in Sec. 8.4.4 in the context of searches. For the moment, let's examine the neutral states' branching ratios, just to get an idea of how they behave. It's easy to suffer plot overload about now, so don't try to absorb every last detail; focus on the general behavior, which you already should be able to guess from the couplings plots.

Figure 8.60 shows the BRs for the CP-even states h and H, cut off at the mass plateaus. They're basically what we would expect: both h and H behave like a SM Higgs of equal mass, except that the various couplings are dialed up or down. M_h can never be above ~ 145 GeV, so it almost never has a significant BR to gauge bosons. Because the fermionic partial widths

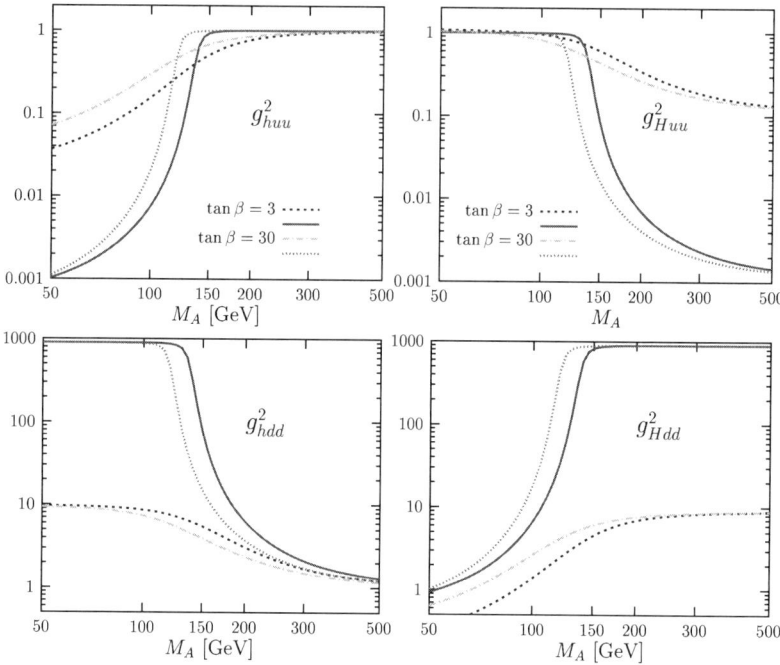

Fig. 8.59. MSSM CP-even Higgs boson couplings to fermions as a function of M_A and for two choices of $\tan\beta$, and for no mixing (darker colors) and maximal mixing (lighter colors). Figures from Ref. [7].

can be enhanced by a factor of $\tan^2\beta$, the rare modes like $\phi \to \gamma\gamma, gg$ tend to be suppressed (and the top quark loop can better cancel the W loop for some parameter choices, suppressing the partial width). The only new features are $H \to hh, AA$ decays, possible for limited parameter choices but making for interesting additional channels.

The pseudoscalar BRs behave similarly, as shown in Fig. 8.61. The new feature here is at small $\tan\beta$, where decays $A \to hZ$ are possible. But otherwise A prefers to decay $\sim 90\%$ to $b\bar{b}$ and $\sim 10\%$ to $\tau^+\tau^-$, unless it is heavy enough to produce top quark pairs. That dominates only at small $\tan\beta$ (large $\cot\beta$), where the up-type coupling dominates. At large $\tan\beta$, $b\bar{b}$ and $\tau^+\tau^-$ both still win by a considerable margin.

There are similar plots for $H^\pm$, but they're not particularly enlightening as its decay patterns are drastically simpler: as far as phenomenology is concerned, it's BR~ 1 to tb when kinematically accessible, $\tau\nu$ if lighter. For low $\tan\beta$ there is a rare BR to $hW^\pm$, but that is predicted to always be difficult to observe.

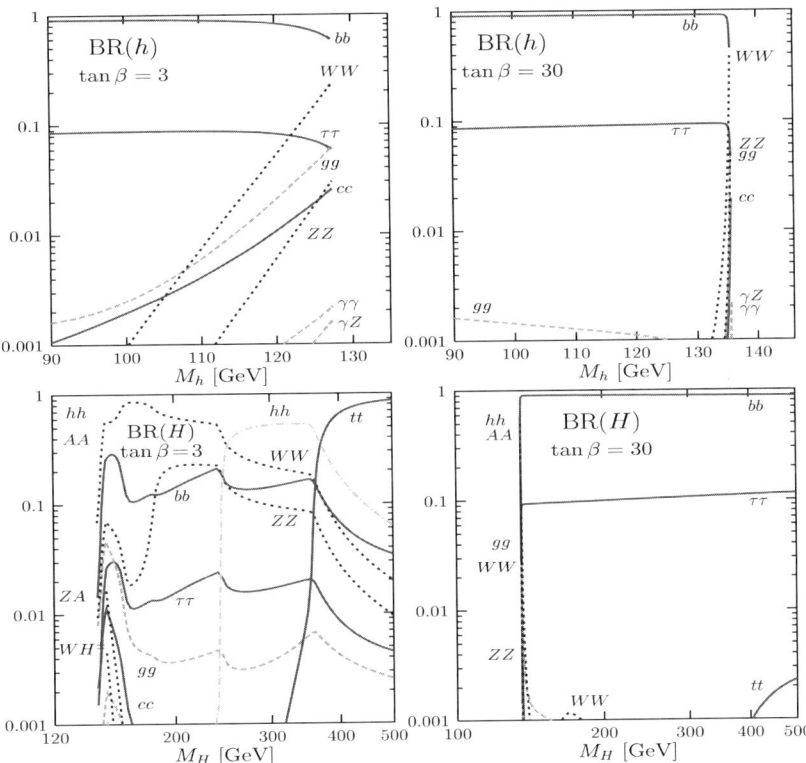

Fig. 8.60. MSSM CP-even Higgs boson branching ratios as a function of M_A for $\tan\beta = 3, 30$. Figures from Ref. [7].

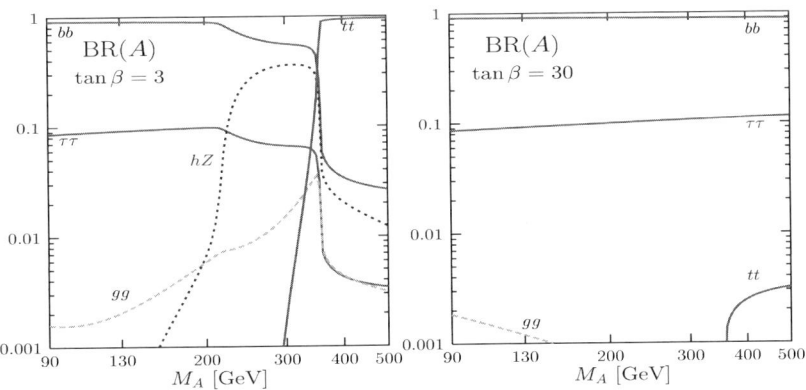

Fig. 8.61. MSSM CP-odd Higgs boson branching ratios as a function of M_A for two choices of $\tan\beta$. Figures from Ref. [7].

All Higgs bosons can decay to SUSY particle pairs if they're light enough, but this is not a very common occurrence across parameter space (especially since so much of it is ruled out already by LEP SUSY searches), so we'll bypass that discussion here.

8.4.4. MSSM Higgs searches

For MSSM Higgs searches past, we start again with LEP. It didn't find anything, but placed various limits. Let's begin with the charged Higgs search, because it's the simplest. This proceeded via H^+H^- pair production (the only mechanism accessible at LEP) and decay to $\tau\nu$ or cs, as there was never kinematic room for tb. Thus, the search had three channels: dual taus, mixed tau plus hadronic decays, and an all-hadronic mode [124]. Because the production mechanism depends on only gauge-fixed couplings, the MSSM charged Higgs search is usually presented as a more general 2HDM search, with limits presented in the $M_{H^\pm}$ v. BR($H^\pm \to \tau^\pm\nu$) plane. Fig. 8.62 summarizes the obtained limits. To translate the general search limits to the MSSM Higgs sector inputs, recall Eq. 8.46, $M_{H^\pm}^2 = M_A^2 + M_W^2$. The difficulty of this search was the low ID efficiency for taus and charm quarks. Unfortunately, there is no final combined limit, but each of the collaborations has published final independent limits [126–129]. Watch the LEP-Higgs web page for updates [130].

The basic neutral Higgs boson search channels are exactly the same as in the SM for each of h and H, to which we add $e^+e^- \to Z^* \to hA/HA$ production via the additional couplings of Table 8.5. Each of the four LEP collaborations presented a multitude of MSSM $h/H/A$ search limits, and there are combined LEP results with CP-conservation [131] and CP-violation (CPX) [131, 132]. However, one should be somewhat wary of what precisely is presented. The results are usually shown as shaded exclusion blobs in either M_A-tanβ space (for a very specific set of additional assumptions) or M_{h_i}-tanβ space, also given some assumptions. There are literally dozens of pages of exclusion plots, depending on what one chooses for the mixing parameter X_t, top quark mass (recall the strong M_h dependence on m_t), stop masses, μ, and so on. This is far too much to show here, because the exclusion contours change so much from assumption to assumption – it's impossible even to select a representative sample without misleading the uninitiated. See e.g. Ref. [133].

The curious student should flip through the plots in Refs. [131, 133] simply to get a feel for how wild this variation is. Observe how much the

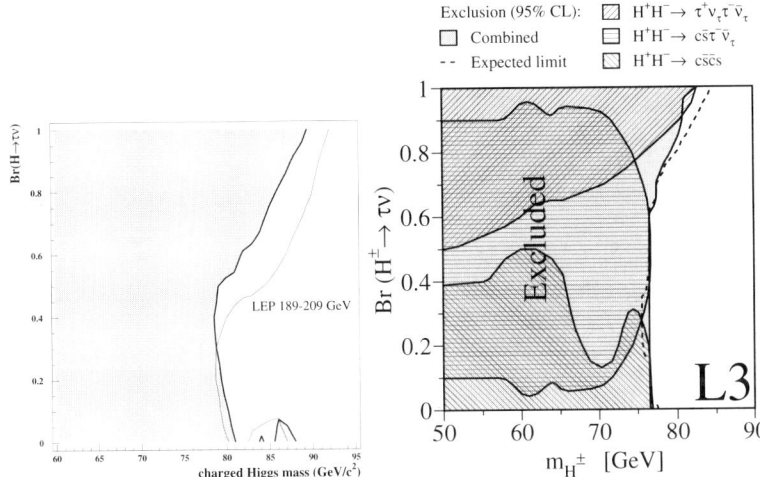

Fig. 8.62. Left: LEP preliminary combined-experiment charged Higgs search 95%CL limits (2001), from Ref. [125]. Right: L3 published limits from 2003, illustrating where each of the three decay channels discussed in the text contributes to the overall limit [128]. There is no final LEP combined limit, but judging from each of the individual limits [126–129], it does not change significantly from the preliminary results.

contours change depending on the top quark mass – it is obviously still fairly poorly measured, as far as fits to supersymmetry go. Note also that the plots are always logarithmic in $\tan\beta$, which compresses the unexcluded large-$\tan\beta$ region, making it appear that parameter space is vastly ruled out in many cases. This simply isn't true. Finally, I should comment that the "theoretically inaccessible" disallowed blobs are even more grossly misleading. All one has to do is move the stop masses up slightly and these retreat dramatically. Perhaps a more logical approach is the model-independent $h/H/A$ search of OPAL [134].

MSSM Higgs Searches at LHC are also mostly variants on the SM search channels, the exceptions being charged Higgses, rare (SUSY or Higgs pair) decay modes, and one new production channel, $b\bar{b}\phi$, which is important at large $\tan\beta$ where the coupling is enhanced to top-quark Yukawa strength. $t\bar{t}\phi$ rates tend to be about the same as the SM for equal mass, or slightly suppressed. WBF h or H rates can only be suppressed relative to the SM, due to the appearance of $\sin^2(\beta - \alpha)$ or $\cos^2(\beta - \alpha)$, respectively. Inclusive rates can change rather dramatically, however, because the b loop can be extremely important. Figure 8.63 shows the cross sections for $gg \to \phi$ as a

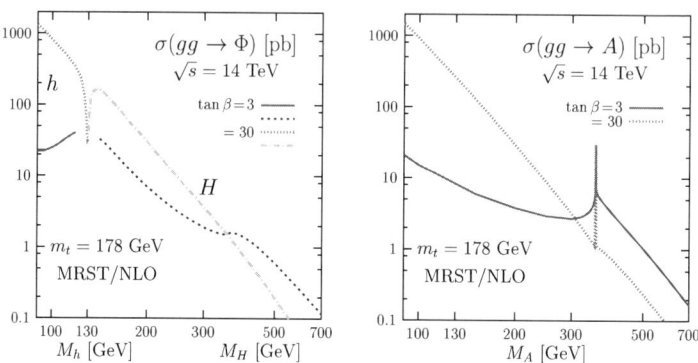

Fig. 8.63. Gluon fusion MSSM Higgs production cross sections at LHC for the CP-even states h and H (left) and the pseudoscalar A (right), for two values of $\tan\beta$. Figures from Ref. [7].

function of the physical masses, for small and large $\tan\beta$. These may be compared with the SM cross sections of Fig. 8.16.

Let's concentrate on the WBF modes, however, as they turn out to be the most interesting. Recall the plateau behavior of h and H masses as a function of M_A (cf. Fig. 8.57), and simultaneously the h and H gauge coupling behavior (cf. Fig. 8.58). The astute student will realize that this implies that WBF Higgs production in an accessible mass region probably always occurs at a good rate, somewhat suppressed but never much so. Figure 8.64 summarizes some of this previous information and goes on to show the cross section times BR to tau pairs (in the two accessible tau decay modes), also as a function of M_A [135]. Indeed, eyeballing the upper and lower rows, it appears that between h and H, there's always a signal in WBF. It may be slightly suppressed, but we know from SM WBF Higgs studies (cf. Sec. 8.2.3.4) that since so little data is required to make an observation, the signal could be suppressed by a factor of several and be detectable. The reason is that in the MSSM the h and H plateau mass ranges are in the "good" region of WBF Higgs observability. Actually, quite a large mass region is observable, but if the MSSM predicted Higgs masses closer to the Z pole, there could be trouble (but LEP would already have discovered such a Higgs).

This bit of luck forms the basis of the MSSM Higgs No-Lose Theorem: at least one of the CP-even Higgs states, h or H, is guaranteed to be observable in WBF at LHC [64, 135]. The original parton-level studies have since been confirmed with full ATLAS detector simulation, and actually im-

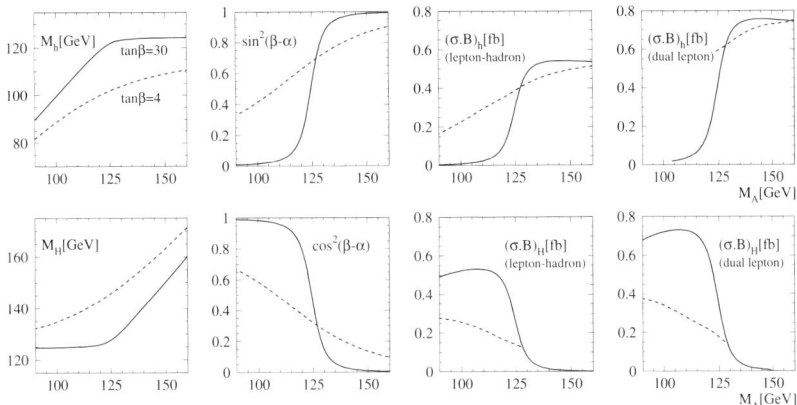

Fig. 8.64. From left to right, each plot as a function of M_A: h/H mass, gauge coupling suppression factor squared, WBF cross section times BR to taus to the lepton-hadron final state, and the same for the dual lepton mode. The upper (lower) row is for $h(H)$. Fig. from Ref. [64].

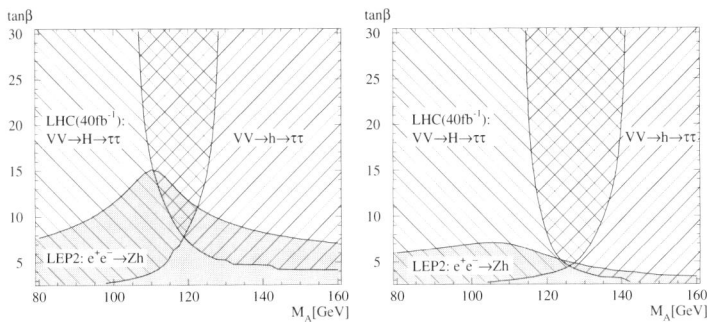

Fig. 8.65. MSSM parameter space coverage of WBF $h/H \to \tau^+\tau^-$ for the no-mixing ($A_t = 0$, left) and maximal mixing ($X_t = \sqrt{6}\, M_{SUSY}$, right) cases [135].

proved [136]. The parton-level coverage plots shown in Fig. 8.65, however, are simpler to grasp. Very little data would be required for discovery, and for some M_A it would be possible to observe both h and H simultaneously.

One caveat: the final state $\tau^+\tau^-$ is not always accessible![s] It's possible to zero out the MSSM down-type fermion coupling at tree level – an interesting exercise for the student. If this happens, $h/H \to \gamma\gamma$ and $h/H \to W^+W^-$ are "large" partial widths, so their BRs take up the

---
[s]There's always fine print...

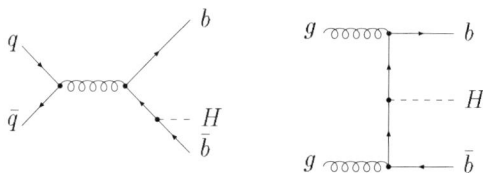

Fig. 8.66. Feynman diagrams for $gg \to b\bar{b}\phi$ production at LHC.

coverage slack [135, 136], saving the No-Lose Theorem. There's been some work on an NMSSM No-Lose Theorem [137–140], which extends the Higgs sector by a complex singlet [6]. The outlook for LHC is promising, but not obviously rock-solid.

The No-Lose Theorem is great for the CP-even states, but what about the other Higgses? I'll gloss over the bulk of searches, since they're mostly variants on the SM ones, and move on to the special case of heavy H/A (towards decoupling) and this new channel $b\bar{b}\phi$. The Feynman diagrams appear in Fig. 8.66. Recall that H has a $\tan\beta$ enhancement to down-type quarks in the decoupling region, and A always has this enhancement. We already know that means that H and A prefer to decay 90% of the time to $b\bar{b}$ and 10% to $\tau^+\tau^-$, but it would be impossible to observe either of those final states in inclusive production, and WBF production is zilch for H in the decoupling region. However, the LHC being essentially a gluon collider, the initial state can create high-energy b pairs, which can then Brem a Higgs, either H or A, which are essentially degenerate (but do not interfere due to the γ_5 coupling). Since the b jets are produced at high-p_T, the H/A must recoil against them, so it also produced with a transverse boost. It's decay products are then not back-to-back, allowing for tau pair reconstruction; $H/A \to \mu^+\mu^-$ may also be used, but is a rare mode. The final state is then $b\bar{b}\tau^+\tau^-$ (or $b\bar{b}\mu^+\mu^-$), which is taggable and distinguishable from mixed QCD-EW backgrounds because the tau pair invariant mass is in the several-hundred GeV region.

Figure 8.67 shows the cross section times BR to tau pairs for 300 GeV Higgs bosons as a function of $\tan\beta$, and also the CMS expected discovery reach for various final states in tau or muon pairs, with only 30 fb^{-1} of luminosity, or about 1/10 of the total LHC data expected. Coverage is not complete, because this mode doesn't produce enough rate at low $\tan\beta$ where there is little coupling enhancement, but is still a significant search tool. The mass resolution achievable for H and A using taus in this mode is

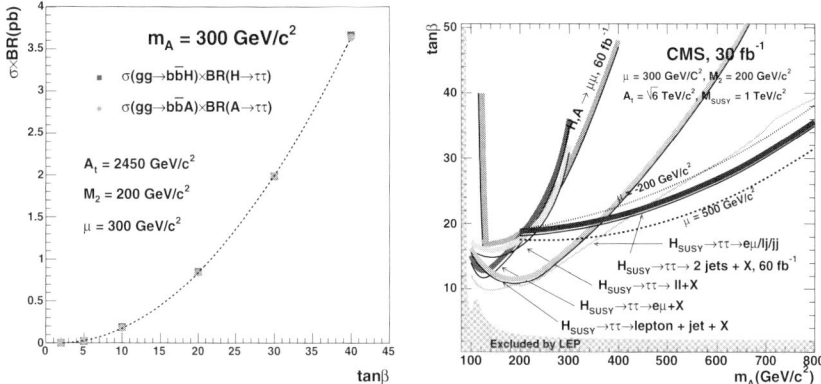

Fig. 8.67. Left: $b\bar{b}\phi$ production cross section at LHC times the BR to tau pairs, as a function of $\tan\beta$ for $M_A = 300$ GeV. Right: expected CMS reach using only 30 fb^{-1} of data for $b\bar{b}H/A \to \tau^+\tau^-, \mu^+\mu^-$ as a function of M_A. Figures from Ref. [141].

even pretty good, on the order of a couple tens of GeV, possibly better. Of course, if the decay to muons is accessible (at very large $\tan\beta$, then mass resolution would be on the order of a GeV.

This would determine M_A quite well, good enough for comparison with theory (at least at first), but what about the other major Higgs parameter, $\tan\beta$? The $b\bar{b}\phi$ production rate is directly proportional to $\tan^2\beta$, so we can measure it using the overall rate, with the mild (but not rock solid) assumption that the ratio of $b\bar{b}$ and $\tau^+\tau^-$ BRs is the ratio of the b and τ squared masses, i.e. that BR$(H/A \to \tau^+\tau^-) \sim 10\%$ [141]. The major sources of uncertainty are this assumption, the machine luminosity uncertainty of $5 - 10\%$, PDF uncertainties of probably about 5%, and higher-order QCD corrections to the production process of probably about 20% [142, 143].

Figure 8.68 shows the CMS expected uncertainty on $\tan\beta$ using this method, as a function of M_A and for 30 or 60 fb^{-1} of data. In general, $10-20\%$ appears achieveable. This is not spectacular, but would be a significant first step toward sorting out the new Higgs sector and presumably comparing to other SUSY discovery measurements. Clearly the higher-order QCD uncertainties dominate, which could probably be improved with better theoretical calculations over the next decade. This will be done if heavy Higgses are discovered.

Now, what about charged Higgs discovery? We know nothing about its phenomenology, because there is no SM analogue. All we do know is the

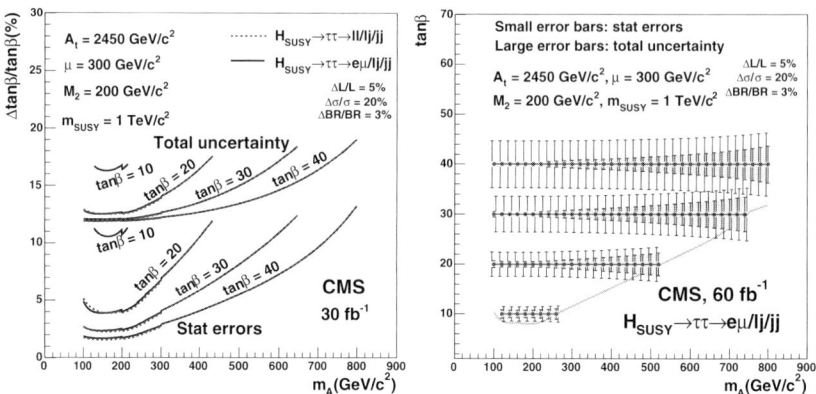

Fig. 8.68. CMS expected precision on $\tan\beta$ at LHC using $b\bar{b}\phi$ production as described in the text. Figures from Ref. [141].

very important fact that, *despite everything else we may see at Tevatron or LHC, the only way to prove the existence of two Higgs doublets is to directly observe the charged Higgs states.* I cannot emphasize this enough. For all we know, an extra neutral state might simply be the residue of an extra Higgs singlet; there could be more to the flavor sector that confuses us when we try to measure Yukawa couplings or $\tan\beta$. Thus, observing the $H^\pm$ states would be a huge qualitative step toward understanding what the Higgs sector is. How would this proceed experimentally?

At Tevatron there is very little energy available for direct charged Higgs production, since it must be produced in association with a top quark (large coupling), as shown in the Feynman diagrams of Fig. 8.69. However, if $M_{H^\pm}$ is small enough, the top quark can decay to $bH^\pm$ followed by

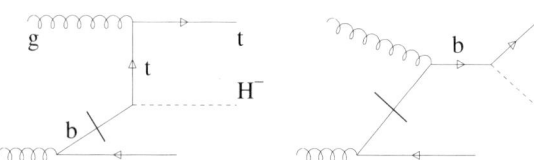

Fig. 8.69. Feynman diagrams for charged Higgs production at hadron colliders. The short line breaking the b quark propagator represents how the process may also be regarded as initiated by a b parton in the proton, rather than from gluon splitting to a b quark pair.

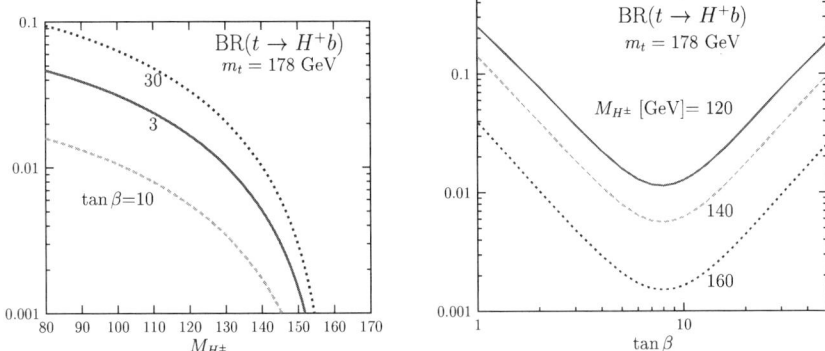

Fig. 8.70. Branching ratio for top quark to bottom quark plus charged Higgs boson, as a function of $M_{H^\pm}$ for a few select values of $\tan\beta$ (left) and as a function of $\tan\beta$ for $M_{H^\pm} = 120$ GeV (right). Figures from Ref. [7].

$H^\pm \to \tau\nu$ if $\tan\beta > 1$, and equally to bc and cs if $\tan\beta < 1$; if $M_{H^\pm} \gtrsim 120$ GeV, then the BR to $W^\pm b\bar{b}$ via a top quark loop becomes significant. Figure 8.70 shows the $t \to bH^\pm$ BR as a function of $M_{H^\pm}$ for a few select $\tan\beta$, and as a function of $\tan\beta$ for $M_{H^\pm} = 120$ GeV. At low $\tan\beta$, the partial width is driven mainly by the top quark Yukawa, while at large $\tan\beta$ it's primarily the bottom quark. Weakness of both Yukawas in the intermediate-$\tan\beta$ regime results in a comparatively reduced top quark partial width (recall Eqs. (8.42,8.43)). For fixed $M_{H^\pm}$, the partial width is symmetric in $\log(\tan\beta)$ about a minimum at $\tan\beta = \sqrt{m_t/m_b}$. Charged Higgs decays to $hW^\pm$ or $AW^\pm$ are generally disallowed in the MSSM from LEP mass limits on h and A.

The Tevatron search proceeds both as appearance (i.e. looking directly for $H^\pm$ in the top quark sample) and disappearance, or missing rate for top quark to $bW^\pm$. Figure 8.71 goes on to show the expected 95% CL limits in the $M_{H^\pm} - \tan\beta$ plane that Tevatron Run I achieved, and Run II might reach depending on how much data it ultimately records. The very slight change between 2 and 10 fb^{-1} reveals that the experiments there are statistics-limited, but not by a great margin.

LHC will search for $tH^\pm$ direct production (Fig. 8.69), covering the mass range $M_{H^\pm} > m_t$. Due to nasty QCD backgrounds, the tb decay will be inaccessible [145], leaving $\tau\nu$ with BR$\sim 10\%$. This is very difficult due to a subtlety of tau decays. Left-handed taus decay to soft leptons [146]. Since neutrinos are left-handed, helicity conservation in scalar decay means all taus are as well. We need a lepton to trigger the event, and it must come

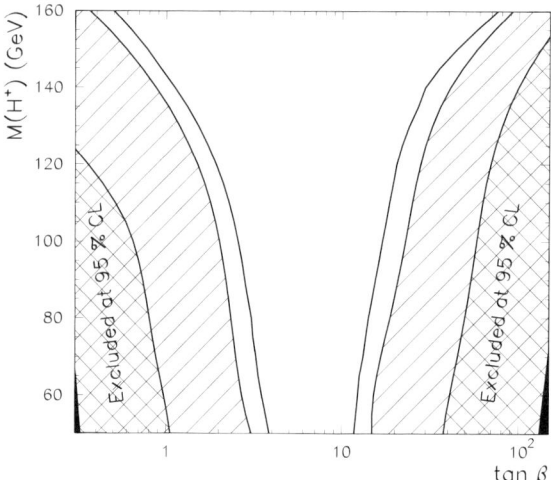

Fig. 8.71. Tevatron Run I 95% CL charged Higgs mass limits (double hatched lines) as a function of $\tan\beta$ from searches for top quark decays to bottom quark plus charged Higgs, and expected limits achievable in Run II (single hatched lines for 2 fb^{-1}, unhatched curves for 10 fb^{-1}). Figure from Ref. [144].

from $H^\pm$ instead of t, so that there is only one source of missing transverse momentum and we can fully reconstruct t, and $H^\pm$ transversely. Only a small fraction of the small rate could pass the necessary detector kinematic cuts to be recorded. This limits the search to large $\tan\beta$ or small $M_{H^\pm}$, where the production rate is largest. Fig. 8.72 shows ATLAS's expected transverse mass distributions for a fairly light and a heavy $H^\pm$.

Finally, we come to the overall picture of MSSM Higgs phenomenology at LHC. Primarily we're concerned with discovering all the states, but especially the charged Higgs as it's the key to confirming the existence of two Higgs doublets. That turns out to be extraordinarily difficult due to a combination of factors, from overwhelming QCD backgrounds to characteristics of left-handed tau decays. Figure 8.73 summarizes the reach for h, H, A and $H^\pm$ [70]. It's reassuring that the No-Lose Theorem holds and we're guaranteed to find at least one of the CP-even states, h or H. However, moderate $\tan\beta$ and the decoupling limit (large M_A) both present significant gaps in coverage to observe any of the additional states. This is especially more apparent once one realizes that the region below the solid black curve is already excluded by LEP, so those LHC access regions don't matter. The figure is from 2001 and needs updating – some significant positive changes exist – but the general picture remains.

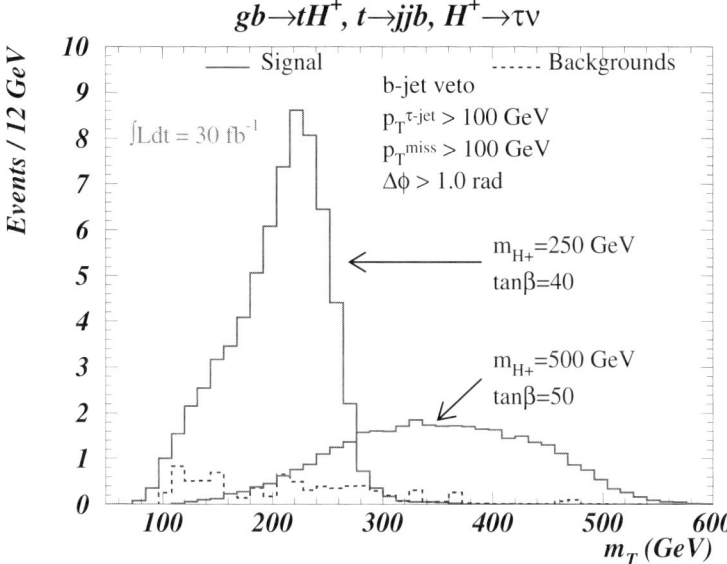

Fig. 8.72. Expected transverse mass distributions for light and heavy $H^{\pm} \to \tau\nu$ at ATLAS [147].

8.4.5. *MSSM Higgs potential*

I've touched on the bits of Higgs gauge and Yukawa couplings in the MSSM that are qualitatively different that the SM: M_A and $\tan\beta$. But we should look at self-couplings more closely, because in a general 2HDM (or the subset MSSM) they are radically different. First, because there are more Higgs bosons, there are more self-couplings – six for the neutral states alone, to be precise: λ_{hhh}, λ_{Hhh}, λ_{HHh}, λ_{HHH}, λ_{hAA}, λ_{HAA}. In the MSSM these are all equal to M_Z^2/v times various mixing angles (which aren't particularly enlightening so I don't show them) plus additional shifts from top quark Yukawa loop corrections. That is, they are all (mostly) gauge parameters. However, in the large-M_A decoupling limit which recovers the SM, $\lambda_{hhh} \to \lambda_{\rm SM}$.

If we discover SUSY, we'd start by assuming it's the MSSM. To measure the MSSM potential in that case, we'd have to observe at least six different Higgs pair production modes to measure the six self-couplings. (Note that I'm leaving out the possible self-couplings involving charged Higgses.) Inclusive Higgs pair production looks generally like it does in the SM, $gg \to \phi_1\phi_2$ via triangle and box loop diagrams as shown in Fig. 8.74, but the b quark loops become important and must be included.

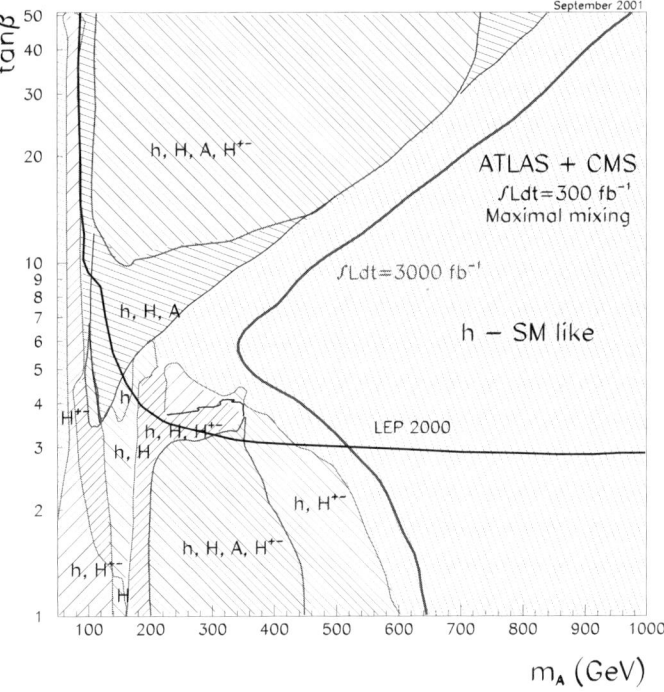

Fig. 8.73. Summary of MSSM Higgs boson discovery reaches at LHC (and extended to SLHC via the solid red line), combining ATLAS and CMS, in the $\tan\beta - M_A$ plane in the maximal mixing scenario. The reach is defined as 5σ discovery in at least one production and decay channel. Below the solid black curve is the region excluded by LEP. Figure from Ref. [70].

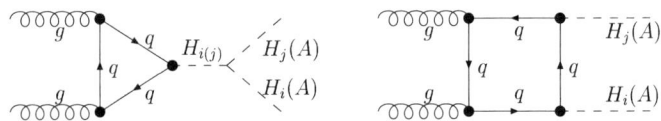

Fig. 8.74. Feynman diagrams for Higgs pair production in a 2HDM like the MSSM. The loops include both top and bottom quarks, and there are six possible processes (see text).

Unfortunately, the box diagram totally swamps the one containing the self-coupling we care about by a factor $\tan^2\beta$, and in any case backgrounds from $H/A b\bar{b}$ production appear to be overwhelming [103]: very generally, LHC would not obtain any λ measurements at all. The one very limited

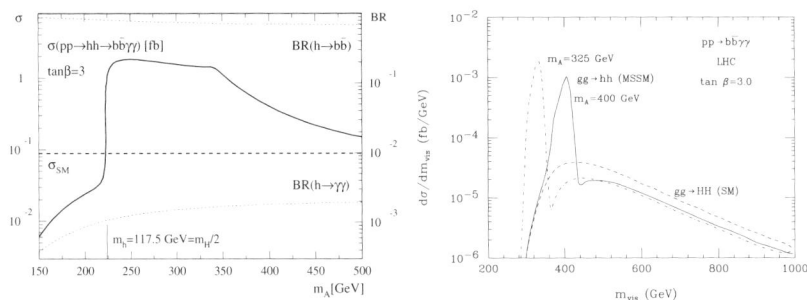

Fig. 8.75. Resonant MSSM Higgs pair production at LHC and decay to $b\bar{b}\gamma\gamma$ final states [103].

exception is that LHC could clearly observe Higgs pair production if it came from resonant heavy Higgs decay, $H/A \to hh$. An example peak is shown in Fig. 8.75. However, this would measure only a BR, at best, not an absolute coupling. Sadly, exactly the same situation exists for Higgs pairs at a future ILC [104].

8.5. Conclusions

The purpose of these lectures has not been to provide exhaustive coverage of all aspects of collider Higgs phenomenology. Rather, it's a solid introduction, focusing on the basics. This includes SM production and decay, mostly at LHC, where we're confident we could discovery a SM-like Higgs, and many non-SM-like variants. I focused on the most important channels which guarantee discovery, and especially in weak boson fusion (WBF) as those are the most powerful (best S/B, distinctive) search channels, covering the broadest range of Higgs mass. I emphasized that our understanding of LHC Higgs physics has changed dramatically from the days of the ATLAS TDR, for example, which is now quite obsolete. However, ATLAS has produced a plethora of Notes and summaries of Notes to cover the changes, and CMS published a fresh TDR [48] in 2006 which covers the changes as well.

We now understand the LHC to be such a spectacular Higgs factory that not only can it discover any mass of SM-like Higgs boson, it can also do an impressive job of measuring all its quantum properties. Granted, Higgs couplings measurements won't be precision-level if the Higgs is light, as expected from EW precision data, but they would nonetheless be absolute couplings measurements. The LHC can even make significant steps toward measuring the SM Higgs potential, at least the Higgs trilinear self-coupling, although depending on M_h it may require precision gauge and Yukawa couplings input from a future e^+e^- collider (an ILC) to control the major systematic uncertainties. I also highlighted where an ILC could make improvements to the LHC's measurements, and where it would be vital to filling in gaps in LHC results.

The final third of the lectures discussed BSM Higgs sectors, but only the 2HDM MSSM Higgs sector in any detail. Many SM Higgs sector extensions are rather simple variants on SM phenomenology, involving factorizable changes in production and decay rates (couplings), mostly arising from mixing angles. This is not general, however, and there are plenty of "exotic" models – Higgs triplets, for example – which would be qualitatively different, but therefore simultaneously distinctive. The popular focus on the MSSM 2HDM is because of several other outstanding questions in particle physics, like dark matter or the theoretical dirty laundry of the SM Higgs sector, which strongly motivate the other new physics.

Students who wish to engage in Higgs phenomenology research should definitely take the time to expand their scope beyond the SM and the MSSM. Other extensions are equally well-motivated, such as Little Higgs, not to mention strong dynamics. But the two well-studied basic models I covered here give one a strong foundation for other BSM Higgs phenomenology by analogy. Happy Higgs hunting!

Acknowledgments

I would like to thank Sally Dawson and the TASI 2006 organizers for the opportunity to give these lectures, and for an extremely pleasant experience at the summer school. Gracious thanks also go to Dan Berdine, John Boersma, Fabio Maltoni, Tilman Plehn, Jürgen Reuter, and especially Steve Martin for proofreading contributions above and beyond the call of duty.

References

[1] B. W. Lee, C. Quigg and H. B. Thacker, Phys. Rev. Lett. **38**, 883 (1977); ibid., Phys. Rev. D **16**, 1519 (1977).
[2] T. Appelquist and M. S. Chanowitz, Phys. Rev. Lett. **59**, 2405 (1987) [Erratum-ibid. **60**, 1589 (1988)].
[3] F. Maltoni, J. M. Niczyporuk and S. Willenbrock, Phys. Rev. D **65**, 033004 (2002).

[4] D. A. Dicus and H. J. He, Phys. Rev. D **71**, 093009 (2005).
[5] D. A. Dicus and H. J. He, Phys. Rev. Lett. **94**, 221802 (2005).
[6] J. F. Gunion, H. E. Haber, G. L. Kane and S. Dawson, "THE HIGGS HUNTER'S GUIDE," SCIPP-89/13, Addison-Wesley, 1989.
[7] A. Djouadi, arXiv:hep-ph/0503172 and arXiv:hep-ph/0503173.
[8] M. Spira, Fortsch. Phys. **46**, 203 (1998) [arXiv:hep-ph/9705337].
[9] J. F. Gunion and H. E. Haber, Nucl. Phys. B **272**, 1 (1986) [Erratum-ibid. B **402**, 567 (1993)].
[10] S. Weinberg, Phys. Rev. D **13**, 974 (1976) and Phys. Rev. D **19**, 1277 (1979).
[11] L. Susskind, Phys. Rev. D **20**, 2619 (1979).
[12] S. Dimopoulos and L. Susskind, Nucl. Phys. B **155**, 237 (1979).
[13] E. Eichten and K. D. Lane, Phys. Lett. B **90**, 125 (1980).
[14] B. Holdom, Phys. Rev. D **24**, 1441 (1981).
[15] C. T. Hill, Phys. Lett. B **266**, 419 (1991) and Phys. Lett. B **345**, 483 (1995).
[16] C. T. Hill and E. H. Simmons, Phys. Rept. **381**, 235 (2003) [Erratum-ibid. **390**, 553 (2004)]; K. Lane, arXiv:hep-ph/0202255.
[17] N. Arkani-Hamed, A. G. Cohen and H. Georgi, Phys. Lett. B **513**, 232 (2001).
[18] E. H. Simmons, R. S. Chivukula, H. J. He, M. Kurachi and M. Tanabashi, AIP Conf. Proc. **857**, 34 (2006) [arXiv:hep-ph/0606019].
[19] For nice reviews of Little Higgs models, see e.g. :
M. Schmaltz and D. Tucker-Smith, arXiv:hep-ph/0502182;
M. Perelstein, Prog. Part. Nucl. Phys. **58**, 247 (2007).
[20] Z. Chacko, H. S. Goh and R. Harnik, Phys. Rev. Lett. **96**, 231802 (2006).
[21] W. M. Yao et al. [Particle Data Group], J. Phys. G **33**, 1 (2006).
[22] A. Djouadi, J. Kalinowski and M. Spira, Comput. Phys. Commun. **108**, 56 (1998).
[23] G. Pocsik and T. Torma, Z. Phys. C **6**, 1 (1980);
T. G. Rizzo, Phys. Rev. D **22**, 722 (1980);
W. Y. Keung and W. J. Marciano, Phys. Rev. D **30**, 248 (1984);
E. Gross, G. Wolf and B. A. Kniehl, Z. Phys. C **63**, 417 (1994) [Err.-ibid. C **66**, 321 (1995)].
[24] T. G. Rizzo, Phys. Rev. D **22**, 178 (1980) [Addendum-ibid. D **22**, 1824 (1980)].
[25] J. R. Ellis, M. K. Gaillard and D. V. Nanopoulos, Nucl. Phys. B **106**, 292 (1976);
M. B. Gavela, G. Girardi, C. Malleville and P. Sorba, Nucl. Phys. B **193**, 257 (1981).
[26] L. Lyons.
[27] E. Gross and A. Klier, arXiv:hep-ex/0211058.
[28] See the ALEPH event displays public web page for this and other pretty pictures:
http://aleph.web.cern.ch/aleph/ALPUB/seminar/wds/Welcome.html

[29] M. Carena et al. [Higgs Working Group Collaboration], arXiv:hep-ph/0010338.
[30] T. Hahn, S. Heinemeyer, F. Maltoni, G. Weiglein and S. Willenbrock, arXiv:hep-ph/0607308; see http://maltoni.web.cern.ch/maltoni/TeV4LHC/SM.html for references to all the specific latest calculations.
[31] U. Aglietti et al., arXiv:hep-ph/0612172.
[32] F. Gianotti, Phys. Rept. **403**, 379 (2004).
[33] L. Babukhadia et al. [CDF & D0 Working Group Members], Phys. Rev. D **66**, 010001 (2002).
[34] Analysis of V. Veszpremi, O. Gonzalez, D. Bortoletto, A. Garfinkel, S.-M. Wang [CDF], Public Note CDF-8842, 2006; see http://www-cdf.fnal.gov/~veszpv/ for the figure.
[35] M. Dittmar and H. K. Dreiner, Phys. Rev. D **55**, 167 (1997).
[36] T. Han and R. J. Zhang, Phys. Rev. Lett. **82**, 25 (1999);
T. Han, A. S. Turcot and R. J. Zhang, Phys. Rev. D **59**, 093001 (1999).
[37] D. L. Rainwater and D. Zeppenfeld, Phys. Rev. D **60**, 113004 (1999) [Erratum-ibid. D **61**, 099901 (2000)].
[38] G. Bernardi [D0 Collaboration], arXiv:hep-ex/0612044.
[39] R. V. Harlander and W. B. Kilgore, Phys. Rev. Lett. **88**, 201801 (2002);
C. Anastasiou and K. Melnikov, Nucl. Phys. B **646**, 220 (2002);
V. Ravindran, J. Smith and W. L. van Neerven, Nucl. Phys. B **665**, 325 (2003).
[40] N. Kauer, Phys. Rev. D **70**, 014020 (2004).
[41] T. Binoth, M. Ciccolini, N. Kauer and M. Kramer, JHEP **0503**, 065 (2005) and **0612**, 046 (2006).
[42] ATLAS TDR, report CERN/LHCC/99-15 (1999).
[43] E. Richter-Was and M. Sapinski, Acta Phys. Polon. B **30** (1999) 1001.
[44] V. Drollinger, T. Muller and D. Denegri, Phys. Rev. D **66**, 010001 (2002).
[45] S. Abdullin et al., Eur. Phys. J. C **39S2** (2005) 41.
[46] W. T. Giele, T. Matsuura, M. H. Seymour and B. R. Webber, FERMILAB-CONF-90-228-T,
published in Snowmass Summer Study 1990:0137-147.
[47] J. Cammin, Ph.D. Thesis [ATLAS], BONN-IR-2004-06
[48] CMS TDR, report CERN/LHCC/2006-001 (2006).
[49] K. Cranmer, B. Quayle, et al., ATL-PHYS-2004-034.
[50] K. Cranmer, private communication, publication forthcoming.
[51] G. L. Kane, G. D. Kribs, S. P. Martin and J. D. Wells, Phys. Rev. D **53**, 213 (1996)
[52] For the early history, applied to heavy Higgs bosons, see the first three citations of Ref. [53].
[53] D. L. Rainwater, R. Szalapski and D. Zeppenfeld, Phys. Rev. D **54**, 6680 (1996).
[54] J. Campbell, R. K. Ellis and D. L. Rainwater, Phys. Rev. D **68**, 094021 (2003).
[55] S. Asai et al., Eur. Phys. J. C **32S2**, 19 (2004).

[56] Y. L. Dokshitzer, V. A. Khoze and S. Troian, in *Proceedings of the 6th International Conference on Physics in Collisions*, p. 365, ed. M. Derrick (World Scientific, 1987);
J. D. Bjorken, Int. J. Mod. Phys. A **7**, 4189 (1992) and Phys. Rev. D **47**, 101 (1993).
[57] V. D. Barger, R. J. N. Phillips and D. Zeppenfeld, Phys. Lett. B **346**, 106 (1995).
[58] D. L. Rainwater, arXiv:hep-ph/9908378.
[59] V. D. Barger, K. m. Cheung, T. Han and R. J. N. Phillips, Phys. Rev. D **42**, 3052 (1990).
[60] V. Del Duca, W. Kilgore, C. Oleari, C. Schmidt and D. Zeppenfeld, Phys. Rev. Lett. **87**, 122001 (2001), Nucl. Phys. B **616**, 367 (2001) and Phys. Rev. D **67**, 073003 (2003).
[61] D. L. Rainwater and D. Zeppenfeld, JHEP **9712**, 005 (1997)
[62] V. Buscher and K. Jakobs, Int. J. Mod. Phys. A **20**, 2523 (2005)
[63] R. K. Ellis, I. Hinchliffe, M. Soldate and J. J. van der Bij, Nucl. Phys. B **297**, 221 (1988).
[64] T. Plehn, D. L. Rainwater and D. Zeppenfeld, Phys. Rev. D **61**, 093005 (2000).
[65] K. Cranmer, private communication.
[66] N. Kauer and D. Zeppenfeld, Phys. Rev. D **65**, 014021 (2002);
N. Kauer, Phys. Rev. D **67**, 054013 (2003) and Phys. Rev. D **70**, 014020 (2004).
[67] S. Dittmaier, P. Uwer, and S. Weinzierl, in preparation.
[68] F. Maltoni, D. L. Rainwater and S. Willenbrock, Phys. Rev. D **66**, 034022 (2002).
[69] V. Kostioukhine, J. Leveque, A. Rozanov, and J.B. de Vivie, ATL-PHYS-2002-019.
[70] F. Gianotti *et al.*[SLHC report], Eur. Phys. J. C **39**, 293 (2004).
[71] J. A. Aguilar-Saavedra *et al.* [ECFA/DESY LC Phys. Wrk. Grp.], arXiv:hep-ph/0106315.
[72] J. F. Gunion, H. E. Haber and R. Van Kooten, arXiv:hep-ph/0301023.
[73] G. Weiglein *et al.* [LHC/LC Study Group], Phys. Rept. **426**, 47 (2006).
[74] C. P. Burgess, J. Matias and M. Pospelov, Int. J. Mod. Phys. A **17**, 1841 (2002).
[75] M. Spira, private communication.
[76] S. P. Martin, arXiv:hep-ph/0701051.
[77] T. Hahn *et al.*, arXiv:hep-ph/0611373.
[78] V. Drollinger and A. Sopczak, Phys. Rev. D **66**, 010001 (2002).
[79] G. Velo and D. Zwanziger, Phys. Rev. **186**, 1337 (1969) and Phys. Rev. **188**, 2218 (1969);
B. Schroer, R. Seiler and J. A. Swieca, Phys. Rev. D **2** (1970) 2927.
[80] C. N. Yang, Phys. Rev. **77**, 242 (1950);
L.D.Landau, Dokl. Akad. Nawk., USSR 60, 207-209 (1948).
[81] E. Accomando *et al.*, arXiv:hep-ph/0608079.
[82] J. R. Dell'Aquila and C. A. Nelson, Phys. Rev. D **33**, 93 (1986).

[83] C. P. Buszello, I. Fleck, P. Marquard and J. J. van der Bij, Eur. Phys. J. C **32**, 209 (2004).
[84] S. Y. Choi, D. J. Miller, M. M. Muhlleitner and P. M. Zerwas, Phys. Lett. B **553**, 61 (2003).
[85] T. Plehn, D. L. Rainwater and D. Zeppenfeld, Phys. Rev. Lett. **88**, 051801 (2002).
[86] W. Buchmuller and D. Wyler, Nucl. Phys. B **268**, 621 (1986).
[87] K. Hagiwara, S. Ishihara, J. Kamoshita and B. A. Kniehl, Eur. Phys. J. C **14**, 457 (2000)
[88] D. J. Miller *et al.*, Phys. Lett. B **505**, 149 (2001).
[89] D. Zeppenfeld, R. Kinnunen, A. Nikitenko, E. Richter-Was, Phys. Rev. D **62**, 013009 (2000).
[90] M. Duhrssen *et al.*, Phys. Rev. D **70**, 113009 (2004).
[91] C. Anastasiou, K. Melnikov and F. Petriello, Phys. Rev. D **72**, 097302 (2005).
[92] P. Garcia-Abia, W. Lohmann and A. Raspereza, LC-PHSM-2000-062 *Prepared for 5th International Linear Collider Workshop, Fermilab, Batavia, Illinois, 24-28 Oct. 2000.*
[93] T. Abe *et al.* [American Linear Collider Working Group], in *Proc. of the APS/DPF/DPB Summer Study on the Future of Particle Physics (Snowmass 2001)* ed. N. Graf, arXiv:hep-ex/0106056.
[94] A. Juste and G. Merino, arXiv:hep-ph/9910301.
[95] K. Desch and M. Schumacher, Eur. Phys. J. C **46**, 527 (2006).
[96] A. Gay, arXiv:hep-ph/0604034.
[97] E. W. N. Glover and J. J. van der Bij, Nucl. Phys. B **309**, 282 (1988).
[98] T. Plehn, M. Spira and P. M. Zerwas, Nucl. Phys. B **479**, 46 (1996) [Erratum-ibid. B **531**, 655 (1998)].
[99] S. Dawson, S. Dittmaier and M. Spira, Phys. Rev. D **58**, 115012 (1998).
[100] A. Djouadi, W. Kilian, M. Muhlleitner and P. M. Zerwas, Eur. Phys. J. C **10**, 45 (1999).
[101] U. Baur, T. Plehn and D. L. Rainwater, Phys. Rev. Lett. **89**, 151801 (2002) and
Phys. Rev. D **67**, 033003 (2003).
[102] A. Dahlhoff, private communication.
[103] U. Baur, T. Plehn and D. L. Rainwater, Phys. Rev. D **69**, 053004 (2004).
[104] A. Djouadi, W. Kilian, M. Muhlleitner and P. M. Zerwas, Eur. Phys. J. C **10**, 27 (1999).
[105] U. Baur, T. Plehn and D. L. Rainwater, Phys. Rev. D **69**, 053004 (2004).
[106] A. De Roeck, *In the Proceedings of 32nd SLAC Summer Institute on Particle Physics (SSI 2004): Natures Greatest Puzzles, Menlo Park, California, 2-13 Aug 2004, pp FRT002.*
[107] E. Accomando *et al.* [CLIC Physics Working Group], arXiv:hep-ph/0412251.
[108] S. Kanemura, S. Kiyoura, Y. Okada, E. Senaha and C. P. Yuan, Phys. Lett. B **558**, 157 (2003).
[109] T. Plehn and M. Rauch, Phys. Rev. D **72**, 053008 (2005).

[110] T. Binoth, S. Karg, N. Kauer and R. Ruckl, Phys. Rev. D **74**, 113008 (2006).
[111] C. T. Hill and E. H. Simmons, Phys. Rept. **381**, 235 (2003) [Erratum-ibid. **390**, 553 (2004)]
[112] G. Cacciapaglia, C. Csaki, C. Grojean and J. Terning, eConf **C040802**, FRT004 (2004)
[Czech. J. Phys. **55**, B613 (2005)].
[113] V. Barger, T. Han, P. Langacker, B. McElrath and P. Zerwas, Phys. Rev. D **67**, 115001 (2003).
[114] K. Hagiwara, R. Szalapski and D. Zeppenfeld, Phys. Lett. B **318**, 155 (1993).
[115] K. Hagiwara, S. Matsumoto and R. Szalapski, Phys. Lett. B **357**, 411 (1995).
[116] R. Szalapski, Phys. Rev. D **57**, 5519 (1998).
[117] M. Beyer et al., Eur. Phys. J. C **48**, 353 (2006).
[118] V. Hankele, G. Klamke, D. Zeppenfeld and T. Figy, Phys. Rev. D **74**, 095001 (2006).
[119] T. D. Lee, Phys. Rev. D **8**, 1226 (1973).
[120] One of the early 2HDMs to be written down was in the Ph.D. dissertation of C. T. Hill (Caltech, 1977), but is unpublished. It may contain the first discussion of the 2HDM potential. Some of those results may be found in a much later publication:
C. T. Hill, C. N. Leung and S. Rao, Nucl. Phys. B **262**, 517 (1985).
[121] H. Huffel and G. Pocsik, Z. Phys. C **8**, 13 (1981).
[122] S. P. Martin, arXiv:hep-ph/9709356.
[123] J. F. Gunion and H. E. Haber, Nucl. Phys. B **272**, 1 (1986) [Erratum-ibid. B **402**, 567 (1993)] and Nucl. Phys. B **278**, 449 (1986).
[124] A. N. Okpara, Ph. D. dissertation, http://www.ub.uni-heidelberg.de/archiv/1873.
[125] [LEP Higgs Working Group for Higgs boson searches], arXiv:hep-ex/0107031.
[126] A. Heister et al. [ALEPH Collaboration], Phys. Lett. B **543**, 1 (2002).
[127] J. Abdallah et al. [DELPHI Collaboration], Eur. Phys. J. C **34**, 399 (2004).
[128] P. Achard et al. [L3 Collaboration], Phys. Lett. B **575**, 208 (2003).
[129] D. Horvath [OPAL Collaboration], Nucl. Phys. A **721**, 453 (2003).
[130] http://lephiggs.web.cern.ch/LEPHIGGS/www/Welcome.html
[131] S. Schael et al. [ALEPH Collaboration], Eur. Phys. J. C **47**, 547 (2006); see citations therein for the individual collaborations' results.
[132] P. Bechtle [LEP Collaboration], PoS **HEP2005**, 325 (2006).
[133] A. Sopczak [ALEPH Collaboration], arXiv:hep-ph/0602136.
[134] G. Abbiendi et al. [OPAL Collaboration], Eur. Phys. J. C **40**, 317 (2005).
[135] T. Plehn, D. L. Rainwater and D. Zeppenfeld, Phys. Lett. B **454**, 297 (1999).
[136] M. Schumacher, arXiv:hep-ph/0410112.
[137] U. Ellwanger, J. F. Gunion and C. Hugonie, arXiv:hep-ph/0111179.

[138] U. Ellwanger, J. F. Gunion, C. Hugonie and S. Moretti, arXiv:hep-ph/0305109.
[139] U. Ellwanger, J. F. Gunion and C. Hugonie, JHEP **0507**, 041 (2005).
[140] S. Moretti, S. Munir and P. Poulose, Phys. Lett. B **644**, 241 (2007).
[141] R. Kinnunen *et al.*, Eur. Phys. J. C **40N5**, 23 (2005); and references therein.
[142] S. Dittmaier, M. Kramer and M. Spira, Phys. Rev. D **70**, 074010 (2004).
[143] S. Dawson, C. B. Jackson, L. Reina and D. Wackeroth, Mod. Phys. Lett. A **21**, 89 (2006).
[144] D. Chakraborty, J. Konigsberg and D. Rainwater, Ann. Rev. Nucl. Part. Sci. **53**, 301 (2003).
[145] K. A. Assamagan *et al.* [Higgs Working Group Collaboration], arXiv:hep-ph/0406152.
[146] K. Hagiwara, A. D. Martin and D. Zeppenfeld, Phys. Lett. B **235**, 198 (1990).
[147] K. A. Assamagan, Y. Coadou and A. Deandrea, Eur. Phys. J. direct C **4**, 9 (2002).

Chapter 9

Z′ Phenomenology and the LHC

Thomas G. Rizzo

Stanford Linear Accelerator Center,
2575 Sand Hill Rd., Menlo Park, CA, 94025,
rizzo@slac.stanford.edu

A brief pedagogical overview of the phenomenology of Z′ gauge bosons is presented. Such particles can arise in various electroweak extensions of the Standard Model (SM). We provide a quick survey of a number of Z′ models, review the current constraints on the possible properties of a Z′ and explore in detail how the LHC may discover and help elucidate the nature of these new particles. We provide an overview of the Z′ studies that have been performed by both ATLAS and CMS. The role of the ILC in determining Z′ properties is also discussed.

9.1. Introduction: What is a Z′ and What is It Not?

To an experimenter, a Z′ is a resonance, which is more massive than the SM Z, observed in the Drell-Yan process $pp(p\bar{p}) \to l^+l^- + X$, where $l=e, \mu$ and, sometimes, τ, at the LHC(or the Tevatron). To a theorist, the production mechanism itself tells us that this new particle is neutral, colorless and self-adjoint, *i.e.*, it is its own antiparticle. However, such a new state could still be interpreted in many different ways. We may classify these possibilities according to the spin of the excitation, *e.g.*, a spin-0 $\tilde{\nu}$ in R-parity violating SUSY,[1] a spin-2 Kaluza-Klein(KK) excitation of the graviton as in the Randall-Sundrum(RS) model,[2,3] or even a spin-1 KK excitation of a SM gauge boson from some extra dimensional model.[4,5] Another possibility for the spin-1 case is that this particle is the carrier of a new force, a new neutral gauge boson arising from an extension of the SM gauge group, *i.e.*, a true Z′, which will be our subject below.[6] Given this discussion it is already clear that once a new Z′-like resonance is discovered it will first be necessary to measure its spin as quickly as possible to have some idea what kind of new physics we are dealing with. As will be discussed below this can be done rather easily with only a few hundred events by measuring the dilepton angular distribution in the reconstructed Z′ rest frame. Thus, a Z′ is a neutral, colorless, self-adjoint, spin-1 gauge boson that is a carrier of a new force.[a]

Once found to be a Z′, the next goal of the experimenter will be to determine as well as possible the couplings of this new state to the particles (mainly fermions) of the SM, *i.e.*, to *identify* which Z′ it is. As we will see there are a huge number of models which predict the existence of a Z′.[6,8] Is this new particle one of those or is it something completely new? How does it fit into a larger theoretical framework?

9.2. Z′ Basics

If our goal is to determine the Z′ couplings to SM fermions, the first question one might ask is 'How many fermionic couplings does a Z′ have?' Since the Z′ is a color singlet its couplings are color-diagonal. Thus (allowing for the possibility of light Dirac neutrinos), in general the Z′ will have 24 distinct couplings-one for each of the two-component SM fields: $u_{L_i}, d_{L_i}, \nu_{L_i}, e_{L_i} + (L \to R)$ with $i = 1 - 3$ labeling the three generations. (Of course, exotic fermions not present in the SM can also occur but we will ignore these for the moment.) For such a generic Z′ these couplings are *non-universal*, *i.e.*, family-dependent and this can result in dangerous flavor changing neutral currents(FCNC) in low-energy processes. The constraints on such beasts are known to be quite strong from both $K - \bar{K}$ and $B_{d,s} - \bar{B}_{d,s}$ mixing[9] as well as from a large number of other low-energy processes. There FCNC are generated by fermion mixing which is needed to diagonalize the corresponding fermion mass matrix. As an example, consider schematically the Z′ coupling to left-handed down-type quarks in the weak basis, *i.e.*, $\bar{d}_{L_i}^0 \eta_i d_{L_i}^0 Z'$, with η_i being a set of coupling parameters whose different values would represent the generational-dependent couplings. For simplicity, now let $\eta_{1,2} = a$ and $\eta_3 = b$ and make the unitary transformation to the physical, mass eigenstate basis, $d_{L_i}^0 = U_{ij} d_{L_j}$. Some algebra leads to FCNC couplings of the type $\sim (b - a) \bar{d}_{L_i} U_{i3}^\dagger U_{3j} d_{L_j} Z'$. Given the existing experimental constraints, since we expect these mixing matrix elements to be of order those in the CKM matrix and a, b to be O(1), the Z′ mass must be huge, ~ 100 TeV or more, and outside the reach of the LHC. Thus un-

---

[a]Distinguishing a Z′ from a spin-1 KK excitation is a difficult subject beyond the scope of the present discussion.[7]

less there is some special mechanism acting to suppress FCNC it is highly likely that a Z′ which is light enough to be observed at the LHC will have *generation-independent* couplings, *i.e.*, now the number of couplings is reduced: $24 \to 8$ (or 7 if neutrinos are Majorana fields and the RH neutrinos are extremely heavy).

Further constraints on the number of independent couplings arise from several sources. First, consider the generator or 'charge' to which the Z′ couples, T'. Within any given model the group theory nature of T' will be known so that one may ask if $[T', T_i] = 0$, with T_i being the usual SM weak isospin generators of $SU(2)_L$. If the answer is in the affirmative, then all members of any SM representation can be labeled by a common eigenvalue of T'. This means that u_L and d_L, *i.e.*, $Q^T = (u,d)_L$, as well as ν_L and e_L, *i.e.*, $L^T = (\nu, e)_L$ (and dropping generation labels), will have identical Z′ couplings so that the number of independent couplings is now reduced from $8 \to 6 (7 \to 5)$. As we will see, this is a rather common occurrence in the case of garden-variety Z′ which originate from extended GUT groups[6] such as $SO(10)$ or E_6. Clearly, models which do not satisfy these conditions lead to Z′ couplings which are at least partially proportional to the diagonal SM isospin generator itself, *i.e.*, $T' = aT_3$.

In UV completed theories a further constraint on the Z′ couplings arises from the requirement of anomaly cancellation. Anomalies can arise from one-loop fermionic triangle graphs with three external gauge boson legs; recall that fermions of opposite chirality contribute with opposite signs to the relevant 'VVA' parts of such graphs. In the SM, the known fermions automatically lead to anomaly cancellation in a generation independent way when the external gauge fields are those of the SM. The existence of the Z′, together with gauge invariance and the existence of gravity, tells us that there are 6 new graphs that must also vanish to make the theory renormalizable thus leading to 6 more constraints on the couplings of the Z′. For example, the graph with an external Z′ and 2 gluons tells us that the sum over the colored fermion's eigenvalues of T' must vanish. We can write these 6 constraints as (remembering to flip signs for RH fields)

$$\sum_{color triplets, i} T'_i = \sum_{isodoublets, i} T'_i = 0$$

$$\sum_i Y_i^2 T'_i = \sum_i Y_i T'^2_i = 0 \qquad (9.1)$$

$$\sum_i T'^3_i = \sum_i T'_i = 0,$$

where here we are summing over various fermion representations. These 6 constraints can be quite restrictive, e.g., if $T' \neq aT_{3L} + bY$, then even in the simplest Z' model, ν_R (not present in the SM!) must exist to allow for anomaly cancellation. More generally, one finds that the existence of new gauge bosons will also require the existence of other new, vector-like (with respect to the SM gauge group) fermions to cancel anomalies, something which happens automatically in the case of extended GUT groups. It is natural in such scenarios that the masses of these new fermions are comparable to that of the Z' itself so that they may also occur as decay products of the Z' thus modifying the various Z' branching fractions. If these modes are present then there are more coupling parameters to be determined.

9.3. Z-Z' Mixing

In a general theory the Z' and the SM Z are not true mass eigenstates due to mixing; in principle, this mixing can arise from two different mechanisms.

In the case where the new gauge group G is a simple new $U(1)'$, the most general set of $SU(2)_L \times U(1)_Y \times U(1)'$ kinetic terms in the original weak basis (here denoted by tilded fields) is

$$\mathcal{L}_K = -\frac{1}{4}W^a_{\mu\nu}W^{\mu\nu}_a - \frac{1}{4}\tilde{B}_{\mu\nu}\tilde{B}^{\mu\nu} - \frac{1}{4}\tilde{Z}'_{\mu\nu}\tilde{Z}'^{\mu\nu} - \frac{\sin\chi}{2}\tilde{Z}'_{\mu\nu}\tilde{B}^{\mu\nu}, \quad (9.2)$$

where $\sin\chi$ is a parameter. Here W^a_μ is the usual $SU(2)_L$ gauge field while $\tilde{B}_\mu, \tilde{Z}_\mu$ are those for $U(1)_Y$ and $U(1)'$, respectively. Such gauge kinetic mixing terms can be induced (if not already present) at the one-loop level if $Tr(T'Y) \neq 0$. Note that if G were a nonabelian group then no such mixed terms would be allowed by gauge invariance. In this basis the fermion couplings to the gauge fields can be schematically written as $\bar{f}(g_L T_a W^a + g_Y Y \tilde{B} + \tilde{g}_{Z'} T' \tilde{Z}')f$. To go to the physical basis, we make the linear transformations $\tilde{B} \to B - \tan\chi Z'$ and $\tilde{Z}' \to Z'/\cos\chi$ which diagonalizes $\mathcal{L}_K$ and leads to the modified fermion couplings $\bar{f}[g_L T_a W^a + g_Y Y B + g_{Z'}(T' + \delta Y)Z']f$ where $g_{Z'} = \tilde{g}_{Z'}/\cos\chi$ and $\delta = -g_Y \tan\chi/g_{Z'}$. Here we see that the Z' picks up an additional coupling proportional to the usual weak hypercharge. $\delta \neq 0$ symbolizes this gauge kinetic mixing[10] and provides a window for its experimental observation. In a GUT framework, being a running parameter, $\delta(M_{GUT}) = 0$, but can it can become non-zero via RGE running at lower mass scales if the low energy sector contains matter in incomplete GUT representations. In most models[10] where this happens, $|\delta(\sim \text{TeV})| \leq 1/2$.

Z-Z' mixing can also occur through the conventional Higgs-induced SSB mechanism (*i.e.*, mass mixing) if the usual Higgs doublet(s), H_i (with vevs v_{D_i}), are *not* singlets under the new gauge group G. In general, the breaking of G requires the introduction of SM singlet Higgs fields, S_j (with vevs v_{S_j}). These singlet vevs should be about an order of magnitude larger than the typical doublet vevs since a Z' has not yet been observed. As usual the Higgs kinetic terms will generate the W, Z and Z' masses which for the neutral fields look like

$$\sum_i \left[\left(\frac{g_L}{c_w} T_{3L} Z + g_{Z'} T' Z'\right) v_{D_i}\right]^2 + \sum_j [g_{Z'} T' v_{S_j} Z']^2, \quad (9.3)$$

where $c_w = \cos\theta_W$. (Note that the massless photon has already been 'removed' from this discussion.) The square of the first term in the first sum produces the square of the usual SM Z boson mass term, $\sim M_Z^2 Z^2$. The square of the last term in this sum plus the square of the second sum produces the corresponding Z' mass term, $\sim M_{Z'}^2 Z'^2$. However, the ZZ' interference piece in the first sum leads to Z-Z' mixing provided $T' H_i \neq 0$ for at least one i; note that the scale of this cross term is set by the doublet vevs and hence is of order $\sim M_Z^2$.

This analysis can be summarized by noting that the interaction above actually generates a mass (squared) matrix in the ZZ' basis:

$$\mathcal{M}^2 = \begin{pmatrix} M_Z^2 & \beta M_Z^2 \\ \beta M_Z^2 & M_{Z'}^2 \end{pmatrix}. \quad (9.4)$$

Note that the symmetry breaking dependent parameter β,

$$\beta = \frac{4 c_w g_{Z'}}{g_L} \left[\sum_i T_{3L_i} T'_i v_{D_i}^2\right] \Big/ \sum_i v_{D_i}^2, \quad (9.5)$$

can be argued to be O(1) or less on rather general grounds. Since this matrix is real, the diagonalization of $\mathcal{M}^2$ proceeds via a simple rotation through a mixing angle ϕ, *i.e.*, by writing $Z = Z_1 \cos\phi - Z_2 \sin\phi$, etc, which yields the mass eigenstates $Z_{1,2}$ with masses $M_{1,2}$; given present data we may expect $r = M_1^2/M_2^2 \leq 0.01 - 0.02$. $Z_1 \simeq Z$ is the state presently produced at colliders, *i.e.*, $M_1 = 91.1875 \pm 0.0021$ GeV, and thus we might also expect that ϕ must be quite small for the SM to work as well as it does. Defining $\rho = M_Z^2/M_1^2$, with M_Z being the would-be mass of the Z if no mixing occurred, we can approximate

$$\phi = -\beta r [1 + (1 + \beta^2) r + O(r^2)] \quad (9.6)$$
$$\delta\rho = \beta^2 r [1 + (1 + 2\beta^2) r + O(r^2)],$$

where $\delta\rho = \rho - 1$, so that β determines the sign of ϕ. We thus expect that both $\delta\rho, |\phi| < 10^{-2}$. In fact, if we are *not* dealing with issues associated with precision measurements[11] then Z-Z' mixing is expected to be so small that it can be safely neglected.

It is important to note that non-zero mixing modifies the predicted SM Z couplings to $\frac{g_L}{c_w}(T_{3L} - x_W Q)c_\phi + g_{Z'}T's_\phi$, where $x_W = \sin^2\theta_W$, which can lead to many important effects. For example, the partial width for $Z_1 \to f\bar{f}$ to lowest order (*i.e.*, apart from phase space, QCD and QED radiative corrections) is now given by

$$\Gamma(Z_1 \to f\bar{f}) = N_c \frac{\rho G_F M_1^3 (v_{eff}^2 + a_{eff}^2)}{6\sqrt{2}\pi}, \qquad (9.7)$$

where N_c is a color factor, ρ is given above and

$$v_{eff} = (T_{3L} - 2x_W Q)c_\phi + \frac{g_{Z'}}{g_L/(2c_w)}(T'_L + T'_R)s_\phi \qquad (9.8)$$

$$a_{eff} = T_{3L}c_\phi + \frac{g_{Z'}}{g_L/(2c_w)}(T'_L - T'_R)s_\phi,$$

and where $T'_{L,R}$ are the eigenvalues of T' for $f_{L,R}$. Other effects that can occur include decay modes such as $Z_2 \to W^+W^-, Z_1 H_i$, where H_i is a light Higgs, which are now induced via mixing. If T' has no T_3 component this is the only way such decays can occur at tree level. In the case of the $Z_2 \to W^+W^-$ mode, an interesting cancellation occurs: the partial width scales as $s_\phi^2 (M_2/M_W)^4$, where the second factor follows from the Goldstone Boson Equivalence Theorem.[12] However, since $s_\phi \simeq -\beta r$ and $r = M_1^2/M_2^2 \simeq M_Z^2/M_2^2$, we find instead that the partial width goes as $\sim \beta^2$ without any additional mass enhancement or suppression factors. The tiny mixing angle induced by small r has been offset by the large M_2/M_W ratio! In specific models, one finds that this small Z-Z' mixing leads to $Z_2 \to W^+W^-$ partial widths which can be comparable to other decay modes. Of course, $Z_2 \to W^+W^-$ can be also be induced at the one-loop level but there the amplitude will be suppressed by the corresponding loop factor as well as possible small mass ratios.

9.4. Some Sample Z' Models

There are many (hundreds of) models on the market which predict a Z' falling into two rather broad categories depending on whether or not they arise in a GUT scenario. The list below is *only* meant to be representative and is very far from exhaustive and I beg pardon if your favorite model is not represented.

The two most popular GUT scenarios are the Left Right Symmetric Model (LRM)[13] and those that come from E_6 grand unification.[6]

(i) In the E_6 case one imagines a symmetry breaking pattern $E_6 \to SO(10) \times U(1)_\psi \to SU(5) \times U(1)_\chi \times U(1)_\psi$. Then $SU(5)$ breaks to the SM and only one linear combination $G = U(1)_\theta = c_\theta U(1)_\psi - s_\theta U(1)_\chi$ remains light at the TeV scale. θ is treated as a free parameter[b] and the particular values $\theta = 0$, $-90°$, $\sin^{-1}\sqrt{(3/8)} \simeq 37.76°$ and $-\sin^{-1}\sqrt{(5/8)} \simeq -52.24°$, correspond to 'special' models called ψ, χ, η and I, respectively. These models are sometimes referred to in the literature as effective rank-5 models (ER5M). In this case, neglecting possible kinetic mixing,

$$g_{Z'}T' = \lambda \frac{g_L}{c_w}\sqrt{\frac{5x_W}{3}}\left(\frac{Q_\psi c_\theta}{2\sqrt{6}} - \frac{Q_\chi s_\theta}{2\sqrt{10}}\right), \qquad (9.9)$$

where $\lambda \simeq 1$ arises from RGE evolution. The parameters $Q_{\psi,\chi}$ originate from the embeddings of the SM fermions into the fundamental **27** representation of E_6. A detailed list of their values can be found in the second paper in[6] with an abbreviated version given in the Table below in LH field notation. Note that this is the *standard* form for this embedding and there are other possibilities.[6] These other choices can be recovered by a shift in the parameter θ. Note further that in addition to the SM fermions plus the RH neutrino, E_6 predicts, per generation, an additional neutral singlet, S^c, along with an electric charge $Q = -1/3$, color triplet, vector-like isosinglet, h, and a color singlet, vector-like isodoublet whose top member has $Q = 0$, H (along with their conjugate fields). These exotic fermions with masses comparable to the Z' cancel the anomalies in the theory and can lead to interesting new phenomenology[6] but we will generally ignore them in our discussion below. In many cases these states are quite heavy and thus will not participate in Z' decays.

(ii) The LRM, based on the low-energy gauge group $SU(2)_L \times SU(2)_R \times U(1)_{B-L}$, can arise from an $SO(10)$ or E_6 GUT. Unlike the case of ER5M, not only is there a Z' but there is also a new charged $W_R^\pm$ gauge boson since here $G = SU(2)$. In general $\kappa = g_R/g_L \neq 1$ is a free parameter but must be $> x_W/(1 - x_W)$ for the existence of real gauge couplings. On occasions, the parameter $\alpha_{LR} = \sqrt{c_w^2 \kappa^2/x_W^2 - 1}$ is also often used. In this case we

---

[b]The reader should be aware that there are several different definitions of this mixing angle in the literature, *i.e.*, Z' = $Z_\chi \cos\beta + z_\psi \sin\beta$ occurs quite commonly.

Table 9.1. Quantum numbers for various SM and exotic fermions in LH notation in E_6 models

Representation	Q_ψ	Q_χ
Q	1	-1
L	1	3
u^c	1	-1
d^c	1	3
e^c	1	-1
ν^c	1	-5
H	-2	-2
H^c	-2	2
h	-2	2
h^c	-2	-2
S^c	4	0

find that

$$g_{Z'}T' = \frac{g_L}{c_w}[\kappa^2 - (1+\kappa^2)x_W]^{-1/2}[x_W T_{3L} + \kappa^2(1-x_W)T_{3R} - x_W Q]. \quad (9.10)$$

The mass ratio of the W' and Z' is given by

$$\frac{M_{Z'}^2}{M_{W'}^2} = \frac{\kappa^2(1-x_W)\rho_R}{\kappa^2(1-x_W) - x_W} > 1, \quad (9.11)$$

with the values $\rho_R = 1(2)$ depending upon whether $SU(2)_R$ is broken by either Higgs doublets (or by triplets). The existence of a $W' = W_R$ with the correct mass ratio to the Z' provides a good test of this model. Note that due to the LR symmetry we need not introduce additional fermions in this model to cancel anomalies although right-handed neutrinos are present automatically. In the E_6 case a variant of this model[14] can be constructed by altering the embeddings of the SM and exotic fermions into the ordinary **10** and **5** representations (called the Alternative LRM, *i.e.*, ALRM).

(*iii*) The Z' in the Little Higgs scenario[15] provides the best non-GUT example. The new particles in these models, *i.e.*, new gauge bosons, fermions and Higgs, are necessary to remove at one-loop the quadratic divergence of the SM Higgs mass and their natures are dictated by the detailed group structure of the particular model. This greatly restricts the possible couplings of such states. With a W' which is essentially degenerate in mass with the Z', the Z' is found to couple like $g_{Z'}T' = (g_L/2)T_{3L}\cot\theta_H$, with θ_H another mixing parameter.

(iv) Another non-GUT example[17] is based on the group $SU(2)_l \times SU(2)_h \times U(1)_Y$ with l, h referring to 'light' and 'heavy'. The first 2 generations couple to $SU(2)_l$ while the third couples to $SU(2)_h$. In this case the Z' and W' are again found to be degenerate and the Z' couples to $g_{Z'}T' = g_L[\cot\Phi T_{3l} - \tan\Phi T_{3h}]$ with Φ another mixing angle. Such a model is a good example of where the Z' couplings are generation dependent.

(v) A final example is a Z' that has couplings which are exactly the same as those of the SM Z (SSM), but is just heavier. This is not a real model but is very commonly used as a 'standard candle' in experimental Z' searches. A more realistic variant of this model is one in which a Z' has *no* couplings to SM fermions in the weak basis but the couplings are then induced in the mass eigenstate basis Z-Z' via mixing. In this case the relevant couplings of the Z' are those of the SM Z but scaled down by a factor of $\sin\phi$.

A nice way to consider rather broad classes of Z' models has recently been described by Carena *et al.*.[18] In this approach one first augments the SM fermion spectrum by adding to it a pair of vector-like (with respect to the SM) fermions, one transforming like L and the other like d^c; this is essentially what happens in the E_6 GUT model. The authors then look for families of models that satisfy the six anomaly constraints with generation-independent couplings. Such an analysis yields several sets of 1-parameter solutions for the generator T' but leaves the coupling $g_{Z'}$ free. The simplest such solution is $T' = B - xL$, with x a free par meter. Some other solutions include $T' = Q + xu_R$ (*i.e.*, $T'(Q) = 1/3$ and $T'(u_R) = x/3$ and all others fixed by anomaly cancellation), $T' = d_R - xu_R$ and $T' = 10 + x\bar{5}$, where '10' and $\bar{5}$ refer to $SU(5)$ GUT assignments.

9.5. What Do We Know Now? Present Z' Constraints

Z' searches are of two kinds: indirect and direct. Important constraints arise from both sources at the present moment though this is likely to change radically in the near future.

9.5.1. *Indirect Z' Searches*

In this case one looks for deviations from the SM that might be associated with the existence of a Z'; this usually involves precision electroweak measurements at, below and *above* the Z-pole. The cross section and forward backward asymmetry, A_{FB}, measurements at LEPII take place at high center of mass energies which are still (far) below the actual Z' mass.

Since such constraints are indirect, one can generalize from the case of a new Z' and consider a more encompassing framework based on contact interactions.[19] Here one 'integrates out' the new physics (since we assume we are at energies below which the new physics is directly manifest) and express its influence via higher-dimensional (usually dim-6) operators. For example, in the dim-6 case, for the process $e^+e^- \to \bar{f}f$, we can consider an effective Lagrangian of the form[19]

$$\mathcal{L} = \mathcal{L}_{SM} + \frac{4\pi}{\Lambda^2(1+\delta_{ef})} \sum_{ij=L,R} \eta_{ij}^f (\bar{e}_i \gamma_\mu e_i)(\bar{f}_j \gamma^\mu f_j), \qquad (9.12)$$

where Λ is called 'the compositeness scale' for historic reasons, δ_{ef} takes care of the statistics in the case of Bhabha scattering, and the η's are chirality structure coefficients which are of order unity. The exchange of many new states can be described in this way and can be analyzed simultaneously. The corresponding parameter bounds can then be interpreted within your favorite model. This prescription can be used for data at all energies as long as these energies are far below Λ.

Z-pole measurements mainly restrict the Z-Z' mixing angle as they are sensitive to small mixing-induced deviations in the SM couplings and not to the Z' mass. LEP and SLD have made very precise measurements of these couplings which can be compared to SM predictions including radiative corrections.[11] An example of this is found in Fig. 9.1 where we see the experimental results for the leptonic partial width of the Z as well as $\sin^2 \theta_{lepton}$ in comparison with the corresponding SM predictions. Deviations in $\sin^2 \theta_{lepton}$ are particularly sensitive to shifts in the Z couplings due to non-zero values of ϕ. Semiquantitatively these measurements strongly suggest that $|\phi| \leq a\ few\ 10^{-3}$, at most, in most Z' models assuming a light Higgs. Performing a global fit to the full electroweak data set, as given, e.g., by the LEPEWWG[11] gives comparable constraints.[8]

Above the Z pole, LEPII data provides strong constraints on Z' couplings and masses but are generally insensitive to small Z-Z' mixing. Writing the couplings as $\sum_i \bar{f}\gamma_\mu(v_{f_i} - a_{f_i}\gamma_5)f Z_i^\mu$ for $i = \gamma, Z, Z'$, the differential cross section for $e^+e^- \to \bar{f}f$ when $m_f = 0$ is just

$$\frac{d\sigma}{dz} = \frac{N_c}{32\pi s} \sum_{i,j} P_{ij}[B_{ij}(1+z^2) + 2C_{ij}z], \qquad (9.13)$$

where

$$\begin{aligned} B_{ij} &= (v_i v_j + a_i a_j)_e (v_i v_j + a_i a_j)_f \\ C_{ij} &= (v_i a_j + a_i v_j)_e (v_i a_j + a_i v_j)_f, \end{aligned} \qquad (9.14)$$

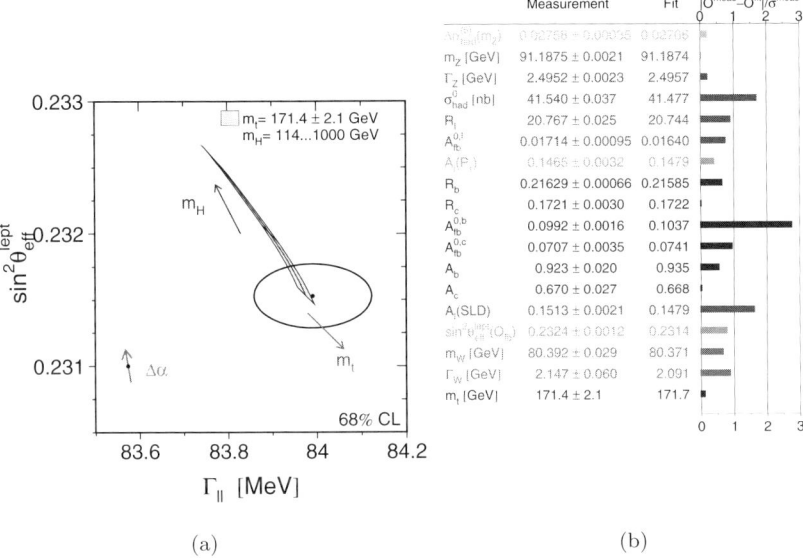

Fig. 9.1. Summer 2006 results from the LEPEWWG. (a) Fit for the Z leptonic partial width and $\sin^2\theta_{lepton}$ in comparison to the SM prediction in the yellow band. (b) Comparison of a number of electroweak measurements with their SM fitted values.

and

$$P_{ij} = s^2 \frac{(s - M_i^2)(s - M_j^2) + \Gamma_i \Gamma_j M_i M_j}{[(s - M_i^2)^2 + \Gamma_i^2 M_i^2][i \to j]}, \quad (9.15)$$

with $\sqrt{s}$ the collision energy, Γ_i being the total widths of the exchanged particles and $z = \cos\theta$, the scattering angle in the CM frame. A_{FB} for any final state fermion f is then given by the ratio of integrals

$$A_{FB}^f = \left[\frac{\int_0^1 dz \frac{d\sigma}{dz} - \int_{-1}^0 dz \frac{d\sigma}{dz}}{'' + ''} \right]. \quad (9.16)$$

If the $e^\pm$ beams are polarized (as at the ILC but not at LEP) one can also define the left-right polarization asymmetry, A_{LR}^f; to this end we let

$$\begin{aligned} B_{ij} &\to B_{ij} + \xi(v_i a_j + a_i v_j)_e (v_i v_j + a_i a_j)_f \\ C_{ij} &\to C_{ij} + \xi(v_i v_j + a_i a_j)_e (v_i a_j + a_i v_j)_f, \end{aligned} \quad (9.17)$$

and then form the ratio

$$A_{LR}^f(z) = P\left[\frac{d\sigma(\xi=+1) - d\sigma(\xi=-1)}{''\quad + \quad''}\right], \quad (9.18)$$

where P is the effective beam polarization.

For a given Z′ mass and couplings the deviations from the SM can then be calculated and compared with data; since no obvious deviations from the SM were observed, LEPII[11] places 95% CL lower bounds on Z′ masses of $673(481, 434, 804, 1787)$ GeV for the $\chi(\psi, \eta, \text{LRM}(\kappa=1), \text{SSM})$ models assuming $\lambda = 1$. Note that since we are far away from the Z′ pole these results are not sensitive to any particular assumed values for the Z′ width as long as it is not too large.

The process $e^+e^- \to W^+W^-$ can also be sensitive to the existence of a Z′, in particular, in the case where there is some substantial Z-Z′ mixing.[20] The main reason for this is the well-known gauge cancellations among the SM amplitudes that maintains unitarity for this process as the center of mass energy increases. The introduction of a Z′ with Z-Z′ mixing induces tiny shifts in the W couplings that modifies these cancellations to some extent and unitarity is not completely restored until energies beyond the Z′ mass are exceeded. As shown by the first authors in Ref. 20, the leading effects from Z-Z′ mixing can be expressed in terms of two s-dependent anomalous couplings for the $WW\gamma$ and WWZ vertices, i.e., $g_{WW\gamma} = e(1+\delta_\gamma)$ and $g_{WWZ} = e(\cot\theta_W + \delta_Z)$ and inserting them into the SM amplitude expressions. The parameters $\delta_{\gamma,Z}$ are sensitive to the Z′ mass, its leptonic couplings, as well as the Z-Z′ mixing angle. In principle, the constraints on anomalous couplings from precision measurements can be used to bound the Z′ parameters in a model dependent way. However, the current data from LEPII[11] is not precise enough to get meaningful bounds. More precise data will, of course, be obtained at both the LHC and ILC.

The measurement of the W mass itself can also provides a constraint on $\delta\rho$ since the predicted W mass is altered by the fact that $M_Z \neq M_{Z_1}$. Some algebra shows that the resulting mass shift is expected to be $\delta M_W = 57.6 \frac{\delta\rho}{10^{-3}}$ MeV. Given that M_W is within $\simeq 30$ MeV of the predicted SM value and the current size of theory uncertainties,[21] strongly suggests that $\delta\rho \leq a\,few\,10^{-3}$ assuming a light Higgs. This is evidence of small r and/or β if a Z′ is actually present.

Below the Z pole many low energy experiments are sensitive to a Z′. Here we give only two examples: (i) The E-158 Polarized Moller scattering experiment[22] essentially measures A_{LR} which is proportional to a coupling combination $\sim -1/2 + 2x_{eff}$ where $x_{eff} = x_W +$ 'new physics'. Here x_W is the running value of $\sin^2\theta_W$ at low Q^2 which is reliable calculable. For a Z' (assuming no mixing) the 'new physics' piece is just $\frac{-1}{\sqrt{2}G_F}\frac{g_{Z'}^2}{M_{Z'}^2}v'_e a'_e$, which can be determined in your favorite model. Given the data,[22] $x_{eff} - x_W = 0.0016 \pm 0.0014$, one finds, e.g., that $M_{Z_\chi} \geq 960\lambda$ GeV at 90% CL. (ii) Atomic Parity Violation(APV) in heavy atoms measures the effective parity violating interaction between electrons and the nucleus and is parameterized via the 'weak charge', Q_W, which is again calculable in your favorite model:

$$Q_W = -4\sum_i \frac{M_Z^2}{M_{Z_i}^2} a_{e_i}[v_{u_i}(2Z+N) + v_{d_i}(2N+Z)], \qquad (9.19)$$

$= -N + Z(1-4x_W) +$ a Z' piece, in the limit of no mixing; here the sum extends over all neutral gauge bosons. The possible shift, ΔQ_W, from the SM prediction then constrains Z' parameters. The highest precision measurements from Cs^{133} yield[23] $\Delta Q_W = 0.45 \pm 0.48$ which then imply (at 95% CL) $M_{Z_\chi} > 1.05\lambda$ TeV and $M_{Z_{LRM}} > 0.67$ TeV for $\kappa = 1$. Note that though both these measurements take place at very low energies, their relative cleanliness and high precision allows us to probe TeV scale Z' masses. Figure 9.2 shows the predicted value of the running $\sin^2\theta_W$[25] together with the experimental results obtained from E-158, APV and NuTeV.[24] The apparent $\sim 3\sigma$ deviation in the NuTeV result remains controversial but is at the moment usually ascribed to our lack of detailed knowledge of, e.g., the strange quark parton densities and not to new physics.

9.5.2. *Direct Z' Searches*

In this case, we rely on the Drell-Yan process at the Tevatron as mentioned above. The present lack of any signal with an integrated luminosity approaching ~ 1 fb^{-1} allows one to place a model-dependent lower bound on the mass of any Z'. The process $p\bar{p} \to l^+l^- + X$ at leading order arises from the parton-level subprocess $q\bar{q} \to l^+l^-$ which is quite similar to the $e^+e^- \to f\bar{f}$ reaction discussed above. The cross section for the inclusive process is described by 4 variables: the collider CM energy, $\sqrt{s}$, the invariant mass of the lepton pair, M, the scattering angle between the q and the l^-, θ^*, and the lepton rapidity in the lab frame, y, which depends on its energy (E) and longitudinal momentum(p_z): $y = \frac{1}{2}\log\left[\frac{E+p_z}{E-p_z}\right]$. For a massless particle, this is the same as the pseudo-rapidity, η. With these variables the triple differential cross section for the Drell-Yan process is

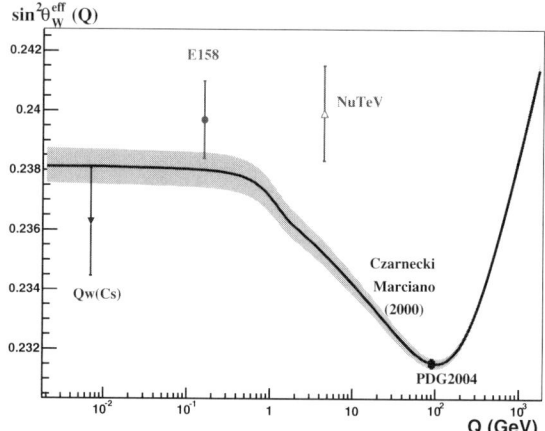

Fig. 9.2. A comparison by E-158 of the predictions for the running value of $\sin^2\theta_W$ with the results of several experiments as discussed in the text.

given by ($z = \cos\theta^*$)

$$\frac{d\sigma}{dM\,dy\,dz} = \frac{K(M)}{48\pi M^3}\sum_q \left[S_q G_q^+(1+z^2) + 2A_q G_q^- z\right], \quad (9.20)$$

where K is a numerical factor that accounts for NLO and NNLO QCD corrections[26] as well as leading electroweak corrections[28] and is roughly of order $\simeq 1.3$ for suitably defined couplings,

$$G_q^\pm = x_a x_b [q(x_a, M^2)\bar{q}(x_b, M^2) \pm q(x_b, M^2)\bar{q}(x_a, M^2)], \quad (9.21)$$

are products of the appropriate parton distribution functions (PDFs), with $x_{a,b} = Me^{\pm y}/\sqrt{s}$ being the relevant momentum fractions, which are evaluated at the scale M^2 and

$$\begin{aligned}S_q &= \sum_{ij} P_{ij}(s\to M^2) B_{ij}(f\to q)\\ A_q &= \sum_{ij} P_{ij}(s\to M^2) C_{ij}(f\to q),\end{aligned} \quad (9.22)$$

with B, C and P as given above. In order to get precise limits (and to measure Z' properties once discovered as we will see later), the NNLO QCD corrections play an important role[26] as do the leading order electroweak radiative corrections.[28] Apart from the machine luminosity errors the largest uncertainty in the above cross section is due to the PDFs. For $M \lesssim 1$ TeV or so these errors are of order $\simeq 5\%$[30] but grow somewhat bigger for larger invariant masses: $\sim 15(25)\%^{31}$ for $M = 3(5)$ TeV. As a point of comparison the corrected SM predictions for the W and Z production cross sections at the Tevatron are seen to agree with the data from both CDF and D0 at the level a few percent.[32]

It is somewhat more useful to perform some of the integrals above in order to make direct comparison with experimental data. To this end we define (for our LHC discussion below)

$$\frac{d\sigma^{\pm}}{dM\,dy} = \left[\int_0^{z_0} \pm \int_{-z_0}^0\right]\frac{d\sigma}{dM\,dy\,dz}, \qquad (9.23)$$

and subsequently

$$\frac{d\sigma^{\pm}}{dM} = \left[\int_{y_{min}}^Y \pm \int_{-Y}^{-y_{min}}\right]\frac{d\sigma^{\pm}}{dM\,dy}. \qquad (9.24)$$

Here Y is cut representing the edge of the central detector acceptance($\simeq 1.1$ for the Tevatron detectors and $\simeq 2.5$ for those at the LHC) with $z_0 = min[\tanh(Y-|y|), 1]$ being the corresponding angular cut. y_{min} is a possible cut employed to define the Z' boost direction which we will return to below. As in the case of e^+e^- collisions above, one can define an $A_{FB}(M) = d\sigma^-/d\sigma^+$.

A Z', being a weakly interacting beast, generally has a rather narrow width to mass ratio, i.e., $\Gamma^2_{Z'}/M^2_{Z'} \ll 1$; e.g., in the case of the SM Z this ratio is $\simeq 10^{-3}$. This being the case, almost the entire Z' event rate comes from a rather narrow window of M values: $M \simeq M_{Z'} \pm 2\Gamma_{Z'}$, or so. In this limit we can approximate the resonance as a δ-function in M and drop all of the SM contributions to the sums above. In this case, pieces of the P_{ij} that go as, e.g., $M^4/|(M^2 - M^2_{Z'}) + iM_{Z'}\Gamma_{Z'}|^2$ can be replaced by $\frac{\pi}{2}\delta(M - M_{Z'})\frac{M^2_{Z'}}{\Gamma_{Z'}}$, up to $\Gamma^2_{Z'}/M^2_{Z'}$ corrections, so that integrals over M can be performed analytically (since the integral over the PDFs is now just a constant factor). In such a limit, the contribution to the cross section for l^+l^- production from the Z' is just $\sigma_{Z'}B(Z' \to l^+l^-)$ with $\sigma_{Z'}$ being the integrated value of the cross section at $M = M_{Z'}$, i.e., at the Z' peak, and B being the leptonic branching fraction of the Z'. This is called the Narrow Width Approximation (NWA). In a similar way, A_{FB} on the Z' pole in the NWA is just the ratio $d\sigma^-/d\sigma^+$ evaluated at $M_{Z'}$; note that this ratio does *not* depend upon what decay modes (other than leptonic) that the Z' might have. Also note that in the NWA, the continuum Drell-Yan background makes no contribution to the event rate. This is a drawback of the NWA

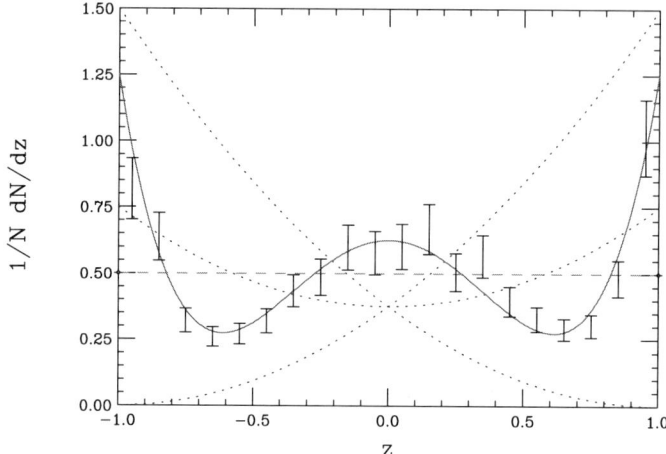

Fig. 9.3. Normalized leptonic angular distribution predicted from the decay of particles with different spin produced in $q\bar{q}$ annihilation. The dashed(solid,dotted) curves are for spin-0(2,1). The generated data corresponds to 1000 events in the spin-2 case.

since it is sometimes important to know the height of the Z' peak relative to this continuum to ascertain the Z' signal significance.

It is evident from the above cross section expressions that the Z' (as well as γ and Z) induced Drell-Yan cross section involves only terms with a particular angular dependence due to the spin-1 nature of the exchanged particles. In the NWA on the Z' pole itself the leptonic angular distribution is seen to behave as $\sim 1+z^2+8A_{FB}z/3$, which is typical of a spin-1 particle. If the Z' had not been a Z' but, say, a $\tilde{\nu}$ in an R-parity violating SUSY model[1] which is spin-0, then the angular distribution on the peak would have been z-independent, i.e., flat(with, of course, $A_{FB} = 0$). This is quite different than the ordinary Z' case. If the Z' had instead been an RS graviton[2] with spin-2, then the $q\bar{q} \to l^+l^-$ part of the cross section would behave as $\sim 1 - 3z^2 + 4z^4$, while the $gg \to l^+l^-$ part would go as $\sim 1 - z^4$, both parts also yielding $A_{FB} = 0$. These distributions are also quite distinctive. Figure 9.3 shows an example of these (normalized) distributions and demonstrates that with less than a few hundred events they are very easily distinguishable. Thus the Z' spin should be well established without much of any ambiguity given sufficient luminosity.

An important lesson from the NWA is that the signal rate for a Z' depends upon B, the Z' leptonic branching fraction. Usually in calculating B one assumes that the Z' decays only to SM fields. Given the possible

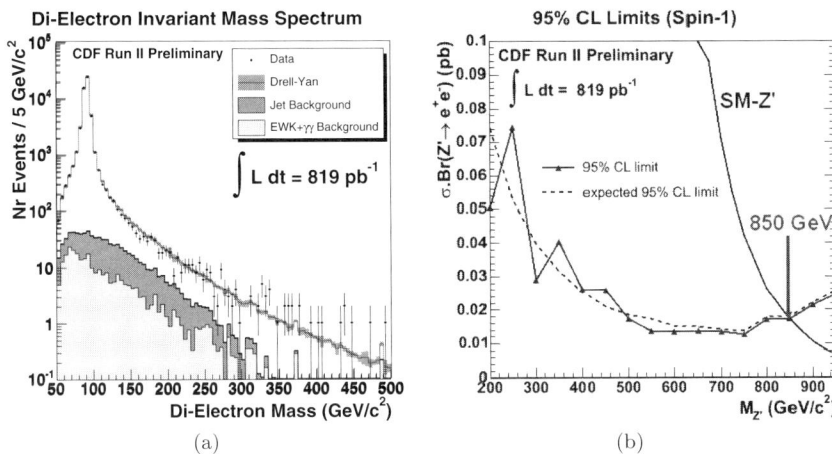

Fig. 9.4. (a) The Drell-Yan distribution as seen by CDF. (b) CDF cross section lower bound in comparison to the predictions for the Z' in the SSM.

existence of SUSY as well as the additional fermions needed in extended electroweak models to cancel anomalies this assumption may be wrong. Clearly Z' decays to these other states would decrease the value of B making the Z' more difficult to observe experimentally.

At the Tevatron only lower bounds on the mass of a Z' exist. These bounds are obtained by determining the 95% CL upper bound on the production cross section for lepton pairs that can arise from new physics as a function of $M(=M_{Z'})$. (Note that this has a slight dependence on the assumption that we are looking for a Z' due to the finite acceptance of the detector.) Then, for any given Z' model one can calculate $\sigma_{Z'}B(Z' \to l^+l^-)$ as a function of $M_{Z'}$ and see at what value of $M_{Z'}$ the two curves cross. At present the best limit comes from CDF although comparable limits are also obtained by D0.[34] The left panel in Fig. 9.4 shows the latest (summer 2006) Drell-Yan spectrum from CDF; the right panel shows the corresponding cross section upper bound and the falling prediction for the Z' cross section in the SSM. Here we see that the lower bound is found to be 850 GeV *assuming* that only SM fermions participate in the Z' decay. For other models an analogous set of theory curves can be drawn and the associated limits obtained.

Figure 9.5 shows the resulting constraints (from a different CDF analysis[35] with a lower integrated luminosity but also employing the A_{FB} observable above the mass of the SM Z) on a number of the models discussed

$E_6 Z'$ Model	Z_χ	Z_ψ	Z_η	Z_I	Z_N	Z_{sec}
Exp. limit (GeV/c^2)	735	725	745	650	710	675
Obs. limit (GeV/c^2)	740	725	745	650	710	680

(a)

Littlest Higgs Z'	$\cot\theta_H=0.3$	$\cot\theta_H=0.5$	$\cot\theta_H=0.7$	$\cot\theta_H=1.0$
Exp. $M_{Z'_H}$ limit (GeV/c^2)	625	765	835	910
Obs. $M_{Z'_H}$ limit (GeV/c^2)	625	760	830	900

(b)

Fig. 9.5. Experimental lower bounds from CDF on a number of Z' models: (a) E_6 models (b) Little Higgs models.

above all assuming Z' decays to SM particles only and no Z-Z' mixing. Looking at these results we see that the Tevatron bounds are generally superior to those from LEPII and are approaching the best that the other precision measurements can do. These bounds would degrade somewhat if we allowed the Z' to have additional decay modes; for example, if B were reduced by a factor of 2 then the resulting search reach would be reduced by 50-100 GeV depending on the model.

The Tevatron will, of course, be continuing to accumulate luminosity for several more years possibly reaching as high as 8 fb^{-1} per experiment. Assuming no signal is found this will increase the Z' search reach lower bound somewhat, $\sim 20\%$, as is shown in Fig. 9.6 from[36]. At this point the

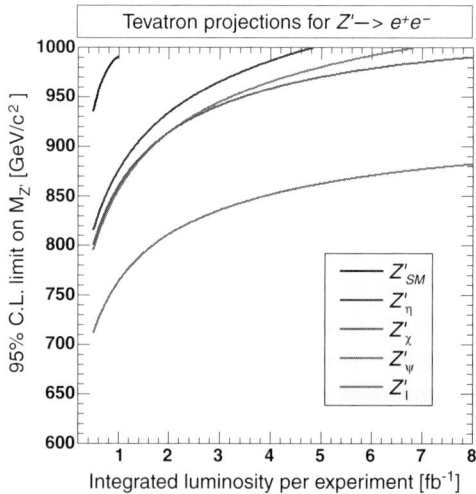

Fig. 9.6. Extrapolation of the Z' reach for a number of different models at the Tevatron as the integrated luminosity increases. Results from CDF and D0 are combined.

search reach at the Tevatron peters out due to the rapidly falling parton densities leaving the mass range above ~ 1 TeV for the LHC to explore.

9.6. The LHC: Z' Discovery and Identification

The search for a Z' at the LHC would proceed in the same manner as at the Tevatron. In fact, since the Z' has such a clean (*i.e.*, dilepton) signal and a sizable cross section it could be one of the first new physics signatures to be observed at the LHC even at relatively low integrated luminosities.[37–39] Figure 9.7 shows both the theoretical anticipated 95% CL lower bound and the 5σ discovery reach for several different Z' models at the LHC for a single leptonic channel as the integrated luminosity is increased; these results are mirrored in detectors studies.[40] Here we see that with only $10-20\,pb^{-1}$ the LHC detectors will clean up any of the low mass region left by the Tevatron below 1 TeV and may actually discover a 1 TeV Z' with luminosities in the $30-100\,pb^{-1}$ range! In terms of discovery, however, to get out to the $\sim 4-5$ TeV mass range will requite $\sim 100\,fb^{-1}$ of luminosity. At such luminosities, the 95% CL bound exceeds the 5σ discovery reach by about 700 GeV. In these plots, we have again assumed that the Z' leptonic branching fraction is determined by decays only to SM fermions. Reducing B by a factor of 2 could reduce these reaches by $\simeq 10\%$ which is not a large effect.

The Z' peak at the LHC should be relatively easy to spot since the SM backgrounds are well understood as shown[38,41] in Fig. 9.8 for a number of

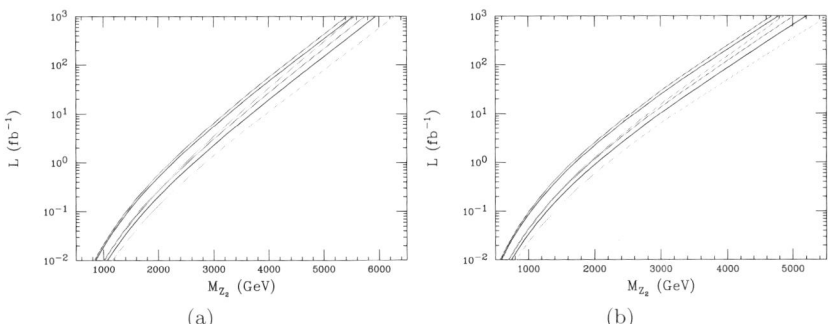

Fig. 9.7. (a) 95% CL lower bound and (b) 5σ discovery reach for a Z' as a function of the integrated luminosity at the LHC for ψ(red), χ(green), η(blue), the LRM with $\kappa = 1$(magenta), the SSM(cyan) and the ALRM(black). Decays to only SM fermions is assumed.

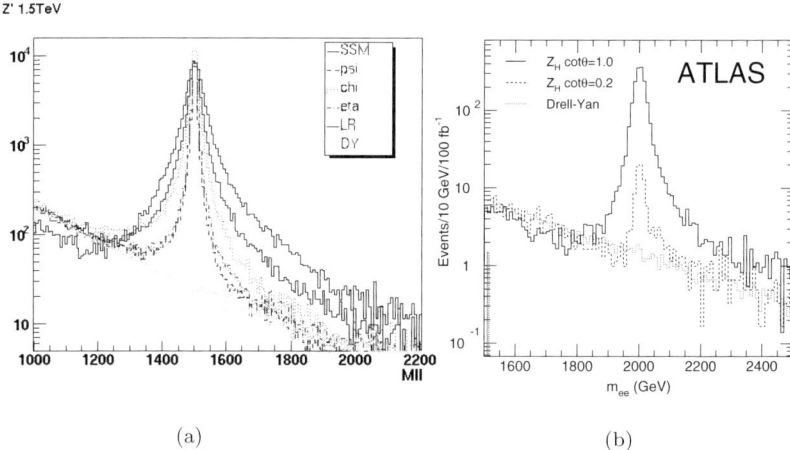

Fig. 9.8. Resonance shapes for a number of Z' models as seen by ATLAS assuming $M_{Z'} = 1.5$ TeV. The continuum is the SM Drell-Yan background.

different Z' models. The one problem that may arise is for the case where the Z' width, $\Gamma_{Z'}$, is far smaller than the experimental dilepton pair mass resolution, δM. Typically in most models, $\Gamma_{Z'}/M_{Z'}$ is of order $\simeq 0.01$ which is comparable to dilepton pair mass resolution, $\delta M/M$, for both ATLAS[42] and CMS.[43] If, however, $\Gamma_{Z'}/M_{Z'} \ll \delta M/M$, then the Z' resonance is smeared out due to the resolution and the cross section peak is reduced by roughly a factor of $\sim \Gamma_{Z'}/\delta M$ making the state difficult to observe. This could happen, e.g., if the Z' (before mixing with the SM Z) had no couplings to SM fields.[44]

Given the huge mass reach of the LHC it is important to entertain the question of how to 'identify' a particular Z' model once such a particle is found. This goes beyond just being able to tell the Z' of Model A from the Z' from model B. As alluded to in the introduction, if a Z'-like object is discovered, the first step will be to determine its spin. Based on the theoretical discussion above this would seem to be rather straightforward and studies of this issue have been performed by both ATLAS[45] and CMS.[46] Generally, one finds that discriminating a spin-1 or spin-2 object from one of spin-0 requires several times more events than does discriminating spin-2 from spin-1. The requirement of a few hundred events, however, somewhat limits the mass range over which such an analysis can be performed. If a particular Z' model has an LHC search reach of 4 TeV, then only for masses below $\simeq 2.5 - 3$ TeV will there be the statistics necessary to perform a

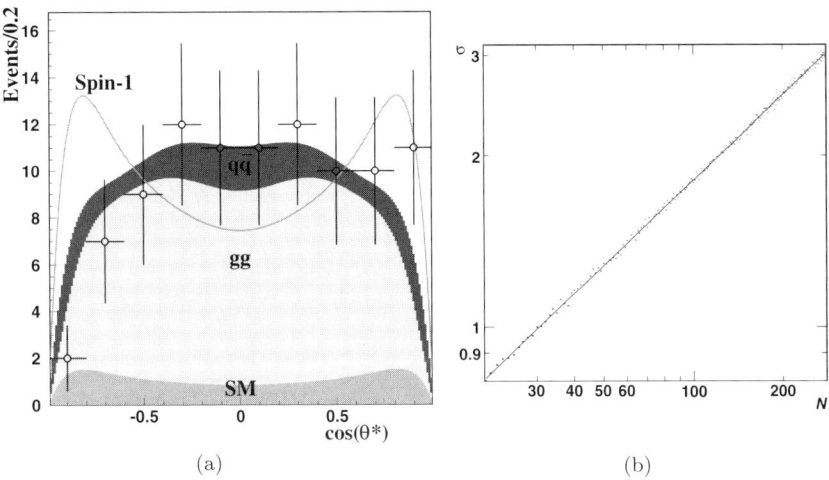

Fig. 9.9. (a) The theoretical predictions for 1.5 TeV SSM Z′ and RS graviton resonance shapes at ATLAS in comparison to the graviton signal data. (b) Differentiation, in σ, of spin-1 and spin-2 resonances at CMS as a function of the number of events assuming a 1.5 TeV mass.

reliable spin determination. Figure 9.9 shows two sample results from this spin analysis. For the ATLAS study in the left panel[45] the lepton angular distribution for a weakly coupled 1.5 TeV KK RS graviton is compared with the expectation for a SSM Z′ of identical mass assuming a luminosity of 100 fb^{-1}. Here one clearly sees the obvious difference and the spin-2 nature of the resonance. In the right panel[46] the results of a CMS analysis is presented with the distinction of a 1.5 TeV Z′ and a KK graviton again being considered. Here one asks for the number of events (N) necessary to distinguish the two cases, at a fixed number of standard deviations, σ, which is seen to grow as (as it should) with $\sqrt{N}$. For example, a 3σ separation is seen to require $\simeq 300$ events.

Once we know that we indeed have a spin-1 object, we next need to 'identify' it, *i.e.*, uniquely determine its couplings to the various SM fermions. (Note that almost all LHC experimental analyses up to now have primarily focused on being able to distinguish models and not on actual coupling extractions.) We would like to be able to do this in as model-independent a way as possible, *e.g.*, we should not assume that the Z′ decays only to SM fields. Clearly this task will require many more events than a simple discovery or even a spin determination and will probably be difficult for a Z′ with a mass much greater than $\simeq 2 - 2.5$ TeV unless

Table 9.2. Results on σ_{ll} and $\sigma_{ll} \times \Gamma_{Z'}$ for all studied models from ATLAS. Here one compares the input values from the generator with the reconstructed values obtained after full detector simulation.

		σ_{ll}^{gen} (fb)	σ_{ll}^{rec} (fb)	$\sigma_{ll}^{rec} \times \Gamma_{rec}$ (fb.GeV)
$M = 1.5$ TeV	SSM	78.4±0.8	78.5±1.8	3550±137
	ψ	22.6±0.3	22.7±0.6	166±15
	χ	47.5±0.6	48.4±1.3	800±47
	η	26.2±0.3	24.6±0.6	212±16
	LR	50.8±0.6	51.1±1.3	1495±72
$M = 4$ TeV	SSM	0.16±0.002	0.16±0.004	19±1
	KK	2.2±0.07	2.2±0.12	331±35

integrated luminosities significantly in excess of 100 fb^{-1} are achieved (as may occur at the LHC upgrade.[47]) Some of the required information can be obtained using the dilepton (i.e., e^+e^- and/or $\mu^+\mu^-$) discovery channel but to obtain more information the examination of additional channels will also be necessary.

In the dilepton mode, three obvious observables present themselves: (i) the cross section, σ_{ll}, on and below the Z' peak (it is generally very small above the peak), (ii) the corresponding values of A_{FB} and (iii) the width, $\Gamma_{Z'}$, of the Z' from resonance peak shape measurements. Recall that while A_{FB} is B insensitive, both σ_{ll} and $\Gamma_{Z'}$ *are* individually sensitive to what we assume about the leptonic branching fraction, B, so that they cannot be used independently. In the NWA, however, one sees that the product of the peak cross section and the Z' width, $\sigma_{ll}\Gamma_{Z'}$, is *independent* of B. (Due to smearing and finite width effects, one really needs to take the product of $d\sigma^+/dM$, integrated around the peak and $\Gamma_{Z'}$.) Table 9.2 from an ATLAS study[48] demonstrates that the product $\sigma_{ll}\Gamma_{Z'}$ can be reliably determined at the LHC in full simulation, reproducing well the original input generator value.

Let us now consider the quantity A_{FB}. At the theory level, the angle θ^* employed above is defined to be that between the incoming q and the outgoing l^-. Experimentally, though the lepton can be charge signed with relative ease, it is not immediately obvious in which direction the initial quark is going, i.e., to determine which proton it came from. However, since the q valence distributions are 'harder' (i.e., have higher average momentum fractions) than the 'softer' $\bar{q}$ sea partons, it is likely[49] that the Z' boost direction will be that of the original q. Of course, this is not *always* true so that making this assumption dilutes the true value of A_{FB} as does, e.g., additional gluon radiation. For the Z' to be boosted, the leptons in the

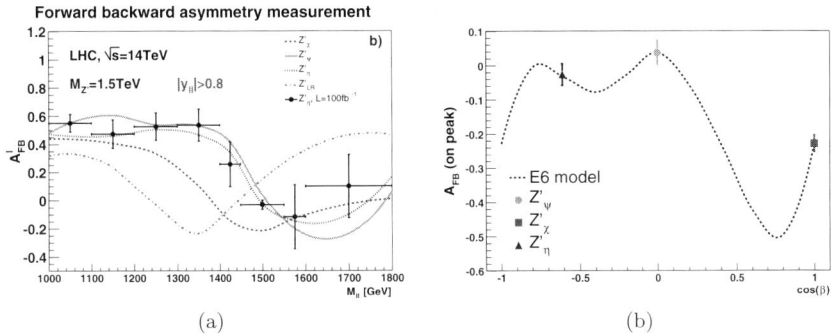

Fig. 9.10. (a) A_{FB} near a 1.5 TeV Z' in a number of models. (b) On-peak differentiation of E_6 models using A_{FB} showing statistical errors for a 1.5 TeV Z'.

final state need to have (significant) rapidity, hence the lower bound in the integration of the cross section expression above. Clearly, a full analysis needs to take these and other experimental issues into account.

The left panel of Fig. 9.10 shows[50] A_{FB} as a function of M in the region near a 1.5 TeV Z' for E_6 model η in comparison with the predictions of several other models. Here we see several features, the first being that the errors on A_{FB} are rather large except on the Z' pole itself due to relatively low statistics even with large integrated luminosities of 100 fb^{-1}; this is particularly true above the resonance. Second, it is clear that A_{FB} both on and off the peak does show some reasonable model sensitivity as was hoped. From the right panel[50] of Fig. 9.10 it is clear that the various special case models of the E_6 family are distinguishable. This is confirmed by more detailed studies performed by both ATLAS[48] and CMS.[51] Figure 9.11 from CMS[51] shows how measurements of the on-peak A_{FB} can be used to distinguish models with reasonable confidence given sufficient statistics (and in the absence of several systematic effects). Table 9.3 from the ATLAS study[48] shows that the original input generator value of the on-peak A_{FB} can be reasonably well reproduced with a full detector simulation, taking dilution and other effects into account.

If a large enough on-peak data sample is available, examining A_{FB} as a function of the lepton rapidity[52] can provide additional coupling information. The reason for this is that u and d quarks have different x distributions so that the weight of $u\bar{u}$ and $d\bar{d}$ induced Z' events changes as the rapidity varies. No detector level studies of this have yet been performed.

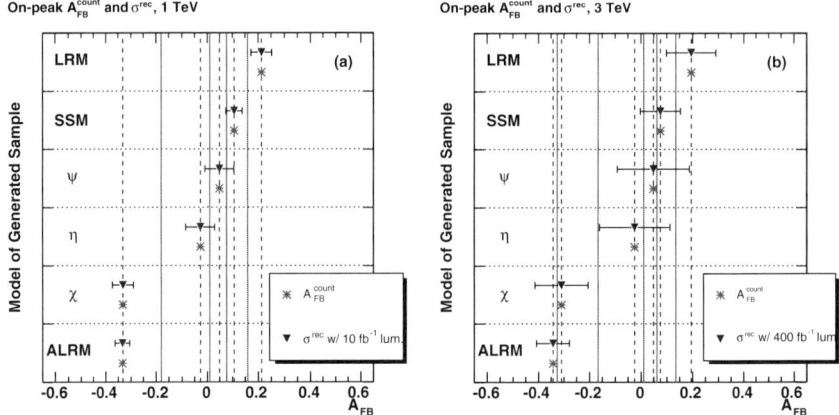

Fig. 9.11. CMS analysis of Z' model differentiation employing A_{FB} assuming $M_{Z'} = 1$ or 3 TeV.

Table 9.3. Measured on-peak A_{FB} for all studied models in the central mass bin from ATLAS. Here the raw value obtained before dilution corrections is labeled as 'Observed'.

Model	$\int \mathcal{L}(fb^{-1})$	Generation	Observed	Corrected
1.5 TeV				
SSM	100	$+0.088 \pm 0.013$	$+0.060 \pm 0.022$	$+0.108 \pm 0.027$
χ	100	-0.386 ± 0.013	-0.144 ± 0.025	-0.361 ± 0.030
η	100	-0.112 ± 0.019	-0.067 ± 0.032	-0.204 ± 0.039
η	300	-0.090 ± 0.011	-0.050 ± 0.018	-0.120 ± 0.022
ψ	100	$+0.008 \pm 0.020$	-0.056 ± 0.033	-0.079 ± 0.042
ψ	300	$+0.010 \pm 0.011$	-0.019 ± 0.019	-0.011 ± 0.024
LR	100	$+0.177 \pm 0.016$	$+0.100 \pm 0.026$	$+0.186 \pm 0.032$
4 TeV				
SSM	10000	$+0.057 \pm 0.023$	-0.001 ± 0.040	$+0.078 \pm 0.051$
KK	500	$+0.491 \pm 0.028$	$+0.189 \pm 0.057$	$+0.457 \pm 0.073$

Off-peak measurements of A_{FB} are also useful although in this case systematics are more important; as shown in the ATLAS study,[48] whose results are shown in Table 9.4, it is more difficult to reproduce the input generator value of this quantity than in the on-peak case.

There are, of course, other observables that one may try to use in the dilepton channel but they are somewhat more subtle. The first possibility[50] is to reconstruct the Z' rapidity distribution from the dilepton final

Table 9.4. Measured off peak, $0.8 < M < 1.4$ TeV, A_{FB} for all studied models from ATLAS using the same nomenclature as above.

Model	$\int \mathcal{L}(fb^{-1})$	Generation	Observed	Corrected
1.5 TeV				
SSM	100	$+0.077 \pm 0.025$	$+0.086 \pm 0.038$	$+0.171 \pm 0.045$
χ	100	$+0.440 \pm 0.019$	$+0.180 \pm 0.032$	$+0.354 \pm 0.039$
η	100	$+0.593 \pm 0.016$	$+0.257 \pm 0.033$	$+0.561 \pm 0.039$
ψ	100	$+0.673 \pm 0.012$	$+0.294 \pm 0.033$	$+0.568 \pm 0.039$
LR	100	$+0.303 \pm 0.022$	$+0.189 \pm 0.033$	$+0.327 \pm 0.040$

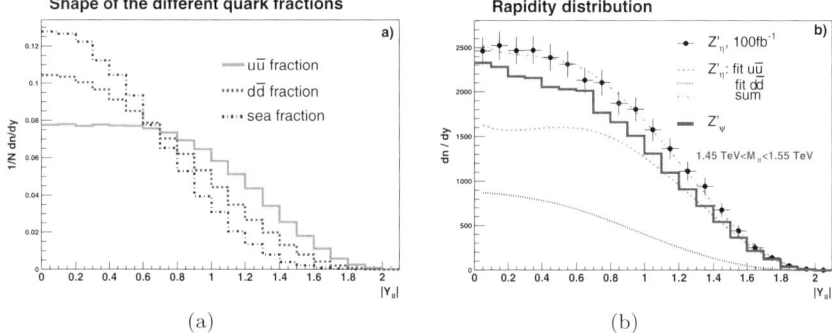

Fig. 9.12. (a) Rapidity distributions for different $q\bar{q}$ induced events. (b) Rapidity distribution differentiation of Z' models.

state. The left panel of Fig. 9.12 reminds us that the Z' rapidity distribution produced by only $u\bar{u}$, $d\bar{d}$ or sea quarks would have a different shape. The particular Z' couplings to quarks induce different weights in these three distributions and so one may hope to distinguish models in this way. An example of this is shown in the right panel of Fig. 9.12. The first analysis[50] of this type considered the quantity $R_{u\bar{u}}$, the fraction of Z' events originating from $u\bar{u}$, as an observable; a similar variable $R_{d\bar{d}}$ can also be constructed. Figure 9.13 from a preliminary ATLAS analysis[53] compares the values of these two parameters extracted via full reconstruction for a 1.5 TeV Z'; here we see that reasonable agreement with the input values of the generator are obtained although the statistical power is not very good. Knowing both $R_{d\bar{d},u\bar{u}}$ and the ratio of the $d\bar{d}$ and $u\bar{u}$ parton densities fairly precisely, one can turn these measurements into a determination of the coupling ratio $(v_u^{'2} + a_u^{'2})/(v_d^{'2} + a_d^{'2})$.

Model	Generation level Fitted values (%)		Reconstruction level Fitted values (%)	
	Prop(Z'←dd)	Prop(Z'←uu)	Prop(Z'←dd)	Prop(Z'←uu)
SSM	41.±10.	52.±12.	22.±16.	60.±16.
χ	62.±12.	29.±14.	79.±17.	17.±19.
η	23.±13.	75.±14.	33.±6.	67.±8.
ψ	36.±12.	61.±13.	32.±15.	62.±17.
LR	57.±4.	43.±14.	53.±13.	46.±15.

Fig. 9.13. Comparison of $R_{q\bar{q}}$ values determined at the generator level and after detector simulation by ATLAS.

A second possibility is to construct the rapidity ratio[54] in the region near the Z' pole:

$$R = \frac{\int_{-y_1}^{y_1} \frac{d\sigma}{dy} dy}{\left[\int_{y_1}^{Y} + \int_{-Y}^{-y_1} \frac{d\sigma}{dy} dy\right]}. \quad (9.25)$$

Here y_1 is some suitable chosen rapidity value $\simeq 1$. R essentially measures the ratio of the cross section in the central region to that in the forward region and is again sensitive to the ratio of u and d quark couplings to the Z'. A detector level study of this observable has yet to be performed.

In addition to the e^+e^- and $\mu^+\mu^-$ discovery channel final states, one might also consider other possibilities, the simplest being $\tau^+\tau^-$. Assuming universality, this channel does not provide anything new unless one can measure the polarization of the τ's, P_τ, on or very near the Z' peak.[55] The statistics for making this measurement can be rather good as the rate for this process is only smaller than that of the discovery mode by the τ pair reconstruction efficiency. In the NWA, $P_\tau = 2v'_e a'_e/(v'^2_e + a'^2_e)$, assuming universality, so that the ratio of v'_e/a'_e can be determined uniquely. Figure 9.14 shows, for purposes of demonstration, the value of P_τ in the E_6 model case where we see that it covers its fully allowed range.

A first pass theoretical study[55] suggests that $\delta P_\tau \simeq 1.5/\sqrt{N}$, with N here being the number of reconstructed τ events. Even for a reconstruction efficiency of 3%, with $M_{Z'}$ not too large $\sim 1-1.5$ TeV, the high luminosity of the LHC should be able to tell us P_τ at the ± 0.05 level. It would be

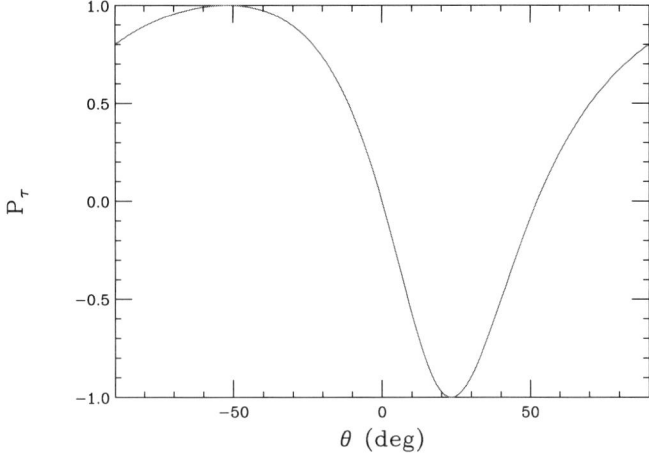

Fig. 9.14. τ polarization asymmetry for a Z' in E_6 models in the NWA.

very good to see a detector study for this observable in the near future to see how well the LHC can really do in this case.

Once we go beyond the dileptons, the next possibility one can imagine is light quark jets from which one might hope to get a handle on the Z' couplings to quarks. The possibility of new physics producing an observable dijet peak at the LHC has been studied in detail by CMS[56]; the essential results are shown in Fig. 9.15. Here we see that for resonances which are color non-singlets, *i.e.*, those which have QCD-like couplings, the rates are sufficiently large as to allow these resonances to be seen above the dijet background. However, for weakly produced particles, such as the SSM Z' shown here, the backgrounds are far too large to allow observation of these decays. Thus it is very unlikely that the dijet channel will provide us with any information on Z' couplings at the LHC.

Another possibility is to consider the heavy flavor decay modes, *i.e.*, Z' $\rightarrow b\bar{b}$ or $t\bar{t}$. Unfortunately, these modes are difficult to observe so that it will be quite unlikely that we will obtain coupling information from them. ATLAS[57] has performed a study of the possibility of observing these modes within the Little Higgs Model context for a Z' in the 1-2 TeV mass range. Figure 9.16 from the ATLAS study demonstrates how difficult observing these decays may really be due to the very large SM backgrounds. It is thus unlikely that these modes will provide any important information except in very special cases.

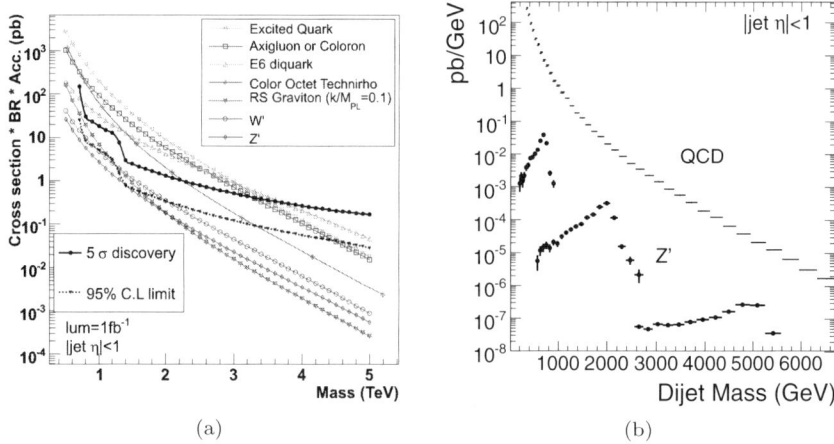

Fig. 9.15. (a) Dijet resonance discovery reach at CMS in comparison to the predictions for a number of models. (b) SSM Z' dijet signal for various masses in comparison with the SM background.

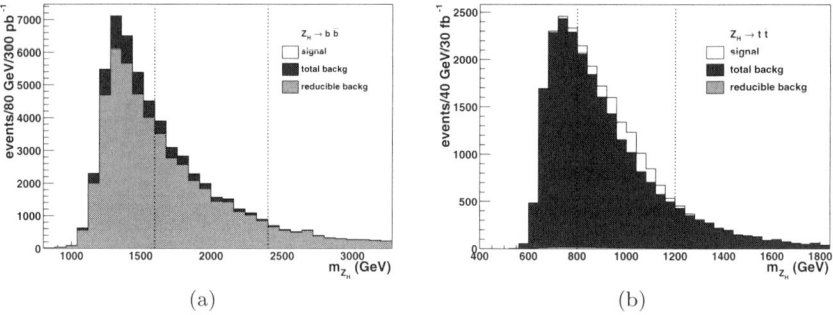

Fig. 9.16. Search for heavy flavor decays of the Z' in the Little Higgs model by ATLAS. $\cot\theta_H = 1$ has been assumed. Z' $\to b\bar{b}$ assuming $M_{Z'} = 2$ TeV and a luminosity of 300 fb^{-1}(a) and $t\bar{t}$(b) for $M_{Z'} = 1$ TeV and a luminosity of 30 fb^{-1}.

Another possible 2-body channel is Z' $\to W^+W^-$, which can occur at a reasonable rate through Z-Z' mixing as discussed above. Clearly the rate for this mode is very highly model dependent. ATLAS[58] has made a preliminary analysis of this mode in the $jjl\nu$ final state taking the Z' to be that of the SSM(for its fermionic couplings) and assuming a large integrated luminosity of 300 fb^{-1}. The mixing parameter β was taken to be unity in the

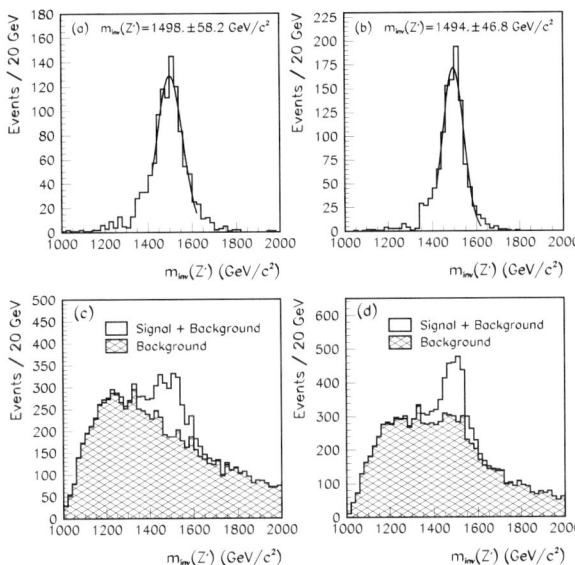

Fig. 9.17. Results of two ATLAS analyses showing the $Z' \to WW$ signal above SM backgrounds and Z' mass reconstruction in this channel for the SSM model assuming $M_{Z'} = 1.5$ TeV and $\beta = 1$.

calculations. The authors of this analysis found that a Z' in the mass range below $\simeq 2.2$ TeV could be observed in this channel given these assumptions. An example is shown in Fig. 9.17 where we clearly see the reconstructed Z' above the SM background. With a full detailed background study an estimate could likely be made of the relevant branching fraction in comparison to that of the discovery mode. This would give important information on the nature of the Z' coupling structure. More study of this mode is needed.

A parallel study was performed by ATLAS[41] for the $Z' \to ZH$ mode which also occurs through mixing as discussed above; this mixing occurs naturally in the Little Higgs model in the absence of T-parity. The results are shown in Fig. 9.18. Here we see that there is a respectable signal over background and the relevant coupling information should be obtainable provided the Z' is not too heavy.

Some rare decays of the Z' may be useful in obtaining coupling information provided the Z' is not too massive. Consider the ratios of Z' partial widths[54,59–61]

$$r_{ff'V} = \frac{\Gamma(Z' \to ff'V)}{\Gamma(Z' \to l^+l^-)}, \qquad (9.26)$$

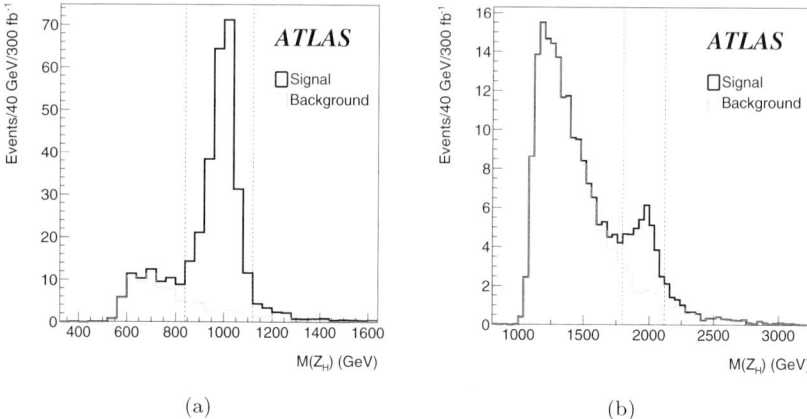

Fig. 9.18. Search study for the decay $Z' \to ZH$ by ATLAS in the Little Higgs model assuming $\cot\theta_H = 0.5$ for the $l^+l^-b\bar{b}$ mode assuming $M_{Z'} = 1$ (a) or 2(b) TeV.

where $V = $ Z,W and $ff' = l^+l^-, l^\pm\nu, \nu\bar{\nu}$, appropriately. The two $\Gamma(Z' \to ff Z)$ (with $f = l, \nu$) partial widths originate from the bremsstrahlung of a SM Z off of either the f or $\bar{f}$ legs and are rather to imagine. Numerically, one finds that for the case $f = l$, little sensitivity to the Z' couplings is obtained so it is not usually considered. Assuming that the SM ν's couple in a left-handed way to the Z', it is clear that $r_{\nu\nu Z} = K_Z v_\nu^{'2}/(v_e^{'2} + a_e^{'2})$, where K_Z is a constant, model-independent factor for any given Z' mass. The signal for this decay is a (reconstructed) Z plus missing p_T with a Jacobean peak at the Z' mass.

$r_{l\nu W}$, on the otherhand, is more interesting; not only can the W be produced as a brem but it can also arise directly if a WWZ' coupling exists. As we saw above this can happen if Z-Z' mixing occurs *or* it can happen if T' is proportional to T_{3L}. If there is no mixing and if T' has no T_{3L} component then one finds the simple relation $r_{l\nu W} = K_W v_\nu^{'2}/(v_e^{'2} + a_e^{'2})$, with K_W another constant factor. Note that now $r_{l\nu W}$ and $r_{\nu\nu Z}$ are proportional to one another and, since T' and T_{3L} commute, one also has $v'_e + a'_e = v'_\nu + a'_\nu = 2v'_\nu$ so that both $r_{l\nu W}$ and $r_{\nu\nu Z}$ are *bounded*, i.e., $0 \leq r_{l\nu W} \leq K_W/2$ and $0 \leq r_{\nu\nu Z} \leq K_Z/2$. Thus, e.g., in E_6 models a short analysis shows that the allowed region in the $r_{l\nu W}, r_{\nu\nu Z}$ plane will be a straight line beginning at the origin and ending at $K_W/2, K_Z/2$. Other common models will lie on this line, such as the LRM and ALRM cases, but some others, e.g., the SSM, will lie elsewhere in this plane signaling the fact that T' contains a

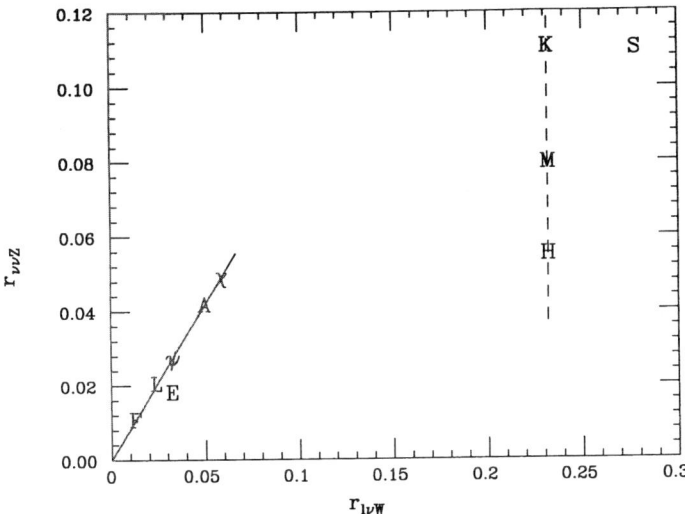

Fig. 9.19. Predictions for the rare decay mode ratios for a number of different models assuming a 1 TeV Z': 'L' is the LRM with $\kappa = 1$, 'S'=SSM, 'A'=ALRM, *etc*. The solid line is the E_6 case.

T_{3L} component. Figure 9.19 from[61] shows a plot of these parameters for a large number of models, the solid line being the just discussed E_6 case and 'S' the SSM result.

While the coupling information provided by these ratios is very useful, the Z' event rates necessary to extract them are quite high in most cases due to their small relative branching fractions. For a Z' much more massive than 1-2 TeV the statistical power of these observables will be lost.

A different way to get at the Z' couplings is to produce it in association with another SM gauge boson, *i.e.*, a photon[62] or a $W^\pm, Z$,[63] with the Z' decaying to dileptons as usual. Taking the ratio of this cross section to that in the discovery channel, we can define the ratios

$$R_{Z'V} = \frac{\sigma(q\bar{q} \to Z'V)B(Z' \to l^+l^-)}{\sigma(q\bar{q} \to Z')B(Z' \to l^+l^-)}, \qquad (9.27)$$

in the NWA with $V = \gamma, W^\pm$, or Z. (For the case $V = g$ there is little coupling sensitivity.[62]) Note that B trivially cancels in this ratio but it remains important for determining statistics. The appearance of an extra particle V in the final state re-weights the combination of couplings which appears in the cross section so that one can get a handle on the vector and axial-vector couplings of the initial u's and d's to the Z'. For example,

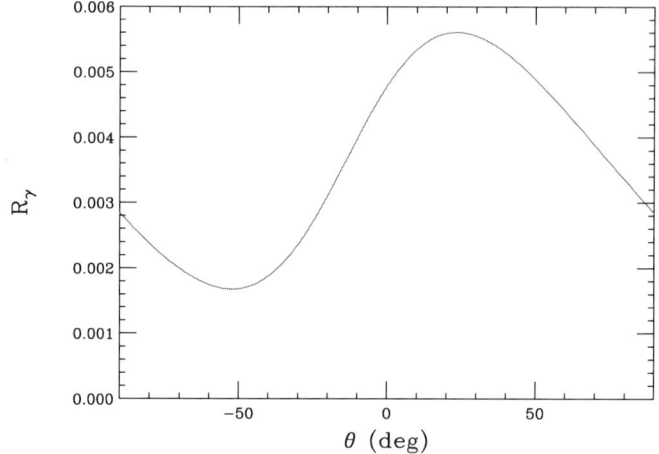

Fig. 9.20. R_γ in E_6 models for a 1 TeV Z' employing a cut $p_T^\gamma > 50$ GeV.

in the simple case of $V = \gamma$, the associated parton level $q\bar{q} \to Z'\gamma$ cross section is proportional to $\sum_i Q_i^2(v_i'^2 + a_i'^2)$ while the simple Z' cross section is proportional to $\sum_i(v_i'^2 + a_i'^2)$. Similarly, for the case $V =$ W, the cross section is found to be proportional to $\sum_i(v_i' + a_i')^2$. Tagging the additional V, when $V \neq \gamma$, may require paying the price of leptonic branching fractions for the W and Z, which is a substantial rate penalty, although an analysis has not yet been performed. For the case of $V = \gamma$, a hard p_T cut on the γ will be required but otherwise the signature is very clean. All the ratios $R_{Z'V}$ are of order a few $\times 10^{-3}$ (or smaller once branching fractions are included) for a Z' mass of 1 TeV and (with fixed cuts) tend to grow with increasing $M_{Z'}$. For example, for a 1 TeV Z' in the E_6 model, the cross section times leptonic branching fraction for the $Z'\gamma$ final state varies in the range 0.65-1.6 fb, depending upon the parameter θ, assuming a photon p_T cut of 50 GeV. R_γ for this case is shown in Fig. 9.20. Generically, with 100 fb^{-1} of luminosity these ratios might be determined at the level of $\simeq 10\%$ for the $M_{Z'} = 1$ TeV case but the quality of the measurement will fall rapidly as $M_{Z'}$ increased due to quickly falling statistics. For much larger masses these ratios are no longer useful. It is possible that the Tevatron will tell us whether such light masses are already excluded.

It is clear from the above discussion that there are many tools available at the LHC for Z' identification. However, many of these are only applicable if the Z' is relatively light. Even if all these observables are available it still

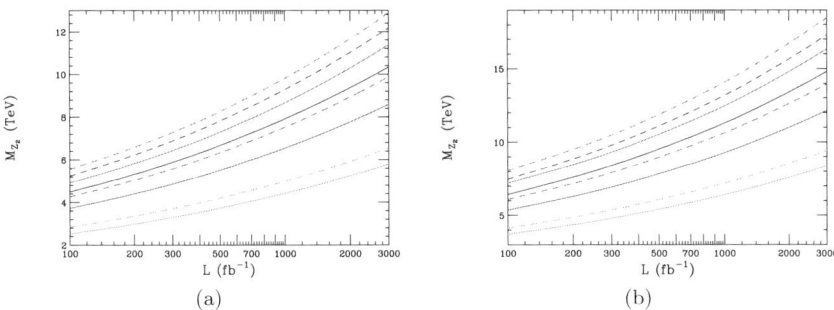

Fig. 9.21. Z' search reach at a $\sqrt{s}$=0.5 TeV(a) or 1 TeV(b) ILC as a function of the integrated luminosity without(solid) or with(dashed) 60% positron beam polarization for models ψ(green), χ(red), SSM(magenta) and LRM with $\kappa = 1$(blue).

remains unclear as to whether or not the complete set of Z' couplings can be extracted from the data with any reliability. A detailed analysis of this situation has yet to be performed. We will probably need a Z' discovery before it is done.

9.7. ILC: What Comes Next

The ILC will begin running a decade or so after the turn on of the LHC. At that point perhaps as much as $\sim 1~ab^{-1}$ or more of integrated luminosity will have been delivered by the LHC to both detectors. From our point of view, the role of the ILC would then be to either extend the Z' search reach (in an indirect manner) beyond that of the LHC or to help identify any Z' discovered at the LHC.[64]

Although the ILC will run at $\sqrt{s} = 0.5 - 1$ TeV, we know from our discussion of LEP Z' searches that the ILC will be sensitive to Z' with masses significantly larger than $\sqrt{s}$. Figure 9.21[65] shows the search reach for various Z' models assuming $\sqrt{s} = 0.5, 1$ TeV as a function of the integrated luminosity both with and without positron beam polarization. Recall that the various final states $e^+e^- \to f\bar{f}$, $f = e, \mu, \tau, c, b, t$ can all be used simultaneously to obtain high Z' mass sensitivity. The essential observables employed here are $d\sigma/dz$ and $A_{LR}(z)$, which is now available since the e^- beam is at least 80% polarized. One can also measure the polarization of τ's in the final state. This figure shows that the ILC will be sensitive to Z' masses in the range $(7-14)\sqrt{s}$ after a couple of years of design luminosity, the exact value depending on the particular Z' model. Thus we see that

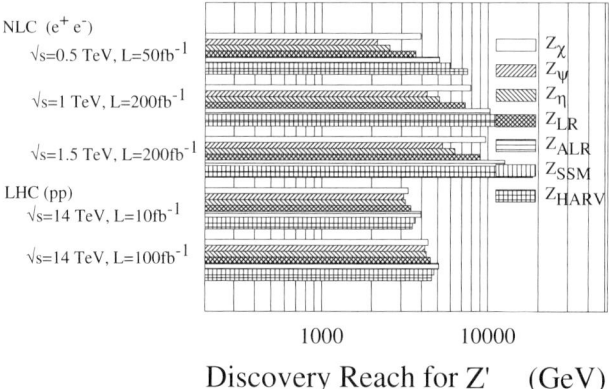

Fig. 9.22. A comparison of LHC direct and ILC indirect Z' search reaches.

it it relatively easy at the ILC to extend the Z' reach beyond the 5-6 TeV value anticipated at the LHC. Figure 9.22 from[66] shows a comparison of the direct Z' search reach at the LHC with the indirect reach at the ILC; note the very modest values assumed here for the ILC integrated luminosities. Here we see explicitly that the ILC has indirect Z' sensitivity beyond the direct reach of the LHC.

In the more optimistic situation where a Z' is discovered at the LHC, the ILC will be essential for Z' identification. As discussed above, it is unclear whether or not the LHC can fully determine the Z' couplings, especially if it were much more massive than $\simeq 1$ TeV.

Once a Z' is discovered at the LHC and its mass is determined, we can use the observed deviations in both $d\sigma/dz$ and $A_{LR}(z)$ at the ILC to determine the Z' couplings channel by channel. For example, assuming lepton universality (which we will already know is applicable from LHC data), we can examine the processes $e^+e^- \to l^+l^-$ using $M_{Z'}$ as an input and determine both v'_e and a'_e (up to a two-fold overall sign ambiguity); a measurement of τ polarization can also contribute in this channel. With this knowledge, we can go on to the $e^+e^- \to b\bar{b}$ channel and perform a simultaneous fit to $v'_{e,b}$ and $a'_{e,b}$; we could then go on to other channels such as $c\bar{c}$ and $t\bar{t}$. In this way *all* of the Z' couplings would be determined. An example of this is shown in Fig. 9.23 from[67] where we see the results of the Z' coupling determinations at the ILC in comparison with the predictions of a number of different models.

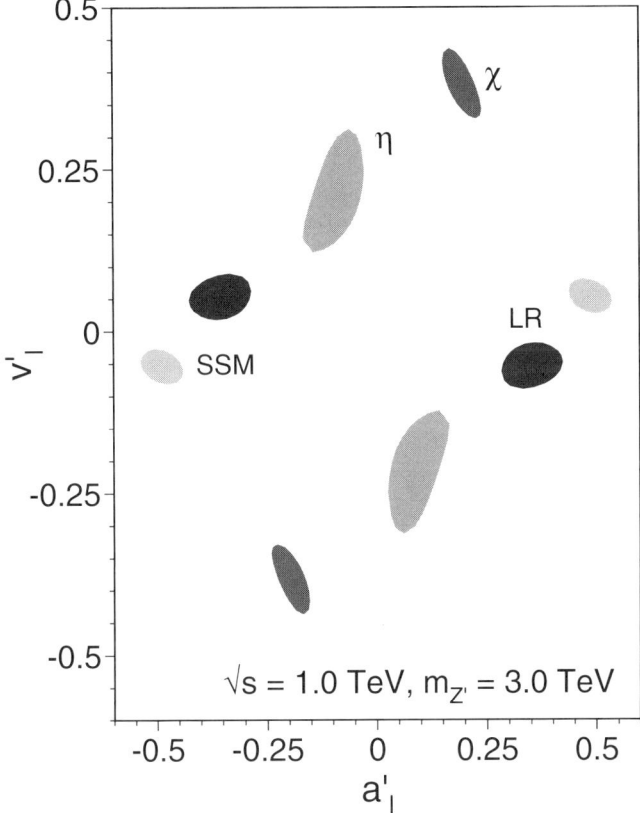

Fig. 9.23. The ability of the ILC to determine the Z' leptonic couplings for a few representative models.

9.8. Summary

The LHC turns on at the end of next year and a reasonable integrated luminosity $\sim 1\ fb^{-1}$ will likely be accumulated in 2008 at $\sqrt{s} = 14$ TeV. The community-wide expectation is that new physics of some kind will be seen relatively 'soon' after this (once the detectors are sufficiently well understood and SM backgrounds are correctly ascertained). Many new physics scenarios predict the existence of a Z' or Z'-like objects. It will then be up to the experimenters (with help from theorists!) to determine what these new states are and how they fit into a larger framework. In our discussion above, we have provided an overview of the tools which experiments at the LHC can employ to begin to address this problem. To complete this program will most likely require input from the ILC.

No matter what new physics is discovered at the LHC the times ahead should prove to be very exciting.

Acknowledgments

The author would like to thank G. Azuelos, D. Benchekroun, C. Berger, K. Burkett, R. Cousins, A. De Roeck, S. Godfrey, R. Harris, J. Hewett, F. Ledroit, L. March, D. Rousseau, S. Willocq, and M. Woods for their input in the preparation of these brief lecture notes. Work supported in part by the Department of Energy, Contract DE-AC02-76SF00515.

References

1. J. L. Hewett and T. G. Rizzo, arXiv:hep-ph/9809525; H. K. Dreiner, P. Richardson and M. H. Seymour, Phys. Rev. D **63**, 055008 (2001) [arXiv:hep-ph/0007228]; B. C. Allanach, M. Guchait and K. Sridhar, Phys. Lett. B **586**, 373 (2004) [arXiv:hep-ph/0311254].
2. L. Randall and R. Sundrum, Phys. Rev. Lett. **83**, 3370 (1999) [arXiv:hep-ph/9905221].
3. H. Davoudiasl, J. L. Hewett and T. G. Rizzo, Phys. Rev. Lett. **84**, 2080 (2000) [arXiv:hep-ph/9909255].
4. I. Antoniadis, Phys. Lett. B **246**, 377 (1990).
5. T. G. Rizzo and J. D. Wells, Phys. Rev. D **61**, 016007 (2000) [arXiv:hep-ph/9906234].
6. For classic reviews of Z' physics, see A. Leike, Phys. Rept. **317**, 143 (1999) [arXiv:hep-ph/9805494]; J. L. Hewett and T. G. Rizzo, Phys. Rept. **183**, 193 (1989); M. Cvetic and S. Godfrey, arXiv:hep-ph/9504216; T. G. Rizzo, "Extended gauge sectors at future colliders: Report of the new gauge boson subgroup," eConf **C960625**, NEW136 (1996) [arXiv:hep-ph/9612440];
7. T. G. Rizzo, JHEP **0306**, 021 (2003) [arXiv:hep-ph/0305077]; G. Azuelos and G. Polesello, Eur. Phys. J. C **39S2**, 1 (2005).
8. W. M. Yao *et al.* [Particle Data Group], J. Phys. G **33**, 1 (2006).
9. K. Cheung, C. W. Chiang, N. G. Deshpande and J. Jiang, "Constraints on flavor-changing Z' models by B/s mixing, Z' production, and arXiv:hep-ph/0604223.
10. K. S. Babu, C. F. Kolda and J. March-Russell, Phys. Rev. D **54**, 4635 (1996) [arXiv:hep-ph/9603212] and Phys. Rev. D **57**, 6788 (1998) [arXiv:hep-ph/9710441]; T. G. Rizzo, Phys. Rev. D **59**, 015020 (1999) [arXiv:hep-ph/9806397]; B. Holdom, Phys. Lett. **B166**, 196 (1986), Phys. Lett. **B259**, 329 (1991), Phys. Lett. **B339**, 114 (1994) and Phys. Lett. **B351**, 279 (1995); F. del Aguila, M. Cvetic and P. Langacker, Phys. Rev. **D52**, 37 (1995);

F. del Aguila, G. Coughan and M. Quiros, Nucl. Phys. **B307**, 633 (1988); F. del Aguila, M. Masip and M. Perez-Victoria, Nucl. Phys. **B456**, 531 (1995); K. Dienes, C. Kolda and J. March-Russell, Nucl. Phys. **B492**, 104 (1997).

11. Results from the LEPEWWG can be found at http://lepewwg.web.cern.ch/LEPEWWG/
12. B. W. Lee, C. Quigg and H. B. Thacker, Phys. Rev. Lett. **38**, 883 (1977).
13. For a classic review and original references, see R.N. Mohapatra, *Unification and Supersymmetry*, (Springer, New York,1986).
14. E. Ma, Phys. Rev. D **36**, 274 (1987).
15. N. Arkani-Hamed, A. G. Cohen and H. Georgi, Phys. Lett. B **513**, 232 (2001) [arXiv:hep-ph/0105239].
16. N. Arkani-Hamed, A. G. Cohen, E. Katz and A. E. Nelson, JHEP **0207**, 034 (2002) [arXiv:hep-ph/0206021].
17. K. R. Lynch, E. H. Simmons, M. Narain and S. Mrenna, Phys. Rev. D **63**, 035006 (2001) [arXiv:hep-ph/0007286].
18. M. Carena, A. Daleo, B. A. Dobrescu and T. M. P. Tait, Phys. Rev. D **70**, 093009 (2004) [arXiv:hep-ph/0408098].
19. E. Eichten, K. D. Lane and M. E. Peskin, Phys. Rev. Lett. **50**, 811 (1983).
20. The possible sensitivity of this reaction has been studied by a large number of authors; see, for example, A. A. Pankov and N. Paver, Phys. Lett. B **393**, 437 (1997) [arXiv:hep-ph/9610509], Phys. Rev. D **48**, 63 (1993), Phys. Lett. B **274**, 483 (1992), and Phys. Lett. B **272**, 425 (1991); R. Najima and S. Wakaizumi, Phys. Lett. B **184**, 410 (1987); P. Kalyniak and M. K. Sundaresan, Phys. Rev. D **35**, 75 (1987); S. Nandi and T. G. Rizzo, Phys. Rev. D **37**, 52 (1988).
21. F. Cossutti, Eur. Phys. J. C **44**, 383 (2005) [arXiv:hep-ph/0505232]. For the most recent status, see, S. Dittmaier, talk given at *Loopfest V*, SLAC, 19-21 June, 2006
22. P. L. Anthony *et al.* [SLAC E158 Collaboration], Phys. Rev. Lett. **95**, 081601 (2005) [arXiv:hep-ex/0504049].
23. J. S. M. Ginges and V. V. Flambaum, "Violations of fundamental symmetries in atoms and tests of unification Phys. Rept. **397**, 63 (2004) [arXiv:physics/0309054].
24. G. P. Zeller *et al.* [NuTeV Collaboration], Phys. Rev. Lett. **88**, 091802 (2002) [Erratum-ibid. **90**, 239902 (2003)] [arXiv:hep-ex/0110059].
25. A. Czarnecki and W. J. Marciano, Int. J. Mod. Phys. A **15**, 2365 (2000) [arXiv:hep-ph/0003049].
26. For a recent analysis and original references, see
27. K. Melnikov and F. Petriello, "Electroweak gauge boson production at hadron colliders through arXiv:hep-ph/0609070.
28. U. Baur and D. Wackeroth, Nucl. Phys. Proc. Suppl. **116**, 159 (2003) [arXiv:hep-ph/0211089];
29. V. A. Zykunov, arXiv:hep-ph/0509315.
30. J. Houston, talk given at the *Workshop on TeV Colliders*, Les Houches, France, 2-20 May 2005.
31. I. Belotelov *et al.*, CMS Note 2006/123.

32. C. Anastasiou, L. J. Dixon, K. Melnikov and F. Petriello, Phys. Rev. D **69**, 094008 (2004) [arXiv:hep-ph/0312266] and Phys. Rev. Lett. **91**, 182002 (2003) [arXiv:hep-ph/0306192];
33. A. D. Martin, R. G. Roberts, W. J. Stirling and R. S. Thorne, Eur. Phys. J. C **35**, 325 (2004) [arXiv:hep-ph/0308087] and Eur. Phys. J. C **28**, 455 (2003) [arXiv:hep-ph/0211080].
34. P. Savard, talk given at the *XXXIII International Conference on High Energy Physics(ICHEP06)*, Moscow, Russia, 26 July - 2 August, 2006; C. Ciobanu, talk given at the *40th Rencontres De Moriond On QCD And High Energy Hadronic Interactions*, La Thuile, Aosta Valley, Italy, 12-19 Mar 2005; K. Burkett, talk given at the *0th Rencontres De Moriond On Electroweak Interactions And Unified Theories*, La Thuile, Aosta Valley, Italy, 2-10 Mar 2005.
35. A. Abulencia *et al.* [CDF Collaboration], Phys. Rev. Lett. **96**, 211801 (2006) [arXiv:hep-ex/0602045].
36. See, for example, the analyses presented in http://www-cdf.fnal.gov/physics/projections/Zprime-CDF.html.
37. R. Alemany, talk given at *Beyond the Standard Model Physics at the LHC*, Cracow, Poland, 3-8 July 2006.
38. S. Willocq, talk given at the *XXXIII International Conference on High Energy Physics(ICHEP06)*, Moscow, Russia, 26 July - 2 August, 2006.
39. O.K. Baker, talk given at the *Third North American ATLAS Physics Workshop*, Boston, MA, 26-28 July, 2006.
40. R. Cousins, J. Mumford and V. Valuev, CMS Note 2006/062.
41. G. Azuelos *et al.*, Eur. Phys. J. C **39S2**, 13 (2005) [arXiv:hep-ph/0402037]; E. Roos, ATL-PHYS-CONF-2006-007.
42. ATLAS Detector and Physics Performance Technical Design Report, http://atlas.web.cern.ch/Atlas/GROUPS/PHYSICS/TDR/access.html.
43. CMS Physics Technical Design Report, https://cmsdoc.cern.ch/cms/cpt/tdr/.
44. See, for example, J. Kumar and J. D. Wells, arXiv:hep-th/0604203 and references therein. See also A. Freitas, Phys. Rev. D **70**, 015008 (2004) [arXiv:hep-ph/0403288].
45. B. C. Allanach, K. Odagiri, M. A. Parker and B. R. Webber, JHEP **0009**, 019 (2000) [arXiv:hep-ph/0006114].
46. R. Cousins, J. Mumford, J. Tucker and V. Valuev, JHEP **0511**, 046 (2005).
47. F. Gianotti *et al.*, "Physics potential and experimental challenges of the LHC luminosity Eur. Phys. J. C **39**, 293 (2005) [arXiv:hep-ph/0204087].
48. M. Schafer, F. Ledroit and B. Trocmé, ATL-PHYS-PUB-2005-010.
49. H. E. Haber, SLAC-PUB-3456 *Presented at 1984 Summer Study on the Design and Utilization of the Superconducting Super Collider, Snowmass, CO, Jun 23 - Jul 23, 1984*
50. M. Dittmar, A. S. Nicollerat and A. Djouadi, Phys. Lett. B **583**, 111 (2004) [arXiv:hep-ph/0307020].
51. R. Cousins, J. Mumford, J. Tucker and V. Valuev, CMS Note 2005/022.
52. J. L. Rosner, Phys. Rev. D **35**, 2244 (1987).

53. J. Morel and F. Ledroit, Talk given at *LPSC-Grenoble*, Grenoble, France, July 2005.
54. F. del Aguila, M. Cvetic and P. Langacker, Phys. Rev. D **48**, 969 (1993) [arXiv:hep-ph/9303299].
55. J. D. Anderson, M. H. Austern and R. N. Cahn, Phys. Rev. Lett. **69**, 25 (1992) and Phys. Rev. D **46**, 290 (1992).
56. K. Gumus, N. Akchurin, S. Esen and R.M. Harris, CMS Note 2006/070
57. S. González de la Hoz,L. March and E. Roos, ATL-PHYS-PUB-2006-003.
58. D. Benchekroun, C. Driouichi and A. Hoummada, Eur. Phys. J. directC **3**, N3 (2001).
59. T. G. Rizzo, Phys. Lett. B **192**, 125 (1987).
60. M. Cvetic and P. Langacker, Phys. Rev. D **46**, 14 (1992).
61. J. L. Hewett and T. G. Rizzo, Phys. Rev. D **47**, 4981 (1993) [arXiv:hep-ph/9206221].
62. T. G. Rizzo, Phys. Rev. D **47**, 956 (1993) [arXiv:hep-ph/9209207].
63. M. Cvetic and P. Langacker, Phys. Rev. D **46**, 4943 (1992) [Erratum-ibid. D **48**, 4484 (1993)] [arXiv:hep-ph/9207216].
64. G. Weiglein *et al.* [LHC/LC Study Group], arXiv:hep-ph/0410364.
65. T. G. Rizzo, arXiv:hep-ph/0303056. Such analyses have been performed by many authors; see, for example, F. Richard, arXiv:hep-ph/0303107 and and work by S. Riemann in J. A. Aguilar-Saavedra *et al.* [ECFA/DESY LC Physics Working Group], "TESLA Technical Design Report Part III: Physics at an e+e- Linear arXiv:hep-ph/0106315; S. Godfrey, P. Kalyniak and A. Tomkins, arXiv:hep-ph/0511335.
66. S. Godfrey, "Search limits for extra neutral gauge bosons at high energy lepton eConf **C960625** (1996) NEW138 [arXiv:hep-ph/9612384] and Phys. Rev. D **51**, 1402 (1995) [arXiv:hep-ph/9411237].
67. S. Riemann, LC-TH-2001-007, http://www.slac.stanford.edu/spires/find/hep/www?r=lc-th-2001-007, *In *2nd ECFA/DESY Study 1998-2001* 1451-1468*

Chapter 10

Neutrinoless Double Beta Decay

Petr Vogel

Kellogg Radiation Laboratory
Caltech, Pasadena, CA 91125, USA[*]

10.1. Introduction - fundamentals of $\beta\beta$ decay

In the recent past neutrino oscillation experiments have convincingly shown that neutrinos have a finite mass. However, in oscillation experiments only the differences of squares of the neutrino masses, $\Delta m^2 \equiv |m_2^2 - m_1^2|$, can be measured, and the results do not depend on the charge conjugation properties of neutrinos, i.e., whether they are Dirac or Majorana fermions. Nevertheless, a lower limit on the absolute value of the neutrino mass scale, $m_{scale} = \sqrt{|\Delta m^2|}$, has been established in this way. Its existence, in turn, is causing a renaissance of enthusiasm in the double beta decay community which is expected to reach and even exceed, in the next generation of experiments, the sensitivity corresponding to this mass scale. Below I review the current status of the double beta decay and the effort devoted to reach the required sensitivity, as well as various issues in theory (or phenomenology) concerning the relation of the $0\nu\beta\beta$ decay rate to the absolute neutrino mass scale and to the general problem of the Lepton Number Violation (LNV).

But before doing that I very briefly summarize the achievements of the neutrino oscillation searches and the role that the search for the neutrinoless double beta decay plays in the elucidation of the pattern of neutrino masses and mixing. In these introductory remarks I use the established terminology, some of which will be defined only later in the text.

There is a consensus that the measurement of atmospheric neutrinos by the SuperKamiokande collaboration[1] can be only interpreted as a conse-

---
[*]email: pxv@caltech.edu

quence of the nearly maximum mixing between ν_μ and ν_τ neutrinos, with the corresponding mass squared difference $|\Delta m_{atm}^2| \sim 2.4 \times 10^{-3}$ eV^2. This finding was confirmed by the K2K experiment[2] that uses accelerator ν_μ beam pointing towards the SuperKamiokande detector 250 km away, as well as by the very recent first result of the MINOS experiment located at the Sudan mine in Minnesota, 735 km away from the Fermilab.[3] Several large long-baseline experiments are being built to further elucidate this discovery, and determine the corresponding parameters more accurately.

At the same time the "solar neutrino puzzle", which has been with us for over thirty years since the pioneering chlorine experiment of Davis,[4] also reached the stage where the interpretation of the measurements in terms of oscillations between the ν_e and some combination of the active, i.e., ν_μ and ν_τ neutrinos, is inescapable. In particular, the juxtaposition of the results of the SNO experiment[5] and SuperKamiokande,[6] together with the earlier solar neutrino flux determination in the gallium experiments,[7,8] leads to that conclusion. The value of the corresponding oscillation parameters, however, remained uncertain, with several "solutions" possible, although the so-called Large Mixing Angle (LMA) solution with $\sin^2 2\theta_{sol} \sim 0.8$ and $\Delta m_{sol}^2 \sim 10^{-4}$ eV^2 was preferred. A decisive confirmation of the "solar" oscillations was provided by the nuclear reactor experiment KamLAND[9,10] that demonstrated that the flux of the reactor $\bar{\nu}_e$ is reduced and its spectrum distorted at the average distance ~ 180 km from nuclear reactors.

The pattern of neutrino mixing is further simplified by the constraint due to the Chooz and Palo Verde reactor neutrino experiments[11,12] which lead to the conclusion that the third mixing angle, θ_{13}, is small, $\sin^2 2\theta_{13} \leq 0.1$. The two remaining possible neutrino mass patterns are illustrated in Fig. 10.1.

Altogether, clearly a *lower* limit for at least one of the neutrino masses, $\sqrt{\Delta m_{atm}^2} \simeq 0.05$ eV has been established. However, the oscillation experiments cannot determine the absolute magnitude of the masses and, in particular, cannot at this stage separate two rather different scenarios, the hierarchical pattern of neutrino masses in which $m \sim \sqrt{\Delta m^2}$ and the degenerate pattern in which $m \gg \sqrt{\Delta m^2}$. It is hoped that the search for the neutrinoless double beta decay, reviewed here, will help in foreseeable future in determining, or at least narrowing down, the absolute neutrino mass scale, and in deciding which of these two possibilities is applicable.

Moreover, the oscillation results do not tell us anything about the properties of neutrinos under charge conjugation. While the charged leptons are Dirac particles, distinct from their antiparticles, neutrinos may be the

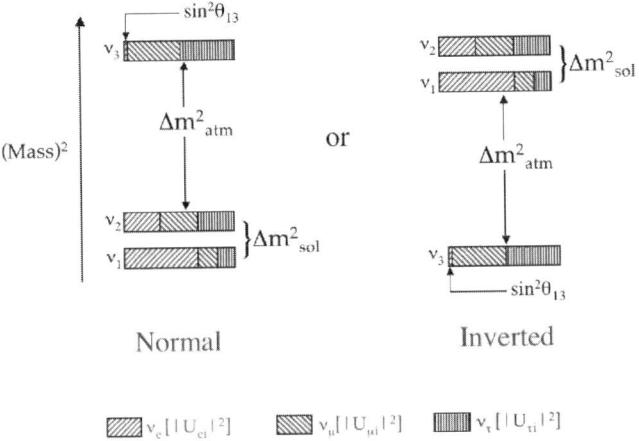

Fig. 10.1. Schematic illustration (mass intervals not to scale) of the decomposition of the neutrino mass eigenstates ν_i in terms of the flavor eigenstates. The two hierarchies cannot be, at this time, distinguished. The small admixture of ν_e into ν_3 is an upper limit.

ultimate neutral particles, as envisioned by Majorana, that are identical to their antiparticles. That fundamental distinction becomes important only for massive particles and becomes irrelevant in the massless limit. Neutrinoless double beta decay proceeds only when neutrinos are massive Majorana particles, hence its observation would resolve the question.

Double beta decay ($\beta\beta$) is a nuclear transition $(Z, A) \rightarrow (Z + 2, A)$ in which two neutrons bound in a nucleus are simultaneously transformed into two protons plus two electrons (and possibly other light neutral particles). This transition is possible and potentially observable because nuclei with even Z and N are more bound than the odd-odd nuclei with the same $A = N + Z$. Analogous transition of two protons into two neutrons are also, in principle, possible in several nuclei, but phase space considerations give preference to the former mode.

An example is shown in Fig. 10.2. The situation shown there is not exceptional. There are eleven analogous cases (candidate nuclei) with the Q-value (i.e., the energy available to leptons) in excess of 2 MeV.

There are two basic modes of the $\beta\beta$ decay. In the two-neutrino mode ($2\nu\beta\beta$) there are two $\bar{\nu}_e$ emitted together with the two e^-. Lepton number is conserved and this mode is allowed in the standard model of electroweak interaction. It has been repeatedly observed by now in a number of cases and proceeds with a typical half-life of $\sim 10^{20}$ years. In contrast, in the

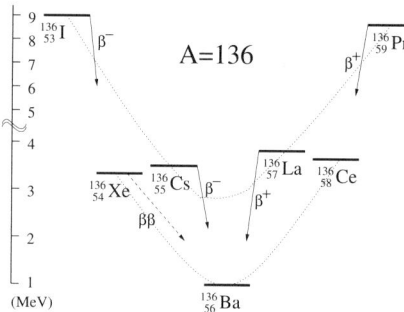

Fig. 10.2. Atomic masses of the isotopes with $A = 136$. Nuclei ^{136}Xe, ^{136}Ba and ^{136}Ce are stable against the ordinary β decay; hence they exist in nature. However, energy conservation alone allows the transition ^{136}Xe $\rightarrow$ ^{136}Ba $+ 2e^-$ (+ possibly other neutral light particles) and the analogous decay of ^{136}Ce with the positron emission.

neutrinoless mode ($0\nu\beta\beta$) only the $2e^-$ are emitted and nothing else. That mode clearly violates the law of lepton number conservation and is forbidden in the standard model. Hence, its observation would be a signal of a "new physics".

The two modes of the $\beta\beta$ decay have some common and some distinct features. The common features are:

- The leptons carry essentially all available energy. The nuclear recoil is negligible, $Q/Am_p \ll 1$.
- The transition involves the 0^+ ground state of the initial nucleus and (in almost all cases) the 0^+ ground state of the final nucleus. In few cases the transition to an excited 0^+ state in the final nucleus is energetically possible, but suppressed by the smaller phase space available. (But the $2\nu\beta\beta$ decay to the excited 0^+ state has been observed in few cases.)
- Both processes are of second order of weak interactions, $\sim G_F^4$, hence inherently slow. The phase space consideration alone (for the $2\nu\beta\beta$ mode $\sim Q^{11}$ and for the $0\nu\beta\beta$ mode $\sim Q^5$) give preference to the $0\nu\beta\beta$ which is, however, forbidden by the lepton number conservation.

The distinct features are:

- In the $2\nu\beta\beta$ mode the two neutrons undergoing the transition are uncorrelated (but decay simultaneously) while in the $0\nu\beta\beta$ the two neutrons are correlated.

- In the $2\nu\beta\beta$ mode the sum electron kinetic energy T_1+T_2 spectrum is continuous and peaked below $Q/2$. As $T_1+T_2 \to Q$ the spectrum approaches zero approximately like $(\Delta E/Q)^6$.
- On the other hand, in the $0\nu\beta\beta$ mode $T_1 + T_2 = Q$ smeared only by the detector resolution.

These last features allow one to separate the two modes experimentally by observing the sum electron spectrum with a good energy resolution, even if the corresponding decay rate for the $0\nu\beta\beta$ mode is much smaller than for the $2\nu\beta\beta$ mode. This is illustrated in Fig. 10.3 where the insert that includes the 0ν peak and the 2ν tail shows the situation for the rate ratio of $1:10^6$ corresponding to the most sensitive current experiments.

Various aspects, both theoretical and experimental, of the $\beta\beta$ decay have been reviewed many times. Here I quote just the more recent review articles,[13-16] earlier references can be found there.

In this introductory section let me make only few general remarks. The existence of the $0\nu\beta\beta$ decay would mean that on the elementary particle level a six fermion lepton number violating amplitude transforming two u quarks into two d quarks and two electrons is nonvanishing. As was first pointed out by Schechter and Valle[17] more than twenty years ago, this fact alone would guarantee that neutrinos are massive Majorana fermions (see

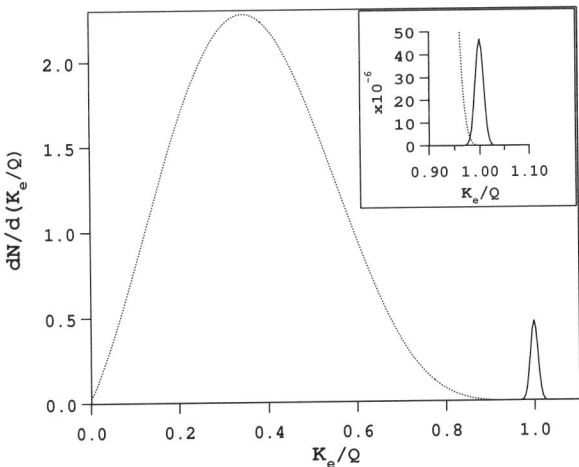

Fig. 10.3. Separating the $0\nu\beta\beta$ mode from the $2\nu\beta\beta$ by the shape of the sum electron spectrum (kinetic energy K_e of the two electrons), including the effect of the 2% resolution smearing. The assumed $2\nu/0\nu$ rate ratio is 10^2, and 10^6 in the insert.

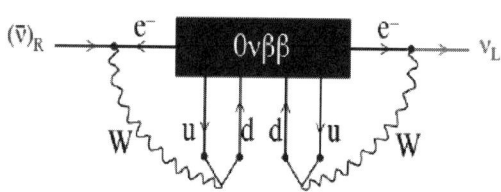

Fig. 10.4. By adding loops involving only standard weak interaction processes the $0\nu\beta\beta$ decay amplitude (the black box) implies the existence of the Majorana neutrino mass.

Fig. 10.4). This qualitative statement (or theorem), unfortunately, does not allow us to deduce the magnitude of the neutrino mass once the rate of the $0\nu\beta\beta$ decay have been determined.

There is no indication at the present time that neutrinos have nonstandard interactions, i.e. they seem to have only interactions carried by the W and Z bosons that are contained in the Standard Electroweak Model. All observed oscillation phenomena can be understood if one assumes that that neutrinos interact exactly the way the Standard Model prescribes, but are massive fermions forcing a generalization of the model. If we accept this, but in addition assume that neutrinos are Majorana particles, we can in fact relate the $0\nu\beta\beta$ decay rate to the quantity related to the absolute neutrino mass. With these caveats that relation can be expressed as

$$\frac{1}{T_{1/2}^{0\nu}} = G^{0\nu}(Q,Z)|M^{0\nu}|^2 \langle m_{\beta\beta} \rangle^2 , \qquad (10.1)$$

where $G^{0\nu}(Q,Z)$ is a phase space factor that depends on the transition Q value and through the Coulomb effect on the emitted electrons on the nuclear charge Z and that can be easily and accurately calculated, $M^{0\nu}$ is the nuclear matrix element that can be evaluated in principle, although with a considerable uncertainty, and finally the quantity $\langle m_{\beta\beta} \rangle$ is the effective neutrino Majorana mass, representing the important particle physics ingredient of the process.

In turn, the effective mass $\langle m_{\beta\beta} \rangle$ is related to the mixing angles θ_{ij} that are determined or constrained by the oscillation experiments, to the absolute neutrino masses m_i of the mass eigenstates ν_i and to the as of now totally unknown additional parameters as fundamental as the mixing angles θ_{ij}, the so-called Majorana phase $\alpha(i)$,

$$\langle m_{\beta\beta}\rangle = |\Sigma_i |U_{ei}|^2 e^{i\alpha(i)} m_i| \ . \tag{10.2}$$

Here U_{ei} are the matrix elements of the first row of the neutrino mixing matrix.

It is straightforward to use the eq. (10.2) and the known neutrino oscillation results in order to relate $\langle m_{\beta\beta}\rangle$ to other neutrino mass dependent quantities. This is illustrated in Fig. 10.5. Traditionally such plot is made as in the left panel. However, the lightest neutrino mass m_{min} is not an observable quantity. For that reason the other two panels show the relation of $\langle m_{\beta\beta}\rangle$ to the sum of the neutrino masses $M = \Sigma m_i$ and also to $\langle m_\beta\rangle$ that represents the parameter that can be determined or constrained in ordinary β decay,

$$\langle m_\beta\rangle^2 = \Sigma_i |U_{ei}|^2 m_i^2 \ . \tag{10.3}$$

Several remarks are in order. First, the observation of the $0\nu\beta\beta$ decay and determination of $\langle m_{\beta\beta}\rangle$, even when combined with the knowledge of M and/or $\langle m_\beta\rangle$ does not allow, in general, to distinguish between the normal and inverted mass orderings. This is a consequence of the fact that the Majorana phases are unknown. In regions in Fig. 10.5 where the two hatched bands overlap it is clear that two solutions with the same $\langle m_{\beta\beta}\rangle$ and the same M (or the same $\langle m_\beta\rangle$) exist and cannot be distinguished.

On the other hand, obviously, if one can determine that $\langle m_{\beta\beta}\rangle \geq 0.1$ eV we would conclude that the mass pattern is degenerate. And in the so far hypothetical case that one could show that $\langle m_{\beta\beta}\rangle \leq 0.01 - 0.02$ eV but nonvanishing nevertheless the normal hierarchy would be established.[a]

It is worthwhile noting that if the inverted mass ordering is realized in nature, (and neutrinos are Majorana particles) the quantity $\langle m_{\beta\beta}\rangle$ is constrained from below by ~ 0.01 eV. This value is within reach of the next generation of experiments. Also, in principle, in the case of the normal hierarchy while all neutrinos could be massive Majorana particles it is still possible that $\langle m_{\beta\beta}\rangle = 0$. Such a situation, however, requires "fine tuning" or reflects a symmetry of some kind.

Let us remark that the $0\nu\beta\beta$ decay is not the only LNV process for which important experimental constraints exist. Examples of the other

---

[a]In that case also the $\langle m_\beta\rangle$ in the right panel would not represent the quatity directly related to the ordinary β decay. There are no realistic ideas, however, how to reach the corresponding sensitivity in ordinary β decay at this time.

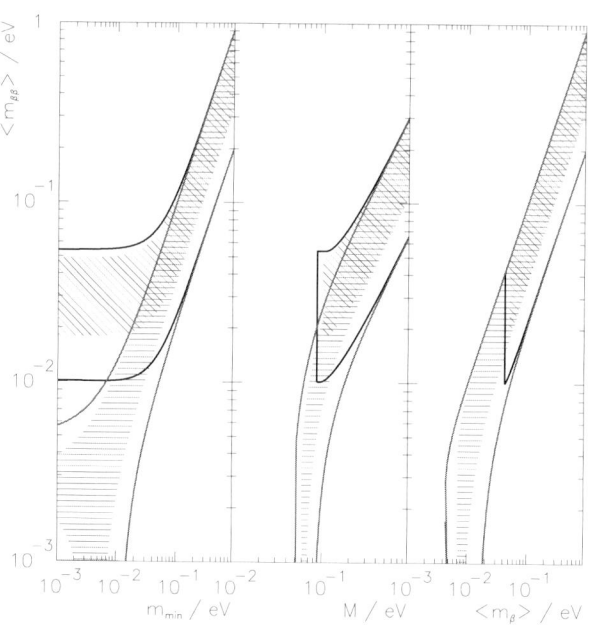

Fig. 10.5. The left panel shows the dependence of $\langle m_{\beta\beta} \rangle$ on the mass of the lightest neutrino $m_{\min}$, the middle one shows the relation between $\langle m_{\beta\beta} \rangle$ and the sum of neutrino masses $M = \Sigma m_i$ determined or constrained by the "observational cosmology", and the right one depicts the relation between $\langle m_{\beta\beta} \rangle$ and the effective mass $\langle m_\beta \rangle$ determined or constrained by the ordinary β decay. In all panels the width of the hatched area is due to the unknown Majorana phases and therefore irreducible. The solid lines indicate the allowed regions by taking into account the current uncertainties in the oscillation parameters; they will shrink as the accuracy improves. The two sets of curves correspond to the normal and inverted hierarchies, they merge above about $\langle m_{\beta\beta} \rangle \geq 0.1$ eV, where the degenerate mass pattern begins.

analogous processes are

$$\mu^- + (Z, A) \to e^+ + (Z-2, A); \text{ exp. branching ratio} \leq 10^{-12},$$
$$K^+ \to \mu^+ \mu^+ \pi^-; \text{ exp. branching ratio} \leq 3 \times 10^{-9},$$
$$\bar{\nu}_e \text{ emission from the Sun; exp. branching ratio} \leq 10^{-4}. \quad (10.4)$$

However, detailed analysis suggests that the study of the $0\nu\beta\beta$ decay is by far the most sensitive test of LNV. In simple terms, this is caused by the amount of tries one can make. A 100 kg $0\nu\beta\beta$ decay source contains $\sim 10^{27}$ nuclei. This can be contrasted with the possibilities of first producing muons or kaons, and then searching for the unusual decay channels. The Fermilab accelerators, for example, produce "a few" $\times 10^{20}$ protons on target per year in their beams and thus correspondingly smaller numbers of muons or kaons.

10.2. Mechanism of the $0\nu\beta\beta$ decay

It has been recognized long time ago that the relation between the $0\nu\beta\beta$ decay rate and the effective Majorana mass $\langle m_{\beta\beta}\rangle$ is to some extent problematic. The assumption leading to the eq. (10.1) is rather conservative, namely that there is an exchange of a virtual light, but massive, Majorana neutrino between the two nucleons undergoing the transition, and that these neutrinos interact by the standard left-handed weak currents. However, that is not the only possible mechanism. LNV interactions involving so far unobserved heavy ($\sim$ TeV) particles can lead to a comparable $0\nu\beta\beta$ decay rate. Thus, in the absence of additional information about the mechanism responsible for the $0\nu\beta\beta$ decay, one could not unambiguously infer $\langle m_{\beta\beta}\rangle$ from the $0\nu\beta\beta$ decay rate.

In general $0\nu\beta\beta$ decay can be generated by (i) light massive Majorana neutrino exchange or (ii) heavy particle exchange (see, e.g. Refs. 18,19), resulting from LNV dynamics at some scale Λ above the electroweak one. The relative size of heavy (A_H) versus light particle (A_L) exchange contributions to the decay amplitude can be crudely estimated as follows:[20]

$$A_L \sim G_F^2 \frac{\langle m_{\beta\beta}\rangle}{\langle k^2\rangle}, \quad A_H \sim G_F^2 \frac{M_W^4}{\Lambda^5}, \quad \frac{A_H}{A_L} \sim \frac{M_W^4 \langle k^2\rangle}{\Lambda^5 \langle m_{\beta\beta}\rangle}, \qquad (10.5)$$

where $\langle m_{\beta\beta}\rangle$ is the effective neutrino Majorana mass, $\langle k^2\rangle \sim (50 \text{ MeV})^2$ is the typical light neutrino virtuality, and Λ is the heavy scale relevant to the LNV dynamics. Therefore, $A_H/A_L \sim O(1)$ for $\langle m_{\beta\beta}\rangle \sim 0.1 - 0.5$ eV and $\Lambda \sim 1$ TeV, and thus the LNV dynamics at the TeV scale leads to similar $0\nu\beta\beta$ decay rate as the exchange of light Majorana neutrinos with the effective mass $\langle m_{\beta\beta}\rangle \sim 0.1 - 0.5$ eV.

Obviously, the lifetime measurement by itself does not provide the means for determining the underlying mechanism. The spin-flip and non-flip exchange can be, in principle, distinguished by the measurement of the single-electron spectra or polarization (see e.g.,[21]). However, in most cases the mechanism of light Majorana neutrino exchange, and of heavy particle exchange cannot be separated by the observation of the emitted electrons. Thus one must look for other phenomenological consequences of the different mechanisms other than observables directly associated with $0\nu\beta\beta$. Here I discuss the suggestion[22] that under natural assumptions the presence of low scale LNV interactions also affects muon lepton flavor violating (LFV) processes, and in particular enhances the $\mu \to e$ conversion compared to the $\mu \to e\gamma$ decay.

The discussion is concerned mainly with the branching ratios $B_{\mu \to e\gamma} = \Gamma(\mu \to e\gamma)/\Gamma_\mu^{(0)}$ and $B_{\mu \to e} = \Gamma_{\rm conv}/\Gamma_{\rm capt}$, where $\mu \to e\gamma$ is normalized to the standard muon decay rate $\Gamma_\mu^{(0)} = (G_F^2 m_\mu^5)/(192\pi^3)$, while $\mu \to e$ conversion is normalized to the corresponding capture rate $\Gamma_{\rm capt}$. The main diagnostic tool in the analysis is the ratio

$$\mathcal{R} = B_{\mu \to e}/B_{\mu \to e\gamma} , \qquad (10.6)$$

and the relevance of our observation relies on the potential for LFV discovery in the forthcoming experiments MEG[23] ($\mu \to e\gamma$) and MECO[24] ($\mu \to e$ conversion)[b] that plan to improve the current limits by several orders of magnitude.

It is useful to formulate the problem in terms of effective low energy interactions obtained after integrating out the heavy degrees of freedom that induce LNV and LFV dynamics. If the scales for both LNV and LFV are well above the weak scale, then one would not expect to observe any signal in the forthcoming LFV experiments, nor would the effects of heavy particle exchange enter $0\nu\beta\beta$ at an appreciable level. In this case, the only origin of a signal in $0\nu\beta\beta$ at the level of prospective experimental sensitivity would be the exchange of a light Majorana neutrino, leading to eq. (10.1), and allowing one to extract $\langle m_{\beta\beta} \rangle$ from the decay rate.

In general, however, the two scales may be distinct, as in SUSY-GUT[25] or SUSY see-saw[26] models. In these scenarios, both the Majorana neutrino mass as well as LFV effects are generated at the GUT scale. The effects of heavy Majorana neutrino exchange in $0\nu\beta\beta$ are, thus, highly suppressed. In contrast, the effects of GUT-scale LFV are transmitted to the TeV-scale by a soft SUSY-breaking sector without mass suppression via renormalization group running of the high-scale LFV couplings. Consequently, such scenarios could lead to observable effects in the upcoming LFV experiments but with an $\mathcal{O}(\alpha)$ suppression of the branching ratio $B_{\mu \to e}$ relative to $B_{\mu \to e\gamma}$ due to the exchange of a virtual photon in the conversion process rather than the emission of a real one, thus $\mathcal{R} \sim 10^{-(2-3)}$ in this case.

The case where the scales of LNV and LFV are both relatively low ($\sim$ TeV) is more subtle. This is the scenario which might lead to observable signals in LFV searches and at the same time generate ambiguities in

---
[b]Even though MECO experiment was recently cancelled, proposals for experiments with similar sensitivity exist elsewhere.

interpreting a positive signal in $0\nu\beta\beta$. Therefore, this is the case where one needs to develop some discriminating criteria.

Denoting the new physics scale by Λ, one has a LNV effective lagrangian of the form

$$\mathcal{L}_{0\nu\beta\beta} = \sum_i \frac{\tilde{c}_i}{\Lambda^5} \tilde{O}_i \qquad \tilde{O}_i = \bar{q}\Gamma_1 q \ \bar{q}\Gamma_2 q \ \bar{e}\Gamma_3 e^c \ , \qquad (10.7)$$

where we have suppressed the flavor and Dirac structures (a complete list of the dimension nine operators $\tilde{O}_i$ can be found in Ref. 19).

For the LFV interactions, one has

$$\mathcal{L}_{\text{LFV}} = \sum_i \frac{c_i}{\Lambda^2} O_i \ , \qquad (10.8)$$

and a complete operator basis can be found in Refs. 27,28. The LFV operators relevant to our analysis are of the following type (along with their analogues with $L \leftrightarrow R$):

$$\begin{aligned} O_{\sigma L} &= \frac{e}{(4\pi)^2} \overline{\ell_{iL}} \, \sigma_{\mu\nu} i \slashed{D} \, \ell_{jL} \, F^{\mu\nu} + \text{h.c.} \\ O_{\ell L} &= \overline{\ell_{iL}} \, \ell^c_{jL} \, \overline{\ell^c_{kL}} \, \ell_{mL} \\ O_{\ell q} &= \overline{\ell_i}\Gamma_\ell \ell_j \ \bar{q}\Gamma_q q \ . \end{aligned} \qquad (10.9)$$

Operators of the type O_σ are typically generated at one-loop level, hence our choice to explicitly display the loop factor $1/(4\pi)^2$. On the other hand, in a large class of models, operators of the type O_ℓ or $O_{\ell q}$ are generated by tree level exchange of heavy degrees of freedom. With the above choices, all non-zero c_i and $\tilde{c}_i$ are nominally of the same size, typically the product of two Yukawa-like couplings or gauge couplings (times flavor mixing matrices).

With the notation established above, the ratio $\mathcal{R}$ of the branching ratios $\mu \to e$ to $\mu \to e+\gamma$ can be written schematically as follows (neglecting flavor indices in the effective couplings and the term with $L \leftrightarrow R$):

$$\mathcal{R} = \frac{\Phi}{48\pi^2} \left| \lambda_1 \, e^2 c_{\sigma L} + e^2 \left(\lambda_2 c_{\ell L} + \lambda_3 c_{\ell q}\right) \log \frac{\Lambda^2}{m_\mu^2} \right. $$
$$\left. + \lambda_4 (4\pi)^2 c_{\ell q} + \ldots \right|^2 / \left[e^2 \left(|c_{\sigma L}|^2 + |c_{\sigma R}|^2\right) \right] \ . \qquad (10.10)$$

In the above formula $\lambda_{1,2,3,4}$ are numerical factors of $O(1)$, while the overall factor $\frac{\Phi}{48\pi^2}$ arises from phase space and overlap integrals of electron and muon wavefunctions in the nuclear field. For light nuclei $\Phi = (ZF_p^2)/(g_V^2 + 3g_A^2) \sim O(1)$ ($g_{V,A}$ are the vector and axial nucleon form factors at zero momentum transfer, while F_p is the nuclear form factor at $q^2 = -m_\mu^2$ [28]). The dots indicate subleading terms, not relevant for our discussion, such as loop-induced contributions to c_ℓ and $c_{\ell q}$ that are analytic in external masses and momenta. In contrast the logarithmically-enhanced loop contribution given by the second term in the numerator of $\mathcal{R}$ plays an essential role. This term arises whenever the operators $O_{\ell L,R}$ and/or $O_{\ell q}$ appear at tree-level in the effective theory and generate one-loop renormalization of $O_{\ell q}$[27] (see Fig. 10.6).

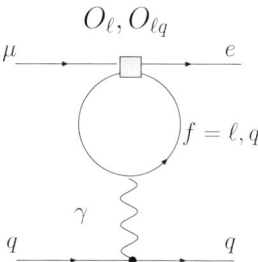

Fig. 10.6. Loop contributions to $\mu \to e$ conversion through insertion of operators O_ℓ or $O_{\ell q}$, generating the large logarithm.

The ingredients in eq. (10.10) lead to several observations: (i) In absence of tree-level $c_{\ell L}$ and $c_{\ell q}$, one obtains $\mathcal{R} \sim (\Phi \lambda_1^2 \alpha)/(12\pi) \sim 10^{-3} - 10^{-2}$, due to gauge coupling and phase space suppression. (ii) When present, the logarithmically enhanced contributions compensate for the gauge coupling and phase space suppression, leading to $\mathcal{R} \sim O(1)$. (iii) If present, the tree-level coupling $c_{\ell q}$ dominates the $\mu \to e$ rate leading to $\mathcal{R} \gg 1$.

Thus, we can formulate our main conclusions regarding the discriminating power of the ratio $\mathcal{R}$:

(1) Observation of both the LFV muon processes $\mu \to e$ and $\mu \to e\gamma$ with relative ratio $\mathcal{R} \sim 10^{-2}$ implies, under generic conditions, that $\Gamma_{0\nu\beta\beta} \sim \langle m_{\beta\beta} \rangle^2$. Hence the relation of the $0\nu\beta\beta$ lifetime to the absolute neutrino mass scale is straightforward.
(2) On the other hand, observation of LFV muon processes with relative ratio $\mathcal{R} \gg 10^{-2}$ could signal non-trivial LNV dynamics at the TeV scale, whose effect on $0\nu\beta\beta$ has to be analyzed on a case by case basis. Therefore, in this scenario no definite conclusion can be drawn based on LFV rates.

(3) Non-observation of LFV in muon processes in forthcoming experiments would imply either that the scale of non-trivial LFV and LNV is above a few TeV, and thus $\Gamma_{0\nu\beta\beta} \sim \langle m_{\beta\beta}\rangle^2$, or that any TeV-scale LNV is approximately flavor diagonal.

The above statements are illustrated using two explicit cases:[22] the minimal supersymmetric standard model (MSSM) with R-parity violation (RPV-SUSY) and the Left-Right Symmetric Model (LRSM).

RPV SUSY — If one does not impose R-parity conservation $[R = (-1)^{3(B-L)+2s}]$, the MSSM superpotential includes, in addition to the standard Yukawa terms, lepton and baryon number violating interactions, compactly written as (see e.g.,[29])

$$W_{RPV} = \lambda_{ijk} L_i L_j E_k^c + \lambda'_{ijk} L_i Q_j D_k^c + \lambda''_{ijk} U_i^c D_j^c D_k^c \\ + \mu'_i L_i H_u \, , \qquad (10.11)$$

where L and Q represent lepton and quark doublet superfields, while E^c, U^c, D^c are lepton and quark singlet superfields. The simultaneous presence of λ' and λ'' couplings would lead to an unacceptably large proton decay rate (for SUSY mass scale $\Lambda_{SUSY} \sim$ TeV), so we focus on the case of $\lambda'' = 0$ and set $\mu' = 0$ without loss of generality. In such case, lepton number is violated by the remaining terms in W_{RPV}, leading to short distance contributions to $0\nu\beta\beta$ [e.g., Fig. 10.7(a)], with typical coefficients [cf. eq. (10.7)]

$$\frac{\tilde{c}_i}{\Lambda^5} \sim \frac{\pi\alpha_s}{m_{\tilde{g}}} \frac{\lambda'^2_{111}}{m_{\tilde{f}}^4} \, ; \, \frac{\pi\alpha_2}{m_\chi} \frac{\lambda'^2_{111}}{m_{\tilde{f}}^4} \, , \qquad (10.12)$$

where α_s, α_2 represent the strong and weak gauge coupling constants, respectively. The RPV interactions also lead to lepton number conserving but lepton flavor violating operators [e.g. Fig. 10.7(b)], with coefficients [cf. eq. (10.8)]

$$\frac{c_\ell}{\Lambda^2} \sim \frac{\lambda_{i11}\lambda^*_{i21}}{m^2_{\tilde{\nu}_i}}, \frac{\lambda^*_{i11}\lambda_{i12}}{m^2_{\tilde{\nu}_i}} \, ,$$

$$\frac{c_{\ell q}}{\Lambda^2} \sim \frac{\lambda'^*_{11i}\lambda'_{21i}}{m^2_{\tilde{d}_i}}, \frac{\lambda'^*_{1i1}\lambda'_{2i1}}{m^2_{\tilde{u}_i}} \, , \qquad (10.13)$$

$$\frac{c_\sigma}{\Lambda^2} \sim \frac{\lambda\lambda^*}{m^2_{\tilde{\ell}}}, \frac{\lambda'\lambda'^*}{m^2_{\tilde{q}}} \, ,$$

where the flavor combinations contributing to c_σ can be found in Ref. 30. Hence, for generic flavor structure of the couplings λ and λ' the underlying

LNV dynamics generate both short distance contributions to $0\nu\beta\beta$ and LFV contributions that lead to $\mathcal{R} \gg 10^{-2}$.

Existing limits on rare processes strongly constrain combinations of RPV couplings, assuming Λ_{SUSY} is between a few hundred GeV and ~ 1 TeV. Non-observation of LFV at future experiments MEG and MECO could be attributed either to a larger Λ_{SUSY} ($>$ few TeV) or to suppression of couplings that involve mixing among first and second generations. In the former scenario, the short distance contribution to $0\nu\beta\beta$ does not compete with the long distance one [see eq. (10.5)], so that $\Gamma_{0\nu\beta\beta} \sim \langle m_{\beta\beta}\rangle^2$. On the other hand, there is an exception to this "diagnostic tool". If the λ and λ' matrices are nearly flavor diagonal, the exchange of superpartners may still make non-negligible contributions to $0\nu\beta\beta$ without enhancing the ratio $\mathcal{R}$.

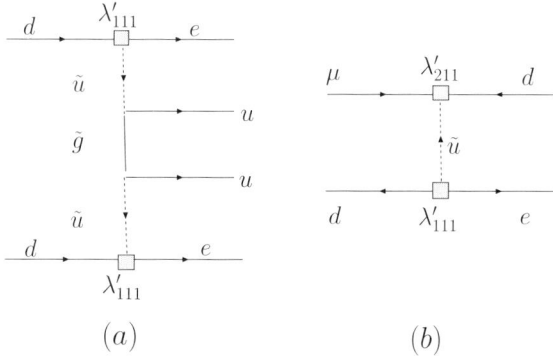

Fig. 10.7. Gluino exchange contribution to $0\nu\beta\beta$ (a), and typical tree-level contribution to $O_{\ell q}$ (b) in RPV SUSY.

LRSM — The LRSM provides a natural scenario for introducing non-sterile, right-handed neutrinos and Majorana masses.[31] The corresponding electroweak gauge group $SU(2)_L \times SU(2)_R \times U(1)_{B-L}$, breaks down to $SU(2)_L \times U(1)_Y$ at the scale $\Lambda \geq \mathcal{O}(\text{TeV})$. The symmetry breaking is implemented through an extended Higgs sector, containing a bi-doublet Φ and two triplets $\Delta_{L,R}$, whose leptonic couplings generate both Majorana neutrino masses and LFV involving charged leptons:

$$\mathcal{L}_Y^{\text{lept}} = -\overline{L_L}^i \left(y_D^{ij} \Phi + \tilde{y}_D^{ij} \tilde{\Phi} \right) L_R^j$$
$$- \overline{(L_L)^c}^i y_M^{ij} \tilde{\Delta}_L L_L^j - \overline{(L_R)^c}^i y_M^{ij} \tilde{\Delta}_R L_R^j . \qquad (10.14)$$

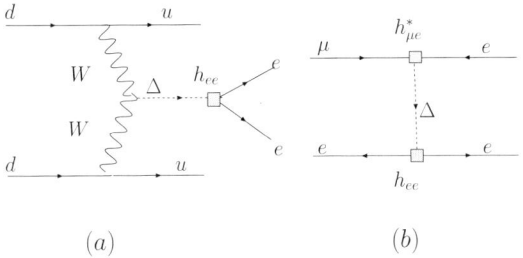

Fig. 10.8. Typical doubly charged Higgs contribution to $0\nu\beta\beta$ (a) and to O_ℓ (b) in the LRSM.

Here $\tilde{\Phi} = \sigma_2 \Phi^* \sigma_2$, $\tilde{\Delta}_{L,R} = i\sigma_2 \Delta_{L,R}$, and leptons belong to two isospin doublets $L^i_{L,R} = (\nu^i_{L,R}, \ell^i_{L,R})$. The gauge symmetry is broken through the VEVs $\langle \Delta^0_R \rangle = v_R$, $\langle \Delta^0_L \rangle = 0$, $\langle \Phi \rangle = \text{diag}(\kappa_1, \kappa_2)$. After diagonalization of the lepton mass matrices, LFV arises from both non-diagonal gauge interactions and the Higgs Yukawa couplings. In particular, the $\Delta_{L,R}$-lepton interactions are not suppressed by lepton masses and have the structure $\mathcal{L} \sim \Delta^{++}_{L,R} \overline{\ell^c_i} h_{ij} (1 \pm \gamma_5) \ell_j + \text{h.c.}$. The couplings h_{ij} are in general non-diagonal and related to the heavy neutrino mixing matrix.[32]

Short distance contributions to $0\nu\beta\beta$ arise from the exchange of both heavy νs and $\Delta_{L,R}$ (Fig. 10.8a), with

$$\frac{\tilde{c}_i}{\Lambda^5} \sim \frac{g_2^4}{M_{W_R}^4} \frac{1}{M_{\nu_R}} \; ; \; \frac{g_2^3}{M_{W_R}^3} \frac{h_{ee}}{M_\Delta^2} \, , \qquad (10.15)$$

where g_2 is the weak gauge coupling. LFV operators are also generated through non-diagonal gauge and Higgs vertices, with[32] (Fig. 10.8b)

$$\frac{c_\ell}{\Lambda^2} \sim \frac{h_{\mu i} h^*_{ie}}{m_\Delta^2} \qquad \frac{c_\sigma}{\Lambda^2} \sim \frac{(h^\dagger h)_{e\mu}}{M_{W_R}^2} \qquad i = e, \mu, \tau \, . \qquad (10.16)$$

Note that the Yukawa interactions needed for the Majorana neutrino mass necessarily imply the presence of LNV and LFV couplings h_{ij} and the corresponding LFV operator coefficients c_ℓ, leading to $\mathcal{R} \sim O(1)$. Again, non-observation of LFV in the next generation of experiments would typically push Λ into the multi-TeV range, thus implying a negligible short distance contribution to $0\nu\beta\beta$. As with RPV-SUSY, this conclusion can be evaded by assuming a specific flavor structure, namely y_M approximately diagonal or a nearly degenerate heavy neutrino spectrum.

In both of these phenomenologically viable models that incorporate LNV and LFV at low scale ($\sim$ TeV), one finds $\mathcal{R} \gg 10^{-2}$.[27,30,32] It is likely that the basic mechanism at work in these illustrative cases is generic: low scale LNV interactions ($\Delta L = \pm 1$ and/or $\Delta L = \pm 2$), which in general contribute to $0\nu\beta\beta$, also generate sizable contributions to $\mu \to e$ conversion, thus enhancing this process over $\mu \to e\gamma$.

In conclusion, the above considerations suggest that the ratio $\mathcal{R} = B_{\mu \to e}/B_{\mu \to e\gamma}$ of muon LFV processes will provide important insight about the mechanism of neutrinoless double beta decay and the use of this process to determine the absolute scale of neutrino mass. Assuming observation of LFV processes in forthcoming experiments, if $\mathcal{R} \sim 10^{-2}$ the mechanism of $0\nu\beta\beta$ is light Majorana neutrino exchange; if $\mathcal{R} \gg 10^{-2}$, there might be TeV scale LNV dynamics, and no definite conclusion on the mechanism of $0\nu\beta\beta$ can be drawn based only on LFV processes.

10.3. Overview of the experimental status of search for $\beta\beta$ decay

The field has a venerable history. The rate of the $2\nu\beta\beta$ decay was first estimated by Maria Goeppert-Mayer already in 1937 in her thesis work suggested by E. Wigner, basically correctly. Yet, first experimental observation in a laboratory experiment was achieved only in 1987, fifty years later. Why it took so long? As pointed out above, the typical half-life of the $2\nu\beta\beta$ decay is $\sim 10^{20}$ years. Yet, its "signature" is very similar to natural radioactivity, present to some extent everywhere, and governed by the half-life of $\sim 10^{10}$ years. So, background suppression is the main problem to overcome when one wants to study either of the $\beta\beta$ decay modes.

During the last two decades the $2\nu\beta\beta$ decay has been observed in "live" laboratory experiments in many nuclei, often by different groups and using different methods. That shows not only the ingenuity of the experimentalists who were able to overcome the background nemesis, but makes it possible at the same time to extract the corresponding 2ν nuclear matrix element from the measured decay rate. In the 2ν mode the half-life is given by

$$1/T_{1/2} = G^{2\nu}(Q,Z)|M^{2\nu}|^2 , \qquad (10.17)$$

where $G^{2\nu}(Q,Z)$ is an easily and accurately calculable phase space factor.

The resulting nuclear matrix elements $M^{2\nu}$, which have the dimension energy^{-1}, are plotted in Fig. 10.9. Note the pronounced shell dependence; the matrix element for ^{100}Mo is almost ten times larger than the one for ^{130}Te. Evaluation of these matrix elements, to be discussed below, is an

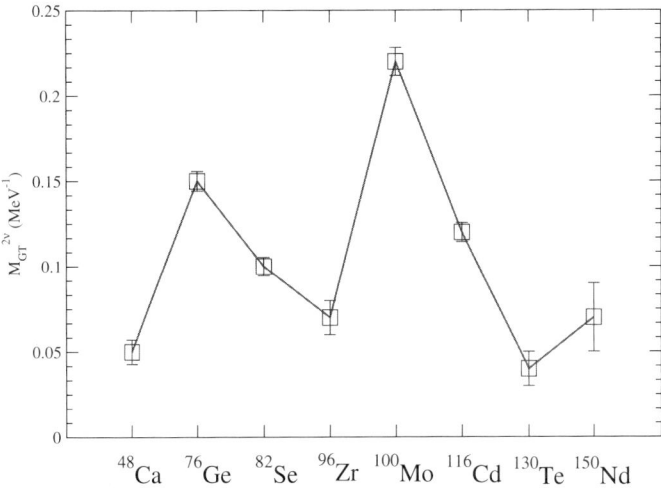

Fig. 10.9. Nuclear matrix elements for the $2\nu\beta\beta$ decay extracted from the measured half-lives.

important test for the nuclear theory models that aim at the determination of the analogous but different quantities for the 0ν neutrinoless mode.

The challenge of detecting the $0\nu\beta\beta$ decay is, at first blush, easier. Unlike the continuous $2\nu\beta\beta$ decay spectrum with a broad maximum at rather low energy where the background suppression is harder, the $0\nu\beta\beta$ decay spectrum is sharply peaked at the known Q value (see Fig. 10.3), at energies that are not immune to the background, but a bit less difficult to manage. However, as also indicated in Fig. 10.3, to obtain interesting results at the present time means to reach sensitivity to the 0ν half-lives that are $\sim 10^6$ times longer than the 2ν decay half-life of the same nucleus. So the requirements of background suppression are correspondingly even more severe.

The historical lessons are illustrated in Fig. 10.10 where the past limits on the $0\nu\beta\beta$ decay half-lives of various candidate nuclei are translated using the eq. (10.1) into the limits on the effective mass $\langle m_{\beta\beta}\rangle$. When plotted in the semi-log plot this figure represents the "Moore's law" of double beta decay, and indicates that, provided that the past trend will continue, the mass scale corresponding to Δm^2_{atm} will be reached in about 10 years. This is also the time scale of significant experiments these days. Indeed, as discussed further, preparations are on the way to reach this sensitivity

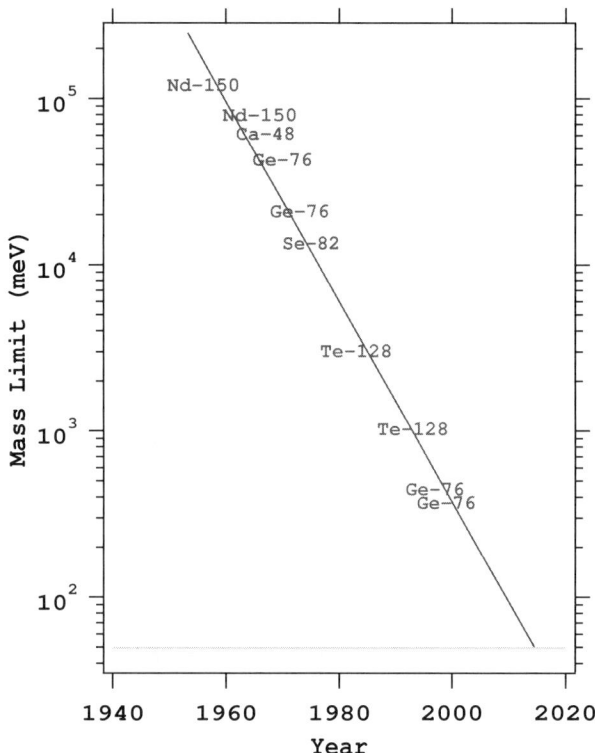

Fig. 10.10. The limit of the effective mass $\langle m_{\beta\beta} \rangle$ extracted from the experimental lower limits on the $0\nu\beta\beta$ decay half-life versus the corresponding year. The gray band near bottom indicates the $\sqrt{\Delta m_{atm}^2}$ value. Figure originally made by S. Elliott.

goal. Note that the figure was made using some assumed values of the corresponding nuclear matrix elements, without including their uncertainty. For such illustrative purposes they are, naturally, irrelevant.

The past search for the neutrinoless double beta decay, illustrated in Fig. 10.10, was driven by the then current technology and the resources of the individual experiments. The goal has been simply to reach sensitivity to longer and longer half-lives. The situation is different, however, now. The experimentalists at the present time can and do use the knowledge summarized in Fig. 10.5 to gauge the aim of their proposals. Based on that figure, the range of the mass parameter $\langle m_{\beta\beta} \rangle$ can be divided into three regions of interest.

- The degenerate mass region where all $m_i \gg \sqrt{\Delta m_{atm}^2}$. In that region $\langle m_{\beta\beta} \rangle \geq 0.1$ eV, corresponding crudely to the 0ν half-lives of 10^{26-27} years. To explore it (in a realistic time frame), ~ 100 kg of the decaying nucleus is needed. Several experiments aiming at such sensitivity are being built and should run and give results within the next 3-5 years. Moreover, this mass region (or a substantial part of it) will be explored, in a similar time frame, by the study of ordinary β decay (in particular of tritium) and by the observational cosmology. These techniques are independent on the Majorana nature of neutrinos. It is easy, but perhaps premature, to envision various scenarios depending on the possible outcome of these measurements.
- The so-called inverted hierarchy mass region where $20 < \langle m_{\beta\beta} \rangle < 100$ meV and the $0\nu\beta\beta$ half-lives are about 10^{27-28} years. (The name is to some extent a misnomer. In that interval one could encounter not only the inverted hierarchy but also a quasi-degenerate but normal neutrino mass ordering. Successful observation of the $0\nu\beta\beta$ decay will not be able to distinguish these possibilities, as I argued above. This is so not only due to the anticipated experimental accuracy, but more fundamentally due to the unknown Majorana phases.) To explore this mass region, $\sim$ ton size sources would be required. Proposals for the corresponding experiments exist, but none has been funded as yet, and presumably the real work will begin depending on the experience with the various ~ 100 kg size sources. Timeline for exploring this mass region is ~ 10 years.
- Normal mass hierarchy region where $\langle m_{\beta\beta} \rangle \leq 10\text{-}20$ meV. To explore this mass region, ~ 100 ton sources would be required. There are no realistic proposals for experiments of this size at present.

Over the last two decades, the methodology for double beta decay experiments has improved considerably. Larger amounts of high-purity enriched parent isotopes, combined with careful selection of all surrounding materials and using deep-underground sites have lowered backgrounds and increased sensitivity. The most sensitive experiments to date use ^{76}Ge, ^{100}Mo, ^{116}Cd, ^{130}Te, and ^{136}Xe. For ^{76}Ge the lifetime limit reached impressive values exceeding 10^{25} years.[33,34] The experimental lifetime limits have been interpreted to yield effective neutrino mass limits typically a few eV and in ^{76}Ge as low as 0.3 - 1.0 eV (the spread reflects an estimate of the uncertainty in the nuclear matrix elements). The sum electron spectrum obtained in the Heidelberg-Moscow[33] experiment is shown in Fig. 10.11

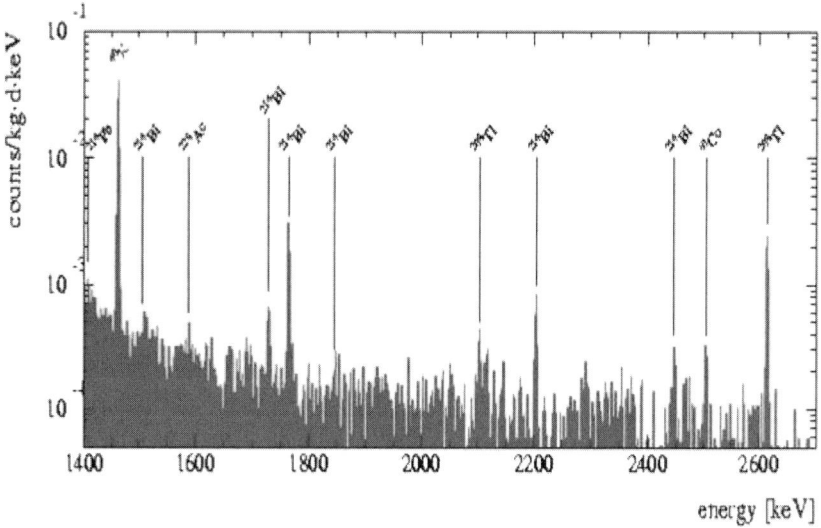

Fig. 10.11. The spectrum recorded in the Heidelberg-Moscow $\beta\beta$ decay experiment on ^{76}Ge. Identified γ lines are indicated.

over a broad energy range, and in Fig. 10.12 over a narrower range in the vicinity of the 0ν Q value of 2039 keV. Some residual natural radioactivity background lines are clearly visible in both figures, and no obvious peak at the 0ν expected position can be seen in Fig. 10.12.

Nevertheless, a subset of members of the Heidelberg-Moscow collaboration reanalyzed the data (and used additional information, e.g. the pulse-shape analysis and a different algorithm in the peak search) and claimed to observe a positive signal corresponding to the effective mass of $\langle m_{\beta\beta}\rangle = 0.39^{+0.17}_{-0.28}$ eV.[35] That report has been followed by a lively discussion. Clearly, such an extraordinary claim with its profound implications, requires extraordinary evidence. It is fair to say that a confirmation, both for the same ^{76}Ge parent nucleus, and better yet also in another nucleus with a different Q value, would be required for a consensus. In any case, if that claim is eventually confirmed, the degenerate mass scenario will be implicated, and eventual positive signal in the analysis of the tritium β decay and/or observational cosmology should be forthcoming. For the neutrinoless $\beta\beta$ decay the next generation of experiments, which use ~ 100 kg of decaying isotopes will, among other things, test this recent claim.

It is beyond the scope of these lecture notes to describe in detail the forthcoming $0\nu\beta\beta$ decay experiments. Rather detailed discussion of them

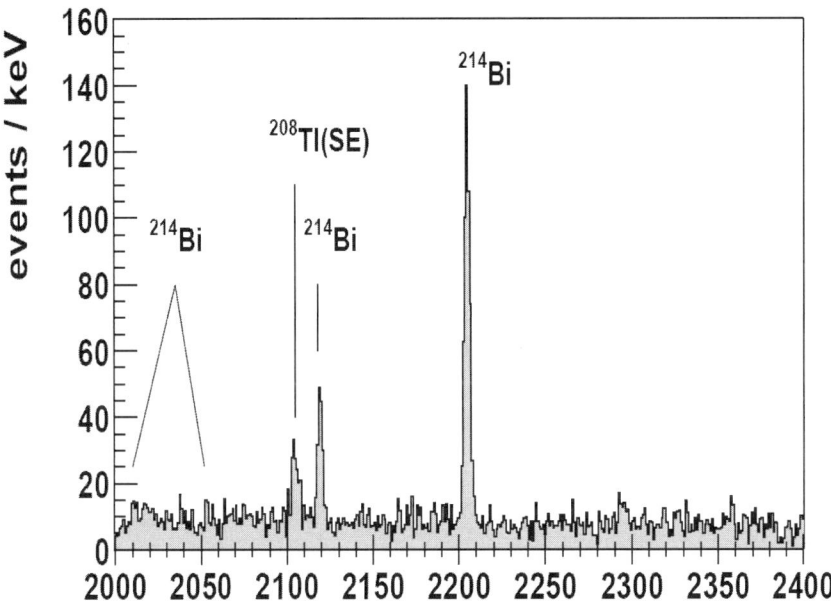

Fig. 10.12. Spectrum of the Heidelberg-Moscow experiment in the vicinity of the $0\nu\beta\beta$ decay value of 2039 keV.

can be found e.g. in Ref. 16. Also, the corresponding chapter of the APS neutrino study[36] has various details. Nevertheless, let me briefly comment on the most advanced of the forthcoming ~ 100 kg source experiments *CUORE, GERDA, EXO*, and *MAJORANA*. All of them are designed to explore all (or at least most) of the degenerate neutrino mass region $\langle m_{\beta\beta} \rangle \geq$ 0.1 eV. If their projected efficiencies and background projections are confirmed, all of them plan to consider scaling up the decaying mass to $\sim$ ton and extend their sensitivity to the "inverted hierarchy" region.

These experiments use different nuclei as a source, ^{76}Ge for *GERDA* and *MAJORANA*, ^{130}Te for *CUORE*, and ^{136}Xe for *EXO*. The requirement of radiopurity of the source material and surrounding auxiliary equipment is common to all of them, as is the placement of the experiment deep underground to shield against cosmic rays. The way the electrons are detected is, however, different. While the germanium detectors with their superb energy resolution have been used for the search of the $0\nu\beta\beta$ decay for a long time, the cryogenic detectors in *CUORE* use the temperature increase associated with an event in the very cold TeO$_2$ crystals, and in the *EXO* experiment a Time Projection Chamber (TPC) uses both scintillation and ionization to detect the events. The *EXO* experiment in its final form (still under development and very challenging) would use a positive identification of the final Ba^+ ion as an ultimate background rejection tool. These four experiments are in various stages of funding and staging. First results are expected in about 3 years, and substantial results within 3-5 years in all of them.

10.4. Nuclear matrix elements

It follows from eq. (10.1) that (i) values of the nuclear matrix elements $M^{0\nu}$ are needed in order to extract the effective neutrino mass from the measured $0\nu\beta\beta$ decay rate, and (ii) any uncertainty in $M^{0\nu}$ causes a corresponding and equally large uncertainty in the extracted $\langle m_{\beta\beta}\rangle$ value. Thus, the issue of an accurate evaluation of the nuclear matrix elements attracts considerable attention.

To see qualitatively where the problems are, let us consider the so-called closure approximation, i.e. a description in which the second order perturbation expression is approximated as

$$M^{0\nu} \equiv \langle \Psi_{final} | \hat{O}^{(0\nu)} | \Psi_{initial} \rangle . \quad (10.18)$$

Now, the challenge is to use an appropriate many-body nuclear model to describe accurately the wave functions of the ground states of the initial and final nuclei, $|\Psi_{initial}\rangle$ and $|\Psi_{final}\rangle$, as well as the appropriate form of the effective transition operator $\hat{O}^{(0\nu)}$ that describes the transformation of two neutrons into two protons correlated by the neutrino propagator, and consistent with the approximations inherent to the nuclear model used.

Common to all methods is the description of the nucleus as a system of nucleons bound in the mean field and interacting by an effective residual interaction. The used methods differ as to the number of nucleon orbits (or shells and subshells) included in the calculations and the complexity of the configurations of the nucleons in these orbits. The two basic approaches used so far for the evaluation of the nuclear matrix elements for both the 2ν and 0ν $\beta\beta$ decay modes are the Quasiparticle Random Phase Approximation (QRPA) and the nuclear shell model (NSM). They are in some sense complementary; QRPA uses a larger set of orbits, but truncates heavily the included configurations, while NSM can include only a rather small set of orbits but includes essentially all possible configurations. NSM also can be tested in a considerable detail by comparing to the nuclear spectroscopy data; in QRPA such comparisons are much more limited.

For the 2ν decay one can relate the various factors entering the calculations to other observables (β strength functions, cross sections of the charge-exchange reactions, etc.), accessible to the experiment. The consistency of the evaluation can be tested in that way. Of course, as pointed out above (see Fig. 10.9) the nuclear matrix elements for this mode are known anyway. Both methods are capable of describing the 2ν matrix elements, at least qualitatively. These quantities, when expressed in natural units based on the sum rules, are very small. Hence their description depends on small components of the nuclear wave functions and is therefore challenging. In QRPA the agreement is achieved if the effective proton-neutron interaction coupling constant (usually called g_{pp}) is slightly (by $\sim$ 10 - 20 %) adjusted.

The theoretical description for the more interesting 0ν mode cannot use any known nuclear observables, since there are no observables directly related to the $M^{0\nu}$. It is therefore much less clear how to properly estimate the uncertainty associated with the calculated values of $M^{0\nu}$, and to judge their accuracy. Since the calculations using QRPA are much simpler, an overwhelming majority of the published calculations uses that method. There are suggestions to use the spread of these published values of $M^{0\nu}$ as a measure of uncertainty.[37] Following this, one would conclude that the uncertainty is quite large, a factor of three or as much as five. But that way of assigning the uncertainty is questionable. Using all or most of the published values of $M^{0\nu}$ means that one includes calculations of uneven quality. Some of them were devoted to the tests of various approximations, and concluded that they are not applicable. Some insist that other data, like the $M^{2\nu}$, are correctly reproduced, other do not pay any attention to such test. Also, different forms of the transition operator $\hat{O}^{0\nu}$ are used, in particular some works include approximately the effect of the short range nucleon-nucleon repulsion, while others neglect it.

In contrast, in Ref. 38 an assesment of uncertainties in the matrix elements $M^{0\nu}$ inherent in the QRPA was made, and it was concluded that with a consistent treatment the uncertainties are much less, perhaps only about 30% (see Fig. 10.13). That calculation uses the known 2ν matrix elements in order to adjust the interaction constant mentioned above. There is a lively debate in the nuclear structure theory community, beyond the scope of these lectures, about this conclusion.

It is of interest also to compare the resulting matrix elements of Rodin *et al.*[38] based on QRPA and its generalizations, and those of the avail-

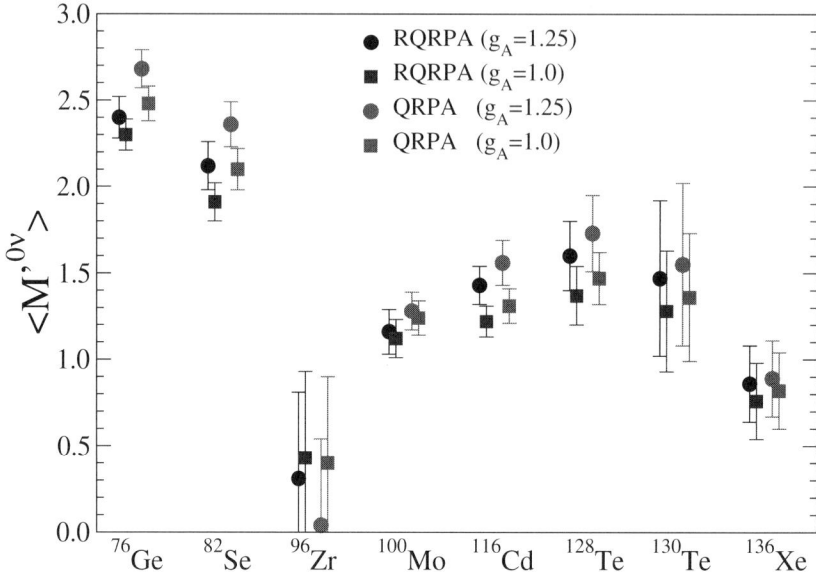

Fig. 10.13. Nuclear matrix elements and their variance for the indicated approximations (see Ref. 38).

able most recent NSM evaluation.[39] Note that the operators used in NSM evaluation do not include the induced nucleon currents that in QRPA reduce the matrix element by about 30%. The QRPA[38] and NSM[39] $M^{0\nu}$ are compared in Table 10.1. In the last column the NSM matrix elements are reduced by 30% to approximately account for the missing terms in the operator, and to make the comparison more meaningful. With this reduction, it seems that QRPA results are a bit larger in the lighter nuclei and a bit smaller in the heavier ones than the NSM results, but basically within the 30% uncertainty estimate. Once the NSM calculations for the intermediate mass nuclei ^{96}Zr, ^{100}Mo and ^{116}Cd become available, one can make a more meaningful comparison of the two methods.

When comparing the results shown in Table 10.1 as well as the results of other calculations (e.g. Refs. 40,41) with Fig. 10.9 it is important to notice a qualitative difference in the behaviour of the 2ν and 0ν matrix elements when going from one nucleus to another one. For 2ν the matrix elements change rapidly, but for the 0ν the variation is much more gentle (^{96}Zr is a notable exception, at least for QRPA). That feature, common to most calculations, if verified, would help tremendously in comparing the results or constraints from one nucleus to another one.

Table 10.1. Comparison of the calculated nuclear matrix elements $M^{0\nu}$ using the QRPA method[38] and the NSM.[39] In the last column the NSM values are reduced, divided by 1.3, to account approximately for the effects of the induced nucleon currents.

Nucleus	QRPA	NSM	NSM/1.3
^{76}Ge	2.3-2.4	2.35	1.80
^{82}Se	1.9-2.1	2.26	1.74
^{96}Zr	0.3-0.4		
^{100}Mo	1.1-1.2		
^{116}Cd	1.2-1.4		
^{130}Te	1.3	2.13	1.64
^{136}Xe	0.6-1.0	1.77	1.36

Once the nuclear matrix elements are fixed (by choosing your favorite set of results), they can be combined with the phase space factors (a complete list is available, e.g. in the monograph[42]) to obtain a half-life prediction for any value of the effective mass $\langle m_{\beta\beta} \rangle$. It turns out that for a fixed $\langle m_{\beta\beta} \rangle$ the half-lives of different candidate nuclei do not differ very much from each other (not more than by factors ~ 3 or so) and, for example, the boundary between the degenerate and inverted hierarchy mass regions corresponds to half-lives $\sim 10^{27}$ years. Thus, the next generation of experiments, discussed above, should reach this region using several candidate nuclei, making the corresponding conclusions less nuclear model dependent.

10.5. Neutrino magnetic moment and the distinction between Dirac and Majorana neutrinos

Neutrino mass and magnetic moments are intimately related. In the orthodox Standard Model neutrinos have a vanishing mass and magnetic moments vanish as well. However, in the minimally extended SM containing gauge-singlet right-handed neutrinos the magnetic moment μ_ν is nonvanishing and proportional to the neutrino mass, but unobservably small,[43]

$$\mu_\nu = \frac{3eG_F}{\sqrt{2}8\pi^2} m_\nu = 3 \times 10^{-19} \mu_B \frac{m_\nu}{1 \text{ eV}} \ . \qquad (10.19)$$

Here μ_B is the electron Bohr magneton, traditionally used as unit also for the neutrino magnetic moments. An experimental observation of a magnetic moment larger than that given in eq. (10.19) would be an uneqivocal indication of physics beyond the minimally extended Standard Model.

Laboratory searches for neutrino magnetic moments are typically based on the obsevation of the $\nu - e$ scattering. Nonvanishing μ_ν will be recognizable only if the corresponding electromagnetic scattering cross section is at least comparable to the well understood weak interaction cross section. The magnitude of μ_ν (diagonal in flavor or transitional) which can be probed in this way is then given by

$$\frac{|\mu_\nu|}{\mu_B} \equiv \frac{G_F m_e}{\sqrt{2}\pi\alpha}\sqrt{m_e T} \sim 10^{-10}\left(\frac{T}{m_e}\right)^{1/2}, \quad (10.20)$$

where T is the electron recoil kinetic energy. Considering realistic values of T, it would be difficult to reach sensitivities below $\sim 10^{-11}\mu_B$. Present limits are about an order of magnitude larger than that.

Limits on μ_ν can also be obtained from bounds on the unobserved energy loss in astrophysical objects. For sufficiently large μ_ν the rate of plasmon decay into the $\nu\bar{\nu}$ pairs would conflict with such bounds. Since plasmons can also decay weakly into the $\nu\bar{\nu}$ pairs, the sensitivity of this probe is again limited by the size of the weak rate, leading to

$$\frac{|\mu_\nu|}{\mu_B} \equiv \frac{G_F m_e}{\sqrt{2}\pi\alpha}\hbar\omega_P, \quad (10.21)$$

where ω_P is the plasmon frequency. Since usually $(\hbar\omega_P)^2 \ll m_e T$ that limit is stronger than that given in eq. (10.20). Current limits on μ_ν based on such considerations are $\sim 10^{-12}\mu_B$.

The interest in μ_ν and its relation to neutrino mass dates from $\sim$1990 when it was suggested that the chlorine data[4] on solar neutrinos show an anticorrelation between the neutrino flux and the solar activity characterized by the number of sunspots. A possible explanation was suggested in Ref. 44 where it was proposed that a magnetic moment $\mu_\nu \sim 10^{-(10-11)}\mu_B$ would cause a precession in solar magnetic field of the neutrinos emitted initially as left-handed ν_e into unobservable right-handed ones. Even though later analyses showed that the correlation with solar activity does not exist, the possibility of a relatively large μ_ν accompanied by a small mass m_ν was widely discussed and various models accomplishing that were suggested.

If a magnetic moment is generated by physics beyond the Standard Model (SM) at an energy scale Λ, we can generically express its value as

$$\mu_\nu \sim \frac{eG}{\Lambda}, \quad (10.22)$$

where e is the electric charge and G contains a combination of coupling constants and loop factors. Removing the photon from the diagram gives a contribution to the neutrino mass of order

$$m_\nu \sim G\Lambda. \tag{10.23}$$

We thus arrive at the relationship

$$m_\nu \sim \frac{\Lambda^2}{2m_e}\frac{\mu_\nu}{\mu_B} \sim \frac{\mu_\nu}{10^{-18}\mu_B}[\Lambda(\text{TeV})]^2 \text{ eV}, \tag{10.24}$$

which implies that it is difficult to simultaneously reconcile a small neutrino mass and a large magnetic moment.

This naïve restriction given in eq. (10.24) can be overcome via a careful choice for the new physics, e.g., by requiring certain additional symmetries.[45-50] Note, however, that these symmetries are typically broken by Standard Model interactions. For Dirac neutrinos such symmetry (under which the left-handed neutrino and antineutrino ν and ν^c transform as a doublet) is violated by SM gauge interactions. For Majorana neutrinos analogous symmetries are not broken by SM gauge interactions, but are instead violated by SM Yukawa interactions, provided that the charged lepton masses are generated via the standard mechanism through Yukawa couplings to the SM Higgs boson. This suggests that the relation between μ_ν and m_ν is different for Dirac and Majorana neutrinos. This distinction can be, at least in principle, exploited experimentally, as shown below.

Earlier, I have quoted the Ref. 17 (see Fig. 10.4) to stress that observation of the $0\nu\beta\beta$ decay would necessarily imply the existence of a novanishing neutrino Majorana mass. Analogous considerations can be applied in this case. By calculating neutrino magnetic moment contributions to m_ν generated by SM radiative corrections, one may obtain in this way general, "naturalness" upper limits on the size of neutrino magnetic moments by exploiting the experimental upper limits on the neutrino mass.

In the case of Dirac neutrinos, a magnetic moment term will generically induce a radiative correction to the neutrino mass of order[51]

$$m_\nu \sim \frac{\alpha}{16\pi}\frac{\Lambda^2}{m_e}\frac{\mu_\nu}{\mu_B} \sim \frac{\mu_\nu}{3\times 10^{-15}\mu_B}[\Lambda(\text{TeV})]^2 \text{ eV}. \tag{10.25}$$

Taking $\Lambda \simeq 1$ TeV and $m_\nu \leq 0.3$ eV, we obtain the limit $\mu_\nu \leq 10^{-15}\mu_B$ (and a more stringent one for larger Λ), which is several orders of magnitude more constraining than current experimental upper limits on μ_ν.

The case of Majorana neutrinos is more subtle, due to the relative flavor symmetries of m_ν and μ_ν respectively. For Majorana neutrinos the transition magnetic moments $[\mu_\nu]_{\alpha\beta}$ (the only possible ones) are antisymmetric in the flavor indices $\{\alpha,\beta\}$, while the mass terms $[m_\nu]_{\alpha\beta}$ are symmetric.

These different flavor symmetries play an important role in the limits, and are the origin of the difference between the magnetic moment constraints for Dirac and Majorana neutrinos.

It has been shown in Ref 52 that the constraints on Majorana neutrinos are significantly weaker than those for Dirac neutrinos,[51] as the different flavor symmetries of m_ν and μ_ν lead to a mass term which is suppressed only by charged lepton masses. This conclusion was reached by considering one-loop mixing of the magnetic moment and mass operators generated by Standard Model interactions. The authors of Ref. 52 found that if a magnetic moment arises through a coupling of the neutrinos to the neutral component of the $SU(2)_L$ gauge boson, the constraints for $\mu_{\tau e}$ and $\mu_{\tau \mu}$ are comparable to present experiment limits, while the constraint on $\mu_{e\mu}$ is significantly weaker. Thus, the analysis of Ref. 52 lead to a bound for the transition magnetic moment of Majorana neutrinos that is less stringent than present experimental limits.

Even more generally it was shown in Ref. 53 that two-loop matching of mass and magnetic moment operators implies stronger constraints than those obtained in[52] if the scale of the new physics $\Lambda \geq 10$ TeV. Moreover, these constraints apply to a magnetic moment generated by either the hypercharge or $SU(2)_L$ gauge boson. In arriving at these conclusions, the most general set of operators that contribute at lowest order to the mass and magnetic moments of Majorana neutrinos was constructed, and model independent constraints which link the two were obtained. Thus the results of Ref. 53 imply completely model independent naturalness bound that – for $\Lambda \geq 100$ TeV – is stronger than present experimental limits (even for the weakest constrained element $\mu_{e\mu}$). On the other hand, for sufficiently low values of the scale Λ the known small values of the neutrino masses do not constrain the magnitude of the transition magnetic moment μ_ν for Majorana neutrinos more than the present experimental limits. Thus, if these conditions are fulfilled, the discovery of μ_ν might be forthcoming any day.

The above result means that an experimental discovery of a magnetic moment near the present limits would signify that (i) neutrinos are Majorana fermions and (ii) new lepton number violating physics responsible for the generation of μ_ν arises at a scale Λ which is well below the see-saw scale. This would have, among other things, implications for the mechanism of the neutrinoless double beta decay and lepton flavor violation as discussed above and in Ref. 22.

10.6. Summary

In these lectures I discussed the status of double beta decay, its relation to the charge conjugation symmetry of neutrinos and to the problem of the lepton number conservation in general. I have shown that if one makes the minimum assumption that the light neutrinos familiar from the oscillation experiments which are interacting by the left-handed weak current are Majorana particles, then the rate of the $0\nu\beta\beta$ decay can be related to the absolute scale of the neutrino mass in a straightforward way.

On the other hand, it is also possible that the $0\nu\beta\beta$ decay is mediated by the exchange of heavy particles. I explained that if the corresponding mass scale of such hypothetical particles is ~ 1 TeV, the corresponding 0ν decay rate could be comparable to the decay rate associated with the exchange of a light neutrino. I further argued that the study of the lepton flavor violation involving $\mu \to e$ conversion and $\mu \to e + \gamma$ decay may be used as a "diagnostic tool" that could help to decide which of the possible mechanisms of the 0ν decay is dominant.

Further, I have shown that the the range of the effective masses $\langle m_{\beta\beta} \rangle$ can be roughly divided into three regions of interest, each corresponding to a different neutrino mass pattern. The region of $\langle m_{\beta\beta} \rangle \geq 0.1$ eV corresponds to the degenerate mass pattern. Its exploration is well advanced, and one can rather confidently expect that it will be explored by several $\beta\beta$ decay experiments in the next 3-5 years. This region of neutrino masses (or most of it) is also accessible to studies using the ordinary β decay and/or the observational cosmology. Thus, if the nature is kind enough to choose this mass pattern, we will have a multiple ways of exploring it.

The region of $0.01 \leq \langle m_{\beta\beta} \rangle \leq 0.1$ eV is often called the "inverted mass hierarchy" region. In fact, both the inverted and the quasi-degenerate but normal mass orderings are possible in this case, and experimentally indistinguishable. Realistic plans to explore this region using the $0\nu\beta\beta$ decay exist, but correspond to a longer time scale of about 10 years. They require much larger, $\sim$ ton size $\beta\beta$ sources and correspondingly even more stringent background suppression.

Finally, the region $\langle m_{\beta\beta} \rangle \leq 0.01$ eV corresponds to the normal hierarchy only. There are no realistic proposals at present to explore this mass region experimentally.

Intimately related to the extraction of $\langle m_{\beta\beta} \rangle$ from the decay rates is the problem of nuclear matrix elements. At present, there is no consensus among the nuclear theorists about their correct values, and the corresponding uncertainty. I argued that the uncertainty is less than some suggest, and that the closeness of the Quasiparticle Random Phase Approximation (QRPA) and Shell Model (NSM) results are encouraging. But this is still a problem that requires further improvements.

In the last part I discussed the neutrino magnetic moments. I have shown that using the Standard Model radiative correction one can calculate the contribution of the magnetic moment to the neutrino mass. That contribution, naturally, should not exceed the experimental upper limit on the neutrino mass. Using this procedure one can show that the magnetic moment of Dirac neutrinos cannot exceed about $10^{-15}\mu_B$, which is several orders of magnitudes less than the current experimental limits on μ_ν. On the other hand, due to the different symmetries of the magnetic moment and mass matrices for Majorana neutrinos, the corresponding constraints are much less restrictive, and do not exceed the current limits. Thus, a discovery of μ_ν near the present experimental limit would indicate that neutrinos are Majorana particles, and the corresponding new physics scale is well below the GUT scale.

Acknowlegment

The original results reported here were obtained in the joint and enjoyable work with a number of collaborators, Nicole Bell, Vincenzo Cirigliano, Steve Elliott, Amand Faessler, Michail Gorchtein, Andriy Kurylov, Gary Prezeau, Michael Ramsey-Musolf, Vadim Rodin, Fedor Šimkovic and Mark Wise. The work was supported in part under U.S. DOE contract DE-FG02-05ER41361.

References

1. T. Kajita and Y. Totsuka, *Rev. Mod. Phys.* **73**, 85–118 (2001); Y. Ashie *et al.*, *Phys. Rev.* **D71**, 112005 (2005).
2. M. H. Ahn, *et al.*, *Phys. Lett. B* **511**, 178–184 (2001); M. H. Ahn *et al.* hep-ex/0606032.
3. MINOS collaboration, hep-ex/0607088.
4. B. T. Cleveland *et al.*, *Astrophys. J.* **496**, 505 (1998).
5. Q. R. Ahmad *et al.*, *Phys. Rev. Lett.* **87**, 071301 (2001).
6. S. Fukuda *et al.*, *Phys. Rev. Lett.* **86**, 5651–5655, (2001); ibid **86**, 5656–5660 (2001).
7. W. Hampel *et al. Phys. Lett.* **B447**, 127 (1999).
8. J. N. Abdurashitov *et al. Phys. Rev.* **C60**, 055801 (1999).
9. K. Eguchi *et al. Phys. Rev. Lett.* **90**, 021802 (2003).

10. T. Araki et al. Phys. Rev. Lett. **94**, 081801 (2005).
11. M. Apollonio et al., Phys. Lett. B **466**, 415–430 (1999).
12. F. Boehm et al., Phys. Rev. **D64**, 112001 (2001).
13. A. Faessler and F. Šimkovic, F. Šimkovic, J. Phys. G **24**, 2139 (1998).
14. J. D. Vergados, Phys. Rep. **361**, 1 (2002).
15. S. R. Elliott and P. Vogel Ann. Rev. Nucl. Part. Sci. **52**, 115 (2002).
16. S. R. Elliott and J. Engel, J. Phys. G **30**, R183 (2004).
17. J. Schechter and J. Valle, Phys. Rev. **D25**, 2951 (1982).
18. R. N. Mohapatra, Phys. Rev. D **34**, 3457 (1986); J. D. Vergados, Phys. Lett. **B184**, 55 (1987); M. Hirsch, H. V. Klapdor-Kleingrothaus and S. G. Kovalenko, Phys. Rev. D **53**, 1329 (1996); M. Hirsch, H. V. Klapdor-Kleingrothaus, and O. Panella, Phys. Lett. **B374**, 7 (1996); A. Fässler, S. Kovalenko, F. Šimkovic and J. Schwieger, Phys. Rev. Lett. **78**, 183 (1997); H. Päs, M. Hirsch, H. V. Klapdor-Kleingrothaus and S. G. Kovalenko, Phys. Lett. **B498**, 35 (2001); F. Šimkovic and A. Fässler, Progr. Part. Nucl. Phys. **48**, 201 (2002).
19. G. Prezeau, M. Ramsey-Musolf and P. Vogel, Phys. Rev. D **68**, 034016 (2003).
20. R. N. Mohapatra, Nucl. Phys. Proc. Suppl. **77**, 376 (1999).
21. M. Doi, T. Kotani and E. Takasugi, Prog. Theor. Phys. Suppl. **83**, 1 (1985).
22. V. Cirigliano, A. Kurylov, M. J. Ramsey-Musolf and P. Vogel, Phys. Rev. Lett **93**, 231802 (2004).
23. G. Signorelli, "The Meg Experiment At Psi: Status And Prospects,"m J. Phys. G **29**, 2027 (2003); see also http://meg.web.psi.ch/docs/index.html.
24. J. L. Popp, NIM **A472**, 354 (2000); hep-ex/0101017.
25. R. Barbieri, L. J. Hall and A. Strumia, Nucl. Phys. B **445**, 219 (1995).
26. F. Borzumati and A. Masiero Phys. Rev. Lett. **57**, 961 (1986).
27. M. Raidal and A. Santamaria, Phys. Lett. B **421**, 250 (1998).
28. R. Kitano, M. Koike and Y. Okada, Phys. Rev. D **66**, 096002 (2002).
29. H. K. Dreiner, in 'Perspectives on Supersymmetry', Ed. by G.L. Kane, World Scientific, 462–479.
30. A. de Gouvea, S. Lola and K. Tobe, Phys. Rev. D **63**, 035004 (2001).
31. R. N. Mohapatra and G. Senjanovic, Phys. Rev. Lett. **44**, 912 (1980).
32. V. Cirigliano, A. Kurylov, M. J. Ramsey-Musolf and P. Vogel, Phys. Rev. **D70**, 075007 (2004).
33. H. V. Klapdor-Kleingrothaus et al. Eur. J. Phys. **A12**, 147 (2001).
34. C. E. Aalseth et al. Phys. Rev. **D65**, 092007 (2002).
35. H. V. Klapdor-Kleingrothaus, A. Dietz, I. V. Krivosheina and). Chvorets, Phys. Lett. **B586**, 198 (2004); Nucl. Inst. Meth **A522**, 371 (2004).
36. C. E. Aalseth et al., hep-ph/0412300.
37. J. N. Bahcall, H. Murayama and C. Pena-Garay, Phys. Rev. **D70**, 033012 (2004).
38. V. A. Rodin, Amand Faessler, F. Šimkovic and Petr Vogel, Phys. Rev. **C68**, 044302(2003); Nucl. Phys. **A766**, 107 (2006).
39. A. Poves, talk at NDM06, http://events.lal.in2p3.fr/conferences/NDM06/.
40. O. Civitarese and J. Suhonen, Nucl. Phys. **A729**, 867 (2003).
41. Aunola M. and Suhonen J., Nucl. Phys. **A643**, 207 (1998).

42. F. Boehm and P. Vogel, *Physics of Massive Neutrinos*, 2nd ed., Cambridge University Press, Cambridge, UK. 1992.
43. W. J. Marciano and A. I. Sanda, *Phys. Lett.* **B67**, 303 (1977); B. W. Lee and R. E. Shrock, *Phys. Rev.* **D16**, 1444 (1977); K. Fujikawa and R. E. Shrock, *Phys. Rev. Lett.* **45**, 963 (1980).
44. M. B. Voloshin, M. I. Vysotskij and L. B. Okun, *Soviet J. of Nucl. Phys.* **44**, 440 (1986).
45. M. B. Voloshin, *Soviet J. of Nucl. Phys.* **48**, 512 (1988).
46. R. Barbieri and R. N. Mohapatra, *Phys. Lett.* **B218**, 225 (1989).
47. H. Georgi and L. Randall, *Phys. Lett.* **B244**, 196 (1990).
48. W. Grimus and H. Neufeld, *Nucl. Phys.* **B351**, 115 (1991).
49. K. S. Babu and R. N. Mohapatra, *Phys. Rev. Lett.* **64**, 1705 (1990).
50. S. M. Barr, E. M. Freie and A. Zee, *Phys. Rev. Lett.* **65**, 2626 (1990).
51. N. F. Bell et al., *Phys. Rev. Lett.* **95**, 151802 (2005).
52. S. Davidson, M. Gorbahn and A. Santamaria, *Phys. Lett.* **B626**, 151 (2005).
53. N. F. Bell et al., Phys. Lett. to be published; hep-ph/0606248.

Chapter 11

Supersymmetry in Elementary Particle Physics

Michael E. Peskin

Stanford Linear Accelerator Center, Stanford University
2575 Sand Hill Road, Menlo Park, California 94025 USA

These lectures give a general introduction to supersymmetry, emphasizing its application to models of elementary particle physics at the 100 GeV energy scale. I discuss the following topics: the construction of supersymmetric Lagrangians with scalars, fermions, and gauge bosons, the structure and mass spectrum of the Minimal Supersymmetric Standard Model (MSSM), the measurement of the parameters of the MSSM at high-energy colliders, and the solutions that the MSSM gives to the problems of electroweak symmetry breaking and dark matter.

11.1. Introduction

11.1.1. Overview

It is an exciting time now in high-energy physics. For many years, ever since the Standard Model was established in the late 1970's, the next logical question in the search for the basic laws of physics has been that of the mechanism by which the weak interaction gauge symmetry is spontaneously broken. This seemed at the time the one important gap that kept the Standard Model from being a complete theory of the strong, weak, and electromagnetic interactions [1–3]. Thirty years later, after many precision experiments at high-energy e^+e^- and hadron colliders, this is still our situation. In the meantime, another important puzzle has been recognized, the fact that 80% of the mass in the universe is composed of 'dark matter', a particle species not included in the Standard Model. Both problems are likely to be solved by new fundamental interactions operating in the energy range of a few hundred GeV. Up to now, there is no evidence from particle physics for such new interactions. But, in the next few years, this situation should change dramatically. Beginning in 2008, the CERN Large Hadron Collider (LHC) should give us access to physics at energies well above 1 TeV and thus should probe the energy region responsible for electroweak symmetry breaking. Over a longer term, we can look forward to precision experiments in e^+e^- annihilation in this same energy region at the proposed International Linear Collider (ILC).

Given this expectation, it is important for all students of elementary particle physics to form concrete ideas of what new phenomena we might find as we explore this new energy region. Of course, we have no way of knowing exactly what we will find there. But this makes it all the more important to study the alternative theories that have been put forward and to understand their problems and virtues.

Many different models of new physics relevant to electroweak symmetry breaking are being discussed at this TASI school. Among these, supersymmetry has pride of place. Supersymmetry (or SUSY) provides an explicit realization of all of the aspects of new physics expected in the hundred GeV energy region. Because SUSY requires only weak interactions to build a realistic theory, it is possible in a model with SUSY to carry out explicit calculations and find the answers that the model gives to all relevant phenomenological questions.

In these lectures, I will give an introduction to supersymmetry as a context for building models of new physics associated with electroweak symmetry breaking. Here is an outline of the material: In Section 2, I will develop appropriate notation and then construct supersymmetric Lagrangians for scalar, spinor, and vector fields. In Section 3, I will define the canonical phenomenological model of supersymmetry, the Minimal Supersymmetric Standard Model (MSSM). I will discuss the quantum numbers of new particles in the MSSM and the connection of the MSSM to the idea of grand unification.

The remaining sections of these lectures will map out the phenomenology of the new particles and interactions expected in models of supersymmetry. I caution you that I will draw only those parts of the map that cover the simplest and most well-studied class of models. Supersymmetry has an enormous parameter space which contains many different scenarios for particle physics, more than I have room to cover here. I will at least try to indicate the possible branches in the path and give references that will help you follow some of the alternative routes.

With this restriction, the remaining sections will proceed as follows: In Section 4, I will compute the mass spectrum of the MSSM from its parameters. I will also discuss the parameters of the MSSM that characterize supersymmetry breaking. In Section 5, I will describe how the MSSM parameters will be measured at the LHC and the ILC. Finally, Section 6 will discuss the answers that supersymmetry gives to the two major questions posed at the beginning of this discussion, the origin of electroweak symmetry breaking, and the origin of cosmic dark matter.

Although I hope that these lectures will be useful to students in studying supersymmetry, there are many other excellent treatments of the subject available. A highly recommended introduction to SUSY is the 'Supersymmetry Primer' by Steve Martin [6]. An excellent presentation of the formalism of supersymmetry is given in the texbook of Wess and Bagger [7]. Supersymmetry has been reviewed at previous TASI schools by Bagger [8], Lykken [9], and Kane [10], among others. Very recently, three textbooks of phenomenological supersymmetry have appeared, by Drees, Godbole, and Roy [11], Binetruy [12], and Baer and Tata [13]. A fourth textbook, by Dreiner, Haber, and Martin [14], is expected soon.

It would be wonderful if all of these articles and books used the same conventions, but that is too much to expect. In these lectures, I will use my own, somewhat ideosyncratic conventions. These are explained in Section 2.1. Where possible, within the philosophy of that section, I have chosen conventions that agree with those of Martin's primer [6].

11.1.2. Motivation and Structure of Supersymmetry

If we propose supersymmetry as a model of electroweak symmetry breaking, we might begin by asking: What is the problem of electroweak symmetry breaking, and what are the alternatives for solving it?

Electroweak symmetry is spontaneously broken in the minimal form of the Standard Model, which I will refer to as the MSM. However, the explanation that the MSM gives for this phenomenon is not satisfactory. The sole source of symmetry breaking is a single elementary Higgs boson field. All mass of quarks, leptons, and gauge bosons arise from the couplings of those particles to the Higgs field.

To generate symmetry breaking, we postulate a potential for the Higgs field

$$V = \mu^2|\varphi|^2 + \lambda|\varphi|^4 , \qquad (11.1)$$

shown in Fig. 11.1. The assumption that $\mu^2 < 0$ is the complete explanation for electroweak symmetry breaking in the MSM. Since μ is a renormalizable coupling of this theory, the value of μ cannot be computed from first principles, and even its sign cannot be predicted.

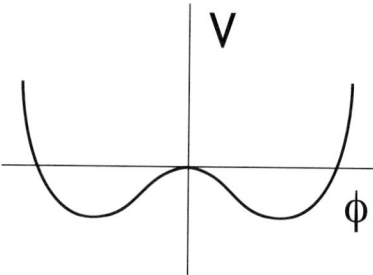

Fig. 11.1. The Standard Model Higgs potential (11.1).

In fact, this explanation has an even worse feature. The parameter μ^2 receives large additive radiative corrections from loop diagrams. For example, the two diagrams shown in Fig. 11.2 are ultraviolet divergent. Supplying a momentum cutoff Λ, the two diagrams contribute

$$\mu^2 = \mu^2_{\text{bare}} + \frac{\lambda}{8\pi^2}\Lambda^2 - \frac{3y_t^2}{8\pi^2}\Lambda^2 + \cdots \qquad (11.2)$$

If we view the MSM as an effective theory, Λ should be taken to be the largest momentum scale at which this theory is still valid. The presence of large additive corrections implies that the criterion $\mu^2 < 0$ is not a simple condition on the underlying parameters of the effective theory. The radiative corrections can easily change the sign of μ^2. Further, if we insist that the MSM has a large range of validity, the corrections become much larger than the desired result. To obtain the Higgs field vacuum expectation value required for the weak interactions, $|\mu|$ should be about 100 GeV. If we insist at the same time that the MSM is valid up to the Planck scale, $\Lambda \sim 10^{19}$ GeV, the formula (11.2) requires a cancellation between the bare value of μ and the radiative corrections in the first 36 decimal places. This problem has its own name, the 'gauge hierarchy problem'. But, to my mind, the absence of a logical explantion for electroweak symmetry breaking in the MSM is already problem enough.

How could we solve this problem? There are two different strategies. One is to look for new strong-couplings dynamics at an energy scale of 1 TeV or below. Then the Higgs field could be composite and its potential could be the result, for example, of pair condensation of fermion constituents. Higgs

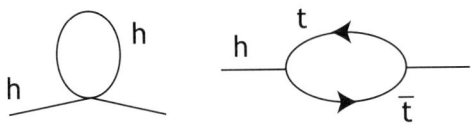

Fig. 11.2. Two Standard Model diagrams that give divergent corrections to the Higgs mass parameter μ^2.

actually proposed that his field was a phenomenological description of a fermion pair condensation mechanism similar to that in superconductivity [4]. Sometime later, Susskind [2] and Weinberg [3] proposed an explicit model of electroweak symmetry breaking by new strong interactions, called 'technicolor'.

Today, this approach is disfavored. Technicolor typically leads to flavor-changing neutral currents at an observable level, and also typically conflicts with the accurate agreement of precision electroweak theory with experiment. Specific models do evade these difficulties, but they are highly constrained [5].

The alternative is to postulate that the electroweak symmetry is broken by a weakly-coupled Higgs field, but that this field is part of a model in which the Higgs potential is computable. In particular, the Higgs mass term $\mu^2|\varphi|^2$ should be generated by well-defined physics within the model. A prerequisite for this is that the μ^2 term not receive additive radiative corrections. This requires that, at high energy, the appearance of a nonzero μ^2 in the Lagrangian should be forbidden by a symmetry of the theory.

There are three ways to arrange a symmetry that forbids the term $\mu^2|\varphi|^2$. We can postulate a symmetry that shifts φ

$$\delta\varphi = \epsilon v \ . \tag{11.3}$$

We can postulate a symmetry that connects φ to a gauge field, whose mass can then forbidden by gauge symmetry

$$\delta\varphi = \epsilon \cdot A \ . \tag{11.4}$$

We can postulate a symmetry that connects φ to a fermion field, whose mass can then be forbidden by a chiral symmetry.

$$\delta\varphi = \epsilon \cdot \psi \ . \tag{11.5}$$

The options (11.3) and (11.4) lead, respectively, to 'little Higgs' models [15–17] and to models with extra space dimensions [18,19]. The third option leads to supersymmetry. This is the route we will now follow.

The symmetry (11.5) looks quite innocent, but it is not. In quantum theory, a symmetry that links a boson with a fermion is generated by a conserved charge Q_α that carries spin-1/2

$$[Q_\alpha, \varphi] = \psi_\alpha, \qquad [Q_\alpha, H] = 0. \tag{11.6}$$

Such a Q_α implies the existence of a conserved 4-vector charge R_m defined by

$$\{Q_\alpha, Q_\beta^\dagger\} = 2\gamma_{\alpha\beta}^m R_m \tag{11.7}$$

(It may not be obvious to you that there is no Lorentz scalar component in this anticommutator, but I will show this in Section 2.1.) The charge R_m is conserved, because both Q and $Q^\dagger$ commute with H. It is nonzero, as we can see by taking the expectation value of (11.7) in any state and setting $\alpha = \beta$

$$\begin{aligned}\langle A | \{Q_\alpha, Q_\alpha^\dagger\} | A \rangle &= \langle A | Q_\alpha Q_\alpha^\dagger | A \rangle + \langle A | Q_\alpha Q_\alpha^\dagger | A \rangle \\ &= \| Q_\alpha | A \rangle \|^2 + \| Q_\alpha^\dagger | A \rangle \|^2 .\end{aligned} \tag{11.8}$$

This expression is non-negative; it can be zero only if Q_α and $Q_\alpha^\dagger$ annihilate every state in the theory.

However, in a relativistic quantum field theory, we do not have the freedom to introduce arbitrary charges that have nontrivial Lorentz transformation properties. Conservation of energy-momentum and angular momentum are already very constraining. For example, in two-body scattering, the scattering amplitude for fixed center of mass energy can only be a function of one variable, the center of mass scattering angle θ. If one adds a second conserved 4-vector charge, almost all values of θ will also be forbidden. Coleman and Mandula proved a stronger version of this statement: In a theory with an addtional conserved 4-vector charge, there can be no scattering at all, and so the theory is trivial [20].

If we would like to have (11.5) as an exact symmetry, then, the only possibility is to set $R_m = P_m$. That is, the square of the fermionic charge Q_α must be *the total energy-momentum of everything*. We started out trying to build a theory in which the fermionic charge acted only on the Higgs field. But now, it seems, the fermionic charge must act on every field in the theory. Everything—quarks, leptons, gauge bosons, even gravitons— must have partners under the symmetry generated by Q_α. Q_α is fermionic and carries spin $\frac{1}{2}$. Then every particle in the theory must have a partner with the opposite statistics and spin differing by $\frac{1}{2}$ unit.

The idea that the transformation (11.5) leads to a profound generalization of space-time symmetry was discovered independently several times in the early 1970's [22,23]. The 1974 paper by Wess and Zumino [24] which gave simple linear realizations of this algebra on multiplets of fields launched the detailed exploration of this symmetry and its application to particle physics.

The pursuit of (11.5) then necessarily leads us to introduce a very large number of new particles. This seems quite daunting. It might be a reason to choose one of the other paths, except that these also lead to new physics models of similarly high complexity. I encourage you to carry on with this line of analysis a bit longer. It will lead to a beautiful structure with many interesting implications for the theory of Nature.

11.2. Formalism of Supersymmetry

11.2.1. Fermions in 4 Dimensions

To work out the full consequences of (11.5), we will need to write this equation more precisely. To do this, we need to set up a formalism that describes relativistic fermions in four dimensions in the most general way. There is no general agreement on the best conventions to use, but every discussion of supersymmetry leans heavily on the particular choices made. I will give my choice of conventions in this section.

There are two basic spin-$\frac{1}{2}$ representations of the Lorentz group. Each is two-dimensional. The transformation laws are those of left- and right-handed Weyl (2-component) fermions,

$$\psi_L \to (1 - i\vec{\alpha} \cdot \vec{\sigma}/2 - \vec{\beta} \cdot \vec{\sigma}/2) \psi_L$$
$$\psi_R \to (1 - i\vec{\alpha} \cdot \vec{\sigma}/2 + \vec{\beta} \cdot \vec{\sigma}/2) \psi_R , \quad (11.9)$$

where $\vec{\alpha}$ is an infinitesimal rotation angle and $\vec{\beta}$ is an infinitesimal boost. The four-component spinor built from these ingredients, $\Psi = (\psi_L, \psi_R)$, is a Dirac fermion.

Define the matrix

$$c = -i\sigma^2 = \begin{pmatrix} 0 & -1 \\ 1 & 0 \end{pmatrix}. \quad (11.10)$$

This useful matrix satisfies $c^2 = -1$, $c^T = -c$. The combination

$$\psi_{1L}^T c \psi_{2L} = -\epsilon_{\alpha\beta} \psi_{1L\alpha} \psi_{2L\beta} \quad (11.11)$$

is the basic Lorentz invariant product of spinors. Many treatments of supersymmetry, for example, that in Wess and Bagger's book [7], represent c implicitly by raising and lowering of spinor indices. I will stick to this more prosaic approach.

Using the identity $\vec{\sigma}c = -c(\vec{\sigma})^T$, it is easy to show that the quantity $(-c\psi_L^*)$ transforms like ψ_R. So if we wish, we can replace every ψ_R by a ψ_L and write all fermions in the theory as left-handed Weyl fermions. With this notation, for example, we would call e_L^- and e_L^+ fermions and e_R^- and e_R^+ antifermions. This convention does not respect parity, but parity is not a symmetry of the Standard Model. The convention of representing all fermions in terms of left-handed Weyl fermions turns out to be very useful for not only for supersymmetry but also for other theories of physics beyond the Standard Model.

Applying this convention, a Dirac fermion takes the form

$$\Psi = \begin{pmatrix} \psi_{1L} \\ -c\psi_{2L}^* \end{pmatrix} \tag{11.12}$$

Write the Dirac matrices in terms of 2×2 matrices as

$$\gamma^m = \begin{pmatrix} 0 & \sigma^m \\ \overline{\sigma}^m & 0 \end{pmatrix} \tag{11.13}$$

with

$$\sigma^m = (1, \vec{\sigma})^m \qquad \overline{\sigma}^m = (1, -\vec{\sigma})^m \qquad c\sigma^m = (\overline{\sigma}^m)^T c \tag{11.14}$$

Then the Dirac Lagrangian can be rewritten in the form

$$\begin{aligned} \mathcal{L} &= \overline{\Psi} i\gamma \cdot \partial \Psi - M\overline{\Psi}\Psi \\ &= \psi_{1L}^\dagger i\overline{\sigma} \cdot \partial \psi_{1L} + \psi_{2L}^\dagger i\overline{\sigma} \cdot \partial \psi_{2L} \\ &\quad - (m\psi_{1L}^T c\psi_{2L} - m^*\psi_{1L}^\dagger c\psi_{2L}^*) \ . \end{aligned} \tag{11.15}$$

For the bilinears in the last line, we can use fermion anticommutation and the antisymmetry of c to show

$$\psi_{1L}^T c\psi_{2L} = +\psi_{2L}^T c\psi_{1L} \ . \tag{11.16}$$

and, similarly,

$$(\psi_{1L}^T c\psi_{2L})^\dagger = \psi_{2L}^\dagger(-c)\psi_{1L}^* = -\psi_{1L}^\dagger c\psi_{2L}^* \ . \tag{11.17}$$

The mass term looks odd, because it is fermion number violating. However, the definition of fermion number is that given in the previous paragraph. The fields ψ_{1L} and ψ_{2L} annihilate, respectively, e_L^- and e_L^+. So this mass term generates the conversion of e_L^- to e_R^-, which is precisely what we would expect a mass term to do.

If we write all fermions as left-handed Weyl fermions, the possibilities for fermion actions are highly restricted. The most general Lorentz-invariant free field Lagrangian takes the form

$$\mathcal{L} = \psi_k^\dagger i\overline{\sigma} \cdot \partial \psi_k - \frac{1}{2}(m_{jk}\psi_j^T c\psi_k - m_{jk}^* \psi_j^\dagger c\psi_k^*) \ . \tag{11.18}$$

where j, k index the fermion fields. Here and in the rest of these lectures, I drop the subscript L. The matrix m_{jk} is a complex symmetric matrix. For a Dirac fermion,

$$m_{jk} = \begin{pmatrix} 0 & m \\ m & 0 \end{pmatrix}_{jk} \tag{11.19}$$

as we have seen in (11.15). This matrix respects the charge

$$Q\psi_1 = +\psi_1 \ , \qquad Q\psi_2 = -\psi_2 \ , \tag{11.20}$$

which is equivalent to the original Dirac fermion number. A Majorana fermion is described in the same formalism by the mass matrix

$$m_{jk} = m\delta_{jk} \ . \tag{11.21}$$

The most general fermion mass is a mixture of Dirac and Majorana terms. We will meet such fermion masses in our study of supersymmetry. These more general mass matrices also occur in other new physics models and in models of the masses of neutrinos.

The SUSY charges are four-dimensional fermions. The minimum set of SUSY charges thus includes one Weyl fermion Q_α and its Hermitian conjugate $Q_\alpha^\dagger$. We can now analyze the anticommutator $\{Q_\alpha, Q_\beta^\dagger\}$. Since the indices belong to different Lorentz representations, this object does not contain a scalar. The indices transform as do the spinor indices of σ^m, and so we can rewrite (11.7) with $R^m = P^m$ as

$$\{Q_\alpha, Q_\beta^\dagger\} = 2\sigma_{\alpha\beta}^m P_m \ . \tag{11.22}$$

It is possible to construct quantum field theories with larger supersymmetry algebras. These must include (11.22), and so the general form is [21]

$$\{Q_\alpha^i, Q_\beta^{\dagger j}\} = 2\sigma_{\alpha\beta}^m P_m \delta^{ij} \ , \tag{11.23}$$

for $i, j = 1 \ldots N$. This relation can be supplemented by a nontrivial anticommutator

$$\{Q_\alpha^i, Q_\beta^j\} = 2\epsilon_{\alpha\beta} Q^{ij} \tag{11.24}$$

where the *central charge* Q^{ij} is antisymmetric in $[ij]$. Theories with $N > 4$ necessarily contain particles of spin greater than 1. Yang-Mills theory with $N = 4$ supersymmetry is an especially beautiful model with exact scale invariance and many other attractive formal properties [25]. In these lectures, however, I will restrict myself to the minimal case of $N = 1$ supersymmetry.

I will discuss supersymmetry transformations using the operation on fields

$$\delta_\xi \Phi = [\xi^T c Q + Q^\dagger c \xi^*, \Phi] \; . \tag{11.25}$$

Note that the operator δ_ξ contains pairs of anticommuting objects and so obeys commutation rather than anticommutation relations. The operator P_m acts on fields as the generator of translations, $P_m = i\partial_m$. Using this, we can rewrite (11.22) as

$$[\delta_\xi, \delta_\eta] = 2i \left(\xi^\dagger \overline{\sigma}^m \eta - \eta^\dagger \overline{\sigma}^m \xi \right) \partial_m \tag{11.26}$$

I will take this equation as the basic (anti-)commutation relation of supersymmetry. In the next two sections, I will construct some representations of this commutation relation on multiplets of fields.

11.2.2. Supersymmetric Lagrangians with Scalars and Fermions

The simplest representation of the supersymmetry algebra (11.26) directly generalizes the transformation (11.5) from which we derived the idea of supersymmetry. The full set of fields required includes a complex-valued boson field ϕ and a Weyl fermion field ψ. These fields create and destroy a scalar particle and its antiparticle, a left-handed massless fermion, and its right-handed antiparticle. Note that the particle content has an equal number of fermions and bosons. This particle content is called a *chiral supermultiplet*.

I will now write out the transformation laws for the fields corresponding to a chiral supermultiplet. It is convenient to add a second complex-valued boson field F that will have no associated particles. Such a field is called an *auxiliary field*. We can then write the transformations that generalize (11.5) as

$$\begin{aligned} \delta_\xi \phi &= \sqrt{2} \xi^T c \psi \\ \delta_\xi \psi &= \sqrt{2} i \sigma^n c \xi^* \partial_n \phi + \sqrt{2} F \xi \\ \delta_\xi F &= -\sqrt{2} i \xi^\dagger \overline{\sigma}^m \partial_m \psi \; . \end{aligned} \tag{11.27}$$

The conjugates of these transformations are

$$\delta_\xi \phi^* = -\sqrt{2}\psi^\dagger c\xi^*$$
$$\delta_\xi \psi^\dagger = \sqrt{2} i \xi^T c\sigma^n \partial_n \phi^* + \sqrt{2}\xi^\dagger F^*$$
$$\delta_\xi F^* = \sqrt{2} i \partial_m \psi^\dagger \overline{\sigma}^m \xi \ . \tag{11.28}$$

These latter transformations define the *antichiral supermultiplet*. I claim that the transformations (11.27) and (11.28), first, satisfy the fundamental commutation relation (11.26) and, second, leave a suitable Lagrangian invariant. Both properties are necessary, and both must be checked, in order for a set of transformations to generate a symmetry group of a field theory.

The transformation laws (11.27) seem complicated. You might wonder if there is a formalism that generates these relations automatically and manipulates them more easily than working with the three distinct component fields (ϕ, ψ, F). In the next section, I will introduce a formalism called *superspace* that makes it almost automatic to work with the chiral supermultiplet. However, the superspace description of the multiplet containing gauge fields is more complicated, and the difficulty of working with superspace becomes exponentially greater in theories that include gravity, higher dimensions, or $N > 1$ supersymmetry. At some stage, one must go back to components. I strongly recommend that you gain experience by working through the component field calculations described in these notes in full detail, however many large pieces of paper that might require.

To verify each of the two claims I have made for (11.27) requires a little calculation. Here is the check of the commutation relation applied to the field ϕ:

$$\begin{aligned}[][\delta_\xi, \delta_\eta]\phi &= \delta_\xi(\sqrt{2}\eta^T c\psi) - (\xi \leftrightarrow \eta) \\ &= \sqrt{2}\eta^T c(\sqrt{2} i \sigma^n c\xi^* \partial_n \phi) - (\xi \leftrightarrow \eta) \\ &= -2i\eta^T (\overline{\sigma}^n)^T \xi^* \partial_n \phi - (\xi \leftrightarrow \eta) \\ &= 2i[\xi^\dagger \overline{\sigma}^n \eta - \eta^\dagger \overline{\sigma}^n \xi]\partial_n \phi \end{aligned}$$
$$\tag{11.29}$$

The check of the commutation relation applied to F is equally straightforward. The check on ψ is a bit lengthier. It requires a *Fierz identity*, that is, a spinor index rearrangement identity. Specifically, we need

$$\eta_\alpha \xi_\beta^\dagger = -\frac{1}{2}(\xi^\dagger \overline{\sigma}_m \eta)\sigma^m_{\alpha\beta} \ , \tag{11.30}$$

which you can derive by writing out the four components explicitly. After some algebra that involves the use of this identity, you can see that the SUSY commutation relation applied to ψ also takes the correct form.

Next, I claim that the Lagrangian

$$\mathcal{L} = \partial^m \phi^* \partial_m \phi + \psi^\dagger i\bar{\sigma} \cdot \partial \psi + F^* F \tag{11.31}$$

is invariant to the transformation (11.27). I will assume that the Lagrangian (11.31) is integrated $\int d^4 x$ and use integration by parts freely. Then

$$\begin{aligned}
\delta_\xi \mathcal{L} &= \partial^m \phi^* \partial_m (\sqrt{2}\xi^T c\psi) + (-\sqrt{2}\partial^m \psi^\dagger c\xi^*)\partial \phi \\
&+ \psi^\dagger i\bar{\sigma} \cdot \partial [\sqrt{2}i\sigma^n c\xi^* \partial_m \phi + \sqrt{2}\xi F] \\
&+ [\sqrt{2}i\partial_n \phi^* \xi^T c\sigma^n + \sqrt{2}\xi^\dagger F^*]i\bar{\sigma} \cdot \partial \psi \\
&+ F^*[-\sqrt{2}i\xi^\dagger \bar{\sigma}^m \partial_m \psi] + [\sqrt{2}i\partial_m \psi^\dagger \bar{\sigma}^m \xi]F \\
&= -\phi^* \sqrt{2}\xi^T c\partial^2 \psi + \sqrt{2}\partial_n \phi^* \xi^T c\sigma^n \bar{\sigma}^m \partial_m \psi \\
&+ \sqrt{2}\psi^\dagger c\xi^* \partial^2 \phi - \sqrt{2}\psi^\dagger \bar{\sigma}^m \sigma^n c\xi^* \partial_m \partial_n \phi \\
&+ \sqrt{2}i\psi^\dagger \bar{\sigma}^m \partial_m F\xi + \sqrt{2}i\partial_m \psi^\dagger \bar{\sigma}^m \xi F \\
&- \sqrt{2}i\xi^\dagger F^* \bar{\sigma}^m \partial_m \psi + \sqrt{2}iF^* \xi^\dagger \bar{\sigma}^m \partial_m \psi \\
&= 0 \,.
\end{aligned} \tag{11.32}$$

In the final expression, the four lines cancel line by line. In the first two lines, the cancellation is made by using the identity $(\bar{\sigma} \cdot \partial)(\sigma \cdot \partial) = \partial^2$.

So far, our supersymmetry Lagrangian is just a massless free field theory. However, it is possible to add rather general interactions that respect the symmetry. Let $W(\phi)$ be an analytic function of ϕ, that is, a function that depends on ϕ but not on ϕ^*. Let

$$\mathcal{L}_W = F\frac{\partial W}{\partial \phi} - \frac{1}{2}\psi^T c\psi \frac{\partial^2 W}{\partial \phi^2} \tag{11.33}$$

I claim that $\mathcal{L}_W$ is invariant to (11.27). Then we can add $(\mathcal{L}_W + \mathcal{L}_W^\dagger)$ to the free field Lagrangian to introduce interactions into the theory. The function W is called the *superpotential*.

We can readily check that $\mathcal{L}_W$ is indeed invariant:

$$\begin{aligned}
\delta_\xi \mathcal{L}_W &= F\frac{\partial^2 W}{\partial \phi^2}(\sqrt{2}\xi^T c\psi) - \sqrt{2}F\xi^T c\psi \frac{\partial^2 W}{\partial \phi^2} \\
&- \sqrt{2}i\xi^\dagger \bar{\sigma}^m \partial_m \psi \frac{\partial W}{\partial \phi} - \psi^T c\sqrt{2}i\sigma^n c\xi^* \partial_n \phi \frac{\partial^2 W}{\partial \phi^2} \\
&- \psi^T c\psi \frac{\partial^3 W}{\partial \phi^3}\sqrt{2}\xi^T c\psi \,.
\end{aligned} \tag{11.34}$$

The second line rearranges to

$$-\sqrt{2}i\xi^\dagger\bar{\sigma}\left(\partial_n\psi\frac{\partial W}{\partial\phi} + \psi\partial_n\phi\frac{\partial^2 W}{\partial\phi^2}\right), \qquad (11.35)$$

which is a total derivative. The third line is proportional to $\psi_\alpha\psi_\beta\psi_\gamma$, which vanishes by fermion antisymmetry since the spinor indices take only two values. Thus it is true that

$$\delta_\xi \mathcal{L}_W = 0. \qquad (11.36)$$

The proofs of invariance that I have just given generalize straightforwardly to systems of several chiral supermultiplets. The requirement on the superpotential is that it should be an analytic function of the complex scalar fields ϕ_k. Then the following Lagrangian is supersymmetric:

$$\mathcal{L} = \partial^m\phi_k^*\partial_m\phi_k + \psi_k^\dagger i\bar{\sigma}\cdot\partial\psi_k + F_k^*F_k + \mathcal{L}_W + \mathcal{L}_W^\dagger, \qquad (11.37)$$

where

$$\mathcal{L}_W = F_k\frac{\partial W}{\partial\phi_k} - \frac{1}{2}\psi_j^T c\psi_k\frac{\partial^2 W}{\partial\phi_j\partial\phi_k}. \qquad (11.38)$$

In this Lagrangian, the fields F_k are Lagrange multipliers. They obey the constraint equations

$$F_k^* = -\frac{\partial W}{\partial\phi_k}. \qquad (11.39)$$

Using these equations to eliminate the F_k, we find an interacting theory with the fields ϕ_k and ψ_k, a Yukawa coupling term proportional to the second derivative of W, as given in (11.38), and the potential energy

$$V_F = \sum_k\left|\frac{\partial W}{\partial\phi_k}\right|^2. \qquad (11.40)$$

I will refer to V_F as the *F-term potential*. Later we will meet a second contribution V_D, the *D-term potential*. These two terms, both obtained by integrating out auxiliary fields, make up the classical potential energy of a general supersymmetric field theory of scalar, fermion, and gauge fields.

The simplest example of the F-term potential appears in the theory with one chiral supermultiplet and the superpotential $W = \frac{1}{2}m\phi^2$. The constraint equation for F is [27]

$$F^* = -m\phi. \qquad (11.41)$$

After eliminating F, we find the Lagrangian

$$\mathcal{L} = \partial^n \phi^* \partial_n \phi - |m|^2 \phi^* \phi + \psi^\dagger i\bar{\sigma}\cdot\partial\psi - \frac{1}{2}(m\psi^T c\psi - m^*\psi^\dagger c\psi^*) \quad (11.42)$$

This is a theory of two free scalar bosons of mass $|m|$ and a free Majorana fermion with the same mass $|m|$. The Majorana fermion has two spin states, so the number of boson and fermion physical states is equal, as required.

The form of the expression (11.40) implies that $V_F \geq 0$, and that $V_F = 0$ only if all $F_k = 0$. This constraint on the potential energy follows from a deeper consideration about supersymmetry. Go back to the anticommutation relation (11.22), evaluate it for $\alpha = \beta$, and take the vacuum expectation value. This gives

$$\langle 0| \{Q_\alpha, Q_\alpha^\dagger\} |0\rangle = \langle 0| (H - P^3) |0\rangle = \langle 0| H |0\rangle , \quad (11.43)$$

since the vacuum expectation value of P^3 vanishes by rotational invariance. Below (11.7), I argued that the left-hand side of this equation is greater than or equal to zero. It is equal to zero if and only if

$$Q_\alpha |0\rangle = Q_\alpha^\dagger |0\rangle = 0 \quad (11.44)$$

The formulae (11.44) give the criterion than the vacuum is invariant under supersymmetry. If this relation is not obeyed, supersymmetry is spontaneously broken. Taking the vacuum expectation value of the transformation law for the chiral representation, we find

$$\langle 0| [\xi^T cQ + Q^\dagger c\xi^*, \psi_k] |0\rangle = \langle 0| \sqrt{2} i\sigma^n \xi^* \partial_n \phi_k + \xi F_k |0\rangle$$
$$= \xi \langle 0| F_k |0\rangle . \quad (11.45)$$

In the last line I have used the fact that the vacuum expectation value of $\phi(x)$ is translation invariant, so its derivative vanishes. The left-hand side of (11.45) vanishes if the vacuum state is invariant under supersymmetry.

The results of the previous paragraph can be summarized in the following way: If supersymmetry is a manifest symmetry of a quantum field theory,

$$\langle 0| H |0\rangle = 0 , \text{ and } \langle 0| F_k |0\rangle = 0 \quad (11.46)$$

for every F field of a chiral multiplet. In complete generality,

$$\langle 0| H |0\rangle \geq 0 . \quad (11.47)$$

The case where $\langle H \rangle$ is positive and nonzero corresponds to spontaneously broken supersymmetry. If the theory has a state satisfying (11.44), this is necesssarily the state in the theory with lowest energy. Thus, supersymmetry can be spontaneously broken only if a supersymmetric vacuum state does not exist[a]

For the moment, we will work with theories that preserve supersymmetry. I will give examples of theories with spontaneous supersymmetry breaking in Section 3.5.

The results we have just derived are exact consequences of the commutation relations of supersymmetry. It must then be true that the vacuum energy of a supersymmetric theory must vanish in perturbation theory. This is already nontrivial for the free theory (11.42). But it is correct. The positive zero point energy of the boson field exactly cancels the negative zero point energy of the fermion field. With some effort, one can show the cancellation also for the leading-order diagrams in an interacting theory. Zumino proved that this cancellation is completely general [29].

I would like to show you another type of cancellation that is also seen in perturbation theory in models with chiral fields. Consider the model with one chiral field and superpotential

$$W = \frac{\lambda}{3}\phi^3 \ . \tag{11.48}$$

After eliminating F, the Lagrangian becomes

$$\mathcal{L} = \partial\phi^*\partial_m\phi + \psi^\dagger i\overline{\sigma}\cdot\partial\psi - \lambda(\phi\psi^T c\psi - \phi^*\psi^\dagger c\psi^*) - \lambda^2|\phi|^4 \ . \tag{11.49}$$

The vertices of this theory are shown in Fig. 11.3(a).

From our experience in (11.2), we might expect to find an adddtive radiative correction to the scalar mass. The corrections to the fermion and scalar mass terms are given by the diagrams in Fig. 11.3(b). Actually, there are no diagrams that correct the fermion mass; you can check that there it is not possible to match the arrows appropriately. For the scalar mass correction, the two diagrams shown contribute

$$-4i\lambda^2 \int \frac{d^4p}{(2\pi)^4}\frac{i}{p^2} + \frac{1}{2}(-2i\lambda)(+2i\lambda)\int \frac{d^4p}{(2\pi)^4} \text{tr}\left[\frac{i\sigma\cdot p}{p^2}c\frac{i\sigma^T\cdot(-p)}{p^2}c\right] \tag{11.50}$$

Using $\sigma\cdot p\overline{\sigma}\cdot p = p^2$ in the second term and then taking the trace, we see that these two contributions cancel precisely. In this way, supersymmetry really does control radiative corrections to the Higgs mass, following the logic that we presented in Section 1.2.

---

[a]It is possible that a supersymmetric vacuum state might exist but that a higher-energy vacuum state might be metastable. A model built on this metastable state would show spontaneous breaking of supersymmetry [26].

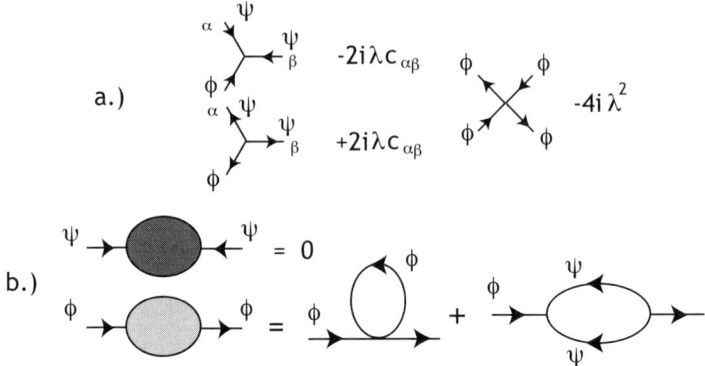

Fig. 11.3. Perturbation theory for the supersymmetric model (11.49): (a) vertices of the model; (b) corrections to the fermion and scalar masses.

In fact, it can be shown quite generally that not only the mass term but the whole superpotential W receives no additive radiative corrections in any order of perturbation theory [30]. For example, the one-loop corrections to quartic terms in the Lagrangian cancel in a simple way that is indicated in Fig. 11.4. The field strength renormalization of chiral fields can be nonzero, so the form of W can be changed by radiative corrections by the rescaling of fields. Examples are known in which W receives additive radiative corrections from nonperturbative effects [31].

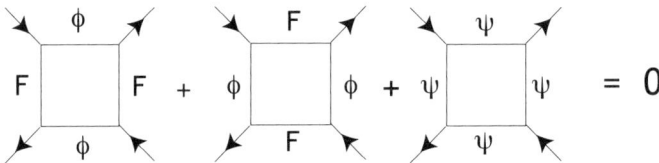

Fig. 11.4. Scheme of cancellations of one-loop corrections to the F-term potential.

11.2.3. Superspace

Because the commutation relations of supersymmetry include the generators of translations, supersymmetry is a space-time symmetry. It is an attractive idea that supersymmetry is the natural set of translations on a generalized space-time with commuting and anticommuting coordinates. In this section, I will introduce the appropriate generalization of space-time and use it to re-derive some of the results of Section 2.2.

Consider, then, a space with four ordinary space-time coordinates x^μ and four anticommuting coordinates $(\theta_\alpha, \bar{\theta}_\alpha)$. I will take the coordinates θ_α to transform as 2-component Weyl spinors; the $\bar{\theta}_\alpha$ are the complex conjugates of the θ_α. This is *superspace*. A *superfield* is a function of these superspace coordinates: $\Phi(x, \theta, \bar{\theta})$.

It is tempting to define supersymmetry transformations as translations $\theta \to \theta + \xi$. However, this does not work. These transformations commute, $[\delta_\xi, \delta_\eta] = 0$, and we have seen in Section 1.2 that this implies that the S-matrix of the resulting field theory must be trivial. To construct a set of transformations with the correct commutation relations, we must write

$$\delta_\xi \Phi = \mathcal{Q}_\xi \Phi \; , \tag{11.51}$$

where

$$\mathcal{Q}_\xi = \left(-\frac{\partial}{\partial \theta} - i\bar{\theta}\bar{\sigma}^m \partial_m \right) \xi + \xi^\dagger \left(\frac{\partial}{\partial \bar{\theta}} + i\bar{\sigma}^m \theta \partial_m \right) \; . \tag{11.52}$$

This is a translation of the fermionic coordinates $(\theta, \bar{\theta})$ plus a translation of the ordinary space-time coordinates proportional to $\theta, \bar{\theta}$. It is straightforward to show that these operators satisfy

$$[\mathcal{Q}_\xi, \mathcal{Q}_\eta] = -2i \left(\xi^\dagger \bar{\sigma}^m \eta - \eta^\dagger \bar{\sigma}^m \xi \right) \partial_m \; . \tag{11.53}$$

Despite the fact that this equation has an extra minus sign on the right-hand side with respect to (11.26), it is the relation that we want. (The difference is similar to that between active and passive transformations.) Combined with the decomposition of the superfield that I will introduce below, this relation will allow us to derive the chiral supermultiplet transformation laws (11.27).

Toward this goal, we need one more ingredient. Define the superspace derivatives

$$D_\alpha = \frac{\partial}{\partial \theta_\alpha} - i(\bar{\theta}\bar{\sigma}^m)_\alpha \partial_m \qquad \bar{D}_\alpha = -\frac{\partial}{\partial \bar{\theta}_\alpha} + i(\sigma^m \theta)_\alpha \partial_m \; , \tag{11.54}$$

such that $(D_\alpha \Phi)^\dagger = \bar{D}_\alpha \Phi^\dagger$. These operators commute with $\mathcal{Q}_\xi$:

$$[D_\alpha, \mathcal{Q}_\xi] = 0 \qquad [\bar{D}_\alpha, \mathcal{Q}_\xi] = 0 \; . \tag{11.55}$$

Thus, we can constrain Φ by the equation

$$D_\alpha \Phi = 0 \quad \text{or} \quad \bar{D}_\alpha \Phi = 0 \; , \tag{11.56}$$

and these constraints are consistent with supersymmetry. What we have just shown is that the general superfield $\Phi(x,\theta,\overline{\theta})$ is a *reducible* representation of supersymmetry. It can be decomposed into a direct sum of three smaller representations, one constrained by the first of the relations (11.56), one constrained by the second of these relations, and the third containing whatever is left over in Φ when these pieces are removed.

Let us begin with the constraint $\overline{D}_\alpha \Phi = 0$. The solution of this equation can be written

$$\Phi(x,\theta,\overline{\theta}) = \Phi(x + i\theta\overline{\sigma}^m\theta, \theta) , \qquad (11.57)$$

that is, this solution is parametrized by a general function of x and θ. Since θ is a two-component anticommuting object, this general function of x and θ can be represented as

$$\Phi(x,\theta) = \phi(x) + \sqrt{2}\theta^T c\psi(x) + \theta^T c\theta F(x) . \qquad (11.58)$$

The field content of this expression is exactly that of the chiral supermultiplet. The supersymmetry transformation of this field should be

$$\delta_\xi \Phi = \mathcal{Q}_\xi \Phi(x + i\theta\overline{\sigma}^m\theta, \theta) . \qquad (11.59)$$

It is straightforward to compute the right-hand side of (11.59) in terms of θ, $\overline{\theta}$, and the component fields of (11.58). The coefficients of powers of θ are precisely the supersymmetry variations given in (11.27). Thus a superfield satisfying

$$\overline{D}_\alpha \Phi = 0 \qquad (11.60)$$

is equivalent to a chiral supermultiplet, and the transformation (11.59) gives the supersymmetry transformation of this multiplet. A superfield satisfying (11.60) is called a *chiral superfield*. Similarly, a superfield satisfying

$$D_\alpha \Phi = 0 \qquad (11.61)$$

is called an *antichiral superfield*. This superfield has a component field decomposition (ϕ^*, ψ^*, F^*), on which $\mathcal{Q}_\xi$ induces the transformation (11.28). I will describe the remaining content of the general superfield Φ in Section 2.5.

A Lagrangian on Minkowski space is integrated over d^4x. A superspace Lagrangian should be also be integrated over the θ coordinates. Integration over fermionic coordinates is defined to be proportional to the coefficient of the highest power of θ. I will define integration over superspace coordinates by the formulae

$$\int d^2\theta\, 1 = \int d^2\theta\, \theta_\alpha = 0 \qquad \int d^2\theta (\theta^T c\theta) = 1 \qquad (11.62)$$

and their conjugates. To use these formulae, expand the superfields in powers of θ and pick out the terms proportional to $(\theta^T c\theta)$. Then, if Φ is a chiral superfield constrained by (11.60) and $W(\Phi)$ is an analytic function of Φ,

$$\int d^2\theta\, \Phi(x,\theta) = F(x)$$

$$\int d^2\theta\, W(\Phi) = F(x)\frac{\partial W}{\partial \phi} - \frac{1}{2}\psi^T c\psi \frac{\partial^2 W}{\partial^2 \phi}, \qquad (11.63)$$

where, in the second line, W on the right-hand side is evaluated with $\Phi = \phi(x)$. With somewhat more effort, one can show

$$\int d^2\theta \int d^2\bar{\theta}\, \Phi^\dagger \Phi = \partial^m \phi^* \partial_m \phi + \psi^\dagger i\bar{\sigma}\cdot\partial\psi + F^*F\,. \qquad (11.64)$$

These formulae produce the invariant Lagrangians of chiral supermultiplets from a superspace point of view. The most general Lagrangian of chiral superfields Φ_k takes the form

$$\mathcal{L} = \int d^4\theta\, K(\Phi,\Phi^\dagger) + \int d^2\theta\, W(\Phi) + \int d^2\bar{\theta}\, (W(\Phi))^\dagger\,, \qquad (11.65)$$

where $W(\Phi)$ is an analytic function of complex superfields and $K(\Phi,\Phi^\dagger)$ is a general real-valued function of the superfields. The Lagrangian (11.37) is generated from this expression by taking $K(\Phi,\Phi^\dagger) = \Phi_k^\dagger \Phi_k$. The most general *renormalizable* Lagrangian of chiral supermultiplets is obtained by taking K to be of this simple form and taking W to be a polynomial of degree at most 3.

Because the integral $d^2\theta$ exposes the Lagrange multiplier F in (11.58), I will refer to a term with this superspace integral as an *F-term*. For similar reasons that will become concrete in the next section, I will call a term with a $d^4\theta$ integral a *D-term*.

In the remainder of these lectures, I will restrict myself to discussing renormalizable supersymmetric theories. But, still, it is interesting to ask what theories we obtain when we take more general forms for K. The Lagrangian for ϕ turns out to be a nonlinear sigma model for which the target space is a complex manifold with the metric [32]

$$g_{m\bar{n}} = \frac{\partial^2}{\partial \Phi^m \partial \Phi^{\dagger \bar{n}}} K(\Phi, \Phi^\dagger) \tag{11.66}$$

A complex manifold whose metric is derived from a potential in this way is called a *Kähler manifold*. The function K is the *Kähler potential*. It is remarkable that, wherever in ordinary quantum field theory we find a general structure from real analysis, the supersymmetric version of the theory has a corresponding complex analytic structure.

Now that we have a Lagrangian in superspace, it is possible to derive Feynman rules and compute Feynman diagrams in superspace. I do not have space here to discuss this formalism; it is discussed, for example, in [7] and [30]. I would like to state one important consequence of this formalism. It turns out that, barring some special circumstances related to perturbation theory anomalies, these Feynman diagrams always generate corrections to the effective Lagrangian that are D-terms,

$$\int d^4\theta \, X(\Phi, \Phi^\dagger) \,. \tag{11.67}$$

The perturbation theory does not produce terms that are integrals $\int d^2\theta$. This leads to an elegant proof of the result cited at the end of the previous section that the superpotential is not renormalized at any order in perturbation theory [30].

11.2.4. Supersymmetric Lagrangians with Vector Fields

To construct a supersymmetric model that can include the Standard Model, we need to be able to write supersymmetric Lagrangians that include Yang-Mills vector fields. In this section, I will discuss how to do that.

To prepare for this discussion, let me present my notation for gauge fields in a general quantum field theory. The couplings of gauge bosons to matter are based on the covariant derivative, which I will write as

$$\mathcal{D}_m \phi = (\partial_m - ig A_m^a t_R^a)\phi \tag{11.68}$$

for a field ϕ that belongs to the representation R of the gauge group G. In this formula, t_R^a are the representation matrices of the generators of G in the representation R. These obey

$$[t_R^a, t_R^b] = i f^{abc} t_R^c \tag{11.69}$$

The coefficients f^{abc} are the *structure constants* of G. They are independent of R; essentially, their values define the multiplication laws of G. They can be taken to be totally antisymmetric.

The generators of G transform under G according to a representation called the *adjoint representation*. I will denote this representation by $R = G$. Its representation matrices are

$$(t_G^a)_{bc} = if^{bac} \tag{11.70}$$

These matrices satisfy (11.69) by virtue of the Jacobi identity. The covariant derivative on a field in the adjoint representation takes the form

$$\mathcal{D}_m \Phi^a = \partial_m \Phi^a + g f^{abc} A_m^b \Phi^c \tag{11.71}$$

The field strengths F_{mn}^a are defined from the covariant derivative (in any representation) by

$$[\mathcal{D}_m, \mathcal{D}_n] = -ig F_{mn}^a t_R^a . \tag{11.72}$$

This gives the familiar expression

$$F_{mn}^a = \partial_m A_n^a - \partial_n A_m^a + g f^{abc} A_m^b A_n^c . \tag{11.73}$$

Now we would like to construct a supersymmetry multiplet that contains the gauge field A_m^a. The fermion in the multiplet should differ in spin by $\frac{1}{2}$ unit. To write a renormalizable theory, we must take this to be a spin-$\frac{1}{2}$ Weyl fermion. I will then define the *vector supermultiplet*

$$(A_m^a, \lambda_\alpha^a, D^a) \tag{11.74}$$

including the gauge field, a Weyl fermion in the adjoint representation of the gauge group, and an auxililary real scalar field, also in the adjoint representation, that will have no independent particle content. The particle content of this multiplet is one massless vector boson, with two transverse polarization states, and one massless fermion and antifermion, for each generator of the gauge group. The fermion is often called a *gaugino*. The number of physical states is again equal between bosons and fermions.

The supersymmetry transformations for this multiplet are

$$\begin{aligned} \delta_\xi A^{am} &= [\xi^\dagger \overline{\sigma}^m \lambda^a + \lambda^{\dagger a} \overline{\sigma}^m \xi] \\ \delta_\xi \lambda^a &= [i\sigma^{mn} F_{mn}^a + D^a]\xi \\ \delta_\xi \lambda^{\dagger a} &= \xi^\dagger [i\overline{\sigma}^{mn} F_{mn}^a + D^a] \\ \delta_\xi D^a &= -i[\xi^\dagger \overline{\sigma}^m \mathcal{D}_m \lambda^a - \mathcal{D}_m \lambda^{\dagger a} \overline{\sigma}^m \xi] \end{aligned} \tag{11.75}$$

where

$$\sigma^{mn} = \frac{1}{4}(\sigma^m \overline{\sigma}^n - \sigma^n \overline{\sigma}^m) . \tag{11.76}$$

I encourage you to verify that these tranformations obey the algebra

$$[\delta_\xi, \delta_\eta] = 2i \left(\xi^\dagger \overline{\sigma}^m \eta - \eta^\dagger \overline{\sigma}^m \xi\right) \partial_m + \delta_\alpha \; , \tag{11.77}$$

where δ_α is a gauge tranformation with the gauge parameter

$$\alpha = -2i(\xi^\dagger \overline{\sigma}^m \eta - \eta^\dagger \overline{\sigma}^m \xi) A_m^a \; . \tag{11.78}$$

Acting on λ^a, the extra term δ_α in (11.77) can be combined with the translation to produce the commutation relation

$$[\delta_\xi, \delta_\eta] \lambda^a = 2i \left(\xi^\dagger \overline{\sigma}^m \eta - \eta^\dagger \overline{\sigma}^m \xi\right) (\mathcal{D}_m \lambda)^a \; . \tag{11.79}$$

This rearrangement applies also for the auxiliary field D^a and for any matter field that tranforms linearly under G. The gauge field A^{am} does not satisfy this last criterion; instead, we find

$$\begin{aligned}[\delta_\xi, \delta_\eta] A_m^a &= 2i(\xi^\dagger \overline{\sigma}^n \eta - \eta^\dagger \overline{\sigma}^n \xi)(\partial_n A_m^a - \mathcal{D}_m A_n) \\ &= 2i(\xi^\dagger \overline{\sigma}^n \eta - \eta^\dagger \overline{\sigma}^n \xi) F_{nm}^a \end{aligned} \tag{11.80}$$

The proof that (11.75) satisfies the supersymmetry algebra is more tedious than for (11.29), but it is not actually difficult. For the transformation of λ^a we need both the Fierz identity (11.30) and the relation

$$\eta_\alpha \xi_\beta - (\xi \leftrightarrow \eta) = -(\xi^T c \sigma_{pq} \eta)(\sigma^{pq} c)_{\alpha\beta} \; . \tag{11.81}$$

The matrices $\sigma^{pq} c$ and $c\overline{\sigma}^{pq}$ are symmetric in their spinor indices.

Again, the transformation laws leave a simple Lagrangian invariant. For the vector supermultiplet, this Lagrangian is that of the renormalizable Yang-Mills theory including the gaugino:

$$\mathcal{L}_F = -\frac{1}{4}(F_{mn}^a)^2 + \lambda^{\dagger a} i \overline{\sigma} \cdot \mathcal{D} \lambda^a + \frac{1}{2}(D^a)^2 \tag{11.82}$$

The kinetic term for D^a contains no derivatives, so this field will be a Lagrange multiplier.

The vector supermultiplet can be coupled to matter particles in chiral supermultiplets. To do this, we must first modify the transformation laws of the chiral supermultiplet so that the commutators of supersymmetry transformations obey (11.77) or (11.79). The modified transformation laws are:

$$\begin{aligned} \delta_\xi \phi &= \sqrt{2} \xi^T c \psi \\ \delta_\xi \psi &= \sqrt{2} i \sigma^n c \xi^* \mathcal{D}_n \phi + \sqrt{2} F \xi \\ \delta_\xi F &= -\sqrt{2} i \xi^\dagger \overline{\sigma}^m \mathcal{D}_m \psi - 2g \xi^\dagger c \lambda^{a*} t^a \phi \end{aligned} \tag{11.83}$$

In this formula, the chiral fields ϕ, ψ, F must belong to the same representation of G, with t^a a representation matrix in that representation. From the transformation laws, we can construct the Lagrangian. Start from (11.31), replace the derivatives by covariant derivatives, add terms to the Lagrangian involving the λ^a to cancel the supersymmetry variation of these terms, and then add terms involving D^a to cancel the remaining supersymmetry variation of the λ^a terms. The result is

$$\mathcal{L}_D = \mathcal{D}^m \phi^* \mathcal{D}_m \phi + \psi^\dagger i \overline{\sigma} \cdot \mathcal{D} \psi + F^* F$$
$$- \sqrt{2} g (\phi^* \lambda^{aT} t^a c \psi - \psi^\dagger c \lambda^{a*} t^a \phi) + g D^a \phi^a t^a \phi \ . \quad (11.84)$$

The proof that this Lagrangian is supersymmetric, $\delta_\xi \mathcal{L} = 0$, is completely straightforward, but it requires a very large sheet of paper.

The gauge invariance of the theory requires the superpotential Lagrangian $\mathcal{L}_W$ to be invariant under G as a global symmetry. Under this condition, $\mathcal{L}_W$, which contains no derivatives, is invariant under (11.83) without modification. The combination of $\mathcal{L}_F$, $\mathcal{L}_D$, and $\mathcal{L}_W$, with W a polynomial of degree at most 3, gives the most general renormalizable supersymmetric gauge theory.

As we did with the F field of the chiral multiplet, it is interesting to eliminate the Lagrange multiplier D^a. For the Lagrangian which is the sum of (11.82) and (11.84), the equation of motion for D^a is

$$D^a = -g\phi^* t^a \phi \ . \quad (11.85)$$

Eliminating D^a gives a second potential energy term proportional to $(D^a)^2$. This is the *D-term potential* promised below (11.40). I will write the result for a theory with several chiral multiplets:

$$V_D = \frac{1}{2} g^2 \left(\sum_k \phi_k^* t^a \phi_k \right)^2 \ . \quad (11.86)$$

As with the F-term potential, $V_D \geq 0$ and vanishes if and only if $D^a = 0$. It can be shown by an argument similar to (11.45) that

$$\langle 0 | D^a | 0 \rangle = 0 \quad (11.87)$$

unless supersymmetry is spontaneously broken.

It makes a nice illustration of this formalism to show how the Higgs mechanism works in supersymmetry. For definiteness, consider a supersymmetric gauge theory with the gauge group $U(1)$.

Introduce chiral supermultiplets ϕ_+, ϕ_-, and X, with charges $+1$, -1, and 0, respectively, and the superpotential

$$W = \lambda(\phi_+\phi_- - v^2)X . \tag{11.88}$$

The $F = 0$ equations are

$$F_X^* = (\phi_+\phi_- - v^2) = 0 \qquad F_\pm^* = \phi_\pm X = 0 . \tag{11.89}$$

To solve these equations, set

$$X = 0 \qquad \phi_+ = v/y \qquad \phi_- = vy , \tag{11.90}$$

where y is a complex-valued parameter. The $D = 0$ equation is

$$\phi_+^\dagger \phi_+ - \phi_-^\dagger \phi_- = 0 . \tag{11.91}$$

This implies $|y| = 1$. So y is a pure phase and can be removed by a $U(1)$ gauge transformation.

Now look at the pieces of the Lagrangian that give mass to gauge bosons, fermions, and scalars. The gauge field receives mass from the Higgs mechanism. To compute the mass, we can look at the scalar kinetic terms

$$\phi_+^\dagger(-\mathcal{D}^2)\phi_+ + \phi_-^\dagger(-\mathcal{D}^2)\phi_- = \cdots + \phi_+^\dagger(g^2A^2)\phi_+ + \phi_-^\dagger(g^2A^2)\phi_- . \tag{11.92}$$

Putting in the vacuum expectation values $\phi_+ = \phi_- = v$, we find

$$m^2 = 4g^2v^2 \tag{11.93}$$

for the vector fields. The mode of the scalar field

$$\delta\phi_+ = \eta/\sqrt{2} \qquad \delta\phi_- = -\eta/\sqrt{2} , \tag{11.94}$$

with η real, receives a mass from the D-term potential energy

$$\frac{g^2}{2}(\phi_+^\dagger\phi_+ - \phi_-^\dagger\phi_-)^2 \tag{11.95}$$

Expanding to quadratic order in η, we see that η also receives the mass $m^2 = 4g^2v^2$. The corresponding mode for η imaginary is the infinitesimal version of the phase rotation of y that we have already gauged away below (11.91). The mode of the fermion fields

$$\delta\psi_+ = \chi/\sqrt{2} \qquad \delta\psi_- = -\chi/\sqrt{2} \tag{11.96}$$

mixes with the gaugino through the term

$$-\sqrt{2}g(\phi_+^\dagger\lambda^T c\psi_+ - \phi_-^\dagger\lambda^T c\psi_-) + h.c. \tag{11.97}$$

Putting in the vacuum expectation values $\phi_+ = \phi_- = v$, we find a Dirac mass with the value

$$m = 2gv \qquad (11.98)$$

In all, we find a massive vector boson, a massive real scalar, and a massive Dirac fermion, all with the mass $m = 2gv$. The system has four physical bosons and four physical fermions, all with the same mass, as supersymmetry requires.

11.2.5. The Vector Supermultiplet in Superspace

The vector supermultiplet has a quite simple representation in superspace. This multiplet turns out to be the answer to the question that we posed in our discussion of superspace in the previous section: When the chiral and antichiral components of a general superfield are removed, what is left over? To analyze this issue, I will write a Lagrangian containing a local symmetry that allows us to gauge away the chiral and antichiral components of this superfield. Let $V(x, \theta, \bar\theta)$ be a real-valued superfield, acted on by a local gauge transformation in superspace

$$\delta V = -\frac{i}{g}(\Lambda - \Lambda^\dagger) \qquad (11.99)$$

where Λ is a chiral superfield and $\Lambda^\dagger$ is its conjugate. Since Λ satisfies (11.60), its expansion in powers of θ contains

$$\Lambda(x, \theta, \bar\theta) = \Lambda(x + i\bar\theta\bar\sigma\theta, \theta) = \alpha(x) + \cdots + i\bar\theta\bar\sigma^m\theta\partial_m\alpha(x) + \cdots \qquad (11.100)$$

The general superfield V contains a term[b]

$$V(x, \theta, \bar\theta) = \cdots + 2\bar\theta\bar\sigma^m\theta A_m(x) + \cdots \qquad (11.101)$$

So the superfield V contains a space-time vector field $A_m(x)$, and under (11.99), A_m transforms as

$$\delta A_m = \frac{1}{g}\partial_m(\mathrm{Re}\,\alpha) \ . \qquad (11.102)$$

This is just what we would like for an Abelian gauge field. So we should accept (11.99) as the generalization of the Abelian gauge transformation to superspace.

The real-valued superfield transforming under (11.99) is called a *vector superfield*. To understand its structure, use the gauge transformation to

---
[b]The factor 2 in this equation is convenient but disagrees with some standard treatments, e.g., [7].

remove all components with powers of θ or $\bar\theta$ only. This choice is called *Wess-Zumino gauge* [33]. What remains after this gauge choice is

$$V(x,\theta,\bar\theta) = 2\bar\theta\bar\sigma^m\theta\, A_m(x) + 2\bar\theta^2\theta^T c\lambda - 2\theta^2\bar\theta^T c\lambda^* + \theta^2\bar\theta^2 D \ . \qquad (11.103)$$

This expression has exactly the field content of the Abelian vector supermultiplet (A_m, λ, D).

This gauge multiplet can be coupled to matter described by chiral superfields. For the moment, I will continue to discuss the Abelian gauge theory. For a chiral superfield Φ with charge Q, the gauge transformation

$$\delta\Phi = iQ\Lambda\Phi \qquad (11.104)$$

contains a standard Abelian gauge transformation with gauge parameter $\operatorname{Re}\alpha(x)$ and also preserves the chiral nature of Φ. Then the superspace Lagrangian

$$\int d^2\theta d^2\bar\theta\ \Phi^\dagger e^{gQV}\Phi \qquad (11.105)$$

is gauge-invariant. Using the representation (11.103) and the rules (11.62), it is straightforward to carry out the integrals explicitly and show that (11.105) reduces to (11.84), with $t^a = Q$ for this Abelian theory.

We still need to construct the pure gauge part of the Lagrangian. To do this, first note that, because a quantity antisymmetrized on three Weyl fermion indices vanishes,

$$\bar D_\alpha \bar D^2 X = 0 \qquad (11.106)$$

for any superfield X. Thus, acting with $\bar D^2$ makes any superfield a chiral superfield. The following is a chiral superfield that also has the property that its leading component is the gaugino field $\lambda(x)$:

$$W_\alpha = -\frac{1}{8}\bar D^2 (Dc)_\alpha V \ . \qquad (11.107)$$

Indeed, working this out in full detail, we find that $W_\alpha = W_\alpha(x + i\bar\theta\sigma\theta, \theta)$, with

$$W_\alpha(x,\theta) = \lambda_\alpha + [(i\sigma^{mn}F_{mn} + D)\theta]_\alpha + \theta^T c\theta\, [\partial_m\lambda^* i\bar\sigma^m c]_\alpha \ . \qquad (11.108)$$

The chiral superfield W_α is the superspace analogue of the electromagnetic field strength. The Lagrangian

$$\int d^2\theta\, \frac{1}{2} W^T c W \qquad (11.109)$$

reduces precisely to the Abelian version of (11.82). It is odd that the kinetic term for gauge fields is an F-term rather than a D-term. It turns out that this term can be renormalized by loop corrections as a consequence of the trace anomaly [34]. However, the restricted form of the correction has implications, both some simple ones that I will discuss later in Section 4.3 and and more profound implications discussed, for example, in [35,36].

I will simply quote the generalizations of these results to the non-Abelian case. The gauge transformation of a chiral superfield in the representation R of the gauge group is

$$\Phi \to e^{i\Lambda^a t^a}\Phi \qquad \Phi^\dagger \to \Phi^\dagger e^{-i\Lambda^{\dagger a} t^a} , \qquad (11.110)$$

where Λ^a is a chiral superfield in the adjoint representation of G and t^a is is the representation of the generators of G in the representation R. The gauge transformation of the vector superfield is

$$e^{gV^a t^a} \to e^{i\Lambda^{\dagger a} t^a} e^{gV^a t^a} e^{-i\Lambda^a t^a} \qquad (11.111)$$

Then the Lagrangian

$$\int d^2\theta d^2\bar\theta\, \Phi^\dagger e^{gV^a t^a}\Phi \qquad (11.112)$$

is locally gauge-invariant. Carrying out the integrals in the gauge (11.103) reduces this Lagrangian to (11.84).

The form of the field strength superfield is rather more complicated than in the Abelian case,

$$W_\alpha^a t^a = -\frac{1}{8g}\overline{D}^2 e^{-gV^a t^a}(Dc)_\alpha e^{gV^a t^a} \qquad (11.113)$$

In Wess-Zumino gauge, this formula does reduce to the non-Abelian version of (11.108),

$$W_\alpha^a(x,\theta) = \lambda_\alpha^a + [(i\sigma^{mn} F_{mn}^a + D^a)\theta]_\alpha + \theta^T c\theta\,[\mathcal{D}_m \lambda^{*a} i\overline\sigma^m c]_\alpha . \qquad (11.114)$$

Then the Lagrangian

$$\int d^2\theta\, \mathrm{tr}[W^T c W] \qquad (11.115)$$

reduces neatly to (11.82).

The most general renormalizable supersymmetric Lagrangian can be built out of these ingredients. We need to put together the Lagrangian (11.115), plus a term (11.112) for each matter chiral superfield, plus a superpotential Lagrangian to represent the scalar field potential energy. These formulae can be generalized to the case of a nonlinear sigma model on a Kähler manifold, with the gauge symmetry associated with an isometry of this target space. For the details, see [7].

11.2.6. R-Symmetry

The structure of the general superspace action for a renormalizable theory of scalar and fermion fields suggests that this theory has a natural continuous symmetry.

The superspace Lagrangian is

$$\mathcal{L} = \int d^2\theta \, \text{tr}[W^T cW] + \int d^4\theta \, \Phi^\dagger e^{gV \cdot t}\Phi + \int d^2\theta \, W(\Phi) + \int d^2\bar{\theta} \, (W(\Phi))^\dagger \,.$$
(11.116)

Consider first the case in which $W(\phi)$ contains only dimensionless parameters and is therefore a cubic polynomial in the scalar fields. Then $\mathcal{L}$ is invariant under the $U(1)$ symmetry

$$\Phi_k(x,\theta) \to e^{-i2\alpha/3}\Phi_k(x, e^{i\alpha}\theta) \,, \quad V^a(x,\theta,\bar{\theta}) \to V^a(x, e^{i\alpha}\theta, e^{-i\alpha}\bar{\theta})$$
(11.117)

or, in components,

$$\phi_k \to e^{-i2\alpha/3}\phi_k \,, \quad \psi_k \to e^{i\alpha/3}\psi_k \,, \quad \lambda^a \to e^{-i\alpha}\lambda^a \,,$$
(11.118)

and the gauge fields are invariant. This transformation is called *R-symmetry*. Under R-symmetry, the charges of bosons and fermions differ by 1 unit, in such a way that that the gaugino and superpotential vertices have zero net charge.

Since all left-handed fermions have the same charge under (11.118), the R-symmetry will have an axial vector anomaly. It can be shown that the R-symmetry current (of dimension 3, spin 1) forms a supersymmetry multiplet together with the supersymmetry current (dimension $\frac{7}{2}$, spin $\frac{3}{2}$) and the energy-momentum tensor (dimension 4, spin 2) [37]. All three currents have perturbation-theory anomalies; the anomaly of the energy-momentum tensor is the trace anomaly, associated with the breaking of scalar invariance by coupling constant renormalization. The R-current anomaly is thus connected to the running of coupling constants and gives a useful formal approach to study this effect in supersymmetric models.

It is often possible to combine the transformation (11.117) with other apparent $U(1)$ symmetries of the theory to define a non-anomalous $U(1)$ R-symmetry. Under such a symmetry, we will have

$$\Phi_k(x,\theta) \to e^{-i\beta_k}\Phi_k(x, e^{i\alpha}\theta) \,, \quad \text{such that} \quad W(x,\theta) \to e^{2i\alpha}W(x, e^{i\alpha}\theta) \,.$$
(11.119)

Such symmetries also often arise in models in which the superpotential has dimensionful coefficients.

In models with extended, $N > 1$, supersymmetry, the R-symmetry group is also extended, to $SU(2)$ for $N = 2$ and to $SU(4)$ for $N = 4$ supersymmetry.

11.3. The Minimal Supersymmetric Standard Model

11.3.1. Particle Content of the Model

Now we have all of the ingredients to construct a supersymmetric generalization of the Standard Model. To begin, let us construct a version of the Standard Model with exact supersymmetry. To do this, we assign the vector fields in the Standard Model to vector supermultiplets and the matter fields of the Standard Model to chiral supermultiplets.

The vector supermultiplets correspond to the generators of $SU(3) \times SU(2) \times U(1)$. In these lectures, I will refer to the gauge bosons of these groups as A_m^a, W_m^a, and B_m, respectively. I will represent the Weyl fermion partners of these fields as $\tilde{g}^a$, $\tilde{w}^a$, $\tilde{b}$. I will call these fields the *gluino*, *wino*, and *bino*, or, collectively, *gauginos*. In the later parts of these lectures, I will drop the tildes over the gaugino fields when they are not needed for clarity.

I will assign the quarks and leptons to be fermions in chiral superfields. I will use the convention presented in Section 1.3 of considering left-handed Weyl fermions as the basic particles and right-handed Weyl fermions as their antiparticles. In the Standard Model, the left-handed fields in a fermion generation have the quantum numbers

$$L = \begin{pmatrix} \nu \\ e \end{pmatrix} \qquad \overline{e} \qquad Q = \begin{pmatrix} u \\ d \end{pmatrix} \qquad \overline{u} \qquad \overline{d} \qquad (11.120)$$

The field $\overline{e}$ is the left-handed positron; the fields $\overline{u}$, $\overline{d}$ are the left-handed antiquarks. The right-handed Standard Model fermion fields are the conjugates of these fields. To make a generalization to supersymmetry, we will extend each of the fields in (11.120)—for each of the three generations—to a chiral supermultiplet. I will use the symbols

$$\tilde{L} \qquad \tilde{\overline{e}} \qquad \tilde{Q} \qquad \tilde{\overline{u}} \qquad \tilde{\overline{d}} \qquad (11.121)$$

to represent both the supermultiplets and the scalar fields in these multiplets. Again, I will drop the tilde if it is unambiguous that I am referring to the scalar partner rather than the fermion. The scalar particles in these supermultiplets are called *sleptons* and *squarks*, collectively, *sfermions*.

What about the Higgs field? The Higgs field of the Standard Model should be identified with a complex scalar component of a chiral supermultiplet. But it is ambiguous what the quantum numbers of this multiplet should be. In the Standard Model, the Higgs field is a color singlet with $I = \frac{1}{2}$, but we can take the hypercharge of this field to be either $Y = +\frac{1}{2}$ or $Y = -\frac{1}{2}$, depending on whether we take the positive hypercharge field or its conjugate to be primary. In a supersymmetric model, the choice matters. The superpotential is an analytic function of superfields, so it can only contain the field, not the conjugate. Then different Higgs couplings will be allowed depending on the choice that we make.

The correct solution to this problem is to include *both* possibilities, That is, we include a Higgs supermultiplet with $Y = +\frac{1}{2}$ and a second Higgs supermultiplet with $Y = -\frac{1}{2}$. I will call the scalar components of these multiplets H_u and H_d, respectively:

$$H_u = \begin{pmatrix} H_u^+ \\ H_u^0 \end{pmatrix} \qquad H_d = \begin{pmatrix} H_d^0 \\ H_d^- \end{pmatrix} \qquad (11.122)$$

I will refer to the Weyl fermion components with these quantum numbers as $\widetilde{h}_u$, $\widetilde{h}_d$. These fields or particles are called *Higgsinos*.

I will argue below that it is necessary to include both Higgs fields in order to obtain all of the needed couplings in the superpotential. However, there is another argument. The axial vector anomaly of one $U(1)$ and two $SU(2)$ currents (Fig. 11.5) must vanish to maintain the gauge invariance of the model. In the Standard Model, the anomaly cancels nontrivially between the quarks and the leptons. In the supersymmetric generalization of the Standard Model, each Higgsino makes a nonzero contribution to this anomaly. These contributions cancel if we include a pair of Higgsinos with opposite hypercharge.

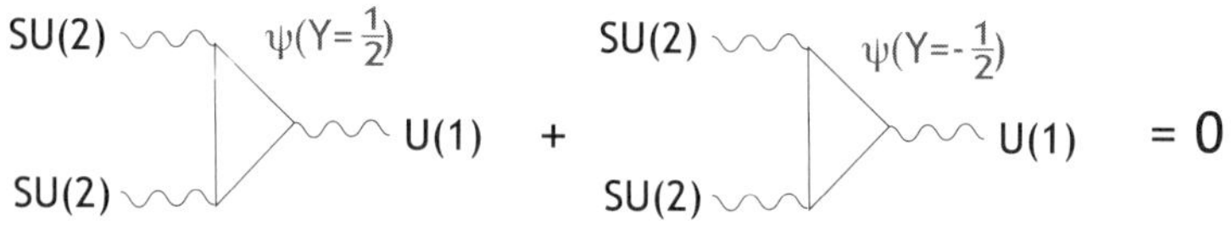

Fig. 11.5. The anomaly cancellation that requires two doublets of Higgs fields in the MSSM.

11.3.2. Grand Unification

Before writing the Lagrangian in detail, I would like to point out that there is an interesting conclusion that follows from the quantum number assignments of the new particles that we have introduced to make the Standard Model supersymmetric.

An attractive feature of the Standard Model is that the quarks and leptons of each generation fill out multiplets of the simple gauge group $SU(5)$. This suggests a very beautiful picture, called *grand unification*, in which $SU(5)$, or a group such as $SO(10)$ or E_6 for which this is a subgroup, is the fundamental gauge symmetry at very short distances. This unified symmetry will be spontaneously broken to the Standard Model gauge group $SU(3) \times SU(2) \times U(1)$.

For definiteness, I will examine the model in which the grand unified symmetry group is $SU(5)$. The generators of $SU(5)$ can be represented as 5×5 Hermitian matrices acting on the 5-dimensional vectors in the fundamental representation. To see how the Standard Model is embedded in $SU(5)$, it is convenient to write these matrices as blocks with 3 and 2 rows and columns. Then the Standard Model generators can be identified as

$$SU(3) : \begin{pmatrix} t^a & \\ & 0 \end{pmatrix}; \quad SU(2) : \begin{pmatrix} 0 & \\ & \sigma^a/2 \end{pmatrix}; \quad U(1) : \sqrt{\frac{3}{5}} \begin{pmatrix} -\frac{1}{3}\mathbf{1} & \\ & \frac{1}{2}\mathbf{1} \end{pmatrix}. \quad (11.123)$$

In these expressions, t^a is an $SU(3)$ generator, $\sigma^a/2$ is an $SU(2)$ generator, and all of these matrices are normalized to $\text{tr}[T^A T^B] = \frac{1}{2}\delta^{AB}$. We should identify the last of these matrices with $\sqrt{3/5}\, Y$.

The symmetry-breaking can be caused by the vacuum expectation value of a Higgs field in the adjoint representation of $SU(5)$. The expectation value

$$\langle \Phi \rangle = V \cdot \begin{pmatrix} -\frac{1}{3}\mathbf{1} & \\ & \frac{1}{2}\mathbf{1} \end{pmatrix} \quad (11.124)$$

commutes with the generators in (11.123) and fails to commute with the off-diagonal generators. So this vacuum expectation value gives mass to the off-diagonal generators and breaks the gauge group to $SU(3) \times SU(2) \times U(1)$.

Matter fermions can be organized as left-handed Weyl fermions in the $SU(5)$ representations $\bar{5}$ and 10. The $\bar{5}$ is the conjugate of the fundamental representation of $SU(5)$; the 10 is the antisymmetric matrix with two 5 indices.

$$\overline{5}:\begin{pmatrix}\overline{d}\\\overline{d}\\\overline{d}\\e\\\nu\end{pmatrix}_L\;;\qquad 10:\begin{pmatrix}0&\overline{u}&\overline{u}&u&d\\&0&\overline{u}&u&d\\&&0&u&d\\&&&0&\overline{e}\\&&&&0\end{pmatrix}_L \qquad (11.125)$$

It is straightforward to check that each entry listed has the quantum numbers assigned to that field in the Standard Model. To compute the hypercharges, we act on the $\overline{5}$ with (-1) times the hypercharge generator in (11.123), and we act on the 10 with the hypercharge generator on each index. This gives the standard results, for example, $Y = +\frac{1}{3}$ for the $\overline{d}$ and $Y = -\frac{1}{3} + \frac{1}{2} = \frac{1}{6}$ for u and d.

The $SU(5)$ covariant derivative is

$$\mathcal{D}_m = (\partial_m - ig_U A_m^A T^A) \;, \qquad (11.126)$$

where g_U is the $SU(5)$ gauge coupling. There is only room for one value here. So this model predicts that the three Standard Model gauge couplings are related by

$$g_3 = g_2 = g_1 = g_U \;, \qquad (11.127)$$

where

$$g_3 = g_s \qquad g_2 = g \qquad g_1 = \sqrt{\frac{5}{3}} g' \;. \qquad (11.128)$$

Clearly, this prediction is not correct for the gauge couplings that we measure in particle physics.

However, there is a way to save this prediction. In quantum field theory, coupling constants are functions of length scale and change their values significantly from one scale to another by renormalization group evolution. It is possible that the values of g', g, and g_s that we measure could evolve at very short distances into values that obey (11.127).

I will now collect the formulae that we need to analyze this question. Let

$$\alpha_i = \frac{g_i^2}{4\pi} \qquad (11.129)$$

for $i = 1, 2, 3$. The one-loop renormalization group equations for gauge couplings are

$$\frac{dg_i}{d\log Q} = -\frac{b_i}{(4\pi)^2} g_i^3 \quad \text{or} \quad \frac{d\alpha_i}{d\log Q} = -\frac{b_i}{(2\pi)} \alpha_i^2 \;. \qquad (11.130)$$

For $U(1)$, the coefficient b_1 is

$$b_1 = -\frac{2}{3}\sum_f \frac{3}{5}Y_f^2 - \frac{1}{3}\sum_b \frac{3}{5}Y_b^2 , \tag{11.131}$$

where the two sums run over the multiplets of left-handed Weyl fermions and complex-valued bosons. The factors $\frac{3}{5}Y^2$ are the squares of the $U(1)$ charges defined by (11.123). For non-Abelian groups, the expressions for the b coefficients are

$$b = -\frac{11}{3}C_2(G) - \frac{2}{3}\sum_f C(r_f) - \frac{1}{3}\sum_b C(r_b) , \tag{11.132}$$

where $C_2(G)$ and $C(r)$ are the standard group theory coefficients. For $SU(N)$,

$$C_2(G) = C(G) = N , \quad C(N) = \frac{1}{2} . \tag{11.133}$$

The solution of the renormalization group equation (11.130) is

$$\alpha^{-1}(Q) = \alpha^{-1}(M) - \frac{b_i}{2\pi}\log\frac{Q}{M} . \tag{11.134}$$

Now consider the situation in which the three couplings g_i become equal at the mass scale M_U, the mass scale of $SU(5)$ symmetry breaking. Let α_U be the value of the α_i at this scale. Using (11.134), we can then determine the Standard Model couplings at any lower mass scale. The three $\alpha_i(Q)$ are determined by two parameters. We can eliminate those parameters and obtain the relation

$$\alpha_3^{-1} = (1+B)\alpha_2^{-1} - B\alpha_1^{-1} \tag{11.135}$$

where

$$B = \frac{b_3 - b_2}{b_2 - b_1} . \tag{11.136}$$

The values of the α_i are known very accurately at $Q = m_Z$ [38]:

$$\alpha_3^{-1} = 8.50\pm0.14 \quad \alpha_2^{-1} = 29.57\pm0.02 \quad \alpha_1^{-1} = 59.00\pm0.02 . \tag{11.137}$$

Inserting these values into (11.135), we find

$$B = 0.716 \pm 0.005 \pm 0.03 . \tag{11.138}$$

In this formula, the first error is that propagated from the errors in (11.137) and the second is my estimate of the systematic error from neglecting the two-loop renormalization group coefficients and other higher-order corrections.

We can compare the value of B in (11.138) to the values of (11.136) from different models. The hypothesis that the three Standard Model couplings unify is acceptable only if the gauge theory that describes physics between m_Z and M_U gives a value of B consistent with (11.138). The minimal Standard Model fails this test. The values of the b_i are

$$b_3 = 11 - \frac{4}{3}n_g$$
$$b_2 = \frac{22}{3} - \frac{4}{3}n_g - \frac{1}{6}n_h$$
$$b_1 = \phantom{\frac{22}{3}} - \frac{4}{3}n_g - \frac{1}{10}n_h \tag{11.139}$$

where n_g is the number of generations and n_h is the number of Higgs doublets. Notice that n_g cancels out of (11.136). This is to be expected. The Standard Model fermions form complete representations of $SU(5)$, and so their renormalization effects cannot lead to differences among the three couplings. For the minimal case $n_h = 1$ we find $B = 0.53$. To obtain a value consistent with (11.138), we need $n_h = 6$.

We can redo this calculation in the minimal supersymmetric version of the Standard Model. First of all, we should rewrite (11.132) for a supersymmetric model with one vector supermultiplet, containing a vector and a Weyl fermion in the adjoint representation, and a set of chiral supermultiplets indexed by k, each with a Weyl fermion and a complex boson. Then (11.132) becomes

$$b_i = \frac{11}{3}C_2(G) - \frac{2}{3}C_2(G) - \left(\frac{2}{3} + \frac{1}{3}\right)\sum_k C(r_k)$$
$$= 3C_2(G) - \sum_k C(r_k) \tag{11.140}$$

The formula (11.131) undergoes a similar rearrangement. Inserting the values of the $C(r_k)$ for the fields of the Standard Model, we find

$$b_3 = 9 - 2n_g$$
$$b_2 = 6 - 2n_g - \frac{1}{2}n_h$$
$$b_1 = - 2n_g - \frac{3}{10}n_h \tag{11.141}$$

For the minimal Higgs content $n_h = 2$, this gives

$$B = \frac{5}{7} = 0.714 \tag{11.142}$$

in excellent agreement with (11.138).

In Fig. 11.6, I show the unification relation pictorially. The three data points on the the left of the figure represent the measured values of the three couplings (11.137). Starting from the values of α_1 and α_2, we can integrate (11.130) up to the scale at which these two couplings converge. Then we can integrate the equation for α_3 back down to $Q = m_Z$ and see whether the result agrees with the measured value. The lower set of curves presents the result for the Standard Model with $n_h = 1$. The upper set of curves shows the result for the supersymmetric extension of the Standard Model with $n_h = 2$. This choice gives excellent agreement with the measured value of α_s.

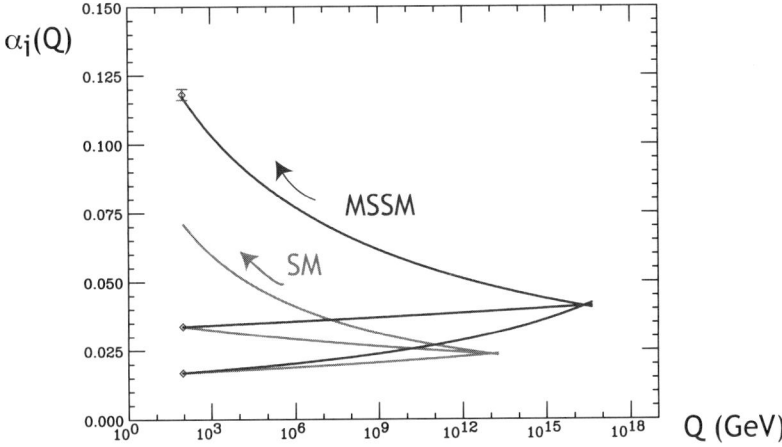

Fig. 11.6. Prediction of the $SU(3)$ gauge coupling α_s from the electroweak coupling constants using grand unification, in the Standard Model and in the MSSM.

Actually, I slightly overstate the case for supersymmetry by ignoring two-loop terms in the renormalization group equations, and also by integrating these equations all the way down to m_Z even though, from searches at high-energy colliders, most of the squarks and gluinos must be heavier than 300 GeV. A more accurate prediction of $\alpha_s(m_Z)$ from the electroweak coupling constants gives a slightly higher value, 0.13 instead of 0.12. However, these corrections could easily be compensated by similar corrections to the upper limit of the integration, following the details of the particle spectrum at the grand unification scale. For a more detailed formal analysis of these corrections, see [39], and for a recent evaluation of their effects, see [40]. It remains a remarkable fact that the minimal supersymmetric extension of the Standard Model is approximately compatible with grand unification 'out of the box', with no need for further model-building.

11.3.3. Construction of the Lagrangian

Now I would like to write the full Lagrangian of the minimal supersymmetric extension of the Standard Model, which I will henceforth call the MSSM.

The kinetic terms and gauge couplings of the MSSM Lagrangian are completely determined by supersymmetry, the choice of the gauge group $SU(3) \times SU(2) \times U(1)$, and the choice of the quantum numbers of the matter fields. The Lagrangian is a sum of terms of the forms (11.82) and (11.84). Up to this point, the only parameters that need to be introduced are the gauge couplings g_1, g_2, and g_3.

Next, we need a superpotential W. The superpotential is the source of nonlinear fermion-scalar interactions, so we should include the appropriate terms to generate the Higgs Yukawa couplings needed to give mass to the quarks and leptons. The appropriate choice is

$$W_Y = y_d^{ij} \overline{d}^i H_{d\alpha} \epsilon_{\alpha\beta} Q_\beta^j + y_e^{ij} \overline{e}^i H_{d\alpha} \epsilon_{\alpha\beta} L_\beta^j - y_u^{ij} \overline{u}^i H_{u\alpha} \epsilon_{\alpha\beta} Q_\beta^j \ . \quad (11.143)$$

The notation for the quark and lepton multiplets is that in (11.120); the indices $i, j = 1, 2, 3$ run over the three generations. The indices $\alpha, \beta = 1, 2$ run over SU(2) isospin indices. Notice that the first two terms require a Higgs field H_d with $Y = -\frac{1}{2}$, while the third term requires a Higgs field H_u with $Y = \frac{1}{2}$. If we leave out one of the Higgs multiplets, some quarks or leptons will be left massless. This is the second argument that requires two Higgs fields in the MSSM.

I have written (11.143) including the most general mixing between left- and right-handed quarks and leptons of different generations. However, as in the minimal Standard Model, we can remove most of this flavor mixing by appropriate field redefinitions. The coupling constants y_d, y_e, y_u are general 3×3 complex-valued matrices. Any such matrix can be diagonalized using two unitary transformations. Thus, we can write

$$y_d = W_d Y_d V_d^\dagger \qquad y_e = W_e Y_e V_e^\dagger \qquad y_u = W_u Y_u V_u^\dagger \ , \quad (11.144)$$

with W_a and V_a 3×3 unitary matrices and Y_a real, positive, and diagonal. The unitary transformations cancel out of the kinetic energy terms and gauge couplings in the Lagrangian, except that the W boson coupling to quarks is transformed

$$gu^\dagger \overline{\sigma}^m dW_m^+ \to gu^\dagger \overline{\sigma}^m (V_u^\dagger V_d) d W_m^+ \ . \tag{11.145}$$

From this equation, we can identify $(V_d^\dagger V_u) = V_{CKM}$, the Cabibbo-Kobayashi-Maskawa weak interaction mixing matrix. The Lagrangian term (11.143) thus introduces the remaining parameters of the Standard Model, the 9 quark and lepton masses (ignoring neutrino masses) and the 4 CKM mixing angles. The field redefinition (11.144) can also induce or shift a QCD theta parameter, so the MSSM, like the Standard Model, has a strong CP problem that requires an axion or another model-building solution [41].

There are several other terms that can be added to W. One possible contribution is a pure Higgs term

$$W_\mu = -\mu H_{d\alpha} \epsilon_{\alpha\beta} H_{u\beta} \ . \tag{11.146}$$

The parameter μ has the dimensions of mass, and consequently this *mu term* provides a supersymmetric contribution to the masses of the Higgs bosons. Because this term is in the superpotential, it does not receive additive raditive corrections. Even in a theory that includes grand unification and energies scale of the order of 10^{16} GeV, we can set the parameter μ to be of order 100 GeV without finding this choice affected by large quantum corrections. We will see in Section 4.2 that the mu term is needed for phenomenological reasons. If $\mu = 0$, a Higgsino state will be massless and should have been detected already in experiments. It is odd that a theory whose fundamental mass scale is the grand unification scale should require a parameter containing a weak interaction mass scale. I will present some models for the origin of this term in Section 3.5.

At this point, we have introduced two new parameters beyond those in the Standard Model. One is the value of μ. The other is the result of the fact that we have two Higgs doublets in the model. The ratio of the Higgs vacuum expectation values

$$\langle H_u \rangle / \langle H_d \rangle \equiv \tan\beta \tag{11.147}$$

will appear in many of the detailed predictions of the MSSM.

There are still more superpotential terms that are consistent with the Standard Model gauge symmetry and quantum numbers. These are

$$W_{\not R} = \eta_1 \epsilon_{ijk} \overline{u}_i \overline{d}_j \overline{d}_k + \eta_2 \overline{d} \epsilon_{\alpha\beta} L_\alpha Q_\beta$$
$$+ \eta_3 \overline{e} \epsilon_{\alpha\beta} L_\alpha L_\beta + \eta_4 \epsilon_{\alpha\beta} L_\alpha H_{u\beta} \ . \tag{11.148}$$

Here i, j, k are color indices, α, β are isospin indices, and arbitrary generation mixing is also possible. These terms violate baryon and lepton number through operators with dimensionless coefficients. In constructing supersymmetric models, it is necessary either to forbid these terms by imposing appropriate discrete symmetries or to arrange by hand that some of the dangerous couplings are extremely small [42].

If baryon number B and lepton number L are conserved in a supersymmetric model, this model respects a discrete symmetry called R-parity,

$$R = (-1)^{3B+L+2J} . \qquad (11.149)$$

Here $(3B)$ is quark number and J is the spin of the particle. This quantity is constructed so that $R = +1$ on the particles of the Standard Model (including the Higgs bosons) and $R = -1$ on their supersymmetry partners. R acts differently on particles of different spin in the same supermultiplet, so R-parity is a discrete subgroup of a continuous R-symmetry.

In a model with grand unification, there will be baryon number and lepton number violation, and so B and L cannot be used as fundamental symmetries. However, we can easily forbid most of the superpotential terms (11.148) by introducing a discrete symmetry that distinguishes the field H_d from the lepton doublets L_i. A similar strategy can be used to forbid the first, 3-quark, term. With these additional discrete symmetries, the MSSM, including all other terms considered up to this point, will conserve R-parity.

11.3.4. The Lightest Supersymmetric Particle

If R-parity is conserved, the lightest supersymmetric particle will be absolutely stable. This conclusion has an important implication for the relation of supersymmetry to cosmology. If a supersymmetric particle is stable for a time longer than the age of the universe, and if this particle is electrically neutral, that particle is a good candidate for the cosmic dark matter. In Sections 6.3 and 6.4, I will discuss in some detail the properties of models in which the lightest Standard Model superpartner is the dark matter particle.

However, this is not the only possibility. Over times much longer than those of particle physics experiments—minutes, years, or billions of years—we need to consider the possibility that the lightest Standard Model superpartner will decay to a particle with only couplngs of gravitational strength. Complete supersymmetric models of Nature must include a superpartner of the graviton, a spin-$\frac{3}{2}$ particle called the *gravitino*. In a model with exact supersymmetry, the gravitino will be massless, but in a model with spontaneously broken supersymmetry, the gravitino acquires a mass through an analogue of the Higgs mechanism. If the supersymmetry breaking is induced by one dominant F-term, the value of this mass is [43]

$$m_{3/2} = \frac{8\pi}{3} \frac{\langle F \rangle}{m_{\rm Pl}} . \qquad (11.150)$$

This expression is of the same order of magnitude as the expressions for Standard Model superpartner masses that I will give in Section 3.6. In string theory and other unified models, there may be additional Standard Model singlet fields with couplings of gravitation strength, called *moduli*, that might also be light enough that long-lived Standard Model superpartners could decay to them.

Supersymmetric models with R-parity conservation and dark matter, then, divide into two classes, according to the identity of the lightest supersymmetric particle—the LSP. On one hand, the LSP could be a Standard Model superpartner. Cosmology requires that this particle is neutral. Several candidates are available, including the fermionic partners of the photon, Z^0, and neutral Higgs bosons and the scalar partner of one of the neutrinos. In all cases, these particles will be weakly interacting; when they are produced at high-energy colliders, they should not make signals in a particle detector. On the other hand, the LSP could be the gravitino or another particle with only gravitational couplings. In that case, the lightest Standard Model superpartner could be a charged particle. Whether this particle is visible or neutral and weakly interacting, its decay should be included in the phenomenology of the model.

11.3.5. Models of Supersymmetry Breaking

There is still one important effect that is missing in our construction of the MSSM. The terms that we have written so far preserve exact supersymmetry. A fully supersymmetric model would contain a massless fermionic partner of the photon and a charged scalar particle with the mass of the electron. These particles manifestly do not exist. So if we wish to build a model of Nature with supersymmetry as a fundamental symmetry, we need to arrange that supersymmetry is spontaneously broken.

From the example of spontaneous symmetry breaking in the Standard Model, we would expect to do this by including in the MSSM a field whose vacuum expectation value leads to supersymmetry breaking. This is not as easy as it might seem. To explain why, I will first present some models of supersymmetry breaking.

The simplest model of supersymmetry breaking is the O'Raifeartaigh model [44], with three chiral supermultiplets ϕ_0, ϕ_1, ϕ_2 interacting through the superpotential

$$W = \lambda\phi_0 + m\phi_1\phi_2 + g\phi_0\phi_1^2 \ . \tag{11.151}$$

This superpotential implies the $F = 0$ conditions

$$0 = F_0^* = \lambda + g\phi_1^2$$
$$0 = F_1^* = m\phi_2 + 2g\phi_0\phi_1$$
$$0 = F_2^* = m\phi_1 \tag{11.152}$$

The first and third equations contradict one another. It is impossible to satisfy both conditions, and so there is no supersymmetric vacuum state. This fulfils the condition for spontaneous supersymmetry breaking that I presented in Section 2.2.

This mechanism of supersymmetry breaking has an unwanted corollary. Because one combination of the scalar fields appears in two different constraints in (11.152), there must be an orthogonal combination that does not appear at all. This means that the F-term potential V_F has a surface of degenerate vacuum states. To see this explicitly, pick a particular vacuum solution

$$\phi_0 = \phi_1 = \phi_2 = 0 \ . \tag{11.153}$$

and expand the potential V_F about this point. There are 6 real-valued boson fields with masses

$$0, \quad 0, \quad m, \quad m, \quad \sqrt{m^2 - 2\lambda g}, \quad \sqrt{m^2 + 2\lambda g} \ . \tag{11.154}$$

These six fields do not pair into complex-valued fields; that is already an indication that supersymmetry is broken. The fermion mass term in (11.38) gives one Dirac fermion mass m and leaves one Weyl fermion massless. This massless fermion is the Goldstone particle associate with spontaneous supersymmetry breaking.

A property of these masses is that the sum rule for fermion and boson masses

$$\text{str}[m^2] = \sum m_f^2 - \sum m_b^2 = 0 \tag{11.155}$$

remains valid even when supersymmetry is broken. This sum rule is the coefficient of the one-loop quadratic divergence in the vacuum energy. Since supersymmetry breaking does not affect the ultraviolet structure of the theory, this coefficient must cancel even if supersymmetry is spontaneously broken [45]. In fact, if Q is a conserved charge in the model, the sum rule is valid in each charge sector $Q = q$:

$$\text{str}_q[m^2] = 0 \ . \tag{11.156}$$

In the O'Raifeartaigh model, supersymmetry is spontaneously broken by a nonzero expectation value of an F term. It is also possible to break supersymmetry with a nonzero expectation value of a D term. The D-term potential V_D typically has zeros. For example, in an $SU(3)$ supersymmetric Yang-Mills theory,

$$V_D = \frac{1}{2} \left(\sum_3 \phi^\dagger t^a \phi - \sum_{\overline{3}} \overline{\phi} t^a \overline{\phi}^\dagger \right)^2 \tag{11.157}$$

and it is easy to find solutions in which the terms in parentheses sum to zero. However, it is not difficult to arrange a V_F such that the solutions of the $F = 0$ conditions do not coincide with the solutions of the $D = 0$ conditions. This leads to spontaneous symmetry breaking, again with the sum rule (11.156) valid at tree level.

Unfortunately, the sum rule (11.156) is a disaster for the prospect of finding a simple model of spontaneously broken supersymmetry that extends the Standard Model. For the charge sector of the d squarks, we would need all down-type squarks to have masses less than 5 GeV. For the charge sector of the charged leptons, we would need all sleptons to have masses less than 2 GeV.

11.3.6. Soft Supersymmetry Breaking

The solution to this problem is to construct models of spontaneously broken supersymmetry using a different strategy from the one that we use for electroweak symmetry breaking in the Standard Model. To break electroweak symmetry, we introduce a Higgs sector whose mass scale is the same as the scale of the fermion and gauge boson masses induced by the symmetry breaking. To break supersymmetry, however, we could introduce a new sector at a much higher mass scale, relying on a weak coupling of the new sector to the Standard Model particles to communicate the supersymmetry breaking terms. In principle, a weak gauge interaction could supply this coupling. However, the default connection is through gravity. Gravity and supergravity couple to all fields. It can be shown that supersymmetry breaking anywhere in Nature is communicated to all other sectors through supergravity couplings.

We are thus led to the following picture, which produces a phenomenologically reasonable supersymmetric extension of the Standard Model: We extend the Standard Model fields to supersymmetry multiplets in the manner described in Section 3.1. We also introduce a *hidden sector* with no direct coupling to quark, leptons, and Standard Model gauge bosons. Supersymmetry is spontaneously broken in this hidden sector. A weak interaction coupling the two sectors then induces a supersymmetry-breaking effective interaction for the Standard Model particles and their superpartners. If Λ is the mass scale of the hidden sector, the supersymmetry breaking mass terms induced for the Standard Model sector are of the order of

$$m \sim \frac{\langle F \rangle}{M} \sim \frac{\Lambda^2}{M} \; ; \qquad (11.158)$$

where M is the mass of the particle responsible for the weak connection between the two sectors. M is called the *messenger scale*. By default, the messenger is supergravity. Then $M = m_{\rm Pl}$ and $\Lambda \sim 10^{11}$ GeV. In this scenario, the superpartners acquire masses of the order of the parameter m in (11.158).

It remains true that the quarks, leptons, and gauge bosons cannot obtain mass until $SU(2) \times U(1)$ is broken. It is attractive to think that the symmetry-breaking terms that give mass to the superpartners cause $SU(2) \times U(1)$ to be spontaneously broken, at more or less the same scale. I will discuss a mechanism by which this can happen in Section 6.1. The weak interaction scale would then not be a fundamental scale in Nature, but rather one that arises dynamically from the hidden sector and its couplings.

The effective interaction that are generated by messenger exchange generally involve simple operators of low mass dimensions, to require the minimal number of powers of M in the denominator. These operators are *soft* perturbations of the theory, and so we say that the MSSM is completed by including *soft supersymmetry-breaking interactions*.

However, the supersymmetry-breaking terms induced in this model will not include all possible low-dimension operators. Since these interactions arise by coupling into a supersymmetry theory, they are formed by starting with a supersymmetric effective action and turning on F and D expectation values as spurions. Only a subset of the possible supersymmetry-breaking terms can be formed in this way [46]. By replacing a superfield Φ by

$\theta^T c\theta \langle F \rangle$, we can convert

$$\int d^4\theta\, K(\Phi,\phi) \to m^2 \phi^\dagger \phi$$

$$\int d^2\theta\, f(\Phi) W^T cW \to m\lambda^T c\lambda$$

$$\int d^2\, W(\Phi,\phi) \to B\phi^2 + A\phi^3 \qquad (11.159)$$

However, as long as the ϕ theory is renormalizable, we cannot generate the terms

$$m\psi^T c\psi\,, \quad C\phi^*\phi^2\,, \qquad (11.160)$$

by turning on expectation values for F and D fields. Thus, we cannot generate supersymmetry-breaking interactions that are mass terms for the fermion field of a chiral multiplet or non-holomorphic cubic terms for the scalar fields.

There is another difficulty with terms of the form (11.160). In models with Standard Model singlet scalar fields, which typically occur in concrete models, these two interactions can generate new quadratic divergences when they appear in loop diagrams [46].

Here is the most general supersymmetry-breaking effective Lagrangian that can be constructed following the rule just given that is consistent with the gauge symmetries of the Standard Model:

$$\begin{aligned}\mathcal{L}_{soft} = &-M_f^2|\widetilde{f}|^2 - \frac{1}{2} m_i \lambda_i^{Ta} c \lambda_i^a \\ &- (A_d y_d \widetilde{\overline{d}} H_{d\alpha} \epsilon_{\alpha\beta} \widetilde{Q}_\beta + A_e y_e \widetilde{\overline{e}} H_{d\alpha} \epsilon_{\alpha\beta} \widetilde{L}_\beta \\ &- A_u y_u \widetilde{\overline{u}} H_{u\alpha} \epsilon_{\alpha\beta} \widetilde{Q}_\beta - B\mu H_{d\alpha} \epsilon_{\alpha\beta} H_{u\beta}) - h.c. \qquad (11.161)\end{aligned}$$

I have made the convention of scaling the A terms with the corresponding Yukawa couplings and scaling the B terms with μ. The parameters A and B then have the dimensions of mass and are expected to be of the order of m in (11.158).

For most of the rest of these lectures, I will represent the effects of the hidden sector and supersymmetry breaking simply by adding (11.161) to the supersymmetric Standard Model. I will then consider the MSSM to be defined by

$$\mathcal{L} = \mathcal{L}_F + \mathcal{L}_D + \mathcal{L}_W + \mathcal{L}_{soft} \qquad (11.162)$$

combining the pieces from (11.82), (11.84), (11.143), (11.146), and (11.161).

There are two problems with this story. The first is the μ term in the MSSM superpotential. This a supersymmetric term, and so μ can be arbitrarily large. To build a successful phenomenology of the MSSM, however, we need to have μ of the order of the weak scale. Ideally, μ should be parametrically equal to (11.158).

There are simple mechanisms that can solve this problem. A fundamental theory that leads to the renormalizable Standard Model at low energies can also contain higher-dimension operators suppressed by the high-energy mass scale. Associate this scale with the messenger scale. Then a supersymmetric higher-dimension operator in the superpotential

$$\int d^2\theta \, \frac{1}{M} S^2 H_d H_u \tag{11.163}$$

leads to a μ term if S acquires a vacuum expectation value. If S is a hidden sector field, we could find [47]

$$\mu = \frac{\langle S^2 \rangle}{M} \sim \frac{\Lambda^2}{M}, \tag{11.164}$$

A supersymmetric higher dimension contribution to the Kähler potential

$$\int d^4\theta \, \frac{1}{M} \Phi^\dagger H_d H_u \tag{11.165}$$

leads to a μ term if Φ acquires a vacuum expectation value in its F term. If Φ is a hidden sector field, we could find [48]

$$\mu = \frac{\langle F_\Phi \rangle}{M} \sim \frac{\Lambda^2}{M}, \tag{11.166}$$

In models with weak-coupling dynamics, higher-dimension operators are associated with the string or Planck scale; then, these mechanisms work most naturally if supergravity is the mediator. However, it is also possible to apply these strategies in models with strong-coupling dynamics in the hidden sector at an intermediate scale.

Generating the μ term typically requires breaking all continuous R-symmetries of the model. This is unfortunate, because an R-symmetry might be helpful phenomenologically, for example, to keep gaugino masses small while allowing sfermion masses to become large, or because it might be difficult to break an R-symmetry using a particular explicit mechanism of supersymmetry breaking. In this case, it is necessary to add Standard Model singlet fields to the MSSM to allow all gaugino and Higgsino fields to acquire nonzero masses. Models of this type are presented in [49,50].

The second problem involves the flavor structure of the soft supersymmetry breaking terms. In writing (11.161), I did not write flavor indices. In principle, these terms could have flavor-mixing that is arbitrary in structure and different from that in (11.143). Then the flavor-mixing would not be transformed away when (11.143) is put into canonical form. However, flavor-mixing from the soft supersymmetry breaking terms is highly constrained by experiment. Contributions such as the one shown in Fig. 11.7 give contributions to K^0, D^0, and B^0 mixing, and to $\tau \to \mu\gamma$ and $\mu \to e\gamma$, that can be large compared to the measured values or limits. Theories of the origin of the soft terms in models of supersymmetry breaking should address this problem. For example, the models of *gauge-mediated* [52] and *anomaly-mediated* [53,54] supersymmetry breaking induce soft terms that depend only on the $SU(2) \times U(1)$ quantum number and are therefore automatically diagonal in flavor. A quite different solution, based on a extension of the MSSM with a continuous R-symmetry, is presented in [51].

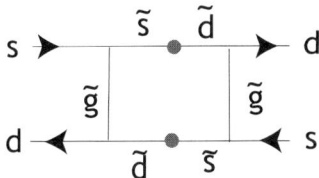

Fig. 11.7. A dangerous contribution to K-$\overline{K}$ mixing involving gluino exchange and flavor mixing in the squark mass matrix.

If I assume that the soft supersymmetry-breaking Lagrangian is diagonal in flavor but is otherwise arbitrary, it introduces 22 new parameters. With arbitrary flavor and CP violation, it introduces over 100 new parameters. This seems a large amount of parameter freedom. I feel that it is not correct, though, to think of these as new fundamental parameters in physics. The soft Lagrangian is computed from the physics of the hidden sector, and so we might expect that these parameters are related to one another as a part of a theory of supersymmetry breaking. Indeed, the values of these parameters are the essential data from which we will infer the properties of the hidden sector and its new high energy interactions.

If supersymmetry is discovered at the weak interaction scale, it will be a key problem to measure the coefficients in the soft Lagrangian and to understand their pattern and implications. Most of my discussion in the next two sections will be devoted to the question of how the soft parameters can be determined from data at the LHC and ILC.

11.4. The Mass Spectrum of the MSSM

11.4.1. Sfermion Masses

Our first task in this program is to ask how the parameters of the MSSM Lagrangian are reflected in the mass spectrum of the superparticles. The relation between the MSSM parameters and the particle masses is surprisingly complicated, even at the tree level. For each particle, we will need to collect all of the pieces of the Lagrangian (11.162) that can contribute to the mass term. Some of these will be direct mass contributions; others will contain Higgs fields and contribute to the masses when these fields obtain their vacuum expectation values. In this discussion, and in the remainder of these lectures, I will ignore all flavor-mixing.

Begin with the squark and slepton masses. For light quarks and leptons, we can ignore the fermion masses and Higgs couplings. Even with this simplification, though, there are two sources for the scalar masses. One is the soft mass term

$$\mathcal{L}_{soft} = -M_f^2 |\widetilde{f}|^2 \ . \tag{11.167}$$

The other comes from the D-term potential. The $SU(2)$ and $U(1)$ potentials contain the cross terms between the Higgs field and sfermion field contributions

$$\begin{aligned} V_D = &\frac{g^2}{2} \cdot 2 \cdot (H_d^\dagger \frac{\sigma^3}{2} H_d + H_u^\dagger \frac{\sigma^3}{2} H_u) \cdot (\widetilde{f}^* t^3 \widetilde{f}) \\ &+ \frac{g'^2}{2} \cdot 2 \cdot (-\frac{1}{2} H_d^\dagger H_d + \frac{1}{2} H_u^\dagger H_u) \cdot (\widetilde{f}^* Y \widetilde{f}) \ . \end{aligned} \tag{11.168}$$

To evalute this expression, we must insert the vacuum expectation values of the two Higgs fields. In terms of the angle β defined in (11.147), these are

$$\langle H_u \rangle = \begin{pmatrix} 0 \\ \frac{1}{\sqrt{2}} v \sin \beta \end{pmatrix} \qquad \langle H_d \rangle = \begin{pmatrix} \frac{1}{\sqrt{2}} v \cos \beta \\ 0 \end{pmatrix}, \tag{11.169}$$

where $v = 246$ GeV so that $m_W = gv/2$.

Inserting the Higgs vevs into the potential (11.168), we find

$$V_D = \tilde{f}^* [\frac{v^2}{4}(\cos^2\beta - \sin^2\beta)(g^2 I^3 - g'^2 Y)]\tilde{f}$$
$$= \tilde{f}^* [\frac{(g^2 + g'^2)v^2}{4}\cos 2\beta\,(I^3 - s_w^2(I^3 + Y))]\tilde{f}$$
$$= \tilde{f}^* [m_Z^2 \cos 2\beta (I^3 - s_w^2 Q)]\tilde{f}\,. \tag{11.170}$$

Then, if we define

$$\Delta_f = (I^3 - s_w^2 Q)\cos 2\beta\, m_Z^2\,, \tag{11.171}$$

the mass of a first- or second-generation sfermion takes the form

$$m_{\tilde{f}}^2 = M_{\tilde{f}}^2 + \Delta_f \tag{11.172}$$

when contributions proportional to fermion masses can be neglected. The D-term contribution can have interesting effects. For example, $SU(2)$ invariance of $M_{\tilde{f}}^2$ implies that

$$m^2(\tilde{e}) - m^2(\tilde{\nu}) = |\cos 2\beta|\, m_Z^2 > 0\,. \tag{11.173}$$

For some choices of parameters, the measurement of this mass difference is a good way to determine $\tan\beta$ [55].

For third-generation fermions, the contributions to the mass term from Yukawa couplings and from A terms can be important. For the $\tilde{b}$ and $\tilde{\bar{b}}$, these contributions come from the terms in the effective Lagrangian

$$|F_b|^2 + |F_{\bar{b}}|^2 = |y_b\,\langle H_d^0\rangle\tilde{b}|^2 + |y_b\tilde{\bar{b}}\,\langle H_d^0\rangle|^2 = m_b^2(|\tilde{b}|^2 + |\tilde{\bar{b}}|^2)$$
$$|F_{Hd}|^2 = (-\mu\,\langle H_d^0\rangle)^*(y_b\tilde{\bar{b}}\tilde{b}) + h.c. = -\mu m_b \tan\beta\,\tilde{\bar{b}}\tilde{b} + h.c.$$
$$-\mathcal{L}_{soft} = A_b y_b\,\langle H_d^0\rangle\tilde{\bar{b}}\tilde{b} = A_b m_b \tilde{\bar{b}}\tilde{b}\,. \tag{11.174}$$

In all, we find a mass matrix with mixing between the two scalar partners of the b quark,

$$\begin{pmatrix}\tilde{b}^* & \tilde{\bar{b}}\end{pmatrix}\mathcal{M}_b^2 \begin{pmatrix}\tilde{b} \\ \tilde{\bar{b}}^*\end{pmatrix}\,, \tag{11.175}$$

with

$$\mathcal{M}_b^2 = \begin{pmatrix} M_{\tilde{b}}^2 + \Delta_b + m_b^2 & m_b(A_b - \mu\tan\beta) \\ m_b(A_b - \mu\tan\beta) & M_{\tilde{\bar{b}}}^2 + \Delta_{\bar{b}} + m_b^2 \end{pmatrix} \tag{11.176}$$

The mass matrix for $\tilde{\tau}, \tilde{\bar{\tau}}$ has the same structure. For $\tilde{t}, \tilde{\bar{t}}$, replace $\tan\beta$ by $\cot\beta$.

The mixing terms in the mass matrices of the third-generation sfermions often play an important role in the qualitative physics of the whole SUSY model. Because of the mixing, one sfermion eigenstate is pushed down in mass. This state is often the lightest squark or even the lightest superparticle in the theory.

11.4.2. Gaugino and Higgsino Masses

In a similar way, we can compute the mass terms for the gauginos and Higgsinos. Since the gauginos and Higgsino have the same quantum numbers after $SU(2) \times U(1)$ breaking, they will mix. We have seen in Section 2.4 that this mixing plays an essential role in the working of the Higgs mechanism in the limit where soft supersymmetry breaking terms are turned off.

The charged gauginos and Higgsinos receive mass from three sources. First, there is a soft SUSY breaking term

$$-\mathcal{L}_{soft} = m_2 \widetilde{w}^{-T} c \widetilde{w}^+ \ . \tag{11.177}$$

The μ superpotential term contributes

$$-\mathcal{L}_W = \mu \widetilde{h}_d^{-T} c \widetilde{h}_u^+ \ . \tag{11.178}$$

The gauge kinetic terms contribute

$$-\mathcal{L} = \sqrt{2}\frac{g}{\sqrt{2}} \left(\langle H_d^0 \rangle \widetilde{w}^{+T} c \widetilde{h}_d^- + \langle H_u^0 \rangle \widetilde{w}^{-T} c \widetilde{h}_u^+ \right) \tag{11.179}$$

Inserting the Higgs field vevs from (11.169), we find the mass term

$$\begin{pmatrix} \widetilde{w}^{-T} & \widetilde{h}_d^{-T} \end{pmatrix} c\, m_C \begin{pmatrix} \widetilde{w}^+ \\ \widetilde{h}_u^+ \end{pmatrix} , \tag{11.180}$$

with

$$m_C = \begin{pmatrix} m_2 & \sqrt{2} m_W \sin\beta \\ \sqrt{2} m_W \cos\beta & \mu \end{pmatrix} . \tag{11.181}$$

The mass matrix for neutral gauginos and Higgsinos also receives contributions from these three sources. In this case, all four of the states

$$(\widetilde{b}, \widetilde{w}^0, \widetilde{h}_d^0, \widetilde{h}_u^0) \tag{11.182}$$

have the same quantum numbers after $SU(2) \times U(1)$ breaking and can mix together. The mass matrix is

$$m_N = \begin{pmatrix} m_1 & 0 & -m_Z c_\beta s_w & m_Z s_\beta s_w \\ 0 & m_2 & m_Z c_\beta c_w & -m_Z s_\beta c_w \\ -m_Z c_\beta s_w & m_Z c_\beta c_w & 0 & -\mu \\ m_Z s_\beta s_w & -m_Z s_\beta c_w & -\mu & 0 \end{pmatrix}. \quad (11.183)$$

The mass eigenstates in these systems are referred to collectively as *charginos* and *neutralinos*. The matrix (11.183) is complex symmetric, so it can be diagonalized by a unitary matrix V_0,[c]

$$m_N = V_0^* D_N V_0^\dagger. \quad (11.184)$$

I will denote the neutralinos as $\widetilde{N}_i^0$, $i = 1, \ldots, 4$, in order of mass with $\widetilde{N}_1^0$ the lightest. Elsewhere in the literature, you will see these states called $\widetilde{\chi}_i^0$ or $\widetilde{Z}_i^0$. The mass eigenstates are related to the weak eigenstates by the transformation

$$\begin{pmatrix} \widetilde{b}^0 \\ \widetilde{w}^0 \\ \widetilde{h}_d^0 \\ \widetilde{h}_u^0 \end{pmatrix} = V_0 \begin{pmatrix} \widetilde{N}_1 \\ \widetilde{N}_2 \\ \widetilde{N}_3 \\ \widetilde{N}_4 \end{pmatrix}. \quad (11.185)$$

Note that the diagonal matrix D_N in (11.184) may have negative or complex-valued elements. If that is true, the physical fermion masses of the $\widetilde{N}_i$ are the absolute values of the corresponding elements of D_N. The phases will appear in the three-point couplings of the $\widetilde{N}_i$ and can lead to observable interference effects. Complex phases in D_N would provide a new source of CP violation.

The chargino mass matrix (11.181) is not symmetric, so in general it is diagonalized by two unitary matrices

$$m_C = V_-^* D_C V_+^\dagger. \quad (11.186)$$

I will denote the charginos as $\widetilde{C}_i^\pm$, $i = 1, 2$, in order of mass with $\widetilde{C}_1^\pm$ the lighter. Elsewhere in the literature, you will see these states called $\widetilde{\chi}_i^\pm$ or $\widetilde{W}_i^\pm$. The mass eigenstates are related to the weak eigenstates by the transformation

$$\begin{pmatrix} \widetilde{w}^+ \\ \widetilde{h}_u^+ \end{pmatrix} = V_+ \begin{pmatrix} \widetilde{C}_1^+ \\ \widetilde{C}_2^+ \end{pmatrix}, \quad \begin{pmatrix} \widetilde{w}^- \\ \widetilde{h}_u^- \end{pmatrix} = V_- \begin{pmatrix} \widetilde{C}_1^- \\ \widetilde{C}_2^- \end{pmatrix}. \quad (11.187)$$

---
[c]Note that this formula is different from that which diagonalizes a Hermitian matrix. A detailed discussion of the diagonalization of mass matrices appearing in SUSY can be found in the Appendix of [56].

It should be noted that μ are must be nonzero. If $\mu = 0$, the determinant of (11.183) vanishes and so the lightest neutralino must be massless. This neutralino will also have a large Higgsino content and thus an order-1 coupling to the Z^0. It is excluded by searches for an excess of invisible Z^0 decays and for $Z^0 \to \widetilde{N}_1 \widetilde{N}_2$. The condition $\mu = 0$ also implies that the lightest chargino has a mass below the current limit of about 100 GeV.

Often, one studies models for which m_1, m_2, and μ are all large compared to m_W and m_Z. The off-diagonal elements that mix the gaugino and Higgsino states are of the order of m_W and m_Z. Thus, if the scale of masses generated by the SUSY breaking terms is large, the mixing is small and the individual eigenstates are mainly gaugino or mainly Higgsino. However, there are two distinct cases. The first is the *gaugino region*, where $m_1, m_2 < |\mu|$. In this region of parameter space, the lightest states $\widetilde{N}_1$, $\widetilde{C}_1$ are mainly gaugino, while the heavy neutralinos and charginos are mainly Higgsino. In the *Higgsino region*, $m_1, m_2 > |\mu|$, the situation is reversed and $\widetilde{N}_1$, $\widetilde{C}_1$ are mainly Higgsino. In this case, the two lightest neutralinos are almost degenerate. In Fig. 11.8, I show the mass eigenvalues as a function of the mass matrix parameters along a line in the parameter space on which the $\widetilde{N}_1$ has a fixed mass of 100 GeV. As we will see in Section 6.4, the exact makeup of the lightest neutralino as a mixture of gaugino and Higgsino components is important to the study of supersymmetric dark matter.

To summarize this discussion, I present in Fig. 11.9 the complete spectrum of new particles in the MSSM at a representative point in its parameter space. Notice that the third-generation sfermions are split off from the others in each group. Note also that the parameter point chosen is in the gaugino region. The lightest superparticle is the $\widetilde{N}_1$. I will discuss the spectrum of Higgs bosons in Section 6.2.

11.4.3. Renormalization Group Evolution of MSSM Parameters

The spectrum shown in Fig. 11.9 appears to have been generated by assigning random values to the soft SUSY breaking parameters. But, actually, I generated this spectrum by making very simple assumptions about the relationships of the soft parameters, at a high energy scale. Specifically, I assumed that the soft SUSY breaking gaugino masses and (separately) the sfermion masses were equal at the scale of grand unification. The structure that you see in the figure is generated by the renormalization group

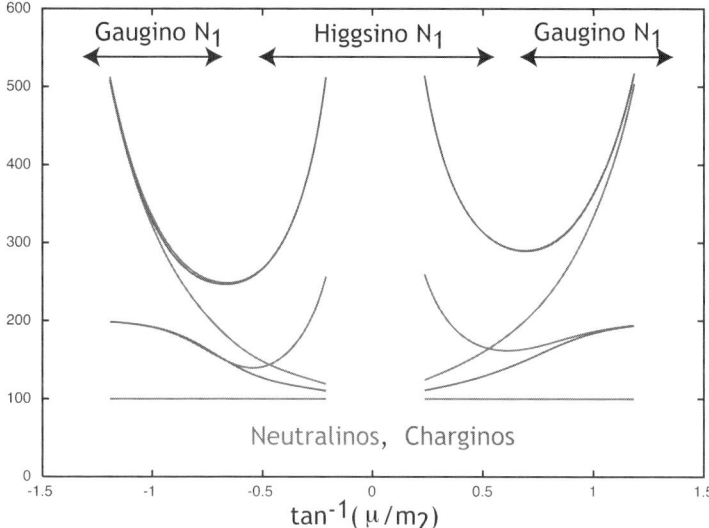

Fig. 11.8. Masses of the four neutralinos and two charginos along a line in the SUSY parameter space on which $m(\widetilde{N}_1^0) = 100$ GeV while the parameter μ moves from large negative to large positive values. The parameter m_1 is set to $m_1 = 0.5 m_2$. Note the approximate degeneracies in the extreme limits of the gaugino and Higgsino regions.

evolution of these parameters from the grand unification scale to the weak scale.

The renomalization group (RG) evolution of soft parameters is likely to play a very important role in the interpretation of measurements of the SUSY particle masses. Essentially, after measuring these masses, it will be necessary to decode the results by running the effective mass parameters up to a higher energy at which their symmetries might become more apparent. The situation is very similar to that of the Standard Model coupling constants, where a renormalization group analysis told us that the apparently random values (11.137) for the coupling constants at the weak scale actually corresponds to a unification of couplings at a much higher scale.

In this section, I will write the most basic RG equations for the soft gaugino and sfermion masses. One further effect, which involves the Yukawa couplings and is important for the third generation, will be discussed later in Section 6.1.

The RG equation for the gaugino masses is especially simple. This

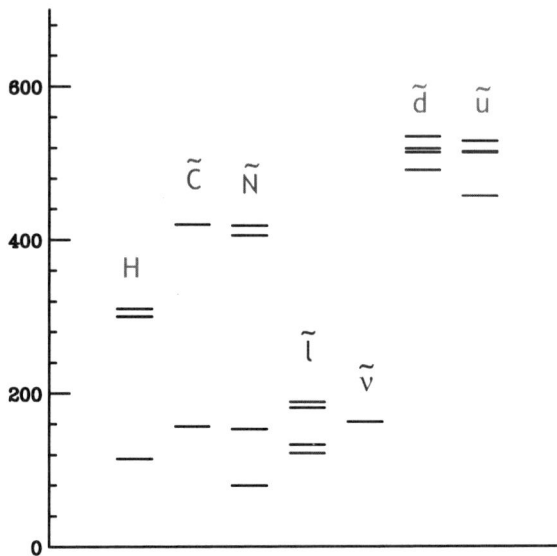

Fig. 11.9. Illustrative spectrum of supersymmetric particles. The columns contain, from the left, the Higgs bosons, the four neutralinos, the two charginos, the charged sleptons, the sneutrinos, the down squarks, and the up squarks. The gluino, not shown, is at about 800 GeV.

is because both the gaugino masses and the gauge couplings arise from the superpotential term (11.115), with the supersymmetry breaking terms arising as shown in (11.159). As I have already noted, this F-term receives a radiative correction proportional to the β function as a consequence of the trace anomaly [34,36]. The corrections are the same for the gauge boson field strength and the gaugino mass. Thus, if gaugino masses and couplings are generated at the scale M, they have the relation after RG running to the scale Q:

$$\frac{m_i(Q)}{m_i(M)} = \frac{\alpha_i(Q)}{\alpha_i(M)} \ . \tag{11.188}$$

If the F term that generates the soft gaugino masses is an $SU(5)$ singlet, the soft gaugino masses will be grand-unified at M. Then, running down to the weak scale, they will have the relation

$$m_1 : m_2 : m_3 = \alpha_1 : \alpha_2 : \alpha_3 = 0.5 : 1 : 3.5 \ . \tag{11.189}$$

This relation of soft gaugino masses is known as *gaugino unification*.

There are other models of the soft gaugino masses that also lead to gaugino unification. In *gauge-mediated SUSY breaking*, the dynamics responsible for SUSY breaking occurs at a scale much lower than the scale associated with mediation by supergravity. At this lower scale M_g (for example, 1000 TeV), some heavy particles with nontrivial $SU(3) \times SU(2) \times U(1)$ quantum numbers acquire masses from SUSY breaking. These fields then couple to gauginos and generate SUSY breaking masses for those particles through the diagram shown in Fig. 11.10(a). The heavy particles must fall into complete $SU(5)$ representations; otherwise, the coupling constant renormalization due to these particles between M_g and the grand unification scale would spoil the grand unification of the gauge couplings. Then the diagram in Fig. 11.10(a) generates soft gaugino masses proportional to $\alpha(M_g)$. Running these parameters down to the weak scale, we derive the relation (11.189) from this rather different mechanism.

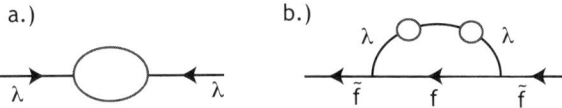

Fig. 11.10. Diagrams that generate the soft mass parameters in gauge mediated supersymmetry breaking: (a.) gaugino masses; (b.) sfermion masses.

Now let us turn to the RG running of soft scalar masses. In principle, there are two contributions, one from the RG rescaling of the soft mass term M_f^2 and one from RG evolution generating M_f^2 from the gaugino mass. The Feynman diagrams that contribute to the RG coefficients are shown in Fig. 11.11. The two one-loop diagrams proportional to M_f^2 cancel. The third diagram, involving the gaugino mass, gives the RG equation

$$\frac{dM_f^2}{d \log Q} = -\frac{2}{\pi} \sum_i \alpha_i(Q) C_2(r_i) m_i^2(Q) , \qquad (11.190)$$

with $i = 1, 2, 3$ and $C_2(r_i)$ the squared charge in the fermion representation r_i under the gauge group i. This equation leads to a positive contribution to M_f^2 as one runs the RG evolution from the messenger scale down to the weak scale. The effect is largest for squarks, for which the SUSY breaking mass is induced from the gluino mass.

As an example of this mechanism of mass generation, assume gaugino unification and assume that $M_f^2 = 0$ for all sfermions at the grand unifica-

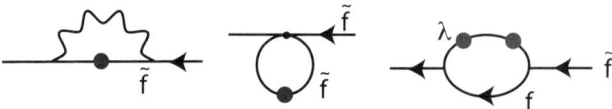

Fig. 11.11. Diagrams that generate the renormalization group evolution of the soft sfermion mass parameters M_f^2.

tion scale. Then the weak scale sfermion masses will be in the ratio
$$M(\widetilde{\overline{e}}) : M(\widetilde{e}) : M(\widetilde{\overline{d}}) : M(\widetilde{\overline{u}}) : M(\widetilde{d}, \widetilde{u}) : m_2$$
$$= 0.5 : 0.9 : 3.09 : 3.10 : 3.24 : 1 \qquad (11.191)$$

This model of fermion mass generation is called *no-scale* SUSY breaking. It has the danger that the lightest stau mass eigenstate could be lighter than than the $\widetilde{N}_1$, leading to problems for dark matter. This problem can be avoided by RG running above the GUT scale [57]. Alternatively, it might actually be that the lightest Standard Model superpartner is a long-lived stau that eventually decays to a tau and a gravitino [58,59].

In gauge-mediated SUSY breaking, the diagram shown in Fig. 11.10(b) leads to the qualitatively similar but distinguishable formula
$$M_f^2 = 2 \sum_i \alpha_i^3(M) C_2(r_i) \cdot \left(\frac{m_2}{\alpha_2}\right)^2 . \qquad (11.192)$$

Each model of SUSY breaking leads to its own set of relations among the various soft SUSY breaking parameters. In general, the relations are predicted for the parameters defined at the messenger scale and must be evolved to the weak scale by RG running to be compared with experiment. Figure 11.12 shows four different sets of high-scale boundary conditions for the RG evolution, and the corresponding evolution to the weak scale. If we can measure the weak-scale values, we could try to undo the evolution and recognize the pattern. This will be a very interesting study for the era in which superparticles are observed at high energy colliders.

There are some features common to these spectra that are general features of the RG evolution of soft parameters:

(1) The pairs of sleptons $\widetilde{\overline{e}}$ and $\widetilde{e}$ can easily acquire a significant mass difference from RG evolution, and they might also have a different initial condition. It is important to measure the mass ratio $m(\widetilde{\overline{e}})/m(\widetilde{e})$ as a diagnostic of the scheme of SUSY breaking.

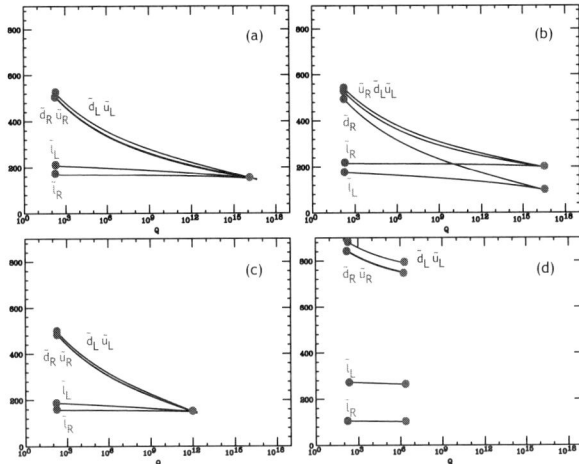

Fig. 11.12. Evolution of squark and slepton masses from the messenger scale down to the weak scale, for four different models of supersymmetry breaking: (a.) universal sfermion masses at the grand unification scale M_U; (b.) sfermion masses at M_U that depend on the $SU(5)$ representation; (c.) universal sfermion masses at an intermediate scale; (d.) gauge mediation from a sector of mass about 1000 TeV.

(2) Gaugino unification is a quantitative prediction of certain schemes of SUSY breaking. It is important to find out whether this relation is correct or not for the real spectrum of superparticles in Nature.

(3) When the RG effects on the squark masses dominate the values of M_f^2 from the initial condition, the various species of squark have almost the same mass and are much heavier than the sleptons. It is important to check whether most or all squarks appear at the same threshold.

11.5. The Measurement of Supersymmetry Parameters

11.5.1. Measurements of the SUSY Spectrum at the ILC

Now that we have discussed the physics that determines the form of the spectrum of superparticles, we turn to the question of how we would determine this spectrum experimentally. This is not as easy as it might seem. In this section, I will consider only models in which the dark matter particle is the $\widetilde{N}_1$, and all other SUSY particles decay to the $\widetilde{N}_1$. This neutral and weakly interacting particle would escape a collider detector unseen. Nevertheless, methods have been worked out not only to measure the masses of superparticles but also to determine mixing angles and other information needed to convert these masses to values of the underlying parameters of the MSSM Lagrangian.

Similar methods apply to other scenarios. For example, in models in which the neutralino decays to a particle with gravitational interactions, one would add that decay, if it is visible, to the analyses that I will present. It is possible in models of this type that the lightest Standard Model superpartner would be a charged slepton that is stable on the time scale of particle physics experiments. That scenario would produce very striking and characteristic events [58].

Most likely, this experimental study of the SUSY spectrum will begin in the next few years with the LHC experiments. However, at a hadron collider like the LHC, much of the kinematic information on superparticle production is missing and so special tricks are needed even to measure the spectrum. The study of supersymmetry should be much more straightforward at an e^+e^- collider such as the planned International Linear Collider (ILC). For this reason, I would like to begin my discussion of the experiments in this section by discussing SUSY spectrum measurements at e^+e^- colliders. More complete reviews of SUSY measurements at linear colliders can be found in [60,61].

I first discuss slepton pair production, beginning with the simplest process, $e^+e^- \to \widetilde{\mu}^+\widetilde{\mu}^-$ and considering successively the production of $\widetilde{\tau}$ and $\widetilde{e}$. Each step will bring in new complexities and will allow new measurements of the SUSY parameters.

The process $e^+e^- \to \widetilde{\mu}^+\widetilde{\mu}^-$, where $\widetilde{\mu}$ is the partner of either the left- or right-handed μ, can be analyzed with the simple formulae for scalar particle-antiparticle production. The cross section for pair production from polarized initial electrons and positrons to final-state scalars with definite $SU(2) \times U(1)$ quantum numbers is given by

$$\frac{d\sigma}{d\cos\theta} = \frac{\pi\alpha^2}{2s}\beta^3 \sin^2\theta\, |f_{ab}|^2\ , \qquad (11.193)$$

where

$$f_{ab} = 1 + \frac{(I_e^3 + s_w^2)(I_\mu^3 + s_w^2)}{c_w^2 s_w^2} \frac{s}{s - m_Z^2} \qquad (11.194)$$

and, in this expression, $I^3 = -\frac{1}{2}, 0$ for $a, b = L, R$. For the initial state, $a = L$ denotes the state $e_L^- e_R^+$ and $a = R$ denotes $e_R^- e_L^+$. For the final state, $b = L$ denotes the $\widetilde{\mu}$, $b = R$ the $\overline{\widetilde{\mu}}$. Notice that this cross section depends strongly on the polarization states:

$$\begin{aligned}|f_{ab}|^2 &= 1.69 \quad e_R^- e_L^+ \to \widetilde{\mu}^+ \widetilde{\mu}^- \\ &= 0.42 \quad e_L^- e_R^+ \to \widetilde{\mu}^+ \widetilde{\mu}^- \\ &= 0.42 \quad e_R^- e_L^+ \to \widetilde{\mu}^+ \widetilde{\mu}^- \\ &= 1.98 \quad e_L^- e_R^+ \to \widetilde{\mu}^+ \widetilde{\mu}^- \end{aligned} \qquad (11.195)$$

The angular distribution is characteristic of pair-production of a spin 0 particle; the normalization of the cross sections picks out the the correct set of $SU(2) \times U(1)$ quantum numbers.

If the smuon is light, its only kinematically allowed decay might be $\widetilde{\mu} \to \mu \widetilde{N}_1^0$. Even if the smuon is heavy, if the $\widetilde{N}_1$ is mainly gaugino, this decay should be important. As noted above, I am assuming that R-parity is conserved and that the $\widetilde{N}_1$ is the lightest particle in the superparticle spectrum. Then events with this decay on both sides will appear as

$$e^+ e^- \to \mu^+ \mu^- + (\text{missing } E \text{ and } p) \qquad (11.196)$$

The spectrum of the observed muons is very simple. Since the $\widetilde{\mu}$ has spin 0, it decays isotropically in its own rest frame. In $e^+ e^-$ production at a definite center of mass energy, the $\widetilde{\mu}$ is produced at a definite energy, and thus with a definite boost, in the lab. The boost of an isotropic distribution is a flat distribution in energy. So, the muon energy distribution should be flat, between endpoints determined by kinematics, as shown in the idealized Fig. 11.13.

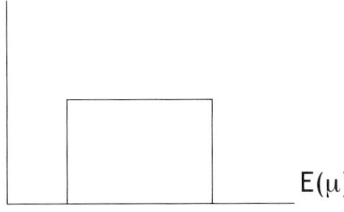

Fig. 11.13. Schematic energy distribution of final-state muons in $e^+ e^- \to \widetilde{\mu}^+ \widetilde{\mu}^-$.

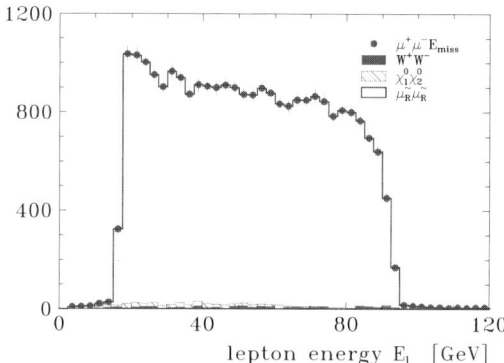

Fig. 11.14. Energy distribution of muons from $e^+e^- \to \widetilde{\mu}^- \widetilde{\mu}^+$ at the ILC, in a simulation by Blair and Martyn that includes realistic momentum resolution and beam effects [63].

The endpoint positions are simple functions of the mass of the $\widetilde{\mu}$ and the mass of the $\widetilde{N}_1$,

$$E_\pm = \gamma(1 \pm \beta) \frac{m^2(\widetilde{\mu}) - m^2(\widetilde{N}_1)}{2m(\widetilde{\mu})} , \qquad (11.197)$$

where $\gamma = E_{\rm CM}/2m(\widetilde{\mu})$, $\beta = (1 - 4m^2(\widetilde{\mu})/E_{\rm CM}^2)^{1/2}$. If we can identify both endpoint positions, we can solve for the two unknown masses. Figure 11.14 shows a simulation of the reconstructed smuon energy distribution from $\widetilde{\mu}$ pair production at the ILC [63]. The high-energy edges of the distributions are rounded because of initial-state radiation in the e^+e^- collision. The experimenters expect to be able to measure this effect and correct for it. Then they should obtain values of the smuon mass to an accuracy of about one hundred MeV, or one part per mil.

A similar analysis applies to $e^+e^- \to \widetilde{\tau}^+\widetilde{\tau}^-$, but there are several complications. First, for the τ system, mixing between the $\widetilde{\tau}$ and the $\widetilde{\widetilde{\tau}}$ might be important, especially if $\tan\beta$ is large. The production cross sections are affected directly by the mixing. For example, to compute the pair-production of the lighter $\widetilde{\tau}$ mass eigenstate from a polarized initial state, $e_R^- e_L^+ \to \widetilde{\tau}_1^- \widetilde{\tau}_1^+$, we must generalize (11.193) to

$$\frac{d\sigma}{d\cos\theta} = \frac{\pi\alpha^2}{2s} \beta^3 \sin^2\theta \, |f_{R1}|^2 , \qquad (11.198)$$

where

$$f_{R1} = f_{RR} \cos^2 \theta_\tau + f_{RL} \sin^2 \theta_\tau \qquad (11.199)$$

and θ_τ is the mixing angle associated with the diagonalization of the $\widetilde{\tau}$ case of (11.176).

Second, while the $\widetilde{\widetilde{\tau}}^-$ can decay to $\tau_R^- \widetilde{b}$ through gauge couplings, this weak eigenstate can also decay to $\tau_L^- \widetilde{h}_d$ through terms proportional to the Yukawa coupling. Both decay amplitudes contribute to the observable decay $\widetilde{\tau}_1 \to \tau \widetilde{N}_1^0$. With the $\widetilde{\tau}$ mixing angle fixed from the measurement of the cross section, the τ polarization in $\widetilde{\tau}$ decays can be used to determine the mixing angles in the diagonalization of the neutralino mass matrix (11.183) [62].

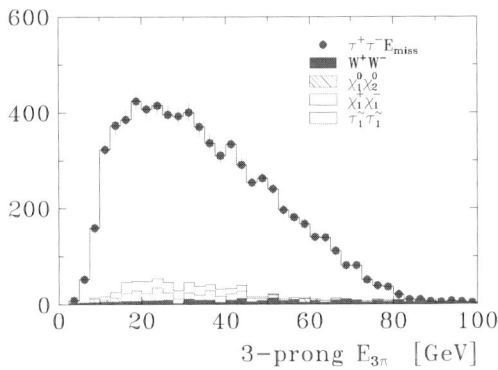

Fig. 11.15. Energy distribution of the three-pion system from $e^+e^- \to \widetilde{\tau}_1^- \widetilde{\tau}_1^+$ at the ILC, with a τ decay to 3π, in a simulation by Blair and Martyn that includes realistic momentum resolution and beam effects. [63].

In Fig. 11.15, I show the distribution of total visible energy in $\widetilde{\tau} \to 3\pi + \nu + \widetilde{N}_1^0$ at the ILC. Though there is no longer a sharp feature at the kinematic endpoint, it is still possible to accurately determine the $\widetilde{\tau}$ mass by fitting the shape of this distribution.

The physics of $e^+e^- \to \widetilde{e}^+\widetilde{e}^-$ brings in further new features. In this case, there is a new Feyman diagram, involving t-channel neutralino exchange. The two diagrams contributing to the cross section for this process are shown in Fig. 11.16. The t-channel diagram turns out to be the more important one, dominating the s-channel gauge boson exchange and generating a large forward peak in selectron production. The cross section for

$e_R^- e_L^+ \to \tilde{e}^- \tilde{e}^+$ is given by another generalization of (11.193),

$$\frac{d\sigma}{d\cos\theta} = \frac{\pi\alpha^2}{2s} \beta^3 \sin^2\theta |\mathcal{F}_{RR}|^2 , \qquad (11.200)$$

where

$$\mathcal{F}_{RR} = f_{RR} - \sum_i \left|\frac{V_{01i}}{c_w}\right|^2 \frac{s}{m_i^2 - t} , \qquad (11.201)$$

with the sum running over neutralino mass eigenstates. The factor V_{01i} is a matrix element of the unitary matrix introduced in (11.184).

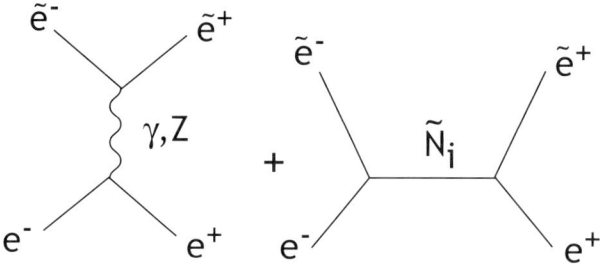

Fig. 11.16. Feynman diagrams contributing to $e^+ e^- \to \tilde{e}^- \tilde{e}^+$.

The t-channel diagram also allows new processes such as $e_L^- e_L^+ \to \tilde{e}^- \tilde{e}^+$. Note the correlation of the initial-state electron and position spins with the identities of the final-state selectrons. A complete set of polarized cross sections for selectron pair production in $e^+ e^-$ and $e^- e^-$ collisions can be found in [64].

The cross sections for chargino and neutralino pair production in $e^+ e^-$ collisions are somewhat more complicated, but still there are interesting things to say about these processes. Chargino pair production is given by the Feynman diagrams shown in Fig. 11.17. These diagrams are just the supersymmetric analogues of the diagrams for $e^+ e^- \to W^+ W^-$. As in that process, the most charcteristic final states are those with a hadronic decay on one side of the event and a leptonic decay on the other side, for example,

$$\tilde{C}_1^+ \to \ell^+ \nu \tilde{N}_1^0 , \quad \tilde{C}_1^- \to d\bar{u}\tilde{N}_1^0 . \qquad (11.202)$$

A typical event of this kind is shown in Fig. 11.18.

The chargino and neutralino production cross sections have a strong dependence on the mixing angles in (11.184) and (11.186) and offer a number

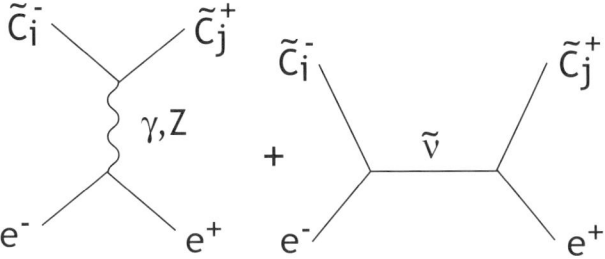

Fig. 11.17. Feynman diagrams contributing to $e^+e^- \to \widetilde{C}_i^- \widetilde{C}_j^+$.

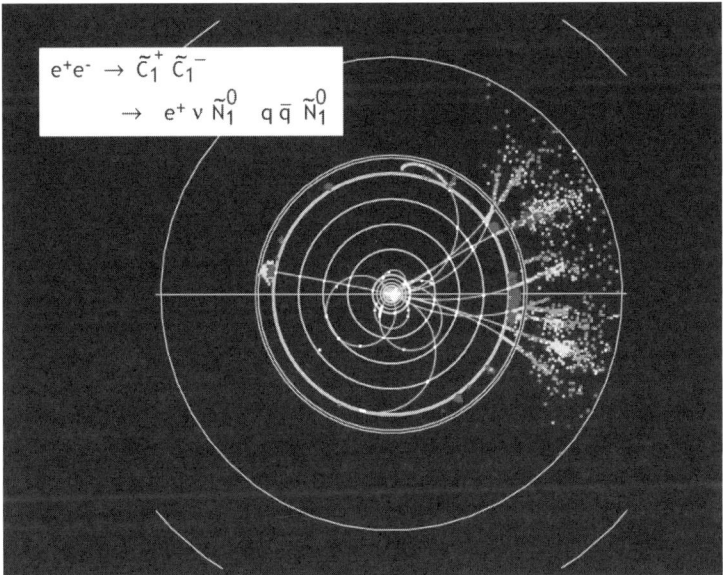

Fig. 11.18. A simulated chargino pair production event at the ILC [65].

of strategies for the determination of these mixing angles. Let me present one such strategy here. Consider the reaction from a polarized initial state $e_R^- e_L^+ \to \widetilde{C}_1^- \widetilde{C}_1^+$. Since we have an initial e_R^-, the t-channel diagram vanishes because the right-handed electron does not couple to the neutrino. Now simplify the s-channel diagram by considering the limit of high energies, $s \gg m_Z^2$. In this limit, it is a good approximation to work with weak gauge eigenstates (B^0, W^0) rather than the mass eigenstates (γ, Z^0). The weak eigenstate basis gives a nice simplification. The initial e_R^- couples only to B^0. But $\widetilde{w}^\pm$ couple only to W^0, so at high energy the s-channel diagram gets contributions only from the Higgsino components of the $\widetilde{C}_1^-$ and $\widetilde{C}_1^+$ eigenstates. If we go to still higher energies, $s \gg m(\widetilde{C}_1)^2$, there is a further simplification. The cross section for $\widetilde{h}_R^- \widetilde{h}_L^+$ production is forward-peaked, and the cross section for $\widetilde{h}_L^- \widetilde{h}_R^+$ production is backward-peaked. Then, the cross section for $e_R^- e_L^+ \to \widetilde{C}_1^- \widetilde{C}_1^+$ takes the form

$$\frac{d\sigma}{d\cos\theta} \sim \frac{\pi\alpha^2}{8c_w^2 s}\left[|V_{+21}|^4(1+\cos\theta)^2 + |V_{-21}|^2(1-\cos\theta)^2\right]. \quad (11.203)$$

In this limit, it is clear that we can read off both of the mixing angles in (11.186) from the shape of this cross section.

The use of high-energy limits simplified this analysis, but the sentivity of this cross section to the chargino mixing angles is not limited to high energy. Even relatively close to threshold, the polarized cross sections for chargino production depend strongly on the chargino mixing angles and can be used to determine their values. In Fig. 11.19, I show contours of constant cross section for $e_R^- e_L^+ \to \widetilde{C}_1^- \widetilde{C}_1^+$ in the (m_2, μ) plane (for $\tan\beta = 4$ and assuming gaugino unification) [66]. The value of this cross section is always a good measure of whether the SUSY parameters in Nature put us in the gaugino or the Higgsino region of Fig. 11.8.

11.5.2. Observation of SUSY at the LHC

Now we turn to supersymmetry production processes at the LHC. This subject, though more difficult, has immediate importance, since the LHC experiments are just about to begin.

The reactions that produce superparticles are typically much more complicated at hadron colliders than at lepton colliders. This is true for several reasons. High energy collisions of hadrons are intrinsically more complicated because the final states include the fragments of the initial hadrons that do not participate in the hard reaction. More importantly, the dominant reactions at hadron colliders are those that involve strongly interacting superparticles. This means that the primary particles are typically the heavier ones in the spectrum, which then decay in several steps. In addition, large backgrounds from QCD obscure the signatures of supersymmetric particle production in many channels.

Because of these difficulties, there is some question whether SUSY particle production can be observed at the LHC. However, as I will explain,

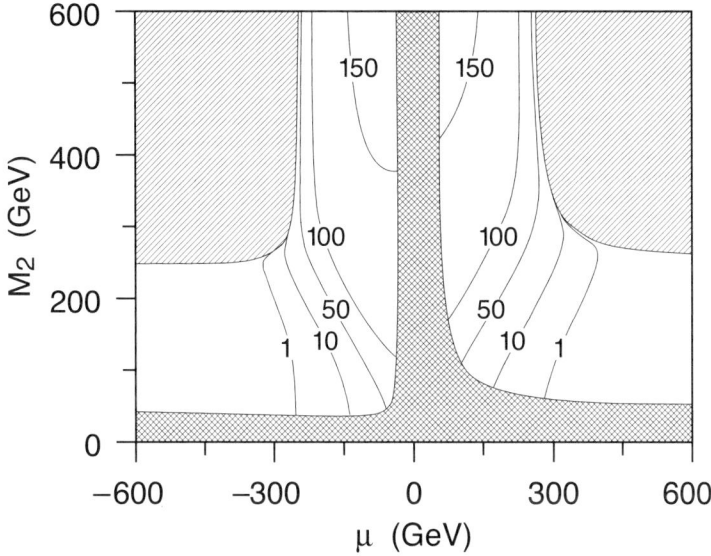

Fig. 11.19. Contours of constant cross section for the process $e_R^- e_L^+ \to C_1^- C_1^+$ (in fb, for $E_{\rm CM} = 500$ GeV), as a function of the underlying SUSY parameters [66]. The region shown is that in which the lightest chargino mass varies from 50 to 200 GeV. For fixed $\widetilde{C}_1^+$ mass, the cross section increases from zero to about 150 fb as we move from the gaugino region into the Higgsino region.

the signatures of supersymmetry are still expected to be striking and characteristic. It is not so clear, though, to what extent it is possible to measure the parameters of the SUSY Lagrangian, as I have described can be done from ILC experiments. This is an important study that still offers much room for new ideas.

The discovery of SUSY particles at the LHC and the measurement of SUSY parameters has been analyzed with simulations at a number of parameter points. Collections of interesting studies can be found in [63,67,68].

The dominant SUSY production processes at the LHC are

$$gg \to \widetilde{g}\widetilde{g}, \widetilde{q}\widetilde{q}^* \qquad gq \to \widetilde{g}\widetilde{q} \qquad (11.204)$$

These cross sections are large—tens of pb in typical cases. The values of numerous SUSY production cross sections at the LHC are shown in Fig. 11.20 [70].

We have seen that the squarks and gluinos are typically the heaviest

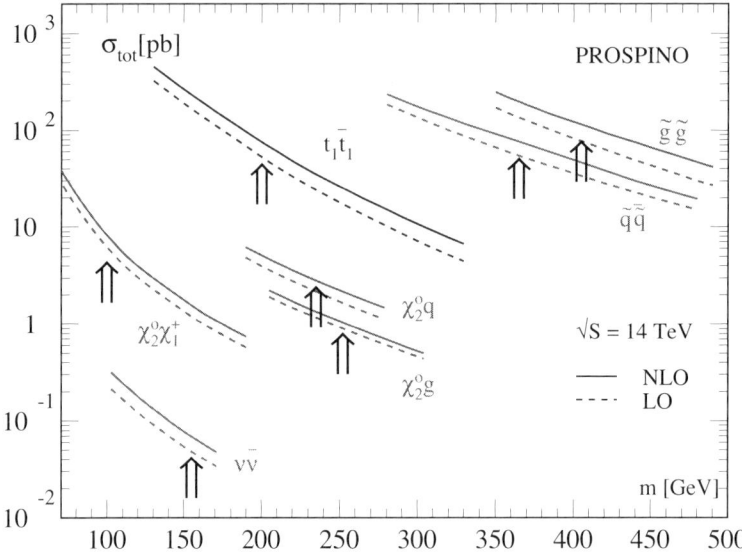

Fig. 11.20. Cross sections for the pair-production of supersymmetric particles at the LHC, from [70].

particles in the supersymmetry spectrum. The gluinos and squarks thus will decay to lighter superparticles. Some of these decays are simple, e.g.,

$$\widetilde{q} \to \overline{q}\widetilde{N}_1^0 \ . \tag{11.205}$$

However, other decays can lead to complex decay chains such as

$$\widetilde{q} \to qN_2^0 \to q(\ell^+\ell^-)\widetilde{N}_1^0 \ , \qquad \widetilde{g} \to u\overline{d}C_1^+ \to u\overline{d}W^+\widetilde{N}_1^0 \ . \tag{11.206}$$

With the assumptions that R-parity is conserved and that the N_1^0 is the LSP, all SUSY decay chains must end with the N_1^0, which is stable and very weakly interacting. SUSY production processes at hadron colliders then have unbalanced visible momentum, accompanied by multiple jets and, possibility, isolated leptons or W and Z bosons. Momentum balance along the beam direction cannot be checked at hadron colliders, because fragments of the initial hadrons exit along the beam directions, but an imbalance of transverse momentum will be visible and can be a characteristic signature of new physics. SUSY events contain this signature and the general large activity characteristic of heavy particle production. A simulated event of this type is shown in Fig. 11.21.

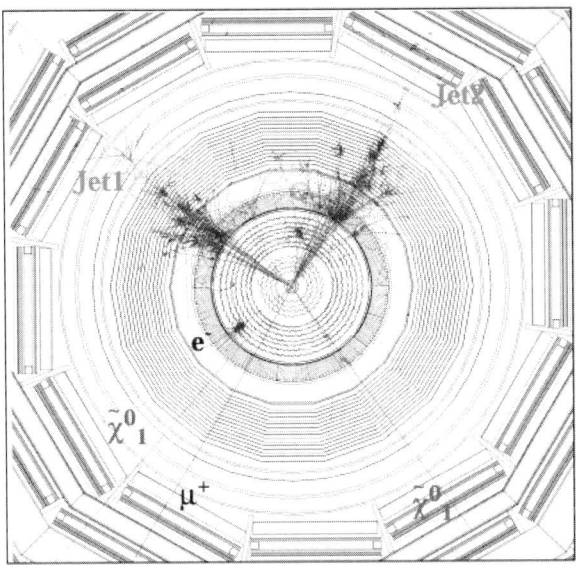

Fig. 11.21. Simulated SUSY particle production event in the CMS detector at the LHC [69].

Figure 11.22 shows a set of estimates given by Tovey and the ATLAS collaboration of the discovery potential for SUSY as a function of the LHC luminosity [71]. The most important backgrounds come from processes that are themselves relatively rare Standard Model reactions with heavy particle production,

$$pp \to (W, Z, t\bar{t}) + \text{jets} . \tag{11.207}$$

With some effort, we can experimentally normalize and control these backgrounds and reliably discovery SUSY production as a new physics process. In the figure, the contours for 5σ excesses of events above these backgrounds for various signatures of SUSY events are plotted as a function of the so-called 'mSUGRA' parameters. The SUSY models considered are defined as follows: Assume gaugino unification with a universal gaugino mass $m_{1/2}$ at the grand unification scale. Assume also that all scalar masses, including the Higgs boson mass parameters, are unified at the grand unification scale at the value m_0. Assume that the A parameter is universal at the grand unification scale; in the figures, the value $A = 0$ is used. Fix the value of $\tan \beta$ at the weak scale. Then it is possible to solve for μ and B, up to a sign, from the condition that electroweak symmetry is broken in such a way as to give the observed value of the Z^0 mass. (I will describe this calculation in Section 6.1.) This gives a 4-parameter subspace of the full 24-dimensional parameter space of the CP- and flavor-conserving MSSM, with the parameters

$$m_0 \,,\, m_{1/2} \,,\, A \,,\, \tan\beta \,,\, \text{sign}(\mu) \,. \qquad (11.208)$$

This subspace is often used to express the results of phenomenological analyses of supersymmetry. In interpreting such results, one should remember that this choice of parameters is used for simplicity rather than being motivated by physics.

The figure shows contours below which the various signatures of supersymmetry significantly modify the Standard Model expectations. For clarity, the contours of constant squark and gluino mass are also plotted. The left-hand plot shows Tovey's results for the missing transverse momentum plus multijets signature at various levels of LHC integrated luminosity. It is remarkable that, in the models in which the squark or gluino mass is below 1 TeV, SUSY should be discoverable with a data sample equivalent to a small fraction of a year of running. The right-hand plot shows the contours for the discovery of a variety of SUSY signals, with up to three leptons plus jets plus missing transverse momentum, with roughly one year of data at the initial design luminosity. The signals are, as I have described, relatively robust with repect to uncertainties in the Standard Model backgrounds. This makes it very likely that, if SUSY is really present in Nature as the explanation of electroweak symmetry breaking, we will discover it at the LHC.

The general characteristics of SUSY events also allow us to estimate the SUSY mass scale in a relatively straightforward way. In Fig. 11.23, I show a correlation pointed out by Hinchliffe and collaborators [72] between the lighter of the squark and gluino masses and the variable

$$M_{eff} = \not{E}_T + \sum_1^4 E_{Ti} \qquad (11.209)$$

given by the sum of the transverse momenta of the four highest E_T jets together with the value of the missing transverse momentum. The correlation applies reasonably well to mSUGRA models. In other models with smaller mass gaps between the squarks and the lightest neutralino, this relation can break down, but M_{eff} still measures the mass difference between the squark or gluino and the $\widetilde{N}_1^0$ [73]. Some more sophisticated techniques for

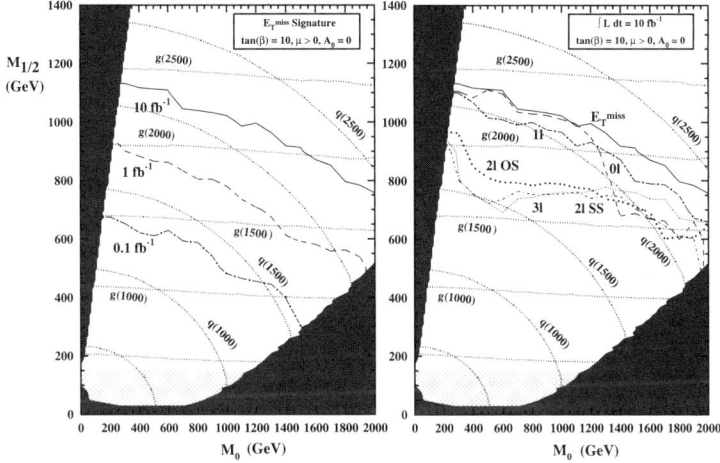

Fig. 11.22. Estimates by the ATLAS collaboration of the observability of various signatures of SUSY at the LHC. The plots refer to models with grand unification and universal sfermion and gaugino masses M_0 and $M_{1/2}$. The left-hand plot shows the region of this parameter space in which it is possible to detect the signature of missing E_T plus multiple jets at various levels of integrated luminosity. The right-hand plot shows the region of this parameter space in which it is possible to detect an excess of events with one or more leptons in addition to jets and missing E_T [71].

determining mass scales in SUSY models from global kinematic variables are described in [74].

11.5.3. Measurements of the SUSY Spectrum at the LHC

So far, I have only discussed the observation of the qualitative features of the SUSY model from global measures of the properties of events. Now I would like to give some examples of analyses in which specific details of the SUSY spectrum are measured with precision at the LHC. The examples that I will discuss involve the decay chain

$$\widetilde{q} \to q \widetilde{N}_2^0 \ , \quad \widetilde{N}_2^0 \to \widetilde{N}_1^0 \ell^+ \ell^- \ , \qquad (11.210)$$

which is typically seen in models in which the gluino is heavier than the squarks and the LSP is gaugino-like.

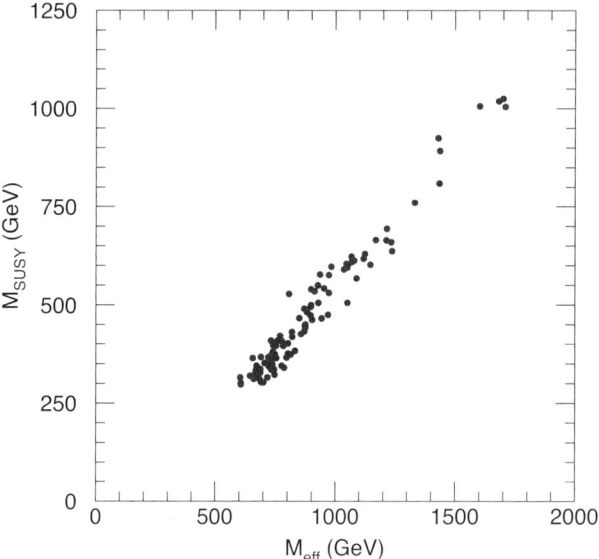

Fig. 11.23. Correlation between the value of the observable (11.209) and the lighter of the squark and gluino masses, from [72].

The decay of the N_2^0 can proceed by any of the mechanisms:

$$\widetilde{N}_2^0 \to \ell^\pm + \widetilde{\ell}^\mp \ , \ \widetilde{\ell}^\mp \to \ell^\mp \widetilde{N}_1^0$$
$$\widetilde{N}_2^0 \to \widetilde{N}_1^0 Z^0 \ , \ Z^0 \to \ell^+ \ell^-$$
$$\widetilde{N}_2^0 \to \widetilde{N}_1^0 Z^{0*} \ , \ Z^{0*} \to \ell^+ \ell^- \ . \qquad (11.211)$$

The last line indicates a virtual Z^0, decaying off-shell. In a model with gaugino unification and heavy Higgsinos, $\widetilde{N}_2$ is mainly $\widetilde{w}^0$ and $\widetilde{N}_1$ is mainly $\widetilde{b}^0$. Then these modes are preferred in the order listed as long as they are kinematically allowed. If the slepton decay is allowed, this is the dominant model. Otherwise, the decay to $\widetilde{N}_1 Z^0$ or other open two-body decays dominate. If no two-body decays are open, the $\widetilde{N}_2$ must decay through three-body processes such as the last line of (11.211).

The decay to an on-shell Z^0 is hard to work with [75], but the other two cases can be explored in depth. It is useful to begin with the *Dalitz plot* associated with the 3-body $(\widetilde{N}_1, \ell^+, \ell^-)$ system. Let

$$x_0 = \frac{2E(\widetilde{N}_1)}{m(\widetilde{N}_2)} \ , \quad x_+ = \frac{2E(\ell^+)}{m(\widetilde{N}_2)} \ , \quad x_- = \frac{2E(\ell^-)}{m(\widetilde{N}_2)} \ , \qquad (11.212)$$

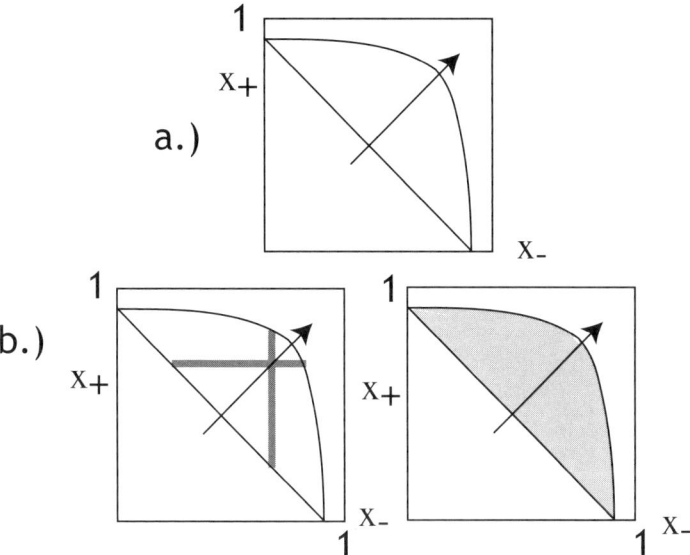

Fig. 11.24. The Dalitz plot describing 3-body neutralino decays, $\widetilde{N}_2^0 \to \widetilde{N}_1^0 \ell^+ \ell^-$.

where the energies are measured in the rest frame of the N_2. The three variables are related by

$$x_0 + x_1 + x_2 = 2 \ . \tag{11.213}$$

The three-body decay phase space is given by

$$\int d\Pi_3 = \frac{m^2(\widetilde{N}_2)}{128\pi^3} \int dx_+ \, dx_- \ ; \tag{11.214}$$

that is, phase space is flat in the variables (11.212). The basic kinematic identities involving the Dalitz plot variables are straightforward to work out, especially if we ignore the masses of the leptons. The kinematically allowed region is a wedge of the (x_+, x_-) plane bounded by the curves

$$x_+ + x_- = 1 - (m(\widetilde{N}_1)/m(\widetilde{N}_2))^2$$
$$(1 - x_+)(1 - x_-) = (m(\widetilde{N}_1)/m(\widetilde{N}_2))^2 \ , \tag{11.215}$$

as shown in Fig. 11.24(a). The invariant masses of two-body combinations are given in terms of the x_a by

$$\frac{m^2(\widetilde{N}_1 \ell^\pm)}{m^2(\widetilde{N}_2)} = (1 - x_\mp) \ , \quad \frac{m^2(\ell^+ \ell^-)}{m^2(\widetilde{N}_2)} = (1 - \frac{m(\widetilde{N}_1)^2}{m(\widetilde{N}_2)^2}) \ . \tag{11.216}$$

I am assuming that the $\widetilde{N}_1$ is stable and weakly interacting. In this case, the $\widetilde{N}_1$ will not be observed in the LHC experiments, and also the frame of the $\widetilde{N}_2$ cannot be readily determined. The only property of this system that is straightforward to measure is the two-body invariant mass $m(\ell^+\ell^-)$. So it is interesting to note that the distribution of this quantity distinguishes the first and third cases in (11.211), in the manner shown in Fig. 11.24(b). In the case of a two-body decay to an intermediate slepton, the decays populate two lines on the Dalitz plot, leading to a sharp discontinuity at the kinematic endpoint. In the case of a three-body decay, the events fill the whole Dalitz plot, producing a distribution with a slope at the endpoint. With a good understanding of the detector resolution in the dilepton invariant mass, these cases can be distinguished experimentally.

In the three-body case, the endpoint of the dilepton mass distribution is exactly

$$m(\widetilde{N}_2) - m(\widetilde{N}_1) , \qquad (11.217)$$

so the observable mass distribution gives a precise measurement of this SUSY mass difference. The shape of the spectrum has more information. For example, for heavy slepton masses, the shape is distinctly different for gaugino-like or Higgsino-like neutralinos. Figure 11.25(a) shows the dilepton mass distribution for an mSUGRA parameter set for which the lightest two neutralinos are gaugino-like [72]. Figure 11.25(b) shows this distribution for a parameter set in which the two lightest neutralinos are Higgsino-like [73].

At the endpoint, the dilepton mass is maximal, and this requires that both the dilepton pair and the N_1 are at rest in the frame of the N_2. By measuring the four-vectors of the leptons, we would then know the N_1 and N_2 four-vectors, up to knowledge of the N_1 mass. It is possible to obtain this mass approximately from other measurements, for example, from the kinematics of $\widetilde{q}$ decays directly to N_1. With this information, we could determine the N_2 four-vector. Now the problem of missing momentum is solved. By adding observed jets to the N_2 four-vector, it is possible to find squarks as resonances [72]. Figure 11.26 shows the result of such an analysis for the SUSY parameter set of Fig. 11.25. The peak just below 300 GeV is a reconstructed $\widetilde{b}$ squark.

The two-body case of $\widetilde{N}_2$ decay is even nicer. In this case, we can see from the right-hand figure in Fig. 11.24(b) that the endpoint of the dilepton mass distribution is not located at the mass difference (11.217) but instead

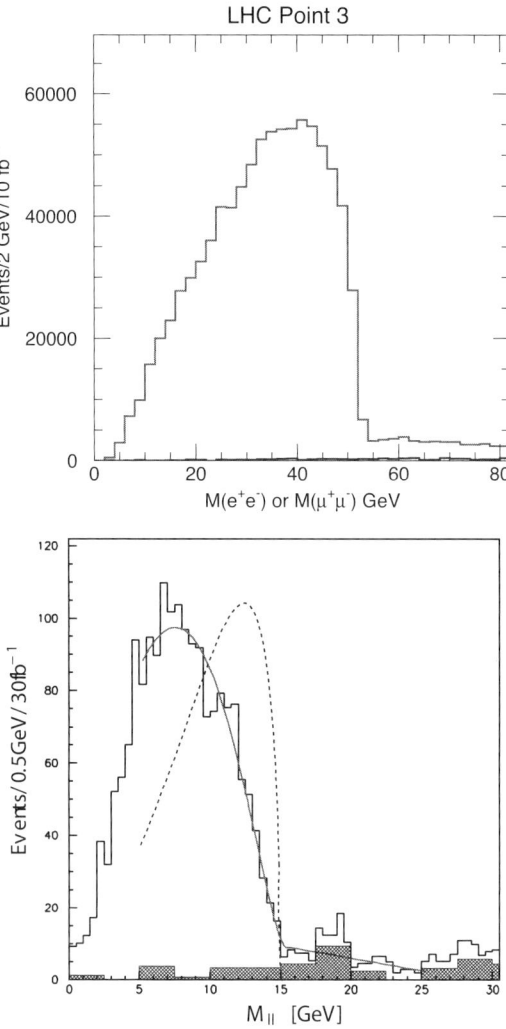

Fig. 11.25. Distribution of the dilepton invariant mass in two supersymmetry models with 3-body neutralino decays: (a.) a model with gaugino-like neutralinos [72], (b.) a model with Higgsino-like neutralinos [73]. In the second figure, the dashed curve indicates the $m(\ell^+\ell^-)$ spectrum expected for gaugino-like neutralinos with the same mass splitting.

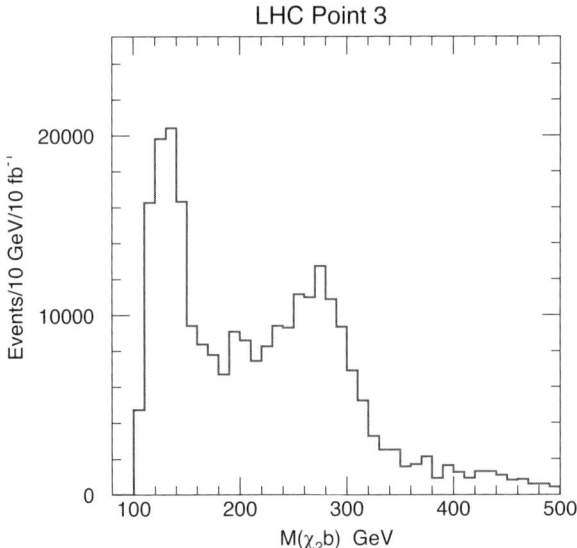

Fig. 11.26. Reconstruction of a squark in the model of Fig. 11.25(a) by combining a dilepton pair at the endpoint of the $m(\ell^+\ell^-)$ distribution, the $\widetilde{N}_1^0$ in the same frame with mass determined from kinematics, and a b-tagged quark jet.

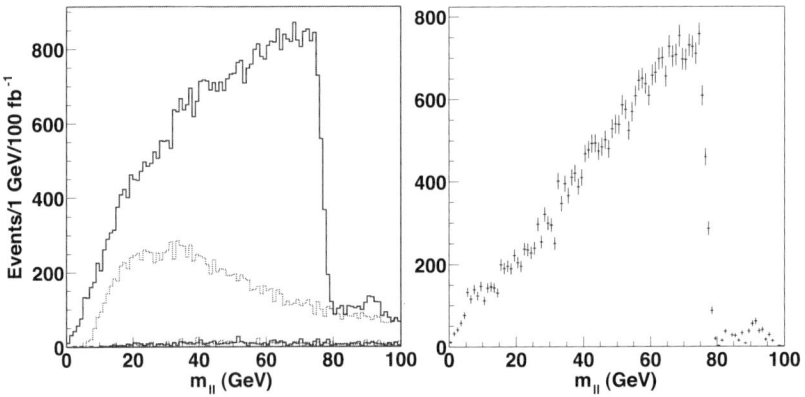

Fig. 11.27. Dilepton mass distribution in a model with two-body $\widetilde{N}_2$ decays, from [63]. The left-hand plot shows the dilepton mass distributions for opposite-sign same-flavor dileptons (solid) and for opposite-sign opposite-flavor dileptons (dashed). The lower histograms give the estimates of the Standard Model background. The right-hand plot shows the difference of the two distributions.

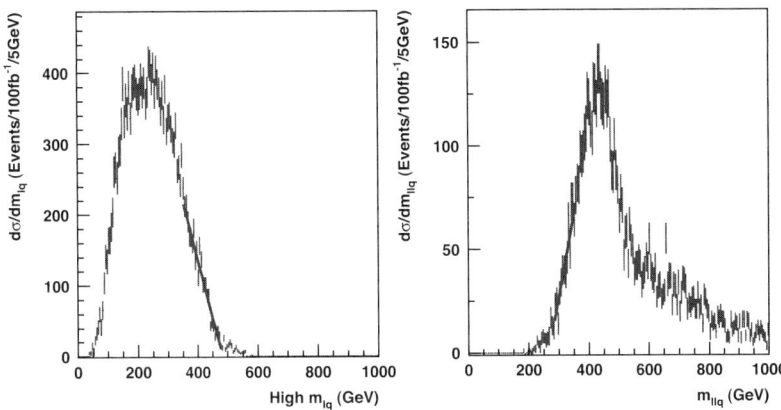

Fig. 11.28. Distributions of mass combinations of leptons and high-p_T jets showing kinematic endpoints in the analysis of [76]: (a.) the higher $m(q\ell)$ combination; (b.) the $m(q\ell^+\ell^-)$ distribution.

at the smaller value

$$m(\ell^+\ell^-) = m(\widetilde{N}_2)\sqrt{1 - \frac{m^2(\widetilde{\ell})}{m^2(\widetilde{N}_2)}}\sqrt{1 - \frac{m^2(\widetilde{N}_1)}{m^2(\widetilde{\ell})}} \ . \tag{11.218}$$

Figure 11.27 shows an example of the dilepton spectrum from a SUSY parameter point in this region [63] The decay $\widetilde{q} \to qN_2$ is also a two-body decay, and there are similar kinematic relations for the upper and lower endpoints of the $(q\ell)$ and $(q\ell\ell)$ invariant mass distributions. These endpoints are likely to be visible in the collider data. Figure 11.28 shows two jet-lepton mass distributions from a similar analysis presented in [76]. In that analysis, it was possible to identify five well-measured kinematic endpoints, from which it was possible to solve (in an overdetermined way) for the four masses $m(N_1)$, $m(\widetilde{\ell})$, $m(N_2)$, $m(\widetilde{q})$.

There is one more case of an $\widetilde{N}_2 \to \widetilde{N}_1$ decay that should be mentioned. If two-body decays of $\widetilde{N}_2$ to sleptons are not kinematically allowed but the decay to $\widetilde{N}_1 h^0$ is permitted, this decay to a Higgs boson will be the dominant $\widetilde{N}_2$ decay. In this case, supersymmetry can provide a copious source of Higgs bosons. Figure 11.29 shows an analysis of a SUSY model in this parameter region [67]. Events with multijets and missing transverse energy are selected. In this sample, the mass distribution of two b-quark-tagged jets is shown. The signature of SUSY selects a sample of events in which the Higgs boson is visible in its dominant decay to $b\bar{b}$.

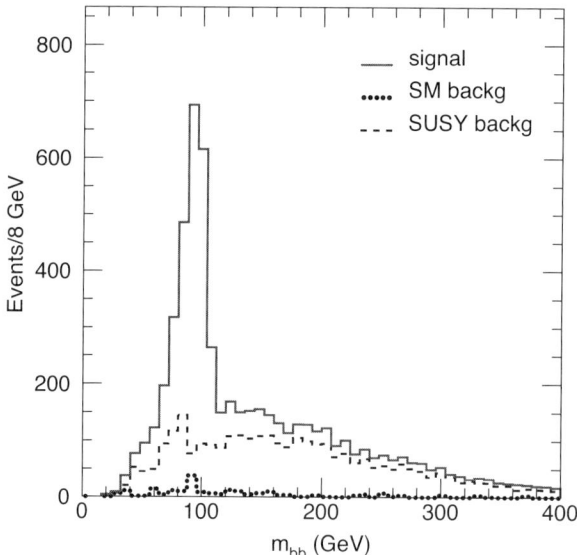

Fig. 11.29. The dijet mass distribution for 2 b-tagged jets at a point in the SUSY parameter space where the decay $\widetilde{N}_2^0 \to h^0 \widetilde{N}_1^0$ is dominant, from [67].

There is much more to say about the measurement of SUSY parameters at the LHC. Some more sophisticated sets of variables are introduced and applied in [76,77]. The question of measuring the spins of superparticles is discussed in [78–81]. And, we have not touched on alternative possibilities for the realization of SUSY, with R-parity violation or charged superparticles that are observed in the LHC experiments as stable particles. A broader overview of SUSY phenomenology at the LHC can be found in the references cited at the beginning of this section.

11.6. Electroweak Symmetry Breaking and Dark Matter in the MSSM

11.6.1. Electroweak Symmetry Breaking in the MSSM

In Section 1.2, I motivated the introduction of SUSY with the claim that SUSY could give an explanation of electroweak symmetry breaking, and for the presence of weakly interacting dark matter in the universe. Now that

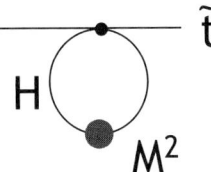

Fig. 11.30. Diagram contributing a term to the renormalization group equation for the soft mass parameter of $\tilde{t}$ proportional to the soft mass parameter for H_u.

we have a detailed understanding of the structure of the MSSM, it is time to come back and discuss these issues.

To present the mechanism of electroweak symmetry breaking in the MSSM, I need to add a term to one of the equations that I derived in Section 4.3. In (11.190), I presented the RG equation for the soft SUSY breaking scalar mass parameters, including renormalization effects from gauge interactions. I remarked that the contributions to this equation from Higgs Yukawa couplings are small for the scalars of the first and second generations. However, for the scalars of the third generation, these corrections can plan an important role.

The F-term interaction

$$\mathcal{L} = -\left|y_t H_u \cdot \tilde{t}\right|^2 \qquad (11.219)$$

leads to a contribution to the RG equations for M_t, the mass parameter of $\tilde{t}$, proportional to M_{Hu}^2, from the diagram shown in Fig. 11.30. The value of the diagram is

$$-iy_t^2 \int \frac{d^4k}{(2\pi)^4} \frac{i}{k^2}(-iM_{Hu}^2)\frac{i}{k^2} = \frac{i}{(4\pi)^2} y_t^2 M_{Hu}^2 \log \Lambda^2 \ . \qquad (11.220)$$

A scalar self-energy diagram is interpreted as $-i\delta m^2$, so this is a *negative* contribution to M_t^2. Each of the scalar fields $(H_u, \tilde{t}, \tilde{\bar{t}})$ gives a similar contribution that renomalizes the soft mass parameter of each of the others. For each correction, there is a counting factor from the number of color or $SU(2)$ degrees of freedom that run around the loop. There is also a correction to each of the scalar masses from the top quark A term. We must also remember that all of these terms add to the positive mass correction from the gaugino loops in Fig. 11.11, of which the gluino loop correction is the most important.

Taking all of these effects into account, we find for the RG equations of the soft mass parameters of H_u, t, and $\bar{t}$

$$\frac{dM_t^2}{d\log Q} = \frac{2}{(4\pi)^2} \cdot 1 \cdot y_t^2[M_t^2 + M_{\bar{t}}^2 + M_{Hu}^2 + A_t^2] - \frac{8}{3\pi}\alpha_3 m_3^2 + \cdots$$

$$\frac{dM_{\bar{t}}^2}{d\log Q} = \frac{2}{(4\pi)^2} \cdot 2 \cdot y_t^2[M_t^2 + M_{\bar{t}}^2 + M_{Hu}^2 + A_t^2] - \frac{8}{3\pi}\alpha_3 m_3^2 + \cdots$$

$$\frac{dM_{Hu}^2}{d\log Q} = \frac{2}{(4\pi)^2} \cdot 3 \cdot y_t^2[M_t^2 + M_{\bar{t}}^2 + M_{Hu}^2 + A_t^2]m_3^2 + \cdots \quad (11.221)$$

The structure is very interesting. The three scalar fields H_u, $\tilde{t}$, and $\tilde{\bar{t}}$ all receive negative corrections to their mass terms as these equations are integrated in the direction of decreasing $\log Q$. If any of these mass terms were to become negative, the corresponding field would have an instability to develop a vacuum expectation value, and the symmetry of the MSSM would be spontaneously broken. The symmetry-breaking we want is that associated with $\langle H_u \rangle \neq 0$. However, it seems equally possible that we could generate $\langle \tilde{\bar{t}} \rangle \neq 0$, which would break color $SU(3)$, or $\langle \tilde{t} \rangle \neq 0$, which would break both $SU(2)$ and $SU(3)$.

If the three mass parameters have similar values at a high mass scale, they race toward negative values according to (11.221). But H_u wins the race, and so the theory predicts the symmetry breaking pattern that is the one observed. In this way, the MSSM leads naturally to electroweak symmetry breaking and realizes the idea that electroweak symmetry breaking is connected to the large value of the top quark-Higgs coupling.

11.6.2. Higgs Boson Masses in the MSSM

Once we expect that $M_u^2 < 0$ at the weak scale, we can work out the details of the Higgs boson spectrum. First, we should write the potential for the Higgs fields H_u, H_d. As in the discussion of Sections 4.1 and 4.2, a number of terms need to be collected from the various pieces of the Lagrangian. The F terms contriubute

$$V_F = \mu^2(H_u^{0*}H_u^0 + H_d^{0*}H_d^0) \quad (11.222)$$

The D terms contribute

$$V_D = \frac{g^2 + g'^2}{8}(H_u^{0*}H_u^0 - H_d^{0*}H_d^0)^2 \quad (11.223)$$

The soft SUSY breaking terms contribute

$$V_{soft} = M_{Hu}^2 H_u^{0*}H_u^0 + M_{Hd}^2 H_d^{0*}H_d^0 - (B\mu H_u^0 H_d^0 + h.c.) \quad (11.224)$$

The sum of these terms gives the complete tree-level Higgs potential. Differentiating this potential with respect to H_u^0 and H_d^0, we obtain the equations that determine the Higgs field vacuum expectation values. If we write these equations with the parametrization of the vacuum expectation values given in (11.169), we find

$$\mu^2 + M_{Hu}^2 = B\mu \cot \beta + \frac{1}{2} m_Z^2 \cos 2\beta$$
$$\mu^2 + M_{Hd}^2 = B\mu \tan \beta - \frac{1}{2} m_Z^2 \cos 2\beta \,, \qquad (11.225)$$

where $m_Z^2 = (g^2 + g'^2)v^2/4$. This system of equations can be solved for μ to give

$$\mu^2 = \frac{M_{Hd}^2 - \tan^2 \beta M_{Hu}^2}{\tan^2 \beta - 1} - \frac{1}{2} m_Z^2 \qquad (11.226)$$

This is, for example, the way that we would determine μ in the mSUGRA parameter space described in Section 5.2.

It is interesting to turn this equation around and write it as an equation for m_Z in terms of the SUSY parameters,

$$m_Z^2 = 2 \frac{M_{Hd}^2 - \tan^2 \beta M_{Hu}^2}{\tan^2 \beta - 1} - 2\mu^2 \,. \qquad (11.227)$$

From this equation, a small value of m_Z would require a cancellation between the Higgs soft mass parameters and μ. The parameter μ sets the mass scale of the Higgsinos, and the Higgs soft mass parameters might be related to other masses of the SUSY scalar particles. Thus, if the masses of the charginos and neutralinos and, perhaps also, the sleptons are not close to m_Z, that disparity must be associated with an apparently unnatural cancellation between different SUSY parameters.

If we prohibit a delicate cancellation in (11.227), we put an upper bound on the SUSY partner masses. To avoid cancellations in more than two decimal places, μ must be less than 700 GeV. Similarly, we find bounds on the Higgs soft masses, and on the parameters that contribute to these masses through the RG equation. This consideration turns out to give a constraint on the gluino mass, $m_3 < 800$ GeV. Assuming gaugino universality, this becomes a condition $m_2 < 250$ GeV that restricts the chargino and neutralino masses. A variety of similar naturalness arguments that constrain the SUSY scale can be found in [82–84]. Though the logic is that of an estimate rather than a rigorous bound, this analysis strongly supports the idea that SUSY partners should be light enough to be discovered at the LHC and at the ILC.

Once we have the Higgs potential and the conditions for the Higgs vacuum expectation values, we can work out the masses of the Higgs bosons by expanding the potential around its minimum. A first step is to identify the combinations of Higgs fields that correspond to physical Higgs bosons. Look first at the charged Higgs bosons. There are two charged Higgs fields in the multiplets H_u, H_d. One linear combination of these fields is the Goldstone boson that is eaten by the W boson as it obtains mass through the Higgs mechanism. The orthogonal linear combination is a physical charged scalar field. If we decompose

$$H_u^+ = \cos\beta H^+ + \sin\beta G^+$$
$$H_d^- = \sin\beta H^- + \sin\beta G^- \qquad (11.228)$$

where $H^- = (H^+)^*$, $G^- = (G^+)^*$, and β is precisely the mixing angle in (11.169), it can be seen that $G^\pm$ are the Goldstone bosons and $H^\pm$ are the physical scalar states.

A similar analysis applies to the neutral components of H_u^0 and H_d^0. These are complex-valued fields. It is appropriate to decomposed them as

$$H_u^0 = \frac{1}{\sqrt{2}}(v\sin\beta + \sin\alpha H^0 + \cos\alpha h^0 + i\cos\beta A^0 + i\sin\beta G^0)$$
$$H_d^0 = \frac{1}{\sqrt{2}}(v\cos\beta + \cos\alpha H^0 - \sin\alpha h^0 + i\sin\beta A^0 - i\cos\beta G^0) \qquad (11.229)$$

The components H^0, h^0 are even under CP; the fields A^0, G^0 are odd under CP. The componet G^0 is the Goldstone boson eaten by the Z^0. The other three fields create physical scalar particles.

Having identified these fields, we can compute their masses. The formulae for the Higgs masses take an especially simple form when they are expressed in terms of the mass of the A^0. For the charged Higgs boson

$$m_{H+}^2 = m_A^2 + m_W^2 \ . \qquad (11.230)$$

For the CP-even scalars, one finds a mass matrix

$$\begin{pmatrix} m_A^2 \sin^2\beta + m_Z^2 \cos^2\beta & -(m_A^2 + m_Z^2)\sin\beta\cos\beta \\ -(m_A^2 + m_Z^2)\sin\beta\cos\beta & m_A^2 \cos^2\beta + m_Z^2 \sin^2\beta \end{pmatrix} \qquad (11.231)$$

The physical scalar masses m_h^2 and m_H^2 are the eigenvalues of this matrix, defined in such a way that $m_h^2 < m_H^2$. The angle α in (11.229) is the mixing angle that defines these eigenstates.

Taking the trace of (11.231), we find the relation
$$m_h^2 + m_H^2 = m_A^2 + m_Z^2 . \qquad (11.232)$$
We can also obtain an upper bound on the lighter Higgs mass m_h^2 by taking the matrix element of (11.231) in the state $(\cos\beta, \sin\beta)$. The bound is a very strong one:
$$m_h^2 \leq m_Z^2 \cos^2 \beta < m_Z^2 . \qquad (11.233)$$
This seems inconsistent with lower bounds on the Higgs boson mass from LEP 2, which exclude $m_h < 114$ GeV for the Standard Model Higgs and for most scenarios of SUSY Higgs bosons [85].[d] However, the one-loop corrections to the tree-level result (11.231) give a significant positive correction
$$\delta m_h^2 = \frac{3}{\pi} \frac{m_t^4}{m_W^2} \sin^4 \beta \log \frac{m_{\tilde{t}} m_{\tilde{t}}}{m_t^2} . \qquad (11.234)$$
This correction can move the mass of the h^0 up to about 130 GeV. The detailed summary of the radiative corrections to the h^0 mass in the MSSM is presented in [88]. A very clear and useful accounting of the major corrections can be found in [89].

It is possible to raise the mass of the h^0 by going outside the MSSM and adding additional $SU(2)$ singlet superfields to the model. However, this strategy is limited by a general constraint coming from grand unification. The requirement that the Higgs couplings do not become strong up to the grand unification scale limit the mass of the Higgs to about 200 GeV [90]. It is possible to raise the mass of the Higgs further only by enlarging the Standard Model gauge group or adding new thresholds that affect unification [91,92].

In the MSSM, we can easily have the situation in which $m_A \gg m_h$. In this limit, the couplings of the h^0 are very close to those of the Standard Model Higgs boson, and the H^0, A^0, and $H^\pm$ are almost degenerate. If $\tan\beta \gg 1$, the heavy neutral Higgs bosons decay dominantly to $b\bar{b}$ and $\tau^+\tau^-$.

Much more about the phenomenology of Higgs bosons in supersymmetry can be found in [93,94].

11.6.3. WIMP Model of Dark Matter

Now we turn to the second problem highlighted in the Introduction, the problem of dark matter in the universe. It has been known from many

---
[d]Some exceptional Higgs decay schemes that escape these bounds are considered in [86,87].

astrophysical measurements that the universe contains enormous amounts of invisible, weakly interacting matter. For an excellent review of the classic astrophysical evidence for this dark matter, see [95].

In the past few years, measurements of the cosmic microwave background have given a new source of evidence for dark matter. Since this data comes from an era in the early universe before the formation of any structure, it argues strongly that the invisible matter is not made of rocks or brown dwarfs but is actually a new, very weakly interacting form of matter. These measurements also determine quite accurately the overall amount of conventional and dark matter in the universe. Let ρ_b, ρ_N, and ρ_Λ be the large-scale energy densities of the universe from baryons, dark matter, and the energy of the vacuum. The data from the microwave background tells us that $\rho_b + \rho_N + \rho_\Lambda = \rho_c$, the 'closure density' corresponding in general relativity to a flat universe, to about 1% accuracy. If $\Omega_i = \rho_i/\rho_c$, the most recent data from the WMAP experiment and other sources gives [96,97]

$$\Omega_b = 0.042 \pm 0.003 \quad \Omega_N = 0.20 \pm 0.02 \quad \Omega_\Lambda = 0.74 \pm 0.02 \ . \tag{11.235}$$

These results present a double mystery. We do not know what particle the dark matter is made of, and we do not have any theory that explains the observed magnitude of the vacuum energy or 'dark energy'.

I believe that supersymmetry will eventually play an essential role in solving the problem of dark energy. In ordinary quantum field theory, the value of the vacuum energy is quartically divergent, so the problem of computing the vacuum energy is not even well-posed. In supersymmetry, there is at least a well-defined zero of the energy associated with exact supersymmetry, which implies $\langle 0| H |0 \rangle = 0$. Unfortunately, in most of today's models of supersymmetry, the vacuum energy is set by the SUSY breaking scale. This gives $\Lambda \sim (10^{11} \text{ GeV})^4$, about 80 orders of magnitude larger than the observed value of the vacuum energy. From this starting point, Λ must be fine-tuned to the scale of eV^4. This is an important problem that needs new insights which, however, I will not provide here.

On the other hand, supersymmetry offers a very definite solution to the problem of the origin of dark matter. We have already noted in Section 3.4 that it is straightforward to arrange that the lightest supersymmetric particle can be absolutely stable. If this particle were produced in the early universe, some density of this type of matter should still be present. In most, but not all, regions of parameter space, the lightest supersymmetric particle is neutral. Candidates include the lightest neutralino, the lightest sneutrino, and the gravitino. In the remainder of these lectures, I will concentrate on the case in which the lightest neutralino is the dark matter particle. For a discussion of the other candidates, see [98].

To begin our discussion, I would like to estimate the cosmic density of dark matter in a more general context. Let me make the following minimal assumptions about the nature of dark matter, that the dark matter particle is stable, neutral, and weakly interacting. To these properties, I would like to add one more, that dark matter particles can be created in pairs at sufficiently high temperature, and that, at some time in the early universe, dark matter particles were in thermal equilibrium. I will refer to a particle satisfying these assumptions as a 'weakly interacting massive particle' or WIMP. The assumption of thermal equilibrium is a strong one that is not satisfied even in many models of supersymmetric dark matter. For some exceptions, see [99,100]. However, let us see what implications follow from these assumptions.

The assumption that WIMPs were once in thermal equilibrium provides a definite initial condition from which to compute the current density of dark matter. In thermal equilibrium at temperture T, we have for the number density of dark matter particles

$$n_{eq} = \frac{g}{(2\pi)^{3/2}} (mT)^{3/2} e^{-m/T} . \tag{11.236}$$

where g is the number of spin degrees of freedom of the massive particle. As the universe expands, the temperature of the universe deccreases and the rate of WIMP pair production becomes very small. But the rate of dark matter pair annihilation also becomes small as the WIMPs separate from one another.

The expansion of the universe is governed by the Hubble constant $H = \dot{a}/a$, where a is the scale factor. Einstein's equations imply that

$$H^2 = \frac{8\pi}{3} \frac{\rho}{m_{\text{Pl}}^2} . \tag{11.237}$$

In a radiation-dominated universe where g_* is the number of relativistic degrees of freedom, $\rho = \pi^2 g_* T^4/30$. Then H is proportional to T^2. In a radiation-dominated universe, the temperature red-shifts as the universe expands, so that $T \sim a^{-1}$. Combining this relation with the equation $H = \dot{a}/a \sim T^2$, we find $t \sim T^{-2} \sim a^2$, that is, $a \sim t^{1/2}$ or $\dot{a}/a = 1/2t$. Setting this expression equal to the explict form of H in (11.237), we find a detailed formula for the time since the start of the radiation-dominated era for cooling to a temperature T,

$$t = \left(\frac{16\pi^3 g_*}{45}\right)^{-1/2} \frac{m_{\text{Pl}}}{T^2} . \qquad (11.238)$$

The evolution of the WIMP density is described by the Boltzmann equation

$$\frac{dn}{dt} = -3Hn - \langle \sigma v \rangle (n^2 - n_{eq}^2) , \qquad (11.239)$$

where H is the Hubble constant, σ is the $\widetilde{N}\widetilde{N}$ annihilation cross section—which appears thermally averaged with the relative velocity of colliding WIMPs—and n_{eq} is the equilibrium WIMP density (11.236). Assume, just for the sake of argument, that the temperature T is of the order of 100 GeV. At this temperature, the Hubble constant has the magnitude $H \sim 10^{-17} T$, so the expansion of the universe is very slow on the scale of typical elementary particle reactions. However, when T becomes less than the WIMP mass m, the WIMP density is exponentially suppressed and so the collision term in the Boltzmann equation is also very small. These two terms are of the same size at the *freezeout* temperature T_F satisfying

$$e^{-m/T_F} \sim \frac{1}{m_{\text{Pl}} m \langle \sigma v \rangle} . \qquad (11.240)$$

At temperatures below T_F, we may neglect the production of WIMPs in particle collisions. The WIMP density is then determined by the expansion of the universe and the residual rate of WIMP pair annihilation. Maybe it is more appropriate to think of T_F as the temperature at which a WIMP density is frozen *in*. To determine the freezeout temperature, we take the logarithm of the right-hand side of (11.240). The result depends only on the order of magnitude of the annihilation cross section. For any interaction of electroweak strength,

$$\xi_F = T_F/m \sim 1/25 . \qquad (11.241)$$

This physical picture suggests a way to estimate the cosmic density of WIMP dark matter. We can take as our initial condition the thermal density of dark matter at freezeout. We then integrate the Boltzmann equation, ignoring the term proportional to n_{eq}^2 associated with the production of WIMP pairs [102].

In analyzing the Boltzmann equation, it is useful normalize the particle density n of dark matter to the density of entropy s. Since the universe expands very slowly, this expansion is very close to adiabatic. Then entropy is conserved,

$$\frac{ds}{dt} = -3Hs .\tag{11.242}$$

In a radiation-dominated universe, $s = 2\pi^2 g_* T^3/45$. Now define

$$Y = \frac{n}{s}, \qquad \xi = \frac{T}{m}, \tag{11.243}$$

the latter as in (11.241). Using the expression (11.238), we can convert the evolution in time to an evolution in temperature or in ξ. Applying these changes of variables and dropping the n_{eq}^2 term, the Boltzmann equation (11.239) rearranges to the form

$$\frac{dY}{d\xi} = C \langle \sigma v \rangle Y^2 , \tag{11.244}$$

where

$$C = \left(\frac{\pi g_*}{45}\right)^{1/2} m m_{\text{Pl}} . \tag{11.245}$$

Let Y_F be the value of Y at $\xi = \xi_F$. If we assume that $\langle \sigma v \rangle$ is approximately constant, since we are at temperatures close to threshold, it is straightforward to integrate this equation to $\xi = 0$, corresponding to late times.

$$Y^{-1} = Y_F^{-1} + C\xi_F \langle \sigma v \rangle . \tag{11.246}$$

The second term typically dominates the first. Then we can put back the value of C in (11.245) and write the final answer in terms of the ratio of the mass density of dark matter to the closure density $\Omega_N = n m_N/\rho_c$. In this way, we find

$$\Omega_N = \frac{s_0}{\rho_c} \left(\frac{45}{\pi g_*}\right)^{1/2} \frac{1}{\xi_F m_{\text{Pl}} \langle \sigma v \rangle} , \tag{11.247}$$

where s_0 is the current entropy density of the universe. Turner and Scherrer observed that this formula gives a value of Ω_N that is usually within 10% of the result from exact integration of the Boltzmann equation [102]. If $\langle\,sigmav\rangle$ has a significant dependence on temperature, the derivation is still correct with the replacement

$$\xi \langle \sigma v \rangle \to \int_0^{\xi_f} d\xi \, \langle \sigma v \rangle (\xi) \tag{11.248}$$

in the denominator of the last term in (11.247).

This is a remarkable relation. Almost every factor in this relation is known from astrophysical measurements. The left-hand side is given by (11.235). On the right-hand side, the entropy density of the universe is dominated by the entropy of the microwave background photons and can be computed from the microwave background temperature. The closure density is known from the measurement of the Hubble constant and the observation that the universe is flat. The parameters g_* and ξ_F are relatively insensitive to the strength of the annihilation cross section, with values $g_* \sim 100$, $\xi_F \sim 1/25$. The mass of the WIMP does not appear explicitly in (11.247). We can then solve for $\langle \sigma v \rangle$. The result is

$$\langle \sigma v \rangle = 1 \text{ pb} . \tag{11.249}$$

This is the value of a typical electroweak cross section at energies of a few hundred GeV. If we convert this value to a mass M of an exchanged particle using the formula

$$\langle \sigma v \rangle = \frac{\pi \alpha^2}{8 M^2} , \tag{11.250}$$

the value (11.249) corresponds to $M = 100$ GeV.

I consider this a truly remarkable result. From a purely astrophysical argument, relying on quite weak and general assumptions, we arrive at the conclusion that there must be new particles at the hundred GeV energy scale. It is probably not a concidence that this argument leads us back to the mass scale of electroweak symmetry breaking.

In our study of supersymmetry, we have found an argument from the physics of electroweak symmetry breaking that predicts the existence of dark matter. As I discussed at the beginning of these lectures, models that explain electroweak symmetry breaking are complex. They typically involve many new particles. It is easily arranged that the lightest of the new particles is neutral. In supersymmetry, there is a reason why the new particles are likely to carry a conserved quantum number (11.149). Other models of electroweak symmetry breaking, such as the extra dimensional and little Higgs models discussed in Section 1.2, have their own reasons to have a complex particle spectrum and discrete symmetries. Then these models lead in their own ways to WIMPs at the hundred GeV mass scale.

A slight extension of this argument adds more interest. In supersymmetry, the sector of new particles includes particles with QCD color. Since the top quark probably plays an essential role in the mechanism of electroweak symmetry breaking, it is very likely that, in any model, some of the new particles will carry color. If these particles have masses below 1 TeV, they have large (10 pb) pair-production cross sections at the LHC. These particles will then decay to the dark matter particle, producting complex events with several hard jets and missing transverse momentum. These mild assumptions thus lead to the conclusion, from any model that follows this general line of argument, that *we should expect exotic events with multiple jets and missing transverse momentum to appear with pb cross sections at the LHC.*

11.6.4. Dark Matter Annihilation in the MSSM

This argument of the previous section gives a very optimistic conclusion for the discovery of new physics at the LHC. However, we have already discussed that the first observation of supersymmetry or another model of new physics will only be the first step in a lengthy experimental program. Once we know that superparticles or other new particles exist, we will need to study them in detail to learn their detailed interactions and, eventually, to work out the underlying Lagrangian that governs their behavior. As we have already discussed in Section 3.5 and 4.3, this Lagrangian can give us a clue to the nature of the ultimate theory at very short distances.

The study of dark matter intersects this program in an interesting way. In principle, once we have discovered supersymmetric particles, we can try to measure their properties and see if these coincide with the properties required from astrophysical detections of dark matter. As we have seen in Section 5.3, the LHC experiments expect to measure the mass of the LSP to about 10% accuracy. These measurements can hopefully be compared to mass measurements at the 20% level that can be expected from astrophysical dark matter detection experiments [103,104]. We would also wish to find out whether the annihilation cross section $\langle \sigma v \rangle$ that is predicted from the supersymmetry parameters measured at colliders agrees with the value (11.249) required to predict the observed WIMP relic density. This comparison turns out to depend in a complex way on the parameters of the underlying supersymmetry theory.

To begin our discussion of the annihilation cross section, we can make a simple model of neutralino annihilation and see how well it works. We have seen in Section 4.3 that the right-handed sleptons are often the lightest charged particles in the supersymmetry spectrum. Consider, then, an idealized parameter set in which the neutralino is a pure bino and pair annihilation is dominated by the slepton exchange diagrams shown in Fig. 11.31. (Away from the pure bino case, there are also s-channel diagrams with Z^0,

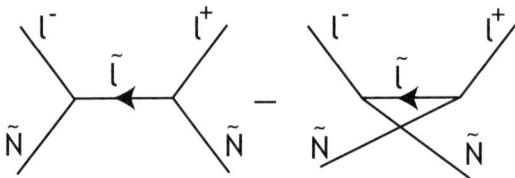

Fig. 11.31. Diagrams giving the simplest scheme of neutralino pair annihilation, leading to the annihilation cross section (11.251).

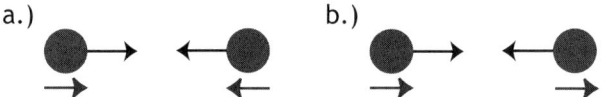

Fig. 11.32. Two possible spin configurations for neutralino annihilation: (a.) spin 0; (b.) spin 1. Because of Fermi statistics, the latter state does not exist in the S-wave.

h^0, H^0, A^0.) In this special limit, the annihilation cross section is given by

$$v \frac{d\sigma}{d\cos\theta} = \pi\alpha^2 m_N^2 \left|\frac{1}{c_w}\right|^2 \left|\frac{1}{m_{\tilde{\ell}}^2 - t} - \frac{1}{m_{\tilde{\ell}}^2 - u}\right|^2, \quad (11.251)$$

where m_N is the $\widetilde{N}_1$ mass. The relative velocity v appears due to the flux factor in the cross section; this factor cancels in σv. I have ignored the lepton masses. This expression is of the order of (11.250) with $M \sim m_N$, except for one unfortunate feature: At threshold, $t = u$ and the cross section vanishes. This leads to a severe suppression, by a factor of

$$v^2 \cdot \left|\frac{m_N^2}{m_{\tilde{\ell}}^2 + m_N^2}\right|^4, \quad (11.252)$$

which is at least of order $\xi_f/16$. So the relic density estimated in this simple way is too large by about a factor of 10.

There is an interesting physics explanation for the vanishing of this cross section at threshold [105]. Neutralinos are spin-$\frac{1}{2}$ fermions, and we might guess from this that, near threshold, they would annihilate in the S-wave either in a spin 0 or in a spin 1 state. The two spin configurations are shown in Fig. 11.32. However, because the neutralino is a Majorana fermion and therefore its own antiparticle, an S-wave state of two neutralinos must be antisymmetric in spin. Hence, the spin 1 S-wave state does not exist However, as we know from pion decay, a spin 0 state can convert to a pair of light leptons only with a helicity flip. Thus, there is an annihilation cross section from the spin 0 S-wave only when lepton masses are included, and even then with the suppression factor m_ℓ^2/m_N^2, which is 10^{-4} even for $\tau^+\tau^-$ final states.

To obtain a realistic value for the neutralino relic density, we have to bring in more complicated mechanisms of neutralino annihilation. These mechanisms are not difficult to find in various regions of the large supersymmetry paramet er space [106–108]. We need to look for annihilation processes that can proceed in the S-wave with full strength. Three possible mechanisms are shown in Fig. 11.33.

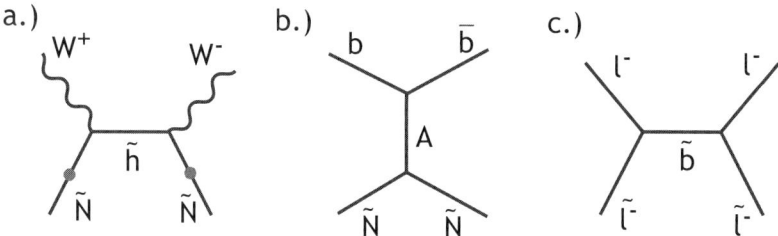

Fig. 11.33. Three mechanisms for obtaining a sufficiently large annihilation cross section to give the observed density of neutralino dark matter: (a.) gaugino-Higgsino mixing, opening the annihilation channels to W^+W^- and Z^0Z^0, (b.) resonance annihilation through the Higgs boson A^0, (c.) co-annihilation with another supersymmetric particle, here taken to be a $\tilde{\ell}$.

Pairs of neutralinos can annihilate in the S-wave into vector bosons. The bino does not couple to W or Z pairs, but if the lightest neutralino has Higgsino or wino content, this reaction can be important. For charginos of mass about 200 GeV, this annihilation cross section can be 50 pb for a pure wino or Higgsino, so only a modest content of these states is needed to give a cross section of 1 pb.

The s-channel exchange of a Higgs boson can provide a mechanism for neutralino annihilation in the spin 0 S-wave. Because this state is CP-odd, it is the boson A^0 that is relevant here. If m_A is close to the neutralino threshold $2m_N$, the cross section has a resonant enhancement. Note that the $\widetilde{N}_1$ annihilation vertex to A arises as a Higgs-Higgsino-gaugino Yukawa term, so this vertex is nonzero only if $\widetilde{N}_1$ has both gaugino and Higgsino content. If $m_A = 2m_N$, the resonance enhancement is at full strength and the cross section can be as large as 50 pb. Thus, it is A boson masses about 20 GeV above or below the threshold that give the desired cross section (11.249).

The final mechanism shown in the figure is *coannihilation*. As we have discussed, the freezeout of the $\widetilde{N}_1$ occurs at a temperature given by $T/m_N \sim 1/25$. So if there is another particle in the supersymmetry spectrum that is within 4% of the $\widetilde{N}_1$ mass, this state will have a number density that remains in equilibrium with the number density of the $\widetilde{N}_1$. If this particle has S-wave annihilation reactions, those reactions can be the dominant mechanisms for the annihilation of supersymmetric particles. For a light slepton, the reactions

$$\widetilde{\ell}^- + \widetilde{N}_1^0 \to \ell^- + \gamma \qquad \widetilde{\ell}^- + \widetilde{\ell}^- \to \ell^- + \ell^- \qquad (11.253)$$

can give significant S-wave annihilation. In [106,109], the lighter stau is invoked as the coannihilating particle. In [110], the lighter top squark is

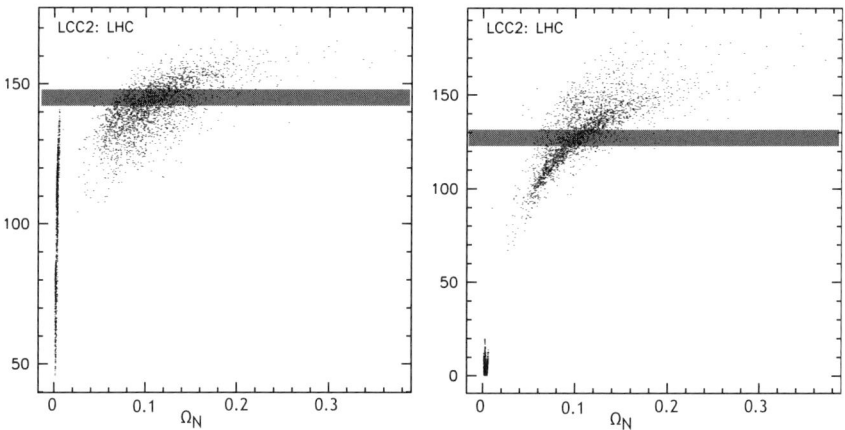

Fig. 11.34. Scatter plot of SUSY parameter points consistent with data from the LHC in the analysis of the parameter set LCC2 from [111]. The horizontal axis show the value of Ω_N at each parameter point. The vertical axes show polarized-beam cross sections measurable at the ILC, in fb: (a.) $\sigma(e_R^- e_L^+ \to \widetilde{C}_1^+ \widetilde{C}_1^-)$, (b.) $\sigma(e_R^- e_L^+ \to \widetilde{N}_2^0 \widetilde{N}_3^0)$. The colored bands show the $\pm 1\sigma$ region allowed after the ILC cross section measurements.

invoked as the coannihilating state. If the lightest neutralinos and charginos are Higgsino-like, chargino coannihilation can also be important.

It is, then, a complex matter to predict the neutralino relic density from microscopic physics. We will first need to learn what particles in the supersymmetry spectrum play the dominant role as particle exchanged in annihilation reactions or as coannihilating species. We will then need to measure the couplings and mixing angles of the important particles, since the dominant annihilation diagrams depend sensitively on these.

Some examples of how measurements at the LHC and ILC can accumulate the relevant information are described in [111]. Figure 11.34 shows a part of the analysis of this paper for a particular SUSY model in which the dominant annihilation reactions are $\widetilde{N}_1\widetilde{N}_1 \to W^+W^-, Z^0 Z^0$. As a first step, the authors constructed numerous supersymmetry parameter sets that were consistent with the mass spectrum of this model as it would be measured at the LHC. These parameter sets included a variety of models in

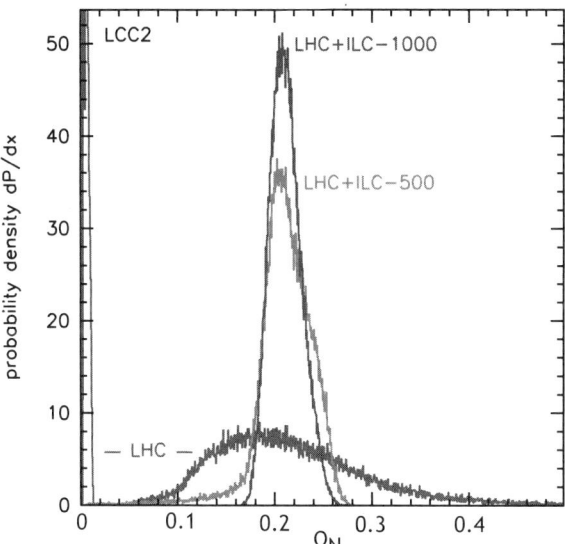

Fig. 11.35. Summary plot for the prediction of Ω_N from collider data for the SUSY parameter set LCC2 considered in [111]. The three curves show the likelihood distributions for the prediction of Ω_N using data from the LHC, the ILC at 500 GeV, and the ILC at 1000 GeV.

which the LSP was dominantly bino and wino. The figure shows scatter plots of the predictions of these models with ILC cross sections for neutralino and chargino pair production on the vertical axis and Ω_N on the horizontal axis. The two cross sections clearly separate the bino- and wino-like solutions. The second of these cross sections is the polarized reaction of chargino pair production for which the cross section is displayed in Fig. 11.19. The horizontal lines represent the accuracy of the measurements of these cross sections expected at the ILC. These measurements select the bino solution and also play an important role in fixing the bino-Higgsino mixing angle which is a crucial input to the annihilation cross sections. In Fig. 11.35, I show the distribution of predictions for Ω_N expected for this model, in the analysis of [111], from the data on SUSY particles that would be obtained from the LHC, from the ILC at a center-of-mass energy of 500 GeV, and from the ILC at a center-of-mass energy of 1000 GeV.

The similar summary plot for another of the models considered in [111] is shown in Fig. 11.36. The model considered in this analysis is one in which the neutralino relic density is set by stau coannihilation. In this

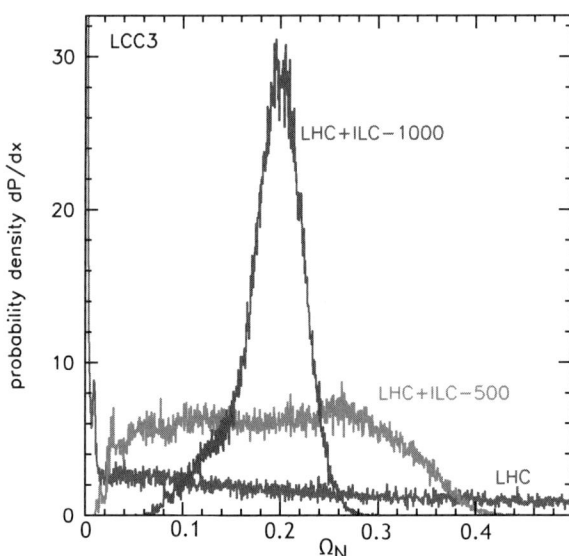

Fig. 11.36. Summary plot for the prediction of Ω_N from collider data for the SUSY parameter set LCC3 of [111]. The notation is as in Fig. 11.35.

model, the stau would be discovered at the LHC, and the stau-neutralino mass difference would be measured to about 10% accuracy at the 500 GeV ILC. However, the annihilation reactions also depend on mixing angles and on the value of $\tan\beta$. In this scenario, these are determined only by ILC measurements of some of the heavier states of the SUSY spectrum.

Collider measurements of the SUSY spectrum can also be used to constrain cross sections of the WIMP that are important for experiments that seek to detect dark matter, for example, the neutralino-proton cross section and the cross section for neutralino pair annihilation to gamma rays. If we can accurately predict these cross sections from collider data, the information about the SUSY spectrum that we learn from colliders will feed back into the astrophysics of dark matter. Some numerical examples that illustrate this are presented in [111].

11.7. Conclusions

In these lectures, I have given an overview of supersymmetry and its application to elementary particle physics. In the early sections of this review, I presented the formalism of SUSY and explained the rules for constructing supersymmetric Lagrangians. Our discussion then became more concrete, focusing on the mass spectrum of the MSSM and the properties of the particle states of the MSSM spectrum. This led us to a discussion of the experimental probes of this spectrum and the possibility of measurement of the parameters of the supersymmetric Lagrangian.

This possibility is now coming very near. As I have discussed in the last sections of this review, supersymmetry gives concrete answers to the major questions about elementary particle physics that we expect to be addressed at the hundred GeV scale—the questions of the origin of electroweak symmetry breaking and the identity of cosmic dark matter. In the next year, the LHC will begin to explore the physics of this mass scale. Supersymmetry is one candidate for what will be found. I hope that, after studying these lectures, you will agree that the picture provided by supersymmetry is highly plausible and even compelling.

Whatever explanations we will learn from the LHC data, our investigation of it will follow the general paradigm that I have described here. In successive stages, we will use data from the LHC and the ILC to learn the mass spectrum of new particles that are revealed at the LHC, to determine their quantum numbers and couplings, and to reconstruct their underlying

Lagrangian. On the basis of the detailed studies of this program that have been carried out for the MSSM, we have the expectation that we will be able to learn the underlying theory of the new particles and to test the specific explanations that this theory gives for the mysteries of the fundamental interactions.

Is supersymmetry just an attractive theory, or is it a part of the true description of elementary particles? We are about to find out.

Acknowledgements

I am grateful to Sally Dawson, Rabi Mohapatra and, especially, to K. T. Mahanthappa for organizing the 2006 TASI Summer School at which these lectures were presented. I thank Howard Haber and Thomas Dumitrescu for instructive comments on the manuscript.

References

[1] A. D. Linde, JETP Lett. **19**, 183 (1974) [Pisma Zh. Eksp. Teor. Fiz. **19**, 320 (1974)].
[2] L. Susskind, Phys. Rev. D **20**, 2619 (1979).
[3] S. Weinberg, Phys. Rev. D **19**, 1277 (1979).
[4] P. W. Higgs, Phys. Rev. Lett. **13**, 508 (1964).
[5] K. D. Lane, arXiv:hep-ph/9401324.
[6] S. P. Martin, arXiv:hep-ph/9709356.
[7] J. Wess and J. Bagger, *Supersymmetry and supergravity*. (Princeton U. Press, 1992).
[8] J. A. Bagger, arXiv:hep-ph/9604232.
[9] J. D. Lykken, arXiv:hep-th/9612114.
[10] G. L. Kane, arXiv:hep-ph/0202185.
[11] M. Drees, R. M. Godbole, and P. Roy, *Theory and Phenomenology of Sparticles*. (World Scientific, 2004).
[12] P. Binetruy, *Supersymmetry: Theory, Experiment, and Cosmology*. (Oxford U. Press, 2004).
[13] H. Baer and X. Tata, *Weak Scale Supersymmetry*. (Cambridge U. Press, 2006).
[14] H. Dreiner, H. E. Haber, and S. P. Martin, to appear.
[15] N. Arkani-Hamed, A. G. Cohen, E. Katz and A. E. Nelson, JHEP **0207**, 034 (2002) [arXiv:hep-ph/0206021].
[16] M. Schmaltz and D. Tucker-Smith, Ann. Rev. Nucl. Part. Sci. **55**, 229 (2005) [arXiv:hep-ph/0502182].
[17] For a pedagogical derivation of origin of the negative μ^2 in little Higgs

models, see M. Perelstein, M. E. Peskin and A. Pierce, Phys. Rev. D **69**, 075002 (2004) [arXiv:hep-ph/0310039].
[18] H. C. Cheng, B. A. Dobrescu and C. T. Hill, Nucl. Phys. B **573**, 597 (2000) [arXiv:hep-ph/9906327]; N. Arkani-Hamed, H. C. Cheng, B. A. Dobrescu and L. J. Hall, Phys. Rev. D **62**, 096006 (2000) [arXiv:hep-ph/0006238];
[19] C. Macesanu, Int. J. Mod. Phys. A **21**, 2259 (2006) [arXiv:hep-ph/0510418].
[20] S. R. Coleman and J. Mandula, Phys. Rev. **159** (1967) 1251.
[21] R. Haag, J. T. Lopuszanski and M. Sohnius, Nucl. Phys. B **88**, 257 (1975).
[22] Yu. A. Golfand and E. P. Likhtman, JETP Lett. **13** (1971) 323 [Pisma Zh. Eksp. Teor. Fiz. **13** (1971) 452].
[23] D. V. Volkov and V. P. Akulov, JETP Lett. **16** (1972) 438 [Pisma Zh. Eksp. Teor. Fiz. **16** (1972) 621].
[24] J. Wess and B. Zumino, Nucl. Phys. B **70** (1974) 39.
[25] For a taste, see N. Beisert, Comptes Rendus Physique **5**, 1039 (2004) [arXiv:hep-th/0409147].
[26] K. Intriligator, N. Seiberg and D. Shih, JHEP **0604**, 021 (2006) [arXiv:hep-th/0602239].
[27] In a common alternative notation, ϕ is written $-A^*$. Then this equation becomes $F = mA$, the *Newton-Witten equation*. See [28].
[28] V. Gates, *et al.*, in *Proceedings of the Workshop on Unified String Theories*, M. Green and D. Gross, eds. (World Scientific, 1986).
[29] B. Zumino, Nucl. Phys. B **89**, 535 (1975).
[30] M. T. Grisaru, W. Siegel and M. Rocek, Nucl. Phys. B **159**, 429 (1979).
[31] I. Affleck, M. Dine and N. Seiberg, Phys. Rev. Lett. **52**, 1677 (1984).
[32] B. Zumino, Phys. Lett. B **87**, 203 (1979).
[33] J. Wess and B. Zumino, Nucl. Phys. B **78**, 1 (1974).
[34] M. T. Grisaru, B. Milewski and D. Zanon, Nucl. Phys. B **266**, 589 (1986).
[35] V. A. Novikov, M. A. Shifman, A. I. Vainshtein and V. I. Zakharov, Nucl. Phys. B **229**, 381 (1983).
[36] N. Arkani-Hamed and H. Murayama, JHEP **0006**, 030 (2000) [arXiv:hep-th/9707133].
[37] S. Ferrara and B. Zumino, Nucl. Phys. B **87**, 207 (1975).
[38] I. Hinchliffe and J. Erler and P. Langacker, in W. M. Yao *et al.* [Particle Data Group], J. Phys. G **33**, 1 (2006).
[39] Y. Yamada, Z. Phys. C **60**, 83 (1993).
[40] M. L. Alciati, F. Feruglio, Y. Lin and A. Varagnolo, JHEP **0503**, 054 (2005) [arXiv:hep-ph/0501086].
[41] M. Dine, arXiv:hep-ph/0011376.
[42] S. Dimopoulos and L. J. Hall, Phys. Lett. B **207**, 210 (1988).
[43] S. Deser and B. Zumino, Phys. Rev. Lett. **38**, 1433 (1977).
[44] L. O'Raifeartaigh, Nucl. Phys. B **96**, 331 (1975).
[45] M. A. Luty, arXiv:hep-th/0509029.
[46] L. Girardello and M. T. Grisaru, Nucl. Phys. B **194**, 65 (1982).
[47] J. E. Kim and H. P. Nilles, Phys. Lett. B **138**, 150 (1984).
[48] G. F. Giudice and A. Masiero, Phys. Lett. B **206**, 480 (1988).
[49] L. J. Hall and L. Randall, Nucl. Phys. B **352**, 289 (1991).

[50] P. J. Fox, A. E. Nelson and N. Weiner, JHEP **0208**, 035 (2002) [arXiv:hep-ph/0206096]; A. E. Nelson, N. Rius, V. Sanz and M. Unsal, JHEP **0208**, 039 (2002) [arXiv:hep-ph/0206102].
[51] G. D. Kribs, E. Poppitz and N. Weiner, arXiv:0712.2039 [hep-ph].
[52] M. Dine, A. E. Nelson, Y. Nir and Y. Shirman, Phys. Rev. D **53**, 2658 (1996) [arXiv:hep-ph/9507378].
[53] G. F. Giudice, M. A. Luty, H. Murayama and R. Rattazzi, JHEP **9812**, 027 (1998) [arXiv:hep-ph/9810442].
[54] L. Randall and R. Sundrum, Nucl. Phys. B **557**, 79 (1999) [arXiv:hep-th/9810155].
[55] J. L. Feng and T. Moroi, Phys. Rev. D **56**, 5962 (1997) [arXiv:hep-ph/9612333].
[56] S. Y. Choi, H. E. Haber, J. Kalinowski and P. M. Zerwas, Nucl. Phys. B **778**, 85 (2007) [arXiv:hep-ph/0612218].
[57] M. Schmaltz and W. Skiba, Phys. Rev. D **62**, 095004 (2000) [arXiv:hep-ph/0004210].
[58] J. L. Feng and T. Moroi, Phys. Rev. D **58**, 035001 (1998) [arXiv:hep-ph/9712499].
[59] J. L. Feng, S. F. Su and F. Takayama, Phys. Rev. D **70**, 063514 (2004) [arXiv:hep-ph/0404198].
[60] T. Abe et al. [American Linear Collider Working Group], in *Proc. of the APS/DPF/DPB Summer Study on the Future of Particle Physics (Snowmass 2001)* ed. N. Graf [arXiv:hep-ex/0106056]
[61] J. L. Feng and M. M. Nojiri, arXiv:hep-ph/0210390.
[62] M. M. Nojiri, Phys. Rev. D **51**, 6281 (1995) [arXiv:hep-ph/9412374].
[63] G. Weiglein et al. [LHC/LC Study Group], Phys. Rept. **426**, 47 (2006) [arXiv:hep-ph/0410364].
[64] M. E. Peskin, Int. J. Mod. Phys. A **13**, 2299 (1998) [arXiv:hep-ph/9803279].
[65] I thank Norman Graf for providing this figure.
[66] J. L. Feng, M. E. Peskin, H. Murayama and X. R. Tata, Phys. Rev. D **52**, 1418 (1995) [arXiv:hep-ph/9502260].
[67] ATLAS Collaboration, *Detector and Physics Performance Technical Design Report*, vol.II. CERN/LHCC/99-14 (1999).
[68] A. Ball, M. Della Negra, A. Petrilli and L. Foa [CMS Collaboration], J. Phys. G **34**, 995 (2007).
[69] http://cmsinfo.cern.ch/outreach/CMSdetectorInfo/NewPhysics/
[70] W. Beenakker, R. Hopker, M. Spira and P. M. Zerwas, Nucl. Phys. B **492**, 51 (1997) [arXiv:hep-ph/9610490]; http://www.ph.ed.ac.uk/~tplehn/prospino/
[71] D. R. Tovey, Eur. Phys. J. direct C **4** (2002) N4.
[72] I. Hinchliffe, F. E. Paige, M. D. Shapiro, J. Soderqvist and W. Yao, Phys. Rev. D **55**, 5520 (1997) [arXiv:hep-ph/9610544].
[73] R. Kitano and Y. Nomura, Phys. Rev. D **73**, 095004 (2006) [arXiv:hep-ph/0602096].
[74] N. Arkani-Hamed, P. Schuster, N. Toro, J. Thaler, L. T. Wang, B. Knuteson and S. Mrenna, arXiv:hep-ph/0703088.

[75] Some models with on-shell gauge bosons in the final state of squark decays are analyzed in J. M. Butterworth, J. R. Ellis and A. R. Raklev, JHEP **0705**, 033 (2007) [arXiv:hep-ph/0702150].

[76] B. C. Allanach, C. G. Lester, M. A. Parker and B. R. Webber, JHEP **0009**, 004 (2000) [arXiv:hep-ph/0007009].

[77] C. G. Lester and D. J. Summers, Phys. Lett. B **463**, 99 (1999) [arXiv:hep-ph/9906349].

[78] A. J. Barr, Phys. Lett. B **596**, 205 (2004) [arXiv:hep-ph/0405052].

[79] T. Goto, K. Kawagoe and M. M. Nojiri, Phys. Rev. D **70**, 075016 (2004) [Erratum-ibid. D **71**, 059902 (2005)] [arXiv:hep-ph/0406317].

[80] J. M. Smillie and B. R. Webber, JHEP **0510**, 069 (2005); [arXiv:hep-ph/0507170]. C. Athanasiou, C. G. Lester, J. M. Smillie and B. R. Webber, JHEP **0608**, 055 (2006) [arXiv:hep-ph/0605286], arXiv:hep-ph/0606212.

[81] A. Alves, O. Eboli and T. Plehn, Phys. Rev. D **74**, 095010 (2006) [arXiv:hep-ph/0605067].

[82] J. R. Ellis, K. Enqvist, D. V. Nanopoulos and F. Zwirner, Mod. Phys. Lett. A **1**, 57 (1986).

[83] R. Barbieri and G. F. Giudice, Nucl. Phys. B **306**, 63 (1988).

[84] J. L. Feng, K. T. Matchev and T. Moroi, Phys. Rev. Lett. **84**, 2322 (2000) [arXiv:hep-ph/9908309]; Phys. Rev. D **61**, 075005 (2000) [arXiv:hep-ph/9909334].

[85] M. M. Kado and C. G. Tully, Ann. Rev. Nucl. Part. Sci. **52**, 65 (2002).

[86] R. Dermisek, J. F. Gunion and B. McElrath, Phys. Rev. D **76**, 051105 (2007) [arXiv:hep-ph/0612031].

[87] S. Chang and N. Weiner, arXiv:0710.4591 [hep-ph].

[88] G. Degrassi, S. Heinemeyer, W. Hollik, P. Slavich and G. Weiglein, Eur. Phys. J. C **28**, 133 (2003) [arXiv:hep-ph/0212020].

[89] H. E. Haber, R. Hempfling and A. H. Hoang, Z. Phys. C **75**, 539 (1997) [arXiv:hep-ph/9609331].

[90] N. Cabibbo, L. Maiani, G. Parisi and R. Petronzio, Nucl. Phys. B **158**, 295 (1979).

[91] P. Batra, A. Delgado, D. E. Kaplan and T. M. P. Tait, JHEP **0402**, 043 (2004) [arXiv:hep-ph/0309149].

[92] R. Harnik, G. D. Kribs, D. T. Larson and H. Murayama, Phys. Rev. D **70**, 015002 (2004) [arXiv:hep-ph/0311349].

[93] J. F. Gunion, H. E. Haber, G. Kane, and S. Dawson, *The Higgs Hunter's Guide*. (Addison-Wesley, 1990).

[94] M. S. Carena and H. E. Haber, Prog. Part. Nucl. Phys. **50**, 63 (2003) [arXiv:hep-ph/0208209].

[95] V. Trimble, Ann. Rev. Astron. Astrophys. **25**, 425 (1987).

[96] D. N. Spergel *et al.* [WMAP Collaboration], Astrophys. J. Suppl. **170**, 377 (2007) [arXiv:astro-ph/0603449].

[97] O.Lahav and A. R. Liddle, in W. M. Yao *et al.* [Particle Data Group], J. Phys. G **33**, 1 (2006).

[98] G. Bertone, D. Hooper and J. Silk, Phys. Rept. **405**, 279 (2005) [arXiv:hep-ph/0404175].

[99] T. Moroi and L. Randall, Nucl. Phys. B **570**, 455 (2000) [arXiv:hep-ph/9906527].
[100] R. Kitano and Y. Nomura, Phys. Lett. B **632**, 162 (2006) [arXiv:hep-ph/0509221].
[101] M. Ibe and R. Kitano, JHEP **0708**, 016 (2007) [arXiv:0705.3686 [hep-ph]].
[102] R. J. Scherrer and M. S. Turner, Phys. Rev. D **33**, 1585 (1986) [Erratum-ibid. D **34**, 3263 (1986)].
[103] E. A. Baltz, J. E. Taylor and L. L. Wai, arXiv:astro-ph/0610731.
[104] A. M. Green, JCAP **0708**, 022 (2007) [arXiv:hep-ph/0703217].
[105] H. Goldberg, Phys. Rev. Lett. **50**, 1419 (1983).
[106] J. R. Ellis, K. A. Olive, Y. Santoso and V. C. Spanos, Phys. Lett. B **565**, 176 (2003) [arXiv:hep-ph/0303043].
[107] J. Edsjo, M. Schelke, P. Ullio and P. Gondolo, JCAP **0304**, 001 (2003) [arXiv:hep-ph/0301106].
[108] H. Baer, A. Belyaev, T. Krupovnickas and X. Tata, JHEP **0402**, 007 (2004) [arXiv:hep-ph/0311351].
[109] R. Arnowitt, B. Dutta and Y. Santoso, Nucl. Phys. B **606**, 59 (2001) [arXiv:hep-ph/0102181].
[110] C. Balazs, M. S. Carena and C. E. M. Wagner, Phys. Rev. D **70**, 015007 (2004) [arXiv:hep-ph/0403224].
[111] E. A. Baltz, M. Battaglia, M. E. Peskin and T. Wizansky, Phys. Rev. D **74**, 103521 (2006) [arXiv:hep-ph/0602187].

TASI 2006 - Students Talks Schedule

Week 1: June 5 - June 9

Time	Monday	Tuesday	Wednesday	Thursday	Friday
**					N. Setzer and S. Spinner (U. Maryland) Predicting the Seesaw Scale Time: 3:45 – 4:25
**					Gabe Shaughnessy (U. Wisconsin) Higgs Sector in Singlet Extended MSSM Time: 4:30 – 5:00
**					
**					
**					

Week 2: June 12 - June 16

Time	Monday	Tuesday	Wednesday	Thursday	Friday
7:15*	Delphine Perrodin (U. Arizona)	Alejandro Jenkins (Caltech)			Chiu Man Ho (U. Pittsburgh) Charged Lepton Mixing & Oscillation from Neutrino Mixing in the Early Universe *Time: 3:45 – 4:15
—	Astrophysical Constraints on higher order theories of gravity.	Limits On A Cosmic "Solid"	PICNIC Starting at 6:00pm	Rouven Essig (Rutgers) Direct Detection of Non-Chiral Dark Matter	
7:45*					
7:50*	Pearl Sandick (U. Minnesota)	Emel Gulez (Ohio State U.)		Ken Hsieh (U. Maryland)	Tommer Wizansky (Stanford U) Determination of Dark Matter Properties at High Energy Colliders *Time: 4:20 – 4:50
—	Cosmological Supernovae: Neutrino Background & Gravitational Wave Signature.	Lattice Determination of form factors for Semi-leptonic B decays	PICNIC Starting at 6:00pm	Dark Matter in QED Models	
8:20*					

Week 3: June 19 - June 23

Time	Monday	Tuesday	Wednesday	Thursday	Friday
7:15	A. Bachri (Oklahoma State U.)	Yingchuan Li (U. Maryland)	Anibal Medina (U. Chicago)	Anupama Atre (U. Wisconsin)	FREE
7:45	Soft Leptogenesis in Left-Right Symmetry, RGE & SUSY Breaking effects.	SO(10) GUT Model, θ_{13} and Leptogenesis.	Soft Leptogenesis in Warped Extra Dimensions	Search for Lepton Number Violation	
7:50	Natalia Shuhmaher (McGill University)	Jing Shu (U. Chicago)	Joachim Kopp (Tech U. Munich)	Haibo Yu (U. Maryland)	FREE
8:20	Undressing some of the hierarchies in Cosmology.	Phase Transition Baryogenesis.	Simulation of Neutrino Oscillation Experiments	Discrete Symmetry in Neutrino Physics and Beyond	

Week 4: June 26 - June 30

Time	Monday	Tuesday	Wednesday	Thursday	Friday
**	John Mason (U Calif. Santa Cruz)	Andrew Noble (Cornell U.)	Guiyo Huang (U. Wisconsin)	Erinn De Pree (William and Mary)	FREE
**	Enhanced Radiative Corrections to Higgs Couplings.	EW Constraints on the littlest Higgs model with T-Parity	Mass variables	Top pair production in Randall-Sundrum Models	
**	*Time: 2:00 – 2:30	*Time: 3:45 – 4:15	*Time: 7:15 – 7:45	*Time: 7:15 – 7:45	
**	Sky Bauman (U. Arizona)	Andrey Katz (Technion Israel)	Frank Tackmann (U. California Berkeley)		FREE
**	KK Masses & Couplings Radiative Corrections to Tree level relations.	Lorentz violation & Superpartner masses.	Flavor Physics & non perturbative effects in $B \to X_s \ell^+ \ell^-$ decays	FREE	
	*Time: 2:40 – 3:10	*Time: 4:20 – 4:50	*Time: 7:50 – 8:20		

Notes: *Please note that Talks on Friday of the second week are taking place in the afternoon.